PLAYS OF THE RESTORATION
AND EIGHTEENTH CENTURY

PLAYS

of the

RESTORATION AND EIGHTEENTH CENTURY

as they were acted at the

THEATRES-ROYAL

by

THEIR MAJESTIES' SERVANTS

EDITED BY

DOUGALD MacMILLAN

and

HOWARD MUMFORD JONES

Ibimus, o socii comitesque!
—Hor. Carm. Lib. I, vii.

Theatra tota reclamant!
—Cic.

I say the stage is the *Mirror of Nature*, and the actors are the *Abstract and brief Chronicles of the Time:* and pray what can a man of sense study better?
—*The Critic.*

HOLT, RINEHART AND WINSTON
NEW YORK · CHICAGO · SAN FRANCISCO
TORONTO · LONDON

COPYRIGHT, 1931, BY
HOLT, RINEHART AND WINSTON, INC.

COPYRIGHT (C) RENEWED, 1959, BY
DOUGALD MACMILLAN
AND
HOWARD MUMFORD JONES

90123 40 19181716

03-006115-6

PRINTED IN THE

UNITED STATES OF AMERICA

TO
ELEANOR DOUGALD AND ROBERT

CONTENTS

	PAGE
THE SIEGE OF RHODES, Part I, by *Sir William Davenant*	3
THE INDIAN QUEEN, by *John Dryden* and *Sir Robert Howard*	27
THE REHEARSAL, by *George Villiers*, Duke of Buckingham [and others]	50
THE MAN OF MODE, by *Sir George Etherege*	82
THE RIVAL QUEENS, by *Nathaniel Lee*	130
ALL FOR LOVE, by *John Dryden*	167
VENICE PRESERVED, by *Thomas Otway*	215
THE SQUIRE OF ALSATIA, by *Thomas Shadwell*	257
LOVE'S LAST SHIFT, by *Colley Cibber*	307
THE RELAPSE, by *Sir John Vanbrugh*	349
THE WAY OF THE WORLD, by *William Congreve*	400
THE FAIR PENITENT, by *Nicholas Rowe*	445
THE BEAUX' STRATAGEM, by *George Farquhar*	475
CATO, by *Joseph Addison*	517
THE CONSCIOUS LOVERS, by *Sir Richard Steele*	548
THE BEGGAR'S OPERA, by *John Gay*	585
THE LONDON MERCHANT, by *George Lillo*	616
DOUGLAS, by *John Home*	646
THE CLANDESTINE MARRIAGE, by *George Colman* and *David Garrick*	673
FALSE DELICACY, by *Hugh Kelly*	717
THE WEST INDIAN, by *Richard Cumberland*	746
SHE STOOPS TO CONQUER, by *Oliver Goldsmith*	788
THE SCHOOL FOR SCANDAL, by *Richard Brinsley Sheridan*	824
THE STRANGER, by *Augustus von Kotzebue*, translated by *Benjamin Thompson*	867
THE PLAIN-DEALER, by *William Wycherley*	897

THE EPISTLE TO THE READER

In preparing this work as well for the reader of taste and discrimination as for the lover of the theater, the editors have taken care to include plays which, in their own days and subsequently, have so often been given representation as to be sure indications of the temper of their respective periods. They have also, except for instances noted at convenient points, reprinted the first editions of the plays, with such changes in spelling, punctuation, and capitals as are called for by the usage of more recent times. In their explanatory and critical notes the editors have, moreover, avoided controverted matter, attempting only to enlighten the page, and leaving to other and more suitable places the discussion of moot questions which, however interesting or illuminating, distract the attention from the play itself. The limitations of space have forced the exclusion of many worthy plays; and the exigencies of historical importance have perhaps compelled the inclusion of works inferior to many others among those included in this volume. It is their hope, however, to have illustrated the annals of the *British* stage from the days of the *second Charles* to the days of *Napoleon* with a representative body of dramatic works.

Though both editors feel themselves responsible for the whole of the volume, the better to divide their task between them, *Mr. Jones* has devoted his labors generally to the Restoration period, *Mr. MacMillan* to the Eighteenth Century. Since the first publication of this work, typographical errors have been corrected. The text of *The Rehearsal* has been newly compared and revised, and is now preserved without those faults that unfortunately were allowed to appear in the earlier printing.

For assistance the editors are under many obligations, and especially to *Professor R. H. Griffith*, Curator of the *Wrenn* Library at the University of Texas; to *Mr. V. Valta Parma* of the Rare Book Room, The Library of Congress; to the Graduate School of the University of North Carolina, for grants-in-aid from the *Smith* Research Fund; to *Mrs. Thornton Shirley Graves*, of Chapel Hill, for the loan of early editions from the library of her late husband, to the officials of the University of Michigan Library, and to *Mrs. Howard Mumford Jones*, for valuable assistance in proof-reading.

THE EDITORS.

Chapel Hill, North Carolina } and { Cambridge, Massachusetts

15 June, 1938

PLAYS OF THE RESTORATION
AND EIGHTEENTH CENTURY

THE SIEGE OF RHODES

PART ONE

By Sir William Davenant

Chief link between two theatrical epochs, William Davenant (later knighted by Charles I) "made his first entry on the stage of this vain world" in Oxford the last of February, 1605/6, and was baptized on March 3. His father, John Davenant, a vintner and a friend of Shakespeare, was mayor of Oxford when he died (1622); his mother possessed beauty, good wit, and conversation. After early training under Edward Sylvester, a noted classical scholar, Davenant lived for a while in Lincoln College, but "wanted much of university learning." Service in the retinues of Frances, Duchess of Richmond, and of Fulke Greville, Lord Brooke, brought him to the court. Prefixed to his earliest play, *The Tragedy of Albovine, King of the Lombards* (1629) are commendatory verses by Edward Hyde (later Earl of Clarendon) and others. The earlier dramas maintain, and sometimes ridicule, the "Platonick love" convention.

Created poet laureate in 1638, Davenant was next appointed "governor" of the company of actors at the Cockpit (1639). A royalist during the Rebellion, he was several times imprisoned, but these years saw the production of the much discussed *Gondibert* (1651), his heroic poem. As the Commonwealth drew to its close, Davenant, apparently protected by Cromwell, took up his rôle of theatrical *entrepreneur*, and at one time may have produced entertainments in four separate theaters. On May 23, 1656, occurred the famous *First Day's Entertainment at Rutland House*, an "opera," the performance of which was semi-private. In the same manner was produced the first version of *The Siege of Rhodes* (September, 1656). After the Restoration, Davenant and Thomas Killigrew were granted patents to "erect" two companies of players (August 21, 1660), and the theater was officially restored. After adapting numerous plays, Davenant concluded a troubled career with his "last exit" in Little Lincoln's Inn Fields April 7, 1668, and was buried in Westminster Abbey, "as if it were the buriall of a poor poet," says Pepys, though Sir John Denham thought it was "the finest coffin that ever he saw." Davenant was three times married.

The best account is by Joseph Knight in the *Dictionary of National Biography*, which should, however, be corrected in the light of discoveries made by Leslie Hotson. See his *Commonwealth and Restoration Stage*, chapter iii. The introductory material in *The Dramatic Works of Sir William Davenant* (5 vols., 1872–3) is of value.

DAVENANT'S DRAMATIC WORKS

(The place and date of first production, when known, are given in parentheses. The date outside the parentheses is the date of publication.)

The Tragedy of Albovine, King of the Lombards (never produced?), 1629.

The Cruel Brother (tragedy) (Blackfriars, 1627/8), 1630.

The Colonel (an early version of The Siege?) (1629).

The Just Italian (Blackfriars, 1629), 1673.

The Wits (comedy) (Blackfriars, 1633/4), 1635.

Love and Honour (tragedy) (Blackfriars, 1634), 1649.

(With Inigo Jones) The Temple of Love (masque) (Whitehall, 1634/5), 1634/5.

News from Plymouth (Globe, 1635), 1673.

The Platonick Lovers (comedy) (Blackfriars, 1635), 1636.

The Triumph of the Prince d'Amour (masque) (Middle Temple, 1635/6), 1635/6.

(With Inigo Jones) Britannia Triumphans (masque) (Whitehall, 1637/8), 1637/8.

The Unfortunate Lovers (Blackfriars, 1638), 1673.

The Fair Favourite (1638), 1673.

The Distress (an early version of The Spanish Lovers?) (1639).

Salmacida Spolia (masque) (Whitehall, 1639/40), 1639/40.

3

The First Day's Entertainment at Rutland House (opera) (Rutland House, 1656), 1656.
The Siege of Rhodes (opera) (Rutland House, Sept., 1656; Cockpit, 1659), 1659 (L.I.F., two parts, June, 1661), 1663.
The Cruelty of the Spaniards in Peru (became part of The Playhouse to be Let) (Cockpit, 1658), 1658.
The History of Sir Francis Drake (became part of The Playhouse to be Let) (Cockpit, 1659), 1659.
The Law Against Lovers (adaptation) (L.I.F., Feb., 1661/2), 1673.
The Playhouse to be Let (L.I.F., 1662?), 1673.
The Rivals (adaptation) (L.I.F., 1662?), 1668.
Macbeth (adaptation) (L.I.F., 1662; D.G., Feb., 1672/3), 1674.
The Man's the Master (adaptation) (L.I.F., March, 1667/8), 1668/9.
(With Dryden) The Tempest (adaptation) (L.I.F., Nov., 1667), 1670.
The Siege (?), 1673.
The Spanish Lovers (see The Distress), 1673.

In the summer of 1522 a huge Turkish army under the command of Solyman moved across Asia Minor to the coast of Caria where they were met by a fleet of 300 ships. This vast armament (the army was 200,000 strong) was destined to reduce the fortress of Rhodes, ships from which threatened the Sultan's communications with Egypt, and were generally piratical. Although abandoned by the western powers, the Grand-Master of the Knights of St. John, Villiers de L'Isle Adam, made every preparation for defence. An iron chain was stretched across the harbor, and outside it, a boom of timber floated to obstruct the Turkish vessels. Houses outside the walls were destroyed in order that they might afford no shelter to the enemy, fresh fortifications were constructed, and the slaves, lest they prove treacherous, were removed from the powder-mills, free men being substituted for them and working day and night. Solyman himself arrived to take charge of operations towards the end of July; and a grand assault in September was repelled with enormous losses. The Sultan resorted to siege tactics. In December the Grand-Master capitulated. Free leave to depart was given the Knights, whose bravery had won Solyman's hearty respect, and, barring some Turkish troops who got out of hand, the terms of the capitulation were honorably fulfilled on both sides.[1]

This in outline is the story which Davenant read in Knolles' great *Historie of the Turkes*, published in London in 1603, and which he resolved to make the subject of an "opera." Adapting the details of the siege to the purposes of a love-and-honor situation, drawing upon other parts of the *Historie* for colorful events and names, he invented other episodes (such as the conflagration of the Grand-Master's palace with which the second part concludes) or borrowed them from French heroic romance and Heywood's *The Fair Maid of the West*, creating a dramatic entertainment which, in Aubrey's phrase, "did affect the eie and eare extremely" and which has become a landmark in the development of the English theater.[2]

The concoction of dramatic entertainment which would avoid the legal ban on plays and yet give pleasure to the cultivated minority was a business in which Davenant showed a practical and canny skill. If the literary value of the poetry in the present "opera" is small, *The Siege of Rhodes* by reason of the relative novelty of its scenery, the use of women actresses, and, above all, its definite employment of the love-and-honor theme is of great significance in the history of the stage. The types developed by Davenant, though he was not the first to use them, became the stock characters of Restoration tragedy and heroic drama. The use of far-away events and romantic coloring is also important; and before we conclude that *The Siege of Rhodes* and its successors in the field of heroic drama are utterly absurd, let us remember that they satisfied the craving of Restoration audiences for color and large utterance; and let us remember also the absurdities of modern costume "movies."

[1] See the amusing sixteenth century wood-cut of the siege of Rhodes reproduced in Stanley Lane-Poole's *Turkey*, p. 171, as well as the pictures of modern (nineteenth century) Rhodes in the same volume.

[2] On Davenant's use of his materials see the articles by Killis Campbell, *Mod. Lang. Notes*, XIII, 177ff.; C. G. Child, *id.*, XIX, 166ff.; and the discussion in J. W. Tupper, *Love and Honour and The Siege of Rhodes by Sir William D'Avenant* (Belles Lettres ed.), Boston, 1909.

THE SIEGE OF RHODES

To the Reader

I may receive disadvantage by this address [1] designed for excuses; for it will too hastily put you in mind that errors are not far off when excuses are at hand; this refers to our representation; and some may be willing to be led to find the blemishes of it, but would be left to their own conduct to discover the beauties, if there be any. Yet I may forewarn you that the defects which I intend to excuse are chiefly such as you cannot reform but only with your purse; that is, by building us a larger room; [2] a design which we began and shall not be left for you to finish, because we have observed that many who are liberal of their understanding when they would issue it out towards discovery of imperfections, have not always money to expend in things necessary towards the making up of perfection. It has been often wished that our scenes (we having obliged ourselves to the variety of five changes, according to the ancient dramatic distinctions made for time) had not been confined to eleven foot in height, [3] and about fifteen in depth, including the places of passage reserved for the music. This is so narrow an allowance for the fleet of Solyman [4] the Magnificent, his army, the Island of Rhodes, and the varieties attending the siege of the city, that I fear you will think we invite you to such a contracted trifle as that of the Caesars carved upon a nut.

As these limits have hindered the splendor of our scene, so we are like to give no great satisfaction in the quantity of our argument, which is in story very copious; but shrinks to a small narration here, because we could not convey it by more than seven persons; being constrained to prevent [5] the length of *recitative* music, as well as to conserve, without encumbrance, the narrowness of the place. Therefore you cannot expect the chief ornaments belonging to a history dramatically digested into turns and counterturns, [6] to double walks, [7] and interweavings of design.

This is expressed to forbid your excess of expectation; but we must take care not to deter you from the hope of some satisfaction; for that were, not only to hang out no bush, [8] but likewise to shut up our doors. Therefore, as you have heard what kind of excellencies you should not expect, so I will in brief (I hope without vanity) give you encouragement by telling you there are some things at least excusable which you may resolve to meet.

---

[1] The address to the reader, as the date subscribed to it shows, seems to indicate that Davenant sent the text of the first version of the play to the printer in advance of performance. On September 3, 1656, he sent a copy to his friend Bulstrode Whitelocke, formerly Master of the Revels for the Society of the Middle Temple, and later Lord Commissioner of the Treasury under Cromwell:

My Lord,
When I consider the nicety of the Times, I fear it may draw a Curtain between your Lordship and our Opera; therefore I have presumed to send your Lordship, hot from the Press, what we mean to represent; making your Lordship my supreme Judge, though I despair to have the Honour of inviting you to be a Spectator. I do not conceive the perusal of it worthy any part of your Lordship's leisure, unless your antient relation to the Muses make you not unwilling to give a little entertainment to Poetry, though in so mean a dress as this and coming from, my Lord,

Your Lordship's
most obedient Servant,
William D'Avenant.

Because of the legal ban on the theater, Whitelocke could not properly go to a playhouse, but Davenant is here obviously making a bid for his support in case of difficulties.

[2] The "cupboard stage" at Rutland House, where the opera was first produced, was simply a large room. The stage at Lisle's Tennis Court, Lincoln's Inn Fields, where the expanded version was given, though presumably more commodious, yet "wanted room for the depth of scenes." See Hotson, *Commonwealth and Restoration Stage*, pp. 120–7.

[3] The exact height noted on Webb's drawings. See *The Burlington Magazine*, XXV (1914), 29, 85, etc., for reproductions of the originals.

[4] As the stage directions indicate, the Turkish fleet, Solyman's army, etc., were simply painted on the back-cloth or back shutters.

[5] Anticipate; i.e., allowance would have to be made for the length of recitative music, which would take up more time than straight dialogue.

[6] A counterturn is an unexpected development of the plot.

[7] A walk is the course of action assigned to one person in a drama—a phrase peculiar to Davenant.

[8] A bush or bunch of ivy hung up as a vintner's sign; a signboard of a tavern.

We conceive, it will not be unacceptable to you if we recompense the narrowness of the room, by containing in it so much as could be conveniently accomplished by art and industry: which will not be doubted in the scenes by those who can judge that kind of illustration and know the excellency of Mr. John Web,[1] who designed and ordered it. The music [2] was composed, and both the vocal and instrumental is exercised by the most transcendent of England in that art, and perhaps not unequal to the best masters abroad; but being *recitative*, and therefore unpractised here, though of great reputation amongst other nations, the very attempt of it is an obligation to our own. The story represented (which will not require much apology because it expects but little praise) is heroical, and notwithstanding the continual hurry and busy agitations of a hot siege, is (I hope) intelligibly conveyed to advance the characters of virtue in the shapes of valor and conjugal love. And though the main argument hath but a single walk,[3] yet perhaps the movings of it will not seem unpleasant. You may inquire, being a reader, why in an heroic argument my numbers are so often diversified and fall into short fractions; considering that a continuation of the usual length of English verse would appear more heroical in reading. But when you are an auditor, you will find that in this I rather deserve approbation than need excuse; for frequent alterations of measure (which cannot be so unpleasant to him that reads as troublesome to him that writes) are necessary to *recitative* music for variation of airs. If what I have said be taken for excuses, I have my intent; because excuses are not always signs of error, but are often modest explanations of things that might otherwise be mistaken. But I have said so much to vindicate myself from having occasion to be excused for the poem that it brings me at last to ask pardon for the length of the epistle.

August 17, 1656   Will. D'Avenant.

To the Right Honorable the Earl of Clarendon,[4]

Lord High Chancellor of England, &c.

My Lord,

Though poems have lost much of their ancient value, yet I will presume to make this a present to your Lordship; and the rather, because poems (if they have anything precious in them) do, like jewels, attract a greater esteem when they come into the possession of great persons than when they are in ordinary hands.

The excuse which men have had for dedication of books has been to protect them from the malice of readers; but a defence of this nature was fitter for your forces when you were early known to learned men (and had no other occasion for your abilities but to vindicate authors) than at this season when you are of extraordinary use to the whole nation.

Yet when I consider how many and how violent they are who persecute dramatic poetry, I will then rather call this a dedication than a present; as not intending by it to pass any kind of obligation, but to receive a great benefit; since I cannot be safe unless I am sheltered behind your Lordship.

Your name is so eminent in the justice which you convey through all the different members of this great empire, that my Rhodians seem to enjoy a better harbor in the pacific Thames, than they had on the Mediterranean; and I have brought Solyman to be arraigned at your tribunal, where you are the censor of his civility and magnificence.

Dramatic poetry meets with the same persecution now from such who esteem themselves the most refined and civil as it ever did from the barbarous. And yet whilst those virtuous enemies deny heroic plays to the gentry, they entertain the people with a seditious farce [5] of their own counterfeit gravity. But I hope you will not be unwilling to receive (in this poetical dress) neither the besieged nor

---

[1] John Webb or Webbe (1611–72), nephew and disciple of Inigo Jones, the architect who designed the scenery.

[2] The music was composed by Henry Lawes, Captain Cooke, Matthew Lock, Dr. Charles Coleman, and Henry Hudson. Cooke and Lock also took part as performers.

[3] Single plot—i.e., no sub-plots. Cf. note 7, p. 5.

[4] Edward Hyde, first Earl of Clarendon (1609–74), statesman and politician, an early friend of Davenant, for whose first play he wrote commendatory verses.

[5] Since the dedication first appeared in the edition of 1663, it is possible that this phrase refers to the insurrection of January, 1661, raised by a fanatic named Venner with thirty followers. Reports of its importance were ludicrously exaggerated. The fanatic Puritans, of course, of whom Venner was one, denied "heroic plays to the gentry."

the besiegers, since they come without their vices; for as others have purged the stage from the corruptions of the art of the drama, so I have endeavored to cleanse it from the corruption of manners; nor have I wanted care to render the ideas of greatness and virtue pleasing and familiar.

In old Rome the magistrates did not only protect but exhibit plays; and, not long since, the two wise cardinals [1] did kindly entertain the great images represented in tragedy by Monsieur Corneille.[2] My Lord, it proceeds from the same mind not to be pleased with princes on the stage, and not to affect them in the throne; for those are ever most inclined to break the mirror who are unwilling to see the images of such as have just authority over their guilt.

In this poem I have revived the remembrance of that fatal desolation [3] which was permitted by Christian princes when they favored the ambition of such as defended the diversity of religions (begot by the factions of learning) in Germany; whilst those who would never admit learning into their empire (lest it should meddle with religion and entangle it with controversy) did make Rhodes defenceless, which was the only fortified academy in Christendom where divinity and arms were equally professed. I have likewise, for variety, softened the martial encounters between Solyman and the Rhodians, with intermingling the conjugal virtues of Alphonso and Ianthe.

If I should proceed, and tell your Lordship of what use theaters have anciently been, and may be now, by heightening the characters of valor, temperance, natural justice,[4] and complacency to government, I should fall into the ill manners and indiscretion of ordinary dedicators, who go about to instruct those from whose abilities they expect protection. The apprehension of this error makes me hasten to crave pardon for what has been already said by,

My Lord,
Your Lordship's most humble
and most obedient servant,
Will. D'Avenant

---

[1] Richelieu and Mazarin.

[2] Until the emergence of Racine, still (1663) the greatest French dramatist.

[3] The Venetians, who should naturally have come to the defence of Rhodes, did not desire to endanger their commercial relations with the Mohammedans; and the other Christian powers, as described in the play, were quarreling among themselves. It is possible that Davenant here intends an oblique hit at religious "factions" in England.

[4] In opposition to the Puritan attack on the theaters, Davenant sets forth an opposite claim.

THE SIEGE OF RHODES

THE PERSONS REPRESENTED

1656		1661
Captain Henry Cook	SOLYMAN THE MAGNIFICENT [1]	Betterton
John Harding	PIRRHUS, *Vizier Bassa* [2]	
Henry Purcell [3]	MUSTAPHA, [a] *Bassa*	
	RUSTAN, [a] *Bassa*	
	HALY, [a] *Eunuch Bassa*	
Gregory Thorndell	VILLERIUS, *Grand Master* [4] *of Rhodes*	Lilliston
Edward Coleman	ALPHONSO, *a Sicilian Duke* [5]	Harris
Matthew Lock [6]	ADMIRAL OF RHODES	Blagden
	ROXOLANA, *wife to Solyman* [7]	Mrs. Davenport
Mrs. Edward Coleman [8]	IANTHE, *wife to Alphonso*	Mrs. Saunderson

Women attendants to Roxolana
Women attendants to Ianthe
Four pages, attendants to Roxolana

THE SCENE: *Rhodes* [9]

The ornament [10] which encompassed the scene consisted of several columns, of gross rustic work,[11] which bore up a large frieze. In the middle of the frieze was a compartment, wherein was written RHODES.[12] The compartment was supported by divers habiliments

---

[1] Solyman II, called the Magnificent, Sultan of the Ottoman Empire, 1520–66.—Captain Henry Cook, musician and royalist, a music teacher, who contributed to Davenant's *Rutland House Entertainment*.

[2] A bassa (bashaw, pacha) is the Turkish term for a military commander or governor. Pirrhus was the general in charge of the Turkish army before the arrival of Solyman.

[3] Spelled *Persill* in the original. Father of the famous Henry Purcell.

[4] Philip Villiers de L'Isle Adam, elected Grand-Master of the Order January 22, 1521.

[5] Davenant read in Knolles' *Historie* that a Spaniard named Alphonsos slipped past the Turks and brought a hundred volunteers from Crete to Rhodes in time for the siege. The name attracted him and he used it.— Edward Coleman was a friend of Pepys and after the Restoration one of the royal musicians.

[6] Besides anthems, Lock is remembered for writing the instrumental music for Dryden and Davenant's perversion of *The Tempest*.

[7] The part is not found in the first version of the play, but the name, or its shorter form, Roxana, soon became a stock term in the theater.

[8] The earliest recorded instance of a woman's appearing on the stage in the period.

[9] There is an excellent description of Rhodes and the sieges in Vertot's *The History of the Knights Hospitallers*, III, 168–70, translated from the French, Edinburgh, 1757.

The editions of 1656 and 1659, from which the list of performers in 1656 is taken, say also that the instrumental music was composed by Dr. Charles Coleman and Mr. George Hudson. It has been lost. Both contributed to the *Rutland House Entertainment* and both were later patronized by the king. In addition the following information is given:

"The Composition of Vocal Musick was performed

The { First Entry / Second Entry / Third Entry / Fourth Entry / Fifth Entry } by { Mr. Henry Lawes / Capt. Henry Cook / Capt. Henry Cook / Mr. Matthew Lock / Mr. Henry Lawes. }

Henry Lawes is of course the friend and associate of Milton in creating *Comus*.

[10] In general the scenery of the play follows the traditions of the court masque and the private theaters, strongly influenced by the practice of the continent. For previous attempts at a "picture-stage" and for the historical significance of Davenant's innovations see "The Origin of the English Picture-Stage" in W. J. Lawrence, *The Elizabethan Playhouse and Other Studies, Second Series*.

[11] Rustic work is masonry characterized by a surface artificially roughened or left rough-hewn, or by having the joints, especially the horizontal ones, deeply sunk. Here it refers of course to the painted imitation of such work.

[12] The practice of painting the name of the place in a central position over the proscenium is continental in origin and was sometimes employed in English masques. A *compartment* refers to an ornamental subdivision of the design.

of war; intermixed with the military ensigns of those several nations who were famous for defence of that island; which were the French, Germans, and Spaniards, the Italians, Avergnois, and English. The renown of the English valor made the Grand-Master Villerius to select their station [1] to be most frequently commanded by himself. The principal enrichment of the frieze was a crimson drapery, whereon several trophies of arms were fixed, those on the right hand representing such as are chiefly in use amongst the western nations; together with the proper cognizance [2] of the Order of the Rhodian Knights; and on the left, such as are most esteemed in the eastern countries; and on an antique shield the crescent of the Ottomans.

The Scene before the First Entry

The curtain being drawn up, a lightsome sky appeared, discovering a maritime coast, full of craggy rocks and high cliffs, with several verdures naturally growing upon such situations; and afar off, the true prospect of the City RHODES, when it was in prosperous estate; with so much view of the gardens and hills about it as the narrowness of the room could allow the scene. In that part of the horizon terminated by the sea was represented the Turkish fleet making towards a promontory some few miles distant from the town.

The Entry is prepared by instrumental music.

THE FIRST ENTRY

Enter ADMIRAL

ADMIRAL. Arm, arm, Villerius, arm!
  Thou hast no leisure to grow old;
Those now must feel thy courage warm,
  Who think thy blood is cold.

Enter VILLERIUS

VILLERIUS. Our Admiral [3] from sea? 5
  What storm transporteth thee?
Or bringst thou storms that can do more
  Than drive an admiral on shore?
  ADMIRAL. Arm, arm, the Bassa's fleet appears;
To Rhodes his course from Chios steers;
  Her shady wings to distant sight 11
  Spread like the curtains of the night.
Each squadron thicker and still darker grows;
The fleet like many floating forests shows.
  VILLERIUS. Arm, arm! Let our drums beat
  To all our out-guards, a retreat; 16
And to our main guards add
Files double lined [4] from the parade.
Send horse to drive [5] the fields;
Prevent what rip'ning summer yields. 20
To all the foe would save
Set fire, or give a secret grave.
  ADMIRAL. I'll to our galley hast[e],
  Untackle ev'ry mast;
Hale 'em within the pier, 25
To range and chain 'em there,
And then behind St. Nic'las' cliffs [6]
Shelter our brigants,[7] land our skiffs.
  VILLERIUS. Our field and bulwark-canon [8]
  mount with hast[e];
Fix to their blocks their brazen bodies fast; 30
Whilst to their foes their iron entrails fly,
Display our colors, raise our standard high!
                      Exit ADMIRAL.

Enter ALPHONSO

ALPHONSO. What various noises do mine ears invade,
And have a consort of confusion made? 34
The shriller trumpet and tempestuous drum:
The deaf'ning clamor from the cannon's womb,
Which through the air like sudden thunder breaks,
Seems calm to soldiers' shouts and women's shrieks.
What danger, rev'rend lord, does this portend?
  VILLERIUS. Danger begins what must in honor end. 40

---

[1] The various "nations" in Rhodes were assigned particular parts of the defences, that of the English being on the north side of the town. There were seven main bastions and eight "nations"; viz., French, English, German, Spanish, Portuguese, Italian, Provenceaux, and Auvergnats.

[2] A device or emblem worn by all the retainers of a noble house or members of a military order. That of the Knights of St. John was a white cross on a red field.

[3] Not necessarily a maritime commander. In the Levant at this period an admiral might be simply a commander.

[4] Doubling the files would increase the depth of the defenders' ranks, at the same time shortening them.

[5] To drive off the animals and devastate the country.

[6] An error of Davenant's. The tower of St. Nicholas stood at one side of the entrance to the harbor, opposite the castle of St. Angelo which defended the other side, but there were no cliffs.

[7] Brigantines; and skiffs are (here) small sea-going boats, adapted for rowing or sailing.

[8] Cannon mounted on the bulwarks or bastions. The heavy artillery as opposed to the "field-guns." Cannon were made of brass in the sixteenth century.

ALPHONSO. What vizards does it wear?
VILLERIUS.   Such, gentle prince,
As cannot fright, but yet must warn you hence.
What can to Rhodes more fatally appear
Than the bright crescents which those ensigns
    wear?
Wise emblems that increasing empire [1] show, 45
Which must be still in nonage and still grow.
All these are yet but the forerunning van
Of the prodigious gross [2] of Solyman.
  ALPHONSO. Pale show those crescents to our
    bloody cross! [3]
Sink not the western kingdoms [4] in our loss? 50
Will not the Austrian eagle [5] moult her wings,
That long hath hovered o'er the Gallic kings?
Whose lilies, too, will wither when we fade,
And th' English lion sink into a shade.
  VILLERIUS. Thou see'st not, whilst so young
    and guiltless, too,   55
That kings mean seldom what their statesmen
    do,
Who measure not the compass of a crown
To fit the head that wears it, but their own,
Still hind'ring peace, because they stewards
    are,
Without account, to that wild spender, War. 60

Enter HIGH MARSHAL OF RHODES

  MARSHAL. Still Christian wars they will
    pursue, and boast
Unjust successes gained, whilst Rhodes is lost,
Whilst we build monuments of death, to shame
Those who forsook us in the chase of fame.
  ALPHONSO. We will endure the colds of
    court delays;   65
Honor grows warm in airy vests [6] of praise.
On rocky Rhodes we will like rocks abide.
  VILLERIUS. Away, away, and hasten to thy
    bride!
'Tis scarce a month since from thy nuptial rites
Thou cam'st to honor here our Rhodian
    knights,   70
To dignify our sacred annual feast. [7]
We love to lodge, not to entomb, a guest.
Honor must yield where reason should prevail.

Aboard, aboard, and hoist up ev'ry sail
That gathers any wind for Sicily!   75
  MARSHAL. Men lose their virtue's pattern,
    losing thee.
Thy bride doth yield her sex no less a light,
But, thy life gone, will set in endless night.
Ye must like stars shine long ere ye expire!
  ALPHONSO. Honor is colder virtue set on fire;
My honor lost, her love would soon decay.
Here for my tomb or triumph I will stay.   82
My sword against proud Solyman I draw,
His cursèd prophet, and his sensual law.
  CHORUS.[8] Our swords against proud Soly-
    man we draw,   85
His cursèd prophet, and his sensual law.
                                        Exeunt

[*Sicily*] [9]

Enter IANTHE, MELOSILE, MADINA (*her two
women*), *bearing two open caskets with
jewels*

  IANTHE. To Rhodes this fatal fleet her
    course does bear.
Can I have love, and not discover fear?
When he, in whom my plighted heart doth live
  (Whom Hymen gave me in reward   90
Of vows, which by with favor heard,
And is the greatest gift he e'er can give)
Shall in a cruel siege imprison'd be,
And I, whom love has bound, have liberty?
Away! Let's leave our flourishing abodes 95
In Sicily, and fly to with'ring Rhodes.
  MELOSILE. Will you convert to instruments
    of war,
To things which to our sex so dreadful are,
Which terror add to Death's detested face,
These ornaments which should your beauty
    grace?   100
  MADINA. Beauty laments! and this ex-
    change abhors!
    Shall all these gems in arms be spent
    Which were by bounteous princes sent
To pay the valor of your ancestors?
  IANTHE. If by their sale my lord may be
    redeemed,   105
Why should they more than trifles be es-
    teemed,
Vainly secured with iron bars and locks?
They are the spawn of shells, and warts of
    rocks.[10]

---

[1] Play on *crescent* (l. 44), meaning growing; and the crescent as the Turkish standard.

[2] Main body of the army, said to have been 200,000.

[3] The cross of the Order was white on a red field, but in view of the incessant fighting was figuratively bloody.

[4] See note 1, p. 12.

[5] France and the Empire were then (1522) at war.

[6] Garments.

[7] The Rhodian Knights were properly the order of St. John of Jerusalem. The Turkish fleet appeared June 26, within the octave of his feast.

[8] Apparently the chorus remains throughout the play taking no part in the action.

[9] There is no shift of scenery, though the locale is now Sicily.

[10] Note the naïve scientific knowledge.

THE SIEGE OF RHODES

MADINA. All, madam, all? Will you from all depart?
IANTHE. Love a consumption learns from chymist's art. 110
Sapphires and harder di'monds must be sold
And turned to softer and more current gold.
With gold we cursèd powder may prepare
Which must consume in smoke and thinner air.
MELOSILE. Thou idol-love, I'll worship thee no more, 115
Since thou dost make us sorrowful and poor.
IANTHE. Go seek out cradles and with childhood dwell
    Where you may still be free
    From Love's self-flattery,
And never hear mistaken lovers tell 120
Of blessings and of joys in such extremes
As never are possessed but in our dreams.
They woo apace, and hasten to be sped,
And praise the quiet of the marriage-bed;
But mention not the storms of grief and care
    When Love does them surprise 126
    With sudden jealousies,
Or they are severed by ambitious war.
MADINA. Love may perhaps the foolish please,
    But he shall quickly leave my heart 130
    When he persuades me to depart
From such a hoard of precious things as these.
IANTHE. Send out to watch the wind! With the first gale
I'll leave thee, Sicily, and, hoisting sail,
Steer straight to Rhodes. For love and I must be 135
Preserved, Alphonso, or else lost with thee.
                            Exeunt

CHORUS

By soldiers of several nations

1. Come, ye termagant Turks,
    If your Bassa dares land ye,
    Whilst the wine bravely works
    Which was brought us from Candy.[1] 140

2. Wealth, the least of our care is,
    For the poor ne'er are undone;
    A vous,[2] Monsieur of Paris,
    To the back-swords of London.

3. Diego,[3] thou in a trice 145
    Shalt advance thy lean belly;
    For their hens and their rice
    Make pillau[4] like a jelly.

4. Let 'em land fine and free,
    For my cap, though an old one, 150
    Such a turban shall be,
    Thou wilt think it a gold one.

5. It is seven to one odds
    They had safer sailed by us:
    Whilst our wine lasts in Rhodes, 155
    They shall water at Chios.

End of the first Entry

The Scene is changed, and the city, Rhodes, appears, beleaguered at sea and land.

The entry is again prepared by instrumental music.

THE SECOND ENTRY

Enter VILLERIUS *and* ADMIRAL

ADMIRAL. The blood of Rhodes grows cold! life must expire!
VILLERIUS. The Duke still warms it with his valor's fire!
ADMIRAL. If he has much in honor's presence done,
Has saved our ensigns, or has others won,
Then he but well by your example wrought, 5
Who well in honor's school his childhood taught.
VILLERIUS. The foe three moons[5] tempestuously has spent
Where we will never yield nor he relent;
Still we but raise what must be beaten down,[6]
Defending walls, yet cannot keep the town; 10
Vent'ring last stakes where we can nothing win;
And, shutting slaughter out, keep famine in.[7]
ADMIRAL. How oft and vainly Rhodes for succor waits

---

[3] Slang term for Spaniard.
[4] Rice boiled with mutton, kid, or fowl, and spiced or flavored.
[5] The besiegers landed late in June; the first assaults (July and August) were unsuccessful; the general assault of September 4, pictured in the play, was repulsed with a loss of 15,000 men. Alphonso's song (p. 12) refers to earlier assaults than that of September.
[6] Solyman's cannon battered at particular parts of the wall until they crumbled. The Rhodians raised fresh walls behind the damaged ones.
[7] After the unsuccessful assault of September, Solyman, as a matter of history, starved the garrison out.

---

[1] Anthony Bosio, uncle to the historian of the Order, sent fifteen brigantines laden with wine from Candia to Rhodes in preparation for the siege.
[2] That for you, Frenchman; the backsword fighters of London are your equals.

From triple diadems and scarlet hats? [1]
Rome keeps her gold, cheaply her warriors
    pays   15
At first with blessings, and at last with praise.
    VILLERIUS. By armies, stowed in fleets, ex-
        hausted Spain [2]
Leaves half her land unploughed, to plough
    the main;
And still would more of the old world subdue,
As if unsatisfied with all the new.   20
    ADMIRAL. France strives to have her lilies
        grow as fair
In others' realms [3] as where they native are.
    VILLERIUS. The English lion ever loves to
        change
His walks, and in remoter forests range. [4]
    CHORUS. All gaining vainly from each
        other's loss,   25
Whilst still the crescent drives away the cross.

        Enter ALPHONSO
ALPHONSO.
1. How bravely fought the fiery French,
    Their bulwark being stormed!
  The colder Almans kept their trench,
    By more than valor warmed.   30

2. The grave Italians paused and fought,
    The solemn Spaniards, too;
  Study'ng more deaths than could be wrought
    By what the rash could do.

3. Th' Avergnian colors high were raised,   35
    Twice ta'en, and twice relieved.
  Our foes, like friends to valor, praised
    The mischiefs they received.

4. The cheerful English got renown;
    Fought merrily and fast: 40
  'Tis time, they cried, to mow them down,
    War's harvest cannot last.

5. If death be rest, here let us die,
    Where weariness is all
  We daily get [5] by victory,   45
    Who must by famine fall.

6. Great Solyman is landed now; [6]
    All fate he seems to be;
  And brings those tempests in his brow
    Which he deserved at sea.   50

    VILLERIUS. He can at most but once pre-
        vail,
Though armed with nations that were brought
    by more
    Gross galleys [7] than would serve to hale
    This island to the Lycian shore.   54
    ADMIRAL. Let us apace do worthily and give
Our story length, though long we cannot live.
    CHORUS. So greatly do that, being dead,
        Brave wonders may be wrought
    By such as shall our story read
    And study how we fought. *Exeunt* 60

        [*Solyman's Camp*] [8]

        Enter SOLYMAN, PIRRHUS
SOLYMAN. What sudden halt [9] hath stayed
    thy swift renown,
O'er-running kingdoms, stopping at a town?
He that will win the prize in honor's race
Must nearer to the goal still mend his pace.
If age thou feel'st, the active camp forbear; 65
In sleepy cities rest, the caves of fear.
Thy mind was never valiant if, when old,
Thy courage cools because thy blood is cold.
    PIRRHUS. How can ambitious manhood be
        expressed
More than by marks of our disdain of rest? 70
What less than toils incessant can, despite
Of cannon, raise these mounts [10] to castle-
    height?
Or less than utmost or unwearied strength
Can draw these lines of batt'ry to that length?
    SOLYMAN. The toils of ants, and mole-hills
        raised, in scorn   75
Of labor, to be levelled with a spurn.
These are the pyramids that show your pains;
But of your army's valor, where remains
One trophy to excuse a bassa's boast?
    PIRRHUS. Valor may reckon what she
        bravely lost;   80

---

[1] The popes and the cardinals. Leo X (d. 1521) proclaimed a crusade against the Turks in 1517, but "nothing resulted from these measures but a profitable compact between himself and the French King," nor did his successor do any better. Leo flattered the vanity of the Emperor Maximilian by appointing him generalissimo of the Christian army and by sending him a consecrated sword and hat, and pursued a similar policy with other warriors.

[2] The Spanish subjects of Charles V complained that Spain was being drained of men and money to pursue political quarrels in Germany and Italy (1519–20).

[3] French armies were fighting in Italy and Navarre.

[4] The English invaded France in June, 1522.

[5] Gain.

[6] July 24, according to most authorities, though Knolles says August 28.

[7] Great galleys.

[8] Here, as elsewhere whenever a change of scene is indicated in brackets, no change of scenery was made.

[9] A paraphrase of Solyman's speech to his soldiers as given by Knolles.

[10] Solyman built two "little hills" opposite the bastion of Italy, ten or twelve feet higher than the walls of Rhodes itself.

Not from successes all her count does raise:
By life well lost we gain a share of praise.
If we in danger's glass [1] all valor see,
And death the farthest step of danger be,
Behold our mount of bodies made a grave; 85
And prize our loss by what we scorned to save.
   SOLYMAN. Away! range [2] all the camp for
     an assault!
Tell them they tread in graves who make a
     halt.
Fat slaves, who have been lulled to a disease,
Crammed out of breath, and crippled by their
     ease! 90
Whose active fathers leapt o'er walls too high
For them to climb. Hence, from my anger fly,
Which is too worthy for thee, being mine,
And must be quenched by Rhodian blood, or
     thine.
               Exit PIRRHUS, *bowing*
  In honor's orb the Christians shine; 95
    Their light in war does still increase;[3]
Though oft misled by mists of wine,
    Or blinder love, the crime of peace.
Bold in adult'ry's frequent change,
    And ev'ry loud, expensive vice; 100
Ebbing out wealth by ways as strange
    As it flowed in by avarice.
Thus vilely they dare live, and yet dare die.
If courage be a virtue, 'tis allowed
But to those few on whom our crowns rely,
    And is condemned as madness in the
      crowd. 106

      Enter MUSTAPHA, IANTHE *veiled*
   MUSTAPHA. Great Sultan, hail! though
     here at land
Lost fools in opposition stand;
Yet thou at sea dost all command.
   SOLYMAN. What is it thou wouldst show,
     and yet dost shroud? 110
   MUSTAPHA. I bring the morning pictured
     in a cloud,
A wealth more worth than all the sea does hide,
Or courts display in their triumphant pride.
   SOLYMAN. Thou seem'st to bring the daugh-
     ter of the night,
And giv'st her many stars to make her bright.
Dispatch my wonder and relate her story. 116
   MUSTAPHA. 'Tis full of fate, and yet has
     much of glory.

---

[1] Looking-glass.
[2] Draw up in ranks.
[3] Note the frequent play on *increase* and *crescent* throughout the play.

A squadron of our galleys that did ply
West from this coast, met two of Sicily,
Both fraught to furnish Rhodes; we gave
    'em chase, 120
And had, but for our number, met disgrace.
For, grappling, they maintained a bloody fight,
Which did begin with day and end with night.
And though this bashful lady then did wear
Her face still veiled, her valor did appear: 125
She urged their courage when they boldly
    fought,
And many shunned the dangers which she
    sought.
   SOLYMAN. Where are the limits thou
     would'st set for praise?
Or to what height wilt thou my wonder raise?
   MUSTAPHA. This is Ianthe, the Sicilian
     flower, 130
Sweeter than buds unfolded in a shower,
Bride to Alphonso, who in Rhodes so long
The theme has been of each heroic song;
And she for his relief those galleys fraught;
Both stowed with what her dow'r and jewels
    bought. 135
   SOLYMAN. O wond'rous virtue of a Christian
     wife!
Advent' ring life's support, and then her life
To save her ruined lord! Bid her unveil!
               IANTHE *steps back*
   IANTHE. It were more honor, Sultan, to
     assail
A public strength against thy forces bent 140
Than to unwall this private tenement,
To which no monarch but my lord has right;
Nor will it yield to treaty or to might:
Where heaven's great law defends him from
    surprise,
This curtain only opens to his eyes. 145
   SOLYMAN. If beauty veiled so virtuous be,
'Tis more than Christian husbands know;
Whose ladies wear their faces free,
    Which they to more than husband[s] show.
   IANTHE. Your bassa swore, and by his
     dreadful law, 150
None but my lord's dear hand this veil should
    draw;
And that to Rhodes I should conducted be,
To take my share of all his destiny.
    Else I had quickly found
    Sure means to get some wound, 155
    Which would in death's cold arms
      My honor instant safety give
    From all those rude alarms
    Which keep it waking whilst I live.

SOLYMAN. Hast thou engaged our prophet's
    plight   160
To keep her beauty from my sight,
And to conduct her person free
To harbor with mine enemy?
    MUSTAPHA. Virtue constrained the priv-
    ilege I gave.
Shall I for sacred virtue pardon crave?   165
    SOLYMAN. I envy not the conquests of thy
    sword:
        Thrive still in wicked war;
But, slave, how did'st thou dare,
In virtuous love, thus to transcend thy lord?
Thou did'st thy utmost virtue show: 170
        Yet somewhat more does rest,
        Not yet by thee expressed,
Which virtue left for me to do.
Thou great example of a Christian wife,
Enjoy thy lord, and give him happy life.   175
        Thy galleys with their freight,
        For which the hungry wait,
Shall straight to Rhodes conducted be;
And as thy passage to him shall be free,
So both m[a]y safe return to Sicily.   180
    IANTHE. May Solyman be ever far
From impious honors of the war;
Since worthy to receive renown
From things repaired, not overthrown.
And when in peace his virtue thrives,   185
Let all the race of loyal wives
Sing this, his bounty, to his glory,
And teach their princes by his story:
Of which, if any victors be,
Let them, because he conquered me,   190
Strip cheerfully each other's brow,
And at his feet their laurel throw.
    SOLYMAN. Straight to the port her galleys
    steer;
Then hail the sentry at the pier.
And though our flags ne'er use to bow,   195
They shall do virtue homage now.
Give fire [1] still as she passes by,
And let our streamers lower fly.
            Exeunt several ways

            CHORUS OF WOMEN

1. Let us live, live! for being dead,
        The pretty spots,   200
        Ribbands and knots,
    And the fine French dress for the head
        No lady wears upon her
        In the cold, cold bed of honor.

[1] Apparently means that a salute is to be fired in
Ianthe's honor as she sails into the harbor of Rhodes.

Beat down our grottoes, and hew down our bowers,
Dig up our arbors, and root up our flowers. 206
Our gardens are bulwarks and bastions become:
Then hang up our lutes, we must sing to the drum.

2.   Our patches and our curls
            (So exact in each station)   210
        Our powders and our purls [2]
        Are now out of fashion.
Hence with our needles, and give us your spades;
We, that were ladies, grow coarse as our maids.
Our coaches have drove us to balls at the court, 215
We now must drive barrows to earth up the port.

    The End of the Second Entry

*The further part of the scene is opened,[3] and a
royal pavilion appears displayed, representing* SOLYMAN'S *imperial throne; and
about it are discerned the quarters of his
bassas and inferior officers.*

*The Entry is again prepared by instrumental
music.*

            THE THIRD ENTRY

    Enter SOLYMAN, PIRRHUS, MUSTAPHA
    SOLYMAN. Pirrhus, draw up our army wide!
Then from the gross [4] two strong reserves di-
    vide;
        And spread the wings,
        As if we were to fight
        In the lost Rhodians' sight   5
        With all the western kings!
Each wing with janizaries line;
The right and left to Haly's sons assign,
The gross to Zangiban.
        The main artillery   10
        With Mustapha shall be.
Bring thou the rear, we lead the van.
    PIRRHUS. It shall be done as early as the
    dawn,
As if the figure by thy hand were drawn.
    MUSTAPHA. We wish that we to ease thee,
    could prevent [5]   15
All thy commands by guessing thy intent.
    SOLYMAN. These Rhodians, who of honor
    boast,
A loss excuse when bravely lost.

[2] "An embroidered and puckered border." (Johnson's
Dictionary.)
[3] That is, the back stage was revealed by drawing
apart the two "shutters" on which the background
for Entry Two was painted.
[4] Main body.
[5] Anticipate.

THE SIEGE OF RHODES

Now they may bravely lose their Rhodes,
Which never played against such odds. 20
Tomorrow let them see our strength and weep
    Whilst they their want of losing blame;
Their valiant folly strives too long to keep
What might be rendered without shame.
  PIRRHUS. 'Tis well our valiant prophet did
    In us not only loss forbid, 26
    But has enjoined us still to get.
    Empire must move apace
    When she begins the race,
And apter is for wings than feet. 30
  MUSTAPHA. They vainly interrupt our speed,
    And civil [1] reason lack,
    To know they should go back
When we determine to proceed.
  PIRRHUS. When to all Rhodes our army does appear 35
    Shall we then make a sudden halt,
    And give a general assault?
  SOLYMAN. Pirrhus, not yet, Ianthe being there:
Let them our valor by our mercy prize.
    The respite of this day 40
    To virtuous love shall pay
A debt long due for all my victories.
  MUSTAPHA. If virtuous beauty can attain such grace
    Whilst she a captive was, and hid,
    What wisdom can his love forbid 45
When virtue's free, and beauty shows her face?
  SOLYMAN. Dispatch a trumpet [2] to the town;
    Summon Ianthe to be gone
    Safe with her lord. When both are free
    And in their course to Sicily, 50
    Then Rhodes shall for that valor mourn
    Which stops the haste of our return.
  PIRRHUS. Those that in Grecian quarries wrought,
    And pioneers [3] from Lycia brought,
    Who like a nation in a throng appear, 55
So great their number is, are landed here.
Where shall they work?
  SOLYMAN.   Upon Philermus Hill. [4]
There, ere this moon her circle fills with days,
They shall, by punished sloth and cherished skill,
    A spacious palace in a castle raise, 60

A neighborhood [5] within the Rhodians' view;
Where, if my anger can not them subdue,
My patience shall out-wait them, whilst they long
Attend [6] to see weak princes make them strong.
There I'll grow old, and die, too, if they have
The secret art to fast me to my grave. 66
                            Exeunt

The Scene is changed to that of the town besieged.

  Enter VILLERIUS, ADMIRAL, ALPHONSO, IANTHE

  VILLERIUS. When we, Ianthe, would this act commend,
    We know no more how to begin
    Than we should do, if we were in,
    How suddenly to make an end. 70
  ADMIRAL. What love was yours which these strong bars of fate
    Were all too weak to separate?
    Which seas and storms could not divide,
    Nor all the dreadful Turkish pride?
Which passed secure, though not unseen, 75
Even double guards of death that lay between.
  VILLERIUS. What more could honor for fair virtue do?
What could Alphonso venture more for you?
  ADMIRAL. With wonder and with shame we must confess,
All we ourselves can do for Rhodes, is less. 80
  VILLERIUS. Nor did your love and courage act alone,
Your bounty, too, has no less wonders done.
And for our guard you have brought wisely down
A troop of virtues to defend the town.
The only troop that can a town defend, 85
Which Heaven before for ruin did intend.
  ADMIRAL. Look here, ye western monarchs, look with shame,
Who fear not a remote, though common, foe;
The cabinet of one illustrious dame
Does more than your exchequers joined did do.
  ALPHONSO. Indeed I think, Ianthe, few 91
    So young and flourishing as you,
    Whose beauties might so well adorn
    The jewels which by them are worn,
    Did ever muskets for them take, 95
    Nor of their pearls did bullets make.

---

[1] Civic.
[2] Trumpeter, frequently used as a messenger or herald.
[3] Solyman sent 60,000 pioneers to the siege.
[4] These are actual details of the siege.
[5] A vicinity.
[6] Wait.

IANTHE. When you, my Lord, are shut up
    here,
        Expense of treasure must appear
        So far from bounty, that, alas!
        It covetous advantage was;   100
        For with small cost I sought to save
        Even all the treasure that I have.
Who would not all her trifling jewels give,
Which but from number can their worth derive,
If she could purchase or redeem with them 105
        One great inestimable gem?
    ADMIRAL. O ripe perfection in a breast so
    young!
    VILLERIUS. Virtue has tuned her heart,
    and wit her tongue.
    ADMIRAL. Though Rhodes no pleasure can
    allow,
I dare secure the safety of it now;   110
        All will so labor to save you
        As that will save the city, too.
    IANTHE. Alas! the utmost I have done
    More than a just reward has won,
If by my lord and you it be but thought   115
I had the care to serve him as I ought.
    VILLERIUS. Brave Duke, farewell, the
    scouts for orders wait,
        And the parade does fill.
    ALPHONSO. Great Master, I'll attend your
    pleasure straight,
        And strive to serve your will.   120
                Exeunt VILLERIUS, ADMIRAL
        Ianthe, after all this praise
        Which fame so fully to you pays,
        For that which all the world beside
        Admires you, I alone must chide. 124
        Are you that kind and virtuous wife,
        Who thus expose your husband's life?
        The hazards both at land and sea
        Through which so boldly thou hast run,
        Did more assault and threaten me   129
        Than all the Sultan could have done.
        Thy dangers, could I them have seen,
        Would not to me have dangers been,
        But certain death; now thou art here
        A danger worse than death I fear.
        Thou hast, Ianthe, honor won,   135
        But mine, alas, will be undone:
        For as thou valiant wert for me,
        I shall a coward grow for thee.
    IANTHE. Take heed, Alphonso, for this care
    of me
        Will to my fame injurious be;   140
        Your love will brighter by it shine,
        But it eclipses mine.

Since I would here before, or with, you fall,
Death needs but beckon when he means to
    call.
    ALPHONSO. Ianthe, even in his you shall
    command,   145
        And this, my strongest passion guide;
        Your virtue will not be denied;
It could even Solyman himself withstand,
        To whom it did so beauteous show
        It seemed to civilize a barb'rous foe. 150
        Of this your strange escape, Ianthe, say
        Briefly the motive and the way.
    IANTHE. Did I not tell you how we fought,
        How I was taken, and how brought
        Before great Solyman? but there   155
        I think we interrupted were.
    ALPHONSO. Yes, but we will not be so here,
        Should Solyman himself appear.
    IANTHE. It seems that what the bassa of
    me said,
Had some respect and admiration bred   160
In Solyman; and this to me increased
The jealousies which honor did suggest.
All that of Turks and tyrants I had heard,
But that I feared not death, I should have
    feared.
I, to excuse my voyage, urged my love   165
To your high worth; which did such pity
    move
That straight his usage did reclaim my fear.
He seemed in civil[1] France, and monarch
    there,
For soon my person, galley, freight were
    free
By his command.
    ALPHONSO.   O wondrous enemy!   170
    IANTHE. These are the smallest gifts his
    bounty knew.
    ALPHONSO. What could he give you more?
    IANTHE.   He gave me you;
And you may homewards now securely go
Through all his fleet.
    ALPHONSO.   But honor says not so.
    IANTHE. If that forbid it, you shall never
    see   175
        That I and that will disagree:
        Honor will speak the same to me.
    ALPHONSO. This Christian Turk amazes me,
    my dear!
        How long, Ianthe, stayed you there?
    IANTHE. Two days with Mustapha.
    ALPHONSO.   How do you say?   180
        Two days and two whole nights? Alas!

[1] Polite.

IANTHE. That it, my lord, no longer was,
   Is such a mercy as too long I stay
   Ere at the altar thanks to heaven I
      pay.
                              Exit IANTHE
ALPHONSO. To heaven, confession should
   prepare the way.   185
She is all harmony, and fair as light,
But brings me discord and the clouds of night.
And Solyman does think heaven's joys to be
In women not so fair as she.
'Tis strange! Dismiss so fair an enemy! 190
   She was his own by right of war,
We are his dogs,[1] and such as she, his angels are.
   O wondrous Turkish chastity!
   Her galleys, freight, and those to send
   Into a town which he would take!   195
   Are we besieged then by a friend?
   Could honor such a present make
   Then, when his honor is at stake?
   Against itself does honor booty play?
   We have the liberty to go away!   200
   Strange above miracle! But who can say,
If in his hands we once should be,
What would become of her? For what of me,
Though Love is blind, even Love may see.
Come back, my thoughts, you must not rove!
For sure Ianthe does Alphonso love!   206
O Solyman, this mystic act of thine
Does all my quiet undermine:
But on thy troops, if not on thee,   209
This sword my cure, and my revenge shall be.
                                    Exit

[*The Scene changes to* SOLYMAN'S *Camp.*]

   Enter ROXOLANA, PIRRHUS, RUSTAN
RUSTAN. You come from sea as Venus came
   before,
And seem that goddess, but mistake her shore.
   PIRRHUS. Her temple did in fruitful Cyprus
      stand;
The Sultan wonders why in Rhodes you land.
   RUSTAN. And by your sudden voyage he
      does fear   215
The tempest of your passion drove you here.
   ROXOLANA. Rustan, I bring more wonder
      than I find;

And it is more than humor bred that wind
   Which with a forward gale
   Did make me hither sail.   220
RUSTAN. He does your forward jealousy
   reprove.
ROXOLANA. Yet jealousy does spring from
   too much love;
   If mine be guilty of excess,
   I dare pronounce it shall grow less.
PIRRHUS. You boldly threaten more than
   we dare hear.   225
ROXOLANA. That which you call your duty
   is your fear.
RUSTAN. We have some valor or our
   wounds are feigned.
ROXOLANA. What has your valor from the
   Rhodians gained?
Unless Ianthe as a prize you boast,   229
Who now has got that heart which I have lost.
Brave conquest, where the taker's self is taken!
   And, as a present, I
   Bring vainly, ere I die,
That heart to him which he has now forsaken.
   RUSTAN. Whispers of eunuchs, and by
      pages brought   235
To Lycia, you have up to story wrought.
   ROXOLANA. Lead to the Sultan's tent!
      Pirrhus, away!
For I dare hear what he himself dares say.
                                    Exeunt

CHORUS

Of Men and Women

MEN. Ye wives all that are, and wives that
   would be,
   Unlearn all ye learn there, of one another,   240
   And all ye have learnt of an aunt or a
      mother:
Then straight hither come, a new pattern to
   see,
Which in a good humor kind fortune did
   send;
A glass for your minds, as well as your faces:
Make haste then and break your own looking-
   glasses;   245
If you see but yourselves, you'll never amend.
   WOMEN. You that would teach us what
      your wives ought to do,
Take heed: there's a pattern in town, too, for
   you.
   Be you but Alphonsos, and we
   Perhaps Ianthes will be.   250

---

[1] Christian "dogs" and Mohammedan "angels," alluding to the familiar noun used by the Mohammedans for the Christians, and to the houris, or beautiful women angels, supposed to be waiting the arrival of the faithful in Paradise.

MEN. Be you but Ianthes, and we
　　Alphonsos a while will be.
BOTH. Let both sides begin then, rather than neither;
Let's both join our hands, and both mend together.
　　　　　　　　　　　　　　Exeunt

End of the Third Entry

The Scene is varied to the prospect of Mount Philermus, artificers appearing at work about that castle which was there, with wonderful expedition, erected by SOLYMAN. *His great army is discovered in the plain below, drawn up in battalia,[1] as if it were prepared for a general assault*

The Entry is again prepared by instrumental music

THE FOURTH ENTRY

Enter SOLYMAN, PIRRHUS, MUSTAPHA

SOLYMAN. Refuse my passport,[2] and resolve to die
Only for fashion's sake, for company?
O costly scruples! But I'll try to be,
Thou stubborn honor, obstinate as thee.　4
My pow'r shalt thou not vanquish by thy will,
I will enforce to live whom thou would'st kill.
PIRRHUS. They in tomorrow's storm will change their mind;
Then, though too late instructed, they shall find
That those who your protection dare reject
No human power dares venture to protect.　10
They are not foes, but rebels, who withstand
The power that does their fate command.
SOLYMAN. O Mustapha, our strength we measure ill,
　　We want the half of what we think we have;
　　For we enjoy the beast-like power to kill,　15
　　But not the god-like power to save.
Who laughs at death, laughs at our highest power;
The valiant man is his own emperor.
MUSTAPHA. Your power to save, you have to them made known,　19
　　Who scorned it with ungrateful pride;

Now, how you can destroy must next be shown;
　　And that the Christian world has tried.
SOLYMAN. 'Tis such a single pair
　　As only equal are
Unto themselves; but many steps above　25
All others who attempt to make up love.
Their lives will noble history afford,
And must adorn my scepter, not my sword.
My strength in vain has with their virtue strove;
In vain their hate would overcome my love.　30
My favors I'll compel them to receive.
Go, Mustapha, and strictest orders give,
Through all the camp, that in assault they spare
(And in the sack of this presumptuous town)
The lives of these two strangers, with a care　35
Above the preservation of their own.
Alphonso has so oft his courage shown
That he to all but cowards must be known.
Ianthe is so fair that none can be
Mistaken, amongst thousands, which is she.　40
　　　　　　　　　　　　　　Exeunt

The Scene returns to that of the town besieged

Enter ALPHONSO, IANTHE

IANTHE. Alphonso, now the danger grows so near,
　　Give her that loves you leave to fear.
　　Nor do I blush this passion to confess,
　　Since it for object has no less
　　Than even your liberty or life;　45
　　I fear not as a woman, but a wife.
　　We were too proud no use to make
　　　Of Solyman's obliging proffer;
　　For why should honor scorn to take
　　　What honor's self does to it offer?　50
ALPHONSO. To be o'ercome by his victorious sword
　　Will comfort to our fall afford;
Our strength may yield to his; but 'tis not fit
　　Our virtue should to his submit;
　　In that, Ianthe, I must be　55
　　Advanced, and greater far than he.
IANTHE. Fighting with him who strives to be your friend,
You not with virtue but with power contend.
ALPHONSO. Forbid it. Heaven, our friends should think that we
Did merit friendship with an enemy.　60

---

[1] In battle array.
[2] Simply "permission of egress"; do not confuse with a modern passport.

IANTHE. He is a foe to Rhodes, and not to
    you.
ALPHONSO. In Rhodes besieged, we must be
    Rhodians too.
IANTHE. 'Twas Fortune that engaged you
    in this war.
ALPHONSO. 'Twas Providence! Heaven's
    pris'ners here we are.
IANTHE. That Providence our freedom does
    restore; 65
The hand that shut, now opens us the door.
    ALPHONSO. Had Heav'n that passport for
        our freedom sent,
It would have chose some better instrument
Than faithless Solyman.
    IANTHE.   O say not so!
To strike and wound the virtue of your foe 70
Is cruelty which war does not allow;
Sure he has better words deserved from you.
    ALPHONSO. From me, Ianthe, no;
What he deserves from you, you best must
    know.
    IANTHE. What means my Lord?
    ALPHONSO.   For I confess I must 75
The poisoned bounties of a foe mistrust:
And when upon the bait I look,
Though all seem fair, suspect the hook.
    IANTHE. He, though a foe, is generous and
        true;
What he hath done declares what he will do. 80
    ALPHONSO. He in two days your high es-
        teem has won;
What he would do I know; who knows what
    he has done?
Done? [*Aside*] Wicked tongue, what hast thou
    said?
What horrid falsehood from thee fled?
O jealousy (if jealousy it be) 85
Would I had here an asp instead of thee!
    IANTHE. Sure you are sick; your words,
        alas!
Gestures, and looks, distempers show.
    ALPHONSO. Ianthe, you may safely pass;
The pass, no doubt, was meant for you. 90
    IANTHE. He's jealous, sure. O virtue, can
        it be?
Have I for this served virtue faithfully?
Alphonso—
    ALPHONSO. Speak, Ianthe, and be free.
    IANTHE. Have I deserved this change?
    ALPHONSO.   Thou dost deserve
So much that emperors are proud to serve 95
    The fair Ianthe; and not dare
    To hurt a land while she is there.

Return, renowned Ianthe, safely home,
    And force thy passage with thine eyes;
    To conquer Rhodes will be a prize 100
Less glorious than by thee to be o'ercome.
But since he longs, it seems, so much to see,
    And be possessed of me,
Tell him, I shall not fly beyond his reach; 104
Would he could dare to meet me in the breach.
                                    Exit

IANTHE. Tell him! tell him? O no, Al-
    phonso, no.
Let never man thy weakness know;
    Thy sudden fall will be a shame
    To man's and virtue's name.
Alphonso's false! for what can falser be 110
Than to suspect that falsehood dwells in me?
Could Solyman both life and honor give?
And can Alphonso me of both deprive?
    Of both, Alphonso; for believe
    Ianthe will disdain to live 115
    So long as to let others see
    Thy true, and her imputed, infamy.
No more let lovers think they can possess
More than a month of happiness.
We thought our hold of it was strong 120
We thought our lease of it was long;
But now, that all may ever happy prove,
    Let never any love.
And yet these troubles of my love to me
Shall shorter than the pleasures be. 125
I'll till tomorrow last; then the assault
Shall finish my misfortune and his fault.
I to my enemies shall doubly owe
For saving me before, for killing now.
                                    Exit

Enter VILLERIUS, ADMIRAL

ADMIRAL. From out the camp a valiant
    Christian slave [1] 130
Escaped, and to our knights assurance gave
    That at the break of day
    Their mine will play.
VILLERIUS. Oft Martiningus [2] struck and
    tried the ground,
And counter-digged, and has the hollows
    found. 135
    We shall prevent
    Their dire intent.

[1] Again, an actual detail from Knolles.
[2] Gabriel Martiningus or Martinengo, a Cretan engineer skillfully sunk counter-mines to thwart the fifty-five mines sunk by the Turks, of which only two were successfully exploded. The Turks were the first to use gun-powder in mining operations at the siege of Malaga in 1487, and were much dreaded in consequence.

Where is the Duke, whose valor strikes to keep
Rhodes still awake, which else would dully
    sleep?
  ADMIRAL. His courage and his reason is
    o'erthrown.   140
  VILLERIUS. Thou sing'st the sad destruction
    of our town.
  ADMIRAL. I met him, wild as all the winds
        When in the ocean they contest;
        And diligent suspicion finds
        He is with jealousy possessed.   145
  VILLERIUS. That arrow, once misdrawn,
    must ever rove.
O weakness, sprung from mightiness of love!
        O pitied crime!
        Alphonso will be overthrown
        Unless we take this ladder down, 150
        Where, though the rounds are broke,
        He does himself provoke
            Too hastily to climb.
  ADMIRAL. Invisibly as dreams, fame's wings
        Fly everywhere;   155
Hov'ring all day o'er palaces of kings,
At night she lodges in the people's ear:
Already they perceive Alphonso wild,
And the belov'd Ianthe grieved.
  VILLERIUS. Let us no more by honor be
    beguiled;   160
This town can never be relieved;
Alphonso and Ianthe being lost,
Rhodes, thou dost cherish life with too much
    cost!
  CHORUS. Away, unchain the streets, un-
    earth the ports.[1]
        Pull down each barricade   165
        Which women's fears have made,
And bravely sally out from all the forts!
Drive back the crescents and advance the
    cross,
Or sink all human empire in our loss!
                                    [*Exeunt*]

            [SOLYMAN'S *Camp*]
    Enter ROXOLANA, PIRRHUS, RUSTAN, *and two
            of her Women*

  ROXOLANA. Not come to see me ere th'
    assault be past?   170
  PIRRHUS. He spoke it not in anger but in
    haste.
  RUSTAN. If mighty Solyman be angry
    grown,
It is not with his empress, but the town.

  [1] That is, the gates of the city had been stopped up
with earth as part of the fortifications.

  ROXOLANA. When stubborn Rhodes does
    him to anger move,
'Tis by detaining there what he does love. 175
  PIRRHUS. He is resolved the city to destroy.
  ROXOLANA. But more resolved Ianthe to
    enjoy.
  RUSTAN. T'avoid the danger cease your
    jealousy.
  ROXOLANA. Tell them of danger who do
    fear to die.
  PIRRHUS. None but yourself dares threaten
    you with death.   180
  FIRST WOMAN. Do not your beauty blast
    with your own breath.
  SECOND WOMAN. You lessen't in your own
    esteem
When of his love you jealous seem.
  FIRST WOMAN. And but a faded beauty
    make it
When you suspect he can forsake it.   185
  SECOND WOMAN. Believe not, Empress,
    that you are decayed,
For so you'll seem by jealous passion swayed.
  ROXOLANA. He follows passion, I pursue my
    reason;
He loves the traitor, and I hate the treason.

            Enter HALY

  HALY. Our foes appear! Th' assault will
    straight begin.   190
They sally out where we must enter in.
        PIRRHUS, RUSTAN *in* CHORUS [2]
  ROXOLANA. Let Solyman forget his way to
    glory,
Increase in conquest and grow less in story.
        That honor which in vain
        His valor shrinks to gain,   195
When from the Rhodians he Ianthe takes,
Is lost in losing me whom he forsakes.
                              Exeunt several ways

            Chorus of Wives
                    1
  FIRST WOMAN. This cursèd jealousy, what is't?
  SECOND WOMAN. 'Tis love that has lost itself
    in a mist.
  THIRD WOMAN. 'Tis love being frighted out of
    his wits.   200
  FOURTH WOMAN. 'Tis love that has a fever got,
    Love that is violently hot,
    But troubled with cold and trembling fits.
    'Tis yet a more unnatural evil:
  CHORUS. 'Tis the god of love, 'tis the god of
    love, possessed with a devil.   205

  [2] This stage direction seems to mean that Haly
Pirrhus, and Rustan sing these two lines together.

FIRST WOMAN. 'Tis rich corrupted wine of love,
  Which sharpest vinegar does prove.
SECOND WOMAN. From all the sweet flowers
  which might honey make,
    It does a deadly poison bring.
THIRD WOMAN. Strange serpent which itself
  doth sting!   210
FOURTH WOMAN. It never can sleep, and
  dreams still awake.
FIFTH WOMAN. It stuffs up the marriage-bed
  with thorns.
CHORUS. It gores itself, it gores itself, with
  imagined horns.

The End of the Fourth Entry

The Scene is changed into a representation of a general assault given to the town, the greatest fury of the army being discerned at the English station.

The Entry is again prepared by instrumental music.

THE FIFTH ENTRY

Enter PIRRHUS

PIRRHUS. Traverse the cannon [1] Mount the
  batt'ries higher!
More gabions,[2] and renew the blinds!
    Like dust they powder spend,
    And to our faces send
The heat of all the element of fire,[3]   5
And to their backs have all the winds.

Enter MUSTAPHA

MUSTAPHA. More ladders, and reliefs [4] to
  scale!
The fire-crooks [5] are too short! Help, help to
  hale!
The battlement is loose, and straight will
  down!
    Point well the cannon, and play fast!   10
    Their fury is too hot to last.
That rampire [6] shakes, they fly into the town.

[1] Turn or point the guns.
[2] Gabions are cylindrical wicker baskets filled with earth and used for fortifying. Blinds are movable structures used as a protection against enemy fire.
[3] Fire so hot that it seems to be the very element of fire itself.
[4] Relieving soldiers, or soldiers from the reserve, to scale the walls.
[5] Firehooks to pull down buildings.
[6] Rampart.

PIRRHUS. March up with those reserves to
  that redoubt!
    Faint slaves! the janizaries [7] reel!
    They bend, they bend! and seem to feel
      The terrors of a rout.   16
MUSTAPHA. Old Zanger halts, and re-enforcement lacks!
PIRRHUS. March on!
MUSTAPHA.   Advance those pikes,[8] and
  charge their backs!

Enter SOLYMAN

SOLYMAN. Those platforms are too low to
  reach!
Haste, haste! call Haly to the breach!   20
Can my domestic janizaries fly!
And not adventure life for victory!
Whose childhood with my palace milk I fed;
Their youth, as if I were their parent, bred.
What is this monster Death that our poor
  slaves,   25
Still vext with toil, are loath to rest in graves?
MUSTAPHA. If life so precious be, why do
  not they,
Who in war's trade can only live by prey,
    Their own afflicted lives expose
    To take the happier from their foes?   30
PIRRHUS. Our troops renew the fight!
    And those that sallied out
      To give the rout
    Are now returned in flight!
SOLYMAN. Follow, follow, follow, make good
  the line!   35
In, Pirrhus, in! Look, we have sprung the
  mine!
                              Exit PIRRHUS
MUSTAPHA. Those desp'rate English ne'er
  will fly!
Their firmness still does hinder others' flight,
    As if their mistresses were by
To see and praise them whilst they fight.   40
SOLYMAN. That flame of valor in Alphonso's eyes
Outshines the light of all my victories!
Those who were slain when they his bulwark
  stormed,
    Contented, fell,
    As vanquished well;   45
Those who were left alive may now,

[7] The janizaries were a crack corps of Christian soldiers, torn from their parents as children, compelled to embrace the Mohammedan faith, and trained at the palace of the Sultan.
[8] Soldiers armed with pikes.

Because their valor is by his reformed,
    Hope to make others bow.
  MUSTAPHA. Ere while I in the English station saw
Beauty, that did my wonder forward draw, 50
Whose valor did my forces back disperse;
Fairer than woman, and than man more fierce;
It showed such courage as disdained to yield,
And yet seemed willing to be killed.
  SOLYMAN. This vision did to me appear, 55
    Which moved my pity and my fear:
It had a dress much like the imag'ry
For heroes drawn, and may Ianthe be.

    Enter PIRRHUS

  PIRRHUS. Fall on! the English stoop [1] when they give fire!
They seem to furl their colors and retire! 60
  SOLYMAN. Advance! I only would the honor have
To conquer two, whom I by force would save.
                          [*Exeunt*]

    Enter ALPHONSO *with his sword drawn*

  ALPHONSO. My reason by my courage is misled!
Why chase I those who would from dying fly,
Enforcing them to sleep amongst the dead, 65
Yet keep myself unslain that fain would die?
Do not the pris'ners whom we take declare
How Solyman proclaimed through all his host,
That they Ianthe's life and mine should spare?
Life ill preserved is worse than basely lost. 70
Mine by dispatch of war he will not take,
But means to leave it ling'ring on the rack,
That in his palace I might live, and know
Her shame, and be afraid to call it so.
Tyrants and devils think all pleasures vain, 75
But what are still derived from others' pain.

    Enter ADMIRAL

  ADMIRAL. Renowned Alphonso, thou hast fought today
As if all Asia were thy valor's prey.
    But now thou must do more
    Than thou hast done before; 80
Else the important life of Rhodes is gone.
  ALPHONSO. Why from the peaceful grave
    Should I still strive to save
The lives of others, that would lose mine own?

---

[1] In l. 169 stoop means to swoop down upon. Here it seems to be used in its usual sense of crouch down.

  ADMIRAL. The soldiers call "Alphonso!"
    thou hast taught 85
The way to all the wonders they have wrought,
    Who now refuse to fight
    But in thy valor's sight.
  ALPHONSO. I would to none example be to fly,
But fain would teach all human kind to die. 90
  ADMIRAL. Haste, haste! Ianthe in disguise
    At th' English bulwark wounded lies;
And in the French our old great master strives
From many hands to rescue many lives.
  ALPHONSO. Ianthe wounded? where? alas!
    Has mourning pity hid her face? 96
Let pity fly, fly far from the oppressed,
Since she removes her lodging from my breast!
  ADMIRAL. You have but two great cruelties to choose
By staying here: you must Ianthe lose 100
    Who ventured life and fame for you;
    Or your great master quite forsake,
    Who to your childhood first did show
    The ways you did to honor take.
  ALPHONSO. Ianthe cannot be 105
    In safer company,
For what will not the valiant English do
When beauty is distressed, and virtue too?
  ADMIRAL. Dispatch your choice, if you will either save,
    Occasion bids you run; 110
    You must redeem the one
And I the other from a common grave.
    Alphonso, haste!
  ALPHONSO. Thou urgest me too fast.
This riddle is too sad and intricate— 115
The hardest that was e'er proposed by Fate.
    Honor and pity have
    Of both too short a time to choose!
    Honor the one would save,
    Pity would not the other lose. 120
  ADMIRAL. Away, brave Duke, away!
    Both perish by our stay.
  ALPHONSO. I to my noble master owe
    All that my youth did nobly do.
    He in war's school my master was, 125
    The ruler of my life;
    She my loved mistress, but, alas,
    My now suspected wife.
  ADMIRAL. By this delay we both of them forsake!
Which of their rescues wilt thou undertake?
  ALPHONSO. Hence, Admiral, and to thy master hie! 131
I will as swiftly to my mistress fly

Through ambush, fire, and all impediments
The witty [1] cruelty of war invents,
For there does yet some taste of kindness last,
Still relishing the virtue that is past.   136
But how, Ianthe, can my sword successful prove,
Where honor stops, and only pity leads my love?
Exeunt several ways

Enter PIRRHUS

PIRRHUS. O sudden change! repulsed in all the heat
Of victory, and forced to lose retreat!   140
Seven crescents,[2] fixed on their redoubts, are gone!
    Horse! horse! we fly
    From victory!
Wheel, wheel from their reserves, and charge our own!
    Divide that wing!   145
    More succor bring!
    Rally the fled,
    And quit our dead!
    Rescue that ensign and that drum!   149
Bold slaves! they to our trenches come,
Though still our army does in posture stay
Drawn up to judge, not act, the business of the day,
As Rome, in theaters, saw fencers play.

Enter MUSTAPHA

MUSTAPHA. Who can be loud enough to give command?
    Stand, Haly, make a stand!   155
Those horses to that carriage span![3] Drive, drive!
    Zanger is shot again, yet still alive!
Coyns for the culv'rin,[4] then give fire
To clear the turnpikes,[5] and let Zanger in!
Look, Pirrhus, look, they all begin   160
To alter their bold count'nance, and retire!
[*Exeunt*]

The Scene returns to that of the Castle on Mount Philermus

Enter SOLYMAN

SOLYMAN. How cowardly my num'rous slaves fall back,

[1] Inventive.
[2] Again, from Knolles.
[3] Hitch those horses to the gun carriage.
[4] A coyn is a wedge used for raising or lowering cannon. A culverin is a large cannon, very long in proportion to its bore.
[5] A turnpike is a revolving cheval-de-frise.

Slow to assault, but dext'rous when they sack!
    Wild wolves in times of peace they are:
    Tame sheep and harmless in the war.
Crowds fit to stop up breaches, and prevail
But so as shoals of herring choke a whale.   167
This dragon-duke so nimbly fought today
As if he wings had got to stoop at prey.
Ianthe is triumphant but not gone,   170
And sees Rhodes still beleaguered, though not won.
Audacious town! thou keep'st thy station still,
And so my castle tarries on that hill,
Where I will dwell till famine enter thee,
And prove more fatal than my sword could be.
Nor shall Ianthe from my favors run,   176
But stay to meet and praise what she did shun.
Exit

The Scene is changed to that of the town besieged.

Enter VILLERIUS, ADMIRAL, IANTHE
She is in a night-gown [6] and a chair is brought in.
  VILLERIUS. Fair virtue, we have found
    No danger in your wound.
    Securely live,   180
    And credit give
    To us, and to the surgeon's art.
  IANTHE. Alas! my wound is in the heart,
    Or else, where'er it be,
    Imprisoned life it comes to free,   185
By seconding a worser wound that hid doth lie.
    What practice can assure
    That patient of a cure,
Whose kind of grief still makes her doubt the remedy?
  ADMIRAL. The wounded that would soon be eased   190
Should keep their spirits tuned and pleased;
    No discords should their mind subdue;
    And who in such distress
    As this ought to express
More joyful harmony than you?   195
'Tis not alone that we assure
    Your certain cure,
But pray remember that your blood's expense
    Was in defence
Of Rhodes, which gained today a most important victory,   200
    For our success, repelling this assault,
    Has taught the Ottomans to halt,
Who may, wasting their heavy body, learn to fly.

[6] Dressing-gown.

[VILLERIUS.][1] Not only this should hasten
  your content,
But you shall joy to know the instrument 205
  That wrought the triumph of this day;
Alphonso did the sally sway,
To whom our Rhodes all that she is does owe,
And all that from her root of hope can grow.
  IANTHE. Has he so greatly done? 210
    Indeed he used to run
As swift in Honor's race as any he
Who thinks he merits wreaths for victory.
This is to all a comfort, and should be,
If he were kind, the greatest joy to me, 215
Where is my altered lord? I cannot tell
If I may ask, if he be safe and well?
For whilst all strangers may his actions boast,
    Who in their songs repeat
    The triumphs he does get, 220
I only must lament his favors lost.
  VILLERIUS. Some wounds he has; none desperate but yours;
Ianthe cured, his own he quickly cures.
  IANTHE. If his be little, mine will soon grow less.
    Ay me! What sword 225
    Durst give my lord
Those wounds which now Ianthe cannot dress?
  ADMIRAL. Ianthe will rejoice when she [does] hear
How greater than himself he [did][2] appear
In rescue of her life; all acts were slight 230
And cold, even in our hottest fight,
    Compared to what he did,
When with death's vizard[3] she her beauty hid.
  VILLERIUS. Love urged his anger, till it made such haste
    And rushed so swiftly in, 235
    That scarcely he did begin
Ere we could say, the mighty work was past.
  IANTHE. All this for me? something he did for you,
    But when his sword begun,
    Much more it would have done 240
If he, alas! had thought Ianthe true.
  ADMIRAL. Be kind, Ianthe, and be well!
    It is too pitiful to tell
    What way of dying he expressed
    When he that letter read 245

[1] By an obvious misprint this speech is assigned to the Admiral in the original.
[2] Again by an obvious misprint, these verbs are reversed in the original.
[3] Visor. Ianthe had donned armor while fighting at the English station.

  You wrote before your wounds were dressed,
When you and we despaired you could recover;
    Then he was more than dead,
And much outwept a husband and a lover.

Enter ALPHONSO *wounded, led in by two Mutes*
  ALPHONSO. Tear up my wounds! I had a passion coarse 250
And rude enough to strengthen jealousy,
But want that more refined and quicker force
Which does out-wrestle nature when we die.
Turn to a tempest all my inward strife.
    Let it not last, 255
    But in a blast
Spend this infectious vapor, life!
  IANTHE. It is my lord! Enough of strength I feel
To bear me to him, or but let me kneel.
He bled for me when he achieved for you 260
This day's success; and much from me is due.
Let me but bless him for his victory,
And hasten to forgive him ere I die.
  ALPHONSO. Be not too rash, Ianthe, to forgive.
    Who knows but I ill use may make 265
    Of pardons which I could not take,
For they may move me to desire to live.
  IANTHE. If aught can make Ianthe worthy grow
Of having power of pard'ning you,
It is because she perfectly does know 270
    That no such power to her is due.
Who never can forget herself, since she
Unkindly did resent your jealousy.
A passion against which you nobly strove;
I know it was but over-cautious love. 275
  ALPHONSO. Accursèd crime! Oh, let it have no name
Till I recover blood to show my shame.
  IANTHE. Why stay we at such distance when we treat?
    As monarchs' children, making love
    By proxy, to each other move, 280
And by advice of tedious councils meet.
  ALPHONSO. Keep back, Ianthe, for my strength does fail
When on thy cheeks I see thy roses pale.
Draw all the curtains, and then lead her in;
Let me in darkness mourn away my sin. 285
    Exeunt

[SOLYMAN'S *Camp*]

Enter [SOLYMAN], ROXOLANA, *and women attendants*

SOLYMAN. Your looks express a triumph at our loss.
ROXOLANA. Can I forsake the crescent for the cross?
SOLYMAN. You wish my spreading crescent shrunk to less.
ROXOLANA. Sultan, I would not lose by your success.
SOLYMAN. You are a friend to the besiegers grown! 290
ROXOLANA. I wish your sword may thrive, Yet would not have you strive
To take Ianthe rather than the town.
SOLYMAN. Too much on wand'ring rumor you rely;
Your foolish women teach you jealousy. 295
FIRST WOMAN. We should too blindly confident appear,
If, when the empress fears, we should not fear.
SECOND WOMAN. The camp does breed that loud report
Which wakens echo in the court.
FIRST WOMAN. The world our duty will approve, 300
If, for our mistress' sake,
We ever are awake
To watch the wand'rings of your love.
SOLYMAN. My war with Rhodes will never have success,
Till I at home, Roxana, make my peace. 305
I will be kind, if you'll grow wise;
Go, chide your whisp'rers and your spies,
Be satisfied with liberty to think,
And, when you should not see me, learn to wink.

[*Exeunt*]

CHORUS OF SOLDIERS

1

With a fine merry gale, 310
Fit to fill ev'ry sail,
They did cut the smooth sea
That our skins they might flea.[1]
Still as they landed, we firked[2] them with sallies;
We did bang their silk shashes,[3] 315
Through sands and through plashes[4]
Till amain they did run to their galleys.

[1] Flay.
[2] Trounced, whipped.
[3] Mohammedan soldiers, particularly the janizaries, wore a silk sash about the waist.
[4] Puddles.

2

They first were so mad
As they jealousies had
That our isle durst not stay, 320
But would float straight away;
For they landed still faster and faster:
And their old bassa, Pirrhus,
Did think he could fear us;
But himself sooner feared our Grand-Master. 325

3

Then the hug'ous[5] great Turk
Came to make us more work,
With enow[6] men to eat
All he meant to defeat;
Whose wonderful worship did confirm us 330
In the fear he would bide here
So long till he died here,
By the castle he built on Philermus.

4

You began the assault
With a very long halt; 335
And, as halting[7] ye came,
So ye went off as lame,
And have left our Alphonso to scoff ye.
To himself, as a dainty,
He keeps his Ianthe, 340
Whilst we drink good wine, and you drink but coffee.

The End of the Fifth Entry

The Curtain is let fall[8]

[5] Huge.
[6] Enough.
[7] Note the pun.
[8] The Second Part of *The Siege of Rhodes* is divided into acts and scenes. The events take place just before the surrender. The famine has become pressing; and the leaders of the army are discussing ways and means of defence, when popular clamor demands that Ianthe be sent to treat with Solyman. Alphonso naturally objects; the Admiral, who has fallen in love with Ianthe, is detailed by Villerius to restrain Alphonso. In Act Two popular clamor increases; Alphonso and the Admiral debate with Villerius the propriety of Ianthe's going to the Turkish camp. For Alphonso's sake that she may preserve his life, no less than for Rhodes, Ianthe is willing to make the attempt. In the camp of the Sultan, meanwhile, Roxolana is still afflicted with jealousy. In Act Three the Sultan detains Ianthe in Roxolana's tent; negotiations are begun with Rhodes; and Alphonso becomes restless and melancholy in Ianthe's absence. In the tent of Roxolana meanwhile, that lady grows furious at the presence of her rival. In Act Four a secret message from Roxolana to Alphonso has aroused all the latter's anxiety; and the leaders resolve that at no cost shall Ianthe be sacrificed to Solyman. In a long scene Roxolana, overcome by Ianthe's virtue, warns her mysteriously against Solyman's designs; Solyman enters and reassures Ianthe of his honorable purpose; and Roxolana con-

fesses to Solyman her fear that the succession of the throne will be denied her son. The Fifth Act opens with a distant view of the Grand-Master's palace on fire; the Rhodians sally out to rescue Ianthe and are defeated, and Alphonso is taken captive. Roxolana, at first repudiating her promises to protect Ianthe, relents and unites the lovers; and Solyman, moved by the general display of virtue, sends them both back to Rhodes on the pleasing condition that Ianthe shall determine the conditions of surrender. It is obvious that the Second Part departs more widely from the actual narrative of the siege than does the First Part.

FINIS

THE INDIAN QUEEN

BY SIR ROBERT HOWARD AND JOHN DRYDEN

(For the life of Dryden see the prefatory material to *All for Love*.)

Sir Robert Howard, who, said Langbaine, was "equally conspicuous for the lustre of his birth and the excellency of his parts," but of whose parts and birth Macaulay acidly remarked that the family was "wonderfully fertile of bad rhymers," was born in 1626, the sixth son of Thomas Howard, first Earl of Berkshire, and Elizabeth, his wife. He received a university education (we are not sure where); and, an ardent royalist, was knighted during the Civil Wars for bravery on the field of battle (1644). Imprisoned under the Commonwealth, Howard rose to prominence after the Restoration; and from 1661 till his death he was (except for a few years) a member of parliament, besides enjoying various lucrative offices. As he had become a Whig, the Revolution of 1688 did not disturb his public career, which, one is tempted to add, included three, and possibly four, marriages. He began his literary course with the publication of the *Poems* of 1660, which are without interest, although a comedy, *The Blind Lady*, was included in the volume. He achieved success, however, with *Foure New Plays* in 1665, of which one, *The Committee*, long held the stage by reason of its comic Irishman, Teague, and another is printed below. Dryden assisted him in writing *The Indian Queen*, but the brothers-in-law differed over theories of the drama, and the quarrel grew bitter with the publication of successive essays on either side. Howard's political prominence would, in any event, have made his works fair game for attack. *The Great Favourite; or, The Duke of Lerma* (1668) is the best constructed of his tragedies; and a rhymed satire, *The Duel of the Stags* (1668) is his only other important work if we except a number of historical works in prose. He died September 3, 1698, and was buried in Westminster Abbey. Howard is a type of the gifted amateur of the seventeenth century; a man, as Evelyn wrote, "pretending to all manner of arts and sciences" and enjoying a moderate talent for the stage, but, though "not ill-natured," one who was ever "insufferably boasting."

See the life of Sir Robert Howard in *The Dictionary of National Biography* by A. H. Bullen; and that prefixed to Carryl Nelson Thurber's edition of *The Committee* (*University of Illinois Studies in Language and Literature*, 1921) for brief accounts with further references.

HOWARD'S DRAMATIC WORKS

The Blind Lady (comedy—never acted), 1660.

The Surprisal (comedy) (T.R. April, 1662).

The Committee (comedy) (T.R. ca. Nov. 1662).

The Indian Queen (tragedy) (T.R. Jan. 1663/4) (with Dryden).

The Vestal Virgin (tragedy) (T.R. 1664?) (the last four published as *Foure New Plays*, 1665).

The Great Favourite; or, The Duke of Lerma (tragedy) (T.R. Feb. 1667/8), 1668 (reprinted with the four above as *Five New Plays*, 1692).

Although the age had tasted heroic drama ere Sir Robert and Mr. Dryden favored it with *The Indian Queen*, the pleasing spectacle of this play with its machines and extravagancies of costume assured the success of the venture, for 'twas "the richest," Mr. Evelyn said, "ever seen in England, or perhaps elsewhere upon a public stage." The wits of the age laid a variety of nations under contribution for the success of heroic drama: the plays of Beaumont and Fletcher, the classical tragedy and heroic romances of the French, the Italian opera and chivalric epic, Spanish drama, and the conventions of Platonic love. As Mr. Dryden wrote, "an heroic play ought to be an imitation, in little, of an heroic poem; and, consequently, . . . love and valour ought to be the subject of it." By "love and valour" genteel taste understood the conflict of the passion of love with the demands of heroic honor, in which conflict, as Mr. Dryden further observed, "all things [are] as far above ordinary proportion of the stage as that is beyond the common words and actions of human life." "An heroic poet," he said, "is not tied to a bare representation of what is true or exceeding probable." Rhyme is thus no true essential; yet from 1660 to 1680 some 42 of the species were written in heroic rhyme.

A later taste may complain that 'tis difficult to consider seriously the vast improbabilities of motive, the sudden shifts of fortune, the sounding rhetoric, and general implausibility of such pieces. It is to be regretted that we cannot behold them acted on the Restoration stage. Seen there, the sounding lines declaimed by actors trained in the school, to whom the attitudes and the language came easily, and embellished by ballets, marching armies, exotic costuming, expensive scenery, and "the frequent use of Drums and Trumpets," these pieces delighted the court, gave them fine sentiments, and let them forget the tedium of life.

What parts of *The Indian Queen* are to be assigned to the two authors it is impossible to say, but the nervous vigor of the verse contrasts sharply with the usual flatness of Sir Robert's poetry; and it is reasonable to believe that the two poets drew up the story together and wrote various scenes apart, but that Mr. Dryden revised the whole.

Montezuma, who "bears fortune to any side he pleases to espouse," is the type of many lover-warriors; and in Zempoalla, with whom Roxolana of *The Siege of Rhodes* may be compared, the dramatists portrayed the passionate and wicked lady whom Mr. Dryden was to show again as Nourmahal in *Aurung-Zebe*. The dramatists killed so many of the characters that only two are left alive with whom to begin the sequel of this play, *The Indian Emperor*, which Mr. Dryden wrote alone; but characters are slaughtered with little compunction in heroic drama. It is to be observed that there is no development in any character, and that for all the sounding lines, the motives of their actions are simple. Nevertheless, *The Indian Queen* is "good theater"; amid its clatter of couplets there are many shrewd maxims and striking sentences after the model of Seneca; and the fable is no more to be disbelieved than that of many modern mystery plays or moving pictures, especially if the latter, like *The Indian Queen*, are compounded of spectacle and movement.

This play was first produced at the Theater Royal in January, 1663/4.

For further discussion of the heroic play see John Dryden's "Essay of Heroick Plays" (1672) often reprinted; Chase, L. N., *The English Heroic Play* (1903); Child, C. G., "The Rise of the Heroic Play," *Modern Language Notes*, 1904, pp. 166–73; Poston, M. L., "The Origin of Heroic Plays," *Modern Language Review*, January, 1921; Pendlebury, B. J., *Dryden's Heroic Plays: A Study of their Origins* (1923).

THE INDIAN QUEEN

DRAMATIS PERSONÆ [1]

The Inca of Peru.
MONTEZUMA, *his General*.
ACACIS, *son to Zempoalla*.
TRAXALLA, *General to Zempoalla*.
GARUCCA, *a faithful subject to Amexia*.
The God of Dreams.
ISMERON, *one of their prophets, a conjuror*.
Officers and Soldiers.

Peruvians and Mexicans.
Priests

AMEXIA, *the lawful Queen of Mexico*.
ZEMPOALLA, *the usurping Indian Queen*.
ORAZIA, *daughter to the Inca*.
Attendants of Ladies.

PROLOGUE

As the music plays a soft air, the curtain rises slowly and discovers an INDIAN BOY *and* GIRL *sleeping under two plantain-trees; and, when the curtain is almost up, the music turns into a tune expressing an alarm, at which the* BOY *wakes and speaks.*

BOY. Wake, wake, Quevira! our soft rest must cease,
And fly together with our country's peace!
No more must we sleep under the plantain shade,
Which neither heat could pierce, nor cold invade;
Where bounteous nature never feels decay, 5
And opening buds drive falling fruits away.
  QUEVIRA. Why should men quarrel here, where all possess
As much as they can hope for by success?—
None can have most, where nature is so kind,
As to exceed man's use, though not his mind. 10
  BOY. By ancient prophecies we have been told,
Our world shall be subdued by one more old;
And, see, that world already's hither come.
  QUEVIRA. If these be they, we welcome then our doom!
Their looks are such that mercy flows from thence, 15
More gentle than our native innocence.
  BOY. Why should we then fear these are enemies,
That rather seem to us like deities?

  QUEVIRA. By their protection let us beg to live;
They came not here to conquer, but forgive.— 20
If so, your goodness may your power express,
And we shall judge both best by our success.

THE INDIAN QUEEN

ACT I

SCENE I

Enter INCA, ORAZIA, MONTEZUMA, ACACIS, PRISONERS, *with* PERUVIANS

  INCA. Thrice have the Mexicans before us fled,
Their armies broke, their prince in triumph led;
Both to thy valor, brave young man, we owe;
Ask thy reward, but such as it may show
It is a king thou hast obliged, whose mind 5
Is large, and, like his fortune, unconfined.
  MONTEZUMA. Young, and a stranger, to your court I came,
There, by your favor, raised to what I am;
I conquer but in right of your great fate,
And so your arms, not mine, are fortunate. 10
  INCA. I am impatient till this debt be paid
Which still increases on me while delayed;
A bounteous monarch to himself is kind.
Ask such a gift as may forever bind
Thy service to my empire and to me. 15
  MONTEZUMA. [*Aside*] What can this gift he bids me ask him be!
Perhaps he has perceived our mutual fires
And now, with ours, would crown his own desires;

---

[1] A list of the original cast seems not to have been preserved.

'Tis so, he sees my service is above
All other payments but his daughter's love. 20
  INCA. So quick to merit, and to take so slow?
I first prevent [1] small wishes, and bestow
This prince, his sword and fortunes, to thy hand;
He's thine unasked; now make thy free demand.
  MONTEZUMA. Here, prince, receive this sword, as only due   25
        (*Gives* ACACIS *his sword*)
To that excess of courage shown in you.—
When you, without demand, a prince bestow,
Less than a prince to ask of you were low.
  INCA. Then ask a kingdom; say where thou wilt reign.
  MONTEZUMA. I beg not empires, those my sword can gain;   30
But for my past and future service, too,
What I have done, and what I mean to do—
For this of Mexico which I have won,
And kingdoms I will conquer yet unknown—
I only ask from fair Orazia's eyes   35
To reap the fruits of all my victories.
  FIRST PERUVIAN. Our Inca's color mounts into his face.
  SECOND PERUVIAN. His looks speak death.
  INCA. Young man of unknown race,
Ask once again; so well thy merits plead,
Thou shalt not die for that which thou hast said;   40
The price of what thou ask'st, thou dost not know;
That gift's too high.
  MONTEZUMA. And all besides too low.
  INCA. Once more I bid thee ask.
  MONTEZUMA. Once more I make the same demand.
  INCA. The Inca bids thee take
Thy choice, what towns, what kingdoms thou wouldst have.   45
  MONTEZUMA. Thou giv'st me only what before I gave.
Give me thy daughter.
  INCA. Thou deserv'st to die.
O thou great author of our progeny,
Thou glorious sun, dost thou not blush to shine,
While such base blood attempts to mix with thine!   50
  MONTEZUMA. That sun thou speak'st of did not hide his face

[1] *Anticipate*, as often in this period.

When he beheld me conquering for his race.
  INCA. My fortunes gave thee thy success in fight!
Convey thy boasted valor from my sight;
I can o'ercome without thy feeble aid.   55
    Exeunt INCA, ORAZIA, *and* PERUVIANS
  MONTEZUMA. And is it thus my services are paid?
Not all his guards—
    (*Offers to go*, ACACIS *holds him*)
  ACACIS. Hold, sir.
  MONTEZUMA. Unhand me.
  ACACIS. No, I must your rage prevent
From doing what your reason would repent;
Like the vast seas, your mind no limits knows,   60
Like them, lies open to each wind that blows.
  MONTEZUMA. Can a revenge that is so just be ill?
  ACACIS. It is Orazia's father you would kill.
  MONTEZUMA. Orazia! how that name has charmed my sword!
  ACACIS. Compose these wild distempers in your breast;   65
Anger, like madness, is appeased by rest.
  MONTEZUMA. Bid children sleep, my spirits boil too high;
But, since Orazia's father must not die,
A nobler vengeance shall my actions guide:
I'll bear the conquest to the conquered side, 70
Until this Inca for my friendship sues,
And proffers what his pride does now refuse.
  ACACIS. Your honor is obliged to keep your trust.
  MONTEZUMA. He broke that bond in ceasing to be just.
  ACACIS. Subjects to kings should more obedience pay.   75
  MONTEZUMA. Subjects are bound, not strangers, to obey.
  ACACIS. Can you so little your Orazia prize,
To give the conquest to her enemies?
Can you so easily forego her sight?
I, that hold liberty more dear than light,   80
Yet to my freedom should my chains prefer,
And think it were well lost to stay with her.
  MONTEZUMA. (*Aside*) How unsuccessfully I still o'ercome!
I brought a rival, not a captive, home;
Yet I may be deceived; but 'tis too late   85
To clear those doubts, my stay brings certain fate.—
Come, prince, you shall to Mexico return,

Where your sad armies do your absence
　　mourn; [1]
And in one battle I will gain you more
Than I have made you lose in three before. 90
　ACACIS. No, Montezuma, though you
　　change your side,
I, as a prisoner, am by honor tied.
　MONTEZUMA. You are my prisoner, and I
　　set you free.
　ACACIS. 'Twere baseness to accept such
　　liberty.
　MONTEZUMA. From him that conquered
　　you it should be sought. 95
　ACACIS. No, but from him for whom my
　　conqueror fought.
　MONTEZUMA. Still you are mine, his gift
　　has made you so.
　ACACIS. He gave me to his general, not his
　　foe.
　MONTEZUMA. How poorly have you pleaded
　　honor's laws!
Yet shun the greatest in your country's
　　cause. 100
　ACACIS. What succor can the captive give
　　the free?
　MONTEZUMA. A needless captive is an
　　enemy.
In painted honor you would seem to shine;
But 'twould be clouded, were your wrongs
　　like mine.
　ACACIS. When choler such unbridled power
　　can have, 105
Thy virtue seems but thy revenge's slave;
If such injustice should my honor stain,
My aid would prove my nation's loss, not
　　gain.
　MONTEZUMA. Be cozened by thy guilty
　　honesty
To make thyself thy country's enemy. 110
　ACACIS. I do not mean in the next fight
　　to stain
My sword in blood of any Mexican,
But will be present in the fatal strife
To guard Orazia's and the Inca's life.
　MONTEZUMA. Orazia's life, fond man! First
　　guard thy own; 115
Her safety she must owe to me alone.
　ACACIS. Your sword, that does such won-
　　ders, cannot be
In an ill cause secure of victory.
　MONTEZUMA. Hark, hark!
　　　　　(*Noise of trampling*)

　ACACIS. What noise is this invades my
　　ear? [2]
Fly, Montezuma, fly! the guards are near; 120
To favor your retreat I'll freely pay
That life which you so frankly gave this
　　day.
　MONTEZUMA. I must retire; but those that
　　follow me
Pursue their deaths, and not their victory.
　　　　　　　　　　Exit MONTEZUMA
　ACACIS. Our quarrels kinder than our
　　friendships prove; 125
You for my country fight, I for your love.
　　　　Enter INCA *and Guards*
　INCA. I was to blame to leave this madman
　　free;
Perhaps he may revolt to the enemy,
Or stay and raise some fatal mutiny.
　ACACIS. Stop your pursuits, for they must
　　pass through me. 130
　INCA. Where is the slave?
　ACACIS.　　　　　　　Gone.
　INCA.　　　　　　　　Whither?
　ACACIS.　　　　　　　　O'er the plain;
Where he may soon the camp, or city,
　　gain.
　INCA. Curse on my dull neglect!
And yet I do less cause of wonder find
That he is gone than that thou stayest be-
　　hind. 135
　ACACIS. My treatment, since you took me,
　　was so free,
It wanted but the name of liberty.
I with less shame can still your captive live
Than take that freedom which you did not
　　give.
　INCA. Thou brave young man, that hast
　　thy years outdone 140
And, losing liberty, hast honor won,
I must myself thy honor's rival make,
And give that freedom which thou would'st
　　not take.
Go, and be safe—
　ACACIS.　　　　But that you may be so—
Your dangers must be past before I go. 145
Fierce Montezuma will for fight prepare,
And bend on you the fury of the war,
Which, by my presence, I will turn away,
If fortune gives my Mexicans the day.
　INCA. Come, then, we are alike to honor
　　just, 150
Thou to be trusted thus, and I to trust.
　　　　　　　　　　　　　Exeunt

---

[1] The original edition reads: "Where your sad Arms
does your absence mourn."

[2] *Ears* in the 1665 edition.

[SCENE II.—Mexico]

Enter ZEMPOALLA, TRAXALLA, *and attendants.*

ZEMPOALLA. O my Acacis!
Does not my grief, Traxalla, seem too rude,
Thus to press out before my gratitude
Has paid my debts to you?—yet it does move
My rage and grief to see those powers above
Punish such men as, if they be divine,   5
They know will most adore, and least repine.
  TRAXALLA. Those that can only mourn
     when they are crossed,
May lose themselves with grieving for the lost.
Rather to your retreated troops appear,
And let them see a woman void of fear;   10
The shame of that may call their spirits home.
Were the prince safe, we were not overcome,
Though we retired. O his too youthful heat,
That thrust him where the dangers are so
     great!
Heaven wanted power his person to protect   15
From that which he had courage to neglect;
But since he's lost, let us draw forth, and pay
His funeral rites in blood, that we are they
May in our fates perform his obsequies,
And make death triumph when Acacis dies. 20
  ZEMPOALLA. That courage thou hast shown
     in fight seems less
Than this, amidst despair to have excess;
Let thy great deeds force fate to change her
     mind;
He that courts fortune boldly makes her kind.
  TRAXALLA. If e'er Traxalla so successful
     proves,   25
May he then say he hopes as well as loves;
And that aspiring passion boldly own
Which gave my prince his fate, and you his
     throne?
I did not feel remorse to see his blood
Flow from the spring of life into a flood; 30
Nor did it look like treason, since to me
You were a sovereign much more great than
     he.
  ZEMPOALLA. He was my brother, yet I
     scorned to pay
Nature's mean debts, but threw those bonds
     away;
When his own issue did my hopes remove,   35
Not only from his empire, but his love,
You, that in all my wrongs then bore a part,
Now need not doubt a place within my heart.
I could not offer you my crown and bed
Till fame and envy with long time were
     dead;   40
But fortune now does happily present
Occasions fit to second my intent.
Your valor may regain the public love,
And make the people's choice their queen's
     approve.
                              (*Shout*)
Hark, hark! What noise is this that strikes
     my ear?   45
  TRAXALLA. 'Tis not a sound that should
     beget a fear;
Such shouts as these have I heard often fly
From conquering armies, crowned with vic-
     tory.
  ZEMPOALLA. Great god of vengeance, here
     I firmly vow,
Make but my Mexicans successful now,   50
And with a thousand feasts thy flames I'll
     feed;
And that[1] I take shall on thy altars bleed;
Princes themselves shall fall, and make thy
     shrine,
Dyed with their blood, in glorious blushes
     shine.

Enter Messenger

  TRAXALLA. How now!   55
What news is this that makes thy haste a
     flight?
  MESSENGER. Such as brings victory with-
     out a fight.
The prince Acacis lives—
  ZEMPOALLA.   Oh, I am blest!—
  MESSENGER. Reserve some joy till I have
     told the rest.
He's safe, and only wants his liberty.   60
But that great man that carries victory
Where'er he goes; that mighty man, by whom
In three set battles we were overcome;
Ill used (it seems) by his ungrateful king,
Does to our camp his fate and valor bring. 65
The troops gaze on him as if some bright star
Shot to their aids; call him the god of war,
Whilst he, as if all conquest did of right
Belong to him, bids them prepare to fight;
Which if they should delay one hour, he
     swears   70
He'll leave them to their dangers, or their
     fears
And shame, which is the ignoble coward's
     choice.
At this the army seemed to have one voice,
United in a shout, and called upon

---

[1] The Scott-Saintsbury edition suggests the substitution of *them* for *that*.

The god-like stranger, "Lead us, lead us
    on." 75
Make haste, great sir, lest you should come
    too late
To share with them in victory, or fate.
    ZEMPOALLA. My general, go; the gods be
    on our side;
Let valor act, but let discretion guide.
                    Exit TRAXALLA
Great god of vengeance, 80
I see thou dost begin to hear me now;
Make me thy offering if I break my vow.
                            Exeunt

ACT II

SCENE I

Enter INCA *and* ORAZIA, *as pursued in battle*

ORAZIA. O fly, sir, fly! Like torrents your
    swift foes
Come rolling on—
    INCA.   The gods can but destroy.
The noblest way to fly is that death shows;
I'll court her now, since victory's grown coy.
    ORAZIA. Death's winged to your pursuit,
    and yet you wait 5
To meet her—
    INCA.   Poor Orazia, time and fate
Must once o'ertake me, though I now should
    fly.
    ORAZIA. Do not meet death; but when it
    comes, then die.

Enter three Soldiers

THIRD SOLDIER. Stand, sir, and yield
    yourself, and that fair prey.
    INCA. You speak to one unpractised to
    obey. 10

Enter MONTEZUMA

MONTEZUMA. Hold, villains, hold, or your
    rude lives shall be
Lost in the midst of your own victory.
These have I hunted for;—nay, do not stare;
Be gone, and in the common plunder share.
                    Exeunt SOLDIERS
How different is my fate from theirs whose
    fame 15
From conquest grows! from conquest grows
    my shame.
    INCA. Why dost thou pause? thou canst
    not give me back,
With fruitless grief, what I enjoyed before.
No more than seas, repenting of a wrack,
Can with a calm our buried wealth restore. 20
    MONTEZUMA. 'Twere vain to own repent-
    ance, since I know
Thy scorn, which did my passions once despise,
Once more would make my swelling anger
    flow,
Which now ebbs lower than your miseries.
The gods, that in my fortunes were unkind, 25
Gave me not sceptres, nor such gilded things;
But whilst I wanted crowns, enlarged my
    mind
To despise sceptres and dispose of kings.
    INCA. Thou art but grown a rebel by suc-
    cess,
And I, that scorned Orazia should be
    tied 30
To thee, my slave, must now esteem thee less;
Rebellion is a greater guilt than pride.
    MONTEZUMA. Princes see others' faults, but
    not their own;
'Twas you that broke that bond and set me
    free;
Yet I attempted not to climb your throne 35
And raise myself, but level you to me.
    ORAZIA. O Montezuma, could thy love
    engage
Thy soul so little, or make banks so low
About thy heart, that thy revenge and rage,
Like sudden floods, so soon should overflow?
Ye gods, how much was I mistaken here! 41
I thought you gentle as the gall-less dove;
But you as humorsome as winds appear,
And subject to more passions than your love.
    MONTEZUMA. How have I been betrayed
    by guilty rage, 45
Which, like a flame, rose to so vast a height,
That nothing could resist, nor yet assuage,
Till it wrapt all things in one cruel fate.
But I'll redeem myself, and act such things,
That you shall blush Orazia was denied; 50
And yet make conquest, though with wearied
    wings,
Take a new flight to your now fainting side.
    INCA. Vain man, what foolish thoughts fill
    thy swelled mind!
It is too late our ruin to recall;
Those that have once great buildings un-
    dermined, 55
Will prove too weak to prop them in their
    fall.

Enter TRAXALLA, *with the former* Soldiers

FIRST SOLDIER. See, mighty sir, where the
    bold stranger stands,

Who snatched these glorious prisoners from
    our hands.
  TRAXALLA. 'Tis the great Inca; seize him
    as my prey,
To crown the triumphs of this glorious day. 60
  MONTEZUMA. Stay your bold hands from
    reaching at what's mine,
If any title springs from victory;
You safer may attempt to rob a shrine,
And hope forgiveness from the deity.

Enter ACACIS

  TRAXALLA. O my dear prince, my joys to
    see you live   65
Are more than all that victory can give.
  ACACIS. How are my best endeavors crossed
    by fate!
Else you had ne'er been lost, or found so late.
Hurried by the wild fury of the fight,
Far from your presence, and Orazia's sight, 70
I could not all that care and duty show
Which, as your captive, mighty prince, I owe.
  INCA. You often have preserved our lives
    this day,
And one small debt with many bounties pay.
But human actions hang on springs that be 75
Too small, or too remote, for us to see.
My glories freely I to yours resign,
And am your prisoner now, that once were
    mine.
  MONTEZUMA. These prisoners, sir, are mine
    by right of war;
And I'll maintain that right, if any dare. 80
  TRAXALLA. Yes, I would snatch them from
    thy weak defence,
But that due reverence which I owe my prince
Permits me not to quarrel in his sight;
To him I shall refer his general's right.
  MONTEZUMA. I knew too well what justice
    I should find   85
From an armed plaintiff, and a judge so kind.
  ACACIS. Unkindly urged, that I should use
    thee so;
Thy virtue is my rival, not my foe;
The prisoners fortune gave thee shall be thine.
  TRAXALLA. Would you so great a prize to
    him resign?   90
  ACACIS. Should he, who boldly for his prey
    designed
To dive the deepest under swelling tides,
Have the less title if he chance to find
The richest jewel that the ocean hides?
They are his due—   95
But in his virtue I repose that trust,

That he will be as kind as I am just.
Dispute not my commands, but go with
    haste,
Rally our men, they may pursue too fast,
And the disorders of the inviting prey   100
May turn again the fortune of the day.
                                Exit TRAXALLA
  MONTEZUMA. How gentle all this prince's
    actions be!
Virtue is calm in him, but rough in me.
  ACACIS. Can Montezuma place me in his
    breast?
  MONTEZUMA. My heart's not large enough
    for such a guest.   105
  ACACIS. See, Montezuma, see, Orazia weeps.
                             (ORAZIA *weeps*)
  MONTEZUMA. Acacis! is he deaf, or, waking,
    sleeps?
He does not hear me, sees me not, nor moves;
How firm his eyes are on Orazia fixed!
Gods, that take care of men, let not our loves
Become divided by their being mixed.   111
  ACACIS. Weep not, fair princess, nor be-
    lieve you are
A prisoner, subject to the chance of war;
Why should you waste the stock of those fair
    eyes,
That from mankind can take their liberties?
And you, great sir, think not a generous
    mind   116
To virtuous princes dares appear unkind
Because those princes are unfortunate,
Since over all men hangs a doubtful fate.
One gains by what another is bereft;   120
The frugal deities have only left
A common bank [1] of happiness below,
Maintained, like nature, by an ebb and flow.
                                      Exeunt

SCENE II

ZEMPOALLA *appears seated upon a throne,
  frowning upon her attendants; then comes
  down and speaks*

  ZEMPOALLA. No more, you that above your
    prince's dare proclaim
With your rebellious breath a stranger's name.
  FIRST PERUVIAN. Dread empress—
  ZEMPOALLA.   Slave, perhaps you
    grieve to see
Your young prince glorious, 'cause he sprang
    from me;

[1] *Bank* means a shelving elevation in the sea or the bed of a river, rising to or near the surface, as in Shakespeare's "*bank* and shoal of time."

THE INDIAN QUEEN

Had he been one of base Amexia's brood, 5
Your tongues, though silent now, had then been loud.

Enter TRAXALLA

Traxalla, welcome; welcomer to me
Than what thou bring'st, a crown and victory.
   TRAXALLA. All I have done is nothing; fluttering fame
Now tells no news but of the stranger's name 10
And his great deeds; 'tis he, they cry, by whom
Not men, but war itself, is overcome;
Who, bold with his success, dares think to have
A prince to wear his chains and be his slave.
   ZEMPOALLA. What prince? 15
   TRAXALLA. The great Peruvian Inca, that of late
In three set battles was so fortunate,
Till this strange man had power to turn the tide,
And carry conquest unto any side.
   ZEMPOALLA. Would you permit a private man to have 20
The great Peruvian Inca for his slave?
Shame to all princes! was it not just now
I made a sacred and a solemn vow
To offer up (if blest with victory)
The prisoners that were took? and they shall die. 25
   TRAXALLA. I soon had snatched from this proud stranger's hand
That too great object for his bold demand,
Had not the prince, your son, to whom I owe
A kind obedience, judged it should be so.
   ZEMPOALLA. I'll hear no more; go quickly, take my guards, 30
And from that man force those usurped rewards;
That prince, upon whose ruins I must rise,
Shall be the gods', but more, my sacrifice.
They, with my slaves, in triumph shall be tied,
While my devotion justifies my pride; 35
Those deities in whom I place my trust
Shall see, when they are kind, that I am just.
                                          Exit
   TRAXALLA. How gladly I obey!
There's something shoots from my enlivened frame,
Like a new soul, but yet without a name, 40
Nor can I tell what the bold guest will prove;
It must be envy, or it must be love:
Let it be either, 'tis the greatest bliss
For man to grant himself, all he dares wish;
For he that to himself himself denies 45
Proves meanly wretched, to be counted wise.
                                       Exit TRAXALLA

[SCENE III]

Enter MONTEZUMA *and* ACACIS

   ACACIS. You wrong me, my best friend, not [1]
to believe
Your kindness gives me joy; and when I grieve,
Unwillingly my sorrows I obey;
Showers sometimes fall upon a shining day.
   MONTEZUMA. Let me, then, share your griefs, that in your fate 5
Would have took part.
   ACACIS.   Why should you ask me that?
Those must be mine, though I have such excess;
Divided griefs increase, and not grow less.
   MONTEZUMA. It does not lessen fate, nor satisfy
The grave, 'tis true, when friends together die, 10
And yet they are unwilling to divide.
   ACACIS. To such a friend nothing can be denied.
You, when you hear my story, will forgive
My grief, and rather wonder that I live.
Unhappy in my title to a throne, 15
Since blood made way for my succession,
Blood of an uncle, too, a prince so free
From being cruel, it taught cruelty.
His queen Amexia then was big with child,
Nor was he gentler than his queen was mild; 20
Th' impatient people longed for what would come
From such a father, bred in such a womb;
When false Traxalla, weary to obey,
Took with his life their joys and hopes away.
Amexia, by the assistance of the night, 25
When this dark deed was acted, took her flight,
Only with true Garucca for her aid;
Since when, for all the searches that were made,
The queen was never heard of more. Yet still
This traitor lives, and prospers by the ill; 30
Nor does my mother seem to reign alone,
But with this monster shares the guilt and throne.

[1] *Nor* in 1665.

Horror chokes up my words; now you'll believe,
'Tis just I should do nothing else but grieve.
    MONTEZUMA. Excellent prince! 35
How great a proof of virtue have you shown,
To be concerned for griefs, though not your own!
    ACACIS. Pray, say no more.

    Enter a Messenger *hastily*

    MONTEZUMA. How now, whither so fast?
    MESSENGER. O sir, I come too slow with all my haste!
The fair Orazia—
    MONTEZUMA. Ha, what dost thou say?
    MESSENGER. Orazia with the Inca's forced away 41
Out of your tent; Traxalla, at the head
Of the rude soldiers, forced the door, and led
Those glorious captives, who on thrones once shined,
To grace the triumph that is now designed. 45
    Exit
    MONTEZUMA. Orazia forced away!—what tempests roll
About my thoughts, and toss my troubled soul!
Can there be gods to see, and suffer this?
Or does mankind make his own fate or bliss,
While every good and bad happens by chance,
Not from their orders, but from ignorance?—
But I will pull a ruin on them all, 52
And turn their triumph to a funeral.
    ACACIS. Be temperate, friend.
    MONTEZUMA. You may as well advise
That I should have less love, as grow more wise. 55
    ACACIS. Yet stay—I did not think to have revealed
A secret which my heart has still concealed;
But, in this cause since I must share with you,
'Tis fit you know—I love Orazia, too!
Delay not then, nor waste the time in words,
Orazia's cause calls only for our swords. 61
    MONTEZUMA. That ties my hand, and turns from thee that rage
Another way, thy blood should else assuage;
The storm on our proud foes shall higher rise,
And, changing, gather blackness as it flies; 65
So, when winds turn, the wandering waves obey,
And all the tempest rolls another way.
    ACACIS. Draw then a rival's sword, as I draw mine,
And, like friends suddenly to part, let's join
In this one act, to seek one destiny; 70
Rivals with honor may together die.
    Exeunt

ACT III

SCENE I

ZEMPOALLA *appears seated upon her* Slaves *in triumph, and the* Indians, *as to celebrate the victory, advance in a warlike dance; in the midst of which triumph,* ACACIS *and* MONTEZUMA *fall in upon them*

ZEMPOALLA *descends from her triumphant throne, and* ACACIS *and* MONTEZUMA *are brought in before her*

    ZEMPOALLA. Shame of my blood, and traitor to thy own,
Born to dishonor, not command, a throne!
Hast thou, with envious eyes, my triumph seen?
Or couldst not see thy mother in the queen?
Couldst thou a stranger above me prefer? 5
    ACACIS. It was my honor made my duty err;
I could not see his prisoners forced away,
To whom I owed my life, and you, the day.
    ZEMPOALLA. Is that young man the warrior so renowned?
    MONTEZUMA. Yes, he that made thy men thrice quit their ground. 10
Do, smile at Montezuma's chains; but know,
His valor gave thee power to use him so.
    TRAXALLA. Grant that it did, what can his merits be
That sought his vengeance, not our victory?
What has thy brutish fury gained us more 15
Than only healed the wounds it gave before?
Die then, for, whilst thou liv'st, wars cannot cease;
Thou mayst bring victory, but never peace.
Like a black storm thou roll'st about us all,
Even to thyself unquiet, till thy fall. 20
    (*Draws to kill him*)
    ACACIS. Unthankful villain, hold!
    TRAXALLA. You must not give him succor, sir.
    ACACIS. Why, then, I must not live.
Posterity shall ne'er report they had
Such thankless fathers, or a prince so bad.
    ZEMPOALLA. You're both too bold to will or to deny: 25

On me alone depends his destiny.
Tell me, audacious stranger, whence could rise
The confidence of this rash enterprise?
    MONTEZUMA. First tell me how you dared
      to force from me
The fairest spoils of my own victory?   30
    ZEMPOALLA. Kill him—hold, must he die?—
      why, let him die;—
Whence should proceed this strange diversity
In my resolves?
Does he command in chains? What would he
    do,
Proud slave, if he were free, and I were so?   35
But is he bound, ye gods, or am I free?
'Tis love, 'tis love, that thus disorder me.
How pride and love tear my divided soul!
For each too narrow, yet both claim it whole;
Love, as the younger, must be forced away.—
Hence with the captives, general, and convey
To several prisons that—young man, and
    this—   42
Peruvian woman.
    TRAXALLA   How concerned she is!
I must know more.
    MONTEZUMA.   Fair princess, why should I
Involve that sweetness in my destiny?   45
I could out-brave my death, were I alone
To suffer, but my fate must pull yours on.
My breast is armed against all sense of fear;
But where your image lies, 'tis tender there.
    INCA. Forbear thy saucy love, she cannot
      be   50
So low but still she is too high for thee.
    ZEMPOALLA. Be gone, and do as I command:
      away!
    MONTEZUMA. I ne'er was truly wretched till
      this day.
    ORAZIA. Think half your sorrows on Orazia
      fall,
And be not so unkind to suffer all;   55
Patience in cowards is tame, hopeless fear,
But in brave minds, a scorn of what they bear.
      [*Exeunt*] INCA, MONTEZUMA,
        ORAZIA, *and* TRAXALLA
    ZEMPOALLA. What grief is this which in your
      face appears?
    ACACIS. The badge of sorrow which my soul
      still wears.
    ZEMPOALLA. Though thy late actions did
      my anger move,   60
It cannot rob thee of a mother's love.
Why shouldst thou grieve?
Grief seldom joined with blooming youth is
    seen.

Can sorrow be where knowledge scarce has
    been?
Fortune does well for heedless youth provide,
But wisdom does unlucky age misguide;   66
Cares are the train of present power and
    state,
But hope lives best that on himself does wait.
O happiest fortune if well understood,
The certain prospect of a future good!   70
    ACACIS. What joy can empire bring me,
      when I know
That all my greatness to your crimes I owe?
    ZEMPOALLA. Yours be the joy, be mine the
      punishment.
    ACACIS. In vain, alas, that wish to heaven
      is sent
For me, if fair Orazia must not live.   75
    ZEMPOALLA. Why should you ask me what
      I cannot give?
She must be sacrificed. Can I bestow
What to the gods, by former vows, I owe?
    ACACIS. O plead not vows; I wish you had
      not shown
You slighted all things sacred for a throne.   80
    ZEMPOALLA. I love thee so, that though fear
      follows still,
And horror urges, all that have been ill,
I could for thee
Act o'er my crimes again, and not repent,
Even when I bore the shame and punish-
    ment.   85
    ACACIS. Could you so many ill acts under-
      take,
And not perform one good one for my sake?
    ZEMPOALLA. Prudence permits not pity
      should be shown
To those that raised the war to shake my
    throne.
    ACACIS. As you are wise, permit me to be
      just;   90
What prudence will not venture, honor must:
We owe our conquest to the stranger's sword,
'Tis just his prisoners be to him restored.
I love Orazia, but a nobler way
Than for my love my honor to betray.   95
    ZEMPOALLA. Honor is but an itch in youth-
      ful blood,
Of doing acts extravagantly good;
We call that virtue which is only heat
That reigns in youth, till age finds out the
    cheat.
    ACACIS. Great actions first did her affections
      move,   100
And I. by greater, would regain her love.

ZEMPOALLA. Urge not a suit which I must still deny;
Orazia and her father both shall die.
Begone, I'll hear no more.
 ACACIS.   You stop your ears [1]—
But though a mother will not, heaven will hear.   105
Like you I vow, when to the powers divine
You pay her guiltless blood, I'll offer mine.
           Exit
 ZEMPOALLA. She dies, this happy rival that enjoys
The stranger's love and all my hopes destroys;
Had she triùmphed, what could she more have done   110
Than robbed the mother and enslaved the son?
Nor will I, at the name of cruel, stay.
Let dull successive monarchs [2] mildly sway;
Their conquering fathers did the laws forsake,
And broke the old ere they the new could make.   115
I must pursue my love; yet love, enjoyed,
Will, with esteem that caused it first, grow less;
But thirst and hunger fear not to be cloyed,
And when they be, are cured by their excess.

     Enter TRAXALLA

 TRAXALLA. [*Aside*] Now I shall see what thoughts her heart conceals;   120
For that which wisdom covers, love reveals.—
Madam, the prisoners are disposed.
 ZEMPOALLA.   They are?
And how fares our young blustering man of war?
Does he support his chains with patience yet?
 TRAXALLA. He and the princess, madam—
 ZEMPOALLA.   Are they met?   125
 TRAXALLA. No; but from whence is all this passion grown?
 ZEMPOALLA. 'Twas a mistake.
 TRAXALLA.   I find this rash unknown
Is dangerous; and, if not timely slain,
May plunge your empire in new wars again.
 ZEMPOALLA. Thank ye; I shall consider.
 TRAXALLA.   Is that all?
The army dote on him, already call   131
You cruel; and, for aught I know, they may
By force unchain, and crown him in a day.
 ZEMPOALLA. You say I have already had their curse
For his bad usage; should I use him worse? 135
 TRAXALLA. Yet once you feared his reputation might
Obscure the prince's in the people's sight.
 ZEMPOALLA. Time will inform us best what course to steer,
But let us not our sacred vows defer:
The Inca and his daughter both shall die. 140
 TRAXALLA. He suffers justly for the war; but why
Should she share his sad fate? A poor pretence,
That birth should make a crime of innocence.
 ZEMPOALLA. Yet we destroy the poisonous viper's young,
Not for themselves, but those from whom they sprung.   145
 TRAXALLA. O no, they die not for their parents' sake,
But for the poisonous seed which they partake.
Once more behold her, and then let her die,
If in that face or person you can see
But any place to fix a cruelty.   150
The heavens have clouds, and spots are in the moon,
But faultless beauty shines in her alone.
 ZEMPOALLA. Beauty has wrought compassion in your mind!
 TRAXALLA. And you to valor are become as kind.
To former services there's something due, 155
Yet be advised—
 ZEMPOALLA. Yes, by myself, not you.
 TRAXALLA. Princes are sacred.
 ZEMPOALLA.   True, whilst they are free;
But power once lost, farewell their sanctity.
'Tis power to which the gods their worship owe,
Which, uncontrolled, makes all things just below.   160
Thou dost the plea of saucy rebels use;
They will be judge of what their prince must choose;
Hard fate of monarchs, not allowed to know
When safe, but as their subjects tell them so.
Then princes but like public pageants move,
And seem to sway because they sit above. 166
           Exit
 TRAXALLA She loves him; in one moment this new guest

---

[1] So in the text, though the rhyme requires the singular.
[2] I.e., inheriting by succession, and therefore legitimate (Scott-Saintsbury).

Has drove me out from this false woman's
  breast;
They that would fetter love with constancy
Make bonds to chain themselves, but leave
  him free. 170
With what impatience I her falsehood bear!
Yet do myself that which I blame in her;
But interest in my own cause makes me see
That act unjust in her, but just in me.
                                    Exit

[SCENE II]

ISMERON *asleep in the scene.*—*Enter*
  ZEMPOALLA

ZEMPOALLA. Ho, Ismeron, Ismeron!
He stirs not; ha, in such a dismal cell
Can gentle sleep with his soft blessings dwell?
Must I feel tortures in a human breast,
While beasts and monsters can enjoy their
  rest? 5
What quiet they possess in sleep's calm bliss!
The lions cease to roar, the snakes to hiss,
While I am kept awake
Only to entertain my miseries.
Or if a slumber steal upon my eyes, 10
Some horrid dream my laboring soul benumbs,
And brings fate to me sooner than it comes.
Fears most oppress when sleep has seized
  upon
The outward parts and left the soul alone.
What envied blessings these cursed things
  enjoy! 15
Next to possess, 'tis pleasure to destroy.
Ismeron! ho, Ismeron, Ismeron! (*Stamps*)
  ISMERON. Who's that, [that] with so loud
    and fierce a call
Disturbs my rest?
  ZEMPOALLA.   She that has none at all,
Nor ever must, unless thy powerful art 20
Can charm the passions of a troubled heart.
  ISMERON. How can you have a discontented
    mind,
To whom the gods have lately been so kind?
  ZEMPOALLA. Their envious kindness how
    can I enjoy,
When they give blessings, and the use de-
  stroy? 25
  ISMERON. Dread empress, tell the cause of
    all your grief;
If art can help, be sure of quick relief.
  ZEMPOALLA. I dreamed before the altar
    that I led
A mighty lion in a twisted thread:
I shook to hold him in so slight a tie, 30
Yet had not power to seek a remedy,
When, in the midst of all my fears, a dove
With hovering wings descended from above,
Flew to the lion, and embraces spread
With wings like clasping arms about his
  head, 35
Making that murmuring noise that cooing
  doves
Use in the soft expression of their loves;
While I, fixed by my wonder gazed to see
So mild a creature with so fierce agree.
At last the gentle dove turned from his head,
And, pecking, tried to break the slender
  thread, 41
Which instantly she severed, and released
From that small bond the fierce and mighty
  beast,
Who presently turned all his rage on me,
And with his freedom brought my destiny. 45
  ISMERON. Dread empress, this strange vision
    you relate
Is big with wonder, and too full of fate,
Without the god's assistance, to expound.
In those low regions where sad night hangs
  round
The drowsy vaults, and where moist vapors
  steep 50
The god's dull brows, that sways the realm of
  sleep;
There all the informing elements repair,
Swift messengers of water, fire, and air,
To give account of actions, whence they came,
And how they govern every mortal frame; 55
How, from their various mixture or their
  strife,
Are known the calms and tempests of our life.
Thence souls, when sleep their bodies over-
  come,
Have some imperfect knowledge of their doom,
From those dark caves those powers shall
  straight appear; 60
Be not afraid, whatever shapes they wear.
  ZEMPOALLA. There's nothing thou canst
    raise can make me start;
A living form can only shake my heart.

  ISMERON. You twice ten hundred deities,
    To whom we daily sacrifice; 65
  You powers that dwell with fate below,
  And see what men are doomed to do,
  Where elements in discord dwell;
  Thou god of sleep, arise and tell
  Great Zempoalla what strange fate 70
  Must on her dismal vision wait.

ZEMPOALLA. How slow these spirits are!
   Call, make them rise,
Or they shall fast from flame and sacrifice.
   ISMERON. Great empress,
Let not your rage offend what we adore, 75
And vainly threaten when we must implore.
Sit, and silently attend—
While my powerful charms I end.

   By the croaking of the toad
   In their caves that makes [1] abode, 80
   Earthy, dun, that pants for breath
   With her swelled sides full of death;
   By the crested adders' pride
   That along the cliffs do glide;
   By the visage fierce and black; 85
   By the death's-head on thy back;
   By the twisted serpents placed
   For a girdle round thy waist;
   By the hearts of gold that deck
   Thy breast, thy shoulders, and thy neck: 90
   From thy sleepy mansion rise,
   And open thy unwilling eyes,
   While bubbling springs their music keep,
   That used to lull thee in thy sleep.

     (*God of Dreams rises*)
GOD. Seek not to know what must not be
   revealed; 95
Joys only flow where fate is most concealed:
Too busy man would find his sorrows more,
If future fortunes he should know before;
For, by that knowledge of his destiny,
He would not live at all, but always die. 100
Inquire not, then, who shall from bonds be
   freed,
Who 'tis shall wear a crown, and who shall
   bleed.
All must submit to their appointed doom;
Fate and misfortune will too quickly come.
Let me no more with powerful charms be
   prest; 105
I am forbid by fate to tell the rest.
     (*The god descends*)
   ZEMPOALLA. Stay, cozener, thou that hat'st
   clear truth like light,
And usest words dark as thy own dull night.
You tyrant gods, do you refuse to free
The soul you gave from its perplexity? 110
Why should we in your mercies still believe,
When you can never pity, though we grieve?
For you have bound yourselves by harsh de-
   crees,
And those, not you, are now the deities.
     (*Sits down sad*)

[1] *Make* in 1665.

ISMERON. She droops under the weight of
   rage and care. 115
You spirits that inhabit in the air,
With all your powerful charms of music try
To bring her soul back to its harmony.

   SONG *is supposed sung by aerial spirits*

Poor mortals that are clogged with earth below,
   Sink under love and care, 120
   While we that dwell in air,
Such heavy passions never know.
   Why then should mortals be
   Unwilling to be free
   From blood, that sullen cloud, 125
   Which shining souls does shroud?
   Then they'll show bright,
   And like us light,
When leaving bodies with their care,
   They slide to us and air. 130

   ZEMPOALLA. Death on these trifles! Can-
   not your art find
Some means to ease the passions of the
   mind?
Or, if you cannot give a lover rest,
Can you force love into a scornful breast?
   ISMERON. 'Tis reason only can make pas-
   sions less; 135
Art gives not new, but may the old, increase;
Nor can it alter love in any breast
That is with other flames before possessed.
   ZEMPOALLA. If this be all your slighted art
   can do,
I'll be a fate both to your gods and you; 140
I'll kindle other flames, since I must burn,
And all their temples into ashes turn.
   ISMERON. Great queen—
   ZEMPOALLA. If you would have this sen-
   tence stayed,
Summon their godheads quickly to your
   aid, 145
And presently compose a charm that may
Love's flames into the stranger's breast con-
   vey,
The captive stranger, he whose sword and
   eyes,
Where'er they strike, meet ready victories;
Make him but burn for me, in flames like
   mine, 150
Victims shall bleed, and feasted altars shine.
If not—
Down go your temples, and your gods shall
   see
They have small use of their divinity.
                              Exeunt

ACT IV

Scene I

The scene opens and discovers Montezuma *sleeping in prison. Enter* Traxalla *leading in* Orazia

Traxalla. Now take your choice, and bid him live or die;
To both show pity or show cruelty.
'Tis you that must condemn, I'll only act;
Your sentence is more cruel than my fact.
  Orazia. You are most cruel to disturb a mind   5
Which to approaching fate was so resigned.
  Traxalla. Reward my passions, and you'll quickly prove
There's none dare sacrifice what I dare love.—
Next to thee, stranger; wake and now resign
The bold pretences of thy love to mine,   10
Or in this fatal minute thou shalt find—
  Montezuma. Death, fool; in that thou mayst be just and kind:
'Twas I that loved Orazia, yet did raise
The storm in which she sinks. Why dost thou gaze,   14
Or stay thy hand from giving that just stroke,
Which, rather than prevent, I would provoke?
When I am dead, Orazia may forgive;
She never must, if I dare wish to live.
  Orazia. Hold, hold—O Montezuma, can you be
So careless of yourself, but more of me?   20
Though you have brought me to this misery,
I blush to say I cannot see you die.
  Montezuma. Can my approaching fate such pity move?
The gods and you at once forgive and love.
  Traxalla. Fond fool, thus to mis-spend that little breath   25
I lent thee to prevent, not hasten, death!
Let her thank you she was unfortunate,
And you thank her for pulling on your fate;
Prove to each other your own destinies.
                                    (*Draws*)

Enter Zempoalla *hastily, and sets a dagger to* Orazia's *breast*

  Zempoalla. Hold, hold, Traxalla, or Orazia dies.—   30
Oh, is't Orazia's name that makes you stay?
'Tis her great power, not mine, that you obey!
Inhuman wretch, dar'st thou the murderer be
Of him that is not yet condemned by me?
  Traxalla. The wretch that gave you all the power you have   35
May venture sure to execute a slave,
And quench a flame your fondness would have burn,
Which may this city into ashes turn,
The nation in your guilty passion lost;
To me ungrateful, to your country most;   40
But this shall be their offering, I their priest.
  Zempoalla. The wounds thou giv'st I'll copy on her breast.
Strike, and I'll open here a spring of blood,
Shall add new rivers to the crimson flood.
How his pale looks are fixed on her!—'tis so.
Oh, does amazement on your spirit grow?   46
What, is your public [1] love Orazia's grown?
Couldst thou see mine, and yet not hide thy own?
Suppose I should strike first, would it not breed
Grief in your public heart to see her bleed?   50
  Traxalla. (*Aside*) She mocks my passions; in her sparkling eyes
Death, and a close dissembled fury lies.
I dare not trust her thus.—If she must die,
The way to her loved life through mine shall lie.
            (*He puts her by, and steps before* Orazia;
            and she runs before Montezuma)
  Zempoalla. And he that does this stranger's fate design   55
Must to his heart a passage force through mine.
  Traxalla. Can fair Orazia yet no pity have?
'Tis just she should her own preserver save.
  Zempoalla. Can Montezuma so ungrateful prove
To her that gave him life and offers love?   60
  Orazia. Can Montezuma live, and live to be
Just to another and unjust to me?
You need not be ungrateful; can she give
A life to you, if you refuse to live?—
Forgive me, Passion; I had rather see   65
You dead than kind to anything but me.
  Montezuma. O my Orazia!
To what new joys and knowledge am I brought!
Are death's hard lessons by a woman taught?
How to despise my fate I always knew,   70
But ne'er durst think, at once, of death and you;

---

[1] The Scott-Saintsbury edition suggests a pun on the meaning of "public" as (1) public prostitute; and (2), ironically, public-spirited.

Yet since you teach this generous jealousy,
I dare not wish your life, if I must die.
How much your love my courage does exceed!
Courage alone would shrink to see you bleed!
    ZEMPOALLA. Ungrateful stranger! thou shalt please thy eyes,   76
And gaze upon Orazia while she dies!—
I'll keep my vow!—It is some joy to see
That my revenge will prove my piety.
    TRAXALLA. Then both shall die!—We have too long withstood,   80
By private passions urged, the public good.
    ZEMPOALLA. (*Aside*) Sure he dissembles; and perhaps may prove
My ruin with his new, ambitious love.
Were but this stranger kind, I'd cross his art,
And give my empire where I gave my heart.—
Yet, thou ungrateful man,   86
Let thy approaching ruin make thee wise.
    MONTEZUMA. Thee, and thy love, and mischief, I despise!
    ZEMPOALLA. (*Aside*) What shall I do? Some way must yet be tried;—
What reasons can she use whom passions guide!   90
    TRAXALLA. (*Aside*) Some black designs are hatching now.—False eyes
Are quick to see another's treacheries.
    ZEMPOALLA. Rash stranger, thus to pull down thy own fate!
    MONTEZUMA. You, and that life you offer me, I hate.

Enter Jailer

    ZEMPOALLA. Here, jailer, take—What title must he have?   95
Slave, slave!—Am I then captive to a slave?—
Why art thou thus unwilling to be free?
    MONTEZUMA. Death will release me from these chains and thee.
    ZEMPOALLA. Here, jailer, take this monster from my sight,
And keep him where it may be always night.
Let none come near him; if thou dost, expect   101
To pay thy life, the price of the neglect.
    MONTEZUMA. I scorn thy pity and thy cruelty,
And should despise a blessing sent from thee.
    ZEMPOALLA. Oh, horror to my soul! take him away!—   105
My rage, like dammed-up streams, swelled by some stay,
Shall from this opposition get new force,
And leave the bound of its old easy course.—

Exeunt MONTEZUMA *and* Jailer

Come, my Traxalla, let us both forgive,
And in these wretches' fate begin to live.   110
The altars shall be crowned with funeral boughs,
Peace-offerings paid,—but with unquiet vows.

Exeunt ZEMPOALLA *and* TRAXALLA

    ORAZIA. How are things ordered, that the wicked should
Appear more kind and gentle than the good?
Her passion seems to make her kinder prove,
And I seem cruel through excess of love.   116
She loves, and would prevent his death; but I,
That love him better, fear he should not die.
My jealousy, immortal as my love,
Would rob my grave below, and me above,   120
Of rest.—Ye gods, if I repine, forgive!
You neither let me die in peace, nor live.

Enter ACACIS, *jailer, and* Indians

    JAILER. They are just gone, sir.
    ACACIS. 'Tis well. Be faithful to my just design,
And all thy prince's fortune shall be thine.   125
    Exit ACACIS
    INDIAN. This shall to the empress.
    Exit Indian
    ORAZIA. What can this mean!
'Twas Prince Acacis, if I durst believe
My sight; but sorrow may like joy deceive.
Each object different from itself appears   130
That comes not to the eyes, but through their tears.

Enter ACACIS, *bringing in* MONTEZUMA

Ha!—
    ACACIS. Here, sir, wear this again.—
    [*Gives a sword*]
Now follow me.
    MONTEZUMA. So, very good.—   135
I dare not think, for I may guess amiss:
None can deceive me while I trust to this.
    Exeunt

SCENE II

Enter ORAZIA, *conducted by two* Indians *with their swords drawn;* MONTEZUMA, ACACIS *whispering* [*to*] *another* Indian

    ACACIS. Think what a weight upon thy faith I lay.
    INDIAN. I ne'er did more unwillingly obey.
    ACACIS. First, Montezuma, take thy liberty.

Thou gav'st me freedom, here I set thee free.
We're equal now.   Madam, the danger's
     great   5
Of close pursuit; to favor your retreat,
Permit we two a little while remain
Behind, while you go softly o'er the plain.
  ORAZIA. Why should I go before?—What's
     your intent?
Where is my father?—Whither am I sent?   10
  ACACIS. Your doubts shall soon be cleared.
     Conduct her on.
                              Exit ORAZIA[1]
So, Montezuma, we are now alone.
That which my honor owed thee I have paid;
As honor was, so love must be obeyed.
I set Orazia, as thy captive, free;   15
But, as my mistress, ask her back from thee.
  MONTEZUMA. Thou hast performed what
     honor bid thee do,
But friendship bars what honor prompts me
     to.—
Friends should not fight.
  ACACIS.   If friendship we profess,
Let us secure each other's happiness.   20
One needs must die, and he shall happy prove
In her remembrance, t'other in her love.
My guards wait near; and, if I fail, they must
Give up Orazia or betray their trust.
  MONTEZUMA. Suppose thou conquer'st,
     wouldst thou wander o'er   25
The south-sea sands or the rough northern
     shore
That parts thy spacious kingdom from Peru,
And, leaving empire, hopeless love pursue?
  ACACIS. By which of all my actions could
     you guess,
Though more your merit, that my love was
     less?   30
What prize can empire with Orazia bear?
Or, where love fills the breast, what room for
     fear?
  MONTEZUMA. Let fair Orazia then the
     sentence give,
Else he may die whom she desires to live.
  ACACIS. Your greater merits bribe her to
     your side;   35
My weaker title must by arms be tried.
  MONTEZUMA. Oh, tyrant love! how cruel
     are thy laws!
I forfeit friendship or betray thy cause.
That person whom I would defend from all
The world, that person by my hand must fall.

---
[1] Whether the two Indians follow Acacis' injunction to "conduct her on" and also go out is not made clear.

  ACACIS. Our lives we to each other's friend-
     ships owe,   41
But love calls back what friendship did be-
     stow;
Love has its cruelties, but friendship, none,
And we now fight in quarrels not our own.
                              (*Fight*)
              Enter ORAZIA
  ORAZIA. What noise is this?—   45
Hold, hold! what cause could be so great,
     to move
This furious hatred?—
  MONTEZUMA.   'Twas our furious love.—
  ACACIS. Love, which I hid till I had set you
     free,
And bought your pardon with my liberty;
That done, I thought I less unjustly might   50
With Montezuma for Orazia fight.
He has prevailed, and I must now confess
His fortune greater, not my passion less;
Yet cannot yield you, till his sword remove
A dying rival that holds fast his love.   55
  ORAZIA. Whoever falls, 'tis my protector
     still,
And then the crime's as great, to die as kill.—
Acacis, do not hopeless love pursue,
But live, and this soft malady subdue.
  ACACIS. You bid me live, and yet command
     me die!   60
I am not worth your care.—Fly, madam, fly!
(While I fall here unpitied) o'er this plain,
Free from pursuit, the faithless[2] mountains
     gain;
And these I charge,
As they would have me think their friendship
     true,   65
Leave me alone, to serve and follow you.
Make haste, fair princess, to avoid that fate
Which does for your unhappy father wait.
  ORAZIA. Is he then left to die, and shall he
     see
Himself forsaken, ere his death, by me?   70
  MONTEZUMA. What would you do?
  ORAZIA.   To prison I'll return,
And there in fetters with my father mourn.
  MONTEZUMA. That saves not his, but throws
     you life away.
  ORAZIA. Duty shall give what nature once
     must pay.
  ACACIS. Life is the gift which heaven and
     parents give,   75

---
[2] Perhaps in the sense of treacherous, though "path-less" would make better sense.

And duty best preserves it, if you live.
 Orazia. I should but further from my
  fountain fly,
And like an unfed stream run on and die.
Urge me no more, and do not grieve to see
Your honor rivalled by my piety.   80
  (*She goes softly off, and often looks back*)
 Montezuma. If honor would not, shame
  would lead the way;
I'll back with her.
  Acacis.   Stay, Montezuma, stay!—
Thy rival cannot let thee go alone,
My love will bear me, though my blood is
  gone.
  (*As they are going off, enter* Zempoalla,
  Traxalla, *the* Indian *that went to tell
  her, and the rest, and seize them*)
 Zempoalla. Seize them!—
 Acacis.   Oh, Montezuma, thou art lost!
 Montezuma. No more, proud heart, thy
  useless courage boast!—   86
Courage, thou curse of the unfortunate,
That [1] canst encounter, not resist, ill fate!—
 Zempoalla. Acacis bleeds!—
What barbarous hand has wounded thus my
  son?   90
 Montezuma. 'Twas I; by my unhappy
  sword 'twas done.—
Thou bleedst, poor prince, and I am left to
  grieve
My rival's fall.
 Traxalla.   He bleeds, but yet may live.
 Acacis. Friendship and love my failing
  strength renew;
I dare not die when I should live for you; 95
My death were now my crime, as it would be
My guilt to live when I have set you free.
Thus I must still remain unfortunate,
Your life and death are equally my fate.
      (Orazia *comes back*)
 Orazia. A noise again!—alas, what do I
  see!   100
Love, thou didst once give place to piety—
Now, piety, let love triumph awhile;—
Here, bind my hands. Come, Montezuma,
  smile
At fortune; since thou sufferest for my sake,
Orazia will her captive's chains partake. 105
 Montezuma. Now, fate, thy worst.
 Zempoalla.   Lead to the temple straight,
A priest and altar for these lovers wait:
They shall be joined, they shall.

[1] Scott-Saintsbury edition suggests interchanging *thou* and *that*.

 Traxalla.   And I will prove
Those joys in vengeance which I want in love.
 Acacis. I'll quench your thirst with blood,
  and will destroy   110
Myself, and with myself, your cruel joy.
Now, Montezuma, since Orazia dies,
I'll fall before thee, the first sacrifice;
My title in her death shall exceed thine,
As much as, in her life, thy hopes did mine,
And when with our mixed blood the altar's
  dyed,   116
Then our new title let the gods decide.
          Exeunt

ACT V

Scene 1

The Scene opens, and discovers the Temple of the Sun, all of gold, and four Priests *in habits of white and red feathers, attending by a bloody altar, as ready for sacrifice.*

Then enter the Guards, Zempoalla, *and* Traxalla; Inca, Orazia, *and* Montezuma, *bound. As soon as they are placed, the* Priest *sings.*

    Song

 You to whom victory we owe,
  Whose glories rise
   By sacrifice,
 And from our fates below;
 Never did your altars shine [2]   5
 Feasted with blood so near divine;
  Princes to whom we bow,
   As they to you.—
Thus you can ravish from a throne,
And by their loss of power declare your own. 10

 Zempoalla. Now to inflict those punishments that are
Due to the authors of invasive war,
Who, to deceive the oppressed world, like
  you
Invent false quarrels to conceal the true.
 Inca. My quarrel was the same that all the
  gods   15
Must have to thee, if there be any odds
Betwixt those titles that are bad or good,
To crowns descended, or usurped by blood.—
Swell not with this success; 'twas not to thee,
But to this man, the gods gave victory. 20
 Montezuma. Since I must perish by my
  own success,

[2] Reads "Never did yet your altars shine" in 1665.

Think my misfortunes more, my crimes the
  less;
And so, forgiving, make me pleased to die,
Thus punished for this guilty victory.
  INCA. Death can make virtue easy; I for-
    give. 25
That word would prove too hard, were I to
  live;
The honor of a prince would then deny,
But in the grave all our distinctions die.
  MONTEZUMA. Forgive me one thing yet;
    to say, I love,
Let it no more your scorn and anger move, 30
Since, dying in one flame, my ashes must
Embrace and mingle with Orazia's dust.
  INCA. Name thy bold love no more, lest
    that last breath
Which should forgive, I stifle with my death.
  ORAZIA. Oh, my dear father! Oh, why may
    not I, 35
Since you gave life to me, for you now die?
  MONTEZUMA. 'Tis I that wrought this [1]
    mischief, ought to fall
A just and willing sacrifice for all.
Now, Zempoalla, be both just and kind,
And, in my fate, let me thy mercy find. 40
Be grateful, then, and grant me that esteem,
That as alive, so dead, I may redeem.
  ORAZIA. O do not for her cruel mercy move;
None should ask pity but from those they love.
    (*Weeps*)
  INCA. Fond girl! to let thy disobedient eyes
Show a concern for him whom I despise. 46
  ORAZIA. How love and nature may divide
    a breast
At once by both their powers severely pressed!
Yet, sir, since love seems less, you may for-
  give;
I would not have you die, nor have him live;
Yet if he dies, alas! what shall I do? 51
I cannot die with him, and live with you.
  MONTEZUMA. How vainly we pursue this
    generous strife,
Parting in death more cruel than in life!—
Weep not, we both shall have one destiny; 55
As in one flame we lived, in one we'll die.
  TRAXALLA. Why do we waste in vain these
    precious hours?
Each minute of his life may hazard ours.
The nation does not live whilst he enjoys
His life, it is his safety that destroys. 60
He shall fall first, and teach the rest to die.
  ZEMPOALLA. Hold!—

[1] *These* in 1665.

Who is it that commands—ha! you, or I?—
Your zeal grows saucy!—sure, you may allow
Your empress freedom first to pay her vow. 65
  TRAXALLA. She may allow—a justice to be
    done
By him that raised his empress to her throne.
  ZEMPOALLA. You are too bold—
  TRAXALLA.   And you, too passionate.
  ZEMPOALLA. Take heed, with his, you urge
    not your own fate.—
For all this pity is now due to me. 70
  MONTEZUMA. I hate thy offered mercy more
    than thee.
  TRAXALLA. Why will not then the fair
    Orazia give
Life to herself, and let Traxalla live?
  MONTEZUMA. Orazia will not live and let
    me die;
She taught me first this cruel jealousy. 75
  ORAZIA. I joy that you have learned it!—
That flame not like immortal love appears,
Where death can cool its warmth or kill its
  fears.
  ZEMPOALLA. What shall I do? am I so
    quite forlorn,
No help from my own pride, nor from his
  scorn! 80
My rival's death may more effectual prove;
He that is robbed of hope may cease to love.—
Here, lead these offerings to their deaths.—
  TRAXALLA.   Let none
Obey but he that will pull on his own!
  ZEMPOALLA. Tempt me not thus; false and
    ungrateful, too! 85
  TRAXALLA. Just as ungrateful and as false
    as you!
  ZEMPOALLA. 'Tis thy false love that fears
    her destiny.
  TRAXALLA. And your false love that fears
    to have him die.
  ZEMPOALLA. Seize the bold traitor!
  TRAXALLA.   What a slighted frown
Troubles your brow! feared nor obeyed by
  none; 90
Come, prepare for sacrifice.

Enter ACACIS *weakly*

  ACACIS. Hold, hold! such sacrifices cannot
    be
Devotions, but a solemn cruelty.
How can the gods delight in human blood?
Think them not cruel, if you think them good.
In vain we ask that mercy which they want, 96
And hope that pity which they hate to grant.

ZEMPOALLA. Retire, Acacis.—
Preserve thyself, for 'tis in vain to waste
Thy breath for them. The fatal vow is past.
ACACIS. To break that vow is juster than
    commit   101
A greater crime by your preserving it.
ZEMPOALLA. The gods themselves their own
    will best express
To like the vow, by giving the success.
ACACIS. If all things by success are under-
    stood,   105
Men that make war grow wicked to be good;
But did you vow, those that were overcome,
And he that conquered, both should share
    one doom?
There's no excuse; for one of these must be
Not your devotion, but your cruelty.   110
TRAXALLA. To that rash stranger, sir, we
    nothing owe;
What he had raised, he strove to overthrow;
That duty lost which should our actions guide,
Courage proves guilt, when merit swells to
    pride.
ACACIS. Darest thou, who didst thy prince's
    life betray,   115
Once name that duty thou hast thrown away?
Like thy injustice to this stranger shown,
To tax him with a guilt that is thy own?—
Can you, brave soldiers, suffer him to die
That gave you life in giving victory?   120
Look but upon this stranger, see those hands
That brought you freedom, fettered up in
    bands.
Not one looks up,—
Lest sudden pity should your hearts surprise,
And steal into their bosoms through their
    eyes.   125
ZEMPOALLA. Why thus, in vain, are thy
    weak spirits pressed?
Restore thyself to thy more needful rest.
ACACIS. And leave Orazia!—
ZEMPOALLA.   Go, you must resign,
For she must be the gods'—not yours nor
    mine.
ACACIS. You are my mother, and my tongue
    is tied   130
So much by duty that I dare not chide.—
Divine Orazia!
Can you have so much mercy to forgive?
I do not ask it with design to live,
But in my death to have my torments cease.
Death is not death when it can bring no
    peace.   136
ORAZIA. I both forgive and pity.—

ACACIS. O say no more, lest words less kind
    destroy
What these have raised in me of peace and
    joy.
You said you did both pity and forgive;   140
You would do neither, should Acacis live.
By death alone the certain way appears
Thus to hope mercy and deserve your tears.
                                (*Stabs himself*)
ZEMPOALLA. O my Acacis!
What cruel cause could urge this fatal deed?—
                                      (*Weeps*)
He faints!—help, help! some help! or he will
    bleed   146
His life, and mine, away!—
Some water there!—Not one stirs from his
    place!
I'll use my tears to sprinkle on his face.
ACACIS. Orazia—   150
ZEMPOALLA. Fond child! why dost thou call
    upon her name?
I am thy mother.
ACACIS.   No, you are my shame.
That blood is shed that you had title in,
And with your title may it end your sin!
Unhappy prince, you may forgive me now,   155
Thus bleeding for my mother's cruel vow.
INCA. Be not concerned for me;
Death's easier than the changes I have seen.
I would not live to trust the world again.
MONTEZUMA. Into my eyes sorrow begins
    to creep;   160
When hands are tied, it is no shame to weep.
ACACIS. Dear Montezuma,
I may be still your friend, though I must
    die
Your rival in her love. Eternity
Has room enough for both; there's no desire
Where to enjoy is only to admire.   166
There we'll meet friends, when this short
    storm is past.
MONTEZUMA. Why must I tamely wait to
    perish last?
ACACIS. Orazia weeps, and my parched
    soul appears
Refreshed by that kind shower of pitying
    tears.   170
Forgive those faults my passion did commit,
'Tis punished with the life that nourished it.
I had no power in this extremity
To save your life, and less to see you die.
My eyes would ever on this object stay,   175
But sinking nature takes the props away.
Kind death,

To end with pleasures all my miseries,
Shuts up your image in my closing eyes.
(Dies)

Enter a Messenger

MESSENGER. To arms, to arms!
TRAXALLA. From whence this sudden fear?
MESSENGER. Stand to your guard, my lord, the danger's near; 181
From every quarter crowds of people meet
And, leaving houses empty, fill the street.
Exit Messenger
TRAXALLA. Fond queen, thy fruitless tears a while defer; 184
Rise, we must join again—Not speak, nor stir!
I hear the people's voice like winds that roar
When they pursue the flying waves to shore.

Enter Second Messenger

SECOND MESSENGER. Prepare to fight, my lord; the banished queen,
With old Garucca, in the streets are [1] seen.
TRAXALLA. We must go meet them or [2] it be too late; 190
Yet, madam, rise! Have you no sense of fate?

Enter Third Messenger

THIRD MESSENGER. King Montezuma their loud shouts proclaim,
The city rings with their new sovereign's name;
The banished queen declares he is her son,
And to his succor all the people run. 195
(ZEMPOALLA rises)
ZEMPOALLA. Can this be true? O love! O fate! have I
Thus doted on my mortal enemy?
TRAXALLA. To my new prince I thus my homage pay;
Your reign is short, young king—
ZEMPOALLA. Traxalla, stay
'Tis to my hand that he must owe his fate,
I will revenge at once my love and hate. 201
(She sets a dagger to MONTEZUMA's breast)
TRAXALLA. Strike, strike, the conquering enemy is near.
My guards are passed while you detain me here.
ZEMPOALLA. Die, then, ungrateful, die! Amexia's son
Shall never triumph on Acacis' throne. 205
Thy death must my unhappy flames remove:

---
[1] Modern usage demands is.
[2] Ere in later editions.

Now where is thy defence—against my love?
(She cuts the cords and gives him the dagger)
TRAXALLA. Am I betrayed?
(He draws and thrusts at MONTEZUMA, [who] puts it by and kills him)
MONTEZUMA. So may all rebels die:
This end has treason joined with cruelty.
ZEMPOALLA. Live thou whom I must love and yet must hate; 210
She gave thee life who knows it brings her fate.
MONTEZUMA. Life is a trifle which I would not take,
But for Orazia's and her father's sake.
Now, Inca, hate me if thou canst; for he
Whom thou hast scorned will die, or rescue thee. 215
(As he goes to attack the guard with Traxalla's sword, enter AMEXIA, GARUCCA, Indians, driving some of the other party before them)
GARUCCA. He lives, ye gods, he lives! great queen, see here
Your coming joys and your departing fear.
AMEXIA. Wonder and joy so fast together flow,
Their haste to pass has made their passage slow;
Like struggling waters in a vessel pent, 220
Who crowding drops choke up the narrow vent.
My son!— (She embraces him)
MONTEZUMA. I am amazed! it cannot be
That fate has such a joy in store for me.
AMEXIA. Can I not gain belief that this is true? 225
MONTEZUMA. It is my fortune I suspect, not you.
GARUCCA. First ask him if he old Garucca know.
MONTEZUMA. My honored father! let me fall thus low.
GARUCCA. Forbear, great prince; 'tis I must pay to you
That adoration as my sovereign's due; 230
For, from my humble race you did not spring;
You are the issue of our murdered king,
Sent by that traitor to his blest abode,
Whom, to be made a king, he made a god.[3]
The story is too full of fate to tell, 235
Or what strange fortune our lost queen befell.

---
[3] The sense is clear, though the grammar is dubious. That traitor and he refer to Traxalla; whom refers to the king.

AMEXIA. That sad relation longer time will crave;
I lived obscure, he bred you in a cave,
But kept the mighty secret from your ear,
Lest heat of blood of some strange course should steer   240
Your youth.
  MONTEZUMA. I owe him all that now I am;
He taught me first the noble thirst of fame,
Showed me the baseness of unmanly fear,
Till the unlicked whelp I plucked from the rough bear,
And made the ounce and tiger give me way
While from their hungry jaws I snatched the prey.   246
'Twas he that charged my young arms first with toils,
And dressed me glorious in my savage spoils.
  GARUCCA. You spent in shady forest all the day,
And joyed, returning, to show me the prey,
To tell the story, to describe the place,   251
With all the pleasures of the boasted chase,
Till fit for arms, I reaved[1] you from your sport,
To train your youth in the Peruvian court.
I left you there, and ever since have been   255
The sad attendant of my exiled queen.
  ZEMPOALLA. My fatal dream comes to my memory;
That lion, whom I held in bonds, was he,
Amexia was the dove that broke his chains.
What now but Zempoalla's death remains?
  MONTEZUMA. Pardon, fair princess, if I must delay   261
My love a while, my gratitude to pay.
Live, Zempoalla—free from dangers live,
For present merits I past crimes forgive.
Oh, might she hope Orazia's pardon, too!   265
  ORAZIA. I would have none condemned for loving you;
In me her merit much her fault o'erpowers;
She sought my life, but she preserved me yours.
  AMEXIA. Taught by my own, I pity her estate,
And wish her penitence, but not her fate.[2]   270
  INCA. I would not be the last to bid her live;
Kings best revenge their wrongs when they forgive.
  ZEMPOALLA. I cannot yet forget what I have been.

Would you give life to her that was a queen?
Must you then give, and must I take? There's yet   275
One way, that's by refusing to be great.
You bid me live—bid me be wretched, too;
Think, think what pride, unthroned, must undergo.
Look on this youth, Amexia, look, and then
Suppose him yours, and bid me live again;
A greater sweetness on these lips there grows   281
Than breath shut out from a new-folded rose;
What lovely charms on these cold cheeks appear!
Could any one hate death, and see it here?
But thou art gone—
  MONTEZUMA.   O that you would believe
Acacis lives in me, and cease to grieve.   286
  ZEMPOALLA. Yes, I will cease to grieve, and cease to be.
His soul stays watching in his wound for me;
All that could render life desired is gone,
Orazia has my life, and you, my throne,   290
And death, Acacis—yet I need not die,
You leave me mistress of my destiny.
In spite of dreams, how am I pleased to see
Heaven's truth or falsehood should depend on me!
But I will help the gods;   295
The greatest proof of courage we can give
Is then to die when we have power to live.
                      (*Kills herself*)
  MONTEZUMA. How fatally that instrument of death
Was hid—
  AMEXIA. She has expired her latest breath.
  MONTEZUMA. But there lies one to whom all grief is due.   300
  ORAZIA. None e'er was so unhappy and so true.
  MONTEZUMA. Your pardon, royal sir.
  INCA.   You have my love.
                      (*Gives him* ORAZIA)
  AMEXIA. The gods, my son, your happy choice approve.
  MONTEZUMA. Come, my Orazia, then, and pay with me
                      (*Leads her to* ACACIS)
Some tears to poor Acacis' memory.   305
So strange a fate for me the gods ordain,
Our clearest sunshine should be mixed with rain;
How equally our joys and sorrows move!

---

[1] Took by force.
[2] I.e., death.

Death's fatal triumphs, joined with those of love.
Love crowns the dead, and death crowns him that lives, 310
Each gains the conquest which the other gives.
Exeunt omnes

EPILOGUE

Spoken by Montezuma

You see what shifts we are enforced to try,
To help our wit with some variety;
Shows may be found that never yet were seen,
'Tis hard to find such wit as ne'er has been.
You have seen all that this old world can do; 5
We therefore try the fortune of the new,
And hope it is below your aim to hit
At untaught nature with your practised wit.
Our naked Indians, then, when wits appear,
Would as soon choose to have the Spaniards here. 10
'Tis true, you have marks enough, the plot, the show,
The poet's scenes, nay, more, the painter's too;
If all this fail, considering the cost,
'Tis a true voyage to the Indies lost.
But if you smile on all, then these designs, 15
Like the imperfect treasure of our mines,[1]
Will pass for current wheresoe'er they go,
When to your bounteous hands their stamps they owe.

[1] Scott-Saintsbury prints *minds*.

THE REHEARSAL

By George Villiers, Second Duke of Buckingham (and Others)

George Villiers, second Duke of Buckingham, was born January 30, 1627/8, at Wallingford House, Westminster, the son of the all-powerful Duke, and Lady Katherine Manners, his wife. On August 23rd his father was assassinated by the fanatic, John Felton; King Charles assured the widow that "he would be a father to her children, and a husband to herself." The young duke and his brother were accordingly educated with Prince Charles, Villiers entering Trinity College, Cambridge, in 1641, of which university he was made a master of arts. But the excitement of the Civil Wars drew him, and from 1642 to 1660 Buckingham's career was highly romantic, involving battle, intrigue, exciting escapes, exile in France, the loss of his estate, imprisonment, and ultimate triumph at the Restoration. In 1657 he married Mary Fairfax, who could not resist the charm of the "most graceful and beautiful person that any Court in Europe ever saw."

His estates restored, Buckingham plunged eagerly into the political, scientific, and literary life of the Restoration. From 1662 to 1670 he was possibly the most powerful political personage in the kingdom, but he fell from power in 1674. Aided by his immense wealth, he undertook to satisfy every whim, to yield to every extravagance. His chaplain was Thomas Sprat, the historian of the Royal Society; Buckingham himself conducted scientific experiments; and his glass manufacture was praised by Evelyn in his *Diary*. He was a lavish patron of literary men, having formed at college a lifelong friendship for Cowley. A poet in his own right, his verses are at any rate respectable, nor did he refrain from political pamphleteering. Because heroic tragedy failed to arouse his critical enthusiasm, he led the most noteworthy attack against it in his play, *The Rehearsal*, in which, however, he was but the principal of a number of collaborators. He wrote other dramatic works, of which only one, *The Chances*, an adaptation from Fletcher, is known to have been produced.

After his disgrace in 1674, Buckingham became involved in various intrigues, and was suspected of more, being distrusted by the very middle class to which he tried to appeal. The accession of James II in 1685 resulted in his permanent retirement from the public stage, and he died April 16, 1687. Though "there was not so much as one farthing to defray the least expense," the funeral was characteristically extravagant. Gifted with all the graces, Buckingham lacked stability; Dryden seized upon the essential weakness of his character in the portrait of Zimri in *Absalom and Achitophel*.

The chief collaborators with Buckingham in *The Rehearsal* were Thomas Sprat (1635–1713), wit and poet, historian of the Royal Society, and later Bishop of Rochester; Samuel Butler (1612–80), the author of *Hudibras;* and Martin Clifford (d. 1677), Master of the Charterhouse from 1671 and author of *A Treatise of Human Reason* (1674).

The standard life is that by Winifred, Lady Burghclere, *George Villiers, Second Duke of Buckingham, 1628–1687: A Study in the History of the Restoration* (1903).

BUCKINGHAM'S DRAMATIC WORKS

The Rehearsal (comedy) (T.R. Dec. 7, 1671), 1672; 1673; 1675, etc.

The Chances (adaptation) (D.L. Dec. 1682), 1682.

Buckingham's other plays seem not to have been produced. They are: *The Restoration* (printed 1714); *The Battle of Sedgmoor* (date unknown); *The Militant Couple* (printed 1705).

Though the former age had produced in *The Knight of the Burning Pestle* (1613) by Sir Francis Beaumont and Mr. Fletcher a burlesque of extravagancies upon the stage, there is little from which a judicious critic might predict the happy appearance of *The Rehearsal* in 1671. As the erudite have pointed out, this play was not in its original the personal attack upon Mr. Dryden which it later became; my lord duke and his friends being first engaged in ridiculing the swelling imaginations of Sir Wm. Davenant, Sir Robert Howard, and Henry Howard, his brother. Particularly did they have in view *The United Kingdoms*, an heroic tragedy by Henry Howard, produced in 1663. Of this first design there are many traces to be discovered in the final version.

Much water flowed under the bridge between the first inception of this burlesque and its final appearance, nor did the wits of the age fail to remark that its construction took "as long as the siege of Troy." In the interval the character of Bilboa, first drawn as a lampoon upon Sir Robert Howard for the intended production of 1664-5 was transmogrified into Mr. Bayes, the image of Mr. Dryden: the change being a tribute to Mr. Dryden's growing reputation in the theater. No less than six of that dramatist's plays are parodied in this comedy; and my lord duke personally supervised the details of the production, and instructed Mr. Lacy, the actor, in the manner of his speech (which was made to imitate Mr. Dryden's as closely as possible) and in the fashion of his dress. But the attacks are by no means confined to Mr. Dryden, and the ingenious have ascertained that at least seventeen plays in all are parodied in *The Rehearsal*. So sweeping an attack, together with the reputation of the authors, the skill of Mr. Lacy, and a desire for novelty, delighted the town; *The Rehearsal* was a prodigious success.

If *The Rehearsal* did not terminate the vogue of heroic tragedy, it exposed the characteristic weaknesses of this way of writing. The debates between love and honor, the tedious points of casuistry, the bombastic language and far-stretched comparisons, the lack of probability in the motivation and catastrophe of these dramas are abundantly satirized in the present comedy. It is to be remarked that a Restoration audience found the play pleasing, and if the taste of the town was touched by the unmotivated actions and sounding style of the heroes of plays seriously intended, it was also tickled by the satire of the Duke of Buckingham. Indeed, since it is possible for the race of men to enjoy contradictory pleasures at one and the same time, *The Rehearsal*, by exposing the weaknesses of a particular genre, paid tribute as well to the vogue of the dramas which it satirized.

So popular was the play that efforts were made, by revising it, to keep abreast of the taste of the times. For this reason the editors, breaking their rule of printing the first edition of the plays in this collection, have preferred the third edition of *The Rehearsal*,[1] following Mr. Montague Summers in this respect, and preferring the mature product of Buckingham's wit (with that of his collaborators) to the first runnings of their muse. The learned are referred to the reprint by the late Edward Arber of the first edition of this play for an earlier version of the comedy. It is to be remarked that a *Key to The Rehearsal*, first published in 1704 in the edition of Samuel Briscoe, is the source from which the ascription of parallel passages has ever since been taken.

The Rehearsal was first produced at Drury Lane Theater December 7, 1671.

Consult the edition of *The Rehearsal* edited by Montague Summers, London, 1916; one by G. R. Noyes in his *Selected Dramas of John Dryden*, New York, 1910; and the reprint by Edward Arber of the first edition, London, 1868.

---

[1] The text is that of the Bridgewater-Huntington copy. For assistance in collating the editors are indebted to the kindness of Mr. L. De L. Wallace, of the University of North Carolina.

THE REHEARSAL

DRAMATIS PERSONÆ[1]

MEN

Bayes	General	Players
Johnson	Lieutenant-General	Soldiers
Smith	Cordelio	Stage-keeper
Two Kings of Brentford	Tom Thimble	Two Heralds
Prince Pretty-man	[Harry]	Four Cardinals
Prince Volscius	Fisherman	Mayor
Gentleman-Usher	Shirley	Judges
Physician	Sun	Sergeants at Arms
Drawcansir	Thunder	[Three Fiddlers]

WOMEN

Amaryllis	Pallas	[Luna]
Cloris	Lightning	Earth
Parthenope		

Attendants of Men and Women

Scene: *Brentford*

PROLOGUE

We might well call this short mock-play of ours
A posy made of weeds instead of flowers;
Yet such have been presented to your noses,
And there are such, I fear, who thought 'em roses.
Would some of 'em were here, to see, this night, 5
What stuff it is in which they took delight.
Here, brisk, insipid rogues, for wit, let fall
Sometimes dull sense; but oft'ner, none at all:
There, strutting heroes, with a grim-faced train,
Shall brave the gods, in King Cambyses'[2] vein. 10
For (changing rules, of late, as if men writ
In spite of reason, nature, art, and wit),
Our poets make us laugh at tragedy,
And with their comedies they make us cry.
Now, critics, do your worst, that here are met; 15
For, like a rook,[3] I have hedged in my bet.[4]
If you approve, I shall assume the state
Of those high-flyers[5] whom I imitate;
And justly too, for I will teach you more
Than ever they would let you know before: 20
I will not only show the feats they do,
But give you all their reasons for 'em too.
Some honor may to me from hence arise;
But if, by my endeavors, you grow wise,
And what you once so praised shall now despise, 25
Then I'll cry out, swelled with poetic rage,
'Tis I, John Lacy,[6] have reformed your stage.

---

[1] The first cast of *The Rehearsal* is not certainly known. Mr. Lacy played the part of Mr. Bayes; the *Key* tells us that Mrs. Anne Reeves was cast as Amaryllis, " who, at that time, was kept by Mr. Bayes" (a doubtful slander), and hints at the actors of other rôles are contained in the text.

[2] The hero of Preston's *A Lamentable Tragedie . . . containing the Life of Cambises, King of Persia* (1570), distinguished by the bombast of his speeches. Cf.

Shakespeare, *I Henry IV*, Act II, scene iv: "I must speak in passion, and I will do it in King Cambyses' vein." Settle produced a ranting play on the same theme in 1666.

[3] Sharper. Cf. "He rooked me."

[4] To bet on both sides of a wager.

[5] Extravagantly ambitious, like the heroes of heroic tragedy.

[6] Lacy (1631–81), the most famous actor in farce and low comedy of the age, who created the rôle of Teague in Howard's *The Committee*. Besides his acting, he was the author of four farces. Tradition is that he mimicked Dryden closely in this present part.

ACT I

Scene 1

Enter JOHNSON *and* SMITH

JOHNSON. Honest Frank! I'm glad to see thee with all my heart: how long hast thou been in town?

SMITH. Faith, not above an hour; and, if I had not met you here, I had gone to look you out; for I long to talk with you freely, of all the strange new things we have heard in the country.

JOHNSON. And, by my troth, I have longed as much to laugh with you, at all the impertinent, dull, fantastical things we are tired out with here.

SMITH. Dull and fantastical! that's an excellent composition. Pray, what are our men of business doing?

JOHNSON. I ne'er enquire after 'em. Thou knowest my humor lies another way. I love to please myself as much and to trouble others as little as I can, and therefore do naturally avoid the company of those solemn fops who, being incapable of reason, and insensible of wit and pleasure, are always looking grave and troubling one another, in hopes to be thought men of business.

SMITH. Indeed, I have ever observed that your grave lookers are the dullest of men.

JOHNSON. Aye, and of birds, and beasts too; your gravest bird is an owl, and your gravest beast is an ass.

SMITH. Well, but how dost thou pass thy time?

JOHNSON. Why, as I use to do—eat and drink as well as I can, have a she-friend to be private with in the afternoon, and sometimes see a play; where there are such things, Frank,—such hideous, monstrous things, that it has almost made me forswear the stage and resolve to apply myself to the solid nonsense of your men of business, as the more ingenious pastime.

SMITH. I have heard, indeed, you have had lately many new plays, and our country wits commend 'em.

JOHNSON. Aye, so do some of our city wits, too; but they are of the new kind of wits.

SMITH. New kind! what kind is that?

JOHNSON. Why, your virtuosi,[1] your civil persons, your drolls—fellows that scorn to imitate nature, but are given altogether to elevate and surprise.

SMITH. Elevate and surprise? Prithee, make me understand the meaning of that.

JOHNSON. Nay, by my troth, that's a hard matter; I don't understand that myself. 'Tis a phrase they have got among them, to express their no-meaning by. I'll tell you, as near as I can, what it is. Let me see; 'tis fighting, loving, sleeping, rhyming, dying, dancing, singing, crying; and everything but thinking and sense.

Mr. BAYES[2] *passes o'er the stage*

BAYES. Your most obsequious and most observant very servant, sir.

JOHNSON. Godso, this is an author! I'll fetch him to you.

SMITH. No, prithee, let him alone.

JOHNSON. Nay, by the Lord, I'll have him. (*Goes after him*) Here he is. I have caught him.—Pray, sir, now for my sake, will you do a favor to this friend of mine?

BAYES. Sir, it is not within my small capacity to do favors, but receive 'em, especially from a person that does wear the honorable title you are pleased to impose, sir, upon this. —Sweet sir, your servant.

SMITH. Your humble servant, sir.

JOHNSON. But wilt thou do me a favor, now?

BAYES. Aye, sir. What is't?

JOHNSON. Why, to tell him the meaning of thy last play.[3]

BAYES. How, sir, the meaning! Do you mean the plot?

JOHNSON. Aye, aye—anything.

BAYES. Faith, sir, the intrigo's now quite out of my head: but I have a new one in my pocket, that I may say is a virgin; 't has never yet been blown upon. I must tell you one thing, 'tis all new wit; and though I say it, a better than my last; and you know well enough how that took. In fine, it shall read, and write, and act, and plot, and show—aye, and pit, box and gallery,[4] 'y gad, with any play in Europe. This morning is its last re-

---

[1] Amateurs of knowledge.

[2] Dryden had been made Poet Laureate (i.e., crowned with bays) in August, 1670. Dryden refers to himself as Bayes (for the name clung to him) in the Epilogue to *All for Love*.

[3] Dryden's *Conquest of Granada*.

[4] According to the *Key to The Rehearsal* by S. Briscoe (1704), this was a favorite expression of Edward Howard at rehearsals. The satire of *The Rehearsal* is aimed not only at Dryden, but at the Howard family with whom he was allied.

hearsal, in their habits and all that, as it is to be acted; and if you and your friend will do it but the honor to see it in its virgin attire, though, perhaps, it may blush, I shall not be ashamed to discover its nakedness unto you. (*Puts his hand in his pocket*) I think it is in this pocket.

JOHNSON. Sir, I confess I am not able to answer you in this new way; but if you please to lead, I shall be glad to follow you; and I hope my friend will do so too.

SMITH. Sir, I have no business so considerable as should keep me from your company.

BAYES. Yes, here it is.—No, cry you mercy! this is my book of drama commonplaces, the mother of many other plays.

JOHNSON. Drama commonplaces! pray, what's that?

BAYES. Why, sir, some certain helps that we men of art have found it convenient to make use of.

SMITH. How, sir, helps for wit?

BAYES. Aye, sir, that's my position. And I do here aver that no man yet the sun e'er shone upon has parts sufficient to furnish out a stage except it were by the help of these my rules.[1]

JOHNSON. What are those rules, I pray?

BAYES. Why, sir, my first rule is the rule of transversion,[2] or *regula duplex*—changing verse into prose, or prose into verse, alternative as you please.

SMITH. Well, but how is this done by a rule, sir?

BAYES. Why, thus, sir—nothing so easy when understood. I take a book in my hand, either at home or elsewhere, for that's all one—if there be any wit in't, as there is no book but has some, I transverse it: that is, if it be prose, put it into verse (but that takes up some time); and if it be verse, put it into prose.

JOHNSON. Methinks, Mr. Bayes, that putting verse into prose should be called transprosing.

BAYES. By my troth, sir, 'tis a very good notion, and hereafter it shall be so.

SMITH. Well, sir, and what d'ye do with it then?

BAYES. Make it my own. 'Tis so changed that no man can know it. My next rule is the rule of record, by way of table-book.[3] Pray, observe.

JOHNSON. We hear you, sir: go on.

BAYES. As thus. I come into a coffee house, or some other place where witty men resort. I make as if I minded nothing (do you mark?), but as soon as any one speaks, pop! I slap it down, and make that, too, my own.

JOHNSON. But, Mr. Bayes, are not you sometimes in danger of their making you restore, by force, what you have gotten thus by art?

BAYES. No, sir, the world's unmindful; they never take notice of these things.

SMITH. But pray, Mr. Bayes, among all your other rules, have you no one rule for invention?

BAYES. Yes, sir, that's my third rule that I have here in my pocket.

SMITH. What rule can that be, I wonder.

BAYES. Why, sir, when I have anything to invent, I never trouble my head about it, as other men do; but presently turn over this book, and there I have, at one view, all that Perseus, Montaigne, Seneca's tragedies, Horace, Juvenal, Claudian, Pliny, Plutarch's *Lives*, and the rest, have ever thought upon this subject; and so, in a trice, by leaving out a few words or putting in others of my own, the business is done.

JOHNSON. Indeed, Mr. Bayes, this is as sure and compendious a way of wit as ever I heard of.

BAYES. Sirs, if you make the least scruple of the efficacy of these my rules, do but come to the play-house and you shall judge of 'em by the effects.

SMITH. We'll follow you, sir. *Exeunt*

[SCENE II]

Enter three Players upon the stage

1ST PLAYER. Have you your part perfect?

2D PLAYER. Yes, I have it without book, but I don't understand how it is to be spoken.

3D PLAYER. And mine is such a one as I can't guess for my life what humor[4] I'm to

---

[1] Cf. the Prologue to Dryden's *The Maiden Queen*:
He who writ this, not without pains and thought
From French and English theatres has brought
The exactest rules by which a play is wrought.

[2] A hit at Dryden's use of the same materials in prose and verse.

[3] Pocket notebook.

[4] In the humors comedy of Jonson and Shadwell, types are supposed to be determined by "the choler, melancholy, phlegm, and blood." When one of these "doth draw All his effects, his spirits, and his powers, In their confluxions, all to run one way, This may be

be in—whether angry, melancholy, merry, or in love. I don't know what to make on't.

1st Player. Phoo! the author will be here presently[1] and he'll tell us all. You must know, this is the new way of writing; and these hard things please forty times better than the old plain way. For, look you, sir, the grand design upon the stage is to keep the auditors in suspense; for to guess presently at the plot and the sense, tires 'em before the end of the first act. Now, here, every line surprises you and brings in new matter. And, then, for scenes, clothes, and dances, we put 'em quite down, all that ever went before us; and those are the things, you know, that are essential to a play.

2d Player. Well, I am not of thy mind, but so it gets us money 'tis no great matter.

Enter Bayes, Johnson, *and* Smith

Bayes. Come, come in, gentlemen. Y'are very welcome, Mr.—a—. Ha' you your part ready?

1st Player. Yes, sir.

Bayes. But do you understand the true humor of it?

1st Player. Aye, sir, pretty well.

Bayes. And Amaryllis,[2] how does she do? Does not her armor become her?

3d Player. Oh, admirably!

Bayes. I'll tell you, now, a pretty conceit. What do you think I'll make 'em call her anon, in this play?

Smith. What, I pray?

Bayes. Why, I'll make 'em call her Armaryllis, because of her armor—ha, ha, ha!

Johnson. That will be very well, indeed.

Bayes. Aye, it's a pretty little rogue; I knew her face would set off armor extremely, and, to tell you true, I writ that part only for her. You must know she is my mistress.

Johnson. Then I know another thing, little Bayes, that thou hast had her, 'y gad.

Bayes. No, 'y gad, not yet, but I'm sure I shall, for I have talked bawdy to her already.

Johnson. Hast thou, faith? Prithee, how was that?

Bayes. Why, sir, there is in the French tongue a certain criticism which, by the variation of the masculine adjective instead of the feminine, makes a quite different signification of the word; as, for example, *Ma vie*[3] is my life; but if before *vie* you put *Mon* instead of *Ma*,[4] you make it bawdy.

Johnson. Very true.

Bayes. Now, sir, I, having observed this, set a trap for her the other day in the tiring-room;[5] for this said I: *Adieu, bel esperansa de ma vie*[6] (which, 'y gad, is very pretty), to which she answered, I vow, almost as prettily every jot. For, said she, *Songes à ma vie, Mounsieur;*[7] whereupon I presently snapped this upon her: *Non, non,* Madam—*songes vous à mon,*[8] by gad, and named the thing directly to her.

Smith. This is one of the richest stories, Mr. Bayes, that ever I heard of.

Bayes. Aye, let me alone, 'y gad, when I get to 'em; I'll nick[9] 'em, I warrant you. But I'm a little nice;[10] for you must know, at this time I am kept by another woman in the city.

Smith. How kept? for what?

Bayes. Why, for a *beau gerson.*[11] I am, i' fackins.[12]

Smith. Nay, then, we shall never have done.

Bayes. And the rogue is so fond of me, Mr. Johnson, that I vow to gad, I know not what to do with myself.

Johnson. Do with thyself! No; I wonder how thou canst make shift to hold out at this rate.

Bayes. O devil, I can toil like a horse; only sometimes it makes me melancholy; and then I vow to gad, for a whole day together I am not able to say you one good thing if it were to save my life.

Smith. That we do verily believe, Mr. Bayes.

Bayes. And that's the only thing, 'y gad, which mads me in my amours; for I'll tell you, as a friend, Mr. Johnson, my acquaint-

---

[1] Immediately.
[2] Played by Mrs. Anne Reeves, who, according to the *Key*, was Dryden's mistress at the time.
[3] My life.
[4] The pun is on the meanings of *vie* and *vit*. The latter has fallen out of respectable French.
[5] Dressing room.
[6] Execrable French for "Good-by, fair hope of my life."
[7] More bad French. "Dream of my life, sir."
[8] The omitted word is again *vit*.
[9] To strike at the right point or time.
[10] Scrupulous. Perhaps also an unconscious pun on the meaning of the word as simple, or silly.
[11] Bad French for *beau garçon*—about equivalent to gigolo here.
[12] In faith.

ances, I hear, begin to give it out that I am dull. Now I am the farthest from it in the whole world, 'y gad; but only, forsooth, they think I am so because I can say nothing.

JOHNSON. Phoo! Pox! That's ill-naturedly done of 'em.

BAYES. Aye, gad, there's no trusting these rogues; but—a—come, let's sit down.—Look you, sirs, the chief hinge of this play, upon which the whole plot moves and turns, and that causes the variety of all the several accidents, which, you know, are the things in nature that make up the grand refinement of a play, is that I suppose two kings[1] to be of the same place—as, for example, at Brentford, for I love to write familiarly. Now the people having the same relations to 'em both, the same affections, the same duty, the same obedience, and all that, are divided among themselves in point of *devoir* and interest, how to behave themselves equally between 'em, these kings differing sometimes in particular, though in the main they agree. (I know not whether I make myself well understood.)

JOHNSON. I did not observe you, sir; pray, say that again.

BAYES. Why, look you, sir (nay, I beseech you, be a little curious[2] in taking notice of this, or else you'll never understand my notion of the thing), the people being embarrassed by their equal ties to both, and the sovereigns concerned in a reciprocal regard, as well to their own interest as the good of the people, may make a certain kind of a—you understand me—upon which there does arise several disputes, turmoils, heart-burnings, and all that.—In fine, you'll apprehend it better when you see it.

Exit, to call the Players

SMITH. I find the author will be very much obliged to the players, if they can make any sense out of this.

Enter BAYES

BAYES. Now, gentlemen, I would fain ask your opinion of one thing. I have made a prologue and an epilogue[3] which may both serve for either (that is, the prologue for the epilogue, or the epilogue for the prologue)—do you mark? Nay, they may both serve too, 'y gad, for any other play as well as this.

SMITH. Very well. That's, indeed, artificial.[4]

BAYES. And I would fain ask your judgments now, which of them would do best for the prologue. For you must know there is in nature but two ways of making very good prologues. The one is by civility, by insinuation, good language, and all that, to—a—in a manner, steal your plaudit from the courtesy of the auditors; the other, by making use of some certain personal things, which may keep a hank[5] upon such censuring persons as cannot otherways, a gad, in nature, be hindered from being too free with their tongues. To which end my first prologue is, that I come out in a long black veil, and a great, huge hangman behind me, with a furred cap and his sword drawn; and there tell 'em plainly that if, out of good nature, they will not like my play, 'y gad, I'll e'en kneel down, and he shall cut my head off. Whereupon they all clapping—a—

SMITH. But suppose they don't.

BAYES. Suppose! Sir, you may suppose what you please, I have nothing to do with your suppose, sir, nor am not at all mortified at it—not at all, sir; 'y gad, not one jot, sir. "Suppose," quoth a!—ha, ha, ha!

Walks away

JOHNSON. Phoo! prithee, Bayes, don't mind what he says. He is a fellow newly come out of the country; he knows nothing of what's the relish,[6] here, of the town.

BAYES. If I writ, sir, to please the country, I should have followed the old plain way: but I write for some persons of quality and peculiar friends of mine, that understand what flame and power in writing is; and they do me the right, sir, to approve of what I do.

JOHNSON. Aye, aye, they will clap, I warrant you; never fear it.

BAYES. I'm sure the design's good; that cannot be denied. And then, for language, 'y gad, I defy 'em all, in nature, to mend it. Besides, sir, I have printed above a hundred sheets of paper,[7] to insinuate the plot into

[1] Probably a hit at *The Conquest of Granada*, in which Mahomet Boabdelin and his traitorous brother Prince Abdalla struggle for the throne. However, the Key suggests Henry Howard's *The United Kingdoms*, which had two kings in it. This play was never printed. Brentford is in the County of Middlesex, close to London.
[2] Careful.
[3] For the writing of which Dryden was famous.
[4] Well contrived.
[5] Hold, influence.
[6] I.e., he knows nothing of what pleases the town.
[7] When Dryden produced *The Indian Emperor*, sequel to *The Indian Queen*, he printed and distributed

the boxes: and withal, have appointed two or three dozen of my friends to be ready in the pit, who, I'm sure, will clap, and so the rest, you know, must follow; and then pray, sir, what becomes of your suppose?—Ha, ha, ha!

JOHNSON. Nay, if the business be so well laid, it cannot miss.

BAYES. I think so, sir, and therefore would choose this to be the prologue. For if I could engage 'em to clap before they see the play, you know 'twould be so much the better, because then they were engaged; for let a man write never so well, there are, now-a-days, a sort of persons they call critics, that, 'y gad, have no more wit in 'em than so many hobby-horses; but they'll laugh you, sir, and find fault, and censure things that, 'y gad, I'm sure they are not able to do themselves—a sort of envious persons that emulate the glories of persons of parts and think to build their fame by calumniating of persons that, 'y gad, to my knowledge, of all persons in the world are, in nature, the persons that do as much despise all that as—a—In fine, I'll say no more of 'em.

JOHNSON. Nay, you have said enough of 'em, in all conscience—I'm sure more than they'll e'er be able to answer.

BAYES. Why, I'll tell you, sir, sincerely, and *bona fide;* were it not for the sake of some ingenious persons and choice female spirits [1] that have a value for me, I would see 'em all hanged, 'y gad, before I would e'er more set pen to paper; but let 'em live in ignorance like ingrates.

JOHNSON. Aye, marry! that were a way to be revenged of 'em, indeed; and, if I were in your place, now, I would do so.

BAYES. No, sir; there are certain ties [2] upon me that I cannot be disengaged from; otherwise, I would. But pray, sir, how do you like my hangman?

SMITH. By my troth, sir, I should like him very well.

BAYES. But how do you like it, sir? for I see you can judge. Would you have it for a prologue, or the epilogue?

JOHNSON. Faith, sir, 'tis so good, let it e'en serve for both.

BAYES. No, no, that won't do. Besides, I have made another.

JOHNSON. What other, sir?

BAYES. Why, sir, my other is Thunder and Lightning.

JOHNSON. That's greater. I'd rather stick to that.

BAYES. Do you think so? I'll tell you then; though there have been many witty prologues written of late, yet I think you'll say this is a *non pareillo.*[3] I'm sure nobody has hit upon it yet. For here, sir, I make my prologue to be dialogue; and as in my first, you see I strive to oblige the auditors by civility, by good nature, good language, and all that, so in this by the other way, *in terrorem,*[4] I choose for the persons Thunder and Lightning. Do you apprehend the conceit?

JOHNSON. Phoo, pox! then you have it cocksure. They'll be hanged before they'll dare to affront an author that has 'em at that lock.[5]

BAYES. I have made, too, one of the most delicate, dainty similies in the whole world, 'y gad, if I knew but how to apply it.

SMITH. Let's hear it, I pray you.

BAYES. 'Tis an allusion to love.

So boar and sow, when any storm is nigh,[6]
Snuff up, and smell it gath'ring in the sky;
Boar beckons sow to trot in chestnut groves,
And there consummate their unfinished loves.
Pensive, in mud, they wallow all alone,
And snore and gruntle to eacn other's moan.

How do you like it now, ha?

JOHNSON. Faith, 'tis extraordinary fine; and very applicable to Thunder and Lightning, methinks, because it speaks of a storm.

BAYES. 'Y gad, and so it does, now I think on't. Mr. Johnson, I thank you, and I'll put it in *profecto.*[7] Come out, Thunder and Lightning.

---

a sheet showing the "Connection of *The Indian Emperor* to *The Indian Queen*," which may be read in Dryden's *Works.*

[1] A hit at the protection given Dryden by Lady Castlemaine.

[2] Dryden had contracted to write three plays a year for the King's Company.

[3] Nonpareil, without equal.

[4] For terror's sake.

[5] Wrestling term; cf. hammerlock.

[6] Cf. *The Conquest of Granada,* Part II, Act I, scene ii:

So two kind turtles, when a storm is nigh,
Look up, and see it gath'ring in the sky;
Each calls his mate to shelter in the groves,
Leaving, in murmurs, their unfinished loves;
Perched on some drooping branch, they sit alone,
And coo, and hearken to each other's moan.

[7] Progress.

Enter Thunder *and* Lightning

THUNDER. I am the bold Thunder.[1]

BAYES. Mr. Cartwright,[2] prithee, speak that a little louder, and with a hoarse voice. "I am the bold Thunder!" Pshaw! speak it me in a voice that thunders it out indeed: *I am the bold Thunder!*

THUNDER. I am the bold Thunder.
LIGHTNING. The brisk Lightning, I.

BAYES. Nay, you must be quick and nimble.—The brisk Lightning, I.—That's my meaning.

THUNDER. I am the bravest Hector of the sky.
LIGHTNING. And I, fair Helen, that made Hector die.
THUNDER. I strike men down.
LIGHTNING. I fire the town.
THUNDER. Let the critics take heed how they grumble,
For then begin I for to rumble.
LIGHTNING. Let the ladies allow us their graces,
Or I'll blast all the paint on their faces,
And dry up their peter [3] to soot.
THUNDER. Let the critics look to't.
LIGHTNING. Let the ladies look to't.
THUNDER. For Thunder will do't.
LIGHTNING. For Lightning will shoot.
THUNDER. I'll give you dash for dash.
LIGHTNING. I'll give you flash for flash.
Gallants, I'll singe your feather.
THUNDER. I'll thunder you together.
BOTH. Look to't, look to't; we'll do't, we'll do't; look to't, we'll do't.

(*Twice or thrice repeated*)
Exeunt Ambo

BAYES. There's no more. 'Tis but a flash of a prologue—a droll.[4]

SMITH. Yes. 'Tis short, indeed, but very terrible.

[1] The following passage is a burlesque of a "Song in Dialogue" between Evening and Jack in *The Slighted Maid* (1663), Act III, by Sir Robert Stapylton, which begins:
　Evening.　I am an Evening dark as night,
　　　　Jack-with-the-Lantern, bring a light
　Jack. (*Within*) Whither, whither, whither?
　Evening.　Hither, hither, hither, etc.
Dryden himself ridiculed the play.
[2] William Cartwright (d. 1686), "a sound actor of much experience and no ordinary merit," whose portly size and loud voice made him the inevitable person to play the part of *Thunder*.
[3] Cosmetic.
[4] A droll was a short, racy, comic scene rounded off with dancing, produced especially during the pre-Restoration period. See Hotson, *Commonwealth and Restoration Stage*, pp. 47ff.

BAYES. Aye, when the simile's in, it will do to a miracle, 'y gad. Come, come, begin the play.

Enter First Player

1ST PLAYER. Sir, Mr. Ivory [5] is not come yet, but he'll be here presently; he's but two doors off.

BAYES. Come then, gentlemen, let's go out and take a pipe of tobacco.　　*Exeunt*

ACT II

SCENE I

Enter BAYES, JOHNSON, *and* SMITH

BAYES. Now, sir, because I'll do nothing here that ever was done before, instead of beginning with a scene that discovers something of the plot, I begin this play with a whisper.[6]

SMITH. Umph! very new, indeed.

BAYES. Come, take your seats. Begin, sirs.

Enter Gentleman-Usher *and* Physician

PHYSICIAN. Sir, by your habit, I should guess you to be the gentleman-usher of this sumptuous place.

USHER. And by your gate and fashion I should almost suspect you rule the healths of both our noble kings, under the notion of physician.

PHYSICIAN. You hit my function right.
USHER. And you, mine.
PHYSICIAN. Then let's embrace.
USHER. Come.
PHYSICIAN. Come.

JOHNSON. Pray, sir, who are those so very civil persons?

BAYES. Why, sir, the gentleman-usher and physician of the two kings of Brentford.

JOHNSON. But, pray then, how comes it to pass that they know one another no better?

BAYES. Phoo! that's for the better carrying on of the plot.

JOHNSON. Very well.

PHYSICIAN. Sir, to conclude,

SMITH. What, before he begins?

BAYES. No, sir; you must know they had been talking of this a pretty while without.

[5] Abraham Ivory had been an actor of women's parts, but through drink had sunk to the rôle of messenger about the theater.
[6] This satire on the "stage whisper" hits at a number of plays of the period.

SMITH. Where? In the tiring-room?

BAYES. Why, aye, sir.—He's so dull!—Come, speak again.

PHYSICIAN. Sir, to conclude, the place you fill has more than amply exacted the talents of a wary pilot, and all these threat'ning storms which, like impregnate clouds, do hover o'er our heads, will (when they once are grasped but by the eye of reason) melt into fruitful showers of blessings on the people.

BAYES. Pray, mark that allegory. Is not that good?

JOHNSON. Yes; that grasping of a storm with the eye is admirable.

PHYSICIAN. But yet some rumors great are stirring; and if Lorenzo should prove false (which none but the great gods can tell), you then perhaps would find that— (*Whispers*)

BAYES. Now he whispers.

USHER. Alone, do you say?

PHYSICIAN. No; attended with the noble— (*Whispers*)

BAYES. Again.

USHER. Who—he in gray?

PHYSICIAN. Yes; and at the head of— (*Whispers*)

BAYES. Pray, mark.

USHER. Then, sir, most certain, 'twill in time appear
These are the reasons that have moved him to't:
First, he— (*Whispers*)

BAYES. Now the other whispers.

USHER. Secondly, they— (*Whispers*)

BAYES. At it still.

USHER. Thirdly and lastly, both he and they— (*Whispers*)

BAYES. Now they both whisper.

Exeunt whispering

—Now, gentlemen, pray tell me true and without flattery, is not this a very odd beginning of a play?

JOHNSON. In troth, I think it is, sir. But why two kings of the same place?

BAYES. Why? because it's new, and that's it I aim at. I despise your Jonson and Beaumont, that borrowed all they writ from nature. I am for fetching it purely out of my own fancy, I.

SMITH. But what think you, sir, of Sir John Suckling?[1]

BAYES. By gad, I am a better poet than he.

SMITH. Well, sir; but pray, why all this whispering?

BAYES. Why, sir (besides that it is new, as I told you before), because they are supposed to be politicians, and matters of state ought not to be divulged.

SMITH. But then, sir, why—

BAYES. Sir, if you'll but respite your curiosity till the end of the fifth act, you'll find it a piece of patience not ill recompensed.

(*Goes to the door*)

JOHNSON. How dost thou like this, Frank? Is it not just as I told thee?

SMITH. Why, I did never, before this, see anything in nature, and all that (as Mr. Bayes says), so foolish but I could give some guess at what moved the fop to do it; but this, I confess, does go beyond my reach.

JOHNSON. It is all alike. Mr. Wintershull[2] has informed me of this play already. And I'll tell thee, Frank, thou shalt not see one scene here worth one farthing or like anything thou canst imagine has ever been the practice of the world. And then, when he comes to what he calls "good language," it is, as I told thee, very fantastical, most abominably dull, and not one word to the purpose.

SMITH. It does surprise me, I'm sure, very much.

JOHNSON. Aye, but it won't do so long; by that time thou hast seen a play or two that I'll show thee, thou wilt be pretty well acquainted with this new kind of foppery.

SMITH. Pox on't, but there's no pleasure in him; he's too gross a fool to be laughed at.

Enter BAYES

JOHNSON. I'll swear, Mr. Bayes, you have done this scene most admirably; though I must tell you, sir, it is a very difficult matter to pen a whisper well.

BAYES. Aye, gentlemen, when you come to write yourselves, o' my word, you'll find it so.

JOHNSON. Have a care of what you say, Mr. Bayes, for Mr. Smith there, I assure you, has written a great many fine things already.

[1] Suckling (1609–42), besides being a Cavalier poet, was also the author of several plays, of which *Aglaura* (1637) is the most important.
[2] William Wintershal (d. 1679), an actor equally distinguished for comedy and tragedy, a member of Killigrew's company at the Theatre Royal.

BAYES. Has he, i'fackins? Why, then, pray, sir, how do you do when you write?

SMITH. Faith, sir, for the most part I am in pretty good health.

BAYES. Aye, but I mean what do you do when you write?

SMITH. I take pen, ink, and paper, and sit down.

BAYES. Now I write standing; that's one thing; and then, another thing is, with what do you prepare yourself?

SMITH. Prepare myself! What the devil does the fool mean?

BAYES. Why, I'll tell you, now, what I do. If I am to write familiar things, as sonnets to Armida, and the like, I make use of stewed prunes only; [1] but when I have a grand design in hand, I ever take physic, and let blood, for, when you would have pure swiftness of thought and fiery flights of fancy, you must have a care of the pensive part. In fine, you must purge the belly.

SMITH. By my troth, sir, this is a most admirable receipt for writing.

BAYES. Aye, 'tis my secret; and in good earnest, I think, one of the best I have.

SMITH. In good faith, sir, and that may very well be.

BAYES. May be, sir? 'Y gad, I'm sure on't: *experto crede Roberto*.[2] But I must give you this caution by the way: be sure you never take snuff when you write.

SMITH. Why so, sir?

BAYES. Why, it spoiled me once, 'y gad, one of the sparkishest plays in all England. But a friend of mine at Gresham College[3] has promised to help me to some spirit of brains and, 'y gad, that shall do my business.

SCENE II

Enter the two Kings, hand in hand [4]

BAYES. Oh, these now are the two kings of Brentford. Take notice of their style; 'twas never yet upon the stage; but, if you like it, I could make a shift, perhaps, to show you a whole play, writ all just so.

[1] Dryden seems to have followed the rules set forth by Mr. Bayes. As to Armida see note 5, p. 65.
[2] Believe that experienced person, Robert (Robert Howard?).
[3] Where the Royal Society first met.
[4] A hit at a scene in Act IV of *Mustapha* (1665) by the Earl of Orrery.

1ST KING. Did you observe their whisper, brother king?

2D KING. I did; and heard besides a grave bird sing
That they intend, sweetheart,[5] to play us pranks.

BAYES. This is now familiar, because they are both persons of the same quality.

SMITH. 'Sdeath, this would make a man spew.

1ST KING. If that design appears,
I'll lug 'em by the ears
Until I make 'em crack.

2D KING. And so will I, i'fack.

1ST KING. You must begin, *mon foy*.[6]

2D KING. Sweet sir, *pardonnes moy*.[7]

BAYES. Mark that. I makes 'em both speak French to show their breeding.

JOHNSON. Oh, 'tis extraordinary fine.

2D KING. Then, spite of Fate, we'll thus combinèd stand;
And, like true brothers, walk still hand in hand.

Exeunt Reges

JOHNSON. This is a very majestic scene indeed.

BAYES. Aye, 'tis a crust, a lasting crust for your rogue critics, 'y gad. I would fain see the proudest of 'em all but dare to nibble at this; 'y gad, if they do, this shall rub their gums for 'em, I promise you. It was I, you must know, that have written a whole play just in this very same style; but it was never acted yet.

JOHNSON. How so?

BAYES. 'Y gad, I can hardly tell you for laughing—ha, ha, ha! It is so pleasant a story—ha, ha, ha!

SMITH. What is't?

BAYES. 'Y gad, the players refused to act it.—Ha, ha, ha!

SMITH. That's impossible.

BAYES. 'Y gad, they did it, sir, point blank refused it, 'y gad.—Ha, ha, ha!

JOHNSON. Fie, that was rude.

BAYES. Rude! Aye, 'y gad, they are the rudest, uncivilest persons, and all that, in the whole world, 'y gad; 'y gad, there's no living with 'em. I have written, Mr. Johnson, I do verily believe, a whole cart-load of things every

[5] A hit at the endearments voiced by Burr in *The Wild Gallant* (1663).
[6] More bad French for "my faith."
[7] Pardon me

whit as good as this; and yet, I vow to gad, these insolent rascals have turned 'em all back upon my hands again.

JOHNSON. Strange fellows, indeed.

SMITH. But pray, Mr. Bayes, how came these two kings to know of this whisper, for, as I remember, they were not present at it?

BAYES. No, but that's the actors' fault, and not mine; for the kings should (a pox take 'em) have popped both their heads in at the door just as the other went off.

SMITH. That, indeed, would ha' done it.

BAYES. Done it! Aye, 'y gad, these fellows are able to spoil the best things in christendom. I'll tell you, Mr. Johnson, I vow to gad, I have been so highly disobliged by the peremptoriness of these fellows, that I'm resolved hereafter to bend my thoughts wholly for the service of the Nursery,[1] and mump [2] your proud players, 'y gad. So. Now Prince Pretty-man comes in, and falls asleep making love to his mistress, which, you know, was a grand intrigue in a late play[3] written by a very honest gentleman, a knight.

SCENE III

Enter PRINCE PRETTY-MAN

PRETTY-MAN. How strange a captive am I grown of late!
Shall I accuse my love, or blame my fate?
My love, I cannot; that is too divine;
And against Fate what mortal dares repine?

Enter CLORIS

—But here she comes.
Sure 'tis some blazing comet, is it not?
           (*Lies down*)

BAYES. Blazing comet! mark that. 'Y gad, very fine.

PRETTY-MAN. But I am so surprised with sleep I cannot speak the rest.   (*Sleeps*)

BAYES. Does not that, now, surprise you, to fall asleep in the nick? His spirits exhale with the heat of his passion, and all that, and —swop! falls asleep, as you see. Now here she must make a simile.

SMITH. Where's the necessity of that, Mr. Bayes?

BAYES. Because she's surprised. That's a general rule: you must ever make a simile when you are surprised,[4] 'tis the new way of writing.

CLORIS. As some tall pine, which we, on Ætna, find
T'have stood the rage of many a boist'rous wind,
Feeling without, that flames within do play
Which would consume his root and sap away,
He spreads his worsted arms unto the skies,
Silently grieves, all pale, repines and dies:
So, shrouded up, your bright eye disappears;
Break forth, bright scorching Sun, and dry my tears.[5]   *Exit*

JOHNSON. Mr. Bayes, methinks this simile wants a little application, too.

BAYES. No, faith, for it alludes to passion, to consuming, to dying, and all that, which, you know, are the natural effects of an amour. But I'm afraid this scene has made you sad, for, I must confess, when I writ it, I wept myself.

SMITH. No, truly, sir, my spirits are almost exhaled too, and I am likelier to fall asleep.

(PRINCE PRETTY-MAN *starts up, and says*)

PRETTY-MAN. It is resolved.   *Exit*

BAYES. That's all.

SMITH. Mr. Bayes, may one be so bold as to ask you a question now, and you not be angry?

BAYES. O Lord, sir, you may ask me anything, what you please. I vow to gad, you do

---

[1] In 1664 Charles II granted W. Legge a patent to establish a nursery or training-school for young actors, which was instituted in Golden Lane as a "feeder" for Killigrew's company. A second in Hatton Garden served as a training school for Davenant's company.
[2] Cheat.
[3] The reference is obscure, but Summers argues that Fanshaw's *To Love Only for Love's Sake* (1617) is meant. See also Arber's edition of *The Rehearsal*, p. 54.

[4] Bishop Percy pointed out in the eighteenth century that in *The Indian Emperor*, Act IV, scene iv, this rule is followed by Almeria who, surprised by misfortune, says:
   All hopes of safety and of love are gone:
   As when some dreadful thunder-clap is nigh,
   The winged fire shoots swiftly through the sky,
   Strikes and consumes ere scarce it does appear,
   And by the sudden ill, prevents the fear;
   Such is my state in this amazing woe:
   It leaves no power to think, much less to do.
[5] Cf. *The Conquest of Granada*, Part I, Act V, scene iii:
   As some fair tulip, by a storm oppressed,
   Shrinks up and folds its silken arms to rest;
   And, bending to the blast, all pale and dead,
   Hears from within the wind sing round its head:
   So shrouded up your beauty disappears;
   Unveil, my love, and lay aside your fears.

me a great deal of honor: you do not know me if you say that, sir.

SMITH. Then, pray, sir, what is it that this prince here has resolved in his sleep?

BAYES. Why, I must confess, that question is well enough asked for one that is not acquainted with this new way of writing. But you must know, sir, that, to outdo all my fellow-writers, whereas they keep their *intrigo* secret till the very last scene before the dance, I now, sir, do you mark me—a—

SMITH. Begin the play and end it, without ever opening the plot at all?

BAYES. I do so; that's the very plain troth on't. Ha, ha, ha! I do, 'y gad. If they cannot find it out themselves, e'en let 'em alone for Bayes, I warrant you. But here, now, is a scene of business. Pray observe it, for I dare say you'll think it no unwise discourse this, nor ill argued. To tell you true, 'tis a discourse I overheard once betwixt two grand, sober, governing persons.

SCENE IV

Enter Gentleman-Usher *and* Physician

USHER. Come, sir; let's state the matter of fact, and lay our heads together.

PHYSICIAN. Right! lay our heads together.[1] I love to be merry sometimes; but when a knotty point comes, I lay my head close to it, with a snuff box in my hand, and then I fegue[2] it away, i'faith.

BAYES. I do just so, 'y gad, always.

USHER. The grand question is, whether they heard us whisper; which I divide thus:—

PHYSICIAN. Yes, it must be divided so indeed.

SMITH. That's very complacent, I swear, Mr. Bayes, to be of another man's opinion before he knows what it is.

BAYES. Nay, I bring in none here but well-bred persons, I assure you.

USHER. I divided the question into when they heard, what they heard, and whether they heard or no.

JOHNSON. Most admirably divided, I swear.

USHER. As to the when, you say just now; so that is answered. Then, as for what. Why, what

[1] The following scene is a hit at Dryden's habit of arguing fine points of logic in verse. See, for example, *The Conquest of Granada*, Part II, Act III, Scene ii.
[2] Drive.

answers itself; for what could they hear but what we talked of? So that naturally and of necessity we come to the last question, *videlicet*, whether they heard or no.

SMITH. This is a very wise scene, Mr. Bayes.

BAYES. Aye, you have it right; they are both politicians.

USHER. Pray, then, to proceed in method, let me ask you that question.

PHYSICIAN. No, you'll answer better; pray let me ask it you.

USHER. Your will must be a law.

PHYSICIAN. Come then, what is it I must ask?

SMITH. This politician, I perceive, Mr. Bayes, has somewhat a short memory.

BAYES. Why, sir, you must know that t'other is the main politician, and this is but his pupil.

USHER. You must ask me whether they heard us whisper.

PHYSICIAN. Well, I do so.

USHER. Say it then.

SMITH. Hey day! here's the bravest work that ever I saw.

JOHNSON. This is mighty methodical!

BAYES. Aye, sir; that's the way: 'tis the way of art; there is no other way, 'y gad, in business.

PHYSICIAN. Did they hear us whisper?

USHER. Why, truly I can't tell. There's much to be said upon the word *whisper*. To whisper, in Latin, is *susurrare*, which is as much as to say, to speak softly. Now if they heard us speak softly, they heard us whisper; but then comes in the *Quomodo*, the how: how did they hear us whisper? Why as to that, there are two ways; the one, by chance or accident; the other, on purpose—that is, with design to hear us whisper.

PHYSICIAN. Nay, if they heard us that way, I'll never give 'em physic more.

USHER. Nor I e'er more will walk abroad before 'em.

BAYES. Pray mark this; for a great deal depend[s] upon it towards the latter end of the play.

SMITH. I suppose that's the reason why you brought in this scene, Mr. Bayes?

BAYES. Partly it was, sir, but I confess I was not unwilling, besides, to show the world a pattern here how men should talk of business.

JOHNSON. You have done it exceeding well indeed.

BAYES. Yes, I think this will do.

PHYSICIAN. Well, if they heard us whisper, they'll turn us out, and nobody else will take us.

SMITH. Not for politicians, I dare answer for it.

PHYSICIAN. Let's then no more ourselves in vain bemoan;
We are not safe until we them unthrone.

USHER. 'Tis right.
And, since occasion now seems debonair,
I'll seize on this, and you shall take that chair.
(They draw their swords and sit down in the two great chairs upon the stage)

BAYES. There's now an odd surprise; the whole state's turn'd quite topsy-turvy,[1] without any puther or stir in the whole world, 'y gad.

JOHNSON. A very silent change of a government, truly, as ever I heard of.

BAYES. It is so. And yet you shall see me bring 'em in again by and by in as odd a way every jot.
(The Usurpers *march out flourishing their swords)*

Enter SHIRLEY[2]

SHIRLEY. Hey ho, hey ho! what a change is here! Hey day, hey day! I know not what to do, nor what to say.[3]   *Exit*

JOHNSON. Mr. Bayes, in my opinion now, that gentleman might have said a little more upon this occasion.

BAYES. No, sir, not at all; for I under-writ his part on purpose to set off the rest.

JOHNSON. Cry you mercy, sir.

SMITH. But pray, sir, how came they to depose the kings so easily?

BAYES. Why, sir, you must know, they long had a design to do it before, but never could put it in practice till now; and, to tell you true, that's one reason why I made 'em whisper so at first.

SMITH. Oh, very well; now I'm fully satisfied.

BAYES. And then, to show you, sir, it was not done so very easily neither, in this next scene you shall see some fighting.

SMITH. Oh, ho! so then you make the struggle to be after the business is done?

BAYES. Aye.

SMITH. Oh, I conceive you. That, I swear, is very natural.

SCENE V

Enter four men at one door, and four at another, with their swords drawn

1ST SOLDIER. Stand![4] Who goes there?
2D SOLDIER. A friend.
1ST SOLDIER. What friend?
2D SOLDIER. A friend to the house.
[1ST SOLDIER.] Fall on!
(They all kill one another. Music strikes)

BAYES. *(To the music)* Hold, hold! *(It ceaseth)* Now, here's an odd surprise: all these dead men you shall see rise up presently, at a certain note that I have made, in *Effaut flat*,[5] and fall a-dancing. Do you hear, dead men? Remember your note in *Effaut flat*. *(To the music)* Play on.—Now, now, now!
(The music play his note, and the dead men rise but cannot get in order)
—O Lord, O Lord!—Out, out, out!—Did ever men spoil a good thing so? no figure, no ear, no time, nothing! Udzookers,[6] you dance worse than the angels in *Harry the Eight*,[7] or the fat spirits in *The Tempest*,[8] 'y gad.

1ST SOLDIER. Why, sir, 'tis impossible to do anything in time to this tune.

BAYES. O Lord, O Lord! Impossible? why, gentlemen, if there be any faith in a person that's a Christian, I sate up two whole nights in composing this air and apting it for the business. For, if you observe, there are two several designs in this tune; it begins swift, and ends slow. You talk of time, and time;

---

[1] The *Key* refers to the "very feeble means" and "slight occasions" which upset princes and governments in plays of the period, and cites Act IV, scene i of Dryden's *Marriage à la Mode* in proof.

[2] A noted stage dancer of the day. His first name is not known.

[3] Cf. *Ormasdes, or Love and Friendship* (1664) by Killigrew, Act V:
  I know not what to say, nor what to think!
  I know not when I sleep, or when I wake.
Also his *Pandora, or The Converts* (1665), Act V:
  My doubts and fears, my reason does dismay,
  I know not what to do nor what to say. (*Key*)

[4] A parody of the opening lines of Act IV, scene i, of *The Maiden Queen* (1667).

[5] F flat.

[6] A meaningless oath, a corruption of "God's wounds."

[7] A production of *Henry VIII* in 1664, seen by Pepys on New Year's Day, was notable for its "shows and processions." The reference is to the scene (Act IV, scene ii, in the Shakespeare-Fletcher text) in which six angels comfort the dying Katherine in a vision.

[8] Revived November 7, 1667, in the Dryden-Davenant version. In the 1701 edition a stage direction to Act III reads "enter eight fat spirits" but this later was taken out. (Summers.)

you shall see me do't. Look you now. (*Lies down flat on his face*) Here I am dead. Now mark my note, *Effaut flat.*—Strike up music. Now.

(*As he rises up hastily, he falls down again*) —Ah, gadsookers! I have broke my nose.[1]

JOHNSON. By my troth, Mr. Bayes, this is a very unfortunate note of yours in *Effaut*.

BAYES. A plague of this damned stage, with your nails and your tenter-hooks,[2] that a gentleman cannot come to teach you to act but he must break his nose, and his face, and the devil and all. Pray, sir, can you help me to a wet piece of brown paper?

SMITH. No indeed, sir; I don't usually carry any about me.

2D SOLDIER. Sir, I'll go get you some within presently.

BAYES. Go, go then; I follow you. Pray, dance out the dance, and I'll be with you in a moment. Remember, you dance like horsemen.

Exit BAYES

SMITH. Like horsemen! What a plague can that be?

(*They dance the dance, but can make nothing of it*)

1ST SOLDIER. A devil! let's try this no longer. Play my dance that Mr. Bayes found fault with so.

Dance, and exeunt

SMITH. What can this fool be doing all this while about his nose?

JOHNSON. Prithee, let's go see. *Exeunt*

ACT III

SCENE I

Enter BAYES *with a paper on his nose, and the two* Gentlemen

BAYES. Now, sirs, this I do because my fancy in this play is to end every act with a dance.[3]

SMITH. Faith, that fancy is very good, but I should hardly have broke my nose for it, though.

JOHNSON. That fancy, I suppose, is new, too.

BAYES. Sir, all my fancies are so. I tread upon no man's heels, but make my flight upon my own wings, I assure you. Now here comes in a scene of sheer wit without any mixture in the whole world, 'y gad, between Prince Pretty-man and his tailor. It might properly enough be called a prize of wit; for you shall see 'em come in upon one another snip, snap, hit for hit, as fast as can be. First one speaks, then presently t'other's upon him slap, with a repartee; then he at him again, dash! with a new conceit, and so eternally, eternally, 'y gad, till they go quite off the stage.

(*Goes to call the* Players)

SMITH. What a plague does this fop mean by his snip snap, hit for hit, and dash?

JOHNSON. Mean? why, he never meant anything in's life. What dost talk of meaning for?

Enter BAYES

BAYES. Why don't you come in?

Enter PRINCE PRETTY-MAN *and* TOM THIMBLE [4]

BAYES. This scene will make you die with laughing, if it be well acted, for 'tis as full of drollery as ever it can hold; 'tis like an orange stuffed with cloves as for conceit.

PRETTY-MAN. But prithee, Tom Thimble, why wilt thou needs marry? If nine tailors make but one man, and one woman cannot be satisfied with nine men, what work art thou cutting out here for thyself, trow?

BAYES. Good!

THIMBLE. Why, an't please your highness, if I can't make up all the work I cut out, I shan't want journeymen enough to help me, I warrant you.

BAYES. Good again.

PRETTY-MAN. I am afraid thy journeymen, though, Tom, won't work by the day, but by the night.

BAYES. Good still.

THIMBLE. However, if my wife sits but cross-legg'd, as I do, there will be no great danger—not half so much as when I trusted you, sir, for your coronation suit.

BAYES. Very good, i'faith.

---

[1] A hit at Sir William Davenant, whose snub nose was often satirized. *The Rehearsal* must not be read as an attack on Dryden only.

[2] A sharp hooked nail used to stretch cloth.

[3] The interpolation of dances and spectacles into his heroic plays was a favorite device of Dryden's.

[4] This scene parodies a scene in Act I of Dryden's *The Wild Gallant* (1663) between Loveby and Will Bibber, a tailor.

PRETTY-MAN. Why, the times then lived upon trust; it was the fashion. You would not be out of time, at such a time as that, sure. A tailor, you know, must never be out of fashion.

BAYES. Right.

THIMBLE. I'm sure, sir, I made your clothes in the Court fashion, for you never paid me yet.

BAYES. There's a bob [1] for the Court.

PRETTY-MAN. Why, Tom, thou art a sharp rogue when thou art angry, I see; thou pay'st me now, methinks.

BAYES. There's pay upon pay! as good as ever was written, 'y gad!

THIMBLE. Aye, sir, in your own coin; you give me nothing but words.

BAYES. Admirable, before gad!

PRETTY-MAN. Well, Tom, I hope shortly I shall have another coin for thee; for now the wars are coming on, I shall grow to be a man of mettle.

BAYES. Oh, you did not do that half enough.
JOHNSON. Methinks he does it admirably.
BAYES. Aye, pretty well, but he does not hit me in't. He does not top his part.

THIMBLE. That's the way to be stamped yourself, sir. I shall see you come home, like an angel [2] for the king's evil, with a hole bored through you.
Exeunt

BAYES. Ha, there he has hit it up to the hilts, 'y gad. How do you like it now, gentlemen? Is not this pure wit?

SMITH. 'Tis "snip snap," sir, as you say, but methinks not pleasant nor to the purpose, for the play does not go on.

BAYES. Play does not go on? I don't know what you mean; why, is not this part of the play?

SMITH. Yes, but the plot stands still.

BAYES. Plot stand still! why, what a devil is the plot good for but to bring in fine things?

SMITH. Oh, I did not know that before.

BAYES. No, I think you did not; nor many things more that I am master of. Now, sir, 'y gad, this is the bane of all us writers: let us soar but never so little above the common pitch, 'y gad, all's spoiled; for the vulgar never understand it. They can never conceive you, sir, the excellency of these things.

JOHNSON. 'Tis a sad fate, I must confess. But you write on still for all that?

BAYES. Write on? I, 'y gad, I warrant you. 'Tis not their talk shall stop me; if they catch me at that lock, I'll give 'em leave to hang me. As long as I know my things are good, what care I what they say?—What, are they gone without singing my last new song? 'Sbud,[3] would it were in their bellies! I'll tell you, Mr. Johnson, if I have any skill in these matters, I vow to gad this song is peremptorily [4] the very best that ever yet was written. You must know it was made by Tom Thimble's first wife after she was dead.

SMITH. How, sir? After she was dead?

BAYES. Aye, sir, after she was dead. Why, what have you to say to that?

JOHNSON. Say? Why, nothing; he were a devil that had anything to say to that!

BAYES. Right.

SMITH. How did she come to die, pray, sir?

BAYES. Phoo! that's no matter—by a fall. But here's the conceit: that upon his knowing she was killed by an accident, he supposes with a sigh that she died for love of him.

JOHNSON. Aye, aye, that's well enough. Let's hear it, Mr. Bayes.

BAYES. 'Tis to the tune of "Farewell, fair Armida,[5] on seas and in battles, in bullets" and all that.

SONG

In swords, pikes, and bullets, 'tis safer to be
Than in a strong castle, remoted from thee;
My death's bruise pray think you gave me, though a fall
Did give it me more, from the top of a wall;
For then, if the moat on her mud would first lay,
And after, before you my body convey,
The blue on my breast when you happen to see,
You'll say with a sigh, there's a true-blue for me.

Ha, rogues! when I am merry, I write these things as fast as hops, 'y gad; for you must know I am as pleasant a debauchee as ever you saw, I am, i'faith.

---

[1] Jeer.
[2] A person suffering from scrofula was touched by the king, when a gold angel (a coin worth about ten shillings) was hung about his neck. Charles II regularly "touched for the king's evil."
[3] A corruption of "God's blood."
[4] Incontrovertibly.
[5] The following song parodies the second stanza of a song by that name written by Dryden and published in 1672, Armida being the Duchess of Richmond.

SMITH. But, Mr. Bayes, how comes this song in here? for methinks there is no great occasion for it.

BAYES. Alack, sir, you know nothing. You must ever interlard your plays with songs, ghosts, and dances if you mean to—a—

JOHNSON. Pit, box, and gallery, Mr. Bayes.

BAYES. 'Y gad and you have nicked it. Hark you, Mr. Johnson, you know I don't flatter; 'y gad, you have a great deal of wit.

JOHNSON. O Lord, sir, you do me too much honor.

BAYES. Nay, nay, come, come, Mr. Johnson, 'y faith this must not be said amongst us that have it. I know you have wit by the judgment you make of this play, for that's the measure I go by; my play is my touchstone. When a man tells me such a one is a person of parts, "Is he so?" say I. What do I do but bring him presently to see this play. If he likes it, I know what to think of him; if not, "your most humble servant, sir, I'll no more of him upon my word; I thank you." I am *clara voyant*,[1] 'y gad. Now, here we go on to our business.

SCENE II

Enter the two Usurpers, *hand in hand*

USHER. But what's become of Volscius the great?
His presence has not graced our courts of late.

PHYSICIAN. I fear some ill, from emulation sprung,
Has from us that illustrious hero wrung.

BAYES. Is not that majestical?

SMITH. Yes, but who a devil is that Volscius?

BAYES. Why, that's a prince I make in love with Parthenope.

SMITH. I thank you, sir.

Enter CORDELIO

CORDELIO. My lieges, news from Volscius the Prince.

USHER. His news is welcome, whatsoe'er it be.

SMITH. How, sir, do you mean—whether it be good or bad?

BAYES. Nay, pray, sir, have a little patience! Godsookers, you'll spoil all my play! Why, sir, 'tis impossible to answer every impertinent question you ask.

SMITH. Cry you mercy, sir.

[1] Clairvoyant.

CORDELIO. His highness, sirs, commanded me to tell you
That the fair person whom you both do know,
Despairing of forgiveness for her fault,
In a deep sorrow, twice she did attempt
Upon her precious life; but, by the care
Of standers-by, prevented was.

SMITH. 'Sheart, what stuff's here!

CORDELIO. At last,
Volscius the great this dire resolve embraced:
His servants he into the country sent,
And he himself to Piccadillé went;
Where he's informed, by letters, that she's dead!

USHER. Dead! Is that possible? Dead!

PHYSICIAN. O ye gods! *Exeunt*

BAYES. There's a smart expression of a passion—"O ye gods!" That's one of my bold strokes, 'y gad.

SMITH. Yes, but who is the fair person that's dead?

BAYES. That you shall know anon, sir.

SMITH. Nay, if we know it at all, 'tis well enough.

BAYES. Perhaps you may find too, by and by, for all this, that she's not dead neither.

SMITH. Marry, that's good news indeed. I am glad of that with all my heart.

BAYES. Now, here's the man brought in that is supposed to have killed her.

(*A great shout within*)

SCENE III

Enter AMARYLLIS *with a book in her hand, and* Attendants

AMARYLLIS. What shout triumphant's that?

Enter a Soldier

SOLDIER. Shy maid, upon the river brink,
Near Twick'nam Town, the false assassinate
Is ta'en.

AMARYLLIS. Thanks to the powers above for this deliverance!
I hope its slow beginning will portend
A forward exit to all future end.

BAYES. Pish, there you are out! To all future end? No, no—to all future *end:* you must lay the accent upon "end," or else you lose the conceit.

SMITH. I see you are very perfect in these matters.

BAYES. Aye, sir; I have been long enough at it, one would think, to know something.

Enter Soldiers *dragging in an old* Fisherman [1]

AMARYLLIS. Villain, what monster did corrupt thy mind
T'attack the noblest soul of human kind?
Tell me who set thee on.
FISHERMAN. Prince Pretty-man.
AMARYLLIS. To kill whom?
FISHERMAN. Prince Pretty-man.
AMARYLLIS. What, did Prince Pretty-man hire you to kill Prince Pretty-man?
FISHERMAN. No; Prince Volscius.
AMARYLLIS. To kill whom?
FISHERMAN. Prince Volscius.
AMARYLLIS. What, did Prince Volscius hire you to kill Prince Volscius?
FISHERMAN. No; Prince Pretty-man.
AMARYLLIS. So!—drag him hence.
Till torture of the rack [2] produce his sense.

Exeunt

BAYES. Mark how I make the horror of his guilt confound his intellects—for he's out at one and t'other; and that's the design of this scene.

SMITH. I see, sir, you have a several design for every scene.

BAYES. Aye, that's my way of writing, and so, sir, I can dispatch you a whole play, before another man, 'y gad, can make an end of his plot.

SCENE IV

BAYES. So, now enter Prince Pretty-man in a rage.—Where the devil is he? Why, Pretty-man! why, when,[3] I say? Oh, fie, fie, fie, fie! all's marred, I vow to gad, quite marred.

Enter PRETTY-MAN

—Phoo, pox! you are come too late, sir; now you may go out again if you please. I vow to gad, Mr.—a—I would not give a button for my play, now you have done this.

PRETTY-MAN. What, sir?

BAYES. What, sir! 'Slife, sir, you should have come out in choler, rous [4] upon the stage, just as the other went off. Must a man be eternally telling you of these things?

JOHNSON. Sure, this must be some very notable matter that he's so angry at.

SMITH. I am not of your opinion.

BAYES. Pish! come, let's hear your part, sir.

PRETTY-MAN.[5] Bring in my father; why d'ye keep him from me?
Although a fisherman, he is my father!
Was ever son yet brought to this distress,
To be, for being a son, made fatherless?
Ah, you just gods, rob me not of a father:
The being of a son take from me rather. *Exit*

SMITH. Well, Ned, what think you now?

JOHNSON. A devil! this is worst of all.—Mr. Bayes, pray what's the meaning of this scene?

BAYES. O, cry you mercy, sir; I purtest I had forgot to tell you. Why, sir, you must know that long before the beginning of this play, this prince was taken by a fisherman.

SMITH. How, sir, taken prisoner?

BAYES. Taken prisoner! O Lord, what a question's there! did ever any man ask such a question? Godsookers, he has put the plot quite out of my head with this damned question. What was I going to say?

JOHNSON. Nay, the Lord knows; I can not imagine.

BAYES. Stay, let me see—taken. O, 'tis true. Why, sir, as I was going to say his highness here, the Prince, was taken in a cradle by a fisherman and brought up as his child.

SMITH. Indeed?

BAYES. Nay, prithee, hold thy peace.—And so, sir, this murder being committed by the river-side, the fisherman upon suspicion was seized, and thereupon the prince grew angry.

SMITH. So, so; now 'tis very plain.

JOHNSON. But, Mr. Bayes, is not this some disparagement to a Prince to pass for a fisherman's son? Have a care of that, I pray.

BAYES. No, no, not at all; for 'tis but for

---

[1] A burlesque of a scene in *Marriage à la Mode*, Act I, in which Polydamas cross questions Hermogenes as to the fate of his wife and child. However, a similar scene from Stapylton's *The Slighted Maid* (already attacked in the "Song in Dialogue" between Thunder and Lightning in Act I of *The Rehearsal*) is quoted by Summers, and in the *Key*.

[2] Polydamas sends Hermogenes to the rack.

[3] Exclamatory; "when are you coming?"

[4] Slap-dash.

[5] Cf. *Marriage à la Mode*, Act I, scene i:

Those I employed have in the neighboring hamlet,
Amongst the fishers' cabins, made discovery
Of some young persons, whose uncommon beauty
And graceful carriage, make it seem suspicious
They are not what they seem.

The whole fisherman passage is a burlesque upon the plot of this play, particularly with reference to the fortunes of Leonidas.

a while. I shall fetch him off again presently, you shall see.

Enter PRETTY-MAN *and* THIMBLE

PRETTY-MAN. By all the gods, I'll set the world on fire
Rather than let 'em ravish hence my sire.
    THIMBLE. Brave, Pretty-man, it is at length revealed
That he is not thy sire who thee concealed.

BAYES. Lo, you now; there, he's off again.
JOHNSON. Admirably done, i' faith.
BAYES. Aye, now the plot thickens very much upon us.
PRETTY-MAN. What oracle this darkness can evince?
Sometimes a fisher's son, sometimes a prince.
It is a secret, great as is the world,
In which I, like the soul, am tossed and hurled.
The blackest ink of fate sure was my lot,
And when she writ my name, she made a blot.
                        Exit

BAYES. There's a blust'ring verse for you now.
SMITH. Yes, sir, but why is he so mightily troubled to find he is not a fisherman's son?
BAYES. Phoo! that is not because he has a mind to be his son, but for fear he should be thought to be nobody's son at all.
SMITH. Nay, that would trouble a man, indeed.
BAYES. So; let me see.

SCENE V

BAYES. (*Reads*) "Enter Prince Volscius going out of town."
SMITH. I thought he had gone to Piccadillé.
BAYES. Yes, he gave it out so, but that was only to cover his design.
JOHNSON. What design?
BAYES. Why, to head the army that lies concealed for him in Knightsbridge.[1]
JOHNSON. I see here's a great deal of plot, Mr. Bayes.
BAYES. Yes, now it begins to break; but we shall have a world of more business anon.

Enter PRINCE VOLSCIUS,[2] CLORIS, AMARYLLIS *and* HARRY *with a riding-cloak and boots*

AMARYLLIS. Sir, you are cruel, thus to leave the town

And to retire to country solitude.
    CLORIS. We hoped this summer that we should at least
Have held the honor of your company.

BAYES. Held the honor of your company! prettily exprest!—Held the honor of your company! Godsookers, these fellows will never take notice of anything.
JOHNSON. I assure you, sir, I admire it extremely; I don't know what he does.
BAYES. Aye, aye, he's a little envious, but 'tis no great matter.—Come!

AMARYLLIS. Pray, let us two this single boon obtain,
That you will here with poor us still remain.[3]
Before your horses come, pronounce our fate;
For then, alas, I fear 'twill be too late.

BAYES. Sad!

VOLSCIUS. Harry, my boots; for I'll go rage among
My blades encamped, and quit this urban throng.

SMITH. But pray, Mr. Bayes, is not this a little difficult, that you were saying e'en now, to keep an army thus concealed in Knightsbridge?
BAYES. In Knightsbridge?—stay.
JOHNSON. No, not if the innkeepers be his friends.
BAYES. His friends! Aye, sir, his intimate acquaintance; or else, indeed, I grant it could not be.
SMITH. Yes, faith, so it might be very easy.
BAYES. Nay, if I do not make all things easy, 'y gad, I'll give you leave to hang me. Now you would think that he is going out of town, but you shall see how prettily I have contrived to stop him presently.
SMITH. By my troth, sir, you have so amazed me that I know not what to think.

Enter PARTHENOPE

VOLSCIUS. Bless me! how frail are all my best resolves!
How, in a moment, is my purpose changed!
Too soon I thought myself secure from love.

---

[1] Across the Tyburn (a small tributary of the Thames).
[2] The following scene is a burlesque of *The English Monsieur*, Act IV, scene ii, a comedy by James Howard acted in 1666. In this scene Comely, about to leave London, is attracted by Elsbeth Pritty, a country lass, and changes his mind.
[3] Cf. "And leaves poor me defenceless here alone," *The Indian Emperor*, Act V, scene ii.

Fair madam, give me leave to ask her name
Who does so gently rob me of my fame:
For I should meet the army out of town,
And, if I fail, must hazard my renown.

PARTHENOPE. My mother, sir, sells ale by the town walls,
And me her dear Parthenope she calls.

BAYES. Now that's the Parthenope I told you of.

JOHNSON. Aye, aye; 'y gad, you are very right.

VOLSCIUS. Can vulgar vestments high-born beauty shroud?[1]
Thou bring'st the morning pictured in a cloud.

BAYES. The morning pictured in a cloud! A godsookers, what a conceit is there!

PARTHENOPE. Give you good ev'n, sir.[2] *Exit*
VOLSCIUS. O inauspicious stars! that I was born
To sudden love and to more sudden scorn!
AMARYLLIS ⎫ —How! Prince Volscius in love?
CLORIS   ⎭ Ha, ha, ha!
Exeunt laughing

SMITH. Sure, Mr. Bayes, we have lost some jest here that they laugh at so.

BAYES. Why did you not observe? He first resolves to go out of town, and then, as he is pulling on his boots, falls in love with her. Ha, ha, ha!

SMITH. Well, and where lies the jest of that?
BAYES. Ha? (*Turns to* JOHNSON)
JOHNSON. Why, in the boots; where should the jest lie?

BAYES. 'Y gad, you are in the right, it does lie in the boots. (*Turns to* SMITH) Your friend and I know where a good jest lies, tho' you don't, sir.

SMITH. Much good do't you, sir.

BAYES. Here, now, Mr. Johnson, you shall see a combat betwixt love and honor. An ancient author[3] has made a whole play on't, but I have dispatched it all in this scene.

(VOLSCIUS *sits down to pull on his boots;*
BAYES *stands by and over acts the part as he speaks it.*)

VOLSCIUS. How has my passion made me Cupid's scoff[4]

This hasty boot is on, the other off,
And sullen lies, with amorous design
To quit loud fame and make that beauty mine.

SMITH. Prithee, mark what pains Mr. Bayes takes to act this speech himself.

JOHNSON. Yes, the fool, I see, is mightily transported with it.

VOLSCIUS. My legs, the emblem of my various thought,
Show to what sad distraction I am brought.
Sometimes with stubborn honor, like this boot,
My mind is guarded, and resolved to do't;
Sometimes again, that very mind, by love
Disarmèd, like this other leg does prove.
Shall I to Honor or to Love give way?
"Go on," cries Honor; tender Love says, "Nay."
Honor aloud commands: "Pluck both boots on";
But softer Love does whisper, "Put on none."
What shall I do? what conduct shall I find
To lead me through this twilight of my mind?
For as bright day with black approach of night
Contending, makes a doubtful, puzzling light,
So does my honor and my love together
Puzzle me so, I can resolve for neither.
(*Goes out hopping with one boot on, and the other off*)

JOHNSON. By my troth, sir, this is as difficult a combat as ever I saw, and as equal; for 'tis determined on neither side.

BAYES. Aye, is't not now, 'y gad, ha? For to go off hip hop, hip hop upon this occasion is a thousand times better than any conclusion in the world, 'y gad.

JOHNSON. Indeed, Mr. Bayes, that hip hop in this place, as you say, does a very great deal.

BAYES. O, all in all, sir; they are these little things that mar or set you off a play; as I remember once in a play of mine, I set off a scene, 'y gad, beyond expectation, only with a petticoat and the belly-ache.[5]

SMITH. Pray, how was that, sir?

BAYES. Why, sir, I contrived a petticoat to be brought in upon a chair (nobody knew how) into a prince's chamber, whose father was not to see it, that came in by chance.

JOHNSON. God's my life, that was a notable contrivance, indeed.

SMITH. Aye; but, Mr. Bayes, how could you contrive the belly-ache?

BAYES. The easiest i'th' world, 'y gad. I'll tell you how: I made the prince sit down upon the petticoat, no more than so, and pretended

---

[1] Cf. *The Siege of Rhodes*, Second Entry, ll. 110–111.
[2] The parody returns to *The English Monsieur*.
[3] Davenant, whose *Love and Honor* was revived in 1661.
[4] A general burlesque on the love and honor debates in heroic drama. For illustrative passages see Arber's edition of *The Rehearsal*, pp. 86–88.
[5] A hit at Act IV, scene i, of Dryden's *The Assignation; or, Love in a Nunnery* (1672).

to his father that he had just then got the belly-ache; whereupon his father went out to call a physician, and his man ran away with the petticoat.

SMITH. Well, and what followed upon that?

BAYES. Nothing, no earthly thing, I vow to gad.

JOHNSON. Oh, my word, Mr. Bayes, there you hit it.

BAYES. Yes, it gave a world of content. And then I paid 'em away besides, for I made 'em all talk bawdy—Ha, ha, ha!—beastly, downright bawdry upon the stage, 'y gad—ha, ha, ha!—but with an infinite deal of wit, that I must say.

JOHNSON. That, aye that, we know well enough, can never fail you.

BAYES. No, 'y gad, can't it. Come, bring in the dance. *Exit to call 'em*

SMITH. Now, the devil take thee for a silly, confident, unnatural, fulsome rogue!

Enter BAYES *and* Players

BAYES. Pray dance well before these gentlemen. You are commonly so lazy, but you should be light and easy, tah, tah, tah.

(*All the while they dance,* BAYES *puts 'em out with teaching 'em*)

Well, gentlemen, you'll see this dance, if I am not deceived, take very well upon the stage when they are perfect in their motions and all that.

SMITH. I don't know how 'twill take, sir, but I am sure you sweat hard for't.

BAYES. Aye, sir, it costs me more pains and trouble to do these things than almost the things are worth.

SMITH. By my troth, I think so, sir.

BAYES. Not for the things themselves, for I could write you, sir, forty of 'em in a day, but, 'y gad, these players are such dull persons that, if a man be not by 'em upon every point and at every turn, 'y gad, they'll mistake you, sir, and spoil all.

Enter a Player

What, is the funeral ready?

PLAYER. Yes, sir.

BAYES. And is the lance filled with wine?

PLAYER. Sir, 'tis just now a-doing.

BAYES. Stay, then, I'll do it myself.

SMITH. Come, let's go with him.

BAYES. A match! But, Mr. Johnson, 'y gad, I am not like other persons; they care not what becomes of their things, so they can but get money for 'em. Now, 'y gad, when I write, if it be not just as it should be in every circumstance, to every particular, 'y gad, I am no more able to endure it; I am not myself, I'm out of my wits and all that; I'm the strangest person in the whole world. For what care I for money? I write for reputation.

Exeunt

ACT IV

SCENE I

Enter BAYES *and the two* Gentlemen

BAYES. Gentlemen, because I would not have any two things alike in this play, the last act beginning with a witty scene of mirth, I make this to begin with a funeral.[1]

SMITH. And is that all your reason for it, Mr. Bayes?

BAYES. No, sir, I have a precedent for it besides. A person of honor and a scholar brought in his funeral just so; and he was one (let me tell you) that knew as well what belonged to a funeral as any man in England, 'y gad.

JOHNSON. Nay, if that be so, you are safe.

BAYES. 'Y gad, but I have another device—a frolic, which I think yet better than all this; not for the plot or characters (for in my heroic plays, I make no difference as to those matters), but for another contrivance.

SMITH. What is that, I pray?

BAYES. Why, I have designed a conquest that cannot possibly, 'y gad, be acted in less than a whole week; and I'll speak a bold word, it shall drum,[2] trumpet, shout and battle, 'y gad, with any the most warlike tragedy we have, either ancient or modern.

JOHNSON. Aye, marry sir, there you say something.

SMITH. And pray, sir, how have you ordered this same frolic of yours?

BAYES. Faith, sir, by the rule of romance.[3] For example: they divided their things into

---

[1] Henry Howard's *The United Kingdoms* (which, as has been mentioned, may have suggested the two kings of Brentford) begins with a funeral.

[2] Dryden defends the use of drums, trumpets, and battles in his *Essay of Heroick Plays*, prefixed to the first part of *The Conquest of Granada*.

[3] The original editions of the French heroic romances ran to many volumes. Dryden's interest in writing plays in two parts (and therefore ten acts) seemed to Buckingham to have the same tedious tendency.

THE REHEARSAL

three, four, five, six, seven, eight, or as many tomes as they please; now I would very fain know what should hinder me from doing the same with my things if I please?

JOHNSON. Nay, if you should not be master of your own works, 'tis very hard.

BAYES. That is my sense. And then, sir, this contrivance of mine has something of the reason of a play in it, too, for as every one makes you five acts to one play, what do me I but make five plays to one plot,[1] by which means the auditors have every day a new thing.

JOHNSON. Most admirably good, i'faith! and must certainly take, because it is not tedious.

BAYES. Aye, sir, I know that; there's the main point. And then, upon Saturday, to make a close of all (for I ever begin upon a Monday), I make you, sir, a sixth play, that sums up the whole matter to 'em, and all that, for fear they should have forgot it.

JOHNSON. That consideration, Mr. Bayes, indeed, I think, will be very necessary.

SMITH. And when comes in your share, pray, sir?

BAYES. The third week.[2]

JOHNSON. I vow, you'll get a world of money.

BAYES. Why, faith, a man must live; and if you don't thus pitch upon some new device, 'y gad, you'll never do it; for this age (take it o' my sword) is somewhat hard to please. But there's one pretty odd passage in the last of these plays, which may be executed two several ways, wherein I'd have your opinion, gentlemen.

JOHNSON. What is't, sir?

BAYES. Why, sir, I make a male person to be in love with a female.

SMITH. Do you mean that, Mr. Bayes, for a new thing?

BAYES. Yes, sir, as I have ordered it. You shall hear. He having passionately loved her through my five whole plays, finding at last that she consents to his love, just after that his mother[3] had appeared to him like a ghost, he kills himself. That's one way. The other is, that she coming at last to love him with as violent a passion as he loved her, she kills herself. Now my question is, which of these two persons should suffer upon this occasion?

JOHNSON. By my troth, it is a very hard case to decide.

BAYES. The hardest in the world, 'y gad; and has puzzled this pate very much. What say you, Mr. Smith?

SMITH. Why, truly, Mr. Bayes, if it might stand with your justice now, I would now spare 'em both.

BAYES. 'Y gad, and I think—ha—why then, I'll make him hinder her from killing herself. Aye, it shall be so.—Come, come, bring in the funeral.

Enter a Funeral, with the two Usurpers *and Attendants*

Lay it down there—no, no, here, sir.—So; now speak.

KING USHER. Set down the funeral pile, and let our grief
Receive from its embraces some relief.

KING PHYSICIAN. Was't not unjust to ravish hence her breath,
And in life's stead to leave us nought but death?
The world discovers now its emptiness,
And by her loss demonstrates we have less.

BAYES. Is not this good language, now? is not that elevate? 'Tis my *non ultra*,[4] 'y gad. You must know they were both in love with her.

SMITH. With her?—with whom?

BAYES. Why, this is Lardella's funeral.

SMITH. Lardella! Aye, who is she?

BAYES. Why, sir, the sister of Drawcansir—a lady that was drowned at sea and had a wave for her winding-sheet.[5]

KING USHER. Lardella, O Lardella, from above
Behold the tragic issues of our love.
Pity us sinking under grief and pain,
For thy being cast away upon the main.

BAYES. Look you now, you see I told you true.

SMITH. Aye, sir, and I thank you for it, very kindly.

BAYES. Aye, 'y gad, but you will not have patience; honest M—a—you will not have patience.

---

[1] There are a number of Restoration plays in two parts; and some even in three.
[2] The author usually received the profits from every third performance of his play.
[3] In the *Conquest of Granada*, Part II, Act IV, scene iii, Almanzor (here burlesqued as Drawcansir), waiting to see Almahide, his mistress, is reproved by the ghost of his mother for his passion.
[4] No further; i.e., my best.
[5] See note 3 above.

JOHNSON. Pray, Mr. Bayes, who is that Drawcansir?

BAYES. Why, sir, a fierce hero that frights his mistress, snubs up kings, baffles armies, and does what he will, without regard to numbers, good manners, or justice.[1]

JOHNSON. A very pretty character.

SMITH. But, Mr. Bayes, I thought your heroes had ever been men of great humanity and justice.

BAYES. Yes, they have been so; but, for my part, I prefer that one quality of singly beating of whole armies above all your moral virtues put together, 'y gad. You shall see him come in presently. (*To the* Players)— Zookers, why don't you read the paper?

KING PHYSICIAN. Oh, cry you mercy.
(*Goes to take the paper*)

BAYES. Pish!—nay, you are such a fumbler. Come, I'll read it myself. (*Takes a paper from off the coffin*)—Stay, it's an ill hand; I must use my spectacles. This, now, is a copy of verses which I make Lardella compose just as she is dying, with design to have it pinned upon her coffin, and so read by one of the usurpers, who is her cousin.

SMITH. A very shrewd design that, upon my word, Mr. Bayes.

BAYES. And what do you think now, I fancy her to make love like, here in the paper?

SMITH. Like a woman. What should she make love like?

BAYES. O' my word you are out though, sir; 'y gad, you are.

SMITH. What then? like a man?

BAYES. No, sir, like a humble bee.

SMITH. I confess, that I should not have fancied.

BAYES. It may be so, sir. But it is, though, in order to the opinion of some of your ancient philosophers who held the transmigration of the soul.

SMITH. Very fine.

BAYES. I'll read the title: "To my dear Couz, King Phys."

SMITH. That's a little too familiar with a king though, sir, by your favor, for a humble bee.

BAYES. Mr. Smith, in other things I grant your knowledge may be above me; but as for Poetry, give me leave to say, I understand that better. It has been longer my practice; it has indeed, sir.

SMITH. Your servant, sir.

BAYES. Pray, mark it.[2] (*Reads*)

Since death my earthly part will thus remove,
I'll come a humble bee to your chaste love.
With silent wings I'll follow you, dear couz;
Or else, before you, in the sun-beams buzz.
And when to melancholy groves you come,
An airy ghost, you'll know me by my hum;
For sound, being air, a ghost does well become.

SMITH. (*After a pause*) Admirable!

BAYES. At night into your bosom I will creep,
And buzz but softly if you chance to sleep;
Yet in your dreams I will pass sweeping by,
And then both hum and buzz before your eye.

JOHNSON. By my troth, that's a very great promise.

SMITH. Yes, and a most extraordinary comfort to boot.

BAYES. Your bed of love, from dangers I will free,
But most, from love of any future bee.
And when with pity your heart-strings shall crack,
With empty arms I'll bear you on my back.

SMITH. A pick-a-pack, a pick-a-pack.

BAYES. Aye, 'y gad, but is not that *tuant*[3] now, ha? is it not *tuant?* Here's the end:

Then, at your birth of immortality,
Like any wingèd archer, hence I'll fly,
And teach you your first flutt'ring in the sky.

JOHNSON. Oh, rare! This is the most natural, refined fancy that ever I heard, I'll swear.

BAYES. Yes, I think for a dead person it is a good enough way of making love; for being

---

[1] An unfavorable description of Almanzor in *The Conquest of Granada*. Dryden defends the character in his prefatory essay.

[2] Cf. Dryden's *Tyrannic Love*, Act III.
I'll come all soul and spirit to your love.
With silent steps I'll follow you all day;
Or else, before you, in the sunbeams play;
I'll lead you thence to melancholy groves,
And there repeat the scenes of our past loves.
At night I will within your curtains peep;
With empty arms embrace you while you sleep;
In gentle dreams I often will be by,
And sweep along before your closing eye.
All dangers from your bed I will remove,
But guard it most from any future love;
And when at last, in pity, you will die,
I'll watch your birth of immortality;
Then, turtle-like, I'll to my mate repair,
And teach you your first flight in open air.

[3] Bad French again: killing.

divested of her terrestrial part, and all that, she is only capable of these little, pretty, amorous designs that are innocent, and yet passionate.—Come, draw your swords.

KING PHYSICIAN. Come sword, come sheath thyself within this breast,
Which only in Lardella's tomb can rest.
KING USHER. Come, dagger, come, and penetrate this heart,
Which cannot from Lardella's love depart.

Enter PALLAS

PALLAS. Hold! stop your murd'ring hands
At Pallas's commands!
For the supposèd dead, O kings,
Forbear to act such deadly things.
Lardella lives: I did but try
If princes for their loves could die.
Such celestial constancy
Shall, by the gods, rewarded be;
And from these funeral obsequies
A nuptial banquet shall arise.

(*The coffin opens, and a banquet is discovered*)

BAYES. So, take away the coffin. Now it's out. This is the very funeral of the fair person which Volscius sent word was dead, and Pallas, you see, has turned it into a banquet.
SMITH. Well, but where is this banquet?
BAYES. Nay, look you, sir, we must first have a dance, for joy that Lardella is not dead. Pray, sir, give me leave to bring in my things properly at least.
SMITH. That, indeed, I had forgot. I ask your pardon.
BAYES. O, d'ye so, sir? I am glad you will confess yourself once in an error, Mr. Smith.

(*Dance*)

KING USHER. Resplendent Pallas, we in thee do find
The fiercest beauty and a fiercer mind;
And since to thee Lardella's life we owe,
We'll supple statues in thy temple grow.
KING PHYSICIAN. Well, since alive Lardella's found,
Let, in full bowls, her health go round.
(*The two* Usurpers *take each of them a bowl in their hands*)
KING USHER. But where's the wine? [1]
PALLAS. That shall be mine.

[1] A parody of a scene in *The Villain* (1663), Act III, in which the host at a tavern draws a meal out of his clothes. The scene may be read in Summers' edition of *The Rehearsal*, pp. 127-32; and in the Arber edition, pp. 100ff.

Lo, from this conquering lance,
Does flow the purest wine of France;
(*Fills the bowls out of her lance*)
And, to appease your hunger, I
Have, in my helmet, brought a pie;
Lastly, to bear a part with these,
Behold a buckler made of cheese. (*Vanish* PALLAS)

BAYES. There's the banquet. Are you satisfied now, sir?
JOHNSON. By my troth, now, that is new, and more than I expected.
BAYES. Yes, I knew this would please you; for the chief art in poetry is to elevate your expectation, and then bring you off some extraordinary way.

Enter DRAWCANSIR

KING PHYSICIAN. What man is this that dares disturb our feast?
DRAWCANSIR. He that dares drink, and for that drink dares die; [2]
And, knowing this, dares yet drink on, am I.

JOHNSON. That is, Mr. Bayes, as much as to say that though he would rather die than not drink, yet he would fain drink for all that, too.
BAYES. Right; that's the conceit on't.
JOHNSON. 'Tis a marvellous good one, I swear.
BAYES. Now there are some critics that have advised me to put out the second *dare*, and print *must* in the place on't, but, 'y gad, I think 'tis better thus a great deal.
JOHNSON. Whoo! a thousand times!
BAYES. Go on, then.
KING USHER. Sir, if you please, we should be glad to know
How long you here will stay, how soon you'll go.

BAYES. Is not that now like a well-bred person, 'y gad? So modest, so gent! [3]
SMITH. Oh, very like.

DRAWCANSIR. You shall not know how long I here will stay; [4]
But you shall know I'll take your bowls away.
(*Snatches the bowls out of the* Kings' *hands and drinks 'em off*)

[2] Cf. *The Conquest of Granada*, Part II, Act IV, scene iii:
He who dares love, and for that love must die,
And knowing this, dares yet love on am I.
[3] Genteel, gentlemanly.
[4] Cf. *The Conquest of Granada*, Part I, Act V, scene iii:
I will not now, if thou wouldst beg me, stay;
But I will take my Almahide away.

SMITH. But, Mr. Bayes, is that, too, modest and gent?

BAYES. No, 'y gad, sir, but it's great.

KING USHER. Though, brother, this grum stranger be a clown,
He'll leave us, sure, a little to gulp down.
DRAWCANSIR. Whoe'er to gulp one drop of this dares think,[1]
I'll stare away his very pow'r to drink.

(*The two* Kings *sneak off the stage, with their Attendants*)

I drink, I huff, I strut, look big and stare;
And all this I can do, because I dare.[2]   *Exit*

SMITH. I suppose, Mr. Bayes, this is the fierce hero you spoke of.

BAYES. Yes, but this is nothing: you shall see him, in the last act, win above a dozen battles, one after another, 'y gad, as fast as they can possible [*sic*] come upon the stage.

JOHNSON. That will be a sight worth the seeing, indeed.

SMITH. But pray, Mr. Bayes, why do you make the kings let him use 'em so scurvily?

BAYES. Phoo! that is to raise the character of Drawcansir.

JOHNSON. O' my word, that was well thought on.

BAYES. Now, sirs, I'll show you a scene indeed; or rather, indeed the scene of scenes. 'Tis an heroic scene.

SMITH. And pray, sir, what's your design in this scene?

BAYES. Why, sir, my design is [3] gilded truncheons, forced conceit, smooth verse, and a rant; in fine, if this scene do not take, 'y gad, I'll write no more. Come, come in, Mr. —a—nay, come in as many as you can. Gentlemen, I must desire you to remove a little, for I must fill the stage.

SMITH. Why fill the stage?

BAYES. Oh, sir, because your heroic verse never sounds well but when the stage is full.

SCENE II

Enter PRINCE PRETTY-MAN *and* PRINCE VOLSCIUS

[BAYES]. Nay, hold, hold! pray, by your leave a little.—Look you, sir, the drift of this scene is somewhat more than ordinary, for I make 'em both fall out because they are not in love with the same woman.

SMITH. Not in love? You mean, I suppose, because they are in love, Mr. Bayes?

BAYES. No, sir; I say not in love. There's a new conceit for you. Now, speak.

PRETTY-MAN. Since fate, Prince Volscius, now has found the way [4]
For our so longed-for meeting here this day,
Lend thy attention to my grand concern.
VOLSCIUS. I gladly would that story from thee learn;
But thou to love dost, Pretty-man, incline:
Yet love in thy breast is not love in mine.

BAYES. Antithesis!—thine and mine.

PRETTY-MAN. Since love itself's the same, why should it be
Diff'ring in you from what it is in me?

BAYES. Reasoning; 'y gad, I love reasoning in verse.[5]

VOLSCIUS.[6] Love takes, chameleon-like, a various dye
From every plant on which itself does lie.

BAYES. Simile!

PRETTY-MAN. Let not thy love the course of nature fright:
Nature does most in harmony delight.
VOLSCIUS. How weak a deity would nature prove
Contending with the pow'rful god of love?

BAYES. There's a great verse!

VOLSCIUS. If incense thou wilt offer at the shrine
Of mighty love, burn it to none but mine.
Her rosy lips eternal sweets exhale,
And her bright flames make all flames else look pale.

BAYES. 'Y gad, that is right.

PRETTY-MAN. Perhaps dull incense may thy love suffice,

---

[1] Same scene:
Thou dar'st not marry her while I'm in sight:
With a bent brow thy priest and thee I'll fright.
[2] Same play, Part II, Act II, scene iii:
Spite of myself I'll stay, fight, love, despair;
And I can do all this because I dare.
[3] In the first edition, the words "Roman Clothes" were inserted before "gilded truncheons." The allusion is to an extravagantly staged revival of Jonson's *Catiline*, December, 1668 (Summers).
[4] This passage is reminiscent of Orrery's *Mustapha* (1665), Act II.
[5] Cf. note 1, p. 62.
[6] In general the debate between Pretty-man and Volscius burlesques the style of the heroic plays of Orrery.

But mine must be adored with sacrifice.
All hearts turn ashes which her eyes control:
The body they consume as well as soul.

VOLSCIUS. My love has yet a power more divine;
Victims her altars burn not, but refine.
Amidst the flames they ne'er give up the ghost,
But with her looks revive still as they roast.
In spite of pain and death, they're kept alive;
Her fiery eyes makes 'em in fire survive.

BAYES. That is as well, 'y gad, as I can do.

VOLSCIUS. Let my Parthenope at length prevail.

BAYES. Civil, 'y gad.

PRETTY-MAN. I'll sooner have a passion for a whale,
In whose vast bulk, though store of oil doth lie,
We find more shape, more beauty, in a fly.

SMITH. That's uncivil, 'y gad.

BAYES. Yes; but as far a fetched fancy though, 'y gad, as e'er you saw.

VOLSCIUS. Soft, Pretty-man, let not thy vain pretence
Of perfect love defame love's excellence.
Parthenope is sure as far above
All other loves as above all is love.

BAYES. Ah! 'y gad, that strikes me.

PRETTY-MAN. To blame my Cloris, gods would not pretend.

BAYES. Now mark.

VOLSCIUS. Were all gods joined, they could not hope to mend [1]
My better choice; for fair Parthenope
Gods would, themselves, un-god themselves to see.

BAYES. Now the rant's a-coming.

PRETTY-MAN. Durst any of the gods be so uncivil,
I'd make that god subscribe himself a devil.

BAYES. Ah, godsookers, that's well writ! (*Scratching his head, his peruke falls off*)

VOLSCIUS. Couldst thou that god from heav'n to earth translate,
He could not fear to want a heav'nly state.
Parthenope, on earth, can heav'n create.

PRETTY-MAN. Cloris does heav'n itself so far excel,
She can transcend the joys of heav'n in hell.

[1] A parody of the extravagant language of Maximin in Dryden's *Tyrannic Love*.

BAYES. There's a bold flight for you now! —'Sdeath, I have lost my peruke!—Well, gentlemen, this is that I never yet saw anyone could write but myself. Here's true spirit and flame all through, 'y gad. So, so; pray clear the stage. (*He puts 'em off the stage*)

JOHNSON. I wonder how the coxcomb has got the knack of writing smooth verse thus.

SMITH. Why, there's no need of brain for this; 'tis but scanning; the labor's in the finger. But where's the sense of it?

JOHNSON. Oh, for that, he desires to be excused; he is too proud a man to creep servilely after sense, I assure you.—But, Mr. Bayes, pray why is this scene all in verse?

BAYES. O sir, the subject is too great for prose.[2]

SMITH. Well said, i'faith. I'll give thee a pot of ale for that answer; 'tis well worth it.

BAYES. Come, with all my heart. "I'll make that god subscribe himself a devil." That single line, 'y gad, is worth all that my brother poets ever writ. Let down the curtain.
Exeunt

ACT V

SCENE I

Enter BAYES *and the two* Gentlemen

BAYES. Now, gentlemen, I will be bold to say, I'll show you the greatest scene that ever England saw. I mean not for words, for those I do not value, but for state, show, and magnificence. In fine, I'll justify it to be as grand to the eye every whit, 'y gad, as that great scene in *Harry the Eight*[3]—and grander too, 'y gad; for, instead of two bishops, I bring in here four cardinals.

The Curtain is drawn up; the two usurping Kings *appear in state,*[4] *with the four* Cardinals, PRINCE PRETTY-MAN, PRINCE VOLSCIUS, AMARYLLIS, CLORIS, PARTHENOPE, *&c. Before them,* Heralds *and* Sergeants at Arms *with maces.*

SMITH. Mr. Bayes, pray what is the reason that two of the cardinals are in hats and the other in caps?

BAYES. Why, sir, because—by gad, I won't

[2] Cf. the opening of Dryden's *Essay of Heroick Plays*.
[3] Cf. note 7, p. 63.
[4] The practice of elaborate stage spectacles during the period was common.

tell you.—Your country friend, sir, grows so troublesome.

KING USHER. Now, sir, to the business of the day.
KING PHYSICIAN. Speak, Volscius.
VOLSCIUS. Dread sovereign lords, my zeal to you must not invade my duty to your son. Let me entreat that great Prince Pretty-man first do speak, whose high preëminence, in all things that do bear the name of good, may justly claim that privilege.

BAYES. Here it begins to unfold. You may perceive, now, that he is his son.
JOHNSON. Yes, sir; and we are very much beholden to you for that discovery.

PRETTY-MAN. Royal father, upon my knees I beg
That the illustrious Volscius first be heard.
VOLSCIUS. That preference is only due to Amaryllis, sir.

BAYES. I'll make her speak very well, by and by; you shall see.

AMARYLLIS. Invincible sovereigns—
(*Soft Music*)
KING USHER. But stay, what sound is this invades our ears?[1]
KING PHYSICIAN. Sure 'tis the music of the moving spheres.
PRETTY-MAN. Behold, with wonder! yonder comes from far,
A god-like cloud and a triumphant car;
In which our two right kings sit one by one,
With virgin vests, and laurel garlands on.
KING USHER. Then, Brother Phys', 'tis time we should be gone.
(*The two* Usurpers *steal out of the throne and go away*)

BAYES. Look you now, did not I tell you that this would be as easy a change as the other?
SMITH. Yes, faith, you did so; though I confess, I could not believe you; but you have brought it about, I see.

(*The two right* Kings of Brentford *descend in the clouds, singing in white garments; and three fiddlers sitting before them, in green*)

BAYES. Now, because the two right kings descend from above, I make 'em sing to the tune and style of our modern spirits.

[1] Cf. *The Indian Queen*, Act I, scene i, l. 119.

1ST KING. Haste, brother king, we are sent from above.[2]
2D KING. Let us move, let us move—
  Move to remove the fate
  Of Brentford's long united state.
1ST KING. Tara, tan tara, full east and by south,
2D KING. We sail with thunder in our mouth;
In scorching noon-day, whilst the traveller stays,
Busy, busy, busy, busy, we bustle along.
Mounted upon warm Phœbus his rays,
  Through the heavenly throng,
  Hasting to those
Who will feast us, at night, with a pig's pettitoes.
1ST KING. And we'll fall with our pate
  In an olio[3] of hate.
2D KING. But now supper's done, the servitors try,
Like soldiers, to storm a whole half-moon pie.
1ST KING. They gather, they gather hot custard in spoons;
But alas, I must leave these half-moons,
And repair to my trusty dragoons.
2D KING. Oh, stay, for you need not as yet go astray;
The tide, like a friend, has brought ships in our way,
And on their high ropes we will play.
Like maggots in filberts, we'll snug[4] in our shell;
  We'll frisk in our shell,
  We'll firk[5] in our shell,
  And farewell.
1ST KING. But the ladies have all inclination to dance,
And the green frogs croak out a coranto[6] of France.

BAYES. Is not that pretty, now? The fiddlers are all in green.
SMITH. Aye, but they play no coranto.
JOHNSON. No, but they play a tune; that's a great deal better.
BAYES. "No coranto," quoth a!—that's a good one, with all my heart!—Come, sing on.

2D KING. Now mortals that hear
  How we tilt and career,
  With wonder will fear
The event of such things as shall never appear.
1ST KING. Stay you to fulfil what the gods have decreed.
2D KING. Then call me to help you if there shall be need.
1ST KING. So firmly resolved is a true Brentford king

[2] A parody of *Tyrannic Love*, Act IV.
[3] Hodgepodge.
[4] Snuggle.
[5] Be lively.
[6] A lively French dance.

To save the distressed and help to 'em bring,
That ere a full pot of good ale you can swallow,
He's here with a whoop, and gone with a holla.

(BAYES *fillips his finger and sings after
'em*)

BAYES. "He's here with a whoop, and gone with a holla." This, sir, you must know, I thought once to have brought in with a conjurer.[1]

JOHNSON. Aye, that would have been better.

BAYES. No, faith, not when you consider it, for thus 'tis more compendious and does the thing every whit as well.

SMITH. Thing!—what thing?

BAYES. Why, bring 'em down again into the throne, sir. What thing would you have?

SMITH. Well; but methinks the sense of this song is not very plain.

BAYES. Plain? why, did you ever hear any people in clouds speak plain? They must be all for flight of fancy, at its full range, without the least check or control upon it. When once you tie up spirits and people in clouds to speak plain, you spoil all.

SMITH. Bless me, what a monster's this!

(*The two* Kings *light out of the clouds and step into the throne*)

1ST KING. Come, now to serious counsel we'll advance.

2D KING. I do agree; but first let's have a dance.

BAYES. Right. You did that very well, Mr. Cartwright. "But first let's have a dance." Pray, remember that; be sure you do it always just so, for it must be done as if it were the effect of thought and premeditation.—"But first, let's have a dance." Pray, remember that.

SMITH. Well, I can hold no longer; I must gag this rogue; there's no enduring of him.

JOHNSON. No, prithee, make use of thy patience a little longer; let's see the end of him now.

(*Dance a grand dance*)

BAYES. This, now, is an ancient dance, of right belonging to the Kings of Brentford, and since derived, with a little alteration, to the Inns of Court.

An Alarm. Enter two Heralds

1ST KING. What saucy groom molests our privacies?

[1] As Dryden does in *Tyrannic Love*, Act IV; and *The Indian Queen*, Act III.

1ST HERALD. The army's at the door and, in disguise,
Desires a word with both your Majesties:

2D HERALD. Having, from Knightsbridge, hither marched by stealth.

2D KING. Bid 'em attend a while and drink our health.

SMITH. How, Mr. Bayes—the army in disguise?

BAYES. Aye, sir, for fear the usurpers might discover them, that went out but just now.

SMITH. Why, what if they had discovered them?

BAYES. Why, then they had broke the design.

1ST KING. Here, take five guineas for those warlike men.[2]

2D KING. And here's five more; that makes the sum just ten.

1ST HERALD. We have not seen so much the Lord knows when.   *Exeunt* Heralds

1ST KING. Speak on, brave Amaryllis.

AMARYLLIS. Invincible sovereigns, blame not my modesty
If at this grand conjuncture—
            (*Drum beat behind the stage*)

1ST KING. What dreadful noise is this that comes and goes?

Enter a Soldier *with his sword drawn*

SOLDIER. Haste hence, great sirs, your royal persons save,
For the event of war no mortal knows!
The army, wrangling for the gold you gave,
First fell to words, and then to handy-blows.
                                    Exit

BAYES. Is not that now a pretty kind of a stanza and a handsome come off?

2D KING. Oh, dangerous estate of sovereign pow'r!
Obnoxious to the change of every hour.

1ST KING. Let us for shelter in our cabinet stay;
Perhaps these threat'ning storms may pass away.
                                    Exeunt

JOHNSON. But, Mr. Bayes, did not you promise us, just now, to make Amaryllis speak very well?

BAYES. Aye, and so she would have done but that they hindered her.

SMITH. How, sir, whether you would or no?

[2] In general this scene parodies *The Conquest of Granada*, Part II, Act I, scene ii. However, other heroic plays have similar scenes.

BAYES. Aye, sir; the plot lay so that, I vow to gad, it was not to be avoided.

SMITH. Marry, that was hard.

JOHNSON. But, pray, who hindered her?

BAYES. Why, the battle, sir, that's just coming in at door. And I'll tell you now a strange thing; though I don't pretend to do more than other men, 'y gad, I'll give you both a whole week to guess how I'll represent this battle.

SMITH. I had rather be bound to fight your battle, I assure you, sir.

BAYES. Whoo! there's it now. Fight a battle? there's the common error. I knew presently where I should have you. Why, pray, sir, do but tell me this one thing: Can you think it a decent thing, in a battle before ladies, to have men run their swords through one another, and all that?

JOHNSON. No, faith, 'tis not civil.

BAYES. Right on the other side: To have a long relation of squadrons here, and squadrons there—what is it but dull prolixity?

JOHNSON. Excellently reasoned, by my troth!

BAYES. Wherefore, sir, to avoid both those indecorums, I sum up my whole battle [1] in the representation of two persons only—no more—and yet so lively that, I vow to gad, you would swear ten thousand men were at it, really engaged. Do you mark me?

SMITH. Yes, sir; but I think I should hardly swear, though, for all that.

BAYES. By my troth, sir, but you would, though, when you see it; for I make 'em both come out in armor, cap-a-pie, with their swords drawn and hung with a scarlet ribbon at their wrists (which, you know, represents fighting enough).

JOHNSON. Aye, aye, so much that, if I were in your place, I would make 'em go out again without ever speaking one word.

BAYES. No, there you are out; for I make each of 'em hold a lute in his hand.

SMITH. How, sir—instead of a buckler?

BAYES. O Lord, O Lord!—Instead of a buckler? Pray, sir, do you ask no more questions. I make 'em, sir, play the battle in *recitativo*. And here's the conceit: just at the very same instant that one sings, the other, sir, recovers you his sword and puts himself in a warlike posture, so that you have at once your ear entertained with music and good language, and your eye satisfied with the garb and accoutrements of war.

SMITH. I confess, sir, you stupefy me.

BAYES. You shall see.

JOHNSON. But, Mr. Bayes, might not we have a little fighting? For I love those plays where they cut and slash one another, upon the stage, for a whole hour together.

BAYES. Why, then, to tell you true, I have contrived it both ways. But you shall have my *recitativo* first.

JOHNSON. Aye, now you are right, there is nothing then can be objected against it.

BAYES. True; and so, 'y gad, I'll make it, too, a tragedy in a trice.

Enter at several doors [2] *the* General *and* Lieutenant-General, *armed cap-a-pie, with each of them a lute in his hand, and his sword drawn and hung with a scarlet ribbon at his wrist*

LIEUTENANT-GENERAL. Villain, thou liest!

GENERAL. Arm, arm, Gonsalvo, arm! What ho!
The lie no flesh can brook, I trow.

LIEUTENANT-GENERAL. Advance, from Acton,
with the musketeers.

GENERAL. Draw down the Chelsea [3] cuirassiers.

LIEUTENANT-GENERAL. The band you boast
of, Chelsea cuirassiers,
Shall, in my Putney pikes, now meet their peers.

GENERAL. Chiswickians agèd, and renowned
in fight,
Join with the Hammersmith brigade.

LIEUTENANT-GENERAL. You'll find my Mortlake boys will do them right,
Unless by Fulham numbers overlaid.

GENERAL. Let the left wing of Twick'nam foot
advance
And line that eastern hedge.

LIEUTENANT-GENERAL. The horse I raised in
Petty-France
Shall try their chance,
And scour the meadows, overgrown with sedge.

GENERAL. Stand! give the word.

LIEUTENANT-GENERAL. Bright sword.

GENERAL. That may be thine,
But 'tis not mine.

[1] Cf. *The Siege of Rhodes*, The Fifth Entry, where seven characters sum up the battle.

[2] For the original of this scene cf. *The Siege of Rhodes*, The First Entry. The use of geographical adjectives for romantic effect is here parodied. See also the openings of The Third Entry and The Fifth Entry in the same play.

[3] In general these places are in, or close to, London. Petty-France was just beyond the city wall.

LIEUTENANT-GENERAL. Give fire, give fire—
at once give fire—
And let those recreant troops perceive mine ire.
   GENERAL. Pursue, pursue! They fly
That first did give the lie.   *Exeunt*
   BAYES. This, now, is not improper, I think, because the spectators know all these towns, and may easily conceive them to be within the dominions of the two kings of Brentford.
   JOHNSON. Most exceeding well designed!
   BAYES. How do you think I have contrived to give a stop to this battle?
   SMITH. How?
   BAYES. By an eclipse—which, let me tell you, is a kind of fancy that was yet never so much as thought of but by myself and one person more that shall be nameless.

Enter Lieutenant-General

LIEUTENANT-GENERAL. What midnight darkness does invade the day,
And snatch the victor from his conquered prey?
Is the Sun weary of this bloody sight,
And winks upon us with the eye of light?
'Tis an eclipse. This was unkind, O Moon,
To clap between me and the Sun so soon.
Foolish Eclipse! thou this in vain hast done;
My brighter honor had eclips'd the Sun.
But now behold eclipses two in one.   *Exit*

   JOHNSON. This is [as] admirable representation of a battle as ever I saw.
   BAYES. Aye, sir. But how would you fancy now to represent an eclipse?
   SMITH. Why, that's to be supposed.
   BAYES. Supposed! Aye, you are ever at your "suppose"—ha, ha, ha! Why, you may as well suppose the whole play. No, it must come in upon the stage, that's certain; but in some odd way that may delight, amuse, and all that. I have a conceit for't that I am sure is new and, I believe, to the purpose.
   JOHNSON. How's that?
   BAYES. Why, the truth is, I took the first hint of this out of a dialogue between Phœbus and Aurora, in *The Slighted Maid*,[1] which, by my troth, was very pretty, but I think you'll confess this is a little better.
   JOHNSON. No doubt on't, Mr. Bayes. A great deal better.
   (BAYES *hugs* JOHNSON, *then turns to Smith*)
   BAYES. Ah, dear rogue! But—a—sir, you have heard, I suppose, that your eclipse of the moon is nothing else but an interposition of the earth between the sun and moon; as likewise your eclipse of the sun is caused by an interlocation of the moon betwixt the earth and sun?
   SMITH. I have heard some such thing, indeed.
   BAYES. Well, sir, then what do me I but make the earth, sun, and moon come out upon the stage and dance the hey-hum? And of necessity by the very nature of this dance, the earth must be sometimes between the sun and the moon, and the moon between the earth and sun; and there you have both your eclipses, by demonstration.
   JOHNSON. That must needs be very fine, truly.
   BAYES. Yes, it is fancy in't. And then, sir, that there may be something in 't too of a joke, I bring 'em in all singing, and make the moon sell the earth a bargain.[2]—Come, come out, eclipse, to the tune of *Tom Tyler*.[3]

Enter Luna

   LUNA. Orbis, O Orbis!
Come to me, thou little rogue Orbis.

Enter the Earth

   ORBIS. Who calls Terra Firma, pray?
   LUNA. Luna that ne'er shines by day.
   ORBIS. What means Luna in a veil?
   LUNA. Luna means to show her tail.

   BAYES. There's the bargain!

Enter Sol *to the tune of* "Robin Hood"

   SOL. Fie, sister, fie! thou mak'st me muse,
      Derry, derry down,
      To see the Orb abuse.
   LUNA. I hope his anger 'twill not move,
Since I showed it out of love.
      Hey down, derry down.
   ORBIS. Where shall I thy true love know,
      Thou pretty, pretty Moon?
   LUNA. To-morrow soon, ere it be noon—
            (*Bis*)
      On Mount Vesuvio.
   SOL. Then I will shine. (*To the tune of* "Trenchmore.")
   ORBIS. And I will be fine.
   LUNA. And I will drink nothing but Lipari wine.
   ALL. And we, etc.

---

[1] For the scene parodied in the following passage consult Summers' edition of *The Rehearsal*, pp. 145–47.

[2] To answer innocent questions vulgarly.

[3] A popular country dance tune, as are Robin Hood and Trenchmore, mentioned below.

(*As they dance the Hey,*[1] BAYES *speaks*)
BAYES. Now the earth's before the moon; now the moon's before the sun; there's the eclipse again.
SMITH. He's mightily taken with this, I see.
JOHNSON. Aye, 'tis so extraordinary! How can he choose?
BAYES. So, now, vanish eclipse, and enter t'other battle, and fight. Here now, if I am not mistaken, you will see fighting enough.

(*A battle is fought between foot and great hobby-horses. At last,* DRAWCANSIR *comes in, and kills 'em all on both sides. All this while the battle is fighting,* BAYES *is telling them when to shout, and shouts with 'em.*)

DRAWCANSIR. Others may boast a single man to kill,
But I the blood of thousands daily spill.
Let petty kings the names of parties know;
Where'er I come, I slay both friend and foe.
The swiftest horsemen my swift rage controls,
And from their bodies drives their trembling souls.
If they had wings and to the gods could fly,
I would pursue, and beat 'em, through the sky;
And make proud Jove, with all his thunder, see
This single arm more dreadful is than he.
Exit

BAYES. There's a brave fellow for you now, sirs. You may talk of your Hector, and Achilles, and I know not who; but I defy all your histories, and your romances, too, to show me one such conqueror as this Drawcansir.
JOHNSON. I swear, I think you may.
SMITH. But, Mr. Bayes, how shall all these dead men go off? for I see none alive to help 'em.[2]
BAYES. Go off! why, as they came on—upon their legs. How should they go off? Why, do you think the people here don't know they are not dead? He is mighty ignorant, poor man; your friend here is very silly, Mr. Johnson, 'y gad, he is. Ha, ha, ha! Come, sir, I'll show you how they shall go off.—Rise, rise, sirs, and go about your business. There's "go off" for you now—ha, ha, ha! Mr. Ivory, a word.—Gentlemen, I'll be with you presently. *Exit*
JOHNSON. Will you so? then we'll be gone.

SMITH. Aye, prithee, let's go, that we may preserve our hearing. One battle more will take mine quite away. *Exeunt*

Enter BAYES *and* Players

BAYES. Where are the gentlemen?
1ST PLAYER. They are gone, sir.
BAYES. Gone! 'Sdeath, this last act is best of all. I'll go fetch 'em again. *Exit*
1ST PLAYER. What shall we do, now he is gone away?
2D PLAYER. Why, so much the better. Then let's go to dinner.[3]
3D PLAYER. Stay, here's a foul piece of paper of his. Let's see what 'tis.
3D or 4TH PLAYER. Aye, aye, come, let's hear it.
3D PLAYER *reads: The Argument of the Fifth Act:*

Cloris, at length, being sensible of Prince Pretty-man's passion, consents to marry him; but just as they are going to church, Prince Pretty-man meeting by chance with old Joan the chandler's widow, and rememb'ring it was she that first brought him acquainted with Cloris, out of a high point of honor break[s] off his match with Cloris and marries old Joan. Upon which, Cloris in despair drowns herself, and Prince Pretty-man discontentedly walks by the river side.

3D PLAYER. This will never do; 'tis just like the rest. Come, let's be gone.
MOST OF THE PLAYERS. Aye, pox on't, let's go away *Exeunt*

Enter BAYES

BAYES. A plague on 'em both for me! they have made me sweat to run after 'em. A couple of senseless rascals that had rather go to dinner than see this play out, with a pox to 'em! What comfort has a man to write for such dull rogues?—[*Calls*] Come Mr.—a—Where are you, sir? come away quick—quick!

Enter Stage-keeper

STAGE-KEEPER. Sir, they are gone to dinner.
BAYES. Yes, I know the gentlemen are gone, but I ask for the players.
STAGE-KEEPER. Why, an't please your worship, sir, the players are gone to dinner, too.

---

[1] A kind of reel or jig.
[2] Since on the Restoration stage the heroes died well forward of the curtain on the projecting apron, the problem of plausibly carrying them off stage was a real one.
[3] As dinner was at noon, we have presumably been attending a morning rehearsal.

BAYES. How! are the players gone to dinner? 'Tis impossible: the players gone to dinner! 'Y gad, if they are, I'll make 'em know what it is to injure a person that does 'em the honor to write for 'em, and all that. A company of proud, conceited, humorous, cross-grained persons, and all that. 'Y gad, I'll make 'em the most contemptible, despicable, inconsiderable persons, and all that, in the whole world for this trick. 'Y gad, I'll be revenged on 'em; I'll sell this play to the other house.

STAGE-KEEPER. Nay, good sir, don't take away the book; you'll disappoint the company that comes to see it acted here this afternoon.[1]

BAYES. That's all one. I must reserve this comfort to myself. My play and I shall go together; we will not part, indeed, sir.

STAGE-KEEPER. But what will the town say, sir?

BAYES. The town! Why, what care I for the town? 'Y gad, the town has used me as scurvily as the players have done. But I'll be revenged on them too; for I'll lampoon 'em all. And since they will not admit of my plays, they shall know what a satirist I am. And so farewell to this stage, 'y gad, forever.
Exit

Enter Players

1ST PLAYER. Come, then, let's set up bills for another play.

2D PLAYER. Aye, aye, we shall lose nothing by this, I warrant you.

1ST PLAYER. I am of your opinion. But before we go let's see Haynes[2] and Shirley practise the last dance, for that may serve us another time.

2D PLAYER. I'll call 'em in; I think they are but in the tiring-room.

(*The dance done*)

1ST PLAYER. Come, come; let's go away to dinner. *Exeunt omnes*

EPILOGUE

The play is at an end, but where's the plot?
That circumstance our poet Bayes forgot,
And we can boast, though 'tis a plotting age,
No place is freer from it than the stage.
The ancients plotted though, and strove to please 5
With sense that might be understood with ease;
They every scene with so much wit did store
That who brought any in, went out with more.
But this new way of wit does so surprise,
Men lose their wits in wond'ring where it lies.
If it be true that monstrous births presage 11
The following mischiefs that afflict the age,
And sad disasters to the state proclaim,
Plays without head or tail may do the same.
Wherefore, for ours, and for the kingdom's peace, 15
May this prodigious way of writing cease.
Let's have at least once in our lives a time
When we may hear some reason, not all rhyme:
We have these ten years felt its influence; 19
Pray, let this prove a year of prose and sense.

[1] Performances began at three in the afternoon.

[2] Joseph Haines (d. 1701), a low comedian and dancer.

THE MAN OF MODE; OR, SIR FOPLING FLUTTER
By Sir George Etherege

Sir George Etherege ("gentle George"), who has been furnished with parents by genealogists in default of better records, was born, either in Bermuda or England, about 1632 or 1633, the son, in all probability, of George Etherege and Mary Powney, his wife. Of his youth almost nothing is known, though he appears to have been in France during the Civil Wars. Upon his return (in 1663?) he seems to have drifted for a time; but his dramatic career begins with the production of *The Comical Revenge; or, Love in a Tub* in March, 1664, a play which Pepys disliked but which, nevertheless, marks an epoch in English comedy. His next play was relatively a failure; Etherege, in the meantime, joining in the wild life of the Restoration rakes. In 1668 he was appointed secretary to the English ambassador to Constantinople, a post which bored him to death, but from which he sent back an admirable report to the government.

Returning some time about 1671, Etherege, after penning some trifles, produced his finest comedy, *The Man of Mode* (1676); and in the same year was involved in a famous scrape with Rochester which resulted in the death of Mr. Downs in a street brawl. Sometime between 1677 and 1680 he married a widow, Mary Arnold, it is said, for her fortune; about the same time he was knighted; and the wits did not fail to comment upon the singular association of events. He also became the lover of Mrs. Barry, the actress, by whom he is said to have had a child. In March, 1685, he was appointed English envoy at Regensburg (Ratisbon), an important diplomatic post which came to him through the patronage of the queen of James II. From this place (which bored him) he sent back the graphic letters preserved in his letter-book, telling how he flaunted the prejudices of the Germans by making an actress his official mistress, with much more in the same vein. The Glorious Revolution cost him his place; and in the spring of 1689 he passed to Paris. His last years are as obscure as his earlier ones; and both the date and the manner of his death are unknown. All that we can confidently say is that he died some time between 1691 and 1693.

Etherege seems to have been a man of personal charm, daring gaiety, and shrewd insight into certain types of character. His contemporary reputation was high, and in *A Trial of the Poets* Apollo is represented as saying that "none had more fancy, sense, judgment and wit" than "gentle George." His morals were the morals of the age.

The latest and most accurate account of Etherege's life is that found in Sybil Rosenfeld, *The Letterbook of Sir George Etherege* (1928), which supersedes all previous biographies. Editions of his works have been edited by A. W. Verity (1888) and H. F. B. Brett-Smith (1927).

ETHEREGE'S DRAMATIC WORKS

The Comical Revenge, or Love in a Tub (comedy) (L.I.F., March, 1664), 1664.

She Would if She Could (comedy) (L.I.F., Feb., 1667/8), 1668.

The Man of Mode or Sir Fopling Flutter (comedy) (D.G., March, 1675/6), 1676

When Mr. Etherege's first play was produced in 1664, our stage stood vastly in need of a new way of humorous writing. Though the comedies of the former age were not without scenes in which genteel folly is held up to ridicule, time, which tarnishes all things, had somewhat dulled their wit; nor had Mr. Dryden or any other poet as yet come forward to hold the mirror up to nature as Mr. Etherege and his friends understood the world. Perceiving in the comedies of the great Molière a complete summary of the follies of the fashionable world, Mr. Etherege apparently resolved to do for London what that poet had done for the court of his great master; and accordingly *Love in a Tub* is commonly accounted the first of our Restoration comedies. Despite the efforts of rival dramatists, our author is an innovator; his characters were novel, his wit was new, the polish of his language not then surpassed, and an easy negligence informed the piece.

In *The Man of Mode* Etherege brought his way of writing to relative perfection. Though he had particularly in mind *Les Précieuses Ridicules* of Molière, from which, in the character of Mascarille, the idea of Sir Fopling Flutter is partly taken, and though he followed that dramatist in his satire of country life from the point of view of the town, his comedy is his own, so truly imaging the polite world that the wits of the day amused themselves in assigning originals to the principal characters, as Lord Rochester for Dorimant, Sir Charles Sedley for Medley, and Mr. Hewitt for Sir Fopling. But as the same characters were assigned to others, it is a tribute to the poet's wit that, as the *Prologue* tells us, "your own follies must supply the stage." The great virtue of *The Man of Mode* is that it remains so true and easy a replica of its own world.

The play is therefore to be called a comedy of manners of a particular period; of which the essential characteristics are witty dialogue, animation in the scenes, a negligent handling of the plot, concentration upon the fashionable world, a certain heartlessness in intrigue, and an easy morality. Sir George "perfectly understood the world," as Mr. Dennis afterward remarked; 'tis the height of polished gallantry in Dorimant to conceal the depth of his affection for Harriet, who, in the game of love, is equal in epigram to Dorimant, and surpasses him in understanding. The amours of Mr. Dorimant give rise, it must be admitted, to a difficult question of morality, and there have not been wanting critics severely to condemn our author for the insensitiveness of his hero. But Mr. Dennis did not find the play notably corrupt; our author took the world as he found it; and if he did not make it better, he has at least amused us by pointing out its follies.

The student seeks therefore in the plays of Sir George Etherege and his followers not for virtue, but for wit, perfectly expressed; for an elegant array of fashionable personages painted in those intrigues which, we must suppose, were the main business of their lives; for an intellectual humor, relieved at intervals by farce, and occasionally softened by sincerity; for a world, in short, small, self-sufficient, artificial, and self-conscious, but a world which brought forth the greatest gallery of comic poets which our literature has to boast.

The Man of Mode was first produced at Dorset Garden Theater, March, 1675–6.

The edition of Etherege's *Works* edited by Brett-Smith contains a valuable critical introduction. The student should also consult the essay in Gosse, *Seventeenth Century Studies* which, though inaccurate in detail, has critical insight; and the chapter on Etherege in Dobrée, *Restoration Comedy*. The unfavorable view of Macaulay in his celebrated essay on the Restoration comic dramatists should not be neglected; nor should Jeremy Collier's earlier attack in his *Short View . . . of the English Stage.*

THE MAN OF MODE;
OR
SIR FOPLING FLUTTER

DRAMATIS PERSONÆ [1]

GENTLEMEN

Mr. Dorimant	Mr. Betterton	Young Bellair	Mr. Jevon
Mr. Medley	Mr. Harris	Sir Fopling Flutter	Mr. Smith
Old Bellair	Mr. Leigh		

GENTLEWOMEN

Lady Townley		Bellinda	Mrs. Betterton
Emilia	Mrs. Twiford	Lady Woodvill	Mrs. Leigh
Mrs. Loveit	Mrs. Barry	Harriet	

WAITING-WOMEN

Pert   Busy

[Swearing Tom], *a Shoemaker*
[Foggy Nan], *an Orange-Woman*
Three Slovenly Bullies
Two Chairmen

Mr. Smirk, *a parson*
Handy, *valet-de-chambre*
Pages, Footmen, etc.

PROLOGUE

By Sir Car Scroope,[2] Baronet

Like dancers on the ropes poor poets fare,
Most perish young, the rest in danger are;
This (one would think) should make our authors wary,
But, gamester-like, the giddy fools miscarry.
A lucky hand or two so tempts 'em on,   5
They cannot leave off play till they're undone.
With modest fears a muse does first begin,
Like a young wench newly enticed to sin;
But tickled once with praise, by her good will,
The wanton fool would never more lie still.   10
  'Tis an old mistress you'll meet here tonight
Whose charms you once have looked on with delight.
But now of late such dirty drabs have known ye,
A muse o'th' better sort's ashamed to own [ye].
Nature well drawn, and wit, must now give place   15
To gaudy nonsense and to dull grimace;
Nor is it strange that you should like so much
That kind of wit, for most of yours is such.
But I'm afraid that while to France we go,
To bring you home fine dresses, dance, and show,
The stage, like you, will but more foppish grow.
Of foreign wares, why should we fetch the scum,   22
When we can be so richly served at home?
For heav'n be thanked, 'tis not so wise an age
But your own follies must supply the stage.   25
Tho' often plowed, there's no great fear the soil
Should barren grow by the too frequent toil;
While at your doors are to be daily found
Such loads of dunghill to manure the ground.
'Tis by your follies that we players thrive,   30
As the physicians by diseases live;

---

[1] The dedication to the Duchess of York is omitted.

[2] Sir Car Scroop, Scroope, or Scrope (1649–80), was one of the host of gentlemen amateurs at court, and a leader of fashion.

And as each year some new distemper reigns,
Whose friendly poison helps t'increase their gains,
So among you there starts up every day
Some new, unheard-of fool for us to play.   35
Then, for your own sakes be not too severe,
Nor what you all admire at home, damn here;
Since each is fond of his own ugly face,
Why should you, when we hold it, break the glass?

ACT I

SCENE I. *A dressing-room. A table covered with a toilet; clothes laid ready*

Enter DORIMANT *in his gown and slippers, with a note in his hand, made up, repeating verses*

DORIMANT.
Now for some ages had the pride of Spain
Made half the sun shine on the world in vain.[1]

(*Then looking on the note* [*he reads*]) "For Mrs. Loveit"—What a dull, insipid thing is a billet-doux written in cold blood, after the heat of the business is over! It is a tax upon good nature which I have here been laboring to pay, and have done it, but with as much regret as ever fanatic paid the Royal Aid [2] or church duties. 'Twill have the same fate, I know, that all my notes to her have had of late; 'twill not be thought kind enough. 'Faith, women are i'the right when they jealously examine our letters, for in them we always first discover our decay of passion.—Hey! Who waits?

Enter HANDY

HANDY. Sir—
DORIMANT. Call a footman.
HANDY. None of 'em are come yet.
DORIMANT. Dogs! Will they ever lie snoring abed till noon?
HANDY. 'Tis all one, sir; if they're up, you indulge 'em so they're ever poaching after whores all the morning.
DORIMANT. Take notice henceforward who's wanting in his duty, the next clap he gets, he shall rot for an example—What vermin are those chattering without?
HANDY. Foggy[3] Nan, the orange-woman, and Swearing Tom, the shoemaker.
DORIMANT. Go, call in that over-grown jade with the flasket of guts before her; fruit is refreshing in a morning.

Exit HANDY
(*Reads*)

It is not that I love you less.[4]
Than when before your feet I lay—

Enter Orange-Woman [*and* HANDY]

How now, double tripe, what news do you bring?
ORANGE-WOMAN. News! Here's the best fruit has come to town t'year; gad, I was up before four o'clock this morning and bought all the choice i'the market.
DORIMANT. The nasty refuse of your shop.
ORANGE-WOMAN. You need not make mouths at it; I assure you, 'tis all culled ware.
DORIMANT. The citizens buy better on a holiday in their walk to Totnam.[5]
ORANGE-WOMAN. Good or bad, 'tis all one. I never knew you commend anything. Lord! would the ladies had heard you talk of 'em as I have done! (*Sets down the fruit*) Here, bid your man give me an angel.[6]
DORIMANT. [*To* HANDY] Give the bawd her fruit again.
ORANGE-WOMAN. Well, on my conscience, there never was the like of you!—God's my life, I had almost forgot to tell you there is a young gentlewoman lately come to town with her mother, that is so taken with you.
DORIMANT. Is she handsome?
ORANGE-WOMAN. Nay, gad, there are few finer women, I tell you but so—and a hugeous fortune, they say.—Here, eat this peach. It comes from the stone; 'tis better than any Newington[7] y'have tasted.
DORIMANT. (*Taking the peach*) This fine woman, I'll lay my life, is some awkward, ill-fashioned country toad who, not having above four dozen of black hairs on her head, has adorned her baldness with a large, white fruz,[8] that she may look sparkishly in the forefront of the King's box at an old play.

---

[1] Dorimant is quoting the opening lines of Waller's poem "Upon a War with Spain and a Fight at Sea." See his *Works*.
[2] Tax.
[3] Puffy.
[4] Waller again. "The Self-Banished," ll. 1–2.
[5] Tottenham, frequented by the lower middle class.
[6] A golden coin worth about 10s.
[7] Newington is in Kent, an orchard district.
[8] Friz of curled hair.

ORANGE-WOMAN. Gad, you'd change your note quickly if you did but see her.

DORIMANT. How came she to know me?

ORANGE-WOMAN. She saw you yesterday at the *Change*.[1] She told me you came and fooled with the woman at the next shop.

DORIMANT. I remember there was a mask observed me, indeed. Fooled, did she say?

ORANGE-WOMAN. Aye; I vow she told me twenty things you said, too, and acted with her head and with her body so like you—

Enter MEDLEY

MEDLEY. Dorimant, my life, my joy, my darling sin! how dost thou?

ORANGE-WOMAN. Lord, what a filthy trick these men have got of kissing one another!
(*She spits*)

MEDLEY. Why do you suffer this cartload of scandal to come near you and make your neighbors think you so improvident to need a bawd?

ORANGE-WOMAN. Good, now we shall have it, you did but want him to help you!—[*To* DORIMANT] Come, pay me for my fruit.

MEDLEY. Make us thankful for it, huswife, bawds are as much out of fashion as gentlemen-ushers; none but old formal ladies use the one, and none but foppish old stagers employ the other. Go, you are an insignificant brandy bottle.

DORIMANT. Nay, there you wrong her; three quarts of Canary is her business.

ORANGE-WOMAN. What you please, gentlemen.

DORIMANT. To him! give him as good as he brings.

ORANGE-WOMAN. Hang him, there is not such another heathen in the town again, except it be the shoemaker without.

MEDLEY. I shall see you hold up your hand at the bar next sessions for murder, huswife; that shoemaker can take his oath you are in fee with the doctors to sell green fruit to the gentry, that the crudities may breed diseases.

ORANGE-WOMAN. Pray give me my money.

DORIMANT. Not a penny! When you bring the gentlewoman hither you spoke of, you shall be paid.

ORANGE-WOMAN. The gentlewoman! the gentlewoman may be as honest as your sisters, for aught I know. Pray, pay me, Mr. Dorimant, and do not abuse me so; I have an honester way of living—you know it.

MEDLEY. Was there ever such a resty[2] bawd!

DORIMANT. Some jade's tricks she has, but she makes amends when she's in good humor. [*To the* ORANGE-WOMAN] Come, tell me the lady's name and Handy shall pay you.

ORANGE-WOMAN. I must not; she forbid me.

DORIMANT. That's a sure sign she would have you.

MEDLEY. Where does she live?

ORANGE-WOMAN. They lodge at my house.

MEDLEY. Nay, then she's in a hopeful way.

ORANGE-WOMAN. Good Mr. Medley, say your pleasure of me, but take heed how you affront my house!—God's my life, in a hopeful way!

DORIMANT. Prithee, peace! What kind of woman's the mother?

ORANGE-WOMAN. A goodly, grave gentlewoman. Lord, how she talks against the wild young men o' the town! As for your part, she thinks you an arrant devil; should she see you, on my conscience she would look if you had not a cloven foot.

DORIMANT. Does she know me?

ORANGE-WOMAN. Only by hearsay; a thousand horrid stories have been told her of you, and she believes 'em all.

MEDLEY. By the character this should be the famous Lady Woodvill and her daughter Harriet.

ORANGE-WOMAN. The devil's in him for guessing, I think.

DORIMANT. Do you know 'em?

MEDLEY. Both very well; the mother's a great admirer of the forms and civility of the last age.

DORIMANT. An antiquated beauty may be allowed to be out of humor at the freedoms of the present. This is a good account of the mother; pray, what is the daughter?

MEDLEY. Why, first, she's an heiress vastly rich.

DORIMANT. And handsome?

MEDLEY. What alteration a twelvemonth may have bred in her I know not, but a year ago she was the beautifullest creature I ever saw: a fine, easy, clean shape; light brown hair in abundance; her features regular; her complexion clear and lively; large, wanton

---

[1] The trading center of London, not the Exchange, which is the financial center.

[2] Restive.

eyes; but above all, a mouth that has made me kiss it a hundred times in imagination; teeth white and even, and pretty, pouting lips, with a little moisture ever hanging on them, that look like the Provence rose fresh on the bush, ere the morning sun has quite drawn up the dew.

DORIMANT. Rapture! mere [1] rapture!

ORANGE-WOMAN. Nay, gad, he tells you true, she's a delicate creature.

DORIMANT. Has she wit?

MEDLEY. More than is usual in her sex, and as much malice. Then she's as wild as you would wish her, and has a demureness in her looks that makes it so surprising.

DORIMANT. Flesh and blood cannot hear this and not long to know her.

MEDLEY. I wonder what makes her mother bring her up to town; an old doting keeper cannot be more jealous of his mistress.

ORANGE-WOMAN. She made me laugh yesterday; there was a judge came to visit 'em, and the old man she told me did so stare upon her, and when he saluted her, smacked so heartily. Who would think it of 'em?

MEDLEY. God a-mercy![2] Judge!

DORIMANT. Do 'em right; the gentlemen of the long robe [3] have not been wanting by their good examples to countenance the crying sin o' the nation.

MEDLEY. Come, on with your trappings; 'tis later than you imagine.

DORIMANT. Call in the shoemaker, Handy.

ORANGE-WOMAN. Good Mr. Dorimant, pay me. Gad, I had rather give you my fruit than stay to be abused by that foul-mouthed rogue; what you gentlemen say, it matters not much, but such a dirty fellow does one more disgrace.

DORIMANT. Give her ten shillings—and be sure you tell the young gentlewoman I must be acquainted with her.

ORANGE-WOMAN. Now do you long to be tempting this pretty creature? Well, heavens mend you!

MEDLEY. Farewell, bog! [4]

[*Exeunt*] ORANGE-WOMAN *and* HANDY

Dorimant, when did you see your *pis-aller*,[5] as you call her—Mrs. Loveit?

DORIMANT. Not these two days.

MEDLEY. And how stand affairs between you?

DORIMANT. There has been great patching of late, much ado; we make a shift to hang together.

MEDLEY. I wonder how her mighty spirit bears it.

DORIMANT. Ill enough, on all conscience; I never knew so violent a creature.

MEDLEY. She's the most passionate in her love and the most extravagant in her jealousy of any woman I ever heard of. What note is that?

DORIMANT. An excuse I am going to send her for the neglect I am guilty of.

MEDLEY. Prithee, read it.

DORIMANT. No; but if you will take the pains, you may.

MEDLEY. (*Reads*)

I never was a lover of business, but now I have a just reason to hate it, since it has kept me these two days from seeing you. I intend to wait upon you in the afternoon, and in the pleasure of your conversation forget all I have suffered during this tedious absence.

This business of yours, Dorimant, has been with a vizard [6] at the playhouse; I have had an eye on you. If some malicious body should betray you, this kind note would hardly make your peace with her.

DORIMANT. I desire no better.

MEDLEY. Why, would her knowledge of it oblige you?

DORIMANT. Most infinitely; next to the coming to a good understanding with a new mistress, I love a quarrel with an old one. But the devil's in't! There has been such a calm in my affairs of late, I have not had the pleasure of making a woman so much as break her fan, to be sullen, or forswear herself, these three days.

MEDLEY. A very great misfortune. Let me see; I love mischief well enough to forward this business myself. I'll about it presently, and though I know the truth of what you've done will set her a-raving, I'll heighten it a little with invention, leave her in a fit o' the mother,[7] and be here again before y'are ready.

DORIMANT. Pray stay; you may spare yourself the labor. The business is undertaken already by one who will manage it with as much address, and I think with a little more malice than you can.

---

[1] Pure.
[2] Thank you (Brett-Smith).
[3] Of the legal profession.
[4] In the sense of "impertinence."
[5] Last resort.
[6] Mask. masked woman.
[7] Hysterics.

MEDLEY. Who i'the devil's name can this be!

DORIMANT. Why, the vizard—that very vizard you saw me with.

MEDLEY. Does she love mischief so well as to betray herself to spite another?

DORIMANT. Not so neither, Medley. I will make you comprehend the mystery. This mask, for a farther confirmation of what I have been these two days swearing to her, made me yesterday at the playhouse make her a promise before her face utterly to break off with Loveit, and, because she tenders [1] my reputation and would not have me do a barbarous thing, has contrived a way to give me a handsome occasion.

MEDLEY. Very good.

DORIMANT. She intends about an hour before me, this afternoon, to make Loveit a visit and, having the privilege by reason of a professed friendship between them, to talk of her concerns.

MEDLEY. Is she a friend?

DORIMANT. Oh, an intimate friend!

MEDLEY. Better and better; pray, proceed.

DORIMANT. She means insensibly to insinuate a discourse of me and artificially [2] to raise her jealousy to such a height that, transported with the first motions of her passion, she shall fly upon me with all the fury imaginable as soon as ever I enter. The quarrel being thus happily begun, I am to play my part, confess and justify all my roguery, swear her impertinence and ill-humor makes her intolerable, tax her with the next fop that comes into my head, and in a huff march away, slight her and leave her to be taken by whosoever thinks it worth his time to lie down before her.

MEDLEY. This vizard is a spark and has a genius that makes her worthy of yourself, Dorimant.

Enter HANDY, *the* Shoemaker, *and* Footman

DORIMANT. You rogue there, who sneak like a dog that has flung down a dish, if you do not mend your waiting, I'll uncase [3] you and turn you loose to the wheel of fortune.— Handy, seal this and let him run with it presently.

Exit Footman [4]

MEDLEY. Since you're resolved on a quarrel, why do you send her this kind note?

DORIMANT. To keep her at home in order to the business. (*To the* Shoemaker) How now, you drunken sot?

SHOEMAKER. 'Zbud, you have no reason to talk; I have not had a bottle of sack of yours in my belly this fortnight.

MEDLEY. The orange-woman says your neighbors take notice what a heathen you are, and design to inform a bishop and have you burned for an atheist.

SHOEMAKER. Damn her, dunghill, if her husband does not remove her, she stinks so, the parish intends to indict him for a nuisance.

MEDLEY. I advise you like a friend—reform your life. You have brought the envy of the world upon you by living above yourself. Whoring and swearing are vices too genteel for a shoemaker.

SHOEMAKER. 'Zbud, I think you men of quality will grow as unreasonable as the women. You would ingross [5] the sins of the nation; poor folks can no sooner be wicked but they're railed at by their betters.

DORIMANT. Sirrah, I'll have you stand i'the pillory for this libel.

SHOEMAKER. Some of you deserve it, I'm sure; there are so many of 'em, that our journeymen nowadays, instead of harmless ballads, sing nothing but your damned lampoons.

DORIMANT. Our lampoons, you rogue?

SHOEMAKER. Nay, good master, why should not you write your own commentaries as well as Cæsar?

MEDLEY. The rascal's read, I perceive.

SHOEMAKER. You know the old proverb— ale and history.[6]

DORIMANT. Draw on my shoes, sirrah.

SHOEMAKER. [*Does so*] Here's a shoe!

DORIMANT. —sits with more wrinkles than there are in an angry bully's forehead!

SHOEMAKER. 'Zbud, as smooth as your mistress's skin does upon her! So; strike your foot in home. 'Zbud, if e'er a monsieur of 'em all make more fashionable ware, I'll be content to have my ears whipped off with my own paring knife.

MEDLEY. And served up in a ragout instead of coxcombs to a company of French shoemakers for a collation.

SHOEMAKER. Hold, hold! Damn 'em, cater-

---

[1] Esteems.
[2] Artfully.
[3] Strip, flay.
[4] In the original the stage direction here also calls for Handy's exit.
[5] Amass.
[6] The proverb is not known.

pillars, let 'em feed upon cabbage. Come master, your health this morning! next my heart now.

DORIMANT. Go, get you home and govern your family better! Do not let your wife follow you to the alehouse, beat your whore, and lead you home in triumph.

SHOEMAKER. 'Zbud, there's never a man i'the town lives more like a gentleman with his wife than I do. I never mind her motions,[1] she never inquires into mine; we speak to one another civilly, hate one another heartily, and because 'tis vulgar to lie and soak together,[2] we have each of us our several [3] settle-bed.

DORIMANT. Give him half a crown.

MEDLEY. Not without he will promise to be bloody drunk.

SHOEMAKER. Tope's [4] the word i'the eye of the world, for my master's honor, Robin.

DORIMANT. Do not debauch my servants, sirrah.

SHOEMAKER. I only tip him the wink; he knows an alehouse from a hovel.

Exit Shoemaker

DORIMANT. [*To* HANDY] My clothes, quickly.

MEDLEY. Where shall we dine to-day?

[*Enter* YOUNG BELLAIR]

DORIMANT. Where you will; here comes a good third man.

YOUNG BELLAIR. Your servant, gentlemen.

MEDLEY. Gentle sir, how will you answer this visit to your honorable mistress? 'Tis not her interest you should keep company with men of sense who will be talking reason.

YOUNG BELLAIR. I do not fear her pardon, do you but grant me yours for my neglect of late.

MEDLEY. Though y'ave made us miserable by the want of your good company, to show you I am free from all resentment, may the beautiful cause of our misfortune give you all the joys happy lovers have shared ever since the world began.

YOUNG BELLAIR. You wish me in heaven, but you believe me on my journey to hell.

MEDLEY. You have a good strong faith, and that may contribute much towards your salvation. I confess I am but of an untoward constitution, apt to have doubts and scruples, and in love they are no less distracting than in religion. Were I so near marriage, I should cry out by fits as I ride in my coach, "Cuckold, cuckold!" with no less fury than the mad fanatic does "glory!" in Bethlem.[5]

YOUNG BELLAIR. Because religion makes some run mad, must I live an atheist?

MEDLEY. Is it not great indiscretion for a man of credit, who may have money enough on his word, to go and deal with Jews, who for little sums make men enter into bonds and give judgments? [6]

YOUNG BELLAIR. Preach no more on this text. I am determined, and there is no hope of my conversion.

DORIMANT. (*To* HANDY, *who is fiddling about him*) Leave your unnecessary fiddling; a wasp that's buzzing about a man's nose at dinner is not more troublesome than thou art.

HANDY. You love to have your clothes hang just, sir.

DORIMANT. I love to be well dressed, sir, and think it no scandal to my understanding.

HANDY. Will you use the essence or orange-flower water? [7]

DORIMANT. I will smell as I do to-day, no offence to the ladies' noses.

HANDY. Your pleasure, sir. [*Exit* HANDY] [8]

DORIMANT. That a man's excellency should lie in neatly tying of a ribband [9] or a cravat! How careful's nature in furnishing the world with necessary coxcombs!

YOUNG BELLAIR. That's a mighty pretty suit of yours, Dorimant.

DORIMANT. I am glad't has your approbation.

YOUNG BELLAIR. No man in town has a better fancy in his clothes than you have.

DORIMANT. You will make me have an opinion of my genius.

MEDLEY. There is a great critic, I hear, in these matters lately arrived piping hot from Paris.

---

[1] Actions.
[2] Drink deeply; "get soaked."
[3] Separate.
[4] Drink hard (a more polite term than "bloody drunk"). The meaning seems to be: "in the polite world the word you would use is tope." *Robin* is a colloquialism for servant, presumably addressed to Handy.
[5] Bethlehem Hospital, where the insane were confined. Oliver Cromwell had a porter afflicted with a religious mania, to whom there are a number of allusions in the period.
[6] Assignments of property.
[7] Essence of oranges, used as a scent.
[8] Handy's exit is not marked in the original text.
[9] Ribbon.

YOUNG BELLAIR. Sir Fopling Flutter, you mean?

MEDLEY. The same.

YOUNG BELLAIR. He thinks himself the pattern of modern gallantry.

DORIMANT. He is indeed the pattern of modern foppery.

MEDLEY. He was yesterday at the play, with a pair of gloves up to his elbows, and a periwig more exactly curled than a lady's head newly dressed for a ball.

YOUNG BELLAIR. What a pretty lisp he has!

DORIMANT. Ho! that he affects in imitation of the people of quality of France.

MEDLEY. His head stands, for the most part, on one side, and his looks are more languishing than a lady's when she lolls at stretch in her coach or leans her head carelessly against the side of a box i'the playhouse.

DORIMANT. He is a person indeed of great acquired follies.

MEDLEY. He is like many others, beholding to his education for making him so eminent a coxcomb. Many a fool had been lost to the world had their indulgent parents wisely bestowed neither learning nor good breeding on 'em.

YOUNG BELLAIR. He has been, as the sparkish word is, "brisk upon the ladies" already. He was yesterday at my Aunt Townley's and gave Mrs. Loveit a catalogue of his good qualities under the character of a complete gentleman, who, according to Sir Fopling, ought to dress well, dance well, fence well, have a genius for love letters, an agreeable voice for a chamber, be very amorous, something discreet, but not overconstant.

MEDLEY. Pretty ingredients to make an accomplished person!

DORIMANT. I am glad he pitched upon Loveit.

YOUNG BELLAIR. How so?

DORIMANT. I wanted a fop to lay to her charge, and this is as pat as may be.

YOUNG BELLAIR. I am confident she loves no man but you.

DORIMANT. The good fortune were enough to make me vain, but that I am in my nature modest.

YOUNG BELLAIR. Hark you, Dorimant. —With your leave, Mr. Medley; 'tis only a secret concerning a fair lady.

MEDLEY. Your good breeding, sir, gives you too much trouble; you might have whispered without all this ceremony.

YOUNG BELLAIR. (*To* DORIMANT) How stand your affairs with Bellinda of late?

DORIMANT. She's a little jilting baggage.

YOUNG BELLAIR. Nay, I believe her false enough, but she's ne'er the worse for your purpose; she was with you yesterday in a disguise at the play.

DORIMANT. There we fell out and resolved never to speak to one another more.

YOUNG BELLAIR. The occasion?

DORIMANT. Want of courage to meet me at the place appointed. These young women apprehend loving as much as the young men do fighting, at first; but once entered, like them too, they all turn bullies straight.

Enter HANDY *to* BELLAIR

HANDY. Sir, your man without desires to speak with you.

YOUNG BELLAIR. Gentlemen, I'll return immediately. *Exit* BELLAIR

MEDLEY. A very pretty fellow this.

DORIMANT. He's handsome, well bred, and by much the most tolerable of all the young men that do not abound in wit.

MEDLEY. Ever well dressed, always complaisant, and seldom impertinent. You and he are grown very intimate, I see.

DORIMANT. It is our mutual interest to be so: it makes the women think the better of his understanding, and judge more favorably of my reputation; it makes him pass upon some for a man of very good sense, and I upon others for a very civil person.

MEDLEY. What was that whisper?

DORIMANT. A thing which he would fain have known, but I did not think it fit to tell him; it might have frightened him from his honorable intentions of marrying.

MEDLEY. Emilia, give her her due, has the best reputation of any young woman about the town who has beauty enough to provoke detraction. Her carriage is unaffected, her discourse modest—not at all censorious nor pretending, like the counterfeits of the age.

DORIMANT. She's a discreet maid, and I believe nothing can corrupt her but a husband.

MEDLEY. A husband?

DORIMANT. Yes, a husband. I have known many a woman make a difficulty of losing a maidenhead, who have afterwards made none of making a cuckold.

MEDLEY. This prudent consideration I am apt to think has made you confirm poor Bellair in the desperate resolution he has taken.

DORIMANT. Indeed, the little hope I found there was of her, in the state she was in, has made me by my advice contribute something towards the changing of her condition.

Enter [YOUNG] BELLAIR

Dear Bellair! By heavens, I thought we had lost thee; men in love are never to be reckoned on when we would form a company.

YOUNG BELLAIR. Dorimant, I am undone; my man has brought the most surprising news i'the world.

DORIMANT. Some strange misfortune has befallen your love?

YOUNG BELLAIR. My father came to town last night and lodges i'the very house where Emilia lies.

MEDLEY. Does he know it is with her you are in love?

YOUNG BELLAIR. He knows I love, but knows not whom, without some officious sot has betrayed me.

DORIMANT. Your Aunt Townley is your confidant and favors the business.

YOUNG BELLAIR. I do not apprehend any ill office from her. I have received a letter, in which I am commanded by my father to meet him at my aunt's this afternoon. He tells me farther he has made a match for me and bids me resolve to be obedient to his will or expect to be disinherited.

MEDLEY. Now's your time, Bellair. Never had lover such an opportunity of giving a generous proof of his passion.

YOUNG BELLAIR. As how, I pray?

MEDLEY. Why, hang an estate, marry Emilia out of hand, and provoke your father to do what he threatens. 'Tis but despising a coach, humbling yourself to a pair of goloshes,[1] being out of countenance when you meet your friends, pointed at and pitied wherever you go by all the amorous fops that know you, and your fame will be immortal.

YOUNG BELLAIR. I could find in my heart to resolve not to marry at all.

DORIMANT. Fie, fie, that would spoil a good jest and disappoint the well-natured town of an occasion of laughing at you.

YOUNG BELLAIR. The storm I have so long expected hangs o'er my head and begins to pour down upon me. I am on the rack and can have no rest till I'm satisfied in what I fear.—Where do you dine?

DORIMANT. At Long's or Locket's.[2]

MEDLEY. At Long's let it be.

YOUNG BELLAIR. I'll run and see Emilia and inform myself how matters stand. If my misfortunes are not so great as to make me unfit for company, I'll be with you.

Exit BELLAIR

Enter a Footman *with a letter*

FOOTMAN. (*To* DORIMANT) Here's a letter, sir.

DORIMANT. The superscription's right: "For Mr. Dorimant."

MEDLEY. Let's see—the very scrawl and spelling of a true-bred whore.

DORIMANT. I know the hand; the style is admirable, I assure you.

MEDLEY. Prithee, read it.

DORIMANT. (*Reads*)

I told a you you dud not love me, if you dud, you wou'd have seen me again ere now. I have no money and am very Mallicolly. Pray send me a Guynie to see the Operies.
  Your Servant to Command,
    Molly

MEDLEY. Pray, let the whore have a favorable answer, that she may spark it [3] in a box and do honor to her profession.

DORIMANT. She shall, and perk up i'the face of quality.—Is the coach at the door?

HANDY. You did not bid me send for it.

(HANDY *offers to go out*)

DORIMANT. Eternal blockhead! Hey, sot—

HANDY. Did you call me, sir?

DORIMANT. I hope you have no just exception to the name, sir?

HANDY. I have sense, sir.

DORIMANT. Not so much as a fly in winter. How did you come, Medley?

MEDLEY. In a chair.

FOOTMAN. You may have a hackney coach if you please, sir.

DORIMANT. I may ride the elephant if I please, sir. Call another chair and let my coach follow to Long's. *Exeunt, singing*
  Be calm, ye great parents, etc.[4]

---

[1] Pattens.
[2] Famous taverns of the day, much frequented by fashionable young men.
[3] Play the fine lady.
[4] Apparently a song of the day.

ACT II

Scene i. [*In lodgings*]

Enter Lady Townley *and* Emilia

Lady Townley. I was afraid, Emilia, all had been discovered.

Emilia. I tremble with the apprehension still.

Lady Townley. That my brother should take lodgings i'the very house where you lie!

Emilia. 'Twas lucky we had timely notice to warn the people to be secret. He seems to be a mighty good-humored old man.

Lady Townley. He ever had a notable smirking way with him.

Emilia. He calls me "rogue," tells me he can't abide me, and does so be-pat me.

Lady Townley. On my word, you are much in his favor then!

Emilia. He has been very inquisitive, I am told, about my family, my reputation, and my fortune.

Lady Townley. I am confident he does not i'the least suspect you are the woman his son's in love with.

Emilia. What should make him, then, inform himself so particularly of me?

Lady Townley. He was always of a very loving temper himself; it may be he has a doting fit upon him—who knows?

Emilia. It cannot be!

Enter Young Bellair

Lady Townley. Here comes my nephew. Where did you leave your father?

Young Bellair. Writing a note within. Emilia, this early visit looks as if some kind jealousy would not let you rest at home.

Emilia. The knowledge I have of my rival gives me a little cause to fear your constancy.

Young Bellair. My constancy! I vow—

Emilia. Do not vow. Our love is frail as is our life and full as little in our power; and are you sure you shall outlive this day?

Young Bellair. I am not; but when we are in perfect health, 'twere an idle thing to fright ourselves with the thoughts of sudden death.

Lady Townley. Pray, what has passed between you and your father i'the garden?

Young Bellair. He's firm in his resolution, tells me I must marry Mrs. Harriet, or swears he'll marry himself and disinherit me. When I saw I could not prevail with him to be more indulgent, I dissembled an obedience to his will, which has composed his passion and will give us time, and I hope, opportunity, to deceive him.

Enter Old Bellair *with a note in his hand*

Lady Townley. Peace, here he comes!

Old Bellair. Harry, take this and let your man carry it for me to Mr. Forbes's chamber—my lawyer i'the Temple.

[*Exit* Young Bellair]

(*To* Emilia) Neighbor, a dod, I am glad to see thee here.—Make much of her, sister; she's one of the best of your acquaintance. I like her countenance and her behavior well; she has a modesty that is not common i'this age—a dod, she has!

Lady Townley. I know her value, brother, and esteem her accordingly.

Old Bellair. Advise her to wear a little more mirth in her face; a dod, she's too serious.

Lady Townley. The fault is very excusable in a young woman.

Old Bellair. Nay, a dod, I like her ne'er the worse. A melancholy beauty has her charms. I love a pretty sadness in a face, which varies now and then, like changeable colors, into a smile.

Lady Townley. Methinks you speak very feelingly, brother.

Old Bellair. I am but five and fifty, sister, you know, an age not altogether unsensible.— (*To* Emilia) Cheer up, sweetheart! I have a secret to tell thee may chance to make thee merry. We three will make collation together anon; i'the meantime, mum, I can't abide you! Go, I can't abide you.—

Enter Young Bellair

Harry, come! You must along with me to my Lady Woodvill's.—I am going to slip the boy at a mistress.

Young Bellair. At a wife, sir, you would say.

Old Bellair. You need not look so glum, sir; a wife is no curse when she brings the blessing of a good estate with her. But an idle town flirt, with a painted face, a rotten reputation, and a crazy fortune, a dod! is the devil and all, and such a one I hear you are in league with.

Young Bellair. I cannot help detraction, sir.

OLD BELLAIR. Out! 'A pize[1] o' their breeches, there are keeping-fools enough for such flaunting baggages, and they are e'en too good for 'em. (*To* EMILIA) Remember 'night.—Go; you're a rogue, you're a rogue!—Fare you well, fare you well!—Come, come, come along, sir!

Exeunt OLD *and* YOUNG BELLAIR

LADY TOWNLEY. On my word, the old man comes on apace. I'll lay my life he's smitten.

EMILIA. This is nothing but the pleasantness of his humor.

LADY TOWNLEY. I know him better than you. Let it work; it may prove lucky.

Enter a Page

PAGE. Madam, Mr. Medley has sent to know whether a visit will not be troublesome this afternoon.

LADY TOWNLEY. Send him word his visits never are so. [*Exit* Page]

EMILIA. He's a very pleasant man.

LADY TOWNLEY. He's a very necessary man among us women; he's not scandalous i'the least, perpetually contriving to bring good company together, and always ready to stop up a gap at ombre.[2] Then, he knows all the little news o'the town.

EMILIA. I love to hear him talk o'the intrigues. Let 'em be never so dull in themselves, he'll make 'em pleasant i'the relation.

LADY TOWNLEY. But he improves things so much one can take no measure of the truth from him. Mr. Dorimant swears a flea or a maggot is not made more monstrous by a magnifying glass than a story is by his telling it.

Enter MEDLEY

EMILIA. Hold, here he comes.

LADY TOWNLEY. Mr. Medley.

MEDLEY. Your servant, madam.

LADY TOWNLEY. You have made yourself a stranger of late.

EMILIA. I believe you took a surfeit of ombre last time you were here.

MEDLEY. Indeed, I had my belly full of that termagant, Lady Dealer. There never was so insatiable a carder,[3] an old gleeker[4] never loved to sit to't like her. I have played with her now at least a dozen times till she's worn out all her fine complexion and her tower[5] would keep in curl no longer.

LADY TOWNLEY. Blame her not, poor woman, she loves nothing so well as a black ace.[6]

MEDLEY. The pleasure I have seen her in when she has had hope in drawing for a matadore.[7]

EMILIA. 'Tis as pretty sport to her as persuading masks off is to you, to make discoveries.

LADY TOWNLEY. Pray, where's your friend Mr. Dorimant?

MEDLEY. Soliciting his affairs; he's a man of great employment—has more mistresses now depending than the most eminent lawyer in England has causes.[8]

EMILIA. Here has been Mrs. Loveit so uneasy and out of humor these two days.

LADY TOWNLEY. How strangely love and jealousy rage in that poor woman!

MEDLEY. She could not have picked out a devil upon earth so proper to torment her; h'as made her break a dozen or two fans already, tear half a score points in pieces, and destroy hoods and knots without number.

LADY TOWNLEY. We heard of a pleasant serenade he gave her t'other night.

MEDLEY. A Danish serenade with kettle-drums and trumpets.

EMILIA. Oh, barbarous!

MEDLEY. What! You are of the number of the ladies whose ears are grown so delicate since our operas[9] you can be charmed with nothing but *flute doux*[10] and French hautboys.[11]

EMILIA. Leave your raillery, and tell us is there any new wit come forth—songs or novels?

MEDLEY. A very pretty piece of gallantry, by an eminent author, called *The Diversions of Brussels*,[12] very necessary to be read by all old ladies who are desirous to improve them-

---

[1] Pox (?).
[2] A card game, usually played by three players.
[3] Gamester.
[4] Card-player.
[5] High headdress.
[6] The ace of spades is high trump in ombre.
[7] One of the three principal trumps in ombre.
[8] Cases.
[9] Italian opera was new in England in the sixteen-seventies.
[10] Or *flutes deux*. An obsolete form of flute.
[11] Properly, *haut bois*, the modern oboe.
[12] *The Diversions of Brussels* is apparently an invention of Medley's active brain. So, too, is *The Art of Affectation*, mentioned below.

selves at questions and commands, blindman's buff, and the like fashionable recreations.

EMILIA. Oh, ridiculous!

MEDLEY. Then there is *The Art of Affectation*, written by a late beauty of quality, teaching you how to draw up your breasts, stretch out your neck, to thrust out your breech, to play with you head, to toss up your nose, to bite your lips, to turn up your eyes, to speak in a silly, soft tone of a voice, and to use all the foolish French words that will infallibly make your person and conversation charming, with a short apology at the latter end in the behalf of young ladies who notoriously wash and paint though they have naturally good complexions.

EMILIA. What a deal of stuff you tell us!

MEDLEY. Such as the town affords, madam. The Russians, hearing the great respect we have for foreign dancing, have lately sent over some of their best balladines,[1] who are now practising a famous ballet which will be suddenly[2] danced at the Bear Garden.[3]

LADY TOWNLEY. Pray forbear your idle stories, and give us an account of the state of love as it now stands.

MEDLEY. Truly, there have been some revolutions in those affairs—great chopping and changing among the old, and some new lovers whom malice, indiscretion, and misfortune have luckily brought into play.

LADY TOWNLEY. What think you of walking into the next room and sitting down before you engage in this business?

MEDLEY. I wait upon you, and I hope (though women are commonly unreasonable) by the plenty of scandal I shall discover, to give you very good content, ladies. *Exeunt*

SCENE II. [*The dressing-room of* MISTRESS LOVEIT]

Enter MRS. LOVEIT *and* PERT, MRS. LOVEIT *putting up a letter, then pulling out a pocket-glass and looking in it*

MRS. LOVEIT. Pert.

PERT. Madam?

MRS. LOVEIT. I hate myself, I look so ill to-day.

PERT. Hate the wicked cause on't, that base man Mr. Dorimant, who makes you torment and vex yourself continually.

MRS. LOVEIT. He is to blame, indeed.

PERT. To blame to be two days without sending, writing, or coming near you, contrary to his oath and covenant! 'Twas to much purpose to make him swear! I'll lay my life there's not an article but he has broken—talked to the vizards i'the pit, waited upon the ladies from the boxes to their coaches, gone behind the scenes, and fawned upon those little insignificant creatures, the players. 'Tis impossible for a man of his inconstant temper to forbear, I'm sure.

MRS. LOVEIT. I know he is a devil, but he has something of the angel yet undefaced in him, which makes him so charming and agreeable that I must love him, be he never so wicked.

PERT. I little thought, madam, to see your spirit tamed to this degree, who banished poor Mr. Lackwit but for taking up another lady's fan in your presence.

MRS. LOVEIT. My knowing of such odious fools contributes to the making of me love Dorimant the better.

PERT. Your knowing of Mr. Dorimant, in my mind, should rather make you hate all mankind.

MRS. LOVEIT. So it does—besides himself.

PERT. Pray, what excuse does he make in his letter?

MRS. LOVEIT. He has had business.

PERT. Business in general terms would not have been a current excuse for another. A modish man is always very busy when he is in pursuit of a new mistress.

MRS. LOVEIT. Some fop has bribed you to rail at him. He had business, I will believe it, and will forgive him.

PERT. You may forgive him anything, but I shall never forgive him his turning me into ridicule, as I hear he does.

MRS. LOVEIT. I perceive you are of the number of those fools his wit had made his enemies.

PERT. I am of the number of those he's pleased to rally, madam, and if we may believe Mr. Wagfan and Mr. Caperwell, he sometimes makes merry with yourself, too. among his laughing companions.

MRS. LOVEIT. Blockheads are as malicious to witty men as ugly women are to the hand-

---
[1] Ballet dancers.
[2] Shortly.
[3] Bear-baiting was a popular sport.

some; 'tis their interest, and they make it their business to defame 'em.

PERT. I wish Mr. Dorimant would not make it his business to defame you.

MRS. LOVEIT. Should he, I had rather be made infamous by him than owe my reputation to the dull discretion of those fops you talk of.

Enter BELLINDA

—Beliinda! (*Running to her*)

BELLINDA. My dear!

MRS. LOVEIT. You have been unkind of late.

BELLINDA. Do not say unkind, say unhappy.

MRS. LOVEIT. I could chide you. Where have you been these two days?

BELLINDA. Pity me rather, my dear, where I have been so tired with two or three country gentlemen, whose conversation has been more unsufferable than a country fiddle.

MRS. LOVEIT. Are they relations?

BELLINDA. No; Welsh acquaintance [1] I made when I was last year at St. Winifred's. They have asked me a thousand questions of the modes and intrigues of the town, and I have told 'em almost as many things for news that hardly were so when their gowns were in fashion.

MRS. LOVEIT. Provoking creatures! How could you endure 'em?

BELLINDA. (*Aside*) Now to carry on my plot. Nothing but love could make me capable of so much falsehood. 'Tis time to begin, lest Dorimant should come before her jealousy has stung her. (*Laughs, and then speaks on*) I was yesterday at a play with 'em, where I was fain to show 'em the living, as the man at Westminster does the dead: "That is Mrs. Such-a-one, admired for her beauty; that is Mr. Such-a-one, cried up for a wit; that is sparkish Mr. Such-a-one, who keeps reverend Mrs. Such-a-one, and there sits fine Mrs. Such-a-one who was lately cast off by my Lord Such-a-one."

MRS. LOVEIT. Did you see Dorimant there?

BELLINDA. I did, and imagine you were with him and have no mind to own it.

MRS. LOVEIT. What should make you think so?

BELLINDA. A lady masked in a pretty dishabille, whom Dorimant entertained with more respect than the gallants do a common vizard.

MRS. LOVEIT. (*Aside*) Dorimant at the play entertaining a mask! Oh, heavens!

BELLINDA. (*Aside*) Good!

MRS. LOVEIT. Did he stay all the while?

BELLINDA. Till the play was done and then led her out, which confirms me it was you.

MRS. LOVEIT. Traitor!

PERT. Now you may believe he has business, and you may forgive him, too.

MRS. LOVEIT. Ingrateful, perjured man!

BELLINDA. You seem so much concerned, my dear, I fear I have told you unawares what I had better have concealed for your quiet.

MRS. LOVEIT. What manner of shape had she?

BELLINDA. Tall and slender. Her motions were very genteel; certainly she must be some person of condition.

MRS. LOVEIT. Shame and confusion be ever in her face when she shows it!

BELLINDA. I should blame your discretion for loving that wild man, my dear, but they say he has a way so bewitching that few can defend their hearts who know him.

MRS. LOVEIT. I will tear him out from mine or die i'the attempt.

BELLINDA. Be more moderate.

MRS. LOVEIT. Would I had daggers, darts, or poisoned arrows in my breast, so I could but remove the thoughts of him from thence!

BELLINDA. Fie, fie! your transports are too violent, my dear; this may be but an accidental gallantry, and 'tis likely ended at her coach.

PERT. Should it proceed farther, let your comfort be, the conduct Mr. Dorimant affects will quickly make you know your rival, ten to one let you see her ruined, her reputation exposed to the town—a happiness none will envy her but yourself, madam.

MRS. LOVEIT. Whoe'er she be, all the harm I wish her is, may she love him as well as I do and may he give her as much cause to hate him.

PERT. Never doubt the latter end of your curse, madam.

MRS. LOVEIT. May all the passions that are raised by neglected love—jealousy, indig-

---

[1] Belinda may have been visiting St. Winifred's Well in Wales; or she may have simply made somebody's acquaintance informally: "Welsh acquaintance."

nation, spite, and thirst of revenge—eternally rage in her soul as they do now in mine. (*Walks up and down with a distracted air*)

Enter a Page

PAGE. Madam, Master Dorimant—
MRS. LOVEIT. I will not see him.
PAGE. I told him you were within, madam.
MRS. LOVEIT. Say you lied—say I'm busy; shut the door—say anything!
PAGE. He's here, madam.

Enter DORIMANT

DORIMANT.
They taste of death who do at heaven arrive;[1]
But we this paradise approach alive.
(*To* [MISTRESS] LOVEIT) What, dancing the galloping nag without a fiddle? (*Offers to catch her by the hand. She flings away and walks on, [he] pursuing her*) I fear this restlessness of the body, madam, proceeds from an unquietness of the mind. What unlucky accident puts you out of humor? A point ill washed, knots spoiled i' the making up, hair shaded awry, or some other little mistake in setting you in order?
PERT. A trifle, in my opinion, sir, more inconsiderable than any you mention.
DORIMANT. O Mrs. Pert! I never knew you sullen enough to be silent; come, let me know the business.
PERT. The business, sir, is the business that has taken you up these two days. How have I seen you laugh at men of business, and now to become a man of business yourself!
DORIMANT. We are not masters of our own affections; our inclinations daily alter. Now we love pleasure, and anon we shall dote on business. Human frailty will have it so, and who can help it?
MRS. LOVEIT. Faithless, inhuman, barbarous man—
DORIMANT. Good! Now the alarm strikes.—
MRS. LOVEIT.—without sense of love, of honor, or of gratitude, tell me, for I will know, what devil masked she was you were with at the play yesterday?
DORIMANT. Faith, I resolved as much as you, but the devil was obstinate and would not tell me.
MRS. LOVEIT. False in this as in your vows to me! You do know.

DORIMANT. The truth is, I did all I could to know.
MRS. LOVEIT. And dare you own it to my face? Hell and furies! (*Tears her fan in pieces*)
DORIMANT. Spare your fan, madam; you are growing hot and will want it to cool you.
MRS. LOVEIT. Horror and distraction seize you! Sorrow and remorse gnaw your soul, and punish all your perjuries to me—(*Weeps*)
DORIMANT.
So thunder breaks the cloud in twain
And makes a passage for the rain.
(*Turning to Bellinda*) Bellinda, you are the devil that has raised this storm; you were at the play yesterday and have been making discoveries to your dear.
BELLINDA. You're the most mistaken man i' the world.
DORIMANT. It must be so, and here I vow revenge; resolve to pursue and persecute you more impertinently than ever any loving fop did his mistress, hunt you i' the park, trace you i' the Mall,[2] dog you in every visit you make, haunt you at the plays and i' the drawing-room, hang my nose in your neck and talk to you whether you will or no, and ever look upon you with such dying eyes till your friends grow jealous of me, send you out of town, and the world suspect your reputation. (*In a lower voice*)—At my Lady Townley's when we go from hence. (*He looks kindly on* BELLINDA)
BELLINDA. I'll meet you there.
DORIMANT. Enough.
MRS. LOVEIT. Stand off! (*Pushing* DORIMANT *away*) You sha' not stare upon her so.
DORIMANT. Good; there's one made jealous already.
MRS. LOVEIT. Is this the constancy you vowed?
DORIMANT. Constancy at my years? 'Tis not a virtue in season; you might as well expect the fruit the autumn ripens i' the spring.
MRS. LOVEIT. Monstrous principle!
DORIMANT. Youth has a long journey to go, madam; should I have set up my rest[3] at the first inn I lodged at, I should never have arrived at the happiness I now enjoy.
MRS. LOVEIT. Dissembler, damned dissembler!
DORIMANT. I am so, I confess. Good nature

---

[1] Dorimant is quoting Waller's "Of Her Chamber."

[2] In St. James's Park. An unnecessary stage direction is omitted a few lines above.

[3] My abode.

and good manners corrupt me. I am honest in my inclinations, and would not, wer't not to avoid offence, make a lady in years believe I think her young—willfully mistake art for nature—and seem as fond of a thing I am weary of as when I doted on't in earnest.

Mrs. Loveit. False man!

Dorimant. True woman!

Mrs. Loveit. Now you begin to show yourself.

Dorimant. Love gilds us over and makes us show fine things to one another for a time, but soon the gold wears off and then again the native brass appears.

Mrs. Loveit. Think on your oaths, your vows, and protestations, perjured man!

Dorimant. I made 'em when I was in love.

Mrs. Loveit. And therefore ought they not to bind? Oh, impious!

Dorimant. What we swear at such a time may be a certain proof of a present passion, but to say truth, in love there is no security to be given for the future.

Mrs. Loveit. Horrid and ingrateful! Begone, and never see me more!

Dorimant. I am not one of those troublesome coxcombs who, because they were once well received, take the privilege to plague a woman with their love ever after. I shall obey you, madam, though I do myself some violence. (*He offers to go and* Mrs. Loveit *pulls him back*)

Mrs. Loveit. Come back! You sha' not go! Could you have the ill-nature to offer it?

Dorimant. When love grows diseased, the best thing we can do is to put it to a violent death. I cannot endure the torture of a ling'ring and consumptive passion.

Mrs. Loveit. Can you think mine sickly?

Dorimant. Oh, it is desperately ill. What worse symptoms are there than your being always uneasy when I visit you, your picking quarrels with me on slight occasions, and in my absence kindly listening to the impertinences of every fashionable fool that talks to you?

Mrs. Loveit. What fashionable fool can you lay to my charge?

Dorimant. Why, the very cock-fool of all those fools—Sir Fopling Flutter.

Mrs. Loveit. I never saw him in my life but once.

Dorimant. The worse woman you, at first sight to put on all your charms, to entertain him with that softness in your voice, and all that wanton kindness in your eyes you so notoriously affect when you design a conquest.

Mrs. Loveit. So damned a lie did never malice yet invent. Who told you this?

Dorimant. No matter. That ever I should love a woman that can dote on a senseless caper, a tawdry French ribband, and a formal cravat!

Mrs. Loveit. You make me mad.

Dorimant. A guilty conscience may do much. Go on—be the game-mistress o' the town, and enter all our young fops at fast as they come from travel.

Mrs. Loveit. Base and scurrilous!

Dorimant. A fine mortifying reputation 'twill be for a woman of your pride, wit, and quality!

Mrs. Loveit. This jealousy's a mere pretence, a cursed trick of your own devising.—I know you.

Dorimant. Believe it and all the ill of me you can, I would not have a woman have the least good thought of me, that can think well of Fopling. Farewell! Fall to, and much good may you do with your coxcomb.

Mrs. Loveit. Stay! Oh stay! and I will tell you all!

Dorimant. I have been told too much already. *Exit* Dorimant

Mrs. Loveit. Call him again!

Pert. E'en let him go—a fair riddance.

Mrs. Loveit. Run, I say! Call him again! I will have him called!

Pert. The devil should call him away first, were it my concern. *Exit* Pert

Bellinda. He's frightened me from the very thoughts of loving men. For heaven's sake, my dear, do not discover what I told you! I dread his tongue as much as you ought to have done his friendship.

Enter Pert

Pert. He's gone, madam.

Mrs. Loveit. Lightning blast him!

Pert. When I told him you desired him to come back, he smiled, made a mouth at me, flung into his coach, and said—

Mrs. Loveit. What did he say?

Pert. "Drive away!" and then repeated verses.

Mrs. Loveit. Would I had made a contract to be a witch when first I entertained this greater devil—Monster—barbarian! I could tear myself in pieces. Revenge—nothing but revenge can ease me! Plague, War, Famine, Fire—all that can bring universal ruin and misery on mankind, with joy I'd perish to have you in my power but this moment!

Exit MRS. LOVEIT

PERT. Follow, madam; leave her not in this outrageous passion! (PERT *gathers up the things*)

BELLINDA. He's given me the proof which I desired of his love, but 'tis a proof of his ill-nature too. I wish I had not seen him use her so.

I sigh to think that Dorimant may be
One day as faithless and unkind to me.

Exeunt

ACT III

SCENE I. LADY WOODVILL'S *lodgings*

Enter HARRIET *and* BUSY, *her woman*

BUSY. Dear madam, let me see that curl in order.

HARRIET. Let me alone; I will shake 'em all out of order.

BUSY. Will you never leave this wildness?

HARRIET. Torment me not.

BUSY. Look! there's a knot falling off.

HARRIET. Let it drop.

BUSY. But one pin, dear madam.

HARRIET. How do I daily suffer under thy officious fingers!

BUSY. Ah, the difference that is between you and my Lady Dapper! How uneasy she is if the least thing be amiss about her!

HARRIET. She is indeed most exact; nothing is ever wanting to make her ugliness remarkable.

BUSY. Jeering people say so.

HARRIET. Her powdering, painting, and her patching never fail in public to draw the tongues and eyes of all the men upon her.

BUSY. She is, indeed, a little too pretending.

HARRIET. That women should set up for beauty as much in spite of nature as some men have done for wit!

BUSY. I hope without offence one may endeavor to make one's self agreeable.

HARRIET. Not when 'tis impossible. Women then ought to be no more fond of dressing than fools should be of talking; hoods and modesty, masks and silence—things that shadow and conceal—they should think of nothing else.

BUSY. Jesu! Madam, what will your mother think is become of you? For heaven's sake go in again!

HARRIET. I won't.

BUSY. This is the extravagant'st thing that ever you did in your life, to leave her and a gentleman who is to be your husband.

HARRIET. My husband! Hast thou so little wit to think I spoke what I meant when I overjoyed her in the country with a low curtsey and "What you please, madam; I shall ever be obedient"?

BUSY. Nay, I know not, you have so many fetches.[1]

HARRIET. And this was one to get her up to London—nothing else, I assure thee.

BUSY. Well, the man, in my mind, is a fine man.

HARRIET. The man indeed wears his clothes fashionably and has a pretty, negligent way with him, very courtly and much affected; he bows, and talks, and smiles so agreeably, as he thinks.

BUSY. I never saw anything so genteel.

HARRIET. Varnished over with good breeding, many a blockhead makes a tolerable show.

BUSY. I wonder you do not like him.

HARRIET. I think I might be brought to endure him, and that is all a reasonable woman should expect in a husband; but there is duty i'the case, and like the haughty Merab[2] I

Find much aversion in my stubborn mind,
which
Is bred by being promised and designed.

BUSY. I wish you do not design your own ruin! I partly guess your inclinations, madam —that Mr. Dorimant—

HARRIET. Leave your prating, and sing some foolish song or other.

BUSY. I will; the song you love so well ever since you saw Mr. Dorimant:

SONG

When first Amintas charmed my heart,
My heedless sheep began to stray;
The wolves soon stole the greatest part,
And all will now be made a prey.

---

[1] Tricks.
[2] See *I Samuel* XIV:49; XVIII, 17–19. Merab also figures in Cowley's *Davideis*, a long epic poem published in 1656, from which Harriet paraphrases ll. 625–6 of Bk. III.

Ah, let not love your thoughts possess,
'Tis fatal to a shepherdess;
The dang'rous passion you must shun,
Or else like me be quite undone.

HARRIET. Shall I be paid down by a covetous parent for a purchase? I need no land; no, I'll lay myself out all in love. It is decreed—

Enter YOUNG BELLAIR

YOUNG BELLAIR. What generous resolution are you in making, madam?
HARRIET. Only to be disobedient, sir.
YOUNG BELLAIR. Let me join hands with you in that—
HARRIET. With all my heart. I never thought I should have given you mine so willingly. Here I, Harriet—
YOUNG BELLAIR. And I, Harry—
HARRIET. Do solemnly protest—
YOUNG BELLAIR. And vow—
HARRIET. That I with you—
YOUNG BELLAIR. And I with you—
BOTH. Will never marry.
HARRIET. A match!
YOUNG BELLAIR. And no match! How do you like this indifference now?
HARRIET. You expect I should take it ill, I see.
YOUNG BELLAIR. 'Tis not unnatural for you women to be a little angry; you miss a conquest, though you would slight the poor man were he in your power.
HARRIET. There are some, it may be, have an eye like Bart'lomew [1]—big enough for the whole fair; but I am not of the number, and you may keep your gingerbread. 'Twill be more acceptable to the lady whose dear image it wears, sir.
YOUNG BELLAIR. But I confess, madam, you came a day after the fair.
HARRIET. You own, then, you are in love?
YOUNG BELLAIR. I do.
HARRIET. The confidence is generous, and in return I could almost find in my heart to let you know my inclinations.
YOUNG BELLAIR. Are you in love?
HARRIET. Yes, with this dear town, to that degree I can scarce endure the country in landscapes and hangings.

YOUNG BELLAIR. What a dreadful thing 'twould be to be hurried back to Hampshire!
HARRIET. Ah, name it not!
YOUNG BELLAIR. As for us, I find we shall agree well enough. Would we could do something to deceive the grave people!
HARRIET. Could we delay their quick proceeding, 'twere well. A reprieve is a good step towards the getting of a pardon.
YOUNG BELLAIR. If we give over the game, we are undone. What think you of playing it on booty? [2]
HARRIET. What do you mean?
YOUNG BELLAIR. Pretend to be in love with one another! 'twill make some dilatory excuses we may feign, pass the better.
HARRIET. Let us do't, if it be but for the dear pleasure of dissembling.
YOUNG BELLAIR. Can you play your part?
HARRIET. I know not what it is to love, but I have made pretty remarks [3] by being now and then where lovers meet. Where did you leave your gravities?
YOUNG BELLAIR. I'th' next room! Your mother was censuring our modern [4] gallant.

Enter OLD BELLAIR *and* LADY WOODVILL

HARRIET. Peace! Here they come; I will lean against this wall and look bashfully down upon my fan, while you, like an amorous spark, modishly entertain me.
LADY WOODVILL. (*To* OLD BELLAIR) Never go about to excuse 'em; come, come, it was not so when I was a young woman.
OLD BELLAIR. A dod, they're something disrespectful—
LADY WOODVILL. Quality was then considered and not rallied by every fleering fellow.
OLD BELLAIR. Youth will have its jest—a dod, it will.
LADY WOODVILL. 'Tis good breeding now to be civil to none but players and Exchange women; [5] they are treated by 'em as much above their condition as others are below theirs.
OLD BELLAIR. Out! A pize on 'em; talk no more! The rogues ha' got an ill habit of preferring beauty no matter where they find it.
LADY WOODVILL. See your son and my daughter; they have improved their acquaintance since they were within.

---

[1] Bartholomew Fair, held annually. Gingerbread cakes were bought and presented by the enamored swains to their mistresses while visiting it.
[2] To play booty is to play a game dishonestly.
[3] Notes.
[4] In the depreciatory sense of trite or common.
[5] Women who frequented the Royal Exchange.

OLD BELLAIR. A dod, methinks they have! Let's keep back and observe.

YOUNG BELLAIR. [*To* HARRIET] Now for a look and gestures that may persuade 'em I am saying all the passionate things imaginable—

HARRIET. Your head a little more on one side. Ease yourself on your left leg and play with your right hand.

YOUNG BELLAIR. Thus, is it not?

HARRIET. Now set your right leg firm on the ground, adjust your belt, then look about you.

YOUNG BELLAIR. A little exercising will make me perfect.

HARRIET. Smile, and turn to me again very sparkish.

YOUNG BELLAIR. Will you take your turn and be instructed?

HARRIET. With all my heart!

YOUNG BELLAIR. At one motion play your fan, roll your eyes, and then settle a kind look upon me.

HARRIET. So.

YOUNG BELLAIR. Now spread your fan, look down upon it, and tell the sticks with a finger!

HARRIET. Very modish!

YOUNG BELLAIR. Clap your hand up to your bosom, hold down your gown, shrug a little, draw up your breasts, and let 'em fall again gently, with a sigh or two, etc.

HARRIET. By the instructions you give, I suspect you for one of those malicious observers who watch people's eyes, and from innocent looks make scandalous conclusions.

YOUNG BELLAIR. I know some, indeed, who out of mere love to mischief are as vigilant as jealousy itself, and will give you an account of every glance that passes at a play and i'th' Circle.[1]

HARRIET. 'Twill not be amiss now to seem a little pleasant.

YOUNG BELLAIR. Clap your fan, then, in both your hands, snatch it to your mouth, smile, and with a lively motion fling your body a little forwards. So—now spread it; fall back on the sudden, cover your face with it and break out into loud laughter. Take up! look grave and fall a-fanning of yourself.—Admirably well acted!

HARRIET. I think I am pretty apt at these matters.

OLD BELLAIR. [*To* LADY WOODVILL] A dod, I like this well!

[1] I.e., in Hyde Park.

LADY WOODVILL. This promises something.

OLD BELLAIR. Come! there is love i'th' case—a dod there is, or will be. [*To* HARRIET] What say you, young lady?

YOUNG BELLAIR. All in good time, sir; you expect we should fall to and love as gamecocks fight, as soon as we are set together? A dod, y'are unreasonable!

OLD BELLAIR. A dod, sirrah, I like thy wit well.

Enter a Servant

SERVANT. The coach is at the door, madam.

OLD BELLAIR. Go, get you and take the air together.

LADY WOODVILL. Will not you go with us?

OLD BELLAIR. Out, a pize! A dod, I ha' business and cannot. We shall meet at night at my sister Townley's.

YOUNG BELLAIR. (*Aside*) He's going to Emilia. I overheard him talk of a collation.[2]

Exeunt

SCENE II. [LADY TOWNLEY'S *drawing-room*]

Enter LADY TOWNLEY, EMILIA, *and* MR. MEDLEY

LADY TOWNLEY. I pity the young lovers we last talked of, though to say truth their conduct has been so indiscreet they deserve to be unfortunate.

MEDLEY. Y'have had an exact account, from the great lady i'th' box down to the little orange wench.

EMILIA. You're a living libel, a breathing lampoon. I wonder you are not torn in pieces.

MEDLEY. What think you of setting up an office of intelligence for these matters? The project may get money.

LADY TOWNLEY. You would have great dealings with country ladies.

MEDLEY. More than Muddiman[3] has with their husbands.

Enter BELLINDA

LADY TOWNLEY. Bellinda, what has been become of you? We have not seen you here of late with your friend Mrs. Loveit.

BELLINDA. Dear creature, I have left her but now so sadly afflicted!

[2] Luncheon
[3] Henry Muddiman (1629–92), a commercial writer, whose "news-letters" were widely subscribed to.

Lady Townley. With her old distemper, jealousy?

Medley. Dorimant has played her some new prank.

Bellinda. Well, that Dorimant is certainly the worst man breathing.

Emilia. I once thought so.

Bellinda. And do you not think so still?

Emilia. No, indeed!

Bellinda. Oh, Jesu!

Emilia. The town does him a great injury, and I will never believe what it says of a man I do not know again, for his sake.

Bellinda. You make me wonder.

Lady Townley. He's a very well-bred man.

Bellinda. But strangely ill-natured.

Emilia. Then, he's a very witty man.

Bellinda. But a man of no principles.

Medley. Your man of principles is a very fine thing, indeed.

Bellinda. To be preferred to men of parts by women who have regard to their reputation and quiet. Well, were I minded to play the fool, he should be the last man I'd think of.

Medley. He has been the first in many ladies' favors, though you are so severe, madam.

Lady Townley. What he may be for a lover, I know not; but he's a very pleasant acquaintance, I am sure.

Bellinda. Had you seen him use Mrs. Loveit as I have done, you would never endure him more—

Emilia. What, has he quarreled with her again?

Bellinda. Upon the slightest occasion; he's jealous of Sir Fopling.

Lady Townley. She never saw him in her life but yesterday, and that was here.

Emilia. On my conscience, he's the only man in town that's her aversion. How horribly out of humor she was all the time he talked to her!

Bellinda. And somebody has wickedly told him—

Emilia. Here he comes.

Enter Dorimant

Medley. Dorimant! you are luckily come to justify yourself.—Here's a lady—

Bellinda. Has a word or two to say to you from a disconsolate person.

Dorimant. You tender [1] your reputation too much, I know, madam, to whisper with me before this good company.

Bellinda. To serve Mrs. Loveit I'll make a bold venture.

Dorimant. Here's Medley—the very spirit of scandal.

Bellinda. No matter!

Emilia. 'Tis something you are unwilling to hear, Mr. Dorimant.

Lady Townley. Tell him, Bellinda, whether he will or no.

Bellinda. (*Aloud*) Mrs. Loveit—

Dorimant. Softly! these are laughers; you do not know 'em.

Bellinda. (*To* Dorimant *apart*) In a word, y'ave made me hate you, which I thought you never could have done.

Dorimant. In obeying your commands.

Bellinda. 'Twas a cruel part you played. How could you act it?

Dorimant. Nothing is cruel to a man who could kill himself to please you. Remember five o'clock to-morrow morning!

Bellinda. I tremble when you name it.

Dorimant. Be sure you come!

Bellinda. I sha' not.

Dorimant. Swear you will!

Bellinda. I dare not.

Dorimant. Swear, I say!

Bellinda. By my life—by all the happiness I hope for—

Dorimant. You will.

Bellinda. I will!

Dorimant. Kind!

Bellinda. I am glad I've sworn. I vow, I think I should ha' failed you else!

Dorimant. Surprisingly kind! In what temper did you leave Loveit?

Bellinda. Her raving was prettily over, and she began to be in a brave way of defying you and all your works. Where have you been since you went from thence?

Dorimant. I looked in at the play.

Bellinda. I have promised, and must return to her again.

Dorimant. Persuade her to walk in the Mall this evening.

Bellinda. She hates the place and will not come.

Dorimant. Do all you can to prevail with her.

Bellinda. For what purpose?

[1] Care for.

DORIMANT. Sir Fopling will be here anon; I'll prepare him to set upon her there before me.

BELLINDA. You persecute her too much, but I'll do all you'll ha' me.

DORIMANT. Tell her plainly 'tis grown too dull a business; I can drudge no longer.

EMILIA. There are afflictions in love, Mr. Dorimant.

DORIMANT. You women make 'em, who are commonly as unreasonable in that as you are at play. Without the advantage be on your side, a man can never quietly give over when he's weary.

MEDLEY. If you would play without being obliged to complaisance, Dorimant, you should play in public places.

DORIMANT. Ordinaries[1] were a very good thing for that, but gentlemen do not of late frequent 'em. The deep play is now in private houses.

(BELLINDA *offering to steal away*)

LADY TOWNLEY. Bellinda, are you leaving us so soon?

BELLINDA. I am going to the Park with Mrs. Loveit, madam. *Exit* BELLINDA

LADY TOWNLEY. This confidence will go nigh to spoil this young creature.

MEDLEY. 'Twill do her good, madam. Young men who are bred up under practising lawyers prove the abler counsel when they come to be called to the bar themselves.

DORIMANT. The town has been very favorable to you this afternoon, my Lady Townley; you used to have an *embarras*[2] of chairs and coaches at your door, an uproar of footmen in your hall, and a noise of fools above here.

LADY TOWNLEY. Indeed, my house is the general rendezvous, and next to the playhouse is the common refuge of all the young, idle people.

EMILIA. Company is a very good thing, madam, but I wonder you do not love it a little more chosen.

LADY TOWNLEY. 'Tis good to have an universal taste; we should love wit, but for variety be able to divert ourselves with the extravagancies of those who want it.

MEDLEY. Fools will make you laugh.

EMILIA. For once or twice, but the repetition of their folly after a visit or two grows tedious and unsufferable.

LADY TOWNLEY. You are a little too delicate, Emilia.

Enter a Page

PAGE. Sir Fopling Flutter, madam, desires to know if you are to be seen.

LADY TOWNLEY. Here's the freshest fool in town, and one who has not cloyed you yet.—Page!

PAGE. Madam?

LADY TOWNLEY. Desire him to walk up.

DORIMANT. Do not you fall on him, Medley, and snub him. Soothe him up in his extravagance; he will show the better.

MEDLEY. You know I have a natural indulgence for fools and need not this caution, sir.

Enter SIR FOPLING FLUTTER *with his* Page *after him*

SIR FOPLING. Page, wait without. (*To* LADY TOWNLEY) Madam, I kiss your hands. I see yesterday was nothing of chance; the *belles assemblées*[3] form themselves here every day. (*To* EMILIA) Lady, your servant.—Dorimant, let me embrace thee! Without lying, I have not met with any of my acquaintance who retain so much of Paris as thou dost—the very air thou hadst when the marquise mistook thee i'th' Tuileries and cried, "Hey, Chevalier!" and then begged thy pardon.

DORIMANT. I would fain wear in fashion as long as I can, sir; 'tis a thing to be valued in men as well as baubles.

SIR FOPLING. Thou art a man of wit and understands[t] the town. Prithee, let thee and I be intimate; there is no living without making some good man the confidant of our pleasures.

DORIMANT. 'Tis true! but there is no man so improper for such a business as I am.

SIR FOPLING. Prithee, why hast thou so modest an opinion of thyself?

DORIMANT. Why, first, I could never keep a secret in my life; and then, there is no charm so infallibly makes me fall in love with a woman as my knowing a friend loves her.—I deal honestly with you.

SIR FOPLING. Thy humor's very gallant, or let me perish! I knew a French count so like thee!

---

[1] Taverns.
[2] Crowd.
[3] Fashionable gatherings.

LADY TOWNLEY. Wit, I perceive, has more power over you than beauty, Sir Fopling, else you would not have let this lady stand so long neglected.

SIR FOPLING. (*To* EMILIA) A thousand pardons, madam; some civilities due of course upon the meeting a long absent friend. The *éclat*[1] of so much beauty, I confess, ought to have charmed me sooner.

EMILIA. The *brilliant*[2] of so much good language, sir, has much more power than the little beauty I can boast.

SIR FOPLING. I never saw anything prettier than this high work on your *point d'Espagne*.[3]

EMILIA. 'Tis not so rich as *point de Venise*.

SIR FOPLING. Not altogether, but looks cooler and is more proper for the season.—Dorimant, is not that Medley?

DORIMANT. The same, sir.

SIR FOPLING. Forgive me, sir; in this *embarras* of civilities I could not come to have you in my arms sooner. You understand an equipage[4] the best of any man in town, I hear.

MEDLEY. By my own you would not guess it.

SIR FOPLING. There are critics who do not write, sir.

MEDLEY. Our peevish poets will scarce allow it.

SIR FOPLING. Damn 'em, they'll allow no man wit who does not play the fool like themselves and show it! Have you taken notice of the *calèche*[5] I brought over?

MEDLEY. Oh, yes! It has quite another air than the English makes.

SIR FOPLING. 'Tis as easily known from an English tumbril as an Inns-of-Court man[6] is from one of us.

DORIMANT. True; there is a *bel air*[7] in *calèches* as well as men.

MEDLEY. But there are few so delicate to observe it.

SIR FOPLING. The world is generally very *grossier*[8] here, indeed.

LADY TOWNLEY. He's very fine.

EMILIA. Extreme proper.

SIR FOPLING. A slight suit I made to appear in at my first arrival—not worthy your consideration, ladies.

DORIMANT. The pantaloon is very well mounted.

SIR FOPLING. The tassels are new and pretty.

MEDLEY. I never saw a coat better cut.

SIR FOPLING. It makes me show long-waisted, and, I think, slender.

DORIMANT. That's the shape our ladies dote on.

MEDLEY. Your breech, though, is a handful too high, in my eye, Sir Fopling.

SIR FOPLING. Peace, Medley, I have wished it lower a thousand times, but a pox on't! 'twill not be.

LADY TOWNLEY. His gloves are well fringed, large, and graceful.

SIR FOPLING. I was always eminent for being *bien gantê*.[9]

EMILIA. He wears nothing but what are originals of the most famous hands in Paris.

SIR FOPLING. You are in the right, madam.

LADY TOWNLEY. The suit?

SIR FOPLING. Barroy.[10]

EMILIA. The garniture?

SIR FOPLING. Le Gras.

MEDLEY. The shoes?

SIR FOPLING. Piccar.

DORIMANT. The periwig?

SIR FOPLING. Chedreux.

LADY TOWNLEY } The gloves?
EMILIA.

SIR FOPLING. Orangerie![11] You know the smell, ladies. Dorimant, I could find in my heart for an amusement to have a gallantry with some of our English ladies.

DORIMANT. 'Tis a thing no less necessary to confirm the reputation of your wit than a duel will be to satisfy the town of your courage.

SIR FOPLING. Here was a woman yesterday—

DORIMANT. Mistress Loveit?

SIR FOPLING. You have named her!

DORIMANT. You cannot pitch on a better for your purpose.

SIR FOPLING. Prithee, what is she?

---

[1] Brilliance.
[2] Brilliancy.
[3] A Spanish lace. Note *point de Venise* in the following line.
[4] Retinue.
[5] In the original, *gallesh*. A light carriage.
[6] Lawyer or law-student.
[7] Fine style.
[8] Coarse, boorish.
[9] Well gloved.
[10] Sir Fopling names a series of Parisian merchants much in fashion for particular goods.
[11] Gloves having an orange scent were much in mode

DORIMANT. A person of quality, and one who has a rest [1] of reputation enough to make the conquest considerable; besides, I hear she likes you, too.

SIR FOPLING. Methoughts she seemed, though, very reserved and uneasy all the time I entertained her.

DORIMANT. Grimace and affectation! You will see her i'th' Mall to-night.

SIR FOPLING. Prithee, let thee and I take the air together.

DORIMANT. I am engaged to Medley, but I'll meet you at Saint James's and give you some information upon the which you may regulate your proceedings.

SIR FOPLING. All the world will be in the Park to-night. Ladies, 'twere pity to keep so much beauty longer within doors and rob the Ring [2] of all those charms that should adorn it.—Hey, page!

Enter Page—

See that all my people be ready.
(and goes out again)
—Dorimant, *a revoir*.[3]
[*Exit* SIR FOPLING.]

MEDLEY. A fine, mettled coxcomb.

DORIMANT. Brisk and insipid.

MEDLEY. Pert and dull.

EMILIA. However you despise him, gentlemen, I'll lay my life he passes for a wit with many.

DORIMANT. That may very well be; Nature has her cheats, stums [4] a brain, and puts sophisticate dulness often on the tasteless multitude for true wit and good humor. Medley, come.

MEDLEY. I must go a little way; I will meet you i'the Mall.

DORIMANT. I'll walk through the Garden thither.—(*To the women*) We shall meet anon and bow.

LADY TOWNLEY. Not to-night. We are engaged about a business the knowledge of which may make you laugh hereafter.

MEDLEY. Your servant, ladies.

DORIMANT. "A revoir," as Sir Fopling says.
Exeunt DORIMANT *and* MEDLEY

LADY TOWNLEY. The old man will be here immediately.

EMILIA. Let's expect [5] him i'th' garden—

LADY TOWNLEY. Go! you are a rogue.

EMILIA. I can't abide you. *Exeunt*

SCENE III. *The Mall*

Enter HARRIET *and* YOUNG BELLAIR, *she pulling him*

HARRIET. Come along.

YOUNG BELLAIR. And leave your mother?

HARRIET. Busy will be sent with a hue and cry after us, but that's no matter.

YOUNG BELLAIR. 'Twill look strangely in me.

HARRIET. She'll believe it a freak of mine and never blame your manners.

YOUNG BELLAIR. What reverend acquaintance is that she has met?

HARRIET. A fellow-beauty of the last king's time, though by the ruins you would hardly guess it.
Exeunt [HARRIET *and* YOUNG BELLAIR]

Enter DORIMANT *and crosses the stage*

Enter YOUNG BELLAIR *and* HARRIET

YOUNG BELLAIR. By this time your mother is in a fine taking.[6]

HARRIET. If your friend Mr. Dorimant were but here now, that she might find me talking with him!

YOUNG BELLAIR. She does not know him, but dreads him, I hear, of all mankind.

HARRIET. She concludes if he does but speak to a woman, she's undone—is on her knees every day to pray Heaven defend me from him.

YOUNG BELLAIR. You do not apprehend [7] him so much as she does?

HARRIET. I never saw anything in him that was frightful.

YOUNG BELLAIR. On the contrary, have you not observed something extreme delightful in his wit and person?

HARRIET. He's agreeable and pleasant, I must own; but he does so much affect being so, he displeases me.

YOUNG BELLAIR. Lord, madam! all he does and says is so easy and so natural!

HARRIET. Some men's verses seem so to the unskillful, but labor i'the one and affecta-

---

[1] Remnant.
[2] In Hyde Park. Cf. the "Circle," Act III, scene i.
[3] Correctly, *au revoir*.
[4] Ferments, giving a false impression of sparkle.

[5] Wait for.
[6] In much excitement.
[7] Fear.

tion in the other to the judicious plainly appear.

YOUNG BELLAIR. I never heard him accused of affectation before.

Enter DORIMANT *and stares upon her*

HARRIET. It passes on the easy town, who are favorably pleased in him to call it humor.

Exeunt YOUNG BELLAIR *and* HARRIET

DORIMANT. 'Tis she! it must be she—that lovely hair, that easy shape, those wanton eyes, and all those melting charms about her mouth which Medley spoke of! I'll follow the lottery and put in for a prize with my friend Bellair.   *Exit* DORIMANT *repeating*

In love the victors from the vanquished fly;
They fly that wound, and they pursue that die.[1]

Enter YOUNG BELLAIR *and* HARRIET; *and after them,* DORIMANT, *at a distance*

YOUNG BELLAIR. Most people prefer Hyde Park to this place.

HARRIET. It has the greater reputation, I confess; but I abominate the dull diversions there—the formal bows, the affected smiles, the silly by-words and amorous tweers[2] in passing. Here one meets with a little conversation now and then.

YOUNG BELLAIR. These conversations have been fatal to some of your sex, madam.

HARRIET. It may be so; because some who want temper have been undone by gaming, must others who have it wholly deny themselves the pleasure of play?

DORIMANT. (*Coming up gently and bowing to her*) Trust me, it were unreasonable, madam.

HARRIET. (*She starts and looks grave*) Lord, who's this?

YOUNG BELLAIR. Dorimant.

DORIMANT. [*Aside*] Is this the woman your father would have you marry?

YOUNG BELLAIR. It is.

DORIMANT. Her name?

YOUNG BELLAIR. Harriet.

DORIMANT. I am not mistaken; she's handsome.

YOUNG BELLAIR. Talk to her; her wit is better than her face. We were wishing for you but now.

DORIMANT. (*To* HARRIET) Overcast with seriousness o'the sudden! A thousand smiles were shining in that face but now; I never saw so quick a change of weather.

HARRIET. (*Aside*) I feel as great a change within; but he shall never know it.

DORIMANT. You were talking of play, madam. Pray, what may be your stint?

HARRIET. A little harmless discourse in public walks, or at most an appointment in a box, bare faced, at the playhouse. You are for masks and private meetings, where women engage for all they are worth, I hear.

DORIMANT. I have been used to deep play, but I can make one at small game when I like my gamester well.

HARRIET. And be so unconcerned you'll ha' no pleasure in't.

DORIMANT. Where there is a considerable sum to be won, the hope of drawing people in makes every trifle considerable.

HARRIET. The sordidness of men's natures, I know, makes 'em willing to flatter and comply with the rich, though they are sure never to be the better for 'em.

DORIMANT. 'Tis in their power to do us good, and we despair not but at some time or other they may be willing.

HARRIET. To men who have fared in this town like you, 'twould be a great mortification to live on hope. Could you keep a Lent for a mistress?

DORIMANT. In expectation of a happy Easter and, though time be very precious, think forty days well lost to gain your favor.

HARRIET. Mr. Bellair, let us walk; 'tis time to leave him. Men grow dull when they begin to be particular.

DORIMANT. Y'are mistaken; flattery will not ensue, though I know you're greedy of the praises of the whole Mall.

HARRIET. You do me wrong.

DORIMANT. I do not. As I followed you, I observed how you were pleased when the fops cried, "She's handsome—very handsome! By God, she is!" and whispered aloud your name. The thousand several forms you put your face into, then, to make yourself more agreeable! How wantonly you played with your head, flung back your locks, and looked smilingly over your shoulder at 'em!

HARRIET. I do not go begging the men's, as you do the ladies', good liking, with a sly softness in your looks and a gentle slowness in your bows as you pass 'em—as thus, sir. (*Acts him*) Is not this like you?

---

[1] From Waller's "To a Friend of the different success of their loves."

[2] Twires, sly glances.

Enter LADY WOODVILL *and* BUSY

YOUNG BELLAIR. Your mother, madam. (*Pulls* HARRIET; *she composes herself*)

LADY WOODVILL. Ah, my dear child Harriet!

BUSY. Now is she so pleased with finding her again she cannot chide her.

LADY WOODVILL. Come away!

DORIMANT. 'Tis now but high Mall,[1] madam—the most entertaining time of the evening.

HARRIET. I would fain see that Dorimant, mother, you so cry out of for a monster; he's in the Mall, I hear.

LADY WOODVILL. Come away then! The plague is here and you should dread the infection.

YOUNG BELLAIR. You may be misinformed of the gentleman.

LADY WOODVILL. Oh, no! I hope you do not know him. He is the prince of all the devils in the town—delights in nothing but in rapes and riots!

DORIMANT. If you did but hear him speak, madam!

LADY WOODVILL. Oh, he has a tongue, they say, would tempt the angels to a second fall.

Enter SIR FOPLING *with his equipage, six* Footmen *and a* Page

SIR FOPLING. Hey! Champagne, Norman, La Rose, La Fleur, La Tour, La Verdure!—Dorimant—

LADY WOODVILL. Here, here he is among this rout!—He names him! Come away, Harriet; come away!

Exeunt LADY WOODVILL, HARRIET, BUSY, *and* YOUNG BELLAIR

DORIMANT. This fool's coming has spoiled all. She's gone, but she has left a pleasing image of herself behind that wanders in my soul—it must not settle there.

SIR FOPLING. What reverie is this? Speak, man!

DORIMANT. Snatched from myself, how far behind
Already I behold the shore![2]

Enter MEDLEY

MEDLEY. Dorimant, a discovery! I met with Bellair.

DORIMANT. You can tell me no news, sir; I know all.

MEDLEY. How do you like the daughter?

DORIMANT. You never came so near truth in your life as you did in her description.

MEDLEY. What think you of the mother?

DORIMANT. Whatever I think of her, she thinks very well of me, I find.

MEDLEY. Did she know you?

DORIMANT. She did not; whether she does now or no, I know not. Here was a pleasant scene towards,[3] when in came Sir Fopling mustering up his equipage, and at the latter end named me and frightened her away.

MEDLEY. Loveit and Bellinda are not far off; I saw 'em alight at St. James's.

DORIMANT. Sir Fopling! Hark you, a word or two. (*Whispers*) Look you do not want assurance.

SIR FOPLING. I never do on these occasions.

DORIMANT. Walk on; we must not be seen together. Make your advantage of what I have told you. The next turn you will meet the lady.

SIR FOPLING. Hey! Follow me all!

Exit SIR FOPLING *and his equipage*

DORIMANT. Medley, you shall see good sport anon between Loveit and this Fopling.

MEDLEY. I thought there was something toward, by that whisper.

DORIMANT. You know a worthy principle of hers?

MEDLEY. Not to be so much as civil to a man who speaks to her in the presence of him she professes to love.

DORIMANT. I have encouraged Fopling to talk to her to-night.

MEDLEY. Now you are here, she will go nigh to beat him.

DORIMANT. In the humor she's in, her love will make her do some very extravagant thing doubtless.

MEDLEY. What was Bellinda's business with you at my Lady Townley's?

DORIMANT. To get me to meet Loveit here in order to an *éclaircissement*.[4] I made some difficulty of it and have prepared this rencounter to make good my jealousy.

MEDLEY. Here they come!

Enter MRS. LOVEIT, BELLINDA, *and* PERT

DORIMANT. I'll meet her and provoke her with a deal of dumb civility in passing by,

---

[1] When the Mall is socially perfection. Cf. "high noon."
[2] Waller again. From "Of Loving at first sight."
[3] Developing.
[4] Explanation.

then turn short and be behind her when Sir Fopling sets upon her—

> See how unregarded now
> That piece of beauty passes.[1]

Exeunt DORIMANT *and* MEDLEY

BELLINDA. How wonderful respectfully he bowed!

PERT. He's always over-mannerly when he has done a mischief.

BELLINDA. Methought, indeed, at the same time he had a strange, despising countenance.

PERT. The unlucky look, he thinks, becomes him.

BELLINDA. I was afraid you would have spoken to him, my dear.

MRS. LOVEIT. I would have died first. He shall no more find me the loving fool he has done.

BELLINDA. You love him still?

MRS. LOVEIT. No!

PERT. I wish you did not.

MRS. LOVEIT. I do not, and I will have you think so. What made you hale me to this odious place, Bellinda?

BELLINDA. I hate to be hulched up [2] in a coach; walking is much better.

MRS. LOVEIT. Would we could meet Sir Fopling now!

BELLINDA. Lord, would you not avoid him?

MRS. LOVEIT. I would make him all the advances that may be.

BELLINDA. That would confirm Dorimant's suspicion, my dear.

MRS. LOVEIT. He is not jealous; but I will make him so, and be revenged a way he little thinks on.

BELLINDA. (*Aside*) If she should make him jealous, that may make him fond of her again. I must dissuade her from it.—Lord, my dear, this will certainly make him hate you.

MRS. LOVEIT. 'Twill make him uneasy, though he does not care for me. I know the effects of jealousy on men of his proud temper.

BELLINDA. 'Tis a fantastic remedy; its operations are dangerous and uncertain.

MRS. LOVEIT. 'Tis the strongest cordial we can give to dying love. It often brings it back when there's no sign of life remaining. But I design not so much the reviving his, as my revenge.

Enter SIR FOPLING *and his equipage*

SIR FOPLING. Hey! Bid the coachman send home four of his horses and bring the coach to Whitehall; I'll walk over the Park. Madam, the honor of kissing your fair hand is a happiness I missed this afternoon at my Lady Townley's.

MRS. LOVEIT. You were very obliging, Sir Fopling, the last time I saw you there.

SIR FOPLING. The preference was due to your wit and beauty.—Madam, your servant; there never was so sweet an evening.

BELLINDA. 'T has drawn all the rabble of the town hither.

SIR FOPLING. 'Tis pity there's not an order made that none but the *beau monde* [3] should walk here.

MRS. LOVEIT. 'Twould add much to the beauty of the place. See what a sort [4] of nasty fellows are coming.

Enter four ill-fashioned fellows, singing:

> 'Tis not for kisses alone, etc.

MRS. LOVEIT. Fo! Their periwigs are scented with tobacco so strong—

SIR FOPLING. It overcomes our pulvilio [5] —methinks I smell the coffee-house they come from.

1ST MAN. Dorimant's convenient,[6] Madam Loveit.

2D MAN. I like the oily buttock [7] with her.

3D MAN. What spruce prig [8] is that?

1ST MAN. A caravan [9] lately come from Paris.

2D MAN. Peace! they smoke.[10]

[*They sing again*]

> There's something else to be done, etc.

All of them coughing; exeunt singing

Enter DORIMANT *and* MEDLEY

DORIMANT. They're engaged.

MEDLEY. She entertains him as if she liked him!

DORIMANT. Let us go forward—seem

---

[1] From a "sonnet" by Suckling.
[2] Doubled up like a hunch back.
[3] Fashionable world.
[4] Troup.
[5] Perfumed powder.
[6] Mistress.
[7] Loose woman.
[8] Coxcomb.
[9] Foolish fellow, person to be cheated.
[10] Suspect.

earnest in discourse and show ourselves; then you shall see how she'll use him.

BELLINDA. Yonder's Dorimant, my dear.

MRS. LOVEIT. I see him. (*Aside*) He comes insulting,[1] but I will disappoint him in his expectation. (*To* SIR FOPLING) I like this pretty, nice humor of yours, Sir Fopling. With what a loathing eye he looked upon those fellows!

SIR FOPLING. I sat near one of 'em at a play to-day and was almost poisoned with a pair of cordovan[2] gloves he wears.

MRS. LOVEIT. Oh, filthy cordovan! How I hate the smell! (*Laughs in a loud, affected way*)

SIR FOPLING. Did you observe, madam, how their cravats hung loose an inch from their neck[s] and what a frightful air it gave 'em?

MRS. LOVEIT. Oh, I took particular notice of one that is always spruced up with a deal of dirty sky-colored ribband.

BELLINDA. That's one of the walking flageolets[3] who haunt the Mall o'nights.

MRS. LOVEIT. Oh, I remember him; he's a hollow tooth enough to spoil the sweetness of an evening.

SIR FOPLING. I have seen the tallest walk the streets with a dainty pair of boxes[4] neatly buckled on.

MRS. LOVEIT. And a little foot-boy at his heels, pocket-high, with a flat cap, a dirty face—

SIR FOPLING. And a snotty nose.

MRS. LOVEIT. Oh, odious!—There's many of my own sex with that Holborn equipage[5] trig[6] to Gray's Inn Walks[7] and now and then travel hither on a Sunday.

MEDLEY. She takes no notice of you.

DORIMANT. Damn her! I am jealous of a counterplot!

MRS. LOVEIT. Your liveries are the finest, Sir Fopling—Oh, that page! that page is the prettili'st dressed—they are all Frenchmen?

SIR FOPLING. There's one damned English blockhead among 'em; you may know him by his mien.

MRS. LOVEIT. Oh, that's he—that's he! What do you call him?

SIR FOPLING. Hey—I know not what to call him—

FOOTMAN. John Trott, madam.

SIR FOPLING. Oh, unsufferable! Trott, Trott, Trott! There's nothing so barbarous as the names of our English servants. What countryman are you, sir?

FOOTMAN. Hampshire, sir.

SIR FOPLING. Then Hampshire be your name. Hey, Hampshire!

MRS. LOVEIT. Oh, that sound, that sound becomes the mouth of a man of quality!

MEDLEY. Dorimant, you look a little bashful on the matter.

DORIMANT. She dissembles better than I thought she could have done.

MEDLEY. You have tempted her with too luscious a bait. She bites at the coxcomb.

DORIMANT. She cannot fall from loving me, to that.

MEDLEY. You begin to be jealous in earnest.

DORIMANT. Of one I do not love—

MEDLEY. You did love her.

DORIMANT. The fit has long been over—

MEDLEY. But I have known men fall into dangerous relapses when they found a woman inclining to another.

DORIMANT. (*To himself*) He guesses the secret of my heart! I am concerned but dare not show it, lest Bellinda should mistrust all I have done to gain her.

BELLINDA. (*Aside*) I have watched his look and find no alteration there. Did he love her, some signs of jealousy would have appeared.

DORIMANT. I hope this happy evening, madam, has reconciled you to the scandalous Mall. We shall have you now hankering here again—

MRS. LOVEIT. Sir Fopling, will you walk?

SIR FOPLING. I am all obedience, madam.

MRS. LOVEIT. Come along then, and let's agree to be malicious on all the ill-fashioned things we meet.

SIR FOPLING. We'll make a critique on the whole Mall, madam.

MRS. LOVEIT. Bellinda, you shall engage—

BELLINDA. To the reserve of our friends, my dear.

---

[1] Exulting.
[2] In England, cordovan leather was made from horsehide.
[3] I. e., itinerant flageolet players.
[4] Overshoes (?).
[5] Mercantile retinue.
[6] Trot.
[7] Gray's Inn, one of the four great Inns of Court, is between Holborn and Theobald's Road in an unfashionable district inhabited by merchants. The gardens were laid out by Francis Bacon.

MRS. LOVEIT. [*To* SIR FOPLING] No, no exceptions.

SIR FOPLING. We'll sacrifice all to our diversion—

MRS. LOVEIT. All—all—

SIR FOPLING. All.

BELLINDA. All? Then let it be.

Exeunt SIR FOPLING, MRS. LOVEIT, BELLINDA, *and* PERT, *laughing*

MEDLEY. Would you had brought some more of your friends, Dorimant, to have been witnesses of Sir Fopling's disgrace and your triumph.

DORIMANT. 'Twere unreasonable to desire you not to laugh at me; but pray, do not expose me to the town this day or two.

MEDLEY. By that time you have hope to have regained your credit?

DORIMANT. I know she hates Fopling and only makes use of him in hope to work on me again. Had it not been for some powerful considerations which will be removed to-morrow morning, I had made her pluck off this mask and show the passion that lies panting under.

Enter a Footman

MEDLEY. Here comes a man from Bellair with news of your last adventure.

DORIMANT. I am glad he sent him. I long to know the consequence of our parting.

FOOTMAN. Sir, my master desires you to come to my Lady Townley's presently and bring Mr. Medley with you. My Lady Woodvill and her daughter are there.

MEDLEY. Then all's well, Dorimant.

FOOTMAN. They have sent for the fiddles and mean to dance. He bid me tell you, sir, the old lady does not know you, and would have you own yourself to be Mr. Courtage. They are all prepared to receive you by that name.

DORIMANT. That foppish admirer of quality, who flatters the very meat at honorable tables and never offers love to a woman below a lady-grandmother?

MEDLEY. You know the character you are to act, I see.

DORIMANT. This is Harriet's contrivance—wild, witty, lovesome, beautiful, and young![1] —Come along, Medley.

---

[1] Brett-Smith suggests that Dorimant is misquoting a line from Waller: "Fierce, goodly, valiant, beautiful and young," from his poem "Of the danger His Majesty . . . escaped . . ."

MEDLEY. This new woman would well supply the loss of Loveit.

DORIMANT. That business must not end so; before to-morrow's sun is set I will revenge and clear it.

And you and Loveit, to her cost, shall find,
I fathom all the depths of womankind.

Exeunt

ACT IV

[SCENE I. LADY TOWNLEY'S *drawing-room*]

The scene opens with fiddlers playing a country dance.

Enter DORIMANT, LADY WOODVILL, YOUNG BELLAIR, *and* MRS. HARRIET, OLD BELLAIR *and* EMILIA, MR. MEDLEY *and* LADY TOWNLEY, *as having just ended the dance*

OLD BELLAIR. So, so, so—a smart bout! a very smart bout, a dod!

LADY TOWNLEY. How do you like Emilia's dancing, brother?

OLD BELLAIR. Not at all—not at all!

LADY TOWNLEY. You speak not what you think, I am sure.

OLD BELLAIR. No matter for that; go, bid her dance no more. It don't become her—it don't become her! Tell her I say so. (*Aside*) A dod, I love her!

DORIMANT. (*To* LADY WOODVILL) All people mingle nowadays, madam, and in public places women of quality have the least respect showed 'em.

LADY WOODVILL. I protest you say the truth, Mr. Courtage.

DORIMANT. Forms and ceremonies, the only things that uphold quality and greatness, are now shamefully laid aside and neglected.

LADY WOODVILL. Well, this is not the women's age. Let 'em think what they will, lewdness is the business now; love was the business in my time.

DORIMANT. The women, indeed, are little beholding to the young men of this age; they're generally only dull admirers of themselves, and make their court to nothing but their periwigs and cravats, and would be more concerned for the disordering of 'em, tho' on a good occasion, than a young maid would be for the tumbling of her head or handkercher.

LADY WOODVILL. I protest you hit 'em.

DORIMANT. They are very assiduous to show themselves at court, well dressed, to the women of quality, but their business is with the stale mistresses of the town, who are prepared to receive their lazy addresses by industrious old lovers who have cast 'em off and make 'em easy.

HARRIET. [*To* MEDLEY] He fits my mother's humor so well, a little more and she'll dance a kissing dance with him anon.

MEDLEY. Dutifully observed, madam.

DORIMANT. [*To* LADY WOODVILL] They pretend to be great critics in beauty. By their talk you would think they liked no face, and yet can dote on an ill one if it belong to a laundress or a tailor's daughter. They cry, "A woman's past her prime at twenty, decayed at four-and-twenty, and unsufferable at thirty."

LADY WOODVILL. Unsufferable at thirty! That they are in the wrong, Mr. Courtage, at five-and-thirty, there are living proofs enough to convince 'em.

DORIMANT. Aye, madam. There's Mrs. Setlooks, Mrs. Droplip, and my Lady Loud; show me among all our opening buds a face that promises so much beauty as the remains of theirs.

LADY WOODVILL. The depraved appetite of this vicious age tastes nothing but green fruit, and loathes it when 'tis kindly [1] ripened.

DORIMANT. Else so many deserving women, madam, would not be so untimely neglected.

LADY WOODVILL. I protest, Mr. Courtage, a dozen such good men as you would be enough to atone for that wicked Dorimant and all the other debauchees of the town. (HARRIET, EMILIA, YOUNG BELLAIR, MEDLEY, *and* LADY TOWNLEY *break out into laughter*)—What's the matter here?

MEDLEY. A pleasant mistake, madam, that a lady has made, occasions a little laughter.

OLD BELLAIR. Come, come; you keep 'em idle! They are impatient till the fiddles play again.

DORIMANT. You are not weary, madam?

LADY WOODVILL. One dance more! I cannot refuse you, Mr. Courtage. (*They dance.* After the dance OLD BELLAIR, *singing and dancing, up to* EMILIA)

EMILIA. You are very active, sir.

OLD BELLAIR. A dod, sirrah! when I was a young fellow I could ha' capered up to my woman's gorget.[2]

DORIMANT. [*To* LADY WOODVILL] You are willing to rest yourself, madam?

LADY TOWNLEY. [*To* MEDLEY] We'll walk into my chamber and sit down.

MEDLEY. Leave us Mr. Courtage; he's a dancer, and the young ladies are not weary yet.

LADY WOODVILL. We'll send him out again.

HARRIET. If you do not quickly, I know where to send for Mr. Dorimant.

LADY WOODVILL. This girl's head, Mr. Courtage, is ever running on that wild fellow.

DORIMANT. 'Tis well you have got her a good husband, madam; that will settle it.

Exeunt LADY TOWNLEY, LADY WOODVILL, *and* DORIMANT

OLD BELLAIR. (*To* EMILIA) A dod, sweetheart, be advised and do not throw thyself away on a young, idle fellow.

EMILIA. I have no such intention, sir.

OLD BELLAIR. Have a little patience! Thou shalt have the man I spake of. A dod, he loves thee and will make a good husband—but no words—

EMILIA. But, sir—

OLD BELLAIR. No answer—out a pize, peace! and think on't.

Enter DORIMANT

DORIMANT. Your company is desired within, sir.

OLD BELLAIR. I go, I go! Good Mr. Courtage, fare you well!—(*To* EMILIA) Go, I'll see you no more!

EMILIA. What have I done, sir?

OLD BELLAIR. You are ugly! you are ugly!—is she not, Mr. Courtage?

EMILIA. Better words or I shan't abide you.

OLD BELLAIR. Out a pize; a dod, what does she say? Hit her a pat for me there.

Exit OLD BELLAIR

MEDLEY. You have charms for the whole family.

DORIMANT. You'll spoil all with some unseasonable jest, Medley.

MEDLEY. You see I confine my tongue and am content to be a bare spectator, much contrary to my nature.

[1] Naturally.

[2] Ruff. Old Bellair could have kicked as high as a woman's neck.

EMILIA. Methinks, Mr. Dorimant, my Lady Woodvill is a little fond of you.

DORIMANT. Would her daughter were!

MEDLEY. It may be you may find her so. Try her—you have an opportunity.

DORIMANT. And I will not lose it. Bellair, here's a lady has something to say to you.

YOUNG BELLAIR. I wait upon her. Mr. Medley, we have both business with you.

DORIMANT. Get you all together then. (*To* HARRIET) That demure curtsey is not amiss in jest, but do not think in earnest it becomes you.

HARRIET. Affectation is catching, I find—from your grave bow I got it.

DORIMANT. Where had you all that scorn and coldness in your look?

HARRIET. From nature, sir; pardon my want of art. I have not learnt those softnesses and languishings which now in faces are so much in fashion.

DORIMANT. You need 'em not; you have a sweetness of your own if you would but calm your frowns and let it settle.

HARRIET. My eyes are wild and wandering like my passions, and cannot yet be tied to rules of charming.

DORIMANT. Women, indeed, have commonly a method of managing those messengers of love. Now they will look as if they would kill, and anon they will look as if they were dying. They point and rebate [1] their glances, the better to invite us.

HARRIET. I like this variety well enough, but hate the set face that always looks as if it would say, "Come, love me"—a woman who at plays makes the *doux yeux* [2] to a whole audience and at home cannot forbear 'em to her monkey.

DORIMANT. Put on a gentle smile and let me see how well it will become you.

HARRIET. I am sorry my face does not please you as it is, but I shall not be complaisant and change it.

DORIMANT. Though you are obstinate, I know 'tis capable of improvement and shall do you justice, madam, if I chance to be at Court when the critics of the circle pass their judgment; for thither you must come.

HARRIET. And expect to be taken in pieces, have all my features examined, every motion censured, and on the whole be condemned to be but pretty, or a beauty of the lowest rate. What think you?

DORIMANT. The women, nay, the very lovers who belong to the drawing-room, will maliciously allow you more than that. They always grant what is apparent, that they may the better be believed when they name concealed faults they cannot easily be disproved in.

HARRIET. Beauty runs as great a risk exposed at Court as wit does on the stage, where the ugly and foolish all are free to censure.

DORIMANT. (*Aside*) I love her and dare not let her know it; I fear she has an ascendant o'er me and may revenge the wrongs I have done her sex. (*To her*) Think of making a party, madam, love will engage.

HARRIET. You make me start! I did not think to have heard of love from you.

DORIMANT. I never knew what 'twas to have a settled ague yet, but now and then have had irregular fits.

HARRIET. Take heed; sickness after long health is commonly more violent and dangerous.

DORIMANT. (*Aside*) I have took the infection from her, and feel the disease now spreading in me. (*To her*) Is the name of love so frightful that you dare not stand it?

HARRIET. 'Twill do little execution out of your mouth on me, I'm sure.

DORIMANT. It has been fatal—

HARRIET. To some easy women, but we are not all born to one destiny. I was informed you use to laugh at love and not make it.

DORIMANT. The time has been, but now I must speak—

HARRIET. If it be on that idle subject, I will put on my serious look, turn my head carelessly from you, drop my lip, let my eyelids fall and hang half o'er my eyes—thus—while you will buzz a speech of an hour long in my ear, and I answer never a word. Why do you not begin?

DORIMANT. That the company may take notice how passionately I make advances of love! And how disdainfully you receive 'em.

HARRIET. When your love's grown strong enough to make you bear being laughed at, I'll give you leave to trouble me with it; till then pray forbear, sir.

---

[1] Blunt.
[2] In the original *deux yeux*, which should probably be corrected to read as in the present text, meaning "fair glances."

Enter Sir Fopling *and others in masks*

Dorimant. What's here—masquerades?

Harriet. I thought that foppery had been left off, and people might have been in private with a fiddle.

Dorimant. 'Tis endeavored to be kept on foot still by some who find themselves the more acceptable the less they are known.

Young Bellair. This must be Sir Fopling.

Medley. This extraordinary habit shows it.

Young Bellair. What are the rest?

Medley. A company of French rascals whom he picked up in Paris and has brought over to be his dancing equipage on these occasions. Make him own himself; a fool is very troublesome when he presumes he is incognito.

Sir Fopling. (*To* Harriet) Do you know me?

Harriet. Ten to one but I guess at you.

Sir Fopling. Are you women as fond of a vizard as we men are?

Harriet. I am very fond of a vizard that covers a face I do not like, sir.

Young Bellair. Here are no masks, you see, sir, but those which came with you. This was intended a private meeting; but because you look like a gentleman, if you will discover yourself and we know you to be such, you shall be welcome.

Sir Fopling. (*Pulling off his mask*) Dear Bellair!

Medley. Sir Fopling! How came you hither?

Sir Fopling. Faith, as I was coming late from Whitehall, after the King's *couchée*,[1] one of my people told me he had heard fiddles at my Lady Townley's, and—

Dorimant. You need not say any more, sir.

Sir Fopling. Dorimant, let me kiss thee.

Dorimant. Hark you, Sir Fopling—

(*Whispers*)

Sir Fopling. Enough, enough, Courtage. —A pretty kind of young woman that, Medley. I observed her in the Mall—more *éveillée*[2] than our English women commonly are. Prithee, what is she?

Medley. The most noted coquetté[3] in town. Beware of her.

Sir Fopling. Let her be what she will, I know how to take my measures. In Paris the mode is to flatter the *prudè*,[4] laugh at the *faux-prudè*, make serious love to the *demi-prudè*, and only rally with the *coquettè*.— Medley, what think you?

Medley. That for all this smattering of mathematics, you may be out in your judgment at tennis.

Sir Fopling. What a *coq-à-l'âne*[5] is this? I talk of women and thou answer'st tennis.

Medley. Mistakes will be for want of apprehension.

Sir Fopling. I am very glad of the acquaintance I have with this family.

Medley. My lady truly is a good woman.

Sir Fopling. Ah, Dorimant—Courtage, I would say—would thou hadst spent the last summer in Paris with me! When thou wert there, La Corneus and Sallyes[6] were the only habitués we had: a comedian would have been a *bonne fortune*.[7] No stranger ever passed his time so well as I did some months before I came over. I was well received in a dozen families where all the women of quality used to visit; I have intrigues to tell thee more pleasant than ever thou read'st in a novel.

Harriet. Write 'em, sir, and oblige us women. Our language wants such little stories.

Sir Fopling. Writing, madam, 's a mechanic part of wit. A gentleman should never go beyond a song or a billet.

Harriet. Bussy[8] was a gentleman.

Sir Fopling. Who, d'Ambois?

Medley. Was there ever such a brisk blockhead!

Harriet. Not d'Ambois, sir, but Rabutin —he who writ the loves of France.

Sir Fopling. That may be, madam; many gentlemen do things that are below 'em.

---

[1] Reception held by a sovereign at bed time.

[2] In the original, *evelié*, which, in view of Sir Fopling's struggle with the language, should perhaps be retained. "Sprightly."

[3] Medley is here satirizing Sir Fopling's French. He means "coquette."

[4] More false French. *Prudè* is meant for "prude"; a *faux-prudè* is a woman falsely prudish; a *demi-prudè* is a farther gradation between the false prude and the "coquetté."

[5] Farrago of nonsense.

[6] Mesdames Corneul and Selles were minor literary ladies in France. (Verity.)

[7] Piece of good luck, desirable man.

[8] Sir Fopling, who is bluffing, confuses the Comte de Bussy (1618–93), the fashionable author of the *Histoire Amoureuse des Gaules*, with the Sieur de Bussy (1549–79), an adventurer whose exploits furnished Chapman with the subject of his tragedy, *Bussy d'Ambois*, still occasionally played in the Restoration. If Etherege expected his audience to get the point, it is a tribute to their literary information.

Damn your authors, Courtage; women are the prettiest things we can fool away our time with.

HARRIET. I hope ye have wearied yourself to-night at Court, sir, and will not think of fooling with anybody here.

SIR FOPLING. I cannot complain of my fortune there, madam.—Dorimant—

DORIMANT. Again!

SIR FOPLING. Courtage—a pox on't! I have something to tell thee. When I had made my court within, I came out and flung myself upon the mat under the state[1] i'th' outward room, i'th' midst of half a dozen beauties who were withdrawn "to jeèr among themselves," as they called it.

DORIMANT. Did you know 'em?

SIR FOPLING. Not one of 'em, by heavens! —not I; but they were all your friends.

DORIMANT. How are you sure of that?

SIR FOPLING. Why, we laughed at all the town—spared nobody but yourself. They found me a man for their purpose.

DORIMANT. I know you are malicious, to your power.

SIR FOPLING. And faith, I had occasion to show it, for I never saw more gaping fools at a ball or on a birthday.

DORIMANT. You learned who the women were?

SIR FOPLING. No matter; they frequent the drawing-room.

DORIMANT. And entertain themselves pleasantly at the expense of all the fops who come there.

SIR FOPLING. That's their bus'ness. Faith, I sifted 'em, and find they have a sort of wit among them—Ah, filthy! (*Pinches a tallow candle*)

DORIMANT. Look, he has been pinching the tallow candle.

SIR FOPLING. How can you breathe in a room where there's grease frying! Dorimant, thou art intimate with my lady; advise her for her own sake and the good company that comes hither, to burn wax lights.

HARRIET. What are these masquerades who stand so obsequiously at a distance?

SIR FOPLING. A set of balladines[2] whom I picked out of the best in France and brought over with a *flute-douce*[3] or two—my servants. They shall entertain you.

HARRIET. I had rather see you dance yourself, Sir Fopling.

SIR FOPLING. And I had rather do it—all the company knows it—but madam—

MEDLEY. Come, come, no excuses, Sir Fopling.

SIR FOPLING. By heavens, Medley—

MEDLEY. Like a woman I find you must be struggled with, before one brings you to what you desire.

HARRIET. (*Aside*) Can he dance?

EMILIA. And fence and sing too, if you'll believe him.

DORIMANT. He has no more excellence in his heels than in his head. He went to Paris a plain, bashful English blockhead, and is returned a fine undertaking[4] French fop.

MEDLEY. I cannot prevail.

SIR FOPLING. Do not think it want of complaisance, madam.

HARRIET. You are too well bred to want that, Sir Fopling. I believe it want of power.

SIR FOPLING. By heavens, and so it is! I have sat up so damned late and drunk so cursed hard since I came to this lewd town, that I am fit for nothing but low dancing now —a *corant*, a *bourrée*, or a *menuet*.[5] But St. Andrè[6] tells me, if I will but be regular, in one month I shall rise again. (*Endeavors at a caper*)—Pox on this debauchery!

EMILIA. I have heard your dancing much commended.

SIR FOPLING. It had the good fortune to please in Paris. I was judged to rise within an inch as high as the basqué[7] in an entry I danced there.

HARRIET. [*To* EMILIA] I am mightily taken with this fool; let us sit.—Here's a seat, Sir Fopling.

SIR FOPLING. At your feet, madam; I can be nowhere so much at ease.—By your leave, gown.

HARRIET. } Ah, you'll spoil it!
EMILIA.

SIR FOPLING. No matter; my clothes are my creatures. I make 'em to make my court to you ladies. Hey! (*Dance*) *Qu'on commencè*[8]—to an English dancer, English mo-

---

[1] Canopy.
[2] See note 1, p. 94.
[3] See note 10, p. 93.
[4] Forward.
[5] Dances of the period, stately in character.
[6] Properly St. Audré, a famous dancer of the period.
[7] He means *basque*, the skirt of a coat.
[8] Begin.

tions. I was forced to entertain this fellow,[1] one of my set miscarrying.—Oh, horrid! Leave your damned manner of dancing and put on the French air. Have you not a pattern before you?—Pretty well!—imitation in time may bring him to something.

After the dance, enter OLD BELLAIR, LADY WOODVILL, *and* LADY TOWNLEY

OLD BELLAIR. Hey, a dod, what have we here—a mumming?

LADY WOODVILL. Where's my daughter—Harriet?

DORIMANT. Here, here, madam! I know not but under these disguises there may be dangerous sparks; I gave the young lady warning.

LADY WOODVILL. Lord! I am much obliged to you, Mr. Courtage.

HARRIET. Lord, how you admire this man!

LADY WOODVILL. What have you to except against him?

HARRIET. He's a fop.

LADY WOODVILL. He's not a Dorimant—a wild extravagant fellow of the times.

HARRIET. He's a man made up of forms and commonplaces sucked out of the remaining lees of the last age.

LADY WOODVILL. He's so good a man that, were you not engaged—

LADY TOWNLEY. You'll have but little night to sleep in.

LADY WOODVILL. Lord, 'tis perfect day.

DORIMANT. (*Aside*) The hour is almost come I appointed Bellinda, and I am not so foppishly in love here to forget. I am flesh and blood yet.

LADY TOWNLEY. I am very sensible, madam.

LADY WOODVILL. Lord, madam!

HARRIET. Look! in what a struggle is my poor mother yonder!

YOUNG BELLAIR. She has much ado to bring out the compliment.

DORIMANT. She strains hard for it.

HARRIET. See, see! her head tottering, her eyes staring, and her under lip trembling—

DORIMANT. Now—now she's in the very convulsions of her civility. (*Aside*) 'Sdeath, I shall lose Bellinda! I must fright her hence; she'll be an hour in this fit of good manners else. (*To* LADY WOODVILL) Do you not know Sir Fopling, madam?

LADY WOODVILL. I have seen that face—Oh, heavens! 'tis the same we met in the Mall! How came he here?

DORIMANT. A fiddle, in this town, is a kind of fop-call; no sooner it strikes up but the house is besieged with an army of masquerades straight.

LADY WOODVILL. Lord! I tremble, Mr. Courtage! For certain, Dorimant is in the company.

DORIMANT. I cannot confidently say he is not. You had best be gone. I will wait upon you; your daughter is in the hands of Mr. Bellair.

LADY WOODVILL. I'll see her before me.—Harriet, come away.

YOUNG BELLAIR.[2] Lights! lights!

LADY TOWNLEY. Light, down there!

OLD BELLAIR. A dod, it needs not—

DORIMANT. [*To the* Servant *entering*] Call my Lady Woodvill's coach to the door quickly.

OLD BELLAIR. Stay, Mr. Medley. Let the young fellows do that duty; we will drink a glass of wine together. 'Tis good after dancing. —What mumming spark is that?

[*Points at* SIR FOPLING]

MEDLEY. He is not to be comprehended in few words.

SIR FOPLING. Hey, La Tour!

MEDLEY. Whither away, Sir Fopling?

SIR FOPLING. I have bus'ness with Courtage.

MEDLEY. He'll but put the ladies into their coach and come up again.

OLD BELLAIR. In the meantime I'll call for a bottle. *Exit* OLD BELLAIR

Enter YOUNG BELLAIR

MEDLEY. Where's Dorimant?

YOUNG BELLAIR. Stol'n home. He has had business waiting him there all this night, I believe, by an impatience I observed in him.

MEDLEY. Very likely; 'tis but dissembling drunkenness, railing at his friends, and then the kind soul will embrace the blessing and forget the tedious expectation.

SIR FOPLING. I must speak with him before I sleep.

---

[1] John Trott, rechristened Hampshire. See Act III, scene iii, p. 108.

[2] Young Bellair, Lady Woodvill, and Harriet apparently exeunt here; and Dorimant exit after "quickly."

THE MAN OF MODE

YOUNG BELLAIR. [*To* MEDLEY] Emilia and I are resolved on that business.

MEDLEY. Peace, here's your father.

Enter OLD BELLAIR *and a* Butler *with a bottle of wine*

OLD BELLAIR. The women are all gone to bed.—Fill, boy. Mr. Medley, begin a health.

MEDLEY. (*Whispers*) To Emilia!

OLD BELLAIR. Out a pize! she's a rogue and I'll not pledge you.

MEDLEY. I know you will.

OLD BELLAIR. A dod, drink it then!

SIR FOPLING. Let us have the new bacchic.

OLD BELLAIR. A dod, that is a hard word. What does it mean, sir?

MEDLEY. A catch or drinking song.

OLD BELLAIR. Let us have it then.

SIR FOPLING. Fill the glasses round and draw up in a body. Hey, music!

(*They sing*)

The pleasures of love and the joys of good wine
To perfect our happiness, wisely we join.
We to beauty all day
Give the sovereign sway
And her favorite nymphs devoutly obey.
At the plays we are constantly making our court,
And when they are ended we follow the sport
To the Mall and the Park,
Where we love till 'tis dark.
Then sparkling champagne
Puts an end to their reign;
It quickly recovers
Poor languishing lovers;
Makes us frolic and gay, and drowns all our sorrow.
But alas! we relapse again on the morrow.
    Let every man stand
    With his glass in his hand,
And briskly discharge at the word of command:
    Here's a health to all those
    Whom to-night we depose!
Wine and beauty by turns great souls should inspire;
Present all together—and now, boys, give fire!

[*They drink*]

OLD BELLAIR. A dod! a pretty business and very merry.

SIR FOPLING. Hark you; Medley, let's you and I take the fiddles and go waken Dorimant.

MEDLEY. We shall do him a courtesy, if it be as I guess. For after the fatigue of this night he'll quickly have his belly full and be glad of an occasion to cry. "Take away, Handy!"

YOUNG BELLAIR. I'll go with you, and there we'll consult about affairs, Medley.

OLD BELLAIR. (*Looks on his watch*) A dod, 'tis six o'clock!

SIR FOPLING. Let's away then.

OLD BELLAIR. Mr. Medley, my sister tells me you are an honest man—and a dod, I love you. Few words and hearty—that's the way with old Harry, old Harry.

SIR FOPLING. [*To his* Servants] Light your flambeaux. Hey!

OLD BELLAIR. What does the man mean?

MEDLEY. 'Tis day, Sir Fopling.

SIR FOPLING. No matter; our serenade will look the greater.   *Exeunt omnes*

SCENE II. DORIMANT'S *lodging. A table, a candle, toilet articles, etc.;* HANDY, *tying up linen*

Enter DORIMANT *in his gown, and* BELLINDA

DORIMANT. Why will you be gone so soon?

BELLINDA. Why did you stay out so late?

DORIMANT. Call a chair,[1] Handy.—What makes you tremble so?

BELLINDA. I have a thousand fears about me. Have I not been seen, think you?

DORIMANT. By nobody but myself and trusty Handy.

BELLINDA. Where are all your people?

DORIMANT. I have dispersed 'em all on sleeveless[2] errands. What does that sigh mean?

BELLINDA. Can you be so unkind to ask me? (*Sighs*) Well—were it to do again—

DORIMANT. We should do it, should we not?

BELLINDA. I think we should—the wickeder man you, to make me love you so well.—Will you be discreet now?

DORIMANT. I will.

BELLINDA. You cannot.

DORIMANT. Never doubt it.

BELLINDA. I never will expect it.

DORIMANT. You do me wrong.

BELLINDA. You have no more power to keep a secret than I had not to trust you with it.

DORIMANT. By all the joys I have had and those I keep in store—[3]

BELLINDA. —You'll do for my sake, what you never did before.

DORIMANT. By that truth thou hast spoken,

---

[1] I.e., a sedan-chair.
[2] Pointless.
[3] Note the rhymed Alexandrines.

a wife shall sooner betray herself to her husband—

BELLINDA. Yet I had rather you should be false in this than in another thing you promised me.

DORIMANT. What's that?

BELLINDA. That you would never see Loveit more but in public places—in the Park, at Court, and plays.

DORIMANT. 'Tis not likely a man should be fond of seeing a damned old play when there is a new one acted.

BELLINDA. I dare not trust your promise.

DORIMANT. You may—

BELLINDA. This does not satisfy me. You shall swear you never will see her more.

DORIMANT. I will, a thousand oaths. By all—

BELLINDA. Hold! You shall not, now I think on't better.

DORIMANT. I will swear!

BELLINDA. I shall grow jealous of the oath and think I owe your truth to that, not to your love.

DORIMANT. Then, by my love; no other oath I'll swear.

Enter HANDY

HANDY. Here's a chair.

BELLINDA. Let me go.

DORIMANT. I cannot.

BELLINDA. Too willingly, I fear.

DORIMANT. Too unkindly feared. When will you promise me again?

BELLINDA. Not this fortnight.

DORIMANT. You will be better than your word.

BELLINDA. I think I shall. Will it make you love me less? (*Starting; fiddles without*)— Hark, what fiddles are these?

DORIMANT. Look out, Handy.

Exit HANDY *and returns*

HANDY. Mr. Medley, Mr. Bellair, and Sir Fopling; they are coming up.

DORIMANT. How got they in?

HANDY. The door was open for the chair.

BELLINDA. Lord, let me fly!

DORIMANT. Here! here down the back stairs! I'll see you into your chair.

BELLINDA. No, no! Stay and receive 'em.— And be sure you keep your word and never see Loveit more. Let it be a proof of your kindness.

DORIMANT. It shall.—Handy, direct her. (*Kissing her hand*) Everlasting love go along with thee. *Exeunt* BELLINDA *and* HANDY

Enter YOUNG BELLAIR, MEDLEY, *and*
SIR FOPLING

YOUNG BELLAIR. Not abed yet?

MEDLEY. You have had an irregular fit, Dorimant.

DORIMANT. I have.

YOUNG BELLAIR. And is it off already?

DORIMANT. Nature has done her part, gentlemen; when she falls kindly to work, great cures are effected in little time, you know.

SIR FOPLING. We thought there was a wench in the case, by the chair that waited. Prithee, make us a *confidancê*.[1]

DORIMANT. Excuse me.

SIR FOPLING. *Lè sagè*[2] Dorimant!—Was she pretty?

DORIMANT. So pretty she may come to keep her coach and pay parish duties if the good humor of the age continue.

MEDLEY. And be of the number of the ladies kept by public-spirited men for the good of the whole town.

SIR FOPLING. Well said, Medley.

(SIR FOPLING *dancing by himself*)

YOUNG BELLAIR. See Sir Fopling dancing!

DORIMANT. You are practising and have a mind to recover, I see.

SIR FOPLING. Prithee, Dorimant, why hast thou not a glass hung up here? A room is the dullest thing without one.

YOUNG BELLAIR. Here is company to entertain you.

SIR FOPLING. But I mean in case of being alone. In a glass a man may entertain himself—

DORIMANT. The shadow of himself, indeed.

SIR FOPLING. —correct the errors of his motions and his dress.

MEDLEY. I find, Sir Fopling, in your solitude you remember the saying of the wise man, and study yourself.

SIR FOPLING. 'Tis the best diversion in our retirements. Dorimant, thou art a pretty fellow and wear'st thy clothes well, but I never saw thee have a handsome cravat. Were they made up like mine, they'd give another air to thy face. Prithee, let me send

[1] Bad French for "tell us your secret."
[2] Prudent.

my man to dress thee but one a day. By heavens, an Englishman cannot tie a ribbon.

DORIMANT. They are something clumsily fisted—

SIR FOPLING. I have brought over the prettiest fellow that ever spread a toilet. He served some time under Merille,[1] the greatest *genie*[2] in the world for a *valet-de-chambre*.

DORIMANT. What, he who formerly belonged to the Duke of Candale?[3]

SIR FOPLING. The same, and got him his immortal reputation.

DORIMANT. Y'have a very fine brandenburg[4] on, Sir Fopling.

SIR FOPLING. It serves to wrap me up after the fatigue of a ball.

MEDLEY. I see you often in it, with your periwig tied up.

SIR FOPLING. We should not always be in a set dress; 'tis more *en cavalier*[5] to appear now and then in a *dessabillée*.[6]

MEDLEY. Pray, how goes your business with Loveit?

SIR FOPLING. You might have answered yourself in the Mall last night. Dorimant, did you not see the advances she made me? I have been endeavoring at a song.

DORIMANT. Already!

SIR FOPLING. 'Tis my *coup d'essai*[7] in English—I would fain have thy opinion of it.

DORIMANT. Let's see it.

SIR FOPLING. Hey, page, give me my song.— Bellair, here; thou hast a pretty voice—sing it.

YOUNG BELLAIR. Sing it yourself, Sir Fopling.

SIR FOPLING. Excuse me.

YOUNG BELLAIR. You learnt to sing in Paris.

SIR FOPLING. I did—of Lambert,[8] the greatest master in the world. But I have my own fault, a weak voice, and care not to sing out of a *ruelle*.[9]

---

[1] Merille, the confidant of the Duc de Candale (Brett-Smith).
[2] Genius.
[3] Duc de Candale (1627-58), a famous French courtier prominent in the *Memoires* of the Comte de Bussy (Brett-Smith).
[4] Dressing gown.
[5] Cavalierly, fashionable.
[6] Undress.
[7] Attempt, trial.
[8] Michel Lambert (1610-96), a favorite musician at the French court.
[9] Bedroom or alcove containing a bed where morning receptions were held. The original has *ruèl*.

DORIMANT. A *ruelle* is a pretty cage for a singing fop, indeed.

YOUNG BELLAIR. (*Reads the song*)

How charming Phyllis is, how fair!
Ah, that she were as willing
To ease my wounded heart of care,
And make her eyes less killing.
I sigh, I sigh, I languish now,
And love will not let me rest;
I drive about the Park and bow,
Still as I meet my dearest.

SIR FOPLING. Sing it! sing it, man; it goes to a pretty new tune which I am confident was made by Baptiste.[10]

MEDLEY. Sing it yourself, Sir Fopling; he does not know the tune.

SIR FOPLING. I'll venture.

(SIR FOPLING *sings*)

DORIMANT. Aye, marry! now 'tis something. I shall not flatter you, Sir Fopling; there is not much thought in't, but 'tis passionate and well turned.

MEDLEY. After the French way.

SIR FOPLING. That I aimed at. Does it not give you a lively image of the thing? Slap down goes the glass, and thus we are at it.

DORIMANT. It does, indeed. I perceive, Sir Fopling, you'll be the very head of the sparks who are lucky in compositions of this nature.

Enter SIR FOPLING'S *Footman*

SIR FOPLING. La Tour, is the bath ready?

FOOTMAN. Yes, sir.

SIR FOPLING. *Adieu don[c], mes chers*.[11]

Exit SIR FOPLING

MEDLEY. When have you your revenge on Loveit, Dorimant?

DORIMANT. I will but change my linen and about it.

MEDLEY. The powerful considerations which hindered, have been removed then?

DORIMANT. Most luckily this morning. You must alone with me; my reputation lies at stake there.

MEDLEY. I am engaged to Bellair.

DORIMANT. What's your business?

MEDLEY. Ma-tri-mony, an't like you.

DORIMANT. It does not, sir.

YOUNG BELLAIR. It may in time, Dorimant. What think you of Mrs. Harriet?

---

[10] Probable Jean Baptist Lully (1633-87), the founder of French opera at the court of Louis XIV, though Jean-Baptiste (ca. 1651-1710), a violinist, may be meant.
[11] Then goodbye, my friends.

DORIMANT. What does she think of me?
YOUNG BELLAIR. I am confident she loves you.
DORIMANT. How does it appear?
YOUNG BELLAIR. Why, she's never well but when she's talking of you—but then, she finds all the faults in you she can. She laughs at all who commend you—but then, she speaks ill of all who do not.
DORIMANT. Women of her temper betray themselves by their over-cunning. I had once a growing quarrel with a lady who would always quarrel with me when I came to see her, and yet was never quiet if I stayed a day from her.
YOUNG BELLAIR. My father is in love with Emilia.
DORIMANT. That is a good warrant for your proceedings. Go on and prosper; I must to Loveit. Medley, I am sorry you cannot be a witness.
MEDLEY. Make her meet Sir Fopling again in the same place and use him ill before me.
DORIMANT. That may be brought about, I think. I'll be at your aunt's anon and give you joy, Mr. Bellair.
YOUNG BELLAIR. You had not best think of Mrs. Harriet too much; without church security there's no taking up there.
DORIMANT. I may fall into the snare, too. But—

The wife will find a difference in our fate;
You wed a woman, I a good estate. *Exeunt*

SCENE III. [*The street before* MRS. LOVEIT'S *house*]

Enter the Chair[men] *with* BELLINDA; *the men set down [the chair] and open it,* BELLINDA *starting*

BELLINDA. (*Surprised*) Lord, where am I? —in the Mall? Whither have you brought me?
1ST CHAIRMAN. You gave us no directions, madam.
BELLINDA. (*Aside*) The fright I was in made me forget it.
1ST CHAIRMAN. We use to carry a lady from the Squire's hither.
BELLINDA. (*Aside*) This is Loveit['s]: I am undone if she sees me.—Quickly, carry me away!
1ST CHAIRMAN. Whither, an't like your honor?
BELLINDA. Ask no questions—

Enter LOVEIT'S Footman

FOOTMAN. Have you seen my lady, madam?
BELLINDA. I am just come to wait upon her.
FOOTMAN. She will be glad to see you, madam. She sent me to you this morning to desire your company, and I was told you went out by five o'clock.
BELLINDA. (*Aside*) More and more unlucky!
FOOTMAN. Will you walk in, madam?
BELLINDA. I'll discharge my chair and follow. Tell your mistress I am here. (*Exit Footman*) Take this (*Gives the* Chairmen *money*), and if ever you should be examined, say you took me up in the Strand over against the Exchange, as you will answer it to Mr. Dorimant.
CHAIRMEN. We will, an't like your honor.
Exeunt Chairmen
BELLINDA. Now to come off, I must on—

In confidence and lies some hope is left;
'Twere hard to be found out in the first theft.
Exit BELLINDA

ACT V

[SCENE I]

Enter MRS. LOVEIT *and* PERT, *her woman*

PERT. Well, in my eyes Sir Fopling is no such despicable person.
MRS. LOVEIT. You are an excellent judge.
PERT. He's as handsome a man as Mr. Dorimant, and as great a gallant.
MRS. LOVEIT. Intolerable! Is't not enough I submit to his impertinences but must I be plagued with yours, too?
PERT. Indeed, madam—
MRS. LOVEIT. 'Tis false, mercenary malice—

Enter her Footman

FOOTMAN. Mrs. Bellinda, madam—
MRS. LOVEIT. What of her?
FOOTMAN. She's below.
MRS. LOVEIT. How came she?
FOOTMAN. In a chair; Ambling Harry brought her.
MRS. LOVEIT. He bring her? His chair stands near Dorimant's door and always brings me from thence.—Run and ask him where he took her up. Go! There is no truth in friendship neither. Women, as well as men, all are false, or all are so to me, at least.

PERT. You are jealous of her, too?
MRS. LOVEIT. You had best tell her I am. 'Twill become the liberty you take of late. This fellow's bringing of her, her going out by five o'clock—I know not what to think.

Enter BELLINDA

Bellinda, you are grown an early riser, I hear.
BELLINDA. Do you not wonder, my dear, what made me abroad so soon?
MRS. LOVEIT. You do not use to be so.
BELLINDA. The country gentlewomen I told you of (Lord, they have the oddest diversions!) would never let me rest till I promised to go with them to the markets this morning to eat fruit and buy nosegays.
MRS. LOVEIT. Are they so fond of a filthy nosegay?
BELLINDA. They complain of the stinks of the town, and are never well but when they have their noses in one.
MRS. LOVEIT. There are essences and sweet waters.
BELLINDA. Oh, they cry out upon perfumes, they are unwholesome; one of 'em was falling into a fit with the smell of these *narolii*.[1]
MRS. LOVEIT. Methinks in compliance you should have had a nosegay, too.
BELLINDA. Do you think, my dear, I could be so loathsome, to trick myself up with carnations and stock gillyflowers? I begged their pardon and told them I never wore anything but orange flowers and tuberose. That which made me willing to go, was a strange desire I had to eat some fresh nectarines.
MRS. LOVEIT. And had you any?
BELLINDA. The best I ever tasted.
MRS. LOVEIT. Whence came you now?
BELLINDA. From their lodgings, where I crowded out of a coach and took a chair to come and see you, my dear.
MRS. LOVEIT. Whither did you send for that chair?
BELLINDA. 'Twas going by empty.
MRS. LOVEIT. Where do these countrywomen lodge, I pray?
BELLINDA. In the Strand over against the Exchange.
PERT. The place is never without a nest of 'em. They are always, as one goes by, fleering[2] in balconies or staring out of windows.

Enter Footman

MRS. LOVEIT. (*To the* Footman) Come hither! (*Whispers*)
BELLINDA. (*Aside*) This fellow by her order has been questioning the chairmen. I threatened 'em with the name of Dorimant; if they should have told truth, I am lost forever.
MRS. LOVEIT. —In the Strand, said you?
FOOTMAN. Yes, madam; over against the Exchange. *Exit* Footman
MRS. LOVEIT. She's innocent, and I am much to blame.
BELLINDA. (*Aside*) I am so frightened my countenance will betray me.
MRS. LOVEIT. Bellinda, what makes you look so pale?
BELLINDA. Want of my usual rest and jolting up and down so long in an odious hackney.

Footman *returns*

FOOTMAN. Madam, Mr. Dorimant.
MRS. LOVEIT. What makes him here?
BELLINDA. (*Aside*) Then I am betrayed, indeed. He's broken his word and I love a man that does not care for me!
MRS. LOVEIT. Lord, you faint, Bellinda!
BELLINDA. I think I shall—such an oppression here on the sudden.
PERT. She has eaten too much fruit I warrant you.
MRS. LOVEIT. Not unlikely.
PERT. 'Tis that lies heavy on her stomach.
MRS. LOVEIT. Have her into my chamber, give her some surfeit water, and let her lie down a little.
PERT. Come, madam, I was a strange devourer of fruit when I was young—so ravenous—
Exeunt BELLINDA *and* PERT *leading her off*
MRS. LOVEIT. Oh, that my love would be but calm awhile, that I might receive this man with all the scorn and indignation he deserves!

Enter DORIMANT

DORIMANT. Now for a touch of Sir Fopling to begin with.—Hey, page, give positive order that none of these people stir. Let the *canaille*[3] wait as they should do. Since noise and nonsense have such powerful charms,

I, that I may successful prove,
Transform myself to what you love.[4]

---
[1] This word is apparently peculiar to Etherege.
[2] Jeering.
[3] Vulgar herd.
[4] Waller again; from "To the mutable fair."

MRS. LOVEIT. If that would do, you need not change from what you are. You can be vain and loud enough.

DORIMANT. But not with so good a grace as Sir Fopling.—"Hey, Hampshire!"—"Oh, that sound, that sound becomes a man of quality!"

MRS. LOVEIT. Is there a thing so hateful as a senseless mimic?

DORIMANT. He's a great grievance to all who, like yourself, madam, love to play the fool in quiet.

MRS. LOVEIT. A ridiculous animal, who has more of the ape than the ape has of the man in him!

DORIMANT. I have as mean an opinion of a sheer mimic as yourself; yet were he all ape, I should prefer him to the gay, the giddy, brisk, insipid, noisy fool you dote on.

MRS. LOVEIT. Those noisy fools, however you despise 'em, have good qualities which weigh more (or ought at least) with us women than all the pernicious wit you have to boast of.

DORIMANT. That I may hereafter have a just value for their merit, pray, do me the favor to name 'em.

MRS. LOVEIT. You'll despise 'em as the dull effects of ignorance and vanity; yet I care not if I mention some. First, they really admire us, while you at best but flatter us well.

DORIMANT. Take heed! Fools can dissemble, too.

MRS. LOVEIT. They may, but not so artificially as you. There is no fear they should deceive us! Then, they are assiduous, sir; they are ever offering us their service, and always waiting on our will.

DORIMANT. You owe that to their excessive idleness. They know not how to entertain themselves at home, and find so little welcome abroad they are fain to fly to you who countenance 'em, as a refuge against solitude they would be otherwise condemned to.

MRS. LOVEIT. Their conversation, too, diverts us better.

DORIMANT. Playing with your fan, smelling to your gloves, commending your hair, and taking notice how 'tis cut and shaded after the new way—

MRS. LOVEIT. Were it sillier than you can make it, you must allow 'tis pleasanter to laugh at others than to be laughed at ourselves, though never so wittily. Then, though they want skill to flatter us, they flatter themselves so well they save us the labor. We need not take that care and pains to satisfy 'em of our love, which we so often lose on you.

DORIMANT. They commonly, indeed, believe too well of themselves, and always better of you than you deserve.

MRS. LOVEIT. You are in the right. They have an implicit faith in us which keeps 'em from prying narrowly into our secrets and saves us from the vexatious trouble of clearing doubts which your subtle and causeless jealousies every moment raise.

DORIMANT. There is an inbred falsehood in women, which inclines 'em still to them whom they may most easily deceive.

MRS. LOVEIT. The man who loves above his quality does not suffer more from the insolent impertinence of his mistress than the woman who loves above her understanding does from the arrogant presumptions of her friend.

DORIMANT. You mistake the use of fools; they are designed for properties, and not for friends. You have an indifferent stock of reputation left yet. Lose it all like a frank gamester on the square; 'twill then be time enough to turn rook[1] and cheat it up again on a good, substantial bubble.[2]

MRS. LOVEIT. The old and the ill-favored are only fit for properties,[3] indeed, but young and handsome fools have met with kinder fortunes.

DORIMANT. They have—to the shame of your sex be it spoken! 'Twas this, the thought of this, made me by a timely jealousy endeavor to prevent the good fortune you are providing for Sir Fopling. But against a woman's frailty all our care is vain.

MRS. LOVEIT. Had I not with a dear experience bought the knowledge of your falsehood, you might have fooled me yet. This is not the first jealousy you have feigned, to make a quarrel with me, and get a week to throw away on some such unknown, inconsiderable slut as you have been lately lurking with at plays.

DORIMANT. Women, when they would break off with a man, never want th' address to turn the fault on him.

[1] Cheat.
[2] Deception.
[3] Patterns of correctness.

Mrs. Loveit. You take a pride of late in using me ill, that the town may know the power you have over me, which now (as unreasonably as yourself) expects that I (do me all the injuries you can) must love you still.

Dorimant. I am so far from expecting that you should, I begin to think you never did love me.

Mrs. Loveit. Would the memory of it were so wholly worn out in me, that I did doubt it, too! What made you come to disturb my growing quiet?

Dorimant. To give you joy of your growing infamy.

Mrs. Loveit. Insupportable! Insulting devil! This from you, the only author of my shame! This from another had been but justice; but from you, 'tis a hellish and inhuman outrage. What have I done?

Dorimant. A thing that puts you below my scorn, and makes my anger as ridiculous as you have made my love.

Mrs. Loveit. I walked last night with Sir Fopling.

Dorimant. You did, madam; and you talked and laughed aloud, "Ha, ha, ha!"—Oh, that laugh! that laugh becomes the confidence of a woman of quality.

Mrs. Loveit. You who have more pleasure in the ruin of a woman's reputation than in the endearments of her love, reproach me not with yourself—and I defy you to name the man who can lay a blemish on my fame.

Dorimant. To be seen publicly so transported with the vain follies of that notorious fop, to me is an infamy below the sin of prostitution with another man.

Mrs. Loveit. Rail on! I am satisfied in the justice of what I did; you had provoked me to't.

Dorimant. What I did was the effect of passion, whose extravagancies you have been willing to forgive.

Mrs. Loveit. And what I did was the effect of a passion you may forgive if you think fit.

Dorimant. Are you so indifferent grown?

Mrs. Loveit. I am.

Dorimant. Nay, then 'tis time to part. I'll send you back your letters you have so often asked for.—I have two or three of 'em about me.

Mrs. Loveit. Give 'em me.

Dorimant. You snatch as if you thought I would not. There! and may the perjuries in 'em be mine if e'er I see you more! (*Offers to go; she catches him*)

Mrs. Loveit. Stay!

Dorimant. I will not.

Mrs. Loveit. You shall.

Dorimant. What have you to say?

Mrs. Loveit. I cannot speak it yet.

Dorimant. Something more in commendation of the fool?—Death, I want patience; let me go!

Mrs. Loveit. I cannot. (*Aside*) I can sooner part with the limbs that hold him.—I hate that nauseous fool; you know I do.

Dorimant. Was it the scandal you were fond of then?

Mrs. Loveit. Y'had raised my anger equal to my love—a thing you ne'er could do before, and in revenge I did—I know not what I did. Would you would not think on't more!

Dorimant. Should I be willing to forget it, I shall be daily reminded of it; 'twill be a commonplace for all the town to laugh at me, and Medley, when he is rhetorically drunk, will ever be declaiming on it in my ears.

Mrs. Loveit. 'Twill be believed a jealous spite. Come, forget it.

Dorimant. Let me consult my reputation; you are too careless of it. (*Pauses*) You shall meet Sir Fopling in the Mall again to-night.

Mrs. Loveit. What mean you?

Dorimant. I have thought on it, and you must. 'Tis necessary to justify my love to the world. You can handle a coxcomb as he deserves when you are not out of humor, madam.

Mrs. Loveit. Public satisfaction for the wrong I have done you? This is some new device to make me more ridiculous.

Dorimant. Hear me!

Mrs. Loveit. I will not.

Dorimant. You will be persuaded.

Mrs. Loveit. Never!

Dorimant. Are you so obstinate?

Mrs. Loveit. Are you so base?

Dorimant. You will not satisfy my love?

Mrs. Loveit. I would die to satisfy that; but I will not, to save you from a thousand racks, do a shameless thing to please your vanity.

Dorimant. Farewell, false woman!

Mrs. Loveit. Do—go!

DORIMANT. You will call me back again.
MRS. LOVEIT. Exquisite fiend, I knew you came but to torment me!

Enter BELLINDA *and* PERT

DORIMANT. (*Surprised*) Bellinda here!
BELLINDA. (*Aside*) He starts and looks pale! The sight of me has touched his guilty soul.
PERT. 'Twas but a qualm, as I said—a little indigestion; the surfeit water did it, madam, mixed with a little *mirabilis*.[1]
DORIMANT. I am confounded, and cannot guess how she came hither!
MRS. LOVEIT. 'Tis your fortune, Bellinda, ever to be here when I am abused by this prodigy of ill-nature.
BELLINDA. I am amazed to find him here. How has he the face to come near you?
DORIMANT. (*Aside*) Here is fine work towards! I never was at such a loss before.
BELLINDA. One who makes a public profession of breach of faith and gratitude—I loathe the sight of him.
DORIMANT. There is no remedy; I must submit to their tongues now, and some other time bring myself off as well as I can.
BELLINDA. Other men are wicked; but then, they have some sense of shame! He is never well but when he triumphs—nay, glories to a woman's face in his villainies.
MRS. LOVEIT. You are in the right, Bellinda, but methinks your kindness for me makes you concern yourself too much with him.
BELLINDA. It does indeed, my dear. His barbarous carriage to you yesterday made me hope you ne'er would see him more, and the very next day to find him here again, provokes me strangely. But because I know you love him, I have done.
DORIMANT. You have reproached me handsomely, and I deserve it for coming hither; but—
PERT. You must expect it, sir. All women will hate you for my lady's sake.
DORIMANT. (*Aside to* BELLINDA) Nay, if she begins too, 'tis time to fly; I shall be scolded to death else.—I am to blame in some circumstances, I confess; but as to the main, I am not so guilty as you imagine. I shall seek a more convenient time to clear myself.

[1] A fashionable strong drink made of spirits of wine and spices

MRS. LOVEIT. Do it now. What impediments are here?
DORIMANT. I want time, and you want temper.
MRS. LOVEIT. These are weak pretenses.
DORIMANT. You were never more mistaken in your life; and so farewell.
(DORIMANT *flings off*)
MRS. LOVEIT. Call a footman, Pert, quickly; I will have him dogged.
PERT. I wish you would not, for my quiet and your own.
MRS. LOVEIT. I'll find out the infamous cause of all our quarrels, pluck her mask off, and expose her bare-faced to the world!
BELLINDA. (*Aside*) Let me but escape this time, I'll never venture more.
MRS. LOVEIT. Bellinda, you shall go with me.
BELLINDA. I have such a heaviness hangs on me with what I did this morning, I would fain go home and sleep, my dear.
MRS. LOVEIT. Death! and eternal darkness! I shall never sleep again. Raging fevers seize the world and make mankind as restless as I am! *Exit* MRS. LOVEIT
BELLINDA. I knew him false and helped to make him so. Was not her ruin enough to fright me from the danger? It should have been, but love can take no warning.
Exit BELLINDA

SCENE II. LADY TOWNLEY'S *house*

Enter MEDLEY, YOUNG BELLAIR, LADY TOWNLEY, EMILIA, *and* [SMIRK], *a* Chaplain

MEDLEY. Bear up, Bellair, and do not let us see that repentance in thine we daily do in married faces.
LADY TOWNLEY. This marriage will strangely surprise my brother when he knows it.
MEDLEY. Your nephew ought to conceal it for a time, madam. Since marriage has lost its good name, prudent men seldom expose their own reputations till 'tis convenient to justify their wives.
OLD BELLAIR. (*Without*) Where are you all there? Out! a dod, will nobody hear?
LADY TOWNLEY. My brother! Quickly, Mr. Smirk, into this closet; you must not be seen yet! (SMIRK *goes into the closet*)

Enter OLD BELLAIR *and* LADY TOWNLEY'S Page

OLD BELLAIR. Desire Mr. Forbes to walk into the lower parlor; I will be with him presently. (*To* YOUNG BELLAIR) Where have you been, sir, you could not wait on me to-day?

YOUNG BELLAIR. About a business.

OLD BELLAIR. Are you so good at business? A dod, I have a business too, you shall dispatch out of hand, sir.—Send for a parson, sister; my Lady Woodvill and her daughter are coming.

LADY TOWNLEY. What need you huddle up things thus?

OLD BELLAIR. Out a pize! youth is apt to play the fool, and 'tis not good it should be in their power.

LADY TOWNLEY. You need not fear your son.

OLD BELLAIR. H'has been idling this morning, and a dod, I do not like him. (*To* EMILIA) How dost thou do, sweetheart?

EMILIA. You are very severe, sir—married in such haste.

OLD BELLAIR. Go to, thou'rt a rogue, and I will talk with thee anon. Here my Lady Woodvill comes.

Enter LADY WOODVILL, HARRIET, *and* BUSY

Welcome, madam; Mr. Forbes [is] below with the writings.

LADY WOODVILL. Let us down and make an end then.

OLD BELLAIR. Sister, show us the way. (*To* YOUNG BELLAIR, *who is talking to* HARRIET) Harry, your business lies not there yet. Excuse him till we have done, lady, and then, a dod, he shall be for thee. Mr. Medley, we must trouble you to be a witness.

MEDLEY. I luckily came for that purpose, sir.

Exeunt OLD BELLAIR, YOUNG BELLAIR, LADY TOWNLEY, *and* LADY WOODVILL

BUSY. What will you do, madam?

HARRIET. Be carried back and mewed up in the country again—run away here—anything rather than be married to a man I do not care for! Dear Emilia, do thou advise me.

EMILIA. Mr. Bellair is engaged, you know.

HARRIET. I do, but know not what the fear of losing an estate may fright him to.

EMILIA. In the desperate condition you are in, you should consult with some judicious man. What think you of Mr. Dorimant?

HARRIET. I do not think of him at all.

BUSY. She thinks of nothing else, I am sure.

EMILIA. How fond your mother was of Mr. Courtage!

HARRIET. Because I contrived the mistake to make a little mirth, you believe I like the man.

EMILIA. Mr. Bellair believes you love him.

HARRIET. Men are seldom in the right when they guess at a woman's mind. Would she whom he loves, loved him no better!

BUSY. (*Aside*) That's e'en well enough, on all conscience.

EMILIA. Mr. Dorimant has a great deal of wit.

HARRIET. And takes a great deal of pains to show it.

EMILIA. He's extremely well fashioned.

HARRIET. Affectedly grave, or ridiculously wild and apish.

BUSY. You defend him still against your mother!

HARRIET. I would not, were he justly rallied, but I cannot hear anyone undeservedly railed at.

EMILIA. Has your woman learned the song you were so taken with?

HARRIET. I was fond of a new thing; 'tis dull at a second hearing.

EMILIA. Mr. Dorimant made it.

BUSY. She knows it, madam, and has made me sing it at least a dozen times this morning.

HARRIET. Thy tongue is as impertinent as thy fingers.

EMILIA. You have provoked her.

BUSY. 'Tis but singing the song and I shall appease her.

EMILIA. Prithee, do.

HARRIET. She has a voice will grate your ears worse than a cat-call, and dresses so ill she's scarce fit to trick up a yeoman's daughter on a holiday. (BUSY *sings*)

SONG

BY SIR C. S.[1]

As Amoret with Phyllis sat,
One evening on the plain,
And saw the charming Strephon wait
To tell the nymph his pain;

The threat'ning danger to remove,
She whispered in her ear,

---

[1] The song is probably by Sir Car Scroope, who wrote the prologue.

"Ah, Phyllis, if you would not love,
This shepherd do not hear!

"None ever had so strange an art,
His passion to convey
Into a list'ning virgin's heart,
And steal her soul away.

"Fly, fly betimes, for fear you give
Occasion for your fate."
"In vain," said she; "in vain I strive!
Alas, 'tis now too late."

Enter DORIMANT

DORIMANT. Music so softens and disarms the mind—
HARRIET. That not one arrow does resistance find.[1]

DORIMANT. Let us make use of the lucky minute, then.
HARRIET. (*Aside, turning from* DORIMANT) My love springs with my blood into my face; I dare not look upon him yet.
DORIMANT. What have we here? the picture of celebrated beauty giving audience in public to a declared lover?
HARRIET. Play the dying fop and make the piece complete, sir.
DORIMANT. What think you if the hint were well improved? The whole mystery of making love pleasantly designed and wrought in a suit of hangings?[2]
HARRIET. 'Twere needless to execute fools in effigy who suffer daily in their own persons.
DORIMANT. (*Aside to* EMILIA) Mrs. Bride, for such I know this happy day has made you—
EMILIA. [*Aside*] Defer the formal joy you are to give me, and mind your business with her. (*Aloud*) Here are dreadful preparations, Mr. Dorimant—writings sealing, and a parson sent for.
DORIMANT. To marry this lady?
BUSY. Condemned she is, and what will become of her I know not, without you generously engage in a rescue.
DORIMANT. In this sad condition, madam, I can do no less than offer you my service.
HARRIET. The obligation is not great; you are the common sanctuary for all young women who run from their relations.
DORIMANT. I have always my arms open to receive the distressed, but I will open my heart and receive you where none yet did ever enter. You have filled it with a secret; might I but let you know it—
HARRIET. Do not speak it if you would have me believe it. Your tongue is so famed for falsehood, 'twill do the truth an injury.
(*Turns away her head*)
DORIMANT. Turn not away, then, but look on me and guess it.
HARRIET. Did you not tell me there was no credit to be given to faces?—that women nowadays have their passions as much at will as they have their complexions, and put on joy and sadness, scorn and kindness, with the same ease they do their paint and patches? Are they the only counterfeits?
DORIMANT. You wrong your own while you suspect my eyes. By all the hope I have in you, the inimitable color in your cheeks is not more free from art than are the sighs I offer.
HARRIET. In men who have been long hardened in sin, we have reason to mistrust the first signs of repentance.
DORIMANT. The prospect of such a heaven will make me persevere and give you marks that are infallible.
HARRIET. What are those?
DORIMANT. I will renounce all the joy I have in friendship and in wine, sacrifice to you all the interest I have in other women—
HARRIET. Hold! Though I wish you devout, I would not have you turn fanatic. Could you neglect these a while and make a journey into the country?
DORIMANT. To be with you, I could live there and never send one thought to London.
HARRIET. Whate'er you say, I know all beyond Hyde Park's a desert to you, and that no gallantry can draw you farther.
DORIMANT. That has been the utmost limit of my love; but now my passion knows no bounds, and there's no measure to be taken of what I'll do for you from anything I ever did before.
HARRIET. When I hear you talk thus in Hampshire, I shall begin to think there may be some little truth enlarged upon.
DORIMANT. Is this all?—Will you not promise me?
HARRIET. I hate to promise; what we do then is expected of us and wants much of the welcome it finds when it surprises.

---

[1] From Waller's "Of my Lady Isabella playing on the lute."
[2] Tapestries to cover the walls.

DORIMANT. May I not hope?
HARRIET. That depends on you and not on me, and 'tis to no purpose to forbid it.
(*Turns to* BUSY)
BUSY. Faith, madam, now I perceive the gentleman loves you, too; e'en let him know your mind and torment yourselves no longer.
HARRIET. Dost think I have no sense of modesty?
BUSY. Think, if you lose this you may never have another opportunity.
HARRIET. May he hate me (a curse that frightens me when I speak it), if ever I do a thing against the rules of decency and honor.
DORIMANT. (*To* EMILIA) I am beholding to you for your good intentions, madam.
EMILIA. I thought the concealing of our marriage from her might have done you better service.
DORIMANT. Try her again.
EMILIA. What are you resolved, madam? The time draws near.
HARRIET. To be obstinate and protest against this marriage.

Enter LADY TOWNLEY *in haste*

LADY TOWNLEY. (*To* EMILIA) Quickly! quickly! let Mr. Smirk out of the closet.
(SMIRK *comes out*)
HARRIET. A parson! Had you laid him in here?
DORIMANT. I knew nothing of him.
HARRIET. Should it appear you did, your opinion of my easiness may cost you dear.

Enter OLD BELLAIR, YOUNG BELLAIR, MEDLEY, *and* LADY WOODVILL

OLD BELLAIR. Out a pize! the canonical hour[1] is almost past. Sister, is the man of God come?
LADY TOWNLEY. He waits your leisure.
OLD BELLAIR. [*To* SMIRK] By your favor, sir.—A dod, a pretty spruce fellow! What may we call him?
LADY TOWNLEY. Mr. Smirk—my Lady Bigot's chaplain.
OLD BELLAIR. A wise woman; a dod, she is. The man will serve for the flesh as well as the spirit. [*To* SMIRK] Please you, sir, to commission a young couple to go to bed together a-God's name.—Harry!
YOUNG BELLAIR. Here, sir.

[1] Hour during which marriage can be legally celebrated.

OLD BELLAIR. Out a pize! Without your mistress in your hand!
SMIRK. Is this the gentleman?
OLD BELLAIR. Yes, sir.
SMIRK. Are you not mistaken, sir?
OLD BELLAIR. A dod, I think not, sir.
SMIRK. Sure, you are, sir?
OLD BELLAIR. You look as if you would forbid the banns, Mr. Smirk. I hope you have no pretension to the lady?
SMIRK. Wish him joy, sir; I have done the good office to-day already.
OLD BELLAIR. Out a pize! What do I hear!
LADY TOWNLEY. Never storm, brother; the truth is out.
OLD BELLAIR. How say you, sir? Is this your wedding day?
YOUNG BELLAIR. It is, sir.
OLD BELLAIR. And a dod, it shall be mine too. (*To* EMILIA) Give me your hand, sweetheart.—What dost thou mean? Give me thy hand, I say.
(EMILIA *kneels and* YOUNG BELLAIR)
LADY TOWNLEY. Come, come! give her your blessing. This is the woman your son loved and is married to.
OLD BELLAIR. Ha! cheated! cozened! and by your contrivance, sister!
LADY TOWNLEY. What would you do with her? She's a rogue and you can't abide her.
MEDLEY. Shall I hit her a pat for you, sir?
OLD BELLAIR. A dod, you are all rogues, and I never will forgive you.
LADY TOWNLEY. Whither? Whither away?
MEDLEY. Let him go and cool awhile.
LADY WOODVILL. (*To* DORIMANT) Here's a business broke out now, Mr. Courtage; I am made a fine fool of.
DORIMANT. You see the old gentleman knew nothing of it.
LADY WOODVIL. I find he did not. I shall have some trick put upon me if I stay in this wicked town any longer.—Harriet! Dear child, where art thou? I'll into the country straight.
OLD BELLAIR. A dod, madam, you shall hear me first.

Enter MRS. LOVEIT *and* BELLINDA

MRS. LOVEIT. Hither my man dogged him.
BELLINDA. Yonder he stands, my dear.
MRS. LOVEIT. (*Aside*) I see him, and with him the face that has undone me. Oh, that

I were but where I might throw out the anguish of my heart! Here, it must rage within and break it.

LADY TOWNLEY. Mrs. Loveit! Are you afraid to come forward?

MRS. LOVEIT. I was amazed to see so much company here in the morning. The occasion sure is extraordinary.

DORIMANT. (*Aside*) Loveit and Bellinda! The devil owes me a shame to-day and I think never will have done paying it.

MRS. LOVEIT. Married, dear Emilia? How am I transported with the news!

HARRIET. (*To* DORIMANT) I little thought Emilia was the woman Mr. Bellair was in love with. I'll chide her for not trusting me with the secret.

DORIMANT. How do you like Mrs. LOVEIT?

HARRIET. She's a famed mistress of yours, I hear.

DORIMANT. She has been on occasion.

OLD BELLAIR. (*To* LADY WOODVILL) A dod, madam, I cannot help it.

LADY WOODVILL. You need make no more apologies, sir.

EMILIA. (*To* MRS. LOVEIT) The old gentleman's excusing himself to my Lady Woodvill.

MRS. LOVEIT. Ha, ha, ha! I never heard of anything so pleasant!

HARRIET. (*To* DORIMANT) She's extremely overjoyed at something.

DORIMANT. At nothing. She is one of those hoiting[1] ladies who gaily fling themselves about and force a laugh when their aching hearts are full of discontent and malice.

MRS. LOVEIT. O Heaven! I was never so near killing myself with laughing.—Mr. Dorimant, are you a brideman?

LADY WOODVILL. Mr. Dorimant!—Is this Mr. Dorimant, madam?

MRS. LOVEIT. If you doubt it, your daughter can resolve you, I suppose.

LADY WOODVILL. I am cheated too—basely cheated!

OLD BELLAIR. Out a pize! what's here? More knavery yet?

LADY WOODVILL. Harriet! On my blessing, come away, I charge you!

HARRIET. Dear mother, do but stay and hear me.

LADY WOODVILL. I am betrayed and thou art undone, I fear.

HARRIET. Do not fear it; I have not, nor

[1] Romping.

never will, do anything against my duty. Believe me, dear mother—do!

DORIMANT. (*To* MRS. LOVEIT) I had trusted you with this secret but that I knew the violence of your nature would ruin my fortune—as now unluckily it has. I thank you, madam.

MRS. LOVEIT. She's an heiress, I know, and very rich.

DORIMANT. To satisfy you, I must give up my interest wholly to my love. Had you been a reasonable woman, I might have secured 'em both and been happy.

MRS. LOVEIT. You might have trusted me with anything of this kind—you know you might. Why did you go under a wrong name?

DORIMANT. The story is too long to tell you now. Be satisfied, this is the business; this is the mask has kept me from you.

BELLINDA. (*Aside*) He's tender of my honor though he's cruel to my love.

MRS. LOVEIT. Was it no idle mistress, then?

DORIMANT. Believe me, a wife to repair the ruins of my estate that needs it.

MRS. LOVEIT. The knowledge of this makes my grief hang lighter on my soul, but I shall never more be happy.

DORIMANT. Bellinda!

BELLINDA. Do not think of clearing yourself with me; it is impossible. Do all men break their words thus?

DORIMANT. Th'extravagant words they speak in love. 'Tis as unreasonable to expect we should perform all we promise then, as to do all we threaten when we are angry. When I see you next—

BELLINDA. Take no notice of me, and I shall not hate you.

DORIMANT. How came you to Mrs. Loveit?

BELLINDA. By a mistake the chairmen made, for want of my giving them directions.

DORIMANT. 'Twas a pleasant one. We must meet again.

BELLINDA. Never!

DORIMANT. Never?

BELLINDA. When we do, may I be as infamous as you are false.

LADY TOWNLEY. Men of Mr. Dorimant's character always suffer in the general opinion of the world.

MEDLEY. You can make no judgment of a witty man from the common fame, considering the prevailing faction, madam.

OLD BELLAIR. A dod. he's in the right.

MEDLEY. Besides, 'tis a common error among women to believe too well of them they know, and too ill of them they don't.

OLD BELLAIR. A dod, he observes well.

LADY TOWNLEY. Believe me, madam, you will find Mr. Dorimant as civil a gentleman as you thought Mr. Courtage.

HARRIET. If you would but know him better—

LADY WOODVILL. You have a mind to know him better? Come away! You shall never see him more.

HARRIET. Dear mother, stay!

LADY WOODVILL. I won't be consenting to your ruin.

HARRIET. Were my fortune in your power—

LADY WOODVILL. Your person is.

HARRIET. Could I be disobedient, I might take it out of yours and put it into his.

LADY WOODVILL. 'Tis that you would be at?—You would marry this Dorimant?

HARRIET. I cannot deny it; I would, and never will marry any other man.

LADY WOODVILL. Is this the duty that you promised?

HARRIET. But I will never marry him against your will.

LADY WOODVILL. (*Aside*) She knows the way to melt my heart. [*Aloud*] Upon yourself light your undoing!

MEDLEY. (*To* OLD BELLAIR) Come, sir, you have not the heart any longer to refuse your blessing.

OLD BELLAIR. A dod, I ha' not.—Rise, and God bless you both! Make much of her, Harry; she deserves thy kindness. (*To* EMILIA) A dod, sirrah, I did not think it had been in thee!

Enter SIR FOPLING *and his* Page

SIR FOPLING. 'Tis a damned windy day. Hey, page, is my periwig right?

PAGE. A little out of order, sir.

SIR FOPLING. Pox o' this apartment! It wants an antechamber to adjust oneself in. (*To* MRS. LOVEIT) Madam, I came from your house, and your servants directed me hither.

MRS. LOVEIT. I shall give order hereafter they shall direct you better.

SIR FOPLING. The great satisfaction I had in the Mall last night has given me much disquiet since.

MRS. LOVEIT. 'Tis likely to give me more than I desire.

SIR FOPLING. What the devil makes her so reserved?—Am I guilty of an indiscretion, madam?

MRS. LOVEIT. You will be—of a great one —if you continue your mistake, sir.

SIR FOPLING. Something's put you out of humor?

MRS. LOVEIT. The most foolish, inconsiderable thing that ever did.

SIR FOPLING. Is it in my power?

MRS. LOVEIT. —To hang or drown it. Do one of 'em and trouble me no more.

SIR FOPLING. So *fieré?*[1] *Serviteur, madam.*[2] —Medley, where's Dorimant?

MEDLEY. Methinks the lady has not made you those advances to-day she did last night, Sir Fopling.

SIR FOPLING. Prithee, do not talk of her!

MEDLEY. She would be a *bonne fortune*.

SIR FOPLING. Not to me at present.

MEDLEY. How so?

SIR FOPLING. An intrigue now would be but a temptation to me to throw away that vigor on one which I mean shall shortly make my court to the whole sex in a ballet.

MEDLEY. Wisely considered, Sir Fopling.

SIR FOPLING. No one woman is worth the loss of a cut in a caper.

MEDLEY. Not when 'tis so universally designed.

LADY WOODVILL. Mr. Dorimant, everyone has spoke so much in your behalf that I can no longer doubt but I was in the wrong.

MRS. LOVEIT. There's nothing but falsehood and impertinence in this world! All men are villains or fools; take example from my misfortunes, Bellinda; if thou wouldst be happy, give thyself wholly up to goodness.

HARRIET. (*To* MRS. LOVEIT) Mr. Dorimant has been your God Almighty long enough; 'tis time to think of another.

MRS. LOVEIT. Jeered by her!—I will lock myself up in my house and never see the world again.

HARRIET. A nunnery is the more fashionable place for such a retreat, and has been the fatal consequence of many a *belle passion*.[3]

MRS. LOVEIT. Hold, heart, till I get home! Should I answer, 'twould make her triumph greater. (*Is going out*)

---

[1] For *fière*, haughty.
[2] Your servant, madam.
[3] Love affair.

DORIMANT. Your hand, Sir Fopling—

SIR FOPLING. Shall I wait upon you, madam?

MRS. LOVEIT. Legion of fools, as many devils take thee! *Exit* MRS. LOVEIT

MEDLEY. Dorimant, I pronounce thy reputation clear; and henceforward when I would know anything of woman, I will consult no other oracle.

SIR FOPLING. Stark mad, by all that's handsome!—Dorimant, thou hast engaged me in a pretty business.

DORIMANT. I have not leisure now to talk about it.

OLD BELLAIR. Out a pize! what does this man of mode do here again?

LADY TOWNLEY. He'll be an excellent entertainment within, brother, and is luckily come to raise the mirth of the company.

LADY WOODVILL. Madam, I take my leave of you.

LADY TOWNLEY. What do you mean, madam?

LADY WOODVILL. To go this afternoon part of my way to Hartley—

OLD BELLAIR. A dod, you shall stay and dine first! Come, we will all be good friends, and you shall give Mr. Dorimant leave to wait upon you and your daughter in the country.

LADY WOODVILL. If his occasions bring him that way, I have now so good an opinion of him, he shall be welcome.

HARRIET. To a great rambling, lone house that looks as if it were not inhabited, the family's so small. There you'll find my mother, an old lame aunt, and myself, sir, perched up on chairs at a distance in a great parlor, sitting moping like four melancholy birds in a spacious volery.[1] Does not this stagger your resolution?

DORIMANT. Not at all, madam. The first time I saw you you left me with the pangs of love upon me, and this day my soul has quite given up her liberty.

HARRIET. This is more dismal than the country! Emilia, pity me, who am going to that sad place. Methinks I hear the hateful noise of rooks already—*Kaw, kaw, kaw!* There's music in the worst cry in London, "My dill and cowcumbers to pickle!"[2]

OLD BELLAIR. Sister, knowing of this matter, I hope you have provided us some good cheer.

LADY TOWNLEY. I have, brother, and the fiddles, too.

OLD BELLAIR. Let 'em strike up, then; the young lady shall have a dance before she departs. (*Dance*)

(*After the dance*)—So! Now we'll in and make this an arrant[3] wedding-day.

(*To the pit*)

And if these honest gentlemen rejoice,
A dod, the boy has made a happy choice.

Exeunt omnes

THE EPILOGUE

BY MR. DRYDEN

Most modern wits such monstrous fools have shown,
They seem'd not of heav'n's making, but their own.
Those nauseous harlequins in farce may pass,
But there goes more to a substantial ass.
Something of man must be exposed to view 5
That, gallants, they may more resemble you.
Sir Fopling is a fool so nicely writ,
The ladies would mistake him for a wit;
And when he sings, talks loud, and cocks,[4] would cry,
"I vow, methinks he's pretty company!" 10
So brisk, so gay, so travelled, so refined
As he, took pains to graft upon his kind.
True fops help nature's work and go to school,
To file and finish God A'mighty's fool.
Yet none Sir Fopling him, or him, can call; 15
He's knight o' th' shire, and represents ye all.
From each he meets, he culls whate'er he can;
Legion's his name, a people in a man.
His bulky folly gathers as it goes
And, rolling o'er you, like a snowball grows.
His various modes, from various fathers follow; 21
One taught the toss,[5] and one the new French wallow.[6]
His sword-knot, this; his cravat, this, designed;
And this, the yard-long snake[7] he twirls behind.

---

[1] Aviary, birdhouse. Why there should be four birds is not clear.
[2] One of the street cries of London.
[3] Thorough.
[4] Either struts; or cocks his hat.
[5] Manner of tossing the head.
[6] Rolling gait.
[7] Tail of his wig.

From one the sacred periwig he gained, 25
Which wind ne'er blew, nor touch of hat prophaned.
Another's diving bow he did adore,
Which with a shog [1] casts all his hair before
Till he with full decorum brings it back,
And rises with a water spaniel's shake. 30
As for his songs (the ladies' dear delight),
Those sure he took from most of you who write.
Yet every man is safe from what he feared,
For no one fool is hunted from the herd.

[1] Shake, jerk.

THE RIVAL QUEENS;

OR,

THE DEATH OF ALEXANDER THE GREAT

By Nathaniel Lee

Nathaniel Lee, who was praised by Dryden for his graphic presentation of the "passions," and whom Rochester unkindly described as a "hot-brained Fustian Fool," was born in 1653, probably in London, and, again probably, the son of the Rev. Richard Lee, a parliamentary divine. Educated at Westminster School where he was "well lasht" by the great Busby, he entered Trinity College, Cambridge, in 1665. After receiving his degree in 1667/8, he was taken up by fashionable society; the Duke of Buckingham brought him to London; and Rochester plunged him into dissipation. Though Lee was an admirable elocutionist, he failed as an actor because of acute nervousness, and took to writing plays. For *Sophonisba*, Lee's second play, Purcell wrote his first music for the stage; *The Rival Queens* established Lee's reputation; the two following plays "took prodigiously"; and Lee met no rebuff until the production of *Lucius Junius Brutus* was stopped on political grounds by the Lord Chamberlain. Indeed, the shadow of political controversy rests on all his later dramas. As Lee's intemperance grew, his aristocratic friends fell away from him; a tendency toward insanity (madness is a favorite theme in his plays) so increased that on November 11, 1684, the poet was confined in Bethlehem Hospital, from which he was not released until 1689. That his mind was not entirely cloudy during these years is evident, however, from various stories regarding his literary activity. Whatever his defects as a man, Lee seems to have held the affection of the actors; and a pension of £10 was granted him from the Theatre Royal. He was still to write *The Massacre of Paris* (1689), in which his faults are less in evidence than in earlier dramas. But life held little more; and he died in a drinking fit, killed or stifled by a fall, and was buried in the church of St. Clement Danes, May 6, 1692. The characteristic judgment of his age on Nathaniel Lee is expressed in the *Session of the Poets*:

"Nat Lee stepped in next in hopes of a prize;
Apollo remembered he had hit once in thrice;
By the rubies in's face he could not deny
But he had as much wit as wine could supply;
Confessed that indeed he had a musical note,
But sometimes strained so hard that he rattled his throat;
Yet owning he had sense, t'encourage him for't,
He made him his Ovid in Augustus's court."

Lee is "Ovid" because he was supposed to be the dramatist of passionate love *par excellence*.

See the life of Lee in the *Dictionary of National Biography* by Sir Sidney Lee, and the references appended.

LEE'S DRAMATIC WORKS

The Tragedy of Nero, Emperor of Rome (D.L., May, 1674), 1675.
Sophonisba (tragedy) (D.L., Apr., 1675), 1676.
Gloriana, or the Court of Augustus Cæsar (tragedy) (D.L., Jan., 1675/6), 1676.
The Rival Queens (tragedy) (D.L., Mar., 1676/7), 1677.
Mithridates, King of Pontus (tragedy) (D.L., Mar. (?) 1677/8), 1678.
Œdipus (with Dryden) (tragedy) (D.G., Jan. (?) 1678/9), 1679.
Cæsar Borgia (tragedy) (D.G., Sept. (?) 1679), 1680.
Theodosius (tragedy) (D.G., Sept. (?) 1680), 1680.
Lucius Junius Brutus (tragedy) (D.G., Dec., 1680), 1681.
The Princess of Cleve[s] (comedy) (D.G., 1681), 1689.
The Duke of Guise (with Dryden) (tragedy) (prohibited), 1683.
Constantine the Great (tragedy) (D.L., Dec., 1683), 1684.
The Massacre of Paris (tragedy) (D.L., Nov., 1689), 1690.

Famous for its acting rôles, filled with occasional flashes of rhetorical splendor, appealing to the women because of its passionate interpretation of love, and to the men by its martial and manly parts, *The Rival Queens* held the boards as long as the tradition of declamatory elocution survived in the theater. So popular was it that, twenty-three years after its first production, Colley Cibber could still write a parody, *The Rival Queans* (1710), which had some success in London, and was popular in Dublin. In later versions the original tragedy was known as *Alexander the Great*, a title which shows the shift of interest in subsequent interpretation. The song, "See the conquering hero comes," the music from Handel's *Joshua*, was interpolated into the second act, some of the more extravagant speeches were curtailed and others were "improved," and the Ghost of Philip was commonly omitted. It was such a version that as late as 1823 was revived by Edmund Kean, who played Alexander to Mrs. Glover's Roxana.

When we try to account for the extraordinary vogue of a play which is justly chargeable with bombast and ridiculous extravagance in certain passages, we are forced to take into account Lee's acute feeling for the theater. By 1676–7 the formula of the rhymed heroic tragedy was beginning to pall. Anticipating Dryden, Lee now tried the experiment of a play in blank verse, eliminated the artificialities of the mere love-and-honor conflict, injected a swelling passion into his love scenes, strove for something like historical accuracy in the story, borrowed a ghost and some supernatural omens from Shakespeare, employed every spectacular device he could crowd into his drama without injury to the plot, and saw to it that every actor had what is known to the profession as "fat" lines. He founded (though his methods were anticipated) the declamatory tragedy in which the eighteenth century was to delight.

His story he happened upon in La Calprenède's "heroic romance," *Cassandre*, translated by Sir Charles Cotterell in 1652, and very popular. For the sake of dramatic unity he fused together the two love-episodes in that novel in which Roxana is concerned: her marriage with Alexander, and her rivalry with Statira for the attentions of Oroondate. He then turned to the classical historians, Quintus Curtius, Plutarch, and Arrian (and possibly to Sir Walter Ralegh's *Historie of the World*) for his historical setting, uniting with material found there several hints from *Cassandre*, out of which he constructed the conspiracy plot. Then he juggled the time elements into a coherent whole and emerged with a play which, with obvious defects, is closer to actual history than such a drama as *The Indian Queen*.

The conflict of love and honor enters the play, but in *The Rival Queens* Lee follows more directly the tradition of French heroic romance: the love interest involves three persons, one of whom destroys the happiness of the others; and, on the death of one lover, the other must also perish. In heroic tragedy, on the contrary, the conflict is resolved happily. Lee found his formula so dramatic that he employed it several times. Moreover, he swept aside the gallantry of the heroic play and substituted the hot speech of passion, speech which shatters the polite conventions of Platonic love. His hero, moreover, is not perfect, but a compound of good and evil. Finally, his "soaring delight in magnificent and imposing historic themes" gave verity to his romantic picture of Alexander's court and to the dark mutterings of the conspirators, who, though, until the end, they contrive very little, furnish effective theatrical contrast to the brilliant scenes of love and oriental magnificence. If one remembers that Lee was only in his twenties when he wrote *The Rival Queens*, the romantic tendency of the play becomes more understandable.

The Rival Queens [1] was first produced at the "New Theatre" in Drury Lane in March, 1676/7, with a brilliant cast.

On the sources of the play see O. Auer, "Ueber einige Dramen Nathaniel Lee's," *Berliner Beiträge*, XXVII, 1904; and Hermann Denker, *Ueber die Quellen von Nath. Lee's Alexander the Great*, Halle, 1903; and for general critical discussion consult A. W. Ward, *History of English Dramatic Literature*, vol. III, and other histories of the drama.

---

[1] The play was originally dedicated to the Earl of Mulgrave. In the dedication, not printed here, Lee commented pessimistically upon the fortunes of a poet in a dissolute age, and paid Mulgrave the usual fulsome compliments.

THE RIVAL QUEENS

DRAMATIS PERSONÆ

ALEXANDER THE GREAT	Mr. Hart
CLYTUS, *Master of his Horse*	Major Mohun
LYSIMACHUS, *Prince of the Blood*	Mr. Griffin
HEPHESTION, *Alexander's Favorite*	Mr. Clarke
CASSANDER, *Son of Antipater* ⎫	Mr. Kynaston
POLYPERCHON, *Commander of the Phalanx* ⎬ *Conspirators*	Mr. Goodman
PHILIP, *Brother to Cassander* ⎭	
THESSALUS, *the Median*	Mr. Wiltshire
PERDICCAS, ⎫	
EUMENES, ⎬ *Great Commanders*	
MELEAGER, ⎭	
ARISTANDER, *a Soothsayer*	
SYSIGAMBIS, *Mother of the Royal Family*	Mrs. Corey
STATIRA, *Daughter of Darius, married to Alexander*	Mrs. Boutell
ROXANA, *Daughter of Cohortanus, first wife of Alexander*	Mrs. Marshall
PARISATIS, *Sister to Statira, in love with Lysimachus*	Mrs. Baker

Attendants, Slaves, Ghost, Dancers, Guards

SCENE: *Babylon*

PROLOGUE

WRITTEN BY SIR CAR SCROOP, BART.[1]

How hard the fate is of the scribbling drudge
Who writes to all, when yet so few can judge!
Wit, like religion, once divine was thought,
And the dull crowd believed as they were taught;
Now each fanatic fool presumes t'explain 5
The text, and does the sacred writ profane;
For, while you wits each other's fall pursue,
The fops usurp the power belongs to you.
You think y'are challenged in each new play-bill,
And here you come for trial of your skill, 10
Where, fencer-like, you one another hurt.
While with your wounds you make the rabble sport.
Others there are that have the brutal will
To murder a poor play, but want the skill.
They love to fight, but seldom have the wit 15
To spy the place where they may thrust and hit;
And therefore, like some bully of the town,
Ne'er stand to draw, but knock the poet down.
With these, like hogs in gardens, it succeeds,
They root up all, and know not flowers from weeds. 20
As for you, sparks, that hither come each day
To act your own, and not to mind our play;
Rehearse your usual follies to the pit,
And with loud nonsense drown the stage's wit;
Talk of your clothes, your last debauches tell,
And witty bargains to each other sell; 26
Gloat on the silly she who, for your sake,
Can vanity and noise for love mistake;
Till the coquette sung in the next lampoon
Is by her jealous friends sent out of town. 30
For in this duelling, intriguing age
The love you make is like the war you wage: ⎤
Y'are still prevented e'er you come t'engage. ⎦
But 'tis not to such trifling foes as you
The mighty Alexander deigns to sue; 35
Ye Persians of the pit he does despise,
But to the men of sense for aid he flies;
On their experienced arms he now depends,
Nor fears he odds, if they but prove his friends;
For as he once a little handful chose 40
The numerous armies of the world t'oppose,
So, backed by you who understand the rules,
He hopes to rout the mighty host of fools.

[1] See the Prologue to *The Man of Mode*, p. 84. Sir Car Scroop was much satirized, and perhaps his complaint that "men of sense" are rare is more than formal here.

ACT I

Scene 1

Enter HEPHESTION, LYSIMACHUS[1] *fighting;* CLYTUS *parting them*

CLYTUS. What, are you madmen! ha!—
  Put up, I say—
Then, mischief's in the bosom of ye both.
  LYSIMACHUS. I have his sword.
  CLYTUS.   But must not have his life.
  LYSIMACHUS. Must not, old Clytus?
  CLYTUS.   Mad Lysimachus, you must not.
  HEPHESTION. Coward flesh! O feeble arm! 5
He dallied with my point, and when I thrust,
He frowned and smiled and foiled me like a
  fencer.
O reverend Clytus, father of the war,
Most famous guard of Alexander's life,[2]
Take pity on my youth and lend a sword. 10
Lysimachus is brave and will not scorn me;
Kill me, or let me fight with him again.
  LYSIMACHUS. There, take thy sword, and
    since thou art resolved
For death, thou hast the noblest from my hand.
  CLYTUS. Stay thee, Lysimachus. Hephestion, hold. 15
I bar you both, my body interposed.
Now let me see which of you dares to strike!
By Jove, ye've stirred the old man; that rash
  arm
That first advances, moves against the gods,
Against the wrath of Clytus, and the will 20
Of our great king whose deputy I stand.
  LYSIMACHUS. Well, I shall take another time.
  HEPHESTION.   And I.
  CLYTUS.   'Tis false.
Another time—what time? what foolish hour?
No time shall see a brave man do amiss.
And what's the noble cause that makes this
  madness? 25
What big ambition blows this dangerous fire?
A cupid's puff, is it not? Woman's breath?
By all our triumphs in the heat of youth,
When towns were sacked and beauties prostrate lay,
When my blood boiled and nature worked me
  high, 30
Clytus ne'er bowed his body to such shame!
The brave will scorn their cobweb arts—The
  souls
Of all that whining, smiling, coz'ning sex
Weigh not one thought of any man of war.
  LYSIMACHUS. I confess our vengeance was
    ill-timed. 35
  CLYTUS. Death! I had rather this right arm
    were lost,
To which I owe my glory, than our king
Should know your fault—what, on this famous day!
  HEPHESTION. I was to blame.
  CLYTUS.   This memorable day!
When our hot master that would tire the
  world, 40
Outride the lab'ring sun, and tread the stars
When he inclined to rest, comes peaceful on,
List'ning to songs; while all his trumpets
  sleep,
And plays with monarchs whom he used to
  drive,
Shall we begin disorders, make new broils? 45
We that have temper learnt, shall we awake
Hushed Mars, the Lion that had left to roar?[3]
  LYSIMACHUS. 'Tis true, old Clytus is an
    oracle.
Put up, Hephestion—did not passion blind
My reason, I on such occasion too 50
Could thus have urged.
  HEPHESTION.   Why is it then we love?
  CLYTUS. Because unmanned.—
Why is not Alexander grown example?
O that a face should thus bewitch a soul
And ruin all that's right and reasonable! 55
Talk be my bane, yet the old man must talk:
Not so he loved when he at Issus fought,
And joined in mighty duel great Darius,
Whom from his chariot flaming all with gems
He hurled to earth, and crushed th' imperial
  crown; 60
Nor could the gods defend their images
Which with the gaudy coach lay overturned.
'Twas not the shaft of love that did the feat—
Cupid had nothing there to do; but now
Two wives he takes, two rival queens disturb
The court; and while each hand does beauty
  hold, 66
Where is there room for glory?
  HEPHESTION.   In his heart.
  CLYTUS.   Well said,
You are his favorite, and I had forgot
Who I was talking to. See, Sysigambis comes
Reading a letter to your princess. Go, 70
Now make your claim while I attend the king.
  Exit

---

[1] In general, the story of the rivalry of Hephestion and Lysimachus follows La Calprenède's *Cassandre*.

[2] Clytus saved Alexander's life at the crossing of the Granicus. See Plutarch, c. xvi; and Act II, ll. 141ff.

[3] Left off roaring.

Enter SYSIGAMBIS, PARISATIS

PARISATIS. Did you not love my father?
    Yes, I see
You did, his very name but mentioned, brings
The tears, howe'er unwilling, to your eyes.
I loved him too; he would not thus have
    forced   75
My trembling heart, which your commands
    may break,
But never bend.
  SYSIGAMBIS. Forbear thy lost complaints;
Urge not a suit which I can never grant.
Behold the royal signet of the king.
Therefore resolve to be Hephestion's wife. 80
  PARISATIS. No. Since Lysimachus has won
    my heart,
My body shall be ashes, e'er another's.
  SYSIGAMBIS. For sixty rolling years, who
    ever stood
The shock of state so unconcerned as I?
This whom I thought to govern, being young,
Heav'n as a plague to power has rendered
    strong;   86
Judge my distresses and my temper prize,
Who, though unfortunate, would still be wise.
  LYSIMACHUS. To let you know that misery
    doth sway   (*Both kneel*)
An humbler fate than yours, see at your feet 90
The lost Lysimachus. O mighty queen,
I have but this to beg: impartial stand;
And since Hephestion serves by your per-
    mission,
Disdain not me who ask your royal leave
To cast a throbbing heart before her feet. 95
  HEPHESTION. A blessing like possession of
    the princess
No services—not crowns, nor all the blood
That circles in our bodies—can deserve;
Therefore I take all helps, much more the
    king's,
And what your majesty vouchsafed to give;
Your word is passed, where all my hopes
    must hang.   101
  LYSIMACHUS. There perish, too—all words
    want sense in love;
But love and I bring such a perfect passion,[1]
So nobly pure, 'tis worthy of her eyes,
Which, without blushing, she may justly
    prize.   105
  HEPHESTION. Such arrogance, should Alex-
    ander woo,
Would lose him all the conquest he has won.

---

[1] Almost word for word from *Cassandre*, III, l, 152.

  LYSIMACHUS. Let not a conquest once be
    named by you,
Who this dispute must to my mercy own.
  SYSIGAMBIS. Rise, brave Lysimachus; He-
    phestion, rise.   110
'Tis true Hephestion first declared his love;
And 'tis as true I promised him my aid.
Your glorious king turned mighty advocate.
How noble therefore were the victory,
If we could vanquish this disordered love? 115
  HEPHESTION. 'Twill never be.
  LYSIMACHUS.   No, I will yet love on,
And hear from Alexander's mouth in what
Hephestion merits more than I.
  SYSIGAMBIS.   I grieve,
And fear the boldness which your love in-
    spires;
But lest her sight should haste your enter-
    prise,   120
'Tis just I take the object from your eyes.
    Exeunt SYSIGAMBIS, PARISATIS
  LYSIMACHUS. She's gone, and see! the day,
    as if her look
Had kindled it, is lost, now she is vanished.
  HEPHESTION. A sudden gloominess and
    horror comes
About me.
  LYSIMACHUS. Let's away to meet the
    king.   125
You know my suit.
  HEPHESTION.   Yonder Cassander comes;
He may inform us.
  LYSIMACHUS.   No, I would avoid him;
There's something in that busy face of his
That shocks my nature.
  HEPHESTION.   Where and what you please.
    Exeunt

Enter CASSANDER

CASSANDER.[2] The morning rises black, the
    low'ring sun,   130
As if the dreadful bus'ness he foreknew,
Drives heavily his sable chariot on;
The face of day now blushes scarlet deep
As if it feared the stroke which I intend,
Like that of Jupiter—lightning and thun-
    der!
The lords above are angry and talk big, 136
Or rather walk the mighty cirque like mourn-
    ers

---

[2] The monolog of Cassander here, and his speeches in Act II, scene i, are obviously reminiscent of *Julius Cæsar*, Act I, scene iii. In general, Lee follows the historians in picturing Cassander.

Clad in long clouds, the robes of thickest night,
And seem to groan for Alexander's fall;
'Tis as Cassander's soul could wish it were, 140
Which, whensoe'er it flies at lofty mischief,
Would startle fate and make all heav'n concerned.
A mad Chaldean [1] in the dead of night
Came to my bedside with a flaming torch;
And bellowing o'er me like a spirit damned,
He cried, Well had it been for Babylon 146
If cursed Cassander never had been born.

Enter THESSALUS, PHILIP, *with letters*

THESSALUS. My lord Cassander.
CASSANDER. Ha! who's there?
PHILIP. Your friends.
CASSANDER. Welcome, dear Thessalus and brother Philip.
Papers—with what contènts?
PHILIP. From Macedon
A trusty slave arrived—great Antipater [2] 151
Writes that your mother labored with you long,
Your birth was slow, and slow is all your life.
CASSANDER. He writes, Dispatch the king—
Craterus comes,
Who in my room must govern Macedon; 155
Let him not live a day—he dies tonight;
And thus my father but forestalls my purpose.
Why am I slow then? If I rode on thunder,
I must a moment have to fall from heaven
Ere I could blast the growth of this colossus.
THESSALUS. The haughty Polyperchon comes this way, 161
A malcontent on whom I lately wrought,
That for a slight affront at Susa given,
Bears Alexander most pernicious hate.
CASSANDER. So when I mocked the Persians that adored him,[3] 165
He struck me in the face, and by the hair
He swung me to his guards to be chastised;
For which, and for my father's weighty cause,
When I abandon what I have resolved,
May I again be beaten like a slave! 170

But lo! where Polyperchon comes. Now fire him
With such complaints that he may shoot to ruin.

Enter POLYPERCHON

POLYPERCHON. Sure I have found those friends dare second me;
I hear fresh murmurs as I pass along.
Yet rather than put up, I'll do't alone. 175
Did not Pausanias,[4] a youth, a stripling,
A beardless boy swelled with inglorious wrong,
For a less cause his father Philip kill?
Peace then, full heart! move like a cloud about,
And when time ripens thee to break, O shed
The stock of all thy poison on his head. 181
CASSANDER. All nations bow their heads with homage down,
And kiss the feet of this exalted man;
The name, the shout, the blast from every mouth
Is Alexander; Alexander bursts 185
Your cheeks, and with a crack so loud
It drowns the voice of heaven; like dogs ye fawn,
The earth's commanders fawn, and follow him;
Mankind starts up to hear his blasphemy;
And if this hunter of the barbarous world 190
But wind himself a god, you echo him
With universal cry.
POLYPERCHON. I echo him?
I fawn? Or fall like a fat eastern slave
And lick his feet? Boys hoot me from the palace
To haunt some cloister with my senseless walk 195
When thus the noble soul of Polyperchon
Lets go the aim of all his actions, honor.
THESSALUS. The king shall slay me, cut me up alive,
Ply me with fire and scourges, rack me worse
Than once he did Philotas,[5] ere I bow. 200
CASSANDER. Curse on thy tongue for mentioning Philotas;
I had rather thou hadst Aristander been,
And to my soul's confusion raised up hell
With all the furies brooding upon horrors,
Than brought Philotas' murder to remembrance. 205

---

[1] Chaldeans were regarded by the ancients as specially versed in magic.
[2] Antipater, the father of Cassander, was made regent of Macedonia in Alexander's absence. When, however, he tried to kill Alexander by sending poison to Alexander's camp, the king removed him and appointed Craterus in his place. Lee assumes in his hearers a knowledge of Greek history. See Quintus Curtius, X, 10, 14; Arrian, VII, 27, 1.
[3] On this incident, see Plutarch, c. lxxiv.
[4] Pausanias, a guardsman, at the instigation of Olympias, the mother of Alexander, and to avenge an insult by one of Philip's generals, assassinated Philip, the father of Alexander, in July 336 B.C.
[5] Philotas was tortured and put to death by Alexander, who suspected him of treachery. Alexander then sent to have Philotas' father, Parmenio, executed.

PHILIP. I saw him racked; a sight so dismal sad
My eyes did ne'er behold.
    CASSANDER.   So dismal! Peace!
It is unutterable. Let me stand
And think upon the tragedy you saw.
By Mars, it comes; aye, now the rack's set forth,   210
Bloody Craterus, his inveterate foe,
With pitiless Hephestion standing by;
Philotas, like an angel seized by fiends,
Is straight disrobed, a napkin [1] ties his head,
His warlike arms with shameful cords are bound,   215
And every slave can now the valiant wound.
    POLYPERCHON. Now by the soul of royal Philip fled,
I dare pronounce young Alexander, who
Would be a god, is cruel as a devil.
    CASSANDER. Oh, Polyperchon, Philip, Thessalus,   220
Did not your eyes rain blood? your spirits burst,
To see your noble fellow-soldier burn;
Yet without trembling or a tear, endure
The torments of the damned? O barbarians,
Could you stand by, and yet refuse to suffer?
Ye saw him bruised, torn, to the bones made bare;   226
His veins wide lanced, and the poor quivering flesh
With pincers from his manly bosom ripped
Till ye discovered the great heart lie panting.
    POLYPERCHON. Why killed we not the king to save Philotas?   230
    CASSANDER. Asses! fools! but asses will bray, and fools be angry.
Why stood ye then like statues? there's the case—
The horror of the sight had turned ye marble.
So the pale Trojans from their weeping walls
Saw the dear body of the godlike Hector,   235
Bloody and soiled, dragged on the famous ground,
Yet senseless stood, nor with drawn weapons ran
To save the great remains of that prodigious man.
    PHILIP. Wretched Philotas! bloody Alexander!
    THESSALUS. Soon after him the great Parmenio [2] fell,   240

[1] Cloth.
[2] See note to l. 200.

Stabbed in his orchard by the tyrant's doom.
But where's the need to mention public loss,
When each receives particular disgrace?
    POLYPERCHON. Late I remember, to a banquet called,
After Alcides' [3] goblet swift had gone   245
The giddy round, and wine had made me bold,
Stirring the spirits up to talk with kings,
I saw Craterus with Hephestion enter
In Persian robes; to Alexander's health
They largely drank; then, turning eastward, fell   250
Flat on the pavement and adored the sun.
Straight to the king they sacred reverence gave
With solemn words: O son of thund'ring Jove,
Young Ammon, live forever! then kissed the ground.
I laughed aloud and, scoffing, asked 'em why
They kissed no harder;—but the king leapt up   256
And spurned me to the earth with this reply:
Do thou!—whilst with his foot he pressed my neck
Till from my ears, my nose, and mouth, the blood
Gushed forth, and I lay foaming on the earth—   260
For which I wish this dagger in his heart.
    CASSANDER. There spoke the spirit of Calisthenes.[4]
Remember he's a man, his flesh as soft
And penetrable as a girl's. We have seen him wounded;
A stone has struck him, yet no thunderbolt:
A pebble felled this Jupiter along;   266
A sword has cut him, a javelin pierced him,
Water will drown him, fire [will] [5] burn him,
A surfeit, nay, a fit of common sickness,
Brings this immortal to the gate of death.   270
    POLYPERCHON. Why should we more delay the glorious business?
Are your hearts firm?
    PHILIP.   Hell can not be more bent
To any ruin than I to the king's.
    THESSALUS.   And I.
    POLYPERCHON. Behold my hand; and if you doubt my truth,

[3] On his mother's side Alexander considered that he was descended from Heracles (Alcides).
[4] A philosopher and historian, either put to death or imprisoned at the order of Alexander. Cf. Plutarch, c. lvi; and Arrian, iv, 14, 3ff. According to the historians Calisthenes incited a group of Alexander's pages to assassinate him, but his guilt is doubtful.
[5] Apparently fallen out to the harm of the meter.

Tear up my breast and lay my heart upon it.
  CASSANDER. Join then, O worthy, hearty,
    noble hands, 276
Fit instruments for such majestic souls;
Remember Hermolaus [1] and be hushed.
  POLYPERCHON. Still as the bosom of the
    desert night,
As fatal planets,[2] or deep, plotting friends. 280
  CASSANDER. Today he comes from Babylon
    to Susa
With proud Roxana.
               Ah! who's that?—look here.

Enter the GHOST OF KING PHILIP,[3] *shaking a truncheon at 'em; walks over the stage*

  CASSANDER. Now by the gods, or furies
    which I ne'er
Believed,—there's one of them arrived to
    shake us.
What art thou? Glaring thing, speak! What,
    the spirit 285
Of our King Philip, or of Polyphemus?
Nay, hurl thy truncheon, second it with
    thunder—
We will abide.—Thessalus, saw you nothing?
  THESSALUS. Yes, and am more amazed
    than you can be.
  PHILIP. 'Tis said that many prodigies were
    seen 290
This morn, but none so horrible as this.
  POLYPERCHON. What can you fear? Though
    the earth yawned so wide
That all the labors of the deep were seen,
And Alexander stood on th' other side,
I'd leap the burning ditch to give him death
Or sink myself forever. Pray, to the busi-
    ness. 296
  CASSANDER. As I was saying, this Roxana,
    whom,
To aggravate my hate to him, I love,
Meeting him as he came triumphant from
The Indies, kept him revelling at Susa; 300
But as I found, a deep repentance since
Turns his affections to the Queen, Statira,
To whom he swore (before he could espouse
    her)
That he would never bed Roxana more.

  POLYPERCHON. How did the Persian queen
    receive the news 305
Of his revolt?
  THESSALUS. With grief incredible!
Great Sysigambis wept, but the young queen
Fell dead amongst her maids; nor could their
    care,
With richest cordials, for an hour or more
Recover life.
  CASSANDER. Knowing how much she loved,
I hoped to turn her all into Medea;[4] 311
For when the first gust of her grief was past,
I entered, and with breath prepared did blow [5]
The dying sparks into a tow'ring flame,
Describing the new love he bears Roxana, 315
Conceiving, not unlikely, that the line
Of dead Darius in her cause might rise.
Is any panther's, lioness's rage
So furious, any torrent's fall so swift
As a wronged woman's hate? Thus far it
    helps 320
To give him troubles which perhaps may end
    him,
And set the court in universal uproar.
But see! it ripens more than I expected;
The scene works up: kill him or kill thyself,
So there be mischief any way, 'tis well. 325
Now change the vizor,[6] every one disperse,
And with a face of friendship meet the king.
                              Exeunt

Enter SYSIGAMBIS, STATIRA, PARISATIS,
    Attendants

  STATIRA. Give me a knife, a draught of
    poison, flames!
Swell, heart, break, break, thou stubborn
    thing!
Now, by the sacred fire, I'll not be held! 330
Why do ye wish me life, yet stifle me
For want of air? pray give me leave to walk.
  SYSIGAMBIS. Is there no reverence to my
    person due?
Darius would have heard me. Trust not
    rumor.
  STATIRA. No, he hates, 335
He loathes the beauties which he has enjoyed.
O, he is false; that great, that glorious man
Is tyrant 'midst of his triumphant spoils,
Is bravely false to all the gods, forsworn.

---

[1] The leader of the conspiracy of the pages. Calisthenes was his tutor. For anticipating Alexander at a boar hunt, he was deprived of his horse and whipped; and in revenge he sought to murder Alexander.
[2] Planets considered as determining human actions, as in astrology.
[3] Lee obviously has in mind the ghost of Hamlet's father. Note that Philip was also murdered.
[4] Classical type of vengeful woman, the subject of plays by Euripides and Seneca.
[5] The love of Cassander for Roxana is part of La Calprenède's story.
[6] *Vizor* in 1677 edition.

Yet who would think it? no, it can not be, 340
It can not—what, that dear, protesting man!
He that has warmed my feet with thousand sighs,
Then cooled 'em with his tears; died on my knees,
Outwept the morning with his dewy eyes,
And groaned and swore the wond'ring stars away. 345
    SYSIGAMBIS. No, 'tis impossible, believe thy mother
That knows him well.
    STATIRA.   Away, and let me die!
O! 'tis my fondness and my easy nature
That would excuse him; but I know he's false.
'Tis now the common talk, the news of the world. 350
False to Statira, false to her that loved him!
That loved him, cruel victor as he was,
And took him, bathed all o'er with Persian blood;
Kissed the dear, cruel wounds, and washed 'em o'er
And o'er in tears—then bound 'em with my hair, 355
Laid him all night upon my panting bosom,
Lulled like a child, and hushed him with my songs.
    PARISATIS. If this be true, ah, who will ever trust
A man again?
    STATIRA. A man! a man! my Parisatis,
Thus with thy hand held up, thus let me swear thee 360
By the eternal body of the sun
Whose body (O forgive the blasphemy)
I loved not half as well as the least part
Of my dear, precious, faithless Alexander;
For I will tell thee, and to warn thee of him,
Not the spring's mouth, not breath of jessamine, 366
Nor violets infant-sweets, nor opening buds
Are half so sweet as Alexander's breast;
From every pore of him a perfume falls;
He kisses softer than a southern wind, 370
Curls like a vine, and touches like a god.
    SYSIGAMBIS. When will thy spirits rest, these transports cease?
    STATIRA. Will you not give me leave to warn my sister?
As I was saying—but I told his sweetness.
Then he will talk, great gods, how he will talk! 375
Even when the joy he sighed for is possessed.

He speaks the kindest words, and looks such things,
Vows with such passion, swears with so much grace
That 'tis a kind of heaven to be deluded by him.
    PARISATIS. But what was it that you would have me swear? 380
    STATIRA. Alas, I had forgot; let me walk by
And weep awhile, and I shall soon remember.
    SYSIGAMBIS. Have patience, child, and give her liberty;
Passions like seas will have their ebbs and flows.
Yet while I see her thus, not all the losses 385
We have received since Alexander's conquest
Can touch my hardened soul; her sorrow reigns
Too fully there.
    PARISATIS.   But what if she should kill herself?
    STATIRA. Roxana then enjoys my perjured love;
Roxana clasps my monarch in her arms; 390
Dotes on my conqueror, my dear lord, my king,
Devours [his][1] lips, eats him with hungry kisses;
She grasps him all, she, the curst happy she!
By heaven, I can not bear it! 'Tis too much!
I'll die, or rid me of the burning torture. 395
I will have remedy, I will, I will,
Or go distracted; madness may throw off
The mighty load, and drown the flaming passion.
Madam, draw near with all that are in presence,
And listen to the vow which here I make. 400
    SYSIGAMBIS. Take heed, my dear Statira, and consider
What desperate love enforces you to swear.
    STATIRA. Pardon me, for I have considered well;
And here I bid adieu to all mankind.
Farewell, ye coz'ners of the easy sex, 405
And thou the greatest, falsest Alexander;
Farewell, thou most belov'd, thou faithless dear;
If I but mention him, the tears will fall.
Sure there is not a letter in his name
But is a charm to melt a woman's eyes. 410
    SYSIGAMBIS. Clear up thy griefs; thy king, thy Alexander,
Comes on to Babylon.
    STATIRA.   Why, let him come,

[1] First edition: *my*.

Joy of all eyes but the forlorn Statira's.
  SYSIGAMBIS. Wilt thou not see him?
  STATIRA.   By heaven, I never will!
That is my vow, my sacred resolution;   415
                                  (*Kneels*)
And when I break it—
  SYSIGAMBIS.   Ah, do not ruin all.
  STATIRA.—May I again be flattered and deluded,
May sudden death and horrid come instead
Of what I wished, and take me unprepared.
  SYSIGAMBIS. Still kneel, and with the same
    breath call again   420
The woeful imprecation thou hast made.
  STATIRA. No, I will publish it through all
    the court;
Then in the bowers of great Semiramis[1]
Forever lock my woes from human view.
  SYSIGAMBIS. Yet be persuaded.
  STATIRA.   Never urge me more, 425
Lest, driv'n to rage, I should my life abhor,
And in your presence put an end to all
The fast calamities that round me fall.
  PARISATIS. O angry heav'n! what have the
    guiltless done?
And where shall wretched Parisatis run? 430
  SYSIGAMBIS. Captives in war, our bodies we
    resigned;
But now made free, love does our spirits bind.
  STATIRA. When to my purposed loneness
    I retire,
Your sight I through the grates shall oft
    desire,
And after Alexander's health enquire.   435
And if this passion can not be removed,
Ask how my resolution he approved,
How much he loves, how much he is beloved;
Then when I hear that all things please him
    well,   439
Thank the good gods, and hide me in my cell.
                                  Exeunt

ACT II

SCENE I

Noise of trumpets sounding far off
The scene draws and discovers a battle of crows
or ravens in the air; an eagle *and a* dragon
meet and fight; the eagle *drops down with
all the rest of the birds, and the* dragon
flies away   Soldiers *walk off, shaking
their heads.*   The *conspirators come forward.*[2]

  CASSANDER. He comes, the fatal glory of the
    world,
The headlong Alexander with a guard
Of thronging crowns, comes on to Babylon,
Though warned, in spite of all the powers
    above
Who by these prodigies foretell his ruin.   5
  POLYPERCHON. Why all this noise because a
    king must die?
Or does heav'n fear, because he swayed the
    earth,
His ghost will war with the high thunderer?
Curse on the babbling fates that can not see
A great man tumble, but they must be talking.[3]   10
  CASSANDER. The spirit of King Philip in
    those arms
We saw him wear passed groaning through
    the court;
His dreadful eyeballs rolled their horror upwards;
He waved his arms and shook his wondrous
    head.
I've heard that at the crowing of the cock   15
Lions will roar and goblins steal away;
But this majestic air stalks steadfast on,
Spite of the morn that calls him from the
    east,
Nor minds the op'ning of the iv'ry door.
  PHILIP. 'Tis certain there was never day
    like this.   20
  CASSANDER. Late as I musing walked behind the palace,
I met a monstrous child that with his hands
Held to his face (which seemed all over eyes)
A silver bowl, and wept it full of blood;
But having spied me, like a cockatrice   25
He glared awhile; then with a shriek so shrill
As all the winds had whistled from his mouth,
He dashed me with the gore he held, and
    vanished.
  POLYPERCHON. That which befell me, though
    'twas horrid, yet
When I consider, it appears ridiculous: 30
For as I passed through by a vacant place,

---

[1] The hanging gardens of Babylon, supposed to have been erected by Queen Semiramis, were one of the seven wonders of the ancient world.

[2] Note the elaborate stage machinery required for the battle of the crows and ravens, characteristic of many plays in this period. Lee took over the details from La Calprenède.

[3] The accumulation of supernatural omens is reminiscent of *Julius Cæsar* and *Macbeth*. Note the verbal echoes of Shakespeare.

I met two women very old and ugly
That wrung their hands, and howled, and
    beat their breasts,
And cried out, Poison! When I asked the
    cause,
They took me by the ears, and with strange
    force   35
Held me to earth, then laughed, and disappeared.
    CASSANDER. O how I love destruction with
    a method
Which none discern but those that weave the
    plot;
Like silkworms we are hid in our own weft,
But we shall burst at last through all the
    strings;   40
And when time calls, come forth in a new form,
Not insects to be trod, but dragons winged.
    THESSALUS. The face of all the court is
    strangely altered;
There's not a Persian I can meet, but stares
As if he were distracted. Oxyartes,[1]   45
Statira's uncle, openly declaimed
Against the perjury of Alexander.
    PHILIP. Others, more fearful, are removed
    to Susa,
Dreading Roxana's rage, who comes i'th' rear
To Babylon.
    CASSANDER. It glads my rising soul   50
That we shall see him racked before he dies.
I know he loves Statira more than life,
And on a crowd of kings in triumph borne
Comes, big with expectation, to enjoy her.
But when he hears the oaths which she has
    ta'en,   55
Her last adieu made public to the world,
Her vowed divorce, how will remorse consume
    him,
Prey like a bird of hell upon his liver!
    POLYPERCHON. To balk his longings and
    delude his lust
Is more than death, 'tis earnest for damnation.   60
    CASSANDER. Then comes Roxana, who must
    help our party;
I know her jealous, bloody, and ambitious.
Sure 'twas the likeness of her heart to mine
And sympathy of natures caused me love her;
'Tis fixed, I must enjoy her, and no way   65
So proper as to make her guilty first.
    POLYPERCHON. To see two rival queens of
    different humors
With a variety of torments vex him!

[1] A Bactrian prince, the father of Roxana.

Enter LYSIMACHUS *and* HEPHESTION

    CASSANDER. Of that anon. But see Lysimachus
And the young favorite. Sort, sort yourselves,[2]   70
And like to other mercenary souls
Adore this mortal god that soon must bleed.
    LYSIMACHUS. Here I will wait the king's
    approach, and stand
His utmost anger if he do me wrong.
    HEPHESTION. That can not be from power
    so absolute   75
And high as his.
    LYSIMACHUS. Well, you and I have done.
    POLYPERCHON. How the court thickens!
        (*Trumpets sound*)
    CASSANDER. Nothing to what it will. Does
    he not come
To hear a thousand thousand embassies
Which from all parts to Babylon are brought
As if the parliament of the world   81
Had met, and he came on, a god, to give
The infinite assembly glorious audience.

Enter CLYTUS, ARISTANDER *in his robes, with a wand*

    ARISTANDER. Haste, reverend Clytus, haste
    and stop the king.
    CLYTUS. He is already entered. Then the
    press   85
Of princes that attend so thick about him
Keep all that would approach, at certain distance.
    ARISTANDER. Though he were hemmed with
    deities, I'd speak to him,
And turn him back from this highway to death.
    CLYTUS. Here place yourself within his
    trumpets' sound.   90
Lo, the Chaldean priests appear; behold
The sacred fire; Nearchus[3] and Eumenes
With their white wands, and dressed in eastern robes
To soothe the king, who loves the Persian mode.
But see, the master of the world appears.   95

Enter ALEXANDER; *all kneel but* CLYTUS

    HEPHESTION. O son of Jupiter, live forever!
    ALEXANDER. Rise, all; and thou, my second
    self, my love,

[2] Adapt yourselves to the immediate circumstances; i.e., hide your feelings. Cf. Shakespeare: "sort thy heart to patience."

[3] Nearchus does not appear among the *dramatis personæ*.

O my Hephestion, raise thee from the earth
Up to my breast, and hide thee in my heart.
Art thou grown cold? Why hang thine arms
　at distance? 100
Hug me, or by heaven thou lov'st me not.
　HEPHESTION. Not love, my lord! Break not
　　the heart you framed
And molded up to such an excellence,
Then stamped on it your own immortal image!
Not love the king! such is not woman's love;
So fond a friendship, such a sacred flame 106
As I must doubt to find in breasts above!
　ALEXANDER. Thou dost, thou lov'st me,
　　crown of all my wars,
Thou dearer to me than my groves of laurel!
I know thou lov'st thy Alexander more 110
Than Clytus does the king. No tears, Hephestion,
I read thy passion in thy manly eyes,
And glory in those planets of my life
Above the rival lights that shine in heaven.
　LYSIMACHUS. I see that death must wait me,
　　yet I'll on. 115
　ALEXANDER. I'll tell thee, friend, and mark
　　it, all ye princes,
Though never mortal man arrived to such
A height as I; yet I would forfeit all,
Cast all my purples and my conquered crowns,
And die to save this darling of my soul. 120
Give me thy hand, share all my sceptres while
I live; and when my hour of fate is come,
I leave thee what thou meritest more than I,
　the world.
　LYSIMACHUS. Dread sir, I cast me at your
　　royal feet.
　ALEXANDER. What, my Lysimachus, whose
　　veins are rich 125
With our illustrious blood? My kinsman, rise.
Is not that Clytus?
　CLYTUS.　　　　Your old faithful soldier.
　ALEXANDER. Come to my hands; thus
　　double arm the King;
And now methinks I stand like the dread god
Who, while his priests and I quaffed sacred
　blood, 130
Acknowledged me his son. My lightning thou,
And thou my mighty thunder.—I have seen
Thy glittering sword outfly celestial fire;
And when I cried, Be gone and execute,
I've seen him run swifter than starting hinds,
Nor bent the tender grass beneath his feet; 136
Swifter than shadows fleeting o'er the fields
Nay, even the winds with all their stock of
　wings

Have puffed behind, as wanting breath to
　reach him. 139
　LYSIMACHUS. But if your majesty—
　CLYTUS.　　　　Who would not lose
The last dear drop of blood for such a king?
　ALEXANDER. Witness, my elder brothers of
　　the sky,
How much I love a soldier.—O my Clytus,
Was it not when we passed the Granicus [1]
Thou didst preserve me from unequal force?
It was when Spithridates and Rhesaces 146
Fell both upon me with two dreadful strokes
And clove my tempered helmet quite in
　sunder,
Then I remember, then thou didst me service;
I think my thunder split them to the navel.
　CLYTUS. To your great self you owe that
　　victory, 151
And sure your arms did never gain a nobler.
　ALEXANDER. By heaven, they never did,
　　for well thou know'st,
And I am prouder to have passed that stream
Than that I drove a million o'er the plain; 155
Can none remember? Yes, I know all must:
When glory like the dazzling eagle stood
Perched on my beaver in the Granic flood;
When Fortune's self my standard trembling
　bore,
And the pale fates stood frighted on the
　shore; 160
When the Immortals on the billows rode,
And I myself appeared the leading god.
　ARISTANDER. But all the honors which your
　　youth has won
Are lost unless you fly from Babylon! [2]
Haste with your chiefs, to Susa take your
　way, 165
Fly for your life; destructive is your stay.
This morning having viewed the angry sky,
And marked the prodigies that threatened
　high,
To our bright god I did for succor fly,
But oh—
　ALEXANDER. What fears thy reverend
　　bosom shake? 170
Or dost thou from some dream of horror wake?
If so, come grasp me with thy shaking hand,
Or fall behind while I the danger stand.

---

[1] The account of Alexander's battle at the river Granicus in which Clytus saved Alexander's life, is historical. See Plutarch, c. xvi.

[2] Alexander was actually warned by a soothsayer on entering Babylon, but Lee depends on La Calprenède for the episode.

ARISTANDER. To Orosmades' cave [1] I did
    repair   174
Where I atoned the dreadful god with prayer;
But as I prayed, I heard long groans within,
And shrieks as of the damned that howl for sin.
I knew the omen, and I feared to stay,
But prostrate on the trembling pavement lay.
When he bodes happiness, he answers mild;
'Twas so of old, and the great image smiled;
But now in abrupt thunder he replied, 182
Loud as rent rocks or roaring seas he cried:
All empires, crowns, glory of Babylon,
Whose head stands wrapped in clouds, must tumble down.   185
    ALEXANDER. If Babylon must fall, what is't to me?
Or can I help immutable decree?
Down then, vast frame, with all thy lofty towers,
Since 'tis so ordered by almighty powers;
Pressed by the Fates, unloose your golden bars,   190
'Tis great to fall the envy of the stars.

    Enter PERDICCAS, MELEAGER

MELEAGER. O horror!
PERDICCAS.   Dire portents!
ALEXANDER.   Out with 'em then;
What, are you ghosts, ye empty shapes of men?
If so, the mysteries of hell unfold,
Be all the scrolls of destiny unrolled, 195
Open the brazen leaves, and let it come;
Point with a thunder-bolt your monarch's doom.
    PERDICCAS. As Meleager and myself in field
Your Persian horse about the army wheeled,
We heard a noise as of a rushing wind, 200
And a thick storm the eye of day did blind;
A croaking noise resounded through the air;
We looked, and saw big ravens battling there;
Each bird of night appeared himself a cloud,
They met and fought, and their wounds rained black blood.   205
    MELEAGER. All, as for honor, did their lives expose;
Their talons clashed, and beaks gave mighty blows,
Whilst dreadful sounds did our scared sense assail
As of small thunder or huge Scythian hail. [2]
    PERDICCAS. Our augurs shook when, with a horrid groan,   210
We thought that all the clouds had tumbled down.
Soldiers and chiefs, who can the wonder tell,
Struck to the ground, promiscuously fell; [3]
While the dark birds, each pond'rous as a shield,
For fifty furlongs hid the fatal field.   215
    ALEXANDER. Be witness for me, all ye powers divine,
If ye be angry, 'tis no fault of mine;
Therefore let furies face me with a band
From hell, my virtue [4] shall not make a stand;
Though all the curtains of the sky be drawn,
And the stars wink, young Ammon shall go on.   221
While my Statira shines, I can not stray;
Love lifts his torch to light me on my way,
And her bright eyes create another day.
    LYSIMACHUS. Ere you remove, be pleased, dread sir, to hear   225
A prince allied to you by blood.
    ALEXANDER.   Speak quickly.
    LYSIMACHUS. For all that I have done for you in war,
I beg the Princess Parisatis.
    ALEXANDER.   Ha—
Is not my word already passed? Hephestion,
I know he hates thee, but he shall not have her;   230
We heard of this before.—Lysimachus,
I here command you nourish no design
To prejudice my person in the man
I love and will prefer to all the world.
    LYSIMACHUS.[5] I never failed to obey your majesty   235
Whilst you commanded what was in my power;
Nor could Hephestion fly more swift to serve
When you commanded us to storm a town
Or fetch a standard from the enemy;
But when you charge me not to love the princess,   240

---

[1] Ormazd, the equivalent of Zeus in Persian mythology.

[2] In the classical poets Scythia is typically a wild and wintry country, and Scythian hail is often referred to.

[3] The sense is not obvious. The passage seems to mean: Who can tell of a wonder like this when, struck to the ground, even soldiers and chiefs fell indiscriminately?

[4] Power, excellence, with no connotation of moral good. Cf. Italian *virtù*.

[5] Lysimachus' speech is taken over almost word for word from La Calprenède, *Cassandre*, III, 2, 161.

I must confess I disobey you, as
I would the gods themselves, should they
    command.
  ALEXANDER. You should, brave sir, hear
    me, and then be dumb:
When by my orders curst Calisthenes
Was as a traitor doomed to live in torments,
Your pity sped him in despite of me.   246
Think not I have forgot your insolence;
No, though I pardoned it; yet if again
Thou dar'st to cross me with another crime,
The bolts of fury shall be doubled on thee; 250
In the mean time think not of Parisatis,
For if thou dost, by Jupiter Ammon,
By my own head, and by King Philip's soul,
I'll not respect that blood of mine thou shar'st,
But use thee as the vilest Macedonian.   255
  LYSIMACHUS. I doubted not at first but I
    should meet
Your indignation, yet my soul's resolved,
And I shall never quit so brave a prize
While I can draw a bow or lift a sword.
  ALEXANDER. Against my life? Ah, was it
    so? How now?   260
'Tis said that I am rash, of hasty humor;
But I appeal to the immortal gods
If ever petty, poor, provincial lord
Had temper like to mine. My slave, whom I
Could tread to clay, dares utter bloody
    threats.   265
  CLYTUS. Contain yourself, dread sir; the
    noble prince,
I see it in his countenance, would die
To justify his truth, but love makes many
    faults.
  LYSIMACHUS. I meant his minion there
    should feel my arm;
Love asks his blood, nor shall he live to
    laugh   270
At my destruction.
  ALEXANDER.   Now be thy own judge:
I pardon thee for my old Clytus' sake,
But if once more thou mention thy rash love,
Or dar'st attempt Hephestion's precious life,
I'll pour such storms of indignation on thee,
Phylotas' rack, Calisthenes' disgrace   276
Shall be delight to what thou shalt endure.

  Enter SYSIGAMBIS, PARISATIS

  HEPHESTION. My lord, the queen comes to
    congratulate
Your safe arrival.
  ALEXANDER.   O thou best of women,
Source of my joy, blest parent of my love! 280

  SYSIGAMBIS. Permit me kneel and give those
    adorations
Which from the Persian family are due:
Have you not raised us from our ruins, high?
And when no hand could help, nor any eye
Behold us with a tear, yours pitied me; 285
You, like a god, snatched us from sorrow's
    gulf,
Fixed us in thrones above our former state.
  PARISATIS. Which, when a soul forgets
    (advanced so nobly),
May it be drowned in deeper misery.
  ALEXANDER. To meet me thus was gener-
    ously done,   290
But still there wants to crown my happiness,
Life of my empire, treasure of my soul,
My dear Statira. O that heavenly beam,
Warmth of my brain and firer of my heart,
Had she but shot to see me, had she met
    me,   295
By this time I had been amongst the gods,
If any ecstasy can make a height,
Or any rapture hurl us to the heavens.
  CLYTUS. [*Aside*] Now who shall dare to tell
    him the queen's vow?
  ALEXANDER. How fares my love? ha—
    neither answer me!   300
Ye raise my wonder. Darkness overwhelm me,
If royal Sysigambis does not weep!
Trembling and horror pierce me cold as ice.
Is she not well? what none, none answer me?
Or is it worse? Keep down, ye rising sighs, 305
And murmur in the hollow of my breast;
Run to my heart and gather more sad wind
That, when the voice of fate shall call you
    forth,
Ye may at one rush from the seat of life
Blow the blood out, and burst like a bladder.
  HEPHESTION. I would relate it, but my
    courage fails me.   311
  ALEXANDER. If she be dead—That "if's"
    impossible!
And let none here affirm it for his soul,
For he that dares but think so damned a lie,
I'll have his body straight empaled before me,
And glut my eyes upon his bleeding entrails.
  CASSANDER. (*Aside*) How will this engine
    of unruly passion   317
Roar when we have rammed him to the mouth
    with poison?
  ALEXANDER. Why stand you all as you
    were rooted here
Like the senseless trees, while to the stupid
    grove   320

I like a wounded lion groan my griefs,
And none will answer—what, not my Hephestion?
If thou hast any love for Alexander,
If ever I obliged thee by my care
When my quick sight has watched thee in the war, 325
Or if to see thee bleed I sent forth cries
And like a mother washed thee with my tears—
If this be true, if I deserve thy love,
Ease me, and tell the cause of my disaster.

HEPHESTION. Your mourning queen (which I had told before, 330
Had you been calm) has no disease but sorrow,
Which was occasioned first by jealous pangs;
She heard (for what can 'scape a watchful lover?)
That you at Susa, breaking all your vows,
Relapsed and, conquered by Roxana's charms,
Gave up yourself, devoted to her arms. 336

ALEXANDER. I know that subtle creature in my riot,
My reason gone, seduced me to her bed;
But when I waked, I shook the Circe off,
Though that enchantress held me by the arm, 340
And wept, and gazed with all the force of love;
Nor grieved I less for that which I had done
Than when at Thais' suit,[1] enraged with wine,
I set the famed Persepolis on fire.

HEPHESTION. Your queen Statira took it so to heart 345
That in the agony of love she swore
Never to see your majesty again;
With dreadful imprecations she confirmed
Her oath, and I much fear that she will keep it.

ALEXANDER. Ha! did she swear? did that sweet creature swear? 350
I'll not believe it! No, she is all softness,
All melting, mild, and calm as a rocked infant,
Nor can you wake her into cries. By heaven,
She is the child of love, and she was born in smiles.

PARISATIS. I and my weeping mother heard her swear. 355

SYSIGAMBIS. And with such fierceness she did aggravate
The foulness of your fault that I could wish
Your majesty would blot her from your breast.

[1] According to legend, Thais, a celebrated Athenian courtesan, urged Alexander during a festival to set fire to Persepolis. See Dryden's poem, *Alexander's Feast*.

ALEXANDER. Blot her? forget her? hurl her from my bosom,
Forever lose that star that gilds my life, 360
Guide of my days, and goddess of my nights!
No, she shall stay with me in spite of vows;
My soul and body both are twisted with her.
The god of love empties his golden quiver,
Shoots every grain of her into my heart; 365
She is all mine; by heaven, I feel her here,
Panting and warm, the dearest, O Statira!

SYSIGAMBIS. Have patience, son, and trust to heaven and me.
If my authority, or the remembrance
Of dead Darius, or her mother's soul 370
Can work upon her, she again is yours.

ALEXANDER. O mother, help me, help your wounded son,
And move the soul of my offended dear;
But fly, haste, ere the sad procession's made
Spend not a thought in a reply—begone, 375
If you would have me live—and, Parisatis,
Hang thou about her knees, wash 'em with tears;
Nay, haste, the breath of gods and eloquence
Of angels go along with you—O, my heart!

Exeunt SYSIGAMBIS *and* PARISATIS

LYSIMACHUS. Now let your majesty, who feel[s] the torments 380
And sharpest pangs of love, encourage mine.

ALEXANDER. Ha—

CLYTUS. Are you a madman? Is this a time?

LYSIMACHUS. Yes; for I see he can not be unjust to me,
Lest something worse befall himself.

ALEXANDER. Why dost thou tempt me thus to thy undoing? 385
Death thou shouldst have, were it not courted so;
But know—to thy confusion—that my word,
Like destiny, admits not a reverse;
Therefore in chains thou shalt behold the nuptials
Of my Hephestion.—Guards, take him prisoner. 390

LYSIMACHUS. I shall not easily resign my sword
Till I have dyed it in my rival's blood.

ALEXANDER. I charge you, kill him not, take him alive;
The dignity of kings is now concerned,
And I will find a way to tame this beast. 395

CLYTUS. Kneel, for I see the lightning in his eyes.

LYSIMACHUS. I neither hope nor ask a
    pardon of him;
But if he should restore my sword, I would
With a new violence run against my rival.
    ALEXANDER. Sure we at last shall conquer
        this fierce lion—   400
Hence from my sight, and bear him to a
    dungeon.
Perdiccas, give this lion to a lion;
None speak for him—fly, stop his mouth,
    away!
    CLYTUS. The king's extremely moved.
    EUMENES.   I dare not speak.
    CLYTUS. This comes of love and women; 'tis
        all madness   405
Yet were I heated now with wine, I should
Be preaching to the king for this rash fool.
    ALEXANDER. Come hither, Clytus, and my
        dear Hephestion;
Lend me your arms; help, for I'm sick o'th'
    sudden.
I fear, betwixt Statira's cruel love   410
And fond Roxana's arts, your king will fall.
    CLYTUS. Better the Persian race were all
        undone.
    HEPHESTION. Look up, my lord, and bend
        not thus your head
As if you'd leave the empire of the world
Which you with toil have won.
    ALEXANDER.   Would I had not,
There's no true joy in such unwieldy for-
    tune.   416
Eternal gazers lasting troubles make;
All find my spots, but few my brightness take.
Stand off, and give me air—
Why was I born a prince, proclaimed a god,
Yet have no liberty to look abroad?   421
Thus palaces in prospect bar the eye
Which, pleased and free, would o'er the
    cottage fly,
O'er flow'ry lands to the gay, distant sky.
Farewell, then, empire and the racks of love;
By all the gods, I will to wilds remove;   426
Stretched like a sylvan god, on grass lie down,
And quite forget that e'er I wore a crown.

ACT III

[SCENE I]

Enter EUMENES, PHILIP, THESSALUS,
    PERDICCAS, LYSIMACHUS, *Guards.*

    EUMENES. Farewell, brave spirit; when you
        come above
Commend us to Philotas and the rest

Of our great friends.
    THESSALUS.   Perdiccas, you are grown
In trust, be thankful for your noble office.
    PERDICCAS. As noble as you sentence me,
        I'd give   5
This arm that Thessalus were so employed.
    LYSIMACHUS. Cease these untimely jars;
        farewell to all,
Fight for the king as I have done, and then
You may be worthy of a death like mine.—
    Lead on.

Enter PARISATIS

    PARISATIS. Ah, my Lysimachus, where are
        you going?   10
Whither? To be devoured? O barbarous
    prince!
Could you expose your life to the king's rage
And yet remember mine was tied to yours?
    LYSIMACHUS. The gods preserve you ever
        from the ills
That threaten me. Live, madam, to enjoy 15
A nobler fortune, and forget this wretch.
I ne'er had worth, nor is it possible
That all the blood which I shall lose this
    day
Should merit this rich sorrow from your
    eyes.
    PARISATIS. The king, I know, is bent to thy
        destruction;   20
Now by command they forced me from his
    knees.
But take this satisfaction in thy death:
No power, command, my mother's, sister's
    tears
Shall cause me to survive thy cruel loss.
    LYSIMACHUS. Live, princess, live; howe'er
        the king disdains me,   25
Perhaps unarmed, and fighting for your
    sake,
I may perform what shall amaze the world,
And force him yet to give you to my arms.
Away, Perdiccas.—Dear Eumenes, take
The princess to your charge.
                Exeunt [PERDICCAS, LYSIMACHUS,
                                         Guards]
    EUMENES.   O cruelty!   30
    PARISATIS. Lead me, Eumenes, lead me
        from the light,
Where I may wait till I his ruin hear,
Then free my soul to meet him in the air.
                Exeunt PARISATIS *and* EUMENES
    PHILIP. See where the jealous, proud Rox-
        ana comes,

A haughty vengeance gathers up her brow.　35
 THESSALUS. Peace, they have raised her to their ends. Observe.

Enter ROXANA, CASSANDER, POLYPERCHON

 ROXANA. O you have ruined me, I shall be mad;
Said you, so passionate? Is't possible?
So kind to her, and so unkind to me?
 CASSANDER. More than your utmost fancy can invent.　40
He swoonèd thrice at hearing of her vow,
And when our care as oft had brought back life,
He drew his sword and offered at his breast.
 POLYPERCHON. Then raised at you with such unheard of curses—
 ROXANA. Away! Begone, and give a whirlwind room,　45
Or I will blow you up like dust! Avaunt!
Madness but meanly represents my toil.
Roxana and Statira, they are names
That must forever jar; eternal discord,
Fury, revenge, disdain, and indignation　50
Tear my swoll'n breast, make way for fire and tempest.
My brain is burst, debate and reason quenched,
The storm is up, and my hot, bleeding heart
Splits with the rack while passions, like the winds,
Rise up to heaven and put out all the stars.　55
What saving hand, O what almighty arm
Can raise me, sinking?
 CASSANDER.　Let your own arm save you.
'Tis in your power; your beauty is almighty.
Let all the stars go out, your eyes can light 'em.
Wake, then, bright planet that should rule the world,　60
Wake like the moon from your too long eclipse,
And we with all the instruments of war,
Trumpets and drums, will help your glorious labor.
 POLYPERCHON. Put us to act, and with a violence
That fits the spirit of a most wronged woman!
Let not Medea's dreadful vengeance stand　66
A pattern more, but draw your own so fierce,
It may forever be original.
 CASSANDER. Touch not, but dash with strokes so bravely bold,

Till you have formed a face of so much horror
That gaping furies may run frighted back;　71
That envy may devour herself for madness,
And sad Medusa's head be turned to stone.[1]
 ROXANA. Yes, we will have revenge, my instruments,
For there is nothing you have said of me　75
But comes far short, wanting of what I am.
When in my nonage I at Zogdia[2] lived,
Amongst my she companions I would reign;
Drew 'em from idleness and little arts
Of coining looks and laying snares for lovers,
Broke all their glasses and their tires[3] tore,　81
Taught 'em like Amazons to ride and chase
Wild beasts in deserts, and to master men.
 CASSANDER. Her looks, her words, her ev'ry motion fires me.
 ROXANA. But when I heard of Alexander's conquests;　85
How with a handful he had millions slain,
Spoiled all the east, their queens his captives made,
Yet with what chastity, and godlike temper,
He saw their beauties and with pity bowed,
Methought I hung upon my father's lips　90
And wished him tell the wondrous tale again;
Left all my sport, the woman now returned,
And sighs uncalled would from my bosom fly;
And all the night, as my Adraste[4] told me,
In slumbers groaned, and murmured, Alexander.　95
 CASSANDER. [*Aside*] Curse on the name! But I will soon remove
That bar of my ambition and my love.
 ROXANA. At last to Zogdia this triumpher came,
And, covered o'er with laurels, forced our city.
At night I by my father's order stood　100
With fifty virgins waiting at a banquet.
But oh! how glad I was to hear his court,
To feel the pressure of his glowing hand,
And taste the dear, the false-protesting lips!

---

[1] The sense of the lines is not obvious. It seems to be: Do not merely touch up or sketch a picture imitated from the classical instance of Medea, but with brave originality strike out a new image of horror by your actions, an image so full of terror it will turn even Medusa's head to stone.
[2] Usually Sogdia, the capital of Bactria, which Alexander captured in 327 B.C. Cf. ll. 98–101 below.
[3] Mirrors; attires: i.e., clothing.
[4] Roxana's nurse.

CASSANDER. Wormwood and hemlock
  henceforth grow about 'em! 105
ROXANA. Gods! that a man should be so
  great and base!
What said he not, when in the bridal bed
He clasped my yielding body in his arms,
When with his fiery lips devouring mine,
And molding with his hand my throbbing
  breast, 110
He swore the globe of heaven and earth were
  vile
To those rich worlds, and talked, and kissed,
  and loved,
And made me shame the morning with my
  blushes.
CASSANDER. Yet after this prove false!
POLYPERCHON.   Horrid perjury!
CASSANDER. Not to be matched!
POLYPERCHON.   O you must find revenge!
CASSANDER. A person of your spirits be
  thus slighted! 116
For whose desire all earth should be too
  little!
ROXANA. And shall the daughter of Darius
  hold him?
That puny girl, that ape of my ambition?
That cried for milk when I was nursed in
  blood! 120
Shall she, made up of wat'ry element,
A cloud, shall she embrace my proper god
While I am cast like lightning at his hand?
No, I must scorn to prey on common things;
Though hurled to earth by this disdainful
  Jove, 125
I will rebound to my own orb of fire,[1]
And with the wrack of all the heav'ns ex-
  pire.
CASSANDER. Now you appear yourself.
  'Tis noble anger.
ROXANA. May the illustrious blood that
  fills my womb
And ripens to be perfect godhead born, 130
Come forth a fury; may Barsina's[2] bastard
Tread it to hell and rule as sovereign lord
When I permit Statira to enjoy
Roxana's right, and strive not to destroy.

[1] In some versions of the Ptolemaic system, the earth is supposed to be surrounded by a sphere of air outside of which is a sphere of fire.
[2] The reference is ambiguous. It may be either Barsine, who was the daughter of Artabazus and the wife of Memnon of Rhodes, who bore a son, Heracles, to Alexander; or it may refer to Statira herself, who was sometimes called Barsine. This is the only reference to the name in the play.

Enter SYSIGAMBIS, STATIRA, *in mourning*

CASSANDER. Behold her going to fulfil her
  vow; 135
Old Sysigambis, whom the king engaged,
Resists and awes her with authority.
ROXANA. 'Twas rashly vowed, indeed, and
  I should pity her.
SYSIGAMBIS. O my Statira, how has passion
  changed thee!
Think if thou drive the king to such ex-
  tremes, 140
What in his fury he may not denounce
Against the poor remains of lost Darius?
STATIRA. I know, I know he will be kind to
  you,
And to my mourning sister for my sake; 144
And tell him how with my departing breath
I railed not, but spoke kindly of his per-
  son,
Nay, wept to think of our divided loves,
And, sobbing, sent at last forgiveness to
  him.
ROXANA. Grant, heav'n, some ease to this
  distracted wretch!
Let her not linger out a life in torments; 150
Be these her last words, and at once dispatch
  her.
SYSIGAMBIS. No, by the everlasting fire I
  swear,
By my Darius' soul, I never more
Will dare to look on Alexander's face,
If you refuse to see him. 155
ROXANA. Curse on that cunning tongue, I
  fear her now.
CASSANDER. No, she's resolved.
STATIRA.   I cast me at your feet
To bathe 'em with my tears; or, if you
  please,
I'll let out life and wash 'em with my
  blood,
But still conjure you not to rack my soul, 160
Nor hurry my wild thoughts to perfect mad-
  ness.
Should now Darius' awful ghost appear,
And my pale mother stand beseeching by,
I would persist to death and keep my vow.
ROXANA. She shows a certain bravery of
  soul 165
Which I should praise in any but my rival.
SYSIGAMBIS. Die, then, rebellious wretch,
  thou art not now
That soft beloved, nor durst thou share my
  blood.

Go hide thy baseness in thy lovely grot,
Ruin thy mother and thy royal house, 170
Pernicious creature! shed the innocent
Blood, and sacrifice to the king's wrath
The lives of all thy people. Fly, begone,
And hide thee where bright virtue never shone.
The day will shun thee, nay the stars that view 175
Mischiefs and murders, deeds to thee not new,
Will start at this.—Go, go, thy crimes deplore,
And never think of Sysigambis more.
[*Exit* Sysigambis]
Roxana. [*Coming forward*] Madam, I hope you will a queen forgive:
Roxana weeps to see Statira grieve. 180
How noble is the brave resolve you make
To quit the world for Alexander's sake!
Vast is your mind, you dare thus greatly die,
And yield the king to one so mean as I.
'Tis a revenge will make the victor smart, 185
And much I fear your death will break his heart.
Statira. You counterfeit a fear and know too well
How much your eyes all beauties else excel.
Roxana, who, though not a princess born,
In chains could make the mighty victor mourn, 190
Forgetting pow'r when wine had made him warm
And senseless, yet even then you knew to charm,
Preserve him by those arts that can not fail,
While I the loss of what I loved bewail.
Roxana. I hope your majesty will give me leave 195
To wait you to the grove where you would grieve,
Where like the turtle you the loss will moan
Of that dear mate, and murmur all alone.
Statira. No, proud triumpher o'er my falling state,
Thou shalt not stay to fill me with my fate. 200
Go to the conquest which your wiles may boast,
And tell the world you left Statira lost.
Go seize my faithless Alexander's hand
(Both hand and heart were once at my command),
Grasp his loved neck, die on his fragrant breast, 205
Love him like me, which can not be expressed—
He must be happy, and you more than blest—
While I in darkness hide me from the day,
That with my mind I may his form survey,
And think so long till I think life away. 210
Roxana. No, sickly virtue, no,
Thou shalt not think, nor thy love's loss bemoan,
Nor shall past pleasures through thy fancy run;
That were to make thee blest as I can be;
But thy no-thought I must, I will decree: 215
As thus, I'll torture thee till thou art mad,
And then no thought to purpose can be had.
Statira. How frail, how cowardly is woman's mind!
We shriek at thunder, dread the rustling wind,
And glitt'ring swords the brightest eyes will blind. 220
Yet when strong jealousy enflames the soul,
The weak will roar, and calms to tempests roll.
Rival, take heed, and tempt me not too far;
My blood may boil, and blushes show a war.
Roxana. When you retire to your romantic cell, 225
I'll make thy solitary mansion hell;
Thou shalt not rest by day nor sleep by night,
But still Roxana shall thy spirit fright.
Wanton in dreams, if thou dar'st dream of bliss,
Thy roving ghost may think to steal a kiss; 230
But when to his sought bed thy wand'ring air
Shall for the happiness it wished, repair,
How will it groan to find thy rival there?
How ghastly wilt thou look, when thou shalt see
Through the drawn curtain that great man and me, 235
Wearied with laughing joys, shot to the soul,
While thou shalt, grinning, stand and gnash thy teeth and howl!
Statira. O barb'rous rage! my tears I can not keep,
But my full eyes in spite of me will weep.

Roxana. The king and I in various pictures
  drawn, 240
Clasping each other, shaded o'er with lawn,
Shall be the daily presents I will send
To help thy sorrow to her journey's end.
And when we hear at last thy hour draws
  nigh,
My Alexander—my dear love—and I 245
Will come and hasten on thy ling'ring fates,
And smile and kiss thy soul out through the
  grates.
Statira. 'Tis well—I thank thee, thou hast
  waked a rage
Whose boiling now no temper can assuage.
I meet thy tides of jealousy with more, 250
Dare thee to [duel],[1] and dash thee o'er and
  o'er.
Roxana. What would you dare?
  Statira. Whatever you dare do.
My warring thoughts the bloodiest tracts
  pursue;
I am by love a fury made, like you.
Kill or be killed, thus acted by despair. 255
  Roxana. Sure, the disdained Statira does
  not dare?
  Statira. Yes, tow'ring, proud Roxana, but
  I dare.
  Roxana. I tow'r indeed o'er thee;
Like a fair wood, the shade of kings I stand
While thou, sick weed, dost but infect the
  land. 260
  Statira. No, like an ivy I will curl thee
  round,
Thy sapless trunk of all its pride confound,
Then, dry and withered, bend thee to the
  ground.
What Sysigambis' threats, objected fears,
My sister's sighs, and Alexander's tears 265
Could not effect, thy rival rage has done;
My soul, whose start at breach of oaths be-
  gun,
Shall to thy ruin, violated, run.
I'll see the king, in spite of all I swore,
Though curst, that thou may'st never see him
  more. 270

Enter Perdiccas, Alexander, Sysigambis,
  Attendants, &c.

  Perdiccas. Madam, your royal mother and
  the king.
  Alexander. O my Statira! O my angry
  dear!

[1] *Dwell* in 1677 edition.

Turn thine eyes on me, I would talk to them.
What shall I say to work upon thy soul?
Where shall I throw me? Whither shall I
  fall? 275
  Statira. For me you shall not fall.
  Alexander. For thee I will;
Before thy feet I'll have a grave dug up,
And perish quick, be buried straight alive;
Give but, as the earth grows heavy on me,
A tender look, and a relenting word; 280
Say but 'twas pity that so great a man,
Who had ten thousand deaths in battle
  'scaped,
For one poor fault so early should remove,
And fall a martyr to the god of love.
  Roxana. Is then Roxana's love and life so
  poor 285
That for another you can choose to die
Rather than live for her? What have I done?
How am I altered since at Susa last
You swore, and sealed it with a thousand
  kisses, 289
Rather than lose Roxanna's smallest charm,
You would forego the conquest of the world?
  Alexander. Madam, you best can tell
  what magic drew
Me to your charms, but let it not be told
For your own sake; take, take that conquered
  world,
Dispose of crowns and scepters as you please;
Let me but have the freedom of an hour 296
To make account with this wronged innocence.
  Statira. You know, my lord, you did com-
  mit a fault;
I ask but this: repeat your crime no more.
  Alexander. O never, never!
  Roxana. Am I rejected then?
  Alexander. Exhaust my treasures, 301
Take all the spoils of the far conquered Indies,
But for the ease of my afflicted soul,
Go where I never may behold thee more.
  Roxana. Yes, I will go, ungrateful as thou
  art, 305
Bane to my life, thou torment of my days,
Thou murd'rer of the world! For as thy sword
Hath cut the lives of thousand thousand men,
So will thy tongue undo all womankind.
But I'll be gone; this last disdain has cured
  me, 310
And I am now grown so indifferent,
I could behold you kiss without a pang,
Nay, take a torch and light you to your bed.
But do not trust me, no, for, if you do,
By all the furies and the flames of love. 315

By love, which is the hottest burning hell,
I'll set you both on fire to blaze forever. *Exit*
   STATIRA. O Alexander, is it possible? Good gods,
That guilt can show so lovely!—Yet I pardon,
Forgive thee all, by thy dear life, I do.   320
   ALEXANDER. Ha, pardon! Saidst thou, pardon me?
   SYSIGAMBIS. Now all my mother's blessings fall about thee,
My best, my most belov'd, my own Statira!
   ALEXANDER. Is it then true that thou hast pardoned me?
And is it given me to touch thy hand   325
And fold thy body in my longing arms?
To gaze upon thy eyes, my happier stars,
To taste thy lip and thy dear, balmy breath,
While ev'ry sigh comes forth so fraught with sweets,
'Tis incense to be offered to a god!   330
   STATIRA. Yes, dear impostor, 'tis most true that I
Have pardoned thee; and 'tis as true that while
I stand in view of thee, thy eyes will wound,
Thy tongue will make me wanton as thy wishes;
And while I feel thy hand, my body glows: 335
Therefore be quick, and take your last adieu,
These your last sighs, and these your parting tears;
Farewell, farewell, a long and last farewell.
   ALEXANDER. O my Hephestion, bear me, or I sink.
   STATIRA. Nay, you may take—(Heav'n! how my heart throbs!)—   340
You may, you may, if yet you think me worthy,
Take from these trembling lips a parting kiss.
   ALEXANDER. No, let me starve first.—Why, Statira, why?
What is the meaning of all this?—O gods!
I know the cause—my working brain divines;   345
You'll say you pardoned, but with this reserve,
Never to make me blest as I have been,
To slumber by the side of that false man,
Nor give a heav'n of beauty to a devil.
Think you not thus? Speak, madam.   350
   SYSIGAMBIS. She is not worthy, son, of so much sorrow.—
Speak comfort to him, speak, my dear Statira,
I ask thee by those tears. Ah, can'st thou e'er
Pretend to love, yet with dry eyes behold him?
   ALEXANDER. Silence more dreadful than severest sounds!   355
Would she but speak, though death, eternal exile
Hung at her lips, yet while her tongue pronounces,
There must be music even in my undoing.
   STATIRA. Still, my loved lord, I can not see you thus,
Nor can I ever yield to share your bed.   360
Or I shall find Roxana in your arms,
And taste her kisses, left upon your lips.
Her cursed embraces have defiled your body,
Nor shall I find the wonted sweetness there,
But artificial smells and [t]aking odors.[1] 365
   ALEXANDER. Yes, obstinate, I will. Madam, you shall,
You shall, in spite of this resistless passion,
Be served; but you must give me leave to think
You never loved—O could I see you thus!
Hell has not half the tortures that you raise.
   CLYTUS. Never did passions combat thus before.   371
   ALEXANDER. O I shall burst
Unless you give me leave to rave a while.
   SYSIGAMBIS. Yet, ere destruction sweep us both away,
Relent, and break through all to pity him.   375
   ALEXANDER. Yes, I will shake this cupid from my arms.
If all the rages of the earth can fright him,
Drown him in the deep bowl of Hercules,[2]
Make the world drunk and then, like Æolus,[3]
When he gave passage to the struggling winds,   380
I'll strike my spear into the reeling globe
To let it blood, set Babylon in a blaze,
And drive this god of flames with more consuming fire.
   STATIRA. My presence will but force him to extremes;
Besides, 'tis death to me to see his pains,   385
Yet stand resolved never to yield again.—
Permit me to remove.
   ALEXANDER.   I charge ye, stay her.
For if she pass, by all the hells I feel,
Your souls, your naked ghosts, shall wait upon her.

---

[1] The 1677 edition has *aking odors*, with a space before the *a* for a dropped letter. *Taking* means "bewitching." Later editions have *stinking odors*.
[2] See Act I, l. 255, note.
[3] See Virgil's *Æneid*, I, 59–87.

O turn thee! turn! thou barb'rous brightness,
 turn! 390
Hear my last words, and see my utmost pang.
But first kneel with me, all my soldiers,
 kneel—
         (All kneel)
Yet lower—prostrate to the earth.—Ah,
 mother, what,
Will you kneel, too? Then let the sun stand
 still
To see himself out-worshipped; not a face 395
Be shown that is not washed all o'er in tears;
But weep as if you here beheld me slain.
 SYSIGAMBIS. Hast thou a heart? or art thou
  savage turned?
But if this posture can not move your mercy,
I never will speak more.
 ALEXANDER.   O my Statira! 400
I swear, my queen, I'll not outlive thy hate,
My soul is still as death.—But one thing more,
Pardon my last extremities, the transports
Of a deep wounded breast, and all is well.
 STATIRA. Rise, and may heaven forgive you
  all, like me. 405
 ALEXANDER. You are too gracious.—
  Clytus, bear me hence;
When I am laid in earth, yield her the world.
There's something here heaves as cold as
 ice
That stops my breath.—Farewell, O gods!
 forever.
 STATIRA. Hold off, and let me run into his
  arms, 410
My dearest, my all love, my lord, my king;
You shall not die, if that the soul and body
Of thy Statira can restore thy life.
Give me thy wonted kindness, bend me,
 break me
With thy embraces.
 ALEXANDER. O the killing joy! 415
O ecstasy! my heart will burst my breast
To leap into thy bosom; but, by heaven,
This night I will revenge me of thy beauties,
For the dear rack I have this day endured;
For all the sighs and tears that I have
 spent, 420
I'll have so many thousand burning loves,
So swell thy lips, so fill me with thy sweet-
 ness,
Thou shalt not sleep nor close thy wand'ring
 eyes.
The smiling hours shall all be loved away,
We'll surfeit all the night, and languish all the
 day. 425

 STATIRA. Nor shall Roxana—
 ALEXANDER.   Let her not be named.—
O mother! how shall I requite your goodness?
And you, my fellow warriors, that could
 weep
For your lost king.—But I invite you all,
My equals in the throne as in the grave, 430
Without distinction to the riot come,
To the king's banquet—
 CLYTUS.   I beg your majesty
Would leave me out.
 ALEXANDER. None, none shall be excused;
All revel out the day, 'tis my command.
Gay as the Persian god ourself will stand 435
With a crowned goblet in our lifted hand.
Young Ammon and Statira shall go round
While antic measures beat the burdened
 ground
And to the vaulted skies our clangors sound.
            Exeunt

ACT IV

[SCENE 1]

Enter CLYTUS *in his Macedonian habit;*
 HEPHESTION, EUMENES, MELEAGER, &c.
 in Persian robes

 CLYTUS. Away, I will not wear these Persian
  robes;
Nor ought the king be angry for the reverence
I owe my country; sacred are her customs,
Which honest Clytus shall preserve to death.
O let me rot in Macedonian rags 5
Rather than shine in fashions of the East.
Then for the adorations he requires
Roast my old body in eternal flames,
Or let him cage me like Calisthenes.
 EUMENES. Dear Clytus, be persuaded.
 HEPHESTION.   You know the king
Is godlike, full of all the richest virtues 11
That ever royal heart possessed; yet you,
Perverse but to one humor, will oppose him.
 CLYTUS. You call it humor! 'tis a pregnant
  one;
By Mars, there's venom in it, burning pride;
And though my life should follow, rather
 than 16
Bear such a hot ambition in my bowels,
I'll rip 'em up to give the poison vent.
 MELEAGER. Was not that Jupiter whom we
  adore,
A man, but for his more than human acts, 20
Advanced to heav'n and worshipped for its
 lord?

HEPHESTION. By all his thunder and his
    sovereign power,
I'll not believe the earth yet ever felt
An arm like Alexander's; not that god
You named, though riding in a car of fire, 25
And drawn by flying horses winged with light-
    ning,
Could in a shorter space do greater deeds,
Drive all the nations, and lay waste the world.
    CLYTUS. There's not a man of war among
    you all
That loves the king like me; yet I'll not
    flatter   30
Nor soothe his vanity; 'tis blameable;
And when the wine works, Clytus' thoughts
    will out.
    HEPHESTION. Then go not to the banquet.
    CLYTUS.   I was called
My minion, was I not, as well as you?
I'll go, my friends, in this old habit thus, 35
And laugh, and drink the King's health
    heartily;
And while you, blushing, bow your heads to
    earth,
And hide 'em in the dust, I'll stand upright,
Straight as a spear, the pillar of my country,
And be by so much nearer to the gods.— 40
But see, the king and all the court appear.

Enter ALEXANDER, SYSIGAMBIS, STATIRA,
    PARISATIS, *&c.*

    PARISATIS. Spare him, O spare Lysimachus
    his life!
I know you will. Kings should delight in
    mercy.
    ALEXANDER. Shield me, Statira, shield me
    from her sorrow.
    PARISATIS. O save him, save him, ere it be
    too late;   45
Speak the kind word before the gaping lion
Swallow him up; let not your soldier perish
But for one rashness which despair did
    cause.
I'll follow thus forever on my knees
And make your way so slippery with tears 50
You shall not pass.—Sister, do you conjure
    him.   (PARISATIS *kneels*)
    ALEXANDER. O mother, take her, take her
    from me;
Her wat'ry eyes assault my very soul,
They shake my best resolve—
    STATIRA.   Did I not break
Through all for you? nay, now, my lord, you
    must.   55

    SYSIGAMBIS. Nor would I make my son so
    bold a prayer,
Had I not first consulted for his honor.
    ALEXANDER. Honor! What honor? has not
    Statira said it?
Were I the king of the blue firmament,
And the bold Titans should again make war,
Though my resistless arrows were made
    ready,   61
By all the gods, she should arrest my hand.
Fly, then, ev'n thou, his rival so beloved,
Fly with old Clytus, snatch him from the jaws
Of the devouring beast, bring him, adorned,
To the king's banquet, fit for loads of honor. 66
    Exeunt HEPHESTION, EUMENES,
        PARISATIS
    STATIRA. O my loved lord! let me embrace
    your knees.
I am not worthy of this mighty passion;
You are too good for goddesses themselves.
No woman, not the sex, is worth a grain 70
Of this illustrious life of my dear master.
Why are you so divine to cause such fond-
    ness
That my heart leaps, and beats, and fain
    would out
To make a dance of joy about your feet?
    ALEXANDER. Excellent woman! no, 'tis im-
    possible   75
To say how much I love thee—Ha! again!
Such ecstasies life can not carry long;
The day comes on so fast, and beamy joy
Darts with such fierceness on me, night will
    follow.
A pale crowned head flew lately glaring by
    me,   80
With two dead hands, which threw a crystal
    globe
From high, that shattered in a thousand
    pieces.
But I will lose these boding dreams in wine;
Then, warm and blushing for my queen's
    embraces,
Bear me with all my heat to thy loved bosom.
    STATIRA. Go, my best love, and cheer your
    drooping spirits;   86
Laugh with your friends, and talk your grief
    away,
While in the bower of great Semiramis
I dress your bed with all the sweets of nature,
And crown it as the altar of my love   90
Where I will lay me down and softly mourn,
But never close my eyes till you return.
    Exeunt STATIRA, SYSIGAMBIS

ALEXANDER. Is she not more than mortal
e'er can wish?
Diana's soul cast in the flesh of Venus!
By Jove, 'tis ominous, our parting is; 95
Her face looked pale, too, as she turned away;
And when I wrung her by the rosy fingers,
Methought the strings of my great heart did crack.
What should it mean?—Forward, Laomedon.
   (ROXANA *meets him, with* CASSANDER,
   POLYPERCHON, PHILIP, *and* THESSALUS)
Why, madam, gaze you thus?
   ROXANA.   For a last look,
   (*She holds his hand*)
And that the memory of Roxana's wrongs
May be forever printed in your mind.   102
   ALEXANDER. O madam, you must let me pass.
   ROXANA.   I will.
But I have sworn that you shall hear me speak,
And mark me well, for fate is in my breath:
Love on the mistress you adore, to death; 106
Still hope, but I fruition will destroy;
Languish for pleasures you shall ne'er enjoy.
Still may Statira's image draw your sight
Like those deluding fires that walk at night;
Lead you through fragrant grots and flow'ry groves,   111
And charm you through deep grass with sleeping loves;
That when your fancy to its height does rise,
The light you loved may vanish from your eyes,
Darkness, despair, and death your wand'ring soul surprise.   115
   ALEXANDER. Away; lead, Meleager, to the banquet.
                        Exit cum suis
ROXANA. So unconcerned! Oh, I could tear my flesh,
Or him, or you, nay, all the world, to pieces.
   CASSANDER. Still keep this spirit up, preserve it still,
Lose not a grain, for such majestic atoms   120
First made the world, and must preserve its greatness.
   ROXANA. I know I am whatever thou canst say;
My soul is pent, and has not elbow room;
'Tis swelled with this last slight beyond all bounds.
O that it had a space might answer to   125
Its infinite desire, where I might stand
And hurl the spheres about like sportive balls!
   CASSANDER. We are your slaves, admirers of your fury.
Command Cassander to obey your pleasure,
And I will on, swift as your nimble eye   130
Scales heav'n; when I am angry with the fates,
No age, nor sex, nor dignity of blood,
No ties of law or nature, not the life
Imperial, though guarded with the gods,
Shall bar Cassander's vengeance. He shall die.
   ROXANA. Ha! shall he die? shall I consent to kill him?   136
To see him clasped in the cold arms of death,
Whom I with such an eagerness have loved?
Do I not bear his image in my womb?
Which, while I meditate and roll revenge,   140
Starts in my body like a fatal pulse,
And strikes compassion through my bleeding bowels.
   POLYPERCHON. The scruples which your love would raise might pass,
Were not the empire of the world considered.
How will the glorious infant in your womb,   145
When time shall teach his tongue, be bound to curse you,
If now you strike not for his coronation!
   CASSANDER. If Alexander lives, you can not reign,
Nor shall your child. Old Sysigambis' head
Will not be idle—sure destruction waits   150
Both you and yours; let not your anger cool,
But give the word: say, Alexander bleeds,
Draw dry the veins of all the Persian race,
And hurl a ruin o'er the East—'tis done.
   POLYPERCHON. Behold the instruments of this great work.   155
   PHILIP. Behold your forward slave.
   THESSALUS.   I'll execute.
   ROXANA. And when this ruin is accomplished,
Shall curst Roxana fly with this dear load?
Where shall she find a refuge from the arms
Of all the successors of this great man?   160
No barb'rous nation will receive a guilt
So much transcending theirs, but drive me out;
The wildest beasts will hunt me from their dens,
And birds of prey molest me in the grave.
   CASSANDER. No, you shall live—pardon the insolence   165
Which this almighty love enforces from me—

You shall live safer, nobler than before
In your Cassander's arms.
    ROXANA. Disgraced Roxana, whither wilt
      thou fall?
I ne'er was truly wretched till this moment:
There's not one mark of former majesty 171
To awe my slave that offers at my honor.
    CASSANDER. Madam, I hope you'll not im-
      pute my passion
To want of that respect which I must bear
    you.
Long have I loved—
    ROXANA. Peace, most audacious villain!
Or I will stab this passion in thy throat. 176
What! shall I leave the bosom of a deity
To clasp a clod, a moving piece of earth
Which a mole heaves? So far art thou be-
    neath me.
    CASSANDER. Your majesty shall hear no
      more my folly. 180
    ROXANA. Nor dare to meet my eyes; for,
      if thou dost,
With a love-glance thy plots are all unravelled,
And your kind thoughts of Alexander told,
Whose life, in spite of all his wrongs to me,
Shall be forever sacred and untouched. 185
    CASSANDER. I know, dread madam, that
      Cassander's life
Is in your hands, so cast to do you service.
    ROXANA. You thought, perhaps, because I
      practised charms
To gain the king, that I had loose desires.
No, 'tis my pride that gives me height of
    pleasure: 190
To see the man by all the world admired
Bowed to my bosom, and my captive there—
Then my veins swell, and my arms grasp the
    poles,
My breasts grow bigger with the vast delight;
'Tis length of rapture and an age of fury. 195
    CASSANDER. By your own life, the greatest
      oath I swear,
Cassander's passion from this time is dumb.
    ROXANA. No, if I were a wanton, I would
      make
Princes the victims of my raging fires;
I, like the changing moon, would have the
    stars 200
My followers, and mantled kings by night
Should wait my call; fine slaves to quench
    my flame,
Who, lest in dreams they should reveal the
    deed,
Still as they came, successively should bleed.

    CASSANDER. To make atonement for the
      highest crime, 205
I beg your majesty will take the life
Of Queen Statira as a sacrifice.
    ROXANA. Rise, thou hast made me ample
      expiation;
Yes, yes, Statira, rival, thou must die;
I know this night is destined for my ruin, 210
And Alexander from the glorious revels
Flies to thy arms.
    PHILIP. The bowers of Semiramis are made
The scene this night of their new-kindled
    loves.
    ROXANA. Methinks I see her yonder (O the
      torment!) 215
Busy for bliss and full of expectation;
She adorns her head, and her eyes give new
    lustre;
Languishes in her glass, tries all her looks;
Steps to the door and listens for his coming;
Runs to the bed, and kneels, and weeps, and
    wishes, 220
Then lays the pillow easy for his head,
Warms it with sighs, and molds it with her
    kisses.
Oh, I am lost! torn with imagination!
Kill me, Cassander, kill me instantly,
That I may haunt her with a thousand
    devils.
    CASSANDER. Why d'ye stop to end her
      while you may? 226
No time so proper as the present now;
While Alexander feasts with all his court,
Give me your eunuchs, half your Zogdian
    slaves,
I'll do the deed; nor shall a waiter 'scape 230
That serves your rival, to relate the news.
    POLYPERCHON. She was committed to
      Eumenes' charge.
    ROXANA. Eumenes dies, and all that are
      about her;
Nor shall I need your aid, you'll love again;
I'll head the slaves myself with this drawn
    dagger 235
To carry death that's worthy of a queen.
A common fate ne'er rushes from my hand;
'Tis more than life to die by my command.
And when she sees
That to my arm her ruin she must owe, 240
Her thankful head will straight be bended
    low,
Her heart shall leap half way to meet the
    blow.
                       Exit ROXANA

CASSANDER. Go thy ways, Semele.[1]—She
   scorns to sin
Beneath a god.—We must be swift; the ruin
We intend, who knows, she may discover?   245
   POLYPERCHON. It must be acted suddenly
      tonight;
Now at the banquet Philip holds his cup.
   PHILIP. And dares to execute. Propose his
      fate.
   CASSANDER. Observe in this small vial
      certain death;
It holds a poison of such deadly force,   250
Should Æsculapius[2] drink it, in five hours
(For then it works) the god himself were
      mortal.
I drew it from Nonarris'[3] horrid spring;
A drop infused in wine will seal his death,   254
And send him howling to the lowest shades.
   PHILIP. Would it were done.
   CASSANDER.   Oh, we shall have him tear
(Ere yet the moon has half her journey rode)
The world to atoms; for it scatters pains
All sorts, and through all nerves, veins,
      arteries,
Ev'n with extremity of frost it burns;   260
Drives the distracted soul about her house,
Which runs to all the pores, the doors of life,
Till she is forced for air to leave her dwelling.
   POLYPERCHON. By Pluto's self, the work is
      wondrous brave!
   CASSANDER. Now separate. Philip and
      Thessalus,   265
Haste to the banquet; at his second call
Give him that fatal draught that crowns the
      night,
While Polyperchon and myself retire.
      Exeunt omnes praeter CASSANDER
Yes, Alexander, now thou pay'st me well;
Blood for a blow is interest indeed.   270
Methinks I am grown taller with the murder,
And, standing straight on this majestic pile,
I hit the clouds and see the world below me.
Oh, 'tis the worst of racks to a brave spirit
To be born base, a vassal, a cursed slave;   275
Now by the project lab'ring in my brain,
'Tis nobler far to be the king of hell,
To head infernal legions, chiefs below,
To let 'em loose for earth, to call 'em in,
And take account of what dark deeds are
      done   280
Than be a subject-god in heav'n unblest,
And without mischief have eternal rest.
               Exit

[SCENE II]

The Scene draws; ALEXANDER *is seen standing
   on a throne with all his commanders
   about him holding goblets in their hands*

   ALEXANDER. To our immortal health and
      our fair queen's!
All drink it deep, and while it flies about,
Mars and Bellona join to make us music.   285
A hundred bulls be offered to the sun,
White as his beams.—Speak the big voice of
      war,
Beat all our drums, and blow our silver trump-
      ets
Till we provoke the gods to act our pleasure
In bowls of nectar and replying thunder.   290
      (*Sound while they drink*)

Enter HEPHESTION, CLYTUS, *leading* LYSI-
   MACHUS *in his shirt, bloody;* PERDICCAS,
   Guard

   CLYTUS. Long live the king, and conquest
      crown his arms
With laurels ever green! Fortune's his slave,
And kisses all that fight upon his side.
   ALEXANDER. Did not I give command you
      should preserve
Lysimachus?
   HEPHESTION. You did.   295
   ALEXANDER. What then portend those
      bloody marks?
   HEPHESTION. Your mercy flew too late.[4]
      Perdiccas had,
According to the dreadful charge you gave,
Already placed the prince in a lone court,
Unarmed, all but his hands, on which he
      wore   300
A pair of gauntlets; such was his desire,
To show in death the difference betwixt
The blood of the Æacides[5] and common men.

---

[1] Semele desired Zeus to visit her in the same splendor in which he was seen by the gods, and was consumed by lightning.

[2] The "blameless physician" of the Homeric poems, who was placed by Zeus among the stars and therefore became immortal.

[3] A misprint for Nonacris, the place where the River Styx took its origin.

[4] The episode of Lysimachus' conflict with the lion is both in La Calprenède and in Quintus Curtius, III, 1, 91–2, 246. Lee seems to have consulted both books.

[5] It is not clear what Lee has in mind. Æacides was the name of Alexander's cousin, the king of Epirus, whom Lee seems to make the father of Lysimachus. The Æacides were also the descendants of Achilles.

CLYTUS. At last the door of an old lion's den
Being drawn up, the horrid beast appeared.
The flames which from his eyes shot gloomy
    red   306
Made the sun start, as the spectators thought
And round 'em cast a day of blood and death.
    HEPHESTION. When we arrived, just as the
      valiant prince
Cried out, O Parisatis, take my life!   310
'Tis for thy sake I go undaunted thus
To be devoured by this most dreadful creature —
    CLYTUS. Then walking forward, the large
      beast descried
His prey, and with a roar that made us pale,
Flew fiercely on him; but the active prince,
Starting aside, avoided his first shock   316
With a slight hurt, and as the lion turned,
Thrust gauntlet, arm and all, into his throat,
And with Herculean force tore forth by th'
    roots
The foaming, bloody tongue; and while the
    savage,   320
Faint with the loss, sunk to the blushing earth
To plough it with his teeth, your conqu'ring
    soldier
Leaped on his back and dashed his skull to
    pieces.
    ALEXANDER. By all my laurels, 'twas a
      godlike act,
And 'tis my glory, as it shall be thine,   325
That Alexander could not pardon thee.
O my brave soldier, think not all the prayers
Of the lamenting queens could move my soul
Like what thou hast performed. Grow to my
    breast!   (*Embraces him*)
    LYSIMACHUS. However love did hurry my
      wild arm,   330
When I was cool, my fev'rish blood did bate,
And as I went to death, I blessed the king.
    ALEXANDER. Lysimachus, we both have
      been transported,
But from this hour be certain of my heart.
A lion be the impress of thy shield,   335
And that gold armor we from Porus [1] won
The king presents thee; but retire to bed,
Thy toils ask rest.
    LYSIMACHUS. I have no wounds to hinder
Of any moment; or, if I had, though mortal,
I'd stand to Alexander's health till all   340

My veins were dry, and fill 'em up again
With that rich blood which makes the gods
    immortal.
    ALEXANDER. Hephestion, thy hand; embrace him close;
Though next my heart you hang, the jewel
    there
(For scarce I know whether my queen be
    dearer),   345
Thou shalt not rob me of my glory, youth,
That must to ages flourish.—Parisatis
Shall now be his that serves me best in
    war.
Neither reply, but mark the charge I give,
And live as friends.—Sound, sound my
    armies' honor!   350
Health to their bodies, and eternal fame
Wait on their memory when those are ashes!
Live all you must, 'tis a god gives you life.
                               (*Sound*)
    (LYSIMACHUS *offers* CLYTUS [2] *a Persian
      robe, and he refuses it*)
    CLYTUS. O vanity!
    ALEXANDER.   Ha! what says Clytus?
      Who am I?
    CLYTUS. The son of good King Philip.
    ALEXANDER.   No, 'tis false;
By all my kindred in the skies,   356
Jove made my mother pregnant.
    CLYTUS.   I ha' done.
    (*Here follows an entertainment of Indian
      singers and dancers. The music flourishes*)
    ALEXANDER. Hold, hold. Clytus, take the
      robe.
    CLYTUS.   Sir, the wine,
The weather's hot; besides, you know my
    humor.
    ALEXANDER. Oh, 'tis not well; I'd burn
      rather than be   360
So singular and froward.
    CLYTUS.   So would I
Burn, hang, or drown, but in a better cause;
I'll drink or fight for sacred majesty
With any here.—Fill me another bowl—
Will you excuse me?
    ALEXANDER.   You will be excused;
But let him have his humor, he is old.   366
    CLYTUS. So was your father, sir.—This to
      his memory!
Sound all the trumpets there.
    ALEXANDER.   They shall not sound

---

[1] *Porcus* in 1677 edition. Porus was the king of the Indian provinces beyond the river Hydaspes, with whom Alexander fought one of his severest battles in 327 B.C.

[2] For the story of the death of Clytus Lee turned to the historians, often translating the exact words of Quintus Curtius in the following scene.

Till the king drinks.—By Mars, I can not taste
A moment's rest for all my years of blood, 370
But one or other will oppose my pleasure.
Sure, I was formed for war, eternal war;
All, all are Alexander's enemies
Which I could tame.—Yes, the rebellious world
Should feel my wrath—but let the sports go on. 375
(*The* Indians *dance*)
LYSIMACHUS. Nay, Clytus, you that could advise—
ALEXANDER.   Forbear.
Let him persist, be positive and proud,
Sullen and dazzled amongst the nobler souls,
Like an infernal spirit that had stole
From hell and mingled with the laughing gods. 380
CLYTUS. When gods grow hot where is the difference
'Twixt them and devils?—Fill me Greek wine, yet fuller,
For I want spirits.
ALEXANDER.   Ha! let me hear a song.
CLYTUS. Music for boys!—Clytus would hear the groans
Of dying persons and horses' neighings; 385
Or if I must be tortured with shrill voices,
Give me the cries of matrons in sacked towns.
HEPHESTION. Lysimachus, the king looks sad. Let us awake him.
—Health to the son of Jupiter Ammon!
Ev'ry man take his goblet in his hand, 390
Kneel all, and kiss the earth with adoration.
ALEXANDER. Sound, sound, that all the universe may hear,
That I could speak like Jove to tell abroad
The kindness of my people.—Rise, O rise,
My hands, my arms, my heart is ever yours.
(*Comes from his throne; all kiss his hands*)
CLYTUS. I did not kiss the earth, nor must your hand. 396
I am unworthy, sir.
ALEXANDER.   I know thou art.
Thou enviest my great honor—sit, my friends—
Nay, I must have a room.—Now let us talk
Of war, for what more fits a soldier's mouth?
And speak, speak freely, or ye do not love me. 401
Who, think you, was the bravest general
That ever led an army to the field?

HEPHESTION. I think the sun himself ne'er saw a chief
So truly great, so fortunately brave 405
As Alexander; not the famed Alcides,
Nor fierce Achilles, who did twice destroy
With their all-conqu'ring arms, the famous Troy.
LYSIMACHUS. Such was not Cyrus.
ALEXANDER.   Oh, you flatter me.
CLYTUS. They do, indeed, and yet ye love 'em for it, 410
But hate old Clytus for his hardy virtue.
Come, shall I speak a man more brave than you,
A better general, and more expert soldier?
ALEXANDER. I should be glad to learn. Instruct me, sir.
CLYTUS. Your father Philip. I have seen him march, 415
And fought beneath his dreadful banner where
The stoutest at this table would ha' trembled.
Nay, frown not, sir; you can not look me dead.
When Greeks joined Greeks, then was the tug of war,
The labored battle sweat, and conquest bled.
Why should I fear to speak a truth more noble 421
Than e'er your father Jupiter Ammon told you?
Philip fought men, but Alexander, women.
ALEXANDER. Spite! By the gods, proud spite, and burning envy!
Is then my glory come to this at last, 425
To vanquish women? Nay, he said the stoutest here
Would tremble at the dangers he has seen.
In all the sickness and the wounds I bore,
When from my reins the javelin's head was cut,
Lysimachus, Hephestion, speak, Perdiccas,
Did I tremble? O the cursèd liar! 431
Did I once shake or groan? or bear myself
Beneath my majesty, my dauntless courage?
HEPHESTION. Wine has transported him.
ALEXANDER.   No, 'tis plain, mere malice.
I was a woman, too, at Oxydrace,[1] 435
When, planting at the walls a scaling ladder,
I mounted, spite of showers of stones, bars, arrows,
And all the lumber which they thundered down,
When you beneath cried out, and spread your arms,
That I should leap among you. Did I so? 440

[1] The bloodiest of Alexander's battles in India.

LYSIMACHUS. Turn the discourse, my lord, the old man raved.
ALEXANDER. Was I a woman when, like Mercury,
I left the walls to fly amongst my foes,
And like a baited lion dyed myself 444
All over with the blood of those bold hunters?
Till, spent with toil, I battled on my knees,
Plucked forth the darts that made my shield a forest,
And hurled 'em back with most unconquered fury.
CLYTUS. 'Twas all bravado, for, before you leaped,
You saw that I had burst the gates in sunder.
ALEXANDER. Did I then turn me like a coward round 451
To seek for succor? Age can not be so base.
That thou wert young again, I would put off
My majesty to be more terrible,
That, like an eagle, I might strike this hare 455
Trembling to earth; shake thee to dust, and tear
Thy heart for this bold lie, thou feeble dotard.
(*He tosses fruit at him as they rise*)
CLYTUS. What, do you pelt me like a boy with apples?
Kill me and bury the disgrace I feel.
I know the reason that you use me so, 460
Because I saved your life at Granicus;
And when your back was turned, opposed my breast
To bold Rhesaces' sword; you hate me for't
You do, proud prince.
ALEXANDER. Away, your breath's too hot.
(*Flings him from him*)
CLYTUS. You hate the benefactor, though you took 465
The gift, your life, from this dishonored Clytus,
Which is the blackest, worst ingratitude.
ALEXANDER. Go, leave the banquet. Thus far I forgive thee.
CLYTUS. Forgive yourself for all your blasphemies,
The riots of a most debauched and blotted life, 470
Philotas' murder—
ALEXANDER. Ha! what said the traitor?
LYSIMACHUS. Eumenes, let us force him thence.
CLYTUS. Away.
HEPHESTION. You shall not tarry. Drag him to the door.

CLYTUS. No, let him send me, if I must be gone,
To Philip, Attalus, Calisthenes, 475
To great Parmenio, to his slaughtered sons,—
Parmenio, who did many brave exploits
Without the king—the king without him nothing.
ALEXANDER. Give me a javelin.
(*Takes one from the guard*)
HEPHESTION. Hold, sir!
ALEXANDER. Off, sirrah, lest
At once I strike through his heart and thine.
LYSIMACHUS. O sacred sir, have but a moment's patience. 481
ALEXANDER. Preach patience to another lion—What,
Hold my arms? I shall be murdered here
Like poor Darius by my own barb'rous subjects.
Perdiccas, sound my trumpets to the camp,
Call my soldiers to the court; nay, haste, 486
For there is treason plotting 'gainst my life,
And I shall perish ere they come to rescue.
LYSIMACHUS and HEPHESTION. Let us all die, ere think so damned a deed.
(*Kneel*)
ALEXANDER. Where is the traitor?
CLYTUS. Sure there's none about you, 490
But here stands honest Clytus, whom the king
Invited to the banquet.
ALEXANDER. Be gone and sup with Philip,
(*Strikes him through*)
Parmenio, Attalus, and Calisthenes;
And let bold subjects learn by thy sad fate
To tempt the patience of a man above 'em. 495
CLYTUS. The rage of wine is drowned in gushing blood.
O Alexander, I have been to blame;
Hate me not after death, for I repent
That so I urged your noblest, sweetest nature.
ALEXANDER. What's this I hear? Say on, my dying soldier. 500
CLYTUS. I should ha' killed myself, had I but lived
To be once sober—now I fall with honor;
My own hand would ha' brought foul death.
Oh, pardon.
(*Dies*)
ALEXANDER. Then I am lost. What has my vengeance done?
Who is it thou hast slain? Clytus. What was he? 505

Thy faithful subject, worthiest counsellor,
Who for saving thee thy life has now
A noble recompense; for one rash word,
For a forgetfulness which wine did work,
The poor, the honest Clytus thou hast slain!
Are these the laws of hospitality?   511
Thy friends will shun thee now, and stand at distance,
Nor dare to speak their minds, nor eat with thee,
Nor drink, lest by thy madness they die, too.
  HEPHESTION. Guards, take the body hence.
  ALEXANDER.   None dare touch him,
For we must never part. Cruel Hephestion,
And you, Lysimachus, that had the power, 517
Yet would not hold me.
  LYSIMACHUS.   Dear sir, we did.
  ALEXANDER.   I know it;
Ye held me like a beast, to let me go
With greater violence—Oh, you have undone me!   520
Excuse it not, you that could stop a lion,
Could not turn me. You should have drawn your swords
And barred my rage with their advancing points;
Made reason glitter in my dazzled eyes
Till I had seen what ruin did attend me: 525
That had been noble, that had showed a friend;
Clytus would so have done to save your lives.
  LYSIMACHUS. When men shall hear how highly you were urged—
  ALEXANDER. No, you have let me stain my rising virtue
Which else had ended brighter than the sun.
Death, hell, and furies! you have sunk my glory!   531
Oh, I am all a blot, which seas of tears
And my heart's blood can never wash away;
Yet 'tis but just I try, and on the point
Still reeking, hurl my black, polluted breast.
  HEPHESTION. O sacred sir, that must not be.
  EUMENES.   Forgive my pious hands.
  LYSIMACHUS. And mine, that dare disarm my master.   537
  ALEXANDER. Yes, cruel men, ye now can show your strength.
Here's not a slave but dares oppose my justice;
Yet I will render all endeavors vain   540
That tend to save my life.—Here I will lie
                      (*Falls*)
Close to his bleeding side, thus kissing him—

These pale, dead lips that have so oft advised me;
Thus bathing o'er his reverend face in tears;
Thus clasping his cold body in my arms 545
Till death like him has made me stiff and horrid.
  HEPHESTION. What shall we do?
  LYSIMACHUS.   I know not; my wounds bleed afresh
With striving with him. Perdiccas, lend's your arm.
          Exeunt PERDICCAS, LYSIMACHUS
  HEPHESTION. Call Aristander hither,
Or Meleager, let's force him from the body.
    (*Cries without:* Arm, Arm, Treason, Treason! *Enter* PERDICCAS, *bloody*)
  PERDICCAS. Haste, all take arms! Hephestion, where's the king?   551
  HEPHESTION. There by old Clytus' side, whom he has slain.
  PERDICCAS. Then misery on misery will fall
Like rolling billows, to advance the storm.
Rise, sacred sir, and haste to aid the queen;
Roxana, filled with furious jealousy,   556
Came with a guard of Zogdian slaves unmarked,
And broke upon me with such sudden rage
That all are perished who resistance made.
I only with these wounds, through clashing spears   560
Have forced my way to give you timely notice.
  ALEXANDER. What says Perdiccas? Is the queen in danger?
  PERDICCAS. She dies unless you turn her fate, and quickly.
Your distance from the palace asks more speed,
And the ascent to th' flying grove is high.   565
  ALEXANDER. Thus from the grave I rise to save my love;
All draw your swords, with wings of lightning move;
When I rush on, sure none will dare to stay,
'Tis beauty calls, and glory shows the way.
                        Exeunt

ACT V

[SCENE I][1]

STATIRA *is discovered sleeping in the Bower of Semiramis. The spirits of* QUEEN STATIRA, *her mother, and* DARIUS *appear standing*

---

[1] The scene of the death of Statira is from La Calprenède, who, however, places it after the death of Alexander.

on each side of her, with daggers threatening her

THEY SING:

DARIUS. Is innocence so void of cares
    That it can undisturbèd sleep
    Amidst the noise of horrid wars
    That make immortal spirits weep?
[QUEEN] STATIRA. No boding crows, nor ravens, come   5
    To warn her of approaching doom?
DARIUS. She walks, as she dreams, in a garden of flowers,
And her hands are employed in the beautiful bowers;
She dreams of the man that is far from the grove,
And all her soft fancy still runs on her love.   10
[QUEEN] STATIRA. She nods o'er the brooks that run purling along,
And the nightingales lull her more fast with a song.
    DARIUS. But see the sad end which the gods have decreed.
[QUEEN] STATIRA. This poinard's thy fate.
DARIUS. My daughter must bleed.   15
CHORUS. Awake then, Statira, awake, for alas! you must die;
Ere an hour be past, you must breathe out your last.
DARIUS. And be such another as I.
[QUEEN] STATIRA. As I.
CHORUS. And be such another as I.   20

STATIRA *sola*

STATIRA. Bless me, ye pow'rs above, and guard my virtue!
I saw, nor was't a dream, I saw and heard
My royal parents; there I saw 'em stand;
My eyes behold their precious images;
I heard their heav'nly voices. Where, O where   25
Fled you so fast, dear shades, from my embraces?
You told me this—this hour should be my last,
And I must bleed.—Away, 'tis all delusion!
Do I not wait for Alexander's coming?
None but my loving lord can enter here,   30
And will he kill me?—Hence, fantastic shadows!
And yet methinks he should not stay thus long.
Why do I tremble thus? If I but stir,
The motion of my robes makes my heart leap.
When will the dear man come, that all my doubts   35
May vanish in his breast? That I may hold him
Fast as my fears can make me, hug him close
As my fond soul can wish; give all my breath
In sighs and kisses; swoon, die away with rapture.
But hark, I hear him—   (*Noise within*)
    Fain I would hide my blushes;
I hear his tread, but dare not go to meet him.   41

Enter ROXANA *with slaves, and a dagger*

ROXANA. At length we've conquered this stupendous height,
These flying groves, whose wonderful ascent
Leads to the clouds.
STATIRA. (*Retires*) Then all the vision's true,
And I must die, lose my dear lord forever.   45
That, that's the murder.
ROXANA.   Shut the brazen gate,
And make it fast with all the massy bars.
I know the king will fly to her relief,
But we have time enough.—Where is my rival?
Appear, Statira, now no more a queen;   50
Roxana calls! Where is your majesty?
STATIRA. And what is she who with such tow'ring pride
Would awe a princess that is born above her?
ROXANA. I like the port imperial beauty bears,
It shows thou hast a spirit fit to fall   55
A sacrifice to fierce Roxana's wrongs.
Be sudden then, put forth these royal breasts
Where our false master has so often languished,
That I may change their milky innocence
To blood, and dye me in a deep revenge.   60
STATIRA. No, barb'rous woman, though I durst meet death
As boldly as our lord, with a resolve
At which thy coward heart would tremble;
Yet I disdain to stand the fate you offer,
And therefore, fearless of thy dreadful threats,   65
Walk thus, regardless, by thee.
ROXANA.   Ha! So stately!
This sure will sink you.
STATIRA.   No, Roxana, no.
The blow you give will strike me to the stars,
But sink my murd'ress in eternal ruin.
ROXANA. Who told you this?
STATIRA.   A thousand spirits tell me.   70
There's not a god but whispers in my ear
This death will crown me with immortal glory.
To die so fair, so innocent, so young

Will make me company for queens above.
   ROXANA. Preach on.
   STATIRA.   While you, the burden of the earth,   75
Fall to the deep, so heavy with thy guilt
That hell itself must groan at thy reception.
While foulest fiends shun thy society,
And thou shalt walk alone, forsaken fury.
   ROXANA. Heaven witness for me, I would spare thy life,   80
If anything but Alexander's love
Were in debate. Come, give me back his heart,
And thou shalt live, live empress of all the world.
   STATIRA. The world is less than Alexander's love;
Yet, could I give it, 'tis not in my power.   85
This I dare promise if you spare my life
Which I disdain to beg: he shall speak kindly.
   ROXANA. Speak! is that all?
   STATIRA.   Perhaps at my request,
And for a gift so noble as my life,
Bestow a kiss.
   ROXANA.   A kiss! no more?
   STATIRA.   O gods!   90
What shall I say to work her to my end?
Fain I would see him—Yes, a little more
Embrace you, and forever be your friend.
   ROXANA. O the provoking word! Your friend! Thou di'st!
Your friend! What, must I bring you then together?   95
Adore your bed, and see you softly laid?
By all my pangs and labors of my love,
This has thrown off all that was sweet and gentle.
Therefore—
   STATIRA. Yet hold thy hand advanced in air.
I see my death is written in thy eyes;   100
Therefore wreak all the lust of vengeance on me,
Wash in my blood, and steep thee in my gore;
Feed like a vulture, tear my bleeding heart.
But O Roxana! that there may appear
A glimpse of justice for thy cruelty,   105
A grain of goodness for a mass of evil,
Give me my death in Alexander's presence.
   ROXANA. Not for the rule of heaven.—
Are you so cunning?
What, you would have him mourn you as you fall?

Take your farewell, and taste such healing kisses   110
As might call back your soul? No, thou shalt fall
Now, and when death has seized thy beauteous limbs,
I'll have thy body thrown into a well,
Buried beneath a heap of stones forever.

Enter a Slave

   SLAVE. Madam, the king with all his captains and his guards   115
Are forcing ope the doors; he threatens thousand deaths
To all that stop his entrance, and I believe
Your eunuchs will obey him.
   ROXANA.   Then I must haste.
                      (*Stabs her*)
   STATIRA. What, is the king so near?
And shall I die so tamely, thus defenceless?   120
O ye good gods, will you not help my weakness?
   ROXANA. They are afar off. (*Stabbing her*)
   STATIRA.   Alas! they are indeed.

Enter ALEXANDER, CASSANDER, POLYPERCHON, Guards *and* Attendants

   ALEXANDER. Oh, harpy! thou shalt reign the queen of devils!
   ROXANA. Do, strike, behold my bosom swells to meet thee;
'Tis full of thine, of veins that run ambition
And I can brave whatever fate you bring.   126
   ALEXANDER. Call our physicians; haste, I'll give an empire
To save her—Oh, my soul, alas! Statira!
These wounds—O gods, are these my promised joys?

Enter Physicians

   STATIRA. My cruel love, my weeping Alexander,   130
Would I had died before you entered here,
For now I ask my heart a hundred questions.
What, must I lose my life, my lord, forever?
   ALEXANDER. Ha! Villains, are they mortal?
—What, retire?
Raise your dashed spirits from the earth, and say,   135
Say she shall live, and I will make you kings.
Give me this one, this poor, this only life,
And I will pardon you for all the wounds

Which your arts widen, all diseases, deaths
Which your damned drugs throw through a ling'ring world. 140
  ROXANA. Rend not your temper; see, a general silence
Confirms the bloody pleasure which I sought. She dies—
  ALEXANDER. And dar'st thou, monster, think to escape?
  STATIRA. Life's on the wing, my love, my lord,
Come to my arms and take the last adieu. 145
Here let me lie and languish out my soul.
  ALEXANDER. Answer me, father, wilt thou take her from me?
What, is the black, sad hour at last arrived
That I must never clasp her body more?
Never more bask in her eyes-shine again? 150
Nor view the loves that played in those dear beams,
And shot me with a thousand thousand smiles?
  STATIRA. Farewell, my dear, my life, my most loved lord,
I swear by Orosmades, 'tis more pleasure,
More satisfaction that I thus die yours 155
Than to have lived another's—Grant me one thing.
  ALEXANDER. All, all—but speak that I may execute
Before I follow thee.
  STATIRA.   Leave not the earth
Before heaven calls you. Spare Roxana's life,
'Twas love of you that caused her give me death. 160
And O sometimes amidst your revels think
Of your poor queen, and ere the cheerful bowl
Salute your lips, crown it with one rich tear,
And I am happy.   (*Dies*)
  ALEXANDER.   Close not thy eyes;
Things of impòrt I have to speak before 165
Thou tak'st thy journey.—Tell the gods I'm coming
To give 'em an account of life and death,
And many other hundred thousand policies
That much concern the government of heaven—
Oh, she is gone! the talking soul is mute! 170
She's hushed—no voice, no music now is heard!
The bower of beauty is more still than death;
The roses fade, and the melodious bird
That waked their sweets has left them now forever.

  ROXANA. 'Tis certain now you never shall enjoy here; 175
Therefore Roxana may have leave to hope
You will at last be kind for all my sufferings,
My torments, racks, for this last, dreadful murder
Which furious love of thee did bring upon me.
  ALEXANDER. O thou vile creature! bear thee from my sight, 180
And thank Statira that thou art alive,
Else thou hadst perished. Yes, I would ha' rent
With my just hands that rock, that marble heart;
I would have dived through seas of blood to find it,
To tear the cruel quarry from its center. 185
  ROXANA. O take me to your arms and hide my blushes!
I love you, spite of all your cruelties;
There is so much divinity about you,
I tremble to approach; yet here's my hold,
Nor will I leave the sacred robe, for such
Is every thing that touches that blest body.
I'll kiss it as the relic of a god, 192
And love shall grasp it with these dying hands.
  ALEXANDER. O that thou wert a man, that I might drive
Thee round the world, and scatter thy contagion, 195
As gods hurl mortal plagues when they are angry.
  ROXANA. Do, drive me, hew me into smallest pieces;
My dust shall be inspired with a new fondness;
Still the love-motes shall play before your eyes
Where'er you go, however you despise. 200
  ALEXANDER. Away, there's not a glance that flies from thee,
But like a basilisk comes winged with death.
  ROXANA. O speak not such harsh words, my royal master,   (*Kneels*)
Look not so dreadful on your kneeling servant;
But take, dear sir, O take me into grace, 205
By the dear babe, the burden of my womb,
That weighs me down when I would follow faster;
My knees are weary and my force is spent.
O do not frown, but clear that angry brow!

Your eyes will blast me, and your words are
    bolts 210
That strike me dead; the little wretch I bear
Leaps frighted at your wrath, and dies within
    me.
  ALEXANDER. O thou hast touched my soul
    so tenderly
That I will raise thee, though thy hands are
    ruin.
Rise, cruel woman, rise, and have a care. 215
O do not hurt that unborn innocence
For whose dear sake I now forgive thee all.
But haste, be gone, fly, fly from these sad
    eyes;
Fly with thy pardon, lest I call it back; 219
Though I forgive thee, I must hate thee ever.
  ROXANA. I go, I fly forever from thy sight;
My mortal injuries have turned my mind,
And I could curse myself for being kind.
If there be any majesty above 224
That has revenge in store for perjured love,
Send, heaven, the swiftest ruin on his head,
Strike the destroyer, lay the victor dead;
Kill the triumpher and avenge my wrong
In height of pomp, while he is warm and
    young;
Bolted with thunder, let him rush along 230
And when in the last pangs of life he lies,
Grant I may stand to dart him with my eyes;
Nay, after death
Pursue his spotted ghost and shoot him as he
    flies. *Exit*
  ALEXANDER. O my fair star, I shall be
    shortly with thee, 235
For I already feel the sad effects
Of those most fatal imprecations.
What means this deadly dew upon my fore-
    head?
My heart, too, heaves.
  CASSANDER. (*Aside*) It will anon be still—
The poison works.
  POLYPERCHON. (*Aside*) I'll see the wished
    effect 240
Ere I remove, and gorge me with revenge.

  Enter PERDICCAS *and* LYSIMACHUS

  PERDICCAS. I beg your majesty will pardon
    me,
A fatal messenger;
Great Sysigambis, hearing Statira's death,
Is now no more; 245
Her last words gave the princess to the brave
Lysimachus, but that which most will strike
    you,
Your dear Hephestion, having drank too
    largely
At your lost feast, is of a surfeit dead.
  ALEXANDER. How, dead? Hephestion dead?
    Alas, the dear 250
Unhappy youth!—But he sleeps happy,
I must wake forever.—This object, this,
This face of fatal beauty
Will stretch my lids with vast, eternal tears—
Who had the care of poor Hephestion's life?
  LYSIMACHUS. Philarda, the Arabian art-
    ist. 256
  ALEXANDER. Fly, Meleager, hang him on a
    cross
That for Hephestion—
But here lies my fate. Hephestion, Clytus,
All my victories forever folded up: 260
In this dear body my banner's lost,
My standard's triumphs gone!
O when shall I be mad? Give order to
The army that they break their shields,
    swords, spears,
Pound their bright armor into dust away. 265
Is there not cause to put the world in mourn-
    ing?
Tear all your robes—he dies that is not naked
Down to the waist, all like the sons of sorrow.
Burn all the spires that seem to kiss the sky;
Beat down the battlements of every city; 270
And for the monument of this loved creature
Root up those bowers and pave 'em all with
    gold.
Draw dry the Ganges, make the Indies poor;
To build her tomb no shrines nor altars
    spare,
But strip the shining gods to make it rare. 275
        Exit
  CASSANDER. Ha! whither now? Follow him,
    Polyperchon.   *Exit* POLYPERCHON
I find Cassander's plot grows full of death;
Murder is playing her great masterpiece,
And the sad sisters sweat, so fast I urge 'em.
O how I hug myself for this revenge! 280
My fancy's great in mischief; for methinks
The night grows dark and the lab'ring ghosts,
For fear that I should find new torments out,
Run o'er the old with most prodigious swift-
    ness.
I see the fatal fruit betwixt the teeth, 285
The sieve brim full, and the swift stone stand
    still.[1]

[1] The reference here is to the punishments of Tanta-
lus and Ixion. See any dictionary of classical mythology.

Enter POLYPERCHON

What, does it work?
   POLYPERCHON.   Speak softly.
   CASSANDER.   Well.
   POLYPERCHON.   It does;
I followed him and saw him swiftly walk
Toward the palace, oftimes looking back
With wat'ry eyes, and calling out, Statira. 290
He stumbled at the gate and fell along;
Nor was he raised with ease by his attendants,
But seemed a greater load than ordinary,
As much more as the dead outweigh the living.
   CASSANDER. Said he nothing?
   POLYPERCHON.   When they took him up,
He sighed, and entered with a strange, wild look, 296
Embraced the princes round, and said he must
Dispatch the business of the world in haste.

Enter PHILIP *and* THESSALUS

   PHILIP. Back, back, all scatter.—With a dreadful shout
I heard him cry, I am but a dead man. 300
   THESSALUS. The poison tears him with that height of horror
That I could pity him.
   POLYPERCHON   Peace—where shall we meet?
   CASSANDER. In Saturn's field
Methinks I see the frighted deities
Ramming more bolts in their big-bellied clouds, 305
And firing all the heavens to drown his noise
Now we should laugh.—But go, disperse yourselves,
While each soul here that fills his noble vessel,
Swells with the murder, works with ruin o'er;
And from the dreadful deed this glory draws:
We killed the greatest man that ever was. 311

[SCENE II]

The scene draws. Enter ALEXANDER *and all his attendants*

   ALEXANDER. Search there, nay, probe me, search my wounded reins;
Pull, draw it out.
   LYSIMACHUS. We have searched, but find no hurt.
   ALEXANDER. O I am shot, a forkèd burning arrow

Sticks 'cross my shoulders; the sad venom flies
Light lightning through my flesh, my blood, my marrow. 316
   LYSIMACHUS. This must be treason.
   PERDICCAS.   Would I could but guess.
   ALEXANDER. Ha! what a change of torments I endure!
A bolt of ice runs hissing through my bowels:
'Tis sure the arm of death; give me a chair; 320
Cover me, for I freeze, [and] [1] my teeth chatter,
And my knees knock together.
   PERDICCAS.   Heaven bless the king!
   ALEXANDER. Ha! who talks of heav'n?
I am all hell; I burn, I burn again—
The war grows wondrous hot; hey for the Tigris! 325
Bear me, Bucephalus, amongst the billows.
Oh, 'tis a noble beast; I would not change him
For the best horse the sun has in his stable;
For they are hot, their mangers full of coals,
Their manes are flakes of lightning, curls of fire, 330
And their red tails like meteors whisk about.
   LYSIMACHUS. Help, all! Eumenes, help, I can not hold him.
   ALEXANDER. Ha, ha ha—I shall die with laughter.
Parmenio, Clytus, dost thou see yon fellow,
That ragged soldier, that poor, tattered Greek? 335
See how he puts to flight the gaudy Persians
With nothing but a rusty helmet on, through which
The grizzly bristles of his pushing beard
Drive 'em like pikes—Ha, ha, ha!
   PERDICCAS. How wild he talks!
   LYSIMACHUS.   Yet warring in his wildness.
   ALEXANDER. Sound, sound, keep your ranks close, ay, now they come. 341
O the brave din, the noble clank of arms!
Charge, charge apace, and let the phalanx move—
Darius comes—ha! let me in, none dare
To cross my fury;—Philotas is unhorsed;—
Ay, 'tis Darius; 345
I see, I know him by the sparkling plumes,
And his gold chariot drawn by ten white horses;
But like a tempest thus I pour upon him—
He bleeds; with that last blow I brought him down;

[1] 1677 ed. omits *and*.

He tumbles, take him, snatch the imperial
    crown—   350
They fly, they fly—follow, follow—Victoria,
    Victoria,
Victoria—Oh, let me sleep.
    PERDICCAS. Let's raise him softly, and bear
      him to his bed.
    ALEXANDER. Hold, the least motion gives
      me sudden death;   354
My vital spirits are quite parched, burnt up
And all my smoky entrails turned to ashes.
    LYSIMACHUS. When you, the brightest star
      that ever shone,
Shall set, it must be night with us forever.
    ALEXANDER. Let me embrace you all before
      I die.   359
Weep not, my dear companions, the good gods
Shall send you in my stead a nobler prince,
One that shall lead you forth with matchless
    conduct.
    LYSIMACHUS. Break not our hearts with
      such unkind expressions.
    PERDICCAS. We will not part with you, nor
      change for Mars.
    ALEXANDER. Perdiccas, take this ring, 365
And see me laid in the temple of Jupiter
    Ammon.
    LYSIMACHUS. To whom does your dread
      majesty bequeath
The empire of the world?
    ALEXANDER.   To him that is most worthy.
    PERDICCAS. When will you, sacred sir, that
      we should give
To your great memory those divine honors
Which such exalted virtue does deserve?   371
    ALEXANDER. When you are all most happy,
      and in peace.
Your hands—O father, if I have discharged
                                          (Rises)
The duty of a man to empire born
If by unwearied toil I have deserved   375
The vast renown of thy adopted son,
Accept this soul which thou didst first in-
    spire,
And with this sigh, thus gives thee back again.
                                          (Dies)
    LYSIMACHUS. Eumenes, cover the fall'n
      majesty.
If there be treason, let us find it out;   380
Lysimachus stands forth to lead you on,
And swears by those most honored, dear
    remains
He will not taste the joys which beauty brings
Till we revenge the greatest, best of kings.

EPILOGUE

Whate'er they mean, yet ought they to be
    cursed
Who this censorious age did polish first:
Who the best play for one poor error blame,
As priests against our ladies' arts declaim,
And for one patch both soul and body damn.
But what does more provoke the actors' rage
(For we must show the grievance of the stage)
Is that our women who adorn each play,
Bred at our cost, become at length your prey;
While green and sour, like trees we bear 'em
    all,   10
But when they're mellow, straight to you they
    fall.
You watch 'em bare and squab, and let 'em
    rest,
But with the first young down you snatch the
    nest.
Pray leave these poaching tricks, if you are
    wise,
Ere we take out our letters of reprize.[1]   15
For we have vowed to find a sort of toys
Known to Blackfriars, a tribe of chipping
    boys:[2]
If once they come, they'll quickly spoil your
    sport;
There's not a lady will receive your court,
But for the youth in petticoats run wild   20
With: "Oh, the archest wag! the sweetest
    child!"
The panting breast, white hands, and lily
    feet
No more shall your palled thoughts with
    pleasure meet.
The woman in boy's clothes all boy shall be,
And never raise your thoughts above the
    knee.   25
Well, if our women knew how false you are,
They would stay here and this new trouble
    spare.
Poor souls, they think all gospel you relate,
Charmed with the noise of settling an es-
    tate;
But when at last your appetites are full,   30
And the tired Cupid grows with action dull,
You'll find some trick to cut off the entail,
And send 'em back to us all worn and stale.
Perhaps they'll find our stage, while they have
    ranged

[1] Letters commissioning a privateer in war.
[2] See the reference to "nurseries," note 1, p. 61.
Chipping means worthless?

To some vile, canting conventicle,[1] changed, 35
Where for the sparks who once resorted there
With their curled wigs that scented all the air,
They'll see grave blockheads with short, greasy hair,
Green aprons, steeple hats, and collar bands;
Dull, sniv'ling rogues that ring, not clap, their hands; 40
Where for gay punks that drew the shining crowd
And misses that in vizards laughed aloud,
They'll hear young sisters sigh, see matrons old
To their chopped cheeks their pickled kerchers [2] hold,
Whose zeal, too, might persuade, in spite to you, 45
Our flying angels to augment their crew,
While Farringdon, their hero, struts about 'em,
And ne'er a damning critic dares to flout 'em.

[1] Nonconformist meeting-house.

[2] Chapped cheeks and handkerchiefs in a sorry plight.

ALL FOR LOVE; OR, THE WORLD WELL LOST

By John Dryden

John Dryden, the greatest literary figure of the Restoration, was born August 9, 1631, in the parsonage house of Aldwincle All Souls, Northamptonshire, the first child of Erasmus and Mary Pickering Dryden, strong Puritans both. Educated at Westminster School under the redoubtable Dr. Busby, and at Trinity College, Cambridge, he went up to London about 1658 where he "set up for a poet." After supporting the Commonwealth in his earlier verses, Dryden accepted the Restoration and became a convinced Royalist, devoting his brilliant satires to the support of the Tory cause, a change made more natural by his marriage to the Lady Elisabeth, sister of Sir Robert Howard, on December 1, 1663. Amid a great deal of hackwork he turned for support to the stage, following Jonson (and to some extent Fletcher) in his first play, *The Wild Gallant* (1663), a prose comedy. Although Dryden was to write a number of comedies, most of them in the coarser tradition of the time, his true vein lay elsewhere; and with the production of *The Indian Queen*, (1664), written with Sir Robert Howard, he began a series of "heroic plays," a genre in which he was to excel. Of these *Aurung-Zebe* (1675), though not wholly typical, is the best. Involved in divers quarrels and rivalries, Dryden examined the theory and practice of the drama in various prose essays, of which *An Essay of Dramatick Poesy* is the most important. In 1678 he produced *All for Love*, written to sustain the nobler traditions of English tragedy, and by general agreement his greatest play. Other dramas followed; but dissatisfaction with the state of the theater, and an increasing interest in party strife gradually led his energies into the field of political and religious controversy. The Revolution of 1688 deprived him of his position as court poet, nor did his conversion to Roman Catholicism (1685) assist his temporal fortunes. After vainly endeavoring to regain his commanding position in the theater, Dryden turned to translation and verse narrative for support. Before his death, it is pleasant to record, he was regarded as the greatest living man of letters, an arbiter to whom any literary dispute might be referred. He died May 1, 1700; his funeral was made the occasion of a splendid tribute, and he was buried in Westminster Abbey.

The standard life of Dryden is that by George Saintsbury in the English Men of Letters series (1881), but the lives by Sir Walter Scott and Samuel Johnson should also be consulted. Mark Van Doren's *The Poetry of John Dryden* (1920) and A. W. Verrall's *Lectures on Dryden* (1914) are recent special studies.

DRYDEN'S DRAMATIC WORKS

The Wild Gallant (comedy) (T.R., Feb. 1662/3), 1669.
The Indian Queen (tragedy) (with Sir Robert Howard) (T.R. Jan. 1663/4), 1665.
The Rival Ladies (comedy) (T.R. June, 1664), 1664.
The Indian Emperor (tragedy) (T.R. April (?) 1665), 1667.
Secret Love (tragi-comedy) (T.R. March 1666/7), 1668.
Sir Martin Mar-All (comedy) (L.I.F. Aug. 1667), 1668.
The Tempest (adaptation) (with Davenant) (L.I.F. Nov. 1667), 1670.
An Evening's Love (comedy) (T.R. June, 1668), 1668.
Tyrannic Love (tragedy) (T.R. June (?) 1669), 1670.
The Conquest of Granada (tragedy); Part I. (T.R. Dec. (?) 1670), Part II (T.R. Jan. 1670/1), 1671.
Marriage à la Mode (comedy) (L.I.F. May (?) 1672), 1673.
The Assignation (comedy) (L.I.F. Nov. (?) 1672), 1673.
Amboyna (tragedy) (L.I.F. June (?) 1673), 1673.
(?) Amorous Adventures (comedy), 1673.
The State of Innocence (opera) (not acted), 1674.
Aurung-Zebe (tragedy) (D.L. Nov. 1675), 1675.
All for Love (tragedy) (D.L. Dec. 1677), 1678.
The Kind Keeper (comedy) (D.G. March, 1677/8), 1679

Œdipus (tragedy) (with Lee) (D.G. Jan. (?) 1678/9), 1679.
Troilus and Cressida (adaptation) (D.G. April (?) 1679), 1679.
The Spanish Friar (tragi-comedy) (D.G. March, 1679/80), 1681.
The Duke of Guise (tragedy) (with Lee) (prohibited), 1683.
Albion and Albianus (opera) (D.G. June, 1685), 1685.
Don Sebastian (tragedy) (D.L. Dec. (?) 1690), 1690.
Amphitryon (comedy) (D.L. Oct. 1690), 1690.
King Arthur (opera) (D.G. Jan. 1691/2), 1691.
Cleomenes (tragedy) (with Southerne?) (D.L. April, 1692), 1692.
Love Triumphant (comedy) (D.L., 1694), 1694.

Whether Mr. Dryden's wit was greatly suited to the stage must remain a matter of debate, but *All for Love*, which he penned to please himself and the Muse, was vastly liked by him, as it was by the genteel audience which first beheld it. It is by the general consent of critics numbered among the noblest of his tragic plays as it is among the noblest examples of Restoration tragedy. This opinion, 'tis true, has been recently questioned,[1] but when allowance is made for the taste of the town in 1677-8, the wonder is not that the play has imperfections, but that Mr. Bayes remained so constant to the better promptings of his genius.

The author has so amply set forth the aim and intention which possessed him in writing this tragedy as to make comment superfluous and addition impertinent. In presuming to correct the errors of the divine Shakespeare while at the same time profiting by his genius, it is, however, to be remarked that Mr. Dryden but followed the practice of the age.

The best of monarchs had scarce returned to Whitehall when the rage of the town for plays compelled the managers to produce such dramas as they could command; and a dearth of new pieces written in the fashionable mode led them to bring forward the productions of the last age with what hasty improvements they might manage. Ridding the tragedy of its inelegancies, Mr. Davenant produced *Hamlet* soon after *The Siege of Rhodes;* and, publishing the play in 1676, purified it (as he thought) from gross improprieties of diction. The *Macbeth* he completely altered, though it is a matter of dispute when he did so; and *Measure for Measure* he new-fashioned as *The Law Against Lovers*.

Following the example of the French, critics of taste and men of understanding next sought to establish the laws of drama as they have been understood by the ancients; and as a knowledge of these spread through the town, 'twas presently seen that the practice of former times had been truly barbarous. In his *Tragedies of the Last Age Considered* (1678) Mr. Rymer convicted these pieces of such great inelegancies as to require, were they to be seen at all, their complete re-fashioning: 'tis remarkable that no "fewer than eleven of (Shakespeare's) plays" were "newly set forth during the four years which followed." But as Mr. Dryden's genius was distinguished by a greater magnanimity of soul than mere scribbling hacks possess, he, and only he, has handled Shakespeare with a becoming reverence.

The author has himself told us, in fashioning his tragedy, that he consulted those of the classic writers who have treated of the loves of Cleopatra and Antony. 'Tis to be feared that he did not study deeply, and to be believed that such was the fascination of Shakespeare's name, he poured into the play, not only such scenes of *Antony and Cleopatra* as he re-wrote, but lines and passages from *Hamlet, Othello, As You Like It*, and others of Shakespeare's dramatic poems, as the learned have since pointed out. But though steeped in this magic, Mr. Dryden is himself throughout; and it is instructive to compare their two styles wherever the actions run parallel.

Mr. Dryden did not forget that the action of a tragedy should be one, its time, within a single revolution of the sun, and its place, the same throughout. A true tragedy must, moreover, represent the conflict of love and honor; which, in the persons of Alexas (love) and Ventidius (honor), is to be seen in this play, the hero being, as it were, caught between them and torn both ways, as he is between the honorable love of Octavia and the lawless passion of Cleopatra, whom, however, the poet has preserved from that fickleness and dishonor which Shakespeare gave her. The love of country is to be seen in Serapion and even in the contemptible Alexas; and indeed no person in the tragedy is without

---

[1] By Dr. Hazelton Spencer in his *Shakespeare Improved*, Cambridge, 1927, pp. 210-21.

a single motive for his actions. If the hero routs no armies, yet armies move in the background of the play, presented upon the stage, as it were, in the single person of Ventidius, whom no luxury can tempt and no flattery persuade. The speeches, though they are often argument while the action stands still, are yet poetry; and the affecting end of the principal characters such as tragedy demands of those who follow unlawful aims.

All for Love was first produced at the Drury Lane Theatre during the winter of 1677-78, probably in December or January.

ALL FOR LOVE;

OR,

THE WORLD WELL LOST

A Tragedy by John Dryden

Written in Imitation of Shakespeare's Style

"Facile est [enim] verbum aliquod ardens, ut ita dicam, notare idque restinctis [iam] animorum incendiis inridere." [1]

PREFACE [2]

The death of Antony and Cleopatra is a subject which has been treated by the greatest wits [3] of our nation, after Shakespeare; and by all so variously that their example has given me the confidence to try myself in this bow of Ulysses [4] amongst the crowd of suitors; and, withal, to take my own measures in aiming at the mark. I doubt not but the same motive has prevailed with all of us in this attempt; I mean the excellency of the moral: for the chief persons represented were famous patterns of unlawful love, and their end accordingly was unfortunate. All reasonable men [5] have long since concluded that the hero of the poem ought not to be a character of perfect virtue, for then he could not without injustice be made unhappy; nor yet altogether wicked, because he could not then be pitied. I have therefore steered the middle course; and have drawn the character of Antony as favorably as Plutarch, Appian, and Dion Cassius would give me leave; the like I have observed in Cleopatra. That which is wanting to work up the pity to a greater height was not afforded me by the story; for the crimes of love which they both committed were not occasioned by any necessity or fatal ignorance but were wholly voluntary; since our passions are, or ought to be, within our power. The fabric of the play is regular enough as to the inferior parts of it; and the unities of time, place, and action more exactly observed than perhaps the English theater requires. Particularly the action is so much one that it is the only of the kind without episode or underplot; every scene in the tragedy conducing to the main design, and every act concluding with a turn of it. The greatest error in the contrivance seems to be in the person of Octavia; for, though I might use the privilege of a poet to introduce her into Alexandria, yet I had not enough considered that the compassion she moved to herself and children was destructive to that which I reserved for Antony and Cleopatra, whose mutual love being founded upon vice, must lessen the favor of the audience to them, when virtue and innocence were oppressed by it. And though I justified Antony in some measure by making Octavia's departure to proceed wholly from herself, yet the force of the first machine [6] still remained; and the dividing of pity, like the cutting of a river into many channels, abated the strength of the natural stream. But this is an objection which none of my critics have urged against me; and therefore I might have let it pass if I could have resolved to have been partial of myself. The faults my enemies have found are rather cavils concerning little and not

---

[1] "It is easy to note some glowing word, if I may say so, and to laugh at it when the fires of the mind are cooled off." Cicero, *Orator ad M. Brutum*, VIII, 27–29.

[2] The dedication to the Earl of Danby is omitted. In it Dryden compliments Danby on his management of the revenues, and pleads for orderly subordination in the commonwealth.

[3] The story of Antony and Cleopatra had formed the subject of a number of plays, such as the *Antony* of Mary, Countess of Pembroke, translated from the French of Garnier in 1592 and reprinted in 1595; Samuel Daniel's *Cleopatra*, 1594, revised in 1623; Thomas May's *Cleopatra*, 1626; and Sir Charles Sedley's *Antony and Cleopatra*, 1677.

[4] Cf. *Odyssey*, bks. xxi–xxii.

[5] See Aristotle, *Poetics*, xiii.

[6] Contrivance.

essential decencies, which a master of the ceremonies may decide betwixt us. The French poets, I confess, are strict observers of these punctilios; they would not, for example, have suffered Cleopatra and Octavia to have met; or, if they had met, there must only have passed betwixt them some cold civilities, but no eagerness of repartee, for fear of offending against the greatness of their characters and the modesty of their sex. This objection I foresaw, and at the same time condemned; for I judged it both natural and probable that Octavia, proud of her new-gained conquest, would search out Cleopatra to triumph over her, and that Cleopatra, thus attacked, was not of a spirit to shun the encounter. And 'tis not unlikely that two exasperated rivals should use such satire as I have put into their mouths; for, after all, though the one were a Roman and the other a queen, they were both women. 'Tis true some actions, though natural, are not fit to be represented; and broad obscenities in words ought in good manners to be avoided: expressions, therefore, are a modest clothing of our thoughts as breeches and petticoats are of our bodies. If I have kept myself within the bounds of modesty, all beyond it is but nicety and affectation, which is no more but modesty depraved into a vice. They betray themselves who are too quick of apprehension in such cases, and leave all reasonable men to imagine worse of them than of the poet.

Honest Montaigne goes yet further: *Nous ne sommes que cérémonie; la cérémonie nous emporte, et laissons la substance des choses. Nous nous tenons aux branches, et abandonnons le tronc et le corps. Nous avons appris aux dames de rougir, oyans seulement nommer ce qu'elles ne craignent aucunement à faire: nous n'osons appeller à droit nos membres, et ne craignons pas de les employer à toute sorte de débauche. La cérémonie nous defend d'exprimer par paroles les choses licites et naturelles, et nous l'en croyons; la raison nous defend de n'en faire point d'illicites et mauvaises, et personne ne l'en croit.*[1] My comfort is that by this opinion my enemies are but sucking critics, who would fain be nibbling ere their teeth are come.

Yet in this nicety of manners does the excellency of French poetry consist. Their heroes are the most civil people breathing; but their good breeding seldom extends to a word of sense; all their wit is in their ceremony; they want the genius which animates our stage; and therefore 'tis but necessary, when they cannot please, that they should take care not to offend. But as the civilest man in the company is commonly the dullest, so these authors, while they are afraid to make you laugh or cry, out of pure good manners make you sleep. They are so careful not to exasperate a critic that they never leave him any work; so busy with the broom, and make so clean a riddance, that there is little left either for censure or for praise. For no part of a poem is worth our discommending where the whole is insipid; as when we have once tasted of palled wine, we stay not to examine it glass by glass. But while they affect to shine in trifles, they are often careless in essentials. Thus their Hippolytus [2] is so scrupulous in point of decency that he will rather expose himself to death than accuse his stepmother to his father; and my critics, I am sure, will commend him for it. But we of grosser apprehensions are apt to think that this excess of generosity is not practicable but with fools and madmen. This was good manners with a vengeance; and the audience is like to be much concerned at the misfortunes of this admirable hero. But take Hippolytus out of his poetic fit, and I suppose he would think it a wiser part to set the saddle on the right horse and choose rather to live with the reputation of a plain-spoken, honest man than to die with the infamy of an incestuous villain. In the meantime we may take notice that where the poet ought to have preserved the character as it was delivered to us by antiquity, when he should have given us the picture of a rough young man of the Amazonian strain, a jolly huntsman, and both by his profession and his early rising a mortal enemy to love, he has chosen to give him the

---

[1] We are nothing but ceremony; ceremony carries us off, and we let go the substance of things. We hold on to the branches, and abandon the trunk and the body. We have taught ladies to blush at merely hearing named what they are not in the least afraid to do; we dare not call our members by their right names, and yet we are not afraid to use them in all sorts of debauchery. Ceremony forbids us to express proper and natural things in words, and we believe it is right; reason forbids us to do anything illicit or bad, and no one believes its counsels. *Essais*, II, xvi, "De la présomption."

[2] Hippolyte in Racine's tragedy, *Phèdre* (1677).

turn of gallantry, sent him to travel from Athens to Paris, taught him to make love, and transformed the Hippolytus of Euripides [1] into Monsieur Hippolyte. I should not have troubled myself thus far with French poets, but that I find our *Chedreux* [2] critics wholly form their judgments by them. But for my part I desire to be tried by the laws of my own country; for it seems unjust to me that the French should prescribe here till they have conquered. Our little sonneteers who follow them have too narrow souls to judge of poetry. Poets themselves are the most proper, though I conclude not the only, critics. But till some genius as universal as Aristotle shall arise, one who can penetrate into all arts and sciences without the practice of them, I shall think it reasonable that the judgment of an artificer in his own art should be preferable to the opinion of another man; at least where he is not bribed by interest or prejudiced by malice. And this, I suppose, is manifest by plain induction. For, first, the crowd cannot be presumed to have more than a gross instinct of what pleases or displeases them. Every man will grant me this; but then, by a particular kindness to himself, he draws his own stake first, and will be distinguished from the multitude of which other men may think him one. But if I come closer to those [3] who are allowed for witty men, either by the advantage of their quality or by common fame, and affirm that neither are they qualified to decide sovereignly concerning poetry, I shall yet have a strong party of my opinion; for most of them severally will exclude the rest, either from the number of witty men, or at least of able judges. But here again they are all indulgent to themselves; and every one who believes himself a wit, that is, every man, will pretend at the same time to a right of judging. But to press it yet farther, there are many witty men, but few poets; neither have all poets a taste of tragedy. And this is the rock on which they are daily splitting. Poetry, which is a picture of nature, must generally please; but it is not to be understood that all parts of it must please every man; therefore is not tragedy to be judged by a witty man whose taste is only confined to comedy. Nor is every man who loves tragedy a sufficient judge of it; he must understand the excellencies of it too, or he will only prove a blind admirer, not a critic. From hence it comes that so many satires on poets and censures of their writings fly abroad. Men of pleasant conversation (at least esteemed so), and endued with a trifling kind of fancy, perhaps helped out with some smattering of Latin, are ambitious to distinguish themselves from the herd of gentlemen by their poetry—

Rarus enim fermè sensus communis in illâ Fortunâ.[4]

And is not this a wretched affectation, not to be contented with what fortune has done for them, and sit down quietly with their estates, but they must call their wits in question and needlessly expose their nakedness to public view, not considering that they are not to expect the same approbation from sober men which they have found from their flatterers after the third bottle? If a little glittering in discourse has passed them on us for witty men, where was the necessity of undeceiving the world? Would a man who has an ill title to an estate but yet is in possession of it—would he bring it of his own accord to be tried at Westminster? We who write, if we want the talent, yet have the excuse that we do it for a poor subsistence; but what can be urged in their defence, who, not having the vocation of poverty to scribble, out of mere wantonness take pains to make themselves ridiculous? Horace [5] was certainly in the right where he said, "That no man is satisfied with his condition." A poet is not pleased because he is not rich; and the rich are discontented because the poets will not admit them of their number. Thus the case is hard with writers: if they succeed not, they must starve; and if they do, some malicious satire is prepared to level them for daring to please without their leave. But while they are so eager to destroy the fame of others, their ambition is manifest in their concernment; some poem of their own is to be produced, and the slaves are to be laid flat with

---

[1] Euripides' *Hippolytus* was much discussed by theorists of tragedy in the seventeenth century.

[2] The name of a fashionable periwig of the day; hence, foppish.

[3] This passage is generally supposed to refer to Rochester.

[4] Common sense, however, is rare in that condition of life.—Juvenal, *Satires*, VIII, 73-4.

[5] See *Satires*, I, i, 1-3.

their faces on the ground that the monarch may appear in the greater majesty.

Dionysius [1] and Nero had the same longings, but with all their power they could never bring their business well about. 'Tis true they proclaimed themselves poets by sound of trumpet; and poets they were upon pain of death to any man who durst call them otherwise. The audience had a fine time on't, you may imagine; they sat in a bodily fear and looked as demurely as they could, for it was a hanging matter to laugh unseasonably; and the tyrants were suspicious, as they had reason, that their subjects had them in the wind; so every man, in his own defence, set as good a face upon the business as he could. It was known beforehand that the monarchs were to be crowned laureates; but when the show was over, and an honest man was suffered to depart quietly, he took out his laughter, which he had stifled, with a firm resolution never more to see an emperor's play, though he had been ten years a-making it. In the meantime the true poets were they who made the best markets; for they had wit enough to yield the prize with a good grace, and not contend with him who had thirty legions.[2] They were sure to be rewarded if they confessed themselves bad writers, and that was somewhat better than to be martyrs for their reputation. Lucan's [3] example was enough to teach them manners; and after he was put to death for overcoming Nero, the emperor carried it without dispute for the best poet in his dominions. No man was ambitious of that grinning honor; for if he heard the malicious trumpeters proclaiming his name before his betters, he knew there was but one way with him. Mæcenas took another course, and we know he was more than a great man, for he was witty too.[4] But finding himself far gone in poetry, which Seneca assures us was not his talent, he thought it his best way to be well with Virgil and with Horace; that at least he might be a poet at the second hand; and we see how happily it has succeeded with him, for his own bad poetry is forgotten and their panegyrics of him still remain. But they who should be our patrons are for no such expensive ways to fame; they have much of the poetry of Mæcenas, but little of his liberality. They are for persecuting Horace and Virgil in the persons of their successors; for such is every man who has any part of their soul and fire, though in a less degree. Some of their little zanies yet go farther; for they are persecutors even of Horace [5] himself, as far as they are able, by their ignorant and vile imitations of him, by making an unjust use of his authority and turning his artillery against his friends. But how would he disdain to be copied by such hands! I dare answer for him, he would be more uneasy in their company than he was with Crispinus,[6] their forefather, in the Holy Way;[7] and would no more have allowed them a place amongst the critics than he would Demetrius the mimic and Tigellius the buffoon:

. . . *Demetri, teque, Tigelli,*
Discipulorum inter jubeo plorare cathedras. [8]

With what scorn would he look down on such miserable translators, who make doggerel of his Latin, mistake his meaning, misapply his censures, and often contradict their own? He is fixed as a landmark to set out the bounds of poetry—

. . . *Saxum antiquum, ingens,* . . .
Limes agro positus, litem ut discerneret arvis.[9]

But other arms than theirs, and other sinews, are required to raise the weight of such an author; and when they would toss him against their enemies—

---

[1] See Diodorus Siculus, XV, vi–vii. For Nero see Suetonius, *Lives of the Cæsars*, VI, xx–xxi; xxiii–xxiv.

[2] Cf. Bacon, *Apothegms*, no. 216 (*Works*, II, 441–2, ed. 1824); or no. 160 in the Spedding edition, XIII, 361.

[3] According to Tacitus (*Annales*, XV), moved by jealousy of Nero, who had forbidden him to recite his poems publicly, Lucan joined the conspiracy of Piso (A.D. 65) against the Emperor; when the conspiracy was discovered, Nero ordered the poet to commit suicide, which he did.

[4] Apparently a reference to the *Epistola*, CI, in which Seneca speaks scornfully of certain verses by Mæcenas on death.

[5] The whole of this passage is a reply to Rochester's *Allusion to the Tenth Satire of Horace*.

[6] Cf. Horace, *Satires*, I, i, iii, iv, and ix. There seems to be no authority for supposing that the bore of the ninth satire is the same as the "blear-eyed Crispinus" of the first.

[7] The *Via Sacra*, the oldest and most famous street in Rome, where Horace met the bore.

[8] I bid you, Demetrius, and you, Tigellius, go whine among the easy chairs of your pupils.—Horace has *discipularum*—female pupils.

[9] A huge and ancient rock placed as the boundary of a field that it might keep disputes away from the fields. *Æneid*, XII, 897–8.

> *Genua labant, gelidus concrevit frigore sanguis.*
> *Tum lapis ipse, viri vacuum per inane volutus,*
> *Nec spatium evasit totum, nec pertulit ictum.*[1]

For my part I would wish no other revenge, either for myself or the rest of the poets, from this rhyming judge of the twelvepenny gallery, this legitimate son of Sternhold,[2] than that he would subscribe his name to his censure or (not to tax him beyond his learning) set his mark. For, should he own himself publicly and come from behind the lion's skin, they whom he condemns would be thankful to him, they whom he praises would choose to be condemned; and the magistrates whom he has elected would modestly withdraw from their employment to avoid the scandal of his nomination. The sharpness of his satire, next to himself, falls most heavily on his friends, and they ought never to forgive him for commending them perpetually the wrong way and sometimes by contraries. If he have a friend whose hastiness in writings is his greatest fault, Horace would have taught him to have minced the matter, and to have called it readiness of thought and a flowing fancy; for friendship will allow a man to christen an imperfection by the name of some neighbor virtue—[3]

> *Vellem in amicitiâ sic erraremus, et isti*
> *Errori nomen virtus posuisset honestum.*[4]

But he would never have allowed him to have called a slow man hasty or a hasty writer a slow drudge, as Juvenal explains it—

> *. . . Canibus pigris, scabieque vetustâ*
> *Lævibus, et siccæ lambentibus ora lucernæ,*
> *Nomen erit, Pardus, Tigris, Leo; si quid adhuc est*
> *Quod fremit in terris violentius.*[5]

Yet Lucretius laughs at a foolish lover even for excusing the imperfections of his mistress—

> *Nigra μελίχοος est, immunda et fœtida ἄκοσμος,*
> *Balba loqui, non quit, Τραυλίζει; muta pudens, est, etc.*[6]

But to drive it *ad Æthiopem cygnum*[7] is not to be endured. I leave him to interpret this by the benefit of his French version on the other side, and without further considering him than I have the rest of my illiterate censors, whom I have disdained to answer because they are not qualified for judges. It remains that I acquaint the reader that I have endeavored in this play to follow the practice of the ancients, who, as Mr. Rymer[8] has judiciously observed, are, and ought to be, our masters. Horace likewise gives it for a rule in his art of poetry—

> *. . . Vos exemplaria Græca*
> *Nocturnâ versate manu, versate diurnâ*[9]

Yet, though their models are regular, they are too little for English tragedy, which requires to be built in a larger compass. I could give an instance in the "Œdipus Tyrannus,"[10] which was the masterpiece of Sophocles; but I reserve it for a more fit occasion, which I hope to have hereafter. In my style I have professed to imitate the divine Shakespeare; which, that I might perform more freely, I have disencumbered myself from rhyme. Not that I condemn my former way, but that this is more proper to my present purpose. I hope I need not to explain myself that I have not copied my author servilely. Words and phrases must of necessity receive a change in succeeding ages, but 'tis almost a miracle that much of his language remains so pure and that he who began dramatic poetry amongst us, untaught by any, and as Ben Jonson[11] tells us, without learning, should by the force of his own genius perform so

---

[1] His knees gave way, his gelid blood froze with cold. Then the very rock, whirled through empty space, the rock of the hero, neither covered the whole distance, nor struck the mark.—*Æneid*, XII, 905-7. The reference is to the fight between Turnus and Æneas.

[2] Thomas Sternhold (1500-40), who, with John Hopkins, made a metrical version of the Psalms long in use in the Anglican church, though it is not distinguished by poetic beauty.

[3] Cf. the closing lines of Rochester's *Allusion*.

[4] I would that we could so err in friendship and that to such error good sense could give an honest name. Horace, *Satires*, I, iii, 41-2.

[5] Lazy dogs, hairless from old mange, licking the edges of a dry lamp, shall have the names of Panther, Tiger, Lion, or whatever else roars more violently over the earth.—Juvenal, *Satires*, VIII, 34-7.

[6] A black girl is called "honey-dark"; a foul and sweaty one, "without love of order." She who stutters and can not speak "has a lisp"; the speechless one is "modest," and so on.—Lucretius, *De Rerum Natura*, IV, 1160; 1164.

[7] We call an Æthiop a swan. Modified from Juvenal, *Satires*, VIII, 333.

[8] Thomas Rymer published his *Tragedies of the Last Age Considered* in 1678.

[9] Turn over the pages of your Greek masters day and night.—Horace, *Ars Poetica*, 268-9.

[10] Dryden and Lee wrote an *Œdipus* in 1678.

[11] Cf. Jonson's lines *To the Memory of My Beloved Master William Shakspeare*, especially 32ff.

much, that in a manner he has left no praise for any who come after him. The occasion is fair, and the subject would be pleasant, to handle the difference of styles betwixt him and Fletcher, and wherein, and how far they are both to be imitated. But since I must not be over-confident of my own performance after him, it will be prudence in me to be silent. Yet I hope I may affirm, and without vanity, that by imitating him I have excelled myself throughout the play; and particularly that I prefer the scene betwixt Antony and Ventidius in the first act to anything which I have written in this kind.

ALL FOR LOVE;
OR,
THE WORLD WELL LOST

DRAMATIS PERSONÆ

MEN

MARK ANTONY	Mr. Hart	ALEXAS, *the Queen's Eunuch*	Mr. Goodman
VENTIDIUS, *his General*	Mr. Mohun	SERAPION, *Priest of Isis*	Mr. Griffin
DOLABELLA, *his Friend*	Mr. Clarke	[MYRIS,] *another Priest*	Mr. Coyash

Servants to Antony

WOMEN

CLEOPATRA, *Queen of Egypt*	Mrs. Boutell	CHARMION }	*Cleopatra's Maids*
OCTAVIA, *Antony's Wife*	Mrs. Corey	IRAS }	

Antony's two little Daughters

PROLOGUE

What flocks of critics hover here today,
As vultures wait on armies for their prey,
All gaping for the carcass of a play!
With croaking notes they bode some dire event
And follow dying poets by the scent.　　5
Ours gives himself for gone; y'have watched your time:
He fights this day unarmed,—without his rhyme;—
And brings a tale which often has been told,
As sad as Dido's, and almost as old.
His hero, whom you wits his bully call,　　10
Bates of his mettle,[1] and scarce rants at all.
He's somewhat lewd; but a well-meaning mind;
Weeps much; fights little; but is wond'rous kind.
In short, a pattern, and companion fit
For all the keeping tonies[2] of the pit.　　15
I could name more: a wife and mistress, too.

Both (to be plain) too good for most of you:
The wife well-natured, and the mistress true;
　Now, poets, if your fame has been his care,
Allow him all the candor you can spare.　　20
A brave man scorns to quarrel once a day,
Like Hectors[3] in at every petty fray.
Let those find fault whose wit's so very small,
They've need to show that they can think at all.
Errors, like straws, upon the surface flow;　　25
He who would search for pearls must dive below.
Fops may have leave to level all they can,
As pigmies would be glad to lop a man.
Half-wits are fleas; so little and so light,
We scarce could know they live, but that they bite.　　30
But as the rich, when tired with daily feasts,
For change become their next poor tenants' guests,
Drink hearty draughts of ale from plain brown bowls
And snatch the homely rasher from the coals,
So you, retiring from much better cheer,　　35
For once may venture to do penance here.
And since that plenteous autumn now is past
Whose grapes and peaches have indulged your taste,

---

[1] Noyes suggests that Dryden is here preparing his audience for an Antony less like Shakespeare's "living and breathing hero" and more like the "conventional lover" of French romances.

[2] Foolish persons, simpletons. Possibly from the disguise of Antony as an idiot in Middleton's *The Changeling* (1623), I, ii.

[3] Bullies; especially applied to disorderly young men who infested the streets of London.

Take in good part, from our poor poet's board,
Such rivelled [1] fruits as winter can afford. 40

SCENE: *Alexandria*

ACT I

SCENE I. *The Temple of Isis*

Enter SERAPION, MYRIS, *Priests of Isis*

SERAPION. Portents and prodigies are grown so frequent
That they have lost their name. Our fruitful Nile
Flowed ere the wonted season with a torrent
So unexpected and so wondrous fierce
That the wild deluge overtook the haste 5
Even of the hinds that watched it. Men and beasts
Were borne above the tops of trees that grew
On the utmost margin of the water-mark.
Then, with so swift an ebb the flood drove backward,
It slipt from underneath the scaly herd: 10
Here monstrous phocæ [2] panted on the shore;
Forsaken dolphins there with their broad tails
Lay lashing the departing waves; hard by them,
Sea-horses, floundering in the slimy mud,
Tossed up their heads, and dashed the ooze about them. 15

Enter ALEXAS *behind them*

MYRIS. Avert these omens, Heaven!
SERAPION. Last night, between the hours of twelve and one,
In a lone aisle of the temple while I walked,
A whirlwind rose that with a violent blast
Shook all the dome; the doors around me clapped; 20
The iron wicket that defends the vault
Where the long race of Ptolemies is laid
Burst open and disclosed the mighty dead.
From out each monument, in order placed,
An armèd ghost starts up: the boy-king [3] last 25
Reared his inglorious head. A peal of groans
Then followed, and a lamentable voice
Cried, "Egypt is no more!" My blood ran back,
My shaking knees against each other knocked;
On the cold pavement down I fell entranced,
And so unfinished left the horrid scene. 31
ALEXAS. (*Showing himself*) And dreamed you this? or did invent the story

To frighten our Egyptian boys withal,
And train them up betimes in fear of priesthood?
SERAPION. My lord, I saw you not, 35
Nor meant my words should reach your ears; but what
I uttered was most true.
ALEXAS. A foolish dream,
Bred from the fumes of indigested feasts
And holy luxury.
SERAPION. I know my duty: 39
This goes no farther.
ALEXAS. 'Tis not fit it should,
Nor would the times now bear it, were it true.
All southern, from yon hills, the Roman camp
Hangs o'er us black and threatening like a storm
Just breaking on our heads. 45
SERAPION. Our faint Egyptians pray for Antony;
But in their servile hearts they own Octavius.
MYRIS. Why then does Antony dream out his hours,
And tempts not fortune for a noble day
Which might redeem what Actium lost? 50
ALEXAS. He thinks 'tis past recovery.
SERAPION. Yet the foe
Seems not to press the siege.
ALEXAS. Oh, there's the wonder.
Mæcenas and Agrippa, who can [4] most
With Cæsar, are his foes. His wife Octavia,
Driven from his house, solicits her revenge; 55
And Dolabella, who was once his friend,
Upon some private grudge now seeks his ruin:
Yet still war seems on either side to sleep.
SERAPION. 'Tis strange that Antony, for some days past,
Has not beheld the face of Cleopatra, 60
But here in Isis' temple lives retired,
And makes his heart a prey to black despair.
ALEXAS. 'Tis true; and we much fear he hopes by absence
To cure his mind of love.
SERAPION. If he be vanquished
Or make his peace, Egypt is doomed to be 65
A Roman province, and our plenteous harvests
Must then redeem [5] the scarceness of their soil.
While Antony stood firm, our Alexandria
Rivaled proud Rome (dominion's other seat),
And Fortune, striding like a vast Colossus, 70
Could fix an equal foot of empire here.

---

[1] Wrinkled.   [2] Seals.   [3] Cleopatra's brother.
[4] Who can accomplish most. An archaism.
[5] May be exchanged for.

ALEXAS. Had I my wish, these tyrants of
  all nature
Who lord it o'er mankind, should perish—
  perish
Each by the other's sword; but, since our will
Is lamely followed by our power, we must 75
Depend on one, with him to rise or fall.
  SERAPION. How stands the queen affected?
  ALEXAS.   Oh, she dotes,
She dotes, Serapion, on this vanquished man,
And winds herself about his mighty ruins;
Whom would she yet forsake, yet yield him up,
This hunted prey, to his pursuer's hands, 81
She might preserve us all; but 'tis in vain—
This changes my designs, this blasts my
  counsels,
And makes me use all means to keep him
  here,
Whom I could wish divided from her arms
Far as the earth's deep center. Well, you
  know   86
The state of things; no more of your ill omens
And black prognostics; labor to confirm[1]
The people's hearts.

Enter VENTIDIUS, *talking aside with a* Gentleman *of* ANTONY'S

  SERAPION. These Romans will o'erhear us.
But who's that stranger? By his warlike port,
His fierce demeanor, and erected look,   91
He's of no vulgar note.
  ALEXAS.   Oh, 'tis Ventidius,
Our emperor's great lieutenant in the East,
Who first showed Rome that Parthia could be
  conquered.
When Antony returned from Syria last, 95
He left this man to guard the Roman frontiers.
  SERAPION. You seem to know him well.
  ALEXAS Too well. I saw him in Cilicia
  first,
When Cleopatra there met Antony.
A mortal foe he was to us and Egypt.   100
But—let me witness to the worth I hate—
A braver Roman never drew a sword;
Firm to his prince, but as a friend, not slave.
He ne'er was of his pleasures; but presides
O'er all his cooler hours and morning counsels:
In short, the plainness, fierceness, rugged
  virtue   106
Of an old true-stamped Roman lives in him.

His coming bodes I know not what of ill
To our affairs. Withdraw, to mark him
  better;
And I'll acquaint you why I sought you here,
And what's our present work.
  (*They withdraw to a corner of the stage;
    and* VENTIDIUS, *with the other, comes
    forward to the front*)
  VENTIDIUS.   Not see him, say you? 111
I say I must and will.
  GENTLEMAN.   He has commanded,
On pain of death, none should approach his
  presence.
  VENTIDIUS. I bring him news will raise his
    drooping spirits,
Give him new life.
  GENTLEMAN.   He sees not Cleopatra. 115
  VENTIDIUS. Would he had never seen her!
  GENTLEMAN. He eats not, drinks not,
    sleeps not, has no use
Of anything but thought; or, if he talks,
'Tis to himself, and then 'tis perfect raving.
Then he defies the world, and bids it pass; 120
Sometimes he gnaws his lip and curses loud
The boy Octavius; then he draws his mouth
Into a scornful smile and cries, "Take all,
The world's not worth my care."
  VENTIDIUS.   Just, just his nature.
Virtue's his path; but sometimes 'tis too
  narrow
For his vast soul; and then he starts out wide,
And bounds into a vice that bears him far 127
From his first course and plunges him in ills;
But when his danger makes him find his fault,
Quick to observe, and full of sharp remorse,
He censures eagerly his own misdeeds,   131
Judging himself with malice to himself,
And not forgiving what as man he did,
Because his other parts are more than man.—
He must not thus be lost.
  (ALEXAS *and the* Priests *come forward*)
  ALEXAS. You have your full instructions,
    now advance;   135
Proclaim your orders loudly.
  SERAPION. Romans, Egyptians, hear the
    queen's command!
Thus Cleopatra bids: Let labor cease;
To pomp and triumphs give this happy day
That gave the world a lord: 'tis Antony's. 140
Live, Antony; and Cleopatra, live!
Be this the general voice sent up to heaven,
And every public place repeat this echo.
  VENTIDIUS. (*Aside*) Fine pageantry!
  SERAPION.   Set out before your doors

---

[1] Strengthen.—The following stage direction should be compared with that about line 197. The Gentleman of Antony is apparently included among the dramatis personæ with the servants of Antony.

The images of all your sleeping fathers, 145
With laurels crowned; with laurels wreathe
   your posts
And strew with flowers the pavement; let
   the priests
Do present [1] sacrifice; pour out the wine
And call the gods to join with you in glad-
   ness.
   VENTIDIUS. Curse on the tongue that bids
      this general joy! 150
Can they be friends of Antony, who revel
When Antony's in danger? Hide, for shame,
You Romans, your great grandsires' images,
For fear their souls should animate their
   marbles,
To blush at their degenerate progeny. 155
   ALEXAS. A love which knows no bounds to
      Antony
Would mark the day with honors when all
   heaven
Labored for him, when each propitious star
Stood wakeful in his orb to watch that hour
And shed his better influence.[2] Her own
   birthday 160
Our queen neglected like a vulgar fate
That passed obscurely by.
   VENTIDIUS.   Would it had slept,
Divided far from his; till some remote
And future age had called it out, to ruin
Some other prince, not him!
   ALEXAS.   Your emperor, 165
Though grown unkind, would be more gentle
   than
To upbraid my queen for loving him too well.
   VENTIDIUS. Does the mute sacrifice upbraid
      the priest?
He knows him not his executioner.
Oh, she has decked his ruin with her love, 170
Led him in golden bands to gaudy slaughter,
And made perdition pleasing. She has left him
The blank of what he was.
I tell thee, eunuch, she has quite unmanned
   him.
Can any Roman see and know him now, 175
Thus altered from the lord of half mankind,
Unbent, unsinewed, made a woman's toy,
Shrunk from the vast extent of all his honors,
And cramped within a corner of the world?
O Antony! 180
Thou bravest soldier and thou best of friends!
Bounteous as nature; next to nature's God!

[1] Immediate.
[2] Referring to the supposed influence of the stars on character or destiny.

Couldst thou but make new worlds, so wouldst
   thou give 'em,
As bounty were thy being: rough in battle
As the first Romans when they went to war;
Yet, after victory, more pitiful 186
Than all their praying virgins left at home!
   ALEXAS. Would you could add to those
      more shining virtues,
His truth to her who loves him.
   VENTIDIUS.   Would I could not!
But wherefore waste I precious hours with
   thee? 190
Thou art her darling mischief, her chief
   engine,
Antony's other fate. Go, tell thy queen
Ventidius is arrived to end her charms.
Let your Egyptian timbrels play alone,
Nor mix effeminate sounds with Roman
   trumpets. 195
You dare not fight for Antony; go pray,
And keep your coward's holiday in temples.
         Exeunt ALEXAS, SERAPION

Re-enter the Gentleman [3] *of* M. ANTONY

   2D GENTLEMAN. The emperor approaches
      and commands
On pain of death that none presume to stay.
   1ST GENTLEMAN. I dare not disobey him.
         (*Going out with the other*)
   VENTIDIUS.   Well, I dare.
But I'll observe him first unseen, and find 201
Which way his humor drives. The rest I'll
   venture.   (*Withdraws*)

Enter ANTONY, *walking with a disturbed motion before he speaks*

   ANTONY. They tell me 'tis my birthday,
      and I'll keep it
With double pomp of sadness.
'Tis what the day deserves which gave me
   breath. 205
Why was I raised the meteor of the world,
Hung in the skies and blazing as I travelled,
Till all my fires were spent, and then cast
   downward
To be trod out by Cæsar?
   VENTIDIUS. (*Aside*)   On my soul,
'Tis mournful, wondrous mournful!
   ANTONY.   Count thy gains.

[3] As Noyes points out, the First Gentleman, who entered with Ventidius, has never left the stage; he proposes to emend the text to read: "Enter a Second Gentleman of M. Antony." The Quarto edition of 1696 and the Folio edition of 1701, however, read: "Re-enter the Gentleman of Antony."

Now, Antony, wouldst thou be born for this!
Glutton of fortune, thy devouring youth 212
Has starved thy wanting age.
    VENTIDIUS. (*Aside*)   How sorrow shakes him!
So now the tempest tears him up by the roots,
And on the ground extends the noble ruin. 215
    ANTONY. (*Having thrown himself down*) Lie there, thou shadow of an emperor;[1]
The place thou pressest on thy mother earth
Is all thy empire now; now it contains thee;
Some few days hence, and then 'twill be too large,
When thou'rt contracted in thy narrow urn,
Shrunk to a few cold ashes; then Octavia 221
(For Cleopatra will not live to see it),
Octavia then will have thee all her own,
And bear thee in her widowed hand to Cæsar;
Cæsar will weep, the crocodile will weep, 225
To see his rival of the universe
Lie still and peaceful there. I'll think no more on't.
Give me some music; look that it be sad.
I'll soothe my melancholy till I swell 229
And burst myself with sighing.— (*Soft music*)
'Tis somewhat to my humor. Stay, I fancy
I'm now turned wild, a commoner of nature;
Of all forsaken and forsaking all,
Live in a shady forest's sylvan scene,
Stretched at my length beneath some blasted oak, 235
I lean my head upon the mossy bark
And look just of a piece as I grew from it;
My uncombed locks, matted like mistletoe,
Hang o'er my hoary face; a murm'ring brook
Runs at my foot.
    VENTIDIUS. [*Aside*] Methinks I fancy 240
Myself there, too.
    ANTONY.   The herd come jumping by me,
And, fearless, quench their thirst while I look on,
And take me for their fellow-citizen.
More of this image, more; it lulls my thoughts.
        (*Soft music again*)
    VENTIDIUS. I must disturb him; I can hold no longer.   (*Stands before him*) 245
    ANTONY. (*Starting up*) Art thou Ventidius?
    VENTIDIUS.   Are you Antony?
I'm liker what I was than you to him
I left you last.
    ANTONY.   I'm angry.
    VENTIDIUS.   So am I.

---

[1] Ll. 216–27 obviously belong to Anthony, and not to Ventidius, as some editions have them.

    ANTONY. I would be private. Leave me.
    VENTIDIUS.   Sir, I love you,
And therefore will not leave you.
    ANTONY.   Will not leave me! 250
Where have you learned that answer? Who am I?
    VENTIDIUS. My emperor; the man I love next Heaven;
If I said more, I think 'twere scarce a sin—
You're all that's good and godlike.
    ANTONY.   All that's wretched.
You will not leave me then?
    VENTIDIUS.   'Twas too presuming
To say I would not; but I dare not leave you,
And 'tis unkind in you to chide me hence 257
So soon, when I so far have come to see you.
    ANTONY. Now thou hast seen me. art thou satisfied?
For, if a friend, thou hast beheld enough; 260
And, if a foe, too much.
    VENTIDIUS. (*Weeping*.) Look, emperor, this is no common dew,
I have not wept this forty years; but now
My mother comes afresh into my eyes;
I cannot help her softness. 265
    ANTONY. By heaven, he weeps! poor, good old man, he weeps!
The big round drops course one another down
The furrows of his cheeks.—Stop them, Ventidius,
Or I shall blush to death: they set my shame,
That caused them, full before me.
    VENTIDIUS.   I'll do my best. 270
    ANTONY. Sure, there's contagion in the tears of friends—
See, I have caught it, too. Believe me, 'tis not
For my own griefs, but thine.—Nay, father!
    VENTIDIUS.   Emperor.
    ANTONY. Emperor! Why, that's the style of victory;
The conqu'ring soldier, red with unfelt wounds, 275
Salutes his general so; but never more
Shall that sound reach my ears.
    VENTIDIUS.   I warrant you.
    ANTONY. Actium, Actium! Oh!—
    VENTIDIUS.   It sits too near you.
    ANTONY. Here, here it lies, a lump of lead by day,
And, in my short, distracted, nightly slumbers,
The hag that rides my dreams.— 281
    VENTIDIUS. Out with it; give it vent.
    ANTONY.   Urge not my shame.
I lost a battle.—

VENTIDIUS. So has Julius done.
ANTONY. Thou favor'st me, and speak'st
   not half thou think'st;
For Julius fought it out, and lost it fairly,   285
But Antony—
VENTIDIUS. Nay, stop not.
   ANTONY.   Antony,—
Well, thou wilt have it,—like a coward fled,
Fled while his soldiers fought; fled first,
   Ventidius.
Thou long'st to curse me, and I give thee
   leave.
I know thou cam'st prepared to rail.
   VENTIDIUS.   I did.   290
   ANTONY. I'll help thee.—I have been a
      man, Ventidius.
   VENTIDIUS. Yes, and a brave one; but—
   ANTONY.   I know thy meaning.
But I have lost my reason, have disgraced
The name of soldier with inglorious ease.
In the full vintage of my flowing honors,   295
Sat still, and saw it pressed by other hands.
Fortune came smiling to my youth, and wooed
   it,
And purple greatness met my ripened years.
When first I came to empire, I was borne   299
On tides of people crowding to my triumphs—
The wish of nations! and the willing world
Received me as its pledge of future peace;
I was so great, so happy, so beloved,
Fate could not ruin me, till I took pains,
And worked against my fortune, chid her
   from me,   305
And turned her loose; yet still she came
   again.
My careless days and my luxurious nights
At length have wearied her, and now she's
   gone,
Gone, gone, divorced for ever.   Help me,
   soldier,
To curse this madman, this industrious fool,
Who labored to be wretched.   Pr'ythee, curse
   me.   311
   VENTIDIUS. No.
   ANTONY.   Why?
   VENTIDIUS.   You are too sensible already
Of what you've done, too conscious of your
   failings;
And, like a scorpion, whipped by others first
To fury, sting yourself in mad revenge.   315
I would bring balm and pour it in your wounds,
Cure your distempered mind and heal your
   fortunes.
ANTONY. I know thou would'st.

VENTIDIUS.   I will.
ANTONY.   Ha, ha, ha, ha!
VENTIDIUS. You laugh.
   ANTONY.   I do, to see officious love
Give cordials to the dead.
   VENTIDIUS.   You would be lost, then?
   ANTONY. I am.
   VENTIDIUS. I say you are not.   Try your
      fortune.   321
   ANTONY. I have, to the utmost.   Dost thou
      think me desperate
Without just cause?   No, when I found all lost
Beyond repair, I hid me from the world,
And learned to scorn it here; which now I do
So heartily, I think it is not worth   326
The cost of keeping.
   VENTIDIUS.   Cæsar thinks not so.
He'll thank you for the gift he could not take.
You would be killed like Tully, would
   you?   Do,
Hold out your throat to Cæsar, and die
   tamely.   330
   ANTONY. No, I can kill myself; and so
      resolve.
   VENTIDIUS. I can die with you, too, when
      time shall serve,
But fortune calls upon us now to live,
To fight, to conquer.
   ANTONY.   Sure, thou dream'st, Ventidius.
   VENTIDIUS. No; 'tis you dream.   You sleep
      away your hours   335
In desperate sloth, miscalled philosophy.
Up, up, for honor's sake!   Twelve legions
   wait you
And long to call you chief.   By painful journeys
I led them, patient both of heat and hunger,
Down from the Parthian marches[1] to the
   Nile.   340
'Twill do you good to see their sunburnt faces,
Their scarred cheeks, and chopped[2] hands.
   There's virtue in them.
They'll sell those mangled limbs at dearer
   rates
Than yon trim bands can buy.
   ANTONY.   Where left you them?
   VENTIDIUS. I said in Lower Syria.
   ANTONY.   Bring them hither;
There may be life in these.
   VENTIDIUS.   They will not come.
   ANTONY. Why didst thou mock my hopes
      with promised aids,   347
To double my despair?   They're mutinous.
   VENTIDIUS. Most firm and loyal.

[1] Boundaries.   [2] Chapped

ANTONY. Yet they will not march
To succor me. O trifler!
   VENTIDIUS. They petition 350
You would make haste to head them.
   ANTONY. I'm besieged.
   VENTIDIUS. There's but one way shut up.
    How came I hither?
   ANTONY. I will not stir.
   VENTIDIUS. They would perhaps desire
A better reason.
   ANTONY. I have never used
My soldiers to demand a reason of 355
My actions. Why did they refuse to march?
   VENTIDIUS. They said they would not fight
    for Cleopatra.
   ANTONY. What was't they said?
   VENTIDIUS. They said they would not fight
    for Cleopatra.
Why should they fight, indeed, to make her
   conquer, 360
And make you more a slave? to gain you
   kingdoms
Which, for a kiss at your next midnight feast,
You'll sell to her? Then she new-names her
   jewels
And calls this diamond such or such a tax;
Each pendant in her ear shall be a province.
   ANTONY. Ventidius, I allow your tongue
    free license 366
On all my other faults; but, on your life,
No word of Cleopatra. She deserves
More worlds than I can lose.
   VENTIDIUS. Behold, you powers,
To whom you have intrusted humankind! 370
See Europe, Afric, Asia, put in balance,
And all weighed down by one light, worth-
   less woman!
I think the gods are Antonies and give,
Like prodigals, this nether world away
To none but wasteful hands.
   ANTONY. You grow presumptuous.
   VENTIDIUS. I take the privilege of plain
    love to speak. 376
   ANTONY. Plain love! plain arrogance, plain
    insolence!
Thy men are cowards; thou, an envious traitor,
Who, under seeming honesty, hast vented
The burden of thy rank, o'erflowing gall. 380
O that thou wert my equal, great in arms
As the first Cæsar was, that I might kill thee
Without a stain to honor!
   VENTIDIUS. You may kill me;
You have done more already,—called me
   traitor.

   ANTONY. Art thou not one?
   VENTIDIUS. For showing you yourself,
Which none else durst have done? But had
   I been 386
That name which I disdain to speak again,
I needed not have sought your abject fortunes,
Come to partake your fate, to die with you.
What hindered me to have led my conquering
   eagles 390
To fill Octavius' bands? I could have been
A traitor then, a glorious, happy traitor,
And not have been so called.
   ANTONY. Forgive me, soldier;
I've been too passionate.
   VENTIDIUS. You thought me false;
Thought my old age betrayed you. Kill me, sir.
Pray, kill me. Yet you need not; your un
   kindness 395
Has left your sword no work.
   ANTONY. I did not think so.
I said it in my rage. Pr'ythee, forgive me.
Why didst thou tempt my anger by discovery
Of what I would not hear?
   VENTIDIUS. No prince but you
Could merit that sincerity I used, 401
Nor durst another man have ventured it;
But you, ere love misled your wandering eyes,
Were sure the chief and best of human race,
Framed in the very pride and boast of nature;
So perfect that the gods who formed you
   wondered 406
At their own skill, and cried—a lucky hit
Has mended our design. Their envy hindered,
Else you had been immortal, and a pattern,
When Heaven would work for ostentation's
   sake 410
To copy out again.
   ANTONY. But Cleopatra—
Go on, for I can bear it now.
   VENTIDIUS. No more.
   ANTONY. Thou dar'st not trust my passion,
    but thou may'st;
Thou only lov'st, the rest have flattered me.
   VENTIDIUS. Heaven's blessing on your
    heart for that kind word! 415
May I believe you love me? Speak again.
   ANTONY. Indeed I do. Speak this, and this,
    and this. (*Hugging him*)
Thy praises were unjust, but I'll deserve them,
And yet mend all. Do with me what thou
   wilt; 419
Lead me to victory! Thou know'st the way.
   VENTIDIUS. And will you leave this—
   ANTONY. Pr'ythee, do not curse her.

And I will leave her; though Heaven knows
    I love
Beyond life, conquest, empire, all but honor;
But I will leave her.
    VENTIDIUS.   That's my royal master;
And—shall we fight?
    ANTONY.   I warrant thee, old soldier.
Thou shalt behold me once again in iron; 426
And at the head of our old troops that beat
The Parthians, cry aloud—Come, follow me!
    VENTIDIUS. Oh, now I hear my emperor!
    In that word
Octavius fell. Gods, let me see that day, 430
And, if I have ten years behind, take all:
I'll thank you for the exchange.
    ANTONY.   O Cleopatra!
    VENTIDIUS. Again?
    ANTONY.   I've done. In that last sigh, she
    went.
Cæsar shall know what 'tis to force a lover
From all he holds most dear.
    VENTIDIUS.   Methinks you breathe
Another soul. Your looks are more divine; 436
You speak a hero, and you move a god.
    ANTONY. Oh, thou hast fired me! My soul's
    up in arms,
And mans each part about me. Once again
That noble eagerness of fight has seized me,
That eagerness with which I darted upward
To Cassius' camp. In vain the steepy hill
Opposed my way; in vain a war of spears 443
Sung round my head and planted all my shield;
I won the trenches while my foremost men
Lagged on the plain below.
    VENTIDIUS.   Ye gods, ye gods, 446
    For such another hour!
    ANTONY.   Come on, my soldier!
Our hearts and arms are still the same. I long
Once more to meet our foes, that thou and I,
Like time and death, marching before our
    troops,   450
May taste fate [1] to them, mow them out a
    passage,
And, entering where the foremost squadrons
    yield,
Begin the noble harvest of the field.   *Exeunt*

ACT II

SCENE I

Enter CLEOPATRA, IRAS, *and* ALEXAS
    CLEOPATRA. What shall I do or whither
    shall I turn?
    ct as tasters of their fortune.

Ventidius has o'ercome, and he will go.
    ALEXAS. He goes to fight for you.
    CLEOPATRA. Then he would see me ere he
        went to fight.
Flatter me not. If once he goes, he's lost, 5
And all my hopes destroyed.
    ALEXAS.   Does this weak passion
Become a mighty queen?
    CLEOPATRA.   I am no queen.
Is this to be a queen, to be besieged
By yon insulting Roman, and to wait
Each hour the victor's chain? These ills are
    small;   10
For Antony is lost, and I can mourn
For nothing else but him. Now come, Oc-
    tavius,
I have no more to lose! Prepare thy bands;
I'm fit to be a captive: Antony
Has taught my mind the fortune of a slave. 15
    IRAS. Call reason to assist you.
    CLEOPATRA.   I have none,
And none would have. My love's a noble
    madness,
Which shows the cause deserved it. Moderate
    sorrow
Fits vulgar love, and for a vulgar man,
But I have loved with such transcendent
    passion,   20
I soared, at first, quite out of reason's view,
And now am lost above it. No, I'm proud
'Tis thus. Would Antony could see me now!
Think you he would not sigh, though he must
    leave me?   24
Sure, he would sigh, for he is noble-natured,
And bears a tender heart. I know him well.
Ah, no, I know him not; I knew him once,
But now 'tis past.
    IRAS.   Let it be past with you.
Forget him, madam.
    CLEOPATRA.   Never, never, Iras.
He once was mine; and once, though now
    'tis gone,   30
Leaves a faint image of possession still.
    ALEXAS. Think him unconstant, cruel, and
        ungrateful.
    CLEOPATRA. I cannot. If I could, those
        thoughts were vain.
Faithless, ungrateful, cruel though he be, 34
I still must love him.

Enter CHARMION
            Now, what news, my Charmion?
Will he be kind? And will he not forsake me?
Am I to live, or die?—nay, do I live?   37

Or am I dead? For when he gave his answer,
Fate took the word, and then I lived or died.
    CHARMION. I found him, madam—
    CLEOPATRA.   A long speech preparing?
If thou bring'st comfort, haste, and give it me,
For never was more need.
    IRAS.   I know he loves you.
    CLEOPATRA. Had he been kind, her eyes
      had told me so
Before her tongue could speak it. Now she studies
To soften what he said; but give me death 45
Just as he sent it, Charmion, undisguised,
And in the words he spoke.
    CHARMION.   I found him, then,
Encompassed round, I think, with iron statues;
So mute, so motionless his soldiers stood,
While awfully he cast his eyes about   50
And every leader's hopes or fears surveyed.
Methought he looked resolved, and yet not pleased.
When he beheld me struggling in the crowd,
He blushed, and bade make way.
    ALEXAS.   There's comfort yet.
    CHARMION. Ventidius fixed his eyes upon
      my passage   55
Severely, as he meant to frown me back,
And sullenly gave place. I told my message,
Just as you gave it, broken and disordered;
I numbered in it all your sighs and tears,
And while I moved your pitiful request, 60
That you but only begged a last farewell,
He fetched an inward groan; and every time
I named you, sighed as if his heart were breaking,
But shunned my eyes and guiltily looked down.
He seemed not now that awful Antony 65
Who shook an armed assembly with his nod;
But, making show as he would rub his eyes,
Disguised and blotted out a falling tear.
    CLEOPATRA. Did he then weep? And was I
      worth a tear?
If what thou hast to say be not as pleasing, 70
Tell me no more, but let me die contented.
    CHARMION. He bid me say, he knew himself so well,
He could deny you nothing if he saw you;
And therefore—
    CLEOPATRA. Thou wouldst say, he would not see me?
    CHARMION. And therefore begged you not
      to use a power   75
Which he could ill resist; yet he should ever
Respect you as he ought.
    CLEOPATRA.   Is that a word
For Antony to use to Cleopatra?
O that faint word, *respect!* how I disdain it!
Disdain myself for loving, after it!   80
He should have kept that word for cold Octavia.
Respect is for a wife. Am I that thing,
That dull, insipid lump, without desires,
And without power to give them?
    ALEXAS.   You misjudge;
You see through love, and that deludes your sight, 85
As what is straight seems crooked through the water.
But I, who bear my reason undisturbed,
Can see this Antony, this dreaded man,
A fearful slave who fain would run away,
And shuns his master's eyes. If you pursue him, 90
My life on't, he still drags a chain along
That needs must clog his flight.
    CLEOPATRA.   Could I believe thee!
    ALEXAS. By every circumstance I know he loves.
True, he's hard pressed by interest and by honor; 94
Yet he but doubts and parleys and casts out
Many a long look for succor.
    CLEOPATRA.   He sends word
He fears to see my face.
    ALEXAS.   And would you more?
He shows his weakness who declines the combat,
And you must urge your fortune. Could he speak
More plainly? To my ears the message sounds— 100
Come to my rescue, Cleopatra, come;
Come, free me from Ventidius—from my tyrant:
See me and give me a pretense to leave him!—
I hear his trumpets. This way he must pass.
Please you, retire a while; I'll work him first, 105
That he may bend more easy.
    CLEOPATRA.   You shall rule me—
But all, I fear, in vain.
                Exit with CHARMION *and* IRAS
    ALEXAS.   I fear so, too,
Though I concealed my thoughts, to make her bold,
But 'tis our utmost means, and fate befriend it!   (*Withdraws*)

ALL FOR LOVE

Enter LICTORS *with fasces, one bearing the eagle; then enter* ANTONY *with* VENTIDIUS, *followed by other commanders*

ANTONY. Octavius is the minion of blind chance 110
But holds from virtue nothing.
  VENTIDIUS.   Has he courage?
  ANTONY. But just enough to season him from coward.[1]
Oh, 'tis the coldest youth upon a charge,
The most deliberate fighter! If he ventures
(As in Illyria once, they say, he did, 115
To storm a town), 'tis when he cannot choose;
When all the world have fixed their eyes upon him,
And then he lives on that for seven years after;
But at a close revenge he never fails.
  VENTIDIUS. I heard you challenged him.
  ANTONY.   I did, Ventidius. 120
What think'st thou was his answer? 'Twas so tame!—
He said he had more ways than one to die;
I had not.
  VENTIDIUS. Poor!
  ANTONY.   He has more ways than one,
But he would choose them all before that one.
  VENTIDIUS. He first would choose an ague or a fever. 125
  ANTONY. No; it must be an ague, not a fever;
He has not warmth enough to die by that.
  VENTIDIUS. Or old age and a bed.
  ANTONY.   Ay, there's his choice,
He would live like a lamp to the last wink,
And crawl upon the utmost verge of life. 130
O Hercules! Why should a man like this,
Who dares not trust his fate for one great action,
Be all the care of Heaven? Why should he lord it
O'er fourscore thousand men, of whom each one
Is braver than himself?
  VENTIDIUS.   You conquered for him. 135
Philippi knows it; there you shared with him
That empire which your sword made all your own.
  ANTONY. Fool that I was, upon my eagle's wings
I bore this wren till I was tired with soaring,
And now he mounts above me. 140
Good heavens, is this—is this the man who braves me?
Who bids my age make way? Drives me before him
To the world's ridge and sweeps me off like rubbish?
  VENTIDIUS. Sir, we lose time; the troops are mounted all.
  ANTONY. Then give the word to march. 145
I long to leave this prison of a town,
To join thy legions, and in open field
Once more to show my face. Lead, my deliverer.

Enter ALEXAS

ALEXAS. Great emperor,
In mighty arms renowned above mankind, 150
But in soft pity to the pressed, a god,
This message sends the mournful Cleopatra
To her departing lord.
  VENTIDIUS.   Smooth sycophant!
  ALEXAS. A thousand wishes and ten thousand prayers,
Millions of blessings wait you to the wars; 155
Millions of sighs and tears she sends you, too,
And would have sent
As many dear embraces to your arms,
As many parting kisses to your lips,
But those, she fears, have wearied you already. 160
  VENTIDIUS. (*Aside*) False crocodile!
  ALEXAS. And yet she begs not now you would not leave her;
That were a wish too mighty for her hopes,
Too presuming for her low fortune and your ebbing love;[2]
That were a wish for her more prosperous days, 165
Her blooming beauty and your growing kindness.
  ANTONY. (*Aside*) Well, I must man it out.—
What would the queen?
  ALEXAS. First, to these noble warriors who attend 168
Your daring courage in the chase of fame,—
Too daring and too dangerous for her quiet,—
She humbly recommends all she holds dear,
All her own cares and fears,—the care of you.
  VENTIDIUS. Yes, witness Actium.

---

[1] This passage may be a slur upon Louis XIV, as Stevens suggests. That king's habit of being present at the sieges of cities which were sure to surrender was especially marked during his two invasions of the Netherlands in 1667 and 1672.

[2] This unmetrical line has been variously dealt. The obvious remedy is to print the first two words as a separate incomplete line.

ANTONY. Let him speak, Ventidius.
ALEXAS. You, when his matchless valor bears him forward
With ardor too heroic, on his foes, 175
Fall down, as she would do, before his feet;
Lie in his way and stop the paths of death.
Tell him this god is not invulnerable,
That absent Cleopatra bleeds in him, 179
And, that you may remember her petition,
She begs you wear these trifles as a pawn
Which, at your wished return, she will redeem
(Gives jewels to the commanders)
With all the wealth of Egypt.
This to the great Ventidius she presents,
Whom she can never count her enemy, 185
Because he loves her lord.
VENTIDIUS. Tell her, I'll none on't;
I'm not ashamed of honest poverty;
Not all the diamonds of the east can bribe
Ventidius from his faith. I hope to see 189
These and the rest of all her sparkling store
Where they shall more deservingly be placed.
ANTONY. And who must wear them then?
VENTIDIUS. The wronged Octavia.
ANTONY. You might have spared that word.
VENTIDIUS. And he, that bribe.
ANTONY. But have I no remembrance?
ALEXAS. Yes, a dear one;
Your slave the queen—
ANTONY. My mistress.
ALEXAS. Then your mistress;
Your mistress would, she says, have sent her soul, 196
But that you had long since; she humbly begs
This ruby bracelet, set with bleeding hearts,
The emblems of her own, may bind your arm.
(Presenting a bracelet)
VENTIDIUS. Now, my best lord,—in honor's name, I ask you, 200
For manhood's sake and for your own dear safety,
Touch not these poisoned gifts,
Infected by the sender; touch them not;
Myriads of bluest plagues lie underneath them,
And more than aconite has dipped the silk.
ANTONY. Nay, now you grow too cynical, Ventidius; 206
A lady's favors may be worn with honor.
What, to refuse her bracelet! On my soul,
When I lie pensive in my tent alone,
'Twill pass the wakeful hours of winter nights
To tell these pretty beads upon my arm, 211
To count for every one a soft embrace,
A melting kiss at such and such a time,
And now and then the fury of her love
When—And what harm's in this?
ALEXAS. None, none, my lord,
But what's to her, that now 'tis past for ever.
ANTONY. *(Going to tie it)* We soldiers are so awkward—help me tie it. 217
ALEXAS. In faith, my lord, we courtiers, too, are awkward
In these affairs: so are all men indeed,
Even I, who am not one. But shall I speak?
ANTONY. Yes, freely.
ALEXAS. Then, my lord, fair hands alone
Are fit to tie it; she who sent it can. 222
VENTIDIUS. Hell! death! this eunuch pander ruins you.
You will not see her?
(ALEXAS *whispers an attendant, who goes out*)
ANTONY. But to take my leave.
VENTIDIUS. Then I have washed an Æthiop.
You're undone; 225
Y'are in the toils; y'are taken; y'are destroyed;
Her eyes do Cæsar's work.
ANTONY. You fear too soon.
I'm constant to myself; I know my strength;
And yet she shall not think me barbarous neither,
Born in the depths of Afric. I'm a Roman,
Bred to the rules of soft humanity. 231
A guest, and kindly used, should bid farewell.
VENTIDIUS. You do not know
How weak you are to her, how much an infant;
You are not proof against a smile or glance;
A sigh will quite disarm you.
ANTONY. See, she comes!
Now you shall find your error.—Gods, I thank you. 237
I formed the danger greater than it was,
And now 'tis near, 'tis lessened.
VENTIDIUS. Mark the end yet.

Enter CLEOPATRA, CHARMION, *and* IRAS

ANTONY. Well, madam, we are met.
CLEOPATRA. Is this a meeting?
Then, we must part?
ANTONY. We must.
CLEOPATRA. Who says we must?
ANTONY. Our own hard fates.
CLEOPATRA. We make those fates ourselves. 242
ANTONY. Yes, we have made them; we have loved each other
Into our mutual ruin.

ALL FOR LOVE

CLEOPATRA. The gods have seen my joys
  with envious eyes; 245
I have no friends in heaven, and all the world,
As 'twere the business of mankind to part us,
Is armed against my love. Even you yourself
Join with the rest; you, you are armed against
  me.
ANTONY. I will be justified in all I do 250
To late posterity, and therefore hear me.
If I mix a lie
With any truth, reproach me freely with it;
Else, favor me with silence.
CLEOPATRA.   You command me,
And I am dumb. 255
VENTIDIUS. [Aside] I like this well; he
  shows authority.
ANTONY. That I derive my ruin
From you alone—
CLEOPATRA.   O heavens! I ruin you!
ANTONY. You promised me your silence,
  and you break it
Ere I have scarce begun.
CLEOPATRA.   Well, I obey you.
ANTONY. When I beheld you first, it was in
  Egypt. 261
Ere Cæsar saw your eyes, you gave me love,
And were too young to know it; that I settled
Your father in his throne was for your sake;
I left the acknowledgment for time to ripen.
Cæsar stepped in and with a greedy hand
Plucked the green fruit ere the first blush of
  red, 267
Yet cleaving to the bough. He was my lord,
And was, beside, too great for me to rival.
But I deserved you first, though he enjoyed
  you. 270
When, after, I beheld you in Cilicia,
An enemy to Rome, I pardoned you.
CLEOPATRA. I cleared myself—
ANTONY.   Again you break your promise.
I loved you still and took your weak excuses,
Took you into my bosom, stained by Cæsar,
And not half mine. I went to Egypt with you,
And hid me from the business of the world,
Shut out inquiring nations from my sight
To give whole years to you. 279
VENTIDIUS. (Aside) Yes, to your shame be't
  spoken.
ANTONY.   How I loved,
Witness, ye days and nights and all your
  hours
That danced away with down upon your feet,
As all your business were to count my passion!
One day passed by and nothing saw but love;
Another came and still 'twas only love. 285
The suns were wearied out with looking on,
And I untired with loving.
I saw you every day, and all the day;
And every day was still but as the first,
So eager was I still to see you more. 290
VENTIDIUS. 'Tis all too true.
ANTONY.   Fulvia, my wife, grew jealous,
As she indeed had reason; raised a war
In Italy to call me back.
VENTIDIUS.   But yet
You went not.
ANTONY.   While within your arms I lay,
The world fell moldering from my hands each
  hour, 295
And left me scarce a grasp—I thank your
  love for't.
VENTIDIUS. Well pushed: that last was
  home.
CLEOPATRA.   Yet may I speak?
ANTONY. If I have urged a falsehood, yes;
  else, not.
Your silence says I have not. Fulvia died
(Pardon, you gods, with my unkindness died);
To set the world at peace I took Octavia, 301
This Cæsar's sister; in her pride of youth
And flower of beauty did I wed that lady,
Whom, blushing, I must praise, because I
  left her.
You called; my love obeyed the fatal sum-
  mons. 305
This raised the Roman arms; the cause was
  yours.
I would have fought by land where I was
  stronger;
You hindered it. Yet, when I fought at sea,
Forsook me fighting; and (O stain to honor!
O lasting shame!) I knew not that I fled, 310
But fled to follow you.
VENTIDIUS. What haste she made to hoist
  her purple sails!
And, to appear magnificent in flight,
Drew half our strength away.
ANTONY.   All this you caused.
And would you multiply more ruins on me?
This honest man, my best, my only friend,
Has gathered up the shipwreck of my for-
  tunes; 317
Twelve legions I have left, my last recruits,
And you have watched the news, and bring
  your eyes
To seize them, too. If you have aught to
  answer, 320
Now speak, you have free leave.

ALEXAS. (*Aside*)　　She stands confounded.
Despair is in her eyes.
　　VENTIDIUS. Now lay a sigh i'th' way to
　　　　stop his passage;
Prepare a tear and bid it for his legions;
'Tis like they shall be sold.　　　　　　325
　　CLEOPATRA. How shall I plead my cause
　　　　when you, my judge,
Already have condemned me? Shall I bring
The love you bore me for my advocate?
That now is turned against me, that destroys
　　me;
For love, once past, is, at the best, forgotten,
But oftener sours to hate. 'Twill please my
　　lord　　　　　　　　　　　　　　　331
To ruin me, and therefore I'll be guilty.
But could I once have thought it would have
　　pleased you,
That you would pry, with narrow searching
　　eyes,
Into my faults, severe to my destruction, 335
And watching all advantages with care
That serve to make me wretched?　Speak,
　　my lord,
For I end here. Though I deserve this usage,
Was it like you to give it?
　　ANTONY.　　　　　　Oh, you wrong me
To think I sought this parting or desired 340
To accuse you more than what will clear my-
　　self
And justify this breach.
　　CLEOPATRA.　　　　Thus low I thank you,
And, since my innocence will not offend,
I shall not blush to own it.
　　VENTIDIUS. (*Aside*)　　　　After this, 344
I think she'll blush at nothing.
　　CLEOPATRA.　　　　　　You seem grieved
(And therein you are kind) that Cæsar first
Enjoyed my love, though you deserved it
　　better.
I grieve for that, my lord, much more than
　　you;
For, had I first been yours, it would have
　　saved
My second choice: I never had been his, 350
And ne'er had been but yours.　But Cæsar
　　first,
You say, possessed my love. Not so, my lord.
He first possessed my person; you, my love.
Cæsar loved me, but I loved Antony.
If I endured him after, 'twas because　　355
I judged it due to the first name of men,
And, half constrained, I gave as to a tyrant
What he would take by force.

　　VENTIDIUS.　　　　　　O Siren! Siren!
Yet grant that all the love she boasts were
　　true,　　　　　　　　　　　　　　　359
Has she not ruined you? I still urge that,
The fatal consequence.
　　CLEOPATRA.　　　　The consequence, indeed,
For I dare challenge him, my greatest foe,
To say it was designed. 'Tis true I loved you,
And kept you far from an uneasy wife,—
Such Fulvia was.　　　　　　　　　　365
Yes, but he'll say you left Octavia for me:—
And can you blame me to receive that love
Which quitted such desert for worthless me?
How often have I wished some other Cæsar,
Great as the first, and as the second, young,
Would court my love to be refused for you!
　　VENTIDIUS. Words, words; but Actium,
　　　　sir; remember Actium.　　　　　372
　　CLEOPATRA. Even there I dare his malice.
　　　　True, I counseled
To fight at sea, but I betrayed you not.
I fled, but not to the enemy. 'Twas fear. 375
Would I had been a man, not to have feared!
For none would then have envied me your
　　friendship,
Who envy me your love.
　　ANTONY.　　　　　We are both unhappy.
If nothing else, yet our ill fortune parts us.
Speak; would you have me perish by my stay?
　　CLEOPATRA. If, as a friend, you ask my
　　　　judgment, go;　　　　　　　　381
If as a lover, stay. If you must perish—
'Tis a hard word—but stay.
　　VENTIDIUS. See now the effects of her so
　　　　boasted love!
She strives to drag you down to ruin with her;
But could she 'scape without you, oh, how
　　soon　　　　　　　　　　　　　　　386
Would she let go her hold and haste to shore
And never look behind!
　　CLEOPATRA.　　　Then judge my love by this.
　　　　　　　(*Giving Antony a writing*)
Could I have borne
A life or death, a happiness or woe　　390
From yours divided, this had given me means.
　　ANTONY. By Hercules, the writing of
　　　　Octavius!
I know it well; 'tis that proscribing hand,
Young as it was, that led the way to mine
And left me but the second place in murder.—
See, see, Ventidius! here he offers Egypt,
And joins all Syria to it as a present;　397
So, in requital, she forsake my fortunes
And join her arms with his.

CLEOPATRA.   And yet you leave me!
You leave me, Antony; and yet I love you,
Indeed I do. I have refused a kingdom;
That is a trifle;   402
For I could part with life, with anything,
But only you. Oh, let me die but with you!
Is that a hard request?
    ANTONY.   Next living with you,
'Tis all that Heaven can give.
    ALEXAS. (*Aside*) He melts; we conquer.
    CLEOPATRA. No; you shall go. Your interest
        calls you hence;   407
Yes, your dear interest pulls too strong for
    these
Weak arms to hold you here.
                        (*Takes his hand*)
Go; leave me, soldier   410
(For you're no more a lover), leave me dying;
Push me, all pale and panting, from your
    bosom,
And, when your march begins, let one run
    after,
Breathless almost for joy, and cry—She's
    dead.
The soldiers shout; you then perhaps may
    sigh   415
And muster all your Roman gravity.
Ventidius chides; and straight your brow
    clears up,
As I had never been.
    ANTONY.   Gods, 'tis too much—
Too much for man to bear.
    CLEOPATRA.   What is't for me, then,
A weak, forsaken woman and a lover?— 420
Here let me breathe my last. Envy me not
This minute in your arms. I'll die apace,
As fast as e'er I can, and end your trouble.
    ANTONY. Die! Rather let me perish;
        loosened nature   424
Leap from its hinges, sink the props of heaven,
And fall the skies to crush the nether world!
My eyes, my soul, my all!   (*Embraces her*)
    VENTIDIUS.   And what's this toy
In balance with your fortune, honor, fame?
    ANTONY. What is't, Ventidius? It out-
        weighs them all;
Why, we have more than conquered Cæsar
    now.   430
My queen's not only innocent, but loves me.
This, this is she who drags me down to ruin!
But could she 'scape without me, with what
    haste
Would she let slip her hold and make to
    shore

And never look behind!   435
Down on thy knees, blasphemer as thou art,
And ask forgiveness of wronged innocence.
    VENTIDIUS. I'll rather die than take it.
        Will you go?
    ANTONY. Go! Whither? Go from all that's
        excellent!   439
Faith, honor, virtue, all good things forbid
That I should go from her who sets my love
Above the price of kingdoms. Give, you gods,
Give to your boy, your Cæsar,
This rattle of a globe to play withal,   444
This gewgaw world, and put him cheaply off.
I'll not be pleased with less than Cleopatra.
    CLEOPATRA. She's wholly yours. My heart's
        so full of joy
That I shall do some wild extravagance
Of love in public, and the foolish world,
Which knows not tenderness, will think me
    mad.   450
    VENTIDIUS. O women! women! women! all
        the gods
Have not such power of doing good to man
As you of doing harm.   *Exit*
    ANTONY.   Our men are armed:—
Unbar the gate that looks to Cæsar's camp.
I would revenge the treachery he meant me;
And long security makes conquest easy. 456
I'm eager to return before I go,
For all the pleasures I have known beat thick
On my remembrance.—How I long for night!
That both the sweets of mutual love may try,
And once triùmph o'er Cæsar [ere] we die.
                                Exeunt

ACT III

SCENE I

At one door enter CLEOPATRA, CHARMION,
    IRAS, *and* ALEXAS, *a train of* Egyptians;
    at the other, ANTONY *and* Romans. *The
    entrance on both sides is prepared by music;
    the trumpets first sounding on* ANTONY'S
    part, then answered by timbrels, etc., on
    CLEOPATRA'S. CHARMION *and* IRAS *hold
    a laurel wreath betwixt them. A dance of*
    Egyptians. *After the ceremony* CLEOPATRA
    crowns ANTONY

    ANTONY. I thought how those white arms
        would fold me in,
And strain me close and melt me into love;
So pleased with that sweet image, I sprung
    forwards,
And added all my strength to every blow.

CLEOPATRA. Come to me, come, my soldier,
    to my arms! 5
You've been too long away from my embraces,
But, when I have you fast and all my own,
With broken murmurs and with amorous sighs
I'll say you were unkind, and punish you, 9
And mark you red with many an eager kiss.
  ANTONY. My brighter Venus!
  CLEOPATRA.   O my greater Mars!
  ANTONY. Thou join'st us well, my love!
Suppose me come from the Phlegræan plains [1]
Where gasping giants lay, cleft by my sword,
And mountain-tops pared off each other blow
To bury those I slew. Receive me, goddess! 16
Let Cæsar spread his subtle nets, like Vulcan;
In thy embraces I would be beheld
By heaven and earth at once;
And make their envy what they meant their sport. 20
Let those who took us blush; I would love on
With awful state, regardless of their frowns,
As their superior god.
There's no satiety of love in thee:
Enjoyed, thou still art new; perpetual spring
Is in thy arms; the ripened fruit but falls, 26
And blossoms rise to fill its empty place,
And I grow rich by giving.

Enter VENTIDIUS, *and stands apart*

  ALEXAS. Oh, now the danger's past, your general comes!
He joins not in your joys, nor minds your triumphs; 30
But with contracted brows looks frowning on,
As envying your success.
  ANTONY. Now, on my soul, he loves me; truly loves me:
He never flattered me in any vice,
But awes me with his virtue. Even this minute 35
Methinks, he has a right of chiding me.—
Lead to the temple—I'll avoid his presence;
It checks too strong upon me.
                   Exeunt the rest
  (*As* ANTONY *is going,* VENTIDIUS *pulls him by the robe*)
  VENTIDIUS.   Emperor!
  ANTONY. (*Looking back*) 'Tis the old argument. I pr'ythee, spare me.

---

[1] Where the battle between the gods and the Titans was supposed to have taken place. Hence the reference to mountain-tops in l. 15.

  VENTIDIUS. But this one hearing, emperor.
  ANTONY.   Let go 40
My robe; or, by my father Hercules—
  VENTIDIUS. By Hercules' father, that's yet greater,
I bring you somewhat you would wish to know.
  ANTONY. Thou see'st we are observed; attend me here, 44
And I'll return.   *Exit*
  VENTIDIUS. I am waning in his favor, yet I love him;
I love this man who runs to meet his ruin;
And sure the gods, like me, are fond of him.
His virtues lie so mingled with his crimes,
As would confound their choice to punish one
And not reward the other.

Enter ANTONY

  ANTONY.   We can conquer,
You see, without your aid. 52
We have dislodged their troops;
They look on us at distance and, like curs
'Scaped from the lion's paws, they bay far off,
And lick their wounds and faintly threaten war. 56
Five thousand Romans with their faces upward
Lie breathless on the plain.
  VENTIDIUS.   'Tis well; and he
Who lost them could have spared ten thousand more.
Yet if, by this advantage, you could gain 60
An easier peace while Cæsar doubts the chance
Of arms—
  ANTONY.   Oh, think not on't, Ventidius!
The boy pursues my ruin, he'll no peace;
His malice is considerate in advantage.
Oh, he's the coolest murderer! so staunch, 65
He kills, and keeps his temper.
  VENTIDIUS.   Have you no friend
In all his army who has power to move him?
Mæcenas, or Agrippa, might do much.
  ANTONY. They're both too deep in Cæsar's interests. 69
We'll work it out by dint of sword, or perish.
  VENTIDIUS. Fain I would find some other.
  ANTONY.   Thank thy love.
Some four or five such victories as this
Will save thy further pains.
  VENTIDIUS. Expect no more—Cæsar is on his guard.
I know, sir, you have conquered against odds.

But still you draw supplies from one poor
    town, 76
And of Egyptians. He has all the world,
And at his back nations come pouring in
To fill the gaps you make. Pray, think again,
  ANTONY. Why dost thou drive me from
    myself, to search 80
For foreign aids?—to hunt my memory,
And range o'er all a waste and barren place
To find a friend? The wretched have no
    friends.—
Yet I had one, the bravest youth of Rome,
Whom Cæsar loves beyond the love of women:
He could resolve his mind as fire does wax, 86
From that hard, rugged image melt him down,
And mold him in what softer form he pleased.
  VENTIDIUS. Him would I see—that man of
    all the world;
Just such a one we want.
  ANTONY. He loved me, too;
I was his soul; he lived not but in me. 91
We were so closed within each other's breasts,
The rivets were not found that joined us first.
That does not reach us yet: we were so mixed
As meeting streams, both to ourselves were
    lost; 95
We were one mass; we could not give or take
But from the same, for he was I, I he.
  VENTIDIUS. (*Aside*) He moves as I would
    wish him.
  ANTONY. After this
I need not tell his name.—'Twas Dolabella.
  VENTIDIUS. He's now in Cæsar's camp.
  ANTONY. No matter where,
Since he's no longer mine. He took unkindly
That I forbade him Cleopatra's sight, 102
Because I feared he loved her. He confessed
He had a warmth which, for my sake, he
    stifled,
For 'twere impossible that two, so one, 105
Should not have loved the same. When he
    departed,
He took no leave, and that confirmed my
    thoughts.
  VENTIDIUS. It argues that he loved you
    more than her,
Else he had stayed. But he perceived you
    jealous,
And would not grieve his friend. I know he
    loves you. 110
  ANTONY. I should have seen him, then,
    ere now.
  VENTIDIUS. Perhaps
He has thus long been laboring for your peace.

  ANTONY. Would he were here!
  VENTIDIUS. Would you
    believe he loved you?
I read your answer in your eyes—you would.
Not to conceal it longer, he has sent 115
A messenger from Cæsar's camp with letters.
  ANTONY. Let him appear.
  VENTIDIUS. I'll bring him instantly.
    Exit VENTIDIUS, [*and*] *re-enters immediately with* DOLABELLA
  ANTONY. 'Tis he himself! himself, by holy
    friendship! (*Runs to embrace him*)
Art thou returned at last, my better half?
Come, give me all myself! Let me not live,
If the young bridegroom, longing for his night,
Was ever half so fond! 122
  DOLABELLA. I must be silent, for my soul
    is busy
About a nobler work: she's new come home,
Like a long-absent man, and wanders o'er
Each room, a stranger to her own, to look
If all be safe.
  ANTONY. Thou hast what's left of me;
For I am now so sunk from what I was,
Thou find'st me at my lowest water-mark.
The rivers that ran in, and raised my fortunes
Are all dried up, or take another course: 131
What I have left is from my native spring.
I've still a heart that swells in scorn of fate
And lifts me to my banks.
  DOLABELLA. Still you are lord of all the
    world to me. 135
  ANTONY. Why, then I yet am so; for thou
    art all.
If I had any joy when thou wert absent,
I grudged it to myself; methought I robbed
Thee of thy part. But, O my Dolabella!
Thou hast beheld me other than I am. 140
Hast thou not seen my morning chambers
    filled
With sceptred slaves who waited to salute me?
With eastern monarchs who forgot the sun
To worship my uprising?—menial kings 144
Ran coursing up and down my palace-yard,
Stood silent in my presence, watched my
    eyes,
And at my least command all started out
Like racers to the goal.
  DOLABELLA. Slaves to your fortune.
  ANTONY. Fortune is Cæsar's now; and what
    am I?
  VENTIDIUS. What you have made yourself;
    I will not flatter. 150
  ANTONY. Is this friendly done?

DOLABELLA. Yes; when his end is so, I
    must join with him;
Indeed, I must; and yet you must not chide;
Why am I else your friend?
    ANTONY.   Take heed, young man,
How thou upbraid'st my love. The queen
    has eyes,   155
And thou, too, hast a soul. Canst thou re-
    member
When, swelled with hatred, thou beheld'st
    her first,
As accessary to thy brother's death?
    DOLABELLA. Spare my remembrance; 'twas
    a guilty day,   159
And still the blush hangs here.
    ANTONY.   To clear herself [1]
For sending him no aid, she came from Egypt.
Her galley down the silver Cydnus rowed,
The tackling silk, the streamers waved with
    gold;
The gentle winds were lodged in purple sails;
Her nymphs, like Nereids, round her couch
    were placed,   165
Where she, another sea-born Venus, lay.
    DOLABELLA. No more; I would not hear it.
    ANTONY.   Oh, you must!
She lay, and leant her cheek upon her hand,
And cast a look so languishingly sweet
As if, secure of all beholders' hearts,   170
Neglecting, she could take them. Boys like
    Cupids
Stood fanning with their painted wings the
    winds
That played about her face; but if she smiled,
A darting glory seemed to blaze abroad,   174
That men's desiring eyes were never wearied,
But hung upon the object. To soft lutes
The silver oars kept time; and while they
    played,
The hearing gave new pleasure to the sight,
And both, to thought. 'Twas heaven, or
    somewhat more:
For she so charmed all hearts, that gazing
    crowds   180
Stood panting on the shore, and wanted
    breath
To give their welcome voice.
Then, Dolabella, where was then thy soul?
Was not thy fury quite disarmed with wonder?
Didst thou not shrink behind me from those
    eyes   185
And whisper in my ear—Oh, tell her not

That I accused her of my brother's death?
    DOLABELLA. And should my weakness be a
    plea for yours?
Mine was an age when love might be excused,
When kindly warmth, and when my springing
    youth,   190
Made it a debt to nature. Yours—
    VENTIDIUS.   Speak boldly.
Yours, he would say, in your declining age,
When no more heat was left but what you
    forced,
When all the sap was needful for the trunk,
When it went down, then you constrained
    the course,   195
And robbed from nature to supply desire;
In you (I would not use so harsh a word)
'Tis but plain dotage.
    ANTONY.   Ha!
    DOLABELLA.   'Twas urged too home.—
But yet the loss was private that I made;
'Twas but myself I lost. I lost no legions;
I had no world to lose, no people's love.
    ANTONY. This from a friend?
    DOLABELLA.   Yes, Antony, a true
    one;   202
A friend so tender that each word I speak
Stabs my own heart before it reach your ear.
Oh, judge me not less kind because I chide!
To Cæsar I excuse you.
    ANTONY.   O ye gods!   206
Have I then lived to be excused to Cæsar?
    DOLABELLA. As to your equal.
    ANTONY.   Well, he's but my equal;
While I wear this, he never shall be more.
    DOLABELLA. I bring conditions from him.
    ANTONY.   Are they noble?
Methinks thou shouldst not bring them else;
    yet he   211
Is full of deep dissembling; knows no honor
Divided from his interest. Fate mistook him,
For nature meant him for an usurer:
He's fit indeed to buy, not conquer, kingdoms.
    VENTIDIUS. Then, granting this,   216
What power was theirs who wrought so hard
    a temper
To honorable terms?
    ANTONY. It was my Dolabella, or some
    god.
    DOLABALLA. Nor I, nor yet Mæcenas, nor
    Agrippa: 220
They were your enemies; and I, a friend,
Too weak alone; yet 'twas a Roman's deed.
    ANTONY. 'Twas like a Roman done: show
    me that man

---

[1] This is Dryden's re-working of the famous descriptive passage in *Antony and Cleopatra*, II, ii, 196-223.

Who has preserved my life, my love, my
    honor; 224
Let me but see his face.
  VENTIDIUS. That task is mine,
And, Heaven, thou know'st how pleasing.
                            Exit VENTIDIUS.
  DOLABELLA. You'll remember
To whom you stand obliged?
  ANTONY. When I forget it,
Be thou unkind, and that's my greatest curse.
My queen shall thank him, too.
  DOLABELLA. I fear she will not.
  ANTONY. But she shall do it—the queen,
    my Dolabella! 230
Hast thou not still some grudgings of thy
    fever?
  DOLABELLA. I would not see her lost.
  ANTONY. When I forsake her,
Leave me, my better stars! for she has truth
Beyond her beauty. Cæsar tempted her,
At no less price than kingdoms, to betray me,
But she resisted all; and yet thou chidest me
For loving her too well. Could I do so? 237
  DOLABELLA. Yes: there's my reason.

Re-enter VENTIDIUS *with* OCTAVIA, *leading*
    ANTONY'S *two little Daughters*

  ANTONY. Where?—Octavia there!
                                (*Starting back*)
  VENTIDIUS. What—is she poison to you?—
    a disease?
Look on her, view her well, and those she
    brings: 240
Are they all strangers to your eyes? has nature
No secret call, no whisper they are yours?
  DOLABELLA. For shame, my lord, if not for
    love, receive them
With kinder eyes. If you confess a man,
Meet them, embrace them, bid them welcome
    to you. 245
Your arms should open, even without your
    knowledge,
To clasp them in; your feet should turn to
    wings,
To bear you to them; and your eyes dart out
And aim a kiss ere you could reach the lips.
  ANTONY. I stood amazed to think how they
    came hither. 250
  VENTIDIUS. I sent for them; I brought them
    in, unknown
To Cleopatra's guards.
  DOLABELLA. Yet are you cold?
  OCTAVIA. Thus long I have attended for
    my welcome,
Which, as a stranger, sure I might expect.
Who am I?
  ANTONY. Cæsar's sister.
  OCTAVIA. That's unkind. 255
Had I been nothing more than Cæsar's sister,
Know, I had still remained in Cæsar's camp.
But your Octavia, your much injured wife,
Though banished from your bed, driven from
    your house,
In spite of Cæsar's sister, still is yours. 260
'Tis true, I have a heart disdains your cold-
    ness,
And prompts me not to seek what you should
    offer;
But a wife's virtue still surmounts that pride.
I come to claim you as my own; to show 264
My duty first; to ask, nay beg, your kindness.
Your hand, my lord; 'tis mine, and I will
    have it. (*Taking his hand*)
  VENTIDIUS. Do, take it; thou deserv'st it.
  DOLABELLA. On my soul,
And so she does; she's neither too submissive,
Nor yet too haughty; but so just a mean
Shows, as it ought, a wife and Roman too.
  ANTONY. I fear, Octavia, you have begged
    my life. 271
  OCTAVIA. Begged it, my lord?
  ANTONY. Yes, begged it, my ambassa-
    dress;
Poorly and basely begged it of your brother.
  OCTAVIA. Poorly and basely I could never
    beg,
Nor could my brother grant. 275
  ANTONY. Shall I, who, to my kneeling slave,
    could say,
Rise up and be a king—shall I fall down
And cry,—Forgive me, Cæsar? Shall I set
A man, my equal, in the place of Jove,
As he could give me being? No—that word
"Forgive" would choke me up 281
And die upon my tongue.
  DOLABELLA. You shall not need it.
  ANTONY. I will not need it. Come, you've
    all betrayed me—
My friend too!—to receive some vile condi-
    tions.
My wife has bought me with her prayers and
    tears, 285
And now I must become her branded slave.
In every peevish mood she will upbraid
The life she gave; if I but look awry,
She cries—I'll tell my brother.
  OCTAVIA. My hard fortune
Subjects me still to your unkind mistakes.

But the conditions I have brought are such
You need not blush to take; I love your honor,
Because 'tis mine. It never shall be said
Octavia's husband was her brother's slave.
Sir, you are free—free, even from her you
　　loathe; 295
For, though my brother bargains for your
　　love,
Makes me the price and cément of your peace,
I have a soul like yours; I cannot take
Your love as alms, nor beg what I deserve.
I'll tell my brother we are reconciled; 300
He shall draw back his troops, and you shall
　　march
To rule the East. I may be dropped at
　　Athens—
No matter where. I never will complain,
But only keep the barren name of wife,
And rid you of the trouble. 305
　　　VENTIDIUS. Was ever such a strife
　　　　of sullen honor!
　　　Both scorn to be obliged.
　　　DOLABELLA. Oh, she has touched
　　　　him in the tenderest part;
(Apart) ⟨ See how he reddens with despite
　　　　and shame,
　　　To be outdone in generosity! 310
　　　VENTIDIUS. See how he winks!
　　　　how he dries up a tear,
　　　That fain would fall!
ANTONY. Octavia, I have heard you, and
　　must praise
The greatness of your soul; 314
But cannot yield to what you have proposed,
For I can ne'er be conquered but by love,
And you do all for duty. You would free me,
And would be dropped at Athens; was't not so?
　　OCTAVIA. It was, my lord.
　　ANTONY.　　　Then I must be obliged
To one who loves me not; who, to herself,
May call me thankless and ungrateful man.—
I'll not endure it—no.
　　VENTIDIUS. (Aside)　　I am glad it pinches
　　　there. 322
　　OCTAVIA. Would you triumph o'er poor
　　　Octavia's virtue?
That pride was all I had to bear me up:
That you might think you owed me for your
　　life, 325
And owed it to my duty, not my love.
I have been injured, and my haughty soul
Could brook but ill the man who slights my
　　bed.
　　ANTONY. Therefore you love me not.

　　OCTAVIA.　　　　Therefore, my lord,
I should not love you.
　　ANTONY.　Therefore you would leave me?
　　OCTAVIA. And therefore I should leave you
　　　—if I could. 331
　　DOLABELLA. Her soul's too great, after
　　　such injuries,
To say she loves; and yet she lets you see it.
Her modesty and silence plead her cause.
　　ANTONY. O Dolabella, which way shall I
　　　turn? 335
I find a secret yielding in my soul;
But Cleopatra, who would die with me,
Must she be left? Pity pleads for Octavia,
But does it not plead more for Cleopatra?
　　VENTIDIUS. Justice and pity both plead for
　　　Octavia; 340
For Cleopatra, neither.
One would be ruined with you, but she first
Had ruined you; the other, you have ruined,
And yet she would preserve you.
In everything their merits are unequal. 345
　　ANTONY. O my distracted soul!
　　OCTAVIA.　　Sweet Heaven, compose it!—
Come, come, my lord, if I can pardon you,
Methinks you should accept it. Look on
　　these—
Are they not yours? or stand they thus
　　neglected 349
As they are mine? Go to him, children, go;
Kneel to him, take him by the hand, speak
　　to him,
For you may speak and he may own you, too,
Without a blush—and so he cannot all
His children. Go, I say, and pull him to me,
And pull him to yourselves from that bad
　　woman. 355
You, Agrippina, hang upon his arms,
And you, Antonia, clasp about his waist.
If he will shake you off, if he will dash you
Against the pavement, you must bear it,
　　children, 359
For you are mine, and I was born to suffer.
　　　　(Here the Children go to him, etc.)
　　VENTIDIUS. Was ever sight so moving?—
　　　Emperor!
　　DOLABELLA.　Friend!
　　OCTAVIA. Husband!
　　BOTH CHILDREN.　Father!
　　ANTONY.　　I am vanquished. Take me,
Octavia—take me, children—share me all.
　　　　　　　　　　(Embracing them)
I've been a thriftless debtor to your loves,
And run out much, in riot, from your stock,

But all shall be amended.
    OCTAVIA.   O blest hour! 366
    DOLABELLA. O happy change!
    VENTIDIUS.   My joy stops at my tongue,
But it has found two channels here for one,
And bubbles out above.
    ANTONY. (*To Octavia*) This is thy triumph.
    Lead me where thou wilt, 370
Even to thy brother's camp.
    OCTAVIA.   All there are yours.

Enter ALEXAS *hastily*

    ALEXAS. The queen, my mistress, sir, and yours—
    ANTONY.   'Tis past.—
Octavia, you shall stay this night. Tomorrow
Cæsar and we are one.
    Exit, leading OCTAVIA; DOLABELLA *and
    the* Children *follow*
    VENTIDIUS. There's news for you! Run, my officious eunuch, 375
Be sure to be the first—haste forward!
Haste, my dear eunuch, haste!   *Exit*
    ALEXAS. This downright fighting fool, this thick-skulled hero,
This blunt, unthinking instrument of death,
With plain, dull virtue has outgone my wit.
Pleasure forsook my earliest infancy; 381
The luxury of others robbed my cradle,
And ravished thence the promise of a man.
Cast out from nature, disinherited
Of what her meanest children claim by kind,
Yet greatness kept me from contempt. That's gone. 386
Had Cleopatra followed my advice,
Then he had been betrayed who now forsakes.
She dies for love, but she has known its joys.
Gods, is this just that I, who know no joys,
Must die because she loves? 391

Enter CLEOPATRA, CHARMION, IRAS,
[*and*] Train

O madam, I have seen what blasts my eyes!
Octavia's here.
    CLEOPATRA.   Peace with that raven's note.
I know it, too, and now am in 394
The pangs of death.
    ALEXAS.   You are no more a queen—
Egypt is lost.
    CLEOPATRA. What tell'st thou me of Egypt?
My life, my soul is lost! Octavia has him!—
O fatal name to Cleopatra's love!
My kisses, my embraces now are hers,
While I—But thou hast seen my rival.
    Speak— 400
Does she deserve this blessing? Is she fair?
Bright as a goddess? and is all perfection
Confined to her?—It is. Poor I was made
Of that coarse matter which, when she was finished,
The gods threw by for rubbish. 405
    ALEXAS. She's indeed a very miracle.
    CLEOPATRA. Death to my hopes, a miracle!
    ALEXAS. (*Bowing*)   A miracle—
I mean, of goodness; for in beauty, madam,
You make all wonders cease.
    CLEOPATRA.   I was too rash.
Take this in part of recompense. But, oh! 410
    (*Giving a ring*)
I fear thou flatterest me.
    CHARMION.   She comes! She's here!
    IRAS. Fly, madam, Cæsar's sister!
    CLEOPATRA. Were she the sister of the thunderer Jove,
And bore her brother's lightning in her eye,
Thus would I face my rival. 415
(*Meets* OCTAVIA *with* VENTIDIUS. OCTAVIA
    bears up to her. Their Trains *come up on
    either side*)
    OCTAVIA. I need not ask if you are Cleopatra,
Your haughty carriage—
    CLEOPATRA.   Shows I am a queen.
Nor need I ask you, who you are.
    OCTAVIA   A Roman:
A name that makes and can unmake a queen.
    CLEOPATRA. Your lord, the man who serves me, is a Roman. 420
    OCTAVIA. He was a Roman, till he lost that name
To be a slave in Egypt; but I come
To free him thence.
    CLEOPATRA. Peace, peace, my lover's Juno.
When he grew weary of that household clog,
He chose my easier bonds.
    OCTAVIA.   I wonder not 425
Your bonds are easy. You have long been practised
In that lascivious art. He's not the first
For whom you spread your snares: let Cæsar witness.
    CLEOPATRA. I loved not Cæsar; 'twas but gratitude
I paid his love. The worst your malice can
Is but to say the greatest of mankind 431
Has been my slave. The next, but far above him

In my esteem, is he whom law calls yours,
But whom his love made mine.
   OCTAVIA. (*Coming up closer to her*) I would
     view nearer   434
That face which has so long usurped my right,
To find the inevitable charms that catch
Mankind so sure, that ruined my dear lord.
   CLEOPATRA. Oh, you do well to search, for
     had you known
But half these charms, you had not lost his
     heart.
   OCTAVIA. Far be their knowledge from a
     Roman lady—   440
Far from a modest wife! Shame of our sex,
Dost thou not blush to own those black en-
     dearments
That make sin pleasing?
   CLEOPATRA.   You may blush, who
     want them.
If bounteous nature, if indulgent heaven
Have given me charms to please the bravest
     man,   445
Should I not thank them? Should I be
     ashamed,
And not be proud? I am, that he has loved
     me.
And when I love not him, heaven change this
     face
For one like that.
   OCTAVIA. Thou lov'st him not so well.
   CLEOPATRA. I love him better, and deserve
     him more.   450
   OCTAVIA. You do not—cannot. You have
     been his ruin.
Who made him cheap at Rome but Cleopatra?
Who made him scorned abroad but Cleopatra?
At Actium, who betrayed him? Cleopatra!
Who made his children orphans, and poor me
A wretched widow? Only Cleopatra.   456
   CLEOPATRA. Yet she who loves him best is
     Cleopatra.
If you have suffered, I have suffered more.
You bear the specious title of a wife
To gild your cause and draw the pitying
     world   460
To favor it. The world condemns poor me,
For I have lost my honor, lost my fame,
And stained the glory of my royal house,
And all to bear the branded name of mistress.
There wants but life, and that, too, I would
     lose   465
For him I love.
   OCTAVIA.   Be't so, then; take thy wish.
                                   Exit with her Train

   CLEOPATRA. And 'tis my wish,
Now he is lost for whom alone I lived.   468
My sight grows dim, and every object dances
And swims before me in the maze of death.
My spirits, while they were opposed, kept up;
They could not sink beneath a rival's scorn,
But now she's gone, they faint.
   ALEXAS.   Mine have had leisure
To recollect their strength and furnish counsel
To ruin her, who else must ruin you.
   CLEOPATRA.   Vain promiser!
Lead me, my Charmion; nay, your hand, too,
     Iras.   476
My grief has weight enough to sink you both.
Conduct me to some solitary chamber,
And draw the curtains round;
Then leave me to myself, to take alone   480
My fill of grief.
There I till death will his unkindness weep
As harmless infants moan themselves asleep.
                                               Exeunt

ACT IV

SCENE I

[*Enter*] ANTONY [*and*] DOLABELLA

   DOLABELLA. Why would you shift it from
     yourself on me?
Can you not tell her you must part?
   ANTONY.   I cannot.
I could pull out an eye and bid it go,
And t'other should not weep. O Dolabella,
How many deaths are in this word, *Depart!*   5
I dare not trust my tongue to tell her so—
One look of hers would thaw me into tears,
And I should melt till I were lost again.
   DOLABELLA. Then let Ventidius—
He's rough by nature.
   ANTONY.   Oh, he'll speak too harshly;
He'll kill her with the news. Thou, only
     thou!   11
   DOLABELLA. Nature has cast me in so soft
     a mould
That but to hear a story feigned for pleasure,
Of some sad lover's death moistens my eyes,
And robs me of my manhood. I should speak
So faintly, with such fear to grieve her heart,
She'd not believe it earnest.
   ANTONY.   Therefore—therefore
Thou, only thou art fit. Think thyself me,
And when thou speak'st (but let it first be
     long),   19
Take off the edge from every sharper sound,

And let our parting be as gently made
As other loves begin. Wilt thou do this?
    DOLABELLA. What you have said so sinks
        into my soul
That, if I must speak, I shall speak just so.
    ANTONY. I leave you then to your sad task.
        Farewell!   25
I sent her word to meet you.
        (*Goes to the door and comes back*)
            I forgot.
Let her be told I'll make her peace with mine.
Her crown and dignity shall be preserved.
If I have power with Cæsar.—Oh, be sure
To think on that!
    DOLABELLA.   Fear not, I will remember.
    (ANTONY *goes again to the door and comes
        back*)
    ANTONY. And tell her, too, how much I
        was constrained;   31
I did not this but with extremest force.
Desire her not to hate my memory,
For I still cherish hers;—insist on that.
    DOLABELLA. Trust me, I'll not forget it.
    ANTONY.   Then that's all.
        (*Goes out and returns again*)
Wilt thou forgive my fondness this once more?
Tell her, though we shall never meet again,
If I should hear she took another love,
The news would break my heart.—Now I
    must go,   39
For every time I have returned, I feel
My soul more tender, and my next command
Would be to bid her stay, and ruin both.
            Exit
    DOLABELLA. Men are but children of a
        larger growth;
Our appetites as apt to change as theirs,
And full as craving, too, and full as vain;   45
And yet the soul, shut up in her dark room,
Viewing so clear abroad, at home sees nothing;
But like a mole in earth, busy and blind,
Works all her folly up and casts it outward
To the world's open view. Thus I discovered,
And blamed, the love of ruined Antony,   51
Yet wish that I were he, to be so ruined.

        Enter VENTIDIUS *above*

    VENTIDIUS. Alone, and talking to himself?
        concerned, too?
Perhaps my guess is right; he loved her once,
And may pursue it still.
    DOLABELLA.   O friendship! friendship!
Ill canst thou answer this; and reason, worse:
Unfaithful in the attempt; hopeless to win;
And, if I win, undone: mere madness all.   58
And yet the occasion's fair. What injury
To him, to wear the robe which he throws by?
    VENTIDIUS. None, none at all. This happens
        as I wish,   61
To ruin her yet more with Antony.

    Enter CLEOPATRA, *talking with* ALEXAS;
        CHARMION, IRAS *on the other side*

    DOLABELLA. She comes! What charms have
        sorrow on that face!
Sorrow seems pleased to dwell with so much
    sweetness;
Yet, now and then, a melancholy smile   65
Breaks loose like lightning in a winter's night,
And shows a moment's day.
    VENTIDIUS. If she should love him, too—
        her eunuch there!
That porc'pisce [1] bodes ill weather. Draw,
    draw nearer,   69
Sweet devil, that I may hear.
    ALEXAS.   Believe me; try
    (DOLABELLA *goes over to* CHARMION *and*
        IRAS; *seems to talk with them*)
To make him jealous; jealousy is like
A polished glass held to the lips when life's
    in doubt;
If there be breath, 'twill catch the damp, and
    show it.
    CLEOPATRA. I grant you, jealousy's a proof
        of love,
But 'tis a weak and unavailing medicine;   75
It puts out the disease, and makes it show,
But has no power to cure.
    ALEXAS. 'Tis your last remedy, and
        strongest, too.
And then this Dolabella—who so fit
To practise on? He's handsome, valiant,
    young,   80
And looks as he were laid for nature's bait
To catch weak women's eyes.
He stands already more than half suspected
Of loving you. The least kind word or glance
You give this youth will kindle him with love;
Then, like a burning vessel set adrift,   86
You'll send him down amain before the wind
To fire the heart of jealous Antony.
    CLEOPATRA. Can I do this? Ah, no. My
        love's so true
That I can neither hide it where it is,   90
Nor show it where it is not. Nature meant me
A wife—a silly, harmless, household dove,
Fond without art, and kind without deceit;

[1] Porcus pisces; porpoise.

But Fortune, that has made a mistress of me,
Has thrust me out to the wide world, un-
    furnished   95
Of falsehood to be happy.
    ALEXAS.   Force yourself.
The event will be, your lover will return
Doubly desirous to possess the good
Which once he feared to lose.
    CLEOPATRA.   I must attempt it,
But oh, with what regret!   100
    Exit ALEXAS. *She comes up to* DOLABELLA
VENTIDIUS. So, now the scene draws near;
    they're in my reach.
    CLEOPATRA. (*To* DOLABELLA) Discoursing
    with my women! Might not I
Share in your entertainment?
    CHARMION.   You have been
The subject of it, madam.
    CLEOPATRA.   How! and how?
    IRAS. Such praises of your beauty!
    CLEOPATRA.   Mere poetry.
Your Roman wits, your Gallus and Tibullus,[1]
Have taught you this from Cytheris and
    Delia.   107
    DOLABELLA. Those Roman wits have never
    been in Egypt;
Cytheris and Delia else had been unsung.
I, who have seen—had I been born a poet,
Should choose a nobler name.
    CLEOPATRA.   You flatter me.
But 'tis your nation's vice. All of your
    country   112
Are flatterers, and false. Your friend's like you.
I'm sure he sent you not to speak these words.
    DOLABELLA. No, madam, yet he sent me—
    CLEOPATRA.   Well, he sent you—
    DOLABELLA. Of a less pleasing errand.
    CLEOPATRA.   How less pleasing?
Less to yourself, or me?
    DOLABELLA.   Madam, to both.
For you must mourn, and I must grieve to
    cause it.   118
    CLEOPATRA. You, Charmion, and your
    fellow, stand at distance.—
(*Aside*) Hold up, my spirits.—Well, now your
    mournful matter,   120
For I'm prepared—perhaps can guess it, too.
    DOLABELLA. I wish you would, for 'tis a
    thankless office

---
[1] Cornelius Gallus (69 or 68–26 B.C.), one of Octavian's generals at the siege of Alexandria, was also a poet who celebrated the charms of Cytheris, a dancing girl, but the poems have been lost. Tibullus (54–19 B.C.) wrote poems celebrating Delia. Both ladies were unfaithful.

To tell ill news; and I, of all your sex,
Most fear displeasing you.
    CLEOPATRA.   Of all your sex
I soonest could forgive you if you should. 125
    VENTIDIUS. Most delicate advances!
    Woman! woman!
Dear, damned, inconstant sex!
    CLEOPATRA.   In the first place,
I am to be forsaken. Is't not so?
    DOLABELLA. I wish I could not answer to
    that question.
    CLEOPATRA. Then pass it o'er because it
    troubles you: 130
I should have been more grieved another
    time.
Next, I'm to lose my kingdom—Farewell,
    Egypt!
Yet, is there any more?
    DOLABELLA.   Madam, I fear
Your too deep sense of grief has turned your
    reason.
    CLEOPATRA. No, no, I'm not run mad; I
    can bear fortune,   135
And love may be expelled by other love,
As poisons are by poisons.
    DOLABELLA.   You o'erjoy me, madam,
To find your griefs so moderately borne.
You've heard the worst; all are not false
    like him.
    CLEOPATRA. No. Heaven forbid they should.
    DOLABELLA.   Some men are constant.
    CLEOPATRA. And constancy deserves re-
    ward, that's certain.   141
    DOLABELLA. Deserves it not, but give it
    leave to hope.
    VENTIDIUS. I'll swear thou hast my leave.
    I have enough.—
But how to manage this! Well, I'll consider.
                                         Exit
    DOLABELLA. I came prepared   145
To tell you heavy news—news which, I
    thought,
Would fright the blood from your pale cheeks
    to hear,
But you have met it with a cheerfulness
That makes my task more easy; and my
    tongue,   149
Which on another's message was employed,
Would gladly speak its own.
    CLEOPATRA.   Hold, Dolabella.
First tell me, were you chosen by my lord?
Or sought you this employment?
    DOLABELLA. He picked me out; and, as his
    bosom friend.

He charged me with his words.
 CLEOPATRA.   The message then
I know was tender, and each accent smooth,
To mollify that rugged word, *Depart*.   157
 DOLABELLA. Oh, you mistake. He chose
  the harshest words;
With fiery eyes and with contracted brows
He coined his face in the severest stamp; 160
And fury shook his fabric like an earthquake;
He heaved for vent, and burst like bellowing
 Ætna
In sounds scarce human—Hence, away, for
 ever,
Let her begone, the blot of my renown,
And bane of all my hopes!   165
 (*All the time of this speech* CLEOPATRA
  *seems more and more concerned till
  she sinks quite down*)
Let her be driven as far as men can think
From man's commèrce! she'll poison to the
 center.
 CLEOPATRA. Oh, I can bear no more!
 DOLABELLA. Help, help!—O wretch! O
  cursèd, cursèd wretch!
What have I done!
 CHARMION.   Help, chafe her temples,
  Iras.   170
 IRAS. Bend, bend her forward quickly.
 CHARMION.   Heaven be praised,
She comes again.
 CLEOPATRA. Oh, let him not approach me.
Why have you brought me back to this
 loathed being,
The abode of falsehood, violated vows,
And injured love? For pity, let me go; 175
For, if there be a place of long repose,
I'm sure I want it. My disdainful lord
Can never break that quiet, nor awake
The sleeping soul with hollowing in my tomb
Such words as fright her hence.—Unkind,
 unkind!   180
 DOLABELLA. (*Kneeling*) Believe me, 'tis
  against myself I speak.
That sure deserves belief—I injured him:
My friend ne'er spoke those words. Oh, had
 you seen
How often he came back, and every time 184
With something more obliging and more kind
To add to what he said; what dear farewells;
How almost vanquished by his love he parted,
And leaned to what unwillingly he left!
I, traitor that I was, for love of you
(But what can you not do, who made me
 false?)   190
I forged that lie; for whose forgiveness kneels
This self-accused, self-punished criminal.
 CLEOPATRA. With how much ease believe
  we what we wish!
Rise, Dolabella, if you have been guilty;
I have contributed, and too much love   195
Has made me guilty too.
The advance of kindness which I made was
 feigned
To call back fleeting love by jealousy,
But 'twould not last. Oh, rather let me lose
Than so ignobly trifle with his heart!   200
 DOLABELLA. I find your breast fenced
  round from human reach,
Transparent as a rock of solid crystal,
Seen through, but never pierced. My friend,
 my friend!
What endless treasure hast thou thrown away
And scattered, like an infant, in the ocean,
Vain sums of wealth, which none can gather
 thence!   206
 CLEOPATRA. Could you not beg
An hour's admittance to his private ear?
Like one who wanders through long barren
 wilds,
And yet foreknows no hospitable inn   210
Is near to succor hunger, eats his fill
Before his painful march:
So would I feed a while my famished eyes
Before we part, for I have far to go,
If death be far, and never must return. 215

[*Enter*] VENTIDIUS *with* OCTAVIA, *behind*

 VENTIDIUS. From hence you may discover—
  Oh, sweet, sweet!
Would you, indeed? The pretty hand in
 earnest?
 DOLABELLA. I will, for this reward.
         (*Takes her hand*)
         Draw it not back,
'Tis all I e'er will beg.
 VENTIDIUS.   They turn upon us.
 OCTAVIA. What quick eyes has guilt!   220
 VENTIDIUS. Seem not to have observed
  them, and go on.
          (*They enter*)
 DOLABELLA. Saw you the emperor, Ven-
  tidius?
 VENTIDIUS. No.
I sought him, but I heard that he was private.
None with him but Hipparchus, his freedman.
 DOLABELLA. Know you his business?
 VENTIDIUS.   Giving him instructions
And letters to his brother Cæsar.

DOLABELLA. Well, 226
He must be found.
   Exeunt DOLABELLA *and* CLEOPATRA
 OCTAVIA. Most glorious impudence!
 VENTIDIUS. She looked, methought,
As she would say—Take your old man, Octavia,
Thank you, I'm better here.—Well, but what use 230
Make we of this discovery?
 OCTAVIA. Let it die.
 VENTIDIUS. I pity Dolabella. But she's dangerous:
Her eyes have power beyond Thessalian charms
To draw the moon from heaven; for eloquence,
The sea-green Syrens taught her voice their flattery; 235
And while she speaks, night steals upon the day,
Unmarked of those that hear. Then she's so charming
Age buds at sight of her, and swells to youth;
The holy priests gaze on her when she smiles,
And with heaved hands, forgetting gravity,
They bless her wanton eyes. Even I, who hate her, 241
With a malignant joy behold such beauty,
And while I curse, desire it. Antony
Must needs have some remains of passion still,
Which may ferment into a worse relapse 245
If now not fully cured. I know, this minute,
With Cæsar he's endeavoring her peace.
 OCTAVIA. You have prevailed:—But for a further purpose   (*Walks off*)
I'll prove how he will relish this discovery.
What, make a strumpet's peace! it swells my heart: 250
It must not, shall not be.
 VENTIDIUS. His guards appear.
Let me begin, and you shall second me.

    Enter ANTONY

 ANTONY. Octavia, I was looking you, my love: 253
What, are your letters ready? I have given
My last instructions.
 OCTAVIA. Mine, my lord, are written.
 ANTONY. Ventidius. (*Drawing him aside*)
 VENTIDIUS. My lord?
 ANTONY. A word in private.—
When saw you Dolabella?
 VENTIDIUS. Now, my lord,
He parted hence; and Cleopatra with him.
 ANTONY. Speak softly.—'Twas by my command he went 259
To bear my last farewell.
 VENTIDIUS. (*Aloud*) It looked indeed
Like your farewell.
 ANTONY. More softly.—My farewell?
What secret meaning have you in those words
Of—my farewell? He did it by my order.
 VENTIDIUS. (*Aloud*) Then he obeyed your order. I suppose
You bid him do it with all gentleness, 265
All kindness, and all—love.
 ANTONY. How she mourned,
The poor forsaken creature!
 VENTIDIUS. She took it as she ought; she bore your parting
As she did Cæsar's, as she would another's,
Were a new love to come.
 ANTONY. (*Aloud*) Thou dost belie her;
Most basely and maliciously belie her. 271
 VENTIDIUS. I thought not to displease you; I have done.
 OCTAVIA. (*Coming up*) You seem disturbed, my lord.
 ANTONY. A very trifle.
Retire, my love.
 VENTIDIUS. It was indeed a trifle.
He sent—
 ANTONY. (*Angrily*) No more. Look how thou disobeyest me; 275
Thy life shall answer it.
 OCTAVIA. Then 'tis no trifle.
 VENTIDIUS. (*To Octavia*) 'Tis less—a very nothing. You too saw it,
As well as I, and therefore 'tis no secret.
 ANTONY. She saw it!
 VENTIDIUS. Yes. She saw young Dolabella—
 ANTONY. Young Dolabella!
 VENTIDIUS. Young, I think him young,
And handsome too, and so do others think him. 281
But what of that? He went by your command,—
Indeed, 'tis probable with some kind message,
For she received it graciously; she smiled;
And then he grew familiar with her hand,
Squeezed it, and worried it with ravenous kisses; 286
She blushed, and sighed, and smiled, and blushed again;
At last she took occasion to talk softly,

And brought her cheek up close, and leaned
  on his; 289
At which, he whispered kisses back on hers;
And then she cried aloud that constancy
Should be rewarded.
  OCTAVIA. This I saw and heard.
  ANTONY. What woman was it whom you
    heard and saw
So playful with my friend? Not Cleopatra?
  VENTIDIUS. Even she, my lord.
  ANTONY. My Cleopatra?
  VENTIDIUS. Your Cleopatra;— 296
Dolabella's Cleopatra;—
Every man's Cleopatra.
  ANTONY. Thou liest.
  VENTIDIUS. I do not lie, my lord.
Is this so strange? Should mistresses be left,
And not provide against a time of change?
You know she's not much used to lonely
    nights. 302
  ANTONY. I'll think no more on't.
I know 'tis false, and see the plot betwixt
    you.—
You needed not have gone this way, Octavia.
What harms it you that Cleopatra's just?
She's mine no more. I see, and I forgive. 307
Urge it no further, love.
  OCTAVIA. Are you concerned
That she's found false?
  ANTONY. I should be, were it so,
For though 'tis past, I would not that the
    world 310
Should tax my former choice, that I loved one
Of so light note, but I forgive you both.
  VENTIDIUS. What has my age deserved that
    you should think
I would abuse your ears with perjury? 314
If Heaven be true, she's false.
  ANTONY. Though heaven and earth
Should witness it, I'll not believe her tainted.
  VENTIDIUS. I'll bring you, then, a witness
From hell to prove her so.—Nay, go not back,
    (*Seeing* ALEXAS *just entering, and starting
      back*)
For stay you must and shall.
  ALEXAS. What means my lord?
  VENTIDIUS. To make you do what most you
    hate,—speak truth. 320
You are of Cleopatra's private counsel,
Of her bed-counsel, her lascivious hours;
Are conscious of each nightly change she makes,
And watch her, as Chaldæans do the moon,
Can tell what signs she passes through, what
    day. 325

  ALEXAS. My noble lord!
  VENTIDIUS. My most illustrious pander,
No fine set speech, no cadence, no turned
    periods,
But a plain homespun truth is what I ask:
I did myself o'erhear your queen make love
To Dolabella. Speak. For I will know 330
By your confession what more passed be-
    twixt them;
How near the business draws to your employ-
    ment;
And when the happy hour.
  ANTONY. Speak truth, Alexas; whether it
    offend
Or please Ventidius, care not. Justify 335
The injured queen from malice. Dare his
    worst.
  OCTAVIA. (*Aside*) See how he gives him
    courage! how he fears
To find her false! and shuts his eyes to truth,
Willing to be misled!
  ALEXAS. As far as love may plead for
    woman's frailty, 340
Urged by desert and greatness of the lover,
So far, divine Octavia, may my queen
Stand even excused to you for loving him
Who is your lord; so far, from brave Ventidius,
May her past actions hope a fair report. 345
  ANTONY. 'Tis well, and truly spoken. Mark,
    Ventidius.
  ALEXAS. To you, most noble emperor, her
    strong passion
Stands not excused, but wholly justified.
Her beauty's charms alone, without her
    crown, 349
From Ind and Meroë [1] drew the distant vows
Of sighing kings; and at her feet were laid
The sceptres of the earth exposed on heaps,
To choose where she would reign.
She thought a Roman only could deserve her,
And of all Romans only Antony; 355
And, to be less than wife to you, disdained
Their lawful passion.
  ANTONY. 'Tis but truth.
  ALEXAS. And yet, though love and your
    unmatched desert
Have drawn her from the due regard of honor,
At last Heaven opened her unwilling eyes
To see the wrongs she offered fair Octavia,
Whose holy bed she lawlessly usurped. 362
The sad effects of this improsperous war
Confirmed those pious thoughts.
  VENTIDIUS. (*Aside*) Oh, wheel you there?

[1] Upper Egypt.

Observe him now; the man begins to mend,
And talk substantial reason.—Fear not,
    eunuch, 366
The emperor has given thee leave to speak.
  ALEXAS. Else had I never dared to offend
    his ears
With what the last necessity has urged
On my forsaken mistress; yet I must not 370
Presume to say her heart is wholly altered.
  ANTONY. No, dare not for thy life, I charge
    thee dare not
Pronounce that fatal word!
  OCTAVIA. (*Aside*) Must I bear this? Good
    Heaven, afford me patience!
  VENTIDIUS. On, sweet eunuch; my dear
    half-man, proceed. 375
  ALEXAS. Yet Dolabella
Has loved her long. He, next my god-like
    lord,
Deserves her best; and should she meet his
    passion,
Rejected as she is by him she loved—
  ANTONY. Hence from my sight! for I can
    bear no more. 380
Let furies drag thee quick to hell; let all
The longer damned have rest; each torturing
    hand
Do thou employ till Cleopatra comes—
Then join thou too, and help to torture her!
    Exit ALEXAS, *thrust out by* ANTONY
  OCTAVIA. 'Tis not well, 385
Indeed, my lord, 'tis much unkind to me,
To show this passion, this extreme con-
    cernment
For an abandoned, faithless prostitute.
  ANTONY. Octavia, leave me. I am much
    disordered.—
Leave me, I say.
  OCTAVIA. My lord!
  ANTONY. I bid you leave me. 390
  VENTIDIUS. Obey him, madam. Best with-
    draw a while,
And see how this will work.
  OCTAVIA. Wherein have I offended you,
    my lord,
That I am bid to leave you? Am I false
Or infamous? Am I a Cleopatra? 395
Were I she,
Base as she is, you would not bid me leave you,
But hang upon my neck, take slight excuses,
And fawn upon my falsehood.
  ANTONY. 'Tis too much,
Too much, Octavia. I am pressed with
    sorrows 400
Too heavy to be borne, and you add more.
I would retire and recollect what's left
Of man within, to aid me.
  OCTAVIA. You would mourn
In private for your love, who has betrayed
    you. 404
You did but half return to me: your kindness
Lingered behind with her. I hear, my lord,
You make conditions for her,
And would include her treaty. Wondrous
    proofs
Of love to me!
  ANTONY. Are you my friend, Ventidius?
Or are you turned a Dolabella too, 410
And let this Fury loose?
  VENTIDIUS. Oh, be advised,
Sweet madam, and retire.
  OCTAVIA. Yes, I will go, but never to return.
You shall no more be haunted with this
    Fury.
My lord, my lord, love will not always last
When urged with long unkindness and disdain.
Take her again whom you prefer to me: 417
She stays but to be called. Poor cozened
    man!
Let a feigned parting give her back your
    heart,
Which a feigned love first got; for injured me,
Though my just sense of wrongs forbid my
    stay, 421
My duty shall be yours.
To the dear pledges of our former love
My tenderness and care shall be transferred,
And they shall cheer, by turns, my widowed
    nights. 425
So, take my last farewell, for I despair
To have you whole, and scorn to take you
    half. *Exit*
  VENTIDIUS. I combat Heaven, which blasts
    my best designs;
My last attempt must be to win her back;
But oh! I fear in vain. *Exit*
  ANTONY. Why was I framed with this
    plain, honest heart, 431
Which knows not to disguise its griefs and
    weakness,
But bears its workings outward to the world?
I should have kept the mighty anguish in,
And forced a smile at Cleopatra's falsehood.
Octavia had believed it, and had stayed. 436
But I am made a shallow-forded stream,
Seen to the bottom; all my clearness scorned,
And all my faults exposed.—See where he
    comes

Enter DOLABELLA

Who has profaned the sacred name of friend,
And worn it into vileness! 441
With how secure a brow, and specious form,
He gilds the secret villain! Sure that face
Was meant for honesty, but Heaven mismatched it,
And furnished treason out with nature's pomp 445
To make its work more easy.
    DOLABELLA.   O my friend!
    ANTONY. Well, Dolabella, you performed my message?
    DOLABELLA. I did, unwillingly.
    ANTONY.   Unwillingly?
Was it so hard for you to bear our parting?
You should have wished it.
    DOLABELLA   Why?
    ANTONY.   Because you love me.
And she received my message with as true,
With as unfeigned a sorrow as you brought it?
    DOLABELLA. She loves you, even to madness.
    ANTONY.   Oh, I know it. 453
You, Dolabella, do not better know
How much she loves me. And should I
Forsake this beauty? This all-perfect creature?
    DOLABELLA. I could not, were she mine.
    ANTONY.   And yet you first
Persuaded me. How come you altered since?
    DOLABELLA. I said at first I was not fit to go:
I could not hear her sighs and see her tears,
But pity must prevail. And so perhaps 461
It may again with you, for I have promised
That she should take her last farewell. And see,
She comes to claim my word.

Enter CLEOPATRA

    ANTONY.   False Dolabella!
    DOLABELLA. What's false, my lord?
    ANTONY   Why, Dolabella's false,
And Cleopatra's false—both false and faithless. 466
Draw near, you well-joined wickedness, you serpents
Whom I have in my kindly bosom warmed,
Till I am stung to death.
    DOLABELLA.   My lord, have I
Deserved to be thus used?
    CLEOPATRA.   Can Heaven prepare
A newer torment? Can it find a curse 471
Beyond our separation?
    ANTONY.   Yes, if fate
Be just, much greater. Heaven should be ingenious
In punishing such crimes. The rolling stone
And gnawing vulture [1] were slight pains, invented 475
When Jove was young, and no examples known
Of mighty ills. But you have ripened sin
To such a monstrous growth 'twill pose the gods
To find an equal torture. Two, two such!—
Oh, there's no further name,—two such! to me, 480
To me, who locked my soul within your breasts,
Had no desires, no joys, no life, but you.
When half the globe was mine, I gave it you
In dowry with my heart; I had no use,
No fruit of all, but you. A friend and mistress 485
Was what the world could give. O Cleopatra!
O Dolabella! how could you betray
This tender heart which with an infant fondness
Lay lulled betwixt your bosoms and there slept,
Secure of injured faith?
    DOLABELLA.   If she has wronged you,
Heaven, hell, and you, revenge it.
    ANTONY.   If she has wronged me!
Thou wouldst evade thy part of guilt. But swear 492
Thou lov'st not her.
    DOLABELLA.   Not so as I love you.
    ANTONY. Not so? Swear, swear, I say, thou dost not love her.
    DOLABELLA. No more than friendship will allow.
    ANTONY.   No more?
Friendship allows thee nothing. Thou art perjured— 496
And yet thou didst not swear thou lov'dst her not,
But not so much, no more. O trifling hypocrite,
Who dar'st not own to her, thou dost not love,
Nor own to me, thou dost. Ventidius heard it;
Octavia saw it.
    CLEOPATRA.   They are enemies. 501
    ANTONY. Alexas is not so. He, he confessed it;

---

[1] Sisyphus was condemned to roll a stone up hill through eternity, which perpetually rolled down again; a vulture was sent by Zeus to devour the liver of Prometheus.

He, who, next hell, best knew it, he avowed it.
Why do I seek a proof beyond yourself?
      (*To* Dolabella)
You, whom I sent to bear my last farewell,
Returned, to plead her stay.
  Dolabella. What shall I answer?
If to have loved, be guilt, then I have sinned;
But if to have repented of that love 508
Can wash away my crime, I have repented.
Yet, if I have offended past forgiveness,
Let not her suffer. She is innocent.
  Cleopatra. Ah, what will not a woman do
  who loves?
What means will she refuse to keep that heart
Where all her joys are placed? 'Twas I en-
  couraged,
'Twas I blew up the fire that scorched his
  soul, 515
To make you jealous, and by that regain you.
But all in vain. I could not counterfeit:
In spite of all the dams, my love broke o'er,
And drowned my heart again: fate took the
  occasion, 519
And thus one minute's feigning has destroyed
My whole life's truth.
  Antony. Thin cobweb arts of falsehood,
Seen, and broke through at first.
  Dolabella. Forgive your mistress.
  Cleopatra. Forgive your friend.
  Antony. You have convinced [1] your-
  selves.
You plead each other's cause. What witness
  have you
That you but meant to raise my jealousy?
  Cleopatra. Ourselves, and Heaven. 526
  Antony. Guilt witnesses for guilt. Hence,
  love and friendship!
You have no longer place in human breasts;
These two have driven you out. Avoid [2] my
  sight! 529
I would not kill the man whom I have loved,
And cannot hurt the woman. But avoid me,
I do not know how long I can be tame,
For, if I stay one minute more, to think
How I am wronged, my justice and revenge
Will cry so loud within me that my pity 535
Will not be heard for either.
  Dolabella. Heaven has but
Our sorrow for our sins, and then delights
To pardon erring man. Sweet mercy seems
Its darling attribute, which limits justice
As if there were degrees in infinite, 540

[1] Convicted
[2] Leave.

And infinite would rather want perfection
Than punish to extent.
  Antony. I can forgive
A foe, but not a mistress and a friend.
Treason is there in its most horrid shape
Where trust is greatest, and the soul, resigned,
Is stabbed by its own guards. I'll hear no
  more.— 546
Hence from my sight forever!
  Cleopatra. How? Forever?
I can not go one moment from your sight,
And must I go forever?
My joys, my only joys, are centered here.
What place have I to go to? My own king-
  dom? 551
That I have lost for you. Or to the Romans?
They hate me for your sake. Or must I
  wander
The wide world o'er, a helpless, banished
  woman,
Banished for love of you—banished from
  you? 555
Aye, there's the banishment! Oh, hear me,
  hear me
With strictest justice, for I beg no favor,
And if I have offended you, then kill me,
But do not banish me.
  Antony. I must not hear you.
I have a fool within me takes your part, 560
But honor stops my ears.
  Cleopatra. For pity hear me!
Would you cast off a slave who followed you?
Who crouched beneath your spurn? [3]—He
  has no pity!
See if he gives one tear to my departure,
One look, one kind farewell. O iron heart!
Let all the gods look down and judge betwixt
  us, 566
If he did ever love!
  Antony. No more.—Alexas!
  Dolabella. A perjured villain!
  Antony. (*To* Cleopatra) Your Alexas,
  yours.
  Cleopatra. Oh, 'twas his plot, his ruinous
  design,
To engage you in my love by jealousy. 570
Hear him. Confront him with me. Let him
  speak.
  Antony. I have, I have.
  Cleopatra. And if he clear me not—
  Antony. Your creature! one who hangs
  upon your smiles!
Watches your eye to say or to unsay 574

[3] Kick.

ALL FOR LOVE

Whate'er you please! I am not to be moved.
  CLEOPATRA. Then must we part? Farewell,
    my cruel lord!
The appearance is against me, and I go,
Unjustified, forever from your sight.
How I have loved, you know; how yet I love,
My only comfort is, I know myself.   580
I love you more, even now you are unkind,
Than when you loved me most; so well, so
    truly
I'll never strive against it but die pleased
To think you once were mine.
  ANTONY. Good heaven, they weep at
    parting!   585
Must I weep too? That calls them innocent.
I must not weep. And yet I must, to think
That I must not forgive.—
Live, but live wretched; 'tis but just you
    should,
Who made me so. Live from each other's
    sight.   590
Let me not hear, you meet. Set all the earth
And all the seas betwixt your sundered loves:
View nothing common but the sun and
    skies.
Now, all take several ways;
And each your own sad fate, with mine,
    deplore: 595
That you were false, and I could trust no
    more.   *Exeunt severally*

ACT V

SCENE I

[*Enter*] CLEOPATRA, CHARMION, [*and*] IRAS

  CHARMION. Be juster, Heaven; such virtue
    punished thus
Will make us think that chance rules all
    above,
And shuffles with a random hand the lots
Which man is forced to draw.
  CLEOPATRA. I could tear out these eyes
    that gained his heart,   5
And had not power to keep it. O the curse
Of doting on, even when I find it dotage!
Bear witness, gods, you heard him bid me go;
You whom he mocked with imprecating vows
Of promised faith!—I'll die! I will not
    bear it.   10
You may hold me—
  (*She pulls out her dagger, and they hold her*)
But I can keep my breath; I can die inward,
And choke this love.

Enter ALEXAS
  IRAS.   Help, O Alexas, help!
The queen grows desperate; her soul struggles
    in her
With all the agonies of love and rage,   15
And strives to force its passage.
  CLEOPATRA.   Let me go.
Art thou here, traitor!—Oh,
Oh, for a little breath, to vent my rage!
Give, give me way, and let me loose upon him.
  ALEXAS. Yes, I deserve it for my ill-timed
    truth.   20
Was it for me to prop
The ruins of a falling majesty?
To place myself beneath the mighty flaw,
Thus to be crushed and pounded into atoms
By its o'erwhelming weight? 'Tis too pre-
    suming   25
For subjects to preserve that wilful power
Which courts its own destruction.
  CLEOPATRA.   I would reason
More calmly with you. Did not you o'errule
And force my plain, direct, and open love
Into these crooked paths of jealousy?   30
Now, what's the event? Octavia is removed,
But Cleopatra's banished. Thou, thou villain,
[Hast] pushed my boat to open sea, to prove
At my sad cost, if thou canst steer it back.
It can not be; I'm lost too far; I'm ruined!—
Hence, thou imposter, traitor, monster,
    devil!—   36
I can no more. Thou, and my griefs, have
    sunk
Me down so low that I want voice to curse
    thee.
  ALEXAS. Suppose some shipwrecked sea
    man near the shore,
Dropping and faint with climbing up the
    cliff;   40
If, from above, some charitable hand
Pull him to safety, hazarding himself
To draw the other's weight, would he look
    back
And curse him for his pains? The case is
    yours;
But one step more, and you have gained the
    height.   45
  CLEOPATRA. Sunk, never more to rise.
  ALEXAS. Octavia's gone, and Dolabella
    banished.
Believe me, madam, Antony is yours.
His heart was never lost, but started off
To jealousy, love's last retreat and covert,   50
Where it lies hid in shades, watchful in silence,

And listening for the sound that calls it back.
Some other, any man ('tis so advanced)
May perfect this unfinished work, which I
(Unhappy only to myself) have left   55
So easy to his hand.
   CLEOPATRA   Look well thou do't: else—
   ALEXAS.   Else what your silence threatens.
      —Anthony
Is mounted up the Pharos, from whose turret
He stands surveying our Egyptian galleys
Engaged with Cæsar's fleet.   Now death or
   conquest!   60
If the first happen, fate acquits my promise;
If we o'ercome, the conqueror is yours.
               (*A distant shout within*)
   CHARMION.   Have comfort, madam.   Did
     you mark that shout?
               (*Second shout nearer*)
   IRAS.   Hark! they redouble it.
   ALEXAS.   'Tis from the port.
The loudness shows it near: Good news, kind
   heavens!   65
   CLEOPATRA.   Osiris make it so!

          Enter SERAPION
   SERAPION.   Where, where's the queen?
   ALEXAS.   How frightfully the holy coward
     stares
As if not yet recovered of the assault,
When all his gods and, what's more dear to
   him,
His offerings were at stake!
   SERAPION.   O horror, horror!
Egypt has been;[1] our latest hour is come; 71
The queen of nations from her ancient seat
Is sunk forever in the dark abyss;
Time has unrolled her glories to the last,
And now closed up the volume.
   CLEOPATRA.   Be more plain.
Say whence thou comest, though fate is in
   thy face,   76
Which from thy haggard eyes looks wildly
   out,
And threatens ere thou speakest.
   SERAPION.   I came from Pharos—
From viewing (spare me, and imagine it)
Our land's last hope, your navy—
   CLEOPATRA.   Vanquished?
   SERAPION.   No.
They fought not.
   CLEOPATRA.   Then they fled!
   SERAPION.   Nor that.   I saw,
With Antony, your well-appointed fleet   82

[1] Cf. *fuit Ilium, Æneid,* II. 325.

Row out; and thrice he waved his hand on
   high,
And thrice with cheerful cries they shouted
   back.
'Twas then false Fortune like a fawning
   strumpet   85
About to leave the bankrupt prodigal,
With a dissembled smile would kiss at parting,
And flatter to the last; the well-timed oars
Now dipt from every bank, now smoothly run
To meet the foe; and soon indeed they met,
But not as foes.   In few, we saw their caps 91
On either side thrown up.   The Egyptian
   galleys,
Received like friends, passed through and
   fell behind
The Roman rear.   And now they all come
   forward,
And ride within the port.
   CLEOPATRA.   Enough, Serapion.
I've heard my doom.—This needed not, you
   gods: 96
When I lost Antony, your work was done.
'Tis but superfluous malice.—Where's my
   lord?
How bears he this last blow?
   SERAPION.   His fury can not be expressed
     by words.   100
Thrice he attempted headlong to have fallen
Full on his foes, and aimed at Cæsar's galley;
Withheld, he raves on you; cries he's betrayed.
Should he now find you—
   ALEXAS.   Shun him.   Seek your safety
Till you can clear your innocence.
   CLEOPATRA.   I'll stay.
   ALEXAS.   You must not.   Haste you to your
     monument,   106
While I make speed to Cæsar.
   CLEOPATRA.   Cæsar!   No,
I have no business with him.
   ALEXAS.   I can work him
To spare your life, and let this madman perish.
   CLEOPATRA.   Base, fawning wretch! wouldst
     thou betray him too?   110
Hence from my sight! I will not hear a traitor.
'Twas thy design brought all this ruin on us.—
Serapion, thou art honest.   Counsel me—
But haste, each moment's precious.
   SERAPION.   Retire.   You must not yet see
     Antony.   115
He who began this mischief,
'Tis just he tempt the danger.   Let him clear
   you;
And, since he offered you his servile tongue,

To gain a poor precarious life from Cæsar
Let him expose that fawning eloquence, 120
And speak to Antony.
    ALEXAS.   O heavens! I dare not;
I meet my certain death.
    CLEOPATRA.   Slave, thou deservest it.—
Not that I fear my lord, will I avoid him;
I know him noble. When he banished me,
And thought me false, he scorned to take my
    life;   125
But I'll be justified, and then die with him.
    ALEXAS. O pity me, and let me follow you!
    CLEOPATRA. To death, if thou stir hence.
        Speak if thou canst
Now for thy life which basely thou wouldst
    save,
While mine I prize at this. Come, good
    Serapion.   130
        Exeunt CLEOPATRA, SERAPION,
            CHARMION, *and* IRAS
    ALEXAS. O that I less could fear to lose this
        being
Which, like a snowball in my coward hand,
The more 'tis grasped, the faster melts away.
Poor reason! what a wretched aid art thou!
For still, in spite of thee, 135
These two long lovers, soul and body, dread
Their final separation. Let me think:
What can I say to save myself from death,
No matter what becomes of Cleopatra.
    ANTONY. (*Within*) Which way? where?
    VENTIDIUS. (*Within*)   This leads to the
        monument,   140
    ALEXAS. Ah me! I hear him; yet I'm un-
        prepared,
My gift of lying's gone;
And this court-devil which I so oft have raised
Forsakes me at my need. I dare not stay,
Yet can not far go hence.   *Exit*

    Enter ANTONY *and* VENTIDIUS

    ANTONY. O happy Cæsar! thou hast men
        to lead: 146
Think not 'tis thou hast conquered Antony,
But Rome has conquered Egypt. I'm be-
    trayed.
    VENTIDIUS. Curse on this treacherous train!
Their soil and heaven infect them all with
    baseness,   150
And their young souls come tainted to the
    world
With the first breath they draw.
    ANTONY. The original villain sure no god
        created;

He was a bastard of the sun,[1] by Nile,
Aped into man; with all his mother's mud
Crusted about his soul.
    VENTIDIUS.   The nation is   156
One universal traitor, and their queen
The very spirit and extract of them all.
    ANTONY. Is there yet left
A possibility of aid from valor?   160
Is there one god unsworn to my destruction?
The least unmortgaged hope? for, if there be,
Methinks I can not fall beneath the fate
Of such a boy as Cæsar.
The world's one half is yet in Antony,   165
And from each limb of it that's hewed away,
The soul comes back to me.
    VENTIDIUS.   There yet remain
Three legions in the town. The last assault
Lopt off the rest. If death be your design—
As I must wish it now—these are sufficient
To make a heap about us of dead foes,   171
An honest pile for burial.
    ANTONY.   They are enough.
We'll not divide our stars, but, side by side,
Fight emulous, and with malicious eyes
Survey each other's acts, so every death   175
Thou giv'st, I'll take on me as a just debt,
And pay thee back a soul.
    VENTIDIUS. Now you shall see I love you.
        Not a word   178
Of chiding more. By my few hours of life,
I am so pleased with this brave Roman fate
That I would not be Cæsar to outlive you.
When we put off this flesh and mount together,
I shall be shown to all the ethereal crowd,—
Lo, this is he who died with Antony!
    ANTONY. Who knows but we may pierce
        through all their troops,   185
And reach my veterans yet? 'tis worth the
    'tempting
To o'erleap this gulf of fate,
And leave our wondering destinies behind.

    Enter ALEXAS, *trembling*

    VENTIDIUS. See, see, that villain!
See Cleopatra stamped upon that face   190
With all her cunning, all her arts of falsehood!
How she looks out through those dissembling
    eyes!
How he has set his countenance for deceit,
And promises a lie before he speaks!
(*Drawing*) Let me despatch him first.

---

[1] According to classical belief, the mud of the Nile had the faculty of spawning life under the rays of the sun.

ALEXAS. O spare me, spare me!
ANTONY. Hold. He's not worth your killing.—On thy life, 196
Which thou may'st keep because I scorn to take it,
No syllable to justify thy queen.
Save thy base tongue its office.
ALEXAS. Sir, she is gone
Where she shall never be molested more
By love, or you.
ANTONY. Fled to her Dolabella! 201
Die, traitor! I revoke my promise! die!
(*Going to kill him*)
ALEXAS. O hold! she is not fled.
ANTONY. She is. My eyes
Are open to her falsehood; my whole life
Has been a golden dream of love and friendship; 205
But, now I wake, I'm like a merchant roused
From soft repose to see his vessel sinking,
And all his wealth cast o'er. Ingrateful woman!
Who followed me but as the swallow summer,
Hatching her young ones in my kindly beams,
Singing her flatteries to my morning wake;
But now my winter comes, she spreads her wings, 212
And seeks the spring of Cæsar.
ALEXAS. Think not so:
Her fortunes have in all things mixed with yours.
Had she betrayed her naval force to Rome,
How easily might she have gone to Cæsar,
Secure by such a bribe.
VENTIDIUS. She sent it first, 217
To be more welcome after.
ANTONY. 'Tis too plain,
Else would she have appeared to clear herself.
ALEXAS. Too fatally she has. She could not bear 220
To be accused by you, but shut herself
Within her monument, looked down and sighed,
While from her unchanged face the silent tears
Dropped, as they had not leave, but stole their parting.
Some undistinguished words she inly murmured; 225
At last she raised her eyes, and, with such looks
As dying Lucrece cast—
ANTONY. My heart forebodes—
VENTIDIUS. All for the best:—go on.

ALEXAS. She snatched her poniard,
And, ere we could prevent the fatal blow,
Plunged it within her breast, then turned to me: 230
Go, bear my lord, said she, my last farewell,
And ask him if he yet suspect my faith.
More she was saying, but death rushed betwixt.
She half pronounced your name with her last breath,
And buried half within her.
VENTIDIUS. Heaven be praised!
ANTONY. Then art thou innocent, my poor dear love? 236
And art thou dead?
O those two words! their sound should be divided:
Hadst thou been false, and died; or hadst thou lived,
And hadst been true—But innocence and death! 240
This shows not well above. Then what am I,
The murderer of this truth, this innocence!
Thoughts can not form themselves in words so horrid
As can express my guilt!
VENTIDIUS. Is't come to this? The gods have been too gracious, 245
And thus you thank them for it!
ANTONY. (*To* ALEXAS) Why stayest thou here?
Is it for thee to spy upon my soul
And see its inward mourning? Get thee hence.
Thou art not worthy to behold what now
Becomes a Roman emperor to perform. 250
ALEXAS. (*Aside*) He loves her still:
His grief betrays it. Good! the joy to find
She's yet alive completes the reconcilement.
I've saved myself and her. But, oh! the Romans!
Fate comes too fast upon my wit, 255
Hunts me too hard, and meets me at each double.
Exit
VENTIDIUS. Would she had died a little sooner, though,
Before Octavia went; you might have treated:
Now 'twill look tame, and would not be received.
Come, rouse yourself, and let's die warm together. 260
ANTONY. I will not fight: there's no more work for war.
The business of my angry hours is done.

VENTIDIUS. Cæsar is at your gates.
ANTONY.   Why, let him enter;
He's welcome now.
VENTIDIUS. What lethargy has crept into
   your soul?   265
ANTONY. 'Tis but a scorn of life, and just
   desire
To free myself from bondage.
VENTIDIUS.   Do it bravely.
   ANTONY. I will; but not by fighting. O
      Ventidius!
What should I fight for now?—my queen is
   dead.   269
I was but great for her; my power, my empire
Were but my merchandise to buy her love,
And conquered kings, my factors. Now she's
   dead,
Let Cæsar take the world,—
An empty circle since the jewel's gone
Which made it worth my strife; my being's
   nauseous;   275
For all the bribes of life are gone away.
   VENTIDIUS. Would you be taken?
   ANTONY.   Yes, I would be taken,
But as a Roman ought,—dead, my Ventidius.
For I'll convey my soul from Cæsar's reach,
And lay down life myself. 'Tis time the world
Should have a lord, and know whom to obey.
We two have kept its homage in suspense,
And bent the globe, on whose each side we
   trod,   283
Till it was dented inwards. Let him walk
Alone upon't: I'm weary of my part.
My torch is out; and the world stands before
   me
Like a black desert at the approach of night.
I'll lay me down and stray no farther on.
   VENTIDIUS. I could be grieved,   289
But that I'll not outlive you. Choose your
   death,
For I have seen him in such various shapes,
I care not which I take—I'm only troubled,
The life I bear is worn to such a rag,
'Tis scarce worth giving. I could wish, indeed,
We threw it from us with a better grace; 295
That, like two lions taken in the toils,
We might at least thrust out our paws and
   wound
The hunters that inclose us.
   ANTONY.   I have thought on it.
Ventidius, you must live.
   VENTIDIUS.   I must not, sir.
   ANTONY. Wilt thou not live to speak some
      good of me?   300

To stand by my fair fame and guard the
   approaches
From the ill tongues of men?
   VENTIDIUS.   Who shall guard mine
For living after you?
   ANTONY.   Say I command it.
   VENTIDIUS. If we die well, our deaths will
      speak themselves,   304
And need no living witness.
   ANTONY.   Thou hast loved me,
And fain I would reward thee. I must die.
Kill me, and take the merit of my death
To make thee friends with Cæsar.
   VENTIDIUS.   Thank your kindness.
You said I loved you; and in recompense
You bid me turn a traitor.—Did I think 310
You would have used me thus?—that I should
   die
With a hard thought of you?
   ANTONY.   Forgive me, Roman.
Since I have heard of Cleopatra's death,
My reason bears no rule upon my tongue,
But lets my thoughts break all at random out.
I've thought better; do not deny me twice.
   VENTIDIUS. By Heaven, I will not.   317
Let it not be to outlive you.
   ANTONY.   Kill me first,
And then die thou; for 'tis but just thou serve
Thy friend before thyself.
   VENTIDIUS.   Give me your hand.
We soon shall meet again. Now, farewell,
   emperor!—   (Embrace)
Methinks that word's too cold to be my last:
Since death sweeps all distinctions, farewell,
   friend!   323
That's all—
I will not make a business of a trifle;
And yet I can not look on you and kill you;
Pray turn your face.
   ANTONY.   I do. Strike home, be sure.
   VENTIDIUS. Home as my sword will reach.
                                 (Kills himself)
   ANTONY. Oh, thou mistak'st;
That wound was none of thine; give it me
   back: 329
Thou robb'st me of my death.
   VENTIDIUS.   I do, indeed;
But think 'tis the first time I e'er deceived you,
If that may plead my pardon.—And you,
   gods,
Forgive me if you will; for I die perjured
Rather than kill my friend.   (Dies)
   ANTONY. Farewell! Ever my leader, even
      in death!   335

My queen and thou have got the start of me,
And I'm [in] the lag of honor.—Gone so soon?
Is death no more? he used him carelessly,
With a familiar kindness; ere he knocked,
Ran to the door and took him in his arms, 340
As who should say—you're welcome at all hours,
A friend need give no warning. Books had spoiled him,
For all the learned are cowards by profession.
'Tis not worth
My farther thought; for death, for aught I know, 345
Is but to think no more. Here's to be satisfied.
                     (*Falls on his sword*)
I've missed my heart. O unperforming hand!
Thou never couldst have erred in a worse time.
My fortune jades me to the last; and death,
Like a great man, takes state, and makes me wait 350
For my admittance—   (*Trampling within*)
            Some, perhaps, from Cæsar
If he should find me living, and suspect
That I played booty [1] with my life! I'll mend
My work ere they can reach me.
                    (*Rises upon his knees*)

Enter CLEOPATRA, CHARMION, [*and*] IRAS

  CLEOPATRA. Where is my lord? where is he?
  CHARMION.   There he lies,
And dead Ventidius by him.
  CLEOPATRA. My fear were prophets; I am come too late.   (*Runs to him*)
O that accursed Alexas!
  ANTONY.   Art thou living?
Or am I dead before I knew, and thou   359
The first kind ghost that meets me?
  CLEOPATRA.   Help me seat him.
Send quickly, send for help!
                  (*They place him in a chair*)
  ANTONY.   I am answered.
We'll live both. Sit thee down, my Cleopatra:
I'll make the most I can of life, to stay
A moment more with thee.
  CLEOPATRA.   How is it with you?
  ANTONY. 'Tis as with a man   365
Removing in a hurry; all packed up,
But one dear jewel that his haste forgot;
And he, for that, returns upon the spur:
So I come back for thee.

[1] *To play booty* is to allow one's adversary at cards to win in order to defraud him later.

  CLEOPATRA. Too long, you heavens, you have been cruel to me: 370
Now show your mended faith, and give me back
His fleeting life!
  ANTONY.   It will not be, my love;
I keep my soul by force.
Say but, thou art not false.
  CLEOPATRA.   'Tis now too late
To say I'm true: I'll prove it, and die with you.   375
Unknown to me, Alexas feigned my death,
Which, when I knew, I hasted to prevent
This fatal consequence. My fleet betrayed
Both you and me.
  ANTONY.   And Dolabella—
  CLEOPATRA.   Scarce
Esteemed before he loved; but hated now.
  ANTONY. Enough. My life's not long enough for more.   381
Thou say'st thou wilt come after: I believe thee,
For I can now believe whate'er thou sayest,
That we may part more kindly.
  CLEOPATRA.   I will come.
Doubt not, my life, I'll come, and quickly too:
Cæsar shall triumph o'er no part of thee. 386
  ANTONY. But grieve not, while thou stayest,
My last disastrous times.
Think we have had a clear and glorious day,
And Heaven did kindly to delay the storm
Just till our close of evening. Ten years' love,
And not a moment lost, but all improved
To the utmost joys,—what ages have we lived?   393
And now to die each other's; and, so dying,
While hand in hand we walk in groves below,
Whole troops of lovers' ghosts shall flock about us,
And all the train be ours.   397
  CLEOPATRA. Your words are like the notes of dying swans,
Too sweet to last. Were there so many hours
For your unkindness, and not one for love?
  ANTONY. No, not a minute.—This one kiss—more worth   401
Than all I leave to Cæsar.   (*Dies*)
  CLEOPATRA.   O tell me so again,
And take ten thousand kisses for that word.
My lord, my lord! speak, if you yet have being;
Sigh to me, if you can not speak; or cast 405
One look! Do anything that shows you live.
  IRAS. He's gone too far to hear you,

And this you see, a lump of senseless clay,
The leavings of a soul.
   CHARMION.   Remember, madam,
He charged you not to grieve.
   CLEOPATRA.   And I'll obey him.
I have not loved a Roman not to know   411
What should become his wife—his wife, my
   Charmion!
For 'tis to that high title I aspire,
And now I'll not die less. Let dull Octavia
Survive to mourn him, dead. My nobler fate
Shall knit our spousals with a tie too strong
For Roman laws to break.
   IRAS.   Will you then die?
   CLEOPATRA. Why shouldst thou make that
   question?   418
   IRAS. Cæsar is merciful.
   CLEOPATRA.   Let him be so
To those that want his mercy. My poor lord
Made no such covenant with him to spare me
When he was dead. Yield me to Cæsar's
   pride?   422
What! to be led in triumph through the streets,
A spectacle to base plebeian eyes,
While some dejected friend of Antony's,   425
Close in a corner, shakes his head, and mutters
A secret curse on her who ruined him?
I'll none of that.
   CHARMION.   Whatever you resolve,
I'll follow, even to death.
   IRAS.   I only feared
For you, but more should fear to live without
   you.   430
   CLEOPATRA. Why, now, 'tis as it should be.
   Quick, my friends,
Despatch. Ere this, the town's in Cæsar's
   hands.
My lord looks down concerned, and fears my
   stay,
Lest I should be surprised.
Keep him not waiting for his love too long.
You, Charmion, bring my crown and richest
   jewels;   436
With them, the wreath of victory I made
(Vain augury!) for him who now lies dead.
You, Iras, bring the cure of all our ills.
   IRAS. The aspics, madam?
   CLEOPATRA.   Must I bid you twice?
         (*Exit* CHARMION *and* IRAS)
'Tis sweet to die when they would force life
   on me,   441
To rush into the dark abode of death,
And seize him first. If he be like my love,
He is not frightful, sure.   444

We're now alone in secrecy and silence;
And is not this like lovers? I may kiss
These pale, cold lips; Octavia does not see me.
And oh! 'tis better far to have him thus
Than see him in her arms.—Oh, welcome,
   welcome!   449

   Enter CHARMION [*and*] IRAS

   CHARMION. What must be done?
   CLEOPATRA.   Short ceremony, friends,
But yet it must be decent. First, this laurel
Shall crown my hero's head: he fell not basely,
Nor left his shield behind him.—Only thou
Couldst triumph o'er thyself; and thou alone
Wert worthy so to triumph.
   CHARMION.   To what end
These ensigns of your pomp and royalty?
   CLEOPATRA. Dull that thou art! why, 'tis
   to meet my love   457
As when I saw him first on Cydnus' bank,
All sparkling, like a goddess; so adorned,
I'll find him once again. My second spousals
Shall match my first in glory. Haste, haste,
   both,   461
And dress the bride of Antony.
   CHARMION.   —'Tis done.
   CLEOPATRA. Now seat me by my lord. I
   claim this place,
For I must conquer Cæsar, too, like him,
And win my share of the world.—Hail, you
   dear relics   465
Of my immortal love!
O let no impious hand remove you hence,
But rest for ever here! Let Egypt give
His death that peace which it denied his
   life.—
Reach me the casket.
   IRAS.   Underneath the fruit
The aspic lies.
   CLEOPATRA. Welcome, thou kind deceiver!
         (*Putting aside the leaves*)
Thou best of thieves, who, with an easy key,
Dost open life and, unperceived by us,   473
Even steal us from ourselves, discharging so
Death's dreadful office better than himself,
Touching our limbs so gently into slumber
That Death stands by, deceived by his own
   image,
And thinks himself but sleep.
   SERAPION. (*Within*)   The queen,
   where is she?
The town is yielded, Cæsar's at the gates.
   CLEOPATRA. He comes too late to invade
   the rights of death.   480

Haste, bare my arm, and rouse the serpent's
    fury.
    (*Holds out her arm, and draws it back*)
Coward flesh,
Wouldst thou conspire with Cæsar to betray
    me
As thou wert none of mine? I'll force thee to
    it,
And not be sent by him,   485
But bring, myself, my soul to Antony.
    (*Turns aside, and then shows her arm
    bloody*)
Take hence. The work is done.
    SERAPION. (*Within*)   Break ope the door
And guard the traitor well.
    CHARMION.   The next is ours.
    IRAS. Now, Charmion, to be worthy
Of our great queen and mistress.   490
    (*They apply the aspics*)
    CLEOPATRA. Already, death, I feel thee in
    my veins.
I go with such a will to find my lord
That we shall quickly meet.
A heavy numbness creeps through every
    limb,   494
And now 'tis at my head. My eyelids fall,
And my dear love is vanished in a mist.—
Where shall I find him—where? O turn me to
    him,
And lay me on his breast!—Cæsar, thy worst.
Now part us, if thou canst.   (*Dies*)
    (IRAS *sinks down at her feet, and dies:*
    CHARMION *stands behind her chair, as
    dressing her head*)

Enter SERAPION, *two* Priests, ALEXAS, *bound,
    Egyptians*

    PRIEST   Behold, Serapion,
What havoc death has made!
    SERAPION.   'Twas what I feared.—
Charmion, is this well done?   501
    CHARMION. Yes, 'tis well done, and like a
    queen, the last
Of her great race. I follow her.
    (*Sinks down* [*and*] *dies*)
    ALEXAS.   'Tis true,
She has done well. Much better thus to die
Than live to make a holiday in Rome.   505
    SERAPION. See, see how the lovers sit in
    state together,
As they were giving laws to half mankind!
The impression of a smile, left in her face,
Shows she died pleased with him for whom
    she lived,   509

And went to charm him in another world.
Cæsar's just entering: grief has now no leisure.
Secure that villain as our pledge of safety
To grace the imperial triumph.—Sleep, blest
    pair,
Secure from human chance, long ages out,
While all the storms of fate fly o'er your tomb;
And fame to late posterity shall tell   516
No lovers lived so great or died so well.
                                                  Exeunt

EPILOGUE

Poets, like disputants when reasons fail,
Have one sure refuge left—and that's to rail.
Fop, coxcomb, fool, are thundered through
    the pit;
And this is all their equipage of wit.   4
We wonder how the devil this difference grows
Betwixt our fools in verse, and yours in
    prose:
For, 'faith, the quarrel rightly understood,
'Tis civil war with their own flesh and blood.
The threadbare author hates the gaudy coat:
And swears at the gilt coach, but swears afoot:
For 'tis observed of every scribbling man,   11
He grows a fop as fast as e'er he can;
Prunes up, and asks his oracle, the glass,
If pink or purple best become his face.
For our poor wretch, he neither rails nor
    prays;   15
Nor likes your wit just as you like his plays;
He has not yet so much of Mr. Bayes.[1]
He does his best; and if he can not please,
Would quietly sue out his *writ of ease*.[2]
Yet, if he might his own grand jury call,   20
By the fair sex he begs to stand or fall.
Let Cæsar's power the men's ambition move,
But grace you him who lost the world for
    love!
Yet if some antiquated lady say,
The last age is not copied in his play;   25
Heaven help the man who for that face must
    drudge,
Which only has the wrinkles of a judge.
Let not the young and beauteous join with
    those;
For should you raise such numerous hosts of
    foes,   29
Young wits and sparks he to his aid must call;
'Tis more than one man's work to please you
    all.

[1] See *The Rehearsal*.
[2] Certificate of discharge from employment.

VENICE PRESERVED;

OR,

A PLOT DISCOVERED

A Tragedy by Thomas Otway

Thomas Otway, son of Humphrey Otway and Elizabeth his wife, was born March 3, 1651/2 in Trotton, Sussex, and educated at Winchester College (1668) and Christ Church College, Oxford (1669-72), but he obtained no degree. Through a friendship with Mrs. Aphra Behn he was allowed a part in *The Forc'd Marriage* in December, 1670, but "the full house put him to such a sweat and tremendous agony," he broke down utterly, and never tried to act again. He went up to London in 1672; and in 1675 saw his first play, *Alcibiades*, produced at Dorset Garden with Betterton and Mrs. Barry, for whom he conceived a hopeless passion, in the cast. The play caught the fancy of Rochester, who brought the young dramatist to the attention of the Duke of York; thenceforth Otway was a consistent Tory. His next play, *Don Carlos*, based on a romance by the Abbé Saint-Réal, which appeared in 1672, was a striking success; it ran for ten nights and "got more money than any preceding tragedy." Otway followed this with two other plays adapted from the French, *Titus and Berenice* and *The Cheats of Scapin*, taken from Racine and Molière respectively, and then tried his hand at an original comedy, *Friendship in Fashion* (1678) which, though it was "very diverting" at the time, is not important. Mrs. Barry in the meantime had become the mistress of Rochester; disappointment and drink had brought Otway to the point of enlisting in the British forces then stationed in Holland. From this service he returned in 1679 to write his first unquestioned masterpiece, *The Orphan*, produced by Betterton and Mrs. Barry in 1680. A duel with Churchill over "an orange wench in the Duke's Playhouse" and a quarrel with Elkanah Settle who, Otway thought, had maligned him in *The Session of the Poets*, enlivened his return. His *Caius Marius*, a strange cooking of Plutarch and Shakespeare, adds nothing to his reputation, but he turned his army experiences to good account in *The Soldier's Fortune* (1681), a comedy. Then Otway rose to his supreme achievement, *Venice Preserved*, produced at Dorset Garden February 9, 1681/2, writing for his idol the part of Belvidera, which she made memorable. *The Atheist*, a comedy, a continuation of his army experiences, was his last play. The Otway legend pictures him struggling against poverty and disappointed love, but it would appear that his earnings as a dramatist were considerable, and that if Mrs. Barry failed to "remember poor Otway," other beauties were kinder. The Byron of the Restoration died in April, 1685, at the age of thirty-three, perhaps of starvation, but almost certainly in an ale-house. Besides his plays, he wrote a group of miscellaneous poems; and some fragments of his passionate love-letters have been preserved.

See the life in the *Dictionary of National Biography;* the life in *The Complete Works of Thomas Otway* by Montague Summers, I: xiii-civ; R. G. Ham, "Otway's Duels with Churchill and Settle," *Modern Language Notes*, XLI, 73-80, February, 1926; and R. G. Ham, "Additional Material for a Life of Thomas Otway," *Notes and Queries*, CL, 75-77.

OTWAY'S DRAMATIC WORKS

Alcibiades (tragedy) (D.G. Sept. 1675), 1675.
Don Carlos, Prince of Spain (tragedy) (D.G. June 1676), 1676.
Titus and Berenice (tragedy) (D.G. Dec. (?) 1676), 1677.
The Cheats of Scapin (farce) (D.G. Dec. (?) 1676), 1677.
Friendship in Fashion (comedy) (D.G. Apr. 1678), 1678.
The History and Fall of Caius Marius (tragedy) (D.G. Oct. (?) 1679), 1680.

The Orphan (tragedy) (D.G. Mar. (?) 1679/80), 1680.
The Soldier's Fortune (comedy) (D.G. Mar. 1680/1), 1681.
Venice Preserved (tragedy) (D.G. Feb. 9, 1681/2), 1682.
The Atheist; or, the Second Part of the Soldier's Fortune (comedy) (D.G. Sept. (?) 1683), 1684.

César Vichard, known as the Abbé Saint-Réal, besides writing *Don Carlos*, from which Mr. Otway drew the plot of his tragedy of that name, was a writer of merit who favored the world in 1674 with *La Conjuration des Espagnols contre Vénise*, Englished in 1675, a work of great fascination which contains some history and much romance. This book falling in Mr. Otway's way, he read therein of the famous conspiracy against the liberties of Venice directed by the Marquis de Bedmar, a very subtle Spaniard, which engaged the abilities of Renault, a Frenchman, Antoine Jaffeir, a Provençal, Captain Jacques Pierre, a corsair, and others whose names furnished the play with its list of characters. This romancer also gave the ingenious dramatist a hint for the character of Aquilina, since he speaks of a Greek courtesan at whose house the conspirators were accustomed to meet, but as well of the friendship between Jaffeir and Pierre as of the infatuation of Senator Antonio for the courtesan, he makes little or nothing, while the unhappy Belvidera is wholly Mr. Otway's invention.

It is also to be remarked that in the years 1677–82 Anthony Cooper, Earl of Shaftesbury, who was in the estimation of some a mighty liberal and in the consideration of others the wickedest man of his time, but who was certainly the first organizer of parties in the kingdom, had maintained an unequal struggle against the encroachment of the Crown upon the liberties of the people. The exposure of the Popish Plot in 1678 had been made the occasion of an attack upon the Duke of York by the Whigs; and the King had seen no opportunity to retaliate until the spring of 1681, when my lord Shaftesbury, the leader of that party, had been imprisoned upon a charge of treason. In November a Whiggish grand jury had refused to bring in a true bill; nevertheless the Earl was held in confinement until February, 1682, the month of Mr. Otway's tragedy. Mr. Dryden had already written his *Absalom and Achitophel: A Poem*, a severe satire upon the person of that nobleman; in his character of Tory and court poet, Mr. Otway, imitating Mr. Dryden in severity interwove allusions ridiculing the Popish Plot with his fable, and in the figures of Renault and Antonio animadverted against that same noble lord, particularly directing the comic under-plot of the tragedy against his vices. By the universal agreement of later writers Mr. Otway was unjust.

The true greatness of *Venice Preserved*, however, lies not in these allusions but in the many romantic beauties of the verse. Although it has been remarked that the conspirators accomplish little, their plotting affords a mysterious background to the tender loves of Jaffeir and his Belvidera and to the no less tender friendship of Jaffeir and Pierre. The personages of the leading characters are presented with great vividness and art, Mr. Otway's genius lying rather in the picturing of the passions than in the regular management of a plot. If the themes of love and honor and of friendship reappear in this tragedy, it is with a wild and romantic poetry thrown over them; and no contrast can be stronger than that between Mr. Otway's treatment of these themes and the formal and argumentative manner of Mr. Dryden in the same kind. Indeed, among all the Restoration dramatists, Mr. Otway most clearly approaches the romantic manner; and it is said with justice that there are in this work many flashes of genius comparable to the divine Shakespeare. The country wherein the tragedy takes place, the liquid verse, the time of the action (which frequently is at night), the extremities to which the principal characters are reduced, are rather Elizabethan than classical; and perhaps for this reason the judicious have thought Mr. Otway's play the finest tragedy of the age. However this may be, it is true that the rôles of Jaffeir, Pierre, and Belvidera attracted the greatest tragic actors of the epoch and of subsequent times; nor has the Austrian dramatist, Hugo von Hofmannsthal, disdained to re-write Mr. Otway's play for the modern theater, omitting much that time hath tarnished, but preserving the principal parts of the story as Mr. Otway conceived them.

The first performance of *Venice Preserved* was given at the Dorset Garden Theatre February 9, 1681/2.

VENICE PRESERVED;

OR,

A PLOT DISCOVERED

DRAMATIS PERSONÆ

Duke of Venice	Mr. David Williams
Priuli, *father to Belvidera, a senator*	Mr. Bowman
Antonio, *a fine speaker in the Senate*	Mr. Leigh
Jaffeir	Mr. Betterton
Pierre	Mr. Smith
Bedamar, [*the Spanish ambassador*]	Mr. Gillo
Renault	Mr. Wiltshire
Spinosa	Mr. Percival
Theodore	
Eliot	
Revillido	
Durand	*Conspirators*
Mezzana	
Brainveil	
Ternon	
[**Retrosi**]	
Brabe	
Belvidera	Mrs. Barry
Aquilina	Mrs. Currer

Two Women, *attendants on Belvidera*
Two Women, *servants to Aquilina*
The Council of Ten
Officer
Guards
Friar
Executioner and Rabble

EPISTLE DEDICATORY

To her Grace the Duchess of Portsmouth [1]

Madam,

Were it possible for me to let the world know how entirely your Grace's goodness has devoted a poor man to your service; were there words enough in speech to express the mighty sense I have of your great bounty towards me; surely I should write and talk of it forever. But your Grace has given me so large a theme, and laid so very vast a foundation, that imagination wants stock to build upon it. I am as one dumb when I would speak of it; and when I strive to write, I want a scale of thought sufficient to comprehend the height of it. Forgive me then, Madam, if (as a poor peasant once made a present of an apple to an emperor) I bring this small tribute. The humble growth of my little garden, and lay it at your feet. Believe it is paid you with the utmost gratitude; believe that so long as I have thought to remember how very much I owe your generous nature, I will ever have a heart that shall be grateful for it too. Your Grace, next Heaven, deserves it amply from

---

[1] Louise de Kéroualle (1649–1734), mistress of Charles II from 1671 until his death in 1685. On 29 July, 1672, she bore the king a son, Charles Lennox, created first Duke of Richmond in August, 1675. She seems to have been without literary tastes. As she was especially unpopular during the trouble over the 'Popish Plot' in 1679, Otway's epistle is the more interesting.

me; that gave me life, but on a hard condition, till your extended favor taught me to prize the gift, and took the heavy burden it was clogged with from me—I mean, hard fortune. When I had enemies that with malicious power kept back and shaded me from those royal beams whose warmth is all I have, or hope to live by, your noble pity and compassion found me where I was far cast backward from my blessing, down in the rear of fortune, called me up, placed me in the shine, and I have felt its comfort. You have in that restored me to my native right, for a steady faith and loyalty to my prince was all the inheritance my father left me, and however hardly my ill fortune deal with me, 'tis what I prize so well that I ne'er pawned it yet, and hope I ne'er shall part with it. Nature and Fortune were certainly in league when you were born; and as the first took care to give you beauty enough to enslave the hearts of all the world, so the other resolved, to do its merit justice, that none but a monarch fit to rule that world should e'er possess it, and in it he had an empire. The young prince [1] you have given him, by his blooming virtues early declares the mighty stock he came from; and as you have taken all the pious care of a dear mother and a prudent guardian to give him a noble and generous education, may it succeed according to his merits and your wishes: may he grow up to be a bulwark to his illustrious father, and a patron to his loyal subjects; with wisdom and learning to assist him whenever called to his councils, to defend his right against the encroachments of republicans in his senates, to cherish such men as shall be able to vindicate the royal cause, that good and fit servants to the crown may never be lost for want of a protector. May he have courage and conduct fit to fight his battles abroad and terrify his rebels at home; and that all these may be yet more sure, may he never, during the springtime of his years, when those growing virtues ought with care to be cherished, in order to their ripening, may he never meet with vicious natures, or the tongues of faithless, sordid, insipid flatterers, to blast 'em. To conclude: may he be as great as the hand of Fortune (with his honor) shall be able to make him; and may your Grace, who are so good a mistress, and so noble a patroness, never meet with a less grateful servant, than,

    Madam,
        Your Grace's entirely
           devoted creature,
              Thomas Otway

PROLOGUE

In these distracted times, when each man dreads
The bloody stratagems of busy heads;
When we have feared three years we know not what,
Till witnesses [2] begin to die o'th' rot,
What made our poet meddle with a plot?
Was't that he fancied, for the very sake
And name of plot, his trifling play might take?
For there's not in't one inch-board [3] evidence,
But 'tis, he says, to reason plain and sense,
And that he thinks a plausible defence.
Were truth by sense and reason to be tried,
Sure all our swearers might be laid aside:
No, of such tools our author has no need,
To make his plot, or make his play succeed;
He, of black bills,[4] has no prodigious tales,
Or Spanish pilgrims [5] cast ashore in Wales;
Here's not one murdered magistrate at least,
Kept rank like ven'son for a city feast,
Grown four days stiff, the better to prepare
And fit his pliant limbs to ride in chair.[6]
Yet here's an army raised, though underground,
But no man seen, nor one commission found;
Here is a traitor [7] too, that's very old,
Turbulent, subtle, mischievous, and bold,
Bloody, revengeful, and to crown his part,

---

[1] The Duke of Richmond, who, however, was not distinguished by principles.

[2] I.e., Titus Oates.

[3] Summers (*Works of Thomas Otway*, III, 271–2) quotes two other instances of this construction. To swear through an inch-board is to swear falsely.

[4] Handbills supposed to be distributed by the Catholic conspirators in the Popish Plot (?).

[5] Spanish Catholics supposed to take part in the uprising.

[6] The reference is to the murder of Sir Edmund Godfrey, which still remains a mystery. Titus Oates swore to the truth of his evidence before Sir Edmund Godfrey, a magistrate, concerning the alleged Popish plot in September, 1678. On October 17 Sir Edmund's body was found in the fields near London. According to one story Sir Edmund was strangled at Somerset House October 12, and, four days later, his body was conveyed in a sedan chair to the fields where it was found.

[7] I.e., Renault.

Loves fumbling with a wench, with all his heart;
Till after having many changes passed,
In spite of age (thanks Heaven) is hanged at last.
Next is a senator[1] that keeps a whore;
In Venice none a higher office bore; 30
To lewdness every night the lecher ran—
Show me, all London, such another man;
Match him at Mother Creswold's[2] if you can.
Oh, Poland, Poland![3] had it been thy lot,
T'have heard in time of this Venetian plot,
Thou surely chosen hadst one king from thence, 36
And honored them as thou hast England since.

ACT I

Scene i

Enter Priuli and Jaffeir

PRIULI. No more! I'll hear no more; be-gone and leave.

JAFFEIR. Not hear me! by my sufferings, but you shall!
My lord, my lord! I'm not that abject wretch
You think me. Patience! where's the distance throws
Me back so far, but I may boldly speak 5
In right, though proud oppression will not hear me!

PRIULI. Have you not wronged me?

JAFFEIR. Could my nature e'er
Have brooked injustice or the doing wrongs,
I need not now thus low have bent myself,
To gain a hearing from a cruel father! 10
Wronged you?

PRIULI. Yes! wronged me, in the nicest point,
The honor of my house; you have done me wrong.
You may remember (for I now will speak,
And urge its baseness) when you first came home
From travel, with such hopes as made you looked on 15
By all men's eyes, a youth of expectation;
Pleased with your growing virtue, I received you,
Courted, and sought to raise you to your merits:
My house, my table, nay, my fortune, too,
My very self, was yours; you might have used me 20
To your best service. Like an open friend,
I treated, trusted you, and thought you mine;
When in requital of my best endeavors,
You treacherously practised to undo me,
Seduced the weakness of my age's darling, 25
My only child, and stole her from my bosom.
Oh, Belvidera!

JAFFEIR. 'Tis to me you owe her;
Childless you had been else, and in the grave,
Your name extinct, nor no more Priuli heard of. 29
You may remember, scarce five years are past
Since in your brigandine you sailed to see
The Adriatic wedded[4] by our Duke,
And I was with you. Your unskilful pilot
Dashed us upon a rock. When to your boat
You made for safety, entrèd first yourself.
The affrighted Belvidera following next, 36
As she stood trembling on the vessel side,
Was by a wave washed off into the deep;
When instantly I plunged into the sea,
And buffeting the billows to her rescue, 40
Redeemed her life with half the loss of mine.
Like a rich conquest in one hand I bore her,
And with the other dashed the saucy waves
That thronged and pressed to rob me of my prize:
I brought her, gave her your despairing arms. 45
Indeed you thanked me, but a nobler gratitude
Rose in her soul; for from that hour she loved me,
Till for her life she paid me with herself.

PRIULI. You stole her from me! Like a thief you stole her,
At dead of night; that cursèd hour you chose
To rifle me of all my heart held dear. 51
May all your joys in her prove false like mine
A sterile fortune and a barren bed
Attend you both; continual discord make
Your days and nights bitter and grievous; still 55

---

[1] Antonio; that is, Shaftesbury.

[2] A notorious procuress of the period, to whom there are a great number of literary allusions.

[3] Shaftesbury had some hope of being elected King of Poland in 1675.

[4] When Pope Alexander III visited Venice in the 12th century, he instituted the famous annual ceremony of marriage between Venice and the sea, modifying a yet earlier ceremony in so doing.

May the hard hand of a vexatious need
Oppress and grind you, till at last you find
The curse of disobedience all your portion.
   JAFFEIR. Half of your curse you have
      bestowed in vain;
Heav'n has already crowned our faithful
      loves   60
With a young boy, sweet as his mother's
      beauty.
May he live to prove more gentle than his
      grandsire,
And happier than his father!
   PRIULI.   Rather live
To bait [1] thee for his bread and din your ears
With hungry cries, whilst his unhappy
      mother   65
Sits down and weeps in bitterness of want.
   JAFFEIR. You talk as if it would please you.
   PRIULI.   'Twould, by heaven!
Once she was dear indeed; the drops that fell
From my sad heart when she forgot her duty,
The fountain of my life was not so precious.
But she is gone; and if I am a man,   71
I will forget her.
   JAFFEIR. Would I were in my grave.
   PRIULI.   And she, too, with thee;
For, living here, you're but my curs'd re-
      membrancers
I once was happy.   75
   JAFFEIR. You use me thus because you
      know my soul
Is fond of Belvidera. You perceive
My life feeds on her, therefore thus you
      treat me.
Oh! could my soul ever have known satiety!
Were I that thief, the doer of such wrongs   80
As you upbraid me with, what hinders me
But I might send her back to you with con-
      tumely,
And court my fortune where she would be
      kinder!
   PRIULI. You dare not do't.—
   JAFFEIR.   Indeed, my lord, I dare not.
My heart, that awes me, is too much my
      master.   85
Three years are past since first our vows
      were plighted,
During which time, the world must bear me
      witness,
I have treated Belvidera like your daughter,
The daughter of a senator of Venice;
Distinction, place, attendance, and observ-
      ance   90

[1] Annoy

Due to her birth, she always has commanded.
Out of my little fortune I've done this,
Because (though hopeless e'er to win your
      nature)
The world might see I loved her for herself,
Not as the heiress of the great Priuli.—   95
   PRIULI. No more!
   JAFFEIR.   Yes! all, and then adieu
      forever!
There's not a wretch that lives on common
      charity
But's happier than me. For I have known
The luscious sweets of plenty; every night
Have slept with soft content about my
      head,   100
And never waked but to a joyful morning;
Yet now must fall like a full ear of corn,
Whose blossom 'scaped, yet's withered in the
      ripening.
   PRIULI. Home, and be humble; study to
      retrench.
Discharge the lazy vermin of thy hall,   105
Those pageants of thy folly;
Reduce the glittering trappings of thy wife
To humble weeds, fit for thy little state.
Then to some suburb cottage both retire;
Drudge to feed loathsome life; get brats,
      and starve—   110
Home, home, I say!   *Exit* PRIULI
   JAFFEIR.   Yes, if my heart would
      let me—
This proud, this swelling heart. Home I
      would go
But that my doors are hateful to my eyes,
Filled and dammed up with gaping creditors,
Watchful as fowlers when their game will
      spring.   115
I have now not fifty ducats in the world;
Yet still I am in love, and pleased with ruin.
O Belvidera! oh, she's my wife—
And we will bear our wayward fate together,
But ne'er know comfort more.

Enter PIERRE [2]

   PIERRE.   My friend, good morrow!
How fares the honest partner of my heart?

[2] According to Saint-Réal Pierre was a Norman "pirate" of courage and experience, who warred on the Turkish galleys and whom Bedamar detached from the service of the Duke of Ossuno and brought to Venice to further the conspiracy. In Saint-Réal's account he is distinguished for bravery, but is a typical professional soldier of the time. His strong friendship for Jaffeir (who was in reality a Provençal brought to the city expressly for the conspiracy) is a dramatic invention of Otway's.

—What, melancholy? not a word to spare
    me? 122
  JAFFEIR. I'm thinking, Pierre, how that
    damned starving quality
Called honesty, got footing in the world.
  PIERRE. Why, pow'rful villainy first set
    it up, 125
For its own ease and safety; honest men
Are the soft, easy cushions on which knaves
Repose and fatten. Were all mankind villains,
They'd starve each other; lawyers would want
    practice,
Cut-throats rewards; each man would kill
    his brother 130
Himself; none would be paid or hanged for
    murder.
Honesty! 'Twas a cheat invented first
To bind the hands of bold deserving rogues,
That fools and cowards might sit safe in
    power, 134
And lord it uncontrolled above their betters.
  JAFFEIR. Then honesty is but a notion?
  PIERRE.   Nothing else;
Like wit, much talked of, not to be defined.
He that pretends to most, too, has least
    share in't;
'Tis a ragged virtue. Honesty!—no more
    on't. 139
  JAFFEIR. Sure, thou art honest!
  PIERRE.   So indeed men think me.
But they're mistaken, Jaffeir; I am a rogue
As well as they—
A fine, gay, bold-faced villain, as thou seest
    me.
'Tis true, I pay my debts when they're con-
    tracted; 144
I steal from no man; would not cut a throat
To gain admission to a great man's purse,
Or a whore's bed. I'd not betray my friend,
To get his place or fortune. I scorn to flatter
A blown-up fool above me, or crush the
    wretch beneath me.
Yet, Jaffeir, for all this, I am a villain! 150
  JAFFEIR. A villain—
  PIERRE.   Yes, a most notorious villain
To see the suff'rings of my fellow creatures,
And own myself a man; to see our senators
Cheat the deluded people with a show
Of liberty, which yet they ne'er must taste
    of! 155
They say by them our hands are free from
    fetters;
Yet whom they please they lay in basest
    bonds;

Bring whom they please to infamy and sorrow;
Drive us like wracks down the rough tide of
    power,
Whilst no hold's left to save us from destruc-
    tion. 160
All that bear this are villains; and I one,
Not to rouse up at the great call of nature,
And check the growth of these domestic
    spoilers,
That makes us slaves and tell us 'tis our
    charter.
  JAFFEIR. O Aquilina! Friend, to lose such
    beauty, 165
The dearest purchase of thy noble labors!
She was thy right by conquest, as by love.
  PIERRE. O Jaffeir! I'd so fixed my heart
    upon her
That wheresoe'er I framed a scheme of life
For time to come, she was my only joy 170
With which I wished to sweeten future cares.
I fancied pleasures, none but one that loves
And dotes as I did, can imagine like 'em.
When in the extremity of all these hopes,
In the most charming hour of expectation, 175
Then when our eager wishes soared the high-
    est,
Ready to stoop and grasp the lovely game,
A haggard owl, a worthless kite of prey,
With his foul wings sailed in and spoiled my
    quarry.
  JAFFEIR. I know the wretch, and scorn
    him as thou hat'st him. 180
  PIERRE. Curse on the common good that's
    so protected,
Where every slave that heaps up wealth
    enough
To do much wrong, becomes a lord of right!
I, who believed no ill could e'er come near me,
Found in the embraces of my Aquilina 185
A wretched, old, but itching senator;
A wealthy fool, that had bought out my title,
A rogue that uses beauty like a lambskin,
Barely to keep him warm. That filthy
    cuckoo, too,
Was in my absence crept into my nest, 190
And spoiling all my brood of noble pleasure.
  JAFFEIR. Didst thou not chase him thence?
  PIERRE.   I did, and drove
The rank old bearded Hirco [1] stinking home.
The matter was complained of in the Senate:
I, summoned to appear, and censured basely,
For violating something they call "privi-
    lege"— 196

[1] From the Latin *hircus*, a he-goat.

This was the recompense of my service.
Would I'd been rather beaten by a coward!
A soldier's mistress, Jaffeir, 's his religion;
When that's profaned, all other ties are broken; 200
That even dissolves all former bonds of service,
And from that hour I think myself as free
To be the foe as ere the friend of Venice.
Nay, dear Revenge, whene'er thou call'st I am ready.
  JAFFEIR. I think no safety can be here for virtue, 205
And grieve, my friend, as much as thou to live
In such a wretched state as this of Venice,
Where all agree to spoil the public good,
And villains fatten with the brave man's labors.
  PIERRE. We have neither safety, unity, nor peace, 210
For the foundation's lost of common good;
Justice is lame as well as blind amongst us;
The laws (corrupted to their ends that make 'em)
Serve but for instruments of some new tyranny,
That every day starts up t'enslave us deeper.
Now could this glorious cause but find out friends 216
To do it right! O Jaffeir! then mightst thou
Not wear these seals of woe upon thy face;
The proud Priuli should be taught humanity,
And learn to value such a son as thou art.
I dare not speak! But my heart bleeds this moment. 221
  JAFFEIR. Curs'd be the cause, though I thy friend be part on't!
Let me partake the troubles of thy bosom,
For I am used to misery, and perhaps
May find a way to sweeten't to thy spirit. 225
  PIERRE. Too soon it will reach thy knowledge—
  JAFFEIR. Then from thee
Let it proceed. There's virtue [1] in thy friendship
Would make the saddest tale of sorrow pleasing,
Strengthen my constancy, and welcome ruin.
  PIERRE. Then thou art ruined!
  JAFFEIR. That I long since knew;
I and ill fortune have been long acquaintance. 231

[1] *Virtus*, power.

  PIERRE. I passed this very moment by thy doors,
And found them guarded by a troop of villains;
The sons of public rapine were destroying;
They told me, by the sentence of the law,
They had commission to seize all thy fortune— 236
Nay, more, Priuli's cruel hand had signed it.
Here stood a ruffian with a horrid face
Lording it o'er a pile of massy plate
Tumbled into a heap for public sale. 240
There was another making villainous jests
At thy undoing. He had ta'en possession
Of all thy ancient, most domestic ornaments,
Rich hangings intermixed and wrought with gold;
The very bed which on thy wedding night
Received thee to the arms of Belvidera, 246
The scene of all thy joys, was violated
By the coarse hands of filthy dungeon villains,
And thrown amongst the common lumber.
  JAFFEIR. Now thanks, Heaven— 250
  PIERRE. Thank Heaven! for what?
  JAFFEIR. That I'm not worth a ducat.
  PIERRE. Curse thy dull stars and the worse fate of Venice!
Where brothers, friends, and fathers, all are false;
Where there's no trust, no truth; where innocence
Stoops under vile oppression, and vice lords it. 255
Hadst thou but seen, as I did, how at last
Thy beauteous Belvidera, like a wretch
That's doomed to banishment, came weeping forth,
Shining through tears, like April suns in showers
That labor to o'ercome the cloud that loads 'em; 260
Whilst two young virgins, on whose arms she leaned,
Kindly looked up, and at her grief grew sad,
As if they catched the sorrows that fell from her.
Even the lewd rabble that were gathered round
To see the sight, stood mute when they beheld her, 265
Governed their roaring throats, and grumbled pity.

I could have hugged the greasy rogues; they
  pleased me.
  JAFFEIR. I thank thee for this story from
    my soul,
Since now I know the worst that can befall me.
Ah, Pierre! I have a heart that could have
  borne 270
The roughest wrong my fortune could have
  done me;
But when I think what Belvidera feels,
The bitterness her tender spirit tastes of,
I own myself a coward. Bear my weakness,
If throwing thus my arms about thy neck, 275
I play the boy and blubber in thy bosom.
Oh, I shall drown thee with my sorrows!
  PIERRE. Burn!
First burn, and level Venice to thy ruin!
What! Starve like beggar's brats in frosty
  weather
Under a hedge, and whine ourselves to death!
Thou, or thy cause, shall never want assistance 281
Whilst I have blood or fortune fit to serve
  thee.
Command my heart: thou art every way its
  master.
  JAFFEIR. No! There's a secret pride in
    bravely dying.
  PIERRE. Rats die in holes and corners,
    dogs run mad; 285
Man knows a braver remedy for sorrow—
Revenge! the attribute of gods. They stamped
  it
With their great image on our natures. Die!
Consider well the cause that calls upon thee,
And if thou'rt base enough, die then; remember 290
Thy Belvidera suffers. Belvidera!
Die—damn first! What, be decently interred
In a church-yard, and mingle thy brave dust
With stinking rogues that rot in winding
  sheets—
Surfeit-slain fools, the common dung o'th'
  soil? 295
  JAFFEIR. Oh!
  PIERRE. Well said! out with't; swear [1]
    a little—

[1] The vast amount of oath-taking and oath-making in the play (there being but one oath in Otway's original) is unusual, and is probably intended as a hit at the perjury of sworn testimony in the Popish Plot. Cf. II, ii, 72ff.; III, ii, 132ff.; IV, ii, 59ff.; IV, ii, 229ff.; V, i, 219ff., and see John Robert Moore, "Contemporary Satire in Otway's *Venice Preserved*," *PMLA*, XLIII, pp. 167–81.

  JAFFEIR. Swear!
By sea and air! by earth, by heaven and hell,
I will revenge my Belvidera's tears! 298
Hark thee, my friend: Priuli—is—a senator!
  PIERRE. A dog!
  JAFFEIR. Agreed.
  PIERRE. Shoot him.
  JAFFEIR. With all my heart.
No more. Where shall we meet at night?
  PIERRE. I'll tell thee:
On the Rialto every night at twelve 302
I take my evening's walk of meditation;
There we two will meet, and talk of precious
  Mischief—
  JAFFEIR. Farewell.
  PIERRE. At twelve.
  JAFFEIR. At any hour; my plagues
Will keep me waking.
        Exit PIERRE
        Tell me why, good Heaven,
Thou mad'st me what I am, with all the spirit,
Aspiring thoughts, and elegant desires 308
That fill the happiest man? Ah! rather why
Didst thou not form me sordid as my fate,
Base-minded, dull, and fit to carry burdens?
Why have I sense to know the curse that's
  on me?
Is this just dealing, Nature?—Belvidera!

Enter BELVIDERA [*with* Attendants]

Poor Belvidera!
  BELVIDERA. Lead me, lead me, my
    virgins,
To that kind voice!—My lord, my love, my
  refuge! 315
Happy my eyes when they behold thy face;
My heavy heart will leave its doleful beating
At sight of thee, and bound with sprightful
  joys.
O, smile, as when our loves were in their
  spring, 319
And cheer my fainting soul!
  JAFFEIR. As when our loves
Were in their spring? has then my fortune
  changed?
Art thou not Belvidera, still the same—
Kind, good, and tender, as my arms first
  found thee?
If thou art altered, where shall I have harbor?
Where ease my loaded heart? oh! where
  complain? 325
  BELVIDERA. Does this appear like change,
    or love decaying,
When thus I throw myself into thy bosom

With all the resolution of a strong truth?
Beats not my heart as 'twould alarm thine
To a new charge of bliss? I joy more in thee
Than did thy mother when she hugged thee
    first, 331
And blessed the gods for all her travail past.
  JAFFEIR. Can there in woman be such
    glorious faith?
Sure, all ill stories of thy sex are false.
Oh, woman! lovely woman! Nature made thee
To temper man; we had been brutes without
    you. 336
Angels are painted fair, to look like you;
There's in you all that we believe of heaven—
Amazing brightness, purity, and truth,
Eternal joy and everlasting love. 340
  BELVIDERA. If love be treasure, we'll be
    wondrous rich;
I have so much, my heart will surely break
    with't.
Vows cannot express it when I would declare
How great's my joy; I'm dumb with the big
    thought.
I swell, and sigh, and labor with my longing.
O lead me to some desert wide and wild, 346
Barren as our misfortunes, where my soul
May have its vent; where I may tell aloud
To the high heavens and every list'ning planet,
With what a boundless stock my bosom's
    fraught; 350
Where I may throw my eager arms about thee,
Give loose to love with kisses, kindling joy,
And let off all the fire that's in my heart.
  JAFFEIR. O Belvidera! double I am a
    beggar—
Undone by fortune, and in debt to thee. 355
Want! worldly want! that hungry, meager
    fiend
Is at my heels, and chases me in view.
Canst thou bear cold and hunger? Can
    these limbs,
Framed for the tender offices of love, 359
Endure the bitter gripes of smarting poverty?
When banished by our miseries abroad,
(As suddenly we shall be) to seek out
(In some far climate where our names are
    strangers)
For charitable succor; wilt thou then,
When in a bed of straw we shrink together,
And the bleak winds shall whistle round our
    heads, 366
Wilt thou then talk thus to me? Wilt thou
    then
Hush my cares thus, and shelter me with love?

  BELVIDERA. Oh, I will love thee, even in
    madness love thee. 369
Tho' my distracted senses should forsake me,
I'd find some intervals when my poor heart
Should 'suage itself, and be let loose to thine.
Tho' the bare earth be all our resting-place,
Its roots our food, some clift our habitation,
I'll make this arm a pillow for thy head; 375
And as thou sighing li'st, and swelled with
    sorrow,
Creep to thy bosom, pour the balm of love
Into thy soul, and kiss thee to thy rest;
Then praise our God, and watch thee till the
    morning.
  JAFFEIR. Hear this, you heavens, and won-
    der how you made her! 380
Reign, reign, ye monarchs that divide the
    world!
Busy rebellion ne'er will let you know
Tranquillity and happiness like mine.
Like gaudy ships, th'obsequious billows fall
And rise again, to lift you in your pride; 385
They wait but for a storm and then devour
    you:
I, in my private bark already wrecked,
Like a poor merchant driven on unknown land,
That had by chance packed up his choicest
    treasure
In one dear casket, and saved only that, 390
  Since I must wander further on the
    shore,
  Thus hug my little, but my precious
    store;
  Resolved to scorn, and trust my fate
    no more. *Exeunt*

ACT II

[SCENE I. AQUILINA'S *house*]

Enter PIERRE *and* AQUILINA

  AQUILINA. By all thy wrongs, thou'rt dearer
    to my arms
Than all the wealth of Venice; prithee, stay
And let us love tonight.
  PIERRE.   No: there's fool,
There's fool about thee. When a woman sells
Her flesh to fools, her beauty's lost to me; 5
They leave a taint, a sully where th'ave
    passed;
There's such a baneful quality about 'em,
Even spoils complexions with their own
    nauseousness.
They infect all they touch; I cannot think

Of tasting any thing a fool has palled. 10
    Aquilina. I loathe and scorn that fool
      thou mean'st, as much
Or more than thou canst. But the beast has
    gold
That makes him necessary; power too,
To qualify my character, and poise me
Equal with peevish virtue, that beholds 15
My liberty with envy: In their hearts,
Are loose as I am; but an ugly power
Sits in their faces, and frights pleasures from
    'em.
    Pierre. Much good may't do you, madam,
      with your senator.
    Aquilina. My senator! why, canst thou
      think that wretch 20
E'er filled thy Aquilina's arms with pleasure?
Think'st thou, because I sometimes give him
    leave
To foil himself at what he is unfit for,
Because I force myself to endure and suffer
    him, 24
Think'st thou I love him? No, by all the joys
Thou ever gav'st me, his presence is my
    penance;
The worst thing an old man can be's a lover—
A mere *memento mori* to poor woman.
I never lay by his decrepit side 29
But all that night I pondered on my grave.
    Pierre. Would he were well sent thither!
    Aquilina.   That's my wish, too,
For then, my Pierre, I might have cause with
    pleasure
To play the hypocrite. Oh! how I could weep
Over the dying dotard, and kiss him too,
In hopes to smother him quite; then, when
    the time 35
Was come to pay my sorrows at his funeral,
(For he has already made me heir to treasures
Would make me out-act a real widow's
    whining)
How could I frame my face to fit my mourning!
With wringing hands attend him to his grave;
Fall swooning on his hearse;[1] take mad
    possession 41
Even of the dismal vault where he lay buried;
There like the Ephesian matron[2] dwell, till
    thou,
My lovely soldier, comest to my deliverance;

Then throwing up my veil, with open arms
And laughing eyes, run to new dawning joy.
    Pierre. No more! I have friends to meet
      me here tonight, 47
And must be private. As you prize my
    friendship,
Keep up[3] your coxcomb. Let him not pry nor
    listen
Nor fisk[4] about the house as I have seen him,
Like a tame mumping[5] squirrel with a bell on.
Curs will be abroad to bite him, if you do. 52
    Aquilina. What friends to meet? may I
      not be of your council?
    Pierre. How! a woman ask questions out
      of bed?
Go to your senator, ask him what passes 55
Amongst his brethren; he'll hide nothing from
    you.
But pump not me for politics. No more!
Give order that whoever in my name
Comes here, receive admittance; so, good
    night.
    Aquilina. Must we ne'er meet again?
      Embrace no more? 60
Is love so soon and utterly forgotten?
    Pierre. As you henceforward treat your
      fool, I'll think on't.
    Aquilina. [*Aside*] Cursed be all fools, and
      doubly cursed myself,
The worst of fools.—I die if he forsakes me;
And how to keep him, heaven or hell instruct
    me.   *Exeunt*

Scene [II.] *The Rialto*

Enter Jaffeir

Jaffeir. I am here; and thus, the shades
    of night around me,
I look as if all hell were in my heart,
And I in hell. Nay, surely, 'tis so with me;
For every step I tread methinks some fiend
Knocks at my breast, and bids it not be
    quiet. 5
I've heard how desperate wretches like myself
Have wandered out at this dead time of night
To meet the foe of mankind in his walk:
Sure, I'm so cursed that, tho' of heaven
    forsaken, 9
No minister of darkness cares to tempt me.
Hell! Hell! why sleepest thou?

---

[1] Bier.
[2] See the *Satyricon* of Petronius or *La Matrone d'Éphèse* of La Fontaine for famous versions of this tale.
[3] Confine.
[4] Run.
[5] Nibbling.

Enter PIERRE

PIERRE. [*Aside*] Sure, I've stayed too long;
The clock has struck, and I may lose my proselyte.
—Speak, who goes there?
    JAFFEIR. A dog that comes to howl
At yonder moon. What's he that asks the question?
    PIERRE. A friend to dogs, for they are honest creatures, 15
And ne'er betray their masters; never fawn
On any that they love not. Well met, friend.
—Jaffeir!
    JAFFEIR. The same. O Pierre! thou'rt come in season: 19
I was just going to pray.
    PIERRE. Ah, that's mechanic;[1]
Priests make a trade on't, and yet starve by't, too.
No praying; it spoils business, and time's precious.
Where's Belvidera?
    JAFFEIR. For a day or two
I've lodged her privately, till I see farther
What fortune will do with me. Prithee, friend, 25
If thou wouldst have me fit to hear good counsel,
Speak not of Belvidera—
    PIERRE. Speak not of her?
    JAFFEIR. Oh, no!
    PIERRE. Nor name her? May be I wish her well. 28
    JAFFEIR. Whom well?
    PIERRE. Thy wife, thy lovely Belvidera.
I hope a man may wish his friend's wife well,
And no harm done!
    JAFFEIR. Y'are merry, Pierre!
    PIERRE. I am so.
Thou shalt smile too, and Belvidera smile;
We'll all rejoice.
    [*Offering gold*] Here's something to buy pins;
Marriage is chargeable.
    JAFFEIR. [*Aside*] I but half wished
To see the devil, and he's here already. 35
—Well!
What must this buy: rebellion, murder, treason?
Tell me which way I must be damned for this.

---

[1] Common, vulgar.

PIERRE. When last we parted, we'd no qualms like these,
But entertained each other's thoughts like men
Whose souls were well acquainted. Is the world 41
Reformed since our last meeting? What new miracles
Have happened? Has Priuli's heart relented?
Can he be honest?
    JAFFEIR. Kind heaven! let heavy curses
Gall his old age! cramps, aches, rack his bones, 45
And bitterest disquiet wring his heart!
Oh, let him live till life become his burden;
Let him groan under't long, linger an age
In the worst agonies and pangs of death,
And find its ease but late!
    PIERRE. Nay, couldst thou not
As well, my friend, have stretched the curse to all 51
The Senate round as to one single villain?
    JAFFEIR. But curses stick not. Could I kill with cursing,
By heaven, I know not thirty heads in Venice
Should not be blasted! Senators should rot
Like dogs on dunghills, but their wives and daughters 56
Die of their own diseases. O for a curse
To kill with!
    PIERRE. Daggers, daggers, are much better.
    JAFFEIR. Ha!
    PIERRE. Daggers.
    JAFFEIR. But where are they?
    PIERRE. Oh, a thousand
May be disposed in honest hands in Venice.
    JAFFEIR. Thou talk'st in clouds.
    PIERRE. But yet a heart half wronged
As thine has been, would find the meaning, Jaffeir. 62
    JAFFEIR. A thousand daggers, all in honest hands,
And have not I a friend will stick one here?
    PIERRE. Yes, if I thought thou wert not to be cherished 65
To a nobler purpose, I'd be that friend.
But thou hast better friends—friends whom thy wrongs
Have made thy friends—friends worthy to be called so.
I'll trust thee with a secret; there are spirits
This hour at work. But as thou art a man
Whom I have picked and chosen from the world, 71

Swear that thou wilt be true to what I utter;
And when I have told thee that which only gods
And men like gods are privy to, then swear
No chance or change shall wrest it from thy bosom. 75
   JAFFEIR. When thou wouldst bind me, is there need of oaths?
(Green-sickness girls lose maiden-heads with such counters!)
For thou'rt so near my heart that thou mayst see
Its bottom, sound its strength and firmness to thee.
Is coward, fool, or villain in my face? 80
If I seem none of these, I dare believe
Thou wouldst not use me in a little cause,
For I am fit for honor's toughest task,
Nor ever yet found fooling was my province;
And for a villainous, inglorious enterprise, 85
I know thy heart so well, I dare lay mine
Before thee, set it to what point thou wilt.
   PIERRE. Nay, it's a cause thou wilt be fond of, Jaffeir,
For it is founded on the noblest basis—
Our liberties, our natural inheritance. 90
There's no religion, no hypocrisy in't:
We'll do the business, and ne'er fast and pray for't;
Openly act a deed the world shall gaze
With wonder at, and envy when 'tis done.
   JAFFEIR. For liberty!
   PIERRE.   For liberty, my friend!
Thou shalt be freed from base Priuli's tyranny, 96
And thy sequestred fortunes healed again.
I shall be freed from opprobrious wrongs
That press me now and bend my spirit downward.
All Venice free, and every growing merit 100
Succeed to its just right: fools shall be pulled
From wisdom's seat—those baleful, unclean birds,
Those lazy owls, who (perched near fortune's top)
Sit only watchful with their heavy wings
To cuff down new-fledged virtues, that would rise 105
To nobler heights, and make the grove harmonious.
   JAFFEIR. What can I do?
   PIERRE.   Canst thou not kill a senator?
   JAFFEIR. Were there one wise or honest, I could kill him

For herding with that nest of fools and knaves.
By all my wrongs, thou talk'st as if revenge
Were to be had, and the brave story warms me. 111
   PIERRE. Swear then!
   JAFFEIR.   I do, by all those glittering stars
And yond great ruling planet of the night!
By all good powers above, and ill below,
By love and friendship, dearer than my life,
No pow'r or death shall make me false to thee! 116
   PIERRE. Here we embrace, and I'll unlock my heart.
A council's held hard by, where the destruction
Of this great empire's hatching: there I'll lead thee!
But be a man for thou art to mix with men
Fit to disturb the peace of all the world, 121
And rule it when it's wildest.
   JAFFEIR.   I give thee thanks
For this kind warning. Yes, I will be a man,
And charge thee, Pierre, whene'er thou see'st my fears
Betray me less, to rip this heart of mine 125
Out of my breast, and show it for a coward's.
Come, let's begone, for from this hour I chase
All little thoughts, all tender human follies
Out of my bosom. Vengeance shall have room— 129
Revenge!
   PIERRE. And liberty!
   JAFFEIR.   Revenge! revenge—
                                Exeunt

[SCENE III.] *The scene changes to* AQUILINA'S *house, the Greek courtesan*

Enter RENAULT [1]

RENAULT. Why was my choice ambition the first ground
A wretch can build on? It's indeed at distance
A good prospect, tempting to the view;
The height delights us, and the mountain top
Looks beautiful, because it's nigh to heaven.

---

[1] In Saint-Réal Bedamar is the real head of the conspiracy, and Renault is his lieutenant. Otway has practically reversed their importance in the interests of his plot; and has given the character "all of the faults and vices popularly attributed to Shaftesbury: excessive ambition, duplicity, an infirm body, licentious tastes, personal cowardice, and a fondness for speechmaking."

But we ne'er think how sandy's the foundation, 6
What storm will batter, and what tempest shake us!
—Who's there?

Enter SPINOSA[1]

SPINOSA. Renault, good morrow! for by this time
I think the scale of night has turned the balance
And weighs up morning. Has the clock struck twelve? 10
RENAULT. Yes, clocks will go as they are set. But man,
Irregular man's ne'er constant, never certain.
I've spent at least three precious hours of darkness,
In waiting dull attendance; 'tis the curse
Of diligent virtue to be mixed, like mine, 15
With giddy tempers, souls but half resolved.
SPINOSA. Hell seize that soul amongst us it can frighten.
RENAULT. What's then the cause that I am here alone?
Why are we not together?

Enter ELIOT

—O sir, welcome!
You are an Englishman: when treason's hatching 20
One might have thought you'd not have been behindhand.
In what whore's lap have you been lolling?
Give but an Englishman his whore and ease,
Beef and a sea-coal fire,[2] he's yours forever.
ELIOT. Frenchman, you are saucy.
RENAULT. How!

Enter BEDAMAR *the ambassador*, THEODORE, BRAINVEIL, DURAND, BRABE, REVILLIDO, MEZZANA, TERNON, RETROSI, *Conspirators*

BEDAMAR. At difference?—fy!
Is this a time for quarrels? Thieves and rogues 26
Fall out and brawl. Should men of your high calling,
Men separated by the choice of providence
From this gross heap of mankind, and set here
In this great assembly as in one great jewel,
T'adorn the bravest purpose it e'er smiled on— 31
Should you like boys wrangle for trifles?
RENAULT. Boys!
BEDAMAR. Renault, thy hand!
RENAULT. I thought I'd given my heart
Long since to every man that mingles here,
But grieve to find it trusted with such tempers, 35
That can't forgive my froward age its weakness.
BEDAMAR. Eliot, thou once hadst virtue; I have seen
Thy stubborn temper bend with godlike goodness,
Not half thus courted. 'Tis thy nation's glory,
To hug the foe that offers brave alliance. 40
Once more embrace, my friends—we'll all embrace.
United thus, we are the mighty engine
Must twist this rooted empire from its basis!
Totters it not already?
ELIOT. Would it were tumbling.
BEDAMAR. Nay, it shall down: this night we seal its ruin. 45

Enter PIERRE

—O Pierre! thou art welcome!
Come to my breast, for by its hopes thou look'st
Lovelily dreadful, and the fate of Venice
Seems on thy sword already. Oh, my Mars!
The poets that first feigned a god of war 50
Sure prophesied of thee.
PIERRE. Friends! was not Brutus,
(I mean that Brutus who in open senate
Stabbed the first Cæsar that usurped the world)
A gallant man?
RENAULT. Yes, and Catiline too,
Tho' story wronged his fame; for he conspired
To prop the reeling glory of his country. 56
His cause was good.
BEDAMAR. And ours as much above it
As, Renault, thou art superior to Cethegus[3]
Or Pierre to Cassius.
PIERRE. Then to what we aim at.
When do we start? or must we talk forever?

---

[1] In Saint-Réal, Spinosa is a spy employed by the Duke of Ossuna to watch Pierre. Bedamar and Renault therefore accused him before the Council of Ten as a spy of the Duke; and he was strangled before the conspiracy neared its climax.

[2] Coal brought to London by sea, as distinguished from charcoal (Summers).

[3] A member of Catiline's conspiracy, put to death by Cicero.

BEDAMAR. No, Pierre, the deed's near birth.
Fate seems to have set 61
The business up and given it to our care.
I hope there's not a heart nor hand amongst us
But is firm and ready.
ALL. All! We'll die with Bedamar.
BEDAMAR. O men,
Matchless as will your glory be hereafter!
The game is for a matchless prize, if won;
If lost, disgraceful ruin.
RENAULT. What can lose it?
The public stock's a beggar; one Venetian 69
Trusts not another. Look into their stores
Of general safety: empty magazines,
A tattered fleet, a murmuring unpaid army,
Bankrupt nobility, a harassed commonalty,
A factious, giddy, and divided senate
Is all the strength of Venice. Let's destroy it. 75
Let's fill their magazines with arms to awe them,
Man out their fleet, and make their trade maintain it;
Let loose the murmuring army on their masters,
To pay themselves with plunder; lop their nobles
To the base roots, whence most of 'em first sprung; 80
Enslave the rout, whom smarting will make humble;
Turn out their droning senate, and possess
That seat of empire which our souls were framed for.
PIERRE. Ten thousand men are armèd at your nod,
Commanded all by leaders fit to guide 85
A battle for the freedom of the world;
This wretched state has starved them in its service,
And by your bounty quickened, they're resolved
To serve your glory and revenge their own.
They've all their different quarters in this city,
Watch for th'alarm, and grumble 'tis so tardy. 91
BEDAMAR. I doubt not, friend, but thy unwearied diligence
Has still kept waking, and it shall have ease.
After this night it is resolved we meet
No more, till Venice own us for her lords.
PIERRE. How lovely the Adriatic whore,
Dressed in her flames, will shine!—devouring flames, 97

Such as shall burn her to the watery bottom
And hiss in her foundation!
BEDAMAR. Now if any
Amongst us that owns this glorious cause 100
Have friends or interest he'd wish to save,
Let it be told. The general doom is sealed,
But I'd forego the hopes of a world's empire,
Rather than wound the bowels of my friend.
PIERRE. I must confess you there have touched my weakness. 105
I have a friend; hear it, such a friend!
My heart was ne'er shut to him. Nay, I'll tell you.
He knows the very business of this hour,
But he rejoices in the cause and loves it:
W'have changed a vow to live and die together, 110
And he's at hand to ratify it here.
RENAULT. How! all betrayed?
PIERRE. No—I've dealt nobly with you.
I've brought my all into the public stock;
I had but one friend, and him I'll share amongst you! 114
Receive and cherish him; or if, when seen
And searched, you find him worthless, as my tongue
Has lodged this secret in his faithful breast,
To ease your fears I wear a dagger here
Shall rip it out again and give you rest.
—Come forth, thou only good I e'er could boast of! 120

Enter JAFFEIR *with a dagger*

BEDAMAR. His presence bears the show of manly virtue.
JAFFEIR. I know you'll wonder all, that thus uncalled
I dare approach this place of fatal councils;
But I am amongst you, and by heaven it glads me
To see so many virtues thus united 125
To restore justice and dethrone oppression.
Command this sword, if you would have it quiet,
Into this breast; but if you think it worthy
To cut the throats of reverend rogues in robes, 129
Send me into the curs'd, assembled Senate:
It shrinks not, tho' I meet a father there.
Would you behold this city flaming? Here's
A hand shall bear a lighted torch at noon
To the arsenal, and set its gates on fire. 134
RENAULT. You talk this well, sir.
JAFFEIR. Nay—by heaven, I'll do this!

Come, come, I read distrust in all you faces,
You fear me a villain, and indeed it's odd
To hear a stranger talk thus at first meeting,
Of matters that have been so well debated;
But I come ripe with wrongs as you with
    councils. 140
I hate this Senate, am a foe to Venice,
A friend to none but men resolved like me
To push on mischief. Oh, did you but know
    me,
I need not talk thus!
    BEDAMAR.   Pierre!—I must embrace
    him;
My heart beats to this man as if it knew him.
    RENAULT. [*Aside*] I never loved these
    huggers.
    JAFFEIR.   Still I see   146
The cause delights me not. Your friends
    survey me
As I were dang'rous—but I come armed
Against all doubts, and to your trust will give
A pledge worth more than all the world can
    pay for.   150
—My Belvidera! Ho! my Belvidera!
    BEDAMAR. What wonder's next?
    JAFFEIR.   Let me entreat you,
As I have henceforth hopes to call ye friends,
That all but the ambassador, this
Grave guide of councils, with my friend that
    owns me,   155
Withdraw awhile to spare a woman's blushes.
    Exeunt all but BEDAMAR, RENAULT, JAF-
        FEIR, PIERRE
    BEDAMAR. Pierre, whither will this cere-
    mony lead us?
    JAFFEIR. My Belvidera! Belvidera!

        Enter BELVIDERA
    BELVIDERA.   Who?
Who calls so loud at this late, peaceful hour?
That voice was wont to come in gentler
    whispers,   160
And fill my ears with the soft breath of love.
Thou hourly image of my thoughts, where
    art thou?
    JAFFEIR. Indeed, 'tis late.
    BELVIDERA.   Oh! I have slept, and
    dreamt,
And dreamt again. Where hast thou been,
    thou loiterer?
Tho' my eyes closed, my arms have still been
    opened,   165
Stretched every way betwixt my broken
    slumbers,
To search if thou wert come to crown my
    rest.
There's no repose without thee. Oh the day
Too soon will break, and wake us to our
    sorrow;
Come, come to bed, and bid thy cares good
    night.   170
    JAFFEIR. O Belvidera! we must change the
    scene
In which the past delights of life were tasted.
The poor sleep little; we must learn to watch
Our labors late, and early every morning,
Midst winter frosts, thin clad and fed with
    sparing,   175
Rise to our toils, and drudge away the day.
    BELVIDERA. Alas! where am I? whither
    is't you lead me?
Methinks I read distraction in your face,
Something less gentle than the fate you tell
    me!
You shake and tremble too! your blood runs
    cold!   180
Heavens, guard my love, and bless his heart
    with patience.
    JAFFEIR. That I have patience, let our fate
    bear witness,
Who has ordained it so that thou and I
(Thou the divinest good man e'er possessed,
And I the wretched'st of the race of man) 185
This very hour, without one tear, must part.
    BELVIDERA. Part! must we part? Oh! am
    I then forsaken?
Will my love cast me off? have my mis-
    fortunes
Offended him so highly that he'll leave me?
Why drag you from me? whither are you
    going?   190
My dear! my life! my love!
    JAFFEIR.   Oh, friends!
    BELVIDERA. Speak to me.
    JAFFEIR.   Take her from my heart,
She'll gain such hold else, I shall ne'er get
    loose.
I charge thee take her, but with tender'st care,
Relieve her troubles, and assuage her sorrows.
    RENAULT. Rise, madam! and command
    amongst your servants.   196
    JAFFEIR. To you, sirs, and your honors,
    I bequeath her,
And with her this. When I prove unworthy—
                      (*Gives a dagger*)
You know the rest—then strike it to her
    heart;   199
And tell her, he who three whole happy years

Lay in her arms and each kind night repeated
The passionate vows of still increasing love,
Sent that reward for all her truth and suf-
  ferings.
  BELVIDERA. Nay, take my life, since he
    has sold it cheaply;   204
Or send me to some distant clime your slave;
But let it be far off, lest my complainings
Should reach his guilty ears, and shake his
  peace.
  JAFFEIR. No, Belvidera, I've contrived thy
    honor;   208
Trust to my faith, and be but Fortune kind
To me, as I'll preserve that faith unbroken,
When next we meet, I'll lift thee to a height
Shall gather all the gazing world about thee
To wonder what strange virtue placed thee
  there.
But if we ne'er meet more—
  BELVIDERA.   Oh, thou unkind one,
Never meet more! Have I deserved this
    from you?   215
Look on me, tell me, tell me, speak, thou dear
  deceiver,
Why am I separated from thy love?
If I am false, accuse me; but if true,   218
Don't, prithee, don't in poverty forsake me,
But pity the sad heart that's torn with parting.
Yet hear me! yet recall me—
  Exeunt RENAULT, BEDAMAR, *and* BEL-
                                      VIDERA
  JAFFEIR.   O my eyes,
Look not that way, but turn yourselves awhile
Into my heart, and be weaned altogether!
—My friend, where art thou?
  PIERRE.   Here, my honor's brother.
  JAFFEIR. Is Belvidera gone?
  PIERRE.   Renault has led her
Back to her own apartment: but, by heaven!
Thou must not see her more till our work's
  over.   22
  JAFFEIR. No.
  PIERRE.   Not for your life.
  JAFFEIR.   O Pierre, wert thou but
    she,
How I could pull thee down into my heart,
Gaze on thee till my eye-strings cracked with
  love,   230
Till all my sinews with its fire extended,
Fixed me upon the rack of ardent longing;
Then swelling, sighing, raging to be blest,
Come like a panting turtle to thy breast;
On thy soft bosom, hovering, bill and play,
Confess the cause why last I fled away: 236

Own' twas a fault, but swear to give it o'er,
And never follow false ambition more.
                                Exeunt ambo

ACT III

[SCENE I. AQUILINA's *house*]

Enter AQUILINA *and her* Maid

  AQUILINA. Tell him I am gone to bed;
tell him I am not at home; tell him I've better
company with me, or anything; tell him in
short I will not see him, the eternal trouble-
5 some, vexatious fool! He's worse company
than an ignorant physician. I'll not be disturbed at these unseasonable hours!
  MAID. But, madam, he's here already, just
entered the doors.
10 AQUILINA. Turn him out again, you unnecessary, useless, giddy-brained ass! If he
will not begone, set the house afire and burn
us both. I'd rather meet a toad in my dish
than that old hideous animal in my chamber
15 to-night.

Enter ANTONIO.[1]

  ANTONIO. Nacky, Nacky, Nacky—how
dost do, Nacky? Hurry durry. I am come,
little Nacky; past eleven a-clock, a late
hour; time in all conscience to go to bed,
20 Nacky—Nacky, did I say? Aye, Nacky;
Aquilina, lina, lina, quilina, quilina, quilina,
Aquilina, Naquilina, Naquilina, Acky, Acky,
Nacky, Nacky, queen Nacky—come, let's
to bed—you fubbs, you pugg, you—you little
25 puss—purree tuzzey—I am a senator.
  AQUILINA. You are a fool, I am sure.
  ANTONIO. May be so, too, sweetheart.
Never the worse senator for all that. Come
Nacky, Nacky, let's have a game at rump,
30 Nacky.
  AQUILINA. You would do well, signior, to
be troublesome here no longer, but leave
me to myself, be sober, and go home, sir.
  ANTONIO. Home, Madonna!
35 AQUILINA. Aye, home, sir. Who am I?
  ANTONIO. Madonna, as I take it you are
my—you are—thou art my little Nicky
Nacky—that's all!
  AQUILINA. I find you are resolved to be
40 troublesome; and so to make short of the

---

[1] The character of Antonio is intended as a personal satire on Shaftesbury. See the article by Moore already referred to.

matter in few words, I hate you, detest you, loathe you, I am weary of you, sick of you—hang you, you are an old, silly, impertinent, impotent, solicitous coxcomb, crazy in your head and lazy in your body, love to be meddling with everything, and if you had not money, you are good for nothing.

ANTONIO. Good for nothing! Hurry durry, I'll try that presently. Sixty-one years old, and good for nothing; that's brave! (*To the Maid*)—Come, come, come, Mistress Fiddle-faddle, turn you out for a season. Go, turn out, I say, it is our will and pleasure to be private some moments—out, out when you are bid to! (*Puts her out and locks the door*)—Good for nothing, you say.

AQUILINA. Why, what are you good for?

ANTONIO. In the first place, madam, I am old, and consequently very wise, very wise, Madonna, d'e mark that? In the second place take notice, if you please, that I am a senator, and when I think fit can make speeches, Madonna. Hurry durry, I can make a speech in the Senate-house now and then—would make your hair stand on end, Madonna.

AQUILINA. What care I for your speeches in the Senate-house? If you would be silent here, I should thank you.

ANTONIO. Why, I can make speeches to thee, too, my lovely Madonna; for example: My cruel fair one (*Takes out a purse of gold, and at every pause shakes it*), since it is my fate that you should with your servant angry prove; tho' late at night—I hope 'tis not too late with this to gain reception for my love.—There's for thee, my little Nicky Nacky—take it, here take it—I say take it, or I'll throw it at your head. How now, rebel!

AQUILINA. Truly, my illustrious senator, I must confess your honor is at present most profoundly eloquent, indeed.

ANTONIO. Very well: come now, let's sit down and think upon't a little. Come sit, I say—sit down by me a little, my Nicky Nacky, hah—(*Sits down*) Hurry durry—"good for nothing!"

AQUILINA. No, sir; if you please, I can know my distance, and stand.

ANTONIO. Stand! How, Nacky, up, and I down? Nay, then, let me exclaim with the poet,

Show me a case more pitiful who can,
A standing woman and a falling man.

Hurry durry—not sit down!—See this, ye gods.—You won't sit down?

AQUILINA. No, sir.

ANTONIO. Then look you now, suppose me a bull, a Basan-bull, the bull of bulls, or any bull. Thus up I get and with my brows thus bent—I broo, I say I broo, I broo, I broo. You won't sit down, will you? —I broo—

(*Bellows like a bull, and drives her about*)

AQUILINA. Well, sir, I must endure this. (*She sits down*) Now your honor has been a bull, pray what beast will your worship please to be next?

ANTONIO. Now I'll be a senator again, and thy lover, little Nicky Nacky! (*He sits by her*) Ah, toad, toad, toad, toad! spit in my face a little, Nacky—spit in my face, prithee, spit in my face, never so little. Spit but a little bit—spit, spit, spit, spit when you are bid, I say; do, prithee, spit—now, now, now, spit. What, you won't spit, will you? then I'll be a dog.

AQUILINA. A dog, my lord?

ANTONIO. Aye, a dog—and I'll give thee this t'other purse to let me be a dog—and to use me like a dog a little. Hurry durry —I will—here 'tis. (*Gives the purse*)

AQUILINA Well, with all my heart. But let me beseech your dogship to play your tricks over as fast as you can, that you may come to stinking the sooner and be turned out of doors as you deserve.

ANTONIO. Aye, aye—no matter for that— that shan't move me. (*He gets under the table*) Now, bough waugh waugh, bough waugh—

(*Barks like a dog*)

AQUILINA. Hold, hold, hold, sir. I beseech you: what is't you do? If curs bite, they must be kicked, sir.—Do you see, kicked thus?

ANTONIO. Aye, with all my heart. Do kick, kick on; now I am under the table, kick again—kick harder—harder yet, bough waugh waugh, waugh, bough—'odd, I'll have a snap at thy shins—bough waugh wough, waugh, bough!—'Odd, she kicks bravely.—

AQUILINA. Nay, then, I'll go another way to work with you; and I think here's an instrument fit for the purpose. (*Fetches a whip and bell*)—What, bite your mistress, sirrah! out, out of doors, you dog, to kennel and be hanged—bite your mistress by the legs, you rogue! (*She whips him*)

ANTONIO. Nay, prithee, Nacky, now thou art too loving! Hurry durry, 'odd! I'll be a dog no longer.

AQUILINA. Nay, none of your fawning and grinning, but be gone, or here's the discipline! What, bite your mistress by the legs, you mongrel? Out of doors—hout hout, to kennel, sirrah! go!

ANTONIO. This is very barbarous usage, Nacky, very barbarous. Look you, I will not go—I will not stir from the door; that I resolve—hurry durry—what, shut me out? (*She whips him out*)

AQUILINA. Aye, and if you come here any more to-night, I'll have my footmen lug you, you cur. What, bite your poor mistress Nacky, sirrah?

Enter MAID

MAID. Heavens, madam! what's the matter? (*He howls at the door like a dog*)

AQUILINA. Call my footmen hither presently.

Enter two FOOTMEN

MAID. They are here already, madam; the house is all alarmed with a strange noise that nobody knows what to make of.

AQUILINA. Go, all of you, and turn that troublesome beast in the next room out of my house—If I ever see him within these walls again without my leave for his admittance, you sneaking rogues, I'll have you poisoned all—poisoned like rats! Every corner of the house shall stink of one of you; go! and learn hereafter to know my pleasure. So now for my Pierre:

Thus when godlike lover was displeased,
We sacrifice our fool and he's appeased.
Exeunt

[SCENE II. *The same*]

Enter BELVIDERA

BELVIDERA. I'm sacrificed! I am sold! betrayed to shame!
Inevitable ruin has inclosed me!
No sooner was I to my bed repaired,
To weigh, and (weeping) ponder my condition,
But the old hoary wretch to whose false care
My peace and honor was entrusted, came
(Like Tarquin) ghastly with infernal lust.
O thou Roman Lucrece! thou couldst find friends to vindicate thy wrong!
I never had but one, and he's proved false;
He that should guard my virtue has betrayed it—
Left me! undone me! Oh, that I could hate him!
Where shall I go? oh, whither, whither wander?

Enter JAFFEIR

JAFFEIR. Can Belvidera want a resting place
When these poor arms are open to receive her?
Oh, 'tis in vain to struggle with desires
Strong as my love to thee; for every moment
I am from thy sight, the heart within my bosom
Moans like a tender infant in its cradle,
Whose nurse had left it. Come, and with the songs
Of gentle love persuade it to its peace.
BELVIDERA. I fear the stubborn wanderer will not own me;
'Tis grown a rebel to be ruled no longer,
Scorns the indulgent bosom that first lulled it,
And like a disobedient child disdains
The soft authority of Belvidera.
JAFFEIR. There was a time—
BELVIDERA. Yes, yes, there was a time
When Belvidera's tears, her cries, and sorrows
Were not despised; when if she chanced to sigh,
Or look but sad—there was indeed a time
When Jaffeir would have ta'en her in his arms,
Eased her declining head upon his breast,
And never left her till he found the cause.
But let her now weep seas,
Cry till she rend the earth, sigh till she burst
Her heart asunder: still he bears it all,
Deaf as the wind, and as the rocks unshaken.
JAFFEIR. Have I been deaf? am I that rock unmoved,
Against whose root tears beat and sighs are sent?
In vain have I beheld thy sorrows calmly!
Witness against me, heavens; have I done this?
Then bear me in a whirlwind back again,
And let that angry dear one ne'er forgive me!
Oh, thou too rashly censur'st of my love!
Couldst thou but think how I have spent this night,

Dark and alone, no pillow to my head, 45
Rest in my eyes, nor quiet in my heart,
Thou wouldst not, Belvidera, sure thou wouldst not
Talk to me thus, but like a pitying angel
Spreading thy wings, come settle on my breast
And hatch warm comfort there ere sorrows freeze it. 50
  BELVIDERA. Why, then, poor mourner, in what baleful corner
Hast thou been talking with that witch, the Night?
On what cold stone hast thou been stretched along,
Gathering the grumbling winds about thy head, 54
To mix with theirs the accents of thy woes?
Oh, now I find the cause my love forsakes me!
I am no longer fit to bear a share
In his concernments: my weak, female virtue
Must not be trusted; 'tis too frail and tender.
  JAFFEIR. O Portia! Portia! what a soul was thine! 60
  BELVIDERA. That Portia was a woman, and when Brutus,
Big with the fate of Rome (Heaven guard thy safety!),
Concealed from her the labors of his mind,
She let him see her blood was great as his,
Flowed from a spring as noble, and a heart
Fit to partake his troubles, as his love. 66
Fetch, fetch that dagger back, the dreadful dower
Thou gav'st last night in parting with me. Strike it
Here to my heart, and as the blood flows from it,
Judge if it run not pure as Cato's daughter's.
  JAFFEIR. Thou art too good, and I indeed unworthy— 71
Unworthy so much virtue. Teach me how
I may deserve such matchless love as thine,
And see with what attention I'll obey thee.
  BELVIDERA. Do not despise me: that's the all I ask. 75
  JAFFEIR. Despise thee! hear me—
  BELVIDERA.   Oh, thy charming tongue
Is but too well acquainted with my weakness;
Knows, let it name but love, my melting heart
Dissolves within my breast, till with closed eyes
I reel into thy arms and all's forgotten. 80
  JAFFEIR. What shall I do?
  BELVIDERA.   Tell me! be just, and tell me
Why dwells that busy cloud upon thy face?
Why am I made a stranger? why that sigh,
And I not know the cause? why, when the world 84
Is wrapped in rest, why chooses then my love
To wander up and down in horrid darkness,
Loathing his bed and these desiring arms?
Why are these eyes bloodshot with tedious watching?
Why starts he now? and looks as if he wished
His fate were finished? Tell me, ease my fears, 90
Lest when we next time meet I want the power
To search into the sickness of thy mind,
But talk as wildly then as thou look'st now.
  JAFFEIR. O Belvidera!
  BELVIDERA. Why was I last night delivered to a villain? 95
  JAFFEIR. Hah, a villain!
  BELVIDERA. Yes! to a villain! Why at such an hour
Meets that assembly all made up of wretches
That look as hell had drawn 'em into league?
Why, I in this hand, and in that a dagger,
Was I delivered with such dreadful ceremonies? 101
"To you, sirs, and to your honor I bequeath her,
And with her this: whene'er I prove unworthy—
You know the rest—then strike it to her heart?"
Oh! why's that *rest* concealed from me? Must I 105
Be made the hostage of a hellish trust?
For such I know I am; that's all my value!
But by the love and loyalty I owe thee,
I'll free thee from the bondage of these slaves;
Straight to the Senate, tell 'em all I know, 110
All that I think, all that my fears inform me.
  JAFFEIR. Is this the Roman virtue? this the blood
That boasts its purity with Cato's daughter?
Would she have e'er betrayed her Brutus?
  BELVIDERA.   No,
For Brutus trusted her; wert thou so kind, 115
What would not Belvidera suffer for thee!
  JAFFEIR. I shall undo myself and tell thee all.
  BELVIDERA. Look not upon me as I am, a woman,

But as a bone,[1] thy wife, thy friend, who long
Has had admission to thy heart, and there 120
Studied the virtues of thy gallant nature.
Thy constancy, thy courage, and thy truth
Have been my daily lesson. I have learnt them,
Am bold as thou, can suffer or despise
The worst of fates for thee, and with thee share them. 125
  JAFFEIR. Oh you divinest powers! look down and hear
My prayers! instruct me to reward this virtue!
Yet think a little ere thou tempt me further,
Think I've a tale to tell will shake thy nature,
Melt all this boasted constancy thou talk'st of 130
Into vile tears and despicable sorrows:
Then if thou shouldst betray me—!
  BELVIDERA.   Shall I swear?
  JAFFEIR. No, do not swear. I would not violate
Thy tender nature with so rude a bond; 134
But as thou hop'st to see me live my days
And love thee long, lock this within thy breast.
I've bound myself by all the strictest sacraments,
Divine and human—
  BELVIDERA.   Speak!—
  JAFFEIR.   To kill thy father—
  BELVIDERA. My father!
  JAFFEIR.   Nay, the throats of the whole senate 139
Shall bleed, my Belvidera. He amongst us
That spares his father, brother, or his friend,
Is damned.   How rich and beauteous will the face
Of ruin look, when these wide streets run blood;
I and the glorious partners of my fortune
Shouting, and striding o'er the prostrate dead,
Still to new waste; whilst thou, far off in safety 146
Smiling, shall see the wonders of our daring;
And when night comes, with praise and love receive me.
  BELVIDERA. Oh!
  JAFFEIR.   Have a care, and shrink not, even in thought,
For if thou dost—
  BELVIDERA.   I know it—thou wilt kill me. 150
Do, strike thy sword into this bosom. Lay me

[1] Boon(?).

Dead on the earth, and then thou wilt be safe.
Murder my father! tho' his cruel nature
Has persecuted me to my undoing,
Driven me to basest wants, can I behold him
With smiles of vengeance, butchered in his age? 156
The sacred fountain of my life destroyed?
And canst thou shed the blood that gave me being?
Nay, be a traitor too, and sell thy country?
Can thy great heart descend so vilely low, 160
Mix with hired slaves, bravoes, and common stabbers,
Nose-slitters, alley-lurking villains? join
With such a crew, and take a ruffian's wages,
To cut the throats of wretches as they sleep?
  JAFFEIR. Thou wrong'st me, Belvidera! I've engaged 165
With men of souls, fit to reform the ills
Of all mankind. There's not a heart amongst them
But's stout as death, yet honest as the nature
Of man first made, ere fraud and vice were fashions.
  BELVIDERA. What's he to whose curs'd hands last night thou gav'st me? 170
Was that well done? Oh! I could tell a story
Would rouse thy lion heart out of its den,
And make it rage with terrifying fury.
  JAFFEIR. Speak on, I charge thee!
  BELVIDERA.   O my love! if e'er
Thy Belvidera's peace deserve thy care, 175
Remove me from this place! Last night, last night!
  JAFFEIR. Distract me not, but give me all the truth.
  BELVIDERA. No sooner wert thou gone, and I alone,
Left in the power of that old son of mischief;
No sooner was I lain on my sad bed, 180
But that vile wretch approached me; loose, unbuttoned,
Ready for violation. Then my heart
Throbbed with its fears. Oh, how I wept and sighed,
And shrunk and trembled; wished in vain for him
That should protect me. Thou, alas, wert gone! 185
  JAFFEIR. Patience, sweet Heaven! till I make vengeance sure.
  BELVIDERA. He drew the hideous dagger forth thou gav'st him,

And with upbraiding smiles he said, "Behold it;
This is the pledge of a false husband's love."
And in my arms then pressed, and would have clasped me; 190
But with my cries I scared his coward heart,
Till he withdrew and muttered vows to hell.
These are thy friends! with these thy life, thy honor,
Thy love—all staked, and all will go to ruin.
    JAFFEIR. No more. I charge thee keep this secret close. 195
Clear up thy sorrows, look as if thy wrongs
Were all forgot, and treat him like a friend,
As no complaint were made. No more; retire,
Retire, my life, and doubt not of my honor;
I'll heal its failings and deserve thy love. 200
    BELVIDERA. Oh, should I part with thee, I fear thou wilt
In anger leave me, and return no more.
    JAFFEIR. Return no more! I would not live without thee
Another night, to purchase the creation.
    BELVIDERA. When shall we meet again?
    JAFFEIR.   Anon at twelve!
I'll steal myself to thy expecting arms, 206
Come like a travelled dove and bring thee peace.
    BELVIDERA. Indeed!
    JAFFEIR.   By all our loves!
    BELVIDERA.   'Tis hard to part:
But sure, no falsehood e'er looked so fairly.
Farewell.—Remember twelve!
                      Exit BELVIDERA
    JAFFEIR.   Let heaven forget me
When I remember not thy truth, thy love.
How cursed is my condition, tossed and jostled 212
From every corner; Fortune's common fool,
The jest of rogues, an instrumental ass
For villains to lay loads of shame upon,
And drive about just for their ease and scorn! 216

              Enter PIERRE

    PIERRE. Jaffeir!
    JAFFEIR.   Who calls?
    PIERRE.   A friend, that could have wished
I'have found thee otherwise employed
What, hunt
A wife on the dull foil![1] sure, a stanch husband

[1] Trail of a hunted animal.

Of all hounds is the dullest! Wilt thou never,
Never be weaned from caudles[2] and confections?
What feminine tale hast thou been listening to,
Of unaired shirts, catarrhs, and tooth-ache got
By thin-soled shoes? Damnation! that a fellow
Chosen to be sharer in the destruction 225
Of a whole people, should sneak thus in corners
To ease his fulsome lusts and fool his mind.
    JAFFEIR. May not a man, then, trifle out an hour
With a kind woman and not wrong his calling? 229
    PIERRE Not in a cause like ours.
    JAFFEIR.   Then, friend, our cause
Is in a damned condition; for I'll tell thee,
That canker-worm called lechery has touched it;
'Tis tainted vilely. Wouldst thou think it? Renault
(That mortified, old, withered, winter rogue)
Loves simple fornication like a priest. 235
I found him out for watering[3] at my wife;
He visited her last night like a kind guardian.
Faith, she has some temptations, that's the truth on't. 238
    PIERRE He durst not wrong his trust!
    JAFFEIR.   'Twas something late, tho',
To take the freedom of a lady's chamber.
    PIERRE. Was she in bed?
    JAFFEIR.   Yes, faith, in virgin sheets
White as her bosom, Pierre, dished neatly up,
Might tempt a weaker appetite to taste. 243
Oh, how the old fox stunk, I warrant thee,
When the rank fit was on him!
    PIERRE.   Patience guide me!
He used no violence?
    JAFFEIR.   No, no! out on't, violence!
Played with her neck, brushed her with his gray beard, 247
Struggled and towzled, tickled her till she squeaked a little,
Maybe, or so—but not a jot of violence—
    PIERRE. Damn him!
    JAFFEIR.   Aye, so say I; but hush, no more on't! 250
All hitherto is well, and I believe
Myself no monster[4] yet, tho' no man knows
What fate he's born to. Sure, 'tis near the hour

[2] Drink for invalids.
[3] Desiring.
[4] Cuckold.

We all should meet for our concluding orders.
Will the ambassador be here in person? 255
    PIERRE. No. He has sent commission to that villain, Renault,
To give the executing charge.
I'd have thee be a man if possible,
And keep thy temper; for a brave revenge
Ne'er comes too late.
    JAFFEIR.   Fear not; I am cool as patience. 260
Had he completed my dishonor, rather
Than hazard the success our hopes are ripe for,
I'd bear it all with mortifying virtue.
    PIERRE. He's yonder, coming this way through the hall; 264
His thoughts seem full.
    JAFFIER. Prithee retire, and leave me
With him alone. I'll put him to some trial,
See how his rotten part will bear the touching.
    PIERRE. Be careful then.   *Exit* PIERRE
    JAFFEIR.   Nay, never doubt, but trust me.
What, be a devil? take a damning oath
For shedding native blood? can there be a sin 270
In merciful repentance? Oh, this villain!

    Enter RENAULT

RENAULT. Perverse and peevish! What a slave is man!
To let his itching flesh thus get the better of him!
Dispatch the tool, her husband—that were well.
—Who's there?
    JAFFEIR.   A man.
    RENAULT.   My friend, my near ally!
The hostage of your faith, my beauteous charge, 276
Is very well.
    JAFFEIR. Sir, are you sure of that?
Stands she in perfect health? beats her pulse even?
Neither too hot nor cold?
    RENAULT.   What means that question?
    JAFFEIR. Oh, women have fantastic constitutions, 280
Inconstant as their wishes, always wavering,
And ne'er fixed. Was it not boldly done
Even at first sight to trust the thing I loved
(A tempting treasure too!) with youth so fierce 284
And vigorous as thine? But thou art honest.
    RENAULT. Who dares accuse me?
    JAFFEIR.   Curs'd be him that doubts
Thy virtue! I have tried it, and declare,
Were I to choose a guardian of my honor,
I'd put it into thy keeping; for I know thee.
    RENAULT. Know me!
    JAFFEIR.   Aye, know thee. There's no falsehood in thee. 290
Thou look'st just as thou art. Let us embrace.
Now wouldst thou cut my throat or I cut thine?
    RENAULT. You dare not do't.
    JAFFEIR.   You lie, sir.
    RENAULT.   How!
    JAFFEIR.   No more.
'Tis a base world, and must reform, that's all.

Enter SPINOSA, THEODORE, ELIOT, REVILLIDO, DURAND, BRAINVEIL, *and the rest of the* CONSPIRATORS

RENAULT. Spinosa! Theodore!
SPINOSA.   The same.
RENAULT.   You are welcome!
SPINOSA. You are trembling, sir.
RENAULT.   'Tis a cold night, indeed, and I am aged, 296
Full of decay and natural infirmities.
We shall be warm, my friend, I hope to-morrow.

    PIERRE *re-enters*

PIERRE. (*Aside*) 'Twas not well done; thou shouldst have stroked him
And not have galled him.
    JAFFEIR. (*Aside*)   Damn him, let him chew on't! 300
Heaven! where am I? beset with cursèd fiends,
That wait to damn me. What a devil's man
When he forgets his nature!—Hush, my heart.
    RENAULT. My friends, 'tis late; are we assembled all? 304
Where's Theodore?
    THEODORE.   At hand.
    RENAULT.   Spinosa?
    SPINOSA.   Here.
RENAULT. Brainveil?
    BRAINVEIL.   I am ready.
    RENAULT.   Durand and Brabe?
    DURAND.   Command us;
We are both prepared!
    RENAULT.   Mezzana, Revillido,
Ternon, Retrosi; oh, you are men, I find,
Fit to behold your fate and meet her summons. 309

To-morrow's rising sun must see you all
Decked in your honors! Are the soldiers ready?
  OMNES. All, all.
    RENAULT. You, Durand, with your thousand must possess
St. Mark's. You, captain, know your charge already;
'Tis to secure the Ducal Palace. You, 315
Brabe, with a hundred more must gain the Secque:[1]
With the like number, Brainveil, to the Procuralle.[2]
Be all this done with the least tumult possible,
Till in each place you post sufficient guards;
Then sheathe your swords in every breast you meet. 320
    JAFFEIR. (*Aside*) Oh, reverend cruelty! damned, bloody villain!
    RENAULT. During this execution, Durand, you
Must in the midst keep your battalia[3] fast.
And, Theodore, be sure to plant the cannon
That may command the streets; whilst Revillido, 325
Mezzana, Ternon and Retrosi, guard you.
This done, we'll give the general alarm,
Apply petards,[4] and force the Ars'nal[5] gates;
Then fire the city round in several places,
Or with our cannon (if it dare resist) 330
Batter't to ruin. But above all I charge you,
Shed blood enough; spare neither sex nor age,
Name nor condition. If there live a senator
After to-morrow, tho' the dullest rogue 334
That e'er said nothing, we have lost our ends.
If possible, let's kill the very name
Of senator, and bury it in blood.
    JAFFEIR. (*Aside*) Merciless, horrid slave!
    —Aye, blood enough!
Shed blood enough, old Renault. How thou charm'st me!
    RENAULT. But one thing more, and then farewell till fate 340
Join us again or separate us ever.

---

[1] The Zecca, or mint, facing the lagoon on the Piazzetta di San Marco. Renault's speech follows closely the details in Saint-Réal.

[2] The residences of the nine Procurators facing the Piazzetta di San Marco. Next to the Doge, the Procurators were the highest officials of the republic of Venice.

[3] Battalions.

[4] A petard is a case containing powder and attached to a plank, the case being placed against gates which it is proposed to break down.

[5] The Arsenal comprised an area about two miles in circuit, and was the key to the power of Venice.

First, let's embrace; Heaven knows who next shall thus
Wing ye together. But let's all remember
We wear no common[6] cause upon our swords:
Let each man think that on his single virtue
Depends the good and fame of all the rest—
Eternal honor or perpetual infamy. 347
Let's remember through what dreadful hazards
Propitious Fortune hitherto has led us,
How often on the brink of some discovery
Have we stood tottering, and yet still kept our ground 351
So well, the busiest searchers ne'er could follow
Those subtle tracks which puzzled all suspicion.
—You droop, sir!
    JAFFEIR. No: with a most profound attention
I've heard it all, and wonder at thy virtue.
    RENAULT. Though there be yet few hours 'twixt them and ruin, 356
Are not the Senate lulled in full security,
Quiet and satisfied, as fools are always?
Never did so profound repose forerun
Calamity so great! Nay, our good fortune
Has blinded the most piercing of mankind,
Strengthened the fearfullest, charmed the most suspectful, 362
Confounded the most subtle; for we live,
We live, my friends, and quickly shall our life
Prove fatal to these tyrants. Let's consider
That we destroy oppression, avarice, 366
A people nursed up equally with vices
And loathsome lusts which Nature most abhors,
And such as without shame she cannot suffer.
    JAFFEIR. (*Aside*) O Belvidera, take me to thy arms, 370
And show me where's my peace, for I've lost it. *Exit* JAFFEIR
    RENAULT. Without the least remorse, then, let's resolve
With fire and sword t'exterminate these tyrants;
And when we shall behold those cursed tribunals,
Stained by the tears and sufferings of the innocent, 375
Burning with flames rather from heaven than ours,
The raging, furious, and unpitying soldier

[6] Ordinary.

Pulling his reeking dagger from the bosoms
Of gasping wretches; death in every quarter,
With all that sad disorder can produce, 380
To make a spectacle of horror—then,
Then let's call to mind, my dearest friends,
That there is nothing pure upon the earth;
That the most valued things have most allays;[1]
And that in change of all those vile enormities
Under whose weight this wretched country labors, 386
The means are only in our hands to crown them.
  PIERRE. And may those powers above that are propitious
To gallant minds, record this cause and bless it.
  RENAULT. Thus happy, thus secure of all we wish for, 390
Should there, my friends, be found amongst us one
False to this glorious enterprise, what fate,
What vengeance were enough for such a villain?
  ELIOT. Death here without repentance, hell hereafter.
  RENAULT. Let that be my lot if as here I stand 395
Lifted by fate amongst her darling sons,
Tho' I had one only brother, dear by all
The strictest ties of nature; tho' one hour
Had given us birth, one fortune fed our wants,
One only love, and that but of each other,
Still filled our minds: could I have such a friend 401
Joined in this cause, and had but ground to fear
Meant foul play, may this right hand drop from me,
If I'd not hazard all my future peace,
And stab him to the heart before you. Who
Would not do less? wouldst not thou, Pierre, the same? 406
  PIERRE. You've singled me, sir, out for this hard question,
As if 'twere started only for my sake!
Am I the thing you fear? Here, here's my bosom;
Search it with all your swords! Am I a traitor? 410
  RENAULT. No, but I fear your late commended friend
Is little less. Come, sirs, 'tis now no time

[1] Alloys.

To trifle with our safety. Where's this Jaffeir?
  SPINOSA. He left the room just now in strange disorder.
  RENAULT. Nay, there is danger in him:[2] I observed him 415
During the time I took for explanation;
He was transported from most deep attention
To a confusion which he could not smother.
His looks grew full of sadness and surprise,
All which betrayed a wavering spirit in him,
That labored with reluctancy and sorrow.
What's requisite for safety must be done 422
With speedy execution; he remains
Yet in our power. I for my own part wear
A dagger.
  PIERRE. Well?
  RENAULT.   And I could wish it—
  PIERRE.   Where?
  RENAULT. Buried in his heart.
  PIERRE.   Away! w'are yet all friends.
No more of this; 'twill breed ill blood amongst us!
  SPINOSA. Let us all draw our swords, and search the house,
Pull him from the dark hole where he sits brooding
O'er his cold fears, and each man kill his share of him. 430
  PIERRE. Who talks of killing? Who's he'll shed the blood
That's dear to me?—Is't you?—or you?— or you, sir?
What, not one speak? how you stand gaping all
On your grave oracle, your wooden god there!
Yet not a word? (*To* RENAULT) Then, sir, I'll tell you a secret: 435
Suspicion's but at best a coward's virtue!
  RENAULT. A coward—

(*Handles his sword*)

[2] As showing the closeness with which Otway followed his source, the following paragraph from Saint-Réal is of interest: "(Renault's) discourse (to the conspirators) was listened to by the assembly with that complacency with which men generally receive sentiments conformable to their own. Nevertheless Renault, who had observed their countenances, remarked that Jaffeir, one of the best friends of the Captain (Pierre), suddenly changed from extreme attention to an anxiety which he endeavoured in vain to conceal, and that there remained in his eyes an expression of astonishment and sadness which proved him overcome by horror. He spoke of it to Pierre, who at first ridiculed it; but after having observed Jaffeir for some time was of the same opinion." (Quoted in Summers' edition, from which the following quotations are also taken.)

PIERRE. Put, put up thy sword, old man,
Thy hand shakes at it. Come, let's heal this breach,
I am too hot. We yet may live friends.
SPINOSA Till we are safe, our friendship cannot be so. 440
PIERRE. Again! Who's that?
SPINOSA. 'Twas I.
THEODORE. And I.
REVILLIDO. And I.
ELIOT. And all.
RENAULT. Who are on my side?
SPINOSA. Every honest sword.
Let's die like men and not be sold like slaves.
PIERRE. One such word more, by heaven, I'll to the Senate
And hang ye all, like dogs in clusters! 445
Why peep your coward swords half out their shells?
Why do you not all brandish them like mine?
You fear to die, and yet dare talk of killing.
RENAULT. Go to the Senate and betray us! Haste,
Secure thy wretched life; we fear to die 450
Less than thou darest be honest.
PIERRE. That's rank falsehood!
Fear'st not thou death? fie, there's a knavish itch
In that salt blood, an utter foe to smarting.
Had Jaffeir's wife proved kind, he had still been true.
Foh—how that stinks? 455
Thou die! thou kill my friend!—or thou—or thou
—Or thou, with that lean, withered, wretched face!
Away! disperse all to your several charges,
And meet to-morrow where your honor calls you;
I'll bring that man whose blood you so much thirst for, 460
And you shall see him venture for you fairly.
—Hence, hence, I say!
Exit RENAULT *angrily*
SPINOSA. I fear we've been to blame,
And done too much.
THEODORE. 'Twas too far urged against the man you loved.
REVILLIDO. Here, take our swords and crush 'em with your feet. 465
SPINOSA. Forgive us, gallant friend.
PIERRE. Nay, now y'have found
The way to melt and cast me as you will.

I'll fetch this friend and give him to your mercy;
Nay, he shall die if you will take him from me.
For your repose I'll quit my heart's jewel,
But would not have him torn away by villains. 471
And spiteful villainy.
SPINOSA. No, may you both
Forever live and fill the world with fame!
PIERRE. Now you are too kind. Whence rose all this discord?
Oh, what a dangerous precipice have we 'scaped! 475
How near a fall was all we had long been building!
What an eternal blot had stained our glories,
If one, the bravest and the best of men,
Had fall'n a sacrifice to rash suspicion,
Butchered by those whose cause he came to cherish! 480
Oh, could you know him all as I have known him,
How good he is, how just, how true, how brave,
You would not leave this place till you had seen him,
Humbled yourselves before him, kissed his feet,
And gained remission for the worst of follies.
Come but to-morrow, all your doubts shall end, 486
And to your loves me better recommend,
That I've preserved your fame, and saved my friend.
Exeunt omnes

ACT IV

[SCENE I.[1] *A street of the city*]

Enter JAFFEIR *and* BELVIDERA

JAFFEIR. Where dost thou lead me? Every step I move,
Methinks I tread upon some mangled limb

[1] Otway seems to have found the material for the first part of this scene in the following paragraph from Saint-Réal: "(Jaffeir's) imagination dwelt upon this picture. It represented in the most lively colours all the cruelty and injustice that would be inevitable on such an occasion. From that moment he heard on all sides the cries of children, trodden under feet, the groans of old men murdered, and the shrieks of women dishonoured. He saw palaces falling, temples on fire, and holy places covered with blood. Venice, sad, unhappy Venice, was no longer present to his eyes . . . but in ashes or in chains swimming in the ensanguined tide of its inhabitants. . . . This sad image pursued

Of a racked friend. O, my dear charming ruin!
Where are we wand'ring?
    BELVIDERA.   To eternal honor;
To do a deed shall chronicle thy name   5
Among the glorious legends of those few
That have saved sinking nations. Thy renown
Shall be the future song of all the virgins
Who by thy piety have been preserved
From horrid violation. Every street   10
Shall be adorned with statues to thy honor.
And at thy feet this great inscription written:
Remember him that propped the fall of Venice.
    JAFFEIR. Rather, remember him who after all
The sacred bonds of oaths and holier friendship   15
In fond compassion to a woman's tears,
Forgot his manhood, virtue, truth, and honor,
To sacrifice the bosom that relieved him.
Why wilt thou damn me?
    BELVIDERA.   O inconstant man!
How will you promise? how will you deceive?
Do, return back, replace me in my bondage,
Tell all thy friends how dangerously thou lov'st me,   22
And let thy dagger do its bloody office.
Oh, that kind dagger, Jaffeir, how 'twill look
Stuck through my heart, drenched in my blood to th'hilts,   25
Whilst these poor dying eyes shall with their tears
No more torment thee! Then thou wilt be free.
Or if thou think'st it nobler, let me live
Till I'm a victim to the hateful lust
Of that infernal devil, that old fiend   30
That's damned himself and would undo mankind:
Last night, my love!
    JAFFEIR.   Name, name it not again.
It shows a beastly image to my fancy
Will wake me into madness. Oh, the villain!
That durst approach such purity as thine   35
On terms so vile! Destruction, swift destruction
Fall on my coward head, and make my name
The common scorn of fools if I forgive him!
If I forgive him? If I not revenge

<small>him night and day. . . . But to betray his friends! and such friends, so intrepid, so intelligent, and each remarkable for some great talent. It would be the work of ages to again unite so large a number of extraordinary men. . . . And how would they perish? By torments more dreadful than any invented by tyrants in past ages."</small>

With utmost rage, and most unstaying fury,
Thy sufferings, thou dear darling of my life, love!   41
    BELVIDERA. Delay no longer then, but to the Senate;
And tell the dismal'st story e'er [was] uttered:
Tell 'em what bloodshed, rapines, desolations,
Have been prepared—how near's the fatal hour!   45
Save thy poor country; save the reverend blood
Of all its nobles, which to-morrow's dawn
Must else see shed. Save the poor, tender lives
Of all those little infants which the swords
Of murderers are whetting for this moment.
Think thou already hear'st their dying screams,   51
Think that thou seest their sad, distracted mothers
Kneeling before thy feet, and begging pity,
With torn, dishevelled hair and streaming eyes,
Their naked, mangled breasts besmeared with blood,   55
And even the milk with which their fondled babes
Softly they hushed, dropping in anguish from 'em.
Think thou seest this, and then consult thy heart.
    JAFFEIR. Oh!
    BELVIDERA. Think too, if thou lose this present minute,   60
What miseries the next day bring upon thee.
Imagine all the horrors of that night,
Murder and rapine, waste and desolation,
Confusedly ranging. Think what then may prove
My lot! The ravisher may then come safe,
And 'midst the terror of the public ruin   66
Do a damned deed—perhaps to lay a train
May catch thy life: then where will be revenge,
The dear revenge that's due to such a wrong?
    JAFFEIR. By all heaven's powers, prophetic truth dwells in thee;   70
For every word thou speak'st strikes through my heart
Like a new light, and shows it how't has wandered.
Just what th'hast made me, take me, Belvidera,
And lead me to the place where I'm to say
This bitter lesson; where I must betray   75

My truth, my virtue, constancy, and friends.
Must I betray my friends? Ah, take me
    quickly,
Secure me well before that thought's renewed.
If I relapse once more, all's lost forever.
  BELVIDERA. Hast thou a friend more dear
      than Belvidera?   80
  JAFFEIR. No, th'art my soul itself, wealth,
      friendship, honor;
All present joys, and earnest of all future,
Are summed in thee. Methinks, when in
    thy arms
Thus leaning on thy breast, one minute's more
Than a long thousand years of vulgar hours.
Why was such happiness not given me pure?
Why dashed with cruel wrongs, and bitter
    wantings?   87
Come, lead me forward now like a tame lamb
To sacrifice; thus in his fatal garlands,
Decked fine, and pleased, the wanton skips
    and plays,   90
Trots by the enticing, flattering priestess'
    side,
And much transported with its little pride,
Forgets his dear companions of the plain
Till by her, bound, he's on the altar lain;
Yet then too hardly bleats, such pleas-
    ure's in the pain.   95

            Enter Officer *and Six* Guards
  OFFICER. Stand! Who goes there?
  BELVIDERA.   Friends.
  JAFFEIR. Friends, Belvidera! Hide me
      from my friends.
By heaven, I'd rather see the face of hell
Than meet the man I love.
  OFFICER.   But what friends are you?
  BELVIDERA. Friends to the Senate and the
      state of Venice.   100
  OFFICER. My orders are to seize on all I find
At this late hour, and bring 'em to the
    Council,
Who now are sitting.
  JAFFEIR.   Sir, you shall be obeyed.
Hold, brutes, stand off! none of your paws
    upon me!
Now the lot's cast, and, Fate, do what thou
    wilt.   *Exeunt guarded*   105

        SCENE [II.] *The Senate-house*
Where appear sitting, the DUKE OF VENICE,
  PRIULI, ANTONIO, *and eight other* Senators
  DUKE. Antony, Priuli, senators of Venice,
Speak; why are we assembled here this night?
What have you to inform us of, concerns
The state of Venice, honor, or its safety?
  PRIULI. Could words express the story I
      have to tell you,   5
Fathers, these tears were useless—these sad
    tears
That fall from my old eyes; but there is cause
We all should weep, tear off these purple
    robes,
And wrap ourselves in sack-cloth, sitting
    down   9
On the sad earth, and cry aloud to heaven.
Heaven knows if yet there be an hour to come
Ere Venice be no more!
  ALL SENATORS.   How!
  PRIULI.   Nay, we stand
Upon the very brink of gaping ruin.
Within this city's formed a dark conspiracy
To massacre us all, our wives and children, 15
Kindred and friends, our palaces and temples
To lay in ashes—nay, the hour, too, fixed;
The swords, for aught I know, drawn even
    this moment,
And the wild waste begun. From unknown
    hands
I had this warning. But if we are men,   20
Let's not be tamely butchered, but do some·
    thing
That may inform the world in after ages,
Our virtue was not ruined, though we were.
(*A noise without* " Room, room, make room for
                          some prisoners!")
  2D SENATOR. Let's raise the city!

            Enter Officer *and* Guard
  PRIULI. Speak there—what disturbance?
  OFFICER. Two prisoners have the guard
      seized in the streets,   26
Who say they come to inform this reverend
    Senate
About the present danger.

        Enter JAFFEIR *and* BELVIDERA, *guarded*
  ALL.   Give 'em entrance—
Well, who are you?
  JAFFEIR.   A villain.
  ANTONIO.   Short and pithy.
The man speaks well.
  JAFFEIR. Would every man that hears me
Would deal so honestly, and own his title.
  DUKE. 'Tis rumored that a plot has been
      contrived   32
Against this state; that you have a share
    in't, too.

If you are a villain, to redeem your honor,
Unfold the truth and be restored with mercy.
 JAFFEIR. Think not that I to save my life
  come hither—   36
I know its value better—but in pity
To all those wretches whose unhappy dooms
Are fixed and sealed. You see me here before
 you,
The sworn and covenanted foe of Venice.
But use me as my dealings may deserve, 41
And I may prove a friend.
 DUKE.   The slave capitulates.
Give him the tortures.
 JAFFEIR.   That you dare not do;
Your fears won't let you, nor the longing itch
To hear a story which you dread the truth of—
Truth which the fear of smart shall ne'er
 get from me.   46
Cowards are scared with threat'nings. Boys
 are whipped
Into confessions: but a steady mind
Acts of itself, ne'er asks the body counsel.
"Give him the tortures!" Name but such a
 thing   50
Again, by heaven, I'll shut these lips forever.
Not all your racks, your engines, or your
 wheels
Shall force a groan away—that you may
 guess at.
 ANTONIO. A bloody-minded fellow, I'll
  warrant;
A damned bloody-minded fellow.   55
 DUKE. Name your conditions.[1]
 JAFFEIR.   For myself, full pardon,
Besides the lives of two and twenty friends
       (*Delivers a list*)
Whose names are here enrolled. Nay, let
 their crimes
Be ne'er so monstrous, I must have the oaths
And sacred promise of this reverend council,
That in a full assembly of the Senate 61

[1] According to Saint-Réal, Jaffeir "sought Barthelemi Comino, secretary of the council of Ten, and told him he had some pressing news to communicate which nearly concerned the safety of the state, but beforehand he wished the Doge and the council to promise him one favour and that they must engage by the most sacred oaths, that the Senate should ratify their promise; that this favour consisted of the lives and safety of twenty-two persons whom he would name, whatever crime they might have committed. But they need not suppose they could force his secret from him by tortures without granting his request, as there were none so horrible that could draw one single word from his mouth. The Ten were assembled in a moment, and they sent immediately to the Doge to receive from him the promise that Jaffeir demanded."

The thing I ask be ratified. Swear this,
And I'll unfold the secrets of your danger.
 ALL. We'll swear.
 DUKE.   Propose the oath.
 JAFFEIR.   By all the hopes
Ye have of peace and happiness hereafter,
Swear!
 ALL.   We all swear.
 JAFFEIR.   To grant me what I've asked,
Ye swear.
 ALL.   We swear.
 JAFFEIR.   And as ye keep the oath,
May you and your posterity be blest 68
Or cursed forever.
 ALL.   Else be cursed forever!
 JAFFEIR. (*Delivers another paper*) Then
here's the list, and with't the full disclose of
all that threatens you.—Now, Fate, thou
hast caught me.   73
 ANTONIO. Why, what a dreadful catalogue
of cut-throats is here! I'll warrant you not
one of these fellows but has a face like a
lion. I dare not so much as read their names
over.
 DUKE. Give orders that all diligent search
  be made
To seize these men; their characters are
 public.   80
The paper intimates their rendezvous
To be at the house of a famed Grecian
 courtesan
Called Aquilina; see that place secured.
 ANTONIO. [*Aside*] What! My Nicky
  Nacky, Hurry Durry,
Nicky Nacky in the plot? I'll make a speech.
—Most noble senators,   86
What headlong apprehension drives you on,
Right noble, wise, and truly solid senators,
To violate the laws and right of nations?
The lady is a lady of renown.   90
'Tis true, she holds a house of fair reception,
And though I say't myself, as many more
Can say as well as I.
 2D SENATOR.   My lord, long speeches
Are frivolous here when dangers are so near us.
We all well know your interest in that lady;
The world talks loud on't.
 ANTONIO.   Verily, I have done.
I say no more.
 DUKE.   But, since he has declared
Himself concerned, pray, captain, take great
 caution
To treat the fair one as becomes her character.   99

And let her bed-chamber be searched with
  decency.
You, Jaffeir, must with patience bear till
  morning
To be our prisoner.
 JAFFEIR.   [*Aside*] Would the chains
  of death
Had bound me fast ere I had known this
  minute!
I've done a deed will make my story hereafter
Quoted in competition with all ill ones. 105
The history of my wickedness shall run
Down through the low traditions of the vulgar,
And boys be taught to tell the tale of Jaffeir.
 DUKE. Captain, withdraw your prisoner.
 JAFFEIR.   Sir, if possible,
Lead me where my own thoughts themselves
  may lose me;   110
Where I may doze out what I've left of life,
Forget myself and this day's guilt and false-
  hood.
Cruel remembrance, how shall I appease thee!
          Exit guarded
(*Noise without* " More traitors; room, room,
      make room there!")
 DUKE. How's this? Guards—
Where are our guards? Shut up the gates;
  the treason's
Already at our doors!

    Enter Officer

 OFFICER.   My lords, more traitors—
Seized in the very act of consultation; 116
Furnished with arms and instruments of mis-
  chief.
Bring in the prisoners.

Enter PIERRE, RENAULT, THEODORE, ELIOT,
  REVILLIDO, *and other* Conspirators, *in
  fetters, guarded*

 PIERRE.   You, the lords and fathers
(As you are pleased to call yourselves) of
 Venice,   119
If you sit here to guide the course of justice,
Why these disgraceful chains upon my limbs
That have so often labored in your service?
Are these the wreaths of triumphs ye bestow
On those that bring you conquests home and
  honors?   125
 DUKE. Go on; you shall be heard, sir.
 ANTONIO. And be hanged too, I hope.
 PIERRE. Are these the trophies I've de-
  served for fighting
Your battles with confederated powers,
When winds and seas conspired to overthrow
  you,
And brought the fleets of Spain to your own
  harbors?   130
When you, great Duke, shrunk trembling in
  your palace,
And saw your wife, th'Adriatic, ploughed
Like a lewd whore by bolder prows than
  yours—
Stepped not I forth, and taught your loose
  Venetians
The task of honor and the way to greatness,
Raised you from your capitulating fears, 136
To stipulate the terms of sued-for peace—
And this my recompense! If I am a traitor,
Produce my charge; or show the wretch
  that's base enough
And brave enough to tell me I am a traitor.
 DUKE. Know you one Jaffeir?
      (*All the* Conspirators *murmur*)
 PIERRE.   Yes, and know his virtue.
His justice, truth, his general worth and
  sufferings   142
From a hard father, taught me first to love him.

   Enter JAFFEIR, *guarded*

 DUKE. See him brought forth.
 PIERRE.   [*Aside*] My friend, too,
  bound? nay, then
Our fate has conquered us, and we must fall
—Why droops the man whose welfare's so
  much mine
They're but one thing? These reverend ty-
  rants, Jaffeir,
Call us all traitors; art thou one, my brother?
 JAFFEIR. To thee I am the falsest, veriest
  slave
That e'er betrayed a generous, trusting friend,
And gave up honor to be sure of ruin. 151
All our fair hopes which morning was to
  have crowned,
Has this curs'd tongue o'erthrown.
 PIERRE.   So! Then all's over.
Venice has lost her freedom; I, my life.
No more. Farewell!
 DUKE.   Say, will you make confession
Of your vile deeds and trust the Senate's
  mercy?
 PIERRE. Curs'd be your Senate; curs'd
  your constitution.
The curse of growing factions and division
Still vex your councils, shake your public
  safety,   159
And make the robes of government you wear

Hateful to you as these base chains to me!
  DUKE. Pardon, or death?
  PIERRE.   Death—honorable death!
  RENAULT. Death's the best thing we ask
    or you can give.
  ALL CONSPIRATORS. No shameful bonds,
    but honorable death!
  DUKE. Break up the council. Captain,
    guard your prisoners.   165
Jaffeir, y'are free, but these must wait for
  judgment.   *Exeunt all the* Senators
  PIERRE. Come, where's my dungeon?
    Lead me to my straw.
It will not be the first time I've lodged hard
To do your Senate service.
  JAFFEIR.   Hold one moment!
  PIERRE. Who's he disputes the judgment
    of the Senate?   170
Presumptuous rebel—on—
              (*Strikes* JAFFEIR)
  JAFFEIR   By heaven, you stir not.
I must be heard, I must have leave to speak!
Thou hast disgraced me, Pierre, by a vile
  blow.
Had not a dagger done thee nobler justice?
But use me as thou wilt, thou canst not
  wrong me,   175
For I am fall'n beneath the basest injuries;
Yet look upon me with an eye of mercy,
With pity and with charity behold me;
Shut not thy heart against a friend's re-
  pentance,   179
But as there dwells a god-like nature in thee,
Listen with mildness to my supplications.
  PIERRE. What whining monk art thou?
    what holy cheat
That wouldst encroach upon my credulous
  ears,
And cant'st thus vilely? Hence! I know
  thee not.
Dissemble and be nasty. Leave me, hypocrite.
  JAFFEIR. Not know me, Pierre?
  PIERRE.   No, I know thee not. What
    art thou?   186
  JAFFEIR. Jaffeir, thy friend, thy once
    loved, valued friend,
Though now deserv'dly scorned, and used
  most hardly.
  PIERRE. Thou Jaffeir! thou my once loved,
    valued friend!
By heavens, thou li'st! The man so called,
  my friend,   190
Was generous, honest, faithful, just, and val-
  iant.

Noble in mind, and in his person lovely,
Dear to my eyes and tender to my heart:
But thou, a wretched, base, false, worthless
  coward,
Poor, even in soul, and loathsome in thy
  aspect,   195
All eyes must shun thee, and all hearts detest
  thee.
Prithee avoid, nor longer cling thus round me
Like something baneful that my nature's
  chilled at.
  JAFFEIR. I have not wronged thee—by
    these tears I have not!
But still am honest, true, and hope, too, val-
  iant;   200
My mind still full of thee; therefore, still
  noble.
Let not thy eyes then shun me, nor thy heart
Detest me utterly. Oh, look upon me!
Look back and see my sad, sincere submis-
  sion!
How my heart swells, as even 'twould burst
  my bosom,   205
Fond of its goal, and laboring to be at thee!
What shall I do, what say to make thee hear
  me?
  PIERRE. Hast thou not wronged me?
    dar'st thou call thyself
Jaffeir, that once loved, valued friend of mine,
And swear thou hast not wronged me?
  Whence these chains?   210
Whence this vile death, which I may meet this
  moment?
Whence this dishonor but from thee, thou
  false one?
  JAFFEIR. —All's true; yet grant one
    thing, and I've done asking.
  PIERRE. What's that?
  JAFFEIR.   To take thy life on such
    conditions
The Council have proposed. Thou and thy
  friends   215
May yet live long, and to be better treated.
  PIERRE. Life! Ask my life? Confess?
    Record myself
A villain for the privilege to breathe
And carry up and down this cursed city
A discontented and repining spirit,   220
Burdensome to itself, a few years longer,
To lose, it may be, at last in a lewd quarrel
For some new friend, treacherous and false
  as thou art?
No, this vile world and I have long been
  jangling,   224

And cannot part on better terms than now,
When only men like thee are fit to live in't.
   JAFFEIR. By all that's just—
   PIERRE.   Swear by some other powers,
For thou hast broke that sacred oath too
   lately.
   JAFFEIR. Then by that hell I merit, I'll
   not leave thee 229
Till to thyself, at least, thou'rt reconciled,
However thy resentments deal with me.
   PIERRE. Not leave me?
   JAFFEIR.   No, thou shalt not force me
   from thee.
Use me reproachfully, and like a slave;
Tread on me, buffet me, heap wrongs on
   wrongs 234
On my poor head, I'll bear it all with patience
Shall weary out thy most unfriendly cruelty,
Lie at thy feet and kiss 'em though they
   spurn me
Till, wounded by my sufferings, thou relent,
And raise me to thy arms with dear forgive-
   ness. 239
   PIERRE. Art thou not—
   JAFFEIR.   What?
   PIERRE.   A traitor?
   JAFFEIR.   Yes.
   PIERRE.   A villain?
   JAFFEIR. Granted.
   PIERRE.   A coward—a most scandal-
   ous coward,
Spiritless, void of honor, one who has sold
Thy everlasting fame for shameless life?
   JAFFEIR. All, all, and more—much more.
   My faults are numberless.
   PIERRE. And wouldst thou have me live
   on terms like thine? 245
Base as thou art false—
   JAFFEIR.   No, 'tis to me that's granted;
The safety of thy life was all I aimed at,
In recompense for faith and trust so broken.
   PIERRE. I scorn it more because preserved
   by thee. 249
And as, when first my foolish heart took pity
On thy misfortunes, sought thee in thy mis-
   eries,
Relieved thy wants, and raised thee from
   thy state
Of wretchedness in which thy fate had
   plunged thee,
To rank thee in my list of noble friends,
All I received in surety for thy truth, 255
Were unregarded oaths—and this, this dag-
   ger,

Given with a worthless pledge thou since
   hast stol'n:
So I restore it back to thee again,
Swearing by all those powers which thou
   hast violated,
Never from this cursed hour to hold com-
   munion, 260
Friendship, or interest with thee, though our
   years
Were to exceed those limited the world.
Take it—farewell!—for now I owe thee
   nothing.
   JAFFEIR. Say thou wilt live, then.
   PIERRE.   For my life, dispose it
Just as thou wilt, because 'tis what I'm tired
   with. 265
   JAFFEIR. O Pierre!
   PIERRE.   No more.
   JAFFEIR.   My eyes won't lose the
   sight of thee,
But languish after thine and ache with gazing.
   PIERRE. Leave me.—Nay, then—thus,
   thus, I throw thee from me,
And curses, great as is thy falsehood, catch
   thee! *Exit*
   JAFFEIR. Amen.—He's gone, my father,
   friend, preserver, 270
And here's the portion he has left me.
                 (*Holds the dagger up*)
This dagger, well remembrèd—with this
   dagger.
I gave a solemn vow of dire importance,
Parted with this and Belvidera together.
Have a care, Mem'ry, drive that thought no
   farther. 275
No, I'll esteem it as a friend's last legacy,
Treasure it up in this wretched bosom,
Where it may grow acquainted with my
   heart,
That when they meet, they start not from
   each other.
—So: now for thinking. A blow; called
   traitor, villain, 280
Coward, dishonorable coward—fogh!
Oh, for a long, sound sleep, and so forget it!
Down, busy devil—

           Enter BELVIDERA

   BELVIDERA.   Whither shall I fly?
Where hide me and my miseries together?
Where's now the Roman constancy I
   boasted? 285
Sunk into trembling fears and desperation!
Not daring to look up to that dear face

Which used to smile even on my faults, but down
Bending these miserable eyes to earth,
Must move in penance, and implore much mercy. 290
JAFFEIR. Mercy!—Kind heaven has surely endless stores
Hoarded for thee of blessings yet untasted;
Let wretches loaded hard with guilt as I am,
Bow [with] the weight, and groan beneath the burden,
Creep with a remnant of that strength th'have left 295
Before the footstool of that heaven th'have injured.
O Belvidera! I'm the wretched'st creature
E'er crawled on earth! Now if thou'st virtue, help me;
Take me into thy arms, and speak the words of peace
To my divided soul that wars within me, 300
And raises every sense to my confusion.
By heaven, I am tottering to the very brink
Of peace, and thou art all the hold I've left.
BELVIDERA. Alas! I know thy sorrows are most mighty.
I know th'hast cause to mourn—to mourn, my Jaffeir, 305
With endless cries, and never-ceasing wailings.
Th'hast lost—
JAFFEIR. Oh, I have lost what can't be counted!
My friend, too, Belvidera, that dear friend,
Who, next to thee, was all my health rejoiced in,
Has used me like a slave—shamefully used me.
'Twould break thy pitying heart to hear the story. 311
What shall I do? resentment, indignation,
Love, pity, fear, and mem'ry, how I've wronged him!
Distract my quiet with the very thought on't,
And tear my heart to pieces in my bosom.
BELVIDERA. What has he done?
JAFFEIR. Thou'dst hate me should I tell thee. 316
BELVIDERA. Why?
JAFFEIR. Oh, he has used me—! Yet, by heaven, I bear it!
He has used me, Belvidera—but first swear
That when I've told thee, thou wilt not loathe me utterly, 320
Though vilest blots and stains appear upon me;
But still at least with charitable goodness,
Be near me in the pangs of my affliction—
Not scorn me, Belvidera, as he has done.
BELVIDERA. Have I then e'er been false that now I'm doubted? 325
Speak, what's the cause I'm grown into distrust?
Why thought unfit to hear my love's complainings?
JAFFEIR. Oh!
BELVIDERA. Tell me.
JAFFEIR. Bear my failings for they're many.
O my dear angel! In that friend I've lost
All my soul's peace; for every thought of him
Strikes my sense hard, and deads in it my brains. 331
Wouldst thou believe it?
BELVIDERA. Speak.
JAFFEIR. Before we parted,
Ere yet his guards had led him to his prison,
Full of severest sorrows for his suff'rings,
With eyes o'erflowing and a bleeding heart
Humbling myself almost beneath my nature,
As at his feet I kneeled and sued for mercy,
Forgetting all our friendship, all the dearness
In which w'have lived so many years together, 339
With a reproachful hand he dashed a blow—
He struck me, Belvidera, by heaven, he struck me,
Buffeted, called me traitor, villain, coward!—
Am I a coward? am I a villain? Tell me:
Th'art the best judge, and mad'st me, if I am so. 344
Damnation—coward!
BELVIDERA. Oh! forgive him, Jaffeir!
And if his sufferings wound thy heart already,
What will they do to-morrow?
JAFFEIR. Hah!
BELVIDERA. To-morrow,
When thou shalt see him stretched in all the agonies
Of a tormenting and a shameful death, 349
His bleeding bowels, and his broken limbs,
Insulted [1] o'er by a vile, butchering villain;
What will thy heart do then? Oh, sure 'twill stream
Like my eyes now.
JAFFEIR. What means thy dreadful story?
Death, and to-morrow? broken limbs and bowels? 354

[1] Exulted.

Insulted o'er by a vile, butchering villain?
By all my fears, I shall start out to madness
With barely guessing if the truth's hid longer.
 BELVIDERA. The faithless senators, 'tis they've decreed it.
They say, according to our friend's request,
They shall have death, and not ignoble bondage; 361
Declare their promised mercy all as forfeited,
False to their oaths, and deaf to intercession.
Warrants are passed for public death to-morrow.
 JAFFEIR. Death! doomed to die! condemned unheard! unpleaded![1] 365
 BELVIDERA. Nay, cruel'st racks and torments are preparing,
To force confessions from their dying pangs.
Oh, do not look so terribly upon me!
How your lips shake, and all your face disordered!
What means my love? 370
 JAFFEIR. Leave me! I charge thee, leave me. Strong temptations
Wake in my heart.
 BELVIDERA.   For what?
 JAFFEIR.   No more, but leave me.
 BELVIDERA. Why?
 JAFFEIR. Oh! by heaven, I love thee with that fondness,
I would not have thee stay a moment longer
Near these cursed hands. Are they not cold upon thee? 375
  (*Pulls the dagger half out of his bosom and puts it back again*)
 BELVIDERA. No, everlasting comfort's in thy arms,
To lean thus on thy breast is softer ease
Than downy pillows decked with leaves of roses.
 JAFFEIR. Alas, thou think'st not of the thorns 'tis filled with:
Fly ere they gall thee. There's a lurking serpent 380
Ready to leap and sting thee to thy heart.
Art thou not terrified?
 BELVIDERA.   No.
 JAFFEIR.   Call to mind
What thou hast done, and whither thou hast brought me.
 BELVIDERA. Hah!

---

[1] Saint-Réal: "However, Jaffeir, in despair at the bad success of his compassion, complained loudly that the Doge and the council of Ten did not keep the word they had given him in favor of his companions."

 JAFFEIR.   Where's my friend? my friend, thou smiling mischief?
Nay, shrink not now—'tis too late. Thou shouldst have fled 385
When thy guilt first had cause, for dire revenge
Is up and raging for my friend. He groans—
Hark, how he groans! His screams are in my ears
Already; see, th'have fixed him on the wheel,
And now they tear him.—Murder! perjured Senate! 390
Murder—Oh!—hark thee, trait'ress, thou hast done this;
Thanks to thy tears and false persuading love.
How her eyes speak! O thou bewitching creature! (*Fumbling for his dagger*)
Madness cannot hurt thee. Come, thou little trembler,
Creep, even into my heart, and there lie safe: 395
'Tis thy own citadel.—Hah—yet stand off!
Heaven must have justice, and my broken vows
Will sink me else beneath its reaching mercy.
I'll wink and then 'tis done—
 BELVIDERA.   What means the lord
Of me, my life and love? What's in thy bosom
Thou grasp'st at so? Nay, why am I thus treated? 401
[*Jaffeir draws the dagger; offers to stab her*]
What wilt thou do?—Ah, do not kill me, Jaffeir!
Pity these panting breasts and trembling limbs
That used to clasp thee when thy looks were milder—
That yet hang heavy on my unpurged soul;
And plunge it not into eternal darkness. 406
 JAFFEIR. No, Belvidera, when we parted last,
I gave this dagger with thee as in trust
To be thy portion if I e'er proved false.
On such condition was my truth believed;
But now 'tis forfeited and must be paid for.
  (*Offers to stab her again*)
 BELVIDERA. (*Kneeling*) Oh, mercy!
 JAFFEIR.   Nay, no struggling.
 BELVIDERA. (*Leaps upon his neck and kisses him*) Now then kill me!
While thus I cling about thy cruel neck,
Kiss thy revengeful lips and die in joys
Greater than any I can guess hereafter. 415

JAFFEIR. I am, I am a coward. Witness't,
    Heaven,
Witness it, Earth, and every being, witness!
'Tis but one blow; yet—by immortal love,
I cannot longer bear a thought to harm thee!
    (*He throws away the dagger and embraces her*)
The seal of providence is sure upon thee, 420
And thou wert born for yet unheard-of
    wonders.
Oh, thou wert either born to save or damn
    me!
By all the power that's given thee o'er my
    soul,
By thy resistless tears and conquering smiles,
By the victorious love that still waits on thee,
Fly to thy cruel father. Save my friend, 426
Or all our future quiet's lost forever.
Fall at his feet; cling round his reverend
    knees;
Speak to him with thy eyes, and with thy
    tears
Melt his hard heart, and wake dead nature
    in him.   430
    Crush him in th'arms, and torture him with
        thy softness:
    Nor, till thy prayers are granted, set him
        free,
    But conquer him, as thou hast vanquished
        me.   *Exeunt ambo*

ACT V

[SCENE I. *A street of the city*]

Enter PRIULI, *solus*

PRIULI. Why, cruel Heaven, have my unhappy days
Been lengthened to this sad one? Oh! dishonor
And deathless infamy is fallen upon me.
Was it my fault? Am I a traitor? No.
But then, my only child, my daughter,
    wedded;   5
There my best blood runs foul, and a disease
Incurable has seized upon my memory,
To make it rot and stink to after ages.
Cursed be the fatal minute when I got her;
Or would that I'd been anything but man,
And raised an issue which would ne'er have
    wronged me.   11
The miserablest creatures (man excepted)
Are the less esteemed though their posterity
Degenerate from the virtues of their fathers;

The vilest beasts are happy in their offsprings,
While only man gets traitors, whores, and
    villains.   16
Cursed be the names, and some swift blow
    from fate
Lay his head deep, where mine may be forgotten!

Enter BELVIDERA *in a long mourning veil*

BELVIDERA. He's there—my father, my
    inhuman father,   19
That, for three years, has left an only child
Exposed to all the outrages of fate
And cruel ruin.—Oh!—
    PRIULI.   What child of sorrow
Art thou, that com'st thus wrapped in weeds
    of sadness,
And mov'st as if thy steps were towards a
    grave?
BELVIDERA. A wretch who from the very
    top of happiness   25
Am fallen into the lowest depths of misery,
And want your pitying hand to raise me up
    again.
    PRIULI. Indeed, thou talk'st as thou hadst
        tasted sorrows.
Would I could help thee.
    BELVIDERA.   'Tis greatly in your power.
The world, too, speaks you charitable, and I,
Who ne'er asked alms before, in that dear
    hope   31
Am come a-begging to you, sir.
    PRIULI.   For what?
    BELVIDERA. Oh, well regard me! Is this
        voice a strange one?
Consider, too, when beggars once pretend
A case like mine, no little will content 'em.
    PRIULI. What wouldst thou beg for?
    BELVIDERA.   Pity and forgiveness.
                            (*Throws up her veil*)
By the kind tender names of child and father
Hear my complaints, and take me to your
    love.   38
    PRIULI. My daughter!
    BELVIDERA.   Yes, your daughter, by a
        mother
Virtuous and noble, faithful to your honor,
Obedient to your will, kind to your wishes,
Dear to your arms. By all the joys she gave
    you,   42
When in her blooming years she was your
    treasure,
Look kindly on me; in my face behold
The lineaments of hers y'have kissed so often,

Pleading the cause of your poor cast-off child.
  PRIULI. Thou art my daughter.
  BELVIDERA.   Yes—and y'have oft told me   47
With smiles of love and chaste, paternal kisses,
I'd much resemblance of my mother.
  PRIULI.   Oh!
Hadst thou inherited her matchless virtues,
I'd been too bless'd.
  BELVIDERA.   Nay, do not call to memory
My disobedience, but let pity enter   52
Into your heart, and quite deface the impression;
For could you think how mine's perplexed, what sadness,
Fears, and despairs distract the peace within me,   55
Oh, you would take me in your dear, dear arms,
Hover with strong compassion o'er your young one,
To shelter me with a protecting wing
From the black gathered storm that's just, just breaking!
  PRIULI. Don't talk thus.
  BELVIDERA.   Yes, I must; and you must hear too.   60
I have a husband—
  PRIULI.   Damn him!
  BELVIDERA.   Oh, do not curse him!
He would not speak so hard a word towards you
On any terms, oh! ere [1] he deal with me.
  PRIULI. Hah! what means my child?
  BELVIDERA. Oh, there's but this short moment   65
'Twixt me and fate. Yet send me not with curses
Down to my grave; afford me one kind blessing
Before we part! Just take me in your arms
And recommend me with a prayer to heaven,
That I may die in peace. And when I'm dead—   70
  PRIULI. How my soul's catched!
  BELVIDERA.   Lay me, I beg you, lay me
By the dear ashes of my tender mother.
She would have pitied me, had fate yet spared her.
  PRIULI. By heaven, my aching heart forebodes much mischief.   74
Tell me thy story, for I'm still thy father.

[1] Becomes *howe'er* in 18th century editions, which is presumably correct.

  BELVIDERA. No, I'm contented.
  PRIULI.   Speak.
  BELVIDERA.   No matter.
  PRIULI.   Tell me.
By yon blest heaven, my heart runs o'er with fondness.
  BELVIDERA. Oh!
  PRIULI.   Utter't.
  BELVIDERA.   Oh, my husband, my dear husband
Carries a dagger in his once kind bosom,
To pierce the heart of your poor Belvidera.
  PRIULI. Kill thee!
  BELVIDERA.   Yes, kill me. When he passed his faith   81
And covenant against your state and Senate,
He gave me up as hostage for his truth,
With me a dagger and a dire commission,
Whene'er he failed, to plunge it through this bosom.   85
I learnt the danger, chose the hour of love
T'attempt his heart, and bring it back to honor.
Great love prevailed and blessed me with success.
He came, confessed, betrayed his dearest friends
For promised mercy. Now they're doomed to suffer,   90
Galled with remembrance of what then was sworn
If they are lost, he vows t'appease the gods
With this poor life, and make my blood th'atonement.
  PRIULI. Heavens!
  BELVIDERA.   Think you saw what passed at our last parting;
Think you beheld him like a raging lion,   95
Pacing the earth, and tearing up his steps,
Fate in his eyes, and roaring with the pain
Of burning fury; think you saw his one hand
Fixed on my throat, while the extended other
Grasped a keen, threat'ning dagger. Oh, 'twas thus   100
We last embraced; when, trembling with revenge,
He dragged me to the ground, and at my bosom
Presented horrid death, cried out, "My friends—
Where are my friends?" swore, wept, raged, threatened, loved—
For he yet loved, and that dear love preserved me   105

To this last trial of a father's pity.
I fear not death, but cannot bear a thought
That that dear hand should do th'unfriendly
  office.
If I was ever then your care, now hear me;
Fly to the Senate, save the promised lives
Of his dear friends, ere mine be made the
  sacrifice. 111
  PRIULI. Oh, my heart's comfort!
  BELVIDERA. Will you not, my father?
Weep not, but answer me.
  PRIULI. By heaven, I will!
Not one of 'em but what shall be immortal.
Canst thou forgive me all my follies past,
I'll henceforth be indeed a father; never,
Never more thus expose, but cherish thee,
Dear as the vital warmth that feeds my life,
Dear as these eyes that weep in fondness
  o'er thee. 119
Peace to thy heart! Farewell.
  BELVIDERA. Go, and remember,
'Tis Belvidera's life her father pleads for.
        Exeunt severally

Enter ANTONIO

  ANTONIO. Hum, hum, hah. Signior Priuli, my lord Priuli, my lord, my lord, my lord.—How we lords love to call one another by our titles.—My lord, my lord, my lord—Pox on him, I am a lord as well as he. And so let him fiddle.—I'll warrant him he's gone to the Senate-house, and I'll be there too, soon enough for somebody. Odd!—here's a tickling speech about the plot. I'll prove there's a plot with a vengeance—would I had it without book. Let me see—"Most reverend senators, That there is a plot, surely by this time, no man that hath eyes or understanding in his head will presume to doubt; 'tis as plain as the light in the cowcumber"—no—hold there—cowcumber does not come in yet—"'tis as plain as the light in the sun, or as the man in the moon, even at noonday. It is, indeed, a pumpkin-plot, which, just as it was mellow, we have gathered; and now we have gathered it, prepared, and dressed it, shall we throw it like a pickled cowcumber out at the window? No! That it is not only a bloody, horrid, execrable, damnable, and audacious plot, but it is, as I may so say, a saucy plot; and we all know, most reverend fathers, that what is sauce for a goose is sauce for a gander: therefore, I say, as those blood-thirsty ganders of the conspiracy would have destroyed us geese of the Senate, let us make haste to destroy them. So I humbly move for hanging"—Hah, hurry durry—I think this will do—tho' I was something out, at first, about the sun and the cowcumber. 156

Enter AQUILINA

  AQUILINA. Good morrow, senator.
  ANTONIO. Nacky, my dear Nacky; morrow, Nacky. Odd, I am very brisk, very merry, very pert, very jovial—ha-a-a-a-a—kiss me, Nacky. How dost thou do, my little Tory, rory strumpet? Kiss me, I say, hussy, kiss me. 163
  AQUILINA. "Kiss me, Nacky!" Hang you, sir!—coxcomb, hang you, sir!
  ANTONIO. Hayty tayty, is it so indeed, with all my heart, faith—(*Sings*) *Hey then, up go we*,[1] faith—*hey then, up go we*, dum dum derum dump.
  AQUILINA. Signior. 170
  ANTONIO. Madonna.
  AQUILINA. Do you intend to die in your bed—?
  ANTONIO. About threescore years hence, much may be done, my dear. 175
  AQUILINA. You'll be hanged, signior.
  ANTONIO. Hanged, sweetheart? Prithee, be quiet. Hanged, quoth-a, that's a merry conceit, with all my heart. Why, thou jok'st, Nacky; thou art given to joking, I'll swear. Well, I protest, Nacky—nay, I must protest, and will protest that I love joking dearly, man.[2] And I love thee for joking, and I'll kiss thee for joking, and touse thee for joking—and odd, I have a devilish mind to take thee aside about that business for joking, too—odd, I have! and (*Sings*) *Hey then, up go we*, dum dum derum dump. 188
  AQUILINA. (*Draws a dagger*) See you this, sir?
  ANTONIO. O laud, a dagger! O laud! it is naturally my aversion! I cannot endure the sight on't; hide it, for heaven's sake! I cannot look that way till it be gone—hide it, hide it, oh, oh, hide it! 195
  AQUILINA. Yes, in your heart I'll hide it.
  ANTONIO. My heart! What, hide a dagger in my heart's blood!

---

[1] A popular song of the day, which exists in a number of versions.
[2] *Man* or *mun*, an interjection addressed either to men or women.

AQUILINA. Yes, in thy heart—thy throat, thou pampered devil!
Thou hast helped to spoil my peace, and I'll have vengeance 199
On thy cursed life for all the bloody Senate,
The perjured, faithless Senate. Where's my lord,
My happiness, my love, my god, my hero?
Doomed by thy accursed tongue, amongst the rest,
T'a shameful wrack? By all the rage that's in me,
I'll be whole years in murdering thee! 205
ANTONIO. Why, Nacky, wherefore so passionate? What have I done? What's the matter, my dear Nacky? Am not I thy love, thy happiness, thy lord, thy hero, thy senator, and everything in the world, Nacky? 211
AQUILINA. Thou! Thinkst thou, thou art fit to meet my joys—
To bear the eager clasps of my embraces?
Give me my Pierre, or—
ANTONIO. Why, he's to be hanged, little Nacky—trussed up for treason, and so forth, child. 217
AQUILINA. Thou li'st! stop down thy throat that hellish sentence,
Or 'tis thy last. Swear that my love shall live,
Or thou art dead!
ANTONIO. Ah-h-h-h.
AQUILINA. Swear to recall his doom—
Swear at my feet, and tremble at my fury. 221
ANTONIO. I do. [*Aside*] Now, if she would but kick a little bit—one kick now, ah-h-h-h.
AQUILINA. Swear, or—
ANTONIO. I do, by these dear fragrant foots and little toes, sweet as—e-e-e-e, my Nacky, Nacky, Nacky.
AQUILINA. How! 228
ANTONIO. Nothing but untie thy shoestring a little, faith and troth; that's all— that's all, as I hope to live, Nacky, that's all. 232
AQUILINA. Nay, then—
ANTONIO. Hold, hold! thy love, thy lord, thy hero
Shall be preserved and safe.
AQUILINA. Or may this poniard
Rust in thy heart!
ANTONIO. With all my soul.
AQUILINA. Farewell—
Exit AQUILINA

ANTONIO. Adieu. Why, what a bloody-minded, inveterate, termagant strumpet have I been plagued with! Oh-h-h, yet more! nay, then, I die, I die—I am dead already. 238
(*Stretches himself out*)

[SCENE II. *A street near* PRIULI'S *house*]

Enter JAFFEIR

JAFFEIR. Final destruction seize on all the world!
Bend down, ye heavens, and shutting round this earth,
Crush the vile globe into its first confusion;
Scorch it with elemental flames to one cursed cinder, 4
And all us little creepers in't, called men,
Burn, burn to nothing. But let Venice burn
Hotter than all the rest: here kindle hell
Ne'er to extinguish, and let souls hereafter
Groan here, in all those pains which mine feels now. 9

Enter BELVIDERA

BELVIDERA. (*Meeting him*) My life—
JAFFEIR. (*Turning from her*) My plague.
BELVIDERA. Nay, then I see my ruin,
If I must die!
JAFFEIR. No, Death's this day too busy;
Thy father's ill-timed mercy came too late.
I thank thee for thy labors, tho', and him, too,
But all my poor, betrayed, unhappy friends
Have summons to prepare for fate's black hour; 15
And yet I live.
BELVIDERA. Then be the next my doom.
I see thou hast passed my sentence in thy heart,
And I'll no longer weep or plead against it;
But with the humblest, most obedient patience
Meet thy dear hands, and kiss 'em when they wound me. 20
Indeed I am willing, but I beg thee do it
With some remorse; and where thou giv'st the blow,
View me with eyes of a relenting love,
And show me pity, for 'twill sweeten justice.
JAFFEIR. Show pity to thee!
BELVIDERA. Yes, and when thy hands,
Charged with my fate, come trembling to the deed. 26

As thou hast done a thousand, thousand dear
    times
To this poor breast when kinder rage has
    brought thee,
When our stinged hearts have leaped to meet
    each other,
And melting kisses sealed our lips together,
When joys have left me gasping in thy arms,
So let my death come now, and I'll not shrink
    from't.   32

    JAFFEIR. Nay, Belvidera, do not fear my
cruelty,
Nor let the thoughts of death perplex thy
    fancy;
But answer me to what I shall demand
With a firm temper and unshaken spirit.
    BELVIDERA. I will when I've done weeping—
    JAFFEIR.   Fie, no more on't!
How long is't since the miserable day   38
We wedded first—
    BELVIDERA.   Oh-h-h.
    JAFFEIR.   Nay, keep in thy tears,
Lest they unman me, too.
    BELVIDERA.   Heaven knows I cannot;
The words you utter sound so very sadly
These streams will follow—
    JAFFEIR.   Come, I'll kiss 'em dry, then.
    BELVIDERA. But was't a miserable day?
    JAFFEIR.   A curs'd one.
    BELVIDERA. I thought it otherwise, and
    you've oft sworn   44
In the transporting hours of warmest love,
When sure you spoke the truth, you've sworn
    you blessed it.
    JAFFEIR. 'Twas a rash oath.
    BELVIDERA.   Then why am I not curs'd
    too?
    JAFFEIR. No, Belvidera; by th'eternal
    truth,   48
I dote with too much fondness.
    BELVIDERA.   Still so kind!
Still then do you, you love me?
    JAFFEIR.   Nature, in her workings,
Inclines not with more ardor to creation
Than I do now towards thee; man ne'er was
    bless'd   52
Since the first pair first met, as I have been.
    BELVIDERA. Then sure you will not curse
    me.
    JAFFEIR.   No, I'll bless thee;
I came on purpose, Belvidera, to bless thee.
'Tis now, I think, three years w'have lived
    together.

    BELVIDERA. And may no fatal minute ever
    part us   57
Till, reverend grown for age and love, we go
Down to one grave as our last bed, together;
There sleep in peace till an eternal morning.
    JAFFEIR. (*Sighing*) When will that be?
    BELVIDERA.   I hope long ages hence.
    JAFFEIR. Have I not hitherto (I beg thee
    tell me   62
Thy very fears) used thee with tender'st love?
Did e'er my soul rise up in wrath against thee?
Did I e'er frown when Belvidera smiled,
Or, by the least unfriendly word, betray   66
A bating passion? Have I ever wronged thee?
    BELVIDERA. No.
    JAFFEIR.   Has my heart, or have my
    eyes e'er wand'rèd
To any other woman?
    BELVIDERA.   Never, never—
I were the worst of false ones, should I accuse
    thee.   70
I own I've been too happy, bless'd above
My sex's charter.
    JAFFEIR. Did I not say I came to bless thee?
    BELVIDERA. Yes.
    JAFFEIR.   Then hear me, bounteous
    heaven!
Pour down your blessings on this beauteous
    head,   75
Where everlasting sweets are always springing,
With a continual giving hand; let peace,
Honor, and safety always hover round her;
Feed her with plenty; let her eyes ne'er see
A sight of sorrow, nor her heart know mourning;   80
Crown all her days with joy, her nights with
    rest
Harmless as her own thoughts, and prop her
    virtue
To bear the loss of one that too much loved,
And comfort her with patience in our parting.
    BELVIDERA. How—parting, parting!
    JAFFEIR.   Yes, forever parting.
I have sworn, Belvidera, by yon heaven   86
That best can tell how much I lose to leave
    thee,
We part this hour forever.
    BELVIDERA.   Oh, call back
Your cruel blessings; stay with me and curse
    me!
    JAFFEIR. No, 'tis resolved.
    BELVIDERA.   Then hear me, too,
    just heaven!   90

Pour down your curses on this wretched
   head
With never-ceasing vengeance; let despair,
Danger, or infamy—nay all, surround me;
Starve me with wantings; let my eyes ne'er
   see
A sight of comfort, nor my heart know
   peace;
But dash my days with sorrow, nights with
   horrors 96
Wild as my own thoughts now, and let loose
   fury
To make me mad enough for what I lose,
If I must lose him.—If I must!—I will not.
Oh, turn and hear me!
   JAFFEIR. Now hold, heart, or
      never! 100
   BELVIDERA. By all the tender days we've
      lived together,
By all our charming nights, and joys that
   crowned 'em,
Pity my sad condition—speak, but speak!
   JAFFEIR. Oh-h-h!
   BELVIDERA. By these arms that now
      cling round thy neck,
By this dear kiss and by ten thousand
   more, 105
By these poor streaming eyes—
   JAFFEIR. Murder! unhold me.
By th'immortal destiny that doomed me
      (*Draws his dagger*)
To this curs'd minute, I'll not live one longer.
Resolve to let me go or see me fall— 109
   BELVIDERA. Hold, sir; be patient.
      (*Passing-bell tolls*)
   JAFFEIR. Hark, the dismal bell
Tolls out for death! I must attend its call, too;
For my poor friend, my dying Pierre, expects
   me.
He sent a message to require I'd see him
Before he died, and take his last forgiveness.
Farewell forever.
      (*Going out, looks back at her*)
   BELVIDERA. Leave thy dagger with me;
Bequeath me something.—Not one kiss at
   parting? 116
O my poor heart, when wilt thou break?
   JAFFEIR. Yet stay!
We have a child, as yet a tender infant.
Be a kind mother to him when I am gone;
Breed him in virtue and the paths of honor,
But let him never know his father's story.
I charge thee guard him from the wrongs my
   fate 122
May do his future fortune or his name.
Now—nearer yet—
      (*Approaching each other*)
   Oh, that my arms were riveted
Thus round thee ever!—But my friends, my
   oath! (*Kisses her*)
This and no more.
   BELVIDERA. Another, sure another,
For that poor little one you've ta'en such care
   of; 127
I'll give't him truly.
   JAFFEIR. [*Kissing her*] So!—now
      farewell.
   BELVIDERA. Forever?
   JAFFEIR. Heaven knows, forever; all good
      angels guard thee. [*Exit.*]
   BELVIDERA. All ill ones sure had charge of
      me this moment. 130
Curs'd be my days, and doubly curs'd my
   nights,
Which I must now mourn out in widowed
   tears.
Blasted be every herb and fruit and tree;
Curs'd be the rain that falls upon the earth,
And may the general curse reach man and
   beast. 135
Oh, give me daggers, fire, or water!
How I could bleed, how burn, how drown,
   the waves
Huzzing and booming round my sinking
   head,
Till I descended to the peaceful bottom! 139
Oh, there's all quiet; here, all rage and fury;
The air's too thin, and pierces my weak
   brain.
I long for thick, substantial sleep. Hell, hell,
Burst from the center, rage and roar aloud
If thou art half so hot, so mad as I am. 144

   Enter PRIULI *and* Servants

Who's there?
   PRIULI. Run, seize and bring her
      safely home. (*They seize her*)
Guard her as you would life. Alas, poor
   creature!
   BELVIDERA. What? To my husband then
      conduct me quickly.
Are all things ready? Shall we die most
   gloriously?
Say not a word of this to my old father.
Murmuring streams, soft shades, and spring-
   ing flowers, 150
Lutes, laurels, seas of milk, and ships of amber.
      Exeunt

SCENE [III] *opening, discovers a scaffold and a wheel prepared for the executing of* PIERRE; *then enter* Officers, PIERRE, *and* Guards, *a* Friar, Executioner, *and a great* Rabble

OFFICER. Room, room there! Stand all by; make room for the prisoner.
PIERRE. My friend not come yet?
FATHER. Why are you so obstinate?
PIERRE. Why you so troublesome, that a poor wretch cannot die in peace, 5
But you, like ravens, will be croaking round him?
FATHER. Yet heaven—
PIERRE. I tell thee, heaven and I are friends.
I ne'er broke peace with't yet by cruel murders,
Rapine, or perjury, or vile deceiving; 9
But lived in moral justice towards all men,
Nor am a foe to the most strong believers,
Howe'er my own short-sighted faith confine me.
FATHER. But an all-seeing Judge—
PIERRE. You say my conscience
Must be mine accuser. I have searched that conscience,
And finds no records there of crimes that scare me. 15
FATHER. 'Tis strange you should want faith.
PIERRE. You want to lead
My reason blindfold, like a hampered lion,
Checked of its nobler vigor then when baited,
Down to obedient tameness; make it couch,
And show strange tricks which you call signs of faith. 20
So silly souls are gulled and you get money.
Away, no more!—Captain, I would hereafter
This fellow wrote no lies of my conversion
Because he has crept upon my troubled hours.

Enter JAFFEIR

JAFFEIR. Hold. Eyes, be dry; heart, strengthen me to bear 25
This hideous sight, and humble me. Take
The last forgiveness of a dying friend,
Betrayed by my vile falsehood to his ruin!
—O Pierre!
PIERRE. Yet nearer.
JAFFEIR. Crawling on my knees,
And prostrate on the earth, let me approach thee. 30
How shall I look up to thy injured face,
That always used to smile with friendship on me?
It darts an air of so much manly virtue,
That I, methinks, look little in thy sight,
And stripes are fitter for me than embraces.
PIERRE. Dear to my arms, though thou hast undone my fame, 36
I cannot forget to love thee. Prithee, Jaffeir,
Forgive that filthy blow my passion dealt thee;
I am now preparing for the land of peace,
And fain would have the charitable wishes 40
Of all good men, like thee, to bless my journey.
JAFFEIR. Good! I am the vilest creature, worse than e'er
Suffered the shameful fate thou art going to taste of.
Why was I sent for to be used thus kindly?
Call, call me villain, as I am; describe 45
The foul complexion of my hateful deeds.
Lead me to the rack, and stretch me in thy stead;
I've crimes enough to give it its full load,
And do it credit. Thou wilt but spoil the use on't,
And honest men hereafter bear its figure 50
About 'em as a charm from treacherous friendship.
OFFICER. The time grows short. Your friends are dead already.
JAFFEIR. Dead!
PIERRE. Yes, dead, Jaffeir; they've all died like men, too,
Worthy their character.
JAFFEIR. And what must I do?
PIERRE. O Jaffeir!
JAFFEIR. Speak aloud thy burdened soul, 56
And tell thy troubles to thy tortured friend.
PIERRE. Friend! Couldst thou yet be a friend, a generous friend,
I might hope comfort from thy noble sorrows.
Heaven knows I want a friend.
JAFFEIR. And I a kind one,
That would not thus scorn my repenting virtue, 61
Or think, when he's to die, my thoughts are idle.
PIERRE. No! Live, I charge thee, Jaffeir.
JAFFEIR. Yes, I will live,
But it shall be to see thy fall revenged 64
At such a rate as Venice long shall groan for.
PIERRE. Wilt thou?
JAFFEIR. I will, by heaven!
PIERRE. Then still thou'rt noble.

And I forgive thee. Oh—yet—shall I trust thee?
JAFFEIR. No: I've been false already.
PIERRE. Dost thou love me?
JAFFEIR. Rip up my heart, and satisfy thy doubtings.
PIERRE. (*He weeps*) Curse on this weakness!
JAFFEIR. Tears! Amazement! Tears!
I never saw thee melted thus before.   71
And know there's something lab'ring in thy bosom
That must have vent; though I'm a villain, tell me.
PIERRE. (*Pointing to the wheel*) Seest thou that engine?
JAFFEIR. Why?   75
PIERRE. Is't fit a soldier who has lived with honor,
Fought nations' quarrels, and been crowned with conquest,
Be exposed a common carcass on a wheel?
JAFFEIR. Hah!
PIERRE. Speak! is't fitting?
JAFFEIR. Fitting?
PIERRE. Yes, is't fitting?
JAFFEIR. What's to be done?
PIERRE. I'd have thee undertake
Something that's noble, to preserve my memory   81
From the disgrace that's ready to attaint it.
OFFICER. The day grows late, sir.
PIERRE. I'll make haste.—O Jaffeir,
Though thou'st betrayed me, do me some way justice.
JAFFEIR. No more of that. Thy wishes shall be satisfied.   85
I have a wife, and she shall bleed; my child, too,
Yield up his little throat, and all t'appease thee— (*Going away,* PIERRE *holds him*)
PIERRE. No, this—
(*He whispers* JAFFEIR)
—no more!
JAFFEIR. Hah! is't then so?
PIERRE. Most certainly.
JAFFEIR. I'll do't.
PIERRE. Remember!
OFFICER. Sir.
PIERRE. Come, now I'm ready.
(*He and* JAFFEIR *ascend the scaffold*)
Captain, you should be a gentleman of honor;   90
Keep off the rabble, that I may have room
To entertain my fate, and die with decency. Come!
(*Takes off his gown.* Executioner *prepares to bind him*)
FATHER. Son!
PIERRE. Hence, tempter!
OFFICER. Stand off, priest!
PIERRE. I thank you, sir.
(*To* JAFFEIR)
You'll think on't?
JAFFEIR. 'Twon't grow stale before tomorrow.   95
PIERRE. Now, Jaffeir! now I am going. Now—
(Executioners *having bound him*)
JAFFEIR. Have at thee,
Thou honest heart. Then—here—
(*Stabs him*)
—And this is well, too.
(*Then stabs himself*)
FATHER. Damnable deed!
PIERRE. Now thou hast indeed been faithful. This was done nobly.—We have deceived the Senate.   101
JAFFEIR. Bravely.
PIERRE. Ha, ha, ha—Oh, oh—   (*Dies*)
JAFFEIR. Now, ye curs'd rulers,
Thus of the blood y'have shed I make libation,
And sprinkle't mingling. May it rest upon you,
And all your race. Be henceforth peace a stranger   106
Within your walls; let plagues and famine waste
Your generations.—Oh, poor Belvidera!
Sir, I have a wife; bear this in safety to her—
A token that with my dying breath I blest her,   110
And the dear little infant left behind me.
I am sick—I am quiet—   (JAFFEIR *dies*)
OFFICER. Bear this news to the Senate,
And guard their bodies till there's farther order.
Heaven grant I die so well—
(*Scene shuts upon them*)

[SCENE IV. *A room in* PRIULI'S *house*]

Soft music. Enter BELVIDERA *distracted, led by two of her* Women, PRIULI, *and* Servants

PRIULI. Strengthen her heart with patience, pitying heaven.
BELVIDERA. Come, come, come, come, come! Nay, come to bed,

Prithee, my love. The winds!—hark, how
  they whistle!
And the rain beats: oh, how the weather
  shrinks me!
You are angry now; who cares? pish, no
  indeed. 5
Choose then. I say you shall not go, you
  shall not!
Whip your ill nature; get you gone then!—
              (JAFFEIR'S Ghost *rises*)
                                    Oh,
Are you returned? See, father, here he's
  come again!
Am I to blame to love him? Oh, thou dear
  one, (Ghost *sinks*)
Why do you fly me? Are you angry still,
  then? 10
Jaffeir! where art thou?—Father, why do
  you do thus?
Stand off, don't hide him from me! He's here
  somewhere.
Stand off, I say!—What, gone? Remember't,
  tyrant!
I may revenge myself for this trick one day.
I'll do't—I'll do't. Renault's a nasty fellow.
Hang him, hang him, hang him! 16

Enter Officers *and others*. Officer *whispers*
        PRIULI
  PRIULI. News—what news?
  OFFICER. Most sad, sir.
Jaffeir, upon the scaffold, to prevent
A shameful death, stabbed Pierre, and next
  himself.
Both fell together.
  PRIULI.   —Daughter—
   (*The* Ghosts *of* JAFFEIR *and* PIERRE *rise
      together, both bloody*)
  BELVIDERA.   Hah, look there!
My husband bloody, and his friend, too!
  —Murder 21
Who has done this? Speak to me, thou sad
  vision;
On these poor trembling knees I beg it.
                         (Ghosts *sink*)
                              Vanished—
Here they went down. Oh, I'll dig, dig the
  den up.
You shan't delude me thus.—Hoa, Jaffeir,
  Jaffeir! 25
Peep up and give me but a look.—I have
  him!
I've got him, father; oh, now how I'll smuggle
  him!

My love! my dear! my blessing! help me,
  help me!
They have hold on me, and drag me to the
  bottom!
Nay—now they pull so hard—farewell—
                         (*She dies*)
  MAID.   She's dead—
Breathless and dead.
  PRIULI.   Then guard me from the
    sight on't. 31
Lead me into some place that's fit for mourn-
  ing,
Where the free air, light, and the cheerful sun
May never enter. Hang it round with black;
Set up one taper that may last a day— 35
As long as I've to live; and there all leave me,
Sparing no tears when you this tale relate,
But bid all cruel fathers dread my fate.
                         Exeunt omnes

            CURTAIN

          EPILOGUE

The text is done, and now for application,
And when that's ended, pass your approba-
  tion.
Though the conspiracy's prevented here,
Methinks I see another hatching there;
And there's a certain faction fain would
  sway, 5
If they had strength enough, and damn
  this play.
But this the author bade me boldly say:
If any take his plainness in ill part,
He's glad on't from the bottom of his heart,
Poets in honor of the truth should write 10
With the same spirit brave men for it fight;
And though against him causeless hatreds
  rise,
And daily where he goes of late he spies
The scowls of sullen and revengeful eyes,
'Tis what he knows with much contempt to
  bear, 15
And serves a cause too good to let him fear.
He fears no poison from an incensed drab,
No ruffian's five-foot-sword, nor rascal's stab,
Nor any other snares of mischief laid,
Not a Rose-alley cudgel-ambuscade,[1] 20

---
[1] On December 18, 1679, as Dryden was returning from Will's Coffee-House through Rose Street, Covent Garden, he was set upon and cudgelled by a gang of ruffians hired for that purpose by Rochester. The affair made a great noise.

From any private cause where malice reigns,
Or general pique all blockheads have to brains:
Nothing shall daunt his pen when truth does call,
No, not the picture-mangler [1] at Guildhall.
The rebel-tribe, of which that vermin's one,
Have now set forward and their course begun;
And while that prince's figure they deface, 27
  As they before had massacred his name,
Durst their base fears but look him in the face,
  They'd use his person as they've used his fame; 30

A face, in which such lineaments they read
Of that great martyr's [2] whose rich blood they shed,
That their rebellious hate they still retain,
And in his son would murder him again. 34
With indignation then, let each brave heart,
Rouse and unite to take his injured part;
Till royal love and goodness call him home,[3]
And songs of triumph meet him as he come;
Till Heaven his honor and our peace restore,
And villains never wrong his virtue more. 40

[1] The Duke of York's picture in Guildhall had been slashed by an unknown person.

[2] Charles I.
[3] When *Venice Preserved* was first produced, the Duke of York was in Scotland. He returned to England the following month (March, 1682).

THE SQUIRE OF ALSATIA

A Comedy by Thomas Shadwell

Thomas Shadwell, who, according to Aubrey, was "counted the best comœdian we have now," and whom Dryden damned to immortality as one who never "deviates into sense," was born, probably in 1641, either at Broomhill House or at Santon Hall, Norfolk, the son of John Shadwell, a royalist lawyer, and Sarah, his wife. He was educated at Bury St. Edmunds and at Gonville and Caius College, Cambridge, which, however, he left without taking a degree. In 1658 he was enrolled in the Middle Temple; he travelled on the continent; and he married Ann Gibbs, an actress in the Duke's Company. His career as a dramatist began with the production of *The Sullen Lovers* (1668), and for the next thirteen years Shadwell was a prolific writer for the theater, a particular success being *The Virtuoso* (1676), a satire on the Royal Society. During this period Shadwell enjoyed the patronage of the Duke of Newcastle. Besides writing occasional verse, Shadwell engaged in controversies with Dryden and Settle over the theory of the drama, particularly of comedy.

A convinced Whig, Shadwell could not avoid the fierce political controversies of the age. Jibes at Catholicism in his comedy, *The Lancashire Witches* (1681) brought forth personal attacks from the Tories, and the squabbles engendered by the Popish Plot, the Exclusion Bill, and the trial of Shaftesbury involved Shadwell in bitter antagonisms. To the Tory satires of Dryden—*Absalom and Achitophel* and *The Medal*—Shadwell replied with vigor and coarseness in *The Medal of John Bayes* (1682), a poem almost certainly his, but nothing availed against Dryden's crushing attack in *MacFlecknoe* and in the second part of *Absalom and Achitophel*. If the artistic honors were Dryden's, Shadwell finally triumphed, when, after the Revolution, through the good offices of the Duke of Dorset, he was appointed Poet Laureate (1689), succeeding his ancient enemy.

The Whig political triumph allowed Shadwell to return to the stage with the production of *The Squire of Alsatia* (1688), a great success, which was followed by *Bury Fair* (1689), a more brilliant, if less representative, comedy. Other plays were less successful, nor did the dramatist excel as a writer of official verse. He died November 19 or 20, 1692, probably from an over-dose of opium. If his person gave occasion for ridicule to the satirists of his age, his conversation was witty, and grave injustice is done him by supposing that Dryden's brilliant lines give us a fair portrait.

The best accounts of Shadwell are Albert S. Borgman, *Thomas Shadwell: His Life and Comedies*, New York, 1928, and Montague Summers' prefatory essay in Vol. I of his edition of the *Works*, 1927. See also W. H. Browne, "Thomas Shadwell," *The Sewanee Review*, XXI:257-76; Bonamy Dobrée, *Restoration Comedy*, 1924; A. W. Ward, *A History of English Dramatic Literature*, III, 455-461, 1899; and A. Nicoll, *A History of Restoration Drama*, pp. 189-98, 1923.

SHADWELL'S DRAMATIC WORKS

The Sullen Lovers (comedy) (L.I.F., May, 1668), 1668.

The Royal Shepherdess (adaptation) (L.I.F., Feb. 25, 1668/9), 1669.

The Humourists (comedy) (L.I.F., Dec., 1670), 1671.

The Hypocrite (comedy) (1671?), never published.

The Miser (adaptation) (T.R., Jan., 1671/2), 1672.

Epsom-Wells (comedy) (D.G., Dec. 2, 1672), 1673.

The Tempest (adaptation) (D.G., Apr., 1674), 1674.

The Triumphant Widow (comedy) (with the Duke of Newcastle) (1674), 1677.

Psyche (opera) (D.G., Feb. 27, 1674/5), 1675.

The Libertine (tragedy) (D.G., June 15, 1675), 1676.

The Virtuoso (comedy) (D.G., May 25, 1676), 1676.

Timon of Athens (adaptation) (D.G., Dec. or Jan., 1677/8), 1678.

A True Widow (comedy) (D.G., Nov. or Dec., 1678), 1679.

The Woman-Captain (comedy) (D.G., before Nov., 1679), 1680.
The Lancashire Witches (comedy) (D.G., Nov. (?), 1681), 1682.
The Squire of Alsatia (comedy) (D.L., May 4 (?), 1688), 1688.
Bury Fair (comedy) (D.L., Apr. (?), 1689), 1689.
The Amorous Bigot (comedy) (D.L., May (?), 1690), 1690.
The Scourers (comedy) (D.L., Dec. or Jan., 1690/1), 1691.
The Volunteers (comedy) (D.L., Dec. (?), 1692), 1693.

The humor of Mr. Shadwell is characteristically Jonsonian, and, though all of his plays are not in this vein, *The Sullen Lovers*, with which he began, *The Virtuoso*, *The Squire of Alsatia*, and *Bury Fair*, with which he concluded the number of his important plays, are all comedies of humors of the Jonsonian kind. As Mr. Shadwell has himself written,

A Humour is the Byass of the Mind
By which with Violence 'tis one way inclin'd:
It makes our Actions lean on one side still;
And in all Changes that way bends the Will.
(Epilogue to *The Humourists*)

More prosaically, he hath defined a humor as "such an Affectation, as misguides Men in Knowledge, Art, or Science, or that causes defection in Manners and Morality, or perverts their Minds in the main Actions of their Lives." In so writing, Mr. Shadwell hath closely followed Mr. Jonson, one of the greatest poets of the former age, who expressed a similar design in his play, *Every Man Out of His Humour*.

If a particular bias of the mind informs Mr. Shadwell's characters, 'tis no less to be noted that he followed his master in those scenes imitative of actual low life, which our own age allows to be realistic. His comedies are pictures; and he has lively expressed the manners and actions of Bury Fair, Whitefriars (in the present play), the Lancashire vulgar, and the habitual language of the London streets. Severe critics have maintained that his scenes were sometimes below the dignity of comedy, but, not to overlook the plays of Plautus and Terence which abound in similar expressions, the student must be grateful to Mr. Shadwell for painting scenes of Restoration life which would otherwise have escaped, and which are invaluable to the historian and the philosopher. Certain it is that our dramatist is the most illustrious follower of Jonson's comedy which his age produced.

The fable of *The Squire of Alsatia* is, apart from the comic scenes, regular, being borrowed from the *Adelphoe* of Terence: as Mr. Langbaine noted in his *Account of the English Dramatic Poets*. In this comedy Demea, a harsh father, keeps one son, Ctesipho, and allows his brother Micio the upbringing of Æschinus, the other. Ctesipho seduces a cithern-player from her master, a slave dealer, and Æschinus hath a love-intrigue with an Athenian lady. At the end, all is discovered, both lovers retain their mistresses, and the more good-humored Micio is preferred by the audience to the harsher father. In Mr. Shadwell's play Demea appears as Sir William, Sir Edward is Micio, and the brothers Belfond correspond to Ctesipho and Æschinus. In addition, Mr. Shadwell borrowed certain scenes from *L'Avare* of Molière.

It is, however, in the scenes of low life that Mr. Shadwell is most himself; and the reader is likely to remember the humors of Alsatia longer than the debate between Sir William and Sir Edward over the education of the boys. The character of Lolpoop (which perhaps owes something to a servant in the *Truculentus* of Plautus) was particularly admired when played; and in the figures of the Alsatians themselves, the language which they use, and the customs which they follow, Mr. Shadwell is an innovator. If the theme of the play is the training of youth, it is surrounded by a continuous and lively action set in the contemporary world of low life which the dramatist hath carefully studied for his purpose.

The Squire of Alsatia was first produced in May, 1688 (probably May 4), at the Drury Lane Theater.

THE SQUIRE OF ALSATIA

Creditur, ex medio quia res arcessit, habere
Sudoris minimum sed habet comœdia tanto
Plus oneris quanto veniæ minus.[1]

Hor. *Ep. ad Aug.* I. lib. 2.

DRAMATIS PERSONÆ

Sir William Belfond — Mr. Leigh
    A gentleman of above £3,000 per annum, who in his youth had been a spark of the town, but married and retired into the country, where he turned to the other extreme, rigid, morose, most sordidly covetous, clownish, obstinate, positive, and froward.

Sir Edward Belfond — Mr. Griffin
    His brother, a merchant who, by lucky hits had gotten a great estate, lives single with ease and pleasure, reasonably and virtuously. A man of great humanity and gentleness and compassion towards mankind; well read in good books, possessed with all gentleman-like qualities.

Belfond, Senior — Mr. Jevon
    Eldest son to Sir William, bred after his father's rustic, swinish manner, with great rigor and severity, upon whom his father's estate is entailed, the confidence of which makes him break out into open rebellion to his father, and become lewd, abominably vicious, stubborn, and obstinate.

Belfond, Junior — Mr. Mountfort
    Second son to Sir William, adopted by Sir Edward, and bred from his childhood by him with all the tenderness and familiarity and bounty and liberty that can be; instructed in all the liberal sciences, and in all gentleman-like education; somewhat given to women, and now and then to good fellowship, but an ingenious, well-accomplished gentleman, a man of honor and of excellent disposition and temper.

Truman — Mr. Bowman
    His friend, a man of honor and fortune.

Cheatly — Mr. Samford
    A rascal who, by reason of debts, dares not stir out of Whitefriars, but there inveigles young heirs in tail, and helps 'em to goods and money upon great disadvantages; is bound for them, and shares with them till he undoes them. A lewd, impudent, debauched fellow, very expert in the cant about the town.

Shamwell — Mr. Powell, Jr.
    Cousin to the Belfonds, an heir who, being ruined by Cheatly, is made a decoy duck for others, not daring to stir out of Alsatia, where he lives; is bound with Cheatly for heirs, and lives upon them, a dissolute, debauched life.

Captain Hackum — Mr. Bright
    A block-headed bully of Alsatia, a cowardly, impudent, blustering fellow, formerly a sergeant in Flanders, run from his colors, retreating into Whitefriars for a very small debt, where, by the Alsatians, he is dubbed a captain, marries one that lets lodgings, sells cherry brandy, and is a bawd.

Scrapeall — Mr. Freeman
    A hypocritical, repeating, praying, psalm-singing, precise fellow, pretending to great piety; a godly knave who joins with Cheatly and supplies young heirs with goods and money.

Attorney to Sir William Belfond — Mr. Powell, Sr.
    Who solicits his business and receives all his packets.

---
[1] Horace, *Epistles*, II, i, 168–70: Men think that because comedy takes its subjects from common life it requires less effort, but it has more obstacles to overcome since the indulgence allowed it is less.

LOLPOOP   Mr. Underhill
    A North-country fellow, servant to Belfond Senior, much displeased at his master's proceedings.
TERMAGANT   Mr. Alexander
    A sharper, brother to Mrs. Termagant.
LA MAR
    French valet de chambre.
[ROGER
    Servant to Belfond, Junior.]
PARSON
    An indebted Alsatian divine.
[RUTH   Mrs. Cory][1]
    A precise governess to Teresia and Isabella.
TERESIA   Mrs. Knight
    Daughter to Scrapeall, in love with, and beloved by, **Truman.**
ISABELLA   Mrs. Mountford
    His niece, in love with, and beloved by, Belfond Junior.
LUCIA   Mrs. Bracegirdle
    The Attorney's daughter, a young, beautiful girl, of a mild and tender disposition, debauched by Belfond Junior.
MRS. TERMAGANT   Mrs. Bowtell
    A neglected mistress of Belfond Junior, by whom he has had a child; a furious, malicious, and revengeful woman, perpetually plaguing him and crossing him in all designs, pursuing him continually with her malice, even to the attempting of his life.
MRS. HACKUM
    Wife to Captain Hackum.
MRS. BETTY
    Lolpoop's whore.
MRS. MARGARET
    His master's whore.
Fiddlers, Constables, Tipstaff, Watch, Sergeant, Musketeers, Rabble, &c.

PROLOGUE [2]

SPOKEN BY MR. MOUNTFORT

How have we in the space of one poor age
Beheld the rise and downfall of the stage!
When, with our king restored, it first arose,
They did each day some good old play expose,
And then it flourished, till, with manna tired, 5
For wholesome food ye nauseous trash desired.
Then rose the whiffling [3] scribblers of those days
Who since have lived to bury all their plays,
And had their issue full as num'rous been
As Priam's,[4] they the fate of all had seen. 10

With what prodigious scarcity of wit
Did the new authors starve the hungry pit!
Infected by the French, you must have rhyme,
Which long to please the ladies' ears did chime.
Soon after this came ranting fustian in, 15
And none but plays upon the fret [5] were seen:
Such roaring bombast stuff, which fops would praise,
Tore our best actors' lungs, cut short their days.
Some in small time did this distemper kill,
And had the savage authors gone on still, 20
Fustian had been a new disease i'th' bill.
When Time, which all things tries, had laid rhyme dead,
The vile usurper, Farce, reigned in its stead.
Then came machines,[6] brought from a neighbor nation: [7]

---

[1] Neither Ruth as a character nor Mrs. Cory as an actress appears in the original edition. Both appear, however, in the 1720 edition of Shadwell's *Works*.

[2] The play is prefaced by a dedication to the Earl of Dorset, here omitted, in which Shadwell speaks of having written the first act at "Copt Hall." In addition, Shadwell furnishes a glossary of cant terms which has been incorporated in the notes.

[3] Trifling.

[4] Priam of Troy had fifty sons and fifty daughters.

[5] High pitched (Summers).

[6] Stage devices. Cf. the elaborate settings of *The Siege of Rhodes* and *The Indian Queen* for examples.

[7] France.

Oh, how we suffered under decoration! 25
If all this stuff has not quite spoiled your taste,
Pray let a comedy once more be graced,
Which does not monsters represent, but men,
Conforming to the rules of Master Ben.[1]
Our author, ever having him in view, 30
At humble distance would his steps pursue.
He to correct, and to inform did write.
If poets aim at nought but to delight,
Fiddlers have to the bays an equal right.
   Our poet found your gentle fathers kind, 35
And now some of his works your favor find.
He'll treat you still with somewhat that is new,
But whether good or bad, he leaves to you.
Bawdy the nicest[2] ladies need not fear,
The quickest fancy shall extract none here. 40
We will not make 'em blush, by which is shown
How much their bought red differs from their own.
No fop, no beau shall just exceptions make,
None but abandoned knaves offense shall take:
Such knaves as he industriously offends, 45
And should be very loth to have his friends.
For you who bring good humor to the play,
We'll do our best to make you laugh today.

ACT I.

SCENE I. [*A street in Whitefriars*]

Enter BELFOND SENIOR, *meeting* SHAMWELL

BELFOND SENIOR. Cousin Shamwell, well met. Good morrow to you.

SHAMWELL. Cousin Belfond, your humble servant. What makes you abroad so early? 'Tis not much past seven.

BELFOND SENIOR. You know we were boozy[3] last night. I am a little hot-headed this morning, and come to take the fresh air here in the Temple Walks.

SHAMWELL. Well, and what do you think of our way of living here? Is not rich, generous wine better than your poor hedge-wine,[4] stummed,[5] or dull March beer? Are not delicate well-bred, well-dressed women better than dairymaids, tenants' daughters, or barefoot strumpets? Streets full of fine coaches better than a yard full of dung-carts? A magnificent tavern than a thatched ale-house? Or the society of brave, honest, witty, merry fellows than the conversation of unthinking, hunting, hawking blockheads, or high-shoed peasants and their wiser cattle?

BELFOND SENIOR. O yes, a world, adad! Ne'er stir, I could never have thought there had been such a gallant place as London. Here I can be drunk over night, and well next morning; can ride in a coach for a shilling as good as a Deputy-Lieutenant's; and such merry wags and ingenious companions—! Well, I vow and swear, I am mightily beholding[6] to you, dear cousin Shamwell. Then for the women! Mercy upon us! so civil and well bred. And I'll swear upon a Bible, finer all of them than knight-baronets' wives with us.

SHAMWELL. And so kind and pleasant!

BELFOND SENIOR. Ay, I vow, pretty rogues! No pride in them in the world, but so courteous and familiar, as I am an honest man, they'll do whatever one would have them presently. Ah, sweet rogues! While in the country, a pize[7] take them! There's such a stir with "pish, fy, nay, Mr. Timothy, what do you do? I vow I'll squeak, never stir, I'll call out," ah hah—

SHAMWELL. And if one of them happen to be with child, there's straight an uproar in the country as if the hundred[8] were sued for a robbery.

BELFOND SENIOR. Ay, so there is. And I am in that fear of my father besides, adad, he'd knock me i'th' head, if he should hear of such a thing. To say truth, he's so terrible to me, I can never enjoy myself for him. Lord! What will he say when he comes to know I am at London? Which he in all his life-time would never suffer me to see, for fear I should be debauched, forsooth; and allows me little or no money at home neither.

SHAMWELL. What matter what he says? Is not every foot of the estate entailed upon you?

BELFOND SENIOR. Well, I'll endur't no longer! If I can but raise money, I'll teach him to use his son like a dog, I'll warrant him.

---

[1] Ben Jonson. See his *Timber* and *Every Man in his Humour* and *Every Man Out of His Humour* especially for precept and example.
[2] Most precise.
[3] Drunk.
[4] Wine of inferior quality, such as would be found at a wayside stopping place.
[5] Re-fermented.

[6] Beholden, obliged.
[7] Pox (?).
[8] Subdivision of a county, having its own court.

SHAMWELL. You can ne'er want that. Take up on the reversion, 'tis a lusty one; and Cheatly will help you to the ready,[1] and thou shalt shine and be as gay as any spruce prig[2] that ever walked the street.

BELFOND SENIOR. Well, adad, you are pleasant men, and have the neatest sayings with you: "ready" and "spruce prig," and abundance of the prettiest witty words.—But sure that Mr. Cheatly is as fine a gentleman as any wears a head, and as ingenious, ne'er stir, I believe he would run down the best scholar in Oxford, and put 'em in a mouse-hole with his wit.

SHAMWELL. In Oxford! Ay, and in London, too.

BELFOND SENIOR. Goodsookers,[3] cousin! I always thought they had been wittiest in the universities.

SHAMWELL. O, fie, cousin. A company of puts,[4] mere puts.

BELFOND SENIOR. "Puts, mere puts!" Very good, I'll swear. Ha, ha, ha!

SHAMWELL. They are all scholar-boys, and nothing else as long as they live there; and yet there are as confident as if they knew everything, when they understand no more beyond Magdalen Bridge than mere Indians. But Cheatly is a rare fellow. I'll speak a bold word: he shall cut a sham[5] or banter with the best wit or poet of 'em all.

BELFOND SENIOR. Good again: "cut a sham or banter!" I shall remember all these quaint words in time. But Mr. Cheatly's a prodigy, that's certain.

SHAMWELL. He is so, and a worthy brave fellow, and the best friend where he takes, and the most sincere of any man breathing.

BELFOND SENIOR. Nay, I must needs say I have found him very frank, and very much a gentleman, and am most extremely obliged to him and you for your great kindness.

SHAMWELL. This morning your clothes and liveries will come home, and thou shalt appear rich and splendid like thyself, and the mobile[6] shall worship thee.

BELFOND SENIOR. The "mobile!" That's pretty.

Enter CHEATLY

Sweet Mr. Cheatly, my best friend, let me embrace thee.

CHEATLY. My sprightly son of timber and of acres! My noble heir, I salute thee! The cole is coming, and shall be brought this morning.

BELFOND SENIOR. Coal? Why, 'tis summer, I need no firing now. Besides, I intend to burn billets.

CHEATLY. My lusty rustic, learn, and be instructed. "Cole" is in the language of the witty, money; the ready, the rhino. Thou shalt be rhinocerical my lad, thou shalt.

BELFOND SENIOR. Admirable, I swear! "Cole, ready, rhino, rhinocerical!" Lord, how long may a man live in ignorance in the country!

SHAMWELL. Ay, but what asses you'll make of the country gentlemen when you go amongst them! 'Tis a providence you are fallen into so good hands.

BELFOND SENIOR. 'Tis a mercy, indeed! How much cole, ready, and rhino shall I have?

CHEATLY. Enough to set thee up to spark it in thy brother's face; and ere thou shalt want the ready, the darby,[7] thou shalt make thy fruitful acres in reversion fly, and all thy sturdy oaks to bend like switches! But thou must squeeze,[8] my lad; squeeze hard, and seal, my bully. Shamwell and I are to be bound with thee.

BELFOND SENIOR. I am mightily beholding to you both, I vow and swear. My uncle, Sir Edward, took my brother when he was a child, and adopted him. Would it had been my lot!

SHAMWELL. He is a noble gentleman, and maintains him in coach and equipage fit for him.

CHEATLY. Thou shalt not see the prig, thy brother, till thou shalt out-jingle him in ready, outshine him in thy ornaments of body, out-spark him in thy coach and liveries; and shalt be so equipped that thou shalt dazzle the whole town with thy outrageous splendor.

BELFOND SENIOR. I vow his tongue is rarely hung!

CHEATLY. Thy brother's heart shall break with envy at thy gallantry; the fops and beaux shall be astonished at thy brightness.

---

[1] Ready money.
[2] Coxcomb.
[3] Variant of gadzooks, a mild oath.
[4] Naïve persons.
[5] To deceive a stupid person. Cf. *banter* on the same line.
[6] Mob.

[7] Ready money.
[8] Squeeze wax, and so set one's seal to a legal document.

What ogling there will be between thee and the blowings![1] Old[2] staring at thy equipage! And every buttock[3] shall fall down before thee!

BELFOND SENIOR. Ha, ha, ha! I vow, you are the pleasantest man I ever met with, and I'll swear, the best friend I ever had in my life; that I must needs say. I was resolved not to let my brother see me till I was in circumstances, d'ye see? And for my father, he is in Holland. My mother's brother died, and left him sole executor. He'll not be here these six weeks.

SHAMWELL. Well, when you see your brother, he'll envy you, and rail at those who made you flourish so. We shall be cast off.

BELFOND SENIOR. Gudsookers, cousin! I take it very unkindly that you should say so. I'll cast off all the relations in the world before I'll part with such true, such loving friends, adad.

Enter CAPTAIN HACKUM

O noble Captain Hackum, your servant; servant, Captain.

HACKUM. Your humble trout,[4] good noble squire. You were brave and boozy last night, i'faith, you were.

BELFOND SENIOR. Yes, really, I was clear,[5] for I do not remember what I did, or where I was. Clear, clear—is not that right?

SHAMWELL. Ay, ay. Why, you broke windows, scoured,[6] broke open a house in Dorset Court, and took a pretty wench, a gentleman's natural,[7] away by force.

CHEATLY. Very true. And this magnanimous spark, this thunderbolt of war, Captain Hackum, laid about him like a hero, as did some other of your friends, or else the watch had mauled us. But we made them scour.

BELFOND SENIOR. Nay, o' my conscience, the captain's mighty valiant; there's terror in that countenance and whiskers. He's a very Scanderberg[8] incarnate. And now you put me in mind, I recollect somewhat of this matter. My shoulders are plaguy sore, and my arms black and blue. But where's the wench, the natural—ha, Captain?

HACKUM. Ah, squire, I led her off. I have her safe for you.

BELFOND SENIOR. But does not the gallant thunder and roar for her?

HACKUM. The scoundrel dares not. He knows me, who never knew fear in my life. For my part, I love magnanimity and honor, and those things, and fighting is one of my recreations.

He that wears a brave soul, and dares honestly do,
Is a herald to himself, and a godfather, too.

BELFOND SENIOR. O brave captain!

CHEATLY. The prigster[9] lugged out[10] in defence of his natural, the captain whipped his porker[11] out, and away rubbed[12] prigster, and called the watch.

BELFOND SENIOR. "Prigster, lugged out, natural, porker, rubbed"—admirable! This is very ingenious conversation! Y'are the purest company! Who would not keep company with the wits? Pox o' the country, I say!

HACKUM. But, squire, I had damned ill luck afterwards: I went up to the gaming ordinary,[13] and lost all my ready, they left me not a rag or sock.[14] Pox o' the tatts,[15] for me! I believe they put the doctor[16] upon me.

BELFOND SENIOR. "Tatts," and "doctor!" What's that?

SHAMWELL. The tools of sharpers—false dice.

HACKUM. Hark you. Prithee, noble squire, equip me with a couple of megs, or two couple of smelts.

BELFOND SENIOR. "Smelts?" What, shall we bespeak another dish of fish for our dinner?

SHAMWELL. No, no, megs are guineas, smelts are half-guineas. He would borrow a couple of guineas.

BELFOND SENIOR. "Megs, smelts!" Ha, ha, ha! Very pretty, by my troth. And so thou shalt, dear Captain. There are two megs, and I vow and swear I am glad to have 'em to pleasure you, adad, I am.

---

[1] Prostitutes; same as blowens.
[2] Used as an intensive. Cf. "high old time."
[3] Prostitute.
[4] "Servant," confidential friend.
[5] "Soused."
[6] Ran away.
[7] Mistress.
[8] Properly, Scanderbeg, a famous Albanian hero, who defeated the Ottoman Turks.
[9] Coxcomb.
[10] Drew his sword.
[11] Sword.
[12] Ran.
[13] Tavern.
[14] Left me not a farthing.
[15] Dice.
[16] A particular false dice which will run **but two or** three chances.

HACKUM. You are so honest a gentleman, quarrel every day, and I'll be your second; once a day, at least. And I'll say this for you, there's not a finer gentleman this day walks the Friars [1]—no dispraise to any man, let him be what he will.

BELFOND SENIOR. Adad, you make me proud, sir.

Enter LOLPOOP

Oh, Lolpoop, where have you been all this morning, sirrah?

LOLPOOP. Why, 'tis but rear.[2] Marry, 'tis meet a bit past eight. By'r lady, yeow were so sow drunken last neeght I had thoughten yeow wouden ha leen [3] a bed aw th' morn. Well, mine eyne ake a-gazing up and down on aw the fine sights; but for aw that, send me north to my own county again.

BELFOND SENIOR. Oh, silly rogue! you are only fit for cattle. Gentlemen, you must excuse him, he knows no better.

LOLPOOP. Marry, better, quotha! By th' mess, this is a life for the deel.[4] To be drunken each night, break windows, roar, sing, and swear i'th' streets; go to loggerheads with the constable and the watch, han [5] harlots in gold and silver lace! Hea'n bless us! and send me a whome [6] again.

BELFOND SENIOR. Peace, you saucy scoundrel, or I'll cudgel you to pap. Sirrah, do not provoke me, I say, do not.

LOLPOOP. Ods-flesh, where's money for aw this? Yeowst be run agraunt [7] soon, and [8] you takken this caurse, Ise tell a that.

BELFOND SENIOR. Take that, sirrah! I'll teach you to mutter. What, my man become my master?

LOLPOOP. Waunds! Give me ten times more, and send me a whome agen at after. What will awd maaster say to this? I mun ne'er see the face of him, I wot.

SHAMWELL. Hang him, rogue! Toss him in a blanket.

CHEATLY. Let me talk with him a little. Come on, fellow.

LOLPOOP. Talk! Well, what sen you?

CHEATLEY. (*Bantering*) Your master being in this matter, to deport his count'nance somewhat obliquely to some principles which others but out of a mature gravity may have weighed, and think too heavy to be undertaken; what does it avail you if you shall precipitate or plunge yourself into affairs as unsuitable to your phys'nomy as they are to your complexion?

LOLPOOP. Hah, what sen yeow? Yeow mistaken me: I am not book-learned. I understand a not.

CHEATLY. No, 'tis the strangest thing! Why, put the case you are indebted to me £20 upon a *scire facias:* [9] I extend this up to an outlawry, upon affidavit upon the *nisi prius;*[10] I plead to all this matter, *non est inventus* upon the panel.[11] What is there to be done more in this case as it lies before the bench but to award out execution upon the *posse comitatus*,[12] who are presently to issue out a *certiorari?* [13]

LOLPOOP. I understand a little of sizes, nisi prizes, affidavi, sussurari! But by the mess, I can not tell what to mack of aw this together, not I.

BELFOND SENIOR. Ha, ha! Puppy! Owl! Loggerhead! O silly country put! Here's a prig, indeed! He'll ne'er find out what 'tis to cut a sham or banter. Well, I swear, sir, vou do it the best of any man in the world.

CHEATLY. No, no, I swear, not I.

BELFOND SENIOR. I protest you do it incomparably.

CHEATLY. Nay, now you compliment. Faith, you make me blush.

LOLPOOP. Sham and banter are heathen Greek to me. But yeow have cut out fine wark for yoursel last neeght. I went to see the hause yeow had brocken. Aw the windows are pood [14] dawn. I asked what was the matter, and by the mass, they haw learnt your nam, too; they saiden Squire Belfond had done it, and ravished a wench, and that they hadden gotten the lord chief justice' warren [15] for you, and wodden bring a pawr of actions against yeow.

[9] A judicial writ.
[10] Another law term, as is *non est inventus*.
[11] Jury.
[12] Citizens summoned by the sheriff to repress disorder.
[13] A judicial writ. Needless to remark, Cheatly's words are mere sound and fury.
[14] Pulled.
[15] Warrant.

[1] Whitefriars, "Alsatia."
[2] Early.
[3] Lain.
[4] Devil.
[5] Have.
[6] Home.
[7] Aground.
[8] An, if.

BELFOND SENIOR. Is this true?

LOLPOOP. Ay, by th' mass.

CHEATLY. No matter. We'll bring you off with a wet finger;[1] trust me for that.

BELFOND SENIOR. Dear friend, I rely upon you for every thing.

SHAMWELL. We value not twenty such things of a rush.

HACKUM. If any of their officers dare invade our privileges,[2] we'll send 'em to hell without bail or mainprize.[3]

LOLPOOP. But I can tella a wor' news than aw this: I ne'er saw flesh alive, and I saw not your father's man, Roger, come out o' th' Temple-yate e'en now. Your father's in town, that's certain.

BELFOND SENIOR. How! my father, say you? 'Tis impossible.

CHEATLY. Courage, my heir in tail:[4] thy father's a poor sneaking tenant for life; thou shalt live better than he can. And if we do contract a debt upon the dirty acres in the north, I have designed for you a fine young lady with a swinging fortune to redeem all. And 'tis impossible, my lad, to miss her.

BELFOND SENIOR. Sir, let me embrace you, and love you. Never man embraced a better friend! *Amicus certus in re incerta cernitur*,[5] as the saying is.

LOLPOOP. Sir, sir, let me speak one word with yeow. Ods-flesh, I'll die the death of a dog and aw these yeow seen here be not rogues, cheats, and pickpockets.

BELFOND SENIOR. Peace, you rascal! Adad, I would not have any of 'em hear for five hundred pounds. You were a dead man.

LOLPOOP. What is the reason they dare not stir out of this privileged place but on Sabbath days?

BELFOND SENIOR. You blockhead, Mr. Cheatly had an alderman's young wife run away with him, is sued for't, and is in fear of a substantial jury of city cuckolds. Shamwell's unnatural father lays wait for him, to apprehend him, and run into the country. The brave and valiant gentleman, Captain Hackum, who is as stout as a lion, beat a judge's son t'other day. And now your questions are fully answered, you put, you.

CHEATLY. Honest Shamwell, thou art a rare fellow. Thy cousin here is the wealthiest caravan[6] we have met with a long time; the hopefullest sealer[7] that ever yet touched wax among us. But we must take off that evil counsellor of his.

Enter Tailor *with a bundle, a* Periwig-maker, Hatter, Shoe-maker

SHAMWELL. I warrant you.—Oh, cousin, here's your tailor with your clothes and liveries, hatter, shoe-maker, periwig-maker.

CHEATLY. All your moveables together. Go into your lodging and fit them. Your new footmen, and your French *valet de chambre* are there. I'll wait on you there presently.

LOLPOOP. Ods-flesh, here's whaint wark![8] By'r lady, this is fine! Whaw, whaw!

BELFOND SENIOR. Get you in, you rogue! An you mutter one word more, adad, I'll mince you, sirrah!—Well, go in, all of you.—Gentlemen, I shall see you presently. [*Exeunt*]

CHEATLY. Immediately.—Let us hug ourselves, my dear rascal, in this adventure. You have done very well to engage him last night in an outrage; and we must take care to put him upon all the expense we can. We must reduce him to have as much need of us as possible.

SHAMWELL. Thou art i' th' right. But, Captain, where's the convenient, the natural?[9]

HACKUM. Why, at my house. My wife has wrought her into a good humor. She is very pretty, and is now pleased to think the Squire will be a better keeper than her former, for he was but a sharper, a tatmonger,[10] and when he wanted money, would kick and beat her most immoderately.

SHAMWELL. Well. I'll say that for the Captain's wife, she's as good an able, discreet woman to carry on an intrigue as ere a woman in the Friars. Nay, better.

HACKUM. Your servant, good Mr. Shamwell. She's a very good woman, thanks be to heaven. I have great comfort in her; she has a cup of the best cherry brandy in the Friars.

[1] With little or no damage.
[2] Within the boundaries of Whitefriars, or at least some portions of it, arrests could not be made by the ordinary officers of the law.
[3] An undertaking that a prisoner shall appear in court at a certain day. Something like "going bond."
[4] Within certain restrictions of inheritance which can not be forfeited.
[5] Cicero, *De Amicitia*—"A friend appears certain in some uncertain affair."
[6] Man to be cheated.
[7] One who gives bonds for goods or money.
[8] Queer work.
[9] Cant terms for mistress.
[10] Cheater at dice.

SHAMWELL. (*Aside*) And commonly a good whore, to boot.—But prithee, Captain, go home, and let her and the young girl prepare to dine with us. We must have a great dinner, and fiddlers at the George,[1] to season the Squire in his new equipage.

HACKUM. Well, well, it shall be done. *Exit*

SHAMWELL. You'll find this fellow a necessary tool in consort with his wife, who is, indeed, a bawd of parts. He is a good ruffian enough, for, though he be not stout, he's impudent, and will roar and keep a filthy pother, which is enough to make fools believe he's stout.

CHEATLY. Let him, and the small fry, pick up the Squire's loose crumbs, while we share in the lusty sums.

Enter SCRAPEALL

Oh, here comes Mr. Scrapeall, with all his zeal—our godly accomplice in all designs. Leave him to me. *Exit* SHAMWELL
Oh, Mr. Scrapeall! Have you brought the money for the Squire?

SCRAPEALL. I come to tell you that my man approacheth with the money and the goods for your Squire.

CHEATLY. I hope you have not burdened him with too many goods at first.

SCRAPEALL. No; but a fourth part. 'Tis true, the goods are somewhat stale, but I will take them off at small under rates. You know I am not seen in furnishing of the goods and money, but only in the buying of the goods. My lawyer accompanieth my man to testify the writings.

CHEATLY. 'Tis as it should be. He is a fat squire; the estate in tail[2] is full £3000 a year. He will yield well.

SCRAPEALL. (*Aside*) This squire is to take to wife a niece I have in charge. His father is to give me £5000 out of her fortune, and the squire's lewdness and prodigality will soon let me deep into his reversion. Besides, his lighting into these hands will make his father, when he finds it, hasten to agree with me for his redemption. I like the business well.—I am going to the man you call Crump,[3] who helpeth solicitors to affidavit-men,[4] and swearers, and bail.

CHEATLY. His office is next door his wardrobe for bail and witnesses. Here he comes. Let's meet him. *Exeunt*

Enter SIR WILLIAM BELFOND *and an* Attorney

SIR WILLIAM. Sure I should know the face of that fellow that's going there into Whitefriars.

ATTORNEY. 'Tis a most notorious one. You have seen him often, this, that most audacious rogue, Cheatly, who has drawn so many young heirs, and undone so many sealers. He's a bolter[5] of Whitefriars.

SIR WILLIAM. It is that villain!

ATTORNEY. I am very glad, sir, you have dispatched your business so soon in Holland.

SIR WILLIAM. I had great success and finished all six weeks, at least, ere I expected; and had time to come by the way of Flanders and see that country, which I desired. And from Newport I came to Dover, and, riding posts from thence, I took a boat to Southwark, and landed just now here at the Temple.[6] But I am troubled you had sent my packet to Holland ere I came.

ATTORNEY. I received none from you of late. No packet has arrived this fortnight from Holland.

SIR WILLIAM. Have you heard no news from my son, nor my steward in the country?

ATTORNEY. None this ten or twelve days.

SIR WILLIAM. That son is all the joy of my life. For him I hurry up and down, take pains, spare,[7] and live hard to raise his fortune.

ATTORNEY. Indeed, I hear he's a fine gentleman, and understands his country affairs as well as e'er a farmer of them all.

SIR WILLIAM. I must confess he proves after my own heart. He's a solid young man, a dutiful child as ever man had, and I think I have done well for him in providing him a wife with such a fortune, which he yet knows nothing of. But will not this godly man, this Mr. Scrapeall, take a farthing less, say you, for his niece?

ATTORNEY. Not a sowce.[8] I have higgled with him as if I were to buy of a horse-courser,

---

[1] An actual tavern in Whitefriars.
[2] Entailed estate; that is, an estate which descends through a particular line of heirs.
[3] Defined in the following clause.
[4] Men willing to make affidavits for a consideration.
[5] Runaway.
[6] Sir William landed at the Temple Stairs, the principal landing place for passengers coming to London up the Thames.
[7] Save.
[8] Sou; i.e., "sous."

and he will not take a farthing less than £5000 for his niece.

SIR WILLIAM. He's a strange mixture, a perpetual sermon-hunter, repeats and sings psalms continually, and prays so loud and vehemently that he is a disturbance to his neighbors; he is so heavenward pious, and seems a very saint of a scrivener.

ATTORNEY. He finds the sweet of that; it gets him many a good trust and executorship.

SIR WILLIAM. Pox on him for a damned godly knave, forsooth! Can not he be contented to sell her whom his own brother committed to his charge, but he must extort so much for her? Well, I must agree with him. I know she has full £20,000 left her, and has been brought up as strictly as my son. Get writings[1] ready. I'll send post for my son Timothy today.

ATTORNEY. They are ready. You may seal in the afternoon, if you please.

SIR WILLIAM. And I will then. I'll detain you no longer. Get my writings ready: I am resolved to settle my other boy well. But my town son afflicts me whene'er I hear him named.

ATTORNEY. Your humble servant, Sir William Belfond. *Exit* Attorney

Enter Servant *to* SIR WILLIAM

SERVANT. Sir, I have been at your brother's house, and they say he is come to some lawyer's chamber in the King's Bench Buildings.

SIR WILLIAM. That's lucky enough. I'll walk here then, and do you watch.

Enter HACKUM *and another* Bully

Who are these? Some inhabitants of Whitefriars; some bullies of Alsatia.

HACKUM. I was plaguy boozy last night with Squire Belfond. We had fiddles, whores, scoured, broke windows, beat watches, and roared like thunder.

BULLY. Ah, I heard you.

SIR WILLIAM. (*Aside*) What says he?

HACKUM. He drinks, whores, swears, sings, roars, rants, and scours with the best of us.

SIR WILLIAM. Sir, with your favor, are you acquainted with young Belfond?

HACKUM. Yes, that I am. (*Aside*) What country put's this?

SIR WILLIAM. What countryman is he, sir?

HACKUM. Prithee, old prigster, why dost

[1] I.e., the marriage contract.

ask? He is a northern man. He has a damned, rustic, miserable rascal to his father, who lives a nasty, brutal life in the country, like a swine. But the Squire will be even with him, I warrant him.

SIR WILLIAM. I have something to say to him, if I could see him.

HACKUM. You, you old prig! You damned country put! You have something to say to him! I am ready to give you satisfaction. Lug out—come, you put! I'll make you scamper!

SIR WILLIAM. D'ye hear, bully rascal? Put up and walk your way, or, by heaven! I'll beat you as long as you're able to be beaten.

BULLY. I'll stand by you. You may easily beat this old fellow.

HACKUM. No man e'er gave me such words, but forfeited his life. I could whip thee through the lungs immediately, but I'll desist at present.—Who the devil would have thought this put durst have drawn a sword?— Well, sir, we shall take a time, sir, another time, sir.

SIR WILLIAM. You lie, you rascal, you will take no time. Here's a fine companion of my son's! *Exeunt* HACKUM *and* Bully

Enter SIR EDWARD BELFOND

SIR EDWARD. Who's this I see? My brother? Sir William Belfond! Your humble servant. You are welcome into England. I looked not for you these six weeks.

SIR WILLIAM. I landed at the Temple Stairs even now. My man has been at your house, and he heard there you were here.

SIR EDWARD. I hope you have done your business.

SIR WILLIAM. Beyond my expectation.

SIR EDWARD. Has your wife's brother done by you in his will as you would have had him?

SIR WILLIAM. Truly, yes. He has made me sole executor, and left my two sons, £5000 to be paid at each of their days of marriage, or at my death.

SIR EDWARD. Well, brother, you are a happy man, for wealth flows in upon you on every side, and riches you account the greatest happiness.

SIR WILLIAM. I find that wealth alone will not make [me] happy. Ah, brother, I must confess it was a kindness in you, when heaven had blessed you with a great estate by merchandise, to adopt my younger son, and take him and breed him from his childhood. But you have been so gentle to him, he is run into all manner of vice and riot; no bounds can hold him, no shame can stop him, no laws nor customs can restrain him.

SIR EDWARD. I am confident you are mistaken. He has as fair a reputation as any gentleman about London. 'Tis true, he's a good fellow, but no sot; he loves mirth and society, without drunkenness; he is, as all young fellows, I believe, are, given to women, but it is in private; and in short keeps as good company as any man in England.

SIR WILLIAM. Your over-weening makes you look through a false glass upon him. Company! Why, he keeps company for the devil! Had you come a minute sooner, you might have seen two of his companions; they were praising him for roaring, swearing, ranting, scouring, whoring, beating watches, breaking windows. I but asked one of 'em if he knew him, and said I had somewhat to say to him; the rogue, the most seeming terrible of the two, told me, if I had anything to say to Squire Belfond, he would give me satisfaction.

SIR EDWARD. What kind of fellow?

SIR WILLIAM. He came out of Whitefriars. He's some Alsatian bully.

SIR EDWARD. 'Tis impossible; he never keeps such company.

SIR WILLIAM. The rogue drew upon me, bid me "Lug out," called me "old prig," "country put," and spoke a particular language which such rogues have made to themselves called canting, as beggars, gipsies, thieves, and jail-birds do; but I made his bullies go away very tamely at the sight of my drawn sword.

SIR EDWARD. I am sure he keeps no such company; it must be some other of his name.

SIR WILLIAM. You make me mad to excuse him thus. The town rings of him. You have ruined him by your indulgence; besides, he throws away money like dirt; his infamy is notorious.

SIR EDWARD. Infamy! Nay, there you wrong him. He does no ungentlemanlike things. Prithee, consider youth a little. What if he does wench a little, and now and then is somewhat extravagant in wine? Where is the great crime? All young fellows that have mettle in them will do the first; and if they have wit and good humor in them, in this drinking country, they will sometimes be forced upon the latter; and he must be a very dull plegmatic lump whom wine will not elevate to some extravagance now and then.

SIR WILLIAM. Will you distract me? What, are drinking and whoring no faults? His courses will break my heart, they bring tears into my eyes so often.

SIR EDWARD. One would think you had been drinking and were maudlin. Think what we ourselves did when we were young fellows. You were a spark, would drink, scour, and wench with the best o'th' town.

SIR WILLIAM. Ay, but I soon repented, married, and settled.

SIR EDWARD. And turned as much to the other extreme; and perhaps I mislike these faults, caused by his heat of youth. But how do you know he may not be reclaimed suddenly?

SIR WILLIAM. Reclaimed? How can he be reclaimed without severity? You should cudgel him and allow him no money; make him not dare to offend you thus. Well, I have a son whom by my strictness I have formed according to my heart. He never puts on his hat in my presence; rises at second course, takes away his plate, says grace, and saves me the charge of a chaplain. Whenever he committed a fault, I mauled him with correction. I'd fain see him once dare to be extravagant! No, he's a good youth, the comfort of my age. I weep for joy to think of him. Good sir, learn to be a father of him that is one; I have a natural care of him you have adopted.

SIR EDWARD. You are his father by nature, I by choice; I took him when he was a child, and bred him with gentleness and that kind of conversation that has made him my friend. He conceals nothing from me, or denies nothing to me. Rigor makes nothing but hypocrites.

SIR WILLIAM. Perhaps, when you begin late; but you should have been severe to him in his childhood, abridged him of liberty and money, and have had him soundly whipped often; he would have blessed you for it afterwards.

SIR EDWARD. Too much straitness to the minds of youth, like too much lacing to the body, will make them grow crooked.

SIR WILLIAM. But no lacing at all will make them swell and grow monsters.

SIR EDWARD. I must govern by love. I had as leave govern a dog as a man, if it must be by fear; this I take to be the difference between a good father to children, and a harsh master over slaves.

SIR WILLIAM. Yes, and see what your government is come to: his vice and prodigality will distract me.

SIR EDWARD. Why should you be so concerned? He is mine, is he not?

SIR WILLIAM. Yes, by adoption, but he is mine by nature.

SIR EDWARD. 'Tis all but custom.

SIR WILLIAM. Mine is a tender care.

SIR EDWARD. Your passion blinds you. I have as tender care as you can have; I have been ever delighted with him from his childhood; he is endeared to me by long custom and familiarity. I have had all the pleasure of a father without the drudgery of getting a son upon a damned wife, whom perhaps I should wish hanged.

SIR WILLIAM. And will you let him run on in his lewdness and prodigality?

SIR EDWARD. He is mine. If he offends, 'tis me; if he squanders away money, 'tis mine; and what need you care? Pray take care of your own; if you will take care of this, too, what do you do but take him from me?

SIR WILLIAM. This you come to always! I take him from you? No, I'd not be troubled with him. Well, let him run on and be ruined, hanged, and damned. I'll never speak a word more about him. Let him go on.

SIR EDWARD. This heat of you will be allayed ere long, I warrant you.

SIR WILLIAM. No, no, let him go on, let him go on. I'll take care of my own at home; and happy were this rake-hell, if he would take example by his brother. But I say no more; I have done—let him go.

SIR EDWARD. Now you are angry, your passion runs away with you.

SIR WILLIAM. No, no, I have done. What would you have more?

SIR EDWARD. Let us go and see him. I'll lay my life you'll find him perusing some good author. He spends his whole morning in study.

SIR WILLIAM. I must into the city, the first thing I do, and get my bills [1] accepted; and then, if you will, we'll see him; and no doubt but we shall find him perusing of some whore or other, instead of a book.

SIR EDWARD. I am not of your opinion.

[1] Of exchange.

But I'll carry [2] you in my coach into the city, and then bring you back to him. He is of so good a disposition, so much a gentleman, and has such worth and honor, that if you knew him as well as I, you'd love him as well as I do.

SIR WILLIAM. Well, well, I hear you, sir. I must send for my son post—I'll show you a son! Well, heaven bless him, I should be weary of this wicked world but for the comforts I find in him. Come along, I'll show you a son. *Exeunt ambo*

ACT II

SCENE I. [BELFOND JUNIOR'S *chambers*]

Enter BELFOND JUNIOR *and* LUCIA

BELFOND JUNIOR. Why dost thou sigh, and show such sadness in thy looks, my pretty miss?

LUCIA. Have I not reason?

BELFOND JUNIOR. Dost thou mislike thy entertainment?

LUCIA. Ah, cruel Belfond, thou hast undone me.

BELFOND JUNIOR. My pretty little rogue, I sooner would undo myself a thousand times.

LUCIA. How I tremble to think what I ha' done! I have made myself forever miserable.

BELFOND JUNIOR. Oh, say not so, dear child! I'll kiss those tears from off thy beauteous eyes. But I shall wrong thy cheeks, on which they fall like precious drops of dew on flowers.

LUCIA. Heaven! What have I done?

BELFOND JUNIOR. No more than what thy mother did before thee; no more than thy whole sex is born to do.

LUCIA. Oh, had I thought you would have been so cruel, I never would have seen your face—I swear I would not.

BELFOND JUNIOR. I swear thou would'st, I know thou would'st. Cruel! No billing turtle [3] e'er was kinder to his tender mate. In billing, cooing, and in gentle murmurs we expressed our kindness; and coo'd and murmured and loved on.

LUCIA. The more unhappy fool was I. Go, go, I hate you now.

BELFOND JUNIOR. O my sweet little one! Thou canst not sure be so unkind. Those

[2] Accompany.
[3] Turtle dove.

pretty tell-tales of thy heart, thy eyes, say better things.

LUCIA. Do they so? I'll be revenged on 'em for't, for they shall never see you more.

BELFOND JUNIOR. Ah, say not so. I had rather much the sun should never shine on me than thou be hidden from my sight. Thou art not sure in earnest?

LUCIA. Yes, sure, I think I am.

BELFOND JUNIOR. No, sweet love, I think thou art not.

LUCIA. Oh, Lord, how shall I look! How shall I bear myself! If any of my friends shall fix their eyes upon me, I shall look down, and blush, and think they know all.

BELFOND JUNIOR. How many fair ones daily do the same, and look demurely as any saints?

LUCIA. They are confident [1] things, I warrant 'em.

BELFOND JUNIOR. Let love be made familiar to thee, and thou wilt bear it better. Thou must see me every day. Canst thou be so hard-hearted to forbear the sight of me?

LUCIA. Perhaps I may desire now and then a look, a sight of thee at some distance. But I will never venture to come near thee more, I vow.

BELFOND JUNIOR. Let me kiss that vow from off thy lips while 'tis warm there. I have it here. 'Tis gone. Thou wilt not kill me, sure? Didst thou not say thou loved'st me?

LUCIA. Yes, I loved too much, or this had never happened. I could not else have been undone.

BELFOND JUNIOR. Undone? Thou art made. Woman is but half a creature till she be joined to man. Now thou art whole and perfect.

LUCIA. Wicked man! Can I be so confident once to come near thee more?

BELFOND JUNIOR. Shouldst thou but fail one day, I never should survive it; and then my ghost will haunt thee. Canst thou look on me, pretty creature, and talk thus?

LUCIA. Well, go thy ways, thou flattering tongue, and those bewitching eyes were made to ruin womankind.

BELFOND JUNIOR. Could I but think thou wert in earnest, these arms should clasp thee ever here. I'd never part with thee.

LUCIA. No, no, now I must be gone; I shall be missed. How shall I get home, and not be known? Sure, everybody will discover me.

BELFOND JUNIOR. Thy mask will cover all. There is a chair [2] below in the entry to carry thee and set thee down where thou wilt.

LUCIA. Farewell, dear, cruel man! And must I come tomorrow morning, say you? No, no.

BELFOND JUNIOR. Yes, yes; tomorrow and tomorrow, and every morning of our lives; I die else.

Enter Footboy

FOOTBOY. Sir, your singing master is coming.

BELFOND JUNIOR. My singing master, Mr. Solfa, is coming.

LUCIA. O Lord, hide me! He is my master, he'll know me! I shall not be able to go by him for trembling.

BELFOND JUNIOR. Pretty miss, into the closet. I'll dispatch him soon.

(LUCIA *goes in*)

Enter Singing Master *and his* daughter

Come, Master, let your daughter sing the song you promised me.

SOLFA. Come, Betty. Please to put in a flute, sir.

BELFOND JUNIOR. Come on.

(*Song with two flutes and a thorough bass* [3])

THE EXPOSTULATION

Still wilt thou sigh, and still in vain
    A cold neglectful nymph adore;
No longer fruitlessly complain,
    But to thyself thyself restore.
In youth thou caught'st this fond disease
    And shouldst abandon it in age;
Some other nymph as well may please,
    Absence or bus'ness disengage.

On tender hearts the wounds of love,
    Like those imprinted on young trees,
Or kill at first, or else they prove
    Larger b'insensible degrees.
Business I tried, she filled my mind;
    On other lips my dear I kissed;
But never solid joy could find,
    Where I my charming Sylvia missed.

Long absence, like a Greenland night,
    Made me but wish for sun the more;
And that inimitable light
    She, none but she, could e'er restore.

[1] Bold.
[2] Sedan chair.
[3] Continuous bass voice part; hence, accompaniment.

She never once regards thy fire,
    Nor ever vents one sigh for thee.
I must the glorious sun admire,
    Though he can never look on me.

Look well, you'll find she's not so rare,
    Much of her former beauty's gone;
My love her shadow larger far
    Is made by her declining sun.
What if her glories faded be,
    My former wounds I must endure:
For should the bow unbended be,
    Yet that can never help the cure.

BELFOND JUNIOR. 'Tis very easy and natural: your daughter sings delicately.

Enter TRUMAN

TRUMAN. Belfond, good morrow to thee. I see thou still tak'st care to melt away thy hours in soft delights.

BELFOND JUNIOR. Honest Truman! All the pleasures and diversions we can invent are little enough to make the farce of life go down.

TRUMAN. And yet what a coil they keep! How busy and industrious are those who are reckoned grave and wise, about this life, as if there were something in it.

BELFOND JUNIOR. Those fools are in earnest, and very solid; they think there's something in't, while wise men know there's nothing to be done here but to make the best of a bad market.

TRUMAN. You are mighty philosophical this morning. But shall I not hear one song as well as you?

BELFOND JUNIOR. Have you set that ode in Horace?

SOLFA. I have.

BELFOND JUNIOR. Then I hope you will be encouraged to set more of them; we then shall be sure of wit and music together, while you great musicians do often take most pains about the silliest words. Prithee, Truman, sing it.

(TRUMAN *sings* Integer vitae sceler isque purus &c.—Hor., Ode 22, l[ib.]1.)

BELFOND JUNIOR. Very well. You have obliged me. Please to accept of this. And, madam, you shall give me leave to show my gratitude by a small present.

SOLFA AND DAUGHTER. Your servant, sir.

Exeunt

TRUMAN. You are so immoderately given to music, methinks it should jostle love out of your thoughts.

BELFOND JUNIOR. Oh, no! Remember Shakespeare: if music be the food of love, play on.[1]—There's nothing nourishes that soft passion like it, it imps[2] his wings, and makes him fly a higher pitch. But, prithee, tell me what news of our dear mistresses? I was never yet so sincerely in love as with my pretty hypocrite. There is a fire in those eyes that strikes like lightning. What a constant churchman she has made of me!

TRUMAN. And mine has made an entire conquest of me! 'Tis the most charming pretty creature that e'er my eyes beheld.

BELFOND JUNIOR. Let us not fall out, like the heroes in *The Rehearsal*,[3] for not being in love with the same woman.

TRUMAN. Nothing could be so fortunate as our difference in this case,—the only one we disagree in.

BELFOND JUNIOR. Thou art in the right. Mine hath so charmed me, I am content to abandon all other pleasures, and live alone for her. She has subdued me even to marriage.

TRUMAN. Mine has no less vanquished me. I'll [sur]render upon discretion. Ah, rogue Belfond, I see by your bed, for all your constant love, you have had a wench this night.

BELFOND JUNIOR. Peace, peace, man. 'Tis dangerous to fast too long, for fear of losing an appetite quite.

TRUMAN. You are a sincere, honest lover, indeed.

BELFOND JUNIOR. Faith, Truman, we may talk of mighty matters; of our honesty and morality; but a young fellow carries that about him that will make him a knave now and then, in spite of his teeth. Besides, I am afraid 'tis impossible for us profane fellows to succeed into that sanctified family.

TRUMAN. You will not say so when you know what progress I have made in our affairs already.

BELFOND JUNIOR. Thou reviv'st my drooping hopes! Tell me, are we like to succeed? Oh, if I can but prevail upon my pretty little churchwoman, I am resolved to conform to her forever!

TRUMAN. Look under my coat! Am I not well habited? with a plain band, bob peruke,[4] and no cuffs.

---

[1] *Twelfth Night*, Act I, scene i, l. 1.
[2] Strengthens.
[3] *The Rehearsal*, Act IV, Scene ii.
[4] A wig with short curls.

BELFOND JUNIOR. Verily, like one of the pure ones.[1]

TRUMAN. Yea. And our frequenting of sermons and lectures (which, heaven knows, we did out of no good, but for the sake of the little ones) has used me to their style. Thus qualified, I got access into the house; having found that their governante[2] is sister to a weaver in the west whom I know, I pretended to be her cousin, and to bring a token sent to her by her brother, and was very welcome to her.

BELFOND JUNIOR. Most fortunate! Why does he keep 'em so strictly? Never to see the face of man?

TRUMAN. Be not troubled at that, 'twill forward our design; they'll be the more earnest to be delivered. But no Italian women are so closely confined; the pure knave intends to sell them, even his daughter, who has a good fortune left her by a widow that was her aunt; and for his niece, he has as good as agreed already with your father for £5000 to marry her to your brother in the country. Her uncle gave her £20,000, and this is the reason for confining 'em, for fear of losing the money.

BELFOND JUNIOR. With my father, say you?

TRUMAN. Most certain. This I learned out of Madam Governante at the first interview.

BELFOND JUNIOR. This is a very odd accident; 'twill make my difficulty greater.

TRUMAN. Not at all. As liars are always readiest to believe lies, I never knew an hypocrite but might easily be cozened by another hypocrite. I have made my way, and I warrant thee a good event. I intend to grow great with the father.

BELFOND JUNIOR. Thy sanguine temper makes thee always hope in every enterprise.

TRUMAN. You might observe, whenever he stared upon them, they would steal a look at us; and by stealth have often twisted eye-beams[3] with us.

BELFOND JUNIOR. The sour and devout look, indeed, seems but put on. There is a pretty warmth and tenderness in their eyes that now and then glides o'er the godly look; like the sun's light, when breaking through a cloud, it swiftly glides upon a field of corn.

[1] I.e., Puritans.
[2] Governess, duenna.
[3] Cf. Donne, "The Ecstasy," ll. 7–8:
Our eye-beams twisted, and did thread
Our eyes upon one double string.

TRUMAN. The air of their faces plainly show[s] they have wit that must despise these trifling forms; their precise looks most surely are constrained.

Enter MRS. TERMAGANT

BELFOND JUNIOR. How. Madam Termagant here! Then we shall have fine work.—What wind blows you hither?

TERMAGANT. How dare you think that I of all womenkind should be used thus?

BELFOND JUNIOR. You mean, not used—that's your grievance.

TERMAGANT. Good Mr. Disdain, I shall spoil your scoffing. Has my love deserved to be thus slighted? I that have refused princes for your sake? Did not all the town court me? And must I choose such an ungrateful wretch?

BELFOND JUNIOR. When you were first in season, you were a little courted by some of quality. Mistresses, like green peas, at first coming, are only had by the rich, but afterwards they come to everybody.

TERMAGANT. Curse on your saucy similes! Was I not yours, and only yours?

BELFOND JUNIOR. I had not faith enough for that; but if you were, I never had any that was mine, and only mine, but I made 'em all mankind's before I had done.

TERMAGANT. Ah, traitor! And you must pick me out to make this base example of. Must I be left?

BELFOND JUNIOR. Left? Yes, sure, left! Why, you were not married to me; I took no lease of your frail tenement; I was but tenant at my own will.

TERMAGANT. Insolent! How dare you thus provoke my fury? Was ever woman's love like mine to thee? Perfidious man! (*Weeps*)

BELFOND JUNIOR. So: after the thunder, thus the heat-drops fall.

TERMAGANT. No; I scorn that thou shouldst bring tears into my eyes.

BELFOND JUNIOR. Why do you come to trouble me?

TERMAGANT. Since I can please no longer, I'll come to plague thee, and if I die before thee, my ghost shall haunt thee.

BELFOND JUNIOR. Indeed, your love was most particular with spitting and scratching, like caterwauling. And in the best of humors you were ever murmuring and complaining: Oh, my head aches, I am so sick; and jealous to madness, too.

Termagant. Oh, devil incarnate!

Truman. Belfond, thou art the most ungentle knight alive.

Termagant. Methinks the pretty child I have had by you should make you less inhumane.

Belfond Junior. Let me have it; I'll breed it up.

Termagant. No, thou shalt never have it while thou livest. I'll pull it limb from limb ere thou shalt have it.

Belfond Junior. This is so unnatural that you will make me so far from thinking it mine, that I shall not believe it yours, but that you have put a false child upon me.

Termagant. Unworthy wretch!

Belfond Junior. When thou art old enough, thy malice and ill humor will qualify thee for a witch, but thou hadst never douceurs [1] enough in thy youth to fit thee for a mistress.

Termagant. How dare you provoke me thus? For what little dirty wench am I thus used? If she be above ground, I'll find her, and tear her eyes out. Hah—by the bed, I see the devil has been here tonight.—Oh, oh, I can not bear it! *(Falls into a fit)*

Truman. Belfond, help the lady, for shame. Lay hold on her.

Belfond Junior. No, no, let her alone; she will not hurt herself, I warrant thee. She is a rare actor. She acts a fit of the mother [2] the best of any one in England. Ha, ha, ha!

Truman. How canst thou be so cruel?

Belfond Junior. What a devil should I do? If a man lies once with a woman, is he bound to do it forever?

Termagant. Oh, oh!

Belfond Junior. Very well, faith; admirably well acted.

Termagant. Is it so? Devil, devil, I'll spoil your *point de Venise* [3] for you. *(Flies at him)*

Belfond Junior. Will you force me to make my footman turn you out?

Enter Footman

Footman. Sir, your father and your uncle are coming hither.

Belfond Junior. 'Sdeath! My father! 'Tis impossible.

[1] Pleasant manners.
[2] Hysterics.
[3] Venetian lace.

Footman. By heaven, 'tis true. They are coming up by this time.

Belfond Junior. Look you, madam, you may, if you will, ruin me, and put me out of all means of doing for you or your child. Try me once more, and get into the bed and cover yourself with the quilt, or I am undone.

Termagant. Villain, you deserve to be ruined. But I love my child too well.

Truman. For heaven's sake, hide yourself in the bed quickly.

Termagant. No, no, I'll run into the closet.

Belfond Junior. Death and hell! I am ruined! There's a young girl there; she'll make yet a worse uproar.

Truman. Peace, let me alone.—Madam, whatever happens, ruin not your self and child inevitably.

Enter Sir William Belfond, Sir Edward, *and* Servants

Sir Edward. Ned, good morrow to thee.

Belfond Junior. Your blessing, sir.

Sir Edward. Heaven bless thee. Here's one unexpected.

Belfond Junior. My father! I beg your blessing, sir.

Sir William. Heaven mend you; it can never bless you in the lewd course you are in.

Belfond Junior. You are misinformed, sir; my courses are not so lewd as you imagine.

Sir William. Do you see? I am misinformed; he'll give me the lie.

Belfond Junior. I would first bite my tongue in pieces, and spit it at you. Whatever little heats of youth I have been guilty of, I doubt not but in short time to please you fully.

Sir Edward. Well said, Ned. I dare swear thou wilt.

Sir William. Good brother Credulous, I thank heaven I am not so.--You were not drunk last night with bullies, and roared and ranted, scoured, broke windows, beat the watch, broke open a house, and forced away a wench in Salisbury Court! [4] This is a fine life! This he calls heats of youth.

Belfond Junior. I was at home by eight o'clock last night, and supped at home; and never keep such company.

Sir William. No, no? You are not called Squire Belfond by the scoundrels, your companions? 'Twas not you—no, no!

[4] Dorset House in Fleet Street. Cf. Act I, scene i.

BELFOND JUNIOR. Not I, upon my faith. I never keep such company, or do such actions. If any one should call me squire, I'd break his head. Some rascal has usurped my name.

SIR EDWARD. Look you, brother, what would you have? This must be some mistake.

SIR WILLIAM. What a devil! You believe this too? Ounds![1] You make me mad! Is there any of our name in England but ourselves? Does he think to flam[2] me with a lie?

BELFOND JUNIOR. I scorn a lie. 'Tis the basest thing a gentleman can be guilty of. All my servants can testify I stirred not out last night.

TRUMAN. I assure you, sir, he was not abroad last night.

SIR WILLIAM. You assure me! Who are you—one of his hopeful companions? No, your clothes are not good enough; you may be his pimp.

TRUMAN. You are the father of my friend, an old gentleman, and a little mad.

SIR WILLIAM. Old! Walk down—I'll try your youth; I'll fight with the bravest ruffian he keeps company with.

SIR EDWARD. Brother, are you mad? Has the country robbed you of all good manners and common sense?

SIR WILLIAM. I had a bout with two of your bullies in the Temple walks.

BELFOND JUNIOR. Whom does he mean? This is a gentleman of estate and quality; he has above £2,000 a year.

SIR EDWARD. You are a mad man. I am ashamed of you.—Sir, I beseech you pardon my brother's passion, which transports him beyond civility.

BELFOND JUNIOR. I know you will for my sake.

TRUMAN. He is the father of my dearest friend. I shall be glad to serve him.

SIR EDWARD. Will you never be of age of discretion? For shame! Use me, your son, and everybody better.

SIR WILLIAM. Well, I must be run down like a tame puppy.

LUCIA. (*Within*) Murder, murder! Help, help! Ah, ah!

(TERMAGANT *pulls* LUCIA *out by the hair; they part them*)

BELFOND JUNIOR. Oh, this damned she-devil!

TERMAGANT. I'll make you an example. Will you see him, whether I will or not, you young whore!

SIR WILLIAM. Here's a son! Here's a fine son! Here's your breeding! Here's a pretty son! Here's a delicate son! Here's a dainty son!

SIR EDWARD. If he be mad, will you be madder?

BELFOND JUNIOR. Turn out this she-bear; turn her out to the rabble.

TERMAGANT. Revenge, you villain, revenge!

Exeunt TERMAGANT *and* Footman

BELFOND JUNIOR. Dear friend, prithee see this innocent girl safe in the chair, from that outrageous strumpet's fury.

Exeunt TRUMAN *and* LUCIA

SIR WILLIAM. Here's a son! Here's a son! Very well, make much of him! Here's the effect of whoring!

BELFOND JUNIOR. No, sir, 'tis the effect of not whoring; this rage is because I have cast her off.

SIR WILLIAM. Yes, yes, for a younger—a sweet reformation! Let me not see your face, nor hear you speak; you will break my heart.

BELFOND JUNIOR. Sir, the young girl was never here before; she brought me linen from the Exchange.

SIR WILLIAM. A fine bawd, her mistress, in the meantime.

BELFOND JUNIOR. This furious wench coming in to rail at me for my leaving her, I was forced to put the other into that closet; and at your coming up, against my will, this run into the same closet.

SIR WILLIAM. Sirrah, most audacious rogue, do you sham me? Do you think you have your uncle to deal with? Avoid my presence, sirrah. Get you out, sirrah.

BELFOND JUNIOR. I am sorry I offended; I obey. *Exit* BELFOND JUNIOR

SIR WILLIAM. I could have found in my heart to have cudgelled him.

SIR EDWARD. Shame of our family! You behave yourself so like a madman and a fool, you will be begged: these fits are more extravagant than anything he can be guilty of. Do you give your son the words of command you use to dogs?

SIR WILLIAM. Justify him, do! He's an excellent son! a very pretty son! a delicate **son**! a discreet son! he is.

---

[1] Shortened form of "by God's wounds."
[2] Cheat, deceive.

Sir Edward. Pray use me better, or I'll assure you, we must never see one another. Besides, I shall entail my estate for want of issue by this son here, upon another's family, if you will treat me thus.

Sir William. (*Aside*) What says he?— Well, brother, I ha' done: his lewdness distracted me! Oh, my poor boy in the country! I long to see him, the great support of my declining age.

Sir Edward. Let us calmly reason: what has your breeding made of him (with your patience) but a blockhead?

Sir William. A blockhead! When he comes, the world shall judge which of us has been the wiser in the education of a son. A blockhead? Why, he knows a sample of any grain as well as e'er a fellow in the north; can handle a sheep or bullock as well as any one; knows his seasons of plowing, sowing, harrowing, laying fallow; understands all sorts of manure; and ne'er a one that wears a head can wrong him in a bargain.

Sir Edward. A very pretty fellow for a gentleman's baily.[1]

Sir William. For his own baily, and to be a rich—

Sir Edward. Swine, and live as nastily, and keep worse company than beasts in a forest.

Sir William. He knows no vice, poor boy.

Sir Edward. He will have his turn to know it, then, as sure as he will have the small pox; and then he'll be fond on't when his brother has left it.

Sir William. I defy the omen; he never whores, nor drinks hard but upon design, as driving a bargain or so; and that I allow him.

Sir Edward. Knavish and designing drunkenness you allow; but not good fellowship for mirth and conversation.

Sir William. Now, brother, pray what have you made your son good for, with your breeding you so much boast of? Let's hear that now. Come on, let's hear.

Sir Edward. First, I bred him at Westminster School till he was master of the Greek and Latin tongues; then I kept him at the university where I instructed him to read the noble Greek and Roman authors.

Sir William. Well, and what use can he make of the noble Greek and Latin but to prate like a pedant, and show his parts over a bottle?

Sir Edward. To make a man fit for the conversation of learned gentlemen is one noble end of study. But those authors make him wiser and honester, sir, to boot.

Sir William. Wiser! Will he ever get sixpence, or improve, or keep his estate by 'em?

Sir Edward. Mean notions. I made him well versed in history.

Sir William. That's a pretty study, indeed! How can there be a true history when we see no man living is able to write truly the history of the last week?

Sir Edward. He, by the way, read natural philosophy, and had insight enough in the mathematics.

Sir William. Natural philosophy! knows nothing! Nor would I give a fart for any mathematician but a carpenter, bricklayer, or measurer of land, or sailor.

Sir Edward. Some moderate skill in it will use a man to reason closely.

Sir William. Very pretty. Reason! Can he reason himself into six shillings by all this?

Sir Edward. He needs it not. But to go on: after three years I removed him from the university (lest he should have too strong a tincture of it) to the Temple;[2] there I got a modest learned lawyer, of little practice, for want of impudence—and there are several such that want, while empty impudent fellows thrive and swagger at the bar; this man I got to instruct my son in some old common law books, the statutes, and the best pleas of the crown, and the constitution of the old true English government.

Sir William. Does he get a shilling by all this? But what a devil made you send him into France, to make an arrant, vain coxcomb of him?

Sir Edward. There he did all his manly exercises; saw two campaigns; studied history, civil laws, and laws of commerce; the language he spoke well ere he went. He made the tour of Italy, and saw Germany and the Low Countries, and returned well skilled in foreign affairs, and a complete accomplished English gentleman.

Sir William. And to know nothing of his own estate but how to spend it. My poor boy has travelled to better purpose, for he

---

[1] Bailiff, chief agent.

[2] Where, in London, young lawyers studied.

has travelled all about my lands, and knows every acre and nook, and the value of it. There's travel for you! Poor boy!

SIR EDWARD. And he enjoys so little of that estate he sees as to be impatient for your death. I dare swear mine wishes my life, next to his own. I have made him a complete gentleman, fit to serve his country in any capacity.

SIR WILLIAM. Serve his country! Pox on his country! 'Tis a country of such knaves 'tis not worth the serving. All those who pretend to serve it, mean nothing but themselves. But among all things, how came you to make him a fiddler, always fluting or scraping? I had as lief hear a jew's-harp.

SIR EDWARD. I love music. Besides, I would have young gentlemen have as many helps to spend their time alone as can be. Most of our youth are ruined by having time lie heavy on their hands, which makes them run into base company to shun themselves.

SIR WILLIAM. And all this gentleman's education is come to drinking, whoring, and debauchery.

Enter Servant *to* SIR WILLIAM

SERVANT. Sir, Mr. Scrapeall is at your attorney's chamber in the Temple, and desires to discourse you.

SIR WILLIAM. Brother, I must go. I shall tell you when I see you next, what is my business with him.

SIR EDWARD. Be sure to dine with me.

SIR WILLIAM. I will. *Exeunt*

[SCENE II]

Enter BELFOND SENIOR, SHAMWELL, CHEATLY, HACKUM, LOLPOOP, French Valet, *two Footmen at the "George" in Whitefriars*

CHEATLY. Now thou look'st like an heir indeed, my lad. When thou cam'st up, thou hadst the scurvy phiz [1] of a mere country put. He did thee a kindness that took thee for a chief constable.

SHAMWELL. Now thou shinest, cousin, like a true Belfond! What! £3,000 a year, entailed, and live like a butcher or a grazier, in the country?

HACKUM. Give you joy, noble sir, now you look like a true gallant squire.

LOLPOOP. Like a squire? Like a puppy, by

[1] Face.

th' mass. Ods-flesh, what will the awd man say? He'll be stark wood.[2]

BELFOND SENIOR. Well, I was the fortunat'st man to light upon such true, such real friends. I had never known any breeding or gentility without you.

SHAMWELL. You buried all your good parts in a sordid, swinish life in the north.

BELFOND SENIOR. My father kept me in ignorance, and would have made a very silly blockheadly put of me. Why, I never heard a gentleman banter, or cut a sham in my life before I saw you, nor ever heard such ingenious discourse.

HACKUM. Nay, the world knows Mr. Cheatly and Mr. Shamwell are as complete gentlemen as ever came within the Friars. And yet we have as fine gentlemen as any in England; we have those here who have broke for £10,000.

BELFOND SENIOR. Well, I protest and vow I am so very fine, I do not know where to look upon myself first; I don't think my lord mayor's son is finer.

CHEATLY. He is a scoundrel compared to thee. There's not a prig at court out-shines thee. Thou shalt strut in the Park, where countesses shall be enamored on thee.

BELFOND SENIOR. I am overjoyed. I can stand no ground! My dear friend Cheatly! My sweet cousin Shamwell! Let me embrace such dear, such loving friends! I could grow to you, methinks, and stick here forever.

(*They embrace*)

LOLPOOP. Ah! Dear, loving dogs! They love him, by'r lady, as a cat loves a mause.

BELFOND SENIOR. What's that you mutter, sirrah? Come hither, sirrah! You are finer than any squire in the country.

LOLPOOP. Pox of finery, I say! Yeow maken a meer ass, an owl o' me. Here are sleeves fit for nought but a miller to steal with when he takes toll;[3] and damned cuffs here, one can not dip one's meat i'th' sauce for them. Ods-flesh, give me my awd clothes again. Would I were a whome in my frock, dressing of my geldings. Poor tits, they wanten me dearly, I warrant a.

BELFOND SENIOR. Well, there's no making a whistle of a pig's tail. This puppy will never learn any breeding. Sirrah, behold me: here's

[2] Mad.
[3] I.e., when he steals grain by concealing it or by falsifying the weight.

a rigging [1] for you. Here's a nab.[2] You never saw such a one in your life.

CHEATLY. A rum[3] nab. It is a beaver of £5.

BELFOND SENIOR. Look you there, blockhead.

LOLPOOP. (*Aside*) Look yeow there, blockhead, I say.

HACKUM. Let me see your porker. Here's a porker! Here's a titler![4] Ha, ha! Oh, how I could whop a prigster through the lungs! Ha, ha! (*Thrusts at* LOLPOOP)

CHEATLY. It cost sixteen louis d'ors[5] in Paris.

HACKUM. Ha, ha!

(*He pushes towards* LOLPOOP)

LOLPOOP. Hawd you, hawd you! And I take kibbo,[6] I'st raddle[7] the bones o' thee, I'se tell a that, for aw th'art a captain mun.

BELFOND SENIOR. Look, sirrah, here's a show, you rogue. Here's a sight of cole, darby, the ready, and the rhino. You rascal, you understand me not! You loggerhead, you silly put, you understand me not! Here are megs and smelts. I ne'er had such a sight of my own in my life. Here are more megs and smelts, you rogue; you understand me not.

LOLPOOP. By'r lady, not I. I understand not this south-country speech, not I.

BELFOND SENIOR. Ah, methinks I could tumble in 'em. But d'ee hear, put, put, put, sirrah. Here's a scout.[8] What's o'clock? What's o'clock, sirrah? Here's a tatler:[9] gold, gold, you rogue. Look on my finger, sirrah, look here: here's a famble,[10] put, put. You don't know what a famble, a scout, or a tatler is, you put.

LOLPOOP. Fine sights for my awd master. Marry, would I were sent from constable to constable, and whipped home again, by'r lady!

BELFOND SENIOR. Let's whet.[11] Bring some wine. Come on, I love a whet. Pray let's huzza; I love huzzaing mightily. But where's your lady, Captain, and the blowen that is to be my natural, my convenient, my pure.

Enter Servants *with bottles*

HACKUM. They're just coming in. Come, Betty.

Enter MRS. HACKUM *and* MRS. MARGARET

MRS. HACKUM. Come in, Mrs. Margaret, come.

MARGARET. I am so ashamed.

BELFOND SENIOR. Madam, your servant. I am very much obliged to your favors.

MRS. HACKUM. I shall be proud to do a gentleman like you any service that lies in my power as a gentlewoman.

BELFOND SENIOR. O Lord, madam, your most humble servant to command. My pretty blowen, let me kiss thee. Thou shalt be my natural. I must rummage thee. She is a pure blowen. My pretty rogue—how happy shall I be? Pox o' the country, I say. Madam Hackum, to testify my gratitude, I make bold to equip you with some megs, smelts, decus's,[12] and Georges.[13]

MRS. HACKUM. I am your faithful servant, and I shall be glad of any occasion whereby to express how ready I am to serve any gentleman or person of quality as becomes a gentlewoman; and upon honor, sir, you shall never find me tardy.

CHEATLY. Come on, sirrah, fill up all the glasses; a health to this pretty lady.

BELFOND SENIOR. Ay, and, i'faith, I'll drink it, pretty rogue.

SHAMWELL. Let them be facers.

BELFOND SENIOR. Facers! What are those? Nay, give the lady and the Captain's lady, too.

MARGARET. No, I can not drink, I am not dry.

MRS. HACKUM. Give it me.

SHAMWELL. There's a facer for you.

(*Drinks the glass clear off, and puts it to his face. All do the like*)

BELFOND SENIOR. Excellent, adad! Come to our facers. It is the prettiest way of drinking! Fill again, we'll have more facers.

(*Fiddles flourish without*)

Ha, boys! The musicians are come. Ha, boys, we'll sing, dance, roar, fling the house out of the windows; and I will manage my pretty natural, my pure blowen here. Huzza! My dear friends Shamwell and Cheatly, I am transported! My pretty natural, kiss me, kiss me! Huzza!

---

[1] Clothes.
[2] Beaver hat.
[3] Good.
[4] Sword.
[5] Gold coins worth about 17s. each.
[6] Cudgel.
[7] Twist.
[8] Watch.
[9] Watch with a striking alarm.
[10] Ring.
[11] Wet our throats.
[12] Crownpiece.
[13] Half-crown.

MARGARET. Nay, pooh, you do so ruffle one's things.

BELFOND SENIOR. I'll ruffle thee more, my little rogue, before I have done with thee. Well, I shall never make you amends, my dear friends. Sirrah, Lolpoop, is not this better than the country, sirrah? Give the rogue a facer to my mistress. Come, fill about the facers. Come on, my lads, stand to't. Huzza! I vow 'tis the prettiest way of drinking, never stir.

Enter four Servants *with four dishes of meat, who cross the stage*

CHEATLY. So here's the prog,[1] here's the dinner coming up. The cloth's laid in the next room. Here's a noble dinner!

BELFOND SENIOR. Ha, boys, we'll sing and roar and huzza like devils.

Enter SIR WILLIAM BELFOND *at the door*

Ounds! Who's here? My father! Lolpoop, Lolpoop, hide me! Give me my Joseph.[2] Let's sneak into the next room.[3]

SHAMWELL. Death! What shall we do? This is the bully's father.

CHEATLY. Let me alone: I warrant you.

HACKUM. This is the old fellow I had like to have had a rubbers[4] with in the morning.

SIR WILLIAM. Is he fallen into these hands? Nay, then, he's utterly lost; his estate is spent before he has it.

CHEATLY. How now, prig, what makes you come into our room?

SIR WILLIAM. I would speak with Squire Belfond.

CHEATLY. Here's no such man.

SIR WILLIAM. Oh, bully, are you there, and my ungracious kinsman, too? Would you bring my son to the gallows! you most notorious seducer of young heirs, I know you, too. I warrant you I'll keep my dear boy in the country far enough from your clutches. In short, I would speak with my rebellious townson, who is here, and bespoke this great dinner.

CHEATLY. (*Bantering*) Why, look you, sir, according to your assertion of things, doubtful in themselves, you must be forced to grant that whatsoever may be, may also as well not be, in their own essential differences and degrees.

SIR WILLIAM. What stuff's this? Where's my son?

CHEATLY. Your question consists of two terms: the one, *ubi*, where; but of that I shall say nothing, because here is no son nor any thing belonging to you, to be the subject of debate at this time; forasmuch as—

SIR WILLIAM. Do you hear me, sir, let me see my son; and offer to banter me, or sham me once more, and I will cut your throat, and cudgel your brace of cowards.

CHEATLY. Nay, then, 'tis time to take a course with you. Help, help! An arrest, an arrest—a baily, a baily!

HACKUM AND SHAMWELL. An arrest, an arrest!

SIR WILLIAM. You dogs! Am I a baily?

CHEATLY. You shall be used like one, you old prig. An arrest!

SIR WILLIAM. Impudent dogs! I must run, or I shall be pulled in pieces. Help, help, an arrest! An arrest!

(*All cry out*, An arrest! *Drawers and some of the rabble come in and join with the cry, which gets into the street; there they cry out, too. He joins the cry, and runs away.* CHEATLY, SHAMWELL, HACKUM, *Drawers follow him, and cry out:* Stop, stop, a baily!)

CHEATLY, SHAMWELL, HACKUM. (*In the street*) Stop, stop, a baily, a baily!

(SIR WILLIAM *runs; the rabble pursue him* [*a*]*cross the stage*)

ACT III

SCENE I. [*Street in front of* SIR EDWARD'S *house*]

Enter MRS. TERMAGANT *and her* Brother

TERMAGANT. As I told you, I have had a child by him; he is my husband by contract, and casts me off; has dishonored me, and made me infamous. Shall you think to game and bully about the town, and not vindicate the honor of your family?

BROTHER. No man shall dare to dishonor our family.

Enter BELFOND JUNIOR

TERMAGANT. If you do not cut his throat, you'll be kicked up and down for a damned coward; and besides, you shall never see a penny of mine more.

---

[1] Meat.
[2] A large cloak.
[3] Belfond Senior and Lolpoop apparently *exeunt*, unseen by Sir William.
[4] Trouble.

BROTHER. I'll fight him, as he be above ground.

TERMAGANT. There, there's the traitor walking before his uncle's door. Be sure, dispatch him; on, I'll withdraw. *Exit*

BROTHER. Do you hear, sir, do you know Mrs. Termagant?

BELFOND JUNIOR. What makes you ask such a familiar question, sir?

BROTHER. I am her brother.

BELFOND JUNIOR. Perhaps so. Well, I do. What then, sir?

BROTHER. Ours is an ancient family as any in England, tho' perhaps unfortunate at present. The Termagants came in with the Conqueror.

BELFOND JUNIOR. It may be so; I am no herald.

BROTHER. And do you think you shall dishonor this family, and debauch my sister, unchastized? You are contracted to her, and have lain with her.

BELFOND JUNIOR. Look you, sir, I see what you would be at; she's mad, and puts you upon this. Let me advise you, 'tis a foolish quarrel.

BROTHER. You debauched her, and have ruined her.

BELFOND JUNIOR. 'Tis false; the silliest coxcombly beau in town had the first of her.

BROTHER. You had a child by her.

BELFOND JUNIOR. Then I have added one to your ancient family that came in with the Normans. Prithee, do not provoke me to take away one from it.

BROTHER. You are contracted to her, and if you will marry her, I will save your life.

BELFOND JUNIOR. 'Tis a lie. I am not contracted to her. Begone, urge me no more.

BROTHER. Draw.

BELFOND JUNIOR. Have at you.

Enter SIR EDWARD BELFOND

SIR EDWARD. Hold! Hold! (BELFOND *strikes up* [*the Brother's*] *heels and disarms him*) Oh, my son, my son! What's the matter? My dear son, art thou not hurt? Let me see.

BELFOND JUNIOR. No, sir, not at all, dear sir. Here, take your sword and begone. Next time you come to trouble me, I'll cut your throat. *Exit* BROTHER

SIR EDWARD. What's the matter, dear Ned? This is about some wench, I warrant.

BELFOND JUNIOR. 'Tis a brother of that furious wench you saw, sir; her violent love is converted into hatred.

SIR EDWARD. You young fellows will never get knowledge but at your own cost. The precepts of the old weigh nothing with you.

BELFOND JUNIOR. Your precepts have ever been sacred to me; and so shall your example be henceforward. You are the best of men, the best of fathers. I have as much honor for you as I can have for human nature, and I love you ten thousand times above my life.

SIR EDWARD. Dear Ned, thou art the greatest joy I have. And believe thy father and thy friend, there's nothing but anxiety in vice. I am not straight-laced, but when I was young, I ne'er knew anything gotten by wenching but duels, claps, and bastards; and every drunken fit is a short madness that cuts off a good part of life.

BELFOND JUNIOR. You have reason,[1] sir, and shall ever be my oracle hereafter.

SIR EDWARD. 'Tis time now to take up, and think of being something in the world. See then, my son, tho' thou shouldst not be over busy to side with parties and with factions, yet that thou takest a care to make some figure in the world, and to sustain that part thy fortune, nature, and education fit thee for.

BELFOND JUNIOR. Your wise advice I'll strive to follow. But I must confess, I am most passionately in love, and am, with your consent, resolved to marry, tho' I will perish ere I do without it.

SIR EDWARD. Be sure to know the humor of the woman; you run a mighty hazard. But if you be valiant enough to venture (which, I must confess, I never was), I'll leave it to your own choice. I know you have so much honor, you will do nothing below your self.

BELFOND JUNIOR. I doubt not of your approbation, but till I can be sure of obtaining her, pardon me if I conceal her name.

Enter SIR WILLIAM BELFOND

SIR EDWARD. Your father comes. Retire a little within hearing till I soften him somewhat. He is much moved, as he always is, I think. ([BELFOND JUNIOR] *retires*)

SIR WILLIAM. Now, brother, as I was saying, I can convince you, your son, your darling, whom you long have fostered in his wickedness, is become the most profligate of all rascals.

[1] *Vous avez raison*—you are right.

Sir Edward. Still upon this subject.

Sir William. 'Tis very well. My mouth must be stopped, and your ears. 'Tis wondrous well. But I have had much ado to escape with life from him and his notorious fellow rogues. As I told you, when I had found that the rogue was with his wicked associates at the "George" in Whitefriars, when they saw I was resolved to see my son, and was rough with 'em, Cheatly and his rogues set up a cry against me: "An arrest! a baily! an arrest!" The mobile and all the rakehells in the house and thereabout the streets assembled; I run, and they had a fair course after me into Fleet Street. Thanks to the vigor I have left, my heels have saved my life. Your infamous rogue would have suffered me to have been sacrificed to the rabble.

Sir Edward. Ha, ha, ha, very pretty, i' faith! It runs very well. Can you tell it over again, think you?

Sir William. Ounds! Am I become your scorn? Your laughter?

BELFOND JUNIOR *appears*

Sir Edward. Ned, you hear all this?

Belfond Junior. Yes, and am distracted to know the meaning of it.

Sir William. Vile parricide! Are you gotten here before me? You are monstrous nimble, sir.

Belfond Junior. By all the powers of heaven! I never was at the "George" in my life.

Sir William. Oh, then they stay for you, you have not yet been there. You'll lose your dinner, 'tis served up—vile wretch!

Belfond Junior. All this is cross purposes to me. I came to my uncle's house from my own lodgings immediately, when you were pleased to banish me your presence, and here have been ever since.

Sir William. Nay, he that will be a thorough villain must be a complete liar. Were not you even now with your associates—rascals at the "George"?

Belfond Junior. No, by heaven! Nor was I ever in the company of any of that gang. I know their infamy too well to be acquainted with their persons.

Sir William. I am not drunk, nor mad; but you will make me one of them.

Belfond Junior. These rascals have gotten somebody to personate me, and are undoubtedly carrying on some cheat in my name.

Sir Edward. Brother, it must be.

Sir William. Yes, yes, no doubt it must be so; and I must be in a dream all this while, I must.

Sir Edward. You say yourself you did not see my son there.

Sir William. No, he was too nimble for me, and got out some back way, to be here before me, so to face down the truth.

Belfond Junior. I'll instantly go thither and discover this imposture that I may suffer no longer for the faults of others.

Sir Edward. Dine first. My dinner's ready.

Belfond Junior. Your pardon, sir, I will go instantly. I can not rest till I have done myself right.

Sir Edward. Let's in and discourse of this matter. Brother, I must say this, I never took him in a lie since he could speak.

Sir William. Took him! no, nor never will take him in anything.

Sir Edward. Let's in—and send your own man with him.

Sir William. It shall be so, though I am convinced already. Is there any of thy name but you, and I, and my two sons, in England?

Belfond Junior. Be pleased to send my footman out to me, sir.

Sir Edward. Have a care of a quarrel, and bringing the Alsatians about your ears. Come, brother.

Exeunt Sir Edward *and* Sir William

Enter Lucia *running,* Termagant *pursuing her*

Lucia. Help, help, help!

Termagant. Now I have found you, you little whore, I'll make you an example!

Lucia. Oh, Lord! are you here! Save me, save me! This barbarous woman threatens to murder me for your sake.

Belfond Junior. Save thee, dear miss![1] That I would at the peril of my life. No danger should make me quit thee, cannons, nor bombs.

Termagant. Damned false fellow! I'll take a time to slit her nose.

Lucia. Oh, heaven! she'll kill me.

Belfond Junior. Thou devil, in thy properest shape of furious and malicious woman! Resolve to leave off this course this moment, or, by heaven! I'll lay thee fast in Bedlam.[2]

[1] Used only for young girls.
[2] Bethlehem Hospital, where lunatics were confined.

Had'st thou fifty brothers, I'd fight with them all, in defence of this dear, pretty miss.

LUCIA. Dear, kind creature! This sweet love of thine, methinks, does make me valiant, and I fear her not so much.

Enter ROGER *and his two* Footmen.

BELFOND JUNIOR. Dear, pretty miss, I'll be thy safeguard.

TERMAGANT. Thou falsest, basest of thy sex, look to see thy child sent thee in pieces, baked in a pie, for so I will.

BELFOND JUNIOR. Though thou hat'st every thing living besides thyself, yet thou has too much tenderness for thy own person to bring it to the gallows. Offer to follow us one step, and I'll set the rabble upon thee. Come, my dear child.

Exeunt [all but TERMAGANT]

TERMAGANT. Thou shalt be dogged, and I'll know who she is. Oh, revenge, revenge! If thou dost not exceed, thou equall'st all the ecstasies of love! *Exit* TERMAGANT

[SCENE II. *Room in the "George" Tavern*]

Enter CHEATLY *and* SHAMWELL

CHEATLY. Thus far our matters go swimmingly. Our squire is debauched and prodigal as we can wish.

SHAMWELL. I told you all England could not afford an heir like this for our purpose, but we must keep him always hot.

CHEATLY. That will be easy. We made him so devilish drunk the first two or three days, the least bumper will warm his addle head afresh at any time. He paid a great fine, and may sit at a little rent. I must be gone for a moment. Our Suffolk heir is nabbed for a small business, and I must find him some sham bail. See the Captain performs his charge. *Exit*

Enter HACKUM

SHAMWELL. Here he comes. See, Captain, you make that blockhead drunk, and do as we directed.

HACKUM. He's almost drunk, and we are in readiness for him. The squire is retired with his natural, so fond.

SHAMWELL. 'Tis well. About your business —I'll be with you soon. *Exit* SHAMWELL

Enter LOLPOOP

HACKUM. Come on, Mr. Lolpoop. You and I'll be merry by ourselves.

LOLPOOP. I must needs say, Captain, yeow are a civil gentleman, but yeow han given me so many bumpers, I am meet [1] drunken already.

HACKUM. Come on, I warrant you. Here's a bumper to the squire's lady.

LOLPOOP. With all my heart.

Enter BETTY

HACKUM. Oh, Mrs. Betty, art thou come? I sent for this pretty rogue to keep you company. She's as pretty a company-keeper as any in the Friars.

LOLPOOP. Odsflesh, what should I do in company with gentlewoman? 'Tis not for such fellees as I.

HACKUM. Have courage, man. You shall have her, and never want such a one while I am your friend.

LOLPOOP. O Lord, I? Do yeow know what yeow saen?

BETTY. A proper, handsome gentleman, I swear.

LOLPOOP. Who, I? No, no. What done yeow mean, forsooth?

BETTY. I vow I have not seen a handsomer. So proper! So well shaped!

LOLPOOP. Oh, Lord, I? I! Yeow jeern me naw.

HACKUM. Why don't you salute her, man?

LOLPOOP. Who—I? By the mass, I dare not be so bold. What! I kiss such a fine gentlewoman!

HACKUM. Kiss—kiss her, man! This town affords us such everywhere! You'll hate the country when you see a little more. Kiss her, I say.

LOLPOOP. I am so hala.[2] I am ashamed.

BETTY. What! Must I do it to you, then?

LOLPOOP. Oh, rare! By th' mass! Whoo kisses daintily? And whoo has a breath like a caw?

HACKUM. Come, t'other bumper. To her health let his be. Here's to you!

LOLPOOP. Thanks, forsooth, and yeow pleasen. (*Drinks to her*)

BETTY. Yes, anything that you do will please me.

(HACKUM *steals out and leaves them together*)

LOLPOOP. Captain! Captain! What, done yeow leave me?

BETTY. What! Are you afraid of me?

[1] Sufficiently.
[2] Lean

LOLPOOP. Nay, by'r lady. I am ashamed, who's farinely[1] a pratty lass! Marry!

BETTY. A handsome man, and ashamed!
(*She edges nearer to him*)

LOLPOOP. Who, I? A handsome man? Nay, nay!

BETTY. A lovely man, I vow. I can not forbear kissing you.

LOLPOOP. O dear! 'Tis your goodness. Odsflesh, whoo loves me! who'll make me stark wood e'en naw! And yeow kissen me, by'r lady, I's kiss yeow.

BETTY. What care I?

LOLPOOP. Looka there naw. Waunds,[2] whoo's a dainty lass, pure white and red! And most of the London lasses are pure white and red. Welly aw like; and I had her in some nook—. Odsflesh, I say no more.

BETTY. I'll stay no longer. Farewell.
(*She retires*)

LOLPOOP. Nay, I's not leave a soo. Marry, whoo's a gallant lass! (*Exit, following her*)

Enter HACKUM

HACKUM. So, he's caught. This will take him off from teasing his master with his damned good counsel.

Enter CHEATLY *and* SHAMWELL

CHEATLY. I have seen our Alsatian attorney, and as substantial bail as can be wished for the redemption of our Suffolk caravan. He's ripe for another judgment; he begins to want the ready much.

SHAMWELL. Scrapeall is provided for him. How now, Captain, what's become of your blockhead?

HACKUM. He's nibbling at the bait; he'll swallow presently.

CHEATLY. But hark you, Shamwell. I have chosen the subtlest and handsomest wench about this town for the great fortune I intend to bestow this hopeful kinsman of yours upon. 'Tis Mrs. Termagant, his brother's cast mistress, who resents her being left to that degree that, tho' she meditates all the revenge besides that woman's nature is capable of against him, yet her heart leapt for joy at this design of marrying his elder brother. If it were for nothing but to plague the younger, and take place of his wife.

SHAMWELL. I have seen her. She will personate a town lady of quality admirably, and be as haughty and impertinent as the best of 'em. Is the lodging, and plate, and things ready for her?

CHEATLY. It is. She comes there this afternoon. She has set her hand to a good, swinging judgment; and thou and I will divide, my lad. And now all we have to do is to preserve him to ourselves from any other correspondence, and at downright enmity with his father and brother; and we must keep him continually hot, as they do in a glass-house,[3] or our work will go backward.

Enter BELFOND SENIOR, MRS. MARGARET, MRS. HACKUM, *and his* Servants

BELFOND SENIOR. Oh, my dear friend and cousin, tread upon my neck; make me your footstool! You have made me a happy man to know plenty and pleasure, good company, good wine, music, fine women. Mrs. Hackum and I have been at bumpers, hand to fist. Here's my pretty natural, my dear, pretty rogue! Adad, she's a rare creature, a delicious creature! And between you and I, dear friend, she has all her goings as well as e'er a blowen in Christendom. Dear Madam Hackum, I am infinitely obliged to you.

MRS. HACKUM. I am glad, sir, she gives your worship content, sir.

BELFOND SENIOR. Content! Ah, my pretty rogue! Pox o' the country, I say, Captain. Captain—here, let me equip you with a quid.[4]

HACKUM. Noble squire, I am your spaniel dog.

BELFOND SENIOR. Pox o' the country, I say! The best team of horses my father has shall not draw me thither again.

SHAMWELL. Be firm to your resolution, and thou'lt be happy.

CHEATLY. If you meet either your father or brother or any from those prigsters, stick up thy countenance, or thou art ruined, my son of promise, my brisk lad in remainder.[5] When one of 'em approaches thee, we'll all pull down our hats and cry bow wow.

BELFOND SENIOR. I warrant you, I am hardened. I knew my brother in the country, but they shan't sham me; they shall find me a smokey[6] thief. I vow 'twill be a very pretty way. "Bow wow"—I warrant thee, I'll do it.

---

[1] Very.
[2] Wounds—i.e., by God's wounds.
[3] Hot-house.
[4] Guinea.
[5] In expectancy of an estate.
[6] Jealous.

Enter BELFOND JUNIOR, *two* Footmen, *and* ROGER

SHAMWELL. Who the devil's here? Your brother! Courage!

CHEATLY. Courage! Be rough and haughty, my bumpkin.

BELFOND SENIOR. Hey, where are all my servants? Call 'em in. (*Captain calls them*)

BELFOND JUNIOR. Who is that in this house here who usurps my name, and is called Squire Belfond?

BELFOND SENIOR. One who is called so without usurping. Bow wow!

BELFOND JUNIOR. Brother! Death! Do I dream? Can I trust my senses? Is this my brother?

BELFOND SENIOR. Ay, ay, I know I am transmogrified,[1] but I am your very brother, Ned.

BELFOND JUNIOR. Could you be so unkind to come to town and not see your nearest kindred, your uncle, and myself?

BELFOND SENIOR. I would not come to disgrace you, till my equipage was all ready. Hey, La Mar, is my coach at the gate next to the "Green Dragon"?

VALET. *Oui, Monsieur.*

BELFOND SENIOR. But I was resolved to give you a visit tomorrow morning.

BELFOND JUNIOR. I should have been glad to have seen you anywhere but here.

BELFOND SENIOR. But here! Why, 'tis as good a tavern as any's in town. Sirrah, fill some bumpers. Here, brother, here's a facer to you. We'll huzza. Call in the fiddlers.

BELFOND JUNIOR, I am struck with astonishment. Not all Ovid's *Metamorphosis*[2] can show such a one as this.

BELFOND SENIOR. I see you wonder at my change. What, would you never have a man learn breeding, adad? Should I always be kept a country bubble,[3] a caravan, a mere put? I am brave and boozy.

BELFOND JUNIOR. 'Slife! He has gotten the cant, too.

BELFOND SENIOR. I shall be clear by and by. T'other bumper, brother.

BELFOND JUNIOR. No, I'll drink no more. I hate drinking between meals.

BELFOND SENIOR. Oh, Lord! Oh, Lord! hate drinking between meals! What company do you keep? But 'tis all one. Here, brother, pray salute this pretty rogue. I manage her, she is my natural, my pure blowen. I am resolved to be like a gentleman, and keep, brother.

BELFOND JUNIOR. (*Aside*) A thorough-paced Whitefriars man!—I never refuse to kiss a pretty woman. (*Salutes her*)

BELFOND SENIOR. This is Mrs. Hackum. I am obliged to her. Pray salute her.

BELFOND JUNIOR. What a pox! Will he make me kiss the bawd, too?

BELFOND SENIOR. Brother, now pray know these gentlemen here; they are the prettiest wits that are in the town, and between you and I, brother, brave, gallant fellows, and the best friends I ever had in my life. This is Mr. Cheatly, and this is my cousin Shamwell.

BELFOND JUNIOR. I know 'em, and am acquainted with their worth.

CHEATLY. Your humble servant, sweet sir.

SHAMWELL. Your servant, cousin.

BELFOND SENIOR. And this is my dear friend, Captain Hackum. There is not a braver fellow under the sun.

BELFOND JUNIOR. By heaven, a downright Alsatian.

BELFOND SENIOR. Come, musicians, strike up; and sing the catch[4] the Captain gave you, and we'll all join, i'faith. We can be merry, brother, and can roar!

HACKUM. 'Tis a very pretty, magnanimous military business upon the victory in Hungary.[5]

Hark, how the Duke of Lorraine comes,
    The brave, victorious soul of war,
With trumpets and with kettle drums
    Like thunder rolling from afar.

On the left wing the conquering horse
    The brave Bavarian Duke does lead;
These heroes with united force
    Fill all the Turkish host with dread.

Their bright caparisons behold;
    Rich habits, streamers, shining arms,
The glittering steel and burnished gold,
    The pomp of war with all its charms.

---

[1] New vamped—London thieves' slang.
[2] Ovid's *Metamorphosis* is a collection of stories of remarkable transformations and changes collected from mythology.
[3] Naive person, fit to be cheated.
[4] A "round" for various voices.
[5] The Turkish army was defeated in Hungary by forces under the command of the Duke of Lorraine and the Elector of Bavaria in August, 1687.

    With solemn march and fatal pace
        They bravely on the foe press on;
    The cannons roar, the shot takes place,
        Whilst smoke and dust obscure the sun.

    The horses neigh, the soldiers shout,
        And now the furious bodies join,
    The slaughter rages all about,
        And men in groans their blood resign.

    The weapons clash, the roaring drum,
        With clangor of the trumpets sound,
    The howls and yells of men o'ercome,
        And from the neighboring hills rebound.

    Now, now the infidels give place,
        Then all in routs they headlong fly,
    Heroes in dust pursue the chase,
        While deaf'ning clamors rend the sky.

BELFOND SENIOR. You see, brother, what company I keep. What's the matter, you are melancholy?

BELFOND JUNIOR. I am not a little troubled, brother, to find you in such cursed company.

BELFOND SENIOR. Hold, brother, if you love your life. They are all stout; but that same Captain has killed his five men.

BELFOND JUNIOR. Stout, say you? This fellow Cheatly is the most notorious rascal and cheat that ever was out of a dungeon; this kinsman, a most silly bubble first, and afterwards, a betrayer of young heirs, of which they have not ruined less than two hundred, and made them run out their estates before they came to them.

BELFOND SENIOR. Brother, do you love your life? The Captain's a lion!

BELFOND JUNIOR. An ass, is he not? He is a ruffian, and cock-bawd to that hen.

CHEATLY. If you were not the brother to my dearest friend, I know what my honor would prompt me to.   (*Walks in a huff*)

SHAMWELL. My dear cousin, thou shalt now find how entirely I am thine. My honor will not let me strike thy brother.

HACKUM. But that the punctilios of honor are sacred to me, which tell me nothing can provoke me against the brother of my noble friend, I had whipped him through the lungs ere this.

BELFOND SENIOR. Well, never man met with such true, such loving friends.

BELFOND JUNIOR. Look you, brother, will this convince you that you are fallen into the hands of fools, knaves, scoundrels, and cowards?

BELFOND SENIOR. Fools! Nay, there I am sure you are out. They are all deep, they are very deep and sharp; sharp as needles, adad; the wittiest men in England. Here's Mr. Cheatly, in the first place, shall sham and banter with you or any one you shall bring for £500 of my money.

BELFOND JUNIOR. Rascally stuff, fit for no places but Ram Alley or Pie Corner.[1]

BELFOND SENIOR. Persuade me to that! They are the merriest companions, and the truest friends to me. 'Tis well for you, adad, that they are so so, for they are all of them as stout as Hector.[2]

BELFOND JUNIOR. This is most amazing.

SHAMWELL. Did I not tell you he would envy your condition, and be very angry with us that put you into't?

CHEATLY. He must needs be a kind brother. We prove ourselves your true friends, and have that respect for your blood that we will let none of it out, where'er we meet it upon any cause.

BELFOND SENIOR. You see, brother, how their love prevails over their valor.

BELFOND JUNIOR. Their valor! Look you, brother, here's valor.

    (*Kicks* CHEATLY *and* SHAMWELL)

CHEATLY. I understand honor and breeding; besides, I have been let blood today.

SHAMWELL. Nothing shall make me transgress the rules of honor, I say.

BELFOND JUNIOR. Here! Where are you, sirrah kill-cow?

    (*Takes* HACKUM *by the nose and leads him*)

HACKUM. 'Tis no matter; I know honor; I know punctilios to a hair. You owe your life to your brother. Besides, I am to be second to a dear friend, and preserve my vigor for his service; but for all that, were he not your brother—

BELFOND JUNIOR. Will not this convince you, brother, of their cowardice?

BELFOND SENIOR. No, I think not, for I am sure they are valiant. This convinces me of their respect and friendship to me. My best friends, let me embrace you. A thousand thanks to you.

BELFOND JUNIOR. [*Aside*] I will redeem him yet from these rascals, if I can.—You are upon the brink of ruin if you go not off with me, and reconcile yourself to my father. I'll undertake it upon good terms.

---

[1] Places within the bounds of Whitefriars.
[2] Here a type of bully. Cf. *hectoring*, Act IV, scene i.

BELFOND SENIOR. No, I thank you. I'll see no father; he shall use me no more like a dog; he shall put upon me no longer. Look you, sir, I have ready, rhino, cole, darby—look here, sir.

BELFOND JUNIOR. Dear brother, let me persuade you to go along with me.

BELFOND SENIOR. You love me! and use my best friends thus? Ne'er stir, I desire none of your company. I'll stick to my friends. I look upon what you have done as an affront to me.

HACKUM. No doubt it is so.

SHAMWELL. That's most certain. You are in the right, cousin.

CHEATLY. We love you but too well—that angers him.

BELFOND JUNIOR. Well, I shall take my leave. You are in your cups. You will wish you had heard me. Rogues, I shall take a course with you.

BELFOND SENIOR. Rogues! They scorn your words.

BELFOND JUNIOR. Fare you well.

BELFOND SENIOR. Fare you well, sir, and you be at that sport.

BELFOND JUNIOR. Roger, do not discover him to my father yet; I'll talk with him cool in a morning first. Perhaps I may redeem him.

ROGER. I'll do it as you would have me.

Exeunt BELFOND JUNIOR, ROGER, *and two* Footmen

BELFOND SENIOR. So now we are free. Dear friends, I never can be grateful enough. But 'tis late; I must show my new coach. Come, ladies. *Exeunt*

[SCENE III. *A street*]

Enter Attorney *and* LUCIA

ATTORNEY. How now, daughter Lucia! Where hast thou been?

LUCIA. I have been at evening prayers at St. Bride's,[1] and am going home through the Temple.

ATTORNEY. Thou art my good girl.

Enter MRS. TERMAGANT

LUCIA. Oh, heaven! Who's here!

ATTORNEY. What's the matter?

LUCIA. I am taken ill on a sudden. I'll run home.

[1] A church in Fleet Street.

TERMAGANT. Stay, stay, thou wicked author of my misfortune.

ATTORNEY. How's this? Stay, Lucia! What mean you, madam? The girl's strangely disordered.

LUCIA. Oh, heaven! I am utterly ruined—beyond redemption.

TERMAGANT. Is she your daughter, sir?

ATTORNEY. She is.

TERMAGANT. Then hear my story. I am contracted with all the solemnity that can be, to Mr. Belfond, the merchant's son; and for this wicked girl he has lately cast me off. And this morning I went to his lodging to inquire a reason for his late carriage to me. I found there in his closet this young, shameless creature, who has been in bed with him.

ATTORNEY. Oh, heaven and earth! Is this true, huswife?

LUCIA. Oh, Lord I—I never saw the gentleman nor her in my life. Oh, she's a confident thing!

TERMAGANT. May all the judgments due to perjury fall on me, if this be not true! I tore her by the hair, and pomelled her to some tune,[2] till that inhuman wretch, Belfond, turned me out of doors, and sent her away in a chair.

LUCIA. O wicked creature! Are you not afraid the earth should open and swallow you up? As I hope to be saved, I never saw her!

TERMAGANT. Though young in years, yet old in impudence! Did I not pursue thee since, in the street, till you run into Belfond's arms just before his father's house? Or I had marked thee for a young whore.

LUCIA. As I hope to live, sir, 'tis all false, every word and tittle of it. I know not what she means.

ATTORNEY. Have I bestowed so much, and taken so much care in thy education, to have no other fruit but this?

LUCIA. Oh, Lord, sir! Why will you believe this wicked woman?

ATTORNEY. No, young impudence! I believe you? What made you ready to swoon at the sight of this lady, but your guilt?

LUCIA. She mistakes me for some other, as she did today, when she pursued me to have killed me, which made me tremble at the sight of her now.

ATTORNEY. And yet you never saw her before! I am convinced. Go, wicked wretch,

[2] To a considerable extent.

go home. This news will kill thy mother. I'll to my chamber, and follow thee.

LUCIA. But if I ever see her, or you either, to be locked from my dear Belfond, I shall deserve whatever you can to me. *Exit*

ATTORNEY. Madam, I beseech you, make as few words as you can of this.

TERMAGANT. I had much rather for my own honor have concealed it. But I shall say no more, provided you will keep her from him.

ATTORNEY. I warrant you, madam, I'll take a course with her. Your servant. *Exit*

Enter CHEATLY

CHEATLY. Madam, your most humble servant. You see I am punctual to my word.

TERMAGANT. You are, sir.

CHEATLY. Come, madam, your lodging, furniture, and everything are ready. Let's lose no time. I'll wait on you thither, where we will consult about our affairs.

TERMAGANT. Come on. It is a rare design, and if it succeeds, I shall sufficiently be revenged on my ungrateful devil.

CHEATLY. I warrant the success. *Exeunt*

[SCENE IV. *A room in* SCRAPEALL'S *house*]

Enter ISABELLA *and* TERESIA

ISABELLA. We must be very careful of this book. My uncle, or our dame governante, will burn it if they find it.

TERESIA. We can not have a pleasant or a witty book, but they serve it so. My father loads us with books such as *The Trial of Man in the Isle of Man, or Manshire; A Treatise on Sabbath-breakers;* and *Health out-drinking, or Life out-healthing Wretches; A Caustick, or Corrosive, for a Seared Conscience.*

ISABELLA. *A Sovereign Ointment for a Wounded Soul; A Cordial for a Sick Sinner; The Nothingness of Good Works; Waxed Boot-Grace for the Sussex Ways of Affliction;* and deal of such stuff. But all novels, romances, or poetry except Quarles and Withers [1] are an abomination. Well, this is a jewel if we can keep it.

Enter RUTH *behind them*

Anger, in hasty words or blows
Itself discharges on our foes;
And sorrow too finds some relief
In tears which wait upon our grief:
Thus every passion but fond love
Unto its own redress does move.

TERESIA. 'Tis sweet poetry. There is a pleasing charm in all he writes.

RUTH. (*She snatches the book*) Yea, there is a charm of Satan's in it. 'Tis vanity and darkness. This book hateth and is contrary to the light; and ye hate the light.

ISABELLA. That's much; and this evening, a little before night, thou blamed'st us for looking out of the window, and threatened to shut the painted sashes.

TERESIA. Now, if thou shut'st those, thou hat'st the light, and not we.

RUTH. Look thee, Teresia, thou art wanton, and so is thy cousin Isabella. Ye seek temptation; you look out of the casement to pick and cull young men, whereby to feed the lust of the eye. Ye may not do it. And look thee, Isbel, and Teresia, if you open the casements once more, I will place ye in the back rooms, and lock the fore rooms up.

TERESIA. We will obey thee, Ruth.

ISABELLA. We will not resist thy power, but prithee, leave us that book.

RUTH. No, it is wanton, and treateth of love. I will instantly commit it to the flames.
Exit

ISABELLA. Shame on this old wall-eyed hypocrite! She is the strictest sort of jailor.

TERESIA. We are as narrowly looked to as if we had been clapped up for treason. We are kept from books, pen, ink, and paper.

ISABELLA. Well, it is a most painful life, to dissemble constantly.

TERESIA. 'Tis well we are often alone, to unbend to one another; one had as good be a player, and act continually, else.

ISABELLA. I can never persuade myself that religion can consist in scurvy, out-of-fashion clothes, stiff constrained behavior, and sour countenances.

TERESIA. A tristful aspect, looking always upon one's nose, with a face full of spiritual pride.

ISABELLA. And when one walks abroad, not to turn one's head to the right or left, but hold it straight forward, like an old, blind mare.

TERESIA. True religion must make one cheerful, and effect one with the most ravishing joy—which must appear in the face, too.

---

[1] Francis Quarles (1592–1644) and George Withers (1588–1667) were regarded as Puritan poets.

ISABELLA. My good mother had the government and brought me up to better things, as thy good aunt did thee.

TERESIA. But we can make no use of our education under this tyranny.

ISABELLA. If we should sing or dance, 'twere worse than murder.

TERESIA. But of all things, why do they keep such a stir to keep us from the conversation of mankind? Sure, there must be more in it than we can imagine; and that makes one have a mind to try.

ISABELLA. Thou hast been so unquiet in thy sleep of late, and so given to sigh and get alone when thou art awake, I fancy thou dost imagine somewhat of it.

TERESIA. Ah, rogue, and I have observed the same in thee. Canst thou not guess at love? Come, confess, and I'll tell thee all.

ISABELLA. Sometimes in my dreams, methinks I am in love. Then a certain youth comes to me, and I grow chill, and pant, and feel a little pain. But 'tis the prettiest thing, methinks! And then I awake and blush, and am afraid.

TERESIA. Very pretty. And when I am awake, when I see one gentleman, methinks I could look through him, and my heart beats like the drums in the camp.

ISABELLA. I dare not ask who 'tis for fear it should be my man, for there are two come often to our church that stare at us continually, and one of them is he.

TERESIA. I have observed them; one who sat by us at church knew them by their names. I am for one of them, too.

ISABELLA. I well remember it.

TERESIA. If it be my man thou lik'st, I'll kill thee.

ISABELLA. And if thou lov'st my man, we must not live together.

TERESIA. Name him.

ISABELLA. Do thou name first.

TERESIA. Let's write their names.

ISABELLA. Agreed. We each have a black-lead pen.[1]

(*They write their papers and give them to one another, at which they both speak together, and start*)

TERESIA. Truman! Mercy on me!
ISABELLA. Belfond! Oh, heavens!

TERESIA. What's this I see? Would I were blind.

ISABELLA. Oh, my Teresia!

TERESIA. Get thee from me.

ISABELLA. 'Tis as it should be. I wrote the wrong name on purpose to discover who was your man more clearly; the other's my beloved; Belfond's my heart's delight.

TERESIA. Say'st thou so, my girl? Good wits jump.[2] I had the same thought with thee. Now 'tis out, Truman for me; and methinks they keep such a staring at us, if we contrive to meet them, we need not despair.

ISABELLA. Nay, they come not for devotion, that's certain; I see that in their eyes. Oh, that they were ordained to free us from this odious jail.

Enter RUTH *and* TRUMAN, *disguised*

RUTH. Go into your chamber. Here is a man cometh about business; ye may not see him.

TERESIA. We go. Come, cousin.

RUTH. Come, friend. Let us retire also.

Exeunt

ACT IV

SCENE I. [BELFOND JUNIOR'S *chambers*]

Enter BELFOND JUNIOR *and* LUCIA

LUCIA. I never more must see the face of a relation.

BELFOND JUNIOR. I warrant thee, my pretty rogue, I'll put thee into that condition, the best of all thy kindred shall visit thee and make their court to thee; thou shalt spark it in the boxes, shine at the Park, and make all the young fellows in the town run mad for thee. Thou shalt never want while I have anything.

LUCIA. I could abandon all the world for thee, if I could think that thou wouldst love me always.

BELFOND JUNIOR. Thou hast so kindly obliged me, I shall never cease to love thee.

LUCIA. Pray heaven I do not repent of it. You were kind to Mrs. Termagant, and sure it must be some barbarous usage which thus provokes her now to all this malice.

BELFOND JUNIOR. She was debauched by the most nauseous coxcomb, the most silly beau and shape about the town; and had cuckolded him with several before I had her. She was, indeed, handsome, but the most

---

[1] Pencil. [2] Tally.

froward, ill-natured creature, always murmuring or scolding, perpetually jealous and exceptious, ever thinking to work her ends by hectoring and daring.

LUCIA. Indeed! Was she such a one? I am sure you were the first that ever had my heart, and you shall be the last.

BELFOND JUNIOR. My dear, I know I had thy virgin heart and I'll preserve it. But for her, her most diverting minutes were unpleasant. Yet for all her malice, which you see, I still maintain her.

LUCIA. Ungrateful creature! She is, indeed, a fury. Should'st thou once take thy love from me, I never should use such ways; silently should mourn and pine away; but never think of once offending thee.

BELFOND JUNIOR. Thou art the prettiest, sweetest, softest creature! And all the tenderest joys that wait on love are ever with thee.

LUCIA. Oh, this is charming kindness! May all the joys on earth be still with thee.

BELFOND JUNIOR. (*Aside*) Now here's a mischief on the other side: for how can a good-natured man think of ever quitting so tender and so kind a mistress, whom no respect but love has thrown into my arms? And yet I must. But I will better her condition.—Oh, how does my friend?

Enter TRUMAN

LUCIA. Oh, Lord! Who's here?

BELFOND JUNIOR. My dear, go to the lodging I have prepared for thee; thou wilt be safe, and I'll wait on thee soon. Who's there?

Enter Servants

Do you wait on this lady's chair, you know whither. [*Exeunt* LUCIA *and* Servants]

TRUMAN. Thou art a pretty fellow, Belfond, to take thy pleasure thus, and put thy friend upon the damned'st drudgery.

BELFOND JUNIOR. What drudgery? A little dissembling?

TRUMAN. Why, that were bad enough, to dissemble myself an ass; but to dissemble love, nay, lust, is the more irksome task a man can undergo.

BELFOND JUNIOR. But prithee come to the point. In short, have we any hopes?

TRUMAN. 'Tis done; the business is done. Whip on your habit; make no words.

BELFOND JUNIOR. I'll put it on in my dressing-room. This news transports me.

TRUMAN. If you had undergone what I have done, 'twould have humbled you. I have enjoyed a lady; but I had as lief have had a Lancashire witch just after she had alighted from a broom-staff. I have been uncivil, and enjoyed the governante in most lewd dalliance.

BELFOND JUNIOR. Thou art a brave fellow, and makest nothing of it.

TRUMAN. Nothing? 'Sdeath, I had rather have stormed a half-moon,[1] I had more pleasure at the battle of Mons.[2]

BELFOND JUNIOR. But hast thou done our work, as well as hers?

TRUMAN. I have. For after the enjoyment of her person had led me into some familiarity with her, I proposed, she accepted, for she is covetous as well as amorous; and she has so far wrought for us that we shall have an interview with our mistresses, whom she says, we shall find very inclinable; and she has promised this night to deliver 'em into our hands.

BELFOND JUNIOR. Thou art a rare friend to me and to thyself. Now farewell, all the vanity of this lewd town. At once I quit it all. Dear rogue, let's in.

TRUMAN. Come in, in, and dress in your habit. *Exeunt*

[SCENE II. *Street*]

Enter SIR WILLIAM, SIR EDWARD, *and* SCRAPEALL

SCRAPEALL. Look you, Sir William, I am glad you like my niece; and I hope also that she may look lovely in your son's eyes.

SIR EDWARD. No doubt but he will be extremely taken with her. Indeed, both she and your daughter are very beautiful.

SIR WILLIAM. He like her! What's matter whether he like her, or no? Is it not enough for him that I do? Is a son, a boy, a jackanapes, to have a will of his own? That were to have him be the father, and me the son. But, indeed, they are both very handsome.

SCRAPEALL. Let me tell you both, Sir William, and Sir Edward, beauty is but vanity,

[1] A form of fortification.
[2] Fought by William III against Luxembourg in August, 1678.

a mere nothing; but they have that which will not fade: they have grace.

SIR EDWARD. (*Aside*) They look like pretty, spirited, witty girls.

SCRAPEALL. I am sorry I must leave ye so soon; I thought to have bidden ye to dinner. But I am to pay down a sum of money upon a mortgage this afternoon. Farewell.

SIR WILLIAM. Farewell, Mr. Scrapeall.

SIR EDWARD. Pray meet my brother at my house at dinner.

SCRAPEALL. Thank you, Sir Edward, I know not but I may.   [*Exit* SCRAPEALL]

SIR EDWARD. The person of this girl is well chosen for your son, if she were not so precise and pure.

SIR WILLIAM. Prithee, what matter what she is; has she not fifteen thousand pounds clear?

SIR EDWARD. For a husband to differ in religion from a wife—

SIR WILLIAM. What, with fifteen thousand pound?

SIR EDWARD. A precise wife will think herself so pure, she will be apt to condemn her husband.

SIR WILLIAM. Ay, but fifteen thousand pound, brother.

SIR EDWARD. You know how intractable misguided zeal and spiritual pride are.

SIR WILLIAM. What, with fifteen thousand pound!

SIR EDWARD. I would not willingly my son should have her.

SIR WILLIAM. Not with fifteen thousand pound?

SIR EDWARD. I see there's no answer to be given to fifteen thousand pound.

SIR WILLIAM. A pox o' this godly knave! It should have been twenty.

SIR EDWARD. Nor would I buy a wife for my son.

SIR WILLIAM. Not if you could have her a good pennyworth? Your son, quoth ye! He is like to make a fine husband. For all your precious son—

SIR EDWARD. Again, brother?

SIR WILLIAM. Look you, brother, you fly out so. Pray, brother, be not passionate; passion drowns one's parts; let us calmly reason; I have fresh matter; have but patience, and hear me speak.

SIR EDWARD. Well, brother, go on, for I see I might as soon stop a tide.

SIR WILLIAM. To be calm and patient: your jewel, though he denied that outrage in Dorset Court, yet he committed it, and was last night hurried before the Lord Chief Justice for it.

SIR EDWARD. It can not be, on my certain knowledge. (*Aside*) I could convince him, but it is not time.

SIR WILLIAM. What a devil! Are all the world mistaken but you?

SIR EDWARD. He was with me all the evening.

SIR WILLIAM. Why, he got bail immediately, and came to you. Ounds, I never saw such a man in my life!

SIR EDWARD. I am assured of the contrary.

SIR WILLIAM. Death and hell! You make me stark mad! You will send me to Bedlam— you will not believe your own senses! I'll hold you a thousand pound.

SIR EDWARD. Brother, remember passion drowns one's parts.

SIR WILLIAM. Well, I am tame, I am cool.

SIR EDWARD. I'll hold you a hundred, which is enough for one brother to win of another.

Enter Attorney

And here's your own attorney comes opportunely enough to hold stakes. I'll bind it with ten.

SIR WILLIAM. Done.

SIR EDWARD. Why, I saw your man Roger, and he says your son found there a rascal that went by his name.

ATTORNEY. Oh, Sir William, I am undone, ruined, made a miserable man!

SIR WILLIAM. What's the matter, man?

ATTORNEY. Though you have been an exceeding good client to me, I have reason to curse one of your family that has ruined mine.

SIR WILLIAM. Pray explain yourself.

ATTORNEY. Oh, sir, your wicked son, your most libidinous son!—

SIR WILLIAM. Look you, brother, d'ye hear? D'ye hear? Do you answer?

ATTORNEY.—has corrupted, debauched my only daughter, whom I had brought up with all the care and charge I could, who was the hopes, the joy of all our family.

SIR WILLIAM. Here's a son! Here's a rare son! Here's a hopeful son! And he were mine, I'd lash him with a dog-whip; I'd cool his courage.

SIR EDWARD. How do you know it is he?

ATTORNEY. I have a witness for it that saw her rise from his bed the other day morning, and last night she ran away to him, and they have lain at a private lodging.

SIR EDWARD. Be well assured ere you conclude, for there is a rascal that has taken my son's name, and has swaggered in and about Whitefriars with Cheatly and that gang of rogues, whom my son will take a course with.

ATTORNEY. Oh, sir, I am too well assured. My wife tears her hair, and I, for my part, shall run distracted.

SIR WILLIAM. Oh, wicked rascal! Oh, my poor Tim! my dear boy Tim! I think each day a year till I see thee.

SIR EDWARD. Sir, I am extremely sorry for this, if it be so; but let me beg of you, play the part of a wise man; blaze not this dishonor abroad, and you shall have all the reparation the case is capable of.

SIR WILLIAM. Reparation for making his daughter a whore? What a pox, can he give her her maidenhead again?

SIR EDWARD. Money shall not be wanting will stop that witness's mouth; and I will give your daughter such a fortune that, were what you believe true and publicly known, she should live above contempt as the world goes now.

ATTORNEY. You speak like the worthy gentleman the world thinks you, but there can be no salve for this sore.

SIR WILLIAM. Why, you are enough to damn forty sons, if you had them: you encourage them to whore. You are fit to breed up youth!

SIR EDWARD. You are mad.—But pray, sir, let me entreat you to go home, and I will wait upon you, and we will consult how to make the best of this misfortune, in which, I assure you, I have a great share.

ATTORNEY. I will submit to your wise advice, sir. My grief has made me forget: here is a letter comes out of the country for you.

Exit Attorney

SIR WILLIAM. For me? 'Tis welcome. Now for news from my dear boy! Now you shall hear, brother. He is a son indeed.

SIR EDWARD. (*Aside*) Yes, a very hopeful one. I will not undeceive him till Ned has tried once more to recover him.

SIR WILLIAM. (*Reads*) "On the tenth of this month your son, my young master, about two of the clock in the morning, rode out with his man, Lolpoop, and notwithstanding all the search and enquiry we can make"— Oh, heaven!—"he can not be found or heard of."

(*He drops the letter, not able to hold it*)

SIR EDWARD. How's this?

SIR WILLIAM. Oh, my poor boy! He is robbed and murdered, and buried in some ditch, or flung into some pond. Oh, I shall never see thee more, dear Tim! The joy and the support of all my life! The only comfort which I had on earth.

SIR EDWARD. Have patience, brother, 'tis nothing but a little ramble in your absence.

SIR WILLIAM. Oh, no. He durst not ramble; he was the dutifullest child! I shall never see his face again. Look you, he goes on: "We have searched and made enquiry in three adjacent counties, and no tidings can be heard of him." What have I done that heaven should thus afflict me?

SIR EDWARD. What if, after all, this son should be he that has made all this noise in Whitefriars, for which mine has been so blamed?

SIR WILLIAM. My son—my son play such pranks? That's likely! One so strictly, so soberly educated? One that's educated your way can not do otherwise.

Enter ROGER

ROGER. Sir, sir, mercy upon me, here's my young master's man, Lolpoop, coming along the streets with a wench.

Enter LOLPOOP, *leading* BETTY *under the arm*

SIR WILLIAM. Oh, heaven! What say you?

SIR EDWARD. (*To himself*) Now it works. Ha, ha, ha!

(SIR WILLIAM *lays hold on* LOLPOOP *ere he or she sees him*)

BETTY. How now! What have you to say to my friend, my dear?

(SIR WILLIAM *and* LOLPOOP *start, and stand amazed at one another; and, after a great pause,* SIR WILLIAM *falls upon* LOLPOOP, *beats the whore, beats* ROGER, *strikes at his brother, and lays about him like a madman; the rabble get all about him*)

SIR WILLIAM. Sirrah, rogue, dog, villain! Whore! And you rogue, rogue! Confound the world! Oh, that the world were all on fire!

SIR EDWARD. Brother, for shame, be more temperate. Are you a madman?

SIR WILLIAM. Plague o' your dull philosophy!

SIR EDWARD. The rabble are gathered together about you.

SIR WILLIAM. Villain, rogue, dog, toad, serpent! Where's my son? Sirrah, you have robbed him and murdered him.

(*He beats* LOLPOOP, *who roars out murder*)

LOLPOOP. Hold, hold, your son is alive, and alive like. He's in London.

SIR WILLIAM. What say you, sirrah? In London? And is he well? Thanks be to heaven for that. Where is he, sirrah?

LOLPOOP. He is in Whitefriars with Mr. Cheatly, his cousin Shamwell, and Captain Hackum.

(SIR WILLIAM *pauses, as amazed; then beats him again*)

SIR WILLIAM. And, you rogue, you damned dog, would you suffer him to keep such company, and commit such villainous actions?

LOLPOOP. Hold, hold, hold, I pray you, sir. I am but a servant. How could I help it, marry?

SIR WILLIAM. You could not help being with a whore yourself, sirrah, sirrah, sirrah! Here, honest mob, course [1] this whore to some purpose. A whore, a whore, a whore!

(*She runs out, the rabble run after and tear her, crying, "A whore! a whore!"*)

SIR EDWARD. This is wisely done! If they murder her, you'll be hanged. I am in commission [2] for Middlesex; I must seek to appease them.

SIR WILLIAM. Sirrah, rogue, bring me to my son instantly, or I'll cut your throat.

Exeunt

[SCENE III. *A room in* SCRAPEALL'S *house*]

Enter ISABELLA, TERESIA, RUTH

ISABELLA. Dear Ruth, thou dost forever oblige us.

TERESIA. And so much that none but our own mothers could ever do it more.

RUTH. Oblige yourselves, and be not silly, coy, and nice. Strike me when the iron's hot, I say. They have great estates, and are both friends. I know both their families and conditions.

[1] Chase.
[2] Sir Edward is commissioned as one of the justices of the peace for Middlesex.

Enter BELFOND JUNIOR *and* TRUMAN

Here they are. Welcome, friends.

TRUMAN. How dost thou?

RUTH. These are the damsels. I will retire and watch, lest the old man surprise us.

Exit RUTH

BELFOND JUNIOR. Look thee, Isabella, I come to confer with thee in a matter which concerneth us both, if thou be'st free.

ISABELLA. Friend, 'tis like I am.

TRUMAN. And mine with thee is of the same nature.

TERESIA. Proceed.

BELFOND JUNIOR. Something within me whispereth that we were made as helps for one another.

TERESIA. They act very well, cousin.

ISABELLA. For young beginners. Come, leave off your Canaanitish dialect and talk like the inhabiters of this world.

TERESIA. We are as arrant hypocrites as the best of you.

ISABELLA. We were bred otherwise than you see, and are able to hear you talk like gentlemen.

TERESIA. You come to our meeting like sparks and beaux, and I never could perceive much devotion in you.

ISABELLA. 'Tis such a pain to dissemble that I am resolved I'll never do it but when I must.

BELFOND JUNIOR. Dear madam, I could wish all forms were laid aside betwixt us. But in short I am most infinitely in love with you, and must be forever miserable if I go without you.

ISABELLA. A frank and hearty declaration, which you make with so much confidence I warrant you have been used to it.

TRUMAN. There is not a difficulty in the world which I would stop at to obtain your love, the only thing on earth could make me happy.

TERESIA. And you are as much in earnest now as you were when you came first to us —even now.

ISABELLA. That's well urged. Can not you gentlemen counterfeit love as well as religion?

BELFOND JUNIOR. Love is so natural it can not be affected.

TRUMAN. To show mine is so, take me at my word: I am ready to [sur]render on discretion.

TERESIA. And was this the reason you frequented our parish church?

BELFOND JUNIOR. Could you think our business was to hear your teacher spin out an hour over a velvet cushion?[1]

ISABELLA. Profane men! I warrant they came to ogle.

TRUMAN. Even so. Our eyes might tell you what we came for.

BELFOND JUNIOR. In short, dear madam, our opportunities are like to be so few, your confinement being so close, that 'tis fit to make use of this. 'Tis not your fortune which I aim at—my uncle will make a settlement equal to it, were it more—but 'tis your charming person.

ISABELLA. And you would have me a fine forward lady, to love *extempore*.[2]

BELFOND JUNIOR. Madam, you have but a few minutes to make use of, and therefore should improve those few. Your uncle has sold you for £5,000 and, for aught I know, you have not this night good for your deliverance.

TRUMAN. Consider, ladies, if you had not better trust a couple of honest gentlemen than an old man that makes his market of you; for I can tell you, you, though his own daughter, are to be sold, too.

TERESIA. But for all that, our consents are to be had.

BELFOND JUNIOR. You can look for nothing but a more strict confinement, which must follow your refusal. Now, if you have the courage to venture an escape, we are the knights that will relieve you.

TRUMAN. I have an estate, madam, equal to your fortune, but I have nothing can deserve your love. But I'll procure your freedom; then use it as you please.

BELFOND JUNIOR. If you are unwilling to trust us, you can trust your governess, whom you shall have with you.

ISABELLA. And what would you and the world say of us for this?

BELFOND JUNIOR. We should adore you; and I am apt to think the world would not condemn your choice.

TRUMAN. But I am sure all the world will condemn your delay, in the condition you are in.

Enter RUTH

RUTH. I see Mr. Scrapeall coming at the end of the street. Begone. I'll bring them to

[1] Pulpit cushion.   [2] At once.

your chamber in the Temple this evening. Haste, haste out at the back door.

BELFOND JUNIOR. This is most unfortunate.

TRUMAN. Dear madam, let me seal my vows.

RUTH. Go, go; begone, begone, friends.

Exeunt

[SCENE IV. *Street outside* SCRAPEALL'S *house*]

Enter SCRAPEALL, *crosses the stage; enter* MRS. TERMAGANT *and her* Brother

TERMAGANT. You see, brother, we have dogged Belfond till we saw him enter the house of this scrivener with his friend Truman, both in disguises; which, with what we have heard even now at the neighboring ale-house, convinces me that 'tis he is to marry the rich niece.

BROTHER. They say she is to be married to the son of Sir William Belfond, and that Sir William gives a great sum of money to her uncle for her. By this it should seem to be the elder son, and not our enemy, who is designed for her.

TERMAGANT. If so, the villain would not at full day go thither.

BROTHER. But 'tis in disguise.

TERMAGANT. With that, I suppose the son pretends to be a Puritan, too, or she would not have him; it must be he. And if you will do as I direct you, I warrant I'll break off this match, and by that, work a[n] exquisite piece of revenge.

BROTHER. I am wholly at your dispose.

TERMAGANT. Now is the time—the door opens. Pursue me with a drawn dagger, with all the seeming fury imaginable, now as the old man comes out.

(SCRAPEALL *passes over the stage.* Brother [*thereupon*] *pursues* [TERMAGANT] *with a drawn dagger; she runs, and gets into the house, and claps the door after her*)

BROTHER. Where is the jade? Deliver her to me, I'll cut her in piecemeal. Deliver her, I say! Well, you will not deliver her? I shall watch her.

[SCENE V.   *Room in* SCRAPEALL'S *house*]

Enter within RUTH, TERESIA, ISABELLA, MRS. TERMAGANT

TERMAGANT. Oh, oh! Where is the murderer? Where is he? I die with fear, I die!

RUTH. Prithee, woman, comfort thyself.

No man shall hurt thee here. Take a sup of this bottle.

(*She pulls out a silver strong-water bottle*)

TERMAGANT. Thou art safe?

ISABELLA. We will defend thee here, as in a castle. But what is the occasion of this man's fury?

TERMAGANT. You are so generous in giving me this succor, and promising my defence, that I am resolved not to conceal it from you, though I must confess I have no reason to boast of it; but I hope your charity will interpret it as well as you can, on my side.

RUTH. Go on; thou need'st not fear.

TERMAGANT. Know, then, I am a gentlewoman whose parents, dying when I was sixteen, left me a moderate fortune, yet able to maintain me like their daughter. I chose an aunt to be my guardian; one of those jolly widows who loves gaming and have great resort in the evenings, at their houses.

RUTH. Good; proceed.

TERMAGANT. There it was my misfortune to be acquainted with a young gentleman whose face, air, mien, shape, wit, and breeding, not I alone, but the whole town admires.

RUTH. Very good.

TERMAGANT. By all his looks, his gestures and addresses he seemed in love with me. The joy that I conceived at this I wanted cunning to conceal; but he must needs perceive it flash in my eyes and kindle in my face; he soon began to court me in such sweet, such charming words as would betray a more experienced heart than mine.

RUTH. Humph. Very well—she speaks notably.

TERMAGANT. There was but little left for him to do, for I had done it all before for him. He had a friend within, too ready to give up the fort; yet I held out as long as I could make defence.

RUTH. Good lackaday! Some men have strange charms, it is confessed.

TERMAGANT. Yet I was safe by solemn mutual oaths, in private contracted. He would have it private because he feared to offend an uncle from whom he had great expectance. But now came all my misery.

RUTH. Alack, alack, I warrant he was false.

TERMAGANT. False as a crocodile. He watched the fatal minute, and he found it and greedily seized upon me, when I trusted to his honor and his oaths; he still swore on that he would marry me, and I sinned on. In short, I had a daughter by him, now three years old, as true a copy as e'er nature drew, beauteous, and witty to a miracle.

RUTH. Nay, men are faithless; I can speak it.

TERESIA. Poor lady! I am strangely concerned for her.

ISABELLA. She was a fool to be catched in so common a snare.

TERMAGANT. From time to time he swore he would marry me, though I must think I am his wife as much as any priest can make me; but still he found excuses about his uncle. I would have patiently waited till his uncle's death, had he been true, but he has thrown me off, abandoned me without so much as a pretended crime.

RUTH. Alack, and well-a-day! It makes me weep.

TERMAGANT. But 'tis for an attorney's daughter, whom he keeps and now is fond of, while he treats me with all contempt and hatred.

ISABELLA. Though she was a fool, yet he's a base, inhuman fellow.

TERESIA. To scorn and hate her for her love to him!

TERMAGANT. By this means my dishonor, which had been yet concealed, became so public my brother, coming from the wars of Hungary, has heard all, has this day fought with the author of my misery, but was disarmed; and now by accident he spied me by your house, I having fled the place where I had lodged, for fear of him; and here the bloody man would have killed me for the dishonor done to his family, which never yet was blemished.

RUTH. Get the chief justice's warrant, and bind him to the peace.

TERESIA. She tells her story well.

ISABELLA. 'Tis a very odd one, but she expresses it so sensible, I can not but believe her.

TERMAGANT. [*Aside*] If they do not ask me who this is, I have told my tale in vain.—Now, ladies, I hope you have charity enough to pardon the weakness of a poor young woman who suffers shame enough within.

TERESIA. We shall be glad to do you what kindness we can.

TERMAGANT. Oh, had you seen this most bewitching person, so beautiful, witty, and well-bred, and full of most gentleman-like qualities, you would be the readier to have compassion on me.

ISABELLA. Pray, who is it?

TERMAGANT. Alas, 'tis no secret; it is Belfond, who calls Sir Edward Belfond father, but is his nephew.

ISABELLA. What do I hear? Was ever woman so unfortunate as I in her first love!

TERESIA. 'Tis most unlucky.

TERMAGANT. [*Aside*] That is the niece; I see 'twas he who was to marry her.

ISABELLA. But I am glad I have thus early heard it; I'll never see his face more.

RUTH. (*Aside*) All this is false: he is a pious man, and true professor. This vile woman will break the match off, and undo my hopes.

TERMAGANT. 'Tis as I thought. He is a ranting blade, a roysterer of the town.

RUTH. Come, you are an idle woman, and belie him. Begone out of the doors—there's the back way, you need not pretend fear of your brother.

TERMAGANT. I am obliged enough in the present defence you gave me. I intended not to trouble you long. But heaven can witness what I say is true.

ISABELLA. Do you hear, cousin? 'Tis most certain, I'll never see him.

RUTH. Go, wicked woman, go. What evil spirit sent thee hither? I say, begone.

TERMAGANT. I go.—[*Aside*] I care not what she says; it works where I would have it.— Your servant, ladies. *Exit*

RUTH. Go, go, thou wicked slanderer.

TERESIA. See him but once, to hear what he can say in his defence.

ISABELLA. Yes, to hear him lie as all the sex will. Persuade me not; I am fixed.

RUTH. Look thee, Isabella—

ISABELLA. I am resolved.

Exit ISABELLA *hastily*

TERESIA. Dear Ruth, thou dearest friend, whom once we took for our most cruel jailor, let's follow, and help me to convince her of her error; but I am resolved, if she be stubborn to undo herself, she shall not ruin me: I will escape.

RUTH. Let us persuade her. *Exeunt*

[SCENE VI. *A room in the "George" Tavern*]

Enter BELFOND SENIOR *and* HACKUM

BELFOND SENIOR. Captain, call all my servants. Why don't they wait?

Enter MARGARET *and* MRS. HACKUM *with a caudle* [1]

Oh, my pure blowen, my convenient, my tackle!

MARGARET. How dost thou, my dear?

MRS. HACKUM. I have brought you a caudle here. There's ambergris [2] in it. 'Tis a rare, refreshing, strengthening thing.

BELFOND SENIOR. What, adad, you take me for a bridegroom? I scorn a caudle; give me some cherry brandy, I'll drink her health in a bumper. Do thee eat this, child.

MRS. HACKUM. I have that at hand—here, sir. (*She fetches the brandy*)

Enter CAPTAIN HACKUM *and* Servants

BELFOND SENIOR. Come, my dear natural, here's a bumper of cherry brandy to thy health; but first let me kiss thee, my dear rogue.

Enter SIR WILLIAM

SIR WILLIAM. Some thunderbolt light on my head! What's this I see?

BELFOND SENIOR. My father!

Enter CHEATLY *and* SHAMWELL

SIR WILLIAM. Hey, here's the whole kennel of hell-hounds!

CHEATLY. Beat up to him—bow, wow!

SHAMWELL. Do not flinch—bow, wow!

BELFOND SENIOR. Bow, wow! Bow, wow!

SIR WILLIAM. Most impudent, abandoned rascal! Let me go, let me come at him! Audacious varlet, how durst thou look on me?

(*He endeavors to fly at his son; footmen hold him*)

BELFOND SENIOR. Go strike your dogs, and call them names; you have nothing to do with me. I am of full age; and I thank heaven, am gotten loose from your yoke. Don't think to put upon me, I'll be kept no longer like a prigster, a silly country put, fit for nothing but to be a bubble, a caravan, or so.

SIR WILLIAM. A most perfect, downright, canting rogue! Am I not your father, sirrah? Sirrah, am I not?

BELFOND SENIOR. Yes, and tenant for lif

[1] Warm drink for sick persons.
[2] Supposed to be strengthening. Mrs. Hackum has prepared what is known as an amber-caudle (Summers).

to my estate in tail, and I'll look to you that you commit no waste. What a pox, did you think to nose[1] me forever, as the saying is? I am not so dark,[2] neither, I am sharp, sharp as a needle. I can smoke[3] now as soon as another.

Sir William. Let me come at him!

Cheatly. So long as you forbear all violence you are safe; but if you strike here, we command the Friars, and we will raise the posse.

Sir William. O villain! thou notorious undoer of young heirs! And thou pernicious wretch, thou art no part of me; have I [not] from thy first swaddling nourished thee and bred thee up with care?

Belfond Senior. Yes, with care to keep your money from me, and bred me in the greatest ignorance, fit for your slave, and not your son. I had been finely dark if I had stayed at home.

Sir William. Were you not educated like a gentleman?

Belfond Senior. No, like a grazier or a butcher. If I had stayed in the country, I had never seen such a nab, such a rum nab, such a modish porker, such spruce and neat accoutrements: here is a tattle, here's a famble, and here's the cole, the ready, the rhino, the darby. I have a lusty cod, old prig. I'd have thee know, and am very rhinocerical: here are megs and smelts, good store, decus's and Georges. The land is entailed, and I will have my snack of it while I am young, adad, I will. Hah!

Sir William. Some mountain cover me and hide my shame forever from the world! Did I not beget thee, rogue?

Belfond Senior. What know I whether you did or not? But 'twas not to use me like a slave. But I am sharp and smokey; I had been purely bred, had I been ruled by you, I should never have known these worthy, ingenious gentlemen, my dear friends. All this fine language had been heathen Greek to me, and I had ne'er been able to have cut a sham or banter while I had lived, adad. Odsookers, I know myself, and will have nothing to do with you.

Sir William. I am astonished!

Belfond Senior. Shall my younger brother keep his coach and equipage, and shine like a spruce prig, and I be your baily in the country? Hie, La Mar, bid my coach be ready at the door; I'll make him know I am elder brother, and I will have the better liveries; and I am resolved to manage my natural, my pure blowen, my convenient, my peculiar, my tackle, my purest pure as the rest of the young gentlemen of the town do.

Sir William. (*Aside*) A most confirmed Alsatian rogue!—Thou most ungracious wretch to break off from me at such a time when I had provided a wife for you, a pretty young lady with fifteen thousand pound down, have settled a great jointure upon her, and a large estate in present on you, the writings all sealed, and nothing wanting but you, whom I had sent for, post, out of the country to marry her!

Belfond Senior. Very likely, that you, who have cudgelled me from my cradle, and made me your slave, and grudged me a crown in my pocket, should do all this.

Cheatly. Believe him not—there's not one word of truth in't.

Shamwell. This is a trick to get you in his power.

Sir William. The writings are all at my attorney's in the Temple; you may go with me and see 'em all; and if you will comply, I'll pardon what is past, and marry you.

Belfond Senior. No, no, I am sharp, as I told you, and smokey; you shall not put upon me, I understand your shams; but to talk fairly, in all occurrences of this nature, which either may, or may not be, according to the different accidents which often intervene upon several opportunities, from whence we may collect either good or bad according to the nature of the things themselves; and forasmuch as whether they be good or bad concerns themselves; and forasmuch as whether they be good or bad concerns only the understanding so far forth as it employs its faculties: now since all this is premised, let us come to the matter in hand.

Sir William. Prodigious impudence! O devil! I'll to my lord chief justice, and with his tipstaff[4] I'll do your business—rogues, dogs, and villains, I will!

Exit in a fury

Cheatly. That was bravely carried on.

Shamwell. Most admirably.

---

[1] Treat impudently
[2] Ignorant.
[3] Suspect.
[4] Constable.

BELFOND SENIOR. Ay, was't not? Don't I begin to banter pretty well? Ha?

CHEATLY. Rarely. But a word in private, my resplendent prig. You see your father resolves to put some trick upon you. Be beforehand with him, and marry this fortune I have prepared. Lose no time but see her, and treat with her, if you like her, as soon as you can.

BELFOND SENIOR. You are in the right. Let not my blowen hear a word. I'll to her instantly.

CHEATLY. Shamwell and I'll go and prepare her for a visit. You know the place.

BELFOND SENIOR. I do. Come along—
Exeunt

[SCENE VII]

Enter CHEATLY, SHAMWELL, *and* MRS. TERMAGANT, *in her fine lodgings*

CHEATLY. Madam, you must carry yourself somewhat stately, but courteously, to the bubble.

SHAMWELL. Somewhat reservedly, and yet so as to give him hopes.

TERMAGANT. I warrant you, let me alone; and if I effect this business, you are the best friends; such friends as I could never yet expect. 'Twill be an exquisite revenge.

CHEATLY. He comes!—Come, noble esquire.

Enter BELFOND SENIOR

Madam, this is the gentleman whom I would recommend to your ladyship's favor, who is ambitious of kissing your hand.

BELFOND SENIOR. Yes, madam, as Mr. Cheatly says, I am ambitious of kissing your hand, and your lip, too, madam; for I vow to gad, madam, there is not a person in the world, madam, has a greater honor for your person. And, madam, I assure you I am a person.

TERMAGANT. My good friend Mr. Cheatly, with whom I trust the management of my small fortune—

CHEATLY. Small fortune! Nay, it is a large one—

TERMAGANT. He's told me of your family and character. To your name I am no stranger, nor to your estate, though this is the first time I have had the honor to see your person.

BELFOND SENIOR. Hold, good madam, the honor lies on my side.—[*Aside*] She's a rare lady, ten times handsomer than my blowens, and here's a lodging and furniture for a queen!
—Madam, if your ladyship please to accept of my affection in an honorable way, you shall find I am no put, no country prigster, nor shall ever want the megs, thes melts, decus's, and Georges, the ready, and the rhino: I am rhinocerical.

TERMAGANT. I want nothing, sir, heaven be thanked.

SHAMWELL. Her worst servants eat in plate, and her maids have all silver chamber-pots.

BELFOND SENIOR. Madam, I beg your pardon. I am somewhat boozy. I have been drinking bumpers and facers till I am almost clear; I have £1,000 a year, and £20,000 worth of wood, which I can turn into coie and ready, and my estate ne'er the worse; there's only the incumbrance of an old fellow upon it, and I shall break his heart suddenly.

TERMAGANT. This is a weighty matter and requires advice, nor is it a sudden work to persuade my heart to love. I have my choice of fortunes.

BELFOND SENIOR. Very like, madam. But Mr. Cheatly and my cousin Shamwell can tell you that my occasions require haste, d'ee see? And therefore I desire you to resolve as soon as conveniently you can.

(*A noise of a tumult without, and blowing of a horn*)

CHEATLY. What's this I hear?

SHAMWELL. They are up in the Friars. Pray heaven, the sheriff's officers be not come.

CHEATLY. 'Slide, 'tis so. Shift for yourselves!—Squire, let me conduct you—This is your wicked father with officers [*Exeunt*]

(*Cry without:* The tipstaff! An arrest! An arrest! *and the horn blows*)

[SCENE VIII. *Street in Whitefriars*]

Enter SIR WILLIAM BELFOND *and a* Tipstaff, *with the* Constable *and his* Watchmen; *and against them the posse of the* Friars *drawn up*, Bankrupts *hurrying to escape*

SIR WILLIAM. Are you mad to resist the tipstaff, the king's authority?

(*They cry out:* An arrest! *Several flock to 'em with all sorts of weapons. Women with fire-forks, spits, paring-shovels, &c.*)

Enter CHEATLY, SHAMWELL, BELFOND SENIOR, *and* HACKUM

CHEATLY. We are too strong for 'em. Stand your ground.

Sir William. We demand that same squire, Cheatly, Shamwell, and Bully Hackum. Deliver them up, and all the rest of you are safe.

Hackum. Not a man.

Sir William. Nay, then, have at you.

Tipstaff. I charge you in the king's name, all to assist me.

Rabble. Fall on!

(*Rabble beat the* Constable *and the rest into the Temple.* Tipstaff *runs away. They take* Sir William *prisoner*)

Cheatly. Come on, thou wicked author of this broil! You are our prisoner.

Sir William. Let me go, rogue.

Shamwell. Now we have you in the Temple, we'll show you the pump first.

Sir William. Dogs, rogues, villains!

Shamwell. To the pump! To the pump!

Hackum. Pump him, pump him!

Belfond Senior. Ah, pump him, pump him, old prig!

Rabble. Pump, pump, to the pump! Huzza!

Enter Belfond Junior, Truman, *and several Gentleman, Porter of the Temple, and* Belfond's *Footmen*

Belfond Junior. What's the matter here?

Truman. The rabble have catched a bailiff.

Belfond Junior. Death and hell! 'tis my father—'tis a gentleman, my father. Gentlemen, I beseech you lend me your hands to his rescue.

Truman. Come on, rascals. Have we caught you? We'll make an example.

(*All draw and fall upon the rabble.* Belfond Senior *runs first away. The* Templers *beat 'em, and take* Cheatly, Shamwell, *and* Hackum *prisoners*)

Belfond Junior. Here! Where are the officers of the Temple? Porter, do you shut the gates into Whitefriars.

Porter. I will, sir.

Belfond Junior. Here's a guinea among ye. See these three rogues well pumped, and let 'em go through the whole course.

Cheatly. Hold, hold,—I am a gentleman!

Shamwell. I am your cousin!

Hackum. Hold, hold, scoundrels, I am a captain!

Belfond Junior. Away with 'em!

Sir William. Away with 'em. Dear son, I am infinitely obliged to you. I ask your pardon for all that I have said against you. I have wronged you.

Belfond Junior. Good sir, reflect not on that. I am resolved, e'er I have done, to deserve your good word.

Sir William. 'Twas ill fortune we have missed my most ungracious rebel, that monster of villainy.

Belfond Junior. Let me alone with him, sir. Upon my honor I will deliver him safe this night. But now let us see the execution.

Sir William. Dear Ned, you bring tears into my eyes. Let me embrace thee, my only comfort now.

Belfond Junior. Good sir, let's on and see the justice of this place. *Exeunt*

ACT V

Scene I. [*Room at the "George" Tavern*]

Enter Cheatly, Shamwell, Hackum

Cheatly. O unmerciful dogs! Were ever gentlemen used thus before? I am drenched into a quartan ague.[1]

Shamwell. My limbs are stiff and numbed all over, but where I am beaten and bruised, there I have some sense left.

Hackum. Dry blows I could have borne magnanimously; but to be made such a sop of—! Besides, I have had the worst of it by wearing my own hair. To be shaved all on one side, and with a lather made of channel dirt instead of a wash-ball![2] I have lost half the best head of hair in the Friars, and a whisker worth fifty pound in its intrinsic value to a commander.

Cheatly. Indeed, your magnanimous phiz is somewhat disfigured by it, Captain.

Shamwell. Your military countenance has lost much of its ornament.

Hackum. I am as disconsolate as a bee that has lost his sting. The other moiety of whisker must follow, then all the terror of my face is gone; that face that used to fright young prigs into submission. I shall now look like an ordinary man.

Cheatly. We'll swinge[3] these rogues with an indictment for a riot and with actions *sans nombre*.[4]

---

[1] Intermittent fever, returning every four days.
[2] Ball of toilet soap.
[3] Chastise.
[4] Numberless.

SHAMWELL. What reparation will that be? I am a gentleman, and can never show my face among my kindred more.

CHEATLY. We that can show our faces after what we have done, may well show 'em after what we have suffered. Great souls are above ordinances, and never can be slaves to fame.

HACKUM. My honor is tender, and this one affront will cost me at least five murders.

CHEATLY. Let's not prate and shiver in cold fits here; but call your wife with the cherry brandy, and let's ask after the squire. If they have taken him, 'tis the worst part of the story.

HACKUM. No, I saw the squire run into the Friars at first. But I'll go fetch some cherry brandy, and that will comfort us.

(Steps in for brandy)

Here's the bottle. Let's drink by word of mouth. *(Drinks)*

CHEATLY. Your cherry brandy is most sovereign[1] and edifying. (CHEATLY *drinks*)

SHAMWELL. Most exceeding comfortable after our Temple-pickling. *(Drinks)*

CHEATLY. A fish has a damned life on't. I shall have that aversion to water after this that I shall scarce ever be cleanly enough to wash my face again.

HACKUM. Well! I'll to the barber's and get myself shaved; then go to the squire, and be new accoutred.

Exit HACKUM

CHEATLY. Dear Shamwell, we must not for a little affliction forget our main business. Our caravan must be well managed. He is now drunk, and when he wakes, will be very fit to be married. Mrs. Termagant has given us a judgment of £2,000 upon that condition.

SHAMWELL. The sooner we dispose of him the better; for all his kindred are bent to retrieve him, and the Temple joining in the war against us, will be too hard for us, so that we must make what we can of him immediately.

CHEATLY. If he should be once cool or irresolute, we have lost him and all our hopes; but when we have sufficiently dipped[2] him, as we shall by this marriage and her judgment, he is our own forever.

SHAMWELL. But what shall we do for our Whitefriars chaplain, our Alsatia divine? I was in search of him before our late misfortune, and the rogue is holed somewhere. I could not find him, and we are undone without him.

CHEATLY. 'Tis true. Pray go instantly and find him out. He dares not stir out of this covert. Beat it well[3] all over for him; you'll find him tappes'd[4] in some ale-house, bawdy-house, or brandy-shop.

SHAMWELL. He's a brave, swinging orthodox, and will marry any couple at any time; he defies licence and canonical hours and all those foolish ceremonies.

CHEATLY. Prithee look after him while I go to prepare the lady.

SHAMWELL. You rogue Cheatly, you have a loving design upon her, you will go to twelve[5] with the squire. If you do, I will have my snack.

CHEATLY. Go, go, you are a wag.

Exeunt severally

[SCENE II]

Enter RUTH, BELFOND JUNIOR, *and* TRUMAN *at* SCRAPEALL'S *house*

RUTH. She told her tale so passionately that Isabella believes every word of it; and is resolved, as she says, never to see thee more.

BELFOND JUNIOR. Oh, this most malicious and most infamous of her sex! There is not the least truth in her accusation.

TRUMAN. That to my knowledge. He is not a man of those principles.

RUTH. I will send them to you if I can; and in the meantime, be upon the watch.

TRUMAN. Take this writing with thee, which is a bond from us to make good our agreement with thee.

RUTH. 'Tis well, and still I doubt not to perform my part. *Exit*

BELFOND JUNIOR. Was ever a man plagued with a wench like me? Well, say what they will, the life of a whoremaster is a foolish, restless, anxious life, and there's an end on't. What can be done with this malicious devil? A man can not offer violence to a woman.

TRUMAN. Steal away her child, and then you may awe her.

BELFOND JUNIOR. I have emissaries abroad to find out the child; but she'll sacrifice that and all the world, to her revenge.

---

[1] Efficacious.
[2] Entangled him in debt.
[3] Hunt well.
[4] Skulking.
[5] Divide equally (Summers).

TRUMAN. You must arrest her upon a swinging action, which she can not get bail for, and keep her till she is humbled.

Enter TERESIA

Madam, I kiss your hands.

TERESIA. You have done well, Mr. Belfond. Here has been a lady whom you have had a child by, were contracted to, and have deserted for an attorney's daughter which you keep. My cousin says she will never see you more.

BELFOND JUNIOR. If this be true, madam, I deserve never to see her more, which would be worse than death to me.

TERESIA. I have prevailed with her once more to see you, and hear what you can say to this. Come, come, cousin.

(*She leads in* ISABELLA)

Look you, cousin, Mr. Belfond denies all this matter.

ISABELLA. I never doubted that. But certainly it is impossible to counterfeit so lively as she did.

BELFOND JUNIOR. Heaven is my witness that her accusation is false. I never was yet contracted to any woman, nor made the least promise, or gave any one the least hope of it; and if I do not demonstrate my innocence to you, I will be content forever to be debarred the sight of you, more prized by me than liberty or life.

ISABELLA. And yet perhaps these very words were said to her.

TRUMAN. Madam, you have not time, if you value your own liberty, to argue any longer. We will carry you to Sir Edward Belfond's; his sister is his housekeeper; and there you may be entertained with safety of your honor.

TERESIA. He is esteemed a worthy gentleman, nor could we choose a better guardian.

ISABELLA. At least, how could you use a woman ill you had a child by?

BELFOND JUNIOR. Not all the malice of mankind can equal hers. I have been frail, I must confess, as others; and though I have provided for her and her child, yet every day she does me all the most outrageous mischief she can possibly conceive. But this has touched me in the tender'st point.

ISABELLA. 'Twould be much for my honor, to put myself into the hands of a known wencher.

BELFOND JUNIOR. Into the hands of one who has abandoned all thoughts of vice and folly, for you.

TRUMAN. Madam, you neither of you trust us. Your governness is with you, and yet we are ready to make good our words by the assistance of the parson.

TERESIA. That's another point. But I'm sure, cousin, there is no dallying about our liberty. If you be in love with your jail, stay; I, for my part, am resolved to go.

BELFOND JUNIOR. My uncle's a virtuous, honorable man; my aunt, his sister, a lady of great piety. Think if you will not be safer there than with your uncle, by whom you are sold for £5,000—to my knowledge to one who is the most debauched, dissolute fellow this day in London.

TERESIA. Liberty, liberty, I say. I'll trust myself and my governess.

Enter RUTH

RUTH. Haste and agree: your father has sent to have supper ready in less than half an hour.

TERESIA. Away, away! I am ready. Cousin, farewell.

BELFOND JUNIOR. For heaven's sake, madam, on my knees I beg you to make use of this occasion, or you have lost yourself; and I, too, shall forever lose you for marriage, which alone can keep me from being the most miserable. You may advise, and all things shall be cleared up to your wish.

TERESIA. Farewell, dear cousin. Let's kiss at parting.

ISABELLA. Sure thou hast not the conscience. Thou wilt not leave me?

TERESIA. By my troth, but I will.

ISABELLA. By my troth, but you shall not, for I'll go with thee.

BELFOND JUNIOR. May all the joys of life forever wait on you.

RUTH. Haste! Haste! Begone— *Exeunt*

[SCENE III. *Room at* SIR EDWARD'S *house*]

Enter SIR WILLIAM BELFOND

SIR WILLIAM. That I should live to this unhappy age! To see the fruit of all my hopes thus blasted! How long like chemists [1] have I watched and toiled? And in the minute when I expected to have seen the projection,[2] all is blown up *in fumo*.[3]

---
[1] Alchemists.
[2] Turning of base metal into gold.
[3] In smoke.

Enter SIR EDWARD

Brother! I am ashamed to look on you, my disappointment is so great. Oh, this most wicked recreant! This perverse and infamous son!

SIR EDWARD. Brother, a wise man is never disappointed. Man's life is like a game at tables;[1] if at any time the cast[2] you most shall need does not come up, let that which comes instead of it be mended by your play.

SIR WILLIAM. How different have been our fates! I left the pleasures of the town to marry, which was no small bondage, had children, which brought more care upon me. For their sakes I lived a rustic, painful, hard, severe, and melancholy life: morose, inhospitable, sparing even necessaries; tenacious, even to griping, for their good. My neighbors shunned me, my friends neglected me, my children hate me and wish my death. Nay, this wicked son in whom I have set up my rest and principally for whose good I thus had lived, has now defeated all my hopes.

SIR EDWARD. 'Twas your own choice. You would not learn from others.

SIR WILLIAM. You have lived ever at ease, indulged all pleasures, and melted down your time in daily feasts and in continual revels; gentle, complaisant, affable and liberal, and at great expense. The world speaks well of you; mankind embrace you; your son loves you and wishes your life as much as he can do his own. But I'll perplex myself no more. I look upon this rascal as an excrement, a wen, or gangrened limb lopped off.

SIR EDWARD. Rather look upon him as a dislocated one, and get him set again. By this time, you see, severity will do nothing. Entice him back to you by love. In short, give him liberty and a good allowance. There now remains no other way to reclaim him; for, like a stone-horse[3] broke in among the mares, no fence hereafter will contain him.

SIR WILLIAM. Brother, I look upon you as a true friend that would not insult[4] upon my folly and presumption; and confess you are nearer to the right than I. Your son, I hope, will be a comfort to me.

SIR EDWARD. I doubt it not. But consider, if you do not reconcile yourself and reclaim yours as I tell you, you lop off the paternal estate, which is all entailed forever upon your family. For, in the course he is, the reversion will be gone in your lifetime.

Enter BELFOND JUNIOR, TRUMAN, ISABELLA, TERESIA, *and* RUTH

BELFOND JUNIOR. Here are my father and my uncle. Mask yourselves, ladies, you must not yet discover who you are.

SIR EDWARD. Yonder's Ned and his friend, with ladies masked. Who should they be?

SIR WILLIAM. Whores, whores, what should they be else? Here's a comfortable sight again! He is incorrigible.

SIR EDWARD. 'Tis you that are incorrigible. How ready are you with your censures!

BELFOND JUNIOR. Sir, pardon the freedom I use with you. I humbly desire protection for these ladies in your house. They are women of honor, I do assure you, and desire to be concealed for some small time. An hour hence I will discover all to you, and you will then approve of what I do.

SIR EDWARD. Dear Ned, I will trust thy honor, and, without any examination, do as you would have me.

SIR WILLIAM. Why, brother, what a pox! will you pimp for your son? What a devil, will you make your house a bawdy-house?

SIR EDWARD. What, will the must never be gotten out of your old vessel? Ladies, be pleased to honor my house, and be assured that while you are there, 'tis yours.

(*He waits on the ladies and* RUTH)

BELFOND JUNIOR. Sir, my friend and I are just now going to do you a service. I'll pawn my life to you, sir, I will retrieve your rebel son and immediately restore him to you, and bring him, as he ought to come, on's knees with a full submission.

SIR WILLIAM. You will oblige me. Thou gain'st upon me hourly, and I begin to love thee more and more.

BELFOND JUNIOR. There's nothing in the world I aim at now but your love; and I will be bold to say, I shortly will deserve it. But this business requires haste, for I have laid everything ready. 'Tis almost bed-time. Come, friend. *Exit with* TRUMAN

SIR WILLIAM. Well, I'll say that for him— he is a good-natured boy; it makes me weep to think how harsh I have been with him. I'll in to my brother and expect the event.

---

[1] Checkers or backgammon.
[2] Of dice.
[3] Stallion.
[4] Exult.

[SCENE IV. *Street in front of* MRS. TERMA-
GANT'S *lodgings*]

Enter BELFOND SENIOR, [CHEATLY], SHAM-
WELL, *and* HACKUM

CHEATLY. I value you not misfortune so long as I have my dear friend still within my arms.

SHAMWELL. My dear, dear cousin! I will hug thee close to me. I feared to have lost thee.

BELFOND SENIOR. How happy am I in the truest, the dearest friends that ever man enjoyed! Well, I was so afflicted for you I was forced to make myself devilish boozy to comfort me.

CHEATLY. Your brother has heard of this great match you are towards. She has to my knowledge (for I do all her law business for her) £1500 a year jointure, and ten thousand pound in plate, money, and jewels; and this damned, envious brother of yours will break it off, if you make not haste and prevent[1] him.

BELFOND SENIOR. My dear friends, you are in the right. Never man met with such before. I'll disappoint the rogue, my brother, and the old prig, my father, and I'll do it instantly.   [*Exeunt*]

[SCENE V]

Scene changes to MRS. TERMAGANT'S *fine lodgings*

Enter BELFOND SENIOR, CHEATLY, SHAMWELL,
HACKUM, Parson, MRS. TERMAGANT,
and her Servants

CHEATLY. Madam, the time permits of no longer deliberation. If you take not this opportunity, my friend here will be ravished from us.

BELFOND SENIOR. Ay, madam, if you take me not now, you will lose me, madam. You will consider what to do.

TERMAGANT. Well, Mr. Cheatly, you dispose of me as you please. I have ever been guided by your wise advice.

SHAMWELL. Come, parson, do your office. Have you your book about ye?

PARSON. What, do you think I am without the tools of my trade?

CHEATLY. Can't you come presently to the joining of hands and leave out the rest of the formalities?

PARSON. Ay, ay. Come, stand forth.

(BELFOND SENIOR *and* MRS. TERMAGANT *stand forth*)

Enter BELFOND JUNIOR, TRUMAN, Constable,
Sergeant, Musketeers

BELFOND JUNIOR. Here they are—seize them all!

CHEATLY. Hell and damnation! We are all undone.

BELFOND SENIOR. Hands off! Let me alone. I am going to be married. You envious rascal, to come just in the nick!

BELFOND JUNIOR. Brother, be satisfied there's nothing but honor meant to you; 'tis for your service.

TERMAGANT. Oh, this accursed wretch, to come in this unlucky minute and ruin all my fortune!

BELFOND SENIOR. She has fifteen hundred a year jointure, and ten thousand pounds in money, &c., and I had been married to her in three minutes.

BELFOND JUNIOR. You have 'scaped the worst of ruins. Resist not; if you do, you shall be carried by head and heels. Your father will receive you, and be kind and give you as good an allowance as ever I had.

SHAMWELL. Where's your warrant?

CONSTABLE. 'Tis here, from my lord chief justice.

BELFOND JUNIOR. Let me see your bride that was to be. Oh, Mrs. Termagant! Oh, horror! horror! What a ruin you have 'scaped! This was my mistress, and still maintained by me. I have a child by her three years old.

TERMAGANT. Impudent villain! how dare you lie so basely!

BELFOND JUNIOR. By heaven, 'tis true.

TERMAGANT. I never saw him in my life before.

BELFOND JUNIOR. Yes, often, to my plague. Brother, if I do not prove this to you, believe me not in aught I e'er shall say.

(TERMAGANT *goes to stab at* BELFOND
JUNIOR. TRUMAN *lays hold on her*)

TRUMAN. Belfond, look to yourself!

BELFOND JUNIOR. Ha! Disarm her. This is another show of her good nature. Brother, give me your hand, I'll wait on you, and you will thank me for your deliverance.

TRUMAN. I am assured you will. You are delivered from the most infamous and destructive villains that ever took sanctuary here.

BELFOND JUNIOR. And from two mischiefs you must have forever sunk under, incest and beggary. Those three are only in the

---

[1] Anticipate.

warrant with my brother. Him I'll wait upon; bring you the rest. Hey! the cry is up! But we are provided.

(*A great noise in the streets, and the horn blowing:* An arrest! An arrest!)

CHEATLY. Undone, undone, all's lost!

SHAMWELL. Ruined! Forever lost!

HACKUM. I am surprised, and can not fight my way through.

BELFOND SENIOR. What! are all these rogues? and that a whore? and am I cheated?

BELFOND JUNIOR. Even so. Come along. Make ready, musketeers. Do you take care of my brother and conduct him with the rest to my uncle's house. I must go before and carry my little mistress, to make up the business with her father.

TRUMAN. I'll do it, I warrant you.

SERGEANT. We are ready.

Exeunt all but MRS. TERMAGANT

TERMAGANT. Oh, vile misfortune! had he but stayed six minutes, I had crowned all my revenge with one brave act in marrying of his brother. Well, I have one piece of vengeance which I will execute or perish. Besides, I'll have his blood, and then I'll die contented. [*Exit*]

SCENE [VI]. *The street*

Enter BELFOND JUNIOR, CHEATLY, SHAMWELL, HACKUM, TRUMAN, Constable, Sergeant, Guards

TRUMAN. What do all these rabble here?

CONSTABLE. Fire amongst 'em.

SERGEANT. Present—!

(*The debtors run up and down, some without their breeches, others without their coats; some out of balconies; some crying out,* Oars, oars! Sculler, five pound for a boat! Ten pound for a boat! Twenty pound for a boat! *The inhabitants all come out armed as before, but as soon as they see the* Musketeers, *they run, and everyone shifts for himself.*)

TRUMAN. Hey, how they run! *Exeunt*

SCENE [VII]

Enter in SIR EDWARD'S *house*, SIR EDWARD BELFOND *and* Attorney

SIR EDWARD. This is the time I appointed my son to bring your daughter hither. The witness is a most malicious, lying wench, and can never have credit. Besides, you know an action will sufficiently stop her mouth; for, were it true, she can never prove what she says.

ATTORNEY. You are right, sir. Next to her being innocent is the concealing of her shame.

Enter BELFOND JUNIOR *and* LUCIA

LUCIA. And can I live to hear my fatal sentence of parting with you? Hold, heart, a little.

BELFOND JUNIOR. It is with some convulsions I am torn from you; but I must marry— I can not help it.

LUCIA. And must I never see you more?

BELFOND JUNIOR. As a lover, never; but your friend I'll be while I have breath.

LUCIA. (*To herself*) Heart, do not swell so. This has awakened me and made me see my crime. Oh, that it had been sooner!

BELFOND JUNIOR. Sir, I beg a thousand pardons that I should attempt to injure your family, for it has gone no farther yet. For any fact, she's innocent, but 'twas no thanks to me—I am not so.—(*Aside*) If a lie be ever lawful, 'tis in this case.

SIR EDWARD. Come, pretty lady, let me present you to your father. Though, as my son says, she's innocent, yet, because his love had gone so far, I present her with £1,500. My son and you shall be trustees for her. Tomorrow you shall have the money.

BELFOND JUNIOR. You are the best of all mankind.

ATTORNEY. All the world speaks your praises justly.

LUCIA. A thousand thanks, sir, for your bounty. And if my father please to pardon me this slip, in which I was so far from fact that I had scarce intention, I will hereafter outlive the strictest nun.

ATTORNEY. Rise; I do pardon you.

SIR EDWARD. That's well. And if they be not kind to you, appeal to me. It will be fit for you to go from hence with the least notice that can be. Tomorrow I'll bring the money.

Exeunt Attorney *and* LUCIA

Who are the ladies you have entrusted me with, Ned?

BELFOND JUNIOR. Scrapeall's niece and daughter. The niece my father was to give £5,000 for, for his son. If you will give me leave, I shall marry her for nothing; and the other will take my friend—

Sir [Edward]. How, Ned! She's a Puritan!

Belfond Junior. No more than you, sir. She was bred otherwise, but was fain to comply for peace. She is beautiful and witty to a miracle, and I beg your consent, for I will die before I marry without it.

Sir Edward. Dear Ned, thou hast it; but what hast thou done with the Alsatians?

Belfond Junior. I have the rogues in custody, and my brother, too, whom I rescued in the very minute he was going to be married to a whore—to my whore, who plagues me continually. I see my father coming; pray prepare him while I prepare my brother for meeting with him. He shall not see me. *Exit*

Enter Sir William Belfond

Sir William. Your servant, brother. No news of Ned yet?

Sir Edward. Oh, yes; he has your son and the three rogues in custody, and will bring them hither. Brother, pray resolve not to lose a son, but use him kindly, and forgive him.

Sir William. I will, brother; and let him spend what he will, I'll come up to London, feast and revel, and never take a minute's care while I breathe, again.

Enter a Servant *to* Sir Edward

Servant. Sir, a young gentleman would speak with you.

Sir Edward. Bid him come in.

Enter Mrs. Termagant *in man's clothes*

Termagant. If you be Sir Edward Belfond, I come to tell you what concerns your honor and my love.

Sir Edward. I am he.

Termagant. Know then, sir, I am informed your brother Sir William Belfond's son is to marry Isabella, the niece of Mr. Scrapeall.

Sir Edward. What then, sir?

Termagant. Then he invades my right. I have been many months contracted to her, and as you are a man of honor, I must tell you we have sealed that contract with mutual enjoyments.

Sir William. How! What, was my son to marry a whore? I'll to this damned fellow instantly, and make him give up my articles.

Sir Edward. Have patience. Be not too rash.

Sir William. Patience! What, to have my son marry a whore?

Sir Edward. Look you, brother, you must stay a moment.

Enter Belfond Junior

Sir William. Oh, Ned, your brother has 'scaped a fine match. This same Isabella is contracted to, and has been enjoyed by, this gentleman, as he calls it. He had liked to have married a whore.

Belfond Junior. Yes, that he had; but I will cut the throat of him that affirms that of Isabella.

Termagant. Sir, I demand the protection of your house.

Sir Edward. Hold, son.

Termagant. (*Aside*) What devil sent him hither at this time?

Belfond Junior. I'll bring them to confront this rogue. What a devil's this? Have we another brother of that devil Termagant's here? *Exit*

Sir Edward. This is a very odd story.

Sir William. Let me go, brother; 'tis true enough. But what makes Ned concerned?

Sir Edward. Let us examine yet farther.

Enter Belfond Junior *with* Isabella, Teresia, *and* Ruth, *and* Truman

Sir William. Look, here they are all! How the devil comes this about?

Termagant. O madam, are you here? I claim your contract, which I suppose will not offend you.

Isabella. What means this impudent fellow? I ne'er saw his face before.

Termagant. Yes, madam, you have seen, and more than seen me often, since we were contracted.

Isabella. What instrument of villainy is this?

Termagant. Nay, if you deny—! Friends, come in.

Enter two Alsatian affidavit men

Friends, do you know this gentlewoman?

First Witness. Yes, she is Mr. Scrapeall's niece.

Second Witness. We were both witness to a contract of marriage between you two.

Isabella. Oh, impious wretches! What conspiracy is this?

Sir William. Can anything be more plain? They seem civil, grave, substantial men.

Belfond Junior. Hold, hold, have I found ye? 'Tis she, it could be no other devil but herself.

(He pulls off her peruke)

Sir William. A woman!

Sir Edward. Secure those witnesses!

Belfond Junior. A woman! No. She has out-sinned her sex, and is a devil. Oh, devil, most complete devil! This is the lady I have been so much of late obliged to.

Isabella. This is she that told us the fine story today.

Teresia. I know her face again, most infamous, lying creature!

Termagant. I am become desperate! Have at thee!

(She snaps a pistol at Belfond, which only flashes in the pan. The ladies shriek)

Belfond Junior. Thank you, madam. Are you not a devil? 'Twas loaden, 'twas well meant, truly.   *(Takes the pistol from her)*

Sir Edward. Lay hold on her. I'll send her to a place where she shall be tamed. I never yet heard of such malice.

Sir William. Dear Ned, thou hast so obliged me, thou melt'st my heart. That thou shouldst steal away those ladies, and save me £5,000! Now I hope, madam, my son Tim shall be your husband without bargain and sale.

Isabella. No, I can assure you, sir, I would never have performed that bargain of my uncle's. We had determined to dispose of ourselves before that, and now are more resolved.

Teresia. We have broken prison by the help of these gentlemen, and I think we must e'en take the authors of our liberty.

Isabella. Will not that be a little hard, cousin, to take their liberty from them who have given it to us?

Sir William. Well, I am disappointed; but I can not blame thee, Ned.

(Truman goes to Teresia)

Enter Belfond Senior

Sir Edward. Your son. Pray use him kindly.

Belfond Senior. I have been betrayed, cheated, and abused. Upon my knees I beg your pardon and never will offend you more; adad, I will not. I thought they had been the honestest, the finest gentlemen in England, and it seems they are rogues, cheats, and blockheads.

Sir William. Rise, Tim. I profess thou makest me weep; thou hast subdued me. I forgive thee. I see all human care is vain. I will allow thee £500 a year, and come and live with ease and pleasure here. I'll feast and revel, and wear myself with pain and care no more.

Belfond Senior. A thousand thanks. I'll ne'er displease you while I live, again; adad, I won't. [*Aside*] Here's an alteration! I ne'er had good word from him before.

Sir William. I would have married you to that pretty lady, but your brother has been too hard for you.

Belfond Senior. She's very pretty. But 'tis no matter; I am in no such haste but I can stay and see the world first.

Sir Edward. Welcome, dear nephew, to my house and me. And now, my dear son, be free, and before all this company, let me know all the encumbrances you have upon you.

Belfond Junior. That good-natured lady is the only one that's heavy upon me. I have her child in my possession, which she says is mine.

Termagant. Has he my child? Then I am undone forever. Oh, cursed misfortune!

Sir Edward. Look you, madam, I will settle an annuity of £100 a year upon you so long as you shall not disturb my son; and for your child, I'll breed her up and provide for her like a gentlewoman. But if you are not quiet, you shall never see her more.

Termagant. You speak like a noble gentleman. I'll strive to compose myself. I am at last subdued, but will not stay to see the triumphs.—   *Exit hastily*

Sir Edward. Well, dear Ned, dost owe any money?

Belfond Junior. No, my dear father, no. You have been too bountiful for that. I have five hundred guineas in my cabinet.

Sir Edward. Now, madam, if you please to accept him for a husband, I will settle fifteen hundred pounds a year on him in present, which shall be your jointure. Besides that, your own money shall be laid out in land and settled on you, too. And at my death the rest of my estate.

Isabella. You do me too much honor; you much out-bid my value.

BELFOND JUNIOR. You best of fathers and of all mankind, I throw myself thus at your feet. Let me embrace your knees and kiss those hands.

SIR EDWARD. Come, rise and kiss these hands.

BELFOND JUNIOR. A long farewell to all the vanity and lewdness of youth. I offer myself at your feet as a sacrifice without a blemish now.

ISABELLA. Rise, I beseech you, rise.

TERESIA. [*To* TRUMAN] Your offers, sir, are better much than I could expect or can deserve.

TRUMAN. That's impossible. The wealth of both the Indies could not buy you from me, I am sure.

RUTH. Come, come, I have been governess, I know their minds. Come, give your hands where you have given your hearts. Here, friend Truman, first take this.

TERESIA. My governess will have it so.

SIR EDWARD. Joy, sir, be ever with you. Please to make my house your own.

ISABELLA. How can I be secure you will not fall to your old courses again?

BELFOND JUNIOR. I have been so sincere in my confessions you can trust me; but I call heaven to witness I will hereafter be entirely yours. I look on marriage as the most solemn vow a man can make; and 'tis by consequence the basest perjury to break it.

RUTH. Come, come, I know your mind, too; take him, take him.

ISABELLA. If fate will have it so.

BELFOND JUNIOR. Let me receive this blessing on my knee.

ISABELLA. You are very devout of late.

SIR EDWARD. A thousand blessings on you both.

SIR WILLIAM. Perpetual happiness attend you both.

BELFOND SENIOR. Brother and madam, I wish you joy from my heart, adad, I do. [*Aside to* BELFOND JUNIOR] Though between you and I, brother, I intend to have my swing at whoring and drinking as you had, before I come to it, though.

SIR EDWARD. Here! Bring in these rogues.

(*The* Constable *brings in* CHEATLY, SHAMWELL, *and* HACKUM)

Come, rascals, I shall take a care to see examples made of you.

CHEATLY. We have substantial bail.

SIR EDWARD. I'll see it shall be substantial bail; it is my lord chief justice's warrant, returnable to none but him. But I will prosecute you, I assure you.

CHEATLY. Squire, dear squire!

HACKUM. Good, noble squire, speak for us.

SHAMWELL. Dear cousin!

BELFOND SENIOR. Oh, rogues! Cousin, you have cozened me; you made a put, a caravan, a bubble of me. I gave a judgment for £1,600 and had but 250, but there's some goods they talk of. But if e'er I be catched again, I'll be hanged.

SIR WILLIAM. Unconscionable villains! the chancery shall relieve us.

SIR EDWARD. I'll rout this knot of most pernicious knaves, for all the privilege of your place. Was ever such impudence suffered in a government? Ireland's conquered; Wales subdued; Scotland united; but there are some few spots of ground in London, just in the face of the government, unconquered yet, that hold in rebellion still. Methinks 'tis strange that places so near the king's palace should be no part of his dominions. 'Tis a shame to the societies of the law to countenance such practices. Should any place be shut against the king's writ, or *posse comitatus?* Take them away, and those two witnesses.

(*The* Constable *and* Watch *hale[s] 'em away*)

BELFOND SENIOR. Away with 'em, rogues, rascals, damned prigs!

SIR EDWARD. Come, ladies, I have sent for some neighbors to rejoice with us. We have fiddles. Let's dance a brisk round or two, and then we'll make a collation.

In the flourish before the dance enter SCRAPEALL

SCRAPEALL. Oh, Sir William, I am undone, ruined! The birds are flown. Read the note they left behind 'em.

SIR WILLIAM. Peace, they are dancing. They have disposed of themselves.

SCRAPEALL. Oh, seed of serpents! Am I cheated then? I'll try a trick of law, you frogs of the bottomless pit, I will, and instantly— What, dancing too? Then they are fallen, indeed!

They dance. Exit SCRAPEALL *hastily*

SIR EDWARD. Come, brother, now who has been in the right, you or I?

SIR WILLIAM. You have. Prithee, do not triumph.
BELFOND JUNIOR. Farewell forever, all the vices of the age!
There is no peace but in a virtuous life,
Nor lasting joy but in a tender wife.
SIR EDWARD. You that would breed your children well, by kindness and liberality endear 'em to you, and teach 'em by example. Severity spoils ten for one it mends: 10
If you'd not have your sons desire your ends,
By gentleness and bounty make those sons your friends.

Exeunt omnes

EPILOGUE

SPOKEN BY MRS. MOUNTFORT

Ye mighty scourers of the narrow seas,
Who suffer not a bark to sail in peace,
But with your tire of culverins [1] ye roar,
Bring 'em by th' lee, and rummage all their store;
Our poet ducked and looked as if half dead 5
At every shot that whistled o'er his head.
Frequent engagements ne'er could make him bold.
He sneaked into a corner of the hold.
Since he submits, pray ease him of his fear,
And with a joint applause bid him appear;
Good critics don't insult and domineer. 11
He fears not sparks, who with brisk dress and mien
Come not to hear or see, but to be seen.

[1] Tier of cannon.

Each prunes himself, and with a languishing eye
Designs to kill a lady by the by 15
Let each fantastic ugly beau and shape,
Little of man, and very much of ape,
Admire himself, and let the poet 'scape.
Ladies, your anger most he apprehends,
And is grown past the age of making friends
Of any of the sex whom he offends. 21
No princess frowns, no hero roars and whines,
Nor his weak sense embroidered with strong lines;
No battles, trumpets, drums; not any die;
No mortal wounds to please your cruelty,
Who like not anything but tragedy, 26
With fond, unnatural extravagances
Stolen from the silly authors of romances.
Let such the chamber-maid's diversions be;
Pray be you reconciled to comedy. 30
For when we make you merry, you must own
You are much prettier than when you frown.
With charming smiles you use to conquer still,
The melancholy look's not apt to kill.
Our poet begs you who adorn this sphere,
This shining circle will not be severe. 36
Here no chit chat, here no tea tables are.
The cant he hopes will not be long unknown,
'Tis almost grown the language of the town.
For fops, who feel a wretched want of wit, 40
Still set up something that may pass for it.
He begs that you will often grace his play,
And let's you know Monday's [2] his visiting day.

[2] The play was produced Friday; the poet was entitled to the profits of the third performance, which would be on Monday.

LOVE'S LAST SHIFT;

OR,

THE FOOL IN FASHION

By Colley Cibber

Fuit hæc sapientia quondam,
Concubitu prohibere vago, dare jura maritis.
Hor. de Art. Poet.[1]

Caius Gabriel Cibber, a Dane by birth, is known to fame as the sculptor of the figures of Raving and Melancholy which adorned the entrance to the old Bedlam hospital, of certain decorations upon St. Paul's Cathedral, and of the pediment of the London Monument. His wife, Jane Colley, claimed descent from William of Wykeham. Their son, Colley Cibber, was one of the most prominent figures on the English stage for forty years. He was born in London, November 6, 1671. He early showed a desire to go upon the stage and, attaching himself to the Theatre Royal in Drury Lane, he was finally hired more or less by accident because he was on the ground. Though he first appeared on the stage in 1691, he made little impression until his appearance in his own *Love's Last Shift* in 1696. Meanwhile he had married and begun to raise a family. His children and his plays followed in rapid succession for years. He also retained his reputation as an actor, creating many parts. In 1710 Cibber became, with Wilks and Dogget, one of the "triumvirate" which managed Drury Lane for a time, and thereafter until his retirement in 1734 he was the principal manager of the theatre as well as a prominent actor and one of its most prolific playwrights.

In 1730 Cibber was appointed Poet Laureate, a post which he filled with considerable satisfaction to himself if to no one else. During his later years he was a well known figure in London public life and society and the second hero of *The Dunciad*, replacing Theobald in the edition of 1742 after many years of quarrel with Pope. In 1740 he published his *An Apology for the Life of Mr. Colley Cibber*, most delightful of autobiographies, which lends color to the witticism, "He seems to have lived his life in order that he might apologize for it." Cibber died December 11, 1757, having retained throughout his eighty-six years the youthful zest for life, the impervious but inoffensive effrontery that one finds in the fops which he portrayed so well. He was thought to be a fool by many people; but even Dr. Johnson, years after Cibber was dead, had to admit that "Colley Cibber, sir, was by no means a blockhead."

See Cibber's *Apology* (edited by R. W. Lowe, 1889), the *Dictionary of National Biography*, De Witt C. Croissant, *Studies in the Work of Colley Cibber* (1912), and *The Life and Times of Colley Cibber* by F. Dorothy Senior (1928).

CIBBER'S PLAYS

(Following is a selected list. Cibber wrote some twenty-six plays.)

Love's Last Shift; or, The Fool in Fashion (comedy) (D.L., Jan., 1696), 1696.
Richard III (altered from Shakespeare) (D.L., c. Feb., 1700), 1700.
She Wou'd and She Wou'd Not (comedy) (D.L., Nov., 1702), 1703.
The Careless Husband (comedy) (D.L., Dec., 1704), 1705.
The Double Gallant (comedy) (Hay., Nov., 1707), 1707.
The Lady's Last Stake; or, The Wife's Resentment (comedy) (Hay., Dec., 1707), 1708.
The Non-Juror (comedy, adapted from Molière's Tartuffe) (D.L., Dec., 1717), 1718.
The Provoked Husband; or, A Journey to

---

[1] This was of old counted wisdom, to prohibit promiscuous intercourse, to grant (legal) rights to married people.—*Ars Pœtica*, 396 and 398. Cibber omits line 397.

London (completion of Vanbrugh's unfinished comedy) (D.L., Jan. 10, 1728), 1728.

Love in a Riddle (ballad opera) (D.L., Jan., 1729), 1729.

Papal Tyranny in the Reign of King John (altered from Shakespeare) (C.G., Feb., 1745), 1745.

In order to create a part for himself young Mr. Cibber wrote a play. As he had made little success of his acting at the Theatre Royal, the company was sceptical as to the success of his efforts as a playwright. But Mr. Southerne, the author of *Oroonoko*, who had "recommended [the comedy] to the patentees," just before the first performance took the author "by the hand and said, 'Young man, I pronounce the play a good one. I will answer for its success, if thou dost not spoil it by thy own action.' Though this," Cibber continues, "might be a fair *salvo* for his favorable judgment of the play, yet, if it were his real opinion of me as an actor, I had the good fortune to deceive him. I succeeded so well in both that people seemed at a loss which they should give the preference to." Thus the author, years later, commented upon his première, adding by way of clinching the argument, "The compliment which my Lord Dorset (then Lord Chamberlain) made me upon it is, I own, what I had rather not suppress, *viz.*, that it was the best first play that any author in his memory had produced, and that for a young fellow to show himself such an actor and such a writer in one day was something extraordinary." And who would go behind the judgment of Mr. Southerne and my Lord Dorset? The successful performance occurred at the Theatre Royal in January, 1696. The young actor established himself as Sir Novelty Fashion; and the young author, probably not aware of his originality but then, as always, uncannily conscious of the beat of the public pulse, instituted a new type of comedy on the English stage.

Love's Last Shift is the first sentimental comedy in the eighteenth century sense of that term. It contains a serious treatment of a serious subject and presents a moral problem the solution of which is happy though the characters involved are at times on the verge of permanent distress. As Cibber artlessly said in his epilogue, "there's not one cuckold made in all this play," a point to be mentioned in the day of Wycherley and Etherege; and foreshadowing comedy for the next hundred years, Cibber reforms his rake, reclaims the libertine, and makes virtue triumphant, all through the appeal to the emotions of pity and gratitude. He points the way for Steele and the rest of the eighteenth century group. That he was himself not especially serious in his protestations of virtue and his picture of the paragon, Amanda, is shown by his gleeful welcome of Vanbrugh's *The Relapse; or, Virtue in Danger*, in which he acted with complete success the next season.

Cibber's first comedy shows, besides the newer element, caught from the spirit of the time, conventions of Restoration comedy in the love intrigue plots, the language, "which, as Mr. Congreve justly said of it, had only in it a great many things that were *like* wit that in reality were *not* wit," the masque at the conclusion, and the character of the fop. Sir Novelty, directly inspired by Sir Foppling Flutter, becomes himself Lord Foppington, perhaps the greatest of a race which includes also Sir Benjamin Backbite and Lord Dundreary.

LOVE'S LAST SHIFT;

OR,

THE FOOL IN FASHION

DRAMATIS PERSONÆ

MEN

SIR WILLIAM WISEWOUD, *a rich old gentleman that fancies himself a great master of his passion, which he only is in trivial matters.* Mr. Johnson

LOVELESS, *of a debauched life, grew weary of his wife in six months, left her, and the town for debts he did not care to pay, and having spent the last part of his estate beyond sea, returns to England in a very mean condition.* Mr. Verbruggen

SIR NOVELTY FASHION, *a coxcomb that loves to be the first in all foppery.* Mr. Cibber

ELDER WORTHY, *a sober gentleman of a fair estate, in love with Hillaria.* Mr. Williams

YOUNG WORTHY, *his brother, of a looser temper, lover to Narcissa.* Mr. Horden

SNAP, *servant to Loveless.* Mr. Pinkethman

SLY, *servant to Young Worthy.* Mr. Bullock

A LAWYER Mr. Mills

WOMEN

AMANDA, *a woman of strict virtue, married to Loveless very young and forsaken by him.* Mrs. Rogers

NARCISSA, *daughter to Sir William Wisewoud, a fortune.* Mrs. Verbruggen

HILLARIA, *his niece.* Mrs. Cibber

FLAREIT, *a kept mistress of Sir Novelty's.* Mrs. Kent

WOMAN TO AMANDA. Mrs. Lucas

MAID TO FLAREIT.

Servants, Sentinels, Porter, Bullies, and Musicians.

The SCENE: *London*

PROLOGUE [1]

BY A FRIEND

Spoken by MR. VERBRUGGEN

Wit bears so thin a crop this duller age,
We're forc'd to glean it from the barren stage.
Ev'n players fledg'd by nobler pens take wing
Themselves, and their own rude composures sing.
Nor need our young one [2] dread a shipwreck here; 5
Who trades without a stock has nought to fear.
In every smile of yours, a prize he draws,
And if you damn him, he's but where he was.

Yet where's the reason for the critic crew
With killing blasts like winter to pursue 10
The tender plant that ripens but for you?
Nature in all her works requires time;
Kindness, and years, 'tis, makes the virgin climb
And shoot and hasten to the expected prime;
And then, if untaught fancy fail to please, 15
Y'instruct the willing pupil by degrees;
By gentle lessons you your joys improve
And mold her awkward passion into love.
Ev'n folly has its growth: few fools are made;
You drudge and sweat for't, as it were a trade. 20
'Tis half the labor of your trifling age
To fashion you fit subjects for the stage.
Well! If our author fail to draw you like
In the first draught, you're not to expect Van Dyck.[3]

---

[1] The dedication of the play to one Richard Norton, of Southwick, Esq., has been omitted. It contains Cibber's statement that the piece is entirely original with him and that its success is the result of his careful consideration of the taste of his audience.

[2] Cibber was twenty-four years old at this time.

[3] Sir Anthony Van Dyck (1599–1641), the famous Flemish painter, worked mainly in London after 1632, largely as a portrait painter.

What, though no master-stroke in this appears, 25
Yet some may find features resembling theirs.
Nor do the bad alone his colors share;
Neglected virtue is at least shown fair;
And that's enough o' conscience for a play'r.
But if you'd have him take a bolder flight 30
And draw your pictures by a truer light,
You must yourselves, by follies yet unknown,
Inspire his pencil[1] and divert the town.
Nor judge by this his genius at a stand,
For time, that makes new fools, may mend his hand. 35

ACT I

[SCENE I]

SCENE: *The Park*

Enter LOVELESS *and* SNAP, *his servant*

LOVELESS. Sirrah! leave your preaching. Your counsel,[2] like an ill clock, either stands still or goes too slow. You ne'er thought my extravagancies amiss while you had your share of them; and now I want money to make myself drunk, you advise me to live sober, you dog. They that will hunt pleasure, as I ha' done, rascal, must never give over in a fair chase.

SNAP. Nay, I knew you would never rest till you had tired your dogs. Ah, sir! what a fine pack of guineas have you had! and yet you would make 'em run till they were quite spent. Would I were fairly turned out of your service! Here we have been three days in town, and I can safely swear I have lived upon picking a hollow tooth ever since.

LOVELESS. Why don't you eat then, sirrah?

SNAP. Even because I don't know where, sir.

LOVELESS. Then stay till I eat, hang-dog, ungrateful rogue, to murmur at a little fasting with me when thou hast been an equal partner of my good fortune.

SNAP. Fortune! It makes me weep to think what you have brought yourself and me to! How well might you ha' lived, sir, had you been a sober man. Let me see! I ha' been in your service just ten years. In the first you married and grew weary of your wife; in the second you whored, drank, gamed, run in debt, mortgaged your estate, and was forced to leave the kingdom; in the third, fourth, fifth, sixth, and seventh you made the tour of Europe, with the state and equipage of a French court favorite, while your poor wife at home broke her heart for the loss of you. In the eighth and ninth you grew poor, and little the wiser, and now in the tenth you are resolved I shall starve with you.

LOVELESS. Despicable rogue, canst not thou bear the frowns of a common strumpet, Fortune?

SNAP. S'bud, I never think of the pearl necklace you gave that damned Venetian strumpet but I wish her hanged in it!

LOVELESS. Why, sirrah! I knew I could not have her without it, and I had a night's enjoyment of her, was worth a pope's revenue for it.

SNAP. Ah, you had better ha' laid out your money here in London; I'll undertake you might have had the whole town over and over for half the price. Besides, sir, what a delicate creature was your wife! She was the only celebrated beauty in town; I'll undertake there were more fops and fools run mad for her, 'Odsbud, she was more plagued with 'em, and more talked of, than a good actress with a maiden-head! Why the devil could not she content you?

LOVELESS. No, sirrah! The world to me is a garden stocked with all sorts of fruit, where the greatest pleasure we can take is in the variety of taste; but a wife is an eternal apple tree—after a pull or two you are sure to set your teeth on edge.

SNAP. And yet I warrant you grudged another man a bit of her, though you valued her no more than you would a half-eaten pippin that had lain a week a-sunning in a parlor window. But see, sir, who's this—for methinks I long to meet with an old acquaintance!

LOVELESS. Ha! Egad, he looks like one, and may be necessary as the case stands with me.—

SNAP. Pray heaven he do but invite us to dinner!

Enter YOUNG WORTHY

LOVELESS. Dear Worthy! Let me embrace thee; the sight of an old friend warms me beyond that of a new mistress.

YOUNG WORTHY. S'death, what bully's this? Sir, your pardon; I don't know you!

---

[1] I.e., brush used by a painter.
[2] The first edition reads *counsel's*, corrected in the first collected edition of Cibber's plays, 1721.

LOVELESS. Faith, Will, I am a little out of repairs at present. But I am all that's left of honest Ned Loveless.

YOUNG WORTHY. Loveless! I am amazed! What means this metamorphosis? Faith, Ned, I am glad to find thee amongst the living, however. How long hast thou been in town?

LOVELESS. About three days. But prithee, Will, how goes the world?

YOUNG WORTHY. Why, like a bowl, it runs on at the old rate; interest is still the jack[1] it aims at; and while it rolls, you know, it must of necessity be often turned upside down. But I doubt, Friend, you have bowled out of the green, have lived a little too fast (*Surveying his dress*) like one that has lost all his ready money, and are forced to be an idle spectator. Prithee, what brought thee at last to England?

LOVELESS. Why, my last hopes, faith, which were to persuade Sir Will[iam][2] Wisewoud (if he be alive), to whom I mortgaged my estate, to let me have five hundred pounds more upon it, or else to get some honest friend to redeem the mortgage and share the overplus! Beside, I thought that London might now be a place of uninterrupted pleasure, for I hear my wife is dead; and to tell you the truth, it was the staleness of her love was the main cause of my going over.

YOUNG WORTHY. (*Aside*) His wife dead, ha! I'm glad he knows no other; I won't undeceive him, lest the rogue should go and rifle her of what she has.—Yes, faith, I was at her burial and saw her take possession of her long home and am sorry to tell you, Ned, she died with grief! Your wild courses broke her heart.

LOVELESS. Why, faith! She was a good-natured fool! That's the truth on it. Well, rest her soul.

SNAP. Now, sir, you are a single man, indeed, for you have neither wife nor estate.

YOUNG WORTHY. But how hast thou improved thy money beyond sea? What hast thou brought over?

LOVELESS. Oh, a great deal of experience.

YOUNG WORTHY. And no money?

SNAP. Not a sou, faith, sir, as my belly can testify.

LOVELESS. But I have a great deal more wit than I had!

SNAP. Not enough to get your estate again or to know where we shall dine today. (*Aside*) Oh, Lord, he don't ask us yet!

YOUNG WORTHY. Why, your rogue's witty, Ned; where didst thou pick him up?

LOVELESS. Don't you remember Snap? Formerly your pimp in ordinary—but he is much improved in his calling, I assure you, sir.

YOUNG WORTHY. I don't doubt it, considering who has been his master.

SNAP. Yes, sir, I was an humble servant of yours, and am still, sir, and should be glad to stand behind your chair at dinner, sir. (*Bows*)

YOUNG WORTHY. Oh, sir, that you may do another time; but today I am engaged upon business; however, there's a meal's meat for you. (*Throws him a guinea*)

SNAP. Bless my eye-sight, a guinea! Sir, is there ever a whore you would have kicked, any old bawd's windows you would have broken? Shall I beat your tailor for disappointing you? Or your surgeon that would be paid for a clap of two years' standing? If you have occasion, you may command your humble servant.—

YOUNG WORTHY. Sweet sir, I am obliged to you, but at present am so happy as to have no occasion for your assistance.—But hark you, Ned, prithee, what hast thou done with thy estate?

LOVELESS. I pawned it to buy pleasure, that is, old wine, young whores, and the conversation of brave fellows as mad as myself. Pox! If a man has appetites, they are torments if not indulged. I shall never complain as long as I have health and vigor; and as for my poverty, why the devil should I be ashamed of that, since a rich man won't blush at his knavery?

YOUNG WORTHY. Faith, Ned, I am as much in love with wickedness as thou canst be, but I am for having it at a cheaper rate than my ruin. Don't it grate you a little to see your friends blush for you?

LOVELESS. It is very odd that people should be more ashamed of others' faults than their own; I never yet could meet with a man that offered me counsel, but had more occasion for it himself.

YOUNG WORTHY. So far you may be in the right, for indeed good counsel is like a home jest, which every busy fool is offering to his fellow, and yet won't take himself.

LOVELESS. Right! Thus have I known a jolly, red-nosed parson at three o'clock in the

---
[1] The small bowl used as a mark in a game of bowls.
[2] The first edition abbreviates, "Will."

morning belch out invectives against late hours and hard drinking, and a canting, hypocritical sinner protest against fornication, when the rogue was himself just crawling out of a flux.

YOUNG WORTHY. Though these are truths, friend, yet I don't see any advantage you can draw from them. Prithee, how will you live now all your money's gone?

LOVELESS. Live! How dost thou live? Thou art but a younger brother, I take it.

YOUNG WORTHY. Oh, very well, sir, though, faith, my father left me but three thousand pounds, one of which I gave for a place at court that I still enjoy; the other two are gone after pleasure, as thou sayest. But besides this, I am supplied by the continual bounty of an indulgent brother; now I am loath to load his good nature too much, and therefore have e'en thought fit, like the rest of my raking brotherhood, to purge out my wild humors with matrimony. By the way, I have taken care to see the dose well sweetened with a swinging portion.

LOVELESS. Ah, Will, you'll find marrying to cure lewdness is like surfeiting to cure hunger—for all the consequence is, you loathe what you surfeit on and are only chaste to her you marry. But prithee, friend, what is thy wife that must be?

YOUNG WORTHY. Why, faith, since I believe the matter is too far gone for any man to postpone me—at least, I am sure, thou wilt not do me an injury to do thyself no good— I'll tell thee: You must know, my mistress is the daughter of that very knight to whom you mortgaged your estate, Sir William Wisewoud.

LOVELESS. Why, she's an heiress and has a thousand pounds a year in her own hands, if she be of age. But I suppose the old man knows nothing of your intentions. Therefore, prithee, how have you had opportunities of promoting your love?

YOUNG WORTHY. Why, thus: You must know, Sir William, being very well acquainted with the largeness of my brother's estate, designs this daughter for him, and to encourage his passion offers him out of his own pocket the additional blessing of five thousand pounds. This offer my brother, knowing my inclinations, seems to embrace; but at the same time is really in love with his niece, who lives with him in the same house; and, therefore, to hide my design from the old gentleman, I pretend visits to his daughter as an intercessor for my brother only, and thus he has given me daily opportunities of advancing my own interest—nay, and I have so contrived it that I design to have the five thousand pounds too.

LOVELESS. How is that possible, since I see no hopes of the old man's consent for you?

YOUNG WORTHY. Have a day's patience, and you'll see the effects on it; in a word, it is so sure that nothing but delays can hinder my success; therefore I am very earnest with my mistress that tomorrow may be the day. But a pox on it! I have two women to prevail with, for my brother quarrels every other day with his mistress, and while I am reconciling him, I lose ground in my own amour.

LOVELESS. Why, has not your mistress told you her mind yet?

YOUNG WORTHY. She will, I suppose, as soon as she knows it herself, for within this week she has changed it as often as her linen and keeps it as secret, too; for she would no more own her love before my face than she would shift herself before my face.

LOVELESS. Pshaw! She shows it the more by striving to conceal it.

YOUNG WORTHY. Nay, she does give me some proofs indeed, for she will suffer nobody but herself to speak ill of me, is always uneasy till I am sent for, never pleased when I am with her, and still jealous when I leave her.

LOVELESS. Well, success to thee, Will; I will send the fiddles to release you from your first night's labor.[1]

YOUNG WORTHY. But hark you, have a care of disobliging the bride, though. Ha! Yonder goes my brother. I am afraid his walking so early proceeds from some disturbance in his love; I must after him and set him right. Dear Ned, you'll excuse me; shall I see you at the Blue Posts between five and six this afternoon?

LOVELESS. With all my heart—but do you hear?—canst not thou lend me the fellow to that same [2] guinea you gave my man; I'll give you my bond if you mistrust me.

YOUNG WORTHY. Oh, sir, your necessity is obligation enough—there it is, and all I have, faith; when I see you at night, you may

---

[1] I.e., serenade on the wedding night, perhaps with a charivari.

[2] "Guineas went then at 30s."—Note in 1721 edition.

command me further. Adieu, at six at farthest. *Exit* YOUNG WORTHY

LOVELESS. Without fail. So! Now, Rascal, you are an hungry, are you! Thou deservest never to eat again. Rogue! Grumble before fortune had quite forsaken us!

SNAP. Ah, dear sir, the thoughts of eating again have so transported me I am resolved to live and die with you.

LOVELESS. Look ye, sirrah, here's that will provide us of a dinner and a brace of whores into the bargain, at least as guineas and whores go now.

SNAP. Ah, good sir, no whores before dinner, I beseech you.

LOVELESS. Well, for once I'll take your advice; for, to say truth, a man is as unfit to follow love with an empty stomach as business with an empty head. Therefore, I think a bit and a bottle won't be amiss first.

The gods of wine and love were ever friends;
For by the help of wine, love gains his ends.
Exeunt

Enter ELDER WORTHY *with a letter*

ELDER WORTHY. How hard is it to find that happiness which our short-sighted passions hope from woman! It is not their cold disdain or cruelty should make a faithful lover curse his stars; that is but reasonable. It is the shadow in our pleasure's picture. Without it love could never be heightened! No, it is their pride and vain desire of many lovers that robs our hope of its imagined rapture; the blind are only happy! For if we look through reason's never erring perspective, we then survey their souls and view the rubbish we were chaffering for. And such I find Hillaria's mind is made of. This letter is an order for the knocking off my fetters, and I'll send it her immediately.

Enter to him YOUNG WORTHY

YOUNG WORTHY. Morrow, brother! (*Seeing the letter.*) What, is your fit returned again? What beau['s] box has Hillaria taken snuff from? What fool has led her from the box to her coach? What fop has she suffered to read a play or novel to her? Or whose money has she indiscreetly won at basset? Come, let's see the ghastly wound she has made in your quiet, that I may know how much claret to prescribe you.

ELDER WORTHY. I have my wound and cure from the same person, I'll assure you—the one from Hillaria's wit and beauty, the other from her pride and vanity.

YOUNG WORTHY. That's what I could never yet find her guilty of. Are you angry at her loving you?

ELDER WORTHY. I am angry at myself for believing she ever did.

YOUNG WORTHY. Have her actions spoke the contrary? Come, you know she loves.

ELDER WORTHY. Indeed she gave a great proof on it last night here in the park, by fastening upon a fool and caressing him before my face, when she might have so easily avoided him.

YOUNG WORTHY. What! And I warrant interrupted you in the middle of your sermon; for I don't question but you were preaching to her. But, prithee, who was the fool she fastened upon?

ELDER WORTHY. One that heaven intended for a man, but the whole business of his life is to make the world believe he is of another species. A thing that affects mightily to ridicule himself, only to give others a kind of necessity of praising him. I can't say he's a slave to every new fashion, for he pretends to be the master of it, and is ever reviving some old or advancing some new piece of foppery; and though it don't take, is still as well pleased, because it then obliges the town to take the more notice of him. He's so fond of a public reputation that he is more extravagant in his attempts to gain it than the fool that fired Diana's temple to immortalize his name.[1]

YOUNG WORTHY. You have said enough to tell me his name is Sir Novelty Fashion.

ELDER WORTHY. The same; but that which most concerns me is that he has the impudence to address to Hillaria, and she vanity enough to discard him.

YOUNG WORTHY. Is this all? Why, thou art as hard to please in a wife as thy mistress in a new gown. How many women have you took in hand and yet can't please yourself at last?

ELDER WORTHY. I had need to have the best goods when I offer so great a price as

---

[1] The temple of Diana at Ephesus was fired by Herostratus in 356 B.C.. The conflagration was said to have occurred on the night in October in which Alexander the Great was born.

marriage for them. Hillaria has some good qualities, but not enough to make a wife of.

YOUNG WORTHY. She has beauty!

ELDER WORTHY. Granted.

YOUNG WORTHY. And money.

ELDER WORTHY. Too much—enough to supply her vanity.

YOUNG WORTHY. She has sense.

ELDER WORTHY. Not enough to believe I am no fool.

YOUNG WORTHY. She has wit.

ELDER WORTHY. Not enough to deceive me.

YOUNG WORTHY. Why, then, you are happy if she can't deceive you.

ELDER WORTHY. Yet she has folly enough to endeavor it. I'll see her no more, and this shall tell her so.

YOUNG WORTHY. Which in an hour's time you'll repent as much as ever—

ELDER WORTHY. As ever I should marrying her.

YOUNG WORTHY. You'll have a damned [meeken][1] look when you are forced to ask her pardon for your ungenerous suspicion and lay the fault upon excess of love.

ELDER WORTHY. I am not so much in love as you imagine.

YOUNG WORTHY. Indeed, sir, you are in love, and that letter tells her so.

ELDER WORTHY. Read it; you'll find the contrary.

YOUNG WORTHY. Prithee, I know what's in it better than thou dost. You say it is to take your leave of her; but I say it is in hopes of a kind, excusive answer. But faith, you mistake her and yourself too. She is too high spirited not to take you at your word; and you are too much in love not to ask her pardon.

ELDER WORTHY. Well, then, I'll not be too rash, but will show my resentment in forbearing my visits.

YOUNG WORTHY. Your visits! Come, I shall soon try what a man of resolution you are, for yonder she comes. Now, let's see if you have power to move.

ELDER WORTHY. I'll soon convince you of that. Farewell. *Exit*

YOUNG WORTHY. Ha! Gone! I don't like that. I am sorry to find him so resolute. But I hope Hillaria has taken too fast hold of his heart to let this fit shake him off. I must to her and make up this breach, for while his amour stands still, I have no hopes of advancing my own. *Exit*

Enter HILLARIA, NARCISSA, *and* AMANDA, *in mourning*

HILLARIA. Well, dear Amanda, thou art the most constant wife I ever heard of, not to shake off the memory of an ill husband after eight or ten years' absence; nay, to mourn, for aught you know, for the living, too, and such a husband that though he were alive would never thank you for it. Why do you persist in such a hopeless grief?

AMANDA. Because it is hopeless! For if he be alive, he is dead to me; his dead affections not virtue's self can e'er retrieve. Would I were with him, though in his grave!

HILLARIA. In my mind, you are much better where you are. The grave! Young widows use to have warmer wishes. But methinks the death of a rich old uncle should be a cordial to your sorrows.

AMANDA. That adds to them, for he was the only relation I had left, and was as tender of me as the nearest! He was a father to me.

HILLARIA. He was better than some fathers to you, for he died just when you had occasion for his estate.

NARCISSA. I have an old father, and the deuce take me!—I think he only lives to hinder me of my occasions. But Lord bless me, madam, how can you be unhappy with two thousand pounds a year in your own possession?

HILLARIA. For my part the greatest reason I think you have to grieve is that you are not sure your husband's dead, for were that confirmed, then indeed there were hopes that one poison might drive out another—you might marry again.

AMANDA. All the comfort of my life is that I can tell my conscience I have been true to virtue.

HILLARIA. And to an extravagant husband that cares not a farthing for you. But come, let's leave this unseasonable talk, and pray give me a little of your advice. What shall I do with this Mr. Worthy? Would you advise me to make a husband of him?

AMANDA. I am but an ill judge of men; the only one I thought myself secure of most cruelly deceived me.

HILLARIA. A losing gamester is fittest to give counsel. What do you think of him?

---

[1] In first edition *meaking*, an obsolete form meaning *made meek*.

AMANDA. Better than of any man I know. I read nothing in him but what is some part of a good man's character.

HILLARIA. He's jealous.

AMANDA. He's a lover.

HILLARIA. He taxes me with a fool.

AMANDA. He would preserve your reputation, and a fool's love ends only in the ruin of it.

HILLARIA. Methinks he's not handsome.

AMANDA. He's a man, madam.

HILLARIA. Why, then, e'en let him make a woman of me.

NARCISSA. (*Smiling*) Pray, madam, what do you think of his brother?

AMANDA. I would not think of him.

NARCISSA. Oh, dear—why, pray?

AMANDA. He puts me in mind of a man too like him, one that had beauty, wit, and falsehood!

NARCISSA. You have hit some part of his character, I must confess, madam; but as to his truth, I'm sure he loves only me.

AMANDA. I don't doubt but he tells you so, nay, and swears it, too.

NARCISSA. O Lord! madam, I hope I may without vanity believe him.

AMANDA. But you will hardly without magic secure him.

NARCISSA. I shall use no spells or charms but this poor face, madam.

AMANDA. And your fortune, madam.

NARCISSA. (*Aside*) Senseless malice.—I know he'd marry me without a groat.

AMANDA. Then he's not the man I take him for.

NARCISSA. Why pray? What do you take him for?

AMANDA. A wild young fellow that loves everything he sees.

NARCISSA. He never loved you yet.

(*Peevishly*)

AMANDA. I hope, madam, he never saw anything in me to encourage him.

NARCISSA. In my conscience you are in the right on it, madam: I dare swear he never did, nor ever would, though he gazed till doomsday.

AMANDA. I hope, madam, your charms will prevent his putting himself to the trial, and I wish he may never—

NARCISSA. Nay, dear madam, no more railing at him, unless you would have me believe you love him.

HILLARIA. Indeed, ladies, you are both in the wrong. You, cousin, in being angry at what you desired, her opinion of your lover; and you, madam, for speaking truth against the man she resolves to love.

NARCISSA. Love him! Prithee, cousin, no more of that old stuff.

HILLARIA. Stuff! Why, don't you own you are to marry him this week? Here he comes; I suppose you'll tell him another thing in his ear.

Enter YOUNG WORTHY

HILLARIA. Mr. Worthy, your servant. You look with the face of business. What's the news, pray?

YOUNG WORTHY. Faith, madam, I have news for you all, and private news, too. But that of the greatest consequence is with this lady. Your pardon, ladies, I'll whisper with you all, one after another.

NARCISSA. Come, cousin, will you walk? The gentleman has business; we shall interrupt him.

HILLARIA. Why, really, cousin, I don't say positively you love Mr. Worthy, but I vow this looks very like jealousy.

NARCISSA. Pish! Lord, Hillaria, you are in a very odd humor today. But to let you see I have no such weak thoughts about me, I'll wait as unconcerned as yourself. (*Aside*) I'll rattle him. [HILLARIA *and* NARCISSA *retire*]

AMANDA. Not unpleasing, say you? Pray, sir, unfold yourself, for I have long despaired of welcome news.

YOUNG WORTHY. Then in a word, madam, your husband, Mr. Loveless, is in town, and has been these three days. I parted with him not an hour ago.

AMANDA. In town! You amaze me! For heaven's sake, go on.

YOUNG WORTHY. Faith, madam, considering Italy and those parts have furnished him with nothing but an improvement of that lewdness he carried over, I can't properly give you joy of his arrival. Besides, he is so very poor that you would take him for an inhabitant of that country. And when I confirmed your being dead, he only shook his head and called you good-natured fool, or to that effect. Nay, though I told him his unkindness broke your heart.

AMANDA. Barbarous man! Not shed a tear upon my grave? But why did you tell him I was dead?

YOUNG WORTHY. Because, madam, I thought you had no mind to have your house plundered, and for another reason, which, if you dare listen to me, perhaps you'll not dislike. In a word, it is such a strategem that will either make him ashamed of his folly or in love with your virtue.

AMANDA. Can there be a hope, when even my death could not move him to a relenting sigh? Yet pray instruct me, sir.

YOUNG WORTHY. You know, madam, it was not above four or five months after you were married but, as most young husbands do, he grew weary of you. Now I am confident it was more an affectation of being fashionably vicious than any reasonable dislike he could either find in your mind or person. Therefore, could you by some artifice pass upon him as a new mistress, I am apt to believe you would find none of the wonted coldness in his love, but a younger heat and fierce desire.

AMANDA. Suppose this done, what would be the consequence?

YOUNG WORTHY. Oh, your having then a just occasion to reproach him with his broken vows, and to let him see the weakness of his deluded fancy, which even in a wife, while unknown, could find those real charms which his blind, ungrateful lewdness would never allow her to be mistress of. After this, I'd have you seem freely to resign him to those fancied raptures which he denied were in a virtuous woman. Who knows but this, with a little submissive eloquence, may strike him with so great sense of shame as may reform his thoughts and fix him yours?

AMANDA. You have revived me, sir. But how can I assure myself he'll like me as a mistress?

YOUNG WORTHY. From your being a new one. Leave the management of all to me. I have a trick shall draw him to your bed, and when he's there, faith, even let him cuckold himself. I'll engage he likes you as a mistress, though he could not as a wife. (*Aside*) At least she'll have the pleasure of knowing the difference between a husband and a lover, without the scandal of the former.

AMANDA. You have obliged me, sir; if I succeed, the glory shall be yours.

YOUNG WORTHY. I'll wait on you at your lodging and consult how I may be farther serviceable to you. But you must put this in a speedy execution, lest he should hear of you and prevent your designs; in the meantime, it is a secret to all the world but yourself and me.

AMANDA. I'll study to be grateful, sir.
[HILLARIA *and* NARCISSA *come forward*]
YOUNG WORTHY. (*To Hillaria*) Now for you, madam.

NARCISSA. (*Aside*) So! I am to be last served! Very well!

YOUNG WORTHY. My brother, madam, confesses he scattered some rough words last night, and I have taken the liberty to tell you, you gave him some provocation.

HILLARIA. That may be; but I'm resolved to be mistress of my actions before marriage, and no man shall usurp a power over me till I give it him.

YOUNG WORTHY. At least, madam, consider what he said as the effect of an impatient passion and give him leave this afternoon to set all right again.

HILLARIA. Well, if I don't find myself out of order after dinner, perhaps I may step into the garden. But I won't promise you, neither.

YOUNG WORTHY. I dare believe you without it. (*To* NARCISSA) Now, madam, I am your humble servant.

NARCISSA. And everybody's humble servant. (*Walks off*)

YOUNG WORTHY. Why, madam, I am come to tell you—

NARCISSA. What success you have had with that lady, I suppose; I don't mind intrigues, sir.

YOUNG WORTHY. I like this jealousy, however, though I scarce know how to appease it. It is business of moment, madam, and may be done in a moment.

NARCISSA. Yours is done with me, sir; but my business is not so soon done as you imagine.

YOUNG WORTHY. In a word, I have very near reconciled my brother and your cousin, and I don't doubt but tomorrow will be the day, if I were but as well assured of your consent for my happiness, too.

NARCISSA. First tell me your discourse with that lady; and afterwards, if you can, look me in the face—Oh, are you studying, sir?

YOUNG WORTHY. [*Aside*] S'death! I must not trust her with it; she'll tell it the whole town for a secret. Pox, never a lie!

NARCISSA. You said it was of the greatest consequence, too.

YOUNG WORTHY. (*Aside*) A good hint, faith. Why, madam, since you will needs force it from me, it was to desire her to advance my interest with you. But all my entreaties could not prevail, for she told me I was unworthy of you. Was not this of consequence, madam?

NARCISSA. Nay, now I must believe you, Mr. Worthy, and I ask your pardon, for she was just railing against you for a husband, before you came.

YOUNG WORTHY. Oh! Madam, a favored lover like a good poem, for the malice of some few, makes the generous temper more admire it.

NARCISSA. Nay, what she said, I must confess, had much the same effects as the coffee critics ridiculing Prince Arthur,[1] for I found a pleasing disappointment in my reading you, and till I see your beauty's equalled I shan't dislike you for a few faults.

YOUNG WORTHY. Then, madam, since you have blessed me with your good opinion let me beg of you, before these ladies, to complete my happiness tomorrow. Let this be the last night of your lying alone.

NARCISSA. What do you mean?

YOUNG WORTHY. To marry you tomorrow, madam.

NARCISSA. Marry me! Who put that in your head?

YOUNG WORTHY. Some small encouragement which my hopes have formed, madam.

NARCISSA. Hopes! Oh insolence! If it once comes to that I don't question but you have been familiar with me in your imagination.[2] Marry you! What, lie in a naked bed with you, trembling by your side, like a tame lamb for sacrifice? Do you think I can be moved to love a man, to kiss him, toy with him, and so forth?

YOUNG WORTHY. (*Aside*) Egad! I find nothing but downright impudence will do with her.—No, madam, it is the man must kiss and toy with you, and so forth. Come, my dear angel, pronounce the joyful word and draw the scene of my eternal happiness. Ah, methinks I'm there already, eager and impatient of approaching bliss! Just laid within the bridal bed, our friends retired, the curtains close drawn around us, no light but Celia's[3] eyes, no noise but her soft, trembling words and broken sighs that plead in vain for mercy. And now a trickling tear steals down her glowing cheek, which tells the rushing lover at length she yields, yet vows she'd rather die, but still submits to the unexperienced joy.
(*Embracing her*)

HILLARIA. What raptures, Mr. Worthy!

YOUNG WORTHY. Only the force of love in imagination, madam.

NARCISSA. Oh, Lord, dear cousin, and madam, let's be gone; I vow he grows rude! Oh, for heaven's sake, I shan't shake off my fright these ten days. Oh, Lord, I will not stay—begone! for I declare I loathe the sight of you. *Exit*

YOUNG WORTHY. I hope you'll stand my friend, madam.

HILLARIA. I'll get her into the garden after dinner. *Exeunt the ladies*

YOUNG WORTHY. I find there's nothing to be done with my lady before company; it is a strange affected piece. But there's no fault in her thousand pounds a year, and that's the loadstone that attracts my heart. The wise and grave may tell us of strange chimeras called virtues in a woman and that they alone are the best dowry; but, faith, we younger brothers are of another mind.

Women are changed from what they were of old;
Therefore let lovers still this maxim hold:
"She's only worth that brings her weight in gold."

Exit

---

[1] Sir Richard Blackmore's "heroic poem," *Prince Arthur*, appeared in 1695. It was in the preface to this poem that Blackmore denounced the dramatists of the day on the score of immorality and indecency. "Coffee critics" are literary gossipers in the coffee houses.

[2] This sentence and the one following were omitted from later editions of the play. In fact, the 1721 edition shows considerable toning down of the language to suit the sensibilities of readers and audiences trained in the fashion initiated with *Love's Last Shift*.

[3] Celia is a common name given by the lover to his mistress in poetry of the period.

ACT II

[SCENE I]

A garden belonging to SIR WILLIAM WISE-WOUD'S *house*

Enter NARCISSA, HILLARIA, *and* SIR NOVELTY FASHION

HILLARIA. Oh, for heaven's sake, no more of this gallantry, Sir Novelty, for I know you say the same to every woman you see.

SIR NOVELTY FASHION. Every one that sees you, madam, must say the same. Your beauty, like the rack, forces every beholder to confess his crime—of daring to adore you.

NARCISSA. Oh, I haven't patience to hear all this. If he be blind, I'll open his eyes. I vow, Sir Novelty, you men of amour are strange creatures: you think no woman worth your while unless you walk over a rival's ruin to her heart. I know nothing has encouraged your passion to my cousin more than her engagement to Mr. Worthy.

HILLARIA. (*Aside*) Poor creature, now is she angry; she hasn't the address of a fop. I nauseate.

SIR NOVELTY FASHION. Oh, madam, as to that, I hope the lady will easily distinguish the sincerity of her adorers, though I must allow Mr. Worthy is infinitely the handsomer person.

NARCISSA. Oh, fie, Sir Novelty, make not such a preposterous comparison.

SIR NOVELTY FASHION. Oh, 'ged, madam, there is no comparison.

NARCISSA. Pardon me, sir; he's an unpolished animal!

SIR NOVELTY FASHION. Why, does your ladyship really think me tolerable?

HILLARIA. (*Aside*) So! She has snapped his heart already.

SIR NOVELTY FASHION. Pray, madam, how do I look today? What, cursedly? I'll warrant with a more hellish complexion than a stale actress at a rehearsal. I don't know, madam—it is true—the town does talk of me, indeed; but, the devil take me, in my mind I am a very ugly fellow!

NARCISSA. Now you are too severe, Sir Novelty.

SIR NOVELTY FASHION. Not I, burn me. For heaven's sake, deal freely with me, madam, and if you can, tell me one tolerable thing about me.

HILLARIA. (*Aside*) It would pose me, I'm sure.

NARCISSA. Oh, Sir Novelty, this is unanswerable; it is hard to know the brightest part of a diamond.

SIR NOVELTY FASHION. You'll make me blush, stop my vitals, madam. (*Aside*) Egad, I always said she was a woman of sense. Strike me dumb, I am in love with her. I'll try her farther.—But, madam, is it possible I may vie with Mr. Worthy—not that he is any rival of mine, madam, for I can assure you my inclinations lie where perhaps your ladyship little thinks.

HILLARIA. (*Aside*) So! Now I am rid of him.

SIR NOVELTY FASHION. But pray tell me, madam—for I really love a severe critic—I am sure you must believe he has a more happy genius in dress. For my part I am but a sloven.

NARCISSA. He a genius! Unsufferable! Why, he dresses worse than a captain of the militia. But you, Sir Novelty, are a true original, the very pink of fashion. I'll warrant there's not a milliner in town but has got an estate by you.

SIR NOVELTY FASHION. I must confess, madam, I am for doing good to my country. For you see this suit, madam—I suppose you are not ignorant what a hard time the ribbon weavers have had since the late mourning.[1] Now my design is to set the poor rogues up again by recommending this sort of trimming. The fancy is pretty well for second mourning. By the way, madam, I had fifteen hundred guineas laid in my hand as a gratuity to encourage it. But, egad, I refused them, being too well acquainted with the consequence of taking a bribe in a national concern.

HILLARIA. A very charitable fashion indeed, Sir Novelty. But how if it should not take?

NARCISSA. Ridiculous! Take? I warrant you in a week the whole town will have it, though perhaps Mr. Worthy will be one of the last of them. He's a mere *valet de chambre* to all fashion and never is in any till his betters have left them off.

SIR NOVELTY FASHION. Nay, 'gad, now I must laugh, for the devil take me if I did not meet him not above a fortnight ago in a coat with buttons no bigger than nutmegs.

HILLARIA. There I must confess you outdo him, Sir Novelty.

[1] Queen Mary had died in 1694.

Sir Novelty Fashion. Oh, dear madam, why mine are not above three inches diameter.

Hillaria. But methinks, Sir Novelty, your sleeve is a little too extravagant.

Sir Novelty Fashion. Nay, madam, there you wrong me; mine does but just reach my knuckles. But my Lord Overdo's covers his diamond ring.

Hillaria. Nay, I confess the fashion may be very useful to you gentlemen that make campaigns; for should you unfortunately lose an arm or so, that sleeve might be very convenient to hide the defect on it.

Sir Novelty Fashion. Ha! I think your ladyship's in the right on it, madam.

(*Hiding his hand in his sleeve*)

Narcissa. Oh, such an air! So becoming a negligence! Upon my soul, Sir Novelty, you'll be the envy of the *beau monde*.

Hillaria. Mr. Worthy! A good fancy were thrown away upon him. But you, sir, are an ornament to your clothes.

Sir Novelty Fashion. Then your ladyship really thinks they are—*bien entendu!* [1]

Hillaria. *A mervielle, monsieur!* [2]

Sir Novelty Fashion. She has almost as much wit as her cousin. I must confess, madam, this coat has had a universal approbation. For this morning I had all the eminent tailors about town at my levee earnestly petitioning for the first measure of it. Now, madam, if you thought it would oblige Mr. Worthy, I would let his tailor have it before any of them.

Narcissa. See, here he comes, and the deuce take me, I think it would be a great piece of good nature, for I declare he looks as rough as a Dutch corporal.[3] Prithee, Sir Novelty, let's laugh at him.

Sir Novelty Fashion. Oh, ged! No, madam, that were too cruel. Why, you know he can't help it. Let's take no notice of him.

Hillaria. (*Aside*) Wretched coxcomb.

Enter Elder Worthy

Elder Worthy. [*Aside*] I find my resolution is but vain; my feet have brought me hither against my will. But sure I can command my tongue, which I'll bite off ere it shall seek a reconciliation. Still so familiar there! But it is no matter; I'll try if I can wear indifference and seem as careless in my love as she is of her honor, which she can never truly know the worth of while she persists to let a fool thus play with it.—Ladies, your humble servant.

Hillaria. (*Aside*) Now can't I forbear fretting his spleen a little?—Oh, Mr. Worthy, we are admiring Sir Novelty and his new suit; did you ever see so sweet a fancy? He is as full of variety as a good play.

Elder Worthy. He's a very pleasant comedy indeed, madam, and dressed with a great deal of good satire, and no doubt may oblige both the stage and the town, especially the ladies.

Hillaria. (*Aside*) So! There's for me!

Sir Novelty Fashion. Oh, ged! Nay, prithee, Tom, you know my humor. Ladies! Stop my vitals, I don't believe there are five hundred in town that ever took any notice of me.

Elder Worthy. Oh, sir, there are some that take so much notice of you that the town takes notice of them for it.

Hillaria. (*Aside*) It works rarely.

Sir Novelty Fashion. How of them, Tom, upon my account? Oh, ged, I would not be the ruin of any lady's reputation for the world. Stop my vitals, I am very sorry for it. Prithee, name but one that has a favorable thought of me, and to convince you that I have no design upon her, I'll instantly visit her in an unpowdered periwig.

Elder Worthy. Nay, she I mean is a woman of sense, too.

Sir Novelty Fashion. Phoo! Prithee, pox, don't banter me. It is impossible; what can she see in me?

Elder Worthy. Oh, a thousand taking qualities. This lady will inform you—come, I'll introduce you. (*Pulls him*)

Sir Novelty Fashion. Oh, ged, no, prithee! Hark you in your ear. I am off of her! Demn me if I be n't; I am, stop my vitals!

Elder Worthy. (*Aside*) Wretched rogue!—Pshaw! No matter, I'll reconcile you. Come—come, madam.

Hillaria. Sir!

Elder Worthy. This gentleman humbly begs to kiss your hands.

Hillaria. He needs not your recommendation, sir.

Elder Worthy. True! A fool recommends

---

[1] Very skillful.
[2] Marvellously, monsieur.
[3] William III had brought Dutch soldiers into England.

himself to your sex, and that's the reason men of common sense live unmarried.

HILLARIA. A fool without jealousy is better than a wit with ill nature.

ELDER WORTHY. A friendly office, seeing your fault is ill nature.

HILLARIA. Believing more than we have is pitiful. You know I hate this wretch, loathe and scorn him.

ELDER WORTHY. Fools have a secret art of pleasing women. If he did not delight you, you would not hazard your reputation by encouraging his love.

HILLARIA. Dares he wrong my reputation?

ELDER WORTHY. He need not. The world will do it for him while you keep him company.

HILLARIA. I dare answer it to the world.

ELDER WORTHY. Then why not to me?

HILLARIA. To satisfy you were a fondness I should never forgive myself.

ELDER WORTHY. To persist in it, is what I'll never forgive.

HILLARIA. Insolence! Is it come to this? Never see me more.

ELDER WORTHY. I have lost the right of you already; there hangs a cloud of folly between you and the woman I once thought you. (*As* HILLARIA *is going off*)

Enter YOUNG WORTHY

YOUNG WORTHY. What to ourselves in passion we propose,
The passion ceasing, does the purpose lose.

Madam, therefore, pray let me engage you to stay a little till your fury is over, that you may see whether you have reason to be angry or no.

SIR NOVELTY FASHION. (*To* NARCISSA) Pray, madam, who is that gentleman?

NARCISSA. Mr. Worthy's brother, sir, a gentleman of no mean parts, I can assure you.

SIR NOVELTY FASHION. I don't doubt it, madam. He has a very good walk.

[SIR NOVELTY *and* NARCISSA *retire*]

HILLARIA. To be jealous of me with a fool is an affront to my understanding.

YOUNG WORTHY. Tamely to resign your reputation to the merciless vanity of a fool were no proof of his love.

HILLARIA. It is questioning my conduct.

YOUNG WORTHY. Why, you let him kiss your hand last night before his face.

HILLARIA. The fool diverted me, and I gave him my hand, as I would lend my money, fan, or handkerchief to a legerdemain [1] that I might see him play all his tricks over.

YOUNG WORTHY. Oh, madam, no juggler is so deceitful as a fop, for while you look his folly in the face, he steals away your reputation with more ease than the other picks your pocket.

HILLARIA. Some fools indeed are dangerous.

YOUNG WORTHY. I grant you your design is only to laugh at him, but that's more than he finds out. Therefore you must expect he will tell the world another story, and it is ten to one but the consequence makes you repent of your curiosity.

HILLARIA. You speak like an oracle; I tremble at the thoughts on it.

YOUNG WORTHY. Here's one shall reconcile your fears. Brother, I have done your business. Hillaria is convinced of her indiscretion and has a pardon ready for your asking it.

ELDER WORTHY. She's the criminal; I have no occasion for it.

YOUNG WORTHY. See, she comes toward you; give her a civil word, at least.

HILLARIA. Mr. Worthy, I'll not be behindhand in the acknowledgment I owe you. I freely confess my folly and forgive your harsh construction of it. Nay, I'll not condemn your want of good nature in not endeavoring, as your brother has done, by mild arguments to convince me of my error.

ELDER WORTHY. Now you vanquish me! I blush to be outdone in generous love! I am your slave; dispose of me as you please.

HILLARIA. No more; from this hour be you the master of my actions and my heart.

ELDER WORTHY. This goodness gives you the power, and I obey with pleasure.

YOUNG WORTHY. So! I find I haven't preached to no purpose! Well, madam, if you find him guilty of love, even let tomorrow be his execution day; make a husband of him, and there's the extent of love's law.

ELDER WORTHY. Brother, I am indebted to you.

YOUNG WORTHY. Well, I'll give you a discharge if you will but leave me but half an hour in private with that lady.

HILLARIA. How will you get rid of Sir Novelty?

YOUNG WORTHY. I'll warrant you; leave him to me.

[1] Juggler.

HILLARIA. Come, Mr. Worthy, as we walk I'll inform you how I intend to sacrifice that wretch to your laughter.

ELDER WORTHY. Not, madam, that I want revenge on so contemptible a creature, but I think you owe this justice to yourself, to let him see, if possible, you never took him for any other than what he really is.

YOUNG WORTHY. Well, pox of your politics, prithee consult of them within.

HILLARIA. We'll obey you, sir.

Exeunt ELDER WORTHY *and* HILLARIA

YOUNG WORTHY. Pray, madam, give me leave to beg a word in private with you; sir, if you please.—

(*To* SIR NOVELTY, *who is taking snuff*)

SIR NOVELTY FASHION. Ay, sir, with all my heart.

YOUNG WORTHY. Sir—

SIR NOVELTY FASHION. Nay, it is right, I'll assure you.   (*Offering his box*)

YOUNG WORTHY. Ay, sir—but now the lady would be alone.

SIR NOVELTY FASHION. Sir!

YOUNG WORTHY. The lady would be alone, sir.

SIR NOVELTY FASHION. I don't hear her say any such thing.

YOUNG WORTHY. Then I tell you so, and I would advise you to believe me.

SIR NOVELTY FASHION. I shall not take your advice, sir. But if you really think the lady would be alone, why—you had best leave her.

YOUNG WORTHY. In short, sir, your company is very unseasonable at present.

SIR NOVELTY FASHION. I can tell you, sir, if you have no more wit than manners, the lady will be but scurvily entertained.

NARCISSA. Oh, fie, gentlemen, no quarrelling before a woman, I beseech you. Pray let me know the business.

SIR NOVELTY FASHION. My business is love, madam.

NARCISSA. And yours, sir?

YOUNG WORTHY. What I hope you are no stranger to, madam. As for that spark, you need take no care of him, for if he stays much longer, I will do his business myself.

NARCISSA. Well, I vow love's a pleasant thing when the men come to cutting of throats once. O 'gad, I'd fain have them fight a little. Methinks Narcissa would sound so great in an expiring lover's mouth. Well, I am resolved Sir Novelty shall not go yet, for I will have the pleasure of hearing myself praised a little, though I don't marry this month for it. Come, gentlemen, since you both say love's your business, e'en plead for yourselves, and he that speaks the greater passion shall have the fairest return.

YOUNG WORTHY. (*Aside*) Oh, the devil! Now is she wrapt with the hopes of a little flattery! There's no remedy but patience. S'death, what piece have I to work upon?

NARCISSA. Come, gentlemen, one at a time. Sir Novelty, what have you to say to me?

SIR NOVELTY FASHION. In the first place, madam, I was the first person in England that was complimented with the name of "Beau," which is a title I prefer before "Right Honorable," for that may be inherited, but this I extorted from the whole nation by my surprising mien and unexampled gallantry.

NARCISSA. So, sir!

SIR NOVELTY FASHION. Then another thing, madam: It has been observed that I have been eminently successful in those fashions I have recommended to the town, and I don't question but this very suit will raise as many ribbon-weavers as ever the clipping or melting trade did goldsmiths.[1]

NARCISSA. (*Aside*) Pish! What does the fool mean? He says nothing of me yet.

SIR NOVELTY FASHION. In short, madam, the cravat string, the garter, the sword knot, the centurine, the b[u]rdash, the steenkirk, the large button, the long sleeve, the plume, and full peruke [2] were all created, cried down, or revived by me. In a word, madam, there has never been anything particularly taking or agreeable for these ten years past, but your humble servant was the author of it.

YOUNG WORTHY. Where the devil will this end?

NARCISSA. This is all extravagant, Sir Novelty; but what have you to say to me, sir?

SIR NOVELTY FASHION. I'll come to you presently, madam, I have just done. Then you must know my coach and equipage are

---

[1] The clipping of gold coins had become so great a scandal that Sir Isaac Newton had just been appointed to the wardenship of the mint to reform the coinage.

[2] These are all articles of clothing or personal adornment. The centurine was a waist-belt, the burdash was either a fringed sash or a kind of cravat, the steenkirk (named by the French in honor of the battle of Steinkirk) was a loosely flowing cravat or neckcloth.

as well known as myself, and since the conveniency of two play houses,[1] I have a better opportunity of showing them, for between every act, whisk! I am gone from one to the other. Oh, what pleasure it is at a good play to go out before half an act's done!

NARCISSA. Why at a good play?

SIR NOVELTY FASHION. Oh, madam, it looks particular and gives the whole audience an opportunity of turning upon me at once. Then do they conclude I have some extraordinary business or a fine woman to go to at least, and then again it shows my contempt of what the dull town think their chiefest diversion. But if I do stay a play out, I always set with my back to the stage.

NARCISSA. Why so, sir?

SIR NOVELTY FASHION. Then everybody will imagine I have been tired with it before, or that I am jealous who talks to who in the King's box. And thus, madam, do I take more pains to preserve a public reputation than ever any lady took after the smallpox to recover her complexion.

NARCISSA. Well, but to the point, what have you to say to me, Sir Novelty?

YOUNG WORTHY. [*Aside*] Now does she expect some compliment shall out-flatter her glass.

SIR NOVELTY FASHION. To you, madam? Why, I have been saying all this to you.

NARCISSA. To what end, sir?

SIR NOVELTY FASHION. Why, all this I have done for your sake.

NARCISSA. What kindness is it to me?

SIR NOVELTY FASHION. Why, madam, don't you think it more glory to be beloved by one eminently particular person, whom all the town knows and talks of, than to be adored by five hundred dull souls that have lived incognito?

NARCISSA. That I must confess is a prevailing argument, but still you haven't told me why you love me.

YOUNG WORTHY. That's a task he has left for me, madam.

SIR NOVELTY FASHION. It is a province I never undertake, I must confess; I think it is sufficient if I tell a lady why she should love me.

NARCISSA. (*Aside*) Hang him! He's too conceited; he's so in love with himself he won't allow a woman the bare comfort of a cold compliment.—Well, Mr. Worthy?

YOUNG WORTHY. Why, madam, I have observed several particular qualities in your ladyship that I have perfectly adored you for, as the majestic toss of your head, your obliging bowed curtsey, your satirical smile, your blushing laugh, your demure look, the careless tie of your hood, the genteel flirt of your fan, the designed accident in your letting fall, and your agreeable manner of receiving it from him that takes it up.

(*What he speaks, she imitates in dumb show. They both offer to take up her fan, and in striving* YOUNG WORTHY *pushes* SIR NOVELTY *on his back.*)

SIR NOVELTY FASHION. (*Adjusting himself*) I hope your ladyship will excuse my disorder, madam. How now?

Enter a Footman *to* SIR NOVELTY

FOOTMAN. Oh, sir, Mrs. Flareit—

SIR NOVELTY FASHION. Ha! Speak lower. What of her?

FOOTMAN. By some unlucky accident has discovered your being here and raves like a mad woman. She's at your lodging, sir, and had broke you above forty pounds worth of china before I came away. She talked of following hither, and if you don't make haste I'm afraid will be here before you can get through the house, sir.

SIR NOVELTY FASHION. [*Aside*] This woman is certainly the devil. Her jealousy is implacable; I must get rid of her, though I give her more for a separate maintenance than her conscience demanded for a settlement before enjoyment.—See the coach ready, and if you meet her, be sure you stop her with some pretended business till I am got away from hence.—Madam, I ask your ladyship ten thousand pardons. There's a person of quality expects me at my lodging upon extraordinary business.

NARCISSA. What, will you leave us, Sir Novelty?

SIR NOVELTY FASHION. As unwillingly as the soul the body. But this is an irresistible occasion. Madam, your most devoted slave. Sir, your most humble servant. Madam, I kiss your hands. Oh, 'gad, no farther, dear sir, upon my soul I won't stir if you do.

YOUNG WORTHY *sees him to the door.*

Exit SIR NOVELTY

---

[1] From 1682 to 1695 Drury Lane had been the sole theatre. In 1695 the Lincoln's Inn Fields theatre was opened by a company under Betterton's management.

YOUNG WORTHY. Nay then, sir, your humble servant.—So! This was a lucky deliverance.

NARCISSA. I overheard the business. You see, Mr. Worthy, a man must be a slave to a mistress sometimes, as well as a wife; yet all can't persuade your sex to a favorable opinion of poor marriage.

YOUNG WORTHY. I long, madam, for an opportunity to convince you of your error; and therefore give me leave to hope tomorrow you will free me from the pain of farther expectation and make a husband of me. Come, I'll spare your blushes, and believe I have already named the day.

NARCISSA. Had not we better consider a little?

YOUNG WORTHY. No, let's avoid consideration; it is an enemy both to love and courage. They that consider much live to be old bachelors and young fighters. No, no, we shall have time enough to consider after marriage. But why are you so serious, madam?

NARCISSA. Not but I do consent tomorrow shall be the day, Mr. Worthy. But I'm afraid you have not loved me long enough to make our marriage be the town talk, for it is the fashion now to be the town talk, and you know one had as good be out of the world as out of the fashion.

YOUNG WORTHY. I don't know, madam, what you call town talk, but it has been in the news-letters above a fortnight ago that we were already married. Besides, the last song I made of you has been sung at the music meeting, and you may imagine, madam, I took no little care to let the ladies and the beaus know who it was made on.

NARCISSA. Well, and what said the ladies?

YOUNG WORTHY. What was most observable, madam, was that while it was singing, my Lady Manlove went out in a great passion.

NARCISSA. Poor jealous animal! On my conscience that charitable creature has such a fund of kind compliance for all young fellows whose love lies dead upon their hands that she has been as great a hindrance to us virtuous women as ever the Bank of England was to city goldsmiths.[1]

YOUNG WORTHY. The reason of that is, madam, because you virtuous ladies pay no interest. I must confess the principal, our health, is a little securer with you.

NARCISSA. Well, and is not that an advantage worth entering into bonds for? Not but I vow we virtuous devils do love to insult a little, and to say truth, it looks too credulous and easy in a woman to encourage a man before he has sighed himself to a skeleton.

YOUNG WORTHY. But heaven be thanked, we are pretty even with you in the end, for the longer you hold us off before marriage, the sooner we fall off after it.

NARCISSA. What, then, you take marriage to be a kind of Jesuit's powder[2] that infallibly cures the fever of love?

YOUNG WORTHY. It is indeed a Jesuit's powder, for the priests first invented it, and only abstained from it because they knew it had a bitter taste, then gilded it over with a pretended blessing and so palmed it upon the unthinking laity.

NARCISSA. Prithee, don't screw your wit beyond the compass of good manners. Do you think I shall be tuned to matrimony by your railing against it? If you have so little stomach to it, I'll even make you fast a week longer.

YOUNG WORTHY. Ay, but let me tell you, madam, it is no policy to keep a lover at a thin diet in hopes to raise his appetite on the wedding night, for then

We come like starving beggars to a feast,
Where unconfined we feed with eager haste,
Till each repeated morsel palls the taste.
Marriage gives prodigals a boundless treasure,
Who squander that which might be lasting pleasure,
And women think they ne'er have over measure.

ACT III

[SCENE I]

SIR WILLIAM WISEWOUD's *house*

Enter AMANDA *and* HILLARIA, *meeting*

AMANDA. My dear, I have news for you.

HILLARIA. I guess at it and would be fain satisfied of the particulars. Your husband is

---

[1] Before the establishment of the Bank of England in 1694 the banking business of London was largely in the hands of the goldsmiths, of whom at one time twenty-seven had shops in Lombard Street. The foundation of the Bank put a stop to the development of private banking firms.

[2] An early name for quinine, introduced into Europe from South America by Jesuit priests.

returned and, I hear, knows nothing of your being alive. Young Worthy has told me of your design upon him.

AMANDA. It is that I wanted your advice in. What think you of it?

HILLARIA. Oh, I admire it. Next to forgetting your husband, it is the best counsel was ever given you, for under the disguise of mistress you may now take a fair advantage of indulging your love, and the little experience you have had of it already has been just enough not to let you be afraid of a man.

AMANDA. Will you never leave your mad humor?

HILLARIA. Not till my youth leaves me. Why should women affect ignorance among themselves? When we converse with men, indeed, modesty and good breeding oblige us not to understand what sometimes we can't help thinking of.

AMANDA. Nay, I don't think the worse of you for what you say, for it is observed that a bragging lover and an over-shy lady are the farthest from what they would seem—the one is as seldom known to receive a favor as the other to resist an opportunity.

HILLARIA. Most women have a wrong sense of modesty, as some men of courage; if you don't fight with all you meet or run from all you see, you are presently thought a coward or an ill woman.

AMANDA. You say true, and it is as hard a matter nowadays for a woman to know how to converse with men as for a man to know when to draw his sword, for many times both sexes are apt to over-act their parts. To me the rules of virtue have been ever sacred, and I am loath to break them by an unadvised understanding. Therefore, dear Hillaria, help me, for I am at a loss. Can I justify, think you, my intended design upon my husband?

HILLARIA. As how, prithee?

AMANDA. Why, if I court and conquer him as a mistress, am I not accessory to his violating the bonds of marriage? For, though I am his wife, yet while he loves me not as such, I encourage an unlawful passion, and though the act be safe, yet his intent is criminal. How can I answer this?

HILLARIA. Very easily, for if he doesn't intrigue with you, he will with somebody else in the meantime, and I think you have as much right to his remains as any one.

AMANDA. Ay, but I am assured the love he will pretend to me is vicious, and it is uncertain that I shall prevent his doing worse elsewhere.

HILLARIA. It is true a certain ill ought not to be done for an uncertain good. But then again, of two evils choose the least, and sure, it is less criminal to let him love you as a mistress than to let him hate you as a wife. If you succeed I suppose you will easily forgive your guilt in the undertaking.

AMANDA. To say truth, I find no argument yet strong enough to conquer my inclination to it. But is there no danger, think you, of his knowing me?

HILLARIA. Not the least, in my opinion. In the first place, he confidently believes you are dead; then he has not seen you these eight or ten years; besides, you were not above sixteen when he left you: this, with the alteration the smallpox have made in you—though not for the worse—I think are sufficient disguises to secure you from his knowledge.

AMANDA. Nay, and to this I may add the considerable amendment of my fortune, for when he left me I had only my bare jointure for a subsistence—besides my strange manner of receiving him.

HILLARIA. That's what I would fain be acquainted with.

AMANDA. I expect further instructions from Young Worthy every moment; then you shall know all, my dear.

HILLARIA. Nay, he will do you no small service, for a thief is the best thief-catcher.

Enter a Servant *to* AMANDA

SERVANT. Madam, your servant is below, who says young Mr. Worthy's man waits at your lodgings with earnest business from his master.

AMANDA. It is well. Come, my dear, I must have your assistance too.

HILLARIA. With all my heart. I love to be at the bottom of a secret, for they say the confidante of any amour has sometimes more pleasure in the observation than the parties concerned in the enjoyment. But methinks you don't look with a good heart upon the business.

AMANDA. I can't help a little concern in a business of such moment, for though my reason tells me my design must prosper, yet my fears say it were happiness too great. Oh, to reclaim the man I'm bound by heaven to love, to expose the folly of a roving mind in pleasing him with what he seemed to loathe were such a sweet revenge for slighted love, so vast a triumph of rewarded constancy as might persuade the looser part of womankind even to forsake themselves and fall in love with virtue.

Re-enter the Servant *to* HILLARIA

SERVANT. Sir Novelty Fashion is below in his coach, madam, and inquires for your ladyship or Madam Narcissa.

HILLARIA. You know my cousin is gone out with my Lady Tattle-tongue. I hope you did not tell him I was within.

SERVANT. No, madam, I did not know if your ladyship would be spoke with, and therefore came to see.

HILLARIA. Then tell him I went with her.

SERVANT. I shall, madam. *Exit* Servant

HILLARIA. You must know, my dear, I have sent to that fury, Mrs. Flareit, whom this Sir Novelty keeps, and have stung her to some purpose with an account of his passion for my cousin. I owed him a quarrel for that he made between Mr. Worthy and me, and I hope her jealousy will severely revenge it; therefore I sent my cousin out of the way because, unknown to her, her name is at the bottom of my design. Here he comes; prithee, my dear, let's go down the back stairs and take coach from the garden.

[*Exeunt*] AMANDA *and* HILLARIA

Re-enter the Servant, *conducting* SIR NOVELTY

SIR NOVELTY FASHION. Both the ladies abroad, say you? Is Sir William within?

SERVANT. Yes, sir. If you please to walk in, I'll acquaint him that you expect him here.

SIR NOVELTY FASHION. Do so, prithee, (*Exit servant*) and in the meantime let me consider what I have to say to him. Hold! In the first place, his daughter is in love with me. Would I marry her? No! Demn it, it is mechanical[1] to marry the woman you love; men of quality should always marry those they never saw. But I hear young Worthy marries her tomorrow, which, if I prevent not, will spoil my design upon her. Let me see—I have it—I'll persuade the old fellow that I would marry her myself, upon which he immediately rejects young Worthy and gives

[1] Vulgar.

me free access to her. Good! What follows upon that? Opportunity, importunity, resistance, force, entreaty, persisting, doubting, swearing, lying, blushes, yielding, victory, pleasure, indifference—Oh here he comes *in ordine ad.*[2]

Enter SIR WILLIAM WISEWOUD

SIR WILLIAM WISEWOUD. Sir Novelty, your servant. Have you any commands for me, sir?

SIR NOVELTY FASHION. I have some proposals to make, sir, concerning your happiness and my own, which perhaps will surprise you. In a word, sir, I am upon the very brink of matrimony.

SIR WILLIAM WISEWOUD. It is the best thing you can pursue, sir, considering you have a good estate.

SIR NOVELTY FASHION. But whom do you think I intend to marry?

SIR WILLIAM WISEWOUD. I can't imagine. Dear sir, be brief, lest your delay transport me into a crime I would avoid, which is impatience. Sir, pray go on.

SIR NOVELTY FASHION. In fine, sir, it is to your very daughter, the fair Narcissa.

SIR WILLIAM WISEWOUD. Humph! Pray, sir, how long have you had this in your head?

SIR NOVELTY FASHION. Above these two hours, sir.

SIR WILLIAM WISEWOUD. Very good. Then you haven't slept upon it?

SIR NOVELTY FASHION. No, nor shan't sleep for thinking on it. Did not I tell you I would surprise you?

SIR WILLIAM WISEWOUD. Oh, you have indeed, sir. I am amazed. I am amazed!

SIR NOVELTY FASHION. Well, sir, and what think you of my proposal?

SIR WILLIAM WISEWOUD. Why, truly, sir, I like it not. But if I did, it is now too late; my daughter is disposed of to a gentleman that she and I like very well. At present, sir, I have a little business; if this be all, your humble servant, I am in haste.

SIR NOVELTY FASHION. Demme! What an insensible blockhead's this? Hold, sir, do you hear—is this all the acknowledgment you make for the honor I designed you?

SIR WILLIAM WISEWOUD. Why, truly, sir,

[2] Perhaps intended for *in ordinem adducere,* to reduce to order, or to straighten all out to the satisfaction of Sir Novelty.

it is an honor that I am not ambitious of. In plain terms, I do not like you for a son-in-law.

SIR NOVELTY FASHION. Now you speak to the purpose, sir. But, prithee, what are thy exceptions to me?

SIR WILLIAM WISEWOUD. Why, in the first place, sir, you have too great a passion for your own person to have any for your wife's. In the next place, you take such an extravagant care in the clothing your body that your understanding goes naked for it. Had I a son so dressed, I should take the liberty to call him an egregious fop.

SIR NOVELTY FASHION. Egad, thou art a comical old gentleman, and I'll tell thee a secret. Understand then, sir, from me, that all young fellows hate the name of fop as women do the name of whore, but, egad, they both love the pleasure of being so. Nay, faith, and it is as hard a matter for some men to be fops, as you call them, as it is for some women to be whores.

SIR WILLIAM WISEWOUD. That's pleasant, in faith. Can't any man be a fop or any woman be a whore that has a mind to it?

SIR NOVELTY FASHION. No, faith, sir, for let me tell you, it is not the coldness of my Lady Freelove's inclination, but her age and wrinkles that won't let her cuckold her husband, and again it is not Sir John Woodlook's aversion to dress, but his want of a fertile genius that won't let him look like a gentleman. Therefore, in vindication of all well-dressed gentlemen, I intend to write a play where my chiefest character shall be a downright English booby that affects to be a beau, without either genius or foreign education, and to call it in imitation of another famous comedy, *He Would If He Could*,[1] and now, I think, you are answered, sir. Have you any exceptions to my birth or family, pray, sir?

SIR WILLIAM WISEWOUD. Yes, sir, I have. You seem to me the offspring of more than one man's labor, for certainly no less than a dancing, singing, and fencing master, with a tailor, milliner, perfumer, peruke-maker, and French *valet de chambre* could be at the begetting of you.

SIR NOVELTY FASHION. All these have been at the finishing of me since I was made.

SIR WILLIAM WISEWOUD. That is, heaven made you a man, and they have made a monster of you. And so farewell to you!

(*He is going*)

SIR NOVELTY FASHION. Hark you, sir, am I to expect no further satisfaction in the proposals I made you?

SIR WILLIAM WISEWOUD. Sir, nothing makes a man lose himself like passion. Now I presume you are young, and consequently rash upon a disappointment; therefore to prevent any difference that may arise by repeating my refusal of your suit, I do not think it convenient to hold any further discourse with you.

SIR NOVELTY FASHION. Nay, faith, thou shalt stay to hear a little more of my mind first.

SIR WILLIAM WISEWOUD. Since you press me, sir, I will rather bear [with][2] than resist you.

SIR NOVELTY FASHION. I doubt, old gentleman, you have such a torrent of philosophy running through your pericranium that it has washed your brains away.

SIR WILLIAM WISEWOUD. Pray, sir, why do you think so?

SIR NOVELTY FASHION. Because you choose a beggarly unaccountable sort of younger-brotherish rake-hell for your son-in-law before a man of quality, estate, good parts, and breeding, demme.

SIR WILLIAM WISEWOUD. Truly, sir, I know neither of the persons to whom these characters belong; if you please to write their names under them, perhaps I may tell you if they be like or no.

SIR NOVELTY FASHION. Why, then, in short, I would have been your son-in-law, and you, it seems, prefer young Worthy before me. Now are your eyes open?

SIR WILLIAM WISEWOUD. Had I been blind, sir, you might have been my son-in-law, and if you were not blind you would not think that I design my daughter for young Worthy. His brother, I think, may deserve her.

SIR NOVELTY FASHION. Then you are not jealous of young Worthy? Humph!

SIR WILLIAM WISEWOUD. No, really, sir, nor of you neither.

SIR NOVELTY FASHION. Give me thy hand; thou art very happy, stop my vitals, for thou dost not see thou art blind. Not jealous of young Worthy? Ha, ha! How now!

---

[1] Etherege's *She Would if She Could* (1668) was one of the first of the Restoration society comedies of manners.

[2] Inserted in later editions.

Enter Sir Novelty's Servant *with a* Porter

Servant. Sir, here's a porter with a letter for your honor.

Porter. I was ordered to give it into your own hands, sir, and expect an answer.

Sir Novelty Fashion. (*Reads*) "Excuse, my dear Sir Novelty, the forced indifference I have shown you, and let me recompense your past sufferings with an hour's conversation after the play at Rosamond's Pond,[1] where you will find an hearty welcome to the arms of your Narcissa!" Unexpected happiness! The arms of your Narcissa! Egad, and when I am there, I'll make myself welcome. Faith, I did not think she was so far gone, neither. But I don't question there are five hundred more in her condition. I have a good mind not to go, faith. Yet, hang it, I will, though only to be revenged of this old fellow! Nay, I'll have the pleasure of making it public, too, for I will give her the music and draw all the town to be witness of my triumph! Where is the lady? (*To the porter*)

Porter. In a hackney coach at the corner of the street.

Sir Novelty Fashion. Enough, tell her I will certainly be there. (*Exit porter*) Well, old gentleman, then you are resolved I shall be no kin to you? Your daughter is disposed of? Humph!

Sir William Wisewoud. You have your answer, sir; you shall be no kin to me.

Sir Novelty Fashion. Farewell, old philosophy, and do you hear, I would advise you to study nothing but the art of patience. You may have an unexpected occasion for it. Hark you, would it not nettle you damnably to hear my son call you grandfather?

Sir William Wisewoud. Sir, notwithstanding this provocation, I am calm, but were I like other men, a slave to passion, I should not forbear calling you impertinent! How I swell with rising vexation! Leave me, leave me; go, sir, go, get you out of my house!
(*Angrily*)

Sir Novelty Fashion. Oh, have a care of passion, dear Diogenes. Ha, ha, ha, ha!

Sir William Wisewoud. So! (*Sighing*) At last I have conquered it. Pray, sir, oblige me with your absence (*Taking off his hat*); I protest I am tired with you. Pray leave my house.   (*Submissively*)

[1] Rosamond's Pond in St. James's Park (filled up in 1770).

Sir Novelty Fashion. Damn your house, your family, your ancestors, your generation, and your eternal posterity.   *Exit*

Sir William Wisewoud. Ah! A fair riddance. How I bless myself that it was not in this fool's power to provoke me beyond that serenity of temper which a wise man ought to be master of. How near are men to brutes when their unruly passions break the bounds of reason? And of all passions anger is the most violent, which often puts me in mind of that admirable saying,

He that strives not to stem his anger's tide
Does a mad horse without a bridle ride.

[Scene II]

The scene changes to St. James's Park

Enter Young Worthy *and* Loveless *as from the tavern*, Snap *following*

Young Worthy. What a sweet evening it is. Prithee, Ned, let's walk a little. Look how lovingly the trees are joined since thou wert here, as if nature had designed this walk for the private shelter of forbidden love.
(*Several crossing the stage*)
Look, here are some for making use of the conveniency.

Loveless. But, hark you, friend, are the women as tame and civil as they were before I left the town? Can they endure the smell of tobacco or vouchsafe a man a word with a dirty cravat on?

Young Worthy. Ay, that they will, for keeping is almost out of fashion, so that now an honest fellow with a promising back need not fear a night's lodging for bare good-fellowship.

Loveless. If whoring be so poorly encouraged, methinks the women should turn honest in their own defense.

Young Worthy. Faith, I don't find there's a whore the less for it; the pleasure of fornication is still the same. All the difference is, lewdness is not so barefaced as heretofore. Virtue is as much debased as our money, for maidenheads are as scarce as our milled half-crowns, and, faith, *Dei gratia* [2] is as hard to be found in a girl of sixteen as round the brims of an old shilling.

[2] By the grace of God, inscribed after the name of the sovereign around the edge of a coin. For the reference to the scarcity of milled coins, see note 1 above, p. 321.

LOVELESS. Well, I find, in spite of law and duty, the flesh will get the better of the spirit. But I see no game yet. Prithee, Will, let's go and take the other bumper to enliven assurance that we may come downright to the business.

YOUNG WORTHY. No, no; what we have in our bellies already, by the help of a little fresh air, will soon be in our pericraniums and work us to a right pitch to taste the pleasures of the night.

LOVELESS. The day thou meanest; my day always breaks at sunset. We wise fellows that know the use of life know, too, that the moon lights men to more pleasures than the sun. The sun was meant for the dull soul of business and poor rogues that have a mind to save candles.

YOUNG WORTHY. Nay, the night was always a friend to pleasure, and that made Diana[1] run a-whoring by the light of her own horns.

LOVELESS. Right, and, prithee, what made Daphne run away from Apollo but that he wore so much daylight about his ears?[2]

YOUNG WORTHY. Ha! Look out, Ned, there's the enemy before you!

LOVELESS. Why, then, as Cæsar said, come follow me. *Exit*

YOUNG WORTHY. I hope it is his wife, whom I desired to meet me here that she might take a view of her soldier before she new-mounted him. *Exit*

Enter MRS FLAREIT and her maid

MAID. I wonder, madam, Sir Novelty don't come yet. I am so afraid he should see Narcissa and find out the trick of your letter.

MRS. FLAREIT. No, no! Narcissa is out of the way. I am sure he won't be long, for I heard the hautboys[3] as they passed by me mention his name; I suppose to make the intrigue more fashionable, he intends to give me the music.

MAID. Suppose he do take you for Narcissa. What advantage do you propose by it?

MRS. FLAREIT. I shall then have a just occasion to quarrel with him for his perfidiousness and so force his pocket to make his peace with me. Besides, my jealousy will not let me rest till I am revenged.

[1] The reference is to the legend of Endymion.— "Horns" are the symbol of cuckoldry.
[2] I.e., as the god of the sun.
[3] Oboe players.

MAID. Jealousy! Why, I have often heard you say you loathed him!

MRS. FLAREIT. It is my pride, not love, that makes me jealous, for, though I don't love him, yet I am incensed to think he dares love another.

MAID. See, madam, here he is, and the music with him.

MRS. FLAREIT. Put on your mask and leave me. (*They mask*)

Enter SIR NOVELTY with the music

SIR NOVELTY FASHION. Here, gentlemen, place yourselves on this spot and pray oblige me with a trumpet sonata. (*The musicians prepare to play.*) This taking a man at his first word is a very new way of preserving reputation, stop my vitals. Nay, and secure one too, for now may we enjoy and grow weary of one another before the town can take any notice of us. (*Mrs. Flareit making towards him.*) Ha, this must be she. I suppose, madam, you are no stranger to the contents of this letter?

MRS. FLAREIT. Dear sir, this place is too public for my acknowledgment, if you please to withdraw to a more private conveniency. *Exeunt*

(*The music prepares to play, and all sorts of people gather about it. Enter at one door NARCISSA, HILLARIA, AMANDA, ELDER WORTHY, and YOUNG WORTHY; at another LOVELESS and SNAP, who talk to the masks*)

ELDER WORTHY. What say you, ladies? Shall we walk homewards? It begins to be dark.

YOUNG WORTHY. Prithee, don't be so impatient; it's light enough to hear the music, I'll warrant you.

AMANDA. Mr. Worthy, you promised me a sight I long for. Is Mr. Loveless among all those?

YOUNG WORTHY. That's he, madam, a-surveying that masked lady.

AMANDA. Ha, is it possible! Methinks I read his vices in his person. Can he be insensible even to the smart of pinching poverty? Pray, sir, your hand—I find myself disordered. It troubles me to think I dare not speak to him after so long an absence.

YOUNG WORTHY. Madam, your staying here may be dangerous; therefore, let me advise you to go home and get all things in order to receive him. About an hour hence will be a convenient time to set my design a-going; till [then] [1] let me beg you to have a little patience. Give me leave, madam, to see you to your coach.

AMANDA. I'll not trouble you, sir; yonder's my cousin Welbred; I'll beg his protection.

Exit

(*The music plays, after which* NARCISSA *speaks*)

NARCISSA. I vow it's very fine, considering what dull souls our nation are. I find it is a harder matter to reform their manners than their government or religion.

ELDER WORTHY. Since the one has been so happily accomplished, I know no reason why we should despair of the other. I hope in a little time to see our youth return from travel big with praises of their own country. But come, ladies, the music's done, I suppose. Shall we walk?

NARCISSA. Time enough; why you have no taste of the true pleasures of the park. I'll warrant you hate as much to ridicule others as to hear yourself praised; for my part, I think a little harmless railing's half the pleasure of one's life.

ELDER WORTHY. I don't love to create myself enemies by observing the weakness of other people. I have more faults of my own than I know how to mend.

NARCISSA. Protect me! How can you see such a medley of human stuffs as [are] [2] here without venting your spleen? Why, look there now, is not it comical to see that wretched creature there with her autumnal face dressed in all the colors of the spring?

ELDER WORTHY. Pray, who is she, madam?

NARCISSA. A thing that won't believe herself out of date, though she was a known woman at the Restoration.

YOUNG WORTHY. Oh, I know her; it is Mrs. Holdout, one that is proud of being an original of fashionable fornication and values herself mightily for being one of the first mistresses that ever kept her coach publicly in England.

HILLARIA. Pray, who's that impudent young fellow there?

ELDER WORTHY. Oh, that's an eternal fan-tearer and a constant persecutor of womankind. He had a great misfortune lately.

NARCISSA. Pray, what was it?

ELDER WORTHY. Why, impudently presuming to cuckold a Dutch officer, he had his fore-teeth kicked out.

OMNES. Ha, ha, ha!

NARCISSA. There's another too, Mr. Worthy; do you know him?

YOUNG WORTHY. That's Beau Noisy, one that brags of favors from my lady, though refused by her woman; that sups with my lord, and borrows his club of his footman; that beats the watch, and is kicked by his companions; that is one day at court, and the next in jail; that goes to church without religion, is valiant without courage, witty without sense, and drunk without measure.

ELDER WORTHY. A very complete gentleman.

HILLARIA. Prithee, cousin, who's that overshy lady there, that won't seem to understand what that brisk young fellow says to her?

NARCISSA. Why, that's my Lady Slylove; that other ceremonious gentleman is her lover. She is so overmodest that she makes a scruple of shifting herself before her woman, but afterwards makes none of doing it before her gallant.

YOUNG WORTHY. Hang her, she's a jest to the whole town, for, though she has been the mother of two by-blows,[3] endeavors to appear as ignorant in all company as if she did not know the distinction of sexes.

NARCISSA. Look, look! Mr. Worthy, I vow, there's the Countess of Incog. out of her dishabille, in a high head, I protest.

YOUNG WORTHY. It is as great a wonder to see her out of an hackney coach as out of debt or—

NARCISSA. Or out of countenance.

YOUNG WORTHY. That, indeed, she seldom changes, for she is never out of a mask and is so well known in it that when she has a mind to be private she goes barefaced.

NARCISSA. But come, cousin, now let's see what monsters the next walk affords.

ELDER WORTHY. With all my heart; it is in our way home.

YOUNG WORTHY. Ladies, I must beg your pardon for a moment; yonder comes one I have a little business with; I'll dispatch it immediately and follow you.

HILLARIA. No, no. We'll stay for you.

---

[1] First edition has *when;* later *then,* which makes better sense, is found.

[2] Inserted in later editions; the first edition has "as here is."

[3] A by-blow is one who comes into the world by a side stroke, a bastard.

NARCISSA. You may, if you please, cousin; but I suppose he will hardly thank you for it.

HILLARIA. What, then you conclude it is a woman's business by his promising a quick dispatch!

YOUNG WORTHY. Madam, in three minutes you shall know the business; if it displease you, condemn me to an eternal absence.

ELDER WORTHY. Come, madam, let me be his security.

NARCISSA. I dare take your word, sir.

Exeunt ELDER WORTHY, HILLARIA, *and* NARCISSA

Enter SLY, *servant to* YOUNG WORTHY

YOUNG WORTHY. Well, how go matters; is she in a readiness to receive him?

SLY. To a hair, sir; every servant has his cue, and all are impatient till the comedy begins.

YOUNG WORTHY. Stand aside a little and let us watch our opportunities.

[*They retire. Enter* SNAP *and* LOVELESS *following a mask*][1]

SNAP. (*To a Mask*) Inquire about half an hour hence for number two at the Gridiron.[2]

MASK. Tomorrow with all my heart, but tonight I am engaged to the chaplain of Colonel Thunder's regiment.

SNAP. What, will you leave me for a mutton-chop, for that's all he'll give you, I'm sure?

MASK. You are mistaken; faith, he keeps me.

SNAP. Not to himself, I'll engage him; yet he may, too, if nobody likes you no better than I do. Hark you, child, prithee when was your smock washed?

MASK. Why dost thou pretend to fresh linen that never wore a clean shirt but of thy mother's own washing? (*Goes from him*)

LOVELESS. What, no adventure, no game, Snap?

SNAP. None, none, sir; I can't prevail with any from the pointhead cloths[3] to the horse-guard whore.

LOVELESS. What a pox! Sure the whores can't smell an empty pocket.

SNAP. No, no, that's certain, sir; they must see it in our faces.

SLY. (*To Loveless*) My dear boy, how is it? Egad, I am glad thou art come to town. My lady expected you above an hour ago, and I am overjoyed I ha' found thee. Come, come, come along; she's impatient till she sees you.

SNAP. Odsbud, sir, follow him; he takes you for another.

LOVELESS. Egad, it looks with the face of an intrigue. I'll humor him. Well, what, shall we go now?

SLY. Ay, ay, now it's pure and[4] dark, you may go undiscovered.

LOVELESS. That's what I would do.

SLY. Odsheart, she longs to see thee, and she is a curious fine creature, you rogue! Such eyes, such lips, and such a tongue between them! Ah, the tip of it will set a man's soul on fire!

LOVELESS. (*Aside*) The rogues make me impatient.

SLY. Come, come, the key, the key, the key, you dear rogue!

SNAP. (*Aside*) Oh, Lord, the key, the key!

LOVELESS. The key? Why sh—sh—sh— should y— y— you have it?

SLY. Ay, ay! Quickly, give's it!

LOVELESS. Why———what the devil! Sure I haven't lost it. Oh, no, gad, it is not there. What the devil shall we do?

SLY. Oons, never stand fumbling; if you have lost it, we must shoot the lock,[5] I think.

LOVELESS. Egad, and so we must, for I haven't it.

SLY. Come, come along, follow me.

LOVELESS. Snap, stand by me, you dog.

SNAP. Ay, ay, sir.

Exeunt SLY, LOVELESS, *and* SNAP

YOUNG WORTHY. Ha, ha! The rogue managed him most dexterously. How greedily he chopped[6] at the bait. What the event will be, heaven knows; but thus far it is pleasant, and since he is safe, I'll venture to divert my company with the story. Poor Amanda, thou well deservest a better husband; thou wert never wanting in thy endeavors to reclaim him; and, faith, considering how a long despair has worn thee,
'Twere pity now thy hopes should not succeed,
This new attempt is *Love's last shift* indeed.

---

[1] This necessary stage direction does not appear in the early editions.
[2] An inn.
[3] I.e., the lady in headdress of point lace.
[4] In the sense of completely, entirely.
[5] The clumsy doorlocks of the period could be broken by shooting a pistol bullet through the keyhole, which was large.
[6] Snapped.

ACT IV

[SCENE I]

The SCENE *continues*

Enter two Bullies *and* Sir William Wisewoud, *observing them*

First Bully. Damn me, Jack, let's after him and fight him; it is not to be put up.

Second Bully. No, damn him, nobody saw the affront, and what need we take notice of it?

First Bully. Why, that's true. But, damn me, I have much ado to forbear cutting his throat.

Sir William Wisewoud. Pray, gentlemen, what's the matter? Why are you in such a passion?

First Bully. What's that to you, sir? What would you have?

Sir William Wisewoud. I hope, sir, a man may ask a civil question.

First Bully. Damn me, sir, we are men of honor; we dare answer any man.

Sir William Wisewoud. But why are you angry, gentlemen? Have you received any wrong?

Second Bully. We have been called rascals, sir, have had the lie given us, and had like to have been kicked.

Sir William Wisewoud. But I hope you were not kicked, gentlemen.

Second Bully. How, sir, we kicked?

Sir William Wisewoud. Nor do I presume that you are rascals.

First Bully. Blood and thunder, sir, let any man say it that wears a head! We rascals!

Sir William Wisewoud. Very good. Since then you are not rascals, he rather was one who maliciously called you so. Pray take my advice, gentlemen; never disturb yourselves for any ill your enemy says of you, for from an enemy the world will not believe it. Now you must know, gentlemen, that a flea-bite is to me more offensive than the severest affront any man can offer me.

First Bully. What, and so you would have us put it up! Damn me, sir, don't preach cowardice to us. We are men of valor; you won't find us cowards, sir.

Second Bully. No, sir, we are no cowards, though you are.

First Bully. Hang him, let him alone; I see a coward in his face.

Sir William Wisewoud. If my face make any reflection, sir, it is against my will.

Second Bully. Prithee, Tom, let's affront him and raise his spleen a little.

Sir William Wisewoud. Raise my spleen! That's more than any man could ever boast of.

First Bully. You lie.

Sir William Wisewoud. I am not angry yet; therefore I do not lie, sir. Now, one of us must lie; I do not lie, *ergo*,—

First Bully. Damn me, sir, have a care! Don't give me the lie. I shan't take it, sir.

Sir William Wisewoud. I need not, sir. You give it yourself.

First Bully. Well, sir, what then? If I make bold with myself, every old puppy shall not pretend to do it.

Sir William Wisewoud. Ha, ha, ha, ha, ha!

First Bully. Damn me, sir, what do you laugh at?

Sir William Wisewoud. To let you see that I am no puppy, sir, for puppies are brutes; now brutes have not risibility, but I laugh; therefore I am no puppy. Ha, ha!

First Bully. Blood and thunder, sir, dare you fight?

Sir William Wisewoud. Not in cool blood, sir, and I confess it is impossible to make me angry.

Second Bully. I'll try that. Hark you, don't you know you are a sniveling old cuckold?

Sir William Wisewoud. No, really, sir.

Second Bully. Why, then, I know you to be one.

Sir William Wisewoud. Look you, sir, my reason weighs this injury, which is so light it will not raise my anger in the other scale.

First Bully. Oons! what a tame old prig's this! I'll give you better weight, then. I know who got all your children.

Sir William Wisewoud. Not so well as my wife, I presume. Now, she tells me it was myself, and I believe her, too.

First Bully. She tells you so because the poor rogue that got them is not able to keep them.

Sir William Wisewoud. Then my keeping them is charity.

First Bully. Blood and thunder, sir, this is an affront to us not to be angry after all these provocations. Damn me, Jack, let's souse him in the canal.

As they lay hold on him
Enter ELDER WORTHY, YOUNG WORTHY, NARCISSA, *and* HILLARIA

YOUNG WORTHY. S'death, what's here? Sir William in the rogues' hands that affronted the ladies. Oh, forbear, forbear!
(*Strikes them*)
ELDER WORTHY. So, gentlemen, I thought you had fair warning before; now you shall pay for it. (*Enter three or four* Sentinels) Hark you, honest soldiers, pray do me the favor to wash these rascals in the canal, and there's a guinea for your trouble.
BULLIES. Damn me, sir, we shall expect satisfaction.
Exeunt [Sentinels], *dragging the* BULLIES
SIR WILLIAM WISEWOUD. Oh, dear gentlemen, I am obliged to you, for I was just going to the canal myself, if you had not come as you did.
ELDER WORTHY. Pray, sir, what had you done to them?
SIR WILLIAM WISEWOUD. Why, hearing the music from my parlor window and being invited by the sweetness of the evening, I e'en took a walk to see if I could meet with you, when the first objects that presented themselves were these bullies, threatening to cut somebody's throat. Now, I, endeavoring to allay their fury, occasioned their giving me scurrilous language, and finding they could not make me as angry as themselves, they offered to fling me into the water.
ELDER WORTHY. I am glad we stepped to your deliverance.
SIR WILLIAM WISEWOUD. Oh, I thank you, gentlemen. I'll e'en go home and recover my fright. Good night, good night to you all.
Exit
ELDER WORTHY. Harry, see Sir William safe to his lodging. (*To his servant*) Well, ladies, I believe it's time for us to be walking, too.[1]
HILLARIA. No, pray let me engage you to stay a little longer. Yonder comes Sir Novelty and his mistress in pursuance of the design I told you of. Pray have a little patience, and you will see the effect on it.
ELDER WORTHY. With all my heart, madam.
(*They stand aside*)

Enter SIR NOVELTY *embracing* MRS. FLAREIT, *masked*

SIR NOVELTY FASHION. Generous creature! This is an unexampled condescension to meet my passion with such early kindness. Thus let me pay my soft acknowledgments.
(*Kisses her hand*)
HILLARIA. You must know he has mistaken her for another.
MRS. FLAREIT. For heaven's sake, let me go. If Hillaria should be at home before me, I am ruined forever.
NARCISSA. Hillaria! What does she mean?
SIR NOVELTY FASHION. Narcissa's reputation shall be ever safe while my life and fortune can protect it.
NARCISSA. O, gad, let me go! Does the impudent creature take my name upon her! I'll pull off her head-clothes.
HILLARIA. Oh, fie, cousin, what an ungenteel revenge would that be! Have a little patience.
NARCISSA. Oh, I am in a flame.
(*Throwing back her hoods*)
MRS. FLAREIT. But will you never see that common creature Flareit more?
SIR NOVELTY FASHION. Never, never! Feed on such homely fare after so rich a banquet?
MRS. FLAREIT. Nay, but you must hate her, too.
SIR NOVELTY FASHION. That I did long ago for her stinking breath! It is true, I have been led away, but I detest a strumpet. I am informed she keeps a fellow under my nose, and for that reason I would not make the settlement I lately gave her some hopes of. But even let her please herself, for now I am wholly yours.
MRS. FLAREIT. Oh, now you charm me! But will you love me ever?
SIR NOVELTY FASHION. Will you be ever kind?
MRS. FLAREIT. Be sure you never see Flareit more.
SIR NOVELTY FASHION. When I do, may this soft hand revenge my perjury.
MRS. FLAREIT. So it shall, villain! (*Strikes him a box on the ear and unmasks*)
OMNES. Ha, ha, ha!
SIR NOVELTY FASHION. Flareit! The devil!
MRS. FLAREIT. What, will nothing but a maidenhead go down with you! Thou miserable, conceited wretch! Foh, my breath

---

[1] The scene of Sir William's encounter with the bullies was later removed from the play, the act beginning with this speech of the Elder Worthy.

stinks, does it! I'm a homely puss, a strumpet not worth your notice! Devil, I'll be revenged.

Sir Novelty Fashion. Damn your revenge. I'm sure I feel it. (*Holding his cheek*)

Narcissa. Really, Sir Novelty, I am obliged to you for your kind thoughts of me and your extraordinary care of my reputation.

Sir Novelty Fashion. 'Sdeath, she here! Exposed to half the town! Well, I must brazen it out, however. (*Walks unconcerned*)

Mrs. Flareit. What, no pretence, no evasion, now!

Sir Novelty Fashion. There's no occasion for any, madam.

Mrs. Flareit. Come, come, swear you knew me all this while.

Sir Novelty Fashion. No, faith, madam, I did not know you, for if I had you would not have found me so furious a lover.

Mrs. Flareit. Furies and hell! Dares the monster own his guilt? This is beyond all sufferance. Thou wretch, thou thing, thou animal, that I—to the everlasting forfeiture of my sense and understanding—have made a man! For till thou knewest me, it was doubted if thou wert of human kind. And dost thou think I'll suffer such a worm as thee to turn against me? No! When I do, may I be cursed to thy embraces all my life and never know a joy beyond thee.

Sir Novelty Fashion. Why, wh—wh—what will your ladyship's fury do, madam?
(*Smiling*)

Mrs. Flareit. Only change my lodging, sir.

Sir Novelty Fashion. I shall keep mine, madam, that you may know where to find me when your fury is over. You see I am good natured. (*Walks by her*)

Mrs. Flareit. (*Aside*) This bravery's affected. I know he loves me, and I'll pierce him to the quick. I have yet a surer way to fool him.

Hillaria. Methinks the knight bears it bravely.

Narcissa. I protest the lady weeps.

Young Worthy. She knows what she does, I'll warrant you.

Elder Worthy. Ay, ay, the fox is a better politician than the lion.[1]

Mrs. Flareit. (*With tears in her eyes. Aside*) Now, woman.—Sir Novelty, pray, sir, let me speak with you.

[1] An idea implied in a number of Æsop's *Fables*.

Sir Novelty Fashion. Ay, madam.

Mrs. Flareit. Before we part—for I find I have irrecoverably lost your love—let me beg of you that from this hour you ne'er will see me more or make any new attempts to deceive my easy temper, for I find my nature's such I shall believe you, though to my utter ruin.

Sir Novelty Fashion. (*Aside*) Pray heaven she be in earnest.

Mrs. Flareit. One thing more, sir. Since our first acquaintance you have received several letters from me. I hope you will be so much a gentleman as to let me have 'em again. Those I have of yours shall be returned tomorrow morning. And now, sir, wishing you as much happiness in her you love as you once pretended I could give you, I take of you my everlasting leave. Farewell, and may your next mistress love you till I hate you.
(*She is going*)

Sir Novelty Fashion. (*Aside*) So! Now must I seem to persuade her.—Nay, prithee, my dear! Why do you struggle so? Whither would you go?

Mrs. Flareit. Pray, sir, give me leave to pass; I can't bear to stay. (*Crying*)

Sir Novelty Fashion. What is it that frightens you?

Mrs. Flareit. Your barbarous usage. Pray, let me go.

Sir Novelty Fashion. Nay, if you are resolved, madam, I won't press you against your will. Your humble servant. (*He leaves her.—Aside*) And a happy riddance, stop my vitals. (Mrs. Flareit *looks back*)

Mrs. Flareit. (*Aside*) Ha, not move to call me back! So unconcerned! Oh, I could tear my flesh, stab every feature in this dull, decaying face that wants a charm to hold him. Damn him! I loathe him too! But shall my pride now fall from such an height and bear the torture unrevenged? No! My very soul's on fire, and nothing but the villain's blood shall quench it. Devil, have at thee.
(*Snatches* Young Worthy's *sword and runs at him*)

Young Worthy. Have a care, sir.

Sir Novelty Fashion. Let her alone, gentlemen; I'll warrant you.
(*He draws and stands upon his guard.*
Young Worthy *takes the sword from her and holds her*)

Mrs. Flareit. Prevented! Oh, I shall

choke with boiling gall. Oh, oh, umh! Let me go! I'll have his blood, his blood, his blood!
(Raving)

SIR NOVELTY FASHION. Let her come, let her come, gentlemen.

MRS. FLAREIT. Death and vengeance, am I become his sport? He's pleased, and smiles to see me rage the more! But he shall find no fiend in hell can match the fury of a disappointed woman! Scorned, slighted, dismissed without a parting pang! Oh, torturing thought! May all the racks mankind e'er gave our easy sex, neglected love, decaying beauty, and hot raging lust light on me if e'er I cease to be the eternal plague of his remaining life, nay, after death, When his [1] black soul lies howling in despair, I'll plunge to hell and be his torment there.
Exit in a fury

ELDER WORTHY. Sure, Sir Novelty, you never loved this lady, if you are so indifferent at parting.

SIR NOVELTY FASHION. Why, faith, Tom, to tell you the truth, her jealousy has been so very troublesome and expensive to me of late that I have these three months sought an opportunity to leave her, but, faith, I had always more respect to my life than to let her know it before.

HILLARIA. Methinks, Sir Novelty, you had very little respect to her life when you drew upon her.

SIR NOVELTY FASHION. Why, what would you have had me done, madam? Complimented her with my naked bosom? No, no! Look you, madam, if she had made any advances, I could have disarmed her in a second at the very first pass. But come, ladies, as we walk, I'll beg your judgments in a particular nice fancy that I intend to appear in the very first week the court is quite out of mourning.

ELDER WORTHY. With all my heart, Sir Novelty. Come, ladies, considering how little rest you'll have tomorrow night, I think it were charity not to keep you up any longer.

YOUNG WORTHY. Nay, as for that matter, the night before a wedding is as unfit to sleep in as the night following. Imagination's a very troublesome bedfellow. Your pardon, ladies, I only speak for myself.

ELDER WORTHY. *(To his* Servant*)* See the coaches ready at St. James' gate. *Exeunt*

[1] The first edition has "when his. his." a misprint.

[SCENE II]

AMANDA'S *House*

Enter two Servants

FIRST SERVANT. Come, come, make haste. Is the supper and the music ready?

SECOND SERVANT. It is, it is. Well, is he come?

FIRST SERVANT. Ay, ay. I came before to tell my lady the news. That rogue Sly managed him rarely; he has been this half hour pretending to pick the lock of the garden door. Well, poor lady, I wish her good luck with him, for she's certainly the best mistress living. Hark you, is the wine strong as she ordered it? Be sure you ply him home, for he must have two or three bumpers to qualify him for her design. See, here he comes. Away to your post.
Exeunt

Enter LOVELESS, *conducted by* SLY, SNAP *stealing after them*

LOVELESS. Where the devil will this fellow lead me? Nothing but silence and darkness! Sure the house is haunted and he has brought me to face the spirit at his wonted hour.

SLY. There, there, in, in. Slip on your night gown and refresh yourself. In the meantime, I'll acquaint my lady that you are here.
Exit

LOVELESS. Snap!

SNAP. Ay, ay, sir, I'll warrant you. *Exeunt*

[SCENE III]

The SCENE *changes to an ante-chamber. A table, light, a night gown, and a periwig lying by. They re-enter*

LOVELESS. Ha, what sweet lodgings are here? Where can this end?

SNAP. Egad, sir, I long to know. Pray heaven we are not deluded hither to be starved. Methinks I wish I had brought the remnants of my dinner with me.

LOVELESS. Hark, I hear somebody coming. Hide yourself, rascal. I would not have you seen.

SNAP. Well, sir, I'll line this trench in case of your being in danger. *(Gets under the table)*

LOVELESS. Ha, this night gown and peruke don't lie here for nothing. I'll make myself agreeable. I have balked many a woman in my time for want of a clean shirt.
(He puts them on)

Enter Servants *with a supper, after them* [Amanda's] [1] *woman*

Loveless. Ha, a supper! Heaven send it be no vision! If the meat be real, I shall believe the lady may prove flesh and blood. Now am I damnably puzzled to know whether this be she or not? Madam—(*He bows*)

Woman. Sir, my lady begs your pardon for a moment.

Loveless. Hm, her lady! Good.

Woman. She's unfortunately detained by some female visitors, which she will dispatch with all the haste imaginable. In the meantime be pleased to refresh yourself with what the house affords. Pray, sir, sit down.

Loveless. Not alone. Madam, you must bear me company.

Amanda's Woman. To oblige you, sir, I'll exceed my commission.

Snap. (*Under the table*) Was there ever so unfortunate a dog! What the devil put it in my head to hide myself before supper? Why, this is worse than being locked into a closet while another man's a-bed with my wife! I suppose my master will take as much care of me, too, as I should of him if I were in his place.

Woman. Sir, my humble service to you.
(*Drinks*)

Loveless. Madam, your humble servant. I'll pledge you. (*Aside to Snap*) Snap, when there's any danger I'll call you; in the meantime, lie still, do you hear?

Snap. Egad, I'll shift for myself then. (*He snatches a flask unseen*) So now I am armed, defiance to all danger!

Loveless. Madam, your lady's health.

Snap. Ay, ay, let it go 'round, I say.
(*Drinks*)

Woman. Well, really, sir, my lady's very happy that she has got loose from her relations, for they were always teasing her about you. But she defies them all now. Come, sir, success to both your wishes. (*Drinks*)

Loveless. Give me a glass. Methinks this health inspires me. My heart grows lighter for the weight of wine. Here, madam—prosperity to the man that ventures most to please her.

---

[1] Early editions read, "after them a Man, Woman." As there is no man present in the scene and as Amanda's woman, so called later, is the woman in question, the emendation seems proper.

Woman. What think you of a song to support this gaiety?

Loveless. With all my heart. (*A song here*) You have obliged me, madam. Egad, I like this girl. She takes off her glass so feelingly I am half persuaded she's of a thirsty love. If her lady don't make a little haste, I shall present my humble service to her.

Enter a Servant, *who whispers to* Amanda's Woman

Woman. Sir, I ask your pardon. My lady has some commands for me; I will return immediately. *Exit*

Loveless. Your servant. Methinks this is a very new method of intriguing.

Snap. Pray heaven it be new, for the old way commonly ended in a good beating. But a pox of danger, I say, and so here's good luck to you, sir.

Loveless. Take heed, rogue, you don't get drunk and discover yourself.

Snap. It must be with a fresh flask, then, for this is expired *supernaculum*.

Loveless. Lie close, you dog. I hear somebody coming. I am impatient till I see this creature. This wine has armed me against all thoughts of danger. Pray heaven she be young, for then she can't want beauty. Ha, here she comes! Now, never-failing impudence assist me.

Enter Amanda, *loosely dressed*

Amanda. Where's my love? Oh, let me fly into his arms and live forever there.

Loveless. My life, my soul! (*Runs and embraces her*) By heaven, a tempting creature. Melting, soft, and warm as my desire. Oh, that I could hide my face forever thus, that undiscovered I might reap the harvest of a ripe desire without the lingering pains of growing love.

(*He kisses her hand*)

Amanda. Look up, my lord, and bless me with a tender look and let my talking eyes inform thee how I have languished for thy absence.

Loveless. Let's retire and chase away our fleeting cares with the raptures of untired love.

Amanda. Bless me, your voice is strangely altered. Ha, defend me! Who's this? Help, help, within there!

Loveless. So, I am discovered! A pox on

my tatling that I could not hold my tongue till I got to her bed chamber.

Enter SLY *and other* Servants

SLY. Did your ladyship call help, madam? What's the matter?

AMANDA. Villain! Slave! Who's this? What ruffian have you brought me here? Dog, I'll have you murdered!

(SLY *looks in his face*)

SLY. Bless me! Oh, Lord! Dear madam, I beg your pardon; as I hope to be saved, madam, it is a mistake. I took him for Mr.—

AMANDA. Be dumb! Eternal blockhead! Here, take this fellow, toss him in a blanket, and let him be turned out of my doors immediately.

SLY. Oh, pray! Dear madam, for heaven's sake, I am a ruined man.

SNAP. [*Aside*] Ah, Snap, what will become of thee? Thou art fallen into the hands of a tigress that has lost her whelp. I have no hopes but in my master's impudence. Heaven strengthen it.

AMANDA. I'll hear no more. Away with him!

Exeunt the servants with SLY

Now, sir, for you. I expected—

LOVELESS. A man, madam, did you not?

AMANDA. Not a stranger, sir, but one that has a right and title to that welcome which by mistake has been given to you.

LOVELESS. Not a husband, I presume? He would not have been so privately conducted to your chamber and in the dark, too.

AMANDA. Whoever it was, sir, it is not your business to examine. But if you would have civil usage, pray be gone.

LOVELESS. To be used civilly, I must stay, madam. There can be no danger with so fair a creature.

AMANDA. I doubt you are mad, sir.

LOVELESS. While my senses have such luscious food before them, no wonder if they are in some confusion, each striving to be foremost at the banquet, and sure my greedy eyes will starve the rest. (*Approaching her*)

AMANDA. Pray, sir, keep your distance lest your feeling, too, be gratified.

SNAP. [*Aside*] Oh, Lord, I would I were a hundred leagues off at sea.

LOVELESS. Then briefly thus, madam: Know I like and love you. Now if you have so much generosity as to let me know what title my pretended rival has to your person or your inclinations, perhaps the little hopes I then may have of supplanting him may make me leave your house. If not, my love shall still pursue you, though to the hazard of my life, which I shall not easily resign while this sword can guard it, madam.

AMANDA. (*Aside*) Oh, were this courage shown but in a better cause, how worthy were the man that owned it!—What is it, sir, that you propose by this unnecessary trifling? Know, then, that I did expect a lover, a man perhaps more brave than you, one that if present would have given you a shorter answer to your question.

LOVELESS. I am glad to hear he's brave, however; it betrays no weakness in your choice. But if you still preserve or raise the joys of love, remove him from your thoughts a moment and in his room receive a warmer heart, a heart that must admire you more than he because my passion's of a fresher date.

AMANDA. What do you take me for?

LOVELESS. A woman, and the most charming of your sex, one whose pointed eyes declare you formed for love, and though your words are flinty, your every look and motion all confess there's a secret fire within you which must sparkle when the steel of love provokes it. Come, now pull away your hand and make me hold it faster.

AMANDA. Nay, now you are rude, sir.

LOVELESS. If love be rudeness, let me be impudent. When we are familiar, rudeness will be love. No woman ever thought a lover rude after she had once granted him the favor.

AMANDA. Pray, sir, forbear.

LOVELESS. How can I when my desire's so violent? Oh, let me snatch the rosy dew from those distilling lips and as you see your power to charm so chide me with your pity. Why do you thus cruelly turn away your face? I own the blessing's worth an age's expectation, but if refused till merited, it is esteemed a debt. Would you oblige your lover, let loose your early kindness?

AMANDA. I shall not take your counsel, sir, while I know a woman's early kindness is as little sign of her generosity as her generosity is a sign of her discretion. Nor would I have you believe I am so ill provided for that I need listen to any man's first addresses.

LOVELESS. Why, madam, would you not drink the first time you had a thirst?

AMANDA. Yes, but not before I had.

LOVELESS. If you can't drink, yet you may kiss the cup, and that may give you inclination.

AMANDA. Your pardon, sir, I drink out of nobody's glass but my own. As the man I love confines himself to me, so my inclination keeps me true to him.

LOVELESS. That's a cheat imposed upon you by your own vanity, for when your back's turned your very chambermaid sips of your leavings and becomes your rival. Constancy in love is all a cheat; women of your understanding know it. The joys of love are only great when they are new, and to make them lasting we must often change.

AMANDA. Suppose it were a fresh lover I now expected.

LOVELESS. Why, then, madam, your expectation's answered, for I must confess I don't take you for an old acquaintance, though somewhere I have seen a face not much unlike you. Come, your arguments are vain, for they are so charmingly delivered they but inspire me the more, as blows in battle raise the brave man's courage. Come, everything pleads for me: your beauty, wit, time, place, opportunity, and my own excess of raging passion.

AMANDA. Stand off—distant as the globes of heaven and earth, that like a falling star I may shoot with greater force into your arms and think it heaven to lie expiring there.

(*She runs into his arms*)

SNAP. [*Aside*] Ah, ah, ah! Rogue, the day's our own.

LOVELESS. Thou sweetest, softest creature heaven ever formed! Thus let me twine myself about thy beauteous limbs till, struggling with the pangs of painful bliss, motionless and mute we yield to conquering love, both vanquished and both victors.

AMANDA. (*Aside*) Can all this heat be real? Oh, why has hateful vice such power to charm while poor, abandoned virtue lies neglected?

LOVELESS. Come, let us surfeit on our newborn raptures. Let's waken sleeping nature with delight, till we may justly say: Now, now, we live!

AMANDA. Come on, let's indulge the transports of our present bliss and bid defiance to our future change of fate. Who waits there?

Enter AMANDA'S *woman*

AMANDA. Bring me word immediately if my apartment's ready, as I ordered it. Oh, I am charmed; I have found the man to please me now, one that can and dares maintain the noble rapture of a lawless love. I own myself a libertine, a mortal foe to that dull thing called virtue, that mere disease of sickly nature. Pleasure's the end of life, and while I'm mistress of myself and fortune, I will enjoy it to the height. Speak freely then— not that I love, like other women, the nauseous pleasure of a little flattery—but answer me like a man that scorns a lie: Does my face invite you, sir? May I, from what you see of me, propose a pleasure to myself in pleasing you?

LOVELESS. By heaven, you may. I have seen all beauties that the sun shines on, but never saw the sun out-shined before; I have measured half the world in search of pleasure, but not returning home, had ne'er been happy.

AMANDA. Spoken like the man I wish might love me. (*Aside*) Pray heaven his words prove true.—Be sure you never flatter me, and when my person tires you, confess it freely. For change whenever you will, I'll change as soon; but while we chance to meet, still let it be with raging fire. No matter how soon it dies, provided the small time it lasts it burn the fiercer.

LOVELESS. Oh, would the blinded world, like us, agree to change, how lasting might the joys of love be! For thus beauty, though stale to one, might somewhere else be new, and while this man were blessed in leaving what he loathed, another were new-ravished in receiving what he ne'er enjoyed.

Re-enter AMANDA'S WOMAN

WOMAN. Madam, everything is according to your order.

LOVELESS. Oh, lead me to the scene of unsupportable delight, rack me with pleasures never known before, till I lie gasping with convulsive passion. This night let us be lavish to our unbounded wishes.
Give all our stock at once to raise the fire,
And revel to the height of loose desire.

Exeunt

WOMAN. Ah, what a happy creature's my lady now! There's many an unsatisfied wife about town would be glad to have her husband as wicked as my master upon the same terms my lady has him. Few women, I'm afraid, would grudge an husband the laying out his stock of love that could receive such considerable interest for it! Well, now shan't I take one wink of sleep for thinking how they'll employ their time tonight. Faith, I must listen if I were to be hanged for it.

(*She listens at the door*)

SNAP. [*Aside*] So! My master's provided for; therefore it is time for me to take care of myself. I have no mind to be locked out of my lodging. I fancy there's room for two in the maid's bed as well as my lady's. This same flask was plaguey strong wine. I find I shall storm if she don't surrender fairly.—By your leave, damsel.

WOMAN. Bless me! Who's this? Oh, Lord, what would you have? Who are you?

SNAP. One that has a right and title to your body, my master having already taken possession of your lady's.

WOMAN. Let me go, or I'll cry out.

SNAP. You lie, you dare not disturb your lady. But the better to secure you, thus I stop your mouth.

(*Kisses her*)

WOMAN. Humph! Lord bless me, is the devil in you, tearing one's things!

SNAP. Then show me your bed-chamber.

WOMAN. The devil shall have you first.

SNAP. He shall have us both together, then. Here will I fix (*Takes her about the neck*) just in this posture till tomorrow morning. In the meantime, when you find your inclination stirring, prithee give me a call, for at present I am very sleepy.

(*He seems to sleep*)

WOMAN. Foh, how he stinks! (*He belches*) Ah, what a whiff was there. The rogue's as drunk as a sailor with a twelve-months' arrears in his pocket, or a Jacobite upon a day of ill news. I'll ha' nothing to say to him. Let me see, how shall I get rid of him? Oh, I have it. I'll soon make him sober, I'll warrant him.—So ho, Mr. What-do-y'-call-'em, where do you intend to lie tonight?

SNAP. Hm, why, where you lay last night, unless you change your lodging.

WOMAN. Well, for once I'll take pity of you. Make no noise, but put out the candles and follow me softly for fear of disturbing my lady.

SNAP. I'll warrant you there's no fear of spoiling her music while we are playing the same tune.

[SCENE IV]

The SCENE *changes to a dark entry, and they re-enter.*

WOMAN. Where are you? Lend me your hand.

SNAP. Here! Here, make haste, my dear concupiscence.

WOMAN. Hold! Stand there a little, while I open the door gently without waking the footmen. (*She feels about and opens a trap door*)

WOMAN. Come along softly, this way.

SNAP. Whereabouts are you?

WOMAN. Here, here, come straight forward.

(*He goes forward and falls into the cellar*)

SNAP. Oh, Lord! Oh, Lord! I have broke my neck.

WOMAN. I am glad to hear him say so; however I should be loath to be hanged for him. How do you, sir?

SNAP. Do you, sir? I am a league under ground.

WOMAN. Whereabouts are you?

SNAP. In hell, I think.

WOMAN. No, no, you are but in the road to it, I dare say. Ah, dear, why will you follow lewd women at this rate, when they lead you to the very gulf of destruction? I knew you would be swallowed up at last. Ha, ha, ha, ha!

SNAP. Ah, you sneering whore!

WOMAN. Shall I fetch you a prayer-book, sir, to arm you against the temptations of the flesh?

SNAP. No, you need but show your own damned ugly face to do that. Hark you, either help me out or I'll hang myself and swear you murdered me.

WOMAN. Nay, if you are so bloody-minded, good night to you, sir.

(*She offers to shut the door over him, and he catches hold on her*)

SNAP. Ah, ah, ah! Have I caught you! Egad, we'll pig together, now.

WOMAN. Oh, Lord! Pray let me go, and I'll do anything.

SNAP. And so you shall before I part with you. (*Pulls her in to him*) And now, master, my humble service to you.

(*He pulls the door over them*)

ACT V

[SCENE I]

The SCENE: SIR WILLIAM WISEWOUD'S *house*

Enter ELDER WORTHY, YOUNG WORTHY, *and a* Lawyer *with writing*

ELDER WORTHY. Are the ladies ready?

YOUNG WORTHY. Hillaria is just gone up to hasten her cousin, and Sir William will be here immediately.

ELDER WORTHY. But hark you, brother, I have considered of it, and pray let me oblige you not to pursue your design upon his five thousand pound; for, in short, it is no better than a cheat and what a gentleman should scorn to be guilty of. Is not it sufficient that I consent to your wronging him of his daughter?

YOUNG WORTHY. Your pardon, brother, I can't allow that a wrong, for his daughter loves me; her fortune, you know, he has nothing to do with, and it's a hard case a young woman shall not have the disposal of her heart. Love's a fever of the mind which nothing but our own wishes can assuage, and I don't question but we shall find marriage a very cooling cordial. And as to the five thousand pounds, it is no more than what he has endeavored to cheat his niece of.

ELDER WORTHY. What do you mean? I take him for an honest man.

YOUNG WORTHY. Oh, very honest! As honest as an old agent to a new-raised regiment. No, faith, I'll say that for him, he will not do an ill thing unless he gets by it. In a word, this so very honest Sir William, as you take him to be, has offered me the refusal of your mistress, and upon condition I will secure him five thousand pounds upon my day of marriage with her, he will secure me her person and ten thousand pounds, the remaining part of her fortune. There's a guardian for you! What think you now, sir?

ELDER WORTHY. Why, I think he deserves to be served in the same kind. I find age and avarice are inseparable! Therefore even make what you can of him, and I will stand by you. But hark you, Mr. Forge, are you sure it will stand good in law if Sir William signs the bond?

LAWYER. In any court in England, sir.

ELDER WORTHY. Then there's your fifty pieces, and if it succeeds, here are as many more in the same pocket to answer them. But mum—here comes Sir William and the ladies.

Enter SIR WILLIAM WISEWOUD, HILLARIA, *and* NARCISSA

SIR WILLIAM WISEWOUD. Good morrow, gentlemen! Mr. Worthy, give you joy! Odso! If my heels were as light as my heart, I should ha' much ado to forbear dancing. Here, here, take her, man. (*Gives him* NARCISSA'S *hand*) She's yours, and so is her thousand pounds a year, and my five thousand pounds shall be yours, too.

YOUNG WORTHY. (*Aside*) You must ask me leave first.

SIR WILLIAM WISEWOUD. Odso! Is the lawyer come?

ELDER WORTHY. He is, and all the writings are ready, sir.

SIR WILLIAM WISEWOUD. Come, come, let's see, man! What's this! Od, this law is a plaguey, troublesome thing, for nowadays it won't let a man give away his own without repeating the particulars five hundred times over, when in former times a man might have held his title to twenty thousand pounds a year in the compass of a horn-book.[1]

LAWYER. That is, sir, because there are more knaves nowadays, and this age is more treacherous and distrustful than heretofore.

SIR WILLIAM WISEWOUD. That is, sir, because there are more lawyers than heretofore. But come, what's this, prithee?

LAWYER. These are the old writings of your daughter's fortune; this is Mr. Worthy's settlement upon her, and this, sir, is your bond for five thousand pounds to him. There wants nothing but filling up the blanks with the parties' names. If you please, sir, I'll do it immediately.

SIR WILLIAM WISEWOUD. Do so.

LAWYER. May I crave your daughter's Christian name? The rest I know, sir.

SIR WILLIAM WISEWOUD. Narcissa! Prithee, make haste.

YOUNG WORTHY. (*Aside to the lawyer*) You know your business.

LAWYER. I'll warrant you, sir.

(*He sits to write*)

SIR WILLIAM WISEWOUD. Mr. Worthy, methinks your brother does not relish your

[1] The horn-books in use in the schools commonly consisted of a single sheet written on both sides;—a contrast to the Lawyer's sheaf of papers.

happiness as he should do. Poor man! I'll warrant he wishes himself in his brother's condition.

YOUNG WORTHY. Not I, I'll assure you, sir.

SIR WILLIAM WISEWOUD. Niece, niece! Have you no pity? Prithee, look upon him a little! Od! He's a pretty young fellow. I am sure he loves you, or he would not have frequented my house so often. Do you think his brother could not tell my daughter his own story without his assistance? Pshaw—waw! I tell you, you were the beauty that made him so assiduous. Come, come, give him your hand, and he'll soon creep into your heart, I'll warrant you. Come, say the word, and make him happy.

HILLARIA. What, to make myself miserable, sir, marry a man without an estate?

SIR WILLIAM WISEWOUD. Hang an estate! True love's beyond all riches! It is all dirt, mere dirt! Besides, haven't you fifteen thousand pounds to your portion?

HILLARIA. I doubt, sir, you would be loath to give him your daughter, though her fortune's larger.

SIR WILLIAM WISEWOUD. 'Od, if he loved her but half so well as he loves you, he should have her for a word speaking.

HILLARIA. But, sir, this asks some consideration.

NARCISSA. You see, Mr. Worthy, what an extraordinary kindness my father has for you.

YOUNG WORTHY. Ay, madam, and for your cousin, too. But I hope with a little of your assistance we shall both be able very shortly to return it.

NARCISSA. Nay, I was always ready to serve Hillaria, for heaven knows I only marry to revenge her quarrel to my father. I cannot forgive his offering to sell her.

YOUNG WORTHY. Oh, you need not take such pains, madam, to conceal your passion for me; you may own it without a blush upon your wedding day.

NARCISSA. My passion! When did you hear me acknowledge any? If I thought you could believe me guilty of such a weakness, though after I had married you, I would never look you in the face.

YOUNG WORTHY. A very pretty humor this, faith. (*Aside*) What a world of unnecessary sins have we two to answer for? For she has told more lies to conceal her love than I have sworn false oaths to promote it —Well, madam, at present I'll content myself with your giving me leave to love.

NARCISSA. Which if I don't give, you'll take, I suppose.

HILLARIA. Well, uncle, I won't promise you I'll go to church and see them married; when we come back, it is ten to one but I surprise you where you least think on.

SIR WILLIAM WISEWOUD. Why, that's well said. Mr. Worthy, now, now's your time. Od, I have so fired her, it is not in her power to deny you, man. To her, to her! I warrant her thy own, boy! You'll keep your word, five thousand pounds upon the day of marriage.

YOUNG WORTHY. I'll give you my bond upon demand, sir.

SIR WILLIAM WISEWOUD. Oh, I dare take your word, sir. Come, lawyer, have you done? Is all ready?

LAWYER. All, sir. This is your bond to Mr. Worthy. Will you be pleased to sign that first, sir?

SIR WILLIAM WISEWOUD. Ay, ay. Let's see: "The condition of this obligation—" (*He reads*) Hm—mm—— Come, lend me the pen. (*Signs*) There, Mr. Worthy, I deliver this as my act and deed to you, and heaven send you a good bargain. Niece, will you witness it? (*Which she does*) Come, lawyer, your fist, too. (*The lawyer witnesses it*)

LAWYER. Now, sir, if you please to sign the jointure.

ELDER WORTHY. Come on. Sir William, I deliver this to you for the use of your daughter. Madam, will you give yourself the trouble once more. (*Hillaria sets her hand*) Come, sir. (*The lawyer does the same*) So now let a coach be called as soon as you please, sir.

SIR WILLIAM WISEWOUD. You may save that charge; I saw your own at the door.

ELDER WORTHY. Your pardon, sir, that would make our business too public, for which reason, Sir William, I hope you will excuse our not taking you along with us.

Exit a Servant

SIR WILLIAM WISEWOUD. Ay, ay, with all my heart. The more privacy, the less expense. But, pray, what time may I expect you back again, for Amanda has sent to me for the writings of her husband's estate? I suppose she intends to redeem the mortgage, and I am afraid she will keep me there till dinner time.

YOUNG WORTHY. Why, about that time she has obliged me to bring some of her nearest friends to be witnesses of her good or evil fortune with her husband. Methinks I long to know her success; if you please, Sir William, we'll meet you there.

SIR WILLIAM WISEWOUD. With all my heart. (*Enter a servant*) Well, is the coach come?

SERVANT. It is at the door, sir.

SIR WILLIAM WISEWOUD. Come, gentlemen, no ceremony. Your time's short.

ELDER WORTHY. Your servant, Sir William.

Exeunt ELDER WORTHY, YOUNG WORTHY, NARCISSA, *and* HILLARIA

SIR WILLIAM WISEWOUD. So! Here's five thousand pounds got with a wet finger! This it is to read mankind. I knew a young lover would never think he gave too much for his mistress. Well, if I don't suddenly meet with some misfortune, I shall never be able to bear this tranquillity of mind. *Exit*

[SCENE II]

The SCENE *changes to* AMANDA'S *house*

Enter AMANDA *sola*

AMANDA. Thus far my hopes have all been answered, and my disguise of vicious love has charmed him even to a madness of impure desire. But now I tremble to pull off the mask, lest bare-faced virtue should fright him from my arms forever. Yet sure there are charms in virtue, nay, stronger and more pleasing far than hateful vice can boast of! Else why have holy martyrs perished for its sake? While lewdness ever gives severe repentance and unwilling death! Good heaven inspire my heart and hang upon my tongue the force of truth and eloquence, that I may lure this wandering falcon back to love and virtue. He comes, and now my dreaded task begins.

Enter LOVELESS *in new clothes*

AMANDA. How fare you, sir? Do you not already think yourself confined? Are you not tired with my easy love?

LOVELESS. Oh, never, never! You have so filled my thoughts with pleasures past that but to reflect on them is still new rapture to my soul, and the bliss must last while I have life or memory.

AMANDA. No flattery, sir! I loved you for your plain dealing; and to preserve my good opinion, tell me, what think you of the grape's persuading juice? Come, speak freely, would not the next tavern-bush [1] put all this out of your head?

LOVELESS. Faith, madam, to be free with you, I am apt to think you are in the right on it, for though love and wine are two very fine tunes, yet they make no music if you play them both together; separately they ravish us. Thus the mistress ought to make room for the bottle, the bottle for the mistress, and both to wait the call of inclination.

AMANDA. That's generously spoken. I have observed, sir, in all your discourse you confess something of a man that has thoroughly known the world. Pray give me leave to ask you of what condition you are whence you came.

LOVELESS. Why, in the first place, madam, by birth I am a gentleman; by ill friends, good wine, and false dice, almost a beggar; but by your servant's mistaking me, the happiest man that ever love and beauty smiled on.

AMANDA. One thing more, sir. Are you married? (*Aside*) Now my fears.

LOVELESS. I was, but very young.

AMANDA. What was your wife?

LOVELESS. A foolish, loving thing that built castles in the air and thought it impossible for a man to forswear himself when he made love.

AMANDA. Was she not virtuous?

LOVELESS. Umph! Yes, faith, I believe she might; I was never jealous of her.

AMANDA. Did you never love her?

LOVELESS. Ah, most damnably at first, for she was within two women of my maidenhead.

AMANDA. What's become of her?

LOVELESS. Why, after I had been from her beyond sea about seven or eight years, like a very loving fool she died of the pip and civilly left me the world free to range in.

AMANDA. Why did you leave her?

LOVELESS. Because she grew stale, and I could not whore in quiet for her. Besides, she was always exclaiming against my extravagancies, particularly my gaming, which she so violently opposed that I fancied a pleasure in it which since I never found, for in one month I lost between eight and ten thousand pounds which I had just before called in to

[1] The bush being out as a sign of a country ale house.

pay my debts. This misfortune made my creditors come so thick upon me that I was forced to mortgage the remaining part of my estate to purchase new pleasure, which I knew I could not do on this side the water amidst the clamors of insatiate duns and the more hateful noise of a complaining wife.

AMANDA. Don't you wish you had taken her counsel, though?

LOVELESS. Not I, faith, madam.

AMANDA. Why so?

LOVELESS. Because it is to no purpose. I am master of more philosophy than to be concerned at what I can't help. But now, madam, pray give me leave to inform myself as far in your condition.

AMANDA. In a word, sir, till you know me thoroughly, I must own myself a perfect riddle to you.

LOVELESS. Nay, nay, I know you are a woman, but in what circumstances, wife or widow?

AMANDA. A wife, sir, a true, a faithful, and a virtuous wife.

LOVELESS. Humph! Truly, madam, your story begins something like a riddle. A virtuous wife, say you? What, and was you never false to your husband?

AMANDA. I never was, by heaven! For him and only him I still love above the world.

LOVELESS. Good again! Pray, madam, don't your memory fail you sometimes? Because I fancy you don't remember what you do overnight.

AMANDA. I told you, sir, I should appear a riddle to you, but if my heart will give me leave, I'll now unloose your fettered apprehension. But I must first amaze you more. Pray, sir, satisfy me in one particular. It is this: What are your undissembled thoughts of virtue? Now, if you can, shake off your loose, unthinking part and summon all your force of manly reason to resolve me.

LOVELESS. Faith, madam, methinks this is a very odd question for a woman of your character. I must confess you have amazed me.

AMANDA. It ought not to amaze you. Why should you think I made a mock of virtue? But last night you allowed my understanding greater than is usual in our sex; if so, can you believe I have no farther sense of happiness than what this empty, dark, and barren world can yield me? No, I have yet a prospect of a sublimer bliss, an hope that carries me to the bright regions of eternal day.

LOVELESS. (*Aside*) Humph! I thought her last night's humor was too good to hold. I suppose by and by she will ask me to go to church with her.—Faith, madam, in my mind this discourse is a little out of the way. You told me I should be acquainted with your condition, and at present that's what I had rather be informed of.

AMANDA. Sir, you shall. But first this question must be answered: Your thoughts of virtue, sir? By all my hopes of bliss hereafter, your answering this pronounces half my good or evil fate forever. But on my knees I beg you, do not speak till you have weighed it well. Answer me with the same truth and sincerity as you would answer heaven at your latest hour.

LOVELESS. Your words confound me, madam. Some wondrous secret surely lies ripened in your breast and seems to struggle for its fatal birth. What is it I must answer you?

AMANDA. Give me your real thoughts of virtue, sir. Can you believe there ever was a woman truly mistress of it, or is it only notion?

LOVELESS. Let me consider, madam. (*Aside*) What can this mean? Why is she so earnest in her demands and begs me to be serious as if her life depended on my answer. I will resolve her, as I ought, as truth and reason and the strange occasion seem to press me.—[*To her*] Most of your sex confound the very name of virtue, for they would seem to live without desires, which could they do, that were not virtue but the defect of unperforming nature, and no praise to them. For who can boast a victory when they have no foe to conquer? Now she alone gives the fairest proofs of virtue whose conscience and whole force of reason can curb her warm desires when opportunity would raise them. That such a woman may be found, I dare believe.

AMANDA. May I believe that from your soul you speak this undissembled truth?

LOVELESS. Madam, you may. But still you rack me with amazement. Why am I asked so strange a question?

AMANDA. I'll give you ease immediately. Since, then, you have allowed a woman may be virtuous, how will you excuse the man who leaves the bosom of a wife so qualified, for the abandoned pleasures of deceitful prostitutes? Ruins her fortune! Condemns her counsel! Loathes her bed and leaves her to the lingering miseries of despair and love, while in return for all these wrongs, she, his poor, forsaken wife, meditates no revenge but what her piercing tears and secret vows to heaven for his conversion yield her—yet still loves on, is constant and unshaken to the last! Can you believe that such a man can live without the stings of conscience and yet be master of his senses? Conscience! Did you never feel the checks of it? Did it never, never tell you of your broken vows?

LOVELESS. That you should ask me this confounds my reason. And yet your words are uttered with such a powerful accent they have awaked my soul and strike my thoughts with horror and remorse.

(*Stands in a fixed posture*)

AMANDA. Then let me strike you nearer, deeper yet—but arm your mind with gentle pity first, or I am lost forever.

LOVELESS. I am all pity, all faith, expectation, and confused amazement. Be kind, be quick, and ease my wonder.

AMANDA. Look on me well. Revive your dead remembrance, and, oh, for pity's sake (*Kneels*) hate me not for loving long, faithfully forgive this innocent attempt of a despairing passion, and I shall die in quiet.

LOVELESS. Ha! Speak on! (*Amazed*)

AMANDA. I would not be! The word's too weighty for my faltering tongue, and my soul sinks beneath the fatal burden. Oh!

(*Falls on the ground*)

LOVELESS. Ha! She faints! Look, fair creature! Behold a heart that bleeds for your distress and fain would share the weight of your oppressing sorrows! Oh, thou hast raised a thought within me that shocks my soul.

AMANDA. It is done. (*Rising*) The conflict's past, and heaven bids me speak undaunted. Know, then, even all the boasted raptures of your last night's love you found in your Amanda's arms. I am your wife.

LOVELESS. Hah!

AMANDA. Forever blessed or miserable, as your next breath shall sentence me.

LOVELESS. My wife! Impossible! Is she not dead? How shall I believe thee?

AMANDA. How time and my afflictions may have altered me, I know not. But here's an indelible confirmation. (*Bares her arm*) These speaking characters, which in their cheerful bloom our early passions mutually recorded.

LOVELESS. Ha! It is here. It is no illusion, but my real name, which seems to upbraid me as a witness of my perjured love. Oh, I am confounded with my guilt and tremble to behold thee. Pray give me leave to think.

(*Turns from her*)

AMANDA. I will. (*Kneels*) But you must look upon me. For only eyes can hear the language of the eyes, and mine have surely the tenderest tale of love to tell that ever misery at the dawn of rising hope could utter.

LOVELESS. I have wronged you. Oh, rise! Basely wronged you! and can I see your face?

AMANDA. One kind, one pitying look cancels those wrongs forever, and, oh, forgive my fond, presuming passion, for from my soul I pardon and forgive you all—all, all but this, the greatest, your unkind delay of love.

LOVELESS. Oh, seal my pardon with thy trembling lips, while with this tender grasp of fond reviving love I seize my bliss and stifle all thy wrongs forever. (*He embraces her*)

AMANDA. No more. I'll wash away their memory in tears of flowing joy.

LOVELESS. Oh, thou hast roused me from my deep lethargy of vice! For hitherto my soul has been enslaved to loose desires, to vain, deluding follies, and shadows of substantial bliss, but now I wake with joy to find my rapture real. Thus let me kneel and pay my thanks to her whose conquering virtue has at last subdued me. Here will I fix, thus prostrate sigh my shame, and wash my crimes in never-ceasing tears of penitence.

AMANDA. Oh, rise! This posture heaps new guilt on me. Now you over-pay me.

LOVELESS. Have I not used thee like a villain? For almost ten long years deprived thee of my love and ruined all thy fortune? But I will labor, dig, beg, or starve to give new proofs of my unfeigned affection.

AMANDA. Forbear this tenderness, lest I repent of having moved your soul so far—you shall not need to beg. Heaven has provided for us beyond its common care. It is now nearly two years since my uncle, Sir William Wealthy, sent you the news of my pretended death. Knowing the extravagance of your temper, he thought it fit you should believe no other of me, and about a month after he had sent you that advice, poor man, he died and left me in the full possession of two thousand pounds a year, which I now cannot offer as a gift because my duty and your lawful right makes you the undisputed master of it.

LOVELESS. How have I labored for my own undoing, while in despite of all my follies, kind heaven resolved my happiness.

Enter Servant *to* AMANDA

SERVANT. Madam, Sir William Wisewoud has sent your ladyship the writings you desired him and says he'll wait upon you immediately.

AMANDA. Now, sir, if you please to withdraw a while, you may inform yourself how fair a fortune you are master of.

LOVELESS. None, none that can outweigh a virtuous mind. While in my arms I thus can circle thee, I grasp more treasure than in a day the posting sun can travel over. Oh, why have I so long been blind to the perfections of thy mind and person? Not knowing thee a wife, I found thee charming beyond the wishes of luxurious love. Is it then a name, a word, shall rob thee of thy worth? Can fancy be a surer guide to happiness than reason? Oh, I have wandered like a benighted wretch and lost myself in life's unpleasing journey. 'Twas heedless fancy first that made me stray, But reason now breaks forth and lights me on my way. *Exeunt*

[SCENE III]

The SCENE *changes to an entry*

Enter three or four Servants

FIRST SERVANT. Prithee, Tom, make haste below there. My lady has ordered dinner at half an hour after one precisely. Look out some of the red[1] that came in last.

(*Two of the* Servants *haul* SNAP *and* AMANDA'S WOMAN *out of the cellar*)

SECOND SERVANT. Come, sir, come out here and show your face.

WOMAN. Oh, I am undone—ruined!

SECOND SERVANT. Pray, sir, who are you, and what was your business, and how in the devil's name came you in here?

SNAP. Why, truly, sir, the flesh led me to the cellar door, but I believe the devil pushed me in. That gentlewoman can inform you better.

[1] Wine.

THIRD SERVANT. Pray, Mrs. Anne, how came you two together in the cellar?

WOMAN. Why, he—he—pu—pu—pulled me in. (*Sobbing*)

THIRD SERVANT. But how the devil came he in?

WOMAN. He fe—fe—fe—fell in.

SECOND SERVANT. How came he into the house?

WOMAN. I do—do—don't know.

SECOND SERVANT. Ah, you are a crocodile. I thought that was the reason I could never get a good word from you. What, in a cellar, too! But come, sir, we will take care of you, however. Bring him along. We will first carry him before my lady and then toss him in a blanket.

SNAP. Nay, but gentlemen, dear gentlemen!
Exeunt

[SCENE III]

[*The* SCENE *changes to* AMANDA'S *house*][2]

Enter LOVELESS, AMANDA, ELDER WORTHY, YOUNG WORTHY, NARCISSA, *and* HILLARIA

ELDER WORTHY. This is indeed a joyful day; we must all congratulate your happiness.

AMANDA. Which while our lives permit us to enjoy, we must still reflect with gratitude on the generous author of it. Sir, we owe you more than words can pay you.

LOVELESS. Words are indeed too weak; therefore let my gratitude be dumb till it can speak in actions.

YOUNG WORTHY. The success of the design I thought on sufficiently rewards me.

HILLARIA. When I reflect upon Amanda's past afflictions, I could almost weep to think of [her][3] unexpected change of fortune.

ELDER WORTHY. Methinks her fair example should persuade all constant wives never to repine at unrewarded virtue. Nay, even my brother being the first promoter of it has atoned for all the looseness of his character.

LOVELESS. I never can return his kindness.

NARCISSA. In a short time, sir, I suppose you'll meet with an opportunity, if you can find a receipt to preserve love after his honeymoon's over.

LOVELESS. The receipt is easily found,

[2] Early editions provide no direction to show that the scene has changed from the entry from which the servants have just departed.

[3] The first edition has *his*, an error later corrected.

madam. Love's a tender plant which can't live out of a warm bed. You must take care with undissembled kindness to keep him from the northern blast of jealousy.

NARCISSA. But I have heard your experienced lovers make use of coldness, and that's more agreeable to my inclination.

LOVELESS. Coldness, madam, before marriage, like throwing a little water upon a clear fire, makes it burn the fiercer, but after marriage you must still take care to lay on fresh fuel.

NARCISSA. Oh fie, sir! How many examples have we of men's hating their wives for being too fond of 'em?

LOVELESS. No wonder, madam. You may stifle a flame by heaping on too great a load.

NARCISSA. Nay, sir, if there be no other way of destroying his passion, for me he may love till doomsday.

ELDER WORTHY. Humph! Don't you smell powder, gentlemen? Sir Novelty is not far off.

LOVELESS. What, not our fellow collegian, I hope, that was expelled the university for beating the proctor?

ELDER WORTHY. The same.

LOVELESS. Does that weed grow still?

ELDER WORTHY. Ay, faith, and as rank as ever, as you shall see, for here he comes.

Enter SIR NOVELTY FASHION

SIR NOVELTY FASHION. Ladies, your humble servant. Dear Loveless, let me embrace thee. I am overjoyed at thy good fortune, stop my vitals. The whole town rings of it already. My Lady Tattletongue has tired a pair of horses in spreading the news about. Hearing, gentlemen, that you were all met upon an extraordinary good occasion, I could not resist this opportunity of joining my joy with yours, for you must know I am.—

NARCISSA. Married, sir?

SIR NOVELTY FASHION. To my liberty, madam. I am just parted from my mistress.

NARCISSA. And pray, sir, how do you find yourself after it?

SIR NOVELTY FASHION. The happiest man alive, madam. Pleasant, easy, gay, light, and free as air! Hah! (*Capers*) I beg your ladyship's pardon, madam, but, upon my soul, I cannot confine my rapture.

NARCISSA. Are you so indifferent, sir?

SIR NOVELTY FASHION. Oh, madam, she's engaged already to a Temple Beau! I saw them in a coach together so fond! And bore it with as unmoved a countenance as Tom Worthy does a thundering jest in a comedy, when the whole house roars at it.

YOUNG WORTHY. Pray, sir, what occasioned your separation?

SIR NOVELTY FASHION. Why, this, sir: You must know she, being still possessed with a brace of implacable devils called revenge and jealousy, dogged me this morning to the chocolate house, where I was obliged to leave a letter for a young, foolish girl that—You will excuse me, sir,—which I had no sooner delivered to the maid of the house, but, whip! she snatches it out of her hand, flew at her like a dragon, tore off her head clothes, flung down three or four sets of lemonade glasses, dashed my Lord Whiffle's chocolate in his face, cut him over the nose, and had like to have strangled me in my own steenkirk.

LOVELESS. Pray, sir, how did this end?

SIR NOVELTY FASHION. Comically, stop my vitals, for in the cloud of powder that she had battered out of the beaux' periwigs I stole away, after which I sent a friend to her with an offer which she readily accepted (three hundred pounds a year during life) provided she would renounce all claims to me and resign my person to my own disposal.

ELDER WORTHY. Methinks, Sir Novelty, you were a little too extravagant in your settlement, considering how the price of women is fallen.

SIR NOVELTY FASHION. Therefore I did it to be the first man should raise their price, for, the devil take me, but the women of the town now come down so low that my very footman, while he kept my place t'other day at the playhouse, carried a mask out of the side-box with him and, stop my vitals, the rogue is now taking physic for it.

Enter the Servant *with* SNAP

FIRST SERVANT. Come, bring him along there.

LOVELESS. How now? Ha! Snap in hold. Pray, let's know the business. Release him, gentlemen.

FIRST SERVANT. Why, an it please you, sir, this fellow was taken in the cellar with my lady's woman. She says he kept her in by force and was rude to her. She stands crying here without and begs her ladyship to do her justice.

AMANDA. Mr. Loveless, we are both the occasion of this misfortune, and for the poor girl's reputation-sake, something should be done.

LOVELESS. Snap, answer me directly, have you lain with this poor girl?

SNAP. Why, truly, sir, imagining you were doing little less with my lady, I must confess, I did commit familiarity with her, or so, sir.

LOVELESS. Then you shall marry her, sir! No reply unless it be your promise.

SNAP. Marry her! Oh, Lord, sir, after I have lain with her? Why, sir, how the devil can you think a man can have any stomach to his dinner after he has had three or four slices off of the spit?

LOVELESS. Well, sirrah, to renew your appetite, and because thou hast been my old acquaintance, I'll give thee an hundred pounds with her and thirty pounds a year during life to set you up in some honest employment.

SNAP. Ah, sir, now I understand you. Heaven reward you! Well, sir, I partly find that the genteel scenes of our lives are pretty well over, and I thank heaven that I have so much grace left that I can repent when I have no more opportunities of being wicked. Come, spouse! (*She enters*) Here's my hand; the rest of my body shall be forthcoming. Ah, little did my master and I think last night that we were robbing our own orchards.

Exeunt [*the* Servants]

ELDER WORTHY. Brother, stand upon your guard. Here comes Sir William.

Enter SIR WILLIAM WISEWOUD

SIR WILLIAM WISEWOUD. Joy, joy to you all! Madam, I congratulate your good fortune. Well, my dear rogue, must not I give thee joy, too? Ha!

YOUNG WORTHY. If you please, sir, but, I confess, I have more than I deserve already.

SIR WILLIAM WISEWOUD. And art thou married?

YOUNG WORTHY. Yes, sir, I am married.

SIR WILLIAM WISEWOUD. Odso, I am glad on it. [*Aside to* YOUNG WORTHY.] I dare swear thou dost not grudge me the five thousand pounds.

YOUNG WORTHY. Not I, really, sir. You have given me all my soul could wish for but the addition of a father's blessing.

(*Kneels with* NARCISSA)

SIR WILLIAM WISEWOUD. Humh! What dost thou mean? I am none of thy father.

YOUNG WORTHY. This lady is your daughter, sir, I hope.

SIR WILLIAM WISEWOUD. Prithee, get up! Prithee, get up! Thou art stark mad! True, I believe she may be my daughter. Well, and so, sir?

YOUNG WORTHY. If she be not, I'm certain she's my wife, sir.

SIR WILLIAM WISEWOUD. Humh! Mr. Worthy, pray, sir, do me the favor to help me understand your brother a little. Do you know anything of his being married?

ELDER WORTHY. Then without any abuse, Sir William, he married your daughter this very morning, not an hour ago, sir.

SIR WILLIAM WISEWOUD. Pray, sir, whose consent had you? Who advised you to it?

YOUNG WORTHY. Our mutual love and your consent, sir, which these writings, entitling her to a thousand pounds a year, and this bond, whereby you have obliged yourself to pay me five thousand pounds upon our day of marriage, are sufficient proofs of.

SIR WILLIAM WISEWOUD. He, he! I gave your brother such a bond, sir.

YOUNG WORTHY. You did so, but the obligation is to me. Look there, sir.

SIR WILLIAM WISEWOUD. Very good! This is my hand, I must confess, sir, and what then?

YOUNG WORTHY. Why, then, I expect my five thousand pounds, sir. Pray, sir, do you know my name?

SIR WILLIAM WISEWOUD. I am not drunk, sir. I am sure it was Worthy, and Jack, or Tom, or Dick, or something.

YOUNG WORTHY. No, sir, I'll show you. It is William. Look you there, sir. You should have taken more care of the lawyer, sir, that filled up the blank.

ELDER WORTHY. So now his eyes are open.

SIR WILLIAM WISEWOUD. And have you married my daughter against my consent and tricked me out of five thousand pounds, sir?

HILLARIA. His brother, sir, has married me, too, with my consent, and I am not tricked out of five thousand pounds.

SIR WILLIAM WISEWOUD. Insulting witch!

Look you, sir, I never had a substantial cause to be angry in my life before, but now I have reason on my side, I will indulge my indignation most immoderately. I must confess, I have not patience to wait the slow redress of a tedious law-suit, therefore am resolved to right myself the nearest way. Draw, draw, sir, you must not enjoy my five thousand pounds, though I fling as much more after it in procuring a pardon for killing you. (*They hold him*) Let me come at him; I'll murder him! I'll cut him! I'll tear him! I'll broil him and eat him! A rogue! A dog! A cursed dog! A cut-throat, murdering dog!

ELDER WORTHY. Oh, fie, Sir William, how monstrous is this passion!

SIR WILLIAM WISEWOUD. You have disarmed me, but I shall find a time to poison him.

LOVELESS. Think better on it, Sir William. Your daughter has married a gentleman, and one whose love entitles him to her person.

SIR WILLIAM WISEWOUD. Ay, but the five thousand pounds, sir! Why, the very report of his having such a fortune will ruin him; I warrant you within this week he will have more duns at his chamber in a morning than a gaming lord after a good night at the groom porters [1] or a poet upon the fourth day [2] of his new play. I shall never be pleased with paying it against my own consent, sir.

HILLARIA. Yet you would have had me done it, Sir William. But, however, I heartily wish you would as freely forgive Mr. Worthy as I do you, sir.

SIR WILLIAM WISEWOUD. I must confess this girl's good nature makes me ashamed of what I have offered. But, Mr. Worthy, I did not expect such usage from a man of your character. I always took you for a gentleman.

ELDER WORTHY. You shall find me no other, sir. Brother, a word with you.

LOVELESS. Sir William, I have some obligations to this gentleman and have so great a confidence in your daughter's merit and his love that I here promise to return you your five thousand pounds if, after the expiration of one year, you are then dissatisfied in his being your son-in-law.

YOUNG WORTHY. But see, brother, he has forstalled your purpose.

ELDER WORTHY. Mr. Loveless, you have been beforehand with me, but you must give me leave to offer Sir William my joint security for what you have promised him.

LOVELESS. With all my heart, sir. Dare you take our bonds, Sir William?

YOUNG WORTHY. Hold gentlemen! I should blush to be obliged to that degree; therefore, Sir William, as the first proof of that respect and duty I owe a father, I here unasked return your bond and will henceforth expect nothing from you but as my conduct shall deserve it.

AMANDA. This is indeed a generous act; methinks it were pity it should go unrewarded.

SIR WILLIAM WISEWOUD. Nay, now you vanquish me. After this I can't suspect your future conduct. There, sir. It is yours; I acknowledge the bond and wish you all the happiness of a bridal bed. Heaven's blessings on you both. Now rise, my boy, and let the world know it was I set you upon your legs again.

YOUNG WORTHY. I'll study to deserve your bounty, sir.

LOVELESS. Now, Sir William, you have shown yourself a father. This prudent action has secured your daughter from the usual consequence of a stolen marriage, a parent's curse. Now she must be happy in her love while you have such a tender care on it.

AMANDA. This is indeed a happy meeting; we all of us have drawn our several prizes in the lottery of human life. Therefore I beg our joys may be united. Not one of us must part this day. The ladies I'll entreat my guests.

LOVELESS. The rest are mine and, I hope, will often be so.

AMANDA. It is yet too soon to dine; therefore, to divert us in the meantime, what think you of a little music, the subject perhaps not improper to this occasion?

ELDER WORTHY. It will oblige us, madam; we are all lovers of it.

The scene draws and discovers LOVE *seated on a throne, attended with a* CHORUS

FAME. Hail! Hail! Victorious Love,
To whom all hearts below
With no less pleasure bow
Than to the thundering Jove
The happy souls above.

---

[1] The groom porter was an officer of the Royal Household who regulated gaming within the precincts of the court. His function seems to have been chiefly to operate the court gambling rooms. The office was abolished under George III.

[2] The author received the profits of the third night's performance of a play.

CHORUS. Hail, *etc.*

Enter REASON

REASON. Cease, cease, fond fools, your empty noise
  And follow not such joys;
  Love gives you but a short-lived bliss,
  But I bestow immortal happiness.
LOVE. Rebellious Reason, talk no more;
  Of all my slaves, I thee abhor;
  But thou, alas, dost strive in vain
  To free the lover from a pleasing chain;
  In spite of Reason, Love shall live and reign.

CHORUS. In spite, *etc.*

(*A martial symphony*)

Enter HONOR

HONOR. What wretch would follow Love's alarms
  When Honor's trumpet sounds to arms?
  Hark, how the warlike notes inspire
  In every breast a glowing fire.
LOVE. Hark, how it swells with love and soft desire.
HONOR. Behold, behold the married state
  By thee too soon betrayed,
  Repenting now too late.

Enter MARRIAGE, *with his yoke*

MARRIAGE. Oh, tell me, cruel God of Love,
  Why didst thou my thoughts possess
  With an eternal round of happiness,
  And yet, alas! I lead a wretched life,
Doomed to this galling yoke—the emblem of a wife.
LOVE. Ungrateful wretch, how darest thou Love upbraid?
  I gave thee raptures in the bridal bed.
MARRIAGE. Long since, alas! the airy vision's fled,
And I with wandering flames my passion feed.
  Oh, tell me, powerful god,
  Where I shall find
  My former peace of mind!
LOVE. Where first I promised thee a happy life,
  There thou shalt find it in a virtuous wife.
LOVE and FAME. Go home, unhappy wretch, and mourn
  For all thy guilty passion past;
  There thou shalt those joys return
  Which shall for ever, ever last.

(*End with the first chorus*)

LOVELESS. It was generously designed, and all my life to come shall show how I approve the moral. Oh, Amanda, once more receive me to thy arms, and while I am there let all the world confess my happiness. By my example taught let every man whose fate has bound him to a married life beware of letting loose his wild desires, for if experience may be allowed to judge, I must proclaim the folly of a wandering passion. The greatest happiness we can hope on earth,

And sure the nearest to the joys above,
Is the chaste rapture of a virtuous love.

EPILOGUE

Spoken by MISS CROSS, *who sang* CUPID [1]

Now, gallants, for the author: first, to you,
Kind city gentlemen, of the middle row,
He hopes you nothing to his charge can lay;
There's not one cuckold made in all this play;
Nay, you must own, if you'll believe your eyes,   5
He draws his pen against your enemies,
For, he declares today, he merely strives
To maul the beaux—because they maul your wives.
  Now, sirs, to you, whose sole religion's drinking,
Whoring, roaring, without the pain of thinking,   10
He fears he's made a fault you'll ne'er forgive,
A crime beyond the hopes of a reprieve.
An honest rake forego the joys of life,
His whores and wine, to embrace a dull-cast [2] wife!
Such out-of-fashion stuff! But then, again, 15
He's lewd for above four acts, gentlemen!
For, faith, he knew, when once he'd changed his fortune
And reformed his vice, 'twas time to drop the curtain.
Four acts for your coarse palates was designed,
But then the ladies' taste is more refined; 20
They, for Amanda's sake, will sure be kind.
Pray, let this figure once your pity move,
Can you resist the pleading God of Love?
In vain my prayers the other sex pursue
Unless your conquering smiles their stubborn hearts subdue.   25

---

[1] That is, Love in the preceding masque.
[2] Later editions have, "dull, chaste," which makes more sense to modern ears, the original expression being obsolete.

THE RELAPSE;

OR,

VIRTUE IN DANGER

Being the sequel of THE FOOL IN FASHION

A COMEDY BY SIR JOHN VANBRUGH

Architect of Blenheim, author of successful comedies, builder and manager of the theatre in the Haymarket, Clarenceux King-of-Arms, Comptroller of Her Majesty's Works, Sir John Vanbrugh was a man of many affairs. In all he was highly regarded; and his contemporaries, differing as they did on the question of his merits in these many fields, all allowed him to be just and honest, a delightful companion and a charming gentleman. Of a family of Flemish extraction whose founder, Sir John's grandfather, had fled to England from religious persecutions probably early in the seventeenth century, allied through his mother with various well born families of England, John Vanbrugh (the name is spelled in several ways) was born in London in 1664 and baptised on January 24th. He was educated at Chester, where his father, Giles Vanbrugh, lived for some years. Later he held commissions in various regiments, attaining the rank of captain. For about two years (1690-92) he was detained in French prisons for reasons which are somewhat obscure, and during his imprisonment in the Bastille he wrote parts of a comedy. Returning to London after his release, he wrote *The Relapse*, in 1696, followed by *Æsop* (Part I, D.L., Dec., 1696; Part II, D.L., March, 1697) and *The Provok'd Wife* (Betterton's company, L.I.F., May, 1697). (Most of his later plays were translations or adaptations from French sources.)

Thus launched upon a career as a playwright, he began the practice of the profession of architecture, in which his best known works are Blenheim, the palace of the Duke of Marlborough at Woodstock, and the Queen's Theatre in the Haymarket, which he managed in partnership with Congreve, 1705-8, and which became the first home of Italian opera in England. Meanwhile Vanbrugh had entered upon his third profession, that of heraldry, becoming Carlisle Herald in 1703 and Clarenceux King-of-Arms the next year. He was already Comptroller of the Board of Works (1702).

The rest of his life was busy, as his many occupations involved him in controversy, litigation, and political agitation, though he was essentially a peaceful, quiet-natured man. He was knighted by George I in 1714. Late in life (1719) he married Henrietta Yarborough. He died March 26, 1726, leaving two sons and a reputation as the greatest writer of comedies of his generation, excepting Mr. Congreve, and the best architect after Sir Christopher Wren.

Biographical information may be found in the D. N. B., in introductions to collections of Vanbrugh's works by W. C. Ward (1893), A. E. H. Swain (in the Mermaid Series), Bonamy Dobrée (1927), in Mr. Dobrée's *Essays in Biography* (1925), and in works there cited.

VANBRUGH'S PLAYS

The Relapse; or, Virtue in Danger. (D.L., Dec., 1696), 1697.

Æsop, Part I (D.L., Dec. (?) 1696), 1697; Part II (D.L., March, 1697), 1702.

The Provok'd Wife (L.I.F., April, 1697), 1709.

The Pilgrim (D.L., *c.* April 29, 1700), 1700.

The False Friend (D.L., Jan., 1701), 1702.

The Country House (D.L., Jan., 1703), 1715.

The Confederacy (Hay., Oct. 30, 1705), 1705.

The Mistake (Hay., Dec. 27, 1706), 1706.

The Cuckold in Conceit (Hay., March 22, 1707) [not published?].

A Journey to London, published (unfinished) 1728. (Completed by Cibber as The Provok'd Husband, D.L., Jan. 10, 1728.)

Captain Vanbrugh, newly commissioned in Lord Berkeley's Marine Regiment of Foot, attended a performance of Mr. Cibber's new comedy, *Love's Last Shift*, at Drury Lane early in the year 1696. He was seemingly amused by the false presentation of human nature contained in the piece. Loveless, the libertine, was to him not the man to be reformed so easily or so permanently as Mr. Cibber's play implied; and London life as it was known to the captain differed from that presented by this new writer of comedy. He wrote a sequel, common report said in six weeks, and presented it to the patentees, to one of whom he was under obligations, in April following. The season was too near its close for the production of a new play; so the first performance was deferred until the next season.

In December *The Relapse* was acted with Mr. Cibber in the rôle of Lord Foppington, his own Sir Novelty Fashion raised to the peerage and reincarnated as the fop by deliberate choice. Loveless and Amanda also appeared again, but the other characters are new. The piece followed the traditions of high comedy rather than the newer tone of its inspirer. Though Amanda preserves her honor, her virtue is sorely tried; and none of the other characters makes any more pretense to that quality than had the fine ladies and gentlemen of Sir George Etherege. Mr. Sheridan attempted to adapt *The Relapse* to the newer mode in his *A Trip to Scarborough* (D.L., Feb. 1777), which had some popularity and is still performed.

The Reverend Jeremy Collier honored *The Relapse* by selecting it as one of his main points of attack in his *A Short View of the Immorality and Profaneness of the English Stage* (1698). Vanbrugh, like his fellow sufferer Congreve, replied to the reformer with *A Short Vindication of* The Relapse *and* The Provok'd Wife *from Immorality and Profaneness* (June, 1698), in which he cleverly and urbanely, but none too effectively, defended his plays and his profession, accusing in his turn the reverend doctor of inability to understand the nature of comedy, and as well, of immorality in his misinterpretation of the Worthy plot. Collier scorns the sudden change in Worthy's attitude toward Amanda, and Vanbrugh replies:

"The world may see by this what a contempt the doctor has for a spark that can make no better use of his mistress than to admire her for her virtue. This methinks is something so very extraordinary in a clergyman that I almost fancy when he and I are fast asleep in our graves, those who shall read what we both have produc'd will be apt to conclude there's a mistake in the tradition about the authors, and that 'twas the reforming divine writ the play and the scandalous poet the remarks upon 't."

But the laurels probably remain with Doctor Collier.

THE PREFACE

To go about to excuse half the defects this abortive brat is come into the world with, would be to provoke the town with a long useless preface, when 'tis, I doubt, sufficiently soured already by a tedious play.

I do therefore (with all the humility of a repenting sinner) confess, it wants everything —but length; and in that, I hope, the severest critic will be pleased to acknowledge I have not been wanting. But my modesty will sure atone for everything, when the world shall know it is so great, I am even to this day insensible of those two shining graces in the play (which some part of the town is pleased to compliment me with)—blasphemy and bawd[r]y.[1]

For my part, I cannot find 'em out. If there were any obscene expressions upon the stage, here they are in the print; for I have dealt fairly, I have not sunk a syllable that could (though by racking of mysteries) be ranged under that head; and yet I believe with a steady faith, there is not one woman of a real reputation in town, but when she has read it impartially over in her closet, will find it so innocent, she'll think it no affront to her prayer book, to lay it upon the same shelf. So to them (with all manner of deference) I entirely refer my cause; and I'm confident they'll justify me against those pretenders to good manners, who, at the same time, have so little respect for the ladies, they would extract a bawdy jest from an ejaculation, to put 'em out of countenance. But I expect to have these well-bred persons always my

[1] This is an allusion to the pre-Collier attacks upon the stage, the chief of which were launched by Sir Richard Blackmore and James Wright.

enemies, since I'm sure I shall never write anything lewd enough to make 'em my friends.

As for the saints (your thorough-paced ones, I mean, with screwed faces and wry mouths) I despair of them, for they are friends to nobody. They love nothing but their altars and themselves. They have too much zeal to have any charity: they make debauches in piety, as sinners do in wine; and are as quarrelsome in their religion, as other people are in their drink; so I hope nobody will mind what they say. But if any man (with flat plod shoes, a little band, greasy hair, and a dirty face, who is wiser than I, at the expense of being forty years older) happens to be offended at a story of a cock and a bull, and a priest and a bulldog, I beg his pardon with all my heart, which, I hope, I shall obtain, by eating my words, and making this public recantation. I do therefore, for his satisfaction, acknowledge I lied, when I said, they never quit their hold; for in that little time I have lived in the world, I thank God I have seen 'em forced to it more than once; but next time I'll speak with more caution and truth, and only say, they have very good teeth.

If I have offended any honest gentlemen of the town, whose friendship or good word is worth the having, I am very sorry for it; I hope they'll correct me as gently as they can, when they consider I have had no other design, in running a very great risk, than to divert (if possible) some part of their spleen, in spite of their wives and their taxes.

One word more about the bawd[r]y, and I have done. I own the first night this thing was acted, some indecencies had like to have happened, but 'twas not my fault.

The fine gentleman of the play,[1] drinking his mistress's health in Nantes brandy, from six in the morning to the time he waddled on upon the stage in the evening, had toasted himself up to such a pitch of vigour, I confess I once gave Amanda for gone, and I am since (with all due respect to Mrs. Rogers) very sorry she scaped; for I am confident a certain lady (let no one take it to herself that's handsome) who highly blames the play, for the barrenness of the conclusion, would then have allowed it a very natural close.

[1] That is, Powell, who played Worthy, a man noted for his intemperance which frequently interfered with his acting.

THE RELAPSE;

OR,

VIRTUE IN DANGER

DRAMATIS PERSONÆ

MEN

SIR NOVELTY FASHION, *newly created Lord Foppington*	Mr. Cibber
YOUNG FASHION, *his Brother*	Mrs. Kent
LOVELESS, *Husband to Amanda*	Mr. Verbruggen
WORTHY, *a Gentleman of the Town*	Mr. Powell
SIR TUNBELLY CLUMSEY, *a Country Gentleman*	Mr. Bullock
SIR JOHN FRIENDLY, *his Neighbour*	Mr. Mills
COUPLER, *a Match-maker*	Mr. Johnson
BULL, *Chaplain to Sir Tunbelly*	Mr. Simson
SYRINGE, *a Surgeon*	Mr. Haynes
LORY, *Servant to Young Fashion*	Mr. Dogget
Shoemaker, Tailor, Periwig-maker, &c.	

WOMEN

AMANDA, *Wife to Loveless*	Mrs. Rogers
BERINTHIA, *her Cousin, a young Widow*	Mrs. Verbruggen
MISS HOYDEN, *a great Fortune, Daughter to Sir Tunbelly*	Mrs. Cross
NURSE, *her Gouvernante*	Mrs. Powell

FIRST PROLOGUE

Spoken by MISS CROSS

Ladies, this play in too much haste was writ,
To be o'ercharged with either plot or wit;
'Twas got, conceived, and born in six weeks' space,[1]
And wit, you know, 's as slow in growth—as grace. 4
Sure it can ne'er be ripened to your taste;
I doubt 'twill prove, our author bred too fast:
For mark 'em well, who with the Muses marry,
They rarely do conceive, but they miscarry.
'Tis the hard fate of those who are big with rhyme, 9
Still to be brought to bed before their time.
Of our late poets Nature few has made;
The greatest part—are only so by trade.
Still want of something brings the scribbling fit; 13
For want of money some of 'em have writ,
And others do't, you see—for want of wit.

Honor, they fancy, summons 'em to write,
So out they lug in wresty Nature's spite,
As some of you spruce beaux do—when you fight.
Yet let the ebb of wit be ne'er so low,
Some glimpse of it a man may hope to show,
Upon a theme so ample—as a beau. 21
So, howsoc'er true courage may decay,
Perhaps there's not one smock-face here to-day,
But's bold as Cæsar—to attack a play,
Nay, what's yet more, with an undaunted face, 25
To do the thing with more heroic grace,
'Tis six to four y'attack the strongest place.
You are such Hotspurs in this kind of venture,
Where there's no breach, just there you needs must enter:
But be advised— 30
E'en give the hero and the critic o'er,
For Nature sent you on another score;—
She formed her beau, for nothing but her whore.

[1] *Love's Last Shift* appeared in January, and the script of *The Relapse* is said to have been in the hands of the managers of the theater by the following April.

PROLOGUE ON THE THIRD DAY

Spoken by Mrs. Verbruggen

Apologies for plays, experience shows,
Are things almost as useless—as the beaux.
Whate'er we say (like them) we neither move
Your friendship, pity, anger, nor your love.
'Tis interest turns the globe: let us but find
The way to please you, and you'll soon be
    kind: 6
But to expect, you'd for our sakes approve,
Is just as though you for their sakes should
    love;
And that, we do confess, we think a task,
Which (though they may impose) we never
    ought to ask. 10
    This is an age, where all things we improve,
But, most of all, the art of making love.
In former days, women were only won
By merit, truth, and constant service done;
But lovers now are much more expert
    grown; 15
They seldom wait, t' approach by tedious
    form;
They're for dispatch, for taking you by storm:
Quick are their sieges, furious are their fires,
Fierce their attacks, and boundless their
    desires.
Before the play's half ended, I'll engage 20
To show you beaux come crowding on the stage,
Who with so little pains have always sped,
They'll undertake to look a lady dead.
How have I shook, and trembling stood with
    awe,
When here, behind the scenes, I've seen 'em
    draw 25
—A comb; that dead-doing weapon to the
    heart,
And turn each powdered hair into a dart!
When I have seen 'em sally on the stage,
Dressed to the war, and ready to engage,
I've mourned your destiny—yet more their
    fate, 30
To think, that after victories so great,
It should so often prove their hard mishap
To sneak into a lane—and get a clap.
But, hush! they're here already; I'll retire,
And leave 'em to you ladies to admire. 35
They'll show you twenty thousand airs and
    graces,
They'll entertain you with their soft grim-
    aces,
Their snuff-box, awkward bows,—and ugly
    faces.
In short, they're after all so much your
    friends,
That lest the play should fail the author's
    ends, 40
They have resolv'd to make you some
    amends.
Between each act (performed by nicest rules)
They'll treat you—with an interlude of fools:
Of which, that you may have the deeper sense,
The entertainment's—at their own expense.

ACT I

Scene [I]—[*A Room in* Loveless's *Country House*] [1]

Enter Loveless *reading*

Loveless. How true is that philosophy,
    which says
Our heaven is seated in our minds!
Through all the roving pleasures of my youth,
(Where nights and days seemed all consumed
    in joy,
Where the false face of luxury 5
Displayed such charms,
As might have shaken the most holy hermit,
And made him totter at his altar.)
I never knew one moment's peace like this.
Here, in this little soft retreat, 10
My thoughts unbent from all the cares of life,
Content with fortune,
Eased from the grating duties of dependence,
From envy free, ambition under foot,
The raging flame of wild destructive lust 15
Reduced to a warm pleasing fire of lawful love,
My life glides on, and all is well within.

Enter Amanda. Loveless *meeting her kindly*
How does the happy cause of my content,
My dear Amanda?
You find me musing on my happy state, 20
And full of grateful thoughts to heaven, and
    you.
    Amanda. Those grateful offerings heaven
    can't receive
With more delight than I do:

---

[1] The first edition lacks most of the scene headings as here given. Vanbrugh's editors, chiefly Leigh Hunt, Ward, Swain, and Dobrée, have differed as to the method of presenting the location of the action. Ward has in general been followed here, the supplied headings appearing in brackets. The same edition has also generally been followed in the printing of the scenes of mixed verse and prose when the first edition was not intelligible as to the division into lines. In cases where Ward and the first edition differ, if the earlier edition is printed so that the intention is clear, it has been followed.

Would I could share with it as well
The dispensations of its bliss,
That I might search its choicest favors out,
And shower 'em on your head for ever!
    LOVELESS. The largest boons that heaven thinks fit to grant,
To things it has decreed shall crawl on earth,
Are in the gift of women formed like you.
Perhaps, when time shall be no more,
When the aspiring soul shall take its flight,
And drop this pond'rous lump of clay behind it,
It may have appetites we know not of,
And pleasures as refined as its desires—
But till that day of knowledge shall instruct me,
The utmost blessing that my thought can reach,   (*Taking her in his arms*)
Is folded in my arms, and rooted in my heart.
    AMANDA. There let it grow for ever!
    LOVELESS. Well said, Amanda—let it be for ever—
Would heaven grant that—
    AMANDA.   'Twere all the heaven I'd ask.
But we are clad in black mortality,
And the dark curtain of eternal night
At last must drop between us.
    LOVELESS.   It must:
That mournful separation we must see.
A bitter pill it is to all; but doubles its ungrateful taste,
When lovers are to swallow it.
    AMANDA. Perhaps that pain may only be my lot,
You possibly may be exempted from it.
Men find out softer ways to quench their fires.
    LOVELESS. Can you then doubt my constancy, Amanda?
You'll find 'tis built upon a steady basis—
The rock of reason now supports my love,
On which it stands so fixed,
The rudest hurricane of wild desire
Would, like the breath of a soft slumbering babe,
Pass by, and never shake it.
    AMANDA. Yet still 'tis safer to avoid the storm;
The strongest vessels, if they put to sea,
May possibly be lost.
Would I could keep you here, in this calm port, for ever!
Forgive the weakness of a woman,
I am uneasy at your going to stay so long in town;
I know its false insinuating pleasures;
I know the force of its delusions;
I know the strength of its attacks;
I know the weak defence of nature;
I know you are a man—and I—a wife.
    LOVELESS. You know then all that needs to give you rest,
For wife's the strongest claim that you can urge.
When you would plead your title to my heart,
On this you may depend. Therefore be calm,
Banish your fears, for they
Are traitors to your peace: beware of 'em,
They are insinuating busy things
That gossip to and fro,
And do a world of mischief where they come.
But you shall soon be mistress of 'em all;
I'll aid you with such arms for their destruction,
They never shall erect their heads again.
You know the business is indispensable, that
obliges me to go for London; and you have
no reason, that I know of, to believe I'm glad
of the occasion. For my honest conscience
is my witness.
I have found a due succession of such charms
In my retirement here with you,
I have never thrown one roving thought that way;
But since, against my will, I'm dragged once more
To that uneasy theater of noise,
I am resolved to make such use on't,
As shall convince you 'tis an old cast mistress,
Who has been so lavish of her favors,
She's now grown bankrupt of her charms,
And has not one allurement left to move me.
    AMANDA. Her bow, I do believe, is grown so weak,
Her arrows (at this distance) cannot hurt you;
But in approaching 'em, you give 'em strength.
The dart that has not far to fly, will put
The best of armor to a dangerous trial.
    LOVELESS. That trial past, and y'are at ease for ever;
When you have seen the helmet proved,
You'll apprehend no more for him that wears it.
Therefore to put a lasting period to your fears,
I am resolved, this once, to launch into temptation:
I'll give you an essay of all my virtues;
My former boon companions of the bottle
Shall fairly try what charms are left in wine:
I'll take my place amongst 'em,
They shall hem me in,
Sing praises to their god, and drink **his glory**:
Turn wild enthusiasts for his sake,

And beasts to do him honor:
Whilst I, a stubborn atheist,
Sullenly look on,
Without one reverend glass to his divinity.
That for my temperance,
Then for my constancy—
　AMANDA.　　　　　Ay, there take heed.
　LOVELESS. Indeed the danger's small.
　AMANDA.　　　And yet my fears are great.
　LOVELESS. Why are you so timorous?
　AMANDA.　　　Because you are so bold.
　LOVELESS. My courage should disperse your apprehensions.
　AMANDA. My apprehensions should alarm your courage.
　LOVELESS. Fie, fie, Amanda! it is not kind thus to distrust me.
　AMANDA. And yet my fears are founded on my love.
　LOVELESS. Your love then is not founded as it ought;
For if you can believe 'tis possible
I should again relapse to my past follies,
I must appear to you a thing
Of such an undigested composition,
That but to think of me with inclination,
Would be a weakness in your taste,
Your virtue scarce could answer.
　AMANDA. 'Twould be a weakness in my tongue,
My prudence could not answer,
If I should press you farther with my fears;
I'll therefore trouble you no longer with 'em.
　LOVELESS. Nor shall they trouble you much longer.
A little time shall show you they were groundless:
This winter shall be the fiery trial of my virtue;
Which, when it once has passed,
You'll be convinced 'twas of no false allay,
There all your cares will end.
　AMANDA.　　　Pray heaven they may.
　　　　　　　　　　Exeunt, hand in hand

SCENE [II]—*Whitehall*

Enter YOUNG FASHION, LORY, *and* WATERMAN
　FASHION. Come, pay the waterman, and take the portmantle.
　LORY. Faith, sir, I think the waterman had as good take the portmantle, and pay himself.
　FASHION. Why, sure there's something left in't!
　LORY. But a solitary old waistcoat, upon honor, sir.
　FASHION. Why, what's become of the blue coat, sirrah?
　LORY. Sir, 'twas eaten at Gravesend; the reckoning came to thirty shillings, and your privy purse was worth but two half-crowns.
　FASHION. 'Tis very well.
　WATERMAN. Pray, master, will you please to dispatch me?
　FASHION. Ay, here, a—canst thou change me a guinea?
　LORY. (*Aside*) Good!
　WATERMAN. Change a guinea, master! Ha! ha! your honor's pleased to compliment.
　FASHION. Egad, I don't know how I shall pay thee then, for I have nothing but gold about me.
　LORY. (*Aside*) Hum, hum!
　FASHION. What dost thou expect, friend?
　WATERMAN. Why, master, so far against wind and tide is richly worth half a piece.
　FASHION. Why, faith, I think thou art a good conscionable fellow. Egad, I begin to have so good an opinion of thy honesty, I care not if I leave my portmantle with thee, till I send thee thy money.
　WATERMAN. Ha! God bless your honour; I should be as willing to trust you, master, but that you are, as a man may say, a stranger to me, and these are nimble times; there are a great many sharpers stirring.—(*Taking up the portmantle*) Well, master, when your worship sends the money, your portmantle shall be forthcoming; my name's Tug; my wife keeps a brandy-shop in Drab-Alley, at Wapping.
　FASHION. Very well; I'll send for't to-morrow.　　　　　　　　　　*Exit* WATERMAN
　LORY. So.—Now, sir, I hope you'll own yourself a happy man, you have outlived all your cares.
　FASHION. How so, sir?
　LORY. Why, you have nothing left to take care of.
　FASHION. Yes, sirrah, I have myself and you to take care of still.
　LORY. Sir, if you could but prevail with somebody else to do that for you, I fancy we might both fare the better for't.
　FASHION. Why, if thou canst tell me where to apply myself, I have at present so little money and so much humility about me, I don't know but I may follow a fool's advice.

LORY. Why then, sir, your fool advises you to lay aside all animosity, and apply to Sir Novelty, your elder brother.

FASHION. Damn my elder brother!

LORY. With all my heart; but get him to redeem your annuity, however.

FASHION. My annuity! 'Sdeath, he's such a dog, he would not give his powder-puff to redeem my soul.

LORY. Look you, sir, you must wheedle him, or you must starve.

FASHION. Look you, sir, I will neither wheedle him, nor starve.

LORY. Why, what will you do then?

FASHION. I'll go into the army.

LORY. You can't take the oaths; you are a Jacobite.[1]

FASHION. Thou may'st as well say I can't take orders because I'm an atheist.

LORY. Sir, I ask your pardon; I find I did not know the strength of your conscience so well as I did the weakness of your purse.

FASHION. Methinks, sir, a person of your experience should have known that the strength of the conscience proceeds from the weakness of the purse.

LORY. Sir, I am very glad to find you have a conscience able to take care of us, let it proceed from what it will; but I desire you'll please to consider, that the army alone will be but a scanty maintenance for a person of your generosity (at least as rents now are paid). I shall see you stand in damnable need of some auxiliary guineas for your *menus plaisirs*;[2] I will therefore turn fool once more for your service, and advise you to go directly to your brother.

FASHION. Art thou then so impregnable a blockhead, to believe he'll help me with a farthing?

LORY. Not if you treat him *de haut en bas*, as you use to do.

FASHION. Why, how wouldst have me treat him?

LORY. Like a trout—tickle him.

FASHION. I can't flatter.

LORY. Can you starve?

FASHION. Yes.

LORY. I can't.—Good-by t'ye, sir—
 (Going)

[1] Supporter of the deposed king, James II, and his son, "the Old Pretender."—Persons who refused to take the oaths of allegiance to the government of William and Mary could not hold civil or military office.

[2] Little pleasures.

FASHION. Stay; thou wilt distract me! What wouldst thou have me say to him?

LORY. Say nothing to him, apply yourself to his favorites, speak to his periwig, his cravat, his feather, his snuff-box, and when you are well with them—desire him to lend you a thousand pounds. I'll engage you'll prosper.

FASHION. 'Sdeath and furies! why was that coxcomb thrust into the world before me? O Fortune! Fortune!—thou art a bitch, by Gad. *Exeunt*

SCENE [III]—*A Dressing-room*

Enter LORD FOPPINGTON *in his nightgown*

LORD FOPPINGTON. Page!

Enter Page

PAGE. Sir!

LORD FOPPINGTON. Sir!—Pray, sir, do me the favor to teach your tongue the title the king has thought fit to honor me with.

PAGE. I ask your lordship's pardon, my lord.

LORD FOPPINGTON. O, you can pronounce the word then? I thought it would have choked you.—D'ye hear?

PAGE. My lord!

LORD FOPPINGTON. Call La Verole: I would dress.—(*Exit* Page. *Solus*)—Well, 'tis an unspeakable pleasure to be a man of quality, strike me dumb!—My lord.—Your lordship! My lord Foppington!—Ah! *c'est quelque chose de beau, que le diable m'emporte!*[3]—Why, the ladies were ready to puke at me whilst I had nothing but Sir Navelty to recommend me to 'em.—Sure, whilst I was but a knight, I was a very nauseous fellow.—Well, 'tis ten thousand pawnd well given, stap my vitals!—

Enter LA VEROLE

LA VEROLE. Me lord, de shoemaker, de tailor, de hosier, de sempstress, de barber, be all ready, if your lordship please to be dress.

LORD FOPPINGTON. 'Tis well, admit 'em.

LA VEROLE. Hey, *messieurs, entrez*.

Enter Tailor, &c.

LORD FOPPINGTON. So, gentlemen, I hope you have all taken pains to show yourselves masters in your professions.

TAILOR. I think I may presume to say, sir—

LA VEROLE. My lord—you clawn, you!

[3] That's something handsome, [or] the devil carry me away.

TAILOR. Why, is he made a lord?—My lord, I ask your lordship's pardon, my lord; I hope, my lord, your lordship will please to own I have brought your lordship as accomplished a suit of clothes as ever peer of England trod the stage in,[1] my lord. Will your lordship please to try 'em now?

LORD FOPPINGTON. Ay; but let my people dispose the glasses so that I may see myself before and behind, for I love to see myself all raund.

Whilst he puts on his clothes, enter YOUNG FASHION *and* LORY

FASHION. Heyday, what the devil have we here? Sure my gentleman's grown a favourite at court, he has got so many people at his levee.

LORY. Sir, these people come in order to make him a favorite at court; they are to establish him with the ladies.

FASHION. Good God! to what an ebb of taste are women fallen, that it should be in the power of a laced coat to recommend a gallant to 'em!

LORY. Sir, tailors and periwig-makers are now become the bawds of the nation; 'tis they debauch all the women.

FASHION. Thou sayest true; for there's that fop now has not by nature wherewithal to move a cook-maid, and by that time these fellows have done with him, egad he shall melt down a countess!—But now for my reception; I'll engage it shall be as cold a one as a courtier's to his friend, who comes to put him in mind of his promise.

LORD FOPPINGTON. (*To his Tailor*) Death and eternal tartures! Sir, I say the packet's too high by a foot.

TAILOR. My lord, if it had been an inch lower, it would not have held your lordship's pocket-handkerchief.

LORD FOPPINGTON. Rat my pocket-handkerchief! have not I a page to carry it? You may make him a packet up to his chin a purpose for it; but I will not have mine come so near my face.

TAILOR. 'Tis not for me to dispute your lordship's fancy.

FASHION. (*To* LORY) His lordship! Lory, did you observe that?

LORY. Yes, sir; I always thought 'twould

end there. Now, I hope, you'll have a little more respect for him.

FASHION. Respect!—Damn him for a coxcomb! now has he ruined his estate to buy a title, that he may be a fool of the first rate; —but let's accost him.—(*To* LORD FOPPINGTON) Brother, I'm your humble servant.

LORD FOPPINGTON. O Lard, Tam! I did not expect you in England.—Brother, I am glad to see you.—(*Turning to his* Tailor) Look you, sir; I shall never be reconciled to this nauseous packet; therefore pray get me another suit with all manner of expedition, for this is my eternal aversion.—Mrs. Calico, are not you of my mind?

SEMPSTRESS. O, directly, my lord! it can never be too low.

LORD FOPPINGTON. You are pasitively in the right on't, for the packet becomes no part of the body but the knee.   *Exit* Tailor

SEMPSTRESS. I hope your lordship is pleased with your steenkirk.

LORD FOPPINGTON. In love with it, stap my vitals!—Bring your bill, you shall be paid to-marrow.

SEMPSTRESS. I humbly thank your honour.
Exit

LORD FOPPINGTON. Hark thee, shoemaker! these shoes an't ugly, but they don't fit me.

SHOEMAKER. My lord, my thinks[2] they fit you very well.

LORD FOPPINGTON. They hurt me just below the instep.

SHOEMAKER. (*Feeling his foot*) My lord, they don't hurt you there.

LORD FOPPINGTON. I tell thee, they pinch me execrably.

SHOEMAKER. My lord, if they pinch you, I'll be bound to be hanged, that's all.

LORD FOPPINGTON. Why, wilt thou undertake to persuade me I cannot feel?

SHOEMAKER. Your lordship may please to feel what you think fit; but that shoe does not hurt you; I think I understand my trade.

LORD FOPPINGTON. Now by all that's great and powerful, thou art an incomprehensible coxcomb! but thou makest good shoes and so I'll bear with thee.

SHOEMAKER. My lord, I have worked for half the people of quality in town these twenty years; and 'twere very hard I should not know when a shoe hurts, and when it don't.

---

[1] Not as actor but as spectator; men of fashion, of course, sat upon the stage itself until Garrick finally succeeded in stopping the custom.

[2] *Sic;* he means methinks.

LORD FOPPINGTON. Well, prithee be gone about thy business. *Exit* Shoemaker (*To the* Hosier) Mr. Mendlegs, a word with you: the calves of these stockings are thickened a little too much. They make my legs look like a chairman's.

MENDLEGS. My lord, my thinks they look mighty well.

LORD FOPPINGTON. Ay, but you are not so good a judge of these things as I am, I have studied 'em all my life; therefore pray let the next be the thickness of a crawn-piece less.—(*Aside*) If the town takes notice my legs are fallen away, 'twill be attributed to the violence of some new intrigue.—(*Exit* MENDLEGS) (*To the* Periwig-maker) Come, Mr. Foretop, let me see what you have done, and then the fatigue of the marning will be over.

FORETOP. My lord, I have done what I defy any prince in Europe to outdo; I have made you a periwig so long, and so full of hair, it will serve you for hat and cloak in all weathers.

LORD FOPPINGTON. Then thou hast made me thy friend to eternity. Come, comb it out.

FASHION. [*Aside to* LORY] Well, Lory, what dost think on't? A very friendly reception from a brother after three years' absence!

LORY. Why, sir, it's your own fault; we seldom care for those that don't love what we love: if you would creep into his heart, you must enter into his pleasures.—Here have you stood ever since you came in, and have not commended any one thing that belongs to him.

FASHION. Nor never shall, whilst they belong to a coxcomb.

LORY. Then, sir, you must be content to pick a hungry bone.

FASHION. No, sir, I'll crack it, and get to the marrow before I have done.

LORD FOPPINGTON. Gad's curse, Mr. Foretop! you don't intend to put this upon me for a full periwig?

FORETOP. Not a full one, my lord! I don't know what your lordship may please to call a full one, but I have crammed twenty ounces of hair into it.

LORD FOPPINGTON. What it may be by weight, sir, I shall not dispute; but by tale, there are not nine hairs of a side.

FORETOP. O lord! O lord! O lord! Why, as Gad shall judge me, your honor's side-face is reduced to the tip of your nose!

LORD FOPPINGTON. My side-face may be in eclipse for aught I know; but I'm sure my full-face is like the full-moon.

FORETOP. Heavens bless my eye-sight— (*Rubbing his eyes*) Sure I look through the wrong end of the perspective; for by my faith, an't please your honor, the broadest place I see in your face does not seem to me to be two inches diameter.

LORD FOPPINGTON. If it did, it would be just two inches too broad; for a periwig to a man should be like a mask to a woman, nothing should be seen but his eyes.

FORETOP. My lord, I have done; if you please to have more hair in your wig, I'll put it in.

LORD FOPPINGTON. Pasitively, yes.

FORETOP. Shall I take it back now, my lord?

LORD FOPPINGTON. No: I'll wear it to-day, though it show such a manstrous pair of cheeks, stap my vitals, I shall be taken for a trumpeter. *Exit* FORETOP

FASHION. Now your people of business are gone, brother, I hope I may obtain a quarter of an hour's audience of you.

LORD FOPPINGTON. Faith, Tam, I must beg you'll excuse me at this time, for I must away to the House of Lards immediately; my lady Teaser's case is to come on to-day, and I would not be absent for the salvation of mankind.—Hey, page!

Enter Page

Is the coach at the door?

PAGE. Yes, my lord.

LORD FOPPINGTON. You'll excuse me, brother. (*Going*)

FASHION. Shall you be back at dinner?

LORD FOPPINGTON. As Gad shall jidge me, I can't tell; for 'tis passible I may dine with some of aur House at Lacket's.[1]

FASHION. Shall I meet you there? For I must needs talk with you.

LORD FOPPINGTON. That I'm afraid mayn't be so praper; far the lards I commonly eat with, are people of a nice conversation; and you know, Tam, your education has been a little at large: but, if you'll stay here, you'll find a family dinner.—(*To* Page) Hey, fellow! What is there for dinner? There's beef: I suppose my brother will eat beef.—Dea Tam, I'm glad to see thee in England, stap my vitals! *Exit with his equipage*.

[1] Locket's, a fashionable tavern near Charing Cross.

FASHION. Hell and furies! is this to be borne?

LORY. Faith, sir, I could almost have given him a knock o' th' pate myself.

FASHION. 'Tis enough; I will now show thee the excess of my passion by being very calm. Come, Lory, lay your loggerhead to mine, and in cool blood let us contrive his destruction.

LORY. Here comes a head, sir, would contrive it better than us both, if he would but join in the confederacy.

Enter COUPLER

FASHION. By this light, old Coupler alive still!—Why, how now, match-maker, art thou here to plague the world with matrimony? You old bawd, how have you the impudence to be hobbling out of your grave twenty years after you are rotten?

COUPLER. When you begin to rot, sirrah, you'll go off like a pippin; one winter will send you to the devil. What mischief brings you home again? Ha! you young lascivious rogue, you. Let me put my hand in your bosom, sirrah.

FASHION. Stand off, old Sodom!

COUPLER. Nay, prithee now, don't be so coy.

FASHION. Keep your hands to yourself, you old dog you, or I'll wring your nose off.

COUPLER. Hast thou then been a year in Italy, and brought home a fool at last? By my conscience, the young fellows of this age profit no more by their going abroad than they do by their going to church. Sirrah, sirrah, if you are not hanged before you come to my years, you'll know a cock from a hen. But, come, I'm still a friend to thy person, though I have a contempt of thy understanding; and therefore I would willingly know thy condition, that I may see whether thou stand'st in need of my assistance: for widows swarm, my boy, the town's infected with 'em.

FASHION. I stand in need of anybody's assistance, that will help me to cut my elder brother's throat, without the risk of being hanged for him.

COUPLER. Egad, sirrah, I could help thee to do him almost as good a turn, without the danger of being burned in the hand for't.[1]

FASHION. Sayest thou so, old Satan? Show me but that, and my soul is thine.

COUPLER. Pox o' thy soul! give me thy warm body, sirrah; I shall have a substantial title to't when I tell thee my project.

FASHION. Out with it then, dear dad, and take possession as soon as thou wilt.

COUPLER. Sayest thou so, my Hephestion?[2] Why, then thus lies the scene.—But hold; who's that? if we are heard we are undone.

FASHION. What, have you forgot Lory?

COUPLER. Who? Trusty Lory, is it thee?

LORY. At your service, sir.

COUPLER. Give me thy hand, old boy. Egad, I did not know thee again; but I remember thy honesty, though I did not thy face; I think thou hadst like to have been hanged once or twice for thy master.

LORY. Sir, I was very near once having that honor.

COUPLER. Well, live and hope; don't be discouraged; eat with him, and drink with him, and do what he bids thee, and it may be thy reward at last, as well as another's.— (*To* YOUNG FASHION) Well, sir, you must know I have done you the kindness to make up a match for your brother.

FASHION. I am very much beholding to you, truly.

COUPLER. You may be, sirrah, before the wedding-day yet. The lady is a great heiress; fifteen hundred pound a year, and a great bag of money; the match is concluded, the writings are drawn, and the pipkin's to be cracked in a fortnight. Now you must know, stripling (with respect to your mother), your brother's the son of a whore.

FASHION. Good!

COUPLER. He has given me a bond of a thousand pounds for helping him to this fortune, and has promised me as much more in ready money upon the day of marriage, which, I understand by a friend, he ne'er designs to pay me. If therefore you will be a generous young dog, and secure me five thousand pounds, I'll be a covetous old rogue, and help you to the lady.

FASHION. Egad, if thou canst bring this about, I'll have thy statue cast in brass. But don't you dote, you old pander you, when you talk at this rate?

COUPLER. That your youthful parts shall judge of. This plump patridge, that I tell you of, lives in the country, fifty miles off, with her honored parents, in a lonely old

---

[1] Minor felons were merely branded in the hand.

[2] Friend and favorite of Alexander. See Lee's *The Rival Queens*.

house which nobody comes near; she never goes abroad, nor sees company at home. To prevent all misfortunes, she has her breeding within doors; the parson of the parish teaches her to play upon the bass-viol, the clerk to sing, her nurse to dress, and her father to dance. In short, nobody can give you admittance there but I; nor can I do it any other way than by making you pass for your brother.

FASHION. And how the devil wilt thou do that?

COUPLER. Without the devil's aid, I warrant thee. Thy brother's face not one of the family ever saw, the whole business has been managed by me, and all the letters go through my hands. The last that was writ to Sir Tunbelly Clumsey (for that's the old gentleman's name), was to tell him, his lordship would be down in a fortnight to consummate. Now, you shall go away immediately, pretend you writ that letter only to have the romantic pleasure of surprising your mistress; fall desperately in love, as soon as you see her; make that your plea for marrying her immediately, and, when the fatigue of the wedding-night's over, you shall send me a swinging purse of gold, you dog you.

FASHION. Egad, old dad, I'll put my hand in thy bosom now.

COUPLER. Ah, you young hot lusty thief, let me muzzle you!—(*Kissing*) Sirrah, let me muzzle you.

FASHION. (*Aside*) Psha, the old lecher!

COUPLER. Well; I'll warrant thou hast not a farthing of money in thy pocket now; no, one may see it in thy face.

FASHION. Not a souse,[1] by Jupiter!

COUPLER. Must I advance then?—Well, sirrah, be at my lodgings in half an hour, and I'll see what may be done; we'll sign, and seal, and eat a pullet, and when I have given thee some farther instructions, thou shalt hoist sail and be gone.—(*Kissing*) T'other buss, and so adieu.

FASHION. Um! psha!

COUPLER. Ah, you young warm dog you, what a delicious night will the bride have on't!
Exit

FASHION. So, Lory; Providence, thou seest at last, takes care of men of merit: we are in a fair way to be great people.

LORY. Ay, sir, if the devil don't step between the cup and the lip, as he uses to do.

[1] Obsolete form for *sou*, the French coin.

FASHION. Why, faith, he has played me many a damned trick to spoil my fortune, and egad I'm almost afraid he's at work about it again now; but if I should tell thee how, thou'dst wonder at me.

LORY. Indeed, sir, I should not.

FASHION. How dost know?

LORY. Because, sir, I have wondered at you so often, I can wonder at you no more.

FASHION. No! what wouldst thou say if a qualm of conscience should spoil my design?

LORY. I would eat my words, and wonder more than ever.

FASHION. Why, faith, Lory, though I am a young rake-hell, and have played many a roguish trick, this is so full-grown a cheat, I find I must take pains to come up to't, I have scruples—

LORY. They are strong symptoms of death; if you find they increase, pray, sir, make your will.

FASHION. No, my conscience shan't starve me neither. But thus far I will hearken to it; before I execute this project, I'll try my brother to the bottom, I'll speak to him with the temper of a philosopher; my reasons (though they press him home) shall yet be clothed with so much modesty, not one of all the truths they urge shall be so naked to offend his sight. If he has yet so much humanity about him as to assist me (though with a moderate aid), I'll drop my project at his feet, and show him I can do for him much more than what I ask he'd do for me. This one conclusive trial of him I resolve to make—

Succeed or no, still victory's my lot;
If I subdue his heart, 'tis well; if not,
I shall subdue my conscience to my plot.
Exeunt

ACT II

SCENE I.—[*London.—A Room in* LOVELESS'S *Lodgings*]

Enter LOVELESS *and* AMANDA

LOVELESS. How do you like these lodgings, my dear? For my part, I am so well pleased with 'em, I shall hardly remove whilst we stay in town, if you are satisfied.

AMANDA. I am satisfied with everything that pleases you; else I had not come to town at all.

LOVELESS. Oh! a little of the noise and bustle of the world sweetens the pleasures of retreat. We shall find the charms of our retirement doubled, when we return to it.

AMANDA. That pleasing prospect will be my chiefest entertainment, whilst (much against my will) I am obliged to stand surrounded with these empty pleasures, which 'tis so much the fashion to be fond of.

LOVELESS. I own most of them are indeed but empty; nay, so empty, that one would wonder by what magic power they act, when they induce us to be vicious for their sakes. Yet some there are we may speak kindlier of. There are delights (of which a private life is destitute) which may divert an honest man, and be a harmless entertainment to a virtuous woman. The conversation of the town is one; and truly (with some small allowances), the plays, I think, may be esteemed another.

AMANDA. The plays, I must confess, have some small charms; and would have more, would they restrain that loose, obscene encouragement to vice, which shocks, if not the virtue of some women, at least the modesty of all.

LOVELESS. But till that reformation can be made, I would not leave the wholesome corn for some intruding tares that grow amongst it. Doubtless the moral of a well-wrought scene is of prevailing force.—Last night there happened one that moved me strangely.

AMANDA. Pray, what was that?

LOVELESS. Why 'twas about—but 'tis not worth repeating.

AMANDA. Yes, pray let me know it.

LOVELESS. No; I think 'tis as well let alone.

AMANDA. Nay, now you make me have a mind to know.

LOVELESS. 'Twas a foolish thing. You'd perhaps grow jealous should I tell it you, though without cause, heaven knows.

AMANDA. I shall begin to think I have cause, if you persist in making it a secret.

LOVELESS. I'll then convince you you have none, by making it no longer so. Know then, I happened in the play to find my very character, only with the addition of a relapse; which struck me so, I put a sudden stop to a most harmless entertainment, which till then diverted me between the acts. 'Twas to admire the workmanship of nature, in the face of a young lady that sat some distance from me, she was so exquisitely handsome!—

AMANDA. So exquisitely handsome!

LOVELESS. Why do you repeat my words, my dear?

AMANDA. Because you seemed to speak 'em with such pleasure, I thought I might oblige you with their echo.

LOVELESS. Then you are alarmed, Amanda?

AMANDA. It is my duty to be so, when you are in danger.

LOVELESS. You are too quick in apprehending for me; all will be well when you have heard me out. I do confess I gazed upon her; nay, eagerly I gazed upon her.

AMANDA. Eagerly! that's with desire.

LOVELESS. No, I desired her not: I viewed her with a world of admiration, but not one glance of love.

AMANDA. Take heed of trusting to such nice distinctions.

LOVELESS. I did take heed; for observing in the play that he who seemed to represent me there was, by an accident like this, unwarily surprised into a net, in which he lay a poor entangled slave, and brought a train of mischiefs on his head, I snatched my eyes away; they pleaded hard for leave to look again, but I grew absolute, and they obeyed.

AMANDA. Were they the only things that were inquisitive? Had I been in your place, my tongue, I fancy, had been curious, too; I should have asked her name, and where she lived (yet still without design).—Who was she, pray?

LOVELESS. Indeed I cannot tell.

AMANDA. You will not tell.

LOVELESS. By all that's sacred then, I did not ask.

AMANDA. Nor do you know what company was with her?

LOVELESS. I do not.

AMANDA. Then I am calm again.

LOVELESS. Why were you disturbed?

AMANDA. Had I then no cause?

LOVELESS. None, certainly.

AMANDA. I thought I had.

LOVELESS. But you thought wrong, Amanda: for turn the case, and let it be your story; should you come home, and tell me you had seen a handsome man, should I grow jealous because you had eyes?

AMANDA. But should I tell you he were exquisitely so; and I had gazed on him with admiration; that I had looked with eager eyes upon him; should you not think 'twere possible

I might go one step farther, and inquire his name?

LOVELESS. (*Aside*) She has reason on her side: I have talked too much; but I must turn it off another way.—(*To* AMANDA) Will you then make no difference, Amanda, between the language of our sex and yours? There is a modesty restrains your tongues, which makes you speak by halves when you commend; but roving flattery gives a loose to ours, which makes us still speak double what we think. You should not, therefore, in so strict a sense, take what I said to her advantage.

AMANDA. Those flights of flattery, sir, are to our faces only: when women once are out of hearing, you are as modest in your commendations as we are. But I shan't put you to the trouble of farther excuses, if you please this business shall rest here. Only give me leave to wish, both for your peace and mine, that you may never meet this miracle of beauty more.

LOVELESS. I am content.

Enter Servant

SERVANT. Madam, there's a young lady at the door in a chair, desires to know whether your ladyship sees company. I think her name is Berinthia.

AMANDA. O dear! 'tis a relation I have not seen these five years. Pray her to walk in.—(*Exit* Servant) Here's another beauty for you. She was young when I saw her last; but I hear she's grown extremely handsome.

LOVELESS. Don't you be jealous now; for I shall gaze upon her, too.

Enter BERINTHIA

(*Aside*)—Ha! by Heavens the very woman!

BERINTHIA. (*Saluting* AMANDA) Dear Amanda, I did not expect to meet with you in town.

AMANDA. Sweet cousin, I'm overjoyed to see you.—(*To* LOVELESS) Mr. Loveless, here's a relation and a friend of mine, I desire you'll be better acquainted with.

LOVELESS. (*Saluting* BERINTHIA) If my wife never desires a harder thing, madam, her request will be easily granted.

BERINTHIA. (*To* AMANDA) I think, madam, I ought to wish you joy.

AMANDA. Joy! Upon what?

BERINTHIA. Upon your marriage: you were a widow when I saw you last.

LOVELESS. You ought rather, madam, to wish me joy upon that, since I am the only gainer.

BERINTHIA. If she has got so good a husband as the world reports, she has gained enough to expect the compliments of her friends upon it.

LOVELESS. If the world is so favorable to me, to allow I deserve that title, I hope 'tis so just to my wife to own I derive it from her.

BERINTHIA. Sir, it is so just to you both, to own you are (and deserve to be) the happiest pair that live in it.

LOVELESS. I'm afraid we shall lose that character, madam, whenever you happen to change your condition.

Enter Servant

SERVANT. Sir, my lord Foppington presents his humble service to you, and desires to know how you do. He but just now heard you were in town. He's at the next door; and if it be not inconvenient, he'll come and wait upon you.

LOVELESS. Lord Foppington!—I know him not.

BERINTHIA. Not his dignity, perhaps, but you do his person. 'Tis Sir Novelty; he has bought a barony, in order to marry a great fortune. His patent has not been passed eight-and-forty hours, and he has already sent how-do-ye's to all the town, to make 'em acquainted with his title.

LOVELESS. Give my service to his lordship, and let him know I am proud of the honour he intends me.—(*Exit* Servant) Sure this addition of quality must have so improved his coxcomb,[1] he can't but be very good company for a quarter of an hour.

AMANDA. Now it moves my pity more than my mirth, to see a man whom nature has made no fool, be so very industrious to pass for an ass.

LOVELESS. No, there you are wrong, Amanda; you should never bestow your pity upon those who take pains for your contempt. Pity those whom nature abuses, but never those who abuse nature.

BERINTHIA. Besides, the town would be robbed of one of its chief diversions, if it should become a crime to laugh at a fool.

AMANDA. I could never yet perceive the town inclined to part with any of its diver-

[1] Cf. his excellency, or his grace.

sions, for the sake of their being crimes; but I have seen it very fond of some I think had little else to recommend 'em.

BERINTHIA. I doubt, Amanda, you are grown its enemy, you speak with so much warmth against it.

AMANDA. I must confess I am not much its friend.

BERINTHIA. Then give me leave to make you mine, by not engaging in its quarrel.

AMANDA. You have many stronger claims than that, Berinthia, whenever you think fit to plead your title.

LOVELESS. You have done well to engage a second, my dear; for here comes one will be apt to call you to an account for your country principles.

Enter LORD FOPPINGTON

LORD FOPPINGTON. (*To* LOVELESS) Sir, I am your most humble servant.

LOVELESS. I wish you joy, my lord.

LORD FOPPINGTON. O Lard, sir!—Madam, your ladyship's welcome to tawn.

AMANDA. I wish your lordship joy.

LORD FOPPINGTON. O Heavens, madam—

LOVELESS. My lord, this young lady is a relation of my wife's.

LORD FOPPINGTON. (*Saluting* BERINTHIA) The beautifullest race of people upon earth, rat me! Dear Loveless, I'm overjoyed to see you have brought your family to tawn again; I am, stap my vitals!—(*Aside*) Far I design to lie with your wife.—(*To* AMANDA) Far Gad's sake, madam, haw has your ladyship been able to sustain thus long, under the fatigue of a country life?

AMANDA. My life has been very far from that, my lord; it has been a very quiet one.

LORD FOPPINGTON. Why, that's the fatigue I speak of, madam. For 'tis impossible to be quiet, without thinking: now thinking is to me the greatest fatigue in the world.

AMANDA. Does not your lordship love reading then?

LORD FOPPINGTON. Oh, passionately, madam.—But I never think of what I read.

BERINTHIA. Why, how can your lordship read without thinking?

LORD FOPPINGTON. O Lard!—can your ladyship pray without devotion, madam?

AMANDA. Well, I must own I think books the best entertainment in the world.

LORD FOPPINGTON. I am so very much of your ladyship's mind, madam, that I have a private gallery, where I walk sometimes; it is furnished with nothing but books and looking-glasses. Madam, I have gilded 'em, and ranged 'em so prettily, before Gad, it is the most entertaining thing in the world to walk and look upon 'em.

AMANDA. Nay, I love a neat library, too; but 'tis, I think, the inside of a book should recommend it most to us.

LORD FOPPINGTON. That, I must confess, I am nat altogether so fand of. Far to mind the inside of a book, is to entertain one's self with the forced product of another man's brain. Naw I think a man of quality and breeding may be much better diverted with the natural sprouts of his own. But to say the truth, madam, let a man love reading never so well, when once he comes to know this tawn, he finds so many better ways of passing the four-and-twenty hours, that 'twere ten thousand pities he should consume his time in that. Far instance, madam, my life; my life, madam, is a perpetual stream of pleasure, that glides through such a variety of entertainments, I believe the wisest of our ancestors never had the least conception of any of 'em. I rise, madam, about ten a-clack. I don't rise sooner, because 'tis the worst thing in the world for the complexion; nat that I pretend to be a beau; but a man must endeavor to look wholesome, lest he make so nauseous a figure in the side-bax, the ladies should be compelled to turn their eyes upon the play. So at ten a-clack, I say, I rise. Naw, if I find 'tis a good day, I resalve to take a turn in the Park, and see the fine women; so huddle on my clothes, and get dressed by one. If it be nasty weather, I take a turn in the chocolate-house: where, as you walk, madam, you have the prettiest prospect in the world; you have looking-glasses all raund you.—But I'm afraid I tire the company.

BERINTHIA. Not at all. Pray go on.

LORD FOPPINGTON. Why then, ladies, from thence I go to dinner at Lacket's, where you are so nicely and delicately served, that, stap my vitals! they shall compose you a dish no bigger than a saucer, shall come to fifty shillings. Between eating my dinner (and washing my mouth, ladies) I spend my time, till I go to the play; where, till nine a-clack, I entertain myself with looking upon the company; and usually dispose of one hour more in leading 'em aut. So there's twelve of the four-and-twenty pretty well over. The other twelve, madam, are disposed of in two articles: in the first four I toast myself drunk, and in t'other eight I sleep myself sober again. Thus, ladies, you see my life is an eternal raund of delights.

LOVELESS. 'Tis a heavenly one indeed.

AMANDA. But I thought, my lord, you beaux spent a great deal of your time in intrigues: you have given us no account of them yet.

LORD FOPPINGTON. (*Aside*) So; she would inquire into my amours.—That's jealousy:—she begins to be in love with me.—(*To* AMANDA) Why, madam,—as to time for my intrigues, I usually make detachments of it from my other pleasures, according to the exigency. Far your ladyship may please to take notice, that those who intrigue with women of quality, have rarely occasion for above half an hour at a time: people of that rank being under those decorums, they can seldom give you a langer view than will just serve to shoot 'em flying. So that the course of my other pleasures is not very much interrupted by my amours.

LOVELESS. But your lordship is now become a pillar of the state; you must attend the weighty affairs of the nation.

LORD FOPPINGTON. Sir,—as to weighty affairs—I leave them to weighty heads. I never intend mine shall be a burden to my body.

LOVELESS. O but you'll find the House will expect your attendance.

LORD FOPPINGTON. Sir, you'll find the House will compound for my appearance.

LOVELESS. But your friends will take it ill if you don't attend their particular causes.

LORD FOPPINGTON. Not, sir, if I come time enough to give 'em my particular vote.

BERINTHIA. But pray, my lord, how do you dispose of yourself on Sundays? for that, methinks, is a day should hang wretchedly upon your hands.

LORD FOPPINGTON. Why, faith, madam—Sunday—is a vile day, I must confess. I intend to move for leave to bring in a bill, that players may work upon it, as well as the hackney coaches. Though this I must say for the government, it leaves us the churches to entertain us.—But then again, they begin so abominable early, a man must rise by candle-light to get dressed by the psalm.

BERINTHIA. Pray which church does your lordship most oblige with your presence?

LORD FOPPINGTON. Oh, St. James's, madam —there's much the best company.

AMANDA. Is there good preaching, too?

LORD FOPPINGTON. Why, faith, madam— I can't tell. A man must have very little to do there that can give an account of the sermon.

BERINTHIA. You can give us an account of the ladies at least?

LORD FOPPINGTON. Or I deserve to be excommunicated.—There is my lady Tattle, my lady Prate, my lady Titter, my lady Leer, my lady Giggle, and my lady Grin. These sit in the front of the boxes, and all church-time are the prettiest company in the world, stap my vitals!—(*To* AMANDA) Mayn't we hope for the honor to see your ladyship added to our society, madam?

AMANDA. Alas, my lord! I am the worst company in the world at church: I'm apt to mind the prayers, or the sermon, or—

LORD FOPPINGTON. One is indeed strangely apt at church to mind what one should not do. But I hope, madam, at one time or other, I shall have the honor to lead your ladyship to your coach there.—(*Aside*) Methinks she seems strangely pleased with everything I say to her.—'Tis a vast pleasure to receive encouragement from a woman before her husband's face.—I have a good mind to pursue my conquest, and speak the thing plainly to her at once. Egad, I'll do't, and that in so cavalier a manner, she shall be surprised at it. —(*Aloud*) Ladies, I'll take my leave; I'm afraid I begin to grow troublesome with the length of my visit.

AMANDA. Your lordship's too entertaining to grow troublesome anywhere.

LORD FOPPINGTON. (*Aside*) That now was as much as if she had said—pray lie with me. I'll let her see I'm quick of apprehension.— (*To* AMANDA) O Lard, madam! I had like to have forgot a secret, I must needs tell your ladyship.—(*To* LOVELESS) Ned, you must not be so jealous now as to listen.

LOVELESS. Not I, my lord; I am too fashionable a husband to pry into the secrets of my wife.

LORD FOPPINGTON. (*To* AMANDA, *squeezing her hand*) I am in love with you to desperation, strike me speechless!

AMANDA. (*Giving him a box o' the ear*) Then

thus I return your passion.—An impudent fool!

LORD FOPPINGTON. Gad's curse, madam, I'm a peer of the realm!

LOVELESS. Hey; what the devil do you affront my wife, sir? Nay then—

(*They draw and fight. The women run shrieking for help*)

AMANDA. Ah! What has my folly done? Help! Murder! help! part 'em, for heaven's sake!

LORD FOPPINGTON. (*Falling back, and leaning upon his sword*) Ah—quite through the body!—stap my vitals!

Enter Servants

LOVELESS. (*Running to him*) I hope I han't killed the fool however.—Bear him up! —Where's your wound?

LORD FOPPINGTON. Just through the guts.

LOVELESS. Call a surgeon there.—Unbutton him quickly.

LORD FOPPINGTON. Ay, pray make haste.

Exit Servant

LOVELESS. This mischief you may thank yourself for.

LORD FOPPINGTON. I may so,—love's the devil indeed, Ned.

Enter SYRINGE *and* Servant

SERVANT. Here's Mr. Syringe, sir, was just going by the door.

LORD FOPPINGTON. He's the welcomest man alive.

SYRINGE. Stand by, stand by, stand by! Pray, gentlemen, stand by. Lord have mercy upon us! did you never see a man run through the body before? Pray, stand by.

LORD FOPPINGTON. Ah, Mr. Syringe—I'm a dead man!

SYRINGE. A dead man and I by!—I should laugh to see that, egad!

LOVELESS. Prithee don't stand prating, but look upon his wound.

SYRINGE. Why, what if I won't look upon his wound this hour, sir?

LOVELESS. Why, then he'll bleed to death, sir.

SYRINGE. Why, then I'll fetch him to life again, sir.

LOVELESS. 'Slife, he's run through the guts, I tell thee.

SYRINGE. Would he were run through the heart, I should get the more credit by his cure. Now I hope you're satisfied?—Come, now let me come at him; now let me come at him.— (*Viewing his wound*) Oons, what a gash is here!—Why, sir, a man may drive a coach and six horses into your body.

LORD FOPPINGTON. Ho!

SYRINGE. Why, what the devil, have you run the gentleman through with a scythe?— (*Aside*) A little prick between the skin and the ribs, that's all.

LOVELESS. Let me see his wound.

SYRINGE. Then you shall dress it, sir; for if anybody looks upon it, I won't.

LOVELESS. Why, thou art the veriest coxcomb I ever saw.

SYRINGE. Sir, I am not master of my trade for nothing.

LORD FOPPINGTON. Surgeon!

SYRINGE. Well, sir.

LORD FOPPINGTON. Is there any hopes?

SYRINGE. Hopes?—I can't tell.—What are you willing to give for your cure?

LORD FOPPINGTON. Five hundred paunds, with pleasure.

SYRINGE. Why, then perhaps there may be hopes. But we must avoid farther delay.— Here; help the gentleman into a chair, and carry him to my house presently, that's the properest place—(*Aside*) to bubble him out of his money.—(*Aloud*) Come, a chair, a chair quickly—there, in with him.

(*They put him into a chair*)

LORD FOPPINGTON. Dear Loveless—adieu! If I die—I forgive thee; and if I live—I hope thou'lt do as much by me. I'm very sorry you and I should quarrel; but I hope here's an end on't, for if you are satisfied—I am.

LOVELESS. I shall hardly think it worth my prosecuting any farther, so you may be at rest, sir.

LORD FOPPINGTON. Thou art a generous fellow, strike me dumb!—(*Aside*) But thou hast an impertinent wife, stap my vitals!

SYRINGE. So, carry him off! carry him off! we shall have him prate himself into a fever by and by; carry him off.

Exit with LORD FOPPINGTON

AMANDA. Now on my knees, my dear, let me ask your pardon for my indiscretion, my own I never shall obtain.

LOVELESS. Oh, there's no harm done: you served him well.

AMANDA. He did indeed deserve it. But I tremble to think how dear my indiscreet resentment might have cost you.

LOVELESS. Oh, no matter, never trouble yourself about that.

BERINTHIA. For heaven's sake, what was't he did to you?

AMANDA. O nothing; he only squeezed me kindly by the hand, and frankly offered me a coxcomb's heart. I know I was to blame to resent it as I did, since nothing but a quarrel could ensue. But the fool so surprised me with his insolence, I was not mistress of my fingers.

BERINTHIA. Now, I dare swear, he thinks you had 'em at great command, they obeyed you so readily.

Enter WORTHY

WORTHY. Save you, save you, good people: I'm glad to find you all alive; I met a wounded peer carrying off. For heaven's sake, what was the matter?

LOVELESS. Oh, a trifle! He would have lain with my wife before my face, so she obliged him with a box o' th' ear, and I run him through the body: that was all.

WORTHY. Bagatelle on all sides. But, pray, madam, how long has this noble lord been a humble servant of yours?

AMANDA. This is the first I have heard on't. So I suppose 'tis his quality more than his love, has brought him into this adventure. He thinks his title an authentic passport to every woman's heart below the degree of a peeress.

WORTHY. He's coxcomb enough to think anything. But I would not have you brought into trouble for him. I hope there's no danger of his life?

LOVELESS. None at all. He's fallen into the hands of a roguish surgeon; I perceive designs to frighten a little money out of him. But I saw his wound, 'tis nothing; he may go to the play to-night, if he pleases.

WORTHY. I am glad you have corrected him without farther mischief. And now, sir, if these ladies have no farther service for you, you'll oblige me if you can go to the place I spoke to you of t'other day.

LOVELESS. With all my heart.—(*Aside*) Though I could wish, methinks, to stay and gaze a little longer on that creature. Good gods, how beautiful she is!—But what have I to do with beauty? I have already had my portion, and must not covet more.—(*To* WORTHY) Come, sir, when you please.

WORTHY. Ladies, your servant.

AMANDA. Mr. Loveless, pray one word with you before you go.

LOVELESS. (*To* WORTHY) I'll overtake you, sir.—(*Exit* WORTHY) What would my dear?

AMANDA. Only a woman's foolish question, —how do you like my cousin here?

LOVELESS. Jealous already, Amanda?

AMANDA. Not at all, I ask you for another reason.

LOVELESS. (*Aside*) Whate'er her reason be, I must not tell her true.—(*To* AMANDA) Why, I confess she's handsome. But you must not think I slight your kinswoman, if I own to you, of all the women who may claim that character, she is the last would triumph in my heart.

AMANDA. I'm satisfied.

LOVELESS. Now tell me why you asked?

AMANDA. At night I will. Adieu.

LOVELESS. I'm yours. (*Kisses her and exit*)

AMANDA. (*Aside*) I'm glad to find he does not like her; for I have a great mind to persuade her to come and live with me.—(*Aloud*) Now, dear Berinthia, let me inquire a little into your affairs: for I do assure you, I am enough your friend to interest myself in everything that concerns you.

BERINTHIA. You formerly have given me such proofs on't, I should be very much to blame to doubt it. I am sorry I have no secrets to trust you with, that I might convince you how entire a confidence I durst repose in you.

AMANDA. Why, is it possible that one so young and beautiful as you should live and have no secrets?

BERINTHIA. What secrets do you mean?

AMANDA. Lovers.

BERINTHIA. Oh, twenty! but not one secret amongst 'em. Lovers in this age have too much honor to do anything underhand; they do all above board.

AMANDA. That now, methinks, would make me hate a man.

BERINTHIA. But the women of the town are of another mind: for by this means a lady may (with the expense of a few coquette glances) lead twenty fools about in a string for two or three years together. Whereas, if she should allow 'em greater favors, and oblige 'em to secrecy, she would not keep one of 'em a fortnight.

AMANDA. There's something indeed in that to satisfy the vanity of a woman, but I can't comprehend how the men find their account in it.

BERINTHIA. Their entertainment, I must confess, is a riddle to me. For there's very few of 'em ever get farther than a bow and an ogle. I have half a score for my share, who follow me all over the town; and at the play, the Park, and the church, do (with their eyes) say the violentest things to me.—But I never hear any more of 'em.

AMANDA. What can be the reason of that?

BERINTHIA. One reason is, they don't know how to go farther. They have had so little practice, they don't understand the trade. But, besides their ignorance, you must know there is not one of my half score lovers but what follows half a score mistresses. Now, their affections being divided amongst so many, are not strong enough for any one to make 'em pursue her to the purpose. Like a young puppy in a warren, they have a flirt at all, and catch none.

AMANDA. Yet they seem to have a torrent of love to dispose of.

BERINTHIA. They have so. But 'tis like the rivers of a modern philosopher, (whose works, though a woman, I have read,) it sets out with a violent stream, splits in a thousand branches, and is all lost in the sands.

AMANDA. But do you think this river of love runs all its course without doing any mischief? Do you think it overflows nothing?

BERINTHIA. O yes; 'tis true, it never breaks into anybody's ground that has the least fence about it; but it overflows all the commons that lie in its way. And this is the utmost achievement of those dreadful champions in the field of love—the beaux.

AMANDA. But prithee, Berinthia, instruct me a little farther; for I'm so great a novice I am almost ashamed on't. My husband's leaving me whilst I was young and fond threw me into that depth of discontent, that ever since I have led so private and recluse a life, my ignorance is scarce conceivable. I therefore fain would be instructed. Not (heaven knows) that what you call intrigues have any charms for me; my love and principles are too well fixed. The practic part of all unlawful love is—

BERINTHIA. Oh, 'tis abominable! But for the speculative; that we must all confess is entertaining. The conversation of all the virtuous women in the town turns upon that and new clothes.

AMANDA. Pray be so just then to me, to believe, 'tis with a world of innocency I would inquire, whether you think those women we call women of reputation, do so really 'scape all other men, as they do those shadows of 'em, the beaux.

BERINTHIA. O no, Amanda; there are a sort of men make dreadful work amongst 'em, men that may be called the beaux' antipathy; for they agree in nothing but walking upon two legs.—These have brains; the beau has none. These are in love with their mistress; the beau with himself. They take care of her reputation; he's industrious to destroy it. They are decent: he's a fop. They are sound; he's rotten. They are men; he's an ass.

AMANDA. If this be their character, I fancy we had here e'en now a pattern of 'em both.

BERINTHIA. His lordship and Mr. Worthy?

AMANDA. The same.

BERINTHIA. As for the lord, he's eminently so; and for the other, I can assure you, there's not a man in town who has a better interest with the women, that are worth having an interest with. But 'tis all private: he's like a back-stair minister at court, who, whilst the reputed favorites are sauntering in the bed-chamber, is ruling the roost in the closet.

AMANDA. He answers then the opinion I had ever of him. Heavens! What a difference there is between a man like him, and that vain nauseous fop, Sir Novelty.—(*Taking her hand*) I must acquaint you with a secret, cousin. 'Tis not that fool alone has talked to me of love. Worthy has been tampering, too. 'Tis true, he has done't in vain: not all his charms or art have power to shake me. My love, my duty, and my virtue, are such faithful guards, I need not fear my heart should e'er betray me. But what I wonder at is this: I find I did not start at his proposal, as when it came from one whom I contemned. I therefore mention his attempt, that I may learn from you whence it proceeds; that vice (which cannot change its nature) should so far change at least its shape, as that the self-same crime proposed from one shall seem a monster gaping at your ruin; when from another it shall look so kind, as though it were your friend, and never meant to harm you. Whence, think you, can this difference proceed? For 'tis not love, heaven knows.

BERINTHIA. O no; I would not for the world believe it were. But possibly, should there a dreadful sentence pass upon you, to undergo the rage of both their passions; the pain you apprehend from one might seem so trivial to the other, the danger would not quite so much alarm you.

AMANDA. Fie, fie, Berinthia! you would indeed alarm me, could you incline me to a thought, that all the merit of mankind combined could shake that tender love I bear my husband. No! he sits triumphant in my heart, and nothing can dethrone him.

BERINTHIA. But should he abdicate again, do you think you should preserve the vacant throne ten tedious winters more in hopes of his return?

AMANDA. Indeed, I think I should. Though I confess, after those obligations he has to me, should he abandon me once more, my heart would grow extremely urgent with me to root him thence, and cast him out forever.

BERINTHIA. Were I that thing they call a slighted wife, somebody should run the risk of being that thing they call—a husband.

AMANDA. O fie, Berinthia! no revenge should ever be taken against a husband. But to wrong his bed is a vengeance, which of all vengeance—

BERINTHIA. Is the sweetest, ha! ha! ha! Don't I talk madly?

AMANDA. Madly, indeed.

BERINTHIA. Yet I'm very innocent.

AMANDA. That I dare swear you are. I know how to make allowances for your humor. You were always very entertaining company; but I find since marriage and widowhood have shown you the world a little, you are very much improved.

BERINTHIA. (*Aside*) Alack a-day, there has gone more than that to improve me, if she knew all!

AMANDA. For heaven's sake, Berinthia, tell me what way I shall take to persuade you to come and live with me?

BERINTHIA. Why, one way in the world there is—and but one.

AMANDA. Pray which is that?

BERINTHIA. It is, to assure me—I shall be very welcome.

AMANDA. If that be all, you shall e'en lie here to-night.

BERINTHIA. To-night!

AMANDA. Yes, to-night.

BERINTHIA. Why, the people where I lodge will think me mad.

AMANDA. Let 'em think what they please.

BERINTHIA. Say you so, Amanda? Why, then they shall think what they please: for I'm a young widow, and I care not what anybody thinks. Ah, Amanda, it's a delicious thing to be a young widow!

AMANDA. You'll hardly make me think so.

BERINTHIA. Puh! because you are in love with your husband: but that is not every woman's case.

AMANDA. I hope 'twas yours, at least.

BERINTHIA. Mine, say ye? Now I have a great mind to tell you a lie, but I should do it so awkwardly you'd find me out.

AMANDA. Then e'en speak the truth.

BERINTHIA. Shall I?—Then after all I did love him, Amanda—as a nun does penance.

AMANDA. Why did not you refuse to marry him, then?

BERINTHIA. Because my mother would have whipped me.

AMANDA. How did you live together?

BERINTHIA. Like man and wife, asunder. He loved the country, I the town. He hawks and hounds, I coaches and equipage. He eating and drinking, I carding and playing. He the sound of a horn, I the squeak of a fiddle. We were dull company at table, worse a-bed. Whenever we met, we gave one another the spleen; and never agreed but once, which was about lying alone.

AMANDA. But tell me one thing, truly and sincerely.

BERINTHIA. What's that?

AMANDA. Notwithstanding all these jars, did not his death at last extremely trouble you?

BERINTHIA. O yes. Not that my present pangs were so very violent, but the after-pains were intolerable. I was forced to wear a beastly widow's band a twelvemonth for't.

AMANDA. Women, I find, have different inclination[s].

BERINTHIA. Women, I find, keep different company. When your husband ran away from you, if you had fallen into some of my acquaintance, 'twould have saved you many a tear. But you go and live with a grandmother, a bishop, and an old nurse; which was enough to make any woman break her heart for her husband. Pray, Amanda, if ever you are a widow again, keep yourself so, as I do.

AMANDA. Why! do you then resolve you'll never marry?
BERINTHIA. O no; I resolve I will.
AMANDA. How so?
BERINTHIA. That I never may.
AMANDA. You banter me.
BERINTHIA. Indeed I don't. But I consider I'm a woman, and form my resolutions accordingly.
AMANDA. Well, my opinion is, form what resolution you will, matrimony will be the end on't.
BERINTHIA. Faith it won't.
AMANDA. How do you know?
BERINTHIA. I'm sure on't.
AMANDA. Why, do you think 'tis impossible for you to fall in love?
BERINTHIA. No.
AMANDA. Nay, but to grow so passionately fond, that nothing but the man you love can give you rest.
BERINTHIA. Well, what then?
AMANDA. Why, then you'll marry him.
BERINTHIA. How do you know that?
AMANDA. Why, what can you do else?
BERINTHIA. Nothing—but sit and cry.
AMANDA. Psha!
BERINTHIA. Ah, poor Amanda! you have led a country life: but if you'll consult the widows of this town, they'll tell you you should never take a lease of a house you can hire for a quarter's warning.[1] *Exeunt*

ACT III

[SCENE I. *A Room in* LORD FOPPINGTON'S *House*]

Enter LORD FOPPINGTON *and* Servant

LORD FOPPINGTON. Hey, fellow, let the coach come to the door.
SERVANT. Will your lordship venture so soon to expose yourself to the weather?
LORD FOPPINGTON. Sir, I will venture as soon as I can, to expose myself to the ladies; though give me my cloak, however: for in that side-box, what between the air that comes in at the door on one side, and the intolerable warmth of the masks on t'other, a man gets so many heats and colds, 'twould destroy the constitution of a harse.
SERVANT. (*Putting on his cloak*) I wish your lordship would please to keep house a little longer; I'm afraid your honor does not well consider your wound.
LORD FOPPINGTON. My wound!—I would not be in eclipse another day, though I had as many wounds in my guts as I have had in my heart. *Exit* Servant

Enter YOUNG FASHION

FASHION. Brother, your servant. How do you find yourself to-day?
LORD FOPPINGTON. So well, that I have ardered my coach to the door: so there's no great danger of death this baut, Tam.
FASHION. I'm very glad of it.
LORD FOPPINGTON. (*Aside*) That I believe's a lie.—(*Aloud*) Prithee, Tam, tell me one thing: did nat your heart cut a caper up to your mauth, when you heard I was run through the bady?
FASHION. Why do you think it should?
LORD FOPPINGTON. Because I remember mine did so, when I heard my father was shat through the head.
FASHION. It then did very ill.
LORD FOPPINGTON. Prithee, why so?
FASHION. Because he used you very well.
LORD FOPPINGTON. Well?—naw, strike me dumb! he starved me. He has let me want a thousand women for want of a thousand paund.
FASHION. Then he hindered you from making a great many ill bargains, for I think no woman is worth money that will take money.
LORD FOPPINGTON. If I were a younger brother, I should think so too.
FASHION. Why, is it possible you can value a woman that's to be bought?
LORD FOPPINGTON. Prithee, why not as well as a padnag?[2]
FASHION. Because a woman has a heart to dispose of; a horse has none.
LORD FOPPINGTON. Look you, Tam, of all things that belang to a woman, I have an aversion to her heart. Far when once a woman has given you her heart, you can never get rid of the rest of her bady.
FASHION. This is strange doctrine. But pray in your amours how is it with your own heart?
LORD FOPPINGTON. Why, my heart in my amours—is like—my heart aut of my amours; *à la glace.* My bady, Tam, is a watch; and

---

[1] I.e., rent by the quarter.

[2] A path-nag, an ambling horse such as would tow a barge on a canal; a spiritless animal.

my heart is the pendulum to it; whilst the finger runs raund to every hour in the circle, that still beats the same time.

FASHION. Then you are seldom much in love?

LORD FOPPINGTON. Never, stap my vitals!

FASHION. Why then did you make all this bustle about Amanda?

LORD FOPPINGTON. Because she was a woman of an insolent virtue, and I thought myself piqued in honour to debauch her.

FASHION. Very well.—(*Aside*) Here's a rare fellow for you, to have the spending of five thousand pounds a year! But now for my business with him.—(*To* LORD FOPPINGTON) Brother, though I know to talk to you of business (especially of money) is a theme not quite so entertaining to you as that of the ladies, my necessities are such, I hope you'll have patience to hear me.

LORD FOPPINGTON. The greatness of your necessities, Tam, is the worst argument in the world for your being patiently heard. I do believe you are going to make me a very good speech, but, strike me dumb! it has the worst beginning of any speech I have heard this twelvemonth.

FASHION. I'm very sorry you think so.

LORD FOPPINGTON. I do believe thou art. But come, let's know thy affair quickly; far 'tis a new play, and I shall be so rumpled and squeezed with pressing through the crawd, to get to my servant, the women will think I have lain all night in my clothes.

FASHION. Why, then, (that I may not be the author of so great a misfortune) my case in a word is this. The necessary expenses of my travels have so much exceeded the wretched income of my annuity, that I have been forced to mortgage it for five hundred pounds, which is spent; so that unless you are so kind to assist me in redeeming it, I know no remedy but to go take a purse.

LORD FOPPINGTON. Why, faith, Tam—to give you my sense of the thing, I do think taking a purse the best remedy in the world: for if you succeed, you are relieved that way; if you are taken—you are relieved t'other.

FASHION. I'm glad to see you are in so pleasant a humor. I hope I shall find the effects on't.

LORD FOPPINGTON. Why, do you then really think it a reasonable thing I should give you five hundred paunds?

FASHION. I do not ask it as a due, brother, I am willing to receive it as a favor.

LORD FOPPINGTON. Thau art willing to receive it anyhaw, strike me speechless! But these are damned times to give money in, taxes are so great, repairs so exorbitant, tenants such rogues, and periwigs so dear, that the devil take me, I am reduced to that extremity in my cash. I have been forced to retrench in that one article of sweet pawder, till I have braught it dawn to five guineas a manth. Naw judge, Tam, whether I can spare you five hundred paunds.

FASHION. If you can't, I must starve, that's all.—(*Aside*) Damn him!

LORD FOPPINGTON. All I can say is, you should have been a better husband.[1]

FASHION. Oons, if you can't live upon five thousand a year, how do you think I should do't upon two hundred?

LORD FOPPINGTON. Don't be in a passion, Tam; far passion is the most unbecoming thing in the world—to the face. Look you, I don't love to say anything to you to make you melancholy; but upon this occasion I must take leave to put you in mind that a running horse does require more attendance than a coach-horse. Nature has made some difference 'twixt you and I.

FASHION. Yes, she has made you older.—(*Aside*) Pox take her!

LORD FOPPINGTON. That is nat all, Tam.

FASHION. Why, what is there else?

LORD FOPPINGTON. (*Looking first upon himself, then upon his brother*) Ask the ladies.

FASHION. Why, thou essence bottle! thou musk cat! dost thou then think thou hast any advantage over me but what Fortune has given thee?

LORD FOPPINGTON. I do—stap my vitals!

FASHION. Now, by all that's great and powerful, thou art the prince of coxcombs!

LORD FOPPINGTON. Sir—I am praud of being at the head of so prevailing a party.

FASHION. Will nothing then provoke thee? Draw, coward!

LORD FOPPINGTON. Look you, Tam, you know I have always taken you for a mighty dull fellow, and here is one of the foolishest plats broke out that I have seen a long time. Your paverty makes your life so burdensome to you, you would provoke me to a quarrel,

---

[1] My lord means that he should have husbanded his money, not his wife, as he has had none.

in hopes either to slip through my lungs into my estate, or to get yourself run through the guts, to put an end to your pain. But I will disappoint you in both your designs; far, with the temper of a philasapher, and the discretion of a statesman—I will go to the play with my sword in my scabbard. *Exit*

FASHION. So! Farewell, snuff-box! And now, conscience, I defy thee.—Lory!

Enter LORY

LORY. Sir!

FASHION. Here's rare news, Lory; his lordship has given me a pill has purged off all my scruples.

LORY. Then my heart's at ease again. For I have been in a lamentable fright, sir, ever since your conscience had the impudence to intrude into your company.

FASHION. Be at peace, it will come there no more: my brother has given it a wring by the nose, and I have kicked it down stairs. So run away to the inn; get the horses ready quickly, and bring 'em to old Coupler's, without a moment's delay.

LORY. Then sir, you are going straight about the fortune?

FASHION. I am. Away! fly, Lory!

LORY. The happiest day I ever saw. I'm upon the wing already. *Exeunt several ways*

SCENE [II]—*A Garden*

Enter LOVELESS *and* Servant

LOVELESS. Is my wife within?

SERVANT. No, sir, she has been gone out this half hour.

LOVELESS. 'Tis well, leave me.
Exit Servant

Solus

Sure fate has yet some business to be done,
Before Amanda's heart and mine must rest;
Else, why amongst those legions of her sex,
Which throng the world,
Should she pick out for her companion
The only one on earth
Whom nature has endow'd for her undoing?
Undoing, was't, I said!—who shall undo her?
Is not her empire fix'd? am I not hers?
Did she not rescue me, a grovelling slave,
When chained and bound by that black tyrant vice,
I labored in his vilest drudgery?
Did she not ransom me, and set me free?
Nay, more: when by my follies sunk
To a poor, tattered, despicable beggar,
Did she not lift me up to envied fortune?
Give me herself, and all that she possessed,
Without a thought of more return,
Than what a poor repenting heart might make her?
Han't she done this? And if she has,
Am I not strongly bound to love her for it?
To love her!—Why, do I not love her then?
By earth and heaven I do!
Nay, I have demonstration that I do:
For I would sacrifice my life to serve her.
Yet hold—if laying down my life
Be demonstration of my love,
What is't I feel in favor of Berinthia?
For should she be in danger, methinks I could incline to risk it for her service too; and yet I do not love her. How then subsists my proof?—Oh, I have found it out! What I would do for one, is demonstration of my love; and if I'd do as much for t'other; if there is demonstration of my friendship—Ay, it must be so. I find I'm very much her friend.— Yet let me ask myself one puzzling question more: Whence springs this mighty friendship all at once? For our acquaintance is of later date. Now friendship's said to be a plant of tedious growth; its root composed of tender fibres, nice in their taste, cautious in spreading, checked with the least corruption in the soil; long ere it take, and longer still ere it appear to do so: whilst mine is in a moment shot so high, and fix'd so fast, it seems beyond the power of storms to shake it. I doubt it thrives too fast. (*Musing*)

Enter BERINTHIA

Ha, she here!—Nay, then take heed, my heart, for there are dangers towards.

BERINTHIA. What makes you look so thoughtful, sir? I hope you are not ill.

LOVELESS. I was debating, madam, whether I was so or not; and that was it which made me look so thoughtful.

BERINTHIA. Is it then so hard a matter to decide? I thought all people had been acquainted with their own bodies, though few people know their own minds.

LOVELESS. What if the distemper, I suspect, be in the mind?

BERINTHIA. Why then I'll undertake to prescribe you a cure.

LOVELESS. Alas! you undertake you know not what.

BERINTHIA. So far at least then allow me to be a physician.

LOVELESS. Nay, I'll allow you so yet farther: for I have reason to believe, should I put myself into your hands, you would increase my distemper.

BERINTHIA. Perhaps I might have reasons from the college not to be too quick in your cure; but 'tis possible I might find ways to give you often ease, sir.

LOVELESS. Were I but sure of that, I'd quickly lay my case before you.

BERINTHIA. Whether you are sure of it or no, what risk do you run in trying?

LOVELESS. Oh! a very great one.

BERINTHIA. How?

LOVELESS. You might betray my distemper to my wife.

BERINTHIA. And so lose all my practice.

LOVELESS. Will you then keep my secret?

BERINTHIA. I will, if it don't burst me.

LOVELESS. Swear.

BERINTHIA. I do.

LOVELESS. By what?

BERINTHIA. By woman.

LOVELESS. That's swearing by my deity. Do it by your own, or I shan't believe you.

BERINTHIA. By man, then.

LOVELESS. I'm satisfied. Now hear my symptoms, and give me your advice. The first were these:
When 'twas my chance to see you at the play,
A random glance you threw at first alarmed me,
I could not turn my eyes from whence the
    danger came.
I gazed upon you till you shot again,
And then my fears came on me.
My heart began to pant, my limbs to tremble,
My blood grew thin, my pulse beat quick, my eyes
Grew hot and dim, and all the frame of nature
Shook with apprehension.
'Tis true, some small recruits of resolution
My manhood brought to my assistance;
And by their help I made a stand a while,
But found at last your arrows flew so thick,
They could not fail to pierce me; so left the
    field,
And fled for shelter to Amanda's arms.
What think you of these symptoms, pray?

BERINTHIA. Feverish, every one of 'em. But what relief, pray, did your wife afford you?

LOVELESS. Why, instantly she let me blood; which for the present much assuaged my flame. But when I saw you, out it burst again, and raged with greater fury than before. Nay, since you now appear, 'tis so increased, that in a moment, if you do not help me, I shall, whilst you look on, consume to ashes. (*Taking hold of her hand*)

BERINTHIA. (*Breaking from him*) O Lard, let me go! 'Tis the plague, and we shall all be infected.

LOVELESS. (*Catching her in his arms, and kissing her*) Then we'll die together, my charming angel!

BERINTHIA. O Ged—the devil's in you!—Lord, let me go, here's somebody coming.

Enter Servant

SERVANT. Sir, my lady's come home, and desires to speak with you. She's in her chamber.

LOVELESS. Tell her I'm coming.—(*Exit* Servant. *To* BERINTHIA) But before I go, one glass of nectar more to drink her health.

BERINTHIA. Stand off, or I shall hate you, by heavens!

LOVELESS. (*Kissing her*) In matters of love, a woman's oath is no more to be minded than a man's.

BERINTHIA. Um—

Enter WORTHY

WORTHY. (*Aside*) Ha! what's here? My old mistress, and so close, i' faith! I would not spoil her sport for the universe.

(*He retires*)

BERINTHIA. O Ged!—Now do I pray to heaven,—(*Exit* LOVELESS *running*) with all my heart and soul, that the devil in hell may take me, if ever—I was better pleased in my life!—This man has bewitched me, that's certain.—(*Sighing*) Well, I am condemned; but, thanks to heaven, I feel myself each moment more and more prepared for my execution. Nay, to that degree, I don't perceive I have the least fear of dying. No, I find, let the executioner be but a man, and there's nothing will suffer with more resolution than a woman. Well, I never had but one intrigue yet—but I confess I long to have another. Pray heaven it end as the first did though, that we may both grow weary at a time; for 'tis a melancholy thing for lovers to outlive one another.

Enter WORTHY

WORTHY. (*Aside*) This discovery's a lucky one, I hope to make a happy use on't. That gentlewoman there is no fool; so I shall be able to make her understand her interest.— (*To* BERINTHIA) Your servant, madam; I need not ask you how you do, you have got so good a color.

BERINTHIA. No better than I used to have, I suppose.

WORTHY. A little more blood in your cheeks.

BERINTHIA. The weather's hot.

WORTHY. If it were not, a woman may have a color.

BERINTHIA. What do you mean by that?

WORTHY. Nothing.

BERINTHIA. Why do you smile then?

WORTHY. Because the weather's hot.

BERINTHIA. You'll never leave roguing, I see that.

WORTHY. (*Putting his finger to his nose*) You'll never leave—I see that.

BERINTHIA. Well, I can't imagine what you drive at. Pray tell me what you mean?

WORTHY. Do you tell me; it's the same thing.

BERINTHIA. I can't.

WORTHY. Guess!

BERINTHIA. I shall guess wrong.

WORTHY. Indeed you won't.

BERINTHIA. Psha! either tell, or let it alone.

WORTHY. Nay, rather than let it alone, I will tell. But first I must put you in mind, that after what has passed 'twixt you and I, very few things ought to be secrets between us.

BERINTHIA. Why, what secrets do we hide? I know of none.

WORTHY. Yes, there are two; one I have hid from you, and t'other you would hide from me. You are fond of Loveless, which I have discovered; and I am fond of his wife—

BERINTHIA. Which I have discovered.

WORTHY. Very well, now I confess your discovery to be true: what do you say to mine?

BERINTHIA. Why, I confess—I would swear 'twere false, if I thought you were fool enough to believe me.

WORTHY. Now I am almost in love with you again. Nay, I don't know but I might be quite so, had I made one short campaign with Amanda. Therefore, if you find 'twould tickle your vanity to bring me down once more to your lure, e'en help me quickly to dispatch her business, that I may have nothing else to do, but to apply myself to yours.

BERINTHIA. Do you then think, sir, I am old enough to be a bawd?

WORTHY. No, but I think you are wise enough to—

BERINTHIA. To do what?

WORTHY. To hoodwink Amanda with a gallant, that she mayn't see who is her husband's mistress.

BERINTHIA. (*Aside*) He has reason.—The hint's a good one.

WORTHY. Well, madam, what think you on't?

BERINTHIA. I think you are so much a deeper politician in these affairs than I am that I ought to have a very great regard to your advice.

WORTHY. Then give me leave to put you in mind, that the most easy, safe, and pleasant situation for your own amour, is the house in which you now are; provided you keep Amanda from any sort of suspicion. That the way to do that, is to engage her in an intrigue of her own, making yourself her confidante. And the way to bring her to intrigue, is to make her jealous of her husband in a wrong place; which the more you foment, the less you'll be suspected. This is my scheme, in short; which if you follow as you should do, my dear Berinthia, we may all four pass the winter very pleasantly.

BERINTHIA. Well, I could be glad to have nobody's sins to answer for but my own. But where there is a necessity—

WORTHY. Right; as you say, where there is a necessity, a Christian is bound to help his neighbor. So, good Berinthia, lose no time, but let us begin the dance as fast as we can.

BERINTHIA. Not till the fiddles are in tune, pray, sir. Your lady's strings will be very apt to fly, I can tell you that, if they are wound up too hastily. But if you'll have patience to screw 'em to their pitch by degrees, I don't doubt but she may endure to be played upon.

WORTHY. Ay, and will make admirable music too, or I'm mistaken. But have you had no private closet discourse with her yet about males and females, and so forth, which may give you hopes in her constitution, for I know her morals are the devil against us?

BERINTHIA. I have had so much discourse

with her, that I believe, were she once cured of her fondness to her husband, the fortress of her virtue would not be so impregnable as she fancies.

WORTHY. What! she runs, I'll warrant you, into that common mistake of fond wives, who conclude themselves virtuous, because they can refuse a man they don't like, when they have got one they do.

BERINTHIA. True; and therefore I think 'tis a presumptuous thing in a woman to assume the name of virtuous, till she has heartily hated her husband, and been soundly in love with somebody else. Whom, if she has withstood,—then—much good may it do her.

WORTHY. Well, so much for her virtue. Now, one word of her inclinations, and every one to their post. What opinion do you find she has of me?

BERINTHIA. What you could wish; she thinks you handsome and discreet.

WORTHY. Good; that's thinking half-seas over. One tide more brings us into port.

BERINTHIA. Perhaps it may, though still remember, there's a difficult bar to pass.

WORTHY. I know there is, but I don't question I shall get well over it, by the help of such a pilot.

BERINTHIA. You may depend upon your pilot, she'll do the best she can; so weigh anchor and begone as soon as you please.

WORTHY. I'm under sail already. Adieu!

BERINTHIA. *Bon voyage!*—(*Exit* WORTHY. [BERINTHIA] *Sola*) So, here's fine work! What a business have I undertaken! I'm a very pretty gentlewoman truly! But there was no avoiding it; he'd have ruined me, if I had refused him. Besides, faith, I begin to fancy there may be as much pleasure in carrying on another body's intrigue as one's own. This at least is certain, it exercises almost all the entertaining faculties of a woman; for there's employment for hypocrisy, invention, deceit, flattery, mischief, and lying.

Enter AMANDA, *her* Woman *following her*

WOMAN. If you please, madam, only to say, whether you'll have me buy 'em or not.

AMANDA. Yes, no, go fiddle! I care not what you do. Prithee leave me.

WOMAN. I have done. *Exit*

BERINTHIA. What in the name of Jove's the matter with you?

AMANDA. The matter, Berinthia! I'm almost mad, I'm plagued to death.

BERINTHIA. Who is it that plagues you?

AMANDA. Who do you think should plague a wife, but her husband?

BERINTHIA. O ho, is it come to that? We shall have you wish yourself a widow by and by.

AMANDA. Would I were anything but what I am! A base, ungrateful man, after what I have done for him, to use me thus!

BERINTHIA. What, he has been ogling now, I'll warrant you!

AMANDA. Yes, he has been ogling.

BERINTHIA. And so you are jealous? Is that all?

AMANDA. That all! Is jealousy then nothing?

BERINTHIA. It should be nothing, if I were in your case.

AMANDA. Why, what would you do?

BERINTHIA. I'd cure myself.

AMANDA. How?

BERINTHIA. Let blood in the fond vein: care as little for my husband as he did for me.

AMANDA. That would not stop his course.

BERINTHIA. Nor nothing else, when the wind's in the warm corner. Look you, Amanda, you may build castles in the air, and fume, and fret, and grow thin and lean, and pale and ugly, if you please. But I tell you, no man worth having is true to his wife, or ever was, or ever will be so.

AMANDA. Do you then really think he's false to me? For I did but suspect him.

BERINTHIA. Think so! I know he's so.

AMANDA. Is it possible? Pray tell me what you know.

BERINTHIA. Don't press me then to name names, for that I have sworn I won't do.

AMANDA. Well, I won't; but let me know all you can without perjury.

BERINTHIA. I'll let you know enough to prevent any wise woman's dying of the pip; and I hope you'll pluck up your spirits, and show upon occasion you can be as good a wife as the best of 'em.

AMANDA. Well, what a woman can do I'll endeavor.

BERINTHIA. Oh, a woman can do a great deal, if once she sets her mind to it. Therefore pray don't stand trifling any longer, and teasing yourself with this and that, and your love and your virtue, and I know not what:

but resolve to hold up your head, get a-tiptoe, and look over 'em all; for to my certain knowledge your husband is a pickeering elsewhere.

AMANDA. You are sure on't?

BERINTHIA. Positively; he fell in love at the play.

AMANDA. Right, the very same. Do you know the ugly thing?

BERINTHIA. Yes, I know her well enough; but she's not such an ugly thing neither.

AMANDA. Is she very handsome?

BERINTHIA. Truly I think so.

AMANDA. Hey ho!

BERINTHIA. What do you sigh for now?

AMANDA. Oh, my heart!

BERINTHIA. (*Aside*) Only the pangs of nature; she's in labor of her love; heaven send her a quick delivery, I'm sure she has a good midwife.

AMANDA. I'm very ill, I must go to my chamber. Dear Berinthia, don't leave me a moment.

BERINTHIA. No, don't fear.—(*Aside*) I'll see you safe brought to bed, I'll warrant you.

Exeunt, AMANDA *leaning upon* BERINTHIA

SCENE [III]—*A Country House*

Enter YOUNG FASHION *and* LORY

FASHION. So, here's our inheritance, Lory, if we can but get into possession. But methinks the seat of our family looks like Noah's ark, as if the chief part on't were designed for the fowls of the air, and the beasts of the field.

LORY. Pray, sir, don't let your head run upon the orders of building here; get but the heiress, let the devil take the house.

FASHION. Get but the house, let the devil take the heiress, I say; as least if she be as old Coupler describes her. But come, we have no time to squander. Knock at the door.— (LORY *knocks two or three times*) What the devil, have they got no ears in this house? Knock harder.

LORY. Egad, sir, this will prove some enchanted castle; we shall have the giant come out by and by with his club, and beat our brains out. (*Knocks again*)

FASHION. Hush! they come.

[SERVANT.] (*From within*) Who is there?

LORY. Open the door and see. Is that your country breeding?

SERVANT. Ay, but two words to a bargain.— Tummas, is the blunderbuss primed?

FASHION. Oons, give 'em good words, Lory; we shall be shot here a fortune-catching.

LORY. Egad, sir, I think y'are in the right on't.—Ho! Mr. What-d'ye-call-um. (Servant *appears at the window with a blunderbuss*)

SERVANT. Weall, naw what's yare business?

FASHION. Nothing, sir, but to wait upon Sir Tunbelly, with your leave.

SERVANT. To weat upon Sir Tunbelly! Why, you'll find that's just as Sir Tunbelly pleases.

FASHION. But will you do me the favor, sir, to know whether Sir Tunbelly pleases or not?

SERVANT. Why, look you, do you see, with good words much may be done.—Ralph, go thy weas, and ask Sir Tunbelly if he pleases to be waited upon. And dost hear? Call to nurse that she may lock up Miss Hoyden before the geat's open.

FASHION. D'ye hear that, Lory?

LORY. Ay, sir, I'm afraid we shall find a difficult job on't. Pray Heaven that old rogue Coupler han't sent us to fetch milk out of the gunroom.

FASHION. I'll warrant thee all will go well. See, the door opens.

Enter SIR TUNBELLY, *with his* Servants *armed with guns, clubs, pitchforks, scythes,* &c.

LORY. (*Running behind his master*) O Lord! O Lord! O Lord! We are both dead men!

FASHION. Take heed, fool! Thy fear will ruin us.

LORY. My fear, sir! 'Sdeath, sir, I fear nothing.—(*Aside*) Would I were well up to the chin in a horsepond!

SIR TUNBELLY. Who is it here has any business with me?

FASHION. Sir, 'tis I, if your name be Sir Tunbelly Clumsey.

SIR TUNBELLY. Sir, my name is Sir Tunbelly Clumsey, whether you have any business with me or not. So you see I am not ashamed of my name—nor my face neither.

FASHION. Sir, you have no cause, that I know of.

SIR TUNBELLY. Sir, if you have no cause neither, I desire to know who you are; for till I know your name, I shall not ask you to come into my house; and when I know your name—'tis six to four I don't ask you neither.

FASHION. (*Giving him a letter*) Sir, I hope you'll find this letter an authentic passport.

SIR TUNBELLY. Cod's my life! I ask your lordship's pardon ten thousand times.—(*To a* Servant) Here, run in a-doors quickly. Get a Scotch-coal fire in the great parlor; set all the Turkey-work chairs in their places; get the great brass candlesticks out, and be sure stick the sockets full of laurel, run!—(*Turning to* YOUNG FASHION) My lord, I ask your lordship's pardon.—(*To other* Servants) And do you hear, run away to nurse, bid her let Miss Hoyden loose again, and if it was not shifting day, let her put on a clean tucker, quick!—(*Exeunt* Servants *confusedly. To* YOUNG FASHION) I hope your honor will excuse the disorder of my family; we are not used to receive men of your lordship's great quality every day. Pray where are your coaches and servants, my lord?

FASHION. Sir, that I might give you and your fair daughter a proof how impatient I am to be nearer akin to you, I left my equipage to follow me, and came away post with only one servant.

SIR TUNBELLY. Your lordship does me too much honor. It was exposing your person to too much fatigue and danger, I protest it was. But my daughter shall endeavor to make you what amends she can; and though I say it that should not say it—Hoyden has charms.

FASHION. Sir, I am not a stranger to them, though I am to her. Common fame has done her justice.

SIR TUNBELLY. My lord, I am common fame's very grateful humble servant. My lord—my girl's young, Hoyden is young, my lord; but this I must say for her, what she wants in art, she has by nature; what she wants in experience, she has in breeding; and what's wanting in her age, is made good in her constitution. So pray, my lord, walk in: pray, my lord, walk in.

FASHION. Sir, I wait upon you. *Exeunt*

[SCENE IV—*A Room in the same*]

MISS HOYDEN *sola*

HOYDEN. Sure, never nobody was used as I am. I know well enough what other girls do, for all they think to make a fool of me. It's well I have a husband coming, or, ecod, I'd marry the baker, I would so! Nobody an knock at the gate, but presently I must be locked up; and here's the young greyhound bitch can run loose about the house all day long, she can; 'tis very well.

NURSE. (*Without; opening the door*) Miss Hoyden! miss! miss! miss! Miss Hoyden!

Enter Nurse

HOYDEN. Well, what do you make such a noise for, ha? what do you din a body's ears for? Can't one be at quiet for you?

NURSE. What do I din your ears for! Here's one come will din your ears for you.

HOYDEN. What care I who's come? I care not a fig who comes, nor who goes, as long as I must be locked up like the ale-cellar.

NURSE. That, miss, is for fear you should be drank before you are ripe.

HOYDEN. Oh, don't trouble your head about that; I'm as ripe as you, though not so mellow.

NURSE. Very well; now have I a good mind to lock you up again, and not let you see my lord to-night.

HOYDEN. My lord! Why, is my husband come?

NURSE. Yes, marry he is, and a goodly person, too.

HOYDEN. (*Hugging* Nurse) O my dear nurse! forgive me this once, and I'll never misuse you again; no, if I do, you shall give me three thumps on the back, and a great pinch by the cheek.

NURSE. Ah, the poor thing, see how it melts. It's as full of good-nature as an egg's full of meat.

HOYDEN. But, my dear nurse, don't lie now; is he come by your troth?

NURSE. Yes, by my truly, is he.

HOYDEN. O Lord! I'll go put on my laced smock, though I'm whipped till the blood run down my heels for't. *Exit running*

NURSE. Eh—the Lord succor thee! How thou art delighted. *Exit after her*

[SCENE V—*Another Room in the same*]

Enter SIR TUNBELLY *and* YOUNG FASHION.

A Servant *with wine*

SIR TUNBELLY. My lord, I am proud of the honor to see your lordship within my doors; and I humbly crave leave to bid you welcome in a cup of sack wine.

FASHION. Sir, to your daughter's health.
(*Drinks*)

Sir Tunbelly. Ah, poor girl, she'll be scared out of her wits on her wedding-night; for, honestly speaking, she does not know a man from a woman but by his beard and his breeches.

Fashion. Sir, I don't doubt but she has a virtuous education, which with the rest of her merit makes me long to see her mine; I wish you would dispense with the canonical hour, and let it be this very night.

Sir Tunbelly. Oh, not so soon neither! that's shooting my girl before you bid her stand. No, give her fair warning, we'll sign and seal to-night, if you please; and this day sevennight—let the jade look to her quarters.

Fashion. This day se'nnight!—why, what, do you take me for a ghost, sir? 'Slife, sir, I'm made of flesh and blood, and bones and sinews, and can no more live a week without your daughter—(Aside) than I can live a month with her.

Sir Tunbelly. Oh, I'll warrant you, my hero; young men are hot, I know, but they don't boil over at that rate, neither. Besides, my wench's wedding-gown is not come home yet.

Fashion. Oh, no matter, sir, I'll take her in her shift.—(Aside) A pox of this old fellow! he'll delay the business till my damned star[1] finds me out and discovers me.—(To Sir Tunbelly) Pray, sir, let it be done without ceremony, 'twill save money.

Sir Tunbelly. Money!—Save money when Hoyden's to be married! Udswoons, I'll give my wench a wedding-dinner, though I go to grass with the King of Assyria[2] for't; and such a dinner it shall be, as is not to be cooked in the poaching of an egg. Therefore, my noble lord, have a little patience, we'll go an look over our deeds and settlements immediately; and as for your bride, though you may be sharp-set before she's quite ready, I'll engage for my girl, she stays your stomach at last. *Exeunt*

ACT IV

Scene I. [*A Room in* Sir Tunbelly Clumsey's *Country House*]

Enter Miss Hoyden *and* Nurse

Nurse. Well, miss, how do you like your husband that is to be?

[1] Unlucky star.
[2] Nebuchadnezzar, King of Babylon, ate grass, though not, as Sir Tunbelly implies, from poverty.

Hoyden. O Lord, nurse! I'm so overjoyed I can scarce contain myself.

Nurse. Oh, but you must have a care of being too fond; for men now-a-days hate a woman that loves 'em.

Hoyden. Love him! why, do you think I love him, nurse? Ecod, I would not care if he were hanged, so I were but once married to him!—No—that which pleases me, is to think what work I'll make when I get to London; for when I am a wife and a lady both, nurse, ecod, I'll flaunt it with the best of 'em.

Nurse. Look, look, if his honor be not coming again to you. Now, if I were sure you would behave yourself handsomely, and not disgrace me that have brought you up, I'd leave you alone together.

Hoyden. That's my best nurse, do as you would be done by; trust us together this once, and if I don't show my breeding from the head to the foot of me, may I be twice married, and die a maid.

Nurse. Well, this once I'll venture you; but if you disparage me—

Hoyden. Never fear, I'll show him my parts, I'll warrant him.—(*Exit* Nurse. *Sola*) These old women are so wise when they get a poor girl in their clutches! but ere it be long, I shall know what's what, as well as the best of 'em.

Enter Young Fashion

Fashion. Your servant, madam; I'm glad to find you alone, for I have something of importance to speak to you about.

Hoyden. Sir (my lord, I meant), you may speak to me about what you please, I shall give you a civil answer.

Fashion. You give me so obliging a one, it encourages me to tell you in few words what I think both for your interest and mine. Your father, I suppose you know, has resolved to make me happy in being your husband, and I hope I may depend upon your consent, to perform what he desires.

Hoyden. Sir, I never disobey my father in anything but eating of green gooseberries.

Fashion. So good a daughter must needs make an admirable wife; I am therefore impatient till you are mine, and hope you will so far consider the violence of my love, that you won't have the cruelty to defer my happiness so long as your father designs it.

Hoyden. Pray, my lord, how long is that?

FASHION. Madam, a thousand year—a whole week.

HOYDEN. A week!—Why, I shall be an old woman by that time.

FASHION. And I an old man, which you'll find a greater misfortune than t'other.

HOYDEN. Why, I thought 'twas to be to-morrow morning, as soon as I was up; I'm sure nurse told me so.

FASHION. And it shall be to-morrow morning still, if you'll consent.

HOYDEN. If I'll consent! Why, I thought I was to obey you as my husband.

FASHION. That's when we are married; till then, I am to obey you.

HOYDEN. Why then, if we are to take it by turns, it's the same thing. I'll obey you now; and when we are married, you shall obey me.

FASHION. With all my heart; but I doubt we must get nurse on our side, or we shall hardly prevail with the chaplain.

HOYDEN. No more we shan't indeed, for he loves her better than he loves his pulpit, and would always be a preaching to her by his good will.

FASHION. Why then, my dear little bed-fellow, if you'll call her hither, we'll try to persuade her presently.

HOYDEN. O Lord, I can tell you a way how to persuade her to anything.

FASHION. How's that?

HOYDEN. Why, tell her she's a wholesome comely woman—and give her half-a-crown.

FASHION. Nay, if that will do, she shall have half a score of 'em.

HOYDEN. O gemini! for half that, she'd marry you herself. I'll run and call her. *Exit*

FASHION. (*Solus*) So, matters go swimmingly. This is a rare girl, i' faith; I shall have a fine time on't with her in London. I'm much mistaken if she don't prove a March hare all the year round. What a scampering chase will she make on't, when she finds the whole kennel of beaux at her tail! Hey to the park, and the play, and the church, and the devil; she'll show 'em sport, I'll warrant 'em. But no matter, she brings an estate will afford me a separate maintenance.

Enter MISS HOYDEN *and* NURSE

How do you do, good mistress nurse? I desired your young lady would give me leave to see you, that I might thank you for your extraordinary care and conduct in her education; pray accept of this small acknowledgment for it at present, and depend upon my farther kindness, when I shall be that happy thing her husband.

NURSE. (*Aside*) Gold, by makings!—[*Aloud*] Your honor's goodness is too great; alas! all I can boast of is, I gave her pure good milk, and so your honor would have said, an you had seen how the poor thing sucked it.—Eh, God's blessing on the sweet face on't! how it used to hang at this poor teat, and suck and squeeze, and kick and sprawl it would, till the belly on't was so full, it would drop off like a leech.

HOYDEN. (*To* Nurse, *taking her angrily aside*) Pray one word with you. Prithee nurse, don't stand ripping up old stories, to make one ashamed before one's love. Do you think such a fine proper gentleman as he cares for a fiddlecome tale of a draggle-tailed girl? If you have a mind to make him have a good opinion of a woman, don't tell him what one did then, tell him what one can do now.—(*To* YOUNG FASHION) I hope your honor will excuse my mismanners to whisper before you; it was only to give some orders about the family.

FASHION. O everything, madam, is to give way to business! Besides, good housewifery is a very commendable quality in a young lady.

HOYDEN. Pray, sir, are the young ladies good housewives at London town? Do they darn their own linen?

FASHION. O no, they study how to spend money, not to save it.

HOYDEN. Ecod, I don't know but that may be better sport than t'other; ha, nurse?

FASHION. Well, you shall have your choice when you come there.

HOYDEN. Shall I?—then by my troth I'll get there as fast as I can.—(*To* NURSE) His honor desires you'll be so kind as to let us be married to-morrow.

NURSE. To-morrow, my dear madam?

FASHION. Yes, to-morrow, sweet nurse, privately; young folks, you know, are impatient, and Sir Tunbelly would make us stay a week for a wedding dinner. Now all things being signed and sealed and agreed, I fancy there could be no great harm in practising a scene or two of matrimony in private, if it were only to give us the better assurance when we come to play it in public.

NURSE. Nay, I must confess stolen pleasures

are sweet; but if you should be married now, what will you do when Sir Tunbelly calls for you to be wed?

HOYDEN. Why then we'll be married again.

NURSE. What, twice, my child?

HOYDEN. Ecod, I don't care how often I'm married, not I.

FASHION. Pray, nurse, don't you be against your young lady's good, for by this means she'll have the pleasure of two wedding-days.

HOYDEN. (*To* Nurse *softly*) And of two wedding-nights, too, nurse.

NURSE. Well, I'm such a tender-hearted fool, I find I can refuse nothing; so you shall e'en follow your own inventions.

HOYDEN. Shall I?—(*Aside*) O Lord, I could leap over the moon!

FASHION. Dear nurse, this goodness of yours shan't go unrewarded; but now you must employ your power with Mr. Bull the chaplain, that he may do us his friendly office too, and then we shall all be happy. Do you think you can prevail with him?

NURSE. Prevail with him!—or he shall never prevail with me, I can tell him that.

HOYDEN. My lord, she has had him upon the hip this seven year.

FASHION. I'm glad to hear it; however, to strengthen your interest with him, you may let him know I have several fat livings in my gift, and that the first that falls shall be in your disposal.

NURSE. Nay, than I'll make him marry more folks than one, I'll promise him.

HOYDEN. Faith do, nurse, make him marry you too, I'm sure he'll do't for a fat living: for he loves eating more than he loves his Bible; and I have often heard him say, a fat living was the best meat in the world.

NURSE. Ay, and I'll make him commend the sauce, too, or I'll bring his gown to a cassock[1] I will so.

FASHION. Well, nurse, whilst you go and settle matters with him, then your lady and I will go take a walk in the garden.

NURSE. I'll do your honor's business in the catching up of a garter. *Exit*

FASHION. (*Giving her his hand*) Come, madam, dare you venture yourself alone with me?

HOYDEN. O dear, yes, sir, I don't think you'll do anything to me I need be afraid on.

Exeunt

[1] Make him live single like a Roman Catholic priest.

[SCENE II. LOVELESS'S *Lodgings*]

Enter AMANDA *and* BERINTHIA

A SONG

I

I smile at Love and all its arts,
  The charming Cynthia cried:
Take heed, for Love has piercing darts,
  A wounded swain replied.
Once free and blest as you are now,
  I trifled with his charms,
I pointed at his little bow,
  And sported with his arms:
Till urged too far, Revenge! he cries,
  A fatal shaft he drew,
It took its passage through your eyes,
  And to my heart it flew.

II

To tear it thence I tried in vain,
  To strive, I quickly found,
Was only to increase the pain,
  And to enlarge the wound.
Ah! much too well, I fear, you know
  What pain I'm to endure,
Since what your eyes alone could do,
  Your heart alone can cure.
And that (grant heaven I may mistake!)
  I doubt is doomed to bear
A burden for another's sake,
  Who ill rewards its care.

AMANDA. Well, now, Berinthia, I'm at leisure to hear what 'twas you had to say to me.

BERINTHIA. What I had to say was only to echo the sighs and groans of a dying lover.

AMANDA. Phu! will you never learn to talk in earnest of anything?

BERINTHIA. Why this shall be in earnest, if you please. For my part, I only tell you matter of fact, you may take it which way you like best; but if you'll follow the women of the town, you'll take it both ways; for when a man offers himself to one of them, first she takes him in jest, and then she takes him in earnest.

AMANDA. I'm sure there's so much jest and earnest in what you say to me, I scarce know how to take it; but I think you have bewitched me, for I don't find it possible to be angry with you, say what you will.

BERINTHIA. I'm very glad to hear it, for I have no mind to quarrel with you, for more reasons than I'll brag of; but quarrel or not, smile or frown, I must tell you what I have suffered upon your account.

AMANDA. Upon my account!

BERINTHIA. Yes, upon yours; I have been forced to sit still and hear you commended for two hours together, without one compliment to myself; now don't you think a woman had a blessed time of that?

AMANDA. Alas! I should have been unconcerned at it; I never knew where the pleasure lay of being praised by the men. But pray who was this that commended me so?

BERINTHIA. One you have a mortal aversion to, Mr. Worthy; he used you like a text, he took you all to pieces, but spoke so learnedly upon every point, one might see the spirit of the church was in him. If you are a woman, you'd have been in an ecstasy to have heard how feelingly he handled your hair, your eyes, your nose, your mouth, your teeth, your tongue, your chin, your neck, and so forth. Thus he preached for an hour, but when he came to use an application, he observed that all these without a gallant were nothing.—Now consider of what has been said, and heaven give you grace to put it in practice.

AMANDA. Alas! Berinthia, did I incline to a gallant (which you know I do not), do you think a man so nice as he could have the least concern for such a plain unpolished thing as I am? It is impossible!

BERINTHIA. Now have you a great mind to put me upon commending you.

AMANDA. Indeed that was not my design.

BERINTHIA. Nay, if it were, it's all one, for I won't do't, I'll leave that to your looking-glass. But to show you I have some good nature left, I'll commend him, and may be that may do as well.

AMANDA. You have a great mind to persuade me I am in love with him.

BERINTHIA. I have a great mind to persuade you, you don't know what you are in love with.

AMANDA. I am sure I am not in love with him, nor never shall be, so let that pass. But you were saying something you would commend him for.

BERINTHIA. Oh! you'd be glad to hear a good character of him, however.

AMANDA. Psha!

BERINTHIA. Psha!—Well, 'tis a foolish undertaking for women in these kind of matters to pretend to deceive one another.—Have not I been bred a woman as well as you?

AMANDA. What then?

BERINTHIA. Why, then I understand my trade so well, that whenever I am told of a man I like, I cry, Psha! But that I may spare you the pains of putting me a second time in mind to commend him, I'll proceed, and give you this account of him. That though 'tis possible he may have had women with as good faces as your ladyship's, (no discredit to it neither), yet you must know your cautious behavior, with that reserve in your humor, has given him his death's wound; he mortally hates a coquette. He says 'tis impossible to love where we cannot esteem; and that no woman can be esteemed by a man who has sense, if she makes herself cheap in the eye of a fool; that pride to a woman is as necessary as humility to a divine; and that far-fetched and dear-bought, is meat for gentlemen as well as for ladies;—in short, that every woman who has beauty may set a price upon herself, and that by under-selling the market, they ruin the trade. This is his doctrine, how do you like it?

AMANDA. So well, that since I never intend to have a gallant for myself, if I were to recommend one to a friend, he should be the man.

Enter WORTHY

Bless me! he's here, pray heaven he did not hear me.

BERINTHIA. If he did, it won't hurt your reputation; your thoughts are as safe in his heart as in your own.

WORTHY. I venture in at an unseasonable time of night, ladies; I hope, if I'm troublesome, you'll use the same freedom in turning me out again.

AMANDA. I believe it can't be late, for Mr. Loveless is not come home yet, and he usually keeps good hours.

WORTHY. Madam, I'm afraid he'll transgress a little to-night; for he told me about half an hour ago, he was going to sup with some company he doubted would keep him out till three or four o'clock in the morning, and desired I would let my servant acquaint you with it, that you might not expect him but my fellow's a blunderhead; so lest he should make some mistake, I thought it my duty to deliver the message myself.

AMANDA. I'm very sorry he should give you that trouble, sir: but—

BERINTHIA. But since he has, will you give me leave, madam, to keep him to play at ombre with us?

AMANDA. Cousin, you know you command my house.

WORTHY. (*To* BERINTHIA) And, madam, you know you command me, though I'm a very wretched gamester.

BERINTHIA. Oh! you play well enough to lose your money, and that's all the ladies require; so without any more ceremony, let us go into the next room and call for the cards.

AMANDA. With all my heart.

Exit WORTHY, *leading* AMANDA

BERINTHIA. (*Sola*) Well, how this business will end heaven knows; but she seems to me to be in as fair a way—as a boy is to be a rogue, when he's put clerk to an attorney.

Exit

SCENE [III]. BERINTHIA'S *Chamber*

Enter LOVELESS *cautiously in the dark*

LOVELESS. So, thus far all's well. I'm got into her bed-chamber, and I think nobody has perceived me steal into the house; my wife don't expect me home till four o'clock; so, if Berinthia comes to bed by eleven, I shall have a chase of five hours. Let me see, where shall I hide myself? Under her bed? No; we shall have her maid searching there for something or other; her closet's a better place, and I have a master-key will open it. I'll e'en in there, and attack her just when she comes to her prayers; that's the most likely to prove her critical minute, for then the devil will be there to assist me.

(*He opens the closet, goes in, and shuts the door after him*)

Enter BERINTHIA, *with a candle in her hand*

BERINTHIA. Well, sure I am the best-natured woman in the world, I that love cards so well (there is but one thing upon earth I love better), have pretended letters to write, to give my friends a *tête-à-tête*. However, I'm innocent, for picquet is the game I set 'em to; at her own peril be it, if she ventures to play with him at any other. But now what shall I do with myself? I don't know how in the world to pass my time; would Loveless were here to *badiner* a little! Well, he's a charming fellow; I don't wonder his wife's so fond of him. What if I should sit down and think of him till I fall asleep, and dream of the Lord knows what? Oh, but then if I should dream we were married, I should be frightened out of my wits!—(*Seeing a book*) What's this book? I think I had best go read. O splenetic! it's a sermon. Well, I'll go into my closet, and read the *Plotting Sisters*.—(*She opens the closet, sees* LOVELESS, *and shrieks out*) O Lord, a ghost! a ghost! a ghost! a ghost!

Enter LOVELESS, *running to her*

LOVELESS. Peace, my dear, it's no ghost; take it in your arms, you'll find 'tis worth a hundred of 'em.

BERINTHIA. Run in again; here's somebody coming.   (LOVELESS *retires as before*)

Enter Maid

MAID. O Lord, madam! what's the matter?

BERINTHIA. O Heavens! I'm almost frightened out of my wits; I thought verily I had seen a ghost, and 'twas nothing but the white curtain, with a black hood pinned up against it: you may begone again; I am the fearfullest fool!   *Exit* Maid

Re-enter LOVELESS

LOVELESS. Is the coast clear?

BERINTHIA. The coast clear! I suppose you are clear,[1] you'd never play such a trick as this else.

LOVELESS. I'm very well pleased with my trick thus far, and shall be so till I have played it out, if it ben't your fault. Where's my wife?

BERINTHIA. At cards.

LOVELESS. With whom?

BERINTHIA. With Worthy.

LOVELESS. Then we are safe enough.

BERINTHIA. Are you so? Some husbands would be of another mind, if he were at cards with their wives.

LOVELESS. And they'd be in the right on't, too: but I dare trust mine.—Besides, I know he's in love in another place, and he's not one of those who court half-a-dozen at a time.

BERINTHIA. Nay, the truth on't is, you'd pity him if you saw how uneasy he is at being engaged with us; but 'twas my malice, I fancied he was to meet his mistress somewhere else, so did it to have the pleasure of seeing him fret.

[1] Drunk.

LOVELESS. What says Amanda to my staying abroad so late?

BERINTHIA. Why, she's as much out of humor as he; I believe they wish one another at the devil.

LOVELESS. Then I'm afraid they'll quarrel at play, and soon throw up the cards.—(*Offering to pull her into the closet*) Therefore, my dear, charming angel, let us make a good use of our time.

BERINTHIA. Heavens! what do you mean?

LOVELESS. Pray what do you think I mean?

BERINTHIA. I don't know.

LOVELESS. I'll show you.

BERINTHIA. You may as well tell me.

LOVELESS. No, that would make you blush worse than t'other.

BERINTHIA. Why, do you intend to make me blush?

LOVELESS. Faith I can't tell that; but if I do, it shall be in the dark. (*Pulling her*)

BERINTHIA. O heavens! I would not be in the dark with you for all the world.

LOVELESS. I'll try that.
(*Puts out the candles*)

BERINTHIA. O Lord! are you mad? What shall I do for light?

LOVELESS. You'll do as well without it.

BERINTHIA. Why, one can't find a chair to sit down.

LOVELESS. Come into the closet, madam, there's moonshine upon the couch.

BERINTHIA. Nay, never pull, for I will not go.

LOVELESS. Then you must be carried.
(*Carrying her*)

BERINTHIA. (*Very softly*) Help! help! I'm ravished! ruined! undone! O Lord, I shall never be able to bear it.

Exit LOVELESS *carrying* BERINTHIA

SCENE [IV]. SIR TUNBELLY'S *House*

Enter MISS HOYDEN, Nurse, YOUNG FASHION, *and* BULL

FASHION. This quick dispatch of yours, Mr. Bull, I take so kindly, it shall give you a claim to my favor as long as I live, I do assure you.

HOYDEN. And to mine, too, I promise you.

BULL. I most humbly thank your honors; and I hope, since it has been my lot to join you in the holy bands of wedlock, you will so well cultivate the soil, which I have craved a blessing on, that your children may swarm about you like bees about a honeycomb.

HOYDEN. Ecod, with all my heart; the more the merrier, I say; ha, nurse?

Enter LORY; *he takes his master hastily aside*

LORY. One word with you, for heaven's sake.

FASHION. What the devil's the matter?

LORY. Sir, your fortune's ruined; and I don't think your life's worth a quarter of an hour's purchase. Yonder's your brother arrived with two coaches and six horses, twenty footmen and pages, a coat worth four-score pound, and periwig down to his knees: so judge what will become of your lady's heart.

FASHION. Death and furies! 'tis impossible!

LORY. Fiends and specters! sir, 'tis true.

FASHION. Is he in the house yet?

LORY. No, they are capitulating with him at the gate. The porter tells him he's come to run away with Miss Hoyden, and has cocked the blunderbuss at him; your brother swears Gad damme, they are a parcel of clawns, and he has a good mind to break off the match; but they have given the word for Sir Tunbelly, so I doubt all will come out presently. Pray, sir, resolve what you'll do this moment, for egad they'll maul you.

FASHION. Stay a little.—(*To* MISS HOYDEN) My dear, here's a troublesome business my man tells me of, but don't be frightened, we shall be too hard for the rogue. Here's an impudent fellow at the gate (not knowing I was come hither *incognito*) has taken my name upon him, in hopes to run away with you.

HOYDEN. O the brazen-faced varlet, it's well we are married, or maybe we might never a been so.

FASHION. (*Aside*) Egad, like enough!—[*Aloud*] Prithee, dear doctor, run to Sir Tunbelly, and stop him from going to the gate before I speak with him.

BULL. I fly, my good lord. *Exit*

NURSE. An't please your honor, my lady and I had best lock ourselves up till the danger be over.

FASHION. Ay, by all means.

HOYDEN. Not so fast, I won't be locked up any more. I'm married.

FASHION. Yes, pray, my dear, do, till we have seized this rascal.

HOYDEN. Nay, if you pray me, I'll do anything. *Exeunt* MISS HOYDEN *and* NURSE

FASHION. Oh! here's Sir Tunbelly coming.—Hark you, sirrah, things are better than you imagine; the wedding's over.

LORY. The devil it is, sir!
FASHION. Not a word, all's safe; but Sir Tunbelly don't know it, nor must not yet; so I am resolved to brazen the business out, and have the pleasure of turning the impostor upon his lordship, which I believe may easily be done.

Enter SIR TUNBELLY, BULL, *and* Servants, *armed*

FASHION. Did you ever hear, sir, of so impudent an undertaking!
SIR TUNBELLY. Never, by the mass! But we'll tickle him, I'll warrant him.
FASHION. They tell me, sir, he has a great many people with him disguised like servants.
SIR TUNBELLY. Ay, ay, rogues enough; but I'll soon raise the posse upon 'em.
FASHION. Sir, if you'll take my advice, we'll go a shorter way to work. I find whoever this spark is, he knows nothing of my being privately here; so if you pretend to receive him civilly, he'll enter without suspicion; and as soon as he is within the gate, we'll whip up the drawbridge upon his back, let fly the blunderbuss to disperse his crew, and so commit him to jail.
SIR TUNBELLY. Egad, your lordship is an ingenious person, and a very great general; but shall we kill any of 'em or not?
FASHION. No, no; fire over their heads only to fright 'em; I'll warrant the regiment scours when the colonel's a prisoner.
SIR TUNBELLY. Then come along, my boys, and let your courage be great—for your danger is but small. *Exeunt*

SCENE [v]. *The Gate*

Enter LORD FOPPINGTON, *with* LA VEROLE *and* Servants

LORD FOPPINGTON. A pax of these bumpkinly people! Will they open the gate, or do they desire I should grow at their moat-side like a willow?—(*To the* Porter) Hey, fellow—prithee do me the favor, in as few words as thou canst find to express thyself, to tell me whether thy master will admit me or not, that I may turn about my coach, and be gone.
PORTER. Here's my master himself now at hand, he's of age, he'll give you his answer.

Enter SIR TUNBELLY *and His* Servants

SIR TUNBELLY. My most noble lord, I crave your pardon for making your honor wait so long; but my orders to my servants have been to admit nobody without my knowledge, for fear of some attempt upon my daughter, the times being full of plots and roguery.
LORD FOPPINGTON. Much caution, I must confess, is a sign of great wisdom: but, stap my vitals, I have got a cold enough to destroy a porter!—He, hem—
SIR TUNBELLY. I am very sorry for't, indeed, my lord; but if your lordship please to walk in, we'll help you to some brown sugar-candy. My lord, I'll show you the way.
LORD FOPPINGTON. Sir, I follow you with pleasure.
(*Exit with* SIR TUNBELLY CLUMSEY. *As* LORD FOPPINGTON'S Servants *go to follow him in, they clap the door against* LA VEROLE)
SERVANTS. (*Within*) Nay, hold you me there, sir.
LA VEROLE. *Jernie die,*[1] *qu'est-ce que veut dire ça?*[2]
SIR TUNBELLY. (*Within*) Fire, porter.
PORTER. (*Fires*) Have among ye, my masters.
LA VEROLE. *Ah, je suis mort!*—
(*The* Servants *all run off*)
PORTER. Not one soldier left, by the mass!

[SCENE VI]. *Scene changes to the Hall*

Enter SIR TUNBELLY, BULL, *and* Servants, *with* LORD FOPPINGTON, *disarmed*

SIR TUNBELLY. Come, bring him along, bring him along!
LORD FOPPINGTON. What the pax do you mean, gentlemen! Is it fair-time, that you are all drunk before dinner?
SIR TUNBELLY. Drunk, sirrah!—Here's an impudent rogue for you! Drunk or sober, bully, I'm a justice of the peace, and know how to deal with strollers.
LORD FOPPINGTON. Strollers!
SIR TUNBELLY. Ay, strollers. Come, give an account of yourself; what's your name, where do you live? do you pay scot and lot? are you a Williamite, or a Jacobite?[3] Come.

[1] Possibly a corruption of *Je renie dieu,* I deny God, an obsolete French expression.
[2] What's that for?
[3] A supporter of King William or of King James. Most people in these years, and indeed until after 1746, constantly expected Jacobite uprisings. See *Henry Esmond,* and Scott's *Waverley* and *Rob Roy.*

Lord Foppington. And why dost thou ask me so many impertinent questions?

Sir Tunbelly. Because I'll make you answer 'em before I have done with you, you rascal you!

Lord Foppington. Before Gad, all the answer I can make thee to 'em is, that thou art a very extraordinary old fellow, stap my vitals!

Sir Tunbelly. Nay, if you are for joking with deputy lieutenants, we'st know how to deal with you. Here, draw a warrant for him immediately.

Lord Foppington. A warrant! What the devil is't thou wouldst be at, old gentleman?

Sir Tunbelly. I would be at you, sirrah (if my hands were not tied as a magistrate), and with these two double fists beat your teeth down your throat, you dog you!

Lord Foppington. And why wouldst thou spoil my face at that rate?

Sir Tunbelly. For your design to rob me of my daughter, villain.

Lord Foppington. Rab thee of thy daughter!—Now do I begin to believe I am a-bed and asleep, and that all this is but a dream.—If it be, 'twill be an agreeable surprise enough to waken by and by; and instead of the impertinent company of a nasty country justice, find myself perhaps in the arms of a woman of quality.—(*To* Sir Tunbelly) Prithee, old father, wilt thou give me leave to ask thee one question?

Sir Tunbelly. I can't tell whether I will or not, till I know what it is.

Lord Foppington. Why, then it is, whether thou didst not write to my Lord Foppington to come down and marry thy daughter?

Sir Tunbelly. Yes, marry did I; and my Lord Foppington is come down, and shall marry my daughter before she's a day older.

Lord Foppington. Now give me thy hand, dear dad; I thought we should understand one another at last.

Sir Tunbelly. This fellow's mad.—Here bind him hand and foot.

(*They bind him down*)

Lord Foppington. Nay, prithee, knight, leave fooling; thy jest begins to grow dull.

Sir Tunbelly. Bind him, I say, he's mad.—Bread and water, a dark room, and a whip may bring him to his senses again.

Lord Foppington. (*Aside*) Egad! if I don't waken quickly, by all I can see, this is like to prove one of the most impertinent dreams that ever I dreamt in my life.

Enter Miss Hoyden *and* Nurse

Hoyden. (*Going up to him*) Is this he that would have run away with me? Fo! how he stinks of sweets!—Pray, father, let him be dragged through the horse-pond.

Lord Foppington. (*Aside*) This must be my wife by her natural inclination to her husband.

Hoyden. Pray, father, what do you intend to do with him, hang him?

Sir Tunbelly. That at least, child.

Nurse. Ay, and it's e'en too good for him, too.

Lord Foppington. (*Aside*) *Madame la gouvernante*, I presume. Hitherto this appears to me to be one of the most extraordinary families that ever one man of quality matched into.

Sir Tunbelly. What's become of my lord, daughter?

Hoyden. He's just coming, sir.

Lord Foppington. (*Aside*) My lord! what does he mean by that now?

Enter Young Fashion *and* Lory

(*Seeing him*) Stap my vitals, Tam! now the dream's out.

Fashion. Is this the fellow, sir, that designed to trick me of your daughter?

Sir Tunbelly. This is he, my lord; how do you like him? Is not he a pretty fellow to get a fortune?

Fashion. I find by his dress he thought your daughter might be taken with a beau.

Hoyden. O gemini! Is this a beau? let me see him again.—Ha! I find a beau's not such an ugly thing neither.

Fashion. (*Aside*) Egad, she'll be in love with him presently; I'll e'en have him sent away to jail.—(*To* Lord Foppington) Sir, though your undertaking shows you are a person of no extraordinary modesty, I suppose you han't confidence enough to expect much favor from me?

Lord Foppington. Strike me dumb, Tam, thou art a very impudent fellow!

Nurse. Look, if the varlet has not the 'frontery to call his lordship plain Thomas!

Bull. The business is, he would feign himself mad, to avoid going to jail.

Lord Foppington. (*Aside*) That must be the chaplain, by his unfolding of mysteries.

Sir Tunbelly. Come, is the warrant writ?

Clerk. Yes, sir.

Sir Tunbelly. Give me the pen, I'll sign it.—So now, constable, away with him.

Lord Foppington. Hold one moment,— pray, gentlemen. My Lord Foppington, shall I beg one word with your lordship?

Nurse. O ho, it's my lord with him now! See how afflictions will humble folks.

Hoyden. Pray, my lord, don't let him whisper too close, lest he bite your ear off.

Lord Foppington. I am not altogether so hungry as your ladyship is pleased to imagine. —(*Aside to* Young Fashion) Look you, Tam, I am sensible I have not been so kind to you as I ought, but I hope you'll forget what's passed, and accept of the five thousand pounds I offer; thou mayst live in extreme splendor with it, stap my vitals!

Fashion. It's a much easier matter to prevent a disease than to cure it; a quarter of that sum would have secured your mistress; twice as much won't redeem her.

(*Leaving him*)

Sir Tunbelly. Well, what says he?

Fashion. Only the rascal offered me a bribe to let him go.

Sir Tunbelly. Ay, he shall go, with a pox to him!—Lead on, constable.

Lord Foppington. One more word, and I have done.

Sir Tunbelly. Before Gad! thou art an impudent fellow, to trouble the court at this rate after thou art condemned; but speak once for all.

Lord Foppington. Why then, once for all; I have at last luckily called to mind that there is a gentleman of this country, who I believe cannot live far from this place, if he were here, would satisfy you, I am Navelty, Baron of Foppington, with five thousand pounds a year, and that fellow there, a rascal not worth a groat.

Sir Tunbelly. Very well; now, who is this honest gentleman you are so well acquainted with?—(*To* Young Fashion) Come, sir, we shall hamper him.

Lord Foppington. 'Tis Sir John Friendly.

Sir Tunbelly. So; he lives within half a mile, and came down into the country but last night; this bold-faced fellow thought he had been at London still, and so quoted him; now we shall display him in his colors: I'll send for Sir John immediately.—Here, fellow, away presently, and desire my neighbor he'll do me the favor to step over, upon an extraordinary occasion.—And in the meanwhile you had best secure this sharper in the gate-house. (*Exit* Servant)

Constable. An't please your worship, he may chance to give us the slip thence. If I were worthy to advise, I think the dog-kennel's a surer place.

Sir Tunbelly. With all my heart; anywhere.

Lord Foppington. Nay, for heaven's sake, sir! do me the favor to put me in a clean room, that I mayn't daub my clothes.

Sir Tunbelly. O, when you have married my daughter, her estate will afford you new ones.—Away with him!

Lord Foppington. A dirty country justice is a barbarous magistrate, stap my vitals!

Exit Constable *with* Lord Foppington

Fashion. (*Aside*) Egad, I must prevent this knight's coming, or the house will grow soon too hot to hold me.—(*To* Sir Tunbelly) Sir, I fancy 'tis not worth while to trouble Sir John upon this impertinent fellow's desire: I'll send and call the messenger back.

Sir Tunbelly. Nay, with all my heart; for, to be sure, he thought he was far enough off, or the rogue would never have named him.

Enter Servant

Servant. Sir, I met Sir John just lighting at the gate; he's come to wait upon you.

Sir Tunbelly. Nay, then, it happens as one could wish.

Fashion. (*Aside*) The devil it does!— Lory, you see how things are, here will be a discovery presently, and we shall have our brains beat out; for my brother will be sure to swear he don't know me: therefore, run into the stable, take the two first horses you can light on, I'll slip out at the back door, and we'll away immediately.

Lory. What, and leave your lady, sir?

Fashion. There's no danger in that as long as I have taken possession; I shall know how to treat with 'em well enough, if once I am out of their reach. Away! I'll steal after thee.

Exit Lory; *his master follows him out at one door, as* Sir John Friendly *enters at t'other*

Enter SIR JOHN

SIR TUNBELLY. Sir John, you are the welcomest man alive; I had just sent a messenger to desire you'd step over, upon a very extraordinary occasion. We are all in arms here.

SIR JOHN. How so?

SIR TUNBELLY. Why, you must know, a finical sort of a tawdry fellow here (I don't know who the devil he is, not I) hearing, I suppose, that the match was concluded between my Lord Foppington and my girl Hoyden, comes impudently to the gate, with a whole pack of rogues in liveries, and would have passed upon me for his lordship; but what does I? I comes up to him boldly at the head of his guards, takes him by the throat, strikes up his heels, binds him hand and foot, dispatches a warrant, and commits him prisoner to the dog-kennel.

SIR JOHN. So; but how do you know but this was my lord? For I was told he set out from London the day before me, with a very fine retinue, and intended to come directly hither.

SIR TUNBELLY. Why, now to show you how many lies people raise in that damned town, he came two nights ago post, with only one servant, and is now in the house with me. But you don't know the cream of the jest yet; this same rogue (that lies yonder neck and heels among the hounds), thinking you were out of the country, quotes you for his acquaintance, and said if you were here, you'd justify him to be Lord Foppington, and I know not what.

SIR JOHN. Pray will you let me see him?

SIR TUNBELLY. Ay, that you shall presently.—Here, fetch the prisoner.

Exit Servant

SIR JOHN. I wish there ben't some mistake in the business.—Where's my lord? I know him very well.

SIR TUNBELLY. He was here just now.—(*To* BULL) See for him, doctor; tell him Sir John is here to wait upon him. *Exit* BULL

SIR JOHN. I hope, Sir Tunbelly, the young lady is not married yet.

SIR TUNBELLY. No, things won't be ready this week. But why do you say you hope she is not married?

SIR JOHN. Some foolish fancies only, perhaps I'm mistaken.

Re-enter BULL

BULL. Sir, his lordship is just rid out to take the air.

SIR TUNBELLY. To take the air! Is that his London breeding, to go take the air when gentlemen come to visit him?

SIR JOHN. 'Tis possible he might want it, he might not be well, some sudden qualm perhaps.

Re-enter Constable, *&c., with* LORD FOPPINGTON

LORD FOPPINGTON. Stap my vitals, I'll have satisfaction!

SIR JOHN. (*Running to him*) My dear Lord Foppington!

LORD FOPPINGTON. Dear Friendly, thou art come in the critical minute, strike me dumb!

SIR JOHN. Why, I little thought I should have found you in fetters.

LORD FOPPINGTON. Why, truly the world must do me the justice to confess, I do use to appear a little more *dégagé*; but this old gentleman, not liking the freedom of my air, has been pleased to skewer down my arms like a rabbit.

SIR TUNBELLY. Is it then possible that this should be the true Lord Foppington at last?

LORD FOPPINGTON. Why, what do you see in his face to make you doubt of it? Sir, without presuming to have any extraordinary opinion of my figure, give me leave to tell you, if you had seen as many lords as I have done, you would not think it impossible a person of a worse *taille* than mine might be a modern man of quality.

SIR TUNBELLY. Unbind him, slaves!—My lord, I'm struck dumb, I can only beg pardon by signs; but if a sacrifice will appease you, you shall have it.—Here pursue this Tartar, bring him back.—Away, I say!—A dog! Oons, I'll cut off his ears and his tail, I'll draw out all his teeth, pull his skin over his head—and—and what shall I do more?

SIR JOHN. He does indeed deserve to be made an example of.

LORD FOPPINGTON. He does deserve to be *chartre*,[1] stap my vitals!

SIR TUNBELLY. May I then hope to have your honor's pardon?

LORD FOPPINGTON. Sir, we courtiers do nothing without a bribe: that fair young lady might do miracles.

[1] I.e., *mis en chartre*, sent to jail (Ward).

Sir Tunbelly. Hoyden! come hither, Hoyden.

Lord Foppington. Hoyden is her name, sir?

Sir Tunbelly. Yes, my lord.

Lord Foppington. The prettiest name for a song I ever heard.

Sir Tunbelly. My lord—here's my girl; she's yours, she has a wholesome body, and a virtuous mind; she's a woman complete, both in flesh and in spirit; she has a bag of milled crowns, as scarce as they are, and fifteen hundred a year stitched fast to her tail: so, go thy ways, Hoyden.

Lord Foppington. Sir, I do receive her like a gentleman.

Sir Tunbelly. Then I'm a happy man, I bless Heaven, and if your lordship will give me leave, I will, like a good Christian at Christmas, be very drunk by way of thanksgiving. Come, my noble peer, I believe dinner's ready; if your honor pleases to follow me, I'll lead you on to the attack of a venison-pasty. *Exit*

Lord Foppington. Sir, I wait upon you.—Will your ladyship do me the favor of your little finger, madam?

Hoyden. My lord, I'll follow you presently, I have a little business with my nurse.

Lord Foppington. Your ladyship's most humble servant.—Come, Sir John; the ladies have *des affaires*.

Exit with Sir John Friendly

Hoyden. So, nurse, we are finely brought to bed! what shall we do now?

Nurse. Ah, dear miss, we are all undone! Mr. Bull, you were used to help a woman to a remedy. *(Crying)*

Bull. Alack-a-day! but it's past my skill now, I can do nothing.

Nurse. Who would have thought that ever your invention should have been drained so dry?

Hoyden. Well, I have often thought old folks fools, and now I'm sure they are so; I have found a way myself to secure us all.

Nurse. Dear lady, what's that?

Hoyden. Why, if you two will be sure to hold your tongues, and not say a word of what's past, I'll e'en marry this lord, too.

Nurse. What! two husbands, my dear?

Hoyden. Why, you have had three, good nurse, you may hold your tongue.

Nurse. Ay, but not altogether, sweet child.

Hoyden. Psha! if you had, you'd ne'er a thought much on't.

Nurse. Oh, but 'tis a sin, sweeting!

Bull. Nay, that's my business to speak to, nurse.—I do confess, to take two husbands for the satisfaction of the flesh, is to commit the sin of exorbitancy; but to do it for the peace of the spirit, is no more than to be drunk by way of physic. Besides, to prevent a parent's wrath, is to avoid the sin of disobedience; for when the parent's angry, the child is froward. So that upon the whole matter, I do think, though miss should marry again, she may be saved.

Hoyden. Ecod, and I will marry again then! and so there's an end of the story.

Exeunt

ACT V

Scene [I].—*London.*—[Coupler's *Lodgings*]

Enter Coupler, Young Fashion, *and* Lory

Coupler. Well, and so Sir John coming in—

Fashion. And so Sir John coming in, I thought it might be manners in me to go out, which I did, and getting on horseback as fast as I could, rid away as if the devil had been at the rear of me. What has happened since, heaven knows.

Coupler. Egad, sirrah, I know as well as heaven.

Fashion. What do you know?

Coupler. That you are a cuckold.

Fashion. The devil I am! By who?

Coupler. By your brother.

Fashion. My brother! which way?

Coupler. The old way; he has lain with your wife.

Fashion. Hell and furies! what dost thou mean?

Coupler. I mean plainly; I speak no parable.

Fashion. Plainly! thou dost not speak common sense, I cannot understand one word thou sayest.

Coupler. You will do soon, youngster. In short, you left your wife a widow, and she married again.

Fashion. It's a lie.

Coupler. Ecod, if I were a young fellow, I'd break your head, sirrah.

Fashion. Dear dad, don't be angry, for I'm as mad as Tom of Bedlam.

COUPLER. [When][1] I had fitted you with a wife, you should have kept her.

FASHION. But is it possible the young strumpet could play me such a trick?

COUPLER. A young strumpet, sir, can play twenty tricks.

FASHION. But prithee instruct me a little farther; whence comes thy intelligence?

COUPLER. From your brother, in this letter; there, you may read it.

FASHION. (*Reads.*)

Dear COUPLER,—(*Pulling off his hat.*) *I have only time to tell thee in three lines, or thereabouts, that there has been the devil. That rascal Tam, having stole the letter thou hadst formerly writ for me to bring to Sir Tunbelly, formed a damnable design upon my mistress, and was in a fair way of success when I arrived. But after having suffered some indignities (in which I have all daubed my embroidered coat), I put him to flight. I sent out a party of horse after him, in hopes to have made him my prisoner, which if I had done, I would have qualified him for the seraglio, stap my vitals!*

The danger I have thus narrowly 'scaped has made me fortify myself against farther attempts, by entering immediately into an association with the young lady, by which we engage to stand by one another as long as we both shall live.

In short, the papers are sealed, and the contract is signed, so the business of the lawyer is achevé; but I defer the divine part of the thing till I arrive at London, not being willing to consummate in any other bed but my own.

Postscript.

'Tis possible I may be in tawn as soon as this letter, far I find this lady is so violently in love with me, I have determined to make her happy with all the dispatch that is practicable, without disordering my coach-harses.

So, here's rare work, i'faith!

LORY. Egad, Miss Hoyden has laid about her bravely!

COUPLER. I think my country-girl has played her part as well as if she had been born and bred in St. James's parish.

FASHION. That rogue the chaplain!

LORY. And then that jade the nurse, sir!

FASHION. And then that drunken sot Lory, sir! that could not keep himself sober to be a witness to the marriage.

LORY. Sir—with respect—I know very few drunken sots that do keep themselves sober.

[1] The first edition has *then* a misprint.

FASHION. Hold your prating, sirrah, or I'll break your head!—Dear Coupler, what's to be done?

COUPLER. Nothing's to be done till the bride and bridegroom come to town.

FASHION. Bride and bridegroom! death and furies! I can't bear that thou shouldst call 'em so.

COUPLER. Why, what shall I call 'em, dog and cat?

FASHION. Not for the world, that sounds more like man and wife than t'other.

COUPLER. Well, if you'll hear of 'em in no language, we'll leave 'em for the nurse and the chaplain.

FASHION. The devil and the witch!

COUPLER. When they come to town—

LORY. We shall have stormy weather.

COUPLER. Will you hold your tongues, gentlemen, or not?

LORY. Mum!

COUPLER. I say when they come, we must find what stuff they are made of, whether the churchman be chiefly composed of the flesh, or the spirit; I presume the former. For as chaplains now go, 'tis probable he eats three pound of beef to the reading of one chapter.—This gives him carnal desires, he wants money, preferment, wine, a whore; therefore we must invite him to supper, give him fat capons, sack and sugar, a purse of gold, and a plump sister. Let this be done, and I'll warrant thee, my boy, he speaks truth like an oracle.

FASHION. Thou art a profound statesman I allow it; but how shall we gain the nurse?

COUPLER. Oh! never fear the nurse, if once you have got the priest; for the devil always rides the hag. Well, there's nothing more to be said of the matter at this time, that I know of; so let us go and inquire if there's any news of our people yet, perhaps they may be come. But let me tell you one thing by the way, sirrah, I doubt you have been an idle fellow; if thou hadst behaved thyself as thou shouldst have done, the girl would never have left thee. *Exeunt*

SCENE [II].—BERINTHIA'S *Apartment*

Enter her Maid, *passing the stage, followed by* WORTHY

WORTHY. Hem, Mrs. Abigail, is your mistress to be spoken with?

ABIGAIL. By you, sir, I believe she may.

WORTHY. Why 'tis by me I would have her spoken with.

ABIGAIL. I'll acquaint her, sir. *Exit*

WORTHY. (*Solus*) One lift more I must persuade her to give me, and then I'm mounted. Well, a young bawd and a handsome one for my money; 'tis they do the execution; I'll never go to an old one, but when I have occasion for a witch. Lewdness looks heavenly to a woman, when an angel appears in its cause; but when a hag is advocate, she thinks it comes from the devil. An old woman has something so terrible in her looks, that whilst she is persuading your mistress to forget she has a soul, she stares hell and damnation full in her face.

Enter BERINTHIA

BERINTHIA. Well, sir, what news brings you?

WORTHY. No news, madam; there's a woman going to cuckold her husband.

BERINTHIA. Amanda?

WORTHY. I hope so.

BERINTHIA. Speed her well!

WORTHY. Ay, but there must be more than a God-speed, or your charity won't be worth a farthing.

BERINTHIA. Why, han't I done enough already?

WORTHY. Not quite.

BERINTHIA. What's the matter?

WORTHY. The lady has a scruple still, which you must remove.

BERINTHIA. What's that?

WORTHY. Her virtue—she says.

BERINTHIA. And do you believe her?

WORTHY. No, but I believe it's what she takes for her virtue; it's some relics of lawful love. She is not yet fully satisfied her husband has got another mistress; which unless I can convince her of, I have opened the trenches in vain; for the breach must be wider, before I dare storm the town.

BERINTHIA. And so I'm to be your engineer?

WORTHY. I'm sure you know best how to manage the battery.

BERINTHIA. What think you of springing a mine? I have a thought just now come into my head, how to blow her up at once.

WORTHY. That would be a thought indeed.

BERINTHIA. Faith, I'll do't; and thus the execution of it shall be. We are all invited to my Lord Foppington's to-night to supper; he's come to town with his bride, and makes a ball, with an entertainment of music. Now, you must know, my undoer here, Loveless, says he must needs meet me about some private business (I don't know what 'tis) before we go to the company. To which end he has told his wife one lie, and I have told her another. But to make her amends, I'll go immediately, and tell her a solemn truth.

WORTHY. What's that?

BERINTHIA. Why, I'll tell her, that to my certain knowledge her husband has a rendezvous with his mistress this afternoon; and that if she'll give me her word she'll be satisfied with the discovery, without making any violent inquiry after the woman, I'll direct her to a place where she shall see 'em meet. Now, friend, this I fancy may help you to a critical minute. For home she must go again to dress. You (with your good breeding) come to wait upon us to the ball, find her all alone, her spirit inflamed against her husband for his treason, and her flesh in a heat from some contemplations upon the treachery, her blood on a fire, her conscience in ice; a lover to draw, and the devil to drive.—Ah, poor Amanda!

WORTHY. (*Kneeling*) Thou angel of light, let me fall down and adore thee!

BERINTHIA. Thou minister of darkness, get up again, for I hate to see the devil at his devotions.

WORTHY. Well, my incomparable Berinthia, how shall I requite you?

BERINTHIA. Oh, ne'er trouble yourself about that: virtue is its own reward. There's a pleasure in doing good, which sufficiently pays itself. Adieu!

WORTHY. Farewell, thou best of women!

Exeunt several ways

Enter AMANDA *meeting* BERINTHIA

AMANDA. Who was that went from you?

BERINTHIA. A friend of yours.

AMANDA. What does he want?

BERINTHIA. Something you might spare him, and be ne'er the poorer.

AMANDA. I can spare him nothing but my friendship; my love already's all disposed of, though, I confess, to one ungrateful to my bounty.

BERINTHIA. Why, there's the mystery! You have been so bountiful, you have cloyed him. Fond wives do by their husbands, as barren wives do by their lapdogs; cram 'em with sweetmeats till they spoil their stomachs.

AMANDA. Alas! had you but seen how passionately fond he has been since our last reconciliation, you would have thought it were impossible he ever should have breathed an hour without me.

BERINTHIA. Ay, but there you thought wrong again, Amanda; you should consider, that in matters of love men's eyes are always bigger than their bellies. They have violent appetites, 'tis true, but they have soon dined.

AMANDA. Well; there's nothing upon earth astonishes me more than men's inconstancy.

BERINTHIA. Now there's nothing upon earth astonishes me less, when I consider what they and we are composed of; for nature has made them children, and us babies.[1] Now, Amanda, now we used our babies you may remember. We were mad to have 'em as soon as we saw 'em; kissed 'em to pieces as soon as we got 'em; then pulled off their clothes, saw 'em naked, and so threw 'em away.

AMANDA. But do you think all men are of this temper?

BERINTHIA. All but one.

AMANDA. Who's that?

BERINTHIA. Worthy.

AMANDA. Why, he's weary of his wife too, you see.

BERINTHIA. Ay, that's no proof.

AMANDA. What can be a greater?

BERINTHIA. Being weary of his mistress.

AMANDA. Don't you think 'twere possible he might give you that, too?

BERINTHIA. Perhaps he might, if he were my gallant; not if he were yours.

AMANDA. Why do you think he should be more constant to me, than he would to you? I'm sure I'm not so handsome.

BERINTHIA. Kissing goes by favor; he likes you best.

AMANDA. Suppose he does. That's no demonstration he would be constant to me.

BERINTHIA. No, that I'll grant you: but there are other reasons to expect it. For you must know after all, Amanda, the inconstancy we commonly see in men of brains, does not so much proceed from the uncertainty of their temper, as from the misfortunes of their love. A man sees perhaps a hundred women he likes well enough for an intrigue, and away; but possibly, through the whole course of his life,

[1] Dolls.

does not find above one who is exactly what he could wish her; now her, 'tis a thousand to one, he never gets. Either she is not to be had at all (though that seldom happens, you'll say), or he wants those opportunities that are necessary to gain her. Either she likes somebody else much better than him, or uses him like a dog, because he likes nobody so well as her. Still something or other Fate claps[2] in the way between them and the woman they are capable of being fond of; and this makes them wander about from mistress to mistress, like a pilgrim from town to town, who every night must have a fresh lodging, and's in haste to be gone in the morning.

AMANDA. 'Tis possible there may be something in what you say; but what do you infer from it as to the man we were talking of?

BERINTHIA. Why, I infer, that you being the woman in the world the most to his humor, 'tis not likely he would quit you for one that is less.

AMANDA. That is not to be depended upon, for you see Mr. Loveless does so.

BERINTHIA. What does Mr. Loveless do?

AMANDA. Why, he runs after something for variety, I'm sure he does not like so well as he does me.

BERINTHIA. That's more than you know, madam.

AMANDA. No, I'm sure on't. I'm not very vain, Berinthia, and yet I'd lay my life, if I could look into his heart, he thinks I deserve to be preferred to a thousand of her.

BERINTHIA. Don't be too positive in that neither; a million to one but she has the same opinion of you. What would you give to see her?

AMANDA. Hang her, dirty trull!—Though I really believe she's so ugly she'd cure me of my jealousy.

BERINTHIA. All the men of sense about town say she's handsome.

AMANDA. They are as often out in those things as any people.

BERINTHIA. Then I'll give you farther proof —all the women about town say she's a fool. Now I hope you're convinced?

AMANDA. Whate'er she be, I'm satisfied he does not like her well enough to bestow anything more than a little outward gallantry upon her.

BERINTHIA. Outward gallantry!—(*Aside*) I can't bear this.—(*To* AMANDA) Don't you

[2] I.e., Fate claps something or other in the way . . .

think she's a woman to be fobbed off so. Come, I'm too much your friend to suffer you should be thus grossly imposed upon by a man who does not deserve the least part about you, unless he knew how to set a greater value upon it. Therefore, in one word, to my certain knowledge, he is to meet her now, within a quarter of an hour, somewhere about that Babylon of wickedness, Whitehall. And if you'll give me your word that you'll be content with seeing her masked in his hand, without pulling her headclothes off, I'll step immediately to the person from whom I have my intelligence, and send you word whereabouts you may stand to see 'em meet. My friend and I'll watch 'em from another place, and dodge 'em to their private lodging; but don't you offer to follow 'em, lest you do it awkwardly, and spoil all. I'll come home to you again as soon as I have earth[ed][1] 'em, and give you an account in what corner of the house the scene of their lewdness lies.

AMANDA. If you can do this, Berinthia, he's a villain.

BERINTHIA. I can't help that; men will be so.

AMANDA. Well, I'll follow your directions, for I shall never rest till I know the worst of this matter.

BERINTHIA. Pray, go immediately and get yourself ready then. Put on some of your woman's clothes, a great scarf and a mask, and you shall presently receive orders.—(*Calls within*) Here, who's there? Get me a chair quickly.

Enter Servant

SERVANT. There are chairs at the door, madam.

BERINTHIA. 'Tis well; I'm coming.

Exit Servant

AMANDA. But pray, Berinthia, before you go, tell me how I may know this filthy thing, if she should be so forward (as I suppose she will) to come to the rendezvous first; for methinks I would fain view her a little.

BERINTHIA. Why, she's about my height; and very well shaped.

AMANDA. I thought she had been a little crooked.

BERINTHIA. O no, she's as straight as I am. But we lose time; come away. *Exeunt*

[1] The first edition has *earth 'em*.

[SCENE III.—YOUNG FASHION'S *Lodgings*]

Enter YOUNG FASHION, *meeting* LORY

FASHION. Well, will the doctor come?

LORY. Sir, I sent a porter to him as you ordered me. He found him with a pipe of tobacco and a great tankard of ale, which he said he would dispatch while I could tell three, and be here.

FASHION. He does not suspect 'twas I that sent for him.

LORY. Not a jot, sir; he divines as little for himself as he does for other folks.

FASHION. Will he bring nurse with him?

LORY. Yes.

FASHION. That's well; where's Coupler?

LORY. He's half-way up the stairs taking breath; he must play his bellows a little, before he can get to the top.

Enter COUPLER

FASHION. Oh, here he is.—Well, Old Phthisic, the doctor's coming.

COUPLER. Would the pox had the doctor!— I'm quite out of wind.—(*To* LORY) Set me a chair, sirrah. Ah!—(*Sits down. To* YOUNG FASHION) Why the plague canst not thou lodge upon the ground-floor?

FASHION. Because I love to lie as near heaven as I can.

COUPLER. Prithee, let heaven alone; ne'er affect tending that way; thy center's downwards.

FASHION. That's impossible! I have too much ill-luck in this world to be damned in the next.

COUPLER. Thou art out in thy logic. Thy major is true, but thy minor is false; for thou art the luckiest fellow in the universe.

FASHION. Make out that.

COUPLER. I'll do't: last night the devil ran away with the parson of Fatgoose living.

FASHION. If he had run away with the parish too, what's that to me?

COUPLER. I'll tell thee what it's to thee.— This living is worth five hundred pounds a-year, and the presentation of it is thine, if thou canst prove thyself a lawful husband to Miss Hoyden.

FASHION. Sayest thou so, my protector? Then, egad, I shall have a brace of evidences here presently.

COUPLER. The nurse and the doctor?

FASHION. The same. The devil himself

won't have interest enough to make 'em withstand it.

COUPLER. That we shall see presently.—Here they come.

Enter NURSE *and* BULL; *they start back, seeing* YOUNG FASHION

NURSE. Ah, goodness, Roger, we are betrayed!

FASHION. (*Laying hold on 'em*) Nay, nay, ne'er flinch for the matter, for I have you safe.—Come, to your trials immediately; I have no time to give you copies of your indictment. There sits your judge.

BOTH. (*Kneeling*) Pray, sir, have compassion on us.

NURSE. I hope, sir, my years will move your pity; I am an aged woman.

COUPLER. That is a moving argument indeed.

BULL. I hope, sir, my character will be considered; I am heaven's ambassador.

COUPLER. Are not you a rogue of sanctity?

BULL. Sir (with respect to my function), I do wear a gown.

COUPLER. Did not you marry this vigorous young fellow to a plump young buxom wench?

NURSE. (*Aside to* BULL) Don't confess, Roger, unless you are hard put to it indeed.

COUPLER. Come, out with't!—Now is he chewing the cud of his roguery, and grinding a lie between his teeth.

BULL. Sir,—I cannot positively say—I say, sir,—positively I cannot say—

COUPLER. Come, no equivocations, no Roman turns upon us. Consider thou standest upon Protestant ground, which will slip from under thee like a Tyburn cart; for in this country we have always ten handmen for one Jesuit.

BULL. (*To* YOUNG FASHION) Pray, sir, then will you but permit me to speak one word in private with nurse.

FASHION. Thou art always for doing something in private with nurse.

COUPLER. But pray let his betters be served before him for once: I would do something in private with her myself.—Lory, take care of this reverend gownman in the next room a little.—Retire, priest.—(*Exit* LORY *with* BULL) Now, virgin, I must put the matter home to you a little: do you think it might not be possible to make you speak truth?

NURSE. Alas, sir! I don't know what you mean by truth.

COUPLER. Nay, 'tis possible thou mayest be a stranger to it.

FASHION. Come, nurse, you and I were better friends when we saw one another last; and I still believe you are a very good woman in the bottom. I did deceive you and your young lady, 'tis true, but I always designed to make a very good husband to her, and to be a very good friend to you. And 'tis possible, in the end, she might have found herself happier, and you richer, than ever my brother will make you.

NURSE. Brother! why is your worship then his lordship's brother?

FASHION. I am; which you should have known, if I durst have stayed to have told you; but I was forced to take horse a little in haste, you know.

NURSE. You were indeed, sir: poor young man, how he was bound to scour for't! Now won't your worship be angry, if I confess the truth to you?—When I found you were a cheat (with respect be it spoken), I verily believed miss had got some pitiful skipjack varlet or other to her husband, or I had ne'er let her think of marrying again.

COUPLER. But where was your conscience all this while, woman? Did not that stare in your face with huge saucer-eyes, and a great horn upon the forehead? Did not you think you should be damned for such a sin?—Ha?

FASHION. Well said, divinity! Press that home upon her.

NURSE. Why, in good truly, sir, I had some fearful thoughts on't, and could never be brought to consent, till Mr. Bull said it was a peckadilla, and he'd secure my soul for a tithe-pig.

FASHION. There was a rogue for you!

COUPLER. And he shall thrive accordingly; he shall have a good living.—Come, honest nurse, I see you have butter in your compound; you can melt. Some compassion you can have of this handsome young fellow.

NURSE. I have, indeed, sir.

FASHION. Why then, I'll tell you what you shall do for me. You know what a warm living here is fallen; and that it must be in the disposal of him who has the disposal of miss. Now if you and the doctor will agree to prove my marriage, I'll present him to it, upon condition he makes you his bride.

NURSE. Naw the blessing of the Lord follow your good worship both by night and by day! —Let him be fetched in by the ears; I'll soon bring his nose to the grindstone.

COUPLER. (*Aside*) Well said, old white-leather!—(*Aloud*) Hey, bring in the prisoner there!

Re-enter LORY *with* BULL

COUPLER. Come, advance, holy man. Here's your duck does not think fit to retire with you into the chancel at this time; but she has a proposal to make to you in the face of the congregation.—Come, nurse, speak for yourself, you are of age.

NURSE. Roger, are not you a wicked man, Roger, to set your strength against a weak woman, and persuade her it was no sin to conceal miss's nuptials? My conscience flies in my face for it, thou priest of Baal! and I find by woful experience, thy absolution is not worth an old cassock; therefore I am resolved to confess the truth to the whole world, though I die a beggar for it. But his worship overflows with his mercy and his bounty; he is not only pleased to forgive us our sins, but designs thou sha't squat thee down in Fat-goose living; and which is more than all, has prevailed with me to become the wife of thy bosom.

FASHION. All this I intend for you, doctor. What you are to do for me I need not tell you.

BULL. Your worship's goodness is unspeakable. Yet there is one thing seems a point of conscience; and conscience is a tender babe. If I should bind myself, for the sake of this living, to marry nurse, and maintain her afterwards, I doubt it might be looked on as a kind of simony.

COUPLER. (*Rising up*) If it were sacrilege, the living's worth it: therefore no more words, good doctor; but with the parish—(*Giving* Nurse *to him*) here—take the parsonage-house. 'Tis true, 'tis a little out of repair; some dilapidations there are to be made good; the windows are broke, the wainscot is warped, the ceilings are peeled, and the walls are cracked; but a little glazing, painting, whitewash, and plaster, will make it last thy time.

BULL. Well, sir, if it must be so, I shan't contend. What Providence orders, I submit to.

NURSE. And so do I, with all humility.

COUPLER. Why, that now was spoke like good people. Come, my turtle-doves, let us go help this poor pigeon to his wandering mate again; and after institution and induction, you shall all go a-cooing together. *Exeunt*

[SCENE IV.—LOVELESS'S *Lodgings*]

Enter AMANDA *in a scarf, &c., as just returned, her* Woman *following her*

AMANDA. Prithee what care I who has been here?

WOMAN. Madam, 'twas my Lady Bridle and my Lady Tiptoe.

AMANDA. My Lady Fiddle and my Lady Faddle! What dost stand troubling me with the visits of a parcel of impertinent women? When they are well seamed with the small-pox, they won't be so fond of showing their faces.—There are more coquettes about this town—

WOMAN. Madam, I suppose they only came to return your ladyship's visit, according to the custom of the world.

AMANDA. Would the world were on fire, and you in the middle on't! Begone! leave me!— (*Exit* Woman) At last I am convinced. My eyes are testimonies of his falsehood. The base, ungrateful, perjured villain!— Good gods! what slippery stuff are men compos'd of!
Sure the account of their creation's false,
And 'twas the woman's rib that they were form'd of.
But why am I thus angry?
This poor relapse should only move my scorn.
'Tis true,
The roving flights of his unfinished youth
Had strong excuses from the plea of nature;
Reason had thrown the reins loose on his neck,
And slipped him to unlimited desire.
If therefore he went wrong, he had a claim
To my forgiveness, and I did him right.
But since the years of manhood rein him in,
And reason, well digested into thought,
Has pointed out the course he ought to run;
If now he strays,
'Twould be as weak and mean in me to pardon,
As it had been in him t'offend. But hold:
'Tis an ill cause indeed, where nothing's to be said for't.
My beauty possibly is in the wane;
Perhaps sixteen has greater charms for him:
Yes, there's the secret. But let him know,
My quiver's not entirely emptied yet,

I still have darts, and I can shoot 'em too;
They're not so blunt, but they can enter still:
The want's not in my power, but in my will.
Virtue's his friend; or, through another's heart,
I yet could find the way to make his smart.
  (*Going off, she meets* WORTHY)
Ha! he here!
Protect me, Heaven! for this looks ominous.

Enter WORTHY [1]

WORTHY. You seem disordered, madam;
I hope there's no misfortune happened to you?
  AMANDA. None that will long disorder me, I hope.
WORTHY. Whate'er it be disturbs you, I would to heaven
'Twere in my power to bear the pain,
Till I were able to remove the cause.
  AMANDA. I hope ere long it will remove itself.
At least, I have given it warning to be gone.
  WORTHY. Would I durst ask, where 'tis the thorn torments you!
Forgive me, if I grow inquisitive;
'Tis only with desire to give you ease.
  AMANDA. Alas! 'tis in a tender part. It can't be drawn without a world of pain: yet out it must; for it begins to fester in my heart.
  WORTHY. If 'tis the sting of unrequited love, remove it instantly: I have a balm will quickly heal the wound.
  AMANDA. You'll find the undertaking difficult: the surgeon, who already has attempted it, has much tormented me.
  WORTHY. I'll aid him with a gentler hand,— if you will give me leave.
  AMANDA. How soft soe'er the hand may be, there still is terror in the operation.
  WORTHY. Some few preparatives would make it easy, could I persuade you to apply 'em. Make home[2] reflections, madam, on your slighted love: weigh well the strength and beauty of your charms: rouse up that spirit women ought to bear, and slight your god, if he neglects his angel. With arms of ice receive his cold embraces, and keep your fire for those who come in flames. Behold a burning lover at your feet, his fever raging in his veins! See how he trembles, how he pants!

See how he glows, how he consumes! Extend the arms of mercy to his aid; his zeal may give him title to your pity, although his merit cannot claim your love.
  AMANDA. Of all my feeble sex, sure I must be the weakest, should I again presume to think on love. (*Sighing*) Alas! my heart has been too roughly treated.
  WORTHY. 'Twill find the greater bliss in softer usage.
  AMANDA. But where's that usage to be found?
  WORTHY. 'Tis here, within this faithful breast; which if you doubt, I'll rip it up before your eyes; lay all its secrets open to your view; And then, you'll see 'twas sound.
  AMANDA. With just such honest words as these, the worst of men deceived me.
  WORTHY. He therefore merits all revenge can do; his fault is such, the extent and stretch of vengeance cannot reach it. Oh! make me but your instrument of justice; you'll find me execute it with such zeal, as shall convince you I abhor the crime.
  AMANDA. The rigor of an executioner has more the face of cruelty than justice: and he who puts the cord about the wretch's neck, is seldom known to exceed him in his morals.
  WORTHY. What proof then can I give you of my truth?
  AMANDA. There is on earth but one.
  WORTHY. And is that in my power?
  AMANDA. It is: and one that would so thoroughly convince me, I should be apt to rate your heart so high, I possibly might purchase 't with a part of mine.
  WORTHY. Then heaven, thou art my friend, and I am blest; for if 'tis in my power, my will I'm sure will reach it. No matter what the terms may be, when such a recompense is offer'd. Oh! tell me quickly what this proof must be! What is it will convince you of my love?
  AMANDA. I shall believe you love me as you ought, if from this moment you forbear to ask whatever is unfit for me to grant.—You pause upon it, sir.—I doubt, on such hard terms, a woman's heart is scarcely worth the having.
  WORTHY. A heart, like yours, on any terms is worth it; 'twas not on that I paused. But I was thinking (*Drawing nearer to her*) whether some things there may not be, which woman cannot grant without a blush, and yet which

---

[1] In some later editions the entire scene between Amanda and Worthy is printed as verse. Here the arrangement follows the first edition.
[2] To the point, direct, as in *home-truth* or *home-thrust*.

men may take without offence. (*Taking her hand*) Your hand, I fancy, may be of the number: Oh, pardon me! if I commit a rape (*Kissing it eagerly*) upon't; and thus devour it with my kisses.

AMANDA. O heavens! let me go.

WORTHY. Never, whilst I have strength to hold you here. (*Forcing her to sit down on a couch*) My life, my soul, my goddess—Oh, forgive me!

AMANDA. Oh whither am I going? Help, heaven, or I am lost.

WORTHY. Stand neuter, gods, this once, I do invoke you.

AMANDA. Then save me, virtue, and the glory's thine.

WORTHY. Nay, never strive.

AMANDA. I will, and conquer, too. My forces rally bravely to my aid, (*Breaking from him*) and thus I gain the day.

WORTHY. Then mine as bravely double their attack; (*Seizing her again*) and thus I wrest it from you. Nay, struggle not; for all's in vain: or death or victory; I am determined.

AMANDA. And so am I: (*Rushing from him*) Now keep your distance, or we part forever.

WORTHY. (*Offering again*) For heaven's sake!—

AMANDA. (*Going*) Nay then, farewell!

WORTHY. Oh stay! and see the magic force of love. (*Kneeling, and holding by her clothes*) Behold this raging lion at your feet, struck dead with fear, and tame as charms can make him. What must I do to be forgiven by you?

AMANDA. Repent, and never more offend.

WORTHY. Repentance for past crimes is just and easy; but sin no more's a task too hard for mortals.

AMANDA. Yet those who hope for heaven must use their best endeavors to perform it.

WORTHY. Endeavors we may use, but flesh and blood are got in t'other scale; and they are ponderous things.

AMANDA. Whate'er they are, there is a weight in resolution sufficient for their balance. The soul, I do confess, is usually so careless of its charge, so soft, and so indulgent to desire, it leaves the reins in the wild hand of nature, who like a Phaeton, drives the fiery chariot, and sets the world on flame. Yet still the sovereignty is in the mind, whene'er it pleases to exert its force. Perhaps you may not think it worth your while to take such mighty pains for my esteem; but that I leave to you.

You see the price I set upon my heart;
Perhaps 'tis dear: but, spite of all your art
You'll find on cheaper terms we ne'er shall part.

Exit

WORTHY. (*Solus*) Sure there's divinity about her! And sh'as dispensed some portion on't to me. For what but now was the wild flame of love, or (to dissect that specious term) the vile, the gross desires of flesh and blood, is in a moment turned to adoration. The coarser appetite of nature's gone, and 'tis, methinks, the food of angels I require. How long this influence may last, heaven knows; but in this moment of my purity, I could on her own terms accept her heart. Yes, lovely woman! I can accept it. For now 'tis doubly worth my care. Your charms are much increased, since thus adorned. When truth's extorted from us, then we own the robe of virtue is a graceful habit.

Could women but our secret counsels scan,
Could they but reach the deep reserves of man,
They'd wear it on, that that of love might last;
For when they throw off one, we soon the other cast.
Their sympathy is such—
The fate of one, the other scarce can fly;
They live together, and together die.

Exit

[SCENE V.—*A Room in* LORD FOPPINGTON'S *House*]

Enter MISS HOYDEN *and* NURSE

HOYDEN. But is it sure and certain, say you, he's my lord's own brother?

NURSE. As sure as he's your lawful husband.

HOYDEN. Ecod, if I had known that in time, I don't know but I might have kept him: for, between you and I, nurse, he'd have made a husband worth two of this I have. But which do you think you should fancy most, nurse?

NURSE. Why, truly, in my poor fancy, madam, your first husband is the prettier gentleman.

HOYDEN. I don't like my lord's shapes, nurse.

NURSE. Why, in good truly, as a body may say, he is but a slam.

HOYDEN. What do you think now he puts me in mind of? Don't you remember a long, loose, shambling sort of a horse my father called Washy?

NURSE. As like as two twin-brothers!

HOYDEN. Ecod, I have thought so a hundred times: faith, I'm tired of him.

NURSE. Indeed, madam, I think you had e'en as good stand to your first bargain.

HOYDEN. Oh, but, nurse, we han't considered the main thing yet. If I leave my lord, I must leave my lady, too; and when I rattle about the streets in my coach, they'll only say, There goes mistress—mistress—mistress what? What's this man's name I have married, nurse?

NURSE. 'Squire Fashion.

HOYDEN. 'Squire Fashion is it?—Well, 'Squire, that's better than nothing. Do you think one could not get him made a knight, nurse?

NURSE. I don't know but one might, madam, when the king's in a good humor.

HOYDEN. Ecod, that would do rarely. For then he'd be as good a man as my father, you know.

NURSE. By'r Lady, and that's as good as the best of 'em.

HOYDEN. So 'tis, faith; for then I shall be my lady, and your ladyship at every word, and that's all I have to care for. Ha, nurse, but hark you me; one thing more, and then I have done. I'm afraid, if I change my husband again, I shan't have so much money to throw about, nurse.

NURSE. Oh, enough's as good as a feast. Besides, madam, one don't know but as much may fall to your share with the younger brother as with the elder. For though these lords have a power of wealth indeed, yet, as I have heard say, they give it all to their sluts and their trulls, who joggle it about in their coaches, with a murrain to 'em! whilst poor madam sits sighing, and wishing, and knotting, and crying, and has not a spare half-crown to buy her a *Practice of Piety*.[1]

HOYDEN. Oh, but for that don't deceive yourself, nurse. For this I must say for my lord, and a—(*Snapping her fingers*) for him; he's as free as an open house at Christmas. For this very morning he told me I should have two hundred a year to buy pins. Now, nurse, if he gives me two hundred a year to buy pins, what do you think he'll give me to buy fine petticoats?

NURSE. Ah, my dearest, he deceives thee faully, and he's no better than a rogue for his pains! These Londoners have got a gibberidge with 'em would confound a gipsy. That which they call pin-money is to buy their wives everything in the 'varsal world, down to their very shoe-ties. Nay, I have heard folks say, that some ladies, if they will have gallants, as they call 'em, are forced to find them out of their pin-money too.

HOYDEN. Has he served me so, say ye?— Then I'll be his wife no longer, so that's fixed. Look, here he comes, with all the fine folk at's heels. Ecod, nurse, these London ladies will laugh till they crack again, to see me slip my collar, and run away from my husband. But, d'ye hear? Pray, take care of one thing: when the business comes to break out, be sure you get between me and my father, for you know his tricks; he'll knock me down.

NURSE. I'll mind him, ne'er fear, madam.

Enter LORD FOPPINGTON, LOVELESS, WORTHY, AMANDA, *and* BERINTHIA

LORD FOPPINGTON. Ladies and gentlemen, you are all welcome.—Loveless, that's my wife; prithee do me the favor to salute her; and dost hear,—(*Aside to him*) if thau hast a mind to try thy fartune, to be revenged of me, I won't take it ill, stap my vitals!

LOVELESS. You need not fear, sir; I'm too fond of my own wife to have the least inclination to yours. (*All salute* MISS HOYDEN)

LORD FOPPINGTON. (*Aside*) I'd give a thousand paund he would make love to her, that he may see she has sense enough to prefer me to him, though his own wife has not.— (*Viewing him*) He's a very beastly fellow, in my opinion.

HOYDEN. (*Aside*) What a power of fine men there are in this London! He that kissed me first is a goodly gentleman, I promise you. Sure those wives have a rare time on't that live here always.

Enter SIR TUNBELLY CLUMSEY, *with* Musicians, Dancers, &c.

SIR TUNBELLY. Come, come in, good people, come in! Come, tune your fiddles, tune your fiddles!—(*To the* hautboys) Bagpipes, make ready there. Come, strike up. (*Sings*)

---

[1] A manual of devotion (Ward).

For this is Hoyden's wedding-day,
And therefore we keep holiday,
And come to be merry.

Ha! there's my wench, i'faith. Touch and take, I'll warrant her; she'll breed like a tame rabbit.

HOYDEN. (*Aside*) Ecod, I think my father's gotten drunk before supper.

SIR TUNBELLY. (*To* LOVELESS *and* WORTHY.) Gentlemen, you are welcome.—(*Saluting* AMANDA *and* BERINTHIA) Ladies, by your leave.—(*Aside*) Ha! they bill like turtles. Udsookers, they set my old blood a-fire; I shall cuckold somebody before morning.

LORD FOPPINGTON. (*To* SIR TUNBELLY) Sir, you being master of the entertainment, will you desire the company to sit?

SIR TUNBELLY. Oons, sir, I'm the happiest man on this side the Ganges!

LORD FOPPINGTON. (*Aside*) This is a mighty unaccountable old fellow.—(*To* SIR TUNBELLY) I said, sir, it would be convenient to ask the company to sit.

SIR TUNBELLY. Sit?—with all my heart.—Come, take your places, ladies; take your places, gentlemen.—Come, sit down, sit down; a pox of ceremony! take your places. (*They sit and the masque begins*)

DIALOGUE BETWEEN CUPID AND HYMEN

1

CUPID. Thou bane to my empire, thou spring of contest,
Thou source of all discord, thou period to rest,
Instruct me, what wretches in bondage can see,
That the aim of their life is still pointed to thee.

2

HYMEN. Instruct me, thou little, impertinent god,
From whence all thy subjects have taken the mode
To grow fond of a change, to whatever it be,
And I'll tell thee why those would be bound who are free.

Chorus

For change, we're for change, to whatever it be,
We are neither contented with freedom nor thee.
  Constancy's an empty sound,
  Heaven, and earth, and all go round,
  All the works of Nature move,
  And the joys of life and love
    Are in variety.

3

CUPID. Were love the reward of a painstaking life,
Had a husband the art to be fond of his wife,
Were virtue so plenty, a wife could afford,
These very hard times, to be true to her lord,
Some specious account might be given of those
Who are tied by the tail, to be led by the nose.

4

But since 'tis the fate of a man and his wife,
To consume all their days in contention and strife;
Since, whatever the bounty of Heaven may create her,
He's morally sure he shall heartily hate her,
I think 'twere much wiser to ramble at large,
And the volleys of love on the herd to discharge.

5

HYMEN. Some color of reason thy counsel might bear,
Could a man have no more than his wife to his share:
Or were I a monarch so cruelly just,
To oblige a poor wife to be true to her trust;
But I have not pretended, for many years past,
By marrying of people, to make 'em grow chaste.

6

I therefore advise thee to let me go on,
Thou'lt find I'm the strength and support of thy throne;
For hadst thou but eyes, thou wouldst quickly perceive it,
  How smoothly the dart
  Slips into the heart
  Of a woman that's wed;
  Whilst the shivering maid
Stands trembling, and wishing, but dare not receive it.

Chorus

For change, &c.

The Masque ended, enter YOUNG FASHION, COUPLER, *and* BULL

SIR TUNBELLY. So; very fine, very fine, i'faith! this is something like a wedding. Now, if supper were but ready, I'd say a short grace; and if I had such a bedfellow as Hoyden to-night—I'd say as short prayers.
(*Seeing* YOUNG FASHION)
How now!—What have we got here? A ghost? Nay, it must be so, for his flesh and blood could never have dared to appear before me.—(*To him*) Ah, rogue!

LORD FOPPINGTON. Stap my vitals, Tam again?

SIR TUNBELLY. My lord, will you cut his throat, or shall I?

LORD FOPPINGTON. Leave him to me, sir, if you please.—Prithee, Tam, be so ingenuous now as to tell me what thy business is here?

FASHION. 'Tis with your bride.

LORD FOPPINGTON. Thau art the impudentest fellow that Nature has yet spawned into the warld, strike me speechless!

FASHION. Why, you know my modesty would have starved me; I sent it a-begging to you, and you would not give it a groat.

LORD FOPPINGTON. And dost thau expect by an excess of assurance to extart a maintenance fram me?

FASHION. (*Taking* MISS HOYDEN *by the hand*) I do intend to extort your mistress from you, and that I hope will prove one.

LORD FOPPINGTON. I ever thaught Newgate or Bedlam would be his fartune, and naw his fate's decided.—Prithee, Loveless, dost know of ever a mad doctor hard by?

FASHION. There's one at your elbow will cure you presently.—(*To* BULL) Prithee, doctor, take him in hand quickly.

LORD FOPPINGTON. Shall I beg the favor of you, sir, to pull your fingers out of my wife's hand?

FASHION. His wife! Look you there; now I hope you are all satisfied he's mad.

LORD FOPPINGTON. Naw is it nat possible far me to penetrate what species of fall it is thau art driving at!

SIR TUNBELLY. Here, here, here, let me beat out his brains, and that will decide all.

LORD FOPPINGTON. No; pray, sir, hold, we'll destray him presently accarding to law.

FASHION. (*To* BULL) Nay, then advance, doctor. Come, you are a man of conscience, answer boldly to the questions I shall ask. Did you not marry me to this young lady before ever that gentleman there saw her face?

BULL. Since the truth must out—I did.

FASHION. Nurse, sweet nurse, were not you a witness to it?

NURSE. Since my conscience bids me speak —I was.

FASHION. (*To* MISS HOYDEN) Madam, am not I your lawful husband?

HOYDEN. Truly I can't tell, but you married me first.

FASHION. Now I hope you are all satisfied?

SIR TUNBELLY. (*Offering to strike him, is held by* LOVELESS *and* WORTHY) Oons and thunder, you lie!

LORD FOPPINGTON. Pray, sir, be calm; the battle is in disarder, but requires more conduct than courage to rally our forces.—Pray, dactor, one word with you.—(*Aside to* BULL) Look you, sir, though I will not presume to calculate your notions of damnation fram the description you give us of hell, yet since there is at least a passibility you may have a pitchfark thrust in your backside, methinks it should not be worth your while to risk your saul in the next warld, for the sake of a begarly yaunger brather, who is nat able to make your bady happy in this.

BULL. Alas! my lord, I have no worldly ends; I speak the truth, heaven knows.

LORD FOPPINGTON. Nay, prithee, never engage heaven in the matter, for by all I can see, 'tis like to prove a business for the devil.

FASHION. Come, pray, sir, all above-board; no corrupting of evidences, if you please. This young lady is my lawful wife, and I'll justify it in all the courts of England; so your lordship (who always had a passion for variety) may go seek a new mistress if you think fit.

LORD FOPPINGTON. I am struck dumb with his impudence, and cannot pasitively tell whether ever I shall speak again or nat.

SIR TUNBELLY. Then let me come and examine the business a little, I'll jerk the truth out of 'em presently. Here, give me my dogwhip.

FASHION. Look you, old gentleman, 'tis in vain to make a noise; if you grow mutinous, I have some friends within call, have swords by their sides above four foot long; therefore be calm, hear the evidence patiently, and when the jury have given their verdict, pass sentence according to law. Here's honest Coupler shall be foreman, and ask as many questions as he pleases.

COUPLER. All I have to ask is, whether nurse persists in her evidence? The parson, I dare swear, will never flinch from his.

NURSE. (*To* SIR TUNBELLY, *kneeling*) I hope in heaven your worship will pardon me. I have served you long and faithfully, but in this thing I was over-reached; your worship, however, was deceived as well as I, and if the wedding-dinner had been ready, you had put madam to bed to him with your own hands.

Sir Tunbelly. But how durst you do this, without acquainting of me?

Nurse. Alas! if your worship had seen how the poor thing begged, and prayed, and clung, and twined about me, like ivy to an old wall, you would say, I who had suckled it and swaddled it, and nursed it both wet and dry, must have had a heart of adamant to refuse it.

Sir Tunbelly. Very well!

Fashion. Foreman, I expect your verdict.

Coupler. Ladies and gentlemen, what's your opinions?

All. A clear case! a clear case!

Coupler. Then, my young folks, I wish you joy.

Sir Tunbelly. (*To* Young Fashion) Come hither, stripling; if it be true then, that thou hast married my daughter, prithee tell me who thou art?

Fashion. Sir, the best of my condition is, I am your son-in-law; and the worst of it is, I am brother to that noble peer there.

Sir Tunbelly. Art thou brother to that noble peer?—Why, then, that noble peer, and thee, and thy wife, and the nurse, and the priest—may all go and be damned together.

Exit

Lord Foppington. (*Aside*) Now, for my part, I think the wisest thing a man can do with an aching heart is to put on a serene countenance; for a philosophical air is the most becoming thing in the world to the face of a person of quality. I will therefore bear my disgrace like a great man, and let the people see I am above an affront.—(*Aloud*) Dear Tam, since things are thus fallen aut, prithee give me leave to wish thee jay; I do it *de bon cœur*, strike me dumb! You have married a woman beautiful in her person, charming in her airs, prudent in her canduct, canstant in her inclinations, and of a nice marality, split my windpipe!

Fashion. Your lordship may keep up your spirits with your grimace if you please; I shall support mine with this lady, and two thousand pound a-year.—(*Taking* Miss Hoyden's *hand*) Come, madam:—

We once again, you see, are man and wife,
And now, perhaps, the bargain's struck for life.
If I mistake, and we should part again,
At least you see you may have choice of men:
Nay, should the war at length such havoc make,
That lovers should grow scarce, yet for your sake,

Kind heaven always will preserve a beau:
  (*Pointing to* Lord Foppington.)
You'll find his lordship ready to come to.
Lord Foppington. Her ladyship shall stap my vitals, if I do.

Exeunt

EPILOGUE

Spoken by Lord Foppington

Gentlemen and Ladies,
These people have regaled you here to-day
(In my opinion) with a saucy play;
In which the author does presume to show,
That coxcomb, *ab origine*—was beau.
Truly, I think the thing of so much weight,
That if some sharp chastisement ben't his fate,
Gad's curse! it may in time destroy the state.
I hold no one its friend, I must confess,
Who would discauntenance your men of dress.
Far, give me leave t'abserve, good clothes are things
Have ever been of great support to kings;
All treasons come from slovens, it is nat
Within the reach of gentle beaux to plat;
They have no gall, no spleen, no teeth, no stings,
Of all Gad's creatures, the most harmless things.
Through all recard, no prince was ever slain
By one who had a feather in his brain.
They're men of too refined an education,
To squabble with a court—for a vile dirt. nation.
I'm very pasitive you never saw
A through republican a finished beau.
Nor, truly, shall you very often see
A Jacobite much better dressed than he.
In shart, through all the courts that I have been in,
Your men of mischief—still are in faul linen.
Did ever one yet dance the Tyburn jig,
With a free air, or a well-pawdered wig?
Did ever highwayman yet bid you stand,
With a sweet bawdy snuff-bax in his hand?
Ar do you ever find they ask your purse
As men of breeding do?—Ladies, Gad's curse!
This author is a dag, and 'tis not fit
You should allow him ev'n one grain of wit:
To which, that his pretense may ne'er be named,
My humble motion is,—he may be damned.

THE WAY OF THE WORLD

A Comedy by William Congreve

*Audire est operæ pretium, procedere recte
Qui mæchos non vultis,*[1]
... metuat doti deprensa.[2]

William Congreve—"the great Mr. Congreve"—was born at Bardsey, near Leeds, the son of an army officer, in 1670, and baptized February 10, 1670. His father was ordered to Ireland, where Congreve was educated, first at Kilkenny School, and then at Trinity College, Dublin, which he entered in 1685, where he acquired an unusual knowledge of the classics. The family removing to England, Congreve became a member of the Middle Temple, joined in the fashionable society of wits, poets, and reigning beauties, and wrote a novel, *Incognita* (1692). His literary rise was rapid; he joined with Dryden and others in a translation of Juvenal and Persius (1693), and in January, 1693, saw his first comedy, *The Old Bachelor* acted with triumphal success at Drury Lane. Subsequent plays enhanced his reputation; *Love for Love*, for example, was chosen to open the new theater in Lincoln's Inn Fields, April 30, 1695, and his solitary tragedy, *The Mourning Bride*, which, according to Johnson, contains "the most poetical paragraph in the whole mass of English poetry," ran for thirteen nights. *The Way of the World*, however, was coolly received, and thereafter (1700) Congreve did little literary work.

In the meantime Congreve had become involved in the controversy over the morality of the stage, being specifically attacked in Jeremy Collier's famous publication, *A Short View of the Immorality and Profaneness of the English Stage* (1697/8), to which he responded in his *Amendments of Mr. Collier's False and Imperfect Citations* (1698), in which he vigorously defended his plays from misrepresentation. He held various honorary appointments under King William and Queen Anne, and was for a time associated with Vanbrugh in the direction of the Queen's Theatre in the Haymarket (1705–6). Although the period of Congreve's important creative work closes in 1700, he was one of the most admired literary figures of the Age of Anne; the Duchess of Marlborough was his patron, Pope, Gay, Swift, Steele, and Voltaire were his friends; and the occasional poem, or essay in *The Tatler* which he wrote, was received with prodigious respect. Moreover, in 1710, Tonson, the great publisher, brought out a collected edition of Congreve's works. Universally lamented, Congreve died January 19, 1729, and was buried with much pomp and ceremony in Westminster Abbey. As a typical man of the world, his later years saw him take up avarice to a mild degree; but, this aside, he left behind him a reputation for polish, wit, and good humor, such as few men of his time possessed. It is curious to note that the Duchess of Marlborough set up a statue of him at her table, which was regularly served with wine at dinner.

The standard life of the dramatist is Edmund Gosse, *Life of William Congreve;* the revised edition (1924) should be used. The life in the *Dictionary of National Biography* is eminently Victorian. The account in Dr. Johnson's *Lives of the Poets* should not be neglected. There is also an important account in the first volume of Congreve's *Complete Works*, edited by Montague Summers (1923).

CONGREVE'S DRAMATIC WORKS

The Old Batchelor (comedy) (T.R., Jan., 1693), 1693.
The Double Dealer (comedy) (T.R., Nov., 1693), 1694.
Love for Love (comedy) (L.I.F., April 30, 1695), 1695.
The Mourning Bride (tragedy) (L.I.F., 1697) 1697.

---

[1] It is worth while for those who do not wish well to adulterers to hear how they are troubled in every way. Horace, *Satires*, I, ii, 37–8. Congreve omits the last phrase.

[2] Being detected, the woman fears for her dowry. Horace, *Satires*, I, ii, 131.

The Way of the World (comedy) (L.I.F., March, 1700), 1700.
The Judgment of Paris (masque) (D.G., March, 1701), 1701.
Semele (opera) (performed as an oratorio with music by Händel, C.G., Feb. 10, 1744), 1710.
(With Vanbrugh and Walsh) Monsieur de Pourceaugnac; or, Squire Trelooby (comedy) (L.I.F., March 30, 1704), 1704.

As Mr. Congreve is the wittiest man that ever wrote our language in the theater, so his plays are the highest peak in the development of Restoration comedy, and 'tis to be regretted that after *The Way of the World* the author writ no more. It is indeed possible that in this comedy the dramatist brought the form (save in the matter of plot) to the highest perfection of which it was capable, so that, despairing of surpassing himself, he abandoned the stage.

The aristocratical spirit of our dramatist led him to disdain the perfecting of a probable plot and to abandon the aid of farce as he perfected his manner. The plot of his second comedy, *The Double Dealer*, is simple; and the interest of the drama is carried forward rather by the witty speeches of the personages than by any surprises in the fable. In his third comedy, *Love for Love*, Mr. Congreve admitted farce in the intrigues of Mrs. Frail and Tattle, and of Ben, Jeremy, and Miss Prue; but in *The Way of the World* the play is all of one piece, 'tis a world of wit and pleasure inhabited only by persons of quality and "deformed neither by realism nor by farce." If the plot be confused, 'tis not inextricable, and the situations but serve for the conversation, which is of such order that, though no one save Mr. Congreve could be thus witty, everyone wishes vainly that he might be. 'Twas Mr. Congreve's design (as expressed in his dedication of the play to my Lord Montague) to polish and refine the language of dialogue, and though the speeches of the characters are always such as appeal to the ear, and the diction is the language of Mr. Congreve's time, there is in the play no superfluous word, and the style may truly be called classical.

Mr. Congreve was doubtless aided by the brilliant casts which were assembled for his plays; nevertheless, despite the lack of care shown in the management of his plots, no one has more artfully used the resources of the stage. By delaying the entrance of Mrs. Millamant until the second act, he arouses expectation to the highest pitch, and only Mr. Congreve could satisfy this expectancy by creating a heroine who is, by universal consent, the most perfect in Restoration drama. Nor is the fifth act, though injudiciously crowded with event, without a constant flow of surprise and reprisal.

The design of the play was to ridicule affected, or false, wit; and though Mr. Congreve expressly disclaims the making the objects of his satire contemptible, 'tis probable that his play came too close to the faults of the town to be wholly agreeable to the audience. The dialogue is, moreover, closely woven, and the repartee (partaking of an agreeable mixture of intellect and humor) demands such attention as in all probability to have exhausted the capacity of its auditors. But although the play is most agreeable in the perusal, it has, since its first failure, been successfully attempted on the stage, and either because of familiarity or because of our greater appreciation of the beauties of stage wit, it has ever pleased when produced. The characters of Mirabell and Mrs. Millamant in particular, and of Lady Wishfort, Foible, Witwoud, and Petulant in the second range are most admirable, but no person in the play, not even excepting Fainall, fails to surprise us with witty observation. 'Tis a comedy of conversation among persons whose lives are spent in the pursuit of pleasure, and no other piece of its time so delightfully instructs us in the way of the world. The piece was first produced at Lincoln's Inn Fields in March, 1700.

There is a wealth of critical material on Congreve. Consult the essays by Lamb, Macaulay, and Meredith (*An Essay on Comedy*), and the more recent work by Bonamy Dobrée, *Restoration Comedy, 1660–1720* (1924). A special study is D. Schmid, *Congreve, sein Leben und seine Lustspiele* (Vienna, 1897); and see Kathleen M. Lynch, *The Social Mode of Restoration Comedy* (1926) and J. W. Krutch, *Comedy and Conscience* (1924).

THE WAY OF THE WORLD

DRAMATIS PERSONÆ [1]

FAINALL, *in love with Mrs. Marwood*, Mr. Betterton
MIRABELL, *in love with Mrs. Millamant* Mr. Verbruggen
WITWOUD } Mr. Bowen
followers of Mrs. Millamant
PETULANT } Mr. Bowman
SIR WILFULL WITWOUD, *half-brother to Witwoud, and nephew to Lady Wishfort* Mr. Underhill
WAITWELL, *servant to Mirabell* Mr. Bright
Dancers, Footmen, and Attendants
LADY WISHFORT, *enemy to Mirabell, for having falsely pretended love to her* Mrs. Leigh

MRS. MILLAMANT, *a fine lady, niece to Lady Wishfort, and loves Mirabell* Mrs. Bracegirdle
MRS. MARWOOD, *friend to Mr. Fainall, and likes Mirabell* Mrs. Barry
MRS. FAINALL, *daughter to Lady Wishfort, and wife to Fainall, formerly friend to Mirabell* Mrs. Bowman
FOIBLE, *woman to Lady Wishfort* Mrs. Willis
MINCING, *woman to Mrs. Millamant* Mrs. Prince
[BETTY, *waiting-maid at a chocolate-house*]
[PEG, *maid to Lady Wishfort*]
[Singer]

SCENE: *London*

[DEDICATION]

TO THE RIGHT HONORABLE RALPH, EARL OF MONTAGUE, ETC.[2]

My Lord,

Whether the world will arraign me of vanity or not, that I have presumed to dedicate this comedy to your Lordship, I am yet in doubt; though it may be it is some degree of vanity even to doubt of it. One who has at any time had the honor of your Lordship's conversation, cannot be supposed to think very meanly of that which he would prefer to your perusal; yet it were to incur the imputation of too much sufficiency, to pretend to such a merit as might abide the test of your Lordship's censure.

Whatever value may be wanting to this play while yet it is mine, will be sufficiently made up to it when it is once become your Lordship's; and it is my security that I cannot have overrated it more by my dedication, than your Lordship will dignify it by your patronage.

That it succeeded on the stage, was almost beyond my expectation; for but little of it was prepared for that general taste which seems now to be predominant in the palates of our audience.

Those characters which are meant to be ridiculed in most of our comedies are of fools so gross that, in my humble opinion, they should rather disturb than divert the well-natured and reflecting part of an audience; they are rather objects of charity than contempt; and instead of moving our mirth, they ought very often to excite our compassion.

This reflection moved me to design some characters which should appear ridiculous not so much through a natural folly (which is incorrigible, and therefore not proper for the stage) as through an affected wit; a wit which at the same time that it is affected, is also false. As there is some difficulty in the formation of a character of this nature, so there is some hazard which attends the progress of its success upon the stage; for many come to a play so overcharged with criticism, that they

---

[1] Because of the vagueness and complexity of the story, it is well to note that Witwoud and Petulant have nothing to do with the plot; and that the attentions of Sir Wilful Witwoud, who is mainly a comic butt, to Mrs. Millamant, have little or no relation to the main intrigue.

[2] Ralph Montagu (1638?–1709), a gallant at the Restoration court, who, however, was favored by William III, by whom he was created Viscount Monthermer and Earl of Montagu in 1689. Congreve's picture of him as a patron of the arts is scarcely justified.

402

very often let fly their censure, when through their rashness they have mistaken their aim. This I had occasion lately to observe; for this play had been acted two or three days before some of these hasty judges could find the leisure to distinguish betwixt the character of a Witwoud and a Truewit.[1]

I must beg your Lordship's pardon for this digression from the true course of this epistle; but that it may not seem altogether impertinent, I beg that I may plead the occasion of it, in part of that excuse of which I stand in need, for recommending this comedy to your protection. It is only by the countenance of your Lordship and the few so qualified, that such who write with care and pains can hope to be distinguished; for the prostituted name of poet promiscuously levels all that bear it.

Terence, the most correct writer in the world, had a Scipio and a Lælius,[2] if not to assist him, at least to support him in his reputation; and notwithstanding his extraordinary merit, it may be their countenance was not more than necessary.

The purity of his style, the delicacy of his turns, and the justness of his characters, were all of them beauties which the greater part of his audience were incapable of tasting; some of the coarsest strokes of Plautus[3]; so severely censured by Horace, were more likely to affect the multitude; such who come with expectation to laugh at the last act of a play, and are better entertained with two or three unseasonable jests, than with the artful solution of the *fable*.

As Terence[4] excelled in his performances, so had he great advantages to encourage his undertakings; for he built most on the foundations of Menander; his plots were generally modelled, and his characters ready drawn to his hand. He copied Menander, and Menander had no less light in the formation of his characters, from the observations of Theophrastus,[5] of whom he was a disciple; and Theophrastus, it is known, was not only the disciple, but the immediate successor, of Aristotle,[6] the first and greatest judge of poetry. These were great models to design by; and the further advantage which Terence possessed, towards giving his plays the due ornaments of purity of style and justness of manners, was not less considerable, from the freedom of conversation which was permitted him with Lælius and Scipio,[7] two of the greatest and most polite men of his age. And indeed the privilege of such a conversation is the only certain means of attaining to the perfection of dialogue.

If it has happened in any part of this comedy that I have gained a turn of style or expression more correct, or at least, more corrigible than in those which I have formerly written, I must, with equal pride and gratitude, ascribe it to the honor of your Lordship's admitting me into your conversation, and that of a society where everybody else was so well worthy of you, in your retirement last summer from the town; for it was immediately after that this comedy was written. If I have failed in my performance, it is only to be regretted, where there were so many not inferior either to a Scipio or a Lælius, that there should be one wanting equal in capacity to a Terence.

If I am not mistaken, poetry is almost the only art which has not yet laid claim to your Lordship's patronage. Architecture and painting, to the great honor of our country, have flourished under your influence and protection. In the meantime, poetry, the eldest sister of all arts, and parent of most, seems to have resigned her birthright, by having neglected to pay her duty to your Lordship, and by permitting others of a later extraction to prepossess that place in your esteem to which none can pretend a better title. Poetry, in its nature, is sacred to the good and great; the relation between them is reciprocal, and they are ever propitious to it. It is the privilege of

---

[1] Leading character in Jonson's *Epicœne*, 1609.

[2] The Roman comic dramatist Terence (B.C. 195-159?) had as his patrons the younger Scipio (Africanus Minor), the patron of poets, and the friend of the younger Lælius, who appears in the dialogues of Cicero. Terence is said to have lived with them on terms of the most remarkable intimacy.

[3] In Horace's *Ars Poetica* that poet finds fault with the Romans for admiring the scurrilous passages in the comedies of Plautus (B.C. 254-184).

[4] Terence went to Greece (where he died) in order to study the comedies of Menander (B.C. 342-291), the chief Athenian dramatist of the "new comedy," which resembled the Jonsonian comedy of humors. Terence followed so closely in his footsteps as to be dubbed by Julius Cæsar a "halved Menander."

[5] Theophrastus (d. B.C. 287), whose *Characters* greatly influenced the "character writing" of the seventeenth century. He was the favorite pupil of Aristotle.

[6] The reference is to Aristotle's treatise on the art of poetry.

[7] Both Lælius and Scipio were enthusiastic students of Greek culture.

poetry to address to them, and it is their prerogative alone to give it protection.

This received maxim is a general apology for all writers who consecrate their labors to great men: but I could wish at this time, that this address were exempted from the common pretence of all dedications; and that I can distinguish your Lordship even among the most deserving, so this offering might become remarkable by some particular instance of respect which should assure your Lordship, that I am, with all due sense of your extreme worthiness and humanity,

    My Lord,

        Your Lordship's most obedient,
        and most obliged servant,
            Will. Congreve.

PROLOGUE

Spoken by Mr. Betterton

Of those few fools who with ill stars are cursed,
Sure scribbling fools called poets, fare the worst:
For they're a sort of fools which Fortune makes,
And after she has made 'em fools, forsakes.
With Nature's oafs 'tis quite a different case,
For Fortune favors all her idiot-race. 6
In her own nest the cuckoo-eggs we find,
O'er which she broods to hatch the changeling-kind.
No portion for her own she has to spare,
So much she dotes on her adopted care. 10
    Poets are bubbles, by the town drawn in,
Suffered at first some trifling stakes to win;
But what unequal hazards do they run!
Each time they write they venture all they've won:
The squire that's buttered [1] still, is sure to be undone. 15
This author heretofore has found your favor;
But pleads no merit from his past behavior.
To build on that might prove a vain presumption,
Should grants, to poets made, admit resumption:
And in Parnassus he must lose his seat, 20
If that be found a forfeited estate.

He owns with toil he wrought the following scenes;
But, if they're naught, ne'er spare him for his pains:
Damn him the more; have no commiseration
For dullness on mature deliberation. 25
He swears he'll not resent one hissed-off scene,
Nor, like those peevish wits, his play maintain,
Who, to assert their sense, your taste arraign.
Some plot we think he has, and some new thought;
Some humor too, no farce—but that's a fault.
Satire, he thinks, you ought not to expect; 31
For so reformed a town who dares correct?
To please, this time, has been his sole pretence,
He'll not instruct, lest it should give offence.
Should he by chance a knave or fool expose,
That hurts none here; sure, here are none of those. 36
In short, our play shall (with your leave to show it)
Give you one instance of a passive poet,
Who to your judgments yields all resignation;
So save or damn, after your own discretion.

ACT I

Scene I. *A chocolate-house*

Mirabell *and* Fainall [*rising from cards*] Betty *waiting*

Mirabell. You are a fortunate man, Mr. Fainall!

Fainall. Have we done?

Mirabell. What you please. I'll play on to entertain you.

Fainall. No, I'll give you your revenge another time, when you are not so indifferent; you are thinking of something else now, and play too negligently. The coldness of a losing gamester lessens the pleasure of the winner.

---

[1] Fulsomely praised. Apparently the first appearance of this word in print.

I'd no more play with a man that slighted his ill fortune than I'd make love to a woman who undervalued the loss of her reputation.

MIRABELL. You have a taste extremely delicate, and are for refining on your pleasures.

FAINALL. Prithee, why so reserved? Something has put you out of humor.

MIRABELL. Not at all. I happen to be grave to-day, and you are gay; that's all.

FAINALL. Confess, Millamant and you quarrelled last night after I left you; my fair cousin has some humors that would tempt the patience of a stoic. What, some coxcomb came in, and was well received by her, while you were by?

MIRABELL. Witwoud and Petulant; and what was worse, her aunt, your wife's mother, my evil genius; or to sum up all in her own name, my old Lady Wishfort came in.

FAINALL. Oh, there it is then! She has a lasting passion for you, and with reason.— What, then my wife was there?

MIRABELL. Yes, and Mrs. Marwood, and three or four more, whom I never saw before. Seeing me, they all put on their grave faces, whispered one another; then complained aloud of the vapors [1] and after fell into a profound silence.

FAINALL. They had a mind to be rid of you.

MIRABELL. For which reason I resolved not to stir. At last the good old lady broke through her painful taciturnity with an invective against long visits. I would not have understood her, but Millamant joining in the argument, I rose, and with a constrained smile, told her I thought nothing was so easy as to know when a visit began to be troublesome. She reddened, and I withdrew without expecting her reply.

FAINALL. You were to blame to resent what she spoke only in compliance with her aunt.

MIRABELL. She is more mistress of herself than to be under the necessity of such a resignation.

FAINALL. What! though half her fortune depends upon her marrying with my lady's approbation?

MIRABELL. I was then in such a humor, that I should have been better pleased if she had been less discreet.

FAINALL. Now I remember, I wonder not they were weary of you; last night was one of their cabal nights. They have 'em three times a week, and meet by turns at one another's apartments, where they come together like the coroner's inquest, to sit upon the murdered reputations of the week. You and I are excluded, and it was once proposed that all the male sex should be excepted; but somebody moved that, to avoid scandal, there might be one man of the community, upon which motion Witwoud and Petulant were enrolled members.

MIRABELL. And who may have been the foundress of this sect? My Lady Wishfort, I warrant, who publishes her detestation of mankind, and, full of the vigor of fifty-five, declares for a friend and ratafia[2]; and let posterity shift for itself, she'll breed no more.

FAINALL. The discovery of your sham addresses to her, to conceal your love to her niece, has provoked this separation; had you dissembled better, things might have continued in the state of nature.

MIRABELL. I did as much as man could, with any reasonable conscience; I proceeded to the very last act of flattery with her, and was guilty of a song in her commendation. Nay, I got a friend to put her into a lampoon and compliment her with the imputation of an affair with a young fellow, which I carried so far that I told her the malicious town took notice that she was grown fat of a sudden; and when she lay in of a dropsy, persuaded her she was reported to be in labor. The devil's in't, if an old woman is to be flattered further, unless a man should endeavor downright personally to debauch her; and that my virtue forbade me. But for the discovery of this amour I am indebted to your friend, or your wife's friend, Mrs. Marwood.

FAINALL. What should provoke her to be your enemy unless she has made you advances which you have slighted? Women do not easily forgive omissions of that nature.

MIRABELL. She was always civil to me till of late. I confess I am not one of those coxcombs who are apt to interpret a woman's good manners to her prejudice, and think that she who does not refuse 'em everything, can refuse 'em nothing.

FAINALL. You are a gallant man, Mirabell; and though you may have cruelty enough not to satisfy a lady's longing, you have too much generosity not to be tender of her honor. Yet

---

[1] The blues, tedium.

[2] A cordial flavored with the kernels of peach, cherry apricot, or almond.

you speak with an indifference which seems to be affected and confesses you are conscious of a negligence.

MIRABELL. You pursue the argument with a distrust that seems to be unaffected and confesses you are conscious of a concern for which the lady is more indebted to you than is your wife.

FAINALL. Fie, fie, friend! If you grow censorious I must leave you.—I'll look upon the gamesters in the next room.

MIRABELL. Who are they?

FAINALL. Petulant and Witwoud.—[*To* BETTY] Bring me some chocolate.

[*Exit* FAINALL]

MIRABELL. Betty, what says your clock?

BETTY. Turned of the last canonical hour,[1] sir. [*Exit* BETTY [2]]

MIRABELL. How pertinently the jade answers me!—(*Looking on his watch*[3])—Ha? almost one o'clock!—Oh, y'are come!

Enter a Servant

Well, is the grand affair over? You have been something tedious.

SERVANT. Sir, there's such coupling at Pancras[4] that they stand behind one another, as 'twere in a country dance. Ours was the last couple to lead up, and no hopes appearing of dispatch—besides, the parson growing hoarse, we were afraid his lungs would have failed before it came to our turn; so we drove round to Duke's-place[5] and there they were riveted in a trice.

MIRABELL. So, so! You are sure they are married?

SERVANT. Married and bedded, sir; I am witness.

MIRABELL. Have you the certificate?

SERVANT. Here it is, sir.

MIRABELL. Has the tailor brought Waitwell's clothes home, and the new liveries?

SERVANT. Yes, sir.

MIRABELL. That's well. Do you go home again, d'ye hear, and adjourn the consummation till further orders. Bid Waitwell shake his ears, and Dame Partlet[6] rustle up her feathers and meet me at one o'clock by Rosamond's Pond,[7] that I may see her before she returns to her lady; and as you tender your ears be secret. [*Exit* SERVANT]

[*Enter* FAINALL]

FAINALL. Joy of your success, Mirabell; you look pleased.

MIRABELL. Aye; I have been engaged in a matter of some sort of mirth, which is not yet ripe for discovery. I am glad this is not a cabal night. I wonder, Fainall, that you, who are married and of consequence should be discreet, will suffer your wife to be of such a party.[8]

FAINALL. Faith, I am not jealous. Besides, most who are engaged are women and relations; and for the men, they are of a kind too contemptible to give scandal.

MIRABELL. I am of another opinion. The greater the coxcomb, always the more the scandal; for a woman who is not a fool, can have but one reason for associating with a man who is one.

FAINALL. Are you jealous as often as you see Witwoud entertained by Millamant?

MIRABELL. Of her understanding I am, if not of her person.

FAINALL. You do her wrong; for, to give her her due, she has wit.

MIRABELL. She has beauty enough to make any man think so; and complaisance enough not to contradict him who shall tell her so.

FAINALL. For a passionate lover, methinks you are a man somewhat too discerning in the failings of your mistress.

---

[1] Hour of legal marriage.

[2] Betty apparently returns to the stage either with Fainall or a little later.

[3] It should be remembered that the watch of the period was a large, turnip-shaped affair.

[4] St. Pancras Church, where marriages could be performed at any time without a license.

[5] Where St. James's Church was situated. Here irregular or "Fleet street" marriages were performed.

[6] I.e., the hen.

[7] In St. James's Park. See the stage direction for Act II.

[8] In order to keep the plot clear, it should be noted that Mirabell is preparing his trick of sending his servant Waitwell, disguised as Sir Rowland, to woo and win Lady Wishfort, who does not wish him to marry Millamant. Lady Wishfort has the power to cut off Millamant from a legacy of six thousand pounds if she marries against her aunt's wishes. Mirabell plans to compel her to acquiesce in his union with Millamant, on pain of making public the humiliating trick that has been played on her. The hypocritical Fainall, however, wants Lady Wishfort to disown Millamant in order that the six thousand pounds may descend to Mrs. Fainall, when Fainall and his mistress, Mrs. Marwood, plan to get possession of the money. (See pp. 413–414.) The student should determine how far in this scene Mirabell detects Fainall's true character.

MIRABELL. And for a discerning man, somewhat too passionate a lover; for I like her with all her faults—nay, like her for her faults. Her follies are so natural, or so artful, that they become her; and those affectations which in another woman would be odious, serve but to make her more agreeable. I'll tell thee, Fainall, she once used me with that insolence, that in revenge I took her to pieces, sifted her, and separated her failings; I studied 'em, and got 'em by rote. The catalogue was so large that I was not without hopes one day or other to hate her heartily: to which end I so used myself to think of 'em, that at length, contrary to my design and expectation, they gave me every hour less and less disturbance, till in a few days it became habitual to me to remember 'em without being displeased. They are now grown as familiar to me as my own frailties, and, in all probability, in a little time longer I shall like 'em as well.

FAINALL. Marry her, marry her! Be half as well acquainted with her charms as you are with her defects, and my life on't, you are your own man again.

MIRABELL. Say you so?

FAINALL. Aye, aye, I have experience: I have a wife, and so forth.

Enter MESSENGER

MESSENGER. Is one Squire Witwoud here?

BETTY. Yes, what's your business?

MESSENGER. I have a letter for him from his brother Sir Wilfull, which I am charged to deliver into his own hands.

BETTY. He's in the next room, friend—that way. [*Exit* Messenger]

MIRABELL. What, is the chief of that noble family in town—Sir Wilfull Witwoud?

FAINALL. He is expected to-day. Do you know him?

MIRABELL. I have seen him; he promises to be an extraordinary person. I think you have the honor to be related to him.

FAINALL. Yes; he is half-brother to this Witwoud by a former wife, who was sister to my Lady Wishfort, my wife's mother. If you marry Millamant, you must call cousins too.[1]

MIRABELL. I had rather be his relation than his acquaintance.

FAINALL. He comes to town in order to equip himself for travel.

MIRABELL. For travel! Why, the man that I mean is above forty.

FAINALL. No matter for that; 'tis for the honor of England, that all Europe should know we have blockheads of all ages.

MIRABELL. I wonder there is not an act of parliament to save the credit of the nation, and prohibit the exportation of fools.

FAINALL. By no means; 'tis better as 'tis. 'Tis better to trade with a little loss, than to be quite eaten up with being overstocked.

MIRABELL. Pray, are the follies of this knight-errant and those of the squire his brother anything related?

FAINALL. Not at all; Witwoud grows by the knight, like a medlar[2] grafted on a crab. One will melt in your mouth, and t'other set your teeth on edge; one is all pulp, and the other all core.

MIRABELL. So one will be rotten before he be ripe, and the other will be rotten without ever being ripe at all.

FAINALL. Sir Wilfull is an odd mixture of bashfulness and obstinacy.—But when he's drunk, he's as loving as the monster in *The Tempest*,[3] and much after the same manner. To give t'other his due, he has something of good nature, and does not always want wit.

MIRABELL. Not always; but as often as his memory fails him, and his commonplace[4] of comparisons. He is a fool with a good memory and some few scraps of other folks' wit. He is one whose conversation can never be approved; yet it is now and then to be endured. He has indeed one good quality—he is not exceptious; for he so passionately affects the reputation of understanding raillery, that he will construe an affront into a jest, and call downright rudeness and ill language, satire and fire.

FAINALL. If you have a mind to finish his picture, you have an opportunity to do it at full length.—Behold the original!

---

[1] This complicated relationship need not be kept in mind to understand the plot.

[2] The fruit of the medlar tree resembles a crab-apple, but is not edible until it begins to decay. See lines 22–24, below.

[3] Caliban, who in Shakespeare's play (Act II, scene ii) becomes very loving to Trinculo and Stephano after they gave him sack to drink. But see in Dryden's *Works* the Dryden-Davenant version, Act III.

[4] A commonplace book was a collection of passages or memoranda.

Enter WITWOUD

WITWOUD. Afford me your compassion, my dears! Pity me, Fainall! Mirabell, pity me!

MIRABELL. I do, from my soul.

FAINALL. Why, what's the matter?

WITWOUD. No letters for me, Betty?

BETTY. Did not a messenger bring you one but now, sir?

WITWOUD. Aye, but no other?

BETTY. No, sir.

WITWOUD. That's hard, that's very hard. —A messenger, a mule, a beast of burden! He has brought me a letter from the fool my brother, as heavy as a panegyric in a funeral sermon, or a copy of commendatory verses from one poet to another. And what's worse, 'tis as sure a forerunner of the author as an epistle dedicatory.

MIRABELL. A fool,—and your brother, Witwoud!

WITWOUD. Aye, aye, my half-brother. My half-brother he is, no nearer, upon honor.

MIRABELL. Then 'tis possible he may be but half a fool.

WITWOUD. Good, good, Mirabell, *le drôle!* [1] Good, good; hang him, don't let's talk of him.—Fainall, how does your lady? Gad, I say anything in the world to get this fellow out of my head. I beg pardon that I should ask a man of pleasure and the town, a question at once so foreign and domestic. But I talk like an old maid at a marriage; I don't know what I say. But she's the best woman in the world.

FAINALL. 'Tis well you don't know what you say, or else your commendation would go near to make me either vain or jealous.

WITWOUD. No man in town lives well with a wife but Fainall.—Your judgment, Mirabell?

MIRABELL. You had better step and ask his wife if you would be credibly informed.

WITWOUD. Mirabell?

MIRABELL. Aye.

WITWOUD. My dear, I ask ten thousand pardons—gad, I have forgot what I was going to say to you!

MIRABELL. I thank you heartily, heartily.

WITWOUD. No, but prithee, excuse me—my memory is such a memory.

MIRABELL. Have a care of such apologies, Witwoud; for I never knew a fool but he affected to complain either of the spleen [2] or his memory.

FAINALL. What have you done with Petulant?

WITWOUD. He's reckoning his money—my money it was. I have no luck to-day.

FAINALL. You may allow him to win of you at play, for you are sure to be too hard for him at repartee. Since you monopolize the wit that is between you, the fortune must be his, of course.

MIRABELL. I don't find that Petulant confesses the superiority of wit to be your talent, Witwoud.

WITWOUD. Come, come, you are malicious now, and would breed debates.—Petulant's my friend, and a very honest fellow, and a very pretty fellow, and has a smattering—faith and troth, a pretty deal of an odd sort of a small wit. Nay, I'll do him justice. I'm his friend, I won't wrong him.—And if he had any judgment in the world, he would not be altogether contemptible. Come, come, don't detract from the merits of my friend.

FAINALL. You don't take your friend to be over-nicely bred?

WITWOUD. No, no, hang him, the rogue has no manners at all, that I must own—no more breeding than a bumbaily [3] that I grant you—'tis pity, faith; the fellow has fire and life.

MIRABELL. What, courage?

WITWOUD. Hum, faith I don't know as to that; I can't say as to that. Yes, faith, in a controversy, he'll contradict anybody.

MIRABELL. Though 'twere a man whom he feared, or a woman whom he loved?

WITWOUD. Well, well, he does not always think before he speaks—we have all our failings. You're too hard upon him—you are, faith. Let me excuse him. I can defend most of his faults, except one or two. One he has, that's the truth on't; if he were my brother, I could not acquit him—that, indeed, I could wish were otherwise.

MIRABELL. Aye, marry, what's that, Witwoud?

WITWOUD. O pardon me!—Expose the infirmities of my friend?—No, my dear, excuse me there.

[1] The droll man.

[2] The spleen was popularly a source of melancholy and ill humor.

[3] Colloquialism for bailiff.

FAINALL. What! I warrant he's unsincere, or 'tis some such trifle.

WITWOUD. No, no, what if he be? 'Tis no matter for that; his wit will excuse that. A wit should no more be sincere than a woman constant; one argues a decay of parts, as t'other of beauty.

MIRABELL. Maybe you think him too positive?

WITWOUD. No, no, his being positive is an incentive to argument, and keeps up conversation.

FAINALL. Too illiterate?

WITWOUD. That? That's his happiness: his want of learning gives him the more opportunities to show his natural parts.

MIRABELL. He wants words?

WITWOUD. Aye, but I like him for that, now; for his want of words gives me the pleasure very often to explain his meaning.

FAINALL. He's impudent?

WITWOUD. No, that's not it.

MIRABELL. Vain?

WITWOUD. No.

MIRABELL. What! He speaks unseasonable truths sometimes, because he has not wit enough to invent an evasion?

WITWOUD. Truths! ha! ha! ha! No, no; since you will have it—I mean, he never speaks truth at all—that's all. He will lie like a chambermaid, or a woman of quality's porter. Now, that is a fault.

Enter Coachman

COACHMAN. Is Master Petulant here, mistress?

BETTY. Yes.

COACHMAN. Three gentlewomen in a coach would speak with him.

FAINALL. O brave Petulant!—three!

BETTY. I'll tell him.

COACHMAN. You must bring two dishes of chocolate and a glass of cinnamon-water.[1]

[*Exit* Coachman]

WITWOUD. That should be for two fasting strumpets, and a bawd troubled with wind. Now you may know what the three are.

MIRABELL. You are very free with your friend's acquaintance.

WITWOUD. Aye, aye, friendship without freedom is as dull as love without enjoyment, or wine without toasting. But to tell you a secret, these are trulls whom he allows coach-hire, and something more, by the week, to call on him once a day at public places.

MIRABELL. How!

WITWOUD. You shall see he won't go to 'em, because there's no more company here to take notice of him.—Why, this is nothing to what he used to do; before he found out this way, I have known him call for himself.

FAINALL. Call for himself! What dost thou mean?

WITWOUD. Mean! Why, he would slip you out of this chocolate-house just when you had been talking to him; as soon as your back was turned—whip, he was gone!—then trip to his lodging, clap on a hood and scarf and a mask, slap into a hackney-coach, and drive hither to the door again in a trice, where he would send in for himself, that is, I mean—call for himself, wait for himself; nay, and what's more, not finding himself, sometimes leave a letter for himself.

MIRABELL. I confess this is something extraordinary.—I believe he waits for himself now, he is so long a-coming.—Oh! I ask his pardon.

Enter PETULANT

BETTY. Sir, the coach stays.

PETULANT. Well, well; I come.—'Sbud,[2] a man had as good be a professed midwife as a professed whoremaster, at this rate! To be knocked up and raised at all hours, and in all places! Pox on 'em, I won't come!—D'ye hear, tell 'em I won't come—let 'em snivel and cry their hearts out.

FAINALL. You are very cruel, Petulant.

PETULANT. All's one, let it pass. I have a humor to be cruel.

MIRABELL. I hope they are not persons of condition that you use at this rate?

PETULANT. Condition! condition's a dried fig if I am not in humor!—By this hand, if they were your—a—a—your what-d'ye-call-'ems themselves, they must wait or rub off, if I want appetite.

MIRABELL. What-d'ye-call-'ems! What are they, Witwoud?

WITWOUD. Empresses, my dear: by your what-d'ye-call-'ems he means sultana queens.

PETULANT. Aye, Roxolanas.[3]

MIRABELL. Cry you mercy.

FAINALL. Witwoud says they are—

---

[1] A drink made by distilling spirits with cinnamon and sugar.

[2] Corruption of "God's blood."

[3] See *The Siege of Rhodes*.

PETULANT. What does he say th' are?
WITWOUD. I? Fine ladies, I say.
PETULANT. Pass on, Witwoud.—Hark'ee, by this light, his relations—two co-heiresses, his cousins, and an old aunt who loves caterwauling better than a conventicle.[1]
WITWOUD. Ha, ha, ha! I had a mind to see how the rogue would come off.—Ha, ha, ha! Gad, I can't be angry with him if he had said they were my mother and my sisters.
MIRABELL. No?
WITWOUD. No; the rogue's wit and readiness of invention charm me. Dear Petulant!
BETTY. They are gone, sir, in great anger.
PETULANT. Enough; let 'em trundle. Anger helps complexion—saves paint.
FAINALL. This continence is all dissembled; this is in order to have something to brag of the next time he makes court to Millamant and swear he has abandoned the whole sex for her sake.
MIRABELL. Have you not left off your impudent pretensions there yet? I shall cut your throat some time or other, Petulant, about that business.
PETULANT. Aye, aye, let that pass—there are other throats to be cut.
MIRABELL. Meaning mine, sir?
PETULANT. Not I—I mean nobody—I know nothing. But there are uncles and nephews in the world—and they may be rivals—what then? All's one for that.
MIRABELL. How! Hark'ee, Petulant, come hither—explain, or I shall call your interpreter.
PETULANT. Explain? I know nothing. Why, you have an uncle, have you not, lately come to town, and lodges by my Lady Wishfort's?
MIRABELL. True.
PETULANT. Why, that's enough—you and he are not friends; and if he should marry and have a child you may be disinherited, ha?
MIRABELL. Where hast thou stumbled upon all this truth?
PETULANT. All's one for that; why, then, say I know something.
MIRABELL. Come, thou art an honest fellow, Petulant, and shalt make love to my mistress; thou sha't, faith. What hast thou heard of my uncle?
PETULANT. I? Nothing, I. If throats are to be cut, let swords clash! snug's the word; I shrug and am silent.

[1] A small assembly.

MIRABELL. Oh, raillery, raillery! Come, I know thou art in the women's secrets.—What, you're a cabalist; I know you stayed at Millamant's last night after I went. Was there any mention made of my uncle or me? Tell me. If thou hadst but good nature equal to thy wit, Petulant, Tony Witwoud, who is now thy competitor in fame, would show as dim by thee as a dead whiting's eye by a pearl of orient [2]; he would no more be seen by thee than Mercury [3] is by the sun. Come, I'm sure thou wo't tell me.
PETULANT. If I do, will you grant me common sense then, for the future?
MIRABELL. Faith, I'll do what I can for thee, and I'll pray that Heaven may grant it thee in the meantime.
PETULANT. Well, hark'ee.
[MIRABELL *and* PETULANT *talk apart*]
FAINALL. [*To* WITWOUD] Petulant and you both will find Mirabell as warm a rival as a lover.
WITWOUD. Pshaw! pshaw! that she laughs at Petulant is plain. And for my part, but that it is almost a fashion to admire her, I should—hark'ee—to tell you a secret, but let it go no further—between friends, I shall never break my heart for her.
FAINALL. How!
WITWOUD. She's handsome; but she's a sort of an uncertain woman.
FAINALL. I thought you had died for her.
WITWOUD. Umh—no—
FAINALL. She has wit.
WITWOUD. 'Tis what she will hardly allow anybody else. Now, demme! I should hate that, if she were as handsome as Cleopatra. Mirabell is not so sure of her as he thinks for.
FAINALL. Why do you think so?
WITWOUD. We stayed pretty late there last night, and heard something of an uncle to Mirabell, who is lately come to town—and is between him and the best part of his [4] estate. Mirabell and he are at some distance, as my Lady Wishfort has been told; and you know she hates Mirabell worse than a

[2] Supposed to be especially brilliant.
[3] The planet Mercury is too close to the sun to be easily visible.
[4] The uncle of Mirabell's who is "between him and the best part of his estate," does not exist, and must not be confused with Sir Wilfull Witwoud. Congreve has neglected to make clear to the audience that this phantom relative is to be personated by the servant, Waitwell. See Act II, p. 417 and Act IV, pp 434 ff.

Quaker hates a parrot,[1] or than a fishmonger hates a hard frost. Whether this uncle has seen Mrs. Millamant or not, I cannot say, but there were items of such a treaty being in embryo; and if it should come to life, poor Mirabell would be in some sort unfortunately fobbed,[2] i'faith.

FAINALL. 'Tis impossible Millamant should hearken to it.

WITWOUD. Faith, my dear, I can't tell; she's a woman, and a kind of humorist.[3]

MIRABELL. [*To* PETULANT] And this is the sum of what you could collect last night?

PETULANT. The quintessence. Maybe Witwoud knows more, he stayed longer. Besides, they never mind him; they say anything before him.

MIRABELL. I thought you had been the greatest favorite.

PETULANT. Aye, *tête-à-tête*, but not in public, because I make remarks.

MIRABELL. Do you?

PETULANT. Aye, aye; pox, I'm malicious, man! Now, he's soft, you know; they are not in awe of him—the fellow's well-bred; he's what you call a—what-d'ye-call-'em, a fine gentleman.—But he's silly withal.

MIRABELL. I thank you. I know as much as my curiosity requires.—Fainall, are you for the Mall?[4]

FAINALL. Aye, I'll take a turn before dinner.

WITWOUD. Aye, we'll all walk in the Park;[5] the ladies talked of being there.

MIRABELL. I thought you were obliged to watch for your brother Sir Wilfull's arrival.

WITWOUD. No, no; he comes to his aunt's, my Lady Wishfort. Pox on him! I shall be troubled with him, too; what shall I do with the fool?

PETULANT. Beg him for his estate, that I may beg you afterwards, and so have but one trouble with you both.

WITWOUD. Oh, rare Petulant! Thou art as quick as fire in a frosty morning. Thou shalt to the Mall with us, and we'll be very severe.

PETULANT. Enough! I'm in a humor to be severe.

MIRABELL. Are you? Pray then, walk by yourselves: let not us be accessory to your putting the ladies out of countenance with your senseless ribaldry, which you roar out aloud as often as they pass by you; and when you have made a handsome woman blush, then you think you have been severe.

PETULANT. What, what? Then let 'em either show their innocence by not understanding what they hear, or else show their discretion by not hearing what they would not be thought to understand.

MIRABELL. But hast not thou then sense enough to know that thou oughtest to be most ashamed thyself when thou hast put another out of countenance?

PETULANT. Not I, by this hand!—I always take blushing either for a sign of guilt or ill breeding.

MIRABELL. I confess you ought to think so. You are in the right, that you may plead the error of your judgment in defence of your practice.

Where modesty's ill manners, 'tis but fit
That impudence and malice pass for wit.

Exeunt

ACT II

SCENE I. *St. James's Park*

Enter MRS. FAINALL *and* MRS. MARWOOD

MRS. FAINALL. Aye, aye, dear Marwood, if we will be happy, we must find the means in ourselves and among ourselves. Men are ever in extremes—either doting or averse. While they are lovers, if they have fire and sense, their jealousies are insupportable; and when they cease to love—(we ought to think at least) they loathe; they look upon us with horror and distaste; they meet us like the ghosts of what we were, and as from such, fly from us.

MRS. MARWOOD. True, 'tis an unhappy circumstance of life, that love should ever die before us and that the man so often should outlive the lover. But say what you will, 'tis better to be left than never to have been loved. To pass our youth in dull indifference, to refuse the sweets of life because they once must leave us, is as preposterous as to wish to have been born old because we one day must be old. For my part, my youth may wear and waste, but it shall never rust in my possession.

MRS. FAINALL. Then it seems you dissem-

---

[1] Presumably because parrots swear.
[2] Cheated.
[3] Unreliable person.
[4] Bordering St. James's Park.
[5] St James's Park. See Act II.

ble an aversion to mankind only in compliance to my mother's humor?

Mrs. Marwood. Certainly. To be free; I have no taste of those insipid dry discourses with which our sex of force must entertain themselves apart from men. We may affect endearments to each other, profess eternal friendships, and seem to dote like lovers; but 'tis not in our natures long to persevere. Love will resume his empire in our breasts and every heart, or soon or late, receive and readmit him as its lawful tyrant.

Mrs. Fainall. Bless me, how have I been deceived! Why, you profess a libertine.

Mrs. Marwood. You see my friendship by my freedom. Come, be as sincere; acknowledge that your sentiments agree with mine.

Mrs. Fainall. Never!

Mrs. Marwood. You hate mankind?

Mrs. Fainall. Heartily, inveterately.

Mrs. Marwood. Your husband?

Mrs. Fainall. Most transcendently; aye, though I say it, meritoriously.

Mrs. Marwood. Give me your hand upon it.

Mrs. Fainall. There.

Mrs. Marwood. I join with you; what I have said has been to try you.

Mrs. Fainall. Is it possible? Dost thou hate those vipers, men?

Mrs. Marwood. I have done hating 'em, and am now come to despise 'em; the next thing I have to do, is eternally to forget 'em.

Mrs. Fainall. There spoke the spirit of an Amazon, a Penthesilea!

Mrs. Marwood. And yet I am thinking sometimes to carry my aversion further.

Mrs. Fainall. How?

Mrs. Marwood. Faith, by marrying; if I could but find one that loved me very well and would be thoroughly sensible of ill usage, I think I should do myself the violence of undergoing the ceremony.

Mrs. Fainall. You would not make him a cuckold?

Mrs. Marwood. No; but I'd make him believe I did, and that's as bad.

Mrs. Fainall. Why had not you as good do it?

Mrs. Marwood. Oh, if he should ever discover it, he would then know the worst and be out of his pain; but I would have him ever to continue upon the rack of fear and jealousy.

Mrs. Fainall. Ingenious mischief! would thou wert married to Mirabell.

Mrs. Marwood. Would I were!

Mrs. Fainall. You change color.

Mrs. Marwood. Because I hate him.

Mrs. Fainall. So do I, but I can hear him named. But what reason have you to hate him in particular?

Mrs. Marwood. I never loved him; he is, and always was, insufferably proud.

Mrs. Fainall. By the reason you give for your aversion, one would think it dissembled; for you have laid a fault to his charge, of which his enemies must acquit him.

Mrs. Marwood. Oh, then it seems you are one of his favorable enemies! Methinks you look a little pale—and now you flush again.

Mrs. Fainall. Do I? I think I am a little sick o' the sudden.

Mrs. Marwood. What ails you?

Mrs. Fainall. My husband. Don't you see him? He turned short upon me unawares, and has almost overcome me.

Enter Fainall *and* Mirabell

Mrs. Marwood. Ha, ha, ha! He comes opportunely for you.

Mrs. Fainall. For you, for he has brought Mirabell with him.

Fainall. [*To* Mrs. Fainall] My dear!

Mrs. Fainall. My soul!

Fainall. You don't look well to-day, child.

Mrs. Fainall. D'ye think so?

Mirabell. He is the only man that does, madam.

Mrs. Fainall. The only man that would tell me so, at least, and the only man from whom I could hear it without mortification.

Fainall. Oh, my dear, I am satisfied of your tenderness; I know you cannot resent anything from me, especially what is an effect of my concern.

Mrs. Fainall. Mr. Mirabell, my mother interrupted you in a pleasant relation last night; I would fain hear it out.

Mirabell. The persons concerned in that affair have yet a tolerable reputation. I am afraid Mr. Fainall will be censorious.

Mrs. Fainall. He has a humor more prevailing than his curiosity, and will willingly dispense with the hearing of one scandalous story, to avoid giving an occasion to make another by being seen to walk with his wife.

This way, Mr. Mirabell, and I dare promise you will oblige us both.

Exeunt MRS. FAINALL *and* MIRABELL

FAINALL. Excellent creature! Well, sure if I should live to be rid of my wife, I should be a miserable man.

MRS. MARWOOD. Aye?

FAINALL. For having only that one hope, the accomplishment of it, of consequence, must put an end to all my hopes; and what a wretch is he who must survive his hopes! Nothing remains when that day comes but to sit down and weep like Alexander when he wanted other worlds to conquer.

MRS. MARWOOD. Will you not follow 'em?

FAINALL. Faith, I think not.

MRS. MARWOOD. Pray, let us; I have a reason.

FAINALL. You are not jealous?

MRS. MARWOOD. Of whom?

FAINALL. Of Mirabell.

MRS. MARWOOD. If I am, is it inconsistent with my love to you that I am tender of your honor?

FAINALL. You would intimate, then, as if [there] were a fellow-feeling between my wife and him.

MRS. MARWOOD. I think she does not hate him to that degree she would be thought.

FAINALL. But he, I fear, is too insensible.

MRS. MARWOOD. It may be you are deceived.

FAINALL. It may be so. I do now begin to apprehend it.

MRS. MARWOOD. What?

FAINALL. That I have been deceived, madam, and you are false.

MRS. MARWOOD. That I am false! What mean you?

FAINALL. To let you know I see through all your little arts.—Come, you both love him, and both have equally dissembled your aversion. Your mutual jealousies of one another have made you clash till you have both struck fire. I have seen the warm confession reddening on your cheeks and sparkling from your eyes.

MRS. MARWOOD. You do me wrong.

FAINALL. I do not. 'Twas for my ease to oversee and wilfully neglect the gross advances made him by my wife, that by permitting her to be engaged, I might continue unsuspected in my pleasures and take you oftener to my arms in full security. But could you think, because the nodding husband would not wake, that e'er the watchful lover slept?

MRS. MARWOOD. And wherewithal can you reproach me?

FAINALL. With infidelity, with loving another—with love of Mirabell.

MRS. MARWOOD. 'Tis false! I challenge you to show an instance that can confirm your groundless accusation. I hate him!

FAINALL. And wherefore do you hate him? He is insensible, and your resentment follows his neglect. An instance!—the injuries you have done him are a proof—your interposing in his love. What cause had you to make discoveries of his pretended passion?—to undeceive the credulous aunt, and be the officious obstacle of his match with Millamant?

MRS. MARWOOD. My obligations to my lady urged me. I had professed a friendship to her, and could not see her easy nature so abused by that dissembler.

FAINALL. What, was it conscience, then? Professed a friendship! Oh, the pious friendships of the female sex!

MRS. MARWOOD. More tender, more sincere, and more enduring than all the vain and empty vows of men, whether professing love to us or mutual faith to one another.

FAINALL. Ha, ha, ha! You are my wife's friend, too.

MRS. MARWOOD. Shame and ingratitude! Do you reproach me? You, you upbraid me? Have I been false to her, through strict fidelity to you, and sacrificed my friendship to keep my love inviolate? And have you the baseness to charge me with the guilt, unmindful of the merit? To you it should be meritorious that I have been vicious: and do you reflect that guilt upon me which should lie buried in your bosom?

FAINALL. You misinterpret my reproof. I meant but to remind you of the slight account you once could make of strictest ties when set in competition with your love to me.

MRS. MARWOOD. 'Tis false; you urged it with deliberate malice! 'Twas spoken in scorn, and I never will forgive it.

FAINALL. Your guilt, not your resentment, begets your rage. If yet you loved, you could forgive a jealousy; but you are stung to find you are discovered.

MRS. MARWOOD. It shall be all discovered. —You too shall be discovered; be sure you shall. I can but be exposed.—If I do it myself I shall prevent your baseness.

FAINALL. Why, what will you do?

MRS. MARWOOD. Disclose it to your wife; own what has passed between us.

FAINALL. Frenzy!

MRS. MARWOOD. By all my wrongs I'll do't!—I'll publish to the world the injuries you have done me, both in my fame and fortune! With both I trusted you,—you, bankrupt in honor, as indigent of wealth.

FAINALL. Your fame I have preserved. Your fortune has been bestowed as the prodigality of your love would have it, in pleasures which we both have shared. Yet, had not you been false, I had ere this repaid it—'tis true. Had you permitted Mirabell with Millamant to have stolen their marriage, my lady had been incensed beyond all means of reconcilement; Millamant had forfeited the moiety of her fortune, which then would have descended to my wife—and wherefore did I marry but to make lawful prize of a rich widow's wealth, and squander it on love and you?

MRS. MARWOOD. Deceit and frivolous pretence!

FAINALL. Death, am I not married? What's pretence? Am I not imprisoned, fettered? Have I not a wife?—nay, a wife that was a widow, a young widow, a handsome widow; and would be again a widow, but that I have a heart of proof, and something of a constitution to bustle through the ways of wedlock and this world! Will you yet be reconciled to truth and me?

MRS. MARWOOD. Impossible. Truth and you are inconsistent—I hate you, and shall forever.

FAINALL. For loving you?

MRS. MARWOOD. I loathe the name of love after such usage; and next to the guilt with which you would asperse me, I scorn you most. Farewell!

FAINALL. Nay, we must not part thus.

MRS. MARWOOD. Let me go.

FAINALL. Come, I'm sorry.

MRS. MARWOOD. I care not—let me go—break my hands, do! I'd leave 'em to get loose.

FAINALL. I would not hurt you for the world. Have I no other hold to keep you here?

MRS. MARWOOD. Well, I have deserved it all.

FAINALL. You know I love you.

MRS. MARWOOD. Poor dissembling!—Oh, that—well, it is not yet—

FAINALL. What? What is it not? What is it not yet? It is not yet too late—

MRS. MARWOOD. No, it is not yet too late—I have that comfort.

FAINALL. It is, to love another.

MRS. MARWOOD. But not to loathe, detest, abhor mankind, myself, and the whole treacherous world.

FAINALL. Nay, this is extravagance!—Come, I ask your pardon—no tears—I was to blame, I could not love you and be easy in my doubts. Pray, forbear—I believe you; I'm convinced I've done you wrong, and any way, every way will make amends. I'll hate my wife yet more, damn her! I'll part with her, rob her of all she's worth, and we'll retire somewhere—anywhere—to another world. I'll marry thee—be pacified.—'Sdeath, they come! Hide your face, your tears.—You have a mask; wear it a moment. This way, this way—be persuaded. *Exeunt*

Enter MIRABELL *and* MRS. FAINALL

MRS. FAINALL. They are here yet.

MIRABELL. They are turning into the other walk.

MRS. FAINALL. While I only hated my husband, I could bear to see him; but since I have despised him, he's too offensive.

MIRABELL. Oh, you should hate with prudence.

MRS. FAINALL. Yes, for I have loved with indiscretion.

MIRABELL. You should have just so much disgust for your husband as may be sufficient to make you relish your lover.

MRS. FAINALL. You have been the cause that I have loved without bounds, and would you set limits to that aversion of which you have been the occasion? Why did you make me marry this man?

MIRABELL. Why do we daily commit disagreeable and dangerous actions? To save that idol, reputation. If the familiarities of our loves had produced that consequence of which you were apprehensive, where could you have fixed a father's name with credit but on a husband? I knew Fainall to be a man lavish of his morals, an interested and professing friend, a false and a designing lover, yet one whose wit and outward fair behavior have gained a reputation with the town enough to make that woman stand excused who has suffered herself to be won by his addresses. A better man ought not to have been sacrificed to the occasion, a worse had not answered to the purpose. When you are weary of him, you know your remedy.

MRS. FAINALL. I ought to stand in some degree of credit with you, Mirabell.

MIRABELL. In justice to you, I have made you privy to my whole design, and put it in your power to ruin or advance my fortune.

MRS. FAINALL. Whom have you instructed to represent your pretended uncle?

MIRABELL. Waitwell, my servant.

MRS. FAINALL. He is an humble servant[1] to Foible, my mother's woman, and may win her to your interest.

MIRABELL. Care is taken for that—she is won and worn by this time. They were married this morning.

MRS. FAINALL. Who?

MIRABELL. Waitwell and Foible. I would not tempt any servant to betray me by trusting him too far. If your mother, in hopes to ruin me, should consent to marry my pretended uncle, he might, like Mosca in *The Fox*,[2] stand upon terms; so I made him sure beforehand.

MRS. FAINALL. So if my poor mother is caught in a contract,[3] you will discover the imposture betimes, and release her by producing a certificate of her gallant's former marriage.

MIRABELL. Yes, upon condition that she consent to my marriage with her niece, and surrender the moiety of her fortune in her possession.

MRS. FAINALL. She talked last night of endeavoring at a match between Millamant and your uncle.

MIRABELL. That was by Foible's direction and my instruction, that she might seem to carry it more privately.

MRS. FAINALL. Well, I have an opinion of your success; for I believe my lady will do anything to get a husband; and when she has this which you have provided for her, I suppose she will submit to anything to get rid of him.

MIRABELL. Yes, I think the good lady would marry anything that resembled a man, though 'twere no more than what a butler could pinch out of a napkin.

MRS. FAINALL. Female frailty! We must all come to it if we live to be old and feel the craving of a false appetite when the true is decayed.

MIRABELL. An old woman's appetite is depraved like that of a girl—'tis the green sickness of a second childhood, and, like the faint offer of a latter spring, serves but to usher in the fall and withers in an affected bloom.

MRS. FAINALL. Here's your mistress.

Enter MRS. MILLAMANT, WITWOUD, *and* MINCING

MIRABELL. Here she comes, i'faith, full sail, with her fan spread and her streamers out, and a shoal of fools for tenders. Ha, no, I cry her mercy!

MRS. FAINALL. I see but one poor empty sculler, and he tows her woman after him.

MIRABELL. (*To* MRS. MILLAMANT) You seem to be unattended, madam. You used to have the *beau monde*[4] throng after you, and a flock of gay fine perukes hovering round you.

WITWOUD. Like moths about a candle.—I had like to have lost my comparison for want of breath.

MRS. MILLAMANT. Oh, I have denied myself airs to-day. I have walked as fast through the crowd—

WITWOUD. As a favorite just disgraced, and with as few followers.

MRS. MILLAMANT. Dear Mr. Witwoud, truce with your similitudes; for I'm as sick of 'em—

WITWOUD. As a physician of a good air.—I cannot help it, madam, though 'tis against myself.

MRS. MILLAMANT. Yet again! Mincing, stand between me and his wit.

WITWOUD. Do, Mrs. Mincing, like a screen before a grate fire.—I confess I do blaze to-day; I am too bright.

MRS. FAINALL. But, dear Millamant, why were you so long?

MRS. MILLAMANT. Long! Lord, have I not made violent haste? I have asked every living thing I met for you; I have inquired after you as after a new fashion.

---

[1] Servant in the sense of suitor.
[2] Mosca is the parasite in Ben Jonson's *Volpone* (1605). See Act V, scene v.
[3] Of marriage.
[4] The polite world.

WILWOUD. Madam, truce with your similitudes.—No, you met her husband, and did not ask him for her.

MRS. MILLAMANT. By your leave, Witwoud, that were like inquiring after an old fashion, to ask a husband for his wife.

WITWOUD. Hum, a hit! a hit! a palpable hit! I confess it.

MRS. FAINALL. You were dressed before I came abroad.

MRS. MILLAMANT. Aye, that's true.—Oh, but then I had—Mincing, what had I? Why was I so long?

MINCING. O mem, your la'ship stayed to peruse a pecquet [1] of letters.

MRS. MILLAMANT. Oh, aye, letters—I had letters—I am persecuted with letters—I hate letters.—Nobody knows how to write letters—and yet one has 'em, one does not know why. They serve one to pin up one's hair.

WITWOUD. Is that the way? Pray, madam, do you pin up your hair with all your letters? I find I must keep copies.

MRS. MILLAMANT. Only with those in verse, Mr. Witwoud; I never pin up my hair with prose. I think I tried once, Mincing.

MINCING. O mem, I shall never forget it.

MRS. MILLAMANT. Aye, poor Mincing tift and tift [2] all the morning.

MINCING. Till I had the cremp in my fingers, I'll vow, mem; and all to no purpose. But when your la'ship pins it up with poetry, it sits so pleasant the next day as anything, and is so pure and so crips.

WITWOUD. Indeed, so "crips"?

MINCING. You're such a critic, Mr. Witwoud.

MRS. MILLAMANT. Mirabell, did you take exceptions last night? Oh, aye, and went away—now I think on't I'm angry—No, now I think on't I'm pleased—for I believe I gave you some pain.

MIRABELL. Does that please you?

MRS. MILLAMANT. Infinitely; I love to give pain.

MIRABELL. You would affect a cruelty which is not in your nature; your true vanity is in the power of pleasing.

MRS. MILLAMANT. Oh, I ask your pardon for that—one's cruelty is one's power; and when one parts with one's cruelty, one parts with one's power; and when one has parted with that, I fancy one's old and ugly.

MIRABELL. Aye, aye, suffer your cruelty to ruin the object of your power, to destroy your lover—and then how vain, how lost a thing you'll be! Nay, 'tis true: you are no longer handsome when you've lost your lover; your beauty dies upon the instant, for beauty is the lover's gift. 'Tis he bestows your charms—your glass is all a cheat. The ugly and the old, whom the looking-glass mortifies, yet after commendation can be flattered by it and discover beauties in it; for that reflects our praises, rather than your face.

MRS. MILLAMANT. Oh, the vanity of these men! Fainall, d'ye hear him? If they did not commend us, we were not handsome! Now you must know they could not commend one, if one was not handsome. Beauty the lover's gift!—Lord, what is a lover, that it can give? Why, one makes lovers as fast as one pleases, and they live as long as one pleases, and they die as soon as one pleases: and then, if one pleases, one makes more.

WITWOUD. Very pretty. Why, you make no more of making of lovers, madam, than of making so many card-matches.

MRS. MILLAMANT. One no more owes one's beauty to a lover, than one's wit to an echo. They can but reflect what we look and say—vain empty things if we are silent or unseen, and want a being.

MIRABELL. Yet to those two vain empty things you owe the two greatest pleasures of your life.

MRS. MILLAMANT. How so?

MIRABELL. To your lover you owe the pleasure of hearing yourselves praised, and to an echo the pleasure of hearing yourselves talk.

WITWOUD. But I know a lady that loves talking so incessantly, she won't give an echo fair play; she has that everlasting rotation of tongue, that an echo must wait till she dies before it can catch her last words.

MRS. MILLAMANT. Oh, fiction!—Fainall, let us leave these men.

MIRABELL. (*Aside to* MRS. FAINALL) Draw off Witwoud.

MRS. FAINALL. Immediately.—[*Aloud*] I have a word or two for Mr. Witwoud.

Exeunt WITWOUD *and* MRS. FAINALL

MIRABELL. [*To* MRS. MILLAMANT] I would beg a little private audience too.—You had the tyranny to deny me last night, though you knew I came to impart a secret to you that concerned my love.

---

[1] Packet.   [2] Arranged.

Mrs. Millamant. You saw I was engaged.

Mirabell. Unkind! You had the leisure to entertain a herd of fools—things who visit you from their excessive idleness, bestowing on your easiness that time which is the encumbrance of their lives. How can you find delight in such society? It is impossible they should admire you; they are not capable —or if they were, it should be to you as a mortification, for sure to please a fool is some degree of folly.

Mrs. Millamant. I please myself. Besides, sometimes to converse with fools is for my health.

Mirabell. Your health! Is there a worse disease than the conversation of fools?

Mrs. Millamant. Yes, the vapors; fools are physic for it, next to asafœtida.

Mirabell. You are not in a course of fools?

Mrs. Millamant. Mirabell, if you persist in this offensive freedom, you'll displease me. —I think I must resolve, after all, not to have you; we shan't agree.

Mirabell. Not in our physic, it may be.

Mrs. Millamant. And yet our distemper, in all likelihood, will be the same; for we shall be sick of one another. I shan't endure to be reprimanded nor instructed; 'tis so dull to act always by advice, and so tedious to be told of one's faults—I can't bear it. Well, I won't have you, Mirabell,—I'm resolved— I think—you may go.—Ha, ha, ha! What would you give, that you could help loving me?

Mirabell. I would give something that you did not know I could not help it.

Mrs. Millamant. Come, don't look grave, then. Well, what do you say to me?

Mirabell. I say that a man may as soon make a friend by his wit, or a fortune by his honesty, as win a woman by plain dealing and sincerity.

Mrs. Millamant. Sententious Mirabell! Prithee, don't look with that violent and inflexible wise face, like Solomon at the dividing of the child in an old tapestry hanging.[1]

Mirabell. You are merry, madam, but I would persuade you for a moment to be serious.

Mrs. Millamant. What, with that face? No, if you keep your countenance, 'tis impossible I should hold mine. Well, after all, there is something very moving in a lovesick face. Ha, ha, ha!—Well, I won't laugh; don't be peevish—Heigho! now I'll be melancholy—as melancholy as a watch-light.[2] Well, Mirabell, if ever you will win me, woo me now.—Nay, if you are so tedious, fare you well; I see they are walking away.

Mirabell. Can you not find in the variety of your disposition one moment—

Mrs. Millamant. To hear you tell me Foible's married, and your plot like to speed? No.[3]

Mirabell. But how came you to know it?

Mrs. Millamant. Without the help of the devil, you can't imagine—unless she should tell me herself. Which of the two it may have been I will leave you to consider; and when you have done thinking of that, think of me. [Exit Mrs. Millamant]

Mirabell. I have something more!—Gone! —Think of you? To think of a whirlwind, though 'twere in a whirlwind, were a case of more steady contemplation—a very tranquillity of mind and mansion. A fellow that lives in a windmill, has not a more whimsical dwelling than the heart of a man that is lodged in a woman. There is no point of the compass to which they cannot turn, and by which they are not turned; and by one as well as another. For motion, not method, is their occupation. To know this, and yet continue to be in love, is to be made wise from the dictates of reason, and yet persevere to play the fool by the force of instinct.—Oh, here come my pair of turtles!—What, billing so sweetly! Is not Valentine's Day over with you yet?

Enter Waitwell *and* Foible

Sirrah Waitwell; why, sure you think you were married for your own recreation, and not for my conveniency.

Waitwell. Your pardon, sir. With submission, we have indeed been solacing in lawful delights; but still with an eye to business, sir. I have instructed her as well as I could. If she can take your directions as readily as my instructions, sir, your affairs are in a prosperous way.

Mirabell. Give you joy, Mrs. Foible.

Foible. Oh, 'las, sir, I'm so ashamed!— I'm afraid my lady has been in a thousand

---

[1] See I Kings, iii:16-28. Tapestries were fashionable wall coverings in the period.

[2] A small candle in a sick room.
[3] The fact that Mrs. Millamant has discovered Mirabell's plan is only incidental to the plot.

inquietudes for me. But I protest, sir, I made as much haste as I could.

WAITWELL. That she did indeed, sir. It was my fault that she did not make more.

MIRABELL. That I believe.

FOIBLE. But I told my lady as you instructed me, sir, that I had a prospect of seeing Sir Rowland, your uncle; and that I would put her ladyship's picture in my pocket to show him, which I'll be sure to say has made him so enamored of her beauty, that he burns with impatience to lie at her ladyship's feet and worship the original.

MIRABELL. Excellent Foible! Matrimony has made you eloquent in love.

WAITWELL. I think she has profited, sir; I think so.

FOIBLE. You have seen Madam Millamant, sir?

MIRABELL. Yes.

FOIBLE. I told her, sir, because I did not know that you might find an opportunity; she had so much company last night.

MIRABELL. Your diligence will merit more—in the meantime— (*Gives [her] money*)

FOIBLE. O dear sir, your humble servant!

WAITWELL. [*Putting forth his hand*] Spouse.

MIRABELL. Stand off, sir, not a penny!—Go on and prosper, Foible—the lease shall be made good and the farm stocked if we succeed.

FOIBLE. I don't question your generosity, sir, and you need not doubt of success. If you have no more commands, sir, I'll be gone; I'm sure my lady is at her toilet, and can't dress till I come.—Oh, dear, [*Looking out*] I'm sure that was Mrs. Marwood that went by in a mask! If she has seen me with you, I'm sure she'll tell my lady. I'll make haste home and prevent her. Your servant, sir.—B'w'y,[1] Waitwell. [*Exit* FOIBLE]

WAITWELL. Sir Rowland, if you please.—The jade's so pert upon her preferment she forgets herself.

MIRABELL. Come, sir, will you endeavor to forget yourself, and transform into Sir Rowland?

WAITWELL. Why, sir, it will be impossible I should remember myself.—Married, knighted, and attended all in one day! 'tis enough to make any man forget himself. The difficulty will be how to recover my acquaintance and familiarity with my former self, and

[1] Shortened form of "God be with you."

fall from my transformation to a reformation into Waitwell. Nay, I shan't be quite the same Waitwell neither; for now, I remember me, I'm married and can't be my own man again.
Aye, there's the grief; that's the sad change of life,
To lose my title, and yet keep my wife.

Exeunt

ACT III

SCENE I. *A room in* LADY WISHFORT'S *house*

LADY WISHFORT *at her toilet*, PEG *waiting*

LADY WISHFORT. Merciful! no news of Foible yet?

PEG. No, madam.

LADY WISHFORT. I have no more patience.—If I have not fretted myself till I am pale again, there's no veracity in me! Fetch me the red—the red, do you hear, sweetheart?—An arrant ash-color, as I am a person! Look you how this wench stirs! Why dost thou not fetch me a little red? Didst thou not hear me, Mopus?[2]

PEG. The red ratafia, does your ladyship mean, or the cherry-brandy?

LADY WISHFORT. Ratafia, fool! No, fool. Not the ratafia, fool—grant me patience!—I mean the Spanish paper,[3] idiot—complexion, darling. Paint, paint, paint!—dost thou understand that, changeling, dangling thy hands like bobbins before thee? Why dost thou not stir, puppet? Thou wooden thing upon wires!

PEG. Lord, madam, your ladyship is so impatient!—I cannot come at the paint, madam; Mrs. Foible has locked it up and carried the key with her.

LADY WISHFORT. A pox take you both!—Fetch me the cherry-brandy then. (*Exit* PEG) I'm as pale and as faint, I look like Mrs. Qualmsick, the curate's wife, that's always breeding.—Wench! Come, come, wench, what art thou doing? Sipping? Tasting?—Save thee, dost thou not know the bottle?

Enter PEG *with a bottle and china cup*

PEG. Madam, I was looking for a cup.

LADY WISHFORT. A cup, save thee! and what a cup hast thou brought!—Dost thou

[2] Mope, dull person.
[3] Used for cosmetic purposes.

take me for a fairy, to drink out of an acorn? Why didst thou not bring thy thimble? Hast thou ne'er a brass thimble clinking in thy pocket with a bit of nutmeg?—I warrant thee. Come, fill, fill!—So—again.—(*One knocks.*)—See who that is.—Set down the bottle first.—Here, here, under the table.— What, wouldst thou go with the bottle in thy hand, like a tapster? As I'm a person, this wench has lived in an inn upon the road before she came to me, like Maritornes [1] the Asturian in *Don Quixote!*—No Foible yet?

PEG. No, madam, Mrs. Marwood.

LADY WISHFORT. Oh, Marwood; let her come in.—Come in, good Marwood.

Enter MRS. MARWOOD

MRS. MARWOOD. I'm surprised to find your ladyship in dishabille at this time of day.

LADY WISHFORT. Foible's a lost thing—has been abroad since morning, and never heard of since.

MRS. MARWOOD. I saw her but now as I came masked through the park, in conference with Mirabell.

LADY WISHFORT. With Mirabell!—You call my blood into my face, with mentioning that traitor. She durst not have the confidence! I sent her to negotiate an affair in which, if I'm detected, I'm undone. If that wheedling villain has wrought upon Foible to detect me, I'm ruined. Oh, my dear friend, I'm a wretch of wretches if I'm detected.

MRS. MARWOOD. O madam, you cannot suspect Mrs. Foible's integrity.

LADY WISHFORT. Oh, he carries poison in his tongue that would corrupt integrity itself! If she has given him an opportunity, she has as good as put her integrity into his hands. Ah, dear Marwood, what's integrity to an opportunity?—Hark! I hear her! [*To* PEG] Go, you thing, and send her in. [*Exit* PEG]
[*To* MRS MARWOOD] Dear friend, retire into my closet, that I may examine her with more freedom.—You'll pardon me, dear friend; I can make bold with you.—There are books over the chimney—Quarles and Prynne, and *The Short View of the Stage,* with Bunyan's works, to entertain you.[2]

Exit MRS. MARWOOD

Enter FOIBLE

LADY WISHFORT. O Foible, where hast thou been? What hast thou been doing?

FOIBLE. Madam, I have seen the party.

LADY WISHFORT. But what hast thou done?

FOIBLE. Nay, 'tis your ladyship has done, and are to do; I have only promised. But a man so enamored—so transported!—Well, if worshipping of pictures be a sin—poor Sir Rowland, I say—

LADY WISHFORT. The miniature has been counted like—but hast thou not betrayed me, Foible? Hast thou not detected me to that faithless Mirabell?—What hadst thou to do with him in the Park? Answer me: has he got nothing out of thee?

FOIBLE. (*Aside*) So the devil has been beforehand with me. What shall I say?— (*Aloud*)—Alas, madam, could I help it if I met that confident thing? Was I in fault? If you had heard how he used me, and all upon your ladyship's account, I'm sure you would not suspect my fidelity. Nay, if that had been the worst, I could have borne; but he had a fling at your ladyship too. And then I could not hold, but i'faith I gave him his own.

LADY WISHFORT. Me? What did the filthy fellow say?

FOIBLE. Oh, madam! 'tis a shame to say what he said—with his taunts and his fleers, tossing up his nose. Humh! (says he) what, you are a hatching some plot (says he), you are so early abroad, or catering (says he), ferreting for some disbanded officer, I warrant.—Half-pay is but thin subsistence (says he)—well, what pension does your lady propose? Let me see (says he); what, she must come down pretty deep now, she's superannuated (says he) and—

LADY WISHFORT. Odds my life, I'll have him—I'll have him murdered! I'll have him poisoned! Where does he eat?—I'll marry a drawer [3] to have him poisoned in his wine. I'll send for Robin [4] from Locket's [5] immediately.

FOIBLE. Poison him! poisoning's too good for him. Starve him, madam, starve him:

---

[1] See *Don Quixote,* Part I, chapter xvi.

[2] Lady Wishfort's library, a very moral one, probably included the *Emblems* of Francis Quarles (1635); William Prynne's *Histrio-Mastix* (1633); Jeremy Collier's *Short View of the Immorality and Profaneness of the English Stage* (1698); and perhaps the *Works* of John Bunyan (1692).

[3] The servant who draws liquor for guests in a tavern.

[4] Colloquial for servant. Cf. "George" for a pullman porter.

[5] A contemporary tavern.

marry Sir Rowland, and get him disinherited. Oh, you would bless yourself to hear what he said!

LADY WISHFORT. A villain! Superannuated!

FOIBLE. Humh (says he), I hear you are laying designs against me too (says he), and Mrs. Millamant is to marry my uncle (he does not suspect a word of your ladyship); but (says he) I'll fit you for that. I warrant you (says he) I'll hamper you for that (says he)—you and your old frippery [1] too (says he); I'll handle you—

LADY WISHFORT. Audacious villain! Handle me, would he durst!—Frippery? old frippery! Was there ever such a foul-mouthed fellow? I'll be married to-morrow; I'll be contracted to-night.

FOIBLE. The sooner the better, madam.

LADY WISHFORT. Will Sir Rowland be here, sayest thou? When, Foible?

FOIBLE. Incontinently, madam. No new sheriff's wife expects the return of her husband after knighthood with that impatience in which Sir Rowland burns for the dear hour of kissing your ladyship's hand after dinner.

LADY WISHFORT. Frippery! superannuated frippery! I'll frippery the villain; I'll reduce him to frippery and rags! a tatterdemalion! I hope to see him hung with tatters, like a Long-lane penthouse [2] or a gibbet thief. A slander-mouthed railer! I warrant the spendthrift prodigal's in debt as much as the million lottery, or the whole court upon a birthday. I'll spoil his credit with his tailor. Yes, he shall have my niece with her fortune, he shall.

FOIBLE. He! I hope to see him lodge in Ludgate [3] first, and angle into Blackfriars for brass farthings with an old mitten.

LADY WISHFORT. Aye, dear Foible; thank thee for that, dear Foible. He has put me out of all patience. I shall never recompose my features to receive Sir Rowland with any economy of face. This wretch has fretted me that I am absolutely decayed. Look, Foible.

FOIBLE. Your ladyship has frowned a little too rashly; indeed, madam. There are some cracks discernible in the white varnish.

LADY WISHFORT. Let me see the glass.—Cracks, sayest thou?—why, I am arrantly flayed—I look like an old peeled wall. Thou must repair me, Foible, before Sir Rowland comes, or I shall never keep up to my picture.

FOIBLE. I warrant you, madam, a little art once made your picture like you, and now a little of the same art [4] must make you like your picture. Your picture must sit for you, madam.

LADY WISHFORT. But art thou sure Sir Rowland will not fail to come? Or will he not fail when he does come? Will he be importunate, Foible, and push? For if he should not be importunate, I shall never break decorums —I shall die with confusion if I am forced to advance.—Oh, no, I can never advance!—I shall swoon if he should expect advances. No, I hope Sir Rowland is better bred than to put a lady to the necessity of breaking her forms. I won't be too coy, neither.—I won't give him despair—but a little disdain is not amiss; a little scorn is alluring.

FOIBLE. A little scorn becomes your ladyship.

LADY WISHFORT. Yes, but tenderness becomes me best—a sort of dyingness—you see that picture has a sort of a—ha, Foible? a swimmingness in the eye—yes, I'll look so.—My niece affects it, but she wants features. Is Sir Rowland handsome? Let my toilet [5] be removed—I'll dress above. I'll receive Sir Rowland here.—Is he handsome? Don't answer me. I won't know; I'll be surprised. I'll be taken by surprise.

FOIBLE. By storm, madam. Sir Rowland's a brisk man.

LADY WISHFORT. Is he? Oh, then he'll importune, if he's a brisk man. I shall save decorums if Sir Rowland importunes. I have a mortal terror at the apprehension of offending against decorums. Oh, I'm glad he's a brisk man!—Let my things be removed, good Foible. [*Exit* LADY WISHFORT]

Enter MRS FAINALL

MRS. FAINALL. Oh, Foible, I have been in a fright lest I should come too late! That devil Marwood saw you in the Park with Mirabell, and I'm afraid will discover it to my lady.

FOIBLE. Discover what, madam?

---

[1] Either cast-off clothes or an old-clothes shop.
[2] Long Lane was given over to old-clothes dealers. A penthouse is a shed with an overhanging roof.
[3] A prison in which debtors were confined, from the windows of which they let down baskets (in this case, an old mitten) on ropes to collect money from the charitable.
[4] The pun is on the meaning of art as "artifice."
[5] Toilet case or service.

MRS. FAINALL. Nay, nay, put not on that strange face! I am privy to the whole design and know that Waitwell, to whom thou wert this morning married, is to personate Mirabell's uncle, and as such, winning my lady, to involve her in those difficulties from which Mirabell only must release her, by his making his conditions to have my cousin and her fortune left to her own disposal.

FOIBLE. Oh, dear madam, I beg your pardon. It was not my confidence in your ladyship that was deficient, but I thought the former good correspondence between your ladyship and Mr. Mirabell might have hindered his communicating this secret.

MRS. FAINALL. Dear Foible, forget that.

FOIBLE. O dear madam, Mr. Mirabell is such a sweet, winning gentleman—but your ladyship is the pattern of generosity.—Sweet lady, to be so good! Mr. Mirabell cannot choose but be grateful. I find your ladyship has his heart still. Now, madam, I can safely tell your ladyship our success: Mrs. Marwood had told my lady, but I warrant I managed myself. I turned it all for the better. I told my lady that Mr. Mirabell railed at her; I laid horrid things to his charge, I'll vow; and my lady is so incensed that she'll be contracted to Sir Rowland to-night, she says. I warrant I worked her up, that he may have her for asking for, as they say of a Welsh maidenhead.[1]

MRS. FAINALL. O rare Foible!

FOIBLE. Madam, I beg your ladyship to acquaint Mr. Mirabell of his success. I would be seen as little as possible to speak to him: besides, I believe Madam Marwood watches me.—She has a month's mind[2]; but I know Mr. Mirabell can't abide her.—[*Enter Footman*] John, remove my lady's toilet.— Madam, your servant: my lady is so impatient I fear she'll come for me if I stay.

MRS. FAINALL. I'll go with you up the back stairs lest I should meet her.   *Exeunt*

Enter MRS. MARWOOD

MRS. MARWOOD. Indeed, Mrs. Engine, is it thus with you? Are you become a go-between of this importance?—Yes, I shall watch you. Why, this wench is the *passe-partout*,[3] a very master-key to everybody's strong-box. My friend Fainall, have you carried it so swimmingly? I thought there was something in it, but it seems it's over with you. Your loathing is not from a want of appetite, then, but from a surfeit. Else you could never be so cool to fall from a principal to be an assistant,—to procure[4] for him! A pattern of generosity, that, I confess. Well, Mr. Fainall, you have met with your match.—O man, man! Woman, woman! The devil's an ass: if I were a painter, I would draw him like an idiot, a driveller with a bib and bells. Man should have his head and horns,[5] and woman the rest of him. Poor simple fiend!—"Madam Marwood has a month's mind, but he can't abide her."— 'Twere better for him you had not been his confessor in that affair, without you could have kept his counsel closer. I shall not prove another pattern of generosity; he has not obliged me to that with those excesses of himself! And now I'll have none of him.— Here comes the good lady, panting ripe, with a heart full of hope, and a head full of care, like any chemist[6] upon the day of projection.[7]

Enter LADY WISHFORT

LADY WISHFORT. Oh, dear Marwood, what shall I say for this rude forgetfulness?—but my dear friend is all goodness.

MRS. MARWOOD. No apologies, dear madam; I have been very well entertained.

LADY WISHFORT. As I'm a person, I am in a very chaos to think I should so forget myself: but I have such an olio[8] of affairs, really I know not what to do.—[*Calls*] Foible!—I expect my nephew, Sir Wilfull, every moment, too.—[*Calls again*] Why, Foible!—He means to travel for improvement.

MRS. MARWOOD. Methinks Sir Wilfull should rather think of marrying than travelling, at his years. I hear he is turned of forty.

LADY WISHFORT. Oh, he's in less danger of being spoiled by his travels—I am against my nephew's marrying too young. It will be time enough when he comes back and has acquired discretion to choose for himself.

MRS. MARWOOD. Methinks Mrs. Milla-

---

[1] Slurs at the Welsh are common in seventeenth century literature.
[2] Desire.
[3] Master-key.
[4] Act as a procuress.
[5] The symbol of a cuckold.
[6] Alchemist.
[7] The day (often determined astrologically) to cast the transmuting substance into the crucible in order to produce gold.
[8] Hodgepodge.

mant and he would make a very fit match. He may travel afterwards.—'Tis a thing very usual with young gentlemen.

LADY WISHFORT. I promise you I have thought on't—and since 'tis your judgment, I'll think on't again. I assure you I will. I value your judgment extremely. On my word, I'll propose it.

Enter FOIBLE

LADY WISHFORT. Come, come, Foible—I had forgot my nephew will be here before dinner. I must make haste.

FOIBLE. Mr. Witwoud and Mr. Petulant are come to dine with your ladyship.

LADY WISHFORT. Oh, dear, I can't appear till I'm dressed! Dear Marwood, shall I be free with you again, and beg you to entertain 'em? I'll make all imaginable haste. Dear friend, excuse me.

[*Exeunt* LADY WISHFORT *and* FOIBLE]

Enter MRS. MILLAMANT *and* MINCING

MRS. MILLAMANT. Sure never anything was so unbred as that odious man!—Marwood, your servant.

MRS. MARWOOD. You have a color; what's the matter?

MRS. MILLAMANT. That horrid fellow, Petulant, has provoked me into a flame: I have broken my fan.—Mincing, lend me yours. Is not all the powder out of my hair?

MRS. MARWOOD. No. What has he done?

MRS. MILLAMANT. Nay, he has done nothing; he has only talked—nay, he has said nothing neither, but he has contradicted everything that has been said. For my part, I thought Witwoud and he would have quarrelled.

MINCING. I vow, mem, I thought once they would have fit.

MRS. MILLAMANT. Well, 'tis a lamentable thing, I swear, that one has not the liberty of choosing one's acquaintance as one does one's clothes.

MRS. MARWOOD. If we had that liberty, we should be as weary of one set of acquaintance, though never so good, as we are of one suit, though never so fine. A fool and a doily stuff[1] would now and then find days of grace, and be worn for variety.

MRS. MILLAMANT. I could consent to wear 'em if they would wear alike; but fools never

[1] A kind of woollen material.

wear out—they are such *drap du Berri*[2] things. Without one could give 'em to one's chambermaid after a day or two!

MRS. MARWOOD. 'Twere better so indeed. Or what think you of the playhouse? A fine, gay, glossy fool should be given there, like a new masking habit, after the masquerade is over and we have done with the disguise. For a fool's visit is always a disguise, and never admitted by a woman of wit but to blind her affair with a lover of sense. If you would but appear barefaced now, and own Mirabell, you might as easily put off Petulant and Witwoud as your hood and scarf. And indeed, 'tis time, for the town has found it; the secret is grown too big for the pretence. 'Tis like Mrs. Primly's great belly; she may lace it down before, but it burnishes[3] on her hips. Indeed, Millamant, you can no more conceal it than my Lady Strammel can her face—that goodly face, which, in defiance of her Rhenish-wine tea,[4] will not be comprehended in a mask.

MRS. MILLAMANT. I'll take my death, Marwood, you are more censorious than a decayed beauty or a discarded toast.—Mincing, tell the men they may come up.—My aunt is not dressing; their folly is less provoking than your malice.   *Exit* MINCING —The town has found it! what has it found? That Mirabell loves me is no more a secret than it is a secret that you discovered it to my aunt, or than the reason why you discovered it is a secret.

MRS. MARWOOD. You are nettled.

MRS. MILLAMANT. You're mistaken. Ridiculous!

MRS. MARWOOD. Indeed, my dear, you'll tear another fan if you don't mitigate those violent airs.

MRS. MILLAMANT. Oh, silly! ha, ha, ha! I could laugh immoderately.—Poor Mirabell! His constancy to me has quite destroyed his complaisance for all the world beside. I swear, I never enjoined it him to be so coy. If I had the vanity to think he would obey me, I would command him to show more gallantry—'tis hardly well-bred to be so particular on one hand, and so insensible on the other. But I despair to prevail, and so let him follow

[2] Properly, *drap de Berri*, woollen cloth formerly made in Berry, France.
[3] Grows stout.
[4] White Rhine wine, taken to reduce corpulence.

his own way. Ha, ha, ha! Pardon me, dear creature, I must laugh—ha, ha, ha!—though I grant you 'tis a little barbarous—ha, ha, ha!

Mrs. Marwood. What pity 'tis, so much fine raillery and delivered with so significant gesture, should be so unhappily directed to miscarry.

Mrs. Millamant. Ha! Dear creature, I ask your pardon. I swear, I did not mind you.

Mrs. Marwood. Mr. Mirabell and you both may think it a thing impossible, when I shall tell him by telling you—

Mrs. Millamant. Oh dear, what? for it is the same thing if I hear it—ha, ha, ha!

Mrs. Marwood. That I detest him, hate him, madam.

Mrs. Millamant. O, Madam! why, so do I—and yet the creature loves me—ha, ha, ha! How can one forbear laughing to think of it. —I am a sibyl if I am not amazed to think what he can see in me. I'll take my death, I think you are handsomer—and within a year or two as young; if you could but stay for me, I should overtake you—but that cannot be.—Well, that thought makes me melancholic.—Now I'll be sad.

Mrs. Marwood. Your merry note may be changed sooner than you think.

Mrs. Millamant. D'ye say so? Then I'm resolved I'll have a song to keep up my spirits.

Enter Mincing

Mincing. The gentlemen stay but to comb,[1] madam, and will wait on you.

Mrs. Millamant. Desire Mrs.——that is in the next room to sing the song I would have learned yesterday.—You shall hear it, madam—not that there's any great matter in it, but 'tis agreeable to my humor.

Song

(Set by Mr. Eccles [2] and sung by Mrs. Hodgson) [3]

1

Love's but the frailty of the mind,
  When 'tis not with ambition joined;
A sickly flame, which, if not fed, expires,
And feeding, wastes in self-consuming fires.

[1] I.e., to comb their wigs.
[2] John Eccles (or Eagles), 1650?–1735, Master of the King's Band, and composer of much incidental music for the theater.
[3] Possibly Mrs. Hudson, a singer attached to the company at L.I.F., is meant.

2

'Tis not to wound a wanton boy
  Or amorous youth, that gives the joy;
But 'tis the glory to have pierced a swain,
For whom inferior beauties sighed in vain.

3

Then I alone the conquest prize,
  When I insult a rival's eyes:
If there's delight in love, 'tis when I see
That heart, which others bleed for, bleed for me.

Enter Petulant *and* Witwoud

Mrs. Millamant. Is your animosity composed, gentlemen?

Witwoud. Raillery, raillery, madam; we have no animosity—we hit off a little wit now and then, but no animosity. The falling out of wits is like the falling out of lovers. We agree in the main, like treble and bass. Ha, Petulant?

Petulant. Aye, in the main—but when I have a humor to contradict—

Witwoud. Aye, when he has a humor to contradict, then I contradict, too. What! I know my cue. Then we contradict one another like two battledores; for contradictions beget one another like Jews.

Petulant. If he says black's black—if I have a humor to say 'tis blue—let that pass—all's one for that. If I have a humor to prove it, it must be granted.

Witwoud. Not positively must—but it may—it may.

Petulant. Yes, it positively must, upon proof positive.

Witwoud. Aye, upon proof positive it must; but upon proof presumptive it only may.— That's a logical distinction now, madam.

Mrs. Marwood. I perceive your debates are of importance and very learnedly handled.

Petulant. Importance is one thing, and learning's another. But a debate's a debate; that I assert.

Witwoud. Petulant's an enemy to learning; he relies altogether on his parts.

Petulant. No, I'm no enemy to learning. It hurts not me.

Mrs. Marwood. That's a sign indeed it's no enemy to you.

Petulant. No, no, it's no enemy to anybody but them that have it.

Mrs. Millamant. Well, an illiterate man's my aversion. I wonder at the impudence of any illiterate man to offer to make love.

WITWOUD. That I confess I wonder at, too.

MRS. MILLAMANT. Ah! to marry an ignorant that can hardly read or write!

PETULANT. Why should a man be any further from being married, though he can't read, than he is from being hanged? The ordinary's[1] paid for setting the psalm,[2] and the parish priest for reading the ceremony. And for the rest which is to follow in both cases, a man may do it without book—so all's one for that.

MRS. MILLAMANT. D'ye hear the creature? —Lord, here's company, I'll be gone.

[*Exeunt* MRS. MILLAMANT *and* MINCING]

Enter SIR WILFULL WITWOUD *in a country riding habit, and* Servant *to* LADY WISHFORT

WITWOUD. In the name of Bartlemew and his fair,[3] what have we here?

MRS. MARWOOD. 'Tis your brother, I fancy. Don't you know him?

WITWOUD. Not I.—Yes, I think it is he—I've almost forgot him; I have not seen him since the Revolution.[4]

SERVANT. (*To* SIR WILFULL) Sir, my lady's dressing. Here's company; if you please to walk in, in the meantime.

SIR WILFULL. Dressing! What, it's but morning here I warrant, with you in London; we should count it towards afternoon in our parts, down in Shropshire.—Why, then belike, my aunt han't dined yet,—ha, friend?

SERVANT. Your aunt, sir?

SIR WILFULL. My aunt, sir! Yes, my aunt, sir, and your lady, sir; your lady is my aunt, sir.—Why, what! Dost thou not know me, friend? Why, then send somebody hither that does. How long hast thou lived with thy lady, fellow,—ha?

SERVANT. A week, sir—longer than anybody in the house, except my lady's woman.

SIR WILFULL. Why, then belike thou dost not know thy lady, if thou seest her,—ha, friend?

SERVANT. Why, truly, sir, I cannot safely swear to her face in a morning, before she is dressed. 'Tis like I may give a shrewd guess at her by this time.

SIR WILFULL. Well, prithee try what thou canst do; if thou canst not guess, inquire her out, dost hear, fellow? And tell her, her nephew, Sir Wilfull Witwoud, is in the house.

SERVANT. I shall, sir.

SIR WILFULL. Hold ye; hear me, friend; a word with you in your ear. Prithee, who are these gallants?

SERVANT. Really, sir, I can't tell; here come so many here, 'tis hard to know 'em all.

[*Exit* Servant]

SIR WILFULL. Oons,[5] this fellow knows less than a starling; I don't think a' knows his own name.

MRS. MARWOOD. Mr. Witwoud, your brother is not behindhand in forgetfulness—I fancy he has forgot you too.

WITWOUD. I hope so—the devil take him that remembers first, I say.

SIR WILFULL. Save you, gentlemen and lady!

MRS. MARWOOD. For shame, Mr. Witwoud; why don't you speak to him?—[*To* SIR WILFULL] And you, sir.

WITWOUD. Petulant, speak.

PETULANT. [*To* SIR WILFULL] And you, sir.

SIR WILFULL. No offense, I hope.

(*Salutes* MRS. MARWOOD)

MRS. MARWOOD. No, sure, sir.

WITWOUD. [*Aside*] This is a vile dog, I see that already. No offence! ha, ha, ha! —To him; to him, Petulant, smoke him.[6]

PETULANT. [*Surveying him round*] It seems as if you had come a journey, sir;—hem, hem.

SIR WILFULL. Very likely, sir, that it may seem so.

PETULANT. No offence, I hope, sir.

WITWOUD. [*Aside*] Smoke the boots, the boots, Petulant, the boots! Ha, ha, ha!

SIR WILFULL. May be not, sir; thereafter as 'tis meant, sir.

PETULANT. Sir, I presume upon the information of your boots.

SIR WILFULL. Why, 'tis like you may, sir: if you are not satisfied with the information of my boots, sir, if you will step to the stable, you may inquire further of my horse, sir.

PETULANT. Your horse, sir? your horse is an ass, sir!

SIR WILFULL. Do you speak by way of offence, sir?

MRS. MARWOOD. The gentleman's merry, that's all, sir.—(*Aside*) 'Slife, we shall have

---

[1] Chaplain.
[2] Selecting the psalm.
[3] The annual Bartholomew Fair in Smithfield
[4] Of 1688.
[5] A contraction of "God's wounds."
[6] To affront a stranger at his coming in.

a quarrel betwixt an horse and an ass before they find one another out.—(*Aloud*) You must not take anything amiss from your friends, sir. You are among your friends here, though it may be you don't know it.—If I am not mistaken, you are Sir Wilfull Witwoud.

Sir Wilfull. Right, lady; I am Sir Wilfull Witwoud—so I write myself. No offence to anybody, I hope—and nephew to the Lady Wishfort of this mansion.

Mrs. Marwood. Don't you know this gentleman, sir?

Sir Wilfull. Hum! What, sure 'tis not—yea, by'r Lady, but 'tis—'sheart, I know not whether 'tis or no—yea, but 'tis, by the Rekin[1] Brother Anthony! What, Tony, i'faith!—what, dost thou not know me? By'r Lady, nor I thee thou art so be-cravated, and so be-periwigged —'Sheart, why dost not speak? art thou overjoyed?

Witwoud. Odso, brother, is it you? Your servant, brother.

Sir Wilfull. Your servant!—why yours, sir. Your servant again—'sheart, and your friend and servant to that—and a (*puff*) — and a—flap-dragon[2] for your service, sir! and a hare's foot and a hare's scut[3] for your service, sir! an you be so cold and so courtly.

Witwoud. No offence, I hope, brother.

Sir Wilfull. 'Sheart, sir, but there is, and much offence!—A pox, is this your Inns o' Court[4] breeding, not to know your friends and your relations, your elders, and your betters?

Witwoud. Why, brother Wilfull of Salop,[5] you may be as short as a Shrewsbury-cake,[6] if you please. But I tell you 'tis not modish to know relations in town. You think you're in the country, where great lubberly brothers slabber[7] and kiss one another when they meet, like a call of sergeants[8]—'tis not the fashion here; 'tis not indeed, dear brother.

Sir Wilfull. The fashion's a fool; and you're a fop, dear brother. 'Sheart, I've suspected this—by'r Lady, I conjectured you were a fop since you began to change the style of your letters, and write on a scrap of paper gilt round the edges, no bigger than a *subpœna*. I might expect this when you left off "Honored Brother," and "hoping you are in good health," and so forth—to begin with a "Rat me, knight, I'm so sick of a last night's debauch—'ods heart," and then tell a familiar tale of a cock and a bull, and a whore and a bottle, and so conclude.—You could write news before you were out of your time,[9] when you lived with honest Pumple Nose, the attorney of Furnival's Inn—you could entreat to be remembered then to your friends round the Rekin. We could have gazettes, then, and Dawks's Letter,[10] and the Weekly Bill,[11] till of late days.

Petulant. 'Slife, Witwoud, were you ever an attorney's clerk? of the family of the Furnivals? Ha, ha, ha!

Witwoud. Aye, aye, but that was but for a while—not long, not long. Pshaw! I was not in my own power then; an orphan, and this fellow was my guardian. Aye, aye, I was glad to consent to that man to come to London. He had the disposal of me then. If I had not agreed to that, I might have been bound 'prentice to a felt-maker in Shrewsbury; this fellow would have bound me to a maker of felts.

Sir Wilfull. 'Sheart, and better than to be bound to a maker of fops—where, I suppose, you have served your time, and now you may set up for yourself.

Mrs. Marwood. You intend to travel, sir, as I'm informed.

Sir Wilfull. Belike I may, madam. I may chance to sail upon the salt seas, if my mind hold.

Petulant. And the wind serve.

Sir Wilfull. Serve or not serve, I shan't ask licence of you, sir; nor the weathercock your companion. I direct my discourse to the lady, sir.—'Tis like my aunt may have told you, madam—yes, I have settled my concerns, I may say now, and am minded to see foreign parts—if an' how that the peace holds, whereby that is, taxes abate.

---

[1] The Wrekin, an extinct volcano in Shropshire.
[2] Contemptuous term from the game of that name.
[3] Tail.
[4] The four sets of buildings in London, and the societies which own them, which have the right of admitting persons to the bar.
[5] Shropshire.
[6] A flat round cake like a biscuit.
[7] Slobber.
[8] When a sergeant-at-law is called to the bar.

[9] As an indentured apprentice.
[10] A news sheet intended for country consumption, half the space being given over to news printed in written characters, and half left blank for personal messages (Stevens).
[11] The bills of mortality for London, then issued weekly.

MRS. MARWOOD. I thought you had designed for France at all adventures.

SIR WILFULL. I can't tell that; 'tis like I may, and 'tis like I may not. I am somewhat dainty in making a resolution because when I make it I keep it. I don't stand shill I, shall I,[1] then; if I say't, I'll do't. But I have thoughts to tarry a small matter in town to learn somewhat of your lingo first, before I cross the seas. I'd gladly have a spice of your French, as they say, whereby to hold discourse in foreign countries.

MRS. MARWOOD. Here's an academy in town for that use.

SIR WILFULL. There is? 'Tis like there may.

MRS. MARWOOD. No doubt you will return very much improved.

WITWOUD. Yes, refined, like a Dutch skipper from a whale-fishing.

Enter LADY WISHFORT *and* FAINALL

LADY WISHFORT. Nephew, you are welcome.

SIR WILFULL. Aunt, your servant.

FAINALL. Sir Wilfull, your most faithful servant.

SIR WILFULL. Cousin Fainall, give me your hand.

LADY WISHFORT. Cousin Witwoud, your servant; Mr. Petulant, your servant; nephew, you are welcome again. Will you drink anything after your journey, nephew, before you eat? Dinner's almost ready.

SIR WILFULL. I'm very well, I thank you, aunt—however, I thank you for your courteous offer. 'Sheart, I was afraid you would have been in the fashion, too, and have remembered to have forgot your relations. Here's your cousin Tony; belike, I mayn't call him brother for fear of offence.

LADY WISHFORT. Oh, he's a rallier, nephew —my cousin's a wit. And your great wits always rally their best friends to choose.[2] When you have been abroad, nephew, you'll understand raillery better.

(FAINALL *and* MRS. MARWOOD *talk apart*)

SIR WILFULL. Why then, let him hold his tongue in the meantime, and rail when that day comes.

Enter MINCING

MINCING. Mem, I am come to acquaint your la'ship that dinner is impatient.

[1] Shilly-shally.
[2] As they please.

SIR WILFULL. Impatient! why, then, belike it won't stay till I pull off my boots.—Sweetheart, can you help me to a pair of slippers?—My man's with his horses, I warrant.

LADY WISHFORT. Fie, fie, nephew! you would not pull off your boots here!—Go down into the hall—dinner shall stay for you.

[*Exit* SIR WILFULL]

My nephew's a little unbred; you'll pardon him, madam.—Gentlemen, will you walk? Marwood?

MRS. MARWOOD. I'll follow you, madam— before Sir Wilfull is ready.

Manent MRS. MARWOOD *and* FAINALL

FAINALL. Why then, Foible's a bawd, an arrant, rank, match-making bawd. And I, it seems, am a husband, a rank husband; and my wife a very errant, rank wife—all in the way of the world. 'Sdeath, to be an anticipated cuckold, a cuckold in embryo! Sure, I was born with budding antlers, like a young satyr or a citizen's child. 'Sdeath! to be outwitted, to be out-jilted—out-matrimony'd!— If I had kept my speed like a stag, 'twere somewhat—but to crawl after, with my horns like a snail, and be outstripped by my wife— 'tis scurvy wedlock.

MRS. MARWOOD. Then shake it off. You have often wished for an opportunity to part, and now you have it. But first prevent their plot—the half of Millamant's fortune is too considerable to be parted with to a foe, to Mirabell.

FAINALL. Damn him! that had been mine, had you not made that fond[3] discovery.—That had been forfeited, had they been married. My wife had added lustre to my horns by that increase of fortune; I could have worn 'em tipped with gold, though my forehead had been furnished like a deputy-lieutenant's hall.[4]

MRS. MARWOOD. They may prove a cap of maintenance[5] to you still, if you can away[6] with your wife. And she's no worse than when you had her—I dare swear she had given up her game before she was married.

[3] Foolish.
[4] I.e., as many times a cuckold as there are horns (of deer) hung up in the country house of a deputy-lieutenant.
[5] A term in heraldry, meaning a cap with two points like horns frequently used in the crests of royal bastards. Mrs. Marwood puns on the meaning of maintenance.
[6] Endure.

FAINALL. Hum! that may be. She might throw up her cards, but I'll be hanged if she did not put pam [1] in her pocket.

MRS. MARWOOD. You married her to keep you; and if you can contrive to have her keep you better than you expected, why should you not keep her longer than you intended?

FAINALL. The means, the means?

MRS. MARWOOD. Discover to my lady your wife's conduct; threaten to part with her! My lady loves her, and will come to any composition to save her reputation. Take the opportunity of breaking it just upon the discovery of this imposture. My lady will be enraged beyond bounds, and sacrifice niece, and fortune, and all, at that conjuncture. And let me alone to keep her warm; if she should flag in her part, I will not fail to prompt her.

FAINALL. Faith, this has an appearance.

MRS. MARWOOD. I'm sorry I hinted to my lady to endeavor a match between Millamant and Sir Wilfull; that may be an obstacle.

FAINALL. Oh, for that matter, leave me to manage him. I'll disable him for that; he will drink like a Dane.[2] After dinner I'll set his hand in.[3]

MRS. MARWOOD. Well, how do you stand affected towards your lady?

FAINALL. Why, faith, I'm thinking of it. —Let me see—I am married already, so that's over. My wife has played the jade with me—well, that's over, too. I never loved her, or if I had, why, that would have been over, too, by this time.—Jealous of her I cannot be, for I am certain; so there's an end of jealousy: weary of her I am, and shall be—no, there's no end of that—no, no, that were too much to hope. Thus far concerning my repose; now for my reputation. As to my own, I married not for it, so that's out of the question; and as to my part in my wife's—why, she had parted with hers before; so bringing none to me, she can take none from me. 'Tis against all rule of play that I should lose to one who has not wherewithal to stake.

MRS. MARWOOD. Besides, you forgot marriage is honorable.

FAINALL. Hum, faith, and that's well thought on. Marriage is honorable, as you say; and if so, wherefore should cuckoldom be a discredit, being derived from so honorable a root?

MRS. MARWOOD. Nay, I know not; if the root be honorable, why not the branches?

FAINALL. So, so; why, this point's clear. —Well, how do we proceed?

MRS. MARWOOD. I will contrive a letter which shall be delivered to my lady at the time when that rascal who is to act Sir Rowland is with her. It shall come as from an unknown hand—for the less I appear to know of the truth, the better I can play the incendiary. Besides, I would not have Foible provoked if I could help it—because you know she knows some passages—nay, I expect all will come out. But let the mine be sprung first, and then I care not if I am discovered.

FAINALL. If the worst come to the worst, I'll turn my wife to grass. I have already a deed of settlement of the best part of her estate, which I wheedled out of her, and that you shall partake at least.

MRS. MARWOOD. I hope you are convinced that I hate Mirabell. Now you'll be no more jealous?

FAINALL. Jealous! No, by this kiss. Let husbands be jealous, but let the lover still believe; or, if he doubt, let it be only to endear his pleasure, and prepare the joy that follows when he proves his mistress true. But let husbands' doubts convert to endless jealousy; or, if they have belief, let it corrupt to superstition and blind credulity. I am single, and will herd no more with 'em. True, I wear the badge, but I'll disown the order. And since I take my leave of 'em, I care not if I leave 'em a common motto to their common crest:

All husbands must or pain or shame endure;
The wise too jealous are, fools too secure.

Exeunt

---

[1] The knave of clubs, the highest trump in the fashionable card game, loo.
[2] An old complaint. Cf. *Hamlet*, Act I, scene iii.
[3] Start him in the game.

ACT IV

SCENE I. [*Scene continues*]

Enter LADY WISHFORT *and* FOIBLE

LADY WISHFORT. Is Sir Rowland coming, sayest thou, Foible? And are things in order?

FOIBLE. Yes, madam, I have put wax lights in the sconces, and placed the footmen in a row in the hall, in their best liveries, with the coachman and postilion to fill up the equipage.

LADY WISHFORT. Have you pulvilled [1] the coachman and postilion, that they may not stink of the stable when Sir Rowland comes by?

FOIBLE. Yes, madam.

LADY WISHFORT. And are the dancers and the music ready, that he may be entertained in all points with correspondence to his passion?

FOIBLE. All is ready, madam.

LADY WISHFORT. And—well—how do I look, Foible?

FOIBLE. Most killing well, madam.

LADY WISHFORT. Well, and how shall I receive him? in what figure shall I give his heart the first impression? There is a great deal in the first impression. Shall I sit?—no, I won't sit—I'll walk—aye, I'll walk from the door upon his entrance, and then turn full upon him—no, that will be too sudden. I'll lie,—aye, I'll lie down—I'll receive him in my little dressing-room; there's a couch—yes, yes, I'll give the first impression on a couch.—I won't lie neither, but loll and lean upon one elbow with one foot a little dangling off, jogging in a thoughtful way—yes—and then as soon as he appears, start, aye, start and be surprised, and rise to meet him in a pretty disorder—yes.—Oh, nothing is more alluring than a levee [2] from a couch. in some confusion; it shows the foot to advantage, and furnishes with blushes, and recomposing airs beyond comparison. Hark! there's a coach.

FOIBLE. 'Tis he, madam.

LADY WISHFORT. Oh, dear, has my nephew made his addresses to Millamant? I ordered him.

FOIBLE. Sir Wilfull is set in drinking, madam, in the parlor.

LADY WISHFORT. Odds my life, I'll send him to her. Call her down, Foible; bring her hither. I'll send him as I go.—When they are together, then come to me, Foible, that I may not be too long alone with Sir Rowland.   [*Exit* LADY WISHFORT]

Enter MRS. MILLAMANT *and* MRS. FAINALL

FOIBLE. Madam, I stayed here to tell your ladyship that Mr. Mirabell has waited this half-hour for an opportunity to talk with you—though my lady's orders were to leave you and Sir Wilfull together. Shall I tell Mr. Mirabell that you are at leisure?

MRS. MILLAMANT. No. What would the dear man have? I am thoughtful, and would amuse myself—bid him come another time.

(*Repeating, and walking about*)

There never yet was woman made
Nor shall, but to be cursed.[3]

That's hard!

MRS. FAINALL. You are very fond of Sir John Suckling to-day, Millamant, and the poets.

MRS. MILLAMANT. He? Aye, and filthy verses—so I am.

FOIBLE. Sir Wilfull is coming, madam. Shall I send Mr. Mirabell away?

MRS. MILLAMANT. Aye, if you please, Foible, send him away, or send him hither—just as you will, dear Foible. I think I'll see him—shall I? Aye, let the wretch come.

Exit FOIBLE
(*Repeating*)

Thyrsis, a youth of the inspired train.[4]

Dear Fainall, entertain Sir Wilfull—thou hast philosophy to undergo a fool. Thou art married and hast patience—I would confer with my own thoughts.

MRS. FAINALL. I am obliged to you that you would make me your proxy in this affair, but I have business of my own.

Enter SIR WILFULL

O Sir Wilfull, you are come at the critical instant. There's your mistress up to the ears in love and contemplation; pursue your point now or never.

SIR WILFULL. Yes; my aunt will have it so—I would gladly have been encouraged with a bottle or two, because I'm somewhat wary at first before I am acquainted.— (*This while* MILLAMANT *walks about repeating to herself*)—But I hope, after a time, I shall break my mind—that is, upon further acquaintance.—So for the present, cousin, I'll take my leave. If so be you'll be so kind to make my excuse, I'll return to my company—

---

[1] Powdered with a scented powder.
[2] Rising.

[3] The quotation is from Sir John Suckling. See his *Works*, ed. W. C. Hazlitt, I, 19.
[4] From Waller's "The Story of Phœbus and Daphne Applied." See his *Poems*, ed. G. Thorn-Drury, I, 52.

MRS. FAINALL. Oh, fie, Sir Wilfull! What! You must not be daunted.

SIR WILFULL. Daunted! No, that's not it; it is not so much for that—for if so be that I set on't, I'll do't. But only for the present, 'tis sufficient till further acquaintance, that's all—your servant.

MRS. FAINALL. Nay, I'll swear you shall never lose so favorable an opportunity if I can help it. I'll leave you together, and lock the door. *Exit*

SIR WILFULL. Nay, nay, cousin—I have forgot my gloves!—What d'ye do?—'Sheart, a' has locked the door indeed, I think. Nay, Cousin Fainall, open the door! Pshaw, what a vixen trick is this?—Nay, now a' has seen me too.—Cousin, I made bold to pass through as it were—I think this door's enchanted!

MRS. MILLAMANT. (*Repeating*)

I prithee spare me, gentle boy,
Press me no more for that slight toy.[1]

SIR WILFULL. Anan?[2] Cousin, your servant.
MRS. MILLAMANT.

—That foolish trifle of a heart.—

Sir Wilfull!

SIR WILFULL. Yes—your servant. No offence, I hope, cousin.

MRS. MILLAMANT. (*Repeating*)

I swear it will do its part,
Though thou dost thine, employ'st thy power and art.

Natural, easy Suckling!

SIR WILFULL. Anan? Suckling. No such suckling neither, cousin, nor stripling: I thank heaven, I'm no minor.

MRS. MILLAMANT. Ah, rustic, ruder than Gothic!

SIR WILFULL. Well, well, I shall understand your lingo one of these days, cousin; in the meanwhile I must answer in plain English.

MRS. MILLAMANT. Have you any business with me, Sir Wilfull?

SIR WILFULL. Not at present, cousin.— Yes, I made bold to see, to come and know if that how you were disposed to fetch a walk this evening; if so be that I might not be troublesome, I would have sought a walk with you.

MRS. MILLAMANT. A walk! what then?

SIR WILFULL. Nay, nothing—only for the walk's sake, that's all.

MRS. MILLAMANT. I nauseate walking; 'tis a country diversion. I loathe the country, and everything that relates to it.

SIR WILFULL. Indeed! ha! Look ye, look ye—you do? Nay, 'tis like you may—here are choice of pastimes here in town, as plays and the like; that must be confessed, indeed.

MRS. MILLAMANT. *Ah, l'étourdi!*[3] I hate the town too.

SIR WILFULL. Dear heart, that's much— ha! that you should hate 'em both! Ha! 'tis like you may; there are some can't relish the town, and others can't away with the country—'tis like you may be one of those, cousin.

MRS. MILLAMANT. Ha, ha, ha! yes, 'tis like I may.—You have nothing further to say to me?

SIR WILFULL. Not at present, cousin.— 'Tis like when I have an opportunity to be more private, I may break my mind in some measure—I conjecture you partly guess— however, that's as time shall try—but spare to speak and spare to speed, as they say.

MRS. MILLAMANT. If it is of no great importance, Sir Wilfull, you will oblige me to leave me; I have just now a little business—

SIR WILFULL. Enough, enough, cousin: yes, yes, all a case.—When you're disposed, when you're disposed. Now's as well as another time, and another time as well as now All's one for that—Yes, yes, if your concerns call you, there's no haste; it will keep cold, as they say. Cousin, your servant.—I think this door's locked.

MRS. MILLAMANT. You may go this way, sir.

SIR WILFULL. Your servant; then with your leave I'll return to my company. *Exit*

MRS. MILLAMANT. Aye, aye; ha, ha, ha!

Like Phœbus sung the no less amorous boy.[4]

Enter MIRABELL

MIRABELL. "Like Daphne she, as lovely and as coy." Do you lock yourself up from me, to make my search more curious, or is this pretty artifice contrived to signify that here the chase must end, and my pursuits be crowned? For you can fly no further.

---

[1] See Suckling's *Works*, ed. cit. I, 22.
[2] What's that?
[3] Giddy, thoughtless.
[4] From the Waller poem cited above. Mirabell caps the quotation in the following line.

Mrs. Millamant. Vanity! No—I'll fly, and be followed to the last moment. Though I am upon the very verge of matrimony, I expect you should solicit me as much as if I were wavering at the grate of a monastery, with one foot over the threshold. I'll be solicited to the very last—nay, and afterwards.

Mirabell. What, after the last?

Mrs. Millamant. Oh, I should think I was poor and had nothing to bestow, if I were reduced to an inglorious ease and freed from the agreeable fatigues of solicitation.

Mirabell. But do not you know that when favors are conferred upon instant [1] and tedious solicitation, that they diminish in their value, and that both the giver loses the grace, and the receiver lessens his pleasure?

Mrs. Millamant. It may be in things of common application; but never, sure, in love. Oh, I hate a lover that can dare to think he draws a moment's air, independent of the bounty of his mistress. There is not so impudent a thing in nature as the saucy look of an assured man, confident of success. The pedantic arrogance of a very husband has not so pragmatical [2] an air. Ah! I'll never marry unless I am first made sure of my will and pleasure.

Mirabell. Would you have 'em both before marriage? or will you be contented with the first now, and stay for the other till after grace?

Mrs. Millamant. Ah! don't be impertinent.—My dear liberty, shall I leave thee? my faithful solitude, my darling contemplation, must I bid you then adieu? Ay-h adieu— my morning thoughts, agreeable wakings, indolent slumbers, all ye *douceurs*, ye *sommeils du matin*,[3] *adieu*.—I can't do't, 'tis more than impossible.—Positively, Mirabell, I'll lie abed in a morning as long as I please.

Mirabell. Then I'll get up in a morning as early as I please.

Mrs. Millamant. Ah? Idle creature, get up when you will—and d'ye hear, I won't be called names after I'm married; positively, I won't be called names.

Mirabell. Names!

Mrs. Millamant. Aye, as wife, spouse, my dear, joy, jewel, love, sweetheart, and the rest of that nauseous cant, in which men and their wives are so fulsomely familiar— I shall never bear that. Good Mirabell, don't let us be familiar or fond, nor kiss before folks, like my Lady Fadler and Sir Francis; nor go to Hyde Park together the first Sunday in a new chariot, to provoke eyes and whispers, and then never to be seen there together again, as if we were proud of one another the first week, and ashamed of one another ever after. Let us never visit together, nor go to a play together; but let us be very strange and well-bred. Let us be as strange as if we had been married a great while, and as well-bred as if we were not married at all.

Mirabell. Have you any more conditions to offer? Hitherto your demands are pretty reasonable.

Mrs. Millamant. Trifles—as liberty to pay and receive visits to and from whom I please; to write and receive letters, without interrogatories or wry faces on your part; to wear what I please, and choose conversation with regard only to my own taste; to have no obligation upon me to converse with wits that I don't like, because they are your acquaintance: or to be intimate with fools, because they may be your relations.—Come to dinner when I please; dine in my dressing-room when I'm out of humor, without giving a reason. To have my closet inviolate; to be sole empress of my tea-table, which you must never presume to approach without first asking leave. And lastly, wherever I am, you shall always knock at the door before you come in. These articles subscribed, if I continue to endure you a little longer, I may by degrees dwindle into a wife.

Mirabell. Your bill of fare is something advanced in this latter account.—Well, have I liberty to offer conditions—that when you are dwindled into a wife, I may not be beyond measure enlarged into a husband?

Mrs. Millamant. You have free leave. Propose your utmost; speak and spare not.

Mirabell. I thank you.—*Imprimis* [4] then, I covenant that your acquaintance be general; that you admit no sworn confidante or intimate of your own sex—no she-friend to screen her affairs under your countenance, and tempt you to make trial of a mutual

---

[1] Urgent.
[2] Officious.
[3] Sweetnesses, morning naps (i.e., beauty sleep).
[4] In the first place.

secrecy. No decoy-duck to wheedle you—a fop scrambling to the play in a mask—[1] then bring you home in a pretended fright, when you think you shall be found out—and rail at me for missing the play and disappointing the frolic which you had, to pick me up and prove my constancy.

MRS. MILLAMANT. Detestable *imprimis!* I go to the play in a mask!

MIRABELL. *Item*, I article, that you continue to like your own face, as long as I shall; and while it passes current with me, that you endeavor not to new-coin it. To which end, together with all vizards for the day, I prohibit all masks for the night, made of oiled-skins and I know not what—hogs' bones, hares' gall, pig-water, and the marrow of a roasted cat. In short, I forbid all commerce with the gentlewoman in what-d'ye-call-it Court. *Item*, I shut my doors against all bawds with baskets, and pennyworths of muslin, china, fans, atlases,[2] etc.—*Item*, when you shall be breeding—

MRS. MILLAMANT. Ah! name it not.

MIRABELL. Which may be presumed, with a blessing on our endeavors—

MRS. MILLAMANT. Odious endeavors!

MIRABELL. I denounce against all strait lacing, squeezing for a shape, till you mould my boy's head like a sugar-loaf, and instead of a man-child, make me father to a crooked billet. Lastly, to the dominion of the tea-table I submit—but with proviso, that you exceed not in your province, but restrain yourself to native and simple tea-table drinks, as tea, chocolate, and coffee; as likewise to genuine and authorized tea-table talk—such as mending of fashions, spoiling reputations, railing at absent friends, and so forth—but that on no account you encroach upon the men's prerogative, and presume to drink healths, or toast fellows: for prevention of which I banish all foreign forces, all auxiliaries to the tea-table, as orange-brandy, all aniseed, cinnamon, citron, and Barbadoes waters, together with ratafia, and the most noble spirit of clary,[3] but for cowslip wine, poppy water, and all dormitives, those I allow.—These provisos admitted, in other things I may prove a tractable and complying husband.

MRS. MILLAMANT. O horrid provisos! filthy strong-waters! I toast fellows! odious men! I hate your odious provisos.

MIRABELL. Then we're agreed. Shall I kiss your hand upon the contract? And here comes one to be a witness to the sealing of the deed.

Enter MRS. FAINALL

MRS. MILLAMANT. Fainall, what shall I do? Shall I have him? I think I must have him.

MRS. FAINALL. Aye, aye, take him, take him; what should you do?

MRS. MILLAMANT. Well then—I'll take my death, I'm in a horrid fright.—Fainall, I shall never say it—well—I think—I'll endure you.

MRS. FAINALL. Fie! fie! Have him, have him, and tell him so in plain terms; for I am sure you have a mind to him.

MRS. MILLAMANT. Are you? I think I have—and the horrid man looks as if he thought so too. Well, you ridiculous thing you, I'll have you—I won't be kissed, nor I won't be thanked—here, kiss my hand though.—So, hold your tongue now; don't say a word.

MRS. FAINALL. Mirabell, there's a necessity for your obedience; you have neither time to talk nor stay. My mother is coming, and in my conscience if she should see you, would fall into fits, and maybe not recover time enough to return to Sir Rowland, who, as Foible tells me, is in a fair way to succeed. Therefore spare your ecstasies for another occasion, and slip down the backstairs, where Foible waits to consult you.

MRS. MILLAMANT. Aye, go, go. In the meantime I suppose you have said something to please me.

MIRABELL. I am all obedience.

[*Exit* MIRABELL]

MRS. FAINALL. Yonder, Sir Wilfull's drunk, and so noisy that my mother has been forced to leave Sir Rowland to appease him; but he

---

[1] In the original, "to wheedle you a fop-scrambling to the play in a mask," which may be correct in the sense: wheedle you to the theater to scramble after a fop.

[2] An atlas is a variety of satin (Summers).

[3] *Orange-brandy* is brandy flavored with orange peel; *aniseed*, a cordial so flavored; *cinnamon* is used for the same purpose; *citron* is citron water, a brandy so flavored; *Barbadoes waters* is a cordial flavored with orange and lemon peelings; *ratafia* (see note 2, p. 405 to Act I); *clary* is composed of brandy, sugar, clary-flowers and cinnamon.

answers her only with singing and drinking. What they may have done by this time I know not, but Petulant and he were upon quarrelling as I came by.

Mrs. Millamant. Well, if Mirabell should not make a good husband, I am a lost thing, for I find I love him violently.

Mrs. Fainall. So it seems, when you mind not what's said to you.—If you doubt him, you had best take up with Sir Wilfull.

Mrs. Millamant. How can you name that superannuated lubber?—Foh!

Enter Witwoud *from drinking*

Mrs. Fainall. So! Is the fray made up, that you have left 'em?

Witwoud. Left 'em? I could stay no longer. I have laughed like ten christ'nings —I am tipsy with laughing. If I had stayed any longer I should have burst—I must have been let out and pieced in the sides like an unfixed camlet.[1]—Yes, yes, the fray is composed; my lady came in like a *noli prosequi*,[2] and stopped their proceedings.

Mrs. Millamant. What was the dispute?

Witwoud. That's the jest; there was no dispute. They could neither of 'em speak for rage, and so fell a sputtering at one another like two roasting apples.

Enter Petulant, *drunk*

Now, Petulant, all's over, all's well. Gad, my head begins to whim it about—Why dost thou not speak? Thou art both as drunk and mute as a fish.

Petulant. Look you, Mrs. Millamant— if you can love me, dear nymph, say it—and that's the conclusion. Pass on, or pass off— that's all.

Witwoud. Thou hast uttered volumes, folios, in less than *decimo sexto*,[3] my dear Lacedemonian.[4] Sirrah Petulant, thou art an epitomizer of words.

Petulant. Witwoud—you are an annihilator of sense.

Witwoud. Thou art a retailer of phrases, and dost deal in remnants of remnants, like a maker of pincushions—thou art in truth

[1] Unsized (i.e., unstiffened) material, originally imported from the Orient, and afterwards shoddily imitated.
[2] Legal term: unwilling to prosecute.
[3] Sixteenmo; a very small size for a book.
[4] The Lacedemonians or Spartans were noted for their laconicism.

(metaphorically speaking) a speaker of shorthand.

Petulant. Thou art (without a figure) just one-half of an ass, and Baldwin [5] yonder, thy half-brother, is the rest.—A Gemini [6] of asses split would make just four of you.

Witwoud. Thou dost bite, my dear mustard seed; kiss me for that.

Petulant. Stand off!—I'll kiss no more males—I have kissed your twin yonder in a humor of reconciliation, till he (*hiccup*) rises upon my stomach like a radish.

Mrs. Millamant. Eh! filthy creature! —What was the quarrel?

Petulant. There was no quarrel—there might have been a quarrel.

Witwoud. If there had been words enow between 'em to have expressed provocation, they had gone together by the ears like a pair of castanets.

Petulant. You were the quarrel.

Mrs. Millamant. Me!

Petulant. If I have a humor to quarrel, I can make less matters conclude premises. —If you are not handsome, what then, if I have a humor to prove it? If I shall have my reward, say so; if not, fight for your face the next time yourself. I'll go sleep.

Witwoud. Do; wrap thyself up like a wood-louse,[7] and dream revenge—and hear me; if thou canst learn to write by tomorrow morning, pen me a challenge.—I'll carry it for thee.

Petulant. Carry your mistress's monkey a spider!—Go, flea dogs, and read romances! —I'll go to bed to my maid. *Exit* [Petulant]

Mrs. Fainall. He's horridly drunk. How came you all in this pickle?

Witwoud. A plot, a plot, to get rid of the knight—your husband's advice, but he sneaked off.

Enter Lady [Wishfort], *and then* Sir Wilfull, *drunk*

Lady Wishfort. Out upon't, out upon't! At years of discretion, and comport yourself at this rantipole rate!

Sir Wilfull. No offence, aunt.

Lady Wishfort. Offence! as I'm a person, I'm ashamed of you. Foh! how you stink of wine! D'ye think my niece will ever endure

[5] The ass in *Reynard the Fox*.
[6] Twins.
[7] Which rolls itself into a ball.

such a borachio! you're an absolute borachio.[1]

SIR WILFULL. Borachio?

LADY WISHFORT. At a time when you should commence an amour and put your best foot foremost—

SIR WILFULL. 'Sheart, an you grutch[2] me your liquor, make a bill—give me more drink, and take my purse—(*Sings*)

    Prithee fill me the glass,
      Till it laugh in my face,
    With ale that is potent and mellow;
    He that whines for a lass,
    Is an ignorant ass,
    For a bumper has not its fellow.

But if you would have me marry my cousin—say the word, and I'll do't. Wilfull will do't; that's the word. Wilfull will do't; that's my crest—My motto I have forgot.

LADY WISHFORT. [*To* MRS. MILLAMANT] My nephew's a little overtaken, cousin, but 'tis with drinking your health.—O' my word, you are obliged to him.

SIR WILFULL. *In vino veritas*,[3] aunt.—If I drunk your health to-day, cousin—I am a Borachio. But if you have a mind to be married, say the word, and send for the piper; Wilfull will do't. If not, dust it away, and let's have t'other round.—Tony!—Odds heart, where's Tony?—Tony's an honest fellow; but he spits after a bumper, and that's a fault.—
(*Sings*)

    We'll drink, and we'll never ha' done, boys,
      Put the glass then around with the sun, boys,
    Let Apollo's example invite us;
    For he's drunk every night,
    And that makes him so bright,
    That he's able next morning to light us.

The sun's a good pimple,[4] an honest soaker; he has a cellar at your Antipodes. If I travel, aunt, I touch at your Antipodes.—Your Antipodes are a good, rascally sort of topsy-turvy fellows: if I had a bumper, I'd stand upon my head and drink a health to 'em.—A match or no match, cousin with the hard name—Aunt, Wilfull will do't. If she has her maidenhead, let her look to't; if she has not, let her keep her own counsel in the meantime, and cry out at the nine months' end.

MRS. MILLAMANT. Your pardon, madam, I can stay no longer—Sir Wilfull grows very powerful. Eh! how he smells! I shall be overcome, if I stay. Come, cousin.

Exeunt MRS. MILLAMANT *and* MRS. FAINALL

LADY WISHFORT. Smells! He would poison a tallow-chandler and his family! Beastly creature, I know not what to do with him!—Travel, quotha! Aye, travel, travel—get thee gone, get thee gone; get thee but far enough, to the Saracens, or the Tartars, or the Turks!—for thou art not fit to live in a Christian commonwealth, thou beastly pagan!

SIR WILFULL. Turks? No; no Turks, aunt. Your Turks are infidels, and believe not in the grape. Your Mahometan, your Mussulman, is a dry stinkard[5]—no offence, aunt. My map says that your Turk is not so honest a man as your Christian. I cannot find by the map that your Mufti is orthodox—whereby it is a plain case that orthodox is a hard word, aunt, and (hiccup)—Greek for claret.—
(*Sings*)

    To drink is a Christian diversion,
    Unknown to the Turk or the Persian:
    Let Mahometan fools
    Live by heathenish rules,
    And be damned over tea-cups and coffee.
    But let British lads sing,
    Crown a health to the king,
    And a fig for your sultan and sophy![6]

Ah, Tony!

Enter FOIBLE, *and whispers* [*to*] LADY WISHFORT

LADY WISHFORT. (*Aside to* FOIBLE) Sir Rowland impatient? Good lack! what shall I do with this beastly tumbril?—(*Aloud*) Go lie down and sleep, you sot!—or, as I'm a person, I'll have you bastinadoed with broomsticks.—Call up the wenches.

Exit FOIBLE

SIR WILFULL. Ahey! wenches; where are the wenches?

LADY WISHFORT. Dear Cousin Witwoud, get him away, and you will bind me to you inviolably. I have an affair of moment that invades me with some precipitation—you will oblige me to all futurity.

WITWOUD. Come, knight.—Pox on him,

---

[1] A Spanish word for winebag; hence, drunkard.
[2] Grudge.
[3] There is truth in wine.
[4] Boon companion (Tupper).
[5] Low fellow. The Koran forbids Mohammedans to drink wine.
[6] Here a general term for a Mohammedan ruler.

I don't know what to say to him.—Will you go to a cock-match?

SIR WILFULL. With a wench, Tony? Is she a shakebag,[1] sirrah? Let me bite your cheek for that.

WITWOUD. Horrible! he has a breath like a bagpipe—Aye, aye; come, will you march, my Salopian?

SIR WILFULL. Lead on, little Tony—I'll follow thee, my Anthony, my Tantony. Sirrah, thou shalt be my Tantony, and I'll be thy pig.[2] (*Sings*)

And a fig for your sultan and sophy.

[*Exeunt* SIR WILFULL *and* WITWOUD]

LADY WISHFORT. This will never do. It will never make a match—at least before he has been abroad.

Enter WAITWELL, *disguised as* SIR ROWLAND

LADY WISHFORT. Dear Sir Rowland, I am confounded with confusion at the retrospection of my own rudeness!—I have more pardons to ask than the pope distributes in the year of jubilee. But I hope, where there is likely to be so near an alliance, we may unbend the severity of decorums and dispense with a little ceremony.

WAITWELL. My impatience, madam, is the effect of my transport; and till I have the possession of your adorable person, I am tantalized on the rack; and do but hang, madam, on the tenter of expectation.

LADY WISHFORT. You have excess of gallantry, Sir Rowland, and press things to a conclusion with a most prevailing vehemence.—But a day or two for decency of marriage—

WAITWELL. For decency of funeral, madam! The delay will break my heart—or, if that should fail, I shall be poisoned. My nephew will get an inkling of my designs, and poison me; and I would willingly starve him before I die—I would gladly go out of the world with that satisfaction.—That would be some comfort to me, if I could but live so long as to be revenged on that unnatural viper!

LADY WISHFORT. Is he so unnatural, say you? Truly, I would contribute much, both to the saving of your life and the accomplishment of your revenge—not that I respect myself, though he has been a perfidious wretch to me.

WAITWELL. Perfidious to you!

LADY WISHFORT. O Sir Rowland, the hours that he has died away at my feet, the tears that he has shed, the oaths that he has sworn, the palpitations that he has felt, the trances and the tremblings, the ardors and the ecstasies, the kneelings and the risings, the heart-heavings and the handgrippings, the pangs and the pathetic regards of his protesting eyes! Oh, no memory can register!

WAITWELL. What, my rival! Is the rebel my rival?—a' dies!

LADY WISHFORT. No, don't kill him at once, Sir Rowland; starve him gradually, inch by inch.

WAITWELL. I'll do't. In three weeks he shall be barefoot; in a month out at knees with begging an alms.—He shall starve upward and upward, till he has nothing living but his head, and then go out in a stink like a candle's end upon a save-all.[3]

LADY WISHFORT. Well, Sir Rowland, you have the way—you are no novice in the labyrinth of love; you have the clue. But as I am a person, Sir Rowland, you must not attribute my yielding to any sinister appetite, or indigestion of widowhood; nor impute my complacency to any lethargy of continence. I hope you do not think me prone to any iteration of nuptials—

WAITWELL. Far be it from me—

LADY WISHFORT. If you do, I protest I must recede—or think that I have made a prostitution of decorums; but in the vehemence of compassion, and to save the life of a person of so much importance—

WAITWELL. I esteem it so—

LADY WISHFORT. Or else you wrong my condescension.

WAITWELL. I do not, I do not—

LADY WISHFORT. Indeed you do.

WAITWELL. I do not, fair shrine of virtue!

LADY WISHFORT. If you think the least scruple of carnality was an ingredient,—

WAITWELL. Dear madam, no. You are all camphor and frankincense, all chastity and odor.

LADY WISHFORT. Or that—

Enter FOIBLE

FOIBLE. Madam, the dancers are ready;

---

[1] Low woman.
[2] The pig is associated with St. Antony in legendary art and lore.
[3] A device for holding a candle end so that it will burn

and there's one with a letter, who must deliver it into your own hands.

LADY WISHFORT. Sir Rowland, will you give me leave? Think favorably, judge candidly, and conclude you have found a person who would suffer racks in honor's cause, dear Sir Rowland, and will wait on you incessantly.

[*Exit* LADY WISHFORT]

WAITWELL. Fie, fie!—What a slavery have I undergone! Spouse, hast thou any cordial? I want spirits.

FOIBLE. What a washy rogue art thou, to pant thus for a quarter of an hour's lying and swearing to a fine lady!

WAITWELL. Oh, she is the antidote to desire! Spouse, thou wilt fare the worse for't—I shall have no appetite to iteration of nuptials this eight-and-forty hours.—By this hand I'd rather be a chairman in the dog-days than act Sir Rowland till this time to-morrow!

Enter LADY WISHFORT, *with a letter*

LADY WISHFORT. Call in the dancers.—Sir Rowland, we'll sit, if you please, and see the entertainment. (*A dance*) Now, with your permission, Sir Rowland, I will peruse my letter.—I would open it in your presence, because I would not make you uneasy. If it should make you uneasy, I would burn it. Speak, if it does—but you may see by the superscription it is like a woman's hand.

FOIBLE. (*Aside to* WAITWELL) By heaven! Mrs. Marwood's, I know it.—My heart aches —get it from her.

WAITWELL. A woman's hand? No, madam, that's no woman's hand; I see that already. That's somebody whose throat must be cut.

LADY WISHFORT. Nay, Sir Rowland, since you give me a proof of your passion by your jealousy, I promise you I'll make a return by a frank communication.—You shall see it—we'll open it together—look you here.—(*Reads*)—"Madam, though unknown to you" —Look you there, 'tis from nobody that I know—"I have that honor for your character, that I think myself obliged to let you know you are abused. He who pretends to be Sir Rowland, is a cheat and a rascal."—Oh, heavens! what's this?

FOIBLE. (*Aside*) Unfortunate, all's ruined!

WAITWELL. How, how! Let me see, let me see!—(*Reads*) "A rascal, and disguised and suborned for that imposture,"—O villainy! O villainy!—"by the contrivance of—"

LADY WISHFORT. I shall faint!—I shall die, I shall die!—Oh!

FOIBLE. (*Aside to* WAITWELL) Say 'tis your nephew's hand—quickly, his plot,—swear it, swear it!

WAITWELL. Here's a villain! Madam, don't you perceive it? Don't you see it?

LADY WISHFORT. Too well, too well! I have seen too much.

WAITWELL. I told you at first I knew the hand.—A woman's hand! The rascal writes a sort of a large hand—your Roman hand.—[1] I saw there was a throat to be cut presently. If he were my son, as he is my nephew, I'd pistol him!

FOIBLE. O treachery!—But are you sure, Sir Rowland, it is his writing?

WAITWELL. Sure? Am I here? Do I live? Do I love this pearl of India? I have twenty letters in my pocket from him in the same character.

LADY WISHFORT. How!

FOIBLE. Oh, what luck it is, Sir Rowland, that you were present at this juncture! This was the business that brought Mr. Mirabell disguised to Madam Millamant this afternoon. I thought something was contriving when he stole by me and would have hid his face.

LADY WISHFORT. How, how!—I heard the villain was in the house, indeed; and now I remember, my niece went away abruptly when Sir Wilfull was to have made his addresses.

FOIBLE. Then, then, madam, Mr. Mirabell waited for her in her chamber; but I would not tell your ladyship to discompose you when you were to receive Sir Rowland.

WAITWELL. Enough; his date is short.

FOIBLE. No, good Sir Rowland, don't incur the law.

WAITWELL. Law! I care not for law. I can but die and 'tis in a good cause.—My lady shall be satisfied of my truth and innocence, though it cost me my life.

LADY WISHFORT. No, dear Sir Rowland, don't fight. If you should be killed, I must never show my face; or hanged—oh, consider my reputation, Sir Rowland!—No, you shan't fight.—I'll go in and examine my niece; I'll make her confess. I conjure you, Sir Rowland, by all your love, not to fight.

WAITWELL. I am charmed, madam; I obey.

[1] I.e., written in bold round letters.

But some proof you must let me give you; I'll go for a black box which contains the writings of my whole estate, and deliver that into your hands.

LADY WISHFORT. Aye, dear Sir Rowland, that will be some comfort. Bring the black box.

WAITWELL. And may I presume to bring a contract to be signed this night? May I hope so far?

LADY WISHFORT. Bring what you will, but come alive, pray, come alive! Oh, this is a happy discovery!

WAITWELL. Dead or alive I'll come—and married we will be in spite of treachery; aye, and get an heir that shall defeat the last remaining glimpse of hope in my abandoned nephew. Come, my buxom widow: Ere long you shall substantial proofs receive, That I'm an errant knight—

FOIBLE. (*Aside*) Or arrant knave.
Exeunt

ACT V

SCENE 1. [*Scene continues*]

LADY WISHFORT *and* FOIBLE

LADY WISHFORT. Out of my house! Out of my house, thou viper, thou serpent, that I have fostered! thou bosom traitress, that I raised from nothing!—Begone, begone, begone, go! go!—That I took from washing of old gauze and weaving of dead hair, with a bleak blue nose over a chafing-dish of starved embers, and dining behind a traverse rag,[1] in a shop no bigger than a birdcage!—Go, go! Starve again! Do, do!

FOIBLE. Dear madam, I'll beg pardon on my knees.

LADY WISHFORT. Away! out, out!—Go, set up for yourself again!—Do, drive a trade, do, with your three-pennyworth of small ware, flaunting upon a packthread under a brandy-seller's bulk, or against a dead wall by a ballad-monger! Go, hang out an old Frisoneer gorget,[2] with a yard of yellow colbertine[3] again, do! An old gnawed mask, two rows of pins, and a child's fiddle; a glass necklace with the beads broken, and a quilted night-cap with one ear! Go, go, drive a trade! —These were your commodities, you treacherous trull! this was the merchandise you dealt in when I took you into my house, placed you next myself, and made you governante[4] of my whole family! You have forgot this, have you, now you have feathered your nest?

FOIBLE. No, no, dear madam. Do but hear me; have but a moment's patience. I'll confess all. Mr. Mirabell seduced me. I am not the first that he has wheedled with his dissembling tongue; your ladyship's own wisdom has been deluded by him—then how should I, a poor ignorant, defend myself? O madam, if you knew but what he promised me, and how he assured me your ladyship should come to no damage!—Or else the wealth of the Indies should not have bribed me to conspire against so good, so sweet, so kind a lady as you have been to me.

LADY WISHFORT. No damage! What, to betray me, and marry me to a cast[5] serving-man! to make me a receptacle, an hospital for a decayed pimp! No damage! O thou frontless impudence, more than a big-bellied actress!

FOIBLE. Pray, do but hear me, madam! He could not marry your ladyship, madam. —No, indeed; his marriage was to have been void in law, for he was married to me first, to secure your ladyship. He could not have bedded your ladyship; for if he had consummated with your ladyship, he must have run the risk of the law, and been put upon his clergy.[6]—Yes, indeed, I inquired of the law in that case before I would meddle or make.

LADY WISHFORT. What, then I have been your property, have I? I have been convenient to you, it seems!—while you were catering for Mirabell, I have been broker for you! What, have you made a passive bawd of me?—This exceeds all precedent! I am brought to fine uses, to become a botcher of second-hand marriages between Abigails and Andrews.[7] I'll couple you! Yes, I'll baste you together, you and your Philander.[8] I'll Duke's-place[9] you, as I'm a person! Your turtle[10] is in custody already: you shall

---

[1] A ragged curtain hung up as a screen.
[2] A woollen kerchief worn over the bosom.
[3] Cheap lace.
[4] Housekeeper.
[5] Cast off, discharged.
[6] Forced to plead benefit of clergy (tested by the ability to read) in order to escape hanging.
[7] Ladies' maids and gentlemen's servants.
[8] Lover.
[9] Cf. note to Act I, p. 406, l. 33.
[10] Turtle dove, lover.

coo in the same cage if there be a constable or warrant in the parish.

Exit LADY WISHFORT

FOIBLE. Oh, that ever I was born! Oh, that I was ever married!—A bride!—aye, I shall be a Bridewell-bride.[1]—Oh!

Enter MRS. FAINALL

MRS. FAINALL. Poor Foible, what's the matter?

FOIBLE. O madam, my lady's gone for a constable! I shall be had to a justice and put to Bridewell to beat hemp. Poor Waitwell's gone to prison already.

MRS. FAINALL. Have a good heart, Foible; Mirabell's gone to give security for him. This is all Marwood's and my husband's doing.

FOIBLE. Yes, yes; I know it, madam. She was in my lady's closet, and overheard all that you said to me before dinner. She sent the letter to my lady, and that missing effect, Mr. Fainall laid this plot to arrest Waitwell when he pretended to go for the papers, and in the meantime Mrs. Marwood declared all to my lady.

MRS. FAINALL. Was there no mention made of me in the letter? My mother does not suspect my being in the confederacy? I fancy Marwood has not told her, though she has told my husband.

FOIBLE. Yes, madam, but my lady did not see that part; we stifled the letter before she read so far—Has that mischievous devil told Mr. Fainall of your ladyship, then?

MRS. FAINALL. Aye, all's out, my affair with Mirabell—everything discovered. This is the last day of our living together, that's my comfort.

FOIBLE. Indeed, madam; and so 'tis a comfort if you knew all—he has been even with your ladyship, which I could have told you long enough since, but I love to keep peace and quietness by my goodwill. I had rather bring friends together than set 'em at distance. But Mrs. Marwood and he are nearer related than ever their parents thought for.

MRS. FAINALL. Sayest thou so, Foible? Canst thou prove this?

FOIBLE. I can take my oath of it, madam; so can Mrs. Mincing. We have had many a fair word from Madam Marwood, to conceal something that passed in our chamber one evening when you were at Hyde Park, and we were thought to have gone a-walking, but we went up unawares—though we were sworn to secrecy, too; Madam Marwood took a book and swore us upon it, but it was but a book of poems. So long as it was not a Bible oath, we may break it with a safe conscience.

MRS. FAINALL. This discovery is the most opportune thing I could wish.—Now, Mincing!

Enter MINCING

MINCING. My lady would speak with Mrs. Foible, mem. Mr. Mirabell is with her; he has set your spouse at liberty, Mrs. Foible, and would have you hide yourself in my lady's closet till my old lady's anger is abated. Oh, my old lady is in a perilous passion at something Mr. Fainall has said; he swears, and my old lady cries. There's a fearful hurricane, I vow. He says, mem, how that he'll have my lady's fortune made over to him, or he'll be divorced.

MRS. FAINALL. Does your lady or Mirabell know that?

MINCING. Yes, mem; they have sent me to see if Sir Wilfull be sober, and to bring him to them. My lady is resolved to have him, I think, rather than lose such a vast sum as six thousand pounds.—Oh, come, Mrs. Foible, I hear my old lady.

MRS. FAINALL. Foible, you must tell Mincing that she must prepare to vouch when I call her.

FOIBLE. Yes, yes, madam.

MINCING. Oh, yes! mem, I'll vouch anything for your ladyship's service, be what it will. [*Exeunt* MINCING *and* FOIBLE]

Enter LADY WISHFORT *and* MRS. MARWOOD

LADY WISHFORT. Oh, my dear friend, how can I enumerate the benefits that I have received from your goodness! To you I owe the timely discovery of the false vows of Mirabell; to you I owe the detection of the imposter Sir Rowland.—And now you are become an intercessor with my son-in-law, to save the honor of my house and compound for the frailties of my daughter. Well, friend, you are enough to reconcile me to the bad world, or else I would retire to deserts and solitudes, and feed harmless sheep by groves and purling streams. Dear

---
[1] I.e., go to the house of correction.

Marwood, let us leave the world, and retire by ourselves and be shepherdesses.

MRS. MARWOOD. Let us first dispatch the affair in hand, madam. We shall have leisure to think of retirement afterwards. Here is one who is concerned in the treaty.

LADY WISHFORT. Oh, daughter, daughter! is it possible thou shouldst be my child, bone of my bone, and flesh of my flesh, and, as I may say, another me, and yet transgress the most minute particle of severe virtue? Is it possible you should lean aside to iniquity, who have been cast in the direct mould of virtue? I have not only been a mould but a pattern for you and a model for you, after you were brought into the world.

MRS. FAINALL. I don't understand your ladyship.

LADY WISHFORT. Not understand? Why, have you not been naught?[1] have you not been sophisticated?[2] Not understand! here I am ruined to compound for[3] your caprices and your cuckoldoms. I must pawn my plate and my jewels, and ruin my niece, and all little enough—

MRS. FAINALL. I am wronged and abused, and so are you. 'Tis a false accusation—as false as hell, as false as your friend there, aye, or your friend's friend, my false husband!

MRS. MARWOOD. My friend, Mrs. Fainall! Your husband my friend? What do you mean?

MRS. FAINALL. I know what I mean, madam, and so do you; and so shall the world at a time convenient.

MRS. MARWOOD. I am sorry to see you so passionate, madam. More temper would look more like innocence. But I have done. I am sorry my zeal to serve your ladyship and family should admit of misconstruction, or make me liable to affronts. You will pardon me, madam, if I meddle no more with an affair in which I am not personally concerned.

LADY WISHFORT. O dear friend, I am so ashamed that you should meet with such returns!—(*To* MRS. FAINALL) You ought to ask pardon on your knees, ungrateful creature; she deserves more from you than all your life can accomplish.—(*To* MRS. MARWOOD) Oh, don't leave me destitute in this perplexity! No, stick to me, my good genius.

MRS. FAINALL. I tell you, madam, you are abused.—Stick to you! aye, like a leech, to suck your best blood—she'll drop off when she's full. Madam, you shan't pawn a bodkin, nor part with a brass counter,[4] in composition for me. I defy 'em all. Let 'em prove their aspersions; I know my own innocence, and dare stand a trial.

[*Exit* MRS. FAINALL]

LADY WISHFORT. Why, if she should be innocent, if she should be wronged after all —ha! I don't know what to think—and I promise you her education has been unexceptionable—I may say it; for I chiefly made it my own care to initiate her very infancy in the rudiments of virtue, and to impress upon her tender years a young odium and aversion to the very sight of men. Aye, friend, she would ha' shrieked if she had but seen a man, till she was in her teens. As I am a person, 'tis true—she was never suffered to play with a male child, though but in coats; nay, her very babies[5] were of the feminine gender. Oh, she never looked a man in the face but her own father, or the chaplain, and him we made a shift to put upon her for a woman, by the help of his long garments and his sleek face,[6] till she was going in her fifteen.

MRS. MARWOOD. 'Twas much she should be deceived so long.

LADY WISHFORT. I warrant you, or she would never have borne to have been catechized by him; and have heard his long lectures against singing and dancing, and such debaucheries; and going to filthy plays, and profane music-meetings, where the lewd trebles squeak nothing but bawdy, and the basses roar blasphemy. Oh, she would have swooned at the sight or name of an obscene play-book!—and can I think, after all this, that my daughter can be naught? What, a whore? and thought it excommunication to set her foot within the door of a playhouse! O dear friend, I can't believe it. No, no! As she says, let him prove it—let him prove it.

MRS. MARWOOD. Prove it, madam? What, and have your name prostituted in a public court—yours and your daughter's reputation worried at the bar by a pack of bawling

---
[1] Naughty.
[2] "Adulterated."
[3] Make up for.
[4] A token in place of money.
[5] Dollbabies.
[6] Ministers of the Established Church wore long black gowns.

lawyers? To be ushered in with an "O yez"[1] of scandal, and have your case opened by an old fumbling lecher in a quoif[2] like a man-midwife; to bring your daughter's infamy to light; to be a theme for legal punsters and quibblers by the statute; and become a jest against a rule of court, where there is no precedent for a jest in any record—not even in Domesday Book; to discompose the gravity of the bench, and provoke naughty interrogatories in more naughty law Latin; while the good judge, tickled with the proceeding, simpers under a grey beard, and fidgets off and on his cushion as if he had swallowed cantharides,[3] or sat upon cow-itch.[4]—

LADY WISHFORT. Oh, 'tis very hard!

MRS. MARWOOD. And then to have my young revellers of the Temple take notes, like 'prentices at a conventicle,[5] and after, talk it all over again in commons, or before drawers[6] in an eating-house.

LADY WISHFORT. Worse and worse!

MRS. MARWOOD. Nay, this is nothing; if it would end here, 'twere well. But it must, after this, be consigned by the shorthand writers to the public press; and from thence be transferred to the hands, nay into the throats and lungs of hawkers, with voices more licentious than the loud flounder-man's,[7] or the woman that cries grey peas. And this you must hear till you are stunned—nay, you must hear nothing else for some days.

LADY WISHFORT. Oh, 'tis insupportable! No, no, dear friend, make it up, make it up; aye, aye, I'll compound. I'll give up all, myself and my all, my niece and her all—anything, everything for composition.

MRS. MARWOOD. Nay, madam, I advise nothing; I only lay before you, as a friend, the inconveniences which perhaps you have overseen. Here comes Mr. Fainall. If he will be satisfied to huddle up all in silence, I shall be glad. You must think I would rather congratulate than condole with you.

LADY WISHFORT. Aye, aye, I do not doubt it, dear Marwood; no, no, I do not doubt it.

[1] Law term; the call made by an officer to preserve silence at the opening of court.
[2] White lawyer's cap.
[3] An aphrodisiac.
[4] The hairy pods of the cowage plant cause intolerable itching.
[5] Apprentices were sometimes sent to church to make notes of the sermon for their masters.
[6] Servants in a tavern.
[7] Referring to the street cries of hucksters.

Enter FAINALL

FAINALL. Well, madam, I have suffered myself to be overcome by the importunity of this lady, your friend; and am content you shall enjoy your own proper estate during life, on condition you oblige yourself never to marry, under such penalty as I think convenient.

LADY WISHFORT. Never to marry!

FAINALL. No more Sir Rowlands; the next imposture may not be so timely detected.

MRS. MARWOOD. That condition, I dare answer, my lady will consent to without difficulty; she has already but too much experienced the perfidiousness of men.—Besides, madam, when we retire to our pastoral solitude we shall bid adieu to all other thoughts.

LADY WISHFORT. Aye, that's true; but in case of necessity, as of health, or some such emergency—

FAINALL. Oh, if you are prescribed marriage, you shall be considered; I only will reserve to myself the power to choose for you. If your physic be wholesome, it matters not who is your apothecary. Next, my wife shall settle on me the remainder of her fortune not made over already, and for her maintenance depend entirely on my discretion.

LADY WISHFORT. This is most inhumanly savage, exceeding the barbarity of a Muscovite husband.

FAINALL. I learned it from his Czarish majesty's[8] retinue, in a winter evening's conference over brandy and pepper, amongst other secrets of matrimony and policy as they are at present practised in the northern hemisphere. But this must be agreed unto, and that positively. Lastly, I will be endowed, in right of my wife, with that six thousand pounds which is the moiety of Mrs. Millamant's fortune in your possession, and which she has forfeited (as will appear by the last will and testament of your deceased husband, Sir Jonathan Wishfort) by her disobedience in contracting herself against your consent or knowledge and by refusing the offered match with Sir Wilfull Witwoud, which you, like a careful aunt, had provided for her.

LADY WISHFORT. My nephew was *non compos*,[9] and could not make his addresses.

[8] Peter the Great visited England in 1697.
[9] Not in his right mind.

FAINALL. I come to make demands—I'll hear no objections.

LADY WISHFORT. You will grant me time to consider?

FAINALL. Yes, while the instrument is drawing, to which you must set your hand till more sufficient deeds can be perfected—which I will take care shall be done with all possible speed. In the meanwhile I will go for the said instrument, and till my return you may balance this matter in your own discretion.

[*Exit* FAINALL]

LADY WISHFORT. This insolence is beyond all precedent, all parallel. Must I be subject to this merciless villain?

MRS. MARWOOD. 'Tis severe indeed, madam, that you should smart for your daughter's wantonness.

LADY WISHFORT. 'Twas against my consent that she married this barbarian, but she would have him, though her year was not out.—Ah! her first husband, my son Languish, would not have carried it thus! Well, that was my choice, this is hers: she is matched now with a witness.—I shall be mad!—Dear friend, is there no comfort for me? must I live to be confiscated at this rebel-rate?—Here come two more of my Egyptian plagues too.[1]

Enter MRS. MILLAMANT *and* SIR WILFULL WITWOUD

SIR WILFULL. Aunt, your servant.

LADY WISHFORT. Out, caterpillar! Call not me aunt! I know thee not!

SIR WILFULL. I confess I have been a little in disguise,[2] as they say.—'Sheart! and I'm sorry for't. What would you have? I hope I have committed no offence, aunt—and if I did I am willing to make satisfaction; and what can a man say fairer? If I have broke anything, I'll pay for't, and it cost a pound. And so let that content for what's past, and make no more words. For what's to come, to pleasure you I'm willing to marry my cousin; so pray let's all be friends. She and I are agreed upon the matter before a witness.[3]

[1] Cf. *Exodus*, chapters vii–x.
[2] Drunk.
[3] Here (as in Lady Wishfort's sudden desire to save Mrs. Fainall's good name), the motivation of Mrs. Millamant's sudden willingness to marry Sir Wilfull does not appear, the whole being part of Mirabell's scheme. It must be confessed that Congreve is far from clear.

LADY WISHFORT. How's this, dear niece! Have I any comfort? Can this be true?

MRS. MILLAMANT. I am content to be a sacrifice to your repose, madam, and to convince you that I had no hand in the plot, as you were misinformed. I have laid my commands on Mirabell to come in person and be a witness that I give my hand to this flower of knighthood; and for the contract that passed between Mirabell and me, I have obliged him to make a resignation of it in your ladyship's presence. He is without, and waits your leave for admittance.

LADY WISHFORT. Well, I'll swear I am something revived at this testimony of your obedience, but I cannot admit that traitor—I fear I cannot fortify myself to support his appearance. He is as terrible to me as a gorgon,[4] if I see him I fear I shall turn to stone, and petrify incessantly.

MRS. MILLAMANT. If you disoblige him, he may resent your refusal and insist upon the contract still. Then 'tis the last time he will be offensive to you.

LADY WISHFORT. Are you sure it will be the last time?—If I were sure of that—shall I never see him again?

MRS. MILLAMANT. Sir Wilfull, you and he are to travel together, are you not?

SIR WILFULL. 'Sheart, the gentleman's a civil gentleman, aunt; let him come in. Why, we are sworn brothers and fellow-travellers.—We are to be Pylades and Orestes,[5] he and I. He is to be my interpreter in foreign parts. He has been overseas once already, and with proviso that I marry my cousin, will cross 'em once again only to bear me company.—'Sheart, I'll call him in. An I set on't once, he shall come in; and see who'll hinder him.

[*Exit* SIR WILFULL]

MRS. MARWOOD. This is precious fooling, if it would pass; but I'll know the bottom of it.

LADY WISHFORT. O dear Marwood, you are not going?

MRS. MARWOOD. Not far, madam; I'll return immediately. [*Exit* MRS. MARWOOD]

[*Re-enter* SIR WILFULL *and*] MIRABELL

SIR WILFULL. Look up, man, I'll stand by you. 'Sbud an she do frown, she can't

[4] The Gorgon's head had power to turn the beholder to stone.
[5] Types of faithful friends from Greek legend. See *The Choephoræ* of Æschylus.

kill you; besides—harkee, she dare not frown desperately, because her face is none of her own. 'Sheart, an she should, her forehead would wrinkle like the coat of a cream-cheese; but mum for that, fellow-traveller.

MIRABELL. If a deep sense of the many injuries I have offered to so good a lady, with a sincere remorse and a hearty contrition, can but obtain the least glance of compassion, I am too happy. Ah, madam, there was a time!—but let it be forgotten—I confess I have deservedly forfeited the high place I once held, of sighing at your feet. Nay, kill me not, by turning from me in disdain. I come not to plead for favor—nay, not for pardon; I am a suppliant only for your pity. I am going where I never shall behold you more—

SIR WILFULL. How, fellow-traveller! you shall go by yourself then.

MIRABELL. Let me be pitied first, and afterwards forgotten.—I ask no more.

SIR WILFULL. By'r Lady, a very reasonable request, and will cost you nothing, aunt! Come, come, forgive and forget, aunt. Why, you must, an you are a Christian.

MIRABELL. Consider, madam, in reality you could not receive much prejudice. It was an innocent device; though I confess it had a face of guiltiness, it was at most an artifice which love contrived—and errors which love produces have ever been accounted venial. At least think it is punishment enough that I have lost what in my heart I hold most dear, that to your cruel indignation I have offered up this beauty, and with her my peace and quiet—nay, all my hopes of future comfort.

SIR WILFULL. An he does not move me, would I may never be o' the quorum! An it were not as good a deed as to drink, to give her to him again, I would I might never take shipping!—Aunt, if you don't forgive quickly, I shall melt, I can tell you that. My contract went no farther than a little mouth glue, and that's hardly dry—one doleful sigh more from my fellow-traveller, and 'tis dissolved.

LADY WISHFORT. Well, nephew, upon your account—Ah, he has a false insinuating tongue!—Well sir, I will stifle my just resentment at my nephew's request. I will endeavor what I can to forget, but on proviso that you resign the contract with my niece immediately.

MIRABELL. It is in writing, and with papers of concern; but I have sent my servant for it, and will deliver it to you with all acknowledgments for your transcendent goodness.

LADY WISHFORT. (*Aside*) Oh, he has witchcraft in his eyes and tongue!—When I did not see him, I could have bribed a villain to his assassination; but his appearance rakes the embers which have so long lain smothered in my breast.

Enter FAINALL *and* MRS. MARWOOD

FAINALL. Your date of deliberation, madam, is expired. Here is the instrument; are you prepared to sign?

LADY WISHFORT. If I were prepared, I am not impowered. My niece exerts a lawful claim, having matched herself by my direction to Sir Wilfull.

FAINALL. That sham is too gross to pass on me—though 'tis imposed on you, madam.

MRS. MILLAMANT. Sir, I have given my consent.

MIRABELL. And, sir, I have resigned my pretensions.

SIR WILFULL. And, sir, I assert my right and will maintain it in defiance of you, sir, and of your instrument. 'Sheart, an you talk of an instrument, sir, I have an old fox [1] by my thigh shall hack your instrument of ram vellum [2] to shreds, sir! It shall not be sufficient for a mittimus [3] or a tailor's measure.[4] Therefore withdraw your instrument, sir, or by'r Lady, I shall draw mine.

LADY WISHFORT. Hold, nephew, hold!

MRS. MILLAMANT. Good Sir Wilfull, respite your valor!

FAINALL. Indeed! Are you provided of a guard, with your single beef-eater [5] there? But I'm prepared for you, and insist upon my first proposal. You shall submit your own estate to my management, and absolutely make over my wife's to my sole use, as pursuant to the purport and tenor of this other covenant.—[*To* MRS. MILLAMANT] I suppose, madam, your consent is not requisite

[1] Sword.
[2] Legal instruments were written on sheepskin.
[3] Writ of commitment to prison.
[4] Sheet on which a tailor writes down his measurements.
[5] A warder of the Tower of London. The warders retained their mediæval uniform; and were not counted as active soldiers.

in this case; nor, Mr. Mirabell, your resignation; nor, Sir Wilfull, your right.—You may draw your fox if you please, sir, and make a bear-garden flourish somewhere else, for here it will not avail. This, my Lady Wishfort, must be subscribed, or your darling daughter's turned adrift, like a leaky hulk, to sink or swim, as she and the current of this lewd town can agree.

LADY WISHFORT. Is there no means, no remedy to stop my ruin? Ungrateful wretch! dost thou not owe thy being, thy subsistence, to my daughter's fortune?

FAINALL. I'll answer you when I have the rest of it in my possession.

MIRABELL. But that you would not accept of a remedy from my hands—I own I have not deserved you should owe any obligation to me; or else perhaps I could advise—

LADY WISHFORT. Oh, what?—what? To save me and my child from ruin, from want, I'll forgive all that's past; nay, I'll consent to anything to come, to be delivered from this tyranny.

MIRABELL. Aye, madam, but that is too late; my reward is intercepted. You have disposed of her who only could have made me a compensation for all my services. But be it as it may, I am resolved I'll serve you! You shall not be wronged in this savage manner.

LADY WISHFORT. How! Dear Mr. Mirabell, can you be so generous at last? But it is not possible. Harkee, I'll break my nephew's match; you shall have my niece yet, and all her fortune, if you can but save me from this imminent danger.

MIRABELL. Will you? I'll take you at your word. I ask no more. I must have leave for two criminals to appear.

LADY WISHFORT. Aye, aye;—anybody, anybody!

MIRABELL. Foible is one, and a penitent.

Enter MRS. FAINALL, FOIBLE, *and* MINCING

MRS. MARWOOD. These corrupt things are brought hither to expose me. [*Aside*] Oh, my shame!

(MIRABELL *and* LADY WISHFORT *go to* MRS. FAINALL *and* FOIBLE)

FAINALL. If it must all come out, why let 'em know it; 'tis but the way of the world. That shall not urge me to relinquish or abate one tittle of my terms; no, I will insist the more.

FOIBLE. Yes, indeed, madam, I'll take my Bible oath of it.

MINCING. And so will I, mem.

LADY WISHFORT. O Marwood, Marwood, art thou false? My friend deceive me? Hast thou been a wicked accomplice with that profligate man?

MRS. MARWOOD. Have you so much ingratitude and injustice to give credit against your friend to the aspersions of two such mercenary trulls?

MINCING. Mercenary, mem? I scorn your words. 'Tis true we found you and Mr. Fainall in the blue garret; by the same token, you swore us to secrecy upon Messalina's poems.[1] Mercenary? No, if we would have been mercenary, we should have held our tongues; you would have bribed us sufficiently.

FAINALL. Go, you are an insignificant thing!—Well, what are you the better for this? Is this Mr. Mirabell's expedient? I'll be put off no longer.—You, thing that was a wife, shall smart for this! I will not leave thee wherewithal to hide thy shame; your body shall be naked as your reputation.

MRS. FAINALL. I despise you and defy your malice!—You have aspersed me wrongfully—I have proved your falsehood! Go, you and your treacherous—I will not name it, but, starve together. Perish!

FAINALL. Not while you are worth a groat, indeed, my dear. Madam, I'll be fooled no longer.

LADY WISHFORT. Ah, Mr. Mirabell, this is small comfort, the detection of this affair.

MIRABELL. Oh, in good time. Your leave for the other offender and penitent to appear, madam.

Enter WAITWELL *with a box of writings*

LADY WISHFORT. O Sir Rowland!—Well, rascal!

WAITWELL. What your ladyship pleases. I have brought the black box at last, madam.

MIRABELL. Give it me. Madam, you remember your promise?

LADY WISHFORT. Aye, dear sir.

MIRABELL. Where are the gentlemen?

WAITWELL. At hand, sir, rubbing their eyes—just risen from sleep.

---

[1] Probably a humorous mispronunciation of *miscellany*, though there are a number of scandalous books with *Messalina* in the title.

FAINALL. 'Sdeath, what's this to me? I'll not wait your private concerns.

Enter PETULANT *and* WITWOUD

PETULANT. How now! What's the matter? Whose hand's out?

WITWOUD. Heyday! What, are you all got together like players at the end of the last act?

MIRABELL. You may remember, gentlemen, I once requested your hands as witnesses to a certain parchment.

WITWOUD. Aye, I do; my hand I remember—Petulant set his mark.

MIRABELL. You wrong him. His name is fairly written, as shall appear.—(*Undoing the box*) You do not remember, gentlemen, anything of what that parchment contained?

WITWOUD. No.

PETULANT. Not I; I writ, I read nothing.

MIRABELL. Very well, now you shall know.—Madam, your promise.

LADY WISHFORT. Aye, aye, sir, upon my honor.

MIRABELL. Mr. Fainall, it is now time that you should know that your lady, while she was at her own disposal, and before you had by your insinuations wheedled her out of a pretended settlement of the greatest part of her fortune—

FAINALL. Sir! pretended!

MIRABELL. Yes, sir. I say that this lady while a widow, having, it seems, received some cautions respecting your inconstancy and tyranny of temper, which from her own partial opinion and fondness of you she could never have suspected—she did, I say, by the wholesome advice of friends and of sages learned in the laws of this land, deliver this same as her act and deed to me in trust, and to the uses within mentioned. You may read if you please—(*Holding out the parchment*) though perhaps what is written on the back may serve your occasions.

FAINALL. Very likely, sir. What's here?—Damnation! (*Reads*) "A deed of conveyance of the whole estate real of Arabella Languish, widow, in trust to Edward Mirabell."—Confusion!

MIRABELL. Even so, sir; 'tis the way of the world, sir,—of the widows of the world. I suppose this deed may bear an elder date than what you have obtained from your lady.

FAINALL. Perfidious fiend! then thus I'll be revenged.

(*Offers to run at* MRS. FAINALL)

SIR WILFULL. Hold, sir! Now you may make your bear-garden flourish somewhere else, sir.

FAINALL. Mirabell, you shall hear of this, sir, be sure you shall.—Let me pass, oaf!

[*Exit* FAINALL]

MRS. FAINALL. Madam, you seem to stifle your resentment; you had better give it vent.

MRS. MARWOOD. Yes, it shall have vent—and to your confusion, or I'll perish in the attempt. [*Exit* MRS. MARWOOD]

LADY WISHFORT. O daughter, daughter! 'Tis plain thou hast inherited thy mother's prudence.

MRS. FAINALL. Thank Mr. Mirabell, a cautious friend, to whose advice all is owing.

LADY WISHFORT. Well, Mr. Mirabell, you have kept your promise—and I must perform mine.—First, I pardon, for your sake, Sir Rowland there, and Foible. The next thing is to break the matter to my nephew—and how to do that—

MIRABELL. For that, madam, give yourself no trouble; let me have your consent. Sir Wilfull is my friend. He has had compassion upon lovers, and generously engaged a volunteer in this action for our service, and now designs to prosecute his travels.

SIR WILFULL. 'Sheart, aunt, I have no mind to marry. My cousin's a fine lady, and the gentleman loves her, and she loves him, and they deserve one another. My resolution is to see foreign parts—I have set on't—and when I'm set on't I must do't. And if these two gentlemen would travel too, I think they may be spared.

PETULANT. For my part, I say little—I think things are best off or on.

WITWOUD. 'Ygad, I understand nothing of the matter; I'm in a maze yet, like a dog in a dancing-school.

LADY WISHFORT. Well, sir, take her, and with her all the joy I can give you.

MRS. MILLAMANT. Why does not the man take me? Would you have me give myself to you over again?

MIRABELL. Aye, and over and over again; (*Kisses her hand*) I would have you as often as possibly I can. Well, Heaven grant I love you not too well; that's all my fear.

SIR WILFULL. 'Sheart, you'll have time

enough to toy after you're married; or if you will toy now, let us have a dance in the meantime, that we who are not lovers may have some other employment besides looking on.

MIRABELL. With all my heart, dear Sir Wilfull. What shall we do for music?

FOIBLE. Oh, sir, some that were provided for Sir Rowland's entertainment are yet within call. (*A dance*) 10

LADY WISHFORT. As I am a person, I can hold out no longer. I have wasted my spirits so to-day already, that I am ready to sink under the fatigue, and I cannot but have some fears upon me yet, that my son Fainall will 15 pursue some desperate course.

MIRABELL. Madam, disquiet not yourself on that account; to my knowledge his circumstances are such he must of force comply. For my part, I will contribute all that in me 20 lies to a reunion; in the meantime, madam— (*To* MRS. FAINALL) let me before these witnesses restore to you this deed of trust. It may be a means, well-managed, to make you live easily together. 25

From hence let those be warned who mean
    to wed,
Lest mutual falsehood stain the bridal bed;
For each deceiver to his cost may find
That marriage-frauds too oft are paid in 30
    kind. *Exeunt omnes*

EPILOGUE

Spoken by MRS. BRACEGIRDLE

After our epilogue this crowd dismisses,
I'm thinking how this play'll be pulled to
    pieces.
But pray consider, ere you doom its fall,
How hard a thing 'twould be to please you all.
There are some critics so with spleen diseased,
They scarcely come inclining to be pleased: 6
And sure he must have more than mortal
    skill,
Who pleases anyone against his will.
Then, all bad poets we are sure are foes,
And how their number's swelled, the town
    well knows: 10
In shoals I've marked 'em judging in the
    pit;
Though they're on no pretense for judgment fit,
But that they have been damned for want
    of wit.
Since when, they by their own offences
    taught,
Set up for spies on plays and finding fault. 15
Others there are whose malice we'd prevent; 16
Such who watch plays with scurrilous
    intent
To mark out who by characters are meant.
And though no perfect likeness they can
    trace,
Yet each pretends to know the copied face. 20
These with false glosses feed their own ill
    nature,
And turn to libel what was meant a satire.
May such malicious fops this fortune find,
To think themselves alone the fools designed!
If any are so arrogantly vain, 25
To think they singly can support a scene,
And furnish fool enough to entertain.
For well the learn'd and the judicious know
That satire scorns to stoop so meanly low
As any one abstracted fop to show. 30
For, as when painters form a matchless face,
They from each fair one catch some different grace,
And shining features in one portrait blend,
To which no single beauty must pretend;
So poets oft do in one piece expose 35
Whole *belles-assemblées*[1] of coquettes and
    beaux.

[1] Polite gatherings.

THE FAIR PENITENT
A Tragedy by Nicholas Rowe

Quin morere, ut merita est, ferroque averte dolorem. Virg[il]. Æn. Lib. 4.[1]

Nicholas Rowe, best known to his own age as the translator of Lucan and to ours as the editor of Shakespeare, was born at Little Barford, Bedfordshire, June 20, 1674, his father being a lawyer of some prominence. The boy was educated at Highgate and at Westminster School under Dr. Busby, but he was shortly withdrawn to study law in the Middle Temple, being admitted to the bar in 1696. But "the *Muses* had stol'n away his Heart from his Infancy"; the death of his father had left him relatively independent; and young Rowe turned to verse-making and to drama, his first play, *The Ambitious Stepmother*, being produced at Lincoln's Inn Fields in 1700. The young dramatist—he was only twenty-six—was handsome, pleasant, and companionable, and presently moved in terms of intimacy with Congreve, Lady Winchelsea, and others. Meantime (1698) he had married Antonia Parsons. A second play, *Tamerlane* (1702), in which William III figures as the conqueror and Louis XIV as Bajazet, was long produced on the fifth of November, the custom not dying out until 1815. Save for one comedy, *The Biter* (1704), Rowe's subsequent dramas were tragic; he began with *The Fair Penitent* (1703) a series of "she-tragedies" with which his name is associated. An ardent Whig, he was rewarded with various government posts; and in 1715 was made Poet Laureate in succession to Nahum Tate. Pleasant tales are told of poetical friends helping him out with the canonical odes which the poet laureate was supposed to present on state occasions. His translation of Lucan was not published until 1719, but his edition of Shakespeare (1709) appeared in his own lifetime. Everybody liked Rowe, whose career is singularly free from the wounds of party strife; and when he died in 1718, it was thought fitting to bury him in Westminster Abbey "over-against Chaucer."

The fullest account of Rowe's life is found in the introduction to *Three Plays . . . by Nicholas Rowe*, edited by J. R. Sutherland (1929). The bibliography appended to the Belles Lettres edition of "The Fair Penitent" and "Jane Shore" (1907) by Sophie C. Hart should also be consulted.

ROWE'S DRAMATIC WORKS

The Ambitious Stepmother (tragedy) (L.I.F., 1700), 1701.
Tamerlane (tragedy) (L.I.F., 1701/2), 1702.
The Fair Penitent (tragedy) (L.I.F., Mar., 1703), 1703.
The Biter (comedy) (L.I.F., Dec., 1704), 1705.
Ulysses (tragedy) (Haymarket, Nov. 22, 1705), 1706.
The Royal Convert (tragedy) (Haymarket, Nov. 27, 1707), 1708.
Jane Shore (tragedy) (D.L., Feb. 2, 1714), 1714.
Lady Jane Gray (tragedy) (D.L., Apr., 1715), 1715.

By the year 1703 the social revolution which had accompanied the coming of good King William to the throne had so far progressed as to involve the theaters. Thither the merchant and his wife cautiously ventured; and 'twas a question with dramatists whether to cling to the heroic conventions and the cynical humors which had vastly delighted the wits and rakes of the preceding age, or to write for the pleasure of the rising citizen class. Dryden, Lee, and Otway had passed away; the line of Restoration comic writers was dying out; and, in this time of confusion, Mr. Rowe stepped forward to soothe the moralist and please the virtuoso.

Mr. Rowe had read *The Fatal Dowry* by Massinger and Field, an old and barbarous play, he thought, in which, however, the virtuous heart was touched by the sufferings of its fair heroine. Casting away so much of the original as could not, without difficulty,

---

[1] Why not die as you deserve, and end the anguish with a sword?—*Æneid*, IV: 547.

be fitted into a tragedy at once moral in its lesson and regular in its construction, he simplified the fable, and translated the language into that soft and flowing declamation which, with his auditors, passed for elegance of diction and chasteness of sentiment. In so doing, in truth, he did not better his original; and was in the first act compelled to make Horatio discourse to Altamont of much that Altamont already knows, purely for the enlightenment of the audience. Nor is the device of the letter in the same act a mechanism of which a nice critic can approve.

Nevertheless *The Fair Penitent* is an important addition to our stage. Mr. Rowe has written "a melancholy tale of private woes" which set a fashion he himself followed in later dramas, and which succeeding dramatists have adopted. As a "she-tragedy" the eighteenth century thought highly of it; man's inhumanity to woman was made the theme of a muse not merely correct but as well pathetic. The moral sentiment is, moreover, properly directed, and the chief culprits, if they involve others in universal ruin, are themselves examples of repentance and punishment. Here was no casuistry (save perhaps in the person of Lothario) to delude the heart.

In the persons of the play, or at least in some of the principal characters, Mr. Rowe undoubtedly achieved theatrical success. The mournful Calista was to be remembered by Mr. Richardson when writing *Clarissa Harlowe* no less than the gay Lothario who, though he no longer treads the boards, has furnished a phrase to the language. In Altamont neither Mr. Rowe's age nor our own has taken much interest, but his faithful friend, Horatio, and Sciolto, the Roman father, are patterns of exemplary virtue, and in Lavinia's fondness for her injured husband the audience beheld a noble lesson of domestic virtue. Mr. Rowe, in short, was writing domestic tragedy for an era which was shortly to patronize *The Tatler* and *The Spectator*, agents of moral reform.

But in traversing new ground, 'tis well to walk softly; and though *The Fair Penitent* is in truth a domestic tragedy, 'tis to be remarked that the characters are well born, their diction elegant, and their deportment lofty. A low and vulgar realism is no part of the play. In view of the taste for spectacle, Mr. Rowe thought it well to supply, in the last act, an appalling picture of melancholy, and to insert at the opening of the scene a song which might strengthen, even at the cost of dramatic truth, the impression of horror. The ensuing debate of Sciolto and Calista over an action already determined is reminiscent of the arguments of the heroic play, as is the multiplicity of deaths with which the play, despite the fewness of its characters, is studded. If the dramatist ventures to imitate the blank verse of a former age, it is but timidly, and the declamation, though soft and swelling, is not remote from the manner of seventeenth-century tragedy.

Saving that he leaned more heavily upon Shakespeare's style, which, however, he greatly watered, Mr. Rowe's subsequent tragedies do not differ greatly from the pattern of *The Fair Penitent*. Of these *Jane Shore* (1714) is by the consent of critics the best known, although *Lady Jane Gray* (1715) has merit. Both are "she-tragedies." *The Royal Convert* (1707), however, is a return to the heroic, and *Ulysses* (1705) is an attempt to combine classical tragedy and Elizabethan.

The Fair Penitent was first produced at Lincoln's Inn Fields, 1703.

For discussions of Rowe see the editions by Sutherland and Hart already cited; A. W. Ward, *A History of English Dramatic Literature;* and the various histories of the drama.

THE FAIR PENITENT

DRAMATIS PERSONÆ

MEN

Sciolto, *a Nobleman of Genoa, Father to Calista.*	Mr. Bowman
Altamont, *a young Lord in love with Calista, and designed her husband by Sciolto.*	Mr. Verbruggen
Horatio, *his friend.*	Mr. Betterton
Lothario, *a young Lord, enemy to Altamont.*	Mr. Powell
Rossano, *his friend.*	Mr. Bail[e]y

WOMEN

Calista, *Daughter to Sciolto.*	Mrs. Barry
Lavinia, *Sister to Altamont, and wife to Horatio.*	Mrs. Bracegirdle
Lucilla, *Confidant[e] to Calista.*	Mrs. Prince

Servants to Sciolto.

SCENE: *Sciolto's Palace and Garden, with some part of the street near it, in Genoa.*

PROLOGUE [1]

Spoken by Mr. Betterton

Long has the fate of kings and empires been [2]
The common bus'ness of the tragic scene,
As if misfortune made the throne her seat,
And none could be unhappy but the great.
Dearly, 'tis true, each buys the crown he wears, 5
And many are the mighty monarch's cares:
By foreign foes and home-bred factions pressed,
Few are the joys he knows, and short his hours of rest.
Stories like these with wonder we may hear,
But far remote, and in a higher sphere, 10
We ne'er can pity what we ne'er can share:
Like distant battles of the Pole and Swede, [3]
Which frugal citizens o'er coffee [4] read,
Careless for who shall fail or who succeed;
Therefore an humbler theme our author chose
A melancholy tale of private woes: 16
No princes here lost royalty bemoan,
But you shall meet with sorrows like your own;
Here see imperious love his vassals treat
As hardly as ambition does the great; 20
See how succeeding passions rage by turns,
How fierce the youth with joy and rapture burns,
And how to death, for beauty lost, he mourns.
Let no nice taste the poet's art arraign [5]
If some frail, vicious characters he feign: 25
Who writes should still let nature be his care,
Mix shades with lights, and not paint all things fair,
But show you men and women as they are.
With deference to the fair he bade me say,
Few to perfection ever found the way; 30
Many in many parts are known t'excel,
But 'twere too hard for one to act all well;
Whom justly life should through each scene commend,
The maid, the wife, the mistress, and the friend: 34
This age, 'tis true, has one great instance seen,
And heaven in justice made that one a Queen.[6]

---

[1] The play was originally dedicated to the Duchess of Ormond, but the dedication is omitted here. In it Rowe comments on the fact that "misfortunes and distress" are "one of the main designs of tragedy," and that "to excite this generous pity" is a sign of success in the dramatist.

[2] Rowe's conscious purpose in writing "a melancholy tale of private woes" apparently called for an explicit statement in the Prologue.

[3] The news of the day concerned the capture of Warsaw by Charles XII in May, 1702, and his subsequent campaigns in North Germany and Poland, resulting in his deposing one King of Poland and his setting up another.

[4] The allusion to the coffee houses should not escape notice.

[5] Those who did not like Rowe's conception of tragedy accused him of picking his heroines out of the gutter. See the extracts of current comment in Sutherland's *Three Plays by Nicholas Rowe*, p. 344.

[6] I.e., Queen Anne.

447

ACT I

SCENE I

SCENE: *A Garden belonging to* SCIOLTO's *Palace*

Enter ALTAMONT *and* HORATIO

ALTAMONT. Let this auspicious day be ever sacred,
No mourning, no misfortunes happen on it;
Let it be marked for triumphs and rejoicings;
Let happy lovers ever make it holy,
Choose it to bless their hopes, and crown their wishes, 5
This happy day that gives me my Calista.
    HORATIO. Yes, Altamont; today thy better stars
Are joined to shed their kindest influence on thee: 8
Sciolto's noble hand, that raised thee first,
Half dead and drooping o'er thy father's grave,
Completes its bounty, and restores thy name
To that high rank and lustre which it boasted
Before ungrateful Genoa had forgot
The merit of thy godlike father's arms;
Before that country which he long had served
In watchful councils, and in winter camps, 16
Had cast off his white age to want and wretchedness,
And made their court to faction [1] by his ruin.
    ALTAMONT. O great Sciolto! O my more than father!
Let me not live but at thy very name 20
My eager heart springs up and leaps with joy!
When I forget the vast, vast debt I owe thee,
Forget (but 'tis impossible!) then let me
Forget the use and privilege of reason,
Be driven from the commerce of mankind 25
To wander in the desert among brutes,
To bear the various fury of the seasons,
The night's unwholesome dew, and noon-day's heat,
To be the scorn of earth and curse of heaven.
    HORATIO. So open, so unbounded was his goodness, 30
It reached ev'n me because I was thy friend.
When that great man I loved, thy noble father,
Bequeathed thy gentle sister to my arms,
His last dear pledge and legacy of friendship,
That happy tie made me Sciolto's son. 35

[1] Flattered a faction in the court by ruining Altamont's father.

He called us his, and with a parent's fondness
Indulged us in his wealth, blessed us with plenty,
Healed all our cares, and sweetened love itself.
    ALTAMONT. By heaven, he found my fortunes so abandoned
That nothing but a miracle could raise 'em. 40
My father's bounty, and the state's ingratitude
Had stripped him bare, nor left him ev'n a grave.
Undone myself, and sinking with his ruin,
I had no wealth to bring, nothing to succor him
But fruitless tears.
    HORATIO.   Yet what thou could'st, thou didst, 45
And didst it like a son; when his hard creditors,
Urged and assisted by Lothario's father
(Foe to thy house, and rival of their greatness),
By sentence of the cruel law, forbid
His venerable corpse to rest in earth, 50
Thou gav'st thyself a ransom for his bones;
With piety uncommon didst give up
Thy hopeful youth to slaves who ne'er knew mercy,
Sour, unrelenting, money-loving villains 54
Who laugh at human nature and forgiveness,
And are like fiends, the factors for destruction.
Heav'n, who beheld the pious act, approved it,
And bade Sciolto's bounty be its proxy
To bless thy filial virtue with abundance.
    ALTAMONT. But see, he comes, the author of my happiness, 60
The man who saved my life from deadly sorrow,
Who bids my days be blessed with peace and plenty,
And satisfies my soul with love and beauty.

Enter SCIOLTO. *He runs to* ALTAMONT *and embraces him*

    SCIOLTO. Joy to thee, Altamont! Joy to myself!
Joy to this happy morn that makes thee mine,
That kindly grants what nature had denied me, 66
And makes me father of a son like thee.
    ALTAMONT. My father! Oh, let me unlade my breast,
Pour out the fullness of my soul before you,
Show ev'ry tender, ev'ry grateful thought 70

This wond'rous goodness stirs. But 'tis impossible,
And utterance all is vile, since I can only
Swear you reign here, but never tell how much.
  SCIOLTO. It is enough; I know thee—thou art honest;
Goodness innate, and worth hereditary 75
Are in thy mind; thy noble father's virtues
Spring freshly forth, and blossom in thy youth.
  ALTAMONT. Thus heaven from nothing raised his fair creation,
And then with wond'rous joy beheld its beauty,
Well pleased to see the excellence he gave. 80
  SCIOLTO. O noble youth! I swear since first I knew thee,
Ev'n from that day of sorrows when I saw thee,
Adorned and lovely in thy filial tears,
The mourner and redeemer of thy father,
I set thee down and sealed thee for my own:
Thou art my son, ev'n near me as Calista. 86
Horatio and Lavinia, too, are mine;
            (*Embraces* HORATIO)
All are my children, and shall share my heart.
But wherefore waste we thus this happy day?
The laughing minutes summon thee to joy,
And with new pleasures court thee as they pass; 91
Thy waiting bride ev'n chides thee for delaying,
And swears thou com'st not with a bridegroom's haste.
  ALTAMONT. Oh! could I hope there was one thought of Altamont,
One kind remembrance in Calista's breast, 95
The winds with all their wings would be too slow
To bear me to her feet. For oh! my father,
Amidst this stream of joy that bears me on,
Blest as I am, and honored in your friendship,
There is one pain that hangs upon my heart.
  SCIOLTO. What means my son?
  ALTAMONT.   When, at your intercession,
Last night Calista yielded to my happiness,
Just e'er we parted, as I sealed my vows
With rapture on her lips, I found her cold
As a dead lover's statue on his tomb; 105
A rising storm of passion shook her breast,
Her eyes a piteous show'r of tears let fall,
And then she sighed as if her heart were breaking.
With all the tend'rest eloquence of love
I begged to be a sharer in her grief; 110
But she, with looks averse and eyes that froze me,
Sadly replied, her sorrows were her own,
Nor in a father's power to dispose of.
  SCIOLTO. Away! it is the cozenage of their sex,
One of the common arts they practise on us,
To sigh and weep then when their hearts beat high 116
With expectation of the coming joy:
Thou hast in camps and fighting fields been bred,
Unknowing in the subtleties of women:
The virgin bride who swoons with deadly fear
To see the end of all her wishes near, 121
When, blushing, from the light and public eyes
To the kind covert of the night she flies,
With equal fires to meet the bridegroom moves, 124
Melts in his arms, and with a loose she loves.
            Exeunt

  Enter LOTHARIO *and* ROSSANO

  LOTHARIO. The father and the husband!
  ROSSANO.   Let them pass,
They saw us not.
  LOTHARIO.   I care not if they did.
Ere long I mean to meet 'em face to face,
And gall 'em with my triumph o'er Calista.
  ROSSANO. You loved her once.
  LOTHARIO.   I liked her, would have married her, 130
But that it pleased her father to refuse me,
To make this honorable fool her husband.
For which, if I forget him, may the shame
I mean to brand his name with, stick on mine.
  ROSSANO. She, gentle soul, was kinder than her father. 135
  LOTHARIO. She was, and oft in private gave me hearing
Till, by long list'ning to the soothing tale,
At length her easy heart was wholly mine.
  ROSSANO. I have heard you oft describe her, haughty, insolent,
And fierce with high disdain; it moves my wonder 140
That virtue thus defended should be yielded
A prey to loose desires.
  LOTHARIO.   Hear, then, I'll tell thee.
Once in a lone and secret hour of night
When ev'ry eye was closed, and the pale moon
And stars alone shone conscious of the theft,
Hot with the Tuscan grape, and high in blood. 146

Hap'ly I stole unheeded to her chamber.
  ROSSANO. That minute sure was lucky.
  LOTHARIO.   Oh, 'twas great.
I found the fond, believing, love-sick maid
Loose, unattired, warm, tender, full of wishes;
Fierceness and pride, the guardians of her
    honor,   151
Were charmed to rest, and love alone was
    waking.
Within her rising bosom all was calm
As peaceful seas that know no storms, and
    only
Are gently lifted up and down by tides. 155
I snatched the glorious, golden opportunity,
And with prevailing, youthful ardor pressed
    her
Till, with short sighs and murmuring reluctance,
The yielding fair one gave me perfect happiness.
Ev'n all the live-long night we passed in bliss,
In ecstasies too fierce to last forever;   161
At length the morn, and cold indifference
    came;
When fully sated with the luscious banquet,
I hastily took leave, and left the nymph
To think on what was past, and sigh alone. 165
  ROSSANO. You saw her soon again?
  LOTHARIO.   Too soon I saw her;
For oh! that meeting was not like the former;
I found my heart no more beat high with
    transport,
No more I sighed and languished for enjoyment;   169
'Twas past, and reason took her turn to reign
While ev'ry weakness fell before her throne.
  ROSSANO. What of the lady?
  LOTHARIO.   With uneasy fondness
She hung upon me, wept, and sighed, and
    swore
She was undone; talked of a priest and marriage,
Of flying with me from her father's power; 175
Called ev'ry saint and blessèd angel down
To witness for her that she was my wife.
I started at that name.
  ROSSANO.   What answer made you?
  LOTHARIO. None; but pretending sudden
    pain and illness,
Escaped the persecution; two nights since, 180
By message urged, and frequent importunity,
Again I saw her. Straight with tears and sighs,
With swelling breasts, with swooning, with
    distraction,
With all the subtleties and pow'rful arts
Of wilful woman lab'ring for her purpose, 185
Again she told the same dull, nauseous tale.
Unmoved, I begged her spare th' ungrateful
    subject,
Since I resolved, that love and peace of mind
Might flourish long inviolate betwixt us,
Never to load it with the marriage chain; 190
That I would still retain her in my heart,
My ever gentle mistress and my friend;
But for those other names of wife and husband,
They only meant ill-nature, cares, and
    quarrels.   194
  ROSSANO. How bore she this reply?
  LOTHARIO.   Ev'n as the earth
When (winds pent up or eating fires beneath,
Shaking the mass) she labors with destruction.
At first her rage was dumb, and wanted words,
But when the storm found way, 'twas wild
    and loud.
Mad [1] as the priestess of the Delphic god, 200
Enthusiastic [2] passion swelled her breast,
Enlarged her voice, and ruffled all her form;
Proud and disdainful of the love I proffered,
She called me "Villain! Monster! Base
    betrayer!"
At last, in very bitterness of soul   205
With deadly imprecations on herself,
She vowed severely ne'er to see me more;
Then bid me fly that minute; I obeyed,
And, bowing, left her to grow cool at leisure.
  ROSSANO. She has relented since, else why
    this message   210
To meet the keeper of her secrets here
This morning?
  LOTHARIO.   See the person whom you
    named.

Enter LUCILLA

Well, my ambassadress, what must we treat
    of?   213
Come you to menace war and proud defiance,
Or does the peaceful olive grace your message?
Is your fair mistress calmer? does she soften?
And must we love again? Perhaps she means
To treat in juncture with her new ally,
And make her husband party to th' agreement.

---

[1] The priestess of the temple to Apollo at Delphi inhaled certain fumes emanating from a crevice in the ground, the gases of which made her "mad" and prophetical.

[2] In the literal sense of god-filled.

LUCILLA. Is this well done, my lord? Have
    you put off 220
All sense of human nature? Keep a little,
A little pity to distinguish manhood,[1]
Lest other men, though cruel, should disclaim you,
And judge you to be numbered with the brutes. 224
    LOTHARIO. I see thou'st learned to rail.
    LUCILLA.   I've learned to weep;
That lesson my sad mistress often gives me;
By day she seeks some melancholy shade
To hide her sorrows from the prying world;
At night she watches all the long, long hours,
And listens to the winds and beating rain, 230
With sighs as loud, and tears that fall as fast.
Then ever and anon she wrings her hands,
And cries, "False, false Lothario!"
    LOTHARIO.   Oh, no more!
I swear thou'lt spoil that pretty face with crying,
And thou hast beauty that may make thy fortune; 235
Some keeping cardinal shall dote upon thee,
And barter his church treasure for thy freshness.
    LUCILLA. What! shall I sell my innocence and youth
For wealth or titles, to perfidious man?
To man, who makes his mirth of our undoing!
The base professed betrayer of our sex! 241
Let me grow old in all misfortunes else
Rather than know the sorrows of Calista.
    LOTHARIO. Does she send thee to chide in her behalf?
I swear thou dost it with so good a grace 245
That I could almost love thee for thy frowning.
    LUCILLA. (*Giving a letter*) Read there, my lord, there, in her own sad lines,
Which best can tell the story of her woes,
That grief of heart which your unkindness gives her.
    LOTHARIO. (*Reads*) "Your cruelty—obedience to my father—give my hand to Altamont." 250
(*Aside*) By heaven! 'tis well; such ever be the gifts
With which I greet the man whom my soul hates.
But to go on!
"—Wish—heart—honor—too faithless—

[1] Show pity that you may be distinguished from the brutes.

weakness—tomorrow—last trouble—lost Calista."—
Women, I see, can change as well as men; 255
She writes me here, forsaken as I am,
That I should bind my brows with mournful willow,
For she has given her hand to Altamont.
Yet tell the fair inconstant—
    LUCILLA.   How, my lord?
    LOTHARIO. Nay, no more angry words; say to Calista, 260
The humblest of her slaves shall wait her pleasure,
If she can leave her happy husband's arms
To think upon so lost a thing as I am.
    LUCILLA. Alas! for pity, come with gentler looks;
Wound not her heart with this unmanly triumph; 265
And though you love her not, yet swear you do,
So shall dissembling once be virtuous in you.
    LOTHARIO. Ha! who comes here?
    LUCILLA.   The bridegroom's friend, Horatio.
He must not see us here. Tomorrow, early,
Be at the garden gate.
    LOTHARIO.   Bear to my love 270
My kindest thoughts, and swear I will not fail her.
    (LOTHARIO *putting up the letter hastily, drops it as he goes out.* Exeunt LOTHARIO *and* ROSSANO *one way, and* LUCILLA *another*)

Enter HORATIO

HORATIO. Sure, 'tis the very error of my eyes:
Walking, I dream, or I behold Lothario;
He seemed conferring with Calista's woman;
At my approach they started, and retired. 275
What business could he have here, and with her?
I know he bears the noble Altamont
Professed and deadly hate—What paper's this?
(*Taking up the letter*) Ha! to Lothario.—
    'Sdeath! Calista's name! (*Opening it.*)
Confusion and misfortune! (*Reads*) 280
"Your cruelty has at length determined me, and I have resolved this morning to yield a perfect obedience to my father, and to give my hand to Altamont, in spite of my weakness for the false

Lothario. I could almost wish I had that heart and that honor to bestow with it which you have robbed me of—"

Damnation!—to the rest— (*Reads again*)
"But oh! I fear, could I retrieve 'em, I should again be undone by the too faithless, yet too lovely Lothario; this is the last weakness of my pen, and tomorrow shall be the last in which I will indulge my eyes. Lucilla shall conduct you, if you are kind enough to let me see you; it shall be the last trouble you shall meet with from
                The lost Calista."

The lost, indeed! for thou art gone as far
As there can be perdition. Fire and sulphur,
Hell is the sole avenger of such crimes.
O that the ruin were but all thy own!   284
Thou wilt ev'n make thy father curse his age;
At sight of this black scroll the gentle Altamont
(For oh! I know his heart is set upon thee)
Shall droop and hang his discontented head
Like merit scorned by insolent authority,
And never grace the public with his virtues.—
Perhaps ev'n now he gazes fondly on her,   291
And thinking soul and body both alike,
Blesses the perfect workmanship of heaven;
Then sighing, to his ev'ry care speaks peace,
And bids his heart be satisfied with happiness.
O wretched husband! while she hangs about thee   296
With idle blandishments, and plays the fond one,
Ev'n then her hot imagination wanders,
Contriving riots and loose shapes of love;
And while she clasps thee close, makes thee a monster.   300
What if I give this paper to her father?
It follows that his justice dooms her dead,
And breaks his heart with sorrow; hard return
For all the good his hand has heaped on us.
Hold, let me take a moment's thought.

              Enter LAVINIA
  LAVINIA.   My lord!
Trust me, it joys my heart that I have found you.   306
Enquiring wherefore you had left the company
Before my brother's nuptial rites were ended,
They told me you had felt some sudden illness.
Where are you sick? Is it your head? your heart?   310
Tell me, my love, and ease my anxious thoughts
That I may tame you gently in my arms,
Soothe you to rest, and soften all your pains.
  HORATIO. It were unjust. No, let me spare my friend,
Lock up the fatal secret in my breast,   315
Nor tell him that which will undo his quiet.
  LAVINIA. What means my lord?
  HORATIO.   Ha! saidst thou, my Lavinia?
  LAVINIA. Alas! you know not what you make me suffer.
Why are you pale? Why did you start and tremble?
Whence is that sigh? And wherefore are your eyes   320
Severely raised to heaven? The sick man thus,
Acknowledging the summons of his fate,
Lifts up his feeble hands and eyes for mercy,
And with confusion thinks upon his audit.
  HORATIO. O no! thou hast mistook my sickness quite,   325
These pangs are of the soul. Would I had met
Sharpest convulsions, spotted pestilences,
Or any other deadly foe to life
Rather than heave beneath this load of thought.
  LAVINIA. Alas, what is it? Wherefore turn you from me?   330
Why did you falsely call me your Lavinia
And swear I was Horatio's better half,
Since now you mourn unkindly by yourself,
And rob me of my partnership of sadness?
Witness, you holy powers, who know my truth,   335
There can not be a chance in life so miserable,
Nothing so very hard but I could bear it
Much rather than my love should treat me coldly,
And use me like a stranger to his heart.
  HORATIO. Seek not to know what I would hide from all,   340
But most from thee. I never knew a pleasure,
Aught that was joyful, fortunate, or good
But straight I ran to bless thee with the tidings,
And laid up all my happiness with thee;
But wherefore, wherefore should I give thee pain?   345
Then spare me, I conjure thee, ask no further;
Allow my melancholy thoughts this privilege,
And let 'em brood in secret o'er their sorrows.
  LAVINIA. It is enough: chide not, and all is well;
Forgive me, if I saw you sad, Horatio,   350

And asked to weep out part of your misfortunes;
I wo' not press to know what you forbid me.
Yet, my loved lord, yet you must grant me this:
Forget your cares for this one happy day,
Devote this day to mirth, and to your Altamont; 355
For his dear sake let peace be in your looks.
Ev'n now the jocund bridegroom wants your wishes,
He thinks the priest has but half blessed his marriage,
Till his friend hails him with the sound of joy.
　HORATIO. O never! never! never! Thou art innocent; 360
Simplicity from ill, pure native truth,
And candor of the mind adorn thee ever;
But there are such, such false ones in the world,
'Twould fill thy gentle soul with wild amazement
To hear their story told.
　LAVINIA.　　　　　False ones, my lord!
　HORATIO. Fatally fair they are, and in their smiles, 366
The graces, little loves, and young desires inhabit;
But all that gaze upon 'em are undone,
For they are false, luxurious in their appetites,
And all the heav'n they hope for is variety:
One lover to another still succeeds, 371
Another and another after that,
And the last fool is welcome as the former,
Till, having loved his hour out, he gives place,
And mingles with the herd that went before him. 375
　LAVINIA. Can there be such? And have they peace of mind?
Have they in all the series of their changing
One happy hour? If women are such things,
How was I formed so different from my sex?
My little heart is satisfied with you, 380
You take up all her room, as in a cottage
Which harbors some benighted princely stranger,
Where the good man, proud of his hospitality,
Yields all his homely dwelling to his guest,
And hardly keeps a corner for himself. 385
　HORATIO. Oh, were they all like thee, men would adore 'em,
And all the bus'ness of their lives be loving;
The nuptial band should be the pledge of peace,
And all domestic cares and quarrels cease;
The world should learn to love by virtuous rules, 390
And marriage be no more the jest of fools.
　　　　　　　　　　　　　　　Exeunt

ACT II

SCENE I

SCENE: *a Hall*

Enter CALISTA *and* LUCILLA

　CALISTA. Be dumb forever, silent as the grave,
Nor let thy fond officious love disturb
My solemn sadness with the sound of joy.
If thou wilt soothe me, tell some dismal tale
Of pining discontent and black despair; 5
For oh! I've gone around through all my thoughts,
But all are indignation, love, or shame,
And my dear peace of mind is lost forever.
　LUCILLA. Why do you follow still that wand'ring fire
That has misled your weary steps and leaves you 10
Benighted in a wilderness of woe?
That false Lothario! Turn from the deceiver.
Turn, and behold where gentle Altamont,
Kind as the softest virgin of our sex,
And faithful as the simple village swain 15
That never knew the courtly vice of changing,
Sighs at your feet, and woos you to be happy.
　CALISTA. Away—I think not of him. My sad soul
Has formed a dismal, melancholy scene,
Such a retreat as I would wish to find; 20
An unfrequented vale, o'ergrown with trees
Mossy and old, within whose lonesome shade
Ravens and birds ill-omened, only dwell;
No sound to break the silence but a brook
That, bubbling, winds among the weeds; no mark 25
Of any human shape that had been there,
Unless the skeleton of some poor wretch
Who had long since, like me by love undone,
Sought that sad place out to despair and die in.
　LUCILLA. Alas, for pity!
　CALISTA.　　　　There I fain would hide me
From the base world, from malice, and from shame; 31
For 'tis the solemn counsel of my soul

Never to live with public loss of honor;
'Tis fixed to die rather than bear the insolence
Of each affected she that tells my story, 35
And blesses her good stars that she is virtuous.
To be a tale for fools! Scorned by the women,
And pitied by the men! Oh, insupportable!
    LUCILLA. Can you perceive the manifest destruction,
The gaping gulf that opens just before you,
And yet rush on, though conscious of the danger? 41
O hear me, hear your ever faithful creature!
By all the good I wish, by all the ill
My trembling heart forebodes, let me entreat you
Never to see this faithless man again: 45
Let me forbid his coming.
    CALISTA.   On thy life
I charge thee, no; my genius drives me on;
I must, I will behold him once again:
Perhaps it is the crisis of my fate,
And this one interview shall end my cares. 50
My lab'ring heart, that swells with indignation,
Heaves to discharge the burden; that once done,
The busy thing shall rest within its cell,
And never beat again.
    LUCILLA.   Trust not to that.
Rage is the shortest passion of our souls: 55
Like narrow brooks that rise with sudden showers,
It swells in haste, and falls again as soon;
Still as it ebbs, the softer thoughts flow in,
And the deceiver, Love, supplies its place.
    CALISTA. I have been wronged enough to arm my temper 60
Against the smooth delusion, but, alas!
(Chide not my weakness, gentle maid, but pity me)
A woman's softness hangs about me still.
Then let me blush, and tell thee all my folly.
I swear I could not see the dear betrayer 65
Kneel at my feet and sigh to be forgiven,
But my relenting heart would pardon all,
And quite forget 'twas he that had undone me.
    LUCILLA. Ye sacred powers whose gracious providence
Is watchful for our good, guard me from men,
From their deceitful tongues, their vows and flatteries; 71
Still let me pass neglected by their eyes,
Let my bloom wither and my form decay,
That none may think it worth his while to ruin me,
And fatal love may never be my bane. 75
    CALISTA. Ha! Altamont? Calista, now be wary,
And guard thy soul's accesses with dissembling,
Nor let this hostile husband's eyes explore
The warring passions and tumultuous thoughts 79
That rage within thee and deform thy reason.

Enter ALTAMONT

    ALTAMONT. Be gone, my cares, I give you to the winds
Far to be borne, far from the happy Altamont;
For from this sacred era of my love
A better order of succeeding days
Come smiling forward, white and lucky all.[1]
Calista is the mistress of the year, 86
She crowns the seasons with auspicious beauty,
And bids ev'n all my hours be good and joyful.
    CALISTA. If I was ever mistress of such happiness,
Oh! wherefore did I play th'unthrifty fool 90
And, wasting all on others, leave myself
Without one thought of joy to give me comfort?
    ALTAMONT. O mighty Love! Shall that fair face profane
This thy great festival with frowns and sadness?
I swear it sha' not be, for I will woo thee 95
With sighs so moving, with so warm a transport,
That thou shalt catch the gentle flame from me,
And kindle into joy.
    CALISTA.   I tell thee, Altamont,
Such hearts as ours were never paired above,
Ill suited to each other; joined, not matched;
Some sullen influ[e]nce, a foe to both, 101
Has wrought this fatal marriage to undo us.
Mark but the frame and temper of our minds,
How very much we differ. Ev'n this day
That fills thee with such ecstasy and transport, 105
To me brings nothing that should make me bless it,
Or think it better than the day before,

[1] By the Romans a fortunate day was supposed to be marked by a white stone. The equivalent of our "red-letter day."

Or any other in the course of time
That dully took its turn, and was forgotten.
 ALTAMONT. If to behold thee as my pledge of happiness, 110
To know none fair, none excellent beside thee;
If still to love thee with unwearied constancy
Through ev'ry season, ev'ry change of life,
Through wrinkled age, through sickness and misfortune,
Be worth the least return of grateful love, 115
Oh, then let my Calista bless this day,
And set it down for happy.
 CALISTA.   'Tis the day
In which my father gave my hand to Altamont;
As such I will remember it forever.

Enter SCIOLTO, HORATIO, *and* LAVINIA, *and Attendants*

 SCIOLTO. Let mirth go on, let pleasure know no pause, 120
But fill up ev'ry minute of this day.
'Tis yours, my children, sacred to your loves;
The glorious sun himself for you looks gay,
He shines for Altamont and for Calista.
Let there be music, let the master touch 125
The sprightly string and softly-breathing flute
Till harmony rouse ev'ry gentle passion,
Teach the cold maid to lose her fears in love,
And the fierce youth to languish at her feet.
Begin. Ev'n age itself is cheered with music,—
It wakes a glad remembrance of our youth, 131
Calls back past joys, and warms us into transport.
 (*Here an entertainment of music and dancing*)

SONG

BY MR. CONGREVE

I

Ah stay! ah turn! ah whither would you fly,
 Too charming, too relentless maid?
I follow not to conquer but to die, 135
 You of the fearful are afraid.

II

In vain I call; for she, like fleeting air
 When pressed by some tempestuous wind,
Flies swifter from the voice of my despair,
 Nor casts one pitying look behind. 140

 SCIOLTO. Take care my gates be open, bid all welcome;
All who rejoice with me today are friends.
Let each indulge his genius, each be glad,
Jocund and free, and swell the feast with mirth.
The spritely bowl shall cheerfully go round,
None shall be grave, nor too severely wise; 146
Losses and disappointments, cares and poverty,
The rich man's insolence, and great man's scorn,
In wine shall be forgotten all. Tomorrow
Will be too soon to think, and to be wretched.
Oh! grant, ye powers, that I may see these happy, 151
 (*Pointing to* ALTAMONT *and* CALISTA)
Completely blest, and I have life enough;
And leave the rest indifferent to fate.
         Exeunt

Manet HORATIO

 HORATIO. What if, while all are here intent on reveling,
I privately went forth and sought Lothario?
This letter may be forged; perhaps the wantonness 156
Of his vain youth, to stain a lady's fame;
Perhaps his malice, to disturb my friend.
Oh, no! my heart forebodes it must be true.
Methought ev'n now I marked the starts of guilt 160
That shook her soul; though damned dissimulation
Screened her dark thoughts, and set to public view
A specious face of innocence and beauty.
Oh, false appearance! What is all our sovereignty,
Our boasted power? When they oppose their arts, 165
Still they prevail, and we are found their fools.
With such smooth looks and many a gentle word
The first fair she beguiled her easy lord;
Too blind with love and beauty to beware,
He fell unthinking in the fatal snare; 170
Nor could believe that such a heav'nly face
Had bargained with the devil to damn her wretched race.
         Exit

SCENE II

SCENE: *the Street near* SCIOLTO'S *Palace*

Enter LOTHARIO *and* ROSSANO

 LOTHARIO. To tell thee, then, the purport of my thoughts:
The loss of this fond paper would not give me

A moment of disquiet, were it not
My instrument of vengeance on this Altamont:
Therefore I mean to wait some opportunity 5
Of speaking with the maid we saw this morning.
   Rossano. I wish you, sir, to think upon the danger
Of being seen; today their friends are round 'em,
And any eye that lights by chance on you 9
Shall put your life and safety to the hazard.
          (*They confer aside*)

       Enter Horatio

   Horatio. Still I must doubt some mystery of mischief,
Some artifice beneath; Lothario's father—
I knew him well; he was sagacious, cunning,
Fluent in words, and bold in peaceful councils,
But of a cold, unactive hand in war. 15
Yet with these coward's virtues he undid
My unsuspecting, valiant, honest friend.
This son, if fame mistakes not, is more hot,
More open and unartful. (*Seeing him*) Ha! he's here!
   Lothario. Damnation! He again!—This second time 20
Today he has crossed me like my evil genius.
   Horatio. I sought you, sir.
   Lothario.   'Tis well then I am found.
   Horatio. 'Tis well you are. The man who wrongs my friend,
To the earth's utmost verge I would pursue;
No place, though e'er so holy, should protect him; 25
No shape that artful fear e'er formed should hide him
Till he fair answer made, and did me justice.
   Lothario. Ha! dost thou know me? that I am Lothario?
As great a name as this proud city boasts of.
Who is this mighty man, then, this Horatio,
That I should basely hide me from his anger,
Lest he should chide me for his friend's displeasure? 32
   Horatio. The brave, 'tis true, do never shun the light;
Just are their thoughts, and open are their tempers,
Freely without disguise they love and hate, 35
Still are they found in the fair face of day,
And heaven and men are judges of their actions.
   Lothario. Such let 'em be of mine; there's not a purpose
Which my soul ever framed or my hand acted,
But I could well have bid the world look on,
And what I once durst do, have dared to justify. 41
   Horatio. Where was this open boldness, this free spirit?
When but this very morning I surprised thee
In base, dishonest privacy, consulting
And bribing a poor, mercenary wretch 45
To sell her lady's secrets, stain her honor,
And with a forged contrivance blast her virtue?
At sight of me thou fled'st.
   Lothario.   Ha! fled from thee?
   Horatio. Thou fled'st, and guilt was on thee; like a thief,
A pilferer descried in some dark corner,
Who there had lodged with mischievous intent 50
To rob and ravage at the hour of rest
And do a midnight murder on the sleepers.
   Lothario. Slave! Villain!
        (*Offers to draw*; Rossano *holds him*)
   Rossano.   Hold, my lord! think where you are,
Think how unsafe and hurtful to your honor
It were to urge a quarrel in this place
And shock the peaceful city with a broil. 55
   Lothario. Then, since thou dost provoke my vengeance, know
I would not for this city's wealth, for all
Which the sea wafts to our Ligurian shore,
But that the joys I reaped with that fond wanton,
The wife of Altamont, should be as public 60
As is the noon-day sun, air, earth, or water,
Or any common benefit of nature.
Think'st thou I meant the shame should be concealed?
Oh, no! by hell and vengeance, all I wanted
Was some fit messenger to bear the news 65
To the dull, doting husband; now I have found him,
And thou art he.
   Horatio.   I hold thee base enough
To break through law, and spurn at sacred order,
And do a brutal injury like this;
Yet mark me well, young lord, I think Calista
Too nice, too noble, and too great of soul 71
To be the prey of such a thing as thou art.
'Twas base and poor, unworthy of a man,

To forge a scroll so villainous and loose 75
And mark it with a noble lady's name.
These are the mean, dishonest arts of cowards,
Strangers to manhood and to glorious dangers,
Who, bred at home in idleness and riot, 79
Ransack for mistresses th' unwholesome stews,
And never know the worth of virtuous love.
    LOTHARIO. Think'st thou I forged the letter?
        Think so still
Till the broad shame comes staring in thy face,
And boys shall hoot the cuckold as he passes.
    HORATIO. Away—no woman could descend
        so low: 85
A skipping, dancing, worthless tribe you are;
Fit only for yourselves, you herd together;
And when the circling glass warms your vain hearts,
You talk of beauties that you never saw,
And fancy raptures that you never knew. 90
Legends of saints who never yet had being,
Or being, ne'er were saints, are not so false
As the fond tales which you recount of love.
    LOTHARIO. But that I do not hold it worth
        my leisure, 94
I could produce such damning proof—
    HORATIO.   'Tis false!
You blast the fair with lies because they scorn you,
Hate you like age, like ugliness and impotence:
Rather than make you blest, they would die virgins,
And stop the propagation of mankind.
    LOTHARIO. It is the curse of fools to be
        secure, 100
And that be thine and Altamont's. Dream on,
Nor think upon my vengeance till thou feel'st it.
    HORATIO. Hold, sir, another word, and
        then—farewell.
Though I think greatly of Calista's virtue, 104
And hold it far beyond thy power to hurt,
Yet, as she shares the honor of my Altamont,
That treasure of a soldier bought with blood
And kept at life's expense, I must not have
(Mark me, young sir) her very name profaned.
Learn to restrain the license of your speech;
'Tis held you are too lavish. When you are met 111
Among your set of fools, talk of your dress,
Of dice, of whores, of horses, and yourselves;
'Tis safer, and becomes your understandings.
    LOTHARIO. What if we pass beyond this
        solemn order? 115
And, in defiance of the stern Horatio,
Indulge our gayer thoughts, let laughter loose,
And use his sacred friendship for our mirth?
    HORATIO. 'Tis well! Sir, you are pleasant—
    LOTHARIO.   By the joys
Which yet my soul has, uncontrolled, pursued,
I would not turn aside from my least pleasure
Though all thy force were armed to bar my way; 122
But like the birds, great Nature's happy commoners,
That haunt in woods, in meads, and flow'ry gardens,
Rifle the sweets, and taste the choicest fruits,
Yet scorn to ask the lordly owners leave. 126
    HORATIO. What liberty has vain, presumptuous youth
That thou should'st dare provoke me unchastised?
But henceforth, boy, I warn thee, shun my walks;
If in the bounds of yon forbidden place 130
Again thou'rt found, expect a punishment
Such as great souls, impatient of an injury,
Exact from those who wrong 'em much, ev'n death,
Or something worse; an injured husband's vengeance
Shall print a thousand wounds, tear thy fine form, 135
And scatter thee to all the winds of heaven.
    LOTHARIO. Is then my way in Genoa prescribed
By a dependent on the wretched Altamont,
A talking sir that brawls for him in taverns,
And vouches for his valor's reputation?—
    HORATIO. Away, thy speech is fouler than
        thy manners! 141
    LOTHARIO. Or if there be a name more vile, his parasite,
A beggar's parasite!—
    HORATIO.   Now learn humanity,
        (*Offers to strike him*; ROSSANO *interposes*)
Since brutes and boys are only taught with blows.
    LOTHARIO. Damnation!   (*They draw*)
    ROSSANO.   Hold, this goes no
        further here, 145
Horatio, 'tis too much; already see
The crowd are gath'ring to us.
    LOTHARIO.   O Rossano!
Or give me way, or thou'rt no more my friend.

ROSSANO. Sciolto's servants, too, have
   ta'en the alarm;   149
You'll be oppressed by numbers. Be advised,
Or I must force you hence; take't on my word,
You shall have justice done you on Horatio.
Put up, my lord.
   LOTHARIO.   This wo' not brook delay; 152
West of the town a mile, among the rocks,
Two hours e'er noon tomorrow I expect thee,
Thy single hand to mine.
   HORATIO.   I'll meet thee there.
   LOTHARIO. Tomorrow, O my better stars!
     tomorrow   155
Exert your influence, shine strongly for me;
'Tis not a common conquest I would gain,
Since love, as well as arms, must grace my
    triumph.
               Exeunt LOTHARIO *and* ROSSANO
   HORATIO. Two hours e'er noon tomorrow!
    Ha, e'er that
He sees Calista! O unthinking fool—
What if I urged her with the crime and danger?
If any spark from heaven remained un-
    quenched   160
Within her breast, my breath perhaps may
    wake it.
Could I but prosper there, I would not doubt
My combat with that loud, vainglorious
    boaster.
Were you, ye fair, but cautious whom ye
    trust,
Did you but think how seldom fools are just,
So many of your sex would not in vain 166
Of broken vows and faithless men complain.
Of all the various wretches love has made,
How few have been by men of sense betrayed!
Convinced by reason, they your power confess,
Pleased to be happy, as you're pleased to
    bless,   171
And conscious of your worth, can never love
    you less.   *Exit*

ACT III

SCENE I

SCENE: *an Apartment in* SCIOLTO'S *Palace*

Enter SCIOLTO *and* CALISTA

   SCIOLTO. Now by my life, my honor, 'tis too
    much!
Have I not marked thee, wayward as thou art,
Perverse and sullen all this day of joy?
When ev'ry heart was cheered, and mirth
    went round,

Sorrow, displeasure, and repining anguish   5
Sat on thy brow like some malignant planet,
Foe to the harvest and the healthy year,
Who scowls adverse, and lowers upon the
    world
When all the other stars, with gentle aspect,
Propitious shine, and meaning good to man.
   CALISTA. Is then the task of duty half per-
    formed?   11
Has not your daughter giv'n herself to Alta-
    mont,
Yielded the native freedom of her will
To an imperious husband's lordly rule
To gratify a father's stern command?   15
   SCIOLTO. Dost thou complain?
   CALISTA.   For pity, do not frown then,
If in despite of all my vowed obedience,
A sigh breaks out, or a tear falls by chance;
For oh! that sorrow which has drawn your
    anger
Is a sad native to Calista's breast,   20
And, once possessed, will never quit its dwell-
    ing
Till life, the prop [of] all, shall leave the build-
    ing
To tumble down and molder into ruin.
   SCIOLTO. Now by the sacred dust of that
    dear saint
That was thy mother, by her wondrous good-
    ness,   25
Her soft, her tender, most complying sweet-
    ness,
I swear some sullen thought that shuns the
    light
Lurks underneath that sadness in thy visage.
But mark me well, though by yon heav'n I
    love thee
As much, I think, as a fond parent can,   30
Yet should'st thou (which the pow'rs above
    forbid)
E'er stain the honor of thy name with infamy,
I cast thee off as one whose impious hands
Had rent asunder nature's nearest ties,
Which, once divided, never join again.   35
Today I have made a noble youth thy hus-
    band;
Consider well his worth, reward his love,
Be willing to be happy, and thou art so.
                                             Exit SCIOLTO
   CALISTA. How hard is the condition of our
    sex,
Through ev'ry state of life the slaves of man!
In all the dear, delightful days of youth   41
A rigid father dictates to our wills,

And deals out pleasure with a scanty hand;
To his, the tyrant husband's reign succeeds;
Proud with opinion of superior reason,   45
He holds domestic bus'ness and devotion
All we are capable to know, and shuts us
Like cloistered idiots from the world's acquaintance,
And all the joys of freedom; wherefore are we
Born with high souls but to assert ourselves,
Shake off this vile obedience they exact,   51
And claim an equal empire o'er the world?

Enter HORATIO

HORATIO. She's here! Yet oh! my tongue is at a loss.
Teach me, some power, that happy art of speech
To dress my purpose up in gracious words   55
Such as may softly steal upon her soul
And never waken the tempestuous passions.
By heaven, she weeps!—Forgive me, fair Calista,
If I presume, on privilege of friendship,
To join my grief to yours, and mourn the evils
That hurt your peace and quench those eyes in tears.   61
  CALISTA. To steal unlooked for on my private sorrow
Speaks not the man of honor nor the friend,
But rather means the spy.
  HORATIO.   Unkindly said!
For oh! as sure as you accuse me falsely,   65
I come to prove myself Calista's friend.
  CALISTA. You are my husband's friend, the friend of Altamont.
  HORATIO. Are you not one? Are you not joined by heaven,
Each interwoven with the other's fate?
Are you not mixed like streams of meeting rivers   70
Whose blended waters are not more distinguished
But roll into the sea, one common flood?
Then who can give his friendship but to one?
Who can be Altamont's, and not Calista's?
  CALISTA. Force, and the wills of our imperious rulers,   75
May bind two bodies in one wretched chain;
But minds will still look back to their own choice.
So the poor captive in a foreign realm
Stands on the shore, and sends his wishes back
To the dear native land from whence he came.
  HORATIO. When souls that should agree to will the same,   81
To have one common object for their wishes,
Look different ways, regardless of each other,
Think what a train of wretchedness ensues:
Love shall be banished from the genial bed,
The nights shall all be lonely and unquiet,
And ev'ry day shall be a day of cares.   87
  CALISTA. Then all the boasted office of thy friendship
Was but to tell Calista what a wretch she is.
Alas! what needed that?
  HORATIO.   Oh! rather say   90
I came to tell her how she might be happy;
To soothe the secret anguish of her soul,
To comfort that fair mourner, that forlorn one,
And teach her steps to know the paths of peace.
  CALISTA. Say thou to whom this paradise is known?   95
Where lies the blissful region? Mark my way to it,
For oh! 'tis sure I long to be at rest.
  HORATIO. Then—to be good is to be happy. —Angels
Are happier than mankind because they are better.   99
Guilt is the source of sorrow; 'tis the fiend,
The avenging fiend, that follows us behind
With whips and stings; the blest know none of this,
But rest in everlasting peace of mind,
And find the height of all their heaven is goodness.
  CALISTA. And what bold parasite's officious tongue   105
Shall dare to tax Calista's name with guilt?
  HORATIO. None should; but 'tis a busy, talking world,
That with licentious breath blows like the wind,
As freely at the palace as the cottage.
  CALISTA. What mystic riddle lurks beneath thy words,   110
Which thou would'st seem unwilling to express,
As if it meant dishonor to my virtue?
Away with this ambiguous, shuffling phrase,
And let thy oracle be understood.
  HORATIO.   Lothario!
  CALISTA. Ha! What would'st thou mean by him?   115
  HORATIO. Lothario and Calista!—Thus they join

Two names which heaven decreed should never
    meet;
Hence have the talkers of this populous city
A shameful tale to tell for public sport,
Of an unhappy beauty, a false fair one, 120
Who plighted to a noble youth her faith
When she had giv'n her honor to a wretch.
  CALISTA. Death! and confusion! Have I
    lived to this?
Thus to be treated with unmanly insolence!
To be a sport of a loose ruffian's tongue! 125
Thus to be used! thus! like the vilest creature
That ever was a slave to vice and infamy.
  HORATIO. By honor and fair truth, you
    wrong me much,
For on my soul, nothing but strong necessity
Could urge my tongue to this ungrateful office:
I came with strong reluctance, as if death 131
Had stood across my way, to save your honor,
Yours and Sciolto's, yours and Altamont's;
Like one who ventures through a burning pile
To save his tender wife with all her brood 135
Of little fondlings from the dreadful ruin.
  CALISTA. Is this, is this the famous friend
    of Altamont,
For noble worth and deeds of arms renowned?
Is this, this tale-bearing, officious fellow
That watches for intelligence from eyes; 140
This wretched Argus of a jealous husband,
That fills his easy ears with monstrous tales,
And makes him toss, and rave, and wreak at
    length
Bloody revenge on his defenseless wife,
Who guiltless dies because her fool ran mad!
  HORATIO. Alas! this rage is vain, for if your
    fame   146
Or peace be worth your care, you must be
    calm,
And listen to the means are left to save 'em.
'Tis now the lucky minute of your fate:
By me [y]our genius speaks, by me it warns
    you   150
Never to see the cursed Lothario more,
Unless you mean to be despised, be shunned
By all our virtuous maids and noble matrons;
Unless you have devoted this rare beauty
To infamy, diseases, prostitution—   155
  CALISTA. Dishonor blast thee, base un-
    mannered slave!
That dar'st forget my birth and sacred sex,
And shock me with the rude, unhallowed
    sound!
  HORATIO. Here kneel, and in the awful
    face of heaven

Breathe out a solemn vow never to see, 160
Nor think, if possible, on him that ruined thee;
Or by my Altamont's dear life, I swear,
This paper!—(*holding her*) nay, you must not
    fly!—This paper,
This guilty paper shall divulge your shame.
  CALISTA. What mean'st thou by that paper?
    What contrivance   165
Hast thou been forging to deceive my father,
To turn his heart against his wretched daugh-
    ter,
That Altamont and thou may share his
    wealth?
A wrong like this will make me ev'n forget
The weakness of my sex.—O for a sword 170
To urge my vengeance on the villainous hand
That forged the scroll!
  HORATIO. (*Showing the letter near*) Behold,
    can this be forged?
See where Calista's name—
  CALISTA. (*Tearing it*)   To atoms thus,
Thus let me tear the vile, detested falsehood,
The wicked, lying evidence of shame.
  HORATIO.   Confusion! 175
  CALISTA. Henceforth, thou officious fool,
Meddle no more, nor dare, ev'n on thy life,
To breathe an accent that may touch my
    virtue:
I am myself the guardian of my honor,
And wo' not bear so insolent a monitor. 180

       Enter ALTAMONT

  ALTAMONT. Where is my life, my love, my
    charming bride,
Joy of my heart, and pleasure of my eyes,
The wish, the care, and bus'ness of my youth?
Oh! let me find her, snatch her to my breast,
And tell her she delays my bliss too long, 185
Till my soft soul ev'n sickens with desire.
Disordered!—and in tears! Horatio, too!
My friend is in amaze!—What can it mean?
Tell me, Calista, who has done thee wrong
That my swift sword may find out the of-
    fender,   190
And do thee ample justice.
  CALISTA.   Turn to him.
  ALTAMONT. Horatio!
  CALISTA.   To that insolent.
  ALTAMONT.   My friend!
Could he do this? He, who was half myself!
One faith has ever bound us, and one reason
Guided our wills: Have I not found him just,
Honest as truth itself? And could he break
The sanctity of friendship? Could he wound

The heart of Altamont in his Calista? 198
  CALISTA. I thought what justice I should
    find from thee!
Go fawn upon him, listen to his tale, 200
Applaud his malice, that would blast my fame,
And treat me like a common prostitute.
Thou art perhaps confederate in his mischief,
And wilt believe the legend, if he tells it.
  ALTAMONT. O impious! What presumptuous
    wretch shall dare 205
To offer at an injury like that?
Priesthood, nor age, nor cowardice itself
Shall save him from the fury of my vengeance.
  CALISTA. The man who dared to do it was
    Horatio!
Thy darling friend! 'Twas Altamont's
    Horatio! 210
But mark me well! While thy divided heart
Dotes on a villain that has wronged me thus,
No force shall drag me to thy hated bed;
Nor can my cruel father's power do more
Than shut me in a cloister; there, well pleased,
Religious hardships will I learn to bear, 216
To fast, and freeze at midnight hours of
    prayer;
Nor think it hard within a lonely cell
With melancholy, speechless saints to dwell;
But bless the day I to that refuge ran 220
Free from the marriage chain, and from that
    tyrant, man. *Exit* CALISTA
  ALTAMONT. She's gone; and as she went,
    ten thousand fires
Shot from her angry eyes, as if she meant
Too well to keep the cruel vow she made.
Now as thou art a man, Horatio, tell me 225
What means this wild confusion in thy looks,
As if thou wert at variance with thyself,
Madness and reason combating within thee,
And thou wert doubtful which should get the
    better?
  HORATIO. I would be dumb forever, but
    thy fate 230
Has otherwise decreed it; thou hast seen
That idol of thy soul, that fair Calista,
Thou hast beheld her tears.
  ALTAMONT. I have seen her weep,
I have seen that lovely one, that dear Calista,
Complaining in the bitterness of sorrow 235
That thou! my friend! Horatio, thou hadst
    wronged her!
  HORATIO. That I have wronged her! Had
    her eyes been fed
From that rich stream which warms her heart,
    and numbered

For ev'ry falling tear a drop of blood,
It had not been too much; for she has ruined
    thee, 240
Ev'n thee, my Altamont! she has undone thee.
  ALTAMONT. Dost thou join ruin with
    Calista's name?
What is so fair, so exquisitely good?
Is she not more than painting can express,
Or youthful poets fancy, when they love? 245
Does she not come, like wisdom or good for-
    tune,
Replete with blessings, giving wealth and
    honor?
The dowry which she brings is peace and
    pleasure,
And everlasting joys are in her arms.
  HORATIO. It had been better thou hadst
    lived a beggar, 250
And fed on scraps at great men's surly doors
Than to have matched with one so false, so
    fatal—
  ALTAMONT. It is too much for friendship
    to allow thee;
Because I tamely bore the wrong thou didst
    her,
Thou dost avow the barb'rous brutal part,
And urge the injury ev'n to my face. 256
  HORATIO. I see she has got possession of
    thy heart,
She has charmed thee, like a siren, to her bed,
With looks of love and with enchanting
    sounds:
Too late the rocks and quicksands will appear.
When thou art wrecked upon the faithless
    shore, 261
Then vainly wish thou hadst not left thy
    friend
To follow her delusion.
  ALTAMONT. If thy friendship
Do churlishly deny my love a room,
It is not worth my keeping, I disclaim it. 265
  HORATIO. Canst thou so soon forget what
    I've been to thee?
I shared the task of nature with thy father,
And formed with care thy unexperienced
    youth
To virtue and to arms.
Thy noble father, O thou light young man!
Would he have used me thus? One fortune
    fed us, 271
For his was ever mine, mine his, and both
Together flourished and together fell.
He called me friend, like thee: would he have
    left me

Thus, for a woman? nay, a vile one too? 275
  ALTAMONT. Thou canst not, dar'st not mean it; speak again,
Say, who is vile? but dare not name Calista.
  HORATIO. I had not spoke at first unless compelled,
And forced to clear myself; but since thus urged,
I must avow I do not know a viler. 280
  ALTAMONT. Thou wert my father's friend, he loved thee well;
A kind of venerable mark of him
Hangs round thee and protects thee from my vengeance:
I can not, dare not lift my sword against thee,
But henceforth never let me see thee more.
                          (*Going out*) 285
  HORATIO. I love thee still, ungrateful as thou art,
And must, and will preserve thee from dishonor,
Ev'n in despite of thee. (*Holds him*)
  ALTAMONT.   Let go my arm.
  HORATIO. If honor be thy care, if thou wouldst live
Without the name of credulous, wittol husband, 290
Avoid thy bride, shun her detested bed,
The joys it yields are dashed with poison.—
  ALTAMONT.   Off!
To urge thee but a minute more is fatal.
  HORATIO. She is polluted! stained!
  ALTAMONT.   Madness and raving!
But hence!
  HORATIO. Dishonored by the man you hate,— 295
  ALTAMONT. I prithee loose me yet, for thy own sake,
If life be worth the keeping,—
  HORATIO.   By Lothario.
  ALTAMONT. Perdition take thee, villain, for the falsehood!
                            (*Strikes him*)
Now nothing but thy life can make atonement.
  HORATIO. (*Draws*) A blow! thou hast used well—
  ALTAMONT   This to my heart— 300
  HORATIO. Yet hold!—By heaven, his father's in his face!
Spite of my wrongs, my heart runs o'er with tenderness,
And I could rather die myself than hurt him.
  ALTAMONT. Defend thyself, for by my much wronged love, 304
I swear the poor evasion shall not save thee
  HORATIO. Yet hold! thou know'st I dare!—
Think how we've lived—
    (*They fight*. ALTAMONT *presses on* HORATIO, *who retires*)
Nay! then 'tis brutal violence! And thus,
Thus nature bids me guard the life she gave.
                               (*They fight*)
LAVINIA *enters and runs between their swords*
  LAVINIA. My brother! my Horatio! Is it possible?
Oh! turn your cruel swords upon Lavinia. 310
If you must quench your impious rage in blood,
Behold, my heart shall give you all her store
To save those dearer streams that flow from yours.
  ALTAMONT. 'Tis well thou hast found a safeguard; none but this,
No power on earth could save thee from my fury. 315
  LAVINIA. O fatal, deadly sound!
  HORATIO.   Safety from thee!
Away, vain boy! Hast thou forgot the reverence
Due to my arm, thy first, thy great example,
Which pointed out thy way to noble daring,
And showed thee what it was to be a man? 320
  LAVINIA. What busy, meddling fiend, what foe to goodness
Could kindle such a discord? Oh! lay by
Those most ungentle looks, and angry weapons,
Unless you mean my griefs and killing fears
Should stretch me out at your relentless feet,
A wretched corse, the victim of your fury. 326
  HORATIO. Ask'st thou what made us foes? 'twas base ingratitude;
'Twas such a sin to friendship as heaven's mercy
That strives with man's untoward, monstrous wickedness,
Unwearied with forgiving, scarce could pardon. 330
He who was all to me, child! brother! friend!
With barb'rous, bloody malice sought my life.
  ALTAMONT. Thou art my sister, and I would not make thee
The lonely mourner of a widowed bed;
Therefore thy husband's life is safe; but warn him 335
No more to know this hospitable roof.
He has but ill repaid Sciolto's bounty:

We must not meet; 'tis dangerous. Farewell.
    (*He is going;* LAVINIA *holds him*)
  LAVINIA. Stay, Altamont, my brother,
    stay, if ever
Nature or what is nearer much than nature,
The kind consent of our agreeing minds, 341
Have made us dear to one another, stay
And speak one gentle word to your Horatio.
Behold, his anger melts, he longs to love you,
To call you friend, then press you hard with
    all   345
The tender, speechless joy of reconcilement.
  ALTAMONT. It can not, sha' not be!—you
    must not hold me.
  LAVINIA. Look kindly then!
  ALTAMONT.   Each minute that I stay
Is a new injury to fair Calista.
From thy false friendship, to her arms I'll
    fly;   350
There if in any pause of love I rest,
Breathless with bliss upon her panting breast,
In broken, melting accents I will swear
Henceforth to trust my heart with none but
    her;
Then own the joys which on her charms at-
    tend,   355
Have more than paid me for my faithless
    friend.
    (ALTAMONT *breaks from* LAVINIA, *and exit*)
  HORATIO. Oh, raise thee, my Lavinia, from
    the earth;
It is too much, this tide of flowing grief,
This wond'rous waste of tears, too much to
    give   359
To an ungrateful friend and cruel brother.
  LAVINIA. Is there not cause for weeping?
    Oh, Horatio!
A brother and a husband were my treasure,
'Twas all the little wealth that poor Lavinia
Saved from the shipwreck of her father's
    fortunes.
One half is lost already; if thou leav'st me,
If thou should'st prove unkind to me as
    Altamont,   366
Whom shall I find to pity my distress,
To have compassion on a helpless wanderer,
And give her where to lay her wretched head?
  HORATIO. Why dost thou wound me with
    thy soft complainings?   370
Though Altamont be false, and use me hardly,
Yet think not I impute his crimes to thee.
Talk not of being forsaken, for I'll keep thee
Next to my heart, my certain pledge of hap-
    piness.

Heaven formed thee gentle, fair, and full of
    goodness,   375
And made thee all my portion here on earth;
It gave thee to me as a large amends
For fortune, friends, and all the world beside.
  LAVINIA. Then you will love me still,
    cherish me ever,
And hide me from misfortune in your bosom?
Here end my cares, nor will I lose one thought
How we shall live, or purchase food and rai-
    ment.   382
The holy Pow'r who clothes the senseless earth
With woods, with fruits, with flow'rs and
    verdant grass,
Whose bounteous hand feeds the whole brute
    creation,   385
Knows all our wants, and has enough to give
    us.
  HORATIO. From Genoa, from falsehood and
    inconstancy,
To some more honest, distant clime we'll go,
Nor will I be beholding to my country
For aught but thee, the partner of my flight.
  LAVINIA. Yes, I will follow thee; forsake
    for thee   391
My country, brother, friends, ev'n all I have;
Though mine's a little all, yet were it more,
And better far, it should be left for thee,
And all that I would keep should be Horatio.
So when the merchant sees his vessel lost, 396
Though richly freighted from a foreign coast,
Gladly for life the treasure he would give,
And only wishes to escape and live.
Gold and his gains no more employ his mind,
But driving o'er the billows with the wind, 401
Cleaves to one faithful plank, and leaves the
    rest behind.   *Exeunt*

ACT IV

SCENE I

SCENE: *a Garden*

Enter ALTAMONT

  ALTAMONT. With what unequal tempers are
    we formed?
One day the soul, supine with ease and full-
    ness,
Revels secure, and fondly tells herself
The hour of evil can return no more;   4
The next, the spirit's palled and, sick of riot,
Turn[s] all to discord, and we hate our beings,
Curse the past joy, and think it folly all,

And bitterness and anguish. O! last night!
What has ungrateful beauty paid me back
For all that mass of friendship which I
    squandered? 10
Coldness, aversion, tears, and sullen sorrow
Dashed all my bliss and damped my bridal
    bed.
Soon as the morning dawned, she vanished
    from me,
Relentless to the gentle call of love.
I have lost a friend, and I have gained—
    a wife! 15
Turn not to thought, my brain; but let me
    find
Some unfrequented shade; there lay me down,
And let forgetful dullness steal upon me
To soften and assuage this pain of thinking.
                                        Exit

    Enter LOTHARIO *and* CALISTA

  LOTHARIO. Weep not, my fair, but let the
    god of love 20
Laugh in thy eyes and revel in thy heart,
Kindle again his torch and hold it high
To light us to new joys; nor let a thought
Of discord or disquiet past, molest thee;
But to a long oblivion give thy cares, 25
And let us melt the present hour in bliss.
  CALISTA. Seek not to soothe me with thy
    false endearments,
To charm me with thy softness; 'tis in vain;
Thou can'st no more betray, nor I be ruined.
The hours of folly and of fond delight 30
Are wasted all, and fled; those that remain
Are doomed to weeping, anguish, and re-
    pentance.
I come to charge thee with a long account
Of all the sorrows I have known already,
And all I have to come;—thou hast undone
    me. 35
  LOTHARIO. Unjust Calista! dost thou call
    it ruin
To love as we have done—to melt, to lan-
    guish,
To wish for somewhat exquisitely happy,
And then be blest ev'n to that wish's height?
To die with joy and straight to live again, 40
Speechless to gaze, and with tumultuous
    transport—
  CALISTA. Oh! let me hear no more; I can
    not bear it,
'Tis deadly to remembrance; let that night,
That guilty night, be blotted from the year;
Let not the voice of mirth or music know it;

Let it be dark and desolate; no stars 46
To glitter o'er it; let it wish for light,
Yet want it still, and vainly wait the dawn;
For 'twas the night that gave me up to shame,
To sorrow, to perfidious, false Lothario. 50
  LOTHARIO. Hear this, ye pow'rs, mark how
    the fair deceiver
Sadly complains of violated truth;
She calls me false, ev'n she, the faithless she,
Whom day and night, whom heav'n and earth
    have heard
Sighing to vow, and tenderly protest 55
Ten thousand times, she would be only
    mine;
And yet, behold, she has giv'n herself away,
Fled from my arms and wedded to another,
Ev'n to the man whom most I hate on earth—
  CALISTA. Art thou so base to upbraid me
    with a crime 60
Which nothing but thy cruelty could cause?
If indignation, raging in my soul,
For thy unmanly insolence and scorn
Urged me to do a deed of desperation,
And wound myself to be revenged on thee, 65
Think whom I should devote to death and
    hell,
Whom curse as my undoer but Lothario!
Hadst thou been just, not all Sciolto's power,
Not all the vows and pray'rs of sighing
    Altamont
Could have prevailed or won me to forsake
    thee. 70
  LOTHARIO. How have I failed in justice or
    in love?
Burns not my flame as brightly as at first?
Ev'n now my heart beats high, I languish
    for thee,
My transports are as fierce, as strong my
    wishes,
As if thou hadst never blest me with thy
    beauty. 75
  CALISTA. How didst thou dare to think that
    I would live
A slave to base desires and brutal pleasures
To be a wretched wanton for thy leisure
To toy and waste an hour of idle time with?
My soul disdains thee for so mean a thought.
  LOTHARIO. The driving storm of passion
    will have way, 81
And I must yield before it; wert thou calm,
Love, the poor criminal, whom thou hast
    doomed,
Has yet a thousand tender things to plead
To charm thy rage and mitigate his fate. 85

THE FAIR PENITENT

Enter behind them ALTAMONT

ALTAMONT. I have lost my peace—Ha! do I live and wake!—

CALISTA. Hadst thou been true, how happy had I been!
Nor Altamont but thou hadst been my lord.
But wherefore named I happiness with thee?
It is for thee, for thee, that I am cursed; 90
For thee my secret soul each hour arraigns me,
Calls me to answer for my virtue stained,
My honor lost to thee; for thee it haunts me
With stern Sciolto's vowing vengeance on me;
With Altamont complaining for his wrongs—

ALTAMONT. (*Coming forward*) Behold him here—

CALISTA. (*Starting*) Ah!—

ALTAMONT. The wretch, whom thou hast made; 96
Curses and sorrows hast thou heaped upon him,
And vengeance is the only good is left.
(*Drawing*)

LOTHARIO. Thou hast ta'en me somewhat unawares, 'tis true,
But love and war take turns like day and night, 100
And little preparation serves my turn,
Equal to both and armed for either field.
We've long been foes, this moment ends our quarrel;
Earth, heaven, and fair Calista judge the combat.

CALISTA. Distraction! Fury! Sorrow! Shame! and death! 105

ALTAMONT. Thou hast talked too much, thy breath is poison to me,
It taints the ambient air; this for my father,
This for Sciolto, and this last for Altamont.
(*They fight;* LOTHARIO *is wounded once or twice, and then falls*)

LOTHARIO. Oh, Altamont, thy genius is the stronger,
Thou hast prevailed!—My fierce, ambitious soul, 110
Declining, droops, and all her fires grow pale;
I conquered in my turn, in love I triumphed;
Those joys are lodged beyond the reach of fate;
That sweet revenge comes smiling to my thoughts, 114
Adorns my fall, and cheers my heart in dying.
(*Dies*)

CALISTA. And what remains for me? Beset with shame,
Encompassed round with wretchedness, there is
But this one way to break the toil and 'scape.
(*She catches up* LOTHARIO'S *sword, and offers to kill herself;* ALTAMONT *runs to her and wrests it from her*)

ALTAMONT. What means thy frantic rage?

CALISTA. Off! let me go.

ALTAMONT. Oh! thou hast more than murdered me; yet still, 120
Still art thou here! and my soul starts with horror
At thought of any danger that may reach thee.

CALISTA. Think'st thou I mean to live? to be forgiven?
Oh, thou hast known but little of Calista.
If thou hadst never heard my name, if only
The midnight moon and silent stars had seen it, 126
I would not bear to be reproached by them,
But dig down deep to find a grave beneath,
And hide me from their beams.

SCIOLTO. (*Within*) What ho! my son!

ALTAMONT. It is Sciolto calls; come near, and find me, 130
The wretched'st thing of all my kind on earth.

CALISTA. Is it the voice of thunder, or my father?
Madness! Confusion! Let the storm come on,
Let the tumultuous roar drive all upon me,
Dash my devoted bark; ye surges, break it;
'Tis for my ruin that the tempest rises. 136
When I am lost, sunk to the bottom low,
Peace shall return and all be calm again.

Enter SCIOLTO

SCIOLTO. Ev'n now Rossano leaped the garden walls—
Ha! Death has been among you—O my fears!
Last night thou hadst a diff'rence with thy friend, 141
The cause thou gav'st me for it was a damned one;
Didst thou not wrong the man who told thee truth?
Answer me quick—

ALTAMONT. Oh! press me not to speak,
Ev'n now my heart is breaking, and the mention 145
Will lay me dead before you; see that body,
And guess my shame! my ruin! Oh, Calista!

SCIOLTO. It is enough! but I am slow to execute,
And justice lingers in my lazy hand;

Thus let me wipe dishonor from my name,
And cut thee from the earth, thou stain to
   goodness.—   151
   (*Offers to kill* CALISTA; ALTAMONT *holds
   him*)
  ALTAMONT. Stay thee, Sciolto, thou rash
   father, stay,
Or turn the point on me and through my
   breast
Cut out the bloody passage to Calista;
So shall my love be perfect, while for her 155
I die for whom alone I wished to live.
  CALISTA. No, Altamont! my heart, that
   scorned thy love
Shall never be indebted to thy pity;
Thus torn, defaced, and wretched as I seem,
Still I have something of Sciolto's virtue. 160
Yes! yes, my father, I applaud thy justice,
Strike home, and I will bless thee for the blow;
Be merciful, and free me from my pain,
'Tis sharp, 'tis terrible, and I could curse
The cheerful day, men, earth, and heaven, and
   thee,   165
Even thee, thou venerable good old man,
For being author of a wretch like me.
  ALTAMONT. Listen not to the wildness of
   her raving,
Remember nature! Should thy daughter's
   murder
Defile that hand so just, so great in arms,
Her blood would rest upon thee to posterity,
Pollute thy name and sully all thy wars.
  CALISTA. Have I not wronged his gentle
   nature much?
And yet behold him pleading for my life.
Lost as thou art to virtue, oh, Calista! 175
I think thou canst not bear to be outdone;
Then haste to die and be obliged no more.
  SCIOLTO. Thy pious care has giv'n me time
   to think,
And saved me from a crime; then rest, my
   sword,
To honor have I kept thee ever sacred, 180
Nor will I stain thee with a rash revenge;
But mark me well, I will have justice done;
Hope not to bear away thy crimes unpunished;
I will see justice executed on thee,
Even to a Roman strictness; and thou, nature,
Or whatsoe'er thou art that plead'st within
   me,   186
Be still, thy tender strugglings are in vain.
  CALISTA. Then am I doomed to live and
   bear your triumph?
To groan beneath your scorn and fierce upbraidings,   189
Daily to be reproached, and have my misery
At morn, at noon, and night told over to me
Lest my remembrance might grow pitiful
And grant a moment's interval of peace—
Is this, is this the mercy of a father?
I only beg to die, and he denies me. 195
  SCIOLTO. Hence from my sight! thy father
   can not bear thee;
Fly with thy infamy to some dark cell
Where on the confines of eternal night
Mourning, misfortunes, cares, and anguish
   dwell;   199
Where ugly shame hides her opprobious head,
And death and hell detested rule maintain;
There howl out the remainder of thy life,
And wish thy name may be no more remembered.
  CALISTA. Yes, I will fly to some such dismal
   place,   204
And be more cursed than you can wish I were;
This fatal form that drew on my undoing,
Fasting and tears and hardship shall destroy,
Nor light nor food nor comfort will I know,
Nor aught that may continue hated life.
Then when you see me meagre, wan, and
   changed,   210
Stretched at my length, and dying in my cave,
On that cold earth I mean shall be my grave,
Perhaps you may relent and, sighing, say,
At length her tears have washed her stains
   away,
At length 'tis time her punishment should
   cease;   215
Die, thou poor, suff'ring wretch, and be at
   peace.
                       Exit CALISTA
  SCIOLTO. Who of my servants wait there?

      Enter two or three Servants

                         On your lives
Take care my doors be guarded well, that none
Pass out or enter but by my appointment.
                      Exeunt Servants
  ALTAMONT. There is a fatal fury in your
   visage,   220
It blazes fierce and menaces destruction;
My father, I am sick of many sorrows,
Ev'n now my easy heart is breaking with 'em,
Yet above all one fear distracts me most,
I tremble at the vengeance which you meditate   225
On the poor, faithless, lovely, dear Calista.

THE FAIR PENITENT

Sciolto. Hast thou not read what brave
    Virginius [1] did?
With his own hand he slew his only daughter
To save her from the fierce Decemvir's lust.
He slew her yet unspotted to prevent   230
The shame which she might know. Then
    what should I do?—
But thou hast tied my hand.—I wo' not kill
    her;
Yet by the ruin she has brought upon us,
The common infamy that brands us both,
She sha' not 'scape.
    Altamont.   You mean that she shall
    die then?   235
    Sciolto. Ask me not what, nor how, I have
    resolved,
For all within is anarchy and uproar.
O Altamont! what a vast scheme of joy
Has this one day destroyed! Well did I hope
This daughter would have blessed my latter
    days;   240
That I should live to see you the world's
    wonder;
So happy, great, and good that none were
    like you,
While I, from busy life and care set free,
Had spent the ev'ning of my age at home
Among a little prattling race of yours: 245
There like an old man talked awhile, and then
Lain down and slept in peace. Instead of this,
Sorrow and shame must bring me to my
    grave;
O damn her! damn her!

Enter a Servant

    Servant.   Arm yourself, my lord: 249
Rossano, who but now escaped the garden,
Has gathered in the street a band of rioters
Who threaten you and all your friends with
    ruin
Unless Lothario be returned in safety.
    Sciolto. By heaven, their fury rises to my
    wish,   254
Nor shall misfortune know my house alone
But thou, Lothario, and thy race shall pay
    me
For all the sorrows which my age is cursed
    with.
I think my name as great, my friends as
    potent
As any in the state; all shall be summoned.

---

[1] The reference is to the famous story of Virginius, who, to protect his daughter from Tarquin ("the fierce Decemvir"), slew her with his own hands.

I know that all will join their hands to ours
And vindicate thy vengeance. Raise the body
And bear it in; his friends shall buy him dearly.
I will have blood for ransom: when our force
Is full and armed, we shall expect thy sword
To join with us, and sacrifice to justice.— 265
    Exit Sciolto. *The body of* Lothario *is
    carried off by* Servants

Manet Altamont

    Altamont. There is a stupid weight upon
    my senses,
A dismal, sullen stillness that succeeds
The storm of rage and grief like silent death
After the tumult and the noise of life.
Would it were death, as sure 'tis wondrous
    like it,   270
For I am sick of living, my soul's palled;
She kindles not with anger or revenge;
Love was th'informing, active fire within;
Now that is quenched, the mass forgets to
    move,   274
And longs to mingle with its kindred earth.
    (*A tumultuous noise with clashing of
    swords, as at a little distance*)

Enter Lavinia *with two* Servants, *their swords
drawn*

    Lavinia. Fly, swiftly fly to my Horatio's
    aid,
Nor lose you[r] vain, officious cares on me;
Bring me my lord, my husband to my arms—
He is Lavinia's life; bring him me safe,   279
And I shall be at ease, be well and happy.
                          Exeunt Servants
    Altamont. Art thou Lavinia? Oh! what
    barb'rous hand
Could wrong thy poor, defenceless innocence,
And leave such marks of more than savage
    fury?
    Lavinia. My brother! Oh, my heart is full
    of fears;   284
Perhaps ev'n now my dear Horatio bleeds.—
Not far from hence, as passing to the port,[2]
By a mad multitude we were surrounded,
Who ran upon us with uplifted swords,   288
And cried aloud for vengeance and Lothario.
My lord with ready boldness stood the shock
To shelter me from danger, but in vain,
Had not a party from Sciolto's palace
Rushed out and snatched me from amidst the
    fray.

---

[2] Gate.

ALTAMONT. What of my friend?
LAVINIA. (*Looking out*)   Ha! by my joys,
    'tis he,   295
He lives, he comes to bless me, he is safe!—

Enter HORATIO *with two or three Servants, their
    swords drawn*

FIRST SERVANT. 'Twere at the utmost
    hazard of your life
To venture forth again till we are stronger;
Their number trebles ours.
    HORATIO.   No matter, let it;
Death is not half so shocking as that traitor.
My honest soul is mad with indignation 300
To think her plainness could be so abused
As to mistake that wretch, and call him friend;
I can not bear the sight.
    ALTAMONT.   Open, thou earth,
Gape wide and take me down to thy dark
    bosom
To hide me from Horatio.
    HORATIO.   Oh, Lavinia, 305
Believe not but I joy to see thee safe.
Would our ill fortune had not drove us hither!
I could ev'n wish we rather had been wrecked
On any other shore than saved on this.
    LAVINIA. Oh, let us bless the mercy that
        preserved us,   310
That gracious pow'r that saved us for each
    other,
And, to adorn the sacrifice of praise,
Offer forgiveness, too; be thou like heaven,
And put away th'offences of thy friend 314
Far, far from thy remembrance.
    ALTAMONT.   I have marked him
To see if one forgiving glance stole hither,
If any spark of friendship were alive
That would by sympathy at meeting glow,
And strive to kindle up the flame anew; 319
'Tis lost, 'tis gone, his soul is quite estranged,
And knows me for its counterpart no more.
    HORATIO. Thou know'st thy rule, thy
        empire in Horatio,
Nor canst thou ask in vain, command in vain
Where nature, reason, nay, where love, is
    judge;
But when you urge my temper to comply 325
With what it most abhors, I can not do it.
    LAVINIA. Where didst thou get this sullen,
        gloomy hate?
It was not in thy nature to be thus;
Come, put it off, and let thy heart be cheer-
    ful,   329
Be gay again, and know the joys of friendship,
The trust, security, and mutual tenderness,
The double joys where each is glad for both;
Friendship, the wealth, the last retreat and
    strength,
Secure against ill fortune and the world.
    HORATIO. I am not apt to take a light
        offence,   335
But, patient of the failings of my friends,
And willing to forgive; but when an injury
Stabs to the heart and rouses my resentment
(Perhaps it is the fault of my rude nature),
I own I can not easily forget it.   340
    ALTAMONT. Thou hast forgot me.
    HORATIO.   No.
    ALTAMONT.   Why are thy
        eyes
Impatient of me, then, scornful and fierce?
    HORATIO. Because they speak the meaning
        of my heart,
Because they are honest and disdain a villain.
    ALTAMONT. I have wronged thee much,
        Horatio.   345
    HORATIO.   True, thou hast;
When I forget it, may I be a wretch
Vile as thyself, a false, perfidious fellow,
An infamous, believing, British husband.
    ALTAMONT. I've wronged thee much, and
        heaven has well avenged it.   350
I have not, since we parted, been at peace,
Nor known one joy sincere; our broken
    friendship
Pursued me to the last retreat of love,
Stood glaring like a ghost and made me cold
    with horror.   354
Misfortunes on misfortunes press upon me,
Swell o'er my head like waves and dash me
    down.
Sorrow, remorse, and shame have torn my
    soul,
They hang like winter on my youthful hopes
And blast the spring and promise of my year.
    LAVINIA. So flowers are gathered to adorn a
        grave,   360
To lose their freshness amongst bones and
    rottenness,
And have their odors stifled in the dust.
Canst thou hear this, thou cruel, hard Ho-
    ratio?
Canst thou behold thy Altamont undone?
That gentle, that dear youth! canst thou be-
    hold him,   365
His poor heart broken, death in his pale visage,
And groaning out his woes, yet stand un-
    moved?

HORATIO. The brave and wise I pity in misfortune,
But when ingratitude and folly suffers,
'Tis weakness to be touched.
ALTAMONT. I wo' not ask thee 370
To pity or forgive me, but confess
This scorn, this insolence of hate is just;
'Tis constancy of mind and manly in thee.
But oh! had I been wronged by thee, Horatio,
There is a yielding softness in my heart 375
Could ne'er have stood it out, but I had ran
With streaming eyes and open arms upon thee,
And pressed thee close, close!
HORATIO. I must hear no more,
The weakness is contagious, I shall catch it,
And be a tame, fond wretch.
LAVINIA. Where wouldst thou go? 380
Wouldst thou part thus? You sha' not, 'tis impossible;
For I will bar thy passage, kneeling thus;
Perhaps thy cruel hand may spurn me off,
But I will throw my body in thy way,
And thou shalt trample o'er my faithful bosom, 385
Tread on me, wound me, kill me e'er thou pass.
ALTAMONT. Urge not in vain thy pious suit, Lavinia,
I have enough to rid me of my pain.
Calista, thou hadst reached my heart before;
To make all sure, my friend repeats the blow.
But in the grave our cares shall be forgotten,
There love and friendship cease. *(Falls)*
(LAVINIA *runs to him and endeavors to raise him*)
LAVINIA. Speak to me, Altamont.
He faints! he dies! Now turn and see thy triumph, 393
My brother! But our cares shall end together;
Here will I lay all down by thy dear side,
Bemoan thy too hard fate, then share it with thee, 396
And never see my cruel lord again.
(HORATIO *runs to* ALTAMONT *and raises him in his arms*)
HORATIO. It is too much to bear! Look up, my Altamont!
My stubborn unrelenting heart has killed him.
Look up and bless me, tell me that thou liv'st.
Oh! I have urged thy gentleness too far. 401
(He revives)
Do thou and my Lavinia both forgive me;
A flood of tenderness comes o'er my soul;
I can not speak!—I love! forgive! and pity thee.—

ALTAMONT. I thought that nothing could have stayed my soul, 405
That long e'er this her flight had reached the stars,
But thy known voice has lured her back again.
Methinks I fain would set all right with thee,
Make up this most unlucky breach, and then
With thine and heaven's forgiveness on my soul, 410
Shrink to my grave and be at ease forever.
HORATIO. By heaven, my heart bleeds for thee; ev'n this moment
I feel thy pangs of disappointed love.
Is it not pity that this youth should fail,
That all this wond'rous goodness should be lost, 415
And the world never know it? Oh, my Altamont!
Give me thy sorrows, let me bear 'em for thee,
And shelter thee from ruin.
LAVINIA. O my brother!
Think not but we will share in all thy woes,
We'll sit all day and tell sad tales of love,
And when we light upon some faithless woman, 421
Some beauty, like Calista, false and fair,
We'll fix our grief and our complaining there;
We'll curse the nymph that drew the ruin on,
And mourn the youth that was like thee undone. *Exeunt*

ACT V

SCENE I

[*The*] *Scene is a room hung with black; on one side, is* LOTHARIO'S *body on a bier; on the other, a table with a skull and other bones, a book, and a lamp on it*

CALISTA *is discovered on a couch in black, her hair hanging loose and disordered; after music and a song, she rises and comes forward*

SONG

Hear, you midnight phantoms, hear,
You who pale and wan appear,
And fill the wretch who wakes, with fear.
You who wander, scream, and groan
Round the mansions once your own, 5
You whom still your crimes upbraid,
You who rest not with the dead;
From the coverts where you stray,

Where you lurk and shun the day,
From the charnel and the tomb   10
Hither haste ye, hither come.

ii

Chide Calista for delay,
Tell her 'tis for her you stay;
Bid her die and come away.
See the sexton with his spade,   15
See the grave already made;
Listen, fair one, to thy knell,
This music is thy passing bell.

CALISTA. 'Tis well! these solemn sounds, this pomp of horror
Are fit to feed the frenzy in my soul;   20
Here's room for meditation, ev'n to madness,
Till the mind burst with thinking; this dull flame
Sleeps in the socket; sure the book was left
To tell me something;—for instruction, then—
He teaches holy sorrow and contrition,   25
And penitence;—is it become an art then?
A trick that lazy, dull, luxurious gown-men [1]
Can teach us to do over? I'll no more on't.
(*Throwing away the book*)
I have more real anguish in my heart
Than all their pedant discipline e'er knew.   30
What charnel has been rifled for these bones?
Fie! this is pageantry;—they look uncouthly,
But what of that, if he or she that owned 'em
Safe from disquiet sit, and smile to see
The farce their miserable relics play?   35
But here's a sight is terrible indeed;
Is this the haughty, gallant, gay Lothario?
That dear perfidious—Ah!—how pale he looks!
How grim with clotted blood, and those dead eyes!   39
Ascend, ye ghosts, fantastic forms of night,
In all your diff'rent, dreadful shapes ascend,
And match the present horror if you can!

Enter SCIOLTO

SCIOLTO. This dead of night, this silent hour of darkness
Nature for rest ordained, and soft repose,
And yet distraction and tumultuous jars   45
Keep all our frighted citizens awake;
The senate, weak, divided, and irresolute,
Want pow'r to succor the afflicted state.
Vainly in words and long debates they're wise,
While the fierce factions scorn their peaceful orders   50

[1] Scholars, or, more specifically, theological scholars.

And drown the voice of law in noise and anarchy.
Amidst the general wreck, see where she stands   (*Pointing to* CALISTA)
Like Helen in the night when Troy was sacked,[2]
Spectatress of the mischief which she made.
CALISTA. It is Sciolto! Be thyself, my soul;
Be strong to bear his fatal indignation   56
That he may see thou art not lost so far
But somewhat still of his great spirit lives
In the forlorn Calista.
SCIOLTO.   Thou wert once
My daughter.
CALISTA.   Happy were it I had died   60
And never lost that name.
SCIOLTO.   That's something yet;
Thou wert the very darling of my age;
I thought the day too short to gaze upon thee,
That all the blessings I could gather for thee
By cares on earth and by my pray'rs to heaven   65
Were little for my fondness to bestow;
Why didst thou turn to folly, then, and curse me?
CALISTA. Because my soul was rudely drawn from yours,
A poor, imperfect copy of my father
Where goodness and the strength of manly virtue   70
Was thinly planted, and the idle void
Filled up with light belief and easy fondness;
It was because I loved and was a woman.
SCIOLTO. Hadst thou been honest, thou hadst been a cherubin;
But of that joy, as of a gem long lost,   75
Beyond redemption gone, think we no more.
Hast thou e'er dared to meditate on death?
CALISTA. I have, as on the end of shame and sorrow.
SCIOLTO. Ha! answer me! say, hast thou coolly thought?
'Tis not the stoic's lessons got by rote,   80
The pomp of words and pedant dissertations
That can sustain thee in that hour of terror:
Books have taught cowards to talk nobly of it,
But when the trial comes, they start and stand aghast;
Hast thou considered what may happen after it?   85
How thy account may stand, and what to answer?

[2] See the *Æneid*, II. 567 ff.

CALISTA. I have turned my eyes inward upon myself
Where foul offence and shame have laid all waste;
Therefore my soul abhors the wretched dwelling, 89
And longs to find some better place of rest.
　SCIOLTO. 'Tis justly thought, and worthy of that spirit
That dwelt in ancient Latian breasts when Rome
Was mistress of the world. I would go on
And tell thee all my purpose, but it sticks
Here at my heart and can not find a way. 95
　CALISTA. Then spare the telling, if it be a pain,
And write the meaning with your poniard here.
　SCIOLTO. O! truly guessed—see'st thou this trembling hand?—(*Holding up a dagger*)
Thrice justice urged—and thrice the slack'ning sinews 99
Forgot their office and confessed the father;
At length the stubborn virtue has prevailed,
It must, it must be so—Oh! take it then,
　　　　　　　(*Giving the dagger*)
And know the rest untaught.
　CALISTA.　　　　　　I understand you.
It is but this, and both are satisfied.
　(*She offers to kill herself;* SCIOLTO *catches hold of her arm*)
　SCIOLTO. A moment—give me yet a moment's space; 105
The stern, the rigid judge has been obeyed;
Now nature and the father claim their turns;
I have held the balance with an iron hand,
And put off ev'ry tender human thought,
To doom my child to death; but spare my eyes
The most unnatural sight lest their strings crack 111
And my old brain split and grow mad with horror.
　CALISTA. Ha! is it possible? And is there yet
Some little, dear remain of love and tenderness
For poor, undone Calista in your heart? 115
　SCIOLTO. Oh! when I think what pleasure I took in thee,
What joys thou gav'st me in thy prattling infancy,
Thy sprightly wit and early blooming beauty,
How have I stood and fed my eyes upon thee.
Then lifted up my hands and, wond'ring, blessed thee; 120
By my strong grief, my heart ev'n melts within me;
I could curse nature and that tyrant, honor,
For making me thy father and thy judge;
Thou art my daughter still.
　CALISTA.　　　　　For that kind word
Thus let me fall, thus humbly to the earth;
Weep on your feet and bless you for this goodness; 126
Oh! 'tis too much for this offending wretch,
This parricide, that murders with her crimes,
Shortens her father's age and cuts him off
E'er little more than half his years be numbered. 130
　SCIOLTO. Would it were otherwise!—but thou must die.—
　CALISTA. That I must die—it is my only comfort;
Death is the privilege of human nature,
And life without it were not worth our taking;
Thither the poor, the pris'ner, and the mourner 135
Fly for relief and lay their burdens down.
Come then, and take me now to thy cold arms,
Thou meagre shade; here let me breathe my last,
Charmed with my father's pity and forgiveness
More than if angels tuned their golden viols
And sung a requiem to my parting soul. 141
　SCIOLTO. I am summoned hence; e'er this my friends expect me.
There is I know not what of sad presàge
That tells me I shall never see thee more;
If it be so, this is our last farewell, 145
And these the parting pangs which nature feels
When anguish rends the heart-strings—
Oh! my daughter!　　　*Exit* SCIOLTO
　CALISTA. Now think thou, cursed Calista, now behold
The desolation, horror, blood, and ruin
Thy crimes and fatal folly spread around 150
That loudly cry for vengeance on thy head;
Yet heaven, who knows our weak, imperfect natures,
How blind with passions and how prone to evil,
Makes not too strict enquiry for offences,
But is atoned by penitence and prayer. 155
Cheap recompense! here 'twould not be received;

Nothing but blood can make the expiation
And cleanse the soul from inbred, deep pollution.
And see—another injured wretch is come
To call for justice from my tardy hand. 160

Enter ALTAMONT

ALTAMONT. Hail to you, horrors! hail, thou house of death!
And thou, the lovely mistress of these shades
Whose beauty gilds the more than midnight darkness
And makes it grateful as the dawn of day.
Oh! take me in, a fellow-mourner with thee;
I'll number groan for groan, and tear for tear; 166
And when the fountain of thy eyes are dry,
Mine shall supply the stream and weep for both.
CALISTA. I know thee well, thou art the injured Altamont,
Thou com'st to urge me with the wrongs I ha' done thee; 170
But now I stand upon the brink of life
And in a moment mean to set me free
From shame and thy upbraiding.
ALTAMONT. Falsely, falsely
Dost thou accuse me; when did I complain,
Or murmur at my fate? For thee I have 175
Forgot the temper of Italian husbands,
And fondness has prevailed upon revenge;
I bore my load of infamy with patience,
As holy men do punishments from heaven,
Nor thought it hard because it came from thee. 180
Oh! then forbid me not to mourn thy loss,
To wish some better fate had ruled our loves,
And that Calista had been mine, and true!
CALISTA. O Altamont, 'tis hard for souls like mine,
Haughty and fierce, to yield they have done amiss; 185
But oh! behold my proud, disdainful heart
Bends to thy gentler virtue; yes, I own
Such is thy truth, thy tenderness and love,
Such are the graces that adorn thy youth 189
That, were I not abandoned to destruction,
With thee I might have lived for ages blest,
And died in peace within thy faithful arms.
ALTAMONT. Then happiness is still within our reach;
Here let remembrance lose our past misfortunes, 194
Tear all records that hold the fatal story;
Here let our joys begin, from hence go on
In long, successive order.
CALISTA. What! In death?
ALTAMONT. Then art thou fixed to die?—
But be it so,
We'll go together; my advent'rous love 199
Shall follow thee to those uncertain beings;
Whether our lifeless shades are doomed to wander
In gloomy groves with discontented ghosts,
Or whether through the upper air we fleet
And tread the fields of light, still I'll pursue thee
Till fate ordains that we shall part no more.
CALISTA. O no! Heaven has some better lot in store 206
To crown thee with; live and be happy long;
Live for some maid that shall deserve thy goodness,
Some kind, unpractised heart that never yet
Has listened to the false ones of thy sex, 210
Nor know the arts of ours; she shall reward thee,
Meet thee with virtues equal to thy own,
Charm thee with sweetness, beauty, and with truth,
Be blest in thee alone, and thou in her.

Enter HORATIO

HORATIO. Now mourn indeed, ye miserable pair, 215
For now the measure of your woes is full.
ALTAMONT. What dost thou mean, Horatio?
HORATIO. O 'tis dreadful;
The great, the good Sciolto dies this moment.
CALISTA. My father!
ALTAMONT. That's a deadly stroke indeed.
HORATIO. Not long ago he privately went forth 220
Attended but by few, and those unbidden;
I heard which way he took and straight pursued him,
But found him compassed by Lothario's faction,
Almost alone amidst a crowd of foes;
Too late we brought him aid and drove them back; 225
E'er that his frantic valor had provoked
The death he seemed to wish for from their swords.
CALISTA. And dost thou bear me yet, thou patient earth?

Dost thou not labor with my murd'rous weight?
And you, ye glitt'ring, heavenly host of stars,
Hide your fair heads in clouds, or I shall blast you, 231
For I am all contagion, death, and ruin,
And nature sickens at me; rest, thou world,
This parricide shall be thy plague no more;
Thus, thus, I set thee free.   (*Stabs herself*)
HORATIO.   O fatal rashness! 235
ALTAMONT. Thou dost instruct me well; to lengthen life
Is but to trifle now.
    (ALTAMONT *offers to kill himself;* HORATIO *prevents him and wrests his sword from him*)
HORATIO.   Ha! what means
The frantic Altamont? Some foe to man
Has breathed on ev'ry breast contagious fury
And epidemic madness.

Enter SCIOLTO, *pale and bloody, supported by Servants*

CALISTA.   Oh, my heart! 240
Well may'st thou fail, for see! the spring that fed
Thy vital stream is wasted and runs low.
My father! will you now at last forgive me,
If, after all my crimes and all your suff'rings,
I call you once again by that dear name? 245
Will you forget my shame and those wide wounds,
Lift up your hand and bless me e'er I go
Down to my dark abode?
    SCIOLTO.   Alas! my daughter!
Thou hast rashly ventured in a stormy sea
Where life, fame, virtue, all were wrecked and lost; 250
But sure thou hast borne thy part in all the anguish,
And smarted with the pain. Then rest in peace;
Let silence and oblivion hide thy name,
And save thee from the malice of posterity;
And may'st thou find with heaven the same forgiveness 255
As with thy father here.—Die, and be happy.
    CALISTA. Celestial sounds! Peace dawns upon my soul,
And ev'ry pain grows less.—O gentle Altamont,
Think not too hardly of me when I'm gone,
But pity me.—Had I but early known 260

Thy wondrous worth, thou excellent young man,
We had been happier both.—Now, 'tis too late,
And yet my eyes take pleasure to behold thee,
Thou art their last dear object.—Mercy, heaven!   (*She dies*)
ALTAMONT. Cold! dead and cold! and yet thou art not changed, 265
But lovely still! Hadst thou a thousand faults,
What heart so hard, what virtue so severe
But at that beauty must of force relented,
Melted to pity, love, and to forgiveness!
    SCIOLTO. Oh! turn thee from that fatal object; Altamont, 270
Come near and let me bless thee e'er I die.
To thee and brave Horatio I bequeath
My fortunes.—Lay me by thy noble father,
And love my memory as thou has done his,
For thou hast been my son.—Oh! gracious heaven! 275
Thou that hast endless blessings still in store
For virtue and for filial piety,
Let grief, disgrace, and want be far away,
But multiply thy mercies on his head;
Let honor, greatness, goodness still be with him, 280
And peace in all his ways.—   (*He dies*)
    ALTAMONT.   Take, take it all;
To thee, Horatio, I resign the gift,
While I pursue my father and my love
And find my only portion in the grave.
    [*He faints*]
HORATIO. The storm of grief bears hard upon his youth 285
And bends him like a drooping flower to earth.
Raise him, and bear him in.
    (ALTAMONT *is carried off*)
By such examples are we taught to prove
The sorrows that attend unlawful love; 289
Death, or some worse misfortunes, soon divide
The injured bridegroom from his guilty bride:
If you would have the nuptial union last,
Let virtue be the bond that ties it fast.
    Exeunt omnes

EPILOGUE

Spoken by MRS. BRACEGIRDLE, who played
                    LAVINIA

You see the tripping dame could find no favor;
Dearly she paid for breach of good behavior.
Nor could her loving husband's fondness save her.

Italian ladies lead but scurvy lives; 4
There's dreadful dealing with eloping wives;
Thus 'tis because these husbands are obeyed
By force of laws which for themselves they made.
With tales of old prescriptions they confine
The right of marriage-rule to their male line,
And huff and domineer by right divine. 10
Had we the pow'r, we'd make the tyrants know
What 'tis to fail in duties which they owe;
We'd teach the saunt'ring squire who loves to roam,
Forgetful of his own dear spouse and home;
Who snores at night supinely by her side, 15
'Twas not for this the nuptial knot was tied.
The plodding pettifogger and the cit[1]
Have learned at least this modern way of wit:
Each ill-bred, senseless rogue, though ne'er so dull,
Has th'impudence to think his wife a fool; 20
He spends the night where merry wags resort,
With joking clubs and eighteen-penny port,
While she, poor soul, 's contented to regale
By a sad sea-coal fire, with wigs [2] and ale. 24
Well may the cuckold-making tribe find grace
And fill an absent husband's empty place:
If you would e'er bring constancy in fashion,
You men must first begin the reformation.
Then shall the golden age of love return,
No turtle [3] for her wand'ring mate shall mourn, 30
No foreign charms shall cause domestic strife,
But ev'ry married man shall toast his wife;
Phyllis shall not be to the country sent,
For carnivals in town to keep a tedious Lent;
Lampoons shall cease, and envious scandal die,
And all shall live in peace like my good man and I. 36

[1] Citizen, used especially of an inhabitant of London within the walls, "The City."

[2] A variety of small cakes. [3] Turtle dove.

THE BEAUX' STRATAGEM

By George Farquhar

George Farquhar, son of a Church of England clergyman in North Ireland, was born in Londonderry in 1677 or 1678. On July 17, 1694, "*annos* 17," he entered Trinity College, Dublin; but lacking funds and finding academic life uncongenial, he left college and turned actor in the theater in Smock Alley. There he met Robert Wilks, who became his life-long friend and the creator of leading parts in his plays. About 1697, Wilks having gone to London, Farquhar also crossed the Irish Sea to become an actor in the metropolis. He soon learned that he could not act, but about the same time he also learned that he could write comedies. His first, *Love and a Bottle*, was produced at the Theatre Royal in 1698. The second, *The Constant Couple*, put on the next year, made Farquhar one of the most popular dramatic authors of the day. The part of Sir Harry Wildair, played by Wilks to the Lady Lurewell of Mrs. Verbruggen, made the fortunes of both actor and author. Farquhar had already secured a commission in the army, but failing to receive the advancement and favors he expected, he turned his attention to the production of his comedies. Though his military career did not lead him to fields of battle or court offices, it sent him on recruiting trips into rural England, the scene of his best plays. His finances were never in a satisfactory condition, however, and his relations with his wife were disappointing; so under care and poverty his health began to fail. By 1706 he was suffering from a "settled illness." Urged on by Wilks, however, he finished his last play, *The Beaux' Stratagem* (Hay., March 8, 1707), shortly after the production of which he died, probably on May 23, 1707.

References: *The Dramatic Works of George Farquhar*. Ed. Alex. Charles Ewald. 2 vols. 1892. Plays "Mermaid Series." Ed. William Archer, 1906, contains: *The Constant Couple, The Twin-Rivals, The Recruiting Officer, The Beaux' Stratagem*.

See also: *The Dictionary of National Biography*, article by Sir Leslie Stephen; D. Schmidt, *George Farquhar, sein leben und seine original dramen*, Wiener Beiträge zur Englischen Philologie, xviii Band, Wien und Leipzig, 1904; John Palmer, *The Comedy of Manners*, 1913.

Farquhar's Dramatic Works

Love and a Bottle (comedy), T.R., Dec., 1698.
The Constant Couple; or, A Trip to the Jubilee (comedy), T.R., 1699.
Sir Harry Wildair: Being the Sequel of the Trip to the Jubilee (comedy), D.L., *c*. April, 1701.
The Inconstant; or, The Way to Win Him (comedy), D.L., *c*. Feb., 1701/2.
The Twin-Rivals (comedy), D.L., Dec. 14, 1702.
The Stage Coach (adaptation from Jean de la Chapelles, in collaboration with P. A. Motteux), L.I.F., *c*. Jan., 1703.
The Recruiting Officer (comedy), D.L., April 8, 1706.
The Beaux' Stratagem (comedy), Hay., March 8, 1706/7.

With the popular, if improvident, "Captain" Farquhar dying a few streets off, his last and sprightliest comedy was put on the stage at Vanbrugh's theater in the Haymarket. His loyal friends, Wilks and Mrs. Oldfield, exerted themselves to do the playwright justice and the piece was a great success. The audience roared and chuckled through the comedy and wept when the epilogue pled for mercy to the "expiring author." Many of them could remember the day in 1698, when in the prologue to a new piece called *Love and a Bottle*, they had been informed,

But our new author has no cause maintain'd,
Let him not lose what he has never gain'd.
Love and a Bottle are his peaceful arms,
Ladies and gallants, have not these some charms?

The young Irishman, who then had but recently come to London, had added something to the manner of Mr. Wycherley and Mr.

Congreve, both still living, and written comedies of the old type in a new way. He had in the following years added popular characters to the English stage; and now on the eve of his death he had produced his best play.

Farquhar has been regarded as the last of the Restoration dramatists in the line of Etherege, Wycherley, Congreve, and Vanbrugh. He is also one of the first writers of eighteenth-century comedy in the line of Cibber and Steele. His earlier plays resemble those of his predecessors and the later ones follow the same lead but with an admixture of the newer spirit. The new movement towards morality accounts to some extent for the change in tone from Vanbrugh to Farquhar, but the romantic temperament of the author himself accentuates the difference. Love in Farquhar's plays is a romantic passion rather than, as it had been earlier, an excuse for intrigue soon consummated and soon ended. Even Sir Harry Wildair, typical of the gay rake of the Restoration, is described as true, in spirit at least, to the wife whom he thinks dead. The romance, incipient in the early plays, is more apparent in *The Beaux' Stratagem*, where Aimwell falls really in love with the heiress whose fortune he had set out to obtain and offers to give her up rather than impose upon her innocence and virtue. *The Beaux' Stratagem*, thus, shows signs of falling over into the sentimentalism of the next generation, and the last Restoration comedy becomes one of the first comedies of sensibility. The Aimwell who can say, "I find myself unequal to the task of villain; she has gained my soul and made it honest like her own," is related as nearly to Richard Steele as to William Wycherley.

The Beaux' Stratagem had, with others of Farquhar's plays, especially *The Constant Couple* and *The Recruiting Officer*, a long and successful stage career. Robert Wilks and Mrs. Oldfield set the example for their successors and almost every important actor and actress for a hundred years appeared in Farquhar's comedies, whose popularity on the stage of the eighteenth century exceeded that of his masters in the comedy of manners.

THE BEAUX' STRATAGEM

ADVERTISEMENT.—The reader may find some faults in this play, which my illness prevented the amending of, but there is great amends made in the representation, which cannot be matched, no more than the friendly and indefatigable care of Mr. Wilks,[1] to whom I chiefly owe the success of the play.—GEORGE FARQUHAR.

DRAMATIS PERSONÆ

MEN

AIMWELL } *Two Gentlemen of broken Fortunes, the first as Master, and the*	Mr. Mills.
ARCHER } *second as Servant*	Mr. Wilks
COUNT BELLAIR, *a French Officer, Prisoner at Lichfield*	Mr. Bowman
SULLEN, *a Country Blockhead, brutal to his wife*	Mr. Verbruggen
FREEMAN, *a Gentleman from London*	Mr. Keen
FOIGARD, *a Priest, Chaplain to the French Officers*	Mr. Bowen
GIBBET, *a Highwayman*	Mr. Cibber
HOUNSLOW } *his Companions*	
BAGSHOT }	
BONIFACE, *Landlord of the Inn*	Mr. Bullock
SCRUB, *servant to Mr. Sullen*	Mr. Norris

WOMEN

LADY BOUNTIFUL, *an old civil, country gentlewoman, that cures all her neighbors of all distempers, and foolishly fond of her son,* SULLEN	Mrs. Powell
DORINDA, *Lady Bountiful's daughter*	Mrs. Bradshaw
MRS. SULLEN, *her Daughter-in-Law*	Mrs. Oldfield
GIPSY, *Maid to the Ladies*	Mrs. Mills
CHERRY, *the Landlord's Daughter in the Inn*	Mrs. Bignal

(Tapster, Coach-passengers, Countryman, Countrywoman, and Servants)

SCENE: *Lichfield*

PROLOGUE

Spoken by MR. WILKS

When strife disturbs, or sloth corrupts an age,
Keen satire is the business of the stage.
When the Plain-Dealer [2] writ, he lashed those crimes, 3
Which then infested most the modish times:
But now, when faction sleeps, and sloth is fled,
And all our youth in active fields are bred;
When, through Great Britain's fair extensive round,
The trumps of fame the notes of UNION sound; [3]
When Anna's sceptre points the laws their course,
And her example gives her precepts force: 10
There scarce is room for satire; all our lays
Must be, or songs of triumph, or of praise.

[1] Robert Wilks (1665?–1732), born at Rathfarnham near Dublin. He first appeared on the stage at Smock Alley Theatre, Dublin, in 1691 as Othello. Later he moved to London and continued to act there and in Dublin. He was a thoroughly competent, though not a brilliant, actor.

[2] William Wycherley (1640?–1716), author of *Love in a Wood* (1672), *The Gentleman Dancing Master* (1673), *The Country Wife* (1675), and *The Plain-Dealer* (1677), all noted for their wit and coarseness.

[3] The Act of Union forming the United Kingdom of Great Britain, uniting England and Scotland under one parliament, became effective March 6. 1707.

But as in grounds best cultivated, tares
And poppies rise among the golden ears,
Our products so, fit for the field or school,
Must mix with Nature's favorite plant—a fool:
A weed that has to twenty summers ran,
Shoots up in stalk, and vegetates to man.
Simpling[1], our author goes from field to field,
And culls such fools as may diversion yield;
And, thanks to Nature, there's no want of those,
For, rain or shine, the thriving coxcomb grows,
Follies to-night we show ne'er lashed before,
Yet such as Nature shows you every hour;
Nor can the pictures give a just offence,
For fools are made for jests to men of sense.

ACT I

Scene i.—*An Inn*

Enter Boniface *running*

Boniface. Chamberlain! maid! Cherry! daughter Cherry! all asleep? all dead?

Enter Cherry *running*

Cherry. Here! here! Why d'ye bawl so, father? d'ye think we have no ears?

Boniface. You deserve to have none, you young minx! The company of the Warrington[2] coach has stood in the hall this hour, and nobody to show them to their chambers.

Cherry. And let 'em wait, father; there's neither redcoat in the coach, nor footman behind it.

Boniface. But they threaten to go to another inn to-night.

Cherry. That they dare not, for fear the coachman should overturn them to-morrow.—Coming! coming!—Here's the London coach arrived.

Enter several People *with trunks, bandboxes, and other luggage, and cross the stage*

Boniface. Welcome, ladies!

Cherry. Very welcome, gentlemen!—Chamberlain, show the Lion and the Rose.[3]

Exit with the company

Enter Aimwell *in riding habit*, Archer *as* Footman *carrying a portmantle*

Boniface. This way, this way, gentlemen!

Aimwell. (*To* Archer) Set down the things; go to the stable, and see my horses well rubbed.

Archer. I shall, sir. *Exit*

Aimwell. You're my landlord, I suppose?

Boniface. Yes, sir; I'm old Will Boniface, pretty well known upon this road, as the saying is.

Aimwell. O Mr. Boniface, your servant!

Boniface. O sir!—What will your honor please to drink, as the saying is.

Aimwell. I have heard your town of Lichfield much famed for ale; I think I'll taste that.

Boniface. Sir, I have now in my cellar ten tun of the best ale in Staffordshire; 'tis smooth as oil, sweet as milk, clear as amber, and strong as brandy; and will be just fourteen year old the fifth day of next March, old style.

Aimwell. You're very exact, I find, in the age of your ale.

Boniface. As punctual, sir, as I am in the age of my children. I'll show you such ale!—Here, tapster, broach number 1706, as the saying is.—Sir, you shall taste my *Anno Domini*.—I have lived in Lichfield, man and boy, above eight-and-fifty years, and, I believe, have not consumed eight-and-fifty ounces of meat.

Aimwell. At a meal, you mean, if one may guess your sense[4] by your bulk.

Boniface. Not in my life, sir. I have fed purely upon ale. I have eat my ale, drank my ale, and I always sleep upon ale.

Enter Tapster *with a bottle and glass,*[5] *and exit*

Now, sir, you shall see!—(*Filling it out*) Your worship's health.—Ha! delicious, delicious! fancy it burgundy, only fancy it, and 'tis worth ten shillings a quart.

Aimwell. (*Drinks*) 'Tis confounded strong!

Boniface. Strong! It must be so, or how should we be strong that drink it?

Aimwell. And have you lived so long upon this ale, landlord?

Boniface. Eight-and-fifty years, upon my credit, sir—but it killed my wife, poor woman, as the saying is.

Aimwell. How came that to pass?

Boniface. I don't know how, sir; she would not let the ale take its natural course, sir; she was for qualifying it every now and then with a dram, as the saying is; and an honest

---

[1] I.e., collecting simples, herbs to compound into home remedies. Cf. Act IV, scene i, p. 498.
[2] On the Mersey near Liverpool.
[3] As in earlier days, the rooms in inns were named.
[4] Your meaning.
[5] Meaning two glasses, as they both drink.

gentleman that came this way from Ireland made her a present of a dozen bottles of usquebaugh—but the poor woman was never well after. But, howe'er, I was obliged to the gentleman, you know.

AIMWELL. Why, was it the usquebaugh that killed her?

BONIFACE. My Lady Bountiful said so. She, good lady, did what could be done; she cured her of three tympanies,[1] but the fourth carried her off. But she's happy, and I'm contented, as the saying is.

AIMWELL. Who's that Lady Bountiful you mentioned?

BONIFACE. Od's my life, sir, we'll drink her health.—(*Drinks*) My Lady Bountiful is one of the best of women. Her last husband, Sir Charles Bountiful, left her worth a thousand pound a year; and, I believe, she lays out one-half on't in charitable uses for the good of her neighbors. She cures rheumatisms, ruptures, and broken shins in men; green sickness, obstructions, and fits of the mother,[2] in women, the king's evil, chincough,[3] and chilblains, in children. In short, she has cured more people in and about Lichfield within ten years than the doctors have killed in twenty; and that's a bold word.

AIMWELL. Has the lady been any other way useful in her generation?

BONIFACE. Yes, sir; she has a daughter by Sir Charles, the finest woman in all our country, and the greatest fortune. She has a son too, by her first husband, Squire Sullen, who married a fine lady from London t'other day; if you please, sir, we'll drink his health.

AIMWELL. What sort of man is he?

BONIFACE. Why, sir, the man's well enough; says little, thinks less, and does—nothing at all, faith. But he's a man of great estate, and values nobody.

AIMWELL. A sportsman, I suppose?

BONIFACE. Yes, sir, he's a man of pleasure; he plays at whisk[4] and smokes his pipe eight-and-forty hours together sometimes.

AIMWELL. And married, you say?

BONIFACE. Ay, and to a curious woman, sir. But he's a—he wants it; here, sir.

(*Pointing to his forehead*)

AIMWELL. He has it there, you mean?

BONIFACE. That's none of my business; he's my landlord, and so a man, you know, would not—But—ecod, he's no better than—Sir, my humble service to you.—(*Drinks*) Though I value not a farthing what he can do to me; I pay him his rent at quarter-day, I have a good running trade, I have but one daughter, and I can give her—but no matter for that.

AIMWELL. You're very happy, Mr. Boniface. Pray, what other company have you in town?

BONIFACE. A power of fine ladies; and then we have the French officers.[5]

AIMWELL. Oh, that's right, you have a good many of those gentlemen. Pray, how do you like their company?

BONIFACE. So well, as the saying is, that I could wish we had as many more of 'em; they're full of money, and pay double for everything they have. They know, sir, that we paid good round taxes for the taking of 'em, and so they are willing to reimburse us a little. One of 'em lodges in my house.

Re-enter ARCHER

ARCHER. Landlord, there are some French gentlemen below that ask for you.

BONIFACE. I'll wait on 'em.—(*Aside to* ARCHER) Does your master stay long in town, as the saying is?

ARCHER. I can't tell, as the saying is.

BONIFACE. Come from London?

ARCHER. No.

BONIFACE. Going to London, mayhap?

ARCHER. No.

BONIFACE. (*Aside*) An odd fellow this.—(*To* AIMWELL) I beg your worship's pardon, I'll wait on you in half a minute.   *Exit*

AIMWELL. The coast's clear, I see.—Now, my dear Archer, welcome to Lichfield.

ARCHER. I thank thee, my dear brother in iniquity.

AIMWELL. Iniquity! prithee, leave canting; you need not change your style with your dress.

ARCHER. Don't mistake me, Aimwell, for 'tis still my maxim, that there is no scandal like rags, nor any crime so shameful as poverty.

AIMWELL. The world confesses it every day in its practice, though men won't own it for

---

[1] *Tympany* was a common equivalent for *tympanites*, distention of the abdomen by gas or air.
[2] Hysterics.
[3] Whooping-cough.
[4] Whist.

[5] Prisoners on parole, taken in Marlborough's campaigns.

their opinion. Who did that worthy lord, my brother, single out of the side-box to sup with him t'other night?

ARCHER. Jack Handycraft, a handsome, well-dressed, mannerly, sharping rogue, who keeps the best company in town.

AIMWELL. Right! And, pray, who married my Lady Manslaughter t'other day, the great fortune?

ARCHER. Why, Nick Marrabone, a professed pickpocket, and a good bowler; but he makes a handsome figure, and rides in his coach, that he formerly used to ride behind.

AIMWELL. But did you observe poor Jack Generous in the Park last week?

ARCHER. Yes, with his autumnal periwig, shading his melancholy face, his coat older than anything but its fashion, with one hand idle in his pocket, and with the other picking his useless teeth; and, though the Mall was crowded with company, yet was poor Jack as single and solitary as a lion in a desert.

AIMWELL. And as much avoided, for no crime upon earth but the want of money.

ARCHER. And that's enough. Men must not be poor; idleness is the root of all evil; the world's wide enough, let 'em bustle. Fortune has taken the weak under her protection, but men of sense are left to their industry.

AIMWELL. Upon which topic we proceed, and I think luckily hitherto. Would not any man swear, now, that I am a man of quality, and you my servant; when if our intrinsic value were known—

ARCHER. Come, come, we are the men of intrinsic value, who can strike our fortunes out of ourselves, whose worth is independent of accidents in life, or revolutions in government; we have heads to get money and hearts to spend it.

AIMWELL. As to our hearts, I grant ye, they are as willing tits as any within twenty degrees; but I can have no great opinion of our heads from the service they have done us hitherto, unless it be that they have brought us from London hither to Lichfield, made me a lord, and you my servant.

ARCHER. That's more than you could expect already. But what money have we left?

AIMWELL. But two hundred pound.

ARCHER. And our horses, clothes, rings, &c.—Why, we have very good fortunes now for moderate people; and, let me tell you besides, that this two hundred pound, with the experience that we are now masters of is a better estate than the ten thousand we have spent. Our friends, indeed, began to suspect that our pockets were low; but we came off with flying colors, showed no signs of want either in word or deed—

AIMWELL. Ay, and our going to Brussels was a good pretence enough for our sudden disappearing; and, I warrant you, our friends imagine that we are gone a-volunteering.

ARCHER. Why, faith, if this prospect fails, it must e'en come to that. I am for venturing one of the hundreds, if you will, upon this knight-errantry; but, in case it should fail, we'll reserve the t'other to carry us to some counterscarp, where we may die, as we lived, in a blaze.

AIMWELL. With all my heart; and we have lived justly, Archer; we can't say that we have spent our fortunes, but that we have enjoyed 'em.

ARCHER. Right! So much pleasure for so much money, we have had our pennyworths; and, had I millions, I would go to the same market again.—Oh London! London!—Well, we have had our share, and let us be thankful: past pleasures, for aught I know, are best, such as we are sure of; those to come may disappoint us.

AIMWELL. It has often grieved the heart of me to see how some inhuman wretches murder their kind fortunes; those that, by sacrificing all to one appetite, shall starve all the rest. You shall have some that live only in their palates, and in their sense of tasting shall drown the other four. Others are only epicures in appearances, such who shall starve their nights to make a figure adays, and famish their own to feed the eyes of others. A contrary sort confine their pleasures to the dark, and contract their spacious acres to the circuit of a muffstring.

ARCHER. Right; but they find the Indies in that spot where they consume 'em. And I think your kind keepers have much the best on't; for they indulge the most senses by one expense. There's the seeing, hearing, and feeling, amply gratified; and some philosophers will tell you that from such a commerce there arises a sixth sense, that gives infinitely more pleasure than the other five put together.

AIMWELL. And to pass to the other extremity, of all keepers I think those the **worst** that keep their money.

ARCHER. Those are the most miserable wights in being: they destroy the rights of nature, and disappoint the blessings of Providence. Give me a man that keeps his five senses keen and bright as his sword; that has 'em always drawn out in their just order and strength, with his reason as commander at the head of 'em; that detaches 'em by turns upon whatever party of pleasure agreeably offers, and commands 'em to retreat upon the least appearance of disadvantage or danger! For my part, I can stick to my bottle while my wine, my company, and my reason, holds good; I can be charmed with Sappho's singing without falling in love with her face; I love hunting, but would not, like Actæon, be eaten up by my own dogs; I love a fine house, but let another keep it; and just so I love a fine woman.

AIMWELL. In that last particular you have the better of me.

ARCHER. Ay, you're such an amorous puppy, that I'm afraid you'll spoil our sport; you can't counterfeit the passion without feeling it.

AIMWELL. Though the whining part be out of doors in town, 'tis still in force with the country ladies: and let me tell you, Frank, the fool in that passion shall outdo the knave at any time.

ARCHER. Well, I won't dispute it now; you command for the day, and so I submit: at Nottingham, you know, I am to be master.

AIMWELL. And at Lincoln, I again.

ARCHER. Then, at Norwich I mount, which, I think shall be our last stage; for, if we fail there, we'll embark for Holland, bid adieu to Venus, and welcome Mars.

AIMWELL. A match!—Mum!

Re-enter BONIFACE

BONIFACE. What will your worship please to have for supper?

AIMWELL. What have you got?

BONIFACE. Sir, we have a delicate piece of beef in the pot, and a pig at the fire.

AIMWELL. Good supper-meat, I must confess. I can't eat beef, landlord.

ARCHER. And I hate pig.

AIMWELL. Hold your prating, sirrah! Do you know who you are?

BONIFACE. Please to bespeak something else; I have everything in the house.

AIMWELL. Have you any veal?

BONIFACE. Veal, sir! We had a delicate loin of veal on Wednesday last.

AIMWELL. Have you got any fish or wildfowl?

BONIFACE. As for fish, truly, sir, we are an inland town and indifferently provided with fish, that's the truth on't; and then for wildfowl—we have a delicate couple of rabbits.

AIMWELL. Get me the rabbits fricasseed.

BONIFACE. Fricasseed! Lard, sir, they'll eat much better smothered with onions.

ARCHER. Psha! damn your onions!

AIMWELL. Again, sirrah!—Well, landlord, what you please. But hold—I have a small charge of money, and your house is so full of strangers, that I believe it may be safer in your custody than mine; for when this fellow of mine gets drunk he minds nothing.— Here, sirrah, reach me the strong-box.

ARCHER. Yes, sir.—(*Aside*) This will give us a reputation. (*Brings the box*)

AIMWELL. Here, landlord; the locks are sealed down both for your security and mine; it holds somewhat above two hundred pound; if you doubt it, I'll count it to you after supper. But be sure you lay it where I may have it at a minute's warning; for my affairs are a little dubious at present; perhaps I may be gone in half an hour, perhaps I may be your guest till the best part of that be spent; and pray order your ostler to keep my horses always saddled. But one thing above the rest I must beg, that you would let this fellow have none of your Anno Domini, as you call it; for he's the most insufferable sot.—Here, sirrah, light me to my chamber.

Exit, lighted by ARCHER

BONIFACE. Cherry! daughter Cherry!

Re-enter CHERRY

CHERRY. D'ye call, father?

BONIFACE. Ay, child, you must lay by this box for the gentleman; 'tis full of money.

CHERRY. Money! all that money! why, sure, father, the gentleman comes to be chosen parliament-man. Who is he?

BONIFACE. I don't know what to make of him; he talks of keeping his horses ready saddled, and of going perhaps at a minute's warning, or staying perhaps till the best part of this be spent.

CHERRY. Ay, ten to one, father, he's a highwayman.

BONIFACE. A highwayman! upon my life,

girl, you have hit it, and this box is some new-purchased booty. Now could we find him out, the money were ours.

CHERRY. He don't belong to our gang.

BONIFACE. What horses have they?

CHERRY. The master rides upon a black.

BONIFACE. A black! ten to one the man upon the black mare! And since he don't belong to our fraternity, we may betray him with a safe conscience; I don't think it lawful to harbor any rogues but my own. Look'ee, child, as the saying is, we must go cunningly to work: proofs we must have. The gentleman's servant loves drink, I'll ply him that way; and ten to one loves a wench—you must work him t'other way.

CHERRY. Father, would you have me give my secret for his?

BONIFACE. Consider, child, there's two hundred pound to boot.—(*Ringing without*) Coming!—coming!—Child, mind your business. *Exit*

CHERRY. What a rogue is my father! My father! I deny it. My mother was a good, generous, free-hearted woman, and I can't tell how far her good-nature might have extended for the good of her children. This landlord of mine, for I think I can call him no more, would betray his guest, and debauch his daughter into the bargain—by a footman too!

Re-enter ARCHER

ARCHER. What footman, pray, mistress, is so happy as to be the subject of your contemplation?

CHERRY. Whoever he is, friend, he'll be but little the better for't.

ARCHER. I hope so, for I'm sure you did not think of me.

CHERRY. Suppose I had?

ARCHER. Why then you're but even with me; for the minute I came in, I was a-considering in what manner I should make love to you.

CHERRY. Love to me, friend!

ARCHER. Yes, child.

CHERRY. Child! manners!—If you kept a little more distance, friend, it would become you much better.

ARCHER. Distance! Good-night, sauce-box.
Going

CHERRY. (*Aside*) A pretty fellow! I like his pride.—Sir, pray, sir, you see, sir, (ARCHER *returns*) I have the credit to be entrusted with your master's fortune here, which sets me a degree above his footman; I hope, sir, you an't affronted?

ARCHER. Let me look you full in the face, and I'll tell you whether you can affront me or no.—'Sdeath, child, you have a pair of delicate eyes, and you don't know what to do with 'em!

CHERRY. Why, sir, don't I see everybody?

ARCHER. Ay, but if some women had 'em, they would kill everybody.—Prithee, instruct me, I would fain make love to you, but I don't know what to say.

CHERRY. Why, did you never make love to anybody before?

ARCHER. Never to a person of your figure, I can assure you, madam. My addresses have been always confined to people within my own sphere; I never aspired as high before. (*Sighs*)

> But you look so bright,[1]
> And are dress'd so tight,
> That a man would swear you're right,
> As arm was e'er laid over.
> Such an air
> You freely wear
> To ensnare,
> As makes each guest a lover!
>
> Since then, my dear, I'm your guest,
> Prithee give me of the best
> Of what is ready drest:
> Since then, my dear, etc.

CHERRY. (*Aside*) What can I think of this man?—Will you give me that song, sir?

ARCHER. Ay, my dear, take it while 'tis warm.—(*Kisses her*) Death and fire! her lips are honeycombs.

CHERRY. And I wish there had been bees too, to have stung you for your impudence.

ARCHER. There's a swarm of Cupids, my little Venus, that has done the business much better.

CHERRY. (*Aside*) This fellow is misbegotten as well as I.—What's your name, sir?

ARCHER. (*Aside*) Name! egad, I have forgot it.—Oh! Martin.

CHERRY. Where were you born?

ARCHER. In St. Martin's parish.

CHERRY. What was your father?

ARCHER. St. Martin's parish.

[1] The first and second editions give only the first two lines of the song.

CHERRY. Then, friend, good night.
ARCHER. I hope not.
CHERRY. You may depend upon't.
ARCHER. Upon what?
CHERRY. That you're very impudent.
ARCHER. That you are very handsome.
CHERRY. That you're a footman.
ARCHER. That you're an angel.
CHERRY. I shall be rude.
ARCHER. So shall I. (*Seizes her hand*)
CHERRY. Let go my hand.
ARCHER. Give me a kiss. (*Kisses her*)
BONIFACE. (*Without*) Cherry! Cherry!
CHERRY. I'mm—my father calls; you plaguy devil, how durst you stop my breath so? Offer to follow me one step, if you dare. *Exit*

ARCHER. A fair challenge, by this light! This is a pretty fair opening of an adventure; but we are knight-errants, and so Fortune be our guide. *Exit*

ACT II

SCENE I.—*A Gallery in* LADY BOUNTIFUL'S *House*

MRS. SULLEN *and* DORINDA, *meeting*

DORINDA. Morrow, my dear sister; are you for church this morning?
MRS. SULLEN. Anywhere to pray; for Heaven alone can help me. But I think Dorinda, there's no form of prayer in the liturgy against bad husbands.
DORINDA. But there's a form of law in Doctors-Commons;[1] and I swear, sister Sullen, rather than see you thus continually discontented, I would advise you to apply to that: for besides the part that I bear in your vexatious broils, as being sister to the husband, and friend to the wife, your example gives me such an impression of matrimony, that I shall be apt to condemn my person to a long vacation all its life. But supposing, madam, that you brought it to a case of separation, what can you urge against your husband? My brother is, first, the most constant man alive.
MRS. SULLEN. The most constant husband, I grant ye.
DORINDA. He never sleeps from you.
MRS. SULLEN. No; he always sleeps with me.

DORINDA. He allows you a maintenance suitable to your quality.
MRS. SULLEN. A maintenance! do you take me, madam, for a hospital child, that I must sit down, and bless my benefactors for meat, drink, and clothes? As I take it, madam, I brought your brother ten thousand pounds, out of which I might expect some pretty things, called pleasures.
DORINDA. You share in all the pleasures that the country affords.
MRS. SULLEN. Country pleasures! racks and torments! Dost think, child, that my limbs were made for leaping of ditches, and clambering over stiles? or that my parents, wisely foreseeing my future happiness in country pleasures, had early instructed me in the rural accomplishments of drinking fat ale, playing at whisk, and smoking tobacco with my husband? or of spreading of plasters, brewing of diet-drinks, and stilling rosemary-water, with the good old gentlewoman my mother-in-law?
DORINDA. I'm sorry, madam, that it is not more in our power to divert you; I could wish, indeed, that our entertainments were a little more polite, or your taste a little less refined. But, pray, madam, how came the poets and philosophers, that labored so much in hunting after pleasure, to place it at last in a country life?
MRS. SULLEN. Because they wanted money, child, to find out the pleasures of the town. Did you ever see a poet or philosopher worth ten thousand pound? If you can show me such a man, I'll lay you fifty pound you'll find him somewhere within the weekly bills.[2] Not that I disapprove rural pleasures, as the poets have painted them; in their landscape, every Phillis has her Corydon, every murmuring stream, and every flowery mead, gives fresh alarms to love. Besides, you'll find that their couples were never married.—But yonder I see my Corydon, and a sweet swain it is, Heaven knows! Come, Dorinda, don't be angry; he's my husband, and your brother; and between both, is he not a sad brute?
DORINDA. I have nothing to say to your part of him—you're the best judge.
MRS. SULLEN. O sister, sister! if ever you marry, beware of a sullen, silent sot, one that's always musing, but never thinks.

---

[1] The ecclesiastical court, which tried cases of marriage and divorce.

[2] The Bills of Mortality for the city of London recorded births and deaths weekly.

There's some diversion in a talking blockhead; and since a woman must wear chains, I would have the pleasure of hearing 'em rattle a little. Now you shall see—but take this by the way: he came home this morning at his usual hour of four, wakened me out of a sweet dream of something else, by tumbling over the tea-table, which he broke all to pieces; after his man and he had rolled about the room, like sick passengers in a storm, he comes flounce into bed, dead as a salmon into a fishmonger's basket; his feet cold as ice, his breath hot as a furnace, and his hands and his face as greasy as his flannel nightcap. O matrimony! He tosses up the clothes with a barbarous swing over his shoulders, disorders the whole economy of my bed, leaves me half naked, and my whole night's comfort is the tuneable serenade of that wakeful nightingale, his nose! Oh, the pleasure of counting the melancholy clock by a snoring husband! But now, sister, you shall see how handsomely, being a well-bred man, he will beg my pardon.

Enter SULLEN

SQUIRE SULLEN. My head aches consumedly.
MRS. SULLEN. Will you be pleased, my dear, to drink tea with us this morning? It may do your head good.
SQUIRE SULLEN. No.
DORINDA. Coffee, brother?
SQUIRE SULLEN. Pshaw!
MRS. SULLEN. Will you please to dress, and go to church with me? The air may help you.
SQUIRE SULLEN. Scrub!

Enter SCRUB

SCRUB. Sir!
SQUIRE SULLEN. What day o' th'week is this?
SCRUB. Sunday, an't please your worship.
SQUIRE SULLEN. Sunday! Bring me a dram; and d'ye hear, set out the venison-pasty, and a tankard of strong beer upon the hall-table; I'll go to breakfast. (*Going*)
DORINDA. Stay, stay, brother, you shan't get off so; you were very naughty last night, and must make your wife reparation; come, come, brother, won't you ask pardon?
SQUIRE SULLEN. For what?
DORINDA. For being drunk last night.
SQUIRE SULLEN. I can afford it, can't I?
MRS. SULLEN. But I can't, sir.

SQUIRE SULLEN. Then you may let it alone.
MRS. SULLEN. But I must tell you, sir, that this is not to be borne.
SQUIRE SULLEN. I'm glad on't.
MRS. SULLEN. What is the reason, sir, that you use me thus inhumanly?
SQUIRE SULLEN. Scrub!
SCRUB. Sir!
SQUIRE SULLEN. Get things ready to shave my head.

Exit, SCRUB *following*

MRS. SULLEN. Have a care of coming near his temples, Scrub, for fear you meet something there that may turn the edge of your razor.—Inveterate stupidity! Did you ever know so hard, so obstinate, a spleen as his? O sister, sister! I shall never ha' good of the beast till I get him to town; London, dear London, is the place for managing and breaking a husband.
DORINDA. And has not a husband the same opportunities there for humbling a wife?
MRS. SULLEN. No, no, child; 'tis a standing maxim in conjugal discipline, that when a man would enslave his wife, he hurries her into the country; and when a lady would be arbitrary with her husband, she wheedles her booby up to town.—A man dare not play the tyrant in London, because there are so many examples to encourage the subject to rebel. O Dorinda! Dorinda! a fine woman may do anything in London: o' my conscience, she may raise an army of forty thousand men.
DORINDA. I fancy, sister, you have a mind to be trying your power that way here in Lichfield; you have drawn the French count to your colors already.
MRS. SULLEN. The French are a people that can't live without their gallantries.
DORINDA. And some English that I know, sister, are not averse to such amusements.
MRS. SULLEN. Well, sister, since the truth must out, it may do as well now as hereafter: I think one way to rouse my lethargic, sottish husband is to give him a rival. Security begets negligence in all people, and men must be alarmed to make 'em alert in their duty. Women are like pictures, of no value in the hands of a fool, till he hears men of sense bid high for the purchase.
DORINDA. This might do, sister, if my brother's understanding were to be convinced into a passion for you; but I fancy, there's a natural aversion of his side; and I fancy,

sister, that you don't come much behind him, if you dealt fairly.

Mrs. Sullen. I own it, we are united contradictions, fire and water: but I could be contented, with a great many other wives, to humor the censorious mob, and give the world an appearance of living well with my husband, could I bring him but to dissemble a little kindness to keep me in countenance.

Dorinda. But how do you know, sister, but that, instead of rousing your husband by this artifice to a counterfeit kindness, he should awake in a real fury?

Mrs. Sullen. Let him: if I can't entice him to the one, I would provoke him to the other.

Dorinda. But how must I behave myself between ye?

Mrs. Sullen. You must assist me.

Dorinda. What, against my own brother?

Mrs. Sullen. He's but half a brother, and I'm your entire friend. If I go a step beyond the bounds of honor, leave me; till then, I expect you should go along with me in everything; while I trust my honor in your hands, you must trust your brother's in mine. The count is to dine here to-day.

Dorinda. 'Tis a strange thing, sister, that I can't like that man.

Mrs. Sullen. You like nothing; your time is not come; love and death have their fatalities, and strike home one time or other. You'll pay for all one day, I warrant ye. But come, my lady's tea is ready, and 'tis almost church time. *Exeunt*

Scene II.—*The Inn*

Enter Aimwell *dressed, and* Archer

Aimwell. And was she the daughter of the house?

Archer. The landlord is so blind as to think so; but I dare swear she has better blood in her veins.

Aimwell. Why dost think so?

Archer. Because the baggage has a pert *je ne sais quoi;* she reads plays, keeps a monkey, and is troubled with vapors.

Aimwell. By which discoveries I guess that you know more of her.

Archer. Not yet, faith; the lady gives herself airs; forsooth, nothing under a gentleman!

Aimwell. Let me take her in hand.

Archer. Say one word more o'that, and I'll declare myself, spoil your sport there, and everywhere else; look ye, Aimwell, every man in his own sphere.

Aimwell. Right; and therefore you must pimp for your master.

Archer. In the usual forms, good sir—after I have served myself.—But to our business. You are so well dressed, Tom, and make so handsome a figure, that I fancy you may do execution in a country church; the exterior part strikes first, and you're in the right to make that impression favorable.

Aimwell. There's something in that which may turn to advantage. The appearance of a stranger in a country church draws as many gazers as a blazing star; no sooner he comes into the cathedral, but a train of whispers runs buzzing round the congregation in a moment: Who is he? Whence comes he? Do you know him? Then I, sir, tips me the verger with half-a-crown; he pockets the simony, and inducts me into the best pew in the church. I pull out my snuff-box, turn myself round, bow to the bishop or the dean, if he be the commanding officer; single out a beauty, rivet both my eyes to hers, set my nose a-bleeding by the strength of imagination, and show the whole church my concern, by my endeavoring to hide it. After the sermon, the whole town gives me to her for a lover; and by persuading the lady that I am a-dying for her, the tables are turned, and she in good earnest falls in love with me.

Archer. There's nothing in this, Tom, without a precedent; but instead of riveting your eyes to a beauty, try and fix 'em upon a fortune; that's our business at present.

Aimwell. Psha! no woman can be a beauty without a fortune. Let me alone, for I am a marksman.

Archer. Tom!

Aimwell. Ay.

Archer. When were you at church before, pray?

Aimwell. Um—I was there at the coronation.

Archer. And how can you expect a blessing by going to church now?

Aimwell. Blessing! nay, Frank, I ask but for a wife. *Exit*

Archer. Truly, the man is not very unreasonable in his demands.

Exit at the opposite door

Enter BONIFACE *and* CHERRY

BONIFACE. Well, daughter, as the saying is, have you brought Martin to confess?

CHERRY. Pray, father, don't put me upon getting anything out of a man; I'm but young, you know, father, and I don't understand wheedling.

BONIFACE. Young! why, you jade, as the saying is, can any woman wheedle that is not young? Your mother was useless at five-and-twenty. Not wheedle! would you make your mother a whore, and me a cuckold, as the saying is? I tell you, his silence confesses it; and his master spends his money so freely, and is so much a gentleman every manner of way, that he must be a highwayman.

Enter GIBBET, *in a cloak*

GIBBET. Landlord, landlord, is the coast clear?

BONIFACE. O Mr. Gibbet, what's the news?

GIBBET. No matter, ask no questions, all fair and honorable.—Here, my dear Cherry.—(*Gives her a bag*) Two hundred sterling pounds, as good as any that ever hanged or saved a rogue; lay 'em by with the rest; and here—three wedding or mourning rings, 'tis much the same, you know—here, two silver-hilted swords; I took those from fellows that never show any part of their swords but the hilts—here is a diamond necklace which the lady hid in the privatest place in the coach, but I found it out—this gold watch I took from a pawn-broker's wife; it was left in her hands by a person of quality, there's the arms upon the case.

CHERRY. But who had you the money from?

GIBBET. Ah! poor woman! I pitied her;—from a poor lady just eloped from her husband. She had made up her cargo, and was bound for Ireland, as hard as she could drive; she told me of her husband's barbarous usage, and so I left her half-a-crown. But I had almost forgot, my dear Cherry, I have a present for you.

CHERRY. What is't?

GIBBET. A pot of ceruse, my child, that I took out of a lady's under-pocket.

CHERRY. What, Mr. Gibbet, do you think that I paint?

GIBBET. Why, you jade, your betters do; I'm sure the lady that I took it from had a coronet upon her handkerchief. Here, take my cloak, and go, secure the premises.

CHERRY. I will secure 'em. *Exit*

BONIFACE. But, heark'ee, where's Hounslow and Bagshot?[1]

GIBBET. They'll be here to-night.

BONIFACE. D'ye know of any other gentlemen o' the pad on this road?

GIBBET. No.

BONIFACE. I fancy that I have two that lodge in the house just now.

GIBBET. The devil! How d'ye smoke 'em?

BONIFACE. Why, the one is gone to church.

GIBBET. That's suspicious, I must confess.

BONIFACE. And the other is now in his master's chamber; he pretends to be servant to the other. We'll call him out and pump him a little.

GIBBET. With all my heart.

BONIFACE. Mr. Martin! Mr. Martin!

Enter ARCHER, *combing a periwig and singing*

GIBBET. The roads are consumed deep, I'm as dirty as old Brentford[2] at Christmas.—A good pretty fellow that. Whose servant are you, friend?

ARCHER. My master's.

GIBBET. Really!

ARCHER. Really.

GIBBET. That's much.—The fellow has been at the bar, by his evasions.—But, pray, sir, what is your master's name?

ARCHER. Tall, all, dall!—(*Sings and combs the periwig*) This is the most obstinate curl—

GIBBET. I ask you his name?

ARCHER. Name, sir—*tall, all, dall!*—I never asked him his name in my life.—*Tall, all, dall!*

BONIFACE. What think you now? (*Aside to* GIBBET)

GIBBET. (*Aside to* BONIFACE) Plain, plain; he talks now as if he were before a judge.—(*To* ARCHER) But, pray, friend, which way does your master travel?

ARCHER. A-horseback.

GIBBET. (*Aside*) Very well again, an old offender, right.—(*To* ARCHER) But, I mean, does he go upwards or downwards?

ARCHER. Downwards, I fear, sir.—*Tall, all!*

GIBBET. I'm afraid my fate will be a contrary way.

---

[1] The names of two heaths near London famous as haunts of highwaymen.
[2] Brentford, a market town in Middlesex, was frequently referred to as a dirty place.

BONIFACE. Ha, ha, ha! Mr. Martin, you're very arch. This gentleman is only travelling towards Chester, and would be glad of your company, that's all.—Come, Captain, you'll stay to-night, I suppose? I'll show you a chamber—come, Captain.

GIBBET. Farewell, friend!

Exit [with BONIFACE]

ARCHER. Captain, your servant.—Captain! a pretty fellow! 'Sdeath, I wonder that the officers of the army don't conspire to beat all scoundrels in red but their own.

Enter CHERRY

CHERRY. (*Aside*) Gone! and Martin here! I hope he did not listen; I would have the merit of the discovery all my own, because I would oblige him to love me.—(*Aloud*) Mr. Martin, who was that man with my father?

ARCHER. Some recruiting sergeant, or whipped-out trooper, I suppose.

CHERRY. (*Aside*) All's safe, I find.

ARCHER. Come, my dear, have you conned over the catechise I taught you last night?

CHERRY. Come, question me.

ARCHER. What is love?

CHERRY. Love is I know not what, it comes I know not how, and goes I know not when.

ARCHER. Very well, an apt scholar.—(*Chucks her under the chin*) Where does love enter?

CHERRY. Into the eyes.

ARCHER. And where go out?

CHERRY. I won't tell ye.

ARCHER. What are the objects of that passion?

CHERRY. Youth, beauty, and clean linen.

ARCHER. The reason?

CHERRY. The two first are fashionable in nature, and the third at court.

ARCHER. That's my dear.—What are the signs and tokens of that passion?

CHERRY. A stealing look, a stammering tongue, words improbable, designs impossible, and actions impracticable.

ARCHER. That's my good child, kiss me.—What must a lover do to obtain his mistress?

CHERRY. He must adore the person that disdains him, he must bribe the chambermaid that betrays him, and court the footman that laughs at him. He must—he must—

ARCHER. Nay, child, I must whip you if you don't mind your lesson; he must treat his—

CHERRY. O ay!—he must treat his enemies with respect, his friends with indifference, and all the world with contempt; he must suffer much, and fear more; he must desire much, and hope little; in short, he must embrace his ruin, and throw himself away.

ARCHER. Had ever man so hopeful a pupil as mine!—Come, my dear, why is Love called a riddle?

CHERRY. Because, being blind, he leads those that see, and, though a child, he governs a man.

ARCHER. Mighty well!—And why is Love pictured blind?

CHERRY. Because the painters out of the weakness or privilege of their art chose to hide those eyes that they could not draw.

ARCHER. That's my dear little scholar, kiss me again.—And why should Love, that's a child, govern a man?

CHERRY. Because that a child is the end of love.

ARCHER. And so ends Love's catechism.—And now, my dear, we'll go in and make my master's bed.

CHERRY. Hold, hold, Mr. Martin! You have taken a great deal of pains to instruct me, and, what d'ye think I have learned by it?

ARCHER. What?

CHERRY. That your discourse and your habit are contradictions, and it would be nonsense in me to believe you a footman any longer.

ARCHER. 'Oons, what a witch it is!

CHERRY. Depend upon this, sir, nothing in this garb shall ever tempt me; for, though I was born to servitude, I hate it. Own your condition, swear you love me, and then—

ARCHER. And then we shall go make the bed?

CHERRY. Yes.

ARCHER. You must know then, that I am born a gentleman, my education was liberal; but I went to London, a younger brother, fell into the hands of sharpers, who stripped me of my money, my friends disowned me, and now my necessity brings me to what you see.

CHERRY. Then take my hand—promise to marry me before you sleep, and I'll make you master of two thousand pounds.

ARCHER. How!

CHERRY. Two thousand pounds that I have this minute in my own custody; so, throw off your livery this instant, and I'll go find a parson.

ARCHER. What said you? a parson!

CHERRY. What! do you scruple?

ARCHER. Scruple! no, no, but—Two thousand pound, you say?

CHERRY. And better.

ARCHER. (*Aside*) 'Sdeath, what shall I do?—But heark'ee, child, what need you make me master of yourself and money, when you may have the same pleasure out of me, and still keep your fortune in your hands.

CHERRY. Then you won't marry me?

ARCHER. I would marry you, but—

CHERRY. O, sweet sir, I'm your humble servant, you're fairly caught! Would you persuade me that any gentleman who could bear the scandal of wearing a livery would refuse two thousand pound, let the condition be what it would? No, no, sir. But I hope you'll pardon the freedom I have taken, since it was only to inform myself of the respect that I ought to pay you.

ARCHER. (*Aside*) Fairly bit, by Jupiter!—Hold! hold!—And have you actually two thousand pounds?

CHERRY. Sir, I have my secrets as well as you; when you please to be more open I shall be more free; and be assured that I have discoveries that will match yours, be what they will. In the meanwhile, be satisfied that no discovery I make shall ever hurt you; but beware of my father!   *Exit*

ARCHER. So! we're like to have as many adventures in our inn as Don Quixote[1] had in his. Let me see—two thousand pounds!—If the wench would promise to die when the money were spent, egad, one would marry her; but the fortune may go off in a year or two, and the wife may live—Lord knows how long. Then an innkeeper's daughter; ay, that's the devil—there my pride brings me off.

For whatsoe'er the sages charge on pride,
The angels' fall, and twenty faults beside,
On earth, I'm sure, 'mong us of mortal call-
    ing,
Pride saves man oft, and woman too, from
    falling.   *Exit*

[1] See *Don Quixote*, **Part I.** Book I, chapters ii and iii.

ACT III

SCENE I.—*The Gallery in* LADY BOUNTIFUL'S *House*

Enter MRS. SULLEN *and* DORINDA

MRS. SULLEN. Ha, ha, ha! my dear sister, let me embrace thee! Now we are friends indeed; for I shall have a secret of yours as a pledge for mine—now you'll be good for something, I shall have you conversable in the subjects of the sex.

DORINDA. But do you think that I am so weak as to fall in love with a fellow at first sight?

MRS. SULLEN. Psha! now you spoil all; why should not we be as free in our friendships as the men? I warrant you the gentleman has got to his confidant already, has avowed his passion, toasted your health, called you ten thousand angels, has run over your lips, eyes, neck, shape, air, and everything in the description that warms their mirth to a second enjoyment.

DORINDA. Your hand, sister, I an't well.

MRS. SULLEN. So—she's breeding already! Come, child, up with it—hem a little—so—now tell me, don't you like the gentleman that we saw at church just now?

DORINDA. The man's well enough.

MRS. SULLEN. Well enough! is he not a demigod, a Narcissus, a star, the man i'the moon?

DORINDA. O sister, I'm extremely ill!

MRS. SULLEN. Shall I send to your mother, child, for a little of her cephalic plaster to put to the soles of your feet, or shall I send to the gentleman for something for you? Come, unlace your stays, unbosom yourself. The man is perfectly a pretty fellow, I saw him when he first came into church.

DORINDA. I saw him too, sister, and with an air that shone, methought, like rays about his person.

MRS. SULLEN. Well said, up with it!

DORINDA. No forward coquette behavior, no airs to set him off, no studied looks nor artful posture,—but nature did it all—

MRS. SULLEN. Better and better!—one touch more—come!

DORINDA. But then his looks—did you observe his eyes?

MRS. SULLEN. Yes, yes, I did—his eyes—well, what of his eyes?

DORINDA. Sprightly, but not wandering;

they seemed to view, but never gazed on anything but me.—And then his looks so humble were, and yet so noble, that they aimed to tell me that he could with pride die at my feet, though he scorned slavery anywhere else.

MRS. SULLEN. The physic works purely!—How d'ye find yourself now, my dear?

DORINDA. Hem! much better, my dear.—Oh, here comes our Mercury! (*Enter* SCRUB) Well Scrub, what news of the gentleman?

SCRUB. Madam, I have brought you a packet of news.

DORINDA. Open it quickly, come.

SCRUB. In the first place I inquired who the gentleman was; they told me he was a stranger. Secondly, I asked what the gentleman was; they answered and said, that they never saw him before. Thirdly, I inquired what countryman he was; they replied, 'twas more than they knew. Fourthly, I demanded whence he came; their answer was, they could not tell. And fifthly, I asked whither he went; and they replied, they knew nothing of the matter,—and this is all I could learn.

MRS. SULLEN. But what do the people say? Can't they guess?

SCRUB. Why, some think he's a spy, some guess he's a mountebank, some say one thing, some another; but for my own part, I believe he's a Jesuit.[1]

DORINDA. A Jesuit! Why a Jesuit?

SCRUB. Because he keeps his horses always ready saddled, and his footman talks French.

MRS. SULLEN. His footman!

SCRUB. Ay, he and the Count's footman were gabbering French like two intriguing ducks in a mill-pond; and I believe they talked of me, for they laughed consumedly.

DORINDA. What sort of livery has the footman?

SCRUB. Livery! Lord, madam, I took him for a captain, he's so bedizened with lace! And then he had tops on his shoes up to his mid leg, a silver-headed cane dangling at his knuckles; he carries his hands in his pockets just so—(*Walks in the French air*) and has a fine long periwig tied up in a bag.—Lord, madam, he's clear another sort of man than I!

MRS. SULLEN. That may easily be.—But what shall we do now, sister?

DORINDA. I have it—this fellow has a world of simplicity, and some cunning; the first hides the latter by abundance.—Scrub!

SCRUB. Madam!

DORINDA. We have a great mind to know who this gentleman is, only for our satisfaction.

SCRUB. Yes, madam, it would be a satisfaction no doubt.

DORINDA. You must go and get acquainted with his footman, and invite him hither to drink a bottle of your ale, because you're butler to-day.

SCRUB. Yes, madam, I am butler every Sunday.

MRS. SULLEN. O brave! Sister, o' my conscience, you understand the mathematics already. 'Tis the best plot in the world; your mother, you know, will be gone to church, my spouse will be got to the ale-house with his scoundrels, and the house will be our own—so we drop in by accident, and ask the fellow some questions ourselves. In the country, you know, any stranger is company, and we're glad to take up with the butler in a country dance, and happy if he'll do us the favor.

SCRUB. O madam, you wrong me! I never refused your ladyship the favor in my life.

Enter GIPSY

GIPSY. Ladies, dinner's upon table.

DORINDA. Scrub, we'll excuse your waiting—go where we ordered you.

SCRUB. I shall. *Exeunt*

SCENE II.—*The Inn*

Enter AIMWELL *and* ARCHER

ARCHER. Well, Tom, I find you're a marksman.

AIMWELL. A marksman! who so blind could be, as not discern a swan among the ravens?

ARCHER. Well, but hark'ee, Aimwell—

AIMWELL. Aimwell! call me Oroondates, Cesario,[2] Amadis[3] all that romance can in a lover paint, and then I'll answer. O Archer! I read her thousands in her looks, she looked like Ceres in her harvest: corn, wine and oil, milk and honey, gardens, groves, and purling streams, played on her plenteous face.

---

[1] Jesuits were suspected at this time of being in the service of the Pretender, plotting against the Hanoverian succession.

[2] Characters in La Calprenède's *Cassandra* and *Cléopâtre*.

[3] Amadis of Gaul, hero of the Spanish romance.

ARCHER. Her face! her pocket, you mean; the corn, wine and oil, lies there. In short, she has ten thousand pound, that's the English on't.

AIMWELL. Her eyes—

ARCHER. Are demi-cannons, to be sure; so I won't stand their battery. (*Going*)

AIMWELL. Pray excuse me, my passion must have vent.

ARCHER. Passion! what a plague, d'ye think these romantic airs will do our business? Were my temper as extravagant as yours, my adventures have something more romantic by half.

AIMWELL. Your adventures!

ARCHER. Yes,

The nymph that with her twice ten hundred pounds,
With brazen engine hot, and quoif clear starched,
Can fire the guest in warming of the bed—

There's a touch of sublime Milton for you, and the subject but an inn-keeper's daughter! I can play with a girl as an angler does with his fish; he keeps it at the end of his line, runs it up the stream, and down the stream, till at last he brings it to hand, tickles the trout, and so whips it into his basket.

Enter BONIFACE

BONIFACE. Mr. Martin, as the saying is— yonder's an honest fellow below, my Lady Bountiful's butler, who begs the honor that you would go home with him and see his cellar.

ARCHER. Do my baise-mains to the gentleman, and tell him I will do myself the honor to wait on him immediately. *Exit* BONIFACE

AIMWELL. What do I hear? Soft Orpheus play, and fair Toftida[1] sing!

ARCHER. Psha! damn your raptures; I tell you, here's a pump going to be put into the vessel, and the ship will get into harbor, my life on't. You say, there's another lady very handsome there?

AIMWELL. Yes, faith.

ARCHER. I'm in love with her already.

AIMWELL. Can't you give me a bill upon Cherry in the meantime?

ARCHER. No, no, friend, all her corn, wine and oil, is ingrossed to my market. And once more I warn you to keep your anchorage clear of mine; for if you fall foul of me, by this light you shall go to the bottom! What, make prize of my little frigate, while I am upon the cruise for you!—

AIMWELL. Well, well, I won't.—(*Exit* ARCHER. *Enter* BONIFACE) Landlord, have you any tolerable company in the house? I don't care for dining alone.

BONIFACE. Yes, sir, there's a captain below, as the saying is, that arrived about an hour ago.

AIMWELL. Gentlemen of his coat are welcome everywhere; will you make him a compliment from me, and tell him I should be glad of his company?

BONIFACE. Who shall I tell him, sir, would—

AIMWELL. (*Aside*) Ha! that stroke was well thrown in!—(*Aloud*) I'm only a traveller like himself, and would be glad of his company, that's all.

BONIFACE. I obey your commands, as the saying is. *Exit*

Enter ARCHER

ARCHER. 'Sdeath! I had forgot: what title will you give yourself?

AIMWELL. My brother's, to be sure; he would never give me anything else, so I'll make bold with his honor this bout!—You know the rest of your cue.

ARCHER. Ay, ay. *Exit*

Enter GIBBET

GIBBET. Sir, I'm yours.

AIMWELL. 'Tis more than I deserve, sir, for I don't know you.

GIBBET. I don't wonder at that, sir, for you never saw me before.—(*Aside*) I hope.

AIMWELL. And pray, sir, how came I by the honor of seeing you now?

GIBBET. Sir, I scorn to intrude upon any gentleman—but my landlord—

AIMWELL. O sir, I ask your pardon; you're the captain he told me of?

GIBBET. At your service, sir.

AIMWELL. What regiment, may I be so bold?

GIBBET. A marching regiment, sir, an old corps.

AIMWELL. (*Aside*) Very old, if your coat be regimental.—You have served abroad, sir?

GIBBET. Yes, sir, in the plantations; 'twas my lot to be sent into the worst service. I would have quitted it indeed, but a man of honor, you know—Besides, 'twas for the good

---

[1] Katherine Tofts, a well-known opera singer. Pope wrote an epigram upon her.

of my country that I should be abroad:—anything for the good of one's country—I'm a Roman for that.

AIMWELL. (*Aside*) One of the first, I'll lay my life.—You found the West Indies very hot, sir?

GIBBET. Ay, sir, too hot for me.

AIMWELL. Pray, sir, han't I seen your face at Will's coffeehouse?

GIBBET. Yes, sir, and at White's too.

AIMWELL. And where is your company now, Captain?

GIBBET. They an't come yet.

AIMWELL. Why, d'ye expect 'em here?

GIBBET. They'll be here to-night, sir.

AIMWELL. Which way do they march?

GIBBET. Across the country.—(*Aside*) The devil's in't, if I han't said enough to encourage him to declare! But I'm afraid he's not right, I must tack about.

AIMWELL. Is your company to quarter in Lichfield?

GIBBET. In this house, sir.

AIMWELL. What! all?

GIBBET. My company's but thin, ha, ha, ha! we are but three, ha, ha, ha!

AIMWELL. You're merry, sir.

GIBBET. Ay, sir, you must excuse me, sir, I understand the world, especially the art of travelling: I don't care, sir, for answering questions directly upon the road—for I generally ride with a charge about me.

AIMWELL. (*Aside*) Three or four, I believe.

GIBBET. I am credibly informed there are highwaymen upon this quarter. Not, sir, that I could suspect a gentleman of your figure—but truly, sir, I have got such a way of evasion upon the road, that I don't care for speaking truth to any man.

AIMWELL. Your caution may be necessary.—Then I presume you're no captain?

GIBBET. Not I, sir. Captain is a good travelling name, and so I take it; it stops a great many foolish inquiries that are generally made about gentlemen that travel, it gives a man an air of something, and makes the drawers obedient:—and thus far I am a captain, and no farther.

AIMWELL. And pray, sir, what is your true profession?

GIBBET. O sir, you must excuse me!—upon my word, sir, I don't think it safe to tell you.

AIMWELL. Ha, ha, ha! upon my word, I commend you. (*Enter* BONIFACE) Well, Mr. Boniface, what's the news?

BONIFACE. There's another gentleman below, as the saying is, that hearing you were but two, would be glad to make the third man, if you would give him leave.

AIMWELL. What is he?

BONIFACE. A clergyman, as the saying is.

AIMWELL. A clergyman! Is he really a clergyman? or is it only his travelling name, as my friend the captain has it?

BONIFACE. O sir, he's a priest, and chaplain to the French officers in town.

AIMWELL. Is he a Frenchman?

BONIFACE. Yes, sir, born at Brussels.

GIBBET. A Frenchman, and a priest! I won't be seen in his company, sir; I have a value for my reputation, sir.

AIMWELL. Nay, but, Captain, since we are by ourselves—Can he speak English, landlord?

BONIFACE. Very well, sir; you may know him, as the saying is, to be a foreigner by his accent, and that's all.

AIMWELL. Then he has been in England before?

BONIFACE. Never, sir; but he's master of languages, as the saying is; he talks Latin—It does me good to hear him talk Latin.

AIMWELL. Then you understand Latin, Mr. Boniface?

BONIFACE. Not I, sir, as the saying is; but he talks it so very fast, that I'm sure it must be good.

AIMWELL. Pray, desire him to walk up.

BONIFACE. Here he is, as the saying is.

Enter FOIGARD

FOIGARD. Save you, gentlemens, both.

AIMWELL. (*Aside*) A Frenchman!—(*To* FOIGARD) Sir, your most humble servant.

FOIGARD. Och, dear joy,[1] I am your most faithful shervant, and yours alsho.

GIBBET. Doctor, you talk very good English, but you have a mighty twang of the foreigner.

FOIGARD. My English is very vell for the vords, but we foreigners, you know, cannot bring our tongues about the pronunciation so soon.

AIMWELL. (*Aside*) A Foreigner! a downright Teague, by this light!—Were you born in France, doctor?

[1] An Irish expression. Foigard's foreign accent is unmistakably Irish.

FOIGARD. I was educated in France, but I was borned at Brussels; I am a subject of the King of Spain, joy.

GIBBET. What King of Spain, sir? Speak![1]

FOIGARD. Upon my shoul, joy, I cannot tell you as yet.

AIMWELL. Nay, Captain, that was too hard upon the doctor; he's a stranger.

FOIGARD. Oh, let him alone, dear joy, I am of a nation that is not easily put out of countenance.

AIMWELL. Come, gentlemen, I'll end the dispute.—Here, landlord, is dinner ready?

BONIFACE. Upon the table, as the saying is.

AIMWELL. Gentlemen—pray—that door—

FOIGARD. No, no, fait, the captain must lead.

AIMWELL. No, doctor, the church is our guide.

GIBBET. Ay, ay, so it is—

Exit foremost, they follow

SCENE III.—*The Gallery in* LADY BOUNTIFUL'S *House*

Enter ARCHER *and* SCRUB *singing, and hugging one another,* SCRUB *with a tankard in his hand.* GIPSY *listening at a distance*

SCRUB. *Tall, all, dall!*—Come, my dear boy, let's have that song once more.

ARCHER. No, no, we shall disturb the family.—But will you be sure to keep the secret?

SCRUB. Pho! upon my honor, as I'm a gentleman.

ARCHER. 'Tis enough. You must know then, that my master is the Lord Viscount Aimwell; he fought a duel t'other day in London, wounded his man so dangerously, that he thinks fit to withdraw till he hears whether the gentleman's wounds be mortal or not. He never was in this part of England before, so he chose to retire to this place— that's all.

GIPSY. (*Aside*) And that's enough for me.
Exit

SCRUB. And where were you when your master fought?

ARCHER. We never know of our masters' quarrels.

SCRUB. No! If our masters in the country here receive a challenge, the first thing they do is to tell their wives; the wife tells the servants, the servants alarm the tenants, and in half an hour you shall have the whole country in arms.

ARCHER. To hinder two men from doing what they have no mind for.—But if you should chance to talk now of my business?

SCRUB. Talk! ay, sir, had I not learned the knack of holding my tongue, I had never lived so long in a great family.

ARCHER. Ay, ay, to be sure there are secrets in all families.

SCRUB. Secrets! ay;—but I'll say no more. Come, sit down, we'll make an end of our tankard: here—(*Gives* ARCHER *the tankard*)

ARCHER. With all my heart; who knows but you and I may come to be better acquainted, eh? Here's your ladies' healths; you have three, I think, and to be sure there must be secrets among 'em.

SCRUB. Secrets! ay, friend.—I wish I had a friend—

ARCHER. Am not I your friend? Come, you and I will be sworn brothers.

SCRUB. Shall we?

ARCHER. From this minute. Give me a kiss: —and now, brother Scrub—

SCRUB. And now, brother Martin, I will tell you a secret that will make your hair stand on end. You must know that I am consumedly in love.

ARCHER. That's a terrible secret, that's the truth on't.

SCRUB. That jade, Gipsy, that was with us just now in the cellar, is the arrantest whore that ever wore a petticoat; and I'm dying for love of her.

ARCHER. Ha, ha, ha!—Are you in love with her person or her virtue, brother Scrub?

SCRUB. I should like virtue best, because it is more durable than beauty; for virtue holds good with some women long, and many a day after they have lost it.

ARCHER. In the country, I grant ye, where no woman's virtue is lost till a bastard be found.

SCRUB. Ay, could I bring her to a bastard, I should have her all to myself; but I dare not put it upon that lay, for fear of being sent for a soldier. Pray, brother, how do you gentlemen in London like that same Pressing Act?

ARCHER. Very ill, brother Scrub; 'tis the worst that ever was made for us. **Formerly**

---

[1] The Spanish succession was unsettled until the Treaty of Utrecht in 1713.

I remember the good days, when we could dun our masters for our wages, and if they refused to pay us, we could have a warrant to carry 'em before a justice: but now if we talk of eating, they have a warrant for us, and carry us before three justices.

Scrub. And to be sure we go, if we talk of eating; for the justices won't give their own servants a bad example. Now this is my misfortune—I dare not speak in the house, while that jade Gipsy dings about like a fury.—Once I had the better end of the staff.

Archer. And how comes the change now?

Scrub. Why, the mother of all this mischief is a priest!

Archer. A priest!

Scrub. Ay, a damned son of a whore of Babylon, that came over hither to say grace to the French officers, and eat up our provisions. There's not a day goes over his head without dinner or supper in this house.

Archer. How came he so familiar in the family?

Scrub. Because he speaks English as if he had lived here all his life, and tells lies as if he had been a traveller from his cradle.

Archer. And this priest, I'm afraid, has converted the affections of your Gipsy.

Scrub. Converted! ay, and perverted, my dear friend: for, I'm afraid, he had made her a whore and a papist! But this is not all; there's the French count and Mrs. Sullen, they're in the confederacy, and for some private ends of their own, to be sure.

Archer. A very hopeful family yours, brother Scrub! I suppose the maiden lady has her lover too?

Scrub. Not that I know. She's the best on 'em, that's the truth on't. But they take care to prevent my curiosity, by giving me so much business, that I'm a perfect slave. What d'ye think is my place in this family?

Archer. Butler, I suppose.

Scrub. Ah, Lord help you! I'll tell you. Of a Monday I drive the coach; of a Tuesday I drive the plough; on Wednesday I follow the hounds; a Thursday I dun the tenants; on Friday I go to market; on Saturday I draw warrants; and a Sunday I draw beer.

Archer. Ha, ha, ha! if variety be a pleasure in life, you have enough on't, my dear brother. But what ladies are those?

Scrub. Ours, ours; that upon the right hand is Mrs. Sullen, and the other is Mrs. Dorinda. Don't mind 'em, sit still, man.

Enter Mrs. Sullen *and* Dorinda

Mrs. Sullen. I have heard my brother talk of my Lord Aimwell; but they say that his brother is the finer gentleman.

Dorinda. That's impossible, sister.

Mrs. Sullen. He's vastly rich, but very close, they say.

Dorinda. No matter for that; if I can creep into his heart, I'll open his breast, I warrant him. I have heard say, that people may be guessed at by the behavior of their servants; I could wish we might talk to that fellow.

Mrs. Sullen. So do I; for I think he's a very pretty fellow. Come this way, I'll throw out a lure for him presently.

(*They walk towards the opposite side of the stage*)

Archer. (*Aside*) Corn, wine, and oil indeed!—But I think the wife has the greatest plenty of flesh and blood; she should be my choice.—Ah, a—Say you so!—(Mrs. Sullen *drops her glove,* Archer *runs, takes it up, and gives it to her*) Madam—your ladyship's glove.

Mrs. Sullen. O sir, I thank you!—(*To* Dorinda) What a handsome bow the fellow has!

Dorinda. Bow! why I have known several footmen come down from London set up here for dancing masters, and carry off the best fortunes in the country.

Archer. (*Aside*) That project, for aught I know, had been better than ours.—Brother Scrub, why don't you introduce me?

Scrub. Ladies, this is the strange gentleman's servant that you see at church to-day; I understood he came from London, and so I invited him to the cellar, that he might show me the newest flourish in whetting my knives.

Dorinda. And I hope you have made much of him?

Archer. O yes, madam; but the strength of your ladyship's liquor is a little too potent for the constitution of your humble servant.

Mrs. Sullen. What! then you don't usually drink ale?

Archer. No, madam; my constant drink is tea, or a little wine and water. 'Tis prescribed me by the physician for a remedy against the spleen.

Scrub. O la! O la! a footman have the spleen!

Mrs. Sullen. I thought that distemper had been only proper to people of quality?

Archer. Madam, like all other fashions it wears out, and so descends to their servants; though in a great many of us, I believe, it proceeds from some melancholy particles in the blood, occasioned by the stagnation of wages.

Dorinda. (*Aside to* Mrs. Sullen) How affectedly the fellow talks!—(*To* Archer) How long, pray, have you served your present master?

Archer. Not long; my life has been mostly spent in the service of the ladies.

Mrs. Sullen. And pray, which service do you like best?

Archer. Madam, the ladies pay best; the honor of serving them is sufficient wages; there is a charm in their looks that delivers a pleasure with their commands, and gives our duty the wings of inclination.

Mrs. Sullen. (*Aside*) That flight was above the pitch of a livery.—And, sir, would not you be satisfied to serve a lady again?

Archer. As a groom of the chamber, madam, but not as a footman.

Mrs. Sullen. I suppose you served as footman before?

Archer. For that reason I would not serve in that post again; for my memory is too weak for the load of messages that the ladies lay upon their servants in London. My Lady Howd'ye, the last mistress I served, called me up one morning, and told me: Martin, go to my Lady Allnight with my humble service; tell her I was to wait on her ladyship yesterday, and left word with Mrs. Rebecca, that the preliminaries of the affair she knows of are stopped till we know the concurrence of the person that I know of, for which there are circumstances wanting which we shall accommodate at the old place; but that in the meantime there is a person about her ladyship, that, from several hints and surmises, was accessory at a certain time to the disappointments that naturally attend things, that to her knowledge are of more importance—

Mrs. Sullen *and* Dorinda. Ha, ha, ha! where are you going, sir?

Archer. Why, I han't half done!—The whole howd'ye was about half an hour long; so I happened to misplace two syllables, and was turned off, and rendered incapable.

Dorinda. (*Aside to* Mrs. Sullen) The pleasantest fellow, sister, I ever saw!—(*To* Archer) But, friend, if your master be married, I presume you still serve a lady?

Archer. No, madam, I take care never to come into a married family; the commands of the master and the mistress are always so contrary, that 'tis impossible to please both.

Dorinda. (*Aside*) There's a main point gained: my lord is not married, I find.

Mrs. Sullen. But I wonder, friend, that in so many good services, you had not a better provision made for you.

Archer. I don't know how, madam. I had a lieutenancy offered me three or four times; but that is not bread, madam—I live much better as I do.

Scrub. Madam, he sings rarely! I was thought to do pretty well here in the country till he came; but alack a day, I'm nothing to my brother Martin!

Dorinda. Does he?—Pray, sir, will you oblige us with a song?

Archer. Are you for passion or humor?

Scrub. O la! he has the purest ballard about a trifle—

Mrs. Sullen. A trifle! pray, sir, let's have it.

Archer. I'm ashamed to offer you a trifle, madam; but since you command me—(*Sings to the tune of* "Sir Simon the King")

> A trifling song you shall hear,[1]
> Begun with a trifle and ended:
> All trifling people draw near,
> And I shall be nobly attended.
>
> Were it not for trifles, a few,
> That lately have come into play,
> The men would want something to do,
> And the women want something to say.
>
> What makes men trifle in dressing?
> Because the ladies (they know)
> Admire, by often possessing,
> That eminent trifle a beau.
>
> When the lover his moments has trifled,
> The trifle of trifles to gain,
> No sooner the virgin is rifled,
> But a trifle shall part 'em again.
>
> What mortal man would be able
> At White's half-an-hour to sit,

[1] Only the first two lines are given in the first and second editions.

Or who could hear a tea-table,
Without talking of trifles for wit?

The Court is from trifles secure,
Gold keys are no trifles, we see!
White rods are no trifles, I'm sure,
Whatever their bearers may be.

But if you will go to the place,
Where trifles abundantly breed,
The levee will show you his Grace [1]
Makes promises trifles indeed.

A coach with six footmen behind,
I count neither trifle nor sin:
But, ye gods! how oft do we find
A scandalous trifle within.

A flask of champagne, people think it
A trifle, or something as bad:
But if you'll contrive how to drink it,
You'll find it no trifle, egad!

A parson's a trifle at sea,
A widow's a trifle in sorrow:
A peace is a trifle to-day:
Who knows what may happen to-morrow!

A black coat a trifle may cloke,
Or to hide it the red may endeavor:
But if once the army is broke,
We shall have more trifles than ever.

The stage is a trifle, they say,
The reason, pray carry along,
Because at every new play,
The house they with trifles so throng.

But with people's malice to trifle,
And to set us all on a foot:
The author of this is a trifle,
And his song is a trifle to boot.

MRS. SULLEN. Very well, sir, we're obliged to you.—Something for a pair of gloves.
(*Offering him money*)
ARCHER. I humbly beg leave to be excused: my master, madam, pays me; nor dare I take money from any other hand, without injuring his honor, and disobeying his commands.
Exit with SCRUB
DORINDA. This is surprising! Did you ever see so pretty a well-bred fellow?
MRS. SULLEN. The devil take him for wearing that livery!
DORINDA. I fancy, sister, he may be some gentleman, a friend of my lord's, that his

[1] Perhaps the Duke of Ormond, who had neglected to keep promises of aid made to Farquhar.

lordship has pitched upon for his courage, fidelity, and discretion, to bear him company in this dress—and who, ten to one, was his second too.
5 MRS. SULLEN. It is so, it must be so, and it shall be so!—for I like him.
DORINDA. What! better than the Count?
MRS. SULLEN. The Count happened to be the most agreeable man upon the place; and
10 so I chose him to serve me in my design upon my husband. But I should like this fellow better in a design upon myself.
DORINDA. But now, sister, for an interview with this lord, and this gentleman; how shall
15 we bring that about?
MRS. SULLEN. Patience! you country ladies give no quarter if once you be entered. Would you prevent their desires, and give the fellows no wishing-time? Look'ee, Dorinda, if my
20 Lord Aimwell loves you or deserves you, he'll find a way to see you, and there we must leave it.—My business comes now upon the tapis. Have you prepared your brother?
DORINDA. Yes, yes.
25 MRS. SULLEN. And how did he relish it?
DORINDA. He said little, mumbled something to himself, promised to be guided by me—but here he comes.

Enter SULLEN

SQUIRE SULLEN. What singing was that I
30 heard just now?
MRS. SULLEN. The singing in your head, my dear; you complained of it all day.
SQUIRE SULLEN. You're impertinent.
MRS. SULLEN. I was ever so, since I became
35 one flesh with you.
SQUIRE SULLEN. One flesh! rather two carcasses joined unnaturally together.
MRS. SULLEN. Or rather a living soul coupled to a dead body.
40 DORINDA. So, this is fine encouragement for me!
SQUIRE SULLEN. Yes, my wife shows you what you must do.
MRS. SULLEN. And my husband shows you
45 what you must suffer.
SQUIRE SULLEN. 'Sdeath, why can't you be silent?
MRS. SULLEN. 'Sdeath, why can't you talk?
SQUIRE SULLEN. Do you talk to any pur-
50 pose?
MRS. SULLEN. Do you think to any purpose?

SQUIRE SULLEN. Sister, heark'ye!—(*Whispers to* DORINDA, *then aloud*) I shan't be home till it be late. *Exit*

MRS. SULLEN. What did he whisper to ye?

DORINDA. That he would go round the back way, come into the closet, and listen as I directed him. But let me beg you once more, dear sister, to drop this project; for as I told you before, instead of awaking him to kindness, you may provoke him to a rage; and then who knows how far his brutality may carry him?

MRS. SULLEN. I'm provided to receive him, I warrant you. But here comes the Count, vanish! (*Exit* DORINDA. *Enter* COUNT BELLAIR) Don't you wonder, Monsieur le Comte, that I was not at church this afternoon?

COUNT BELLAIR. I more wonder, madam, that you go dere at all, or how you dare to lift those eyes to heaven that are guilty of so much killing.

MRS. SULLEN. If Heaven, sir, has given to my eyes, with the power of killing, the virtue of making a cure, I hope the one may atone for the other.

COUNT BELLAIR. Oh, largely, madam, would your ladyship be as ready to apply the remedy as to give the wound? Consider, madam, I am doubly a prisoner; first to the arms of your general, then to your more conquering eyes. My first chains are easy, there a ransom may redeem me; but from your fetters I never shall get free.

MRS. SULLEN. Alas, sir! why should you complain to me of your captivity, who am in chains myself? You know, sir, that I am bound, nay, must be tied up in that particular that might give you ease. I am like you, a prisoner of war,—of war, indeed! I have given my parole of honor; would you break yours to gain your liberty?

COUNT BELLAIR. Most certainly I would, were I a prisoner among the Turks; dis is your case; you're a slave, madam, slave to the worst of Turks, a husband.

MRS. SULLEN. There lies my foible, I confess; no fortifications, no courage, conduct, nor vigilancy, can pretend to defend a place, where the cruelty of the governor forces the garrison to mutiny.

COUNT BELLAIR. And where de besieger is resolved to die before de place.—Here will I fix;—(*Kneels*) with tears, vows, and prayers assault your heart, and never rise till you surrender; or if I must storm—Love and St. Michael!—And so I begin the attack—

MRS. SULLEN. Stand off!—(*Aside*) Sure he hears me not!—And I could almost wish he—did not!—The fellow makes love very prettily. —But, sir, why should you put such a value upon my person, when you see it despised by one that knows it so much better?

COUNT BELLAIR. He knows it not, though he possesses it; if he but knew the value of the jewel he is master of, he would always wear it next his heart, and sleep with it in his arms.

MRS. SULLEN. But since he throws me unregarded from him—

COUNT BELLAIR. And one that knows your value well comes by and takes you up, is it not justice? (*Goes to lay hold on her*)

Enter SULLEN *with his sword drawn*

SQUIRE SULLEN. Hold, villain, hold!

MRS. SULLEN. (*Presenting a pistol*) Do you hold!

SQUIRE SULLEN. What! murther your husband, to defend your bully!

MRS. SULLEN. Bully! for shame, Mr. Sullen! Bullies wear long swords, the gentleman has none, he's a prisoner, you know. I was aware of your outrage, and prepared this to receive your violence; and, if occasion were, to preserve myself against the force of this other gentleman.

COUNT BELLAIR. O madam, your eyes be bettre firearms than your pistol; they nevre miss.

SQUIRE SULLEN. What! court my wife to my face!

MRS. SULLEN. Pray, Mr. Sullen, put up; suspend your fury for a minute.

SQUIRE SULLEN. To give you time to invent an excuse!

MRS. SULLEN. I need none.

SQUIRE SULLEN. No, for I heard every syllable of your discourse.

COUNT BELLAIR. Ay! and begar, I tink the dialogue was vera pretty.

MRS. SULLEN. Then I suppose, sir, you heard something of your own barbarity?

SQUIRE SULLEN. Barbarity! Oons, what does the woman call barbarity? Do I ever meddle with you?

MRS. SULLEN. No.

SQUIRE SULLEN. As for you, sir, I shall take another time.

Count Bellair. Ah, begar, and so must I.

Squire Sullen. Look'ee, madam, don't think that my anger proceeds from any concern I have for your honor, but for my own; and if you can contrive any way of being a whore without making me a cuckold, do it and welcome.

Mrs. Sullen. Sir, I thank you kindly: you would allow me the sin but rob me of the pleasure. No, no, I'm resolved never to venture upon the crime without the satisfaction of seeing you punished for't.

Squire Sullen. Then will you grant me this, my dear? Let anybody else do you the favor but that Frenchman, for I mortally hate his whole generation.
Exit

Count Bellair. Ah, sir, that be ungrateful, for begar, I love some of yours. Madam— *(Approaching her)*

Mrs. Sullen. No, sir.

Count Bellair. No, sir! Garzoon, madam, I am not your husband.

Mrs. Sullen. 'Tis time to undeceive you, sir. I believed your addresses to me were no more than an amusement, and I hope you will think the same of my complaisance; and to convince you that you ought, you must know that I brought you hither only to make you instrumental in setting me right with my husband, for he was planted to listen by my appointment.

Count Bellair. By your appointment?

Mrs. Sullen. Certainly.

Count Bellair. And so, madam, while I was telling twenty stories to part you from your husband, begar, I was bringing you together all the while?

Mrs. Sullen. I ask your pardon, sir, but I hope this will give you a taste of the virtue of the English ladies.

Count Bellair. Begar, madam, your virtue be vera great, but garzoon, your honeste be vera little.

Enter Dorinda

Mrs. Sullen. Nay, now, you're angry, sir.

Count Bellair. Angry!—Fair Dorinda (*Sings* Dorinda *the Opera Tune,*[1] *and addresses to* Dorinda) Madam, when your ladyship

[1] Possibly the opera *Camilla*, by M. A. Buononcini (D.L., March 30, 1706), but no song beginning thus is found there.

want a fool, send for me. *Fair Dorinda, Revenge, &c.*
Exit singing

Mrs. Sullen. There goes the true humor of his nation—resentment with good manners, and the height of anger in a song! Well, sister, you must be judge, for you have heard the trial.

Dorinda. And I bring in my brother guilty.

Mrs. Sullen. But I must bear the punishment. 'Tis hard, sister.

Dorinda. I own it; but you must have patience.

Mrs. Sullen. Patience! the cant of custom —Providence sends no evil without a remedy. Should I lie groaning under a yoke I can shake off, I were accessary to my ruin, and my patience were no better than self-murder.

Dorinda. But how can you shake off the yoke? Your divisions don't come within the reach of the law for a divorce.

Mrs. Sullen. Law! what law can search into the remote abyss of nature? What evidence can prove the unaccountable disaffections of wedlock? Can a jury sum up the endless aversions that are rooted in our souls, or can a bench give judgment upon antipathies?

Dorinda. They never pretended, sister; they never meddle, but in case of uncleanness.

Mrs. Sullen. Uncleanness! O sister! casual violation is a transient injury, and may possibly be repaired; but can radical hatreds be ever reconciled? No, no, sister; Nature is the first lawgiver; and when she has set tempers opposite, not all the golden links of wedlock nor iron manacles of law, can keep 'em fast.

Wedlock we own ordained by Heaven's decree,
But such as Heaven ordained it first to be;—
Concurring tempers in the man and wife
As mutual helps to draw the load of life.
View all the works of Providence above:
The stars with harmony and concord move;
View all the works of Providence below:
The fire, the water, earth and air, we know,
All in one plant agree to make it grow.
Must man, the chiefest work of art divine,
Be doomed in endless discord to repine?
No, we should injure Heaven by that surmise:
Omnipotence is just, were man but wise.
Exeunt

ACT IV

SCENE I.—*Scene continues*

Enter MRS. SULLEN

MRS. SULLEN. Were I born an humble Turk, where women have no soul nor property, there I must sit contented. But in England, a country whose women are its glory, must women be abused? Where women rule, must women be enslaved? Nay, cheated into slavery, mocked by a promise of comfortable society into a wilderness of solitude! I dare not keep the thought about me. Oh, here comes something to divert me.

Enter a COUNTRYWOMAN

WOMAN. I come, an't please your ladyship—you're my Lady Bountiful, an't ye?

MRS. SULLEN. Well, good woman, go on.

WOMAN. I come seventeen long mail to have a cure for my husband's sore leg.

MRS. SULLEN. Your husband! what, woman, cure your husband!

WOMAN. Ay, poor man, for his sore leg won't let him stir from home.

MRS. SULLEN. There, I confess, you have given me a reason. Well, good woman, I'll tell you what you must do. You must lay your husband's leg upon a table, and with a chopping-knife you must lay it open as broad as you can; then you must take out the bone, and beat the flesh soundly with a rolling-pin; then take salt, pepper, cloves, mace and ginger, some sweet herbs, and season it very well; then roll it up like brawn, and put it into the oven for two hours.

WOMAN. Heavens reward your ladyship! I have two little babies too that are piteous bad with the graips, an't please ye.

MRS. SULLEN. Put a little pepper and salt in their bellies, good woman. (*Enter* LADY BOUNTIFUL) I beg your ladyship's pardon for taking your business out of your hands; I have been a-tampering here a little with one of your patients.

LADY BOUNTIFUL. Come, good woman, don't mind this mad creature; I am the person that you want, I suppose. What would you have, woman?

MRS. SULLEN. She wants something for her husband's sore leg.

LADY BOUNTIFUL. What's the matter with his leg, goody?

WOMAN. It comes first, as one might say, with a sort of dizziness in his foot, then he had a kind of laziness in his joints, and then his leg broke out, and then it swelled, and it closed again, and then it broke out again, and then it festered, and then it grew better, and then it grew worse again.

MRS. SULLEN. Ha, ha, ha!

LADY BOUNTIFUL. How can you be merry with the misfortunes of other people?

MRS. SULLEN. Because my own make me sad, madam.

LADY BOUNTIFUL. The worst reason in the world, daughter; your own misfortunes should teach you to pity others.

MRS. SULLEN. But the woman's misfortunes and mine are nothing alike; her husband is sick, and mine, alas! is in health.

LADY BOUNTIFUL. What! would you wish your husband sick?

MRS. SULLEN. Not of a sore leg, of all things.

LADY BOUNTIFUL. Well, good woman, go to the pantry, get your bellyful of victuals, then I'll give you a receipt of diet-drink for your husband. But d'ye hear, goody, you must not let your husband move too much.

WOMAN. No, no, madam, the poor man's inclinable enough to lie still. *Exit*

LADY BOUNTIFUL. Well, daughter Sullen, though you laugh, I have done miracles about the country here with my receipts.

MRS. SULLEN. Miracles indeed, if they have cured anybody; but I believe, madam, the patient's faith goes farther toward the miracle than your prescription.

LADY BOUNTIFUL. Fancy helps in some cases; but there's your husband, who has as little fancy as anybody, I brought him from death's door.

MRS. SULLEN. I suppose, madam, you made him drink plentifully of ass's milk.

Enter DORINDA, *runs to* MRS. SULLEN

DORINDA. News, dear sister! news! news!

Enter ARCHER, *running*

ARCHER. Where, where is my Lady Bountiful?—Pray, which is the old lady of you three?

LADY BOUNTIFUL. I am.

ARCHER. O madam, the fame of your ladyship's charity, goodness, benevolence, skill and ability, have drawn me hither to implore your ladyship's help in behalf of my unfortunate master, who is this moment breathing his last.

LADY BOUNTIFUL. Your master! where is he?

ARCHER. At your gate, madam. Drawn by the appearance of your handsome house to view it nearer, and walking up the avenue within five paces of the courtyard, he was taken ill of a sudden with a sort of I know not what, but down he fell, and there he lies.

LADY BOUNTIFUL. Here, Scrub, Gipsy, all run, get my easychair downstairs, put the gentleman in it, and bring him in quickly! quickly!

ARCHER. Heaven will reward your ladyship for this charitable act.

LADY BOUNTIFUL. Is your master used to these fits?

ARCHER. O yes, madam, frequently: I have known him have five or six of a night.

LADY BOUNTIFUL. What's his name?

ARCHER. Lord, madam, he's a-dying! a minute's care or neglect may save or destroy his life.

LADY BOUNTIFUL. Ah, poor gentleman!—Come, friend, show me the way; I'll see him brought in myself.   *Exit with* ARCHER

DORINDA. O sister, my heart flutters about strangely! I can hardly forbear running to his assistance.

MRS. SULLEN. And I'll lay my life he deserves your assistance more than he wants[1] it. Did not I tell you that my lord would find a way to come at you? Love's his distemper, and you must be the physician; put on all your charms, summon all your fire into your eyes, plant the whole artillery of your looks against his breast, and down with him.

DORINDA. O sister! I'm but a young gunner; I shall be afraid to shoot, for fear the piece should recoil, and hurt myself.

MRS. SULLEN. Never fear! You shall see me shoot before you, if you will.

DORINDA. No, no, dear sister; you have missed your mark so unfortunately, that I sha'n't care for being instructed by you.

Enter AIMWELL, *in a chair, carried by* ARCHER *and* SCRUB: LADY BOUNTIFUL *and* GIPSY *following;* AIMWELL *counterfeiting a swoon*

LADY BOUNTIFUL. Here, here, let's see the hartshorn drops.—Gipsy, a glass of fair water!

[1] In the sense of *needs*.

His fit's very strong.—Bless me, how his hands are clenched!

ARCHER. For shame, ladies, what d'ye do? why don't you help us?—(*To* DORINDA) Pray, madam, take his hand, and open it, if you can, whilst I hold his head. (DORINDA *takes his hand*)

DORINDA. Poor gentleman!—Oh!—he has got my hand within his, and he squeezes it unmercifully—

LADY BOUNTIFUL. 'Tis the violence of his convulsion, child.

ARCHER. Oh, madam, he's perfectly possessed in these cases—he'll bite if you don't have a care.

DORINDA. Oh, my hand! my hand!

LADY BOUNTIFUL. What's the matter with the foolish girl? I have got this hand open you see with a great deal of ease.

ARCHER. Ay, but, madam, your daughter's hand is somewhat warmer than your ladyship's, and the heat of it draws the force of the spirits that way.

MRS. SULLEN. I find, friend, you're very learned in these sorts of fits.

ARCHER. 'Tis no wonder, madam, for I'm often troubled with them myself; I find myself extremely ill at this minute.
        (*Looking hard at* MRS. SULLEN)

MRS. SULLEN. (*Aside*) I fancy I could find a way to cure you.

LADY BOUNTIFUL. His fit holds him very long.

ARCHER. Longer than usual, madam.—Pray, young lady, open his breast, and give him air.

LADY BOUNTIFUL. Where did his illness take him first, pray?

ARCHER. To-day, at church, madam.

LADY BOUNTIFUL. In what manner was he taken?

ARCHER. Very strangely, my lady. He was of a sudden touched with something in his eyes, which, at the first, he only felt, but could not tell whether 'twas pain or pleasure.

LADY BOUNTIFUL. Wind, nothing but wind!

ARCHER. By soft degrees it grew and mounted to his brain; there his fancy caught it, there formed it so beautiful, and dressed it up in such gay, pleasing colors, that his transported appetite seized the fair idea, and straight conveyed it to his heart. That hospitable seat of life sent all its sanguine spirits forth to meet, and opened all its sluicy gates to take the stranger in.

LADY BOUNTIFUL. Your master should never go without a bottle to smell to.—Oh,—he recovers!—The lavender water—some feathers to burn under his nose—Hungary water to rub his temples.—Oh, he comes to himself! —Hem a little, sir, hem.—Gipsy! bring the cordial-water.

(AIMWELL *seems to awake in amaze*)

DORINDA. How d'ye, sir?

AIMWELL. Where am I? (*Rising*)
Sure I have pass'd the gulf of silent death,
And now I land on the Elysian shore!—
Behold the goddess of those happy plains,
Fair Proserpine—Let me adore thy bright divinity.

(*Kneels to* DORINDA, *and kisses her hand*)

MRS. SULLEN. So, so, so! I knew where the fit would end!

AIMWELL. Eurydice perhaps—
How could thy Orpheus keep his word,
And not look back upon thee?
No treasure but thyself could sure have bribed him
To look one minute off thee.

LADY BOUNTIFUL. Delirious, poor gentleman!

ARCHER. Very delirious, madam, very delirious.

AIMWELL. Martin's voice, I think.

ARCHER. Yes, my lord.—How does your lordship?

LADY BOUNTIFUL. Lord! did you mind that, girls?

AIMWELL. Where am I?

ARCHER. In very good hands, sir. You were taken just now with one of your old fits, under the trees, just by this good lady's house; her ladyship had you taken in, and has miraculously brought you to yourself, as you see—

AIMWELL. I am so confounded with shame, madam, that I can now only beg pardon, and refer my acknowledgments for your ladyship's care till an opportunity offers of making some amends. I dare be no longer troublesome.— Martin, give two guineas to the servants.

(*Going*)

DORINDA. Sir, you may catch cold by going so soon into the air; you don't look, sir, as if you were perfectly recovered.

(*Here* ARCHER *talks to* LADY BOUNTIFUL *in dumb show*)

AIMWELL. That I shall never be, madam; my present illness is so rooted that I must expect to carry it to my grave.

MRS. SULLEN. Don't despair, sir; I have known several in your distemper shake it off with a fortnight's physic.

LADY BOUNTIFUL. Come, sir, your servant has been telling me that you're apt to relapse if you go into the air: your good manners sha'n't get the better of ours—you shall sit down again, sir. Come, sir, we don't mind ceremonies in the country. Here, sir, my service t'ye.—You shall taste my water; 'tis a cordial I can assure you, and of my own making—drink it off, sir.—(AIMWELL *drinks*) And how d'ye find yourself now, sir?

AIMWELL. Somewhat better—though very faint still.

LADY BOUNTIFUL. Ay, ay, people are always faint after these fits.—Come, girls, you shall show the gentleman the house.—'Tis but an old family building, sir; but you had better walk about, and cool by degrees, than venture immediately into the air. You'll find some tolerable pictures.—Dorinda, show the gentleman the way. I must go to the poor woman below. *Exit*

DORINDA. This way, sir.

AIMWELL. Ladies, shall I beg leave for my servant to wait on you, for he understands pictures very well?

MRS. SULLEN. Sir, we understand originals as well as he does pictures, so he may come along.

Exeunt all but SCRUB, AIMWELL *leading* DORINDA

Enter FOIGARD

FOIGARD. Save you, Master Scrub!

SCRUB. Sir, I won't be saved your way—I hate a priest, I abhor the French, and I defy the devil. Sir, I'm a bold Briton, and will spill the last drop of my blood to keep out popery and slavery.

FOIGARD. Master Scrub, you would put me down in politics, and so I would be speaking with Mrs. Shipsy.

SCRUB. Good Mr. Priest, you can't speak with her; she's sick, sir, she's gone abroad, sir, she's—dead two months ago, sir.

Enter GIPSY

GIPSY. How now, impudence! how dare you talk so saucily to the doctor?—Pray, sir, don't take it ill; for the common people of England are not so civil to strangers, as—

SCRUB. You lie! you lie! 'tis the common people that are civilest to strangers.

GIPSY. Sirrah, I have a good mind to—get you out, I say!

SCRUB. I won't.

GIPSY. You won't, sauce-box!—Pray, doctor, what is the captain's name that came to your inn last night?

SCRUB. (*Aside*) The captain! ah, the devil, there she hampers me again; the captain has me on one side, and the priest on t'other: so between the gown and the sword, I have a fine time on't.—But, *Cedunt arma togæ*.[1] (*Going*)

GIPSY. What, sirrah, won't you march.

SCRUB. No my dear, I won't march—but I'll walk.—(*Aside*) And I'll make bold to listen a little too.

(*Goes behind the side-scene, and listens*)

GIPSY. Indeed, doctor, the Count has been barbarously treated, that's the truth on't.

FOIGARD. Ah, Mrs. Gipsy, upon my shoul, now, gra, his complainings would mollify the marrow in your bones, and move the bowels of your commiseration! He veeps, and he dances, and he fistles, and he swears, and he laughs, and he stamps, and he sings: in conclusion, joy, he's afflicted *à la Française*, and a stranger would not know whider to cry or to laugh with him.

GIPSY. What would you have me do, doctor?

FOIGARD. Noting, joy, but only hide the Count in Mrs. Sullen's closet when it is dark.

GIPSY. Nothing! is that nothing? It would be both a sin and a shame, doctor.

FOIGARD. Here is twenty Lewidores, joy, for your shame; and I will give you an absolution for the shin.

GIPSY. But won't that money look like a bribe?

FOIGARD. Dat is according as you shall tauk it. If you receive the money beforehand, 'twill be, *logicè*, a bribe; but if you stay till afterwards, 'twill be only a gratification.

GIPSY. Well, doctor, I'll take it *logicè*. But what must I do with my conscience, sir?

FOIGARD. Leave dat wid me, joy; I am your priest, gra; and your conscience is under my hands.

GIPSY. But should I put the Count into the closet—

FOIGARD. Vel, is dere any shin for a man's being in a closhet? One may go to prayers in a closhet.

GIPSY. But if the lady should come into her chamber, and go to bed?

FOIGARD. Vel, and is dere any shin in going to bed, joy?

GIPSY. Ay, but if the parties should meet, doctor?

FOIGARD. Vel den—the parties must be responsable. Do you be after putting the Count in the closhet, and leave the shins wid themselves. I will come with the Count to instruct you in your chamber.

GIPSY. Well, doctor, your religion is so pure! Methinks I'm so easy after an absolution, and can sin afresh with so much security, that I'm resolved to die a martyr to't. Here's the key of the garden door, come in the back way when 'tis late, I'll be ready to receive you; but don't so much as whisper, only take hold of my hand; I'll lead you, and do you lead the Count and follow me. *Exeunt*

Enter SCRUB

SCRUB. What witchcraft now have these two imps of the devil been a-hatching here? There's twenty Lewidores; I heard that, and saw the purse.—But I must give room to my betters. *Exit*

Enter AIMWELL, *leading* DORINDA, *and making love in dumb show;* MRS. SULLEN *and* ARCHER

MRS. SULLEN. (*To* ARCHER) Pray, sir, how d'ye like that piece?

ARCHER. Oh, 'tis Leda! You find, madam, how Jupiter comes disguised to make love—

MRS. SULLEN. But what think you there of Alexander's battles?

ARCHER. We want only a Le Brun,[2] madam, to draw greater battles, and a greater general of our own. The Danube, madam, would make a greater figure in a picture than the Granicus; and we have our Ramilies to match their Arbela.[3]

MRS. SULLEN. Pray, sir, what head is that in the corner there?

---

[1] Arms yield to the toga. The toga was the garment of a civilian.

[2] Charles Le Brun (1619–1690), French historical painter, designed the Gobelin tapestries for Louis XIV.

[3] Victories of Alexander and Marlborough respectively.

ARCHER. O madam, 'tis poor Ovid in his exile.

MRS. SULLEN. What was he banished for?

ARCHER. His ambitious love, madam.—(*Bowing*) His misfortune touches me.

MRS. SULLEN. Was he successful in his amours?

ARCHER. There he has left us in the dark.—He was too much a gentleman to tell.

MRS. SULLEN. If he were secret, I pity him.

ARCHER. And if he were successful, I envy him.

MRS. SULLEN. How d'ye like that Venus over the chimney?

ARCHER. Venus! I protest, madam, I took it for your picture; but now I look again, 'tis not handsome enough.

MRS. SULLEN. Oh, what a charm is flattery! If you would see my picture, there it is, over that cabinet. How d'ye like it?

ARCHER. I must admire anything, madam, that has the least resemblance of you. But, methinks, madam—(*He looks at the picture and* MRS. SULLEN *three or four times, by turns*) Pray, madam, who drew it?

MRS. SULLEN. A famous hand, sir.

(*Here* AIMWELL *and* DORINDA *go off*)

ARCHER. A famous hand, madam!—Your eyes, indeed, are featured there; but where's the sparkling moisture, shining fluid, in which they swim? The picture, indeed, has your dimples; but where's the swarm of killing Cupids that should ambush there? The lips too are figured out; but where's the carnation dew, the pouting ripeness, that tempts the taste in the original?

MRS. SULLEN. (*Aside*) Had it been my lot to have matched with such a man!

ARCHER. Your breasts too—presumptuous man! what, paint Heaven!—À *propos*, madam, in the very next picture is Salmoneus, that was struck dead with lightning, for offering to imitate Jove's thunder; I hope you served the painter so, madam?

MRS. SULLEN. Had my eyes the power of thunder, they should employ their lightning better.

ARCHER. There's the finest bed in that room, madam! I suppose 'tis your ladyship's bed-chamber.

MRS. SULLEN. And what then, sir?

ARCHER. I think the quilt is the richest that ever I saw. I can't at this distance, madam, distinguish the figures of the embroidery; will you give me leave, madam—?

(*Goes into the chamber*)

MRS. SULLEN. The devil take his impudence!—Sure, if I gave him an opportunity, he durst not offer it?—I have a great mind to try.—(*Going in, returns*) 'Sdeath, what am I doing?—And alone, too!—Sister! sister!

(*Runs out*)

ARCHER. (*Coming out*) I'll follow her close—For where a Frenchman durst attempt to storm,
A Briton sure may well the work perform.

(*Going*)

Enter SCRUB

SCRUB. Martin! brother Martin!

ARCHER. O brother Scrub, I beg your pardon, I was not a-going: here's a guinea my master ordered you.

SCRUB. A guinea! hi! hi! hi! a guinea! eh—by this light it is a guinea! But I suppose you expect one and twenty shillings in change?

ARCHER. Not at all; I have another for Gipsy.

SCRUB. A guinea for her! Faggot and fire for the witch! Sir, give me that guinea, and I'll discover a plot.

ARCHER. A plot!

SCRUB. Ay, sir, a plot, and a horrid plot! First, it must be a plot, because there's a woman in't: secondly, it must be a plot, because there's a priest in't: thirdly, it must be a plot, because there's French gold in't: and fourthly, it must be a plot, because I don't know what to make on't.[1]

ARCHER. Nor anybody else, I'm afraid, brother Scrub.

SCRUB. Truly, I'm afraid so too; for where there's a priest and a woman, there's always a mystery and a riddle. This I know, that here has been the doctor with a temptation in one hand and an absolution in the other, and Gipsy has sold herself to the devil; I saw the price paid down, my eyes shall take their oath on't.

ARCHER. And is all this bustle about Gipsy?

SCRUB. That's not all; I could hear but a word here and there; but I remember they mentioned a Count, a closet, a back-door, and a key.

ARCHER. The Count!—Did you hear nothing of Mrs. Sullen?

[1] All the elements requisite to a plot in the year 1707.

SCRUB. I did hear some word that sounded that way; but whether it was Sullen or Dorinda, I could not distinguish.

ARCHER. You have told this matter to nobody, brother?

SCRUB. Told! no, sir, I thank you for that; I'm resolved never to speak one word, pro nor con, till we have a peace.

ARCHER. You're i'the right, brother Scrub. Here's a treaty afoot between the Count and the lady: the priest and the chambermaid are the plenipotentiaries. It shall go hard but I find a way to be included in the treaty.—Where's the doctor now?

SCRUB. He and Gipsy are this moment devouring my lady's marmalade in the closet.

AIMWELL. (*Without*) Martin! Martin!

ARCHER. I come, sir, I come.

SCRUB. But you forgot the other guinea, brother Martin.

ARCHER. Here, I **give** it with all my heart.

SCRUB. And I take it with all my soul.— (*Exit* ARCHER) Ecod, I'll spoil your plotting, Mrs. Gipsy! and if you should set the captain upon me, these two guineas will buy me off.
Exit

Enter MRS. SULLEN *and* DORINDA, *meeting*

MRS. SULLEN. Well, sister!

DORINDA. And well, sister!

MRS. SULLEN. What's become of my lord?

DORINDA. What's become of his servant?

MRS. SULLEN. Servant! he's a prettier fellow, and a finer gentleman by fifty degrees, than his master.

DORINDA. O' my conscience, I fancy you could beg that fellow at the gallows-foot!

MRS. SULLEN. O' my conscience I could, provided I could put a friend of yours in his room.

DORINDA. You desired me, sister, to leave you when you transgressed the bounds of honor.

MRS. SULLEN. Thou dear censorious country girl! what dost mean? You can't think of the man without the bedfellow, I find.

DORINDA. I don't find anything unnatural in that thought: while the mind is conversant with flesh and blood, it must conform to the humors of the company.

MRS. SULLEN. How a little love and good company improves a woman! Why, child, you begin to live—you never spoke before.

DORINDA. Because I was never spoke to.— My lord has told me that I have more wit and beauty than any of my sex; and truly I begin to think the man is sincere.

MRS. SULLEN. You're in the right, Dorinda; pride is the life of a woman, and flattery is our daily bread; and she's a fool that won't believe a man there, as much as she that believes him in anything else. But I'll lay you a guinea that I had finer things said to me than you had.

DORINDA. Done! What did your fellow say to ye?

MRS. SULLEN. My fellow took the picture of Venus for mine.

DORINDA. But my lover took me for Venus herself.

MRS. SULLEN. Common cant! Had my spark called me a Venus directly, I should have believed him a footman in good earnest.

DORINDA. But my lover was upon his knees to me.

MRS. SULLEN. And mine was upon his tiptoes to me.

DORINDA. Mine vowed to die for me.

MRS. SULLEN. Mine swore to die with me.

DORINDA. Mine spoke the softest moving things.

MRS. SULLEN. Mine had his moving things too.

DORINDA. Mine kissed my hand ten thousand times.

MRS. SULLEN. Mine has all that pleasure to come.

DORINDA. Mine offered marriage.

MRS. SULLEN. O Lard! d'ye call that a moving thing?

DORINDA. The sharpest arrow in his quiver, my dear sister! Why, my ten thousand pounds may lie brooding here this seven years, and hatch nothing at last but some ill-natured clown like yours! Whereas, if I marry my Lord Aimwell, there will be title, place, and precedence, the Park, the play, and the drawing-room, splendor, equipage, noise, and flambeaux.—Hey, my Lady Aimwell's servants there!—Lights, lights to the stairs!— My Lady Aimwell's coach put forward!— Stand by, make room for her ladyship!— Are not these things moving?—What! melancholy of a sudden?

MRS. SULLEN. Happy, happy sister! your angel has been watchful for your happiness, whilst mine has slept, regardless of his charge. Long smiling years of circling joys for you, but not one hour for me! (*Weeps*)

DORINDA. Come, my dear, we'll talk of something else.

MRS. SULLEN. O Dorinda! I own myself a woman, full of my sex; a gentle, generous soul, easy and yielding to soft desires; a spacious heart, where love and all his train might lodge. And must the fair apartment of my breast be made a stable for a brute to lie in?

DORINDA. Meaning your husband, I suppose?

MRS. SULLEN. Husband! no; even husband is too soft a name for him.—But, come, I expect my brother here to-night or to-morrow; he was abroad when my father married me; perhaps he'll find a way to make me easy.

DORINDA. Will you promise not to make yourself easy in the meantime, with my lord's friend?

MRS. SULLEN. You mistake me, sister. It happens with us as among the men, the greatest talkers are the greatest cowards; and there's a reason for it; those spirits evaporate in prattle, which might do more mischief if they took another course.—Though, to confess the truth, I do love that fellow;—and if I met him dressed as he should be, and I undressed as I should be—look'ye, sister, I have no supernatural gifts—I can't swear I could resist the temptation; though I can safely promise to avoid it; and that's as much as the best of us can do. *Exeunt*

SCENE II.—*The Inn*

Enter AIMWELL *and* ARCHER, *laughing*

ARCHER. And the awkward kindness of the good motherly old gentlwoman—

AIMWELL. And the coming easiness of the young one—'Sdeath, 'tis pity to deceive her!

ARCHER. Nay, if you adhere to those principles, stop where you are.

AIMWELL. I can't stop, for I love her to distraction.

ARCHER. 'Sdeath, if you love her a hair's breadth beyond discretion, you must go no farther.

AIMWELL. Well, well, anything to deliver us from sauntering away our idle evenings at White's, Tom's, or Will's, and be stinted to bare looking at our old acquaintance, the cards, because our impotent pockets can't afford us a guinea for the mercenary drabs.

ARCHER. Or be obliged to some purse-proud coxcomb for a scandalous bottle, where we must not pretend to our share of the discourse, because we can't pay our club o'th' reckoning.—Damn it, I had rather sponge upon Morris, and sup upon a dish of bohea scored behind the door![1]

AIMWELL. And there expose our want of sense by talking criticisms, as we should our want of money by railing at the government.

ARCHER. Or be obliged to sneak into the side-box, and between both houses steal two acts of a play, and because we han't money to see the other three, we come away discontented, and damn the whole five.[2]

AIMWELL. And ten thousand such rascally tricks—had we outlived our fortunes among our acquaintance.—But now—

ARCHER. Ay, now is the time to prevent all this:—strike while the iron is hot.—This priest is the luckiest part of our adventure; he shall marry you, and pimp for me.

AIMWELL. But I should not like a woman that can be so fond of a Frenchman.

ARCHER. Alas, sir, necessity has no law. The lady may be in distress; perhaps she has a confounded husband, and her revenge may carry her farther than her love. Egad, I have so good an opinion of her, and of myself, that I begin to fancy strange things; and we must say this for the honor of our women, and indeed of ourselves, that they do stick to their men as they do to their *Magna Charta*. If the plot lies as I suspect, I must put on the gentleman.—But here comes the doctor—I shall be ready. *Exit*

Enter FOIGARD

FOIGARD. Sauve you, noble friend.

AIMWELL. O sir, your servant! Pray, doctor, may I crave your name?

FOIGARD. Fat naam is upon me! My naam is Foigard, joy.

AIMWELL. Foigard! A very good name for a clergyman. Pray, Doctor Foigard, were you ever in Ireland?

FOIGARD. Ireland! No, joy. Fat sort of plaace is dat saam Ireland? Dey say de people are catched dere when dey are young.

---

[1] I.e., run up an account at a public house.
[2] Persons who left the theater after one act paid nothing.

AIMWELL. And some of 'em when they're old:—as for example.—(*Takes* FOIGARD *by the shoulder*) Sir, I arrest you as a traitor against the government; you're a subject of England, and this morning showed me a commission, by which you served as chaplain in the French army. This is death by our law, and your reverence must hang for't.

FOIGARD. Upon my shoul, noble friend, dis is strange news you tell me! Fader Foigard a subject of England! de son of a burgomaster of Brussels a subject of England! Ubooboo—

AIMWELL. The son of a bog-trotter in Ireland! Sir, your tongue will condemn you before any bench in the kingdom.

FOIGARD. And is my tongue all your evidensh, joy?

AIMWELL. That's enough.

FOIGARD. No, no, joy, for I vil never spake English no more.

AIMWELL. Sir, I have other evidence.—Here, Martin!

Enter ARCHER

You know this fellow?

ARCHER. (*In a brogue*) Saave you, my dear cussen, how does your health?

FOIGARD. (*Aside*) Ah! upon my shoul dere is my countryman, and his brogue will hang mine.—(*To* ARCHER) *Mynhhr, Ick wet neat watt hey zacht, Ick universton ewe neat, sacramant!* [1]

AIMWELL. Altering your language won't do, sir; this fellow knows your person, and will swear to your face.

FOIGARD. Faash! fey, is dere a brogue upon my faash too?

ARCHER. Upon my soulvation, dere ish, joy!—But cussen Mackshane, vil you not put a remembrance upon me?

FOIGARD. (*Aside*) Mackshane! by St. Paatrick, dat ish naame [2] sure enough.

AIMWELL. (*Aside to* ARCHER) I fancy, Archer, you have it.

FOIGARD. The devil hang you, joy! by fat acquaintance are you my cussen?

ARCHER. Oh, de devil hang yourshelf, joy! you know we were little boys togeder upon de school, and your fostermoder's son was married upon my nurse's chister, joy, and we are Irish cussens.

[1] Presumably intended to represent Flemish: "Sir, I do not know what he says; I understand you not, truly."

[2] *Sic* in the first edition. Meaning *my name*?

FOIGARD. De devil taak de relation! Vel, joy, and fat school was it?

ARCHER. I tinks it was—aay,—'twas Tipperary.

FOIGARD. No, no, joy; it vas Kilkenny.

AIMWELL. That's enough for us—self-confession. Come, sir, we must deliver you into the hands of the next magistrate.

ARCHER. He sends you to jail, you're tried next assizes, and away you go swing into purgatory.

FOIGARD. And is it so wid you, cussen?

ARCHER. It vil be sho wid you, cussen, if you don't immediately confess the secret between you and Mrs. Gipsy. Look'ee, sir, the gallows or the secret, take your choice.

FOIGARD. The gallows! upon my shoul I hate that saame gallow, for it is a diseash dat is fatal to our family. Vel den, dere is nothing, shentlemens, but Mrs. Shullen would spaak wid the Count in her chamber at midnight and dere is no haarm, joy, for I am to conduct the Count to the plash myshelf.

ARCHER. As I guessed.—Have you communicated the matter to the Count?

FOIGARD. I have not sheen him since.

ARCHER. Right again! Why then, doctor—you shall conduct me to the lady instead of the Count.

FOIGARD. Fat, my cussen to the lady! upon my shoul, gra, dat is too much upon the brogue.

ARCHER. Come, come, doctor; consider we have got a rope about your neck, and if you offer to squeak, we'll stop your windpipe, most certainly. We shall have another job for you in a day or two, I hope.

AIMWELL. Here's company coming this way; let's into my chamber, and there concert our affair farther.

ARCHER. Come, my dear cussen, come along. *Exeunt*

Enter BONIFACE, HOUNSLOW *and* BAGSHOT *at one door,* GIBBET *at the opposite*

GIBBET. Well, gentlemen, 'tis a fine night for our enterprise.

HOUNSLOW. Dark as hell.

BAGSHOT. And blows like the devil; our landlord here has showed us the window where we must break in, and tells us the plate stands in the wainscot cupboard in the parlor.

BONIFACE. Ay, ay, Mr. Bagshot, as the

saying is, knives and forks, and cups and cans, and tumblers and tankards. There's one tankard, as the saying is, that's near upon as big as me; it was a present to the squire from his godmother, and smells of nutmeg and toast like an East-India ship.

HOUNSLOW. Then you say we must divide at the stair-head?

BONIFACE. Yes, Mr. Hounslow, as the saying is. At one end of that gallery lies my Lady Bountiful and her daughter, and at the other Mrs. Sullen. As for the squire—

GIBBET. He's safe enough, I have fairly entered him, and he's more than half seas over already. But such a parcel of scoundrels are got about him now, that, egad, I was ashamed to be seen in his company.

BONIFACE. 'Tis now twelve, as the saying is —gentlemen, you must set out at one.

GIBBET. Hounslow, do you and Bagshot see our arms fixed, and I'll come to you presently.

HOUNSLOW AND BAGSHOT. We will.

Exeunt

GIBBET. Well, my dear Bonny, you assure me that Scrub is a coward?

BONIFACE. A chicken, as the saying is. You'll have no creature to deal with but the ladies.

GIBBET. And I can assure you, friend, there's a great deal of address and good manners in robbing a lady; I am the most a gentleman that way that ever travelled the road.— But, my dear Bonny, this prize will be a galleon, a Vigo business.[1]—I warrant you we shall bring off three or four thousand pound.

BONIFACE. In plate, jewels, and money, as the saying is, you may.

GIBBET. Why then, Tyburn, I defy thee! I'll get up to town, sell off my horse and arms, buy myself some pretty employment in the household, and be as snug and as honest as any courtier of 'em all.

BONIFACE. And what think you then of my daughter Cherry for a wife?

GIBBET. Look'ee, my dear Bonny—Cherry is the Goddess I adore, as the song goes; but it is a maxim that man and wife should never have it in their power to hang one another; for if they should, the Lord have mercy on 'um both!

Exeunt

[1] The destruction of the Spanish fleet by the English and Dutch off Vigo took place in 1702.

ACT V

SCENE I.—*Scene continues*

Knocking without, enter BONIFACE

BONIFACE. Coming! coming!—A coach and six foaming horses at this time o'night! Some great man, as the saying is, for he scorns to travel with other people.

Enter SIR CHARLES FREEMAN

SIR CHARLES. What, fellow! a public house, and abed when other people sleep!

BONIFACE. Sir, I an't abed, as the saying is.

SIR CHARLES. Is Mr. Sullen's family abed, think'ee?

BONIFACE. All but the squire himself, sir, as the saying is—he's in the house.

SIR CHARLES. What company has he?

BONIFACE. Why, sir, there's the constable, Mr. Gage, the exciseman, the hunchbacked barber, and two or three other gentlemen.

SIR CHARLES. (*Aside*) I find my sister's letters gave me the true picture of her spouse.

Enter SULLEN, *drunk*

BONIFACE. Sir, here's the squire.

SQUIRE SULLEN. The puppies left me asleep —Sir!

SIR CHARLES. Well, sir.

SQUIRE SULLEN. Sir, I'm an unfortunate man—I have three thousand pound a year, and I can't get a man to drink a cup of ale with me.

SIR CHARLES. That's very hard.

SQUIRE SULLEN. Ay, sir; and unless you have pity upon me, and smoke one pipe with me, I must e'en go home to my wife, and I had rather go to the devil by half.

SIR CHARLES. But I presume, sir, you won't see your wife tonight; she'll be gone to bed. You don't use to lie with your wife in that pickle?

SQUIRE SULLEN. What! not lie with my wife! Why, sir, do you take me for an atheist or a rake?

SIR CHARLES. If you hate her, sir, I think you had better lie from her.

SQUIRE SULLEN. I think so too, friend. But I'm a justice of peace, and must do nothing against the law.

SIR CHARLES. Law! As I take it, Mr. Justice, nobody observes law for law's sake, only for the good of those for whom it was made.

SQUIRE SULLEN. But, if the law orders me to send you to jail, you must lie there, my friend.

SIR CHARLES. Not unless I commit a crime to deserve it.

SQUIRE SULLEN. A crime! oons, an't I married?

SIR CHARLES. Nay, sir, if you call marriage a crime, you must disown it for a law.

SQUIRE SULLEN. Eh! I must be acquainted with you, sir.—But, sir, I should be very glad to know the truth of this matter.

SIR CHARLES. Truth, sir, is a profound sea, and few there be that dare wade deep enough to find out the bottom on't. Besides, sir, I'm afraid the line of your understanding mayn't be long enough.

SQUIRE SULLEN. Look'ee, sir, I have nothing to say to your sea of truth, but if a good parcel of land can entitle a man to a little truth, I have as much as any he in the country.

BONIFACE. I never heard your worship, as the saying is, talk so before.

SQUIRE SULLEN. Because I never met with a man that I liked before.

BONIFACE. Pray, sir, as the saying is, let me ask you one question: are not man and wife one flesh?

SIR CHARLES. You and your wife, Mr. Guts, may be one flesh, because ye are nothing else; but rational creatures have minds that must be united.

SQUIRE SULLEN. Minds!

SIR CHARLES. Ay, minds, sir: don't you think that the mind takes place of the body?

SQUIRE SULLEN. In some people.

SIR CHARLES. Then the interest of the master must be consulted before that of his servant.

SQUIRE SULLEN. Sir, you shall dine with me to-morrow!—Oons, I always thought that we were naturally one.

SIR CHARLES. Sir, I know that my two hands are naturally one, because they love one another, kiss one another, help one another in all the actions of life; but I could not say so much if they were always at cuffs.

SQUIRE SULLEN. Then 'tis plain that we are two.

SIR CHARLES. Why don't you part with her, sir?

SQUIRE SULLEN. Will you take her, sir?

SIR CHARLES. With all my heart.

SQUIRE SULLEN. You shall have her to-morrow morning, and a venison-pasty into the bargain.

SIR CHARLES. You'll let me have her fortune too?

SQUIRE SULLEN. Fortune! why, sir, I have no quarrel at her fortune: I only hate the woman, sir, and none but the woman shall go.

SIR CHARLES. But her fortune, sir—

SQUIRE SULLEN. Can you play at whisk, sir?

SIR CHARLES. No, truly, sir.

SQUIRE SULLEN. Not at all-fours?

SIR CHARLES. Neither.

SQUIRE SULLEN. (*Aside*) Oons! where was this man bred?—Burn me, sir! I can't go home, 'tis but two a clock.

SIR CHARLES. For half an hour, sir, if you please; but you must consider 'tis late.

SQUIRE SULLEN. Late! that's the reason I can't go to bed—Come, sir! *Exeunt*

Enter CHERRY, *runs across the stage, and knocks at* AIMWELL'S *chamber-door. Enter* AIMWELL *in his nightcap and gown*

AIMWELL. What's the matter? You tremble, child, you're frighted.

CHERRY. No wonder, sir.—But, in short, sir, this very minute a gang of rogues are gone to rob my Lady Bountiful's house.

AIMWELL. How!

CHERRY. I dogged 'em to the very door, and left 'em breaking in.

AIMWELL. Have you alarmed anybody else with the news?

CHERRY. No, no, sir, I wanted to have discovered the whole plot, and twenty other things, to your man Martin; but I have searched the whole house, and can't find him! Where is he?

AIMWELL. No matter, child; will you guide me immediately to the house?

CHERRY. With all my heart, sir; my Lady Bountiful is my godmother, and I love Mrs. Dorinda so well—

AIMWELL. Dorinda! the name inspires me! The glory and the danger shall be all my own. —Come, my life, let me but get my sword. *Exeunt*

SCENE II.—*A Bedchamber in* LADY BOUNTIFUL'S *House*

Enter Mrs. SULLEN *and* DORINDA *undressed. A table and lights*

DORINDA. 'Tis very late, sister—no news of your spouse yet?

Mrs. Sullen. No, I'm condemned to be alone till towards four, and then perhaps I may be executed with his company.

Dorinda. Well, my dear, I'll leave you to your rest. You'll go directly to bed, I suppose?

Mrs. Sullen. I don't know what to do.—Heigh-ho!

Dorinda. That's a desiring sigh, sister.

Mrs. Sullen. This is a languishing hour, sister.

Dorinda. And might prove a critical minute, if the pretty fellow were here.

Mrs. Sullen. Here! what, in my bedchamber at two o'clock o'th' morning, I undressed, the family asleep, my hated husband abroad, and my lovely fellow at my feet!—O 'gad, sister!

Dorinda. Thoughts are free, sister, and them I allow you.—So, my dear, good night.

Mrs. Sullen. A good rest to my dear Dorinda!—(*Exit* Dorinda) Thoughts free! are they so? Why, then, suppose him here, dressed like a youthful, gay, and burning bridegroom, (*Here* Archer *steals out of the closet*) with tongue enchanting, eyes bewitching, knees imploring.—(*Turns a little on one side and sees* Archer *in the posture she describes*)—Ah!—(*Shrieks and runs to the other side of the stage*) Have my thoughts raised a spirit?—What are you, sir?—a man or a devil?

Archer. A man, a man, madam. (*Rising*)

Mrs. Sullen. How shall I be sure of it?

Archer. Madam, I'll give you demonstration this minute. (*Takes her hand*)

Mrs. Sullen. What, sir! do you intend to be rude?

Archer. Yes, madam, if you please.

Mrs. Sullen. In the name of wonder, whence came ye?

Archer. From the skies, madam—I'm a Jupiter in love, and you shall be my Alcmena.

Mrs. Sullen. How came you in?

Archer. I flew in at the window, madam; your cousin Cupid lent me his wings, and your sister Venus opened the casement.

Mrs. Sullen. I'm struck dumb with admiration!

Archer. And I—with wonder.

(*Looks passionately at her*)

Mrs. Sullen. What will become of me?

Archer. How beautiful she looks!—The teeming jolly Spring smiles in her blooming face, and, when she was conceived, her mother smelt to roses, looked on lilies—

Lilies unfold their white, their fragrant charms,
When the warm sun thus darts into their arms.

(*Runs to her*)

Mrs. Sullen. Ah! (*Shrieks*)

Archer. Oons, madam, what d'ye mean? You'll raise the house.

Mrs. Sullen. Sir, I'll wake the dead before I bear this!—What! approach me with the freedoms of a keeper! I'm glad on't, your impudence has cured me.

Archer. If this be impudence,—(*Kneels*) I leave to your partial self; no panting pilgrim, after a tedious, painful voyage, e'er bowed before his saint with more devotion.

Mrs. Sullen. (*Aside*) Now, now, I'm ruined if he kneels!—Rise, thou prostrate engineer, not all thy undermining skill shall reach my heart.—Rise, and know, I am a woman without my sex; I can love to all the tenderness of wishes, sighs, and tears—but go no farther. Still, to convince you that I'm more than woman, I can speak my frailty, confess my weakness even for you—but—

Archer. For me! (*Going to lay hold on her*)

Mrs. Sullen. Hold, sir! build not upon that; for my most mortal hatred follows if you disobey what I command you now.—Leave me this minute.—(*Aside*) If he denies I'm lost.

Archer. Then you'll promise—

Mrs. Sullen. Anything another time.

Archer. When shall I come?

Mrs. Sullen. To-morrow—when you will.

Archer. Your lips must seal the promise.

Mrs. Sullen. Psha!

Archer. They must! they must!—(*Kisses her*) Raptures and paradise!—And why not now, my angel? the time, the place, silence, and secrecy, all conspire—And the now conscious stars have preordained this moment for my happiness. (*Takes her in his arms*)

Mrs. Sullen. You will not! cannot, sure!

Archer. If the sun rides fast, and disappoints not mortals of to-morrow's dawn, this night shall crown my joys.

Mrs. Sullen. My sex's pride assist me!

ARCHER. My sex's strength help me!
MRS. SULLEN. You shall kill me first!
ARCHER. I'll die with you.
     (*Carrying her off*)
MRS. SULLEN. Thieves! thieves! murther!—

Enter SCRUB *in his breeches and one shoe*
SCRUB. Thieves! thieves! murder! popery!
ARCHER. Ha! the very timorous stag will kill in rutting time.
    (*Draws, and offers to stab* SCRUB)
SCRUB. (*Kneeling*) O pray, sir, spare all I have, and take my life!
MRS. SULLEN. (*Holding* ARCHER's *hand*) What does the fellow mean?
SCRUB. O madam, down upon your knees, you marrowbones!—he's one of 'em.
ARCHER. Of whom?
SCRUB. One of the rogues—I beg your pardon, sir,—of the honest gentlemen that just now are broke into the house.
ARCHER. How!
MRS. SULLEN. I hope you did not come to rob me?
ARCHER. Indeed I did, madam, but I would have taken nothing but what you might ha' spared; but your crying "Thieves" has waked this dreaming fool, and so he takes 'em for granted.
SCRUB. Granted! 'tis granted, sir, take all we have.
MRS. SULLEN. The fellow looks as if he were broke out of Bedlam.
SCRUB. Oons, madam, they're broke into the house with fire and sword! I saw them, heard them, they'll be here this minute.
ARCHER. What, thieves?
SCRUB. Under favor, sir, I think so.
MRS. SULLEN. What shall we do, sir?
ARCHER. Madam, I wish your ladyship a good night.
MRS. SULLEN. Will you leave me?
ARCHER. Leave you! Lord, madam, did not you command me to be gone just now, upon pain of your immortal hatred?
MRS. SULLEN. Nay, but pray, sir—
    (*Takes hold of him*)
ARCHER. Ha, ha, ha! now comes my turn to be ravished.—You see now, madam, you must use men one way or other; but take this by the way, good madam, that none but a fool will give you the benefit of his courage, unless you'll take his love along with it.—How are they armed, friend?
SCRUB. With sword and pistol, sir.
ARCHER. Hush!—I see a dark lantern coming through the gallery.—Madam, be assured I will protect you, or lose my life.
MRS. SULLEN. Your life! no, sir, they can rob me of nothing that I value half so much; therefore, now, sir, let me entreat you to be gone.
ARCHER. No, madam, I'll consult my own safety for the sake of yours; I'll work by stratagem. Have you courage enough to stand the appearance of 'em!
MRS. SULLEN. Yes, yes, since I have 'scaped your hands, I can face anything.
ARCHER. Come hither, brother Scrub! don't you know me?
SCRUB. Eh, my dear brother, let me kiss thee.   (*Kisses* ARCHER)
ARCHER. This way—here—
(ARCHER *and* SCRUB *hide behind the bed*)

Enter GIBBET, *with a dark lantern in one hand, and a pistol in t'other*

GIBBET. Ay, ay, this is the chamber, and the lady alone.
MRS. SULLEN. Who are you, sir? what would you have? d'ye come to rob me?
GIBBET. Rob you! alack a day, madam, I'm only a younger brother, madam; and so, madam, if you make a noise, I'll shoot you through the head; but don't be afraid, madam. —(*Laying his lantern and pistol upon the table*) These rings, madam—don't be concerned, madam, I have a profound respect for you, madam! Your keys, madam—don't be frighted, madam, I'm the most of a gentleman.—(*Searching her pockets*) This necklace, madam—I never was rude to a lady;—I have a veneration—for this necklace—
   (*Here* ARCHER *having come round and seized the pistol, takes* GIBBET *by the collar, trips up his heels, and claps the pistol to his breast*)
ARCHER. Hold, profane villain, and take the reward of thy sacrilege!
GIBBET. Oh! pray, sir, don't kill me; I an't prepared.
ARCHER. How many is there of 'em, Scrub?
SCRUB. Five-and-forty, sir.
ARCHER. Then I must kill the villain, to have him out of the way.
GIBBET. Hold, hold, sir; we are but three, upon my honor.

ARCHER. Scrub, will you undertake to secure him?

SCRUB. Not I, sir; kill him, kill him!

ARCHER. Run to Gipsy's chamber, there you'll find the doctor; bring him hither presently.—(*Exit* SCRUB, *running*) Come, rogue, if you have a short prayer, say it.

GIBBET. Sir, I have no prayer at all; the government has provided a chaplain to say prayers for us on these occasions.

MRS. SULLEN. Pray, sir, don't kill him; you fright me as much as him.

ARCHER. The dog shall die, madam, for being the occasion of my disappointment.—Sirrah, this moment is your last.

GIBBET. Sir, I'll give you two hundred pound to spare my life.

ARCHER. Have you no more, rascal?

GIBBET. Yes, sir, I can command four hundred, but I must reserve two of 'em to save my life at the sessions.

Enter SCRUB *with* FOIGARD

ARCHER. Here, doctor—I suppose Scrub and you between you may manage him. Lay hold of him, doctor. (FOIGARD *lays hold of* GIBBET)

GIBBET. What! turned over to the priest already!—Look'ye, doctor, you come before your time; I an't condemned yet, I thank ye.

FOIGARD. Come, my dear joy, I vill secure your body and your shoul too; I vill make you a good catholic, and give you an absolution.

GIBBET. Absolution! Can you procure me a pardon, doctor?

FOIGARD. No, joy.

GIBBET. Then you and your absolution may go to the devil!

ARCHER. Convey him into the cellar, there bind him:—take the pistol, and if he offers to resist, shoot him through the head—and come back to us with all the speed you can.

SCRUB. Ay, ay; come, doctor—do you hold him fast, and I'll guard him.

(*Exit* FOIGARD *with* GIBBET, SCRUB *following*)

MRS. SULLEN. But how came the doctor.

ARCHER. In short, madam—(*Shrieking without*) 'Sdeath! the rogues are at work with the other ladies—I'm vexed I parted with the pistol; but I must fly to their assistance.—Will you stay here, madam, or venture yourself with me?

MRS. SULLEN. (*Taking him by the arm*) Oh, with you, dear sir, with you. *Exeunt*

SCENE III

Another apartment in the same house

Enter HOUNSLOW *dragging in* LADY BOUNTIFUL, *and* BAGSHOT *haling in* DORINDA; *the rogues with swords drawn*

HOUNSLOW. Come, come, your jewels, mistress!

BAGSHOT. Your keys, your keys, old gentlewoman!

Enter AIMWELL *and* CHERRY

AIMWELL. Turn this way, villains! I durst engage an army in such a cause.
(*He engages 'em both*)

DORINDA. O madam, had I but a sword to help the brave man!

LADY BOUNTIFUL. There's three or four hanging up in the hall; but they won't draw. I'll go fetch one, however. *Exit*

Enter ARCHER *and* MRS. SULLEN

ARCHER. Hold, hold, my lord! every man his bird, pray. (*They engage man to man, the rogues are thrown and disarmed*)

CHERRY. (*Aside*) What! the rogues taken! then they'll impeach my father; I must give him timely notice. (*Runs out*)

ARCHER. Shall we kill the rogues?

AIMWELL. No, no, we'll bind them.

ARCHER. Ay, ay.—(*To* MRS. SULLEN *who stands by him*) Here, madam, lend me your garter.

MRS. SULLEN. (*Aside*) The devil's in this fellow! he fights, loves, and banters, all in a breath.—Here's a cord that the rogues brought with 'em, I suppose.

ARCHER. Right, right, the rogue's destiny, a rope to hang himself.—Come, my lord—this is but a scandalous sort of an office, (*Binding the rogues together*) if our adventures should end in this sort of hangman-work; but I hope there is something in prospect, that—(*Enter* SCRUB) Well, Scrub, have you secured your Tartar?

SCRUB. Yes, sir, I left the priest and him disputing about religion.

AIMWELL. And pray carry these gentlemen to reap the benefit of the controversy.
(*Delivers the prisoners to* SCRUB, *who leads 'em out*)

MRS. SULLEN. Pray, sister, how came my lord here?

DORINDA. And pray how came the gentleman here?

MRS. SULLEN. I'll tell you the greatest piece of villainy— (*They talk in dumb show*)

AIMWELL. I fancy, Archer, you have been more successful in your adventures than the housebreakers.

ARCHER. No matter for my adventure, yours is the principal.—Press her this minute to marry you—now while she's hurried between the palpitation of her fear and the joy of her deliverance, now, while the tide of her spirits are at high-flood—throw yourself at her feet, speak some romantic nonsense or other—address her like Alexander in the height of his victory, confound her senses, bear down her reason, and away with her.— The priest is now in the cellar, and dare not refuse to do the work.

Enter LADY BOUNTIFUL

AIMWELL. But how shall I get off without being observed?

ARCHER. You a lover, and not find a way to get off!—Let me see—

AIMWELL. You bleed, Archer.

ARCHER. 'Sdeath, I'm glad on't; this wound will do the business. I'll amuse the old lady and Mrs. Sullen about dressing my wound, while you carry off Dorinda.

LADY BOUNTIFUL. Gentlemen, could we understand how you would be gratified for the services—

ARCHER. Come, come, my lady, this is no time for compliments; I'm wounded, madam.

LADY BOUNTIFUL AND MRS. SULLEN. How! Wounded!

DORINDA. I hope, sir, you have received no hurt.

AIMWELL. None but what you may cure.— (*Makes love in dumb show*)

LADY BOUNTIFUL. Let me see your arm, sir—I must have some powder-sugar to stop the blood.—O me! an ugly gash, upon my word, sir! You must go into bed.

ARCHER. Ay, my lady, a bed would do very well.—(*To* MRS. SULLEN) Madam, will you do me the favor to conduct me to a chamber?

LADY BOUNTIFUL. Do, do, daughter— while I get the lint and the probe and the plaster ready.

(*Runs out one way,* AIMWELL *carries off* DORINDA *another*)

ARCHER. Come, madam, why don't you obey your mother's commands?

MRS. SULLEN. How can you, after what is passed, have the confidence to ask me?

ARCHER. And if you go to that, how can you, after what is passed, have the confidence to deny me? Was not this blood shed in your defence, and my life exposed for your protection? Look'ye, madam, I'm none of your romantic fools, that fight giants and monsters for nothing; my valor is downright Swiss;[1] I'm a soldier of fortune, and must be paid.

MRS. SULLEN. 'Tis ungenerous in you, sir, to upbraid me with your services!

ARCHER. 'Tis ungenerous in you, madam, not to reward 'em.

MRS. SULLEN. How! at the expense of my honor?

ARCHER. Honor! can honor consist with ingratitude? If you would deal like a woman of honor, do like a man of honor. D'ye think I would deny you in such a case?

Enter a Servant

SERVANT. Madam, my lady ordered me to tell you that your brother is below at the gate. *Exit*

MRS. SULLEN. My brother! Heavens be praised!—Sir, he shall thank you for your services, he has it in his power.

ARCHER. Who is your brother, madam?

MRS. SULLEN. Sir Charles Freeman.— You'll excuse me, sir; I must go and receive him. *Exit*

ARCHER. Sir Charles Freeman! 'Sdeath and hell! my old acquaintance! Now unless Aimwell has made good use of his time, all our fair machine goes souse into the sea like the Eddystone.[2] *Exit*

SCENE IV.—*The Gallery in the same*

Enter AIMWELL *and* DORINDA

DORINDA. Well, well, my lord, you have conquered; your late generous action will, I hope, plead for my easy yielding; though I must own, your lordship had a friend in the fort before.

AIMWELL. The sweets of Hybla dwell upon her tongue!—Here, doctor—

[1] Mercenary soldiers.
[2] Eddystone Lighthouse, in the Channel off Plymouth Harbor. The first lighthouse was destroyed in a storm in 1703.

Enter FOIGARD, *with a book*

FOIGARD. Are you prepared boat?

DORINDA. I'm ready. But first, my lord, one word—I have a frightful example of a hasty marriage in my own family; when I reflect upon't, it shocks me. Pray, my lord, consider a little—

AIMWELL. Consider! do you doubt my honor or my love?

DORINDA. Neither: I do believe you equally just as brave: and were your whole sex drawn out for me to choose, I should not cast a look upon the multitude if you were absent. But, my lord, I'm a woman; colors, concealments may hide a thousand faults in me—therefore know me better first. I hardly dare affirm I know myself, in anything except in love.

AIMWELL. (*Aside*) Such goodness who could injure! I find myself unequal to the task of villain; she has gained my soul, and made it honest like her own—I cannot, cannot hurt her.—Doctor, retire.— (*Exit* FOIGARD) Madam, behold your lover and your proselyte, and judge of my passion by my conversion!—I'm all a lie, nor dare I give a fiction to your arms; I'm all counterfeit, except my passion.

DORINDA. Forbid it, Heaven! a counterfeit!

AIMWELL. I am no lord, but a poor needy man, come with a mean, a scandalous design to prey upon your fortune; but the beauties of your mind and person have so won me from myself, that, like a trusty servant, I prefer the interest of my mistress to my own.

DORINDA. Sure I have had the dream of some poor mariner, a sleepy image of a welcome port, and wake involved in storms!—Pray, sir, who are you?

AIMWELL. Brother to the man whose title I usurped, but stranger to his honor or his fortune.

DORINDA. Matchless honesty!—Once I was proud, sir, of your wealth and title, but now am prouder that you want it; now I can show my love was justly levelled, and had no aim but love.—Doctor, come in. (*Enter* FOIGARD *at one door*, GIPSY *at another, who whispers to* DORINDA) (*To* FOIGARD) Your pardon, sir, we shannot want you now.—(*To* AIMWELL) Sir, you must excuse me—I'll wait on you presently. *Exit with* GIPSY

FOIGARD. Upon my shoul, now, dis is foolish. *Exit*

AIMWELL. Gone! and bid the priest depart!—It has an ominous look.

Enter ARCHER

ARCHER. Courage, Tom!—Shall I wish you joy?

AIMWELL. No.

ARCHER. Oons, man, what ha' you been doing?

AIMWELL. O Archer! my honesty, I fear, has ruined me.

ARCHER. How!

AIMWELL. I have discovered myself.

ARCHER. Discovered! and without my consent? What! have I embarked my small remains in the same bottom with yours, and you dispose of all without my partnership?

AIMWELL. O Archer! I own my fault.

ARCHER. After conviction—'tis then too late for pardon.—You may remember, Mr. Aimwell, that you proposed this folly: as you begun, so end it. Henceforth I'll hunt my fortune single—so farewell!

AIMWELL. Stay, my dear Archer, but a minute.

ARCHER. Stay! what, to be despised, exposed, and laughed at! No, I would sooner change conditions with the worst of the rogues we just now bound, than bear one scornful smile from the proud knight that once I treated as my equal.

AIMWELL. What knight?

ARCHER. Sir Charles Freeman, brother to the lady that I had almost—but no matter for that, 'tis a cursed night's work, and so I leave you to make the best on't. (*Going*)

AIMWELL. Freeman!—One word, Archer. Still I have hopes; methought she received my confession with pleasure.

ARCHER. 'Sdeath, who doubts it?

AIMWELL. She consented after to the match; and still I dare believe she will be just.

ARCHER. To herself, I warrant her, as you should have been.

AIMWELL. By all my hopes, she comes, and smiling comes!

Enter DORINDA *mighty gay*

DORINDA. Come, my dear lord—I fly with impatience to your arms—the minutes of my absence was a tedious year. Where's this tedious priest?

Enter FOIGARD

ARCHER. Oons, a brave girl!

DORINDA. I suppose, my lord, this gentleman is privy to our affairs?

ARCHER. Yes, yes, madam; I'm to be your father.

DORINDA. Come, priest, do your office.

ARCHER. Make haste, make haste, couple 'em any way.—(*Takes* AIMWELL'S *hand*) Come, madam, I'm to give you—

DORINDA. My mind's altered; I won't.

ARCHER. Eh!—

AIMWELL. I'm confounded!

FOIGARD. Upon my shoul, and sho is my-shelf.

ARCHER. What's the matter now, madam?

DORINDA. Look'ye, sir, one generous action deserves another.—This gentleman's honor obliged him to hide nothing from me; my justice engages me to conceal nothing from him. In short, sir, you are the person that you thought you counterfeited; you are the true Lord Viscount Aimwell, and I wish your lordship joy.—Now, priest, you may be gone; if my lord is pleased now with the match, let his lordship marry me in the face of the world.

AIMWELL AND ARCHER. What does she mean?

DORINDA. Here's a witness for my truth.

Enter SIR CHARLES FREEMAN *and* MRS. SULLEN

SIR CHARLES. My dear Lord Aimwell, I wish you joy.

AIMWELL. Of what?

SIR CHARLES. Of your honor and estate. Your brother died the day before I left London; and all your friends have writ after you to Brussels;—among the rest I did myself the honor.

ARCHER. Heark'ye, sir knight, don't you banter now?

SIR CHARLES. 'Tis truth, upon my honor.

AIMWELL. Thanks to the pregnant stars that formed this accident!

ARCHER. Thanks to the womb of time that brought it forth!—away with it!

AIMWELL. Thanks to my guardian angel that led me to the prize.

(*Taking* DORINDA'S *hand*)

ARCHER. And double thanks to the noble Sir Charles Freeman.—My lord, I wish you joy.—My lady, I wish you joy.—Egad, Sir Freeman, you're the honestest fellow living!—'Sdeath, I'm grown strange airy upon this matter.—My lord, how d'ye?—A word, my lord; don't you remember something of a previous agreement, that entitles me to the moiety of this lady's fortune, which I think will amount to five thousand pound?

AIMWELL. Not a penny, Archer; you would ha' cut my throat just now, because I would not deceive this lady.

ARCHER. Ay, and I'll cut your throat again, if you should deceive her now.

AIMWELL. That's what I expected; and to end the dispute, the lady's fortune is ten thousand pounds, we'll divide stakes: take the ten thousand pounds or the lady.

DORINDA. How! is your lordship so indifferent?

ARCHER. No, no, no, madam! his lordship knows very well that I'll take the money; I leave you to his lordship, and so we're both provided for.

Enter COUNT BELLAIR

COUNT BELLAIR. Mesdames et Messieurs, I am your servant trice humble! I hear you be rob here.

AIMWELL. The ladies have been in some danger, sir.

COUNT BELLAIR. And, begar, our inn be rob too!

AIMWELL. Our inn! by whom?

COUNT BELLAIR. By the landlord, begar!—Garzoon, he has rob himself, and run away?

ARCHER. Robbed himself!

COUNT BELLAIR. Ay, begar, and me too of a hundre pound.

ARCHER. A hundred pound?

COUNT BELLAIR. Yes, that I owed him.

AIMWELL. Our money's gone, Frank.

ARCHER. Rot the money! my wench is gone.—(*To* COUNT BELLAIR) *Savez-vous quel quechose de Mademoiselle Cherry?*

Enter a Fellow *with a strong box and a letter*

FELLOW. Is there one Martin here?

ARCHER. Ay, ay—who wants him?

FELLOW. I have a box here, and letter for him. (*Gives the box and letter to* ARCHER *and exit*)

ARCHER. Ha, ha, ha! what's here? Legerdemain!—By this light, my lord, our money again!—But this unfolds the riddle.—(*Opening the letter, reads*) Hum, hum, hum!—Oh, 'tis for the public good, and must be communicated to the company. (*Reads*)

MR. MARTIN,

My father being afraid of an impeachment

by the rogues that are taken to-night, is gone off; but if you can procure him a pardon, he will make great discoveries that may be useful to the country. Could I have met you instead of your master to-night, I would have delivered myself into your hands, with a sum that much exceeds that in your strong-box, which I have sent you, with an assurance to my dear Martin that I shall ever be his most faithful friend till death. CHERRY BONIFACE

There's a billet-doux for you! As for the father, I think he ought to be encouraged; and for the daughter—pray, my lord, persuade your bride to take her into her service instead of Gipsy.

AIMWELL. I can assure you, madam, your deliverance was owing to her discovery.

DORINDA. Your command, my lord, will do without the obligation. I'll take care of her.

SIR CHARLES. This good company meets opportunely in favor of a design I have in behalf of my unfortunate sister. I intend to part her from her husband—gentlemen, will you assist me?

ARCHER. Assist you! 'sdeath, who would not?

COUNT BELLAIR. Assist! garzoon, we all assist!

Enter SULLEN *and* SCRUB

SQUIRE SULLEN. What's all this? They tell me, spouse, that you had like to have been robbed.

MRS. SULLEN. Truly, spouse, I was pretty near it—had not these two gentlemen interposed.

SQUIRE SULLEN. How came these gentlemen here?

MRS. SULLEN. That's his way of returning thanks, you must know.

COUNT BELLAIR. Garzoon, the question be àpropos for all dat.

SIR CHARLES. You promised last night, sir, that you would deliver your lady to me this morning.

SQUIRE SULLEN. Humph!

ARCHER. Humph! what do you mean by humph? Sir, you shall deliver her! In short, sir, we have saved you and your family; and if you are not civil, we'll unbind the rogues, join with 'um, and set fire to your house. What does the man mean? not part with his wife!

COUNT BELLAIR. Ay, garzoon, de man no understan common justice.

MRS. SULLEN. Hold, gentlemen! All things here must move by consent; compulsion would spoil us. Let my dear and I talk the matter over, and you shall judge it between us.

SQUIRE SULLEN. Let me know first who are to be our judges. Pray, sir, who are you?

SIR CHARLES. I am Sir Charles Freeman, come to take away your wife.

SQUIRE SULLEN. And you, good sir?

AIMWELL. Charles,[1] Viscount Aimwell, come to take away your sister.

SQUIRE SULLEN. And you, pray, sir?

ARCHER. Francis Archer, esquire, come—

SQUIRE SULLEN. To take away my mother, I hope. Gentlemen, you're heartily welcome; I never met with three more obliging people since I was born!—And now, my dear, if you please, you shall have the first word.

ARCHER. And the last, for five pound!

MRS. SULLEN. Spouse!

SQUIRE SULLEN. Rib!

MRS. SULLEN. How long have we been married?

SQUIRE SULLEN. By the almanac, fourteen months; but by my account, fourteen years.

MRS. SULLEN. 'Tis thereabout by my reckoning.

COUNT BELLAIR. Garzoon, their account will agree.

MRS. SULLEN. Pray, spouse, what did you marry for?

SQUIRE SULLEN. To get an heir to my estate.

SIR CHARLES. And have you succeeded?

SQUIRE SULLEN. No.

ARCHER. The condition fails of his side.— Pray, madam, what did you marry for?

MRS. SULLEN. To support the weakness of my sex by the strength of his, and to enjoy the pleasures of an agreeable society.

SIR CHARLES. Are your expectations answered?

MRS. SULLEN. No.

COUNT BELLAIR. A clear case! a clear case!

SIR CHARLES. What are the bars to your mutual contentment?

MRS. SULLEN. In the first place, I can't drink ale with him.

SQUIRE SULLEN. Nor can I drink tea with her.

MRS. SULLEN. I can't hunt with you.

SQUIRE SULLEN. Nor can I dance with you.

[1] He was Tom in Act II and earlier in this act. Of course his name may have been Charles Thomas.

Mrs. Sullen. I hate cocking and racing.
Squire Sullen. And I abhor ombre and piquet.
Mrs. Sullen. Your silence is intolerable.
Squire Sullen. Your prating is worse.
Mrs. Sullen. Have we not been a perpetual offence to each other? a gnawing vulture at the heart?
Squire Sullen. A frightful goblin to the sight?
Mrs. Sullen. A porcupine to the feeling?
Squire Sullen. Perpetual wormwood to the taste?
Mrs. Sullen. Is there on earth a thing we could agree in?
Squire Sullen. Yes—to part.
Mrs. Sullen. With all my heart.
Squire Sullen. Your hand.
Mrs. Sullen. Here.
Squire Sullen. These hands joined us, these shall part.—Away!
Mrs. Sullen. North.
Squire Sullen. South.
Mrs. Sullen. East.
Squire Sullen. West—far as the poles asunder.
Count Bellair. Begar, the ceremony be vera pretty.
Sir Charles. Now, Mr. Sullen, there wants only my sister's fortune to make us easy.
Squire Sullen. Sir Charles, you love your sister, and I love her fortune; every one to his fancy.
Archer. Then you won't refund?
Squire Sullen. Not a stiver.
Archer. Then I find, madam, you must e'en go to your prison again.
Count Bellair. What is the portion?
Sir Charles. Ten thousand pound, sir.
Count Bellair. Garzoon, I'll pay it, and she shall go home wid me.
Archer. Ha, ha, ha! French all over.—Do you know, sir, what ten thousand pound English is?
Count Bellair. No, begar, not justement.
Archer. Why, sir, 'tis a hundred thousand livres!
Count Bellair. A hundre tousand livres! A garzoon, me canno' do't! Your beauties and their fortunes are both too much for me.
Archer. Then I will.—This night's adventure has proved strangely lucky to us all—for Captain Gibbet in his walk had made bold, Mr. Sullen, with your study and escritoire, and had taken out all the writings of your estate, all the articles of marriage with your lady, bills, bonds, leases, receipts to an infinite value; I took 'em from him, and I deliver 'em to Sir Charles.

(*Gives* Sir Charles Freeman *a parcel of papers and parchments*)

Squire Sullen. How, my writings!—my head aches consumedly.—Well, gentlemen, you shall have her fortune, but I can't talk. If you have a mind, Sir Charles, to be merry, and celebrate my sister's wedding and my divorce, you may command my house—but my head aches consumedly.—Scrub, bring me a dram.
Archer. (*To* Mrs. Sullen) Madam, there's a country dance to the trifle that I sung to-day; your hand, and we'll lead it up.

Here a Dance

Archer. 'Twould be hard to guess which of these parties is the better pleased, the couple joined, or the couple parted: the one rejoicing in hopes of an untasted happiness, and the other in their deliverance from an experienced misery.
Both happy in their several states we find,
Those parted by consent, and those conjoined.
Consent, if mutual, saves the lawyer's fee—
Consent is law enough to set you free.

EPILOGUE

Designed to be Spoke in the "Beaux' Stratagem"

If to our play your judgment can't be kind,
Let its expiring author pity find: [1]
Survey his mournful case with melting eyes,
Nor let the bard be damned before he dies.
Forbear, you fair, on his last scene to frown,
But his true exit with a plaudit crown;
Then shall the dying poet cease to fear
The dreadful knell, while your applause he hears.
At Leuctra [2] so the conquering Theban died,
Claimed his friends' praises, but their tears denied:

[1] Cf. Farquhar's "Advertisement," which preceded the printed play.
[2] Ancient village in Bœotia, scene of a battle between the Thebans and the Spartans (371 B.C.). Epaminondas, the Theban general, died, however, in 362 B.C., at the Battle of Mantineia.

Pleased in the pangs of death, he greatly thought
Conquest with loss of life but cheaply bought.
The difference this,—the Greek was one would fight,
As brave, though not so gay, as Serjeant Kite;[1]

[1] Hero of Farquhar's own *The Recruiting Officer*.

Ye sons of Will's,[2] what's that to those who write? 15
To Thebes alone the Grecian owed his bays;
You may the bard above the hero raise,
Since yours is greater than Athenian praise.

[2] Will's coffee-house, patronized by Dryden, was famous as a resort of men of letters.

CATO

A Tragedy by Joseph Addison

Ecce spectaculum dignum, ad quod respiciat, intentus operi suo, Deus! Ecce par Deo dignum, vir fortis cum malā fortunā compositus! Non video, inquam, quid habeat in terris Jupiter pulchrius, si convertere animum velit, quam ut spectet Catonem, jam partibus non semel fractis, nihilominus inter ruinas publicas erectum. Sen. de Divin. Prov.[1]

Joseph Addison was the son of the Reverend Lancelot Addison, Rector of Milston, Wiltshire, later Dean of Lichfield; he was born at Milston, May 1, 1672. He attended schools at Amesbury, near his birthplace, Salisbury, and Lichfield. After a short term at the Charterhouse, where he met Steele, Addison went to Queen's College, Oxford, in 1687. Two years later he transferred to Magdalen, where he was made a Master of Arts in 1693, and where he held a Fellowship from 1697 to 1711. From 1699 to 1703 he traveled on the Continent. Upon his return to England he entered the world of literature and politics. His first chance in life came in 1704 when he was asked to write a poem commemorating the successes of the Duke of Marlborough, which he did in *The Campaign*, the elegant couplets of which have placed their author in the first rank of Augustan poets. In 1706 he became an Under-Secretary of State, the first of several public offices which he held under the various Whig governments of Queen Anne and George I. His first dramatic effort, *Rosamond*, an English opera "after the Italian manner," was performed in 1707, a practical expression of his opposition to the too-powerful Italian influence on the English stage. Addison soon became a prominent figure in the politico-literary circles of London, a member of the famous Kit-Kat Club, and friend of the foremost persons of the day, including Pope and Swift. From 1709 to 1712 with his friend Steele he engaged as editor or contributor in the publication of the *Tatler* and the *Spectator*. Here our author's peculiar genius enabled him to set forth in its most favorable light that prose which is the "model of the middle style," pure and exact, equable and easy. In 1713 the production of his tragedy, *Cato*, confirmed him in his position as one of the great men of letters of the time. In 1716 he became one of His Majesty's Principal Secretaries of State, crowning a career of political aspiration, and husband of the Countess Dowager of Warwick, fulfilling a desire cherished for many years. In this year, also, he favored the stage with his moral comedy, *The Drummer*, which, produced anonymously, met with small success. His later years were spent as the center of a circle of admirers at Button's coffee-house, where, according to Pope, he gave his little senate laws. He died on June 17, 1719, at Holland House and was buried in Westminster Abbey.

REFERENCES: Editions of Addison's works by Tickell (1723), Hurd (1854–56).

Biographies by Samuel Johnson (in *Lives of the Poets*), Lucy Aikin (1843), W. J. Courthope (1884), Bonamy Dobrée in *Essays in Biography* (1925), &c.

ADDISON'S DRAMATIC WORKS

Rosamond (opera) (D.L., March 3, 1707), 1707.
Cato. A Tragedy. (D.L., April 14, 1713), 1713.
The Drummer; or, The Haunted House (comedy) (D.L., March 10, 1716), 1716.

Political feeling was running high in 1712. The Tories were suspected, more or less rightly, of plotting with the Pretender; the Queen was thought, naturally enough, to have Jacobite sympathies; and the Whigs were endeavoring to recover from the disadvantage at which they had been placed by the disgrace of Marlborough the year before. The notion

---

[1] Behold a sight worthy of being regarded by a god intent upon his own work! Behold a pair worthy of a god, a brave man matched with evil fortune! I do not see, I declare, what more beautiful sight Jupiter could find on earth, if he should wish to turn his mind to it, than the spectacle of Cato, after his party had been more than once broken, erect amidst the ruins of the republic. Seneca. *De Div. Prov.*, 6.

of a drama about a banished leader of such undoubted integrity as Cato appealed to the patriotic instincts of certain Whig leaders; and Mr. Addison was known to have in his possession an almost completed draft of such a play, which he could be persuaded to finish. He waived his rights to pecuniary reward from the tragedy, which was produced at Drury Lane, April 14, 1713, with great splendor and unprecedented success. Booth at last became the greatest living actor, and Mrs. Oldfield added new jewels to her crown. Though produced at Whig instigation the Tories seized an opportunity to share in the glory. A prologue to the tragedy was written by Mr. Pope, the friend of Harley and St. John. The epilogue, however, was done by the Whig, Dr. Garth. Whigs and Tories vied with each other in applauding the virtuous sententiousness of the great Mr. Addison's verses on liberty and a falling state. Pope, in a letter to Trumbull, April 30, 1713, describes the occasion in these words: "Cato was not so much the wonder of Rome in his day as he is of Britain in ours; and though all the foolish industry possible had been used to make it thought a party play, yet what the author said of another may the most properly be applied to him on this occasion:

Envy itself is dumb, in wonder lost,
And factions strive who shall applaud him most! [1]

The numerous and violent claps of the Whig party on the one side of the theater were echoed back by the Tories on the other, while the author sweated behind the scenes with concern to find their applause proceeding more from the hand than the head. This was the case, too, with the Prologue-writer [Pope himself], who was clapped into a staunch Whig at the end of every two lines."

[1] *The Campaign*, ll. 45–46.

Few critics can hope to excel Dr. Johnson on the subject of *Cato*. "About things on which the public thinks long," he says, "it commonly attains to think right; and of *Cato* it has not been unjustly determined that it is rather a poem in dialogue than a drama, rather a succession of just sentiments in elegant language than a representation of natural affections, or of any state probable or possible in human life. Nothing here 'excites or assuages emotion;' here is 'no magical power of raising fantastic terror or wild anxiety.' The events are expected without solicitude and are remembered without joy or sorrow. Of the agents we have no care; we consider not what they are doing or what they are suffering; we only wish to know what they have to say. Cato is a being above our solicitude, a man of whom the gods take care and whom we leave to their care with heedless confidence. To the rest neither gods nor men can have much attention, for there is not one among them that strongly attracts either affection or esteem. But they are made vehicles of such sentiments and such expressions that there is scarcely a scene in the play which the reader does not wish to impress upon his memory."

The absurdities of the play, most of them pointed out by John Dennis at the time, the ridiculous observance of the unity of place for one, are too palpable to need comment. But, as Dr. Johnson said and as Addison himself probably felt, the "just sentiments in elegant language," the chaste stoicism of Cato, and the undoubted advocacy of a sane and ordered existence, with the strict adherence to classical principles, all made *Cato* the supreme example of Augustan pseudo-classical tragedy.

CATO

DRAMATIS PERSONÆ

MEN

Cato [1]	Mr. Booth	Portius ⎫ Sons of Cato [4]	Mr. Powell
Lucius, *a Senator* [2]	Mr. Keen	Marcus ⎭	Mr. Rian
Sempronius, *a Senator*	Mr. Mills	Decius, *Ambassador from Cæsar*	Mr. Bowman
Juba,[3] *Prince of Numidia*	Mr. Wilks		
Syphax, *General of the Numidians*	Mr. Cibber		

Mutineers, Guards, &c.

WOMEN

Marcia,[5] *Daughter to Cato*   Mrs. Oldfield   Lucia, *Daughter to Lucius*   Mrs. Porter

Scene: *a large Hall in the Governor's Palace of Utica*

PROLOGUE

By Mr. Pope [6]

Spoken by Mr. Wilks [7]

To wake the soul by tender strokes of art,
To raise the genius, and to mend the heart,
To make mankind in conscious virtue bold,
Live o'er each scene, and be what they behold:
For this the Tragic Muse first trod the stage,
Commanding tears to stream thro' every age;
Tyrants no more their savage nature kept, 7
And foes to virtue wondered how they wept.
Our author shuns by vulgar springs to move
The hero's glory, or the virgin's love;   10
In pitying love we but our weakness show,
And wild ambition well deserves its woe.
Here tears shall flow from a more gen'rous cause,
Such tears as patriots shed for dying laws:
He bids your breasts with ancient ardor rise,
And calls forth Roman drops from British eyes.   16
Virtue confessed in human shape he draws,
What Plato thought, and god-like Cato was:
No common object to your sight displays,   19
But what with pleasure heaven itself surveys;
A brave man struggling in the storms of fate,
And greatly falling with a falling state!
While Cato gives his little senate laws,[8]
What bosom beats not in his country's cause?
Who sees him act, but envies ev'ry deed?   25

---

[1] Marcus Porcius Cato (95–46 B.C.), called "Uticensis" to distinguish him from "the Censor," his great-grandfather, opposed corruption in Roman public life and took sides with Cicero against Cæsar on the question of the Catilinian conspiracy. He further opposed the first triumvirate; but, forced by circumstances to take sides, he favored Pompey. After the defeat of Pompey's adherents at Pharsalia (48), separating himself from the main body of the republicans, Cato led the remnant of his followers to Utica, where he shut himself up until the arrival of Cæsar. As resistance was impossible, he sent his followers to Europe in ships and stabbed himself when they were safely embarked. For this act he was made the patron saint of the Roman stoics. Lucan refers to him as a model of virtue and disinterestedness.

Addison based his plot on Plutarch's life of Cato the Younger, though Plutarch relates only the main outline of historical events.

[2] Possibly Lucius Cæsar, a relation of Julius Cæsar mentioned by Plutarch as being with Cato.

[3] Juba II, King of Numidia. He was carried to Rome by Cæsar for his triumph, but later was educated by Augustus and married to Cleopatra Semele, daughter of Antony and Cleopatra. He was replaced on his father's throne and lived until 19 or 24 A.D. He was known as a writer of valuable historical and geographic works.

[4] Plutarch mentions only one son of Cato.

[5] Cato's daughter, better known as Portia, married Marcus Junius Brutus, one of the assassins of Cæsar.

[6] Despite his strained relations with Addison, Pope was willing to have his name connected with a production that would most certainly be a success.

[7] Robert Wilks, who acted the part of Juba.

[8] Compare Pope's description of Atticus found in the "Epistle to Dr. Arbuthnot," ll. 193–214.

Who hears him groan, and does not wish to
    bleed?
Ev'n when proud Cæsar 'midst triumphal cars,
The spoils of nations, and the pomp of wars,
Ignobly vain, and impotently great,
Showed Rome her Cato's figure drawn in
    state,   30
As her dead father's rev'rend image past,
The pomp was darkened, and the day o'ercast,
The triumph ceased,—tears gushed from ev'ry
    eye,
The world's great victor past unheeded by;
Her last good man dejected Rome adored,   35
And honored Cæsar's less than Cato's sword.

   Britains attend: Be worth like this ap-
    proved,
And show you have the virtue to be moved.
With honest scorn the first famed Cato
    viewed [1]
Rome learning arts from Greece, whom she
    subdued; [2]   40
Our scene precariously subsists too long
On French translation, and Italian song. [3]
Dare to have sense yourselves; assert the stage,
Be justly warmed with your own native rage.
Such plays alone should please a British ear,
As Cato's self had not disdained to hear.   46

ACT I

Scene 1

Portius, Marcus

Portius. The dawn is over-cast, the morn-
    ing low'rs,
And heavily in clouds brings on the day,
The great, th' important day; big with the fate
Of Cato and of Rome.—Our father's death
Would fill up all the guilt of civil war,   5
And close the scene of blood. Already Cæsar
Has ravaged more than half the globe, and
    sees
Mankind grown thin by his destructive sword:
Should he go further, numbers would be
    wanting   9

---

[1] Cato the Elder (234–149 b.c.), called "the Censor," great-grandfather of the subject of this play.

[2] This line is almost a literal translation of Horace's Epistle to Augustus lines 156–7, *Epistles*, Book II, i.

[3] Cf. Addison's own comments upon Italian opera in *The Spectator*, nos. 5, 13 (the account of "Signior Nicolini's combat with a lion in the Haymarket"), 18 (an account of Italian opera and its progress on the English stage), 22, 28, 29, 31, 39, etc.

To form new battles, and support his crimes.
Ye gods, what havoc does ambition make
Among your works!
   Marcus. Thy steady temper, Portius,
Can look on guilt, rebellion, fraud, and Cæsar,
In the calm lights of mild philosophy;   14
I'm tortured, even to madness, when I think
On the proud victor: ev'ry time he's named
Pharsalia rises to my view!—I see
Th' insulting tyrant, prancing o'er the field
Strowed with Rome's citizens, and drenched in
    slaughter,   19
His horse's hoofs wet with patrician blood!
Oh, Portius, is there not some chosen curse,
Some hidden thunder in the stores of heaven,
Red with uncommon wrath, to blast the man,
Who owes his greatness to his country's ruin?
   Portius. Believe me, Marcus, 'tis an im-
    pious greatness,   25
And mixed with too much horror to be en-
    vied:
How does the luster of our father's actions,
Through the dark cloud of ills that cover him,
Break out, and burn with more triumphant
    brightness!
His sufferings shine, and spread a glory round
    him;   30
Greatly unfortunate, he fights the cause
Of honor, virtue, liberty, and Rome.
His sword ne'er fell but on the guilty head;
Oppression, tyranny, and pow'r usurped,
Draw all the vengeance of his arm upon 'em.
   Marcus. Who knows not this? But what
    can Cato do   36
Against a world, a base degen'rate world,
That courts the yoke, and bows the neck to
    Cæsar?
Pent up in Utica he vainly forms
A poor epitome of Roman greatness,   40
And, covered with [4] Numidian guards, directs
A feeble army, and an empty senate,
Remnants of mighty battles fought in vain.
By heavens, such virtues, joined with such
    success,
Distract my very soul: our father's fortune
Would almost tempt us to renounce his pre-
    cepts.   46
   Portius. Remember what our father oft
    has told us:
The ways of heaven are dark and intricate;
Puzzled in mazes, and perplext with errors,
Our understanding traces 'em in vain,   50
Lost and bewildered in the fruitless search;

---

[4] I.e., protected by.

Nor sees with how much art the windings run,
Nor where the regular confusion ends.
> MARCUS. These are suggestions of a mind
> at ease. 54

Oh, Portius, didst thou taste but half the griefs
That wring my soul, thou couldst not talk
thus coldly.
Passion unpitied, and successless love,
Plant daggers in my heart, and aggravate
My other griefs. Were but my Lucia kind!—
> PORTIUS. (*Aside*) Thou see'st not that thy
> brother is thy rival. 60

But I must hide it, for I know thy temper.—
Now Marcus, now, thy virtue's on the proof:
Put forth thy utmost strength, work ev'ry
nerve,
And call up all thy father in thy soul: 64
To quell the tyrant love, and guard thy heart
On this weak side, where most our nature fails,
Would be a conquest worthy Cato's son.
> MARCUS. Portius, the counsel which I cannot take,

Instead of healing, but upbraids my weakness.
Bid me for honor plunge into a war 70
Of thickest foes, and rush on certain death,
Then shalt thou see that Marcus is not slow
To follow glory, and confess his father.
Love is not to be reasoned down, or lost
In high ambition, and a thirst of greatness; 75
'Tis second life, it grows into the soul,
Warms ev'ry vein, and beats in ev'ry pulse,
I feel it here: My resolution melts—
> PORTIUS. Behold young Juba, the Numidian
> prince! 79

With how much care he forms himself to glory,
And breaks the fierceness of his native temper
To copy out our father's bright example.
He loves our sister Marcia, greatly loves her,
His eyes, his looks, his actions all betray it:
But still the smothered fondness burns within
him. 85
When most it swells, and labors for a vent,
The sense of honor and desire of fame
Drive the big passion back into his heart.
What, shall an African, shall Juba's heir
Reproach great Cato's son, and show the
world 90
A virtue wanting in a Roman soul?
> MARCUS. Portius, no more! your words leave
> stings behind 'em.

Whene'er did Juba, or did Portius, show
A virtue that has cast me at a distance,[1]
And thrown me out in the pursuits of honor?

[1] I.e., outdistanced me.

> PORTIUS. Marcus, I know thy gen'rous
> temper well, 96

Fling but th' appearance of dishonor on it,
It straight takes fire, and mounts into a blaze.
> MARCUS. A brother's suff'rings claim a
> brother's pity.
> PORTIUS. Heav'n knows I pity thee! Behold
> my eyes 100

Ev'n whilst I speak.—Do they not swim in
tears?
Were but my heart as naked to thy view,
Marcus would see it bleed in his behalf.
> MARCUS. Why then dost treat me with
> rebukes, instead 104

Of kind condoling cares, and friendly sorrow?
> PORTIUS. O Marcus, did I know the way
> to ease

Thy troubled heart, and mitigate thy pains,
Marcus, believe me, I could die to do it.
> MARCUS. Thou best of brothers, and thou
> best of friends! 109

Pardon a weak distempered soul, that swells
With sudden gusts, and sinks as soon in calms,
The sport of passions:—But Sempronius
comes:
He must not find this softness hanging on
me. [*Exeunt*]

SCENE II

Enter SEMPRONIUS

> SEMPRONIUS. (*Aside*) Conspiracies no sooner
> should be formed

Than executed. What means Portius here?
I like not that cold youth. I must dissemble,
And speak a language foreign to my heart.

[*Enter* PORTIUS]

Good morrow, Portius! let us once embrace,
Once more embrace; whilst yet we both are
free. 6
To-morrow should we thus express our friendship,
Each might receive a slave into his arms.
This sun perhaps, this morning sun's the last,
That e'er shall rise on Roman liberty. 10
> PORTIUS. My father has this morning called
> together

To this poor hall his little Roman senate,
(The leavings of Pharsalia) to consult
If yet he can oppose the mighty torrent
That bears down Rome, and all her gods,
before it, 15
Or must at length give up the world to Cæsar.

SEMPRONIUS. Not all the pomp and majesty
　　of Rome
Can raise her senate more than Cato's pres-
　ence.
His virtues render our assembly awful,　　19
They strike with something like religious fear,
And make ev'n Cæsar tremble at the head
Of armies flushed with conquest: O my Portius,
Could I but call that wondrous man my father,
Would but thy sister Marcia be propitious
To thy friend's vows: I might be blessed
　　indeed!　　25
　　PORTIUS. Alas! Sempronius, wouldst thou
　　　talk of love
To Marcia whilst her father's life's in danger?
Thou might'st as well court the pale trembling
　vestal,
When she beholds the holy flame expiring.
　　SEMPRONIUS. The more I see the wonders
　　　of thy race,　　30
The more I'm charmed: Thou must take heed,
　my Portius!
The world has all its eyes on Cato's son.
Thy father's merit sets thee up to view,
And shows thee in the fairest point of light,
To make thy virtues, or thy faults, conspicu-
　ous.　　35
　　PORTIUS. Well dost thou seem to check
　　　my ling'ring here
On this important hour. I'll straight away,
And while the fathers of the senate meet
In close debate to weigh th' events of war,
I'll animate the soldier's drooping courage, 40
With love of freedom and contempt of life:
I'll thunder in their ears their country's cause,
And try to rouse up all that's Roman in 'em.
'Tis not in mortals to command success,
But we'll do more, Sempronius; we'll deserve
　it.　　　　　　　　　　　　*Exit*　　45

SEMPRONIUS *solus*

Curse on the stripling! How he apes his
　sire,
Ambitiously sententious!—But I wonder
Old Syphax comes not; his Numidian genius
Is well disposed to mischief, were he prompt
And eager on it; but he must be spurred,　50
And ev'ry moment quickened to the course.
—Cato has used me ill. He has refused
His daughter Marcia to my ardent vows.
Besides, his baffled arms, and ruined cause
Are bars to my ambition. Cæsar's favor,　55
That showers down greatness on his friends,
　will raise me

To Rome's first honors. If I give up Cato,
I claim in my reward his captive daughter.
But Syphax comes!—

SCENE III

SYPHAX, SEMPRONIUS

　　SYPHAX.—Sempronius, all is ready,
I've sounded my Numidians, man by man,
And find 'em ripe for a revolt.—They all
Complain aloud of Cato's discipline
And wait but the command to change their
　master.　　5
　　SEMPRONIUS. Believe me, Syphax, there's
　　　no time to waste;
Ev'n whilst we speak, our conqueror comes on,
And gathers ground upon us ev'ry moment.
Alas! thou know'st not Cæsar's active soul,
With what a dreadful course he rushes on　10
From war to war. In vain has nature formed
Mountains and oceans to oppose his passage;
He bounds o'er all, victorious in his march.
The Alps and Pyreneans sink before him;
Through winds, and waves, and storms, he
　works his way,　　15
Impatient for the battle. One day more
Will set the victor thundering at our gates.
But tell me, hast thou yet drawn o'er young
　Juba?
That still would recommend thee more to
　Cæsar,
And challenge better terms.
　　SYPHAX.　　　　　　Alas! he's lost,　20
He's lost, Sempronius; all his thoughts are full
Of Cato's virtues. But I'll try once more
(For ev'ry instant I expect him here)
If yet I can subdue those stubborn principles
Of faith, of honor, and I know not what,　25
That have corrupted his Numidian temper,
And struck th' infection into all his soul.
　　SEMPRONIUS. Be sure to press upon him
　　　ev'ry motive.
Juba's surrender, since his father's death,
Would give up Africk into Cæsar's hands 30
And make him lord of half the burning zone.
　　SYPHAX. But is it true, Sempronius, that
　　　your senate
Is called together? Gods! Thou must be
　cautious!
Cato has piercing eyes, and will discern
Our frauds unless they're covered thick with
　art.　　35
　　SEMPRONIUS. Let me alone, good Syphax,
　　　I'll conceal

My thoughts in passion ('tis the surest way);
I'll bellow out for Rome and for my country,
And mouth at Cæsar till I shake the senate.
Your cold hypocrisy's a stale device,   40
A worn-out trick. Wouldst thou be thought
  in earnest,
Clothe thy feigned zeal in rage, in fire, in fury!
  SYPHAX. In troth, thou'rt able to instruct
    grey hairs,
And teach the wily African deceit!
  SEMPRONIUS. Once more, be sure to try thy
    skill on Juba.   45
Meanwhile I'll hasten to my Roman soldiers,
Inflame the mutiny, and underhand
Blow up their discontents till they break out
Unlooked for and discharge themselves on
  Cato.   49
Remember, Syphax, we must work in haste.
O think what anxious moments pass between
The birth of plots, and their last fatal periods.
Oh! 'tis a dreadful interval of time,
Filled up with horror all, and big with death!
Destruction hangs on ev'ry word we speak, 55
On ev'ry thought, 'till the concluding stroke
Determines all, and closes our design.   *Exit*

SYPHAX *solus*

I'll try if yet I can reduce to reason
This head-strong youth, and make him spurn
  at Cato.
The time is short, Cæsar comes rushing on
  us—   60
But hold! young Juba sees me and approaches.

SCENE IV

JUBA, SYPHAX

  JUBA. Syphax, I joy to meet thee thus alone.
I have observed of late thy looks are fall'n,
O'ercast with gloomy cares, and discontent;
Then tell me, Syphax, I conjure thee, tell me,
What are the thoughts that knit thy brow in
  frowns,   5
And turn thine eye thus coldly on thy prince?
  SYPHAX. 'Tis not my talent to conceal my
    thoughts,
Or carry smiles and sunshine in my face,
When discontent sits heavy at my heart.
I have not yet so much the Roman in me.   10
  JUBA. Why dost thou cast out such un-
    generous terms
Against the lords and sov'reigns of the world?
Dost thou not see mankind fall down before
  them,
And own the force of their superior virtue?
Is there a nation in the wilds of Africk,   15
Amidst our barren rocks and burning sands,
That does not tremble at the Roman name?
  SYPHAX. Gods! where's the worth that sets
    this people up
Above your own Numidia's tawny sons!
Do they with tougher sinews bend the bow?
Or flies the javelin swifter to its mark,   21
Launched from the vigor of a Roman arm?
Who like our active African instructs
The fiery steed, and trains him to his hand?
Or guides in troops th' embattled elephant,
Loaden with war? These, these are arts, my
  prince,   26
In which your Zama [1] does not stoop to Rome.
  JUBA. These all are virtues of a meaner
    rank,
Perfections that are placed in bones and
  nerves.
A Roman soul is bent on higher views: [2]   30
To civilize the rude unpolished world,
And lay it under the restraint of laws;
To make man mild, and sociable to man;
To cultivate the wild licentious savage
With wisdom, discipline, and lib'ral arts;   35
Th' embellishments of life. Virtues like these,
Make human nature shine, reform the soul,
And break our fierce barbarians into men.
  SYPHAX. Patience kind heavens!—Excuse an
    old man's warmth.
What are these wond'rous civilizing arts,   40
This Roman polish, and this smooth be-
  havior,
That render man thus tractable and tame?
Are they not only to disguise our passions,
To set our looks at variance with our thoughts,
To check the starts and sallies of the soul,
And break off all its commerce with the
  tongue;   46
In short, to change us into other creatures
Than what our nature and the gods designed
  us?
  JUBA. To strike thee dumb, turn up thy
    eyes to Cato!   49
There may'st thou see to what a godlike height
The Roman virtues lift up mortal man.

---

[1] Zama was the capital of Numidia.
[2] Lines 30–35 paraphrase Virgil, Æneid VI, ll. 851–3, which Dryden translated thus:
"But Rome, 'tis thine alone with awful sway,
To rule mankind, and make the world obey,
Disposing peace and war by thy own majestic **way;**
To tame the proud, the fetter'd slave to free:
These are imperial arts, and worthy thee."

While good, and just, and anxious for his
    friends,
He's still severely bent against himself;
Renouncing sleep, and rest, and food, and
    ease,
He strives with thrift and hunger, toil and
    heat;   55
And when his fortune sets before him all
The pomps and pleasures that his soul can
    wish,
His rigid virtue will accept of none.
    SYPHAX. Believe me, prince, there's not an
    African
That traverses our vast Numidian deserts 60
In quest of prey and lives upon his bow,
But better practises these boasted virtues.
Coarse are his meals, the fortune of the chase;
Amidst the running stream he slacks his
    thirst;   64
Toils all the day, and at th' approach of night
On the first friendly bank he throws him down,
Or rests his head upon a rock 'till morn;
Then rises fresh, pursues his wonted game,
And if the following day he chance to find
A new repast or an untasted spring, 70
Blesses his stars, and thinks it luxury.
    JUBA. Thy prejudice, Syphax, won't discern
What virtues grow from ignorance and choice,
Nor how the hero differs from the brute.
But grant that others could with equal glory
Look down on pleasures, and the baits of
    sense;   76
Where shall we find the man that bears
    affliction,
Great and majestic in his griefs, like Cato?
Heavens, with what strength, what steadiness
    of mind,
He triumphs in the midst of all his suff'rings!
How does he rise against a load of woes, 81
And thank the gods that throw the weight
    upon him!
    SYPHAX. 'Tis pride, rank pride, and haughti-
    ness of soul!
I think the Romans call it stoicism.
Had not your royal father thought so highly
Of Roman virtue, and of Cato's cause, 86
He had not fall'n by a slave's hand, inglorious:
Nor would his slaughtered army now have
    lain
On Africk's sands, disfigured with their
    wounds,
To gorge the wolves and vultures of Numidia.
    JUBA. Why dost thou call my sorrows up
    afresh?   91
My father's name brings tears into my eyes.
    SYPHAX. Oh, that you'd profit by your
    father's ills!
    JUBA. What wouldst thou have me do?
    SYPHAX.   Abandon Cato.
    JUBA. Syphax, I should be more than twice
    an orphan   95
By such a loss.
    SYPHAX.   Ay, there's the tie that binds
    you!
You long to call him father. Marcia's charms
Work in your heart unseen, and plead for
    Cato.
No wonder you are deaf to all I say.
    JUBA. Syphax, your zeal becomes impor-
    tunate;   100
I've hitherto permitted it to rave,
And talk at large; but learn to keep it in,
Lest it should take more freedom than I'll give
    it.
    SYPHAX. Sir, your great father never used
    me thus.
Alas, he's dead! But can you e'er forget 105
The tender sorrows, and the pangs of nature,
The fond embraces, and repeated blessings,
Which you drew from him in your last fare-
    well?
Still must I cherish the dear, sad, remem-
    brance,
At once to torture, and to please my soul.
The good old king, at parting, wrung my
    hand,   111
(His eyes brim full of tears) then sighing cried,
"Prithee be careful of my son!"—His grief
Swelled up so high, he could not utter more.
    JUBA. Alas, thy story melts away my soul.
That best of fathers! how shall I discharge
The gratitude and duty, which I owe him!
    SYPHAX. By laying up his counsels in your
    heart.   118
    JUBA. His counsels bade me yield to thy
    directions.
Then, Syphax, chide me in severest terms;
Vent all thy passion, and I'll stand its shock
Calm and unruffled as a summer sea 122
When not a breath of wind flys o'er its surface.
    SYPHAX. Alas, my prince, I'd guide you to
    your safety.
    JUBA. I do believe thou would'st; but tell
    me how?   125
    SYPHAX. Fly from the fate that follows
    Cæsar's foes.
    JUBA. My father scorned to do it.
    SYPHAX.   And therefore died.

JUBA. Better to die ten thousand thousand deaths,
Than wound my honor.
SYPHAX.   Rather say your love.
JUBA. Syphax, I've promised to preserve my temper.   130
Why wilt thou urge me to confess a flame,
I long have stifled, and would fain conceal?
   SYPHAX. Believe me, prince, tho' hard to conquer love,
'Tis easy to divert and break its force: 134
Absence might cure it, or a second mistress
Light up another flame, and put out this.
The glowing dames of Zama's royal court
Have faces flushed with more exalted charms;
The sun, that rolls his chariot o'er their heads,
Works up more fire and color in their cheeks:
Were you with these, my prince, you'd soon forget   141
The pale, unripened, beauties of the north.
   JUBA. 'Tis not a set of features, or complexion,
The tincture of a skin, that I admire.
Beauty soon grows familiar to the lover,
Fades in his eye and palls upon the sense.   146
The virtuous Marcia towers above her sex;
True, she is fair, (Oh, how divinely fair!)
But still the lovely maid improves her charms
With inward greatness, unaffected wisdom,
And sanctity of manners. Cato's soul   151
Shines out in every thing she acts or speaks,
While winning mildness and attractive smiles
Dwell in her looks, and with becoming grace
Soften the rigor of her father's virtues.   155
   SYPHAX. How does your tongue grow wanton in her praise!
But on my knees I beg you would consider—

Enter MARCIA *and* LUCIA

   JUBA. Hah! Syphax, is't not she!—She moves this way:
And with her Lucia, Lucius's fair daughter.
My heart beats thick—I prithee, Syphax, leave me.   160
   SYPHAX. [*Aside*] Ten thousand curses fasten on 'em both!
Now will this woman with a single glance
Undo, what I've been lab'ring all this while.
                                        Exit

SCENE V

JUBA, MARCIA, LUCIA

   JUBA. Hail, charming maid! How does thy beauty smooth
The face of war, and make ev'n horror smile!
At sight of thee my heart shakes off its sorrows;
I feel a dawn of joy break in upon me,   4
And for a while forget th' approach of Cæsar.
   MARCIA. I should be grieved, young prince, to think my presence
Unbent your thoughts, and slackened 'em to arms,
While, warm with slaughter, our victorious foe
Threatens aloud, and calls you to the field.
   JUBA. O Marcia, let me hope thy kind concerns   10
And gentle wishes follow me to battle!
The thought will give new vigor to my arm,
Add strength and weight to my descending sword,
And drive it in a tempest on the foe.
   MARCIA. My prayers and wishes always shall attend   15
The friends of Rome, the glorious cause of virtue,
And men approved of by the gods and Cato.
   JUBA. That Juba may deserve thy pious cares,
I'll gaze forever on thy godlike father,
Transplanting, one by one, into my life   20
His bright perfections, till I shine like him.
   MARCIA. My father never at a time like this
Would lay out his great soul in words, and waste
Such precious moments.
   JUBA.   Thy reproofs are just,
Thou virtuous maid; I'll hasten to my troops,
And fire their languid souls with Cato's virtue.
If e'er I lead them to the field, when all   27
The war shall stand ranged in its just array,
And dreadful pomp, then will I think on thee!
O lovely maid, then will I think on thee!   30
And, in the shock of charging hosts, remember
What glorious deeds should grace the man, who hopes
For Marcia's love.   *Exit*

SCENE VI

LUCIA, MARCIA

   LUCIA.   Marcia, you're too severe:
How could you chide the young, good-natured prince,
And drive him from you with so stern an air,
A prince that loves and dotes on you to death?
   MARCIA. 'Tis therefore, Lucia, that I chide him from me.

His air, his voice, his looks, and honest soul
Speak all so movingly in his behalf,
I dare not trust myself to hear him talk.
 Lucia. Why will you fight against so sweet a passion,
And steel your heart to such a world of charms? 10
 Marcia. How, Lucia, would'st thou have me sink away
In pleasing dreams, and lose myself in love,
When ev'ry moment Cato's life's at stake?
Cæsar comes armed with terror and revenge,
And aims his thunder at my father's head.
Should not the sad occasion swallow up 16
My other cares, and draw them all into it?
 Lucia. Why have not I this constancy of mind,
Who have so many griefs to try its force?
Sure, nature formed me of her softest mold,
Enfeebled all my soul with tender passions, 21
And sunk me even below my own weak sex.
Pity and love, by turns, oppress my heart.
 Marcia. Lucia, disburden all thy cares on me, 24
And let me share thy most retired distress;
Tell me who raises up this conflict in thee?
 Lucia. I need not blush to name them, when I tell thee
They're Marcia's brothers, and the sons of Cato.
 Marcia. They both behold thee with their sister's eyes, 29
And often have revealed their passion to me.
But tell me, whose address thou favorest most?
I long to know, and yet I dread to hear it.
 Lucia. Which is it Marcia wishes for?
 Marcia.   For neither—
And yet for both—the youths have equal share 34
In Marcia's wishes, and divide their sister:
But tell me which of them is Lucia's choice?
 Lucia. Marcia, they both are high in my esteem,
But in my love—Why wilt thou make me name him?
Thou know'st it is a blind and foolish passion,
Pleased and disgusted with it knows not what— 40
 Marcia. O Lucia, I'm perplexed! O tell me which
I must hereafter call my happy brother?
 Lucia. Suppose 'twere Portius, could you blame my choice?
—O Portius, thou hast stolen away my soul!
With what a graceful tenderness he loves! 45
And breathes the softest, the sincerest vows!
Complacency, and truth, and manly sweetness
Dwell ever on his tongue, and smooth his thoughts.
Marcus is over-warm, his fond complaints
Have so much earnestness and passion in them, 50
I hear him with a secret kind of horror,
And tremble at his vehemence of temper.
 Marcia. Alas poor youth! How canst thou throw him from thee?
Lucia, thou know'st not half the love he bears thee;
Whene'er he speaks of thee, his heart's in flames; 55
He sends out all his soul in ev'ry word,
And thinks, and talks, and looks like one transported.
Unhappy youth! how will thy coldness raise
Tempests and storms in his afflicted bosom!
I dread the consequence.
 Lucia.   You seem to plead 60
Against your brother Portius.
 Marcia.   Heaven forbid!
Had Portius been the unsuccessful lover,
The same compassion would have fall'n on him.
 Lucia. Was ever virgin love distressed like mine?
Portius himself oft falls in tears before me,
As if he mourned his rival's ill success, 66
Then bids me hide the motions of my heart,
Nor show which way it turns. So much he fears
The sad effects, that it would have on Marcus.
 Marcia. He knows too well how easily he's fired, 70
And would not plunge his brother in despair,
But waits for happier times and kinder moments.
 Lucia. Alas, too late I find myself involved
In endless griefs and labyrinths of woe,
Born to afflict my Marcia's family, 75
And sow dissension in the hearts of brothers.
Tormenting thought! It cuts into my soul.
 Marcia. Let us not, Lucia, aggravate our sorrows,
But to the gods permit [1] th' event of things.
Our lives, discolored with our present woes,
May still grow bright, and smile with happier hours. 81

[1] In the Latin sense of the word: entrust. *Event* means *outcome*.

So the pure limpid stream, when foul with
   stains
Of rushing torrents and descending rains,
Works itself clear, and as it runs, refines;
Till by degrees the floating mirror shines, 85
Reflects each flower that on the border grows,
And a new heaven in its fair bosom shows.
                                  Exeunt

ACT II

Scene I. *The Senate*

Sempronius. Rome still survives in this
   assembled senate!
Let us remember we are Cato's friends,
And act like men who claim that glorious title.
   Lucius. Cato will soon be here, and open
      to us   4
Th' occasion of our meeting. Hark! he comes!
               (*A sound of trumpets*)
May all the guardian gods of Rome direct him!

Enter Cato

   Cato. Fathers, we once again are met in
      council.   7
Cæsar's approach has summoned us together,
And Rome attends her fate from our resolves.
How shall we treat this bold aspiring man?
Success still follows him, and backs his crimes.
Pharsalia gave him Rome; Egypt has since
Received his yoke, and the whole Nile is
   Cæsar's.   13
Why should I mention Juba's overthrow,
And Scipio's death?[1] Numidia's burning sands
Still smoke with blood. 'Tis time we should
   decree
What course to take. Our foe advances on us,
And envies us ev'n Libya's sultry deserts.
Fathers, pronounce your thoughts: are they
   still fixed
To hold it out, and fight it to the last?   20
Or are your hearts subdued at length and
   wrought
By time and ill success to a submission?
Sempronius, speak.
   Sempronius.   My voice is still for war.
Gods, can a Roman senate long debate   24
Which of the two to choose, slavery or death!
No, let us rise at once, gird on our swords,
And, at the head of our remaining troops,
Attack the foe, break through the thick array
Of his thronged legions, and charge home upon
   him.
Perhaps some arm, more lucky than the rest,
May reach his heart, and free the world from
   bondage.   31
Rise, fathers, rise! 'tis Rome demands your
   help;
Rise, and revenge her slaughtered citizens,
Or share their fate! The corps of half her
   senate
Manure the fields of Thessaly,[2] while we 35
Sit here, delib'rating in cold debates,
If we should sacrifice our lives to honor,
Or wear them out in servitude and chains.
Rouse up for shame! Our brothers of Phar-
   salia
Point at their wounds, and cry aloud—To
   battle!   40
Great Pompey's shade complains that we are
   slow,
And Scipio's ghost walks unrevenged amongst
   us!
   Cato. Let not a torrent of impetuous zeal
Transport thee thus beyond the bounds of
   reason.
True fortitude is seen in great exploits   45
That justice warrants, and that wisdom
   guides;
All else is tow'ring frenzy and distraction.
Are not the lives of those who draw the sword
In Rome's defence entrusted to our care?
Should we thus lead them to a field of slaugh-
   ter,   50
Might not th' impartial world with reason say
We lavished at our deaths the blood of
   thousands,
To grace our fall, and make our ruin glorious?
Lucius, we next would know what's your
   opinion.
   Lucius. My thoughts, I must confess, are
      turned on peace.   55
Already have our quarrels filled the world
With widows and with orphans; Scythia
   mourns[3]
Our guilty wars, and earth's remotest regions
Lie half unpeopled by the feuds of Rome.
'Tis time to sheath the sword, and spare
   mankind.   60
It is not Cæsar, but the gods, my fathers;
The gods declare against us, and repel

---

[1] Cæsar had shortly before defeated Scipio and the elder Juba, killing according to Plutarch fifty thousand of his enemies in a single day. See Plutarch's life of Cæsar.

[2] Where the battle of Pharsalia was fought.

[3] Pompey the Great invaded Scythia and **marched almost to the Caucasus,** 66–64 B.C.

Our vain attempts. To urge the foe to battle
(Prompted by blind revenge and wild despair)
Were to refuse th' awards of providence, 65
And not to rest in heaven's determination.
Already have we shown our love to Rome,
Now let us show submission to the gods.
We took up arms, not to revenge ourselves,
But free the commonwealth; when this end
  fails, 70
Arms have no further use. Our country's
  cause,
That drew our swords, now wrests 'em from
  our hands,
And bids us not delight in Roman blood,
Unprofitably shed; what men could do
Is done already: heaven and earth will witness,
If Rome must fall, that we are innocent. 76
  SEMPRONIUS. This smooth discourse and
  mild behavior oft
Conceal a traitor.—Something whispers me
All is not right.—(*Aside to* CATO) Cato, be-
  ware of Lucius.
  CATO. Let us appear nor rash nor diffident:
Immod'rate valor swells into a fault, 81
And fear, admitted into public councils,
Betrays like treason. Let us shun 'em both.
Fathers, I cannot see that our affairs,
Are grown thus desp'rate. We have bulwarks
  round us; 85
Within our walls are troops inured to toil
In Africk's heats, and seasoned to the sun;
Numidia's spacious kingdom lies behind us,
Ready to rise at its young prince's call. 89
While there is hope, do not distrust the gods;
But wait at least till Cæsar's near approach
Force us to yield. 'Twill never be too late
To sue for chains, and own a conqueror.
Why should Rome fall a moment ere her time?
No, let us draw her term of freedom out 95
In its full length, and spin it to the last.
So shall we gain still one day's liberty;
And let me perish, but, in Cato's judgment,
A day, an hour of virtuous liberty,
Is worth a whole eternity in bondage. 100

Enter MARCUS

  MARCUS. Fathers, this moment, as I
    watched the gates
Lodged on my post, a herald is arrived
From Cæsar's camp, and with him comes
  old Decius,
The Roman knight; he carries in his looks
Impatience, and demands to speak with
  Cato. 105

  CATO. By your permission, fathers, bid him
    enter. *Exit* MARCUS
Decius was once my friend, but other pros-
  pects
Have loosed those ties, and bound him fast
  to Cæsar.
His message may determine our resolves.

SCENE II

DECIUS, CATO

  DECIUS. Cæsar sends health to Cato—
  CATO.   Could he send it
To Cato's slaughtered friends, it would be
  welcome.
Are not your orders to address the senate?
  DECIUS. My business is with Cato. Cæsar
    sees
The straits to which you're driven; and, as he
  knows 5
Cato's high worth, is anxious for your life.
  CATO. My life is grafted on the fate of Rome.
Would he save Cato, bid him spare his coun-
  try.
Tell your dictator this; and tell him, Cato
Disdains a life which he has power to offer.
  DECIUS. Rome and her senators submit to
    Cæsar; 11
Her generals and her consuls are no more
Who checked his conquests and denied his
  triumphs.
Why will not Cato be this Cæsar's friend?
  CATO. Those very reasons thou hast urged,
    forbid it. 15
  DECIUS. I've orders to expostulate,
And reason with you, as from friend to friend.
Think on the storm that gathers o'er your
  head,
And threatens ev'ry hour to burst upon it.
Still may you stand high in your country's
  honors; 20
Do but comply, and make your peace with
  Cæsar.
Rome will rejoice, and cast its eyes on Cato,
As on the second of mankind.
  CATO.   No more!
I must not think of life on such conditions.
  DECIUS. Cæsar is well acquainted with
    your virtues, 25
And therefore sets this value on your life:
Let him but know the price of Cato's friend-
  ship,
And name your terms.
  CATO.   Bid him disband his legions,

Restore the commonwealth to liberty,
Submit his actions to the public censure, 30
And stand the judgment of a Roman senate.
Bid him do this, and Cato is his friend.
    DECIUS. Cato, the world talks loudly of your wisdom—
    CATO. Nay more, tho' Cato's voice was ne'er employed
To clear the guilty, and to varnish crimes, 35
Myself will mount the rostrum in his favor,
And strive to gain his pardon from the people.
    DECIUS. A style like this becomes a conqueror.
    CATO. Decius, a style like this becomes a Roman.
    DECIUS. What is a Roman, that is Cæsar's foe? 40
    CATO. Greater than Cæsar; he's a friend to virtue.
    DECIUS. Consider, Cato, you're in Utica,
And at the head of your own little senate;
You don't now thunder in the capitol, 44
With all the mouths of Rome to second you.
    CATO. Let him consider that, who drives us hither:
'Tis Cæsar's sword has made Rome's senate little,
And thinned its ranks. Alas, thy dazzled eye
Beholds this man in a false glaring light,
Which conquest and success have thrown upon him; 50
Didst thou but view him right, thou'dst see him black
With murder, treason, sacrilege, and crimes
That strike my soul with horror but to name 'em.
I know thou look'st on me as on a wretch 54
Beset with ills and covered with misfortunes;
But, by the gods I swear, millions of worlds
Should never buy me to be like that Cæsar.
    DECIUS. Does Cato send this answer back to Cæsar,
For all his gen'rous cares and proffered friendship?
    CATO. His cares for me are insolent and vain. 60
Presumptuous man! The gods take care of Cato.
Would Cæsar show the greatness of his soul?
Bid him employ his care for these my friends,
And make good use of his ill-gotten power,
By shelt'ring men much better than himself.
    DECIUS. Your high, unconquered heart makes you forget 66

You are a man. You rush on your destruction.
But I have done. When I relate hereafter
The tale of this unhappy embassy,
All Rome will be in tears.   *Exit* DECIUS

SCENE III

SEMPRONIUS, LUCIUS, CATO

    SEMPRONIUS. Cato, we thank thee.
The mighty genius of immortal Rome
Speaks in thy voice; thy soul breathes liberty.
Cæsar will shrink to hear the words thou utter'st, 4
And shudder in the midst of all his conquests.
    LUCIUS. The senate owns its gratitude to Cato,
Who with so great a soul consults its safety,
And guards our lives, while he neglects his own.
    SEMPRONIUS. Sempronius gives no thanks on this account.
Lucius seems fond of life; but what is life? 10
'Tis not to stalk about, and draw fresh air
From time to time, or gaze upon the sun;
'Tis to be free. When liberty is gone,
Life grows insipid, and has lost its relish. 14
O could my dying hand but lodge a sword
In Cæsar's bosom and revenge my country,
By heavens I could enjoy the pangs of death,
And smile in agony.
    LUCIUS.   Others perhaps
May serve their country with as warm a zeal,
Tho' 'tis not kindled into so much rage. 20
    SEMPRONIUS. This sober conduct is a mighty virtue
In lukewarm patriots.
    CATO.   Come! No more, Sempronius,
All here are friends to Rome, and to each other.
Let us not weaken still the weaker side,
By our divisions.
    SEMPRONIUS.   Cato, my resentments 25
Are sacrificed to Rome.—I stand reproved.
    CATO. Fathers, 'tis time you come to a resolve.
    LUCIUS. Cato, we all go into your opinion.
Cæsar's behavior has convinced the senate
We ought to hold it out till terms arrive. 30
    SEMPRONIUS. We ought to hold it out till death; but, Cato,
My private voice is drowned amid the senate's.
    CATO. Then let us rise, my friends, and strive to fill
This little interval, this pause of life, 34

(While yet our liberty and fates are doubtful)
With resolution, friendship, Roman brav'ry,
And all the virtues we can crowd into it;
That heaven may say, it ought to be prolonged.
Fathers, farewell—The young Numidian prince
Comes forward, and expects to know our councils. *Exeunt* SENATORS 40

SCENE IV

CATO, JUBA

CATO. Juba, the Roman senate has resolved,
Till time give better prospects, still to keep
The sword unsheathed and turn its edge on Cæsar. 3
JUBA. The resolution fits a Roman senate.
But, Cato, lend me for a while thy patience,
And condescend to hear a young man speak.
My father, when some days before his death
He ordered me to march for Utica
(Alas, I thought not then his death so near!)
Wept o'er me, pressed me in his aged arms, 10
And, as his griefs gave way, "My son," said he,
"Whatever fortune shall befall thy father,
Be Cato's friend; he'll train thee up to great
And virtuous deeds. Do but observe him well,
Thou'lt shun misfortunes, or thou'lt learn to bear 'em." 15
CATO. Juba, thy father was a worthy prince,
And merited, alas! a better fate;
But heaven thought otherwise.
    JUBA. My father's fate,
In spite of all the fortitude that shines
Before my face, in Cato's great example, 20
Subdues my soul, and fills my eyes with tears.
CATO. It is an honest sorrow and becomes thee.
JUBA. My father drew respect from foreign climes.
The kings of Africk sought him for their friend;
Kings far remote, that rule, as fame reports,
Behind the hidden sources of the Nile, 26
In distant worlds, on t'other side the sun;
Oft have their black ambassadors appeared,
Loaden with gifts, and filled the courts of Zama.
CATO. I am no stranger to thy father's greatness. 30
JUBA. I would not boast the greatness of my father,
But point out new alliances to Cato.
Had we not better leave this Utica,
To arm Numidia in our cause, and court 34
Th' assistance of my father's pow'rful friends?
Did they know Cato, our remotest kings
Would pour embattled multitudes about him;
Their swarthy hosts would darken all our plains,
Doubling the native horror of the war,
And making death more grim.
    CATO. And canst thou think 40
Cato will fly before the sword of Cæsar?
Reduced like Hannibal, to seek relief
From court to court, and wander up and down,
A vagabond in Africk![1]
    JUBA. Cato, perhaps
I'm too officious, but my forward cares 45
Would fain preserve a life of so much value.
My heart is wounded, when I see such virtue
Afflicted by the weight of such misfortunes.
CATO. Thy nobleness of soul obliges me.
But know, young prince, that valor soars above 50
What the world calls misfortune and affliction.
These are not ills; else would they never fall
On heaven's first fav'rites, and the best of men.
The gods, in bounty, work up storms about us,
That give mankind occasion to exert 55
Their hidden strength, and throw out into practice
Virtues which shun the day and lie concealed
In the smooth seasons and the calms of life.
JUBA. I'm charmed whene'er thou talk'st!
I pant for virtue!
And all my soul endeavors at perfection. 60
CATO. Dost thou love watchings, abstinence, and toil,
Laborious virtues all? Learn them from Cato.
Success and fortune must thou learn from Cæsar.
JUBA. The best good fortune that can fall on Juba, 64
The whole success, at which my heart aspires
Depends on Cato.
    CATO. What does Juba say?
Thy words confound me.
    JUBA. I would fain retract them.

---

[1] Alarmed by Hannibal's patriotic activities as a Carthaginian magistrate, the Roman government forced that general into the exile in which he died. The appropriateness of Cato's reference arises from the fact that Hannibal was decisively defeated at Zama (202 B.C.).

Give 'em me back again. They aimed at
    nothing.
  Cato. Tell me thy wish, young prince; make
    not my ear
A stranger to thy thoughts.
  Juba.   Oh, they're extravagant; 70
Still let me hide them.
  Cato.   What can Juba ask
That Cato will refuse!
  Juba.   I fear to name it.
Marcia—inherits all her father's virtues.
  Cato. What wouldst thou say?
  Juba.   Cato, thou hast a daughter.
  Cato. Adieu, young prince! I would not
    hear a word   75
Should lessen thee in my esteem. Remember
The hand of fate is over us, and heaven
Exacts severity from all our thoughts.
It is not now a time to talk of aught   79
But chains, or conquest; liberty, or death.
                                         Exit

Scene v

Spyhax, Juba

  Syphax. How's this, my prince! What,
    covered with confusion?
You look as if yon stern philosopher
Had just now chid you.
  Juba.   Syphax, I'm undone!
  Syphax. I know it well.
  Juba.   Cato thinks meanly of me.
  Syphax. And so will all mankind.
  Juba.   I've opened to him 5
The weakness of my soul, my love for Marcia.
  Syphax. Cato's a proper person to entrust
A love-tale with.
  Juba. Oh, I could pierce my heart,
My foolish heart! Was ever wretch like Juba?
  Syphax. Alas, my prince, how are you
    changed of late!   10
I've known young Juba rise, before the sun,
To beat the thicket where the tiger slept,
Or seek the lion in his dreadful haunts;
How did the color mount into your cheeks,
When first you roused him to the chase!
    I've seen you,   15
Ev'n in the Lybian dog-days, hunt him down,
Then charge him close, provoke him to the
    rage
Of fangs and claws, and stooping from your
    horse,
Rivet the panting savage to the ground.
  Juba. Prithee, no more!

  Syphax.   How would the old king smile
To see you weigh the paws, when tipped with
    gold,   21
And throw the shaggy spoils about your
    shoulders!
  Juba. Syphax, this old man's talk (tho'
    honey flowed
In ev'ry word) would now lose all its sweet-
    ness.
Cato's displeased, and Marcia lost forever! 25
  Syphax. Young prince, I yet could give you
    good advice.
Marcia might still be yours.
  Juba.   What say'st thou, Syphax?
By heavens, thou turn'st me all into atten-
    tion.
  Syphax. Marcia might still be yours.
  Juba.   As how, dear Syphax?
  Syphax. Juba commands Numidia's hardy
    troops,   30
Mounted on steeds, unused to the restraint
Of curbs or bits, and fleeter than the winds.
Give but the word, we'll snatch this damsel
    up,
And bear her off.
  Juba.   Can such dishonest thoughts
Rise up in man! Wouldst thou seduce my
    youth   35
To do an act that would destroy my honor?
  Syphax. Gods, I could tear my beard to
    hear you talk!
Honor's a fine imaginary notion,
That draws in raw and unexperienced men
To real mischiefs, while they hunt a shadow.
  Juba. Wouldst thou degrade thy prince
    into a ruffian?   41
  Syphax. The boasted ancestors of these
    great men,
Whose virtues you admire, were all such
    ruffians.
This dread of nations, this almighty Rome,
That comprehends in her wide empire's
    bounds   45
All under heaven, was founded on a rape.
Your Scipios, Cæsars, Pompeys, and your
    Catos,
(These gods on earth) are all the spurious
    brood
Of violated maids, of ravished Sabines.
  Juba. Syphax, I fear that hoary head of
    thine   50
Abounds too much in our Numidian wiles.
  Syphax. Indeed, my prince, you want to
    know the world,

You have not read mankind; your youth
    admires
The throws[1] and swellings of a Roman soul,
Cato's bold flights, th' extravagance of virtue.
    JUBA. If knowledge of the world makes
        men perfidious,   56
May Juba ever live in ignorance!
    SYPHAX. Go, go, you're young.
    JUBA.   Gods, must I tamely bear
This arrogance unanswered! Thou'rt a traitor,
A false old traitor.
    SYPHAX. (*Aside*)   I have gone too far.   60
    JUBA. Cato shall know the baseness of thy
        soul.
    SYPHAX. (*Aside*) I must appease this storm,
        or perish in it.—
Young prince, behold these locks, that are
    grown white
Beneath a helmet in your father's battles.
    JUBA. Those locks shall ne'er protect thy
        insolence.   65
    SYPHAX. Must one rash word, th' infirmity
        of age,
Throw down the merit of my better years?
This the reward of a whole life of service!
—(*Aside*) Curse on the boy! How steadily he
    hears me!
    JUBA. Is it because the throne of my fore-
        fathers   70
Still stands unfilled, and that Numidia's
    crown
Hangs doubtful yet, whose head it shall en-
    close,
Thou thus presumest to treat thy prince with
    scorn?
    SYPHAX. Why will you rive my heart with
        such expressions?
Does not old Syphax follow you to war?   75
What are his aims? Why does he load with
    darts
His trembling hand, and crush beneath a
    casque
His wrinkled brows? What is it he aspires to?
Is it not this, to shed the slow remains,
His last poor ebb of blood, in your defence?
    JUBA. Syphax, no more! I would not hear
        you talk.   81
    SYPHAX. Not hear me talk! What, when
        my faith to Juba,
My royal master's son, is called in ques-
    tion?
My prince may strike me dead, and I'll be
    dumb;

[1] I.e., the high flights, extravagancies.

But whilst I live I must not hold my tongue,
And languish out old age in his displeasure.
    JUBA. Thou know'st the way too well into
        my heart,   87
I do believe thee loyal to thy prince.
    SYPHAX. What greater instance can I give?
        I've offered
To do an action, which my soul abhors,   90
And gain you whom you love at any price.
    JUBA. Was this thy motive? I have been
        too hasty.
    SYPHAX. And 'tis for this my prince has
        called me traitor.
    JUBA. Sure thou mistakest, I did not call
        thee so.
    SYPHAX. You did indeed, my prince, you
        called me traitor;   95
Nay, further, threatened you'd complain to
    Cato.
Of what, my prince, would you complain to
    Cato?
That Syphax loves you, and would sacrifice
His life, nay more, his honor in your service.
    JUBA. Syphax, I know thou lov'st me, but
        indeed   100
Thy zeal for Juba carried thee too far.
Honor's a sacred tie, the law of kings,
The noble mind's distinguishing perfection,
That aids and strengthens virtue where it
    meets her,
And imitates her actions where she is not: 105
It ought not to be sported with.
    SYPHAX.   By heavens
I'm ravished when you talk thus, tho' you
    chide me!
Alas, I've hitherto been used to think
A blind, officious zeal to serve my king
The ruling principle, that ought to burn 110
And quench all others in a subject's heart.
Happy the people, who preserve their honor
By the same duties, that oblige their prince!
    JUBA. Syphax, thou now begin'st to speak
        thyself.   114
Numidia's grown a scorn among the nations
For breach of public vows. Our Punic[2] faith
Is infamous, and branded to a proverb.
Syphax, we'll join our cares, to purge away
Our country's crimes, and clear her reputation.
    SYPHAX. Believe me, prince, you make old
        Syphax weep   120
To hear you talk—but 'tis with tears of joy.
If e'er your father's crown adorn your brows,

[2] The Romans regarded the Carthaginians as treacherous liars.

Numidia will be blest by Cato's lectures.
>JUBA. Syphax, thy hand! We'll mutually forget
The warmth of youth, and frowardness of age.
Thy prince esteems thy worth, and loves thy person. 126
If e'er the scepter comes into my hand,
Syphax shall stand the second in my kingdom.
>SYPHAX. Why will you overwhelm my age with kindness?
My joy grows burdensome, I sha'n't support it. 130
>JUBA. Syphax, farewell. I'll hence, and try to find
Some blest occasion that may set me right
In Cato's thoughts. I'd rather have that man
Approve my deeds, than worlds for my admirers. *Exit*

SYPHAX *solus*

Young men soon give, and soon forget, affronts; 135
Old age is slow in both—A false old traitor!
Those words, rash boy, may chance to cost thee dear.
My heart had still some foolish fondness for thee;
But hence! 'tis gone. I give it to the winds.
Cæsar, I'm wholly thine—

SCENE VI

SYPHAX, SEMPRONIUS

SYPHAX. All hail, Sempronius!
Well, Cato's senate is resolved to wait
The fury of a siege, before it yields.
>SEMPRONIUS. Syphax, we both were on the verge of fate.
Lucius declared for peace, and terms were offered 5
To Cato by a messenger from Cæsar.
Should they submit, ere our designs are ripe,
We both must perish in the common wreck,
Lost in a gen'ral undistinguished ruin.
>SYPHAX. But how stands Cato?
>SEMPRONIUS. Thou hast seen Mount Atlas! 10
While storms and tempests thunder on its brows,
And oceans break their billows at its feet,
It stands unmoved, and glories in its height.
Such is that haughty man; his tow'ring soul,
'Midst all the shocks and injuries of fortune,
Rises superior, and looks down on Cæsar. 16

SYPHAX. But what's this messenger?
>SEMPRONIUS. I've practised with him,
And found a means to let the victor know
That Syphax and Sempronius are his friends.
But let me now examine in my turn: 20
Is Juba fixed?
>SYPHAX. Yes,—but it is to Cato.
I've tried the force of ev'ry reason on him,
Soothed and caressed, been angry, soothed again,
Laid safety, life, and int'rest in his sight, 24
But all are vain, he scorns them all for Cato.
>SEMPRONIUS. Come, 'tis no matter, we shall do without him.
He'll make a pretty figure in a triumph,
And serve to trip before the victor's chariot.
Syphax, I now may hope thou hast forsook
Thy Juba's cause, and wishest Marcia mine.
>SYPHAX. May she be thine as fast as thou wouldst have her! 31
>SEMPRONIUS. Syphax, I love that woman; tho' I curse
Her and myself, yet spite of me, I love her.
>SYPHAX. Make Cato sure, and give up Utica,
Cæsar will ne'er refuse thee such a trifle. 35
But are thy troops prepared for a revolt?
Does the sedition catch from man to man,
And run among their ranks?
>SEMPRONIUS. All, all is ready.
The factious leaders are our friends, that spread
Murmurs and discontents among the soldiers.
They count their toilsome marches, long fatigues, 41
Unusual fastings, and will bear no more
This medley of philosophy and war.
Within an hour they'll storm the senate-house.
>SYPHAX. Meanwhile I'll draw up my Numidian troops 45
Within the square, to exercise their arms,
And, as I see occasion, favor thee.
I laugh to think how your unshaken Cato
Will look aghast, while unforeseen destruction
Pours in upon him thus from every side. 50
So, where our wide Numidian wastes extend,
Sudden, th' impetuous hurricanes descend,
Wheel through the air, in circling eddies play,
Tear up the sands, and sweep whole plains away.
The helpless traveller, with wild surprise,
Sees the dry desert all around him rise, 56
And, smothered in the dusty whirlwind dies.
Exeunt

ACT III

Scene I

MARCUS, *and* PORTIUS

MARCUS. Thanks to my stars, I have not ranged about
The wilds of life, ere I could find a friend;
Nature first pointed out my Portius to me,
And early taught me, by her secret force,
To love thy person, ere I knew thy merit; 5
Till what was instinct, grew up into friendship.
PORTIUS. Marcus, the friendships of the world are oft
Confed'racies in vice, or leagues of pleasure;
Ours has severest virtue for its basis, 9
And such a friendship ends not but with life.
MARCUS. Portius, thou know'st my soul in all its weakness;
Then prithee spare me on its tender side;
Indulge me but in love, my other passions
Shall rise and fall by virtue's nicest rules.
PORTIUS. When love's well-timed, 'tis not a fault to love. 15
The strong, the brave, the virtuous, and the wise,
Sink in the soft captivity together.
I would not urge thee to dismiss thy passion,
(I know 'twere vain) but to suppress its force,
Till better times may make it look more graceful. 20
MARCUS. Alas! thou talk'st like one who never felt
Th' impatient throbs and longings of a soul
That pants and reaches after distant good.
A lover does not live by vulgar time. 24
Believe me, Portius, in my Lucia's absence
Life hangs upon me, and becomes a burden;
And yet, when I behold the charming maid,
I'm ten times more undone; while hope, and fear,
And grief, and rage, and love, rise up at once,
And with variety of pain distract me. 30
PORTIUS. What can thy Portius do to give thee help?
MARCUS. Portius, thou oft enjoy'st the fair one's presence;
Then undertake my cause and plead it to her
With all the strength and heats of eloquence
Fraternal love and friendship can inspire. 35
Tell her thy brother languishes to death
And fades away and withers in his bloom;
That he forgets his sleep and loathes his food,
That youth and health and war are joyless to him. 39
Describe his anxious days and restless nights
And all the torments that thou seest me suffer.
PORTIUS. Marcus, I beg thee give me not an office,
That suits with me so ill. Thou know'st my temper.
MARCUS. Wilt thou behold me sinking in my woes?
And wilt thou not reach out a friendly arm
To raise me from amidst this plunge of sorrows? 46
PORTIUS. Marcus, thou canst not ask what I'd refuse.
But here, believe me, I've a thousand reasons—
MARCUS. I know thou'lt say my passion's out of season,
That Cato's great example and misfortunes
Should both conspire to drive it from my thoughts. 51
But what's all this to one who loves like me!
Oh Portius, Portius, from my soul I wish
Thou didst but know thyself what 'tis to love!
Then wouldst thou pity and assist thy brother.
PORTIUS. (*Aside*) What should I do! If I disclose my passion 56
Our friendship's at an end. If I conceal it,
The world will call me false to a friend and brother.
MARCUS. But see where Lucia, at her wonted hour,
Amid the cool of yon high marble arch, 60
Enjoys the noon-day breeze! Observe her, Portius!
That face, that shape, those eyes, that heaven of beauty!
Observe her well, and blame me if thou can'st.
PORTIUS. She sees us, and advances—
MARCUS. I'll withdraw,
And leave you for a while. Remember, Portius, 65
Thy brother's life depends upon thy tongue.
Exit

Scene II

LUCIA, PORTIUS

LUCIA. Did not I see your brother Marcus here?
Why did he fly the place, and shun my presence?

PORTIUS. Oh, Lucia, language is too faint
    to show
His rage of love; it preys upon his life;
He pines, he sickens, he despairs, he dies: 5
His passions and his virtues lie confused
And mixed together in so wild a tumult
That the whole man is quite disfigured in him.
Heavens! would one think 'twere possible for
    love
To make such ravage in a noble soul! 10
Oh, Lucia, I'm distressed! My heart bleeds
    for him;
Ev'n now, while thus I stand blest in thy
    presence,
A secret damp of grief comes o'er my thoughts,
And I'm unhappy, tho' thou smilest upon me.
    LUCIA. How wilt thou guard thy honor, in
        the shock 15
Of love and friendship! Think betimes, my
    Portius,
Think how the nuptial tie, that might ensure
Our mutual bliss, would raise to such a height
Thy brother's griefs, as might perhaps destroy
    him.
    PORTIUS. Alas, poor youth! What dost you
        think, my Lucia? 20
His gen'rous, open, undesigning heart
Has begged his rival to solicit for him.
Then do not strike him dead with a denial,
But hold him up in life, and cheer his soul
With the faint glimm'ring of a doubtful
    hope. 25
Perhaps, when we have passed these gloomy
    hours,
And weathered out the storm that beats upon
    us—
    LUCIA. No, Portius, no! I see thy sister's
        tears,
Thy father's anguish, and thy brother's
    death,
In the pursuit of our ill-fated loves. 30
And, Portius, here I swear, to heaven I swear,
To heaven, and all the pow'rs that judge
    mankind,
Never to mix my plighted hands with thine,
While such a cloud of mischiefs hangs about
    us. 34
But to forget our loves, and drive thee out
From all my thoughts, as far—as I am able.
    PORTIUS. What hast thou said! I'm
        thunder-struck!—Recall
Those hasty words, or I am lost forever.
    LUCIA. Has not the vow already passed my
        lips?

The gods have heard it, and 'tis sealed in
    heaven. 40
May all the vengeance, that was ever poured
On perjured heads, o'erwhelm me, if I break
    it!
    PORTIUS. (*After a pause*) Fixed in astonish-
        ment, I gaze upon thee;
Like one just blasted by a stroke from heaven,
Who pants for breath, and stiffens, yet alive
In dreadful looks, a monument of wrath! 46
    LUCIA. At length I've acted my severest
        part,
I feel the woman breaking in upon me,
And melt about my heart! My tears will flow.
But oh I'll think no more! The hand of fate
Has torn thee from me, and I must forget
    thee. 51
    PORTIUS. Hard-hearted, cruel maid!
    LUCIA.   Oh stop those sounds,
Those killing sounds! Why dost thou frown
    upon me?
My blood runs cold, my heart forgets to heave,
And life itself goes out at thy displeasure.
The gods forbid us to indulge our loves, 56
But oh! I cannot bear thy hate and live!
    PORTIUS. Talk not of love, thou never
        knew'st its force.
I've been deluded, led into a dream
Of fancied bliss. O Lucia, cruel maid! 60
Thy dreadful vow, loaden with death, still
    sounds
In my stunned ears. What shall I say or do?
Quick, let us part! Perdition's in thy presence,
And horror dwells about thee!—Hah, she
    faints!
Wretch that I am! what has my rashness
    done! 65
Lucia, thou injured innocence! thou best
And loveli'st of thy sex! awake, my Lucia,
Or Portius rushes on his sword to join thee.
—Her imprecations reach not to the tomb,
They shut not out society in death—[1] 70
But hah! She moves! Life wanders up and
    down
Through all her face, and lights up ev'ry
    charm.
    LUCIA. O Portius, was this well—to frown
        on her
That lives upon thy smiles! to call in doubt
The faith of one expiring at thy feet, 75
That loves thee more than ever woman loved!
—What do I say? My half-recovered sense

---

[1] Her vow cannot keep them separated after death seems to be his meaning.

Forgets the vow in which my soul is bound.
Destruction stands betwixt us! We must part.
　PORTIUS. Name not the word, my frighted
　　thoughts run back,　　　　　　　　80
And startle into madness at the sound.
　LUCIA. What wouldst thou have me do?
　　Consider well
The train of ills our love would draw behind it.
Think, Portius, think, thou see'st thy dying
　brother
Stabbed at his heart, and all besmeared with
　blood,　　　　　　　　　　　　　　85
Storming at heaven and thee! Thy awful sire
Sternly demands the cause, th' accursed
　cause,
That robs him of his son! Poor Marcia
　trembles,
Then tears her hair, and frantic in her griefs
Calls out on Lucia! What could Lucia
　answer?　　　　　　　　　　　　　90
Or how stand up in such a scene of sorrow!
　PORTIUS. To my confusion and eternal
　　grief,
1 must approve the sentence that destroys
　me.
The mist that hung about my mind clears up;
And now, athwart the terrors that thy vow
Has planted round thee, thou appear'st more
　fair,　　　　　　　　　　　　　　96
More amiable, and risest in thy charms.
Loveli'st of women! Heaven is in thy soul,
Beauty and virtue shine forever round thee,
Bright'ning each other! Thou art all divine!
　LUCIA. Portius, no more! Thy words shoot
　　thro' my heart,　　　　　　　　　101
Melt my resolves, and turn me all to love.
Why are those tears of fondness in thy eyes?
Why heaves thy heart? Why swells thy soul
　with sorrow?
It softens me too much.—Farewell, my Por-
　tius,　　　　　　　　　　　　　　105
Farewell, tho' death is in the word, forever!
　PORTIUS. Stay, Lucia, stay! What dost
　　thou say? Forever?
　LUCIA. Have I not sworn? If, Portius, thy
　　success
Must throw thy brother on his fate, farewell,—
Oh, how shall I repeat the word—forever! 110
　PORTIUS. Thus o'er the dying lamp th'
　　unsteady flame
Hangs quiv'ring on a point, leaps off by fits,
And falls again, as loath to quit its hold.
—Thou must not go, my soul still hovers
　o'er thee

And can't get loose.
　LUCIA. If the firm Portius shake　　115
To hear of parting, think what Lucia suffers!
　PORTIUS. 'Tis true; unruffled and serene
　　I've met
The common accidents of life, but here
Such an unlooked-for storm of ills falls on me,
It beats down all my strength. I cannot bear
　it.　　　　　　　　　　　　　　120
We must not part.
　LUCIA. What dost thou say? Not part?
Hast thou forgot the vow that I have made?
Are there not heavens, and gods, and thunder
　o'er us!
—But see! Thy brother Marcus bends this
　way!　　　　　　　　　　　　　124
I sicken at the sight. Once more, farewell,
Farewell, and know thou wrong'st me, if thou
　think'st
Ever was love, or ever grief, like mine.　*Exit*

SCENE III

MARCUS, PORTIUS

　MARCUS. Portius, what hopes? How stands
　　she? Am I doomed
To life or death?
　PORTIUS.　　What wouldst thou have me
　　say?
　MARCUS. What means this pensive posture?
　　Thou appear'st
Like one amazed and terrified.
　PORTIUS.　　　　　　　　I've reason.
　MARCUS. Thy down-cast looks and thy
　　disordered thoughts　　　　　　　5
Tell me my fate. I ask not the success
My cause has found.
　PORTIUS. I'm grieved I undertook it.
　MARCUS. What? Does the barb'rous maid
　　insult my heart,
My aching heart and triumph in my pains?
That I could cast her from my thoughts for-
　ever!　　　　　　　　　　　　　10
　PORTIUS. Away! You're too suspicious in
　　your griefs;
Lucia, though sworn never to think of love,
Compassionates your pains, and pities you.
　MARCUS. Compassionates my pains, and
　　pities me!　　　　　　　　　　14
What is compassion when 'tis void of love!
Fool that I was to choose so cold a friend
To urge my cause! Compassionates my pains!
Prithee what art, what rhet'ric did'st thou use
To gain this mighty boon? She pities me! 19

To one that asks the warm returns of love,
Compassion's cruelty, 'tis scorn, 'tis death—
  PORTIUS. Marcus, no more! Have I deserved this treatment?
  MARCUS. What have I said! O Portius, O forgive me!
A soul exasp'rated in ills falls out
With ev'ry thing, its friend, itself—But hah!
What means that shout, big with the sounds of war? 26
What new alarm?
  PORTIUS.   A second, louder yet
Swells in the winds and comes more full upon us.
  MARCUS. Oh, for some glorious cause to fall in battle!
Lucia, thou hast undone me! Thy disdain
Has broke my heart; 'tis death must give me ease. 31
  PORTIUS. Quick, let us hence; who knows if Cato's life
Stand sure? O Marcus, I am warmed, my heart
Leaps at the trumpet's voice, and burns for glory. *Exeunt*

SCENE IV

Enter SEMPRONIUS *with the Leaders of the Mutiny*

  SEMPRONIUS. At length the winds are raised, the storm blows high,
Be it your care, my friends, to keep it up
In its full fury, and direct it right,
Till it has spent itself on Cato's head.
Meanwhile I'll herd among his friends, and seem 5
One of the number, that whate'er arrive,
My friends and fellow-soldiers may be safe.
                                      Exit
  1ST LEADER. We all are safe! Sempronius is our friend;
Sempronius is as brave a man as Cato. 9
But hark! He enters. Bear up boldly to him;
Be sure you beat him down, and bind him fast:
This day will end our toils, and give us rest.
Fear nothing, for Sempronius is our friend.

SCENE V

Enter CATO, SEMPRONIUS, LUCIUS, PORTIUS, *and* MARCUS

  CATO. Where are these bold, intrepid sons of war,
That greatly turn their backs upon the foe,
And to their general send a brave defiance?
  SEMPRONIUS. (*Aside*) Curse on their dastard souls, they stand astonished!
  CATO. Perfidious men! and will you thus dishonor 5
Your past exploits, and sully all your wars?
Do you confess 'twere not a zeal for Rome,
Nor love of liberty, nor thirst of honor,
Drew you thus far; but hopes to share the spoil 9
Of conquered towns, and plundered provinces?
Fired with such motives you do well to join
With Cato's foes, and follow Cæsar's banners.
Why did I 'scape th' envenomed aspic's rage,
And all the fiery monsters of the desert, 14
To see this day? Why could not Cato fall
Without your guilt? Behold, ungrateful men,
Behold my bosom naked to your swords,
And let the man that's injured strike the blow. 18
Which of you all suspects that he is wronged,
Or thinks he suffers greater ills than Cato?
Am I distinguished from you but by toils,
Superior toils, and heavier weight of cares!
Painful pre-eminence!
  SEMPRONIUS.   (*Aside*) By heavens they droop!
Confusion to the villains! All is lost.
  CATO. Have you forgotten Lybia's burning waste, 25
Its barren rocks, parched earth and hills of sand,
Its tainted air, and all its broods of poison?
Who was the first to explore th' untrodden path,
When life was hazarded in ev'ry step?
Or, fainting in the long laborious march, 30
When on the banks of an unlooked-for stream
You sunk the river with repeated draughts,
Who was the last in all your host that thirsted?
  SEMPRONIUS. If some penurious source by chance appeared,
Scanty of waters, when you scooped it dry, 35
And offered the full helmet up to Cato,
Did he not dash th' untasted moisture from him?
Did not he lead you through the mid-day sun,
And clouds of dust? Did not his temples glow
In the same sultry winds and scorching heats?
  CATO. Hence, worthless men! Hence, and complain to Cæsar 41
You could not undergo the toils of war,
Nor bear the hardships that your leader bore.

Lucius. See, Cato, see th' unhappy men!
　They weep!　44
Fear and remorse and sorrow for their crime
Appear in ev'ry look, and plead for mercy.
　Cato. Learn to be honest men, give up
　　your leaders,
And pardon shall descend on all the rest.
　Sempronius. Cato, commit these wretches
　　to my care.
First let 'em each be broken on the rack, 50
Then, with what life remains, impaled, and
　left
To writhe at leisure round the bloody stake.
There let 'em hang, and taint the southern
　wind.
The partners of their crime will learn obedience,
When they look up and see their fellow-
　traitors　55
Stuck on a fork, and black'ning in the sun.
　Lucius. Sempronius, why, why wilt thou
　　urge the fate
Of wretched men?
　Sempronius.　How! wouldst thou clear[1]
　　rebellion!
Lucius, (good man) pities the poor offenders
That would imbrue their hands in Cato's
　blood.　60
　Cato. Forbear, Sempronius!—See they
　　suffer death,
But in their deaths remember they are men.
Strain not the laws to make their tortures
　grievous.
Lucius, the base degen'rate age requires
Severity, and justice in its rigor;　65
This awes an impious, bold, offending world,
Commands obedience, and gives force to laws.
When by just vengeance guilty mortals perish,
The gods behold their punishment with
　pleasure,
And lay th' uplifted thunderbolt aside.　70
　Sempronius. Cato, I execute thy will with
　　pleasure.
　Cato. Meanwhile we'll sacrifice to liberty.
Remember, O my friends, the laws, the rights,
The gen'rous plan of power delivered down,
From age to age, by your renowned forefathers,　75
(So dearly bought, the price of so much blood)
O let it never perish in your hands!
But piously transmit it to your children.
Do thou, great liberty, inspire our souls, 79

[1] Pardon.

And make our lives in thy possession happy,
Or our deaths glorious in thy just defence.
　　　　　　　Exeunt Cato, &c.

Scene VI

Sempronius *and the Leaders of the Mutiny*

　1st Leader. Sempronius, you have
　　acted like yourself,
One would have thought you had been half
　in earnest.
　Sempronius. Villain, stand off!　Base
　　grov'ling worthless wretches,
Mongrels in faction, poor faint-hearted traitors!
　2d Leader. Nay, now you carry it too
　　far, Sempronius.　5
Throw off the mask, there are none here but
　friends.
　Sempronius. Know, villains, when such
　　paltry slaves presume
To mix in treason, if the plot succeeds,
They're thrown neglected by.　But if it fails,
They're sure to die like dogs, as you shall do.
Here, take these factious monsters, drag 'em
　forth　11
To sudden death.

Enter Guards

　1st Leader. Nay, since it comes to
　　this—
　Sempronius. Dispatch 'em quick, but first
　　pluck out their tongues,
Lest with their dying breath they sow
　sedition.
　　　　Exeunt Guards *with the* Leaders

Scene VII

Syphax *and* Sempronius

　Syphax. Our first design, my friend, has
　　proved abortive;
Still there remains an after-game to play.
My troops are mounted; their Numidian
　steeds
Snuff up the wind, and long to scow'r the
　desert.
Let but Sempronius head us in our flight,　5
We'll force the gate where Marcus keeps his
　guard,
And hew down all that would oppose our
　passage.
A day will bring us into Cæsar's camp.

SEMPRONIUS. Confusion! I have failed of half my purpose.
Marcia, the charming Marcia's left behind!
    SYPHAX. How? Will Sempronius turn a woman's slave! 11
    SEMPRONIUS. Think not thy friend can ever feel the soft
Unmanly warmth, and tenderness of love.
Syphax, I long to clasp that haughty maid,
And bend her stubborn virtue to my passion;
When I have gone thus far, I'd cast her off.
    SYPHAX. Well said! that's spoken like thyself, Sempronius. 17
What hinders then, but that thou find her out,
And hurry her away by manly force?
    SEMPRONIUS. But how to gain admission? for access 20
Is given to none but Juba, and her brothers.
    SYPHAX. Thou shalt have Juba's dress, and Juba's guards.
The doors will open, when Numidia's prince
Seems to appear before the slaves, that watch them.
    SEMPRONIUS. Heavens, what a thought is there! Marcia's my own! 25
How will my bosom swell with anxious joy,
When I behold her struggling in my arms,
With glowing beauty, and disordered charms,
While fear and anger, with alternate grace,
Pant in her breast, and vary in her face! 30
So Pluto, seized of Proserpine, conveyed
To hell's tremendous gloom th' affrighted maid,
There grimly smiled, pleased with the beauteous prize,
Nor envied Jove his sunshine and his skies.

ACT IV

SCENE I

LUCIA and MARCIA

LUCIA. Now tell me, Marcia, tell from thy soul,
If thou believ'st 'tis possible for woman
To suffer greater ills than Lucia suffers?
    MARCIA. O Lucia, Lucia, might my bigswoln [1] heart 4
Vent all its griefs, and give a loose to sorrow,
Marcia could answer thee in sighs, keep pace
With all thy woes, and count out tear for tear.
    LUCIA. I know thou'rt doomed alike, to be beloved

[1] Heavy with grief.

By Juba, and thy father's friend Sempronius;
But which of these has pow'r to charm like Portius! 10
    MARCIA. Still must I beg thee not to name Sempronius?
Lucia, I like not that loud boist'rous man.
Juba to all the brav'ry of a hero
Adds softest love, and more than female sweetness;
Juba might make the proudest of our sex,
Any of womankind, but Marcia, happy. 16
    LUCIA. And why not Marcia? Come, you strive in vain
To hide your thoughts from one, who knows too well
The inward glowings of a heart in love.
    MARCIA. While Cato lives, his daughter has no right 20
To love or hate, but as his choice directs.
    LUCIA. But should this father give you to Sempronius?
    MARCIA. I dare not think he will; but if he should—
Why wilt thou add to all the griefs I suffer
Imaginary ills, and fancied tortures? 25
I hear the sound of feet! They march this way!
Let us retire, and try if we can drown
Each softer thought in sense of present danger.
When love once pleads admission to our hearts
(In spite of all the virtue we can boast) 30
The woman that deliberates is lost. *Exeunt*

SCENE II

Enter SEMPRONIUS, *dressed like* JUBA, *with* Numidian Guards

SEMPRONIUS. The deer is lodged. I've tracked her to her covert.
Be sure you mind the word, and when I give it,
Rush in at once, and seize upon your prey.
Let not her cries or tears have force to move you. 4
—How will the young Numidian rave, to see
His mistress lost? If aught could glad my soul,
Beyond th' enjoyment of so bright a prize,
'Twould be to torture that young, gay barbarian.
—But heark, what noise! Death to my hopes! 'Tis he;
'Tis Juba's self! there is but one way left—
He must be murdered, and a passage cut 11

Through those his guards.—Hah, dastards,
    do you tremble!
Or act like men, or by yon azure heaven—

Enter JUBA

JUBA. What do I see? Who's this, that
    dares usurp
The guards and habit of Numidia's prince?
    SEMPRONIUS. One that was born to scourge
    thy arrogance,   16
Presumptuous youth!
    JUBA.   What can this mean?
    Sempronius!
    SEMPRONIUS. My sword shall answer thee.
    Have at thy heart.
    JUBA. Nay, then beware thy own, proud,
    barbarous man!
    (SEMPRONIUS *falls, his* Guards *surrender*)
    SEMPRONIUS. Curse on my stars! Am I then
    doomed to fall   20
By a boy's hand, disfigured in a vile
Numidian dress, and for a worthless woman?
Gods, I'm distracted! This my close of life!
O for a peal of thunder that would make
Earth, sea, and air, and heaven, and Cato
    tremble!   (*Dies*) 25
    JUBA. With what a spring his furious soul
    broke loose,
And left the limbs still quiv'ring on the
    ground!
Hence let us carry off those slaves to Cato,
That we may there at length unravel all
This dark design, this mystery of fate.   30
    Exit JUBA *with* Prisoners

SCENE III

Enter LUCIA *and* MARCIA

LUCIA. Sure 'twas the clash of swords; my
    troubled heart
Is so cast down, and sunk amidst its sorrows;
It throbs with fear, and aches at ev'ry sound.
O Marcia, should thy brothers for my sake!—
I die away with horror at the thought.   5
    MARCIA. See, Lucia, see! Here's blood!
    Here's blood and murder!
Hah! a Numidian! Heavens preserve the
    prince!
The face lies muffled up within the garment.
But hah! death to my sight! a diadem   9
And purple robes! O gods! 'tis he, 'tis he!
Juba, the loveliest youth that ever warmed
A virgin's heart, Juba lies dead before us!
    LUCIA. Now, Marcia, now call up to thy
    assistance
Thy wonted strength and constancy of mind;
Thou canst not put it to a greater trial.   15
    MARCIA. Lucia, look here, and wonder at
    my patience.
Have I not cause to rave, and beat my breast,
To rend my heart with grief, and run dis-
    tracted!
    LUCIA. What can I think or say to give thee
    comfort?
    MARCIA. Talk not of comfort, 'tis for lighter
    ills: 20
Behold a sight, that strikes all comfort dead.

Enter JUBA *listening*

I will indulge my sorrows, and give way
To all the pangs and fury of despair;
That man, that best of men, deserved it from
    me.
    JUBA. What do I hear? and was the false
    Sempronius   25
That best of men? O had I fall'n like him,
And could have thus been mourned, I had
    been happy!
    LUCIA. Here will I stand, companion in
    thy woes,
And help thee with my tears; when I behold
A loss like thine, I half forget my own.   30
    MARCIA. 'Tis not in fate to ease my tor-
    tured breast,
This empty world, to me a joyless desert,
Has nothing left to make poor Marcia happy.
    JUBA. I'm on the rack! Was he so near her
    heart?
    MARCIA. Oh he was all made up of love
    and charms,   35
Whatever maid could wish, or man admire.
Delight of ev'ry eye! When he appeared,
A secret pleasure gladdened all that saw him;
But when he talked, the proudest Roman
    blushed   39
To hear his virtues, and old age grew wise.
    JUBA. I shall run mad—
    MARCIA.   O Juba! Juba! Juba!
    JUBA. What means that voice? Did she
    not call on Juba?
    MARCIA. Why do I think on what he was!
    he's dead!
He's dead, and never knew how much I loved
    him.
Lucia, who knows but his poor bleeding heart,
Amidst its agonies, remembered Marcia,   46
And the last words he uttered called me cruel!
Alas, he knew not, hapless youth, he knew not
Marcia's whole soul was full of love and Juba!

JUBA. Where am I! Do I live, or am indeed
What Marcia thinks! All is Elysium round
  me! 51
  MARCIA. Ye dear remains of the most loved
    of men!
Nor modesty nor virtue here forbid
A last embrace, while thus—
  JUBA. See, Marcia, see,
    (*Throwing himself before her*)
The happy Juba lives! He lives to catch 55
That dear embrace, and to return it too
With mutual warmth and eagerness of love.
  MARCIA. With pleasure and amaze, I stand
    transported!
Sure 'tis a dream! Dead and alive at once!
If thou art Juba, who lies there?
  JUBA. A wretch 60
Disguised like Juba on a cursed design.
The tale is long, nor have I heard it out;
Thy father knows it all. I could not bear
To leave thee in the neighborhood of death,
But flew, in all the haste of love, to find thee.
I found thee weeping, and confess this once,
Am wrapped with joy to see my Marcia's
  tears. 67
  MARCIA. I've been surprised in an un-
    guarded hour,
But must not now go back. The love, that lay
Half-smothered in my breast, has broke
  through all 70
Its weak restraints, and burns in its full
  luster;
I cannot, if I would, conceal it from thee.
  JUBA. I'm lost in ecstasy! And dost thou
    love,
Thou charming maid?
  MARCIA. And dost thou live to
    ask it?
  JUBA. This, this is life indeed! Life worth
    preserving! 75
Such life as Juba never felt till now!
  MARCIA. Believe me, prince, before I
    thought thee dead,
I did not know myself how much I loved
  thee.
  JUBA. O fortunate mistake!
  MARCIA. O happy Marcia!
  JUBA. My joy! my best beloved! my only
    wish! 80
How shall I speak the transport of my soul!
  MARCIA. Lucia, thy arm! Oh let me rest
    upon it!—
The vital blood, that had forsook my heart,
Returns again in such tumultuous tides.
It quites o'ercomes me. Lead to my apart-
  ment.— 85
O prince! I blush to think what I have said,
But fate has wrested the confession from me;
Go on, and prosper in the paths of honor,
Thy virtue will excuse my passion for thee,
And make the gods propitious to our love. 90
    Exeunt MARCIA *and* LUCIA
  JUBA. I am so blessed, I fear 'tis all a dream.
Fortune, thou now hast made amends for all
Thy past unkindness. I absolve my stars.
What tho' Numidia add her conquered towns
And provinces to swell the victor's triumph?
Juba will never at his fate repine; 96
Let Cæsar have the world, if Marcia's mine.
    Exit

SCENE IV

A March at a Distance

Enter CATO *and* LUCIUS

  LUCIUS. I stand astonished! What, the bold
    Sempronius!
That still broke foremost through the crowd
  of patriots,
As with a hurricane of zeal transported,
And virtuous ev'n to madness—
  CATO. Trust me, Lucius,
Our civil discords have produced such crimes,
Such monstrous crimes, I am surprised at
  nothing. 6
—O Lucius, I am sick of this bad world!
The daylight and the sun grow painful to me.

Enter PORTIUS

But see where Portius comes! What means
  this haste?
Why are thy looks thus changed?
  PORTIUS. My heart is grieved. 10
I bring such news as will afflict my father.
  CATO. Has Cæsar shed more Roman blood?
  PORTIUS. Not so.
The traitor Syphax, as within the square
He exercised his troops, the signal given,
Flew off at once with his Numidian horse 15
To the south gate, where Marcus holds the
  watch.
I saw, and called to stop him, but in vain;
He tossed his arm aloft, and proudly told me,
He would not stay and perish like Sempronius.
  CATO. Perfidious men! But haste my son,
    and see 20
Thy brother Marcus acts a Roman's part.
    Exit PORTIUS

—Lucius, the torrent bears too hard upon
 me:
Justice gives way to force; the conquered
 world
Is Cæsar's; Cato has no business in it.
    Lucius. While pride, oppression, and in-
 justice reign, 25
The world will still demand her Cato's
 presence.
In pity to mankind, submit to Cæsar,
And reconcile thy mighty soul to life.
    Cato. Would Lucius have me live to swell
 the number 29
Of Cæsar's slaves, or by a base submission
Give up the cause of Rome, and own a tyrant?
    Lucius. The victor never will impose on
 Cato
Ungen'rous terms. His enemies confess
The virtues of humanity are Cæsar's.
    Cato. Curse on his virtues! They've un-
 done his country. 35
Such popular humanity is treason—
But see young Juba! the good youth appears
Full of the guilt of his perfidious subjects.
    Lucius. Alas, poor prince! his fate deserves
 compassion.

Enter Juba

Juba. I blush, and am confounded to ap-
 pear 40
Before thy presence, Cato.
    Cato.   What's thy crime?
    Juba. I'm a Numidian.
    Cato.   And a brave one too.
Thou hast a Roman soul.
    Juba.   Hast thou not heard
Of my false countrymen?
    Cato.   Alas, young prince,
Falsehood and fraud shoot up in ev'ry soil,
The product of all climes—Rome has its
 Cæsars. 46
    Juba. 'Tis gen'rous thus to comfort the
 distressed.
    Cato. 'Tis just to give applause where 'tis
 deserved;
Thy virtue, prince, has stood the test of
 fortune,
Like purest gold, that, tortured in the furnace,
Comes out more bright, and brings forth all
 its weight. 51
    Juba. What shall I answer thee? My
 ravished heart
O'erflows with secret joy: I'd rather gain
Thy praise, O Cato, than Numidia's empire.

Re-enter Portius

Portius. Misfortune on misfortune! Grief
 on grief! 55
My brother Marcus—
    Cato.   Hah! what has he done?
Has he forsook his post? Has he giv'n way?
Did he look tamely on, and let 'em pass?
    Portius. Scarce had I left my father, but
 I met him
Borne on the shields of his surviving soldiers,
Breathless and pale, and covered o'er with
 wounds. 61
Long, at the head of his few faithful friends,
He stood the shock of a whole host of foes,
Till obstinately brave, and bent on death,
Oppressed with multitudes, he greatly fell. 65
    Cato. I'm satisfied.
    Portius.   Nor did he fall before
His sword had pierced through the false heart
 of Syphax.
Yonder he lies. I saw the hoary traitor
Grin in the pangs of death and bite the ground.
    Cato. Thanks to the gods! my boy has
 done his duty. 70
—Portius, when I am dead, be sure thou
 place
His urn near mine.
    Portius. Long may they keep asunder!
    Lucius. O Cato, arm thy soul with all its
 patience;
See where the corpse of thy dead son ap-
 proaches!
The citizens and senators, alarmed, 75
Have gathered round it, and attend it weep-
 ing.

Cato meeting the Corpse

Cato. Welcome, my son! Here lay him
 down, my friends,
Full in my sight, that I may view at leisure
The bloody corpse, and count those glorious
 wounds.
—How beautiful is death, when earned by
 virtue! 80
Who would not be that youth? What pity
 is it
That we can die but once to serve our country!
—Why sits this sadness on your brows, my
 friends?
I should have blushed if Cato's house had
 stood
Secure, and flourished in a civil war. 85
—Portius, behold thy brother, and remember

Thy life is not thy own, when Rome demands it.
JUBA. (*Aside*) Was ever man like this!
CATO.   Alas my friends!
Why mourn you thus? Let not a private loss
Afflict your hearts. 'Tis Rome requires our tears.   90
The mistress of the world, the seat of empire,
The nurse of heroes, the delight of gods,
That humbled the proud tyrants of the earth,
And set the nations free, Rome is no more.
O liberty! O virtue! O my country!   95
JUBA. (*Aside*) Behold that upright man! Rome fills his eyes
With tears, that flowed not o'er his own dead son.
CATO. Whate'er the Roman virtue has subdued,
The sun's whole course, the day and year, are Cæsar's.
For him the self-devoted Decii died,   100
The Fabii[1] fell, and the great Scipio's[2] conquered;
Ev'n Pompey fought for Cæsar. Oh my friends!
How is the toil of fate, the work of ages,
The Roman empire fall'n! O curst ambition!
Fall'n into Cæsar's hands! Our great forefathers   105
Had left him nought to conquer but his country.
JUBA. While Cato lives, Cæsar will blush to see
Mankind enslaved, and be ashamed of empire.
CATO. Cæsar ashamed! Has not he seen Pharsalia!
LUCIUS. Cato, 'tis time thou save thyself and us.   110
CATO. Lose not a thought on me. I'm out of danger.
Heaven will not leave me in the victor's hand.
Cæsar shall never say: "I conquered Cato."
But oh! my friends, your safety fills my heart
With anxious thoughts. A thousand secret terrors,   115
Rise in my soul! How shall I save my friends!
'Tis now, O Cæsar, I begin to fear thee.
LUCIUS. Cæsar has mercy, if we ask it of him.
CATO. Then ask it, I conjure you! Let him know   119

Whate'er was done against him, Cato did it.
Add, if you please, that I request it of him,
That I myself, with tears, request it of him,
The virtue of my friends may pass unpunished.
—Juba, my heart is troubled for thy sake.
Should I advise thee to regain Numidia,   125
Or seek the Conqueror?—
JUBA.   If I forsake thee
Whilst I have life, may heaven abandon Juba!
CATO. Thy virtues, prince, if I foresee aright,
Will one day make thee great;[3] at Rome, hereafter,
'Twill be no crime to have been Cato's friend.
Portius, draw near! My son, thou oft hast seen   131
Thy sire engaged in a corrupted state,
Wrestling with vice and faction. Now thou see'st me
Spent, overpowered, despairing of success;
Let me advise thee to retreat betimes   135
To thy paternal seat, the Sabine field,
Where the great Censor[4] toiled with his own hands,
And all our frugal ancestors were blessed
In humble virtues and a rural life.
There live retired, pray for the peace of Rome,
Content thyself to be obscurely good.[5]   141
When vice prevails, and impious men bear sway,
The post of honor is a private station.
PORTIUS. I hope my father does not recommend
A life to Portius that he scorns himself.   145
CATO. Farewell, my friends! if there be any of you
Who dare not trust the victor's clemency,
Know, there are ships prepared by my command,
(Their sails already op'ning to the winds)
That shall convey you to the wished-for port.
Is there aught else, my friends, I can do for you?   151
The conqueror draws near. Once more farewell!
If e'er we meet hereafter, we shall meet
In happier climes, and on a safer shore,
Where Cæsar never shall approach us more.
There the brave youth, with love of virtue fired,   (*Pointing to his dead son*) 156

---

[1] Famous families of republican Rome.
[2] Publius Cornelius Africanus Major conquered Carthage in the Second Carthaginian War.
[3] See note 3, p. 519.
[4] Cato the Elder when not in public service devoted himself to agriculture.
[5] I.e., good in an obscure station in life.

Who greatly in his country's cause expired,
Shall know he conquered. The firm patriot
    there
(Who made the welfare of mankind his care)
Tho' still by faction, vice, and fortune,
    crossed,   160
Shall find the gen'rous labor was not lost.

ACT V

SCENE I

CATO *solus, sitting in a thoughtful posture; in his hand Plato's Book on the Immortality of the Soul.*[1] *A drawn sword on the table by him*

CATO. It must be so—Plato, thou reason'st well!—
Else whence this pleasing hope, this fond desire,
This longing after immortality?
Or whence this secret dread, and inward horror,   4
Of falling into nought? Why shrinks the soul
Back on herself, and startles at destruction?
'Tis the divinity that stirs within us;
'Tis heaven itself, that points out an hereafter,
And intimates eternity to man.
Eternity! thou pleasing, dreadful, thought!
Through what variety of untried being,   11
Through what new scenes and changes must we pass!
The wide, th' unbounded prospect, lies before me;
But shadows, clouds, and darkness, rest upon it.
Here will I hold. If there's a pow'r above us,
(And that there is all nature cries aloud 16
Through all her works) he must delight in virtue;
And that which he delights in, must be happy.
But when! or where!—This world was made for Cæsar.   19
I'm weary of conjectures—This must end 'em.
            (*Laying his hand on his sword*)
Thus am I double armed: my death and life,
My bane and antidote are both before me:
This in a moment brings me to an end;
But this informs me I shall never die.
The soul, secured in her existence, smiles 25

[1] Addison apparently has the *Phædo* of Plato in mind. The audience, of course, cannot tell what book is in Cato's hand. The following speech, however, is a rapid summary of the Platonic argument.

At the drawn dagger, and defies its point.
The stars shall fade away, the sun himself
Grow dim with age, and nature sink in years;
But thou shalt flourish in immortal youth,
Unhurt amidst the war of elements,   30
The wrecks of matter, and the crush of worlds.
What means this heaviness that hangs upon me?
This lethargy that creeps through all my senses?
Nature oppressed, and harrassed out with care,   34
Sinks down to rest. This once I'll favor her.
That my awakened soul may take her flight,
Renewed in all her strength and fresh with life,
An off'ring fit for heaven. Let guilt or fear
Disturb man's rest; Cato knows neither of 'em.
Indiff'rent in his choice to sleep or die. 40

SCENE II

CATO, PORTIUS

CATO. But hah! How's this, my son? Why this intrusion?
Were not my orders that I would be private?
Why am I disobeyed?
    PORTIUS.   Alas, my father!
What means this sword, this instrument of death?
Let me convey it hence!
    CATO.   Rash youth, forbear! 5
    PORTIUS. O let the pray'rs, th' entreaties of your friends,
Their tears, their common danger, wrest it from you.
    CATO. Wouldst thou betray me? Wouldst thou give me up
A slave, a captive, into Cæsar's hands?
Retire and learn obedience to a father,   10
Or know, young man!—
    [PORTIUS. Look not thus sternly on me;
You know I'd rather die than disobey you.
    CATO. 'Tis well! Again I'm master of myself,
Now, Cæsar, let thy troops beset our gates,
And bar each avenue, thy gath'ring fleets 15
O'er-spread the sea, and stop up ev'ry port;
Cato shall open to himself a passage,
And mock thy hopes—][2]
    PORTIUS.   O sir, forgive your son,

[2] The lines enclosed in brackets are lacking in the first edition.

Whose grief hangs heavy on him! O my father!
How am I sure it is not the last time 20
I e'er shall call you so! Be not displeased,
O be not angry with me whilst I weep,
And, in the anguish of my heart, beseech you
To quit the dreadful purpose of your soul! 24
   CATO. Thou hast been ever good and dutiful.
                              (*Embracing him*)
Weep not, my son. All will be well again.
The righteous gods, whom I have sought to please,
Will succor Cato, and preserve his children.
   PORTIUS. Your words give comfort to my drooping heart.
   CATO. Portius, thou may'st rely upon my conduct. 30
Thy father will not act what misbecomes him.
But go, my son, and see if aught be wanting
Among thy father's friends; see them embarked;
And tell me if the winds and seas befriend them.
My soul is quite weighed down with care, and asks 35
The soft refreshment of a moment's sleep.
                                       Exit
   PORTIUS. My thoughts are more at ease, my heart revives.

SCENE III

PORTIUS *and* MARCIA

   PORTIUS. O Marcia, O my sister, still there's hope!
Our father will not cast away a life
So needful to us all, and to his country.
He is retired to rest, and seems to cherish
Thoughts full of peace. He has dispatched me hence 5
With orders that bespeak a mind composed,
And studious for the safety of his friends.
Marcia, take care that none disturb his slumbers.   *Exit*
   MARCIA. O ye immortal powers, that guard the just,
Watch round his couch, and soften his repose, 10
Banish his sorrows, and becalm his soul
With easy dreams; remember all his virtues!
And show mankind that goodness is your care.

SCENE IV

LUCIA *and* MARCIA

   LUCIA. Where is your father, Marcia, where is Cato?
   MARCIA. Lucia, speak low, he is retired to rest.
Lucia, I feel a gently-dawning hope
Rise in my soul. We shall be happy still.
   LUCIA. Alas, I tremble when I think on Cato, 5
In every view, in every thought I tremble!
Cato is stern, and awful as a god,
He knows not how to wink at human frailty,
Or pardon weakness that he never felt.
   MARCIA. Though stern and awful to the foes of Rome, 10
He is all goodness, Lucia, always mild,
Compassionate, and gentle to his friends.
Filled with domestic tenderness, the best,
The kindest father! I have ever found him
Easy, and good, and bounteous to my wishes.
   LUCIA. 'Tis his consent alone can make us blessed. 16
Marcia, we both are equally involved
In the same intricate, perplexed, distress.
The cruel hand of fate, that has destroyed
Thy brother Marcus, whom we both lament—
   MARCIA. And ever shall lament, unhappy youth! 21
   LUCIA. Has set my soul at large, and now I stand
Loose of my vow. But who knows Cato's thoughts?
Who knows how yet he may dispose of Portius,
Or how he has determined of thyself? 25
   MARCIA. Let him but live! commit the rest to heaven.

Enter LUCIUS

   LUCIUS. Sweet are the slumbers of the virtuous man!
O Marcia, I have seen thy godlike father:
Some pow'r invisible supports his soul, 29
And bears it up in all its wonted greatness.
A kind refreshing sleep is fall'n upon him.
I saw him stretched at ease, his fancy lost
In pleasing dreams; as I drew near his couch,
He smiled, and cried, "Cæsar, thou can'st not hurt me."
   MARCIA. His mind still labors with some dreadful thought. 35

Lucius. Lucia, why all this grief, these floods of sorrow?
Dry up thy tears, my child, we all are safe
While Cato lives.—His presence will protect us.

Enter Juba

Juba. Lucius, the horsemen are returned from viewing 39
The number, strength, and posture of our foes,
Who now encamp within a short hour's march.
On the high point of yon bright western tower
We ken them from afar; the setting sun
Plays on their shining arms and burnished helmets,
And covers all the field with gleams of fire.
Lucius. Marcia, 'tis time we should awake thy father. 46
Cæsar is still disposed to give us terms,
And waits at distance till he hears from Cato.

Enter Portius

Portius, thy looks speak somewhat of importance.
What tidings dost thou bring? Methinks I see
Unusual gladness sparkling in thy eyes. 51
Portius. As I was hasting to the port, where now
My father's friends, impatient for a passage,
Accuse the ling'ring winds, a sail arrived
From Pompey's son, who through the realms of Spain 55
Calls out for vengeance on his father's death,
And rouses the whole nation up to arms.[1]
Were Cato at their head, once more might Rome
Assert her rights, and claim her liberty.
But hark! What means that groan! O give me way, 60
And let me fly into my father's presence.
Exit
Lucius. Cato, amidst his slumbers, thinks on Rome,
And in the wild disorder of his soul
Mourns o'er his country. Hah! a second groan!—
Heaven guard us all—
Marcia. Alas, 'tis not the voice 65
Of one who sleeps! 'Tis agonizing pain.
'Tis death is in that sound—

[1] Gnæus Pompeius Magnus, with his brother Sextus, collected an army in Spain, where he was defeated by Cæsar 45 b.c.

Re-enter Portius
Portius. O sight of woe
O Marcia, what we feared is come to pass!
Cato is fall'n upon his sword—
Lucia. O Portius,
Hide all the horrors of thy mournful tale, 70
And let us guess the rest.
Portius. I've raised him up,
And placed him in his chair, where pale, and faint,
He gasps for breath, and, as his life flows from him,
Demands to see his friends. His weeping servants, 74
Obsequious to his orders, bear him hither.
(*The back scene opens, and discovers* Cato)
Marcia. O heaven assist me in this dreadful hour
To pay the last sad duties to my father.
Juba. These are thy triumphs, thy exploits, O Cæsar!
Lucius. Now is Rome fall'n indeed!
(Cato *brought forward in his chair*)
Cato. Here set me down—
Portius come near me—are my friends embarked? 80
Can any thing be thought of for their service?
Whilst I yet live, let me not live in vain.
—O Lucius, art thou here?—Thou art too good!—
Let this our friendship live between our children; 84
Make Portius happy in thy daughter Lucia.
Alas poor man, he weeps!—Marcia, my daughter—
—O bend me forward!—Juba loves thee, Marcia.
A senator of Rome, while Rome survived,
Would not have matched his daughter with a king,
But Cæsar's arms have thrown down all distinction; 90
Whoe'er is brave and virtuous, is a Roman—
—I'm sick to death—O when shall I get loose
From this vain world, th' abode of guilt and sorrow!—
—And yet methinks a beam of light breaks in
On my departing soul. Alas, I fear 95
I've been too hasty. O ye pow'rs that search
The heart of man and weigh his inmost thoughts,
If I have done amiss, impute it not!—
The best may err, but you are good, and—oh! (*Dies*)

Lucius. There fled the greatest soul that
　　ever warmed　　　　　　　　　　　100
A Roman breast. O Cato! O my friend!
Thy will shall be religiously observed.
But let us bear this awful corpse to Cæsar,
And lay it in his sight, that it may stand
A fence betwixt us and the victor's wrath;
Cato, tho' dead, shall still protect his friends.
　From hence, let fierce contending nations
　　know　　　　　　　　　　　　　　107
What dire effects from civil discord flow.
'Tis this that shakes our country with alarms,
And gives up Rome a prey to Roman arms,
Produces fraud, and cruelty, and strife,
And robs the guilty world of Cato's life.
　　　　　　　　　　　　Exeunt omnes

EPILOGUE

By Dr. Garth [1]

Spoken by Mrs. Porter [2]

What odd fantastic things we women do!
Who would not listen when young lovers
　woo?
But die a maid, yet have the choice of two!
Ladies are often cruel to their cost;
To give you pain, themselves they punish
　most.　　　　　　　　　　　　　　5
Vows of virginity should well be weighed;
Too oft they're cancelled, tho' in convents
　made.
Would you revenge such rash resolves—
　you may:　　　　　　　　　　　　8
Be spiteful—and believe the thing we say,
We hate you when you're easily said nay.

---

[1] Pope's Tory prologue was countered by the Whigs with an epilogue by Samuel Garth (1661-1719), a Whig and a popular physician, author of a poem called *The Dispensary* (1699).
[2] As Lucia.

How needless, if you knew us, were your fears?
Let love have eyes, and beauty will have
　ears.
Our hearts are formed, as you yourselves
　would choose,
Too proud to ask, too humble to refuse:
We give to merit, and to wealth we sell;　15
He sighs with most success that settles well.
The woes of wedlock with the joys we mix;
'Tis best repenting in a coach and six.
　Blame not our conduct, since we but pursue
Those lively lessons we have learned from
　you:　　　　　　　　　　　　　　20
Your breasts no more the fire of beauty
　warms,
But wicked wealth usurps the pow'r of charms;
What pains to get the gaudy thing you hate,
To swell in show, and be a wretch in state!
At plays you ogle, at the Ring [3] you bow;　25
Even churches are no sanctuaries now.
There, golden idols all your vows receive;
She is no goddess that has nought to give.
Oh, may once more the happy age appear,
When words were artless, and the thoughts
　sincere;　　　　　　　　　　　　30
When gold and grandeur were unenvied
　things,
And courts less coveted than groves and
　springs.
Love then shall only mourn when truth com-
　plains,
And constancy feel transport in its chains.　34
Sighs with success their own soft anguish tell,
And eyes shall utter what the lips conceal:
Virtue again to its bright station climb,
And beauty fear no enemy but time.
The fair shall listen to desert alone,
And every Lucia find a Cato's son.　　　40

---

[3] In Hyde Park.

THE CONSCIOUS LOVERS

A Comedy by Sir Richard Steele

Illud genus narrationis quod in personis positum est, debet habere sermonis festivitatem, animorum dissimilitudinem, gravitatem, lenitatem, spem, metum, suspicionem, desiderium, dissimulationem, misericordiam, rerum varietates, fortunæ commutationem, insperatum incommodum, subitam letitiam, jucundum exitum rerum.—Cic. Rhetor. ad Herenn. Lib. i.[1]

Richard Steele was born in Dublin, March 12 (?), 1672. Little is known of his parents, who died when he was a small boy, leaving him to the care of an uncle, Henry Gascoigne. In 1684 he was admitted to the Charterhouse, and he entered Christ's Church College, Oxford, in 1689. He was later made a postmaster of Merton, but leaving the University without taking a degree, he enlisted in the army as a cadet and was ultimately promoted to a captaincy. His literary career began while he was in the army with the publication of *The Christian Hero* (1701), which was followed by his three early comedies. These dramatic ventures failed to make for Steele the place in the world which he expected. His appointment as Gazetteer in 1707 marks the beginning of his connection with official politics, which was to continue for most of his active life; it marks also his entry into the world of journalism. In 1709 he began the publication of *The Tatler*, followed by *The Spectator*, on the basis of which rests the chief reputation of Steele and his life-long friend and collaborator, Addison. In 1714, with the actors, Wilks, Cibber, Dogget, and Booth, Steele became one of the managers of the theater in Drury Lane, a position which he held in one way or another for the rest of his life. His later years were saddened by domestic, public, and pecuniary difficulties, by the quarrel with Addison, and by the deaths of his wife and most of his children. He himself died, after a long retirement and illness, at Carmarthen, Wales, the home of his wife's family, Sept. 1, 1729.

References: Aitken, George A., *The Life of Richard Steele*, 2 vols., 1889. Dobson, Austin, *Richard Steele* (English Worthies Series), 1886.

STEELE'S DRAMATIC WORKS

The Funeral; or, Grief à-la-Mode (comedy) (D.L., *c.* Dec., 1701), 1702.
The Lying Lover; or, The Ladies' Friendship (comedy) (D.L., Dec. 2, 1703), 1704.
The Tender Husband; or, The Accomplish'd Fools (comedy) (D.L., April 23, 1705), 1705.
The Conscious Lovers (comedy) (D.L., Nov. 7, 1722), 1723.

Rumor early in 1722 said that Sir Richard Steele was at work upon a new play, a report which doubtless enheartened persons interested in the theater, for it had been long since a first-rate play had appeared. The managers of the theater, particularly Cibber, were frequently subjected to attacks in the papers charging them with such bad practices as altering old plays for the worse and rejecting new ones which should have been given a trial. It had been seventeen years since Steele's last play had appeared and in the meantime the author had become a person of consequence. Theater-goers with long memories could perhaps recall the series of moral comedies with which Captain Steele had in those years endeavored to "enliven his character." One of them, indeed, *The Lying Lover*, had been "damned for its piety." Rumor proved to be correct, and Sir Richard's fourth and last comedy appeared at Drury Lane on November 7, 1722, "with new scenes, and all the characters new drest." Two titles,

---

[1] That kind of narrative which is represented by persons [*i.e.*, on the stage] ought to be marked by gaiety of dialogue, diversity of characters, gravity, tenderness, hope, fear, suspicion, desire, concealment, pity, variety of events, change of fortune, unexpected disaster, sudden joy, [and] a happy ending.—Cicero, *de Rhetor. ad Herennium*, I, 8.

This motto implies the attitude of sentimental comedy as written by Steele and his followers. They placed the emphasis upon *gravitatem, lenitatem,* and *misericordiam*.

"The Fine Gentleman" and "The Unfashionable Lovers," seem to have been rejected before the play was called "The Conscious Lovers." The best cast available was put into action: Mrs. Oldfield as Indiana, Booth as young Bevil, Cibber as Tom, and Mrs. Younger as Phillis; and these names give color to the author's statement, made later in the preface to the published play, that "it was in every part excellently perform'd." It ran for eighteen nights and was given eight additional representations before the end of the season.

The Conscious Lovers represents Steele's ideal of comedy. "The whole," he says, "was writ for the sake of the scene in the fourth act wherein Mr. Bevil evades the quarrel with his friend." The defense of Restoration comedy had been that it had held folly and vice up to scorn, satirized them as things to be avoided; Steele, on the other hand, presented virtuous characters to be emulated by the audience. He hopes that the scene of the averted duel "may have some effect upon the Goths and Vandals that frequent the theatres." In this respect, and since the play is based upon the *Andria* (B.C. 167) of Terence, *The Conscious Lovers* marks the climax of the first stage in the development of sentimental comedy, characterized by the presentation of a moral problem and the sentimental misinterpretation of Plautus and Terence. Earlier writers of comedy had thought it in their province to make the audience laugh; Steele had expressed his idea on this phase of the subject in the epilogue to *The Lying Lover* in the following lines:

Our too advent'rous author soared to-night
Above the little praise, mirth to excite,
And chose with pity to chastise delight.
For laughter's a distorted passion, born
Of sudden self-esteem and sudden scorn;
Which, when 'tis o'er, the men in pleasure wise,
Both him that moved it and themselves despise;
While generous pity of a painted woe
Makes us ourselves both more approve and know.

In writing *The Conscious Lovers* he had been guided by this principle, and it is said that he inserted the comic parts of Tom and Phillis only at the insistence of Colley Cibber, who thought the play without some lightening elements would be too solemn for an English audience. In spite of these characters the play has earned the praise bestowed upon it by Parson Adams, who pronounced it the only comedy fit for a Christian to see, thinking that it contained "some things almost solemn enough for a sermon."

THE PREFACE [1]

This comedy has been received with universal acceptance, for it was in every part excellently performed; and there needs no other applause of the actors, but that they excelled according to the dignity and difficulty of the character they represented. But this great favor done to the work in acting, renders the expectation still the greater from the author, to keep up the spirit in the representation of the closet, or any other circumstance of the reader, whether alone or in company; to which I can only say, that it must be remembered a play is to be seen and is made to be represented with the advantage of action, nor can appear but with half the spirit, without it; for the greatest effect of a play in reading is to excite the reader to go see it; and when he does so, it is then a play has the effect of example and precept.

The chief design of this was to be an innocent performance, and the audience have abundantly showed how ready they are to support what is visibly intended that way; nor do I make any difficulty to acknowledge, that the whole was writ for the sake of the scene of the fourth act, wherein Mr. Bevil evades the quarrel with his friend, and hope it may have some effect upon the Goths and Vandals that frequent the theatres, or a more polite audience may supply their absence.

But this incident, and the case of the father and daughter, are esteemed by some people no subjects of comedy; but I cannot be of their mind; for any thing that has its foundation in happiness and success, must be allowed to be the object of comedy, and sure it must be an improvement of it, to introduce a joy too exquisite for laughter, that can have no

[1] The DEDICATION, to George I, is not reprinted here, though it appears in the first edition of the play, as it contains chiefly Steele's thanks to the King for favors bestowed upon him.
The PREFACE is important as presenting Steele's own attitude towards the play and sentimental comedy as a species. The emphasis upon the pathetic atmosphere and the indebtedness to Terence show clearly the position of the writers of sentimental comedy of this period.

spring out in delight, which is the case of this young lady. I must, therefore, contend, that the tears which were shed on that occasion flowed from reason and good sense, and that men ought not to be laughed at for weeping, till we are come to a more clear notion of what is to be imputed to the hardness of the head, and the softness of the heart; and I think it was very politely said of Mr. Wilks to one who told him there was a general weeping for Indiana, "I'll warrant he'll fight never the worse for that." To be apt to give way to the impressions of humanity is the excellence of a right disposition and the natural working of a well-turned spirit. But as I have suffered by critics who are got no farther than to inquire whether they ought to be pleased or not, I would willingly find them properer matter for their employment, and revive here a song which was omitted for want of a performer, and designed for the entertainment of Indiana; Signor Carbonelli [1] instead of it played on the fiddle, and it is for want of a singer that such advantageous things are said of an instrument which were designed for a voice. The song is the distress of a love-sick maid and may be a fit entertainment for some small critics to examine whether the passion is just, or the distress male or female.

[1] A violinist popular on the London stage at this time.

I

From place to place forlorn I go,
  With downcast eyes a silent shade;
Forbidden to declare my woe;
  To speak, till spoken to, afraid.

II

My inward pangs, my secret grief,
  My soft consenting looks betray.
He loves, but gives me no relief.
  Why speaks not he who may?

It remains to say a word concerning Terence, and I am extremely surprised to find what Mr. Cibber told me prove a truth, that what I valued myself so much upon, the translation of him, should be imputed to me as a reproach. Mr. Cibber's zeal for the work, his care and application in instructing the actors, and altering the disposition of the scenes, when I was through sickness unable to cultivate such things myself, has been a very obliging favor and friendship to me. For this reason, I was very hardly persuaded to throw away Terence's celebrated funeral, and take only the bare authority of the young man's character, and how I have worked it into an Englishman, and made use of the same circumstances of discovering a daughter when we least hoped for one, is humbly submitted to the learned reader.

THE CONSCIOUS LOVERS

DRAMATIS PERSONÆ

MEN

Sir John Bevil	Mr. Mills	Cimberton, *a coxcomb*	Mr. Griffin
Mr. Sealand	Mr. Williams	Humphrey, *an old servant to Sir John*	Mr. Shepard
Bevil, Junior, *in love with Indiana*	Mr. Booth	Tom, *servant to Bevil, jun.*	Mr. Cibber
Myrtle, *in love with Lucinda*	Mr. Wilks	Daniel, *a country boy, servant to Indiana*	Mr. Theo. Cibber

WOMEN

Mrs. Sealand, *second wife to Sealand*	Mrs. Moore	Lucinda, *Sealand's daughter by his second wife*	Mrs. Booth
Isabella, *sister to Sealand*	Mrs. Thurmond	Phillis, *maid to Lucinda*	Mrs. Younger
Indiana, *Sealand's daughter by his first wife*	Mrs. Oldfield		

Scene: *London*

PROLOGUE

By Mr. Welsted [1]

Spoken by Mr. Wilks

To win your hearts, and to secure your praise,
The comic writers strive by various ways;
By subtle stratagems they act their game,
And leave untried no avenue to fame.
One writes the spouse a beating from his wife;
And says each stroke was copied from the life.
Some fix all wit and humor in grimace,   7
And make a livelihood of Pinkey's [2] face.
Here, one gay show and costly habits tries,
Confiding to the judgment of your eyes;   10
Another smuts his scene (a cunning shaver)
Sure of the rakes' and of the wenches' favor.
Oft have these arts prevailed; and one may guess,
If practised o'er again, would find success.
But the bold sage, the poet of to-night,   15
By new and desp'rate rules resolved to write;
Fain would he give more just applauses rise,
And please by wit that scorns the aids of vice;
The praise he seeks, from worthier motives springs,

Such praise, as praise to those that give, it brings.   20
Your aid, most humbly sought, then Britons lend,
And liberal mirth, like liberal men, defend.
No more let ribaldry, with licence writ,
Usurp the name of eloquence or wit;
No more let lawless farce uncensured go,   25
The lewd dull gleanings of a Smithfield [3] show.
'Tis yours, with breeding to refine the age,
To chasten wit, and moralize the stage.   28
Ye modest, wise and good, ye fair, ye brave,
To-night the champion of your virtues save,
Redeem from long contempt the comic name,
And judge politely for your country's fame.

ACT I

Scene I

Sir John Bevil's *house*

Enter Sir John Bevil *and* Humphrey

Sir John. Have you ordered that I should not be interrupted while I am dressing?

Humphrey. Yes, sir. I believed you had something of moment to say to me.

Sir John. Let me see, Humphrey; I think it is now full forty years since I first took thee to be about myself.

---

[1] Leonard Welsted (1688–1747), a poet, author of occasional verse and one play, is famous because of his quarrel with Pope. He is mentioned in *The Dunciad* and in the *Epistle to Dr. Arbuthnot*.

[2] William Pinkethman, a popular actor of low comedy parts, acted from 1692 to 1724.

[3] Smithfield, in the heart of the City, near St. Paul's and the Charterhouse, was the scene of Bartholomew Fair.

HUMPHREY. I thank you, sir, it has been an easy forty years; and I have passed 'em without much sickness, care, or labor.

SIR JOHN. Thou hast a brave constitution; you are a year or two older than I am, sirrah.

HUMPHREY. You have ever been of that mind, sir.

SIR JOHN. You knave, you know it; I took thee for thy gravity and sobriety in my wild years.

HUMPHREY. Ah, sir! our manners were formed from our different fortunes, not our different age. Wealth gave a loose to your youth, and poverty put a restraint upon mine.

SIR JOHN. Well, Humphrey, you know I have been a kind master to you. I have used you, for the ingenuous nature I observed in you from the beginning, more like an humble friend than a servant.

HUMPHREY. I humbly beg you'll be so tender of me as to explain your commands, sir, without any farther preparation.

SIR JOHN. I'll tell thee then. In the first place, this wedding of my son's, in all probability (shut the door) will never be at all.

HUMPHREY. How, sir! not be at all? For what reason is it carried on in appearance?

SIR JOHN. Honest Humphrey, have patience; and I'll tell thee all in order. I have myself, in some part of my life lived, indeed, with freedom, but, I hope without reproach. Now, I thought liberty would be as little injurious to my son; therefore, as soon as he grew towards man, I indulged him in living after his own manner. I knew not how, otherwise, to judge of his inclination; for what can be concluded from a behavior under restraint and fear? But what charms me above all expression is that my son has never in the least action, the most distant hint or word, valued himself upon that great estate of his mother's, which, according to our marriage settlement, he has had ever since he came to age.

HUMPHREY. No, sir; on the contrary, he seems afraid of appearing to enjoy it, before you or any belonging to you. He is as dependent and resigned to your will, as if he had not a farthing but what must come from your immediate bounty. You have ever acted like a good and generous father, and he like an obedient and grateful son.

SIR JOHN. Nay, his carriage is so easy to all with whom he converses, that he is never assuming, never prefers himself to others, nor ever is guilty of that rough sincerity which a man is not called to, and certainly disobliges most of his acquaintance; to be short, Humphrey, his reputation was so fair in the world, that old Sealand, the great India merchant, has offered his only daughter, and sole heiress to that vast estate of his, as a wife for him. You may be sure I made no difficulties, the match was agreed on, and this very day named for the wedding.

HUMPHREY. What hinders the proceeding?

SIR JOHN. Don't interrupt me. You know, I was last Thursday at the masquerade. My son, you may remember, soon found us out. He knew his grandfather's habit, which I then wore, and though it was the mode in the last age, yet the maskers, you know, followed us as if we had been in the most monstrous figures in that whole assembly.

HUMPHREY. I remember indeed a young man of quality in the habit of a clown that was particularly troublesome.

SIR JOHN. Right. He was too much what he seemed to be. You remember how impertinently he followed and teased us and would know who we were.

HUMPHREY. (*Aside*) I know he has a mind to come into that particular.

SIR JOHN. Ay, he followed us, till the gentleman who led the lady in the Indian mantle presented that gay creature to the rustic and bid him, like Cymon in the fable,[1] grow polite by falling in love and let that worthy old gentleman alone, meaning me. The clown was not reformed, but rudely persisted, and offered to force off my mask. With that the gentleman throwing off his own, appeared to be my son, and in his concern for me, tore off that of the nobleman. At this, they seized each other; the company called the guards; and in the surprise, the lady swooned away, upon which my son quitted his adversary and had now no care but of the lady. When raising her in his arms, "Art thou gone," cried he, "forever? Forbid it, heaven!" She revives at his known voice, and with the most familiar though modest

[1] Dryden's fable of *Cymon and Iphigenia*, from *Fables, Ancient and Modern*. The clown is made a gentleman by his love for the lady. Garrick used this fable as the source of his *Cymon, A Dramatic Romance*, D.L., 1767.

gesture hangs in safety over his shoulder weeping, but wept as in the arms of one before whom she could give herself a loose, were she not under observation. While she hides her face in his neck, he carefully conveys her from the company.

HUMPHREY. I have observed this accident has dwelt upon you very strongly.

SIR JOHN. Her uncommon air, her noble modesty, the dignity of her person, and the occasion itself, drew the whole assembly together, and I soon heard it buzzed about, she was the adopted daughter of a famous sea officer, who had served in France. Now this unexpected and public discovery of my son's so deep concern for her—

HUMPHREY. Was what I suppose alarmed Mr. Sealand in behalf of his daughter to break off the match.

SIR JOHN. You are right. He came to me yesterday, and said he thought himself disengaged from the bargain, being credibly informed my son was already married, or worse, to the lady at the masquerade. I palliated matters and insisted on our agreement; but we parted with little less than a direct breach between us.

HUMPHREY. Well, sir, and what notice have you taken of all this to my young master?

SIR JOHN. That's what I wanted to debate with you. I have said nothing to him yet; but look you, Humphrey: if there is so much in this amour of his that he denies my summons to marry, I have cause enough to be offended; and then by my insisting upon his marrying today, I shall know how far he is engaged to this lady in masquerade, and from thence only shall be able to take my measures. In the meantime, I would have you find out how far that rogue his man is let into his secret. He, I know, will play tricks as much to cross me as to serve his master.

HUMPHREY. Why do you think so of him, sir? I believe he is no worse than I was for you at your son's age.

SIR JOHN. I see it in the rascal's looks. But I have dwelt on these things too long. I'll go to my son immediately, and while I'm gone, your part is to convince his rogue Tom that I am in earnest. I'll leave him to you.

Exit SIR JOHN BEVIL

HUMPHREY. Well, though this father and son live as well together as possible, yet their fear of giving each other pain is attended with constant mutual uneasiness. I'm sure I have enough to do to be honest and yet keep well with them both. But they know I love 'em, and that makes the task less painful, however. —Oh, here's the prince of poor coxcombs, the representative of all the better fed than taught.—Ho! ho! Tom, whither so gay and so airy this morning?

Enter TOM, *singing*

TOM. Sir, we servants of single gentlemen are another kind of people than you domestic ordinary drudges that do business. We are raised above you. The pleasures of board wages, tavern dinners, and many a clear gain. Vails,[1] alas! you never heard or dreamed of.

HUMPHREY. Thou hast follies and vices enough for a man of ten thousand a year, though 'tis but as t'other day that I sent for you to town, to put you into Mr. Sealand's family that you might learn a little before I put you to my young master, who is too gentle for training such a rude thing as you were into proper obedience. You then pulled off your hat to every one you met in the street like a bashful great awkward cub as you were. But your great oaken cudgel when you were a booby became you much better than that dangling stick at your button, now you are a fop. That's fit for nothing, except it hangs there to be ready for your master's hand when you are impertinent.

TOM. Uncle Humphrey, you know my master scorns to strike his servants. You talk as if the world was now just as it was when my old master and you were in your youth, when you went to dinner because it was so much o'clock, when the great blow [2] was given in the hall at the pantry door, and all the family came out of their holes in such strange dresses and formal faces as you see in the pictures in our long gallery in the country.

HUMPHREY. Why, you wild rogue!

TOM. You could not fall to your dinner till a formal fellow in a black gown said something over the meat, as if the cook had not made it ready enough.

HUMPHREY. Sirrah, who do you prate after? Despising men of sacred characters! I hope you never heard my good young master talk so like a profligate?

[1] Tips, gratuities.
[2] Dinner gong.

Tom. Sir, I say you put upon me, when I first came to town, about being orderly, and the doctrine of wearing shams[1] to make linen last clean a fortnight, keeping my clothes fresh, and wearing a frock within doors.

Humphrey. Sirrah, I gave you those lessons because I supposed at that time your master and you might have dined at home every day and cost you nothing. Then you might have made a good family servant, but the gang you have frequented since at chocolate houses and taverns, in a continual round of noise and extravagance—

Tom. I don't know what you heavy inmates call noise and extravagance, but we gentlemen, who are well fed, and cut a figure, sir, think it a fine life, and that we must be very pretty fellows who are kept only to be looked at.

Humphrey. Very well, sir, I hope the fashion of being lewd and extravagant, despising of decency and order, is almost at an end, since it is arrived at persons of your quality.

Tom. Master Humphrey, Ha! ha! you were an unhappy lad to be sent up to town in such queer days as you were. Why, now, sir, the lackeys are the men of pleasure of the age; the topgamesters and many a laced coat about town have had their education in our party-colored regiment. We are false lovers; have a taste of music, poetry, *billet-doux*, dress, politics; ruin damsels; and when we are weary of this lewd town, and have a mind to take up, whip into our masters' wigs and linen, and marry fortunes.

Humphrey. Hey-day!

Tom. Nay, sir, our order is carried up to the highest dignities and distinctions; step but into the Painted Chamber,[2] and by our titles you'd take us all for men of quality. Then again, come down to the Court of Requests, and you see us all laying our broken heads together for the good of the nation; and though we never carry a question *nemine contradicente*,[3] yet this I can say with a safe conscience (and I wish every gentleman of our cloth could lay his hand upon his heart and say the same) that I never took so much as a single mug of beer for my vote in all my life.

Humphrey. Sirrah, there is no enduring your extravagance. I'll hear you prate no longer. I wanted to see you, to enquire how things go with your master, as far as you understand them. I suppose he knows he is to be married today.

Tom. Ay, sir, he knows it, and is dressed as gay as the sun; but, between you and I, my dear, he has a very heavy heart under all that gaiety. As soon as he was dressed I retired, but overheard him sigh in the most heavy manner. He walked thoughtfully to and fro in the room, then went into his closet;[4] when he came out, he gave me this for his mistress, whose maid you know—

Humphrey. Is passionately fond of your fine person.

Tom. The poor fool is so tender and loves to hear me talk of the world, and the plays, operas and *ridottos*[5] for the winter; the parks and Belsize[6] for our summer diversions; and, "Lard!" says she, "you are so wild—But you have a world of humor—"

Humphrey. Coxcomb! Well, but why don't you run with your master's letter to Mrs. Lucinda, as he ordered you?

Tom. Because Mrs. Lucinda is not so easily come at as you think for.

Humphrey. Not easily come at? Why, sirrah, are not her father and my old master agreed that she and Mr. Bevil are to be one flesh before tomorrow morning?

Tom. It's no matter for that; her mother, it seems, Mrs. Sealand, has not agreed to it; and you must know, Mr. Humphrey, that in that family the grey mare is the better horse.

Humphrey. What dost thou mean?

Tom. In one word, Mrs. Sealand pretends to have a will of her own and has provided a relation of hers, a stiff, starched philosopher and a wise fool, for her daughter; for which reason for these ten days past she has suffered no message nor letter from my master to come near her.

Humphrey. And where had you this intelligence?

---

[1] False shirt-fronts and sleeves.

[2] The Painted Chamber in the old Palace of Westminster was near the House of Lords and the old Court of Requests mentioned below. It was decorated with mural paintings. Here servants waited for their masters who were attending the House.

[3] Unanimously.

[4] Any small room; in this case a writing-room or study.

[5] Entertainments of music and dancing, first introduced at the Opera House in 1722. They formed a favorite amusement of the century.

[6] Belsize House, in Hampstead, was a place of amusement resembling Vauxhall and Ranelagh of a later date

Tom. From a foolish, fond soul, that can keep nothing from me,—one that will deliver this letter, too, if she is rightly managed.

Humphrey. What! Her pretty handmaid, Mrs. Phillis?

Tom. Even she, sir; this is the very hour, you know, she usually comes hither, under pretense of a visit to your housekeeper, forsooth, but in reality to have a glance at—

Humphrey. Your sweet face, I warrant you.

Tom. Nothing else in nature. You must know I love to fret and play with the little wanton.—

Humphrey. Play with the little wanton! What will this world come to!

Tom. I met her this morning in a new manteau [1] and petticoat, not a bit the worse for her lady's wearing; and she has always new thoughts and new airs with new clothes;—then she never fails to steal some glance or gesture from every visitant at their house, and is, indeed, the whole town of coquettes at second hand. But here she comes. In one motion she speaks and describes herself better than all the words in the world can.

Humphrey. Then I hope, dear sir, when your own affair is over, you will be so good as to mind your master's with her.

Tom. Dear Humphrey, you know my master is my friend and those are people I never forget—

Humphrey. Sauciness itself! But I'll leave you to do your best for him. *Exit*

Enter Phillis

Phillis. Oh, Mr. Thomas, is Mrs. Sugarkey at home?—Lard, one is almost ashamed to pass along the streets. The town is quite empty, and nobody of fashion left in it; and the ordinary people do so stare to see anything dressed like a woman of condition, as it were on the same floor with them, pass by. Alas! Alas! it is a sad thing to walk. Oh, Fortune! Fortune!

Tom. What! a sad thing to walk? Why, Madam Phillis, do you wish yourself lame?

Phillis. No, Mr. Tom, but I wish I were generally carried in a coach or chair and of a fortune neither to stand nor go, but to totter, or slide, to be shortsighted, or to stare, to fleer in the face, to look distant, to observe, to overlook, yet all become me; and, if I was

rich, I could twire [2] and loll as well as the best of them. Oh, Tom! Tom! is it not a pity that you should be so great a coxcomb and I so great a coquette, and yet be such poor devils as we are?

Tom. Mrs. Phillis, I am your humble servant for that—

Phillis. Yes, Mr. Thomas, I know how much you are my humble servant, and know what you said to Mrs. Judy upon seeing her in one of her lady's cast manteaus: That anyone would have thought her the lady and that she had ordered the other to wear it till it sat easy, for now only it was becoming;—to my lady it was only a covering, to Mrs. Judy it was a habit. This you said after somebody or other. Oh, Tom! Tom! thou art as false and as base as the best gentleman of them all; but, you wretch, talk to me no more on the old odious subject. Don't, I say.

Tom. I know not how to resist your commands, madam. (*In a submissive tone, retiring*)

Phillis. Commands about parting are grown mighty easy to you of late.

Tom. (*Aside*) Oh, I have her; I have nettled and put her into the right temper to be wrought upon and set a-prating.—Why truly, to be plain with you, Mrs. Phillis, I can take little comfort of late in frequenting your house.

Phillis. Pray, Mr. Thomas, what is it all of a sudden offends your nicety at our house?

Tom. I don't care to speak particulars, but I dislike the whole.

Phillis. I thank you, sir, I am a part of that whole.

Tom. Mistake me not, good Phillis.

Phillis. Good Phillis! Saucy enough. But however—

Tom. I say, it is that thou art a part, which gives me pain for the disposition of the whole. You must know, madam, to be serious, I am a man at the bottom of prodigious nice honor. You are too much exposed to company at your house. To be plain, I don't like so many that would be your mistress's lovers whispering to you.

Phillis. Don't think to put that upon me. You say this because I wrung you to the heart when I touched your guilty conscience about Judy.

Tom. Ah, Phillis! Phillis! If you but knew my heart!

Phillis. I know too much on't.

[1] A loose upper garment worn by women at this time.

[2] Ogle.

Tom. Nay then, poor Crispo's [1] fate and mine are one.—Therefore give me leave to say, or sing at least, as he does upon the same occasion—
Se vedette, &c. (sings)
Phillis. What, do you think I'm to be fobbed off with a song? I don't question but you have sung the same to Mrs. Judy, too.
Tom. Don't disparage your charms, good Phillis, with jealousy of so worthless an object; besides she is a poor hussy, and if you doubt the sincerity of my love, you will allow me true to my interest. You are a fortune, Phillis—
Phillis. What would the fop be at now? In good time indeed, you shall be setting up for a fortune!
Tom. Dear Mrs. Phillis, you have such a spirit that we shall never be dull in marriage, when we come together. But I tell you, you are a fortune; you have an estate in my hands.
(He pulls out a purse. She eyes it)
Phillis. What pretense have I to what is in your hands, Mr. Tom?
Tom. As thus: there are the hours, you know, when a lady is neither pleased or displeased, neither sick or well, when she lolls and loiters, when she's without desires from having more of everything than she knows what to do with.
Phillis. Well, what then?
Tom. When she has not life enough to keep her bright eyes quite open, to look at her own dear image in the glass.
Phillis. Explain thyself, and don't be so fond of thy own prating.
Tom. There are also prosperous and good-natured moments, as when a knot or a patch is happily fixed, when the complexion particularly flourishes.
Phillis. Well, what then? I have not patience!
Tom. Why then—or on the like occasions—we servants who have skill to know how to time business, see when such a pretty folded thing as this *(shows a letter)* may be presented, laid, or dropped, as best suits the present humor. And, madam, because it is a long, wearisome journey to run through all the several stages of a lady's temper, my master, who is the most reasonable man in the world, presents you this to bear your charges on the road. *(Gives her the purse)*
Phillis. Now you think me a corrupt hussy.
Tom. Oh, fie, I only think you'll take the letter.
Phillis. Nay, I know you do, but I know my own innocence. I take it for my mistress's sake.
Tom. I know it, my pretty one, I know it.
Phillis. Yes, I say I do it, because I would not have my mistress deluded by one who gives no proof of his passion; but I'll talk more of this, as you see me on my way home.—No, Tom, I assure thee, I take this trash of thy master's, not for the value of the thing, but as it convinces me he has a true respect for my mistress. I remember a verse to the purpose.
They may be false who languish and complain,
But they who part with money never feign.
Exeunt

Scene II

Bevil Junior's *Lodgings*

Bevil Junior. *Reading*

Bevil. These moral writers practise virtue after death. This charming *Vision of Mirza!* [2] Such an author consulted in a morning, sets the spirit for the vicissitudes of the day better than the glass does a man's person. But what a day have I to go through! To put on an easy look with an aching heart.—If this lady my father urges me to marry should not refuse me, my dilemma is insupportable. But why should I fear it? Is not she in equal distress with me? Has not the letter I have sent her this morning confessed my inclination to another? Nay, have I not moral assurances of her engagements, too, to my friend Myrtle? It's impossible but she must give in to it; for sure to be denied is a favor any man may pretend to. It must be so.—Well then, with the assurance of being rejected, I think I may confidently say to my father I am ready to marry her.—Then let me resolve upon (what I am not very good at, though it is) an honest dissimulation.

Enter Tom

Tom. Sir John Bevil, sir, is in the next room.

---

[1] Crispo is the hero of the opera by Buononcini discussed by Indiana and Bevil in Act II, scene ii.

[2] *The Spectator* No. 159. Cf. Mr. Addison's statement of his own purpose, *Spectator* No. 10.

BEVIL. Dunce! Why did not you bring him in?

TOM. I told him, sir, you were in your closet.

BEVIL. I thought you had known, sir, it was my duty to see my father anywhere.
(*Going himself to the door*)

TOM. (*Aside*) The devil's in my master! He has always more wit than I have.

BEVIL, JUNIOR, *introducing* SIR JOHN

BEVIL. Sir, you are the most gallant, the most complaisant of all parents.—Sure 'tis not a compliment to say these lodgings are yours.—Why would you not walk in, sir?

SIR JOHN. I was loth to interrupt you unseasonably on your wedding-day.

BEVIL. One to whom I am beholden for my birth-day might have used less ceremony.

SIR JOHN. Well, son, I have intelligence you have writ your mistress this morning. It would please my curiosity to know the contents of a wedding-day letter, for courtship must then be over.

BEVIL. I assure you, sir, there was no insolence in it, upon the prospect of such a vast fortune's being added to our family, but much acknowledgment of the lady's greater desert.

SIR JOHN. But, dear Jack, are you in earnest in all this? And will you really marry her?

BEVIL. Did I ever disobey any command of yours, sir? Nay, any inclination that I saw you bent upon?

SIR JOHN. Why, I can't say you have, son; but methinks in this whole business you have not been so warm as I could have wished you. You have visited her, it's true, but you have not been particular. Every one knows you can say and do as handsome things as any man; but you have done nothing but lived in the general; been complaisant only.

BEVIL. As I am ever prepared to marry if you bid me, so I am ready to let it alone if you will have me.

HUMPHREY *enters unobserved*

SIR JOHN. Look you there now! Why, what am I to think of this so absolute and indifferent a resignation?

BEVIL. Think? That I am still your son, sir.—Sir, you have been married, and I have not. And you have, sir, found the inconvenience there is, when a man weds with too much love in his head. I have been told, sir, that at the time you married, you made a mighty bustle on the occasion. There was challenging and fighting, scaling walls—locking up the lady—and the gallant under arrest for fear of killing all his rivals. Now, sir, I suppose you having found the ill consequences of these strong passions and prejudices in preference of one woman to another in case of a man's becoming a widower—

SIR JOHN. How is this!

BEVIL. I say, sir, experience has made you wiser in your care of me,—for, sir, since you lost my dear mother, your time has been so heavy, so lonely, and so tasteless that you are so good as to guard me against the like unhappiness by marrying me prudentially by way of bargain and sale. For, as you well judge, a woman that is espoused for a fortune is yet a better bargain if she dies; for then a man still enjoys what he did marry, the money, and is disencumbered of what he did not marry, the woman.

SIR JOHN. But pray, sir, do you think Lucinda, then, a woman of such little merit?

BEVIL. Pardon me, sir, I don't carry it so far neither; I am rather afraid I shall like her too well. She has for one of her fortune a great many needless and superfluous good qualities.

SIR JOHN. I am afraid, son, there's something I don't see yet, something that's smothered under all this raillery.

BEVIL. Not in the least, sir. If the lady is dressed and ready, you see I am. I suppose the lawyers are ready, too.

HUMPHREY. (*Aside*) This may grow warm if I don't interpose.—Sir, Mr. Sealand is at the coffee-house and has sent to speak with you.

SIR JOHN. Oh! that's well! Then I warrant the lawyers are ready. Son, you'll be in the way, you say—

BEVIL. If you please, sir, I'll take a chair and go to Mr. Sealand's, where the young lady and I will await your leisure.

SIR JOHN. By no means—The old fellow will be so vain, if he sees—

BEVIL. Ay—But the young lady, sir, will think me so indifferent—

HUMPHREY. (*Aside to* BEVIL, JUN.) Ay—There you are right. Press your readiness to go to the bride. He won't let you.

BEVIL. (*Aside to* HUMPHREY) Are you sure of that?

HUMPHREY. (*Aside*) How he likes being prevented.

Sir John. No, no. You are an hour or two too early. (*Looking at his watch*)

Bevil. You'll allow me, sir, to think it too late to visit a beautiful, virtuous young woman in the pride and bloom of life, ready to give herself to my arms and to place her happiness or misery for the future in being agreeable or displeasing to me, is a—Call a chair.

Sir John. No, no, no, dear Jack; this Sealand is a moody old fellow. There's no dealing with some people but by managing with indifference. We must leave to him the conduct of this day. It is the last of his commanding his daughter.

Bevil. Sir, he can't take it ill that I am impatient to be hers.

Sir John. Pray let me govern in this matter. You can't tell how humorsome old fellows are. There's no offering reason to some of 'em, especially when they are rich. (*Aside*) If my son should see him before I've brought old Sealand into better temper, the match would be impracticable.

Humphrey. Pray, sir, let me beg you to let Mr. Bevil go.—(*Aside to* Sir John) See whether he will or not. (*Then to* Bevil) Pray, sir, command yourself; since you see my master is positive, it is better you should not go.

Bevil. My father commands me as to the object of my affections, but I hope he will not as to the warmth and height of them.

Sir John. [*Aside*] So! I must even leave things as I found them. And in the meantime, at least, keep old Sealand out of his sight.— Well, son, I'll go myself and take orders in your affair. You'll be in the way, I suppose, if I send to you. I'll leave your old friend with you.—Humphrey, don't let him stir, d'ye hear.—Your servant, your servant.

Exit Sir John

Humphrey. I have had a sad time on't, sir, between you and my master. I see you are unwilling, and I know his violent inclinations for the match. I must betray neither and yet deceive you both for your common good. Heaven grant a good end of this matter. But there is a lady, sir, that gives your father much trouble and sorrow. You'll pardon me.

Bevil. Humphrey, I know thou art a friend to both and in that confidence I dare tell thee: —That lady is a woman of honor and virtue. You may assure yourself I never will marry without my father's consent. But give me leave to say, too, this declaration does not come up to a promise that I will take whomever he pleases.

Humphrey. Come, sir, I wholly understand you. You would engage my services to free you from this woman whom my master intends you to make way in time for the woman you have really a mind to.

Bevil. Honest Humphrey, you have always been an useful friend to my father and myself; I beg you continue your good offices and don't let us come to the necessity of a dispute; for, if we should dispute, I must either part with more than life or lose the best of fathers.

Humphrey. My dear master, were I but worthy to know this secret that so near concerns you, my life, my all, should be engaged to serve you. This, sir, I dare promise, that I am sure I will and can be secret. Your trust, at worst, but leaves you where you were; and if I cannot serve you, I will at once be plain and tell you so.

Bevil. That's all I ask. Thou hast made it now my interest to trust thee. Be patient, then, and hear the story of my heart.

Humphrey. I am all attention, sir.

Bevil. You may remember, Humphrey, that in my last travels my father grew uneasy at my making so long a stay at Toulon.

Humphrey. I remember it; he was apprehensive some woman had laid hold of you.

Bevil. His fears were just; for there I first saw this lady. She is of English birth. Her father's name was Danvers, a younger brother of an ancient family and originally an eminent merchant of Bristol, who upon repeated misfortunes was reduced to go privately to the Indies. In this retreat Providence again grew favorable to his industry and in six years' time, restored him to his former fortunes. On this he sent directions over that his wife and little family should follow him to the Indies. His wife, impatient to obey such welcome orders, would not wait the leisure of a convoy but took the first occasion of a single ship, and with her husband's sister only and this daughter, then scarce seven years old, undertook the fatal voyage. For here, poor creature, she lost her liberty and life. She and her family with all they had were unfortunately taken by a privateer from Toulon. Being thus made a prisoner, though as such not ill treated, yet the fright, the shock, and cruel disappointment seized with such violence upon her unhealthy frame she sickened, pined, and died at sea.

HUMPHREY. Poor soul! O the helpless infant!

BEVIL. Her sister yet survived and had the care of her. The captain too proved to have humanity and became a father to her; for having himself married an English woman and being childless, he brought home into Toulon this her little country-woman, presenting her with all her dead mother's moveables of value to his wife to be educated as his own adopted daughter.

HUMPHREY. Fortune here seemed again to smile on her.

BEVIL. Only to make her frowns more terrible; for in his height of fortune this captain, too, her benefactor, unfortunately was killed at sea and dying intestate, his estate fell wholly to an advocate, his brother, who coming soon to take possession, there found among his other riches this blooming virgin at his mercy.

HUMPHREY. He durst not, sure, abuse his power!

BEVIL. No wonder if his pampered blood was fired at the sight of her. In short, he loved. But when all arts and gentle means had failed to move, he offered, too, his menaces in vain, denouncing vengeance on her cruelty, demanding her to account for all her maintenance from her childhood, seized on her little fortune as his own inheritance and was dragging her by violence to prison when Providence at the instant interposed and sent me, by miracle, to relieve her.

HUMPHREY. 'Twas Providence indeed; but pray, sir, after all this trouble, how came this lady at last to England?

BEVIL. The disappointed advocate, finding she had so unexpected a support, on cooler thoughts descended to a composition[1]; which I without her knowledge secretly discharged.

HUMPHREY. That generous concealment made the obligation double.

BEVIL. Having thus obtained her liberty, I prevailed not without some difficulty, to see her safe to England, where no sooner arrived, but my father, jealous of my being imprudently engaged, immediately proposed this other fatal match that hangs upon my quiet.

HUMPHREY. I find, sir, you are irrecoverably fixed upon this lady.

[1] Compromise.

BEVIL. As my vital life dwells in my heart. And yet, you see—what I do to please my father: walk in this pageantry of dress, this splendid covering of sorrow—But, Humphrey, you have your lesson.

HUMPHREY. Now, sir, I have but one material question—

BEVIL. Ask it freely.

HUMPHREY. Is it, then, your own passion for this secret lady, or hers for you, that gives you this aversion to the match your father has proposed?

BEVIL. I shall appear, Humphrey, more romantic in my answer than in all the rest of my story; for though I dote on her to death and have no little reason to believe she has the same thoughts for me; yet in all my acquaintance and utmost privacies with her I never once directly told her that I loved.

HUMPHREY. How was it possible to avoid it?

BEVIL. My tender obligations to my father have laid so inviolable a restraint upon my conduct that till I have his consent to speak, I am determined on that subject to be dumb forever.

HUMPHREY. Well, sir, to your praise be it spoken, you are certainly the most unfashionable lover in Great Britain.

Enter TOM

TOM. Sir, Mr. Myrtle's at the next door and if you are at leisure will be glad to wait on you.

BEVIL. Whenever he pleases—Hold, Tom! Did you receive no answer to my letter?

TOM. Sir, I was desired to call again, for I was told her mother would not let her be out of her sight; but about an hour hence, Mrs. Lettice said I should certainly have one.

BEVIL. Very well. *Exit* TOM

HUMPHREY. Sir, I will take another opportunity. In the meantime, I think it only proper to tell you that from a secret I know you may appear to your father as forward as you please to marry Lucinda without the least hazard of its coming to a conclusion.—Sir, your most obedient servant.

BEVIL. Honest Humphrey, continue but my friend in this exigence and you shall always find me yours. (*Exit* HUMPHREY) I long to hear how my letter has succeeded with Lucinda; but I think it cannot fail, for at worst were it possibly she could take it ill, her resentment of my indifference may as probably occasion a delay as her taking it right.—Poor

Myrtle! What terrors must he be in all this while? Since he knows she is offered to me and refused to him, there is no conversing or taking any measures with him for his own service. But I ought to bear with my friend and use him as one in adversity.

All his disquiets by my own I prove
The greatest grief's perplexity in love.

Exit

ACT II

SCENE I. *Scene continues*

Enter BEVIL, JUNIOR, *and* TOM

TOM. Sir, Mr. Myrtle.
BEVIL. Very well.—Do you stop again and wait for an answer to my letter. *Exit* TOM

Enter MYRTLE

BEVIL. Well, Charles, why so much care in thy countenance? Is there any thing in this world deserves it? You, who used to be so gay, so open, so vacant![1]

MYRTLE. I think we have of late changed complexions. You, who used to be much the graver man, are now all air in your behavior. But the cause of my concern may, for ought I know, be the same object that gives you all this satisfaction. In a word, I am told that you are this day (and your dress confirms me in it) to be married to Lucinda.

BEVIL. You are not misinformed. Nay, put not on the terrors of a rival till you hear me out. I shall disoblige the best of fathers if I don't seem ready to marry Lucinda; and you know I have ever told you you might make use of my secret resolution never to marry her for your own service as you please. But I am now driven to the extremity of immediately refusing or complying unless you help me to escape the match.

MYRTLE. Escape? Sir, neither her merit or her fortune are below your acceptance. Escaping do you call it!

BEVIL. Dear sir, do you wish I should desire the match?

MYRTLE. No, but such is my humorous and sickly state of mind since it has been able to relish nothing but Lucinda, that though I must owe my happiness to your aversion to this marriage I can't bear to hear her spoken of with levity or unconcern.

BEVIL. Pardon me, sir, I shall transgress that way no more. She has understanding, beauty, shape, complexion, wit—

MYRTLE. Nay, my dear Bevil, don't speak of her as if you loved her, neither.

BEVIL. Why then, to give you ease at once, though I allow Lucinda to have good sense, wit, beauty, and virtue, I know another in whom these qualities appear to me more amiable than in her.

MYRTLE. There you spoke like a reasonable and good-natured friend. When you acknowledge her merit and own your prepossession for another, at once, you gratify my fondness and cure my jealousy.

BEVIL. But all this while you take no notice, you have no apprehension of another man that has twice the fortune of either of us.

MYRTLE. Cimberton! Hang him! A formal, philosophical, pedantic coxcomb—For the sot, with all these crude notions of divers things, under the direction of great vanity and very little judgment, shows his strongest bias is avarice, which is so predominant in him that he will examine the limbs of his mistress with the caution of a jockey and pays no more compliment to her personal charms than if she were a mere breeding animal.

BEVIL. Are you sure that is not affected? I have known some women sooner set on fire by that sort of negligence than by—

MYRTLE. No, no! Hang him, the rogue has no art; it is pure simple insolence and stupidity.

BEVIL. Yet, with all this, I don't take him for a fool.

MYRTLE. I own the man is not a natural;[2] he has a very quick sense though very slow understanding. He says indeed many things that want only the circumstances of time and place to be very just and agreeable.

BEVIL. Well, you may be sure of me, if you can disappoint him; but my intelligence says the mother has actually sent for the conveyancer to draw articles for his marriage with Lucinda, though those for mine are, by her father's orders, ready for signing. But it seems she has not thought fit to consult either him or his daughter in the matter.

MYRTLE. Pshaw! A poor troublesome woman—Neither Lucinda nor her father will ever be brought to comply with it. Besides,

---
[1] Carefree.
[2] Idiot.

I am sure Cimberton can make no settlement upon her without the concurrence of his great uncle, Sir Geoffry, in the West.

BEVIL. Well, sir, and I can tell you that's the very point that is now laid before her council,—to know whether a firm settlement can be made without this uncle's actually joining in it. Now pray consider, sir, when my affair with Lucinda comes, as it soon must, to an open rupture, how are you sure that Cimberton's fortune may not then tempt her father too to hear his proposals?

MYRTLE. There you are right indeed. That must be provided against. Do you know who are her council?

BEVIL. Yes. For your service I have found out that too. They are Sergeant Bramble and old Target—By the way, they are neither of 'em known in the family; now I was thinking why you might not put a couple of false counsel upon her to delay and confound matters a little. Besides, it may probably let you into the bottom of her whole design against you.

MYRTLE. As how, pray?

BEVIL. Why can't you slip on a black wig and a gown and be old Bramble yourself?

MYRTLE. Ha! I don't dislike it! But what shall I do for a brother in the case?

BEVIL. What do you think of my fellow, Tom? The rogue's intelligent and is a good mimic. All his part will be but to stutter heartily, for that's old Target's case. Nay, it would be an immoral thing to mock him were it not that his impertinence is the occasion of its breaking out to that degree. The conduct of the scene will chiefly lie upon you.

MYRTLE. I like it of all things. If you'll send Tom to my chambers, I will give him full instructions. This will certainly give me occasion to raise difficulties, to puzzle, or confound her project for a while at least.

BEVIL. I'll warrant you success. So far we are right, then. And now, Charles, your apprehension of my marrying her is all you have to get over.

MYRTLE. Dear Bevil, though I know you are my friend, yet when I abstract myself from my own interest in the thing, I know no objection she can make to you, or you to her, and therefore hope—

BEVIL. Dear Myrtle, I am as much obliged to you for the cause of your suspicion as I am offended at the effect; but be assured I am taking measures for your certain security and that all things with regard to me will end in your entire satisfaction.

MYRTLE. Well, I'll promise you to be as easy and as confident as I can, though I cannot but remember that I have more than life at stake on your fidelity. (*Going*)

BEVIL. Then depend upon it, you have no chance against you.

MYRTLE. Nay, no ceremony. You know I must be going. *Exit* MYRTLE

BEVIL. Well, this is another instance of the perplexities which arise too in faithful friendship. We must often in this life go on in our good offices even under the displeasure of those to whom we do them in compassion to their weaknesses and mistakes. But all this while poor Indiana is tortured with the doubt of me. She has no support or comfort but in my fidelity, yet sees me daily pressed to marriage with another. How painful in such a crisis must be every hour she thinks on me! I'll let her see, at least, my conduct to her is not changed. I'll take this opportunity to visit her; for, though the religious [1] vow I have made to my father restrains me from ever marrying without his approbation, yet that confines me not from seeing a virtuous woman that is the pure delight of my eyes and the guiltless joy of my heart. But the best condition of human life is but a gentler mercy.

To hope for perfect happiness is vain,
And love has ever its allays of pain.
Exit

[SCENE II. INDIANA's *Lodgings*]

Enter ISABELLA *and* INDIANA *in her own lodgings*

ISABELLA. Yes, I say 'tis artifice, dear child. I say to thee again and again, 'tis all skill and management.

INDIANA. Will you persuade me there can be an ill design in supporting me in the condition of a woman of quality, attended, dressed, and lodged like one; in my appearance abroad and my furniture at home, every way in the most sumptuous manner, and he that does it has an artifice, a design in it?

ISABELLA. Yes, yes.

INDIANA. And all this without so much as explaining to me that all about me comes from him!

ISABELLA. Aye, aye. The more for that,

[1] I.e., solemn.

that keeps the title to all you have the more in him.

INDIANA. The more in him! He scorns the thought.

ISABELLA. Then—he—he—he—he—

INDIANA. Well, be not so eager. If he is an ill man, let us look into his stratagems. Here is another of them. (*Showing a letter*) Here's two hundred and fifty pound in bank notes, with these words, "To pay for the set of dressing plate which will be brought home to-morrow." Why, dear aunt, now here's another piece of skill for you, which I own I cannot comprehend,—and it is with a bleeding heart I hear you say anything to the disadvantage of Mr. Bevil. When he is present, I look upon him as one to whom I owe my life and the support of it. Then again, as the man who loves me with sincerity and honor. When his eyes are cast another way and I dare survey him, my heart is painfully divided between shame and love. Oh! could I tell you!

ISABELLA. Ah! You need not. I imagine all this for you.

INDIANA. This is my state of mind in his presence; and when he is absent, you are ever dinning my ears with notions of the arts of men,—that his hidden bounty, his respectful conduct, his careful provision for me, after his preserving me from the utmost misery are certain signs he means nothing but to make I know not what of me.

ISABELLA. Oh! You have a sweet opinion of him, truly.

INDIANA. I have, when I am with him, ten thousand things besides my sex's natural decency and shame to suppress my heart that yearns to thank him, to praise, to say it loves him. I say thus it is with me while I see him; and in his absence I am entertained with nothing but your endeavors to tear this amiable image from my heart and in its stead to place a base dissembler, an artful invader of my happiness, my innocence, my honor.

ISABELLA. Ah poor soul! Has not his plot taken? Don't you die for him? Has not the way he has taken been the most proper with you? Oh, ho! He has sense and has judged the thing right.

INDIANA. Go on then, since nothing can answer you. Say what you will of him. Heigh ho!

ISABELLA. Heigh ho, indeed! It is better to say so, as you are now than as many others are. There are among the destroyers of women, the gentle, the generous, the mild, the affable, the humble who all soon after their success in their designs turn to the contrary of those characters. I will own to you, Mr. Bevil carries his hypocrisy the best of any man living, but still he is a man and therefore a hypocrite. They have usurped an exemption from shame for any baseness, any cruelty, towards us. They embrace without love; they make vows without conscience of obligation; they are partners, nay, seducers to the crime wherein they pretend to be less guilty.

INDIANA. (*Aside*) That's truly observed.— But what's all this to Bevil?

ISABELLA. This it is to Bevil and all mankind. Trust not those who will think the worse of you for your confidence in them. Serpents who lie in wait for doves. Won't you be on your guard against those who would betray you? Won't you doubt those who would condemn you for believing 'em? Take it from me, fair and natural dealing is to invite injuries; 'tis bleating to escape wolves who would devour you! Such is the world;— (*Aside*) and such (since the behavior of one man to myself) have I believed all the rest of the sex.

INDIANA. I will not doubt the truth of Bevil, I will not doubt it. He has not spoken it by an organ that is given to lying. His eyes are all that have ever told me that he was mine. I know his virtue, I know his filial piety and ought to trust his management with a father to whom he has uncommon obligations. What have I to be concerned for? My lesson is very short. If he takes me forever, my purpose of life is only to please him. If he leaves me (which Heaven avert) I know he'll do it nobly, and I shall have nothing to do but to learn to die, after worse than death has happened to me.

ISABELLA. Ay, do; persist in your credulity! Flatter yourself that a man of his figure and fortune will make himself the jest of the town and marry a handsome beggar for love.

INDIANA. The town! I must tell you, madam, the fools that laugh at Mr. Bevil will but make themselves more ridiculous. His actions are the result of thinking and he has sense enough to make even virtue fashionable.

ISABELLA. O' my conscience, he has turned

her head! Come, come! If he were the honest fool you take him for, why has he kept you here these three weeks without sending you to Bristol in search of your father, your family, and your relations?

INDIANA. I am convinced he still designs it and that nothing keeps him here but the necessity of not coming to a breach with his father in regard to the match he has proposed him. Beside, has he not writ to Bristol, and has not he advice that my father has not been heard of there almost these twenty years?

ISABELLA. All sham, mere evasion. He is afraid if he should carry you thither your honest relations may take you out of his hands and so blow up all his wicked hopes at once.

INDIANA. Wicked hopes! Did I ever give him any such?

ISABELLA. Has he ever given you any honest ones? Can you say in your conscience he has ever once offered to marry you?

INDIANA. No; but by his behavior I am convinced he will offer it the moment 'tis in his power or consistent with his honor to make such a promise good to me.

ISABELLA. His honor!

INDIANA. I will rely upon it. Therefore [I] desire you will not make my life uneasy by these ungrateful jealousies of one to whom I am, and wish to be, obliged, for from his integrity alone, I have resolved to hope for happiness.

ISABELLA. Nay! I have done my duty. If you won't see, at your peril be it—

INDIANA. Let it be! This is his hour of visiting me.

ISABELLA. (*Apart*) Oh, to be sure, keep up your form! Don't see him in a bed chamber. This is pure prudence,[1] when she is liable wherever he meets her to be conveyed where'er he pleases.

INDIANA. All the rest of my life is but waiting till he comes. I only live when I'm with him. *Exit*

ISABELLA. Well, go thy ways, thou willful innocent! I once had almost as much love for a man who poorly left me to marry an estate. And I am now, against my will, what they call an old maid; but I will not let the peevishness of that condition grow upon me,— only keep up the suspicion of it to prevent this creature's being any other than a virgin except upon proper terms. *Exit*

[1] Prudery.

Re-enter INDIANA *speaking to a servant*

INDIANA. Desire Mr. Bevil to walk in.— Design! Impossible! A base, designing mind could never think of what he hourly puts in practice.—And yet, since the late rumor of his marriage, he seems more reserved than formerly. He sends in, too, before he sees me, to know if I am at leisure. Such new respect may cover coldness in the heart. It certainly makes me thoughtful. I'll know the worst at once; I'll lay such fair occasions in his way that it shall be impossible to avoid an explanation, for these doubts are insupportable! But see! He comes and clears them all!

Enter BEVIL JUNIOR

BEVIL. Madam, your most obedient! I am afraid I broke in upon your rest last night. 'Twas very late before we parted, but 'twas your own fault. I never saw you in such agreeable humor.

INDIANA. I am extremely glad we were both pleased, for I thought I never saw you better company.

BEVIL. Me, madam! You rally. I said very little.

INDIANA. But I am afraid you heard me say a great deal, and when a woman is in the talking vein the most agreeable thing a man can do, you know, is to have patience to hear her.

BEVIL. Then it's pity, madam, you should ever be silent, that we might be always agreeable to one another.

INDIANA. If I had your talent or power to make my actions speak for me, I might indeed be silent and yet pretend to something more than the agreeable.

BEVIL. If I might be vain of anything in my power, madam, 'tis that my understanding, from all your sex, has marked you out as the most deserving object of my esteem.

INDIANA. Should I think I deserve this, 'twere enough to make my vanity forfeit the very esteem you offer me.

BEVIL. How so, madam?

INDIANA. Because esteem is the result of reason; and to deserve it from good sense the height of human glory. Nay, I had rather a man of honor should pay me that than all the homage of a sincere and humble love.

BEVIL. You certainly distinguish right, madam. Love often kindles from external merit only—

INDIANA. But esteem arises from a higher source, the merit of the soul.

BEVIL. True. And great souls only can deserve it. *(Bowing respectfully)*

INDIANA. Now I think they are greater still that can so charitably part with it.

BEVIL. Now, madam, you make me vain, since the utmost pride and pleasure of my life is that I esteem you,—as I ought.

INDIANA. *(Aside)* As he ought! Still more perplexing! He neither saves nor kills my hope.

BEVIL. But, madam, we grow grave, methinks. Let's find some other subject. Pray how did you like the opera last night?

INDIANA. First, give me leave to thank you for my tickets.

BEVIL. O, your servant, madam! But pray tell me, you, now, who are never partial to the fashion, I fancy, must be the properest judge of a mighty dispute among the ladies, that is, whether *Crispo* or *Griselda*[1] is the more agreeable entertainment.

INDIANA. With submission now, I cannot be a proper judge of this question.

BEVIL. How so, madam?

INDIANA. Because I find I have a partiality for one of them.

BEVIL. Pray which is that?

INDIANA. I do not know—There's something in that rural cottage of Griselda, her forlorn condition, her poverty, her solitude, her resignation, her innocent slumbers, and that lulling *dolce sogno*[2] that's sung over her. It had an effect upon me, that—In short I never was so well deceived at any of them.

BEVIL. Oh! Now then I can account for the dispute. *Griselda*, it seems, is the distress of an injured, innocent woman; *Crispo*, that only of a man in the same condition; therefore the men are mostly concerned for Crispo, and, by a natural indulgence, both sexes for Griselda.

INDIANA. So that judgment, you think, ought to be for one though fancy and complaisance have got ground for the other. Well! I believe you will never give me leave to dispute with you on any subject, for I own *Crispo* has its charms for me too, though in the main all the pleasure the best opera gives us is but mere sensation. Methinks it's pity the mind can't have a little more share in the entertainment. The music's certainly fine; but, in my thoughts, there's none of your composers come up to old Shakespeare and Otway.

BEVIL. How, madam! Why if a woman of your sense were to say this in a drawing-room—

Enter a Servant

SERVANT. Sir, here's Signior Carbonelli says he waits your commands in the next room.

BEVIL. À propos, you were saying yesterday, madam, you had a mind to hear him. Will you give him leave to entertain you now?

INDIANA. By all means! Desire the gentleman to walk in. *Exit* Servant

BEVIL. I fancy you will find something in this hand that is uncommon.

INDIANA. You are always finding ways, Mr. Bevil, to make life seem less tedious to me. *(Enter* MUSIC MASTER*)* When the gentleman pleases.

After a sonata[3] *is played,* BEVIL *waits on the master to the door, &c.*

BEVIL. You smile, madam, to see me so complaisant to one whom I pay for his visit. Now I own I think it is not enough barely to pay those whose talents are superior to our own. (I mean such talents as would become our condition if we had them.) Methinks we ought to do something more than barely gratify them for what they do at our command only because their fortune is below us.

INDIANA. You say I smile. I assure you it was a smile of approbation, for indeed I cannot but think it the distinguishing part of a gentleman to make his superiority of fortune as easy to his inferiors as he can.—*(Aside)* Now, once more to try him.—I was saying just now I believed you would never let me dispute with you and I dare say it will always be so. However I must have your opinion upon a subject which created a debate between my aunt and me just before you came hither. She would needs have it that no man ever does any extraordinary kindness or service for a woman but for his own sake.

BEVIL. Well, madam! Indeed I can't but be of her mind.

INDIANA. What, though he should maintain

---

[1] Both Italian operas by Buononcini, produced at the Haymarket, 1722.

[2] Sweet dream.

[3] At this time any musical composition for instruments not the conventionalized sonata of modern music.

and support her without demanding anything of her on her part?

BEVIL. Why, madam, is making an expense in the service of a valuable woman (for such I must suppose her) though she should never do him any favor, nay, though she should never know who did her such service, such a mighty heroic business?

INDIANA. Certainly! I should think he must be a man of an uncommon mold.

BEVIL. Dear madam, why so? 'Tis but at best a better taste in experience to bestow upon one whom he may think one of the ornaments of the whole creation to be conscious that from his superfluity an innocent, a virtuous spirit is supported above the temptations and sorrows of life. That he sees satisfaction, health, and gladness in her countenance while he enjoys the happiness of seeing her,—as that I will suppose too, or he must be too abstracted, too insensible—I say, if he is allowed to delight in that prospect—Alas, what mighty matter is there in all this?

INDIANA. No mighty matter in so disinterested a friendship!

BEVIL. Disinterested! I can't think him so. Your hero, madam, is no more than what every gentleman ought to be and I believe very many are. He is only one who takes more delight in reflections than in sensations. He is more pleased with thinking than eating; that's the utmost you can say of him. Why, madam, a greater expense than all this men lay out upon an unnecessary stable of horses.

INDIANA. Can you be sincere in what you say?

BEVIL. You may depend upon it, if you know any such man, he does not love dogs inordinately.

INDIANA. No, that he does not.

BEVIL. Nor cards, nor dice.

INDIANA. No.

BEVIL. Nor bottle companions.

INDIANA. No.

BEVIL. Nor loose women.

INDIANA. No, I'm sure he does not.

BEVIL. Take my word then, if your admired hero is not liable to any of these kinds of demands there's no such preëminence in this as you imagine. Nay, this way of expense you speak of is what exalts and raises him that has a taste for it; and, at the same time, his delight is incapable of satiety, disgust, or penitence.

INDIANA. But still I insist his having no private interest in the action makes it prodigious, almost incredible.

BEVIL. Dear madam, I never knew you more mistaken. Why, who can be more an usurer than he who lays out his money in such valuable purchases? If pleasure be worth purchasing, how great a pleasure is it to him who has a true taste of life to ease an aching heart, to see the human countenance lighted up into smiles of joy on the receipt of a bit of ore which is superfluous and otherwise useless in a man's own pocket? What could a man do better with his cash? This is the effect of an humane disposition, where there is only a general type of nature and common necessity. What then must it be when we serve an object of merit, of admiration!

INDIANA. Well! The more you argue against it, the more I shall admire the generosity.

BEVIL. Nay, nay! Then, madam, 'tis time to fly after a declaration that my opinion strengthens my adversary's argument. I had best hasten to my appointment with Mr. Myrtle and be gone while we are friends and—before things are brought to an extremity.—

Exit carefully

Enter ISABELLA

ISABELLA. Well, madam, what think you of him now, pray?

INDIANA. I protest, I begin to fear he is wholly disinterested in what he does for me. On my heart, he has no other view but the mere pleasure of doing it and has neither good or bad designs upon me.

ISABELLA. Ah, dear niece, don't be in fear of both! I'll warrant you, you will know time enough that he is not indifferent.

INDIANA. You please me when you tell me so, for if he has any wishes towards me I know he will not pursue them but with honor.

ISABELLA. I wish I were as confident of one as t'other. I saw the respectful downcast of his eye when you catched him gazing at you during the music. He, I warrant, was surprised as if he had been taken stealing your watch. Oh, the dissembled guilty look!

INDIANA. But did you observe any such thing, really? I thought he looked most charmingly graceful! How engaging is modesty in a man when one knows there is a great mind within. So tender a confusion, and yet in other respects so much himself, so collected, so dauntless, so determined!

ISABELLA. Ah! Niece! There is a sort of bashfulness which is the best engine to carry on a shameless purpose. Some men's modesty serves their wickedness as hypocrisy gains the respect due to piety. But I will own to you there is one hopeful symptom, if there could be such a thing as a disinterested lover. But it's all a perplexity, till—till—till—

INDIANA. Till what?

ISABELLA. Till I know whether Mr. Myrtle and Mr. Bevil are really friends or foes. And that I will be convinced of before I sleep. For you shall not be deceived.

INDIANA. I'm sure I never shall if your fears can guard me. In the meantime, I'll wrap myself up in the integrity of my own heart nor dare to doubt of his.

As conscious honor all his actions steers,
So conscious innocence dispels my fears.

Exeunt

ACT III

SCENE I. SEALAND'S *House*

Enter TOM *meeting* PHILLIS

TOM. Well, Phillis!—What, with a face as if you had never seen me before—(*Aside*) What a work have I to do now? She has seen some new visitant at their house whose airs she has catched and is resolved to practise them upon me. Numberless are the changes she'll dance through before she'll answer this plain question; *videlicet*, "Have you delivered my master's letter to your lady?" Nay, I know her too well to ask an account of it in an ordinary way. I'll be in my airs as well as she.—Well, madam, as unhappy as you are at present pleased to make me, I would not in the general be any other than what I am. I would not be a bit wiser, a bit richer, a bit taller, a bit shorter than I am at this instant.

(*Looking steadfastly at her*)

PHILLIS. Did ever anybody doubt, Master Thomas, but that you were extremely satisfied with your sweet self?

TOM. I am indeed. The thing I have least reason to be satisfied with is my fortune and I am glad of my poverty. Perhaps if I were rich I should overlook the finest woman in the world, that wants nothing but riches to be thought so.

PHILLIS. (*Aside*) How prettily was that said! But I'll have a great deal more before I'll say one word.

TOM. I should perhaps have been stupidly above her had I not been her equal and by not being her equal never had an opportunity of being her slave. I am my master's servant for hire; I am my mistress's, from choice, would she but approve my passion.

PHILLIS. I think it's the first time I ever heard you speak of it with any sense of anguish, if you really do suffer any.

TOM. Ah, Phillis, can you doubt after what you have seen?

PHILLIS. I know not what I have seen, nor what I have heard; but since I'm at leisure, you may tell me when you fell in love with me, how you fell in love with me, and what you have suffered or are ready to suffer for me.

TOM. (*Aside*) Oh, the unmerciful jade! When I'm in haste about my master's letter— But I must go through it.—Ah, too well I remember when and how, and on what occasion I was first surprised. It was on the first of April, one thousand, seven hundred and fifteen; I came into Mr. Sealand's service. I was then a hobble-de-hoy and you a pretty little tight girl, a favorite handmaid of the housekeeper. At that time we neither of us knew what was in us. I remember I was ordered to get out of the window, one pair of stairs, to rub the sashes clean. The person employed on the inner side was your charming self, whom I had never seen before.

PHILLIS. I think I remember the silly accident. What made ye, you oaf, ready to fall down into the street?

TOM. You know, I warrant you. You could not guess what surprised me. You took no delight when you immediately grew wanton in your conquest and put your lips close and breathed upon the glass, and when my lips approached a dirty cloth you rubbed against my face and hid your beauteous form. When I again drew near, you spit and rubbed and smiled at my undoing.

PHILLIS. What silly thoughts you men have!

TOM. We were Pyramus and Thisbe—but ten times harder was my fate. Pyramus could peep only through a wall; I saw her, saw my Thisbe in all her beauty, but as much kept from her as if a hundred walls between, for there was more, there was her will against me. Would she but yet relent! Oh, Phillis,

Phillis, shorten my torment and declare you pity me.

PHILLIS. I believe it's very sufferable. The pain is not so exquisite but that you may bear it a little longer.

TOM. Oh, my charming Phillis, if all depended on my fair one's will I could with glory suffer. But, dearest creature, consider our miserable state.

PHILLIS. How! Miserable!

TOM. We are miserable to be in love and under the command of others than those we love,—with that generous passion in the heart, to be sent to and fro on errands, called, checked and rated for the meanest trifles. Oh, Phillis, you don't know how many china cups and glasses my passion for you has made me break. You have broke my fortune as well as my heart.

PHILLIS. Well, Mr. Thomas, I cannot but own to you that I believe your master writes and you speak the best of any men in the world. Never was woman so well pleased with a letter as my young lady was with his, and this is an answer to it. (*Gives him a letter*)

TOM. This was well done, my dearest. Consider we must strike some livelihood for ourselves by closing their affairs. It will be nothing for them to give us a little being of our own, some small tenement out of their large possessions. Whatever they give us, 'twill be more than what they keep for themselves. One acre with Phillis would be worth a whole county without her.

PHILLIS. O, could I but believe you!

TOM. If not the utterance, believe the touch of my lips.

(*Kisses her*)

PHILLIS. There's no contradicting you; how closely you argue, Tom!

TOM. And will closer in due time. But I must hasten with this letter, to hasten towards the possession of you.—Then, Phillis, consider how I must be revenged; look to it of all your skittishness, shy looks, and at best but coy compliances.

PHILLIS. Oh, Tom! You grow wanton and sensual, as my lady calls it. I must not endure it. Oh! Foh! You are a man, an odious, filthy male creature; you should behave, if you had a right sense or were a man of sense like Mr. Cimberton, with distance and indifference; or let me see some other becoming hard word, with seeming in——in——inadvert-

ency, and not rush on one as if you were seizing a prey. But hush! The ladies are coming. Good Tom, don't kiss me above once and be gone. Lard, we have been fooling and toying and not considered the main business of our masters and mistresses.

TOM. Why, their business is to be fooling and toying as soon as the parchments are ready.

PHILLIS. Well remembered! Parchments! My lady, to my knowledge is preparing writings between her coxcomb cousin Cimberton and my mistress, though master has an eye to the parchments already prepared between your master, Mr. Bevil, and my mistress; and I believe my mistress herself has signed and sealed in her heart to Mr. Myrtle.—Did I not bid you kiss me but once and be gone? But I know you won't be satisfied.

TOM. No, you smooth creature, how should I! (*Kissing her hand*)

PHILLIS. Well, since you are so humble, or so cool, as to ravish my hand only, I'll take my leave of you like a great lady and you a man of quality. (*They salute formally*)

TOM. Pox of all this state.

(*Offers to kiss her more closely*)

PHILLIS. No, prithee, Tom, mind your business. We must follow that interest which will take, but endeavor at that which will be most for us and we like most.—O, here's my young mistress! (TOM *taps her neck behind and kisses his fingers*) Go, ye liquorish fool!

Exit

Enter LUCINDA

LUCINDA. Who was that you was [1] hurrying away?

PHILLIS. One that I had no mind to part with.

LUCINDA. Why did you turn him away then?

PHILLIS. For your ladyship's service, to carry your ladyship's letter to his master. I could hardly get the rogue away.

LUCINDA. Why, has he so little love for his master?

PHILLIS. No; but he has so much love for his mistress.

LUCINDA. But I thought I heard him kiss you. Why do you suffer that?

PHILLIS. Why, madam, we vulgar take it to be a sign of love; we servants, we poor

---

[1] The polite form of the verb in the eighteenth century.

people that have nothing but our persons to bestow or treat for are forced to deal and bargain by way of sample; and therefore, as we have no parchments or wax necessary in our agreements. we squeeze with our hands and seal with our lips to ratify vows and promises.

LUCINDA. But can't you trust one another without such earnest down?

PHILLIS. We don't think it safe any more than you gentry to come together without deeds executed.

LUCINDA. Thou art a pert, merry hussy.

PHILLIS. I wish, madam, your lover and you were as happy as Tom and your servant are.

LUCINDA. You grow impertinent.

PHILLIS. I have done, madam; and I won't ask you what you intend to do with Mr. Myrtle, what your father will do with Mr. Bevil, nor what you all, especially my lady, mean by admitting Mr. Cimberton as particularly here as if he were married to you already. Nay, you are married actually as far as people of quality are.

LUCINDA. How's that?

PHILLIS. You have different beds in the same house.

LUCINDA. Pshaw! I have a very great value for Mr. Bevil, but I have absolutely put an end to his pretensions in the letter I gave you for him. But my father, in his heart, still has a mind to him, were it not for this woman they talk of; and I am apt to imagine he is married to her or never designs to marry at all.

PHILLIS. Then Mr. Myrtle—

LUCINDA. He had my parents' leave to apply to me and by that has won me and my affections. Who is to have this body of mine without 'em, it seems is nothing to me. My mother says it's indecent for me to let my thoughts stray about the person of my husband. Nay, she says a maid rigidly virtuous, though she may have been where her lover was a thousand times should not have made observations enough to know him from another man when she sees him in a third place.

PHILLIS. That is more than the severity of a nun, for not to see when one may, is impossible; not to see when one can't, is very easy. At this rate, madam, there are a great many whom you have not seen who—

LUCINDA. Mamma says the first time you see your husband should be at the instant he is made so, when your father with the help of the minister gives you to him; then you are to observe and take notice of him because then you are to obey him.

PHILLIS. But does not my lady remember you are to love as well as obey?

LUCINDA. To love is a passion, 'tis a desire, and we must have no desires. Oh! I cannot endure the reflection. With what insensibility on my part, with what more than patience, have I been exposed and offered to some awkward booby or other in every county of Great Britain.

PHILLIS. Indeed, madam, I wonder I never heard you speak of it before with this indignation.

LUCINDA. Every corner of the land has been presented me with a wealthy coxcomb. As fast as one treaty has gone off, another has come on till my name and person have been the tittle tattle of the whole town. What is this world come to? No shame left! To be bartered for like the beasts of the fields and that in such an instance as coming together to an entire familiarity and union of soul and body. Oh! and this without being so much as well-wishers to each other but for the increase of fortune.

PHILLIS. But, madam, all these vexations will end very soon in one for all. Mr. Cimberton is your mother's kinsman and three hundred years an older gentleman than any lover you ever had, for which reason, with that of his prodigious large estate, she is resolved on him and has sent to consult the lawyers accordingly. Nay, has (whether you know it or no) been in treaty with Sir Geoffry, who to join in the settlement has accepted of a sum to do it and is every moment expected in town for that purpose.

LUCINDA. How did you get all this intelligence?

PHILLIS. By an art I have, I thank my stars, beyond all the waiting-maids in Great Britain, the art of listening, madam, for your ladyship's service.

LUCINDA. I shall soon know as much as you do. Leave me, leave me, Phillis begone. Here, here, I'll turn you out. My mother says I must not converse with my servants, though I must converse with no one else. (*Exit* PHILLIS) How unhappy are we who are born to great fortunes! No one looks at us with indifference or acts towards us on the foot of plain dealing; yet by all I have been heretofore offered to or treated for I have been used with the most agreeable of all abuses, flattery; but now by this phlegmatic fool I am used as nothing, or a mere thing. He, forsooth, is too wise, too learned, to have any regard to desires; and I know not what the learned oaf calls sentiments of love and passion.—Here he comes with my mother. It's much if he looks at me, or if he does takes no more notice of me than of any other movable in the room.

Enter MRS. SEALAND *and* MR. CIMBERTON

MRS. SEALAND. How do I admire this noble, this learned taste of yours and the worthy regard you have to our own ancient and honorable house in consulting a means to keep the blood as pure and as regularly descended as may be.

CIMBERTON. Why, really, madam, the young women of this age are treated with discourses of such a tendency and their imaginations so bewildered in flesh and blood that a man of reason can't talk to be understood. They have no ideas of happiness but what are more gross than the gratification of hunger and thirst.

LUCINDA. (*Aside*) With how much reflection he is a coxcomb!

CIMBERTON. And in truth, madam, I have considered it as a most brutal custom that persons of the first character in the world should go as ordinarily and with as little shame to bed as to dinner with one another. They proceed to the propagation of the species as openly as to the preservation of the individual.

LUCINDA. (*Aside*) She that willingly goes to bed to thee must have no shame, I'm sure.

MRS. SEALAND. Oh, cousin Cimberton! Cousin Cimberton! How abstracted, how refined, is your sense of things! But, indeed it is too true, there is nothing so ordinary as to say in the best governed families, my master and lady are gone to bed. One does not know but it might have been said of one's self. (*Hiding her face with her fan*)

CIMBERTON. Lycurgus, madam, instituted otherwise among the Lacedemonians. The whole female world was pregnant, but none but the mothers themselves knew by whom. Their meetings were secret and the amorous congress always by stealth, and no such professed doings between the sexes as are tolerated among us under the audacious word, marriage.

MRS. SEALAND. Oh, had I lived in those days and been a matron of Sparta, one might with less indecency have had ten children according to that modest institution than one under the confusion of our modern, barefaced manner.

LUCINDA. (*Aside*) And yet, poor woman, she has gone through the whole ceremony and here I stand a melancholy proof of it.

MRS. SEALAND. We will talk then of business. That girl walking about the room there is to be your wife. She has, I confess, no ideas, no sentiments, that speak her born of a thinking mother.

CIMBERTON. I have observed her. Her lively look, free air, and disengaged [1] countenance speak her very—

LUCINDA. Very what?

CIMBERTON. If you please, madam, to set her a little that way.

MRS. SEALAND. Lucinda, say nothing to him; you are not a match for him. When you are married, you may speak to such a husband when you're spoken to. But I am disposing of you above yourself every way.

CIMBERTON. Madam, you cannot but observe the inconveniences I expose myself to in hopes that your ladyship will be the consort of my better part. As for the young woman, she is rather an impediment than a help to a man of letters and speculation. Madam, there is no reflection, no philosophy, can at all times subdue the sensitive life, but the animal shall sometimes carry away the man. Ha! Ay, the vermilion of her lips!

LUCINDA. Pray, don't talk of me thus.

CIMBERTON. The pretty enough—pant of her bosom.

LUCINDA. Sir! Madam, don't you hear him?

CIMBERTON. Her forward chest.

LUCINDA. Intolerable!

CIMBERTON. High health—

LUCINDA. The grave, easy impudence of him!

CIMBERTON. Proud heart—

LUCINDA. Stupid coxcomb!

CIMBERTON. I say, madam, her impatience while we are looking at her throws out all

[1] I.e., dégagée,—free, easy.

attractions,—her arms, her neck—What a spring in her step!

LUCINDA. Don't you run me over thus, you strange unaccountable!

CIMBERTON. What an elasticity in her veins and arteries!

LUCINDA. I have no veins, no arteries!

MRS. SEALAND. Oh, child, hear him, he talks finely. He's a scholar, he knows what you have.

CIMBERTON. The speaking invitation of her shape, the gathering of herself up, and the indignation you see in the pretty little thing—Now, I am considering her, on this occasion, but as one that is to be pregnant.

LUCINDA. (*Aside*) The familiar, learned, unseasonable puppy!

CIMBERTON. And pregnant undoubtedly she will be yearly. I fear I shan't for many years have discretion enough to give her one fallow season.

LUCINDA. Monster! There's no bearing it. The hideous sot! There's no enduring it, to be thus surveyed like a steed at sale.

CIMBERTON. At sale! She's very illiterate. But she's very well limbed too. Turn her in; I see what she is. *Exit* LUCINDA *in a rage*

MRS. SEALAND. Go, you creature, I am ashamed of you.

CIMBERTON. No harm done. You know, madam, the better sort of people, as I observed to you treat by their lawyers of weddings (*adjusting himself at the glass*) and the woman in the bargain, like the mansion-house in the sale of the estate, is thrown in, and what that is, whether good or bad, is not at all considered.

MRS. SEALAND. I grant it and therefore make no demand for her youth and beauty and every other accomplishment, as the common world think 'em, because she is not polite.

CIMBERTON. Madam, I know your exalted understanding, abstracted as it is from vulgar prejudices, will not be offended when I declare to you I marry to have an heir to my estate and not to beget a colony or a plantation. This young woman's beauty and constitution will demand provision for a tenth child at least.

MRS. SEALAND. (*Aside*) With all that wit and learning, how considerate! What an economist!—Sir, I cannot make her other than she is, or say she is much better than the other young women of this age or fit for much besides being a mother; but I have given directions for the marriage settlements, and Sir Geoffry Cimberton's counsel is to meet ours here at this hour, concerning his joining in the deed, which, when executed, makes you capable of settling what is due to Lucinda's fortune. Herself, as I told you, I say nothing of.

CIMBERTON. No, no, no, indeed, madam, it is not usual and I must depend upon my own reflection and philosophy not to overstock my family.

MRS. SEALAND. I cannot help her, cousin Cimberton; but she is for aught I see, as well as the daughter of anybody else.

CIMBERTON. That is very true, madam.

Enter a Servant *who whispers* [*to*] MRS. SEALAND

MRS. SEALAND. The lawyers are come and now we are to hear what they have resolved as to the point whether it's necessary that Sir Geoffry should join in the settlement, as being what they call in the remainder. But, good cousin, you must have patience with 'em. These lawyers, I am told, are of a different kind, one is what they call a chamber-counsel, the other a pleader. The conveyancer is slow from an imperfection in his speech and therefore shunned the bar, but extremely passionate and impatient of contradiction. The other is as warm as he but has a tongue so voluble and a head so conceited he will suffer nobody to speak but himself.

CIMBERTON. You mean old Sergeant Target and Counsellor Bramble? I have heard of 'em.

MRS. SEALAND. The same. Show in the gentlemen. *Exit* Servant

Re-enter Servant *introducing* MYRTLE *and* TOM *disguised as* BRAMBLE *and* TARGET

MRS. SEALAND. Gentlemen, this is the party concerned, Mr. Cimberton; and I hope you have considered of the matter.

TARGET. Yes, madam, we have agreed that it must be by indent—dent—dent—dent—

BRAMBLE. Yes, madam, Mr. Sergeant and myself have agreed as he is pleased to inform you, that it must be by an indenture tripartite, and tripartite let it be, for Sir Geoffry must needs be a party. Old Cimberton in the year 1619 says in that ancient roll in Mr.

Sergeant's hands, as recourse being thereto had, will more at large appear—

TARGET. Yes, and by the deeds in your hands it appears that—

BRAMBLE. Mr. Sergeant, I beg of you to make no inferences upon what is in our custody, but to speak to the titles in your own deeds. I shall not show that deed till my client is in town.

CIMBERTON. You know best your own methods.

MRS. SEALAND. The single question is whether the entail is such that my cousin, Sir Geoffry, is necessary in this affair?

BRAMBLE. Yes, as to the lordship of Tretriplet but not as to the messuage of Grimgribber.

TARGET. I say that Gr—Gr—that Gr—Gr—Grimgribber, Grimgribber is in us. That is to say the remainder thereof as well as that of Tr—Tr—Triplet.

BRAMBLE. You go upon the deed of Sir Ralph, made in the middle of the last century, precedent to that in which old Cimberton made over the remainder and made it pass to the heirs general, by which your client comes in; and I question whether the remainder even of Tretriplet is in him. But we are willing to waive that and give him a valuable consideration. But we shall not purchase what is in us forever, as Grimgribber is, at the rate as we guard against the contingent of Mr. Cimberton having no son. Then we know Sir Geoffry is the first of the collateral male line in this family; yet—

TARGET. Sir, Gr—Gr—ber is—

BRAMBLE. I apprehend you very well and your argument might be of force and we would be inclined to hear that in all its parts. But, sir, I see very plainly what you are going into. I tell you it is as probable a contingent that Sir Geoffry may die before Mr. Cimberton as that he may outlive him.

TARGET. Sir, we are not ripe for that yet, but I must say—

BRAMBLE. Sir, I allow you the whole extent of that argument; but that will go no farther than as to the claimants under old Cimberton. I am of opinion that according to the instruction of Sir Ralph he could not dock the entail and then create a new estate for the heirs general.

TARGET. Sir, I have not patience to be told that, when Gr—Gr—ber—

BRAMBLE. I will allow it to you, Mr. Sergeant; but there must be the word "heirs forever" to make such an estate as you pretend.

CIMBERTON. I must be impartial, though you are counsel for my side of the question. Were it not that you are so good as to allow him what he has not said, I should think it very hard you should answer him without hearing him. But, gentlemen, I believe you have both considered this matter and are firm in your different opinions. 'Twere better, therefore, you proceeded according to the particular sense of each of you and gave your thoughts distinctly to writing. And you see, sirs, pray let me have a copy of what you say in English.

BRAMBLE. Why, what is all we have been saying? In English!—Oh, but I forgot myself, you're a wit.—But however, to please you, sir, you shall have it in as plain terms as the law will admit of.

CIMBERTON. But I would have it, sir, without delay.

BRAMBLE. That, sir, the law will not admit of. The courts are sitting at Westminster, and I am this moment obliged to be at every one of them, and 'twould be wrong if I should not be in the Hall to attend one of 'em at least, the rest would take it ill else. Therefore, I must leave what I have said to Mr. Sergeant's consideration, and I will digest his arguments on my part, and you shall hear from me again, sir. *Exit* BRAMBLE

TARGET. Agreed, agreed.

CIMBERTON. Mr. Bramble is very quick. He parted a little abruptly.

TARGET. He could not bear my argument, I pinched him to the quick about that Gr—Gr—ber.

MRS. SEALAND. I saw that, for he durst not so much as hear you. I shall send to you, Mr. Sergeant, as soon as Sir Geoffry comes to town, and then I hope all may be adjusted.

TARGET. I shall be at my chambers at my usual hours. *Exit*

CIMBERTON. Madam, if you please, I'll now attend you to the tea table, where I shall hear from your ladyship reason and good sense after all this law and gibberish.

MRS. SEALAND. 'Tis a wonderful thing, sir, that men of professions do not study to talk the substance of what they have to say in the language of the rest of the world. Sure they'd find their account in it.

CIMBERTON. They might, perhaps, madam, with people of your good sense; but with the generality 'twould never do. The vulgar would have no respect for truth and knowledge if they were exposed to naked view.
Truth is too simple, of all art bereaved.
Since the world will,—why let it be deceived.

Exeunt

ACT IV

SCENE I. BEVIL, JUNIOR'S *Lodgings*

BEVIL, JUNIOR, *with a letter in his hand followed by* TOM

TOM. Upon my life, sir, I know nothing of the matter. I never opened my lips to Mr. Myrtle about anything of your honor's letter to Madam Lucinda.

BEVIL. What's the fool in such a fright for? I don't suppose you did. What I would know is whether Mr. Myrtle showed any suspicion or asked you any questions, to lead you to say casually that you had carried any such letter for me this morning.

TOM. Why, sir, if he did ask me any questions, how could I help it?

BEVIL. I don't say you could. Oaf, I am not questioning you, but him. What did he say to you?

TOM. Why, sir, when I came to his chambers to be dressed for the lawyer's part your honor was pleased to put me upon, he asked me if I had been at Mr. Sealand's this morning. So I told him, sir, I often went thither,—because, sir, if I had not said that he might have thought there was something more in my going now than at another time.

BEVIL. Very well!—(*Aside*) The fellow's caution, I find, has given him this jealousy.—Did he ask you no other questions?

TOM. Yes, sir, now I remember, as we came away in the hackney coach from Mr. Sealand's, "Tom," says he, "as I came in to your master this morning, he bade you go for an answer to a letter he had sent. Pray did you bring him any?" says he. "Ah," says I, "sir, your honor is pleased to joke with me; you have a mind to know whether I can keep a secret or no!"

BEVIL. And so, by showing him you could, you told him you had one.

TOM. (*Confused*) Sir—

BEVIL. What mean actions does jealousy make a man stoop to! How poorly has he used art [1] with a servant to make him betray his master! Well, and when did he give you this letter for me?

TOM. Sir, he writ it before he pulled off his lawyer's gown at his own chambers.

BEVIL. Very well; and what did he say when you brought him my answer to it?

TOM. He looked a little out of humor, sir, and said it was very well.

BEVIL. I knew he would be grave upon't. Wait without.

TOM. Humh! 'Gad, I don't like this. I am afraid we are all in the wrong box here. *Exit*

BEVIL. I put on a serenity while my fellow was present, but I have never been more thoroughly disturbed. This hot man! To write me a challenge on supposed artificial dealing when I professed myself his friend! I can live contented without glory, but I cannot suffer shame. What's to be done? But first let me consider Lucinda's letter again.

(*Reads*)

SIR:

I hope it is consistent with the laws a woman ought to impose upon herself to acknowledge that your manner of declining a treaty of marriage in our family and desiring the refusal may come from hence, has something more engaging in it than the courtship of him who, I fear, will fall to my lot except your friend exerts himself for our common safety and happiness. I have reasons for desiring Mr. Myrtle may not know of this letter till hereafter and am your most obliged, humble servant,

Lucinda Sealand

Well, but the postscript. (*Reads*)

I won't, upon second thoughts, hide anything from you. But my reason for concealing this is that Mr. Myrtle has a jealousy of temper which gives me some terrors; but my esteem for him inclines me to hope that only an ill effect which sometimes accompanies a tender love, and what may be cured by a careful and unblameable conduct.

Thus has this lady made me her friend and confidant and put herself, in a kind, under my protection. I cannot tell him immediately the purport of her letter except I could cure him of the violent and untractable passion and jealousy and so serve him and her by disobliging her in the article of secrecy more that I should be complying with her direc-

[1] Artifice.

tions. But then this dueling, which custom has imposed upon every man who would live with reputation and honor in the world! How must I preserve myself from imputations there? He'll, forsooth, call it or think it fear, if I explain without fighting. But this letter,— I'll read it again:

Sir:
You have used me basely in corresponding and carrying on a treaty where you told me you were indifferent. I have changed my sword since I saw you, which advertisement I thought proper to send you against the next meeting between you and the injured

Charles Myrtle.

Enter TOM

TOM. Mr. Myrtle, sir. Would your honor please to see him?

BEVIL. Why, you stupid creature! Let Mr. Myrtle wait at my lodgings! Show him up. (*Exit* TOM) Well, I am resolved upon my carriage to him. He is in love and in every circumstance of life a little distrustful, which I must allow for—But here he is.

Enter TOM *introducing* MYRTLE

BEVIL. Sir, I am extremely obliged to you for this honor. But, sir, you, with your very discerning face, leave the room. (*Exit* TOM) Well, Mr. Myrtle, your commands with me?

MYRTLE. The time, the place, our long acquaintance and many other circumstances which affect me on this occasion oblige me without farther ceremony or conference to desire you would not only, as you already have, acknowledge the receipt of my letter but also comply with the request in it. I must have farther notice taken of my message than these half lines: "I have yours. I shall be at home."

BEVIL. Sir, I own I have received a letter from you in a very unusual style; but, as I design everything in this matter shall be your own action, your own seeking, I shall understand nothing but what you are pleased to confirm face to face and I have already forgot the contents of your epistle.

MYRTLE. This cool manner is very agreeable to the abuse you have already made of my simplicity and frankness; and I see your moderation tends to your own advantage and not mine, to your own safety, not consideration of your friend.

BEVIL. My own safety, Mr. Myrtle!

MYRTLE. Your own safety, Mr. Bevil.

BEVIL. Look you, Mr. Myrtle, there's no disguising that I understand what you would be at. But, sir, you know I have often dared to disapprove of the directions a tyrant custom has introduced to the breach of all laws both divine and human.

MYRTLE. Mr. Bevil, Mr. Bevil, it would be a good first principle in those who have so tender a conscience that way to have as much abhorrence of doing injuries as—

BEVIL. As what?

MYRTLE. As fear of answering for 'em.

BEVIL. As fear of answering for 'em! But that apprehension is just or blameable according to the object of that fear. I have often told you in confidence of heart, I abhorred the daring to offend the Author of Life and rushing into His presence. I say, by the very same act, to commit the crime against Him and immediately to urge on to His tribunal.

MYRTLE. Mr. Bevil, I must tell you, this coolness, this gravity, this show of confidence shall never cheat me of my mistress. You have, indeed, the best excuse for life, the hopes of possessing Lucinda. But consider, sir, I have as much reason to be weary of it, if I am to lose her; and my first attempt to recover her, shall be to let her see the dauntless man who is to be her guardian and protector.

BEVIL. Sir, show me but the least glimpse of argument that I am authorized by my own hand to vindicate any lawless insult of this nature and I will show thee—to chastise thee hardly deserves the name of courage, slight, inconsiderate man! There is, Mr. Myrtle, no such terror in quick anger; and you shall, you know not why, be cool, as you have, you know not why, been warm.

MYRTLE. Is the woman one loves so little occasion of anger? You perhaps, who know not what it is to love, who have your ready, your commodious, your foreign trinket for your loose hours; and from your fortune, your specious outward carriage, and other lucky circumstances as easy a way to the possession of a woman of honor, you know nothing of what it is to be alarmed, to be distracted with anxiety and terror of losing more than life. Your marriage, happy man, goes on like common business; and in the interim you have your rambling captive, your

Indian princess, for your soft moments of dalliance, your convenient, your ready Indiana.

BEVIL. You have touched me beyond the patience of man; and I'm excusable, in the guard of innocence (or from the infirmity of human nature, which will bear no more) to accept your invitation and observe your letter. Sir, I'll attend you!

Enter TOM

TOM. Did you call, sir? I thought you did. I heard you speak aloud.

BEVIL. Yes, go call a coach.

TOM. Sir,—master,—Mr. Myrtle,—friends, —gentlemen—What d'ye mean? I am but a servant, or—

BEVIL. Call a coach. (*Exit* TOM. *A long pause, walking sullenly by each other*) (*Aside*) Shall I, though provoked to the uttermost, recover myself at the entrance of a third person and that my servant, too, and not have respect enough to all I have ever been receiving from infancy, the obligation to the best of fathers, to an unhappy virgin too, whose life depends on mine?

(*Shutting the door. To* MYRTLE)

I have, thank heaven, had time to recollect myself and shall not, for fear of what such a rash man as you think of me, keep longer unexplained the false appearances under which your infirmity of temper makes you suffer, when perhaps too much regard to a false point of honor makes me prolong that suffering.

MYRTLE. I am sure Mr. Bevil cannot doubt but I had rather have satisfaction from his innocence than his sword.

BEVIL. Why, then, would you ask it first that way?

MYRTLE. Consider, you kept your temper yourself no longer than till I spoke to the disadvantage of her you loved.

BEVIL. True. But let me tell you I have saved you from the most exquisite distress even though you had succeeded in the dispute. I know you so well that I am sure to have found this letter about a man you had killed would have been worse than death to yourself. Read it. [*Aside*] When he is thoroughly mortified and shame has got the better of jealousy, when he has seen himself thoroughly he will deserve to be assisted towards obtaining Lucinda.

MYRTLE. [*Aside*] With what a superiority has he turned the injury on me as the aggressor! I begin to fear I have been too far transported. "A treaty in our family—" Is not that saying too much? I shall relapse— But I find on the postscript, "—something like jealousy—" With what face can I see my benefactor, my advocate, whom I have treated like a betrayer?—Oh, Bevil, with what words shall I—

BEVIL. There needs none; to convince is much more than to conquer.

MYRTLE. But can you—

BEVIL. You have o'erpaid the inquietude you gave me in the change I see in you towards me. Alas, what machines are we! Thy face is altered to that of another man, to that of my companion, my friend.

MYRTLE. That I could be such a precipitant wretch!

BEVIL. Pray, no more.

MYRTLE. Let me reflect how many friends have died by the hands of friends for the want of temper; and you must give me leave to say again and again how much I am beholden to that superior spirit you have subdued me with. What had become of one of us, or perhaps both, had you been as weak as I was and as incapable of reason?

BEVIL. I congratulate to us both the escape from ourselves and hope the memory of it will make us dearer friends than ever.

MYRTLE. Dear Bevil, your friendly conduct has convinced me there is nothing manly but what is conducted by reason and agreeable to the practice of virtue and justice. And yet how many have been sacrificed to that idol, the unreasonable opinion of men! Nay, they are so ridiculous in it that they often use their swords against each other with dissembled anger and real fear.

Betrayed by honor and compelled by shame,
They hazard being to preserve a name,
Nor dare enquire into the dread mistake,
Till plunged in sad eternity they wake.

Exeunt

SCENE [II.] *St. James's Park*

Enter SIR JOHN BEVIL *and* MR. SEALAND

SIR JOHN. Give me leave, however, Mr. Sealand, as we are upon a treaty for uniting our families, to mention only the business of an ancient house. Genealogy and descent are to be of some consideration in an affair of this sort.

MR. SEALAND. Genealogy and descent! Sir, there has been in our family a very large one. There was Galfrid, the father of Edward, the father of Ptolomy,[1] the father of Crassus, the father of Earl Richard, the father of Henry the marquis, the father of Duke John—

SIR JOHN. What, do you rave, Mr. Sealand? All these great names in your family?

MR. SEALAND. These? Yes, sir. I have heard my father name 'em all, and more.

SIR JOHN. Ay, sir, and did he say they were all in your family?

MR. SEALAND. Yes, sir, he kept 'em all. He was the greatest cocker[2] in all England. He said Duke John won him many battles and never lost one.

SIR JOHN. Oh, sir, your servant! You are laughing at my laying any stress upon descent; but I must tell you, sir, I never knew anyone but he that wanted that advantage turn it into ridicule.

MR. SEALAND. And I never knew anyone who had many better advantages put that into his account. But, Sir John, value yourself as you please upon your ancient house; I am to talk freely of everything you are pleased to put into your bill of rates on this occasion. Yet, sir, I have made no objections to your son's family. 'Tis his morals that I doubt.

SIR JOHN. Sir, I can't help saying that what might injure a citizen's credit may be no stain to a gentleman's honor.

MR. SEALAND. Sir John, the honor of a gentleman is liable to be tainted by as small a matter as the credit of a trader; we are talking of a marriage and in such a case the father of a young woman will not think it an addition to the honor or credit of her lover that he is a keeper—

SIR JOHN. Mr. Sealand, don't take upon you to spoil my son's marriage with any woman else.

MR. SEALAND. Sir John, let him apply to any woman else and have as many mistresses as he pleases—

SIR JOHN. My son, sir, is a discreet and sober gentleman—

MR. SEALAND. Sir, I never saw a man that wenched soberly and discreetly that ever left it off. The decency observed in the practice hides even from the sinner the iniquity of it. They pursue it, not that their appetites hurry them away, but, I warrant you, because 'tis their opinion they may do it.

SIR JOHN. Were what you suspect a truth— Do you design to keep your daughter a virgin till you find a man unblemished that way?

MR. SEALAND. Sir, as much a cit[3] as you take me for, I know the town and the world; and give me leave to say that we merchants are a species of gentry that have grown into the world this last century and are as honorable and almost as useful as you landed folks that have always thought yourselves so much above us, for your trading, forsooth, is extended no farther than a load of hay or a fat ox. You are pleasant people, indeed, because you are bred up to be lazy; therefore, I warrant you, industry is dishonorable.

SIR JOHN. Be not offended, sir. Let us go back to our point.

MR. SEALAND. Oh, not at all offended! But I don't love to leave any part of the account unclosed. Look you, Sir John, comparisons are odious and more particularly so on occasions of this kind when we are projecting races that are to be made out of both sides of the comparisons.

SIR JOHN. But my son, sir, is in the eye of the world a gentleman of merit.

MR. SEALAND. I own to you I think him so. But, Sir John, I am a man exercised and experienced in chances and disasters. I lost in my earlier years a very fine wife and with her a poor little infant; this makes me, perhaps, over cautious to preserve the second bounty of providence to me and be as careful as I can of this child. You'll pardon me, my poor girl, sir, is as valuable to me as your boasted son to you.

SIR JOHN. Why, that's one very good reason, Mr. Sealand, why I wish my son had her.

MR. SEALAND. There is nothing but this strange lady here, this *incognita*, that can be objected to him. Here and there a man falls in love with an artful creature and gives up all the motives of life to that one passion.

SIR JOHN. A man of my son's understanding cannot be supposed to be one of them.

MR. SEALAND. Very wise men have been so enslaved; and when a man marries with one of them upon his hands, whether moved from the demand of the world or slighter

---

[1] *Sic*, but doubtless intended for Ptolemy.
[2] Owner of fighting cocks.
[3] Citizen in a depreciatory sense.

reasons, such a husband soils with his wife for a month perhaps; then, "Good b'w'y', madam!" The show's over. Ah! John Dryden points out such a husband to a hair where he says,

"And while abroad so prodigal the dolt is,
Poor spouse at home as ragged as a colt is." [1]

Now, in plain terms, sir, I shall not care to have my poor girl turned a-grazing, and that must be the case when—

SIR JOHN. But pray consider, sir, my son—

MR. SEALAND. Look you, sir, I'll make the matter short. This unknown lady, as I told you, is all the objection I have to him. But one way or other, he is, or has been, certainly engaged to her. I am therefore resolved this very afternoon to visit her. Now from her behavior or appearance I shall soon be let into what I may fear or hope for.

SIR JOHN. Sir, I am very confident there can be nothing enquired into relating to my son that will not upon being understood turn to his advantage.

MR. SEALAND. I hope that as sincerely as you believe it. Sir John Bevil, when I am satisfied in this great point, if your son's conduct answers the character you give of him, I shall wish your alliance more than that of any gentleman in Great Britain, and so your servant. *Exit*

SIR JOHN. He is gone in a way but barely civil; but his great wealth and the merit of his only child, the heiress of it, are not to be lost for a little peevishness—(*Enter* HUMPHREY) Oh, Humphrey, you are come in a seasonable minute. I want to talk to thee and to tell thee that my head and heart are on the rack about my son.

HUMPHREY. Sir, you may trust his discretion; I am sure you may.

SIR JOHN. Why, I do believe I may, and yet I am in a thousand fears when I lay this vast wealth before me. When I consider his prepossessions, either generous to a folly in an honorable love or abandoned past redemption in a vicious one, and from the one or the other his insensibility to the fairest prospect towards doubling our estate. A father who knows how useful wealth is and how necessary even to those who despise it, I say a father, Humphrey, a father cannot bear it.

[1] From Dryden's Prologue to *The Disappointment* by Southerne, ll. 54–5.

HUMPHREY. Be not transported, sir. You will grow incapable of taking any resolution in your perplexity.

SIR JOHN. Yet, as angry as I am with him, I would not have him surprised in any thing. This mercantile rough man may go grossly into the examination of this matter and talk to the gentlewoman so as to—

HUMPHREY. No, I hope not in an abrupt manner.

SIR JOHN. No, I hope not! Why, dost thou know anything of her, or of him, or of anything of it, or of all of it?

HUMPHREY. My dear master, I know so much that I told him this very day you had reason to be secretly out of humor about her.

SIR JOHN. Did you go so far? Well, what said he to that?

HUMPHREY. His words were, looking upon me steadfastly, "Humphrey," says he, "that woman is a woman of honor."

SIR JOHN. How! Do you think he is married to her or designs to marry her?

HUMPHREY. I can say nothing to the latter; but he says he can marry no one without your consent while you are living.

SIR JOHN. If he said so much, I know he scorns to break his word with me.

HUMPHREY. I am sure of that.

SIR JOHN. You are sure of that? Well, that's some comfort. Then I have nothing to do but to see the bottom of this matter during this present ruffle [2]—Oh, Humphrey!

HUMPHREY. You are not ill, I hope, sir.

SIR JOHN. Yes, a man is very ill that's in a very ill humor. To be a father is to be in care for one whom you oftener disoblige than please by that very care. Oh, that sons could know the duty to a father before they themselves are fathers! But perhaps you'll say now that I am one of the happiest fathers in the world; but, I assure you, that of the very happiest is not a condition to be envied.

HUMPHREY. Sir, your pain arises not from the thing itself but your particular sense of it. You are overfond, nay, give me leave to say you are unjustly apprehensive from your fondness. My master Bevil never disobliged you and he will, I know he will, do everything you ought to expect.

SIR JOHN. He won't take all this money with this girl. For ought I know he will, forsooth, have so much moderation as to

[2] Trouble, annoyance.

think he ought not to force his liking for any consideration.

HUMPHREY. He is to marry her, not you; he is to live with her, not you, sir.

SIR JOHN. I know not what to think. But I know nothing can be more miserable than to be in this doubt. Follow me; I must come to some resolution. *Exeunt*

SCENE [III.] BEVIL JUNIOR'S *Lodgings*

Enter TOM *and* PHILLIS

TOM. Well, madam, if you must speak with Mr. Myrtle, you shall. He is now with my master in the library.

PHILLIS. But you must leave me alone with him, for he can't make me a present nor I so handsomely take anything from him before you. It would not be decent.

TOM. It will be very decent, indeed, for me to retire and leave my mistress with another man.

PHILLIS. He is a gentleman and will treat one properly—

TOM. I believe so, but, however, I won't be far off and therefore will venture to trust you. I'll call him to you. *Exit*

PHILLIS. What a deal of pother and sputter here is between my mistress and Mr. Myrtle from mere punctilio! I could any hour of the day get her to her lover and would do it. But she, forsooth, will allow no plot to get him; but, if he can come to her, I know she will be glad of it. I must, therefore, do her an acceptable violence and surprise her into his arms. I am sure I go by the best ruse imaginable. If she were my maid, I should think her the best servant in the world for doing so by me.

Enter MYRTLE *and* TOM

Oh sir! You and Mr. Bevil are fine gentlemen to let a lady remain under such difficulties as my poor mistress and no[t] attempt to set her at liberty or release her from the danger of being instantly married to Cimberton.

MYRTLE. Tom has been telling—But what is to be done?

PHILLIS. What is to be done! When a man can't come at his mistress! Why can't you fire our house or the next house to us to make us run out and you take us?

MYRTLE. How, Mrs. Phillis—

PHILLIS. Ay! Let me see that rogue deny to fire a house, make a riot, or any other little thing when there were no other way to come at me.

TOM. I'm obliged to you, madam.

PHILLIS. Why, don't we hear every day of people's hanging themselves for love, and won't they venture the hazard of being hanged for love? Oh, were I a man—

MYRTLE. What manly thing would you have me undertake, according to your ladyship's notion of a man?

PHILLIS. Only be at once what one time or other you may be and wish to be or must be.

MYRTLE. Dear girl, talk plainly to me and consider, I in my condition can't be in very good humor. You say to be at once what I must be.

PHILLIS. Ay, ay! I mean no more than to be an old man. I saw you do it very well at the masquerade. In a word, old Sir Geoffry Cimberton is every hour expected in town to join the deeds and settlements for marrying Mr. Cimberton. He is half blind, half lame, half dumb; though as to his passions and desires, he is as warm and ridiculous as when in the heat of youth.

TOM. Come to business and don't keep the gentleman in suspense for the pleasure of being courted as you serve me.

PHILLIS. I saw you at the masquerade act such a one to perfection. Go and put on that very habit and come to our house as Sir Geoffry. There is not one there but myself knows his person. I was born in the parish where he is lord of the manor. I have seen him often and often at church in the country. Do not hesitate, but come hither. They will think you bring a certain security against Mr. Myrtle and you bring Mr. Myrtle. Leave the rest to me. I leave this with you and expect—They don't, I told you, know you; they think you out of town, which you had as good be forever, if you lose this opportunity. I must be gone; I know I am wanted at home.

MYRTLE. My dear Phillis!

(*Catches and kisses her and gives her money*)

PHILLIS. O fie! My kisses are not my own; you have committed violence; but I'll carry 'em to the right owner. (*Tom kisses her*) Come, see me down stairs (*to* TOM) and leave the lover to think of his last game for the prize.

Exeunt TOM *and* PHILLIS

MYRTLE. I think I will instantly attempt this wild expedient. The extravagance of it will make me less suspected and it will give me opportunity to assert my own right to Lucinda, without whom I cannot live. But I am so mortified at this conduct of mine towards poor Bevil. He must think meanly of me. I know not how to reassume myself and be in spirit enough for such an adventure as this. Yet I must attempt it if it be only to be near Lucinda under her perplexities; and sure
The next delight to transport, with the fair,
Is to relieve her in her hours of care. *Exit*

ACT V

SCENE I. SEALAND'S *House*

Enter PHILLIS *with lights, before* MYRTLE *disguised like old* SIR GEOFFRY, *supported* [1] *by* MRS. SEALAND, LUCINDA, *and* CIMBERTON

MRS. SEALAND. Now I have seen you thus far, Sir Geoffry, will you excuse me a moment while I give my necessary orders for your accommodation? *Exit*

MYRTLE. I have not seen you, Cousin Cimberton, since you were ten years old; and as it is incumbent on you to keep up our name and family, I shall, upon very reasonable terms, join with you in a settlement to that purpose. Though I must tell you, cousin, this is the first merchant that has married into our house.

LUCINDA. (*Aside*) Deuce on 'em! Am I a merchant because my father is?

MYRTLE. But is he directly a trader at this time?

CIMBERTON. There's no hiding the disgrace, sir; he trades to all parts of the world.

MYRTLE. We never had one of our family before who descended from persons that did anything.

CIMBERTON. Sir, since it is a girl that they have, I am, for the honor of the family, willing to take it in again and to sink her into our name and no harm done.

MYRTLE. 'Tis prudently and generously resolved. Is this the young thing?

CIMBERTON. Yes, sir.

PHILLIS. Good madam, don't be out of humor, but let them run to the utmost of their extravagance. Hear them out.

[1] Assisted.

MYRTLE. Can't I see her nearer? My eyes are but weak.

PHILLIS. Beside, I am sure the uncle has something worth your notice. I'll take care to get off the young one and leave you to observe what may be wrought out of the old one for your good. *Exit*

CIMBERTON. Madam, this old gentleman, your great uncle, desires to be introduced to you and to see you nearer. Approach, sir!

MYRTLE. By your leave, young lady— (*Puts on spectacles*) Cousin Cimberton, she has exactly that sort of neck and bosom for which my sister Gertrude was so much admired in the year sixty one, before the French dresses first discovered anything in women below the chin.

LUCINDA. (*Aside*) What a very odd situation am I in? Though I cannot but be diverted at the extravagance of their humors equally suitable to their age. Chin, quotha! I don't believe my passionate lover there knows whether I have one or not. Ha! Ha!

MYRTLE. Madam, I would not willingly offend, but I have a better glass—
(*Pulls out a large one*)

Enter PHILLIS *to* CIMBERTON

PHILLIS. Sir, my lady desires to show the apartment to you that she intends for Geoffry.

CIMBERTON. Well, sir, by that time you have sufficiently gazed and sunned yourself in the beauties of my spouse there, I will wait on you again.

[*Exeunt*] CIMBERTON *and* PHILLIS

MYRTLE. Were it not, madam, that I might be troublesome, there is something of importance, though we are alone, which I would say more safe from being heard.

LUCINDA. There is something in this old fellow, methinks, that raises my curiosity.

MYRTLE. To be free, madam, I as heartily condemn this kinsman of mine as you do and am sorry to see so much beauty and merit devoted by your parents to so insensible a possessor.

LUCINDA. Surprising! I hope then, sir, you will not contribute to the wrong you are so generous as to pity, whatever may be the interest of your family.

MYRTLE. This hand of mine shall never be employed to sign anything against your good and happiness.

LUCINDA. I am sorry, sir, it is not in my

power to make you proper acknowledgments; but there is a gentleman in the world whose gratitude will, I am sure, be worthy of the favor.

MYRTLE. All the thanks I desire, madam, are in your power to give.

LUCINDA. Name them and command them.

MYRTLE. Only, madam, that the first time you are alone with your lover you will with open arms receive him.

LUCINDA. As willingly as his heart could wish it.

MYRTLE. Thus then he claims your promise! O Lucinda!

LUCINDA. O! A cheat! a cheat! a cheat!

MYRTLE. Hush! 'Tis I, 'tis I, your lover, Myrtle himself, madam.

LUCINDA. O bless me, what a rashness and folly to surprise me so! But hush—My mother—

Enter MRS. SEALAND, CIMBERTON, *and* PHILLIS

MRS. SEALAND. How now! What's the matter?

LUCINDA. O madam, as soon as you left the room, my uncle fell into a sudden fit, and— and—so I cried out for help to support him and conduct him to his chamber.

MRS. SEALAND. That was kindly done! Alas, sir, how do you find yourself?

MYRTLE. Never was so taken in so odd a way in my life. Pray lead me. Oh, I was talking here—pray carry me—to my cousin Cimberton's young lady—

MRS. SEALAND. (*Aside*) My Cousin Cimberton's young lady! How zealous he is even in his extremity for the match! A right Cimberton!

(CIMBERTON *and* LUCINDA *lead him as one in pain, &c.*)

CIMBERTON. Pox, Uncle! You will pull my ear off.

LUCINDA. Pray, uncle! You will squeeze me to death.

MRS. SEALAND. No matter, no matter! He knows not what he does. Come, sir, shall I help you out?

MYRTLE. By no means; I'll trouble nobody but my young cousins here.

(*They lead him off*)

PHILLIS. But pray, madam, does your ladyship intend that Mr. Cimberton shall really marry my young mistress at last? I don't think he likes her.

MRS. SEALAND. That's not material! Men of his speculation are above desires, but be it as it may. Now I have given old Sir Geoffry the trouble of coming up to sign and seal with what countenance can I be off?

PHILLIS. As well as with twenty others, madam. It is the glory and honor of a great fortune to live in continual treaties and still to break off. It looks great, madam.

MRS. SEALAND. True, Phillis. Yet to return our blood again into the Cimberton's is an honor not to be rejected. But were you not saying that Sir John Bevil's creature, Humphrey, has been with Mr. Sealand?

PHILLIS. Yes, madam. I overheard them agree that Mr. Sealand should go himself and visit this unknown lady that Mr. Bevil is so great with; and if he found nothing there to fright him, that Mr. Bevil should still marry my young mistress.

MRS. SEALAND. How! Nay, then, he shall find she is my daughter as well as his. I'll follow him this instant and take the whole family along with me. The disputed power of disposing of my own daughter shall be at an end this very night. I'll live no longer in anxiety for a little hussy that hurts my appearance wherever I carry [1] her and for whose sake I seem to be at all regarded and that in the best of my days.

PHILLIS. Indeed, madam, if she were married, your ladyship might very well be taken for Mr. Sealand's daughter.

MRS. SEALAND. Nay, when the chit has not been with me, I have heard the men say as much. I'll no longer cut off the greatest pleasure of a woman's life, the shining in assemblies, by her forward anticipation of the respect that's due to her superior. She shall down to Cimberton Hall. She shall, she shall!

PHILLIS. I hope, madam, I shall stay with your ladyship.

MRS. SEALAND. Thou shalt, Phillis, and I'll place thee then more about me. But order chairs immediately. I'll be gone this minute.

Exeunt

SCENE [II.] *Charing Cross*

Enter MR. SEALAND *and* HUMPHREY

MR. SEALAND. I am very glad, Mr. Humphrey, that you agree with me that it is for

[1] In the sense of conduct.

our common good I should look into this matter.

HUMPHREY. I am indeed of that opinion, for there is no artifice, nothing concealed, in our family which ought in justice to be known. I need not desire you, sir, to treat the lady with care and respect.

MR. SEALAND. Master Humphrey, I shall not be rude, though I design to be a little abrupt and come into the matter at once to see how she will bear upon a surprise.

HUMPHREY. That's the door, sir. I wish you success. (*While* HUMPHREY *speaks,* SEALAND *consults his table-book*)[1] I am less concerned what happens there because I hear Mr. Myrtle is well lodged as old Sir Geoffry; so I am willing to let this gentleman employ himself here to give them time at home, for I am sure 'tis necessary for the quiet of our family Lucinda were well disposed of out of it, since Mr. Bevil's inclination is so much otherwise engaged. *Exit*

MR. SEALAND. I think this is the door. (*Knocks*) I'll carry this matter with an air of authority to enquire though I make an errand to begin discourse. (*Knocks again, and enter a foot-boy*) So, young man! Is your lady within?

BOY. Alack, sir, I am but a country boy. I don't know whether she is or noa; but an you'll stay a bit, I'll goa and ask the gentle-woman that's with her.

MR. SEALAND. Why, sirrah, though you are a country boy, you can see, can't you? You know whether she is at home when you see her, don't you?

BOY. Nay, nay, I'm not such a country lad neither, master, to think she's at home because I see her. I have been in town but a month and I lost one place already for believing my own eyes.

MR. SEALAND. Why, sirrah, have you learnt to lie already?

BOY. Ah, master, things that are lies in the country are not lies at London. I begin to know my business a little better than so. But an you please to walk in, I'll call a gentle-woman to you that can tell you for certain. She can make bold to ask my lady herself.

MR. SEALAND. O, then, she is within, I find, though you dare not say so.

BOY. Nay, nay! That's neither here nor there. What matter whether she is within or no, if she has not a mind to see anybody.

[1] Memorandum book.

MR. SEALAND. I can't tell, sirrah, whether you are arch or simple, but however, get me a direct answer, and here's a shilling for you.

BOY. Will you please to walk in? I'll see what I can do for you.

MR. SEALAND. I see you will be fit for your business in time, child. But I expect to meet with nothing but extraordinaries in such a house.

BOY. Such a house! Sir, you han't seen it yet. Pray walk in.

MR. SEALAND. Sir, I'll wait upon you.

Exeunt

SCENE [III]. INDIANA'S *House*

Enter ISABELLA

ISABELLA. What anxiety do I feel for this poor creature! What will be the end of her? Such a languishing unreserved passion for a man that at last must certainly leave or ruin her! And perhaps both! Then the aggravation of the distress is that she does not believe he will,—not but I must own if they are both what they would seem they are made for one another as much as Adam and Eve were, for there is no other of their kind but themselves. (*Enter* BOY) So, Daniel! What news with you?

BOY. Madam, there's a gentleman below would speak with my lady.

ISABELLA. Sirrah, don't you know Mr. Bevil yet?

BOY. Madam, 'tis not the gentleman who comes every day and asks for you and won't go in till he knows whether you are with her or no.

ISABELLA. Ha! That's a particular I did not know before. Well, be it who it will, let him come up to me.

Exit BOY, *and re-enters with* MR. SEALAND. ISABELLA *looks amazed*

MR. SEALAND. Madam, I can't blame your being a little surprised to see a perfect stranger make a visit and—

ISABELLA. I am indeed surprised!—[*Aside*] I see he does not know me.

MR. SEALAND. You are very prettily lodged here, madam; in troth, you seem to have everything in plenty. (*Aside and looking about*) A thousand a year, I warrant you, upon this pretty nest of rooms and the dainty one within them.

ISABELLA. (*Apart*) Twenty years, it seems, have less effect in the alteration of a man of thirty than a girl of fourteen. He's almost still the same; but, alas, I find by other men as well as himself I am not what I was. As soon as he spoke I was convinced 'twas he. How shall I contain my surprise and satisfaction? He must not know me yet.

Mr. Sealand. Madam, I hope I don't give you any disturbance, but there's a young lady here with whom I have a particular business to discourse, and I hope she will admit me to that favor.

Isabella. Why, sir, have you had any notice concerning her? I wonder who could give it you.

Mr. Sealand. That, madam, is fit only to be communicated to herself.

Isabella. Well, sir, you shall see her.— [*Aside*] I find he knows nothing as yet, nor shall he from me. I am resolved I will observe this interlude, this sport of nature and of fortune.—You shall see her presently, sir, for now I am as a mother and will trust her with you. *Exit*

Mr. Sealand. As a mother! Right. That's the old phrase for one of those commode [1] ladies, who lend out beauty for hire to young gentlemen that have pressing occasions. But here comes the precious lady herself. In truth, a very fine sightly woman—

Enter Indiana

Indiana. I am told, sir, you have some affair that requires your speaking with me.

Mr. Sealand. Yes, madam. There came into my hands a bill drawn by Mr. Bevil, which is payable tomorrow; and he in the intercourse of business sent it to me, who have cash of his and desired me to send a servant with it; but I have made bold to bring you the money myself.

Indiana. Sir! Was that necessary?

Mr. Sealand. No, madam; but, to be free with you, the fame of your beauty and the regard which Mr. Bevil is a little too well known to have for you, excited my curiosity.

Indiana. Too well known to have for me! Your sober appearance, sir, which my friend described, made me expect no rudeness, or absurdity at least.—Who's there? Sir, if you pay the money to a servant 'twill be as well.

Mr. Sealand. Pray, madam, be not offended. I came hither on an innocent, nay a virtuous, design; and if you will have patience to hear me it may be as useful to you, as you are in friendship with Mr. Bevil, as to my only daughter, whom I was this day disposing of.

Indiana. You make me hope, sir, I have mistaken you. I am composed again. Be free, say on—(*Aside*) what I am afraid to hear.

Mr. Sealand. I feared, indeed, an unwarranted passion here, but I did not think it was in abuse of so worthy an object, so accomplished a lady as your sense and mine bespeak. But the youth of our age care not what merit and virtue they bring to shame so they gratify.—

Indiana. Sir! You are going into very great errors; but as you are pleased to say you see something in me that has changed at least the color of your suspicions, so has your appearance altered mine; and made me earnestly attentive to what has any way concerned you to enquire into my affairs and character.

Mr. Sealand. [*Aside*] How sensibly, with what an air she talks!

Indiana. Good sir, be seated and tell me tenderly. Keep all your suspicions concerning me alive, that you may in a proper and prepared way acquaint me why the care of your daughter obliges a person of your seeming worth and fortune to be thus inquisitive about a wretched, helpless, friendless—(*weeping*) But I beg your pardon. Though I am an orphan, your child is not; and your concern for her, it seems, has brought you hither. I'll be composed. Pray go on, sir.

Mr. Sealand. How could Mr. Bevil be such a monster to injure such a woman?

Indiana. Sir, you wrong him. He has not injured me. My support is from his bounty.

Mr. Sealand. Bounty! When gluttons give high prices for delicates,[2] they are prodigious bountiful!

Indiana. Still, still you will persist in that error.—But my own fears tell me all.—You are the gentleman, I suppose, for whose happy daughter he is designed a husband by his good father; and he has perhaps consented to the overture. He was here this morning dressed beyond his usual plainness, nay most sumptuously, and he is to be perhaps, this night a bridegroom.

Mr. Sealand. I own he was intended such. But, madam, on your account, I have deter-

[1] Accommodating.
[2] I.e., delicacies.

mined to defer my daughter's marriage till I am satisfied from your own mouth of what nature are the obligations you are under to him.

INDIANA. His actions, sir, his eyes have only made me think he designed to make me the partner of his heart. The goodness and gentleness of his demeanor made me misinterpret all. 'Twas my own hope, my own passion, that deluded me. He never made one amorous advance to me. His large heart and bestowing hand have only helped the miserable. Nor know I why, but from his mere delight in virtue that I have been his care, the object on which to indulge and please himself with pouring favors.

MR. SEALAND. Madam, I know not why it is, but I, as well as you, am, methinks, afraid of entering into the matter I came about; but 'tis the same thing as if we had talked never so distinctly. He ne'er shall have a daughter of mine.

INDIANA. If you say this from what you think of me, you wrong yourself and him. Let not me, miserable though I may be, do injury to my benefactor. No, sir, my treatment ought rather to reconcile you to his virtues. If to bestow without a prospect of return, if to delight in supporting what might perhaps be thought an object of desire with no other view than to be her guard against those who would not be so disinterested; if these actions, sir, can in a careful parent's eye commend him to a daughter, give yours, sir, give her to my honest, generous Bevil. What have I to do but sigh and weep, to rave, run wild, a lunatic in chains or hid in darkness, mutter in distracted starts and broken accents my strange, strange story!

MR. SEALAND. Take comfort, madam.

INDIANA. All my comfort must be to expostulate in madness, to relieve with frenzy my despair and shrieking to demand of fate why—why was I born to such variety of sorrows!

MR. SEALAND. If I have been the least occasion—

INDIANA. No! 'Twas heaven's high will, I should be such. To be plundered in my cradle! Tossed on the seas and even there an infant captive! To lose my mother, hear but of my father! To be adopted, lose my adopter; then plunged again in worse calamities!

MR. SEALAND. An infant captive!

INDIANA. Yet then, to find the most charming of mankind once more to set me free from what I thought the last distress, to load me with his services, his bounties, and his favors, to support my very life in a way that stole at the same time my soul itself from me.

MR. SEALAND. And has young Bevil been this worthy man?

INDIANA. Yet then again, this very man to take another! Without leaving me the right, the pretense of easing my fond heart with tears! For, oh, I can't reproach him, though the same hand that raised me to this height, now throws me down the precipice.

MR. SEALAND. Dear lady! O yet one moment's patience. My heart grows full with your affliction. But yet there's something in your story that—

INDIANA. My portion here is bitterness and sorrow.

MR. SEALAND. Do not think so. Pray answer me. Does Bevil know your name and family?

INDIANA. Alas, too well! O, could I be any other thing than what I am! I'll tear away all traces of my former self, my little ornaments, the remains of my first state, the hints of what I ought to have been—

(*In her disorder she throws away a bracelet, which* SEALAND *takes up and looks earnestly on it*)

MR. SEALAND. Ha! What's this? My eyes are not deceived. It is, it is the same! The very bracelet which I bequeathed my wife at our last mournful parting.

INDIANA. What said you, sir! Your wife! Whither does my fancy carry me? What means this unfelt motion at my heart? And yet again my fortune but deludes me, for if I err not, sir, your name is Sealand but my lost father's name was—

MR. SEALAND. Danvers, was it not?

INDIANA. What new amazement! That is indeed my family.

MR. SEALAND. Know then, when my misfortunes drove me to the Indies, for reasons too tedious now to mention, I changed my name of Danvers into Sealand.

Enter ISABELLA

ISABELLA. If yet there wants an explanation of your wonder, examine well this face. Yours, sir, I well remember. Gaze on and read in me your sister Isabella!

Mr. Sealand. My sister!

Isabella. But here's a claim more tender yet,—your Indiana, sir, your long lost daughter.

Mr. Sealand. O my child, my child!

Indiana. All-gracious heaven! Is it possible? Do I embrace my father!

Mr. Sealand. And do I hold thee—These passions are too strong for utterance. Rise, rise, my child, and give my tears their way. O my sister! *(Embracing her)*

Isabella. Now, dearest niece, my groundless fears, my painful cares no more shall vex thee. If I have wronged thy noble lover with too hard suspicions, my just concern for thee I hope will plead my pardon.

Mr. Sealand. O, make him then the full amends and be yourself the messenger of joy. Fly this instant! Tell him all these wondrous turns of providence in his favor. Tell him I have now a daughter to bestow which he no longer will decline, that this day he still shall be a bridegroom; nor shall a fortune, the merit which his father seeks, be wanting. Tell him the reward of all his virtues waits on his acceptance. *(Exit* Isabella*)* My dearest Indiana! *(Turns and embraces her)*

Indiana. Have I then at last a father's sanction on my love! His bounteous hand to give and make my heart a present worthy of Bevil's generosity.

Mr. Sealand. O my child, how are our sorrows past o'erpaid by such a meeting! Though I have lost so many years of soft paternal dalliance with thee, yet, in one day, to find thee thus and thus bestow thee in such perfect happiness is ample, ample reparation! And yet again the merit of thy lover!

Indiana. Oh, had I spirit left to tell you of his actions! How strongly filial duty has suppressed his love, and how concealment still has doubled all his obligations! The pride, the joy of this alliance, sir, would warm your heart as he has conquered mine.

Mr. Sealand. How laudable is love when born of virtue! I burn to embrace him—

Indiana. See, sir, my aunt already has succeeded and brought him to your wishes.

Enter Isabella *with* Sir John Bevil, Bevil, Junior, Mrs. Sealand, Cimberton, Myrtle, *and* Lucinda

Sir John. *(Entering)* Where, where's this scene of wonder?—Mr. Sealand, I congratulate, on this occasion, our mutual happiness. Your good sister, sir, has with the story of your daughter's fortune filled us with surprise and joy! Now all exceptions are removed; my son has now avowed his love and turned all former jealousies and doubts to approbation; and, I am told, your goodness has consented to reward him.

Mr. Sealand. If, sir, a fortune equal to his father's hopes can make this object worthy his acceptance.

Bevil. I hear your mention, sir, of fortune with pleasure only as it may prove the means to reconcile the best of fathers to my love. Let him be provident, but let me be happy! My ever-destined, my acknowledged wife!
(Embracing Indiana*)*

Indiana. Wife! O my ever loved! My lord, my master!

Sir John. I congratulate myself as well as you that I had a son who could under such disadvantages discover your great merit.

Mr. Sealand. O, Sir John, how vain, how weak is human prudence! What care, what foresight, what imagination could contrive such blest events to make our children happy as Providence in one short hour has laid before us!

Cimberton. *(To* Mrs. Sealand*)* I am afraid, madam, Mr. Sealand is a little too busy for our affair. If you please, we'll take another opportunity.

Mrs. Sealand. Let us have patience, sir.

Cimberton. But we make Sir Geoffry wait, madam.

Myrtle. O sir, I am not in haste.

(During this, Bevil *presents* Lucinda *to* Indiana*)*

Mr. Sealand. But here, here's our general benefactor! Excellent young man that could be at once a lover to her beauty and a parent to her virtue!

Bevil. If you think that an obligation, sir, give me leave to overpay myself in the only instance that can now add to my felicity by begging you to bestow this lady on Mr. Myrtle.

Mr. Sealand. She is his without reserve. I beg he may be sent for. Mr. Cimberton, notwithstanding you never had my consent, yet there is since I last saw you another objection to your marriage with my daughter.

Cimberton. I hope, sir, your lady has concealed nothing from me?

MR. SEALAND. Troth, sir, nothing but what was concealed from myself, another daughter who has an undoubted title to half my estate.

CIMBERTON. How, Mr. Sealand! Why then, if half Mrs. Lucinda's fortune is gone, you 5 can't say that any of my estate is settled upon her. I was in treaty for the whole, but if that is not to be come at, to be sure there can be no bargain. Sir, I have nothing to do but to take my leave of your good lady, my cousin, 10 and beg pardon for the trouble I have given this old gentleman.

MYRTLE. That you have, Mr. Cimberton, with all my heart. (*Discovers himself*)

OMNES. Mr. Myrtle! 15

MYRTLE. And I beg pardon of the whole company that I assumed the person of Sir Geoffry only to be present at the danger of this lady's being disposed of and in her utmost exigence to assert my right to her, which if her 20 parents will ratify, as they once favored my pretensions, no abatement of fortune shall lessen her value to me.

LUCINDA. Generous man!

MR. SEALAND. If, sir, you can overlook the 25 injury of being in treaty with one who as meanly left her as you have generously asserted your right in her, she is yours.

LUCINDA. Mr. Myrtle, though you have ever had my heart, yet now I find I love you 30 more because I bring you less.

MYRTLE. We have much more than we want, and I am glad any event has contributed to the discovery of our real inclinations to each other. 35

MRS. SEALAND. (*Aside*) Well! However, I'm glad the girl's disposed of any way.

BEVIL. Myrtle, no longer rivals now but brothers!

MYRTLE. Dear Bevil, you are born to 40 triumph over me! But now our competition ceases. I rejoice in the preëminence of your virtue and your alliance adds charms to Lucinda.

SIR JOHN. Now ladies and gentlemen, you 45 have set the world a fair example. Your happiness is owing to your constancy and merit, and the several difficulties you have struggled with evidently show,

Whate'er the generous mind itself denies,
The secret care of Providence supplies.
Exeunt

EPILOGUE

BY MR. WELSTED

Intended to be spoken by INDIANA

Our author, whom entreaties cannot move,
Spite of the dear coquetry that you love,
Swears he'll not frustrate (so he plainly means)
By a loose epilogue, his decent scenes.
Is it not, sirs, hard fate I meet to-day 5
To keep me rigid [1] still beyond the play?
And yet I'm saved a world of pains that way.
I now can look, I now can move at ease,
Nor need I torture these poor limbs to please,
Nor with the hand or foot attempt surprise,
Nor wrest my features, nor fatigue my eyes.
Bless me! What freakish gambols have I played! 12
What motions tried and wanton looks betrayed,
Out of pure kindness all to overrule
The threatened hiss, and screen some scribbling fool!
With more respect I'm entertained tonight.
Our author thinks I can with ease delight. 17
My artless looks while modest graces arm,
He says I need but to appear and charm.
A wife so formed, by these examples bred,
Pours joy and gladness round the marriage bed.
Soft source of comfort, kind relief from care,
And 'tis her best perfection to be fair.
The nymph with Indiana's worth who vies
A nation will behold with Bevil's eyes. 25

[1] Strictly decorous.

THE BEGGAR'S OPERA
By John Gay

Nos hæc novimus esse nihil.—Mart.[1]

John Gay, youngest son of William Gay, was born in 1685 and baptized in Barnstaple, Devonshire, Old Church on September 16. His parents died while he was a small boy, and he lived with an uncle, Thomas Gay. After a short apprenticeship to a mercer in London, Gay gave up trade and decided to become a poet. His early attempts proving not particularly successful, he sought the patronage of the great, and became successively secretary to Aaron Hill, "domestic steward" to the Duchess of Monmouth, and secretary to Lord Clarendon, Tory envoy extraordinary to Hanover in 1714. These employments were short-lived, however, and with the accession of the Whigs to power early in the summer of 1714, Gay was again thrown upon his own resources. He had already published several of his poems, among them "Rural Sports" (1713) and "The Shepherd's Week" (1714), and produced two unsuccessful plays, *The Wife of Bath* (D.L., May 15, 1713) and *The What D'Ye Call It* (D.L., Feb. 23, 1715). In 1716 he published *Trivia, or The Art of Walking the Streets of London* and wrote, in collaboration with Pope and Arbuthnot, the scurrilous *Three Hours After Marriage* (D.L., Jan. 16, 1717). Charming and improvident, he spent the rest of his life living, for the most part, on his friends, who evinced astonishing devotion to him, and attempting to secure government posts. With a sinecure in view he wrote the *Fables*, which appeared in 1727, dedicated to Prince William, Duke of Cumberland, aged six, for whose amusement they were "invented." The post offered to Gay, however, on the death of George I, that of Gentleman Usher to the Princess Louisa, two years old, was not what he expected and was declined. Gay's first period of prosperity had been brought to an abrupt close by the bursting of the South Sea Bubble in 1720. Faithful friends, however, came to his assistance; and the Duke and Duchess of Queensberry managed his affairs thereafter, saving for him the greater portion of the small fortune which came to him as the result of the success of *The Beggar's Opera* (1728) and *Polly* (forbidden by the Lord Chamberlain to be performed but published by subscription, 1729). With the Queensberrys Gay spent his last years petted and cared for in every way. He was the intimate friend of Pope, Arbuthnot and Swift, of Mrs. Howard, later Lady Suffolk, and many other persons of prominence. He died Dec. 4, 1732, and was buried in Westminster Abbey, where an elaborate monument was erected to his memory by the Queensberrys, bearing the affectionate epitaph by Pope.

References: *Poems of John Gay.* (Muses Library) 1893. With introduction by John Underwood. Melville, Lewis, *Life and Letters of John Gay.* 1921. Schultz, W. E., *Gay's Beggar's Opera.* 1923.

Gay's Dramatic Works

The Mohocks. A Tragi-Comical Farce. 8vo, 1712. [Never acted?]
The Wife of Bath (comedy) (D.L., May 15, 1713), 1713.
The What D'Ye Call It, A Tragi-Comi-Pastoral Farce (D.L., Feb. 23, 1715), 1715.
Three Hours After Marriage (comedy; with Pope and Arbuthnot) (D.L., Jan. 16, 1717), 1717.
Dione (pastoral), 4to, 1720. [Apparently never acted.]
The Captives (tragedy) (D.L., Jan. 15, 1724), 1724.
The Beggar's Opera (ballad opera) (L.I.F., Jan. 29, 1728), 1728.
Polly: An Opera. Being the Second Part of The Beggar's Opera. 4to, 1729. [First acted 1777 (?) altered by Colman (?).]
Acis and Galatea: An English Pastoral Opera. (L.I.F., March 26, 1731), 1732. [Music by Händel.]
Achilles (ballad opera) (C.G., Feb. 10, 1733), 1733.

---

[1] We know these things to be nothing (Martial, XIII, ii, 8).

The Distress'd Wife (comedy) (C.G., March 5, 1734), 1743.
The Rehearsal at Goatham. 8vo, 1754.

Gay's pastorals, burlesquing those of Ambrose Philips, having had some vogue, Dean Swift wrote to Mr. Pope in 1716, "What think you of a Newgate pastoral, among the whores and thieves there?" Though the suggestion was probably passed on to "our friend Gay," some ten years passed before the "Newgate pastoral" was begun. By the end of 1727, however, the play was nearly finished, the indolent Gay having been spurred on by the advice and assistance of Pope and the Queensberrys at home and the letters of Swift from Ireland. The completed manuscript was shown to Mr. Congreve, who said, "It would either take greatly or be damned confoundedly." Cibber, at Drury Lane, fearing the latter alternative, refused to produce it; so the new piece was carried to Rich at Lincoln's Inn Fields. There was considerable difference of opinion as to the merit of this novel entertainment. Fearing his reputation, Quin, the old actor, refused the part of Macheath, which was given to Walker, to the greater glory of all concerned.

On the evening of January 29, 1728, the play was ready, equipped with an orchestral accompaniment and overture by Dr. Pepusch. The world of fashion packed the house. Among those present were Pope, the Queensberrys, and others of Gay's friends; the dukes of Argyll and Bolton were there, as was also Sir Robert Walpole, loudly applauding the hits at himself and giving Walker a purse to show that he was untouched by Gay's thrusts. For a while the fate of the play was undecided; but it was said that when Mrs. Fenton as Polly sang the song "O ponder well," Pope and his companions "were very much encouraged by hearing the Duke of Argyll, who sat in the next box to us, say: 'It will do—it must do!—I see it in the eyes of them!'" It did do. It ran for sixty-two nights, making a record for its time, and it was by all odds, then and thereafter, the most popular play of the eighteenth century. Immediately after the early performances The Beggar's Opera became the fad of all London. Its songs were on every tongue, its characters were depicted on fans, screens, and playing cards, and its two leading interpreters, Walker and Mrs. Fenton, were sought after and fêted by the fashionable world for the rest of the season.

The influence of The Beggar's Opera was wide and powerful. Though it is not the first comic opera in English, it is by far the earliest truly successful one; and it is the first ballad opera; that is, "an opera which makes use mainly of old ballad airs, instead of specially composed music." It also introduced to the English stage a type which persisted well into the nineteenth century. Dr. Johnson says of Gay, "He had not in any degree the *mens divinior*, the dignity of genius. Much, however, must be allowed to the author of a new species of composition, though it be not of the highest kind." This new species of composition retained its popularity until it was displaced by the type of the Gilbert and Sullivan operetta.

The satire in The Beggar's Opera, which undoubtedly added spice to it for its first audiences, is found in four forms, social, political, literary, and musical. To begin with, Gay is satirizing Italian opera, which had come near to driving all other forms of theatrical entertainment from the stage and had rendered them quite unfashionable. Gay's attack upon Italian opera is found in ridicule of the affectation and ornamentation of the music and its usual libretto, chiefly seen in the use of recitative and the elaborate distribution of lines among the characters in several of the songs and in the introduction and final scene between the Player and the Beggar. The Beggar apologizes for not making his opera "throughout unnatural, like those in vogue." Gay's literary burlesque is general rather than specific or detailed like that of Fielding's *Tom Thumb*, which came a few years later. Gay burlesques three types of literature popular at the time: (1) heroic drama and sentimental comedy, (2) "affectedly tender songs of the period," and (3) contemporary romance. This burlesque overlaps in many cases, the classes being not always themselves clearly distinguishable.

The social satire of The Beggar's Opera is comprehensive, including in its general attack upon corruption and social degeneracy specific allusion to fashionable vices such as the keeping of mistresses, ideas of marriage and widowhood, the worship of power and money, the propensity for gambling at card games, and the custom of excessive drinking, particularly of gin, newly introduced. But, excepting possibly the burlesque of Italian opera, the political satire probably appealed most to Gay's contemporaries. Even here one finds less specific satire than one expects. In its own day the play was considered by some a satire of government in general rather than, as others believed, a direct attack upon the administration of Walpole. The opera is filled with scattered references to the court and the government, and it contains an elaborate picture of organized dishonesty in the extended metaphor of the gang. The allusions to Walpole, constituting a revolving satire in at least three characters in the play, Robin of Bagshot, Peachum, and Macheath, are manifested in three ways: (1) by the use of proper names; (2) by the relations of Peachum and Lockit; and (3) by Macheath's relations to Polly and Lucy.

Before the production of *The Beggar's Opera*, Gay was already known as a writer of songs, and the opera enhanced his reputation. The play contains sixty-nine songs, all of them subjective, "in character," and definitely contributing to the action of the play. The ballad originals used by Gay are found chiefly in two collections, Thomas D'Urfey's *Wit and Mirth; or, Pills to Purge Melancholy* (1699 and later editions) and *The Dancing Master* by J. Playford, H. Playford, or Pearson (1652 and later editions). As many of the original songs are smutty in varying degrees, a knowledge of the original words doubtless added to the mirth of early audiences.

THE BEGGAR'S OPERA

DRAMATIS PERSONÆ

Men

Peachum		Mr. Hippisley
Lockit		Mr. Hall
Macheath		Mr. Walker
Filch		Mr. Clark
Jeremy Twitcher	⎫	Mr. H. Bullock
Crook-Fingered Jack	⎪	Mr. Houghton
Wat Dreary	⎪	Mr. Smith
Robin of Bagshot	⎬ *Macheath's gang*	Mr. Lacy
Nimming[1] Ned	⎪	Mr. Pit
Harry Padington	⎪	Mr. Eaton
Matt of the Mint	⎪	Mr. Spiller
Ben Budge	⎭	Mr. Morgan
Beggar		Mr. Chapman
Player		Mr. Milward

Women

Mrs. Peachum		Mrs. Martin
Polly Peachum		Mrs. Fenton
Lucy Lockit		Mrs. Egleton
Diana Trapes		Mrs. Martin
Mrs. Coaxer	⎫	Mrs. Holiday
Dolly Trull	⎪	Mrs. Lacy
Mrs. Vixen	⎪	Mrs. Rice
Betty Doxy	⎬ *Women of the town*	Mrs. Rogers
Jenny Diver	⎪	Mrs. Clarke
Mrs. Slammekin	⎪	Mrs. Morgan
Suky Tawdry	⎪	Mrs. Palin
Molly Brazen	⎭	Mrs. Sallee

Constables, Drawers, Turnkey, etc.

INTRODUCTION

Beggar, Player

Beggar. If poverty be a title to poetry, I am sure nobody can dispute mine. I own myself of the company of beggars, and I make one at their weekly festivals at St. Giles's.[2] I have a small yearly salary for my catches and am welcome to a dinner there whenever I please, which is more than most poets can say.

Player. As we live by the muses, 'tis but (5) gratitude in us to encourage poetical merit wherever we find it. The muses, contrary to all other ladies, pay no distinction to dress, and never partially mistake the pertness of embroidery for wit, nor the modesty of want for dulness. Be the author who he will, we (10) push his play as far as it will go. So (though you are in want) I wish you success heartily.

Beggar. This piece, I own, was originally writ for the celebrating the marriage of James Chanter and Moll Lay, two most excellent (15) ballad-singers. I have introduced the similes

---

[1] The obsolete verb *to nim* means to steal, filch, or pilfer.

[2] St. Giles's: the parish of St. Giles in Holborn, a squalid district, in which in 1665 the Great Plague started. Condemned criminals on their way to be hanged at Tyburn were given their last cup of ale from the steps of St.-Giles-in-the-Fields, in High Street. It was also a favorite resort of beggars off duty.

PEACHUM. But make haste to Newgate,[1] boy, and let my friends know what I intend; for I love to make them easy one way or other.

FILCH. When a gentleman is long kept in suspense, penitence may break his spirit ever after. Besides, certainty gives a man a good air upon his trial, and makes him risk another without fear or scruple. But I'll away, for 'tis a pleasure to be the messenger of comfort to friends in affliction. *Exit*

Scene III

Peachum

PEACHUM. But 'tis now high time to look about me for a decent execution against next sessions. I hate a lazy rogue, by whom one can get nothing till he is hanged. A register of the gang: (*Reading*) "Crook-fingered Jack. A year and a half in the service." Let me see how much the stock owes to his industry; one, two, three, four, five gold watches, and seven silver ones.—A mighty clean-handed fellow! —Sixteen snuff-boxes, five of them of true gold. Six dozen of handkerchiefs, four silver-hilted swords, half a dozen of shirts, three tie-periwigs, and a piece of broadcloth.—Considering these are only the fruits of his leisure hours, I don't know a prettier fellow, for no man alive hath a more engaging presence of mind upon the road. "Wat Dreary, alias Brown Will"—an irregular dog, who hath an underhand way of disposing of his goods. I'll try him only for a sessions or two longer upon his good behavior. "Harry Padington"—a poor petty-larceny rascal, without the least genius; that fellow, though he were to live these six months, will never come to the gallows with any credit. "Slippery Sam"—he goes off the next sessions, for the villain hath the impudence to have views of following his trade as a tailor, which he calls an honest employment. "Matt of the Mint"—listed not above a month ago, a promising sturdy fellow, and diligent in his way: somewhat too bold and hasty, and may raise good contributions on the public, if he does not cut himself short by murder. "Tom Tipple"—a guzzling, soaking sot, who is always too drunk to stand himself, or to make others stand. A cart is absolutely necessary for him. "Robin of Bagshot, alias Gorgon, alias Bob Bluff, alias Carbuncle, alias Bob Booty!—"[2]

Scene IV

Peachum, Mrs. Peachum

MRS. PEACHUM. What of Bob Booty, husband? I hope nothing bad hath betided him. You know, my dear, he's a favorite customer of mine. 'Twas he made me a present of this ring.

PEACHUM. I have set his name down in the black list, that's all, my dear; he spends his life among women, and as soon as his money is gone, one or other of the ladies will hang him for the reward, and there's forty pound lost to us forever.

MRS. PEACHUM. You know, my dear, I never meddle in matters of death; I always leave those affairs to you. Women indeed are bitter bad judges in these cases, for they are so partial to the brave that they think every man handsome who is going to the camp or the gallows.

AIR III—*Cold and raw, etc.*

If any wench Venus's girdle wear,
  Though she be never so ugly;
Lilies and roses will quickly appear,
  And her face look wond'rous smugly.
Beneath the left ear so fit but a cord,
  (A rope so charming a zone is!)
The youth in his cart hath the air of a lord,
  And we cry, There dies an Adonis!

But really, husband, you should not be too hard-hearted, for you never had a finer, braver set of men than at present. We have not had a murder among them all, these seven months. And truly, my dear, that is a great blessing.

PEACHUM. What a dickens is the woman always a-whimp'ring about murder for? No gentleman is ever looked upon the worse for killing a man in his own defence; and if business cannot be carried on without it, what would you have a gentleman do?

MRS. PEACHUM. If I am in the wrong, my

---

[1] An infamous old prison, demolished 1902–3. It was connected with the Old Bailey, the court building, and was occupied by prisoners before and after trial. The condemned cell housed such famous men as Jack Sheppard before their last rides to Tyburn. The site is now partially occupied by the Central Criminal Court.

[2] These and the following remarks about Robin of Bagshot were taken as referring to Sir Robert Walpole, whose coarseness, conviviality, partiality to women, and general corruption were well known. Bagshot Heath, south of the City of London, at this time was infested with highwaymen.

Air V—*Of all the simple things we do, etc.*

A maid is like the golden ore,
    Which hath guineas intrinsical in't;
Whose worth is never known, before
    It is tried and impressed in the mint.
A wife's like a guinea in gold,
    Stamped with the name of her spouse;
Now here, now there; is bought, or is sold;
    And is current in every house.

Scene VI

Mrs. Peachum, Filch

Mrs. Peachum. Come hither, Filch. I am as fond of this child as though my mind misgave me he were my own. He hath as fine a hand at picking a pocket as a woman, and is as nimble-fingered as a juggler. If an unlucky session does not cut the rope of thy life, I pronounce, boy, thou wilt be a great man in history. Where was your post last night, my boy?

Filch. I plied at the opera, madam; and considering 'twas neither dark nor rainy, so that there was no great hurry in getting chairs and coaches, made a tolerable hand on't. These seven handkerchiefs, madam.

Mrs. Peachum. Colored ones, I see. They are of sure sale from our warehouse at Redriff[1] among the seamen.

Filch. And this snuff-box.

Mrs. Peachum. Set in gold! A pretty encouragement this to a young beginner.

Filch. I had a fair tug at a charming gold watch. Pox take the tailors for making the fobs so deep and narrow. It stuck by the way, and I was forced to make my escape under a coach. Really, madam, I fear, I shall be cut off in the flower of my youth, so that every now and then (since I was pumped)[2] I have thoughts of taking up and going to sea.

Mrs. Peachum. You should go to Hockley-in-the-Hole[3] and to Marybone, child, to learn valor. These are the schools that have bred so many brave men. I thought, boy, by this time, thou hadst lost fear as well as shame.—Poor lad! how little does he know as yet of the Old Bailey![4] For the first fact I'll insure thee from being hanged; and going to sea, Filch, will come in time enough upon a sentence of transportation. But now since you have nothing better to do, even go to your book, and learn your catechism; for really a man makes but an ill figure in the ordinary's paper,[5] who cannot give a satisfactory answer to his questions. But, hark you, my lad. Don't tell me a lie; for you know I hate a liar. Do you know of anything that hath passed between Captain Macheath and our Polly?

Filch. I beg you, madam, don't ask me; for I must either tell a lie to you or to Miss Polly —for I promised her I would not tell.

Mrs. Peachum. But when the honor of our family is concerned—

Filch. I shall lead a sad life with Miss Polly if ever she come to know that I told you. Besides, I would not willingly forfeit my own honor by betraying anybody.

Mrs. Peachum. Yonder comes my husband and Polly. Come, Filch, you shall go with me into my own room, and tell me the whole story. I'll give thee a glass of a most delicious cordial that I keep for my own drinking.

Exeunt

Scene VII

Peachum, Polly

Polly. I know as well as any of the fine ladies how to make the most of myself and of my man too. A woman knows how to be mercenary, though she hath never been in a court or at an assembly. We have it in our natures, papa. If I allow Captain Macheath some trifling liberties, I have his watch and other visible marks of his favor to show for it. A girl who cannot grant some things, and refuse what is most material, will make but a poor hand of her beauty, and soon be thrown upon the common.

Air VI—*What shall I do to show how much I love her, etc.*

Virgins are like the fair flower in its luster,[6]
    Which in the garden enamels the ground;
Near it the bees in play flutter and cluster,
    And gaudy butterflies frolic around.
But, when once plucked 'tis no longer alluring;
    To Covent-garden[7] 'tis sent (as yet sweet),

---

[1] East of London near the docks.

[2] Young pickpockets were not infrequently held beneath the pump. Cf. *Trivia*, III, 74.

[3] A resort where bear-baitings and bull-baitings were held.

[4] The criminal court for London and Middlesex.

[5] The report of the chaplain who examined prisoners with a view to securing confessions.

[6] Once attributed, probably wrongly, to Sir Charles Hanbury Williams.

[7] The London flower-market.

There fades, and shrinks, and grows past all
  enduring,
Rots, stinks, and dies, and is trod under feet.

PEACHUM. You know, Polly, I am not against your toying and trifling with a customer in the way of business, or to get out a secret or so. But if I find out that you have played the fool and are married, you jade you, I'll cut your throat, hussy! Now you know my mind.

SCENE VIII

PEACHUM, POLLY, MRS. PEACHUM

MRS. PEACHUM *in a very great passion*

AIR VII—*Oh London is a fine town*

Our Polly is a sad slut! nor heeds what we taught
  her.
I wonder any man alive will ever rear a daughter!
For she must have both hoods and gowns, and
  hoops to swell her pride,
With scarfs and stays, and gloves and lace; and
  she will have men beside;
And when she's dressed with care and cost, all-
  tempting fine and gay,
As men should serve a cowcumber, she flings herself away.

You baggage, you hussy! you inconsiderate jade! Had you been hanged, it would not have vexed me, for that might have been your misfortune; but to do such a mad thing by choice! The wench is married, husband.

PEACHUM. Married! The captain is a bold man, and will risk anything for money; to be sure, he believes her a fortune!—Do you think your mother and I should have lived comfortably so long together, if ever we had been married? Baggage!

MRS. PEACHUM. I knew she was always a proud slut; and now the wench has played the fool and married because, forsooth, she would do like the gentry. Can you support the expense of a husband, hussy, in gaming, drinking, and whoring? Have you money enough to carry on the daily quarrels of man and wife about who shall squander most? There are not many husbands and wives who can bear the charges of plaguing one another in a handsome way. If you must be married, could you introduce nobody into our family but a highwayman? Why, thou foolish jade, thou wilt be as ill used, and as much neglected, as if thou hadst married a lord!

PEACHUM. Let not your anger, my dear, break through the rules of decency, for the captain looks upon himself in the military capacity, as a gentleman by his profession. Besides what he hath already, I know he is in a fair way of getting, or of dying; and both these ways, let me tell you, are most excellent chances for a wife.—Tell me, hussy, are you ruined or no?

MRS. PEACHUM. With Polly's fortune, she might very well have gone off to a person of distinction. Yes, that you might, you pouting slut!

PEACHUM. What, is the wench dumb? Speak, or I'll make you plead by squeezing out an answer from you. Are you really bound wife to him, or are you only upon liking?

(*Pinches her*)

POLLY. (*Screaming*) Oh!

MRS. PEACHUM. How the mother is to be pitied who hath handsome daughters! Locks, bolts, bars, and lectures of morality are nothing to them; they break through them all. They have as much pleasure in cheating a father and mother as in cheating at cards.

PEACHUM. Why, Polly, I shall soon know if you are married, by Macheath's keeping from our house.

POLLY.

AIR VIII—*Grim king of the ghosts, etc.*

Can love be controlled by advice?
  Will Cupid our mothers obey?
Though my heart were as frozen as ice,
  At his flame 'twould have melted away.

When he kissed me, so closely he pressed,
  'Twas so sweet that I must have complied,
So I thought it both safest and best
  To marry, for fear you should chide.

MRS. PEACHUM. Then all the hopes of our family are gone for ever and ever!

PEACHUM. And Macheath may hang his father- and mother-in-law, in hope to get into their daughter's fortune!

POLLY. I did not marry him (as 'tis the fashion) coolly and deliberately for honor or money—but I love him.

MRS. PEACHUM. Love him! Worse and worse! I thought the girl had been better bred. O husband, husband! her folly makes me mad! my head swims! I'm distracted! I can't support myself—Oh! (*Faints*)

PEACHUM. See, wench, to what a condition you have reduced your poor mother! a glass of cordial, this instant. How the poor woman takes it to heart! (*Polly goes out and returns with it*) Ah, hussy, now this is the only comfort your mother has left!

POLLY. Give her another glass, sir; my mama drinks double the quantity whenever she is out of order.—This, you see, fetches her.

MRS. PEACHUM. The girl shows such a readiness, and so much concern, that I could almost find in my heart to forgive her.

AIR IX—*O Jenny, O Jenny, where hast thou been*
  O Polly, you might have toyed and kissed;
  By keeping men off, you keep them on.

POLLY.
    But he so teased me,
    And he so pleased me,
  What I did, you must have done—

MRS. PEACHUM. Not with a highwayman. You sorry slut!

PEACHUM. A word with you, wife. 'Tis no new thing for a wench to take a man without consent of parents. You know 'tis the frailty of woman, my dear.

MRS. PEACHUM. Yes, indeed, the sex is frail. But the first time a woman is frail, she should be somewhat nice, methinks, for then or never is the time to make her fortune. After that, she hath nothing to do but to guard herself from being found out, and she may do what she pleases.

PEACHUM. Make yourself a little easy; I have a thought shall soon set all matters again to rights. Why so melancholy, Polly? Since what is done cannot be undone, we must all endeavor to make the best of it.

MRS. PEACHUM. Well, Polly, as far as one woman can forgive another, I forgive thee.—Your father is too fond of you, hussy.

POLLY. Then all my sorrows are at an end.

MRS. PEACHUM. A mighty likely speech in troth, for a wench who is just married.

POLLY.
  AIR X—*Thomas, I cannot, etc.*
    I, like a ship in storms, was tossed,
    Yet afraid to put into land;
    For seized in the port, the vessel's lost,
    Whose treasure is contraband.
      The waves are laid,
      My duty's paid,
    Oh, joy beyond expression!
      Thus, safe ashore,
      I ask no more,
    My all is in my possession.

PEACHUM. I hear customers in t'other room. Go, talk with 'em, Polly; but come to us again as soon as they are gone.—But, hark ye, child, if 'tis the gentleman who was here yesterday about the repeating watch, say, you believe we can't get intelligence of it till tomorrow—for I lent it to Suky Straddle, to make a figure with it to-night at a tavern in Drury Lane. If t'other gentleman calls for the silver-hilted sword, you know beetle-browed Jemmy hath it on, and he doth not come from Tunbridge [1] till Tuesday night; so that it cannot be had till then. (*Exit Polly*)

SCENE IX

PEACHUM, MRS. PEACHUM

PEACHUM. Dear wife, be a little pacified. Don't let your passion run away with your senses. Polly, I grant you, hath done a rash thing.

MRS. PEACHUM. If she had had only an intrigue with the fellow, why, the very best families have excused and huddled up a frailty of that sort. 'Tis marriage, husband, that makes it a blemish.

PEACHUM. But money, wife, is the true fuller's earth for reputations; there is not a spot or a stain but what it can take out. A rich rogue nowadays is fit company for any gentleman, and the world, my dear, hath not such a contempt for roguery as you imagine. I tell you, wife, I can make this match turn to our advantage.

MRS. PEACHUM. I am very sensible, husband, that Captain Macheath is worth money, but I am in doubt whether he hath not two or three wives already, and then if he should die in a session or two, Polly's dower would come into dispute.

PEACHUM. That, indeed, is a point which ought to be considered.

  AIR XI—*A soldier and a sailor*
  A fox may steal your hens, sir,
  A whore your health and pence, sir
  Your daughter rob your chest, sir,
  Your wife may steal your rest, sir,
    A thief your goods and plate.
  But this is all but picking;
  With rest, pence, chest, and chicken,
  It ever was decreed, sir,
  If lawyer's hand is fee'd, sir,
    He steals your whole state.

[1] North of the City.

The lawyers are bitter enemies to those in our way. They don't care that anybody should get a clandestine livelihood but themselves.

SCENE X

MRS. PEACHUM, PEACHUM, POLLY

POLLY. 'Twas only Nimming Ned. He brought in a damask window-curtain, a hoop petticoat, a pair of silver candlesticks, a periwig, and one silk stocking, from the fire that happened last night.

PEACHUM. There is not a fellow that is cleverer in his way and saves more goods out of fire, than Ned. But now, Polly, to your affair; for matters must not be left as they are. You are married then, it seems?

POLLY. Yes, sir.

PEACHUM. And how do you propose to live, child?

POLLY. Like other women, sir,—upon the industry of my husband.

MRS. PEACHUM. What, is the wench turned fool? A highwayman's wife, like a soldier's, hath as little of his pay as of his company.

PEACHUM. And had not you the common views of a gentlewoman in your marriage, Polly?

POLLY. I don't know what you mean, sir.

PEACHUM. Of a jointure, and of being a widow.

POLLY. But I love him, sir; how then could I have thoughts of parting with him?

PEACHUM. Parting with him! Why, that is the whole scheme and intention of all marriage articles. The comfortable estate of widowhood is the only hope that keeps up a wife's spirits. Where is the woman who would scruple to be a wife, if she has it in her power to be a widow whenever she pleased? If you have any views of this sort, Polly, I shall think the match not so very unreasonable.

POLLY. How I dread to hear your advice! Yet I must beg you to explain yourself.

PEACHUM. Secure what he hath got, have him peached [1] the next sessions, and then at once you are made a rich widow.

POLLY. What, murder the man I love! The blood runs cold at my heart at the very thought of it.

PEACHUM. Fie, Polly! What hath murder to do in the affair? Since the thing sooner or later must happen, I dare say the captain himself would like that we should get the reward for his death sooner than a stranger. Why, Polly, the captain knows that as 'tis his employment to rob, so 'tis ours to take robbers; every man in his business. So that there is no malice in the case.

MRS. PEACHUM. Ay, husband, now you have nicked the matter. To have him peached is the only thing could ever make me forgive her.

POLLY.

AIR XII—*Now ponder well, ye parents dear*
    Oh, ponder well! be not severe;
      So save a wretched wife!
    For on the rope that hangs my dear
      Depends poor Polly's life.

MRS. PEACHUM. But your duty to your parents, hussy, obliges you to hang him. What would many a wife give for such an opportunity!

POLLY. What is a jointure, what is a widowhood to me? I know my heart. I cannot survive him.

AIR XIII—*Le printemps rappelle aux armes*
    The turtle thus with plaintive crying,
      Her lover dying,
    The turtle thus with plaintive crying,
      Laments her dove.
    Down she drops, quite spent with sighing;
    Pair'd in death, as pair'd in love.

Thus, sir, it will happen to your poor Polly.

MRS. PEACHUM. What, is the fool in love in earnest then? I hate thee for being particular. Why, wench, thou art a shame to thy very sex.

POLLY. But hear me, mother,—if you ever loved—

MRS. PEACHUM. Those cursed play-books she reads have been her ruin. One word more, hussy, and I shall knock your brains out, if you have any.

PEACHUM. Keep out of the way, Polly, for fear of mischief, and consider of what is proposed to you.

MRS. PEACHUM. Away, hussy! Hang your husband, and be dutiful.

SCENE XI

MRS. PEACHUM, PEACHUM, POLLY *listening*

MRS. PEACHUM. The thing, husband, must and shall be done. For the sake of intelligence,

[1] Indicted.

we must take other measures and have him peached the next session without her consent. If she will not know her duty, we know ours.

PEACHUM. But really, my dear, it grieves one's heart to take off a great man. When I consider his personal bravery, his fine stratagem, how much we have already got by him, and how much more we may get, methinks I can't find in my heart to have a hand in his death. I wish you could have made Polly undertake it.

MRS. PEACHUM. But in a case of necessity— our own lives are in danger.

PEACHUM. Then, indeed, we must comply with the customs of the world, and make gratitude give way to interest. He shall be taken off.

MRS. PEACHUM. I'll undertake to manage Polly.

PEACHUM. And I'll prepare matters for the Old Bailey. *Exeunt*

SCENE XII

POLLY

POLLY. Now I'm a wretch, indeed—methinks I see him already in the cart, sweeter and more lovely than the nosegay in his hand! —I hear the crowd extolling his resolution and intrepidity!—What volleys of sighs are sent from the windows of Holborn, that so comely a youth should be brought to disgrace!—I see him at the tree! The whole circle are in tears! —even butchers weep!—Jack Ketch[1] himself hesitates to perform his duty, and would be glad to lose his fee, by a reprieve. What then will become of Polly? As yet I may inform him of their design, and aid him in his escape. It shall be so!—But then he flies, absents himself, and I bar myself from his dear, dear conversation! That too will distract me. If he keep out of the way, my papa and mama may in time relent, and we may be happy. If he stays, he is hanged, and then he is lost forever! He intended to lie concealed in my room till the dusk of the evening. If they are abroad, I'll this instant let him out, lest some accident should prevent him.

Exit, and returns

[1] The hangman, from one of that name who died in 1686.

SCENE XIII

POLLY, MACHEATH

AIR XIV—*Pretty Parrot, say*

MACHEATH.
    Pretty Polly, say,
    When I was away,
Did your fancy never stray
    To some newer lover?

POLLY.
    Without disguise,
    Heaving sighs,
    Doating eyes,
My constant heart discover.
    Fondly let me loll!

MACHEATH.
    O pretty, pretty Poll.

POLLY. And are *you* as fond as ever, my dear?

MACHEATH. Suspect my honor, my courage —suspect anything but my love. May my pistols miss fire, and my mare slip her shoulder while I am pursued, if I ever forsake thee!

POLLY. Nay, my dear, I have no reason to doubt you, for I find in the romance you lent me, none of the great heroes were ever false in love.

MACHEATH.
AIR XV—*Pray, fair one, be kind*

    My heart was so free,
    It roved like the bee,
Till Polly my passion requited;
    I sipped each flower,
    I changed ev'ry hour,
But here ev'ry flower is united.

POLLY. Were you sentenced to transportation, sure, my dear, you could not leave me behind you,—could you?

MACHEATH. Is there any power, any force that could tear me from thee? You might sooner tear a pension out of the hands of a courtier, a fee from a lawyer, a pretty woman from a looking glass, or any woman from quadrille. But to tear me from thee is impossible!

AIR XVI—*Over the hills and far away*

Were I laid on Greenland's coast,
    And in my arms embraced my lass;
Warm amidst eternal frost,
    Too soon the half year's night would pass.

POLLY.
Were I sold on Indian soil,
    Soon as the burning day was closed,
I could mock the sultry toil,
    When on my charmer's breast reposed.

MACHEATH. And I would love you all the day,
POLLY. Every night would kiss and play,
MACHEATH. If with me you'd fondly stray
POLLY. Over the hills and far away.

POLLY. Yes, I would go with thee. But oh!—how shall I speak it? I must be torn from thee. We must part.
MACHEATH. How! Part!
POLLY. We must, we must. My papa and mama are set against thy life. They now, even now are in search after thee. They are preparing evidence against thee. Thy life depends upon a moment.

AIR XVII—*'Gin thou wert mine awn thing*
Oh, what pain it is to part!
Can I leave thee, can I leave thee?
Oh, what pain it is to part!
Can thy Polly ever leave thee?
But lest death my love should thwart
And bring thee to the fatal cart,
Thus I tear thee from my bleeding heart!
Fly hence, and let me leave thee.

One kiss and then,—one kiss. Begone,—farewell.
MACHEATH. My hand, my heart, my dear, is so riveted to thine, that I cannot unloose my hold.
POLLY. But my papa may intercept thee, and then I should lose the very glimmering of hope. A few weeks, perhaps, may reconcile us all. Shall thy Polly hear from thee?
MACHEATH. Must I then go?
POLLY. And will not absence change your love?
MACHEATH. If you doubt it, let me stay—and be hanged.
POLLY. Oh, how I fear! how I tremble!—Go—but when safety will give you leave, you will be sure to see me again; for till then Polly is wretched. (*Parting, and looking back at each other with fondness; he at one door, she at the other*)

MACHEATH.
AIR XVIII—*Oh the broom, etc.*
The miser thus a shilling sees,
Which he's obliged to pay,
With sighs resigns it by degrees,
And fears 'tis gone for aye.

POLLY.
The boy, thus, when his sparrow's flown,
The bird in silence eyes;

But soon as out of sight 'tis gone,
Whines, whimpers, sobs, and cries.

ACT II

SCENE I. *A tavern near Newgate*

JEREMY TWITCHER, CROOK-FINGERED JACK, WAT DREARY, ROBIN OF BAGSHOT, NIMMING NED, HARRY PADINGTON, MATT OF THE MINT, BEN BUDGE, *and the rest of the gang, at the table, with wine, brandy, and tobacco*

BEN. But prithee, Matt, what is become of thy brother Tom? I have not seen him since my return from transportation.
MATT. Poor brother Tom had an accident this time twelve-month, and so clever a made[1] fellow he was, that I could not save him from those flaying rascals the surgeons; and now, poor man, he is among the anatomies at Surgeons' Hall.[2]
BEN. So, it seems, his time was come.
JEREMY. But the present time is ours, and nobody alive hath more. Why are the laws levelled at us? Are we more dishonest than the rest of mankind? What we win, gentlemen, is our own by the law of arms and the right of conquest.
JACK. Where shall we find such another set of practical philosophers, who to a man are above the fear of death?
WAT. Sound men, and true!
ROBIN. Of tried courage, and indefatigable industry!
NED. Who is there here that would not die for his friend?
HARRY. Who is there here that would betray him for his interest?
MATT. Show me a gang of courtiers that can say as much.
BEN. We are for a just partition of the world, for every man hath a right to enjoy life.
MATT. We retrench the superfluities of mankind. The world is avaricious, and I hate avarice. A covetous fellow, like a jackdaw, steals what he was never made to enjoy, for the sake of hiding it. These are the robbers of mankind, for money was made for the freehearted and generous; and where is the injury

[1] Well made.
[2] Under the law bodies of convicts were used for dissection by medical students.

of taking from another, what he hath not the heart to make use of?

JEREMY. Our several stations for the day are fixed. Good luck attend us! Fill the glasses.

MATT.

AIR I—*Fill ev'ry glass, etc.*

Fill ev'ry glass, for wine inspires us,
    And fires us,
With courage, love, and joy.
Women and wine should life employ.
Is there aught else on earth desirous?

CHORUS.

Fill ev'ry glass, etc.

SCENE II

To them enter MACHEATH

MACHEATH. Gentlemen, well met. My heart hath been with you this hour, but an unexpected affair hath detained me. No ceremony, I beg you.

MATT. We were just breaking up to go upon duty. Am I to have the honor of taking the air with you, sir, this evening upon the heath? I drink a dram now and then with the stage-coachmen in the way of friendship and intelligence, and I know that about this time there will be passengers upon the Western Road who are worth speaking with.

MACHEATH. I was to have been of that party—but—

MATT. But what, sir?

MACHEATH. Is there any man who suspects my courage?—

MATT. We have all been witnesses of it.—

MACHEATH. My honor and truth to the gang?

MATT. I'll be answerable for it.

MACHEATH. In the division of our booty, have I ever shown the least marks of avarice or injustice?

MATT. By these questions something seems to have ruffled you. Are any of us suspected?

MACHEATH. I have a fixed confidence, gentlemen, in you all, as men of honor, and as such I value and respect you. Peachum is a man that is useful to us.

MATT. Is he about to play us any foul play? I'll shoot him through the head.

MACHEATH. I beg you, gentlemen, act with conduct and discretion. A pistol is your last resort.

MATT. He knows nothing of this meeting.

MACHEATH. Business cannot go on without him. He is a man who knows the world, and is a necessary agent to us. We have had a slight difference, and till it is accommodated I shall be obliged to keep out of his way. Any private dispute of mine shall be of no ill consequence to my friends. You must continue to act under his direction, for the moment we break loose from him, our gang is ruined.

MATT. As a bawd to a whore, I grant you, he is to us of great convenience.

MACHEATH. Make him believe I have quitted the gang, which I can never do but with life. At our private quarters I will continue to meet you. A week or so will probably reconcile us.

MATT. Your instructions shall be observed. 'Tis now high time for us to repair to our several duties; so till the evening at our quarters in Moor-fields [1] we bid you farewell.

MACHEATH. I shall wish myself with you. Success attend you.

(*Sits down melancholy at the table*)

MATT.

AIR II—*March in Rinaldo,*[2] *with drums and trumpets*

Let us take the road.
    Hark! I hear the sound of coaches!
    The hour of attack approaches,
To your arms, brave boys, and load.

    See the ball I hold!
Let the chymists [3] toil like asses,
Our fire their fire surpasses,
    And turns all our lead to gold.

(*The gang, ranged in the front of the stage, load their pistols, and stick them under their girdles, then go off singing the first part in chorus*)

SCENE III

MACHEATH, DRAWER

MACHEATH. What a fool is a fond wench! Polly is most confoundedly bit—I love the sex. And a man who loves money might be as well contented with one guinea, as I with one woman. The town perhaps hath been as much

---

[1] Just outside London Wall on the north.
[2] An opera by Händel, Haymarket, 1711.
[3] Alchemists. The references are to the transmutation of metals by "projection."

obliged to me, for recruiting it with free-hearted ladies, as to any recruiting officer in the army. If it were not for us, and the other gentlemen of the sword, Drury Lane [1] would be uninhabited.

AIR III—*Would you have a young virgin, etc.*
If the heart of a man is depressed with cares,
The mist is dispelled when a woman appears;
Like the notes of a fiddle, she sweetly, sweetly
Raises the spirits, and charms our ears.
Roses and lilies her cheeks disclose,
But her ripe lips are more sweet than those.
    Press her,
    Caress her
    With blisses,
    Her kisses
Dissolve us in pleasure and soft repose.

I must have women. There is nothing unbends the mind like them. Money is not so strong a cordial for the time. Drawer!—

Enter DRAWER

Is the porter gone for all the ladies, according to my directions?

DRAWER. I expect him back every minute. But you know, sir, you sent him as far as Hockley-in-the-Hole for three of the ladies, for one in Vinegar Yard, and for the rest of them somewhere about Lewkner's Lane.[2] Sure some of them are below, for I hear the bar bell. As they come I will show them up. Coming! coming!   *Exit*

SCENE IV

MACHEATH, MRS. COAXER, DOLLY TRULL, MRS. VIXEN, BETTY DOXY, JENNY DIVER, MRS. SLAMMEKIN, SUKY TAWDRY, *and* MOLLY BRAZEN

MACHEATH. Dear Mrs. Coaxer, you are welcome. You look charmingly to-day. I hope you don't want the repairs of quality, and lay on paint.—Dolly Trull! kiss me, you slut; are you as amorous as ever, hussy? You are always so taken up with stealing hearts, that you don't allow yourself time to steal anything else. Ah Dolly, thou wilt ever be a coquette.—Mrs. Vixen, I'm yours! I always loved a woman of wit and spirit; they make charming mistresses, but plaguy wives.—

[1] Famous not only for the theater but for the lodgings of women of the town.
[2] Widely separated sections of London, but all known as resorts of the lowest classes.

Betty Doxy! come hither, hussy. Do you drink as hard as ever? You had better stick to good, wholesome beer; for in troth, Betty, strong waters will, in time, ruin your constitution. You should leave those to your betters. —What! and my pretty Jenny Diver too! As prim and demure as ever! There is not any prude, though ever so high bred, hath a more sanctified look, with a more mischievous heart. Ah! thou art a dear artful hypocrite!—Mrs. Slammekin! as careless and genteel as ever! all you fine ladies, who know your own beauty, affect an undress.—But see, here's Suky Tawdry come to contradict what I was saying. Everything she gets one way, she lays out upon her back. Why, Suky, you must keep at least a dozen tally-men.—Molly Brazen! (*She kisses him*) That's well done. I love a free-hearted wench. Thou hast a most agreeable assurance, girl, and art as willing as a turtle.[3]— But heark! I hear music. The harper is at the door. "If music be the food of love, play on." [4] Ere you seat yourselves, ladies, what think you of a dance? Come in.

Enter HARPER

Play the French tune that Mrs. Slammekin was so fond of.
(*A dance à la ronde in the French manner; near the end of it this song and chorus*)

AIR IV—*Cotillion*
Youth's the season made for joys,
 Love is then our duty;
She alone who that employs,
 Well deserves her beauty.
  Let's be gay,
  While we may,
Beauty's a flower despised in decay.

Youth's the season, etc.

Let us drink and sport to-day,
 Ours is not to-morrow.
Love with youth flies swift away,
 Age is nought but sorrow.
  Dance and sing,
  Time's on the wing,
Life never knows the return of spring.

CHORUS.
  Let us drink, etc.

MACHEATH. Now pray, ladies, take your places. Here, fellow. (*Pays the Harper*) Bid the drawer bring us more wine. (*Exit* HARPER)

[3] Turtledove.
[4] *Twelfth Night*, Act I, scene i, l. 1.

If any of the ladies choose gin, I hope they will be so free to call for it.

JENNY. You look as if you meant me. Wine is strong enough for me. Indeed, sir, I never drink strong waters but when I have the colic.

MACHEATH. Just the excuse of the fine ladies! Why, a lady of quality is never without the colic. I hope, Mrs. Coaxer, you have had good success of late in your visits among the mercers.

MRS. COAXER. We have so many interlopers. Yet, with industry, one may still have a little picking. I carried a silver-flowered lute-string and a piece of black padesoy[1] to Mr. Peachum's lock but last week.

MRS. VIXEN. There's Molly Brazen hath the ogle[2] of a rattlesnake. She riveted a linen-draper's eye so fast upon her, that he was nicked of three pieces of cambric before he could look off.

MOLLY BRAZEN. Oh, dear madam! But sure nothing can come up to your handling of laces! And then you have such a sweet deluding tongue! To cheat a man is nothing; but the woman must have fine parts indeed who cheats a woman!

MRS. VIXEN. Lace, madam, lies in a small compass, and is of easy conveyance. But you are apt, madam, to think too well of your friends.

MRS. COAXER. If any woman hath more art than another, to be sure, 'tis Jenny Diver. Though her fellow be never so agreeable, she can pick his pocket as coolly as if money were her only pleasure. Now, that is a command of the passions uncommon in a woman!

JENNY. I never go to the tavern with a man but in the view of business. I have other hours, and other sort of men for my pleasure. But had I your address, madam—

MACHEATH. Have done with your compliments, ladies, and drink about. You are not so fond of me, Jenny, as you use to be.

JENNY. 'Tis not convenient, sir, to show my kindness among so many rivals. 'Tis your own choice, and not the warmth of my inclination, that will determine you.

AIR V—*All in a misty morning, etc.*
Before the barn-door crowing,
  The cock by hens attended,
His eyes around him throwing,
  Stands for a while suspended.
Then one he singles from the crew,
  And cheers the happy hen;
With "How do you do," and "How do you do,"
  And "How do you do" again.

MACHEATH. Ah Jenny! thou art a dear slut.

TRULL. Pray, madam, were you ever in keeping?

TAWDRY. I hope, madam, I han't been so long upon the town but I have met with some good fortune as well as my neighbors.

TRULL. Pardon me, madam, I meant no harm by the question; 'twas only in the way of conversation.

TAWDRY. Indeed, madam, if I had not been a fool, I might have lived very handsomely with my last friend. But upon his missing five guineas, he turned me off. Now, I never suspected he had counted them.

SLAMMEKIN. Who do you look upon, madam, as your best sort of keepers?

TRULL. That, madam, is thereafter as they be.

SLAMMEKIN. I, madam, was once kept by a Jew; and bating their religion, to women they are a good sort of people.

TAWDRY. Now for my part, I own I like an old fellow; for we always make them pay for what they can't do.

VIXEN. A spruce prentice, let me tell you, ladies, is no ill thing; they bleed freely.[3] I have sent at least two or three dozen of them in my time to the plantations.[4]

JENNY. But to be sure, sir, with so much good fortune as you have had upon the road, you must be grown immensely rich.

MACHEATH. The road, indeed, hath done me justice, but the gaming-table hath been my ruin.

JENNY.

AIR VI—*When once I lay with another man's wife, etc.*

The gamesters and lawyers are jugglers alike,[5]
  If they meddle, your all is in danger:
Like gypsies, if once they can finger a souse,
  Your pockets they pick, and they pilfer your house,
And give your estate to a stranger.

(*She takes up his pistol. Tawdry takes up the other*)

[1] Fashionable fabrics. [2] Eye.
[3] Cf. Lillo's *The London Merchant*.
[4] I.e., they were transported as convicts to America.
[5] This song was credited by popular opinion to Gay's friend William Fortescue, Master of the Rolls.

These are the tools of men of honor. Cards and dice are only fit for cowardly cheats, who prey upon their friends.

TAWDRY. This, sir, is fitter for your hand. Besides your loss of money, 'tis a loss to the ladies. Gaming takes you off from women. How fond could I be of you!—but before company, 'tis ill-bred,

MACHEATH. Wanton hussies!

JENNY. I must and will have a kiss, to give my wine a zest.

(*They take him about the neck, and make signs to Peachum and Constables, who rush in upon him*)

SCENE V

To them PEACHUM *and* CONSTABLES

PEACHUM. I seize you, sir, as my prisoner.

MACHEATH. Was this well done, Jenny? Women are decoy ducks: who can trust them? Beasts, jades, jilts, harpies, furies, whores!

PEACHUM. Your case, Mr. Macheath, is not particular. The greatest heroes have been ruined by women. But, to do them justice, I must own they are a pretty sort of creatures, if we could trust them. You must now, sir, take your leave of the ladies, and if they have a mind to make you a visit, they will be sure to find you at home. This gentleman, ladies, lodges in Newgate. Constables, wait upon the captain to his lodgings.

MACHEATH

AIR VII—*When first I laid siege to my Chloris, etc.*

At the tree I shall suffer with pleasure,
At the tree I shall suffer with pleasure;
    Let me go where I will,
    In all kinds of ill,
I shall find no such furies as these are.

PEACHUM. Ladies, I'll take care the reckoning shall be discharged.

(*Exit* MACHEATH, *guarded, with* PEACHUM *and* CONSTABLES.

SCENE VI

The Women *remain*

VIXEN. Look ye, Mrs. Jenny; though Mr. Peachum may have made a private bargain with you and Suky Tawdry for betraying the captain, as we were all assisting, we ought all to share alike.

COAXER. I think Mr. Peacham, after so long an acquaintance, might have trusted me as well as Jenny Diver.

SLAMMEKIN. I am sure at least three men of his hanging, and in a year's time too, (if he did me justice) should be set down to my account.

TRULL. Mrs. Slammekin, that is not fair. For you know one of them was taken in bed with me.

JENNY. As far as a bowl of punch or a treat, I believe Mrs. Suky will join with me. As for anything else, ladies, you cannot in conscience expect it.

SLAMMEKIN. Dear madam—

TRULL. I would not for the world—

SLAMMEKIN. 'Tis impossible for me—

TRULL. As I hope to be saved, madam—

SLAMMEKIN. Nay, then I must stay here all night.—

TRULL. Since you command me.

Exeunt with great ceremony

SCENE VII. *Newgate*

LOCKIT, TURNKEYS, MACHEATH, CONSTABLES

LOCKIT. Noble captain, you are welcome. You have not been a lodger of mine this year and half. You know the custom, sir. Garnish,[1] captain, garnish! Hand me down those fetters there.

MACHEATH. Those, Mr. Lockit, seem to be the heaviest of the whole set! With your leave, I should like the further pair better.

LOCKIT. Look ye, captain, we know what is fittest for our prisoners. When a gentleman uses me with civility, I always do the best I can to please him.—Hand them down, I say.—We have them of all prices,[2] from one guinea to ten, and 'tis fitting every gentleman should please himself.

MACHEATH. I understand you, sir. (*Gives money*) The fees here are so many, and so exorbitant, that few fortunes can bear the expense of getting off handsomely, or of dying like a gentleman.

LOCKIT. Those, I see, will fit the captain better. Take down the further pair. Do but examine them, sir,—never was better work. How genteelly they are made! They will fit as easy as a glove, and the nicest man in Eng-

[1] Fee me.
[2] A cruel and extortionate method of making prisoners pay to be relieved of discomfort or actual torture.

land might not be ashamed to wear them. (*He puts on the chains*) If I had the best gentleman in the land in my custody, I could not equip him more handsomely. And so, sir—I now leave you to your private meditations.

Scene VIII

Macheath

Air VIII—*Courtiers, courtiers, think it no harm, etc.*

Man may escape from rope and gun;
Nay, some have outlived the doctor's pill;
Who takes a woman must be undone,
  That basilisk is sure to kill.

The fly that sips treacle is lost in the sweets,
So he that tastes woman, woman, woman,
He that tastes woman, ruin meets.

To what a woeful plight have I brought myself! Here must I (all day long, till I am hanged) be confined to hear the reproaches of a wench who lays her ruin at my door. I am in the custody of her father, and to be sure if he knows of the matter, I shall have a fine time on't betwixt this and my execution. But I promised the wench marriage. What signifies a promise to a woman? Does not a man in marriage itself promise a hundred things that he never means to perform? Do all we can, women will believe us; for they look upon a promise as an excuse for following their own inclinations.—But here comes Lucy, and I cannot get from her. Would I were deaf!

Scene IX

Macheath, Lucy

Lucy. You base man, you, how can you look me in the face after what hath passed between us?—See here, perfidious wretch, how I am forced to bear about the load of infamy you have laid upon me—O Macheath! thou hast robbed me of my quiet—to see thee tortured would give me pleasure.

Air IX—*A lovely lass to a friar came, etc.*

Thus when a good housewife sees a rat
  In a trap in the morning taken,
With pleasure her heart goes pit-a-pat
  In revenge for her loss of bacon.
    Then she throws him
    To the dog or cat,
To be worried, crushed, and shaken.

Macheath. Have you no bowels, no tenderness, my dear Lucy, to see a husband in these circumstances?

Lucy. A husband!

Macheath. In every respect but the form, and that, my dear, may be said over us at any time. Friends should not insist upon ceremonies. From a man of honor, his word is as good as his bond.

Lucy. 'Tis the pleasure of all you fine men to insult the women you have ruined.

Air X—*'Twas when the sea was roaring, etc.*

How cruel are the traitors
  Who lie and swear in jest,
To cheat unguarded creatures
  Of virtue, fame, and rest!

Whoever steals a shilling
  Through shame the guilt conceals;
In love, the perjured villain
  With boasts the theft reveals.

Macheath. The very first opportunity my dear, (have but patience) you shall be my wife in whatever manner you please.

Lucy. Insinuating monster! And so you think I know nothing of the affair of Miss Polly Peachum. I could tear thy eyes out!

Macheath. Sure, Lucy, you can't be such a fool as to be jealous of Polly!

Lucy. Are you not married to her, you brute, you?

Macheath. Married! Very good. The wench gives it out only to vex thee, and to ruin me in thy good opinion. 'Tis true I go to the house; I chat with the girl, I kiss her, I say a thousand things to her (as all gentlemen do) that mean nothing, to divert myself; and now the silly jade hath set it about that I am married to her, to let me know what she would be at. Indeed, my dear Lucy, these violent passions may be of ill consequence to a woman in your condition.

Lucy. Come, come, captain, for all your assurance, you know that Miss Polly hath put it out of your power to do me the justice you promised me.

Macheath. A jealous woman believes everything her passion suggests. To convince you of my sincerity, if we can find the ordinary, I shall have no scruples of making you my wife—and I know the consequence of having two at a time.

Lucy. That you are only to be hanged, and so get rid of them both.

MACHEATH. I am ready, my dear Lucy, to give you satisfaction—if you think there is any in marriage. What can a man of honor say more?

LUCY. So then it seems—you are not married to Miss Polly.

MACHEATH. You know, Lucy, the girl is prodigiously conceited. No man can say a civil thing to her, but (like other fine ladies) her vanity makes her think he's her own for ever and ever.

AIR XI—*The sun had loosed his weary teams, etc.*

    The first time at the looking-glass
      The mother sets her daughter,
    The image strikes the smiling lass
      With self-love ever after.
    Each time she looks, she, fonder grown,
      Thinks ev'ry charm grows stronger.
    But alas, vain maid, all eyes but your own
      Can see you are not younger.

When women consider their own beauties, they are all alike unreasonable in their demands; for they expect their lovers should like them as long as they like themselves.

LUCY. Yonder is my father. Perhaps this way we may light upon the ordinary,[1] who shall try if you will be as good as your word; for I long to be made an honest woman.

                                  Exeunt

SCENE X. [*Lockit's room in Newgate*]

PEACHUM, LOCKIT *with an account-book*[2]

LOCKIT. In this last affair, brother Peachum, we are agreed. You have consented to go halves in Macheath.

PEACHUM. We shall never fall out about an execution. But as to that article, pray how stands our last year's account?

LOCKIT. If you will run your eye over it, you'll find 'tis fair and clearly stated.

PEACHUM. This long arrear of the government is very hard upon us! Can it be expected that we should hang our acquaintance for nothing, when our betters will hardly save theirs without being paid for it? Unless the people in employment pay better, I promise them for the future, I shall let other rogues live besides their own.

LOCKIT. Perhaps, brother, they are afraid these matters may be carried too far. We are treated, too, by them with contempt, as if our profession were not reputable.

PEACHUM. In one respect, indeed, our employment may be reckoned dishonest, because, like great statesmen, we encourage those who betray their friends.

LOCKIT. Such language, brother, anywhere else might turn to your prejudice. Learn to be more guarded, I beg you.

AIR XII—*How happy are we, etc.*[3]

    When you censure the age,
      Be cautious and sage,
    Lest the courtiers offended should be.
      If you mention vice or bribe,
      'Tis so pat to all the tribe
    Each cries—That was levelled at me.

PEACHUM. Here's poor Ned Clincher's name, I see. Sure, brother Lockit, there was a little unfair proceeding in Ned's case; for he told me in the condemned hold, that for value received, you had promised him a session or two longer without molestation.

LOCKIT. Mr. Peachum, this is the first time my honor was ever called in question.

PEACHUM. Business is at an end, if once we act dishonorably.

LOCKIT. Who accuses me?

PEACHUM. You are warm, brother.

LOCKIT. He that attacks my honor, attacks my livelihood. And this usage, sir, is not to be borne.

PEACHUM. Since you provoke me to speak, I must tell you too, that Mrs. Coaxer charges you with defrauding her of her information-money, for the apprehending of curl-pated Hugh. Indeed, indeed, brother, we must punctually pay our spies, or we shall have no information.

LOCKIT. Is this language to me, sirrah? Who have saved you from the gallows, sirrah!
                        (*Collaring each other*)

PEACHUM. If I am hanged, it shall be for ridding the world of an arrant rascal.

LOCKIT. This hand shall do the office of the halter you deserve, and throttle you, you dog!
                          (*They break apart*)

PEACHUM. —Brother, brother, we are both in the wrong. We shall be both losers in the

---

[1] Chaplain.
[2] This scene was taken by early audiences to refer to a quarrel between Walpole and Townshend, who besides being colleagues in the government were also brothers-in-law. Whether the reference is to a specific quarrel or not, the scene probably was meant to reflect the general condition of the government.
[3] Supposed by some to have been written by Swift.

dispute—for you know we have it in our power to hang each other. You should not be so passionate.

LOCKIT. Nor you so provoking.

PEACHUM. 'Tis our mutual interest; 'tis for the interest of the world we should agree. If I said anything, brother, to the prejudice of your character, I ask pardon.

LOCKIT. Brother Peachum, I can forgive as well as resent. Give me your hand. Suspicion does not become a friend.

PEACHUM. I only meant to give you occasion to justify yourself. But I must now step home, for I expect the gentleman about this snuff-box that Filch nimmed two nights ago in the park. I appointed him at this hour.

Exit

SCENE XI

LOCKIT, LUCY

LOCKIT. Whence come you, hussy?

LUCY. My tears might answer that question.

LOCKIT. You have then been whimpering and fondling, like a spaniel, over the fellow that hath abused you.

LUCY. One can't help love; one can't cure it. 'Tis not in my power to obey you, and hate him.

LOCKIT. Learn to bear your husband's death like a reasonable woman. 'Tis not the fashion, nowadays, so much as to affect sorrow upon these occasions. No woman would ever marry if she had not the chance of mortality for a release. Act like a woman of spirit, hussy, and thank your father for what he is doing.

Lucy.

AIR XIII—*Of a noble race was Shenkin*

Is then his fate decreed, sir?
    Such a man can I think of quitting?
When first we met, so moves me yet,
    Oh, see how my heart is splitting!

LOCKIT. Look ye, Lucy—there is no saving him—so, I think, you must ev'n do like other widows,—buy yourself weeds, and be cheerful.

AIR XIV

You'll think, ere many days ensue,
    This sentence not severe;
I hang your husband, child, 'tis true,
    But with him hang your care.
        Twang dang dillo dee.

Like a good wife, go moan over your dying husband; that, child, is your duty.—Consider girl, you can't have the man and the money too—so make yourself as easy as you can by getting all you can from him. *Exeunt*

SCENE XII. [*Another part of the prison*]

LUCY, MACHEATH

LUCY. Though the ordinary was out of the way to-day, I hope, my dear, you will, upon the first opportunity, quiet my scruples.—Oh, sir!—my father's hard heart is not to be softened, and I am in the utmost despair.

MACHEATH. But if I could raise a small sum—would not twenty guineas, think you, move him?—Of all the arguments in the way of business, the perquisite is the most prevailing.—Your father's perquisites for the escape of prisoners must amount to a considerable sum in the year. Money well timed and properly applied, will do anything.

AIR XV—*London ladies*

If you at an office solicit your due,
    And would not have matters neglected;
You must quicken the clerk with the perquisite too,
    To do what his duty directed.
Or would you the frowns of a lady prevent,
    She too has this palpable failing,
The perquisite softens her into consent;
    That reason with all is prevailing.

LUCY. What love or money can do shall be done, for all my comfort depends upon your safety.

SCENE XIII

LUCY, MACHEATH, POLLY [1]

POLLY. Where is my dear husband?—Was a rope ever intended for this neck?—Oh, let me throw my arms about it, and throttle thee with love!—Why dost thou turn away from me?—'Tis thy Polly—'tis thy wife.

MACHEATH. Was there ever such an unfortunate rascal as I am!

LUCY. Was there ever such another villain!

POLLY. O Macheath! was it for this we parted? Taken! imprisoned! tried! hanged!—cruel reflection! I'll stay with thee till death—

[1] This triangle was construed, if not so intended, into a satire on Walpole's relations with Maria Skerritt, whom he married after the death of Lady Walpole.

no force shall tear thy dear wife from thee now.—What means my love?—not one kind word!—not one kind look! Think what thy Polly suffers to see thee in this condition.

AIR XVI—*All in the downs, etc.*
  Thus when the swallow, seeking prey,
    Within the sash is closely pent,
  His consort, with bemoaning lay,
    Without, sits pining for th'event.
  Her chattering lovers all around her skim;
  She heeds them not (poor bird!)—her soul's with him.

MACHEATH. (*Aside*) I must disown her.— The wench is distracted.

LUCY. Am I then bilked of my virtue? Can I have no reparation? Sure, men were born to lie, and women to believe them. O villain! villain!

POLLY. Am I not thy wife? Thy neglect of me, thy aversion to me, too severely proves it. —Look on me. Tell me; am I not thy wife?

LUCY. Perfidious wretch!

POLLY. Barbarous husband!

LUCY. Hadst thou been hanged five months ago, I had been happy.

POLLY. And I too. If you had been kind to me till death, it would not have vexed me— and that's no very unreasonable request (though from a wife) to a man who hath not above seven or eight days to live.

LUCY. Art thou then married to another? Hast thou two wives, monster?

MACHEATH. If women's tongues can cease for an answer—hear me.

LUCY. I won't! Flesh and blood can't bear my usage.

POLLY, Shall I not claim my own? Justice bids me speak.

MACHEATH.

AIR XVII—*Have you heard of a frolicsome ditty, etc.*
  How happy I could be with either,
    Were t'other dear charmer away!
  But while you thus teaze me together,
    To neither a word will I say;
      But tol de rol, etc.

POLLY. Sure, my dear, there ought to be some preference shown to a wife! At least she may claim the appearance of it.—He must be distracted with his misfortunes, or he could not use me thus!

LUCY. O villain, villain! thou hast deceived me—I could even inform against thee with pleasure. Not a prude wishes more heartily to have facts against her intimate acquaintance, than I now wish to have facts against thee. I would have her satisfaction, and they should all out.

AIR XVIII—*Irish Trot*
POLLY. I'm bubbled.[1]
LUCY.   —I'm bubbled!
POLLY. Oh how I am troubled!
LUCY. Bamboozled, and bit!
POLLY.   —My distresses are doubled.
LUCY.
When you come to the tree, should the hangman refuse,
These fingers, with pleasure, could fasten the noose.
POLLY. I'm bubbled, etc.

MACHEATH. Be pacified, my dear Lucy!— This is all a fetch of Polly's to make me desperate with you in case I get off. If I am hanged, she would fain have the credit of being thought my widow.—Really, Polly, this is no time for a dispute of this sort; for whenever you are talking of marriage, I am thinking of hanging.

POLLY. And hast thou the heart to persist in disowning me?

MACHEATH. And hast thou the heart to persist in persuading me that I am married? Why, Polly, dost thou seek to aggravate my misfortunes?

LUCY. Really, Miss Peachum, you but expose yourself. Besides, 'tis barbarous in you to worry a gentleman in his circumstances.

POLLY.

AIR XIX
  Cease your funning,
    Force or cunning
  Never shall my heart trepan.
    All these sallies
    Are but malice
  To seduce my constant man.
    'Tis most certain,
    By their flirting,
  Women oft have envy shown;
    Pleased to ruin
    Others' wooing;
  Never happy in their own!

LUCY. Decency, madam, methinks, might teach you to behave yourself with some reserve with the husband while his wife is present.

MACHEATH. But, seriously, Polly, this is carrying the joke a little too far.

[1] Cheated. Cf. the South Sea Bubble.

LUCY. If you are determined, madam, to raise a disturbance in the prison, I shall be obliged to send for the turnkey to show you the door. I am sorry, madam, you force me to be so ill-bred.

POLLY. Give me leave to tell you, madam; these forward airs don't become you in the least, madam. And my duty, madam, obliges me to stay with my husband, madam.

LUCY.

AIR XX—*Good-morrow, gossip Joan*
Why, how now, Madam Flirt?
 If you thus must chatter;
And are for flinging dirt,
 Let's try who best can spatter!
  Madam Flirt!

POLLY.
Why, how now, saucy jade;
 Sure the wench is tipsy!
How can you see me made (*To him*)
 The scoff of such a gipsy?
  Saucy jade! (*To her*)

SCENE XIV

LUCY, MACHEATH, POLLY, PEACHUM

PEACHUM. Where's my wench? Ah hussy! hussy!—Come you home, you slut; and when your fellow is hanged, hang yourself, to make your family some amends.

POLLY. Dear, dear father, do not tear me from him! I must speak; I have more to say to him. (*To* MACHEATH) Oh! twist thy fetters about me, that he may not haul me from thee!

PEACHUM. Sure, all women are alike! If ever they commit the folly, they are sure to commit another by exposing themselves.—Away—not a word more—you are my prisoner now, hussy!

POLLY. (*Holding* MACHEATH, PEACHUM *pulling her.*)

AIR XXI—*Irish howl*
No power on earth can e'er divide
The knot that sacred love hath tied.
When parents draw against our mind,
The true-love's knot they faster bind.
 Oh, oh ray, oh amborah—Oh, oh, etc.

Exeunt POLLY *and* PEACHUM

SCENE XV

LUCY, MACHEATH

MACHEATH. I am naturally compassionate, wife, so that I could not use the wench as she deserved, which made you at first suspect there was something in what she said.

LUCY. Indeed, my dear, I was strangely puzzled.

MACHEATH. If that had been the case, her father would never have brought me into this circumstance. No, Lucy,—I had rather die than be false to thee.

LUCY. How happy am I if you say this from your heart! For I love thee so, that I could sooner bear to see thee hanged than in the arms of another.

MACHEATH. But couldst thou bear to see me hanged?

LUCY. O Macheath, I can never live to see that day.

MACHEATH. You see, Lucy; in the account of love you are in my debt, and you must now be convinced that I rather choose to die than to be another's. Make me, if possible, love thee more, and let me owe my life to thee. If you refuse to assist me, Peachum and your father will immediately put me beyond all means of escape.

LUCY. My father, I know, hath been drinking hard with the prisoners, and I fancy he is now taking his nap in his own room. If I can procure the keys, shall I go off with thee, my dear?

MACHEATH. If we are together, 'twill be impossible to lie concealed. As soon as the search begins to be a little cool, I will send to thee—till then, my heart is thy prisoner.

LUCY. Come then, my dear husband—owe thy life to me—and though you love me not—be grateful. But that Polly runs in my head strangely.

MACHEATH. A moment of time may make us unhappy forever.

LUCY.

AIR XXII—*The lass of Patie's mill, etc.*
I like the fox shall grieve,
 Whose mate hath left her side,
Whom hounds, from morn till eve,
 Chase o'er the country wide,
Where can my lover hide?
 Where cheat the weary pack?
If love be not his guide,
 He never will come back!

ACT III

SCENE I. *Newgate*

LOCKIT, LUCY

LOCKIT. To be sure, wench, you must have been aiding and abetting to help him to this escape.

Lucy. Sir, here hath been Peachum and his daughter Polly, and to be sure they know the ways of Newgate as well as if they had been born and bred in the place all their lives. Why must all your suspicion light upon me?

Lockit. Lucy, Lucy, I will have none of these shuffling answers.

Lucy. Well then—if I know anything of him, I wish I may be burnt!

Lockit. Keep your temper, Lucy, or I shall pronounce you guilty.

Lucy. Keep yours, sir. I do wish I may be burnt, I do. And what can I say more to convince you.

Lockit. Did he tip handsomely? How much did he come down with? Come, hussy, don't cheat your father, and I shall not be angry with you. Perhaps you have made a better bargain with him than I could have done. How much, my good girl?

Lucy. You know, sir, I am fond of him, and would have given money to have kept him with me.

Lockit. Ah, Lucy! thy education might have put thee more upon thy guard; for a girl in the bar of an ale-house is always besieged.

Lucy. Dear sir, mention not my education —for 'twas to that I owe my ruin.

Air I—*If love's a sweet passion, etc.*

When young, at the bar you first taught me to score,
And bid me be free of my lips, and no more.
I was kissed by the parson, the squire, and the sot;
When the guest was departed, the kiss was forgot.
But his kiss was so sweet, and so closely he prest,
That I languished and pined till I granted the rest.

If you can forgive me, sir, I will make a fair confession, for to be sure he hath been a most barbarous villain to me.

Lockit. And so you have let him escape, hussy, have you?

Lucy. When a woman loves, a kind look, a tender word can persuade her to anything, and I could ask no other bribe.

Lockit. Thou wilt always be a vulgar slut, Lucy. If you would not be looked upon as a fool, you should never do anything but upon the foot of interest. Those that act otherwise are their own bubbles.

Lucy. But love, sir, is a misfortune that may happen to the most discreet woman, and in love we are all fools alike. Notwithstanding all he swore, I am now fully convinced that Polly Peachum is actually his wife. Did I let him escape (fool that I was!) to go to her? Polly will wheedle herself into his money, and then Peachum will hang him, and cheat us both.

Lockit. So I am to be ruined, because, forsooth, you must be in love!—a very pretty excuse!

Lucy. I could murder that impudent happy strumpet! I gave him his life, and that creature enjoys the sweets of it. Ungrateful Macheath!

Air II—*South-sea Ballad*

My love is all madness and folly,
 Alone I lie,
 Toss, tumble, and cry;
What a happy creature is Polly!
Was e'er such a wretch as I!
With rage I redden like scarlet,
That my dear, inconstant varlet,
 Stark blind to my charms,
 Is lost in the arms
Of that jilt, that inveigling harlot! [1]
This, this my resentment alarms.

Lockit. And so, after all this mischief, I must stay here to be entertained with your caterwauling, mistress Puss! Out of my sight, wanton strumpet! You shall fast and mortify yourself into reason, with now and then a little handsome discipline to bring you to your senses. Go! *Exit* Lucy

SCENE II

LOCKIT

—Peachum then intends to outwit me in this affair, but I'll be even with him. The dog is leaky in his liquor; so I'll ply him that way, get the secret from him, and turn this affair to my own advantage. Lions, wolves, and vultures don't live together in herds, droves, or flocks. Of all animals of prey, man is the only sociable one. Every one of us preys upon his neighbor, and yet we herd together. Peachum is my companion, my friend. According to the custom of the world, indeed, he may quote thousands of precedents for cheating me. And shall not I make use of the privilege of friendship to make him a return?

[1] These three lines are repeated in the first and third editions. In many of the songs repetition is required to make the words fit the airs, but the early editions usually do not indicate it.

AIR III—*Packington's Pound*

Thus gamesters united in friendship are found,
Though they know that their industry all is a cheat;
They flock to their prey at the dice-box's sound,
And join to promote one another's deceit.
    But if by mishap
      They fail of a chap,
To keep in their hands, they each other entrap.
Like pikes, lank with hunger, who miss of their ends,
They bite their companions, and prey on their friends.

Now, Peachum, you and I, like honest tradesmen, are to have a fair trial which of us two can over-reach the other. (*Calls*) Lucy!

Enter LUCY

Are there any of Peachum's people now in the house?

LUCY. Filch, sir, is drinking a quartern of strong waters in the next room with Black Moll.

LOCKIT. Bid him come to me.

Exit LUCY

SCENE III

LOCKIT, FILCH

LOCKIT. Why, boy, thou lookest as if thou wert half starved—like a shotten [1] herring.

FILCH. One had need have the constitution of a horse to go through the business. Since the favorite child-getter was disabled by a mishap, I have picked up a little money by helping the ladies to a pregnancy against their being called down to sentence. But if a man cannot get an honest livelihood any easier way, I am sure 'tis what I can't undertake for another session.

LOCKIT. Truly, if that great man should tip off, 'twould be an irreparable loss. The vigor and prowess of a knight-errant never saved half of the ladies in distress that he hath done. —But, boy, canst thou tell me where thy master is to be found?

FILCH. At his lock, sir, at the Crooked Billet.

LOCKIT. Very well. I have nothing more with you. (*Exit* FILCH) I'll go to him there, for I have many important affairs to settle with him; and in the way of those transactions, I'll artfully get into his secret, so that Macheath shall not remain a day longer out o' my clutches.

SCENE IV. *A gaming-house*

MACHEATH *in a fine tarnished coat*, BEN BUDGE, MATT OF THE MINT

MACHEATH. I am sorry, gentlemen, the road was so barren of money. When my friends are in difficulties, I am always glad that my fortune can be serviceable to them. (*Gives them money*) You see, gentlemen, I am not a mere court friend, who professes everything and will do nothing.

AIR IV—*Lillibullero*

The modes of the court so common are grown,
    That a true friend can hardly be met;
Friendship for interest is but a loan,
    Which they let out for what they can get.
      'Tis true, you find
      Some friends so kind,
Who will give you good counsel themselves to defend.
      In sorrowful ditty,
      They promise, they pity,
But shift you, for money, from friend to friend.

But we, gentlemen, have still honor enough to break through the corruptions of the world. And while I can serve you, you may command me.

BEN. It grieves my heart that so generous a man should be involved in such difficulties as oblige him to live with such ill company, and herd with gamesters.

MATT. See the partiality of mankind! One man may steal a horse, better than another look over a hedge. Of all mechanics, of all servile handicrafts-men, a gamester is the vilest. But yet, as many of the quality are of the profession, he is admitted amongst the politest company. I wonder we are not more respected.

MACHEATH. There will be deep play tonight at Marybone and consequently money may be picked up upon the road. Meet me there, and I'll give you the hint who is worth setting.

MATT. The fellow with a brown coat with narrow gold binding, I am told, is never without money.

MACHEATH. What do you mean, Matt? Sure you will not think of meddling with him! He's a good honest kind of a fellow, and one of us.

---

[1] A herring that has spawned and, having no roe, is of no value. Cf. *1 Henry IV*, Act II, scene iv.

BEN. To be sure, sir, we will put ourselves under your direction.

MACHEATH. Have an eye upon the money-lenders. A rouleau[1] or two would prove a pretty sort of an expedition. I hate extortion.

MATT. These rouleaus are very pretty things. I hate your bank bills. There is such a hazard in putting them off.

MACHEATH. There is a certain man of distinction who in his time hath nicked me out of a great deal of the ready. He is in my cash, Ben. I'll point him out to you this evening, and you shall draw upon him for the debt.—The company are met; I hear the dice-box in the other room. So, gentlemen, your servant! You'll meet me at Marybone. *Exeunt*

SCENE V. PEACHUM'S *lock. A table with wine, brandy, pipes and tobacco*

PEACHUM, LOCKIT

LOCKIT. The Coronation account,[2] brother Peachum, is of so intricate a nature, that I believe it will never be settled.

PEACHUM. It consists, indeed, of a great variety of articles. It was worth to our people, in fees of different kinds, above ten installments. This part of the account, brother, that lies open before us.

LOCKIT. A lady's tail[3] of rich brocade—that, I see, is disposed of—

PEACHUM. To Mrs. Diana Trapes, the tally-woman,[4] and she will make a good hand on't in shoes and slippers, to trick out young ladies upon their going into keeping.

LOCKIT. But I don't see any article of the jewels.

PEACHUM. Those are so well known that they must be sent abroad. You'll find them entered under the article of exportation. As for the snuff-boxes, watches, swords, etc., I thought it best to enter them under their several heads.

LOCKIT. Seven and twenty women's pockets complete, with the several things therein contained—all sealed, numbered, and entered.

PEACHUM. But, brother, it is impossible for us now to enter upon this affair.—We should have the whole day before us.—Besides, the account of the last half-year's plate is in a book by itself, which lies at the other office.

LOCKIT. Bring us then more liquor.—To-day shall be for pleasure—tomorrow for business.—Ah, brother, those daughters of ours are two slippery hussies. Keep a watchful eye upon Polly, and Macheath in a day or two shall be our own again.

LOCKIT.

AIR V—*Down in the North Country, etc.*

What gudgeons are we men!
Ev'ry woman's easy prey,
Though we have felt the hook, again
We bite and they betray.
The bird that hath been trapped,
When he hears his calling mate,
To her he flies, again he's clapped
Within the wiry grate.

PEACHUM. But what signifies catching the bird if your daughter Lucy will set open the door of the cage?

LOCKIT. If men were answerable for the follies and frailities of their wives and daughters, no friends could keep a good correspondence together for two days.—This is unkind of you, brother; for among good friends, what they say or do goes for nothing.

Enter A SERVANT

SERVANT. Sir, here's Mrs. Diana Trapes wants to speak with you.

PEACHUM. Shall we admit her, brother Lockit?

LOCKIT. By all means—she's a good customer, and a fine-spoken woman—and a woman who drinks and talks so freely, will enliven the conversation.

PEACHUM. Desire her to walk in.

Exit SERVANT

SCENE VI

PEACHUM, LOCKIT, MRS. TRAPES

PEACHUM. Dear Mrs. Dye, your servant—one may know by your kiss, that your gin is excellent.

TRAPES. I was always very curious[5] in my liquors.

LOCKIT. There is no perfumed breath like it. I have been long acquainted with the flavor of those lips—han't I, Mrs. Dye?

TRAPES. Fill it up.—I take as large draughts of liquor as I did of love.—I hate a flincher in either.

---

[1] Gold coins rolled into a packet.
[2] The pickings from the crowd at the coronation of George II the preceding year.
[3] Train.
[4] A woman who sells on credit,—on the installment plan.
[5] Particular.

AIR VI—*A shepherd kept sheep, etc.*

In the days of my youth I could bill like a dove,
    fa, la, la, etc.
Like a sparrow at all times was ready for love,
    fa, la, la, etc.
The life of all mortals in kissing should pass,
Lip to lip while we're young—then the lip to the
    glass, fa, etc.

But now, Mr. Peachum, to our business.—If you have blacks of any kind, brought in of late; mantoes[1]—velvet scarfs—petticoats—let it be what it will, I am your chap—for all my ladies are very fond of mourning.

PEACHUM. Why, look ye, Mrs. Dye—you deal so hard with us, that we can afford to give the gentlemen who venture their lives for the goods, little or nothing.

TRAPES. The hard times oblige me to go very near in my dealing. To be sure, of late years I have been a great sufferer by the parliament.—Three thousand pounds would hardly make me amends.—The act for destroying the Mint[2] was a severe cut upon our business—till then, if a customer stepped out of the way—we knew where to have her. No doubt you know Mrs. Coaxer—there's a wench now (till to-day) with a good suit of clothes of mine upon her back, and I could never set eyes upon her for three months together. Since the act, too, against imprisonment for small sums, my loss there too hath been very considerable; and it must be so, when a lady can borrow a handsome petticoat, or a clean gown, and I not have the least hank[3] upon her! And, o' my conscience, nowadays most ladies take a delight in cheating, when they can do it with safety!

PEACHUM. Madam, you had a handsome gold watch of us t'other day for seven guineas. Considering we must have our profit—to a gentleman upon the road, a gold watch will be scarce worth the taking.

TRAPES. Consider, Mr. Peachum, that watch was remarkable and not of very safe sale. If you have any black velvet scarfs—they are handsome winter wear, and take with most gentlemen who deal with my customers. 'Tis I that put the ladies upon a good foot. 'Tis not youth or beauty that fixes their price. The gentlemen always pay according to their dress, from half a crown to two guineas;[4] and yet those hussies make nothing of bilking me. Then, too, allowing for accidents.—I have eleven fine customers now down under the surgeon's hands; what with fees and other expenses, there are great goings-out, and no comings-in, and not a farthing to pay for at least a month's clothing. We run great risks—great risks, indeed.

PEACHUM. As I remember, you said something just now of Mrs. Coaxer.

TRAPES. Yes, sir. To be sure, I stripped her of a suit of my own clothes about two hours ago, and have left her as she should be, in her shift, with a lover of hers, at my house. She called him upstairs as he was going to Marybone in a hackney coach. And I hope, for her sake and mine, she will persuade the captain to redeem her, for the captain is very generous to the ladies.

LOCKIT. What captain?

TRAPES. He thought I did not know him—an intimate acquaintance of yours, Mr. Peachum—only Captain Macheath—as fine as a lord.

PEACHUM. To-morrow, dear Mrs. Dye, you shall set your own price upon any of the goods you like. We have at least half a dozen velvet scarfs, and all at your service. Will you give me leave to make you a present of this suit of nightclothes for your own wearing?—But are you sure it is Captain Macheath?

TRAPES. Though he thinks I have forgot him, nobody knows him better. I have taken a great deal of the captain's money in my time at second-hand, for he always loved to have his ladies well dressed.

PEACHUM. Mr. Lockit and I have a little business with the captain—you understand me—and we will satisfy you for Mrs. Coaxer's debt.

LOCKIT. Depend upon it—we will deal like men of honor.

TRAPES. I don't enquire after your affairs—so whatever happens, I wash my hands on't. It hath always been my maxim, that one friend should assist another.—But if you please, I'll take one of the scarfs home with me. 'Tis always good to have something in hand.

---

[1] Manteaus.
[2] The Mint of Southwark, destroyed by act of Parliament in 1723, had been a favorite resort of criminals.
[3] Curb, or restraining hold.
[4] The ladies' remuneration depends more on their dress than on their natural beauty.

Scene VII. *Newgate*

Lucy

Lucy. Jealousy, rage, love, and fear are at once tearing me to pieces. How I am weather-beaten and shattered with distresses!

Air VII—*One evening, having lost my way, etc.*

I'm like a skiff on the ocean tossed,
Now high, now low, with each billow borne;
With her rudder broke, and her anchor lost,
    Deserted and all forlorn.
While thus I lie rolling and tossing all night,
That Polly lies sporting on seas of delight!
    Revenge, revenge, revenge,
Shall appease my restless sprite.

—I have the ratsbane ready. I run no risk; for I can lay her death upon the gin, and so many die of that naturally that I shall never be called in question. But say I were to be hanged—I never could be hanged for anything that would give me greater comfort than the poisoning that slut.

Enter Filch

Filch. Madam, here's our Miss Polly come to wait upon you.
Lucy. Show her in.

Scene VIII

Lucy, Polly

Lucy. Dear madam, your servant. I hope you will pardon my passion when I was so happy to see you last. I was so overrun with the spleen, that I was perfectly out of myself. And really when one hath the spleen, everything is to be excused by a friend.

Air VIII—*Now Roger, I'll tell thee, because thou'rt my son, etc.*

When a wife's in her pout,
  (As she's sometimes, no doubt);
The good husband, as meek as a lamb,
    Her vapors to still,
    First grants her her will,
And the quieting draught is a dram.
Poor man! And the quieting draught is a dram.

—I wish all our quarrels might have so comfortable a reconciliation.
Polly. I have no excuse for my own behavior, madam, but my misfortunes. And really, madam, I suffer too upon your account.
Lucy. But, Miss Polly—in the way of friendship, will you give me leave to propose a glass of cordial to you?
Polly. Strong waters are apt to give me the headache; I hope, madam, you will excuse me.
Lucy. Not the greatest lady in the land could have better in her closet, for her own private drinking. You seem mighty low in spirits, my dear.
Polly. I am sorry, madam, my health will not allow me to accept of your offer. I should not have left you in the rude manner I did when we met last, madam, had not my papa hauled me away so unexpectedly. I was indeed somewhat provoked, and perhaps might use some expressions that were disrespectful. But really, madam, the captain treated me with so much contempt and cruelty, that I deserved your pity, rather than your resentment.
Lucy. But since his escape, no doubt, all matters are made up again.—Ah Polly! Polly! 'tis I am the unhappy wife, and he loves you as if you were only his mistress.
Polly. Sure, madam, you cannot think me so happy as to be the object of your jealousy! A man is always afraid of a woman who loves him too well—so that I must expect to be neglected and avoided.
Lucy. Then our cases, my dear Polly, are exactly alike. Both of us, indeed, have been too fond.

Air IX—*O Bessy Bell*

Polly. A curse attends that woman's love,
  Who always would be pleasing.
Lucy. The pertness of the billing dove,
  Like tickling, is but teasing.
Polly. What then in love can woman do?
Lucy. If we grow fond they shun us.
Polly. And when we fly them, they pursue.
Lucy. But leave us when they've won us.

Lucy. Love is so very whimsical in both sexes, that it is impossible to be lasting. But my heart is particular, and contradicts my own observation.
Polly. But really, mistress Lucy, by his last behavior, I think I ought to envy you. When I was forced from him, he did not shew the least tenderness. But perhaps he hath a heart not capable of it.

Air X—*Would fate to me Belinda give*

Among the men, coquets we find,
Who court by turns all womankind;
And we grant all their hearts desired,
When they are flattered and admired.

The coquets of both sexes are self-lovers, and that is a love no other whatever can dispossess. I fear, my dear Lucy, our husband is one of those.

Lucy. Away with these melancholy reflections!—indeed, my dear Polly, we are both of us a cup too low. (*Going*) Let me prevail upon you to accept of my offer.

>Air XI—*Come, sweet lass, etc.*
>Come, sweet lass,
>Let's banish sorrow
>'Till to-morrow;
>Come, sweet lass,
>Let's take a chirping glass.
>Wine can clear
>The vapors of despair;
>And make us light as air;
>Then drink, and banish care.

I can't bear, child, to see you in such low spirits. And I must persuade you to what I know will do you good. (*Aside*) I shall now soon be even with the hypocritical strumpet.
Exit Lucy

Scene ix

Polly

Polly. All this wheedling of Lucy cannot be for nothing—at this time too, when I know she hates me! The dissembling of a woman is always the forerunner of mischief. By pouring strong waters down my throat, she thinks to pump some secret out of me. I'll be upon my guard and won't taste a drop of her liquor, I'm resolved.

Scene x

Lucy, *with strong waters;* Polly

Lucy. Come, Miss Polly.

Polly. Indeed, child, you have given yourself trouble to no purpose.—You must, my dear, excuse me.

Lucy. Really, Miss Polly, you are as squeamishly affected about taking a cup of strong waters as a lady before company. I vow, Polly, I shall take it monstrously ill if you refuse me.—Brandy and men (though women love them never so well) are always taken by us with some reluctance—unless 'tis in private.

Polly. I protest, madam, it goes against me. What do I see! Macheath again in custody!—Now every glimmering of happiness is lost. (*Drops the glass of liquor on the ground*)

Lucy. (*Aside*) Since things are thus, I am glad the wench hath escaped: for by this event, 'tis plain, she was not happy enough to deserve to be poisoned.

Scene xi

Lockit, Macheath, Peachum, Lucy, Polly

Lockit. Set your heart to rest, captain.—You have neither the chance of love, or money for another escape; for you are ordered to be called down upon your trial immediately.

Peachum. Away, hussies!—This is not a time for a man to be hampered with his wives. You see, the gentleman is in chains already.

Lucy. O husband, husband, my heart longed to see thee; but to see thee thus distracts me!

Polly. Will not my dear husband look upon his Polly? Why hadst thou not flown to me for protection? With me thou hadst been safe.

>Air XII—*The last time I went o'er the moor*

Polly. Hither, dear husband, turn your eyes.
Lucy. Bestow one glance to cheer me.
Polly. Think, with that look, thy Polly dies.
Lucy. Oh shun me not—but hear me.
Polly. 'Tis Polly sues.
Lucy. —'Tis Lucy speaks.
Polly. Is thus true love requited?
Lucy. My heart is bursting.
Polly. —Mine too breaks.
Lucy. Must I?
Polly. —Must I be slighted?

Macheath. What would you have me say, ladies?—You see, this affair will soon be at an end without my disobliging either of you.

Peachum. But the settling this point, captain, might prevent a lawsuit between your two widows.

Macheath.

>Air XIII—*Tom Tinker's my true love*
>Which way shall I turn me? How can I decide?
>Wives, the day of our death, are as fond as a bride.
>One wife is too much for most husbands to hear,
>But two at a time there's no mortal can bear.
>This way, and that way, and which way I will,
>What would comfort the one, t'other wife would take ill.

Polly. (*Aside*) But if his own misfortunes have made him insensible to mine—a father

THE BEGGAR'S OPERA

sure will be more compassionate.—(*To* PEACHUM) Dear, dear sir, sink the material evidence, and bring him off at his trial! Polly upon her knees begs it of you.

AIR XIV—*I am a poor shepherd undone*

> When my hero in court appears,
>   And stands arraigned for his life;
> Then think of poor Polly's tears;
>   For ah! poor Polly's his wife.
> Like the sailor he holds up his hand,
> Distressed on the dashing wave.
> To die a dry death at land,
>   Is as bad as a wat'ry grave.
>   And alas, poor Polly;
>   Alack, and well-a-day!
>   Before I was in love,
>   Oh, every month was May!

LUCY. (*To Lockit*) If Peachum's heart is hardened, sure you, sir, will have more compassion on a daughter. I know the evidence is in your power. How can you be a tyrant to me? (*Kneeling*)

AIR XV—*Ianthe the lovely, etc.*

When he holds up his hand arraigned for his life,
Oh, think of your daughter, and think I'm his wife!
What are cannons, or bombs, or clashing of swords?
For death is more certain by witnesses' words.
Then nail up their lips; that dread thunder allay;
And each month of my life will hereafter be May.

LOCKIT. Macheath's time is come, Lucy. We know our own affairs; therefore let us have no more whimpering or whining.

AIR [1]—*A cobbler there was, etc.*

Ourselves, like the great, to secure a retreat,
When matters require it, must give up our gang.
  And good reason why,
  Or instead of the dry,
  Ev'n Peachum and I,
Like poor petty rascals, might hang, hang;
Like poor petty rascals might hang.

PEACHUM. Set your heart at rest, Polly. Your husband is to die to-day! therefore, if you are not already provided, 'tis high time to look about for another.—There's comfort for you, you slut.

LOCKIT. We are ready, sir, to conduct you to the Old Bailey.

[1] Not in early issues of the first edition but added in the last impression and retained in later editions

MACHEATH.
AIR XVI—*Bonny Dundee*

The charge is prepared; the lawyers are met,
The judges all ranged (a terrible show!).
I go, undismayed—for death is a debt,
A debt on demand. So, take what I owe.
Then farewell, my love—dear charmers, adieu.
Contented I die—'tis the better for you.
Here ends all dispute the rest of our lives,
  For this way at once I please all my wives.

—Now, gentlemen, I am ready to attend you.
Exeunt MACHEATH, LOCKIT *and* PEACHUM

SCENE XII

LUCY, POLLY, FILCH

POLLY. Follow them, Filch, to the court; and when the trial is over, bring me a particular account of his behavior, and of everything that happened.—You'll find me here with Miss Lucy. *Exit* FILCH
But why is all this music?

LUCY. The prisoners whose trials are put off till next sessions are diverting themselves.

POLLY. Sure there is nothing so charming as music! I'm fond of it to distraction! But alas! now, all mirth seems an insult upon my affliction.—Let us retire, my dear Lucy, and indulge our sorrows.—The noisy crew, you see, are coming upon us. *Exeunt*

(*A dance of prisoners in chains, etc.*)

SCENE XIII. *The condemned hold*

MACHEATH *in a melancholy posture*

AIR XVII—*Happy groves*
  O cruel, cruel, cruel case!
  Must I suffer this disgrace?

AIR XVIII—*Of all the girls that are so smart*
  Of all the friends in time of grief,
    When threat'ning death looks grimmer,
  Not one so sure can bring relief,
    As this best friend, a brimmer.
(*Drinks*)

AIR XIX—*Britons, strike home*
Since I must swing,—I scorn, I scorn to wince or whine.
(*Rises*)

AIR XX—*Chevy Chase*
  But now again my spirits sink;
  I'll raise them high with wine.
(*Drinks a glass of wine*)

AIR XXI—*To old Sir Simon the king*
 But valor the stronger grows,
 The stronger liquor we're drinking.
 And how can we feel our woes,
 When we've left the trouble of thinking?
       (*Drinks*)

AIR XXII—*Joy to great Cæsar*
 If thus—a man can die.
 Much bolder with brandy.
  (*Pours out a bumper of brandy*)

AIR XXIII—*There was an old woman*
So I drink off this bumper.—And now I can stand
 the test.
And my comrades shall see that I die as brave as
 the best.
       (*Drinks*)

AIR XXIV—*Did you ever hear of a gallant sailor*
 But can I leave my pretty hussies,
 Without one tear, or tender sigh?

AIR XXV—*Why are mine eyes still flowing*
 Their eyes, their lips, their busses,
 Recall my love.—Ah, must I die?

  AIR XXVI—*Greensleeves*
Since laws were made for ev'ry degree,[1]
To curb vice in others, as well as me,
I wonder we han't better company,
 Upon Tyburn tree!
But gold from law can take out the sting;
And if rich men like us were to swing,
'Twould thin the land, such numbers to string
 Upon Tyburn tree!

   (*Enter a* JAILOR)

JAILOR. Some friends of yours, captain, desire to be admitted.—I leave you together.
        Exit

   SCENE XIV

MACHEATH, BEN BUDGE, MATT OF THE MINT

MACHEATH. For my having broke prison, you see, gentlemen, I am ordered immediate execution. The sheriff's officers, I believe, are now at the door. That Jemmy Twitcher should peach me, I own, surprised me! 'Tis a plain proof that the world is all alike, and that even our gang can no more trust one another than other people. Therefore, I beg you, gentlemen, look well to yourselves, for in all probability you may live some months longer.

MATT. We are heartily sorry, captain, for your misfortune.—But 'tis what we must all come to.

MACHEATH. Peachum and Lockit, you know, are infamous scoundrels. Their lives are as much in your power, as yours are in theirs. Remember your dying friend!—'Tis my last request. Bring those villains to the gallows before you, and I am satisfied.

MATT. We'll do't.

  [*Re-enter* JAILOR]

JAILOR. Miss Polly and Miss Lucy entreat a word with you.

MACHEATH. Gentlemen, adieu.
  Exeunt BEN, MATT, *and* JAILOR

   SCENE XV

  LUCY, MACHEATH, POLLY

MACHEATH. My dear Lucy—my dear Polly! Whatsoever hath passed between us is now at an end. If you are fond of marrying again, the best advice I can give you is to ship yourselves off for the West Indies, where you'll have a fair chance of getting a husband apiece —or by good luck, two or three, as you like best.

POLLY. How can I support this sight!

LUCY. (*Aside*) There is nothing moves one so much as a great man in distress.

AIR XXVII—*All you that must take a leap, etc.*

LUCY. Would I might be hanged!
POLLY.   —And I would so too!
LUCY. To be hanged with you.
POLLY.   —My dear, with you.
MACHEATH. Oh, leave me to thought! I fear! I doubt!
I tremble! I droop!—See, my courage is out.
    (*Turns up the empty bottle*)
POLLY. No token of love?
MACHEATH.   —See, my courage is out.
    (*Turns up the empty pot*)
LUCY. No token of love?
POLLY.   Adieu.
LUCY.   Farewell!
MACHEATH. But hark! I hear the toll of the bell!
CHORUS. Tol de rol lol, etc.

  [*Enter* JAILOR]

JAILOR. Four women more, captain, with a child apiece! See, here they come.

---

[1] Pope or Swift was said by contemporaries to have written this song.

Enter WOMEN *and* CHILDREN

MACHEATH. What—four wives more!—This is too much.—Here, tell the Sheriff's officers I am ready. *Exit* MACHEATH *guarded*

SCENE XVI

To them enter PLAYER *and* BEGGAR

PLAYER. But, honest friend, I hope you don't intend that Macheath shall be really executed.

BEGGAR. Most certainly, sir. To make the piece perfect, I was for doing strict poetical justice. Macheath is to be hanged; and for the other personages of the drama, the audience must have supposed they were all either hanged or transported.

PLAYER. Why then, friend, this is a downright deep tragedy. The catastrophe is manifestly wrong, for an opera must end happily.

BEGGAR. Your objection, sir, is very just, and is easily removed; for you must allow that in this kind of drama, 'tis no matter how absurdly things are brought about. So—you rabble there! run and cry a reprieve!—let the prisoner be brought back to his wives in triumph.

PLAYER. All this we must do, to comply with the taste of the town.

BEGGAR. Through the whole piece you may observe such a similitude of manners in high and low life, that it is difficult to determine whether (in the fashionable vices) the fine gentlemen imitate the gentlemen of the road, or the gentlemen of the road the fine gentlemen. Had the play remained as I at first intended, it would have carried a most excellent moral. 'Twould have shown that the lower sort of people have their vices in a degree as well as the rich, and that they are punished for them.

SCENE XVII

To them MACHEATH, *with rabble, etc.*

MACHEATH. So it seems I am not left to my choice, but must have a wife at last.—Look ye, my dears, we will have no controversy now. Let us give this day to mirth, and I am sure she who thinks herself my wife will testify her joy by a dance.

ALL. Come, a dance—a dance!

MACHEATH. Ladies, I hope you will give me leave to present a partner to each of you. And (if I may without offence) for this time, I take Polly for mine. [*To* POLLY] And for life, you slut, for we were really married. As for the rest—but at present keep your own secret.

A Dance

AIR XXVIII—*Lumps of pudding, etc.*

Thus I stand like the Turk, with his doxies around;
From all sides their glances his passion confound:
For black, brown, and fair, his inconstancy burns,
And the different beauties subdue him by turns.
Each calls forth her charms, to provoke his desires;
Though willing to all, with but one he retires.
But think of this maxim, and put off your sorrow,
The wretch of to-day may be happy to-morrow.

CHORUS. But think of this maxim, etc.

THE LONDON MERCHANT;

OR,

THE HISTORY OF GEORGE BARNWELL

By George Lillo

*Learn to be wise from others' harm
And you shall do full well.*
  Old Ballad of The Lady's Fall.

Son of a Dutch jeweller living in the neighborhood of Moorfields, London, and his English wife, George Lillo, himself a London merchant, was born Feb. 4, 1693. He was brought up to his father's business in the pursuit of which he spent most of his life. The family were dissenters, a fact which may account for Lillo's late interest in the stage. At the age of thirty-seven he produced his first play, *Silvia; or, The Country Burial*, a decidedly moral ballad opera. His other plays, by which he gained some reputation as a man of letters, followed at more or less regular intervals until his death Sept. 3, 1739. He was buried in the vault of St. Leonard's, Shoreditch. Little else is known about him. His class interests are displayed in his two best tragedies, *The London Merchant* and *Fatal Curiosity*, and his Dutch extraction probably in the masque written to celebrate the royal marriage into the house of Orange. He was said by his contemporaries to be an unassuming, exemplary, pleasant little man. He was probably fairly successful in business and he is said to have made several thousand pounds by the success of his *The London Merchant*.

References: George Lillo. *The London Merchant and Fatal Curiosity*. Edited by A. W. Ward (Belles-Lettres Series).

LILLO'S DRAMATIC WORKS

Silvia; or, The Country Burial (ballad opera) (L.I.F., Nov. 10, 1730), 1730.
  The London Merchant; or, The History of George Barnwell (domestic tragedy) (D.L., June 22, 1731), 1731.
  The Christian Hero (tragedy) (D.L., Jan. 13, 1734/5), 1735.
  Fatal Curiosity. A True Tragedy of three Acts (domestic tragedy) (Hay., May 27, 1736), 1737.
  Marina. . . . from Pericles, Prince of Tyre (altered from Shakespeare) (C.G., Aug. 1, 1738), 1738.
  Elmerick; or, Justice Triumphant (tragedy) (D.L., Feb. 23, 1739/40), 1740.
  Britannia and Batavia (masque) written probably in 1734; never produced; printed, 8vo, 1740.
  Arden of Faversham (adaptation) (D.L., July, 1759), 1762.

Copies of the old ballad of George Barnwell were being sold on the streets of London in anticipation of a new play on the subject which was to appear at Drury Lane on June 22, 1731. According to the story, spectators arrived at the theater armed with copies of the ballad and determined to make the new tragedy ridiculous by comparing it with its source; but those who came to damn remained to weep, so affected were they by the simple pathos of this new form of dramatic entertainment. The acting of the younger Mr. Cibber, supported by his wife and his sister, Mrs. Charke, filled the audience with tearful admiration. The piece became a part of the repertory at Drury Lane, where the custom soon developed of putting it on during the holidays of Christmas and Easter as a special form of moral entertainment for London apprentices and as a horrible example of what would happen to them if they did not behave themselves. In this position *The London Merchant; or, The History of George Barnwell* remained on the boards for considerably over a century.

A new domestic tragedy had not been seen on the London stage for many a year before Lillo's first successful effort appeared. The Elizabethan examples like *Arden of Faversham* and *A Woman Killed with Kindness* were remote and forgotten; even Mr. Rowe's verse tragedies belonged to the early years of the century. Comedy had, indeed, turned to the affairs of common life and was in a fair way to make itself indistinguishable from tragedy in its sentimental moralizing and its all but tragic conclusion; Lillo, however, produced the first domestic tragedy in England under the influence of the sentimental school. The original title of the play, *The Merchant; or, The True History of George Barnwell*, changed during the original run, indicates the author's desire to have the events recorded looked upon as actual happenings. The ballad source was regarded as a true record. (It is to be found in Percy's *Reliques* and in Professor Child's collection of ballads.)

The significance of the play lies in the choice of form and subject, the prose being a distinct step in the direction of realism in tragedy, though much of this prose can be scanned as blank verse; and the characters and story being in line with the development of a literature of the lower middle class best illustrated in the period by *Pamela*, which, with Lillo's play, marks an epoch in English literature. The direct influence of *The London Merchant* in England, however, is not as profound as one would expect. It inspired only one other domestic tragedy of note, Edward Moore's *The Gamester* (D.L., 1753), which probably owes as much of its fame to the acting of Garrick as to any excellence of its own; most of the rest of English drama of the century is comic. On the Continent, however, through Diderot and Lessing, Lillo influenced the development of that domestic drama which was to find its way back to England late in the century chiefly in the dramas of Kotzebue and to determine indirectly the course of English dramatic literature from Lillo's day to ours.

[DEDICATION]

TO

SIR JOHN EYLES, BAR.[1] Member of Parliament for, and Alderman of, the City of *London*, and Sub-Governor of the *South-Sea* Company

Sir,

If tragic poety be, as Mr. Dryden[2] has some where said, the most excellent and most useful kind of writing, the more extensively useful the moral of any tragedy is, the more excellent that piece must be of its kind.

I hope I shall not be thought to insinuate that this, to which I have presumed to prefix your name, is such; that depends on its fitness to answer the end of tragedy, the exciting of the passions in order to the correcting such of them as are criminal, either in their nature, or through their excess. Whether the following scenes do this in any tolerable degree, is, with the deference that becomes one who would not be thought vain, submitted to your candid and impartial judgment.

What I would infer is this, I think, evident truth: that tragedy is so far from losing its dignity by being accommodated to the circumstances of the generality of mankind that it is more truly august in proportion to the extent of its influence, and the numbers that are properly affected by it. As it is more truly great to be the instrument of good to many, who stand in need of our assistance, than to a very small part of that number.

If princes, &c., were alone liable to misfortunes arising from vice or weakness in themselves or others there would be good reason for confining the characters in tragedy to those of superior rank; but, since the contrary is evident, nothing can be more reasonable than to proportion the remedy to the disease.

I am far from denying that tragedies founded on any instructive and extraordinary events in history or a well-invented fable where the persons introduced are of the highest rank are without their use, even to the bulk of the audience. The strong contrast between a *Tamerlane* and a *Bajazet*,[3] may have its weight with an unsteady people and contribute to the fixing of them in the interest of a prince of the character of the former, when, thro' their own levity or the arts of designing men, they are rendered factious and uneasy though they have the highest reason to be satisfied. The sentiments and example of a *Cato*,[4] may inspire his spectators with a just sense of the value of liberty when

---

[1] Sir John Eyles, Bart., member of a prominent City family, had been Lord Mayor in 1727.
[2] Cf. Dryden's *Discourse concerning the Original and Progress of Satire* and *Essay of Dramatick Poesy*.
[3] Characters in Nicholas Rowe's *Tamerlane* (1702), where they represent William III and Louis XIV. Rowe's play, not Marlowe's *Tamburlaine the Great* was known to the eighteenth century.
[4] Addison's *Cato, q.v.*

Though this phrase does not occur, Dryden's general idea might be construed to resemble Lillo's contention.

they see that honest patriot prefer death to an obligation from a tyrant who would sacrifice the constitution of his country and the liberties of mankind to his ambition or revenge. I have attempted, indeed, to enlarge the province of the graver kind of poetry, and should be glad to see it carried on by some abler hand. Plays founded on moral tales in private life may be of admirable use by carrying conviction to the mind with such irresistible force as to engage all the faculties and powers of the soul in the cause of virtue by stifling vice in its first principles. They who imagine this to be too much to be attributed to tragedy must be strangers to the energy of that noble species of poetry. Shakespeare, who has given such amazing proofs of his genius in that as well as in comedy, in his *Hamlet*, has the following lines:

Had he the motive and the cause for passion
That I have, he would drown the stage with tears
And cleave the general ear with horrid speech;
Make mad the guilty, and appall the free,
Confound the ignorant, and amaze indeed
The very faculty of eyes and ears.

And farther, in the same speech,

I've heard that guilty creatures at a play,
Have, by the very cunning of the scene,
Been so struck to the soul that presently
They have proclaim'd their malefactions.

Prodigious! yet strictly just. But I shan't take up your valuable time with my remarks; only give me leave just to observe that he seems so firmly persuaded of the power of a well wrote piece to produce the effect here ascribed to it, as to make Hamlet venture his soul on the event, and rather trust that, than a messenger from the other world, tho' it assumed, as he expresses it, his noble father's form, and assured him that it was his spirit. I'll have, says Hamlet, grounds more relative.

... The Play's the thing
Wherein I'll catch the conscience of the king.

Such plays are the best answers to them who deny the lawfulness of the stage.
Considering the novelty of this attempt, I thought it would be expected from me to say something in its excuse; and I was unwilling to lose the opportunity of saying something of the usefulness of tragedy in general, and what may be reasonably expected from the farther improvement of this excellent kind of poetry.

Sir, I hope you will not think I have said too much of an art, a mean specimen of which I am ambitious enough to recommend to your favor and protection. A mind conscious of superior worth as much despises flattery as it is above it. Had I found in myself an inclination to so contemptible a vice, I should not have chose Sir John Eyles for my patron. And indeed the best writ panegyric, tho' strictly true, must place you in a light, much inferior to that in which you have long been fixed by the love and esteem of your fellow citizens, whose choice of you for one of their representatives in Parliament, has sufficiently declared their sense of your merit. Nor hath the knowledge of your worth been confined to the City. The proprietors in the South-Sea Company, in which are included numbers of persons as considerable for their rank, fortune, and understanding as any in the kingdom, gave the greatest proof of their confidence in your capacity and probity when they chose you Sub-Governor of their company, at a time when their affairs were in the utmost confusion, and their properties in the greatest danger.[1] Nor is the court insensible of your importance. I shall not therefore attempt your character, nor pretend to add any thing to a reputation so well established.

Whatever others may think of a dedication, wherein there is so much said of other things and so little of the person to whom it is addressed, I have reason to believe that you will the more easily pardon it on that very account.

I am, sir,
Your most obedient
humble servant,
George Lillo

[1] After the collapse of the South-Sea Bubble in 1720, it was proposed to confiscate the estates of the directors to reimburse the losers. The company was reorganized by Walpole.

THE LONDON MERCHANT;
OR,
THE HISTORY OF GEORGE BARNWELL

DRAMATIS PERSONÆ

MEN

THOROWGOOD	Mr. Bridgwater	TRUEMAN	Mr. W. Mills
BARNWELL, *Uncle to George*	Mr. Roberts	BLUNT	Mr. R. Wetherilt
GEORGE BARNWELL	Mr. Cibber, Jun.		

WOMEN

MARIA	Mrs. Cibber	LUCY	Mrs. Charke
MILLWOOD	Mrs. Butler		

Officers *with their* Attendants, Keeper, *and* Footmen

SCENE: *London, and an adjacent Village*

PROLOGUE

Spoke BY MR. CIBBER, JUN.

The tragic muse, sublime, delights to show
Princes distressed, and scenes of royal woe;
In awful pomp, majestic, to relate
The fall of nations or some hero's fate,
That sceptered chiefs may by example know
The strange vicissitude of things below; 6
What danger on security attend;
How pride and cruelty in ruin end;
Hence Providence supreme to know; and own
Humanity adds glory to a throne. 10
    In ev'ry former age, and foreign tongue,
With native grandeur thus the goddess sung.
Upon our stage indeed with wished success
You've sometimes seen her in a humbler dress,
Great only in distress. When she complains
In Southerne's, Rowe's, or Otway's moving
    strains [1] 16
The brillant drops that fall from each bright
    eye,
The absent pomp with brighter gems supply.
Forgive us then, if we attempt to show
In artless strains a tale of private woe. 20
A London prentice ruined is our theme,
Drawn from the famed old song that bears
    his name.
We hope your taste is not so high to scorn
A moral tale esteemed e'er you were born,

Which for a century of rolling years 25
Has filled a thousand-thousand eyes with
    tears.
If thoughtless youth to warn and shame the
    age
From vice destructive well becomes the stage,
If this example innocence secure,
Prevents our guilt, or by reflection cure, 30
If Millwood's dreadful guilt, and sad despair,
Commend the virtue of the good and fair,
Though art be wanting, and our numbers fail,
Indulge th' attempt in justice to the tale.

ACT I

SCENE I. *A Room in* THOROWGOOD'S *House*

[*Enter*] THOROWGOOD *and* TRUEMAN

TRUEMAN. Sir, the packet from Genoa is arrived. (*Gives letters*)
THOROWGOOD. Heaven be praised, the storm that threatened our royal mistress, pure re-5 ligion, liberty, and laws is for a time diverted; the haughty and revengeful Spaniard, disappointed of the loan on which he depended from Genoa, must now attend the slow return of wealth from his new world to supply his 10 empty coffers, e'er he can execute his purposed invasion of our happy island; [2] by which means

---

[1] Southerne, Rowe, and Otway all wrote tragedies inclining towards the domestic rather than the heroic.

[2] These allusions date the action some time before the sailing of the Spanish Armada, 1588. The references to the Spaniards and true religion throughout the play show Lillo's own religious inclinations.

time is gained to make such preparations on our part as may, Heaven concurring, prevent his malice or turn the meditated mischief on himself.

TRUEMAN. He must be insensible indeed who is not affected when the safety of his country is concerned.—Sir, may I know by what means,—if I am too bold—

THOROWGOOD. Your curiosity is laudable; and I gratify it with the greater pleasure because from thence you may learn how honest merchants, as such, may sometimes contribute to the safety of their country as they do at all times to its happiness; that if hereafter you should be tempted to any action that has the appearance of vice or meanness in it, upon reflecting on the dignity of our profession, you may with honest scorn reject whatever is unworthy of it.

TRUEMAN. Should Barnwell or I, who have the benefit of your example, by our ill conduct bring any imputation on that honorable name, we must be left without excuse.

THOROWGOOD. You compliment, young man.— (TRUEMAN *bows respectfully*) Nay, I'm not offended. As the name of merchant never degrades the gentleman, so by no means does it exclude him; only take heed not to purchase the character of complaisant at the expense of your sincerity.—But to answer your question,—the bank of Genoa had agreed, at excessive interest and on good security, to advance the King of Spain a sum of money sufficient to equip his vast armada, of which our peerless Elizabeth (more than in name the mother of her people), being well informed, sent Walsingham,[1] her wise and faithful secretary, to consult the merchants of this loyal city, who all agreed to direct their several agents to influence, if possible, the Genoese to break their contract with the Spanish court. 'Tis done, the state and bank of Genoa, having maturely weighed and rightly judged of their true interest, prefer the friendship of the merchants of London to that of a monarch who proudly styles himself King of both Indies.

TRUEMAN. Happy success of prudent councils. What an expense of blood and treasure is here saved!—Excellent queen! O how unlike to former princes, who made the danger of foreign enemies a pretense to oppress their subjects, by taxes great and grievous to be borne.

THOROWGOOD. Not so our gracious queen, whose richest exchequer is her people's love as their happiness her greatest glory.

TRUEMAN. On these terms to defend us, is to make our protection a benefit worthy her who confers it, and well worth our acceptance. Sir, have you any commands for me at this time?

THOROWGOOD. Only to look carefully over the files to see whether there are any tradesmen's bills unpaid; and if there are, to send and discharge 'em. We must not let artificers lose their time, so useful to the public and their families, in unnecessary attendance.

[*Exit* TRUEMAN]

SCENE II

THOROWGOOD *and* MARIA, [*who enters.*]

THOROWGOOD. Well, Maria, have you given orders for the entertainment? I would have it in some measure worthy the guests. Let there be plenty, and of the best, that the courtiers, though they should deny us citizens politeness, may at least commend our hospitality.

MARIA. Sir, I have endeavored not to wrong your well-known generosity by an ill-timed parsimony.

THOROWGOOD. Nay, 'twas a needless caution; I have no cause to doubt your prudence.

MARIA. Sir! I find myself unfit for conversation at present. I should but increase the number of the company, without adding to their satisfaction.

THOROWGOOD. Nay, my child, this melancholy must not be indulged.

MARIA. Company will but increase it. I wish you would dispense with my absence;[2] solitude best suits my present temper.

THOROWGOOD. You are not insensible that it is chiefly on your account these noble lords do me the honor so frequently to grace my board; should you be absent, the disappointment may make them repent their condescension and think their labor lost.

MARIA. He that shall think his time or honor lost in visiting you, can set no real value on your daughter's company, whose only merit is that she is yours. The man of quality, who chooses to converse with a gentle-

---

[1] Sir Francis Walsingham (c. 1530-1590), Elizabeth's secretary of state and leader of the war party.

[2] The reverse, obviously, is meant.

man and merchant of your worth and character, may confer honor by so doing, but he loses none.

THOROWGOOD. Come, come, Maria, I need not tell you that a young gentleman may prefer your conversation to mine, yet intend me no disrespect at all; for though he may lose no honor in my company, 'tis very natural for him to expect more pleasure in yours. I remember the time when the company of the greatest and wisest man in the kingdom would have been insipid and tiresome to me, if it had deprived me of an opportunity of enjoying your mother's.

MARIA. Yours no doubt was as agreeable to her; for generous minds know no pleasure in society but where 'tis mutual.

THOROWGOOD. Thou know'st I have no heir, no child, but thee; the fruits of many years' successful industry must all be thine. Now it would give me pleasure great as my love, to see on whom you would bestow it. I am daily solicited by men of the greatest rank and merit for leave to address you, but I have hitherto declined it, in hopes that by observation I should learn which way your inclination tends; for as I know love to be essential to happiness in the marriage state, I had rather my approbation should confirm your choice than direct it.

MARIA. What can I say? How shall I answer as I ought this tenderness, so uncommon even in the best of parents; but you are without example; yet had you been less indulgent, I had been most wretched. That I look on the crowd of courtiers that visit here with equal esteem but equal indifference you have observed, and I must needs confess; yet had you asserted your authority, and insisted on a parent's right to be obeyed, I had submitted, and to my duty sacrificed my peace.

THOROWGOOD. From your perfect obedience in every other instance, I feared as much; and therefore would leave you without a bias in an affair wherein your happiness is so immediately concerned.

MARIA. Whether from a want of that just ambition that would become your daughter or from some other cause I know not; but I find high birth and titles don't recommend the man who owns them, to my affections.

THOROWGOOD. I would not that they should, unless his merit recommends him more. A noble birth and fortune, though they make not a bad man good, yet they are a real advantage to a worthy one, and place his virtues in the fairest light.

MARIA. I cannot answer for my inclinations, but they shall ever be submitted to your wisdom and authority; and as you will not compel me to marry where I cannot love, so love shall never make me act contrary to my duty. Sir, have I your permission to retire?

THOROWGOOD. I'll see you to your chamber.

[*Exeunt*]

SCENE III. *A Room in* MILLWOOD'S *house*

[*Discovered*] MILLWOOD. *Lucy waiting*

MILLWOOD. How do I look to-day, Lucy?

LUCY. O, killingly, madam!—A little more red, and you'll be irresistible!—But why this more than ordinary care of your dress and complexion? What new conquest are you aiming at?

MILLWOOD. A conquest would be new indeed!

LUCY. Not to you, who make 'em every day,—but to me.—Well! 'tis what I'm never to expect,—unfortunate as I am:—But your wit and beauty—

MILLWOOD. First made me a wretch, and still continue me so.—Men, however generous or sincere to one another, are all selfish hypocrites in their affairs with us. We are no otherwise esteemed or regarded by them, but as we contribute to their satisfaction.

LUCY. You are certainly, madam, on the wrong side in this argument. Is not the expense all theirs? And I am sure it is our own fault if we haven't our share of the pleasure.

MILLWOOD. We are but slaves to men.

LUCY. Nay, 'tis they that are slaves most certainly; for we lay them under contribution.

MILLWOOD. Slaves have no property; no, not even in themselves.—All is the victor's.

LUCY. You are strangely arbitrary in your principles, madam.

MILLWOOD. I would have my conquests complete, like those of the Spaniards in the New World, who first plundered the natives of all the wealth they had, and then condemned the wretches to the mines for life to work for more.

LUCY. Well, I shall never approve of your scheme of government. I should think it much more politic, as well as just, to find *my* subjects an easier employment.

MILLWOOD. It's a general maxim among the knowing part of mankind that a woman without virtue, like a man without honor or honesty, is capable of any action, though never so vile; and yet what pains will they not take, what arts not use, to seduce us from our innocence and make us contemptible and wicked even in their own opinions? Then is it not just, the villains, to their cost, should find us so.—But guilt makes them suspicious, and keeps them on their guard; therefore we can take advantage only of the young and innocent part of the sex, who, having never injured women, apprehend no injury from them.

LUCY. Ay, they must be young indeed.

MILLWOOD. Such a one, I think, I have found.—As I've passed through the City, I have often observed him receiving and paying considerable sums of money; from thence I conclude he is employed in affairs of consequence.

LUCY. Is he handsome?

MILLWOOD. Ay, ay, the stripling is well made.

LUCY. About—

MILLWOOD. Eighteen—

LUCY. Innocent, handsome, and about eighteen.—You'll be vastly happy.—Why, if you manage well, you may keep him to yourself these two or three years.

MILLWOOD. If I manage well, I shall have done with him much sooner; having long had a design on him, and meeting him yesterday, I made a full stop and gazing, wishfully on his face, asked him his name. He blushed, and bowing very low, answered, George Barnwell. I begged his pardon for the freedom I had taken, and told him that he was the person I had long wished to see, and to whom I had an affair of importance to communicate at a proper time and place. He named a tavern; I talked of honor and reputation, and invited him to my house. He swallowed the bait, promised to come, and this is the time I expect him. (*Knocking at the door*) Somebody knocks,—d'ye hear? I am at home to nobody to-day, but him.— [*Exit* LUCY]

SCENE IV

MILLWOOD

MILLWOOD. Less affairs must give way to those of more consequence; and I am strangely mistaken if this does not prove of great importance to me and him, too, before I have done with him.—Now, after what manner shall I receive him? Let me consider—What manner of person am I to receive?—He is young, innocent, and bashful; therefore I must take care not to shock him at first.—But then, if I have any skill in physiognomy, he is amorous, and, with a little assistance, will soon get the better of his modesty.—I'll trust to nature, who does wonders in these matters.—If to seem what one is not, in order to be the better liked for what one really is; if to speak one thing, and mean the direct contrary, be art in a woman, I know nothing of nature.

SCENE V

[*Enter*] *to her,* BARNWELL *bowing very low,* [*and*] LUCY *at a distance*

MILLWOOD. Sir, the surprise and joy!—

BARNWELL. Madam.—

MILLWOOD. This is such a favor,— (*Advancing*)

BARNWELL. Pardon me, madam,—

MILLWOOD. So unhoped for,—

(*Still advances.* BARNWELL *salutes her, and retires in confusion*)

MILLWOOD. To see you here—Excuse the confusion—

BARNWELL. I fear I am too bold.—

MILLWOOD. Alas, sir! All my apprehensions proceed from my fears of your thinking me so.—Please, sir, to sit.—I am as much at a loss how to receive this honor as I ought, as I am surprised at your goodness in conferring it.

BARNWELL. I thought you had expected me.—I promised to come.

MILLWOOD. That is the more surprising; few men are such religious observers of their word.

BARNWELL. All who are honest are.

MILLWOOD. To one another:—But we silly women are seldom thought of consequence enough to gain a place in your remembrance.

(*Laying her hand on his, as by accident*)

BARNWELL. (*Aside*) Her disorder is so great, she don't perceive she has laid her hand on mine.—Heaven! how she trembles!—What can this mean!

MILLWOOD. The interest I have in all that relates to you (the reason of which you shall know hereafter) excites my curiosity; and, were I sure you would pardon my presumption, I should desire to know your real sentiments on a very particular affair.

BARNWELL. Madam, you may command my poor thoughts on any subject;—I have none that I would conceal.
MILLWOOD. You'll think me bold.
BARNWELL. No, indeed.
MILLWOOD. What then are your thoughts of love?
BARNWELL. If you mean the love of women, I have not thought of it [at] all.—My youth and circumstances make such thoughts improper in me yet. But if you mean the general love we owe to mankind, I think no one has more of it in his temper than myself.—I don't know that person in the world whose happiness I don't wish, and wouldn't promote, were it in my power.—In an especial manner I love my uncle, and my master, but above all my friend.
MILLWOOD. You have a friend then whom you love?
BARNWELL. As he does me, sincerely.
MILLWOOD. He is, no doubt, often blessed with your company and conversation.—
BARNWELL. We live in one house together, and both serve the same worthy merchant.
MILLWOOD. Happy, happy youth!—Who e'er thou art, I envy thee, and so must all who see and know this youth.—What I have lost, by being formed a woman!—I hate my sex, myself.—Had I been a man, I might, perhaps, have been as happy in your friendship as he who now enjoys it:—But as it is,—Oh!—
BARNWELL. (*Aside*) I never observed women before, or this is sure the most beautiful of her sex.—You seem disordered, madam! May I know the cause?
MILLWOOD. Do not ask me.—I can never speak it, whatever is the cause;—I wish for things impossible;—I would be a servant, bound to the same master as you are, to live in one house with you.
BARNWELL. (*Aside*) How strange, and yet how kind, her words and actions are!—And the effect they have on me is as strange.—I feel desires I never knew before;—I must be gone, while I have power to go.—Madam, I humbly take my leave.—
MILLWOOD. You will not sure leave me so soon!
BARNWELL. Indeed I must.
MILLWOOD. You cannot be so cruel!—I have prepared a poor supper, at which I promised myself your company.
BARNWELL. I am sorry I must refuse the honor that you designed me;—but my duty to my master calls me hence.—I never yet neglected his service. He is so gentle and so good a master that should I wrong him, though he might forgive me, I never should forgive myself.
MILLWOOD. Am I refused, by the first man, the second favor I ever stooped to ask?—Go then, thou proud, hard-hearted youth.—But know, you are the only man that could be found, who would let me sue twice for greater favors.
BARNWELL. (*Aside*) What shall I do!—How shall I go or stay!
MILLWOOD. Yet do not, do not, leave me. I wish my sex's pride would meet your scorn; but when I look upon you, when I behold those eyes,—oh! spare my tongue, and let my blushes speak. This flood of tears to that will force their way, and declare—what woman's modesty should hide.
BARNWELL. Oh, heavens! she loves me, worthless as I am; her looks, her words, her flowing tears confess it. And can I leave her then? Oh, never, never! Madam, dry up those tears. You shall command me always; I will stay here for ever, if you'd have me.
LUCY. (*Aside*) So! she has wheedled him out of his virtue of obedience already and will strip him of all the rest one after another till she has left him as few as her ladyship or myself.
MILLWOOD. Now you are kind, indeed; but I mean not to detain you always: I would have you shake off all slavish obedience to your master;—but you may serve him still.
LUCY. Serve him still!—Aye, or he'll have no opportunity of fingering his cash, and then he'll not serve your end, I'll be sworn.

SCENE VI

[*Enter to them*] BLUNT

BLUNT. Madam, supper's on the table.
MILLWOOD. Come, sir, you'll excuse all defects. My thoughts were too much employed on my guest to observe the entertainment.
[*Exeunt* MILLWOOD *and* BARNWELL]

SCENE VII

[*Manent*] LUCY *and* BLUNT

BLUNT. What! is all this preparation, this elegant supper, variety of wines and music, for the entertainment of that young fellow!
LUCY. So it seems.

BLUNT. What, is our mistress turned fool at last! She's in love with him, I suppose.

LUCY. I suppose not, but she designs to make him in love with her if she can.

BLUNT. What will she get by that? He seems under age, and can't be supposed to have much money.

LUCY. But his master has; and that's the same thing, as she'll manage it.

BLUNT. I don't like this fooling with a handsome young fellow; while she's endeavoring to ensnare him, she may be caught herself.

LUCY. Nay, were she like me, that would certainly be the consequence;—for, I confess, there is something in youth and innocence that moves me mightily.

BLUNT. Yes, so does the smoothness and plumpness of a patridge move a mighty desire in the hawk to be the destruction of it.

LUCY. Why, birds are their prey, as men are ours; though, as you observed, we are sometimes caught ourselves. But that, I dare say, will never be the case with our mistress.

BLUNT. I wish it may prove so; for you know we all depend upon her. Should she trifle away her time with a young fellow that there's nothing to be got by, we must all starve.

LUCY. There's no danger of that, for I am sure she has no view in this affair but interest.

BLUNT. Well, and what hopes are there of success in that?

LUCY. The most promising that can be.—'Tis true, the youth has his scruples; but she'll soon teach him to answer them, by stifling his conscience.—O, the lad is in a hopeful way, depend upon't. [*Exeunt*]

SCENE VIII. [*Another room in* MILLWOOD's *house*]

[*Discovered*] BARNWELL *and* MILLWOOD *at an entertainment*

BARNWELL. What can I answer! All that I know is, that you are fair and I am miserable.

MILLWOOD. We are both so, and yet the fault is in ourselves.

BARNWELL. To ease our present anguish, by plunging into guilt, is to buy a moment's pleasure with an age of pain.

MILLWOOD. I should have thought the joys of love as lasting as they are great. If ours prove otherwise, 'tis your inconstancy must make them so.

BARNWELL. The law of Heaven will not be reversed; and that requires us to govern our passions.

MILLWOOD. To give us sense of beauty and desires, and yet forbid us to taste and be happy, is cruelty to nature. Have we passions only to torment us!

BARNWELL. To hear you talk, tho' in the cause of vice, to gaze upon your beauty, press your hand, and see your snow-white bosom heave and fall, enflames my wishes; my pulse beats high, my senses all are in a hurry, and I am on the rack of wild desire; yet for a moment's guilty pleasure, shall I lose my innocence, my peace of mind, and hopes of solid happiness?

MILLWOOD. Chimeras all,—
Come on with me and prove,
No joy's like woman, kind, nor heaven like love.

BARNWELL. I would not, yet I must on.
Reluctant thus, the merchant quits his ease
And trusts to rocks and sands and stormy seas;
In hopes some unknown golden coast to find,
Commits himself, tho' doubtful, to the wind,
Longs much for joys to come, yet mourns
   those left behind.
[*Exeunt*]

ACT II

SCENE I. *A Room in* THOROWGOOD'S *House*

[*Enter*] BARNWELL

BARNWELL. How strange are all things round me! Like some thief, who treads forbidden ground, fearful I enter each apartment of this well-known house. To guilty love, as if that was too little, already have I added breach of trust. A thief! Can I know myself that wretched thing, and look my honest friend and injured master in the face? Though hypocrisy may a while conceal my guilt, at length it will be known, and public shame and ruin must ensue. In the meantime, what must be my life? Ever to speak a language foreign to my heart; hourly to add to the number of my crimes in order to conceal 'em. Sure, such was the condition of the grand apostate,[1] when first he lost his purity; like me disconsolate he wandered, and while yet in heaven, bore all his future hell about him.
[*Enter* TRUEMAN]

[1] Lucifer.

Scene ii

Barnwell *and* Trueman

Trueman. Barnwell! O how I rejoice to see you safe! So will our master and his gentle daughter, who during your absence often inquired after you.

Barnwell. (*Aside*) Would he were gone, his officious love will pry into the secrets of my soul.

Trueman. Unless you knew the pain the whole family has felt on your account, you can't conceive how much you are beloved. But why thus cold and silent? When my heart is full of joy for your return, why do you turn away? Why thus avoid me? What have I done? How am I altered since you saw me last? Or rather what have you done, and why are you thus changed, for I am still the same?

Barnwell. (*Aside*) What have I done indeed?

Trueman. Not speak nor look upon me.

Barnwell. (*Aside*) By my face he will discover all I would conceal; methinks already I begin to hate him.

Trueman. I cannot bear this usage from a friend, one whom till now I ever found so loving, whom yet I love, though this unkindness strikes at the root of friendship, and might destroy it in any breast but mine.

Barnwell. I am not well. (*Turning to him*) Sleep has been a stranger to these eyes since you beheld them last.

Trueman. Heavy they look indeed, and swollen with tears; now they o'erflow; rightly did my sympathizing heart forebode last night when thou wast absent something fatal to our peace.

Barnwell. Your friendship engages you too far. My troubles, whate'er they are, are mine alone; you have no interest in them, nor ought your concern for me give you a moment's pain.

Trueman. You speak as if you knew of friendship nothing but the name. Before I saw your grief I felt it. Since we parted last I have slept no more than you, but, pensive in my chamber, sat alone and spent the tedious night in wishes for your safety and return; e'en now, though ignorant of the cause, your sorrow wounds me to the heart.

Barnwell. 'Twill not be always thus. Friendship and all engagements cease, as circumstances and occasions vary; and since you once may hate me, perhaps it might be better for us both that now you loved me less.

Trueman. Sure I but dream! Without a cause would Barnwell use me thus? Ungenerous and ungrateful youth, farewell.—I shall endeavor to follow your advice,—(*Going*) Yet stay, perhaps I am too rash, and angry when the cause demands compassion. Some unforeseen calamity may have befallen him, too great to bear.

Barnwell. [*Aside*] What part am I reduced to act; 'tis vile and base to move his temper thus, the best of friends and men.

Trueman. I am to blame, prithee forgive me, Barnwell. Try to compose your ruffled mind, and let me know the cause that thus transports you from yourself, my friendly counsel may restore your peace.

Barnwell. All that is possible for man to do for man, your generous friendship may effect; but here even that's in vain.

Trueman. Something dreadful is laboring in your breast. O give it vent and let me share your grief! 'Twill ease your pain should it admit no cure and make it lighter by the part I bear.

Barnwell. Vain supposition! My woes increase by being observed; should the cause be known they would exceed all bounds.

Trueman. So well I know thy honest heart, guilt cannot harbor there.

Barnwell. (*Aside*) O torture insupportable!

Trueman. Then why am I excluded? Have I a thought I would conceal from you?

Barnwell. If still you urge me on this hated subject, I'll never enter more beneath this roof, nor see your face again.

Trueman. 'Tis strange. But I have done; say but you hate me not.

Barnwell. Hate you!—I am not that monster yet.

Trueman. Shall our friendship still continue?

Barnwell. It's a blessing I never was worthy of, yet now must stand on terms; and but upon conditions can confirm it.

Trueman. What are they?

Barnwell. Never hereafter, though you should wonder at my conduct, desire to know more than I am willing to reveal.

Trueman. 'Tis hard, but upon any conditions I must be your friend.

BARNWELL. Then, as much as one lost to himself can be another's, I am yours.
(Embracing)
TRUEMAN. Be ever so, and may heaven restore your peace.
BARNWELL. Will yesterday return? We have heard the glorious sun, that till then incessant rolled, once stopped his rapid course and once went back. The dead have risen; and parched rocks poured forth a liquid stream to quench a people's thirst. The sea divided and formed walls of water while a whole nation passed in safety through its sandy bosom. Hungry lions have refused their prey; and men unhurt have walked amidst consuming flames; but never yet did time once past, return.
TRUEMAN. Though the continued chain of time has never once been broke, nor ever will, but uninterrupted must keep on its course till lost in eternity it ends there where it first begun; yet as heaven can repair whatever evils time can bring upon us, he who trusts heaven ought never to despair. But business requires our attendance, business the youth's best preservative from ill, as idleness [is] his worst of snares. Will you go with me?
BARNWELL. I'll take a little time to reflect on what has past, and follow you.
[Exit TRUEMAN*]*

SCENE III

BARNWELL

I might have trusted Trueman to have applied to my uncle to have repaired the wrong I have done my master; but what of Millwood? Must I expose her too? Ungenerous and base! Then heaven requires it not. But heaven requires that I forsake her. What! Never see her more! Does heaven require that! I hope I may see her, and heaven not be offended. Presumptuous hope! Dearly already have I proved my frailty; should I once more tempt heaven, I may be left to fall never to rise again. Yet shall I leave her, forever leave her, and not let her know the cause? She who loves me with such a boundless passion? Can cruelty be duty? I judge of what she then must feel, by what I now endure. The love of life and fear of shame, opposed by inclination strong as death or shame, like wind and tide in raging conflict met, when neither can prevail, keep me in doubt. How then can I determine?
[Enter THOROWGOOD*]*

SCENE IV

THOROWGOOD *and* BARNWELL

THOROWGOOD. Without a cause assigned, or notice given, to absent yourself last night was a fault, young man, and I came to chide you for it, but hope I am prevented. That modest blush, the confusion so visible in your face, speak grief and shame. When we have offended heaven, it requires no more; and shall man, who needs himself to be forgiven, be harder to appease? If my pardon or love be of moment to your peace, look up, secure of both.
BARNWELL. *(Aside)* This goodness has o'ercome me.—O sir! You know not the nature and extent of my offence; and I should abuse your mistaken bounty to receive 'em. Though I had rather die than speak my shame; though racks could not have forced the guilty secret from my breast, your kindness has.
THOROWGOOD. Enough, enough! Whate'er it be, this concern shows you're convinced, and I am satisfied. How painful is the sense of guilt to an ingenuous mind!—some youthful folly, which it were prudent not to enquire into. When we consider the frail condition of humanity, it may raise our pity, not our wonder, that youth should go astray; when reason, weak at the best when opposed to inclination, scarce formed, and wholly unassisted by experience, faintly contends, or willingly becomes the slave of sense. The state of youth is much to be deplored, and the more so because they see it not; they being then to danger most exposed, when they are least prepared for their defence.
BARNWELL. It will be known, and you recall your pardon and abhor me.
THOROWGOOD. I never will; so heaven confirm to me the pardon of my offences. Yet be upon your guard in this gay, thoughtless season of your life; now, when the sense of pleasure's quick, and passion high, the voluptuous appetites, raging and fierce, demand the strongest curb; take heed of a relapse. When vice becomes habitual, the very power of leaving it is lost.
BARNWELL. Hear me, then, on my knees confess.

THOROWGOOD. I will not hear a syllable more upon this subject; it were not mercy, but cruelty, to hear what must give you such torment to reveal.

BARNWELL. This generosity amazes and distracts me.

THOROWGOOD. This remorse makes thee dearer to me than if thou hadst never offended; whatever is your fault, of this I'm certain, 'twas harder for you to offend than me to pardon. [*Exit* THOROWGOOD]

SCENE V

BARNWELL

BARNWELL. Villain, villain, villain! basely to wrong so excellent a man. Should I again return to folly?—detested thought!—But what of Millwood then? Why, I renounce her; I give her up; the struggle's over, and virtue has prevailed. Reason may convince, but gratitude compels. This unlooked for generosity has saved me from destruction (*Going*)

SCENE VI

To him a Footman

FOOTMAN. Sir, two ladies, from your uncle in the country, desire to see you.

BARNWELL. (*Aside*) Who should they be? Tell them I'll wait upon 'em.

SCENE VII

BARNWELL

BARNWELL. Methinks I dread to see 'em. Guilt, what a coward hast thou made me? Now everything alarms me. [*Exit*]

SCENE VIII. *Another room in* THOROWGOOD'S *house*

[*Discovered*] MILLWOOD *and* LUCY, *and to them* [*enters*] *a* Footman

FOOTMAN. Ladies, he'll wait upon you immediately.

MILLWOOD. 'Tis very well. I thank you.

[*Enter* BARNWELL]

SCENE IX

BARNWELL, MILLWOOD, *and* LUCY

BARNWELL. Confusion! Millwood!

MILLWOOD. That angry look tells me that here I'm an unwelcome guest; I feared as much,—the unhappy are so everywhere.

BARNWELL. Will nothing but my utter ruin content you?

MILLWOOD. Unkind and cruel! lost myself, your happiness is now my only care.

BARNWELL. How did you gain admission?

MILLWOOD. Saying we were desired by your uncle to visit and deliver a message to you, we were received by the family without suspicion, and with much respect directed here.

BARNWELL. Why did you come at all?

MILLWOOD. I never shall trouble you more; I'm come to take my leave forever. Such is the malice of my fate, I go hopeless, despairing ever to return. This hour is all I have left me. One short hour is all I have to bestow on love and you, for whom I thought the longest life too short.

BARNWELL. Then we are met to part forever?

MILLWOOD. It must be so; yet think not that time or absence ever shall put a period to my grief or make me love you less; though I must leave you, yet condemn me not.

BARNWELL. Condemn you? No, I approve your resolution, and rejoice to hear it; 'tis just, 'tis necessary. I have well weighed, and found it so.

LUCY. (*Aside*) I'm afraid the young man has more sense than she thought he had.

BARNWELL. Before you came I had determined never to see you more.

MILLWOOD. (*Aside*) Confusion!

LUCY. (*Aside*) Ay! we are all out; this is a turn so unexpected, that I shall make nothing of my part; they must e'en play the scene betwixt themselves.

MILLWOOD. 'Twas some relief to think, though absent, you would love me still; but to find, though fortune had been kind, that you, more cruel and inconstant, had resolved to cast me off. This, as I never could expect, I have not learnt to bear.

BARNWELL. I am sorry to hear you blame in me a resolution that so well becomes us both.

MILLWOOD. I have reason for what I do, but you have none.

BARNWELL. Can we want a reason for parting, who have so many to wish we never had met?

MILLWOOD. Look on me, Barnwell; am I deformed or old, that satiety so soon succeeds enjoyment? Nay, look again; am I not she whom yesterday you thought the fairest and the kindest of her sex, whose hand, trembling with ecstasy, you pressed and molded thus, while on my eyes you gazed with such delight, as if desire increased by being fed?

BARNWELL. No more! Let me repent my former follies, if possible, without remembering what they were.

MILLWOOD. Why?

BARNWELL. Such is my frailty that 'tis dangerous.

MILLWOOD. Where is the danger, since we are to part?

BARNWELL. The thought of that already is too painful.

MILLWOOD. If it be painful to part, then I may hope at least you do not hate me?

BARNWELL. No,—no,—I never said I did!—O my heart!

MILLWOOD. Perhaps you pity me?

BARNWELL. I do, I do, indeed, I do.

MILLWOOD. You'll think upon me?

BARNWELL. Doubt it not while I can think at all.

MILLWOOD. You may judge an embrace at parting too great a favor, though it would be the last? (*He draws back*) A look shall then suffice,—farewell forever.

[*Exeunt* MILLWOOD *and* LUCY]

SCENE X

BARNWELL

BARNWELL. If to resolve to suffer be to conquer, I have conquered. Painful victory!

SCENE XI

BARNWELL, MILLWOOD *and* LUCY [*who return*]

MILLWOOD. One thing I had forgot. I never must return to my own house again. This I thought proper to let you know, lest your mind should change, and you should seek in vain to find me there. Forgive me this second intrusion; I only came to give you this caution, and that, perhaps, was needless.

BARNWELL. I hope it was, yet it is kind, and I must thank you for it.

MILLWOOD. My friend, your arm. (*To* LUCY) Now I am gone forever. (*Going*)

BARNWELL. One thing more;—sure, there's no danger in my knowing where you go? If you think otherwise—

MILLWOOD. Alas! (*Weeping*)

LUCY. (*Aside*) We are right I find, that's my cue.—Ah; dear sir, she's going she knows not whither; but go she must.

BARNWELL. Humanity obliges me to wish you well; why will you thus expose yourself to needless troubles?

LUCY. Nay, there's no help for it. She must quit the town immediately, and the kingdom as soon as possible; it was no small matter, you may be sure, that could make her resolve to leave you.

MILLWOOD. No more, my friend; since he for whose dear sake alone I suffer, and am content to suffer, is kind and pities me. Where'er I wander through wilds and deserts, benighted and forlorn, that thought shall give me comfort.

BARNWELL. For my sake! O tell me how; which way am I so cursed as to bring such ruin on thee?

MILLWOOD. No matter, I am contented with my lot.

BARNWELL. Leave me not in this incertainty.

MILLWOOD. I have said too much.

BARNWELL. How, how am I the cause of your undoing?

MILLWOOD. 'Twill but increase your troubles.

BARNWELL. My troubles can't be greater than they are.

LUCY. Well, well, sir, if she won't satisfy you, I will.

BARNWELL. I am bound to you beyond expression.

MILLWOOD. Remember, sir, that I desired you not to hear it.

BARNWELL. Begin, and ease my racking expectation.

LUCY. Why you must know, my lady here was an only child; but her parents dying while she was young, left her and her fortune, (no inconsiderable one, I assure you) to the care of a gentleman who has a good estate of his own.

MILLWOOD. Ay, ay, the barbarous man is rich enough;—but what are riches when compared to love?

LUCY. For a while he performed the office of a faithful guardian, settled her in a house, hired her servants;[1]—but you have seen in what manner she lived, so I need say no more of that.

[1] I.e., hired servants for her.

MILLWOOD. How I shall live hereafter, heaven knows.

LUCY. All things went on as one could wish, till, some time ago, his wife dying, he fell violently in love with his charge, and would fain have married her. Now the man is neither old nor ugly, but a good, personable sort of a man, but I don't know how it was, she could never endure him, that he brought in an account of his executorship, wherein he makes her debtor to him.—[1]

MILLWOOD. A trifle in itself, but more than enough to ruin me, whom, by this unjust account, he had stripped of all before.

LUCY. Now she having neither money nor friend, except me, who am as unfortunate as herself, he compelled her to pass his account, and give bond for the sum he demanded; but still provided handsomely for her and continued his courtship, till, being informed by his spies (truly I suspect some in her own family) that you were entertained at her house, and stayed with her all night, he came this morning raving, and storming like a madman, talks no more of marriage (so there's no hopes of making up matters that way) but vows her ruin, unless she'll allow him the same favor that he supposes she granted you.

BARNWELL. Must she be ruined, or find her refuge in another's arms?

MILLWOOD. He gave me but an hour to resolve in, that's happily spent with you;—and now I go.—

BARNWELL. To be exposed to all the rigors of the various seasons; the summer's parching heat, and winter's cold; unhoused to wander friendless through the unhospitable world, in misery and want; attended with fear and danger, and pursued by malice and revenge, wouldst thou endure all this for me, and can I do nothing, nothing to prevent it?

LUCY. 'Tis really a pity, there can be no way found out.

BARNWELL. O where are all my resolutions now? Like early vapors, or the morning dew, chased by the sun's warm beams they're vanished and lost, as though they had never been.

LUCY. Now I advised her, sir, to comply with the gentleman, that would not only put an end to her troubles, but make her fortune at once.

BARNWELL. Tormenting fiend, away!—I had rather perish, nay, see her perish, than

[1] The sense would be clearer if "that" were omitted.

have her saved by him; I will myself prevent her ruin, though with my own. A moment's patience, I'll return immediately.— [Exit]

SCENE XII

MILLWOOD and LUCY

LUCY. 'Twas well you came, or, by what I can perceive, you had lost him.

MILLWOOD. That, I must confess, was a danger I did not foresee; I was only afraid he should have come without money. You know a house of entertainment like mine, is not kept with nothing.

LUCY. That's very true; but then you should be reasonable in your demands; 'tis pity to discourage a young man.

[Enter BARNWELL]

SCENE XIII

BARNWELL, MILLWOOD, and LUCY

BARNWELL. (Aside) What am I about to do! Now you, who boast your reason all sufficient, suppose yourselves in my condition, and determine for me, whether it's right to let her suffer for my faults, or, by this small addition to my guilt, prevent the ill effects of what is past.

LUCY. (Aside) These young sinners think everything in the ways of wickedness so strange,—but I could tell him that this is nothing but what's very common; for one vice as naturally begets another, as a father a son. But he'll find out that himself, if he lives long enough.

BARNWELL. Here take this, and with it purchase your deliverance; return to your house, and live in peace and safety.

MILLWOOD. So I may hope to see you there again.

BARNWELL. Answer me not,—but fly,—lest, in the agonies of my remorse, I take again what is not mine to give, and abandon thee to want and misery.

MILLWOOD. Say but you'll come.—

BARNWELL. You are my fate, my heaven, or my hell. Only leave me now, dispose of me hereafter as you please.

[Exeunt MILLWOOD and LUCY]

SCENE XIV

BARNWELL

What have I done? Were my resolutions founded on reason, and sincerely made? why then has heaven suffered me to fall? I sought

not the occasion; and, if my heart deceives me not, compassion and generosity were my motives. Is virtue inconsistent with itself, or are vice and virtue only empty names? Or do they depend on accidents beyond our power to produce, or to prevent, wherein we have no part, and yet must be determined by the event?—But why should I attempt to reason? All is confusion, horror, and remorse; —I find I am lost, cast down from all my late erected hopes and plunged again in guilt, yet scarce know how or why—
Such undistinguished horrors make my brain, Like hell, the seat of darkness, and of pain.
[*Exit*]

ACT III

Scene i

[*Enter*] Thorowgood *and* Trueman

Thorowgood. Methinks I would not have you only learn the method of merchandize and practise it hereafter merely as a means of getting wealth. 'Twill be well worth your pains to study it as a science. See how it is founded in reason and the nature of things. How it has promoted humanity, as it has opened and yet keeps up an intercourse between nations far remote from one another in situation, customs, and religion; promoting arts, industry, peace and plenty, by mutual benefits diffusing mutual love from pole to pole.

Trueman. Something of this I have considered, and hope, by your assistance, to extend my thoughts much farther. I have observed those countries where trade is promoted and encouraged do not make discoveries to destroy, but to improve mankind by love and friendship, to tame the fierce, and polish the most savage, to teach them the advantages of honest traffic by taking from them with their own consent their useless superfluities, and giving them in return what, from their ignorance in manual arts, their situation, or some other accident they stand in need of.

Thorowgood. 'Tis justly observed. The populous east, luxuriant, abounds with glittering gems, bright pearls, aromatic spices, and health-restoring drugs. The late found western world glows with unnumbered veins of gold and silver ore. On every climate, and on every country, heaven had bestowed some good peculiar to itself. It is the industrious merchant's business to collect the various blessings of each soil and climate, and, with the product of the whole, to enrich his native country.

Well! I have examined your accounts. They are not only just, as I have always found them, but regularly kept, and fairly entered. I commend your diligence. Method in business is the surest guide. He who neglects it frequently stumbles, and always wanders perplexed, uncertain, and in danger. Are Barnwell's accounts ready for my inspection? He does not use to be the last on these occasions.

Trueman. Upon receiving your orders he retired, I thought in some confusion. If you please, I'll go and hasten him. I hope he hasn't been guilty of any neglect.

Thorowgood. I'm now going to the Exchange; let him know, at my return, I expect to find him ready. [*Exeunt*]

Scene ii

[*Enter*] Maria *with a book* [*; she*] *sits and reads*

Maria. How forcible is truth! The weakest mind, inspired with love of that, fixed and collected in itself, with indifference beholds the united force of earth and hell opposing. Such souls are raised above the sense of pain, or so supported that they regard it not. The martyr cheaply purchases his heaven. Small are his sufferings, great is his reward; not so the wretch who combats love with duty, when the mind, weakened and dissolved by the soft passion, feeble and hopeless opposes its own desire. What is an hour, a day, a year of pain, to a whole life of tortures, such as these?

[*Enter* Trueman]

Scene iii

Trueman *and* Maria

Trueman. O, Barnwell! O, my friend, how art thou fallen!

Maria. Ha! Barnwell! What of him? Speak, say what of Barnwell?

Trueman. 'Tis not to be concealed. I've news to tell of him that will afflict your generous father, yourself, and all who knew him.

Maria. Defend us, Heaven!

Trueman. I cannot speak it.—See there.
(*Gives a letter*, Maria *reads*)

Maria.
Trueman,
I know my absence will surprise my honored master, and yourself; and the more, when you

shall understand that the reason of my withdrawing, is my having embezzled part of the cash with which I was entrusted. After this, 'tis needless to inform you that I intend never to return again. Though this might have been known by examining my accounts; yet, to prevent that unnecessary trouble, and to cut all fruitless expectations of my return, I have left this from the lost George Barnwell.

TRUEMAN. Lost indeed! Yet how he should be guilty of what he there charges himself withal, raises my wonder equal to my grief. Never had youth a higher sense of virtue. Justly he thought, and as he thought he practised; never was life more regular than his; an understanding uncommon at his years; an open, generous, manliness of temper; his manners easy, unaffected and engaging.

MARIA. This and much more you might have said with truth.—He was the delight of every eye, and joy of every heart that knew him.

TRUEMAN. Since such he was, and was my friend, can I support his loss? See, the fairest and happiest maid this wealthy city boasts, kindly condescends to weep for thy unhappy fate, poor, ruined Barnwell!

MARIA. Trueman, do you think a soul so delicate as his, so sensible of shame, can e'er submit to live a slave to vice?

TRUEMAN. Never, never! So well I know him, I'm sure this act of his, so contrary to his nature, must have been caused by some unavoidable necessity.

MARIA. Is there no means yet to preserve him?

TRUEMAN. O! that there were!—But few men recover reputation lost, a merchant never. Nor would he, I fear, though I should find him, ever be brought to look his injured master in the face.

MARIA. I fear as much,—and therefore would never have my father know it.

TRUEMAN. That's impossible.

MARIA. What's the sum?

TRUEMAN. 'Tis considerable.—I've marked it here, to show it, with the letter, to your father, at his return.

MARIA. If I should supply the money, could you so dispose of that, and the account, as to conceal this unhappy mismanagement from my father?

TRUEMAN. Nothing more easy.—But can you intend it? Will you save a helpless wretch from ruin? Oh! 'twere an act worthy such exalted virtue as Maria's.—Sure, heaven in mercy to my friend inspired the generous thought!

MARIA. Doubt not but I would purchase so great a happiness at a much dearer price.—But how shall he be found?

TRUEMAN. Trust to my diligence for that.—In the meantime, I'll conceal his absence from your father, or find such excuses for it, that the real cause shall never be suspected.

MARIA. In attempting to save from shame, one whom we hope may yet return to virtue, to heaven and you, the judges of this action, I appeal, whether I have done anything misbecoming my sex and character.

TRUEMAN. Earth must approve the deed, and heaven, I doubt not, will reward it.

MARIA. If heaven succeed it, I am well rewarded. A virgin's fame is sullied by suspicion's slightest breath; and therefore as this must be a secret from my father and the world for Barnwell's sake; for mine, let it be so to him.

SCENE IV. MILLWOOD's *House*

[*Discovered*] LUCY *and* BLUNT

LUCY. Well! what do you think of Millwood's conduct now?

BLUNT. I own it is surprising. I don't know which to admire most, her feigned, or his real passion, though I have sometimes been afraid that her avarice would discover her:—But his youth and want of experience make it the easier to impose on him.

LUCY. No, it is his love. To do him justice, notwithstanding his youth, he don't want understanding; but you men are much easier imposed on in these affairs than your vanity will allow you to believe. Let me see the wisest of you all as much in love with me as Barnwell is with Millwood, and I'll engage to make as great a fool of him.

BLUNT. And all circumstances considered, to make as much money of him, too.

LUCY. I can't answer for that. Her artifice in making him rob his master at first, and the various stratagems, by which she has obliged him to continue in that course, astonish even me, who know her so well.

BLUNT. But then you are to consider that the money was his master's.

LUCY. There was the difficulty of it. Had

it been his own, it had been nothing. Were the world his, she might have it for a smile. But these golden days are done; he's ruined, and Millwood's hopes of farther profits there are at an end.

BLUNT. That's no more than we all expected.

LUCY. Being called by his master to make up his accounts, he was forced to quit his house and service, and wisely flies to Millwood for relief and entertainment.

BLUNT. I have not heard of this before! How did she receive him?

LUCY. As you would expect. She wondered what he meant, was astonished at his impudence, and, with an air of modesty peculiar to herself swore so heartily that she never saw him before that she put me out of countenance.

BLUNT. That's much indeed! But how did Barnwell behave?

LUCY. He grieved, and at length, enraged at this barbarous treatment, was preparing to be gone; and, making toward the door, showed a bag of money, which he had stolen from his master,—the last he's ever like to have from thence.

BLUNT. But then Millwood?

LUCY. Aye, she, with her usual address, returned to her old arts of lying, swearing, and dissembling. Hung on his neck, and wept, and swore 'twas meant in jest, till the easy fool, melted into tears, threw the money into her lap, and swore he had rather die than think her false.

BLUNT. Strange infatuation!

LUCY. But what followed was stranger still. As doubts and fears followed by reconcilement ever increase love where the passion is sincere, so in him it caused so wild a transport of excessive fondness, such joy, such grief, such pleasure, and such anguish, that nature in him seemed sinking with the weight, and the charmed soul disposed to quit his breast for hers.—Just then, when every passion with lawless anarchy prevailed, and reason was in the raging tempest lost, the cruel, artful Millwood prevailed upon the wretched youth to promise what I tremble but to think on.

BLUNT. I am amazed! What can it be?

LUCY. You will be more so to hear it is to attempt the life of his nearest relation, and best benefactor.

BLUNT. His uncle, whom we have often heard him speak of as a gentleman of a large estate and fair character in the country where he lives?

LUCY. The same. She was no sooner possessed of the last dear purchase of his ruin, but her avarice, insatiate as the grave, demands this horrid sacrifice, Barnwell's near relation; and unsuspected virtue must give too easy means to seize the good man's treasure, whose blood must seal the dreadful secret, and prevent the terrors of her guilty fears.

BLUNT. Is it possible she could persuade him to do an act like that! He is, by nature, honest, grateful, compassionate, and generous. And though his love and her artful persuasions have wrought him to practise what he most abhors; yet we all can witness for him with what reluctance he has still complied! So many tears he shed o'er each offence, as might, if possible, sanctify theft, and make a merit of a crime.

LUCY. 'Tis true, at the naming the murder of his uncle, he started into rage; and, breaking from her arms, where she till then had held him with well dissembled love and false endearments, called her cruel monster, devil; and told her she was born for his destruction. She thought it not for her purpose to meet his rage with rage, but affected a most passionate fit of grief, railed at her fate, and cursed her wayward stars, that still her wants should force her to press him to act such deeds as she must needs abhor as well as he; but told him necessity had no law and love no bounds; that therefore he never truly loved, but meant in her necessity to forsake her. Then kneeled and swore, that since by his refusal he had given her cause to doubt his love, she never would see him more, unless, to prove it true, he robbed his uncle to supply her wants and murdered him to keep it from discovery.

BLUNT. I am astonished! What said he?

LUCY. Speechless he stood; but in his face you might have read that various passions tore his very soul. Oft he in anguish threw his eyes towards heaven, and then as often bent their beams on her; then wept and groaned and beat his breast; at length, with horror not to be expressed, he cried, "Thou cursed fair! have I not given dreadful proofs of love? What drew me from my youthful innocence to stain my then unspotted soul but love?

What caused me to rob my gentle master but cursed love? What makes me now a fugitive from his service, loathed by myself, and scorned by all the world, but love? What fills my eyes with tears, my soul with torture, never felt on this side death before? Why love, love, love! And why, above all, do I resolve (for, tearing his hair, he cried, I do resolve!) to kill my uncle?"

BLUNT. Was she not moved? It makes me weep to hear the sad relation.

LUCY. Yes, with joy that she had gained her point. She gave him no time to cool, but urged him to attempt it instantly. He's now gone; if he performs it and escapes, there's more money for her; if not, he'll ne'er return, and then she's fairly rid of him.

BLUNT. 'Tis time the world was rid of such a monster.—

LUCY. If we don't do our endeavors to prevent this murder, we are as bad as she.

BLUNT. I'm afraid it is too late.

LUCY. Perhaps not. Her barbarity to Barnwell makes me hate her. We've run too great a length with her already. I did not think her or myself so wicked, as I find upon reflection we are.

BLUNT. 'Tis true, we have all been too much so. But there is something so horrid in murder that all other crimes seem nothing when compared to that. I would not be involved in the guilt of that for all the world.

LUCY. Nor I, heaven knows; therefore let us clear ourselves by doing all that is in our power to prevent it. I have just thought of a way that, to me, seems probable, Will you join with me to detect this cursed design?

BLUNT. With all my heart. How else shall I clear myself? He who knows of a murder intended to be committed and does not discover it in the eye of the law and reason is a murderer.

LUCY. Let us lose no time; I'll acquaint you with the particulars as we go.

SCENE V. *A walk at some distance from a county seat.*

[*Enter*] BARNWELL

BARNWELL. A dismal gloom obscures the face of day; either the sun has slipped behind a cloud, or journeys down the west of heaven with more than common speed to avoid the sight of what I'm doomed to act. Since I set forth on this accursed design, where'er I tread, methinks, the solid earth trembles beneath my feet. Yonder limpid stream, whose hoary fall has made a natural cascade, as I passed by, in doleful accents seemed to murmur, "Murder." The earth, the air, the water, seem concerned; but that's not strange, the world is punished, and nature feels the shock when Providence permits a good man's fall! Just heaven! Then what should I be! for him that was my father's only brother, and since his death has been to me a father, who took me up an infant, and an orphan, reared me with tenderest care, and still indulged me with most paternal fondness; yet here I stand avowed his destined murderer!—I stiffen with horror at my own impiety; 'tis yet unperformed. What if I quit my bloody purpose and fly the place! (*Going, then stops*)—But whither, O whither, shall I fly! My master's once friendly doors are ever shut against me; and without money Millwood will never see me more, and life is not to be endured without her! She's got such firm possession of my heart, and governs there with such despotic sway! Aye, there's the cause of all my sin and sorrow. 'Tis more than love; 'tis the fever of the soul and madness of desire. In vain does nature, reason, conscience, all oppose it; the impetuous passion bears down all before it, and drives me on to lust, to theft, and murder.—Oh conscience! feeble guide to virtue, who only shows us when we go astray, but wants the power to stop us in our course. —Ha! in yonder shady walk I see my uncle. He's alone. Now for my disguise. (*Plucks out a visor*) This is his hour of private meditation. Thus daily he prepares his soul for heaven, whilst I—but what have I to do with heaven! —Ha! No struggles, Conscience.— Hence! Hence remorse, and ev'ry thought that's good;

The storm that lust began must end in blood.

(*Puts on the visor, and draws a pistol*)

SCENE VI. *A close walk in a wood*

[*Enter*] UNCLE

UNCLE. If I was superstitious, I should fear some danger lurked unseen, or death were nigh. A heavy melancholy clouds my spirits; my imagination is filled with gashly [1] forms of dreary graves, and bodies changed by death,

[1] Ghastly.

when the pale lengthened visage attracts each weeping eye, and fills the musing soul at once with grief and horror, pity and aversion. I will indulge the thought. The wise man prepares himself for death by making it familiar to his mind. When strong reflections hold the mirror near, and the living in the dead behold their future selves, how does each inordinate passion and desire cease or sicken at the view! The mind scarce moves; the blood, curdling and chilled, creeps slowly through the veins, fixed, still, and motionless, like the solemn object of our thoughts. We are almost at present what we must be hereafter, till curiosity awakes the soul, and sets it on inquiry.—

Scene VII

Uncle, [enter] George Barnwell at a distance

Uncle. O death, thou strange mysterious power, seen every day, yet never understood but by the incommunicative dead, what art thou? The extensive mind of man, that with a thought circles the earth's vast globe, sinks to the center, or ascends above the stars; that worlds exotic finds, or thinks it finds, thy thick clouds attempts to pass in vain; lost and bewildered in the horrid gloom, defeated she returns more doubtful than before; of nothing certain, but of labor lost.[1]

(*During this speech,* Barnwell *sometimes presents the pistol, and draws it back again; at last he drops it,—at which his uncle starts, and draws his sword*)

Barnwell. Oh, 'tis impossible!

Uncle. A man so near me, armed and masked!

Barnwell. Nay, then there's no retreat.

(*Plucks a poinard from his bosom, and stabs him*)

Uncle. Oh! I am slain! All gracious heaven, regard the prayer of thy dying servant! Bless with thy choicest blessings my dearest nephew, forgive my murderer, and take my fleeting soul to endless mercy.

(Barnwell *throws off his mask, runs to him, and, kneeling by him, raises and chafes him*)

Barnwell. Expiring saint! Oh, murdered,

[1] This confused speech seems to mean that man, an exotic in the world, finds it vain to pass beyond the thick clouds of death; bewildered by the extensity of the universe, the soul returns, defeated, from her quest, more doubtful than before.

martyred uncle! Lift up your dying eyes, and view your nephew in your murderer. O do not look so tenderly upon me! Let indignation lighten from your eyes, and blast me ere you die. By heaven, he weeps in pity of my woes. Tears, tears, for blood! The murdered, in the agonies of death, weeps for his murderer! O, speak your pious purpose, pronounce my pardon then, and take me with you!—He would, but cannot. O why, with such fond affection do you press my murdering hand!— What! will you kiss me! (*Kisses him.*—Uncle *groans and dies*) He's gone forever, and oh! I follow.—(*Swoons away upon his uncle's dead body*) Do I still live to press the suffering bosom of the earth? Do I still breathe, and taint with my infectious breath the wholesome air? Let Heaven, from its high throne, in justice or in mercy, now look down on that dear murdered saint, and me the murderer. And, if his vengeance spares, let pity strike and end my wretched being.—Murder the worst of crimes, and parricide the worst of murders, and this the worst of parricides! Cain, who stands on record from the birth of time, and must to its last final period, as accursed, slew a brother favored above him. Detested Nero, by another's hand, dispatched a mother, that he feared and hated. But I, with my own hand, have murdered a brother, mother, father, and a friend; most loving and beloved. This execrable act of mine's without a parallel.—O may it ever stand alone!—the last of murders, as it is the worst.—

The rich man thus, in torment and despair,
Preferred his vain, but charitable prayer.
The fool, his own soul lost, would fain be wise
For others' good; but heaven his suit denies.
By laws and means well known we stand or fall,
And one eternal rule remains for all.

ACT IV

Scene I. [Thorowgood's *house*]

[*Enter*] Maria

Maria. How falsely do they judge who censure or applaud, as we're afflicted or rewarded here! I know I am unhappy, yet cannot charge myself with any crime more than the common frailties of our kind that should provoke just heaven to mark me out for sufferings so uncommon and severe. Falsely to accuse ourselves, heaven must abhor; then it is just and right that innocence should suffer, for heaven must be just in all its ways. Perhaps by that they are kept from moral evils, much worse than penal, or more improved in virtue; or may not the lesser ills that they sustain, be the means of greater good to others? Might all the joyless days and sleepless nights that I have passed, but purchase peace for thee—

Thou dear, dear cause of all my grief and pain,
Small were the loss, and infinite the gain:
Tho' to the grave in secret love I pine,
So life, and fame, and happiness were thine.

[*Enter* TRUEMAN]

SCENE II

TRUEMAN *and* MARIA

MARIA. What news of Barnwell?

TRUEMAN. None.—I have sought him with the greatest diligence, but all in vain.

MARIA. Doth my father yet suspect the cause of his absenting himself?

TRUEMAN. All appeared so just and fair to him, it is not possible he ever should; but his absence will no longer be concealed. Your father's wise; and though he seems to hearken to the friendly excuses, I would make for Barnwell, yet, I am afraid, he regards 'em only as such, without suffering them to influence his judgment.

MARIA. How does the unhappy youth defeat all our designs to serve him! Yet I can never repent what we have done. Should he return, 'twill make his reconciliation with my father easier, and preserve him from future reproach from a malicious, unforgiving world.

SCENE III

[*Enter*] *to them* THOROWGOOD *and* LUCY

THOROWGOOD. This woman here has given me a sad, (and bating some circumstances) too probable account of Barnwell's defection.

LUCY. I am sorry, sir, that my frank confession of my former unhappy course of life should cause you to suspect my truth on this occasion.

THOROWGOOD. It is not that; your confession has in it all the appearance of truth. (*To them*) Among many other particulars, she informs me that Barnwell had been influenced to break his trust, and wrong me, at several times, of considerable sums of money; now, as I know this to be false, I would fain doubt the whole of her relation, too dreadful to be willingly believed.

MARIA. Sir, your pardon; I find myself on a sudden so indisposed, that I must retire. —(*Aside*) Providence opposes all attempts to save him.—Poor ruined Barnwell!—Wretched lost Maria!— [*Exit* MARIA]

SCENE IV

THOROWGOOD, TRUEMAN *and* LUCY

THOROWGOOD. How am I distressed on every side! Pity for that unhappy youth, fear for the life of a much valued friend—and then my child—the only joy and hope of my declining life. Her melancholy increases hourly and gives me painful apprehensions of her loss.—O Trueman! this person informs me, that your friend, at the instigation of an impious woman, is gone to rob and murder his venerable uncle.

TRUEMAN. O execrable deed! I am blasted with the horror of the thought.

LUCY. This delay may ruin all.

THOROWGOOD. What to do or think I know not; that he ever wronged me, I know is false; the rest may be so too, there's all my hope.

TRUEMAN. Trust not to that, rather suppose all true than lose a moment's time; even now the horrid deed may be a-doing—dreadful imagination! or it may be done, and we are vainly debating on the means to prevent what is already past

THOROWGOOD. [*Aside*] This earnestness convinces me that he knows more than he has yet discovered. What ho! Without there! who waits?

SCENE V

[*Enter*] *to them* a Servant

THOROWGOOD. Order the groom to saddle the swiftest horse, and prepare himself to set out with speed. An affair of life and death demands his diligence. [*Exit* SERVANT]

SCENE VI

THOROWGOOD, TRUEMAN *and* LUCY

THOROWGOOD. For you, whose behavior on this occasion I have no time to commend as it deserves, I must engage your farther assistance.—Return and observe this Millwood till I come. I have your directions, and will follow you as soon as possible. [*Exit* Lucy]

SCENE VII

THOROWGOOD *and* TRUEMAN

THOROWGOOD. Trueman, you, I am sure, would not be idle on this occasion.

[*Exit* THOROWGOOD]

SCENE VIII
TRUEMAN

He only who is a friend can judge of my distress. [*Exit*]

SCENE IX. MILLWOOD'S *house*

[*Enter*] MILLWOOD

MILLWOOD. I wish I knew the event of his design; the attempt without success would ruin him. Well! what have I to apprehend from that? I fear too much. The mischief being only intended, his friends, in pity of his youth, turn all their rage on me. I should have thought of that before. Suppose the deed done; then, and then only, I shall be secure; or what if he returns without attempting it at all?

SCENE X

MILLWOOD, *and* BARNWELL *bloody*

MILLWOOD. But he is here, and I have done him wrong; his bloody hands show he has done the deed, but show he wants the prudence to conceal it.

BARNWELL. Where shall I hide me? Whither shall I fly to avoid the swift unerring hand of justice?

MILLWOOD. Dismiss those fears; though thousands had pursued you to the door, yet being entered here, you are safe as innocence; I have such a cavern, by art so cunningly contrived, that the piercing eyes of jealousy and revenge may search in vain, nor find the entrance to the safe retreat. There will I hide you if any danger's near.

BARNWELL. O hide me from myself if it be possible, for while I bear my conscience in my bosom, tho' I were hid where man's eye never saw, nor light e'er dawned, 'twere all in vain. For that inmate, that impartial judge, will try, convict, and sentence me for murder; and execute me with never-ending torments. Behold these hands all crimsoned o'er with my dear uncle's blood! Here's a sight to make a statue start with horror or turn a living man into a statue.

MILLWOOD. Ridiculous! Then it seems you are afraid of your own shadow; or what's less than a shadow, your conscience.

BARNWELL. Though to man unknown I did the accursed act, what can we hide from heaven's omniscient eye?

MILLWOOD. No more of this stuff; what advantage have you made of his death, or what advantage may yet be made of it? Did you secure the keys of his treasure? Those no doubt were about him? What gold, what jewels, or what else of value have you brought me?

BARNWELL. Think you I added sacrilege to murder? Oh! had you seen him as his life flowed from him in a crimson flood, and heard him praying for me by the double name of nephew and of murderer; alas, alas! he knew not then that his nephew was his murderer; how would you have wished as I did, tho' you had a thousand years of life to come, to have given them all to have lengthened his one hour. But being dead, I fled the sight of what my hands had done, nor could I, to have gained the empire of the world, have violated by theft his sacred corpse.

MILLWOOD. Whining preposterous canting villain! to murder your uncle, rob him of life, nature's first, last, dear prerogative, after which there's no injury—then fear to take what he no longer wanted! and bring to me your penury and guilt. Do you think I'll hazard my reputation, nay my life, to entertain you?

BARNWELL. Oh!—Millwood!—This from thee?—But I have done, if you hate me, if you wish me dead; then are you happy,—for oh! 'tis sure my grief will quickly end me.

MILLWOOD. [*Aside*] In his madness he will discover all, and involve me in his ruin; we are on a precipice from whence there's no retreat for both.—Then to preserve myself—(*Pauses*) There is no other way;—'tis dreadful, but reflection comes too late when danger's pressing, and there's no room for choice. It must be done. (*Stamps*)

SCENE XI

[*Enter*] *to them a* Servant

MILLWOOD. Fetch me an officer and seize this villain; he has confessed himself a murderer. Should I let him escape, I justly might be thought as bad as he. [*Exit* SERVANT]

SCENE XII

MILLWOOD *and* BARNWELL

BARNWELL. O Millwood! sure thou dost not, cannot mean it. Stop the messenger, upon my knees I beg you, call him back. 'Tis fit I die indeed, but not by you. I will this instant deliver myself into the hands of justice; indeed I will, for death is all I wish. But thy ingratitude so tears my wounded soul, 'tis worse ten thousand times than death with torture!

MILLWOOD. Call it what you will, I am willing to live; and live secure; which nothing but your death can warrant.

BARNWELL. If there be a pitch of wickedness that seats the author beyond the reach of vengeance, you must be secure. But what remains for me but a dismal dungeon, hard-galling fetters, an awful trial, and ignominious death, justly to fall unpitied and abhorred? —After death to be suspended between heaven and earth, a dreadful spectacle, the warning and horror of a gaping crowd. This I could bear, nay wish not to avoid, had it but come from any hand but thine.—

[*Enter* BLUNT, Officer *and* Attendants]

SCENE XIII

MILLWOOD, BARNWELL, BLUNT, Officer *and* Attendants

MILLWOOD. Heaven defend me! Conceal a murderer! Here, sir, take this youth into your custody; I accuse him of murder and will appear to make good my charge.

(*They seize him*)

BARNWELL. To whom, of what, or how shall I complain? I'll not accuse her; the hand of heaven is in it, and this, the punishment of lust and parricide! Yet heaven, that justly cuts me off, still suffers her to live, perhaps to punish others. Tremendous mercy! So friends are cursed with immortality to be the executioners of heaven—

Be warned, ye youths, who see my sad despair,
Avoid lewd women, false as they are fair;
By reason guided, honest joys pursue;
The fair, to honor, and to virtue true,
Just to herself, will ne'er be false to you.
By my example learn to shun my fate,

(How wretched is the man who's wise too late!)
Ere innocence, and fame, and life be lost,
Here purchase wisdom cheaply, at my cost.

[*Exeunt*]

SCENE XIV

[*Manent*] MILLWOOD *and* BLUNT

MILLWOOD. Where's Lucy? Why is she absent at such a time?

BLUNT. Would I had been so too, thou devil!

MILLWOOD. Insolent! This to me?

BLUNT. The worst that we know of the devil is, that he first seduces to sin, and then betrays to punishment. [*Exit* BLUNT]

SCENE XV

MILLWOOD

MILLWOOD. They disapprove of my conduct, and mean to take this opportunity to set up for themselves. My ruin is resolved; I see my danger, but scorn both it and them. I was not born to fall by such weak instruments.

[*Enter* THOROWGOOD]

SCENE XVI

THOROWGOOD *and* MILLWOOD

THOROWGOOD. Where is the scandal of her own sex, and curse of ours?

MILLWOOD. What means this insolence? Who do you seek?

THOROWGOOD. Millwood.

MILLWOOD. Well, you have found her then. I am Millwood.

THOROWGOOD. Then you are the most impious wretch that e'er the sun beheld.

MILLWOOD. From your appearance I should have expected wisdom and moderation, but your manners belie your aspect. What is your business here? I know you not.

THOROWGOOD. Hereafter you may know me better; I am Barnwell's master.

MILLWOOD. Then you are master to a villain, which, I think, is not much to your credit.

THOROWGOOD. Had he been as much above thy arts as my credit is superior to thy malice, I need not blush to own him.

MILLWOOD. My arts? I don't understand you, sir! If he has done amiss, what's that to me? Was he my servant, or yours? You should have taught him better.

THOROWGOOD. Why should I wonder to find such uncommon impudence in one arrived to such a height of wickedness! When innocence is banished, modesty soon follows. Know, sorceress, I'm not ignorant of any of your arts by which you first deceived the unwary youth. I know how, step by step, you've led him on, reluctant and unwilling, from crime to crime to this last horrid act which you contrived and by your cursed wiles even forced him to commit, and then betrayed him.

MILLWOOD. (*Aside*) Ha! Lucy has got the advantage of me, and accused me first; unless I can turn the accusation, and fix it upon her and Blunt, I am lost.

THOROWGOOD. Had I known your cruel design sooner, it had been prevented. To see you punished as the law directs, is all that now remains. Poor satisfaction, for he, innocent as he is compared to you, must suffer too. But heaven, who knows our frame, and graciously distinguishes between frailty and presumption, will make a difference, though man cannot, who sees not the heart, but only judges by the outward action.

MILLWOOD. I find, sir, we are both unhappy in our servants. I was surprised at such ill treatment, from a gentleman of your appearance without cause, and therefore too hastily returned it, for which I ask your pardon. I now perceive you have been so far imposed on, as to think me engaged in a former correspondence with your servant, and, some way or other, accessory to his undoing.

THOROWGOOD. I charge you as the cause, the sole cause of all his guilt, and all his suffering, of all he now endures, and must endure, till a violent and shameful death shall put a dreadful period to his life and miseries together.

MILLWOOD. 'Tis very strange; but who's secure from scandal and detraction? So far from contributing to his ruin, I never spoke to him till since that fatal accident, which I lament as much as you. 'Tis true, I have a servant, on whose account he has of late frequented my house; if she has abused my good opinion of her, am I to blame? Hasn't Barnwell done the same by you?

THOROWGOOD. I hear you; pray go on.

MILLWOOD. I have been informed he had a violent passion for her, and she for him; but I always thought it innocent; I know her poor and given to expensive pleasures. Now who can tell but she may have influenced the amorous youth to commit this murder, to supply her extravagancies? It must be so. I now recollect a thousand circumstances that confirm it. I'll have her and a man servant that I suspect as an accomplice, secured immediately. I hope, sir, you will lay aside your ill-grounded suspicions of me, and join to punish the real contrivers of this bloody deed.
(*Offers to go*)

THOROWGOOD. Madam, you pass not this way. I see your design, but shall protect them from your malice.

MILLWOOD. I hope you will not use your influence and the credit of your name to screen such guilty wretches. Consider, sir, the wickedness of persuading a thoughtless youth to such a crime.

THOROWGOOD. I do, and of betraying him when it was done.

MILLWOOD. That which you call betraying him, may convince you of my innocence. She who loves him, though she contrived the murder, would never have delivered him into the hands of justice, as I, struck with the horror of his crimes, have done.

THOROWGOOD. [*Aside*] How should an unexperienced youth escape her snares? The powerful magic of her wit and form might betray the wisest to simple dotage and fire the blood that age had froze long since. Even I, that with just prejudice came prepared, had, by her artful story, been deceived, but that my strong conviction of her guilt makes even a doubt impossible.—Those whom subtly you would accuse, you know are your accusers; and what proves unanswerably, their innocence, and your guilt—they accused you before the deed was done, and did all that was in their power to have prevented it.

MILLWOOD. Sir, you are very hard to be convinced; but I have such a proof, which, when produced, will silence all objections.
[*Exit*]

SCENE XVII

THOROWGOOD, [*and enter*] LUCY, TRUEMAN, BLUNT, Officers, &c.

LUCY. Gentlemen, pray place yourselves, some on one side of that door, and some on the other; watch her entrance, and act as your prudence shall direct you.—This way—

(to THOROWGOOD) and note her behavior; I have observed her, she's driven to the last extremity, and is forming some desperate resolution.—I guess at her design.—

SCENE XVIII

[Enter] to them, MILLWOOD with a Pistol,— TRUEMAN secures her

TRUEMAN. Here thy power of doing mischief ends, deceitful, cruel, bloody woman!

MILLWOOD. Fool, hypocrite, villain!—Man! thou can'st not call me that.

TRUEMAN. To call thee woman were to wrong the sex, thou devil!

MILLWOOD. That imaginary being is an emblem of thy cursed sex collected. A mirror, wherein each particular man may see his own likeness and that of all mankind!

TRUEMAN. Think not, by aggravating the fault of others, to extenuate thy own, of which the abuse of such uncommon perfections of mind and body is not the least.

MILLWOOD. If such I had, well may I curse your barbarous sex, who robbed me of 'em, ere I knew their worth, then left me, too late, to count their value by their loss! Another and another spoiler came, and all my gain was poverty and reproach. My soul disdained, and yet disdains, dependence and contempt. Riches, no matter by what means obtained, I saw, secured the worst of men from both; I found it therefore necessary to be rich; and, to that end, I summoned all my arts. You call 'em wicked; be it so, they were such as my conversation with your sex had furnished me withal.

THOROWGOOD. Sure none but the worst of men conversed with thee.

MILLWOOD. Men of all degrees and all professions I have known, yet found no difference, but in their several capacities; all were alike wicked to the utmost of their power. In pride, contention, avarice, cruelty, and revenge, the reverend priesthood were my unerring guides. From suburb-magistrates,[1] who live by ruined reputations, as the unhospitable natives of Cornwall do by shipwrecks,[2] I learned that to charge my innocent neighbors with my crimes was to merit their protection; for to screen the guilty, is the less scandalous, when many are suspected, and detraction, like darkness and death, blackens all objects and levels all distinction. Such are your venal magistrates, who favor none but such as, by their office, they are sworn to punish. With them, not to be guilty is the worst of crimes; and large fees privately paid is every needful virtue.

THOROWGOOD. Your practice has sufficiently discovered your contempt of laws, both human and divine; no wonder then that you should hate the officers of both.

MILLWOOD. I hate you all, I know you, and expect no mercy; nay, I ask for none; I have done nothing that I am sorry for; I followed my inclinations and that the best of you does every day. All actions are alike natural and indifferent to man and beast, who devour, or are devoured, as they meet with others weaker or stronger than themselves.

THOROWGOOD. What pity it is, a mind so comprehensive, daring and inquisitive, should be a stranger to religion's sweet, but powerful charms.

MILLWOOD. I am not fool enough to be an atheist, though I have known enough of men's hypocrisy to make a thousand simple women so. Whatever religion is in itself, as practised by mankind, it has caused the evils you say it was designed to cure. War, plague, and famine [have] [3] not destroyed so many of the human race, as this pretended piety has done, and with such barbarous cruelty, as if the only way to honor heaven were to turn the present world into hell.

THOROWGOOD. Truth is truth, though from an enemy and spoke in malice. You bloody, blind, and superstitious bigots, how will you answer this?

MILLWOOD. What are your laws, of which you make your boast, but the fool's wisdom and the coward's valor; the instrument and screen of all your villainies, by which you punish in others what you act yourselves, or would have acted, had you been in their circumstances? The judge who condemns the poor man for being a thief had been a thief himself had he been poor. Thus you go on deceiving and being deceived, harassing, plaguing, and destroying one another; but women are your universal prey.

[1] Magistrates outside the City were notoriously corrupt.

[2] The natives of Cornwall were formerly notorious for murdering persons shipwrecked on their rocky coast. Lillo seems to have been impressed by this custom; cf. allusions and implications in his *Fatal Curiosity*.

[3] *Has* in the text.

Women, by whom you are, the source of joy,
With cruel arts you labor to destroy.
A thousand ways our ruin you pursue,
Yet blame in us those arts, first taught by you.
O may, from hence, each violated maid,
By flattering, faithless, barb'rous man betrayed;
When robbed of innocence and virgin fame
From your destruction raise a nobler name;
To right their sex's wrongs devote their mind,
And future Millwoods prove to plague mankind.

ACT V

SCENE I. *A room in a prison*

[*Enter*] THOROWGOOD, BLUNT *and* LUCY

THOROWGOOD. I have recommended to Barnwell a reverend divine whose judgment and integrity I am well acquainted with; nor has Millwood been neglected, but she, unhappy woman, still obstinate, refuses his assistance.

LUCY. This pious charity to the afflicted well becomes your character; yet pardon me, sir, if I wonder you were not at their trial.

THOROWGOOD. I knew it was impossible to save him, and I and my family bear so great a part in his distress, that to have been present would have aggravated our sorrows without relieving his.

BLUNT. It was mournful, indeed. Barnwell's youth and modest deportment as he passed drew tears from every eye. When placed at the bar and arraigned before the reverend judges, with many tears and interrupting sobs he confessed and aggravated his offences, without accusing, or once reflecting on, Millwood, the shameless author of his ruin, who, dauntless and unconcerned, stood by his side, viewing with visible pride and contempt the vast assembly, who all with sympathizing sorrow wept for the wretched youth. Millwood, when called upon to answer, loudly insisted upon her innocence, and made an artful and a bold defence; but finding all in vain, the impartial jury and the learned bench concurring to find her guilty, how did she curse herself, poor Barnwell, us, her judges, all mankind; but what could that avail? She was condemned, and is this day to suffer with him.

THOROWGOOD. The time draws on; I am going to visit Barnwell, as you are Millwood.

LUCY. We have not wronged her, yet I dread this interview. She's proud, impatient, wrathful, and unforgiving. To be the branded instruments of vengeance, to suffer in her shame, and sympathize with her in all she suffers, is the tribute we must pay for our former ill-spent lives, and long confederacy with her in wickedness.

THOROWGOOD. Happy for you it ended when it did. What you have done against Millwood, I know, proceeded from a just abhorrence of her crimes, free from interest, malice, or revenge. Proselytes to virtue should be encouraged. Pursue your proposed reformation, and know me hereafter for your friend.

LUCY. This is a blessing as unhoped for as unmerited, but heaven, that snatched us from impending ruin, sure intends you as its instrument to secure us from apostasy.

THOROWGOOD. With gratitude to impute your deliverance to heaven is just. Many, less virtuously disposed than Barnwell was, have never fallen in the manner he has done,— may not such owe their safety rather to Providence than to themselves? With pity and compassion let us judge him. Great were his faults, but strong was the temptation. Let his ruin learn [1] us diffidence, humanity and circumspection; for we, who wonder at his fate, perhaps had we like him, been tried,—like him, we had fallen, too.

SCENE II. *A dungeon, a table and lamp*

[*Enter*] THOROWGOOD, [*to*] BARNWELL *reading*

THOROWGOOD. See there the bitter fruits of passion's detested reign and sensual appetite indulged. Severe reflections, penitence, and tears!

BARNWELL. [*Rising*] My honored, injured master, whose goodness has covered me a thousand times with shame, forgive this last unwilling disrespect,—indeed I saw you not.

THOROWGOOD. 'Tis well. I hope you were better employed in viewing [2] of yourself; your journey's long, your time for preparation almost spent. I sent a reverend divine to teach you to improve it and should be glad to hear of his success.

BARNWELL. The word of truth, which he recommended for my constant companion in

[1] Modern usage requires *teach*.
[2] Examining.

this my sad retirement, has at length removed the doubts I labored under. From thence I've learned the infinite extent of heavenly mercy; that my offences, though great, are not unpardonable; and that 'tis not my interest only, but my duty, to believe and to rejoice in that hope. So shall heaven receive the glory, and future penitents the profit of my example.

THOROWGOOD. Go on. How happy am I who live to see this!

BARNWELL. 'Tis wonderful that words should charm despair, speak peace and pardon to a murderer's conscience; but truth and mercy flow in every sentence, attended with force and energy divine. How shall I describe my present state of mind? I hope in doubt, and trembling I rejoice. I feel my grief increase, even as my fears give way. Joy and gratitude now supply more tears than the horror and anguish of despair before.

THOROWGOOD. These are the genuine signs of true repentance, the only preparatory, certain way to everlasting peace. O the joy it gives to see a soul formed and prepared for heaven! For this the faithful minister devotes himself to meditation, abstinence, and prayer, shunning the vain delights of sensual joys, and daily dies that others may live forever. For this he turns the sacred volumes o'er, and spends his life in painful search of truth. The love of riches and the lust of power, he looks on with just contempt and detestation; who only counts for wealth the souls he wins, and whose highest ambition is to serve mankind. If the reward of all his pains be to preserve one soul from wandering or turn one from the error of his ways, how does he then rejoice and own his little labors over-paid!

BARNWELL. What do I owe for all your generous kindness! But though I cannot, heaven can, and will, reward you.

THOROWGOOD. To see thee thus is joy too great for words. Farewell! Heaven strengthen thee! Farewell!

BARNWELL. Oh, sir, there's something I could say, if my sad swelling heart would give me leave.

THOROWGOOD. Give it vent a while and try.

BARNWELL. I had a friend ('tis true I am unworthy) yet methinks your generous example might persuade—could I not see him once before I go from whence there's no return?

THOROWGOOD. He's coming, and as much thy friend as ever; but I'll not anticipate his sorrow. (*Aside*) Too soon he'll see the sad effect of his contagious ruin. This torrent of domestic misery bears too hard upon me; I must retire to indulge a weakness I find impossible to overcome.—Much loved—and much lamented youth,—farewell! Heaven strengthen thee! Eternally farewell!

BARNWELL. The best of masters and of men, farewell—While I live, let me not want your prayers!

THOROWGOOD. Thou shalt not;—thy peace being made with Heaven, death's already vanquished; bear a little longer the pains that attend this transitory life, and cease from pain forever. [*Exit*]

SCENE III

BARNWELL

BARNWELL. I find a power within that bears my soul above the fears of death, and, spite of conscious shame and guilt, gives me a taste of pleasure more than mortal.

SCENE IV

[*Enter*] *to him* TRUEMAN *and* Keeper

KEEPER. Sir, there's the prisoner. [*Exit*]

SCENE V

BARNWELL *and* TRUEMAN

BARNWELL. Trueman,—my friend, whom I so wished to see, yet now he's here I dare not look upon him. (*Weeps*)

TRUEMAN. O Barnwell! Barnwell!

BARNWELL. Mercy! Mercy! gracious Heaven! for death, but not for this, was I prepared!

TRUEMAN. What have I suffered since I saw you last!—What pain has absence given me! But oh! to see thee thus!

BARNWELL. I know it is dreadful! I feel the anguish of thy generous soul,—but I was born to murder all who love me. (*Both weep*)

TRUEMAN. I came not to reproach you;—I thought to bring you comfort,—but I'm deceived, for I have none to give;—I came to share thy sorrow, but cannot bear my own.

BARNWELL. My sense of guilt, indeed, you cannot know; 'tis what the good and innocent like you can ne'er conceive; but other griefs at present I have none but what I feel for you. In your sorrow I read you love me still, but yet methinks 'tis strange, when I consider what I am.

TRUEMAN. No more of that. I can remember nothing but thy virtue, thy honest, tender friendship, our former happy state and present misery. O had you trusted me when first the fair seducer tempted you, all might have been prevented!

BARNWELL. Alas, thou know'st not what a wretch I've been! Breach of friendship was my first and least offence. So far was I lost to goodness,—so devoted to the author of my ruin,—that had she insisted on my murdering thee,—I think,—I should have done it.

TRUEMAN. Prithee, aggravate thy faults no more.

BARNWELL. I think I should! Thus good and generous as you are, I should have murdered you!

TRUEMAN. We have not yet embraced, and may be interrupted. Come to my arms.

BARNWELL. Never, never will I taste such joys on earth; never will I so soothe my just remorse. Are those honest arms and faithful bosom fit to embrace and to support a murderer? These iron fetters only shall clasp and flinty pavement bear me. (*Throwing himself on the ground*) Even these too good for such a bloody monster!

TRUEMAN. Shall fortune sever those whom friendship joined! Thy miseries cannot lay thee so low, but love will find thee. (*Lies down by him*) Upon this rugged couch then let us lie, for well it suits our most deplorable condition. Here will we offer to stern calamity, this earth the altar, and ourselves the sacrifice. Our mutual groans shall echo to each other through the dreary vault. Our sighs shall number the moments as they pass,—and mingling tears communicate such anguish as words were never made to express.

BARNWELL. Then be it so. Since you propose an intercourse of woe, pour all your griefs into my breast,—and in exchange take mine. (*Embracing*) Where's now the anguish that you promised? You've taken mine, and make me no return.—Sure peace and comfort dwell within these arms, and sorrow can't approach me while I'm here! This, too, is the work of Heaven, who, having before spoke peace and pardon to me, now sends thee to confirm it. O take, take some of the joy that overflows my breast!

TRUEMAN. I do, I do. Almighty Power, how have you made us capable to bear, at once, the extremes of pleasure and pain?

SCENE VI

[*Enter*] *to them*, Keeper

KEEPER. Sir.
TRUEMAN. I come.   [*Exit* Keeper]

SCENE VII

BARNWELL *and* TRUEMAN

BARNWELL. Must you leave me? Death would soon have parted us forever.

TRUEMAN. O, my Barnwell, there's yet another task behind:—Again your heart must bleed for others' woes.

BARNWELL. To meet and part with you, I thought was all I had to do on earth! What is there more for me to do or suffer?

TRUEMAN. I dread to tell thee, yet it must be known.—Maria—

BARNWELL. Our master's fair and virtuous daughter!

TRUEMAN. The same.

BARNWELL. No misfortune, I hope, has reached that lovely maid! Preserve her, Heaven, from every ill, to show mankind that goodness is your care.

TRUEMAN. Thy, thy misfortunes, my unhappy friend, have reached her. Whatever you and I have felt, and more, if more be possible, she feels for you.

BARNWELL. (*Aside*) I know he doth abhor a lie, and would not trifle with his dying friend.—This is, indeed, the bitterness of death!

TRUEMAN. You must remember, for we all observed it, for some time past, a heavy melancholy weighed her down. Disconsolate she seemed, and pined and languished from a cause unknown; till hearing of your dreadful fate, the long stifled flame blazed out. She wept, she wrung her hands, and tore her hair, and in the transport of her grief discovered her own lost state, whilst she lamented yours.

BARNWELL. Will all the pain I feel restore thy ease, lovely unhappy maid? (*Weeping*) Why didn't you let me die and never know it?

TRUEMAN. It was impossible; she makes no secret of her passion for you, and is determined to see you ere you die. She waits for me to introduce her.   [*Exit*]

Scene VIII

BARNWELL

BARNWELL. Vain busy thoughts be still! What avails it to think on what I might have been. I now am what I've made myself.

Scene IX

[*Enter*] *to him,* TRUEMAN *and* MARIA

TRUEMAN. Madam, reluctant I lead you to this dismal scene. This is the seat of misery and guilt. Here awful justice reserves her public victims. This is the entrance to shameful death.

MARIA. To this sad place, then, no improper guest, the abandoned, lost Maria brings despair; and see! the subject and the cause of all this world of woe! Silent and motionless he stands, as if his soul had quitted her abode, and the lifeless form alone was left behind; yet that so perfect, that beauty and death, ever at enmity, now seem united there.

BARNWELL. I groan, but murmur not. Just Heaven, I am your own; do with me what you please.

MARIA. Why are your streaming eyes still fixed below as though thou'dst give the greedy earth thy sorrows, and rob me of my due? Were happiness within your power, you should bestow it where you pleased; but in your misery I must and will partake.

BARNWELL. Oh! say not so, but fly, abhor, and leave me to my fate. Consider what you are! How vast your fortune, and how bright your fame! Have pity on your youth, your beauty, and unequalled virtue, for which so many noble peers have sighed in vain. Bless with your charms some honorable lord. Adorn with your beauty; and, by your example, improve the English court, that justly claims such merit; so shall I quickly be to you as though I had never been.

MARIA. When I forget you, I must be so, indeed. Reason, choice, virtue, all forbid it. Let women like Millwood if there be more such women smile in prosperity and in adversity forsake. Be it the pride of virtue to repair or to partake the ruin such have made.

TRUEMAN. Lovely, ill-fated maid! Was there ever such generous distress before? How must this pierce his grateful heart and aggravate his woes!

BARNWELL. Ere I knew guilt or shame, when fortune smiled, and when my youthful hopes were at the highest; if then to have raised my thoughts to you, had been presumption in me, never to have been pardoned, think how much beneath yourself you condescend to regard me now.

MARIA. Let her blush, who, professing love, invades the freedom of your sex's choice and meanly sues in hopes of a return. Your inevitable fate hath rendered hope impossible as vain. Then why should I fear to avow a passion so just and so disinterested?

TRUEMAN. If any should take occasion from Millwood's crimes to libel the best and fairest part of the creation, here let them see their error. The most distant hopes of such a tender passion from so bright a maid might add to the happiness of the most happy and make the greatest proud. Yet here 'tis lavished in vain. Though by the rich present the generous donor is undone, he on whom it is bestowed receives no benefit.

BARNWELL. So the aromatic spices of the East, which all the living covet and esteem, are with unavailing kindness wasted on the dead.

MARIA. Yes, fruitless is my love, and unavailing all my sighs and tears. Can they save thee from approaching death, from such a death? O terrible idea! What is her misery and distress, who sees the first last object of her love, for whom alone she'd live, for whom she'd die a thousand, thousand deaths if it were possible, expiring in her arms? Yet she is happy, when compared to me. Were millions of worlds mine, I'd gladly give them in exchange for her condition. The most consummate woe is light to mine. The last of curses to other miserable maids, is all I ask; and that's denied me.

TRUEMAN. Time and reflection cure all ills.

MARIA. All but this; his dreadful catastrophe virtue herself abhors. To give a holiday to suburb slaves; and, passing, entertain[1] the savage herd who, elbowing each other for a sight, pursue and press upon him like his fate. A mind with piety and resolution armed may smile on death. But public ignominy! everlasting shame! shame the death of souls! to die a thousand times and yet survive even death itself, in never-dying infamy, is this to be endured? Can I, who live in him, and must each

[1] Entertain as he passes by on the way to execution.

hour of my devoted life feel all these woes renewed, can I endure this!—

TRUEMAN. Grief has impaired her spirits; she pants, as in the agonies of death.

BARNWELL. Preserve her, Heaven, and restore her peace,—nor let her death be added to my crime,—(*Bell tolls*) I am summoned to my fate.

SCENE X

[*Enter*] *to them*, KEEPER

KEEPER. The officers attend you, sir. Mrs. Millwood is already summoned.

BARNWELL. Tell 'em I'm ready. And now, my friend, farewell. (*Embracing*) Support and comfort the best you can this mourning fair. No more. Forget not to pray for me. (*Turning to* MARIA) Would you, bright excellence, permit me the honor of a chaste embrace, the last happiness this world could give were mine. (*She inclines towards him; they embrace*) Exalted goodness! O turn your eyes from earth and me to heaven, where virtue like yours is ever heard. Pray for the peace of my departing soul.—Early my race of wickedness began, and soon has reached the summit, ere nature has finished her work, and stamped me man. Just at the time that others begin to stray, my course is finished! Though short my span of life, and few my days, yet count my crimes for years, and I have lived whole ages. Justice and mercy are in heaven the same. Its utmost severity is mercy to the whole, thereby to cure man's folly and presumption, which else would render even infinite mercy vain and ineffectual. Thus justice in compassion to mankind cuts off a wretch like me,—by one such example to secure thousands from future ruin.
If any youth, like you,[1] in future times,
Shall mourn my fate, though he abhor my crimes;
Or tender maid, like you, my tale shall hear,
And to my sorrows give a pitying tear:
To each such melting eye, and throbbing heart,
Would gracious heaven this benefit impart,
Never to know my guilt, nor feel my pain;
Then must you own, you ought not to complain;
Since you nor weep, nor shall I die, in vain.

[*Exeunt* Keeper *and* BARNWELL]

[1] Pointing into the audience.

SCENE XI

TRUEMAN, BLUNT, *and* LUCY

LUCY. Heart-breaking sight! O wretched, wretched Millwood!

TRUEMAN. You came from her then—how is she disposed to meet her Fate?

BLUNT. Who can describe unalterable woe?

LUCY. She goes to death encompassed with horror, loathing life, and yet afraid to die; no tongue can tell her anguish and despair.

TRUEMAN. Heaven be better to her than her fears; may she prove a warning to others, a monument of mercy in herself.

LUCY. O sorrow insupportable! Break, break, my heart!

TRUEMAN. In vain
With bleeding hearts and weeping eyes we show
A human gen'rous sense of others' woe;
Unless we mark what drew their ruin on,
And by avoiding that, prevent our own.[2]

EPILOGUE [3]

Written by COLLEY CIBBER, ESQ.; and Spoke by MRS. CIBBER [4]

Since Fate has robbed me of the hopeless youth,
For whom my heart had hoarded up its truth;
By all the laws of love and honor, now,
I'm free again to choose,—and one of you.

But soft! With caution first I'll round me peep;
Maids, in my case, should look before they leap:

[2] This is the last scene of the play as originally produced. Certain later editions contain a scene at the place of execution. It can hardly be regarded as adding to the artistic effect.
[3] An excellent example of the vulgar, comic epilogue which frequently followed serious plays in the seventeenth and eighteenth centuries and against which many dramatists protested. See the epilogues to *The Conscious Lovers* and *Douglas*.
[4] In the character of Maria, of course. The poor taste of this feature would hardly be tolerated by modern audiences. Mrs. Cibber was the first wife of Theophilus Cibber, not to be confused with her more famous successor.

Here's choice enough, of various sorts, and hue,
The cit, the wit, the rake cocked up in cue,[1]
The fair spruce mercer, and the tawny[2] Jew. 9

Suppose I search the sober gallery. No,
There's none but prentices,—and cuckolds all a row;
And these, I doubt, are those that make 'em so.[3] (*Points to the boxes*)

'Tis very well, enjoy the jest. But you,
Fine powdered sparks, nay, I'm told 'tis true,
Your happy spouses—can make cuckolds too. 15

'Twixt you and them, the diff'rence this perhaps,
The cit's ashamed whene'er his duck he traps;
But you, when madam's tripping, let her fall,
Cock up your hats, and take no shame at all.

What if some savored poet I could meet?
Whose love would lay his laurels at my feet?
No,—painted passion real love abhors,— 22
His flame would prove the suit of creditors.[4]

Not to detain you then with longer pause,
In short; my heart to this conclusion draws,
I yield it to the hand, that's loudest in applause. 26

[1] With hat tipped over the queue of his wig.
[2] Yellow, referring to the yellow head dress which Jews had been compelled to wear.
[3] This is the well-worn joke based on a frequent theme in Restoration comedy, the seduction of the citizen's wife by the courtier.
[4] The poet would be seeking a means of support.

DOUGLAS

A Tragedy by John Home

Non ego sum vates, sed prisci conscius ævi.[1]

John Home, son of the town clerk of Leith, Alexander Home, was born at Leith, Sept. 22, 1722. He was educated for the Church of Scotland and was ready to assume the duties of a minister of the Kirk when "the forty-five" gave him a chance to exercise his military predilections. He joined a Whig corps and was captured by the Jacobites at Falkirk. He escaped, however, and spent the remaining few weeks of the rebellion in seclusion pursuing his favorite study of classical history. The troubles over, Home was inducted into the living of Athelstaneford, near Edinburgh, where he lived until the uproar caused by his play, *Douglas*, caused him to resign his living and move to London to write plays under the patronage of Lord Bute and to secure a pension from George III. In 1779 he returned to Scotland, where he spent the rest of his days as a respected member of a famous literary circle which had included among its members David Hume and Henry Mackenzie. Home's mental faculties had suffered as a result of injuries following a fall from his horse in 1778, while he was for a second time serving in the army; but he continued his literary and historical work, publishing in 1802 his *History of the Rebellion of 1745*. He died September 5, 1808, remembered as the author of *Douglas* long after his other dramatic works had passed into oblivion.

The best contemporary biography of Home is that by Henry Mackenzie, which appears as an introduction to the 1822 edition of Home's works. Among recent studies is Alice E. Gipson's *John Home*, Yale University dissertation, 1916.

HOME'S DRAMATIC WORKS

Douglas (tragedy) (Canongate, Edinburgh, Dec. 14, 1756; C.G., March 14, 1757), 1757.
Agis (tragedy) (D.L., Feb. 21, 1758), 1758. (Written before Douglas.)
The Siege of Aquileia (tragedy) (D.L., Feb. 21, 1760), 1760.
The Fatal Discovery (tragedy) (D.L., Feb. 23, 1769), 1769.
Alonzo (tragedy) (D.L., Feb. 27, 1773), 1773.
Alfred (tragedy) (C.G., Jan. 21, 1778), 1778.

Garrick, at Drury Lane, refused the Reverend John Home's second tragedy, *Douglas*, completed a few years before by the minister of Athelstaneford. The manager maintained that like its predecessor *Agis* it was unfit for theatrical representation. Mr. Home, however, moved in the best learned society of Edinburgh, and Garrick's opposition aroused Scottish pride. It was decided, therefore, that *Douglas* should have a trial in Edinburgh. A group of gentlemen, friends of the author, arranged with West Digges, manager of the theater and himself a favorite actor with Scotch audiences, to put the play upon the stage. It appeared, with Digges as Norval, at the Canongate Theater, December 14, 1756, before a crowded house, in which was the now famous man who exclaimed, "Whaur's yer Wully Shakespeare noo!". In the words of the Rev. Dr. Carlyle, "The town was in an uproar of exultation that a Scotchman did write a tragedy of the first rate, and that its merits were submitted to them." The undoubted success of *Douglas* probably influenced Rich to accept Home's tragedy and produce it at Covent Garden, March 14, 1757, with Peg Woffington and Spranger Barry in the leading parts. From that time forth for a good century it remained in favor and served as a vehicle for all the great declaimers of the English and American stages, male and female, as well as a few "infant" actors, among whom are included Master Betty and John Howard Payne.

The performance and publication of *Douglas* precipitated a passionate controversy in Edinburgh over the propriety of ministerial dramatic authorship and the wickedness of the stage in general. As pamphlets appeared from all sides, Home and his defenders were

---

[1] I am not a prophet, but I understand a former age.

made the subject of investigation and action by the Kirk. Having resigned his living, of his own accord, Home departed to London, where his later plays were produced with varying success, which, however, never equalled that of *Douglas*.

Douglas is a romantic tragedy, in which are combined medieval subject-matter, picturesque language, passionate speech and action, with a classical regularity of form (each act constituting a definite movement in the action) and a strict observance of the unities. It is by all odds after Rowe, the best poetic drama of the century, and no subsequent English tragedy in verse has had so long and successful a stage history. The sources of the plot are the well-known ballad of *Gil Morrice.* in the story of which Home made minor alterations, changing the name of the heroine from Lady Barnard (or Barnet) to Lady Randolph after the first run at Edinburgh; and *Merope*, Aaron Hill's adaptation of Voltaire's tragedy (D.L., 1749). Though the historical background of the play is indefinite and somewhat confusing, Home produced an atmosphere of Scottish antiquity by historical allusions and the frequent introduction of Scotch place-names. The excellence of the play is found in its genuine passion and fervid language, which contrast vividly with the cold conventionality of contemporary pseudo-Augustan tragedies like Johnson's *Irene*. In this respect, as well as in setting and theme, *Douglas* forecasts the drama of the Romantic Movement.

DOUGLAS

DRAMATIS PERSONÆ

EDINBURGH	[MEN]	LONDON
Mr. Younger	LORD RANDOLPH	Mr. Ridout
Mr. Love	GLENALVON	Mr. Smith
Mr. Digges	NORVAL, *Douglas*	Mr. Barry
Mr. Hayman	STRANGER	Mr. Sparks

WOMEN

Mrs. Ward	MATILDA, LADY RANDOLPH	Mrs. Woffington
Mrs. Hopkins	ANNA	Mrs. Vincent

PROLOGUE,[1]

Spoken by MR. SPARKS

In ancient times, when Britain's trade was arms,
And the loved music of her youth, alarms;
A god-like race sustained fair England's fame:
Who has not heard of gallant Percy's name?
Ay, and of Douglas?[2] Such illustrious foes 5
In rival Rome and Carthage never rose!
From age to age bright shone the British fire,
And every hero was a hero's sire.
When powerful fate decreed one warrior's doom,
Up sprung the phœnix from his parent's tomb.
But whilst these generous rivals fought and fell, 11
These generous rivals loved each other well:
Though many a bloody field was lost and won,
Nothing in hate, in honor all was done.
When Percy, wronged, defied his prince or peers, 15
Fast came the Douglas with his Scottish spears;
And, when proud Douglas made his king his foe,
For Douglas, Percy bent his English bow. 18
Expelled[3] their native homes by adverse fate,
They knocked alternate at each other's gate:
Then blazed the castle, at the midnight hour,
For him whose arms had shook its firmest tower.
This night a Douglas your protection claims;
A wife! a mother! Pity's softest names:
The story of her woes indulgent hear, 25
And grant your suppliant all she begs, a tear.
In confidence she begs; and hopes to find
Each English breast, like noble Percy's, kind.

PROLOGUE,

Spoken at EDINBURGH

In days of classic fame, when Persia's Lord[4]
Opposed his millions to the Grecian sword,
Flourished the state of Athens, small her store,
Rugged her soil, and rocky was her shore,
Like Caledonia's; yet she gained a name 5
That stands unrivaled in the rolls of fame.
Such proud pre-eminence not valor gave,
(For who than Sparta's dauntless sons more brave?)[5]
But learning, and the love of every art,
That Virgin Pallas and the Muse impart. 10
Above the rest the Tragic Muse admired
Each Attic breast with noblest passions fired.
In peace their poets with their heroes shared
Glory, the hero's and the bard's reward.
The Tragic Muse each glorious record kept, 15
And, o'er the kings she conquered, Athens wept.[6]
Here let me cease, impatient for the scene;

---

[1] This is the London prologue. The prologue which was spoken at Edinburgh, which follows in most of the editions of the play, being decidedly nationalistic in tone, was not suited to a London audience.

[2] Home's reference is to the two famous ballads of "The Battle of Otterburne" and "The Hunting of the Cheviot," on which see the seventieth *Spectator*.

[3] Expelled from.

[4] Xerxes. [5] Leonidas.
[6] See the *Persai* of Æschylus.—ORIGINAL NOTE.

To you I need not praise the Tragic Queen:
Oft has this audience soft compassion shown
To woes of heroes, heroes not their own.   20
This night our scenes no common tear demand,
He comes, the hero of your native land!
Douglas, a name through all the world renowned,
A name that rouses like the trumpet's sound!
Oft have your fathers, prodigal of life,   25
A Douglas followed through the bloody strife;
Hosts have been known at that dread time to yield
And, Douglas dead, his name hath won the field.
Listen attentive to the various tale,
Mark if the author's kindred [1] feelings fail;   30
Swayed by alternate hopes, alternate fears,
He waits the test of your congenial tears.
If they shall flow, back to the Muse he flies,
And bids your heroes in succession rise;   34
Collects the wand'ring warriors as they roam,
Douglas assures them of a welcome home.

ACT I

The court of a castle surrounded with woods [2]

Enter LADY RANDOLPH

LADY RANDOLPH.   Ye woods and wilds, whose melancholy gloom
Accords with my soul's sadness, and draws forth
The voice of sorrow from my bursting heart,
Farewell a while: I will not leave you long;
For in your shades I deem some spirit dwells,
Who from the chiding stream, or groaning oak,
Still hears and answers to Matilda's moan.   7
O, Douglas, Douglas! if departed ghosts
Are e'er permitted to review this world,
Within the circle of that wood thou art,   10
And with the passion of immortals hear'st
My lamentation; hear'st thy wretched wife
Weep for her husband slain, her infant lost.
My brother's timeless death I seem to mourn,
Who perished with thee on this fatal day.   15
To thee I lift my voice; to thee address
The plaint which mortal ear has never heard.
O disregard me not; though I am called
Another's now, my heart is wholly thine.

[1] Home was distantly connected with the Douglas family.
[2] The scene seems, from various references to locations, to be laid near Carron Water, on the northwest coast of Scotland.

Incapable of change, affection lies   20
Buried, my Douglas, in thy bloody grave.—
But Randolph comes, whom fate had made my lord,
To chide my anguish, and defraud the dead.

Enter LORD RANDOLPH

LORD RANDOLPH.   Again these weeds of woe!
Say, dost thou well
To feed a passion which consumes thy life?   25
The living claim some duty; vainly thou
Bestow'st thy cares upon the silent dead.
LADY RANDOLPH.   Silent, alas! is he for whom I mourn:
Childless, without memorial of his name,
He only now in my remembrance lives.   30
This fatal day stirs my time-settled sorrow—
Troubles afresh the fountain of my heart.
LORD RANDOLPH.   When was it pure of sadness! These black weeds
Express the wonted color of thy mind,   34
Forever dark and dismal.   Seven long years
Are passed, since we were joined by sacred ties:
Clouds all the while have hung upon thy brow,
Nor broke, nor parted by one gleam of joy.
Time, that wears out the trace of deepest anguish,
As the sea smooths the prints made in the sand,   40
Has passed o'er thee in vain.
LADY RANDOLPH.   If time to come
Should prove as ineffectual, yet, my lord,
Thou can'st not blame me.   When our Scottish youth
Vied with each other for my luckless love,
Oft I besought them, I implored them all   45
Not to assail me with my father's aid,
Nor blend their better destiny with mine;
For melancholy had congealed my blood,
And froze affection in my chilly breast.
At last my sire, roused with the base attempt
To force me from him, which thou rend'redst vain,   51
To his own daughter bowed his hoary head,
Besought me to commiserate his age,
And vowed he should not, could not, die in peace,
Unless he saw me wedded, and secured   55
From violence and outrage.   Then, my lord!
In my extreme distress I called on thee,
Thee I bespake, professed my strong desire
To lead a single, solitary life,
And begged thy nobleness, not to demand   60
Her for a wife whose heart was dead to love.

How thou persisted'st after this, thou know'st,
And must confess that I am not unjust,
Nor more to thee than to myself injurious.
 LORD RANDOLPH. That I confess; yet ever
  must regret   65
The grief I cannot cure. Would thou wert not
Composed of grief and tenderness alone,
But hadst a spark of other passions in thee,
Pride, anger, vanity, the strong desire
Of admiration, dear to womankind;   70
These might contend with, and allay thy
 grief,
As meeting tides and currents smooth our frith.
 LADY RANDOLPH. To such a cause the hu-
  man mind oft owes
Its transient calm, a calm I envy not.
 LORD RANDOLPH. Sure thou art not the
  daughter of Sir Malcolm: 75
Strong was his rage, eternal his resentment:
For when thy brother fell, he smiled to hear
That Douglas' son in the same field was slain.
 LADY RANDOLPH. Oh! rake not up the ashes
  of my fathers;
Implacable resentment was their crime, 80
And grievous has the expiation been.
Contending with the Douglas, gallant lives
Of either house were lost; my ancestors
Compelled at last, to leave their ancient seat
On Tiviot's [1] pleasant banks; and now, of them
No heir is left. Had they not been so stern, 86
I had not been the last of all my race.
 LORD RANDOLPH. Thy grief wrests to its
  purposes my words.
I never asked of thee that ardent love,
Which in the breasts of fancy's children burns.
Decent affection and complacent kindness 91
Were all I wished for; but I wished in vain.
Hence with the less regret my eyes behold
The storm of war that gathers o'er this land: [2]
If I should perish by the Danish sword, 95
Matilda would not shed one tear the more.
 LADY RANDOLPH. Thou dost not think so;
  woeful as I am,
I love thy merit, and esteem thy virtues.
But whither goest thou now?
 LORD RANDOLPH.   Straight to the camp,
Where every warrior on the tip-toe stands
Of expectation, and impatient asks   101
Each who arrives, if he is come to tell
The Danes are landed.

[1] The River Teviot is in the Lowlands. Lady Randolph has been removed into the less pleasant Highlands.
[2] Home has apparently no single Danish invasion in mind.

 LADY RANDOLPH.   O! may adverse winds,
Far from the coast of Scotland, drive their
 fleet!
And every soldier of both hosts return 105
In peace and safety to his pleasant home!
 LORD RANDOLPH. Thou speak'st a woman's,
  hear a warrior's wish:
Right from their native land, the stormy
 north,
May the wind blow, till every keel is fixed
Immovable in Caledonia's strand!   110
Then shall our foes repent their bold invasion,
And roving armies shun the fatal shore.
 LADY RANDOLPH. War I detest; but war
  with foreign foes,
Whose manners, language, and whose looks
 are strange,
Is not so horrid, nor to me so hateful, 115
As that which with our neighbors oft we wage.
A river here, there an ideal [3] line,
By fancy drawn, divides the sister kingdoms.[4]
On each side dwells a people similar,
As twins are to each other; valiant both: 120
Both for their valor famous through the world.
Yet will they not unite their kindred arms,
And, if they must have war, wage distant war,
But with each other fight in cruel conflict.
Gallant in strife, and noble in their ire, 125
The battle is their pastime. They go forth
Gay in the morning, as to summer sport;
When ev'ning comes, the glory of the morn,
The youthful warrior, is a clod of clay.
Thus fall the prime of either hapless land; 130
And such the fruit of Scotch and English wars.
 LORD RANDOLPH. I'll hear no more: this
  melody would make
A soldier drop his sword, and doff his arms,
Sit down and weep the conquests he has made;
Yea, (like a monk) sing rest and peace in
 heaven   135
To souls of warriors in his battles slain.
Lady, farewell: I leave thee not alone;
Yonder comes one whose love makes duty
 light.   *Exit*

Enter ANNA

 ANNA. Forgive the rashness of your Anna's
  love:
Urged by affection, I have thus presumed 140
To interrupt your solitary thoughts;
And warn you of the hours that you neglect,
And lose in sadness.

[3] Imaginary.
[4] I.e., England and Scotland.

DOUGLAS

LADY RANDOLPH.   So to lose my hours
Is all the use I wish to make of time.
　ANNA. To blame thee, lady, suits not with
　　my state: 145
But sure I am, since death first preyed on
　man,
Never did sister thus a brother mourn.
What had your sorrows been if you had lost,
In early youth, the husband of your heart?
　LADY RANDOLPH. Oh!   150
　ANNA. Have I distressed you with officious
　　love,
And ill-timed mention of your brother's fate?
Forgive me, lady; humble though I am,
The mind I bear partakes not of my fortune.
So fervently I love you, that to dry   155
These piteous tears, I'd throw my life away.
　LADY RANDOLPH. What power directed thy
　　unconscious tongue
To speak as thou hast done? to name—
　ANNA.   I know not:
But since my words have made my mistress
　tremble,
I will speak so no more; but silent mix 160
My tears with hers.
　LADY RANDOLPH. No, thou shalt not be
　　silent.
I'll trust thy faithful love, and thou shalt be
Henceforth the instructed partner of my
　woes.
But what avails it? Can thy feeble pity
Roll back the flood of never-ebbing time? 165
Compel the earth and ocean to give up
Their dead alive?
　ANNA.   What means my noble mistress?
　LADY RANDOLPH. Didst thou not ask what
　　had my sorrows been,
If I in early youth had lost a husband?—
In the cold bosom of the earth is lodged, 170
Mangled with wounds, the husband of my
　youth;
And in some cavern of the ocean lies
My child and his!
　ANNA. O! lady, most revered!
The tale wrapt up in your amazing words 174
Deign to unfold.
　LADY RANDOLPH.   Alas! an ancient feud,
Hereditary evil, was the source
Of my misfortunes. Ruling fate decreed,
That my brave brother should in battle save
The life of Douglas' son, our house's foe:
The youthful warriors vowed eternal friend-
　ship.   180
To see the vaunted sister of his friend

Impatient, Douglas to Balarmo[1] came,
Under a borrowed name.—My heart he gained;
Nor did I long refuse the hand he begged:
My brother's presence authorized our mar-
　riage.   185
Three weeks, three little weeks, with wings of
　down,
Had o'er us flown, when my loved lord was
　called
To fight his father's battles; and with him,
In spite of all my tears, did Malcolm go.
Scarce were they gone, when my stern sire was
　told   190
That the false stranger was Lord Douglas'
　son.
Frantic with rage, the baron drew his sword,
And questioned me. Alone, forsaken, faint,
Kneeling beneath his sword, falt'ring, I took
An oath equivocal, that I ne'er would   195
Wed one of Douglas' name.—Sincerity,
Thou first of virtues, let no mortal leave
Thy onward path! although the earth should
　gape,
And from the gulf of hell destruction cry,
To take dissimulation's winding way.   200
　ANNA. Alas! how few of woman's fearful
　　kind
Durst own a truth so hardy!
　LADY RANDOLPH.   The first truth
Is easiest to avow. This moral learn,
This precious moral, from my tragic tale.—
In a few days the dreadful tidings came, 205
That Douglas and my brother both were
　slain.
My lord! my life! my husband!—Mighty God!
What had I done to merit such affliction?
　ANNA. My dearest lady! many a tale of
　　tears
I've listened to; but never did I hear   210
A tale so sad as this.
　LADY RANDOLPH.   In the first days
Of my distracting grief, I found myself—
As women wish to be who love their lords.
But who durst tell my father? The good priest
Who joined our hands, my brother's ancient
　tutor,   215
With his loved Malcolm, in the battle fell:—
They two alone were privy to the marriage.
On silence and concealment I resolved,
Till time should make my father's fortune
　mine.
That very night on which my son was born,

[1] Balarmo is apparently Home's invention, no such castle being known.

My nurse, the only confidante I had, 221
Set out with him to reach her sister's house:
But nurse, nor infant, have I ever seen,
Or heard of, Anna, since that fatal hour.
My murdered child!—Had thy fond mother feared 225
The loss of thee, she had loud fame defied,
Despised her father's rage, her father's grief,
And wandered with thee through the scorning world.

ANNA. Not seen nor heard of! then perhaps he lives.

LADY RANDOLPH. No. It was dark December: wind and rain 230
Had beat all night. Across the Carron [1] lay
The destined road; and in its swelling flood
My faithful servant perished with my child.
O hapless son! of a most hapless sire!—
But they are both at rest; and I alone 235
Dwell in this world of woe, condemned to walk,[2]
Like a guilt-troubled ghost, my painful rounds:
Nor has despiteful fate permitted me
The comfort of a solitary sorrow.
Though dead to love, I was compelled to wed
Randolph, who snatched me from a villain's arms; 241
And Randolph now possesses the domains,
That by Sir Malcolm's death on me devolved;
Domains, that should to Douglas' son have given
A baron's title, and a baron's power. 245
Such were my soothing thoughts, while I bewailed
The slaughtered father of a son unborn.
And when that son came, like a ray from heaven,
Which shines and disappears; alas! my child!
How long did thy fond mother grasp the hope
Of having thee, she knew not how, restored.
Year after year hath worn her hope away; 252
But left still undiminished her desire.

ANNA. The hand,[3] that spins the uneven thread of life,
May smooth the length that's yet to come of yours. 255

LADY RANDOLPH. Not in this world: I have considered well

[1] The River Carron empties into Loch Carron, or Carron Water, an arm of the sea on the northwest coast, opposite the Isle of Skye.
[2] One catches every now and then echoes of Shakespearean phraseology.
[3] Clotho, one of the Fates.

Its various evils, and on whom they fall.
Alas! how oft does goodness wound itself,
And sweet affection prove the spring of woe!
O! had I died when my loved husband fell!
Had some good angel opened to me the book
Of Providence, and let me read my life, 262
My heart had broke, when I beheld the sum
Of ills, which one by one I have endured.

ANNA. That God, whose ministers good angels are, 265
Hath shut the book in mercy to mankind.

But we must leave this theme: Glenalvon comes.
I saw him bend on you his thoughtful eyes;
And hitherward he slowly stalks his way.

LADY RANDOLPH. I will avoid him. An ungracious person 270
Is doubly irksome in an hour like this.

ANNA. Why speaks my lady thus of Randolph's heir?

LADY RANDOLPH. Because he's not the heir of Randolph's virtues.
Subtle and shrewd, he offers to mankind
An artificial image of himself; 275
And he with ease can vary to the taste
Of different men its features.[4] Self-denied,
And master of his appetites he seems:
But his fierce nature, like a fox chained up,
Watches to seize unseen the wished-for prey.
Never were vice and virtue poised so ill, 281
As in Glenalvon's unrelenting mind.
Yet is he brave and politic in war,
And stands aloft in these unruly times.
Why I describe him thus I'll tell hereafter:
Stay and detain him till I reach the castle. 286

Exit LADY RANDOLPH

ANNA. O happiness! where art thou to be found?
I see thou dwellest not with birth and beauty,
Though graced with grandeur, and in wealth arrayed:
Nor dost thou, it would seem, with virtue dwell; 290
Else had this gentle lady missed thee not.

Enter GLENALVON

GLENALVON. What dost thou muse on, meditating maid?
Like some entranced and visionary seer,
On earth thou stand'st, thy thoughts ascend to heaven.

ANNA. Would that I were, e'en as thou say'st, a seer, 295

[4] I.e., the features of the image.

To have my doubts by heavenly vision cleared!
GLENALVON. What dost thou doubt of?
    what hast thou to do
With subjects intricate? thy youth, thy
    beauty,
Cannot be questioned: think of these good
    gifts;
And then thy contemplations will be pleasing.
ANNA. Let women view yon monument of
    woe,   301
Then boast of beauty. Who so fair as she?
But I must follow; this revolving day
Awakes the memory of her ancient woes.
                                    Exit ANNA
GLENALVON. (*Solus.*) So! Lady Randolph
    shuns me: by and by   305
I'll woo her as the lion woos his bride.
The deed's a-doing now, that makes me lord
Of these rich valleys, and a chief of power.
The season is most apt: my sounding steps
Will not be heard amidst the din of arms. 310
Randolph has lived too long; his better fate
Had the ascendant once, and kept me down.
When I had seized the dame, by chance he
    came,
Rescued, and had the lady for his labor.
I 'scaped unknown; a slender consolation! 315
Heaven is my witness that I do not love
To sow in peril, and let others reap
The jocund harvest. Yet I am not safe:
By love, or something like it, stung, inflamed,
Madly I blabbed my passion to his wife, 320
And she has threatened to acquaint him of it.
The way of woman's will I do not know;
But well I know the baron's wrath is deadly.
I will not live in fear: the man I dread
Is as a Dane to me; ay, and the man   325
Who stands betwixt me and my chief desire.
No bar but he; she has no kinsman near;
No brother in his sister's quarrel bold;
And for the righteous cause, a stranger's
    cause,
I know no chief that will defy Glenalvon. *Exit*

ACT II

A court, &c. as before

Enter Servants *and a* Stranger *at one door,
and* LADY RANDOLPH *and* ANNA *at another*

LADY RANDOLPH. What means this clamor?
    Stranger, speak secure;
Hast thou been wronged? Have these rude
    men presumed
To vex the weary traveller on his way?
1ST SERVANT. By us no stranger ever suf-
    fered wrong:
This man with outcry wild had called us forth;
So sore afraid he cannot speak his fears. 6

Enter LORD RANDOLPH *and a* Young Man,
with their swords drawn and bloody

LADY RANDOLPH. Not vain the stranger's
    fears!—How fares my lord?
LORD RANDOLPH. That it fares well, thanks
    to this gallant youth,
Whose valor saved me from a wretched
    death!—
As down the winding dale I walked alone, 10
At the cross way four armed men attacked me:
Rovers, I judge, from the licentious camp;
Who would have quickly laid Lord Randolph
    low,
Had not this brave and generous stranger
    come,
Like my good angel, in the hour of fate, 15
And, mocking danger, made my foes his own.
They turned upon him; but his active arm
Struck to the ground, from whence they rose
    no more,
The fiercest two; the others fled amain,
And left him master of the bloody field. 20
Speak, Lady Randolph; upon beauty's tongue
Dwell accents pleasing to the brave and bold;
Speak, noble dame, and thank him for thy
    lord.
LADY RANDOLPH. My lord, I cannot speak
    what now I feel.
My heart o'erflows with gratitude to heaven;
And to this noble youth, who, all unknown 26
To you and yours, deliberated not,
Nor paused at peril, but, humanely brave,
Fought on your side, against such fearful odds.
Have you yet learned of him whom we should
    thank?   30
Whom call the savior of Lord Randolph's
    life?
LORD RANDOLPH. I asked that question,
    and he answered not:
But I must know who my deliverer is.
                            (*To the* Stranger)
STRANGER. A low-born man, of parentage
    obscure,
Who nought can boast but his desire to be 35
A soldier, and to gain a name in arms.
LORD RANDOLPH. Whoe'er thou art, thy
    spirit is ennobled
By the great King of kings! Thou art ordained

And stamped a hero by the sovereign hand
Of Nature! Blush not, flower of modesty, 40
As well as valor, to declare thy birth.
    STRANGER. My name is Norval; on the Grampian hills [1]
My father feeds his flocks, a frugal swain,
Whose constant cares were to increase his store,
And keep his only son, myself, at home, 45
For I had heard of battles, and I longed
To follow to the field some warlike lord;
And heaven soon granted what my sire denied.
This moon which rose last night, round as my shield,
Had not yet filled her horns, when, by her light, 50
A band of fierce barbarians, from the hills,
Rushed like a torrent down upon the vale,
Sweeping our flocks and herds. The shepherds fled
For safety and for succor. I alone, 54
With bended bow, and quiver full of arrows,
Hovered about the enemy, and marked
The road he took, then hastened to my friends,
Whom, with a troop of fifty chosen men,
I met advancing. The pursuit I led,
Till we o'ertook the spoil-encumbered foe. 60
We fought and conquered. Ere a sword was drawn,
An arrow from my bow had pierced their chief,
Who wore that day the arms which now I wear.
Returning home in triumph, I disdained
The shepherd's slothful life; and having heard
That our good king had summoned his bold peers 66
To lead their warriors to the Carron side,
I left my father's house, and took with me
A chosen servant to conduct my steps:—
Yon trembling coward, who forsook his master. 70
Journeying with this intent, I passed these towers,
And, heaven-directed, came this day to do
The happy deed that gilds my humble name.
    LORD RANDOLPH. He is as wise as brave.
Was ever tale
With such a gallant modesty rehearsed? 75

My brave deliverer! thou shalt enter now
A nobler list, and in a monarch's sight
Contend with princes for the prize of fame.
I will present thee to our Scottish king,
Whose valiant spirit ever valor loved.— 80
Ha, my Matilda! wherefore starts that tear?
    LADY RANDOLPH. I cannot say: for various affections,
And strangely mingled, in my bosom swell;
Yet each of them may well command a tear.
I joy that thou art safe; and I admire 85
Him and his fortunes who hath wrought thy safety;
Yea, as my mind predicts, with thine his own.
Obscure and friendless, he the army sought,
Bent upon peril, in the range of death
Resolved to hunt for fame, and with his sword 90
To gain distinction which his birth denied.
In this attempt unknown he might have perished,
And gained, with all his valor, but oblivion.
Now, graced by thee, his virtue serves no more
Beneath despair. The soldier now of hope 95
He stands conspicuous; fame and great renown
Are brought within the compass of his sword.
On this my mind reflected, whilst you spoke,
And blessed the wonder-working Lord of heaven.
    LORD RANDOLPH. Pious and grateful ever are thy thoughts! 100
My deeds shall follow where thou point'st the way.
Next to myself, and equal to Glenalvon,
In honor and command shall Norval be.
    NORVAL. I know not how to thank you.
Rude I am 104
In speech and manners: never till this hour
Stood I in such a presence; yet, my lord,
There's something in my breast, which makes me bold
To say that Norval ne'er will shame thy favor.
    LADY RANDOLPH. I will be sworn thou wilt not. Thou shalt be 109
My knight; and ever, as thou didst to-day,
With happy valor guard the life of Randolph.
    LORD RANDOLPH. Well hast thou spoke.
Let me forbid reply.   (*To Norval*)
We are thy debtors still; thy high desert
O'ertops our gratitude. I must proceed,
As was at first intended. to the camp. 115

---

[1] The Grampian Mountains stretch across the central part of Scotland from Argyll to Aberdeen. This speech of Norval was once perhaps, Shakespeare excluded, the most famous speech in English drama. It was a favorite of young declaimers.

Some of my train, I see, are speeding hither,
Impatient, doubtless, of their lord's delay.
Go with me, Norval, and thine eyes shall see
The chosen warriors of thy native land,
Who languish for the fight, and beat the air
With brandished swords.
  NORVAL. Let us begone, my lord. 121
  LORD RANDOLPH. (*To Lady Randolph*)
About the time that the declining sun
Shall his broad orbit o'er yon hills suspend,
Expect us to return. This night once more
Within these walls I rest; my tent I pitch 125
To-morrow in the field.—Prepare the feast.
Free is his heart who for his country fights:
He in the eve of battle may resign
Himself to social pleasure; sweetest then,
When danger to a soldier's soul endears 130
The human joy that never may return.
Exeunt all except LADY RANDOLPH *and* ANNA
  LADY RANDOLPH. His parting words have
   struck a fatal truth.
O Douglas, Douglas! tender was the time
When we two parted, ne'er to meet again!
How many years of anguish and despair 135
Has heaven annexed to those swift-passing
  hours
Of love and fondness! Then my bosom's flame,
Oft, as blown back by the rude breath of fear,
Returned, and with redoubled ardor blazed.
  ANNA. May gracious heaven pour the
   sweet balm of peace 140
Into the wounds that fester in your breast!
For earthly consolation cannot cure them.
  LADY RANDOLPH. One only cure can heaven
   itself bestow;
A grave—that bed in which the weary rest.
Wretch that I am! Alas! why am I so? 145
At every happy parent I repine!
How blest the mother of yon gallant Norval!
She for a living husband bore her pains, 148
And heard him bless her when a man was born:
She nursed her smiling infant on her breast;
Tended the child, and reared the pleasing boy.
She, with affection's triumph, saw the youth
In grace and comeliness surpass his peers:
Whilst I to a dead husband bore a son,
And to the roaring waters gave my child. 155
  ANNA. Alas, alas! why will you thus re-
   sume
Your grief afresh? I thought that gallant
  youth
Would for a while have won you from your
  woe.
On him intent you gazèd, with a look

Much more delighted, than your pensive eye
Has deigned on other objects to bestow. 161
  LADY RANDOLPH. Delighted, say'st thou?
   Oh! even there mine eye
Found fuel for my life-consuming sorrow.
I thought, that had the son of Douglas lived,
He might have been like this young gallant
  stranger, 165
And paired with him in features and in shape.
In all endowments, as in years, I deem,
My boy with blooming Norval might have
  numbered.
Whilst thus I mused, a spark from fancy fell
On my sad heart, and kindled up a fondness
For this young stranger, wand'ring from his
  home, 171
And like an orphan cast upon my care.
I will protect thee (said I to myself),
With all my power, and grace with all my
  favor.
  ANNA. Sure heaven will bless so generous a
   resolve. 175
You must, my noble dame, exert your power:
You must awake: devices will be framed,
And arrows pointed at the breast of Norval.
  LADY RANDOLPH. Glenalvon's false and
   crafty head will work
Against a rival in his kinsman's love, 180
If I deter him not: I only can.
Bold as he is, Glenalvon will beware
How he pulls down the fabric that I raise.
I'll be the artist of young Norval's fortune.
'Tis pleasing to admire! most apt was I 185
To this affection in my better days;
Though now I seem to you shrunk up, retired
Within the narrow compass of my woe.
Have you not sometimes seen an early flower
Open its bud, and spread its silken leaves, 190
To catch sweet airs, and odors to bestow;
Then, by the keen blast nipt, pull in its leaves,
And, though still living, die to scent and
  beauty?
Emblem of me: affliction, like a storm, 194
Hath killed the forward blossoms of my heart.

   Enter GLENALVON

  GLENALVON. Where is my dearest kinsman,
   noble Randolph?
  LADY RANDOLPH. Have you not heard,
   Glenalvon, of the base—
  GLENALVON. I have: and that the villains
   may not 'scape,
With a strong band I have begirt the wood:
If they lurk there, alive they shall be taken,

And torture force from them th' important
    secret, 201
Whether some foe of Randolph hired their
    swords,
Or if—
    LADY RANDOLPH. That care becomes a
    kinsman's love.—
I have a counsel for Glenalvon's ear.
                      Exit ANNA
    GLENALVON. To him your counsels are
    commands. 205
    LADY RANDOLPH. I have not found so; thou
    art known to me.
    GLENALVON. Known!
    LADY RANDOLPH. And most certain is my
    cause of knowledge.
    GLENALVON. What do you know? By the
    most blessed cross,
You much amaze me. No created being,
Yourself except, durst thus accost Glenalvon.
    LADY RANDOLPH. Is guilt so bold? and dost
    thou make a merit 211
Of thy pretended meekness? This to me,
Who, with a gentleness which duty blames,
Have hitherto concealed what, if divulged,
Would make thee nothing; or, what's worse
    than that, 215
An outcast beggar, and unpitied too?
For mortals shudder at a crime like thine.
    GLENALVON. Thy virtue awes me. First
    of womankind!
Permit me yet to say that the fond man
Whom love transports beyond strict virtue's
    bounds, 220
If he is brought by love to misery,
In fortune ruined, as in mind forlorn,
Unpitied cannot be. Pity's the alms
Which on such beggars freely is bestowed:
For mortals know that love is still their lord,
And o'er their vain resolves advances still, 226
As fire, when kindled by our shepherds, moves
Through the dry heath before the fanning
    wind.
    LADY RANDOLPH. Reserve these accents for
    some other ear.
To love's apology I listen not. 230
Mark thou my words; for it is meet thou
    should'st.
His brave deliverer Randolph here retains.
Perhaps his presence may not please thee well;
But, at thy peril, practise aught against him:
Let not thy jealousy attempt to shake 235
And loosen the good root he has in Randolph;
Whose favorites I know thou hast supplanted.

Thou look'st at me, as if thou fain would'st pry
Into my heart. 'Tis open as my speech.
I give this early caution; and put on 240
The curb, before thy temper breaks away.
The friendless stranger my protection claims:
His friend I am, and be not thou his foe. *Exit*

          Manet GLENALVON

    GLENALVON. Child that I was, to start at
    my own shadow,
And be the shallow fool of coward conscience!
I am not what I have been, what I should be.
The darts of destiny have almost pierced 247
My marble heart. Had I one grain of faith
In holy legends, and religious tales,
I should conclude there was an arm above 250
That fought against me, and malignant turned,
To catch myself, the subtle snare I set.
Why, rape and murder are not simple means!
Th' imperfect rape to Randolph gave a spouse;
And the intended murder introduced 255
A favorite to hide the sun from me;
And, worst of all, a rival. Burning hell!
This were thy center, if I thought she loved him!
'Tis certain she contemns me; nay, commands
    me,
And waves the flag of her displeasure o'er me,
In his behalf. And shall I thus be braved? 261
Curbed, as she calls it, by dame chastity?
Infernal fiends, if any fiends there are
More fierce than hate, ambition, and revenge,
Rise up, and fill my bosom with your fires, 265
And policy remorseless! Chance may spoil
A single aim; but perseverance must
Prosper at last. For chance and fate are
    words:
Persistive wisdom in the fate of man.
Darkly a project peers upon my mind, 270
Like the red moon when rising in the east,
Crossed and divided by strange-colored clouds.
I'll seek the slave who came with Norval
    hither,
And for his cowardice was spurned from him.
I've known a follower's rankled bosom breed
Venom most fatal to his heedless lord. *Exit*

ACT III

A court, etc., as before

Enter ANNA

    ANNA. Thy vassals, Grief! great nature's
    order break,
And change the noon-tide to the midnight
    hour.

Whilst Lady Randolph sleeps, I will walk
  forth,
And taste the air that breathes on yonder
  bank.
Sweet may her slumbers be! Ye ministers   5
Of gracious heaven who love the human race,
Angels and seraphs who delight in goodness,
Forsake your skies, and to her couch descend!
There from her fancy chase those dismal forms
That haunt her waking; her sad spirit charm
With images celestial, such as please   11
The bless'd above upon their golden beds.

Enter Servant

SERVANT. One of the vile assassins is se-
  cured.
We found the villain lurking in the wood:
With dreadful imprecations he denies   15
All knowledge of the crime. But this is not
His first essay; these jewels were concealed
In the most secret places of his garment;
Belike the spoils of some that he has mur-
  dered.
ANNA. Let me look on them! Ha! here is a
  heart,   20
The chosen crest of Douglas' valiant name!
These are no vulgar jewels.—Guard the
  wretch.   *Exit* ANNA

Enter Servants *with a* Prisoner

PRISONER. I know no more than does the
  child unborn
Of what you charge me with.
FIRST SERVANT.   You say so, sir!
But torture soon shall make you speak the
  truth.   25
Behold, the lady of Lord Randolph comes;
Prepare yourself to meet her just revenge.

Enter LADY RANDOLPH *and* ANNA

ANNA. Summon your utmost fortitude, be-
  fore   28
You speak with him. Your dignity, your fame,
Are now at stake. Think of the fatal secret,
Which in a moment from your lips may fly.
LADY RANDOLPH. Thou shalt behold me,
  with a desperate heart,
Hear how my infant perished. See, he kneels.
        (*The* Prisoner *kneels*)
PRISONER. Heaven bless that countenance
  so sweet and mild!
A judge like thee makes innocence more bold.
O save me, lady! from these cruel men,   36
Who have attacked and seized me; who accuse
Me of intended murder. As I hope
For mercy at the judgment-seat of God,
The tender lamb, that never nipped the grass,
Is not more innocent than I of murder.   41
  LADY RANDOLPH. Of this man's guilt what
    proof can ye produce?
  FIRST SERVANT. We found him lurking in
    the hollow glen.
When viewed and called upon, amazed he fled.
We overtook him, and inquired from whence
And what he was: he said he came from far,
And was upon his journey to the camp.   47
Not satisfied with this, we searched his clothes,
And found these jewels, whose rich value plead
Most powerfully against him. Hard he seems,
And old in villainy. Permit us try   51
His stubbornness against the torture's force.
  PRISONER. O, gentle lady! by your lord's
    dear life,
Which these weak hands, I swear, did ne'er
  assail;
And by your children's welfare, spare my age!
Let not the iron tear my ancient joints,   56
And my grey hairs bring to the grave with
  pain.
  LADY RANDOLPH. Account for these; thine
    own they cannot be:
For these, I say: be steadfast to the truth;
Detected falsehood is most certain death.   60
  (ANNA *removes the* Servants *and returns*)
  PRISONER. Alas! I'm sore beset! let never
    man,
For sake of lucre, sin against his soul!
Eternal justice is in this most just!
I, guiltless now, must former guilt reveal.
  LADY RANDOLPH. O! Anna, hear!—Once
    more I charge thee speak   65
The truth direct: for these to me foretell
And certify a part of thy narration;
With which, if the remainder tallies not,
An instant and a dreadful death abides thee.
  PRISONER. Then, thus adjured, I'll speak to
    you as just   70
As if you were the minister of heaven,
Sent down to search the secret sins of men.
Some eighteen years ago, I rented land
Of brave Sir Malcolm, then Balarmo's lord;
But falling to decay, his servants seized   75
All that I had, and then turned me and mine
(Four helpless infants and their weeping
  mother,)
Out to the mercy of the winter winds.
A little hovel by the river's side

Received us: there hard labor, and the skill 80
In fishing, which was formerly my sport,
Supported life. Whilst thus we poorly lived,
One stormy night, as I remember well,
The wind and rain beat hard upon our roof:
Red came the river down, and loud and oft 85
The angry spirit of the water shrieked.
At the dead hour of night was heard the cry
Of one in jeopardy. I rose, and ran
To where the circling eddy of a pool,
Beneath the ford, used oft to bring within 90
My reach whatever floating thing the stream
Had caught. The voice was ceased; the person lost:
But, looking sad and earnest on the waters,
By the moon's light I saw, whirled round and round,
A basket: soon I drew it to the bank, 95
And nestled curious there an infant lay.
  LADY RANDOLPH. Was he alive?
  PRISONER.   He was.
  LADY RANDOLPH. Inhuman that thou art!
How could'st thou kill what waves and tempests spared?
  PRISONER. I was not inhuman.
  LADY RANDOLPH.   Didst thou not? 100
  ANNA. My noble mistress, you are moved too much.
This man has not the aspect of stern murder;
Let him go on, and you, I hope, will hear
Good tidings of your kinsman's long lost child.
  PRISONER. The needy man who has known better days, 105
One whom distress has spited at the world,
Is he whom tempting fiends would pitch upon
To do such deeds, as make the prosperous men
Lift up their hands, and wonder who could do them:
And such a man was I, a man declined, 110
Who saw no end of black adversity.
Yet, for the wealth of kingdoms, I would not
Have touched that infant with a hand of harm.
  LADY RANDOLPH. Ha! dost thou say so?
Then perhaps he lives!
  PRISONER. Not many days ago he was alive. 115
  LADY RANDOLPH. O God of heaven! Did he then die so lately?
  PRISONER. I did not say he died; I hope he lives.
Not many days ago these eyes beheld
Him, flourishing in youth, and health, and beauty.
  LADY RANDOLPH. Where is he now?
  PRISONER.   Alas! I know not where.
  LADY RANDOLPH. Oh, fate! I fear thee still. Thou riddler, speak 121
Direct and clear; else I will search thy soul.
  ANNA. Permit me, ever honored! Keen impatience,
Though hard to be restrained, defeats itself.—
Pursue thy story with a faithful tongue, 125
To the last hour that thou didst keep the child.
  PRISONER. Fear not my faith, though I must speak my shame.
Within the cradle where the infant lay
Was stowed a mighty store of gold and jewels;
Tempted by which, we did resolve to hide, 130
From all the world, this wonderful event,
And like a peasant breed the noble child.
That none might mark the change of our estate,
We left the country, traveled to the north,
Bought flocks and herds, and gradually brought forth 135
Our secret wealth. But God's all-seeing eye
Beheld our avarice, and smote us sore:
For one by one all our own children died,
And he, the stranger, sole remained the heir
Of what indeed was his. Fain then would I,
Who with a father's fondness loved the boy,
Have trusted him, now in the dawn of youth,
With his own secret: but my anxious wife, 143
Foreboding evil, never would consent.
Meanwhile the stripling grew in years and beauty; 145
And, as we oft observed, he bore himself,
Not as the offspring of our cottage blood;
For nature will break out; mild with the mild,
But with the froward he was fierce as fire,
And night and day he talked of war and arms. 150
I set myself against his warlike bent;
But all in vain, for when a desperate band
Of robbers from the savage mountains came—
  LADY RANDOLPH.   Eternal Providence! What is thy name?
  PRISONER. My name is Norval; and my name he bears. 155
  LADY RANDOLPH. 'Tis he; 'tis he himself! It is my son!
O, sovereign mercy! 'Twas my child I saw!—
No wonder, Anna, that my bosom burned.
  ANNA. Just are your transports: ne'er was woman's heart

Proved with such fierce extremes. High-fated
    dame! 160
But yet remember that you are beheld
By servile eyes; your gestures may be seen
Impassioned, strange; perhaps your words
    o'er-heard.
    LADY RANDOLPH. Well dost thou counsel,
        Anna. Heaven bestow 164
On me that wisdom which my state requires!
    ANNA. The moments of deliberation pass,
And soon you must resolve. This useful man
Must be dismissed in safety, ere my lord
Shall with his brave deliverer return.
    PRISONER. If I, amidst astonishment and
        fear, 170
Have of your words and gestures rightly
    judged,
Thou art the daughter of my ancient master;
The child I rescued from the flood is thine.
    LADY RANDOLPH. With thee dissimulation
        now were vain.
I am indeed the daughter of Sir Malcolm; 175
The child thou rescued'st from the flood is
    mine.
    PRISONER. Bless'd be the hour that made
        me a poor man!
My poverty hath saved my master's house!
    LADY RANDOLPH. Thy words surprise me:
        sure thou dost not feign!
The tear stands in thine eye: such love from
    thee 180
Sir Malcolm's house deserved not; if aright
Thou told'st the story of thy own distress.
    PRISONER. Sir Malcolm of our barons was
        the flower;
The fastest friend, the best, the kindest
    master:
But ah! he knew not of my sad estate. 185
After that battle, where his gallant son,
Your own brave brother, fell, the good old
    lord
Grew desperate and reckless of the world;
And never, as he erst was wont, went forth
To overlook the conduct of his servants. 190
By them I was thrust out, and them I blame:
May heaven so judge me as I judged my
    master!
And God so love me as I love his race!
    LADY RANDOLPH. His race shall yet re-
        ward thee. On thy faith
Depends the fate of thy loved master's house.
Remember'st thou a little lonely hut, 196
That like a holy hermitage appears
Among the cliffs of Carron?

    PRISONER.   I remember
The cottage of the cliffs.
    LADY RANDOLPH.   'Tis that I mean:
There dwells a man of venerable age, 200
Who in my father's service spent his youth:
Tell him I sent thee, and with him remain,
Till I shall call upon thee to declare,
Before the king and nobles, what thou now
To me hast told. No more but this, and thou
Shalt live in honor all thy future days; 206
Thy son so long shall call thee father still,
And all the land shall bless the man who saved
The son of Douglas, and Sir Malcolm's heir.
Remember well my words; if thou should'st
    meet 210
Him whom thou call'st thy son, still call him
    so;
And mention nothing of his nobler father.
    PRISONER. Fear not that I shall mar so
        fair a harvest,
By putting in my sickle ere 'tis ripe.
Why did I leave my home and ancient dame?
To find the youth, to tell him all I knew, 216
And make him wear these jewels in his arms,
Which might, I thought, be challenged, and
    so bring
To light the secret of his noble birth.
    (LADY RANDOLPH *goes towards the* Servants)
    LADY RANDOLPH. This man is not the as-
        sassin you suspected, 220
Though chance combined some likelihoods
    against him.
He is the faithful bearer of the jewels
To their right owner, whom in haste he seeks.
'Tis meet that you should put him on his way,
Since your mistaken zeal hath dragged him
    hither. 225
        Exeunt Stranger *and* Servants
    LADY RANDOLPH. My faithful Anna! dost
        thou share my joy?
I know thou dost. Unparalleled event!
Reaching from heaven to earth, Jehovah's
    arm
Snatched from the waves, and brings to me
    my son!
Judge of the widow, and the orphan's father,
Accept a widow's and a mother's thanks 231
For such a gift!—What does my Anna think
Of the young eaglet of a valiant nest?
How soon he gazed on bright and burning
    arms,
Spurned the low dunghill where his fate had
    thrown him, 235
And towered up to the region of his sire!

ANNA. How fondly did your eyes devour
  the boy!
Mysterious nature, with the unseen cord
Of powerful instinct, drew you to your own.
  LADY RANDOLPH. The ready story of his
    birth believed   240
Suppressed my fancy quite; nor did he owe
To any likeness my so sudden favor:
But now I long to see his face again,
Examine every feature, and find out
The lineaments of Douglas, or my own. 245
But most of all I long to let him know
Who his true parents are, to clasp his neck,
And tell him all the story of his father.
  ANNA. With wary caution you must bear
    yourself
In public, lest your tenderness break forth,
And in observers stir conjectures strange. 251
For, if a cherub in the shape of woman
Should walk this world, yet defamation would,
Like a vile cur, bark at the angel's train.—
To-day the baron started at your tears. 255
  LADY RANDOLPH. He did so, Anna! Well
    thy mistress knows
If the least circumstance, note of offence,
Should touch the baron's eye, his sight would
  be
With jealousy disordered. But the more
It does behove me instant to declare   260
The birth of Douglas, and assert his rights.
This night I purpose with my son to meet,
Reveal the secret, and consult with him:
For wise he is, or my fond judgment errs. 264
As he does now, so looked his noble father,
Arrayed in nature's ease; his mien, his speech,
Were sweetly simple, and full oft deceived
Those trivial mortals who seem always wise.
But, when the matter matched his mighty
  mind,
Up rose the hero; on his piercing eye   270
Sat observation; on each glance of thought
Decision followed, as the thunderbolt
Pursues the flash.
  ANNA.   That demon haunts you still:
Behold Glenalvon.
  LADY RANDOLPH.   Now I shun him not.
This day I braved him in behalf of Norval:
Perhaps too far: at least my nicer fears 276
For Douglas thus interpret.

  Enter GLENALVON

  GLENALVON.   Noble dame!
The hov'ring Dane at last his men hath
  landed.

No band of pirates; but a mighty host,
That come to settle where their valor con-
  quers;   280
To win a country, or to lose themselves.
  LADY RANDOLPH. But whence comes this
    intelligence, Glenalvon?
  GLENALVON. A nimble courier sent from
    yonder camp
To hasten up the chieftains of the north,
Informed me, as he passed, that the fierce
  Dane   285
Had on the eastern coast of Lothian landed,
Near to that place where the sea-rock im-
  mense,
Amazing Bass,¹ looks o'er a fertile land.
  LADY RANDOLPH. Then must this western
    army march to join
The warlike troops that guard Edina's towers.²
  GLENALVON. Beyond all question. If im-
    pairing time   291
Has not effaced the image of a place
Once perfect in my breast, there is a wild
Which lies to westward of that mighty rock,
And seems by nature formèd for the camp
Of water-wafted armies, whose chief strength
Lies in firm foot, unflanked with warlike
  horse.   297
If martial skill directs the Danish lords,
There inaccessible their army lies
To our swift-scow'ring horse; the bloody
  field   300
Must man to man, and foot to foot, be fought.
  LADY RANDOLPH. How many mothers shall
    bewail their sons!
How many widows weep their husbands slain!
Ye dames of Denmark! even for you I feel,
Who, sadly sitting on the sea-beat shore, 305
Long look for lords that never shall return.
  GLENALVON. Oft has the unconquered
    Caledonian sword
Widowed the north. The children of the slain
Come, as I hope, to meet their fathers' fate.
The monster war, with her infernal brood, 310
Loud yelling fury, and life-ending pain,
Are objects suited to Glenalvon's soul.
Scorn is more grievous than the pains of
  death:

[1] The Bass Rock stands about a mile and a half off the south bank of the Firth of Forth near the mouth. It is some twenty miles east of Edinburgh and eight north-west of Dunbar. There is no record of an important Danish invasion landing on or near this tiny island.
[2] Edwin, King of Northumbria, built Edinburgh Castle about 617. The old Scottish name of the town was Dunedin (hill of Edwin).

Reproach more piercing than the pointed
    sword.
LADY RANDOLPH. I scorn thee not, but
    when I ought to scorn; 315
Nor e'er reproach, but when insulted virtue
Against audacious vice asserts herself.
I own thy worth, Glenalvon; none more apt
Than I to praise thine eminence in arms,
And be the echo of thy martial fame. 320
No longer vainly feed a guilty passion;
Go and pursue a lawful mistress, Glory.
Upon the Danish crests redeem thy fault,
And let thy valor be the shield of Randolph.
GLENALVON. One instant stay, and hear
    an altered man. 325
When beauty pleads for virtue, vice abashed
Flies its own colors, and goes o'er to virtue.
I am your convert; time will shew how truly:
Yet one immediate proof I mean to give.
That youth, for whom your ardent zeal to-day
Somewhat too haughtily defied your slave,
Amidst the shock of armies I'll defend, 332
And turn death from him with a guardian arm.
Sedate by use, my bosom maddens not
At the tumultuous uproar of the field. 335
LADY RANDOLPH. Act thus, Glenalvon, and
    I am thy friend:
But that's thy least reward. Believe me, sir,
The truly generous is the truly wise;
And he, who loves not others, lives unblest.
    Exit LADY RANDOLPH [*and* ANNA]
GLENALVON. (*Solus*.) Amen! and virtue is
    its own reward!— 340
I think that I have hit the very tone
In which she loves to speak. Honeyed assent,
How pleasant art thou to the taste of man,
And woman also! Flattery direct
Rarely disgusts. They little know mankind
Who doubt its operation: 'tis my key, 346
And opes the wicket of the human heart.
How far I have succeeded now, I know not:
Yet I incline to think her stormy virtue
Is lulled awhile. 'Tis her alone I fear: 350
Whilst she and Randolph live, and live in faith
And amity, uncertain is my tenure.
Fate o'er my head suspends disgrace and
    death,
By that weak hair, a peevish female's will.
I am not idle; but the ebbs and flows 355
Of fortune's tide cannot be calculated.
That slave of Norval's I have found most
    apt:
I showed him gold, and he has pawned his soul
To say and swear whatever I suggest.

Norval, I'm told, has that alluring look, 360
'Twixt man and woman, which I have ob-
    served
To charm the nicer and fantastic dames,
Who are, like Lady Randolph, full of virtue.
In raising Randolph's jealousy, I may 364
But point him to the truth. He seldom errs,
Who thinks the worst he can of womankind.
    Exit

ACT IV

[*A court, etc., as, before*] *Flourish of trumpets*

Enter LORD RANDOLPH, *attended*

LORD RANDOLPH. Summon a hundred
    horse, by break of day,
To wait our pleasure at the castle gate.

Enter LADY RANDOLPH

LADY RANDOLPH. Alas! my lord! I've heard
    unwelcome news:
The Danes are landed.
    LORD RANDOLPH. Ay, no inroad this
Of the Northumbrian, bent to take a spoil: 5
No sportive war, no tournament essay
Of some young knight resolved to break a
    spear,
And stain with hostile blood his maiden arms.
The Danes are landed: we must beat them
    back,
Or live the slaves of Denmark.
    LADY RANDOLPH. Dreadful times! 10
    LORD RANDOLPH. The fenceless[1] villages
    are all forsaken;
The trembling mothers, and their children,
    lodged
In wall-girt towers and castles, whilst the men
Retire indignant. Yet, like broken waves,
They but retire more awful to return. 15
LADY RANDOLPH. Immense, as fame re-
    ports, the Danish host!
LORD RANDOLPH. Were it as numerous as
    loud fame reports,
An army knit like ours would pierce it through:
Brothers, that shrink not from each other's
    side,
And fond companions, fill our warlike files: 20
For his dear offspring, and the wife he loves,
The husband and the fearless father arm.
In vulgar breasts heroic ardor burns,
And the poor peasant mates his daring lord.
LADY RANDOLPH. Men's minds are tem-
    pered, like their swords, for war; 25

---

[1] I.e., defenceless.

Lovers of danger, on destruction's brink
They joy to rear erect their daring forms.
Hence, early graves; hence, the lone widow's life;
And the sad mother's grief-embittered age.—
Where is our gallant guest?
    LORD RANDOLPH.   Down in the vale   30
I left him, managing a fiery steed,
Whose stubborness had foiled the strength and skill
Of every rider. But behold he comes,
In earnest conversation with Glenalvon.—

Enter NORVAL *and* GLENALVON

Glenalvon! with the lark arise; go forth,   35
And lead my troops that lie in yonder vale:
Private I travel to the royal camp.
Norval, thou goest with me. But say, young man!
Where didst thou learn so to discourse of war,
And in such terms, as I o'erheard to-day?   40
War is no village science, nor its phrase
A language taught amongst the shepherd swains.
    NORVAL. Small is the skill my lord delights to praise
In him he favors.—Hear from whence it came:
Beneath a mountain's brow, the most remote
And inaccessible by shepherds trod,   46
In a deep cave dug by no mortal hand
A hermit lived, a melancholy man,
Who was the wonder of our wand'ring swains.
Austere and lonely, cruel to himself,   50
Did they report him; the cold earth his bed,
Water his drink, his food the shepherd's alms.
I went to see him, and my heart was touched
With rev'rence and with pity. Mild he spake,
And, entering on discourse, such stories told
As made me oft revisit his sad cell,   56
For he had been a soldier in his youth,
And fought in famous battles, when the peers
Of Europe, by the bold Godfredo [1] led,
Against the usurping infidel displayed   60
The cross of Christ, and won the Holy Land.
Pleased with my admiration, and the fire
His speech struck from me, the old man would shake

---
[1] Godefroy de Bouillon (1061?–1100) was leader of the French in the Crusade of the Princes (1096). This allusion dates the action of the play probably about the middle of the twelfth century. However, Danish invasions of Scotland were well over by this date.

His years away, and act his young encounters.
Then, having showed his wounds, he'd sit him down,   65
And all the live-long day discourse of war.
To help my fancy, in the smooth green turf
He cut the figures of the marshalled hosts;
Described the motion, and explained the use
Of the deep column, and the lengthened line,
The square, the crescent, and the phalanx firm.
For all that Saracen or Christian knew   72
Of war's vast art, was to this hermit known.
    LORD RANDOLPH. Why did this soldier in a desert hide
Those qualities that should have graced a camp?
    NORVAL. That too at last I learned. Unhappy man!   76
Returning homeward by Messina's port,
Loaded with wealth and honors bravely won,
A rude and boist'rous captain of the sea   79
Fastened a quarrel on him. Fierce they fought;
The stranger fell, and with his dying breath
Declared his name and lineage. "Mighty God!"
The soldier cried, "My brother! Oh my brother!"
    LADY RANDOLPH. His brother!
    NORVAL. Yes; of the same parents born,
His only brother. They exchanged forgiveness: 85
And happy, in my mind, was he that died;
For many deaths has the survivor suffered.
In the wild desert on a rock he sits,
Or on some nameless stream's untrodden banks,
And ruminates all day his dreadful fate.   90
At times, alas! not in his perfect mind,
Holds dialogues with his loved brother's ghost
And oft each night forsakes his sullen couch
To make sad orisons for him he slew.
    LADY RANDOLPH. To what mysterious woes are mortals born!   95
In this dire tragedy, were there no more
Unhappy persons? Did the parents live?
    NORVAL. No; they were dead; kind heaven had closed their eyes
Before their son had shed his brother's blood.
    LORD RANDOLPH. Hard is his fate; for he was not to blame!   100
There is a destiny in this strange world,
Which oft decrees an undeserved doom:
Let schoolmen tell us why.—From whence these sounds?   (*Trumpets at a distance*)

Enter an Officer

OFFICER. My lord, the trumpets of the
  Troops of Lorn:[1]
The valiant leader hails the noble Randolph.
  LORD RANDOLPH. Mine ancient guest! Does
    he the warriors lead? 106
Has Denmark roused the brave old knight to
  arms?
  OFFICER. No; worn with warfare, he re-
signs the sword.
His eldest hope, the valiant John of Lorn,
Now leads his kindred bands.
  LORD RANDOLPH.   Glenalvon, go,
With hospitality's most strong request 111
Entreat the chief.   *Exit* GLENALVON
  OFFICER. My lord, requests are vain.
He urges on impatient of delay,
Stung with the tidings of the foe's approach.
  LORD RANDOLPH. May victory sit on the
    warrior's plume! 115
Bravest of men! his flocks and herds are safe;
Remote from war's alarms his pastures lie.
By mountains inaccessible secured;
Yet foremost he into the plain descends,
Eager to bleed in battles not his own. 120
Such were the heroes of the ancient world,—
Contemners they of indolence and gain,
But still, for love of glory and of arms,
Prone to encounter peril, and to lift
Against each strong antagonist the spear. 125
I'll go and press the hero to my breast.
                        Exit RANDOLPH

Manent LADY RANDOLPH *and* NORVAL

  LADY RANDOLPH. The soldier's loftiness,
    the pride and pomp
Investing awful war, Norval, I see,
Transport thy youthful mind.
  NORVAL.   Ah! should they not?
Blest be the hour I left my father's house! 130
I might have been a shepherd all my days,
And stole obscurely to a peasant's grave.
Now, if I live, with mighty chiefs I stand;
And, if I fall, with noble dust I lie.
  LADY RANDOLPH. There is a gen'rous spirit
    in thy breast, 135

[1] As the historical John of Lorn fought with Bruce in 1309, Home apparently hoped the audience would telescope history, or else assume that some progenitor of the famous John of Lorn would be understood. Generally speaking, his picture of the gathering of the clans to repulse the Danes has a vague resemblance to the gathering to repulse the Norwegian king, Haakon IV, defeated at the battle of Largs (on the western coast) in 1263.

That could have well sustained a prouder
  fortune.
This way with me; under yon spreading beech,
Unseen, unheard, by human eye or ear,
I will amaze thee with a wondrous tale.
  NORVAL. Let there be danger, lady, with
    the secret, 140
That I may hug it to my grateful heart,
And prove my faith. Command my sword
  my life;
These are the sole possessions of poor Norval.
  LADY RANDOLPH. Know'st thou these gems?
  NORVAL. Durst I believe mine eyes, 145
I'd say I knew them, and they were my
  father's.
  LADY RANDOLPH. Thy father's, say'st
    thou? Ah! they were thy father's!
  NORVAL. I saw them once and curiously in-
    quired
Of both my parents whence such splendor
  came;
But I was checked and more could never learn.
  LADY RANDOLPH. Then learn of me, thou
    art not Norval's son. 151
  NORVAL. Not Norval's son!
  LADY RANDOLPH.   Nor of a shepherd
    sprung.
  NORVAL. Lady, who am I then?
  LADY RANDOLPH.   Noble thou art;
For noble was thy sire!
  NORVAL.   I will believe— 154
O, tell me farther! Say, who was my father?
  LADY RANDOLPH. Douglas!
  NORVAL.   Lord Douglas whom today
    I saw?
  LADY RANDOLPH. His younger brother.
  NORVAL.   And in yonder camp—
  LADY RANDOLPH. Alas!
  NORVAL.   You make me tremble—Sighs
    and tears!—
Lives my brave father?
  LADY RANDOLPH.   Ah! too brave indeed!
He fell in battle ere thyself was born. 160
  NORVAL. Ah me, unhappy! ere I saw the
    light?
But does my mother live? I may conclude,
From my own fate, her portion has been sor-
  row.
  LADY RANDOLPH. She lives; but wastes her
    life in constant woe, 164
Weeping her husband slain, her infant lost.
  NORVAL. You that are skilled so well in the
    sad story
Of my unhappy parents, and with tears

Bewail their destiny, now have compassion
Upon the offspring of the friends you loved.
O! tell me who, and where my mother is? 170
Oppressed by a base world, perhaps she bends
Beneath the weight of other ills than grief;
And, desolate, implores of heaven the aid
Her son should give. It is, it must be so—
Your countenance confesses that she's
   wretched. 175
O, tell me her condition! Can the sword—
Who shall resist me in a parent's cause?
   LADY RANDOLPH. Thy virtue ends her
   woes.—My son! my son!
I am thy mother, and the wife of Douglas!
               (*Falls upon his neck*)
   NORVAL. O heaven and earth, how won-
   drous is my fate! 180
Art thou my mother? Ever let me kneel!
   LADY RANDOLPH. Image of Douglas!
   Fruit of fatal love!
All that I owe thy sire, I pay to thee.
   NORVAL. Respect and admiration still pos-
   sess me,
Checking the love and fondness of a son: 185
Yet I was filial to my humble parents.
But did my sire surpass the rest of men,
As thou excellest all of womankind?
   LADY RANDOLPH. Arise, my son! In me
   thou dost behold 189
The poor remains of beauty once admired:
The autumn of my days is come already;
For sorrow made my summer haste away.
Yet in my prime I equalled not thy father:
His eyes were like the eagle's, yet sometimes
Liker the dove's; and, as he pleased, he won
All hearts with softness, or with spirit awed.
   NORVAL. How did he fall? Sure 'twas a
   bloody field 197
When Douglas died. O! I have much to ask.
   LADY RANDOLPH. Hereafter thou shalt hear
   the lengthened tale
Of all thy father's and thy mother's woes. 200
At present this: Thou art the rightful heir
Of yonder castle, and the wide domains
Which now Lord Randolph, as my husband,
   holds.
But thou shalt not be wronged; I have the
   power 204
To right thee still: before the king I'll kneel,
And call Lord Douglas to protect his blood.
   NORVAL. The blood of Douglas will protect
   itself.
   LADY RANDOLPH. But we shall need both
   friends and favor, boy,

To wrest the lands and lordship from the grip
Of Randolph and his kinsman. Yet I think
My tale will move each gentle heart to pity;
My life incline the virtuous to believe. 212
   NORVAL. To be the son of Douglas is to me
   Inheritance enough. Declare my birth,
And in the field I'll seek for fame and fortune.
   LADY RANDOLPH. Thou dost not know what
   perils and injustice 216
Await the poor man's valor. O, my son!
The noblest blood of all the land's abashed,
Having no lackey but pale poverty.
Too long hast thou been thus attended, Doug-
   las! 220
Too long hast thou been deemed a peasant's
   child.
The wanton heir of some inglorious chief
Perhaps has scorned thee, in the youthful
   sports,
Whilst thy indignant spirit swelled in vain!
Such contumely [1] thou no more shalt bear:
But how I purpose to redress thy wrongs 226
Must be hereafter told. Prudence directs
That we should part before yon chief's return,
Retire, and from thy rustic follower's hand
Receive a billet, which thy mother's care, 230
Anxious to see thee, dictated before
This casual opportunity arose
Of private conference. Its purport mark;
For, as I there appoint, we meet again.
Leave me, my son! and frame thy manners
   still 235
To Norval's, not to noble Douglas', state.
   NORVAL. I will remember. Where is Norval
   now,
That good old man?
   LADY RANDOLPH. At hand concealed he lies,
An useful witness. But beware, my son,
Of yon Glenalvon; in his guilty breast 240
Resides a villain's shrewdness, ever prone
To false conjecture. He hath grieved my
   heart.
   NORVAL. Has he, indeed?—Then let yon
   false Glenalvon
Beware of me.   *Exit* DOUGLAS

       Manet LADY RANDOLPH

   LADY RANDOLPH. There burst the smoth-
   ered flame!—
O! thou all righteous and eternal King! 245
Who father of the fatherless art called,
Protect my son! Thy inspiration, Lord!
Hath filled his bosom with that sacred fire

[1] Pronounced contume′ly.

Which in the breast of his forefathers burned:
Set him on high, like them, that he may shine
The star and glory of his native land! 251
Then let the minister of death descend,
And bear my willing spirit to its place
Yonder they come.—How do bad women find
Unchanging aspects to conceal their guilt?
When I, by reason and by justice urged, 256
Full hardly can dissemble with these men
In nature's pious cause?

Enter LORD RANDOLPH *and* GLENALVON

LORD RANDOLPH. Yon gallant chief,
Of arms enamoured, all repose disclaims.
 LADY RANDOLPH. Be not, my lord, by his
  example swayed; 260
Arrange the business of to-morrow now,
And, when you enter, speak of war no more.
      Exit LADY RANDOLPH

Manent LORD RANDOLPH *and* GLENALVON

 LORD RANDOLPH. 'Tis so, by heaven! her
  mien, her voice, her eye,
And her impatience to be gone, confirm it.
 GLENALVON. He parted from her now: be-
  hind the mount, 265
Amongst the trees, I saw him glide along.
 LORD RANDOLPH. For sad sequestered vir-
  tue she's renowned.—
 GLENALVON. Most true, my lord.—
 LORD RANDOLPH. Yet, this distinguished
  dame
Invites a youth, the acquaintance of a day,
Alone to meet her at the midnight hour. 270
This assignation, (*Shows a letter*) the assassin
 freed,
Her manifest affection for the youth,
Might breed suspicion in a husband's brain,
Whose gentle consort all for love had wedded;
Much more in mine. Matilda never loved me.
Let no man, after me, a woman wed, 276
Whose heart he knows he has not; though she
 brings
A mine of gold, a kingdom for her dowry.
For let her seem, like the night's shadowy
 queen,
Cold and contemplative—he cannot trust her:
She may, she will, bring shame and sorrow on
 him; 281
The worst of sorrows, and the worst of shames!
 GLENALVON. Yield not, my lord, to such
  afflicting thoughts;
But let the spirit of a husband sleep,
Till your own senses make a sure conclusion.

This billet must to blooming Norval go: 286
At the next turn awaits my trusty spy;
I'll give it him refitted for his master.
In the close thicket take your secret stand;
The moon shines bright, and your own eyes
 may judge 290
Of their behavior.
 LORD RANDOLPH Thou dost counsel well.
 GLENALVON. Permit me now to make one
  slight essay.
Of all the trophies which vain mortals boast,
By wit, by valor, or by wisdom won, 294
The first and fairest, in a young man's eye,
Is woman's captive heart. Successful love
With glorious fumes intoxicates the mind!
And the proud conqueror in triumph moves,
Air-borne, exalted above vulgar men.
 LORD RANDOLPH. And what avails this
  maxim?
 GLENALVON. Much, my lord, 300
Withdraw a little: I'll accost young Norval,
And with ironical derisive counsel
Explore his spirit. If he is no more
Than humble Norval, by thy favor raised,
Brave as he is, he'll shrink astonished from me:
But if he be the fav'rite of the fair, 306
Loved by the first of Caledonia's dames,
He'll turn upon me, as the lion turns
Upon the hunter's spear.
 LORD RANDOLPH. 'Tis shrewdly thought.
 GLENALVON. When we grow loud, draw
  near. But let my lord 310
His rising wrath restrain. *Exit* RANDOLPH

Manet GLENALVON

 GLENALVON. 'Tis strange, by heaven!
That she should run full tilt her fond career,
To one so little known. She, too, that seemed
Pure as the winter stream, when ice embossed
Whitens its course. Even I did think her
 chaste, 315
Whose charity exceeds not. Precious sex!
Whose deeds lascivious pass Glenalvon's
 thoughts!

NORVAL *appears*

His port I love; he's in a proper mood
To chide the thunder, if at him it roared.—
Has Norval seen the troops?
 NORVAL. The setting sun 320
With yellow radiance lightened all the vale;
And as the warriors moved, each polished
 helm.

Corslet, or spear, glanced back his guilded
    beams.
The hill they climbed, and halting at its top,
Of more than mortal size, towering, they
    seemed   325
An host angelic, clad in burning arms.
    GLENALVON. Thou talk'st it well; no leader
    of our host
In sounds more lofty speaks of glorious war.
    NORVAL. If I shall e'er acquire a leader's
    name,
My speech will be less ardent. Novelty   330
Now prompts my tongue, and youthful ad-
    miration
Vents itself freely; since no part is mine
Of praise pertaining to the great in arms.
    GLENALVON. You wrong yourself, brave
    sir; your martial deeds
Have ranked you with the great. But mark
    me, Norval;   335
Lord Randolph's favor now exalts your youth
Above his veterans of famous service.
Let me, who know these soldiers, counsel you:
Give them all honor; seem not to command;
Else they will scarcely brook your late sprung
    power,   340
Which nor alliance props, nor birth adorns.
    NORVAL. Sir, I have been accustomed all
    my days
To hear and speak the plain and simple
    truth:
And though I have been told that there are
    men
Who borrow friendship's tongue to speak their
    scorn,   345
Yet in such language I am little skilled.
Therefore I thank Glenalvon for his counsel,
Although it sounded harshly. Why remind
Me of my birth obscure? Why slur my power
With such contemptuous terms?
    GLENALVON.   I did not mean
To gall your pride, which now I see is great.
    NORVAL. My pride!
    GLENALVON.   Suppress it as you wish to
    prosper: 352
Your pride's excessive. Yet, for Randolph's
    sake,
I will not leave you to its rash direction.
If thus you swell, and frown at high-born men,
Will high-born men endure a shepherd's scorn?
    NORVAL. A shepherd's scorn!
    GLENALVON.   Yes, if you presume
To bend on soldiers these disdainful eyes, 358
As if you took the measure of their minds.

And said in secret, "You're no match for
    me!"—
What will become of you?
    NORVAL. (*Aside.*)   If this were told!— 361
Hast thou no fears for thy presumptuous self?
    GLENALVON. Ha! Dost thou threaten me?
    NORVAL.   Didst thou not hear?
    GLENALVON. Unwillingly I did; a nobler foe
Had not been questioned thus. But such as
    thee—
    NORVAL. Whom dost thou think me?
    GLENALVON.   Norval.
    NORVAL.   So I am—
And who is Norval in Glenalvon's eyes? 367
    GLENALVON. A peasant's son, a wand'ring
    beggar-boy;
At best no more, even if he speaks the truth.
    NORVAL. False as thou art, dost thou sus-
    pect my truth?   370
    GLENALVON. Thy truth! Thou'rt all a lie;
    and false as hell
Is the vain-glorious tale thou told'st to Ran-
    dolph.
    NORVAL. If I were chained, unarmed, and
    bed-rid old,
Perhaps I should revile. But as I am,
I have no tongue to rail. The humble Norval
Is of a race who strive not but with deeds. 376
Did I not fear to freeze thy shallow valor,
And make thee sink too soon beneath my
    sword,
I'd tell thee—what thou art. I know thee well.
    GLENALVON. Dost thou know Glenalvon,
    born to command   380
Ten thousand slaves like thee!—
    NORVAL.   Villain, no more:
Draw and defend thy life, I did design
To have defied thee in another cause;
But heaven accelerates its vengeance on thee.
Now for my own and Lady Randolph's
    wrongs.   385

    Enter LORD RANDOLPH

    LORD RANDOLPH. Hold, I command you
    both. The man that stirs
Makes me his foe.
    NORVAL.   Another voice than thine
That threat had vainly sounded, noble Ran-
    dolph.
    GLENALVON. Hear him, my lord; he's
    wond'rous condescending!
Mark the humility of shepherd Norval!   390
    NORVAL. Now you may scoff in safety.
                       (*Sheathes his sword*)

LORD RANDOLPH. Speak not thus,
Taunting each other; but unfold to me
The cause of quarrel, then I judge betwixt
    you.
NORVAL. Nay, my good lord, though I re-
    vere you much,
My cause I plead not, nor demand your judg-
    ment.   395
I blush to speak; I will not, cannot speak
Th' opprobrious words that I from him have
    borne.
To the liege-lord of my dear native land
I owe a subject's homage; but even him
And his high arbitration I'd reject.   400
Within my bosom reigns another lord;
Honor, sole judge and umpire of itself.
If my free speech offend you, noble Randolph,
Revoke your favors, and let Norval go
Hence as he came, alone but not dishonored.
    LORD RANDOLPH. Thus far I'll mediate
    with impartial voice: 406
The ancient foe of Caledonia's land
Now waves his banners o'er her frighted
    fields;
Suspend your purpose, till your country's arms
Repel the bold invader: then decide   410
The private quarrel.
    GLENALVON.   I agree to this.
    NORVAL.   And I.

Enter Servant

    SERVANT. The banquet waits.
    LORD RANDOLPH. We come.
                                      Exit with Servant
    GLENALVON.   Norval,
Let not our variance mar the social hour,
Nor wrong the hospitality of Randolph.
Nor frowning anger, nor yet wrinkled hate,
Shall stain my countenance. Smooth thou thy
    brow;   416
Nor let our strife disturb the gentle dame.
    NORVAL. Think not so lightly, sir, of my
    resentment.
When we contend again, our strife is mortal.
                                               Exeunt

ACT V

The Wood

Enter DOUGLAS

DOUGLAS. This is the place, the center of
    the grove;
Here stands the oak, the monarch of the wood.
How sweet and solemn is this midnight
    scene!

The silver moon, unclouded, holds her way
Through skies where I could count each little
    star.   5
The fanning west wind scarcely stirs the
    leaves;
The river rushing o'er its pebbled bed,
Imposes silence with a stilly sound.
In such a place as this, at such an hour,
If ancestry [1] can be in aught believed,   10
Descending spirits have conversed with man,
And told the secrets of the world unknown.

Enter OLD NORVAL

    OLD NORVAL. 'Tis he. But what if he
    should chide me hence?
His just reproach I fear.
                (DOUGLAS *turns and sees him.*)
                              Forgive, forgive!
Can'st thou forgive the man, the selfish man,
Who bred Sir Malcolm's heir a shepherd's
    son?   16
    DOUGLAS. Kneel not to me; thou art my
    father still.
Thy wished-for presence now completes my
    joy.
Welcome to me, my fortunes thou shalt share,
And ever honored with thy Douglas live.   20
    OLD NORVAL. And dost thou call me
    father? O my son!
I think that I could die to make amends
For the great wrong I did thee. 'Twas my
    crime
Which in the wilderness so long concealed
The blossom of thy youth.
    DOUGLAS.   Not worse the fruit,
That in the wilderness the blossom blowed.   26
Amongst the shepherds, in the humble cot,
I learned some lessons, which I'll not forget
When I inhabit yonder lofty towers;
I, who was once a swain, will ever prove   30
The poor man's friend; and, when my vassals
    bow,
Norval shall smooth the crested pride of
    Douglas.
    OLD NORVAL. Let me but live to see thine
    exaltation!
Yet grievous are my fears. O leave this place,
And those unfriendly towers.
    DOUGLAS.   Why should I leave them?
    OLD NORVAL. Lord Randolph and his kins-
    man seek your life.   36
    DOUGLAS. How know'st thou that?
    OLD NORVAL.   I will inform you how.

---
[1] Not genealogy, but ancient lore or superstition.

When evening came, I left the secret place
Appointed for me by your mother's care,
And fondly trod in each accustomed path   40
That to the castle leads. Whilst thus I ranged,
I was alarmed with unexpected sounds
Of earnest voices. On the persons came;
Unseen I lurked, and overheard them name
Each other as they talked, Lord Randolph
    this,   45
And that Glenalvon. Still of you they spoke,
And of the lady; threat'ning was their speech,
Though but imperfectly my ear could hear it.
'Twas strange, they said, a wonderful dis-
    covery;
And ever and anon they vowed revenge.   50
    DOUGLAS. Revenge! for what?
    OLD NORVAL.   For being what you are,
Sir Malcolm's heir; how else have you of-
    fended?
When they were gone, I hied me to my cot-
    tage,
And there sat musing how I best might find
Means to inform you of their wicked pur-
    pose.   55
But I could think of none. At last perplexed,
I issued forth, encompassing the tower
With many a weary step and wishful look.
Now Providence hath brought you to my
    sight,
Let not your too courageous spirit scorn   60
The caution which I give.
    DOUGLAS.   I scorn it not.
My mother warned me of Glenalvon's base-
    ness;
But I will not suspect the noble Randolph.
In our encounter with the vile assassins,   64
I marked his brave demeanor: him I'll trust.
    OLD NORVAL. I fear you will, too far.
    DOUGLAS.   Here in this place,
I wait my mother's coming. She shall know
What thou hast told: her counsel I will follow;
And cautious ever are a mother's counsels.
You must depart; your presence may prevent
Our interview.
    OLD NORVAL. My blessing rest upon thee!
O may heaven's hand, which saved thee from
    the wave,   72
And from the sword of foes, be near thee still;
Turning mischance, if aught hangs o'er thy
    head,
All upon mine!   *Exit* OLD NORVAL
    DOUGLAS. He loves me like a parent;   75
And must not, shall not, lose the son he loves,
Although his son has found a nobler father.—

Eventful day! how hast thou changed my
    state!
Once on the cold and winter shaded side
Of a bleak hill mischance had rooted me,   80
Never to thrive, child of another soil,
Transplanted now to the gay sunny vale,
Like the green thorn of May my fortune
    flowers.
Ye glorious stars! high heaven's resplendent
    host!
To whom I oft have of my lot complained,
Hear and record my soul's unaltered wish!   86
Dead or alive, let me but be renowned!
May heaven inspire some fierce gigantic Dane,
To give a bold defiance to our host!
Before he speaks it out I will accept;   90
Like Douglas conquer, or like Douglas die.

    Enter LADY RANDOLPH

    LADY RANDOLPH. My son! I heard a
    voice—
    DOUGLAS.   —The voice was mine.
    LADY RANDOLPH. Didst thou complain
    aloud to Nature's ear,
That thus in dusky shades, at midnight hours,
By stealth the mother and the son should
    meet?   95
    (*Embracing him*)
    DOUGLAS. No; on this happy day, this bet-
    ter birthday,
My thoughts and words are all of hope and
    joy.
    LADY RANDOLPH. Sad fear and melancholy
    still divide
The empire of my breast with hope and joy.
Now hear what I advise.
    DOUGLAS.   First, let me tell   100
What may the tenor of your counsel change.
    LADY RANDOLPH. My heart forbodes some
    evil!
    DOUGLAS.   'Tis not good.—
At eve, unseen by Randolph and Glenalvon,
The good old Norval in the grove o'erheard
Their conversation; oft they mentioned me
With dreadful threat'nings; you they some-
    times named.   106
'Twas strange, they said, a wonderful discov-
    ery;
And ever and anon they vowed revenge.
    LADY RANDOLPH. Defend us, gracious God!
    we are betrayed!
They have found out the secret of thy birth;
It must be so. That is the great discovery.   111
Sir Malcolm's heir is come to claim his own;

And [they][1] will be revenged. Perhaps even now,
Armed and prepared for murder, they but wait
A darker and more silent hour, to break 115
Into the chamber where they think thou sleep'st.
This moment, this, heaven hath ordained to save thee!
Fly to the camp, my son!
    DOUGLAS.   And leave you here?
No: to the castle let us go together,
Call up the ancient servants of your house, 120
Who in their youth did eat your father's bread;
Then tell them loudly that I am your son.
If in the breasts of men one spark remains
Of sacred love, fidelity, or pity,
Some in your cause will arm. I ask but few 125
To drive those spoilers from my father's house.
    LADY RANDOLPH. O Nature, Nature! what can check thy force?—
Thou genuine offspring of the daring Douglas!
But rush not on destruction: save thyself,
And I am safe. To me they mean no harm. 130
Thy stay but risks thy precious life in vain.
That winding path conducts thee to the river.
Cross where thou seest a broad and beaten way,
Which running eastward leads thee to the camp.
Instant demand admittance to Lord Douglas.
Show him these jewels which his brother wore.
Thy look, thy voice, will make him feel the truth, 137
Which I by certain proof will soon confirm.
    DOUGLAS. I yield me, and obey: but yet my heart
Bleeds at this parting. Something bids me stay, 140
And guard a mother's life. Oft have I read
Of won'drous deeds by one bold arm achieved.
Our foes are two—no more, let me go forth,
And see if any shield can guard Glenalvon.
    LADY RANDOLPH. If thou regard'st thy mother, or reverest 145
Thy father's mem'ry, think of this no more.
One thing I have to say before we part;
Long wert thou lost; and thou art found, my child,
In a most fearful season. War and battle
I have great cause to dread. Too well I see

[1] The first Edinburgh edition reads *he;* all other editions have *they,* which is obviously the better reading.

Which way the current of thy temper sets: 151
To-day I've found thee. Oh! my long-lost hope!
If thou to giddy valor givest the rein,
To-morrow I may lose my son forever.
The love of thee, before thou saw'st the light,
Sustained my life when thy brave father fell.
If thou shalt fall, I have nor love nor hope 157
In this waste world! My son, remember me!
    DOUGLAS. What shall I say? How can I give you comfort?
The God of battles of my life dispose 160
As may be best for you; for whose dear sake
I will not bear myself as I resolved.
But yet consider, as no vulgar name
That which I boast sounds amongst martial men,
How will inglorious caution suit my claim? 165
The post of fate unshrinking I maintain.
My country's foes must witness who I am.
On the invaders' heads I'll prove my birth,
Till friends and foes confess the genuine strain.
If in this strife I fall, blame not your son, 170
Who, if he lives not honored, must not live.
    LADY RANDOLPH. I will not utter what my bosom feels.
Too well I love that valor which I warn.
Farewell, my son! my counsels are but vain;
                  (*Embracing*)
And as high heaven hath willed it, all must be.
            (*They are about to separate*)
Gaze not on me, thou wilt mistake the path;
I'll point it out again.

Just as they are separating, enter from the Wood
    LORD RANDOLPH *and* GLENALVON

    LORD RANDOLPH.   Not in her presence.
    Exeunt, at different sides, DOUGLAS *and*
                     LADY RANDOLPH
Now—
    GLENALVON. I'm prepared.
    LORD RANDOLPH. No; I command thee stay. 178
I go alone: it never shall be said
That I took odds to combat mortal man.
The noblest vengeance is the most complete.
                    Exit LORD RANDOLPH
(GLENALVON *makes some steps to the same side of the stage, listens and speaks*)
    GLENALVON. Demons of death, come, settle on my sword, 182
And to a double slaughter guide it home!
The lover and the husband both must die.
    (LORD RANDOLPH *behind the scenes*

LORD RANDOLPH. Draw, villain! draw.
DOUGLAS. Assail me not, Lord Randolph!
Not, as thou lovest thyself.
      (*Clashing of swords*)
GLENALVON. Now is the time. 186
      (*Running out*)

Enter LADY RANDOLPH *at the opposite side of the stage, faint and breathless*

LADY RANDOLPH. Lord Randolph, hear me; all shall be thine own:
But spare! Oh spare my son!

Enter DOUGLAS *with a sword in each hand.*

DOUGLAS. My mother's voice!
I can protect thee still.
 LADY RANDOLPH. He lives, he lives!
For this, for this to heaven eternal praise!
But sure I saw thee fall.
 DOUGLAS. It was Glenalvon. 191
Just as my arm had mastered Randolph's sword,
The villain came behind me; but I slew him.
 LADY RANDOLPH. Behind thee! Ah, thou'rt wounded! O my child,
How pale thou look'st! And shall I lose thee now?   195
DOUGLAS. Do not despair: I feel a little faintness;
I hope it will not last. (*Leans upon his sword*)
 LADY RANDOLPH. There is no hope!
And we must part! the hand of death is on thee!
O my belovèd child! O Douglas, Douglas!
    (DOUGLAS *growing more and more faint*)
DOUGLAS. Too soon we part; I have not long been Douglas.   200
O destiny! hardly thou deal'st with me:
Clouded and hid, a stranger to myself,
In low and poor obscurity I lived.
 LADY RANDOLPH. Has heaven preserved thee for an end like this?
DOUGLAS. O had I fall'n as my brave fathers fell,   205
Turning with great effort the tide of battle!
Like them I should have smiled and welcomed death.
But thus to perish by a villain's hand!
Cut off from nature's and from glory's course,
Which never mortal was so fond to run. 210
 LADY RANDOLPH. Hear, justice! hear! stretch thy avenging arm. (DOUGLAS *falls*)
DOUGLAS. Unknown I die; no tongue shall speak of me.

Some noble spirits, judging by themselves,
May yet conjecture what I might have proved,
And think life only wanting to my fame: 215
But who shall comfort thee?
 LADY RANDOLPH. Despair! despair!
DOUGLAS. O, had it pleased high heaven to let me live
A little while!—My eyes that gaze on thee
Grow dim apace! my mother!—O, my mother!
      (*Dies*)

Enter LORD RANDOLPH *and* ANNA

LORD RANDOLPH. Thy words, the words of truth, have pierced my heart. 220
I am the stain of knighthood and of arms.
Oh! if my brave deliverer survives
The traitor's sword—
 ANNA. Alas! look there, my lord.
LORD RANDOLPH. The mother and her son!
How curst I am!
Was I the cause? No: I was not the cause.
Yon matchless villain did seduce my soul
To frantic jealousy.
 ANNA. My lady lives: 227
The agony of grief hath but suppressed
A while her powers.
 LORD RANDOLPH. But my deliverer's dead!
The world did once esteem Lord Randolph well;   230
Sincere of heart, for spotless honor famed:
And in my early days, glory I gained
Beneath the holy banner of the cross.
Now past the noon of life, shame comes upon me;
Reproach, and infamy, and public hate, 235
Are near at hand; for all mankind will think
That Randolph basely stabbed Sir Malcolm's heir.   (LADY RANDOLPH *recovering*)
 LADY RANDOLPH. Where am I now? still in this wretched world!
Grief cannot break a heart so hard as mine.
My youth was worn in anguish; but youth's strength,   240
With hope's assistance, bore the brunt of sorrow,
And trained me on to be the object, now,
On which Omnipotence displays itself,
Making a spectacle, a tale of me,
To awe its vassal, man.
 LORD RANDOLPH. O misery! 245
Amidst thy raging grief I must proclaim
My innocence.
 LADY RANDOLPH. Thy innocence!
 LORD RANDOLPH. My guilt

Is innocence, compared with what thou
    think'st it.
  LADY RANDOLPH. Of thee I think not: what
    have I to do
With thee, or anything? My son! my son!
My beautiful! my brave! how proud was I
Of thee, and of thy valor! My fond heart 252
O'erflowed this day with transport, when I
    thought
Of growing old amidst a race of thine,
Who might make up to me their father's child-
    hood,   255
And bear my brother's and my husband's
    name:
Now all my hopes are dead! A little while
Was I a wife! a mother not so long!
What am I now?—I know—But I shall be
That only whilst I please; for such a son 260
And such a husband make a woman bold.
                              (*Runs out*)
  LORD RANDOLPH. Follow her, Anna: I my-
    self would follow,
But in this rage she must abhor my presence.
                              Exit ANNA

             Enter OLD NORVAL

  OLD NORVAL. I hear the voice of woe;
    heaven guard my child!
  LORD RANDOLPH. Already is the idle gap-
    ing crowd,   265
The spiteful vulgar, come to gaze on Ran-
    dolph?
Begone!
  OLD NORVAL. I fear thee not. I will not go.
Here I'll remain. I'm an accomplice, lord,
With thee in murder. Yes, my sins did help
To crush down to the ground this lovely
    plant.   270
O noblest youth that ever yet was born!
Sweetest and best, gentlest and bravest spirit
That ever blessed the world! Wretch that I
    am,
Who saw that noble spirit swell and rise
Above the narrow limits that confined it, 275
Yet never was by all thy virtues won
To do thee justice, and reveal the secret,
Which, timely known, had raised thee far
    above
The villain's snare! Oh! I am punished now!
These are the hairs that should have strewed
    the ground,   280
And not the locks of Douglas.
(*Tears his hair, and throws himself upon the
                           body of* DOUGLAS)

  LORD RANDOLPH. I know thee now: thy
    boldness I forgive;
My crest is fall'n. For thee I will appoint
A place of rest, if grief will let thee rest.
I will reward, although I cannot punish. 285
Curst, curst Glenalvon, he escaped too well,
Though slain and baffled by the hand he
    hated.
Foaming with rage and fury to the last,
Cursing his conqueror the felon died.

             Enter ANNA

  ANNA. My lord! my lord!
  LORD RANDOLPH.   Speak: I can hear of
    horror.   290
  ANNA. Horror indeed!
  LORD RANDOLPH.   Matilda?—
  ANNA.   Is no more.
She ran, she flew like lightning up the hill,
Nor halted till the precipice she gained,
Beneath whose low'ring top the river falls,
Engulfed in rifted rocks: thither she came,
As fearless as the eagle lights upon it, 296
And headlong down—
  LORD RANDOLPH.   'Twas I! alas! 'twas I
That filled her breast with fury; drove her
    down
The precipice of death! Wretch that I am!
  ANNA. O had you seen her last despairing
    look!   300
Upon the brink she stood, and cast her eyes
Down on the deep: then lifting up her head
And her white hands to heaven, seeming to
    say,
Why am I forced to this? she plunged herself
Into the empty air.
  LORD RANDOLPH.   I will not vent,
In vain complaints, the passion of my soul.
Peace in this world I never can enjoy.   307
These wounds the gratitude of Randolph
    gave.
They speak aloud, and with the voice of
    fate
Denounce my doom. I am resolved. I'll go
Straight to the battle, where the man that
    makes   311
Me turn aside, must threaten worse than
    death.—
Thou, faithful to thy mistress, take this ring,
Full warrant of my power. Let every rite
With cost and pomp upon their funerals
    wait: 315
For Randolph hopes he never shall return.
                                 Exeunt

EPILOGUE

[Spoken by Mr. Barry][1]

An epilogue I asked; but not one word [2]
Our bard will write. He vows 'tis most absurd
With comic wit to contradict the strain
Of tragedy, and make your sorrows vain.
Sadly he says, that pity is the best, 5
The noblest passion of the human breast,
For when its sacred streams the heart o'er-
   flow,
In gushes pleasure with the tide of woe;
And when its waves retire, like those of
   Nile,
They leave behind them such a golden soil, 10
That there the virtues without culture grow,
There the sweet blossoms of affection blow.
These were his words:—void of delusive art
I felt them; for he spoke them from his heart.
Nor will I now attempt, with witty folly, 15
To chase away celestial melancholy.

[1] The Edinburgh edition lacks this statement, though it contains the Epilogue. Barry, who spoke the Epilogue in London, is generally supposed to have written it, though John Jackson in *The Scottish Stage* assumes that it was written by Home. The present editors have been unable to ascertain what epilogue, if any, was spoken at the first Edinburgh performances. None of the early editions give such an epilogue, nor do Mackenzie or the historians such as Genest, Dibdin, Lawson, and Gipson, mention it.

[2] Compare this epilogue with that to *The London Merchant*, p. 644.

THE CLANDESTINE MARRIAGE,

A Comedy by George Colman and David Garrick

Huc adhibe vultus, et in una parce duobus:
Vivat, et ejusdem simus uterque parens! Ovid.[1]

George Colman (1732–1794) was born at Florence, where his father, Francis Colman, was British envoy to the court of Tuscany. His mother was Mary Gumley, sister to Mrs. Pulteney, later Countess of Bath. Colman's father died in 1733 and the boy was reared under the direction and patronage of his uncle-in-law, William Pulteney, Lord Bath. He attended Westminster School and Christ Church College, Oxford, where he took his A. B. in 1755. He contributed "A Vision" to Hawkesworth's *The Adventurer;* and, with Bonnell Thornton, conducted *The Connoisseur* (1754–1756). Though he had been entered at Lincoln's Inn and was called to the bar in 1755, Colman's fondness for the theater prevented his following his profession with any success. Despite the opposition of his family, he began to write for the stage. His early pieces met with great success, particularly *The Jealous Wife* (1761) and *The Clandestine Marriage*, written in collaboration with Garrick, with whom he had previously formed a warm friendship. The rest of his long career on the stage is taken up with managerial duties and the tasks of authorship. He wrote or adapted some thirty-five plays. He managed Covent Garden from 1767 to 1774, having bought Rich's patent; in 1776 he took over Foote's patent at the Haymarket, where he reigned until he was incapacitated by a stroke of paralysis in 1785. As his faculties were considerably impaired, he spent his last years in confinement, slowly growing more and more feeble in mind and body. He died August 14, 1794. At the time of his death his son, known as *the younger* Colman, had already begun to gain the reputation as a dramatist which he was to enhance in the next generation.

See the *Dictionary of National Biography* and references there cited. Histories of Covent Garden and the Haymarket theaters also contain accounts of Colman's managerial career.

David Garrick (1717–1779) was born at the Angel Inn, Hereford, where his father, a captain in the army, was engaged on recruiting duty. David's grandfather had been a French Huguenot refugee, a fact which, accounting for the Gallic strain in the actor's blood, may explain some of his temperamental vagaries which distressed or amused his friends in later years. His mother, Arabella Clough, was the daughter of a vicar of Lichfield. David was sent to the Lichfield grammar school and later to the school of Samuel Johnson, eight years his senior, whose friendship for "Davy" has become a matter of tradition. In 1737 Garrick went to London with Johnson. He tried several methods of gaining a livelihood, but his undoubted capacities led him upon the stage. He appeared here and there without much success until Gifford put him into the part of Richard III at Goodman's Fields, October 19, 1741. From this time on the story of Garrick's career is practically equivalent to a history of the English stage until his death. He appeared at Drury Lane in 1742; and, except for one season (1746) when he was at Covent Garden, he retained his connection with that theater for thirty-four years, becoming joint owner with Lacy and active manager in 1747. In 1749 he married Marie Violelli, a dancer at the Haymarket. He had a successful career as actor-manager and author until his retirement in 1776. He died wealthy and respected on January 20, 1779, and was buried with great pomp in Westminster Abbey.

As the greatest actor in England, not only of his own day but, by reputation, of all time, Garrick was the friend of most eminent persons of the time, a member of the Literary Club, intimate associate of Johnson, Burke,

---

[1] *Huc . . . duobus,*—Turn hither thy countenance, and in one spare us both.—Ovid, *Amores* II, 13, 15. The second line of the motto, "*Vivat . . . parens*," the editors have been unable to trace to its source. It means: let her live, and each will be her parent.

Reynolds, and others. His portrait was painted by Hogarth, Reynolds, and Gainsborough as well as a number of less known artists. As a prosperous manager, Garrick was concerned in the revision of many plays produced in his theater. He also was sole author of a number of plays, mostly short farces and occasional pieces, and collaborator with Colman in *The Clandestine Marriage*.

See the *Dictionary of National Biography* and the two best contemporary biographies of Garrick by Thomas Davies and Arthur Murphy. See also Boswell's *Life of Johnson* and accounts of the eighteenth-century stage.

COLMAN'S DRAMATIC WORKS
(SELECTED LIST)

Polly Honeycombe; A Dramatic Novel (farce) (D.L., Dec. 5, 1760), 1760.

The Jealous Wife (comedy) (D.L., Feb. 12, 1761), 1761.

The Clandestine Marriage (comedy, with David Garrick) (D.L., Feb. 20, 1766), 1766.

The Portrait (burletta) (C.G., Nov. 22, 1770), 1770.

New Brooms! An Occasional Prelude (D.L., Sept. 21, 1776), 1776.

(A complete list will be found in A. Nicoll's *A History of Late Eighteenth Century Drama*.)

GARRICK'S DRAMATIC WORKS
(SELECTED LIST)

The Lying Valet (comedy), Goodman's Fields (Nov. 30, 1741), 1741.

Miss in her Teens; or, The Medley of Lovers (farce) (C.G., Jan. 17, 1747), 1747.

The Clandestine Marriage (comedy, with George Colman) (D.L., Feb. 20, 1766), 1766.

Cymon. A Dramatic Romance (dramatic opera) (D.L., Jan. 2, 1767), 1767.

A Peep Behind the Curtain; or, The New Rehearsal (burlesque) (D.L., Oct. 23, 1767), 1767.

Bon Ton; or, High Life Above Stairs (farce) (D.L., March 18, 1775), 1775.

(Also various occasional pieces and adaptations of Shakespeare, et al. Cf. lists given by Nicoll, *Biographia Dramatica*, etc.)

Having come up to London to pursue the law, Colman formed a friendship with Garrick about 1755. By 1760 their relations were such that Garrick produced Colman's first play, *Polly Honeycombe*, as his own to conceal Colman's participation from his family. At some time after the production of *The Jealous Wife* in 1761, they began writing *The Clandestine Marriage*. The composition of the play seems to have taken some time, and in the meanwhile Garrick made one of his customary journeys to the continent. Soon after his return, the play was ready; it appeared with success at Drury Lane, February 20, 1766. Colman had apparently expected his collaborator and manager to play the part of Lord Ogleby, but Garrick, pleading ill health and advancing years, which made him, he said, unequal to the strain of a new part, declined; and Lord Ogleby fell to the share of King, "a comedian of rising merit," says Benjamin Victor, "who by his excellent performance of Lord Ogleby established his reputation." Garrick's refusal of the rôle caused the beginning of the coolness between the collaborators which widened into an actual breach when Colman became one of the managers of Covent Garden. "The great run of the comedy," says Tom Davies, however, "soon reconciled Mr. Colman to his disappointment."

About the play, Davies also remarks, "It has been observed, and I believe justly, that there has been no dramatick piece, since the days of Beaumont and Fletcher, written by two authors, in which wit, fancy, character, and humour, are so happily blended, that the texture of the whole might well be supposed to be woven by one hand, as in this comedy." The basic conception of the play seems to have been Colman's, as were also the characters, except Canton and Brush, who are particularly in Garrick's line.[1] Garrick is supposed also to have written the levée scene, in Act II, and Act V. Contemporary charges of plagiarism from the Rev. James Townley's *False Concord* (C.G., March 20, 1764; not printed) were brought but are of little worth, even if true; and of *The Clandestine Marriage* Colman has just claim to the credit of principal authorship.

Though containing unmistakable sentimental elements, *The Clandestine Marriage* is chiefly comedy of manners, standing with *The Jealous Wife* and the comedies of Sheridan and Arthur Murphy as evidence that the later years of the century were not entirely devoid of comic spirit. In fact, *The Clandestine Marriage* was no mean competitor with *The School for Scandal* in their own day; and in this case posterity might well follow the critical lead of the eighteenth century.

[1] Cf. J. M. Beatty, Jr., "Garrick, Colman, and *The Clandestine Marriage*," *Mod. Lang. Notes*, xxxvi, 129–41. Also see A. Nicoll's *A History of Late Eighteenth Century Drama* (1927), p. 168, n. 3.

THE CLANDESTINE MARRIAGE,

ADVERTISEMENT.—Hogarth's [1] "Marriage-à-la-mode" has before furnished materials to the author of a novel, published some years ago, under the title of *The Marriage Act;* [2] but as that writer pursued a very different story and, as his work was chiefly designed for a political satire, very little use could be made of it for the service of this comedy.

In justice to the person who has been considered as the sole author, the party who has hitherto lain concealed thinks it incumbent on him to declare that the disclosure of his name was, by his own desire, reserved till the publication of the piece.

Both the authors, however, who have before been separately honored with the indulgence of the public, now beg leave to make their joint acknowledgments for the very favorable reception of *The Clandestine Marriage*.[3]

DRAMATIS PERSONÆ [4]

Lord Ogleby	Mr. King	Brush	Mr. Palmer
Sir John Melvil	Mr. Holland	Sergeant Flower	Mr. Love
Sterling	Mr. Yates	Traverse	Mr. Lee
Lovewell	Mr. Powell	Trueman	Mr. Aickin
Canton	Mr. Baddeley		
Mrs. Heidelberg	Mrs. Clive [5]	Betty	Mrs. [Abington][6]
Miss Sterling	Miss Pope	Chambermaid	Miss Plym
Fanny	Mrs. Palmer	Trusty	Miss Mills

PROLOGUE

Written by Mr. Garrick,

And Spoken by Mr. Holland [7]

Poets and painters, who from Nature draw
Their best and richest stores, have made this law:
That each should neighborly assist his brother,
And steal with decency from one another.

To-night, your matchless Hogarth gives the thought, 5
Which from his canvas to the stage is brought.
And who so fit to warm the poet's mind,
As he who pictured morals and mankind?
But not the same their characters and scenes;
Both labor for one end, by different means;
Each, as it suits him, takes a separate road,

---

[1] William Hogarth (1697–1764), most original of English painters, produced *Marriage à la Mode* in 1745. It is a series of pictures showing fashionable married life in the satiric manner characteristic of the artist.

[2] A political novel by John Shebbeare, M.D. (1709–1788), published anonymously, 2 vols., 1754 "in which the ruin of female honour, the contempt of the clergy, the destruction of private and public liberty, . . . are considered, in a series of interesting adventures."

[3] In place of the last two paragraphs here reprinted, the Advertisement in later editions was concluded as follows:
"Some friends, and some enemies, have endeavoured to allot distinct portions of this play to each of the Authors. Each, however, considers himself as responsible for the whole; and though they have, on other occasions, been separately honoured with the indulgence of the publick, it is with peculiar pleasure they now make their joint acknowledgements for the very favourable reception of *The Clandestine Marriage*."

[4] The cast was the best that could at the time be assembled for comedy at D.L. Notice how often the same names appear, particularly here and in *The School for Scandal*.

[5] Mrs. Heidelberg was the last new part of importance except one, Lady Fuzz in Garrick's *A Peep Behind the Curtain*, of the great Kitty Clive, famous in comedy for forty years (1728–1769). She created some seventy rôles besides, of course, acting many old favorites.

[6] Mrs. Abington played Betty in the play and Miss Crotchet in the epilogue. Her name appeared on the bills; but, apparently ashamed of the small parts, she would not allow it to be printed in the published play; consequently in the first edition its place is taken by a heavy line.

[7] Charles Holland (1733–1769), a handsome and popular actor, who imitated Garrick, acted at D.L. 1755–1769.

675

Their one great object, *Marriage-à-la-Mode!*
Where titles deign with cits to have and hold,
And change rich blood for more substantial
    gold!   14
And honored trade from interest turns aside,
To hazard happiness for titled pride.
The painter dead, yet still he charms the eye;
While England lives, his fame can never die:
But he, who *struts his hour upon the stage*,[1]
Can scarce extend his fame for half an age;
Nor pen nor pencil can the actor save,   21
The art, and artist, share one common grave.
  Oh, let me drop one tributary tear,
On poor Jack Falstaff's grave, and Juliet's
    bier!
You to their worth must testimony give;   25
'Tis in your hearts alone their fame can live.
Still as the scenes of life will shift away,
The strong impressions of their art decay.
Your children cannot feel what you have
    known;
They'll boast of Quins and Cibbers of their
    own;   30
The greatest glory of our happy few,
Is to be felt, and be approved by *you*.

ACT I

Scene [I]. *A room in* Sterling's *house*

Miss Fanny *and* Betty *meeting*

Betty. (*Running in*) Ma'am! Miss Fanny! ma'am!
Fanny. What's the matter, Betty!
Betty. Oh la, ma'am! as sure as I'm alive, here is your husband—
Fanny. Hush, my dear Betty! if anybody in the house should hear you, I am ruined.
Betty. Mercy on me! it has frighted me to such a degree that my heart is come up to my mouth. But as I was a-saying, ma'am, here's that dear, sweet—
Fanny. Have a care, Betty.
Betty. Lord! I'm bewitched, I think. But, as I was a saying, ma'am, here's Mr. Lovewell just come from London.
Fanny. Indeed!
Betty. Yes, indeed, and indeed, ma'am, he is. I saw him crossing the court-yard in his boots.
Fanny. I am glad to hear it. But pray now, my dear Betty, be cautious. Don't mention that word again, on any account. You know,

[1] Cf. *Macbeth*, Act V, scene v.

we have agreed never to drop any expressions of that sort, for fear of an accident.
Betty. Dear ma'am, you may depend upon me. There is not a more trustier creature on 5 the face of the earth, than I am. Though I say it, I am as secret as the grave; and if it's never told, till I tell it, it may remain untold till doom's-day for Betty.
Fanny. I know you are faithful, but in our 10 circumstances we cannot be too careful.
Betty. Very true, ma'am! and yet I vow and protest, there's more plague than pleasure with a secret, especially if a body mayn't mention it to four or five of one's particular 15 acquaintance.
Fanny. Do but keep this secret a little while longer, and then, I hope, you may mention it to anybody. Mr. Lovewell will acquaint the family with the nature of our situation as soon 20 as possible.
Betty. The sooner the better, I believe; for if he does not tell it, there's a little tell-tale, I know of, will come and tell it for him.
Fanny. Fie, Betty!   (*Blushing*)
25 Betty. Ah! you may well blush; but you're not so sick, and so pale, and so wan, and so many qualms—
Fanny. Have done! I shall be quite angry with you.
30 Betty. Angry! bless the dear puppet! I am sure I shall love it as much as if it was my own. I meant no harm, heaven knows.
Fanny. Well, say no more of this; it makes me uneasy. All I have to ask of you, is to be 35 faithful and secret, and not to reveal this matter till we disclose it to the family ourselves.
Betty. Me reveal it! If I say a word, I wish I may be burned. I would not do you 40 any harm for the world; and as for Mr. Lovewell, I am sure I have loved the dear gentleman, ever since he got a tide-waiter's[2] place for my brother. But let me tell you both, you must leave off your soft looks to each 45 other, and your whispers, and your glances, and your always sitting next to one another at dinner, and your long walks together in the evening. For my part, if I had not been in the secret, I should have known you were a pair 50 of *loviers* at least, if not man and wife, as—
Fanny. See there now! again. Pray be careful.

[2] A customs officer who boards incoming ships to prevent evasions of duties.

BETTY. Well, well, nobody hears me. Man and wife. I'll say no more. What I tell you is very true, for all that—

LOVEWELL. (*Calling within*) William!

BETTY. Hark! I hear your husband—

FANNY. What!

BETTY. I say, here comes Mr. Lovewell. Mind the caution I give you. I'll be whipped now, if you are not the first person he sees or speaks to in the family. However, if you choose it, it's nothing at all to me; as you sow, you must reap; as you brew, so you must bake. I'll e'en slip down the back-stairs, and leave you together. *Exit*

FANNY *alone*

I see, I see I shall never have a moment's ease till our marriage is made public. New distresses crowd in upon me every day. The solicitude of my mind sinks my spirits, preys upon my health, and destroys every comfort of my life. It shall be revealed, let what will be the consequence.

Enter LOVEWELL

LOVEWELL. My love! How's this? In tears? Indeed, this is too much. You promised me to support your spirits, and to wait the determination of our fortune with patience. For my sake, for your own, be comforted! Why will you study to add to our uneasiness and perplexity?

FANNY. Oh, Mr. Lovewell! the indelicacy of a secret marriage grows every day more and more shocking to me. I walk about the house like a guilty wretch. I imagine myself the object of the suspicion of the whole family; and am under the perpetual terrors of a shameful detection.

LOVEWELL. Indeed, indeed, you are to blame. The amiable delicacy of your temper, and your quick sensibility, only serve to make you unhappy. To clear up this affair properly to Mr. Sterling, is the continual employment of my thoughts. Everything now is in a fair train. It begins to grow ripe for a discovery and I have no doubt of its concluding to the satisfaction of ourselves, of your father, and the whole family.

FANNY. End how it will, I am resolved it shall end soon, very soon. I would not live another week in this agony of mind, to be mistress of the universe.

LOVEWELL. Do not be too violent neither. Do not let us disturb the joy of your sister's marriage with the tumult this matter may occasion! I have brought letters from Lord Ogleby and Sir John Melvil to Mr. Sterling. They will be here this evening; and, I dare say, within this hour.

FANNY. I am sorry for it.

LOVEWELL. Why so?

FANNY. No matter; only let us disclose our marriage immediately!

LOVEWELL. As soon as possible.

FANNY. But directly.

LOVEWELL. In a few days, you may depend on it.

FANNY. To-night; or to-morrow morning.

LOVEWELL. That, I fear, will be impracticable.

FANNY. Nay, but you must.

LOVEWELL. Must! Why?

FANNY. Indeed, you must. I have the most alarming reasons for it.

LOVEWELL. Alarming indeed! for they alarm me, even before I am acquainted with them. What are they?

FANNY. I cannot tell you.

LOVEWELL. Not tell me?

FANNY. Not at present. When all is settled, you shall be acquainted with everything.

LOVEWELL. Sorry they are coming! Must be discovered! What can this mean! Is it possible you can have any reasons that need be concealed from me?

FANNY. Do not disturb yourself with conjectures; but rest assured, that though you are unable to divine the cause, the consequence of a discovery, be it what it will, cannot be attended with half the miseries of the present interval.

LOVEWELL. You put me upon the rack. I would do anything to make you easy. But you know your father's temper. Money (you will excuse my frankness) is the spring of all his actions, which nothing but the idea of acquiring nobility or magnificence can ever make him forego; and these he thinks his money will purchase. You know too your aunt's, Mrs. Heidelberg's, notions of the splendor of high life, her contempt for everything that does not relish of what she calls *quality*, and that from the vast fortune in her hands, by her late husband, she absolutely governs Mr. Sterling and the whole family. Now, if they should come to the knowledge of this affair too abruptly, they might, perhaps, be incensed beyond all hopes of reconciliation.

FANNY. But if they are made acquainted with it otherwise then by ourselves, it will be ten times worse: and a discovery grows every day more probable. The whole family have long suspected our affection. We are also in the power of a foolish maid-servant; and if we may even depend on her fidelity, we cannot answer for her discretion. Discover it, therefore, immediately, lest some accident should bring it to light, and involve us in additional disgrace.

LOVEWELL. Well, well; I meant to discover it soon, but would not do it too precipitately. I have more than once sounded Mr. Sterling about it, and will attempt him more seriously the next opportunity. But my principal hopes are these. My relationship to Lord Ogleby, and his having placed me with your father, have been, you know, the first links in the chain of this connection between the two families; in consequence of which, I am at present in high favor with all parties. While they all remain thus well-affected to me, I propose to lay our case before the old lord; and if I can prevail on him to mediate in this affair, I make no doubt but he will be able to appease your father; and, being a lord and a man of quality, I am sure he may bring Mrs. Heidelberg into good-humor at any time. Let me beg you, therefore, to have but a little patience, as, you see, we are upon the very eve of a discovery, that must probably be to our advantage.

FANNY. Manage it your own way. I am persuaded.

LOVEWELL. But, in the meantime, make yourself easy.

FANNY. As easy as I can, I will. We had better not remain together any longer at present. Think of this business, and let me know how you proceed.

LOVEWELL. Depend on my care! But pray, be cheerful.

FANNY. I will.

As she is going out, enter STERLING

STERLING. Hey-day! who have we got here?

FANNY. (*Confused*) Mr. Lovewell, sir!

STERLING. And where are you going, hussy?

FANNY. To my sister's chamber, sir! *Exit*

STERLING. Ah, Lovewell! What! always getting my foolish girl yonder into a corner? Well, well; let us but once see her elder sister fast married to Sir John Melvil, we'll soon provide a good husband for Fanny, I warrant you.

LOVEWELL. Would to heaven, sir, you would provide her one of my recommendation!

STERLING. Yourself, eh, Lovewell?

LOVEWELL. With your pleasure, sir.

STERLING. Mighty well!

LOVEWELL. And I flatter myself, that such a proposal would not be very disagreeable to Miss Fanny.

STERLING. Better and better!

LOVEWELL. And if I could but obtain your consent, sir—

STERLING. What! you marry Fanny! No, no; that will never do, Lovewell. You're a good boy, to be sure; I have a great value for you—but can't think of you for a son-in-law. There's no *stuff* in the case; no money, Lovewell!

LOVEWELL. My pretensions to fortune, indeed, are but moderate, but though not equal to splendor, sufficient to keep us above distress. Add to which, that I hope by diligence to increase it; and have love, honor—

STERLING. But not the *stuff*, Lovewell! Add one little round *o* to the sum-total of your fortune, and that will be the finest thing you can say to me. You know I've a regard for you—would do anything to serve you—anything on the footing of friendship; but—

LOVEWELL. If you think me worthy of your friendship, sir, be assured that there is no instance in which I should rate your friendship so highly.

STERLING. Psha! psha! that's another thing, you know. Where money or interest is concerned, friendship is quite out of the question.

LOVEWELL. But where the happiness of a daughter is at stake, you would not scruple, sure, to sacrifice a little to her inclinations.

STERLING. Inclinations! why, you would not persuade me that the girl is in love with you; eh, Lovewell?

LOVEWELL. I cannot absolutely answer for Miss Fanny, sir; but am sure that the chief happiness or misery of my life depends entirely upon her.

STERLING. Why, indeed now, if your kinsman Lord Ogleby, would come down handsomely for you—But that's impossible—No, no; 'twill never do; I must hear no more of this. Come, Lovewell, promise me that I shall hear no more of this.

LOVEWELL. (*Hesitating*) I am afraid, sir, I should not be able to keep my word with you, if I did promise you.

STERLING. Why, you would not offer to marry her without my consent! Would you, Lovewell?

LOVEWELL. Marry her, sir! (*Confused*)

STERLING. Ay, marry her, sir! I know very well that a warm speech or two from such a dangerous young spark as you are, would go much farther towards persuading a silly girl to do what she has more than a month's mind [1] to do, than twenty grave lectures from fathers or mothers, or uncles or aunts, to prevent her. But you would not, sure, be such a base fellow, such a treacherous young rogue, as to seduce my daughter's affections, and destroy the peace of my family in that manner. I must insist on it, that you give me your word not to marry her without my consent.

LOVEWELL. Sir—I—I—as to that—I—I—I beg, sir—Pray, sir, excuse me on this subject at present.

STERLING. Promise then, that you will carry this matter no further without my approbation.

LOVEWELL. You may depend on it, sir, that it shall go no further.

STERLING. Well, well, that's enough; I'll take care of the rest, I warrant you. Come, come, let's have done with this nonsense! What's doing in town? Any news upon 'Change?

LOVEWELL. Nothing material.

STERLING. Have you seen the currants, the soap, and Madeira, safe in the warehouses? Have you compared the goods with the invoice and bills of lading, and are they all right?

LOVEWELL. They are, sir!

STERLING. And how are stocks?

LOVEWELL. Fell one and a half this morning.

STERLING. Well, some good news from America,[2] and they'll be up again. But how are Lord Ogleby and Sir John Melvil? When are we to expect them?

LOVEWELL. Very soon, sir. I came on purpose to bring you their commands. Here are letters from both of them. (*Giving letters*)

STERLING. Let me see, let me see. 'Slife, how his lordship's letter is perfumed! It takes my breath away. (*Opening it*) And French paper too! with a fine border of flowers and flourishes, and a slippery gloss on it that dazzles one's eyes. *My dear Mr. Sterling.* (*reading*) Mercy on me! His lordship writes a worse hand than a boy at his exercise. But how's this? Eh! *With you to-night,* (*reading*) *Lawyers to-morrow morning.* To-night! That's sudden indeed. Where's my sister Heidelberg? She should know of this immediately.—Here, John! Harry! Thomas! (*Calling the servants*) Hark ye, Lovewell!

LOVEWELL. Sir!

STERLING. Mind now, how I'll entertain his lordship and Sir John. We'll show your fellows at the other end [3] of the town how we live in the city. They shall eat gold, and drink gold, and lie in gold. Here, Cook! Butler! (*Calling*) What signifies your birth and education, and titles? Money, money! That's the stuff that makes the great man in this country.

LOVEWELL. Very true, sir.

STERLING. True, sir? Why then, have done with your nonsense of love and matrimony. You're not rich enough to think of a wife yet. A man of business should mind nothing but his business. Where are these fellows? John! Thomas! (*Calling*) Get an estate, and a wife will follow of course. Ah, Lovewell! an English merchant is the most respectable character in the universe.[4] 'Slife, man, a rich English merchant may make himself a match for the daughter of a nabob. Where are all my rascals? Here, William! *Exit calling*

LOVEWELL *alone*

[LOVEWELL.] So! As I suspected. Quite averse to the match, and likely to receive the news of it with great displeasure. What's best to be done? Let me see! Suppose I get Sir John Melvil to interest himself in this affair. He may mention it to Lord Ogleby with a better grace than I can, and more probably prevail on him to interfere in it. I can open my mind also more freely to Sir John. He told me, when I left him in town, that he had something of consequence to communicate, and that I could be of use to him. I am glad of it, for the confidence he reposes in me, and the serv-

[1] Strong desire.
[2] American readers will remember that the Stamp Act had been passed during the year preceding the performance of this play, and that relations with the colonies were strained. Two days after the first performance of the piece the Stamp Act was repealed (Feb. 22, 1766).
[3] I.e., the West End.
[4] The difference between Colman's attitude towards the English merchant and Lillo's is worthy of notice.

ice I may do him, will ensure me his good offices. Poor Fanny! it hurts me to see her so uneasy, and her making a mystery of the cause adds to my anxiety. Something must be done upon her account, for, at all events, her solicitude shall be removed. *Exit*

[SCENE II]

Scene changes to another chamber

Enter MISS STERLING *and* MISS FANNY

MISS STERLING. Oh, my dear sister, say no more! This is downright hypocrisy. You shall never convince me that you don't envy me beyond measure. Well, after all, it is extremely natural. It is impossible to be angry with you.

FANNY. Indeed, sister, you have no cause.

MISS STERLING. And you really pretend not to envy me?

FANNY. Not in the least.

MISS STERLING. And you don't in the least wish that you were just in my situation?

FANNY. No, indeed, I don't. Why should I?

MISS STERLING. Why should you? What! on the brink of marriage, fortune, title—But I had forgot; there's that dear sweet creature Mr. Lovewell in the case. You would not break your faith with your true love now for the world, I warrant you.

FANNY. Mr. Lovewell! always Mr. Lovewell! Lord, what signifies Mr. Lovewell, sister?

MISS STERLING. Pretty peevish soul! Oh my dear, grave, romantic sister! A perfect philosopher in petticoats! Love and a cottage, eh, Fanny! Ah, give me indifference and a coach and six!

FANNY. And why not the coach and six, without the indifference? But, pray, when is this happy marriage of yours to be celebrated? I long to give you joy.

MISS STERLING. In a day or two; I can't tell exactly. Oh, my dear sister!—(*Aside*) I must mortify her a little.—I know you have a pretty taste. Pray, give me your opinion of my jewels. How d'ye like the style of this esclavage?[1] (*Showing jewels*)

FANNY. Extremely handsome indeed, and well fancied.

MISS STERLING. What d'ye think of these bracelets? I shall have a miniature of my father, set round with diamonds, to one, and Sir John's to the other. And this pair of earrings, set transparent! Here, the tops, you see, will take off to wear in a morning, or in an undress. How d'ye like them?

(*Shows jewels*)

FANNY. Very much, I assure you. Bless me, sister, you have a prodigious quantity of jewels; you'll be the very queen of diamonds.

MISS STERLING. Ha! ha! ha! very well, my dear! I shall be as fine as a little queen indeed. I have a bouquet to come home to-morrow, made up of diamonds, and rubies, and emeralds, and topazes, and amethysts; jewels of all colors, green, red, blue, yellow, intermixed; the prettiest thing you ever saw in your life! The jeweller says, I shall set out with as many diamonds as anybody in town, except Lady Brilliant, and Polly What-d'ye-call-it [2] Lord Squander's kept mistress.

FANNY. But what are your wedding-clothes, sister?

MISS STERLING. Oh, white and silver, to be sure, you know. I bought them at Sir Joseph Lutestring's, and sat above an hour in the parlor behind the shop, consulting Lady Lutestring about gold and silver stuffs, on purpose to mortify her.

FANNY. Fy, sister! How could you be so abominably provoking?

MISS STERLING. Oh, I have no patience with the pride of your city-knights' ladies. Did you never observe the airs of Lady Lutestring, drest in the richest brocade out of her husband's shop, playing crownwhist at Haberdasher's Hall, while the civil, smirking Sir Joseph, with a smug wig trimmed round his broad face as close as a new-cut yew-hedge, and his shoes so black that they shine again, stands all day in his shop, fastened to his counter like a bad shilling?

FANNY. Indeed, indeed, sister, this is too much. If you talk at this rate, you will be a byword in the city. You must never venture on the inside of Temple-Bar [3] again.

MISS STERLING. Never do I desire it; never, my dear Fanny, I promise you. Oh, how I long to be transported to the dear regions of Grosvenor Square,[4] far, far from the dull dis-

---

[1] A sort of chain, usually ornamented with precious stones, which hangs on the breast in a semi-circle.

[2] Many actresses, after the original Lavinia Fenton, had been translated from the rôle of Polly Peachum to the intimate society of certain peers.

[3] The division between the city and the West End, Westminster, the fashionable part of London.

[4] In the heart of the West End. The "dull districts" are in the commercial part of the city.

tricts of Aldersgate, Cheap, Candlewick, and Farringdon Without and Within! My heart goes pit-a-pat at the very idea of being introduced at court, gilt chariot! piebalded horses! laced liveries! and then the whispers buzzing round the circle, "Who is that young lady? Who is she?" "Lady Melvil, ma'am!" Lady Melvil! my ears tingle at the sound. And then at dinner, instead of my father perpetually asking, "Any news upon 'Change?" to cry, "Well, Sir John! anything new from Arthur's?[1]" or to say to some other woman of quality, "Was your ladyship at the Duchess of Rubber's last night? Did you call in at Lady Thunder's? In the immensity of crowd, I swear I did not see you! Scarce a soul at the opera last Saturday! Shall I see you at Carlisle House[2] next Thursday?" Oh, the dear beau-monde! I was born to move in the sphere of the great world.

FANNY. And so, in the midst of all this happiness, you have no compassion for me; no pity for us poor mortals in common life.

MISS STERLING. (*Affectedly*) You? You're above pity. You would not change conditions with me; you're over head and ears in love, you know. Nay, for that matter, if Mr. Lovewell and you come together, as I doubt not you will, you will live very comfortably, I dare say. He will mind his business, you'll employ yourself in the delightful care of your family, and once in a season perhaps you'll sit together in a front-box at a benefit play, as we used to do at our dancing-master's, you know; and perhaps I may meet you in the summer with some other citizens at Tunbridge. For my part, I shall always entertain a proper regard for my relations. You shan't want my countenance, I assure you.

FANNY. Oh, you're too kind, sister!

Enter MRS. HEIDELBERG

MRS. HEIDELBERG. (*At entering*) Here this evening! I vow and pertest we shall scarce have time to provide for them! Oh, my dear! (*To* MISS STERLING) I am glad to see you're not quite in dish-abille. Lord Ogleby and Sir John Melvil will be here to-night.

MISS STERLING. To-night, ma'am?

MRS. HEIDELBERG. Yes, my dear, to-night. Do put on a smarter cap, and change those ordinary ruffles! Lord, I have such a deal to do, I shall scarce have time to slip on my Italian lutestring. Where is this dawdle of a housekeeper? (*Enter* MRS. TRUSTY) Oh, here, Trusty! do you know that people of qualaty are expected here this evening?

TRUSTY. Yes, ma'am.

MRS. HEIDELBERG. Well! do you be sure now that everything is done in the most genteelest manner, and to the honor of the famaly.

TRUSTY. Yes, ma'am.

MRS. HEIDELBERG. Well, but mind what I say to you.

TRUSTY. Yes, ma'am.

MRS. HEIDELBERG. His lordship is to lie in the chintz bedchamber; d'ye hear? And Sir John in the blue damask room. His lordship's valet-de-shamb in the opposite.—

TRUSTY. But Mr. Lovewell is come down, and you know that's his room, ma'am.

MRS. HEIDELBERG. Well, well, Mr. Lovewell may make shift; or get a bed at the George. But hark you, Trusty!

TRUSTY. Ma'am!

MRS. HEIDELBERG. Get the great dining-room in order as soon as possible. Unpaper the curtains, take the civers off the couch and the chairs, and put the china figures on the mantlepiece immediately. [And set them o'nodding as soon as his lordship comes in, d'ye hear, Trusty?][3]

TRUSTY. Yes, ma'am.

MRS. HEIDELBERG. Be gone then! Fly, this instant! Where's my brother Sterling?

TRUSTY. Talking to the butler, ma'am.

MRS. HEIDELBERG. Very well. (*Exit* TRUSTY). Miss Fanny! I pertest I did not see you before! Lord, child, what's the matter with you?

FANNY. With me? Nothing, ma'am.

MRS. HEIDELBERG. Bless me! Why your face is as pale, and black, and yellow—of fifty colors, I pertest. And then you have drest yourself as loose and as big—I declare there is not such a thing to be seen now, as a

[1] Robert Arthur became proprietor of White's Chocolate House in St. James's Street, meeting place of the famous White's Club, in 1736. The club was a favorite gambling resort of the aristocracy.

[2] Previously the residence of the Earls of Carlisle, in Soho Square, Carlisle House was from 1762 or '63 the scene of Mrs. Cornelys's famous assemblies, patronized by royalty and frequented only by persons of the highest quality. Here were given also balls, *soirées*, concerts, and masquerades.

[3] This interesting bit does not appear in the first edition. The sentence was added later and is found in the 1777 edition.

young woman with a fine waist; you all make yourselves as round as Mrs. Deputy Barter. Go, child! you know the qualaty will be here by and by; go, and make yourself a little more fit to be seen. (*Exit* FANNY) She is gone away in tears; absolutely crying, I vow and pertest. This ridiculous love! We must put a stop to it. It makes a perfect nataral of the girl.

MISS STERLING. (*Affectedly*) Poor soul! she can't help it.

MRS. HEIDELBERG. Well, my dear! Now I shall have an opportunity of convincing you of the absurdity of what you was telling me concerning Sir John Melvil's behavior to you.

MISS STERLING. Oh, it gives me no manner of uneasiness. But, indeed, ma'am, I cannot be persuaded but that Sir John is an extremely cold lover. Such distant civility, grave looks, and lukewarm professions of esteem for me and the whole family! I have heard of flames and darts, but Sir John's is a passion of mere ice and snow.

MRS. HEIDELBERG. Oh, fie, my dear! I am perfectly ashamed of you. That's so like the notions of your poor sister! What you complain of as coldness and indifference, is nothing but the extreme gentilaty of his address, an exact picture of the manners of qualaty.

MISS STERLING. Oh, he is the very mirror of complaisance! full of formal bows and set speeches! I declare, if there was any violent passion on my side, I should be quite jealous of him.

MRS. HEIDELBERG. I say jealus indeed! Jealus of who, pray?

MISS STERLING. My sister Fanny. She seems a much greater favorite than I am, and he pays her infinitely more attention, I assure you.

MRS. HEIDELBERG. Lord! d'ye think a man of fashion, as he is, can't distinguish between the genteel and the wulgar part of the famaly? Between you and your sister, for instance; or me and my brother? Be advised by me, child! It is all politeness and good breeding. Nobody knows the qualaty better than I do.

MISS STERLING. In my mind the old lord, his uncle, has ten times more gallantry about him than Sir John. He is full of attention to the ladies, and smiles, and grins, and leers, and ogles, and fills every wrinkle in his old wizen face with comical expressions of tenderness. I think he would make an admirable sweetheart.

Enter STERLING

STERLING. (*At entering*) No fish? Why the pond was dragged but yesterday morning; there's carp and tench in the boat. Pox on't, if that dog Lovewell had any thought, he would have brought down a turbot, or some of the land-carriage mackerel.

MRS. HEIDELBERG. Lord, brother, I am afraid his lordship and Sir John will not arrive while it is light.

STERLING. I warrant you. But, pray, sister Heidelberg, let the turtle be dressed to-morrow, and some venison; and let the gardener cut some pine-apples, and get out some ice. I'll answer for wine, I warrant you: I'll give them such a glass of Champagne as they never drank in their lives; no, not at a duke's table.

MRS. HEIDELBERG. Pray now, brother, mind how you behave. I am always in a fright about you with people of qualaty. Take care that you don't fall asleep directly after supper, as you commonly do. Take a good deal of snuff; and that will keep you awake; and don't burst out with your horrible loud horse-laughs. It is monstrous wulgar.

STERLING. Never fear, sister! Who have we here?

MRS. HEIDELBERG. It is Mons. Cantoon, the Swish gentleman, that lives with his lordship, I vow and pertest.

Enter CANTON

STERLING. Ah, mounseer! your servant. I am very glad to see you, mounseer.

CANTON. Mosh oblige to Mons. Sterling. Ma'am, I am yours! Matemoiselle, I am yours! (*Bowing round*)

MRS. HEIDELBERG. Your humble servant, Mr. Cantoon!

CANTON. I kiss your hands, Matam!

STERLING. Well, mounseer! and what news of your good family? When are we to see his lordship and Sir John?

CANTON. Mons. Sterling, Milor Ogelby and Sir Jean Melvil will be here in one quarter-hour.

STERLING. I am glad to hear it.

MRS. HEIDELBERG. Oh, I am perdigious glad to hear it. Being so late, I was afeard of some accident. Will you please to have anything, Mr. Cantoon, after your journey?

CANTON. No, I tank you, ma'am.

MRS. HEIDELBERG. Shall I go and show you the apartments, sir?

CANTON. Yo do me great honeur, ma'am.
MRS. HEIDELBERG. Come then! (*To* MISS STERLING) Come, my dear! *Exeunt*

Manet STERLING

STERLING. Pox on't, it's almost dark! It will be too late to go round the garden this evening. However, I will carry them to take a peep at my fine canal at least; that I am determined. *Exit*

ACT II

SCENE [I]. *An anti-chamber to* LORD OGLEBY'S *bedchamber. Table with chocolate, and small case for medicines.*

Enter BRUSH, *my* LORD'S *valet-de-chambre, and* STERLING'S *Chambermaid*

BRUSH. You shall stay, my dear, I insist upon it.

CHAMBERMAID. Nay, pray, sir, don't be so positive; I can't stay indeed.

BRUSH. You shall take one cup to our better acquaintance.

CHAMBERMAID. I seldom drinks chocolate; and if I did, one has no satisfaction, with such apprehensions about one. If my lord should wake, or the Swish gentleman should see one, or Madam Heidelberg should know of it, I should be frighted to death! Besides, I have had my tea already this morning. I'm sure I hear my lord! (*In a fright*)

BRUSH. No, no, madam; don't flutter yourself. The moment my lord wakes, he rings his bell, which I answer sooner or later, as it suits my convenience.

CHAMBERMAID. But should he come upon us without ringing—

BRUSH. I'll forgive him, if he does. This key (*Takes a phial out of the case*) locks him up till I please to let him out.

CHAMBERMAID. Law, sir! that's 'potecary's stuff.

BRUSH. It is so. But without this he can no more get out of bed, than he can read without spectacles. (*Sips*) What with qualms, age, rheumatism, and a few surfeits in his youth, he must have a great deal of brushing, oiling, screwing, and winding-up, to set him a-going for the day.

CHAMBERMAID. (*Sips*) That's prodigious, indeed! (*Sips*) My lord seems quite in a decay.

BRUSH. Yes, he's quite a spectacle (*Sips*), a mere corpse, till he is revived and refreshed from our little magazine here. When the restorative pills, and cordial waters warm his stomach, and get into his head, vanity frisks in his heart, and then he sets up for the lover, the rake, and the fine gentleman.

CHAMBERMAID. (*Sips*) Poor gentleman! But should the Swish gentleman come upon us— (*Frightened*)

BRUSH. Why then, the English gentleman would be very angry. No foreigner must break in upon my privacy. (*Sips*) But, I can assure you, Monsieur Canton is otherwise employed. He is obliged to skim the cream of half-a-score newspapers for my lord's breakfast. Ha, ha, ha! Pray, madam, drink your cup peaceably! My lord's chocolate is remarkably good; he won't touch a drop but what comes from Italy.

CHAMBERMAID. (*Sipping*) 'Tis very fine indeed (*Sips*), and charmingly perfumed! It smells for all the world like our young ladies' dressing-boxes.

BRUSH. You have an excellent taste, madam; and I must beg of you to accept of a few cakes for your own drinking (*Takes 'em out of a drawer in the table*), and in return, I desire nothing but to taste the perfume of your lips. (*Kisses her*) A small return of favors, madam, will make, I hope, this country and retirement agreeable to both. (*He bows, she curtsies*) Your young ladies are fine girls, faith (*Sips*), tho', upon my soul, I am quite of my old lord's mind about them; and, were I inclined to matrimony, I should take the youngest. (*Sips*)

CHAMBERMAID. Miss Fanny's the most affablest and the most best-natered creter!

BRUSH. And the eldest a little haughty, or so?

CHAMBERMAID. More haughtier and prouder than Saturn[1] himself. But this I say quite confidential to you, for one would not hurt a young lady's marriage, you know. (*Sips*)

BRUSH. By no means; but you can't hurt it with us; we don't consider tempers; we want money, Mrs. Nancy. Give us enough of that, we'll abate you a great deal in other particulars. Ha, ha, ha! (*Bell rings*)

CHAMBERMAID. Bless me, here's somebody! Oh, 'tis my lord! Well, your servant, Mr. Brush, I'll clean the cups in the next room.

BRUSH. Do so; but never mind the bell.

[1] I.e., Satan.

I shan't go this half-hour. Will you drink tea with me in the afternoon?

CHAMBERMAID. Not for the world, Mr. Brush. I'll be here to set all things to rights, but I must not drink tea, indeed; and so your servant!

Exit Maid, *with tea-board. Bell rings again*

BRUSH. It is impossible to stupefy one's self in the country for a week, without some little flirting with the abigails.[1] This is much the handsomest wench in the house, except the old citizen's youngest daughter, and I have not time enough to lay a plan for her. (*Bell rings*) And now I'll go to my lord, for I have nothing else to do. (*Going*)

Enter CANTON, *with newspapers in his hand*

CANTON. Monsieur Brush! Maistre Brush! My lor stirra yet?

BRUSH. He has just rung his bell; I am going to him.

CANTON. Depêchez-vous donc.[2] *Exit* BRUSH (*Puts on spectacles*) I wish the deviel had all dese papiers; I forget as fast as I read. *De Advertise* put out of my head de *Gazette;* de *Gazette,* de *Chronique;* and so dey all go *l'un après l'autre!*[3] I must get some *nouvelle* for my lor, or he'll be *enragé contre moi. Voyons!*[4] (*Reads in the papers*) Here is nothing but Anti-Sejanus & advertise! (*Enter* Maid, *with chocolate things*) Vat you vant, child?

CHAMBERMAID. Only the chocolate things, sir.

CANTON. O ver well! Dat is good girl, and ver prit too! *Exit* Maid

LORD OGLEBY. (*Within*) Canton, he, he! (*Coughs*) Canton!

CANTON. I come, my lor! Vat shall I do? I have no news. He will make great *tintamarrel!*[5]

LORD OGLEBY. (*Within*) Canton, I say, Canton! Where are you?

Enter LORD OGLEBY, *leaning on* BRUSH

CANTON. Here, my lor! I ask pardon, my lor! I have not finish de papiers.

LORD OGLEBY. Dem your pardon, and your papiers. I want you here, Canton.

CANTON. Den I run, dat is all.

(*Shuffles along;* LORD OGLEBY *leans upon* CANTON *too, and comes forward*)

[1] Women servants.   [2] Then hurry up.
[3] One after the other.
[4] Angry with me. Let's see!   [5] Racket.

LORD OGLEBY. You Swiss are the most unaccountable mixture: You have the language and the impertinence of the French, with the laziness of Dutchmen.

CANTON. 'Tis very true, my lor! I can't help—

LORD OGLEBY. (*Cries out*) O *diavolo!*

CANTON. You are not in pain, I hope, my lor.

LORD OGLEBY. Indeed, but I am, my lor! That vulgar fellow Sterling, with his city politeness, would force me down his slope last night to see a clay-colored ditch, which he calls a canal; and what with the dew, and the east-wind, my hips and shoulders are absolutely screwed to my body.

CANTON. A littel *vèritable eau d'arquibusade*[6] vil set all to right again.

(*My lord sits down,* BRUSH *gives chocolate*)

LORD OGLEBY. Where are the palsy-drops, Brush?

BRUSH. Here, my lord. (*Pouring out*)

LORD OGLEBY. *Quelle nouvelle avez-vous,*[7] Canton?

CANTON. A great deal of *papier,* but no news at all.

LORD OGLEBY. What! nothing at all, you stupid fellow?

CANTON. Yes, my lor, I have little advertise here vil give you more *plaisir* den all de lyes about nothing at all. *La voilà!*[8]

(*Puts on his spectacles*)

LORD OGLEBY. Come, read it, Canton, with good emphasis, and good discretion.

CANTON. I vil, my lor. (CANTON *reads*) "Dere is no question, but dat de Cosmetique Royale vil utterlie take away all heats, pimps, frecks & oder eruptions of de skin, and likewise de wrinque of old age, &c. &c. A great deal more, my lor! Be sure to ask for de Cosmetique Royale, signed by de docteur own hand. Dere is more *raison* for dis caution dan good men vil tink.—*Eh bien,*[9] my lor!"

LORD OGLEBY. *Eh bien,* Canton! Will you purchase any?

CANTON. For you, my lor?

LORD OGLEBY. For me, you old puppy! For what?

CANTON. My lor?

LORD OGLEBY. Do I want cosmeticks?

[6] Harquebusade water, a lotion for wounds.
[7] What news have you?
[8] There it is.
[9] Well!

CANTON. My lor?

LORD OGLEBY. Look in my face! Come, be sincere! Does it want the assistance of art?

CANTON. (*With his spectacles*) *En verité, non!*[1] 'Tis very smoose and brillian'. But I tote dat you might take a litt' by way of prevention.

LORD OGLEBY. You thought like an old fool, monsieur, as you generally do. The surfeit-water, Brush! (BRUSH *pours out*) What do you think, Brush, of this family we are going to be connected with? Eh!

BRUSH. Very well to marry in, my lord; but it would not do to live with.

LORD OGLEBY. You are right, Brush. There is no washing the blackamoor white. Mr. Sterling will never get rid of Blackfriars;[2] always taste of the borachio;[3] and the poor woman his sister is so busy and so notable, to make one welcome, that I have not yet got over her first reception; it almost amounted to suffocation! I think the daughters are tolerable. Where's my cephalic snuff?

(BRUSH *gives him a box*)

CANTON. Day tink so of you, my lor, for day look at nothing else, *ma foi*.

LORD OGLEBY. Did they? Why, I think they did a little. Where's my glass? (BRUSH *puts one on the table*) The youngest is delectable. (*Takes snuff*)

CANTON. O, *oui*, my lor; very delect, inteed; she made *doux yeux*[4] at you, my lor.

LORD OGLEBY. She was particular. The eldest, my nephew's lady, will be a most valuable wife; she has all the vulgar spirits of her father and aunt, happily blended with the termagant qualities of her deceased mother.—Some pepper-mint-water, Brush!— How happy is it, Cant, for young ladies in general, that people of quality overlook everything in a marriage contract, but their fortune.

CANTON. *C'est bien heureux, et commode aussi.*[5]

LORD OGLEBY. Brush, give me that pamphlet by my bed-side. (BRUSH *goes for it*) Canton, do you wait in the anti-chamber, and let nobody interrupt me till I call you.

[1] Truly, no!
[2] Blackfriars is the section of the City of London formerly the property of the Black Friars. It is between Ludgate Hill and the river. Here it means bourgeois, of the merchant class.
[3] A borachio is a Spanish wine-bag. The term sometimes means a drunkard; or in this case, probably, a dealer in imported wines, a merchant.
[4] To make *doux yeux* is to ogle.
[5] It is very fortunate, and convenient, too.

CANTON. Mush goot may do your lordship!
Exit

LORD OGLEBY. (*To* BRUSH, *who brings the pamphlet*) And now, Brush, leave me a little to my studies. *Exit* BRUSH

LORD OGLEBY *alone*

[LORD OGLEBY.] What can I possibly do among these women here, with this confounded rheumatism? It is a most grievous enemy to gallantry and address. (*Gets off his chair*) He!—Courage, my lor! By heavens, I'm another creature! (*Hums and dances a little*) It will do, faith! Bravo, my lor! these girls have absolutely inspired me. If they are for a game of romps—*Me voilà prêt!*[6] (*Sings and dances*) Oh, that's an ugly twinge! but it's gone. I have rather too much of the lily this morning in my complexion; a faint tincture of the rose will give a delicate spirit to my eyes for the day. (*Unlocks a drawer at the bottom of the glass, and takes out rouge; while he's painting himself, a knocking at the door*) Who's there? I won't be disturbed.

CANTON. (*Without*) My lor, my lor, here is Monsieur Sterling to pay his *devoir*[7] to you this morn in your *chambre*.

LORD OGLEBY. (*Softly*) What a fellow! (*Aloud*) I am extremely honored by Mr. Sterling. Why don't you see him in, monsieur?—I wish he was at the bottom of his stinking canal.—(*Door opens*) Oh, my dear Mr. Sterling, you do me a great deal of honor.

Enter STERLING *and* LOVEWELL [*with* CANTON]

STERLING. I hope, my lord, that your lordship slept well in the night. I believe there are no better beds in Europe than I have. I spare no pains to get 'em, nor money to buy 'em. His majesty, God bless him, don't sleep upon a better, out of his palace; and if I said *in* too, I hope no treason, my lord.

LORD OGLEBY. Your beds are like everything else about you, incomparable! They not only make one rest well, but give one spirits, Mr. Sterling.

STERLING. What say you then, my lord, to another walk in the garden?[8] You must see my water by day-light, and my walks, and

[6] There, I'm ready.
[7] Respects.
[8] The new fashion in gardening is a constant source of merriment on the stage of the eighteenth century. Artificial ruins, grottoes, ponds, and wild, "Gothic" scenery are frequently referred to.

my slopes, and my clumps, and my bridge, and my flowering-trees, and my bed of Dutch tulips. Matters looked but dim last night, my lord. I feel the dew in my great toe; but I would put on a cut shoe, that I might be able to walk you about. I may be laid up tomorrow.

LORD OGLEBY. (*Aside*) I pray heaven you may!

STERLING. What say you, my lord?

LORD OGLEBY. I was saying, sir, that I was in hopes of seeing your young ladies at breakfast. Mr. Sterling, they are, in my mind, the finest tulips in this part of the world. He, he!

CANTON. *Bravissimo*, my lor! Ha, ha, he!

STERLING. They shall meet your lordship in the garden; we won't lose our walk for them, I'll take you a little round before breakfast, and a larger before dinner, and in the evening you shall go the Grand Tower,[1] as I call it. Ha, ha, ha!

LORD OGLEBY. Not a-foot, I hope, Mr. Sterling! Consider your gout, my good friend! You'll certainly be laid by the heels for your politeness. He, he, he!

CANTON. Ha, ha, ha! 'Tis admirable, *en verité!* (*Laughing very heartily*)

STERLING. If my young man (*To* LOVEWELL) here, would but laugh at my jokes, which he ought to do, as mounseer does at yours, my lord, we should be all life and mirth.

LORD OGLEBY. What say you, Cant, will you take my kinsman into your tuition? You have certainly the most companionable laugh I ever met with, and never out of tune.

CANTON. But when your lordship is out of spirit.

LORD OGLEBY. Well said, Cant! But here comes my nephew, to play his part. (*Enter* SIR JOHN MELVIL) Well, Sir John, what news from the island of love? Have you been sighing and serenading this morning?

SIR JOHN. I am glad to see your lordship in such spirits this morning.

LORD OGLEBY. I'm so sorry to see you so dull, sir. What poor things, Mr. Sterling, these *very* young fellows are! They make love with faces as if they were burying the dead, though, indeed, a marriage sometimes may be properly called a burying of the living. Eh, Mr. Sterling?

STERLING. Not if they have enough to live upon, my lord. Ha, ha, ha!

CANTON. [*Aside*] Dat is all monsieur Sterling t'ink of.

SIR JOHN. (*Apart*) Prithee, Lovewell, come with me into the garden; I have something of consequence for you, and I must communicate it directly.

LOVEWELL. (*Apart*) We'll go together.— If your lordship and Mr. Sterling please, we'll prepare the ladies to attend you in the garden.

Exeunt SIR JOHN *and* LOVEWELL

STERLING. My girls are always ready; I make 'em rise soon and to-bed early. Their husbands shall have them with good constitutions, and good fortunes, if they have nothing else, my lord.

LORD OGLEBY. Fine things, Mr. Sterling!

STERLING. Fine things, indeed, my lord! Ah, my lord, had not you run off your speed in your youth, you had not been so crippled in your age, my lord.

LORD OGLEBY. Very pleasant, I protest! He, he, he! (*Half-laughing*)

STERLING. Here's mounseer now, I suppose, is pretty near your lordship's standing; but having little to eat, and little to spend, in his own country, he'll wear three of your lordship out. Eating and drinking kills us all.

LORD OGLEBY. Very pleasant, I protest! (*Aside*) What a vulgar dog!

CANTON. My lor so old as me! He is shicken to me; and look like a boy to *pauvre* me.

STERLING. Ha, ha, ha! Well said, mounseer! Keep to that, and you'll live in any country of the world. Ha, ha, ha! But, my lord, I will wait upon you into the garden; we have but a little time to breakfast. I'll go for my hat and cane, fetch a little walk with you, my lord, and then for the hot rolls and butter!

Exit STERLING

LORD OGLEBY. I shall attend you with pleasure. Hot rolls and butter, in July! I sweat with the thoughts of it. What a strange beast it is!

CANTON. *C'est un barbare.*[2]

LORD OGLEBY. He is a vulgar dog; and if there was not so much money in the family, which I can't do without, I would leave him and his hot rolls and butter directly. Come along, monsieur!

Exeunt LORD OGLEBY *and* CANTON

---

[1] Young men completed their education by "going the Grand Tour" through France, Italy, Switzerland, and down the Rhine.

[2] He's a barbarian.

[SCENE II]

Scene changes to the garden

Enter SIR JOHN MELVIL *and* LOVEWELL

LOVEWELL. In my room this morning? Impossible.

SIR JOHN. Before five this morning, I promise you.

LOVEWELL. On what occasion?

SIR JOHN. I was so anxious to disclose my mind to you, that I could not sleep in my bed. But I found that you could not sleep neither; the bird was flown and the nest long since cold. Where were you, Lovewell?

LOVEWELL. Pho! prithee! ridiculous!

SIR JOHN. Come now! which was it? Miss Sterling's maid? A pretty little rogue! Or Miss Fanny's abigail? a sweet soul too! or—

LOVEWELL. Nay, nay, leave trifling, and tell me your business.

SIR JOHN. Well, but where was[1] you, Lovewell?

LOVEWELL. Walking—writing—What signifies where I was?

SIR JOHN. Walking! Yes, I dare say. It rained as hard as it could pour. Sweet refreshing showers to walk in! No, no, Lovewell. Now would I give twenty pounds, to know which of the maids—

LOVEWELL. But your business! Your business, Sir John.

SIR JOHN. Let me a little into the secrets of the family.

LOVEWELL. Psha!

SIR JOHN. Poor Lovewell! he can't bear it, I see. She charged you not to kiss and tell; eh, Lovewell! However, though you will not honor me with your confidence, I'll venture to trust you with mine. What d'ye think of Miss Sterling?

LOVEWELL. What do I think of Miss Sterling?

SIR JOHN. Ay; what d'ye think of her?

LOVEWELL. An odd question! But I think her a smart, lively girl, full of mirth and sprightliness.

SIR JOHN. All mischief and malice, I doubt.

LOVEWELL. How?

SIR JOHN. But her person! What d'ye think of that?

LOVEWELL. Pretty and agreeable.

SIR JOHN. A little grisette thing.

LOVEWELL. What is the meaning of all this?

SIR JOHN. I'll tell you. You must know, Lovewell, that notwithstanding all appearances—(*seeing* LORD OGLEBY, &c.) We are interrupted. When they are gone, I'll explain.

Enter LORD OGLEBY, STERLING, MRS. HEIDELBERG, MISS STERLING, *and* FANNY

LORD OGLEBY. Great improvements, indeed, Mr. Sterling! Wonderful improvements! The four seasons in lead, the flying Mercury, and the basin with Neptune in the middle, are all in the very extreme of fine taste. You have as many rich figures as the man at Hyde-Park-Corner.[2]

STERLING. The chief pleasure of a country-house is to make improvements, you know, my lord. I spare no expense, not I. This is quite another-guess sort of a place than it was when I first took it, my lord. We were surrounded with trees. I cut down above fifty, to make the lawn before the house, and let in the wind and sun; smack smooth, as you see. Then I made a greenhouse out of the old laundry, and turned the brew-house into a pinery. The high octagon summer-house, you see yonder, is raised on the mast of a ship, given me by an East-India captain, who has turned many a thousand of my money. It commands the whole road. All the coaches and chariots, and chaises, pass and repass under your eye. I'll mount you up there in the afternoon, my lord. 'Tis the pleasantest place in the world to take a pipe and a bottle; and so you shall say, my lord.

LORD OGLEBY. Ay, or a bowl of punch, or a can of flip, Mr. Sterling, for it looks like a cabin in the air. If flying chairs were in use, the captain might make a voyage to the Indies in it still, if he had but a fair wind.

CANTON. Ha, ha, ha, ha!

MRS. HEIDELBERG. My brother's a little comacal in his ideas, my lord, but you'll excuse him. I have a little gothic dairy, fitted up entirely in my own taste. In the evening, I shall hope for the honor of your lordship's company to take a dish of tea there, or a sullabub warm from the cow.

LORD OGLEBY. I have every moment a fresh opportunity of admiring the elegance of Mrs.

---

[1] The bad grammar was corrected to *were* in later editions, though *you was* is the polite form throughout the century.

[2] A man who sold plaster of Paris statuettes.

Heidelberg, the very flower of delicacy, and cream of politeness.

MRS. HEIDELBERG. Oh, my lord!

LORD OGLEBY. Oh, madam!
(*Leering at each other*)

STERLING. How d'ye like these close walks, my lord?

LORD OGLEBY. A most excellent serpentine! It forms a perfect maze, and winds like a true lover's knot.

STERLING. Ay, here's none of your straight lines here; but all taste—zig-zag—crinkum-crankum—in and out—right and left—to and again—twisting and turning like a worm, my lord!

LORD OGLEBY. Admirably laid out indeed, Mr. Sterling! one can hardly see an inch beyond one's nose anywhere in these walks. You are a most excellent economist of your land, and make a little go a great way. It lies together in as small parcels as if it were placed in pots out at your window in Gracechurch Street.

CANTON. Ha, ha, ha, ha!

LORD OGLEBY. What d'ye laugh at, Canton?

CANTON. Ah! *que cette similitude est drôle!* [1] So clever what you say, mi lor!

LORD OGLEBY. (*To* FANNY) You seem mightily engaged, madam. What are those pretty hands so busily employed about?

FANNY. Only making up a nosegay, my lord! Will your lordship do me the honor of accepting it? (*Presenting it*)

LORD OGLEBY. I'll wear it next my heart, madam!—(*Apart*) I see the young creature dotes on me!

MISS STERLING. Lord, sister! you've loaded his lordship with a bunch of flowers as big as the cook or the nurse carry to town on Monday morning for a beaupot.[2] Will your lordship give me leave to present you with this rose, and a sprig of sweet-briar?

LORD OGLEBY. The truest emblems of yourself, madam, all sweetness and poignancy!—(*Apart*) A little jealous, poor soul!

STERLING. Now my lord, if you please, I'll carry you to see my ruins.

MRS. HEIDELBERG. You'll absolutely fatigue his lordship with overwalking, brother!

LORD OGLEBY. Not at all, madam! We're in the garden of Eden, you know, in the region of perpetual spring, youth, and beauty.
(*Leering at the women*)

[1] How funny that comparison is.   [2] Bouquet.

MRS. HEIDELBERG. (*Apart*) Quite the man of qualaty, I pertest!

CANTON. Take-a my arm, mi lor!
(LORD OGLEBY *leans on him*)

STERLING. I'll only show his lordship my ruins, and the cascade, and the Chinese bridge, and then we'll go in to breakfast.

LORD OGLEBY. Ruins, did you say, Mr. Sterling?

STERLING. Ay, ruins, my lord, and they are reckoned very fine ones too! You would think them ready to tumble on your head. It has just cost me a hundred and fifty pounds to put my ruins in thorough repair. This way, if your lordship pleases.

LORD OGLEBY. (*Going, stops*) What steeple's that we see yonder? the parish-church, I suppose.

STERLING. Ha, ha, ha! that's admirable. It is no church at all, my lord! It is a spire that I have built against a tree, a field or two off, to terminate the prospect. One must always have a church, or an obelisk, or a something, to terminate the prospect, you know. That's a rule in taste, my lord!

LORD OGLEBY. Very ingenious, indeed! For my part, I desire no finer prospect than this I see before me. (*Leering at the women*) Simple, yet varied; bounded, yet extensive. Get away, Canton! (*Pushing away* CANTON) I want no assistance; I'll walk with the ladies.

STERLING. This way, my lord!

LORD OGLEBY. Lead on, sir! we young folks here will follow you. Madam! Miss Sterling! Miss Fanny! I attend you.

Exit, after STERLING *gallanting the ladies*

CANTON. (*Following*) He is cock o'de game, ma foy!   *Exit*

Manent SIR JOHN MELVIL *and* LOVEWELL

SIR JOHN. At length, thank heaven, I have an opportunity to unbosom. I know you are faithful, Lovewell, and flatter myself you would rejoice to serve me.

LOVEWELL. Be assured, you may depend on me.

SIR JOHN. You must know then notwithstanding all appearances, that this treaty of marriage between Miss Sterling and me will come to nothing.

LOVEWELL. How!

SIR JOHN. It will be no match, Lovewell.

LOVEWELL. No match?

SIR JOHN. No.

LOVEWELL. You amaze me. What should prevent it?

SIR JOHN. I.

LOVEWELL. You! wherefore?

SIR JOHN. I don't like her.

LOVEWELL. Very plain indeed! I never supposed that you were extremely devoted to her from inclination, but thought you always considered it as a matter of convenience, rather than affection.

SIR JOHN. Very true. I came into the family without any impressions on my mind, with an unimpassioned indifference, ready to receive one woman as soon as another. I looked upon love, serious, sober love, as a chimæra, and marriage as a thing of course; as you know most people do. But I, who was lately so great an infidel in love, am now one of its sincerest votaries. In short, my defection from Miss Sterling proceeds from the violence of my attachment to another.

LOVEWELL. Another! So, so! Here will be fine work. And pray who is she?

SIR JOHN. Who is she! Who can she be, but Fanny, the tender, amiable, engaging Fanny?

LOVEWELL. Fanny! What Fanny?

SIR JOHN. Fanny Sterling; her sister. Is not she an angel, Lovewell?

LOVEWELL. Her sister?—Confusion!—You must not think of it, Sir John.

SIR JOHN. Not think of it? I can think of nothing else. Nay, tell me, Lovewell, was it possible for me to be indulged in a perpetual intercourse with two such objects as Fanny and her sister, and not find my heart led by insensible attraction towards her? You seem confounded! why don't you answer me?

LOVEWELL. Indeed, Sir John, this event gives me infinite concern.

SIR JOHN. Why so? Is not she an angel, Lovewell?

LOVEWELL. I foresee that it must produce the worst consequences. Consider the confusion it must unavoidably create. Let me persuade you to drop these thoughts in time.

SIR JOHN. Never, never, Lovewell!

LOVEWELL. You have gone too far to recede. A negotiation, so nearly concluded, cannot be broken off with any grace. The lawyers, you know, are hourly expected; the preliminaries almost finally settled between Lord Ogleby and Mr. Sterling; and Miss Sterling herself ready to receive you as a husband.

SIR JOHN. Why the banns have been published, and nobody has forbidden them, 'tis true. But you know either of the parties may change their minds, even after they enter the church.

LOVEWELL. You think too lightly of this matter. To carry your addresses so far, and then to desert her, and for her sister too! It will be such an affront to the family, that they can never put up with it.

SIR JOHN. I don't think so, for, as to my transferring my passion from her to her sister, so much the better; for then, you know, I don't carry my affections out of the family.

LOVEWELL. Nay, but prithee be serious, and think better of it.

SIR JOHN. I have thought better of it already, you see. Tell me honestly, Lovewell! Can you blame me? Is there any comparison between them?

LOVEWELL. As to that now—why that—is just—just as it may strike different people. There are many admirers of Miss Sterling's vivacity.

SIR JOHN. Vivacity! A medley of Cheapside pertness, and Whitechapel pride. No, no, if I do go so far into the city for a wedding-dinner, it shall be upon turtle at least.

LOVEWELL. But I see no probability of success; for granting that Mr. Sterling would have consented to it at first, he cannot listen to it now. Why did not you break this affair to the family before?

SIR JOHN. Under such embarrassed circumstances as I have been, can you wonder at my irresolution or perplexity? Nothing but despair, the fear of losing my dear Fanny, could bring me to a declaration even now. And yet, I think I know Mr. Sterling so well, that, strange as my proposal may appear, if I can make it advantageous to him as a money-transaction, as I am sure I can, he will certainly come into it.

LOVEWELL. But even suppose he should,—which I very much doubt,—I don't think Fanny herself would listen to your addresses.

SIR JOHN. You are deceived a little in that particular.

LOVEWELL. You'll find I am in the right.

SIR JOHN. I have some little reason to think otherwise.

LOVEWELL. You have not declared your passion to her already?

SIR JOHN. Yes, I have.

LOVEWELL. Indeed! And—and—and how did she receive it?

SIR JOHN. I think it is not very easy for me to make my addresses to any women, without receiving some little encouragement.

LOVEWELL. Encouragement! Did she give you any encouragement?

SIR JOHN. I don't know what you call *encouragement;*—but she blushed—and cried—and desired me not to think of it any more, upon which I pressed her hand—kissed it—swore she was an angel—and I could see it tickled her to the soul.

LOVEWELL. And did she express no surprise at your declaration?

SIR JOHN. Why, faith, to say the truth, she was a little surprised; and she got away from me too, before I could thoroughly explain myself. If I should not meet with an opportunity of speaking to her, I must get you to deliver a letter from me.

LOVEWELL. I! A letter! I had rather have nothing—

SIR JOHN. Nay, you promised me your assistance; and I am sure you cannot scruple to make yourself useful on such an occasion. You may, without suspicion, acquaint her verbally of my determined affection for her, and that I am resolved to ask her father's consent.

LOVEWELL. As to that, I—your commands, you know—that is, if she—Indeed, Sir John, I think you are in the wrong.

SIR JOHN. Well, well, that's my concern. Ha! there she goes, by heaven! along that walk yonder, d'ye see? I'll go to her immediately.

LOVEWELL. You are too precipitate. Consider what you are doing.

SIR JOHN. I would not lose this opportunity for the universe.

LOVEWELL. Nay, pray don't go! Your violence and eagerness may overcome her spirits. The shock will be too much for her.
(Detaining him)

SIR JOHN. Nothing shall prevent me. Ha! now she turns into another walk. Let me go! *(Breaks from him)* I shall lose her. *(Going, turns back)* Be sure now to keep out of the way! If you interrupt us, I shall never forgive you. *Exit hastily*

LOVEWELL *alone*

[LOVEWELL.] 'Sdeath! I can't bear this. In love with my wife! Acquaint me with his passion for her! Make his addresses before my face! I shall break out before my time. This was the meaning of Fanny's uneasiness. She could not encourage him; I am sure she could not. Ha, they are turning into the walk, and coming this way. Shall I leave the place?—Leave him to solicit my wife! I can't submit to it. They come nearer and nearer—If I stay, it will look suspicious.—It may betray us, and incense him.—They are here.—I must go!—I am the most unfortunate fellow in the world. *Exit*

Enter FANNY *and* SIR JOHN

FANNY. Leave me, Sir John, I beseech you leave me! Nay, why will you persist to follow me with idle solicitations, which are an affront to my character, and an injury to your own honor?

SIR JOHN. I know your delicacy, and tremble to offend it; but let the urgency of the occasion be my excuse! Consider, madam, that the future happiness of my life depends on my present application to you! Consider that this day must determine my fate; and these are perhaps the only moments left me to incline you to warrant my passion, and to entreat you not to oppose the proposals I mean to open to your father.

FANNY. For shame, for shame, Sir John! Think of your previous engagements! Think of your own situation, and think of mine! What have you discovered in my conduct that might encourage you to so bold a declaration? I am shocked that you should venture to say so much, and blush that I should even dare to give it a hearing. Let me be gone!

SIR JOHN. Nay, stay, madam! But one moment! Your sensibility is too great. Engagements! What engagements have even been pretended on either side than those of family-convenience? I went on in the trammels of matrimonial negotiation, with a blind submission to your father and Lord Ogleby; but my heart soon claimed a right to be consulted. It has devoted itself to you, and obliges me to plead earnestly for the same tender interest in yours.

FANNY. Have a care, Sir John! Do not mistake a depraved will for a virtuous inclination. By these common pretenses of the heart, half of our sex are made fools, and a greater part of yours despise them for it.

SIR JOHN. Affection, you will allow, is involuntary. We cannot always direct it to the object on which it should fix; but, when it is once inviolably attached, inviolably as mine is to you, it often creates reciprocal affection. When I last urged you on this subject, you heard me with more temper, and I hoped with some compassion.

FANNY. You deceived yourself. If I forbore to exert a proper spirit, nay, if I did not even express the quickest resentment of your behavior, it was only in consideration of that respect I wish to pay you, in honor to my sister; and be assured, sir, woman as I am, that my vanity could reap no pleasure from a triumph that must result from the blackest treachery to her. (*Going*)

SIR JOHN. One word, and I have done. (*Stopping her*) Your impatience and anxiety, and the urgency of the occasion, oblige me to be brief and explicit with you. I appeal therefore from your delicacy to your justice. Your sister, I verily believe, neither entertains any real affection for me, or tenderness for you. Your father, I am inclined to think, is not much concerned by means of which of his daughters the families are united. Now as they cannot, shall not, be connected otherwise than by my union with you, why will you, from a false delicacy, oppose a measure so conducive to my happiness, and, I hope, your own? I love you, most passionately and sincerely love you—and hope to propose terms agreeable to Mr. Sterling. If then you don't absolutely loathe, abhor, and scorn me—if there is no other happier man—

FANNY. Hear me, sir; hear my final determination—Were my father and sister as insensible as you are pleased to represent them; were my heart forever to remain disengaged to any other; I could not listen to your proposals. What! you on the very eve of a marriage with my sister; I living under the same roof with her, bound not only by the laws of friendship and hospitality, but even the ties of blood, to contribute to her happiness, and not to conspire against her peace—the peace of a whole family—and that my own too! Away! away, Sir John!—At such a time, and in such circumstances, your addresses only inspire me with horror.—Nay, you must detain me no longer.—I will go.

SIR JOHN. Do not leave me in absolute despair! Give me a glimpse of hope!
(*Falling on his knees*)

FANNY. I cannot. Pray, Sir John!
(*Struggling to go*)

SIR JOHN. Shall this hand be given to another? (*Kissing her hand*) No—I cannot endure it.—My whole soul is yours, and the whole happiness of my life is in your power.

Enter MISS STERLING

FANNY. Ha! my sister is here. Rise, for shame, Sir John!

SIR JOHN. (*Rising*) Miss Sterling!

MISS STERLING. I beg pardon, sir! You'll excuse me, madam! I have broke in upon you a little unopportunely, I believe—but I did not mean to interrupt you—I only came, sir, to let you know that breakfast waits, if you have finished your morning's devotions.

SIR JOHN. I am very sensible, Miss Sterling, that this may appear particular,[1] but—

MISS STERLING. Oh, dear, Sir John, don't put yourself to the trouble of an apology. The thing explains itself.

SIR JOHN. It will soon, madam! In the meantime, I can only assure you of my profound respect and esteem for you, and make no doubt of convincing Mr. Sterling of the honor and integrity of my intentions. And—and—your humble servant, madam!
Exit in confusion

Manent FANNY *and* MISS STERLING

MISS STERLING. Respect? Insolence! Esteem? Very fine truly! And you, madam! my sweet, delicate, innocent, sentimental sister! will you convince my papa too of the integrity of your intentions?

FANNY. Do not upbraid me, my dear sister! Indeed, I don't deserve it. Believe me, you can't be more offended at his behavior than I am, and I am sure it cannot make you half so miserable.

MISS STERLING. Make me miserable! you are mightily deceived, madam! it gives me no sort of uneasiness, I assure you. A base fellow! As for you, miss, the pretended softness of your disposition, your artful good-nature, never imposed upon me. I always knew you to be sly, and envious, and deceitful.

FANNY. Indeed you wrong me.

MISS STERLING. Oh, you are all goodness, to be sure! Did not I find him on his knees before you? Did not I see him kiss your sweet hand? Did not I hear his protestations? Was

---

[1] In the obsolete sense of strange.

not I witness of your dissembled modesty? No, no, my dear! Don't imagine that you can make a fool of your elder sister so easily.

FANNY. Sir John, I own, is to blame; but I am above the thoughts of doing you the least injury.

MISS STERLING. We shall try that, madam! I hope, miss, you'll be able to give a better account to my papa and my aunt—for they shall both know of this matter, I promise you. *Exit*

FANNY *alone*

[FANNY.] How unhappy I am! My distresses multiply upon me. Mr. Lovewell must now become acquainted with Sir John's behavior to me, and in a manner that may add to his uneasiness. My father, instead of being disposed by fortunate circumstances to forgive any transgression, will be previously incensed against me. My sister and my aunt will become irreconcilably my enemies, and rejoice in my disgrace. Yet, at all events, I am determined on a discovery. I dread it, and am resolved to hasten it. It is surrounded with more horrors every instant, as it appears every instant more necessary. *Exit*

ACT III

[SCENE I.] *A Hall*

Enter a servant leading in SERJEANT FLOWER, *and* Counsellors TRAVERSE *and* TRUEMAN, *all booted*

SERVANT. This way, if you please, gentlemen! My master is at breakfast with the family at present; but I'll let him know, and he will wait on you immediately.

FLOWER. Mighty well, young man, mighty well.

SERVANT. Please to favor me with your names.

FLOWER. Let Mr. Sterling know, that Mr. Serjeant Flower, and [two][1] other gentlemen of the bar, are come to wait on him according to his appointment.

SERVANT. I will, sir. (*Going*)

FLOWER. And harkee, young man! (Servant *returns*) Desire my servant—Mr. Serjeant Flower's servant—to bring in my green and gold saddle-cloth and pistols, and lay them down here in the hall with my portmanteau.

SERVANT. I will, sir. *Exit*

Manent Lawyers

FLOWER. Well, gentlemen! the settling these marriage articles falls conveniently enough, almost just on the eve of the circuits.—Let me see, the Home, the Midland, Oxford, and Western—ay, we can all cross the country well enough to our several destinations.—Traverse, when do you begin at Hertford?

TRAVERSE. The day after to-morrow.

FLOWER. That is commission-day[2] with us at Warwick too.—But my clerk has retainers for every cause[3] in the paper, so it will be time enough if I am there the next morning.—Besides, I have about half a dozen cases that have lain by me ever since the spring assizes, and I must tack opinions to them before I see my country clients again; so I will take the evening before me—and then, *currente calamo*,[4] as I say—eh, Traverse!

TRAVERSE. True, Mr. Serjeant—[and the easiest thing in the world too—for those country attorneys are such ignorant dogs, that in case of the devise of an estate to A. and his heirs forever, they'll make a query, whether he takes in fee or in tail.][5]

FLOWER. Do you expect to have much to do on the Home circuit these assizes?

TRAVERSE. Not much *nisi prius*[6] business, but a good deal on the crown side, I believe. The jails are brimfull—and some of the felons in good circumstances, and likely to be tolerable clients.—Let me see! I am engaged for three highway robberies, two murders, one forgery, and half a dozen larcenies, at Kingston.

FLOWER. A pretty decent jail-delivery!—Do you expect to bring off Darkin, for the robbery on Putney Common? Can you make out your *alibi?*

TRAVERSE. Oh, no! the crown witnesses are sure to prove our identity. We shall certainly be hanged; but that don't signify. But, Mr. Serjeant, have you much to do? Any remarkable cause on the Midland this circuit?

---

[1] First edition has *three*. It is possible that at one time during the composition of the play the authors had another lawyer in the group; if so, he was removed before the production.

[2] The first day of assizes, when the commission authorizing the judge to hold them is read.

[3] Case.

[4] With running pen.

[5] Lacking in first edition.

[6] Here this phrase means civil as opposed to **criminal** action.

FLOWER. Nothing very remarkable—except two rapes, and Rider and Western at Nottingham, for *crim. con.*[1]—but, on the whole, I believe a good deal of business.—Our associate tells me, there are above thirty *venires*[2] for Warwick.

TRAVERSE. Pray, Mr. Serjeant, are you concerned in Jones and Thomas, at Lincoln?

FLOWER. I am—for the plaintiff.

TRAVERSE. And what do you think on't?

FLOWER. A non-suit.

TRAVERSE. I thought so.

FLOWER. Oh, no manner of doubt on't—*luce clarius*[3]—we have no right in us; we have but one chance.

TRAVERSE. What's that?

FLOWER. Why, my Lord Chief does not go the circuit this time, and my brother Puzzle being in the commission,[4] the cause will come on before him.

TRUEMAN. Ay, that may do, indeed, if you can but throw dust in the eyes of the defendant's counsel.

FLOWER. True.—Mr. Trueman, I think you are concerned for Lord Ogleby in this affair?
(*To* TRUEMAN)

TRUEMAN. I am, sir—I have the honor to be related to his lordship, and hold some courts for him in Somersetshire, go the Western circuit, and attend the sessions at Exeter, merely because his lordship's interest and property lie in that part of the kingdom.

FLOWER. Ha!—And pray, Mr. Trueman, how long have you been called to the bar?

TRUEMAN. About nine years and three quarters.

FLOWER. Ha!—I don't know that I ever had the pleasure of seeing you before. I wish you success, young gentleman!

Enter STERLING

STERLING. Oh, Mr. Serjeant Flower, I am glad to see you. Your servant, Mr. Serjeant! Gentlemen, your servant!—Well, are all matters concluded? Has that snail-paced conveyancer, old Ferret of Gray's Inn, settled the articles at last? Do you approve of what he has done? Will his tackle hold? tight and strong?—eh, master Serjeant?

FLOWER. My friend Ferret's slow and sure, sir. But then, *serius aut citius*, as we say—sooner or later, Mr. Sterling, he is sure to put his business out of hand as he should do.—My clerk has brought the writings, and all other instruments along with him, and the settlement is, I believe, as good a settlement, as any settlement on the face of the earth!

STERLING. But that damned mortgage of sixty thousand pounds. There don't appear to be any other incumbrances, I hope?

TRAVERSE. I can answer for that, sir, and that will be cleared off immediately on the payment of the first part of Miss Sterling's portion. You agree, on your part, to come down with eighty thousand pound.—

STERLING. Down on the nail.—Ay, ay, my money is ready to-morrow, if he pleases. He shall have it in India-bonds, or notes, or how he chooses.—Your lords, and your dukes, and your people at the court end of the town, stick at payments sometimes,—debts unpaid, no credit lost with them—but no fear of us substantial fellows—eh, Mr. Serjeant?

FLOWER. Sir John having last term according to agreement, levied a fine, and suffered a recovery, has thereby cut off the entail of the Ogleby estate for the better effecting the purposes of the present intended marriage; on which above-mentioned Ogleby estate, a jointure of two thousand pound *per annum* is secured to your eldest daughter, now Elizabeth Sterling, spinster, and the whole estate, after the death of the aforesaid earl, descends to the heirs male of Sir John Melvil, on the body of the aforesaid Elizabeth Sterling lawfully to be begotten.

TRAVERSE. Very true—and Sir John is to be put in immediate possession of as much of his lordship's Somersetshire estate, as lies in the manors of Hogmore and Cranford, amounting to between two and three thousands *per annum* and, at the death of Mr. Sterling, a further sum of seventy thousand—

Enter SIR JOHN MELVIL

STERLING. Ah, Sir John! Here we are—hard at it—paving the road to matrimony. We'll have no jolts; all upon the nail, as easy as the new pavement! First the lawyers, then comes the doctor! Let us but dispatch the

---

[1] Criminal conversation; i.e., adultery.
[2] A legal order summoning a jury; or the men so summoned as juries for particular cases. Here it means that over thirty groups have been called to pick juries from.
[3] Clearer than day.
[4] The justices authorized to hold court on a particular circuit.

long-robe, we shall soon set pudding-sleeves [1] to work, I warrant you.

Sir John. I am sorry to interrupt you, sir, but I hope that both you and these gentlemen will excuse me. Having something very particular for your private ear, I took the liberty of following you, and beg you will oblige me with an audience immediately.

Sterling. Ay, with all my heart!—Gentlemen, Mr. Serjeant, you'll excuse it. Business must be done, you know. The writings will keep cold till to-morrow morning.

Flower. I must be at Warwick, Mr. Sterling, the day after.

Sterling. Nay, nay, I shan't part with you to-night, gentlemen, I promise you. My house is very full, but I have beds for you all, beds for your servants, and stabling for all your horses.—Will you take a turn in the garden, and view some of my improvements before dinner? Or will you amuse yourselves in the green with a game of bowls and a cool tankard? My servants shall attend you. Do you choose any other refreshment? Call for what you please; do as you please, make yourselves quite at home, I beg of you.—Here—Thomas! Harry! William! Wait on these gentlemen!—(*Follows the lawyers out, bawling and talking, and then returns to* Sir John) And now, sir, I am entirely at your service. What are your commands with me, Sir John?

Sir John. After having carried the negotiation between our families to so great a length, after having assented so readily to all your proposals, as well as received so many instances of your cheerful compliance with the demands made on our part, I am extremely concerned, Mr. Sterling, to be the involuntary cause of any uneasiness.

Sterling. Uneasiness! What uneasiness? Where business is transacted as it ought to be, and the parties understand one another, there can be no uneasiness. You agree, on such and such conditions, to receive my daughter for a wife; on the same conditions I agree to receive you as a son-in-law; and as to all the rest, it follows of course, you know, as regularly as the payment of a bill after acceptance.

Sir John. Pardon me, sir; more uneasiness has arisen than you are aware of. I am myself, at this instant, in a state of inexpressible embarrassment; Miss Sterling, I know, is extremely disconcerned, too; and unless you will oblige me with the assistance of your friendship, I foresee the speedy progress of discontent and animosity through the whole family.

Sterling. What the deuce is all this? I don't understand a single syllable.

Sir John. In one word then—it will be absolutely impossible for me to fulfill my engagements in regard to Miss Sterling.

Sterling. How, Sir John! Do you mean to put an affront upon my family? What! refuse to—

Sir John. Be assured, sir, that I neither mean to affront, nor forsake your family. My only fear is, that you should desert me; for the whole happiness of my life depends on my being connected with your family, by the nearest and tenderest ties in the world.

Sterling. Why, did not you tell me, but a moment ago, that it was absolutely impossible for you to marry my daughter?

Sir John. True. But you have another daughter, sir—

Sterling. Well!

Sir John. Who has obtained the most absolute dominion over my heart. I have already declared my passion to her; nay, Miss Sterling herself is also apprised of it, and if you will but give a sanction to my present addresses, the uncommon merit of Miss Sterling will no doubt recommend her to a person of equal, if not superior rank to myself, and our families may still be allied by my union with Miss Fanny.

Sterling. Mighty fine, truly! Why, what the plague do you make of us, Sir John? Do you come to market for my daughter, like servants at a statute-fair? [2] Do you think that I will suffer you, or any man in the world, to come into my house, like the Grand Signior,[3] and throw the handkerchief first to one, and then to t'other, just as he pleases? Do you think I drive a kind of African slave-trade with them? and—

Sir John. A moment's patience, sir! Nothing but the excess of my passion for Miss Fanny should have induced me to take any step that had the least appearance of any disrespect to any part of your family; and

---

[1] "Hippocrates sleeve," the sleeve of a doctor's gown, is a variety of pudding-bag, or straining bag. The fellows of the universities were sometimes referred to as sleeves; here the meaning is the clergyman, doctor of divinity. The long-robe, of course, is the lawyer.

[2] The annual fair for hiring servants.
[3] The Sultan of Turkey.

even now I am desirous to atone for my transgression, by making the most adequate compensation that lies in my power.

STERLING. Compensation! What compensation can you possibly make in such a case as this, Sir John?

SIR JOHN. Come, come, Mr. Sterling; I know you to be a man of sense, a man of business, a man of the world. I'll deal frankly with you; and you shall see that I don't desire a change of measures for my own gratification, without endeavoring to make it advantageous to you.

STERLING. What advantage can your inconstancy be to me, Sir John?

SIR JOHN. I'll tell you, sir.—You know that by the articles at present subsisting between us, on the day of my marriage with Miss Sterling, you agree to pay down the gross sum of eighty thousand pounds.

STERLING. Well!

SIR JOHN. Now, if you will but consent to my waiving that marriage—

STERLING. I agree to your waiving that marriage? Impossible, Sir John.

SIR JOHN. I hope not, sir; as, on my part, I will agree to waive my right to thirty thousand pounds of the fortune I was to receive with her.

STERLING. Thirty thousand, d'ye say?

SIR JOHN. Yes, sir; and accept of Miss Fanny with fifty thousand, instead of fourscore.

STERLING. Fifty thousand! (*Pausing*)

SIR JOHN. Instead of fourscore.

STERLING. Why—why—there may be something in that. Let me see! Fanny with fifty thousand, instead of Betsey with fourscore! But how can this be, Sir John? For you know I am to pay this money into the hands of my Lord Ogleby; who, I believe—between you and me, Sir John—is not overstocked with ready money at present; and threescore thousand of it, you know, is to go to pay off the present incumbrances on the estate, Sir John.

SIR JOHN. That objection is easily obviated. —Ten of the twenty thousand, which would remain as a surplus of the fourscore, after paying off the mortgage, was intended by his lordship for my use, that we might set off with some little *éclat* on our marriage; and the other ten for his own.—Ten thousand pounds, therefore, I shall be able to pay you immediately; and for the remaining twenty thousand, you shall have a mortgage on that part of the estate which is to be made over to me, with whatever security you shall require for the regular payment of the interest, till the principal is duly discharged.

STERLING. Why, to do you justice, Sir John, there is something fair and open in your proposal; and since I find you do not mean to put an affront upon the family—

SIR JOHN. Nothing was ever farther from my thoughts, Mr. Sterling.—And after all, the whole affair is nothing extraordinary—such things happen every day—and as the world has only heard generally of a treaty between the families, when this marriage takes place, nobody will be the wiser, if we have but discretion enough to keep our own counsel.

STERLING. True, true; and since you only transfer from one girl to the other, it is no more than transferring so much stock, you know.

SIR JOHN. The very thing.

STERLING. Odso, I had quite forgot! We are reckoning without our host here. There is another difficulty—

SIR JOHN. You alarm me! What can that be?

STERLING. I can't stir a step in this business, without consulting my sister Heidelberg. The family has very great expectations from her, and we must not give her any offence.

SIR JOHN. But if you come into this measure, surely, she will be so kind as to consent—

STERLING. I don't know that. Betsey is her darling, and I can't tell how far she may resent any slight that seems to be offered to her favorite niece. However, I'll do the best I can for you. You shall go and break the matter to her first; and, by that time that I may suppose that your rhetoric has prevailed on her to listen to reason, I will step in to reinforce your arguments.

SIR JOHN. I'll fly to her immediately! You promise me your assistance?

STERLING. I do.

SIR JOHN. Ten thousand thanks for it! And now success attend me! (*Going*)

STERLING. Harkee, Sir John! (SIR JOHN *returns*) Not a word of the thirty thousand to my sister, Sir John.

SIR JOHN. Oh, I am dumb, I am dumb, sir. (*Going*)

STERLING. You remember it is thirty thousand.

Sir John. To be sure I do. (*Going*)
Sterling. But, Sir John! one thing more. (Sir John *returns*) My lord must know nothing of this stroke of friendship between us.
Sir John. Not for the world. Let me alone! Let me alone! (*Offering to go*)
Sterling. (*Holding him*) And, when every thing is agreed, we must give each other a bond to be held fast to the bargain.
Sir John. To be sure. A bond, by all means; a bond, or whatever you please!
Exit hastily

Sterling *alone*

[Sterling.] I should have thought of more conditions; he's in a humor to give me everything. Why, what mere children are your fellows of quality; that cry for a plaything one minute, and throw it by the next! as changeable as the weather, and as uncertain as the stocks. Special fellows to drive a bargain; and yet they are to take care of the interest of the nation, truly! Here does this whirligig man of fashion offer to give up thirty thousand pounds in hard money, with as much indifference as if it was a china orange. By this mortgage, I shall have a hold on his *terra firma;* and if he wants more money, as he certainly will, let him have children by my daughter or no, I shall have his whole estate in a net, for the benefit of my family. Well; thus it is, that the children of citizens who have acquired fortunes, prove persons of fashion; and thus it is, that persons of fashion, who have ruined their fortunes, reduce the next generation to cits! *Exit*

[Scene ii]

Scene changes to another apartment

Enter Mrs. Heidelberg *and* Miss Sterling

Miss Sterling. This is your gentle-looking, soft-speaking, sweet-smiling, affable Miss Fanny for you!

Mrs. Heidelberg. My Miss Fanny! I disclaim her. With all her arts, she never could insinuate herself into my good graces,—and yet she has a way with her, that deceives man, woman, and child, except you and me, niece.

Miss Sterling. O, ay; she wants nothing but a crook in her hand, and a lamb under her arm, to be a perfect picture of innocence and simplicity.

Mrs. Heidelberg. Just as I was drawn at Amsterdam, when I went over to visit my husband's relations![1]

Miss Sterling. And then she's so mighty good to servants—"Pray, John, do this—pray, Tom, do that—thank you, Jenny"—and then so humble to her relations—"To be sure, papa! —as my aunt pleases—my sister knows best—" But, with all her demureness and humility, she has no objection to be Lady Melvil, it seems, nor to any wickedness that can make her so.

Mrs. Heidelberg. She Lady Melvil? Compose yourself, niece. I'll ladyship her indeed! a little creppin', cantin'—She shan't be the better for a farden of my money. But, tell me, child, how does this intriguing with Sir John corruspond with her partiality to Lovewell? I don't see a concatunation here.

Miss Sterling. There I was deceived, madam. I took all their whisperings and stealing into corners to be the mere attraction of vulgar minds; but, behold! their private meetings were not to contrive their own insipid happiness, but to conspire against mine. But I know whence proceeds Mr. Lovewell's resentment to me. I could not stoop to be familiar with my father's clerk, and so I have lost his interest.

Mrs. Heidelberg. My spurrit to a T! My dear child! (*Kissing her*) Mr. Heidelberg lost his election for member of parliament, because I would not demean myself to be slobbered about by drunken shoemakers, beastly cheesemongers, and greasy butchers and tallow-chandlers. However, niece, I can't help diffurring a little in opinion from you in this matter. My experunce and sagucity makes me still suspect, that there is something more between her and that Lovewell, notwithstanding this affair of Sir John. I had my eye upon them the whole time of breakfast. Sir John, I observed, looked a little confounded, indeed, though I knew nothing of what had passed in the garden. You seemed to sit upon thorns, too. But Fanny and Mr. Lovewell made quite another-guess sort of a figur; and were as perfect a pictur of two distressed lovers, as if it had been drawn by Raphael Angelo. As to Sir John and Fanny, I want a matter of fact.

Miss Sterling. Matter of fact, madam? Did not I come unexpectedly upon them?

[1] Many ladies of the period had themselves portrayed as shepherdesses.

Was not Sir John kneeling at her feet, and kissing her hand? Did not he look all love, and she all confusion? Is not that matter of fact? And did not Sir John, the moment that papa was called out of the room to the lawyer-men, get up from breakfast, and follow him immediately? And, I warrant you that by this time he has made proposals to him to marry my sister. Oh, that some other person, an earl, or a duke, would make his addresses to me, that I might be revenged on this monster!

MRS. HEIDELBERG. Be cool, child! You *shall* be Lady Melvil, in spite of all their caballins, if it costs me ten thousand pounds to turn the scale. Sir John may apply to my brother, indeed; but I'll make them all know who governs in this fammaly.

MISS STERLING. As I live, madam, yonder comes Sir John. A base man! I can't endure the sight of him. I'll leave the room this instant. (*Disordered*)

MRS. HEIDELBERG. Poor thing! Well, retire to your own chamber, child; I'll give it him, I warrant you; and by and by I'll come and let you know all that has passed between us.

MISS STERLING. Pray do, madam!—(*Looking back*)—A vile wretch! *Exit in a rage*

Enter SIR JOHN MELVIL

SIR JOHN. Your most obedient humble servant, madam! (*Bowing very respectfully*)

MRS. HEIDELBERG. Your servant, Sir John! (*Dropping a half-curtsy, and pouting*)

SIR JOHN. Miss Sterling's manner of quitting the room on my approach, and the visible coolness of your behavior to me, madam, convince me that she has acquainted you with what passed this morning.

MRS. HEIDELBERG. I am very sorry, Sir John, to be made acquainted with anything that should induce me to change the opinion which I could always wish to entertain of a person of quallaty. (*Pouting*)

SIR JOHN. It has always been my ambition to merit the best opinion from Mrs. Heidelberg; and when she comes to weigh all circumstances, I flatter myself—

MRS. HEIDELBERG. You *do* flatter yourself, if you imagine that I can approve of your behavior to my niece, Sir John. And give me leave to tell you, Sir John, that you have been drawn into an action much beneath you, Sir John; and that I look upon every injury offered to Miss Betty Sterling, as an affront to myself, Sir John. (*Warmly*)

SIR JOHN. I would not offend you for the world, madam! But when I am influenced by a partiality for another, however ill-founded, I hope your discernment and good sense will think it rather a point of honor to renounce engagements, which I could not fulfill so strictly as I ought; and that you will excuse the change in my inclinations, since the new object, as well as the first, has the honor of being your niece, madam.

MRS. HEIDELBERG. I disclaim her as a niece, Sir John; Miss Sterling disclaims her as a sister; and the whole fammaly must disclaim her for her monstrous baseness and treachery.

SIR JOHN. Indeed she has been guilty of none, madam: Her hand and heart are, I am sure, entirely at the disposal of yourself, and Mr. Sterling. (*Enter* STERLING *behind*) And, if you should not oppose my inclinations, I am sure of Mr. Sterling's consent, madam.

MRS. HEIDELBERG. Indeed!

SIR JOHN. Quite certain, madam.

STERLING. (*Behind*) So! they seem to be coming to terms already. I may venture to make my appearance.

MRS. HEIDELBERG. To marry Fanny? (STERLING *advances by degrees*)

SIR JOHN. Yes, madam.

MRS. HEIDELBERG. My brother has given his consent, you say?

SIR JOHN. In the most ample manner, with no other restriction than the failure of your concurrence, madam. (*Sees* STERLING) Oh, here's Mr. Sterling, who will confirm what I have told you.

MRS. HEIDELBERG. What! Have you consented to give up your own daughter in this manner, brother?

STERLING. Give her up! No, not give her up, sister; only in case that you—(*Apart to* SIR JOHN) Zounds, I am afraid you have said too much, Sir John!

MRS. HEIDELBERG. Yes, yes; I see now that it is true enough what my niece told me. You are all plottin' and caballin' against her. Pray, does Lord Ogleby know of this affair?

SIR JOHN. I have not yet made him acquainted with it, madam.

MRS. HEIDELBERG. No, I warrant you; I thought so. And so his lordship and myself truly, are not to be consulted 'till the last

STERLING. What! did not you consult my lord? Oh, fie, for shame, Sir John!

SIR JOHN. Nay, but, Mr. Sterling—

MRS. HEIDELBERG. We, who are the persons of most consequence and experunce in the two fammalies, are to know nothing of the matter, 'till the whole is as good as concluded upon. But his lordship, I am sure, will have more generosaty than to countenance such a perceeding: And I could not have expected such behavior from a person of your quallaty, Sir John! And as for you, brother—

STERLING. Nay, nay, but hear me, sister!

MRS. HEIDELBERG. I am perfectly ashamed of you! Have you no spurrit, no more concern for the honor of our fammaly than to consent—

STERLING. Consent? I consent? As I hope for mercy, I never gave my consent. Did I consent, Sir John?

SIR JOHN. Not absolutely, without Mrs. Heidelberg's concurrence. But, in case of her approbation—

STERLING. Ay, I grant you, if my sister approved. But that's quite another thing, you know. (*To* MRS. HEIDELBERG)

MRS. HEIDELBERG. Your sister approve, indeed! I thought you knew her better, brother Sterling! What! approve of having your eldest daughter returned upon your hands, and exchanged for the younger? I am surprised how you could listen to such a scandalus proposal.

STERLING. I tell you, I never did listen to it. Did not I say that I would be governed entirely by my sister, Sir John, and, unless she agreed to your marrying Fanny—

MRS. HEIDELBERG. I agree to his marrying Fanny? Abominable! The man is absolutely out of his senses! Can't that wise head of yours foresee the consequence of all this, brother Sterling? Will Sir John take Fanny without a fortune? No! After you have settled the largest part of your property on your youngest daughter can there be an equal portion left for the eldest? No! Does not this overturn the whole systum of the fammaly? Yes, yes, yes! You know I was always for my niece Betsey's marrying a person of the very first quallaty; that was my maxum; and, therefore, much the largest settlement was of course to be made upon her. As for Fanny, if she could, with a fortune of twenty or thirty thousand pounds, get a knight, or a member of parliament, or a rich common-council-man, for a husband, I thought it might do very well.

SIR JOHN. But if a better match should offer itself, why should not it be accepted, madam?

MRS. HEIDELBERG. What, at the expense of her elder sister? Oh fie, Sir John! How could you bear to hear of such an indignaty, brother Sterling?

STERLING. I! Nay, I shan't hear of it, I promise you. I can't hear of it, indeed, Sir John.

MRS. HEIDELBERG. But you *have* heard of it, brother Sterling; you know you have; and sent Sir John to propose it to me. But if you can give up your daughter, I shan't forsake my niece, I assure you. Ah! if my poor dear Mr. Heidelberg, and our sweet babes, had been alive, he would not have behaved so.

STERLING. Did I, Sir John? Nay, speak!— (*Apart to* SIR JOHN) Bring me off, or we are ruined.

SIR JOHN. Why to be sure, to speak the truth—

MRS. HEIDELBERG. To speak the truth, I'm ashamed of you both. But have a care what you are about, brother, have a care, I say! The lawyers are in the house, I hear; and if everything is not settled to my liking, I'll have nothing more to say to you, if I live these three hundred years. I'll go over to Holland, and settle with Mr. Vanderspracken, my poor husband's first-cousin, and my own fammaly shall never be the better for a farden of my money, I promise you. *Exit*

Manent SIR JOHN *and* STERLING

STERLING. I thought so. I knew she never would agree to it.

SIR JOHN. 'Sdeath, how unfortunate! What can we do, Mr. Sterling?

STERLING. Nothing.

SIR JOHN. What, must our agreement break off, the moment it is made then?

STERLING. It can't be helped, Sir John. The family, as I told you before, have great expectations from my sister; and if this matter proceeds, you hear yourself that she threatens to leave us. My brother Heidelberg was a warm man, a very warm man, and died worth a plum[1] at least,—a plum! ay, I warrant you, he died worth a plum and a half.

[1] £100,000.

Sir John. Well; but if I—

Sterling. And then, my sister has three or four very good mortgages, a deal of money in the three per cents. and old South-Sea annuities, besides large concerns in the Dutch and French funds. The greatest part of all this she means to leave to our family.

Sir John. I can only say, sir—

Sterling. Why, your offer of the difference of thirty thousand, was very fair and handsome, to be sure, Sir John.

Sir John. Nay, but I am even willing to—

Sterling. Ay, but if I was to accept it against her will, I might lose above a hundred thousand; so you see the balance is against you, Sir John.

Sir John. But is there no way, do you think of prevailing on Mrs. Heidelberg to grant her consent?

Sterling. I am afraid not. However, when her passion is a little abated—for she's very passionate—you may try what can be done. But you must not use my name any more, Sir John.

Sir John. Suppose I was to prevail on Lord Ogleby to apply to her, do you think that would have any influence over her?

Sterling. I think he would be more likely to persuade her to it than any other person in the family. She has a great respect for Lord Ogleby. She loves a lord.

Sir John. I'll apply to him this very day. And, if he should prevail on Mrs. Heidelberg, I may depend on your friendship, Mr. Sterling?

Sterling. Ay, ay, I shall be glad to oblige you, when it is in my power; but as the account stands now, you see it is not upon the figures. And so your servant, Sir John. *Exit*

Sir John Melvil *alone*

[Sir John.] What a situation am I in! Breaking off with her whom I was bound by treaty to marry; rejected by the object of my affections; and embroiled with this turbulent woman, who governs the whole family. And yet opposition, instead of smothering, increases my inclination. I must have her. I'll apply immediately to Lord Ogleby; and if he can but bring over the aunt to our party, her influence will overcome the scruples and delicacy of my dear Fanny, and I shall be the happiest of mankind! *Exit*

ACT IV

[Scene I.] *A room*

Enter Sterling, Mrs. Heidelberg, *and* Miss Sterling

Sterling. What! Will you send Fanny to town, sister?

Mrs. Heidelberg. To-morrow morning. I've given orders about it already.

Sterling. Indeed?

Mrs. Heidelberg. Posatively.

Sterling. But consider, sister, at such a time as this, what an odd appearance it will have.

Mrs. Heidelberg. Not half so odd as her behavior, brother. This time was intended for happiness, and I'll keep no incendiaries here to destroy it. I insist on her going off to-morrow morning.

Sterling. I'm afraid this is all your doing, Betsey.

Miss Sterling. No, indeed, papa; my aunt knows that it is not. For all Fanny's baseness to me, I am sure I would not do or say anything to hurt her with you or my aunt for the world.

Mrs. Heidelberg. Hold your tongue, Betsey! I will have my way. When she is packed off, everything will go on as it should do.—Since they are at their intrigues, I'll let them see that we can act with vigur on our part, and the sending her out of the way shall be the purliminary step to all the rest of my perceedings.

Sterling. Well, but, sister—

Mrs. Heidelberg. It does not signify talking, brother Sterling; for I'm resolved to be rid of her, and I will. Come along, child! (*To* Miss Sterling) The post-shay shall be at the door by six o'clock in the morning; and if Miss Fanny does not get into it, why *I* will; and so there's an end of the matter.

(*Bounces out, with* Miss Sterling. Mrs. Heidelberg *returns*)

Mrs. Heidelberg. One word more, brother Sterling! I expect that you will take your eldest daughter in your hand, and make a formal complaint to Lord Ogleby of Sir John Melvil's behavior. Do this, brother; show a proper regard for the honor of your fammaly yourself, and I shall throw in my mite to the raising of it. If not—But now you know my mind. So act as you please, and take the consequences. *Exit*

STERLING *alone*

[STERLING.] The devil's in the woman for tyranny; mothers, wives, mistresses, or sisters, they always will govern us. As to my sister Heidelberg, she knows the strength of her purse, and domineers upon the credit of it.— "I will do this"—and "you shall do that"— and "you must do t'other, or else the fammaly shan't have a farden of"—(*Mimicking*)—So absolute with her money! But, to say the truth, nothing but money *can* make us absolute, and so we must e'en make the best of her.

[SCENE II]

Scene changes to the garden

Enter LORD OGLEBY *and* CANTON

LORD OGLEBY. What! mademoiselle Fanny to be sent away! Why? Wherefore? What's the meaning of all this?

CANTON. *Je ne sais pas.*[1] I know noting of it.

LORD OGLEBY. It can't be; it shan't be. I protest against the measure. She's a fine girl, and I had much rather that the rest of the family were annihilated than that she should leave us. Her vulgar father, that's the very abstract of 'Change-Alley—the aunt, that's always endeavoring to be a fine lady— and the pert sister, forever showing that she is one—are horrid company indeed, and without her would be intolerable. Ah, *la petite Fanchon!*[2] She's the thing. Isn't she, Cant?

CANTON. Dere is very good sympatie *entre vous*[3] and dat young lady, mi lor.

LORD OGLEBY. I'll not be left among these Goths and Vandals, your Sterlings, your Heidelbergs, and Devilbergs. If she goes, I'll positively go too.

CANTON. In de same post-chay, mi lor? You have no object[4] to dat, I believe, nor mademoiselle neider too, ha, ha, ha!

LORD OGLEBY. Prithee hold thy foolish tongue, Cant! Does thy Swiss stupidity imagine that I can[5] see and talk with a fine girl without desires? My eyes are involuntarily attracted by beautiful objects; I fly as naturally to a fine girl—

CANTON. As de fine girl to you, mi lor. Ha, ha, ha! you alway fly togedre like un pair de pigeons.

LORD OGLEBY. Like un pair de pigeons— (*Mocks him*)—*Vous êtes un sot,*[6] Mons. Canton. Thou art always dreaming of my intrigues, and never seest me *badiner,*[7] but you suspect mischief, you old fool, you.

CANTON. I am fool, I confess, but not always fool in dat, mi lor. He, he, he!

LORD OGLEBY. He, he, he! Thou art incorrigible, but thy absurdities amuse one. Thou art like my rappee[8] here (*Takes out his box*), a most ridiculous superfluity, but a pinch of thee now and then is a most delicious treat.

CANTON. You do me great honeur, mi lor.

LORD OGLEBY. 'Tis fact, upon my soul. Thou art properly my cephalic snuff, and art no bad medicine against megrims, vertigoes, and profound thinking. Ha, ha, ha!

CANTON. Your flatterie, mi lor, vil make me too prode.

LORD OGLEBY. The girl has some little partiality for me, to be sure; but prithee, Cant, is not that Miss Fanny yonder?

CANTON. (*Looking with a glass*)[9] *En verité,* 'tis she, mi lor; 'tis one of de pigeons, de pigeons *d'amour.*

LORD OGLEBY. Don't be ridiculous, you old monkey. (*Smiling*)

CANTON. I am monkée, I am ole, but I have eye, I have ear, and a little understand, now and den.

LORD OGLEBY. *Taisez vous, bête!*[10]

CANTON. *Elle vous attend,*[11] mi lor. She vil make-a love to you.

LORD OGLEBY. Will she? Have at her then! A fine girl can't oblige me more. Egad, I find myself a little *enjoué!*[12] Come along, Cant! she is but in the next walk; but there is such a deal of this damned crinkum-crankum, as Sterling calls it, that one sees people for half an hour before one can get to them. *Allons, Mons. Canton, allons donc!*[13]

Exeunt, singing in French

[SCENE III]

Another part of the garden

LOVEWELL *and* FANNY

LOVEWELL. My dear Fanny, I cannot bear your distress! It overcomes all my resolutions, and I am prepared for the discovery.

---

[1] I do not know. [2] The little Fanny.
[3] Between you. [4] Objection.
[5] *Sic.*, though the meaning is obviously *cannot*.
[6] You are a fool. [7] Trifle, dally.
[8] Snuff. [9] An eye-glass.
[10] Hold your tongue, brute!
[11] She waits for you. [12] Lively.
[13] Come on. Mr. Canton. come on then.

FANNY. But how can it be effected before my departure?

LOVEWELL. I'll tell you. Lord Ogleby seems to entertain a visible partiality for you; and notwithstanding the peculiarities of his behavior, I am sure that he is humane at the bottom. He is vain to an excess; but withal extremely good-natured, and would do anything to recommend himself to a lady. Do you open the whole affair of our marriage to him immediately. It would come with more irresistible persuasion from you than from myself; and I doubt not but you'll gain his friendship and protection at once. His influence and authority will put an end to Sir John's solicitations, remove your aunt's and sister's unkindness and suspicions, and, I hope, reconcile your father and the whole family to our marriage.

FANNY. Heaven grant it! Where is my lord?

LOVEWELL. I have heard him and Canton since dinner singing French songs under the great walnut-tree by the parlor door. If you meet with him in the garden, you may disclose the whole immediately.

FANNY. Dreadful as the task is, I'll do it. Anything is better than this continual anxiety.

LOVEWELL. By that time the discovery is made, I will appear to second you. Ha! here comes my lord! Now, my dear Fanny, summon up all your spirits, plead our cause powerfully, and be sure of success. (*Going*)

FANNY. Ah, don't leave me!

LOVEWELL. Nay, you must let me.

FANNY. Well, since it must be so, I'll obey you, if I have the power. Oh, Lovewell!

LOVEWELL. Consider, our situation is very critical. To-morrow morning is fixed for your departure, and if we lose this opportunity we may wish in vain for another. He approaches. I must retire. Speak, my dear Fanny, speak, and make us happy!   *Exit*

FANNY. (*Alone*) Good heaven, what a situation am I in! What shall I do? What shall I say to him? I am all confusion.

Enter LORD OGLEBY *and* CANTON

LORD OGLEBY. To see so much beauty so solitary, madam, is a satire upon mankind, and 'tis fortunate that one man has broke in upon your reverie for the credit of our sex. I say one, madam, for poor Canton here, from age and infirmities, stands for nothing.

CANTON. Noting at all, inteed.

FANNY. Your lordship does me great honor. I had a favor to request, my lord!

LORD OGLEBY. A favor, madam! To be honored with your commands, is an inexpressible favor done to me, madam.

FANNY. If your lordship could indulge me with the honor of a moment's—(*Aside*) What is the matter with me?

LORD OGLEBY. (*To* CANTON) The girl's confused—He! Here's something in the wind, faith.—I'll have a tête-a-tête with her. *Allez vous en!* [1]

CANTON. I go. Ah, *pauvre mademoiselle!* [2] mi lor, have *pitié* upon the poor *pigeone!*

LORD OGLEBY. I'll knock you down, Cant, if you're impertinent.   (*Smiling*)

CANTON. Den I must avay—(*Shuffles along*) You are mosh please, for all dat.
                        (*Aside, and exit*)

FANNY. (*Aside*) I shall sink with apprehension.

LORD OGLEBY. What a sweet girl! She's a civilized being, and atones for the barbarism of the rest of the family.

FANNY. My lord! I—
                (*She curtsies, and blushes*)

LORD OGLEBY. (*Addressing her*) I look upon it, madam, to be one of the luckiest circumstances of my life, that I have this moment the honor of receiving your commands, and the satisfaction of confirming with my tongue, what my eyes perhaps have but too weakly expressed—that I am, literally—the humblest of your servants.

FANNY. I think myself greatly honored by your lordship's partiality to me; but it distresses me, that I am obliged in my present situation to apply to it for protection.

LORD OGLEBY. I am happy in your distress, madam, because it gives me an opportunity to show my zeal. Beauty to me is a religion, in which I was born and bred a bigot, and would die a martyr.—(*Aside*) I'm in tolerable spirits, faith!

FANNY. There is not perhaps at this moment a more distressed creature than myself. Affection, duty, hope, despair, and a thousand different sentiments, are struggling in my bosom; and even the presence of your lordship, to whom I have flown for protection, adds to my perplexity.

[1] You go in.
[2] Poor girl.

Lord Ogleby. Does it, madam? Venus forbid! (*Aside and smiling*) My old fault; the devil's in me, I think, for perplexing young women.—Take courage, madam! Dear Miss Fanny, explain. You have a powerful advocate in my breast, I assure you—my heart, madam. I am attached to you by all the laws of sympathy, and delicacy. By my honor, I am.

Fanny. Then I will venture to unburden my mind. Sir John Melvil, my lord, by the most misplaced, and mistimed declaration of affection for me, has made me the unhappiest of women.

Lord Ogleby. How, madam! Has Sir John made his addresses to you?

Fanny. He has, my lord, in the strongest terms. But I hope it is needless to say, that my duty to my father, love to my sister, and regard to the whole family, as well as the great respect I entertain for your lordship, (*Curtsying*) made me shudder at his addresses.

Lord Ogleby. Charming girl!—Proceed, my dear Miss Fanny, proceed!

Fanny. In a moment—give me leave, my lord! But if what I have to disclose should be received with anger or displeasure—

Lord Ogleby. Impossible, by all the tender powers! Speak, I beseech you, or I shall divine the cause before you utter it.

Fanny. Then, my lord, Sir John's addresses are not only shocking to me in themselves, but are more particularly disagreeable to me at this time—as—as— (*Hesitating*)

Lord Ogleby. As what, madam?

Fanny. As—pardon my confusion—I am entirely devoted to another.

Lord Ogleby. (*Aside*) If this is not plain, the devil's in it.—But tell me, my dear Miss Fanny, for I must know, tell me the how, the when, and where—Tell me—

Enter Canton *hastily*

Canton. Mi lor, mi lor, mi lor!

Lord Ogleby. Damn your Swiss impertinence! How durst you interrupt me in the most critical melting moment that ever love and beauty honored me with?

Canton. I demande *pardonne*, mi lor! Sir John Melvil, mi lor, sent me to beg you do him de honeur to speak a little to your lordship.

Lord Ogleby. I'm not at leisure.—I'm busy.—Get away, you stupid old dog, you Swiss rascal, or I'll—

Canton. *Fort bien*,[1] mi lor.

Canton *goes out on tiptoe*

Lord Ogleby. By the laws of gallantry, madam, this interruption should be death; but as no punishment ought to disturb the triumph of the softer passions, the criminal is pardoned and dismissed. Let us return, madam, to the highest luxury of exalted minds—a declaration of love from the lips of beauty!

Fanny. [*Aside*] The entrance of a third person has a little relieved me, but I cannot go through with it—and yet I must open my heart with a discovery, or it will break with its burthen.

Lord Ogleby. (*Aside*) What passion in her eyes! I am alarmed to agitation.—I presume, madam (and as you have flattered me, by making me a party concerned, I hope you'll excuse the presumption) that—

Fanny. Do you excuse my making you a party concerned, my lord! and let me interest your heart in my behalf, as my future happiness or misery in a great measure depend—

Lord Ogleby. Upon me, madam?

Fanny. Upon you, my lord. (*Sighs*)

Lord Ogleby. There's no standing this. I have caught the infection; her tenderness dissolves me. (*Sighs*)

Fanny. And should you too severely judge of a rash action, which passion prompted, and modesty has long concealed—

Lord Ogleby. (*Taking her hand*) Thou amiable creature, command my heart, for it is vanquished! Speak but thy virtuous wishes, and enjoy them!

Fanny. I cannot, my lord,—indeed, I cannot. Mr. Lovewell must tell you my distresses; and when you know them, pity and protect me! *Exit in tears*

Lord Ogleby alone

[Lord Ogleby.] How the devil could I bring her to this? It is too much—too much—I can't bear it—I must give way to this amiable weakness—(*Wipes his eyes*) My heart overflows with sympathy, and I feel every tenderness I have inspired—(*Stifles the tear*) How blind have I been to the desolation I have made! How could I possibly imagine, that a little partial attention and tender civil-

[1] Very well.

ities to this young creature should have gathered to this burst of passion! Can I be a man, and withstand it? No—I'll sacrifice the whole sex to her.—But here comes the father, quite *àpropos*. I'll open the matter immediately, settle the business with him and take the sweet girl down to Ogleby House to-morrow morning. But, what the devil! Miss Sterling too! What mischief's in the wind now?

Enter STERLING *and* MISS STERLING

STERLING. My lord, your servant! I am attending my daughter here, upon rather a disagreeable affair. Speak to his lordship, Betsey!

LORD OGLEBY. Your eyes, Miss Sterling— for I always read the eyes of a young lady— betray some little emotion. What are your commands, madam?

MISS STERLING. I have but too much cause for my emotion, my lord!

LORD OGLEBY. I cannot commend my kinsman's behavior, madam; he has behaved like a false knight, I must confess. I have heard of his apostasy; Miss Fanny has informed me of it.

MISS STERLING. Miss Fanny's baseness has been the cause of Sir John's inconstancy.

LORD OGLEBY. Nay, now, my dear Miss Sterling, your passion transports you too far. Sir John may have entertained a passion for Miss Fanny; but, believe me, my dear Miss Sterling, believe me, Miss Fanny has no passion for Sir John. She has a passion, indeed, a most tender passion! She has opened her whole soul to me, and I know where her affections are placed. *(Conceitedly)*

MISS STERLING. Not upon Mr. Lovewell, my lord; for I have great reason to think that her seeming attachment to him, is, by his consent, made use of as a blind to cover her designs upon Sir John.

LORD OGLEBY. Lovewell! No, poor lad! She does not think of him. *(Smiling)*

MISS STERLING. Have a care, my lord, that both the families are not made the dupes of Sir John's artifice, and my sister's dissimulation! You don't know her—indeed, my lord, you don't know her—a base, insinuating, perfidious—It is too much! She has been beforehand with me, I perceive. Such unnatural behavior to me! But, since I see I can have no redress, I am resolved that some way or other I will have revenge. *Exit*

Manent LORD OGLEBY *and* STERLING

STERLING. This is foolish work, my lord!

LORD OGLEBY. I have too much sensibility to bear the tears of beauty.

STERLING. It is touching indeed, my lord; and very moving for a father.

LORD OGLEBY. To be sure, sir! You must be distressed beyond measure! Wherefore, to divert your too exquisite feelings, suppose we change the subject, and proceed to business.

STERLING. With all my heart, my lord!

LORD OGLEBY. You see, Mr. Sterling, we can make no union in our families, by the proposed marriage.

STERLING. And very sorry I am to see it, my lord.

LORD OGLEBY. Have you set your heart upon being allied to our house, Mr. Sterling?

STERLING. 'Tis my only wish, at present, my *omnium*, as I may call it.

LORD OGLEBY. Your wishes shall be fulfilled.

STERLING. Shall they, my lord? But how— how?

LORD OGLEBY. I'll marry in your family.

STERLING. What! My sister Heidelberg?

LORD OGLEBY. You throw me into a cold sweat, Mr. Sterling. No, not your sister; but your daughter.

STERLING. My daughter!

LORD OGLEBY. Fanny! Now the murder's out!

STERLING. What, *you*, my lord!

LORD OGLEBY. Yes—I, I, Mr. Sterling!

STERLING. No, no, my lord—That's too much. *(Smiling)*

LORD OGLEBY. Too much? I do not comprehend you.

STERLING. What, you, my lord, marry my Fanny?—Bless me, what will the folks say?

LORD OGLEBY. Why, what will they say?

STERLING. That, you're a bold man, my lord—that's all.

LORD OGLEBY. Mr. Sterling, this may be city wit, for aught I know—Do you court my alliance?

STERLING. To be sure, my lord.

LORD OGLEBY. Then I'll explain. My nephew won't marry your eldest daughter— nor I neither. Your youngest daughter won't marry him. I will marry your youngest daughter—

STERLING. What! with a youngest daughter's fortune, my lord?

LORD OGLEBY. With any fortune, or no fortune at all, sir. Love is the idol of my heart, and the demon Interest sinks before him. So, sir, as I said before, I will marry your youngest daughter; your youngest daughter will marry me—

STERLING. Who told you so, my lord?

LORD OGLEBY. Her own sweet self, sir.

STERLING. Indeed?

LORD OGLEBY. Yes, sir; our affection is mutual; your advantage double and treble—your daughter will be a countess directly—I shall be the happiest of beings—and you'll be father to an earl instead of a baronet.

STERLING. But what will my sister say,—and my daughter?

LORD OGLEBY. I'll manage that matter. Nay, if they won't consent, I'll run away with your daughter, in spite of you.

STERLING. Well said, my lord! Your spirit's good! I wish you had my constitution! But, if you'll venture, I have no objection, if my sister has none.

LORD OGLEBY. I'll answer for your sister, sir. *Apropos!* the lawyers are in the house. I'll have articles drawn, and the whole affair concluded to-morrow morning.

STERLING. Very well; and I'll dispatch Lovewell to London immediately for some fresh papers I shall want; and I shall leave you to manage matters with my sister. You must excuse me, my lord, but I can't help laughing at the match! He, he, he! What will folks say? *Exit*

LORD OGLEBY. What a fellow am I going to make a father of? He has no more feeling than the post in his warehouse. But Fanny's virtues tune me to rapture again, and I won't think of the rest of the family.

Enter LOVEWELL *hastily*

LOVEWELL. I beg your lordship's pardon, my lord! Are you alone, my lord?

LORD OGLEBY. No, my lord, I am not alone! I am in company, the best company!

LOVEWELL. My lord!

LORD OGLEBY. I never was in such exquisite enchanting company since my heart first conceived, or my senses tasted pleasure.

LOVEWELL. Where are they, my lord?
(*Looking about*)

LORD OGLEBY. In my mind, sir.

LOVEWELL. What company have you there, my lord? (*Smiling*)

LORD OGLEBY. My own ideas, sir, which so crowd upon my imagination and kindle it to such a delirium of ecstasy, that wit, wine, music, poetry, all combined, and each perfection, are but mere mortal shadows of my felicity.

LOVEWELL. I see that your lordship is happy, and I rejoice at it.

LORD OGLEBY. You *shall* rejoice at it, sir; my felicity shall not selfishly be confined, but shall spread its influence to the whole circle of my friends. I need not say, Lovewell, that you shall have your share of it.

LOVEWELL. Shall I, my lord?—Then I understand you—you have heard—Miss Fanny has informed you—

LORD OGLEBY. She has—I have heard, and she shall be happy—'Tis determined.

LOVEWELL. Then I have reached the summit of my wishes.—And will your lordship pardon the folly?

LORD OGLEBY. O yes, poor creature, how could she help it?—'Twas unavoidable—Fate and necessity.

LOVEWELL. It was indeed, my lord! Your kindness distracts me!

LORD OGLEBY. And so it did the poor girl, faith.

LOVEWELL. She trembled to disclose the secret, and declare her affections?

LORD OGLEBY. The world, I believe, will not think her affections ill placed.

LOVEWELL. (*Bowing*) You are too good, my lord! And do you really excuse the rashness of the action?

LORD OGLEBY. From my very soul, Lovewell.

LOVEWELL. Your generosity overpowers me. (*Bowing*) I was afraid of her meeting with a cold reception.

LORD OGLEBY. More fool you then! "Who pleads her cause with never failing beauty,
Here finds a full redress."
(*Strikes his breast*) She's a fine girl, Lovewell.

LOVEWELL. Her beauty, my lord, is her least merit. She has an understanding—

LORD OGLEBY. Her choice convinces me of that.

LOVEWELL. (*Bowing*) That's your lordship's goodness. Her choice was a disinterested one.

LORD OGLEBY. No—no—not altogether. It began with interest, and ended in passion.

LOVEWELL. Indeed, my lord, if you were

acquainted with her goodness of heart, and generosity of mind, as well as you are with the inferior beauties of her face and person—

Lord Ogleby. I am so perfectly convinced of their existence, and so totally of your mind touching every amiable particular of that sweet girl, that were it not for the cold unfeeling impediments of the law, I would marry her to-morrow morning.

Lovewell. My lord!

Lord Ogleby. I would, by all that's honorable in man, and amiable in woman!

Lovewell. Marry her! Who do you mean, my lord?

Lord Ogleby. Miss Fanny Sterling, that is—the Countess of Ogleby, that shall be.

Lovewell. I am astonished.

Lord Ogleby. Why, could you expect less from me?

Lovewell. I did not expect this, my lord.

Lord Ogleby. Trade and accounts have destroyed your feeling.

Lovewell. No, indeed, my lord. (*Sighs*)

Lord Ogleby. The moment that love and pity entered my breast, I was resolved to plunge into matrimony, and shorten the girl's tortures. I never do anything by halves; do I, Lovewell?

Lovewell. No, indeed, my lord! (*Sighs*) What an accident!

Lord Ogleby. What's the matter, Lovewell? Thou seem'st to have lost thy faculties. Why don't you wish me joy, man?

Lovewell. O, I do, my lord. (*Sighs*)

Lord Ogleby. She said that you would explain what she had not power to utter. But I wanted no interpreter for the language of love.

Lovewell. But has your lordship considered the consequences of your resolution?

Lord Ogleby. No, sir; I am above consideration, when my desires are kindled.

Lovewell. But consider the consequences, my lord, to your nephew Sir John.

Lord Ogleby. Sir John has considered no consequences himself, Mr. Lovewell.

Lovewell. Mr. Sterling, my lord, will certainly refuse his daughter to Sir John.

Lord Ogleby. Sir John has already refused Mr. Sterling's daughter.

Lovewell. But what will become of Miss Sterling, my lord?

Lord Ogleby. What's that to you? You may have her, if you will. I depend upon Mr. Sterling's city-philosophy, to be reconciled to Lord Ogleby's being his son-in-law, instead of Sir John Melvil, Baronet. Don't you think that your master may be brought to that, without having recourse to his calculations? Eh, Lovewell?

Lovewell. But, my lord, that is not the question.

Lord Ogleby. Whatever is the question, I'll tell you my answer. I am in love with a fine girl, whom I resolve to marry. (*Enter* Sir John Melvil) What news with you, Sir John? You look all hurry and impatience, like a messenger after a battle!

Sir John. After a battle, indeed, my lord. I have this day had a severe engagement, and, wanting your lordship as an auxiliary, I have at last mustered up resolution to declare, what my duty to you and to myself have demanded from me some time.

Lord Ogleby. To the business then, and be as concise as possible; for I am upon the wing. Eh, Lovewell?

(*He smiles, and* Lovewell *bows*)

Sir John. I find 'tis in vain, my lord, to struggle against the force of inclination.

Lord Ogleby. Very true, nephew; I am your witness, and will second the motion. Shan't I, Lovewell?

(*Smiles, and* Lovewell *bows*)

Sir John. Your lordship's generosity encourages me to tell you, that I cannot marry Miss Sterling.

Lord Ogleby. I am not at all surprised at it; she's a bitter potion, that's the truth of it; but as you were to swallow it, and not I, it was your business, and not mine. Anything more?

Sir John. But this, my lord; that I may be permitted to make my addresses to the other sister.

Lord Ogleby. O, yes, by all means. Have you any hopes there, nephew? Do you think he'll succeed, Lovewell?

(*Smiles, and winks at* Lovewell)

Lovewell. I think not, my lord. (*Gravely*)

Lord Ogleby. [*Aside*] I think so too, but let the fool try.

Sir John. Will your lordship favor me with your good offices to remove the chief obstacle to the match, the repugnance of Mrs. Heidelberg?

Lord Ogleby. Mrs. Heidelberg! Had not you better begin with the young lady first?

It will save you a great deal of trouble; won't it, Lovewell? (*Smiles*) But, do what you please; it will be the same thing to me, won't it, Lovewell? (*Conceitedly*) Why don't you laugh at him?

LOVEWELL. I do, my lord. (*Forces a smile*)

SIR JOHN. And your lordship will endeavor to prevail on Mrs. Heidelberg to consent to my marriage with Miss Fanny?

LORD OGLEBY. I'll speak to Mrs. Heidelberg about the adorable Fanny, as soon as possible.

SIR JOHN. Your generosity transports me.

LORD OGLEBY. (*Aside*) Poor fellow, what a dupe! He little thinks who's in possession of the town.

SIR JOHN. And your lordship is not offended at this seeming inconstancy?

LORD OGLEBY. Not in the least. Miss Fanny's charms will even excuse infidelity! I look upon women as the *feræ naturæ*[1]—lawful game—and every man who is qualified, has a natural right to pursue them; Lovewell as well as you, and I as well as either of you. Every man shall do his best, without offence to any. What say you, kinsmen?

SIR JOHN. You have made me happy, my lord.

LOVEWELL. And me, I assure you, my lord.

LORD OGLEBY. And I am superlatively so. *Allons donc!* to horse and away, boys! You to your affairs, and I to mine! (*Sings*) *Suivons l'amour!*[2]   *Exeunt severally*

ACT V

[SCENE I.] FANNY'S *apartment*

Enter LOVEWELL *and* FANNY, *followed by* BETTY

FANNY. Why did you come so soon, Mr. Lovewell? The family is not yet in bed; and Betty certainly heard somebody listening near the chamber door.

BETTY. My mistress is right, sir! Evil spirits are abroad; and I am sure you are both too good, not to expect mischief from them.

LOVEWELL. But who can be so curious, or so wicked?

BETTY. I think we have wickedness and curiosity enough in this family, sir, to expect the worst.

FANNY. I do expect the worst. Prithee, Betty, return to the outward door, and listen if you hear anybody in the gallery; and let us know directly.

BETTY. I warrant you, madam. The Lord bless you both!   *Exit*

FANNY. What did my father want with you this evening?

LOVEWELL. He gave me the key of his closet, with orders to bring from London some papers relating to Lord Ogleby.

FANNY. And why did you not obey him?

LOVEWELL. Because I am certain that his lordship has opened his heart to him about you, and those papers are wanted merely on that account. But as we shall discover all to-morrow, there will be no occasion for them, and it would be idle in me to go.

FANNY. Hark! hark! Bless me, how I tremble! I feel the terrors of guilt. Indeed, Mr. Lovewell, this is too much for me.

LOVEWELL. And for me too, my sweet Fanny. Your apprehensions make a coward of me. But what can alarm you? Your aunt and sister are in their chambers, and you have nothing to fear from the rest of the family.

FANNY. I fear everybody, and everything, and every moment! My mind is in continual agitation and dread! Indeed, Mr. Lovewell, this situation may have very unhappy consequences.   (*Weeps*)

LOVEWELL. But it shan't. I would rather tell our story this moment to all the house, and run the risk of maintaining you by the hardest labor, than suffer you to remain in this dangerous perplexity. What! shall I sacrifice all my best hopes and affections, in your dear health and safety, for the mean, and in such a case, the meanest consideration—of our fortune! Were we to be abandoned by all our relations, we have that in our hearts and minds, will weigh against the most affluent circumstances. I should not have proposed the secrecy of our marriage, but for your sake; and with hopes that the most generous sacrifice you have made to love and me, might be less injurious to you, by waiting a lucky moment of reconciliation.

FANNY. Hush! hush! for heaven sake, my dear Lovewell, don't be so warm! Your gen-

---

[1] Wild animals.

[2] Let's follow love! The opening words of a song.

erosity gets the better of your prudence; you will be heard, and we shall be discovered. I am satisfied; indeed I am! Excuse this weakness, this delicacy—this what you will. My mind's at peace,—indeed, it is! Think no more of it, if you love me!

LOVEWELL. That one word has charmed me, as it always does, to the most implicit obedience; it would be the worst of ingratitude in me to distress you a moment. (*Kisses her*)

Re-enter BETTY

BETTY. (*In a low voice*) I'm sorry to disturb you.

FANNY. Ha! what's the matter?

LOVEWELL. Have you heard anybody?

BETTY. Yes, yes, I have; and they have heard *you* too, or I am mistaken.—If they had *seen* you too, we should have been in a fine quandary.

FANNY. Prithee, don't prate now, Betty!

LOVEWELL. What did you hear?

BETTY. I was preparing myself, as usual, to take me a little nap—

LOVEWELL. A nap!

BETTY. Yes, sir, a nap; for I watch much better so than wide awake; and when I had wrapped this handkerchief round my head, for fear of the earache from the keyhole. I thought I heard a kind of a sort of a buzzing, which I first took for a gnat, and shook my head two or three times, and went so with my hand—

FANNY. Well, well—and so—

BETTY. And so, madam, when I heard Mr. Lovewell a little loud, I heard the buzzing louder too; and pulling off my handkerchief softly, I could hear this sort of noise—

(*Makes an indistinct noise like speaking*)

FANNY. Well, and what did they say?

BETTY. Oh! I could not understand a word of what was said.

LOVEWELL. The outward door is locked?

BETTY. Yes; and I bolted it too, for fear of the worst.

FANNY. Why did you? They must have heard you if they were near.

BETTY. And I did it on purpose, madam, and coughed a little too, that they might not hear Mr. Lovewell's voice. When I was silent, they were silent, and so I came to tell you.

FANNY. What shall we do?

LOVEWELL. Fear nothing; we know the worst; it will only bring on our catastrophe a little too soon. But Betty might fancy this noise; she's in the conspiracy, and can make a man of a mouse at any time.

BETTY. I can distinguish a man from a mouse, as well as my betters! I'm sorry you think so ill of me, sir.

FANNY. He compliments you; don't be a fool! Now you have set her tongue a-running, she'll mutter for an hour. (*To* LOVEWELL) I'll go and harken myself. *Exit*

BETTY. (*Half aside, and muttering*) I'll turn my back upon no girl, for sincerity and service.

LOVEWELL. Thou art the first in the world for both; and I will reward you soon, Betty, for one and the other.

BETTY. I'm not marcenary neither—I can live on a little, with a good carreter.

Re-enter FANNY

FANNY. All seems quiet. Suppose, my dear, you go to your own room. I shall be much easier then, and to-morrow we will be prepared for the discovery.

BETTY. (*Half aside, and muttering*) You may discover, if you please; but for my part, I shall still be secret.

LOVEWELL. Should I leave you now, if they still are upon the watch, we shall lose the advantage of our delay. Besides, we should consult upon to-morrow's business. Let Betty go to her own room, and lock the outward door after her; we can fasten this; and when she thinks all safe, she may return and let me out as usual.

BETTY. Shall I, madam?

FANNY. Do let me have my way to-night, and you shall command me ever after. I would not have you surprised here for the world! Pray leave me! I shall be quite myself again, if you will oblige me.

LOVEWELL. I live only to oblige you, my sweet Fanny! I'll be gone this moment.
(*Going*)

FANNY. Let us listen first at the door, that you may not be intercepted. Betty shall go first, and if they lay hold of her—

BETTY. They'll have the wrong sow by the ear, I can tell them that. (*Going hastily*)

FANNY. Softly, softly, Betty! Don't venture out, if you hear a noise. Softly, I beg of you! See, Mr. Lovewell, the effects of indiscretion!

LOVEWELL. But love, Fanny, makes amends for all! *Exeunt all, softly*

[SCENE II]

Scene changes to a gallery, which leads to several bed-chambers

Enter MISS STERLING, *leading* MRS. HEIDELBERG *in a night-cap*

MISS STERLING. This way, dear madam, and then I'll tell you all.

MRS. HEIDELBERG. Nay, but niece—consider a little—don't drag me out in this figur—let me put on my fly-cap![1] If any of my lord's fammaly, or the counsellors at law, should be stirring, I should be perdigus disconcarted.

MISS STERLING. But, my dear madam, a moment is an age, in my situation. I am sure my sister has been plotting my disgrace and ruin in that chamber. Oh, she's all craft and wickedness.

MRS. HEIDELBERG. Well, but softly, Betsey!—You are all in emotion,—your mind is too much flustrated,—you can neither eat nor drink, nor take your natural rest.—Compose yourself, child; for if we are not as warysome as they are wicked, we shall disgrace ourselves and the whole fammaly.

MISS STERLING. We are disgraced already, madam. Sir John Melvil has forsaken me; my lord cares for nobody but himself; or if for anybody, it is my sister; my father, for the sake of a better bargain, would marry me to a 'Change-broker; so that if you, madam, don't continue my friend—if you forsake me—if I am to lose my best hopes and consolation—in your tenderness—and affections—I had better—at once—give up the matter—and let my sister enjoy—the fruits of her treachery—trample with scorn upon the rights of her elder sister, the will of the best of aunts, and the weakness of a too-interested father.

(*She pretends to be bursting into tears all this speech*)

MRS. HEIDELBERG. Don't, Betsey—keep up your spurrit.—I hate whimpering.—I am your friend—depend upon me in every partickler—but be composed, and tell me what new mischief you have discovered.

MISS STERLING. I had no desire to sleep, and would not undress myself, knowing that my Machiavel[ian] sister would not rest till she had broke my heart: I was so uneasy that I could not stay in my room; but when I thought all the house was quiet, I sent my maid to discover what was going forward, she immediately came back and told me, that they were in high consultation; that she had heard only, for it was in the dark, my sister's maid conduct Sir John Melvil to her mistress, and then lock the door.

MRS. HEIDELBERG. And how did you conduct yourself in this dalimma?

MISS STERLING. I returned with her, and could hear a man's voice, though nothing that they said distinctly; and you may depend upon it, that Sir John is now in that room, that they have settled the matter, and will run away together before morning, if we don't prevent them.

MRS. HEIDELBERG. Why, the brazen slut! Has she got her sister's husband (that is to be) locked up in her chamber! At night too!—I tremble at the thoughts!

MISS STERLING. Hush, madam! I hear something.

MRS. HEIDELBERG. You frighten me—let me put on my fly-cap.—I would not be seen in this figur for the world!

MISS STERLING. 'Tis dark, madam; you can't be seen.

MRS. HEIDELBERG. I pertest there's a candle coming, and a man too!

MISS STERLING. Nothing but servants. Let us retire a moment! (*They retire*)

Enter BRUSH, *half-drunk, laying hold of the* Chambermaid, *who has a candle in her hand*

CHAMBERMAID. Be quiet, Mr. Brush! I shall drop down with terror!

BRUSH. But, my sweet, and most amiable chambermaid, if you have no love, you may hearken to a little reason; that cannot possibly do your virtue any harm.

CHAMBERMAID. But you will do me harm, Mr. Brush, and a great deal of harm too.—Pray, let me go.—I am ruined if they hear you.—I tremble like an asp.[2]

BRUSH. But they sha'n't hear us—and if you have a mind to be ruined, it shall be the making of your fortune, you little slut, you!—Therefore, I say it again, if you have no love, hear a little reason!

CHAMBERMAID. I wonder at your impurence, Mr. Brush, to use me in this manner, this is not the way to keep me company, I assure you. You are a town rake, I see; and now you are a little in liquor, you fear nothing.

---

[1] A headdress, apparently with strings or side pieces hanging down, popular in the 1760's and '70's.

[2] Aspen.

BRUSH. Nothing, by heavens, but your frowns, most amiable chambermaid. I am a little electrified, that's the truth on't; I am not used to drink port, and your master's is so heady, that a pint of it oversets a claret-drinker.

CHAMBERMAID. Don't be rude! Bless me, I shall be ruined! What will become of me?

BRUSH. I'll take care of you, by all that's honorable.

CHAMBERMAID. You are a base man, to use me so! I'll cry out, if you don't let me go. That is Miss Sterling's chamber, that Miss Fanny's, and that Madam Heidelberg's.
(*Pointing*)

BRUSH. And that my Lord Ogleby's, and that my lady What-d'ye-callem's. I don't mind such folks when I'm sober, much less when I am whimsical—rather above that too.

CHAMBERMAID. More shame for you, Mr. Brush! You terrify me! You have no modesty.

BRUSH. O, but I have, my sweet spider-brusher! For instance, I reverence Miss Fanny; she's a most delicious morsel, and fit for a prince. With all my horrors of matrimony, I could marry her myself; but, for her sister—

MISS STERLING. There, there, madam; all in a story!

CHAMBERMAID. Bless me, Mr. Brush! I heard something!

BRUSH. Rats, I suppose, that are gnawing the old timbers of this execrable old dungeon. If it were mine, I would pull it down, and fill your fine canal up with the rubbish; and then I should get rid of two damned things at once.

CHAMBERMAID. Law! law! how you blaspheme! We shall have the house upon our head for it.

BRUSH. No, no, it will last our time. But, as I was saying, the elder sister—Miss Jezebel—

CHAMBERMAID. —is a fine young lady, for all your evil tongue.

BRUSH. No; we have smoked her already; and unless she marries our old Swiss, she can have none of us.—No, no, she won't do.—We are a little too nice.

CHAMBERMAID. You're a monstrous rake, Mr. Brush, and don't care what you say.

BRUSH. Why, for that matter, my dear, I am a little inclined to mischief; and if you won't have pity upon me, I will break open that door and ravish Mrs. Heidelberg.

MRS. HEIDELBERG. (*Coming forward*) There's no bearing this.—You profligate monster!

CHAMBERMAID. Ha! I am undone!

BRUSH. Zounds! Here she is, by all that's monstrous. (*Runs off*)

MISS STERLING. A fine discourse you have had with that fellow!

MRS. HEIDELBERG. And a fine time of night it is to be here with that drunken monster!

MISS STERLING. What have you to say for yourself?

CHAMBERMAID. I can say nothing—I am so frightened, and so ashamed—but indeed I am vartuous—I am vartuous indeed.

MRS. HEIDELBERG. Well, well—don't tremble so; but tell us what you know of this horrable plot here.

MISS STERLING. We'll forgive you, if you'll discover all.

CHAMBERMAID. Why, madam, don't let me betray my fellow-servants! I shan't sleep in my bed, if I do.

MRS. HEIDELBERG. Then you shall sleep somewhere else to-morrow night.

CHAMBERMAID. O dear! what shall I do?

MRS. HEIDELBERG. Tell us this moment, or I'll turn you out of doors directly.

CHAMBERMAID. Why, our butler has been treating us below in his pantry. Mr. Brush forced us to make a kind of holiday night of it.

MISS STERLING. Holiday! for what?

CHAMBERMAID. Nay, I only made one.

MISS STERLING. Well, well; but upon what account?

CHAMBERMAID. Because, as how, madam, there was a change in the family, they said; that his honor, Sir John, was to marry Miss Fanny instead of your ladyship.

MISS STERLING. And so you made a holiday for that—very fine!

CHAMBERMAID. I did not make it, ma'am.

MRS. HEIDELBERG. But do you know nothing of Sir John's being to run away with Miss Fanny to-night?

CHAMBERMAID. No, indeed, ma'am!

MISS STERLING. Nor of his being now locked up in my sister's chamber?

CHAMBERMAID. No, as I hope for marcy, ma'am.

MRS. HEIDELBERG. Well, I'll put an end to all this directly. Do you run to my brother Sterling—

CHAMBERMAID. Now, ma'am! 'Tis so very late, ma'am—

MRS. HEIDELBERG. I don't care how late it is. Tell him there are thieves in the house—that the house is o'fire—tell him to come here immediately—go, I say!

CHAMBERMAID. I will, I will; though I'm frightened out of my wits. *Exit*

MRS. HEIDELBERG. Do you watch here, my dear; and I'll put myself in order to face them. We'll plot 'em, and counter-plot 'em too. *Exit into her chamber*

MISS STERLING. I have as much pleasure in this revenge, as in being made a countess! Ha! they are unlocking the door. Now for it!
(*Retires*)

FANNY'S *door is unlocked, and* BETTY *comes out with a candle.* MISS STERLING *approaches her*

BETTY. (*Calling within*) Sir, sir!—now's your time! All's clear. (*Seeing* MISS STERLING) Stay, stay! not yet! We are watched!

MISS STERLING. And so you are, Madam Betty. (MISS STERLING *lays hold of her, while* BETTY *locks the door, and puts the key into her pocket*)

BETTY. (*Turning round*) What's the matter, madam?

MISS STERLING. Nay, that you shall tell my father and aunt, madam.

BETTY. I am no tell-tale, madam, and no thief; they'll get nothing from me.

MISS STERLING. You have a great deal of courage, Betty; and, considering the secrets you have to keep, you have occasion for it.

BETTY. My mistress shall never repent her good opinion of me, ma'am.

Enter STERLING

STERLING. What is all this? What's the matter? Why am I disturbed in this manner?

MISS STERLING. This creature, and my distresses, sir, will explain the matter.

Re-enter MRS. HEIDELBERG *with another head-dress*

MRS. HEIDELBERG. Now I'm prepared for the rancounter! Well, brother, have you heard of this scene of wickedness?

STERLING. Not I—but what is it? speak!—I was got into my little closet—all the lawyers were in bed, and I had almost lost my senses in the confusion of Lord Ogleby's mortgages, when I was alarmed with a foolish girl, who could hardly speak; and whether it's fire or thieves, or murder, or a rape, I am quite in the dark.

MRS. HEIDELBERG. No, no, there's no rape, brother! All parties are willing, I believe.

MISS STERLING. Who's in that chamber? (*Detaining* BETTY, *who seemed to be stealing away*)

BETTY. My mistress.

MISS STERLING. And who is with your mistress?

BETTY. Why, who should there be?

MISS STERLING. Open the door then and let us see!

BETTY. The door is open, madam. (MISS STERLING *goes to the door*) I'll sooner die than peach! *Exit hastily*

MISS STERLING. The door's locked; and she has got the key in her pocket.

MRS. HEIDELBERG. There's impudence, brother! piping hot from your daughter Fanny's school!

STERLING. But, zounds! what is all this about? You tell me of a sum-total, and you don't produce the particulars.

MRS. HEIDELBERG. Sir John Melvil is locked up in your daughter's bed-chamber. There is the particular!

STERLING. The devil he is! That's bad!

MISS STERLING. And he has been there some time too.

STERLING. Ditto.

MRS. HEIDELBERG. Ditto! worse and worse, I say. I'll raise the house, and expose him to my lord and the whole fammaly!

STERLING. By no means! We shall expose ourselves, sister! The best way is to insure privately. Let me alone! I'll make him marry her to-morrow morning.

MISS STERLING. Make him marry her! This is beyond all patience! You have thrown away all your affection, and I shall do as much by my obedience. Unnatural fathers make unnatural children. My revenge is in my own power, and I'll indulge it. Had they made their escape, I should have been exposed to the derision of the world; but the deriders shall be derided; and so—Help! Help, there! Thieves! Thieves!

MRS. HEIDELBERG. Tit-for-tat, Betsey! You are right, my girl!

STERLING. Zounds! You'll spoil all! You'll raise the whole family. The devil's in the girl!

MRS. HEIDELBERG. No, no; the devil's in *you*, brother. I am ashamed of your principles. What! would you connive at your daughter's being locked up with her sister's husband? Help! thieves! thieves! I say. (*Cries out*)

STERLING. Sister, I beg you!—Daughter, I command you!—If you have no regard for me, consider yourselves!—We shall lose this opportunity of ennobling our blood, and getting above twenty per cent. for our money.

MISS STERLING. What, by my disgrace and my sister's triumph! I have a spirit above such mean considerations; and, to show you that it is not a low-bred, vulgar, 'Changealley spirit—Help! Help! Thieves! Thieves! Thieves! I say.

STERLING. Ay, ay, you may save your lungs! The house is in an uproar!—Women at best have no discretion; but, in a passion, they'll fire a house, or burn themselves in it, rather than not be revenged.

Enter CANTON, *in a night-gown and slippers*

CANTON. Eh, diable! vat is de raison of dis great noise, dis *tintamarre?*

STERLING. Ask those ladies, sir; 'tis of their making.

LORD OGLEBY (*Calls within*) Brush! Brush! Canton! where are you? What's the matter? (*Rings a bell*) Where are you?

STERLING. 'Tis my lord calls, Mr. Canton.

CANTON. I come, mi lor! *Exit*

(LORD OGLEBY *still rings*)

SERJEANT FLOWER (*Calls within*) A light! A light here!—Where are the servants? Bring a light for me and my brothers.

STERLING. Lights here! Lights for the gentlemen! *Exit*

MRS. HEIDELBERG. My brother feels, I see—Your sister's turn will come next.

MISS STERLING. Ay, ay, let it go round, madam; it is the only comfort I have left.

Re-enter STERLING, *with lights, before* SERJEANT FLOWER (*with one boot and a slipper*) *and* TRAVERSE

STERLING. This way, sir! This way, gentlemen!

FLOWER. Well, but, Mr. Sterling, no danger, I hope. Have they made a burglarious entry? Are you prepared to repulse them? I am very much alarmed about thieves at circuit-time. They would be particularly severe with us gentlemen of the bar.

TRAVERSE. No danger, Mr. Sterling; no trespass, I hope?

STERLING. None, gentlemen, but of those ladies' making.

MRS. HEIDELBERG. You'll be ashamed to know, gentlemen, that all your labors and studies about this young lady are thrown away. Sir John Melvil is at this moment locked up with this lady's younger sister.

FLOWER. The thing is a little extraordinary, to be sure: but, why were we to be frightened out of our beds for this? Could not we have tried this cause to-morrow morning?

MISS STERLING. But, sir, by to-morrow morning, perhaps, even your assistance would not have been of any service.—The birds, now in that cage, would have flown away.

Enter LORD OGLEBY (*in his robe-de-chambre, night-cap, &c.*) *leaning on* CANTON

LORD OGLEBY. I had rather lose a limb than my night's rest! What's the matter with you all?

STERLING. Ay, ay, 'tis all over! Here's my lord, too.

LORD OGLEBY. What's all this shrieking and screaming? Where's my angelic Fanny? She's safe, I hope!

MRS. HEIDELBERG. Your angelic Fanny, my lord, is locked up with your angelic nephew in that chamber.

LORD OGLEBY. My nephew! then will I be excommunicated.

MRS. HEIDELBERG. Your nephew, my lord, has been plotting to run away with the younger sister; and the younger sister has been plotting to run away with your nephew; and if we had not watched them and called up the fammaly, they had been upon the scamper to Scotland by this time.

LORD OGLEBY. Look'ee, ladies!—I know that Sir John has conceived a violent passion for Miss Fanny; and I know too that Miss Fanny has conceived a violent passion for another person; and I am so well convinced of the rectitude of her affections, that I will support them with my fortune, my honor, and my life.—Eh, shan't I, Mr. Sterling? (*Smiling*) What say you?

STERLING. (*Sulkily*) To be sure, my lord.— (*Aside*) These bawling women have been the ruin of everything.

LORD OGLEBY. But come, I'll end this business in a trice. If you, ladies, will compose yourselves, and Mr. Sterling will insure Miss Fanny from violence, I will engage to draw her from her pillow with a whisper through the keyhole.

Mrs. Heidelberg. The horrid creaturs!—I say, my lord, break the door open.

Lord Ogleby. Let me beg of your delicacy not to be too precipitate!—Now to our experiment! (*Advancing towards the door*)

Miss Sterling. Now what will they do?—My heart will beat through my bosom.

Enter Betty, *with the key*

Betty. There's no occasion for breaking open doors, my lord; we have done nothing that we ought to be ashamed of, and my mistress shall face her enemies.

(*Going to unlock the door*)

Mrs. Heidelberg. There's impudence!

Lord Ogleby. The mystery thickens. Lady of the bed-chamber! (*To* Betty) Open the door, and entreat Sir John Melvil (for these ladies will have it that he is there) to appear and answer to high crimes and misdemeanors. Call Sir John Melvil into court!

Enter Sir John Melvil *on the other side*

Sir John. I am here, my lord.

Mrs. Heidelberg. Heyday!

Miss Sterling. Astonishment!

Sir John. What is all this alarm and confusion? There is nothing but hurry in the house; what is the reason of it?

Lord Ogleby. Because you have been in that chamber.—*Have* been! Nay, you *are* there at this moment, as these ladies have protested; so don't deny it!

Traverse. This is the clearest *alibi* I ever knew, Mr. Serjeant.

Flower. *Luce clarius*.

Lord Ogleby. Upon my word, ladies, if you have often these frolics, it would be really entertaining to pass a whole summer with you. But, come! (*To* Betty) open the door, and entreat your amiable mistress to come forth, and dispel all our doubts with her smiles.

Betty. (*Opening the door*) Madam, you are wanted in this room. (*Pertly*)

Enter Fanny, *in great confusion*

Miss Sterling. You see she's ready dressed —and what confusion she's in!

Mrs. Heidelberg. Ready to pack off, bag and baggage! Her guilt confounds her!

Flower. Silence in the court, ladies!

Fanny. I *am* confounded, indeed, madam!

Lord Ogleby. Don't droop, my beauteous lily! but with your own peculiar modesty declare your state of mind. Pour conviction into their ears, and raptures into mine.

(*Smiling*)

Fanny. I am at this moment the most unhappy—most distressed—The tumult is too much for my heart—and I want the power to reveal a secret, which to conceal has been the misfortune and misery of my—my—

(*Faints away*)

Lord Ogleby. She faints! Help, help! for the fairest, and best of women! ⎫
Betty. (*Running to her*) Oh my ⎬ (*Speaking all at once*)
dear mistress! help, help, there! ⎪
Sir John. Ha! let me fly to her assistance. ⎭

Lovewell *rushes out from the chamber*

Lovewell. My Fanny in danger! I can contain no longer.—Prudence were now a crime; all other cares were lost in this! Speak, speak to me, my dearest Fanny! Let me but hear thy voice! Open your eyes, and bless me with the smallest sign of life!

(*During this speech they are all in amazement*)

Miss Sterling. Lovewell!—I am easy.

Heidelberg. I am thunderstruck!

Lord Ogleby. I am petrified!

Sir John. And I undone!

Fanny. (*Recovering*) O Lovewell!—even supported by thee, I dare not look my father nor his lordship in the face.

Sterling. What now! Did not I send you to London, sir?

Lord Ogleby. Eh!—What!—How's this?—By what right and title have you been half the night in that lady's bed-chamber?

Lovewell. By that right which makes me the happiest of men; and by a title which I would not forego, for any the best of kings could give.

Betty. I could cry my eyes out to hear his magnimity.

Lord Ogleby. I am annihilated!

Sterling. I have been choked with rage and wonder; but now I can speak. Zounds, what have you to say to me? Lovewell, you are a villain. You have broke your word with me-

FANNY. Indeed, sir, he has not. You forbade him to think of me, when it was out of his power to obey you; we have been married these four months.

STERLING. And he shan't stay in my house four hours. What baseness and treachery! As for you, you shall repent this step as long as you live, madam.

FANNY. Indeed, sir, it is impossible to conceive the tortures I have already endured in consequence of my disobedience. My heart has continually upbraided me for it; and though I was too weak to struggle with affection; I feel that I must be miserable forever without your forgiveness.

STERLING. Lovewell, you shall leave my house directly;—and you shall follow him, madam. (*To* FANNY)

LORD OGLEBY. And if they do, I will receive them into mine. Look ye, Mr. Sterling, there have been some mistakes, which we had all better forget for our own sakes; and the best way to forget is to forgive the cause of them; which I do from my soul.—Poor girl! I swore to support her affection with my life and fortune;—'tis a debt of honor, and must be paid. You swore as much too, Mr. Sterling; but your laws in the city will excuse *you*, I suppose; for you never strike a balance without errors excepted.

STERLING. I am a father, my lord; but for the sake of all other fathers, I think I ought not to forgive her, for fear of encouraging other silly girls like herself to throw themselves away without the consent of their parents.

LOVEWELL. I hope there will be no danger of that, sir. Young ladies with minds like my Fannys, would startle at the very shadow of vice; and when they know to what uneasiness only an indiscretion has exposed her, her example, instead of encouraging, will rather serve to deter them.

MRS. HEIDELBERG. Indiscretion, quotha! a mighty pretty delicat word to express disobedience!

LORD OGLEBY. For my part, I indulge my own passions too much, to tyrannize over those of other people. Poor souls, I pity them. And you must forgive them too. Come, come, melt a little of your flint, Mr. Sterling.

STERLING. Why, why—as to that, my lord—to be sure he is a relation of yours, my lord—what say *you*, sister Heidelberg?

MRS. HEIDELBERG. The girl's ruined, and I forgive her.

STERLING. Well—so do I then. Nay, no thanks!—(*To* LOVEWELL *and* FANNY, *who seem preparing to speak*) There's an end of the matter.

LORD OGLEBY. But, Lovewell, what makes you dumb all this while?

LOVEWELL. Your kindness, my lord. I can scarce believe my own senses—they are all in a tumult of fear, joy, love, expectation, and gratitude! I ever was, and am now more bound in duty to your lordship. For you, Mr. Sterling, if every moment of my life, spent gratefully in your service, will in some measure compensate the want of fortune, you perhaps will not repent your goodness to me. And you, ladies, I flatter myself, will not for the future suspect me of artifice and intrigue. —I shall be happy to oblige and serve you. As for you, Sir John—

SIR JOHN. No apologies to me, Lovewell! I do not deserve any. All I have to offer in excuse of what has happened, is my total ignorance of your situation. Had you dealt a little more openly with me, you would have saved me, and yourself, and that lady, (who I hope will pardon my behavior) a great deal of uneasiness. Give me leave, however, to assure you, that light and capricious as I may have appeared, now my infatuation is over, I have sensibility enough to be ashamed of the part I have acted, and honor enough to rejoice at your happiness.

LOVEWELL. And now, my dearest Fanny, though we are seemingly the happiest of beings, yet all our joys will be damped, if his lordship's generosity and Mr. Sterling's forgiveness should not be succeeded by the indulgence, approbation, and consent of these, our best benefactors. (*To the audience*)

EPILOGUE

Written by Mr. Garrick
The Music by Mr. Barthelemon [1]

CHARACTERS OF THE EPILOGUE

Lord Minum	Mr. Dodd
Colonel Trill	Mr. Vernon
Sir Patrick Mahony	Mr. Moody
Miss Crotchet	Mrs. [Abington]
Mrs. Quaver	Mrs. Lee
First Lady	Mrs. Bradshaw
Second Lady	Miss Mills [2]
Third Lady	Mrs. Dorman

Scene, *an assembly*

Several persons at cards, at different tables; among the rest, Colonel Trill, Lord Minum, Mrs. Quaver, Sir Patrick Mahony

At the quadrille table

Colonel Trill. Ladies, with leave!
Second Lady. Pass!
Third Lady. Pass!
Mrs. Quaver. You must do more.
Colonel Trill. Indeed I can't.
Mrs. Quaver. I play in hearts.
Colonel Trill. Encore!
Second Lady. What luck!
Colonel Trill. To-night at Drury-lane is played
A comedy, and *toute nouvelle*—a spade!
Is not Miss Crotchet at the play?
Mrs. Quaver. My niece 5
Has made a party, sir, to damn the piece.

At the whist table

Lord Minum. I hate a playhouse—Trump!
—It makes me sick.
First Lady. We're two by honors, ma'am.
Lord Minum. And we th' odd trick.
Pray do you know the author, Colonel Trill?
Colonel Trill. I know no poets, heaven be praised!—Spadille. 10
First Lady. I'll tell you who, my lord!
(*Whispers my lord*)
Lord Minum. What, he again?
"And dwell such daring souls in little men?"

Be whose it will, they down our throats will cram it!
Colonel Trill. O, no.—I have a club—the best.—We'll damn it.
Mrs. Quaver. O bravo, colonel! music is my flame. 15
Lord Minum. And mine, by Jupiter!—We've won the game.
Colonel Trill. What, do you love all musick?
Mrs. Quaver. No, not Handel's.
And nasty plays—
Lord Minum. Are fit for Goths and Vandals. (*Rise from the table and pay*)

From the piquette table

Sir Patrick. Well, faith and troth! that Shakespeare was no fool!
Colonel Trill. I'm glad you like him, sir!—So ends the pool! 20
(*Pay and rise from the table*)

Song by the Colonel
I hate all their nonsense,
 Their Shakespeares and Jonsons,
Their plays, and their playhouse, and bards:
 'Tis singing, not saying;
 A fig for all playing, 25
But playing, as we do, at cards!

I love to see Jonas,
 Am pleased too with Comus; [3]
Each well the spectator rewards.
 So clever, so neat in 30
 Their tricks, and their cheating!
Like them we would fain deal our cards.

Sir Patrick. King Lare is touching!—And how fine to see
Ould Hamlet's ghost!—"To be, or not to be."—
What are your op'ras to Othello's roar? 35
Oh, he's an angel of a blackmoor!
Lord Minum. What, when he chokes his wife?—
Colonel Trill. And calls her whore?
Sir Patrick. King Richards calls his horse
 —and then Macbeth,
Whene'er he murders—takes away the breath.
My blood runs cold at every syllable, 40
To see the dagger—that's invisible.
(*All laugh*)

Sir Patrick. Laugh if you please, a pretty play—
Lord Minum. Is pretty.

---

[1] François Hippolite Barthélemon (1741–1808), a French violinist, came to England in 1765. He was leader of the opera band, director of music at Vauxhall, and a popular composer of operas, chamber pieces, etc.
[2] The Dramatic Works of 1777 has "Miss Pearce."
[3] Dr. John Dalton's adaptation of Milton's masque.

SIR PATRICK. And when there's wit in't—
COLONEL TRILL.   To be sure 'tis witty.
SIR PATRICK. I love the playhouse now—
  so light and gay,
With all those candles, they have ta'en away! [1]
  (*All laugh*)
For all your game, what makes it so much
  brighter?   46
  COLONEL TRILL. Put out the lights, and
    then—
  LORD MINUM   'Tis so much lighter.
SIR PATRICK. Pray do you mane, sirs, more
  than you express?
COLONEL TRILL. Just as it happens—
LORD MINUM.   Either more, or less.
MRS. QUAVER. An't you ashamed, sir?
                              (*To* SIR PATRICK)
  SIR PATRICK.   Me!—I seldom blush:
For little Shakespeare, faith, I'd take a
  push!   51
  LORD MINUM. News, news! here comes Miss
    Crotchet from the play.

       Enter MISS CROTCHET

MRS. QUAVER. Well, Crotchet, what's the
  news?
MISS CROTCHET.   We've lost the day.
COLONEL TRILL. Tell us, dear miss, all you
  have heard and seen.
MISS CROTCHET. I'm tired—a chair—here,
  take my capuchin! [2]   55
LORD MINUM. And isn't it damn'd, miss?
MISS CROTCHET.   No, my lord, not quite:
But we shall damn it.
  COLONEL TRILL.   When?
  MISS CROTCHET.   To-morrow night.
There is a party of us, all of fashion,
Resolved to exterminate this vulgar pas-
  sion:
A playhouse, what a place!—I must forswear
  it.   60
A little mischief only makes one bear it.
Such crowds of city folks!—so rude and press-
  ing!
And their horse-laughs, so hideously distress-
  ing!

[1] An allusion to Garrick's new method of lighting the stage. In 1765 Garrick had introduced from France the device of lighting not by means of hoops of candles suspended above the actors' heads, as had been the practice, but by strips of lights behind the proscenium arch and the wings, hidden from the audience but lighting the stage directly, known as side-lighting. This is Garrick's great contribution to English stage craft, at this time in its first season.
[2] A wrap resembling a monk's cassock and hood.

Whene'er we hissed, they frowned and fell
  a-swearing,
Like their own Guildhall giants [3]—fierce and
  staring!   65
  COLONEL TRILL. What said the folks of
    fashion? were they cross?
  LORD MINUM. The rest have no more judg-
    ment than my horse.
  MISS CROTCHET. Lord Grimley swore 'twas
    execrable stuff.
Says one, why so, my lord?—My lord took
  snuff.
In the first act Lord George began to doze   70
And criticized the author—through his nose;
So loud indeed, that as his lordship snored,
The pit turned round, and all the brutes en-
  cored.
Some lords, indeed, approved the author's
  jokes.
  LORD MINUM. We have among us, miss,
    some foolish folks.   75
  MISS CROTCHET. Says poor Lord Simper—
    well, now to my mind
The piece is good;—but he's both deaf and
  blind.
  SIR PATRICK. Upon my soul a very pretty
    story!
And quality appears in all its glory!—
There was some merit in the piece, no
  doubt.   80
  MISS CROTCHET. O, to be sure!—if one
    could find it out.
  COLONEL TRILL. But tell us, miss, the sub-
    ject of the play.
  MISS CROTCHET. Why, 'twas a marriage—
    yes, a marriage—stay!
A lord, an aunt, two sisters, and a merchant—
A baronet—ten lawyers—a fat sergeant,   85
Are all produced—to talk with one another;
And about something make a mighty pother;
They all go in, and out; and to, and fro;
And talk, and quarrel—as they come and
  go—
Then go to bed, and then get up—and then—
Scream, faint, scold, kiss,—and go to bed
  again.   (*All laugh*)   91
Such is the play!—Your judgment! never
  sham it.
  COLONEL TRILL. Oh, damn it!
  MRS. QUAVER.   Damn it!
  FIRST LADY.   Damn it!
  MISS CROTCHET.   Damn it!
  LORD MINUM.   Damn it!

[3] Statues of Gog and Magog in the Guildhall.

SIR PATRICK. Well, faith, you speak your minds, and I'll be free; 94
Good night! this company's too good for me. *(Going)*
COLONEL TRILL. Your judgment, dear Sir Patrick, makes us proud. *(All laugh)*
SIR PATRICK. Laugh if you please, but pray don't laugh too loud. *Exit*

RECITATIVE

COLONEL TRILL. Now the barbarian's gone, Miss, tune your tongue,
And let us raise our spirits high with song!

RECITATIVE

MISS CROTCHET. Colonel, *de tout mon cœur*—[1]
    I've one in *petto*, 100
Which you shall join, and make it a *duetto*.

RECITATIVE

LORD MINUM. *Bella signora, et amico mio!*
I too will join, and then we'll make a *trio*.

[1] With all my heart.

COLONEL TRILL. Come all, and join the full-mouthed chorus, 104
And drive all Tragedy and Comedy before us.
(All the company rise, and advance to the front of the stage)

AIR

COLONEL TRILL. Would you ever go to see a Tragedy?
MISS CROTCHET. Never, never.
COLONEL TRILL. A Comedy?
LORD MINUM. Never, never,
    Live for ever!
    Tweedle-dum and tweedle-dee!

COLONEL TRILL, LORD MINUM AND MISS CROTCHET. Live for ever!
    Tweedle-dum and tweedle-dee!

CHORUS

Would you ever go to see, *etc.*

FALSE DELICACY

By Hugh Kelly

Hugh Kelly (1739-1777), son of a Dublin tavern-keeper, born at Killarney, received little education and was early apprenticed to a stay maker. At his father's house he became acquainted with some of the actors of Dublin and contracted a fondness for the stage and literature. In 1760 he came to London to make a living by his literary efforts. After about a year in the metropolis, he secured various sorts of literary hack-work, at which, having gained some reputation, he continued until the production of his first play. About 1761 he married a needlewoman, whose good-nature Goldsmith is said to have admired and whose ill-tempered sister he is also said at one time to have wanted to marry. Kelly published a novel in 1767, *Memoirs of a Magdalen, or the History of Louisa Mildmay,* which was fairly successful and was translated into French in 1800. By this time Kelly had come into contact with some of the literary figures of the day, but Goldsmith and others are said to have treated him with contempt. *False Delicacy,* Kelly's first play, was read by Garrick in September, 1767, and that manager joined with the playwright in his rivalry with Goldsmith. The comedy was produced the following January, and Kelly's fortune was temporarily made. He was given a post as newspaper writer for the government of Lord North and later, perhaps, a pension. His political connections, however, operated to his disadvantage in the production of his later plays, some of which were opposed bitterly by the adherents of John Wilkes, an opposition which necessitated their production anonymously or under the names of false authors. In 1774 Kelly gave up literature for the bar, at which he made no success. His failure led him into debt, which in turn led to drink, and Kelly died in Gough Square, Fleet Street, Feb. 3, 1777, leaving a widow and five children, the youngest only a few weeks old. On May 29 a benefit performance of *A Word to the Wise* was put on for the heirs, with a prologue by Dr. Johnson, at Covent Garden; and in 1778 appeared by subscription Kelly's *Works,* printed for the widow, with an anonymous life and a portrait by Hugh Hamilton.

See also the *Dictionary of National Biography* and the references there cited.

KELLY'S DRAMATIC WORKS

L'Amour A-la-Mode; or, Love-à-la-Mode (farce), published 1760, attributed to Kelly.
False Delicacy (comedy) (D.L., Jan. 23, 1768), 1768. (Parts ascribed to Garrick.)
A Word to the Wise (comedy) (D.L., March 3, 1770), 1770.
Clementina (tragedy) (C.G., Feb. 23, 1771), 1771. (Produced anonymously.)
The School for Wives (comedy) (D.L., Dec. 11, 1773), 1774. (Produced as if by Major,—later Sir William,—Addington.)
The Romance of an Hour (comedy) (C.G., Dec. 2, 1774), 1774.
The Man of Reason (comedy) (C.G., Feb. 9, 1776), not published.

False Delicacy, a new comedy by Hugh Kelly, known already in literary circles as contributor to various periodicals and as author of theatrical criticism which, in the manner of *The Rosciad,* had offended most of the actors at Drury Lane, was brought out at that theater, January 23, 1768. The play had been in Garrick's hands since the preceding fall and that great physician of plays had probably touched it up, particularly in the speeches of the more lively comic characters of Mrs. Harley and Mr. Cecil. The manager had also exerted every effort to insure the success of the production, even going so far as to persuade Mrs. Dancer to forgive Kelly's offense in his attack upon the actors and to perform the part of the lively widow. The comedy, being written in the popular sentimental mode and, though artificial, rather entertaining and extremely well acted, was an immediate success. Three thousand copies of the printed play were sold before 2 P. M. on the day of publication and before the end of the

717

season the booksellers disposed of ten thousand copies. The author's profits were something like £700.

Six days after the first performance of *False Delicacy*, Goldsmith's *The Good-Natured Man* appeared at Covent Garden and failed. Critics have long lamented the poor taste of a public which could prefer Kelly to Goldsmith and have denounced Garrick as meanly preventing the success of Goldsmith by rushing Kelly's play before the public, knowing what the result would be. As a matter of fact neither of the two authors was known widely or well at the time, and neither had previously written a play. Though much maligned by posterity, *False Delicacy* probably deserved its original success; and had it not been for *She Stoops to Conquer*, *The Good-Natured Man* would long since have been forgotten. Goldsmith surpassed himself, but Kelly never exceeded the limits set by *False Delicacy*.

Kelly and Cumberland have long been coupled as the exemplars of sentimental comedy; and *False Delicacy* is one of the best examples of its type. It is artificial, "high," aphoristic, done in the French philosophical manner. Lord Winworth says at the end of the play, expressing the author's attitude, "The stage should be a school of morality;" and Kelly did his best to put his theory into practice. Though itself sentimental in manner, *False Delicacy* mildly ridicules the sentiment which it embodies; and through the words and actions of Cecil and Mrs. Harley, whether written by Garrick or not, it presents a delightful comment upon that "delicacy" which, if the play be rightly interpreted, is always false. Compared with the heavy, forced morality of Cumberland's dramas, *False Delicacy* is light and natural. Viewed without undue bias and somewhat in the spirit of its century it is not a bad play.

FALSE DELICACY

DRAMATIS PERSONÆ

MEN

COLONEL RIVERS	Mr. Holland	LORD WINWORTH	Mr. Reddish
CECIL	Mr. King	SIDNEY	Mr. Cautherly
SIR HARRY NEWBURG	Mr. J. Palmer		

Footmen, MR. WRIGHT, &c.

WOMEN

LADY BETTY LAMBTON	Mrs. Abington	MRS. HARLEY	Mrs. Dancer
MISS MARCHMONT	Mrs. Baddeley	SALLY	Miss Reynolds
MISS RIVERS	Mrs. Jefferies		

SCENE: *Richmond.* TIME: *The time of representation*

PROLOGUE [1]

Written by DAVID GARRICK, ESQ.
Spoken by MR. KING

I'm vexed—quite vexed—and you'll be vexed
 —that's worse
To deal with stubborn scribblers! there's the
 curse!
Write moral plays—the blockhead!—why,
 good people,
You'll soon expect this house to wear a steeple!
For our fine piece, to let you into facts,   5
Is quite a sermon,—only preached in acts.
You'll scarce believe me, 'till the proof appears,
But even I, Tom Fool, must shed some tears:
Do, ladies, look upon me,—nay, no simp'-
 ring—
Think you this face was ever made for
 whimp'ring?   10
Can I, a cambric handkerchief display,—
Thump my unfeeling breast, and roar
 away?
"Why, this is comical" perhaps he'll say.
Resolving this strange awkward bard to pump,
I asked him what he meant.—He, somewhat
 plump,   15
New pursed his belly, and his lips thus biting,
I must keep up the dignity of writing!

[1] The short dedication, to Garrick, is omitted. In the prologue Garrick makes fun of sentimental, moral plays in the same way that he did later in his prologue to *She Stoops to Conquer*, q. v.

You may; but, if you do, sir, I must tell ye,
You'll not keep up that dignity of belly.
Still he preached on.—"Bards of a former age
Held up abandoned pictures on the stage,   21
Spread out their wit, with fascinating art,
And catched the fancy, to corrupt the heart;
But, happy change!—in these more moral
 days,
You cannot sport with virtue, even in plays;
On virtue's side his pen the poet draws,   26
And boldly asks a hearing for his cause."
Thus did he prance, and swell.—The man
 may prate,
And feed these whimsies in his addle pate,
That you'll protect his muse, because she's
 good,   30
A virgin, and so chaste!—O lud! O lud!
No muse the critic beadle's lash escapes,
Though virtuous, if a dowdy, and a trapes:
If his come forth, a decent likely lass,
You'll speak her fair, and grant the proper
 pass.   35
Or should his brain be turned with wild pretences;
In three hours time, you'll bring him to his
 senses;
And well you may, when in your power you
 get him;
In that short space, you blister, bleed, and
 sweat him.   39
Among the Turks, indeed, he'd run no danger,
They sacred hold a madman, and a stranger.

ACT I

SCENE 1. *An Apartment at* LADY BETTY LAMBTON'S

Enter SIDNEY *and* WINWORTH

SIDNEY. Still I can't help thinking but Lady Betty Lambton's refusal was infinitely more the result of an extraordinary delicacy, than the want of affection for your lordship.

WINWORTH. O, my dear cousin, you are very much mistaken; I am not one of those coxcombs who imagine a woman doesn't know her own mind; or who, because they were treated with civility by a lady who has rejected their addresses, suppose she is secretly debating in their favor. Lady Betty is a woman of sense, and must consequently despise coquetry or affectation.

SIDNEY. Why, she always speaks of you with the greatest respect.

WINWORTH. Respect!—Why, she always speaks of you with the greatest respect; does it therefore follow that she loves you? No, Charles! I have, for some time you know, ceased to trouble Lady Betty with my solicitations; and I see myself honored with her friendship, though I haven't been so happy as to merit her heart. For this reason, I have no doubt of her assistance on the present occasion, and, I am certain I shall please her by making my addresses to Miss Marchmont.

SIDNEY. Miss Marchmont is, indeed, a very deserving young woman.

WINWORTH. Next to Lady Betty I never saw one so formed to my wishes; besides, during the whole period of my fruitless attendance, she seemed so interested for my success, and expressed so hearty a concern for my disappointment, that I have considered her with an eye of more than common friendship ever since.—But what's the matter with you, Charles? You seem to have something upon your spirits.

SIDNEY. Indeed, my lord, you are mistaken; I am only attentive.

WINWORTH. O, is that all!—This very day I purpose to request Lady Betty's interest with Miss Marchmont; for, unhappily circumstanced as she is with regard to fortune, she possesses an uncommon share of delicacy, and may possibly think herself insulted by the offer of a rejected heart. Lady Betty, in that case, will save her the pain of a supposed disrespect, and me the mortification of a new repulse. But I beg your pardon, Charles, I am forgetting the cause of friendship, and shall now step up stairs to Colonel Rivers about your affair. Ah, Sidney! you have no difficulties to obstruct the completion of your wishes, and a few days must make you one of the happiest men in England. *Exit*

SIDNEY. (*Looking after him*) A few days make me one of the happiest men in England! A likely matter, truly! Little does he know how passionately I admire the very woman to whom he is immediately going with an offer of his person and fortune. The marriage with Miss Rivers, I see, is unavoidable; and I am almost pleased that I never obtained any encouragement from Miss Marchmont, as I should now be reduced to the painful alternative, either of giving up my own hopes, or of opposing the happiness of such a friend.

Enter MRS. HARLEY *and* MISS MARCHMONT

MRS. HARLEY. O here, my dear girl, is the sweet swain, *in propria persona*. Only mind what a funeral-sermon face the creature has, notwithstanding the agreeable prospects before him. Well, of all things in the world, defend me, I say, from a sober husband!

SIDNEY. You are extremely welcome, Mrs. Harley, to divert yourself—

MRS. HARLEY. He speaks, too, in as melancholy a tone as a passing-bell. Lord, Lord, what can Colonel Rivers see in the wretch, to think of him for a son-in-law? Only look, Miss Marchmont, at this love-exciting countenance! Observe the Cupids that ambush in these eyes! These lips, to be sure, are fraught with the honey of Hybla. Go, you lifeless devil you,—go, try to get a little animation into this unfortunate face of yours.

SIDNEY. Upon my word, my face is very much obliged to you.

MISS MARCHMONT. You are a mad creature, my dear; and yet I envy your spirits prodigiously.

MRS. HARLEY. And so you ought. But for all that, you and Lady Betty are unaccountably fond of those half-souled fellows, who are as mechanically regular as so many pieces of clock-work, and never strike above once an hour upon a new observation, who are so sentimental, and so dull, so wise and so drowsy. Why, I thought Lady Betty had already a sufficient quantity of lead in her family, without taking in this lump to increase the weight of it.

MISS MARCHMONT. What can she possibly mean, Mr. Sidney?

SIDNEY. 'Tis impossible to guess, madam. The lively widow will still have her laugh without sparing anybody.

MRS. HARLEY. Why surely, my dear, you can't forget the counterpart of poor Dismal here, that elaborate piece of dignified dulness, Lady Betty's cousin, Lord Hectic, who, through downright fondness, is continually plaguing his poor wife, and rendering her the most miserable woman in the world, from an extraordinary desire of promoting her happiness.

MISS MARCHMONT. And isn't there a great deal to say in extenuation of an error which proceeds from a principle of real affection?

MRS. HARLEY. Affection! ridiculous! but you shall have an instance of this wonderful affection. T'other day I dined at his house; and, though the weather was intolerably warm, the table was laid in a close room, with a fire large enough to roast an ox for a country corporation.[1]

SIDNEY. Well, and so—

MRS. HARLEY. In a great chair, near the fire-side, sat poor Lady Hectic, wrapped up in as many fur-cloaks as would baffle the severity of a winter in Siberia. On my entrance I expressed a proper concern for her illness, and asked the nature of her complaint. She told me she complained of nothing but the weight of her dress, and the intolerable heat of the apartment, adding that she had been caught in a little shower the preceding evening, which terrified Lord Hectic out of his wits; and so, for fear she might run the chance of a slight cold, he exposed her to the hazard of absolute suffocation.

SIDNEY. Upon my word, Miss Marchmont, she has a pretty manner of turning things.

MISS MARCHMONT. Really, I think so.

MRS. HARLEY. Well, unable to bear either the tyranny of this preposterous fondness any longer, or the intolerable heat of his room, I made my escape the moment the cloth was removed; and shan't be surprised if, before the conclusion of the summer, he is brought before his peers, for having murdered his poor lady, out of downright affection.

[1] I.e., a county corporation,—a town which, with the surrounding country, has been given the rights of a county.

SIDNEY. A very uncommon death, Mrs. Harley, among people of quality.

Enter a Footman

FOOTMAN. (*To* SIDNEY) Lord Winworth, sir, desires the favor of your company above. The person is come with the writings from the Temple.

SIDNEY. I'll wait upon him immediately.

MRS. HARLEY. Ay, pray do, you are the fittest company in the world for each other. If Colonel Rivers was of my mind, he'd turn you instantly adrift, and listen to the overtures of Sir Harry Newburg.

SIDNEY. I really believe you have a fancy to me yourself; you're so constantly abusing me. *Exit*

MRS. HARLEY. I, you odious creature!

MISS MARCHMONT. Now you mention Sir Harry, my dear, isn't it rather extraordinary for him to think of Miss Rivers, when he knows of the engagements between her and Mr. Sidney—especially as her father has such an objection to the wildness of his character?

MRS. HARLEY. What, you are still at your sober reflections, I see, and are for scrutinizing into the morals of a lover. The women truly would have a fine time of it, if they were never to be married till they found men of unexceptionable characters.

MISS MARCHMONT. Nay, I don't want to lessen Sir Harry's merit in the least,—he has his good qualities as well as his faults, and is no way destitute of understanding; but still his understanding is a fashionable one, and pleads the knowledge of everything right to justify the practice of many things not strictly warrantable.

MRS. HARLEY. Why, I never heard anything to his prejudice, but some fashionable liberties which he has taken with the ladies.

MISS MARCHMONT. And, in the name of wonder, what would you desire to hear!

MRS. HARLEY. Come, come, Hortensia, we women are unaccountable creatures; the greatest number of us by much love a fellow for having a little modish wildness about him; and if we are such fools as to be captivated with the vices of the men, we ought to be punished for the depravity of our sentiments.

Enter RIVERS *and* LADY BETTY

RIVERS. I tell you, sister, they can read the parchments very well without our assistance.

and I have been so fatigued with looking over papers all the morning that I am heartily sick of your indentures witnessing, your *forasmuch's*, *likewise's*, *also's*, and *notwithstanding's*, and I must take a turn in the garden to recover myself. *Exit*

LADY BETTY. Nay, I only spoke, because I imagined our being present would be more agreeable to Lord Winworth. But I wonder Sir Harry doesn't come; he promised to be here by ten, and I want to see his cousin Cecil mightily.

MISS MARCHMONT. What, Lady Betty, does Mr. Cecil come with him here this morning?

LADY BETTY. He does, my dear. He arrived at Sir Harry's last night, and (*Ironically*) I want to see if his late journey to France has any way improved the elegance of his appearance.

MRS. HARLEY. Well, I shall be glad to see him, too; for, notwithstanding his disregard of dress, and freedom of manner, there is a something right in him that pleases me prodigiously.

MISS MARCHMONT. A something right, Mrs. Harley! He is one of the worthiest creatures in the world.

LADY BETTY. O, Hortensia, he ought to be a favorite of yours, for I don't know anybody who possesses a higher place in his good opinion.

MISS MARCHMONT. 'Twould be odd, indeed, if he wasn't a favorite of mine. He was my father's best friend; gave him a considerable living, you know; and, when he died, would have provided very kindly for me, if your generosity, Lady Betty, hadn't rendered his goodness wholly unnecessary.

LADY BETTY. Poh! poh! no more of this.

MRS. HARLEY. [I][1] wish there was a possibility of making him dress like a gentleman. But I am glad he comes with Sir Harry—for though they have a great regard for each other, they are continually wrangling, and form a contrast which is often extremely diverting—

Enter a Footman

FOOTMAN. Sir Harry Newburg and Mr. Cecil, madam.

LADY BETTY. O, here they are! Show them in. *Exit Footman*

MRS. HARLEY. Now for it!

MISS MARCHMONT. Hush, they are here.

[*Enter* SIR HARRY NEWBURG *and* MR. CECIL][2]

SIR HARRY. Ladies, your most obedient.—

CECIL. Ah, girls! Give me a kiss each of you instantly.—Lady Betty, I am heartily glad to see you. I have a budget full of compliments for you, from several of your friends at Paris—

LADY BETTY. Did you meet any of them at Paris?

CECIL. I did,—and, what was worse, I met them in every town I passed through. But the English are a great commercial nation, you know, and their fools, like their broad cloths, are exported in large quantities to all parts of Europe.

SIR HARRY. What? And they found you a fool so much above the market price, that they have returned you upon the hands of your country? Here, ladies, is a head for you, piping hot from Paris.

CECIL. And here, ladies, is a head for you, like the Alps.

SIR HARRY. Like the Alps, ladies! How do you make that out?

CECIL. Why it's always white,[3] and always barren; 'tis constantly covered with snow, but never produces anything profitable.

MRS. HARLEY. O say no more upon that head, I beseech you.

LADY BETTY. Indeed, Sir Harry, I think they're too hard upon you.

MRS. HARLEY. Why, I think so too—especially my friend Cecil, who, with that unfortunate shock of hair, has no great right to be considered as a standard for dress in this country.

CECIL. Ah, widow, there are many heads in this country with much more extraordinary things upon them than my unfortunate shock of hair, as you call it. What do you think of these wings, for instance, that cover the ears of my cousin Mercury?

SIR HARRY. Death! don't spoil my hair.

CECIL. You see this fellow is so tortured upon the wheel of fashion, that a single touch immediately throws him into agonies. Now,

---

[1] The *I* is lacking in the first edition; an obvious error.

[2] This necessary stage direction, though implied, has been omitted from early editions.

[3] White, not with years, but with hair powder. This and the reference to the "wings" which cover Sir Harry's ears are indicative of Cecil's attitude toward the elegance of that gentleman's wigs.

my dress is as easy as 'tis simple, and five minutes—

SIR HARRY. With the help of your five fingers equips you at any time for the drawing-room,—Ha! ha! ha!

CECIL. And isn't it better than being five hours under the paws of your hair-dresser?

LADY BETTY. But custom, Mr. Cecil!

CECIL. Men of sense have nothing to do with custom; and 'tis more their business to set wise examples than to follow foolish ones.

MRS. HARLEY. But don't you think the world will be apt to laugh a little, Mr. Cecil?

CECIL. I can't help the want of understanding among mankind.

SIR HARRY. The blockhead thinks there's nothing due to the general opinion of one's country.

CECIL. And none but blockheads, like you, would mind the foolish opinions of any country.

LADY BETTY. Well! Mr. Cecil must take his own way, I think; so come along, ladies, let us go into the garden, and send my brother to Sir Harry to settle the business about Theodora.

CECIL. Theodora! What a charming name for the romance of a circulating library! I wonder, Lady Betty, your brother wouldn't call his girl Deborah, after her grandmother?—

MRS. HARLEY. Deborah! O, I should hate such an old fashioned name abominably.

CECIL. And I hate this new fashion of calling our children by pompous appellations. By and by we shan't have a Ralph or a Roger, a Bridget or an Alice, remaining in the kingdom. The dregs of the people have adopted this unaccountable custom, and a fellow who keeps a little alehouse at the bottom of my avenue in the country, has no less than an Augustus Frederick, a Scipio Africanus, and a Matilda Wilhelmina Leonora, in his family.

MRS. HARLEY. Upon my word, a very pretty string of Christian names.

LADY BETTY. Well, Sir Harry, you and Mr. Cecil dine with us. Come, ladies, let us go to the garden.

MRS. HARLEY. I positively won't go without Mr. Cecil, for I must have somebody to laugh at.

CECIL. And so must I, widow; therefore I won't lose this opportunity of being in your company.

Exeunt Ladies, *and followed by* CECIL, *who meets* RIVERS *entering*

CECIL. Ah, colonel, I am heartily glad to see you.

RIVERS. My dear Cecil, you are welcome home again.

CECIL. There's my wise kinsman wants a word with you. *Exit*

SIR HARRY. Colonel, your most obedient. I am come upon the old business; for unless I am allowed to entertain hope of Miss Rivers, I shall be the most miserable of human beings.

RIVERS. Sir Harry, I have already told you by letter; and I now tell you personally, I cannot listen to your proposals.

SIR HARRY. No, sir?

RIVERS. No, sir! I have promised my daughter to Mr. Sidney; do you know that, sir?

SIR HARRY. I do; but what then? Engagements of this kind, you know.—

RIVERS. So then, you do know I promised her to Mr. Sidney?

SIR HARRY. I do; but I also know that matters are not finally settled between Mr. Sidney and you; and I moreover know that his fortune is by no means equal to mine; therefore—

RIVERS. Sir Harry, let me ask you one question, before you make your consequence.

SIR HARRY. A thousand, if you please, sir.

RIVERS. Why, then, sir, let me ask you what you have ever observed in me, or my conduct, that you desire me so familiarly to break my word? I thought, sir, you considered me as a man of honor.

SIR HARRY. And so I do, sir, a man of the nicest honor.

RIVERS. And yet, sir, you ask me to violate the sanctity of my word and tell me, indirectly, that it is my interest to be a rascal—

SIR HARRY. I really don't understand you, colonel. I thought, when I was talking to you, I was talking to a man who knew the world; and, as you have not yet signed—

RIVERS. Why, this is mending matters with a witness! And so you think, because I am not legally bound, I am under no necessity of keeping my word! Sir Harry, laws were never made for men of honor; they want no bond but the rectitude of their own sentiments, and laws are of no use but to bind the villains of society.

SIR HARRY. Well! But, my dear colonel, if you have no regard for me, show some little regard for your daughter.

RIVERS. Sir Harry, I show the greatest

regard for my daughter by giving her to a man of honor; and I must not be insulted with any farther repetition of your proposals.

SIR HARRY. Insult you, colonel! Is the offer of my alliance an insult? Is my readiness to make what settlements you think proper—

RIVERS. Sir Harry, I should consider the offer of a kingdom an insult, if it was to be purchased by the violation of my word. Besides, though my daughter shall never go a beggar to the arms of her husband, I would rather see her happy than rich; and if she has enough to provide handsomely for a young family, and something to spare for the exigencies of a worthy friend, I shall think her as affluent as if she was mistress of Mexico.

SIR HARRY. Well, colonel, I have done, but I believe—

RIVERS. Well, Sir Harry, and as our conference is done, we will, if you please, retire to the ladies. I shall be always glad of your acquaintance, though I can't receive you as a son-in-law; for a union of interest I look upon as a union of dishonor; and consider a marriage for money, at best, but a legal prostitution. *Exeunt*

ACT II

[SCENE I]

A Garden

Enter LADY BETTY *and* MRS. HARLEY

MRS. HARLEY. Lord, Lord, my dear you're enough to drive one out of one's wits. I tell you, again and again, he's as much yours as ever; and was I in your situation, he should be my husband to-morrow morning.

LADY BETTY. Dear Emmy, you mistake the matter strangely.—Lord Winworth is no common man; nor would he have continued his silence so long upon his favorite subject, if he had the least inclination to renew his addresses. His pride has justly taken the alarm at my insensibility; and he will not, I am satisfied, run the hazard of another refusal.

MRS. HARLEY. Why, then, in the name of wonder, if he was so dear to you, could you prodigally trifle with your own happiness, and repeatedly refuse him?

LADY BETTY. I have repeatedly told you, because I was a fool, Emmy. Till he withdrew his addresses, I knew not how much I esteemed him; my unhappiness in my first marriage, you know, made me resolve against another. And you are also sensible I have frequently argued that a woman of real delicacy should never admit a second impression on her heart.

MRS. HARLEY. Yes, and I always thought you argued very foolishly. I am sure I ought to know, for I have been twice married; and though I loved my first husband very sincerely, there was not a woman in England who could have made the second a better wife. Nay, for that matter, if another was to offer himself to-morrow, I am not altogether certain that I should refuse listening—

LADY BETTY. You are a strange creature.

MRS. HARLEY. And aren't you a much stranger, in declining to follow your own inclinations when you could have consulted them so highly, to the credit of your good sense, and the satisfaction of your whole family? But it isn't yet too late; and if you will be advised by me, everything shall end as happily as you can wish.

LADY BETTY. Well, let me hear your advice.

MRS. HARLEY. Why this, then. My lord, you know, has requested that you would indulge him with half an hour's private conversation some time this morning.

LADY BETTY. Well!

MRS. HARLEY. This is a liberty he hasn't taken these three months, and he must design something by it. Now as he can design nothing but to renew his addresses, I would advise you to take him at the very first word, for fear your delicacy, if it has time to consider, should again shew you the strange impropriety of second marriages.

LADY BETTY. But suppose this should not be his business with me?

MRS. HARLEY. Why, then, we'll go another way to work. I, as a sanguine friend of my lord's, can give him a distant hint of matters, exacting, at the same time, a promise of the most inviolable secrecy; and assuring him you would never forgive me, if you had the least idea of my having acquainted him with so important a—

LADY BETTY. And so you would have me—

MRS. HARLEY. Why not? This is the very step I should take myself, if I was in your situation.

LADY BETTY. Maybe so. But 'tis a step which I shall never take. What! would you have me lost to all feeling? Would you have me meanly make use of chambermaid-artifices for a husband?

MRS. HARLEY. I would only have you happy, my dear. And where the man of one's heart is at stake, I don't think we ought to stand so rigidly upon trifles.

LADY BETTY. Trifles, Emmy! Do you call the laws of delicacy trifles? She that violates these—

MRS. HARLEY. Poh! poh! she that violates— What a work there is with you sentimental folks! Why, don't I tell you that my lord shall never know anything of your concern in the design?

LADY BETTY. But shan't I know it myself, Emmy! And how can I escape the justice of my own reflections?

MRS. HARLEY. Well, thank heaven, my sentiments are not sufficiently refined to make me unhappy.

LADY BETTY. I can't change my sentiments, my dear Emmy, nor would I, if I could. Of this, however, be certain, that unless I have Lord Winworth without courting him, I shall never have him at all. But be silent to all the world upon this matter, I conjure you, particularly to Miss Marchmont; for she has been so strenuous an advocate for my lord, that the concealment of it from her might give her some doubts of my friendship; and I should be continually uneasy, for fear my reserve should be considered as an indirect insult upon her circumstances.

MRS. HARLEY. Well, the devil take this delicacy; I don't know anything it does besides making people miserable. And yet somehow, foolish as it is, one can't help liking it. But yonder I see Sir Harry and Mr. Cecil.

LADY BETTY. Let us withdraw then, my dear; they may detain us; and, till this interview is over, I shall be in a continual agitation; yet I am strangely apprehensive of a disappointment, Emmy—and if— (*Going*)

MRS. HARLEY. Lady Betty!

LADY BETTY. What do you say?

MRS. HARLEY. Do you still think there is anything extremely preposterous in second marriages?

LADY BETTY. You are intolerably provoking.— *Exeunt*

Enter CECIL and SIR HARRY

CECIL. Well, didn't I tell you the moment you opened this affair to me, that the colonel was a man of too much sense to give his daughter to a coxcomb?

SIR HARRY. But what if I should tell you, that his daughter shall be still mine, and in spite of his teeth?

CECIL. Prithee explain, kinsman.

SIR HARRY. Why suppose Miss Rivers should have no very strong objection to this unfortunate figure of mine?

CECIL. Why even your vanity can't think that a young lady of her good sense can possibly be in love with you?

SIR HARRY. What, you think that no likely circumstance, I see?

CECIL. I do, really. Formerly indeed the women were fools enough to be caught by the frippery of externals; and so a fellow neither picked a pocket, nor put up with an affront, he was a dear toad, a sweet creature, and a wicked devil. Nay, the wicked devil was quite an angel of a man; and, like another Alexander, in proportion to the number of wretches which he made, he constantly increased the luster of his reputation till at last, having conquered all his worlds, he sat down with that celebrated ruffian, and wept because he could commit no farther outrages upon society.

SIR HARRY. O, my good moralizing cousin, you'll find yourself cursedly out in your politics; and I shall convince you in a few hours, that a handsome suit on the back of a sprightly young fellow, will still do more among the women than all your sentiment and slovenliness.

CECIL. What, would you persuade me that Miss Rivers will go off with you?

SIR HARRY. You have hit the mark for once in your life, my sweet-tempered mouther of morality. The dear Theodora—

CECIL. The dear Theodora! And so, Harry, you imagine, that by the common maxims of fashionable life, you may appear to be a friend to the colonel, at the very moment you are going to rob him of his daughter. For shame, kinsman, for shame! Have some pride, if you have no virtue, and don't smile in a man's face when you want to do him the greatest of all injuries,—don't Harry—

SIR HARRY. Cecil, I scorn a base action as much as you, or as much as any man; but I love Miss Rivers honorably. I ask nothing from her father; and as her person is her own, she has a right to bestow it where she pleases

CECIL. I am answered. Her person is her own, and she has a right to be miserable her own way. I acknowledge it and will not discover your secret to her father.

SIR HARRY. Discover it to her father! Why, sure, you wouldn't think of it. Take care, Cecil, take care! I do, indeed, love you better than any man in the world, and I know you have a friendship, a cordial friendship for me; but the happiness of my whole life is at stake, and must not be destroyed by any of your unaccountable peculiarities.

CECIL. Harry, you know I would at any time rather promote your happiness than obstruct it. And you also know, that if I die without children, you shall have a principal part of my fortune; but damn it, I wish you had not used the mask of friendship to steal this young lady away from her relations. 'Tis hard that their good-nature must be turned against their peace, and hard, because her whole family treat you with regard, that you should offer them the greatest insult imaginable.

SIR HARRY. Dear Cecil, I am more to be pitied than condemned in this transaction. When I first endeavored to make myself agreeable to Miss Rivers, I imagined her family would readily countenance my addresses; and when I succeeded in that endeavor, I had not time to declare myself in form, before her father entered into this engagement with Sidney. The moment I heard it mentioned, I wrote to him, offering him a *carte blanche*;[1] and this morning a repetition of my offer was treated with contempt. I have therefore been forced into the measure you disapprove so much; but I hope my conduct, in the character of the son-in-law, will amply atone for any error in my behavior as a friend.

CECIL. Well, well, we must make the best of a bad market; her father has no right to force her inclinations; 'tis equally cruel and unjust. Therefore you may depend upon my utmost endeavors not only to assist you in carrying her off, but in appeasing all family resentments, for, really, you are so often in the wrong, that one must stand by you a little when you are in the right; so I shall be ready for you, kinsman.

SIR HARRY. Why, Cecil, this is honest—this is really friendly—and you shall abuse me a whole twelvemonth without my answering a syllable. But for the present I must leave you. Yonder I see Miss Rivers.—We have some little matters to talk of.—You understand me—and now— *Exit*

CECIL. For a torrent of rapture and nonsense! What egregious puppies does this unaccountable love make of young fellows: Nay, for that matter, what egregious puppies does it not make of old ones? *Ecce signum!*[2] 'Tis a comfort, though, that nobody knows I am a puppy in this respect but myself. Here was I, fancying that all the partiality I felt for poor Hortensia Marchmont proceeded from my friendship for her father; when, upon an honest examination into my own heart, I find it principally arises from my regard for herself. I was in hopes a change of objects would have driven the baggage out of my thoughts, and I went to France; but I am come home with a settled resolution of asking her to marry a slovenly rascal of fifty, who is, to be sure, a very likely swain for a young lady to fall in love with. But who knows! The most sensible women have sometimes strange tastes; and yet it must be a very strange taste that can possibly approve of my overtures. I'll go cautiously to work, however,—and solicit her as for a friend of my own age and fortune; so that if she refuses me, which is probable enough, I shan't expose myself to her contempt. What a ridiculous figure is an old fool sighing at the feet of a young woman! Zounds, I wonder how the grey-headed dotards have the impudence to ask a blooming girl of twenty to throw herself upon a moving mummy, or a walking skeleton. *Exit*

[SCENE II]

The scene changes to an apartment in LADY BETTY'S *house*

Enter LADY BETTY *and* MRS. HARLEY

LADY BETTY. You can't think, Emmy, how my spirits are agitated! I wonder what my lord can want with me?

MRS. HARLEY. Well, well, try and collect yourself a little. He is just coming up. I must retire. Courage, my dear creature, this once, and the day's our own, I warrant you. *Exit*

Enter WINWORTH, *bowing very low*

LADY BETTY. [*Aside*] Here he is! Bless me, what a flutter I am in!

---

[1] I.e., the right to make his own terms.

[2] Behold an instance.

WINWORTH. Your ladyship's most obedient.
LADY BETTY. Won't your lordship be seated?—(*Aside*) He seems excessively confused.
WINWORTH. I have taken the liberty, madam—(*Aside*) How she awes me, now I am alone with her!
LADY BETTY. My lord!
WINWORTH. I say, madam, I have taken the liberty to—
LADY BETTY. I beg, my lord, you won't consider an apology in the least—
WINWORTH. Your ladyship is extremely obliging,—and yet I am fearful—
LADY BETTY. I hope your lordship will consider me as a friend, and therefore lay aside this unnecessary ceremony.
WINWORTH. I do consider you, madam, as a friend;—as an inestimable friend—and I am this moment come to solicit you upon a subject of the utmost importance to my happiness.
LADY BETTY. (*Aside*) Lord! what is he going to say?
WINWORTH. Madam!—
LADY BETTY. I say, my lord, that you cannot speak to me on any subject of importance without engaging my greatest attention.
WINWORTH. You honor me too much, madam.
LADY BETTY. Not in the least, my lord—for there is not a person in the world who wishes your happiness with greater cordiality.
WINWORTH. You eternally oblige me, madam—and I can now take courage to tell you, that my happiness, in a most material degree, depends upon your ladyship.
LADY BETTY. On me, my lord?—Bless me!
WINWORTH. Yes, madam, on your ladyship.
LADY BETTY. (*Aside*) Mrs. Harley was right, and I shall sink with confusion.
WINWORTH. 'Tis on this business, madam, I have taken the liberty of requesting the present interview,—and as I find your ladyship so generously ready—
LADY BETTY. Why, my lord, I must confess—I say, I must acknowledge, my lord,—that if your happiness depends upon me—I should not be very much pleased to see you miserable.
WINWORTH. Your ladyship is benignity itself;—but as I want words to express my sense of this obligation, I shall proceed at once to my request, nor trespass upon your patience by an ineffectual compliment to your generosity.
LADY BETTY. If you please, my lord.
WINWORTH. Then, madam, my request is, that I may have your consent—
LADY BETTY. This is so sudden, my lord!—so unexpected!
WINWORTH. Why, madam, it is so;—yet, if I could but engage your acquiescence, I might still think of a double union on the day which makes my cousin happy—
LADY BETTY. My lord, I really don't know how to answer. Doesn't your lordship think this is rather precipitating matters?
WINWORTH. No man, madam, can be too speedy in promoting his happiness. If, therefore, I might presume to hope for your concurrence, I wouldn't altogether—
LADY BETTY. My concurrence, my lord! Since it is so essentially necessary to your peace, I cannot refuse any longer. Your great merit will justify so immediate a compliance and I shall stand excused of all—
WINWORTH. Then, madam, I don't despair of the lady's—
LADY BETTY. My lord?
WINWORTH. I know your ladyship can easily prevail upon her to overlook an immaterial punctilio; and, therefore—
LADY BETTY. The lady, my lord?
WINWORTH. Yes, madam! Miss Marchmont, if she finds my addresses supported by your ladyship, will, in all probability, be easily induced to receive them;—and then, your ladyship knows—
LADY BETTY. Miss Marchmont! my lord!
WINWORTH. Yes, madam, Miss Marchmont. Since your final disapprobation of those hopes which I was once presumptuous enough to entertain of calling your ladyship mine, the anguish of a rejected passion has rendered me inconceivably wretched; and I see no way of mitigating the severity of my situation, but in the esteem of this amiable woman, who knows how tenderly I have been attached to you, and whose goodness will induce her, I am well convinced, to alleviate, as much as possible, the greatness of my disappointment.
LADY BETTY. Your lordship is undoubtedly right in your opinion—and I am infinitely concerned to have been the involuntary cause of uneasiness to you; but Miss Marchmont, my lord—she will merit your utmost—
WINWORTH. I know she will, madam—and

it rejoices me to see you so highly pleased with my intention.

LADY BETTY. O, I am quite delighted with it.

WINWORTH. I knew I should please you by it.

LADY BETTY. You can't imagine how you have pleased me!

WINWORTH. How noble is this goodness!—Then, madam, I may expect your ladyship will be my advocate. The injustice which Fortune has done Miss Marchmont's merit, obliges me to act with a double degree of circumspection; for, when virtue is unhappily plunged into difficulties, 'tis entitled to an additional share of veneration.

LADY BETTY. (*Aside*) How has my folly undone me!

WINWORTH. I will not trespass any longer upon your ladyship's leisure than just to observe, that though I have solicited your friendship on this occasion, I must, nevertheless, beg you will not be too much my friend. I know Miss Marchmont would make any sacrifice to oblige you; and if her gratitude should appear in the least concerned—This is a nice point, my dear Lady Betty, and I must not wound the peace of any person's bosom, to recover the tranquillity of my own.
Exit

Enter MRS. HARLEY, *who speaks*

MRS. HARLEY. Well, my dear, is it all over?

LADY BETTY. It is all over indeed, Emmy.

MRS. HARLEY. But why that sorrowful tone—and melancholy countenance? Mustn't I wish you joy?

LADY BETTY. O, I am the most miserable woman in the world! Would you believe it? The business of this interview was to request my interest in his favor with Miss Marchmont.

MRS. HARLEY. With Miss Marchmont!—Then there is not one atom of sincere affection in the universe.

LADY BETTY. As to that, I have reason to think his sentiments for me are as tender as ever.

MRS. HARLEY. He gives you a pretty proof of his tenderness, truly, when he asks your assistance to marry another woman!

LADY BETTY. Had you but seen his confusion—

MRS. HARLEY. He might well be confused, when, after courting you these three years, he could think of another; and that, too, at the very moment in which you were ready to oblige him.

LADY BETTY. There has been a sort of fatality in the affair—and I am punished but too justly. The woman that wants candor, where she is addressed by a man of merit, wants a very essential virtue; and she who can delight in the anxiety of a worthy mind, is little to be pitied when she feels the sharpest stings of anxiety in her own.

MRS. HARLEY. But what do you intend to do with regard to this extraordinary request of Lord Winworth? Will you really suffer him to marry Miss Marchmont?

LADY BETTY. Why, what can I do? If it was improper for me, before I knew anything of his design in regard to Miss Marchmont, to insinuate the least desire of hearing him again on the subject of his heart, 'tis doubly improper now, when I see he has turned his thoughts on another woman, and when this woman, besides, is one of my most valuable friends.

MRS. HARLEY. Well, courage, Lady Betty. We aren't yet in a desperate situation. Miss Marchmont loves you as herself and wouldn't, I dare say, accept the first man in the world, if it gave you the least uneasiness. I'll go to her, therefore, this very moment, tell her at once how the case is; and, my life for it, her obligations to you—

LADY BETTY. Stay, Emmy. I conjure you, stay—and, as you value my peace of mind, be forever silent on this subject! Miss Marchmont has no obligations to me; since our acquaintance I have been the only person obliged; she has given me a power of serving the worthiest young creature in the world, and so far has laid me under the greatest obligation.

MRS. HARLEY. Why, my dear—

LADY BETTY. But suppose I could be mean enough to think an apartment in my house, a place in my chariot, a seat at my table, and a little annuity in case of my decease, were obligations, when I continually enjoy such a happiness as her friendship and her company. Do you think they are obligations which should make a woman of her fine sense reject the most amiable man existing, especially in her circumstances, where he has the additional recommendation of an elevated rank and an affluent fortune? This would be exacting interest with a witness for trifles; and, instead of having any little merit to claim from my behavior to her, I should be the most inexorable of all usurers.

MRS. HARLEY. Well, but suppose Miss Marchmont should not like my lord?

LADY BETTY. Not like him!—Why will you suppose an impossibility?

MRS. HARLEY. But let us suppose it, for argument sake.

LADY BETTY. Why I cannot say but it would please me above all things; for still, Emmy, I am a woman, and feel this unexpected misfortune with the keenest sensibility. It kills me to think of his being another's; but if he must, I would rather see him hers than any woman's in the universe. But I'll talk no more upon this subject till I acquaint her with his proposal; and yet, Emmy, how severe a trial must I go through!

MRS. HARLEY. Ay, and you most richly deserve it. *Exeunt*

ACT III

[SCENE I]

LADY BETTY's *garden*

SIR HARRY, MISS RIVERS, *and* SALLY, *cross at the head of the stage;* COLONEL RIVERS *observing them*

RIVERS. In close conversation with Sir Harry this half hour, at the remotest part of the garden! Why, what am I to think of all this? Doesn't she know I have refused him? Doesn't she know herself engaged to Sidney? There's something mean and pitiful in suspicion. But still there is something that alarms me in this affair; and who knows how far the happiness of my child may be at stake? Women, after all, are strange things; they have more sense than we generally allow them, but they have also more vanity. 'Tisn't for want of understanding they err, but through an insatiable love of flattery. They know very well when they are committing a fault, but destruction wears so bewitching a form that they rebel against the sense of their own conviction and never trouble themselves about consequences till they are actually undone. But here they come. I don't like this listening; yet the meanness of the action must for once be justified by the necessity.

(*Retires behind a clump of trees*)

Enter MISS RIVERS, SIR HARRY, *and* SALLY

MISS RIVERS. Indeed, Sir Harry, you upbraid me very unjustly. I feel the refusal which my father has given you severely; nevertheless, I must not consent to your proposal. An elopement would, I am sure, break his heart; and as he is wholly ignorant of my partiality for you, I cannot accuse him of unkindness.

RIVERS. (*Behind*) So! so! so! so!

SIR HARRY. Why then, my dear Miss Rivers, wouldn't you give me leave to mention the prepossession with which you honor me to the old gentleman?

RIVERS. The old gentleman!

MISS RIVERS. Because I was in hopes my father would have listened to your application, without putting me to the painful necessity of acknowledging my sentiments in your favor; and because I feared that unless the application was approved, on account of its intrinsic generosity, there was nothing which could possibly work upon the firmness of his temper.

RIVERS. Well said, daughter!

SALLY. The firmness of your father's temper, madam! The obstinacy you should say!—Sir Harry, as I live and breathe, there isn't so obstinate, so perverse, and so peevish an old devil in all England.

RIVERS. Thank you, Mrs. Sally!

MISS RIVERS. Sally, I insist that when you speak of my father, you always speak of him with respect. 'Tisn't your knowledge of secrets which shall justify these freedoms; for I would rather everything was discovered this minute, than hear him mentioned with so impudent a familiarity by his servants.

SALLY. Well, madam, I beg pardon; but you know the colonel, where he once determines, is never to be altered; so call this steadiness of temper by what name you please, 'tis likely to make you miserable, unless you embrace the present opportunity, and go off, like a woman of spirit, with the object of your affections.

RIVERS. What a damned jade it is!

SIR HARRY. Indeed, my dear Miss Rivers, Sally advises you like a true friend; and I am satisfied your own good sense must secretly argue on her side the question. The only alternative you have is to fly and be happy, or stay and be miserable. You have yourself acknowledged, my ever adorable—

RIVERS. O damn your adorables!

SIR HARRY. I say, madam, you have yourself acknowledged, that there is no hope whatsoever of working upon the colonel's tenderness, by acquainting him with our mutual affection. On the contrary, 'tis likely that, had he the least suspicion of my being honored with your regard, he would drag you instantly to his favorite Sidney, who is so utterly insensible of your merit, and who, if he has a passion for anybody, is, I am confident, devoted to Miss Marchmont.

RIVERS. Why, what a lie has the rascal trumped up here against poor Sidney?

MISS RIVERS. Dear Sir Harry, what would you have me do?

RIVERS. There!—Her dear Sir Harry!

SIR HARRY. My ever adorable Miss Rivers—

RIVERS. No, she can't stand these ever-adorables.

SIR HARRY. This excess of filial affection is extremely amiable; but it ought by no means to render you forgetful of what is due to yourself. Consider, madam, if you have been treated with tenderness, you have repaid that tenderness with duty, and have so far discharged this mighty obligation.

RIVERS. A pretty method of settling accounts, truly!

MISS RIVERS. Don't, my dear Sir Harry, speak in this negligent manner of my father.

RIVERS. Kind creature!

SIR HARRY. From what I have urged you must see, madam, that though you are so ready to sacrifice your peace for your father, he sets a greater value upon a trifling promise than upon your happiness. Judge, therefore, whether his repose should be dearer to you than your own; and judge too, whether to prevent the breach of his word, you should vow eternal tenderness to a man you must eternally detest, and violate even your veracity to kill the object of your love?

MISS RIVERS. Good heaven, what shall I do?

SALLY. Do, madam! Go off, to be sure.

RIVERS. I'll wring that hussy's head off.

SIR HARRY. On my knees, madam, let me beg you will consult your own happiness, and, in your own, the happiness of your father.

RIVERS. Ay, now he kneels, 'tis all over.

SIR HARRY. The colonel, madam, has great sensibility, and the consciousness that he himself has been the cause of your unhappiness, will fill him with endless regret. Whereas, by escaping with me, the case will be utterly otherwise. When he sees we are inseparably united, and hears with how unabating an assiduity I labor to merit the blessing of your hand, a little time will necessarily make us friends; and I have great hopes that, before the end of three months, we shall be the favorites of the whole family.

RIVERS. You'll be cursedly mistaken, though.

SIR HARRY. But speak, my dear Miss Rivers—speak, and pronounce my fate.

MISS RIVERS. Sir Harry, you have convinced me;—

RIVERS. Ay, I knew he would.

MISS RIVERS. And provided you here give me a solemn assurance, that the moment we are married you will employ every possible method of effecting a reconciliation—

SIR HARRY. You consent to go off with me the first opportunity. A thousand thanks, my angel, for this generous condescension!—and when—

MISS RIVERS. There is no occasion for professions, Sir Harry. I rely implicitly on your tenderness and your honor.

SALLY. Dear madam, you have transported your poor Sally by this noble resolution.

RIVERS. I dare say she has; but I may chance to cool your transport in a horsepond.

MISS RIVERS. I am obliged to you, Sally, for the part you take in my affairs, and I purpose that you shall be the companion of my flight.

SALLY. Shall I, madam! You are too good;—and I am sure I shouldn't like to live in my old master's house, when you are out of the family.

RIVERS. Don't be uneasy on that account.

SIR HARRY. Suffer me now, my dear Miss Rivers, since you have been thus generously kind, to inform you, that a coach and six will be ready punctually at twelve, at the side of the little paddock, at the back of Lady Betty's garden. There's a close walk,[1] you know, from the garden to the place, and I'll meet you at the spot to conduct you to the coach.

MISS RIVERS. Well, I am strangely apprehensive! But I'll be there. However, 'tis now high time for us to separate; my father's eyes are generally everywhere, and I am impatient,

[1] A private walk, enclosed by walls or hedges.

since it is determined, 'till our design is executed.

RIVERS. O, I don't in the least doubt it.

SIR HARRY. 'Till twelve, then, farewell, my charmer.

MISS RIVERS. You do what you will with me.

Exeunt separately [*except* COLONEL RIVERS]

RIVERS. (*Coming forward*) You do what you will with me! Why what a fool, what an idiot was I, even to suppose I had a daughter? From the moment of her birth to this cursed hour, I have labored, I have toiled for [her] [1] happiness; and now, when I fancied myself sure of her tenderest affection, she casts me off for ever. By and by, I shall have this fellow at my feet, entreating my forgiveness; and the world will think me an unfeeling monster, if I don't give him my estate, as a reward for having blasted my dearest expectations. The world will think it strange that I should not promote his felicity, because he has utterly destroyed mine; and my dutiful daughter will be surprised if the tender ties of nature are not strictly regarded in my conduct, though she has violated the most sacred of them all in her own. Death and hell! who would be a father?—There is yet one way left,—and, if that fails,—why, I never had a daughter.—
Exit

[SCENE II]

The Scene changes to an apartment

Enter MISS MARCHMONT *and* CECIL

MISS MARCHMONT. Nay, now, sir, I must tax you with unkindness;—know something that may possibly be of consequence to my welfare,—and yet decline to tell me! Is this consistent with the usual friendship which I have met with from Mr. Cecil?

CECIL. Look'e, Hortensia, 'tis because I set a very great value on your esteem, that I find this unwillingness to explain myself.

MISS MARCHMONT. Indeed, sir, you grow every moment more and more mysterious.—

CECIL. Well then, Hortensia, if I thought you wouldn't be offended,—I—

MISS MARCHMONT. I am sure, sir, you will never say any thing to give me a reasonable cause of offence. I know your kindness for me too well, sir.

[1] *Her* was inserted after the first edition was printed; it certainly improves the meaning of the sentence.

CECIL. Where is the need of *sirring* me at every word? I desire you will lay aside this ceremony, and treat me with the same freedom you do everybody else; these *sirs* are so cold, and so distant—

MISS MARCHMONT. Indeed, sir, I can't so easily lay aside my respect as you imagine, for I have long considered you as a father.

CECIL. As a father!—but that's a light in which I don't want to be considered. (*Aside*) As a father indeed! O she's likely to think me a proper husband for her, I can see that already!

MISS MARCHMONT. Why not, sir? Your years, your friendship for my father, and your partiality for me, sufficiently justify the propriety of my epithet.

CECIL. (*Aside*) My years! Yes, I thought my years would be an invincible obstacle.

MISS MARCHMONT. But pray, sir,—to the business upon which you wanted to speak with me. You don't consider I am all this time upon the rack of my sex's curiosity.

CECIL. Why, then, Hortensia,—I will proceed to the business—and ask you, in one word,—if you have any disinclination to be married?

MISS MARCHMONT. This is proceeding to business indeed, sir. But ha! ha! ha! pray, who have you designed me as a husband?

CECIL. Why, what do you think of a man about my age?

MISS MARCHMONT. Of your age, sir?

CECIL. Yes, of my age.

MISS MARCHMONT. Why, sir, what would you advise me to think of him?

CECIL. That isn't the question, for all your arch significance of manner, madam.

MISS MARCHMONT. O I am sure you would never recommend him to me as a husband, sir!

CECIL. So!—and why not, pray?

MISS MARCHMONT. Because I am sure you have too great a regard for me.

CECIL. (*Aside*) She gives me rare encouragement.—But do you imagine it impossible for such a husband to love you very tenderly?

MISS MARCHMONT. No, sir! But do you imagine it possible for me to love him very tenderly? You see I have caught your own frankness, sir, and answer with as much ease as you question me.

CECIL. (*Aside*) How lucky it was that I did not open myself directly to her!—O I should have been most purely contemptible!

Miss Marchmont. But pray, sir, have you, in reality, any meaning by these questions? Is there actually anybody who has spoken to you on my account?

Cecil. Hortensia, there is a fellow, a very foolish fellow, for whom I have some value, that entertains the sincerest affection for you.

Miss Marchmont. Then, indeed, sir, I am very unhappy, for I cannot encourage the addresses of anybody.

Cecil. No!

Miss Marchmont. O, sir! I had but two friends in the world, yourself and Lady Betty; and I am, with justice, apprehensive that neither will consider me long with any degree of regard. Lady Betty has a proposal from Lord Winworth of the same nature with yours, in which I fear she will strongly interest herself; and I must be under the painful necessity of disobliging you both, from an utter impossibility of listening to either of your recommendations.

Cecil. I tell you, Hortensia, not to alarm yourself.

Miss Marchmont. Dear sir, I have always considered you with reverence, and it would make me inconceivably wretched, if you imagined I was actuated upon this occasion by any ridiculous singularity of sentiment. I would do much to please you, and I scarcely know what I should refuse to Lady Betty's request; but, sir, though it distresses me exceedingly to discover it, I must tell you I have not a heart to dispose of.

Cecil. How's this?

Miss Marchmont. At the same time, I must, however, tell you, that my affections are so placed as to make it wholly impossible for me ever to change my situation. This acknowledgment of a prepossession, sir, may be inconsistent with the nice reserve which is proper for my sex; but it is necessary to justify me in a case where my gratitude might be reasonably suspected; and when I recollect to whom it is made, I hope it will be doubly entitled to an excuse.

Cecil. Your candor, Hortensia, needs no apology; but as you have trusted me thus far with your secret, mayn't I know why you can have no prospect of being united to the object of your affections?

Miss Marchmont. Because, sir, he is engaged to a most deserving young lady, and will be married to her in a few days. In short, Mr. Sidney is the man for whom I entertain this secret partiality. You see, therefore, that my partiality is hopeless; but you see, at the same time, how utterly improper it would be for me to give a lifeless hand to another while he is entirely master of my affections. It would be a meanness, of which I think myself incapable; and I should be quite unworthy the honor of any deserving hand, if, circumstanced in this manner, I could basely stoop to accept it.

Cecil. You interest me strangely in your story, Hortensia! But has Sidney any idea—

Miss Marchmont. None in the least. Before the match with Miss Rivers was in agitation, he made addresses to me, though privately; and, I must own, his tenderness, joined to his good qualities, soon gave me impressions in his favor. But, sir, I was a poor orphan, wholly dependent upon the generosity of others, and he was a younger brother of family, great in his birth, but contracted in his circumstances. What could I do? It was not in my power to make his fortune, and I had too much pride, or too much affection, to think of destroying it.

Cecil. You are a good girl, a very good girl; but surely if Lady Betty knows anything of this matter, there can be no danger of her recommending Lord Winworth so earnestly to your attention.

Miss Marchmont. There, sir, is my principal misfortune.—Lady Betty is, of all persons, the least proper to be made acquainted with it. Her heart is in the marriage between Miss Rivers and Mr. Sidney; and had she the least idea of my sentiments for him, or of his inclination for me, I am positive it would immediately frustrate the match. On this account, sir, I have carefully concealed the secret of my wishes, and on this account I must still conceal it. My heart shall break before it shall be worthless; and I should detest myself forever if I was capable of establishing my own peace at the expense of my benefactress's first wish, and the desire of her whole family.

Cecil. Zounds, what can be the matter with my eyes!

Miss Marchmont. My life was marked out early by calamity, and the first light I beheld, was purchased with the loss of a mother. The grave snatched away the best of fathers, just as I came to know the value of such a blessing; and hadn't it been for the exalted goodness of others, I, who once experienced the unspeakable pleasure of relieving the necessitous, had myself, perhaps, felt the immediate want of bread. And shall I ungratefully sting the bosom which has thus benevolently cherished me? Shall I basely wound the peace of those who have rescued me from despair;—and stab at their tranquillity, in the very moment they honor me with protection?—O, Mr. Cecil! they deserve every sacrifice which I can make. May the benignant hand of Providence shower endless happiness upon their heads; and may the sweets of still-increasing felicity be their portion, whatever becomes of me!

CECIL. Hortensia, I can't stay with you. My eyes are exceedingly painful of late. What the devil can be the matter with them?—But let me tell you before I go, that you shall be happy after all; that you shall, I promise you. But I see Lady Betty coming this way and I cannot enter into explanations; yet, do you hear, don't suppose I am angry with you for refusing my friend; don't suppose such a thing, I charge you; for he has too much pride to force himself upon any woman, and too much humanity to make any woman miserable. He is, besides, a very foolish fellow, and it doesn't signify—

Exit

Enter LADY BETTY

LADY BETTY. Well, my dear Hortensia, I am come again to ask you what you think of Lord Winworth. We were interrupted before, and I want, as soon as possible, for the reason I hinted, to know your real opinion of him.

MISS MARCHMONT. You have long known my real opinion of him, Lady Betty. You know I always thought him a very amiable man.

LADY BETTY. (*With impatience*) Do you think him an amiable man?

MISS MARCHMONT. The whole world thinks as I do in this respect,—yet—

LADY BETTY. (*Aside*) Ay, she loves him, 'tis plain; and there is no hope after this declaration.—His lordship merits your good opinion, I assure you, Miss Marchmont.

MISS MARCHMONT. (*Aside*) Yes, I see by this ceremony that she is offended at my coolness to the proposal.

LADY BETTY. I have hinted to you, Miss Marchmont, that my lord requested I would exert my little interest with you in his favor.

MISS MARCHMONT. The little interest your ladyship has with me;—the little interest—

LADY BETTY. Don't be displeased with me, my dear Hortensia,—I know my interest with you is considerable.—I know you love me.

MISS MARCHMONT. I would sacrifice my life for you, Lady Betty, for what had that life been without your generosity?

LADY BETTY. If you love me, Hortensia, never mention anything of this nature.

MISS MARCHMONT. You are too good—

LADY BETTY. But to my Lord Winworth. He has earnestly requested I would become his advocate with you. He has entirely got the better of his former attachments, and there can be no doubt of his making you an excellent husband.

MISS MARCHMONT. His lordship does me infinite honor;—nevertheless—

LADY BETTY. (*Eagerly*) Nevertheless, what, my dear?

MISS MARCHMONT. I say, notwithstanding I think myself highly honored by his sentiments in my favor,—'tis utterly impossible for me to return his affection.

LADY BETTY. (*Surprised*) Impossible for you to return his affection!

MISS MARCHMONT. (*Aside*) I knew what an interest she would take in this affair.

LADY BETTY. And do you really say you can't give him a favorable answer?—(*Aside*) How fortunate!

MISS MARCHMONT. I do, my dear Lady Betty;—I can honor, I can reverence him—but I cannot feel that tenderness for his person, which I imagine to be necessary both for his happiness and my own.

LADY BETTY. Upon my word, my dear, you are extremely difficult in your choice; and if Lord Winworth is not capable of inspiring you with tenderness,—I don't know who is likely to succeed; for, in my opinion, there is not a man in England possessed of more personal accomplishments.

MISS MARCHMONT. And yet, great as these accomplishments are, my dear Lady Betty, they never excited your tenderness.—

LADY BETTY. Why, all this is very true, my dear;—but, though I felt no tenderness,—yet I—to be sure, I—that is—I say, nevertheless—(*Aside*) This is beyond my hopes!

MISS MARCHMONT. (*Aside*) She's distressed that I decline the proposal.—Her friendship for us both is generously warm; and she imagines I am equally insensible to his merit, and to my own interest.

LADY BETTY. Well, my dear, I see your emotion, and I heartily beg your pardon for saying so much. I should be inexpressibly concerned if I thought you made any sacrifice on this occasion to me. My lord, to be sure, possesses a very high place in my esteem,—but—

MISS MARCHMONT. Dear Lady Betty, what can I do? I see you are offended with me,—and yet—

LADY BETTY. I offended with you, my dear! Far from it; I commend your resolution extremely, since my lord is not a man to your taste.—Offended with you! why should I take the liberty to be offended with you?—A presumption of that nature—

MISS MARCHMONT. Indeed, Lady Betty, this affair makes me very unhappy.

LADY BETTY. Indeed, my dear, you talk very strangely. So far from being sorry that you have refused my lord—I am pleased—infinitely pleased,—that is, since he was not agreeable to you. Be satisfied your acceptance of him would have given me no pleasure in the world;—I assure you it wouldn't:—on the contrary, as matters are situated, I wouldn't for the world have you give him the smallest encouragement. *Exit*

MISS MARCHMONT. (*Alone*) I see she's greatly disappointed at my refusal of an offer so highly to my advantage.—I see, moreover, she's grieved that his lordship should meet with a second repulse, and from a quarter, too, where the generosity of his proposal might be reasonably expected to promise it success. How surprised she seemed, when I told her he couldn't make an impression on my heart, and how eagerly she endeavored to convince me that she was pleased with my conduct, not considering that this very eagerness was a manifest proof of her dissatisfaction!—She is more interested in this affair than I even thought she would be,—and I should be completely miserable if she could suspect me of ingratitude. As she was so zealous for the match, I was certainly to blame in declining it. 'Tis not yet, however, too late. She has been a thousand parents to me, and I will not regard my own wishes, when they are any way opposite to her inclinations. Poor Mr. Cecil! Make me happy after all! How? Impossible!—for I was born to nothing but misfortune. *Exit*

ACT IV

[SCENE I.]

An apartment at LADY BETTY's *house*

Enter LADY BETTY *and* MRS. HARLEY

LADY BETTY. Thus far, my dear Emmy, there is a gleam of hope. She determined, positively determined, against my lord; and even suspected so little of my partiality for him, that she appeared under the greatest anxiety lest I should be offended with her for refusing him. And yet, shall I own my folly to you?

MRS. HARLEY. Pray do, my dear.—You'll scarcely believe it, but I have follies of my own sometimes.

LADY BETTY. Why you quite surprise me!

MRS. HARLEY. 'Tis very true for all that.—But to your business.

LADY BETTY. Why then, greatly as I dreaded her approbation of the proposal, I was secretly hurt at her insensibility to the personal attractions of his lordship.

MRS. HARLEY. I don't doubt it, my dear. We think all the world should love what we are in love with ourselves.

LADY BETTY. You are right. And though I was happy to find her resolution so agreeable to my wishes, my pride was not a little piqued to find it possible for her to refuse a man upon whom I had so ardently placed my own affection. The surprise which I felt on this account, threw a warmth into my expressions, and made the generous girl apprehensive that I was offended with her.

MRS. HARLEY. Well, this is a strange world we live in. That a woman without a shilling should refuse an earl with a fine person and a great estate, is the most surprising affair I ever heard of. Perhaps, Lady Betty, my lord may take it in his head to go round the family. If he should, my turn is next, and I assure you he shall meet with a very different reception.

LADY BETTY. Then you wouldn't be cruel, Emmy?

MRS. HARLEY. Why, no, not very cruel. I might give myself a few airs at first; I might blush a little, and look down, wonder what he could find in me to attract his attention; then pulling up my head, with a toss of disdain, desire him, if ever he spoke to me on that subject again,—

LADY BETTY. Well!

MRS. HARLEY. To have a licence in his pocket;—that's all.—I would make sure work of it at once, and leave it to your elevated minds to deal in delicate absurdities.—But I have a little anecdote for you, which proves, beyond a doubt, that you are as much as ever in possession of Lord Winworth's affection.

LADY BETTY. What is it, my dear Emmy?

MRS. HARLEY. Why, about an hour ago, my woman, it seems, and Arnold, my lord's man, had a little conversation on this unexpected proposal to Miss Marchmont, in which Arnold said, "Never tell me of your Miss Marchmonts, Mrs. Nelson; between ourselves—but let it go no farther—Lady Betty is still the woman; and a sweet creature she is, that's the truth on't, but a little fantastical and does not know her own mind—"

LADY BETTY. I'll assure you!—Why Mr. Arnold is a wit.

MRS. HARLEY. Well, but hear him out:— "Mrs. Nelson, I know as much of my lord's mind as anybody; let him marry whom he pleases, he'll never be rightly happy but with her ladyship; and I'd give a hundred guineas, with all my soul, that it could be a match." These Nelson tells me were his very words. Arnold is an intelligent fellow, and much in the confidence of his master.

LADY BETTY. Indeed, I always thought my lord happy in so excellent a servant. This intelligence is worth a world, my dear Emmy!—

Enter MISS MARCHMONT

MISS MARCHMONT. I have been looking for your ladyship.

LADY BETTY. Have you any thing particular, my dear Hortensia!—But why that gloom upon your features? What gives you uneasiness, my sweet girl? Speak, and make me happy by saying it is in my power to oblige you.

MISS MARCHMONT. 'Tis in your power, my dear Lady Betty, to oblige me highly, by forgiving the ungrateful disregard which I just now showed to your recommendation of Lord Winworth;—

MRS. HARLEY. (*Aside*) Now will I be hanged if she doesn't undo everything by a fresh stroke of delicacy.

LADY BETTY. My dear!

MISS MARCHMONT. And by informing his lordship that I am ready to pay a proper obedience to your commands.

MRS. HARLEY. (*Aside*) O the devil take this elevation of sentiment!

LADY BETTY. A proper obedience to my commands, my dear! I really don't understand you.

MISS MARCHMONT. I see how generously you are concerned for fear I should upon this occasion offer violence to my inclination. But, Lady Betty, I should be infinitely more distressed by the smallest act of ingratitude to you, than by any other misfortune. I am therefore ready, in obedience to your wishes, to accept of his lordship; and if I can't make him a fond wife, I will, at least, make him a dutiful one.

MRS. HARLEY. (*Aside*) Now her delicacy is willing to be miserable.

LADY BETTY. How could you ever imagine, my dear Hortensia, that your rejection of Lord Winworth could possibly give me the smallest offence? I have a great regard for his lordship, 'tis true, but I have a great regard for you also and would by no means wish to see his happiness promoted at your expense. Think of him, therefore, no more, and be assured you oblige me in an infinitely higher degree by refusing, than accepting him.

MISS MARCHMONT. The more I see your ladyship's tenderness and delicacy, the more I see it necessary to give an affirmative to Lord Winworth's proposal. Your generosity must not get the better of my gratitude.

MRS. HARLEY. (*Aside*) Did ever two fools plague one another so heartily with their delicacy and sentiment?—Dear Lady Betty, why don't you deal candidly with her?—

LADY BETTY. Her happiness makes it necessary now, and I will.

MRS. HARLEY. Ay, there's some sense in this.—

LADY BETTY. Your uncommon generosity, my dear Hortensia, has led you into an error.—

MISS MARCHMONT. Not in the least, Lady Betty.

LADY BETTY. Still, Hortensia, you are running into very great mistakes. My esteem for Lord Winworth, let me now tell you,—

Enter LORD WINWORTH

LORD WINWORTH. Ladies, your most obedient.—As I entered, Lady Betty, I heard you pronounce my name. May I presume to ask, if you were talking to Miss Marchmont on the business I took the liberty of communicating to you this morning?

MRS. HARLEY. (*Aside*) Ay, now 'tis all over, I see.

LADY BETTY. Why, to be candid, my lord, I have mentioned your proposal.

LORD WINWORTH. Well, my dear Miss Marchmont, and may I flatter myself that Lady Betty's interposition will induce you to be propitious to my hopes? The heart now offered to you, madam, is a grateful one, and will retain an eternal sense of your goodness. Speak, therefore, my dear Miss Marchmont, and kindly say you condescend to accept it.

MRS. HARLEY. (*Aside*) So—here will be a comfortable piece of work.—I'll e'en retire, and leave them to the consequences of their ridiculous delicacy. *Exit*

MISS MARCHMONT. I know not what to say, my lord. You have honored me, greatly honored me,—but Lady Betty will acquaint you with my determination.

LADY BETTY. I acquaint him, my dear—surely you are yourself the most proper to—(*Aside*) I shall run distracted!

MISS MARCHMONT. Indeed, madam, I can't speak to his lordship on this subject.

LADY BETTY. And I assure you, Hortensia, 'tis a subject upon which I do not choose to enter.

LORD WINWORTH. If you had a kind answer from Miss Marchmont, Lady Betty, I am sure you would enter upon it readily. But I see her reply very clearly in your reluctance to acquaint me with it.—

MISS MARCHMONT. Why, madam, will you force me to—

LADY BETTY. And why, Hortensia—(*Aside*) What am I going to say?

LORD WINWORTH. Don't, my dear ladies, suffer me to distress you any longer. To your friendship, madam, I am as much indebted (*Addressing himself to* LADY BETTY) as if I had been successful; and I sincerely wish Miss Marchmont that happiness with a more deserving man, which I find it impossible for her to confer on me. (*Going*)

LADY BETTY. (*Aside*) Now I have some hope.

MISS MARCHMONT. My lord, I entreat your stay.

LADY BETTY. Don't call his lordship back, my dear; it will have an odd appearance.

Enter LORD WINWORTH

MISS MARCHMONT. He is come back; and I must tell him what your unwillingness to influence my inclinations, makes you decline.

LORD WINWORTH. Your commands, madam?

LADY BETTY. (*Aside*) Now I am undone again!

MISS MARCHMONT. I am in such a situation, my lord, that I can scarcely proceed. Lady Betty is cruelly kind to me; but as I know her wishes—

LADY BETTY. My wishes, Miss Marchmont! Indeed, my dear, there is such a mistake—

MISS MARCHMONT. There is no mistaking your ladyship's goodness; you are fearful to direct my resolution, and I should be unkind to distress your friendship any longer.

LADY BETTY. (*Half aside and sighing*) You do distress me indeed, Miss Marchmont.

LORD WINWORTH. I am all expectation, madam!

MISS MARCHMONT. I am compelled by gratitude to both, and from affection to my dear Lady Betty, to break through the common forms imposed on our sex, and to declare that I have no will but her ladyship's.

LADY BETTY. (*Aside*) This is so provoking!

LORD WINWORTH. Ten thousand thanks for this condescending goodness, madam,—a goodness which is additionally dear to me, as the result of your determination is pronounced by your own lips.

MISS MARCHMONT. Well, Lady Betty, I hope I have answered your wishes now.

LADY BETTY. You cannot conceive how sensibly I am touched with your behavior, my dear. (*Sighs*)

MISS MARCHMONT. You feel too much for me, Lady Betty.

LADY BETTY. Why I do feel something, my dear. This unexpected event has filled my heart—and I am a little agitated. But come, my dear, let us now go to the company.

MISS MARCHMONT. How generously, madam, do you interest yourself for my welfare!

LORD WINWORTH. And for the welfare of all her friends!

LADY BETTY. Your lordship is too good—

LORD WINWORTH. But the business of her life is to promote the happiness of others, and she is constantly rewarded in the exercise of her own benignity.

LADY BETTY. You can't imagine how I am rewarded upon the present occasion, I assure your lordship. *Exeunt*

[SCENE II]

The paddock behind LADY BETTY'S *Garden*

Enter MISS RIVERS *and* SALLY

SALLY. Dear madam, don't terrify yourself with such gloomy reflections.

MISS RIVERS. O Sally, you can't conceive my distress in this critical situation! An elopement, even from a tyrannical father, has something in it which must shock a delicate mind; but when a woman flies from the protection of a parent who merits the utmost return of her affection she must be insensible indeed, if she does not feel the sincerest regret. If he shouldn't forgive me!

SALLY. Dear madam, he must forgive you! Aren't you his child?

MISS RIVERS. And therefore I shouldn't disoblige him. I am half distracted, and I almost repent the promise I gave Sir Harry, when I consider how much my character may be lessened by this step, and recollect how it is likely to affect my unfortunate father.

SALLY. But I wonder where Sir Harry can be all this time.

MISS RIVERS. I wish he was come.

SALLY. Courage, madam! I hear him coming.

MISS RIVERS. It must be he; let's run and meet him.—

Enter RIVERS. SALLY *shrieks and runs off*

MISS RIVERS. My father!

RIVERS. Yes, Theodora,—your poor, abandoned, miserable father.

MISS RIVERS. Oh sir!

RIVERS. Little, Theodora, did I imagine I should ever have cause to lament the hour of your birth; and less did I imagine, when you arrived at an age to be perfectly acquainted with your duty, you would throw every sentiment of duty off. In what, my dear, has your unhappy father been culpable, that you cannot bear his society any longer? What has he done to forfeit either your esteem or your affection? From the moment of your birth to this unfortunate hour, he has labored to promote your happiness. But how has his solicitude on that account been rewarded? You now fly from these arms which have cherished you with so much tenderness when gratitude, generosity, and nature should have twined me round your heart.

MISS RIVERS. Dear sir!

RIVERS. Look back, infatuated child, upon my whole conduct since your approach to maturity. Haven't I contracted my own enjoyments on purpose to enlarge yours, and watched your very looks to anticipate your inclinations? Have I ever, with the obstinacy of other fathers, been partial in favor of any man to whom you made the slightest objection?—Or have I ever shown the least design of forcing your wishes to my own humor or caprice? On the contrary, hasn't the engagement I have entered into been carried on seemingly with your own approbation? And haven't you always appeared reconciled, at least, to a marriage with Mr. Sidney?

MISS RIVERS. I am so ashamed of myself.

RIVERS. How then, Theodora, have I merited a treatment of this nature? You have understanding, my dear, though you want filial affection; and my arguments must have weight with your reason, however my tranquility may be the object of your contempt. I loved you, Theodora, with the warmest degree of paternal tenderness, and flattered myself the proofs I every day gave of that tenderness, had made my peace of mind a matter of some importance to my child.—But alas! a paltry compliment from a coxcomb undoes the whole labor of my life; and the daughter whom I looked upon as the support of my declining years betrays me in the unsuspecting hour of security, and rewards with her person the assassin who stabs me to the heart.—

MISS RIVERS. Hear me, dear sir, hear me!—

RIVERS. I do not come here, Theodora, to stop your flight, or put the smallest impediment in the way of your wishes. Your person is your own, and I scorn to detain even my daughter by force, where she is not bound to me by inclination. Since, therefore, neither duty nor discretion, a regard for my peace, nor a solicitude for your own welfare, are able to detain you, go to this man, who has taught you to obliterate the sentiments of nature, and gained a ready way to your heart, by expressing a contempt for your father. Go to him boldly, my child, and laugh at the pangs which tear this unhappy bosom. Be uniformly culpable, nor add the baseness of a despicable flight to the unpardonable want of a filial affection. (*Going*)

MISS RIVERS. I am the most miserable creature in the world!—

RIVERS. (*Returns*) One thing more, Theodora,—and then farewell forever. Though you come here to throw off the affection of a child, I will not quit this place before I discharge the duty of a parent, even to a romantic extravagance, and provide for your welfare, while you plunge me into the most poignant of all distress. In the doting hours of paternal blandishment, I have often promised you a fortune of twenty thousand pounds, whenever you changed your situation. This promise was, indeed, made when I thought you incapable either of ingratitude or dissimulation, and when I fancied your person would be given where there was some reasonable prospect of your happiness. But still it was a promise, and shall be faithfully discharged. Here then in this pocket-book are notes[1] for that sum. (MISS RIVERS *shows an unwillingness to receive the pocket-book*) Take it,—but never see me more. Banish my name eternally from your remembrance; and when a little time shall remove me from a world which your conduct has rendered insupportable, boast an additional title, my dear, to your husband's regard, by having shortened the life of your miserable father. *Exit*

Enter SALLY

SALLY. What, madam, is he gone?

MISS RIVERS. How could I be such a monster, such an unnatural monster, as ever to think of leaving him!—But come, Sally, let us go into the house.

SALLY. Go into the house, madam! Why aren't we to go off with Sir Harry?

MISS RIVERS. This insensible creature has been my confidante too! O I shall eternally detest myself!

Enter SIR HARRY *and* CECIL

SIR HARRY. I beg a thousand pardons, my dear Miss Rivers, for detaining you. An unforeseen accident prevented me from being punctual;—but the carriage is now ready, and a few hours will whirl us to the summit of felicity. My cousin Cecil is kindly here to assist us, and—

MISS RIVERS. Sir Harry, I can never forsake my father.

SIR HARRY. Madam!

MISS RIVERS. By some accident he discovered our design and came to this spot while I was trembling with expectation of your appearance.

SIR HARRY. Well, my dear creature!

MISS RIVERS. Here, in a melancholy but resolute voice, he expatiated on the infamy of my intended flight, and mentioned my want of affection for him in terms that pierced my very soul. Having done this, he took an abrupt leave, and, scorning to detain me by force, forsook me to the course of my own inclinations.

SIR HARRY. Well, my angel, and since he has left you to follow your own inclinations, you will not, surely, hesitate to—

MISS RIVERS. Sir Harry, unloose my hand; the universe wouldn't bribe me now to go off with you. O, Sir Harry! if you regarded your own peace, you would cease this importunity; for is it possible that a woman can make a valuable wife, who has proved an unnatural daughter!

SIR HARRY. But consider your own happiness, my dear Miss Rivers!

MISS RIVERS. My own happiness, Sir Harry!—What a wretch must the woman be who can dream of happiness, while she wounds the bosom of her father!

CECIL. [*Aside*] What a noble girl! I shall love her myself for her sense and goodness.

SALLY. (*Aside to* SIR HARRY) She won't consent, I know, Sir Harry; so, if the coach is at hand, it will be the best way to carry her off directly.

SIR HARRY. Then, my dear Miss Rivers, there is no hope—

MISS RIVERS. Sir Harry, I must not hear you.—This parting is a kind of death.—

SIR HARRY. Part, madam!—By all that's gracious, we must not part! My whole soul is unalterably fixed upon you; and since neither tenderness for yourself, nor affection for me, persuade you to the only measure which can promote our mutual felicity, you

[1] Kelly evidently thought that it was unsafe for her to have so much cash on her person as in later editions we find "Here . . . is a security."

must forgive the despair that forces you from hence and commits a momentary disrespect to avoid a lasting unhappiness.

MISS RIVERS. Hear me, Sir Harry! I conjure you hear me!

SIR HARRY. Let me but remove you from this place, madam, and I'll hear everything. —Cecil, assist me.

MISS RIVERS. O, Mr. Cecil, I rely upon your honor to save and protect me!

CECIL. And it shall, madam.—For shame, kinsman, unhand the lady!

SIR HARRY. Unhand her, what do you mean, Cecil?

CECIL. What do I mean? I mean to protect the lady. What should a man of honor mean?

MISS RIVERS. (*Breaking from* SIR HARRY) Dear Mr. Cecil, don't let him follow me.

(*She runs off*)

SALLY. (*Following*) I'll give her warning this moment, that's the short and the long of it. *Exit*

SIR HARRY. Mr. Cecil, this is no time for trifling. Didn't you come here to assist me in carrying the lady off?

CECIL. With her own inclinations, kinsman;—but as they are now on the other side of the question, so am I, too. You must not follow her, Sir Harry.

SIR HARRY. Zounds! but I will.

CECIL. Zounds! but you shan't. Look'e, Harry, I came here to assist the purposes of a man of honor, not to abet the violence of a ruffian. Your friends of the world, your fashionable friends, may, if they please, support one another's vices; but I am a friend only to the virtues of a man; and where I sincerely esteem him, I always endeavor to make him honest in spite of his teeth.

SIR HARRY. An injury like this—

CECIL. Harry!—Harry!—Don't advance. I am not to be terrified, you know, from the support of what is just; and though you may think it very brave to fight in the defence of a bad action, it will do but little credit either to your understanding or your humanity.

SIR HARRY. Dear Cecil, there's no answering that. Your justice and your generosity overpower me. You have restored me to myself. It was mean, it was unmanly, it was infamous to think of using force. But I was distracted;—nay, I am distracted now, and must entirely rely upon your assistance to recover her.

CECIL. As far as I can act with honesty, Harry, you may depend upon me;—but let me have no more violence, I beg of you.

SIR HARRY. Don't mention it, Cecil;—I am heartily ashamed—

CECIL. And I am heartily glad of it.

SIR HARRY. Pray let us go to my house and consult a little. What a contemptible figure do I make!

CECIL. Why, pretty well, I think; but to be less so, put up your sword, Harry.

SIR HARRY. She never can forgive me.

CECIL. If she does, she will scarcely deserve to be forgiven herself.

SIR HARRY. Don't, Cecil; 'tis ungenerous to be so hard upon me. I own my fault, and you should encourage me, for every coxcomb has not so much modesty.

CECIL. Why, so I will, Harry; for modesty, I see, as yet, sits upon you but very awkwardly. *Exeunt*

ACT V

[SCENE I]

An apartment at LADY BETTY'S

Enter RIVERS *and* SIDNEY

SIDNEY. I am deeply sensible of Miss Rivers's very great merit, sir; but—

RIVERS. But what, sir?

SIDNEY. Hear me with temper, I beseech you, colonel.

RIVERS. Hear you with temper! I don't know whether I shall be able to hear you with temper;—but go on, sir.

SIDNEY. Miss Rivers, independent of her very affluent fortune, colonel, has beauty and merit which would make her alliance a very great honor to the first family in the kingdom. —But notwithstanding my admiration of her beauty, and my reverence for her merit, I find it utterly impossible to profit either by her goodness or your generosity.

RIVERS. How is all this, sir! Do you decline a marriage with my daughter?

SIDNEY. A marriage with Miss Rivers, sir, was once the object of my highest ambition; and, had I been honored with her hand, I should have studied to show my sensibility of a blessing so invaluable;—but at that time, I did not suppose my happiness to be incompatible with hers. I am now convinced that it is so, and it becomes me much better to give up my own hopes, than to offer the smallest violence to her inclinations.

RIVERS. Death and hell, sir! What do you mean by this behavior? Shall I prefer your alliance to any man's in England? Shall my daughter even express a readiness to marry you, and shall you, after this, insolently tell me you don't choose to accept her?

SIDNEY. Dear colonel, you totally misconceive my motive; and I am sure, upon reflection, you will rather approve than condemn it. A man of common humanity, sir, in a treaty of marriage, should consult the lady's wishes as well as his own; and if he can't make her happy, he will scorn to make her miserable.

RIVERS. Scorn to make her miserable! Why the fellow's mad, I believe. Doesn't the girl absolutely consent to have you? Would you have her drag you to the altar by force? Would you have her fall at your feet, and beg of you, with tears, to pity one of the finest women, with one of the best fortunes, in England?

SIDNEY. Your vehemence, sir, prevents you from considering this matter in a proper light. Miss Rivers is sufficiently unhappy in losing the man of her heart; but her distress must be greatly aggravated, if, in the moment she is most keenly sensible of this loss, she is compelled to marry another. Besides, colonel, I must have my feelings too. There is something shocking in an union with a woman whose affections we know to be alienated; and 'tis difficult to say which is most entitled to contempt, he that stoops to accept of a pre-engaged mind, or he that puts up with a prostituted person.

RIVERS. Mighty well, sir! Mighty well! But let me tell you, Mr. Sidney,—that under this specious appearance of generosity, I can easily see your motive for this refusal of my daughter; let me tell you, I can easily see your motive, sir;—and let me tell you, that the person who is in possession of your affections, shall no longer find an asylum in this house.

SIDNEY. Colonel, if I had not been always accustomed to respect you, and if I did not even consider this insult as a kind of compliment, I don't know how I should put up with it. As to your insinuation, you must be more explicit before I can understand you.

RIVERS. Miss Marchmont, sir. Do you understand me now, sir? If Miss Marchmont had not been in the case, my daughter had not received this insult. Sir Harry was right; and had not I been ridiculously besotted with your hypocritical plausibility, I might have seen it sooner; but your cousin shall know of your behavior, and then, sir, you shall answer me as a man.

SIDNEY. Miss Marchmont, colonel, is greatly above this illiberal reflection; as for myself, I shall be always ready to justify an action which I know to be right, though I should be sorry ever to meet you but in the character of a friend. *Exit*

RIVERS. (*Alone*) Well! well! well! But it doesn't signify,—it doesn't signify,—it doesn't signify;—I won't put myself in a passion about it;—I won't put myself in a passion about it.—I'll tear the fellow piece-meal.— Zounds! I don't know what I'll do. *Exit*

Enter MRS. HARLEY *and* CECIL

CECIL. Why, this is better and better.

MRS. HARLEY. What a violent passion he's in!

CECIL. This is the very thing I could wish. 'Twill advance a principal part of our project rarely.—Well, isn't Sidney a noble young fellow and doesn't he richly deserve the regard which my poor little girl entertains for him?

MRS. HARLEY. Why, really, I think he does. But how secretly my Lady Sentimental carried matters! O, I always said that your grave, reflecting, moralizing damsels, were a thousand times more susceptible of tender impressions than those lively, open-hearted girls who talk away at random, and seem ready to run off with every man that happens to fall into their company.

CECIL. I don't know, widow, but there may be some truth in this; you see, at least, I have such a good opinion of a madcap, that you are the first person I have made acquainted with the secret.

MRS. HARLEY. Well, and haven't I returned the compliment, by letting you into my design about Lady Betty and Lord Winworth?

CECIL. What a ridiculous bustle is there here about delicacy and stuff! Your people of refined sentiments are the most troublesome creatures in the world to deal with, and their friends must even commit a violence upon their nicety, before they can condescend to study their own happiness. But have you done as we concerted?

MRS. HARLEY. Yes; I have pretended to Lady Betty that my lord desires to speak with her privately on business of the utmost importance; and I have told his lordship that she wants to see him, to disclose a secret that must entirely break off the intended marriage with Miss Marchmont.

CECIL. What an awkward figure they must make, each imagining that the other has desired the interview and expecting every moment to be told something of consequence! But you have not given either the least hint of Hortensia's secret inclination for Sidney?

MRS. HARLEY. How could you possibly suppose such a thing?

CECIL. Well, well, to your part of the business then, while I find out the colonel, and try what I can do with him for my rattle-pated Sir Harry.

MRS. HARLEY. O never doubt my assiduity in an affair of this nature! *Exeunt*

[SCENE II]

Enter LADY BETTY, *in another apartment*

LADY BETTY. What can he want with me, I wonder?—Speak with me again in private, and upon business of the utmost importance! He has spoken sufficiently to me already upon his business of importance to make me miserable for ever. But the fault is my own, and I have nobody to blame but myself.—Bless me! here he is.

Enter WINWORTH

WINWORTH. Madam, your most devoted! I come in obedience to your commands to—

LADY BETTY. My commands, my lord?

WINWORTH. Yes, madam, your message has alarmed me prodigiously; and you cannot wonder if I am a little impatient for an explanation.

LADY BETTY. Impatient for an explanation, my lord!

WINWORTH. Yes, madam, the affair is of the nearest concern to my happiness, and the sooner you honor me with—

LADY BETTY. Honor you with what, my lord?

WINWORTH. My dear Lady Betty, this reserve is unkind, especially as you know how uneasy I must be till I hear from yourself—

LADY BETTY. Really, my lord, I am quite astonished!—Uneasy till you hear from myself!—Impatient for an explanation!—I beg your lordship will tell me what is the meaning of all this?

WINWORTH. Surely, madam, you cannot so suddenly change your kind intentions.

LADY BETTY. My kind intentions, my lord!

WINWORTH. I would not, madam, be too presuming, but, as I know your ladyship's goodness, I flatter myself that—

LADY BETTY. Your lordship is all a mystery! —I beg you will speak out; for upon my word I don't understand these half sentences.

WINWORTH. Why, madam, Mrs. Harley has told me—

LADY BETTY. (*With eagerness*) What has she told you, my lord?

WINWORTH. She has told me of the secret, madam, which you have to disclose, that must entirely break off my marriage with Miss Marchmont.

LADY BETTY. Has she then betrayed my weakness?

WINWORTH. Madam, I hope you won't think your generous intentions in my favor a weakness; for be assured that the study of my whole life—

LADY BETTY. I did not think that Mrs. Harley could be capable of such an action; but since she has told you of the only circumstances which I ever wished to be concealed, I cannot deny my partiality for your lordship.

WINWORTH. Madam!

LADY BETTY. This secret was trusted with her, and her alone; but though she has ungenerously discovered it, her end will still be disappointed. I acknowledge that I prize your lordship above all the world; but even to obtain you, I will not be guilty of a baseness, nor promote my own happiness by an act of injustice to Miss Marchmont.

WINWORTH. I am the most unfortunate man in the world! And does your ladyship really honor me with any degree of a tender partiality?

LADY BETTY. This question is needless, my lord, after what Mrs. Harley has acquainted you with.

WINWORTH. Mrs. Harley, madam, has not acquainted me with particulars of any nature—

LADY BETTY. No!

WINWORTH. No.—And happy as this discovery would have made me at any other time, it now distresses me beyond expression, since the engagements I have just entered into with Miss Marchmont, put it wholly out of my power to receive any benefit from the knowledge of your sentiments.—O Lady Betty! had you been generously candid when I solicited the blessing of your hand, how much had I been indebted to your goodness! But now, think what my situation is, when, in the moment I am sensible of your regard, I must give you up for ever.

Enter CECIL *and* MRS. HARLEY *from opposite places*

MRS. HARLEY. (*Repeating ludicrously*) "Who can behold such beauty, and be silent!"
CECIL. (*In the same accent*) "Desire first taught us words."—
MRS. HARLEY. "Man, when created, wander'd up and down,
CECIL. "Forlorn and silent as his vassal beasts;
MRS. HARLEY. "But when a heav'n-born maid like you appear'd,
CECIL. "Strange pleasure fill'd his eyes, and seiz'd his heart,
MRS. HARLEY. "Unloos'd his tongue,
CECIL. "And his first talk was love." (*Both*) Ha! ha! ha!
WINWORTH. Pray, Mr. Cecil, what is the meaning of this whimsical behavior?
LADY BETTY. The nature of this conduct, Mrs. Harley, bears too strong a resemblance to a late disingenuity, for me to wonder at.
MRS. HARLEY. What disingenuity, my dear?
LADY BETTY. Why, pray, madam, what secret had I to disclose to his lordship?
MRS. HARLEY. The secret which you have disclosed, my dear! (*Curtsying*)
CECIL. I beg, my lord, that we mayn't interrupt your heroics, "when, in the moment you are sensible of her regard,—you must give her up for ever."—A very moving speech, Mrs. Harley!—I am sure it almost makes me cry to repeat it.
WINWORTH. Mr. Cecil, listening is—
MRS. HARLEY. What, are we going to have a quarrel?—
CECIL. O, yes; your lover is a mere nobody without a little bloodshed. Two or three duels give a wonderful addition to his character.
LADY BETTY. Why, what is the meaning of all this?

CECIL. You shall know in a moment, madam;—so walk in, good people,—walk in, and see the most surprising pair of true lovers, who have too much sense[1] to be wise, and too much delicacy to be happy.
MRS. HARLEY. Walk in,—walk in.

Enter RIVERS, MISS RIVERS, MISS MARCHMONT, SIR HARRY *and* SIDNEY

LADY BETTY. O, Emmy! is this behaving like a friend?
MRS. HARLEY. Yes, and like a true friend, as you shall see presently.
RIVERS. My lord, I give you joy, joy heartily.—We have been posted for some time, under the direction of Marshal Cecil and General Harley, in the next room, who have acquainted us with everything; and I feel the sincerest satisfaction to think the perplexities of to-day have so fortunate a conclusion.
WINWORTH. The perplexities of to-day are not yet concluded, colonel.
MISS MARCHMONT. O Lady Betty, why wouldn't you trust me with your secret? I have been the innocent cause of great uneasiness to you, and yet my conduct entirely proceeded from the greatness of my affection.
LADY BETTY. I know it, my dear,—I know it well—but were you to give up Lord Winworth this moment,—be assured that I wouldn't accept of any sacrifice made at the expense of your happiness.
CECIL. At the expense of her happiness!— O, is that all?—Come here, master Sobersides (*To* SIDNEY) and come here, Madam Gravity (*To* MISS MARCHMONT) come here, I say!— I suppose, my lord, I suppose, Lady Betty, that you already know from what very manly motives Sidney, here, has declined the marriage with Miss Rivers?
WINWORTH. I do; and though I lament the impossibility of a relation to the colonel's family, I cannot but admire his behavior on that occasion.
LADY BETTY. And I think it extremely generous.
MRS. HARLEY. Come, Cecil, stand by a little; you shan't have the whole management of this discovery.
CECIL. Did you ever see such a woman!
MRS. HARLEY. Well, my lord and Lady Betty, since we have agreed thus far, you

[1] I.e., sensibility.

must know that Mr. Sidney's behavior has produced more good consequences than you can imagine.—In the first place, it has enabled Colonel Rivers, without a breach of his word,—

CECIL. To give his daughter to my foolish kinsman.

MRS. HARLEY. You won't hold your tongue.

CECIL. And, in the next place, it has enabled Mr. Sidney.—

MRS. HARLEY. To marry Miss Marchmont.

CECIL. Ay, she will have the last word.—For it seems that between these two turtles there has long subsisted—

MRS. HARLEY. A very tender affection,—

CECIL. The devil's in her tongue!—she has the speed of me.

WINWORTH. What an unexpected felicity!

LADY BETTY. I am all amazement!

RIVERS. Well, well, my dear sister,—no wondering about it;—at a more convenient time you shall know particulars; for the present let me tell you, that now I am cool, and that matters have been properly explained to me, I am not only satisfied but charmed with Mr. Sidney's behavior, though it has prevented the first wish of my heart; and I hope that his lordship and you, by consenting to his marriage with Miss Marchmont, will immediately remove every impediment in the way of your own happiness.

WINWORTH. If my own happiness was not to be promoted by such a step, I should instantly give my consent;—and therefore, my dear Miss Marchmont, if I have Lady Betty's approbation and your own concurrence, I here bestow this hand upon as deserving a young man as any in the universe. This is the only atonement I can make for the uneasiness I have given you; and if your happiness is any way proportioned to your merit, I need not wish you a greater share of felicity.

SIDNEY. What shall I say, my lord?

WINWORTH. Say nothing, Charles; for if you only knew how exquisite a satisfaction I receive on this occasion, you would rather envy my feelings than think yourself under an obligation. And now, my dear Lady Betty, if I might presume—

LADY BETTY. That I may not be censured any longer, I here declare my hand your lordship's, whenever you think proper to demand it; for I am now convinced the greatest proof which a woman can give of her own worth, is to entertain an affection for a man of honor and understanding.

WINWORTH. This goodness, madam, is too great for acknowledgment.

LADY BETTY. And now, my dear Theodora, let me congratulate with you. I rejoice that your inclinations are consulted in the most important circumstance of your life; and I am sure Sir Harry will not be wanting in gratitude for the partiality which you have shown in his favor.

MISS RIVERS. Dear madam, you oblige me infinitely.

SIR HARRY. And as for me, Lady Betty, it is so much my inclination to deserve the partiality with which Miss Rivers has honored me, as well as to repay the goodness of her family, that I shall have little merit in my gratitude to either. I have been wild, I have been inconsiderate, but I hope I never was despicable; and I flatter myself I shan't be wanting in acknowledgment only to those who have laid me under the greatest of all obligations.

RIVERS. Sir Harry, say no more. My girl's repentance has been so noble; your cousin Cecil's behavior has been so generous; and I believe you, after all, to be a man of such principle, that next to Sidney, I don't know who I should prefer to you for a son-in-law. But you must think a little for the future, and remember, that it is a poor excuse for playing the fool, to be possessed of a good understanding.

WINWORTH. Well, there seems but one thing remaining undone:—I just now took the liberty of exercising a father's right over Miss Marchmont, by disposing of her hand; 'tis now necessary for me—

CECIL. Hold, my lord;—I guess what you are about, but you shan't monopolize generosity, I assure you.—I have a right to show my friendship, as well as your lordship; so, after your kinsman's marriage, whatever you have a mind to do for him shall be equalled, on my part, for Miss Marchmont; guinea for guinea, as far as you will, and let's see who tires first in going through with it.

WINWORTH. A noble challenge, and I accept it.

LADY BETTY. No, there's no bearing this.—

MISS MARCHMONT. Speak to them, Mr. Sidney, for I cannot.

SIDNEY. I wish I had words to declare my sense of this goodness.

RIVERS. I didn't look upon myself as a very pitiful fellow, but I am strangely sunk in my own opinion, since I have been a witness of this transaction.

CECIL. Why, what the devil is there in all this to wonder at? People of fortune often throw away thousands at the hazard table to make themselves miserable, and nobody ever accuses them of generosity.

WINWORTH. Mr. Cecil is perfectly right; and he is the best manager of a fortune who is most attentive to the wants of the deserving.

MRS. HARLEY. Why now all is as it should be,—all is as it should be!—This is the triumph of good sense over delicacy.—I could cry for downright joy.—I wonder what ails me!—This is all my doing!

CECIL. No,—part of it is mine;—and I think it extremely happy for your people of refined sentiments to have friends with a little common understanding.

RIVERS. Sister, I always thought you a woman of sense.

MRS. HARLEY. Yes, she has been a long time intimate with me, you know.

CECIL. Well said, sauce-box!

SIR HARRY. If this story was to be represented on the stage, the poet would think it his duty to punish me for life, because I was once culpable.

WINWORTH. That would be very wrong. The stage should be a school of morality; and the noblest of all lessons is the forgiveness of injuries.

RIVERS. True, my lord.—But the principal moral to be drawn from the transactions of to-day is, that those who generously labor for the happiness of others, will, sooner or later, arrive at happiness themselves.

EPILOGUE

Written by DAVID GARRICK, ESQ. Spoken by MRS. DANCER

When with the comic muse a bard hath dealing,
The traffic thrives when there's a mutual feeling;
Our author boasts, that well he chose his plan,
False Modesty!—Himself, an Irishman.
As I'm a woman somewhat prone to satire, 5
I'll prove it all a bull, what he calls nature;
And you I'm sure, will join before you go,
To maul False Modesty,—from Dublin ho!
Where are these Lady Lambtons to be found?
Not in these riper times, on English ground. 5
Among the various flowers which sweetly blow,
To charm the eyes, at Almack's and Soho,[1]
Pray does that weed, false delicacy, grow?
O No.—
Among the fair of fashion; common breeding,
Is there one bosom, where love lies a-bleeding?[2] 16
In olden times your gran'ams unrefined,
Tied up the tongue, put padlocks on the mind;
O, ladies, thank your stars there's nothing now confined.
In love, you English men,—there's no concealing, 20
Are most, like Winworth, simple in your dealing;
But Britons, in their natures as their names,
Are different as the Shannon, Tweed, and Thames.
As the Tweed flows, the bonny Scot proceeds,
Wunds slaw, and sure, and nae obstruction heeds; 25
Though oft repulsed, his purpose still hauds fast,
Sticks like a burr, and wuns the lass at last.
The Shannon, rough and vigorous, pours along,
Like the bold accents of brave Paddy's tongue:
"Arrah, dear creature—can you scorn me so?
Cast your sweet eyes upon me, top and toe! 31
Not fancy me?—Pooh!—that's all game and laughter,
First marry me, my jew'l—ho!—you'll love me after."
Like his own Thames, honest John Trot, their brother,
More quick than one, and much less bold than t'other, 35
Gentle not dull, his loving arms will spread;
But stopped—in willows hides his bashful head;

[1] Almack's was a popular club and dance hall; Soho is the district in which were Carlisle House and other resorts of society.

[2] An allusion to Beaumont and Fletcher's *Philaster; or, Love Lies a-Bleeding* (1608), known at this time through Colman's alteration (D.L., October 8, 1763), which was still popular enough to be reprinted in 1780.

John leaves his home, resolved to tell his pain;
Hesitates—"I—love"—"Fye, Sir—'tis in vain,—"
John blushes, turns him round, and whistles home again. 40

Well! is my painting like?—Or do you doubt it?—
What say you to a trial?—let's about it.
Let Cupid lead three Britons to the field,
And try which first can make a damsel yield
What say you to a widow?—Smile consent,
And she'll be ready for experiment.

THE WEST INDIAN

A Comedy by Richard Cumberland

Richard Cumberland, son of Denison Cumberland, Rector of Stanwick, Northamptonshire, later Bishop of Clonfert in Ireland, was born in the house of his maternal grandfather, the great Dr. Richard Bentley, in Cambridge, Feb. 19, 1732. He was descended from a long line of learned gentlemen and clergymen. He studied, generally with success, in school at Bury St. Edmund and at Westminster and entered Trinity College, Cambridge, in 1745. After taking his degree he became secretary to Lord Halifax, going with him in 1761 to Ireland as Ulster secretary when Halifax was appointed Lord Lieutenant. Cumberland's political career was brief. He lost favor with his patron and turned to writing plays as a means of supporting his growing family. Between 1762 and his death he produced some fifty plays, various poems, three novels, and his *Memoirs* (1806). His reputation as an important playwright after the production of *The West Indian*, together with the position of his family, placed him in the best of London society. Though not himself a member, he knew most of the great men of Johnson's club and was the friend of many other eminent persons. He was thought to be the inspiration of Sir Fretful Plagiary in Sheridan's *The Critic* (1779). Whether this is true or not, the characterization certainly fitted in many respects. Cumberland died, respected and honored but in poverty, May 7, 1811.

See Williams, S. T., *Richard Cumberland, His Life and Dramatic Works*. New Haven, 1917; and the same author's "The Dramas of Richard Cumberland, 1779-1785" (*Mod. Lang. Notes*, xxxvi, 403-408), "The Early Sentimental Dramas of Richard Cumberland" (*Mod. Lang. Notes*, xxxvi, 160-165), and "Richard Cumberland's *West Indian*" (*Mod. Lang. Notes*, xxxv, 413-417).

CUMBERLAND'S DRAMATIC WORKS

(Cumberland wrote something over 50 plays: 26 sentimental comedies, 9 tragedies, 7 operas or musical entertainments, 5 alterations or adaptations, and 3 occasional pieces. Those listed below are regarded as his best. Cf. S. T. Williams, *Richard Cumberland*, pp. 331 ff.)

The Brothers (comedy) (C.G., Dec. 2, 1769), 1770.
The West Indian (comedy) (D.L., Jan. 19, 1771), 1771.
The Fashionable Lover (comedy) (D.L., Jan. 20, 1772), 1772.
The Note of Hand; or, Trip to Newmarket (farce) (D.L., Feb. 9, 1774), 1774.
The Mysterious Husband (domestic tragedy), (C.G., Jan. 28, 1783), 1783.
The Jew (comedy) (D.L., May 8, 1794), 1794.
The Wheel of Fortune (comedy) (D.L., Feb. 28, 1795), 1795.

Mr. Cumberland's *The West Indian* achieved immediate success. What if the hero did resemble Fielding's Tom Jones a little more closely than was perhaps necessary, the play was English in tone and it contained a remarkably well done stage Irishman, admirably acted by Moody. "Its success," says Benjamin Victor, "exceeded that of any comedy within the memory of the oldest man living." "There was," he continues, "the same demand for places in the boxes and the same crowding to get into the pit and galleries at the twenty-sixth representation as on the first night." The author's importunate flattery of Garrick had at last had its reward to the benefit of both author and manager. Garrick had seen *The Brothers* in 1769 at Covent Garden and had begun to think that perhaps this Cumberland might do something after all. So he had encouraged him and had gone over *The West Indian* carefully himself, giving it that expert attention which had saved the careers of so many plays. At last *The West Indian* was ready and it appeared at Drury Lane on Saturday, Jan. 19, 1771. Goldsmith's feeble protest against sentimental comedy in *The Good-Natured Man* had been silenced effectively by Kelly's *False Delicacy;* and now anti-sentimental plays like Colman's *The Jealous Wife* (1761) would have to share favor with the work of a new dramatist. As the popularity of *The West Indian* increased with successive performances, it had an initial run of thirty nights before the end of the season. The audiences and critics who praised Mr. Cumberland's highly moral, but not tearful, comedy, welcoming the author as one of the bright lights of the drama, fortunately did not know that, though they were to see new plays from the same elegant pen for the next forty years, never again was the learned gentleman to strike the note of popular appeal then resounding through theatrical London. Therefore, in a later age, he is remembered as Sir Fretful Plagiary and as the author of one play.

The play itself is the supreme example of English sentimental comedy. It follows the tradition established by Steele with *The Conscious Lovers* rather than the sententiously tearful manner of the French adopted by Hugh Kelly. *The West Indian* has all the characteristics of its type,—the rake reformed, virtue rescued from distress and rewarded, vice exposed and disposed of, avarice outwitted, and honorable simplicity triumphant. The resulting combination pleased; and though long since forgotten, the play deserved the position which it held for two generations as one of the most popular of comedies.

THE WEST INDIAN

DRAMATIS PERSONÆ

MEN

STOCKWELL	Mr. Aickin	STUKELY	Mr. J. Aickin
BELCOUR	Mr. King	FULMER	Mr. Baddely
CAPTAIN DUDLEY	Mr. Packer	VARLAND	Mr. Parsons
CHARLES DUDLEY	Mr. Cautherly	Servant to STOCKWELL	Mr. Wheeler
MAJOR O'FLAHERTY	Mr. Moody		

WOMEN

LADY RUSPORT	Mrs. Hopkins	LUCY	Mrs. Love
CHARLOTTE RUSPORT	Mrs. Abington	Housekeeper belonging to STOCKWELL	Mrs. Bradshaw
LOUISA, *daughter to* DUDLEY	Mrs. Baddely		
MRS. FULMER	Mrs. Egerton		

Clerks belonging to STOCKWELL; servants, sailors, negroes, &c.

SCENE: *London*

PROLOGUE

Spoken by MR. REDDISH [1]

Critics, hark forward! noble game and new;
A fine West Indian started full in view:
Hot as the soil, the clime which gave him birth,
You'll run him on a burning scent to earth;
Yet don't devour him in his hiding place;   5
Bag him; he'll serve you for another chase;
For sure that country has no feeble claim,
Which swells your commerce and supports your fame.
And in this humble sketch, we hope you'll find
Some emanations of a noble mind,   10
Some little touches, which, tho' void of art,
May find perhaps their way into your heart.
Another hero your excuse implores,
Sent by your sister kingdom to your shores,
Doomed by religion's too severe command   15
To fight for bread against his native land:
A brave, unthinking, animated rogue,
With here and there a touch upon the brogue;
Laugh, but despise him not, for on his lip
His errors lie; his heart can never trip.   20
Others there are—but may we not prevail
To let the gentry tell their own plain tale?
Shall they come in? They'll please you if they can;   23
If not, condemn the bard—but spare the *Man*.
For speak, think, act, or write in angry times,
A wish to please is made the worst of crimes;
Dire slander now with black envenomed dart,
Stands ever armed to stab you to the heart.
  Rouse, Britons, rouse for honor of your isle,
Your old good humor; and be seen to smile.
You say we write not like our fathers—true,
Nor were our fathers half so strict as you,   32
Damned not each error of the poet's pen,
But judging man, remembered they were men.
Awed into silence by the time's abuse,
Sleeps many a wise, and many a witty, muse;
We that for mere experiment come out   37
Are but the light armed rangers on the scout;
High on Parnassus' lofty summit stands
The immortal camp; there lie the chosen bands!   40
But give fair quarter to us puny elves,
The giants then will sally forth themselves,
With wit's sharp weapons vindicate the age,
And drive ev'n *Arthur's* magic [2] from the stage.

[1] Samuel Reddish (1735–1785), a second-rate actor, who appeared in various rôles at D.L. (1767–1777) and C.G. (1778–1779). He lost his mind and died in a mad-house at York.

[2] Dryden's *King Arthur, or The British Worthy* (1691) with alterations by Garrick and additional music by Dr. Arne was revived at D.L., Dec. 13, 1770. As it was performed twenty-one times during the season it was probably still "running" when *The West Indian* appeared. It contains an enchanted wood and other magical elements.

THE WEST INDIAN

ACT I

SCENE I. *A merchant's counting house*

In an inner room, set off by glass doors, are discovered several clerks employed at their desks. A writing table in the front room. STOCKWELL *is discovered reading a letter.* STUKELY *comes gently out of the back room and observes him some time before he speaks*

STUKELY. He seems disordered. Something in that letter, and I'm afraid of an unpleasant sort. He has many ventures of great account at sea, a ship richly freighted for Barcelona, another for Lisbon, and others expected from Cadiz of still greater value. Besides these, I know he has many deep concerns in foreign bottoms and underwritings to a vast amount. I'll accost him.—Sir! Mr. Stockwell!

STOCKWELL. Stukely!—Well, have you shipped the cloths?

STUKELY. I have, sir; here's the bill of lading, and copy of the invoice; the assortments are all compared. Mr. Traffick will give you the policy upon 'Change.

STOCKWELL. 'Tis very well. Lay these papers by, and no more business for a while. Shut the door, Stukely; I have had long proof of your friendship and fidelity to me; a matter of most intimate concern lies on my mind, and 'twill be a sensible relief to unbosom myself to you. I have just now been informed of the arrival of the young West Indian I have so long been expecting. You know who I mean.

STUKELY. Yes, sir; Mr. Belcour, the young gentleman who inherited old Belcour's great estates in Jamaica.

STOCKWELL. Hush, not so loud; come a little nearer this way. This Belcour is now in London; part of his baggage is already arrived, and I expect him every minute. Is it to be wondered at if his coming throws me into some agitation, when I tell you, Stukely, he is my son?

STUKELY. Your son!

STOCKWELL. Yes, sir, my only son. Early in life I accompanied his grandfather to Jamaica as his clerk. He had an only daughter somewhat older than myself, the mother of this gentleman. It was my chance (call it good or ill) to engage her affections; and, as the inferiority of my condition made it hopeless to expect her father's consent, her fondness provided an expedient and we were privately married. The issue of that concealed engagement is, as I have told you, this Belcour.

STUKELY. That event, surely, discovered your connection.

STOCKWELL. You shall hear. Not many days after our marriage old Belcour set out for England; and during his abode here my wife was, with great secrecy, delivered of this son. Fruitful in expedients to disguise her situation without parting from her infant, she contrived to have it laid at her door as a foundling. After some time her father returned, having left me here. In one of those favorable moments that decide the fortunes of prosperous men, this child was introduced; from that instant he treated him as his own, gave him his name, and brought him up in his family.

STUKELY. And did you never reveal this secret either to old Belcour or your son?

STOCKWELL. Never.

STUKELY. Therein you surprise me. A merchant of your eminence and a member of the British parliament might surely aspire without offence to the daughter of a planter. In this case, too, natural affection would prompt to a discovery.

STOCKWELL. Your remark is obvious; nor could I have persisted in this painful silence but in obedience to the dying injunctions of a beloved wife. The letter you found me reading conveyed those injunctions to me. It was dictated in her last illness and almost in the article of death. (You'll spare me the recital of it.) She there conjures me in terms as solemn as they are affecting never to reveal the secret of our marriage or withdraw my son while her father survived.

STUKELY. But on what motives did your unhappy lady found these injunctions?

STOCKWELL. Principally, I believe, from apprehension on my account, lest old Belcour, on whom at her decease I wholly depended, should withdraw his protection; in part from consideration of his repose, as well knowing the discovery would deeply affect his spirit, which was haughty, vehement, and unforgiving; and lastly, in regard to the interest of her infant, whom he had warmly adopted and for whom, in case of a discovery, everything was to be dreaded from his resentment. And, indeed, though the alteration in my condition might have justified me in discovering myself, yet I always thought my son safer in trusting to the caprice than to the justice of his grandfather. My judgment has not suffered by the event. Old Belcour is dead and has bequeathed his whole estate to him we are speaking of.

STUKELY. Now then you are no longer bound to secrecy.

STOCKWELL. True; but before I publicly reveal myself, I could wish to make some experiment of my son's disposition. This can be only done by letting his spirit take its course without restraint; by these means I think I shall discover much more of his real character under the title of his merchant than I should under that of his father.

SCENE II

A Sailor *enters, ushering in several* black servants, *carrying portmanteaus, trunks, &c.*

SAILOR. Save your honor! Is your name Stockwell, pray?

STOCKWELL. It is.

SAILOR. Part of my master Belcour's baggage an't please you. There's another cargo not far astern of us, and the cockswain has got charge of the dumb creatures.

STOCKWELL. Pr'ythee, friend, what dumb creatures do you speak of? Has Mr. Belcour brought over a collection of wild beasts?

SAILOR. No, Lord love him; no, not he. Let me see; there's two green monkies, a pair of grey parrots, a Jamaica sow and pigs, and a mangrove [1] dog; that's all.

STOCKWELL. Is that all?

SAILOR. Yes, your honor; yes that's all; bless his heart. A'might have brought over the whole island if he would; a didn't leave a dry eye in it.

STOCKWELL. Indeed! Stukely, show 'em where to bestow their baggage. Follow that gentleman.

SAILOR. Come, bear a hand, my lads, bear a hand.   *Exit with* STUKELY *and* Servants

STOCKWELL. If the principal tallies with his purveyors, he must be a singular spectacle in this place. He has a friend, however, in this seafaring fellow. 'Tis no bad prognostic of a man's heart when his shipmates give him a good word.   *Exit*

[1] Apparently a humorous perversion of "mongrel." A mangrove is a tropical tree.

SCENE III

Scene changes to a drawing-room. A Servant *discovered setting the chairs by, &c. A* Woman Servant *enters to him*

HOUSEKEEPER. Why, what a fuss does our good master put himself in about this West Indian. See what a bill of fare I've been forced to draw out; seven and nine I'll assure you, and only a family dinner as he calls it. Why, if my Lord Mayor was expected, there couldn't be a greater to-do about him.

SERVANT. I wish to my heart you had but seen the loads of trunks, boxes, and portmanteaus he has sent hither. An ambassador's baggage, with all the smuggled goods of his family, does not exceed it.

HOUSEKEEPER. A fine pickle he'll put the house into. Had he been master's own son and a Christian Englishman, there could not be more rout than there is about this Creolian, as they call 'em.

SERVANT. No matter for that; he's very rich and that's sufficient. They say he has rum and sugar enough belonging to him to make all the water in the Thames into punch. But I see my master coming.   *Exeunt*

SCENE IV

STOCKWELL *enters, followed by a* Servant

STOCKWELL. Where is Mr. Belcour? Who brought this note from him?

SERVANT. A waiter from the London Tavern, sir. He says the young gentleman is just dressed and will be with you directly.

STOCKWELL. Show him in when he arrives.

SERVANT. I shall, sir. (*Aside*) I'll have a peep at him first, however. I've a great mind to see this outlandish spark. The sailor says he'll make rare doings amongst us.

STOCKWELL. You need not wait. Leave me. (*Exit* Servant) Let me see.   (*Reads*)

Sir,
I write to you under the hands of the hairdresser. As soon as I have made myself decent and slipped on some fresh clothes, I will have the honor of paying you my devoirs.   Yours,
Belcour.

He writes at his ease, for he's unconscious to whom his letter is addressed; but what a palpitation does it throw my heart into, a father's heart! 'Tis an affecting interview. When my eyes meet a son whom yet they never saw, where shall I find constancy to support it? Should he resemble his mother, I am overthrown. All the letters I have had from him, for I industriously drew him into correspondence with me, bespeak him of quick and ready understanding. All the reports I ever received give me favorable impressions of his character, wild, perhaps, as the manner of his country is, but, I trust, not frantic [1] or unprincipled.

SCENE V

Servant enters

SERVANT. Sir, the foreign gentleman is come.

Another Servant

SERVANT. Mr. Belcour.

BELCOUR *enters*

STOCKWELL. Mr. Belcour, I'm rejoiced to see you. You're welcome to England!

BELCOUR. I thank you heartily, good Mr. Stockwell. You and I have long conversed at a distance; now we are met, and the pleasure this meeting gives me amply compensates for the perils I have run through in accomplishing it.

STOCKWELL. What perils, Mr. Belcour? I could not have thought you would have met a bad passage at this time o' year.

BELCOUR. Nor did we. Courier-like, we came posting to your shores upon the pinions of the swiftest gales that ever blew. 'Tis upon English ground all my difficulties have arisen; 'tis the passage from the riverside I complain of.

STOCKWELL. Ay, indeed! What obstructions can you have met between this and the riverside?

BELCOUR. Innumerable! Your town's as full of defiles as the island of Corsica; and I believe they are as obstinately defended. So much hurry, bustle, and confusion on your quays; so many sugar-casks, porter-butts, and common-council-men in your streets, that unless a man marched with artillery in his front, 'tis more than the labor of a Hercules can effect to make any tolerable way through your town.

STOCKWELL. I am sorry you have been so incommoded.

BELCOUR. Why, faith, 'twas all my own

[1] Affected by extreme folly.

fault. Accustomed to a land of slaves and out of patience with the whole tribe of custom-house extortioners, boatmen, tidewaiters,[2] and water-bailiffs[2] that beset me on all sides worse than a swarm of mosquitoes, I proceeded a little too roughly to brush them away with my rattan. The sturdy rogues took this in dudgeon and beginning to rebel, the mob chose different sides and a furious scuffle ensued, in the course of which my person and apparel suffered so much that I was obliged to step into the first tavern to refit before I could make my approaches in any decent trim.

STOCKWELL. (*Aside*) All without is as I wish. Dear Nature, add the rest and I am happy.— Well, Mr. Belcour, 'tis a rough sample you have had of my countrymen's spirit, but I trust you will not think the worse of them for it.

BELCOUR. Not at all, not at all. I like 'em the better. Was I only a visitor, I might, perhaps, wish them a little more tractable; but as a fellow subject and a sharer in their freedom I applaud their spirit though I feel the effects of it in every bone in my skin.

STOCKWELL. (*Aside*) That's well; I like that well. How gladly I could fall upon his neck and own myself his father.

BELCOUR. Well, Mr. Stockwell, for the first time in my life here am I in England, at the fountainhead of pleasure, in the land of beauty, of arts, and elegancies. My happy stars have given me a good estate, and the conspiring winds have blown me hither to spend it.

STOCKWELL. To use it, not to waste it, I should hope; to treat it, Mr. Belcour, not as a vassal, over whom you have a wanton and despotic power, but as a subject, which you are bound to govern with a temperate and restrained authority.

BELCOUR. True, sir; most truly said. Mine's a commission, not a right. I am the offspring of distress, and every child of sorrow is my brother. While I have hands to hold, therefore, I will hold them open to mankind. But, sir, my passions are my masters; they take me where they will; and oftentimes they leave to reason and to virtue nothing but my wishes and my sighs.

STOCKWELL. Come, come, the man who can accuse, corrects himself.

[2] Customs officers.

BELCOUR. Ah! that's an office I am weary of. I wish a friend would take it up. I would to heaven you had leisure for the employ; but did you drive a trade to the four corners of the world, you would not find the task so toilsome as to keep me free from faults.

STOCKWELL. Well, I am not discouraged; this candor tells me I should not have the fault of self-conceit to combat; that, at least, is not amongst the number.

BELCOUR. No; if I knew that man on earth who thought more humbly of me than I do of myself, I would take up his opinion and forego my own.

STOCKWELL. And, was I to choose a pupil, it should be one of your complexion; so if you'll come along with me, we'll agree upon your admission and enter on a course of lectures directly.

BELCOUR. With all my heart. *Exeunt*

SCENE VI. *Scene changes to a room in* LADY RUSPORT'S *house*

LADY RUSPORT *and* CHARLOTTE

LADY RUSPORT. Miss Rusport, I desire to hear no more of Captain Dudley and his destitute family. Not a shilling of mine shall ever cross the hands of any of them. Because my sister chose to marry a beggar, am I bound to support him and his posterity?

CHARLOTTE. I think you are.

LADY RUSPORT. You think I am; and pray where do you find the law that tells you so?

CHARLOTTE. I am not proficient enough to quote chapter and verse; but I take charity to be a main clause in the great statute of Christianity.

LADY RUSPORT. I say charity, indeed! And pray, miss, are you sure that it is charity, pure charity which moves you to plead for Captain Dudley? Amongst all your pity do you find no spice of a certain anti-spiritual passion called love? Don't mistake yourself; you are no saint, child, believe me; and I am apt to think the distresses of old Dudley and of his daughter into the bargain would never break your heart if there was not a certain young fellow of two-and-twenty in the case, who by the happy recommendation of a good person and the brilliant appointments of an ensigncy, will, if I am not mistaken, cozen you out of a fortune of twice twenty thousand pounds as soon as ever you are of age to bestow it upon him.

CHARLOTTE. A nephew of your ladyship's can never want any other recommendation with me; and, if my partiality for Charles Dudley is acquitted by the rest of the world, I hope Lady Rusport will not condemn me for it.

LADY RUSPORT. I condemn you! I thank heaven, Miss Rusport, I am no ways responsible for your conduct; nor is it any concern of mine how you dispose of yourself. You are not my daughter; and when I married your father, poor Sir Stephen Rusport, I found you a forward spoiled miss of fourteen, far above being instructed by me.

CHARLOTTE. Perhaps your ladyship calls this instruction.

LADY RUSPORT. You're strangely pert; but it's no wonder. Your mother, I'm told, was a fine lady and according to the modern style of education you was brought up. It was not so in my young days. There was then some decorum in the world, some subordination, as the great Locke expresses it. Oh! 'twas an edifying sight to see the regular deportment observed in our family. No giggling, no gossiping, was going on there; my good father, Sir Oliver Roundhead, never was seen to laugh himself nor ever allowed it in his children.

CHARLOTTE. Ay; those were happy times, indeed.

LADY RUSPORT. But in this forward age, we have coquettes in the eggshell and philosophers in the cradle, girls of fifteen that lead the fashion in new caps and new opinions, that have their sentiments and their sensations; and the idle fops encourage 'em in it. O' my conscience, I wonder what it is the men can see in such babies.

CHARLOTTE. True, madam; but all men do not overlook the maturer beauties of your ladyship's age. Witness that admirer, Major Dennis O'Flaherty; there's an example of some discernment. I declare to you, when your ladyship is by, the major takes no more notice of me that if I was part of the furniture of your chamber.

LADY RUSPORT. The major, child, has traveled through various kingdoms and climates and has more enlarged notions of female merit than falls to the lot of an English homebred lover. In most other countries no woman on your side forty would ever be named in a polite circle.

CHARLOTTE. Right, madam; I've been told that in Vienna they have coquettes upon crutches and Venuses in their grand climacteric. A lover there celebrates the wrinkles, not the dimples, in his mistress's face. The major, I think, has served in the imperial army.

LADY RUSPORT. Are you piqued, my young madam? Had my sister Louisa now yielded to the addresses of one of Major O'Flaherty's person and appearance, she would have had some excuse; but to run away, as she did, at the age of sixteen, too, with a man of old Dudley's sort —

CHARLOTTE. Was, in my opinion, the most venial trespass that ever girl of sixteen committed. Of a noble family, an engaging person, strict honor, and sound understanding, what accomplishment was there wanting in Captain Dudley but that which the prodigality of his ancestors had deprived him of?

LADY RUSPORT. They left him as much as he deserves. Hasn't the old man captain's half-pay? And is his son not an ensign?

CHARLOTTE. An ensign! Alas, poor Charles! Would to heaven he knew what my heart feels and suffers for his sake.

Servant *enters*

SERVANT. Ensign Dudley to wait upon your ladyship.

LADY RUSPORT. Who! Dudley! What can have brought him to town?

CHARLOTTE. Dear madam, 'tis Charles Dudley. 'Tis your nephew.

LADY RUSPORT. Nephew! I renounce him as my nephew. Sir Oliver renounced him as his grandson. Wasn't he son of the eldest daughter and only male descendant of Sir Oliver; and didn't he cut him off with a shilling? Didn't the poor, dear, good man leave his whole fortune to me, except a small annuity to my maiden sister, who spoiled her constitution with nursing him? And, depend upon it, not a penny of that fortune shall ever be disposed of otherwise than according to the will of the donor. (CHARLES DUDLEY *enters*) So, young man, whence come you? What brings you to town?

CHARLES. If there is any offence in my coming to town, your ladyship is in some degree responsible for it, for part of my errand was to pay my duty here.

LADY RUSPORT. I hope you have some better excuse than all this.

CHARLES. 'Tis true, madam, I have other motives; but, if I consider my trouble repaid by the pleasure I now enjoy, I should hope my aunt would not think my company the less welcome for the value I set upon hers.

LADY RUSPORT. Coxcomb! And where is your father, child, and your sister? Are they in town too?

CHARLES. They are.

LADY RUSPORT. Ridiculous! I don't know what people do in London who have no money to spend in it.

CHARLOTTE. Dear madam, speak more kindly to your nephew. How can you oppress a youth of his sensibility?

LADY RUSPORT. Miss Rusport, I insist upon your retiring to your apartment. When I want your advice I'll send to you. (*Exit* CHARLOTTE) So you have put on a red coat, too, as well as your father. 'Tis plain what value you set upon the good advice Sir Oliver used to give you. How often has he cautioned you against the army?

CHARLES. Had it pleased my grandfather to enable me to have obeyed his caution, I would have done it; but you well know how destitute I am; and 'tis not to be wondered at if I prefer the service of my king to that of any other master.

LADY RUSPORT. Well, well, take your own course; 'tis no concern of mine. You never consulted me.

CHARLES. I frequently wrote to your ladyship but could obtain no answer; and, since my grandfather's death, this is the first opportunity I have had of waiting upon you.

LADY RUSPORT. I must desire you not to mention the death of that dear, good man in my hearing. My spirits cannot support it.

CHARLES. I shall obey you. Permit me to say that, as that event has richly supplied you with the materials of bounty, the distresses of my family can furnish you with objects of it.

LADY RUSPORT. The distresses of your family, child, are quite out of the question at present. Had Sir Oliver been pleased to consider them, I should have been well content; but he has absolutely taken no notice of you in his will, and that to me must and

sentimental

shall be law. Tell your father and your sister I totally disapprove of their coming to town.

CHARLES. Must I tell my father that, before your ladyship knows the motive that brought him hither? Allured by the offer to exchanging, for a commission on full pay, the veteran after thirty years service, prepared to encounter the fatal heats of Senegambia [1] but wants a small supply to equip him for the expedition.

Servant enters

SERVANT. Major O'Flaherty to wait upon your ladyship.

MAJOR [O'FLAHERTY] *enters*

O'FLAHERTY. Spare your speeches, young man. Don't you think her ladyship can take my word for that? I hope, madam, 'tis evidence enough of my being present when I've the honor of telling you myself.

LADY RUSPORT. Major O'Flaherty! I am rejoiced to see you. Nephew Dudley, you perceive I'm engaged.

CHARLES. I shall not intrude upon your ladyship's more agreeable engagements. I presume I have my answer.

LADY RUSPORT. Your answer, child! What answer can you possibly expect, or how can your romantic father suppose that I am to abet him in all his idle and extravagant undertakings? Come, major, let me show you the way into my dressing room; and let us leave this young adventurer to his meditations.
Exit

O'FLAHERTY. I follow you, my lady.— Young gentleman, your obedient! [*Aside*] Upon my conscience, as fine a young fellow as I would wish to clap my eyes on. He might have answered my salute, however—Well, let it pass. Fortune, perhaps, frowns upon the poor lad. She's a damned slippery lady and very apt to jilt us poor fellows that wear cockades in our hats.[2] Fare thee well, honey, whoever thou art.
Exit

CHARLES. So much for the virtues of a puritan. Out upon it, her heart is flint; yet that woman, that aunt of mine, without one worthy particle in her composition would, I dare be sworn, as soon set her foot in a pest-house as in a playhouse. (*Going*)

MISS RUSPORT *enters to him*

CHARLOTTE. Stop, stay a little, Charles. Whither are you going in such haste?

CHARLES. Madam! Miss Rusport, what are your commands?

CHARLOTTE. Why so reserved? We had used to answer to no other names than those of Charles and Charlotte.

CHARLES. What ails you? You've been weeping.

CHARLOTTE. No, no; or if I have—your eyes are full, too; but I have a thousand things to say to you; before you go, tell me, I conjure you, where you are to be found. Here, give me your direction; write it upon the back of this visiting ticket.[3] Have you a pencil?

CHARLES. I have. But why should you desire to find us out? 'Tis a poor, little, inconvenient place; my sister has no apartment fit to receive you in.

Servant enters

SERVANT. Madam, my lady desires your company directly.

CHARLOTTE. I am coming. Well, have you wrote it? Give it me. O Charles! Either you do not, or you will not, understand me.

Exeunt severally

ACT II

SCENE I. *A room in* FULMER'S *house*

FULMER *and* MRS. FULMER

MRS. FULMER. Why, how you sit, musing and moping, sighing and desponding! I'm ashamed of you, Mr. Fulmer. Is this the country you described to me, a second Eldorado, rivers of gold and rocks of diamonds? You found me in a pretty snug retired way of life at Bologne, out of the noise and bustle of the world and wholly at my ease; you, indeed, was upon the wing, with a fiery persecution[4] at your back; but, like a true son of Loyola,[5] you had then a thousand ingenious devices to repair your fortune; and this your

---

[1] Senegambia was formerly the name of the region on the west coast of Africa between the Senegal and Gambia rivers. The term was not used after the latter part of the nineteenth century.

[2] I.e., soldiers.

[3] Card.

[4] The fear of Roman Catholics at this period culminated in the Gordon Riots (1780).

[5] Ignatius de Loyola (1491-1556), founder of the Society of Jesus. The Jesuits were popularly supposed to be crafty and false.

native country was to be the scene of your performances. Fool that I was to be inveigled into it by you; but, thank heaven, our partnership is revocable. I am not your wedded wife, praised be my stars! for what have we got, whom have we gulled but ourselves; which of all your trains has taken fire? even this poor expedient of your bookseller's shop seems abandoned, for if a chance customer drops in, who is there, pray, to help him to what he wants?

FULMER. Patty, you know it is not upon slight grounds that I despair; there had used to be a livelihood to be picked up in this country, both for the honest and dishonest. I have tried each walk and am likely to starve at last. There is not a point to which the wit and faculty of man can turn that I have not set mine to; but in vain. I am beat through every quarter of the compass.

MRS. FULMER. Ah! common efforts all! Strike me a master stroke, Mr. Fulmer, if you wish to make any figure in this country.

FULMER. But where, how, and what? I have blustered for prerogative; I have bellowed for freedom; I have offered to serve my country; I have engaged to betray it. A master stroke, truly! Why, I have talked treason, writ treason, and if a man can't live by that, he can live by nothing. Here I set up as a bookseller; why, men left off reading; and if I was to turn butcher, I believe, o' my conscience, they'd leave off eating.

CAPT. DUDLEY *crosses the stage*

MRS. FULMER. Why there now's your lodger old Captain Dudley, as he calls himself. There's no flint without fire; something might be struck out of him, if you'd the wit to find the way.

FULMER. Hang him, an old, dry-skinned curmudgeon; you may as well think to get truth out of a courtier or candor out of a critic. I can make nothing of him. Besides, he's poor and therefore not to our purpose.

MRS. FULMER. The more fool he! Would any man be poor that had such a prodigy in his possession?

FULMER. His daughter, you mean? She is indeed uncommonly beautiful.

MRS. FULMER. Beautiful! Why she need only be seen to have the first men in the kingdom at her feet. Egad, I wish I had the leasing of her beauty. What would some of our young nabobs[1] give—?

FULMER. Hush; here comes the captain. Good girl, leave us to ourselves, and let me try what I can make of him.

MRS. FULMER. Captain, truly; i' faith I'd have a regiment, had I such a daughter, before I was three months older. *Exit*

SCENE II

CAPT. DUDLEY *enters to him*

FULMER. Captain Dudley, good morning to you.

DUDLEY. Mr. Fulmer, I have borrowed a book from your shop; 'tis the sixth volume of my deceased friend Tristram.[2] He is a flattering writer to us poor soldiers; and the divine story of Le Fevre, which makes part of the book, in my opinion of it, does honor not to its author only, but to human nature.

FULMER. He is an author I keep in the way of trade, but one I never relished. He is much too loose and profligate for my taste.

DUDLEY. That's being too severe. I hold him to be a moralist in the noblest sense. He plays, indeed, with the fancy and sometimes perhaps too wantonly; but while he thus designedly masks his main attack, he comes at once upon the heart, refines, amends it, softens it, beats down each selfish barrier from about it, and opens every sluice of pity and benevolence.

FULMER. We of the catholic persuasion are not much bound to him.—Well, sir, I shall not oppose your opinion; a favorite author is like a favorite mistress; and there, you know, captain, no man likes to have his taste arraigned.

DUDLEY. Upon my word, sir, I don't know what a man likes in that case. 'Tis an experiment I never made.

FULMER. Sir! Are you serious?

DUDLEY. 'Tis of little consequence whether you think so.

FULMER. (*Aside*) What a formal old prig it is.—I apprehend you, sir; you speak with caution; you are married?

DUDLEY. I have been.

---

[1] The use of this word to mean a person who had returned from India with a fortune was new at this time.
[2] Laurence Sterne's *The Life and Opinions of Tristram Shandy, Gent.*, nine volumes, 1759-1767. Sterne had died in 1768.

FULMER. And this young lady, which accompanies you—

DUDLEY. Passes for my daughter.

FULMER. (*Aside*) Passes for his daughter! Humph—She is exceedingly beautiful, finely accomplished, of a most enchanting shape and air—

DUDLEY. You are much too partial; she has the greatest defect a woman can have.

FULMER. How so, pray?

DUDLEY. She has no fortune.

FULMER. Rather say that you have none; and that's a sore defect in one of your years, Captain Dudley. You've served, no doubt?

DUDLEY. (*Aside*) Familiar coxcomb! But I'll humor him.

FULMER. (*Aside*) A close old fox! But I'll unkennel him.

DUDLEY. Above thirty years I've been in the service, Mr. Fulmer.

FULMER. I guessed as much; I laid it at no less. Why 'tis a wearisome time; 'tis an apprenticeship to a profession, fit only for a patriarch. But preferment must be closely followed. You never could have been so far behind-hand in the chase unless you had palpably mistaken your way. You'll pardon me, but I begin to perceive you have lived in the world, not with it.

DUDLEY. It may be so; and you perhaps can give me better counsel. I am now soliciting a favor, an exchange to a company on full pay, nothing more; and yet I meet a thousand bars to that; though, without boasting, I should think the certificate of services which I sent in might have purchased that indulgence to me.

FULMER. Who thinks or cares about 'em? Certificate of services, indeed! Send in a certificate of your fair daughter; carry her in your hand with you.

DUDLEY. What! Who! My daughter! Carry my daughter; well, and what then?

FULMER. Why then your fortune's made, that's all.

DUDLEY. I understand you; and this you call knowledge of the world? Despicable knowledge; but, sirrah, I will have you know— (*Threatening him*)

FULMER. Help! Who's within? Would you strike me, sir; would you lift up your hand against a man in his own house?

DUDLEY. In a church, if he dare insult the poverty of a man of honor.

FULMER. Have a care what you do. Remember there is such a thing in law as assault and battery; ay, and such trifling forms as warrants and indictments.

DUDLEY. Go, sir; you are too mean for my resentment. 'Tis that, and not the law, protects you. Hence!

FULMER (*Aside*) An old, absurd, incorrigible blockhead! I'll be revenged of him.
Exit

SCENE III

YOUNG DUDLEY *enters to him*

CHARLES. What's the matter, sir? Sure I heard an outcry as I entered the house.

DUDLEY. Not unlikely; our landlord and his wife are forever wrangling.—Did you find your aunt [Rusport][1] at home?

CHARLES. I did.

DUDLEY. And what was your reception?

CHARLES. Cold as our poverty and her pride could make it.

DUDLEY. You told her the pressing occasion I had for a small supply to equip me for this exchange; has she granted me the relief I asked?

CHARLES. Alas! Sir, she has peremptorily refused it.

DUDLEY. That's hard; that's hard, indeed! My petition was for a small sum. She has refused it, you say? Well, be it so. I must not complain. Did you see the broker about the insurance on my life?

CHARLES. There again I am the messenger of ill news; I can raise no money, so fatal is the climate. Alas! that ever my father should be sent to perish in such a place!

SCENE IV

MISS DUDLEY *enters hastily*

DUDLEY. Louisa, what's the matter? You seem frightened.

LOUISA. I am, indeed. Coming from Miss Rusport's, I met a young gentleman in the streets who has beset me in the strangest manner.

CHARLES. Insufferable! Was he rude to you?

LOUISA. I cannot say he was absolutely rude to me, but he was very importunate to speak to me, and once or twice attempted to lift up my hat. He followed me to the corner of the street and there I gave him the slip.

[1] The first edition has *Dudley*, obviously an error.

THE WEST INDIAN

DUDLEY. You must walk no more in the streets, child, without me or your brother.

LOUISA. O Charles! Miss Rusport desires to see you directly. Lady Rusport is gone out, and she has something particular to say to you.

CHARLES. Have you any commands for me, sir?

DUDLEY. None, my dear. By all means wait upon Miss Rusport. Come, Louisa, I shall desire you to go up to your chamber and compose yourself. *Exeunt*

SCENE V

BELCOUR *enters, after peeping in at the door*

BELCOUR. Not a soul, as I'm alive. Why, what an odd sort of a house this is! Confound the little jilt; she has fairly given me the slip. A plague upon this London. I shall have no luck in it. Such a crowd, such a hurry, and such a number of shops, and one so like the other, that whether the wench turned into this house or the next, or whether she went up stairs or down stairs, (for there's a world above and a world below, it seems) I declare, I know no more than if I was in the Blue Mountains.[1] In the name of all the devils at once, why did she run away? If every handsome girl I meet in this town is to lead me such a wild goose chase, I had better have stayed in the torrid zone. I shall be wasted to the size of a sugar cane. What shall I do? Give the chase up? Hang it, that's cowardly. Shall I, a true-born son of Phœbus, suffer this little nimble-footed Daphne to escape me?— "Forbid it, honor, and forbid it, love." Hush! hush! here she comes! Oh! the devil! What tawdry thing have we got here?

MRS. FULMER *enters to him*

MRS. FULMER. Your humble servant, sir.
BELCOUR. Your humble servant, madam.
MRS. FULMER. A fine summer's day, sir.
BELCOUR. Yes, ma'am, and so cool that if the calendar didn't call it July, I should swear it was January.
MRS. FULMER. Sir!
BELCOUR. Madam!
MRS. FULMER. Do you wish to speak to Mr. Fulmer, sir?
BELCOUR. Mr. Fulmer, madam? I haven't the honor of knowing such a person.

[1] A mountain range in Jamaica.

MRS. FULMER. No, I'll be sworn, have you not? Thou art much too pretty a fellow, and too much of a gentleman to be an author thyself, or to have anything to say to those that are so. 'Tis the captain, I suppose, you are waiting for.

BELCOUR. I rather suspect it is the captain's wife.

MRS. FULMER. The captain has no wife, sir.

BELCOUR. No wife? I'm heartily sorry for it, for then she's his mistress; and that I take to be the more desperate case of the two. Pray, madam, wasn't there a lady just now turned into your house? 'Twas with her I wished to speak.

MRS. FULMER. What sort of a lady, pray?

BELCOUR. One of the loveliest sort my eyes ever beheld; young, tall, fresh, fair; in short, a goddess.

MRS. FULMER. Nay, but dear, dear sir, now I'm sure you flatter, for 'twas me you followed into the shop door this minute.

BELCOUR. You! No, no, take my word for it, it was not you, madam.

MRS. FULMER. But what is it you laugh at?

BELCOUR. Upon my soul, I ask your pardon; but it was not you, believe me; be assured it wasn't.

MRS. FULMER. Well, sir, I shall not contend for the honor of being noticed by you. I hope you think you wouldn't have been the first man that noticed me in the streets; however, this I'm positive of, that no living woman but myself has entered these doors this morning.

BELCOUR. Why, then I'm mistaken in the house, that's all, for 'tis not humanly possible I can be so far out in the lady. (*Going*)

MRS. FULMER. [*Aside*] Coxcomb! But hold —a thought occurs; as sure as can be he has seen Miss Dudley.—A word with you, young gentleman; come back.

BELCOUR. Well, what's your pleasure?

MRS. FULMER. You seem greatly captivated with this young lady. Are you apt to fall in love thus at first sight?

BELCOUR. Oh, yes. 'Tis the only way I ever can fall in love. Any man may tumble into a pit by surprise; none but a fool would walk into one by choice.

MRS. FULMER. You are a hasty lover, it seems. Have you spirit to be a generous one? They that will please the eye mustn't spare the purse.

BELCOUR. Try me; put me to the proof; bring me to an interview with the dear girl that has thus captivated me and see whether I have spirit to be grateful.

MRS. FULMER. But how, pray, am I to know the girl you have set your heart on?

BELCOUR. By an undescribable grace that accompanies every look and action that falls from her. There can be but one such woman in the world and nobody can mistake that one.

MRS. FULMER. Well, if I should stumble upon this angel in my walks, where am I to find you? What's your name?

BELCOUR. Upon my soul, I can't tell you my name.

MRS. FULMER. Not tell me! Why so?

BELCOUR. Because I don't know it myself; as yet I have no name.

MRS. FULMER. No name!

BELCOUR. None. A friend, indeed, lent me his; but he forbade me to use it on any unworthy occasion.

MRS. FULMER. But where is your place of abode?

BELCOUR. I have none. I never slept a night in England in my life.

MRS. FULMER. Hey-dey!

SCENE VI

FULMER *enters*

FULMER. A fine case, truly, in a free country; a pretty pass things are come to, if a man is to be assaulted in his own house.

MRS. FULMER. Who has assaulted you, my dear?

FULMER. Who! why this Captain Drawcansir,[1] this old Dudley, my lodger; but I'll unlodge him; I'll unharbor him, I warrant.

MRS. FULMER. Hush! Hush! Hold your tongue, man. Pocket the affront and be quiet. I've a scheme on foot will pay you for a hundred beatings. Why, you surprise me, Mr. Fulmer; Captain Dudley assault you! Impossible!

FULMER. Nay, I can't call it an absolute assault; but he threatened me.

MRS. FULMER. Oh, was that all? I thought how it would turn out—A like[ly] thing, truly for a person of his obliging compassionate turn. No, no, poor Captain Dudley, he has sorrows and distresses enough of his own to employ his spirits without setting them against other people. Make it up as fast as you can. Watch this gentleman out; follow him wherever he goes and bring me word who and what he is; be sure you don't lose sight of him. I've other business in hand. *Exit*

BELCOUR. Pray, sir, what sorrows and distresses have befallen this old gentleman you speak of?

FULMER. Poverty, disappointment, and all the distresses attendant thereupon: sorrow enough of all conscience. I soon found how it was with him by his way of living, low enough of all reason; but what I overheard this morning put it out of all doubt.

BELCOUR. What did you overhear this morning?

FULMER. Why, it seems he wants to join his regiment and has been beating the town over to raise a little money for that purpose upon his pay. But the climate, I find, where he is going is so unhealthy that nobody can be found to lend him any.

BELCOUR. Why, then, your town is a damned good-for-nothing town, and I wish I had never come into it.

FULMER. That's what I say, sir; the hardheartedness of some folks is unaccountable. There's an old Lady Rusport, a near relation of this gentleman's; she lives hard by here, opposite to Stockwell's, the great merchant; he sent her a begging, but to no purpose; though she is as rich as a Jew, she would not furnish him with a farthing.

BELCOUR. Is the captain at home?

FULMER. He is up stairs, sir.

BELCOUR. Will you take the trouble to desire him to step hither? I want to speak to him.

FULMER. I'll send him to you directly. [*Aside*] I don't know what to make of this young man; but, if I live, I will find him out, or know the reason why. *Exit*

BELCOUR. I've lost the girl, it seems; that's clear. She was the first object of my pursuit; but the case of this poor officer touches me; and, after all, there may be as much true delight in rescuing a fellow creature from distress as there would be in plunging one into it.— But let me see; it's a point that must be managed with some delicacy.—*A propos!* there's pen and ink.—I've struck upon a method that will do. (*Writes*) Ay, ay, this is the very thing; 'twas devilish lucky I happened to have these

[1] See *The Rehearsal*, Act V.

THE WEST INDIAN

bills about me. There, there, fare you well; I'm glad to be rid of you. You stood a chance of being worse applied, I can tell you.

(*Encloses and seals paper*)

Scene VII

Fulmer *brings in* Dudley

FULMER. That's the gentleman, sir. [*Aside*] I shall make bold, however, to lend an ear.

DUDLEY. Have you any commands for me, sir?

BELCOUR. Your name is Dudley, sir?

DUDLEY. It is.

BELCOUR. You command a company, I think, Captain Dudley?

DUDLEY. I did. I am now on half-pay.

BELCOUR. You've served some time?

DUDLEY. A pretty many years. Long enough to see some people of more merit, and better interest than myself, made general officers.

BELCOUR. Their merit I may have some doubt of; their interest I can readily give credit to; there is little promotion to be looked for in your profession, I believe, without friends, captain?

DUDLEY. I believe so too. Have you any other business with me, may I ask?

BELCOUR. Your patience for a moment. I was informed you was about to join your regiment in distant quarters abroad.

DUDLEY. I have been soliciting an exchange to a company on full-pay quartered at James's Fort, in Senegambia; but I'm afraid I must drop the undertaking.

BELCOUR. Why so, pray?

DUDLEY. Why so, sir? 'Tis a home question for a perfect stranger to put; there is something very particular in all this.

BELCOUR. If it is not impertinent, sir, allow me to ask you what reason you have for despairing of success.

DUDLEY. Why, really, sir, mine is an obvious reason for a soldier to have—Want of money; simply that.

BELCOUR. May I beg to know the sum you have occasion for?

DUDLEY. Truly, sir, I cannot exactly tell you on a sudden; nor is it, I suppose, of any great consequence to you to be informed; but I should guess, in the gross, that two hundred pounds would serve.

BELCOUR. And do you find a difficulty in raising that sum upon your pay? 'Tis done every day.

DUDLEY. The nature of the climate makes it difficult. I can get no one to insure my life.

BELCOUR. Oh! that's a circumstance may make for you, as well as against. In short, Captain Dudley, it so happens that I can command the sum of two hundred pounds. Seek no farther; I'll accommodate you with it upon easy terms.

DUDLEY. Sir! do I understand you rightly? —I beg your pardon; but am I to believe that you are in earnest?

BELCOUR. What is your surprise? Is it an uncommon thing for a gentleman to speak truth; or is it incredible that one fellow creature should assist another?

DUDLEY. I ask your pardon—May I beg to know to whom? Do you propose this in the way of business?

BELCOUR. Entirely. I have no other business on earth.

DUDLEY. Indeed! you are not a broker, I'm persuaded.

BELCOUR. I am not.

DUDLEY. Nor an army agent, I think?

BELCOUR. I hope you will not think the worst of me for being neither. In short, sir, if you will peruse this paper, it will explain to you who I am and upon what terms I act. While you read it, I will step home and fetch the money; and we will conclude the bargain without loss of time. In the meanwhile, good day to you.   *Exit hastily*

DUDLEY. Humph! there's something very odd in all this.—Let me see what we've got here.—This paper is to tell me who he is and what are his terms. In the name of wonder, why has he sealed it! Hey-dey! what's here? Two bank notes, of a hundred each! I can't comprehend what this means. Hold; here's a writing; perhaps that will show me. "Accept this trifle; pursue your fortune and prosper." —Am I in a dream? Is this a reality?

Scene VIII

Enter Major O'Flaherty

MAJOR. Save you, my dear! Is it you now that are Captain Dudley, I would ask?— [DUDLEY *rushes to the door and looks out.*] Whuh! What's the hurry the man's in? If 'tis the lad that run out of the shop you would overtake, you might as well stay where you are. By my soul, he's as nimble as a Croat;[1] you are a full hour's march in his rear.—Ay, faith, you may as well turn back and give over the pursuit. Well, Captain Dudley, if that's your name, there's a letter for you. Read, man, read it; and I'll have a word with you after you've done.

DUDLEY. More miracles on foot! So, so, from Lady Rusport.

O'FLAHERTY. You're right, it is from her ladyship.

DUDLEY. Well, sir, I have cast my eye over it; 'tis short and peremptory; are you acquainted with the contents?

O'FLAHERTY. Not at all, my dear, not at all.

DUDLEY. Have you any message from Lady Rusport?

O'FLAHERTY. Not a syllable, honey. Only when you've digested the letter, I've a bit of a message to deliver you from myself.

DUDLEY. And may I beg to know who yourself is?

O'FLAHERTY. Dennis O'Flaherty, at your service; a poor major of grenadiers, nothing better.

DUDLEY. So much for your name and title, sir. Now be so good as to favor me with your message.

O'FLAHERTY. Why, then, captain, I must tell you I have promised Lady Rusport you shall do whatever it is she bids you to do in that letter there.

DUDLEY. Ay, indeed; have you undertaken so much, major, without knowing either what she commands or what I can perform?

O'FLAHERTY. That's your concern, my dear, not mine; I must keep my word, you know.

DUDLEY. Or else, I suppose, you and I must measure swords?

O'FLAHERTY. Upon my soul, you've hit it.

DUDLEY. That would hardly answer to either of us. You and I have probably had enough of fighting in our time before now.

O'FLAHERTY. Faith and troth, Master Dudley, you may say that. 'Tis thirty years, come the time, that I have followed the trade, and in a pretty many countries.—Let me see— In the war before last[2] I served in the Irish Brigade, d'ye see? There, after bringing off the French monarch, I left his service with a British bullet in my body and this ribband in my button-hole. Last war[3] I followed the fortunes of the German eagle, in the corps of grenadiers; there I had my belly-full of fighting and a plentiful scarcity of everything else. After six and twenty engagements, great and small, I went off with this gash on my skull and a kiss of the empress queen's[4] sweet hand (Heaven bless it) for my pains. Since the peace, my dear, I took a little turn with the Confederates in Poland[5]—but such another set of madcaps!—By the Lord Harry, I never knew what it was they were scuffling about.

DUDLEY. Well, major, I won't add another action to the list. You shall keep your promise with Lady Rusport. She requires me to leave London; and you may take what credit you please from my compliance.

O'FLAHERTY. Give me your hand, my dear boy. This will make her my own; when that's the case, we shall be brothers you know and we'll share her fortune between us.

DUDLEY. Not so, major. The man who marries Lady Rusport will have a fair title to her whole fortune without division. But I hope your expectations of prevailing are founded upon good reasons.

O'FLAHERTY. Upon the best grounds in the world. First I think she will comply because she is a woman; secondly, I am persuaded she won't hold out long because she's a widow; and thirdly, I make sure of her because I've married five wives and never failed yet; and for what I know, they're all alive and merry at this very hour.

DUDLEY. Well, sir, go on and prosper. If you can inspire Lady Rusport with half your charity, I shall think you deserve all her fortune. At present, I must beg your excuse. Good morning to you. *Exit*

O'FLAHERTY. A good, sensible man, and very much of a soldier. I did not care if I was better acquainted with him; but 'tis an awkward kind of counter for that. The English, I observe, are close friends but distant acquaintance. I suspect the old lady has not

---

[1] The major, having served in the Seven Years' War, had, presumably, met Croatian soldiers in the Austrian service.

[2] War of the Austrian Succession, 1740–1748. An Irish brigade in French service fought against George II at Dettingen, and see Smollett's *Roderick Random*, the hero of which was also present in the French army.

[3] The Seven Years' War (1756–1763).

[4] Maria Theresa (1717–1780). Empress of Austria and Queen of Hungary.

[5] An abortive Polish uprising in 1768 was known as the Confederation of the Bar.

been over generous to poor Dudley. I shall give her a little touch about that. Upon my soul, I know but one excuse a person can have for giving nothing, and that is, like myself, having nothing to give. *Exit*

SCENE IX. *Scene changes to* LADY RUSPORT'S *house. A dressing-room*

MISS RUSPORT *and* LUCY

CHARLOTTE. Well, Lucy, you've dislodged the old lady at last; but methought you was a tedious time about it.

LUCY. A tedious time, indeed! I think they who have least to spare contrive to throw the most away. I thought I should never have got her out of the house.

CHARLOTTE. Why, she's as deliberate in canvassing every article of her dress as an ambassador would be in settling the preliminaries of a treaty.

LUCY. There was a new hood and handkerchief that had come express from Holborn-Hill on the occasion, that took as much time in adjusting—

CHARLOTTE. As they did in making, and she was as vain of them as an old maid of a young lover.

LUCY. Or a young lover of himself. Then, madam, this being a visit of ceremony to a person of distinction at the west end of the town, the old state chariot was dragged forth on the occasion, with strict charges to dress out the box with the leopard skin hammer-cloth.

CHARLOTTE. Yes, and to hang the false tails on the miserable stumps of the old crawling cattle. Well, well, pray heaven the crazy affair don't break down again with her! At least till she gets to her journey's end.—But where's Charles Dudley? Run down, dear girl, and be ready to let him in. I think he's as long in coming as she was in going.

LUCY. Why, indeed, madam, you seem the more alert of the two, I must say. *Exit*

CHARLOTTE. Now, the deuce take the girl for putting that notion into my head. I'm sadly afraid Dudley does not like me. So much encouragement as I have given him to declare himself! I never could get a word from him on the subject. This may be very honorable, but upon my life it's very provoking. By the way, I wonder how I look to-day. Oh! shockingly, hideously pale! like a witch. This is the old lady's glass, and she has left some of her wrinkles on it. How frightfully have I put on my cap, all awry! and my hair dressed so unbecomingly! Altogether I'm a most complete fright.

SCENE X

CHARLES DUDLEY *comes in unobserved*

CHARLES. That I deny.

CHARLOTTE. Ah!

CHARLES. Quarrelling with your glass, cousin? Make it up; make it up and be friends. It cannot compliment you more than by reflecting you as you are.

CHARLOTTE. Well, I vow, my dear Charles, that is delightfully said and deserves my very best curtsy. Your flattery, like a rich jewel, has a value not only from its superior luster but from its extreme scarceness. I verily think this is the only civil speech you ever directed to my person in your life.

CHARLES. And I ought to ask pardon of your good sense for having done it now.

CHARLOTTE. Nay, now you relapse again. Don't you know if you keep well with a woman on the great score of beauty, she'll never quarrel with you on the trifling article of good sense? But anything serves to fill up a dull yawning hour with an insipid cousin. You have brighter moments and warmer spirits for the dear girl of your heart.

CHARLES. Oh! fie upon you, fie upon you!

CHARLOTTE. You blush, and the reason is apparent. You are a novice at hypocrisy; but no practice can make a visit of ceremony pass for a visit of choice. Love is ever before its time; friendship is apt to lag a little after it. Pray, Charles, did you make any extraordinary haste hither?

CHARLES. By your question, I see you acquit me of the impertinence of being in love.

CHARLOTTE. But why impertinence? Why the impertinence of being in love? You have one language for me, Charles, and another for the woman of your affection.

CHARLES. You are mistaken. The woman of my affection shall never hear any other language from me than what I use to you.

CHARLOTTE. I am afraid, then, you'll never make yourself understood by her.

CHARLES. It is not fit I should. There is no need of love to make me miserable. 'Tis wretchedness enough to be a beggar.

CHARLOTTE. A beggar do you call yourself! O Charles, Charles, rich in every merit and accomplishment, whom may you not aspire to? And why think you so unworthily of our sex as to conclude there is not one to be found with sense to discern your virtue and generosity to reward it?

CHARLES. You distress me. I must beg to hear no more.

CHARLOTTE. Well, I can be silent.—[*Aside*] Thus does he always serve me whenever I am about to disclose myself to him.

CHARLES. Why do you not banish me and my misfortunes forever from your thoughts?

CHARLOTTE. Ay, wherefore do I not, since you never allowed me a place in yours? But go, sir. I have no right to stay you. Go where your heart directs you, go to the happy, the distinguished fair one.

CHARLES. Now, by all that's good, you do me wrong. There is no such fair one for me to go to, nor have I an acquaintance amongst the sex, yourself excepted, which answers to that description.

CHARLOTTE. Indeed!

CHARLES. In very truth. There then let us drop the subject. May you be happy though I never can!

CHARLOTTE. O, Charles, give me your hand. If I have offended you, I ask your pardon. You have been long acquainted with my temper, and know how to bear with its infirmities.

CHARLES. Thus, my dear Charlotte, let us seal our reconciliation (*Kissing her hand*). Bear with thy infirmities! By heaven, I know not any one failing in thy whole composition, except that of too great a partiality for an undeserving man.

CHARLOTTE. And you are now taking the very course to augment that failing. A thought strikes me. I have a commission that you must absolutely execute for me. I have immediate occasion for the sum of two hundred pounds. You know my fortune is shut up till I am of age. Take this paltry box; it contains my ear-rings and some other baubles I have no use for; carry it to our opposite neighbor, Mr. Stockwell. I don't know where else to apply. Leave it as a deposit in his hands and beg him to accommodate me with the sum.

CHARLES. Dear Charlotte, what are you about to do? How can you possibly want two hundred pounds?

CHARLOTTE. How can I possibly do without it, you mean? Doesn't every lady want two hundred pounds? Perhaps I have lost it at play; perhaps I mean to win as much to it; perhaps I want it for two hundred different uses.

CHARLES. Pooh! pooh! all this is nothing; don't I know you never play?

CHARLOTTE. You mistake. I have a spirit to set not only this trifle but my whole fortune upon a stake; therefore make no wry faces, but do as I bid you. You will find Mr. Stockwell a very honorable gentleman.

LUCY *enters in haste*

LUCY. Dear madam, as I live, here comes the old lady in a hackney-coach.

CHARLOTTE. The old chariot has given her a second tumble. Away with you; you know your way out without meeting her. Take the box and do as I desire you.

CHARLES. I must not dispute your orders. Farewell! *Exeunt* CHARLES *and* CHARLOTTE

SCENE XI

LADY RUSPORT *enters leaning on* MAJOR O'FLAHERTY'S *arm*

O'FLAHERTY. Rest yourself upon my arm; never spare it; 'tis strong enough. It has stood harder service than you can put it to.

LUCY. Mercy upon me, what's the matter? I am frightened out of my wits. Has your ladyship had an accident?

LADY RUSPORT. O Lucy! The most untoward one in nature. I know not how I shall repair it.

O'FLAHERTY. Never go about to repair it, my lady. Even build a new one; 'twas but a crazy piece of business at best.

LUCY. Bless me, is the old chariot broke down with you again?

LADY RUSPORT. Broke, child? I don't know what might have been broke, if, by great good fortune, this obliging gentleman had not been at hand to assist me.

LUCY. Dear madam, let me run and fetch you a cup of the cordial drops.

LADY RUSPORT. Alas! Sir, ever since I lost my husband, my poor nerves have been shook to pieces. There hangs his beloved picture; that precious relic, and a plentiful jointure, is all that remains to console me for the best of men.

O'FLAHERTY. Let me see. I' faith a comely personage. By his fur cloak I suppose he was in the Russian service, and by the gold chain round his neck I should guess he had been honored with the order of St. Catharine.[1]

LADY RUSPORT. No, no. He meddled with no St. Catharines. That's the habit he wore in his mayoralty. Sir Stephen was Lord Mayor of London. But he is gone and has left me a poor, weak, solitary widow behind him.

O'FLAHERTY. By all means, then, take a strong, able, hearty man to repair his loss. If such a plain fellow as one Dennis O'Flaherty can please you, I think I may venture to say, without any disparagement to the gentleman in the fur gown there—

LADY RUSPORT. What are you going to say? Don't shock my ears with any comparisons, I desire.

O'FLAHERTY. Not I, by my soul. I don't believe there's any comparison in the case.

Enter LUCY *with the drops*

LADY RUSPORT. Oh, are you come? Give me the drops. I'm all in a flutter.

O'FLAHERTY. Hark'e, sweetheart, what are those same drops? Have you any more left in the bottle? I don't care if I took a little sip of them myself.

LUCY. Oh! Sir, they are called the cordial restorative elixir, or the nervous golden drops. They are only for ladies' cases.

O'FLAHERTY. Yes, yes, my dear, there are gentlemen as well as ladies that stand in need of those same golden drops. They'd suit my case to a tittle. *Exit* LUCY

LADY RUSPORT. Well, major, did you give old Dudley my letter, and will the silly man do as I bid him and be gone?

O'FLAHERTY. You are obeyed; he's on the march.

LADY RUSPORT. That's well. You have managed this matter to perfection. I didn't think he would have been so easily prevailed upon.

O'FLAHERTY. At the first word; no difficulty in life. 'Twas the very thing he was determined to do before I came. I never met a more obliging gentleman.

LADY RUSPORT. Well, 'tis no matter, so I am but rid of him and his distresses. Would you believe it, Major O'Flaherty, it was but this morning he sent a-begging to me for money to fit him out upon some wild-goose expedition to the coast of Africa, I know not where.

O'FLAHERTY. Well, you sent him what he wanted?

LADY RUSPORT. I sent him what he deserved, a flat refusal.

O'FLAHERTY. You refused him!

LADY RUSPORT. Most undoubtedly.

O'FLAHERTY. You sent him nothing!

LADY RUSPORT. Not a shilling.

O'FLAHERTY. Good morning to you—Your servant— *(Going)*

LADY RUSPORT. Heyday! What ails the man? Where are you going?

O'FLAHERTY. Out of your house before the roof falls on my head—to poor Dudley, to share the little modicum that thirty years hard service has left me. I wish it was more for his sake.

LADY RUSPORT. Very well, sir. Take your course. I shan't attempt to stop you. I shall survive it; it will not break my heart if I never see you more.

O'FLAHERTY. Break your heart! No, o' my conscience will it not—You preach and you pray and you turn up your eyes, and all the while you're as hard-hearted as a hyena. A hyena, truly! By my soul there isn't in the whole creation so savage an animal as a human creature without pity. *Exit*

LADY RUSPORT. A hyena, truly! Where did the fellow blunder upon that word? Now the deuce take him for using it and the macaronies[2] for inventing it.

ACT III

SCENE I. *A room in* STOCKWELL'S *house*

STOCKWELL *and* BELCOUR

STOCKWELL. Gratify me so far, however, Mr. Belcour, as to see Miss Rusport. Carry her the sum she wants and return the poor girl her box of diamonds, which Dudley left in my hands. You know what to say on the occasion better than I do. That part of your

---

[1] An error of Cumberland's, as this order (founded 1714 by Peter the Great as the Order of Rescue) was for women. The reference should be, in all probability, to the Order of St. George, founded 1769, for military service, by Catherine the Great.

[2] Fops of the period.

commission I leave to your own discretion and you may season it with what gallantry you think fit.

BELCOUR. You could not have pitched upon a greater bungler at gallantry than myself if you had rummaged every company in the city and the whole court of aldermen into the bargain. Part of your errand, however, I will do; but whether it shall be with an ill grace or a good one depends upon the caprice of a moment, the humor of the lady, the mode of our meeting, and a thousand undefinable small circumstances that nevertheless determine us upon all the great occasions of life.

STOCKWELL. I persuade myself you will find Miss Rusport an ingenuous, worthy, animated girl.

BELCOUR. Why, I like her the better as a woman, but name her not to me as a wife! No, if ever I marry, it must be to a staid, sober, considerate damsel with blood in her veins as cold as a turtle's, quick of scent as a vulture when danger's in the wind, wary and sharp-sighted as a hawk when treachery is on foot. With such a companion at my elbow forever whispering in my ear, "Have a care of this man; he's a cheat. Don't go near that woman; she's a jilt. Over head there's a scaffold, under foot there's a well." Oh! sir, such a woman might lead me up and down this great city without difficulty or danger; but with a girl of Miss Rusport's complexion, heaven and earth! Sir, we should be duped, undone, and distracted in a fortnight.

STOCKWELL. Ha! ha! ha! Why you are become wondrous circumspect of a sudden, pupil; and if you can find such a prudent damsel as you describe, you have my consent. Only beware how you choose; discretion is not the reigning quality amongst the fine ladies of the present time; and I think in Miss Rusport's particular I have given you no bad counsel.

BELCOUR. Well, well, if you'll fetch me the jewels, I believe I can undertake to carry them to her; but as for the money, I'll have nothing to do with that. Dudley would be your fittest ambassador on that occasion, and, if I mistake not, the most agreeable to the lady.

STOCKWELL. Why, indeed, from what I know of the matter, it may not improbably be destined to find its way into his pockets.
Exit

BELCOUR. Then depend upon it, these are not the only trinkets she means to dedicate to Captain Dudley. As for me, Stockwell indeed wants me to marry; but till I can get this bewitching girl, this incognita, out of my head, I can never think of any other woman.

Servant enters and delivers a letter

Hey-day! Where can I have picked up a correspondent already? 'Tis a most execrable manuscript.—Let me see.—Martha Fulmer—Who is Martha Fulmer? Pshaw! I won't be at the trouble of deciphering her damned pothooks. Hold, hold, hold! What have we got here?

Dear Sir,

I've discovered the lady you was so much smitten with, and can procure you an interview with her. If you can be as generous to a pretty girl as you was to a paltry old captain, (How did she find that out?) you need not despair. Come to me immediately. The lady is now in my house and expects you.

Yours,
Martha Fulmer.

O thou dear, lovely, and enchanting paper, which I was about to tear into a thousand scraps, devoutly I entreat thy pardon. I have slighted thy contents, which are delicious, slandered thy characters, which are divine; and all the atonement I can make is implicitly to obey thy mandates.

STOCKWELL *returns*

STOCKWELL. Mr. Belcour, here are the jewels; this letter encloses bills for the money; and, if you will deliver it to Miss Rusport, you'll have no farther trouble on that score.

BELCOUR. Ah, sir! the letter which I've been reading disqualifies me for delivering the letter which you have been writing. I have other game on foot. The loveliest girl my eyes ever feasted upon is started in view, and the world cannot now divert me from pursuing her.

STOCKWELL. Hey-dey! What has turned you thus on a sudden?

BELCOUR. A woman; one that can turn and overturn me and my tottering resolutions every way she will. Oh, sir, if this is folly in me, you must rail at nature; you must chide the sun, that was vertical at my birth and would not wink upon my nakedness but swaddled me in the broadest, hottest glare of his meridian beams.

STOCKWELL. Mere[1] rhapsody; mere childish rhapsody; the libertine's familiar plea—Nature made us, 'tis true, but we are the responsible creators of our own faults and follies.

BELCOUR. Sir!

STOCKWELL. Slave of every face you meet, some hussy has inveigled you, some handsome profligate, (the town is full of them) and when once fairly bankrupt in constitution, as well as fortune, nature no longer serves as your excuse for being vicious, necessity, perhaps, will stand your friend, and you'll reform.

BELCOUR. You are severe.

STOCKWELL. It fits me to be so. It well becomes a father—I would say a friend—(*Aside*) How strangely I forget myself. How difficult it is to counterfeit indifference and put a mask upon the heart. I've struck him hard; he reddens.

BELCOUR. How could you tempt me so? Had you not inadvertently dropped the name of father, I fear our friendship, short as it has been, would scarce have held me. But even your mistake I reverence. Give me your hand. 'Tis over.

STOCKWELL. Generous young man, let me embrace you.—How shall I hide my tears?—I have been to blame; because I bore you the affection of a father, I rashly took up the authority of one. I ask your pardon. Pursue your course; I have no right to stop it.—What would you have me do with these things?

BELCOUR. This, if I might advise; carry the money to Miss Rusport immediately; never let generosity wait for its materials; that part of the business presses. Give me the jewels; I'll find an opportunity of delivering them into her hands; and your visit may prepare the way for my reception. *Exit*

STOCKWELL. Be it so. Good morning to you. Farewell, advice! Away he goes upon the wing for pleasure. What passions he awakens in me! He pains, yet pleases me, affrights, offends, yet grows upon my heart. His very failings set him off. Forever trespassing, forever atoning. I almost think he would not be so perfect, were he free from fault. I must dissemble longer; and yet how painful the experiment! Even now he's gone upon some wild adventure, and who can tell what mischief may befall him! O Nature, what it is to be a father! Just such a thoughtless, headlong thing was I when I beguiled his mother into love. *Exit*

SCENE II. *Scene changes to* FULMER's *house*

FULMER *and his wife*

FULMER. I tell you, Patty, you are a fool to think of bringing him and Miss Dudley together; 'twill ruin everything and blow your whole scheme up to the moon at once.

MRS. FULMER. Why, sure, Mr. Fulmer, I may be allowed to rear a chicken of my own hatching, as they say. Who first sprung the thought but I, pray? Who contrived the plot? Who proposed the letter, but I, I?

FULMER. And who dogged the gentleman home? Who found out his name, fortune, connection, that he was a West Indian, fresh landed, and full of cash, a gull to our heart's content, a hot-brained, headlong spark that would run into our trap like a wheat-ear under a turf?

MRS. FULMER. Hark! He's come. Disappear, march; and leave the field open to my machinations. *Exit* FULMER

SCENE III

BELCOUR *enters to her*

BELCOUR. O, thou dear minister to my happiness, let me embrace thee! Why thou art my polar star, my propitious constellation, by which I navigate my impatient bark into the port of pleasure and delight.

MRS. FULMER. Oh, you men are fly[2] creatures! Do you remember now, you cruel, what you said to me this morning?

BELCOUR. All a jest, a frolic; never think on't; bury it forever in oblivion. Thou! Why thou, art all over nectar and ambrosia, powder of pearl and odor of roses; thou hast the youth of Hebe, the beauty of Venus, and the pen of Sappho. But, in the name of all that's lovely, where's the lady? I expected to find her with you.

MRS. FULMER. No doubt you did, and these raptures were designed for her, but where have you loitered? The lady's gone; you are too late. Girls of her sort are not to be kept waiting like negro slaves in your sugar plantations.

[1] Pure. [2] Sharp.

Belcour. Gone; whither is she gone? Tell me that I may follow her.

Mrs. Fulmer. Hold, hoid! Not so fast, young gentleman. This is a case of some delicacy. Should Captain Dudley know that I introduced you to his daughter, he is a man of such scrupulous honor—

Belcour. What do you tell me! Is she daughter to the old gentleman I met here this morning?

Mrs. Fulmer. The same; him you was so generous to.

Belcour. There's an end of the matter then at once. It shall never be said of me that I took advantage of the father's necessities to trepan the daughter. *(Going)*

Mrs. Fulmer. *(Aside)* So, so, I've made a wrong cast. He's one of your conscientious sinners I find, but I won't lose him thus—Ha! ha! ha!

Belcour. What is it you laugh at?

Mrs. Fulmer. Your absolute inexperience. Have you lived so very little time in this country as not to know that between young people of equal ages the term "sister" often is a cover for that of mistress? This young lady is, in that sense of the word, sister to young Dudley and consequently daughter to my old lodger.

Belcour. Indeed! Are you serious?

Mrs. Fulmer. Can you doubt it? I must have been pretty well assured of that before I invited you hither.

Belcour. That's true. She cannot be a woman of honor, and Dudley is an unconscionable young rogue to think of keeping one fine girl in pay by raising contributions on another. He shall therefore give her up. She is a dear, bewitching, mischievous little devil; and he shall positively give her up.

Mrs. Fulmer. Ay, now the freak has taken you again. I say, give her up. There's one way, indeed, and certain of success.

Belcour. What's that?

Mrs. Fulmer. Out-bid him. Never dream of out-blust'ring him. Buy out his lease of possession and leave her to manage his ejectment.

Belcour. Is she so venal? Never fear me then. When beauty is the purchase, I shan't think much of the price.

Mrs. Fulmer. All things, then, will be made easy enough. Let me see. Some little genteel present to begin with. What have you got about you? Ay, search; I can bestow it to advantage. There's no time to be lost.

Belcour. Hang it, confound it; a plague upon't, say I! I haven't a guinea left in my pocket. I parted from my whole stock here this morning and have forgot to supply myself since.

Mrs. Fulmer. Mighty well. Let it pass then. There's an end. Think no more of the lady, that's all.

Belcour. Distraction! Think no more of her? Let me only step home and provide myself. I'll be back with you in an instant.

Mrs. Fulmer. Pooh, pooh! That's a wretched shift. Have you nothing of value about you? Money's a coarse slovenly vehicle, fit only to bribe electors in a borough. There are more graceful ways of purchasing a lady's favors; rings, trinkets, jewels!

Belcour. Jewels! Gadso, I protest I had forgot. I have a case of jewels. But they won't do; I must not part from them. No, no, they are appropriated. They are none of my own.

Mrs. Fulmer. Let me see, let me see! Ay, now, this were something like. Pretty creatures, how they sparkle! These would ensure success.

Belcour. Indeed!

Mrs. Fulmer. These would make her your own forever.

Belcour. Then the deuce take 'em for belonging to another person. I could find in my heart to give 'em the girl and swear I've lost them.

Mrs. Fulmer. Ay, do, say they were stolen out of your pocket.

Belcour. No, hang it, that's dishonorable. Here, give me the paltry things. I'll write you an order on my merchant for double their value.

Mrs. Fulmer. An order! No; order for me no orders upon merchants, with their value received and three days grace, their noting, protesting, and endorsing, and all their counting-house formalities. I'll have nothing to do with them. Leave your diamonds with me and give your order for the value of them to the owner. The money would be as good as the trinkets, I warrant you.

Belcour. Hey! How! I never thought of that; but a breach of trust; 'tis impossible. I never can consent; therefore give me the jewels back again.

Mrs. Fulmer. Take 'em. I am now to tell you the lady is in this house.

Belcour. In this house?

Mrs. Fulmer. Yes, sir, in this very house; but what of that? You have got what you like better, your toys, your trinkets. Go, go. Oh! you're a man of notable spirit, are you not?

Belcour. Provoking creature! Bring me to the sight of the dear girl and dispose of me as you think fit.

Mrs. Fulmer. And of the diamonds too?

Belcour. Damn 'em. I would there was not such a bauble in nature! But come, come, dispatch. If I had the throne of Delhi, I should give it to her.

Mrs. Fulmer. Swear to me then that you will keep within bounds. Remember she passes for the sister of young Dudley. Oh! If you come to your flights and your rhapsodies, she'll be off in an instant.

Belcour. Never fear me.

Mrs. Fulmer. You must expect to hear her talk of her father, as she calls him, and her brother, and your bounty to the family.

Belcour. Ay, ay, never mind what she talks of, only bring her.

Mrs. Fulmer. You'll be prepared upon that head?

Belcour. I shall be prepared, never fear. Away with you!

Mrs. Fulmer. But hold, I had forgot. Not a word of the diamonds. Leave that matter to my management.

Belcour. Hell and vexation! Get out of the room, or I shall run distracted. (*Exit* Mrs. Fulmer) Of a certain, Belcour, thou art born to be the fool of woman. Sure, no man sins with so much repentance, or repents with so little amendment as I do. I cannot give away another person's property; honor forbids me; and I positively cannot give up the girl. Love, passion, constitution, everything protests against that. How shall I decide? I cannot bring myself to break a trust and I am not at present in the humor to baulk my inclinations. Is there no middle way? Let me consider—There is, there is! My good genius has presented me with one, apt, obvious, honorable. The girl shall not go without her baubles, I'll not go without the girl, Miss Rusport shan't lose her diamonds, I'll save Dudley from destruction, and every party shall be a gainer by the project.

Scene IV. Mrs. Fulmer *introducing* Miss Dudley

Mrs. Fulmer. Miss Dudley, this is the worthy gentleman you wish to see; this is Mr. Belcour.

Louisa. (*Aside*) As I live, the very man that beset me in the streets.

Belcour. (*Aside*) An angel, by this light! Oh I am gone past all retrieving!

Louisa. Mrs. Fulmer, sir, informs me you are the gentleman from whom my father has received such civilities.

Belcour. Oh! never name 'em.

Louisa. Pardon me, Mr. Belcour, they must be both named and remembered; and if my father was here—

Belcour. I am much better pleased with his representative.

Louisa. That title is my brother's, sir. I have no claim to it.

Belcour. I believe it.

Louisa. But as neither he nor my father were fortunate enough to be at home, I could not resist the opportunity—

Belcour. Nor I neither, by my soul, madam. Let us improve it, therefore. I am in love with you to distraction. I was charmed at the first glance; I attempted to accost you; you fled; I followed but was defeated of an interview. At length I have obtained one and seize the opportunity of casting my person and my fortune at your feet.

Louisa. You astonish me! Are you in your senses, or do you make a jest of my misfortunes? Do you ground pretenses on your generosity, or do you make a practice of this folly with every woman you meet?

Belcour. Upon my life, no. As you are the handsomest woman I ever met, so you are the first to whom I ever made the like professions. As for my generosity, madam, I must refer you on that score to this good lady, who, I believe, has something to offer in my behalf.

Louisa. Don't build upon that, sir. I must have better proofs of your generosity than the mere divestment of a little superfluous dross before I can credit the sincerity of professions so abruptly delivered.

Exit hastily

Belcour. Oh! Ye gods and goddesses, how her anger animates her beauty!

(*Going out*)

Mrs. Fulmer. Stay, sir. If you stir a step

after her, I renounce your interest forever. Why you'll ruin everything.

BELCOUR. Well, I must have her, cost what it will. I see she understands her own value though. A little superfluous dross, truly! She must have better proofs of my generosity.

MRS. FULMER. 'Tis exactly as I told you. Your money she calls dross. She's too proud to stain her fingers with your coin. Bait your hook well with jewels. Try that experiment, and she's your own.

BELCOUR. Take 'em. Let me go. Lay 'em at her feet. I must get out of the scrape as I can. My propensity is irresistible. There! You have 'em; they are yours; they are hers; but remember they are a trust; I commit them to her keeping till I can buy 'em off with something she shall think more valuable. Now tell me when shall I meet her?

MRS. FULMER. How can I tell that? Don't you see what an alarm you have put her into? Oh! You are a rare one! But go your ways for this while. Leave her to my management and come to me at seven this evening; but remember not to bring empty pockets with you—Ha! ha! ha! *Exeunt severally*

SCENE V. LADY RUSPORT'S *House*

MISS RUSPORT *enters, followed by a* Servant

CHARLOTTE. Desire Mr. Stockwell to walk in. *Exit* Servant

STOCKWELL *enters*

STOCKWELL. Madam, your most obedient servant. I am honored with your commands by Captain Dudley and have brought the money with me as you directed. I understand the sum you have occasion for is two hundred pounds.

CHARLOTTE. It is, sir; I am quite confounded at your taking this trouble upon yourself, Mr. Stockwell.

STOCKWELL. There is a bank-note, madam, to the amount. Your jewels are in safe hands and will be delivered to you directly. If I had been happy in being better known to you, I should have hoped you would not have thought it necessary to place a deposit in my hands for so trifling a sum as you have now required me to supply you with.

CHARLOTTE. The baubles I sent you may very well be spared; and, as they are the only security in my present situation I can give you, I could wish you would retain them in your hands. When I am of age, which, if I live a few months, I shall be, I will replace your favor with thanks.

STOCKWELL. It is obvious, Miss Rusport, that your charms will suffer no impeachment by the absence of these superficial ornaments; but they should be seen in the suite of a woman of fashion, not as creditors to whom you are indebted for your appearance, but as subservient attendants, which help to make up your equipage.

CHARLOTTE. Mr. Stockwell is determined not to wrong the confidence I reposed in his politeness.

STOCKWELL. I have only to request, madam, that you allow Mr. Belcour, a young gentleman in whose happiness I particularly interest myself, to have the honor of delivering you the box of jewels.

CHARLOTTE. Most gladly. Any friend of yours cannot fail of being welcome here.

STOCKWELL. I flatter myself you will not find him totally undeserving your good opinion. An education not of the strictest kind and strong animal spirits are apt sometimes to betray him into youthful irregularities; but an high principle of honor and an uncommon benevolence, in the eye of candor, will, I hope, atone for any faults by which these good qualities are not impaired.

CHARLOTTE. I dare say Mr. Belcour's behavior wants no apology. We've no right to be over-strict in canvassing the morals of a common acquaintance.

STOCKWELL. I wish it may be my happiness to see Mr. Belcour in the list, not of your common, but of your particular acquaintance, of your friends, Miss Rusport.—I dare not be more explicit.

CHARLOTTE. Nor need you, Mr. Stockwell. I shall be studious to deserve his friendship; and, though I have long since unalterably placed my affections on another, I trust I have not left myself insensible to the merits of Mr. Belcour and hope that neither you nor he will, for that reason, think me less worthy your good opinion and regards.

STOCKWELL. Miss Rusport, I sincerely wish you happy. I have no doubt you have placed your affection on a deserving man, and I have no right to combat you in your choice. *Exit*

CHARLOTTE. How honorable is that behavior! Now, if Charles was here, I should be happy. The old lady is so fond of her new Irish acquaintance that I have the whole house at my disposal. *Exit* CHARLOTTE

SCENE VI

BELCOUR *enters, preceded by a* Servant

SERVANT. I ask your honor's pardon; I thought my young lady was here. Who shall I inform her would speak to her?

BELCOUR. Belcour is my name, sir; and pray beg your lady to put herself in no hurry on my account, for I'd sooner see the devil than see her face. (*Exit* Servant) In the name of all that's mischievous, why did Stockwell drive me hither in such haste? A pretty figure, truly, I shall make, an ambassador without credentials. Blockhead that I was to charge myself with her diamonds. Officious, meddling puppy! Now they are irretrievably gone. That suspicious jade Fulmer wouldn't part even with a sight of them though I would have ransomed 'em at twice their value. Now must I trust to my poor wits to bring me off, a lamentable dependence. Fortune be my helper! Here comes the girl.—If she is noble-minded, as she is said to be, she will forgive me; if not, 'tis a lost cause, for I have not thought of one word in my excuse.

SCENE VII

CHARLOTTE *enters*

CHARLOTTE. Mr. Belcour, I'm proud to see you. Your friend, Mr. Stockwell, prepared me to expect this honor, and I am happy in the opportunity of being known to you.

BELCOUR. (*Aside*) A fine girl, by my soul! Now what a cursed hang-dog do I look like!

CHARLOTTE. You are newly arrived in this country, sir?

BELCOUR. Just landed, madam; just set a-shore with a large cargo of Muscovado sugars, rum-puncheons, mahogany slabs, wet sweet-meats, and green paroquets.

CHARLOTTE. May I ask you how you like London, sir?

BELCOUR. To admiration. I think the town and the town's folk are exactly suited; 'tis a great, rich, overgrown, noisy, tumultuous place. The whole morning is a bustle to get money, and the whole afternoon is a hurry to spend it.

CHARLOTTE. Are these all the observations you have made?

BELCOUR. No, madam; I have observed the women are very captivating and the men very soon caught.

CHARLOTTE. Ay, indeed! Whence do you draw that conclusion?

BELCOUR. From infallible guides. The first remark I collect from what I now see, the second from what I now feel.

CHARLOTTE. Oh, the deuce take you! But to waive this subject; I believe, sir, this was a visit of business, not compliment, was it not?

BELCOUR. [*Aside*] Ay; now comes my execution.

CHARLOTTE. You have some foolish trinkets of mine, Mr. Belcour, haven't you?

BELCOUR. (*Aside*) No, in truth; they are gone in search of a trinket still more foolish than themselves.

CHARLOTTE. Some diamonds I mean, sir; Mr. Stockwell informed me you was charged with them.

BELCOUR. Oh, yes, madam; but I have the most treacherous memory in life—Here they are! Pray put them up; they're all right; you need not examine 'em. (*Gives a box*)

CHARLOTTE. Hey-dey! right, sir! Why these are not my diamonds; these are quite different; and, as it should seem, of much greater value.

BELCOUR. Upon my life I'm glad on't, for then I hope you value them more than your own.

CHARLOTTE. As a purchaser I should, but not as an owner; you mistake, these belong to somebody else.

BELCOUR. 'Tis yours, I'm afraid, that belong to somebody else.

CHARLOTTE. What is it you mean? I must insist upon your taking 'em back again.

BELCOUR. Pray, madam, don't do that. I shall infallibly lose them. I have the worst luck with diamonds of any man living.

CHARLOTTE. That you might well say, was you to give me these in the place of mine; but pray, sir, what is the reason of all this? Why have you changed the jewels? And where have you disposed of mine?

BELCOUR. Miss Rusport, I cannot invent a lie for my life; and, if it was to save it, I couldn't tell one. I am an idle, dissipated, unthinking fellow, not worth your notice: in short, I am a West Indian; and you must try me according to the charter of my colony, not by a jury of English spinsters. Truth is, I have given away your jewels. Caught with a pair of sparkling eyes whose luster blinded theirs, I served your property as I should my own and lavished it away. Let me not totally despair of your forgiveness. I frequently do wrong, but never with impunity. If your displeasure is added to my own, my punishment will be too severe. When I parted from the jewels, I had not the honor of knowing their owner.

CHARLOTTE. Mr. Belcour, your sincerity charms me; I enter at once into your character, and I make all the allowances for it you can desire. I take your jewels for the present because I know there is no other way of reconciling you to yourself; but if I give way to your spirit in one point, you must yield to mine in another; remember I will not keep more than the value of my own jewels. There is no need to be pillaged by more than one woman at a time, sir.

BELCOUR. Now may every blessing that can crown your virtues and reward your beauty be showered upon you; may you meet admiration without envy, love without jealousy, and old age without malady! May the man of your heart be ever constant and you never meet a less penitent or less grateful offender than myself.

Servant *enters and delivers a letter*

CHARLOTTE. Does your letter require such haste?

SERVANT. I was bade to give it into your own hands, madam.

CHARLOTTE. From Charles Dudley, I see—Have I your permission? Good heaven, what do I read! Mr. Belcour you are concerned in this—

Dear Charlotte, in the midst of our distress Providence has cast a benefactor in our way after the most unexpected manner. A young West Indian, rich, and with a warmth of heart peculiar to his climate, has rescued my father from his troubles, satisfied his wants, and enabled him to accomplish his exchange. When I relate to you the manner in which this was done, you will be charmed. I can only now add that it was by chance we found out that his name is Belcour and that he is a friend of Mr. Stockwell's. I lose not a moment's time in making you acquainted with this fortunate event for reasons which delicacy obliges me to suppress; but, perhaps, if you have not received the money on your jewels, you will not think it necessary now to do it. I have the honor to be,

  Dear Madam,
    most faithfully yours,
      Charles Dudley.

Is this your doing, sir? Never was generosity so worthily exerted.

BELCOUR. Or so greatly overpaid.

CHARLOTTE. After what you have now done for this noble, but indigent, family, let me not scruple to unfold the whole situation of my heart to you. Know then, sir, (and don't think the worse of me for the frankness of my declaration) that such is my attachment to the son of that worthy officer whom you relieved that the moment I am of age and in possession of my fortune I should hold myself the happiest of women to share it with young Dudley.

BELCOUR. Say you so, madam! Then let me perish if I don't love and reverence you above all womankind; and, if such is your generous resolution, never wait till you're of age. Life is too short, pleasure too fugitive; the soul grows narrower every hour. I'll equip you for your escape; I'll convoy you to the man of your heart, and away with you then to the first hospitable parson that will take you in.

CHARLOTTE. O blessed be the torrid zone forever whose rapid vegetation quickens nature into such benignity! These latitudes are made for politics and philosophy; friendship has no root in this soil. But had I spirit to accept your offer, which is not improbable, wouldn't it be a mortifying thing for a fond young girl to find herself mistaken and sent back to her home like a vagrant? And such, for what I know, might be my case.

BELCOUR. Then he ought to be proscribed the society of mankind for ever.—(*Aside*) Ay ay, 'tis the sham sister makes him thus indifferent; twill be a meritorious office to take that girl out of the way.

SCENE VIII

Servant *enters*

SERVANT. Miss Dudley to wait on you, madam.

BELCOUR. Who?

SERVANT. Miss Dudley.

CHARLOTTE. What's the matter, Mr. Belcour? Are you frighted at the name of a pretty girl? 'Tis the sister of him we were speaking of.—Pray admit her.

BELCOUR. (*Aside*) The sister! So, so; he has imposed upon her too.—This is an extraordinary visit truly. Upon my soul the assurance of some folks is not to be accounted for.

CHARLOTTE. I insist upon your not running away. You'll be charmed with Louisa Dudley.

BELCOUR. Oh, yes, I am charmed with her.

CHARLOTTE. You've seen her then, have you?

BELCOUR. Yes, yes, I've seen her.

CHARLOTTE. Well, isn't she a delightful girl?

BELCOUR. Very delightful.

CHARLOTTE. Why, you answer as if you was in a court of justice. O' my conscience! I believe you are caught; I've a notion she has tricked you out of your heart.

BELCOUR. I believe she has, and out of your jewels; for to tell you the truth, she's the very person I gave 'em to.

CHARLOTTE. You gave her my jewels! Louisa Dudley my jewels? Admirable, inimitable! Oh the sly little jade! But hush, here she comes. I don't know how I shall keep my countenance. (LOUISA *enters*) My dear, I'm rejoiced to see you. How d'ye do? I beg leave to introduce Mr. Belcour, a very worthy friend of mine. I believe, Louisa, you have seen him before.

LOUISA. I have met the gentleman.

CHARLOTTE. You have met the gentleman. Well, sir, and you have met the lady. In short, you have met each other. Why, then, don't you speak to each other? How you both stand, tongue-tied and fixed as statues!—Ha, ha, ha! Why you'll fall asleep by-and-by.

LOUISA. Fie upon you; fie upon you! Is this fair?

BELCOUR. (*Aside*) Upon my soul, I never looked so like a fool in my life. The assurance of that girl puts me quite down.

CHARLOTTE. Sir—Mr. Belcour—Was it your pleasure to advance anything? Not a syllable. Come, Louisa, women's wit, they say, is never at a loss.—Nor you neither? Speechless both? Why you was merry enough before this lady came in.

LOUISA. I am sorry I have been any interruption to your happiness, sir.

BELCOUR. Madam.

CHARLOTTE. Madam! Is that all you can say? But come, my dear girl, I won't tease you. *Apropos*, I must show you what a fine present this dumb gentleman has made me. Are not these handsome diamonds?

LOUISA. Yes, indeed, they seem very fine; but I am no judge of these things.

CHARLOTTE. Oh, you wicked little hypocrite, you are no judge of these things, Louisa; you have no diamonds, not you.

LOUISA. You know I haven't, Miss Rusport; you know those things are infinitely above my reach.

CHARLOTTE. Ha! ha! ha!

BELCOUR. [*Aside*] She does tell a lie with an admirable countenance, that's true enough.

LOUISA. What ails you, Charlotte? What impertinence have I been guilty of that you should find it necessary to humble me at such a rate? If you are happy, long may you be so; but surely it can be no addition to it to make me miserable.

CHARLOTTE. So serious! There must be some mystery in this.—Mr. Belcour, will you leave us together? You see I treat you with all the familiarity of an old acquaintance already.

BELCOUR. Oh, by all means; pray command me. Miss Rusport, I'm your most obedient! By your condescension in accepting those poor trifles, I am under eternal obligations to you.— Miss Dudley, I shall not offer a word on that subject. You despise finery; you have a soul above it; I adore your spirit. I was rather unprepared for meeting you here; but I shall hope for an opportunity of making myself better known to you. *Exit*

SCENE IX

CHARLOTTE *and* LOUISA

CHARLOTTE. Louisa Dudley, you surprise me. I never saw you act thus before. Can't you bear a little innocent raillery before the man of your heart?

LOUISA. The man of my heart, madam? Be assured I never was so visionary to aspire to any man whom Miss Rusport honors with her choice.

CHARLOTTE. My choice, my dear! Why are we playing at cross purposes. How entered it into your head that Mr. Belcour was the man of my choice?

LOUISA. Why, didn't he present you with those diamonds?

CHARLOTTE. Well; perhaps he did—and pray, Louisa, have you no diamonds?

LOUISA. I, diamonds, truly! Who should give me diamonds?

CHARLOTTE. Who, but this very gentleman. *Apropos*, here comes your brother!

SCENE X

CHARLES *enters*

[CHARLOTTE.] I insist upon referring our dispute to him. Your sister and I, Charles, have a quarrel. Belcour, the hero of your letter, has just left us. Somehow or other, Louisa's bright eyes have caught him; and the poor fellow's fallen desperately in love with her—(don't interrupt me, hussy)—Well that's excusable enough, you'll say; but the jet [1] of the story is that this hair-brained spark, who does nothing like other people, has given her the very identical jewels which you pledged for me to Mr. Stockwell; and will you believe that this little demure slut made up a face and squeezed out three or four hypocritical tears because I rallied her about it?

CHARLES. I'm all astonishment! Louisa, tell me without reserve has Mr. Belcour given you any diamonds?

LOUISA. None, upon my honor.

CHARLES. Has he made any professions to you?

LOUISA. He has, but altogether in a style so whimsical and capricious that the best which can be said of them is to tell you that they seemed more the result of good spirits than good manners.

CHARLOTTE. Ay, ay, now the murder's out; he's in love with her, and she has no very great dislike to him. Trust to my observation, Charles, for that. As to the diamonds, there's some mistake about them, and you must clear it up. Three minutes conversation with him will put everything in a right train. Go, go, Charles; 'tis a brother's business. About it instantly. Ten to one, you'll find him over the way at Mr. Stockwell's.

CHARLES. I confess I'm impatient to have the case cleared up. I'll take your advice, and find him out. Good-bye to you.

CHARLOTTE. Your servant. [*Exit* CHARLES] My life upon it, you'll find Belcour a man of honor. Come, Louisa, let us adjourn to my dressing-room. I've a little business to transact with you before the old lady comes up to tea and interrupts us.

ACT IV

SCENE I. FULMER'S *house*

FULMER *and* MRS. FULMER

FULMER. Patty, wasn't Mr. Belcour with you?

MRS. FULMER. He was, and is now shut up in my chamber in high expectation of an interview with Miss Dudley. She's at present with her brother and 'twas with some difficulty I persuaded my hot-headed spark to wait 'till he has left her.

FULMER. Well, child, and what then?

MRS. FULMER. Why then, Mr. Fulmer, I think it will be time for you and me to steal a march and be gone.

FULMER. So this is all the fruit of your ingenious project—a shameful overthrow or a sudden flight.

MRS. FULMER. Why, my project was a mere impromptu and can at worst but quicken our departure a few days. You know we have fairly outlived our credit here and a trip to Boulogne is no ways unseasonable. Nay, never droop, man.—Hark! hark! here's enough to bear charges. (*Showing a purse*)

FULMER. Let me see. Let me see. This weighs well. This is of the right sort. Why, your West Indian bled freely.

MRS. FULMER. But that's not all. Look here! Here are the sparklers! (*Showing the jewels*) Now what d'ye think of my performances? Hah! a foolish scheme, isn't it?—A silly woman—?

FULMER. Thou art a Judith, a Joan of Arc, and I'll march under thy banners, girl, to the world's end. Come let's be gone; I've little to regret. My creditors may share the old books amongst them. They'll have occasion for philosophy to support their loss. They'll find enough upon my shelves. The world is my library; I read mankind.—Now, Patty, lead the way.

MRS. FULMER. *Adieu*, Belcour! *Exeunt*

SCENE II

[*The scene continues*]

CHARLES DUDLEY *and* LOUISA

CHARLES. Well, Louisa, I confess the force of what you say. I accept Miss Rusport's

---
[1] Gist.

bounty and when you see my generous Charlotte, tell her—But have a care, there is a selfishness even in gratitude when it is too profuse; to be over-thankful for any one favor is in effect to lay out for another. The best return I could make my benefactress would be never to see her more.

LOUISA. I understand you.

CHARLES. We that are poor, Louisa, should be cautious. For this reason, I would guard you against Belcour, at least till I can unravel the mystery of Miss Rusport's diamonds. I was disappointed of finding him at Mr. Stockwell's and am now going in search of him again. He may intend honorably, but I confess to you I am staggered. Think no more of him, therefore, for the present. Of this be sure: while I have life and you have honor, I will protect you or perish in your defense.

Exit

LOUISA. Think of him no more! Well, I'll obey; but, if a wandering, uninvited thought should creep by chance into my bosom, must I not give the harmless wretch a shelter? Oh! yes; the Great Artificer of the human heart knows every thread He wove into its fabric, nor puts His work to harder uses than it was made to bear. My wishes then, my guiltless ones I mean, are free. How fast they spring within me at that sentence! Down, down, ye busy creatures! Whither would you carry me? Ah! there is one amongst you, a forward, new intruder that in the likeness of an offending, generous man grows into favor with my heart. Fie, fie upon it! Belcour pursues, insults me; yet such is the fatality of my condition that what should rouse resentment only calls up love.

SCENE III

BELCOUR *enters to her*

BELCOUR. Alone, by all that's happy!

LOUISA. Ah!

BELCOUR. Oh! shriek not, start not, stir not, loveliest creature! But let me kneel and gaze upon your beauties.

LOUISA. Sir,—Mr. Belcour,—rise! What is it you do?

BELCOUR. See, I obey you. Mold me as you will; behold your ready servant! New to your country, ignorant of your manners, habits, and desires, I put myself into your hands for instruction. Make me only such as you can like yourself, and I shall be happy.

LOUISA. I must not hear this, Mr. Belcour. Go. Should he that parted from me but this minute now return, I tremble for the consequences.

BELCOUR. Fear nothing. Let him come. I love you, madam. He'll find it hard to make me unsay that.

LOUISA. You terrify me. Your impetuous temper frightens me. You know my situation. It is not generous to pursue me thus.

BELCOUR. True; I do know your situation, your real one, Miss Dudley, and I am resolved to snatch you from it. 'Twill be a meritorious act. The old captain shall rejoice; Miss Rusport shall be made happy; and even he, even your beloved brother, with whose resentment you threaten me, shall in the end applaud and thank me. Come; thou art a dear, enchanting girl, and I'm determined not to live a minute longer without thee.

LOUISA. Hold, are you mad? I see you are a bold, assuming man and know not where to stop.

BELCOUR. Who that beholds such beauty can? By heaven, you put my blood into a flame. Provoking girl! is it within the stretch of my fortune to content you? What is it you can further ask that I am not ready to grant?

LOUISA. Yes, with the same facility that you bestowed upon me Miss Rusport's diamonds. For shame! For shame! was that a manly story?

BELCOUR. So! so? these devilish diamonds meet me everywhere.—Let me perish if I meant you any harm. Oh! I could tear my tongue out for saying a word about the matter.

LOUISA. Go to her then, and contradict it. Till that is done, my reputation is at stake.

BELCOUR. [*Aside*] Her reputation! Now she has got upon that she'll go on forever.—What is there I will not do for your sake? I will go to Miss Rusport.

LOUISA. Do so; restore her own jewels to her, which I suppose you kept back for the purpose of presenting others to her of a greater value; but for the future, Mr. Belcour, when you would do a gallant action to that lady, don't let it be at my expense.

BELCOUR. [*Aside*] I see where she points. She is willing enough to give up Miss Rusport's diamonds now that she finds she shall be a gainer by the exchange. Be it so! 'tis what

I wished.—Well, madam, I will return Miss Rusport her own jewels, and you shall have others of tenfold their value.

LOUISA. No, sir, you err most widely; it is my good opinion, not my vanity, which you must bribe.

BELCOUR. [*Aside*] Why, what the devil would she have now?—Miss Dudley, it is my wish to obey and please you, but I have some apprehension that we mistake each other.

LOUISA. I think we do. Tell me, then, in few words what it is you aim at.

BELCOUR. In few words, then, and in plain honesty, I must tell you: so entirely am I captivated with you that, had you but been such as it would have become me to have called my wife, I had been happy in knowing you by that name. As it is, you are welcome to partake my fortune; give me in return your person. Give me pleasure, give me love, free, disencumbered, anti-matrimonial love.

LOUISA. Stand off and let me never see you more.

BELCOUR. Hold, hold, thou dear, tormenting, tantalizing girl! Upon my knees I swear you shall not stir till you've consented to my bliss.

LOUISA. Unhand me, sir. O Charles! protect me, rescue me, redress me. *Exit*

SCENE IV

CHARLES DUDLEY *enters*

CHARLES. How's this? Rise, villain, and defend yourself.

BELCOUR. Villain!

CHARLES. The man who wrongs that lady is a villain.—Draw!

BELCOUR. Never fear me, young gentleman; brand me for a coward if I balk you.

CHARLES. Yet hold! Let me not be too hasty. Your name, I think, is Belcour?

BELCOUR. Well, sir.

CHARLES. How is it, Mr. Belcour, you have done this mean, unmanly wrong. Beneath the mask of generosity to give this fatal stab to our domestic peace? You might have had my thanks, my blessing; take my defiance now. 'Tis Dudley speaks to you, the brother, the protector of that injured lady.

BELCOUR. The brother? Give yourself a truer title.

CHARLES. What is't you mean?

BELCOUR. Come, come, I know both her and you. I found you, sir, (but how or why I know not) in the good graces of Miss Rusport —(yes, color at the name!) I gave you no disturbance there, never broke in upon you in that rich and plenteous quarter, but, when I could have blasted all your projects with a word, spared you, in foolish pity spared you, nor roused her from the fond credulity in which your artifice had lulled her.

CHARLES. No, sir, nor boasted to her of the splendid present you had made my poor Louisa; the diamonds, Mr. Belcour. How was that? What can you plead to that arraignment?

BELCOUR. You question me too late. The name of Belcour and of villain never met before. Had you enquired of me before you uttered that rash word, you might have saved yourself or me a mortal error. Now, sir, I neither give nor take an explanation; so, come on! (*They fight*)

SCENE V

LOUISA, *and afterwards* O'FLAHERTY

LOUISA. Hold, hold, for heaven's sake hold! Charles! Mr. Belcour! Help! Sir, sir, make haste, they'll murder one another.

Enter O'FLAHERTY

O'FLAHERTY. [*Throwing up their swords*] Hell and confusion! What's all this uproar for? Can't you leave off cutting one another's throats and mind what the poor girl says to you? You've done a notable thing, haven't you, both, to put her into such a flurry? I think o' my conscience, she's the most frighted of the three.

CHARLES. Dear Louisa, recollect yourself. Why did you interfere? 'Tis in your cause.

BELCOUR. [*Aside*] Now could I kill him for caressing her.

O'FLAHERTY. O sir, your most obedient! You are the gentleman I had the honor of meeting here before; you was then running off at full speed like a Calmuck.[1] Now you are tilting and driving like a Bedlamite with this lad here that seems as mad as yourself. 'Tis pity but your country had a little more employment for you both.

BELCOUR. Mr. Dudley, when you've re-

---

[1] The Kalmucks are members of Tartar tribes of Russian Astrakhan or western China. They are largely nomadic and raise cattle and horses.

covered the lady, you know where I am to be found. *Exit*

O'FLAHERTY. Well, then, can't you stay where you are and that will save the trouble of looking after you? Yon volatile fellow thinks to give a man the meeting by getting out of his way. By my soul 'tis a roundabout method that of his. But I think he called you Dudley. Hark'ee, young man, are you son of my friend the old captain?

CHARLES. I am. Help me to convey this lady to her chamber, and I shall be more at leisure to answer your questions.

O'FLAHERTY. Ay, will I. Come along, pretty one. If you've had wrong done you, young man, you need look no further for a second. Dennis O'Flaherty's your man for that; but never draw your sword before a woman, Dudley; damn it, never, while you live, draw your sword before a woman. *Exeunt*

SCENE VI. LADY RUSPORT'S *house*

LADY RUSPORT *and* Servant

SERVANT. An elderly gentleman, who says his name is Varland, desires leave to wait on your ladyship.

LADY RUSPORT. Show him in. The very man I wish to see,—Varland. He was Sir Oliver's solicitor and privy to all his affairs. He brings some good tidings, some fresh mortgage or another bond come to light; they start up every day. (VARLAND *enters*) Mr. Varland, I'm glad to see you. You're heartily welcome, honest Mr. Varland. You and I haven't met since our late irreparable loss. How have you passed your time this age?

VARLAND. Truly, my lady, ill enough. I thought I must have followed good Sir Oliver.

LADY RUSPORT. Alack-a-day, poor man! Well, Mr. Varland, you find me here overwhelmed with trouble and fatigue, torn to pieces with a multiplicity of affairs, a great fortune poured upon me unsought for and unexpected. 'Twas my good father's will and pleasure it should be so, and I must submit.

VARLAND. Your ladyship inherits under a will made in the year forty-five, immediately after Captain Dudley's marriage with your sister.

LADY RUSPORT. I do so, Mr. Varland; I do so.

VARLAND. I well remember it; I engrossed every syllable; but I am surprised to find your ladyship set so little store by this vast accession.

LADY RUSPORT. Why, you know, Mr. Varland, I am a moderate woman. I had enough before; a small matter satisfies me; and Sir Stephen Rusport (heaven be his portion!) took care I shouldn't want that.

VARLAND. Very true; very true, he did so; and I am overjoyed at finding your ladyship in this disposition, for, truth to say, I was not without apprehension the news I have to communicate would have been of some prejudice to your ladyship's tranquillity.

LADY RUSPORT. News, sir! What news have you for me?

VARLAND. Nay, nothing to alarm you; a trifle, in your present way of thinking. I have a will of Sir Oliver's you have never seen.

LADY RUSPORT. A will! Impossible! How came you by it, pray?

VARLAND. I drew it up, at his command, in his last illness. It will save you a world of trouble. It gives his whole estate from you to his grandson, Charles Dudley.

LADY RUSPORT. To Dudley? His estate to Charles Dudley? I can't support it! I shall faint! You've killed me, you vile man! I never shall survive it!

VARLAND. Look'ee there now! I protest I thought you would have rejoiced at being clear of the encumbrance.

LADY RUSPORT. 'Tis false; 'tis all a forgery concerted between you and Dudley. Why else did I never hear of it before?

VARLAND. Have patience, my lady, and I'll tell you. By Sir Oliver's direction, I was to deliver this will into no hands but his grandson Dudley's. The young gentleman happened to be then in Scotland. I was dispatched thither in search of him. The hurry and fatigue of my journey brought on a fever by the way, which confined me in extreme danger for several days. Upon my recovery, I pursued my journey, found that young Dudley had left Scotland in the interim, and now am directed hither, where, as soon as I can find him, doubtless, I shall discharge my conscience and fulfil my commission.

LADY RUSPORT. Dudley then, as yet, knows nothing of this will?

VARLAND. Nothing; that secret remains with me.

LADY RUSPORT. (*Aside*) A thought occurs;

by this fellow's talking of his conscience, I should guess it was upon sale.—Come, Mr. Varland, if 'tis as you say, I must submit. I was somewhat flurried at first and forgot myself; I ask your pardon. This is no place to talk business; step with me into my room. We will there compare the will and resolve accordingly.—[*Aside*] Oh! would your fever had you and I had your paper! *Exeunt*

Scene VII

Miss Rusport, Charles, *and* O'Flaherty

CHARLOTTE. So, so! My lady and her lawyer have retired to close confabulation. Now, major, if you are the generous man I take you for, grant me one favor.

O'FLAHERTY. Faith will I, and not think much of my generosity neither; for, though it may not be in my power to do the favor you ask, look you, it can never be in my heart to refuse it.

CHARLES. (*Aside*) Could this man's tongue do justice to his thoughts, how eloquent would he be!

CHARLOTTE. Plant yourself then in that room. Keep guard for a few moments upon the enemy's motions in the chamber beyond; and, if they should attempt a sally, stop their march a moment, till your friend here can make good his retreat down the back stairs.

O'FLAHERTY. A word to the wise! I'm an old campaigner. Make the best use of your time and trust me for tying the old cat up to the picket.

CHARLOTTE. Hush! hush! not so loud.

CHARLES. 'Tis the office of a sentinel, major, you have undertaken rather than that of a field-officer.

O'FLAHERTY. 'Tis the office of a friend, my dear boy; and, therefore, no disgrace to a general. *Exit*

Scene VIII

Charles *and* Charlotte

CHARLOTTE. Well, Charles, will you commit yourself to me for a few minutes?

CHARLES. Most readily; and let me, before one goes by, tender you the only payment I can ever make for your abundant generosity.

CHARLOTTE. Hold, hold! so vile a thing as money must not come between us. What shall I say! O Charles! O Dudley! What difficulties have you thrown upon me! Familiarly as we have lived, I shrink at what I'm doing; and, anxiously as I have sought this opportunity, my fears almost persuade me to abandon it.

CHARLES. You alarm me!

CHARLOTTE. Your looks and actions have been so distant and at this moment are so deterring, that, was it not for the hope that delicacy, and not disgust, inspires this conduct in you, I should sink with shame and apprehension; but time presses, and I must speak and plainly too—Was you now in possession of your grandfather's estate, as justly you ought to be, and was you inclined to seek a companion for life, should you, or should you not, in that case, honor your unworthy Charlotte with your choice?

CHARLES. My unworthy Charlotte! So judge me, heaven, there is not a circumstance on earth so valuable as your happiness, so dear to me as your person; but to bring poverty, disgrace, reproach from friends, ridicule from all the world upon a generous benefactress, thievishly to steal into an open, unreserved, ingenuous heart. O Charlotte! dear, unhappy girl, it is not to be done.

CHARLOTTE. Nay, now you rate too highly the poor advantages fortune alone has given me over you. How otherwise could we bring our merits to any balance? Come, my dear Charles, I have enough; make that enough still more by sharing it with me. Sole heiress of my father's fortune, a short time will put it in my disposal. In the meanwhile you will be sent to join your regiment. Let us prevent a separation by setting out this very night for that happy country where marriage still is free.[1] Carry me this moment to Belcour's lodgings.

CHARLES. Belcour's?—(*Aside*) The name is ominous; there's murder in it. Bloody inexorable honor!

CHARLOTTE. D'ye pause? Put me in his hands while you provide the means for our escape. He is the most generous, the most honorable of men.

CHARLES. Honorable! most honorable!

CHARLOTTE. Can you doubt it? Do you

---

[1] In Scotland there were no restrictions on marriage, the contracting parties merely expressing their desire to be married in the presence of witnesses. English couples eloped to Gretna Green and were married by the blacksmith, the toll-keeper, or the ferryman.

demur? Have you forgot your letter? Why, Belcour 'twas that prompted me to this proposal, that promised to supply the means, that nobly offered his unasked assistance—

O'FLAHERTY *enters hastily*

O'FLAHERTY. Run, run, for holy St. Antony's sake, to horse and away! The conference is broke up, and the old lady advances upon a full piedmontese trot, within pistol-shot of your encampment.

CHARLOTTE. Here, here, down the back-stairs! O, Charles, remember me!

CHARLES. Farewell! Now, now I feel myself a coward. *Exit*

CHARLOTTE. What does he mean?

O'FLAHERTY. Ask no questions but be gone. [*Exit* CHARLOTTE] She has cooled the lad's courage and wonders he feels like a coward. There's a damned deal of mischief brewing between this hyena and her lawyer. Egad, I'll step behind this screen and listen. A good soldier must sometimes fight in ambush as well as open field. (*Retires*)

SCENE IX

LADY RUSPORT *and* VARLAND

LADY RUSPORT. Sure I heard somebody. Hark! No; only the servants going down the back-stairs. Well, Mr. Varland, I think then we are agreed; you'll take my money, and your conscience no longer stands in your way.

VARLAND. Your father was my benefactor; his will ought to be sacred; but if I commit it to the flames, how will he be the wiser? Dudley, 'tis true, has done me no harm; but five thousand pounds will do me much good. So, in short, madam, I take your offer. I will confer with my clerk, who witnessed the will, and to-morrow morning put it into your hands upon condition you put five thousand good pounds into mine.

LADY RUSPORT. 'Tis a bargain. I'll be ready for you. Farewell. *Exit*

VARLAND. Let me consider—Five thousand pounds prompt payment for destroying this scrap of paper not worth five farthings. 'Tis a fortune easily earned. Yes; and 'tis another man's fortune easily thrown away. 'Tis a good round sum to be paid down at once for a bribe, but 'tis a damned rogue's trick in me to take it.

O'FLAHERTY. (*Aside*) So, so! this fellow speaks truth to himself, though he lies to other people—But hush!

VARLAND. 'Tis breaking the trust of my benefactor. That's a foul crime, but he's dead and can never reproach me with it; and 'tis robbing young Dudley of his lawful patrimony; that's a hard case, but he's alive and knows nothing of the matter.

O'FLAHERTY. (*Aside*) These lawyers are so used to bring off the rogueries of others that they are never without an excuse for their own.

VARLAND. Were I assured now that Dudley would give me half the money for producing this will that Lady Rusport does for concealing it, I would deal with him and be an honest man at half price. I wish every gentleman of my profession could lay his hand on his heart and say the same thing.

O'FLAHERTY. [*Advancing*] A bargain, old gentleman! Nay, never start, nor stare. You wasn't afraid of your own conscience; never be afraid of me.

VARLAND. Of you, sir; who are you, pray?

O'FLAHERTY. I'll tell you who I am. You seem to wish to be honest but want the heart to set about it. Now I am the very man in the world to make you so, for, if you do not give me up that paper this very instant, by the soul of me, fellow, I will not leave one whole bone in your skin that shan't be broken.

VARLAND. What right have you, pray, to take this paper from me?

O'FLAHERTY. What right have you, pray, to keep it from young Dudley? I don't know what it contains, but I am apt to think it will be safer in my hands than in yours; therefore give it me without more words and save yourself a beating. Do now; you had best.

VARLAND. Well, sir, I may as well make a grace of necessity. There! I have acquitted my conscience at the expense of five thousand pounds.

O'FLAHERTY. Five thousand pounds! Mercy upon me! When there are such temptations in the law, can we wonder if some of the corps are a disgrace to it?

VARLAND. Well, you have got the paper; if you are an honest man, give it to Charles Dudley.

O'FLAHERTY. An honest man! Look at me, friend. I am a soldier. This is not the livery of a knave. I am an Irishman, honey; mine is not the country of dishonor. Now, sirrah, be gone. If you enter these doors or give Lady Rusport the least item of what has passed, I will cut off both your ears and rob the pillory of its due.

VARLAND. I wish I was once fairly out of his sight. *Exeunt*

SCENE X

A room in STOCKWELL'S *house*

STOCKWELL. I must disclose myself to Belcour. This noble instance of his generosity, which old Dudley has been relating, allies me to him at once. Concealment becomes too painful. I shall be proud to own him for my son.—But see, he's here.

BELCOUR *enters and throws himself on a sofa*

BELCOUR. O my cursed tropical constitution! Would to heaven I had been dropped upon the snows of Lapland and never felt the blessed influence of the sun, so had I never burnt with these inflammatory passions!

STOCKWELL. So, so, you seem disordered, Mr. Belcour.

BELCOUR. Disordered, sir! Why did I ever quit the soil in which I grew? What evil planet drew me from that warm sunny region where nature walks without disguise into this cold, contriving, artificial country?

STOCKWELL. Come, sir, you've met a rascal. What o'that? General conclusions are illiberal.

BELCOUR. No, sir, I've met reflection by the way; I've come from folly, noise, and fury and met a silent monitor.—Well, well, a villain! 'twas not to be pardoned—Pray never mind me, sir.

STOCKWELL. [*Aside*] Alas! my heart bleeds for him.

BELCOUR. [*Aside*] And yet I might have heard him. Now plague upon that blundering Irishman for coming in as he did; the hurry of the deed might palliate the event. Deliberate execution has less to plead.—Mr. Stockwell. I am bad company to you.

STOCKWELL. Oh, sir, make no excuse. I think you have not found me forward to pry into the secrets of your pleasures and pursuits. 'Tis not my disposition; but there are times when want of curiosity would be want of friendship.

BELCOUR. Ah, sir, mine is a case wherein you and I shall never think alike. The punctilious rules by which I am bound are not to be found in your ledgers nor will pass current in the counting-house of a trader.

STOCKWELL. 'Tis very well, sir; if you think I can render you any service, it may be worth your trial to confide in me. If not, your secret is safer in your own bosom.

BELCOUR. That sentiment demands my confidence. Pray sit down by me. You must know I have an affair of honor on my hands with young Dudley, and, though I put up with no man's insult, yet I wish to take away no man's life.

STOCKWELL. I know the young man and am apprised of your generosity to his father. What can have bred a quarrel between you?

BELCOUR. A foolish passion on my side and a haughty provocation on his. There is a girl, Mr. Stockwell, whom I have unfortunately seen, of most uncommon beauty. She has withal an air of so much natural modesty that had I not had good assurance of her being an attainable wanton, I declare I should as soon have thought of attempting the chastity of Diana.

Servant enters

STOCKWELL. Hey-dey, do you interrupt us?

SERVANT. Sir, there's an Irish gentleman will take no denial. He says he must see Mr. Belcour directly upon business of the last consequence.

BELCOUR. Admit him. 'Tis the Irish officer that parted us and brings me young Dudley's challenge. I should have made a long story of it, and he'll tell it to you in three words.

O'FLAHERTY *enters*

O'FLAHERTY. Save you, my dear; and you, sir! I have a little bit of a word in private for you.

BELCOUR. Pray deliver your commands. This gentleman is my intimate friend.

O'FLAHERTY. Why, then, Ensign Dudley will be glad to measure swords with you yonder at the London Tavern, in Bishopsgate Street, at nine o'clock.—You know the place.

BELCOUR. I do and shall observe the appointment.

O'FLAHERTY. Will you be of the party, sir? We shall want a fourth hand.

STOCKWELL. Savage as the custom is, I close with your proposal, and though I am not fully informed of the occasion of your quarrel, I shall rely on Mr. Belcour's honor for the justice of it and willingly stake my life in his defence.

O'FLAHERTY. Sir, you're a gentleman of honor, and I shall be glad of being better known to you.—But hark'e, Belcour, I had like to have forgot part of my errand. There is the money you gave old Dudley. You may tell it over, faith; 'tis a receipt in full. Now the lad can put you to death with a safe conscience and when he has done that job for you, let it be a warning how you attempt the sister of a man of honor.

BELCOUR. The sister?

O'FLAHERTY. Ay, the sister; 'tis English, is it not? Or Irish; 'tis all one. You understand me, his sister, or Louisa Dudley, that's her name I think, call her what you will. By St. Patrick, 'tis a foolish piece of business, Belcour, to go about to take away a poor girl's virtue from her, when there are so many to be met in this town who [would] have disposed of theirs to your hands. *Exit*

STOCKWELL. Why, I am thunderstruck! What is this you have done, and what is the shocking business in which I have engaged? If I understood him right, 'tis the sister of young Dudley you've been attempting. You talked to me of a professed wanton! The girl he speaks of has beauty enough to inflame your desires, but she has honor, innocence, and simplicity to awe the most licentious passion. If you have done that, Mr. Belcour, I renounce you, I abandon you, I forswear all fellowship or friendship with you forever.

BELCOUR. Have patience for a moment. We do indeed speak of the same person, but she is not innocent; she is not young Dudley's sister.

STOCKWELL. Astonishing! Who told you this?

BELCOUR. The woman where she lodges. The person who put me on the pursuit and contrived our meetings.

STOCKWELL. What woman? What person?

BELCOUR. Fulmer her name is. I warrant you I did not proceed without good grounds.

STOCKWELL. Fulmer, Fulmer? Who waits? (*A Servant enters*) Send Mr. Stukely hither directly; I begin to see my way into this dark transaction. Mr. Belcour, Mr. Belcour, you are no match for the cunning and contrivances of this intriguing town. (STUKELY *enters*) Prythee, Stukely, what is the name of the woman and her husband who were stopped upon suspicion of selling stolen diamonds at our next-door neighbor's, the jeweller?

STUKELY. Fulmer.

STOCKWELL. So'

BELCOUR. Can you procure me a sight of those diamonds?

STUKELY. They are now in my hand. I was desired to show them to Mr. Stockwell.

STOCKWELL. Give 'em to me.—What do I see? As I live, the very diamonds Miss Rusport sent hither and which I intrusted to you to return.

BELCOUR. Yes, but I betrayed that trust and gave 'em Mrs. Fulmer to present to Miss Dudley.

STOCKWELL. With a view, no doubt, to bribe her to compliance.

BELCOUR. I own it.

STOCKWELL. For shame, for shame! And 'twas this woman's intelligence [1] you relied upon for Miss Dudley's character?

BELCOUR. I thought she knew her. By heaven, I would have died sooner than have insulted a woman of virtue or a man of honor.

STOCKWELL. I think you would, but mark the danger of licentious courses; you are betrayed, robbed, abused, and but for this providential discovery, in a fair way of being sent out of the world with all your follies on your head.—Dear Stukely, go to my neighbor; tell him I have an owner for the jewels and beg him to carry the people under custody to the London Tavern and wait for me there. (*Exit* STUKELY) I fear the law does not provide a punishment to reach the villainy of these people; but how in the name of wonder could you take anything on the word of such an informer?

BELCOUR. Because I had not lived long enough in your country to know how few informers' words are to be taken. Persuaded as I was of Miss Dudley's guilt, I must own to you I was staggered with the appearance of such innocence, especially when I saw her admitted into Miss Rusport's company.

STOCKWELL. Good heaven! Did you meet her at Miss Rusport's, and could you doubt her being a woman of reputation?

BELCOUR. By you perhaps such a mistake could not have been made, but in a perfect stranger I hope it is venial. I did not know what artifices young Dudley might have used

[1] In the sense of information.

to conceal her character. I did not know what disgrace attended the detection of it.

STOCKWELL. I see it was a trap laid for you, which you have narrowly escaped. You addressed a woman of honor with all the loose incense of a profane admirer, and you have drawn upon you the resentment of a man of honor who thinks himself bound to protect her. Well, sir, you must atone for this mistake.

BELCOUR. To the lady the most penitent submission I can make is justly due, but in the execution of an act of justice it never shall be said my soul was swayed by the least particle of fear. I have received a challenge from her brother. Now, though I would give my fortune, almost my life itself, to purchase her happiness, yet I cannot abate her one scruple of my honor. I have been branded with the name of villain.

STOCKWELL. Ay, sir, you mistook her character and he mistook yours; error begets error.

BELCOUR. Villain, Mr. Stockwell, is a harsh word.

STOCKWELL. It is a harsh word and should be unsaid.

BELCOUR. Come, come, it shall be unsaid.

STOCKWELL. Or else what follows? Why the sword is drawn and to heal the wrongs you have done to the reputation of the sister, you make an honorable amends by murdering the brother.

BELCOUR. Murdering!

STOCKWELL. 'Tis thus religion writes and speaks the word. In the vocabulary of modern honor there is no such term.—But come, I don't despair of satisfying the one without alarming the other. That done, I have a discovery to unfold that you will then I hope be fitted to receive.

ACT V

SCENE I. *The London Tavern*

O'FLAHERTY, STOCKWELL, CHARLES, *and* BELCOUR

O'FLAHERTY. Gentlemen, well met! You understand each other's minds, and as I see you have brought nothing but your swords, you may set to without any further ceremony.

STOCKWELL. You will not find us backward in any worthy cause; but before we proceed any further, I would ask this young gentleman whether he has any explanation to require of Mr. Belcour.

CHARLES. Of Mr. Belcour, none. His actions speak for themselves; but to you, sir, I would fain propose one question.

STOCKWELL. Name it.

CHARLES. How is it, Mr. Stockwell, that I meet a man of your character on this ground?

STOCKWELL. I will answer you directly, and my answer shall not displease you. I come hither in defence of the reputation of Miss Dudley, to redress the injuries of an innocent young lady.

O'FLAHERTY. By my soul, the man knows he's to fight, only he mistakes which side he's to be of.

STOCKWELL. You are about to draw your sword to refute a charge against your sister's honor. You would do well, if there were no better means within reach; but the proofs of her innocence are lodged in our bosoms; and if we fall, you destroy the evidence that most effectually can clear her fame.

CHARLES. How's that, sir?

STOCKWELL. This gentleman could best explain it to you, but you have given him an undeserved name that seals his lips against you. I am not under the same inhibition, and if your anger can keep cool for a few minutes, I desire I may call in two witnesses who will solve all difficulties at once. Here, waiter! Bring those people in that are without.

O'FLAHERTY. Out upon it, what need is there for so much talking about the matter? Can't you settle your differences first and dispute about 'em afterwards?

FULMER *and* MRS. FULMER *brought in*

CHARLES. Fulmer and his wife in custody?

STOCKWELL. Yes, sir, these are your honest landlord and landlady, now in custody for defrauding this gentleman of certain diamonds intended to have been presented to your sister. Be so good, Mrs. Fulmer, to inform the company why you so grossly scandalized the reputation of an innocent lady by persuading Mr. Belcour that Miss Dudley was not the sister, but the mistress, of this gentleman.

MRS. FULMER. Sir, I don't know what right you have to question me, and I shall not answer till I see occasion.

STOCKWELL. Had you been as silent heretofore, madam, it would have saved you some trouble; but we don't want your confession.

This letter, which you wrote to Mr. Belcour, will explain your design; and these diamonds, which of right belong to Miss Rusport, will confirm your guilt. The law, Mrs. Fulmer, will make you speak, though I can't. Constable, take charge of your prisoners.

FULMER. Hold a moment. Mr. Stockwell, you are a gentleman that knows the world, and a member of parliament. We shall not attempt to impose upon you. We know we are open to the law, and we know the utmost it can do against us. Mr. Belcour has been ill used, to be sure, and so has Miss Dudley; and, for my own part, I always condemned the plot as a very foolish plot, but it was the child of Mrs. Fulmer's brain and she would not be put out of conceit with it.

MRS. FULMER. You are a very foolish man, Mr. Fulmer; so prythee, hold your tongue.

FULMER. Therefore, as I was saying, if you send her to Bridewell,[1] it won't be amiss; and if you give her a little wholesome discipline, she may be the better for that, too. But for me, Mr. Stockwell, who am a man of letters, I must beseech you, sir, not to bring any disgrace upon my profession.

STOCKWELL. 'Tis you, Mr. Fulmer, not I, that disgrace your profession; therefore be gone, nor expect that I will betray the interests of mankind so far as to show favor to such incendiaries. Take 'em away; I blush to think such wretches should have the power to set two honest men at variance.

Exeunt FULMER, &c.

CHARLES. Mr. Belcour, we have mistaken each other; let us exchange forgiveness. I am convinced you intended no affront to my sister, and I ask your pardon for the expression I was betrayed into.

BELCOUR. 'Tis enough, sir. The error began on my side, and was Miss Dudley here, I would be the first to atone.

STOCKWELL. Let us all adjourn to my house and conclude the evening like friends. You will find a little entertainment ready for you; and, if I am not mistaken, Miss Dudley and her father will make part of our company. Come, major, do you consent?

O'FLAHERTY. Most readily, Mr. Stockwell; a quarrel well made up is better than a victory hardly earned. Give me your hand, Belcour; o' my conscience you are too honest for the country you live in. [*To* CHARLES] And now, my dear lad, since peace is concluded on all sides, I have a discovery to make to you, which you must find out for yourself, for deuce take me if I rightly comprehend it, only that your aunt Rusport is in a conspiracy against you, and a vile rogue of a lawyer, whose name I forget at the bottom of it.

CHARLES. What conspiracy? Dear major, recollect yourself.

O'FLAHERTY. By my soul, I've no faculty at recollecting myself; but I've a paper somewhere about me that will tell you more of the matter than I can. When I get to the merchant's, I will endeavor to find it.

CHARLES. Well, it must be in your own way; but I confess you have thoroughly roused my curiosity.

Exeunt

SCENE II. STOCKWELL'S *house*

CAPT. DUDLEY, LOUISA, *and* STUKELY

DUDLEY. And are those wretches, Fulmer and his wife, in safe custody?

STUKELY. They are in good hands. I accompanied them to the tavern, where your son was to be, and then went in search of you. You may be sure Mr. Stockwell will enforce the law against them as far as it will go.

DUDLEY. What mischief might their cursed machinations have produced but for this timely discovery!

LOUISA. Still, I am terrified. I tremble with apprehension lest Mr. Belcour's impetuosity and Charles's spirit should not wait for an explanation, but drive them both to extremes before the mistake can be unraveled.

STUKELY. Mr. Stockwell is with them, madam, and you have nothing to fear. You cannot suppose he would ask you hither for any other purpose but to celebrate their reconciliation and to receive Mr. Belcour's atonement.

DUDLEY. No, no, Louisa, Mr. Stockwell's honor and discretion guard us against all danger or offence. He well knows we will endure no imputation on the honor of our family and he certainly has invited us to receive satisfaction on that score in an amicable way.

LOUISA. Would to heaven they were returned!

---

[1] Bridewell was the famous house of correction for vagabonds and loose women. It stood in the district between Fleet Street and the Thames and had formerly been a royal residence.

STUKELY. You may expect them every minute; and see, madam, agreeable to your wish, they are here. *Exit*

SCENE III

CHARLES *enters, and afterwards* STOCKWELL *and* O'FLAHERTY

LOUISA. O Charles, O brother, how could you serve me so? How could you tell me you was going to Lady Rusport's and then set out with a design of fighting Mr. Belcour? But where is he; where is your antagonist?

STOCKWELL. Captain, I am proud to see you, and you, Miss Dudley, do me particular honor. We have been adjusting, sir, a very extraordinary and dangerous mistake, which I take for granted my friend Stukely has explained to you.

DUDLEY. He has. I have too good an opinion of Mr. Belcour to believe he could be guilty of a designed affront to an innocent girl, and I am much too well acquainted with your character to suppose you could abet him in such design. I have no doubt, therefore, all things will be set to rights in very few words when we have the pleasure of seeing Mr. Belcour.

STOCKWELL. He has only stepped into the counting-house and will wait upon you directly. You will not be over strict, madam, in weighing Mr. Belcour's conduct to the minutest scruple. His manners, passions, and opinions are not as yet assimilated to this climate. He comes amongst you a new character, an inhabitant of a new world; and both hospitality as well as pity recommend him to our indulgence.

SCENE IV

BELCOUR *enters, bows to* MISS DUDLEY

BELCOUR. I am happy and ashamed to see you. No man in his senses would offend you. I forfeited mine and erred against the light of the sun when I overlooked your virtues; but your beauty was predominant and hid them from my sight. I now perceive I was the dupe of a most improbable report and humbly entreat your pardon.

LOUISA. Think no more of it; 'twas a mistake.

BELCOUR. My life has been composed of little else. 'Twas founded in mystery and has continued in error. I was once given to hope, Mr. Stockwell, that you was to have delivered me from these difficulties, but either I do not deserve your confidence or I was deceived in my expectations.

STOCKWELL. When this lady has confirmed your pardon, I shall hold you deserving of my confidence.

LOUISA. That was granted the moment it was asked.

BELCOUR. To prove my title to his confidence honor me so far with yours as to allow me a few minutes conversation in private with you. (*She turns to her father*)

DUDLEY. By all means, Louisa. Come, Mr. Stockwell, let us go into another room.

CHARLES. And now, Major O'Flaherty, I claim your promise of a sight of the paper that is to unravel this conspiracy of my aunt Rusport's. I think I have waited with great patience.

O'FLAHERTY. I have been endeavoring to call to mind what it was I overheard. I've got the paper and will give you the best account I can of the whole transaction. *Exeunt*

SCENE V

BELCOUR *and* LOUISA

BELCOUR. Miss Dudley, I have solicited this audience to repeat to you my penitence and confusion. How shall I atone? What reparation can I make to you and virtue?

LOUISA. To me there's nothing due, nor anything demanded of you but your more favorable opinion for the future if you should chance to think of me. Upon the part of virtue I'm not empowered to speak; but if hereafter, as you range through life, you should surprise her in the person of some wretched female, poor as myself and not so well protected, enforce not your advantage, complete not your licentious triumph, but raise her, rescue her from shame and sorrow, and reconcile her to herself again.

BELCOUR. I will, I will. By bearing your idea ever present in my thoughts, virtue shall keep an advocate within me. But tell me, loveliest, when you pardon the offence, can you, all perfect as you are, approve of the offender? As I now cease to view you in that false light I lately did, can you, and in the fullness of your bounty will you, cease also to reflect upon the libertine addresses I have paid you and look upon me as your reformed, your rational admirer?

Louisa. Are sudden reformations apt to last; and how can I be sure the first fair face you meet will not ensnare affections so unsteady and that I shall not lose you lightly as I gained you.

Belcour. Because, though you conquered me by surprise, I have no inclination to rebel; because, since the first moment I saw you, every instant has improved you in my eyes; because, by principle as well as passion, I am unalterably yours. In short, there are ten thousand causes for my love to you. Would to heaven I could plant one in your bosom that might move you to return it!

Louisa. Nay, Mr. Belcour—

Belcour. I know I am not worthy your regard; I know I'm tainted with a thousand faults, sick of a thousand follies; but there's a healing virtue in your eyes that makes recovery certain. I cannot be a villain in your arms.

Louisa. That you can never be. Whomever you shall honor with your choice, my life upon't, that woman will be happy. It is not from suspicion that I hesitate; it is from honor. 'Tis the severity of my condition; it is the world that never will interpret fairly in our case.

Belcour. Oh, what am I, and who in this wide world concerns himself for such a nameless, such a friendless thing as I am? I see, Miss Dudley, I've not yet obtained your pardon.

Louisa. Nay, that you are in full possession of.

Belcour. Oh, seal it with your hand then, loveliest of women; confirm it with your heart. Make me honorably happy, and crown your penitent not with your pardon only but your love.

Louisa. My love!—

Belcour. By heaven, my soul is conquered with your virtues more than my eyes are ravished with your beauty. Oh, may this soft, this sensitive alarm be happy, be auspicious! Doubt not, deliberate not, delay not. If happiness be the end of life, why do we slip a moment?

Scene vi

O'Flaherty *enters and afterwards* Dudley *and* Charles *with* Stockwell

O'Flaherty. Joy, joy, joy! Sing, dance, leap, laugh for joy! Ha' done making love and fall down on your knees to every saint in the calendar, for they're all on your side and honest St. Patrick at the head of them.

Charles. O Louisa, such an event! By the luckiest chance in life we have discovered a will of my grandfather's made in his last illness, by which he cuts off my Aunt Rusport with a small annuity and leaves me heir to his whole estate, with a fortune of fifteen thousand pounds to yourself.

Louisa. What is it you tell me? O sir, instruct me to support this unexpected turn of fortune. (*To her father*)

Dudley. Name not fortune; 'tis the work of Providence, 'tis the justice of heaven that would not suffer innocence to be oppressed, nor your base aunt to prosper in her cruelty and cunning.

(*A Servant whispers to* Belcour, *and he goes out*)

O'Flaherty. You shall pardon me, Captain Dudley, but you must not overlook St. Patrick neither, for by my soul if he had not put it into my head to slip behind the screen when your righteous aunt and the lawyer were plotting together, I don't see how you would ever have come at the paper there that Master Stockwell is reading.

Dudley. True, my good friend, you are the father of this discovery, but how did you contrive to get this will from the lawyer?

O'Flaherty. By force, my dear, the only way of getting anything from a lawyer's clutches.

Stockwell. Well, major, when he brings his action of assault and battery against you, the least Dudley can do is to defend you with the weapons you have put into his hands.

Charles. That I am bound to do; and after the happiness I shall have in sheltering a father's age from the vicissitudes of life, my next delight will be in offering you an asylum in the bosom of your country.

O'Flaherty. And upon my soul, my dear, 'tis high time I was there, for 'tis now thirty long years since I sat foot in my native country, and by the power of St. Patrick I swear I think it's worth all the rest of the world put together.

Dudley. Ay, major, much about that time have I been beating the round of service, and 'twere well for us both to give over. We have stood many a tough gale and abundance of hard blows, but Charles shall lay us up in a private, but safe, harbor, where we'll rest from our labors and peacefully wind up the remainder of our days.

O'FLAHERTY. Agreed, and you may take it as proof of my esteem, young man, that Major O'Flaherty accepts a favor at your hands, for, by heaven, I'd sooner starve than say I thank you to the man I despise. But I believe you are an honest lad, and I'm glad you've trounced the old cat, for on my conscience I believe I must otherwise have married her myself to have let you in for a share of her fortune.

STOCKWELL. Hey-dey, what's become of Belcour?

LOUISA. One of your servants called him out just now and seemingly on some earnest occasion.

STOCKWELL. I hope, Miss Dudley, he has atoned to you as a gentleman ought.

LOUISA. Mr. Belcour, sir, will always do what a gentleman ought, and in my case I fear only you will think he has done too much.

STOCKWELL. What has he done, and what can be too much? (*Aside*) Pray heaven it may be as I wish!

DUDLEY. Let us hear it, child.

LOUISA. With confusion for my own unworthiness, I confess to you he has offered me—

STOCKWELL. Himself.

LOUISA. 'Tis true.

STOCKWELL. [*Aside*] Then I am happy; all my doubts, my cares are over, and I may own him for my son.—Why, these are joyful tidings. Come, my good friend, assist me in disposing your lovely daughter to accept this returning prodigal. He is no unprincipled, no hardened libertine. His love for you and virtue is the same.

DUDLEY. 'Twere vile ingratitude in me to doubt his merit. What says my child?

O'FLAHERTY. Begging your pardon, now, 'tis a frivolous sort of a question, that of yours; for you may see plainly enough by the young lady's looks that she says a great deal, though she speaks never a word.

CHARLES. Well, sister, I believe the major has fairly interpreted the state of your heart.

LOUISA. I own it; and what must that heart be which love, honor, and beneficence like Mr. Belcour's can make no impression on?

STOCKWELL. I thank you. What happiness has this hour brought to pass!

O'FLAHERTY. Why don't we all sit down to supper then and make a night on't?

STOCKWELL. Hold, here comes Belcour.

SCENE VII

BELCOUR *introducing* MISS RUSPORT

BELCOUR. Mr. Dudley, here is a fair refugee, who properly comes under your protection, for she is equipped for Scotland; but your good fortune, which I have related to her, seems inclined to save you both the journey.—Nay, madam, never go back; you are amongst friends.

CHARLES. Charlotte!

CHARLOTTE. The same. That fond, officious girl that haunts you everywhere; that persecuting spirit—

CHARLES. Say rather that protecting angel; such you have been to me.

CHARLOTTE. O Charles, you have an honest but proud heart!

CHARLES. Nay, chide me not, dear Charlotte.

BELCOUR. Seal up her lips then; she is an adorable girl; her arms are open to you; and love and happiness are ready to receive you.

CHARLES. Thus then I claim my dear, my destined wife. (*Embracing her*)

SCENE VIII

LADY RUSPORT *enters*

LADY RUSPORT. Hey-dey! Mighty fine! Wife truly! Mighty well! Kissing, embracing —Did ever anything equal this? Why you shameless hussy!—But I won't condescend to waste a word upon you.—You, sir, you, Mr. Stockwell, you fine, sanctified, fair-dealing man of conscience, is this the principle you trade upon? Is this your neighborly system, to keep a house of reception for run-away daughters and young beggarly fortune-hunters?

O'FLAHERTY. Be advised now, and don't put yourself in such a passion; we were all very happy till you came.

LADY RUSPORT. Stand away, sir. Haven't I a reason to be in a passion?

O'FLAHERTY. Indeed, honey, and you have, if you knew all.

LADY RUSPORT. Come, madam, I have found out your haunts; dispose yourself to return home with me. Young man, let me never see you within my doors again. Mr. Stockwell, I shall report your behavior, depend on it.

STOCKWELL. Hold! Madam, I cannot consent to lose Miss Rusport's company this evening, and I am persuaded you won't insist upon it. 'Tis an unmotherly action to interrupt your daughter's happiness in this manner, believe me it is.

LADY RUSPORT. Her happiness! upon my word! And I suppose it's an unmotherly action to interrupt her ruin, for what but ruin must it be to marry a beggar? (*To* CAPTAIN DUDLEY) I think my sister had proof of that, sir, when she made choice of you.

DUDLEY. Don't be too lavish of your spirits, Lady Rusport.

O'FLAHERTY. By my soul you'll have occasion for a sip of the cordial elixir by and by.

STOCKWELL. It don't appear to me, madam, that Mr. Dudley can be called a beggar.

LADY RUSPORT. But it appears to me, Mr. Stockwell. I am apt to think a pair of colors cannot furnish settlement quite sufficient for the heiress of Sir Stephen Rusport.

CHARLOTTE. But a good estate in aid of a commission may do something.

LADY RUSPORT. A good estate, truly! Where should he get a good estate, pray?

STOCKWELL. Why, suppose a worthy old gentleman on his death-bed should have taken it in mind to leave him one—

LADY RUSPORT. Hah! What's that you say?

O'FLAHERTY. O ho! You begin to smell a plot, do you?

STOCKWELL. Suppose there should be a paper in the world that runs thus:—"I do hereby give and bequeath all my estates, real and personal, to Charles Dudley, son of my late daughter Louisa, &c., &c., &c."

LADY RUSPORT. Why, I am thunder-struck! By what contrivance, what villainy, did you get possession of that paper?

STOCKWELL. There was no villainy, madam, in getting possession of it. The crime was in concealing it, none in bringing it to light.

LADY RUSPORT. Oh, that cursed lawyer, Varland!

O'FLAHERTY. You may say that, faith; he is a cursed lawyer, and a cursed piece of work I had to get the paper from him. Your ladyship now was to have paid him five thousand pounds for it. I forced him to give it to me of his own accord for nothing at all, at all.

LADY RUSPORT. Is it you that have done this? Am I foiled by your blundering contrivances, after all?

O'FLAHERTY. 'Twas a blunder, faith, but as natural a one as if I'd made it o' purpose.

CHARLES. Come, let us not oppress the fallen. Do right even now and you shall have no cause to complain.

LADY RUSPORT. Am I become an object of your pity then? Insufferable! Confusion light amongst you! Marry and be wretched! Let me never see you more. *Exit*

CHARLOTTE. She is outrageous. I suffer for her and blush to see her thus exposed.

CHARLES. Come, Charlotte, don't let this angry woman disturb our happiness. We will save her in spite of herself. Your father's memory shall not be stained by the discredit of his second choice.

CHARLOTTE. I trust implicitly to your discretion and am in all things yours.

BELCOUR. Now, lovely but obdurate, does not this example soften?

LOUISA. What can you ask for more? Accept my hand, accept my willing heart.

BELCOUR. O bliss inutterable! Brother, father, friend, and you the author of this general joy—

O'FLAHERTY. Blessing of St. Patrick upon us all! 'Tis a night of wonderful and surprising ups and downs. I wish we were all fairly set down to supper and there was an end on't.

STOCKWELL. Hold for a moment! I have yet one word to interpose.—Entitled by my friendship to a voice in your disposal, I have approved your match. There yet remains a father's consent to be obtained.

BELCOUR. Have I a father?

STOCKWELL. You have a father. Did not I tell you I had a discovery to make? Compose yourself; you have a father, who observes, who knows, who loves you.

BELCOUR. Keep me no longer in suspense. My heart is softened for the affecting discovery, and nature fits me to receive his blessing.

STOCKWELL. I am your father.

BELCOUR. My father? Do I live?

STOCKWELL. I am your father.

BELCOUR. It is too much; my happiness o'erpowers me. To gain a friend and find a father is too much. I blush to think how little I deserve you. (*They embrace*)

DUDLEY. See, children, how many new

relations spring from this night's unforeseen events to endear us to each other.

O'FLAHERTY. O my conscience, I think we shall be all related by and bye.

STOCKWELL. How happily has this evening concluded, and yet how threatening was its approach! Let us repair to the supper room, where I will unfold to you every circumstance of my mysterious story. Yes, Belcour, I have watched you with a patient but enquiring eye; and I have discovered through the veil of some irregularities, a heart beaming with benevolence, an animated nature, fallible indeed, but not incorrigible; and your election of this excellent young lady makes me glory in acknowledging you to be my son.

BELCOUR. I thank you, and in my turn glory in the father I have gained. Sensibly impressed with gratitude for such extraordinary dispensations, I beseech you, amiable Louisa, for the time to come, whenever you perceive me deviating into error or offence, bring only to my mind the providence of this night, and I will turn to reason and obey.

EPILOGUE

Written by D. G., ESQ.[1]

Spoken by MRS. ABINGTON

N. B. The lines in italics are to be spoken in a catechise tone

Confess, good folks, has not Miss Rusport shown
Strange whims for SEVENTEEN HUN-
  DRED SEVENTY-ONE?
What pawn her jewels!—There's a precious plan!
To extricate from want a brave *old* man;
And fall in love with poverty and honor;   5
A girl of fortune, fashion!—Fie upon her.
But do not think we females of the stage,
So dead to the refinements of the age,
That we agree with our old fashioned poet:
I am point blank against him, and I'll show it: 10
And that my tongue may more politely run,
Make me a lady—Lady Blabington.
Now, with a rank and title to be free,
I'll make a catechism—and you shall see,
What is the *veritable Beaume*[2] *de Vie*:   15

As I change place, I stand for that, or this,
My lady questions first—then answers miss.
                (*She speaks as my lady*)
"Come, tell me, child, what were our modes and dress,
In those strange times of that old fright Queen Bess?"—
And now for Miss—
        (*She changes place, and speaks for miss*)
        When Bess was England's queen,
Ladies were dismal beings, seldom seen;   21
They rose betimes, and breakfasted as soon
On beef and beer, then studied Greek till noon;
Unpainted cheeks with blush of health did glow,
Beruffed and fardingaled from top to toe,   25
Nor necks, nor ancles would they ever show.
Learned Greek!—(*Laughs*)—Our outside head takes half a day;
Have we much time to dress the *inside*, pray?
No heads dressed *à la Grecque;* the ancients quote,
There may be learning in a *papillote*[3]   30
Cards are our classics; and I, Lady B,
In learning will not yield to any she,
Of the late founded *female* university.[4]
But now for Lady Blab—
                (*Speaks as my lady*)
        "Tell me, Miss Nancy,
What sports and what employments did they fancy?"   (*Speaks as miss*)   35
The vulgar creatures seldom left their houses,
But taught their children, worked, and loved their spouses;
The use of cards at Christmas only knew,
They played for little, and their games were few,
One-and-thirty, Put, All fours, and Lantera Loo;[5]   40
They bore a race of martals stout and boney,
And never heard the name of Macaroni.
                (*Speaks as my lady*)
"Oh brava, brava! that's my pretty dear—
Now let a modern, modish fair appear;
No more of these old dowdy maids and wives,
Tell how superior beings pass their lives."—
                (*Speaks as miss*)
Till noon they sleep, from noon till night they dress,   47
From night till morn they game it more or less,

[1] David Garrick, of course. Spoken by Mrs. Abington as Charlotte Rusport.

[2] *Beaume*, i.e., *baume* which means *balm*.

[3] Curl paper.

[4] Possibly an allusion to the Blue-Stocking Club. Garrick, author of this epilogue, was a frequent visitor of the club, if not actually a member.

[5] All card games known in the sixteenth or seventeenth centuries and therefore old fashioned.

Next night the same sweet course of joy run o'er,
Then the night after as the night before, 50
And the night after that, encore, encore!—
                    (*She comes forward*)
Thus with our cards we *shuffle* off all sorrow,
To-morrow, and to-morrow, and to-morrow![1]
We *deal apace*, from youth unto our prime,
To the last moment of our *tabby*-time; 55

[1] A paraphrase of *Macbeth*, V, v, 19–23.

And all our yesterdays, from rout and drum,
Have lighted fools with empty pockets home.
Thus do our lives with rapture roll away,
Not with the nonsense of our author's play;
This is true life—true spirit—give it praise;
Don't snarl and sigh for good Queen Bess's
   days: 61
For all you look so sour, and bend the brow,
You all rejoice with me, you're living now.

SHE STOOPS TO CONQUER

OR

THE MISTAKES OF A NIGHT

A Comedy by Oliver Goldsmith

Oliver Goldsmith was born at Pallas, near Ballymahon, Longford, Ireland, November 10, 1728 (?),[1] fifth child of the Rev. Charles Goldsmith, curate of Kilkenny West and a farmer. The poverty of the family affected Goldsmith's entire career, though it apparently failed to encourage him to industrious exertions. Aided by his uncle-in-law, Thomas Contarine, he attended schools at Athlone and Edgeworthstown; and on June 11, 1745,[2] he entered Trinity College, Dublin, as a sizar. From this time until about 1760 Goldsmith's career, though interesting to biographers and students of his work, is confused and unsettled. He did, however, take his degree in 1750; and two years later, he went to Edinburgh to study medicine. An aversion to his new abode or a desire to wander carried him in 1753 to the Continent, ostensibly to complete his study of medicine at Leyden. He traveled over the Continent, according to the well known story "disputing his passage through Europe," visiting universities and joining in debates. After three years he was back in England destitute.

For several years after 1756 he lived in or near London as an usher in a school and a literary hack. His *Enquiry into the Present State of Polite Learning in Europe*, published in 1759, attracted attention; and he soon became the contributor to periodicals, novelist, and poet, the friend of Percy and Johnson and member of "The Club," familiar to posterity. In 1767 he wrote *The Good-Natured Man*, which was produced, after much disappointment to the author and much controversy among his friends, by Colman at Covent Garden, January 29, 1768, a week after the first performance of Kelly's *False Delicacy* (at Drury Lane), a comedy once much traduced by Goldsmith's admirers as a poor thing little meriting the success it achieved. The failure of *The Good-Natured Man*, probably deserved, was laid to the poor taste of audiences and the hostility of Garrick. Goldsmith, however, established his fame as a dramatist with the production of *She Stoops to Conquer*, March 15, 1773, at Covent Garden. He died April 14, 1774, and was buried in the Temple. The Literary Club erected a monument to him in Westminster Abbey.

REFERENCES:—lives, memoirs, etc., by Percy (1801), Prior (1837), Forster (1877), Black (1878), Dobson (1899). See also Boswell's *Johnson*, and other contemporary memoirs. More recently have appeared articles and detailed studies by Katharine C. Balderston, R. S. Crane, and others.

GOLDSMITH'S DRAMATIC WORKS

The Good-Natured Man (comedy) (C.G., Jan. 29, 1768), 1768.

She Stoops to Conquer; or, The Mistakes of a Night (comedy) (C.G., March 15, 1773), 1773.

The Grumbler (farce), C.G., May 8, 1773 [Adaptation of Sedley's translation of Bruey's *Le Grondeur*. Acted once, never printed.]

As Dr. Goldsmith's *The Good-Natured Man*, appearing at Covent Garden a week after *False Delicacy* at Drury Lane in 1768, had been a failure, Mr. Colman doubted the wisdom of producing a second comedy by the same author, particularly as it, too, was not written in the prevailing mode. Mr. Garrick, also, would have nothing to do with it. Successful pieces not quite in the sentimental manner had, it was true, been written by Arthur Murphy and by Mr. Colman himself;

---

[1] The date of Goldsmith's birth has occasioned some controversy. Evidence in support of Katharine C. Balderston's contention in favor of 1730 instead of the conventionally accepted date will be found in her *The History and Sources of Percy's Memoir of Goldsmith* (1926), and T. L. S., Nov. 8, 1928, March 7, and March 14, 1929.

[2] Cf. Miss Balderston's letter, T. L. S., March 7, 1929.

but the popular playwrights of the time were Mr. Cumberland and Mr. Kelly. In the summer of 1771, Dr. Goldsmith had begun a new comedy, which was started on its round of the managers upon its completion. Colman kept it for more than a year without making up his mind. By January, 1773, the author importuned for a verdict, which at the insistence of Dr. Johnson was at last rendered; and the play, much against Mr. Colman's judgment, was put into rehearsal. Although Smith and Woodward, the two masters of comedy at Covent Garden, threw up their parts after the early rehearsals, the many difficulties were overcome and the comedy, *She Stoops to Conquer;* or, *The Mistakes of a Night,* as they had at last decided to call it, appeared on March 15, 1773. Dr. Johnson and his friends had organized a party to see their colleague's play through. Applauding vociferously, if not always judiciously, they fairly clapped it into success and lasting fame. It appeared twelve times during the rest of the season, being chosen to close with on May 31. "I know of no comedy for many years," said Dr. Johnson, "that has answered so much the great end of comedy,—making an audience merry." And he, as usual, was right. Though not the best comedy of the century, it is certainly the merriest.

"When I undertook to write a comedy," says Goldsmith in his preface to *The Good-Natured Man,* "I confess I was strongly prepossessed in favour of the poets of the last age, and strove to imitate them. The term *genteel comedy* was then unknown amongst us, and little more was desired by an audience than nature and humour, in whatever walks of life they were most conspicuous." With these words in view we should judge *She Stoops to Conquer* and estimate its position in English comedy. Though Goldsmith failed of his purpose in his first play, he succeeded admirably at last; and "nature and humour" are more pronounced in *She Stoops to Conquer* than in any comedy since the Elizabethans, whom Goldsmith meant when he said "the poets of the last age." The resemblance of the play to *The Beaux' Stratagem* is obvious and has often been remarked; but Goldsmith resembles no other Restoration dramatist than Farquhar, who has in himself something of the Elizabethan as well as of Wycherley and Etherege, with whom Goldsmith has nothing in common. That Goldsmith founded no school, had no successor, produced almost no effect on the drama of his day is perhaps regrettable. More than the two plays of a charming and incomprehensible Irishman were needed to check the course of sentimentalism, and one can hardly expect a dawn of Shakespearean comedy in "the twilight of the Augustans."

[DEDICATION]

To SAMUEL JOHNSON, LL.D.

Dear Sir,

By inscribing this slight performance to you, I do not mean so much to compliment you as myself. It may do me some honor to inform the public that I have lived many years in intimacy with you. It may serve the interests of mankind also to inform them that the greatest wit may be found in a character without impairing the most unaffected piety.

I have, particularly, reason to thank you for your partiality to this performance. The undertaking a comedy, not merely sentimental, was very dangerous; and Mr. Colman, who saw this piece in its various stages, always thought it so. However I ventured to trust it to the public; and though it was necessarily delayed till late in the season, I have every reason to be grateful.

I am, Dear Sir,
Your most sincere friend,
And admirer,
Oliver Goldsmith.

SHE STOOPS TO CONQUER

OR

THE MISTAKES OF A NIGHT

DRAMATIS PERSONÆ

MEN

SIR CHARLES MARLOW,	Mr. Gardener	HASTINGS,	Mr. Dubellamy
YOUNG MARLOW (*his Son*),	Mr. Lewes	TONY LUMPKIN,	Mr. Quick
HARDCASTLE,	Mr. Shuter	[DIGGORY,	Mr. Saunders] [1]

WOMEN

MRS. HARDCASTLE,	Mrs. Green	MISS NEVILLE,	Mrs. Kniveton
MISS HARDCASTLE,	Mrs. Bulkely	MAID,	Miss Willems.

Landlord, Servants, &c. &c.

PROLOGUE

BY DAVID GARRICK, ESQ.

Enter MR. WOODWARD,[2] *dressed in black and holding a handkerchief to his eyes.*

Excuse me, sirs, I pray—I can't yet speak—
I'm crying now—and have been all the week!
'*Tis not alone this mourning suit*, good masters;
I've *that within*[3]—for which there are no plasters!
Pray would you know the reason why I'm crying?　　　　　　　　　　　　　　　5
The comic Muse, long sick, is now a-dying!
And if she goes, my tears will never stop;
For as a player, I can't squeeze out one drop.
I am undone, that's all—shall lose my bread—
I'd rather, but that's nothing—lose my head.
When the sweet maid is laid upon the bier,　11
Shuter[4] and I shall be chief mourners here.
To her a mawkish drab of spurious breed,
Who deals in sentimentals will succeed!
Poor Ned and I are dead to all intents,　　15
We can as soon speak Greek as sentiments!
Both nervous grown, to keep our spirits up,
We now and then take down a hearty cup.
What shall we do?—If comedy forsake us!
They'll turn us out, and no one else will take us.　　　　　　　　　　　　　　20
But why can't I be moral?—Let me try:
My heart thus pressing—fixed my face and eye—
With a sententious look, that nothing means,
(Faces are blocks, in sentimental scenes)
Thus I begin:—"All is not gold that glitters,
Pleasure seems sweet, but proves a glass of bitters.　　　　　　　　　　　　　26
When ign'rance enters, folly is at hand;
Learning is better far than house and land.
Let not your virtue trip, who trips may stumble,
And virtue is not virtue, if she tumble."　30
I give it up—morals won't do for me;
To make you laugh I must play tragedy.
One hope remains—hearing the maid was ill,
A doctor comes this night to show his skill.
To cheer her heart and give your muscles motion,　　　　　　　　　　　　　35
He in five draughts prepared, presents a potion:
A kind of magic charm—for be assured,
If you will swallow it, the maid is cured;
But desperate the doctor, and her case is,
If you reject the dose, and make wry faces! 40
This truth he boasts, will boast it while he lives,
No poisonous drugs are mixed in what he gives;

---

[1] Lacking in the first issue of the first edition, but added in the second issue.

[2] Woodward (d. 1777) was long a popular actor in London. He had previously been at D.L. under Garrick, where he played Harlequin as "Lun, Jr.," in competition with Rich, who as "Lun" was Harlequin at C.G. Woodward refused the part of Tony, giving Quick his first taste of popular favor.

[3] Paraphrase of *Hamlet*, I, ii, 77 ff.

[4] Edward ("Ned") Shuter had appeared prominently as Croaker in *The Good-Natured Man*, and now was playing Mr. Hardcastle. He was a popular actor of low comedy, a fact which gives added point to the allusions here to "genteel" comedy.

790

Should he succeed, you'll give him his degree;
If not, within[1] he will receive no fee!
The college, you, must his pretensions back,
Pronounce him regular, or dub him quack. 46

ACT I

SCENE [I]. *A chamber in an old-fashioned house*

Enter MRS. HARDCASTLE *and* MR. HARDCASTLE

MRS. HARDCASTLE. I vow, Mr. Hardcastle, you're very particular. Is there a creature in the whole country but ourselves that does not take a trip to town now and then to rub off the rust a little? There's the two Miss Hoggs and our neighbor, Mrs. Grigsby, go to take a month's polishing every winter.

HARDCASTLE. Ay, and bring back vanity and affectation to last them the whole year. I wonder why London cannot keep its own fools at home. In my time, the follies of the town crept slowly among us, but now they travel faster than a stage-coach. Its fopperies come down, not only as inside passengers, but in the very basket.[2]

MRS. HARDCASTLE. Ay, *your* times were fine times, indeed; you have been telling us of *them* for many a long year. Here we live in an old rumbling mansion that looks for all the world like an inn, but that we never see company. Our best visitors are old Mrs. Oddfish, the curate's wife, and little Cripplegate, the lame dancing-master. And all our entertainment your old stories of Prince Eugene and the Duke of Marlborough.[3] I hate such old-fashioned trumpery.

HARDCASTLE. And I love it. I love everything that's old: old friends, old times, old manners, old books, old wine; and I believe, Dorothy, (*taking her hand*) you'll own I have been pretty fond of an old wife.

MRS. HARDCASTLE. Lord, Mr. Hardcastle, you're for ever at your Dorothy's and your old wife's. You may be a Darby, but I'll be

[1] That is, if the play fails the author receives nothing for his labors.
[2] The overhanging back compartment on the outside of a stage-coach, meant to carry luggage but sometimes used for passengers.
[3] Prince Eugene of Savoy (1663–1736) and John Churchill, first Duke of Marlborough (1650–1722), commanding generals of the Austrian and English armies against the French in the War of the Spanish Succession.

no Joan, I promise you. I'm not so old as you'd make me, by more than one good year. Add twenty to twenty, and make money of that.

HARDCASTLE. Let me see; twenty added to twenty makes just fifty and seven.

MRS. HARDCASTLE. It's false, Mr. Hardcastle; I was but twenty when I was brought to bed of Tony, that I had by Mr. Lumpkin, my first husband; and he's not come to years of discretion yet.

HARDCASTLE. Nor ever will, I dare answer for him. Ay, you have taught *him* finely.

MRS. HARDCASTLE. No matter. Tony Lumpkin has a good fortune. My son is not to live by his learning. I don't think a boy wants much learning to spend fifteen-hundred a year.

HARDCASTLE. Learning, quotha! A mere composition of tricks and mischief.

MRS. HARDCASTLE. Humor, my dear; nothing but humor. Come, Mr. Hardcastle, you must allow the boy a little humor.

HARDCASTLE. I'd sooner allow him an horse-pond. If burning the footmen's shoes, frightening the maids, and worrying the kittens be humor, he has it. It was but yesterday he fastened my wig to the back of my chair, and when I went to make a bow, I popped my bald head in Mrs. Frizzle's face.

MRS. HARDCASTLE. And am I to blame? The poor boy was always too sickly to do any good. A school would be his death. When he comes to be a little stronger, who knows what a year or two's Latin may do for him?

HARDCASTLE. Latin for him! A cat and fiddle. No, no, the ale-house and the stable are the only schools he'll ever go to.

MRS. HARDCASTLE. Well, we must not snub the poor boy now, for I believe we shall not have him long among us. Anybody that looks in his face may see he's consumptive.

HARDCASTLE. Ay, if growing too fat be one of the symptoms.

MRS. HARDCASTLE. He coughs sometimes.

HARDCASTLE. Yes, when his liquor goes the wrong way.

MRS. HARDCASTLE. I'm actually afraid of his lungs.

HARDCASTLE. And truly so am I; for he sometimes whoops like a speaking trumpet —(*Tony hallooing behind the scenes*)—O there he goes—A very consumptive figure, truly.

Enter TONY, *crossing the stage*

MRS. HARDCASTLE. Tony, where are you going, my charmer? Won't you give papa and I a little of your company, lovee?

TONY. I'm in haste, mother; I cannot stay.

MRS. HARDCASTLE. You shan't venture out this raw evening, my dear. You look most shockingly.

TONY. I can't stay, I tell you. The Three Pigeons expects me down every moment. There's some fun going forward.

HARDCASTLE. [*Aside*] Ay, the ale-house, the old place. I thought so.

MRS. HARDCASTLE. A low, paltry set of fellows.

TONY. Not so low neither. There's Dick Muggins, the exciseman, Jack Slang, the horse doctor, Little Aminadab that grinds the music box, and Tom Twist that spins the pewter platter.

MRS. HARDCASTLE. Pray, my dear, disappoint them for one night at least.

TONY. As for disappointing *them*, I should not so much mind; but I can't abide to disappoint *myself*.

MRS. HARDCASTLE. (*Detaining him*) You shan't go.

TONY. I will, I tell you.

MRS. HARDCASTLE. I say you shan't.

TONY. We'll see which is strongest, you or I. *Exit, hauling her out*

HARDCASTLE, *solus*

HARDCASTLE. Ay, there goes a pair that only spoil each other. But is not the whole age in a combination to drive sense and discretion out of doors? There's my pretty darling Kate; the fashions of the times have almost infected her, too. By living a year or two in town, she is as fond of gauze and French frippery as the best of them.

Enter MISS HARDCASTLE

HARDCASTLE. Blessings on my pretty innocence! Dressed out as usual, my Kate. Goodness! What a quantity of superfluous silk thou has got about thee, girl! I could never teach the fools of this age that the indigent world could be clothed out of the trimmings of the vain.

MISS HARDCASTLE. You know our agreement, sir. You allow me the morning to receive and pay visits and to dress in my own manner; and in the evening I put on my housewife's dress to please you.

HARDCASTLE. Well, remember I insist on the terms of our agreement; and, by the bye, I believe I shall have occasion to try your obedience this very evening.

MISS HARDCASTLE. I protest, sir, I don't comprehend your meaning.

HARDCASTLE. Then to be plain with you, Kate, I expect the young gentleman I have chosen to be your husband, from town this very day. I have his father's letter in which he informs me his son is set out and that he intends to follow himself shortly after.

MISS HARDCASTLE. Indeed! I wish I had known something of this before. Bless me, how shall I behave? It's a thousand to one I shan't like him. Our meeting will be so formal and so like a thing of business that I shall find no room for friendship or esteem.

HARDCASTLE. Depend upon it, child, I'll never control your choice; but Mr. Marlow, whom I have pitched upon, is the son of my old friend, Sir Charles Marlow, of whom you have heard me talk so often. The young gentleman had been bred a scholar and is designed for an employment in the service of his country. I am told he's a man of excellent understanding.

MISS HARDCASTLE. Is he?

HARDCASTLE. Very generous.

MISS HARDCASTLE. I believe I shall like him.

HARDCASTLE. Young and brave.

MISS HARDCASTLE. I'm sure I shall like him.

HARDCASTLE. And very handsome.

MISS HARDCASTLE. My dear papa, say no more; (*kissing his hand*) he's mine, I'll have him.

HARDCASTLE. And to crown all, Kate, he's one of the most bashful and reserved young fellows in all the world.

MISS HARDCASTLE. Eh! you have frozen me to death again. That word "reserved" has undone all the rest of his accomplishments. A reserved lover, it is said, always makes a suspicious husband.

HARDCASTLE. On the contrary, modesty seldom resides in a breast that is not enriched with nobler virtues. It was the very feature in his character that struck me.

MISS HARDCASTLE. He must have more striking features to catch me, I promise you. However, if he be so young, so handsome, and so everything, as you mention, I believe he'll do still. I think I'll have him.

HARDCASTLE. Ay, Kate, but there is still an obstacle. It's more than an even wager he may not have *you*.

MISS HARDCASTLE. My dear papa, why will you mortify one so?—Well, if he refuses, instead of breaking my heart at his indifference, I'll only break my glass for its flattery, set my cap to some newer fashion, and look out for some less difficult admirer.

HARDCASTLE. Bravely resolved! In the meantime I'll go prepare the servants for his reception; as we seldom see company they want as much training as a company of recruits, the first day's muster. *Exit*

MISS HARDCASTLE, *sola*

MISS HARDCASTLE. Lud, this news of papa's puts me all in a flutter. Young, handsome; these he put last, but I put them foremost. Sensible, good-natured; I like that. But then, reserved and sheepish, that's much against him. Yet can't he be cured of his timidity by being taught to be proud of his wife? Yes, and can't I—But I vow I'm disposing of the husband before I have secured the lover.

Enter MISS NEVILLE

MISS HARDCASTLE. I'm glad you're come, Neville, my dear. Tell me, Constance, how do I look this evening? Is there anything whimsical about me? Is it one of my well looking days, child? Am I in face to-day?

MISS NEVILLE. Perfectly, my dear. Yet now I look again—bless me!—sure, no accident has happened among the canary birds or the gold fishes. Has your brother or the cat been meddling? Or has the last novel been too moving?

MISS HARDCASTLE. No; nothing of all this. I have been threatened—I can scarce get it out—I have been threatened with a lover.

MISS NEVILLE. And his name—
MISS HARDCASTLE. Is Marlow.
MISS NEVILLE. Indeed!
MISS HARDCASTLE. The son of Sir Charles Marlow.

MISS NEVILLE. As I live, the most intimate friend of Mr. Hastings, *my* admirer. They are never asunder. I believe you must have seen him when we lived in town.

MISS HARDCASTLE. Never.

MISS NEVILLE. He's a very singular character, I assure you. Among women of reputation and virtue, he is the modestest man alive; but his acquaintance give him a very different character among creatures of another stamp. You understand me.

MISS HARDCASTLE. An odd character, indeed. I shall never be able to manage him. What shall I do? Pshaw, think no more of him, but trust to occurrences for success. But how goes on your own affair, my dear? Has my mother been courting you for my brother Tony, as usual?

MISS NEVILLE. I have just come from one of our agreeable *tête-à-têtes*. She has been saying a hundred tender things and setting off her pretty monster as the very pink of perfection.

MISS HARDCASTLE. And her partiality is such that she actually thinks him so. A fortune like yours is no small temptation. Besides, as she has the sole management of it, I'm not surprised to see her unwilling to let it go out of the family.

MISS NEVILLE. A fortune like mine, which chiefly consists in jewels, is no such mighty temptation. But at any rate if my dear Hastings be but constant, I make no doubt to be too hard for her at last. However, I let her suppose that I am in love with her son, and she never once dreams that my affections are fixed upon another.

MISS HARDCASTLE. My good brother holds out stoutly. I could almost love him for hating you so.

MISS NEVILLE. He is a good-natured creature at bottom, and I'm sure would wish to see me married to anybody but himself. But my aunt's bell rings for our afternoon's walk round the improvements. *Allons*. Courage is necessary as our affairs are critical.

MISS HARDCASTLE. Would it were bed time and all were well! *Exeunt*

SCENE [II]. *An alehouse room. Several shabby fellows, with punch and tobacco.* TONY *at back of the table, a little higher than the rest, a mallet in his hand*

OMNES. Hurrea, hurrea, hurrea, bravo.
FIRST FELLOW. Now, gentlemen, silence for a song. The squire is going to knock himself down for a song.
OMNES. Ay, a song, a song.

TONY. Then I'll sing you, gentlemen, a song I made upon this ale-house, the Three Pigeons.

SONG

Let school-masters puzzle their brain
   With grammar, and nonsense, and learning;
Good liquor, I stoutly maintain
   Gives genius a better discerning.
Let them brag of their heathenish gods,
   Their Lethes, their Styxes, and Stygians;
Their Quis, and their Quæs, and their Quods,[1]
   They're all but a parcel of pigeons.
            Toroddle, toroddle, toroll.

When Methodist preachers come down,
   A preaching that drinking is sinful,
I'll wager the rascals a crown,
   They always preach best with a skinful.
But when you come down with your pence,
   For a slice of their scurvy religion,
I'll leave it to all men of sense,
   But you, my good friend, are the pigeon.
            Toroddle, toroddle, toroll.

Then come, put the jorum about,
   And let us be merry and clever,
Our hearts and our liquors are stout,
   Here's the Three Jolly Pigeons for ever.
Let some cry up woodcock or hare,
   Your bustards, your ducks, and your widgeons;
But of all of the birds in the air,
   Here's a health to the Three Jolly Pigeons.
            Toroddle, toroddle, toroll.

OMNES. Bravo, bravo.

FIRST FELLOW. The squire has got spunk in him.

SECOND FELLOW. I loves to hear him sing, bekays he never gives us nothing that's *low*.

THIRD FELLOW. O damn anything that's *low*, I cannot bear it.

FOURTH FELLOW. The genteel thing is the genteel thing at any time. If so be that a gentleman bees in a concatenation accordingly.

THIRD FELLOW. I like the maxum if it, Master Muggins. What, tho' I am obligated to dance a bear, a man may be a gentleman for all that. May this be my poison if my bear ever dances but to the very genteelest of tunes, "Water Parted," or the minuet in *Ariadne*.[2]

---

[1] The nominative singular of the Latin relative pronoun is *qui, quæ, quod*.

[2] "Water Parted" is a song in Arne's *Artaxerxes* (C.G., Feb. 2, 1762). The minuet is found at the end of the overture to Handel's *Ariadne*. In reading this scene one should remember that *The Good-Natured Man* had been damned because it was "low."

SECOND FELLOW. What a pity it is the squire is not come to his own. It would be well for all the publicans within ten miles round of him.

TONY. Ecod and so it would, Master Slang. I'd then show what it was to keep choice of company.

SECOND FELLOW. O he takes after his own father for that. To be sure old squire Lumpkin was the finest gentleman I ever set my eyes on. For winding the straight horn, or beating a thicket for a hare or a wench he never had his fellow. It was a saying in the place, that he kept the best horses, dogs, and girls in the whole county.

TONY. Ecod, and when I'm of age, I'll be no bastard, I promise you. I have been thinking of Bett Bouncer and the miller's grey mare to begin with. But come, my boys, drink about and be merry, for you pay no reckoning. Well, Stingo, what's the matter?

Enter LANDLORD

LANDLORD. There be two gentlemen in a post-chaise at the door. They have lost their way upo' the forest; and they are talking something about Mr. Hardcastle.

TONY. As sure as can be, one of them must be the gentleman that's coming down to court my sister. Do they seem to be Londoners?

LANDLORD. I believe they may. They look woundily like Frenchmen.

TONY. Then desire them to step this way, and I'll set them right in a twinkling. (*Exit* Landlord) Gentlemen, as they mayn't be good enough company for you, step down for a moment, and I'll be with you in the squeezing of a lemon.   *Exeunt* MOB

TONY solus

TONY. Father-in-law has been calling me whelp and hound this half year. Now if I pleased, I could be so revenged upon the old grumbletonian. But then I'm afraid!—afraid of what? I shall soon be worth fifteen hundred a year, and let him frighten me out of *that* if he can.

Enter LANDLORD, *conducting* MARLOW *and* HASTINGS

MARLOW. What a tedious, uncomfortable day have we had of it! We were told it was but forty miles across the country, and we have come above three score.

HASTINGS. And all, Marlow, from that unaccountable reserve of yours that would not let us enquire more frequently on the way.

MARLOW. I own, Hastings, I am unwilling to lay myself under an obligation to every one I meet; and often, stand the chance of an unmannerly answer.

HASTINGS. At present, however, we are not likely to receive any answer.

TONY. No offence, gentlemen. But I'm told you have been enquiring for one Mr. Hardcastle, in those parts. Do you know what part of the country you are in?

HASTINGS. Not in the least, sir, but I should thank you for information.

TONY. Nor the way you came?

HASTINGS. No, sir; but if you can inform us—

TONY. Well, gentlemen, if you know neither the road you are going, nor where you are, nor the road you came, the first thing I have to inform you is, that—You have lost your way.

MARLOW. We wanted no ghost to tell us that.

TONY. Pray, gentlemen, may I be so bold as to ask the place from whence you came?

MARLOW. That's not necessary towards directing us where we are to go.

TONY. No offence; but question for question is all fair you know. Pray, gentlemen, is not this same Hardcastle a cross-grained, old-fashioned, whimsical fellow, with an ugly face, a daughter, and a pretty son?

HASTINGS. We have not seen the gentleman, but he has the family you mention.

TONY. The daughter, a tall, trapesing, trolloping, talkative maypole—the son, a pretty, well-bred, agreeable youth that everybody is fond of?

MARLOW. Our information differs in this. The daughter is said to be well bred and beautiful; the son, an awkward booby, reared up and spoiled at his mother's apron-string.

TONY. He-he-hem—Then, gentlemen, all I have to tell you is that you won't reach Mr. Hardcastle's house this night, I believe.

HASTINGS. Unfortunate!

TONY. It's a damned long, dark, boggy, dirty, dangerous way. Stingo, tell the gentlemen the way to Mr. Hardcastle's; (*winking upon the* Landlord) Mr. Hardcastle's of Quagmire Marsh, you understand me.

LANDLORD. Master Hardcastle's! Lack-a-daisy, my masters, you're come a deadly deal wrong! When you came to the bottom of the hill, you should have crossed down Squash-lane.

MARLOW. Cross down Squash-lane!

LANDLORD. Then you were to keep straight forward, 'till you came to four roads.

MARLOW. Come to where four roads meet!

TONY. Ay; but you must be sure to take only one of them.

MARLOW. O sir, you're facetious.

TONY. Then keeping to the right, you are to go sideways till you come upon Crack-skull common. There you must look sharp for the track of the wheel and go forward till you come to farmer Murrain's barn. Coming to the farmer's barn, you are to turn to the right, and then to the left, and then to the right about again, till you find out the old mill—

MARLOW. Zounds, man! we could as soon find out the longitude!

HASTINGS. What's to be done, Marlow?

MARLOW. This house promises but a poor reception; though perhaps the landlord can accommodate us.

LANDLORD. Alack, master, we have but one spare bed in the whole house.

TONY. And to my knowledge, that's taken up by three lodgers already. (*After a pause, in which the rest seem disconcerted*) I have hit it. Don't you think, Stingo, our landlady could accommodate the gentlemen by the fire-side, with—three chairs and a bolster?

HASTINGS. I hate sleeping by the fire-side.

MARLOW. And I detest your three chairs and a bolster.

TONY. You do, do you?—Then, let me see—what—if you go on a mile further, to the Buck's Head, the old Buck's Head on the hill, one of the best inns in the whole county!

HASTINGS. O ho! so we have escaped an adventure for this night, however.

LANDLORD. (*Apart to* TONY) Sure, you ben't sending them to your father's as an inn, be you?

TONY. Mum, you fool you. Let *them* find that out. (*To them*) You have only to keep on straight forward till you come to a large old house by the road side. You'll see a pair of large horns over the door. That's the sign. Drive up the yard and call stoutly about you.

HASTINGS. Sir, we are obliged to you. The servants can't miss the way?

TONY. No, no. But I tell you, though, the landlord is rich and going to leave off business; so he wants to be thought a gentleman, saving your presence, he, he, he, he'll be for giving you his company, and ecod, if you mind him, he'll persuade you that his mother was an alderman and his aunt a justice of peace.

LANDLORD. A troublesome old blade, to be sure; but a keeps as good wine and beds as any in the whole country.

MARLOW. Well, if he supplies us with these, we shall want no further connection. We are to turn to the right, did you say?

TONY. No, no; straight forward. I'll just step myself and show you a piece of the way. (*To the landlord*) Mum.

LANDLORD. Ah, bless your heart, for a sweet, pleasant—damned mischievous son of a whore. *Exeunt*

ACT II

SCENE, *the parlor of an old-fashioned house*

Enter HARDCASTLE, *followed by three or four awkward* Servants

HARDCASTLE. Well, I hope you're perfect in the table exercise I have been teaching you these three days. You all know your posts and your places and can show that you have been used to good company, without ever stirring from home.

OMNES. Ay, ay.

HARDCASTLE. When company comes, you are not to pop out and stare, and then run in again, like frightened rabbits in a warren.

OMNES. No, no.

HARDCASTLE. You, Diggory, whom I have taken from the barn, are to make a show at the side-table; and you, Roger, whom I have advanced from the plow, are to place yourself behind *my* chair. But you're not to stand so, with your hands in your pockets. Take your hands from your pockets, Roger; and from your head, you blockhead you. See how Diggory carries his hands. They're a little too stiff, indeed, but that's no great matter.

DIGGORY. Ay, mind how I hold them. I learned to hold my hands this way when I was upon drill for the militia. And so being upon drill—

HARDCASTLE. You must not be so talkative, Diggory. You must be all attention to the guests. You must hear us talk and not think of talking; you must see us drink and not think of drinking; you must see us eat and not think of eating.

DIGGORY. By the laws, your worship, that's perfectly unpossible. Whenever Diggory sees yeating going forward, ecod, he's always wishing for a mouthful himself.

HARDCASTLE. Blockhead! Is not a belly full in the kitchen as good as a belly full in the parlor? Stay your stomach with that reflection.

DIGGORY. Ecod, I thank your worship, I'll make a shift to stay my stomach with a slice of cold beef in the pantry.

HARDCASTLE. Diggory, you are too talkative. Then if I happen to say a good thing, or tell a story at table, you must not all burst out a-laughing, as if you made part of the company.

DIGGORY. Then, ecod, your worship must not tell the story of Ould Grouse in the gunroom. I can't help laughing at that—he! he! he!—for the soul of me. We have laughed at that these twenty years—ha! ha! ha!

HARDCASTLE. Ha! ha! ha! The story is a good one. Well, honest Diggory, you may laugh at that—but still remember to be attentive. Suppose one of the company should call for a glass of wine, how will you behave? A glass of wine, sir, if you please (*to* DIGGORY) —Eh, why don't you move?

DIGGORY. Ecod, your worship, I never have courage till I see the eatables and drinkables brought upo' the table, and then I'm as bauld as a lion.

HARDCASTLE. What, will nobody move?

FIRST SERVANT. I'm not to leave this pleace.

SECOND SERVANT. I'm sure it's no pleace of mine.

THIRD SERVANT. Nor mine, for sartain.

DIGGORY. Wauns, and I'm sure it canna be mine.

HARDCASTLE. You numbskulls! and so while, like your betters, you are quarreling for places, the guests must be starved. O you dunces! I find I must begin all over again. —But don't I hear a coach drive into the yard? To your posts, you blockheads. I'll

go in the meantime and give my old friend's son a hearty reception at the gate.
Exit HARDCASTLE

DIGGORY. By the elevens,[1] my pleace is gone quite out of my head.

ROGER. I know that my pleace is to be everywhere.

FIRST SERVANT. Where the devil is mine?

SECOND SERVANT. My pleace is to be no where at all; and so I'ze go about my business.

Exeunt Servants, *running about as if frightened, different ways*

Enter Servant *with candles, showing in* MARLOW *and* HASTINGS

SERVANT. Welcome, gentlemen, very welcome. This way.

HASTINGS. After the disappointments of the day, welcome once more, Charles, to the comforts of a clean room and a good fire. Upon my word, a very well-looking house; antique, but creditable.

MARLOW. The usual fate of a large mansion. Having first ruined the master by good housekeeping, it at last comes to levy contributions as an inn.

HASTINGS. As you say, we passengers are to be taxed to pay all these fineries. I have often seen a good sideboard, or a marble chimney-piece, though not actually put in the bill, enflame a reckoning confoundedly.

MARLOW. Travellers, George, must pay in all places. The only difference is, that in good inns, you pay dearly for luxuries; in bad inns, you are fleeced and starved.

HASTINGS. You have lived pretty much among them. In truth, I have been often surprised that you, who have seen so much of the world, with your natural good sense and your many opportunities, could never yet acquire a requisite share of assurance.

MARLOW. The Englishman's malady. But tell me, George, where could I have learned that assurance you talk of? My life has been chiefly spent in a college or an inn, in seclusion from that lovely part of the creation that chiefly teach men confidence. I don't know that I was ever familiarly acquainted with a single modest woman—except my mother, but among females of another class, you know—

[1] A phrase of uncertain origin and doubtful meaning.

HASTINGS. Ay, among them you are impudent enough of all conscience.

MARLOW. They are of *us*, you know.

HASTINGS. But in the company of women of reputation I never saw such an idiot, such a trembler; you look for all the world as if you wanted an opportunity of stealing out of the room.

MARLOW. Why, man, that's because I *do* want to steal out of the room. Faith, I have often formed a resolution to break the ice and rattle away at any rate. But I don't know how. A single glance from a pair of fine eyes has totally overset my resolution. An impudent fellow may counterfeit modesty, but I'll be hanged if a modest man can ever counterfeit impudence.

HASTINGS. If you could but say half the fine things to them that I have heard you lavish upon the bar-maid of an inn, or even a college bedmaker—

MARLOW. Why, George, I can't say fine things to them. They freeze, they petrify me. They may talk of a comet, or a burning mountain, or some such bagatelle. But to me, a modest woman, dressed out in all her finery, is the most tremendous object of the whole creation.

HASTINGS. Ha, ha, ha! At this rate, man, how can you ever expect to marry?

MARLOW. Never, unless, as among kings and princes, my bride were courted by proxy. If, indeed, like an Eastern bridegroom, one were to be introduced to a wife he never saw before, it might be endured. But to go through all the terrors of a formal courtship, together with the episode of aunts, grandmothers, and cousins, and at last to blurt out the broad staring question of, *madam, will you marry me?* No, no, that's a strain much above me, I assure you.

HASTINGS. I pity you. But how do you intend behaving to the lady you are come down to visit at the request of your father?

MARLOW. As I behave to all ladies. Bow very low; answer yes, or no, to all her demands. But for the rest, I don't think I shall venture to look in her face till I see my father's again.

HASTINGS. I'm surprised that one who is so warm a friend can be so cool a lover.

MARLOW. To be explicit, my dear Hastings, my chief inducement down was to be instrumental in forwarding your happiness, not my own. Miss Neville loves you, the family don't know you; as my friend you are sure of a reception, and let honor do the rest.

HASTINGS. My dear Marlow! But I'll suppress the emotion. Were I a wretch, merely seeking to carry off a fortune, you should be the last man in the world I would apply to for assistance. But Miss Neville's person is all I ask, and that is mine, both from her deceased father's consent and her own inclination.

MARLOW. Happy man! You have talents and art to captivate any woman. I'm doomed to adore the sex and yet to converse with the only part of it I despise. This stammer in my address and this awkward prepossessing visage of mine can never permit me to soar above the reach of a milliner's prentice or one of the duchesses of Drury-lane.[1] Pshaw! this fellow here to interrupt us.

Enter HARDCASTLE

HARDCASTLE. Gentlemen, once more you are heartily welcome. Which is Mr. Marlow? Sir, you're heartily welcome. It's not my way, you see, to receive my friends with my back to the fire. I like to give them a hearty reception in the old style at my gate. I like to see their horses and trunks taken care of.

MARLOW. (*Aside*) He has got our names from the servants already. (*To him*) We approve your caution and hospitality, sir. (*To Hastings*) I have been thinking, George, of changing our traveling dresses in the morning. I am grown confoundedly ashamed of mine.

HARDCASTLE. I beg, Mr. Marlow, you'll use no ceremony in this house.

HASTINGS. I fancy, [Charles][2] you're right. The first blow is half the battle. I intend opening the campaign with the white and gold.

HARDCASTLE. Mr. Marlow—Mr. Hastings—gentlemen—pray be under no constraint in this house. This is Liberty Hall, gentlemen. You may do just as you please here.

MARLOW. Yet, George, if we open the campaign too fiercely at first, we may want ammunition before it is over. I think to reserve the embroidery to secure a retreat.

HARDCASTLE. Your talking of a retreat, Mr. Marlow, puts me in mind of the Duke of Marlborough, when we went to besiege Denain.[3] He first summoned the garrison.

MARLOW. Don't you think the *ventre d'or* waistcoat will do with the plain brown?

HARDCASTLE. He first summoned the garrison, which might consist of about five thousand men—

HASTINGS. I think not. Brown and yellow mix but very poorly.

HARDCASTLE. I say, gentlemen, as I was telling you, he summoned the garrison, which might consist of about five thousand men—

MARLOW. The girls like finery.

HARDCASTLE. Which might consist of about five thousand men, well appointed with stores, ammunition, and other implements of war. Now, says the Duke of Marlborough, to George Brooks, that stood next to him:—(You must have heard of George Brooks) "I'll pawn my dukedom," says he, "but I take that garrison without spilling a drop of blood." So—

MARLOW. What, my good friend, if you gave us a glass of punch in the meantime it would help us to carry on the siege with vigor.

HARDCASTLE. Punch, sir! (*Aside*) This is the most unaccountable kind of modesty I ever met with.

MARLOW. Yes, sir, punch. A glass of warm punch, after our journey, will be comfortable. This is Liberty Hall, you know.

HARDCASTLE. Here's cup, sir.

MARLOW. (*Aside*) So this fellow, in his Liberty Hall, will only let us have just what he pleases.

HARDCASTLE. (*Taking the cup*) I hope you'll find it to your mind. I have prepared it with my own hands, and I believe you'll own the ingredients are tolerable. Will you be so good as to pledge me, sir? Here, Mr. Marlow, here is to our better acquaintance. (*Drinks*)

MARLOW. (*Aside*) A very impudent fellow this! But he's a character and I'll humor him a little.—Sir, my service to you. (*Drinks*)

HASTINGS. (*Aside*) I see this fellow wants to give us his company, and forgets he's an innkeeper before he has learned to be a gentleman.

MARLOW. From the excellence of your cup, my old friend, I suppose you have a good deal

---

[1] Not actresses. Drury Lane contained, besides the theatre, lodgings patronized by women of the town. (Cf. *The Beggar's Opera*, II, iii.)

[2] The first edition has *George*, obviously an error.

[3] The allies were defeated at Denain by the French in 1712.

of business in this part of the country. Warm work, now and then, at elections, I suppose.

HARDCASTLE. No, sir, I have long given that work over. Since our betters have hit upon the expedient of electing each other, there's no business *for us that sell ale*.[1]

HASTINGS. So, then, you have no turn for politics, I find.

HARDCASTLE. Not in the least. There was a time, indeed, I fretted myself about the mistakes of government, like other people; but finding myself every day grow more angry and the government growing no better, I left it to mend itself. Since that, I no more trouble my head about Heyder Ally or Ally Cawn than about "Ally Croaker."[2] Sir, my service to you.

HASTINGS. So that with eating above stairs and drinking below, with receiving your friends within and amusing them without, you lead a good, pleasant, bustling life of it.

HARDCASTLE. I do stir about a great deal, that's certain. Half the differences of the parish are adjusted in this very parlor.

MARLOW. (*After drinking*) And you have an argument in your cup, old gentleman, better than any in Westminster Hall.

HARDCASTLE. Ay, young gentleman, that, and a little philosophy.

MARLOW. (*Aside*) Well, this is the first time I ever heard of an innkeeper's philosophy.

HASTINGS. So then, like an experienced general, you attack them on every quarter. If you find their reason manageable, you attack it with your philosophy; if you find they have no reason, you attack them with this. Here's your health, my philosopher.

(*Drinks*)

HARDCASTLE. Good, very good, thank you; ha, ha. Your generalship puts me in mind of Prince Eugene, when he fought the Turks at the battle of Belgrade.[3] You shall hear.

MARLOW. Instead of the battle of Belgrade, I believe it's almost time to talk about supper. What has your philosophy got in the house for supper?

HARDCASTLE. For supper, sir! (*Aside*) Was ever such a request to a man in his own house!

MARLOW. Yes, sir, supper, sir; I begin to feel an appetite. I shall make devilish work to-night in the larder, I promise you.

HARDCASTLE. (*Aside*) Such a brazen dog sure never my eyes beheld. (*To him*) Why really, sir, as for supper I can't well tell. My Dorothy and the cook-maid settle these things between them. I leave these kind of things entirely to them.

MARLOW. You do, do you?

HARDCASTLE. Entirely. By the bye, I believe they are in actual consultation upon what's for supper this moment in the kitchen.

MARLOW. Then I beg they'll admit *me* as one of their privy council. It's a way I have got. When I travel, I always choose to regulate my own supper. Let the cook be called. No offence, I hope, sir.

HARDCASTLE. O no, sir, none in the least; yet I don't know how. Our Bridget, the cook-maid, is not very communicative upon these occasions. Should we send for her, she might scold us all out of the house.

HASTINGS. Let's see your list of the larder then. I ask it as a favor. I always match my appetite to my bill of fare.

MARLOW. (*To* HARDCASTLE, *who looks at them with surprise*) Sir, he's very right, and it's my way too.

HARDCASTLE. Sir, you have a right to command here.—Here, Roger, bring us the bill of fare for to-night's supper. I believe it's drawn out.—Your manner, Mr. Hastings, puts me in mind of my uncle, Colonel Wallop. It was a saying of his that no man was sure of his supper till he had eaten it.

HASTINGS. (*Aside*) All upon the high ropes! His uncle a colonel! We shall soon hear of his mother being a justice of peace.[4] But let's hear the bill of fare.

MARLOW. (*Perusing*) What's here? For the first course; for the second course; for the dessert. The devil, sir, do you think we have brought down the whole Joiners Company, or the Corporation of Bedford, to eat up such a supper? Two or three little things, clean and comfortable, will do.

HASTINGS. But let's hear it.

---

[1] I.e., ordinary people. Hardcastle refers humorously to himself as an innkeeper, using a common expression.

[2] Hyder Ali, Sultan of Mysore (d. 1782), the occasion of one of Burke's most famous speeches; Ally Cawn, Sultan of Bengal; "Ally Croaker," a popular Irish song.

[3] The Turks were defeated, 1717.

[4] A stage direction presumably should state that Roger brings the bill of fare, which had been prepared for the cook's guidance.

MARLOW. (*Reading*) For the first course at the top, a pig and prune sauce.

HASTINGS. Damn your pig, I say.

MARLOW. And damn your prune sauce, say I.

HARDCASTLE. And yet, gentlemen, to men that are hungry, pig and prune sauce is very good eating.

MARLOW. At the bottom, a calf's tongue and brains.

HASTINGS. Let your brains be knocked out, my good sir; I don't like them.

MARLOW. Or you may clap them on a plate by themselves; I do.

HARDCASTLE. (*Aside*) Their impudence confounds me. (*To them*) Gentlemen, you are my guests; make what alterations you please. Is there anything else you wish to retrench or alter, gentlemen?

MARLOW. Item: A pork pie, a boiled rabbit and sausages, a florentine,[1] a shaking pudding, and a dish of tiff—taff—taffety cream!

HASTINGS. Confound your made dishes! I shall be as much at a loss in this house as at a green and yellow dinner at the French ambassador's table. I'm for plain eating.

HARDCASTLE. I'm sorry, gentlemen, that I have nothing you like, but if there be anything you have a particular fancy to—

MARLOW. Why, really, sir, your bill of fare is so exquisite that any one part of it is full as good as another. Send us what you please. So much for supper. And now to see that our beds are aired and properly taken of.

HARDCASTLE. I entreat you'll leave all that to me. You shall not stir a step.

MARLOW. Leave that to you! I protest, sir, you must excuse me. I always look to these things myself.

HARDCASTLE. I must insist, sir, you'll make yourself easy on that head.

MARLOW. You see I'm resolved on it. (*Aside*) A very troublesome fellow this, as ever I met with.

HARDCASTLE. Well, sir, I'm resolved at least to attend you. (*Aside*) This may be modern modesty, but I never saw anything look so like old-fashioned impudence.

Exeunt MARLOW *and* HARDCASTLE

HASTINGS *solus*

HASTINGS. So I find this fellow's civilities begin to grow troublesome. But who can be angry at those assiduities which are meant to please him? Ha! what do I see? Miss Neville, by all that's happy!

Enter MISS NEVILLE

MISS NEVILLE. My dear Hastings! To what unexpected good fortune, to what accident, am I to ascribe this happy meeting?

HASTINGS. Rather let me ask the same question, as I could never have hoped to meet my dearest Constance at an inn.

MISS NEVILLE. An inn! Sure you mistake! My aunt, my guardian lives here. What could induce you to think this house an inn?

HASTINGS. My friend, Mr. Marlow, with whom I came down, and I have been sent here as to an inn, I assure you. A young fellow, whom we accidentally met at a house hard by directed us hither.

MISS NEVILLE. Certainly it must be one of my hopeful cousin's tricks, of whom you have heard me talk so often. Ha! ha! ha! ha!

HASTINGS. He whom your aunt intends for you? He of whom I have such just apprehensions?

MISS NEVILLE. You have nothing to fear from him, I assure you. You'd adore him if you knew how heartily he despises me. My aunt knows it too, and has undertaken to court me for him, and actually begins to think she has made a conquest.

HASTINGS. Thou dear dissembler! You must know, my Constance, I have just seized this happy opportunity of my friend's visit here to get admittance into the family. The horses that carried us down are now fatigued with their journey, but they'll soon be refreshed; and then if my dearest girl will trust in her faithful Hastings, we shall soon be landed in France, where even among slaves the laws of marriage are respected.

MISS NEVILLE. I have often told you that though ready to obey you, I yet should leave my little fortune behind with reluctance. The greatest part of it was left me by my uncle, the India Director,[2] and chiefly consists in jewels. I have been for some time persuading my aunt to let me wear them. I fancy I'm very near succeeding. The instant they are

---

[1] A meat pie. Shaking pudding is quaking pudding, a sort of jelly. Taffety, or taffeta, cream may be velvet cream. All are old-fashioned dishes.

[2] A director of the East India Company, consequently a wealthy man.

put into my possession you shall find me ready to make them and myself yours.

Hastings. Perish the baubles! Your person is all I desire. In the meantime, my friend Marlow must not be let into his mistake. I know the strange reserve of his temper is such that if abruptly informed of it, he would instantly quit the house before our plan was ripe for execution.

Miss Neville. But how shall we keep him in the deception? Miss Hardcastle is just returned from walking; what if we still continue to deceive him?—This, this way—

(*They confer*)

Enter Marlow

Marlow. The assiduities of these good people tease me beyond bearing. My host seems to think it ill manners to leave me alone and so he claps not only himself but his old-fashioned wife on my back. They talk of coming to sup with us too; and then, I suppose, we are to run the gauntlet through all the rest of the family.—What have we got here!

Hastings. My dear Charles! Let me congratulate you!—The most fortunate accident! —Who do you think is just alighted?

Marlow. Cannot guess.

Hastings. Our mistresses, boy, Miss Hardcastle and Miss Neville. Give me leave to introduce Miss Constance Neville to your acquaintance. Happening to dine in the neighborhood, they called, on their return to take fresh horses here. Miss Hardcastle has just stepped into the next room and will be back in an instant. Wasn't it lucky? Eh!

Marlow. (*Aside*) I have just been mortified enough of all conscience; and here comes something to complete my embarrassment.

Hastings. Well! But wasn't it the most fortunate thing in the world?

Marlow. Oh! yes. Very fortunate—a most joyful encounter—But our dresses, George, you know, are in disorder—What if we should postpone the happiness till to-morrow?— To-morrow at her own house—It will be every bit as convenient—And rather more respectful—To-morrow let it be.

(*Offering to go*)

Miss Neville. By no means, sir. Your ceremony will displease her. The disorder of your dress will show the ardor of your impatience. Besides, she knows you are in the house and will permit you to see her.

Marlow. O! the devil! How shall I support it? Hem! hem! Hastings, you must not go. You are to assist me, you know. I shall be confoundedly ridiculous. Yet, hang it! I'll take courage. Hem!

Hastings. Pshaw, man! It's but the first plunge and all's over. She's but a woman, you know.

Marlow. And of all women, she that I dread most to encounter!

Enter Miss Hardcastle *as returned from walking, a bonnet, &c.*

Hastings. (*Introducing them*) Miss Hardcastle, Mr. Marlow, I'm proud of bringing two persons of such merit together, that only want to know to esteem each other.

Miss Hardcastle. (*Aside*) Now, for meeting my modest gentleman with a demure face and quite in his own manner. (*After a pause, in which he appears very uneasy and disconcerted*) I'm glad of your safe arrival, sir—I'm told you had some accidents by the way.

Marlow. Only a few, madam. Yes, we had some. Yes, madam, a good many accidents, but should be sorry—madam—or rather glad of any accidents—that are so agreeably concluded. Hem!

Hastings. (*To him*) You never spoke better in your whole life. Keep it up, and I'll insure you the victory.

Miss Hardcastle. I'm afraid you flatter, sir. You that have seen so much of the finest company can find little entertainment in an obscure corner of the country.

Marlow. (*Gathering courage*) I have lived, indeed, in the world, madam; but I have kept very little company. I have been but an observer upon life, madam, while others were enjoying it.

Miss Neville. But that, I am told, is the way to enjoy it at last.

Hastings. (*To him*) Cicero never spoke better. Once more, and you are confirmed in assurance for ever.

Marlow. (*To him*) Hem! Stand by me then, and when I'm down, throw in a word or two to set me up again.

Miss Hardcastle. An observer, like you, upon life were, I fear, disagreeably employed, since you must have had much more to censure than to approve.

Marlow. Pardon me, madam. I was

always willing to be amused. The folly of most people is rather an object of mirth than uneasiness.

HASTINGS. (*To him*) Bravo, bravo! Never spoke so well in your whole life.—Well! Miss Hardcastle, I see that you and Mr. Marlow are going to be very good company. I believe our being here will but embarrass the interview.

MARLOW. Not in the least, Mr. Hastings. We like your company of all things. (*To him*) Zounds! George, sure you won't go? How can you leave us?

HASTINGS. Our presence will but spoil conversation, so we'll retire to the next room. (*To him*) You don't consider, man, that we are to manage a little *tête-à-tête* of our own. *Exeunt*

MISS HARDCASTLE. (*After a pause*) But you have not been wholly an observer, I presume, sir; the ladies, I should hope, have employed some part of your addresses.

MARLOW. (*Relapsing into timidity*) Pardon me, madam, I—I—I—as yet have studied—only—to—deserve them.

MISS HARDCASTLE. And that, some say, is the worst way to obtain them.

MARLOW. Perhaps so, madam. But I love to converse only with the more grave and sensible part of the sex.—But I'm afraid I grow tiresome.

MISS HARDCASTLE. Not at all, sir; there is nothing I like so much as grave conversation myself. I could hear it forever. Indeed I have often been surprised how a man of *sentiment* could admire those light, airy pleasures, where nothing reaches the heart.

MARLOW. It's—a disease—of the mind, madam. In the variety of tastes there must be some who wanting a relish—for—um—a—um—

MISS HARDCASTLE. I understand you, sir. There must be some, who wanting a relish for refined pleasures, pretend to despise what they are incapable of tasting.

MARLOW. My meaning, madam, but infinitely better expressed. And I can't help observing—a—

MISS HARDCASTLE. (*Aside*) Who could ever suppose this fellow impudent upon some occasions? (*To him*) You were going to observe, sir—

MARLOW. I was observing, madam—I protest, madam, I forget what I was going to observe.

MISS HARDCASLTE. (*Aside*) I vow and so do I. (*To him*) You were observing, sir, that in this age of hypocrisy something about hypocrisy, sir.

MARLOW. Yes, madam. In this age of hypocrisy there are few who upon strictest enquiry do not—a—a—a—

MISS HARDCASTLE. I understand you perfectly, sir.

MARLOW. (*Aside*) Egad! and that's more than I do myself.

MISS HARDCASTLE. You mean that in this hypocritical age there are few that do not condemn in public what they practise in private and think they pay every debt to virtue when they praise it.

MARLOW. True, madam; those who have most virtue in their mouths, have least of it in their bosoms. But I'm sure I tire you, madam.

MISS HARDCASTLE. Not in the least, sir; there's something so agreeable and spirited in your manner, such life and force—Pray, sir, go on.

MARLOW. Yes, madam. I was saying—that there are some occasions—when a total want of courage, madam, destroys all the—and puts us—upon—a—a—a—

MISS HARDCASTLE. I agree with you entirely, a want of courage upon some occasions assumes the appearance of ignorance and betrays us when we most want to excel. I beg you'll proceed.

MARLOW. Yes, madam. Morally speaking, madam—But I see Miss Neville expecting us in the next room. I would not intrude for the world.

MISS HARDCASTLE. I protest, sir, I never was more agreeably entertained in all my life. Pray go on.

MARLOW. Yes, madam. I was—but she beckons us to join her. Madam, shall I do myself the honor to attend you?

MISS HARDCASTLE. Well, then, I'll follow.

MARLOW. (*Aside*) This pretty, smooth dialogue has done for me. *Exit*

MISS HARDCASTLE *sola*

MISS HARDCASTLE. Ha! ha! ha! Was there ever such a sober, sentimental interview? I'm certain he scarce looked in my face the whole time. Yet the fellow, but for his unaccountable bashfulness, is pretty well, too. He has good sense, but then so buried in his fears that it fatigues one more than ignorance. If I could teach him a little confidence, it would be doing somebody that I know of a piece of service. But who is that somebody?—That, faith, is a question I can scarce answer. *Exit*

Enter TONY *and* MISS NEVILLE, *followed by* MRS. HARDCASTLE *and* HASTINGS

TONY. What do you follow me for, cousin Con? I wonder how you're not ashamed to be so very engaging.[1]

MISS NEVILLE. I hope, cousin, one may speak to one's own relations and not be to blame.

TONY. Ay, but I know what sort of a relation you want to make me though; but it won't do. I tell you, cousin Con, it won't do; so I beg you'll keep your distance. I want no nearer relationship.

(*She follows,* coquetting *him to the back scene*)

MRS. HARDCASTLE. Well! I vow, Mr. Hastings, you are very entertaining. There's nothing in the world I love to talk of so much as London and the fashions, though I was never there myself.

HASTINGS. Never there! You amaze me! From your air and manner, I concluded you had been bred all your life either at Ranelagh, St. James's, or Tower Wharf.[2]

MRS. HARDCASTLE. O! Sir, you're only pleased to say so. We country persons can have no manner at all. I'm in love with the town and that serves to raise me above some of our neighboring rustics; but who can have a manner that has never seen the Pantheon, the Grotto Gardens, the Borough, and such places where the nobility chiefly resort? All I can do, is to know every *tête-à-tête* from the *Scandalous Magazine*[3] and have all the fashions, as they come out, in a letter from the two Miss Rickets of Crooked-lane. Pray how do you like this head, Mr. Hastings?

HASTINGS. Extremely elegant and *degagé*, upon my word, madam. Your *friseur* is a Frenchman, I suppose?

[1] Persuasive, importunate.
[2] To contemporary audiences, the appeal of these allusions lay in the fact that though Ranelagh and St. James's were resorts of the nobility, Tower Wharf was in the disreputable east end of the City. The same thing is true of Mrs. Hardcastle's speech below, the Borough (Southwark) being far removed, literally and figuratively, from the center of fashion.
[3] These *tête-à-tête* portraits were more or less scandalous biographies, referred to also in the opening scene of *The School for Scandal*. a. v.

MRS. HARDCASTLE. I protest I dressed it myself from a print in the *Ladies' Memorandum-book* for the last year.

HASTINGS. Indeed! Such a head in a side-box at the playhouse would draw as many gazers as my Lady May'ress at a City Ball.

MRS. HARDCASTLE. I vow, since innoculation began,[4] there is no such thing to be seen as a plain woman; so one must dress a little particular or one may escape in the crowd.

HASTINGS. But that can never be your case, madam, in any dress. (*Bowing*)

MRS. HARDCASTLE. Yet, what signifies *my* dressing when I have such a piece of antiquity by my side as Mr. Hardcastle. All I can say will never argue down a single button from his clothes. I have often wanted him to throw off his great flaxen wig, and where he was bald, to plaster it over like my Lord Pately, with powder.

HASTINGS. You are right, madam; for, as among the ladies, there are none ugly, so among the men there are none old.

MRS. HARDCASTLE. But what do you think his answer was? Why, with his usual Gothic vivacity, he said I only wanted him to throw off his wig to convert it into a *tête* for my own wearing.

HASTINGS. Intolerable! At your age you may wear what you please and it must become you.

MRS. HARDCASTLE. Pray, Mr. Hastings, what do you take to be the most fashionable age about town?

HASTINGS. Some time ago, forty was all the mode; but I'm told the ladies intend to bring up fifty for the ensuing winter.

MRS. HARDCASTLE. Seriously? Then I shall be too young for the fashion.

HASTINGS. No lady begins to put on jewels till she's past forty. For instance, miss there, in a polite circle, would be considered as a child, as a mere maker of samplers.

MRS. HARDCASTLE. And yet Mrs. Niece thinks herself as much a woman and is as fond of jewels as the oldest of us all.

HASTINGS. Your niece, is she? And that young gentleman, a brother of yours, I should presume?

MRS. HARDCASTLE. My son, sir. They are contracted to each other. Observe their little sports. They fall in and out ten times

[4] Innoculation against smallpox was introduced into England by Lady Mary Wortley Montagu in 1718.

a day, as if they were man and wife already. (*To them*) Well, Tony, child, what soft things are you saying to your cousin Constance this evening?

TONY. I have been saying no soft things; but that it's very hard to be followed about so. Ecod! I've not a place in the house now that's left to myself but the stable.

MRS. HARDCASTLE. Never mind him, Con, my dear. He's in another story behind your back.

MISS NEVILLE. There's something generous in my cousin's manner. He falls out before faces to be forgiven in private.

TONY. That's a damned confounded—crack.

MRS. HARDCASTLE. Ah! he's a sly one. Don't you think they're like each other about the mouth, Mr. Hastings? The Blenkinsop mouth to a *T*. They're of a size too. Back to back, my pretties, that Mr. Hastings may see you. Come, Tony.

TONY. You had as good not make me, I tell you. (*Measuring*)

MISS NEVILLE. O lud! he has almost cracked my head.

MRS. HARDCASTLE. O the monster! For shame, Tony. You a man, and behave so!

TONY. If I'm a man, let me have my fortin. Ecod! I'll not be made a fool of no longer.

MRS. HARDCASTLE. Is this, ungrateful boy, all that I'm to get for the pains I have taken in your education? I have rocked you in your cradle and fed that pretty mouth with a spoon! Did not I work that waistcoat to make you genteel? Did not I prescribe for you every day and weep while the receipt was operating?

TONY. Ecod! you had no reason to weep, for you have been dosing me ever since I was born. I have gone through every receipt in the complete huswife ten times over; and you have thoughts of coursing me through Quincy[1] next spring. But, ecod! I tell you I'll not be made a fool of no longer.

MRS. HARDCASTLE. Wasn't it all for your good, viper? Wasn't it all for your good?

TONY. I wish you'd let me and my good alone then. Snubbing this way when I'm in spirits! If I'm to have any good, let it come of itself; not to keep dinging it, dinging it into one so.

MRS. HARDCASTLE. That's false; I never

[1] Quincy was the author of the popular *Complete English Dispensatory*.

see you when you're in spirits. No, Tony, you then go to the alehouse or kennel. I'm never to be delighted with your agreeable, wild notes, unfeeling monster!

TONY. Ecod! Mamma, your own notes are the wildest of the two.

MRS. HARDCASTLE. Was ever the like? But I see he wants to break my heart, I see he does.

HASTINGS. Dear madam, permit me to lecture the young gentleman a little. I'm certain I can persuade him to his duty.

MRS. HARDCASTLE. Well! I must retire. Come, Constance, my love. You see, Mr. Hastings, the wretchedness of my situation. Was ever poor woman so plagued with a dear, sweet, pretty, provoking, undutiful boy.

Exeunt MRS. HARDCASTLE *and* MISS NEVILLE.

HASTINGS, TONY

TONY. (*Singing*) There was a young man riding by, and fain would have his will. Rang do didlo dee.——Don't mind her. Let her cry. It's the comfort of her heart. I have seen her and sister cry over a book for an hour together, and they said they liked the book the better the more it made them cry.

HASTINGS. Then you're no friend to the ladies, I find, my pretty young gentleman?

TONY. That's as I find 'um.

HASTINGS. Not to her of your mother's choosing, I dare answer? And yet she appears to me a pretty, well-tempered girl.

TONY. That's because you don't know her as well as I. Ecod! I know every inch about her; and there's not a more bitter, cantankerous toad in all Christendom.

HASTINGS. (*Aside*) Pretty encouragement this for a lover!

TONY. I have seen her since the height of that. She has as many tricks as a hare in a thicket or a colt the first day's breaking.

HASTINGS. To me she appears sensible and silent!

TONY. Ay, before company. But when she's with her playmates, she's as loud as a hog in a gate.

HASTINGS. But there is a meek modesty about her that charms me.

TONY. Yes, but curb her never so little, she kicks up and you're flung in a ditch.

HASTINGS. Well, but you must allow her a

little beauty.—Yes, you must allow her some little beauty.

TONY. Bandbox! She's all a made up thing, mun. Ah! could you but see Bet Bouncer of these parts, you might then talk of beauty. Ecod, she has two eyes as black as sloes, and cheeks as broad and red as a pulpit cushion. She'd make two of she.

HASTINGS. Well, what say you to a friend that would take this bitter bargain off your hands?

TONY. Anon.

HASTINGS. Would you thank him that would take Miss Neville and leave you to happiness and your dear Betsy?

TONY. Ay; but where is there such a friend, for who would take *her?*

HASTINGS. I am he. If you will but assist me, I'll engage to whip her off to France and you shall never hear more of her.

TONY. Assist you! Ecod, I will, to the last drop of my blood. I'll clap a pair of horses to your chaise that shall trundle you off in a twinkling, and may be get you a part of her fortin beside, in jewels that you little dream of.

HASTINGS. My dear squire, this looks like a lad of spirit.

TONY. Come along then, and you shall see more of my spirit before you have done with me.
(Singing)
We are the boys
That fears no noise
Where the thundering cannons roar.
Exeunt

ACT III

[*The scene continues*]

Enter HARDCASTLE *solus*

HARDCASTLE. What could my old friend, Sir Charles, mean by recommending his son as the modestest young man in town? To me he appears the most impudent piece of brass that ever spoke with a tongue. He has taken possession of the easy chair by the fireside already. He took off his boots in the parlor and desired me to see them taken care of. I'm desirous to know how his impudence affects my daughter.—She will certainly be shocked at it.

Enter MISS HARDCASTLE, *plainly dressed*

HARDCASTLE. Well, my Kate, I see you have changed your dress as I bid you; and yet, I believe, there was no great occasion.

MISS HARDCASTLE. I find such a pleasure, sir, in obeying your commands, that I take care to observe them without ever debating their propriety.

HARDCASTLE. And yet, Kate, I sometimes give you some cause, particularly when I recommended my *modest* gentleman to you as a lover to-day.

MISS HARDCASTLE. You taught me to expect something extraordinary, and I find the original exceeds the description.

HARDCASTLE. I was never so surprised in my life! He has quite confounded all my faculties!

MISS HARDCASTLE. I never saw anything like it. And a man of the world, too!

HARDCASTLE. Ay, he learned it all abroad.— What a fool was I, to think a young man could earn modesty by traveling! He might as soon learn wit at a masquerade.

MISS HARDCASTLE. It seems all natural to him.

HARDCASTLE. A good deal assisted by bad company and a French dancing-master.

MISS HARDCASTLE. Sure you mistake, papa! A French dancing-master could never have taught him that timid look,—that awkward address,—that bashful manner—

HARDCASTLE. Whose look? Whose manner, child?

MISS HARDCASTLE. Mr. Marlow's. His *mauvaise honte*,[1] his timidity, struck me at the first sight.

HARDCASTLE. Then your first sight deceived you; for I think him one of the most brazen first sights that ever astonished my senses.

MISS HARDCASTLE. Sure, sir, you rally! I never saw anyone so modest.

HARDCASTLE. And can you be serious? I never saw such a bouncing, swaggering puppy since I was born. Bully Dawson[2] was but a fool to him.

MISS HARDCASTLE. Surprising! He met me with a respectful bow, a stammering voice, and a look fixed on the ground.

HARDCASTLE. He met me with a loud voice, a lordly air, and a familiarity that made my blood freeze again.

MISS HARDCASTLE. He treated me with

[1] False shame.
[2] A well known ruffian in the early years of the century. Sir Roger de Coverley "kicked Bully Dawson in a public coffee-house for calling him 'youngster.'"— *Spectator*, No. 2.

diffidence and respect; censured the manners of the age, admired the prudence of girls that never laughed, tired me with apologies for being tiresome; then left the room with a bow, and, "Madam, I would not for the world detain you."

HARDCASTLE. He spoke to me as if he knew me all his life before, asked twenty questions, and never waited for an answer, interrupted my best remarks with some silly pun, and when I was in my best story of the Duke of Marlborough and Prince Eugene, he asked if I had not a good hand at making punch. Yes, Kate, he asked your father if he was a maker of punch!

MISS HARDCASTLE. One of us must certainly be mistaken.

HARDCASTLE. If he be what he has shown himself, I'm determined he shall never have my consent.

MISS HARDCASTLE. And if he be the sullen thing I take him, he shall never have mine.

HARDCASTLE. In one thing then we are agreed—to reject him.

MISS HARDCASTLE. Yes. But upon conditions. For if you should find him less impudent and I more presuming; if you find him more respectful and I more importunate—I don't know—the fellow is well enough for a man. Certainly we don't meet many such at a horse race in the country.

HARDCASTLE. If we should find him so—but that's impossible. The first appearance has done my business. I'm seldom deceived in that.

MISS HARDCASTLE. And yet there may be many good qualities under that first appearance.

HARDCASTLE. Ay, when a girl finds a fellow's outside to her taste, she then sets about guessing the rest of his furniture. With her, a smooth face stands for good sense and a genteel figure for every virtue.

MISS HARDCASTLE. I hope, sir, a conversation begun with a compliment to my good sense won't end with a sneer at my understanding?

HARDCASTLE. Pardon me, Kate. But if young Mr. Brazen can find the art of reconciling contradictions, he may please us both, perhaps.

MISS HARDCASTLE. And as one of us must be mistaken, what if we go to make further discoveries?

HARDCASTLE. Agreed. But depend on't I'm in the right.

MISS HARDCASTLE. And depend on't I'm not much in the wrong. *Exeunt*

Enter TONY *running in with a casket*

TONY. Ecod! I have got them. Here they are. My cousin Con's necklaces, bobs, and all. My mother shan't cheat the poor souls out of their fortune neither. O! my genius, is that thou?

Enter HASTINGS

HASTINGS. My dear friend, how have you managed with your mother? I hope you have amused her with pretending love for your cousin, and that you are willing to be reconciled at last? Our horses will be refreshed in a short time, and we shall soon be ready to set off.

TONY. And here's something to bear your charges by the way. (*Giving the casket*) Your sweetheart's jewels. Keep them, and hang those, I say, that would rob you of one of them.

HASTINGS. But how have you procured them from your mother?

TONY. Ask me no questions, and I'll tell you no fibs. I procured them by the rule of thumb. If I had not a key to every drawer in mother's bureau, how could I go to the alehouse so often as I do? An honest man may rob himself of his own at any time.

HASTINGS. Thousands do it every day. But to be plain with you; Miss Neville is endeavoring to procure them from her aunt this very instant. If she succeeds, it will be the most delicate way at least of obtaining them.

TONY. Well, keep them, till you know how it will be. But I know how it will be well enough; she'd as soon part with the only sound tooth in her head.

HASTINGS. But I dread the effects of her resentment when she finds she has lost them.

TONY. Never you mind her resentment. Leave *me* to manage that. I don't value her resentment the bounce of a cracker.[1] Zounds! Here they are. Morrice.[2] Prance.

Exit HASTINGS

TONY, MRS. HARDCASTLE, MISS NEVILLE

MRS. HARDCASTLE. Indeed, Constance, you amaze me. Such a girl as you want jewels?

[1] Report of a fire cracker.   [2] Dance away.

It will be time enough for jewels, my dear, twenty years hence, when your beauty begins to want repairs.

MISS NEVILLE. But what will repair beauty at forty, will certainly improve it at twenty, madam.

MRS. HARDCASTLE. Yours, my dear, can admit of none. That natural blush is beyond a thousand ornaments. Besides, child, jewels are quite out at present. Don't you see half the ladies of our acquaintance, my Lady Kill-day-light and Mrs. Crump and the rest of them, carry their jewels to town and bring nothing but paste and marcasites[1] back.

MISS NEVILLE. But who knows, madam, but somebody that shall be nameless would like me best with all my little finery about me?

MRS. HARDCASTLE. Consult your glass, my dear, and then see if with such a pair of eyes you want any better sparklers. What do you think, Tony, my dear, does your cousin Con want any jewels, in your eyes, to set off her beauty?

TONY. That's as thereafter may be.

MISS NEVILLE. My dear aunt, if you knew how it would oblige me.

MRS. HARDCASTLE. A parcel of old-fashioned rose and table-cut things.[2] They would make you look like the court of king Solomon at a puppet-show. Besides, I believe I can't readily come at them. They may be missing for aught I know to the contrary.

TONY. (*Apart to* MRS. HARDCASTLE) Then why don't you tell her so at once, as she's longing for them? Tell her they're lost. It's the only way to quiet her. Say they're lost, and call me to bear witness.

MRS. HARDCASTLE. (*Apart to* TONY) You know, my dear, I'm only keeping them for you. So if I say they're gone, you'll bear me witness, will you? He! he! he!

TONY. Never fear me. Ecod! I'll say I saw them taken out with my own eyes.

MISS NEVILLE. I desire them but for a day, madam. Just to be permitted to show them as relics, and then they may be locked up again.

MRS. HARDCASTLE. To be plain with you, my dear Constance, if I could find them, you should have them. They're missing, I assure you. Lost, for aught I know; but we must have patience wherever they are.

MISS NEVILLE. I'll not believe it; this is but a shallow pretense to deny me. I know they're too valuable to be so slightly kept, and as you are to answer for the loss.

MRS. HARDCASTLE. Don't be alarmed, Constance. If they be lost, I must restore an equivalent. But my son knows they are missing and not to be found.

TONY. That I can bear witness to. They are missing and not to be found, I'll take my oath on't.

MRS. HARDCASTLE. You must learn resignation, my dear; for though we lose our fortune, yet we should not lose our patience. See me, how calm I am.

MISS NEVILLE. Ay, people are generally calm at the misfortunes of others.

MRS. HARDCASTLE. Now, I wonder a girl of your good sense should waste a thought upon such trumpery. We shall soon find them; and in the meantime you shall make use of my garnets till your jewels be found.

MISS NEVILLE. I detest garnets.

MRS. HARDCASTLE. The most becoming things in the world to set off a clear complexion. You have often seen how well they look upon me. You *shall* have them. *Exit*

MISS NEVILLE. I dislike them of all things. You shan't stir.—Was ever anything so provoking to mislay my own jewels and force me to wear her trumpery!

TONY. Don't be a fool. If she gives you the garnets, take what you can get. The jewels are your own already. I have stolen them out of her bureau and she does not know it. Fly to your spark; he'll tell you more of the matter. Leave me to manage *her*.

MISS NEVILLE. My dear cousin!

TONY. Vanish. She's here and has missed them already. [*Exit* MISS NEVILLE][3] Zounds! How she fidgets and spits about like a Catherine-wheel.

Enter MRS. HARDCASTLE

MRS. HARDCASTLE. Confusion! thieves! robbers! We are cheated, plundered, broke open, undone.

TONY. What's the matter, mamma? I hope nothing has happened to any of the good family!

MRS. HARDCASTLE. We are robbed. My

---

[1] Ornaments made of marcasite, or iron pyrites, sometimes called fools' gold.

[2] Gems cut in the old-fashioned manner with relatively few facets.

[3] No stage direction appears here in the text.

bureau has been broke open, the jewels taken out, and I'm undone.

TONY. Oh! is that all? Ha, ha, ha! By the laws I never saw it better acted in my life. Ecod, I thought you was ruined in earnest. Ha, ha, ha!

MRS. HARDCASTLE. Why, boy, I *am* ruined in earnest. My bureau has been broke open and all taken away.

TONY. Stick to that; ha, ha, ha; stick to that. I'll bear witness, you know, call me to bear witness.

MRS. HARDCASTLE. I tell you, Tony, by all that's precious, the jewels are gone, and I shall be ruined for ever.

TONY. Sure I know they're gone, and I am to say so.

MRS. HARDCASTLE. My dearest Tony, but hear me. They're gone, I say.

TONY. By the laws, mamma, you make me for to laugh, ha, ha! I know who took them well enough, ha, ha, ha!

MRS. HARDCASTLE. Was there ever such a blockhead, that can't tell the difference between jest and earnest. I tell you I'm not in jest, booby.

TONY. That's right, that's right. You must be in a bitter passion and then nobody will suspect either of us. I'll bear witness that they are gone.

MRS. HARDCASTLE. Was there ever such a cross-grained brute, that won't hear me? Can you bear witness that you're no better than a fool? Was ever poor woman so beset with fools on one hand and thieves on the other?

TONY. I can bear witness to that.

MRS. HARDCASTLE. Bear witness again, you blockhead you, and I'll turn you out of the room directly. My poor niece, what will become of *her!* Do you laugh, you unfeeling brute, as if you enjoyed my distress?

TONY. I can bear witness to that.

MRS. HARDCASTLE. Do you insult me, monster? I'll teach you to vex your mother, I will.

TONY. I can bear witness to that.

(*He runs off; she follows him*)

Enter MISS HARDCASTLE *and* MAID

MISS HARDCASTLE. What an unaccountable creature is that brother of mine, to send them to the house as an inn! Ha, ha! I don't wonder at his impudence.

MAID. But what is more, madam, the young gentleman, as you passed by in your present dress, asked me if you were the barmaid. He mistook you for the barmaid, madam.

MISS HARDCASTLE. Did he? Then as I live I'm resolved to keep up the delusion. Tell me, Pimple, how do you like my present dress. Don't you think I look something like Cherry in the *Beaux' Stratagem?*

MAID. It's the dress, madam, that every lady wears in the country, but when she visits or receives company.

MISS HARDCASTLE. And are you sure he does not remember my face or person?

MAID. Certain of it.

MISS HARDCASTLE. I vow I thought so; for though we spoke for some time together, yet his fears were such that he never once looked up during the interview. Indeed, if he had, my bonnet would have kept him from seeing me.

MAID. But what do you hope from keeping him in his mistake?

MISS HARDCASTLE. In the first place, I shall be *seen*, and that is no small advantage to a girl who brings her face to market. Then I shall make perhaps an acquaintance, and that's no small victory gained over one who never addresses any but the wildest of her sex. But my chief aim is to take my gentleman off his guard, and like an invisible champion of romance examine the giant's force before I offer combat.

MAID. But are you sure you can act your part and disguise your voice so that he may mistake that, as he has already mistaken your person?

MISS HARDCASTLE. Never fear me. I think I have got the true bar cant.—Did your honor call?—Attend the Lion,[1] there.—Pipes and tobacco for the Angel.—The Lamb has been outrageous this half hour.

MAID. It will do, madam. But he's here.

Exit Maid

Enter MARLOW

MARLOW. What a bawling in every part of the house! I have scarce a moment's repose. If I go to the best room, there I find my host and his story. If I fly to the gallery, there we have my hostess with her curtsy down to the ground. I have at last got a moment to myself, and now for recollection.

(*Walks and muses*)

---

[1] Names of rooms in an imaginary inn.

Miss Hardcastle. Did you call, sir? Did your honor call?

Marlow. (*Musing*) As for Miss Hardcastle, she's too grave and sentimental for me.

Miss Hardcastle. Did your honor call? (*She still places herself before him, he turning away*)

Marlow. No, child. (*Musing*) Besides, from the glimpse I had of her, I think she squints.

Miss Hardcastle. I'm sure, sir, I heard the bell ring.

Marlow. No, no. (*Musing*) I have pleased my father, however, by coming down; and I'll to-morrow please myself by returning.
(*Taking out his tablets [1] and perusing*)

Miss Hardcastle. Perhaps the other gentleman called, sir.

Marlow. I tell you, no.

Miss Hardcastle. I should be glad to know, sir. We have such a parcel of servants.

Marlow. No, no, I tell you. (*Looks full in her face*) Yes, child, I think I did call. I wanted—I wanted—I vow, child, you are vastly handsome.

Miss Hardcastle. O la, sir, you'll make one ashamed.

Marlow. Never saw a more sprightly malicious eye. Yes, yes, my dear, I did call. Have you got any of your—a—what d'ye call it in the house?

Miss Hardcastle. No, sir, we've been out of that these ten days.

Marlow. One may call in this house, I find, to very little purpose. Suppose I should call for a taste, just by way of trial, of the nectar of your lips; perhaps I might be disappointed in that too.

Miss Hardcastle. Nectar! nectar! That's a liquor there's no call for in these parts. French, I suppose. We keep no French wines here, sir.

Marlow. Of true English growth, I assure you.

Miss Hardcastle. Then it's odd I should not know it. We brew all sorts of wine in this house, and I have lived here these eighteen years.

Marlow. Eighteen years! Why one would think, child, you kept the bar before you were born. How old are you?

Miss Hardcastle. O! sir, I must not tell my age. They say women and music should never be dated.

Marlow. To guess at this distance, you can't be much above forty. (*Approaching*) Yet nearer I don't think so much. (*Approaching*) By coming close to some women they look younger still; but when we come very close indeed— (*Attempting to kiss her*)

Miss Hardcastle. Pray, sir, keep your distance. One would think you wanted to know one's age as they do horses, by mark of mouth.

Marlow. I protest, child, you use me extremely ill. If you keep me at this distance, how is it possible you and I can be ever acquainted?

Miss Hardcastle. And who wants to be acquainted with you? I want no such acquaintance, not I. I'm sure you did not treat Miss Hardcastle that was here a while ago in this obstropalous manner. I'll warrant me, before her you looked dashed, and kept bowing to the ground, and talked for all the world as if you was before a justice of peace.

Marlow. (*Aside*) Egad! she has hit it, sure enough. (*To her*) In awe of her, child? Ha! ha! ha! A mere, awkward, squinting thing? No, no. I find you don't know me. I laughed and rallied her a little, but I was unwilling to be too severe. No, I could not be too severe, curse me!

Miss Hardcastle. O! Then, sir, you are a favorite, I find, among the ladies?

Marlow. Yes, my dear, a great favorite. And yet, hang me, I don't see what they find in me to follow. At the Ladies Club in town, I'm called their agreeable Rattle. Rattle, child, is not my real name, but one I'm known by. My name is Solomons. Mr. Solomons, my dear, at your service.
(*Offering to salute her*)

Miss Hardcastle. Hold, sir; you were introducing me to your club, not to yourself. And you're so great a favorite there, you say?

Marlow. Yes, my dear. There's Mrs. Mantrap, Lady Betty Blackleg, the Countess of Sligo, Mrs. Langhorns, old Miss Biddy Buckskin, and your humble servant, keep up the spirit of the place.

Miss Hardcastle. Then it's a very merry place, I suppose.

Marlow. Yes, as merry as cards, suppers, wine, and old women can make us.

Miss Hardcastle. And their agreeable Rattle, ha, ha, ha!

[1] Memorandum-book

MARLOW. (*Aside*) Egad! I don't quite like this chit. She looks knowing, methinks. You laugh, child!

MISS HARDCASTLE. I can't but laugh to think what time they all have for minding their work or their family.

MARLOW. (*Aside*) All's well, she don't laugh at me. (*To her*) Do *you* ever work, child?

MISS HARDCASTLE. Ay, sure. There's not a screen or a quilt in the whole house but what can bear witness to that.

MARLOW. Odso! Then you must show me your embroidery. I embroider and draw patterns myself a little. If you want a judge of your work, you must apply to me.

(*Seizing her hand*)

MISS HARDCASTLE. Ay, but the colors don't look well by candle light. You shall see all in the morning. (*Struggling*)

MARLOW. And why not now, my angel? Such beauty fires beyond the power of resistance.—Pshaw! the father here! My old-luck. I never nicked seven [1] that I did not throw ames ace [2] three times following.

Exit MARLOW

Enter HARDCASTLE, *who stands in surprise*

HARDCASTLE. So, madam! So I find *this* is your *modest* lover. This is your humble admirer that kept his eyes fixed on the ground and only adored at humble distance. Kate, Kate, art thou not ashamed to deceive your father so?

MISS HARDCASTLE. Never trust me, dear papa, but he's still the modest man I first took him for; you'll be convinced of it as well as I.

HARDCASTLE. By the hand of my body, I believe his impudence is infectious! Didn't I see him seize your hand? Didn't I see him haul you about like a milkmaid? And now you talk of his respect and his modesty, forsooth!

MISS HARDCASTLE. But if I shortly convince you of his modesty, that he has only the faults that will pass off with time, and the virtues that will improve with age, I hope you'll forgive him.

HARDCASTLE. The girl would actually make one run mad! I tell you I'll not be convinced. I am convinced. He has scarcely been three hours in the house, and he has already encroached on all my prerogatives. You may like his impudence and call it modesty, but my son-in-law, madam, must have very different qualifications.

MISS HARDCASTLE. Sir, I ask but this night to convince you.

HARDCASTLE. You shall not have half the time, for I have thoughts of returning him this very hour.

MISS HARDCASTLE. Give me that hour then, and I hope to satisfy you.

HARDCASTLE. Well, an hour let it be then. But I'll have no trifling with your father. All fair and open, do you mind me?

MISS HARDCASTLE. I hope, sir, you have ever found that I considered your commands as my pride, for your kindness is such that my duty as yet has been inclination. *Exeunt*

ACT IV

[*The scene continues*]

Enter HASTINGS *and* MISS NEVILLE

HASTINGS. You surprise me! Sir Charles Marlow expected here this night? Where have you had your information?

MISS NEVILLE. You may depend upon it. I just saw his letter to Mr. Hardcastle, in which he tells him he intends setting out a few hours after his son.

HASTINGS. Then, my Constance, all must be completed before he arrives. He knows me; and should he find me here, would discover my name and perhaps my designs to the rest of the family.

MISS NEVILLE. The jewels, I hope, are safe.

HASTINGS. Yes, yes. I have sent them to Marlow, who keeps the keys of our baggage. In the meantime, I'll go to prepare matters for our elopement. I have had the squire's promise of a fresh pair of horses, and if I should not see him again will write him further directions. *Exit*

MISS NEVILLE. Well! success attend you. In the meantime, I'll go amuse my aunt with the old pretense of a violent passion for my cousin. *Exit*

Enter MARLOW *followed by a* Servant

MARLOW. I wonder what Hastings could mean by sending me so valuable a thing as a casket to keep for him, when he knows the

---

[1] In the game of hazard, seven was a winning throw.
[2] Ambs-ace,—both aces, the lowest throw.

only place I have is the seat of a post-chaise at an inn door. Have you deposited the casket with the landlady as I ordered you? Have you put it into her own hands?

SERVANT. Yes, your honor.

MARLOW. She said she'd keep it safe, did she?

SERVANT. Yes, she said she'd keep it safe enough; she asked me how I came by it, and she said she had a great mind to make me give an account of myself. *Exit* Servant.

MARLOW. Ha! ha! ha! They're safe, however. What an unaccountable set of beings have we got amongst! This little barmaid though, runs in my head most strangely and drives out the absurdities of all the rest of the family. She's mine, she must be mine, or I'm greatly mistaken.

Enter HASTINGS

HASTINGS. Bless me! I quite forgot to tell her that I intended to prepare at the bottom of the garden. Marlow here, and in spirits, too!

MARLOW. Give me joy George! Crown me, shadow me with laurels! Well, George, after all, we modest fellows don't want for success among the women.

HASTINGS. Some women, you mean. But what success has your honor's modesty been crowned with now, that it grows so insolent upon us?

MARLOW. Didn't you see the tempting, brisk, lovely, little thing that runs about the house with a bunch of keys to its girdle?

HASTINGS. Well! And what then?

MARLOW. She's mine, you rogue you. Such fire, such motion, such eyes, such lips—But, egad! She would not let me kiss them, though.

HASTINGS. But are you so sure, so very sure of her?

MARLOW. Why, man, she talked of showing me her work above-stairs, and I am to improve the pattern.

HASTINGS. But how can *you*, Charles, go about to rob a woman of her honor?

MARLOW. Pshaw! Pshaw! We all know the honor of the barmaid of an inn. I don't intend to *rob* her, take my word for it; there's nothing in this house I shan't honestly *pay* for.

HASTINGS. I believe the girl has virtue.

MARLOW. And if she has, I should be the last man in the world that would attempt to corrupt it.

HASTINGS. You have taken care, I hope, of the casket I sent you to lock up? It's in safety?

MARLOW. Yes, yes. It's safe enough. I have taken care of it. But how could you think the seat of a post-coach at an inn door a place of safety? Ah! numbskull! I have taken better precautions for you than you did for yourself.—I have—

HASTINGS. What!

MARLOW. I have sent it to the landlady to keep for you.

HASTINGS. To the landlady!

MARLOW. The landlady.

HASTINGS. You did!

MARLOW. I did. She's to be answerable for its forthcoming, you know.

HASTINGS. Yes, she'll bring it forth, with a witness.

MARLOW. Wasn't I right? I believe you'll allow that I acted prudently upon this occasion?

HASTINGS. (*Aside*) He must not see my uneasiness.

MARLOW. You seem a little disconcerted though, methinks. Sure nothing has happened?

HASTINGS. No, nothing. Never was in better spirits in all my life. And so you left it with the landlady, who, no doubt, very readily undertook the charge?

MARLOW. Rather too readily. For she not only kept the casket, but, through her great precaution, was going to keep the messenger too. Ha! ha! ha!

HASTINGS. He! he! he! They're safe, however.

MARLOW. As a guinea in a miser's purse.

HASTINGS. (*Aside*) So now all my hopes of fortune are at an end, and we must set off without it. (*To him*) Well, Charles, I'll leave you to your meditations on the pretty barmaid, and, he! he! he! may you be as successful for yourself as you have been for me. *Exit*

MARLOW. Thank ye, George! I ask no more. Ha! ha! ha!

Enter HARDCASTLE

HARDCASTLE. I no longer know my own house. It's turned all topsey-turvy. His servants have got drunk already. I'll bear it no longer, and yet, from my respect for his father, I'll be calm. (*To him*) Mr. Marlow, your servant. (*Bowing low*)

MARLOW. Sir, your humble servant. (*Aside*) What's to be the wonder now?

HARDCASTLE. I believe, sir, you must be sensible, sir, that no man alive ought to be more welcome than your father's son, sir. I hope you think so?

MARLOW. I do from my soul, sir. I don't want much entreaty. I generally make my father's son welcome wherever he goes.

HARDCASTLE. I believe you do, from my soul, sir. But though I say nothing to your own conduct, that of your servants is insufferable. Their manner of drinking is setting a very bad example in this house, I assure you.

MARLOW. I protest, my very good sir, that's no fault of mine. If they don't drink as they ought *they* are to blame. I ordered them not to spare the cellar. I did, I assure you. (*To the side scene*) Here, let one of my servants come up. (*To him*) My positive directions were that, as I did not drink myself, they should make up for my deficiencies below.

HARDCASTLE. Then they had your orders for what they do! I'm satisfied!

MARLOW. They had, I assure. You shall hear from one of themselves.

Enter Servant *drunk*

MARLOW. You, Jeremy! Come forward, sirrah! What were my orders? Were you not told to drink freely, and call for what you thought fit, for the good of the house?

HARDCASTLE. (*Aside*) I begin to lose my patience.

JEREMY. Please your honor, liberty and Fleet-street [1] for ever! Though I'm but a servant, I'm as good as another man. I'll drink for no man before supper, sir, dammy! Good liquor will sit upon a good supper, but a good supper will not sit upon—hiccup—upon my conscience, sir.

MARLOW. You see, my old friend, the fellow is as drunk as he can possibly be. I don't know what you'd have more, unless you'd have the poor devil soused in a beer-barrel.

HARDCASTLE. [*Aside*] Zounds! He'll drive me distracted if I contain myself any longer.—Mr. Marlow! Sir, I have submitted to your insolence for more than four hours, and I see no likelihood of its coming to an end. I'm now resolved to be master here, sir, and I desire that you and your drunken pack may leave my house directly.

MARLOW. Leave your house!—Sure you jest, my good friend? What, when I'm doing what I can to please you?

HARDCASTLE. I tell you, sir, you don't please me; so I desire you'll leave my house.

MARLOW. Sure, you cannot be serious? At this time o'night, and such a night? You only mean to banter me?

HARDCASTLE. I tell you, sir, I'm serious; and now that my passions are roused, I say this house is mine, sir; this house is mine, and I command you to leave it directly.

MARLOW. Ha! ha! ha! A puddle in a storm. I shan't stir a step, I assure you. (*In a serious tone*) This your house, fellow! It's my house. This is my house. Mine, while I choose to stay. What right have you to bid me leave this house, sir? I never met with such impudence, curse me, never in my whole life before.

HARDCASTLE. Nor I, confound me if I ever did. To come to my house, to call for what he likes, to turn me out of my own chair, to insult the family, to order his servants to get drunk, and then to tell me "This house is mine, sir." By all that's impudent, it makes me laugh. Ha! ha! ha! Pray, sir, (*Bantering*) as you take the house, what think you of taking the rest of the furniture? There's a pair of silver candlesticks, and there's a fire screen, and here's a pair of brazen-nosed bellows, perhaps you may take a fancy to them?

MARLOW. Bring me your bill, sir, bring me your bill, and let's make no more words about it.

HARDCASTLE. There are a pair of prints, too. What think you of "The Rake's Progress" [2] for your own apartment?

MARLOW. Bring me your bill, I say; and I'll leave you and your infernal house directly.

HARDCASTLE. Then there's a mahogany table that you may see your own face in.

MARLOW. My bill, I say.

HARDCASTLE. I had forget the great chair, for your own particular slumbers after a hearty meal.

MARLOW. Zounds! Bring me my bill, I say, and let's hear no more on't.

HARDCASTLE. Young man, young man, from your father's letter to me, I was taught to

---

[1] Early audiences may have seen in this an allusion to John Wilkes and the Middlesex election case, the election cry of Wilkes' followers being "Wilkes and liberty."

[2] Hogarth's famous series of engravings, published 1735.

SHE STOOPS TO CONQUER

expect a well-bred, modest man, as a visitor here, but now I find him no better than a coxcomb and a bully; but he will be down here presently, and shall hear more of it.

Exit

MARLOW. How's this! Sure I have not mistaken the house! Everything looks like an inn. The servants cry, "Coming!" The attendance is awkward; the barmaid, too, to attend us. But she's here, and will further inform me.—Whither so fast, child? A word with you.

Enter MISS HARDCASTLE

MISS HARDCASTLE. Let it be short then. I'm in a hurry. (*Aside*) I believe he begins to find out his mistake, but it's too soon quite to undeceive him.

MARLOW. Pray, child, answer me one question. What are you, and what may your business in this house be?

MISS HARDCASTLE. A relation of the family, sir.

MARLOW. What? A poor relation?

MISS HARDCASTLE. Yes, sir. A poor relation appointed to keep the keys and to see that the guests want nothing in my power to give them.

MARLOW. That is, you act as the barmaid of this inn.

MISS HARDCASTLE. Inn! O law!—What brought that in your head? One of the best families in the county keep an inn! Ha! ha! ha! Old Mr. Hardcastle's house an inn!

MARLOW. Mr. Hardcastle's house! Is this house Mr. Hardcastle's house, child?

MISS HARDCASTLE. Ay, sure. Whose else should it be?

MARLOW. So then all's out, and I have been damnably imposed on. O, confound my stupid head, I shall be laughed at over the whole town. I shall be stuck up in *caricatura* in all the print-shops. The Dullissimo Maccaroni. To mistake this house of all others for an inn, and my father's old friend for an inn-keeper. What a swaggering puppy must he take me for! What a silly puppy do I find myself! There again, may I be hanged, my dear, but I mistook you for the barmaid.

MISS HARDCASTLE. Dear me! dear me! I'm sure there's nothing in my *behavior* to put me upon a level with one of that stamp.

MARLOW. Nothing, my dear, nothing. But I was in for a list of blunders and could not help making you a subscriber. My stupidity saw everything the wrong way. I mistook your assiduity for assurance and your simplicity for allurement. But it's over.—This house I no more show *my* face in.

MISS HARDCASTLE. I hope, sir, I have done nothing to disoblige you. I'm sure I should be sorry to affront any gentleman who has been so polite and said so many civil things to me. I'm sure I should be sorry (*Pretending to cry*) if he left the family upon my account. I'm sure I should be sorry, [if] people said anything amiss, since I have no fortune but my character.

MARLOW. (*Aside*) By heavens, she weeps. This is the first mark of tenderness I ever had from a modest woman, and it touches me. (*To her*) Excuse me, my lovely girl, you are the only part of the family I leave with reluctance. But to be plain with you, the difference of our birth, fortune, and education make an honorable connection impossible; and I can never harbor a thought of seducing simplicity that trusted in my honor, or bring ruin upon one whose only fault was being too lovely.

MISS HARDCASTLE. (*Aside*) Generous man. I now begin to admire him. (*To him*) But I'm sure my family is as good as Miss Hardcastle's, and though I'm poor, that's no misfortune to a contented mind, and until this moment, I never thought that it was bad to want a fortune.

MARLOW. And why now, my pretty simplicity?

MISS HARDCASTLE. Because it puts me at a distance from one that if I had a thousand pounds, I would give it all to.

MARLOW. (*Aside*) This simplicity bewitches me so that if I stay I'm undone. I must make one bold effort, and leave her. (*To her*) Your partiality in my favor, my dear, touches me most sensibly, and were I to live for myself alone, I could easily fix my choice. But I owe too much to the opinion of the world, too much to the authority of a father, so that— I can scarcely speak it—it affects me. Farewell.

Exit

MISS HARDCASTLE. I never knew half his merit till now. He shall not go if I have power or art to detain him. I'll still preserve the character in which I stooped to conquer, but will undeceive my papa, who, perhaps, may laugh him out of his resolution.

Exit

Enter TONY, MISS NEVILLE

TONY. Ay, you may steal for yourselves the next time. I have done my duty. She has got the jewels again, that's a sure thing; but she believes it was all a mistake of the servants.

MISS NEVILLE. But, my dear cousin, sure you won't forsake us in this distress. If she in the least suspects that I am going off, I shall certainly be locked up or sent to my aunt Pedigree's, which is ten times worse.

TONY. To be sure, aunts of all kinds are damned bad things. But what can I do? I have got you a pair of horses that will fly like Whistlejacket, and I'm sure you can't say but I have courted you nicely before her face. Here she comes. We must court a bit or two more, for fear she should suspect us.

(*They retire and seem to fondle*)

Enter MRS. HARDCASTLE

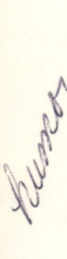

MRS. HARDCASTLE. Well, I was greatly fluttered, to be sure. But my son tells me it was all a mistake of the servants. I shan't be easy, however, till they are fairly married, and then let her keep her own fortune. But what do I see! Fondling together, as I'm alive. I never saw Tony so sprightly before.—Ah! I have caught you, my pretty doves! What, billing, exchanging stolen glances, and broken murmurs. Ah!

TONY. As for murmurs, mother, we grumble a little now and then, to be sure. But there's no love lost between us.

MRS. HARDCASTLE. A mere sprinkling, Tony, upon the flame, only to make it burn brighter.

MISS NEVILLE. Cousin Tony promises to give us more of his company at home. Indeed, he shan't leave us any more. It won't leave us, cousin Tony, will it?

TONY. O! it's a pretty creature. No, I'd sooner leave my horse in a pound than leave you when you smile upon one so. Your laugh makes you so becoming.

MISS NEVILLE. Agreeable cousin! Who can help admiring that natural humor, that pleasant, broad, red, thoughtless,—(*Patting his cheek*)—Ah! it's a bold face.

MRS. HARDCASTLE. Pretty innocence!

TONY. I'm sure I always loved cousin Con's hazel eyes, and her pretty, long fingers that she twists this way and that over the haspicholls,[1] like a parcel of bobbins.

[1] Harpsichord.

MRS. HARDCASTLE. Ah, he would charm the bird from the tree. I was never so happy before. My boy takes after his father, poor Mr. Lumpkin, exactly. The jewels, my dear Con, shall be yours incontinently. You shall have them. Isn't he a sweet boy, my dear? You shall be married tomorrow, and we'll put off the rest of his education, like Dr. Drowsy's sermons, to a fitter opportunity.

Enter DIGGORY

DIGGORY. Where's the squire? I have got a letter for your worship.

TONY. Give it to my mamma. She reads all my letters first.

DIGGORY. I had orders to deliver it into your own hands.

TONY. Who does it come from?

DIGGORY. Your worship mun ask that o' the letter itself.

TONY. I could wish to know, though.

(*Turning the letter and gazing at it*)

MISS NEVILLE. (*Aside*) Undone, undone. A letter to him from Hastings. I know the hand. If my aunt sees it, we are ruined for ever. I'll keep her employed a little if I can. (*To* MRS. HARDCASTLE) But I have not told you, madam, of my cousin's smart answer just now to Mr. Marlow. We so laughed— You must know, madam—This way a little, for he must not hear us. (*They confer*)

TONY. (*Still gazing*) A damned cramp piece of penmanship as ever I saw in my life. I can read your print-hand very well. But here there are such handles and shanks and dashes that one can scarce tell the head from the tail. *To Anthony Lumpkin, Esquire.* It's very odd, I can read the outside of my letters, where my own name is, well enough. But when I come to open it, it's all—buzz. That's hard, very hard; for the inside of the letter is always the cream of the correspondence.

MRS. HARDCASTLE. Ha, ha, ha! Very well! Very well! And so my son was too hard for the philosopher.

MISS NEVILLE. Yes, madam; but you must hear the rest, madam. A little more this way, or he may hear us. You'll hear now how he puzzled him again.

MRS. HARDCASTLE. He seems strangely puzzled now himself, methinks.

TONY. (*Still gazing*) A damned up-and-down hand, as if it was disguised in liquor. (*Reading*) *Dear Sir.* Ay, that's that. Then there's an

M, and a *T*, and an *S*, but whether the next be an *izzard* or an *R*, confound me, I cannot tell.

MRS. HARDCASTLE. What's that, my dear? Can I give you any assistance?

MISS NEVILLE. Pray, aunt, let me read it. Nobody reads a cramped hand better than I. (*Twitching the letter from her*) Do you know who it is from?

TONY. Can't tell, except from Dick Ginger, the feeder.

MISS NEVILLE. Ay, so it is, (*Pretending to read*) Dear Squire, Hoping that you're in health, as I am at this present. The gentlemen of the Shake-bag club has cut the gentlemen of Goose-Green quite out of feather. The odds—um—odd battle—um—long fighting—um—here, here, it's all about cocks and fighting; it's of no consequence; here, put it up, put it up.

(*Thrusting the crumpled letter upon him*)

TONY. But I tell you, miss, it's of all the consequence in the world. I would not lose the rest of it for a guinea. Here, mother, do you make it out. Of no consequence!

(*Giving* MRS. HARDCASTLE *the letter*)

MRS. HARDCASTLE. How's this. (*Reads*) "Dear Squire, I'm now waiting for Miss Neville with a post-chaise and pair at the bottom of the garden, but I find my horses yet unable to perform the journey. I expect you'll assist us with a pair of fresh horses, as you promised. Dispatch is necessary, as the hag (aye, *the hag!*) your mother will otherwise suspect us. Yours, Hastings." Grant me patience! I shall run distracted! My rage chokes me!

MISS NEVILLE. I hope, madam, you'll suspend your resentment for a few moments and not impute to me any impertinence or sinister design that belongs to another.

MRS. HARDCASTLE. (*Curtsying very low*) Fine spoken, madam, you are most miraculously polite and engaging and quite the very pink of courtesy and circumspection, madam. (*Changing her tone*) And you, you great ill-fashioned oaf, with scarce sense enough to keep your mouth shut! Were you, too, joined against me? But I'll defeat all your plots in a moment. As for you, madam, since you have got a pair of fresh horses ready, it would be cruel to disappoint them. So, if you please, instead of running away with your spark, prepare, this very moment to run off with *me*.

Your old aunt Pedigree will keep you secure, I'll warrant me. You too, sir, may mount your horse and guard us upon the way. Here, Thomas, Roger, Diggory! I'll show you that I wish you better than you do yourselves.

Exit

MISS NEVILLE. So now I'm completely ruined.

TONY. Ay, that's a sure thing.

MISS NEVILLE. What better could be expected from being connected with such a stupid fool and after all the nods and signs I made him.

TONY. By the laws, miss, it was your own cleverness and not my stupidity that did your business. You were so nice and so busy with your Shake-Bags and Goose-Greens that I thought you could never be making believe.

Enter HASTINGS

HASTINGS. So, sir, I find by my servant that you have shown my letter and betrayed us. Was this well done, young gentleman?

TONY. Here's another. Ask miss there who betrayed you. Ecod, it was her doing, not mine.

Enter MARLOW

MARLOW. So I have been finely used here among you. Rendered contemptible, driven into ill manners, despised, insulted, laughed at.

TONY. Here's another. We shall have old Bedlam broke loose presently.

MISS NEVILLE. And there, sir, is the gentleman to whom we all owe every obligation.

MARLOW. What can I say to him, a mere boy, an idiot, whose ignorance and age are a protection.

HASTINGS. A poor contemptible booby that would but disgrace correction.

MISS NEVILLE. Yet with cunning and malice enough to make himself merry with all our embarrassments.

HASTINGS. An insensible cub.

MARLOW. Replete with tricks and mischief.

TONY. Baw! Damme, but I'll fight you both one after the other,—with baskets.[1]

MARLOW. As for him, he's below resentment. But your conduct, Mr. Hastings, requires an explanation. You knew of my mistakes; yet would not undeceive me.

HASTINGS. Tortured as I am with my own

[1] Basket-hilt swords; i.e., with a basket-like protection for the hand.

disappointments, is this a time for explanations? It is not friendly, Mr. Marlow.

MARLOW. But, sir,—

MISS NEVILLE. Mr. Marlow, we never kept on your mistake, till it was too late to undeceive you. Be pacified.

Enter Servant

SERVANT. My mistress desires you'll get ready immediately, madam. The horses are putting to. Your hat and things are in the next room. We are to go thirty miles before morning. *Exit Servant*

MISS NEVILLE. Well, well; I'll come presently.

MARLOW. (*To* HASTINGS) Was it well done, sir, to assist in rendering me ridiculous? To hang me out for the scorn of all my acquaintance? Depend upon it, sir, I shall expect an explanation.

HASTINGS. Was it well done, sir, if you're upon that subject to deliver what I entrusted to yourself to the care of another, sir?

MISS NEVILLE. Mr. Hastings! Mr. Marlow! Why will you increase my distress by this groundless dispute? I implore, I entreat you—

Enter Servant

SERVANT. Your cloak, madam. [*Giving it*] My mistress is impatient.

MISS NEVILLE. I come. Pray be pacified. (*Exit* Servant) If I leave you thus, I shall die with apprehension.

Enter Servant

SERVANT. Your fan, muff, and gloves, madam. [*Handing them to her*] The horses are waiting.

MISS NEVILLE. O, Mr. Marlow; if you knew what a scene of constraint and ill-nature lies before me, I'm sure it would convert your resentment into pity.

MARLOW. I'm so distracted with a variety of passions that I don't know what to do. Forgive me, madam. George, forgive me. You know my hasty temper and should not exasperate it.

HASTINGS. The torture of my situation is my only excuse.

MISS NEVILLE. Well, my dear Hastings, if you have that esteem for me that I think, that I am sure you have, your constancy for three years will but increase the happiness of our future connection. If—

MRS. HARDCASTLE. (*Within*) Miss Neville! Constance, why Constance, I say!

MISS NEVILLE. I'm coming. Well, constancy. Remember, constancy is the word. *Exit*

HASTINGS. My heart! How can I support this! To be so near happiness, and such happiness!

MARLOW. (*To* TONY) You see, young gentleman, the effects of your folly. What might be amusement to you is here disappointment and even distress.

TONY. (*From a reverie*) Ecod, I have hit it. It's here. Your hands. Yours and yours, my poor Sulky. My boots there, ho! Meet me two hours hence at the bottom of the garden; and if you don't find Tony Lumpkin a more good-natured fellow than you thought for, I'll give you leave to take my best horse and Bet Bouncer into the bargain. Come along. My boots ho! *Exeunt*

ACT V

[SCENE I]

Scene continues

Enter HASTINGS *and* Servant

HASTINGS. You saw the old lady and Miss Neville drive off, you say.

SERVANT. Yes, your honor. They went off in a post coach, and the young squire went on horseback. They're thirty miles off by this time.

HASTINGS. Then all my hopes are over.

SERVANT. Yes, sir. Old Sir Charles is arrived. He and the old gentleman of the house have been laughing at Mr. Marlow's mistake this half hour. They are coming this way.

HASTINGS. Then I must not be seen. So now to my fruitless appointment at the bottom of the garden. This is about the time. *Exit*

Enter SIR CHARLES *and* HARDCASTLE

HARDCASTLE. Ha, ha, ha! The peremptory tone in which he sent forth his sublime commands!

SIR CHARLES. And the reserve with which I suppose he treated all your advances!

HARDCASTLE. And yet he might have seen something in me above a common inn-keeper, too.

Sir Charles. Yes, Dick, but he mistook you for an uncommon inn-keeper, ha, ha, ha!

Hardcastle. Well, I'm in too good spirits to think of anything but joy. Yes, my dear friend, this union of our families will make our personal friendships hereditary; and tho' my daughter's fortune is but small—

Sir Charles. Why, Dick, will you talk of fortune to me? My son is possessed of more than a competence already, and can want nothing but a good and virtuous girl to share his happiness and increase it. If they like each other, as you say they do—

Hardcastle. If, man! I tell you they do like each other. My daughter as good as told me so.

Sir Charles. But girls are apt to flatter themselves, you know.

Hardcastle. I saw him grasp her hand in the warmest manner myself; and here he comes to put you out of your *if's*, I warrant him.

Enter Marlow

Marlow. I come, sir, once more, to ask pardon for my strange conduct. I can scarce reflect on my insolence without confusion.

Hardcastle. Tut, boy, a trifle. You take it too gravely. An hour or two's laughing with my daughter will set all to rights again. She'll never like you the worse for it.

Marlow. Sir, I shall be always proud of her approbation.

Hardcastle. Approbation is but a cold word, Mr. Marlow; if I am not deceived, you have something more than approbation thereabouts. You take me.

Marlow. Really, sir, I have not that happiness.

Hardcastle. Come, boy, I'm an old fellow, and know what's what, as well as you that are younger. I know what has past between you; but mum.

Marlow. Sure, sir, nothing has past between us but the most profound respect on my side, and the most distant reserve on her's. You don't think, sir, that my impudence has been past upon all the rest of the family.

Hardcastle. Impudence! No, I don't say that—not quite impudence—though girls like to be played with, and rumpled a little too, sometimes. But she has told no tales, I assure you.

Marlow. I never gave her the slightest cause.

Hardcastle. Well, well, I like modesty in its place well enough. But this is over-acting, young gentleman. You *may* be open. Your father and I will like you the better for it.

Marlow. May I die, sir, if I ever—

Hardcastle. I tell you, she don't dislike you; and as I'm sure you like her—

Marlow. Dear sir—I protest, sir—

Hardcastle. I see no reason why you should not be joined as fast as the parson can tie you.

Marlow. But hear me, sir—

Hardcastle. Your father approves the match. I admire it; every moment's delay will be doing mischief, so—

Marlow. But why won't you hear me? By all that's just and true, I never gave Miss Hardcastle the slightest mark of my attachment, or even the most distant hint to suspect me of affection. We had but one interview, and that was formal, modest, and uninteresting.

Hardcastle. (*Aside*) This fellow's formal modest impudence is beyond bearing.

Sir Charles. And you never grasped her hand, or made any protestations!

Marlow. As heaven is my witness, I came down in obedience to your commands. I saw the lady without emotion, and parted without reluctance. I hope you'll exact no further proofs of my duty, nor prevent me from leaving a house in which I suffer so many mortifications. *Exit*

Sir Charles. I'm astonished at the air of sincerity with which he parted.

Hardcastle. And I'm astonished at the deliberate intrepidity of his assurance.

Sir Charles. I dare pledge my life and honor upon his truth.

Hardcastle. Here comes my daughter, and I would stake my happiness upon her veracity.

Enter Miss Hardcastle

Hardcastle. Kate, come hither, child. Answer us sincerely and without reserve; has Mr. Marlow made you any professions of love and affection?

Miss Hardcastle. The question is very abrupt, sir! But since you require unreserved sincerity, I think he has.

Hardcastle. (*To* Sir Charles) You see.

Sir Charles. And pray, madam, have you and my son had more than one interview?

MISS HARDCASTLE. Yes, sir, several.
HARDCASTLE. (*To* SIR CHARLES) You see.
SIR CHARLES. But did he profess any attachment?
MISS HARDCASTLE. A lasting one.
SIR CHARLES. Did he talk of love?
MISS HARDCASTLE. Much, sir.
SIR CHARLES. Amazing! And all this formally?
MISS HARDCASTLE. Formally.
HARDCASTLE. Now, my friend, I hope you are satisfied.
SIR CHARLES. And how did he behave, madam?
MISS HARDCASTLE. As most professed admirers do. Said some civil things of my face, talked much of his want of merit, and the greatness of mine; mentioned his heart, gave a short tragedy speech, and ended with pretended rapture.
SIR CHARLES. Now I'm perfectly convinced, indeed. I know his conversation among women to be modest and submissive. This forward, canting, ranting manner by no means describes him, and I am confident, he never sat for the picture.
MISS HARDCASTLE. Then what, sir, if I should convince you to your face of my sincerity? If you and my papa, in about half an hour, will place yourselves behind that screen, you shall hear him declare his passion to me in person.
SIR CHARLES. Agreed. And if I find him what you describe, all my happiness in him must have an end. *Exit*
MISS HARDCASTLE. And if you don't find him what I describe, I fear my happiness must never have a beginning. *Exeunt*

[SCENE II]

Scene changes to the back of the garden

Enter HASTINGS

HASTINGS. What an idiot am I, to wait here for a fellow, who probably takes a delight in mortifying me. He never intended to be punctual, and I'll wait no longer. What do I see? It is he, and perhaps with news of my Constance!

Enter TONY, *booted and spattered*

HASTINGS. My honest squire! I now find you a man of your word. This looks like friendship.

TONY. Ay, I'm your friend, and the best friend you have in the world, if you knew but all. This riding by night, by the bye, is cursedly tiresome. It has shook me worse than the basket of a stage coach.
HASTINGS. But how? Where did you leave your fellow travellers? Are they in safety? Are they housed?
TONY. Five and twenty miles in two hours and a half is no such bad driving. The poor beasts have smoked for it. Rabbit me, but I'd rather ride forty miles after a fox, than ten with such *varment*.
HASTINGS. Well, but where have you left the ladies? I die with impatience!
TONY. Left them! Why, where should I leave them, but where I found them?
HASTINGS. This is a riddle.
TONY. Riddle me this then. What's that goes round the house, and round the house, and never touches the house?
HASTINGS. I'm still astray.
TONY. Why that's it, man! I have led them astray. By jingo, there's not a pond or slough within five miles of the place but they can tell the taste of.
HASTINGS. Ha, ha, ha, I understand; you took them in a round, while they supposed themselves going forward. And so you have at last brought them home again?
TONY. You shall hear. I first took them down Featherbed-lane, where we stuck fast in the mud. I then rattled them crack over the stones of Up-and-down-Hill. I then introduced them to the gibbet on Heavy-tree Heath, and from that, with a circumbendibus, I fairly lodged them in the horsepond at the bottom of the garden.
HASTINGS. But no accident, I hope!
TONY. No, no! Only mother is confoundedly frightened. She thinks herself forty miles off. She's sick of the journey, and the cattle can scarce crawl. So if your own horses be ready, you may whip off with cousin, and I'll be bound that no soul here can budge a foot to follow you.
HASTINGS. My dear friend, how can I be grateful?
TONY. Ay, now its "dear friend," "noble squire." Just now, it was all "idiot," "cub," and "run me through the guts." Damn *your* way of fighting, I say. After we take a knock in this part of the country, we kiss and be friends. But if you had run me through the

guts, then I should be dead, and you might go kiss the hangman.

HASTINGS. The rebuke is just. But I must hasten to relieve Miss Neville; if you keep the old lady employed, I promise to take care of the young one. *Exit* HASTINGS.

TONY. Never fear me! Here she comes. Vanish! She's got from the pond, and draggled up to the waist like a mermaid.

Enter MRS. HARDCASTLE

MRS. HARDCASTLE. Oh, Tony, I'm killed! Shook! Battered to death! I shall never survive it. That last jolt that laid us against the quickset hedge has done my business.

TONY. Alack, mama, it was all your own fault. You would be for running away by night, without knowing one inch of the way.

MRS. HARDCASTLE. I wish we were at home again. I never met so many accidents in so short a journey. Drenched in the mud, overturned in a ditch, stuck fast in a slough, jolted to a jelly, and at last to lose our way. Whereabouts do you think we are, Tony?

TONY. By my guess we should be upon Crackskull common, about forty miles from home.

MRS. HARDCASTLE. O lud! O lud! the most notorious spot in all the country. We only want a robbery to make a complete night on't.

TONY. Don't be afraid, mama, don't be afraid! Two of the five that kept here are hanged, and the other three may not find us. Don't be afraid.—Is that a man that's galloping behind us? No; its only a tree. Don't be afraid!

MRS. HARDCASTLE. The fright will certainly kill me.

TONY. Do you see anything like a black hat moving behind the thicket?

MRS. HARDCASTLE. O death!

TONY. No, it's only a cow. Don't be afraid, mama; don't be afraid!

MRS. HARDCASTLE. As I'm alive, Tony, I see a man coming towards us. Ah! I'm sure on't! If he perceives us we are undone.

TONY. (*Aside*) Father-in-law, by all that's unlucky, come to take one of his night walks. (*To her*) Ah, it's a highwayman, with pistols as long as my arm. A damned ill-looking fellow.

MRS. HARDCASTLE. Good heaven, defend us! He approaches!

TONY. Do you hide yourself in that thicket, and leave me to manage him. If there be any danger I'll cough and cry hem. When I cough be sure to keep close.

(MRS. HARDCASTLE *hides behind a tree in the back scene*)

Enter MR. HARDCASTLE

HARDCASTLE. I'm mistaken, or I heard voices of people in want of help.—Oh, Tony, is that you? I did not expect you so soon back. Are your mother and her charge in safety?

TONY. Very safe, sir, at my aunt Pedigree's. Hem!

MRS. HARDCASTLE. (*From behind*) Ah, death! I find there's danger!

HARDCASTLE. Forty miles in three hours; sure, that's too much, my youngster.

TONY. Stout horses and willing minds make short journies, as they say. Hem!

MRS. HARDCASTLE. (*From behind*) Sure, he'll do the dear boy no harm!

HARDCASTLE. But I heard a voice here; I should be glad to know from whence it came?

TONY. It was I, sir, talking to myself, sir. I was saying that forty miles in four hours was very good going. Hem! As to be sure it was. Hem! I have got a sort of cold by being out in the air. We'll go in, if you please. Hem.

HARDCASTLE. But if you talked to yourself, you did not answer yourself. I am certain I heard two voices, and resolved (*Raising his voice*) to find the other out.

MRS. HARDCASTLE. (*From behind*) Oh! he's coming to find me out! Oh!

TONY. What need you go, sir, if I tell you? Hem! I'll lay down my life for the truth—hem—I'll tell you all, sir! (*Detaining him*)

HARDCASTLE. I tell you, I will not be detained! I insist on seeing. It's in vain to expect I'll believe you.

MRS. HARDCASTLE. (*Running forward from behind*) O lud, he'll murder my poor boy, my darling! Here, good gentleman, whet your rage upon me. Take my money, my life, but spare that young gentleman, spare my child, if you have any mercy!

HARDCASTLE. My wife, as I'm a Christian! From whence can she come, or what does she mean!

MRS. HARDCASTLE. (*Kneeling*) Take compassion on us, good Mr. Highwayman. Take our money, our watches, all we have, but spare our lives! We will never bring you to justice, indeed we won't, good Mr. Highwayman!

HARDCASTLE. I believe the woman's out of her senses.—What, Dorothy, don't you know *me*?

MRS. HARDCASTLE. Mr. Hardcastle, as I'm alive! My fears blinded me. But who, my dear, could have expected to meet you here, in this frightful place, so far from home? What has brought you to follow us?

HARDCASTLE. Sure, Dorothy, you have not lost your wits. So far from home, when you are within forty yards of your own door? (*To him*) This is one of your old tricks, you graceless rogue you! (*To her*) Don't you know the gate, and the mulberry tree, and don't you remember the horsepond, my dear?

MRS. HARDCASTLE. Yes, I shall remember the horsepond as long as I live; I have caught my death in it. (*To* TONY) And it is to you, you graceless varlet, I owe all this! I'll teach you to abuse your mother, I will!

TONY. Ecod, mother, all the parish says you have spoiled me, and so you may take the fruits on't.

MRS. HARDCASTLE. I'll spoil you, I will!
Follows him off the stage

HARDCASTLE. There's morality, however, in his reply. *Exit*

Enter HASTINGS *and* MISS NEVILLE

HASTINGS. My dear Constance, why will you deliberate thus? If we delay a moment, all is lost forever. Pluck up a little resolution, and we shall soon be out of the reach of her malignity.

MISS NEVILLE. I find it impossible! My spirits are so sunk with the agitations I have suffered, that I am unable to face any new danger. Two or three years patience will at last crown us with happiness.

HASTINGS. Such a tedious delay is worse than inconstancy. Let us fly, my charmer! Let us date our happiness from this very moment! Perish fortune! Love and content will increase what we possess beyond a monarch's revenue. Let me prevail!

MISS NEVILLE. No, Mr. Hastings, no! Prudence once more comes to my relief, and I will obey its dictates. In the moment of passion, fortune may be despised, but it ever produces a lasting repentance. I'm resolved to apply to Mr. Hardcastle's compassion and justice for redress.

HASTINGS. But tho' he had the will, he has not the power to relieve you.

MISS NEVILLE. But he has influence, and upon that I am resolved to rely.

HASTINGS. I have no hopes. But since you persist, I must reluctantly obey you. *Exeunt*

[SCENE III]

Scene changes [*to the parlor*]

Enter SIR CHARLES *and* MISS HARDCASTLE

SIR CHARLES. What a situation am I in! If what you say appears, I shall then find a guilty son. If what he says be true, I shall then lose one that, of all others, I most wished for a daughter.

MISS HARDCASTLE. I am proud of your approbation, and to show I merit it, if you place yourselves as I directed, you shall hear his explicit declaration. But he comes.

SIR CHARLES. I'll to your father, and keep him to the appointment. *Exit* SIR CHARLES

Enter MARLOW

MARLOW. Though prepared for setting out, I come once more to take leave, nor did I, till this moment, know the pain I feel in the separation.

MISS HARDCASTLE. (*In her own natural manner*) I believe these sufferings cannot be very great, sir, which you can so easily remove. A day or two longer, perhaps, might lessen your uneasiness, by showing the little value of what you now think proper to regret.

MARLOW. (*Aside*) This girl every moment improves upon me. (*To her*) It must not be, madam. I have already trifled too long with my heart. My very pride begins to submit to my passion. The disparity of education and fortune, the anger of a parent, and the contempt of my equals, begin to lose their weight; and nothing can restore me to myself, but this painful effort of resolution.

MISS HARDCASTLE. Then go, sir. I'll urge nothing more to detain you. Tho' my family be as good as hers you came down to visit, and my education, I hope, not inferior, what are these advantages without equal affluence? I must remain contented with the slight approbation of imputed merit; I must have only the mockery of your addresses, while all your serious aims are fixed on fortune.

Enter HARDCASTLE *and* SIR CHARLES *from behind*

SIR CHARLES. [*To* HARDCASTLE] Here, behind this screen!

HARDCASTLE. Ay, ay, make no noise. I'll engage my Kate covers him with confusion at last.

MARLOW. By heavens, madam, fortune was ever my smallest consideration. Your beauty at first caught my eye; for who could see that without emotion! But every moment that I converse with you, steals in some new grace, heightens the picture, and gives it stronger expression. What at first seemed rustic plainness, now appears refined simplicity. What seemed forward assurance, now strikes me as the result of courageous innocence, and conscious virtue.

SIR CHARLES. What can it mean! He amazes me.

HARDCASTLE. I told you how it would be. Hush!

MARLOW. I am now determined to stay, madam, and I have too good an opinion of my father's discernment, when he sees you, to doubt his approbation.

MISS HARDCASTLE. No, Mr. Marlow, I will not, cannot detain you. Do you think I could suffer a connection in which there is the smallest room for repentance? Do you think I would take the mean advantage of a transient passion, to load you with confusion? Do you think I could ever relish that happiness, which was acquired by lessening yours?

MARLOW. By all that's good, I can have no happiness but what's in your power to grant me! Nor shall I ever feel repentance, but in not having seen your merits before. I will stay, even contrary to your wishes; and though you should persist to shun me, I will make my respectful assiduities atone for the levity of my past conduct.

MISS HARDCASTLE. Sir, I must entreat you'll desist. As our acquaintance began, so let it end, in indifference. I might have given an hour or two to levity, but seriously, Mr. Marlow, do you think I could ever submit to a connection, where *I* must appear mercenary, and *you* imprudent? Do you think I could ever catch at the confident addresses of a secure admirer?

MARLOW. (*Kneeling*) Does this look like security? Does this look like confidence? No, madam, every moment shows me your merit, only serves to increase my diffidence and confusion. Here let me continue—

SIR CHARLES. [*Discovering himself and* HARDCASTLE] I can hold it no longer!—Charles, Charles, how hast thou deceived me! Is this your indifference, your uninteresting conversation!

HARDCASTLE. Your cold contempt! your formal interview! What have you to say now?

MARLOW. That I'm all amazement! What can it mean?

HARDCASTLE. It means that you can say and unsay things at pleasure. That you can address a lady in private, and deny it in public; that you have one story for us, and another for my daughter.

MARLOW. Daughter! This lady your daughter?

HARDCASTLE. Yes, sir, my only daughter. My Kate, whose else should she be?

MARLOW. Oh, the devil!

MISS HARDCASTLE. Yes, sir, that very identical tall squinting lady you were pleased to take me for. (*Curtesying*) She that you addressed as the mild, modest, sentimental man of gravity, and the bold forward agreeable Rattle of the ladies club; ha, ha, ha.

MARLOW. [*Aside*] Zounds, there's no bearing this; it's worse than death.

MISS HARDCASTLE. In which of your characters, sir, will you give us leave to address you? As the faltering gentleman, with looks on the ground, that speaks just to be heard, and hates hypocrisy; or the loud confident creature, that keeps it up with Mrs. Mantrap, and old Miss Biddy Buckskin, till three in the morning; ha, ha, ha!

MARLOW. [*Aside*] O, curse on my noisy head! I never attempted to be impudent yet, that I was not taken down. I must be gone.

HARDCASTLE. By the hand of my body, but you shall not. I see it was all a mistake, and I am rejoiced to find it. You shall not, sir, I tell you. I know she'll forgive you. Won't you forgive him, Kate? We'll all forgive you! Take courage, man!

(*They retire, she tormenting him, to the back scene*)

Enter MRS. HARDCASTLE *and* TONY

MRS. HARDCASTLE. So, so, they're gone off! Let them go; I care not.

HARDCASTLE. Who gone?

MRS. HARDCASTLE. My dutiful niece and

her gentleman, Mr. Hastings, from town. He who came down with our modest visitor here.

Sir Charles. Who,—my honest George Hastings? As worthy a fellow as lives, and the girl could not have made a more prudent choice.

Hardcastle. Then, by the hand of my body, I'm proud of the connection.

Mrs. Hardcastle. Well, if he has taken away the lady, he has not taken her fortune; that remains in this family to console us for her loss.

Hardcastle. Sure Dorothy you would not be so mercenary?

Mrs. Hardcastle. Ay, that's my affair, not yours.

[Hardcastle.][1] But you know if your son, when of age, refuses to marry his cousin, her whole fortune is then at her own disposal.

[Mrs.] Hardcastle. Ay, but he's not of age, and she has not thought proper to wait for his refusal.

Enter Hastings *and* Miss Neville

Mrs. Hardcastle. (*Aside*) What, returned so soon; I begin not to like it.

Hastings. (*To* Hardcastle) For my late attempt to fly off with your niece, let my present confusion be my punishment. We are now come back, to appeal from your justice to your humanity. By her father's consent, I first paid her my addresses, and our passions were first founded in duty.

Miss Neville. Since his death, I have been obliged to stoop to dissimulation to avoid oppression. In an hour of levity, I was ready even to give up my fortune to secure my choice. But I'm now recovered from the delusion, and hope from your tenderness what is denied me from a nearer connection.

Mrs. Hardcastle. Pshaw, pshaw, this is all but the whining end of a modern novel.

Hardcastle. Be it what it will, I'm glad they're come back to reclaim their due. Come hither, Tony boy! Do you refuse this lady's hand whom I now offer you?

Tony. What signifies my refusing? You know I can't refuse her till I'm of age, father.

Hardcastle. While I thought concealing your age, boy, was likely to conduce to your improvement, I concurred with your mother's desire to keep it secret. But since I find she turns it to a wrong use, I must now declare, you have been of age these three months.

Tony. Of age! Am I of age, father?

Hardcastle. Above three months.

Tony. Then you'll see the first use I'll make of my liberty. (*Taking* Miss Neville's *hand*) Witness all men by these presents, that I, Anthony Lumpkin, Esquire, of Blank place, refuse you, Constantia Neville, spinster, of no place at all, for my true and lawful wife. So Constance Neville may marry whom she pleases, and Tony Lumpkin is his own man again.

Sir Charles. O brave squire!

Hastings. My worthy friend!

Mrs. Hardcastle. My undutiful offspring!

Marlow. Joy, my dear George, I give you joy sincerely! And could I prevail upon my little tyrant here to be less arbitrary, I should be the happiest man alive, if you would return me the favor.

Hastings. (*To* Miss Hardcastle) Come, madam, you are now driven to the very last scene of all your contrivances. I know you like him, I'm sure he loves you, and you must and shall have him.

Hardcastle. (*Joining their hands*) And I say so too! And, Mr. Marlow, if she makes as good a wife as she was a daughter, I don't believe you'll ever repent your bargain. So now to supper! To-morrow we shall gather all the poor of the parish about us, and the Mistakes of the Night shall be crowned with a merry morning; so, boy, take her; and as you have mistaken in the mistress, my wish is, that you may never be mistaken in the wife.

EPILOGUE [2]

By Dr. Goldsmith

[Spoken by Mrs. Bulkely]

Well, having stooped to conquer with
    success,
And gained a husband without aid from dress,
Still as a bar-maid, I could wish it too,
As I have conquered him to conquer you.
And let me say, for all your resolution,   5
That pretty bar-maids have done execution.
Our life is all a play, composed to please,

---

[1] This speech-tag is lacking in the first edition and Mrs. Hardcastle's next speech is assigned to Mr. Hardcastle. The correction has been made in most later editions of the play.

[2] Goldsmith wrote two other epilogues for the play; they will be found among his collected poems.

"We have our exits and our entrances."[1]
The first act shows the simple country maid,
Harmless and young, of everything afraid; 10
Blushes when hired and with unmeaning action,
I hopes as how to give you satisfaction.
Her second act displays a livelier scene,—
The unblushing bar-maid of a country inn.
Who whisks about the house, at market caters,
Talks loud, coquettes the guests, and scolds the waiters, 16
Next the scene shifts to town, and there she soars,
The chop-house toast[2] of ogling connoisseurs.
On squires and cits she there displays her arts, 19
And on the gridiron broils her lovers' hearts—
And as she smiles, her triumphs to complete,
Even Common-Councilmen forget to eat.
The fourth act shows her wedded to the 'Squire,
And madam now begins to hold it higher,
Pretends to taste, at opera cries *caro*, 25
And quits her "Nancy Dawson,"[3] for *Che Faro*.[4]
Dotes upon dancing, and in all her pride,
Swims round the room, the Heinel[5] of Cheapside;
Ogles and leers with artificial skill,
Till, having lost in age the power to kill, 30
She sits all night at cards and ogles at spadille.
Such, thro' our lives, the eventful history—
The fifth and last act still remains for me.

[1] Parody of *As You Like It*, II, vii, 141; and the rest of the epilogue carries out the figure.
[2] The lunch-room beauty.
[3] A popular song of the day, now sometimes found in Mother Goose rhymes.
[4] An aria in Glück's *Orfeo*, (1764).
[5] "Madame" Heinel was a German dancer popular among the fashionable set at the time.

The bar-maid now for your protection prays,
Turns female barrister, and pleads for Bayes.[6]

EPILOGUE[7]

To be Spoken in the Character of Tony Lumpkin

By J. Craddock, Esq.[8]

Well—now all's ended—and my comrades gone,
Pray what becomes of mother's nonly son?
A hopeful blade!—in town I'll fix my station,
And try to make a bluster in the nation.
As for my cousin Neville, I renounce her; 5
Off—in a crack—I'll carry big Bet Bouncer.
Why should not I in the great world appear?
I soon shall have a thousand pounds a year;
No matter what a man may here inherit,
In London—'gad, they've some regard to spirit. 10
I see the horses prancing up the streets
And big Bet Bouncer bobs to all she meets;
Then hoiks to jiggs and pastimes every night—
Not to the plays—they say it a'n't polite,
To Sadler's Wells perhaps, or Operas go, 15
And once, by chance, to the roratorio.
Thus here and there, for ever up and down,
We'll set the fashions, too, to half the town;
And then at auctions—money ne'er regard,
Buy pictures like the great, ten pounds a yard; 20
Zounds, we shall make these London gentry say,
We know what's damned genteel, as well as they.

[6] See *The Rehearsal*.
[7] This came too late to be spoken. ORIGINAL NOTE.
[8] Joseph Craddock, of Gumley, Leicestershire, a member of Goldsmith's circle. He died in 1826, aged 85. His *Memoirs* were published in 1828.

THE SCHOOL FOR SCANDAL[1]

A Comedy by Richard Brinsley Sheridan

Richard Brinsley Butler Sheridan was born in Dublin, October 30, 1751. His father, son of Swift's friend, was Thomas Sheridan, a popular actor and manager of the Theatre Royal, Dublin. His mother, Mrs. Frances (Chamberlaine) Sheridan, is remembered as an admirer of Richardson, and as authoress of a novel, *Memoirs of Sidney Bidulph* (1760), and of several small comedies, which served in part as inspiration for her son's work. As the Sheridans left Ireland in 1758, Richard grew up in England, in school at Harrow and after his mother's death in 1766, in London with his father. In 1770 Thomas Sheridan moved to Bath, where his son's career began with his romantic love affair with Elizabeth Linley, daughter of the prominent musician and herself a concert singer of great popularity. She and Sheridan were married April 13, 1773, and set up housekeeping in London with next to nothing and no prospects. Fortunately, however, the young member of the Middle Temple wrote a comedy, *The Rivals*, which, after opening without much luck at Convent Garden, was revised and succeeded. Within six years Sheridan had risen to the first position as a dramatist; he was manager and part owner of Drury Lane, having succeeded Garrick in 1776; and he had acquired, as the friend of Burke and Johnson, a recognized place in the literary life of London as well as a membership in the Literary Club. He was also on the threshold of a long and brilliant career in politics.

Sheridan entered parliament in 1780, allying himself with the Whigs, led by Fox and Burke, with whom he was associated for the rest of their common lives. He held office for a short while, as Under Secretary of State in 1782 and as Secretary to the Treasury in 1783, but like the other two great Whigs of the period, he spent most of his life in opposition. The height of his career was reached in the trial of Warren Hastings, whom Sheridan prosecuted from the beginning of the impeachment proceedings in 1787 to the close of the trial in 1794. Though less known to posterity than those of his colleagues, his speeches gained for Sheridan a reputation among his contemporaries as an orator second to none.

Mrs. Sheridan died in 1792, leaving one son, Thomas (1775–1817), and an infant daughter, who died within a few weeks; and three years later Sheridan married Esther Jane Ogle, daughter of the Dean of Winchester, by whom he had one child, Charles Brinsley (1796–1843). His two marriages were happy; and his domestic life, for one in his position as a man of fashion, a member of the circle of the Prince of Wales and a friend of Fox, was singularly tranquil.

During his membership of the House of Commons, Sheridan continued to manage Drury Lane with considerable success. He rebuilt the theater between 1792 and 1794, incurring large debts in the process. In 1809 the theater was burned in a famous fire which destroyed not only the theater but also Sheridan's hopes of recovering his fortune. His last years were passed in obscurity and comparative poverty. He lost his seat in parliament in 1812, and his friends are accused of having deserted him in his distresses. He died July 7, 1816; and, though bailiffs were said to have attended at his house during his last illness, he was buried with great pomp in Westminster Abbey.

[1] The text here reprinted is that of the 1821 edition of Sheridan's dramatic works published by John Murray and containing an "Advertisement" by Thomas Moore. Readers interested in textual matters are referred to R. C. Rhodes, *The Plays and Poems of R. B. Sheridan* (1928), and references there cited.

See W. Fraser Rae's *Sheridan, a Biography*, 2 vols., 1896; and lives by Thomas Moore (1825), Mrs. Oliphant (1883, English Men of Letters), L. C. Sanders (n. d., Great Writers Series), and R. C. Rhodes (1933).

SHERIDAN'S DRAMATIC WORKS [1]

The Rivals (comedy) (C.G., Jan. 17, 1775), 1775.
St. Patrick's Day; or, The Scheming Lieutenant (farce) (C.G., May 2, 1775), 1788.
The Duenna (comic opera) (C.G., Nov. 21, 1775) 1783.
A Trip to Scarborough, altered from Vanbrugh's The Relapse (comedy) (D.L., Feb. 24, 1777), 1781.
The School for Scandal (comedy) (D.L., May 8, 1777), 1777 (?).
The Camp, A Musical Entertainment, D.L., Oct. 15, 1778. (Attributed to Richard Tickell; certainly partly by Sheridan, perhaps with the assistance of General Burgoyne. Cf. Rhodes, The Plays and Poems of R. B. Sheridan, vol. ii.)
The Critic; or, A Tragedy Rehearsed (burlesque) (D.L., Oct. 30, 1779), 1781.
Songs, Duetts, Choruses, &c. In a New and Appropriate Entertainment Called the Glorious First of June (entertainment) (D.L., July 2, 1794), 1794. (By Sheridan and James Cobb, with various other contributors.)
Songs, Duetts, Choruses, &c., in an Occasional Entertainment called Cape St. Vincent; or, British Valour Triumphant (entertainment) (D.L., March, 1797), 1797. (Alteration of The Glorious First of June.)
Pizarro. . . . Taken from the German Drama of Kotzebue and adapted to the English Stage (tragedy) (D.L., May 24, 1799), 1799.

The School for Scandal "was so admirably acted that tho' it has continued on the acting list at Drury Lane from that time to this [1830] and been several times represented at Covent Garden and the Haymarket, yet no new performer has ever appeared in any one of the principal characters that was not inferior to the person who acted it originally." Thus the Rev. John Genest summed up the opinion of his generation that no play could be better acted than had been The School for Scandal at Drury Lane on May 8, 1777. Mr. Sheridan, the brilliant young manager, had outdone himself and, indeed, all English comedy since Congreve. Not only had he cast his play with the greatest possible care but he had given his cast a superb play to perform. The comedy was, in the words of

[1] Many of the early editions of Sheridan's plays were pirated. Space does not permit differentiation between pirated and authorized editions here. See A. Nicoll's A History of Late Eighteenth Century Drama and R. C. Rhodes' (ed.) The Plays and Poems of R. B. Sheridan (1928).

Mr. Sheridan's biographer, "the slow result of many and doubtful experiments, gradually unfolding beauties unforeseen even by him who produced them, and arriving at length, step by step, at perfection;" and perfection it has long been regarded.

The comedy is composed of two plays, called earlier "The Slanderers" and "The Teazles," which were later joined by their author to form The School for Scandal. The joints are discernible; but the flow of witty speech, the satire, the triumph of the screen scene, are likely to blind one to minor defects. The play represents the typical high comedy of its time, verging in one direction upon Restoration comedy of manners and falling in the other into the usual sentimentalism of the comedy of sensibility. One of the brothers Surface is a true sentimental hero, a rake reformed, at the same time that the other is the most complete satiric presentation of the man of sentiment in eighteenth century drama. The scandal scenes and the Lady Teazle seduction plot are reminiscent of Restoration comedy, as are the witty servant, Trip, and the dialogue, while the Charles-Maria love affair and Sir Oliver, the benevolent and sentimental old gentleman, with Rowley, the faithful family servant, are true to that type of sentimental comedy since the day of Steele.

Though Mr. Sheridan's contemporaries thought that no actor could exceed the original in any part in the play, most actors of comedy have attempted to do so; and many stage beauties from that day to this have added to the conquests of the incomparable Lady Teazle.

The complications of the plot of The School for Scandal will seem less baffling to the average reader if he notices that the various scenes of the first three acts frequently represent simultaneous action. The two plots, first, that hinging upon Lady Sneerwell's love for Charles and her consequent scandalous libels of Lady Teazle and involving the last named lady's relations with Joseph Surface, and, secondly, that of Sir Oliver's testing of his nephews, should be kept separately in mind until the screen scene, in which Sheridan with a brilliant *coup* brings all together. The movements of Snake, too, should not go unobserved.

THE SCHOOL FOR SCANDAL

DRAMATIS PERSONÆ

SIR PETER TEAZLE	Mr. King	SNAKE	Mr. Packer
SIR OLIVER SURFACE	Mr. Yates	CARELESS	Mr. Farren
JOSEPH SURFACE	Mr. Palmer	SIR [TOBY] BUMPER [2]	Mr. Gawdry
CHARLES [SURFACE] [1]	Mr. Smith		
CRABTREE	Mr. Parsons	LADY TEAZLE	Mrs. Abington
SIR BENJAMIN BACKBITE	Mr. Dodd	MARIA	Miss P. Hopkins
ROWLEY	Mr. Aickin	LADY SNEERWELL	Miss Sherry
MOSES	Mr. Baddeley	MRS. CANDOUR	Miss Pope
TRIP	Mr. Lamash		

PROLOGUE

WRITTEN BY MR. GARRICK

[SPOKEN BY MR. KING] [3]

A school for scandal! tell me, I beseech you,
Needs there a school this modish art to teach you?
No need of lessons now, the knowing think;
We might as well be taught to eat and drink.
Caused by a dearth of scandal, should the vapors   5
Distress our fair ones, let them read the papers;
Their powerful mixtures such disorders hit,
Crave what you will,—there's *quantum sufficit*.[4]
"Lord!" cries my Lady Wormwood, who loves tattle   9
And puts much salt and pepper in her prattle,
Just risen at noon, all night at cards when threshing,
Strong tea and scandal,—"Bless me, how refreshing!
Give me the papers, Lisp,—how bold and free!   (*Sips*)
Last night Lord L. (*Sips*) was caught with Lady D.
For aching head what charming sal volatile!   (*Sips*) 15
If Mrs. B. will still continue flirting,
We hope she'll draw, or we'll undraw *the curtain.*
Fine satire, poz![5] In public all abuse it,
But by ourselves (*Sips*) our praise we can't refuse it.
Now, Lisp, read you,—there at that dash and star."   20
"Yes, ma'am. *A certain lord had best beware,*
Who lives not twenty miles from Grosvenor Square,
For, should he Lady W. find willing,
Wormwood is bitter—" "Oh! that's me! the villain!
Throw it behind the fire and never more   25
Let that vile paper come within my door."
Thus at our friends we laugh, who feel the dart;
To reach our feelings, we ourselves must smart.
Is our young bard so young to think that he
Can stop the full spring-tide of calumny?   30
Knows he the world so little, and its trade?
Alas! the devil's sooner raised than laid.
So strong, so swift, the monster there's **no** gagging;
Cut Scandal's head off, still the tongue is wagging. 34

---

[1] In the Murray edition this character is listed simply as *Charles*. The obvious addition has here been made.

[2] In Murray and in many other editions this character is called Sir *Harry* Bumper. He was not named in the early playbills; and the best editions list him as Sir Toby.

[3] Rhodes, who takes his text of Garrick's Prologue from *The Town and Country Magazine* for June, 1777, prints the statement, not found in most editions of the play, that King spoke the Prologue.

[4] Enough, plenty, a pharmacist's phrase.

[5] Positively.

Proud of your smiles once lavishly bestowed,[1]
Again our young Don Quixote takes the road;
To show his gratitude he draws his pen
And seeks this hydra, Scandal, in his den.
For your applause all perils he would through,—
He'll fight (that's write) a cavalliero true, 40
Till every drop of blood (that's ink) is spilt for you.

ACT I

Scene i. Lady Sneerwell's *House*

Discovered, Lady Sneerwell *at the dressing table;* Snake *drinking chocolate*

Lady Sneerwell. The paragraphs, you say, Mr. Snake, were all inserted?

Snake. They were, madam; and as I copied them myself in a feigned hand, there can be no suspicion whence they came.

Lady Sneerwell. Did you circulate the report of Lady Brittle's intrigue with Captain Boastall?

Snake. That's in as fine a train as your ladyship could wish. In the common course of things, I think it must reach Mrs. Clackitt's ears within four-and-twenty hours; and then, you know, the business is as good as done.

Lady Sneerwell. Why, truly, Mrs. Clackitt has a very pretty talent and a great deal of industry.

Snake. True, madam, and has been tolerably successful in her day. To my knowledge, she has been the cause of six matches being broken off and three sons being disinherited; of four forced elopements and as many close confinements; nine separate maintenances and two divorces. Nay, I have more than once traced her causing a *tête-à-tête* in the *Town and Country Magazine*[2] when the parties, perhaps, had never seen each other's face before in the course of their lives.

Lady Sneerwell. She certainly has talents, but her manner is gross.

Snake. 'Tis very true. She generally de-signs well, has a free tongue and a bold invention; but her coloring is too dark and her outlines often extravagant.[3] She wants that delicacy of tint and mellowness of sneer which distinguish your ladyship's scandal.

Lady Sneerwell. You are partial, Snake.

Snake. Not in the least; everybody allows that Lady Sneerwell can do more with a word or look than many can with the most labored detail, even when they happen to have a little truth on their side to support it.

Lady Sneerwell. Yes, my dear Snake; and I am no hypocrite to deny the satisfaction I reap from the success of my efforts. Wounded myself in the early part of my life by the envenomed tongue of slander, I confess I have since known no pleasure equal to the reducing others to the level of my own reputation.

Snake. Nothing can be more natural. But, Lady Sneerwell, there is one affair in which you have lately employed me, wherein, I confess, I am at a loss to guess your motives.

Lady Sneerwell. I conceive you mean with respect to my neighbor, Sir Peter Teazle, and his family?[4]

Snake. I do. Here are two young men to whom Sir Peter has acted as a kind of guardian since their father's death, the eldest possessing the most amiable character and universally well spoken of, the youngest, the most dissipated and extravagant young fellow in the kingdom, without friends or character; the former an avowed admirer of your ladyship and apparently your favorite; the latter attached to Maria, Sir Peter's ward, and confessedly beloved by her. Now, on the face of these circumstances, it is utterly unaccountable to me why you, the widow of a city knight,[5] with a good jointure, should not close with the passion of a man of such character and expectations as Mr. Surface; and more so, why you should be so uncommonly earnest to destroy the mutual attachment subsisting between his brother Charles and Maria.

Lady Sneerwell. Then at once to unravel

---

[1] Once lavishly bestowed upon *The Rivals*, two years before.

[2] A feature of *The Town and Country Magazine* was a series of "Memoirs" or "Histories," containing imaginary conversations, and a "Tête-à-tête," or picture showing the principals in vignette; the tone of these sketches was, of course, scandalous. Rhodes has identified one of them which appeared in January, 1777, as detailing the career of Mrs. Abington, the original Lady Teazle. (See Rhodes' edition, II, 14.)

[3] Snake describes her technique as if it were that of a painter.

[4] This awkward exposition, though conveying desirable information to the audience, slows up the opening of the play in a manner which would hardly be allowed by modern technique. It is one of the ill-concealed joints between the two plots of the comedy.

[5] A merchant, knighted because of some office which he held, as distinguished from a knight of the court.

this mystery, I must inform you that love has no share whatever in the intercourse between Mr. Surface and me.

SNAKE. No!

LADY SNEERWELL. His real attachment is to Maria, or to her fortune; but finding in his brother a favored rival, he has been obliged to mask his pretensions and profit by my assistance.

SNAKE. Yet still I am more puzzled why you should interest yourself in his success.

LADY SNEERWELL. Heavens! how dull you are! Cannot you surmise the weakness which I hitherto, through shame, have concealed even from you? Must I confess that Charles, that libertine, that extravagant, that bankrupt in fortune and reputation,—that he it is for whom I am thus anxious and malicious, and to gain whom I would sacrifice everything?

SNAKE. Now, indeed, your conduct appears consistent; but how came you and Mr. Surface so confidential?

LADY SNEERWELL. For our mutual interest. I have found him out a long time since. I know him to be artful, selfish, and malicious,— in short, a sentimental knave, while with Sir Peter, and indeed with all his acquaintance, he passes for a youthful miracle of prudence, good sense, and benevolence.

SNAKE. Yes! Yet Sir Peter vows he has not his equal in England; and, above all, he praises him as a man of sentiment.

LADY SNEERWELL. True; and with the assistance of his sentiment and hypocrisy he has brought Sir Peter entirely into his interest with regard to Maria, while poor Charles has no friend in the house, though I fear he has a powerful one in Maria's heart, against whom we must direct our schemes.

Enter Servant

SERVANT. Mr. Surface.

LADY SNEERWELL. Show him up.

Exit Servant

Enter JOSEPH SURFACE

JOSEPH SURFACE. My dear Lady Sneerwell, how do you do to-day? Mr. Snake, your most obedient.

LADY SNEERWELL. Snake has just been rallying me on our mutual attachment; but I have informed him of our real views. You know how useful he has been to us, and, believe me, the confidence is not ill placed.

JOSEPH SURFACE. Madam, it is impossible for me to suspect a man of Mr. Snake's sensibility and discernment.

LADY SNEERWELL. Well, well, no compliments now; but tell me when you saw your mistress, Maria,—or what is more material to me, your brother.

JOSEPH SURFACE. I have not seen either since I left you; but I can inform you that they never meet. Some of your stories have taken a good effect on Maria.

LADY SNEERWELL. Ah, my dear Snake, the merit of this belongs to you. But do your brother's distresses increase?

JOSEPH SURFACE. Every hour. I am told he has had another execution in the house yesterday. In short, his dissipation and extravagance exceed anything I have ever heard of.

LADY SNEERWELL. Poor Charles!

JOSEPH SURFACE. True, madam, notwithstanding his vices, one can't help feeling for him. Poor Charles! I'm sure I wish it were in my power to be of any essential service to him, for the man who does not share in the distresses of a brother, even though merited by his own misconduct, deserves—

LADY SNEERWELL. O lud! you are going to be moral and forget that you are among friends.

JOSEPH SURFACE. Egad, that's true! I'll keep that sentiment till I see Sir Peter. However, it is certainly a charity to rescue Maria from such a libertine, who, if he is to be reclaimed, can be so only by a person of your ladyship's superior accomplishments and understanding.

SNAKE. I believe, Lady Sneerwell, here's company coming. I'll go and copy the letter I mentioned to you. Mr. Surface, your most obedient.

JOSEPH SURFACE. Sir, your very devoted.— (*Exit* SNAKE) Lady Sneerwell, I am very sorry you have put any farther confidence in that fellow.

LADY SNEERWELL. Why so?

JOSEPH SURFACE. I have lately detected him in frequent conference with old Rowley, who was formerly my father's steward and has never, you know, been a friend of mine.

LADY SNEERWELL. And do you think he would betray us?

JOSEPH SURFACE. Nothing more likely. Take my word for 't, Lady Sneerwell, that fellow hasn't virtue enough to be faithful even to his own villainy. Ah, Maria!

Enter MARIA

LADY SNEERWELL. Maria, my dear, how do you do? What's the matter?
MARIA. Oh! there's that disagreeable lover of mine, Sir Benjamin Backbite, has just called at my guardian's with his odious uncle, Crabtree; so I slipped out and ran hither to avoid them.
LADY SNEERWELL. Is that all?
JOSEPH SURFACE. If my brother Charles had been of the party, madam, perhaps you would not have been so much alarmed.
LADY SNEERWELL. Nay, now you are too severe, for I dare swear the truth of the matter is, Maria heard you were here. But, my dear, what has Sir Benjamin done that you should avoid him so?
MARIA. Oh, he has done nothing; but 'tis for what he has said. His conversation is a perpetual libel on all his acquaintance.
JOSEPH SURFACE. Ay, and the worst of it is, there is no advantage in not knowing him, for he'll abuse a stranger just as soon as his best friend; and his uncle's as bad.
LADY SNEERWELL. Nay, but we should make allowance; Sir Benjamin is a wit and a poet.
MARIA. For my part, I own, madam, wit loses its respect with me when I see it in company with malice. What do you think, Mr. Surface?
JOSEPH SURFACE. Certainly, madam. To smile at the jest which plants a thorn in another's breast is to become a principal in the mischief.
LADY SNEERWELL. Psha, there's no possibility of being witty without a little ill nature. The malice of a good thing is the barb that makes it stick. What's your opinion, Mr. Surface?
JOSEPH SURFACE. To be sure, madam, that conversation where the spirit of raillery is suppressed will ever appear tedious and insipid.
MARIA. Well, I'll not debate how far scandal may be allowable; but in a man, I am sure, it is always contemptible. We have pride, envy, rivalship, and a thousand motives to depreciate each other; but the male slanderer must have the cowardice of a woman before he can traduce one.

Enter Servant

SERVANT. Madam, Mrs. Candour is below and, if your ladyship's at leisure, will leave her carriage.
LADY SNEERWELL. Beg her to walk in. (*Exit* Servant) Now, Maria, here is a character to your taste, for though Mrs. Candour is a little talkative, everybody allows her to be the best natured and best sort of woman.
MARIA. Yes, with a very gross affectation of good-nature and benevolence, she does more mischief than the direct malice of old Crabtree.
JOSEPH SURFACE. I' faith that's true, Lady Sneerwell. Whenever I hear the current running against the characters of my friends, I never think them in such danger as when Candour undertakes their defence.
LADY SNEERWELL. Hush!—Here she is.

Enter MRS. CANDOUR

MRS. CANDOUR. My dear Lady Sneerwell, how have you been this century? Mr. Surface, what news do you hear,—though indeed it is no matter, for I think one hears nothing else but scandal.
JOSEPH SURFACE. Just so, indeed, ma'am.
MRS. CANDOUR. Oh, Maria, child! What, is the whole affair off between you and Charles? His extravagance, I presume—the town talks of nothing else.
MARIA. I am very sorry, ma'am, the town is not better employed.
MRS. CANDOUR. True, true, child; but there's no stopping people's tongues. I own I was hurt to hear it, as I indeed was to learn from the same quarter that your guardian, Sir Peter, and Lady Teazle have not agreed lately as well as could be wished.
MARIA. 'Tis strangely impertinent for people to busy themselves so.
MRS. CANDOUR. Very true, child, but what's to be done? People will talk; there's no preventing it. Why, it was but yesterday I was told that Miss Gadabout had eloped with Sir Filigree Flirt. But, Lord, there's no minding what one hears, though, to be sure, I had this from very good authority.
MARIA. Such reports are highly scandalous.
MRS. CANDOUR. So they are, child,— shameful, shameful! But the world is so censorious, no character escapes. Lord, now who would have suspected your friend, Miss Prim, of an indiscretion? Yet such is the ill

nature of people that they say her uncle stopped her last week just as she was stepping into the York diligence with her dancing master.

MARIA. I'll answer for 't there are no grounds for that report.

MRS. CANDOUR. Ah, no foundation in the world, I dare swear; no more probably than for the story circulated last month of Mrs. Festino's affair with Colonel Cassino,— though, to be sure, that matter was never rightly cleared up.

JOSEPH SURFACE. The license of invention some people take is monstrous indeed.

MARIA. 'Tis so; but in my opinion those who report such things are equally culpable.

MRS. CANDOUR. To be sure they are; tale bearers are as bad as the tale makers. 'Tis an old observation and a very true one; but what's to be done, as I said before? How will you prevent people from talking? To-day, Mrs. Clackitt assured me Mr. and Mrs. Honeymoon were at last become mere man and wife like the rest of their acquaintance. She likewise hinted that a certain widow in the next street had got rid of her dropsy and recovered her shape in a most surprising manner. And at the same time Miss Tattle, who was by, affirmed that Lord Buffalo had discovered his lady at a house of no extraordinary fame; and that Sir H[arry] Boquet and Tom Saunter were to measure swords on a similar provocation. But, Lord, do you think I would report these things! No, no! Tale bearers as I said before, are just as bad as the tale makers.

JOSEPH SURFACE. Ah! Mrs. Candour, if everybody had your forbearance and good nature!

MRS. CANDOUR. I confess, Mr. Surface, I cannot bear to hear people attacked behind their backs; and when ugly circumstances come out against our acquaintance, I own I always love to think the best. By the by, I hope 'tis not true that your brother is absolutely ruined.

JOSEPH SURFACE. I am afraid his circumstances are very bad indeed, ma'am.

MRS. CANDOUR. Ah, I heard so; but you must tell him to keep up his spirits. Everybody almost is in the same way. Lord Spindle, Sir Thomas Splint, Captain Quinze, and Mr. Nickit,—all up,[1] I hear, within this week; so, if Charles is undone, he'll find half his acquaintance ruined too; and that, you know, is a consolation.

JOSEPH SURFACE. Doubtless, ma'am, a very great one.

Enter Servant

SERVANT. Mr. Crabtree and Sir Benjamin Backbite. *Exit*

LADY SNEERWELL. So, Maria, you see your lover pursues you. Positively you shan't escape.

Enter CRABTREE and SIR BENJAMIN BACKBITE

CRABTREE. Lady Sneerwell, I kiss your hand. Mrs. Candour, I don't believe you are acquainted with my nephew, Sir Benjamin Backbite? Egad, ma'am, he has a pretty wit and is a pretty poet too, isn't he, Lady Sneerwell?

SIR BENJAMIN. Oh, fie, uncle!

CRABTREE. Nay, egad, it's true; I back him at a rebus or a charade against the best rhymer in the kingdom. Has your ladyship heard the epigram he wrote last week on Lady Frizzle's feather catching fire?—Do, Benjamin, repeat it, or the charade you made last night extempore at Mrs. Drowzie's *conversazione*. Come, now, your first is the name of a fish, your second a great naval commander, and—

SIR BENJAMIN. Uncle, now, prithee—

CRABTREE. I' faith, ma'am, 'twould surprise you to hear how ready he is at all these sort of things.

LADY SNEERWELL. I wonder, Sir Benjamin, you never publish anything.

SIR BENJAMIN. To say truth, ma'am, 'tis very vulgar to print; and, as my little productions are mostly satires and lampoons on particular people, I find they circulate more by giving copies in confidence to the friends of the parties. However, I have some love elegies, which, when favored with this lady's smiles, I mean to give the public.

[*Bowing to MARIA*][2]

CRABTREE. 'Fore heaven, ma'am, they'll immortalize you!—You will be handed down to posterity like Petrarch's Laura or Waller's Sacharissa.[3]

---

[1] I.e., arrested for debt or "sold up."

[2] Clearness seems to demand some stage direction, and the one supplied is appropriate and better than "Pointing," which is found in some editions.

[3] Laura was the heroine of the sonnet cycle of Francesco Petrarca (1304-1374), the first great poet of the Italian Renaissance. Edmund Waller (1606-1687) ad-

SIR BENJAMIN. Yes, madam, I think you will like them when you shall see them on a beautiful quarto page, where a neat rivulet of text shall meander through a meadow of margin. 'Fore gad they will be the most elegant things of their kind!

CRABTREE. But, ladies, that's true—Have you heard the news?

MRS. CANDOUR. What, sir, do you mean the report of—

CRABTREE. No, ma'am, that's not it. Miss Nicely is going to be married to her own footman.

MRS. CANDOUR. Impossible!

CRABTREE. Ask Sir Benjamin.

SIR BENJAMIN. 'Tis very true, ma'am. Everything is fixed and the wedding liveries bespoke.

CRABTREE. Yes; and they do say there were pressing reasons for it.

LADY SNEERWELL. Why, I have heard something of this before.

MRS. CANDOUR. It can't be—And I wonder anyone should believe such a story of so prudent a lady as Miss Nicely.

SIR BENJAMIN. O lud! ma'am, that's the very reason 'twas believed at once. She has always been so cautious and so reserved that everybody was sure there was some reason for it at bottom.

MRS. CANDOUR. Why, to be sure, a tale of scandal is as fatal to the credit of a prudent lady of her stamp as a fever is generally to those of the strongest constitutions. But there is a sort of puny, sickly reputation that is always ailing, yet will outlive the robuster characters of a hundred prudes.

SIR BENJAMIN. True, madam, there are valetudinarians in reputation as well as in constitution, who, being conscious of their weak part, avoid the least breath of air and supply their want of stamina by care and circumspection.

MRS. CANDOUR. Well, but this may be all a mistake. You know, Sir Benjamin, very trifling circumstances often give rise to the most injurious tales.

CRABTREE. That they do, I'll be sworn, ma'am. Did you ever hear how Miss Piper came to lose her lover and her character last summer at Tunbridge? Sir Benjamin, you remember it?

SIR BENJAMIN. Oh, to be sure,—the most whimsical circumstance.

LADY SNEERWELL. How was it, pray?

CRABTREE. Why, one evening at Mrs. Ponto's assembly the conversation happened to turn on the breeding of Nova Scotia sheep in this country. Says a young lady in company, " I have known instances of it, for Miss Letitia Piper, a first cousin of mine, had a Nova Scotia sheep that produced her twins." "What," cries the Lady Dowager Dundizzy, who, you know, is as deaf as a post, "has Miss Piper had twins?" This mistake, as you may imagine, threw the whole company into a fit of laughter. However, 'twas next morning everywhere reported, and in a few days believed by the whole town, that Miss Letitia Piper had actually been brought to bed of a fine boy and a girl; and in less than a week there were some people who could name the father and the farm-house where the babies were put to nurse.

LADY SNEERWELL. Strange, indeed!

CRABTREE. Matter of fact, I assure you.— O lud, Mr. Surface, pray is it true that your uncle, Sir Oliver, is coming home?

JOSEPH SURFACE. Not that I know of, indeed, sir.

CRABTREE. He has been in the East Indies a long time. You can scarcely remember him, I believe? Sad comfort, whenever he returns, to hear how your brother has gone on.

JOSEPH SURFACE. Charles has been imprudent, sir, to be sure; but I hope no busy people have already prejudiced Sir Oliver against him. He may reform.

SIR BENJAMIN. To be sure, he may. For my part, I never believed him to be so utterly void of principle as people say; and, though he has lost all his friends, I am told nobody is better spoken of by the Jews.

CRABTREE. That's true, egad, nephew. If the Old Jewry was a ward, I believe Charles would be an alderman. No man is more popular there, 'fore gad! I hear he pays as many annuities as the Irish tontine;[1] and that whenever he is sick, they have prayers

dressed poems to Lady Dorothy Sidney under the name of "Sacharissa."

[1] The tontines in Great Britain of the years 1773, 1775, 1777, arranged by act of the Irish parliament, were government loans negotiated by the process of selling annuities to subscribers at whose deaths the capital became the property of the government. The system was invented by an Italian banker, Lorenzo Tonti, in the seventeenth century.

for the recovery of his health in all the synagogues.

SIR BENJAMIN. Yet no man lives in greater splendor. They tell me that when he entertains his friends he will sit down to dinner with a dozen of his own securities, have a score of tradesmen waiting in the antechamber, and an officer behind every guest's chair.

JOSEPH SURFACE. This may be entertaining to you, gentlemen, but you pay very little regard to the feelings of a brother.

MARIA. (*Aside*) Their malice is intolerable! —Lady Sneerwell, I must wish you a good morning; I'm not very well. *Exit*

MRS. CANDOUR. O dear, she changes color very much!

LADY SNEERWELL. Do, Mrs. Candour, follow her. She may want assistance.

MRS. CANDOUR. That I will, with all my soul, ma'am. Poor dear girl, who knows what her situation may be! *Exit*

LADY SNEERWELL. 'Twas nothing but that she could not bear to hear Charles reflected on, notwithstanding their difference.

SIR BENJAMIN. The young lady's *penchant* is obvious.

CRABTREE. But, Benjamin, you must not give up the pursuit for that. Follow her and put her into good humor. Repeat her some of your own verses. Come, I'll assist you.

SIR BENJAMIN. Mr. Surface, I did not mean to hurt you; but depend on 't your brother is utterly undone.

CRABTREE. O lud, ay! Undone as ever man was! Can't raise a guinea!

SIR BENJAMIN. And everything sold, I'm told, that was moveable.

CRABTREE. I have seen one that was at his house. Not a thing left but some empty bottles that were overlooked and the family pictures, which I believe are framed in the wainscots.

SIR BENJAMIN. And I'm very sorry also to hear some bad stories against him. (*Going*)

CRABTREE. Oh, he has done many mean things, that's certain.

SIR BENJAMIN. But, however, as he's your brother— (*Going*)

CRABTREE. We'll tell you all another opportunity.

Exeunt CRABTREE *and* SIR BENJAMIN

LADY SNEERWELL. Ha! ha! 'tis very hard for them to leave a subject they have not quite run down.

JOSEPH SURFACE. And I believe the abuse was no more acceptable to your ladyship than Maria.

LADY SNEERWELL. I doubt her affections are farther engaged than we imagine. But the family are to be here this evening; so you may as well dine where you are and we shall have an opportunity of observing farther. In the meantime, I'll go and plot mischief and you shall study sentiment. *Exeunt*

SCENE II. SIR PETER'S *House*

Enter SIR PETER

SIR PETER. When an old bachelor marries a young wife, what is he to expect? 'Tis now six months since Lady Teazle made me the happiest of men,—and I have been the most miserable dog ever since! We tiffed a little going to church and fairly quarreled before the bells had done ringing. I was more than once nearly choked with gall during the honeymoon and had lost all comfort in life before my friends had done wishing me joy. Yet I chose with caution,—a girl bred wholly in the country, who never knew luxury beyond one silk gown nor dissipation above the annual gala of a race ball. Yet she now plays her part in the extravagant fopperies of the fashion and the town with as ready a grace as if she never had seen a bush or a grass-plot out of Grosvenor Square. I am sneered at by all my acquaintance and paragraphed in the newspapers. She dissipates my fortune and contradicts all my humors; yet the worst of it is, I doubt[1] I love her, or I should never bear all this. However, I'll never be weak enough to own it.

Enter ROWLEY

ROWLEY. Oh, Sir Peter, your servant! How is it with you, sir?

SIR PETER. Very bad, Master Rowley, very bad. I meet with nothing but crosses and vexations.

ROWLEY. What can have happened to trouble you since yesterday?

SIR PETER. A good question to a married man!

ROWLEY. Nay, I'm sure your lady, Sir Peter, can't be the cause of your uneasiness.

SIR PETER. Why, has anybody told you she was dead?

ROWLEY. Come, come, Sir Peter, you love

[1] Doubt not, believe.

her, notwithstanding your tempers don't exactly agree.

SIR PETER. But the fault is entirely hers, Master Rowley. I am myself the sweetest tempered man alive and hate a teasing temper; and so I tell her a hundred times a day.

ROWLEY. Indeed!

SIR PETER. Ay; and what is very extraordinary in all our disputes she is always in the wrong. But Lady Sneerwell and the set she meets at her house encourage the perverseness of her disposition. Then, to complete my vexation, Maria, my ward, whom I ought to have the power over, is determined to turn rebel too and absolutely refuses the man whom I have long resolved on for her husband, meaning, I suppose, to bestow herself on his profligate brother.

ROWLEY. You know, Sir Peter, I have always taken the liberty to differ with you on the subject of these two young gentlemen. I only wish you may not be deceived in your opinion of the elder. For Charles, my life on 't, he will retrieve his errors yet. Their worthy father, once my honored master, was at his years nearly as wild a spark; yet when he died, he did not leave a more benevolent heart to lament his loss.

SIR PETER. You are wrong, Master Rowley. On their father's death, you know, I acted as a kind of guardian to them both till their uncle Sir Oliver's liberality gave them an early independence. Of course, no person could have more opportunities of judging of their hearts, and I was never mistaken in my life. Joseph is indeed a model for the young men of the age. He is a man of sentiment and acts up to the sentiments he professes; but for the other, take my word for 't, if he had any grain of virtue by descent, he has dissipated it with the rest of his inheritance. Ah! my old friend Sir Oliver will be deeply mortified when he finds how part of his bounty has been misapplied.

ROWLEY. I am sorry to find you so violent against the young man, because this may be the most critical period of his fortune. I came hither with news that will surprise you.

SIR PETER. What? Let me hear!

ROWLEY. Sir Oliver is arrived and at this moment in town.

SIR PETER. How! You astonish me! I thought you did not expect him this month.

ROWLEY. I did not; but his passage has been remarkably quick.

SIR PETER. Egad, I shall rejoice to see my old friend. 'Tis fifteen years since we met. We have had many a day together. But does he still enjoin us not to inform his nephews of his arrival?

ROWLEY. Most strictly. He means, before it is known, to make some trial of their dispositions.

SIR PETER. Ah! There needs no art to discover their merits. He shall have his way; but, pray, does he know I am married?

ROWLEY. Yes, and will soon wish you joy.

SIR PETER. What, as we drink health to a friend in a consumption? Ah! Oliver will laugh at me. We used to rail at matrimony together, and he has been steady to his text. Well, he must be soon at my house, though— I'll instantly give orders for his reception. But, Master Rowley, don't drop a word that Lady Teazle and I ever disagree.

ROWLEY. By no means.

SIR PETER. For I should never be able to stand Noll's jokes; so I'll have him think, Lord forgive me! that we are a very happy couple.

ROWLEY. I understand you; but then you must be very careful not to differ while he is in the house with you.

SIR PETER. Egad, and so we must,—and that's impossible. Ah! Master Rowley, when an old bachelor marries a young wife, he deserves—No, the crime carries its punishment along with it. *Exeunt*

ACT II

SCENE I. SIR PETER'S *House*

Enter SIR PETER *and* LADY TEAZLE

SIR PETER. Lady Teazle, Lady Teazle, I'll not bear it!

LADY TEAZLE. Sir Peter, Sir Peter, you may bear it or not as you please; but I ought to have my own way in everything, and, what's more, I will, too. What though I was educated in the country, I know very well that women of fashion in London are accountable to nobody after they are married.

SIR PETER. Very well, ma'am, very well; so a husband is to have no influence, no authority?

LADY TEAZLE. Authority! No, to be sure!

If you wanted authority over me, you should have adopted me and not married me. I am sure you were old enough.

SIR PETER. Old enough! Ay, there it is. Well, well, Lady Teazle, though my life may be made unhappy by your temper, I'll not be ruined by your extravagance.

LADY TEAZLE. My extravagance! I'm sure I'm not more extravagant then a woman of fashion ought to be.

SIR PETER. No, no, madam, you shall throw away no more sums on such unmeaning luxury. 'Slife! to spend as much to furnish your dressing-room with flowers in winter as would suffice to turn the Pantheon[1] into a greenhouse a..d give a *fête champêtre*[2] at Christmas.

LADY TEAZLE. And am I now to blame, Sir Peter, because flowers are dear in cold weather? You should find fault with the climate, and not with me. For my part, I'm sure I wish it was spring all the year round and that roses grew under our feet!

SIR PETER. Oons, madam! If you had been born to this, I shouldn't wonder at your talking thus; but you forget what your situation was when I married you.

LADY TEAZLE. No, no, I don't. 'Twas a very disagreeable one, or I should never have married you.

SIR PETER. Yes, yes, madam, you were then in somewhat a humbler style,—the daughter of a plain country squire. Recollect, Lady Teazle, when I saw you first, sitting at your tambour[3] in a pretty figured linen gown with a bunch of keys at your side, your hair combed smooth over a roll and your apartment hung round with fruits in worsted of your own working.

LADY TEAZLE. Oh, yes! I remember it very well, and a curious life I led. My daily occupation to inspect the dairy, superintend the poultry, make extracts from the family receipt-book, and comb my Aunt Deborah's lap-dog.

SIR PETER. Yes, yes, ma'am, 'twas so indeed.

LADY TEAZLE. And then you know, my evening amusements! To draw patterns for ruffles, which I had not materials to make up; to play Pope Joan[4] with the curate; to read a sermon to my aunt; or to be stuck down to an old spinet to strum my father to sleep after a fox-chase.

SIR PETER. I am glad you have so good a memory. Yes, madam, these were the recreations I took you from; but now you must have your coach,—*vis-à-vis*,[5]—and three powdered footmen before your chair, and in the summer a pair of white cats[6] to draw you to Kensington Gardens. No recollection, I suppose, when you were content to ride double behind the butler on a docked coach-horse.

LADY TEAZLE. No—I swear I never did that. I deny the butler and the coach-horse.

SIR PETER. This, madam, was your situation; and what have I done for you? I have made you a woman of fashion, of fortune, of rank,—in short, I have made you my wife.

LADY TEAZLE. Well, then, and there is but one thing more you can make me to add to the obligation, that is—

SIR PETER. My widow, I suppose?

LADY TEAZLE. Hem! hem!

SIR PETER. I thank you, madam; but don't flatter yourself; for, though your ill conduct may disturb my peace, it shall never break my heart, I promise you. However, I am equally obliged to you for the hint.

LADY TEAZLE. Then why will you endeavor to make yourself so disagreeable to me and thwart me in every little elegant expense?

SIR PETER. 'Slife, madam, I say; had you any of these little elegant expenses when you married me?

LADY TEAZLE. Lud, Sir Peter, would you have me be out of the fashion?

SIR PETER. The fashion, indeed! What had you to do with the fashion before you married me?

LADY TEAZLE. For my part, I should think you would like to have your wife thought a woman of taste.

SIR PETER. Ay! There again! Taste! Zounds, madam, you had no taste when you married me!

LADY TEAZLE. That's very true, indeed, Sir Peter; and, having married you, I should never pretend to taste again, I allow. But now, Sir Peter, since we have finished our

---

[1] A concert hall, with tea-rooms, etc., in Oxford Street, opened in 1770 and a favorite resort of the fashionable world at this time; cf. Fanny Burney's *Evelina*.
[2] Outdoor entertainment
[3] Embroidery frame.
[4] An old game of cards, not fashionable at this time.
[5] An elegant coach in which the occupants, usually four in number, faced each other.
[6] Ponies.

daily jangle, I presume I may go to my engagement at Lady Sneerwell's.

SIR PETER. Ay, there's another precious circumstance! A charming set of acquaintance you have made there!

LADY TEAZLE. Nay, Sir Peter, they are all people of rank and fortune and remarkably tenacious of reputation.

SIR PETER. Yes, egad, they are tenacious of reputation with a vengeance, for they don't choose anybody should have a character but themselves! Such a crew! Ah, many a wretch has rid on a hurdle[1] who has done less mischief than these utterers of forged tales, coiners of scandal, and clippers of reputation.

LADY TEAZLE. What, would you restrain the freedom of speech!

SIR PETER. Ah! they have made you just as bad as any one of the society.

LADY TEAZLE. Why, I believe I do bear a part with a tolerable grace. But I vow I bear no malice against the people I abuse. When I say an ill-natured thing, 'tis out of pure good humor; and I take it for granted they deal exactly in the same manner with me. But, Sir Peter, you know you promised to come to Lady Sneerwell's, too.

SIR PETER. Well, well, I'll call in just to look after my own character.

LADY TEAZLE. Then, indeed, you must make haste after me, or you'll be too late. So good by to ye! *Exit*

SIR PETER. So I have gained much by my intended expostulation! Yet with what a charming air she contradicts everything I say, and how pleasantly she shows her contempt for my authority! Well, though I can't make her love me, there is great satisfaction in quarreling with her; and I think she never appears to such advantage as when she is doing everything in her power to plague me.
Exit

SCENE II. *At* LADY SNEERWELL'S

Enter LADY SNEERWELL, MRS. CANDOUR, CRABTREE, SIR BENJAMIN BACKBITE, *and* JOSEPH SURFACE

LADY SNEERWELL. Nay, positively, we will hear it.

JOSEPH SURFACE. Yes, yes, the epigram, by all means.

[1] Rail.

SIR BENJAMIN. O plague on it, uncle! 'Tis mere nonsense.

CRABTREE. No, no! 'Fore gad, very clever for an extempore!

SIR BENJAMIN. But, ladies, you should be acquainted with the circumstance. You must know that one day last week as Lady Betty Curricle was taking the dust in Hyde Park in a sort of duodecimo phaëton, she desired me to write some verses on her ponies, upon which I took out my pocketbook and in one moment produced the following:—

Sure never were seen two such beautiful ponies;
Other horses are clowns, but these macaronies.
To give them this title I'm sure can't be wrong,
Their legs are so slim and their tails are so long.

CRABTREE. There, ladies, done in the smack of a whip and on horseback too!

JOSEPH SURFACE. A very Phœbus mounted! Indeed, Sir Benjamin!

SIR BENJAMIN. Oh, dear sir! Trifles, trifles.

Enter LADY TEAZLE *and* MARIA

MRS. CANDOUR. I must have a copy.

LADY SNEERWELL. Lady Teazle, I hope we shall see Sir Peter?

LADY TEAZLE. I believe he'll wait on your ladyship presently.

LADY SNEERWELL. Maria, my love, you look grave. Come, you shall sit down to piquet with Mr. Surface.

MARIA. I take very little pleasure in cards; however I'll do as you please.

LADY TEAZLE. (*Aside*) I am surprised Mr. Surface should sit down with her; I thought he would have embraced this opportunity of speaking to me before Sir Peter came.

MRS. CANDOUR. Now, I'll die; but you are so scandalous I'll forswear your society.

LADY TEAZLE. What's the matter, Mrs. Candour?

MRS. CANDOUR. They'll not allow our friend Miss Vermilion to be handsome.

LADY SNEERWELL. Oh, surely she is a pretty woman.

CRABTREE. I am very glad you think so, ma'am.

MRS. CANDOUR. She has a charming, fresh color.

LADY TEAZLE. Yes, when it is fresh put on.

MRS. CANDOUR. Oh, fie! I'll swear her color is natural. I have seen it come and go.

LADY TEAZLE. I dare swear you have.

ma'am; it goes off at night and comes again in the morning.

SIR BENJAMIN. True, ma'am, it not only comes and goes; but what's more, egad, her maid can fetch and carry it!

MRS. CANDOUR. Ha, ha, ha! How I hate to hear you talk so! But surely, now, her sister is, or was, very handsome.

CRABTREE. Who? Mrs. Evergreen? O Lord! She's six-and-fifty if she's an hour!

MRS. CANDOUR. Now positively you wrong her; fifty-two or fifty-three in the utmost,— and I don't think she looks more.

SIR BENJAMIN. Ah! There's no judging by her looks unless one could see her face.

LADY SNEERWELL. Well, well, if Mrs. Evergreen does take some pains to repair the ravages of time, you must allow she effects it with great ingenuity; and surely that's better than the careless manner in which the widow Ochre chalks her wrinkles.

SIR BENJAMIN. Nay, now, Lady Sneerwell, you are severe upon the widow. Come, come, 'tis not that she paints so ill; but, when she has finished her face, she joins it so badly to her neck that she looks like a mended statue in which the connoisseur may see at once that the head's modern though the trunk's antique.

CRABTREE. Ha! ha! ha! Well said, nephew!

MRS. CANDOUR. Ha! ha! ha! Well, you make me laugh; but I vow I hate you for it. What do you think of Miss Simper?

SIR BENJAMIN. Why, she has very pretty teeth.

LADY TEAZLE. Yes; and on that account, when she is neither speaking nor laughing, which very seldom happens, she never absolutely shuts her mouth, but leaves it always on a-jar, as it were; thus—

(Shows her teeth)

MRS. CANDOUR. How can you be so ill natured?

LADY TEAZLE. Nay, I allow even that's better than the pains Mrs. Prim takes to conceal her losses in front. She draws her mouth till it positively resembles the aperture of a poor's-box,[1] and all her words appear to slide out edgewise, as it were; thus: *How do you do, madam? Yes, madam.*

LADY SNEERWELL. Very well, Lady Teazle. I see you can be a little severe.

LADY TEAZLE. In defence of a friend it is but justice. But here comes Sir Peter to spoil our pleasantry.

Enter SIR PETER

SIR PETER. Ladies, your most obedient.— *(Aside)* Mercy on me, here is the whole set! A character dead at every word, I suppose.

MRS. CANDOUR. I am rejoiced you are come, Sir Peter. They have been so censorious, and Lady Teazle as bad as any one.

SIR PETER. That must be very distressing to you, Mrs. Candour, I dare swear.

MRS. CANDOUR. Oh, they will allow good qualities to nobody, not even good nature to our friend Mrs. Pursy.

LADY TEAZLE. What, the fat dowager who was at Mrs. Quadrille's last night?

MRS. CANDOUR. Nay, her bulk is her misfortune; and, when she takes so much pains to get rid of it, you ought not to reflect on her.

LADY SNEERWELL. That's very true, indeed.

LADY TEAZLE. Yes, I know she almost lives on acids and small whey; laces herself by pulleys; and often in the hottest noon in summer you may see her on a little squat pony, with her hair plaited up behind like a drummer's and puffing round the Ring [2] on a full trot.

MRS. CANDOUR. I thank you, Lady Teazle, for defending her.

SIR PETER. Yes, a good defence, truly.

MRS. CANDOUR. Truly, Lady Teazle is as censorious as Miss Sallow.

CRABTREE. Yes, and she is a curious being to pretend to be censorious, an awkward gawky without any one good point under heaven.

MRS. CANDOUR. Positively you shall not be so very severe. Miss Sallow is a near relation of mine by marriage, and, as for her person, great allowance is to be made; for, let me tell you, a woman labors under many disadvantages who tries to pass for a girl of six-and-thirty.

LADY SNEERWELL. Though, surely, she is handsome still; and for the weakness in her eyes, considering how much she reads by candlelight, it is not to be wondered at.

MRS. CANDOUR. True, and then as to her manner; upon my word, I think it is particularly graceful, considering she never had the least education; for you know her mother was

---

[1] A box with a slit in the top placed in the vestibule of a church to receive offerings for charity.

[2] The fashionable drive in Hyde Park.

a Welsh milliner and her father a sugar-baker at Bristol.

SIR BENJAMIN. Ah! you are both of you too good natured!

SIR PETER. (*Aside*) Yes, damned good natured! This their own relation! Mercy on me!

MRS. CANDOUR. For my part, I own I cannot bear to hear a friend ill spoken of.

SIR PETER. No, to be sure!

SIR BENJAMIN. Oh, you are of a moral turn. Mrs. Candour and I can sit for an hour and hear Lady Stucco talk sentiment.

LADY TEAZLE. Nay, I vow Lady Stucco is very well with the dessert after dinner, for she's just like the French fruit[1] one cracks for mottoes, made up of paint and proverb.

MRS. CANDOUR. Well, I never will join in ridiculing a friend; and so I constantly tell my cousin Ogle, and you all know what pretensions she has to be critical on beauty.

CRABTREE. Oh, to be sure, she has herself the oddest countenance that ever was seen; 'tis a collection of features from all the different countries of the globe.

SIR BENJAMIN. So she has, indeed! An Irish front—

CRABTREE. Caledonian locks—

SIR BENJAMIN. Dutch nose—

CRABTREE. Austrian lips—

SIR BENJAMIN. Complexion of a Spaniard—

CRABTREE. And teeth *à la Chinoise*—

SIR BENJAMIN. In short, her face resembles a *table d'hôte* at Spa,—where no two guests are of a nation—

CRABTREE. Or a congress at the close of a general war,—wherein all the members, even to her eyes, appear to have a different interest, and her nose and chin are the only parties likely to join issue.

MRS. CANDOUR. Ha! ha! ha!

SIR PETER. (*Aside*) Mercy on my life! A person they dine with twice a week!

LADY SNEERWELL. Go, go! You are a couple of provoking toads.

MRS. CANDOUR. Nay, but I vow you shall not carry the laugh off so, for give me leave to say that Mrs. Ogle—

SIR PETER. Madam, madam, I beg your pardon. There's no stopping these good gentlemen's tongues. But when I tell you, Mrs. Candour, that the lady they are abusing is a particular friend of mine, I hope you'll not take her part.

LADY SNEERWELL. Ha! ha! ha! Well said, Sir Peter! But you are a cruel creature,—too phlegmatic yourself for a jest, and too peevish to allow wit in others.

SIR PETER. Ah, madam, true wit is more nearly allied to good nature than your ladyship is aware of.

LADY TEAZLE. True, Sir Peter. I believe they are so near akin that they can never be united.

SIR BENJAMIN. Or rather, madam, suppose them to be man and wife because one seldom sees them together.

LADY TEAZLE. But Sir Peter is such an enemy to scandal I believe he would have it put down by parliament.

SIR PETER. 'Fore heaven, madam, if they were to consider the sporting with reputation of as much importance as poaching on manors and pass an act for the preservation of fame,[2] I believe I would thank them for the bill.

LADY SNEERWELL. O lud, Sir Peter, would you deprive us of our privileges?

SIR PETER. Ay, madam; and then no person should be permitted to kill characters and run down reputations but qualified old maids and disappointed widows.

LADY SNEERWELL. Go, you monster!

MRS. CANDOUR. But, surely, you would not be quite so severe on those who only report what they hear!

SIR PETER. Yes, madam, I would have law merchant[3] for them, too; and in all cases of slander currency, whenever the drawer of the lie was not to be found, the injured parties should have a right to come on any of the indorsers.

CRABTREE. Well, for my part, I believe there never was a scandalous tale without some foundation.

SIR PETER. O, nine out of ten of the malicious inventions are founded on some ridiculous misrepresentation.

LADY SNEERWELL. Come, ladies, shall we sit down to cards in the next room?

Enter Servant, *who whispers* SIR PETER

SIR PETER. (*To* Servant) I'll be with them

---

[1] Artificial fruits containing sentiments on slips of paper, like the "crackers" of a later age

[2] In some editions Sir Peter's meaning is made clear by the addition of "as well as game."

[3] Mercantile law, which makes indorsers liable for debts if the principals fail to pay.

directly. (*Exit* Servant. *Aside*) I'll get away unperceived.

LADY SNEERWELL. Sir Peter, you are not going to leave us?

SIR PETER. Your ladyship must excuse me; I'm called away by particular business. But I leave my character behind me.   *Exit*

SIR BENJAMIN. Well—certainly, Lady Teazle, that lord of yours is a strange being. I could tell you some stories of him would make you laugh heartily if he were not your husband.

LADY TEAZLE. Oh, pray don't mind that; come, do let's hear them.

(*Joins the rest of the company going into the next room,* [*who*] *exeunt, except* JOSEPH SURFACE *and* MARIA

JOSEPH SURFACE. Maria, I see you have no satisfaction in this society.

MARIA. How is it possible I should? If to raise malicious smiles at the infirmities or misfortunes of those who have never injured us be the province of wit or humor, Heaven grant me a double portion of dulness!

JOSEPH SURFACE. Yet they appear more ill-natured than they are; they have no malice at heart.

MARIA. Then is their conduct still more contemptible; for, in my opinion, nothing could excuse the [intemperance][1] of their tongues but a natural and uncontrollable bitterness of mind.

JOSEPH SURFACE. Undoubtedly, madam; and it has always been a sentiment of mine that to propagate a malicious truth wantonly is more despicable than to falsify from revenge. But can you, Maria, feel thus for others and be unkind to me alone? Is hope to be denied the tenderest passion?

MARIA. Why will you distress me by renewing this subject?

JOSEPH SURFACE. Ah, Maria, you would not treat me thus and oppose your guardian, Sir Peter's will, but that I see that profligate Charles is still a favored rival.

MARIA. Ungenerously urged! But whatever my sentiments are for that unfortunate young man, be assured I shall not feel more bound to give him up because his distresses have lost him the regard even of a brother.

JOSEPH SURFACE. Nay, but, Maria, do not leave me with a frown. By all that's honest I swear—(*Kneels. Enter* LADY TEAZLE, *Aside*) Gad's life, here's Lady Teazle.—You must not—no, you shall not—for though I have the greatest regard for Lady Teazle—

MARIA. Lady Teazle!

JOSEPH SURFACE. Yet were Sir Peter to suspect—

LADY TEAZLE *comes forward*

LADY TEAZLE. [*Aside*] What is this, pray? Does he take her for me?—Child, you are wanted in the next room. (*Exit* MARIA) What is all this, pray?

JOSEPH SURFACE. Oh, the most unlucky circumstance in nature! Maria has somehow suspected the tender concern I have for your happiness and threatened to acquaint Sir Peter with her suspicions, and I was just endeavoring to reason with her when you came in.

LADY TEAZLE. Indeed! but you seemed to adopt a very tender mode of reasoning. Do you usually argue on your knees?

JOSEPH SURFACE. Oh, she's a child and I thought a little bombast—But, Lady Teazle, when are you to give me your judgment on my library, as you promised?

LADY TEAZLE. No, no; I begin to think it would be imprudent, and you know I admit you as a lover no farther than fashion sanctions.

JOSEPH SURFACE. True—a mere Platonic *cicisbeo*,[2]—what every wife is entitled to.

LADY TEAZLE. Certainly, one must not be out of the fashion. However, I have so many of my country prejudices left that, though Sir Peter's ill humor may vex me ever so, it shall never provoke me to—

JOSEPH SURFACE. The only revenge in your power. Well, I applaud your moderation.

LADY TEAZLE. Go! You are an insinuating wretch! But we shall be missed. Let us join the company.

JOSEPH SURFACE. But we had best not return together.

LADY TEAZLE. Well, don't stay, for Maria shan't come to hear any more of your reasoning, I promise you.   *Exit*

JOSEPH SURFACE. A curious dilemma my politics have run me into! I wanted at first only to ingratiate myself with Lady Teazle that she might not be my enemy with Maria;

---

[1] Murray's edition has *interference*, which makes doubtful sense. *Intemperance* is the reading in Rhodes.

[2] An Italian word meaning *gallant*, more specifically the lover of a married woman.

and I have, I don't know how, become her serious lover. Sincerely I begin to wish I had never made such a point of gaining so very good a character, for it has led me into so many cursed rogueries that I doubt I shall be exposed at last.   *Exit*

Scene iii. Sir Peter Teazle's [*house*]

Enter Rowley *and* Sir Oliver Surface

Sir Oliver. Ha! ha! ha! so my old friend is married, hey? A young wife from the country! Ha! ha! ha! that he should have stood bluff [1] to old bachelor so long and sink into a husband at last!

Rowley. But you must not rally him on the subject, Sir Oliver; 'tis a tender point, I assure you, though he has been married only seven months.

Sir Oliver. Then he has been just half a year on the stool of repentance! Poor Peter! But you say he has entirely given up Charles—never sees him, hey?

Rowley. His prejudice against him is astonishing, and I am sure greatly increased by a jealousy of him with Lady Teazle, which he has industriously been led into by a scandalous society in the neighborhood who have contributed not a little to Charles's ill name. Whereas the truth is, I believe, if the lady is partial to either of them, his brother is the favorite.

Sir Oliver. Ay, I know there are a set of malicious, prating, prudent gossips, both male and female, who murder characters to kill time and will rob a young fellow of his good name before he has years to know the value of it. But I am not to be prejudiced against my nephew by such, I promise you. No, no; if Charles has done nothing false or mean, I shall compound for his extravagance.

Rowley. Then, my life on 't, you will reclaim him. Ah, sir, it gives me new life to find that your heart is not turned against him and that the son of my good old master has one friend, however, left.

Sir Oliver. What! Shall I forget, Master Rowley, when I was at his years myself? Egad, my brother and I were neither of us very prudent youths; and yet I believe you have not seen many better men than your old master was?

[1] Firm.

Rowley. Sir, 'tis this reflection gives me assurance that Charles may yet be a credit to his family. But here comes Sir Peter.

Sir Oliver. Egad, so he does. Mercy on me, he's greatly altered and seems to have a settled, married look! One may read *husband* in his face at this distance.

Enter Sir Peter

Sir Peter. Ha! Sir Oliver, my old friend! Welcome to England a thousand times!

Sir Oliver. Thank you, thank you, Sir Peter! And i' faith I am glad to find you well, believe me!

Sir Peter. Oh, 'tis a long time since we met,—fifteen years, I doubt, Sir Oliver, and many a cross accident in the time.

Sir Oliver. Ay, I have had my share. But, what! I find you are married, hey? Well, well, it can't be helped; and so—I wish you joy with all my heart!

Sir Peter. Thank you, thank you, Sir Oliver. Yes, I have entered into—the happy state; but we'll not talk of that now.

Sir Oliver. True, true, Sir Peter. Old friends should not begin on grievances at first meeting. No, no, no.

Rowley. [*Aside to* Sir Oliver] Take care, pray, sir.

Sir Oliver. Well, so one of my nephews is a wild fellow, hey?

Sir Peter. Wild! Ah, my old friend, I grieve for your disappointment there. He's a lost young man, indeed. However, his brother will make you amends; Joseph is, indeed, what a youth should be,—everybody in the world speaks well of him.

Sir Oliver. I am sorry to hear it; he has too good a character to be an honest fellow. "Everybody speaks well of him!" Psha! then he has bowed as low to knaves and fools as to the honest dignity of genius and virtue.

Sir Peter. What, Sir Oliver! Do you blame him for not making enemies?

Sir Oliver. Yes, if he has merit enough to deserve them.

Sir Peter. Well, well,—you'll be convinced when you know him. 'Tis edification to hear him converse; he professes the noblest sentiments.

Sir Oliver. Oh, plague of his sentiments! If he salutes me with a scrap of morality in his mouth, I shall be sick directly. But, however, don't mistake me, Sir Peter; I don't mean to defend Charles's errors; but before I form my judgment of either of them, I intend to make a trial of their hearts; and my old friend Rowley and I have planned something for the purpose.

ROWLEY. And Sir Peter shall own for once he has been mistaken.

SIR PETER. Oh, my life on Joseph's honor!

SIR OLIVER. Well, come, give us a bottle of good wine, and we'll drink the lads' health and tell you our scheme.

SIR PETER. *Allons,* then!

SIR OLIVER. And don't, Sir Peter, be so severe against your old friend's son. Odds, my life! I am not sorry that he has run out of the course a little. For my part, I hate to see prudence clinging to the green suckers of youth; 'tis like ivy round a sapling and spoils the growth of the tree. *Exeunt*

ACT III

SCENE I. SIR PETER TEAZLE'S *house*

Enter SIR PETER TEAZLE, SIR OLIVER SURFACE, *and* ROWLEY

SIR PETER. Well, then, we will see this fellow first and have our wine afterwards. But how is this, Master Rowley? I don't see the jet [1] of your scheme.

ROWLEY. Why, sir, this Mr. Stanley, [whom] [2] I was speaking of, is nearly related to them by their mother. He was once a merchant in Dublin but has been ruined by a series of undeserved misfortunes. He has applied by letter to both Mr. Surface and Charles. From the former he has received nothing but evasive promises of future service, while Charles has done all that his extravagance has left him power to do; and he is at this time endeavoring to raise a sum of money, part of which, in the midst of his own distresses, I know he intends for the service of poor Stanley.

SIR OLIVER. Ah! he is my brother's son.

SIR PETER. Well, but how is Sir Oliver personally to—

ROWLEY. Why, sir, I will inform Charles and his brother that Stanley has obtained permission to apply personally to his friends; and, as they have neither of them ever seen him, let Sir Oliver assume his character and he will have a fair opportunity of judging at least of the benevolence of their dispositions. And, believe me, sir, you will find in the youngest brother one who, in the midst of folly and dissipation, has still, as our immortal bard expresses it,—

a heart to pity and a hand,
Open as day for melting charity.[3]

SIR PETER. Psha! What signifies his having an open hand or purse either when he has nothing left to give? Well, well, make the trial, if you please. But where is the fellow whom you brought for Sir Oliver to examine relative to Charles's affairs?

ROWLEY. Below, waiting his commands, and no one can give him better intelligence. This, Sir Oliver, is a friendly Jew, who, to do him justice, has done everything in his power to bring your nephew to a proper sense of his extravagance.

SIR PETER. Pray, let us have him in.

ROWLEY. (*Apart to* Servant) Desire Mr. Moses to walk upstairs.

SIR PETER. But, pray, why should you suppose he will speak the truth?

ROWLEY. Oh, I have convinced him that he has no chance of recovering certain sums advanced to Charles but through the bounty of Sir Oliver, who, he knows, has arrived, so that you may depend on his fidelity to his own interests. I have also another evidence in my power, one Snake, whom I have detected in a matter little short of forgery and shall speedily produce him to remove some of your prejudices.

SIR PETER. I have heard too much on that subject.

ROWLEY. Here comes the honest Israelite. (*Enter* MOSES) This is Sir Oliver.

SIR OLIVER. Sir, I understand you have lately had great dealings with my nephew Charles.

MOSES. Yes, Sir Oliver, I have done all I could for him; but he was ruined before he came to me for assistance.

SIR OLIVER. That was unlucky, truly, for you have had no opportunity of showing your talents.

MOSES. None at all. I hadn't the pleasure

---

[1] Point.
[2] Murray's edition has *who,* but the grammar has been corrected in various early editions.
[3] *2nd Henry IV,* IV, iv, 31–32. The correct line, given in some early editions but not in others, is "a tear for pity, . . ."

of knowing his distresses till he was some thousands worse than nothing.

SIR OLIVER. Unfortunate, indeed! But I suppose you have done all in your power for him, honest Moses?

MOSES. Yes, he knows that. This very evening I was to have brought him a gentleman from the city who does not know him and will, I believe, advance him some money.

SIR PETER. What, one Charles has never had money from before!

MOSES. Yes. Mr. Premium, of Crutched Friars, formerly a broker.

SIR PETER. Egad, Sir Oliver, a thought strikes me! Charles, you say, does not know Mr. Premium?

MOSES. Not at all.

SIR PETER. Now then, Sir Oliver, you may have a better opportunity of satisfying yourself than by an old, romancing tale of a poor relation. Go with my friend Moses and represent Premium, and then, I'll answer for it, you'll see your nephew in all his glory.

SIR OLIVER. Egad, I like this idea better than the other, and I may visit Joseph afterwards as old Stanley.

SIR PETER. True,—so you may.

ROWLEY. Well, this is taking Charles rather at a disadvantage, to be sure. However, Moses, you understand Sir Peter and will be faithful?

MOSES. You may depend upon me. This is near the time I was to have gone.

SIR OLIVER. I'll accompany you as soon as you please, Moses. But hold! I have forgot one thing,—how the plague shall I be able to pass for a Jew?

MOSES. There's no need. The principal is Christian.

SIR OLIVER. Is he? I'm very sorry to hear it; but then, again, an't I rather too smartly dressed to look like a money-lender?

SIR PETER. Not at all; 'twould not be out of character, if you went in your own carriage, would it, Moses?

MOSES. Not in the least.

SIR OLIVER. Well, but how must I talk? There's certainly some cant of usury and mode of treating that I ought to know.

SIR PETER. Oh, there's not much to learn. The great point, as I take it, is to be exorbitant enough in your demands. Hey, Moses?

MOSES. Yes, that's a very great point.

SIR OLIVER. I'll answer for 't I'll not be wanting in that. I'll ask him eight or ten per cent. on the loan at least.

MOSES. If you ask him no more than that, you'll be discovered immediately.

SIR OLIVER. Hey! what, the plague! how much then?

MOSES. That depends upon the circumstances. If he appears not very anxious for the supply, you should require only forty or fifty per cent.; but if you find him in great distress and want the moneys very bad, you may ask double.

SIR PETER. A good honest trade you're learning, Sir Oliver!

SIR OLIVER. Truly, I think so,—and not unprofitable.

MOSES. Then you know, you haven't the moneys yourself but are forced to borrow them of an old friend.

SIR OLIVER. Oh! I borrow it of a friend, do I?

MOSES. And your friend is an unconscionable dog; but you can't help that.

SIR OLIVER. My friend an unconscionable dog, is he?

MOSES. Yes, and he himself has not the moneys by him but is forced to sell stock at a great loss.

SIR OLIVER. He is forced to sell stock at a great loss, is he? Well, that's very kind of him.

SIR PETER. I'faith, Sir Oliver—Mr. Premium, I mean—you'll soon be master of the trade. But, Moses, would not you have him run out a little against the annuity bill?[1] That would be in character, I should think.

MOSES. Very much.

ROWLEY. And lament that a young man now must be at years of discretion before he is suffered to ruin himself?

MOSES. Ay, great pity!

SIR PETER. And abuse the public for allowing merit to an act whose only object is to snatch misfortune and imprudence from the rapacious gripe of usury and give the minor a chance of inheriting his estate without being undone by coming into possession.

SIR OLIVER. So, so—Moses shall give me farther particulars as we go together.

SIR PETER. You will not have much time, for your nephew lives hard by.

---

[1] The Annuity Bill, passed in May, 1777, was designed to protect minors against the sellers of annuities. It required, among other things, that grants of annuities be registered.

SIR OLIVER. Oh, never fear! My tutor appears so able that though Charles lived in the next street, it must be my own fault if I am not a complete rogue before I turn the corner.

Exit with MOSES

SIR PETER. So, now, I think Sir Oliver will be convinced. You are partial, Rowley, and would have prepared Charles for the other plot.

ROWLEY. No, upon my word, Sir Peter.

SIR PETER. Well, go bring me this Snake, and I'll hear what he has to say presently. I see Maria and want to speak with her. (*Exit* ROWLEY) I should be glad to be convinced my suspicions of Lady Teazle and Charles were unjust. I have never yet opened my mind on this subject to my friend Joseph. I am determined I will do it; he will give me his opinion sincerely. (*Enter* MARIA) So, child, has Mr. Surface returned with you?

MARIA. No, sir. He was engaged.

SIR PETER. Well, Maria, do you not reflect the more you converse with that amiable young man what return his partiality for you deserves?

MARIA. Indeed, Sir Peter, your frequent importunity on this subject distresses me extremely. You compel me to declare that I know no man who has ever paid me a particular attention whom I would not prefer to Mr. Surface.

SIR PETER. So—here's perverseness! No, no, Maria, 'tis Charles only whom you would prefer. 'Tis evident his vices and follies have won your heart.

MARIA. This is unkind, sir. You know I have obeyed you in neither seeing or corresponding with him. I have heard enough to convince me that he is unworthy my regard. Yet I cannot think it culpable, if, while my understanding severely condemns his vices, my heart suggests some pity for his distresses.

SIR PETER. Well, well, pity him as much as you please, but give your heart and hand to a worthier object.

MARIA. Never to his brother.

SIR PETER. Go, perverse and obstinate! But take care, madam; you have never yet known what the authority of a guardian is. Don't compel me to inform you of it.

MARIA. I can only say, you shall not have just reason. 'Tis true, by my father's will I am for a short period bound to regard you as his substitute, but must cease to think you so when you would compel me to be miserable.

Exit

SIR PETER. Was ever man so crossed as I am, everything conspiring to fret me! I had not been involved in matrimony a fortnight before her father, a hale and hearty man, died, on purpose, I believe, for the pleasure of plaguing me with the care of his daughter.— But here comes my helpmate! She appears in great good humor. How happy I should be if I could tease her into loving me, though but a little!

Enter LADY TEAZLE

LADY TEAZLE. Lud, Sir Peter, I hope you haven't been quarreling with Maria? It is not using me well to be ill-humored when I am not by.

SIR PETER. Ah, Lady Teazle, you might have the power to make me good humored at all times.

LADY TEAZLE. I am sure I wish I had, for I want you to be in a charming, sweet temper at this moment. Do be good humored now and let me have two hundred pounds, will you?

SIR PETER. Two hundred pounds! What, ain't I to be in a good humor without paying for it? But speak to me thus and, i' faith, there's nothing I could refuse you. You shall have it, but seal me a bond for the repayment.

LADY TEAZLE. Oh, no! There,—my note of hand will do as well. (*Offering her hand*)

SIR PETER. And you shall no longer reproach me with not giving you an independent settlement. I mean shortly to surprise you. But shall we always live thus, hey?

LADY TEAZLE. If you please. I'm sure I don't care how soon we leave off quarreling provided you'll own you were tired first.

SIR PETER. Well, then let our future contest be who shall be most obliging.

LADY TEAZLE. I assure you, Sir Peter, good nature becomes you. You look now as you did before we were married, when you used to walk with me under the elms and tell me stories of what a gallant you were in your youth and chuck me under the chin and ask me if I thought I could love an old fellow who would deny me nothing—didn't you?

SIR PETER. Yes, yes, and you were as kind and attentive—

LADY TEAZLE. Ay, so I was, and would

always take your part when my acquaintance used to abuse you and turn you into ridicule.

Sir Peter. Indeed!

Lady Teazle. Ay, and when my cousin Sophy has called you a stiff, peevish old bachelor and laughed at me for thinking of marrying one who might be my father, I have always defended you and said I didn't think you so ugly by any means; and I dared say you'd make a very good sort of husband.

Sir Peter. And you prophesied right; and we shall now be the happiest couple—

Lady Teazle. And never differ again?

Sir Peter. No, never. Though at the same time, indeed, my dear Lady Teazle, you must watch your temper very seriously, for in all our quarrels, my dear, if you recollect, my love, you always began first.

Lady Teazle. I beg your pardon, my dear Sir Peter. Indeed you always gave the provocation.

Sir Peter. Now see, my angel! Take care! Contradicting isn't the way to keep friends.

Lady Teazle. Then don't you begin it, my love.

Sir Peter. There, now, you—you—are going on. You don't perceive, my life, that you are just doing the very thing which you know always makes me angry.

Lady Teazle. Nay, you know if you will be angry without any reason, my dear—

Sir Peter. There, now you want to quarrel again.

Lady Teazle. No, I'm sure I don't; but if you will be so peevish—

Sir Peter. There now! Who begins first?

Lady Teazle. Why, you to be sure. I said nothing; but there's no bearing your temper.

Sir Peter. No, no, madam! The fault's in your own temper.

Lady Teazle. Ay, you are just what my cousin Sophy said you would be.

Sir Peter. Your cousin Sophy is a forward, impertinent gipsy.

Lady Teazle. You are a great bear, I'm sure, to abuse my relations.

Sir Peter. Now may all the plagues of marriage be doubled on me if ever I try to be friends with you any more!

Lady Teazle. So much the better.

Sir Peter. No, no, madam. 'Tis evident you never cared a pin for me and I was a madman to marry you,— a pert, rural coquette that had refused half the honest squires in the neighborhood.

Lady Teazle. And I am sure I was a fool to marry you,—an old dangling bachelor, who was single at fifty only because he never could meet with anyone who would have him.

Sir Peter. Ay, ay, madam; but you were pleased enough to listen to me. You never had such an offer before.

Lady Teazle. No? Didn't I refuse Sir Tivy Terrier, who everybody said would have been a better match, for his estate is just as good as yours and he has broke his neck since we have been married?

Sir Peter. I have done with you, madam! You are an unfeeling, ungrateful—But there's an end of everything. I believe you capable of everything that is bad. Yes, madam, I now believe the reports relative to you and Charles, madam. Yes, madam, you and Charles are, not without grounds—

Lady Teazle. Take care, Sir Peter! You had better not insinuate any such thing! I'll not be suspected without cause, I promise you.

Sir Peter. Very well, madam, very well! A separate maintenance as soon as you please. Yes, madam, or a divorce! I'll make an example of myself for the benefit of all old bachelors. Let us separate, madam.

Lady Teazle. Agreed, agreed! And now, my dear, Sir Peter, we are of a mind once more, we may be the happiest couple and never differ again, you know. Ha, ha, ha! Well, you are going to be in a passion, I see, and I shall only interrupt you; so bye, bye! *Exit*

Sir Peter. Plagues and tortures! Can't I make her angry either? Oh, I am the most miserable fellow! But I'll not bear her presuming to keep her temper. No! She may break my heart, but she shan't keep her temper. *Exit*

Scene ii. Charles Surface's *House*

Enter Trip, Moses, *and* Sir Oliver Surface

Trip. Here, Master Moses! If you'll stay a moment, I'll try whether—What's the gentleman's name?

Sir Oliver. (*Aside to* Moses) Mr. Moses, what is my name?

Moses. Mr. Premium.

Trip. Premium. Very well.

Exit, taking snuff

SIR OLIVER. To judge by the servants, one wouldn't believe the master was ruined. But what! Sure, this was my brother's house?

MOSES. Yes, sir; Mr. Charles bought it of Mr. Joseph, with the furniture, pictures, &c., just as the old gentleman left it. Sir Peter thought it a piece of extravagance in him.

SIR OLIVER. In my mind, the other's economy in selling it to him was more reprehensible by half.

Enter TRIP

TRIP. My master says you must wait, gentlemen. He has company and can't speak with you yet.

SIR OLIVER. If he knew who it was wanted to see him, perhaps he would not send such a message?

TRIP. Yes, yes, sir; he knows you are here. I did not forget little Premium. No, no, no.

SIR OLIVER. Very well; and I pray, sir, what may be your name?

TRIP. Trip, sir; my name is Trip, at your service.

SIR OLIVER. Well, then, Mr. Trip, you have a pleasant sort of place here, I guess.

TRIP. Why, yes. Here are three or four of us pass our time agreeably enough; but then our wages are sometimes a little in arrear, and not very great either, but fifty pounds a year and find our own bags and bouquets.[1]

SIR OLIVER. (*Aside*) Bags and bouquets! Halters and bastinadoes!

TRIP. And *à propos*, Moses, have you been able to get me that little bill discounted?

SIR OLIVER. (*Aside*) Wants to raise money too! Mercy on me! has his distresses too, I warrant, like a lord and affects creditors and duns.

MOSES. 'Twas not to be done, indeed, Mr. Trip.

TRIP. Good lack, you surprise me! My friend Brush has indorsed it, and I thought when he put his name at the back of a bill 'twas the same as cash.

MOSES. No, 'twouldn't do.

TRIP. A small sum,—but twenty pounds. Harkee, Moses, do you think you couldn't get it me by way of annuity?

SIR OLIVER. (*Aside*) An annuity! Ha, ha! A footman raise money by way of annuity! Well done, luxury, egad!

MOSES. Well, but you must insure you. place.

TRIP. Oh, with all my heart! I'll insure my place and my life too, if you please.

SIR OLIVER. (*Aside*) It's more than I would your neck.

MOSES. But is there nothing you could deposit?

TRIP. Why, nothing capital of my master's wardrobe has dropped lately; but I could give you a mortgage on some of his winter clothes with equity of redemption before November; or you shall have the reversion of the French velvet or a post-obit on the blue and silver. These I should think, Moses, with a few pairs of point ruffles as collateral security—Hey, my little fellow?

MOSES. Well, well. (*Bell rings*)

TRIP. Egad, I heard the bell! I believe, gentlemen, I can now introduce you. Don't forget the annuity, little Moses. This way, gentlemen; I'll insure my place, you know.

SIR OLIVER. (*Aside*) If the man be a shadow of the master, this is a temple of dissipation indeed.
Exeunt

SCENE III. [*Another room*]

CHARLES SURFACE, CARELESS, &c., &c., *at a table with wine, &c.*

CHARLES. 'Fore heaven, 'tis true! There's the great degeneracy of the age. Many of our acquaintance have taste, spirit, and politeness; but, plague on't, they won't drink.

CARELESS. It is so, indeed, Charles. They go into all the substantial luxuries of the table and abstain from nothing but wine and wit. Oh, certainly society suffers by it intolerably, for now instead of the social spirit of raillery that used to mantle over a glass of bright Burgundy, their conversation is become just like the Spa-water they drink, which has all the pertness and flatulency of champagne without the spirit or flavor.

1ST GENTLEMAN. But what are they to do who love play better than wine?

CARELESS. True! There's Sir Harry diets himself for gaming and is now under a hazard regimen.

CHARLES SURFACE. Then he'll have the worst of it. What! you wouldn't train a horse for the course by keeping him from corn?[2] For my part, egad, I am never so successful

---

[1] Bag wigs and shoulder bouquets were worn by footmen.

[2] Wheat or other grain.

as when I am a little merry. Let me throw on a bottle of champagne and I never lose.

CARELESS. At least I never feel my losses, which is exactly the same thing.

2D GENTLEMAN. Ay, that I believe.

CHARLES. And then, what man can pretend to be a believer in love who is an abjurer of wine? 'Tis the test by which the lover knows his own heart. Fill a dozen bumpers to a dozen beauties and she that floats atop is the maid that has bewitched you.

CARELESS. Now then, Charles, be honest and give us your real favorite.

CHARLES. Why, I have withheld her only in compassion to you. If I toast her, you must give a round of her peers, which is impossible—on earth.

CARELESS. Oh, then, we'll find some canonized vestals or heathen goddesses that will do, I warrant!

CHARLES. Here, then, bumpers, you rogues! Bumpers! Maria! Maria!

SIR [TOBY] BUMPER. Maria who?

CHARLES. Oh, damn the surname! 'Tis too formal to be registered in love's calendar. But now, Sir [Toby], beware! We must have beauty superlative.

CARELESS. Nay, never study, Sir [Toby]. We'll stand to the toast though your mistress should want an eye and you know you have a song will excuse you.

SIR [TOBY]. Egad, so I have, and I'll give him the song instead of the lady. (*Sings*)

Here's to the maiden of bashful fifteen;
  Here's to the widow of fifty;
Here's to the flaunting, extravagant quean,
  And here's to the housewife that's thrifty.
CHORUS.   Let the toast pass,
      Drink to the lass,—
I'll warrant she'll prove an excuse for the glass!

Here's to the charmer whose dimples we prize;
  Now to the maid who has none, sir!
Here's to the girl with a pair of blue eyes,
  And here's to the nymph with but one, sir!
CHORUS.   Let the toast pass, &c.

Here's to the maid with a bosom of snow!
  Now to her that's as brown as a berry!
Here's to the wife with a face full of woe,
  And now to the girl that is merry!
CHORUS.   Let the toast pass, &c.

For let 'em be clumsy, or let 'em be slim,
  Young or ancient, I care not a feather:

So fill a pint bumper quite up to the brim,
  And let us e'en toast them together!
CHORUS.   Let the toast pass, &c.

ALL. Bravo! Bravo!

Enter TRIP *and whispers* CHARLES SURFACE

CHARLES. Gentlemen, you must excuse me a little. Careless, take the chair, will you?

CARELESS. Nay, pr'ythee, Charles, what now? This is one of your peerless beauties, I suppose, has dropped in by chance?

CHARLES. No, faith! To tell you the truth, 'tis a Jew and a broker, who are come by appointment.

CARELESS. Oh, damn it, let's have the Jew in.

1ST GENTLEMAN. Ay, and the broker too, by all means.

2D GENTLEMAN. Yes, yes, the Jew and the broker!

CHARLES. Egad, with all my heart! Trip, bid the gentlemen walk in. (*Exit* TRIP) Though there's one of them a stranger, I can tell you.

CARELESS. Charles, let us give them some generous Burgundy and perhaps they'll grow conscientious.

CHARLES. Oh, hang 'em, no! Wine does but draw forth a man's natural qualities; and to make them drink would only be to whet their knavery.

Enter TRIP, SIR OLIVER, *and* MOSES

CHARLES. So, honest Moses! Walk in, pray, Mr. Premium. That's the gentleman's name, isn't it, Moses?

MOSES. Yes, sir.

CHARLES. Set chairs, Trip.—Sit down, Mr. Premium.—Glasses, Trip.—Sit down, Moses. —Come, Mr. Premium, I'll give you a sentiment: here's *Success to usury!* Moses, fill the gentleman a bumper.

MOSES. Success to usury! (*Drinks*)

CARELESS. Right, Moses! Usury is prudence and industry, and deserves to succeed.

SIR OLIVER. Then—here's—all the success it deserves! (*Drinks*)

CARELESS. No, no, that won't do! Mr. Premium, you have demurred at the toast and must drink it in a pint bumper.

1ST GENTLEMAN. A pint bumper at least!

MOSES. Oh, pray, sir, consider! Mr. Premium's a gentleman.

CARELESS. And therefore loves good wine.

2ND GENTLEMAN. Give Moses a quart glass.

This is mutiny and a high contempt for the chair.

CARELESS. Here, now for 't! I'll see justice done, to the last drop of my bottle.

SIR OLIVER. Nay, pray, gentlemen! I did not expect this usage.

CHARLES. No, hang it, you shan't. Mr. Premium's a stranger.

SIR OLIVER. (*Aside*) Odd! I wish I was well out of their company.

CARELESS. Plague on 'em then! If they won't drink, we'll not sit down with them. Come, Toby, the dice are in the next room. Charles, you'll join us when you have finished your business with the gentlemen?

CHARLES. I will! I will!(*Exeunt* [Gentlemen]) Careless!

CARELESS. (*Returning*) Well?

CHARLES. Perhaps I may want you.

CARELESS. Oh, you know I am always ready. Word, note, or bond, 'tis all the same to me! *Exit*

MOSES. Sir, this is Mr. Premium, a gentleman of the strictest honor and secrecy, and always performs what he undertakes. Mr. Premium, this is—

CHARLES. Psha! Have done! Sir, my friend Moses is a very honest fellow but a little slow at expression. He'll be an hour giving us our titles. Mr. Premium, the plain state of the matter is this: I am an extravagant young fellow who wants to borrow money; you I take to be a prudent old fellow who have got money to lend. I am blockhead enough to give fifty per cent. sooner than not have it; and you, I presume, are rogue enough to take a hundred if you can get it. Now, sir, you see we are acquainted at once and may proceed to business without farther ceremony.

SIR OLIVER. Exceeding frank, upon my word. I see, sir, you are not a man of many compliments.

CHARLES. Oh, no, sir! Plain dealing in business I always think best.

SIR OLIVER. Sir, I like you the better for it. However, you are mistaken in one thing. I have no money to lend, but I believe I could procure some of a friend; but then he's an unconscionable dog, isn't he, Moses?

MOSES. But you can't help that.

SIR OLIVER. And must sell stock to accommodate you, mustn't he, Moses?

MOSES. Yes, indeed! You know I always speak the truth and scorn to tell a lie.

CHARLES. Right! People that speak truth generally do. But these are trifles, Mr. Premium. What, I know money isn't to be bought without paying for 't!

SIR OLIVER. Well, but what security could you give? You have no land, I suppose?

CHARLES. Not a mole-hill, nor a twig, but what's in the bough-pots [1] out of the window!

SIR OLIVER. Nor any stock, I presume?

CHARLES. Nothing but live stock,—and that's only a few pointers and ponies. But, pray, Mr. Premium, are you acquainted at all with any of my connections?

SIR OLIVER. Why, to say truth, I am.

CHARLES. Then you must know that I have a devilish rich uncle in the East Indies, Sir Oliver Surface, from whom I have the greatest expectations.

SIR OLIVER. That you have a wealthy uncle, I have heard; but how your expectations will turn out is more, I believe, than you can tell.

CHARLES. Oh, no! There can be no doubt! They tell me I'm a prodigious favorite and that he talks of leaving me everything.

SIR OLIVER. Indeed! This is the first I've heard of it.

CHARLES. Yes, yes, 'tis just so. Moses knows 'tis true, don't you, Moses?

MOSES. Oh, yes! I'll swear to 't.

SIR OLIVER. (*Aside*) Egad, they'll persuade me presently I'm at Bengal.

CHARLES. Now I propose, Mr. Premium, if it's agreeable to you, a post-obit on Sir Oliver's life, though at the same time the old fellow has been so liberal to me that I give you my word I should be very sorry to hear that anything had happened to him.

SIR OLIVER. Not more than I should, I assure you. But the bond you mention happens to be just the worst security you could offer me,—for I might live to a hundred and never see the principal.

CHARLES. Oh, yes, you would! The moment Sir Oliver dies, you know, you would come on me for the money.

SIR OLIVER. Then I believe I should be the most unwelcome dun you ever had in your life.

CHARLES. What! I suppose you're afraid that Sir Oliver is too good a life?

SIR OLIVER. No, indeed I am not, though I have heard he is as hale and healthy as any man of his years in Christendom.

[1] Bouquets or window-boxes.

CHARLES. There, again, now you are misinformed. No, no, the climate has hurt him considerably, poor uncle Oliver. Yes, yes, he breaks apace, I'm told, and is so much altered lately that his nearest relations don't know him.

SIR OLIVER. No! Ha, ha, ha! So much altered lately that his nearest relations don't know him! Ha, ha, ha! Egad! Ha, ha, ha!

CHARLES. Ha, ha! You're glad to hear that, little Premium?

SIR OLIVER. No, no, I'm not.

CHARLES. Yes, yes, you are! Ha, ha, ha! You know that mends your chance.

SIR OLIVER. But I'm told Sir Oliver is coming over. Nay, some say he is actually arrived.

CHARLES. Psha! sure I must know better than you whether he's come or not. No, no, rely on't, he's at this moment at Calcutta, isn't he, Moses?

MOSES. Oh, yes, certainly.

SIR OLIVER. Very true, as you say, you must know better than I, though I have it from pretty good authority, haven't I, Moses?

MOSES. Yes, most undoubted!

SIR OLIVER. But, sir, as I understand you want a few hundreds immediately, is there nothing you could dispose of?

CHARLES. How do you mean?

SIR OLIVER. For instance, now, I have heard that your father left behind him a great quantity of massy old plate.

CHARLES. O Lud! that's gone long ago. Moses can tell you how better than I can.

SIR OLIVER (*Aside*) Good lack, all the family race-cups and corporation bowls![1]—Then it was also supposed that his library was one of the most valuable and compact.

CHARLES. Yes, yes, so it was,—vastly too much so for a private gentleman. For my part, I was always of a communicative disposition; so I thought it a shame to keep so much knowledge to myself.

SIR OLIVER. (*Aside*) Mercy upon me! Learning that had run in the family like an heirloom!—Pray what are become of the books?

CHARLES. You must inquire of the auctioneer, Master Premium, for I don't believe even Moses can direct you.

MOSES. I know nothing of books.

[1] Trophies, and testimonial bowls presented by the city for distinguished services.

SIR OLIVER. So, so, nothing of the family property left, I suppose?

CHARLES. Not much, indeed, unless you have a mind to the family pictures. I have got a room full of ancestors above; and if you have a taste for paintings, egad, you shall have 'em a bargain.

SIR OLIVER. Hey! What the devil? Sure, you wouldn't sell your forefathers, would you?

CHARLES. Every man of them to the best bidder.

SIR OLIVER. What! Your great-uncles and aunts?

CHARLES. Ay, and my great-grandfathers and grandmothers too.

SIR OLIVER. (*Aside*) Now I give him up!—What the plague, have you no bowels for your own kindred? Odd's life, do you take me for Shylock in the play that you would raise money of me on your own flesh and blood?

CHARLES. Nay, my little broker, don't be angry. What need you care if you have your money's worth?

SIR OLIVER. Well, I'll be the purchaser. I think I can dispose of the family canvas. (*Aside*) Oh, I'll never forgive him for this, never!

Enter CARELESS

CARELESS. Come, Charles; what keeps you?

CHARLES. I can't come yet. I' faith, we are going to have a sale above stairs. Here's little Premium will buy all my ancestors.

CARELESS. Oh, burn your ancestors!

CHARLES. No, he may do that afterwards if he pleases. Stay, Careless, we want you. Egad, you shall be auctioneer; so come along with us.

CARELESS. Oh, have with you, if that's the case. Handle a hammer as well as a dice-box!

SIR OLIVER. (*Aside*) Oh, the profligates!

CHARLES. Come, Moses, you shall be appraiser if we want one. Gad's life, little Premium, you don't seem to like the business.

SIR OLIVER. Oh, yes, I do, vastly! Ha, ha, ha! Yes, yes, I think it a rare joke to sell one's family by auction. Ha, ha! (*Aside*) Oh, the prodigal!

CHARLES. To be sure! When a man wants money, where the plague should he get assistance if he can't make free with his own relations? *Exeunt*

ACT IV

SCENE I. *Picture room at* CHARLES'S

Enter CHARLES SURFACE, SIR OLIVER SURFACE, MOSES, *and* CARELESS

CHARLES. Walk in, gentlemen, pray walk in. Here they are, the family of the Surfaces up to the Conquest.

SIR OLIVER. And, in my opinion, a goodly collection.

CHARLES. Ay, ay, these are done in the true spirit of portrait-painting; no *volontière grace* or expression. Not like the works of your modern Raphaels,[1] who give you the strongest resemblance, yet contrive to make your portrait independent of you, so that you may sink the original and not hurt the picture. No, no; the merit of these is the inveterate likeness,—all stiff and awkward as the originals and like nothing in human nature besides.

SIR OLIVER. Ah! We shall never see such figures of men again.

CHARLES. I hope not! Well, you see, Master Premium, what a domestic character I am; here I sit of an evening surrounded by my family. But come, get into your pulpit, Mr. Auctioneer; here's an old, gouty chair of my grandfather's will answer the purpose.

CARELESS. Ay, ay, this will do. But, Charles, I haven't a hammer; and what's an auctioneer without his hammer!

CHARLES. Egad, that's true! What parchment have we here? Oh, our genealogy in full. Here, Careless, you shall have no common bit of mahogany; here's the family tree for you, you rogue! This shall be your hammer, and now you may knock down my ancestors with their own pedigree.

SIR OLIVER. (*Aside*) What an unnatural rogue! An *ex post facto* parricide!

CARELESS. Yes, yes, here's a list of your generation, indeed. Faith, Charles, this is the most convenient thing you could have found for the business, for 'twill serve not only as a hammer but a catalogue into the bargain. Come, begin! A-going, a-going, a-going!

CHARLES. Bravo, Careless! Well, here's my great-uncle, Sir Richard Raveline, a marvellous good general in his day, I assure you. He served in all the Duke of Marlborough's wars and got that cut over his eye at the battle of Malplaquet.[2] What say you, Mr. Premium? Look at him. There's a hero! Not cut out of his feathers as your modern clipped captains are, but enveloped in wig and regimentals as a general should be. What do you bid?

MOSES. Mr. Premium would have you speak.

CHARLES. Why, then, he shall have him for ten pounds, and I'm sure that's not dear for a staff officer.

SIR OLIVER. (*Aside*) Heaven deliver me! His famous uncle Richard for ten pounds!— Very well, sir, I take him at that.

CHARLES. Careless, knock down my uncle Richard.—Here, now, is a maiden sister of his, my great-aunt Deborah, done by Kneller,[3] thought to be in his best manner, and a very formidable likeness. There she is, you see, a shepherdess feeding her flock. You shall have her for five pounds ten,—the sheep are worth the money.

SIR OLIVER. (*Aside*) Ah, poor Deborah, a woman who set such a value on herself!— Five pounds ten—She's mine.

CHARLES. Knock down my aunt Deborah! Here, now, are two that were a sort of cousins of theirs. You see, Moses, these pictures were done some time ago when beaux wore wigs and the ladies their own hair.

SIR OLIVER. Yes, truly, head-dresses appear to have been a little lower in those days.

CHARLES. Well, take that couple for the same.

MOSES. 'Tis a good bargain.

CHARLES. Careless!—This now, is a grandfather of my mother's, a learned judge, well known on the western circuit. What do you rate him at, Moses?

MOSES. Four guineas.

CHARLES. Four guineas! Gad's life, you don't bid me the price of his wig. Mr. Premium, you have more respect for the woolsack.[4] Do let us knock his lordship down at fifteen.

---

[1] I.e., perhaps, Sir Joshua Reynolds, Gainsborough, and Romney, all of whom painted portraits whose originals have been "sunk," without hurting the pictures.

[2] Marlborough's victory over the French in 1709, in which his losses more than doubled those of his enemies, who were actually encouraged by their defeat.

[3] Sir Godfrey Kneller (1648–1723) the fashionable portrait painter of the early years of the century. His work is pleasant but insipid and monotonous.

[4] The Woolsack, emblem of the source of England's

Sir Oliver. By all means.

Careless. Gone!

Charles. And these are two brothers of his, William and Walter Blunt, Esquires, both members of parliament and noted speakers; and what's very extraordinary, I believe this is the first time they were ever bought or sold.

Sir Oliver. That is very extraordinary, indeed! I'll take them at your own price for the honor of parliament.

Careless. Well said, little Premium! I'll knock them down at forty.

Charles. Here's a jolly fellow! I don't know what relation, but he was mayor of Manchester; take him at eight pounds.

Sir Oliver. No, no; six will do for the mayor.

Charles. Come, make it guineas,[1] and I'll throw you the two aldermen there into the bargain.

Sir Oliver. They're mine.

Charles. Careless, knock down the mayor and aldermen. But, plague on 't, we shall be all day retailing in this manner. Do let us deal wholesale, what say you, little Premium? Give me three hundred pounds for the rest of the family in the lump.

Careless. Ay, ay, that will be the best way.

Sir Oliver. Well, well, anything to accommodate you. They are mine. But there is one portrait which you have always passed over.

Careless. What, that ill-looking little fellow over the settee?

Sir Oliver. Yes, sir, I mean that, though I don't think him so ill-looking a little fellow by any means.

Charles. What, that? Oh, that's my uncle Oliver. 'Twas done before he went to India.

Careless. Your uncle Oliver! Gad, then you'll never be friends, Charles. That, now, is as stern a looking rogue as ever I saw, an unforgiving eye and a damned disinheriting countenance! An inveterate knave, depend on 't, don't you think so, little Premium?

Sir Oliver. Upon my soul, sir, I do not. I think it is as honest a looking face as any in the room, dead or alive. But I suppose uncle Oliver goes with the rest of the lumber?

Charles. No, hang it! I'll not part with poor Noll. The old fellow has been very good to me, and, egad, I'll keep his picture while I've a room to put it in.

Sir Oliver. (*Aside*) The rogue's my nephew after all!—But, sir, I have somehow taken a fancy to that picture.

Charles. I'm sorry for't, for you certainly will not have it. Oons, haven't you got enough of them?

Sir Oliver. (*Aside*) I forgive him for everything!—But, sir, when I take a whim in my head, I don't value money. I'll give you as much for that as for all the rest.

Charles. Don't tease me, master broker. I tell you I'll not part with it, and there's an end of it.

Sir Oliver. (*Aside*) How like his father the dog is!—Well, well, I have done. (*Aside*) I did not perceive it before, but I think I never saw such a striking resemblance.—Here's a draft for your sum.

Charles. Why, 'tis for eight hundred pounds!

Sir Oliver. You will not let Sir Oliver go?

Charles. Zounds, no! I tell you once more.

Sir Oliver. Then never mind the difference, we'll balance that another time. But give me your hand on the bargain. You are an honest fellow, Charles—I beg pardon, sir, for being so free.—Come, Moses.

Charles. Egad, this is a whimsical old fellow!—But hark'ee, Premium, you'll prepare lodgings for these gentlemen.

Sir Oliver. Yes, yes, I'll send for them in a day or two.

Charles. But hold! Do, now, send a genteel conveyance for them, for, I assure you, they were most of them used to ride in their own carriages.

Sir Oliver. I will, I will,—for all but little Oliver.

Charles. Ay, all but the little nabob.

Sir Oliver. You're fixed on that?

Charles. Peremptorily.

Sir Oliver. (*Aside*) A dear extravagant rogue!—Good day! Come, Moses. (*Aside*) Let me hear now who dares call him profligate!

Exeunt Sir Oliver *and* Moses

Careless. Why, this is the oddest genius of the sort I ever met with.

Charles. Egad, he's the prince of brokers, I think. I wonder how Moses got acquainted

---

wealth in old days, serves as the seat of the Lord Chancellor in the House of Lords. The term here implies the legal profession.

[1] A pound is twenty shillings, a guinea twenty-one.

with so honest a fellow. Ha! here's Rowley.—Do, Careless, say I'll join the company in a few moments.

CARELESS. I will, but don't let that old blockhead persuade you to squander any of that money on old, musty debts or any such nonsense, for tradesmen, Charles, are the most exorbitant fellows.

CHARLES. Very true, and paying them is only encouraging them.

CARELESS. Nothing else.

CHARLES. Ay, ay, never fear. (*Exit* CARELESS) So, this was an odd old fellow, indeed. Let me see, two-thirds of this is mine by right, five hundred and thirty odd pounds. 'Fore heaven, I find one's ancestors are more valuable relations than I took them for! [*Bowing to the pictures*] Ladies and gentlemen, your most obedient and very grateful servant. (*Enter* ROWLEY) Ha, old Rowley! Egad, you are just come in time to take leave of your old acquaintance.

ROWLEY. Yes, I heard they were a-going. But I wonder you can have such spirits under so many distresses.

CHARLES. Why, there's the point, my distresses are so many that I can't afford to part with my spirits; but I shall be rich and splenetic, all in good time. However, I suppose you are surprised that I am not more sorrowful at parting with so many near relations. To be sure, 'tis very affecting; but you see they never move a muscle; so why should I?

ROWLEY. There's no making you serious a moment.

CHARLES. Yes, faith, I am so now. Here, my honest Rowley, here get me this changed directly and take a hundred pounds of it immediately to old Stanley.

ROWLEY. A hundred pounds! Consider only—

CHARLES. Gad's life, don't talk about it! Poor Stanley's wants are pressing and, if you don't make haste, we shall have someone call that has a better right to the money.

ROWLEY. Ah, there's the point! I never will cease dunning you with the old proverb—

CHARLES. "Be just before you're generous."—Why, so I would if I could; but Justice is an old, lame, hobbling beldame, and I can't get her to keep pace with Generosity for the soul of me.

ROWLEY. Yet, Charles, believe me, one hour's reflection—

CHARLES. Ay, ay, that's very true; but hark'ee, Rowley, while I have, by heaven I'll give; so damn your economy. And now for hazard!
Exeunt

SCENE II. *The parlor*

Enter SIR OLIVER SURFACE *and* MOSES

MOSES. Well, sir, I think, as Sir Peter said, you have seen Mr. Charles in high glory; 'tis great pity he's so extravagant.

SIR OLIVER. True, but he would not sell my picture.

MOSES. And loves wine and women so much.

SIR OLIVER. But he would not sell my picture.

MOSES. And games so deep.

SIR OLIVER. But he would not sell my picture. Oh, here's Rowley!

Enter ROWLEY

ROWLEY. So, Sir Oliver, I find you have made a purchase—

SIR OLIVER. Yes, yes, our young rake has parted with his ancestors like old tapestry.

ROWLEY. And here he has commissioned me to re-deliver you part of the purchase money. I mean, though, in your necessitous character of old Stanley.

MOSES. Ah, there's the pity of all; he is so damned charitable.

ROWLEY. And left a hosier and two tailors in the hall, who, I'm sure, won't be paid; and this hundred would satisfy them.

SIR OLIVER. Well, well, I'll pay his debts and his benevolence, too. But now I am no more a broker, and you shall introduce me to the elder brother as old Stanley.

ROWLEY. Not yet awhile. Sir Peter, I know, means to call there about this time.

Enter TRIP

TRIP. Oh, gentlemen, I beg pardon for not showing you out. This way.—Moses, a word.
Exit with MOSES

SIR OLIVER. There's a fellow for you! Would you believe it, that puppy intercepted the Jew on our coming and wanted to raise money before he got to his master!

ROWLEY. Indeed!

SIR OLIVER. Yes, they are now planning an annuity business. Ah, Master Rowley, in my days servants were content with the follies of their masters when they were worn a little

threadbare, but now they have their vices like their birthday clothes,[1] with the gloss on.
Exeunt

SCENE III. *A library* [*in* JOSEPH SURFACE'S *house*]

Enter JOSEPH SURFACE *and* Servant

JOSEPH SURFACE. No letter from Lady Teazle?

SERVANT. No, sir.

JOSEPH SURFACE. I am surprised she has not sent if she is prevented from coming. Sir Peter certainly does not suspect me. Yet I wish I may not lose the heiress through the scrape I have drawn myself into with the wife. However, Charles's imprudence and bad character are great points in my favor.

(*Knocking heard without*)

SERVANT. Sir, I believe that must be Lady Teazle.

JOSEPH SURFACE. Hold! See whether it is or not before you go to the door. I have a particular message for you if it should be my brother.

SERVANT. 'Tis her ladyship, sir. She always leaves her chair at a milliner's in the next street.

JOSEPH SURFACE. Stay, stay! Draw that screen before the window. That will do. My opposite neighbor is a maiden lady of so curious a temper. (*Servant draws the screen and exit*) I have a difficult hand to play in this affair. Lady Teazle has lately suspected my views on Maria, but she must by no means be let into that secret,—at least, till I have her more in my power.

Enter LADY TEAZLE

LADY TEAZLE. What, sentiment in soliloquy now? Have you been very impatient? O lud! don't pretend to look grave. I vow I couldn't come before.

JOSEPH SURFACE. O madam, punctuality is a species of constancy very unfashionable in a lady of quality.

LADY TEAZLE. Upon my word, you ought to pity me. Do you know Sir Peter is grown so ill-natured to me of late, and so jealous of Charles too! That's the best of the story, isn't it?

JOSEPH SURFACE. (*Aside*) I am glad my scandalous friends keep that up.

LADY TEAZLE. I am sure I wish he would let Maria marry him and then, perhaps, he would be convinced; don't you, Mr. Surface?

JOSEPH SURFACE. (*Aside*) Indeed I do not.— Oh, certainly I do! for then my dear Lady Teazle would also be convinced how wrong her suspicions were of my having any design on the silly girl.

LADY TEAZLE. Well, well, I'm inclined to believe you. But isn't it provoking to have the most ill-natured things said of one? And there's my friend Lady Sneerwell has circulated I don't know how many scandalous tales of me, and all without any foundation too. That's what vexes me.

JOSEPH SURFACE. Ay, madam, to be sure, that's the provoking circumstance,—without foundation. Yes, yes, there's the mortification, indeed; for, when a scandalous story is believed against one, there certainly is no comfort like the consciousness of having deserved it.

LADY TEAZLE. No, to be sure, then I'd forgive their malice. But to attack me, who am really so innocent and who never say an ill-natured thing of anybody,—that is, of any friend; and then Sir Peter, too, to have him so peevish and so suspicious, when I know the integrity of my own heart,—indeed, 'tis monstrous!

JOSEPH SURFACE. But, my dear Lady Teazle, 'tis your own fault if you suffer it. When a husband entertains a groundless suspicion of his wife and withdraws his confidence from her, the original compact is broken; and she owes it to the honor of her sex to endeavor to outwit him.

LADY TEAZLE. Indeed! So that, if he suspects me without cause, it follows that the best way of curing his jealousy is to give him reason for it?

JOSEPH SURFACE. Undoubtedly,—for your husband should never be deceived in you; and in that case it becomes you to be frail in compliment to his discernment.

LADY TEAZLE. To be sure, what you say is very reasonable, and when the consciousness of my innocence.—

JOSEPH SURFACE. Ah, my dear madam, there is the great mistake! 'Tis this very conscious innocence that is of the greatest prejudice to you. What is it makes you negligent

---

[1] Birthday clothes were elegant costumes for the celebration of the king's birthday, one of the traditional occasions for the creation of new peers and the announcement of other honors.

of forms and careless of the world's opinion? Why, the consciousness of your own innocence. What makes you thoughtless in your conduct and apt to run into a thousand little imprudences? Why, the consciousness of your own innocence. What makes you impatient of Sir Peter's temper and outrageous at his suspicions? Why, the consciousness of your own innocence.

LADY TEAZLE. 'Tis very true.

JOSEPH SURFACE. Now, my dear Lady Teazle, if you would but make a trifling *faux pas*, you can't conceive how cautious you would grow and how ready to humor and agree with your husband.

LADY TEAZLE. Do you think so?

JOSEPH SURFACE. Oh, I am sure on't! And then you would find all scandal cease at once, for, in short, your character at present is like a person in a plethora, absolutely dying from too much health.

LADY TEAZLE. So, so; then I perceive your prescription is that I must sin in my own defense and part with my virtue to preserve my reputation?

JOSEPH SURFACE. Exactly so, upon my credit, ma'am.

LADY TEAZLE. Well, certainly this is the oddest doctrine and the newest receipt for avoiding calumny!

JOSEPH SURFACE. An infallible one, believe me. Prudence, like experience, must be paid for.

LADY TEAZLE. Why, if my understanding were once convinced—

JOSEPH SURFACE. Oh, certainly, madam, your understanding should be convinced. Yes, yes,—heaven forbid I should persuade you to do anything you thought wrong. No, no, I have too much honor to desire it.

LADY TEAZLE. Don't you think we may as well leave honor out of the question?

JOSEPH SURFACE. Ah, the ill effects of your country education, I see, still remain with you.

LADY TEAZLE. I doubt they do, indeed; and I will fairly own to you that if I could be persuaded to do wrong, it would be by Sir Peter's ill usage sooner than your honorable logic after all.

JOSEPH SURFACE. Then, by this hand, which he is unworthy of—(*Taking her hand. Enter Servant*) 'Sdeath, you blockhead, what do you want?

SERVANT. I beg your pardon, sir, but I thought you would not choose Sir Peter to come up without announcing him.

JOSEPH SURFACE. Sir Peter! Oons,—the devil!

LADY TEAZLE. Sir Peter! O lud! I'm ruined! I'm ruined!

SERVANT. Sir, 'twasn't I let him in.

LADY TEAZLE. Oh, I'm quite undone! What will become of me now, Mr. Logic? Oh, he's on the stairs—I'll get behind here, and if ever I'm so imprudent again—

(*Goes behind the screen*)

JOSEPH SURFACE. Give me that book.

(*Sits down. Servant pretends to adjust his chair*)

Enter SIR PETER TEAZLE

SIR PETER. Ay, ever improving himself! Mr. Surface, Mr. Surface—

JOSEPH SURFACE. Oh, my dear Sir Peter, I beg your pardon. (*Gaping, throws away the book*) I have been dozing over a stupid book. Well, I am much obliged to you for this call. You haven't been here, I believe, since I fitted up this room. Books, you know, are the only things I am a coxcomb in.

SIR PETER. 'Tis very neat indeed. Well, well, that's proper; and you can make even your screen a source of knowledge,—hung, I perceive, with maps.

JOSEPH SURFACE. Oh, yes, I find great use in that screen.

SIR PETER. I dare say you must, certainly, when you want to find anything in a hurry.

JOSEPH SURFACE. (*Aside*) Ay, or to hide anything in a hurry either.

SIR PETER. Well, I have a little private business—

JOSEPH. (*To* Servant) You need not stay.

SERVANT. No, sir. *Exit*

JOSEPH SURFACE. Here's a chair, Sir Peter. I beg—

SIR PETER. Well, now we are alone, there's a subject, my dear friend, on which I wish to unburden my mind to you, a point of the greatest moment to my peace; in short, my good friend, Lady Teazle's conduct of late has made me very unhappy.

JOSEPH SURFACE. Indeed! I am very sorry to hear it.

SIR PETER. Ay, 'tis but too plain she has not the least regard for me; but, what's worse, I have pretty good authority to suppose she has formed an attachment to another.

JOSEPH SURFACE. Indeed! You astonish me!

SIR PETER. Yes, and, between ourselves, I think I've discovered the person.

JOSEPH SURFACE. How! You alarm me exceedingly.

SIR PETER. Ay, my dear friend, I knew you would sympathize with me!

JOSEPH SURFACE. Yes, believe me, Sir Peter, such a discovery would hurt me just as much as it would you.

SIR PETER. I am convinced of it. Ah, it is a happiness to have a friend whom we can trust even with one's family secrets. But have you no guess who I mean?

JOSEPH SURFACE. I haven't the most distant idea. It can't be Sir Benjamin Backbite!

SIR PETER. Oh, no! What say you to Charles?

JOSEPH SURFACE. My brother? Impossible!

SIR PETER. Oh, my dear friend, the goodness of your own heart misleads you. You judge of others by yourself.

JOSEPH SURFACE. Certainly, Sir Peter, the heart that is conscious of its own integrity is ever slow to credit another's treachery.

SIR PETER. True, but your brother has no sentiment. You never hear him talk so.

JOSEPH SURFACE. Yet I can't but think Lady Teazle herself has too much principle.

SIR PETER. Ay, but what is principle against the flattery of a handsome, lively young fellow?

JOSEPH SURFACE. That's very true.

SIR PETER. And then, you know, the difference of our ages makes it very improbable that she should have any great affection for me; and, if she were to be frail, and I were to make it public, why, the town would only laugh at me, the foolish old bachelor who had married a girl.

JOSEPH SURFACE. That's true, to be sure. They would laugh.

SIR PETER. Laugh, ay! And make ballads and paragraphs and the devil knows what of me.

JOSEPH SURFACE. No, you must never make it public.

SIR PETER. But then, again, that the nephew of my old friend, Sir Oliver, should be the person to attempt such a wrong, hurts me more nearly.

JOSEPH SURFACE. Ay, there's the point. When ingratitude barbs the dart of injury, the wound has double danger in it.

SIR PETER. Ay! I that was, in a manner, left his guardian, in whose house he had been so often entertained, who never in my life denied him—my advice!

JOSEPH SURFACE. Oh, 'tis not to be credited! There may be a man capable of such baseness, to be sure; but, for my part, till you can give me positive proofs, I cannot but doubt it. However, if it should be proved on him, he is no longer a brother of mine; I disclaim kindred with him; for the man who can break the laws of hospitality and tempt the wife of his friend, deserves to be branded as the pest of society.

SIR PETER. What a difference there is between you! What noble sentiments!

JOSEPH SURFACE. Yet I cannot suspect Lady Teazle's honor.

SIR PETER. I am sure I wish to think well of her and to remove all ground of quarrel between us. She has lately reproached me more than once with having made no settlement on her, and, in our last quarrel, she almost hinted that she should not break her heart if I was dead. Now, as we seem to differ in our ideas of expense, I have resolved she shall have her own way and be her own mistress in that respect for the future; and, if I were to die, she will find I have not been inattentive to her interest while living. Here, my friend, are the drafts of two deeds, which I wish to have your opinion on. By one, she will enjoy eight hundred a year independent while I live; and, by the other, the bulk of my fortune at my death.

JOSEPH SURFACE. This conduct, Sir Peter, is indeed truly generous. (*Aside*) I wish it may not corrupt my pupil.

SIR PETER. Yes, I am determined she shall have no cause to complain, though I would not have her acquainted with the latter instance of my affection yet awhile.

JOSEPH SURFACE. (*Aside*) Nor I, if I could help it.

SIR PETER. And now, my dear friend, if you please, we will talk over the situation of your hopes with Maria.

JOSEPH SURFACE. (*Softly*) Oh, no, Sir Peter! Another time, if you please.

SIR PETER. I am sensibly chagrined at the little progress you seem to make in her affections.

JOSEPH SURFACE. (*Softly*) I beg you will not mention it. What are my disappointments when your happiness is in debate! (*Aside*) 'Sdeath, I shall be ruined every way!

SIR PETER. And though you are averse to my acquainting Lady Teazle with your passion for Maria, I'm sure she's not your enemy in the affair.

JOSEPH SURFACE. Pray, Sir Peter, now oblige me. I am really too much affected by the subject we have been speaking of to bestow a thought on my own concerns. The man who is entrusted with his friend's distresses can never—(*Enter* Servant) Well, sir?

SERVANT. Your brother, sir, is speaking to a gentleman in the street and says he knows you are within.

JOSEPH SURFACE. 'Sdeath, you blockhead! I'm not within. I'm out for the day.

SIR PETER. Stay—Hold! A thought has struck me. You shall be at home.

JOSEPH SURFACE. Well, well, let him up. (*Exit* Servant. *Aside*) He'll interrupt Sir Peter, however.

SIR PETER. Now, my good friend, oblige me, I entreat you. Before Charles comes, let me conceal myself somewhere; then do you tax him on the point we have been talking, and his answer may satisfy me at once.

JOSEPH SURFACE. Oh, fie, Sir Peter! Would you have me join in so mean a trick? To trepan my brother too!

SIR PETER. Nay, you tell me you are sure he is innocent. If so, you do him the greatest service by giving him an opportunity to clear himself, and you will set my heart at rest. Come, you shall not refuse me. Here, behind the screen will be—Hey! What the devil! There seems to be one listener here already! I'll swear I saw a petticoat!

JOSEPH SURFACE. Ha! ha! ha! Well, this is ridiculous enough. I'll tell you, Sir Peter, though I hold a man of intrigue to be a most despicable character, yet, you know, it does not follow that one is to be an absolute Joseph either.[1] Hark'ee, 'tis a little French milliner, a silly rogue that plagues me; and having some character to lose, on your coming, sir, she ran behind the screen.

SIR PETER. Ah, you rogue,—But, egad, she has overheard all I have been saying of my wife.

JOSEPH SURFACE. Oh, 'twill never go any farther, you may depend upon it!

[1] An allusion to the story of Joseph and Potiphar's wife (*Genesis* 39).

SIR PETER. No? Then, faith, let her hear it out.—Here's a closet will do as well.

JOSEPH SURFACE. Well, go in there.

SIR PETER. Sly rogue! Sly rogue!
(*Going into the closet*)

JOSEPH SURFACE. A narrow escape, indeed! And a curious situation I'm in, to part man and wife in this manner.

LADY TEAZLE. (*Peeping*) Couldn't I steal off?

JOSEPH SURFACE. Keep close, my angel!

SIR PETER. (*Peeping*) Joseph, tax him home!

JOSEPH SURFACE. Back, my dear friend!

LADY TEAZLE. [*Peeping*] Couldn't you lock Sir Peter in?

JOSEPH SURFACE. Be still, my life!

SIR PETER. (*Peeping*) You're sure the little milliner won't blab?

JOSEPH SURFACE. In, in, my good Sir Peter! —'Fore gad, I wish I had a key to the door!

Enter CHARLES SURFACE

CHARLES. Holla, brother, what has been the matter? Your fellow would not let me up at first. What, have you had a Jew or a wench with you?

JOSEPH SURFACE. Neither, brother, I assure you.

CHARLES. But what has made Sir Peter steal off? I thought he had been with you.

JOSEPH SURFACE. He was, brother; but, hearing you were coming, he did not choose to stay.

CHARLES. What, was the old gentleman afraid I wanted to borrow money of him?

JOSEPH SURFACE. No, sir; but I am sorry to find, Charles, you have lately given that worthy man grounds for great uneasiness.

CHARLES. Yes, they tell me I do that to a great many worthy men. But how so, pray?

JOSEPH SURFACE. To be plain with you, brother, he thinks you are endeavoring to gain Lady Teazle's affections from him.

CHARLES. Who, I? O lud, not I, upon my word. Ha! ha! ha! ha! so the old fellow has found out that he has got a young wife, has he? Or, what's worse, Lady Teazle has found out she has an old husband?

JOSEPH SURFACE. This is no subject to jest on, brother. He who can laugh—

CHARLES. True, true, as you were going to say—Then, seriously, I never had the least idea of what you charge me with, upon my honor.

JOSEPH SURFACE. (*Aloud*) Well, it will give Sir Peter great satisfaction to hear this.

CHARLES. To be sure, I once thought the lady seemed to have taken a fancy to me; but, upon my soul, I never gave her the least encouragement. Besides, you know my attachment to Maria.

JOSEPH SURFACE. But, sure, brother, even if Lady Teazle had betrayed the fondest partiality for you—

CHARLES. Why, look'ee, Joseph, I hope I shall never deliberately do a dishonorable action; but if a pretty woman was purposely to throw herself in my way, and that pretty woman married to a man old enough to be her father—

JOSEPH SURFACE. Well?

CHARLES. Why, I believe I should be obliged to borrow a little of your morality, that's all. But, brother, do you know now that you surprise me exceedingly by naming me with Lady Teazle; for, i' faith, I always understood you were her favorite.

JOSEPH SURFACE. Oh, for shame, Charles! This retort is foolish.

CHARLES. Nay, I swear I have seen you exchange such significant glances—

JOSEPH SURFACE. Nay, nay, sir, this is no jest.

CHARLES. Egad, I'm serious! Don't you remember one day when I called here—

JOSEPH SURFACE. Nay, pr'ythee, Charles—

CHARLES. And found you together—

JOSEPH SURFACE. Zounds, sir, I insist—

CHARLES. And another time when your servant—

JOSEPH SURFACE. Brother, brother, a word with you! (*Aside*) Gad, I must stop him.

CHARLES. Informed, I say, that—

JOSEPH SURFACE. Hush! I beg your pardon, but Sir Peter has overhead all we have been saying. I knew you would clear yourself, or I should not have consented.

CHARLES. How, Sir Peter! Where is he?

JOSEPH SURFACE. Softly! There!

(*Points to the closet*)

CHARLES. Oh, 'fore heaven, I'll have him out. Sir Peter, come forth!

JOSEPH SURFACE. No, no—

CHARLES. I say, Sir Peter, come into court! (*Pulls in* SIR PETER) What! My old guardian! What, turn inquisitor and take evidence *incog.?*

SIR PETER. Give me your hand, Charles. I believe I have suspected you wrongfully; but you mustn't be angry with Joseph. 'Twas my plan.

CHARLES. Indeed!

SIR PETER. But I acquit you. I promise you I don't think near so ill of you as I did. What I have heard has given me great satisfaction.

CHARLES. Egad, then, 'twas lucky you didn't hear any more. (*Apart to* JOSEPH) Wasn't it, Joseph?

SIR PETER. Ah, you would have retorted on him.

CHARLES. Ah, ay, that was a joke.

SIR PETER. Yes, yes, I know his honor too well.

CHARLES. But you might as well have suspected him as me in this matter, for all that. (*Apart to* JOSEPH) Mightn't he, Joseph?

SIR PETER. Well, well, I believe you.

JOSEPH SURFACE. (*Aside*) Would they were both out of the room!

Enter Servant *and whispers* JOSEPH

SIR PETER. And in future, perhaps, we may not be such strangers.   *Exit* Servant

JOSEPH SURFACE. Gentlemen, I beg pardon. I must wait on you down stairs. Here is a person come on particular business.

CHARLES. Well, you can see him in another room. Sir Peter and I have not met a long time, and I have something to say to him.

JOSEPH SURFACE. (*Aside*) They must not be left together.—I'll send this man away and return directly. (*Apart to* SIR PETER *and goes out*) Sir Peter, not a word of the French milliner.

SIR PETER. (*Apart to* JOSEPH) I! Not for the world.—Ah, Charles, if you associated more with your brother, one might indeed hope for your reformation. He is a man of sentiment. Well, there is nothing in the world so noble as a man of sentiment.

CHARLES. Psha, he is too moral by half; and so apprehensive of his good name, as he calls it, that I suppose he would as soon let a priest into his house as a wench.

SIR PETER. No, no! Come, come! You wrong him. No, no, Joseph is no rake, but he is no such saint either, in that respect. (*Aside*) I have a great mind to tell him. We should have such a laugh at Joseph.

CHARLES. Oh, hang him, he's a very anchorite, a young hermit.

Sir Peter. Hark'ee, you must not abuse him. He may chance to hear of it again, I promise you.

Charles. Why, you won't tell him?

Sir Peter. No, but—This way. (*Aside*) Egad, I'll tell him.—Hark'ee, have you a mind to have a good laugh at Joseph?

Charles. I should like it, of all things.

Sir Peter. Then, i' faith, we will! I'll be quit with him for discovering me. He had a girl with him when I called.

Charles. What! Joseph? You jest.

Sir Peter. Hush! A little French milliner, and the best of the jest is she's in the room now.

Charles. The devil she is!

Sir Peter. Hush, I tell you! (*Points*)

Charles. Behind the screen? 'Slife let's unveil her!

Sir Peter. No, no, he's coming. You shan't, indeed!

Charles. Oh, egad, we'll have a peep at the little milliner!

Sir Peter. Not for the world! Joseph will never forgive me.

Charles. I'll stand by you—

Sir Peter. Odds, here he is!

Joseph Surface *enters just as* Charles Surface *throws down the screen*

Charles. Lady Teazle, by all that's wonderful!

Sir Peter. Lady Teazle, by all that's damnable!

Charles. Sir Peter, this is one of the smartest French milliners I ever saw. Egad, you seem all to have been diverting yourselves here at hide and seek, and I don't see who is out of the secret. Shall I beg your ladyship to inform me? Not a word! Brother, will you be pleased to explain this matter? What! Is morality dumb too? Sir Peter, though I found you in the dark, perhaps you are not so now! All mute!—Well, though I can make nothing of the affair, I suppose you perfectly understand one another; so I'll leave you to yourselves. (*Going*) Brother, I'm sorry to find you have given that worthy man grounds for so much uneasiness. Sir Peter, there's nothing in the world so noble as a man of sentiment!

Exit Charles. *They stand for some time looking at each other*

Joseph Surface. Sir Peter, notwithstanding—I confess, that appearances are against me,—if you will afford me your patience, I make no doubt—but I shall explain everything to your satisfaction.

Sir Peter. If you please, sir.

Joseph Surface. The fact is, sir, that Lady Teazle, knowing my pretensions to your ward Maria,—I say, sir, Lady Teazle, being apprehensive of the jealousy of your temper,—and knowing my friendship to the family,—she, sir, I say—called here,—in order that—I might explain these pretensions: but on your coming,—being apprehensive.—as I said,—of your jealousy, she withdrew; and this, you may depend on it, is the whole truth of the matter.

Sir Peter. A very clear account, upon my word, and I dare swear the lady will vouch for every particle of it.

Lady Teazle. For not one word of it, Sir Peter.

Sir Peter. How! Don't you think it worth while to agree in the lie?

Lady Teazle. There is not one syllable of truth in what that gentleman has told you.

Sir Peter. I believe you, upon my soul, ma'am.

Joseph Surface. (*Aside*) 'Sdeath, madam, will you betray me?

Lady Teazle. Good Mr. Hypocrite, by your leave, I'll speak for myself.

Sir Peter. Ay, let her alone, sir; you'll find she'll make out a better story than you, without prompting.

Lady Teazle. Hear me, Sir Peter! I came here on no matter relating to your ward and even ignorant of this gentleman's pretensions to her. But I came, seduced by his insidious arguments, at least to listen to his pretended passion, if not to sacrifice your honor to his baseness.

Sir Peter. Now, I believe the truth is coming, indeed.

Joseph Surface. The woman's mad!

Lady Teazle. No, sir; she has recovered her senses and your own arts have furnished her with the means. Sir Peter, I do not expect you to credit me, but the tenderness you expressed for me when I am sure you could not think I was a witness to it has so penetrated to my heart that had I left this place without the shame of this discovery my future life should have spoken the sincerity of my grati tude. As for that smooth-tongued hypocrite, who would have seduced the wife of his too credulous friend while he affected honorable addresses to his ward, I behold him now in a light so truly despicable that I shall never again respect myself for having listened to him. *Exit*

JOSEPH SURFACE. Notwithstanding all this, Sir Peter, heaven knows—

SIR PETER. That you are a villain, and so I leave you to your conscience. *Exit*

JOSEPH SURFACE. (*Following* SIR PETER) You are too rash, Sir Peter. You shall hear me. The man who shuts out conviction by refusing to— *Exit*

ACT V

SCENE I. *The library*

Enter JOSEPH SURFACE *and* Servant

JOSEPH SURFACE. Mr. Stanley! And why should you think I would see him? You must know he comes to ask something.

SERVANT. Sir, I should not have let him in, but that Mr. Rowley came to the door with him.

JOSEPH SURFACE. Psha, blockhead! To suppose that I should now be in a temper to receive visits from poor relations! Well, why don't you show the fellow up?

SERVANT. I will, sir. Why, sir, it was not my fault that Sir Peter discovered my lady—

JOSEPH SURFACE. Go, fool! (*Exit* Servant) Sure, Fortune never played a man of my policy such a trick before. My character with Sir Peter, my hopes with Maria, destroyed in a moment! I'm in a rare humor to listen to other people's distresses. I shan't be able to bestow even a benevolent sentiment on Stanley.—So here he comes and Rowley with him. I must try to recover myself and put a little charity into my face, however. *Exit*

Enter SIR OLIVER SURFACE *and* ROWLEY

SIR OLIVER. What, does he avoid us? That was he, was it not?

ROWLEY. It was, sir. But I doubt you are come a little too abruptly. His nerves are so weak that the sight of a poor relation may be too much for him. I should have gone first to break it to him.

SIR OLIVER. Oh, plague of his nerves! Yet this is he whom Sir Peter extols as a man of the most benevolent way of thinking.

ROWLEY. As to his way of thinking, I cannot pretend to decide; for, to do him justice, he appears to have as much speculative benevolence as any private gentleman in the kingdom, though he is seldom so sensual as to indulge himself in the exercise of it.

SIR OLIVER. Yet he has a string of charitable sentiments at his fingers' ends.

ROWLEY. Or, rather, at his tongue's end, Sir Oliver, for I believe there is no sentiment he has such faith in as that "Charity begins at home."

SIR OLIVER. And his, I presume, is of that domestic sort which never stirs abroad at all.

ROWLEY. I doubt you'll find it so. But he's coming. I mustn't seem to interrupt you; and you know immediately as you leave him, I come in to announce your arrival in your real character.

SIR OLIVER. True, and afterwards you'll meet me at Sir Peter's.

ROWLEY. Without losing a moment. *Exit*

SIR OLIVER. I don't like the complaisance of his features.

Enter JOSEPH SURFACE

JOSEPH SURFACE. Sir, I beg you ten thousand pardons for keeping you a moment waiting. Mr. Stanley, I presume.

SIR OLIVER. At your service.

JOSEPH SURFACE. Sir, I beg you will do me the honor to sit down.—I entreat you, sir.

SIR OLIVER. Dear sir,—there's no occasion. (*Aside*) Too civil by half.

JOSEPH SURFACE. I have not the pleasure of knowing you, Mr. Stanley, but I am extremely happy to see you look so well. You were nearly related to my mother, I think, Mr. Stanley?

SIR OLIVER. I was, sir; so nearly that my present poverty, I fear, may do discredit to her wealthy children, else I should not have presumed to trouble you.

JOSEPH SURFACE. Dear sir, there needs no apology! He that is in distress, though a stranger, has a right to claim kindred with the wealthy. I am sure I wish I was of that class and had it in my power to offer you even a small relief.

SIR OLIVER. If your uncle, Sir Oliver, were here, I should have a friend.

JOSEPH SURFACE. I wish he was, sir, with all my heart. You should not want an advocate with him, believe me, sir.

Sir Oliver. I should not need one; my distresses would recommend me. But I imagined his bounty would enable you to become the agent of his charity.

Joseph Surface. My dear sir, you were strangely misinformed. Sir Oliver is a worthy man, a very worthy man; but avarice, Mr. Stanley, is the vice of age. I will tell you, my good sir, in confidence what he has done for me has been a mere nothing, though people I know have thought otherwise; and, for my part, I never chose to contradict the report.

Sir Oliver. What! Has he never transmitted you bullion, rupees, pagodas?[1]

Joseph Surface. Oh, dear sir, nothing of the kind! No, no, a few presents now and then,—china, shawls, congou tea,[2] avadavats,[3] and Indian crackers,[4]—little more, believe me.

Sir Oliver. (*Aside*) Here's gratitude for twelve thousand pounds! Avadavats and Indian crackers!

Joseph Surface. Then, my dear sir, you have heard, I doubt not, of the extravagance of my brother. There are very few who would credit what I have done for that unfortunate young man.

Sir Oliver. (*Aside*) Not I, for one!

Joseph Surface. The sums I have lent him! Indeed I have been exceedingly to blame; it was an amiable weakness; however, I don't pretend to defend it; and now I feel it doubly culpable since it has deprived me of the pleasure of serving you, Mr. Stanley, as my heart dictates.

Sir Oliver. (*Aside*) Dissembler!—Then, sir, you can't assist me?

Joseph Surface. At present it grieves me to say I cannot; but whenever I have the ability, you may depend upon hearing from me.

Sir Oliver. I am extremely sorry—

Joseph Surface. Not more than I, believe me. To pity without the power to relieve is still more painful than to ask and be denied.

Sir Oliver. Kind sir, your most obedient, humble servant!

Joseph Surface. You leave me deeply

[1] Indian coins, one, silver, worth about two shillings; the other, gold, then valued at about eight shillings.
[2] A black Chinese tea.
[3] Small Indian song-birds with red and black plumage.
[4] A variety of small fire crackers wrapped in colored paper.

affected, Mr. Stanley.—William, be ready to open the door.

Sir Oliver. Oh, dear sir, no ceremony.

Joseph Surface. Your very obedient!

Sir Oliver. Sir, your most obsequious!

Joseph Surface. You may depend upon hearing from me whenever I can be of service.

Sir Oliver. Sweet sir, you are too good!

Joseph Surface. In the meantime I wish you health and spirits.

Sir Oliver. Your ever grateful and perpetual humble servant!

Joseph Surface. Sir, yours as sincerely!

Sir Oliver. (*Aside*) Charles, you are my heir!
Exit

Joseph Surface. This is one bad effect of a good character; it invites application from the unfortunate, and there needs no small degree of address to gain the reputation of benevolence without incurring the expense. The silver ore of pure charity is an expensive article in the catalogue of a man's good qualities, whereas the sentimental French plate I use instead of it, makes just as good a show and pays no tax.

Enter Rowley

Rowley. Mr. Surface, your servant! I was apprehensive of interrupting you, though my business demands immediate attention, as this note will inform you.

Joseph Surface. Always happy to see Mr. Rowley. (*Reads the letter*) Sir Oliver Surface! My uncle arrived!

Rowley. He is, indeed; we have just parted. Quite well after a speedy voyage and impatient to embrace his worthy nephew.

Joseph Surface. I am astonished!—William, stop Mr. Stanley, if he's not gone!

Rowley. Oh, he's out of reach, I believe.

Joseph Surface. Why did you not let me know this when you came in together?

Rowley. I thought you had particular business. But I must be gone to inform your brother and appoint him here to meet your uncle. He will be with you in a quarter of an hour.

Joseph Surface. So he says. Well, I am strangely overjoyed at his coming. (*Aside*) Never, to be sure, was anything so damned unlucky!

Rowley. You will be delighted to see how well he looks.

JOSEPH SURFACE. Ah, I'm overjoyed to hear it.—(*Aside*) Just at this time!

ROWLEY. I'll tell him how impatiently you expect him.

JOSEPH SURFACE. Do, do! Pray give him my best duty and affection. Indeed, I cannot express the sensations I feel at the thought of seeing him. (*Exit* ROWLEY) Certainly his coming just at this time is the cruellest piece of ill fortune. *Exit*

SCENE II. SIR PETER TEAZLE'S

Enter MRS. CANDOUR *and* Maid

MAID. Indeed, ma'am, my lady will see nobody at present.

MRS. CANDOUR. Did you tell her it was her friend Mrs. Candour?

MAID. Yes, ma'am; but she begs you will excuse her.

MRS. CANDOUR. Do go again. I shall be glad to see her if it be only for a moment, for I am sure she must be in great distress. (*Exit* Maid) Dear heart, how provoking! I'm not mistress of half the circumstances! We shall have the whole affair in the newspapers with the names of the parties at length before I have dropped the story at a dozen houses. (*Enter* SIR BENJAMIN BACKBITE) Oh, Sir Benjamin, you have heard, I suppose—

SIR BENJAMIN. Of Lady Teazle and Mr. Surface—

MRS. CANDOUR. And Sir Peter's discovery—

SIR BENJAMIN. Oh, the strangest piece of business, to be sure!

MRS. CANDOUR. Well, I never was so surprised in my life. I am so sorry for all parties, indeed.

SIR BENJAMIN. Now, I don't pity Sir Peter at all; he was so extravagantly partial to Mr. Surface.

MRS. CANDOUR. Mr. Surface! Why, 'twas with Charles Lady Teazle was detected.

SIR BENJAMIN. No, no, I tell you; Mr. Surface is the gallant.

MRS. CANDOUR. No such thing! Charles is the man. 'Twas Mr. Surface brought Sir Peter on purpose to discover them.

SIR BENJAMIN. I tell you I had it from one—

MRS. CANDOUR. And I have it from one—

SIR BENJAMIN. Who had it from one, who had it—

MRS. CANDOUR. From one immediately. But here comes Lady Sneerwell; perhaps she knows the whole affair.

Enter LADY SNEERWELL

LADY SNEERWELL. So, my dear Mrs. Candour, here's a sad affair of our friend Lady Teazle.

MRS. CANDOUR. Ay, my dear friend, who would have thought—

LADY SNEERWELL. Well, there is no trusting appearances, though, indeed, she was always too lively for me.

MRS. CANDOUR. To be sure, her manners were a little too free; but then she was so young!

LADY SNEERWELL. And had, indeed, some good qualities.

MRS. CANDOUR. So she had, indeed. But have you heard the particulars?

LADY SNEERWELL. No; but everybody says that Mr. Surface—

SIR BENJAMIN. Ay, there, I told you Mr. Surface was the man.

MRS. CANDOUR. No, no; indeed, the assignation was with Charles.

LADY SNEERWELL. With Charles? You alarm me, Mrs. Candour!

MRS. CANDOUR. Yes, yes; he was the lover. Mr. Surface, to do him justice, was only the informer.

SIR BENJAMIN. Well, I'll not dispute with you, Mrs. Candour; but, be it which it may, I hope that Sir Peter's wound will not—

MRS. CANDOUR. Sir Peter's wound! Oh, mercy! I didn't hear a word of their fighting.

LADY SNEERWELL. Nor I, not a syllable.

SIR BENJAMIN. No? What, no mention of the duel?

MRS. CANDOUR. Not a word.

SIR BENJAMIN. Oh, yes. They fought before they left the room.

LADY SNEERWELL. Pray let us hear.

MRS. CANDOUR. Ay, do oblige us with the duel.

SIR BENJAMIN. "Sir," says Sir Peter, immediately after the discovery, "you are a most ungrateful fellow."

MRS. CANDOUR. Ay, to Charles—

SIR BENJAMIN. No, no, to Mr. Surface. "A most ungrateful fellow; and old as I am, sir," says he, "I insist on immediate satisfaction."

MRS. CANDOUR. Ay, that must have been

to Charles, for 'tis very unlikely Mr. Surface should fight in his own house.

SIR BENJAMIN. Gad's life, ma'am, not at all,—"giving me immediate satisfaction!" On this, ma'am, Lady Teazle, seeing Sir Peter in such danger, ran out of the room in strong hysterics and Charles after her calling out for hartshorn and water; then, madam, they began to fight with swords—

Enter CRABTREE

CRABTREE. With pistols, nephew, pistols! I have it from undoubted authority.

MRS. CANDOUR. Oh, Mr. Crabtree, then it is all true?

CRABTREE. Too true, indeed, madam, and Sir Peter is dangerously wounded—

SIR BENJAMIN. By a thrust in second [1] quite through his left side—

CRABTREE. By a bullet lodged in the thorax.

MRS. CANDOUR. Mercy on me! Poor Sir Peter!

CRABTREE. Yes, madam, though Charles would have avoided the matter if he could.

MRS. CANDOUR. I knew Charles was the person.

SIR BENJAMIN. My uncle, I see, knows nothing of the matter.

CRABTREE. But Sir Peter taxed him with the basest ingratitude—

SIR BENJAMIN. That I told you, you know—

CRABTREE. Do, nephew, let me speak! And insisted on immediate—

SIR BENJAMIN. Just as I said—

CRABTREE. Odd's life, nephew, allow others to know something too! A pair of pistols lay on the bureau (for Mr. Surface, it seems, had come home the night before late from Salt-hill,[2] where he had been to see the Montem with a friend who has a son at Eton) so, unluckily, the pistols were left charged.

SIR BENJAMIN. I heard nothing of this.

CRABTREE. Sir Peter forced Charles to take one, and they fired, it seems, pretty nearly together. Charles's shot took effect, as I tell you, and Sir Peter's missed; but what is very extraordinary, the ball struck a little bronze Shakespeare that stood over the fireplace, grazed out of the window at a right angle and wounded the postman, who was just coming to the door with a double letter [3] from Northamptonshire.

SIR BENJAMIN. My uncle's account is more circumstantial, I confess; but I believe mine is the true one, for all that.

LADY SNEERWELL. (*Aside*) I am more interested in this affair than they imagine and must have better information. *Exit*

SIR BENJAMIN. Ah, Lady Sneerwell's alarm is very easily accounted for.

CRABTREE. Yes, yes, they certainly do say—But that's neither here nor there.

MRS. CANDOUR. But, pray, where is Sir Peter at present?

CRABTREE. Oh, they brought him home, and he is now in the house, though the servants are ordered to deny him.

MRS. CANDOUR. I believe so, and Lady Teazle, I suppose, attending him.

CRABTREE. Yes, yes; and I saw one of the faculty [4] enter just before me.

SIR BENJAMIN. Hey! Who comes here?

CRABTREE. Oh, this is he, the physician, depend on't.

MRS. CANDOUR. Oh, certainly, it must be the physician; and now we shall know.

Enter SIR OLIVER SURFACE

CRABTREE. Well, doctor, what hopes?

MRS. CANDOUR. Ay, doctor, how's your patient?

SIR BENJAMIN. Now, doctor, isn't it a wound with a smallsword?

CRABTREE. A bullet lodged in the thorax, for a hundred!

SIR OLIVER. Doctor? A wound with a smallsword? And a bullet in the thorax?—Oons, are you mad, good people?

SIR BENJAMIN. Perhaps, sir, you are not a doctor?

SIR OLIVER. Truly, I am to thank you for my degree, if I am.

CRABTREE. Only a friend of Sir Peter's, then, I presume. But, sir, you must have heard of his accident.

SIR OLIVER. Not a word.

---

[1] Properly *seconde*, a technical term in fencing, a position in parrying.

[2] Salthill is a hill near Eton to which the boys of the school formerly went on every third Whit-Tuesday for a ceremony, which is accompanied by festivities resembling a carnival. It is known as Montem, from the phrase "processus ad montem." (Cf. Disraeli's *Coningsby*, where the occasion is described in great detail.) This allusion dates the time of action of *The School for Scandal* as about the first of June, Whitsunday being fifty days after Easter.

[3] A letter so heavy that it required double postage
[4] Medical profession.

CRABTREE. Not of his being dangerously wounded?
SIR OLIVER. The devil he is!
SIR BENJAMIN. Run through the body—
CRABTREE. Shot in the breast—
SIR BENJAMIN. By one Mr. Surface—
CRABTREE. Ay, the younger—
SIR OLIVER. Hey, what the plague! You seem to differ strangely in your accounts; however you agree that Sir Peter is dangerously wounded.
SIR BENJAMIN. Oh, yes, we agree there.
CRABTREE. Yes, yes, I believe there can be no doubt of that.
SIR OLIVER. Then, upon my word, for a person in that situation he is the most imprudent man alive, for here he comes, walking as if nothing at all was the matter. (*Enter* SIR PETER TEAZLE) Odd's heart, Sir Peter, you are come in good time, I promise you, for we had just given you over.
SIR BENJAMIN. (*Aside to* CRABTREE) Egad, uncle, this is the most sudden recovery!
SIR OLIVER. Why, man, what do you out of bed with a smallsword through your body and a bullet lodged in your thorax?
SIR PETER. A smallsword and a bullet!
SIR OLIVER. Ay! These gentlemen would have killed you without law or physic, and wanted to dub me a doctor to make me an accomplice.
SIR PETER. Why, what is all this?
SIR BENJAMIN. We rejoice, Sir Peter, that the story of the duel is not true and are sincerely sorry for your other misfortune.
SIR PETER. (*Aside*) So, so! All over the town already.
CRABTREE. Though, Sir Peter, you were certainly vastly to blame to marry at your years.
SIR PETER. Sir, what business is that of yours?
MRS. CANDOUR. Though, indeed, as Sir Peter made so good a husband, he's very much to be pitied.
SIR PETER. Plague on your pity, ma'am! I desire none of it.
SIR BENJAMIN. However, Sir Peter, you must not mind the laughing and jests you will meet with on the occasion.
SIR PETER. Sir, sir, I desire to be master in my own house.
CRABTREE. 'Tis no uncommon case, that's one comfort.
SIR PETER. I insist on being left to myself. Without ceremony, I insist on your leaving my house directly.
MRS. CANDOUR. Well, well, we are going; and depend on't, we'll make the best report of it we can. *Exit*
SIR PETER. Leave my house!
CRABTREE. And tell how hardly you've been treated. *Exit*
SIR PETER. Leave my house!
SIR BENJAMIN. And how patiently you bear it. *Exit*
SIR PETER. Fiends! Vipers! Furies! Oh, that their own venom would choke them!
SIR OLIVER. They are very provoking indeed, Sir Peter.

Enter ROWLEY

ROWLEY. I heard high words. What has ruffled you, sir?
SIR PETER. Psha, what signifies asking? Do I ever pass a day without my vexations?
ROWLEY. Well, I'm not inquisitive.
SIR OLIVER. Well, Sir Peter, I have seen both my nephews in the manner we proposed.
SIR PETER. A precious couple they are!
ROWLEY. Yes, and Sir Oliver is convinced that your judgment was right, Sir Peter.
SIR OLIVER. Yes, I find Joseph is indeed the man, after all.
ROWLEY. Ay, as Sir Peter says, he is a man of sentiment.
SIR OLIVER. And acts up to the sentiments he professes.
ROWLEY. It certainly is edification to hear him talk.
SIR OLIVER. Oh, he's a model for the young men of the age! But how's this, Sir Peter, you don't join us in your friend Joseph's praise as I expected?
SIR PETER. Sir Oliver, we live in a damned wicked world, and the fewer we praise the better.
ROWLEY. What, do you say so, Sir Peter, who were never mistaken in your life?
SIR PETER. Psha! Plague on you both! I see by your sneering you have heard the whole affair. I shall go mad among you!
ROWLEY. Then, to fret you no longer, Sir Peter, we are indeed acquainted with it all. I met Lady Teazle coming from Mr. Surface's so humbled that she deigned to request me to be her advocate with you.

Sir Peter. And does Sir Oliver know all this?

Sir Oliver. Every circumstance.

Sir Peter. What? Of the closet and the screen, hey?

Sir Oliver. Yes, yes, and the little French milliner. Oh, I have been vastly diverted with the story! Ha! ha! ha!

Sir Peter. 'Twas very pleasant.

Sir Oliver. I never laughed more in my life, I assure you. Ah! ah! ah!

Sir Peter. Oh, vastly diverting! Ha! ha! ha!

Rowley. To be sure, Joseph with his sentiments! Ha! ha! ha!

Sir Peter. Yes, yes, his sentiments! Ha! ha! ha! Hypocritical villain!

Sir Oliver. Ay, and that rogue Charles to pull Sir Peter out of the closet! Ha! ha! ha!

Sir Peter. Ha! ha! 'Twas devilish entertaining, to be sure!

Sir Oliver. Ha! ha! ha! Egad, Sir Peter, I should like to have seen your face when the screen was thrown down! Ha! ha!

Sir Peter. Yes, yes, my face when the screen was thrown down! Ha! ha! ha! Oh, I must never show my head again!

Sir Oliver. But come, come, it isn't fair to laugh at you neither, my old friend, though, upon my soul, I can't help it.

Sir Peter. Oh, pray don't restrain your mirth on my account. It does not hurt me at all. I laugh at the whole affair myself. Yes, yes, I think being a standing jest for all one's acquaintance a very happy situation. Oh, yes, and then of a morning to read the paragraphs about Mr. S—, Lady T—, and Sir P— will be so entertaining.

Rowley. Without affectation, Sir Peter, you may despise the ridicule of fools. But I see Lady Teazle going towards the next room. I am sure you must desire a reconciliation as earnestly as she does.

Sir Oliver. Perhaps my being here prevents her coming to you. Well, I'll leave honest Rowley to mediate between you; but he must bring you all presently to Mr. Surface's, where I am now returning, if not to reclaim a libertine, at least to expose hypocrisy.

Sir Peter. Ah, I'll be present at your discovering yourself there with all my heart, though 'tis a vile unlucky place for discoveries.

Rowley. We'll follow. *Exit* Sir Oliver

Sir Peter. She is not coming here, you see, Rowley.

Rowley. No, but she has left the door of that room open, you perceive. See, she is in tears.

Sir Peter. Certainly a little mortification appears very becoming in a wife. Don't you think it will do her good to let her pine a little?

Rowley. Oh, this is ungenerous in you!

Sir Peter. Well, I know not what to think. You remember the letter I found of hers evidently intended for Charles?

Rowley. A mere forgery, Sir Peter, laid in your way on purpose. This is one of the points which I intend Snake shall give you conviction of.

Sir Peter. I wish I were once satisfied of that. She looks this way. What a remarkably elegant turn of the head she has! Rowley, I'll go to her.

Rowley. Certainly.

Sir Peter. Though, when it is known that we are reconciled, people will laugh at me ten times more.

Rowley. Let them laugh and retort their malice only by showing them you are happy in spite of it.

Sir Peter. I' faith, so I will! And, if I'm not mistaken, we may yet be the happiest couple in the country.

Rowley. Nay, Sir Peter, he who once lays aside suspicion—

Sir Peter. Hold, Master Rowley! If you have any regard for me, never let me hear you utter anything like a sentiment. I have had enough of them to serve me the rest of my life. *Exeunt*

Scene III. *The library*

Enter Joseph Surface *and* Lady Sneerwell

Lady Sneerwell. Impossible! Will not Sir Peter immediately be reconciled to Charles and, of course, no longer oppose his union with Maria? The thought is distraction to me!

Joseph Surface. Can passion furnish a remedy?

Lady Sneerwell. No, nor cunning neither. Oh, I was a fool, an idiot, to league with such a blunderer!

Joseph Surface. Sure, Lady Sneerwell, I am the greatest sufferer; yet you see I bear the accident with calmness.

Lady Sneerwell. Because the disappointment doesn't reach your heart; your interest only attached you to Maria. Had you felt for her what I have for that ungrateful libertine, neither your temper nor hypocrisy could prevent your showing the sharpness of your vexation.

JOSEPH SURFACE. But why should your reproaches fall on me for this disappointment?

LADY SNEERWELL. Are you not the cause of it? Had you not a sufficient field for your roguery in imposing upon Sir Peter and supplanting his brother but you must endeavor to seduce his wife? I hate such an avarice of crimes. 'Tis an unfair monopoly and never prospers.

JOSEPH SURFACE. Well, I admit I have been to blame. I confess I deviated from the direct road of wrong, but I don't think we're so totally defeated neither.

LADY SNEERWELL. No?

JOSEPH SURFACE. You tell me you have made a trial of Snake since we met and that you still believe him faithful to us?

LADY SNEERWELL. I do believe so.

JOSEPH SURFACE. And that he has undertaken, should it be necessary, to swear and prove that Charles is at this time contracted by vows and honor to your ladyship, which some of his former letters to you will serve to support?

LADY SNEERWELL. This, indeed, might have assisted.

JOSEPH SURFACE. Come, come; it is not too late yet. (*Knocking at the door*) But hark! This is probably my uncle, Sir Oliver. Retire to that room; we'll consult farther when he is gone.

LADY SNEERWELL. Well, but if he should find you out, too?

JOSEPH SURFACE. Oh, I have no fear of that. Sir Peter will hold his tongue for his own credit's sake. And you may depend on it I shall soon discover Sir Oliver's weak side.

LADY SNEERWELL. I have no diffidence [1] of your abilities; only be constant to one roguery at a time. *Exit*

JOSEPH SURFACE. I will, I will! So! 'Tis confounded hard, after such bad fortune, to be baited by one's confederate in evil. Well, at all events, my character is so much better than Charles's that I certainly—Hey! What! This is not Sir Oliver but old Stanley again. Plague on 't that he should return to tease me

[1] Doubt. an obsolete meaning.

just now! I shall have Sir Oliver come and find him here, and—(*Enter* SIR OLIVER SURFACE) Gad's life, Mr. Stanley, why have you come back to plague me at this time? You must not stay now, upon my word.

SIR OLIVER. Sir, I hear your uncle Oliver is expected here and, though he has been so penurious to you, I'll try what he'll do for me.

JOSEPH SURFACE. Sir, 'tis impossible for you to stay now; so I must beg—Come any other time and I promise you, you shall be assisted.

SIR OLIVER. No. Sir Oliver and I must be acquainted.

JOSEPH SURFACE. Zounds, sir! Then I must insist on your quitting the room directly.

SIR OLIVER. Nay, sir—

JOSEPH SURFACE. Sir, I insist on 't!—Here William, show this gentleman out. Since you compel me, sir, not one moment—This is such insolence! (*Going to push him out*)

Enter CHARLES SURFACE

CHARLES. Heyday! What's the matter now? What the devil? Have you got hold of my little broker here! Zounds, brother, don't hurt little Premium. What's the matter, my little fellow?

JOSEPH SURFACE. So, he has been with you too, has he?

CHARLES. To be sure, he has. Why, he's as honest a little—But sure, Joseph, you have not been borrowing money too, have you?

JOSEPH SURFACE. Borrowing? No! But, brother, you know we expect Sir Oliver here every—

CHARLES. O Gad, that's true! Noll mustn't find the little broker here, to be sure!

JOSEPH SURFACE. Yet Mr. Stanley insists—

CHARLES. Stanley! Why his name's Premium.

JOSEPH SURFACE. No, sir, Stanley.

CHARLES. No, no, Premium!

JOSEPH SURFACE. Well, no matter which, but—

CHARLES. Ay, ay, Stanley or Premium, 'tis the same thing, as you say; for I suppose he goes by half a hundred names besides A. B. at the coffee-house. (*Knocking*)

JOSEPH SURFACE. 'Sdeath, here's Sir Oliver at the door! Now, I beg, Mr. Stanley—

CHARLES. Ay, ay, and I beg, Mr. Premium—

SIR OLIVER. Gentlemen—

JOSEPH SURFACE. Sir, by heaven, you shall go!
CHARLES. Ay, out with him, certainly!
SIR OLIVER. This violence—
JOSEPH SURFACE. Sir, 'tis your own fault.
CHARLES. Out with him, to be sure!
(*Both forcing* SIR OLIVER *out*)

Enter SIR PETER *and* LADY TEAZLE, MARIA, *and* ROWLEY

SIR PETER. My old friend, Sir Oliver—Hey! What in the name of wonder? Here are two dutiful nephews! Assault their uncle at a first visit!
LADY TEAZLE. Indeed, Sir Oliver, 'twas well we came in to rescue you.
ROWLEY. Truly it was, for I perceive, Sir Oliver, the character of old Stanley was no protection to you.
SIR OLIVER. Nor of Premium either. The necessities of the former could not extort a shilling from that benevolent gentleman; and, now, egad, I stood a chance of faring worse than my ancestors and being knocked down without being bid for.
JOSEPH SURFACE. Charles!
CHARLES. Joseph!
JOSEPH SURFACE. 'Tis now complete!
CHARLES. Very!
SIR OLIVER. Sir Peter, my friend, and Rowley, too, look on that elder nephew of mine. You know what he has already received from my bounty; and you know how gladly I would have regarded half my fortune as held in trust for him. Judge then my disappointment in discovering him to be destitute of faith, charity, and gratitude!
SIR PETER. Sir Oliver, I should be more surprised at this declaration if I had not myself found him to be mean, treacherous, and hypocritical.
LADY TEAZLE. And if the gentleman pleads not guilty to these, pray let him call me to his character.
SIR PETER. Then, I believe, we need add no more. If he knows himself, he will consider it as the most perfect punishment that he is known to the world.
CHARLES. (*Aside*) If they talk this way to honesty, what will they say to me, by and by?
SIR OLIVER. As for that prodigal, his brother there—
CHARLES. (*Aside*) Ay, now comes my turn. The damned family pictures will ruin me!

JOSEPH SURFACE. Sir Oliver—uncle, will you honor me with a hearing?
CHARLES. (*Aside*) Now, if Joseph would make one of his long speeches, I might recollect myself a little.
SIR OLIVER. (*To* JOSEPH) I suppose you would undertake to justify yourself entirely?
JOSEPH SURFACE. I trust I could.
SIR OLIVER. (*To* CHARLES) Well, sir, and you could justify yourself, too, I suppose?
CHARLES. Not that I know of, Sir Oliver.
SIR OLIVER. What? Little Premium has been let too much into the secret, I suppose?
CHARLES. True, sir; but they were family secrets and should not be mentioned again, you know.
ROWLEY. Come, Sir Oliver, I know you cannot speak of Charles's follies with anger.
SIR OLIVER. Odd's heart, no more I can, nor with gravity either. Sir Peter, do you know the rogue bargained with me for all his ancestors, sold me judges and generals by the foot and maiden aunts as cheap as broken china?
CHARLES. To be sure, Sir Oliver, I did make a little free with the family canvas, that's the truth on 't. My ancestors may rise in judgment against me, there's no denying it; but believe me sincere when I tell you, and upon my soul I would not say so if I was not, that if I do not appear mortified at the exposure of my follies, it is because I feel at this moment the warmest satisfaction in seeing you, my liberal benefactor.
SIR OLIVER. Charles, I believe you. Give me your hand again. The ill-looking little fellow over the settee has made your peace.
CHARLES. Then, sir, my gratitude to the original is still increased.
LADY TEAZLE. Yet I believe, Sir Oliver, here is one whom Charles is still more anxious to be reconciled to.
SIR OLIVER. Oh, I have heard of his attachment there; and, with the young lady's pardon, if I construe right, that blush—
SIR PETER. Well, child, speak your sentiments!
MARIA. Sir, I have little to say, but that I shall rejoice to hear that he is happy. For me, whatever claim I had to his attention, I willingly resign to one who has a better title.
CHARLES. How, Maria!
SIR PETER. Heyday! What's the mystery

now? While he appeared an incorrigible rake, you would give your hand to no one else; and now that he is likely to reform I'll warrant you won't have him!

MARIA. His own heart and Lady Sneerwell know the cause.

CHARLES. Lady Sneerwell!

JOSEPH SURFACE. Brother, it is with great concern I am obliged to speak on this point, but my regard for justice compels me, and Lady Sneerwell's injuries can no longer be concealed. (*Opens the door*)

Enter LADY SNEERWELL

SIR PETER. So! Another French milliner! Egad, he has one in every room in the house, I suppose!

LADY SNEERWELL. Ungrateful Charles! Well may you be surprised and feel for the indelicate situation your perfidy has forced me into.

CHARLES. Pray, uncle, is this another plot of yours? For, as I have life, I don't understand it.

JOSEPH SURFACE. I believe, sir, there is but the evidence of one person more necessary to make it extremely clear.

SIR PETER. And that person, I imagine, is Mr. Snake. Rowley, you were perfectly right to bring him with us, and pray let him appear.

ROWLEY. Walk in, Mr. Snake. (*Enter* SNAKE) I thought his testimony might be wanted; however, it happens unluckily that he comes to confront Lady Sneerwell, not to support her.

LADY SNEERWELL. A villain! Treacherous to me at last! Speak, fellow, have you, too, conspired against me?

SNAKE. I beg your ladyship ten thousand pardons. You paid me extremely liberally for the lie in question, but I unfortunately have been offered double to speak the truth.

SIR PETER. Plot and counter-plot, egad!

LADY SNEERWELL. The torments of shame and disappointment on you all!

LADY TEAZLE. Hold, Lady Sneerwell! Before you go, let me thank you for the trouble you and that gentleman have taken in writing letters from me to Charles and answering them yourself; and let me also request you to make my respects to the scandalous college, of which you are president, and inform them that Lady Teazle, licentiate, begs leave to return the diploma they granted her, as she leaves off practice and kills characters no longer.

LADY SNEERWELL. You too, madam! Provoking! Insolent! May your husband live these fifty years! *Exit*

SIR PETER. Oons, what a fury!

LADY TEAZLE. A malicious creature, indeed!

SIR PETER. Hey! Not for her last wish?

LADY TEAZLE. Oh, no!

SIR OLIVER. Well, sir, and what have you to say now?

JOSEPH SURFACE. Sir, I am so confounded to find that Lady Sneerwell could be guilty of suborning Mr. Snake in this manner to impose on us all that I know not what to say. However, lest her revengeful spirit should prompt her to injure my brother, I had certainly better follow her directly. *Exit*

SIR PETER. Moral to the last drop!

SIR OLIVER. Ay, and marry her, Joseph, if you can. Oil and vinegar! Egad you'll do very well together.

ROWLEY. I believe we have no more occasion for Mr. Snake at present?

SNAKE. Before I go, I beg pardon once for all, for whatever uneasiness I have been the humble instrument of causing to the parties present.

SIR PETER. Well, well, you have made atonement by a good deed at last.

SNAKE. But I must request of the company that it shall never be known.

SIR PETER. Hey! What the plague! Are you ashamed of having done a right thing once in your life?

SNAKE. Ah, sir, consider. I live by the badness of my character. I have nothing but my infamy to depend on; and, if it were once known that I had been betrayed into an honest action, I should lose every friend I have in the world.

SIR OLIVER. Well, well, we'll not traduce you by saying anything in your praise, never fear. *Exit* SNAKE

SIR PETER. There's a precious rogue!

LADY TEAZLE. See, Sir Oliver, there needs no persuasion now to reconcile your nephew and Maria.

SIR OLIVER. Ay, ay, that's as it should be; and, egad, we'll have the wedding tomorrow morning.

CHARLES. Thank you, dear uncle.

SIR PETER. What, you rogue! Don't you ask the girl's consent first?

CHARLES. Oh, I have done that a long time
—a minute ago, and she has looked *yes*.

MARIA. For shame, Charles! I protest, Sir Peter, there has not been a word—

SIR OLIVER. Well then, the fewer the better. May your love for each other never know abatement!

SIR PETER. And may you live as happily together as Lady Teazle and I intend to do!

CHARLES. Rowley, my old friend, I am sure you congratulate me; and I suspect that I owe you much.

SIR OLIVER. You do, indeed, Charles.

ROWLEY. If my efforts to serve you had not succeeded, you would have been in my debt for the attempt; but deserve to be happy and you overpay me!

SIR PETER. Ay, honest Rowley always said you would reform.

CHARLES. Why, as to reforming, Sir Peter, I'll make no promises, and that I take to be a proof that I intend to set about it. But here shall be my monitor, my gentle guide. Ah, can I leave the virtuous path those eyes illumine?
Though thou, dear maid, shouldst waive thy
    beauty's sway,
Thou still must rule, because I will obey.
An humble fugitive from Folly view,
No sanctuary near but love and you.
                (*To the audience*)
You can, indeed, each anxious fear remove,
For even Scandal dies, if you approve!

EPILOGUE

BY MR. COLMAN

Spoken by LADY TEAZLE

I, who was late so volatile and gay,
Like a trade-wind must now blow all one way,
Bend all my cares, my studies, and my vows,
To one dull, rusty weathercock,—my spouse!
So wills our virtuous bard,—the motley Bayes
Of crying epilogues and laughing plays! 6
Old bachelors who marry smart young wives
Learn from our play to regulate your lives;
Each bring his dear to town, all faults upon
    her,—
London will prove the very source of honor.
Plunged fairly in, like a cold bath it serves, 11
When principles relax, to brace the nerves.
Such is my case; and yet I must deplore
That the gay dream of dissipation's o'er.
And say, ye fair, was ever lively wife, 15
Born with a genius for the highest life,
Like me untimely blasted in her bloom,
Like me condemned to such a dismal doom?
Save money, when I just knew how to waste
    it!
Leave London, just as I began to taste it! 20
    Must I then watch the early-crowing cock,
The melancholy ticking of a clock;
In a lone rustic hall forever pounded,[1]
With dogs, cats, rats, and squalling brats
    surrounded?
With humble curate can I now retire, 25
(While good Sir Peter boozes with the squire)
And at backgammon mortify my soul,
That pants for loo or flutters at a vole?[2]
Seven's near the main![3] Dear sound that
    must expire, 29
Lost at hot cockles[4] round a Christmas fire.
The transient hour of fashion too soon spent,
Farewell the tranquil mind, farewell content![5]
Farewell the plumèd head, the cushioned *tête*,
That takes the cushion from its proper seat!
That spirit-stirring drum! Card drums, I
    mean, 35
Spadille, odd trick, pam, basto, king and
    queen!
And you, ye knockers that with brazen throat
The welcome visitors' approach denote,
Farewell all quality of high renown,
Pride, pomp, and circumstance of glorious
    town! 40
Farewell! Your revels I partake no more,
And Lady Teazle's occupation's o'er!
All this I told our bard; he smiled and said
    'twas clear,
I ought to play deep tragedy next year. 44
Meanwhile he drew wise morals from his play,
And in these solemn periods stalked away:—
"Blessed were the fair like you, her faults
    who stopped,
And closed her follies when the curtain
    dropped!
No more in vice or error to engage 49
Or play the fool at large on life's great stage."

---

[1] Confined in a pound, said of animals.
[2] Loo is the fashionable game of cards of the eighteenth century; a vole is a "grand slam," taking all the tricks.
[3] The main was the number which the caster of dice attempted to throw, his "point.' Seven, of course, is one of the most probable combinations with two dice.
[4] An old, childish game.
[5] This and the following ten lines parody *Othello's* soliloquy, III, iii, 347–357.

THE STRANGER

A Drama in Five Acts

Translated from the German of Augustus von Kotzebue

By Benjamin Thompson, Esq.

August Friedrich Ferdinand von Kotzebue was born at Weimar, May 3, 1761. After studying law at Duisburg, he practised his profession in Germany and Russia for a while, but deserted it for the theater and politics. At one time he was dramatist to the court theater at Vienna, and later he became director of the German Theater at St. Petersburg, in which office he was patronized by the Czar, Paul I. Returning to Germany, Kotzebue found that his open derision of Goethe and his undisguised opposition to the liberal movement made him so unpopular in his birthplace that he deemed it advisable to move. He was known at this time as the greatest living German dramatist, having written some two hundred plays, besides novels, histories, and miscellaneous sketches. He was popularly regarded as superior to Goethe as a dramatist and was in England called the "German Shakespeare." The young liberals detested him, however, and one of them, a theological student named Karl Ludwig Sand, murdered him at Mannheim, March 23, 1817.

See H. Dörnig, *A von Kotzebues Leben*, 1830; W. von Kotzebue, *A von Kotzebue*, 1881; Rabany, Charles, *Kotzebue, sa vie et sons temps, ses œuvres dramatiques*, 1893: and see, on the general craze for German melodrama and sentimentality, Sellier, Walter, *Kotzebue in England*, 1901.

Benjamin Thompson (born 1776?), the son of a merchant of Kingston-upon-Hull, was educated for the law, but, disliking his profession, went as his father's agent to Hamburg, where he translated a number of German plays into English. The translations, mostly from Kotzebue, were published as *The German Theatre*, in six volumes, containing twenty plays, "dedicated by permission to Her Grace The Duchess of Devonshire," in 1801. After his return to England, Thompson's two original plays were produced at Drury Lane, *Godolphin* (Oct. 12, 1812) and *Oberon's Oath* (May 21, 1816). Both were failures. His disappointment over the reception of his last play is said to have killed him. He died May 26, 1816.

See *The Biographia Dramatica*, *The Gentleman's Magazine* (1816), and *The Dictionary of National Biography*.

PLAYS BY KOTZEBUE PRODUCED IN LONDON
1798–1800

(Only the versions produced are listed; various unacted translations of many plays were published. Stage versions were frequently based upon other translations, as noticed below.)

1. Menschenhass und Reue as The Stranger (D.L., March 24, 1798) by Benjamin Thompson.
2. Das Kind der Liebe; oder, der Strassenräuber aus kindlicher Liebe as Lovers' Vows (C.G., Oct. 11, 1798) by Mrs. Inchbald from Stephen Porter's Lovers' Vows; or, The Child of Love, from (?) Anne Plumptre's The Natural Son.
3. Der Bruderzwist as The Birth-Day (C.G., April 8, 1799) by Thomas John Dibdin from The Birth-Day by an unknown translator.
4. Der Graf von Burgund as The Count of Burgundy (C.G., April 12, 1799) by Alexander Pope [1] from Anne Plumptre.
5. Die Witwe und das Reitfpferd as The Horse and the Widow (C.G., May 4, 1799) by Dibdin from Plumptre's The Widow and the Riding Horse.
6. Die Spanier in Peru; oder, Rolla's Tod as Pizarro (D.L., May 24, 1799) by R. B. Sheridan from Plumptre's The Spaniards in Peru.
7. Der Opfertod as Family Distress (Hay., June 15, 1799) by H. Neuman from his own Self-Immolation.
8. Armuth und Edelsinn as Sighs; or, the Daughter (Hay., July 30, 1799) by Prince Hoare from Maria Geisweiler's Poverty and Nobleness of Mind.
9. Das Schreibepult; oder, die Gefahren der Jugend as The Wise Man of the East (C.G., Nov. 30, 1799) by Mrs. Inchbald from The Writing Desk (anon.)
10. Johannah von Montfaucon as Joanna of Montfaucon (C.G., Jan. 16, 1800) by Richard Cumberland from Maria Geisweiler.

[1] An actor, not the great poet of Twickenham.

The following plays by Kotzebue, though translated earlier, were produced only after 1800: La Peyrouse; Edouard in Schottland, oder, die Nacht eines Fluchtlings; Graf Benjowsky, oder, die Verschwörung auf Kamtschatka; Die Sonnen-Jungfrau; Blind Geladen; and Rehbock, oder, die schuldlosen Schuldbewussten, this last at C.G. during the season 1823–24.

The vogue of German drama in England at the close of the eighteenth century is most obviously attested by the extraordinary popularity of translations from Kotzebue of which the highest in popular favor were *The Stranger*, and Sheridan's *Pizarro* (D.L., May 24, 1799). The "Kotzebue fever" was at its height from 1798 to 1800, during which years the plays of "the German Shakespeare" furnished materials for translators and adapters, and subjects for more or less original dramatists. Though the absurdity of the German fashion was recognized by some, and though Canning, Ellis, and Frere ridiculed its sensationalism and sentimentality in *The Rovers* (*The Anti-Jacobin*, 1798), the populace applauded German plays in the theaters and the judicious perused them, in translation, in their libraries. The appeal was twofold: the romantic temper of German drama coincided with the *Zeitgeist* of the period of *Lyrical Ballads;* and sociological themes frequently employed by Kotzebue, were sure of a welcome by readers of *The Rights of Women* and *Political Justice*. Although Kotzebue's plays usually end happily, in the conventional sense, those known in England are not generally comedies but serious studies of serious problems, resembling later social problem plays and, at least in the case of *The Stranger*, raising questions as to their propriety as public entertainment.

The Stranger, Benjamin Thompson's translation of *Menschenhass und Reue*, with the addition of a couple of songs and some dances and considerably shortened from its German original, illustrates the type, of which it is probably the best example. Its very real theatricality, a quality common to most of Kotzebue's plays, probably accounts to some extent for its popularity in its own day; but at Drury Lane, March 24, 1798, the production was brilliant. Mrs. Siddons and her accomplished brother, then at the height of their powers, wrung the hearts of their audiences in a fashion which in itself, when one considers their vehicle, is the greatest possible tribute to the extreme virtuosity of the Kemble family. As they were also ably supported, the palpable absurdities of the dialogue and characterization were more than compensated by the acting.

ADVERTISEMENT

Various reports were circulated respecting this piece when it was first performed. Another translator,[1] in an address to the public, asserted that he had been "ungenerously treated" by the proprietors of the Theatre Royal, Drury Lane, and laid to their charge "the undisguised appropriation of the whole of *his* play," which they had previously refused and returned to him. I should have thought this account too contemptible for notice, had it not in some degree influenced the opinions of several respectable periodical critics, who finding it impossible to credit so preposterous a charge ascribed to superior interest the preference which had been given to my translation. This conjecture is, however, erroneous, for at the time I transmitted *The Stranger* to Drury Lane Theatre, I was totally unknown to any of the proprietors and had no introduction to them but through the play itself. Mr. Grubb, to whom I sent it with a few lines, put it into the hands of Mr. Sheridan, who was so kind as to improve its effect by several alterations and additions.[2] To both these gentlemen I acknowledge my grateful obligations and also return sincere thanks to the several performers for their exertions.

B. T.

Nottingham, Dec. 26, 1799.

[1] August Schink, whose translation, *The Stranger*, went through five editions in 1798 but was never produced. George Papendinck also published *The Stranger; or, Misanthropy and Repentance,* . . . Faithfully translated, entire. from the German . . ., 1798.

[2] Sheridan's additions probably consist chiefly of the addition of the vaudeville scenes at the end of Act II and the beginning of Act IV. See D. MacMillan, "Sheridan's Share in *The Stranger*," *Modern Language Notes*, XLV, 2.

THE STRANGER

DRAMATIS PERSONÆ

MEN
THE STRANGER	Mr. Kemble
COUNT WINTERSEN	Mr. Barrymore
BARON STEINFORT	Mr. Palmer
MR. SOLOMON	Mr. Wewitzer
PETER	Mr. Suett
TOBIAS	Mr. Aickin
FRANCIS	Mr. R. Palmer
GEORGE	Mr. Webb
COUNT'S SON, 5 years old	Master Wells
STRANGER'S SON, 5 years old	Master Stokeley

WOMEN
MRS. HALLER	Mrs Siddons
COUNTESS WINTERSEN	Mrs. Goodall
CHARLOTTE	Miss Stuart
ANNETTE	Mrs. Bland
SAVOYARD	Miss Leake
MAID	Mrs. Jones.
STRANGER'S DAUGHTER, 4 years old	Miss Beton

Tenants, Servants, Dancers, &c.

PROLOGUE

Written by W. LINLEY, ESQ.[1]

Spoken by MR. BARRYMORE

When first the Comic Muse with forceful art
Essayed to triumph o'er the yielding heart,
With trembling zeal at Fancy's awful shrine
Graceful she bent, and claimed the wreath divine.
"To me," she cries, "the mingled powers belong 5
Of wit, of humor, dance, and social song;
Mine the glad task to check the rising sigh,
And wipe the glistening drop from Beauty's eye;
On me the blooming loves and graces smile,
And crown with eager praise my cheerful toil.
The Tragic Muse, too oft thy favorite care, 11
May sanction, still, the unobtruding tear;
May wake to passion, or to pity move,
Rouse to despair, or melt the soul to love:
But oh! how sweetly beaming through the maze 15
Of fictioned grief, Thalia darts her rays!
With double zest she feeds the listening ear,
And rapture dawns through Pity's transient tear."
"Equal in power," the impartial goddess cried,
"Ye both are suitors, both to be denied; 20
Nor can the wreath on either head be wove,
When both have equal claim to grace and love!
But go; collect your powers; that path explore
Which leads to Albion's still united shore!
There, if near Drury's walls you chance to stray, 25
And meet a timid *Stranger* on his way,
Give to my fearful charge your equal aid;
Protect and guide him through the scenic shade,
And as my favorite Shakespeare struck the lyre,
Warmed by an equal portion of your fire, 30
Still with impartial zeal your force employ
And ope to him the source of grief and joy."
Thus Fancy spoke; each Muse reclined her head;
A hesitating blush their cheeks o'erspread.
Have they then deigned to prop our Author's cause? 35
What's to decide the question? Your applause!

---

[1] William Linley (1771-1835), Sheridan's brother-in-law, composer and author of novels, songs, and other verses.

This prologue presents reasons for the existence of that form, neither comedy nor tragedy, which as "drama" became the predominating form in the nineteenth and early twentieth centuries.

ACT I

Scene I

The skirts of Count Wintersen's park. The park gates in the center. On one side a low lodge among the trees. On the other in the background a peasant's hut.

Enter PETER

PETER. Pooh! Pooh! Never tell me! I'm a clever lad, for all father's crying out every minute, "Peter!" and "Stupid Peter!" But I say Peter is not stupid, though father will always be so wise. First, I talk too much; then I talk too little; and if I talk a bit to myself, he calls me driveller. Now, I like best to talk to myself, for I never contradict myself; and I don't laugh at myself, as other folks do. That laughing is often a plaguy teasing custom. To be sure, when Mrs. Haller laughs one can bear it well enough; there is a sweetness even in her reproof that somehow— But lud! I had near forgot what I was sent about. Yes, then they would have laughed at me indeed! (*Draws a green purse from his pocket*) I am to carry this money to old Tobias; and Mrs. Haller said I must be sure not to blab or say that she had sent it. Well, well, she may be easy for that matter; not a word shall drop from my lips. Mrs. Haller is charming, but silly, if father is right, for father says, "He that spends his money is not wise; but he that gives it away is stark mad."

Enter STRANGER *from the lodge, with his arms folded, his head hanging down, followed by* FRANCIS. *At sight of* PETER, STRANGER *stops and looks suspiciously at him.* PETER *stands opposite to him with his mouth wide open. At length he takes off his hat, scrapes a bow, and goes into the hut*

STRANGER. Who is that?
FRANCIS. The steward's son.
STRANGER. Of the castle?
FRANCIS. Yes.
STRANGER. (*After a pause*) You were speaking last night—
FRANCIS. Of the old countryman?
STRANGER. Ay.
FRANCIS. You would not hear me out.
STRANGER. Proceed.
FRANCIS. He is poor.
STRANGER. Who told you so?
FRANCIS. He himself.
STRANGER. (*With acrimony*) Ay, ay; he knows how to tell his story, no doubt.
FRANCIS. And to impose, you think?
STRANGER. Right.
FRANCIS. This man does not.
STRANGER. Fool!
FRANCIS. A feeling fool is better than a cold sceptic.
STRANGER. False!
FRANCIS. Charity begets gratitude.
STRANGER. False!
FRANCIS. And blesses the giver more than the receiver.
STRANGER. True!
FRANCIS. Well, sir, this countryman—
STRANGER. Has he complained to you?
FRANCIS. Yes.
STRANGER. He who is really unhappy never complains. (*Pauses*) Francis, you have had means of education beyond your lot in life, and hence you are encouraged to attempt imposing on me. But go on.
FRANCIS. His only son has been taken from him.
STRANGER. Taken from him?
FRANCIS. By the exigency of the times, for a soldier.
STRANGER. Ay!
FRANCIS. The old man is poor.
STRANGER. 'Tis likely.
FRANCIS. Sick and forsaken.
STRANGER. I cannot help him.
FRANCIS. Yes.
STRANGER. How?
FRANCIS. By money. He may buy his son's release.
STRANGER. I'll see him myself.
FRANCIS. Do so.
STRANGER. But if he prove an impostor!
FRANCIS. He is not.
STRANGER. In that hut?
FRANCIS. In that hut. (STRANGER *goes into the hut*) A good master, though one almost loses the use of speech by living with him. A man kind and clear, though I cannot understand him. He rails against the whole world and yet no beggar leaves his door unsatisfied. I have now lived three years with him and yet I know not who he is. A hater of society, no doubt; but not by Providence intended so. Misanthropy in his *head*, not in his *heart*.

Enter STRANGER *and* PETER *from the hut*
PETER. Pray walk on.
STRANGER. (*To* FRANCIS) Fool!
FRANCIS. So soon returned?
STRANGER. What should I do there?
FRANCIS. Did you not find it as I said?
STRANGER. This lad I found.
FRANCIS. What has he to do with your charity?
STRANGER. The old man and he understand each other perfectly well.
FRANCIS. How?
STRANGER. What were this boy and the countryman doing?
FRANCIS. (*Smiling and shaking his head*) Well, you shall hear. (*To* PETER) Young man, what were you doing in that hut?
PETER. Doing? Nothing.
FRANCIS. Well, but you couldn't go there for nothing.
PETER. And why not, pray? But I did go there for nothing, though. Do you think one must be paid for everything? If Mrs. Haller were to give me but a smiling look, I'd jump up to my neck in the great pond for nothing.
FRANCIS. It seems then Mrs. Haller sent you?
PETER. Why, yes—but I'm not to talk about it.
FRANCIS. Why so?
PETER. How should I know? "Look you," says Mrs. Haller, "Master Peter, be so good as not to mention it to anybody." (*With much consequence*) "Master Peter, be so good—" Hi! hi! hi! "Master Peter, be so—" Hi! hi! hi!
FRANCIS. Oh, that is quite a different thing. Of course you must be silent, then.
PETER. I know that, and so I am too. For I told old Tobias, says I, "Now you're not to think as how Mrs. Haller sent the money; for I shall not say a word about that as long as I live," says I.
FRANCIS. There you were very right. Did you carry him much money?
PETER. I don't know; I didn't count it. It was in a bit of a green purse. Mayhap it may be some little matter that she has scraped together in the last fortnight.
FRANCIS. And why just in the last fortnight?
PETER. Because about a fortnight since, I carried him some money before.
FRANCIS. From Mrs. Haller?

PETER. Ay, sure; who else think you? Father's not such a fool. He says it is our bounden duty as Christians to take care of our money and not give anything away, especially in summer; for then, he says, there's herbs and roots enough in conscience to satisfy all the reasonable hungry poor. But I say father's wrong, and Mrs. Haller's right.
FRANCIS. Yes, yes. But this Mrs. Haller seems a strange woman, Peter.
PETER. Ay, at times she is plaguy odd. Why, she'll sit and cry a whole day through without anyone's knowing why. Ay, and yet, some how or other, whenever she cries, I always cry too, without knowing why.
FRANCIS. (*To* STRANGER) Are you satisfied?
STRANGER. Rid me of that babbler.
FRANCIS. Good day, Master Peter.
PETER. You're not going yet, are you?
FRANCIS. Mrs. Haller will be waiting for an answer.
PETER. So she will. And I have another place or two to call at. (*Takes off his hat to* STRANGER) Servant, sir! (STRANGER *nods.* PETER *turns to* FRANCIS *in a half whisper*) He's angry, I suppose, because he can get nothing out of me.
FRANCIS. It almost seems so.
PETER. Ay, I'd have him know that I'm no blab. *Exit*
FRANCIS. Now, sir?
STRANGER. What do you want?
FRANCIS. Were you not wrong, sir?
STRANGER. Hem!
FRANCIS. Can you still doubt?
STRANGER. I'll hear no more! Who is this Mrs. Haller? Why do I always follow her path? Go where I will, whenever I try to do good, she has always been before me.
FRANCIS. You should rejoice at that.
STRANGER. Rejoice?
FRANCIS. Surely. That there are other good and charitable people in the world beside yourself.
STRANGER. Oh, yes!
FRANCIS. Why not seek to be acquainted with her? I saw her yesterday in the garden up at the castle. Mr. Solomon, the steward, says she has been unwell and confined to her room almost ever since we have been here. But one would not think it to look at her, for a more beautiful creature I never saw.
STRANGER. So much the worse. Beauty is a mask.

FRANCIS. In her it seems a mirror of the soul. Her charities—

STRANGER. Pshaw! Talk not to me of her charities. All women wish to be conspicuous, in town by their wit, in the country by their heart.

FRANCIS. 'Tis immaterial in what way good is done.

STRANGER. No, 'tis not immaterial.

FRANCIS. To this poor old man at least.

STRANGER. He needs no assistance of mine.

FRANCIS. His most urgent wants Mrs. Haller, indeed, relieved; but whether she has, or could, have given as much as would purchase liberty for the son, the prop of his age—

STRANGER. Silence! I will not give him a doit! (*In a peevish tone*) You interest yourself very warmly in his behalf. Perhaps you are to be a sharer in the gift?

FRANCIS. Sir, sir, that did not come from your heart.

STRANGER. (*Recollecting himself*) Forgive me!

FRANCIS. Poor master! How must the world have used you before it could have instilled this hatred of mankind, this constant doubt of honesty and virtue!

STRANGER. Leave me to myself! (*Throws himself on a seat; takes from his pocket "Zimmerman on Solitude"* [1] *and reads.*)

FRANCIS. (*Aside and surveying him*) Again reading! Thus it is from morn to night. To him nature has no beauty, life no charm. For three years I have never seen him smile. What will be his fate at last? Nothing diverts him. Oh, if he would but attach himself to any living thing, were it an animal, for something man must love!

Enter TOBIAS *from the hut*

TOBIAS. Oh, how refreshing after seven long weeks to feel these warm sunbeams again! Thanks, thanks, bounteous heaven for the joy I taste. (*Presses his cap between his hands, looks up, and prays.* STRANGER *lets his book drop and observes him attentively.*)

[1] Johann Georg Zimmerman (1728–1795), born at Brugg, canton of Berne, Switzerland, sentimental philosopher, who lived most of his life in Germany, published *Solitude* in four volumes, 1784, 1786. The work contains chapters on "Influence of solitude upon the mind," "Influence of solitude upon the heart," "General advantages of retirement," etc. Of course, the audience could not know what he read; but the purchaser of the printed play could, and rejoiced to see a congenial friend in the volume.

FRANCIS. (*To* STRANGER) This old man's share of earthly happiness can be but little; yet mark how grateful he is for his portion of it.

STRANGER. Because, though old, he is but a child in the leading-strings of hope.

FRANCIS. Hope is the nurse of life.

STRANGER. And her cradle is the grave. (TOBIAS *replaces his cap and approaches.*)

FRANCIS. I wish you joy. I am glad to see you are so much recovered.

TOBIAS. Thank you. Heaven and the assistance of a kind lady have saved me for another year or two.

FRANCIS. How old are you, pray?

TOBIAS. Seventy-six. To be sure I can expect but little joy before I die. Yet, there is another and a better world.

FRANCIS. To the unfortunate, then, death is scarce an evil?

TOBIAS. Am I so unfortunate? Do I not enjoy this glorious morning? Am I not in health again? Believe me, sir, he who, leaving the bed of sickness, for the first time breathes the fresh, pure air, is at that moment the happiest of his maker's creatures.

FRANCIS. Yet 'tis a happiness that fails upon enjoyment.

TOBIAS. True; but less so in old age. Some fifty years ago my father left me this cottage. I was a strong lad and took an honest wife. Heaven blessed my farm with rich crops and my marriage with five children. This lasted nine or ten years. Two of my children died. I felt it sorely. The land was afflicted with a famine. My wife assisted me in supporting our family; but four years after, she left our dwelling for a better place. And of my five children only one son remained.[2] This was blow upon blow. It was long before I regained my fortitude. At length resignation and religion had their effect. I again attached myself to life. My son grew and helped me in my work. Now the state has called him away to bear a musket. This is to me a loss, indeed. I can work no more. I am old and weak; and, true it is, but for Mrs. Haller I must have perished.

FRANCIS. Still, then, life has its charms for you?

TOBIAS. Why not, while the world holds anything that's dear to me? Have not I a son?

[2] This son, later called a lad, must be over forty years old.

FRANCIS. Who knows that you will ever see him more? He may be dead.

TOBIAS. Alas, he may! But as long as I am not sure of it, he lives to me; and if he falls, 'tis in his country's cause. Nay, should I lose him, still I should not wish to die. Here is the hut in which I was born. Here is the tree that grew with me; and (I am almost ashamed to confess it) I have a dog I love.

FRANCIS. A dog?

TOBIAS. Yes! Smile if you please, but hear. My benefactress once came to my hut herself some time before you fixed here. The poor animal, unused to see the form of elegance and beauty enter the door of penury, growled at her. "I wonder you keep that surly, ugly animal, Mr. Tobias," said she; "you, who have hardly food enough for yourself." "Ah, madam," I replied, "if I now part with him, are you sure what else will love me?" She was pleased with my answer.

FRANCIS. (*To* STRANGER) Excuse me, sir, but I wish you had listened.

STRANGER. I have listened.

FRANCIS. Then, sir, I wish you would follow this poor old man's example.

STRANGER. (*Pauses*) Here, take this book and lay it on my desk. (FRANCIS *goes into the lodge with the book*) How much has Mrs. Haller given you?

TOBIAS. Oh, sir, she has given me so much that I can look towards winter without fear.

STRANGER. No more?

TOBIAS. What could I do with more?—Ah, true! I might—

STRANGER. I know it. You might buy your son's release. There! (*Presses a heavy purse into his hand and exit.*)

TOBIAS. What is all this? (*Opens the purse and finds it full of gold*) Merciful heaven! (*Enter* FRANCIS. TOBIAS *runs to meet him*) Now look, sir! Is confidence in heaven unrewarded?

FRANCIS. I wish you joy! My master gave you this!

TOBIAS. Yes, your noble master. Heaven reward him!

FRANCIS. Just like him. He sent me with his book that no one might be witness to his bounty.

TOBIAS. He would not even take my thanks. He was gone before I could speak.

FRANCIS. Just his way!

TOBIAS. Now, sir, I'll go as quick as these old legs will bear me. What a delightful errand! I go to release my Robert! How the lad will rejoice! There is a girl, too, in the village that will rejoice with him. Oh, Providence, how good art thou! Years of distress never can efface the recollection of former happiness; but one joyful moment drives from the memory an age of misery. *Exit*

FRANCIS. (*Looks after him*) Why am I not wealthy? 'Sdeath! why am I not a prince! I never thought myself envious, but I feel I am. Yes, I must envy those who, with the will, have the power to do good. *Exit*

SCENE II

An antechamber in Wintersen Castle. Enter a MAID *meeting* FOOTMEN *with table and chairs.*

MAID. Why, George! Harry! Where have you been loitering? Put down these things. Mrs. Haller has been calling for you this half-hour.

GEORGE. Well, here I am then. What does she want with me?

MAID. That she will tell you yourself. Here she comes.

Enter MRS. HALLER, *with a letter, a* MAID *following*

MRS. HALLER. Very well; if those things are done, let the drawing-room be made ready immediately. (*Exeunt* MAIDS) And, George, run immediately into the park and tell Mr. Solomon I wish to speak with him. (*Exit* FOOTMAN) I cannot understand this. I do not learn whether their coming to this place be but the whim of a moment or a plan for a longer stay. If the latter, farewell, solitude! Farewell, study, farewell! Yes, I must make room for gaiety and mere frivolity. Yet could I willingly submit to all; but should the countess give me new proofs of her attachment, perhaps of her respect, oh, how will my conscience upbraid me! Or (I shudder at the thought) if this seat be visited by company and chance should conduct hither any of my former acquaintance—Alas! alas! how wretched is the being who fears the sight of any one fellow creature! But, oh, superior misery, to dread still more the presence of a former friend! Who's there?

Enter PETER

PETER. Nobody. It's only me.
MRS. HALLER. So soon returned?
PETER. Sharp lad, ain't I? On the road I've had a bit of talk too, and—
MRS. HALLER. But you have observed my directions?
PETER. Oh, yes, yes. I told old Tobias as how he would never know as long as he lived that the money came from you.
MRS. HALLER. You found him quite recovered, I hope?
PETER. Ay, sure did I. He's coming out to-day for the first time.
MRS. HALLER. I rejoice to hear it.
PETER. He said that he was obliged to you for all, and before dinner would crawl up to thank you.
MRS. HALLER. Good Peter, do me another service.
PETER. Ay, a hundred if you'll only let me have a good long stare at you.
MRS. HALLER. With all my heart! Observe when old Tobias comes and send him away. Tell him I am busy, or asleep, or unwell, or what you please.
PETER. I will, I will!
SOLOMON. (*Without*) There, there, go to the post-office.
MRS. HALLER. Oh, here comes Mr. Solomon.
PETER. What! Father? Ay, so there is. Father's a main clever man. He knows what's going on all over the world.
MRS. HALLER. No wonder, for you know he receives as many letters as a prime minister and all his secretaries.

Enter SOLOMON

SOLOMON. Good morning, good morning to you, Mrs. Haller. It gives me infinite pleasure to see you look so charmingly well. You have had the goodness to send for your humble servant. Any news from the great city? There are very weighty matters in agitation. I have my letters too.
MRS. HALLER. (*Smiling*) I think, Mr. Solomon, you must correspond with the four quarters of the globe?
SOLOMON. Beg pardon, not with the whole world, Mrs. Haller. But—(*Consequentially*) to be sure I have correspondents on whom I can rely in the chief cities of Europe, Asia, Africa, and America.
MRS. HALLER. And yet I have my doubts whether you know what is to happen this very day at this very place.
SOLOMON. At this very place? Nothing material. We meant to have sown a little barley today, but the ground is too dry. And the sheep-shearing is not to be till to-morrow.
PETER. No, nor the bear-baiting till—
SOLOMON. Hold your tongue, blockhead! Get about your business.
PETER. Blockhead! There again! I suppose I'm not to open my mouth. (*To* MRS. HALLER) Good-bye! *Exit*
MRS. HALLER. The count will be here to-day.
SOLOMON. How! What!
MRS. HALLER. With his lady and his brother-in-law, Baron Steinfort.
SOLOMON. My letters say nothing of this. You are laughing at your humble servant.
MRS. HALLER. You know, sir, I'm not much given to jesting.
SOLOMON. Peter!—Good lack-a-day! His Right Honorable Excellency Count Wintersen and her Right Honorable Excellency the Countess Wintersen and his Honorable Lordship Baron Steinfort—And, Lord have mercy, nothing in proper order! Here, Peter! Peter!

Enter PETER

PETER. Well, now, what's the matter again?
SOLOMON. Call all the house together directly! Send to the gamekeeper; tell him to bring some venison. Tell Rebecca to uncase the furniture and take the covering from the Venetian looking-glasses that her right honorable ladyship, the countess, may look at her gracious countenance. And tell the cook to let me see him without loss of time. And tell John to catch a brace or two of carp. And tell—and tell—and tell—tell Frederick to friz my Sunday wig. Mercy on us! Tell—There—Go! (*Exit* PETER) Heavens and earth, so little of the new furnishing of this old castle is completed! Where are we to put his honorable lordship the baron?
MRS. HALLER. Let him have the little chamber at the head of the stairs; it is a neat room and commands a beautiful prospect.
SOLOMON. Very right, very right. But that room has always been occupied by the count's private secretary. Suppose—Hold, I have it! You know the little lodge at the end of the park? We can thrust the secretary into that.

Mrs. Haller. You forget, Mr. Solomon, you told me that the stranger lived there.

Solomon. Pshaw! What have we to do with the stranger? Who told him to live there? He must turn out.

Mrs. Haller. That would be unjust, for you said that you let the dwelling to him; and by your own account he pays well for it.

Solomon. He does, he does. But nobody knows who he is. The devil himself can't make him out. To be sure, I lately received a letter from Spain, which informed me that a spy had taken up his abode in this country and from the description—

Mrs. Haller. A spy! Ridiculous! Everything I have heard bespeaks him to be a man who may be allowed to dwell anywhere. His life is solitude and silence.

Solomon. So it is.

Mrs. Haller. You tell me, too, he does much good and in private.

Solomon. That he does.

Mrs. Haller. He hurts nothing, not the worm in his way.

Solomon. That he does not.

Mrs. Haller. He troubles no one.

Solomon. True, true!

Mrs. Haller. Well, what do you want more?

Solomon. I want to know who he is. If the man would only converse a little, one might have an opportunity of *pumping;* but if one meets him in the lime walk or by the river, it is nothing but, "Good morrow!" and off he marches. Once or twice I have contrived to edge in a word: "Fine day." "Yes." "Taking a little exercise, I perceive." "Yes." And off again like a shot. The devil take such close fellows, say I. And, like master like man; not a syllable do I know of that mumps, his servant, except that his name is Francis.

Mrs. Haller. You are putting yourself into a passion and quite forgetting who are expected.

Solomon. So I do! Mercy on us! There now, you see what misfortunes arise from not knowing people.

Mrs. Haller. (*Looking at her watch*) Twelve o'clock already! If his lordship has stolen an hour from his usual sleep, the family must soon be here. I go to my duty; you will attend to yours, Mr. Solomon. *Exit*

Solomon. Yes, I'll look after my duty, never fear. There goes another of the same class. Nobody knows who she is again. However, thus much I do know of her, that her right honorable ladyship, the countess, all at once popped her into the house like a blot of ink upon a sheet of paper. But why, wherefore, or for what reason, not a soul can tell. "She is to manage the family within doors." She to manage! Fire and faggots! Haven't I managed everything within and without most reputable these twenty years? I must own I grow a little old and she does take a deal of pains. But all this she learned of me. When she first came here, mercy on us! She didn't even know that linen was made of flax. But what was to be expected from one who has no foreign correspondence!

ACT II

Scene I

A drawing-room in the castle, with a pianoforte, harp, music, book-stand, sofas, chairs, tables, &c.

Enter Solomon

Solomon. Well, for once I think I have the advantage of Madam Haller. Such a dance have I provided to welcome their excellencies, and she quite out of the secret. And such a hornpipe by the little brunette! I'll have a rehearsal first, though; and then surprise their honors after dinner. (*Flourish of rural music without.*)

Peter. (*Without*) Stop! Not yet, not yet! But make way there, make way, my good friends, tenants, and villagers. John! George! Frederick! Good friends, make way!

Solomon. It is not the count. It's only Baron Steinfort. Stand back, I say, and stop the music!

Enter Baron Steinfort *ushered in by* Peter *and* Footmen. Peter *mimics and apes his father*

Solomon. I have the honor to introduce to your lordship myself, Mr. Solomon, who blesses the hour in which fortune allows him to become acquainted with the Honorable Baron Steinfort, brother-in-law of his Right Honorable Excellency, Count Wintersen, my noble master.

Peter. Bless our noble master!

Baron. (*Aside*) Old and young, I see they'll allow me no peace.—Enough, enough, good

Mr. Solomon. I am a soldier. I pay but few compliments and require as few from others.

Solomon. I beg, my lord—We do live in the country, to be sure; but we are acquainted with the reverence due to exalted personages.

Peter. Yes, we are acquainted with exalted personages.

Baron. What is to become of me? Well, well, I hope we shall be better acquainted. You must know, Mr. Solomon, I intend to assist for a couple of months, at least, in attacking the well-stocked cellars of Wintersen.

Solomon. Why not whole years, my lord? Inexpressible would be the satisfaction of your humble servant. And, though I say it, well stocked, indeed, are our cellars. I have, in every respect, here managed matters in so frugal and provident a way that his right honorable excellency the count will be astonished. (*Baron sits on the sofa, not listening*) Extremely sorry it is not in my power to entertain his lordship.

Peter. Extremely sorry.

Solomon. Where can Mrs. Haller have hid herself?

Baron. Mrs. Haller? Who is she?

Solomon. Why, who she is, I can't exactly tell your lordship.

Peter. No, nor I.

Solomon. None of my correspondents give any account of her. She is here in the capacity of a kind of a superior housekeeper. Methinks I hear her silver voice upon the stairs. I will have the honor of sending her to your lordship in an instant.

Baron. Oh, don't trouble yourself.

Solomon. No trouble, whatever! I remain, at all times, your lordship's most obedient, humble, and devoted servant. *Exit bowing*

Peter. Devoted servant. *Exit bowing*

Baron. Now for a fresh plague. Now I am to be tormented by some chattering, old, ugly hag till I am stunned with her noise and officious hospitality. O, patience, what a virtue art thou! (*Enter* Mrs. Haller *with a becoming curtesy. Baron rises and returns bow in confusion. Aside.*) No, old she is not. (*Casts another glance at her*) No, by Jove, nor ugly.

Mrs. Haller. I rejoice, my lord, in thus becoming acquainted with the brother of my benefactress.

Baron. Madam, that title shall be doubly valuable to me since it gives me an introduction equally to be rejoiced at.

Mrs. Haller. (*Without attending to the compliment*) This lovely weather, then, has enticed the count from the city?

Baron. Not exactly that. You know him. Sunshine or clouds are to him alike as long as eternal summer reigns in his own heart and family.

Mrs. Haller. The count possesses a most cheerful and amiable philosophy. Ever in the same happy humor, ever enjoying each minute of his life. But you must confess, my lord, that he is a favorite child of fortune and has much to be grateful to her for, not merely because she has given him birth and riches but for a native sweetness of temper never to be acquired and a graceful suavity of manners, whose school must be the mind. And, need I enumerate among fortune's favors the hand and affections of your accomplished sister?

Baron. (*More and more struck as her understanding opens upon him*) True, madam. My good, easy brother, too, seems fully sensible of his happiness and is resolved to retain it. He has quitted the service to live here. I am afraid he may soon grow weary of Wintersen and retirement.

Mrs. Haller. I should trust not. They who bear a cheerful and unreproaching conscience into solitude surely must increase the measure of their own enjoyments; they quit the poor, precarious, the dependent pleasures, which they borrowed from the world, to draw a real bliss from that exhaustless source of true delight, the fountain of a pure, unsullied heart.

Baron. Has retirement long possessed so lovely an advocate?

Mrs. Haller. I have lived here three years.

Baron. And never felt a secret wish for the society you left and must have adorned.

Mrs. Haller. Never!

Baron. To feel thus belongs either to a very rough or a very polished soul. The first sight convinced me in which class I am to place you.

Mrs. Haller. (*With a sigh*) There may, perhaps, be a third case.

Baron. Indeed, madam, I wish not to be thought forward, but women always seemed to me less calculated for retirement than men. We have a thousand employments, a thousand amusements, which you have not.

MRS. HALLER. Dare I ask what they are?
BARON. We ride, we hunt, we play,—read,—write—
MRS. HALLER. The noble employments of the chase and the still more noble employment of play, I grant you.
BARON. Nay, but dare I ask what are your employments for a day?
MRS. HALLER. Oh, my lord, you cannot imagine how quickly time passes when a certain uniformity guides the minutes of your life. How often do I ask, "Is Saturday come again so soon?" On a bright, cheerful morning, my books and breakfast are carried out upon the grass-plot. Then is the sweet picture of reviving industry and eager innocence always new to me. The birds' notes, so often heard, still waken new ideas; the herds are led into the fields; the peasant bends his eye upon his plough. Everything loves and moves, and in every creature's mind it seems as it were morning. Towards evening I begin to roam abroad from the park into the meadows; and sometimes, returning, I pause to look at the village boys and girls as they play. Then do I bless their innocence and pray to heaven those laughing, thoughtless hours could be their lot forever.
BARON. This is excellent! But these are summer amusements. The winter, the winter!
MRS. HALLER. Why forever picture winter like old age, torpid, tedious, and uncheerful? Winter has its own delights; this is the time to instruct and mend the mind by reading and reflection. At this season, too, I often take my harp and amuse myself by playing or singing the little favorite airs that remind me of the past or solicit hope for the future.
BARON. Happy indeed are they who can thus create and vary their own pleasures and employments.

Enter PETER

PETER. Well—well—pray now,—I was ordered—I can keep him back no longer. He will come in.
MRS. HALLER. Who is it you mean?
PETER. Why, old Tobias.

Enter TOBIAS, *forcing his way*

TOBIAS. I must, good heaven, I must!
MRS. HALLER. (*Confused*) I have no time at present—I—I—you see I am not alone.
TOBIAS. Oh, this good gentleman will forgive me.
BARON. What do you want?
TOBIAS. To return thanks. Even charity is a burden if one cannot be grateful for it.
MRS. HALLER. To-morrow, good Tobias, to-morrow!
BARON. Nay, no false delicacy, madam. Allow him to vent the feelings of his heart and permit me to witness a scene which convinces me even more powerfully than your conversation how nobly you employ your time. Speak, old man.
TOBIAS. Oh, lady, that each word which drops from my lips might call down a blessing on your head! I lay forsaken and dying in my hut; not even bread nor hope remained. Oh, then you came in the form of an angel, brought medicines to me; and your sweet, consoling voice did more than those. I am recovered. To-day, for the first time, I have returned thanks in the presence of the sun, and now come to you, noble lady. Let me drop my tears upon your charitable hand. For your sake heaven has blessed my latter days. The stranger, too, who lives near me has given me a purse of gold to buy my son's release. I am on my way to the city; I shall purchase my Robert's release. Then I shall have an honest daughter-in-law. And you, if ever after that you pass our happy cottage, oh, what must you feel when you say to yourself, "This is my work!"
MRS. HALLER. (*In a tone of entreaty*) Enough, Tobias, enough!
TOBIAS. I beg pardon. I cannot utter what is breathing in my breast. There is one who knows it. May His blessing and your own heart reward it! (*Exit,* PETER *following.*
MRS. HALLER *casts her eyes upon the ground and contends against the confusion of an exalted soul when surprised in a good action.* BARON *stands opposite her and from time to time casts a glance at her in which his heart is swimming.*)
MRS. HALLER. (*Endeavoring to bring about a conversation*) I suppose, my lord, we may expect the count and countess every moment now?
BARON. Not just yet, madam. He travels at his leisure. I am selfish, perhaps, in not being anxious for his speed. The delay has procured me a delight which I never shall forget.

MRS. HALLER. (*Smiling*) You satirize mankind, my lord.

BARON. How so?

MRS. HALLER. In supposing such scenes to be uncommon.

BARON. I confess I was little prepared for such an acquaintance as yourself. I am extremely surprised. When Solomon told me your name and situation, how could I suppose that—

MRS. HALLER. My name?—Yes—(*Aside*) I don't wish to make it of greater consequence than it is.

BARON. Pardon my curiosity. You have been, or are married?

MRS. HALLER. (*Suddenly sinking from her cheerful raillery into mournful gloom*) I have been married, my lord.

BARON. (*Whose enquiries evince his curiosity, yet are restrained within the bounds of the nicest respect*) A widow, then?

MRS. HALLER. I beseech you—there are strings in the human heart which touched will sometimes utter dreadful discord. I beseech you—

BARON. I understand you. I see you know how to conceal everything except your perfections.

MRS. HALLER. My perfections, alas! (*Rural music without*) But I hear the happy tenantry announce the count's arrival. Your pardon, my lord; I must attend them. *Exit*

BARON. Excellent creature! What is she, and what can be her history? I must seek my sister instantly. How strong and how sudden is the interest I feel for her! But it is a feeling I ought to check. And yet, why so? Whatever are the emotions she has inspired, I am sure they arise from the perfections of her mind, and never shall they be met with unworthiness in mine. *Exit*

SCENE II

The Lawn

SOLOMON *and* PETER *are discovered arranging the tenantry. Rural music. Enter* COUNT *and* COUNTESS WINTERSEN, *the latter leading a child, the* BARON, MRS. HALLER, CHARLOTTE, *and servants following*

SOLOMON. Welcome, ten thousand welcomes, your excellencies. Some little preparation made for welcome, too. But that will be seen anon.

COUNT. Well, here we are! Heaven bless our advance and retreat! Mrs. Haller, I bring you an invalid who in future will swear by no flag but yours.

MRS. HALLER. Mine flies for retreat and rural happiness.

COUNT. But not without retreating Graces and retiring Cupids too.

COUNTESS. (*Who has in the meantime kindly embraced* MRS. HALLER *and by her been welcomed to Wintersen*) My dear count, you forget that I am present.

COUNT. Why, in the name of chivalry, how can I do less than your gallant brother, the baron, who has been so kind as nearly to kill my four greys in order to be here five minutes before me?

BARON. Had I known all the charms of this place, you should have said so with justice.

COUNTESS. Don't you think William much grown?

MRS. HALLER. The sweet boy! (*She stoops to kiss him, and deep melancholy overshadows her countenance.*)

COUNT. Well, Solomon, you've provided a good dinner?

SOLOMON. As good as haste would allow, please your right honorable excellency.

PETER. Yes, as good as—(COUNT *goes aside with* SOLOMON.)

BARON. Tell me, I conjure you, sister, what jewel you have thus buried in the country?

COUNTESS. Ha! ha! ha! What, brother, you caught at last!

BARON. Answer me.

COUNTESS. Well, her name is Mrs. Haller.

BARON. That I know, but—

COUNTESS. But! But I know no more myself.

BARON. Jesting apart, I wish to know.

COUNTESS. And, jesting apart, I wish you would not plague me. I have at least a hundred thousand important things to do. Heavens! The vicar may come to pay his respects to me before I have been at my toilet. Of course, I must consult my looking-glass on the occasion. Come, William, will you help to dress me, or stay with your father?

WILLIAM. I had rather stay here.

COUNT. We'll take care of him.

COUNTESS. Come, Mrs. Haller.

Exit with MRS. HALLER, CHARLOTTE *following*

THE STRANGER

BARON. (*Aside and going*) I am in a very singular humor.

COUNT. Whither so fast, good brother?

BARON. To my apartment; I have letters to—I—

COUNT. Psha! Stay! Let us take a turn in the park together.

BARON. Excuse me. I am not perfectly well. I should be but bad company. I—

Exit. The tenantry retire

COUNT. Well, Solomon, you're as great a fool as ever, I see.

SOLOMON. Ha! ha! At your right honorable excellency's service.

COUNT. (*Points to* PETER) Who is that ape in the corner?

SOLOMON. Ape! Oh, that is—with respect to your excellency be it spoken, the son of my body, by name, Peter. (PETER *bows*.)

COUNT. So, so! Well, how goes all on?

SOLOMON. Well and good, well and good. Your excellency will see how I've improved the park. You'll not know it again. A hermitage here, serpentine walks there, an obelisk, a ruin,[1] and all so sparingly, all done with the most economical economy.

COUNT. Well, I'll have a peep at your obelisk and ruins while they prepare for dinner.

SOLOMON. I have already ordered it and will have the honor of attending your right honorable excellency.

COUNT. Come, lead the way. Peter, attend your young master to the house; we must not tire him.   *Exit, conducted by* SOLOMON

PETER. This way, your little excellency, and we shall see the bridge as we go by and the new boat with all the fine ribbons and streamers. This way, your little excellency.

Exit, leading the child

SCENE III

The Antechamber

Enter MRS. HALLER

MRS. HALLER. What has thus alarmed and subdued me? My tears flow, my heart bleeds. Already had I apparently overcome my chagrin; already had I at least assumed that easy gaiety once so natural to me, when the sight of this child in an instant overpowered me. When the countess called him William—Oh! she knew not that she plunged a pogniard in my heart. I have a William, too, who must be as tall as this, if he be still alive. Ah, yes! If he be still alive! His little sister, too. Why, Fancy, dost thou rack me thus? Why dost thou image my poor children, fainting in sickness and crying to their mother? To the mother who has abandoned them? (*Weeps*) What a wretched outcast am I! And that just to-day I should be doomed to feel these horrible emotions! Just to-day when disguise was so necessary!

Enter CHARLOTTE, *bellowing at the door*

CHARLOTTE. Your servant, Mrs. Haller. I beg, madam, I may have a room fit for a respectable person.

MRS. HALLER. The chamber into which you have been shown is, I think, a very neat one.

CHARLOTTE. A very neat one is it? Up the back stairs and over the laundry! I shall never be able to close my eyes.

MRS. HALLER. (*Very mildly*) I slept there a whole year.

CHARLOTTE. Did you? Then I advise you to remove into it again, and the sooner the better. I'd have you to know, madam, there is a material difference between certain persons and certain persons. Much depends upon the manner in which one has been educated. I think, madam, it would be only proper if you resigned your room to me.

MRS. HALLER. If the countess desires it, certainly.

CHARLOTTE. The countess! Very pretty, indeed! Would you have me think of plaguing her ladyship with such trifles? I shall order my trunk to be carried wherever I please.

MRS. HALLER. Certainly; only not into my chamber.

CHARLOTTE. Provoking creature! But how could I expect to find breeding among creatures born of they know not whom and coming they know not whence?

MRS. HALLER. The remark is very just.

Enter PETER *in haste*

PETER. Oh lud! Oh lud! Oh lud! Oh lud!

MRS. HALLER. What's the matter?

---

[1] See note on *The Clandestine Marriage.* p. 685. n. 8.

PETER. The child has fallen into the river! His little excellency is drowned!
MRS. HALLER. Who? What?
PETER. His honor, my young master.
MRS. HALLER. Drowned?
PETER. Yes.
MRS. HALLER. Dead?
PETER. No, he's not dead.
MRS. HALLER. Well, well, then softly. You will alarm the countess.

Enter the BARON

BARON. What is the matter? Why all this noise?
PETER. Noise? Why—
MRS. HALLER. Be not alarmed, my lord. Whatever may have happened, the dear child is now at least safe. You said so, I think, master Peter.
PETER. Why, to be sure, his little excellency is not hurt, but he's very wet through, and the count is taking him by the garden door to the house.
BARON. Right, that the countess may not be alarmed. But tell us, young man, how could it happen?
PETER. From beginning to end?
MRS. HALLER. Never mind the particulars. You attended the dear child?
PETER. True, and he would see the boat and streamers. I turned round only for a moment, and then, oh, how I was scared to see him borne down the river!
BARON. And then you drew him out again directly?
PETER. No, I didn't; 'twas the deepest part; and I never could swim in my life. But I called and bawled as loud as I could. I believe you might have heard me down in the village.
MRS. HALLER. Ay, and so the people came immediately to his assistance?
PETER. No, they didn't; but the stranger came, that lives yonder, close by old Toby, and never speaks a syllable. Odsbodlikins! What a devil of a fellow it is! With a single spring, bounces he slap into the torrent, sails and dives about like a duck, gets me hold of the little angel's hair, and, heaven bless him! pulls him safe to dry land. Ha! ha! ha!
BARON. I think I hear them.
MRS. HALLER. Is the stranger with them?
PETER. Oh lud, no! He ran away. His excellency wanted to thank him and all that, but he was off; vanished like a ghost.

Enter SOLOMON

SOLOMON. Oh! thou careless varlet! I disown you! What an accident might have happened! And how you have terrified his excellency! But I beg pardon—(*Bows*) His right honorable excellency, the count, requests your—
BARON. We come. *Exit with* MRS. HALLER
CHARLOTTE. Ha! ha! ha! Why, Mr. Solomon, you seem to have a hopeful pupil.
SOLOMON. Ah! sirrah!
CHARLOTTE. But, Mr. Solomon, why were you not nimble enough to have saved his young lordship?
SOLOMON. Not in time, my sweet miss. Besides, mercy on us, I should have sunk like a lump of lead; and I happened to have a letter of consequence in my pocket, which would have been made totally illegible, a letter from Constantinople, written by Chevallier—what's his name? (*Draws a letter from his pocket, and putting it up again directly, drops it.* PETER *takes it up slyly and unobserved*) It contains momentous matter, I assure you. The world will be astonished when it comes to light, and not a soul will suppose that old Solomon had a finger in the pie.
CHARLOTTE. No, that I believe.
SOLOMON. But I must go and see to the cellar. Miss, your most obedient servant. *Exit*
CHARLOTTE. (*With pride*) Your servant, Mr. Solomon.
PETER. Here's the letter from Constantinople. I wonder what it can be about. Now for it! (*Opens it*)
CHARLOTTE. Ay, let us have it.
PETER. (*Reads*) "If so be you say so, I'll never work for you, never no more. Considering as how your Sunday waistcoat has been turned three times, it doesn't look amiss; and I've charged as little as any tailor of 'em all. You say I must pay for the buckram; but I say, I'll be damned if I do. So no more from your loving nephew, Timothy Twist."— From Constantinople! Why, cousin Tim writ it.
CHARLOTTE. Cousin Tim! Who is he?
PETER. Good lack! Don't you know cousin Tim? Why, he's one of the best tailors in all—

CHARLOTTE. A tailor! No, sir, I do not know him. My father was state-coachman and wore his highness's livery. *Exit*

PETER. (*Mimicking*) "My father was state-coachman and wore his highness's livery." Well, and cousin Tim could have made his highness's livery, if you go to that. (*Going*)

Enter SOLOMON

SOLOMON. Peter, you ninny, stay where you are. Is that chattering girl gone? Didn't I tell you we would have to practice our dance? And they are all ready on the lawn. Mark me, I represent the count and you the baron. *Exit with affected dignity.* PETER *follows, mimicking*

SCENE IV

The lawn

Seats placed. Rustic music. Dancers are discovered as ready to perform. SOLOMON *and* PETER *enter and seat themselves. A dance, in which the dancers pay their reverence to* SOLOMON *and* PETER *as they pass. At the end* SOLOMON *and* PETER *strut off before the dancers*

ACT III

SCENE I

The skirts of the park and lodge, &c., as before. The STRANGER *is discovered on a seat reading. Enter* FRANCIS

FRANCIS. Dinner is ready.
STRANGER. I want no dinner.
FRANCIS. I've got something good.
STRANGER. Eat it yourself.
FRANCIS. You are not hungry?
STRANGER. No.
FRANCIS. Nor I. The heat takes away all appetite.
STRANGER. Yes.
FRANCIS. I'll put it by; perhaps at night—
STRANGER. Perhaps.
FRANCIS. (*After a pause*) Dear sir, dare I speak?
STRANGER. Speak.
FRANCIS. You have done a noble action.
STRANGER. What?
FRANCIS. You have saved a fellow-creature's life.
STRANGER. Peace.

FRANCIS. Do you know who he was?
STRANGER. No.
FRANCIS. The only son of Count Wintersen.
STRANGER. Immaterial.
FRANCIS. A gentleman, by report, worthy and benevolent as yourself.
STRANGER. (*Angry*) Silence! Dare you flatter me?
FRANCIS. As I look to heaven for mercy, I speak from my heart. When I observe how you are doing good around you, how you are making every individual's wants your own, and are yet yourself unhappy, alas! my heart bleeds for you.
STRANGER. I thank you, Francis. I can only thank you. Yet share this consolation with me:—my sufferings are unmerited.
FRANCIS. My poor master!
STRANGER. Have you forgotten what the old man said this morning? "There is another and a better world!" Oh, 'twas true. Then let us hope with fervency and yet endure with patience. What's here?

Enter CHARLOTTE *from the park gate*

CHARLOTTE. I presume, sir, you are the strange gentleman that drew my young master out of the water? (STRANGER *stares at her*) Or (*To* FRANCIS) are you he? (FRANCIS *makes a wry face*) Are the creatures both dumb? (*Looks at them both by turns; they stare at her*) Surely old Solomon has fixed two statues here, by way of ornament, for of any use there is no sign. (*Approaches* FRANCIS) No, this is alive and breathes; yes, and moves its eyes. (*Bawls in his ear*) Good friend!
FRANCIS. I'm not deaf.
CHARLOTTE. Nor dumb, I perceive at last. Is yon lifeless thing your master?
FRANCIS. That honest, silent gentleman is my master.
CHARLOTTE. The same that saved the young count's life?
FRANCIS. The same.
CHARLOTTE. (*To* STRANGER) Sir, my master and mistress, the count and countess, present their respectful compliments and request the honor of your company at family supper this evening.
STRANGER. I shall not come.
CHARLOTTE. But you'll scarce send such an uncivil answer as this? The count is overpowered with gratitude. You have saved his son's life.

STRANGER. I did it willingly.

CHARLOTTE. And won't accept of "I thank you" in return?

STRANGER. No.

CHARLOTTE. You are really cruel, sir, I must tell you. There are three of us ladies at the castle, and we are all dying with curiosity to know who you are. (*Exit* STRANGER) The master is crabbed enough. However, let me try what I can make of the man. Pray, sir? (FRANCIS *turns his back to her*) The beginning promises little enough. Friend, why won't you look at me?

FRANCIS. I like to look at green trees better than green eyes.

CHARLOTTE. Green eyes, you monster! Who told you that my eyes were green? Let me tell you there have been sonnets made on my eyes before now.

FRANCIS. Glad to hear it.

CHARLOTTE. To the point then at once. What is your master?

FRANCIS. A man.

CHARLOTTE. I surmised as much. But what's his name?

FRANCIS. The same as his father's.

CHARLOTTE. Not unlikely; and his father was—

FRANCIS. Married.

CHARLOTTE. To whom?

FRANCIS. To a woman.

CHARLOTTE. (*Enraged*) I'll tell you what. Who your master is, I see I shall not learn, and I don't care; but I know what you are.

FRANCIS. Well, what am I?

CHARLOTTE. A bear! *Exit*

FRANCIS. Thank you!—Now to see how habit and example corrupt one's manners. I am naturally the civilest-spoken fellow in the world to the pretty, prattling rogues; yet, following my master's humor, I've rudely driven this wench away.

Enter STRANGER

STRANGER. Is that woman gone?
FRANCIS. Yes.
STRANGER. Francis.
FRANCIS. Sir?
STRANGER. We must be gone too.
FRANCIS. But whither?
STRANGER. I don't care.
FRANCIS. I'll attend you.
STRANGER. To any place?
FRANCIS. To death.

STRANGER. Heaven grant it,—to me at least. There is peace.

FRANCIS. Peace is everywhere. Let the storm rage without, if the heart be but at rest. Yet I think we are very well where we are. The situation is inviting, and nature is lavish of her beauties and of her bounties too.

STRANGER. But I am not a wild beast to be stared at and sent for as a show. Is it fit I should be?

FRANCIS. Another of your interpretations! That a man, the life of whose only son you have saved, should invite you to his house, seems to me not very unnatural.

STRANGER. I will not be invited to any house.

FRANCIS. For once methinks you might submit. You'll not be asked a second time.

STRANGER. Proud wretches! They believe the most essential service is requited if one may but have the honor of sitting at their table. Let us be gone.

FRANCIS. Yet hold, sir. This bustle will soon be over. Used to the town, the count and his party will soon be tired of simple nature; and you will again be freed from observation.

STRANGER. Not from yours.

FRANCIS. This is too much. Do I deserve your doubts?

STRANGER. Am I in the wrong?

FRANCIS. You are, indeed!

STRANGER. Francis, my servant, you are my only friend. (*Giving his hand*)

FRANCIS. That title makes amends for all! (*Kisses it*)

STRANGER. But look, Francis; there are uniforms and gay dresses in the walk again. No, I must be gone. Here I'll stay no longer.

FRANCIS. Well then, I'll tie up my bundle.

STRANGER. The sooner the better! They come this way. Now must I shut myself in my hovel and lose this fine breeze. Nay, if they be your high-bred class of all, they may have impudence enough to walk into my chamber. Francis, I shall lock the door. (*Goes into the lodge, locks the door, and fastens the shutters*)

FRANCIS. And I'll be your sentinel. Should these people be as inquisitive as their maid, I must summon my whole stock of impertinence. But their questions and my answers need little study. They can learn nothing of the stranger from me for the best of all possible reasons,—I know nothing myself.

Enter BARON *and* COUNTESS

COUNTESS. There is a strange face. The servant probably.

BARON. Friend, can we speak to your master?

FRANCIS. No.

BARON. Only for a few minutes.

FRANCIS. He has locked himself in his room.

COUNTESS. Tell him a lady waits for him.

FRANCIS. Then he's sure not to come.

COUNTESS. Does he hate our sex?

FRANCIS. He hates the whole human race, but woman particularly.

COUNTESS. And why?

FRANCIS. He may perhaps have been deceived.

COUNTESS. This is not very courteous.

FRANCIS. My master is not over-courteous; but when he sees a chance of saving a fellow creature's life, he'll attempt it at the peril of his own.

BARON. You are right. Now hear the reason of our visit. The wife and brother-in-law of the man whose child your master has saved wish to acknowledge their obligations to him.

FRANCIS. That he dislikes. He only wishes to live unnoticed.

COUNTESS. He appears to be unfortunate.

FRANCIS. Appears!

COUNTESS. An affair of honor, perhaps, or some unhappy attachment may have—

FRANCIS. They may.

COUNTESS. Be this as it may, I wish to know who he is.

FRANCIS. So do I.

COUNTESS. What, don't you know him yourself?

FRANCIS. Oh, I know him well enough. I mean his real self, his heart, his soul, his worth, his honor. Perhaps you think one knows a man when one is acquainted with his name and person?

COUNTESS. 'Tis well said, friend; you please me much. And now I should like to know you. Who are you?

FRANCIS. Your humble servant. *Exit*

COUNTESS. Nay, now, this is affectation! A desire to appear singular! Everyone wishes to make himself distinguished. One sails round the world; another creeps into a hovel.

BARON. And the man apes his master!

COUNTESS. Come, brother, let us seek the count. He and Mrs. Haller turned into the lawn. (*Going*)

BARON. Stay! First a word or two, sister! I am in love.

COUNTESS. For the hundredth time.

BARON. For the first time in my life.

COUNTESS. I wish you joy.

BARON. Till now you have evaded my inquiries. Who is she? I beseech you, sister, be serious. There is a time for all things.

COUNTESS. Bless us! Why you look as if you were going to raise a spirit. Don't fix your eyes so earnestly. Well, if I am to be serious, I obey. I do not know who Mrs. Haller is, as I have already told you; but what I do know of her shall not be concealed from you. It may now be three years ago when one evening about twilight a lady was announced, who wished to speak to me in private. Mrs. Haller appeared with all that grace and modesty which have enchanted you. Her features at that moment bore keener marks of the sorrow and confusion which have since settled into gentle melancholy. She threw herself at my feet and besought me to save a wretch who was on the brink of despair. She told me she had heard much of my benevolence and offered herself as a servant to attend me. I endeavored to dive into the cause of her sufferings, but in vain. She concealed her secret, yet opened to me more and more each day a heart chosen by virtue as her temple and an understanding improved by the most refined attainments. She no longer remained my servant but became my friend and, by her own desire, has ever since resided here. (*Curtesying*) Brother, I have done.

BARON. Too little to satisfy my curiosity; yet enough to make me realize my project. Sister, lend me your aid. I would marry her.

COUNTESS. You!

BARON. I!

COUNTESS. Baron Steinfort!

BARON. For shame! If I understand you!

COUNTESS. Not so harsh and not so hasty! Those great sentiments of contempt of inequality in rank are very fine in a romance; but we happen not to be inhabitants of an ideal world. How could you introduce her to the circle we live in? You surely would not attempt to present her to—

BARON. Object as you will, my answer is.

"I love!" Sister, you see a man before you who—

COUNTESS. Who wants a wife.

BARON. No; who has deliberately poised advantage against disadvantage, domestic ease and comfort against the false gaieties of fashion. I can withdraw into the country. I need no honors to make my tenants happy, and my heart will teach me to make their happiness my own. With such a wife as this, children who resemble her, and fortune enough to spread comfort around me, what would the soul of man have more?

COUNTESS. This is all vastly fine. I admire your plan; only you seem to have forgotten one trifling circumstance.

BARON. And that is?

COUNTESS. Whether Mrs. Haller will have you or not.

BARON. There, sister, I want your assistance. (*Seizing her hand*) Good Henrietta!

COUNTESS. Well, here's my hand. I'll do all I can for you. St! We had near been overheard. They are coming. Be patient and obedient.

Enter COUNT *and* MRS. HALLER *leaning on his arm*

COUNT. Upon my word, Mrs. Haller, you are a nimble walker. I should be sorry to run a race with you.

MRS. HALLER. Custom, my lord. You need only take the same walk every day for a month.

COUNT. Yes, if I wanted to resemble my greyhounds.—But what said the stranger?

COUNTESS. He gave Charlotte a flat refusal, and you see his door and even his shutters are closed against us.

COUNT. What an unaccountable being! But it won't do. I must show my gratitude one way or other. Steinfort, we will take the ladies home and then you shall try once again to see him. You can talk to these oddities better than I can.

BARON. If you wish it, with all my heart.

COUNT. Thank you, thank you! Come, ladies; come Mrs. Haller. *Exeunt*

SCENE II

A close walk in the garden

Enter COUNTESS *and* MRS. HALLER

COUNTESS. Well, Mrs. Haller, how do you like the man that just now left us?

MRS. HALLER. Who?

COUNTESS. My brother.

MRS. HALLER. He deserves to be your brother.

COUNTESS. (*Curtesying*) Your most obedient! That shall be written in my pocket-book.[1]

MRS. HALLER. Without flattery, then, madam, he appears to be most amiable.

COUNTESS. Good; and a handsome man?

MRS. HALLER. (*With indifference*) Oh, yes.

COUNTESS. "Oh, yes." It sounded almost like, "Oh, no!" But I must tell you that he looks upon you to be a handsome woman. (MRS. HALLER *smiles*) You make no reply to this.

MRS. HALLER. What shall I reply? Derision never fell from your lips, and I am little calculated to support it.

COUNTESS. As little as you are calculated to be the cause of it. No, I was in earnest. Now?

MRS. HALLER. You confuse me. But why should I play the prude? I will own there was a time when I thought myself handsome. 'Tis past. Alas! the enchanting beauties of a female countenance arise from peace of mind. The look which captivates an honorable man must be reflected from a noble soul.

COUNTESS. Then heaven grant my bosom may ever hold as pure a heart as now those eyes bear witness lives in yours!

MRS. HALLER. (*With sudden wildness*) Oh! Heaven forbid!

COUNTESS. (*Astonished*) How!

MRS. HALLER. (*Checking her tears*) Spare me! I am a wretch. The suffering of three years can give no claim to your friendship. No, not even to your compassion. Oh, spare me! (*Going*)

COUNTESS. Stay, Mrs. Haller! For the first time I beg your confidence. My brother loves you.

MRS. HALLER. (*Starting and gazing full in the face of the Countess*) For mirth, too much,—for earnest, too mournful!

COUNTESS. I revere that modest blush. Discover to me who you are. You risk nothing. Pour all your griefs into a sister's bosom. Am I not kind? And can I not be silent?

MRS. HALLER. Alas! But a frank reliance on a generous mind is the greatest sacrifice to

[1] Memorandum-book.

be offered by true repentance. This sacrifice I will offer. (*Hesitating*) Did you never hear—pardon me. Did you never hear—Oh, how shocking is it to unmask a deception which alone has recommended me to your regard! But it must be so. Madam,—Fie, Adelaide, does pride become you? Did you never hear of the Countess Waldbourg?

Countess. I think I did hear at a neighboring court of such a creature. She plunged an honorable husband into misery. She ran away with a villain.

Mrs. Haller. She did, indeed. (*Falls at the feet of the Countess*) Do not cast me from you.

Countess. For heaven's sake! You are—

Mrs. Haller. I am that wretch.

Countess. (*Turning from her with horror*) Ha! Begone! (*Going, her heart draws her back*) Yet, she is unfortunate, she is unfriended. Her image is repentance. Her life the proof. She has wept away her fault in three years' agony. Be still a while, remorseless prejudice, and let the genuine feelings of my soul avow, "They do not truly honor virtue who can insult the erring heart that would return to her sanctuary!" (*Looking with sorrow on her*) Rise, I beseech you, rise! My husband and my brother may surprise us. I promise to be silent. (*Raising her*)

Mrs. Haller. Yes, you will be silent—But, oh, Conscience! Conscience! Thou never wilt be silent. (*Clasping her hand*) Do not cast me from you.

Countess. Never! Your lonely life, your silent anguish and contrition may at length atone your crime. And never shall you want an asylum where your patience may lament your loss.

Mrs. Haller. Yes, I have lost him. But—I had children, too.

Countess. Enough! Enough!

Mrs. Haller. Oh, madam—I would only know whether they are alive or dead. That, for a mother, is not much.

Countess. Compose yourself.

Mrs. Haller. Oh! had you known my husband when I first beheld him! I was then scarcely sixteen years of age.

Countess. And your marriage?

Mrs. Haller. A few months after.

Countess. And your flight?

Mrs. Haller. I lived three years with him.

Countess. Oh, my friend! Your crime was youth and inexperience. Your heart never was, never could be concerned in it.

Mrs. Haller. Oh, spare me! My conscience never martyrs me so horribly as when I catch my thoughts in search of an excuse. No, nothing can palliate my guilt, and the only consolation left me is to acquit the man I wronged and own I erred without a cause of fair complaint.

Countess. And this is the mark of true repentance. Alas! my friend, when superior sense, recommended, too, by superior charms of person, assail a young, though wedded—

Mrs. Haller. Ah, not even that excuse is left me! In all that merits admiration, respect, and love, he was far, far beneath my husband. But to attempt to account for my infatuation —I cannot bear it! 'Tis true, I thought my husband's manner grew colder to me; I knew that his expenses and his confidence in deceitful friends had embarrassed his means and clouded his spirits; yet I thought he denied me pleasures and amusements still within our reach. My vanity was mortified. My confidence not courted. The serpent-tongue of my seducer promised everything. But never could such arguments avail, till, assisted by forged letters and the treachery of a servant whom I most confided in, he fixed the belief that my lord was false and that all the coldness I complained of was disgust to me and love for another, all his home retrenchments but the means of satisfying a rival's luxury. Maddened with this conviction (conviction it was, for artifice was most ingenious in its proof,) I left my children, father, husband, to follow—a villain.

Countess. But with such a heart, my friend could not remain long in her delusion?

Mrs. Haller. Long enough to make sufficient penitence impossible. 'Tis true that in a few weeks the delirium was at an end. Oh, what were my sensations when the mist dispersed before my eyes! I called for my husband, but in vain. I listened for the prattle of my children, but in vain.

Countess. Check the recollection! I guess the end! You left your seducer?

Mrs. Haller. I did and fled to you, to you, who have given me a spot where I might weep and who will give me a spot where I may die.

Countess. (*Embracing her*) Here, here, on this bosom only shall your future tears be shed; and may I, dear sufferer, make you again familiar with hope!

MRS. HALLER. Oh, impossible!

COUNTESS. Have you never heard of your children?

MRS. HALLER. Never!

COUNTESS. We must endeavor to gain some account of them. We must—hold! My husband and my brother! Oh, my poor brother! I had quite forgotten him. Quick, dear Mrs. Haller, wipe your eyes. Let us meet them.

MRS. HALLER. Madam, I'll follow. Allow me a moment to compose myself. (*Exit*
COUNTESS) I pause! Oh, yes,—to compose myself. (*Ironically*) She thinks little it is but to gain one solitary moment to vent my soul's remorse. Once the purpose of my unsettled mind was self-destruction. Heaven knows how I sued for hope and resignation. I did trust my prayers were heard—Oh, spare me further trial! I feel, I feel, my heart and brain can bear no more. *Exit*

ACT IV

SCENE I

The skirts of the park, lodge, &c., as before. A table spread with fruits, &c. FRANCIS *discovered placing the supper*

FRANCIS. I know he loves to have his early supper in the fresh air; and, while he sups, not that I believe anything can amuse him, yet I will try my little Savoyards' pretty voices. I have heard him speak as if he loved music. (*Music without*) Oh, here they are!

Enter ANNETTE *and* SAVOYARD *playing*

1

To welcome mirth and harmless glee,[1]
We rambling minstrels, blithe and free,
With song the laughing hours beguile,
 And wear a never-fading smile;
  Where'er we roam
  We find a home,
And greeting to reward our toil.

2

We sing of love, its hopes and fears,
Of perjured swains and damsels' tears,
Of eyes that speak the heart's warm glow,
Of sighs that tell the bosom's woe.
  O'er hills and plains
  We breathe our strains
Through summer's heat and winter's snow.

3

No anxious griefs disturb our rest,
No busy cares annoy our breast;
Fearless we sink in soft repose,
While night her sable mantle throws.
  We grateful lay,
  Hail rising day
That rosy health and peace bestows.

During the duet, STRANGER *looks from the lodge window, and at the conclusion he comes out*

STRANGER. What mummery is this?

FRANCIS. I hope it might amuse you, sir.

STRANGER. Amuse *me?* Fool!

FRANCIS. Well then, I wished to amuse myself a little. I don't think my recreations are so very numerous.

STRANGER. That's true, my poor fellow; indeed they are not. Let them go on. (*Sits*) I'll listen.

FRANCIS. But to please you, poor master, I fear it must be a sadder strain. Annette, have you none but these cheerful songs?

ANNETTE. O plenty! If you are dolefully given, we can be as sad as night. I'll sing you an air Mrs. Haller taught me the first year she came to the castle.

1

I have a silent sorrow here,[2]
 A grief I'll ne'er impart;
It breathes no sigh; it sheds no tear;
 But it consumes my heart!
This cherished woe, this loved despair,
 My lot forever be;
So, my soul's lord, the pangs I bear
 Be never known by thee!

2

And when pale characters of death
 Shall mark this altered cheek;
When my poor, wasted, trembling breath
 My life's last hope would speak;
I shall not raise my eyes to heav'n
 Nor mercy ask for me;
My soul despairs to be forgiv'n
 Unpardoned, love, by thee.

[1] For the words of this duet, the translator is obliged to John Grubb, Esq., and for the music to Mr. Shaw.—ORIGINAL NOTE.

[2] For the words of this song [the translator] is indebted to R. B. Sheridan, Esq., M. P., and for the music to her Grace the Duchess of Devonshire.—ORIGINAL NOTE.

STRANGER. (*Surprised and moved*) Oh! I have heard that air before, but 'twas with other words. Francis, share our supper with your friends. I need none. (*Enters the lodge*)

FRANCIS. So I feared. Well, my pretty favorites, here are refreshments. So? Disturbed again? Now will this gentleman call for more music and make my master mad? Return when you observe this man is gone. (*Exeunt* SAVOYARDS. FRANCIS *sits and eats*) I was in hopes that I might at least eat my supper peaceably in the open air; but they follow at our heels like bloodhounds.

Enter BARON

BARON. My good friend, I must speak to your master.

FRANCIS. Can't serve you.

BARON. Why not?

FRANCIS. It's forbidden.

BARON. (*Offers money*) There. Announce me.

FRANCIS. Want no money.

BARON. Well, only announce me then.

FRANCIS. I will announce you, sir; but it won't avail! I shall be abused and you rejected. However, we can but try. (*Going*)

BARON. I only ask half a minute. (FRANCIS *goes into the lodge*) But when he comes, how am I to treat him? I never encountered a misanthrope before. I have heard of instructions as to conduct in society, but how I am to behave towards a being who loathes the whole world and his own existence, I have never learned.

Enter STRANGER

STRANGER. Now, what's your will?

BARON. I beg pardon, sir, for—(*Suddenly recognizing him*) Charles!

STRANGER. Steinfort! (*They embrace*)

BARON. Is it really you, my dear friend?

STRANGER. It is.

BARON. Merciful heavens! How you are altered!

STRANGER. The hand of misery lies heavy on me. But how came you here? What want you?

BARON. Strange! Here I was ruminating how to address this mysterious recluse. He appears and proves to be my old and dearest friend.

STRANGER. Then you were not sent in search of me, nor knew that I lived here?

BARON. As little as I know who lives on the summit of Caucasus. You this morning saved the life of my brother-in-law's son; a grateful family wishes to behold you in its circle. You refused my sister's messenger; therefore, to give more weight to the invitation, I was deputed to be the bearer of it. And thus has fortune restored to me a friend whom my heart has so long missed and whom my heart just now so much requires.

STRANGER. Yes, I am your friend, your sincere friend. You are a true man, an uncommon man. Towards you my heart is still the same. But, if this assurance be of any value to you, go. Leave me and return no more.

BARON. Stay! All that I see and hear of you is inexplicable. 'Tis you; but these, alas, are not the features which once enchanted every female bosom, beamed gaiety through all society, and won you friends before your lips were opened! Why do you avert your face? Is the sight of a friend become hateful? Or do you fear that I should read in your eye what passes in your soul? Where is that open look of fire, which at once penetrated into every heart and revealed your own?

STRANGER. (*With asperity*) My look penetrate into every heart? Ha! ha! ha!

BARON. Oh, heavens! Rather may I never hear you laugh than in such a tone! Charles! What has happened to you?

STRANGER. Things that happen every day, occurrences heard of in every street. Steinfort, if I am not to hate you, ask me not another question. If I am to love you, leave me.

BARON. Oh, Charles, awake the faded ideas of past joys! Feel that a friend is near! Recollect the days we passed in Hungary, when we wandered arm in arm upon the banks of the Danube, while nature opened our hearts and made us enamored of benevolence and friendship. In those blessed moments you gave me this seal as a pledge of your regard. Do you remember it?

STRANGER. Yes.

BARON. Am I since that time become less worthy of your confidence?

STRANGER. No.

BARON. Charles, it grieves me that I am thus compelled to enforce my rights upon you. Do you know this scar?

STRANGER. Comrade! Friend! It received and resisted the stroke aimed at my life. I have not forgotten it. Alas, you knew not what a wretched present you then made me.

BARON. Speak then, I beseech you!

STRANGER. You cannot help me.

BARON. Then I can mourn with you.

STRANGER. That I hate. Besides, I cannot weep.

BARON. Then give me words instead of tears. Both relieve the heart.

STRANGER. My heart is like a close-shut sepulchre. Let what is within it moulder and decay. Why open the wretched charnel-house to spread pestilence around?

BARON. How horrid are your looks! For shame! A man like you thus to crouch beneath the chance of fortune.

STRANGER. Steinfort! I did think the opinion of all mankind was alike indifferent to me; but I feel that it is not so. My friend, you shall not quit me without learning how I have been robbed of every joy which life afforded. Listen! Much misery may be contained in few words. Attracted by my native country, I quitted you and the service. What pleasing pictures did I draw of a life employed in improving society and diffusing happiness. I fixed on Cassel to be my abode. All went on admirably. I found friends. At length, too, I found a wife, a lovely, innocent creature, scarce sixteen years of age. Oh, how I loved her! She bore me a son and a daughter. Both were endowed by nature with the beauty of their mother. Ask me not how I loved my wife and children! Yes, then I was really happy. (*Wiping his eyes*) Ha! A tear! I could not have believed it. Welcome, my friends! 'Tis long since we have known each other. Well, my story is nearly ended. One of my friends, for whom I became engaged, treacherously lost me more than half my fortune. This hurt me. I was obliged to retrench my expenses. Contentment needs but little. I forgave him. Another friend, a villain to whom I was attached heart and soul, whom I had assisted with my means and promoted by my interest, this *fiend* seduced my wife and bore her from me. Tell me, sir, is this enough to justify my hatred of mankind and palliate my seclusion from the world? Kings, laws, tyranny, or guilt can but imprison me or kill me! But, O God! O God! Oh, what are chains or death compared to the tortures of a deceived yet doting husband!

BARON. To lament the loss of a faithless wife is madness.

STRANGER. Call it what you please, say what you please, I love her still.

BARON. And where is she?

STRANGER. I know not, nor do I wish to know.

BARON. And your children?

STRANGER. I left them in a small town hard by.

BARON. But why did you not keep your children with you? They would have amused you in many a dreary hour.

STRANGER. Amused! Oh, yes, while their likeness to their mother would every hour remind me of my past happiness! No! For three years I have never seen them. I hate that any human creature should be near me, young or old. Had not ridiculous habits made a servant necessary, I should long since have discharged him, though he is not the worst among the bad.

BARON. Such too often is the consequence of great alliances. Therefore, Charles, I have resolved to take a wife from a lower rank of life.

STRANGER. You marry! Ha! ha! ha!

BARON. You shall see her. She is in the house where you are expected. Come with me.

STRANGER. What! I mix again with the world!

BARON. To do a generous action without requiring thanks is noble and praiseworthy. But so obstinately to avoid those thanks as to make the kindness a burden is affectation.

STRANGER. Leave me! Leave me! Everyone tries to form a circle of which he may be the center. As long as there remains a bird in these woods to greet the rising sun with its melody, I shall court no other society.

BARON. Do as you please to-morrow, but give me your company this evening.

STRANGER. (*Resolutely*) No.

BARON. Not though it were in your own power by this single visit to secure the happiness of your friend for life?

STRANGER. Ha! then I must—But how?

BARON. You shall sue in my behalf to Mrs. Haller. You have the talent of persuasion.

STRANGER. I! My dear Steinfort!

BARON. The happiness or misery of your friend depends upon it. I'll contrive that you shall speak to her alone. Will you?

STRANGER. These are pretenses. But I'll come, however, on one condition.

BARON. Name it.

STRANGER. That you allow me to be gone to-morrow without endeavoring to detain me.

BARON. Go! Whither?

STRANGER. No matter! Promise this or I will not come.

BARON. Well, I do promise.

STRANGER. I have directions to give my servant.

BARON. In half an hour then we shall expect you. Remember you have given your word.

STRANGER. I have! (*Exit* BARON. STRANGER *walks up and down thoughtful and melancholy*) Francis!

Enter FRANCIS

FRANCIS. Sir!

STRANGER. I shall leave this place to-morrow.

FRANCIS. With all my heart.

STRANGER. Perhaps to go into another land.

FRANCIS. With all my heart again!

STRANGER. Perhaps into another quarter of the globe.

FRANCIS. With all my heart still. Into which quarter?

STRANGER. Wherever heaven directs! Away, away from Europe! From this cultivated moral lazaret! Do you hear, Francis? To-morrow early.

FRANCIS. Very well.

STRANGER. But first I have an errand for you. Hire that carriage in the village; drive to the town hard by; you may be back by sunset. I shall give you a letter to a widow who lives there. With her you will find two children. They are mine.

FRANCIS. (*Astonished*) Your children, sir!

STRANGER. Take them and bring them hither.

FRANCIS. Your children, sir?

STRANGER. Yes, mine! Is it so very inconceivable?

FRANCIS. That I should have been three years in your service and never have heard them mentioned is somewhat strange.

STRANGER. Pshaw!

FRANCIS. You have been married then?

STRANGER. Go, and prepare for our journey.

FRANCIS. That I can do in five minutes.

Exit

STRANGER. I shall come and write the letter directly.—Yes, I'll take them with me. I'll accustom myself to the sight of them. The innocents! They shall not be poisoned by the refinements of society. Rather let them hunt their daily sustenance upon some desert island with their bow and arrow, or creep like torpid Hottentots into a corner and stare at each other. Better to do nothing than to do evil. Fool that I was to be prevailed upon once more to exhibit myself among these apes! What a ridiculous figure shall I be, and in the capacity of a suitor too! Pshaw! He cannot be serious. 'Tis but a friendly artifice to draw me from my solitude. Why did I promise him? Well, my sufferings have been many; and, to oblige a friend, why should I not add another painful hour to the wretched calendar of my life? I'll go, I'll go! *Exit*

SCENE II

The Antechamber. Enter CHARLOTTE

CHARLOTTE. No, indeed, my lady, if you choose to bury yourself in the country, I shall take my leave. I am not calculated for a country life. And, to sum up all, when I think of this Mrs. Haller—

Enter SOLOMON

SOLOMON. (*Overhearing her last words*) What of Mrs. Haller, my sweet miss?

CHARLOTTE. Why, Mr. Solomon, who is Mrs. Haller? You know everything; you hear everything.

SOLOMON. I have received no letters from any part of Europe on the subject, miss.

CHARLOTTE. But who is to blame? The count and countess. She dines with them, and at this very moment is drinking tea with them. Is this proper?

SOLOMON. By no means.

CHARLOTTE. Shouldn't a count in all his actions show a certain degree of pride and pomposity?

SOLOMON. To be sure! To be sure he should!

CHARLOTTE. No, I won't submit to it. I'll tell her ladyship when I dress her to-morrow that either Mrs. Haller or I must quit the house.

SOLOMON. (*Seeing the* BARON) St!

Enter BARON

BARON. Didn't I hear Mrs. Haller's name here?

SOLOMON. (*Confused*) Why—yes—we—we—

BARON. Charlotte, tell my sister I wish to see her as soon as the tea-table is removed.

CHARLOTTE. (*Aside to* SOLOMON) Either she or I go; that I'm determined. *Exit*

BARON. May I ask what it was you were saying?

SOLOMON. Why, please your honorable lordship, we were talking here and there,—this and that—

BARON. I almost begin to suspect some secret.

SOLOMON. Secret! Heaven forbid! Mercy on us, no! I should have had letters on the subject if there had been a secret.

BARON. Well then, since it was no secret, I presume I may know your conversation.

SOLOMON. You do us great honor, my lord. Why then, at first we were making a few commonplace observations. Miss Charlotte remarked that we all had our faults. I said, "Yes." Soon after I remarked that the best persons in the world were not without their weaknesses. She said, "Yes."

BARON. If you referred to Mrs. Haller's faults and weaknesses, I am desirous to hear more.

SOLOMON. Sure enough, sir, Mrs. Haller is an excellent woman; but she's not an angel, for all that. I am an old, faithful servant to his excellency the count, and therefore it is my duty to speak when anything is done disadvantageous to his interest.

BARON. Well!

SOLOMON. For instance, now, his excellency may think he has at least some score of dozens of the old six-and-twenty hock. Mercy on us! There are not ten dozen bottles left; and not a drop has gone down my throat, I'll swear.

BARON. (*Smiling*) Mrs. Haller has not drank it, I suppose?

SOLOMON. Not she herself, for she never drinks wine. But if anybody be ill in the village, any poor woman lying-in, that might think herself well off with common Rhenish, away goes a bottle of the six-and-twenty! Innumerable are the times that I've reproved her; but she always answers me snappishly that she will be responsible for it.

BARON. So will I, Mr. Solomon.

SOLOMON. Oh, with all my heart, your honorable lordship. It makes no difference to me. I had the care of the cellar twenty years and can safely take my oath that I never gave the poor a single drop in the whole course of my trust.

BARON. How extraordinary is this woman!

SOLOMON. Extraordinary! One can make nothing of her. To-day the vicar's wife is not good enough for her. To-morrow you may see her sitting with all the women in the village. To be sure, she and I agree pretty well; for, between me and your honorable lordship, she has cast an eye upon my son Peter.

BARON. Has she?

SOLOMON. Yes. Peter's no fool, I assure you. The schoolmaster is teaching him to write. Would your honorable lordship please to see a specimen? I'll go for his copy-book. He makes his pot-hooks capitally.

BARON. Another time, another time. Good-bye for the present, Mr. Solomon. (SOLOMON *bows without attempting to go*) Good day, Mr. Solomon.

SOLOMON. (*Not understanding the hint*) Your honorable lordship's most obedient servant.

BARON. This is too bad. Mr. Solomon, I wish to be alone.

SOLOMON. As your lordship commands. If the time should seem long in my absence and your lordship wishes to hear the newest from the seat of war, you need only send for old Solomon. I have letters from Leghorn, Cape Horn, and every known part of the habitable globe. *Exit*

BARON. Tedious old fool! Yet hold. Did he not speak in praise of Mrs. Haller? Pardoned be his rage for news and politics. (*Enter* COUNTESS) Well, sister, have you spoken to her?

COUNTESS. I have; and if you do not steer for another haven, you will be doomed to drive upon the ocean for ever.

BARON. Is she married?

COUNTESS. I don't know.

BARON. Is she of a good family?

COUNTESS. I can't tell.

BARON. Does she dislike me?

COUNTESS. Excuse my making a reply.

BARON. I thank you for your sisterly affection and the explicitness of your communications. Luckily I placed little reliance on either and have found a friend who will save your ladyship all further trouble.

COUNTESS. A friend?
BARON. Yes, the stranger who saved your son's life this morning proves to be my intimate friend.
COUNTESS. What's his name?
BARON. I don't know.
COUNTESS. Is he of a good family?
BARON. I can't tell.
COUNTESS. Will he come hither?
BARON. Excuse my making a reply.
COUNTESS. Well, the retort is fair,—but insufferable.
BARON. You can't object to the *da capo*[1] of your own composition.

Enter COUNT *and* MRS. HALLER

COUNT. Zounds! Do you think I am Xenocrates,[2] or like the poor sultan with marble legs?[3] There you leave me *tête-à-tête* with Mrs. Haller as if my heart were a mere flint. So you prevailed, brother. The stranger will come then, it seems?
BARON. I expect him every minute.
COUNTESS. I'm so glad to hear it. One companion more; however, in the country we never can have too many.
BARON. This gentleman will not exactly be an addition to your circle, for he leaves this place to-morrow.
COUNT. But he won't I think. Now, Lady Wintersen, summon all your charms. There is no art in conquering us poor devils; but this strange man, who does not care a doit for you all together, is worth your efforts. Try your skill. I shan't be jealous.
COUNTESS. I allow the conquest to be worth the trouble. But what Mrs. Haller has not been able to effect in three months ought not to be attempted by me.
MRS. HALLER. (*Jocosely*) O yes, madam. He has given me no opportunity of trying the force of my charms, for I have never once happened to see him.
COUNT. Then he's a blockhead and you an idler.
SOLOMON. (*Without*) This way, sir. This way.

Enter SOLOMON

SOLOMON. The stranger begs leave to have the honor—
COUNT. Welcome, welcome! Show him the way. (*Exit* SOLOMON. *Count turns to meet the* STRANGER *whom he conducts in by the hand*) My dear sir—Lady Wintersen! Mrs. Haller!
MRS. HALLER, *as soon as she sees the* STRANGER, *shrieks and swoons in the arms of the* BARON *and* COUNTESS. *The* STRANGER *casts a look at her and, struck with astonishment and horror, rushes out of the room. The* BARON *and* COUNTESS *bear* MRS. HALLER *off,* COUNT *following in great surprise.*

ACT V

SCENE I

The Antechamber. Enter BARON

BARON. Oh, deceitful hope! Thou phantom of future happiness! To thee have I stretched out my arms and thou hast vanished into air! Wretched Steinfort! The mystery is solved. She is the wife of my friend. Enough! Not by idle disputation but by deeds will I contradict what Wintersen just now asserted.[4] I cannot myself be happy; but I may, perhaps, be able to reunite two lovely souls whom cruel fate has severed. Ha! They are here. I must propose it instantly.

Enter COUNTESS *and* MRS. HALLER

COUNTESS. Into the garden, my dear friend! Into the air!
MRS. HALLER. I am quite well. Do not alarm yourselves on my account.
BARON. Madam, pardon my intrusion; but to lose a moment may be fatal. He means to quit the country to-morrow. We must devise means to reconcile you to—the stranger.

---

[1] Repetition.
[2] The Greek philosopher (396–314, B.C.), rector of the Athenian Academy, a man known for his austere life.
[3] The unfortunate sultan is found in *The Arabian Nights*, the story of the young king of the Black Islands.
[4] This sentence is rendered unintelligible, presumably by the excision of the first part of the scene as it appears in the German original, where the Baron's speech beginning "O die täuschende Hoffnung!" follows a page of dialogue with the Count. In this scene, which is lacking in the published form of Thompson's translation, the Baron accuses the Count of acting upon very egotistical principles. The Count replies, "Ach, lieber Herr Bruder! Egoisten sind wir alle; der eine mehr, der andere weniger! Der eine lässt seinen Egoismus nackend laufen, der andere hängt ihm ein Mäntelchen um." This **seems to be** "what Wintersen just now asserted."

MRS. HALLER. How, my lord? You seem acquainted with my history?

BARON. I am. Waldbourg has been my friend ever since we were boys. We served together from the rank of cadet. We have been separated seven years. Chance brought us this day together and his heart was open to me.

MRS. HALLER. Now do I feel what it is to be in the presence of an honest man when I dare not meet his eyes. (*Hides her face*)

BARON. If sincere repentance, if years without reproach, do not give us a title to man's forgiveness, what must we expect hereafter? No, lovely penitent, your contrition is complete. Error, for a moment, wrested from slumbering virtue the dominion of your heart; but she awoke and, with a look, banished her enemy for ever. I know my friend. He has the firmness of a man, but with it the gentlest feelings of your sex. I hasten to him. With the fire of pure disinterested friendship will I enter on this work, that when I look back upon my past life I may derive from this good action consolation in disappointment and even resignation in despair.
(*Going*)

MRS. HALLER. Oh, stay! What would you do? No! Never! My husband's honor is sacred to me. I love him unutterably; but never, never can I be his wife again, even if he were generous enough to pardon me.

BARON. Madam! Can you, countess, be serious?

MRS. HALLER. Not that title, I beseech you. I am not a child who wishes to avoid deserved punishment. What were my penitence if I hoped advantage from it beyond the consciousness of atonement for past offence.

COUNTESS. But if your husband himself—

MRS. HALLER. Oh, he will not. He cannot! And let him rest assured I never will replace my honor at the expense of his.

BARON. He still loves you.

MRS. HALLER. Loves me! Then he must not—No, he must purify his heart from a weakness which would degrade him!

BARON. Incomparable woman! I go to my friend,—perhaps for the last time. Have you not one word to send him?

MRS. HALLER. Yes, I have two requests to make. Often, when in excess of grief, I have despaired of every consolation, I have thought I should be easier if I might behold my husband once again, acknowledge my injustice to him, and take a gentle leave of him forever. This, therefore, is my first request,—a conversation for a few short minutes, if he does not quite abhor the sight of me. My second request is—O, not to see, but to hear some account of my poor children.

BARON. If humanity and friendship can avail, he will not for a moment delay your wishes.

COUNTESS. Heaven be with you!

MRS. HALLER. And my prayers.

Exit BARON

COUNTESS. Come, my friend, come into the air till he returns with hope and consolation.

MRS. HALLER. O, my heart, how thou art afflicted! My husband! My little ones! Past joys and future fears—Oh, dearest madam, there are moments in which we live years! Moments which steal the roses from the cheek of health and plough deep furrows in the brow of youth.

COUNTESS. Banish these sad reflections. Come, let us walk. The sun will set soon; let nature's beauties dissipate anxiety.

MRS. HALLER. Alas! Yes, the setting sun is a proper scene for me.

COUNTESS. Never forget a morning will succeed.
Exeunt

SCENE II

The skirts of the park, lodge, &c., as before

Enter BARON

BARON. On earth there is but one such pair. They shall not be parted. Yet, what I have undertaken is not so easy as I at first hoped. What can I answer when he asks me whether I would persuade him to renounce his character and become the derision of society? For he is right. A faithless wife is a dishonor; and to forgive her is to share her shame. What though Adelaide may be an exception, a young, deluded girl who has so long and so sincerely repented; yet what cares an unfeeling world for this? The world! He has quitted it. 'Tis evident he loves her still, and upon this assurance builds my sanguine heart the hope of a happy termination to an honest enterprise.

Enter FRANCIS *with two children,* WILLIAM *and* AMELIA

FRANCIS. Come along, my pretty ones. Come!

WILLIAM. Is it far to home?

FRANCIS. No, we shall be there directly, now.

BARON. Hold! Whose children are these?

FRANCIS. My master's.

WILLIAM. Is that my father?

BARON. It darts like lightning through my brain! A word with you. I know you love your master. Strange things have happened here. Your master has found his wife again.

FRANCIS. Indeed! Glad to hear it.

BARON. Mrs. Haller—

FRANCIS. Is she his wife? Still more glad to hear it.

BARON. But he is determined to go from her.

FRANCIS. Oh!

BARON. We must try to prevent it.

FRANCIS. Surely.

BARON. The unexpected appearance of the children may perhaps assist us.

FRANCIS. How so?

BARON. Hide yourself with them in that hut. Before a quarter of an hour is past you shall know more.

FRANCIS. But—

BARON. No more questions, I entreat you. Time is precious.

FRANCIS. Well, well. Questions are not much in my way. Come, children.

WILLIAM. Why, I thought you told me I should see my father.

FRANCIS. So you shall, my dear. Come, moppets. (*Goes into the hut with children*)

BARON. Excellent! I promise myself much from this little artifice. If the mild look of the mother fails, the innocent smiles of these his own children will surely find the way to his heart. (*Taps at the door.* STRANGER *comes out*) Charles, I wish you joy!

STRANGER. Of what?

BARON. You have found her again.

STRANGER. Show a bankrupt the treasure which he once possessed and then congratulate him on the amount!

BARON. Why not, if it be in your power to retrieve the whole?

STRANGER. I understand you; you are a negotiator from my wife. It won't avail.

BARON. Learn to know your wife better. Yes, I am a messenger from her, but without power to treat. She, who loves you unutterably, who without you can never be happy, renounces your forgiveness because, as she thinks, your honor is incompatible with such a weakness.

STRANGER. Pshaw! I am not to be caught.

BARON. Charles! Consider well—

STRANGER. Steinfort, let me explain all this. I have lived here four months. Adelaide knew it.

BARON. Knew it! She never saw you till today.

STRANGER. That she may make fools believe. Hear further: she knows too that I am not a common sort of man, that my heart is not to be attacked in the usual way. She, therefore, framed a nice, deep-concerted plan. She played a charitable part, but in such a way that it always reached my ears. She played a pious, modest, reserved part in order to excite my curiosity. And at last, today, she plays the prude. She refuses my forgiveness in order by this generous device to extort it from my compassion.

BARON. Charles! I have listened to you with astonishment. This is weakness only to be pardoned in a man who has often been deceived by the world. Your wife has expressly and steadfastly declared that she will not accept of your forgiveness even if you yourself were weak enough to offer it.

STRANGER. What then has brought you hither?

BARON. More than one reason. First, I am come in my own name as your friend and comrade to conjure you solemnly not to spurn this creature from you, for, by my soul, you will not find her equal.

STRANGER. Give yourself no further trouble.

BARON. Be candid, Charles. You love her still.

STRANGER. Alas, yes!

BARON. Her sincere repentance has long since obliterated her crime.

STRANGER. Sir, a wife once induced to forfeit her honor must be capable of a second crime.

BARON. Not so, Charles. Ask your own heart what portion of the blame may be your own.

STRANGER. Mine!

BARON. Yours! Who told you to marry a thoughtless, inexperienced girl? One scarce expects established principles at twenty-five in a man; yet you require them in a girl of sixteen. But of this no more! She has erred; she has repented; and during three years her conduct has been so far above reproach that even the piercing eye of calumny has not discovered a speck upon this radiant orb.

STRANGER. Now, were I to believe all this,—for I confess I would willingly believe it,—yet can she never again be mine. (*With extreme asperity*) Oh, what a feast would it be for the painted dolls when I appeared among them with my runaway wife upon my arm! What mocking, whispering, and pointing! Never! Never! Never!

BARON. Enough! As a friend I have done my duty. I now appear as Adelaide's ambassador. She requests one moment's conversation; she wishes once again to see you and never more. You cannot deny her this only, this last request.

STRANGER. Oh, I understand this, too. She thinks my firmness will be melted by her tears. She is mistaken. She may come.

BARON. She will come to make you feel how much you mistake her. I go for her.

STRANGER. Another word. Give her this paper and these jewels. They belong to her.
(*Presenting them*)

BARON. That you may do yourself. *Exit*

STRANGER. The last anxious moment of my life draws near. I shall see her once again, see her on whom my soul dotes. Is this the language of an injured husband? Alas! alas! what is the principle which we call honor? Is it a feeling of the heart or a mere quibble in the brain? I must be resolute; it cannot be otherwise. Let me speak solemnly yet mildly and beware that nothing of reproach escape my lips. Yes, her penitence is real. She shall not be obliged to live in mean dependence; she shall be mistress of herself and have enough to—(*Looks round and shudders*) Ha, they come! Awake, insulted pride! Protect me, injured honor!

Enter MRS. HALLER, COUNTESS, *and* BARON

MRS. HALLER. (*Advances slowly and in a tremor*. COUNTESS *attempts to support her*) Leave me now, I beseech you. (*Approaches* STRANGER, *who with averted countenance and in extreme agitation awaits her address*) My lord!

STRANGER. (*With gentle, tremulous utterance and face turned away*) What would you with me, Adelaide?

MRS. HALLER. (*Much agitated*) No, for heaven's sake! I was not prepared for this. Oh, that tone cuts to my heart! Adelaide! No! For heaven's sake! Harsh tones alone are suited to a culprit's ear.

STRANGER. (*Endeavoring to give his voice firmness*) Well, madam?

MRS. HALLER. Oh! If you will ease my heart, if you will spare and pity me, use reproaches.

STRANGER. Reproaches! Here they are upon my sallow cheek, here in my hollow eye, here in my faded form. These reproaches I could not spare you.

MRS. HALLER. Were I a hardened sinner, this forbearance would be charity; but I am a suffering penitent and it overpowers me. Alas! then I must be the herald of my own shame. For where shall I find peace till I have eased my soul by my confession?

STRANGER. No confession, madam! I release you from every humiliation. I perceive you feel that we must part forever.

MRS. HALLER. I know it. Nor come I here to supplicate your pardon; nor has my heart contained a ray of hope that you would grant it. All I dare ask is that you will not curse my memory.

STRANGER. (*Moved*) No, Adelaide, I do not curse you. No, I shall never curse you.

MRS. HALLER. (*Agitated*) From the inward conviction that I am unworthy of your name, I have, during three years, abandoned it. But this is not enough; you must have that redress which will enable you to choose another,—another wife, in whose untainted arms may heaven protect your hours in bliss! This paper will be necessary for the purpose; it contains a written acknowledgment of my guilt. (*Offers it trembling*)

STRANGER. (*Tearing it*) Perish the record forever. No, Adelaide, you only have possessed my heart; and without shame I confess it, you alone will reign there forever. Your own sensations of virtue, your resolute honor, forbid you to profit by my weakness; and even if—Now, by heaven, this is beneath a man! But—Never, never, will another fill Adelaide's place here.

MRS. HALLER. (*Trembling*) Then nothing now remains but that one sad, hard, just word,—farewell!

STRANGER. A moment's stay. For some months we have without knowing it lived near each other. I have learned much good of you. You have a heart open to the wants of your fellow creatures. I am happy that it is so. You shall not be without the power of gratifying your benevolence. I know you have a spirit that must shrink from a state of obligation. This paper, to which the whole remnant of my fortune is pledged, secures you independence, Adelaide; and let the only recommendation of the gift be that it will administer to you the means of indulging in charity the divine propensity of your nature.

MRS. HALLER. Never! By the labor of my hands must I earn my sustenance. A morsel of bread moistened with the tear of penitence will suffice my wishes and exceed my merits. It would be an additional reproach to think that I served myself, or even others, from the bounty of him whom I had so basely injured.

STRANGER. Take it, madam, take it!

MRS. HALLER. I have deserved this. But I throw myself upon your generosity. Have compassion on me!

STRANGER. (*Aside*) Villain, of what a woman hast thou robbed me! (*Puts up the paper*) Well, madam, I respect your sentiments and withdraw my request, but on this one condition, that if you ever should be in want of anything, I shall be the first and only person in the world to whom you will make application.

MRS. HALLER. I promise it, my lord.

STRANGER. And now I may at least desire you to take back what is your own,—your jewels. (*Gives her the casket*)

MRS. HALLER. (*Opens it with violent agitation and her tears burst upon it*) How well do I recollect the sweet evening when you gave me these! That evening my father joined our hands and joyfully I pronounced the oath of eternal fidelity. It is broken. This locket you gave me on my birthday. 'Tis five years since. That was a happy day! We had a country feast. How cheerful we all were! This bracelet I received after my William was born! No! I cannot keep these, unless you wish that the sight of them should be an incessant reproach to my almost broken heart.
(*Gives them back*)

STRANGER. (*Aside*) I must go. My soul and pride will hold no longer. (*Turning towards her*) Farewell!

MRS. HALLER. Oh, but one minute more! An answer to but one more question. Feel for a mother's heart! Are my children still alive?

STRANGER. They are alive.

MRS. HALLER. And well?

STRANGER. They are well.

MRS. HALLER. God be praised! William must be much grown?

STRANGER. I believe so.

MRS. HALLER. What! Have you not seen them! And little Amelia, is she still your favorite? (*The* STRANGER, *who is in violent agitation throughout this scene, remains in silent contention between honor and affection*) Oh, if you knew how my heart has hung upon them for these three long, dreadful years, how I have sat at evening twilight, first fancying William, then Amelia, on my lap! Oh, allow me to behold them once again. Let me once more kiss the features of their father in his babes and I will kneel to you and part with them forever.

STRANGER. Willingly, Adelaide. This very night. I expect the children every minute. They have been brought up near this spot. I have already sent my servant for them. He might before this time have returned. I pledge my word to send them to the castle as soon as they arrive. There, if you please, they may remain till daybreak to-morrow. Then they must go with me. (*A pause*)

(*The* COUNTESS *and* BARON, *who at a little distance have listened to the whole conversation with the warmest sympathy, exchange signals.* BARON *goes into the hut and soon returns with* FRANCIS *and the children. He gives the boy to the* COUNTESS, *who places herself behind* MRS. HALLER. *He himself walks with the girl behind the* STRANGER)

MRS. HALLER. In this world then—we have no more to say. (*Summoning all her resolution*) Farewell! (*Seizing his hand*) Forget a wretch who will never forget you. (*Kneels*) Let me press this hand once more to my lips,—this hand which once was mine.

STRANGER. (*Raising her*) No humiliation, Adelaide! (*Shakes her hand*) Farewell!

MRS. HALLER. A last farewell!

STRANGER. The last.

MRS. HALLER. And when my penance shall have broken my heart, when we again meet in a better world—

STRANGER. There, Adelaide, you may be mine again.

(*Their hands lie in each other; their eyes mournfully meet each other. They stammer another "Farewell" and part; but as they are going she encounters the boy and he the girl*)

CHILDREN. Dear father! Dear mother!

(*They press the children in their arms with speechless affection; then tear themselves away, gaze at each other, spread their arms, and rush into an embrace. The children run and cling round their parents. The curtain falls*)

EPILOGUE

Written by M. G. LEWIS, ESQ., M. P.[1]

Spoken by MR. SUETT AS A GYPSY

In Norwood's [2] spell-fraught shades and haunted bow'rs,
From public eye remote, I pass my hours;
There gives this magic crutch imperial sway,
And shirtless tribes their tag-rag queen obey.
Silence! I wave my wand! With rev'rence view it   5
And hear the oracles of Goody Suett!
Hark! hark! How many female tongues I hear
Lisp, "Oh! my stars! The Gypsy queen, my dear!
A person of great fashion, I'll assure ye;   9
But what the devil brings her now to Drury?"
Peace and I'll tell you. Yet without a shilling
To speak the gypsy tribe is seldom willing.
Nor holds the Sybil o'er old Nick command
Unless with silver first you cross her hand.   14
A different mode, I own, suits best with me;
'Till answered your demands, I'll ask no fee,
But hope to find you, when my art is shown,
Instead of crossing my hand, clap your own.
Know, in my secret grot retired of late
A spell I cast to learn this drama's fate,   20
When, lo! the cave was filled with sulphrous smoke
And distant hisses midnight's slumber broke!
I marked the omens dire with doubt and fear,
Saddled my broomstick, and straight hurried here
Dame Haller's cause to plead in accents humble;   25
For I, like her, have known what 'tis to stumble.
When youth my cheeks with roses loved to deck
And auburn ringlets graced my iv'ry neck,
Then did my artless bosom dare to harbor
Too fond a flame for a too faithless barber!   30
Great were his charms, too great for words to state 'em;
Sweeter his manners were then rose pomatum;
But ah! though seeming candor graced his looks,
His heart was falser than his own peruques!
Oft at my feet in amrous grief he knelt,   35
Oft painted pangs and flames he never felt.
I strove to fly, but vain was each endeavor;
I listened, loved, and was undone forever!
Excuse these tears! and let my pray'rs prevailing,
Induce you to forgive Dame Haller's failing.
The malice of her foes with plaudits stem,   41
Nor when her spouse absolves do you condemn.
Should vou refuse me, dread my vengeance; dread
My imps at midnight shrieking round your bed!
Dread too—But Hecate calls! I must away,   45
Though I've a thousand things still left to say;
But as my stay cannot be now protracted,
I'll tell you more next time this play is acted.

---

[1] Matthew Gregory Lewis (1775–1818), famous as the author of *The Monk*, M. P. for Hindon, Wiltshire, 1796–1802, was also author of a large number of tales, romances, and plays.

[2] Norwood is a hilly, well wooded section of London, lying on the southwestern outskirts of Lambeth.

NOTE

The Plain-Dealer, by William Wycherley, has been added to this collection of plays at the request of teachers using the book as a text. To avoid repaging, it has been placed at the end of the volume.

NOTE

THE PLAIN-DEALER [1]

By William Wycherley

*Ridiculum acri
Fortius et melius magnas plerumque secat res.*[2]
HORAT.

Known to his own age as "manly Wycherley" and to the Victorian period as the most immoral of Restoration comic writers, William Wycherley, the eldest son of Daniel Wycherley of Clive Hall, Shropshire, and Bethia Shrimpton, his wife, was born on his father's manor some time in 1640. The father was a royalist country gentleman of the old school, delighting in lawsuits and living to be eighty-one. Apparently no love was lost between him and his brilliant offspring. The boy was taught the classics at home and at fifteen sent for polishing to France, where he frequented the provincial salon of the former Mlle. de Rambouillet, now Madame de Montausier, a *précieuse*. In France Wycherley became a Roman Catholic. He returned at the Restoration to enter Oxford, but left the university almost immediately (November, 1660?) to become a member of the Inner Temple.

The young man of twenty now entered upon his worldly career as a dramatist and man about town. His first publication (if it was his) was a poem, *Hero and Leander in Burlesque* (1669), a travesty in a genre then popular, which the world has agreed to forget. According to his own account, he had already written his first plays, but this is doubtful. The brilliant success of *Love in a Wood* in the autumn of 1671 made Wycherley famous, and he "became acquainted with several of the most celebrated wits both of the Court and the Town." The favors of the beautiful Duchess of Cleveland soon followed. The story of their first meeting is flavored with Restoration piquancy. Wycherley also adroitly won the favor of Buckingham, a declared pretender to the lady's affections.

After *The Gentleman Dancing Master* other plays followed at two-year intervals. During the decade of the seventies the dramatist was at the height of his fame and fortune, living the life of the Restoration to the full. But in 1678 he fell dangerously ill; neither a royal visit to his bedside nor a winter in France brought back what the illness cost him in health and memory, and thereafter, despite his secret marriage to Laetitia Moore, widow of the Earl of Drogheda in 1680, from which he would normally have profited, the story of his life is the story of gradual decay. The king resented the secrecy of the marriage; his wife proved to be insanely jealous; and her death involved him in distressing lawsuits, as a consequence of which he spent some years in prison.

The dramatist was rescued in 1685 through the bounty of James II, who pensioned him. His great reputation remained, but his last years were clouded by vanity and the decline of his creative power. The chief literary activity of his old age was the publication of his poems (1704). The revision of his manuscripts by the young Alexander Pope in 1706-10 proved unhappy on both sides. Eleven days before his death, probably to thwart a designing nephew, Wycherley married a second time. He died December 31, 1715. One may apply to the close of his life a pathetic passage in Prior; he lingered on

> As some old actor loads the scene,
> Unwilling to retire, though weary.

Consult the life in the *Dictionary of National Biography* by G. A. Aitken; that prefixed to *The Complete Works of William Wycherley* (Nonesuch

---

[1] The editors wish gratefully to acknowledge the kindness of Mr. V. Valta Parma in collating this text with the copy of the first edition of the play in the Congressional Library.

[2] Ridicule usually determines great matters better and more forcibly than does gravity. Horace, *Satires*, I, x, 14-15.

Press), 4 vols., 1924, edited by Montague Summers; and the work by Perromat mentioned below.

WYCHERLEY'S DRAMATIC WORKS

Love in a Wood (comedy) (D.L. before Oct., 1671), 1672.
The Gentleman Dancing Master (comedy) (?L.I.F., 1671?; D.G., Jan.? 1672), 1673.
The Country Wife (comedy) (D.L., Jan., 1674/5), 1675.
The Plain-Dealer (comedy) (D.L., 1676), 1677.

The reputation of Mr. Wycherley as a dramatist is vast, but the repute of his immorality is as great, especially since the celebrated essay of Mr. Macaulay fixed upon him the glory or the opprobrium of being the most vicious of Restoration comic writers. But of this dramatist it may be said that he but spoke out more freely than did his fellow-writers, and further, that this evil reputation is founded upon one half of his work only. *Love in a Wood* is not licentious, unless Mr. Etherege be so; and of *The Gentleman Dancing Master*, it may be said that 'tis only a Spanish comedy of intrigue translated to our English stage. *The Country Wife* and *The Plain-Dealer* are, in their language, plain spoken, but as it was the design of the latter to deal plainly with the faults of the age, the language is part of the design; and, though *The Country Wife* turns upon a humorous idea which no other dramatist has been bold enough to employ, the present age hath patronized books in prose which are more licentious, since they treat seriously what Wycherley viewed with scornful laughter.

A more modern writer divides mankind into the tender-minded and the tough-minded. Mr. Wycherley is clearly of the latter group of philosophers. His thought has been profoundly molded by the *libertin* thinkers of France, and he participates in that cruel disillusion respecting mankind which led my Lord Rochester to the extreme of cynicism. There are in this poet's later plays but few amiable persons; nor is the fidelity of the disguised Fidelia, or the faithfulness of Freeman to his friend, in *The Plain-Dealer*, of that heroic kind which insensibly lures men to follow virtue. Mr. Wycherley involves the one in a scarcely credible love-deception, and the other in a love-intrigue ruthlessly pursued and cruelly victorious. For this dramatist, 'tis apparent, virtue may be desirable, but in a world of weakness and folly, few there are that find it.

The Country Wife and *The Plain-Dealer* are rival claimants for the honor of being Mr. Wycherley's masterpiece. *The Country Wife* is perhaps inferior to its successor in the variety of its scenes and personages. Borrowing freely from Molière, the poet has yet remolded everything that he has taken; his play is thoroughly British, if we except the Fidelia-Olivia story, which not even the example of Shakespeare in *Twelfth Night* can quite make probable. There is in this play a rich variety, and the student may amuse himself by tracing out its elements. The scenes in Westminster-hall are executed with a bustle and realism which parallels Mr. Shadwell's comedies; and the comedy of humors has helped to create the Widow Blackacre, her son, and other personages. The talk of the fashionable characters, when they deal in human types, is that of men and women conversant with the "character writing" of the day. The intrigue itself, with its plot and counter-plot, especially in the last two acts, is to be associated with the Spanish comedy of intrigue, which Mr. Wycherley had already employed in *The Gentleman Dancing Master;* the influence of Molière has been profound upon Manly and his mistress, and in the conversations of Manly and his Freeman. If *Le Misanthrope* suffers from thinness of plot, that of *The Plain-Dealer* suffers by the uneven distribution of events over the play, the end being especially huddled together, but is nevertheless testimony to this writer's wide observation and vigor of description. Mr. Wycherley's world is a cruel world; the laughter is not silvery, but scornful; and the mood is fundamentally one of weariness and disillusion with an age grown old and cold and dreary.

Besides the celebrated essay of Macaulay on the Restoration dramatists and more modern treatises dealing with the period, the student should consult Johannes Klette, *William Wycherley's Leben und dramatische Werke*, Münster, 1883; and Charles Perromat, *William Wycherley: Sa Vie—Son Œuvre*, Paris, 1921. The edition of Wycherley in the "Mermaid Series", ed. W. C. Ward, contains the Macaulay essay, with corrections by the editor. There is also an interesting discussion of Wycherley in Taine's *History of English Literature*, valuable in its comparison of English and French comedy.

THE PLAIN-DEALER

To My Lady B———[1]

Madam,

Though I never had the honor to receive a favor from you, nay, or be known to you, I take the confidence of an author to write to you a *billet-doux* dedicatory; which is no new thing, for by most dedications it appears that authors, though they praise their patrons from top to toe, and seem to turn 'em inside out, know 'em as little as sometimes their patrons their books, though they read 'em out; and if the poetical daubers did not write the name of the man or woman on top of the picture, 'twere impossible to guess whose it were. But you, madam, without the help of a poet, have made yourself known and famous in the world; and, because you do not want it, are therefore most worthy an epistle dedicatory. And this play claims naturally your protection, since it has lost its reputation with the ladies of stricter lives in the playhouse; and (you know) when men's endeavors are discountenanced and refused by the nice coy women of honor, they come to you, to you, the great and noble patroness of rejected and bashful men, of which number I profess myself to be one, though a poet, a dedicating poet; to you, I say, madam, who have as discerning a judgment, in what's obscene or not, as any quick-sighted civil person of 'em all, and can make as much of a double-meaning saying as the best of 'em; yet would not, as some do, make nonsense of a poet's jest, rather than not make it bawdy: by which they show they as little value wit in a play as in a lover, provided they can bring t'other thing about. Their sense, indeed, lies all one way, and therefore are only for that in a poet which is moving, as they say; but what do they mean by that word *moving*? Well, I must not put 'em to the blush, since I find I can do't. In short, madam, you would not be one of those who ravish a poet's innocent words, and make 'em guilty of their own naughtiness (as 'tis termed) in spite of his teeth;[2] nay, nothing is secure from the power of their imaginations; no, not their husbands, whom they cuckold with themselves, by thinking of other men; and so make the lawful matrimonial embraces adultery, wrong husbands and poets in thought and word, to keep their own reputations. But your ladyship's justice, I know, would think a woman's arraigning and damning a poet for her own obscenity like her crying out a rape, and hanging a man for giving her pleasure, only that she might be thought not to consent to't; and so to vindicate her honor, forfeits her modesty. But you, madam, have too much modesty to pretend to't; though you have as much to say for your modesty as many a nicer she; for you never were seen at this play, no, not the first day; and 'tis no matter what people's lives have been, they are unquestionably modest who frequent not this play. For, as Mr. Bay[e]s[3] says of his, that it is the only touchstone[4] of men's wit and understanding; mine is, it seems, the only touchstone of women's virtue and modesty. But hold [!] that touchstone is equivocal, and, by the strength of a lady's imagination, may become something that is not civil; but your ladyship, I know, scorns to misapply a touchstone. And, madam, though you have not seen this play, I hope (like other nice ladies) you will rather read it; yet, lest the chambermaid or page should not be trusted, and their indulgence could gain no further admittance for it than to their ladies' lobbies or outward rooms, take it into your care and protection; for, by your recommendation and procurement, it may have the honor to get into their closets; for what they renounce in public often entertains 'em there, with your help

---

[1] "Lady" or "Mother" Bennett, a noted procuress of the day. The student should consult Pepys' *Diary*, sub Bennett.

[2] In spite of him.

[3] Dryden. The quotation is from *The Rehearsal*, Act III, scene i, l. 50.

[4] Some equivoque on "touchstone" is intended, the significance of which has been lost.

especially. In fine, madam, for these and many other reasons, you are the fittest patroness or judge of this play; for you show no partiality to this or that author; for from some, many ladies will take a broad jest as cheerfully as from the watermen, and sit at some downright filthy plays (as they call 'em) as well satisfied, and as still, as a poet could wish 'em elsewhere; therefore it must be the doubtful obscenity of my plays alone they take exceptions at, because it is too bashful for 'em: and, indeed, most women hate men for attempting to halves on their chastity; and bawdy, I find, like satire, should be home, not to have it taken notice of. But, now I mention satire, some there are who say, " 'Tis the plain-dealing of the play, not the obscenity; 'tis taking off the ladies' masks, not offering at their petticoats, which offends 'em:" and generally they are not the handsomest, or most innocent, who are the most angry at being discovered:

Nihil est audacius illis Deprensis; iram atq[ue] animos a crimine sumunt.[1]

Pardon, madam, the quotation, for a dedication can no more be without ends of Latin, than flattery; and 'tis no matter whom it is writ to; for an author can as easily (I hope) suppose people to have more understanding and languages than they have, as well as more virtues. But why the devil should any of the few modest and handsome be alarmed? —(for some there are who, as well as any, deserve those attributes, yet refrain not from seeing this play, nor think it any addition to their virtue to set up for it in a playhouse, lest there it should look too much like acting). But why, I say, should any at all of the truly virtuous be concerned, if those who are not so are distinguished from 'em? For by that mask of modesty which women wear promiscuously in public, they are all alike, and you can no more know a kept wench from a woman of honor by her looks than by her dress; for those who are of quality without honor (if any such there are) they have their quality to set off their false modesty, as well as their false jewels; and you must no more suspect their countenances for counterfeit than their pendants, though, as the plain-dealer Montaigne says, *Els envoy[ent] leur conscience au bordel, et tiennent leur continence en règle:*[2] but those who act as they look, ought not to be scandalized at the reprehension of others' faults, lest they tax themselves with 'em, and by too delicate and quick an apprehension not only make that obscene which I meant innocent, but that satire on all, which was intended only on those who deserved it. But, madam, I beg your pardon for this digression to civil women and ladies of honor, since you and I shall never be the better for 'em; for a comic poet and a lady of your profession make most of the other sort; and the stage and your houses, like our plantations,[3] are propagated by the least nice women; and, as with the ministers of justice, the vices of the age are our best business. But now I mention public persons, I can no longer defer doing you the justice of a dedication, and telling you your own, who are, of all public-spirited people, the most necessary, most communicative, most generous, and hospitable. Your house has been the house of the people; your sleep still disturbed for the public; and when you arose, 'twas that others might lie down, and you waked that others might rest; the good you have done is unspeakable. How many young unexperienced heirs have you kept from rash, foolish marriages, and from being jilted for their lives by the worst sort of jilts, wives! How many unbewitched widowers' children have you preserved from the tyranny of stepmothers! How many old dotards from cuckoldage, and keeping other men's wenches and children! How many adulteries and unnatural sins have you prevented! In fine, you have been a constant scourge to the old lecher, and often a terror to the young: you have made concupiscence its own punishment, and extinguished lust with lust, like blowing up of houses to stop the fire.

Nimirum propter continentiam, incontinentia Necessaria est, incendium ignibus extinguitur.[4]

---

[1] There is no effrontery like that of a woman caught; her guilt fills her with wrath and violence. Juvenal, *Satires*, VI, 283–84.

[2] "They send their Consciences to the Stews, and keep a starch'd Countenance." Montaigne, *Essais*, III, 5 (Cotton's translation). This passage is found in vol. III, p. 321, of the edition of Montaigne ed. Courbet and Royer, Paris, 1875, and should be read in its context. The whole essay (purporting to discuss some verses of Virgil, but really discussing the sexual problem) has influenced the tone and substance of Wycherley's dedication.

[3] Colonies.

[4] Apparently it is for the love of continence that incontinence is necessary, and fire is extinguished by

There's Latin for you again, madam; I protest to you, as I am an author, I cannot help it; nay, I can hardly keep myself from quoting Aristotle and Horace, and talking to you of the rules of writing (like the French authors), to show you and my readers I understand 'em, in my epistle, lest neither of you should find it out by the play; and according to the rules of dedications, 'tis no matter whether you understand or no what I quote or say to you of writing; for an author can as easily make any one a judge or critic in an epistle, as an hero in his play. But, madam, that this may prove to the end a true epistle dedicatory, I'd have you know 'tis not without a design upon you, which is in the behalf of the fraternity of Parnassus, that songs and sonnets may go at your houses, and in your liberties,[1] for guineas and half-guineas; and that wit, at least with you, as of old, may be the price of beauty, and so you will prove a true encourager of poetry; for love is a better help to it than wine; and poets, like painters, draw better after the life than by fancy. Nay, in justice, madam, I think a poet ought to be as free of your houses, as of the play-houses; since he contributes to the support of both, and is as necessary to such as you, as a ballad-singer to the pick-purse, in convening the cullies at the theatres, to be picked up and carried to supper and bed at your houses. And, madam, the reason of this motion of mine is, because poor poets can get no favor in the tiring-rooms,[2] for they are no keepers, you know; and folly and money, the old enemies of wit, are even too hard for it on its own dunghill: and for other ladies, a poet can least go to the price of them. Besides, his wit, which ought to recommend him to 'em, is as much an obstruction to his love, as to his wealth or preferment; for most women now-a-days apprehend wit in a lover, as much as in a husband; they hate a man that knows 'em, they must have a blind easy fool, whom they can lead by the nose; and, as the Scythian women[3] of old, must baffle a man, and put out his eyes, ere they will lie with him; and then, too, like thieves, when they have plundered and stripped a man, leave him. But if there should be one of an hundred of those ladies generous enough to give herself to a man that has more wit than money, (all things considered) he would think it cheaper coming to you for a mistress, though you made him pay his guinea; as a man in a journey (out of good husbandry) had better pay for what he has in an inn, than lie on free-cost[4] at a gentleman's house.

In fine, madam, like a faithful dedicator, I hope I have done myself right in the first place, then you, and your profession, which in the wisest and most religious government of the world is honored with the public allowance; and in those that are thought the most uncivilized and barbarous is protected and supported by the ministers of justice; and of you, madam, I ought to say no more here, for your virtues deserve a poem rather than an epistle, or a volume entire to give the world your memoirs, or life at large; and which (upon the word of an author that has a mind to make an end of his dedication) I promise to do, when I write the annals of our British love, which shall be dedicated to the ladies concerned, if they will not think them something too obscene, too; when your life, compared with many that are thought innocent, I doubt not, may vindicate you, and me, to the world, for the confidence I have taken in this address to you; which then may be thought neither impertinent nor immodest; and whatsoever your amorous misfortunes have been, none can charge you with that heinous, and worst of women's crimes, hypocrisy; nay, in spite of misfortunes or age, you are the same woman still; though most of your sex grow Magdalens at fifty, and as a solid French author has it,

Après le plaisir, vient la peine;
Après la peine, la vertu.[5]

But sure an old sinner's continency is much like a gamester's forswearing play when he had lost all his money; and modesty is a kind

---

flames. Tertullian, *De Pudicitia*, i, but Wycherley found this passage in the Montaigne essay, and followed Montaigne's mis-reading of *extinguitur* for *extinguetur*.

[1] Districts exempt from the jurisdiction of the customary law officers.

[2] Dressing rooms.

[3] Apparently a borrowing from Montaigne: "Les femmes Scythes creuoyent les yeux a touts leurs esclaues & prisonniers de guere, pour s'en seruir plus librement & Couuertement." (Courbet et Royer ed., III, 348.)

[4] Lie gratis.

[5] After pleasure comes pain; after pain, comes virtue. The source of the quotation has not been found.

of a youthful dress, which, as it makes a young woman more amiable, makes an old one more nauseous: a bashful old woman is like an hopeful old man; and the affected chastity of antiquated beauties is rather a reproach than an honor to 'em, for it shows the men's virtue only, not theirs. But you, in fine, madam, are no more an hypocrite than I am when I praise you; therefore I doubt not will be thought (even by yours and the play's enemies, the nicest ladies) to be the fittest patroness for,

Madam,
Your ladyship's most obedient,
faithful, humble servant, and
THE PLAIN-DEALER.

THE PLAIN-DEALER

THE PERSONS

MANLY — Mr. Hart
Of an honest, surly, nice humor, supposed first, in the time of the Dutch war,[1] to have procured the command of a ship, out of honor, not interest; and choosing a sea-life only to avoid the world.

FREEMAN — Mr. Kynaston
Manly's Lieutenant, a gentleman well educated, but of a broken fortune, a complier with the age.

VERNISH — Mr. Griffin
Manly's bosom and only friend.

NOVEL — Mr. Clark
A pert railing Coxcomb, and an admirer of novelties, makes love to Olivia.

MAJOR OLDFOX — Mr. Cartwright
An old impertinent Fop, given to scribbling, makes love to the Widow Blackacre.

MY LORD PLAUSIBLE — Mr. Haines
A ceremonious, supple, commending Coxcomb, in love with Olivia.

JERRY BLACKACRE — Mr. Charlton
A true raw Squire, under age, and his mother's government, bred to the law.

OLIVIA — Mrs. Marshall
Manly's Mistress.

FIDELIA — Mrs. Boutell
In love with Manly, and followed him to sea in man's clothes.

ELIZA — Mrs. Knep
Cousin to Olivia.

LET[T]ICE — Mrs. Knight
Olivia's Woman.

THE WIDOW BLACKACRE — Mrs. Cory
A petulant, litigious Widow, always in law, and Mother to Squire Jerry.

Lawyers, Knights of the Post,[2] Bailiffs, an Alderman, a Bookseller's 'Prentice, a Footboy, Sailors, Waiters, and Attendants.

THE SCENE: *London*

PROLOGUE

SPOKEN BY THE PLAIN-DEALER

I, the Plain-Dealer, am to act to-day,
And my rough part begins before the play.
First, you who scribble, yet hate all that write,
And keep each other company in spite,
As rivals in your common mistress, fame, 5
And with faint praises one another damn;
'Tis a good play, we know, you can't forgive,
But grudge yourselves the pleasure you receive:
Our scribbler therefore bluntly bid me say,
He would not have the wits pleased here to-day. 10
Next, you, the fine, loud gentlemen o' th' pit,
Who damn all plays, yet, if y'ave any wit,
'Tis but what here you spunge [3] and daily get;
Poets, like friends to whom you are in debt,
You hate; and so rooks laugh, to see undone 15

---

[1] The Naval War with Holland, 1665–67, in which Manly lost his ship.

[2] A knight of the post is one who gets his living by giving false evidence or furnishing false bail.

[3] In allusion to the curious regulation that any person entering a Restoration theatre, and leaving before the end of the act in progress was not required to pay (Summers).

Those pushing gamesters whom they live
    upon.
Well, you are sparks, and still will be i' th'
    fashion;
Rail then at plays, to hide your obligation.
Now, you shrewd judges, who the boxes
    sway,
Leading the ladies' hearts and sense as-
    tray,   20
And, for their sakes, see all, and hear no
    play;
Correct your cravats, foretops, lock behind;[1]
The dress and breeding of the play ne'er
    mind;
Plain-dealing is, you'll say, quite out of fash-
    ion;
You'll hate it here, as in a dedication;   25
And your fair neighbors, in a limning poet,
No more than in a painter will allow it.
Pictures, too, like the ladies will not please;
They must be drawn too here like goddesses.
You, as at Lely's[2] too, would truncheon
    wield,
And look like heroes in a painted field;   31
But the coarse dauber of the coming scenes
To follow life and nature only means,
Displays you as you are, makes his fine
    woman
A mercenary jilt, and true to no man;   35
His men of wit and pleasure of the age
Are as dull rogues as ever cumber'd stage:
He draws a friend only to custom just,
And makes him naturally break his trust.
I, only, act a part like none of you,   40
And yet, you'll say, it is a fool's part, too:
An honest man who, like you, never winks
At faults; but, unlike you, speaks what he
    thinks:
The only fool who ne'er found patron yet,
For truth is now a fault as well as wit.   45
And where else, but on stages, do we see
Truth pleasing, or rewarded honesty?
Which our bold poet does this day in me.
If not to th' honest, be to th' prosp'rous kind:
Some friends at court let the Plain-Dealer
    find.   50

---

[1] The cravat of the period of lace, linen, or muslin edged with lace terminated in long, flowing ends, the arrangement of which was a matter of profound concern to the well-dressed man. The foretop is a lock of hair arranged ornamentally on the forehead.

[2] Sir Peter Lely (1618–80), the court painter, who had just been knighted. The reference is to portraits of men in which the subject is represented as holding a truncheon as an emblem of authority.

ACT I

SCENE I. CAPTAIN MANLY'S *Lodging*

Enter CAPTAIN MANLY, *surlily, and my* LORD PLAUSIBLE, *following him; and two Sailors behind*

MANLY. Tell not me, my good Lord Plausible, of your decorums, supercilious forms, and slavish ceremonies; your little tricks, which you, the spaniels of the world, do daily over and over, for and to one another; not out of love or duty, but your servile fear.

LORD PLAUSIBLE. Nay, i' faith, i' faith, you are too passionate, and I must humbly beg your pardon and leave to tell you, they are the arts and rules the prudent of the world walk by.

MANLY. Let 'em. But I'll have no leading-strings, I can walk alone; I hate a harness, and will not tug on in a faction, kissing my leader behind, that another slave may do the like to me.

LORD PLAUSIBLE. What, will you be singular then, like nobody? follow love, and esteem nobody?

MANLY. Rather than be general, like you; follow everybody, court and kiss everybody, though perhaps at the same time you hate everybody.

LORD PLAUSIBLE. Why, seriously, with your pardon, my dear friend—

MANLY. With your pardon, my no friend, I will not, as you do, whisper my hatred or my scorn, call a man fool or knave by signs or mouths over his shoulder, whilst you have him in your arms; for such as you, like common whores and pickpockets, are only dangerous to those you embrace.

LORD PLAUSIBLE. Such as I! Heavens defend me!—upon my honor—

MANLY. Upon your title, my lord, if you'd have me believe you.

LORD PLAUSIBLE. Well, then, as I am a person of honor, I never attempted to abuse or lessen any person in my life.

MANLY. What, you were afraid?

LORD PLAUSIBLE. No; but seriously, I hate to do a rude thing; no, faith, I speak well of all mankind.

MANLY. I thought so; but know, that speaking well of all mankind is the worst kind of detraction; for it takes away the reputation of the few good men in the world.

by making all alike. Now, I speak ill of most men, because they deserve it,—I that can do a rude thing, rather than an unjust thing.

LORD PLAUSIBLE. Well, tell not me, my dear friend, what people deserve; I ne'er mind that. I, like an author in a dedication, never speak well of a man for his sake, but my own; I will not disparage any man, to disparage myself; for to speak ill of people behind their backs, is not like a person of honor; and, truly, to speak ill of 'em to their faces, is not like a complaisant person. But if I did say or do an ill thing to any body, it should be sure to be behind their backs, out of pure good manners.

MANLY. Very well; but I, that am an unmannerly sea-fellow, if I ever speak well of people (which is very seldom indeed), it should be sure to be behind their backs; and if I would say or do ill to any, it should be to their faces. I would jostle a proud, strutting, overlooking coxcomb, at the head of his sycophants, rather than put out my tongue at him when he were past me; would frown in the arrogant, big, dull face of an overgrown knave of business, rather than vent my spleen against him when his back were turned; would give fawning slaves the lie whilst they embrace or commend me; cowards whilst they brag; call a rascal by no other title, though his father had left him a duke's; laugh at fools aloud before their mistresses; and must desire people to leave me, when their visits grow at last as troublesome as they were at first impertinent.

LORD PLAUSIBLE. I would not have my visits troublesome.

MANLY. The only way to be sure not to have 'em troublesome, is to make 'em when people are not at home; for your visits, like other good turns, are most obliging when made or done to a man in his absence. A pox! why should any one, because he has nothing to do, go and disturb another man's business?

LORD PLAUSIBLE. I beg your pardon, my dear friend. What, you have business?

MANLY. If you have any, I would not detain your lordship.

LORD PLAUSIBLE. Detain me, dear sir! I can never have enough of your company.

MANLY. I'm afraid I should be tiresome. I know not what you think.

LORD PLAUSIBLE. Well, dear sir, I see you would have me gone.

MANLY. (Aside) But I see you won't.

LORD PLAUSIBLE. Your most faithful—

MANLY. God be w'ye, my lord.

LORD PLAUSIBLE. Your most humble—

MANLY. Farewell.

LORD PLAUSIBLE. And eternally—

MANLY. And eternally ceremony—(Aside) Then the devil take thee eternally!

LORD PLAUSIBLE. You shall use no ceremony, by my life.

MANLY. I do not intend it.

LORD PLAUSIBLE. Why do you stir then?

MANLY. Only to see you out of doors, that I may shut 'em against more welcomes.

LORD PLAUSIBLE. Nay, faith, that shan't pass upon your most faithful, humble servant.

MANLY. (Aside) Nor this any more upon me.

LORD PLAUSIBLE. Well, you are too strong for me.

MANLY. (Aside) I'd sooner be visited by the plague; for that only would keep a man from visits, and his doors shut.

Exit, thrusting out my LORD PLAUSIBLE

Manent SAILORS

1ST SAILOR. Here's a finical fellow, Jack! What a brave fair-weather captain of a ship he would make!

2ND SAILOR. He a captain of a ship! it must be when she's in the dock then; for he looks like one of those that get the king's commissions for hulls [1] to sell a king's ship, when a brave fellow has fought her almost to a longboat.[2]

1ST SAILOR. On my conscience then, Jack, that's the reason our bully tar sunk our ship: not only that the Dutch might not have her, but that the courtiers, who laugh at wooden legs, might not make her prize.

2ND SAILOR. A pox of his sinking, Tom! we have made a base, broken, short voyage of it.

1ST SAILOR. Ay, your brisk dealers in honor always make quick returns with their ship to the dock, and their men to the hospitals. 'Tis, let me see, just a month since we set out of the river, and the wind was almost as cross to us as the Dutch.[3]

---

[1] I.e., authority to sell a dismantled vessel.
[2] Fought her until she was well-nigh dismantled.
[3] Manly's ship was defeated by the Dutch in an engagement.

2ND SAILOR. Well, I forgive him sinking my own poor truck,[1] if he would but have given me time and leave to have saved black Kate of Wapping's [2] small venture.

1ST SAILOR. Faith, I forgive him, since, as the purser told me, he sunk the value of five or six thousand pound of his own, with which he was to settle himself somewhere in the Indies;[3] for our merry lieutenant was to succeed him in his commission for the ship back; for he was resolved never to return again for England.

2ND SAILOR. So it seemed, by his fighting.

1ST SAILOR. No; but he was a-weary of this side of the world here, they say.

2ND SAILOR. Ay, or else he would not have bid so fair for a passage into t'other.

1ST SAILOR. Jack, thou think'st thyself in the forecastle, thou'rt so waggish; but I tell you, then, he had a mind to go live and bask himself on the sunny side of the globe.

2ND SAILOR. What, out of any discontent? for he's always as dogged as an old tarpaulin, when hindered of a voyage by a young pantaloon captain.[4]

1ST SAILOR. 'Tis true, I never saw him pleased but in the fight; and then he looked like one of us coming from the pay-table, with a new lining to our hats under our arms.

2ND SAILOR. A pox! he's like the Bay of Biscay, rough and angry, let the wind blow where 'twill.

1ST SAILOR. Nay, there's no more dealing with him, than with the land in a storm, no near—

2ND SAILOR. 'Tis a hurry-durry blade.[5] Dost thou remember after we had tugged hard the old leaky longboat to save his life, when I welcomed him ashore, he gave me a box on the ear, and called me fawning waterdog?

Enter MANLY, *and* FREEMAN

1ST SAILOR. Hold thy peace, Jack, and stand by; the foul weather's coming.

MANLY. You rascals! dogs! how could this tame thing get through you?

1ST SAILOR. Faith, to tell your honor the truth, we were at hob in the hall,[6] and whilst my brother and I were quarrelling about a cast,[7] he slunk by us.

2ND SAILOR. He's a sneaking fellow, I warrant for't.

MANLY. Have more care for the future, you slaves; go, and with drawn cutlasses stand at the stair-foot, and keep all that ask for me from coming up; suppose you were guarding the scuttle to the powder-room. Let none enter here, at your and their peril.

1ST SAILOR. No, for the danger would be the same: you would blow them and us up, if we should.

2ND SAILOR. Must no one come to you, sir?

MANLY. No man, sir.

1ST SAILOR. No man, sir; but a woman then, an't like your honor—

MANLY. No woman neither, you impertinent dog! Would you be pimping? A seapimp is the strangest monster she has.

2ND SAILOR. Indeed, an't like your honor, 'twill be hard for us to deny a woman anything, since we are so newly come on shore.

1ST SAILOR. We'll let no old woman come up, though it were our trusting landlady at Wapping.

MANLY. Would you be witty, you brandy casks you? You become a jest as ill as you do a horse. Begone, you dogs! I hear a noise on the stairs.

Exeunt SAILORS

FREEMAN. Faith, I am sorry you would let the fop go, I intended to have had some sport with him.

MANLY. Sport with him! A pox, then, why did you not stay? You should have enjoyed your coxcomb, and had him to yourself, for me.

FREEMAN. No, I should not have cared for him without you neither; for the pleasure which fops afford is like that of drinking, only good when 'tis shared; and a fool, like a bottle, which would make you merry in company, will make you dull alone. But how the devil could you turn a man of his quality down stairs? You use a lord with very little ceremony, it seems.

MANLY. A lord! What, thou art one of those who esteem men only by the marks and value fortune has set upon 'em, and never

[1] Commodities.
[2] A part of London close to the docks, frequented by sailors.
[3] Here, the East Indies is apparently meant.
[4] Foppish courtiers without naval experience were sometimes appointed to the command of ships. Pantaloons were worn by the fashionable courtiers.
[5] Boisterous fellow.

[6] A game played with round pins, resembling quoits.
[7] Throw.

consider intrinsic worth! But counterfeit honor will not be current with me. I weigh the man, not his title; 'tis not the king's stamp can make the metal better, or heavier. Your lord is a leaden shilling, which you may bend every way, and debases the stamp he bears, instead of being raised by't.—Here again, you slaves?

Enter SAILORS

1ST SAILOR. Only to receive farther instructions, an't like your honor.—What if a man should bring you money, should we turn him back?

MANLY. All men, I say: must I be pestered with you, too? You dogs, away!

2ND SAILOR. Nay, I know one man your honor would not have us hinder coming to you, I'm sure.

MANLY. Who's that? speak quickly, slaves.

2ND SAILOR. Why, a man that should bring you a challenge; for though you refuse money, I'm sure you love fighting too well to refuse that.

MANLY. Rogue! rascal! dog!

Kicks the SAILORS *out.*

FREEMAN. Nay, let the poor rogues have their forecastle jests; they cannot help 'em in a fight, scarce when a ship's sinking.

MANLY. Damn their untimely jests! a servant's jest is more sauciness than his counsel.

FREEMAN. But what, will you see nobody? not your friends?

MANLY. Friends!—I have but one, and he, I hear, is not in town; nay, can have but one friend, for a true heart admits but of one friendship, as of one love; but in having that friend, I have a thousand; for he has the courage of men in despair, yet the diffidency and caution of cowards; the secrecy of the revengeful, and the constancy of martyrs; one fit to advise, to keep a secret, to fight and die for his friend. Such I think him; for I have trusted him with my mistress in my absence; and the trust of beauty is sure the greatest we can show.

FREEMAN. Well, but all your good thoughts are not for him alone, I hope? Pray, what d'ye think of me for a friend?

MANLY. Of thee! Why, thou art a latitudinarian [1] in friendship, that is, no friend; thou dost side with all mankind, but wilt suffer for none. Thou art indeed like your Lord Plausible, the pink of courtesy, therefore hast no friendship: for ceremony and great professing renders friendship as much suspected as it does religion.

FREEMAN. And no professing, no ceremony at all in friendship, were as unnatural and as undecent as in religion; and there is hardly such a thing as an honest hypocrite, who professes himself to be worse than he is, unless it be yourself; for though I could never get you to say you were my friend, I know you'll prove so.

MANLY. I must confess, I am so much your friend, I would not deceive you; therefore must tell you, not only because my heart is taken up, but according to your rules of friendship, I cannot be your friend.

FREEMAN. Why, pray? [2]

MANLY. Because he that is, you'll say, a true friend to a man, is a friend to all his friends. But you must pardon me, I cannot wish well to pimps, flatterers, detractors, and cowards, stiff nodding knaves, and supple, pliant, kissing fools. Now, all these I have seen you use like the dearest friends in the world.

FREEMAN. Ha, ha, ha!—What, you observed me, I warrant, in the galleries at Whitehall, doing the business of the place? Pshaw! Court professions, like court promises, go for nothing, man. But, faith, could you think I was a friend to all those I hugged, kissed, flattered, bowed to? Ha! ha!—

MANLY. You told 'em so, and swore it, too; I heard you.

FREEMAN. Ay, but when their backs were turned, did I not tell you they were rogues, villains, rascals, whom I despised and hated?

MANLY. Very fine! But what reason had I to believe you spoke your heart to me, since you professed deceiving so many?

FREEMAN. Why, don't you know, good captain, that telling truth is a quality as prejudicial to a man that would thrive in the world, as square play to a cheat, or true love to a whore? Would you have a man speak truth to his ruin? You are severer than the

---

[1] This word had special topical significance in Wycherley's day, since the latitudinarian movement (the latitudinarians were Anglicans who, though attached to Episcopalian forms, regarded them as indifferent) was a problem of importance.

[2] The scene from this point on closely follows Molière's *Le Misanthrope*, Act I, scene i.

law, which requires no man to swear against himself. You would have me speak truth against myself, I warrant, and tell my promising friend, the courtier, he has a bad memory?

MANLY. Yes.

FREEMAN. And so make him remember to forget my business? And I should tell the great lawyer, too, that he takes oft[e]ner fees to hold his tongue, than to speak?

MANLY. No doubt on't.

FREEMAN. Ay, and have him hang or ruin me, when he should come to be a judge, and I before him. And you would have me tell the new officer, who bought his employment lately, that he is a coward?

MANLY. Ay.

FREEMAN. And so get myself cashiered, not him, he having the better friends, though I the better sword? And I should tell the scribbler of honor,[1] that heraldry were a prettier and fitter study for so fine a gentleman than poetry?

MANLY. Certainly.

FREEMAN. And so find myself mauled in his next hired lampoon. And you would have me tell the holy lady, too, she lies with her chaplain.

MANLY. No doubt on't.

FREEMAN. And so draw the clergy upon my back, and want a good table to dine at sometimes. And by the same reason too, I should tell you that the world thinks you a mad man, a brutal, and have you cut my throat, or worse, hate me. What other good success of all my plain-dealing could I have, than what I've mentioned?

MANLY. Why, first, your promising courtier would keep his word out of fear of more reproaches, or at least would give you no more vain hopes: your lawyer would serve you more faithfully; for he, having no honor but his interest, is truest still to him he knows suspects him. The new officer would provoke thee to make him a coward, and so be cashiered, that thou, or some other honest fellow, who had more courage than money, might get his place; the noble sonnetteer would trouble thee no more with his madrigals; the praying lady would leave off railing at wenching before thee, and not turn away her chambermaid for her own known frailty with thee; and I, instead of hating thee, should love thee for thy plain-dealing; and in lieu of being mortified, am proud that the world and I think not well of one another.

FREEMAN. Well, doctors differ. You are for plain-dealing, I find; but against your particular notions, I have the practice of the whole world. Observe but any morning what people do when they get together on the Exchange, in Westminster-hall,[2] or the galleries in Whitehall.[3]

MANLY. I must confess, there they seem to rehearse Bay[e]s's grand dance:[4] here you see a bishop bowing low to a gaudy atheist; a judge to a door-keeper; a great lord to a fishmonger, or a scrivener with a jack-chain about his neck; a lawyer to a sergeant-at-arms; a velvet physician to a threadbare chemist; and a supple gentleman-usher to a surly beefeater;[5] and so tread round in a preposterous huddle of ceremony to each other, they can hardly hold their solemn false countenances.

FREEMAN. Well, they understand the world.

MANLY. Which I do not, I confess.

FREEMAN. But, sir, pray believe the friendship I promise you real, whatsoever I have professed to others. Try me, at least.

MANLY. Why, what would you do for me?

FREEMAN. I would fight for you.

MANLY. That you would do for your own honor; but what else?

FREEMAN. I would lend you money, if I had it.

MANLY. To borrow more of me another time. That were but putting your money to interest; a usurer would be as good a friend. But what other piece of friendship?

FREEMAN. I would speak well of you to your enemies.

MANLY. To encourage others to be your friends, by a show of gratitude; but what else?

FREEMAN. Nay, I would not hear you ill spoken of behind your back by my friend.

MANLY. Nay, then, thou'rt a friend, indeed; but it were unreasonable to expect it from thee, as the world goes now, when new friends, like new mistresses, are got by disparaging old ones.

Enter FIDELIA [*disguised as* MANLY'S *page*]

---

[1] Gentleman author.
[2] See Act III.
[3] I.e., the royal palace.
[4] See *The Rehearsal*, Act V, scene i.
[5] Guard of the Tower of London.

But here comes another, will say as much at least.—Dost not thou love me devilishly too, my little volunteer, as well as he or any man can?

FIDELIA. Better than any man can love you, my dear captain.

MANLY. Look you there, I told you so.

FIDELIA. As well as you do truth or honor, sir; as well.

MANLY. Nay, good young gentleman, enough, for shame! Thou hast been a page, by thy flattering and lying, to one of those praying ladies who love flattery so well they are jealous of it; and wert turned away for saying the same things to the old housekeeper for sweetmeats, as you did to your lady; for thou flatterest everything and everybody alike.

FIDELIA. You, dear sir, should not suspect the truth of what I say of you, though to you. Fame, the old liar, is believed when she speaks wonders of you; you cannot be flattered, sir, your merit is unspeakable.

MANLY. Hold, hold, sir, or I shall suspect worse of you, that you have been a cushion-bearer to some state-hypocrite, and turned away by the chaplains, for out-flattering their probation-sermons [1] for a benefice.

FIDELIA. Suspect me for anything, sir, but the want of love, faith, and duty to you, the bravest, worthiest of mankind; believe me, I could die for you, sir.

MANLY. Nay, there you lie, sir; did I not see thee more afraid in the fight than the chaplain of the ship, or the purser that bought his place?

FIDELIA. Can he be said to be afraid, that ventures to sea with you?

MANLY. Fie! fie! no more; I shall hate thy flattery worse than thy cowardice, nay, than thy bragging.

FIDELIA. Well, I own, then, I was afraid, mightily afraid; yet for you I would be afraid again, an hundred times afraid. Dying is ceasing to be afraid; and that I could do, sure, for you, and you'll believe me one day.

(*Weeps.*)

FREEMAN. Poor youth! believe his eyes, if not his tongue; he seems to speak truth with them.

MANLY. What, does he cry? A pox on't! a maudlin flatterer is as nauseously troublesome as a maudlin drunkard. No more, you little milksop, do not cry, I'll never make thee afraid again; for of all men, if I had occasion, thou shouldst not be my second; and when I go to sea again, thou shalt venture thy life no more with me.

FIDELIA. Why, will you leave me behind then?—(*Aside.*) If you would preserve my life, I'm sure you should not.

MANLY. Leave thee behind! Ay, ay, thou art a hopeful youth for the shore only; here thou wilt live to be cherished by fortune and the great ones; for thou mayst easily come to outflatter a dull poet, outlie a coffee-house or gazette-writer, outswear a knight of the post, outwatch a pimp, outfawn a rook, out-promise a lover, outrail a wit, and outbrag a sea-captain. All this thou canst do, because thou'rt a coward, a thing I hate; therefore thou'lt do better with the world than with me; and these are the good courses you must take in the world. There's good advice, at least, at parting; go, and be happy with't.

FIDELIA. Parting, sir! Oh let me not hear that dismal word!

MANLY. If my words frighten thee, begone the sooner; for, to be plain with thee, cowardice and I cannot dwell together.

FIDELIA. And cruelty and courage never dwelt together sure, sir. Do not turn me off to shame and misery; for I am helpless and friendless.

MANLY. Friendless! there are half a score friends for thee then. (*Offers her gold.*) I leave myself no more: they'll help thee a little. Begone, go, I must be cruel to thee (if thou call'st it so) out of pity.

FIDELIA. If you would be cruelly pitiful, sir, let it be with your sword, not gold. *Exit.*

Enter first SAILOR

1ST SAILOR. We have, with much ado, turned away two gentlemen, who told us forty times over their names were Mr. Novel and Major Oldfox.

MANLY. Well, to your post again.—(*Exit* SAILOR.) But how come those puppies coupled always together?

FREEMAN. Oh, the coxcombs keep each other company, to show each other, as Novel calls it; or, as Oldfox says, like two knives, to whet one another.

MANLY. And set other people's teeth on edge.

Enter second SAILOR

---

[1] Sermons preached as a test of the candidate's fitness for some ecclesiastical preferment.

2ND SAILOR. Here is a woman, an't like your honor, scolds and bustles with us to come in, as much as a seaman's widow at the Navy office. Her name is Mrs. Blackacre.

MANLY. That fiend, too!

FREEMAN. The Widow Blackacre, is it not? that litigious she-pettifogger, who is at law and difference with all the world; but I wish I could make her agree with me in the church: they say she has fifteen hundred pounds a year jointure, and the care of her son, that is, the destruction of his estate.

MANLY. Her lawyers, attorneys, and solicitors have fifteen hundred pound a year, whilst she is contented to be poor, to make other people so; for she is as vexatious as her father was, the great attorney, nay, as a dozen Norfolk attorneys,[1] and as implacable an adversary as a wife suing for alimony, or a parson for his tithes; and she loves an Easter term,[2] or any term, not as other country ladies do, to come up to be fine, cuckold their husbands, and take their pleasure; for she has no pleasure but in vexing others, and is usually clothed and daggled[3] like a bawd in disguise, pursued through alleys by sergeants.[4] When she is in town, she lodges in one of the inns of Chancery,[5] where she breeds her son, and is herself his tutoress in law-French; and for her country abode, though she has no estate there, she chooses Norfolk. But, bid her come in, with a pox to her! she is Olivia's kinswoman, and may make me amends for her visit, by some discourse of that dear woman. *Exit* SAILOR

Enter WIDOW BLACKACRE, *with a mantle and a green bag, and several papers in the other hand,* JERRY BLACKACRE, *her son, in a gown, laden with green bags, following her*

WIDOW. I never had so much to do with a judge's doorkeeper, as with yours; but—

MANLY. But the incomparable Olivia, how does she since I went?

WIDOW. Since you went, my suit—

MANLY. Olivia, I say, is she well?

WIDOW. My suit, if you had not returned—

MANLY. Damn your suit! how does your cousin Olivia?

WIDOW. My suit, I say, had been quite lost; but now—

MANLY. But now, where is Olivia? in town? for—

WIDOW. For to-morrow we are to have a hearing.

MANLY. Would you'd let me have a hearing to-day!

WIDOW. But why won't you hear me?

MANLY. I am no judge, and you talk of nothing but suits; but, pray tell me, when did you see Olivia?

WIDOW. I am no visitor, but a woman of business; or if I ever visit, 'tis only the Chancery-lane ladies, ladies towards the law; and not any of your lazy, good-for-nothing flirts, who cannot read law-French,[6] though a gallant writ it. But as I was telling you, my suit—

MANLY. Damn these impertinent, vexatious people of business, of all sexes! They are still troubling the world with the tedious recitals of their lawsuits; and one can no more stop their mouths than a wit's when he talks of himself, or an intelligencer's[7] when he talks of other people.

WIDOW. And a pox of all vexatious, impertinent lovers! they are still perplexing the world with the tedious narrations of their love-suits, and discourses of their mistresses! You are as troublesome to a poor widow of business, as a young coxcombly [rhyming][8] lover.

MANLY. And thou art as troublesome to me, as a rook to a losing gamester, or a young putter of cases to his mistress and sempstress, who has love in her head for another.

WIDOW. Nay, since you talk of putting of cases, and will not hear me speak, hear our Jerry a little; let him put our case to you, for the trial's to-morrow; and since you are my chief witness, I would have your memory

---

[1] Norfolk was supposed to be an especially litigious district.
[2] One of the four terms during which courts of law are sitting.
[3] Bedraggled.
[4] The selected upper class of barristers are known as sergeants. On the other hand, the lady may have been pursued by officers charged with the duty of arresting offenders, or of summoning them into court.
[5] Social and educational associations of lawyers inferior to, but organized on the plan of. the larger Inns of Court.
[6] A corrupt Norman-French formerly much employed in English legal writings. Its influence is to be seen in Jerry Blackacre's legal jargon.
[7] Either a police spy or a newsmonger is meant.
[8] The first edition has "rithming," changed, in later editions, to "riming."

refreshed and your judgment informed, that you may not give your evidence improperly.—Speak out, child.

JERRY. Yes, forsooth. Hem! hem! John-a-Stiles—[1]

MANLY. You may talk, young lawyer, but I shall no more mind you, than a hungry judge does a cause after the clock has struck one.

FREEMAN. Nay, you'll find him as peevish, too.

WIDOW. No matter. Jerry, go on.—Do you observe it then, sir; for I think I have seen you in a gown once. Lord, I could hear our Jerry put cases all day long! Mark him, sir.

JERRY. John-a-Stiles—no—there are first, Fitz, Pere, and Ayle,[2]—no, no, Ayle, Pere, and Fitz; Ayle is seised in fee [3] of Blackacre; John-a-Stiles disseises [4] Ayle; Ayle makes claim, and the disseisor dies; then the Ayle—no, the Fitz—

WIDOW. No, the Pere, sirrah.

JERRY. Oh, the Pere! ay, the Pere, sir, and the Fitz—no, the Ayle,—no, the Pere and the Fitz, sir, and—

MANLY. Damn Pere, Mere, and Fitz, sir!

WIDOW. No, you are out, child.—Hear me, captain, then. There are Ayle, Pere, and Fitz; Ayle is seised in fee of Blackacre; and, being so seised, John-a-Stiles disseises the Ayle; Ayle makes claim, and the disseisor dies; and then the Pere re-enters—(to JERRY) the Pere, sirrah, the Pere—and the Fitz enters upon the Pere, and the Ayle brings his writ of disseisin in the post; [5] and the Pere brings his writ of disseisin in the Pere, and—

MANLY. Canst thou hear this stuff, Freeman? I could as soon suffer a whole noise of flatterers at a great man's levee in a morning; but thou hast servile complacency enough to listen to a quibbling statesman in disgrace, nay, and be beforehand with him, in laughing at his dull no-jest; but I— (Offering to go out)

WIDOW. Nay, sir, hold! Where's the subpœna, Jerry? I must serve you, sir. You are required, by this, to give your testimony—

MANLY. I'll be forsworn to be revenged on thee.

Exit MANLY, *throwing away the subpœna*

WIDOW. Get you gone, for a lawless companion!—Come, Jerry, I had almost forgot, we were to meet at the master's at three. Let us mind our business still, child.

JERRY. Ay, forsooth, e'en so, let's.

FREEMAN. Nay, madam, now I would beg you to hear me a little, a little of my business.

WIDOW. I have business of my own calls me away, sir.

FREEMAN. My business would prove yours too, dear madam.

WIDOW. Yours would be some sweet business, I warrant. What, 'tis no Westminster Hall business? Would you have my advice?

FREEMAN. No, faith, 'tis a little Westminster Abbey business. I would have your consent.

WIDOW. O fie, fie, sir! to me such discourse, before my dear minor there!

JERRY. Ay, ay, mother, he would be taking livery and seisin of your jointure,[6] by digging the turf; [7] but I'll watch your waters,[8] bully, i'fac.—Come away, mother.

Exit JERRY, *haling away his Mother*

Manet FREEMAN. *Enter to him* FIDELIA

FIDELIA. Dear sir, you have pity; beget but some in our captain for me.

FREEMAN. Where is he?

FIDELIA. Within; swearing as much as he did in the great storm, and cursing you, and sometimes sinks into calms and sighs, and talks of his Olivia.

FREEMAN. He would never trust me to see her. Is she handsome?

FIDELIA. No, if you'll take my word; but I am not a proper judge.

FREEMAN. What is she?

FIDELIA. A gentlewoman, I suppose, but of as mean a fortune as beauty; but her relations would not suffer her to go with him to the Indies: and his aversion to this side of the world, together with the late opportunity of commanding the convoy, would not let him stay here longer, though to enjoy her.

FREEMAN. He loves her mightily then.

FIDELIA. Yes, so well, that the remainder of

---

[1] I.e., John Doe.
[2] Jerry's legal jargon need not be taken too seriously. Fitz means "son;" pere, "father," and ayle is "grandfather."
[3] Owns.
[4] Dispossesses.
[5] A special writ to secure repossession of land.
[6] I.e., to secure legal possession of your holdings.
[7] Legal action necessary to symbolize the taking possession of property.
[8] Watch closely.

his fortune (I hear about five or six thousand pounds) he has left her, in case he had died by the way, or before she could prevail with her friends to follow him, which he expected she should do, and has left behind him his great bosom friend to be her convoy to him.

FREEMAN. What charms has she for him, if she be not handsome?

FIDELIA. He fancies her, I suppose, the only woman of truth and sincerity in the world.

FREEMAN. No common beauty, I confess.

FIDELIA. Or else sure he would not have trusted her with so great a share of his fortune in his absence; I suppose (since his late loss) all he has.

FREEMAN. Why, has he left it in her own custody?

FIDELIA. I am told so.

FREEMAN. Then he has showed love to her indeed, in leaving her, like an old husband that dies as soon as he has made his wife a good jointure.—But I'll go in to him, and speak for you, and know more from him of his Olivia. *Exit*

Manet FIDELIA *sola*

FIDELIA. His Olivia, indeed, his happy Olivia,
Yet she was left behind, when I was with him;
But she was ne'er out of his mind or heart.
She has told him she loved him; I have show'd it,
And durst not tell him so, till I had done,
Under this habit, such convincing acts
Of loving friendship for him, that through it
He first might find out both my sex and love;
And, when I'd had him from his fair Olivia,
And this bright world of artful beauties here,
Might then have hoped, he would have look'd on me,
Amongst the sooty Indians; and I could
To choose there live his wife, where wives are forced
To live no longer, when their husbands die;
Nay, what's yet worse, to share 'em whilst they live
With many rival wives. But here he comes,
And I must yet keep out of his sight, not
To lose it for ever. *Exit*

Enter MANLY *and* FREEMAN

FREEMAN. But pray what strange charms has she that could make you love?

MANLY. Strange charms, indeed! She has beauty enough to call in question her wit or virtue, and her form would make a starved hermit a ravisher; yet her virtue and conduct would preserve her from the subtle lust of a pampered prelate. She is so perfect a beauty, that art could not better it, nor affectation deform it; yet all this is nothing. Her tongue as well as face ne'er knew artifice; nor ever did her words or looks contradict her heart. She is all truth, and hates the lying, masking, daubing world, as I do; for which I love her, and for which I think she dislikes not me; for she has often shut out of her conversation for mine, the gaudy fluttering parrots of the town, apes and echoes of men only, and refused their commonplace, pert chat, flattery, and submissions, to be entertained with my sullen bluntness, and honest love. And, last of all, swore to me, since her parents would not suffer her to go with me, she would stay behind for no other man; but follow me, without their leave, if not to be obtained. Which oath—

FREEMAN. Did you think she would keep?

MANLY. Yes; for she is not (I tell you) like other women, but can keep her promise, though she has sworn to keep it. But, that she might the better keep it, I left her the value of five or six thousand pound, for women's wants are generally their most importunate solicitors to love or marriage.

FREEMAN. And money summons lovers more than beauty, and augments but their importunity, and their number; so makes it the harder for a woman to deny 'em. For my part, I am for the French maxim:[1] "If you would have your female subjects loyal, keep 'em poor."—But in short, that your mistress may not marry, you have given her a portion.

MANLY. She had given me her heart first, and I am satisfied with the security; I can never doubt her truth and constancy.

FREEMAN. It seems you do, since you are fain to bribe it with money. But how come you to be so diffident of the man that says he loves you, and not doubt the woman that says it?

MANLY. I should (I confess) doubt the love of any other woman but her, as I do the friendship of any other man but him I have trusted; but I have such proofs of their faith as cannot deceive me.

[1] The source of this maxim has not been found.

FREEMAN. Cannot!

MANLY. Not but I know that generally no man can be a great enemy but under the name of friend; and if you are a cuckold, it is your friend only that makes you so, for your enemy is not admitted to your house; if you are cheated in your fortune, 'tis your friend that does it, for your enemy is not made your trustee; if your honor or good name be injured, 'tis your friend that does it still, because your enemy is not believed against you. Therefore, I rather choose to go where honest, downright barbarity is professed, where men devour one another like generous hungry lions and tigers, not like crocodiles; where they think the devil white, of our complexion; and I am already so far an Indian. But if your weak faith doubts this miracle of a woman, come along with me, and believe; and thou wilt find her so handsome, that thou, who art so much my friend, wilt have a mind to lie with her, and so will not fail to discover what her faith and thine is to me.

When we're in love, the great adversity,
Our friends and mistresses at once we try.

ACT II

SCENE I. OLIVIA'S *Lodging*

Enter OLIVIA, ELIZA, [*and*] LETTICE

OLIVIA. Ah, cousin, what a world 'tis we live in! I am so weary of it.

ELIZA. Truly, cousin, I can find no fault with it, but that we cannot always live in't; for I can never be weary of it.

OLIVIA. O hideous! you cannot be in earnest sure, when you say you like the filthy world.

ELIZA. You cannot be in earnest sure, when you say you dislike it.

OLIVIA. You are a very censorious creature, I find.

ELIZA. I must confess, I think we women as often discover where we love by railing, as men when they lie by their swearing; and the world is but a constant keeping gallant, whom we fail not to quarrel with when anything crosses us, yet cannot part with't for our hearts.

LETTICE. A gallant indeed, madam, whom ladies first make jealous, and then quarrel with it for being so; for if, by her indiscretion, a lady be talked of for a man, she cries presently, "'Tis a censorious world!"; if, by her vanity, the intrigue be found out, "'Tis a prying, malicious world!"; if, by her overfondness, the gallant proves unconstant, "'Tis a false world!"; and if, by her niggardliness, the chambermaid tells, "'Tis a perfidious world!" But that, I'm sure, your ladyship cannot say of the world yet, as bad as 'tis.

OLIVIA. But I may say, "'Tis a very impertinent world!"—Hold your peace.—And, cousin, if the world be a gallant, 'tis such an one as is my aversion. Pray name it no more.

ELIZA. But is it possible the world, which has such variety of charms for other women, can have none for you? Let's see—first, what d'ye think of dressing and fine clothes?

OLIVIA. Dressing! Fie, fie, 'tis my aversion.—[*To* LETTICE.] But come hither, you dowdy; methinks you might have opened this toure[1] better. O hideous! I cannot suffer it! D'ye see how't fits?

ELIZA. Well enough, cousin, if dressing be your aversion.

OLIVIA. 'Tis so: and for variety of rich clothes, they are more my aversion.

LETTICE. Ay, 'tis because your ladyship wears 'em too long; for indeed a gown, like a gallant, grows one's aversion, by having too much of it.

OLIVIA. Insatiable creature! I'll be sworn I have had this not above three days, cousin, and within this month have made some six more.

ELIZA. Then your aversion to 'em is not altogether so great.

OLIVIA. Alas! 'tis for my woman only I wear 'em, cousin.

LETTICE. If it be for me only, madam, pray do not wear 'em.

ELIZA. But what d'ye think of visits—balls?

OLIVIA. Oh, I detest 'em!

ELIZA. Of plays?

OLIVIA. I abominate 'em; filthy, obscene, hideous things!

ELIZA. What say you to masquerading in the winter, and Hyde Park in the summer?

OLIVIA. Insipid pleasures I taste not.

ELIZA. Nay, if you are for more solid pleasure, what think you of a rich young husband?

OLIVIA. O horrid! marriage! what a pleas-

[1] Curled hair worn across the forehead.

ure you have found out! I nauseate it of all things.

LETTICE. But what does your ladyship think then of a liberal, handsome, young lover?

OLIVIA. A handsome young fellow, you impudent! Begone, out of my sight. Name a handsome young fellow to me! foh, a hideous, handsome, young fellow I abominate! (*Spits*)

ELIZA. Indeed! But let's see—will nothing please you? what d'ye think of the court?

OLIVIA. How? the court! the court, cousin! my aversion, my aversion, my aversion of all aversions!

ELIZA. How? the court! where—

OLIVIA. Where sincerity is a quality as out of fashion, and as unprosperous, as bashfulness: I could not laugh at a quibble, though it were a fat privy-counsellor's; nor praise a lord's ill verses, though I were myself the subject; nor an old lady's young looks, though I were her woman; nor sit to a vain young simile-maker, though he flattered me. In short, I could not gloat upon a man when he comes into a room, and laugh at him when he goes out. I cannot rail at the absent, to flatter the standers-by; I—

ELIZA. Well, but railing now is so common, that 'tis no more malice, but the fashion; and the absent think they are no more the worse for being railed at, than the present think they are the better for being flattered; and for the court—

OLIVIA. Nay, do not defend the court; for you'll make me rail at it, like a trusting citizen's widow.

ELIZA. Or like a Holborn lady,[1] who could not get into the last ball, or was out of countenance in the drawing-room[2] the last Sunday of her appearance there; for none rail at the court but those who cannot get into it, or else who are ridiculous when they are there; and I shall suspect you were laughed at when you were last there, or would be a maid of honor.

OLIVIA. I a maid of honor! To be a maid of honor were yet of all things my aversion.

ELIZA. In what sense am I to understand you? But, in fine, by the word aversion, I'm sure you dissemble; for I never knew woman yet that used it who did not. Come, our tongues belie our hearts more than our pocket-glasses do our faces. But methinks we ought to leave off dissembling, since 'tis grown of no use to us; for all wise observers understand us now-a-days, as they do dreams, almanacs, and Dutch gazettes,[3] by the contrary; and a man no more believes a woman, when she says she has an aversion for him, than when she says she'll cry out.

OLIVIA. O filthy! hideous! Peace, cousin, or your discourse will be my aversion; and you may believe me.

ELIZA. Yes; for if anything be a woman's aversion, 'tis plain-dealing from another woman; and perhaps that's your quarrel to the world; for that will talk, as your woman says.

OLIVIA. Talk? not of me sure; for what men do I converse with? what visits do I admit?

Enter BOY

BOY. Here's the gentleman to wait upon you, madam.

OLIVIA. On me! you little, unthinking fop, d'ye know what you say?

BOY. Yes, madam, 'tis the gentleman that comes every day to you, who—

OLIVIA. Hold your peace, you heedless little animal, and get you gone.—(*Exit* BOY) This country boy, cousin, takes my dancing-master, tailor, or the spruce milliner, for visitors.

LETTICE. No, madam; 'tis Mr. Novel, I'm sure, by his talking so loud. I know his voice too, madam.

OLIVIA. You know nothing, you buffle-headed,[4] stupid creature you; you would make my cousin believe I receive visits. But if it be Mr.—what did you call him?

LETTICE. Mr. Novel, madam, he that—

OLIVIA. Hold your peace, I'll hear no more of him; but if it be your Mr.—(I can't think of his name again) I suppose he has followed my cousin hither.

ELIZA. No, cousin, I will not rob you of the honor of the visit: 'tis to you, cousin, for I know him not.

OLIVIA. Nor did I ever hear of him before, upon my honor, cousin; besides, ha'n't I told you that visits and the business of visits, flat-

---

[1] City lady.
[2] I.e., an evening reception at the king's palace of Whitehall.
[3] Supposed to be proverbially unintelligible. Note the various hits at the Dutch in the play, showing that the wounds of war still rankle.
[4] Stupid.

tery and detraction, are my aversion? D'ye think, then, I would admit such a coxcomb as he is, who, rather than not rail, will rail at the dead, whom none speak ill of; and, rather than not flatter, will flatter the poets of the age, whom none will flatter; who affects novelty as much as the fashion and is as fantastical as changeable and as well known as the fashion; who likes nothing but what is new, nay, would choose to have his friend or his title a new one? In fine, he is my aversion.

ELIZA. I find you do know him, cousin, at least, have heard of him.

OLIVIA. Yes, now I remember, I have heard of him.

ELIZA. Well, but since he is such a coxcomb, for heaven's sake, let him not come up. Tell him, Mrs. Lettice, your lady is not within.

OLIVIA. No, Lettice, tell him my cousin is here, and that he may come up; for, notwithstanding I detest the sight of him, you may like his conversation; and though I would use him scurvily, I will not be rude to you in my own lodging. Since he has followed you hither, let him come up, I say.

ELIZA. Very fine! Pray let him go to the devil, I say, for me. I know him not, nor desire it. Send him away, Mrs. Lettice.

OLIVIA. Upon my word, she shan't. I must disobey your commands to comply with your desires. Call him up, Lettice.

ELIZA. Nay, I'll swear she shall not stir on that errand.   (*Holds* LETTICE)

OLIVIA. Well then, I'll call him myself for you, since you will have it so.—
                        (*Calls out at the door*)
Mr. Novel, sir, sir!

Enter NOVEL

NOVEL. Madam, I beg your pardon; perhaps you were busy. I did not think you had company with you.

ELIZA. (*Aside*) Yet he comes to me, cousin!

OLIVIA.—Chairs there.   (*They sit*)

NOVEL. Well, but, madam, d'ye know whence I come now?

OLIVIA. From some melancholy place, I warrant, sir, since they have lost your good company.

ELIZA. So?

NOVEL. From a place where they have treated me at dinner with so much civility and kindness, a pox on 'em! that I could hardly get away to you, dear madam.

OLIVIA. You have a way with you so new and obliging, sir!

ELIZA. (*Apart to* OLIVIA) You hate flattery, cousin.

NOVEL. Nay, faith, madam, d'ye think my way new? Then you are obliging, madam. I must confess, I hate imitation, to do anything like other people. All that know me do me the honor to say, I am an original, faith; but, as I was saying, madam, I have been treated to-day with all the ceremony and kindness imaginable at my Lady Autumn's; but the nauseous old woman at the upper end of her table—

OLIVIA. Revives the old Grecian custom,[1] of serving in a death's head with their banquets.

NOVEL. Ha, ha! fine, just, i'faith; nay, and new. 'Tis like eating with the ghost in "The Libertine;"[2] she would frighten a man from her dinner with her hollow invitations, and spoil one's stomach—

OLIVIA. To meat, or women. I detest her hollow cherry cheeks; she looks like an old coach new painted: affecting an unseemly smugness, whilst she is ready to drop in pieces.

ELIZA. (*Apart to* OLIVIA) You hate detraction, I see, cousin!

NOVEL. But the silly old fury, whilst she affects to look like a woman of this age, talks—

OLIVIA. Like one of the last; and as passionately as an old courtier who has outlived his office.

NOVEL. Yes, madam; but pray let me give you her character. Then she never counts her age by the years, but—

OLIVIA. By the masques she has lived to see.

NOVEL. Nay then, madam, I see you think a little harmless railing too great a pleasure for any but yourself; and therefore I've done.

---

[1] Wycherley's memory has here telescoped an author's nationality with what he says of another country. Herodotus (11:78) ascribes the custom mentioned in the text to the Egyptians.

[2] A Play by Shadwell (1675) on the Don Juan theme. In Act IV, scene iii, the ghost of Don John's father banquets with him and invites him to a return feast at the ancestral tomb (Act V, scene ii). The allusion was probably inserted after the first production of *The Plain-Dealer.*

Olivia. Nay, faith, you shall tell me who you had there at dinner.

Novel. If you would hear me, madam.

Olivia. Most patiently; speak, sir.

Novel. Then, we had her daughter—

Olivia. Ay, her daughter, the very disgrace to good clothes, which she always wears but to heighten her deformity, not mend it; for she is still most splendidly, gallantly ugly, and looks like an ill piece of daubing in a rich frame.

Novel. So! But have you done with her, madam? And can you spare her to me a little now?

Olivia. Ay, ay, sir.

Novel. Then, she is like—

Olivia. She is, you'd say, like a city bride, the greater fortune, but not the greater beauty, for her dress.

Novel. Well: yet have you done, madam? Then she—

Olivia. Then she bestows as unfortunately on her face all the graces in fashion, as the languishing eye, the hanging or pouting lip; but as the fool is never more provoking than when he aims at wit, the ill-favored of our sex are never more nauseous than when they would be beauties, adding to their natural deformity the artificial ugliness of affectation.

Eliza. So, cousin, I find one may have a collection of all one's acquaintances' pictures as well at your house as at Mr. Lely's; only the difference is, there we find 'em much handsomer than they are, and like; here, much uglier, and like; and you are the first of the profession of picture-drawing I ever knew without flattery.

Olivia. I draw after the life; do nobody wrong, cousin.

Eliza. No, you hate flattery and detraction!

Olivia. But, Mr. Novel, who had you besides at dinner?

Novel. Nay, the devil take me if I tell you, unless you will allow me the privilege of railing in my turn.—But, now I think on't, the women ought to be your province, as the men are mine: and you must know, we had him whom—

Olivia. Him, whom—

Novel. What, invading me already? And giving the character, before you know the man?

Eliza. No, that is not fair, though it be usual.

Olivia. I beg your pardon, Mr. Novel; pray go on.

Novel. Then, I say, we had that familiar coxcomb who is at home wheresoe'er he comes.

Olivia. Ay, that fool—

Novel. Nay then, madam, your servant; I'm gone. Taking a fool out of one's mouth is worse than taking the bread out of one's mouth.

Olivia. I've done; your pardon, Mr. Novel; pray proceed.

Novel. I say, the rogue, that he may be the only wit in company, will let nobody else talk, and—

Olivia. Ay, those fops who love to talk all themselves are of all things my aversion.

Novel. Then you'll let me speak, madam, sure. The rogue, I say, will force his jest upon you; and I hate a jest that's forced upon a man, as much as a glass.

Eliza. Why, I hope, sir, he does not expect a man of your temperance in jesting should do him reason?

Novel. What, interruption from this side, too! I must then—

(*Offers to rise.* Olivia *holds him*)

Olivia. No, sir.—You must know, cousin, that fop he means, though he talks only to be commended, will not give you leave to do't.

Novel. But, madam—

Olivia. He a wit! Hang him, he's only an adopter of straggling jests and fatherless lampoons; by the credit of which he eats at good tables, and so, like the barren beggar-woman, lives by borrowed children.[1]

Novel. Madam—

Olivia. And never was author of anything but his news; but that is still all his own.

Novel. Madam, pray—

Olivia. An eternal babbler; and makes no more use of his ears, than a man that sits at a play by his mistress, or in fop-corner.[2] He's, in fine, a base detracting fellow, and is my aversion.—But who else prithee, Mr. Novel, was there with you? Nay, you shan't stir.

Novel. I beg your pardon, madam; I cannot stay in any place where I'm not allowed a little christian liberty of railing.

Olivia. Nay, prithee, Mr. Novel, stay; and though you should rail at me, I would

---

[1] I.e., by kidnapping(?)
[2] That part of the pit near the stage frequented by the fops.

hear you with patience. Prithee, who else was there with you?

NOVEL. Your servant, madam.

OLIVIA. Nay, prithee tell us, Mr. Novel, prithee do.

NOVEL. We had nobody else.

OLIVIA. Nay, faith, I know you had. Come, my Lord Plausible was there too, who is, cousin, a—

ELIZA. You need not tell me what he is, cousin; for I know him to be a civil, good-natured, harmless gentleman, that speaks well of all the world, and is always in good-humor; and—

OLIVIA. Hold, cousin, hold, I hate detraction; but I must tell you, cousin, his civility is cowardice, his good-nature, want of wit; and he has neither courage nor sense to rail: and for his being always in humor, 'tis because he is never dissatisfied with himself. In fine, he is my aversion; and I never admit his visits beyond my hall.

NOVEL. No, he visit you! Damn him, cringing, grinning rogue! If I should see him coming up to you, I would make bold to kick him down again.—Ha!—

Enter my LORD PLAUSIBLE

My dear lord, your most humble servant.

(*Rises and salutes* PLAUSIBLE, *and kisses him*)

ELIZA. (*Aside*) So! I find kissing and railing succeed each other with the angry men as well as with the angry women; and their quarrels are like love-quarrels, since absence is the only cause of them; for as soon as the man appears again, they are over.

LORD PLAUSIBLE. Your most faithful, humble servant, generous Mr. Novel; and, madam, I am your eternal slave, and kiss your fair hands; which I had done sooner, according to your commands, but—

OLIVIA. No excuses, my lord.

ELIZA. (*Apart*) What, you sent for him then, cousin?

NOVEL. (*Aside*) Ha! invited!

OLIVIA. I know you must divide yourself; for your good company is too general a good to be engrossed by any particular friend.

LORD PLAUSIBLE. O Lord, madam, my company! your most obliged, faithful, humble servant. But I could have brought you good company indeed, for I parted at your door with two of the worthiest, bravest men—

OLIVIA. Who were they, my lord?

NOVEL. Who do you call the worthiest, bravest men, pray?

LORD PLAUSIBLE. Oh, the wisest, bravest gentlemen! men of such honor and virtue! of such good qualities! ah—

ELIZA. (*Aside*) This is a coxcomb that speaks ill of all people a different way, and libels everybody with dull praise, and commonly in the wrong place; so makes his panegyrics abusive lampoons.

OLIVIA. But pray let me know who they were?

LORD PLAUSIBLE. Ah! such patterns of heroic virtue! such—

NOVEL. Well, but who the devil were they?

LORD PLAUSIBLE. The honor of our nation! the glory of our age! Ah, I could dwell a twelvemonth on their praise; which indeed I might spare by telling their names: Sir John Current and Sir Richard Court-Title.

NOVEL. Court-Title![1] Ha, ha!

OLIVIA. And Sir John Current! Why will you keep such a wretch company, my lord?

LORD PLAUSIBLE. O madam, seriously you are a little too severe; for he is a man of unquestioned reputation in everything.

OLIVIA. Yes, because he endeavors only with the women to pass for a man of courage, and with the bullies for a wit; with the wits for a man of business, and with the men of business for a favorite at court; and at court for good city-security.

NOVEL. And for Sir Richard, he—

LORD PLAUSIBLE. He loves your choice, picked company, persons that—

OLIVIA. He loves a lord indeed; but—

NOVEL. Pray, dear madam, let me have but a bold stroke or two at his picture. He loves a lord, as you say, though—

OLIVIA. Though he borrowed his money, and ne'er paid him again.

NOVEL. And would bespeak a place three days before at the back-end of a lord's coach to Hyde Park.

LORD PLAUSIBLE. Nay, i'faith, i'faith, you are both too severe.

OLIVIA. Then to show yet more his passion for quality, he makes love to that fulsome coach-load of honor, my Lady Goodly, for he is always at her lodging.

[1] Note the influence of the "character" writers in the descriptions of types in this scene.

LORD PLAUSIBLE. Because it is the conventicle-gallant,[1] the meeting-house of all the fair ladies and glorious superfine beauties of the town.

NOVEL. Very fine ladies! there's first—

OLIVIA. Her honor, as fat as an hostess.

LORD PLAUSIBLE. She is something plump indeed, a goodly, comely, graceful person.

NOVEL. Then there's my Lady Frances, what d'ye call her? as ugly—

OLIVIA. As a citizen's lawfully begotten daughter.

LORD PLAUSIBLE. She has wit in abundance, and the handsomest heel, elbow, and tip of an ear, you ever saw.

NOVEL. Heel and elbow! ha, ha! And there's my Lady Betty, you know—

OLIVIA. As sluttish and slatternly as an Irish woman bred in France.

LORD PLAUSIBLE. Ah, all she has hangs with a loose air, indeed, and becoming negligence.

ELIZA. You see all faults with lovers' eyes, I find, my lord.

LORD PLAUSIBLE. Ah, madam, your most obliged, faithful, humble servant to command! But you can say nothing, sure, against the superfine mistress—

OLIVIA. I know who you mean. She is as censorious and detracting a jade as a superannuated sinner.

LORD PLAUSIBLE. She has a smart way of raillery, 'tis confessed.

NOVEL. And then, for Mrs. Grideline—

LORD PLAUSIBLE. She, I'm sure, is—

OLIVIA. One that never spoke ill of anybody, 'tis confessed; for she is as silent in conversation as a country lover, and no better company than a clock, or a weatherglass; for if she sounds, 'tis but once an hour, to put you in mind of the time of day, or to tell you 'twill be cold or hot, rain or snow.

LORD PLAUSIBLE. Ah, poor creature! she's extremely good and modest.

NOVEL. And for Mrs. Bridlechin, she's—

OLIVIA. As proud as a churchman's wife.

LORD PLAUSIBLE. She's a woman of great spirit and honor, and will not make herself cheap, 'tis true.

NOVEL. Then Mrs. Hoyden, that calls all people by their surnames, and is—

OLIVIA. As familiar a duck—

NOVEL. As an actress in the tiring room. There, I was once beforehand with you, madam.

LORD PLAUSIBLE. Mrs. Hoyden! a poor, affable, good-natured soul! But the divine Mrs. Trifle comes thither too; sure her beauty, virtue, and conduct, you can say nothing to.

OLIVIA. No!

NOVEL. No!—Pray let me speak, madam.

OLIVIA. First, can any one be called beautiful that squints?

LORD PLAUSIBLE. Her eyes languish a little, I own.

NOVEL. Languish! ha, ha!

OLIVIA. Languish!—Then, for her conduct, she was seen at "The Country Wife,"[2] after the first day. There's for you, my lord.

LORD PLAUSIBLE. But, madam, she was not seen to use her fan all the play long, turn aside her head, or by a conscious blush discover more guilt than modesty.

OLIVIA. Very fine! Then you think a woman modest that sees the hideous "Country Wife" without blushing or publishing her detestation of it? D'ye hear him, cousin?

ELIZA. Yes, and am, I must confess, something of his opinion, and think, that as an over-conscious fool at a play, by endeavoring to show the author's want of wit, exposes his own to more censure, so may a lady call her own modesty in question, by publicly cavilling with the poet's; for all those grimaces of honor, and artificial modesty, disparage a woman's real virtue, as much as the use of white and red does the natural complexion: and you must use very, very little, if you would have it thought your own.

OLIVIA. Then you would have a woman of honor with passive looks, ears, and tongue, undergo all the hideous obscenity she hears at nasty plays?

ELIZA. Truly, I think a woman betrays her want of modesty, by showing it publicly in a playhouse, as much as a man does his want of courage by a quarrel there; for the truly modest and stout say least, and are least exceptious, especially in public.

OLIVIA. O hideous! Cousin, this cannot be your opinion; but you are one of those who have the confidence to pardon the filthy play.

---

[1] Probably used here to mean: gallant assembly or gathering.

[2] *The Country Wife* was produced in January, 1674/5. In connection with this scene the student should read Act II, scene v of Molière's *Le Misanthrope*, and his *La Critique de l'Ecole des Femmes*

ELIZA. Why, what is there of ill in't, say you?

OLIVIA. O fie! fie! fie! would you put me to the blush anew? call all the blood into my face again? But to satisfy you then; first, the clandestine obscenity in the very name of Horner.

ELIZA. Truly, 'tis so hidden, I cannot find it out, I confess.

OLIVIA. O horrid! Does it not give you the rank conception or image of a goat, a town-bull, or a satyr? nay, what is yet a filthier image than all the rest, that of an eunuch?[1]

ELIZA. What then? I can think of a goat, a bull, or satyr, without any hurt.

OLIVIA. Ay; but cousin, one cannot stop there.

ELIZA. I can, cousin.

OLIVIA. O no; for when you have those filthy creatures in your head once, the next thing you think, is what they do; as their defiling of honest men's beds and couches, rapes upon sleeping and waking country virgins, under hedges, and on haycocks; nay, farther—

ELIZA. Nay, no farther, cousin. We have enough of your comment on the play, which will make me more ashamed than the play itself.

OLIVIA. Oh, believe me, 'tis a filthy play! and you may take my word for a filthy play as soon as another's; but the filthiest thing in that play, or any other play, is—

ELIZA. Pray keep it to yourself, if it be so.

OLIVIA. No, faith, you shall know it; I'm resolved to make you out of love with the play. I say, the lewdest, filthiest thing is his china;[2] nay, I will never forgive the beastly author his china, he has quite taken away the reputation of poor china itself, and sullied the most innocent and pretty furniture of a lady's chamber; insomuch that I was fain to break all my defiled vessels. You see I have none left; nor you, I hope.

ELIZA. You'll pardon me, I cannot think the worse of my china for that of the play-house.

OLIVIA. Why, you will not keep any now, sure! 'Tis now as unfit an ornament for a lady's chamber as the pictures that come from Italy and other hot countries, as appears by their nudities, which I always cover, or scratch out, whereso'er I find 'em. But china! out upon't, filthy china! nasty, debauched china!

ELIZA. All this will not put me out of conceit with china, nor the play, which is acted to-day, or another of the same beastly author's, as you call him, which I'll go see.

OLIVIA. You will not, sure! nay, you sha' not venture your reputation by going, and mine by leaving me alone with two men here: nay, you'll disoblige me forever, if— (*Pulls her back*)

ELIZA. I stay!—Your servant.

Exit ELIZA

OLIVIA. Well—but, my lord, though you justify everybody, you cannot in earnest uphold so beastly a writer, whose ink is so smutty, as one may say.

LORD PLAUSIBLE. Faith, I dare swear the poor man did not think to disoblige the ladies by any amorous, soft, passionate, luscious saying in his play.

OLIVIA. Foy, my lord! But what think you, Mr. Novel, of the play? though I know you are a friend to all that are new.

NOVEL. Faith, madam, I must confess, the new plays would not be the worse for my advice, but I could never get the silly rogues, the poets, to mind what I say; but I'll tell you what counsel I gave the surly fool you spake of.

OLIVIA. What was't?

NOVEL. Faith, to put his play into rhythm;[3] for rhythm you know, often makes mystical nonsense pass with the critics for wit, and a double-meaning saying with the ladies, for soft, tender, and moving passion. But now I talk of passion, I saw your old lover this morning—Captain— (*Whispers*)

Enter CAPTAIN MANLY, FREEMAN, *and* FIDELIA *standing behind*

OLIVIA. Whom?—nay, you need not whisper.

MANLY. We are luckily got hither unobserved!—How! in a close conversation with these supple rascals, the outcasts of sempstresses' shops!

---

[1] Horner, in *The Country Wife*, by pretending to be impotent, tricks the husbands of various women.

[2] See *The Country Wife*, Act IV, scene iii. The point of this not very edifying conversation is that Olivia's mock-modesty interprets the text of *The Country Wife* in the worst possible light.

[3] Rhyme (?)

FREEMAN. Faith, pardon her, captain, that, since she could no longer be entertained with your manly bluntness and honest love, she takes up with the pert chat and commonplace flattery of these fluttering parrots of the town, apes and echoes of men only.

MANLY. Do not you, sir, play the echo too, mock me, dally with my own words, and show yourself as impertinent as they are.

FREEMAN. Nay, captain—

FIDELIA. Nay, lieutenant, do not excuse her; methinks she looks very kindly upon 'em both, and seems to be pleased with what that fool there says to her.

MANLY. You lie, sir! and hold your peace, that I may not be provoked to give you a worse reply.

OLIVIA. Manly returned, d'ye say! And is he safe?   (*Whispers to* PLAUSIBLE)

NOVEL. My lord saw him too. Hark you, my lord!

MANLY. (*Aside*) She yet seems concerned for my safety, and perhaps they are admitted now here but for their news of me; for intelligence indeed is the common passport of nauseous fools, when they go their round of good tables and houses.

OLIVIA. I heard of his fighting only, without particulars, and confess I always loved his brutal courage, because it made me hope it might rid me of his more brutal love.

MANLY. (*Apart*) What's that?

OLIVIA. But is he at last returned, d'ye say, unhurt?

NOVEL. Ay, faith, without doing his business; for the rogue has been these two years pretending to a wooden leg, which he would take from fortune as kindly as the staff[1] of a marshal of France, and rather read his name in a gazette—

OLIVIA. Than in the entail of a good estate.

MANLY. (*Apart*) So!—

NOVEL. I have an ambition, I must confess, of losing my heart before such a fair enemy as yourself, madam; but that silly rogues should be ambitious of losing their arms, and—

OLIVIA. Looking like a pair of compasses.

NOVEL. But he has no use of his arms but to set 'em on kimbow,[2] for he never pulls off his hat, at least not to me, I'm sure; for you must know, madam, he has a fanatical hatred to good company: he can't abide me.

LORD PLAUSIBLE. Oh, be not so severe to him, as to say he hates good company; for I assure you he has a great respect, esteem, and kindness for me.

MANLY. [*Aside*] That kind, civil rogue has spoken yet ten thousand times worse of me than t'other.

OLIVIA. Well, if he be returned, Mr. Novel, then shall I be pestered again with his boist'rous sea-love; have my alcove smell like a cabin, my chamber perfumed with his tarpaulin Brandenburgh;[3] and hear volleys of brandy-sighs, enough to make a fog in one's room. Foh! I hate a lover that smells like Thames Street![4]

MANLY. (*Aside*) I can bear no longer, and need hear no more.—[*To* OLIVIA] But since you have these two pulvillio[5] boxes, these essence-bottles, this pair of muskcats[6] here, I hope I may venture to come yet nearer you.

OLIVIA. Overheard us then?

NOVEL. (*Aside*) I hope he heard me not.

LORD PLAUSIBLE. Most noble and heroic captain, your most obliged, faithful, humble servant.

NOVEL. Dear tar, thy humble servant.

MANLY. Away!—Madam—

OLIVIA. (*Thrusts* NOVEL *and* PLAUSIBLE *on each side*) Nay, I think I have fitted you[7] for list'ning.

MANLY. You have fitted me for believing you could not be fickle, though you were young; could not dissemble love, though 'twas your interest; nor be vain,[8] though you were handsome; nor break your promise, though to a parting lover; nor abuse your best friend, though you had wit; but I take not your contempt of me worse than your esteem or civility for these things here, though you know 'em.

NOVEL. Things!

LORD PLAUSIBLE. Let the captain rally a little.

---

[1] Emblem of the authority of a French marshal.
[2] Arms a-kimbo.
[3] Dressing-gown.
[4] A street along the Thames River, permeated by river-smells.
[5] Sweet-scented powder.
[6] The oil secreted by this animal is used as the base of perfumes.
[7] Got even with you.
[8] The first edition has "in vain," apparently a misprint.

MANLY. Yes, things! Canst thou be angry, thou thing?   (*Coming up to* NOVEL)

NOVEL. No, since my lord says you speak in raillery; for though your sea-raillery be something rough, yet, I confess, we use one another, too, as bad every day at Locket's,[1] and never quarrel for the matter.

LORD PLAUSIBLE. Nay, noble captain, be not angry with him.—(*Whispers to* MANLY) A word with you, I beseech you—

OLIVIA. (*Aside*) Well, we women, like the rest of the cheats of the world, when our cullies[2] or creditors have found us out, and will or can trust no longer, pay debts and satisfy obligations with a quarrel, the kindest present a man can make to his mistress, when he can make no more presents. For oftentimes in love, as at cards, we are forced to play foul, only to give over the game; and use our lovers like the cards,—when we can get no more by 'em, throw 'em up in a pet upon the first dispute.

MANLY. My lord, all that you have made me know by your whispering, which I knew not before, is, that you have a stinking breath; there's a secret for your secret.

LORD PLAUSIBLE. Pshaw! pshaw!

MANLY. But, madam, tell me, pray, what was't about this spark could take you? Was it the merit of his fashionable impudence, the briskness of his noise, the wit of his laugh, his judgment, or fancy in his garniture? or was it a well-trimmed glove, or the scent of it, that charmed you?

NOVEL. Very well, sir; 'gad, these sea-captains make nothing of dressing. But let me tell you, sir, a man by his dress, as much as by anything, shows his wit and judgment, nay, and his courage too.

FREEMAN. How his courage, Mr. Novel?

NOVEL. Why, for example, by red breeches, tucked-up hair or peruke, a greasy broad belt, and now-a-days a short sword.

MANLY. Thy courage will appear more by thy belt than thy sword, I dare swear.—Then, madam, for this gentle piece of courtesy, this man of tame honor, what could you find in him? Was it his languishing affected tone? his mannerly look? his second-hand flattery? the refuse of the playhouse tiring-rooms? or his slavish obsequiousness in watching at the door of your box at the playhouse, for your hand to your chair? or his jaunty way of playing with your fan? or was it the gunpowder spot[3] on his hand, or the jewel in his ear, that purchased your heart?

OLIVIA. Good jealous captain, no more of your—

LORD PLAUSIBLE. No, let him go on, madam, for perhaps he may make you laugh; and I would contribute to your pleasure any way.

MANLY. Gentle rogue!

OLIVIA. No, noble captain, you cannot sure think anything could take me more than that heroic title of yours, captain; for you know we women love honor inordinately.

NOVEL. Ha, ha! faith, she is with thee, bully, for thy raillery.

MANLY. (*Aside to* NOVEL) Faith, so shall I be with you, no bully, for your grinning.

OLIVIA. Then, that noble lion-like mien of yours, that soldier-like, weather-beaten complexion, and that manly roughness of your voice; how can they otherwise than charm us women, who hate effeminacy!

NOVEL. Ha, ha! faith I can't hold from laughing.

MANLY. (*Aside to* NOVEL) Nor shall I from kicking anon.

OLIVIA. And then, that captain-like carelessness in your dress, but especially your scarf; 'twas just such another, only a little higher tied, made me in love with my tailor as he passed by my window the last training-day,[4] for we women adore a martial man, and you have nothing wanting to make you more one, or more agreeable, but a wooden leg.

LORD PLAUSIBLE. Nay, i'faith, there your ladyship was a wag, and it was fine, just, and well rallied.

NOVEL. Ay, ay, madam, with you ladies, too, martial men must needs be very killing.

MANLY. Peace, you Bartholomew-fair buffoons! and be not you vain that these laugh on your side, for they will laugh at their own dull jests; but no more of 'em, for I will only suffer now this lady to be witty and merry.

OLIVIA. You would not have your panegyric interrupted. I go on then to your humor. Is there anything more agreeable than the pretty sullenness of that? than the great-

---

[1] A tavern of the period frequented by the beaux.
[2] Simpletons.
[3] A beauty spot produced by the use of gunpowder.
[4] Day for military exercises by the train-bands, or militia.

ness of your courage? which most of all appears in your spirit of contradiction, for you dare give all mankind the lie; and your opinion is your only mistress, for you renounce that too, when it becomes another man's.

NOVEL. Ha, ha! I cannot hold, I must laugh at thee, tar, faith!

LORD PLAUSIBLE. And i'faith, dear captain, I beg your pardon, and leave to laugh at you, too, though I protest I mean you no hurt; but when a lady rallies, a stander-by must be complaisant, and do her reason in laughing. Ha, ha!

MANLY. Why, you impudent, pitiful wretches, you presume sure upon your effeminacy to urge me; for you are in all things so like women, that you may think it in me a kind of cowardice to beat you.

OLIVIA. No hectoring, good captain.

MANLY. Or, perhaps, you think this lady's presence secures you; but have a care, she has talked herself out of all the respect I had for her; and by using me ill before you, has given me a privilege of using you so before her; but if you would preserve your respect to her, and not be beaten before her, go, begone immediately.

NOVEL. Begone! what?

LORD PLAUSIBLE. Nay, worthy, noble, generous, captain—

MANLY. Begone, I say!

NOVEL. Begone again! to us, begone!

MANLY. No chattering, baboons, instantly begone, or—

MANLY puts 'em out of the room: NOVEL struts, PLAUSIBLE cringes.

NOVEL. Well, madam, we'll go make the cards ready in your bedchamber. Sure you will not stay long with him.

Exeunt PLAUSIBLE [and] NOVEL

OLIVIA. Turn hither your rage, good captain Swaggerhuff, and be saucy with your mistress, like a true captain; but be civil to your rivals and betters, and do not threaten anything but me here; no, not so much as my windows; nor do not think yourself in the lodgings of one of your suburb mistresses [1] beyond the Tower.[2]

MANLY. Do not give me cause to think so; for those less infamous women part with their lovers, just as you did from me, with unforced vows of constancy and floods of willing tears; but the same winds bear away their lovers and their vows; and for their grief, if the credulous unexpected fools return, they find new comforters, fresh cullies, such as I found here. The mercenary love of those women, too, suffer[s] shipwreck with their gallants' fortunes; now you have heard chance has used me scurvily, therefore you do too. Well, persevere in your ingratitude, falsehood, and disdain; have constancy in something, and I promise you to be as just to your real scorn as I was to your feigned love; and henceforward will despise, contemn, hate, loathe, and detest you most faithfully.

Enter LETTICE

OLIVIA. Get the ombre-cards [3] ready in the next room, Lettice, and—

(Whispers to LETTICE)

FREEMAN. Bravely resolved, captain!

FIDELIA. And you'll be sure to keep your word, I hope, sir.

MANLY. I hope so too.

FIDELIA. Do you but hope it, sir? If you are not as good as your word, 'twill be the first time you ever bragged, sure.

MANLY. She has restored my reason with my heart.

FREEMAN. But now you talk of restoring, captain, there are other things, which next to one's heart, one would not part with; I mean your jewels and money, which it seems she has, sir.

MANLY. What's that to you, sir?

FREEMAN. Pardon me, whatsoever is yours, I have a share in't, I'm sure, which I will not lose for asking, though you may be too generous or too angry now to do't yourself.

FIDELIA. Nay, then I'll make bold to make my claim, too.

(Both going towards OLIVIA)

MANLY. Hold, you impertinent, officious fops—*(Aside)* How have I been deceived!

FREEMAN. Madam, there are certain appurtenances to a lover's heart, called jewels, which always go along with it.

FIDELIA. And which, with lovers, have no value in themselves, but from the heart they come with. Our captain's, madam, it seems you scorn to keep, and much more will those worthless things without it, I am confident.

[1] Loose women. [2] I.e., in Wapping. [3] Ombre requires only forty cards.

OLIVIA. A gentleman so well made as you are may be confident—us easy women could not deny you anything you ask, if 'twere for yourself; but, since 'tis for another, I beg your leave to give him my answer.—(*Aside*) An agreeable young fellow this!—and would not be my aversion!—(*Aside to* MANLY) Captain, your young friend here has a very persuading face, I confess; yet you might have asked me yourself for those trifles you left with me, which (hark you a little, for I dare trust you with the secret: you are a man of so much honor, I'm sure)—I say then, not expecting your return, or hoping ever to see you again, I have delivered your jewels to—

MANLY. Whom?

OLIVIA. My husband.

MANLY. Your husband!

OLIVIA. Ay, my husband; for, since you could leave me, I am lately and privately married to one, who is a man of so much honor and experience in the world, that I dare not ask him for your jewels again, to restore 'em to you; lest he should conclude you never would have parted with 'em to me on any other score but the exchange of my honor, which rather than you'd let me lose, you'd lose, I'm sure, yourself, those trifles of yours.

MANLY. Triumphant impudence! but married, too!

OLIVIA. Oh, speak not so loud, my servants know it not: I am married; there's no resisting one's destiny, or love, you know.

MANLY. Why, did you love him, too?

OLIVIA. Most passionately; nay, love him now, though I have married him, and he, me, which mutual love I hope you are too good, too generous a man to disturb, by any future claim, or visits to me. 'Tis true, he is now absent in the country, but returns shortly; therefore I beg of you, for your own ease and quiet, and my honor, you will never see me more.

MANLY. I wish I never had seen you.

OLIVIA. But if you should ever have anything to say to me hereafter, let that young gentleman there be your messenger.

MANLY. You would be kinder to him; I find he should be welcome.

OLIVIA. Alas, his youth would keep my husband from suspicions, and his visits from scandal; for we women may have pity for such as he, but no love; and I already think you do not well to spirit him away to sea; and the sea is already but too rich with the spoils of the shore.

MANLY. (*Aside*) True, perfect woman! If I could say anything more injurious to her now, I would; for I could outrail a bilked whore, or a kicked coward; but, now I think on't, that were rather to discover my love than hatred; and I must not talk, for something I must do.

OLIVIA. (*Aside*) I think I have given him enough of me now, never to be troubled with him again.—

Enter LETTICE

Well, Lettice, are the cards and all ready within? I come then.—Captain, I beg your pardon. You will not make one at ombre?

MANLY. No, madam, but I'll wish you a little good luck before you go.

OLIVIA. No, if you would have me thrive, curse me; for that you'll do heartily, I suppose.

MANLY. Then, if you will have it so, may all the curses light upon you, women ought to fear, and you deserve!—First, may the curse of loving play attend your sordid covetousness, and fortune cheat you, by trusting to her, as you have cheated me; the curse of pride, or a good reputation, fall on your lust; the curse of affectation on your beauty; the curse of your husband's company on your pleasures; and the curse of your gallant's disappointments in his absence; and the curse of scorn, jealousy, or despair on your love; and then the curse of loving on!

OLIVIA. And, to requite all your curses, I will only return you your last; may the curse of loving me still fall upon your proud, hard heart, that could be so cruel to me in these horrid curses! But heaven forgive you!

Exit OLIVIA

MANLY. Hell and the devil reward thee!

FREEMAN. Well, you see now, mistresses, like friends, are lost by letting 'em handle your money; and most women are such kind of witches, who can have no power over a man, unless you give 'em money; but when once they have got any from you, they never leave you till they have all. Therefore I never dare give a woman a farthing.

MANLY. Well, there is yet this comfort: by losing one's money with one's mistress, a man is out of danger of getting another; of being made prize again by love, who, like a pirate, takes you by spreading false colors: but when once you have run your ship a-ground, the treacherous picaroon luffs [1]; so by your ruin you save yourself from slavery at least.

Enter BOY

BOY. Mrs. Lettice, here's Madam Blackacre come to wait upon her honor.

[*Exeunt* LETTICE *and* BOY]

MANLY. D'ye hear that? Let us be gone before she comes; for henceforward I'll avoid the whole damned sex for ever, and woman as a sinking ship.

Exeunt MANLY *and* FIDELIA

FREEMAN. And I'll stay, to revenge on her your quarrel to the sex; for out of love to her jointure, and hatred to business, I would marry her, to make an end of her thousand suits, and my thousand engagements, to the comfort of two unfortunate sorts of people, my plaintiffs and her defendants, my creditors and her adversaries.

Enter WIDOW BLACKACRE, *led in by* MAJOR OLDFOX, *and* JERRY BLACKACRE *following, laden with green bags.*

WIDOW. 'Tis an arrant sea-ruffian; but I'm glad I met with him at last, to serve him again, major; for the last service was not good in law. Boy, duck, Jerry, where is my paper of memorandums? Give me, child, so. Where is my cousin Olivia now, my kind relation?

FREEMAN. Here is one that would be your kind relation, madam.

WIDOW. What mean you, sir?

FREEMAN. Why, faith, (to be short) to marry you, widow.

WIDOW. Is not this the wild, rude person we saw at Captain Manly's?

JERRY. Ay, forsooth, an't please.

WIDOW. What would you? What are you? Marry me!

FREEMAN. Ay, faith; for I am a younger brother, and you are a widow.

WIDOW. You are an impertinent person; and go about your business.

FREEMAN. I have none, but to marry thee, widow.

WIDOW. But I have other business, I'd have you to know.

FREEMAN. But you have no business a-nights, widow; and I'll make you pleasanter business than any you have; for a-nights, I assure you, I am a man of great business; for the business—

WIDOW. Go, I'm sure you're an idle fellow.

FREEMAN. Try me but, widow, and employ me as you find my abilities and industry.

OLDFOX. Pray be civil to the lady, Mr.—— She is a person of quality, a person that is no person—

FREEMAN. Yes, but she's a person that is a widow. Be you mannerly to her, because you are to pretend only to be her squire, to arm her to her lawyer's chambers; but I will be impudent and bawdy, for she must love and marry me.

WIDOW. Marry come up, you saucy, familiar Jack! You think, with us widows, 'tis no more than up, and ride. Gad forgive me! now-a-days, every idle, young, hectoring, roaring companion, with a pair of turned red breeches, and a broad back, thinks to carry away any widow of the best degree; but I'd have you to know, sir, all widows are not got, like places at court, by impudence and importunity only.

OLDFOX. No, no, soft, soft, you are a young man, and not fit—

FREEMAN. For a widow? Yes, sure, old man, the fitter.

OLDFOX. Go to, go to; if others had not laid in their claims before you—

FREEMAN. Not you, I hope.

OLDFOX. Why not I, sir? Sure I am a much more proportionable match for her than you, sir; I, who am an elder brother, of a comfortable fortune, and of equal years with her.

WIDOW. How's that, you unmannerly person? I'd have you to know, I was born but in *Ann' undec' Caroli prim'*.[2]

OLDFOX. Your pardon, lady, your pardon; be not offended with your very [humble] servant.—But I say, sir, you are a beggarly younger brother, twenty years younger than her, without any land or stock, but your great stock of impudence; therefore what pretension can you have to her?

FREEMAN. You have made it for me: first, because I am a younger brother.

WIDOW. Why, is that a sufficient plea to a relict? How appears it, sir? by what foolish custom?

---

[1] I.e., the treacherous pirate turns his ship nearer to the wind in order to avoid running aground.

[2] In the eleventh year of the reign of Charles I.

FREEMAN. By custom time out of mind only. Then, sir, because I have nothing to keep me after her death, I am the likelier to take care of her life. And for my being twenty years younger than her, and having a sufficient stock of impudence, I leave it to her whether they will be valid exceptions to me in her widow's law or equity.

OLDFOX. Well, she has been so long in chancery, that I'll stand to her equity and decree [1] between us.—(*Aside to* WIDOW BLACKACRE) Come, lady, pray snap up this young snap at first, or we shall be troubled with him. Give him a city-widow's answer, that is, with all the ill-breeding imaginable.— Come, madam.

WIDOW. Well, then, to make an end of this foolish wooing, for nothing interrupts business more: first, for you, major—

OLDFOX. You declare in my favor, then?

FREEMAN. What, direct the court!—(*To* JERRY) Come, young lawyer, thou sha't be a counsel for me.

JERRY. Gad, I shall betray your cause then, as well as an older lawyer; never stir.

WIDOW. First, I say, for you, major, my walking hospital of an ancient foundation, thou bag of mummy,[2] that wouldst fall asunder, if 'twere not for thy cerecloths—

OLDFOX. How, lady?

FREEMAN. Ha, ha!—

JERRY. Hey, brave mother! use all suitors thus, for my sake.

WIDOW. Thou withered, hobbling, distorted cripple; nay, thou art a cripple all over: wouldst thou make me the staff of thy age, the crutch of thy decrepidness? Me—

FREEMAN. Well said, widow! Faith, thou wouldst make a man love thee now, without dissembling.

WIDOW. Thou senseless, impertinent, quibbling, drivelling, feeble, paralytic, impotent, fumbling, frigid nincompoop!

JERRY. Hey, brave mother, for calling of names, i'fac!

WIDOW. Wouldst thou make a caudlemaker, a nurse of me? Can't you be bedrid without a bed-fellow? Won't your swanskins,[3] furs, flannels, and the scorched trencher,[4] keep you warm there? Would you have me your Scotch warming-pan,[5] with a pox to you! Me—

OLDFOX. O Heavens!

FREEMAN. I told you I should be thought the fitter man, major.

JERRY. Ay, you old fobus,[6] and you would have been my guardian, would you, to have taken care of my estate, that half of't should never come to me, by letting long leases at pepper-corn rents?[7]

WIDOW. If I would have married an old man, 'tis well known I might have married an earl, nay, what's more, a judge, and been covered the winter nights with the lambskins, which I prefer to the ermines[8] of nobles. And dost thou think I would wrong my poor minor there for you?

FREEMAN. Your minor is a chopping[9] minor, God bless him!

(*Strokes* JERRY *on the head*)

OLDFOX. Your minor may be a major[10] of horse or foot, for his bigness; and it seems you will have the cheating of your minor to yourself.

WIDOW. Pray, sir, bear witness: cheat my minor! I'll bring my action of the case for the slander.

FREEMAN. Nay, I would bear false witness for thee now, widow, since you have done me justice, and have thought me the fitter man for you.

WIDOW. Fair and softly, sir, 'tis my minor's case, more than my own; and I must do him justice now on you.

FREEMAN. How?

OLDFOX. So then.

WIDOW. You are, first, (I warrant) some renegado from the inns of court and the law: and thou'lt come to suffer for't by the law, that is, be hanged.

JERRY. Not about your neck, forsooth, I hope.

FREEMAN. But, madam—

OLDFOX. Hear the court.

WIDOW. Thou art some debauched, drunken, lewd, hectoring, gaming companion, and want'st some widow's old

---

[1] The court of Chancery issues decrees in equity cases.
[2] Pulpy substance.
[3] A kind of flannel.
[4] Round, flat board used as a warming pan.
[5] A wench.
[6] Fool.
[7] Nominal rents.
[8] The point lies in the association of lambskin with lawyers, and ermine with the robes of nobles.
[9] Strapping.
[10] The point of the pun lies in the meaning of major as (1) elder; and (2) military officer.

gold [1] to nick [2] upon; but I thank you, sir, that's for my lawyers.

FREEMAN. Faith, we should ne'er quarrel about that; for guineas [1] would serve my turn. But, widow—

WIDOW. Thou art a foul-mouthed boaster of thy lust, a mere braggadocio of thy strength for wine and women, and wilt belie thyself more than thou dost women, and art every way a base deceiver of women; and would deceive me, too, would you?

FREEMAN. Nay, faith, widow, this is judging without seeing the evidence.

WIDOW. I say, you are a worn-out whoremaster at five-and-twenty, both in body and fortune; and cannot be trusted by the common wenches of the town, lest you should not pay 'em; nor by the wives of the town lest you should pay 'em; so you want women, and would have me your bawd to procure 'em for you.

FREEMAN. Faith, if you had any good acquaintance, widow, 'twould be civilly done of thee; for I am just come from sea.

WIDOW. I mean, you would have me keep you, that you might turn keeper; for poor widows are only used like bawds by you; you go to church with us, but to get other women to lie with. In fine, you are a cheating, chousing [3] spendthrift; and having sold your own annuity, would waste my jointure.

JERRY. And make havoc of our estate personal, and all our old gilt plate; I should soon be picking up all our mortgaged apostle-spoons, [4] bowls, and beakers, out of most of the ale-houses betwixt Hercules' Pillars and the Boatswain in Wapping; [5] nay, and you'd be scouring [6] amongst my trees, and make 'em knock down one another, like routed reeling watchmen at midnight. Would you so, bully?

FREEMAN. Nay, prithee, widow, hear me.

WIDOW. No, sir; I'd have you to know, thou pitiful, paltry, lath-backed fellow, if I would have married a young man, 'tis well known I could have had any young heir in Norfolk, nay, the hopefull'st young man this day at the King's-bench bar; [7] I that am a relict and executrix of known plentiful assets and parts, who understand myself and the law. And would you have me under covert-baron [8] again? No, sir, no covert-baron for me.

FREEMAN. But, dear widow, hear me. I value you only, not your jointure.

WIDOW. Nay, sir, hold there; I know your love to a widow is covetousness of her jointure; and a widow, a little stricken in years, with a good jointure, is like an old mansion-house in a good purchase, never valued, but take one, take t'other: and perhaps, when you are in possession, you'd neglect it, let it drop to the ground, for want of necessary repairs or expenses upon't.

FREEMAN. No, widow, one would be sure to keep all tight, when one is to forfeit one's lease by dilapidation. [9]

WIDOW. Fie! fie! I neglect my business with this foolish discourse of love. Jerry, child, let me see the list of the jury; I'm sure my cousin Olivia has some relations amongst 'em. But where is she?

FREEMAN. Nay, widow, but hear me—one word only.

WIDOW. Nay, sir, no more, pray; I will no more hearken again to your foolish love-motions, than to offers of arbitration.

Exeunt WIDOW [BLACKACRE] *and* JERRY

FREEMAN. Well, I'll follow thee yet; for he that has a pretension at court, or to a widow, must never give over for a little ill-usage.

OLDFOX. Therefore, I'll get her by assiduity, patience, and long sufferings, which you will not undergo; for you idle young fellows leave off love when it comes to be business; and industry gets more women than love.

FREEMAN. Ay, industry, the fool's and old man's merit; but I'll be industrious too, and make a business on't, and get her by law, wrangling, and contests, and not by sufferings: and, because you are no dangerous rival, I'll give thee counsel, major:

---

[1] The point of this comparison lies in the fact that guineas were first coined in 1663.

[2] Cheat.

[3] Same as cheating.

[4] Spoons with the figures of the apostles in their handles, valued because they were given by sponsors at baptism.

[5] The Hercules' Pillars was an inn in the Hyde Park part of London; hence, the phrase is equivalent to "from one end of town to the other."

[6] Roistering; possibly here in its derived sense of cutting down.

[7] The court of King's Bench was the highest ordinary common-law court in the kingdom.

[8] Law French, meaning: under the authority of a husband.

[9] To forfeit a lease by allowing the property to fall out of repair.

If you litigious widow e'er would gain,
Sigh not to her, but by the law complain;
To her, as to a bawd, defendant sue
With statutes, and make justice pimp for you.

Exeunt

ACT III

SCENE I. *Westminster Hall* [1]

Enter MANLY *and* FREEMAN, *two Sailors behind*

MANLY. I hate this place, worse than a man that has inherited a chancery suit. I wish I were well out on't again.

FREEMAN. Why, you need not be afraid of this place, for a man without money needs no more fear a crowd of lawyers than a crowd of pickpockets.

MANLY. This, the reverend of the law would have thought the palace or residence of Justice; but, if it be, she lives here with the state of a Turkish emperor, rarely seen; and besieged rather than defended by her numerous black-guard [2] here.

FREEMAN. Methinks 'tis like one of their own halls in Christmas time, whither from all parts fools bring their money, to try by the dice (not the worst judges) whether it shall be their own or no; but after a tedious fretting and wrangling, they drop away all their money on both sides; and, finding neither the better, at last go emptily and lovingly away together to the tavern, joining their curses against the young lawyer's box, that sweeps all, like the old ones.

MANLY. Spoken like a revelling Christmas lawyer.

FREEMAN. Yes, I was one, I confess, but was fain to leave the law, out of conscience, and fall to making false musters: [3] rather choose to cheat the king than his subjects; plunder rather than take fees.

MANLY. Well, a plague and a purse-famine light on the law; and that female limb of it who dragged me hither to-day! But prithee, go see if, in that crowd of daggled gowns there, (*Pointing to a crowd of lawyers at the end of the stage*) thou canst find her. *Exit* FREEMAN

Manet MANLY

How hard it is to be an hypocrite!
At least to me, who am but newly so.
I thought it once a kind of knavery,
Nay, cowardice, to hide one's faults; but now
The common frailty, love, becomes my shame.
He must not know I love th' ungrateful still,
Lest he contemn me more than she; for I,
It seems, can undergo a woman's scorn,
But not a man's—

Enter to him FIDELIA

FIDELIA. Sir, good sir, generous captain.

MANLY. Prithee, kind impertinence, leave me. Why should'st thou follow me, flatter my generosity now, since thou know'st I have no money left? If I had it I'd give it thee, to buy my quiet.

FIDELIA. I never followed yet, sir, reward or fame, but you alone; nor do I now beg anything but leave to share your miseries. You should not be a niggard of 'em, since, methinks, you have enough to spare. Let me follow you now, because you hate me, as you have often said.

MANLY. I ever hated a coward's company, I must confess.

FIDELIA. Let me follow you till I am none, then; for you, I'm sure, will [go] through such worlds of dangers, that I shall be inured to 'em; nay, I shall be afraid of your anger more than danger, and so turn valiant out of fear. Dear captain, do not cast me off till you have tried me once more. Do not, do not go to sea again without me.

MANLY. Thou to sea! to court, thou fool; remember the advice I gave thee: thou art a handsome spaniel, and canst fawn naturally. Go, busk [4] about, and run thyself into the next great man's lobby; first fawn upon the slaves without, and then run into the lady's bedchamber; thou mayst be admitted, at last, to tumble her bed. Go, seek, I say, and lose me; for I am not able to keep thee; I have not bread for myself.

FIDELIA. Therefore I will not go, because then I may help and serve you.

---

[1] This scene will become clearer if the student remembers that in Westminster Hall three of the principal courts of the kingdom of England held their sessions; and that the walls of Westminster Hall were lined with stalls for the selling of merchandise.

[2] The double entendre lies in the fact that lawyers wore black gowns, and that the Turkish emperor was supposed to have a swarthy bodyguard.

[3] The fraudulent inclusion on a muster-roll of names of men not available for service, with a view of drawing their pay.

[4] Cruise.

MANLY. Thou!

FIDELIA. I warrant you, sir; for, at worst, I could beg or steal for you.

MANLY. Nay, more bragging! Dost thou not know there's venturing your life in stealing? Go, prithee, away: thou art as hard to shake off as that flattering, effeminating mischief, love.

FIDELIA. Love did you name? Why, you are not so miserable as to be yet in love, sure?

MANLY. No, no, prithee away, begone, or—(*Aside*) I had almost discovered my love and shame; well, if I had? that thing could not think the worse of me—or if he did?—no—yes, he shall know it—he shall—but then I must never leave him, for they are such secrets that make parasites and pimps lords of their masters; for any slavery or tyranny is easier than love's.—Come hither. Since thou art so forward to serve me, hast thou but resolution enough to endure the torture of a secret, for such, to some, is insupportable?

FIDELIA. I would keep it as safe as if your dear, precious life depended on't.

MANLY. Damn your dearness! It concerns more than my life,—my honor.

FIDELIA. Doubt it not, sir.

MANLY. And do not discover it, by too much fear of discovering it; but have a great care you let not Freeman find it out.

FIDELIA. I warrant you, sir. I am already all joy with the hopes of your commands; and shall be all wings in the execution of 'em. Speak quickly, sir.

MANLY. You said you would beg for me.

FIDELIA. I did, sir.

MANLY. Then you shall beg for me.

FIDELIA. With all my heart, sir.

MANLY. That is, pimp for me.

FIDELIA. How, sir?

MANLY. D'ye start! Think'st thou, thou couldst do me any other service? Come, no dissembling honor. I know you can do it handsomely, thou wert made for't. You have lost your time with me at sea, you must recover it.

FIDELIA. Do not, sir, beget yourself more reasons for your aversion to me, and make my obedience to you a fault; I am the unfittest in the world to do you such a service.

MANLY. Your cunning arguing against it shows but how fit you are for it. No more dissembling; here, I say, you must go use it for me to Olivia.

FIDELIA. To her, sir?

MANLY. Go flatter, lie, kneel, promise, anything to get her for me. I cannot live unless I have her. Didst thou not say thou wouldst do anything to save my life? And she said you had a persuading face.

FIDELIA. But did you not say, sir, your honor was dearer to you than your life? And would you have me contribute to the loss of that, and carry love from you to the most infamous, most false, and—

MANLY. And most beautiful!—
(*Sighs aside*)

FIDELIA. Most ungrateful woman that ever lived; for sure she must be so, that could desert you so soon, use you so basely, and so lately too. Do not, do not forget it, sir, and think—

MANLY. No, I will not forget it, but think of revenge. I will lie with her out of revenge. Go, begone, and prevail for me, or never see me more.

FIDELIA. You scorned her last night.

MANLY. I know not what I did last night; I dissembled last night.

FIDELIA. Heavens!

MANLY. Begone, I say, and bring me love or compliance back, or hopes at least, or I'll never see thy face again, by—

FIDELIA. Oh, do not swear, sir! first hear me.

MANLY. I am impatient, away! you'll find me here till twelve. (*Turns away*)

FIDELIA. Sir—

MANLY. Not one word, no insinuating argument more, or soothing persuasion; you'll have need of all your rhetoric with her: go strive to alter her, not me; begone.

Exit MANLY *at the end of the stage*

Manet FIDELIA

FIDELIA. Should I discover to him now my sex,
And lay before him his strange cruelty,
'Twould but incense it more.—No, 'tis not time.
For his love must I then betray my own?
Were ever love or chance, till now, severe?
Or shifting woman posed with such a task?
Forced to beg that which kills her, if obtained,
And give away her lover not to lose him!
Exit FIDELIA

Enter WIDOW BLACKACRE *in the middle of half-a-dozen lawyers, whispered to by a fellow in black,* JERRY BLACKACRE *following the crowd*

WIDOW. Offer me a reference,[1] you saucy companion you! d'ye know who you speak to? Art thou a solicitor in chancery, and offer a reference? A pretty fellow! Mr. Serjeant Ploddon, here's a fellow has the impudence to offer me a reference!

SERJEANT PLODDON. Who's that has the impudence to offer a reference within these walls?

WIDOW. Nay, for a splitter of causes to do't!

SERJEANT PLODDON. No, madam; to a lady learned in the law, as you are, the offer of a reference were to impose upon you.

WIDOW. No, no, never fear me for a reference, Mr. Serjeant. But come, have you not forgot your brief? Are you sure you shan't make the mistake of—hark you—(*Whispers*) Go then, go to your court of common-pleas,[2] and say one thing over and over again: you do it so naturally, you'll never be suspected for protracting time.

SERJEANT PLODDON. Come, I know the course of the court, and your business.

Exit SERJEANT PLODDON

WIDOW. Let's see, Jerry, where are my minutes? Come, Mr. Quaint, pray go talk a great deal for me in chancery; let your words be easy, and your sense hard; my cause requires it. Branch[3] it bravely, and deck my cause with flowers, that the snake may lie hidden. Go, go, and be sure you remember the decree of my Lord Chancellor, *Tricesimo quart'*[4] of the queen.

QUAINT. I will, as I see cause, extenuate or examplify matter of fact; baffle truth with impudence; answer exceptions with questions, though never so impertinent; for reasons give 'em words; for law and equity, tropes and figures; and so relax and enervate the sinews of their argument with the oil of my eloquence. But when my lungs can reason no longer, and not being able to say anything more for our cause, say everything of our adversary, whose reputation, though never so clear and evident in the eye of the world, yet with sharp invectives—

WIDOW. Alias, Billingsgate.

QUAINT. With poignant and sour invectives, I say, I will deface, wipe out, and obliterate his fair reputation, even as a record with the juice of lemons;[5] and tell such a story, (for, the truth on't is, all that we can do for our client in chancery, is telling a story,) a fine story, a long story, such a story—

WIDOW. Go, save thy breath for the cause; talk at the bar, Mr. Quaint. You are so copiously fluent, you can weary any one's ears sooner than your own tongue. Go, weary our adversaries' counsel, and the court. Go, thou art a fine-spoken person. Adad, I shall make thy wife jealous of me, if you can but court the court into a decree for us. Go, get you gone, and remember—(*Whispers. Exit* QUAINT)—Come, Mr. Blunder, pray bawl soundly for me, at the King's-bench; bluster, sputter, question, cavil; but be sure your argument be intricate enough to confound the court; and then you do my business. Talk what you will, but be sure your tongue never stand still; for your own noise will secure your sense from censure. 'Tis like coughing or hemming when one has got the belly-ache, which stifles the unmannerly noise. Go, dear rogue, and succeed; and I'll invite thee, ere it be long, to more soused venison.

BLUNDER. I'll warrant you, after your verdict, your judgment shall not be arrested upon if's and and's. [*Exit*]

WIDOW. Come, Mr. Petulant, let me give you some new instructions for our cause in the Exchequer. Are the barons[6] sat?

PETULANT. Yes, no; may be they are, may be they are not: what know I? what care I?

WIDOW. Heyday! I wish you would but snap up the counsel on t'other side anon at the bar as much; and have a little more patience with me, that I might instruct you a little better.

PETULANT. You instruct me! What is my brief for, mistress?

---

[1] To offer a reference means to offer to submit a disputed matter to a Master in Chancery, with a view to settlement. The widow, on the other hand, wishes to continue her suit.

[2] A court for the trial of civil cases formerly sitting in Westminster Hall.

[3] Ornament.

[4] In the 34th year of the reign of the queen [Elizabeth].

[5] Used for making writing invisible.

[6] The chief Baron of the Exchequer, and five judges called the barons of the exchequer, sat originally as a court in matters of revenue, but by this date as a regular common-law court.

WIDOW. Ay, but you seldom read your brief but at the bar, if you do it then.

PETULANT. Perhaps I do, perhaps I don't, and perhaps 'tis time enough. Pray hold yourself contented, mistress.

WIDOW. Nay, if you go there too, I will not be contented, sir; though you, I see, will lose my cause for want of speaking, I wo' not. You shall hear me, and shall be instructed. Let's see your brief.

PETULANT. Send your solicitor to me. Instructed by a woman! I'd have you to know, I do not wear a bar-gown [1] — !

WIDOW. By a woman! And I'd have you to know, I am no common woman; but a woman conversant in the laws of the land, as well as yourself, though I have no bar-gown.

PETULANT. Go to, go to, mistress, you are impertinent, and there's your brief for you. Instruct me! (*Flings her breviate at her*)

WIDOW. Impertinent to me, you saucy Jack, you! You return my breviate,[2] but where's my fee? You'll be sure to keep that, and scan that so well, that if there chance to be but a brass half-crown in't, one's sure to hear on't again. Would you would but look on your breviate half so narrowly! But pray give me my fee, too, as well as my brief.

PETULANT. Mistress, that's without precedent. When did a counsel ever return his fee, pray? And you are impertinent, and ignorant, to demand it.

WIDOW. Impertinent again, and ignorant, to me! Gadsbodikins,[3] you puny upstart in the law, to use me so! you green-bag [4] carrier, you murderer of unfortunate causes, the clerk's ink is scarce off of your fingers,—you that newly come from lamp-blacking the judges' shoes, and are not fit to wipe mine; you call me impertinent and ignorant! I would give thee a cuff on the ear, sitting the courts,[5] if I were ignorant. Marry gep,[6] if it had not been for me, thou hadst been yet but a hearing counsel [7] at the bar. *Exit* PETULANT

[1] Lawyer's gown; hence, lawyer.
[2] About equivalent to legal brief.
[3] Corruption meaning: by the little body of God.
[4] Bags for carrying legal documents were formerly made of green cloth. A green-bag carrier is therefore a clerk; or (depreciatively) a lawyer.
[5] Apparently the widow, in her anger, has omitted some word before "sitting" such as "during."
[6] Corruption of: by St. Mary of Egypt.
[7] Probably a student in the Inns-of-Court, who had not yet been admitted to the privilege of pleading in court.

Enter MR. BUTTONGOWN, *crossing the stage in haste*

Mr. Buttongown, Mr. Buttongown, whither so fast? What, won't you stay till we are heard?

BUTTONGOWN. I cannot, Mrs. Blackacre, I must be at the council, my lord's cause stays there for me.

WIDOW. And mine suffers here.

BUTTONGOWN. I cannot help it.

WIDOW. I'm undone.

BUTTONGOWN. What's that to me?

WIDOW. Consider the five-pound fee, if not my cause. That was something to you.

BUTTONGOWN. Away, away! pray be not so troublesome, mistress, I must be gone.

WIDOW. Nay, but consider a little. I am your old client, my lord but a new one; or let him be what he will, he will hardly be a better client to you than myself. I hope you believe I shall be in law as long as I live; therefore am no despicable client. Well, but go to your lord; I know you expect he should make you a judge one day; but I hope his promise to you will prove a true lord's promise. But that he might be sure to fail you, I wish you had his bond for't.

BUTTONGOWN. But what, will you yet be thus impertinent, mistress?

WIDOW. Nay, I beseech you, sir, stay; if it be but to tell me my lord's case; come, in short—

BUTTONGOWN. Nay, then—
Exit BUTTONGOWN

WIDOW. Well, Jerry, observe, child, and lay it up for hereafter. These are those lawyers who, by being in all causes, are in none; therefore if you would have 'em for you, let your adversary fee 'em; for he may chance to depend upon 'em; and so, in being against thee, they'll be for thee.

JERRY. Ay, mother, they put me in mind of the unconscionable wooers of widows, who undertake briskly their matrimonial business for their money; but when they have got it once, let who's will drudge for them. Therefore have a care of 'em, forsooth: there's advice for your advice.

WIDOW. Well said, boy.—Come, Mr. Splitcause, pray go see when my cause in Chancery comes on; and go speak with Mr. Quillit in the King's-bench, and Mr. Quirk in the Common-pleas, and see how our matters go there.

Enter Major Oldfox

Oldfox. Lady, a good and propitious morning to you; and may all your causes go as well as if I myself were judge of 'em!

Widow. Sir, excuse me, I am busy, and cannot answer compliments in Westminster Hall.—Go, Mr. Splitcause, and come to me again to that bookseller's; there I'll stay for you, that you may be sure to find me.

Oldfox. No, sir, come to the other bookseller's.—I'll attend your ladyship thither.

Exit Splitcause

Widow. Why to the other?

Oldfox. Because he is my bookseller, lady.

Widow. What, to sell you lozenges for your catarrh? or medicines for your corns? What else can a major deal with a bookseller for?

Oldfox. Lady, he prints for me.

Widow. Why, are you an author?

Oldfox. Of some few essays; deign you, lady, to peruse 'em.—(*Aside*) She is a woman of parts, and I must win her by showing mine.

[*They cross the stage to the bookstall*]

Bookseller's Boy. Will you see Culpepper,[1] mistress? *Aristotle's Problems?*[2] *The Complete Midwife?*

Widow. No; let's see Dalton, Hughs, Shepherd, Wingate.[3]

Boy. We have no law books.

Widow. No? you are a pretty bookseller then.

Oldfox. Come, have you e'er a one of my essays left?

Boy. Yes, sir, we have enough, and shall always have 'em.

Oldfox. How so?

Boy. Why, they are good, steady, lasting ware.

Oldfox. Nay, I hope they will live; let's see.—Be pleased, madam, to peruse the poor endeavors of my pen; for I have a pen, though I say it, that— (*Gives her a book*)

Jerry. Pray let me see *St. George for Christendom*, or, *The Seven Champions of England*.[4]

Widow. No, no; give him *The Young Clerk's Guide*.[5]—What, we shall have you read yourself into a humor of rambling and fighting, and studying military discipline, and wearing red breeches!

Oldfox. Nay, if you talk of military discipline, show him my *Treatise of the Art Military*.

Widow. Hold; I would as willingly he should read a play.

Jerry. Oh, pray forsooth, mother, let me have a play!

Widow. No, sirrah; there are young students of the law enough spoiled already by plays. They would make you in love with your laundress. or, what's worse, some queen of the stage that was a laundress; and so turn keeper before you are of age. (*Several crossing the stage*) But stay, Jerry, is not that Mr. What d'ye-call-him, that goes there, he that offered to sell me a suit in chancery for five hundred pounds, for a hundred down, and only paying the clerk's fees?

Jerry. Ay, forsooth, 'tis he.

Widow. Then stay here, and have a care of the bags, whilst I follow him.—Have a care of the bags, I say.

Jerry. And do you have a care, forsooth, of the statute against champerty,[6] I say.

Exit Widow [Blackacre]

Enter Freeman *to them*

Freeman. (*Aside*) So, there's a limb of my widow, which was wont to be inseparable from her. She can't be far.—How now, my pretty son-in-law that shall be, where's my widow?

Jerry. My mother, but not your widow, will be forthcoming presently.

Freeman. Your servant, major. What, are you buying furniture for a little sleeping closet, which you miscall a study? For you do only by your books, as by your wenches, bind 'em up neatly and make 'em fine, for other people to use 'em. And your bookseller is properly your upholsterer, for he furnishes your room, rather than your head.

Oldfox. Well, well, good sea-lieutenant,

---

[1] Nicholas Culpepper (1616–54), astrologer and herbalist.

[2] A popular, and often reprinted, work by J. Reynhard de Emingen. *The Complete Midwife* (1663) is by Culpepper.

[3] Legal writers whose books were then much used.

[4] Jerry confuses two titles—*St. George for England* is a popular ballad: and *The Seven Champions of Christendom*, a popular prose romance, originally in black letter.

[5] *The Young Clerk's Guide* by E. Cocker (1631–75), first published in 1660 and often reprinted, was a book of legal forms.

[6] Illegal assistance given a party to a suit by a third person, on condition of receiving all or a portion of the property under litigation, in case of success.

study you your compass; that's more than your head can deal with.—(*Aside*) I will go find out the widow, to keep her out of his sight, or he'll board her, whilst I am treating a peace. *Exit* OLDFOX

Manent FREEMAN, JERRY

JERRY. [*To the* BOOKSELLER'S BOY] Nay, prithee, friend, now let me have but *The Seven Champions*. You shall trust me no longer than till my mother's Mr. Splitcause comes; for I hope he'll lend me wherewithal to pay for't.

FREEMAN. Lend thee! here, I'll pay him. Do you want money, squire? I'm sorry a man of your estate should want money.

JERRY. Nay, my mother will ne'er let me be at age: and till then, she says—

FREEMAN. At age! why, you are at age already to have spent an estate, man. There are younger than you have kept their women these three years, have had half a dozen claps, and lost as many thousand pounds at play.

JERRY. Ay, they are happy sparks! Nay, I know some of my schoolfellows, who, when we were at school, were two years younger than me; but now, I know not how, are grown men before me, and go where they will, and look to themselves; but my curmudgeonly mother won't allow me wherewithal to be a man of myself with.

FREEMAN. Why, there 'tis; I knew your mother was in the fault. Ask but your schoolfellows what they did to be men of themselves.

JERRY. Why, I know they went to law with their mothers; for they say, there's no good to be done upon a widow mother, till one goes to law with her; but mine is as plaguy a lawyer as any's of our inn. Then would she marry too, and cut down my trees. Now, I should hate, man, to have my father's wife kissed and slapped, and t'other thing, too, (you know what I mean) by another man; and our trees are the purest,[1] tall, even, shady twigs, by my fa—

FREEMAN. Come, squire, let your mother and your trees fall as she pleases, rather than wear this gown and carry green bags all thy life, and be pointed at for a Tony.[2] But you shall be able to deal with her yet the common way; thou shalt make false love to some lawyer's daughter, whose father, upon the hopes of thy marrying her, shall lend thee money and law to preserve thy estate and trees; and thy mother is so ugly nobody will have her, if she cannot cut down thy trees.

JERRY. Nay, if I had but anybody to stand by me, I am as stomachful as another.

FREEMAN. That will I. I'll not see any hopeful young gentleman abused.

BOY. (*Aside*) By any but yourself.

JERRY. The truth on't is, mine's as arrant a widow-mother to her poor child as any's in England. She won't so much as let one have sixpence in one's pocket to see a motion,[3] or the dancing of the ropes, or—

FREEMAN. Come, you shan't want money; there's gold for you.

JERRY. O lord, sir, two guineas! D'ye lend me this? Is there no trick in't? Well, sir, I'll give you my bond for security.

FREEMAN. No, no; thou hast given me thy face for security. Anybody would swear thou dost not look like a cheat. You shall have what you will of me; and if your mother will not be kinder to you, come to me, who will.

JERRY. (*Aside*) By my fa—he's a curious fine gentleman!—But will you stand by one?

FREEMAN. If you can be resolute.

JERRY. Can be resolved! Gad, if she gives me but a cross word, I'll leave her to-night, and come to you. But now I have got money, I'll go to Jack-of-all-Trades, at t'other end of the Hall, and buy the neatest, purest[4] things—

FREEMAN. And I'll follow the great boy, and my blow at his mother. Steal away the calf, and the cow will follow you.

Exit JERRY, *followed by* FREEMAN

Enter, on the other side, MANLY, WIDOW BLACKACRE, *and* [MAJOR] OLDFOX

MANLY. Damn your cause! can't you lose it without me? which you are like enough to do, if it be, as you say, an honest one. I will suffer no longer for't.

WIDOW. Nay, captain, I tell you, you are my prime witness; and the cause is just now coming on, Mr. Splitcause tells me. Lord, methinks you should take a pleasure

---

[1] Best. [2] Simpleton.

[3] Puppet show.

[4] Here about equivalent to "nicest."

in walking here, as half you see now do; for they have no business here, I assure you.

MANLY. Yes; but I'll assure you then, their business is to persecute me. But d'ye think I'll stay any longer, to have a rogue, because he knows my name, pluck me aside and whisper a news-book secret [1] to me with a stinking breath? A second come piping angry from the court, and sputter in my face his tedious complaints against it? A third law-coxcomb, because he saw me once at a reader's [2] dinner, come and put me a long law case, to make a discovery of his indefatigable dulness and my wearied patience? A fourth, a most barbarous civil rogue, who will keep a man half an hour in the crowd with a bowed body, and a hat off, acting the reformed sign [3] of the Salutation tavern, to hear his bountiful professions of service and friendship, whilst he cares not if I were damned, and I am wishing him hanged out of my way?—I'd as soon run the gauntlet, as walk t'other turn.

Enter to them JERRY BLACKACRE *without his bags, but laden with trinkets, which he endeavors to hide from his Mother, and followed at a distance by* FREEMAN

WIDOW. Oh, are you come, sir? But where have you been, you ass? And how come you thus laden?

JERRY. Look here, forsooth, mother; now here's a duck, here's a boar-cat, and here's an owl.

Making a noise with catcalls [4] and other such like instruments.

WIDOW. Yes, there is an owl, sir.

OLDFOX. He's an ungracious bird, indeed.

WIDOW. But go, thou trangame,[5] and carry back those trangames, which thou hast stolen or purloined; for nobody would trust a minor in Westminster Hall, sure.

JERRY. Hold yourself contented, forsooth: I have these commodities by a fair bargain and sale; and there stands my witness, and creditor.

WIDOW. How's that? What, sir, d'ye

[1] Newspaper secret—i.e., no secret at all.
[2] A lecturer on law at one of the Inns of Court. The title is now honorary.
[3] The Salutation Tavern was in Billingsgate, the sign being a man bowing low (Summers).
[4] Whistles (instruments).
[5] Toy.

think to get the mother by giving the child a rattle?—But where are my bags, my writings, you rascal?

JERRY. (*Aside*) Oh, law! where are they indeed!

WIDOW. How, sirrah? speak, come—

MANLY. (*Apart to him*) You can tell her, Freeman, I suppose.

FREEMAN. (*Apart to him*) 'Tis true, I made one of your salt-water sharks steal 'em whilst he was eagerly choosing his commodities, as he calls 'em, in order to my design upon his mother.

WIDOW. Won't you speak? Where were you, I say, you son of a—an unfortunate woman?—Oh, major, I'm undone! They are all that concern my estate, my jointure, my husband's deed of gift, my evidences for all my suits now depending! What will become of them?

FREEMAN. (*Aside*) I'm glad to hear this.—They'll be safe, I warrant you, madam.

WIDOW. O where? where? Come, you villain, along with me, and show me where.

Exeunt WIDOW [BLACKACRE,] JERRY, *and* OLDFOX.

Manent MANLY, FREEMAN

MANLY. Thou hast taken the right way to get a widow, by making her great boy rebel; for when nothing will make a widow marry, she'll do't to cross her children. But canst thou in earnest marry this harpy, this volume of shrivelled blurred parchments and law, this attorney's desk?

FREEMAN. Ay, ay; I'll marry and live honestly; that is, give my creditors, not her, due benevolence, pay my debts.

MANLY. Thy creditors, you see, are not so barbarous as to put thee in prison; and wilt thou commit thyself to a noisome dungeon for thy life? which is the only satisfaction thou canst give thy creditors by this match?

FREEMAN. Why, is not she rich?

MANLY. Ay; but he that marries a widow for her money, will find himself as much mistaken as the widow that marries a young fellow for due benevolence, as you call it.

FREEMAN. Why, d'ye think I shan't deserve wages? I'll drudge faithfully.

MANLY. I tell thee again, he that is the slave in the mine has the least propriety in the ore. You may dig, and dig; but if thou wouldst have her money, rather get to be her trustee than her husband; for a true widow will make over her estate to anybody, and cheat herself, rather than be cheated by her children or a second husband.

Enter to them JERRY, *running in a fright*
JERRY. O law! I'm undone, I'm undone! My mother will kill me.—You said you'd stand by one.
FREEMAN. So I will, my brave squire, I warrant thee.
JERRY. Ay, but I dare not stay till she comes; for she's as furious, now she has lost her writings, as a bitch when she has lost her puppies.
MANLY. The comparison's handsome!
JERRY. Oh, she's here!

Enter WIDOW BLACKACRE *and* [MAJOR] OLDFOX

FREEMAN. (*To the Sailor*[1]) Take him, Jack, and make haste with him to your master's lodging; and be sure you keep him up till I come.   *Exeunt* JERRY *and* Sailor.
WIDOW. O my dear writings! Where's this heathen rogue, my minor?
FREEMAN. Gone to drown or hang himself.
WIDOW. No, I know him too well; he'll ne'er be *felo de se*[2] that way: but he may go and choose a guardian of his own head, and so be *felo de ses biens*,[3] for he has not yet chosen one.
FREEMAN. (*Aside*) Say you so? And he shan't want one.
WIDOW. But, now I think on't, 'tis you, sir, have put this cheat upon me; for there is a saying, "Take hold of a maid by her smock, and a widow by her writings, and they cannot get from you." But I'll play fast and loose with you yet, if there be law; and my minor and writings are not forthcoming, I'll bring my action of detinue or trover.[4] But first, I'll try to find out this guardianless, graceless villain. Will you jog, major?
MANLY. If you have lost your evidence, I hope your causes cannot go on, and I may be gone?
WIDOW. O no; stay but a making-water while, (as one may say) and I'll be with you again.
Exeunt WIDOW [BLACKACRE] *and* [MAJOR] OLDFOX.

Manent MANLY [*and*] FREEMAN

FREEMAN. Well; sure I am the first man that ever began a love-intrigue in Westminster Hall.
MANLY. No, sure; for the love to a widow generally begins here: and as the widow's cause goes against the heir or executors, the jointure-rivals[5] commence their suit to the widow.
FREEMAN. Well; but how, pray, have you passed your time here, since I was forced to leave you alone? You have had a great deal of patience.
MANLY. Is this a place to be alone, or have patience in? But I have had patience indeed; for I have drawn upon me, since I came, but three quarrels and two law-suits.
FREEMAN. Nay, faith, you are too cursed to be let loose in the world; you should be tied up again in your sea-kennel, called a ship. But how could you quarrel here?
MANLY. How could I refrain? A lawyer talked peremptorily and saucily to me, and as good as gave me the lie.
FREEMAN. They do it so often to one another at the bar, that they make no bones on't elsewhere.
MANLY. However, I gave him a cuff on the ear; whereupon he jogs two men, whose backs were turned to us, (for they were reading at a bookseller's) to witness I struck him, sitting the courts; which office they so readily promised, that I called 'em rascals and knights of the post. One of 'em presently calls two other absent witnesses, who were coming towards us at a distance; whilst the other, with a whisper, desires to know my name, that he might have satisfaction by way of challenge, as t'other by way of writ; but if it were not rather to direct his brother's writ, than his own challenge.—There, you see, is one of my quarrels, and two of my lawsuits.
FREEMAN. So!—and the other two?
MANLY. For advising a poet to leave off

---
[1] The Sailor has entered earlier.
[2] Suicide.
[3] Literally: "felon of his own goods." The estates of suicides formerly went to the king.
[4] Detinue is a legal action to recover a chattel wrongfully detained; trover is a legal action to recover the value of the chattel illegally appropriated to another
[5] Rival heirs.

writing, and turn lawyer, because he is dull and impudent, and says or writes nothing now but by precedent.

FREEMAN. And the third quarrel?

MANLY. For giving more sincere advice to a handsome, well-dressed young fellow, (who asked it, too) not to marry a wench that he loved, and I had lain with.

FREEMAN. Nay, if you will be giving your sincere advice to lovers and poets, you will not fail of quarrels.

MANLY. Or, if I stay in this place; for I see more quarrels crowding upon me. Let's be gone, and avoid 'em.

Enter NOVEL *at a distance, coming towards them*

A plague on him, that sneer is ominous to us; he is coming upon us and we shall not be rid of him.

NOVEL. Dear bully, don't look so grum upon me; you told me just now, you had forgiven me a little harmless raillery upon wooden legs last night.

MANLY. Yes, yes, pray begone, I am talking of business.

NOVEL. Can't I hear it? I love thee, and will be faithful, and always—

MANLY. Impertinent! 'Tis business that concerns Freeman only.

NOVEL. Well, I love Freeman too, and would not divulge his secret.—Prithee speak, prithee, I must—

MANLY. Prithee let me be rid of thee, I must be rid of thee.

NOVEL. Faith, thou canst hardly, I love thee so. Come, I must know the business.

MANLY. (*Aside*) So, I have it now.—Why, if you needs will know it, he has a quarrel, and his adversary bids him bring two friends with him: now, I am one, and we are thinking who we shall have for a third.

Several crossing the stage

NOVEL. A pox, there goes a fellow owes me an hundred pound, and goes out of town to-morrow. I'll speak with him, and come to you presently. *Exit* NOVEL

MANLY. No, but you won't.

FREEMAN. You are dext'rously rid of him.

Enter [MAJOR] OLDFOX

MANLY. To what purpose, since here comes another as impertinent? I know by his grin he is bound hither.

OLDFOX. Your servant, worthy, noble captain. Well, I have left the widow, because she carried me from your company; for, faith, captain, I must needs tell thee thou art the only officer in England, who was not an Edge-hill [1] officer, that I care for.

MANLY. I'm sorry for't.

OLDFOX. Why, wouldst thou have me love them?

MANLY. Anybody, rather than me.

OLDFOX. What! you are modest, I see; therefore, too, I love thee.

MANLY. No, I am not modest, but love to brag myself, and can't patiently hear you fight over the last civil war; therefore, go look out the fellow I saw just now here, that walks with his stockings and sword out at heels, and let him tell you the history of that scar on his cheek, to give you occasion to show yours, got in the field at Bloomsbury,[2] not that at Edgehill. Go to him, poor fellow, he is fasting, and has not yet the happiness this morning to stink of brandy and tobacco. Go, give him some to hear you; I am busy.

OLDFOX. Well, egad, I love thee now, boy, for thy surliness. Thou art no tame captain, I see, that will suffer—

MANLY. An old fox.

OLDFOX. All that shan't make me angry. I consider that thou art peevish, and fretting at some ill success at law. Prithee, tell me what ill luck you have met with here.

MANLY. You.

OLDFOX. Do I look like the picture of ill luck? Gadsnouns,[3] I love thee more and more. And shall I tell thee what made me love thee first?

MANLY. Do; that I may be rid of that damned quality and thee.

OLDFOX. 'Twas thy wearing that broad sword there.

MANLY. Here, Freeman, let's change. I'll never wear it more.

OLDFOX. How! you won't, sure. Prithee, don't look like one of our holiday captains [4] now-a-days, with a bodkin by your side, your martinet rogues.[5]

---

[1] A battle was fought between Royalist and Parliamentary forces at Edgehill in 1642.
[2] Duels were often fought in this part of London.
[3] Corruption of "By God's wounds."
[4] Cf. pantaloon captain, p. 906, ll. 24–25.
[5] Colonel Martinet, a French tactician, greatly improved military drill and tactics. He was especially noted for his management of the crossing of the Rhine by Louis XIV in 1672.

MANLY. (*Aside*) Oh, then there's hopes.— What, d'ye find fault with Martinet? Let me tell you, sir, 'tis the best exercise in the world; the most ready, most easy, most graceful exercise that ever was used, and the most—

OLDFOX. Nay, nay, sir, no more; sir, your servant. If you praise Martinet once, I have done with you, sir.—Martinet! Martinet!—
Exit OLDFOX

FREEMAN. Nay, you have made him leave you as willingly as ever he did an enemy; for he was truly for the king and parliament: for the parliament, in their list[1]; and for the king, in cheating 'em of their pay, and never hurting the king's party in the field.

Enter a Lawyer *towards them*

MANLY. A pox! this way; here's a lawyer I know, threat'ning us with another greeting.

LAWYER. Sir, sir, your very servant; I was afraid you had forgotten me.

MANLY. I was not afraid you had forgotten me.

LAWYER. No, sir; we lawyers have pretty good memories.

MANLY. You ought to have, by your wits.

LAWYER. Oh, you are a merry gentleman, sir; I remember you were merry when I was last in your company.

MANLY. I was never merry in thy company, Mr. Lawyer, sure.

LAWYER. Why, I'm sure you joked upon me, and shammed me all night long.

MANLY. Shammed! prithee, what barbarous law-term is that?

LAWYER. Shamming! Why, don't you know that? 'tis all our way of wit, sir.

MANLY. I am glad I do not know it then. Shamming! What does he mean by't, Freeman!

FREEMAN. Shamming is telling you an insipid dull lie with a dull face, which the sly wag, the author, only laughs at himself; and making himself believe 'tis a good jest, puts the sham only upon himself.

MANLY. So, your lawyer's jest, I find, like his practice, has more knavery than wit in't. I should make the worst shammer in England; I must always deal ingenuously, as I will with you, Mr. Lawyer, and advise you to be seen rather with attorneys and solicitors, than such fellows as I am; they will credit your practice more.

LAWYER. No, sir, your company's an honor to me.

MANLY. No, faith; go this way, there goes an attorney; leave me for him; let it be never said a lawyer's civility did him hurt.

LAWYER. No, worthy, honored sir; I'll not leave you for any attorney, sure.

MANLY. Unless he had a fee in his hand.

LAWYER. Have you any business here, sir? Try me. I'd serve you sooner than any attorney breathing.

MANLY. Business!—(*Aside*) So, I have thought of a sure way.—Yes, faith, I have a little business.

LAWYER. Have you so, sir? in what court, sir? what is't, sir? Tell me but how I may serve you, and I'll do't, sir, and take it for as great an honor—

MANLY. Faith, 'tis for a poor orphan of a sea officer of mine, that has no money; but if it could be followed *in forma pauperis*,[2] and when the legacy's recovered—

LAWYER. *Forma pauperis*, sir!

MANLEY. Ay, sir.

Several crossing the stage

LAWYER. Mr. Bumblecase, Mr. Bumblecase! a word with you.—Sir, I beg your pardon at present; I have a little business—

MANLY. Which is not *in forma pauperis*.
Exit Lawyer

FREEMAN. So, you have now found a way to be rid of people without quarrelling?

Enter Alderman

MANLY. But here's a city rogue will stick as hard upon us, as if I owed him money.

ALDERMAN. Captain, noble sir, I am yours heartily, d'ye see; why should you avoid your old friends?

MANLY. And why should you follow me? I owe you nothing.

ALDERMAN. Out of my hearty respects to you; for there is not a man in England—

MANLY. Thou wouldst save from hanging with the expense of a shilling only.

ALDERMAN. Nay, nay, but, captain, you are like enough to tell me—

---

[1] List of royalists whose property was proscribed by parliament during the Civil War and after.

[2] To sue *in forma pauperis* is to apply to the court for permission to proceed in a suit without paying costs because of poverty.

MANLY. Truth, which you won't care to hear; therefore you had better go talk with somebody else.

ALDERMAN. No, I know nobody can inform me better of some young wit, or spend-thrift, that has a good dipped[1] seat and estate in Middlesex, Hertfordshire, Essex, or Kent, any of these would serve my turn. Now, if you knew of such an one, and would but help—

MANLY. You to finish his ruin.

ALDERMAN. I'faith, you should have a snip—

MANLY. Of your nose, you thirty-in-the-hundred[2] rascal; would you make me your squire setter,[3] your bawd for manors?

(*Takes him by the nose*)

ALDERMAN. Oh!

FREEMAN. Hold, or here will be your third law-suit.

ALDERMAN. Gads-precious,[4] you hectoring person you, are you wild? I meant you no hurt, sir: I begin to think, as things go, land-security best, and have, for a convenient mortgage, some ten, fifteen, or twenty thousand pound by me.

MANLY. Then go lay it out upon an hospital, and take a mortgage of heaven, according to your city custom; for you think, by laying out a little money, to hook in that, too, hereafter. Do, I say, and keep the poor you've made by taking forfeitures, that heaven may not take yours.

ALDERMAN. No, to keep the cripples you make this war. This war spoils our trade.

MANLY. Damn your trade! 'tis the better for't.

ALDERMAN. What, will you speak against our trade?

MANLY. And dare you speak against the war, our trade?

ALDERMAN. (*Aside*) Well, he may be a convoy[5] of ships I am concerned in.—Come, captain, I will have a fair correspondency with you, say what you will.

MANLY. Then, prithee, be gone.

ALDERMAN. No, faith; prithee, captain, let's go drink a dish of laced coffee, and talk of the times. Come, I'll treat you; nay, you shall go, for I have no business here.

MANLY. But I have.

ALDERMAN. To pick up a man to give thee a dinner? Come, I'll do thy business for thee.

MANLY. Faith, now I think on't, so you may, as well as any man; for 'tis to pick up a man to be bound with me to one who expects city security for—

ALDERMAN. Nay, then your servant, captain; business must be done.

MANLY. Ay, if it can; but hark you, alderman, without you—

ALDERMAN. Business, sir, I say, must be done; and there's an officer of the treasury I have an affair with— *Exit Alderman*

MANLY. You see now what the mighty friendship of the world is; what all ceremony, embraces, and plentiful professions come to! You are no more to believe a professing friend than a threat'ning enemy; and as no man hurts you, that tells you he'll do you a mischief, no man, you see, is your servant, who says he is so. Why the devil, then, should a man be troubled with the flattery of knaves. if he be not a fool or cully; or with the fondness of fools, if he be not a knave or cheat?

FREEMAN. Only for his pleasure; for there is some in laughing at fools, and disappointing knaves.

MANLY. That's a pleasure, I think, would cost you too dear, as well as marrying your widow to disappoint her; but, for my part, I have no pleasure by 'em but in despising 'em, wheresoe'er I meet 'em; and then the pleasure of hoping so to be rid of 'em. But now my comfort is, I am not worth a shilling in the world, which all the world shall know; and then I'm sure I shall have none of 'em come near me.

FREEMAN. A very pretty comfort, which I think you pay too dear for.—But is the twenty pound gone since the morning?

MANLY. To my boat's crew.—Would you have the poor, honest, brave fellows want?

FREEMAN. Rather than you or I.

MANLY. Why, art thou without money, thou who art a friend to everybody?

FREEMAN. I ventured my last stake upon the squire to nick him of his mother; and cannot help you to a dinner, unless you will go dine with my lord—

MANLY. No, no; the ordinary[6] is too dear

---

[1] Mortgaged.
[2] To pay thirty on the hundred of a debt.
[3] Decoy for trusting squires.
[4] Shortened, corrupt form of: By God's precious wounds.
[5] I.e., captain of an armed ship sent to convoy merchant vessels to port.
[6] Tavern.

for me, where flattery must pay for my dinner. I am no herald, or poet.

FREEMAN. We'll go then to the bishop's—

MANLY. There you must flatter the old philosophy.[1] I cannot renounce my reason for a dinner.

FREEMAN. Why, then let's go to your alderman's.

MANLY. Hang him, rogue! that were not to dine; for he makes you drunk with lees of sack before dinner, to take away your stomach: and there you must call usury and extortion God's blessings, or the honest turning of the penny; hear him brag of the leather breeches in which he trotted first to town, and make a greater noise with his money in his parlor, than his cashiers do in his counting-house, without hopes of borrowing a shilling.

FREEMAN. Ay, a pox on't! 'tis like dining with the great gamesters; and when they fall to their common dessert, see the heaps of gold drawn on all hands, without going to twelve. Let us go to my Lady Goodly's.

MANLY. There, to flatter her looks, you must mistake her grandchildren for her own; praise her cook, that she may rail at him; and feed her dogs, not yourself.

FREEMAN. What d'ye think of eating with your lawyer, then?

MANLY. Eat with him! damn him! To hear him employ his barbarous eloquence in a reading[2] upon the two-and-thirty good bits in a shoulder of veal, and be forced yourself to praise the cold bribe-pie that stinks, and drink law-French wine as rough and harsh as his law-French. A pox on him! I'd rather dine in the Temple-rounds or walks,[3] with the knights without noses, or the knights of the post, who are honester fellows, and better company. But let us home and try our fortune; for I'll stay no longer here, for your damned widow.

FREEMAN. Well, let us go home then; for I must go for my damned widow, and look after my new damned charge. Three or four hundred year ago a man might have dined in this Hall.[4]

MANLY. But now the lawyer only here is fed; And, bully-like, by quarrels gets his bread.

Exeunt

ACT IV

SCENE I. MANLY's *Lodgings*

Enter MANLY *and* FIDELIA

MANLY. Well, there's success in thy face. Hast thou prevailed? say.

FIDELIA. As I could wish, sir.

MANLY. So; I told thee what thou wert fit for, and thou wouldst not believe me. Come, thank me for bringing thee acquainted with thy genius. Well, thou hast mollified her heart for me?

FIDELIA. No, sir, not so; but what's better.

MANLY. How? what's better!

FIDELIA. I shall harden your heart against her.

MANLY. Have a care, sir; my heart is too much in earnest to be fooled with, and my desire at height, and needs no delays to incite it. What, you are too good a pimp already, and know how to endear pleasure by withholding it? But leave off your page's bawdy-house tricks, sir, and tell me, will she be kind?

FIDELIA. Kinder than you could wish, sir.

MANLY. So, then: well, prithee, what said she?

FIDELIA. She said—

MANLY. What? thou'rt so tedious. Speak comfort to me; what?

FIDELIA. That of all things you were her aversion.

MANLY. How!

FIDELIA. That she would sooner take a bedfellow out of an hospital, and diseases into her arms, than you.

MANLY. What?

FIDELIA. That she would rather trust her honor with a dissolute debauched hector,[5] nay worse, with a finical baffled coward, all over loathsome with affectation of the fine gentleman.

MANLY. What's all this you say?

FIDELIA. Nay, that my offers of your love to her were more offensive, than when parents woo their virgin-daughters to the enjoyment of riches only; and that you were in all circumstances as nauseous to her as a husband on compulsion.

[1] The "old philosophy" may refer to the bishop's beliefs as opposed to the fashionable rationalism of the day or (less probably) to the bishop himself.
[2] Lecture.
[3] The Inns of Courts in Fleet Street occupied grounds formerly belonging to the Knights Templars.
[4] Westminster Hall had been formerly a royal banqueting place.
[5] Bully.

MANLY. Hold! I understand you not.
FIDELIA. (*Aside*) So, 'twill work, I see.
MANLY. Did you not tell me—
FIDELIA. She called you ten thousand ruffians.
MANLY. Hold, I say.
FIDELIA. Brutes—
MANLY. Hold.
FIDELIA. Sea-monsters—
MANLY. Damn your intelligence! Hear me a little now.
FIDELIA. Nay, surly coward she called you, too.
MANLY. Won't you hold yet? Hold, or—
FIDELIA. Nay, sir, pardon me; I could not but tell you she had the baseness, the injustice, to call you coward, sir; coward, coward, sir.
MANLY. Not yet?
FIDELIA. I've done.—Coward, sir.
MANLY. Did not you say, she was kinder than I could wish her?
FIDELIA. Yes, sir.
MANLY. How then?—O—I understand you now. At first she appeared in rage and disdain, the truest sign of a coming woman; but at last you prevailed, it seems: did you not?
FIDELIA. Yes, sir.
MANLY. So then, let's know that only; come, prithee, without delays. I'll kiss thee for that news beforehand.
FIDELIA. (*Aside*) So; the kiss I'm sure is welcome to me, whatsoe'er the news will be to you.
MANLY. Come, speak, my dear volunteer.
FIDELIA. (*Aside*) How welcome were that kind word too, if it were not for another woman's sake!
MANLY. What, won't you speak? You prevailed for me at last, you say?
FIDELIA. No, sir.
MANLY. No more of your fooling, sir. It will not agree with my impatience or temper.
FIDELIA. Then not to fool you, sir, I spoke to her for you, but prevailed for myself; she would not hear me when I spoke in your behalf, but bid me say what I would in my own, though she gave me no occasion, she was so coming, and so was kinder, sir, than you could wish; which I was only afraid to let you know, without some warning.
MANLY. How's this? Young man, you are of a lying age; but I must hear you out, and if —

FIDELIA. I would not abuse you, and cannot wrong her by any report of her, she is so wicked.
MANLY. How, wicked! had she the impudence, at the second sight of you only—
FIDELIA. Impudence, sir! oh, she has impudence enough to put a court out of countenance, and debauch a stews.
MANLY. Why, what said she?
FIDELIA. Her tongue, I confess, was silent; but her speaking eyes gloated such things, more immodest and lascivious than ravishers can act, or women under a confinement think.
MANLY. I know there are [those] whose eyes reflect more obscenity than the glasses in alcoves; but there are others who use a little art with their looks, to make 'em seem more beautiful, not more loving; which vain young fellows like you are apt to interpret in their own favor, and to the lady's wrong.
FIDELIA. Seldom, sir. Pray, have you a care of gloating eyes; for he that loves to gaze upon 'em, will find at last a thousand fools and cuckolds in 'em instead of cupids.
MANLY. Very well, sir.—But what, you had only eye-kindness from Olivia?
FIDELIA. I tell you again, sir, no woman sticks there; eye-promises of love they only keep; nay, they are contracts which make you sure of 'em. In short, sir, she, seeing me, with shame and amazement dumb, unactive, and resistless, threw her twisting arms about my neck, and smothered me with a thousand tasteless kisses. Believe me, sir, they were so to me.
MANLY. Why did you not avoid 'em then?
FIDELIA. I fenced [1] with her eager arms, as you did with the grapples of the enemy's fireship; and nothing but cutting 'em off could have freed me.
MANLY. Damned, damned woman, that could be so false and infamous! and damned, damned heart of mine, that cannot yet be false, though so infamous! What easy, tame, suffering, trampled things does that little god of talking cowards make of us! but—
FIDELIA. (*Aside*) So! it works, I find, as I expected.
MANLY. But she was false to me before, she told me so herself, and yet I could not quite believe it; but she was, so that her second falseness is a favor to me, not an injury, in revenging me upon the man that

[1] Parried.

wronged me first of her love. Her love!—a whore's, a witch's love!—But what, did she not kiss well, sir?—I'm sure I thought her lips—but I must not think of 'em more—but yet they are such I could still kiss—grow to—and then tear off with my teeth, grind 'em into mammocks,[1] and spit 'em into her cuckold's face.

FIDELIA. (*Aside*) Poor man, how uneasy is he! I have hardly the heart to give him so much pain, though withal I give him a cure, and to myself new life.

MANLY. But what, her kisses sure could not but warm you into desire at last, or a compliance with hers at least?

FIDELIA. Nay, more, I confess—

MANLY. What more? speak.

FIDELIA. All you could fear had passed between us, if I could have been made to wrong you, sir, in that nature.

MANLY. Could have been made! you lie, you did.

FIDELIA. Indeed, sir, 'twas impossible for me; besides, we were interrupted by a visit; but I confess, she would not let me stir till I promised to return to her again within this hour, as soon as it should be dark; by which time she would dispose of her visit, and her servants, and herself, for my reception, which I was fain to promise, to get from her.

MANLY. Ha!

FIDELIA. But if ever I go near her again, may you, sir, think me as false to you, as she is; hate and renounce me, as you ought to do her, and, I hope, will do now.

MANLY. Well, but now I think on't, you shall keep your word with your lady. What, a young fellow, and fail the first, nay, so tempting an assignation!

FIDELIA. How, sir?

MANLY. I say, you shall go to her when 'tis dark, and shall not disappoint her.

FIDELIA. I, sir! I should disappoint her more by going; for—

MANLY. How so?

FIDELIA. Her impudence and injustice to you will make me disappoint her love, loathe her.

MANLY. Come, you have my leave; and if you disgust her, I'll go with you, and act love, whilst you shall talk it only.

FIDELIA. You, sir! nay, then I'll never go near her. You act love, sir! You must but

[1] Small pieces.

act it indeed, after all I have said to you. Think of your honor, sir, love!—

MANLY. Well, call it revenge, and that is honorable. I'll be revenged on her; and thou shalt be my second.

FIDELIA. Not in a base action, sir, when you are your own enemy. O go not near her, sir; for heaven's sake, for your own, think not of it!

MANLY. How concerned you are! I thought I should catch you. What, you are my rival at last, and are in love with her yourself; and have spoken ill of her out of your love to her, not me; and therefore would not have me go to her!

FIDELIA. Heaven witness for me, 'tis because I love you only, I would not have you go to her.

MANLY. Come, come, the more I think on't, the more I'm satisfied you do love her. Those kisses, young man, I knew were irresistible; 'tis certain.

FIDELIA. There is nothing certain in the world, sir, but my truth and your courage.

MANLY. Your servant, sir. Besides, false and ungrateful as she has been to me, and though I may believe her hatred to me great as you report it, yet I cannot think you are so soon and at that rate beloved by her, though you may endeavor it.

FIDELIA. Nay, if that be all, and you doubt it still, sir, I will conduct you to her; and, unseen, your ears shall judge of her falseness, and my truth to you, if that will satisfy you.

MANLY. Yes, there is some satisfaction in being quite out of doubt; because 'tis that alone withholds us from the pleasure of revenge.

FIDELIA. Revenge! What revenge can you have, sir? Disdain is best revenged by scorn; and faithless love, by loving another and making her happy with the other's losings; which, if I might advise—

Enter FREEMAN

MANLY. Not a word more.

FREEMAN. What, are you talking of love yet, captain? I thought you had done with't.

MANLY. Why, what did you hear me say?

FREEMAN. Something imperfectly of love, I think.

MANLY. I was only wondering why fools, rascals, and desertless wretches, should still have the better of men of merit with all women, as much as with their own common mistress, Fortune.

FREEMAN. Because most women, like Fortune, are blind, seem to do all things in jest, and take pleasure in extravagant actions. Their love deserves neither thanks, or blame, for they cannot help it. 'Tis all sympathy; therefore, the noisy, the finical, the talkative, the cowardly, and effeminate, have the better of the brave, the reasonable, and man of honor; for they have no more reason in their love, or kindness, than Fortune herself.

MANLY. Yes, they have their reason. First, honor in a man they fear too much to love; and sense in a lover upbraids their want of it; and they hate anything that disturbs their admiration of themselves; but they are of that vain number, who had rather show their false generosity, in giving away profusely to worthless flatterers, than in paying just debts. And, in short, all women, like Fortune (as you say) and rewards, are lost by too much meriting.

FIDELIA. All women, sir! Sure there are some who have no other quarrel to a lover's merit, but that it begets their despair of him.

MANLY. Thou art young enough to be credulous; but we—

Enter 1ST SAILOR

1ST SAILOR. Here are now below, the scolding daggled gentlewoman, and that Major Old—Old—Fop, I think you call him.

FREEMAN. Oldfox:—prithee bid 'em come up, with your leave, captain, for now I can talk with her upon the square, if I shall not disturb you. [*Exit* SAILOR]

MANLY. No; for I'll begone. Come, volunteer.

FREEMAN. Nay, pray stay; the scene between us will not be so tedious to you as you think. Besides, you shall see how I have rigged my squire out, with the remains of my shipwrecked wardrobe; he is under your sea valet-de-chambre's hands, and by this time dressed, and will be worth your seeing. Stay, and I'll fetch my fool.

MANLY. No; you know I cannot easily laugh; besides, my volunteer and I have business abroad.

Exeunt MANLY [*and*] FIDELIA *on one side;* FREEMAN *on t'other.*

Enter MAJOR OLDFOX *and* WIDOW BLACKACRE

WIDOW. What, nobody here! Did not the fellow say he was within?

OLDFOX. Yes, lady; and he may be perhaps a little busy at present; but if you think the time long till he comes, (*unfolding papers*) I'll read you here some of the fruits of my leisure, the overflowings of my fancy and pen.—(*Aside*) To value me right, she must know my parts.—Come—

WIDOW. No, no; I have reading work enough of my own in my bag, I thank you.

OLDFOX. Ay, law, madam; but here is a poem, in blank verse, which I think a handsome declaration of one's passion.

WIDOW. Oh, if you talk of declarations, I'll show you one of the prettiest penned things, which I mended, too, myself, you must know.

OLDFOX. Nay, lady, if you have used yourself so much to the reading of harsh law, that you hate smooth poetry, here is a character for you, of—

WIDOW. A character! Nay, then I'll show you my bill in chancery here, that gives you such a character of my adversary, makes him as black—

OLDFOX. Pshaw! away, away, lady! But if you think the character too long, here is an epigram, not above twenty lines, upon a cruel lady, who decreed her servant should hang himself, to demonstrate his passion.

WIDOW. Decreed! if you talk of decreeing, I have such a decree here, drawn by the finest clerk—

OLDFOX. O lady, lady, all interruption, and no sense between us, as if we were lawyers at the bar! But I had forgot, Apollo and Littleton [1] never lodge in a head together. If you hate verses, I'll give you a cast of my politics in prose. 'Tis "A Letter to a Friend in the Country;" which is now the way of all such sober, solid persons as myself, when they have a mind to publish their disgust to the times; though perhaps, between you and I, they have no friend in the country. And sure a politic, serious person may as well have a feigned friend in the country to write to, as well as an idle poet a feigned mistress to write

---

[1] Sir Thomas Littleton (1402–81), author of Littleton's *Tenures* (1481), a classic of legal exposition, especially famous in an edition containing commentaries by Sir Edward Coke, first published in 1628.

to. And so here is my letter to a friend, or no friend, in the country, concerning the late conjuncture of affairs, in relation to coffee-houses; or "The Coffee-man's Case."

WIDOW. Nay, if your letter have a case in't, 'tis something; but first I'll read you a letter of mine to a friend in the country, called a letter of attorney.

Enter to them FREEMAN *and* JERRY BLACKACRE *in an old gaudy suit and red breeches of* FREEMAN'S

OLDFOX. (*Aside*) What, interruption still! O the plague of interruption! worse to an author than the plague of critics.

WIDOW. What's this I see? Jerry Blackacre, my minor, in red breeches! What, hast thou left the modest, seemly garb of gown and cap for this? and have I lost all my good inns-of-chancery breeding upon thee then? and thou wilt go a-breeding thyself from our inn of chancery and Westminster Hall, at coffee-houses, and ordinaries, play-houses, tennis-courts, and bawdy-houses?

JERRY. Ay, ay, what then? perhaps I will; but what's that to you? Here's my guardian and tutor now, forsooth, that I am out of your huckster's hands.

WIDOW. How! thou hast not chosen him for thy guardian yet?

JERRY. No, but he has chosen me for his charge, and that's all one; and I'll do anything he'll have me, and go all the world over with him; to ordinaries, and bawdy-houses, or anywhere else.

WIDOW. To ordinaries and bawdy-houses! Have a care, minor, thou wilt enfeeble there thy estate and body. Do not go to ordinaries and bawdy-houses, good Jerry.

JERRY. Why, how come you to know any ill by bawdy-houses? You never had any hurt by 'em, had you, forsooth? Pray hold yourself contented; if I do go where money and wenches are to be had, you may thank yourself; for you used me so unnaturally, you would never let me have a penny to go abroad with; nor so much as come near the garret where your maidens lay; nay, you would not so much as let me play at hotcockles[1] with 'em, nor have any recreation with 'em though one should have kissed you behind, you were so unnatural a mother, so you were.

FREEMAN. Ay, a very unnatural mother, faith, squire.

WIDOW. But, Jerry, consider thou art yet but a minor; however, if thou wilt go home with me again, and be a good child, thou shalt see—

FREEMAN. Madam, I must have a better care of my heir under age, than so; I would sooner trust him alone with a stale waiting-woman and a parson, than with his widow-mother and her lover or lawyer.

WIDOW. Why, thou villain, part mother and minor! rob me of my child and my writings! but thou shalt find there's law; and as in the case of ravishment of guard[2]!—Westminster the Second.

OLDFOX. Young gentleman, squire, pray be ruled by your mother and your friends.

JERRY. Yes, I'll be ruled by my friends, therefore not by my mother, so I won't. I'll choose him for my guardian till I am of age; nay, maybe, for as long as I live.

WIDOW. Wilt thou so, thou wretch? And when thou'rt of age, thou wilt sign, seal, and deliver too, wilt thou?

JERRY. Yes, marry will I, if you go there too.

WIDOW. O do not squeeze wax,[3] son; rather go to ordinaries and bawdy-houses, than squeeze wax. If thou dost that, farewell the goodly manor of Blackacre, with all its woods, underwoods, and appurtenances[4] whatever! Oh, oh! (*Weeps.*)

FREEMAN. Come, madam, in short, you see I am resolved to have a share in the estate, yours or your son's; if I cannot get you, I'll keep him, who is less coy, you find; but if you would have your son again, you must take me too. Peace or war? love or law? You see my hostage is in my hand. I'm in possession.

WIDOW. Nay, if one of us must be ruined, e'en let it be him. By my body, a good one! Did you ever know yet a widow marry or not marry for the sake of her child? I'd have you to know, sir, I shall be hard enough for you both yet, without marrying you, if Jerry won't be ruled by me. What say you, booby, will you be ruled? speak.

JERRY. Let one alone, can't you?

---

[1] A country game, in which one player lies face downward and tries to guess who strikes his back.

[2] Properly, *de gard*—the illegal taking away of a ward.

[3] Slang term, meaning to affix seals to legal papers, and used here with an implication of recklessness.

[4] Legal terms descriptive of an estate.

WIDOW. Wilt thou choose him for guardian, whom I refuse for husband?

JERRY. Ay, to choose, I thank you.

WIDOW. And are all my hopes frustrated? Shall I never hear thee put cases again to John the butler, or our vicar? never see thee amble the circuit with the judges; and hear thee, in our town-hall, louder than the crier?

JERRY. No, for I have taken my leave of lawyering and pettifogging.

WIDOW. Pettifogging! thou profane villain, hast thou so? Pettifogging!—then you shall take your leave of me, and your estate too; thou shalt be an alien to me and it forever. Pettifogging!

JERRY. Oh, but if you go there too, mother, we have the deeds and settlements, I thank you. Would you cheat me of my estate, i'fac?

WIDOW. No, no, I will not cheat your little brother Bob; for thou wert not born in wedlock.

FREEMAN. How's that?

JERRY. How? What quirk has she got in her head now?

WIDOW. I say thou canst not, shalt not inherit the Blackacres estate.

JERRY. Why? Why, forsooth? What d'ye mean, if you go there to[o]?

WIDOW. Thou art but my base[1] child; and according to the law, canst not inherit it. Nay, thou art not so much as bastard eigne.[2]

JERRY. What, what? Am I then the son of a whore, mother?

WIDOW. The law says—

FREEMAN. Madam, we know what the law says; but have a care what you say. Do not let your passion to ruin your son ruin your reputation.

WIDOW. Hang reputation, sir! am not I a widow? have no husband, nor intend to have any? Nor would you, I suppose, now have me for a wife. So I think now I'm revenged on my son and you, without marrying, as I told you.

FREEMAN. But consider, madam.

JERRY. What, have you no shame left in you, mother?

WIDOW. (*Aside to* OLDFOX) Wonder not at it, major. 'Tis often the poor pressed widow's case, to give up her honor to save her jointure; and seem to be a light woman, rather than marry, as some young men, they say, pretend to have the filthy disease, and lose their credit with most women, to avoid the importunities of some.

FREEMAN. But one word with you, madam.

WIDOW. No, no, sir. Come, major, let us make haste now to the Prerogative-court.[3]

OLDFOX. But, lady, if what you say be true, will you stigmatize your reputation on record? and if it be not true, how will you prove it?

WIDOW. Pshaw! I can prove anything; and for my reputation, know, major, a wise woman will no more value her reputation in disinheriting a rebellious son of a good estate, than she would in getting him, to inherit an estate.

Exeunt WIDOW [BLACKACRE] *and* [MAJOR] OLDFOX

FREEMAN. Madam!—We must not let her go so, squire.

JERRY. Nay, the devil can't stop her though, if she has a mind to't. But come, bully-guardian, we'll go and advise with three attorneys, two proctors, two solicitors, and a shrewd man of Whitefriars,[4] neither attorney, proctor, or solicitor, but as pure a pimp to the law as any of 'em; and sure all they will be hard enough for her, for I fear, bully-guardian, you are too good a joker to have any law in your head.

FREEMAN. Thou'rt in the right on't, squire; I understand no law; especially that against bastards, since I'm sure the custom is against that law, and more people get estates by being so, than lose 'em. *Exeunt*

[SCENE II.]

The scene changes to OLIVIA'S *Lodging*

Enter Lord PLAUSIBLE *and* Boy *with a candle*

LORD PLAUSIBLE. Little gentleman, your most obedient, faithful, humble servant. Where, I beseech you, is that divine person, your noble lady?

BOY. Gone out, my lord; but commanded me to give you this letter.

(*Gives him a letter*)

Enter to him NOVEL

---

[1] Bastard.
[2] Eldest son born out of wedlock.
[3] A court formerly held by either of the two English archbishops.
[4] Shyster lawyer. On the peculiar position of Whitefriars in English legal topography, see Shadwell's *The Squire of Alsatia*.

Lord Plausible. (*Aside*) Which he must not observe.— (*Puts it up*)

Novel. Hey, boy, where is thy lady?

Boy. Gone out, sir; but I must beg a word with you. (*Gives him a letter, and exit*)

Novel. For me? So.—(*Puts up the letter*) Servant, servant, my lord; you see the lady knew of your coming, for she is gone out.

Lord Plausible. Sir, I humbly beseech you not to censure the lady's good breeding. She has reason to use more liberty with me than with any other man.

Novel. How, viscount, how?

Lord Plausible. Nay, I humbly beseech you, be not in choler; where there is most love, there may be most freedom.

Novel. Nay, then 'tis time to come to an eclaircissement with you, and to tell you, you must think no more of this lady's love.

Lord Plausible. Why, under correction, dear sir?

Novel. There are reasons, reasons, viscount.

Lord Plausible. What, I beseech you, noble sir?

Novel. Prithee, prithee, be not impertinent, my lord; some of you lords are such conceited, well-assured, impertinent rogues!

Lord Plausible. And you noble wits are so full of shamming and drolling, one knows not where to have you seriously.

Novel. Well, you shall find me in bed with this lady one of these days.

Lord Plausible. Nay, I beseech you, spare the lady's honor; for hers and mine will be all one shortly.

Novel. Prithee, my lord, be not an ass. Dost thou think to get her from me? I have had such encouragements—

Lord Plausible. I have not been thought unworthy of 'em.

Novel. What, not like mine! Come to an eclaircissement, as I said.

Lord Plausible. Why, seriously then, she has told me, viscountess sounded prettily.

Novel. And me, that Novel was a name she would sooner change hers for than for any title in England.

Lord Plausible. She has commended the softness and respectfulness of my behavior.

Novel. She has praised the briskness of my raillery, of all things, man.

Lord Plausible. The sleepiness of my eyes she liked.

Novel. Sleepiness! dulness, dulness. But the fierceness of mine she adored.

Lord Plausible. The brightness of my hair she liked.

Novel. The brightness! no, the greasiness, I warrant. But the blackness and lustre of mine she admires.

Lord Plausible. The gentleness of my smile.

Novel. The subtilty of my leer.

Lord Plausible. The clearness of my complexion.

Novel. The redness of my lips.

Lord Plausible. The whiteness of my teeth.

Novel. My jaunty way of picking them.

Lord Plausible. The sweetness of my breath.

Novel. Ha, ha!—Nay, then she abused you, 'tis plain; for you know what Manly said:—the sweetness of your pulvillio she might mean; but for your breath! ha, ha, ha! Your breath is such, man, that nothing but tobacco can perfume; and your complexion nothing could mend but the small-pox.

Lord Plausible. Well, sir, you may please to be merry; but, to put you out of all doubt, sir, she has received some jewels from me of value.

Novel. And presents from me; besides what I presented her jauntily, by way of ombre, of three or four hundred pound value, which I'm sure are the earnest-pence for our love-bargain.

Lord Plausible. Nay, then, sir, with your favor, and to make an end of all your hopes, look you there, sir, she has writ to me—

Novel. How! how! well, well, and so she has to me; look you there—

([*They*] *deliver to each other their letters*)

Lord Plausible. What's here?

Novel. How's this?

(*Reads out*)—"My dear lord,—You'll excuse me for breaking my word with you, since 'twas to oblige, not offend you; for I am only gone abroad but to disappoint Novel, and meet you in the drawing-room[1]; where I expect you with as much impatience as when I used to suffer Novel's visits—the most impertinent fop that ever affected the name of a wit, therefore not capable, I hope, to give you

[1] See note 2, p. 914.

jealousy; for, for your sake alone, you saw I renounced an old lover, and will do all the world. Burn the letter, but lay up the kindness of it in your heart, with your—Olivia." Very fine! but pray let's see mine.

LORD PLAUSIBLE. I understand it not; but sure she cannot think so of me.

NOVEL. (*Reads the other letter*) Humh! hah!—"meet—for your sake"—umh—"quitted an old lover—world—burn—in your heart—with your—Olivia." Just the same, the names only altered.

LORD PLAUSIBLE. Surely there must be some mistake, or somebody has abused her and us.

NOVEL. Yes, you are abused, no doubt on't, my lord; but I'll to Whitehall, and see.

LORD PLAUSIBLE. And I, where I shall find you are abused.

NOVEL. Where, if it be so, for our comfort, we cannot fail of meeting with fellow-sufferers enough; for, as Freeman said of another, she stands in the drawing-room, like the glass, ready for all comers, to set their gallantry by her: and, like the glass too, lets no man go from her unsatisfied with himself.

Exeunt ambo

Enter OLIVIA *and* Boy

OLIVIA. Both here, and just gone?

BOY. Yes, madam.

OLIVIA. But are you sure neither saw you deliver the other a letter?

BOY. Yes, yes, madam, I am very sure.

OLIVIA. Go then to the Old Exchange,[1] to Westminster, Holborn, and all the other places I told you of; I shall not need you these two hours: begone, and take the candle with you, and be sure you leave word again below, I am gone out, to all that ask.

BOY. Yes, madam. *Exit*

OLIVIA. And my new lover will not ask, I'm sure; he has his lesson, and cannot miss me here, though in the dark, which I have purposely designed, as a remedy against my blushing gallant's modesty; for young lovers, like gamecocks, are made bolder by being kept without light.

Enter her husband VERNISH, *as from a journey*

VERNISH. (*Softly*) Where is she? Darkness everywhere!

[1] Gresham's, or the Royal, Exchange.

OLIVIA. What! come before your time? My soul! my life! your haste has augmented your kindness; and let me thank you for it thus, and thus—(*embracing and kissing him*). And though, my soul, the little time since you left me has seemed an age to my impatience, sure it is yet but seven—

VERNISH. How! who's that you expected after seven?

OLIVIA. [*Aside*] Ha! my husband returned! and have I been throwing away so many kind kisses on my husband, and wronged my lover already?

VERNISH. Speak, I say, who was't you expected after seven?

OLIVIA. (*Aside*) What shall I say?—oh—Why 'tis but seven days, is it, dearest, since you went out of town? and I expected you not so soon.

VERNISH. No, sure, 'tis but five days since I left you.

OLIVIA. Pardon my impatience, dearest, I thought 'em seven at least.

VERNISH. Nay, then—

OLIVIA. But, my life, you shall never stay half so long from me again; you shan't indeed, by this kiss you shan't.

VERNISH. No, no; but why alone in the dark?

OLIVIA. Blame not my melancholy in your absence.—But, my soul, since you went, I have strange news to tell you: Manly is returned.

VERNISH. Manly returned! Fortune forbid!

OLIVIA. Met with the Dutch in the channel, fought, sunk his ship, and all he carried with him. He was here with me yesterday.

VERNISH. And did you own our marriage to him?

OLIVIA. I told him I was married to put an end to his love and my trouble; but to whom, is yet a secret kept from him and all the world. And I have used him so scurvily, his great spirit will ne'er return to reason it farther with me. I have sent him to sea again, I warrant.

VERNISH. 'Twas bravely done. And sure he will now hate the shore more than ever, after so great a disappointment. Be you sure only to keep a while our great secret, till he be gone; in the mean time, I'll lead the easy, honest fool by the nose, as I used to do; and whilst he stays, rail with him at thee; and when he's gone, laugh with thee at him.

But have you his cabinet of jewels safe? Part not with a seed-pearl to him, to keep him from starving.

OLIVIA. Nor from hanging.

VERNISH. He cannot recover 'em; and, I think, will scorn to beg 'em again.

OLIVIA. But, my life, have you taken the thousand guineas he left in my name out of the goldsmith's [1] hands?

VERNISH. Ay, ay; they are removed to another goldsmith's.

OLIVIA. Ay, but, my soul, you had best have a care he find not where the money is; for his present wants, as I'm informed, are such as will make him inquisitive enough.

VERNISH. You say true, and he knows the man, too; but I'll remove it to-morrow.

OLIVIA. To-morrow! O do not stay till to-morrow; go to-night, immediately.

VERNISH. Now I think on't, you advise well, and I will go presently.

OLIVIA. Presently! instantly! I will not let you stay a jot.

VERNISH. I will then, though I return not home till twelve.

OLIVIA. Nay, though not till morning, with all my heart. Go, dearest; I am impatient till you are gone.—(*Thrusts him out*) So, I have at once now brought about those two grateful businesses which all prudent women do together, secured money and pleasure; and now all interruptions of the last are removed. Go, husband, and come up, friend; just the buckets in the well; the absence of one brings the other; but I hope, like them too, they will not meet in the way, jostle, and clash together.

Enter FIDELIA *and* MANLY, *treading softly and staying behind at some distance*

So, are you come? (but not the husband-bucket, I hope, again).—(*Softly*) Who's there? my dearest?

FIDELIA. My life—

OLIVIA. Right, right.—Where are thy lips? Here, take the dumb and best welcomes, kisses and embraces; 'tis not a time for idle words. In a duel of love, as in others, parleying shows basely. Come, we are alone; and now the word is only satisfaction, and defend not thyself.

MANLY. (*Aside*) How's this? Wuh, she makes love like a devil in a play; and in this

[1] The goldsmith of the period also acted as a banker.

darkness, which conceals her angel's face, if I were apt to be afraid, I should think her a devil.

OLIVIA. (FIDELIA *avoiding her*) What, you traverse ground,[2] young gentleman!

FIDELIA. I take breath only.

MANLY. (*Aside*) Good Heavens! how was I deceived!

OLIVIA. Nay, you are a coward; what, are you afraid of the fierceness of my love?

FIDELIA. Yes, madam, lest its violence might presage its change; and I must needs be afraid you would leave me quickly, who could desert so brave a gentleman as Manly.

OLIVIA. Oh, name not his name! for in a time of stolen joys, as this is, the filthy name of husband were not a more allaying sound.

MANLY. (*Aside*) There's some comfort yet.

FIDELIA. But did you not love him?

OLIVIA. Never! How could you think it?

FIDELIA. Because he thought it, who is a man of that sense, nice discerning, and diffidency, that I should think it hard to deceive him.

OLIVIA. No; he that distrusts most the world, trusts most to himself, and is but the more easily deceived, because he thinks he can't be deceived. His cunning is like the coward's sword, by which he is oft'ner worsted than defended.

FIDELIA. Yet, sure, you used no common art to deceive him.

OLIVIA. I knew he loved his own singular moroseness so well, as to dote upon any copy of it; wherefore I feigned an hatred to the world, too, that he might love me in earnest; but, if it had been hard to deceive him, I'm sure 'twere much harder to love him. A dogged, ill-mannered—

FIDELIA. (*Aside to* MANLY) D'ye hear her, sir? pray, hear her.

OLIVIA.—surly, untractable, snarling brute! He! a mastiff dog were as fit a thing to make a gallant of.

MANLY. (*Aside*) Ay, a goat, or monkey, were fitter for thee.

FIDELIA. I must confess, for my part, though my rival, I cannot but say he has a manly handsomeness in's face and mien.

OLIVIA. So has a Saracen in the sign.[3]

FIDELIA. Is proper, and well made.

OLIVIA. As a drayman.

[2] To shift from side to side in fencing.
[3] I.e., in the sign of the Saracen's Head tavern.

FIDELIA. Has wit.
OLIVIA. He rails at all mankind.
FIDELIA. And undoubted courage.
OLIVIA. Like the hangman's; can murder a man when his hands are tied. He has cruelty, indeed; which is no more courage, than his railing is wit.
MANLY. (Aside) Thus women, and men like women, are too hard for us, when they think we do not hear 'em; and reputation, like other mistresses, is never true to a man in his absence.
FIDELIA. He is—
OLIVIA. Prithee, no more of him; I thought I had satisfied you enough before that he could never be a rival for you to apprehend; and you need not be more assured of my aversion to him, but by the last testimony of my love to you, which I am ready to give you. Come, my soul, this way— (Pulls FIDELIA)
FIDELIA. But, madam, what could make you dissemble love to him, when 'twas so hard a thing for you, and flatter his love to you?
OLIVIA. That which makes all the world flatter and dissemble, 'twas his money. I had a real passion for that. Yet I loved not that so well, as for it to take him; for, as soon as I had his money, I hastened his departure, like a wife, who, when she has made the most of a dying husband's breath, pulls away the pillow.
MANLY. [Aside] Damned money! its master's potent rival still; and like a saucy pimp, corrupts, itself, the mistress it procures for us.
OLIVIA. But I did not think with you, my life, to pass my time in talking. Come hither, come; yet stay, till I have locked a door in the other room, that might chance to let us in some interruption; which reciting poets or losing gamesters fear not more than I at this time do.   Exit OLIVIA
FIDELIA. Well, I hope you are now satisfied, sir, and will be gone, to think of your revenge?
MANLY. No, I am not satisfied, and must stay to be revenged.
FIDELIA. How, sir? You'll use no violence to her, I hope, and forfeit your own life, to take away hers? That were no revenge.
MANLY. No, no, you need not fear: my revenge shall only be upon her honor, not her life.
FIDELIA How, sir? her honor? O heavens! consider, sir, she has no honor. D'ye call that revenge? Can you think of such a thing? But reflect, sir, how she hates and loathes you.
MANLY. Yes, so much she hates me, that it would be a revenge sufficient to make her accessary to my pleasure, and then let her know it.
FIDELIA. No, sir, no; to be revenged on her now, were to disappoint her. Pray, sir, let us begone.   (Pulls MANLY)
MANLY. Hold off! What, you are my rival then! and therefore you shall stay, and keep the door for me, whilst I go in for you; but when I'm gone, if you dare to stir off from this very board, or breathe the least murmuring accent, I'll cut her throat first; and if you love her, you will not venture her life.—Nay, then I'll cut your throat too; and I know you love your own life at least.
FIDELIA. But, sir; good sir!
MANLY. Not a word more, lest I begin my revenge on her by killing you.
FIDELIA. But are you sure 'tis revenge that makes you do this? how can it be?
MANLY. Whist! [1]
FIDELIA. 'Tis a strange revenge, indeed.
MANLY. If you make me stay, I shall keep my word, and begin with you. No more.
    Exit MANLY, at the same door OLIVIA went

Manet FIDELIA

FIDELIA. O heav'ns! is there not punishment enough
In loving well, if you will have't a crime,
But you must add fresh torments daily to't,
And punish us like peevish rivals still,
Because we fain would find a heaven here?
But did there never any love like me,
That untried tortures, you must find me out?
Others, at worst, you force to kill themselves;
But I must be self-murd'ress of my love,
Yet will not grant me pow'r to end my life,
My cruel life; for when a lover's hopes
Are dead and gone, life is unmerciful.
    (*Sits down and weeps*)

Enter MANLY *to her*

MANLY. [*Aside*] I have thought better on't; I must not discover myself now I am without witnesses; for if I barely should publish it, she would deny it with as much impudence as

[1] Keep still.

she would act it again with this young fellow here.—Where are you?

FIDELIA. Here—oh—now I suppose we may be gone.

MANLY. I will, but not you; you must stay and act the second part of a lover, that is, talk kindness to her.

FIDELIA. Not I, sir.

MANLY. No disputing, sir, you must; 'tis necessary to my design of coming again to-morrow night.

FIDELIA. What, can you come again then hither?

MANLY. Yes; and you must make the appointment, and an apology for your leaving her so soon; for I have said not a word to her; but have kept your counsel, as I expect you should do mine. Do this faithfully, and I promise you here, you shall run my fortune still, and we will never part as long as we live; but if you do not do it, expect not to live.

FIDELIA. 'Tis hard, sir; but such a consideration will make it easier. You won't forget your promise, sir?

MANLY. No, by heav'ns! But I hear her coming. *Exit*

Enter OLIVIA *to* FIDELIA

OLIVIA. Where is my life? Run from me already! You do not love me, dearest; nay, you are angry with me, for you would not so much as speak a kind word to me within. What was the reason?

FIDELIA. I was transported too much.

OLIVIA. That's kind; but come, my soul, what make you here? Let us go in again; we may be surprised in this room, 'tis so near the stairs.

FIDELIA. No, we shall hear the better here, if anybody should come up.

OLIVIA. Nay, I assure you, we shall be secure enough within: come, come—

FIDELIA. I am sick, and troubled with a sudden dizziness; cannot stir yet.

OLIVIA. Come, I have spirits within.

FIDELIA. Oh!—don't you hear a noise, madam?

OLIVIA. No, no, there is none; come, come. (*Pulls her*)

FIDELIA. Indeed there is; and I love you so much, I must have a care of your honor, if you wo' not, and go; but to come to you to-morrow night, if you please.

OLIVIA. With all my soul; but you must not go yet; come, prithee.

FIDELIA. Oh!—I'm now sicker, and am afraid of one of my fits.

OLIVIA. What fits?

FIDELIA. Of the falling sickness; and I lie generally an hour in a trance; therefore pray consider your honor for the sake of my love, and let me go, that I may return to you often.

OLIVIA. But will you be sure then to come to-morrow night?

FIDELIA. Yes.

OLIVIA. Swear.

FIDELIA. By our past kindness!

OLIVIA. Well, go your ways then, if you will, you naughty creature, you.—(*Exit* FIDELIA) These young lovers, with their fears and modesty, make themselves as bad as old ones to us; and I apprehend their bashfulness more than their tattling.

FIDELIA *returns*

FIDELIA. O madam, we're undone! There was a gentleman upon the stairs, coming up with a candle, which made me retire. Look you, here he comes!

Enter VERNISH, *and his* MAN *with a light*

OLIVIA. How! my husband! Oh, undone indeed! This way. *Exit*

VERNISH. Ha! You shall not 'scape me so, sir. (*Stops* FIDELIA)

FIDELIA. (*Aside*) O heav'ns! more fears, plagues, and torments yet in store!

VERNISH. Come, sir, I guess what your business was here; but this must be your business now. Draw! (*Draws*)

FIDELIA. Sir—

VERNISH. No expostulations; I shall not care to hear of't. Draw!

FIDELIA. Good sir!

VERNISH. How, you rascal! not courage to draw, yet durst do me the greatest injury in the world? Thy cowardice shall not save thy life. (*Offers to run at* FIDELIA)

FIDELIA. O hold, sir, and send but your servant down, and I'll satisfy you, sir, I could not injure you as you imagine.

VERNISH. Leave the light and begone.— *Exit* SERVANT
Now, quickly, sir, what you've to say, or—

FIDELIA. I am a woman, sir, a very unfortunate woman.

VERNISH. How! a very handsome woman, I'm sure then. Here are witnesses of't too, I confess—(*Pulls off her peruke and feels her breasts*)—(*Aside*) Well, I'm glad to find the tables turned, my wife in more danger of cuckolding than I was.

FIDELIA. Now, sir, I hope you are so much a man of honor, as to let me go, now I have satisfied you, sir.

VERNISH. When you have satisfied me, madam, I will.

FIDELIA. I hope, sir, you are too much a gentleman to urge those secrets from a woman which concern her honor. You may guess my misfortune to be love by my disguise; but a pair of breeches could not wrong you, sir.

VERNISH. I may believe love has changed your outside, which could not wrong me; but why did my wife run away?

FIDELIA. I know not, sir; perhaps because she would not be forced to discover me to you, or to guide me from your suspicions, that you might not discover me yourself; which ungentlemanlike curiosity I hope you will cease to have, and let me go.

VERNISH. Well, madam, if I must not know who you are, 'twill suffice for me only to know certainly what you are; which you must not deny me. Come, there is a bed within, the proper rack for lovers; and if you are a woman, there you can keep no secrets; you'll tell me there all, unasked. Come. (*Pulls her*)

FIDELIA. Oh! what d'ye mean? Help! oh!—

VERNISH. I'll show you; but 'tis in vain to cry out. No one dares help you, for I am lord here.

FIDELIA. Tyrant here!—But if you are master of this house, which I have taken for a sanctuary, do not violate it yourself.

VERNISH. No, I'll preserve you here, and nothing shall hurt you, and will be as true to you as your disguise; but you must trust me then. Come, come.

FIDELIA. Rather than you shall drag me to a [deed][1] so horrid and so shameful, I'll die here a thousand deaths.—But you do not look like a ravisher, sir.

VERNISH. Nor you like one would put me to't; but if you will—

FIDELIA. Oh! oh! help! help!—

Enter SERVANT

VERNISH. You saucy rascal, how durst you come in, when you heard a woman squeak?

[1] The first edition has *death*.

That should have been your cue to shut the door.

SERVANT. I come, sir, to let you know, the alderman coming home immediately after you were at his house, has sent his cashier with the money, according to your note.

VERNISH. Damn his money! Money never came to any, sure, unseasonably, till now. Bid him stay.

SERVANT. He says, he cannot a moment.

VERNISH. Receive it you, then.

SERVANT. He says, he must have your receipt for it. He is in haste, for I hear him coming up, sir.

VERNISH. Damn him! Help me in here then with this dishonorer of my family.

FIDELIA. Oh! oh!

SERVANT. You say she is a woman, sir.

VERNISH. No matter, sir: must you prate?

FIDELIA. Oh heav'ns! is there—

(*They thrust her in, and lock the door*)

VERNISH. Stay there, my prisoner; you have a short reprieve.

I'll fetch the gold, and that she can't resist, For with a full hand 'tis we ravish best.

Exeunt

ACT V

SCENE I. ELIZA'S *Lodgings*

Enter OLIVIA *and* ELIZA

OLIVIA. Ah, cousin, nothing troubles me, but that I have given the malicious world its revenge, and reason now to talk as freely of me as I used to do of it.

ELIZA. Faith, then, let not that trouble you; for, to be plain, cousin, the world cannot talk worse of you than it did before.

OLIVIA. How, cousin? I'd have you to know, before this *faux pas*, this trip of mine, the world could not talk of me.

ELIZA. Only that you mind other people's actions so much that you take no care of your own, but to hide 'em; that, like a thief, because you know yourself most guilty, you impeach your fellow-criminals first, to clear yourself.

OLIVIA. O wicked world!

ELIZA. That you pretend an aversion to all mankind in public, only that their wives and mistresses may not be jealous, and hinder you of their conversation in private.

OLIVIA. Base world!

ELIZA. That abroad you fasten quarrels upon innocent men for talking of you, only to bring 'em to ask your pardon at home, and to become dear friends with them, who were hardly your acquaintance before.

OLIVIA. Abominable world!

ELIZA. That you condemn the obscenity of modern plays, only that you may not be censured for never missing the most obscene of the old ones.

OLIVIA. Damned world!

ELIZA. That you deface the nudities of pictures, and little statues, only because they are not real.[1]

OLIVIA. Oh, fie, fie, fie! hideous, hideous, cousin! the obscenity of their censures makes me blush!

ELIZA. The truth of 'em, the naughty world would say now.

Enter LETTICE *hastily*

LETTICE. O, madam! here is that gentleman coming up who now, you say, is my master.

OLIVIA. O, cousin! whither shall I run? protect me, or—

(OLIVIA *runs away, and stands at a distance*)

Enter VERNISH

VERNISH. Nay, nay, come—

OLIVIA. Oh, sir, forgive me!

VERNISH. Yes, yes, I can forgive you being alone in the dark with a woman in man's clothes; but have a care of a man in woman's clothes.

OLIVIA. (*Aside*) What does he mean? He dissembles, only to get me into his power; or has my dear friend made him believe he was a woman? My husband may be deceived by him, but I'm sure I was not.

VERNISH. Come, come, you need not have lain out of your house for this; but perhaps you were afraid, when I was warm with suspicions, you must have discovered who she was.—And, prithee, may I not know it?

OLIVIA. She was—(*Aside*) I hope he has been deceived; and since my lover has played the card, I must not renounce.[2]

VERNISH. Come, what's the matter with thee? If I must not know who she is, I'm satisfied without. Come hither.

OLIVIA. Sure, you do know her; she has told you herself, I suppose.

VERNISH. No, I might have known her better but that I was interrupted by the goldsmith, you know, and was forced to lock her into your chamber, to keep her from his sight; but, when I returned, I found she was got away by tying the window-curtains to the balcony, by which she slid down into the street; for, you must know, I jested with her, and made her believe I'd ravish her; which she apprehended, it seems, in earnest.

OLIVIA. Then she got from you?

VERNISH. Yes.

OLIVIA. And is quite gone?

VERNISH. Yes.

OLIVIA. I'm glad on't—otherwise you had ravished her, sir? But how darest thou go so far, as to make her believe you would ravish her? Let me understand that, sir. What! there's guilt in your face, you blush, too; nay, then you did ravish her, you did, you base fellow! What, ravish a woman in the first month of our marriage! 'Tis a double injury to me, thou base, ungrateful man! wrong my bed already, villain! I could tear out those false eyes, barbarous, unworthy wretch!

ELIZA. So, so!—

VERNISH. Prithee hear, my dear.

OLIVIA. I will never hear you, my plague, my torment!

VERNISH. I swear—prithee, hear me.

OLIVIA. I have heard already too many of your false oaths and vows, especially your last in the church. O wicked man! and wretched woman that I was! I wish I had then sunk down into a grave, rather than to have given you my hand, to be led to your loathsome bed. Oh—oh— (*Seems to weep*)

VERNISH. So, very fine! just a marriage-quarrel! which, though it generally begins by the wife's fault, yet, in the conclusion, it becomes the husband's; and whosoever offends at first, he only is sure to ask pardon at last. My dear—

OLIVIA. My devil!—

VERNISH. Come, prithee be appeased, and go home; I have bespoken our supper betimes, for I could not eat till I found you. Go, I'll give you all kind of satisfactions; and one, which uses to be a reconciling one, two hundred of those guineas I received last night, to do what you will with.

---

[1] The dialogue closely follows a passage in *Le Misanthrope*, Act III, scene v.
[2] Revoke.

OLIVIA. What, would you pay me for being your bawd?

VERNISH. Nay, prithee no more; go, and I'll thoroughly satisfy you when I come home; and then, too, we will have a fit of laughter at Manly, whom I am going to find at the Cock in Bow-street, where I hear he dined. Go, dearest, go home.

ELIZA. (*Aside*) A very pretty turn, indeed, this!

VERNISH. Now, cousin, since by my wife I have that honor and privilege of calling you so, I have something to beg of you, too; which is, not to take notice of our marriage to any whatever yet a while, for some reasons very important to me; and next, that you will do my wife the honor to go home with her; and me the favor to use that power you have with her in our reconcilement.

ELIZA. That, I dare promise, sir, will be no hard matter. Your servant.

(*Exit* VERNISH)

—Well, cousin, this, I confess, was reasonable hypocrisy; you were the better for't.

OLIVIA. What hypocrisy?

ELIZA. Why, this last deceit of your husband was lawful, since in your own defence.

OLIVIA. What deceit? I'd have you to know I never deceived my husband.

ELIZA. You do not understand me, sure; I say, this was an honest come-off, and a good one; but 'twas a sign your gallant had had enough of your conversation, since he could so dext'rously cheat your husband in passing for a woman.

OLIVIA. What d'ye mean, once more, with my gallant, and passing for a woman?

ELIZA. What do you mean? You see your husband took him for a woman.

OLIVIA. Whom?

ELIZA. Heyday! Why, the man he found you with, for whom last night you were so much afraid; and who, you told me—

OLIVIA. Lord, you rave sure!

ELIZA. Why, did not you tell me last night—

OLIVIA. I know not what I might tell you last night, in a fright.

ELIZIA. Ay, what was that fright for? for a woman? Besides, were you not afraid to see your husband just now? I warrant, only for having been found with a woman! Nay, did you not just now, too, own your false step, or trip, as you called it, which was with a woman too? Fie, this fooling is so insipid, 'tis offensive!

OLIVIA. And fooling with my honor will be more offensive. Did you not hear my husband say he found me with a woman in man's clothes? And d'ye think he does not know a man from a woman?

ELIZA. Not so well, I'm sure, as you do; therefore I'd rather take your word.

OLIVIA. What, you grow scurrilous, and are, I find, more censorious than the world! I must have a care of you, I see.

ELIZA. No, you need not fear yet, I'll keep your secret.

OLIVIA. My secret! I'd have you to know, I have no need of confidants, though you value yourself upon being a good one.

ELIZA. O admirable confidence! You show more in denying your wickedness, than other people in glorying in't.

OLIVIA. Confidence, to me! to me such language! nay, then I'll never see your face again.—(*Aside*) I'll quarrel with her, that people may never believe I was in her power; but take for malice all the truth she may speak against me.—Lettice, where are you? Let us be gone from this censorious, ill woman.

ELIZA. (*Aside*) Nay, thou shalt stay a little, to damn thyself quite.—One word first, pray, madam; can you swear that whom your husband found you with—

OLIVIA. Swear! ay, that whosoever 'twas that stole up, unknown, into my room, when 'twas dark, I know not whether man or woman, by heav'ns! by all that's good! or, may I never more have joys here, or in the other world! Nay, may I eternally—

ELIZA. Be damned. So, so, you are damned enough already by your oaths; and I enough confirmed; and now you may please to be gone. Yet take this advice with you, in this plain-dealing age, to leave off forswearing yourself; for when people hardly think the better of a woman for her real modesty, why should you put that great constraint upon yourself to feign it?

OLIVIA. O hideous, hideous advice! Let us go out of the hearing of it. She will spoil us, Lettice.

Exeunt OLIVIA *and* LETTICE *at one door*, ELIZA *at t'other*

[SCENE II]

The scene changes to the Cock *in Bow Street.
A table and bottles.*

[*Enter*] MANLY *and* FIDELIA

MANLY. How! saved her honor by making her husband believe you were a woman! 'Twas well, but hard enough to do, sure.

FIDELIA. We were interrupted before he could contradict me.

MANLY. But can't you tell me, d'ye say, what kind of man he was?

FIDELIA. I was so frightened, I confess, I can give no other account of him, but that he was pretty tall, round-faced, and one, I'm sure, I ne'er had seen before.

MANLY. But she, you say, made you swear to return to-night?

FIDELIA. But I have since sworn, never to go near her again; for the husband would murder me, or worse, if he caught me again.

MANLY. No, I'll go with you, and defend you to-night, and then I'll swear, too, never to go near her again.

FIDELIA. Nay, indeed, sir, I will not go, to be accessary to your death too. Besides, what should you go again, sir, for?

MANLY. No disputing, or advice, sir; you have reason to know I am unalterable. Go, therefore, presently, and write her a note, to inquire if her assignation with you holds; and if not to be at her own house, where else; and be importunate to gain admittance to her to-night. Let your messenger, ere he deliver your letter, inquire first if her husband be gone out. Go, 'tis now almost six of the clock; I expect you back here before seven, with leave to see her then. Go, do this dext'rously, and expect the performance of my last night's promise, never to part with you.

FIDELIA. Ay, sir; but will you be sure to remember that?

MANLY. Did I ever break my word? Go, no more replies, or doubts.   *Exit* FIDELIA

Enter FREEMAN *to* MANLY

Where hast thou been?

FREEMAN. In the next room, with my Lord Plausible and Novel.

MANLY. Ay, we came hither, because 'twas a private house; but with thee, indeed, no house can be private, for thou hast that pretty quality of the familiar fops of the town, who, in an eating-house, always keep company with all people in't but those they came with.

FREEMAN. I went into their room, but to keep them, and my own fool, the squire, out of your room; but you shall be peevish now, because you have no money. But why the devil won't you write to those we were speaking of? Since your modesty, or your spirit, will not suffer you to speak to 'em, to lend you money, why won't you try 'em at last that way?

MANLY. Because I know 'em already, and can bear want better than denials, nay, than obligations.

FREEMAN. Deny you! they cannot. All of 'em have been your intimate friends.

MANLY. No, they have been people only I have obliged particularly

FREEMAN. Very well; therefore you ought to go to 'em the rather, sure.

MANLY. No, no. Those you have obliged most, most certainly avoid you, when you can oblige 'em no longer; and they take your visits like so many duns. Friends, like mistresses, are avoided for obligations past.

FREEMAN. Pshaw! but most of 'em are your relations; men of great fortune and honor.

MANLY. Yes; but relations have so much honor as to think poverty taints the blood, and disown their wanting kindred; believing, I suppose, that as riches at first makes a gentleman, the want of 'em degrades him. But damn 'em! now I am poor, I'll anticipate their contempt, and disown them.

FREEMAN. But you have many a female acquaintance whom you have been liberal to, who may have a heart to refund to you a little, if you would ask it. They are not all Olivias.

MANLY. Damn thee! how couldst thou think of such a thing? I would as soon rob my footman of his wages. Besides 'twere in vain too; for a wench is like a box in an ordinary,[1] receives all people's money easily but there is no getting, nay, shaking any out again; and he that fills it is sure never to keep the key.

FREEMAN. Well, but noble captain, would you make me believe that you, who know half the town, have so many friends, and

---

[1] A wooden box used in a tavern in place of the modern cash register.

have obliged so many, can't borrow fifty or an hundred pound?

MANLY. Why, noble lieutenant, you who know all the town, and call all you know friends, methinks should not wonder at it; since you find ingratitude too. For how many lords' families (though descended from blacksmiths or tinkers) hast thou called great and illustrious? how many ill tables call[ed] good eating? how many noisy coxcombs, wits? how many pert, [cocking][1] cowards stout? how many tawdry, affected rogues well-dressed? how many perukes admired? and how many ill verses applauded? and yet canst not borrow a shilling. Dost thou expect I, who always spoke truth, should?

FREEMAN. Nay, now you think you have paid me; but hark you, captain, I have heard of a thing called grinning honor, but never of starving honor.

MANLY. Well, but it has been the fate of some brave men; and if they won't give me a ship again, I can go starve anywhere, with a musket on my shoulder.

FREEMAN. Give you a ship! why, you will not solicit it.

MANLY. If I have not solicited it by my services, I know no other way.

FREEMAN. Your servant, sir; nay, then I'm satisfied, I must solicit my widow the closer, and run the desperate fortune of matrimony on shore. *Exit.*

Enter, to MANLY, VERNISH

MANLY. How!—Nay, here is a friend, indeed; and he that has him in his arms can know no wants.   (*Embraces* VERNISH)

VERNISH. Dear sir! and he that is in your arms is secure from all fears whatever: nay, our nation is secure by your defeat at sea, and the Dutch that fought against you have proved enemies to themselves only, in bringing you back to us.

MANLY. Fie, fie! this from a friend? and yet from any other 'twere insufferable. I thought I should never have taken anything ill from you.

VERNISH. A friend's privilege is to speak his mind, though it be taken ill.

MANLY. But your tongue need not tell me you think too well of me; I have found it

[1] "Coaching" in the first edition. "Cocking," the emendation found in several other editions, is about equivalent to "cocky."

from your heart, which spoke in actions, your unalterable heart. But Olivia is false, my friend, which I suppose is no news to you.

VERNISH. (*Aside*) He's in the right on't.

MANLY. But couldst thou not keep her true to me?

VERNISH. Not for my heart, sir.

MANLY. But could you not perceive it at all before I went? Could she so deceive us both?

VERNISH. I must confess, the first time I knew it was three days after your departure, when she received the money you had left in Lombard-street in her name; and her tears did not hinder her, it seems, from counting that. You would trust her with all, like a true, generous lover!

MANLY. And she, like a mean, jilting—

VERNISH. Trait'rous—

MANLY. Base—

VERNISH. Damned—

MANLY. Covetous—

VERNISH. Mercenary whore.—(*Aside*) I can hardly hold from laughing.

MANLY. Ay, a mercenary whore indeed, for she made me pay her before I lay with her.

VERNISH. How!—Why, have you lain with her?

MANLY. Ay, ay.

VERNISH. Nay, she deserves you should report it at least, though you have not.

MANLY. Report it! by heav'n, 'tis true!

VERNISH. How! sure not.

MANLY. I do not use to lie, nor you to doubt me.

VERNISH. When?

MANLY. Last night, about seven or eight of the clock.

VERNISH. Ha!—(*Aside*) Now I remember, I thought she spake as if she expected some other rather than me. A confounded whore, indeed!

MANLY. But what, thou wonder'st at it! Nay, you seem to be angry, too.

VERNISH. I cannot but be enraged against her, for her usage of you. Damned, infamous, common jade!

MANLY. Nay, her cuckold, who first cuckolded me in my money, shall not laugh all himself; we will do him reason, shan't we?

VERNISH. Ay, ay.

MANLY. But thou dost not, for so great a friend, take pleasure enough in your friend's revenge, methinks.

VERNISH. Yes, yes; I'm glad to know it, since you have lain with her.

MANLY. Thou canst not tell me who that rascal, her cuckold, is?

VERNISH. No.

MANLY. She would keep it from you, I suppose.

VERNISH. Yes, yes—

MANLY. Thou wouldst laugh, if thou knew'st but all the circumstances of my having her. Come, I'll tell thee.

VERNISH. Damn her! I care not to hear any more of her.

MANLY. Faith, thou shalt. You must know—

Enter FREEMAN *backwards, endeavoring to keep out* NOVEL, LORD PLAUSIBLE, JERRY [BLACKACRE], *and* [MAJOR] OLDFOX, *who all press in upon him*

FREEMAN. I tell you, he has a wench with him, and would be private.

MANLY. Damn 'em! a man can't open a bottle in these eating-houses, but presently you have these impudent, intruding, buzzing flies and insects in your glass.—Well, I'll tell thee all anon. In the mean time, prithee, go to her, but not from me, and try if you can get her to lend me but an hundred pound of my money, to supply my present wants; for I suppose there is no recovering any of it by law.

VERNISH. Not any; think not of it; nor by this way neither.

MANLY. Go try, at least.

VERNISH. I'll go; but I can satisfy you beforehand 'twill be to no purpose. You'll no more find a refunding wench—

MANLY. Than a refunding lawyer; indeed their fees alike scarce ever return. However, try her; put it to her.

VERNISH. Ay, ay, I'll try her; put it to her home with a vengeance. *Exit* VERNISH

Manent cæteri

NOVEL. Nay, you shall be our judge, Manly.—Come, major, I'll speak it to your teeth; if people provoke me to say bitter things to their faces, they must take what follows, though, like my Lord Plausible, I'd rather do't civilly behind their backs.

MANLY. Nay, thou art a dangerous rogue, I've heard, behind a man's back.

LORD PLAUSIBLE. You wrong him sure, noble captain; he would do a man no more harm behind his back than to his face.

FREEMAN. I am of my lord's mind.

MANLY. Yes, a fool, like a coward, is the more to be feared behind a man's back, more than a witty man; for, as a coward is more bloody than a brave man, a fool is more malicious than a man of wit.

NOVEL. A fool, tar,—a fool! nay, thou art a brave sea-judge of wit! a fool! Prithee, when did you ever find me want something to say, as you do often?

MANLY. Nay, I confess thou art always talking, roaring, or making a noise; that I'll say for thee.

NOVEL. Well, and is talking a sign of a fool?

MANLY. Yes, always talking, especially, too, if it be loud and fast, is the sign of a fool.

NOVEL. Pshaw! talking is like fencing, the quicker the better; run 'em down, run 'em down, no matter for parrying; push on still, sa, sa, sa! no matter whether you argue in form, push in guard [1] or no.

MANLY. Or hit, or no; I think thou always talk'st without thinking, Novel.

NOVEL. Ay, ay; studied play's the worse, to follow the allegory, as the old pedant says.

OLDFOX. A young fop!

MANLY. I ever thought the man of most wit, had been like him of most money, who has no vanity in showing it everywhere, whilst the beggarly pusher of his fortune has all he has about him still, only to show.

NOVEL. Well, sir, and makes a very pretty show in the world, let me tell you; nay, a better than your close hunks. A pox, give me ready money in play! what care I for a man's reputation? what are we the better for your substantial, thrifty curmudgeon in wit, sir?

OLDFOX. Thou art a profuse young rogue indeed.

NOVEL. So much for talking, which, I think I have proved a mark of wit; and so is railing, roaring, and making a noise; for railing is satire, you know; and roaring and making a noise, humor.

Enter to them FIDELIA, *taking* MANLY *aside, and showing him a paper*

FIDELIA. The hour is betwixt seven and eight exactly. 'Tis now half an hour after six.

MANLY. Well, go then to the piazza, and

[1] Term from fencing.

wait for me; as soon as it is quite dark, I'll be with you. I must stay here yet a while for my friend.—(*Exit* FIDELIA) But is railing satire, Novel?

FREEMAN. And roaring and making a noise, humor?

NOVEL. What, won't you confess there's humor in roaring and making a noise?

FREEMAN. No.

NOVEL. Nor in cutting napkins and hangings?

MANLY. No, sure.

NOVEL. Dull fops!

OLDFOX. O rogue, rogue, insipid rogue!—Nay, gentlemen, allow him those things for wit; for his parts lie only that way.

NOVEL. Peace, old fool! I wonder not at thee; but that young fellows should be so dull, as to say there's no humor in making a noise, and breaking windows! I tell you, there's wit and humor too, in both; and a wit is as well known by his frolic, as by his simile.

OLDFOX. Pure rogue! there's your modern wit for you! Wit and humor in breaking of windows! There's mischief, if you will, but no wit, or humor.

NOVEL. Prithee, prithee, peace, old fool! I tell you, where there is mischief, there's wit. Don't we esteem the monkey a wit amongst beasts, only because he's mischievous? And let me tell you, as good-nature is a sign of a fool, being mischievous is a sign of wit.

OLDFOX. O rogue, rogue! pretend to be a wit, by doing mischief and railing!

NOVEL. Why, thou, old fool, hast no other pretence to the name of a wit, but by railing at new plays!

OLDFOX. Thou, by railing at that facetious, noble way of wit, quibbling!

NOVEL. Thou call'st thy dulness gravity; and thy dozing, thinking.

OLDFOX. You, sir, your dulness, spleen; and you talk much, and say nothing.

NOVEL. Thou read'st much, and understand'st nothing, sir.

OLDFOX. You laugh loud, and break no jest.

NOVEL. You rail, and nobody hangs himself; and thou hast nothing of the satyr but in thy face.

OLDFOX. And you have no jest, but your face, sir.

NOVEL. Thou art an illiterate pedant.

OLDFOX. Thou art a fool, with a bad memory.

MANLY. Come, a pox on you both! You have done like wits now; for you wits, when you quarrel, never give over till you prove one another fools.

NOVEL. And you fools have never any occasion of laughing at us wits but when we quarrel. Therefore, let us be friends, Oldfox.

MANLY. They are such wits as thou art, who make the name of a wit as scandalous as that of bully; and signify a loud-laughing, talking, incorrigible coxcomb, as bully a roaring, hardened coward.

FREEMAN. And would have his noise and laughter pass for wit, as t'other his huffing and blust'ring for courage.

Enter VERNISH

MANLY. Gentlemen, with your leave, here is one I would speak with; and I have nothing to say to you. (*Puts 'em out of the room*)

Manent MANLY, VERNISH

VERNISH. I told you 'twas in vain to think of getting money out of her. She says, if a shilling would do't, she would not save you from starving or hanging, or what you would think worse, begging or flattering; and rails so at you, one would not think you had lain with her.

MANLY. O friend, never trust for that matter a woman's railing; for she is no less a dissembler in her hatred than her love; and as her fondness of her husband is a sign he's a cuckold, her railing at another man is a sign she lies with him.

VERNISH. (*Aside*) He's in the right on't. I know not what to trust to.

MANLY. But you did not take any notice of it to her, I hope?

VERNISH. So!—(*Aside*) Sure he is afraid I should have disproved him by an inquiry of her. All may be well yet.

MANLY. What hast thou in thy head that makes thee seem so unquiet?

VERNISH. Only this base, impudent woman's falseness; I cannot put her out of my head.

MANLY. O my dear friend, be not you too sensible of my wrongs; for then I shall feel 'em, too, with more pain, and think 'em unsufferable. Damn her, her money, and that ill-natured whore, too, Fortune herself! But if thou wouldst ease a little my present trouble, prithee go borrow me somewhere else some money. I can trouble thee.

VERNISH. You trouble me, indeed, most sensibly, when you command me anything I cannot do. I have lately lost a great deal of money at play, more than I can yet pay; so that not only my money, but my credit, too, is gone, and know not where to borrow; but could rob a church for you.—(*Aside*) Yet would rather end your wants by cutting your throat.

MANLY. Nay, then I doubly feel my poverty, since I'm incapable of supplying thee.

Embraces VERNISH

VERNISH. But, methinks, she that granted you the last favor, (as they call it) should not deny you anything—

NOVEL. Hey, tarpaulin, have you done?

NOVEL *looks in, and retires again*

VERNISH. I understand not that point of kindness, I confess.

MANLY. No, thou dost not understand it, and I have not time to let you know all now; for these fools, you see, will interrupt us; but anon, at supper, we'll laugh at leisure together at Olivia's cuckold, who took a young fellow, that goes between his wife and me, for a woman.

VERNISH. Ha!

MANLY. Senseless, easy rascal! 'twas no wonder she chose him for a husband; but she thought him, I thank her, fitter than me, for that blind, bearing office.

VERNISH. (*Aside*) I could not be deceived in that long woman's hair tied up behind, nor those infallible proofs, her pouting, swelling breasts. I have handled too many, sure, not to know 'em.

MANLY. What, you wonder the fellow could be such a blind coxcomb?

VERNISH. Yes, yes—

NOVEL. Nay, prithee, come to us, Manly. Gad, all the fine things one says in their company are lost without thee.

NOVEL *looks in again, and retires*

MANLY. Away, fop! I'm busy yet.—You see we cannot talk here at our ease; besides, I must be gone immediately, in order to meeting with Olivia again to-night.

VERNISH. To-night! it cannot be, sure—

MANLY. I had an appointment just now from her.

VERNISH. For what time?

MANLY. At half an hour after seven precisely.

VERNISH. Don't you apprehend the husband?

MANLY. He! snivelling gull! he a thing to be feared! a husband! the tamest of creatures!

VERNISH. (*Aside*) Very fine!

MANLY. But, prithee, in the mean time, go try to get me some money. Though thou art too modest to borrow for thyself, thou canst do anything for me, I know. Go; for I must be gone to Olivia. Go, and meet me here, anon.—Freeman, where are you?

Exit MANLY

Manet VERNISH

VERNISH. Ay, I'll meet with you, I warrant; but it shall be at Olivia's. Sure, it cannot be. She denies it so calmly, and with that honest, modest assurance, it can't be true—and he does not use to lie—but belying a woman when she won't be kind, is the only lie a brave man will least scruple. But then the woman in man's clothes, whom he calls a man!—Well, but by her breasts I know her to be a woman—but then again, his appointment from her, to meet with him to-night! I am distracted more with doubt than jealousy. Well, I have no way to disabuse or revenge myself, but by going home immediately, putting on a riding-suit, and pretending to my wife the same business which carried me out of town last, requires me again to go post to Oxford to-night. Then, if the appointment he boasts of be true, it's sure to hold; and I shall have an opportunity either of clearing her, or revenging myself on both. Perhaps she is his wench, of an old date, and I am his cully, whilst I think him mine; and he has seemed to make his wench rich, only that I might take her off his hands. Or if he has but lately lain with her, he must needs discover by her my treachery to him; which I'm sure he will revenge with my death, and which I must prevent with his, if it were only but for fear of his too just reproaches; for I must confess, I never had till now any excuse but that of int'rest, for doing ill to him. *Exit* VERNISH

Re-enter MANLY *and* FREEMAN

MANLY. Come hither; only, I say, be sure you mistake not the time. You know the house exactly where Olivia lodges; 'tis just hard by.

FREEMAN. Yes, yes.

MANLY. Well then, bring 'em all, I say, thither, and all you know that may be then in the house; for the more witnesses I have of her infamy, the greater will be my revenge: and be sure you come straight up to her chamber without more ado. Here, take the watch; you see 'tis above a quarter past seven; be there in half an hour exactly.

FREEMAN. You need not doubt my diligence or dexterity; I am an old scourer,[1] and can naturally beat up a wench's quarters that won't be civil. Shan't we break her windows, too?

MANLY. No, no; be punctual only.

Exeunt ambo

Enter WIDOW BLACKACRE, *and two Knights of the Post; a Waiter with wine*

WIDOW. Sweetheart, are you sure the door was shut close, that none of those roysters saw us come in?

WAITER. Yes, mistress; and you shall have a privater room above, instantly.

Exit Waiter

WIDOW. You are safe enough, gentlemen; for I have been private in this house ere now, upon other occasions, when I was something younger. Come, gentlemen; in short, I leave my business to your care and fidelity: and so, here's to you.

1ST KNIGHT. We were ungrateful rogues if we should not be honest to you; for we have had a great deal of your money.

WIDOW. And you have done me many a good job for't; and so, here's to you again.

2ND KNIGHT. Why, we have been perjured but six times for you.

1ST KNIGHT. Forged but four deeds, with your husband's last deed of gift.

2ND KNIGHT. And but three wills.

1ST KNIGHT. And counterfeited hands and seals to some six bonds; I think that's all, brother.

WIDOW. Ay, that's all, gentlemen; and so, here's to you again.

2ND KNIGHT. Nay, 'twould do one's heart good to be forsworn for you. You have a conscience in your ways, and pay us well.

1ST KNIGHT. You are in the right on't, brother; one would be damned for her with all one's heart.

2ND KNIGHT. But there are rogues, who make us forsworn for 'em; and when we come to be paid, they'll be forsworn, too, and not pay us our wages, which they promised with oaths sufficient.

[1] Roisterer.

1ST KNIGHT. Ay, a great lawyer that shall be nameless bilked me, too.

WIDOW. That was hard, methinks, that a lawyer should use gentlemen witnesses no better.

1ST KNIGHT. A lawyer! d'ye wonder a lawyer should do't? I was bilked by a reverend divine, that preaches twice on Sundays, and prays half an hour still before dinner.

WIDOW. How! a conscientious divine, and not pay people for damning themselves! Sure then, for all his talking, he does not believe damnation. But come, to our business. Pray be sure to imitate exactly the flourish at the end of this name. (*Pulls out a deed or two*)

1ST KNIGHT. O he's the best in England at untangling a flourish, madam.

WIDOW. And let not the seal be a jot bigger. Observe well the dash too, at the end of this name.

2ND KNIGHT. I warrant you, madam.

WIDOW. Well, these and many other shifts, poor widows are put to sometimes; for everybody would be riding a widow, as they say, and breaking into her jointure. They think marrying a widow an easy business, like leaping the hedge where another has gone over before. A widow is a mere gap, a gap with them.

Enter to them MAJOR OLDFOX, *with two Waiters. The Knights of the Post huddle up the writings*

What, he here! Go then, go, my hearts, you have your instructions.

Ex[eunt] Knights of the Post

OLDFOX. Come, madam, to be plain with you, I'll be fobbed off no longer.—(*Aside*) I'll bind her and gag her but she shall hear me.—[*To the Waiters.*] Look you, friends, there's the money I promised you; and now do you what you promised me. Here are my garters, and here's a gag.—[*To the Widow*] You shall be acquainted with my parts, lady, you shall.

WIDOW. Acquainted with your parts! A rape! a rape!—What, will you ravish me?

The Waiters tie her to the chair, gag her, and ex[eunt]

OLDFOX. Yes, lady, I will ravish you; but it shall be through the ear, lady, the ear only, with my well-penned acrostics.

Enter to them FREEMAN, JERRY BLACKACRE, *three Bailiffs, a Constable, and his Assistants, with the two Knights of the Post*

What, shall I never read my things undisturbed again?

JERRY. O law! my mother bound hand and foot, and gaping as if she rose before her time to-day!

FREEMAN. What means this, Oldfox?—But I'll release you from him; you shall be no man's prisoner but mine. Bailiffs, execute your writ.   (FREEMAN *unties her*)

OLDFOX. Nay, then, I'll be gone, for fear of being bail, and paying her debts, without being her husband.   *Exit* OLDFOX

1ST BAILIFF. We arrest you in the king's name, at the suit of Mr. Freeman, guardian to Jeremiah Blackacre, esquire, in an action of ten thousand pounds.

WIDOW. How, how! in a choke-bail action![1] What, and the pen-and-ink gentlemen taken too!—Have you confessed, you rogues?

1ST KNIGHT. We needed not to confess; for the bailiffs dogged us hither to the very door, and overheard all that you and we said.

WIDOW. Undone, undone then! No man was ever too hard for me till now. Jerry, child, wilt thou vex again the womb that bore thee?

JERRY. Ay, for bearing me before wedlock, as you say. But I'll teach you call a Blackacre a bastard, though you were never so much my mother.

WIDOW. (*Aside*) Well, I'm undone! not one trick left? no law-mesh imaginable?—[*To* FREEMAN] Cruel sir, a word with you, I pray.

FREEMAN. In vain, madam; for you have no other way to release yourself, but by the bonds of matrimony.

WIDOW. How, sir, how! that were but to sue out an habeas-corpus, for a removal from one prison to another. Matrimony!

FREEMAN. Well, bailiffs, away with her.

WIDOW. O stay, sir! can you be so cruel as to bring me under covert-baron again, and put it out of my power to sue in my own name? Matrimony to a woman is worse than excommunication, in depriving her of the benefit of the law; and I would rather be deprived of life. But hark you, sir, I am contented you should hold and enjoy my person by lease or

[1] An action of such importance that no bail can be allowed.

patent, but not by the spiritual patent called a licence; that is, to have the privileges of a husband without the dominion; that is, *Durante beneplacito*.[2] In consideration of which, I will out of my jointure secure you an annuity of three hundred pounds a year, and pay your debts; and that's all you younger brothers desire to marry a widow for, I'm sure.

FREEMAN. Well, widow, if—

JERRY. What! I hope, bully-guardian, you are not making agreements without me?

FREEMAN. No, no. First, widow, you must say no more that he is a son of a whore; have a care of that. And then, he must have a settled exhibition of forty pounds a year, and a nag of assizes,[3] kept by you, but not upon the common; and have free ingress, egress, and regress to and from your maids' garret.

WIDOW. Well, I can grant all that too.

JERRY. Ay, ay, fair words butter no cabbage; but guardian, make her sign, sign and seal; for otherwise, if you knew her as well as I, you would not trust her word for a farthing.

FREEMAN. I warrant thee, squire.—Well, widow, since thou art so generous, I will be generous too; and if you'll secure me four hundred pound a year, but during your life, and pay my debts, not above a thousand pound, I'll bate you your person, to dispose of as you please.

WIDOW. Have a care, sir, a settlement without a consideration is void in law. You must do something for't.

FREEMAN. Prithee, then, let the settlement on me be called alimony; and the consideration, our separation. Come; my lawyer, with writings ready drawn, is within, and in haste. Come.

WIDOW. But, what, no other kind of consideration, Mr. Freeman? Well, a widow, I see, is a kind of sinecure, by custom of which the unconscionable incumbent enjoys the profits, without any duty, but does that still elsewhere.   *Ex[eunt] omnes*

[SCENE III.]

The scene changes to OLIVIA's *Lodging*

Enter OLIVIA *with a candle in her hand*

OLIVIA. So, I am now prepared once more for my timorous young lover's reception. My

[2] During pleasure.
[3] Jerry is to have forty pounds a year income, a horse of his own to ride to court, and opportunity to pasture the animal on the family property.

husband is gone; and go thou out too, thou next interrupter of love.—(*Puts out the candle*) Kind darkness, that frees us lovers from scandal and bashfulness, from the censure of our gallants and the world!—So, are you there?

Enter to OLIVIA, FIDELIA, *followed softly by* MANLY

Come, my dear punctual lover, there is not such another in the world; thou hast beauty and youth to please a wife; address and wit, to amuse and fool a husband; nay, thou hast all things to be wished in a lover, but your fits. I hope, my dear, you won't have one to-night; and that you may not, I'll lock the door, though there be no need of it, but to lock out your fits; for my husband is just gone out of town again. Come, where are you? (*Goes to the door and locks it*)

MANLY. (*Aside*) Well, thou hast impudence enough to give me fits too, and make revenge itself impotent, hinder me from making thee yet more infamous, if it can be.

OLIVIA. Come, come, my soul, come.

FIDELIA. Presently, my dear; we have time enough sure.

OLIVIA. How? time enough! True lovers can no more think they ever have time enough, than love enough. You shall stay with me all night; but that is but a lover's moment. Come.

FIDELIA. But won't you let me give you and myself the satisfaction of telling you how I abused your husband last night?

OLIVIA. Not when you can give me, and yourself too, the satisfaction of abusing him again to-night. Come!

FIDELIA. Let me but tell you how your husband—

OLIVIA. O name not his, or Manly's more loathsome name, if you love me! I forbid 'em last night: and you know I mentioned my husband but once, and he came. No talking, pray; 'twas ominous to us. You make me fancy a noise at the door already, but I'm resolved not to be interrupted. (*A noise at the door*) Where are you? Come, for rather than lose my dear expectation now, though my husband were at the door, and the bloody ruffian, Manly, here in the room, with all his awful insolence, I would give myself to this dear hand, to be led away to heavens of joys, which none but thou canst give. But what's this noise at the door? So, I told you what talking would come to.—(*The noise at the door increases*) Ha!—O Heavens, my husband's voice!— (OLIVIA *listens at the door*)

MANLY. (*Aside*) Freeman is come too soon.

OLIVIA. Oh, 'tis he!—Then here's the happiest minute lost that ever bashful boy or trifling woman fooled away! I'm undone! my husband's reconcilement too was false, as my joy, all delusion. But come this way, here's a back door.—(*Exit, and returns*) The officious jade has locked us in, instead of locking others out; but let us then escape your way, by the balcony; and whilst you pull down the curtains, I'll fetch from my closet what next will best secure our escape. I have left my key in the door, and 'twill not suddenly be broke open. *Exit*

A noise as it were people forcing the door

MANLY. Stir not, yet fear nothing.

FIDELIA. Nothing but your life, sir.

MANLY. We shall now know this happy man she calls husband.

OLIVIA *re-enters*

OLIVIA. Oh, where are you? What, idle with fear? Come, I'll tie the curtains, if you will hold. Here, take this cabinet and purse, for it is thine, if we escape;—(MANLY *takes from her the cabinet and purse*)—therefore let us make haste. *Exit* OLIVIA

MANLY. 'Tis mine, indeed, now again, and it shall never escape more from me, to you at least.

(*The door broken open, enter* VERNISH *alone, with a dark-lantern and a sword, running at* MANLY, *who draws, puts by the thrust, and defends himself, whilst* FIDELIA *runs at* VERNISH *behind*)

VERNISH. (*With a low voice*) So, there I'm right, sure—

MANLY. (*Softly*) Sword and dark-lantern, villain, are some odds; but—

VERNISH. (*With a low voice*) Odds! I'm sure I find more odds than I expected. What, has my insatiable two seconds at once? but—

(*Whilst they fight,* OLIVIA *re-enters, tying two curtains together*)

OLIVIA. Where are you now?—What, is he entered then, and are they fighting?— Oh, do not kill one that can make no defence! —(MANLY *throws* VERNISH *down and disarms him*) How! but I think he has the better on't.

Here's his scarf, 'tis he.—So, keep him down still: I hope thou hast no hurt, my dearest?
(*Embracing* MANLY)

Enter to them FREEMAN, LORD PLAUSIBLE, NOVEL, JERRY BLACKACRE, *and the* WIDOW BLACKACRE, *lighted in by the two Sailors with torches*

Ha!—what?—Manly! and have I been thus concerned for him, embracing him? and has he his jewels again, too? What means this? Oh, 'tis too sure, as well as my shame! which I'll go hide for ever.
(*Offers to go out,* MANLY *stops her*)

MANLY. No, my dearest; after so much kindness as has passed between us, I cannot part with you yet.—Freeman, let nobody stir out of the room; for notwithstanding your lights, we are yet in the dark, till this gentleman please to turn his face.—(*Pulls* VERNISH *by the sleeve*) How! Vernish! art thou the happy man then? Thou! thou! speak, I say; but thy guilty silence tells me all.—Well, I shall not upbraid thee; for my wonder is striking me as dumb as thy shame has made thee. But what? my little volunteer hurt, and fainting!

FIDELIA. My wound, sir, is but a slight one in my arm; 'tis only my fear of your danger, sir, not yet well over.

MANLY. But what's here? More strange things!—(*Observing* FIDELIA'S *hair untied behind, and without a peruke, which she lost in the scuffle*) What means this long woman's hair, and face! Now all of it appears too beautiful for a man; which I still thought womanish indeed! What, you have not deceived me too, my little volunteer?

OLIVIA. (*Aside*) Me she has, I'm sure.
MANLY. Speak!

Enter ELIZA *and* LETTICE

ELIZA. What, cousin, I am brought hither by your woman, I suppose, to be a witness of the second vindication of your honor?

OLIVIA. Insulting is not generous. You might spare me, I have you.

ELIZA. Have a care, cousin, you'll confess anon too much: and I would not have your secrets.

MANLY. (*To* FIDELIA) Come, your blushes answer me sufficiently, and you have been my volunteer in love.

FIDELIA. I must confess I needed no compulsion to follow you all the world over; which I attempted in this habit, partly out of shame to own my love to you, and fear of a greater shame, your refusal of it; for I knew of your engagement to this lady, and the constancy of your nature; which nothing could have altered but herself.

MANLY. Dear madam, I desired you to bring me out of confusion, and you have given me more. I know not what to speak to you, or how to look upon you; the sense of my rough, hard, and ill usage of you, (though chiefly your own fault) gives me more pain now 'tis over, than you had when you suffered it: and if my heart, the refusal of such a woman, (*pointing to* OLIVIA) were not a sacrifice to profane your love, and a greater wrong to you than ever yet I did you, I would beg of you to receive it, though you used it as she has done; for though it deserved not from her the treatment she gave it, it does from you.

FIDELIA. Then it has had punishment sufficient from her already, and needs no more from me; and, I must confess, I would not be the only cause of making you break your last night's oath to me, of never parting with me; if you do not forget or repent it.

MANLY. Then take for ever my heart, and this with it; (*gives her the cabinet*) for 'twas given to you before, and my heart was before your due; I only beg leave to dispose of these few.—Here, madam, I never yet left my wench unpaid.
(*Takes some of the jewels, and offers 'em to* OLIVIA; *she strikes 'em down:* PLAUSIBLE *and* NOVEL *take 'em up*)

OLIVIA. So it seems, by giving her the cabinet.

LORD PLAUSIBLE. These pendants appertain to your most faithful humble servant.

NOVEL. And this locket is mine; my earnest for love, which she never paid; therefore my own again.

WIDOW. By what law, sir, pray?—Cousin Olivia, a word. What, do they make a seizure on your goods and chattels, *vi et armis?* [1] Make your demand, I say, and bring your trover, bring your trover. I'll follow the law for you.

[1] By force of arms.

OLIVIA. And I my revenge.
Exit OLIVIA

MANLY. (*To* VER[NISH]) But 'tis, my friend, in your consideration most, that I would have returned part of your wife's portion; for 'twere hard to take all from thee, since thou hast paid so dear for't, in being such a rascal. Yet thy wife is a fortune without a portion; and thou art a man of that extraordinary merit in villainy, the world and fortune can never desert thee, though I do; therefore be not melancholy. Fare you well, sir.—(*Ex[it]* VERNISH *doggedly*) Now, madam, (*turning to* FIDELIA) I beg your pardon for lessening the present I made you; but my heart can never be lessened. This, I confess, was too small for you before; for you deserve the Indian world; and I would now go thither, out of covetousness for your sake only.

FIDELIA. Your heart, sir, is a present of that value, I can never make any return to't; (*Pulling* MANLY *from the company*) but I can give you back such a present as this, which I got by the loss of my father, a gentleman of the north, of no mean extraction, whose only child I was, therefore left me in the present possession of two thousand pounds a year; which I left, with multitudes of pretenders, to follow you, sir; having in several public places seen you, and observed your actions thoroughly, with admiration, when you were too much in love to take notice of mine, which yet was but too visible. The name of my family is Grey, my other, Fidelia. The rest of my story you shall know when I have fewer auditors.

MANLY. Nay, now, madam, you have taken from me all power of making you any compliment on my part; for I was going to tell you, that for your sake only I would quit the unknown pleasure of a retirement; and rather stay in this ill world of ours still, though odious to me, than give you more frights again at sea, and make again too great a venture there, in you alone. But if I should tell you now all this, and that your virtue (since greater than I thought any was in the world) had now reconciled me to't, my friend here would say, 'tis your estate that has made me friends with the world.

FREEMAN. I must confess I should; for I think most of our quarrels to the world are just such as we have to a handsome woman: only because we cannot enjoy her as we would do.

MANLY. Nay, if thou art a plain-dealer too, give me thy hand; for now I'll say, I am thy friend indeed; and for your two sakes, though I have been so lately deceived in friends of both sexes,—

I will believe there are now in the world
Good-natured friends, who are not prostitutes,
And handsome women worthy to be friends;
Yet, for my sake, let no one e'er confide
In tears, or oaths, in love, or friend untried.

Ex[eunt] omnes

EPILOGUE

SPOKEN BY THE WIDOW BLACKACRE

To you, the judges learnéd in stage-laws,
Our poet now, by me, submits his cause;
For with young judges, such as most of you,
The men by women best their bus'ness do.
And, truth on't is, if you did not sit here,
To keep for us a term throughout the year,
We could not live by'r tongues; nay, but for you,
Our chamber-practice would be little too.
And 'tis not only the stage-practiser
Who by your meeting gets her living here;
For as in Hall of Westminster
Sleek sempstress vends amidst the courts her ware;
So, while we bawl, and you in judgment sit,
The visor-mask sells linen, too, i' th' pit.
Oh, many of your friends, besides us here,
Do live by putting off their sev'ral ware.
Here's daily done the great affair o' th' nation;
Let love and us then ne'er have long vacation.
But hold; like other pleaders I have done
Not my poor client's bus'ness, but my own.
Spare me a word, then, now for him. First know,
Squires of the long robe, he does humbly show
He has a just right in abusing you,
Because he is a Brother-Templar, too:
For at the bar you rally one another;
And, "fool," and "knave," is swallowed from a brother:
If not the poet here, the Templer spare,
And maul him when you catch him at the bar.
From you, our common modish censurers,
Your favor, not your judgment, 'tis he fears:
Of all loves begs you then to rail, find fault;
For plays, like women, by the world are thought
(When you speak kindly of 'em) very naught